WEBSTER'S II NEW RIVERSIDE DESK DICTIONARY

HOME AND OFFICE EDITION

Houghton Mifflin Company Boston

Library of Congress Cataloging-in-Publication Data

Webster's II new Riverside desk dictionary.

"An abridgment of Webster's II new Riverside university dictionary"—Pref.

1. English language—Dictionaries. I. Riverside Publishing Company. II. Webster's II new Riverside university dictionary. III. Title: Webster's two new Riverside desk dictionary. IV. Title: Webster's 2 new Riverside desk dictionary.

PE1628.W55165 1988 423 88-845

ISBN 0-395-48368-9

Manufactured in the United States of America

Table of Contents

Preface

This *Webster's II New Riverside Desk Dictionary* is an abridgment of *Webster's II New Riverside University Dictionary.* Like the parent volume, this book traces its lineage to the American lexicographer whose name, more than any other, is associated with lexicography on this continent.

As Noah Webster's intent was to create a lexicon specific to the New World, reflecting and serving a unique American culture, so the intent of the present volume is to mirror what our language is and to convey that information in a form appropriate to an inexpensive dictionary. Included are words not in other books of this type, regionalisms, scientific and technical terms, and biographic and geographic entries. Fine line drawings illustrate particular points.

In America, smaller dictionaries have earned positions of importance among students, home users, business users, and all those who want a lexicon in narrower compass than the university-level dictionary. In *Webster's II New Riverside Desk Dictionary* that lexicon is especially authoritative and is expressed with a directness and clarity that meet the special needs of this audience. Our A-Z word list is augmented by a variety of aids designed to help readers and writers and to communicate to them something of the richness and charm of our language.

A style guide shows how to punctuate and capitalize, with examples as well as rules. A list of clichés and redundancies will alert users to those denizens of the lexical wilderness we desire to avoid. A special section on foreign words and phrases provides a list of many terms not yet naturalized into English but often encountered nevertheless. Synonym lists provide an obvious resource for enrichment of expression. Words with principally Canadian usage are noted. Attractive word histories convey the antecedents of key words and their allure as elements of a language that has grown and continues to grow.

Webster's II New Riverside Desk Dictionary is based on the Houghton Mifflin electronic lexical data base. This is additional evidence of the opportunity the new technology affords of creating a range of sound dictionaries to respond to the many specific requirements of individual groups of users.

Perhaps this edition especially well realizes Noah Webster's dream of a lexicon serving, as he predicted, "*three hundred millions of people,* who are destined to occupy, and I hope, to adorn the vast territory within our jurisdiction."

Abbreviations and Symbols in this Dictionary

abbr.	abbreviation
A.D.	in the year of the Lord
adj.	adjective
adv.	adverb
Alta.	Alberta
Amer.	American
amp	ampere(s)
Anat.	Anatomy
approx.	approximately
Apr.	April
Astron.	Astronomy
Aug.	August
Austral.	Australian
bbl	barrel(s)
B.C.	before Christ
B.C.	British Columbia
Biochem.	Biochemistry
Biol.	Biology
Bot.	Botany
Brit.	British
bu	bushel(s)
C	Celsius; centigrade; central
c.	circa
Can.	Canadian
Cap.	capital
cent.	century; centuries
cg	centigram(s)
Chem.	Chemistry
cm	centimeter(s)
compar.	comparative
Computer Sci.	Computer Science
conj.	conjunction
cu	cubic
D.C.	District of Columbia
Dec.	December
def. art.	definite article
dwt.	pennyweight
E	east, eastern
EC	east-central
Ecol.	Ecology
Elect.	Electricity
Electron.	Electronics
Engineer.	Engineering
esp.	especially
F	Fahrenheit
Feb.	February
fl.	flourished
fl oz	fluid ounce(s)
ft	foot, feet
g	gram(s)
gal	gallon(s)
gen.	generally
Geol.	Geology
Gk. Myth.	Greek Mythology
gr	grain(s)
in.	inch(es)
indef. art.	indefinite article
interj.	interjection
Ir.	Irish
Is.	Island(s)
Jan.	January
Jul.	July
Jun.	June
kg	kilogram(s)
kl	kiloliter(s)
km	kilometer(s)
kph	kilometers per hour
kw	kilowatt(s)
kwh	kilowatt-hour(s)
L	liter(s)
lb	pound(s)
m	meter(s)
Man.	Manitoba
Mar.	March
Math.	Mathematics
Med.	Medicine
Meteorol.	Meteorology
mg	milligram(s)
Microbiol.	Microbiology
min	minute(s)
mm	millimeter(s)

mph	miles per hour
Mt.	Mount, Mountain
Mts.	Mountains
Mus.	Music
Myth.	Mythology
N	north, northern
n.	noun
Naut.	Nautical
N.B.	New Brunswick
NC	north-central
NE	northeast, northeastern
Norse Myth.	Norse Mythology
Nov.	November
N.S.	Nova Scotia
NW	northwest; northwestern
N.W.T.	Northwest Territories
Obs.	Obsolete
occas.	occasionally
Oct.	October
Ont.	Ontario
orig.	originally
oz	ounce(s)
Pathol.	Pathology
P.E.I.	Prince Edward Island
Philos.	Philosophy
pl.	plural
pl.n.	plural noun
Pop.	population
p.p.	past participle
pref.	prefix
prep.	preposition
prob.	probably
pron.	pronoun
Psychiat.	Psychiatry
Psychoanal.	Psychoanalysis
p.t.	past tense
qt	quart(s)
Que.	Quebec
R.	River
Rom.Cath. Ch.	Roman Catholic Church
Rom. Myth.	Roman Mythology
rpm	revolutions per minute
S	south, southern
Sask.	Saskatchewan
SC	south-central
Scot.	Scottish
SE	southeast, southeastern
sec	second(s)
Sept.	September
sing.	singular
So. Afr.	South African
specif.	specifically
sq	square
St.	Saint
suff.	suffix
superl.	superlative
SW	southwest, southwestern
t	ton(s)
ult.	ultimately
U.S.	United States
USSR	Union of Soviet Socialist Republics
usu.	usually
v.	verb
var.	variant
vars.	variants
w	watt(s)
W	west, western
WC	west-central
yd	yard(s)

Symbols

&	and
°	degree
′	minute
%	per cent
†	*Regional*
″	second

Pronunciation Key

ă	pat
ā	pay
âr	care
ä	father
b	bib
ch	church
d	deed, milled
ĕ	pet
ē	bee
f	fife, phase, rough
g	gag
h	hat
hw	which
ĭ	pit
ī	pie, by
îr	pier
j	judge, gem
k	kick, cat, pique
l	lid, needle
m	mum
n	no, sudden
ng	thing
ŏ	pot, horrid
ō	toe, hoarse

ô	caught, paw, for
oi	noise
o͝o	took
o͞o	boot
ou	out
p	pop
r	roar
s	sauce
sh	ship, dish
t	tight, stopped
th	thin
th	this
ŭ	cut
ûr	urge, term, firm word, heard
v	valve
w	with
y	yes
yo͞o	abuse, use
z	zebra, xylem
zh	vision, pleasure, garage
ə	about, item, edible, gallop, circus
ər	butter

Foreign

œ	*French* feu, *German* schön
ü	*French* tu, *German* über
KH	*Scottish* loch, *German* ich
N	*French* bon

Stress

Primary stress ′
phil·os′o·phy

Secondary stress ′
phil′o·soph′i·cal

Aa

a or **A** (ā) *n., pl.* **a's** or **A's.** **1.** The 1st letter of the English alphabet. **2.** A speech sound represented by the letter *a.* **3.** Something with the shape of the letter A. **4.** The 1st in a series. **5.** The highest grade or rank. **6.** *Mus.* The 6th tone in the scale of C major. **7. A** A human blood type of the ABO group.

a[1] (ə; ā *when stressed*) *indef. art.* **1.** Used before nouns and noun phrases that denote a single, but unspecified, person or thing <*a* mountain><*a* woman> **2.** Used before terms, as *few* or *many,* denoting number <*a* hundred animals><just *a* few of the players> **3.** The same <people of *a* kind> **4.** Any <not *a* bite to eat> **5. a.** Used before a proper name to denote a type or a member of a class <the strength of *a* Hercules> **b.** Used before a mass noun to indicate a single type or example <*a* dark beer>

a[2] (ə) *prep.* In or for each or every : per <twice *a* day><two dollars *a* yard>

†**a**[3] (ə; ă *when stressed*) *v. Regional.* Have <We'd *a* come if it hadn't rained.>

A *abbr.* **1.** *also* **a, A.** acre. **2.** ammeter. **3.** ampere. **4.** area.

a. *abbr.* **1.** acceleration. **2.** adjective. **3.** answer. **4.** *also* **A.** are (measurement).

A. *abbr.* **1.** alto. **2.** America; American.

A.A. *abbr.* Associate in Arts.

aard•vark *n.* A burrowing insectivorous mammal, *Orycteropus afer,* of S Africa, with a stocky, hairy body and a long, tubular snout.

aard•wolf (ärd'woolf') *n.* A hyenalike mammal, *Proteles cristatus,* of S and E Africa, that has gray fur with black stripes and feeds chiefly on termites and insect larvae.

Aar•on (âr'ən, ăr'-). Hebrew high priest. **—Aar•on'ic** (â-rŏn'ĭk, ăr-ŏn'-), **Aar•on'i•cal** *adj.*

AB (ā'bē') *n.* A human blood type of the ABO group.

A.B. *abbr.* Bachelor of Arts.

a•ba (ə-bä', ä-bä') *n.* A loose-fitting, often sleeveless garment made of woven camel or goat hair, worn by Arabs.

aba

ab•a•ca (ăb'ə-kä') *n.* A Philippine plant, *Musa textilis,* whose leafstalks are the source of Manila hemp.

a•back (ə-băk') *adv.* **—take aback.** To startle : dumbfound.

ab•a•cus (ăb'ə-kəs) *n., pl.* **-cus•es** *or* **-ci** (-sī'). A frame holding parallel rods strung with movable beads that is used for manual computation.

a•baft (ə-băft') *adv. Naut.* Toward the stern. **—a•baft'** *prep.*

ab•a•lo•ne (ăb'ə-lō'nē) *n.* A large, edible marine gastropod of the genus *Haliotis,* with an ear-shaped shell.

a•ban•don (ə-băn'dən) *v.* **1.** To desert : forsake. **2.** To give up completely : surrender. ☆**syns:** DESIST, DISCONTINUE, FORSWEAR, LEAVE, QUIT, RENOUNCE, STOP —*n.* **1.** A complete surrender to feeling or impulse. **2.** Unlimited enthusiasm. **—a•ban'don•ment** *n.*

a•ban•doned (ə-băn'dənd) *adj.* **1.** Forsaken. **2.** Recklessly unrestrained.

a•base (ə-bās') *v.* **a•based, a•bas•ing.** To lower in rank or prestige : humiliate. **—a•base'ment** *n.*

a•bash (ə-băsh') *v.* To embarrass : disconcert. **—a•bash'ment** *n.*

a•ba•sia (ə-bā'zhə) *n.* Dysfunction of muscular coordination in walking.

a•bate (ə-bāt') *v.* **a•bat•ed, a•bat•ing.** To decrease in amount, intensity, or degree. **—a•bat'a•ble** *adj.* **—a•bate'ment** *n.*

ab•at•toir (ăb'ə-twär') *n.* A slaughterhouse.

ab•bé (ăb'ā', ă-bā') *n.* The French title of an ecclesiastical figure.

ab•bess (ăb'ĭs) *n.* The superior of a convent.

ab•bey (ăb'ē) *n., pl.* **-beys.** **1.** A convent or monastery. **2.** An abbey church.

ab•bot (ăb'ət) *n.* The superior of a monastery.

abbr. *or* **abbrev.** *abbr.* abbreviation.

ab•bre•vi•ate (ə-brē'vē-āt') *v.* **-at•ed, -at•ing.** **1.** To shorten. **2.** To shorten (a word or phrase) to a form representing the entire word or phrase. **—ab•bre'vi•a'tion** *n.* **—ab•bre'vi•a'tor** *n.*

ABC (ā'bē'sē') *n., pl.* **ABC's.** **1.** *often* **ABC's.** The alphabet. **2. ABC's.** Fundamentals of reading and writing.

ab•di•cate (ăb'dĭ-kāt') *v.* **-cat•ed, -cat•ing.** To relinquish (power or responsibility) formally. **—ab'di•ca•ble** (-kə-bəl) *adj.* **—ab'di•ca'tion** *n.* **—ab'di•ca'tor** *n.*

ab•do•men (ăb'də-mən, ăb-dō'mən) *n.* **1.** The part of the mammalian body that is between the thorax and the pelvis and encloses the viscera. **2.** The major posterior part of an arthropod's body. **—ab•dom'i•nal** (-dŏm'ə-nəl) *adj.* **—ab•dom'i•nal•ly** *adv.*

ab•duct (ăb-dŭkt') *v.* To kidnap. **—ab•duc'tion** *n.* **—ab•duc'tor** *n.*

a•beam (ə-bēm') *adv.* At right angles to a ship's keel.

A•bel (ā'bəl). Son of Adam and Eve, killed by his brother, Cain.

a•bele (ə-bēl') *n.* A poplar, *Populis alba,* that has leaves with whitish undersides.

a•bed (ə-bĕd') *adv.* In bed.

Ab•er•deen An•gus (ăb'ər-dēn ăng'gəs) *n.* Any of a breed of black, hornless beef cattle orig. developed in Scotland.

ab•er•ra•tion (ăb'ə-rā'shən) *n.* **1.** A departure from the normal, usual, or expected. **2.** Mental disorder. **3.** Blurring or distortion of an image. **—ab•ber'rance, ab•ber'ran•cy** *n.* **—ab•er'rant** *adj.*

a•bet (ə-bĕt') *v.* **a•bet•ted, a•bet•ting.** To incite, encourage, or assist, esp. in wrongdoing. **—a•bet'ment** *n.* **—a•bet'tor, a•bet'ter** *n.*

a•bey•ance (ə-bā'əns) *n.* The state of being temporarily set aside : suspension. ☆**syns:** DORMANCY, INTERMISSION, LATENCY, QUIESCENCE, REMISSION, SUSPENSION **—a•bey'ant** *adj.*

ab•hor (ăb-hôr') *v.* **-horred, -hor•ring.** To consider with horror or disgust : loathe. **—ab•hor'rence** *n.* **—ab•hor'rer** *n.*

ab•hor•rent (ăb-hôr'ənt, -hŏr'-) *adj.* Disgusting : loathsome. **—ab•hor'rent•ly** *adv.*

a•bide (ə-bīd') *v.* **a•bode** (ə-bōd') *or* **a•bid•ed, a•bid•ing.** **1.** To tolerate : endure. **2.** To remain : stay. **3.** To dwell : sojourn. **—abide by.** To comply with <*abide* by her decision> **—a•bid'ance** *n.* **—a•bid'er** *n.*

a•bid•ing (ə-bī'ding) *adj.* Long-lasting : enduring <*abiding* love>

Ab•i•djan (ăb'ĭ-jän'). Cap. of Ivory Coast. *Pop.* 685,800.

a•bil•i•ty (ə-bĭl'ĭ-tē) *n., pl.* **-ties.** **1.** Physical or mental power to perform. **2.** A skill or talent. ☆**syns:** ADEPTNESS, COMMAND, CRAFT, EXPERTISE, EXPERTNESS, KNACK, KNOW-HOW, MASTERY, PROFICIENCY, SKILL

-ability or **-ibility** *suff.* Ability, inclination, or suitability for a specified action or condition <teach*ability*><wear*ability*>

ab in•i•ti•o (ăb' ĭ-nĭsh'ē-ō') *adv.* From the beginning.

ab•ject (ăb'jĕkt', ăb-jĕkt') *adj.* **1.** Contemptible : despicable <an *abject* coward> **2.** Miserable : wretched <*abject* poverty> **—ab'ject'ly** *adv.* **—ab•ject'ness, ab•jec'tion** *n.*

ab•jure (ăb-jŏŏr') *v.* **-jured, -jur•ing.** **1.** To recant solemnly : repudiate. **2.** To renounce under oath : forswear. **—ab'ju•ra'tion** *n.* **—ab•jur'er** *n.*

ab•la•tion (ă-blā'shən) *n.* **1.** Surgical removal of a body part. **2.** *Aerospace.* Dissipation of heat generated by atmospheric friction. **—ab•late'** *v.*

ab•la•tive (ăb'lə-tĭv) *adj.* Of or relating to a grammatical case designating separation, direction away from, and sometimes manner or agency, used in some Indo-European languages. **—ab'la•tive** *n.*

a•blaze (ə-blāz') *adj.* **1.** Being on fire : blazing. **2.** Radiantly bright : glowing.

a•ble (ā'bəl) *adj.* **a•bler, a•blest.** **1.** Having sufficient ability or resources. **2.** Capable or talented. **—a•ble•ness** *n.* **—a'bly** *adv.*

-able *or* **-ible** *suff.* **1.** Capable or worthy of undergoing a specified action <wash*able*> **2.** Inclined or given to a specified state <blam*able*>

a•ble-bod•ied (ā'bəl-bŏd'ēd) *adj.* Physically healthy and strong : sound.

able-bodied seaman *or* **able seaman** *n.* A seaman certified for all seaman's duties.

a•bloom (ə-blōōm') *adj.* Being in bloom : flowering.

ab•lu•tion (ə-blōō'shən) *n.* A cleansing of the body.

ABM (ā'bē-ĕm') *n.* Antiballistic missile.

ab•ne•ga•tion (ăb'nĭ-gā'shən) *n.* Self-denial : renunciation.

ab•nor•mal (ăb-nôr'məl) *adj.* Not normal : irregular. ☆**syns:**

ABERRANT, ANOMALOUS, ATYPICAL, DEVIANT, PRETERNATURAL, UNNATURAL **—ab′nor·mal′i·ty** (-măl′ĭ-tē) *n.* **—ab·nor′mal·ly** *adv.*

abnormal psychology *n.* Psychopathology.

a·board (ə-bôrd′, ə-bōrd′) *adv.* On board a passenger vehicle, as a ship, train, or aircraft. **—a·board′** *prep.*

a·bode (ə-bōd′) *n.* A habitation.

a·bol·ish (ə-bŏl′ĭsh) *v.* **1.** To put an end to. : annul. **2.** To destroy completely : annihilate. **—a·bol′ish·a·ble** *adj.* **—a·bol′ish·er** *n.* **—a·bol′ish·ment** *n.*

ab·o·li·tion (ăb′ə-lĭsh′ən) *n.* **1.** An abolishing. **2.** *often* **Abolition.** The prohibition of slavery in the U.S. **—ab′o·li′tion·ar′y** *adj.* **—ab·o·li·tion·ism** *n.* **—ab′o·li′tion·ist** *n.*

A-bomb (ā′bŏm′) *n.* An atomic bomb.

a·bom·i·na·ble (ə-bŏm′ə-nə-bəl) *adj.* Utterly loathsome : detestable. **—a·bom′i·na·bly** *adv.*

abominable snowman *n.* A hirsute manlike creature allegedly inhabiting the high Himalayas.

a·bom·i·nate (ə-bŏm′ə-nāt′) *v.* **-nat·ed, -nat·ing.** To regard as abominable : detest. **—a·bom′i·na′tion** *n.*

ab·o·rig·i·nal (ăb′ə-rĭj′ə-nəl) *adj.* **1.** Being of the earliest of its type : indigenous. **2.** Of or relating to aborigines. **—ab′o·rig′i·nal** *n.* **—ab′o·rig′i·nal·ly** *adv.*

ab·o·rig·i·ne (ăb′ə-rĭj′ə-nē) *n.* **1.** An indigenous inhabitant of a region. **2. aborigines.** The flora and fauna native to an area.

a·born·ing (ə-bôr′nĭng, -bōr′-) *adv.* While coming into being or getting started <a poem that died *aborning*>

a·bort (ə-bôrt′) *v.* **1.** To terminate or cause to terminate a pregnancy prematurely. **2.** To terminate (an operation or procedure) before completion. **—a·bort′** *n.*

a·bor·tion (ə-bôr′shən) *n.* **1.** Induced termination of pregnancy before the fetus can survive. **2.** A fatally premature expulsion of a fetus from the womb. **3.** Something malformed. **—a·bor′tive** *adj.* **—a·bor′tive·ly** *adv.* **—a·bor′tive·ness** *n.*

ABO system (ā′bē′ō′) *n.* The antigenic system of human blood, which, by functioning genetically as an allelic unit, produces the 4 human blood groups or types, A, B, AB, and O.

a·bound (ə-bound′) *v.* **1.** To be plentiful in amount. **2.** To be fully supplied : teem.

a·bout (ə-bout′) *adv.* **1.** Approximately <traveled *about* a year> **2.** Here and there. **3.** In the area : near. *—prep.* **1.** In reference to : concerning. **2.** Close or near to. **3.** Ready <*about* to begin> **4.** On all sides of : surrounding.

a·bout-face (ə-bout′fās′, ə-bout′fās′) *n.* A reversal of direction, attitude, or standpoint. **—a·bout′-face′** *v.*

a·bove (ə-bŭv′) *adv.* **1.** In or to a higher place or position. **2.** In an earlier part of a text. *—prep.* **1.** Over or higher than. **2.** Upstream or uphill from. **3.** Superior to. *—adj.* Appearing or stated earlier.

a·bove·board (ə-bŭv′bôrd′, -bōrd′) *adv.* & *adj.* Without trickery or deceit.

▲word history: *Aboveboard* is a compound of *above* and *board*. It is recorded as early as the 17th cent. as a gambler's term. If the gambler's hands were above the board or gaming table then presumably he could not surreptitiously change the cards or indulge in other forms of cheating.

abr. *abbr.* abridge; abridgment.

ab·ra·ca·dab·ra (ăb′rə-kə-dăb′rə) *n.* **1.** A magical word once held to avert disease or disaster. **2.** Nonsensical talk : gibberish.

a·brade (ə-brād′) *v.* **a·brad·ed, a·brad·ing. 1.** To rub off or wear away by friction : erode. **2.** To irritate. **—a·bra′sion** *n.*

A·bra·ham (ā′brə-hăm′). Hebrew patriarch.

a·bra·sive (ə-brā′sĭv, -zĭv) *adj.* **1.** Causing abrasion. **2.** Causing irritation <an *abrasive* voice> **—a·bra′sive** *n.* **—a·bra′sive·ly** *adv.* **—a·bra′sive·ness** *n.*

a·breast (ə-brĕst′) *adv.* & *adj.* **1.** Side by side <lined up four *abreast*> **2.** Up to date with <*abreast* of the news>

a·bridge (ə-brĭj′) *v.* **a·bridged, a·bridg·ing. 1.** To reduce the length of : condense <*abridge* a book> **2.** To diminish. **3.** To curtail. **—a·bridg′er** *n.* **—a·bridg′ment, a·bridge′ment** *n.*

a·broach (ə-brōch′) *adj.* **1.** Opened so that a liquid, as wine, can be let out. **2.** Moving about : astir.

a·broad (ə-brôd′) *adv.* & *adj.* **1.** In or to a foreign country. **2.** Covering a large area : widely. **3.** Away from one's home.

ab·ro·gate (ăb′rə-gāt′) *v.* **-gat·ed, -gat·ing.** To abolish or annul by authority : nullify. **—ab′ro·ga′tion** *n.*

a·brupt (ə-brŭpt′) *adj.* **1.** Unexpected : sudden. **2.** Rudely curt : brusque. **3.** Steep <an *abrupt* cliff> **—a·brupt′ly** *adv.* **—a·brupt′ness** *n.*

ab·scess (ăb′sĕs′) *n.* A localized collection of pus surrounded by inflammation.

ab·scis·sa (ăb-sĭs′ə) *n., pl.* **-sas** *or* **-scis·sae** (-sĭs′ē). The coordinate of a point from the *y*–axis measured along a line parallel to the x–axis.

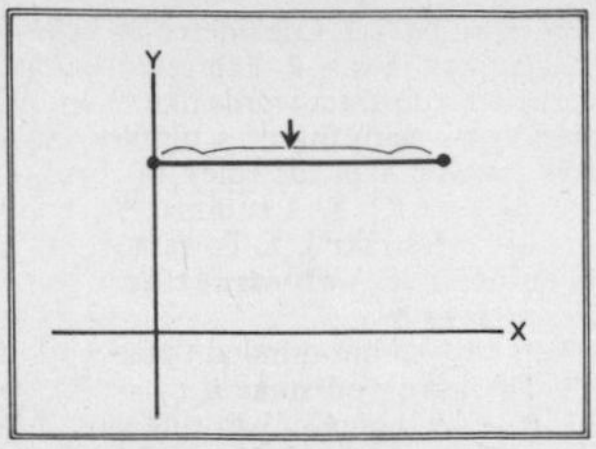

abscissa

ab·scis·sion (ăb-sĭzh′ən) *n.* **1.** An act of cutting off. **2.** The process by which plant parts are shed. **—ab·scise′** (-sīz′) *v.*

ab·scond (ăb-skŏnd′) *v.* To leave quickly and secretly and hide, esp. from the law.

ab·sence (ăb′səns) *n.* **1.** The condition or a period of being away. **2.** Lack <*abscence* of curiosity>

ab·sent (ăb′sənt) *adj.* **1.** Not present : missing. **2.** Not existent : lacking. **3.** Inattentive. *—v.* (ăb-sĕnt′). To keep (oneself) away. **—ab′sen·tee′** *n.* **—ab′sent·ly** *adv.*

ab·sen·tee·ism (ăb′sən-tē′ĭz′əm) *n.* Habitual failure to appear, esp. for work or school.

ab·sent-mind·ed (ăb′sənt-mīn′dĭd) *adj.* **1.** Preoccupied. **2.** Chronically forgetful. **—ab′sent-mind′ed·ly** *adv.* **—ab′sent-mind′ed·ness** *n.*

absent without leave *adj.* Absent without official permission from military duties but without the intention to desert.

ab·sinthe *also* **ab·sinth** (ăb′sĭnth) *n.* A liqueur flavored with anise and wormwood.

ab·so·lute (ăb′sə-lo͞ot′) *adj.* **1.** Perfect in nature or quality : complete. **2.** Not mixed : pure <*absolute* alcohol> **3. a.** Not limited by restrictions or exceptions : unconditional <*absolute* freedom> **b.** Not limited by constitutional provisions or other restraints <an *absolute* ruler> **4.** Positive : certain <*absolute* truth> **5.** *Physics.* **a.** Pertaining to measurements derived from basic relationships of space, mass, and time. **b.** Pertaining to absolute temperature. ☆***syns:*** ABSOLUTISTIC, ARBITRARY, AUTOCRATIC, DESPOTIC, DICTATORIAL, MONOCRATIC, TOTALITARIAN, TYRANNICAL **—ab′so·lute′ly** *adv.* **—ab′so·lute′ness** *n.*

absolute alcohol *n.* Ethyl alcohol with no more than 1% water.

absolute pitch *n.* **1.** The precise pitch of a tone as established by its frequency. **2.** The ability to remember the pitches of tones precisely and reliably.

absolute scale *n.* A scale of temperature with absolute zero as the minimum and scale units equal in magnitude to centigrade degrees.

absolute temperature *n.* Temperature measured on the absolute scale.

absolute value *n.* The numerical value or magnitude of a quantity, as of a negative integer, without regard to its sign.

absolute zero *n.* The temperature at which substances possess no thermal energy, equal to –273.15°C or –459.67°F.

ab·so·lu·tion (ăb′sə-lo͞o′shən) *n.* *Rom. Cath. Ch.* Formal remission of sin imparted by a priest.

ab·so·lut·ism (ăb′sə-lo͞o′tĭz′əm) *n.* Government in which all power is vested in a single ruler : despotism. **—ab′so·lut′ist** *n.* **—ab′so·lut·is′tic** *adj.*

ab·solve (ăb-zŏlv′, -sŏlv′) *v.* **-solved, -solv·ing. 1.** To clear of blame or guilt. **2.** To relieve of an obligation. **—ab·solv′a·ble** *adj.* **—ab·solv′er** *n.*

ab·sorb (ăb-sôrb′, -zôrb′) *v.* **1.** To take in : soak in or up. **2.** To assimilate <*absorbed* odd notions in childhood> **3.** *Chem. & Physics.* To retain wholly, without reflection or transmission, what is taken in. **4.** To occupy completely : engross. **—ab·sorb′a·bil′i·ty** *n.* **—ab·sorb′a·ble** *adj.* **—ab·sorb′er** *n.* **—ab·sorb′ing·ly** *adv.*

ab·sorb·ent (ăb-sôr′bənt, -zôr′-) *adj.* Capable of absorbing <*absorbent* cotton> **—ab·sorb′en·cy** *n.* **—ab·sorb′ent** *n.*

ab·sorp·tion (ăb-sôrp′shən, -zôrp′-) *n.* **1.** The act or process of absorbing. **2.** Mental concentration. **—ab·sorp′tive** *adj.*

absorption spectrum *n.* *Physics.* The spectrum of dark lines and bands observed when radiation traverses an absorbing medium.

ab·stain (ăb-stān′) *v.* To refrain from something voluntarily. **—ab·stain′er** *n.* **—ab·sten′tion** *n.*

ab·ste·mi·ous (ăb-stē′mē-əs) *adj.* Consuming food and drink in moderation : temperate. **—ab·ste′mi·ous·ly** *adv.* **—ab·ste′mi·ous·ness** *n.*

ab·sti·nence (ăb′stə-nəns) *n.* **1.** Denial of the appetites. **2.** Habitual abstaining from alcoholic beverages or specified foods. **—ab′sti·nent** *adj.* **—ab′sti·nent·ly** *adv.*

ab·stract (ăb'străkt', ăb-străkt') *adj.* **1.** Considered apart from concrete existence <an *abstract* idea> **2.** Expressed without reference to a specific instance <*abstract* words like "honesty" and "beauty"> **3.** Designating a painting or sculpture whose intellectual and affective content depends soley on intrinsic form : nonobjective. —*n.* (ăb'străkt'). **1.** A summary. **2.** Something abstract, as a term. —*v.* (ăb-străkt'). **1.** To remove. **2.** To steal. **3.** (ăb'străkt') To summarize. **—ab·stract'er** *n.* **—ab·stract'ly** *adv.* **—ab·stract'ness** *n.*
ab·stract·ed (ăb-străk'tĭd) *adj.* Absent-minded : preoccupied. **—ab·stract'ed·ly** *adv.* **—ab·stract'ed·ness** *n.*
abstract expressionism *n.* A school of painting that flourished after World War II until the early 1960's, marked by the exclusion of representational content. **—abstract expressionist** *n.*
ab·strac·tion (ăb-străk'shən) *n.* **1.** The act or process of separating or removing. **2.** An abstract idea. **3.** Preoccupation : absent-mindedness. **4.** An abstract work of art.
ab·struse (ăb-stro͞os') *adj.* Not easily understood : recondite. **—ab·struse'ly** *adv.* **—ab·struse'ness** *n.*
ab·surd (ăb-sûrd', -zûrd') *adj.* Ridiculously incongruous or unreasonable. —*n.* **1.** Existence in a meaningless and irrational universe in which an individual's life has no meaning or purpose. **2.** The literary genre dealing with the theme of an absurd universe. **—ab·surd'i·ty, ab·surd'ness** *n.* **—ab·surd'ly** *adv.*
▲word history: *Absurdus* in Latin meant "silly" and "irrational" just as *absurd* does in English, but its literal sense was "out of tune." It was used figuratively outside the realm of music and acoustics to mean "out of harmony with reason."
A·bu Dha·bi (ä'bo͞o dä'bē). Sheikdom in E. Arabia and cap. of United Arab Emirates. *Pop.* 347,000.
a·bu·li·a *also* **a·bou·li·a** (ə-bo͞o'lē-ə, ə-byo͞o'-) *n.* Impairment of the ability to act or decide independently. **—a·bu'lic** (-lĭk) *adj.*
a·bun·dant (ə-bŭn'dənt) *adj.* Plentifully supplied : rich <an *abundant* harvest> **—a·bun'dance** *n.* **—a·bun'dant·ly** *adv.*
a·buse (ə-byo͞oz') *v.* **a·bused, a·bus·ing. 1.** To use improperly : misuse. **2.** To maltreat. **3.** To assail with insults : revile. ☆**syns:** MISAPPLY, MISAPPROPRIATE, MISEMPLOY, MISUSE, PERVERT —*n.* (ə-byo͞os'). **1.** Improper use : misuse. **2.** Physical maltreatment. **3.** Coarse or insulting language. **—a·bus'er** *n.* **—a·bu'sive** *adj.* **—a·bu'sive·ly** *adv.* **—a·bu'sive·ness** *n.*
a·but (ə-bŭt') *v.* **a·but·ted, a·but·ting.** To border upon : adjoin. **—a·but'ter** *n.*
a·but·ment (ə-bŭt'mənt) *n.* A structure that supports, as at the end of a bridge.
a·bysm (ə-bĭz'əm) *n.* An abyss.
a·bys·mal (ə-bĭz'məl) *adj.* Immeasurably deep or extreme : profound <*abysmal* ignorance> **—a·bys'mal·ly** *adv.*
a·byss (ə-bĭs') *n.* **1. a.** The primeval chaos. **b.** The bottomless pit : hell. **2.** A yawning gulf. **3.** An immeasurably profound depth or void <vast *abysses* of the galaxies>
Ab·ys·sin·i·an cat (ăb'ĭ-sĭn'ē-ən) *n.* A short-haired cat with a reddish-brown coat tipped with black markings.
Ac *symbol for* ACTINIUM.
a·ca·cia (ə-kā'shə) *n.* A chiefly tropical tree of the genus *Acacia* with compound leaves and tight small yellow or white flower clusters.
acad. *abbr.* **1.** academic. **2.** academy.
ac·a·deme (ăk'ə-dēm') *also* **ac·a·de·mi·a** (-dē'mē-ə) *n.* **1.** The academic environment. **2.** Academic life.
ac·a·dem·ic (ăk'ə-dĕm'ĭk) *adj.* **1.** Of or relating to a school. **2.** Pertaining to liberal or classical rather than technical or vocational education. **3.** Not practical : theoretical. **—ac'a·dem'i·cal·ly** *adv.*
academic freedom *n.* Freedom to pursue and teach relevant knowledge without interference, as from public officials.
ac·a·dem·i·cism (ăk'ə-dĕm'ĭ-sĭz'əm) *also* **a·cad·e·mism** (ə-kăd'ə-mĭz'əm) *n.* Traditional formalism, particularly in art.
a·cad·e·my (ə-kăd'ə-mē) *n., pl.* **-mies. 1.** A school for a special field of study. **2.** A private secondary school. **3.** An association of scholars or artists. **—ac'a·de·mi'cian** (ăk'ə-də-mĭsh'ən) *n.*
a·can·thus (ə-kăn'thəs) *n.* **1.** A plant of the genus *Acanthus*, native to the Mediterranean region, with large thistlelike leaves. **2.** Ornamentation patterned after acanthus leaves.
A·ca·pul·co (ăk'ə-po͝ol'kō). City on the Pacific coast of S Mexico. *Pop.* 421,100.
a·cau·date (ā-kô'dāt') *also* **a·cau·dal** (ā-kôd'l) *adj.* Having no tail.
a cap·pel·la (ä' kə-pĕl'ə) *adv. Mus.* Without instrumental accompaniment <sing *a capella*>
ac·cede (ăk-sēd') *v.* **-ced·ed, -ced·ing. 1.** To give consent : agree. **2.** To come into a public office or dignity. **—ac·ced'ence** *n.*
ac·cel·er·an·do (ä-chĕl'ə-rän'dō, ăk-sĕl'ə-) *adv. Mus.* Gradually quickening in tempo. Used as a direction. **—ac·cel'er·an·do** *adj.* & *n.*
ac·cel·er·ate (ăk-sĕl'ə-rāt') *v.* **-at·ed, -at·ing. 1.** To increase the speed of. **2.** To bring about sooner. **—ac·cel·er·a'tion** *n.* **—ac·cel'er·a'tive** *adj.*
ac·cel·er·a·tor (ăk-sĕl'ə-rā'tər) *n.* **1.** A mechanical device, esp. the gas pedal of a vehicle, that increases speed. **2.** *Physics.* A device, such as an electrostatic generator or cyclotron, for accelerating charged particles.
ac·cel·er·om·e·ter (ăk-sĕl'ə-rŏm'ĭ-tər) *n.* A device for measuring acceleration.
ac·cent (ăk'sĕnt') *n.* **1.** Vocal stress or emphasis accorded a particular syllable, word, or phrase. **2.** A characteristic pronunciation <a British *accent*> **3.** A mark or symbol placed over a vowel in certain languages to indicate its quality. —*v.* **1.** To stress the pronunciation of. **2.** To stress : emphasize.
ac·cen·tu·ate (ăk sĕn'cho͞o-āt') *v.* **-at·ed, -at·ing. 1.** To pronounce with an accent. **2.** To emphasize. **—ac·cen'tu·a'tion** *n.*
ac·cept (ăk-sĕpt') *v.* **1.** To receive willingly. **2.** To admit to a group or place. **3.** To answer affirmatively <I *accept* your invitation.> **4.** To consent to pay, as by a signed agreement.
ac·cept·a·ble (ăk-sĕp'tə-bəl) *adj.* Adequate : satisfactory <an *acceptable* grade> **—ac·cept'a·bil'i·ty, ac·cept'a·ble·ness** *n.* **—ac·cept'a·bly** *adv.*
ac·cep·tance (ăk-sĕp'təns) *n.* **1. a.** The act or process of accepting. **b.** The state of being accepted or acceptable. **2.** An accepted time draft or bill of exchange.
ac·cep·ta·tion (ăk'sĕp-tā'shən) *n.* The usual or accepted meaning, as of a word.
ac·cess (ăk'sĕs') *n.* **1.** A means of approaching : passage. **2.** The right to enter or use <has *access* to official documents> **3.** A sudden outburst <an *access* of weeping>
ac·ces·si·ble (ăk-sĕs'ə-bəl) *adj.* **1.** Easily approached, entered, or obtainable. **2.** Susceptible <*accessible* to flattery> **—ac·ces'si·bil'i·ty** *n.* **—ac·ces'si·bly** *adv.*
ac·ces·sion (ăk-sĕsh'ən) *n.* **1.** The attainment of rank or dignity. **2. a.** An increase by means of something added. **b.** An addition. **—ac·ces'sion·al** *adj.*
ac·ces·so·ry *also* **ac·ces·sa·ry** (ăk-sĕs'ə-rē) *n., pl.* **-ries. 1.** A supplementary part : adjunct. **2.** Something nonessential but useful or decorative. **3.** One who aids or abets a lawbreaker in the commission of a crime but is not present at the time of the crime. **—ac·ces'so·ry** *adj.*
accessory fruit *n.* A fruit, as the pear, that develops from floral parts and the ovary.
access time *n. Computer Sci.* The time lag between a request for information stored in a computer and its delivery.
ac·ci·dence (ăk'sĭ-dəns, -dĕns') *n.* The section of morphology dealing with word inflections.
ac·ci·dent (ăk'sĭ-dənt, -dĕnt') *n.* **1.** An unexpected, undesirable event <a car *accident*> **2.** Something occurring unexpectedly or unintentionally. **3.** A nonessential circumstance or attribute. **4.** Fortune : chance.
ac·ci·den·tal (ăk'sĭ-dĕn'tl) *adj.* **1.** Occurring unexpectedly and unintentionally : by chance. **2.** Not intrinsic : nonessential. ☆**syns:** CASUAL, CHANCE, CONTINGENT, FLUKY, FORTUITOUS, INADVERTENT —*n. Mus.* A chromatically altered note not belonging to the key signature. **—ac'ci·den'tal·ly** *adv.*
ac·ci·dent-prone (ăk'sĭ-dənt-prōn') *adj.* Susceptible to having a greater than average number of accidents.
ac·cip·i·ter (ăk-sĭp'ĭ-tər) *n.* A hawk of the genus *Accipiter*, with a long tail and short wings. **—ac·cip'i·trine'** (-trīn', -trĭn) *adj.*

accipiter

ac·claim (ə-klām') *v.* **1.** To salute or hail : applaud. **2.** To shout approval. **—ac·claim'** *n.* **—ac·claim'er** *n.*
ac·cla·ma·tion (ăk'lə-mā'shən) *n.* **1.** An expression of enthusiastic approval. **2.** An oral vote, esp. an enthusiastic one of approval taken without formal ballot. **—ac·clam'a·to'ry** *adj.*

ac·cli·mate (ə-klī′mĭt, ăk′lə-māt′) *v.* **-mat·ed, -mat·ing.** To accustom or become accustomed to new surroundings or circumstances : adapt. **—ac′cli·ma′tion** *n.*
ac·cli·ma·tize (ə-klī′mə-tīz′) *v.* **-tized, -tiz·ing.** To acclimate. **—ac·cli′ma·tiz′er** *n.* **—ac·cli′ma·ti·za′tion** *n.*
ac·cliv·i·ty (ə-klĭv′ĭ-tē) *n., pl.* **-ties.** An upward slope.
ac·co·lade (ăk′ə-lād′, ăk′ə-läd′) *n.* **1.** An embrace of salutation. **2.** Approval : praise.
ac·com·mo·date (ə-kŏm′ə-dāt′) *v.* **-dat·ed, -dat·ing. 1.** To do a service for : oblige. **2.** To supply with (e.g., lodging). **3.** To have enough space for. **4.** To adapt : adjust. **5.** To reconcile, as differences : settle.
ac·com·mo·dat·ing (ə-kŏm′ə-dā′tĭng) *adj.* Willing to help. **—ac·com′mo·dat′ing·ly** *adv.*
ac·com·mo·da·tion (ə-kŏm′ə-dā′shən) *n.* **1.** The act of accommodating or the state of being accommodated. **2.** Something that fulfills a need : convenience. **3. accommodations.** Lodgings.
ac·com·pa·ni·ment (ə-kŭm′pə-nə-mənt, ə-kŭmp′nə-) *n.* **1.** Something that accompanies : concomitant. **2.** An embellishment : complement. **3.** *Mus.* An instrumental or vocal part that supports a solo part.
ac·com·pa·ny (ə-kŭm′pə-nē, ə-kŭmp′nē) *v.* **-nied, -ny·ing. 1.** To go with as a companion. **2.** To supplement. **3.** *Mus.* To play an accompaniment (for).
ac·com·plice (ə-kŏm′plĭs) *n.* One who aids and abets a lawbreaker in a criminal act.
ac·com·plish (ə-kŏm′plĭsh) *v.* To succeed in doing : achieve. ☆***syns:*** ACHIEVE, ATTAIN, REACH, REALIZE, SCORE **—ac·com′plish·a·ble** *adj.*
ac·com·plished (ə-kŏm′plĭsht) *adj.* **1.** Completed : finished. **2.** Skilled : expert. **3.** Socially adept : poised.
ac·com·plish·ment (ə-kŏm′plĭsh-mənt) *n.* **1.** The act of accomplishing or state of being accomplished. **2.** Something successfully achieved. **3.** Social poise.
ac·cord (ə-kôrd′) *v.* **1.** To cause to conform, agree, or harmonize. **2.** To grant : give. **3.** To be in agreement, unity, or harmony. *—n.* **1.** Agreement : harmony. **2. a.** Settlement of conflicting opinions. **b.** Settlement of points of issue between nations. **—of (one's) own accord.** Voluntarily. **—ac·cor′dance** *n.* **—ac·cor′dant** *adj.* **—ac·cor′dant·ly** *adv.*
ac·cord·ing·ly (ə-kôr′dĭng-lē) *adv.* **1.** Correspondingly. **2.** Consequently : therefore.
according to *prep.* **1.** On the authority of <*according to* informed sources> **2.** In keeping with <*according to* plan> **3.** As determined by <lined up *according to* height>
ac·cor·di·on (ə-kôr′dē-ən) *n.* A portable musical instrument with a small keyboard and free metal reeds that sound when air is forced past them by pleated bellows. **—ac·cor′di·on·ist** *n.*
ac·cost (ə-kôst′, ə-kŏst′) *v.* To approach and address first.
ac·couche·ment (ä′-ko͞osh-mäN′) *n.* Parturition.
†ac·count (ə-kount′) *n.* **1. a.** A narrative or record of events. **b.** A written or oral explanation. **2.** A detailed list. **3.** An exact list of monetary transactions. **4.** A business relationship involving the exchange of money or credit. *—v.* To consider or esteem. **—account for.** To explain. **—on account.** In partial payment for. **—on account of. 1.** Because of. **2.** *Regional.* Because.
ac·count·a·ble (ə-koun′tə-bəl) *adj.* Responsible : answerable. **—ac·count′a·bil′i·ty, ac·count′a·ble·ness** *n.* **—ac·count′a·bly** *adv.*
ac·count·ant (ə-koun′tənt) *n.* An expert in accounting. **—ac·count′an·cy** *n.*
account executive *n.* An advertising executive who manages client accounts.
ac·count·ing (ə-koun′tĭng) *n.* The bookkeeping methods involved in making a financial record of business transactions and in the preparation of statements concerning the assets, liabilities, and operating results of a business.
ac·cou·ter (ə-ko͞o′tər) *v.* To outfit and equip, as for military duty. **—ac·cou′ter·ments** *or* **ac·cou′tre·ments** *pl. n.*
ac·cou·tre (ə-ko͞o′tər) *v. esp. Brit. var. of* ACCOUTER.
Ac·cra (ăk′rə, ə-krä′). Cap. of Ghana. *Pop.* 633,800.
ac·cred·it (ə-krĕd′ĭt) *v.* **1.** To attribute to : credit. **2.** To certify as meeting a prescribed standard. **—ac·cred′i·ta′tion** *n.*
ac·cre·tion (ə-krē′shən) *n.* **1.** Growth or increase by gradual external accumulation. **2.** The product of accretion. **—ac·crete′** *v.* **—ac·cre′tion·ar′y, ac·cre′tive** *adj.*
accretion disk *n.* A ring of interstellar material surrounding a celestial object with an intense gravitational field, as a black hole.
ac·crue (ə-kro͞o′) *v.* **-crued, -cru·ing. 1.** To come to someone or something as a gain. **2.** To increase by regular growth, as interest on capital. **—ac·cru′al** *n.*
acct. account.
ac·cul·tur·ate (ə-kŭl′chə-rāt′) *v.* **-at·ed, -at·ing.** To change or cause to change by the process of acculturation.
ac·cul·tur·a·tion (ə-kŭl′chə-rā′shən) *n.* **1.** Modification of one culture as a result of contact with a different, esp. a more advanced, culture. **2.** The process by which the culture of a society is instilled from infancy onward.
ac·cu·mu·late (ə-kyo͞o′myə-lāt′) *v.* **-lat·ed, -lat·ing.** To amass or gather : mount up. **—ac·cu′mu·la·ble** *adj.* **—ac·cu′mu·la′tion** *n.* **—ac·cu′mu·la′tor** *n.*
ac·cu·rate (ăk′yər-ĭt) *adj.* Having no errors : correct. ☆***syns:*** CORRECT, EXACT, FAITHFUL, PRECISE, PROPER, RIGHT, TRUE, VERACIOUS, VERIDICAL. **—ac′cu·ra·cy, ac′cu·rate·ness** *n.* **—ac′cu·rate·ly** *adv.*
ac·curs·ed (ə-kûr′sĭd, ə-kûrst′) *also* **ac·curst** (ə-kûrst′) *adj.* **1.** Under a curse : doomed. **2.** Abominable : damnable. **—ac·curs′ed·ly** *adv.*
ac·cu·sa·tion (ăk′yo͞o-zā′shən) *n.* **1.** An act of accusing. **2.** An allegation. **3.** *Law.* A formal charge of a punishable offense brought before a court. ☆***syns:*** CHARGE, DENOUNCEMENT, DENUNCIATION, IMPUTATION, INCRIMINATION, INDICTMENT.
ac·cu·sa·tive (ə-kyo͞o′zə-tĭv) *adj.* Of or relating to the case of a noun, pronoun, adjective, or participle that is the direct object of a verb or the object of certain prepositions. *—n.* The accusative case.
▲word history: The connection between accusation and grammatical case is not immediately evident. The Latin verb *accusare,* the source of English *accuse,* means "to call to account," esp. in the sense of answering a legal charge. *Accusativus* is an adjective derived from *accusare,* and it is the source of English *accusative. Accusativus* at bottom means "pertaining to an accusation," and it seems an odd choice for the name of a grammatical category. But *accusativus,* which has only the grammatical, not the legal meaning in Latin, is a translation of the Greek word *aitiatikē,* which means both "causal" and "accusative," being itself derived from *aitia,* "accusation," "guilt," "cause." Thus the accusative case is the case of something caused or brought about by the verb.
ac·cuse (ə-kyo͞oz′) *v.* **-cused, -cus·ing. 1.** To charge with a shortcoming or error. **2.** To bring charges against. **—ac′cu·sa′tion** *n.* **—ac·cus′er** *n.* **—ac·cus′ing·ly** *adv.*
ac·cus·tom (ə-kŭs′təm) *v.* To familiarize, as by constant use, practice, or habit.
ac·cus·tomed (ə-kŭs′təmd) *adj.* Usual, characteristic, or normal.
AC/DC (ā′sē-dē′sē) *adj. Slang.* BISEXUAL 3.
ace (ās) *n.* **1.** A playing card, die, or domino with 1 spot. **2.** A point scored by one's opponent failing to return a serve in racket games. **3.** A military pilot who has shot down 5 or more enemy planes. **4.** An expert in a given field. *—v.* **aced, ac·ing.** To get the better of : surpass. **—ace in the hole.** A hidden advantage.
†a·ce·qui·a (ə-sā′kē-ə, ä-sä′-) *n. SW U.S.* An irrigation canal.
ac·er·ate (ăs′ə-rāt′) *also* **ac·er·at·ed** (-rā′tĭd) *adj. Biol.* Pointed at 1 end like a needle.
a·cerb (ə-sûrb′) *adj.* **1.** Having a bitter or sour taste. **2.** Sharp or bitter in temper, mood, or expression. **—a·cer′bi·ty** *n.*
ac·er·bate (ăs′ər-bāt′) *v.* **-bat·ed, -bat·ing.** To irritate : annoy.
ac·er·ose (ăs′ə-rōs′) *adj.* Sharp-pointed and slender, as a pine needle.
ac·e·tate (ăs′ĭ-tāt′) *n.* **1.** A salt or ester of acetic acid. **2.** Cellulose acetate or derivative products.
a·ce·tic (ə-sē′tĭk, ə-sĕt′ĭk) *adj.* Of, relating to, or containing acetic acid or vinegar.
acetic acid *n.* A clear, colorless organic acid with a pungent odor, used in making rubber, plastics, and photographic chemicals.
ac·e·tone (ăs′ĭ-tōn′) *n.* A colorless, volatile, highly flammable liquid used as a solvent.
a·cet·y·lene (ə-sĕt′l-ēn′, -ĭn) *n.* A colorless, extremely flammable or explosive gas used for metal welding.
a·ce·tyl·sal·i·cyl·ic acid (ə-sēt′l-săl′ĭ-sĭl′ĭk) *n.* Aspirin.
ache (āk) *v.* **ached, ach·ing. 1.** To suffer a dull, steady pain. **2.** *Informal.* To long for something : yearn. **—ach′i·ness** *n.* **—ache** *n.* **—ach′y** *adj.*
a·chieve (ə-chēv′) *v.* **a·chieved, a·chiev·ing.** To accomplish or attain by work or effort. **—a·chiev′a·ble** *adj.* **—a·chieve′ment** *n.* **—a·chiev′er** *n.*
A·chil·les (ə-kĭl′ēz) *n. Gk. Myth.* The hero of Homer's *Iliad.*
Achilles' heel *n.* A vulnerable point : weakness.
Achilles jerk *n.* Reflex plantar flexion in response to a blow to the Achilles tendon.
Achilles tendon *n.* The large tendon extending from the heel bone to the calf muscle of the leg.
ach·ro·mat·ic (ăk′rə-măt′ĭk) *adj.* **1.** Designating color, such

as a neutral gray, that has zero saturation and therefore no hue. **2.** Refracting light without spectral color separation. **—ach'ro·mat'i·cal·ly** *adv.* **—a·chro'ma·tism, ach'ro·ma·tic'i·ty** *n.*

a·chro·mic (ā-krō'mĭk) *adj.* Colorless.

ac·id (ăs'ĭd) *n.* **1.** *Chem.* Any of a large group of substances that when dissolved in water are capable of turning blue litmus to red, of reacting with a base to form water and a salt, and have a characteristic sour taste. **2.** A sour-tasting substance. **3.** *Slang.* LSD. *—adj.* **1.** *Chem.* Of or relating to an acid. **2.** Sour-tasting. **3.** Biting, sarcastic, or scornful <*acid* prose> **—a·cid'ic** (ə-sĭd'ĭk) *adj.* **—a·cid'i·ty, ac'id·ness** *n.* **—ac'id·ly** *adv.*

ac·id·head (ăs'ĭd-hĕd') *n.* *Slang.* A user of LSD.

a·cid·i·fy (ə-sĭd'ə-fī') *v.* **-fied, -fy·ing.** To make or become acid. **—a·cid'i·fi'a·ble** *adj.* **—a·cid'i·fi·ca'tion** *n.*

ac·i·do·sis (ăs'ĭ-dō'sĭs) *n.* An abnormal increase in the acidity of the blood. **—ac'i·dot'ic** (ăs'ĭ-dŏt'ĭk) *adj.*

acid precipitation *n.* Precipitation abnormally high in sulfuric and nitric acid content caused by industrial pollution.

acid rain *n.* Acid precipitation falling as rain.

acid rock *n.* Rock music with lyrics suggesting drug-related experiences.

acid test *n.* A decisive test.

a·cid·u·late (ə-sĭj'o͞o-lāt') *v.* **-lat·ed, -lat·ing.** To make or become somewhat acid. **—a·cid'u·la'tion** *n.*

a·cid·u·lous (ə-sĭj'ə-ləs, ə-sĭd'yə-) *adj.* Acid in taste or manner : caustic.

ack. *abbr.* acknowledge; acknowledgement.

ack-ack (ăk'ăk') *n.* *Slang.* **1.** An antiaircraft gun. **2.** Antiaircraft fire.

ac·knowl·edge (ăk-nŏl'ĭj) *v.* **-edged, -edg·ing. 1.** To admit the existence, reality, or truth of. **2. a.** To express recognition of <*acknowledged* our presence> **b.** To express gratitude for. **3.** To report the receipt of. ☆**syns:** ADMIT, ALLOW, AVOW, CONCEDE, CONFESS, GRANT *v.* **—ac·knowl'edge·a·ble** *adj.* **—ac·knowl'edg·ment, ac·knowl'edge·ment** *n.*

ac·knowl·edged (ăk-nŏl'ĭjd) *adj.* Commonly recognized or accepted.

a·clin·ic line (ā-klĭn'ĭk) *n.* The magnetic equator.

ac·me (ăk'mē) *n.* The point of attainment : peak.

ac·ne (ăk'nē) *n.* An inflammatory disease of the glands, causing pimples esp. on the face.

ac·o·lyte (ăk'ə-līt') *n.* **1.** One who assists a priest at Mass. **2.** An attendant or follower.

ac·o·nite (ăk'ə-nīt') *n.* **1.** The monkshood. **2.** The dried root of *Aconite napellus* used medicinally.

a·corn (ā'kôrn', ā'kərn) *n.* The nut of the oak tree, usu. set in a woody, cuplike base.

acorn squash *n.* An acorn-shaped squash with a ridged rind and yellow flesh.

a·cot·y·le·don (ā-kŏt'l-ēd'n) *n.* A plant, as a moss or fern, that does not have seed leaves. **—a·cot'y·le'don·ous** *adj.*

a·cous·tic (ə-ko͞o'stĭk) *also* **a·cous·ti·cal** (-stĭ-kəl) *adj.* **1.** Of or relating to sound, the sense of hearing, or the science of sound. **2. a.** Designed to aid in hearing. **b.** Absorbing sound <*acoustic* tile> **—a·cous'ti·cal·ly** *adv.*

a·cous·tics (ə-ko͞o'stĭks) *n.* **1.** (*sing. in number*). The scientific study of sound. **2.** (*pl. in number*). The total effect of sound, esp. in an enclosed space.

ac·quaint (ə-kwānt') *v.* To familiarize or inform <*acquainted* us with the facts>

ac·quain·tance (ə-kwān'təns) *n.* **1.** Knowledge or information. **2.** A person whom one knows. **—ac·quain'tance·ship'** *n.*

ac·qui·esce (ăk'wē-ĕs') *v.* **-esced, -esc·ing.** To comply without overt protest. **—ac'qui·es'cence** *n.* **—ac'qui·es'cent** *adj.* **—ac'qui·es'cent·ly** *adv.*

ac·quire (ə-kwīr') *v.* **-quired, -quir·ing. 1.** To secure possession or control of : get. **2.** To come to have <*acquire* immunity> **—ac·quir'a·ble** *adj.* **—ac·quire'ment** *n.*

acquired antibody *n.* An antibody produced by an immune response as compared with one occurring naturally.

acquired immune deficiency syndrome *n.* AIDS.

acquired immunity *n.* Immunity developed during a lifetime.

ac·qui·si·tion (ăk'wĭ-zĭsh'ən) *n.* **1.** The act of acquiring. **2.** Something acquired.

ac·quis·i·tive (ə-kwĭz'ĭ-tĭv) *adj.* Eager to gain and possess : greedy. **—ac·quis'i·tive·ly** *adv.* **—ac·quis'i·tive·ness** *n.*

ac·quit (ə-kwĭt') *v.* **-quit·ted, -quit·ting. 1.** To clear of a charge. **2.** To conduct (oneself). **—ac·quit'tal** *n.* **—ac·quit'ter** *n.*

a·cre (ā'kər) *n.* **1.** See MEASUREMENT TABLE. **2. acres.** Landed property : estate.

▲word history: The Old English word *æcer*, of which *acre* is the direct descendent, meant simply "field," esp. a field of cultivated land. The word acquired the meaning of "a unit of land measurement" because it was used specifically to mean a field as large as a man could plow in a day. The size of such a field was fixed during medieval times at 4,840 sq yd, which is still the size of a modern acre. Old English *æcer* is descended from the same Indo-European form as Latin *ager* and Greek *agros*, which both mean "field." The Modern English spelling comes from Old French *acre*, an alteration of the Latin form.

a·cre·age (ā'kər-ĭj) *n.* Area of land in acres.

ac·rid (ăk'rĭd) *adj.* **1.** Having a harsh taste or smell. **2.** Acrimonious : caustic. **—a·crid'i·ty** (ə-krĭd'ĭ-tē), **ac'rid·ness** *n.* **—ac'rid·ly** *adv.*

ac·ri·mo·ny (ăk'rə-mō'nē) *n.* Ill-natured animosity, esp. harshness in manner or tone. **—ac'ri·mo'ni·ous** *adj.* **—ac'ri·mo'ni·ous·ly** *adv.* **—ac'ri·mo'ni·ous·ness** *n.*

ac·ro·bat (ăk'rə-băt') *n.* One skilled in gymnastic feats. **—ac'ro·bat'ic** *adj.* **—ac'ro·bat'i·cal·ly** *adv.*

ac·ro·bat·ics (ăk'rə-băt'ĭks) *n.* (*sing. or pl. in number*). The feats of an acrobat.

ac·ro·meg·a·ly (ăk'rō-mĕg'ə-lē) *n.* Pathological enlargement of the bones of the hands, feet, and face. **—ac'ro·me·gal'ic** *adj.* & *n.*

ac·ro·nym (ăk'rə-nĭm') *n.* A word formed from the initial letters or parts of a series of words, as *radar* for *ra*dio *d*etecting *a*nd *r*anging.

ac·ro·pho·bi·a (ăk'rə-fō'bē-ə) *n.* Abnormal fear of heights.

a·crop·o·lis (ə-krŏp'ə-lĭs) *n.* The fortified height or citadel of an ancient Greek city, esp. the Athenian citadel.

a·cross (ə-krôs', ə-krŏs') *prep.* **1.** On, at, or from the other side of <*across* the road> **2.** So as to cross <draw a line *across* the paper> *—adv.* From one side to the other <The street was empty and I ran *across.*>

a·cross-the-board (ə-krôs'*th*ə-bôrd', -bōrd', ə-krŏs'-) *adj.* **1.** Designating win, place, or show in 1 bet on the same contestant. **2.** Including all categories or members.

a·cros·tic (ə-krô'stĭk, ə-krŏs'tĭk) *n.* A poem or series of lines in which certain letters in each line form a name, motto, etc.

a·cryl·ic (ə-krĭl'ĭk) *n.* **1.** Acrylic resin. **2.** Acrylic fiber. **3.** A paint containing acrylic resin.

acrylic fiber *n.* A synthetic fiber polymerized from acrylonitrile.

acrylic resin *n.* A thermoplastic used to produce synthetic rubbers and lightweight plastics.

ac·ry·lo·ni·trile (ăk'rə-lō-nī'trəl, -trēl', -trīl) *n.* A liquid organic compound used to make acrylic rubber and fibers.

act (ăkt) *n.* **1.** The process of doing : action. **2.** Something done : deed. **2. a.** A theatrical performance that forms part of a longer presentation. **b.** One of the major divisions of a play or opera. **3.** A manifestation of insincerity : pose. **4.** An enactment, as of a legislature. *—v.* **1.** To assume the dramatic role of <*acted* Hamlet> **2.** To conduct oneself : behave. **3.** To take action <We *acted* quickly.> **4.** To behave affectedly : pretend. **5.** To function : serve <a hedge *acting* as a windbreak> **6.** To take effect <hoped the pill would *act*> **—act up.** To misbehave or malfunction. **—act'a·bil'i·ty** *n.* **—act'a·ble** *adj.*

ACTH (ā'sē'tē-āch') *n.* A pituitary hormone used to stimulate secretion of adrenal cortex hormones, as cortisone : adrenocorticotropic hormone.

ac·tin (ăk'tĭn) *n.* A muscle protein active in muscular contraction.

act·ing (ăk'tĭng) *adj.* Temporarily assuming the authority, duties, or function of another. *—n.* The occupation or performance of an actor.

actinic ray *n.* Photochemically active radiation.

ac·ti·nide (ăk'tə-nīd') *n.* Any of a series of radioactive elements with atomic numbers ranging from 89 (actinium) through 103 (lawrencium).

ac·ti·nism (ăk'tə-nĭz'əm) *n.* The intrinsic property in radiation that produces photochemical activity. **—ac·tin'ic** *adj.* **—ac·tin'i·cal·ly** *adv.*

ac·tin·i·um (ăk-tĭn'ē-əm) *n.* *Symbol* **Ac** A highly radioactive metallic element found in uranium ores.

ac·tin·o·gen (ăk-tĭn'ō-jən) *n.* A radioactive element.

ac·ti·non (ăk'tə-nŏn') *n.* A radioactive inert gaseous isotope of radon.

ac·tion (ăk'shən) *n.* **1.** The process of acting or doing. **2.** An act or deed. **3.** A movement or sequence of movements. **4.** *often* **actions.** Behavior : conduct. **5.** The plot of a story or play. **6. a.** The operating parts of a mechanism. **b.** The way such parts operate. **7.** A lawsuit. **8.** Combat. **9.** Significant or exciting activity.

ac·tion·a·ble (ăk'shə-nə-bəl) *adj.* Giving cause for a legal suit or action. **—ac'tion·a·bly** *adv.*

ac·ti·vate (ăk'tə-vāt') *v.* **-vat·ed, -vat·ing. 1.** To set in motion. 2. To create or organize (e.g., a military unit). 3. To purify (sewage) by aeration. 4. *Chem.* To accelerate a reaction in. 5. *Physics.* To make (a substance) radioactive. **–ac′ti·va′tion** *n.* **–ac′ti·va′tor** *n.*

ac·tive (ăk′tĭv) *adj.* 1. In action : moving. 2. Capable of functioning. 3. Causing action or change. 4. Participating <take an *active* role> 5. In a state of action <an *active* geyser> 6. Marked by energy : lively. 7. Expressing action rather than a state of being <an *active* verb such as "run" or "speak"> **–ac′tive·ly** *adv.* **–ac′tive·ness** *n.*

active immunity *n.* Long-lasting immunity to a disease due to antibody production by the organism.

ac·tiv·ism (ăk′tĭv-ĭz′əm) *n.* The practice based on direct action to effect changes in social conditions, government, etc. **–ac′tiv·ist** *n.*

ac·tiv·i·ty (ăk-tĭv′ĭ-tē) *n., pl.* **-ties.** 1. The state of being active. 2. Energetic action. 3. A form of supervised action, as in education or recreation.

act of God *n. Law.* An unforeseeable occurrence caused by nature, as a flood.

ac·to·my·o·sin (ăk′tə-mī′ə-sĭn) *n.* A system of actin and myosin that is responsible for muscular expansion and contraction.

ac·tor (ăk′tər) *n.* 1. A theatrical performer. 2. A participant.

ac·tress (ăk′trĭs) *n.* A woman who is a theatrical performer.

Acts of the Apostles *pl.n.* (*sing. in number*). See BIBLE TABLE.

ac·tu·al (ăk′chōō-əl) *adj.* 1. Existing in fact or reality <*actual*, not ideal, conditions> 2. Existing or acting at the present moment : current. **–ac′tu·al′i·ty** *n.* **–ac′tu·al·i·za′tion** *n.* **–ac′tu·al·ize′** *v.* **–ac′tu·al·ly** *adv.*

ac·tu·ar·y (ăk′chōō-ĕr′ē) *n., pl.* **-ies.** A statistician who computes insurance risks and premiums. **–ac′tu·ar′i·al** *adj.*

ac·tu·ate (ăk′chōō-āt′) *v.* **-at·ed, -at·ing.** 1. To put into action or motion. 2. To stimulate : motivate. **–ac′tu·a′tion** *n.* **–ac′tu·a′tor** *n.*

ac·u·ate (ăk′yōō-āt′) *adj.* Pointed at the tip.

a·cu·i·ty (ə-kyōō′ĭ-tē) *n.* Perceptual keenness.

a·cu·men (ə-kyōō′mən, ăk′yə-) *n.* Accuracy and quickness of judgment.

ac·u·punc·ture (ăk′yŏŏ-pŭngk′chər) *n.* A traditional Chinese technique of puncturing the body with fine needles to treat disease or relieve pain.

a·cute (ə-kyōōt′) *adj.* 1. Sharply pointed. 2. Keenly perceptive or discerning : shrewd. 3. Sensitive. 4. Extremely serious or significant : crucial <an *acute* food shortage> 5. Extremely severe or sharp, as pain. 6. *Med.* Reaching a crisis rapidly. Used of a disease. 7. *Geom.* Describing angles less than 90°. **–a·cute′ly** *adv.* **–a·cute′ness** *n.*

acute accent *n.* A mark indicating: a. Primary stress of a spoken sound or syllable. b. Sound quality or vowel length.

ad (ăd) *n.* An advertisement.

A.D. *abbr. Lat.* anno Domini (in the year of the Lord); usu. small capitals A.D.

ad·age (ăd′ĭj) *n.* A short maxim : proverb.

a·da·gio (ə-dä′jō, -jē-ō′) *adv.* Slowly. Used as a musical direction. *–adj.* Slower than andante in tempo. *–n., pl.* **-gios.** 1. An adagio movement in music. 2. The slow section of a pas de deux in ballet.

Ad·am (ăd′əm) *n.* The 1st man and progenitor of humankind as described in the Old Testament.

ad·a·mant (ăd′ə-mənt, -mănt′) *n.* A legendary stone thought to be impenetrable. *–adj.* Resolute : unyielding. **–ad′a·mant·ly** *adv.*

Ad·ams (ăd′əmz). 1. **John.** 1735–1826. 2nd U.S. President (1797–1801). 2. **John Quincy.** 1767–1848. 6th U.S. President (1825–29). **–Ad′am·so′ni·an** *adj.*

Adam's apple *n.* The projection of the largest laryngeal cartilage at the front of the throat, esp. in men.

a·dapt (ə-dăpt′) *v.* To adjust or become adjusted to a specified use or situation. **–a·dapt′a·bil′i·ty, a·dapt′a·ble·ness** *n.* **–a·dapt′a·ble** *adj.*

ad·ap·ta·tion (ăd′ăp-tā′shən) *n.* 1. a. The state of being adapted. b. The process of adapting. 2. An adjustment. **–ad′ap·ta′tion·al** *adj.* **–ad′ap·ta′tion·al·ly** *adv.*

a·dapt·er *also* **a·dap·tor** (ə-dăp′tər) *n.* A device used to effect operative compatability between different parts of an apparatus.

a·dap·tive (ə-dăp′tĭv) *adj.* Capable of adapting. **–a·dap′tive·ly** *adv.* **–a·dap′tive·ness** *n.*

adaptive radiation *n.* The evolution of a relatively unspecialized species into several related species characterized by different specializations that fit them for life in various environments.

add (ăd) *v.* 1. To unite or join so as to increase in size, quantity, or scope : append. 2. To combine (e.g., a column of figures) to form a sum. 3. To say or write further. **–add up.** To be reasonable : make sense. **–add up to.** To mean : indicate.

add. *abbr.* 1. addendum. 2. addition; additional. 3. address.

ad·dax (ăd′ăks′) *n.* An antelope, *Addax nasomaculatus,* of Africa, with spirally twisted horns.

add·ed-val·ue tax (ăd′ĭd-văl′yōō) *n.* Value-added tax.

ad·dend (ăd′ĕnd′, ə-dĕnd′) *n.* Any of a set of numbers to be added.

ad·den·dum (ə-dĕn′dəm) *n., pl.* **-da** (-də). Something added, esp. a supplement to a book.

add·er[1] (ăd′ər) *n.* One that adds, esp. a computer device that performs arithmetic addition.

ad·der[2] (ăd′ər) *n.* 1. Any of various Old World snakes of the family Viperidae. 2. Any of several nonvenomous snakes of North America.

ad·dict (ə-dĭkt′) *v.* To surrender (oneself) habitually or compulsively to something, as caffeine or alcohol. *–n.* (ăd′ĭkt). One who is addicted, esp. to narcotics. **–ad·dic′tion** *n.* **–ad·dic′tive** *adj.*

Ad·dis Ab·a·ba (ăd′dĭs ä′bə-bä, ăd′ĭs ăb′ə-bə). Cap. of Ethiopia *Pop.* 1,125,340.

ad·di·tion (ə-dĭsh′ən) *n.* 1. The act or process of adding. 2. Something added. 3. The process of combining sets of numbers to find their sum. **–in addition.** As well as : also. **–in addition to.** Besides. **–ad·di′tion·al** *adj.* **–ad·di′tion·al·ly** *adv.*

ad·di·tive (ăd′ĭ-tĭv) *adj.* Involving addition. *–n.* A substance added in smallish amounts to something else to alter it.

ad·dle (ăd′l) *v.* **-dled, -dling.** 1. To make or become confused. 2. To become rotten, as an egg.

ad·dress (ə-drĕs′) *v.* 1. To speak to. 2. To make a formal speech to. 3. To mark with a destination <*address* an envelope> 4. To direct the efforts or attention of (oneself). *–n.* 1. A spoken or written communication. 2. A speech. 3. (*also* ăd′rĕs′). The location of a person or organization. 4. (*also* ăd′res′). The indication of destination, as on mail or parcels. 5. *Computer Sci.* A number in information storage or retrieval assigned to a specific memory location. 6. Skillfulness. **–ad′dress·ee′** *n.*

ad·duce (ə-dōōs′, ə-dyōōs′, ă-) *v.* **-duced, -duc·ing.** To give or offer as an example or means of proof. ☆**syns:** ADVANCE, CITE, LAY, PRESENT

-ade *suff.* 1. A sweetened beverage <lime*ade*> 2. The act of <block*ade*>

A·dé·lie penguin (ə-dā′lē) *n.* A common, medium-sized Antarctic penguin, *Pygoscelis adeliae.*

A·den (äd′n, ād′n). Cap. of Southern Yemen, on NW shore of the **Gulf of Aden.** *Pop.* 264,326.

ad·e·nine (ăd′n-ēn′, -ĭn) *n.* A purine derivative that is a constituent of nucleic acid in organs such as the spleen and pancreas.

ad·e·noid (ăd′n-oid′) *n. often* **adenoids.** Lymphoid tissue growths in the nose above the throat. **–ad′e·noid′, ad′e·noi′dal** *adj.*

a·den·o·sine (ə-dĕn′ə-sēn′) *n.* An organic compound that is a structural component of nucleic acids.

adenosine di·phos·phate (dī-fŏs′fāt′) *n.* ADP.

adenosine mon·o·phos·phate (mŏn′ō-fŏs′fāt′) *n.* AMP.

adenosine tri·phos·phate (trī-fŏs′fāt′) *n.* ATP.

a·dept (ə-dĕpt′) *adj.* Highly skilled : expert. *–n.* (ăd′ĕpt′). A highly skilled person. **–a·dept′ly** *adv.* **–a·dept′ness** *n.*

ad·e·quate (ăd′ĭ-kwĭt) *adj.* 1. Able to fill a requirement. 2. Barely sufficient or satisfactory. **–ad′e·qua·cy, ad′e·quate·ness** *n.* **–ad′e·quate·ly** *adv.*

à deux (ä′ dœ′) *adj.* Involving 2 individuals, esp. in private <a picnic *à deux*>

ad·here (ăd-hîr′) *v.* **-hered, -her·ing.** 1. To stick fast or together : cling. 2. To support or be devoted to. 3. To follow without deviation. **–ad·her′ence** *n.* **–ad·her′ent** *adj. & n.*

ad·he·sion (ăd-hē′zhən) *n.* 1. The act or state of adhering. 2. An abnormal condition in which bodily tissues are united by fibrous tissue.

ad·he·sive (ăd-hē′sĭv) *adj.* 1. Tending to adhere : sticky. 2. Made so as to adhere. **–ad·he′sive** *n.* **–ad·he′sive·ly** *adv.* **–ad·he′sive·ness** *n.*

ad hoc (ăd hŏk′) *adj. & adv.* For a specific case, situation, or purpose <formed an *ad hoc* committee>

ad hom·i·nem (ăd hŏm′ə-nĕm′) *adj. & adv.* Appealing to prejudice or emotion rather than reason <an *ad hominem* debate>

ad·i·a·bat·ic (ăd′ē-ə-băt′ĭk, ī′dī-ə-) *adj.* Of, pertaining to, or designating a reversible thermodynamic process executed at constant entropy. **–ad′i·a·bat′i·cal·ly** *adv.*

a·dieu (ə-dōō′, ə-dyōō′) *interj.* Good-by. *–n., pl.* **a·dieus** or **a·dieux** (ə-dōōz′, ə-dyōōz′). A farewell.

ad in•fi•ni•tum (ăd ĭn′fə-nī′təm) *adj. & adv.* Without limit or end : forever.

a•di•os (ä′dē-ōs′, ăd′ē-) *interj.* Good-by.

ad in•ter•im (ăd ĭn′tər-əm) *adj. & adv.* In the meantime.

ad•i•pose (ăd′ə-pōs′) *adj.* Of or pertaining to animal fat : fatty. **—ad′i•pos′i•ty** (-pŏs′ĭ-tē) *n.*

Ad•i•ron•dack Mountains (ăd′ə-rŏn′dăk′). Range of the Appalachian system in NE N.Y.

adj. *abbr.* **1.** adjacent. **2.** adjective. **3.** adjourned. **4.** adjunct.

ad•ja•cent (ə-jā′sənt) *adj.* **1.** Close to : nearby <the house and *adjacent* pond> **2.** Next to : adjoining. ☆***syns:*** ABUTTING, ADJOINING, BORDERING, CONTIGUOUS, JUXTAPOSED, MEETING, TOUCHING **—ad•ja′cen•cy** *n.* **—ad•ja′cent•ly** *adv.*

adjacent angle *n.* Either of 2 angles having a common side and a common vertex.

ad•jec•tive (ăj′ĭk-tĭv) *n.* A word used to describe a noun or limit its meaning. **—ad′jec•ti′val** (-tī′vəl) *adj.* **—ad′jec•ti′val•ly** *adv.*

ad•join (ə-join′) *v.* **1.** To be next to. **2.** To be in or nearly in contact.

ad•join•ing (ə-joi′nĭng) *adj.* Bordering : contiguous.

ad•journ (ə-jûrn′) *v.* **1.** To suspend until a later stated time or indefinitely. **2.** To move from one location to another. **—ad•journ′ment** *n.*

ad•judge (ə-jŭj′) *v.* **-judged, -judg•ing. 1.** To determine by judicial procedure : adjudicate. **2.** To regard or consider.

ad•ju•di•cate (ə-jo͞o′dĭ-kāt′) *v.* **-cat•ed, -cat•ing.** To hear, determine, and settle (a case) by judicial procedure. **—ad•ju′di•ca′tion** *n.* **—ad•ju′di•ca′tive** *adj.* **—ad•ju′di•ca′tor** *n.*

ad•junct (ăj′ŭngkt′) *n.* One connected to another in a dependent or subordinate position.

ad•jure (ə-jo͝or′) *v.* **-jured, -jur•ing.** To command solemnly : ask urgently. **—ad′ju•ra′tion** *n.*

ad•just (ə-jŭst′) *v.* **1.** To alter to match or fit. **2.** To bring into correct relationship. **3.** To conform or adapt. **4.** To make accurate by regulating. **5.** To settle (a claim or debt). ☆***syns:*** ATTUNE, FIX, REGULATE, SET **—ad•just′a•ble** *adj.* **—ad•just′er, ad•jus′tor** *n.* **—ad•just′ment** *n.*

ad•ju•tant (ăj′ə-tənt) *n.* **1.** An administrative staff officer who assists a commanding officer. **2.** An assistant. **3.** The marabou. **—ad′ju•tan•cy** *n.*

ad lib (ăd lĭb′) *adv.* In an improvisatory manner : spontaneously.

ad-lib (ăd-lĭb′) *v.* **-libbed, -lib•bing.** *Informal.* To improvise and deliver extemporaneously. **—ad-lib′** *n. & adj.*

ad loc. *abbr. Lat.* ad locum (or at the place).

ad•man (ăd′măn′) *n. Informal.* A person in the advertising business.

admin. *abbr.* administration; administrator.

ad•min•is•ter (ăd-mĭn′ĭ-stər) *v.* **1.** To direct : manage. **2. a.** To give as a remedy <*administer* a tranquilizer> **b.** To give (e.g., a sacrament) formally. **3.** To mete out. **4.** To tender (e.g., an oath). **5.** To manage or dispose of (a trust or estate). ☆***syns:*** ADMINISTRATE, DIRECT, GOVERN, HEAD, MANAGE, RUN, SUPERINTEND **—ad•min′is•trant** *n. & adj.*

ad•min•is•trate (ăd-mĭn′ĭ-strāt′) *v.* **-trat•ed, -trat•ing, -trates.** To administer.

ad•min•is•tra•tion (ăd-mĭn′ĭ-strā′shən) *n.* **1.** The act of administering. **2.** Management. **3.** *often* **Administration.** The executive branch of a government. **4.** The term of office of an executive officer or body. **5.** *Law.* The managing of a trust or estate. **—ad•min′is•tra′tive** *adj.* **—ad•min′is•tra′tive•ly** *adv.*

ad•min•is•tra•tor (ăd-mĭn′ĭ-strā′tər) *n.* **1.** One who administers : executive. **2.** *Law.* One who administers an estate.

ad•mi•ra•ble (ăd′mər-ə-bəl) *adj.* Worthy of admiration. ☆***syns:*** COMMENDABLE, ESTIMABLE, LAUDABLE, MERITORIOUS, PRAISEWORTHY **—ad′mi•ra•ble•ness** *n.* **—ad′mir•a•bly** *adv.*

ad•mi•ral (ăd′mər-əl) *n.* **1.** The commander in chief of a fleet or navy. **2.** An Admiral of the Fleet. **3.** A naval officer of the next to the highest rank.

Admiral of the Fleet *n.* The highest rank in the U.S. Navy.

ad•mi•ral•ty (ăd′mər-əl-tē) *n., pl.* **-ties. 1.** A court exercising jurisdiction over maritime cases. **2. Admiralty.** The department of the British government that formerly controlled naval affairs.

†ad•mire (ăd-mīr′) *v.* **-mired, -mir•ing. 1.** To regard with wonder and delighted approval. **2.** To have a high opinion of : esteem. **3.** *Regional.* To be pleased. **—ad′mi•ra′tion** (-mə-rā′shən) *n.* **—ad•mir′er** *n.* **—ad•mir′ing•ly** *adv.*

ad•mis•si•ble (ăd-mĭs′ə-bəl) *adj.* Capable of being accepted or allowed. **—ad•mis′si•bil′i•ty, ad•mis′si•ble•ness** *n.*

ad•mis•sion (ăd-mĭsh′ən) *n.* **1.** The act of admitting or the state of being admitted. **2.** A confession of wrongdoing. **3.** The right to enter : access. **4.** An entrance fee. **—ad•mis′sive** *adj.*

ad•mit (ăd-mĭt′) *v.* **-mit•ted, -mit•ting. 1.** To allow to enter. **2.** To serve as an entrance. **3.** To accommodate <The room *admits* 45.> **4.** To afford possibility for : allow <a question that *admits* of more than one answer> **5.** To acknowledge or confess <*admit* the truth> **6.** To concede <had to *admit* we were wrong>

ad•mit•tance (ăd-mĭt′ns) *n.* Permission to enter. **—ad•mit′ted•ly** *adv.*

ad•mix•ture (ăd-mĭks′chər) *n.* **1.** A combination, mixture, or blend. **2.** Something added in mixing. **—ad•mix′** *v.*

ad•mon•ish (ăd-mŏn′ĭsh) *v.* **1.** To reprove mildly but seriously. **2.** To warn against something : caution. ☆***syns:*** REBUKE, REPRIMAND, REPROACH, REPROVE **—ad•mon′ish•er** *n.* **—ad′mo•ni′tion, ad•mon′ish•ment** *n.* **—ad•mon′i•to′ry** *adj.*

ad nau•se•am (ăd nô′zē-əm) *adv.* To a sickening or ridiculous degree <rambled on *ad nauseam*>

ad•noun (ăd′noun′) *n.* An adjective used as a noun, as in *the bold and the brave.* **—ad•nom′i•nal** (ăd-nŏm′ə-nəl) *adj.*

a•do (ə-do͞o′) *n.* Fuss.

a•do•be (ə-dō′bē) *n.* **1.** A sun-dried brick of clay and straw. **2.** Clay from which these bricks are made. **3.** A structure of adobe.

ad•o•les•cence (ăd′l-ĕs′əns) *n.* The period of physical and psychological development between puberty and maturity. **—ad′o•les′cent** *n. & adj.*

A•don•is (ə-dŏn′ĭs, ə-dō′nĭs) *n.* **1.** *Gk. Myth.* A youth loved by Aphrodite. **2. adonis.** A very handsome young man.

a•dopt (ə-dŏpt′) *v.* **1.** To take (a child) into one's family legally and raise as one's own. **2.** To take and follow by choice or assent. **3.** To vote to accept <*adopt* a proposal> **4.** To take up and make one's own, as an idea. **—a•dopt′a•ble** *adj.* **—a•dopt′er** *n.* **—a•dop′tion** *n.*

a•dop•tive (ə-dŏp′tĭv) *adj.* Acquired by adoption <*adoptive* parents> **—a•dop′tive•ly** *adv.*

a•dor•a•ble (ə-dôr′ə-bəl, ə-dōr′-) *adj.* **1.** *Informal.* Charming : delightful. **2.** *Archaic.* Worthy of adoration. **—a•dor′a•bil′i•ty, a•dor′a•ble•ness** *n.* **—a•dor′a•bly** *adv.*

a•dore (ə-dôr′, ə-dōr′) *v.* **a•dored, a•dor•ing. 1.** To worship as divine. **2.** To love or revere deeply. **3.** *Informal.* To like a lot. **—ad′o•ra′tion** *n.* **—a•dor′er** *n.* **—a•dor′ing•ly** *adv.*

a•dorn (ə-dôrn′) *v.* **1.** To decorate with or as if with ornaments. **2.** To enhance. **—a•dorn′ment** *n.*

ADP (ā′dē′pē′) *n.* An ester that is an adenosine derivative formed in cells and converted to ATP for the storage of energy.

ad rem (ăd rĕm′) *adj.* Relevant to the point at issue : pertinent. **—ad rem** *adv.*

a•dre•nal (ə-drē′nəl) *adj.* Of or relating to the adrenal glands or their secretions.

adrenal gland *n.* Either of 2 endocrine glands above each kidney.

A•dren•a•lin (ə-drĕn′ə-lĭn). A trademark for a preparation of adrenaline.

a•dren•a•line (ə-drĕn′ə-lĭn) *n.* Epinephrine.

ad•re•no•cor•ti•co•trop•ic hormone (ə-drē′nō-kôr′tĭ-kō-trŏp′ĭk, -trō′pĭk) *also* **ad•re•no•cor•ti•co•troph** (ə-drē′nō-kôr′tĭ-kō′trōf) *or* **ad•re•no•cor•ti•co•tro•phin** (-kôr′tĭ-kō-trō′fən) *n.* ACTH.

A•dri•a•tic Sea (ā′drē-ăt′ĭk). Arm of the Mediterranean between Italy and the Balkan Peninsula.

a•drift (ə-drĭft′) *adv. & adj.* **1.** Without being anchored. **2.** Without purpose.

a•droit (ə-droit′) *adj.* **1.** Dexterous : deft. **2.** Skillful and adept, esp. in difficult circumstances. **—a•droit′ly** *adv.* **—a•droit′ness** *n.*

ad•sorb (ăd-sôrb′, -zôrb′) *v.* To collect and hold (gas or vapor) on the surface of a solid. **—ad•sorp′tion** *n.* **—ad•sorp′tive** *adj.*

ad•u•late (ăj′o͝o-lāt′) *v.* **-lat•ed, -lat•ing.** To praise excessively or servilely. **—ad′u•la′tion** *n.* **—ad′u•la′tor** *n.* **—ad′u•la•to′ry** (-lə-tôr′ē, -tōr′ē) *adj.*

a•dult (ə-dŭlt′, ăd′ŭlt′) *n.* One who has attained maturity or legal age. —*adj.* **1.** Mature. **2.** Intended for or befitting mature persons. **—a•dult′hood′** *n.*

a•dul•ter•ate (ə-dŭl′tə-rāt′) *v.* **-at•ed, -at•ing.** To make impure, spurious, or inferior by adding improper ingredients. **—a•dul′ter•ant** *n. & adj.* **—a•dul′ter•a′tion** *n.* **—a•dul′ter•a′tor** *n.*

a•dul•ter•y (ə-dŭl′tə-rē, -trē) *n., pl.* **-ries.** Voluntary sexual intercourse between a married person and a partner other than the lawful spouse. **—a•dul′ter•er** *n.* **—a•dul′ter•ess** *n.* **—a•dul′ter•ous** *adj.* **—a•dul′ter•ous•ly** *adv.*

ad•um•brate (ăd′əm-brāt′, ə-dŭm′-) *v.* **-brat•ed, -brat•ing. 1.** To give a sketchy outline of. **2.** To give signs of in advance.

☆**syns:** FORESHADOW, PREFIGURE, PRESAGE **—ad'um·bra'tion** *n.* **—ad·um'bra·tive** (-brə-tĭv) *adj.*

a·dust (ə-dŭst') *adj.* **1.** Burned. **2.** Melancholy.
▲word history: *Adust,* which has etymologically nothing to do with *dust,* acquired the meaning "burned" directly from its Latin source but came to mean "melancholy" through its use in early medical writings. Dryness, heat, and a burnt color of the body and its components, like the blood, certain organs, and the skin, were considered symptoms of a melancholy temperament.

adv. *abbr.* adverb; adverbial.

adv. or **advt.** *abbr.* advertisement.

ad va·lo·rem (ăd' və-lôr'əm, -lōr'-) *adj.* According to the value <*ad valorem* taxes on imported goods>

ad·vance (ăd-văns') *v.* **-vanced, -vanc·ing. 1.** To move or cause to move forward. **2.** To propose. **3.** To aid the progress of. **4.** To promote. **5.** To make occur sooner : hasten. **6.** To raise in rate or amount. **7.** To pay (e.g., money) before legally due. *—n.* **1.** The act or process of moving forward. **2.** Progress or improvement. **3.** An increase in price or value. **4. advances.** Personal approaches to gain favor, acquaintance, or an agreement. **5.** Money paid before it is legally due. *—adj.* **1.** Made or given ahead of time : prior. **2.** Going before. **—advance on** (or **upon**). To move against. **—in advance. 1.** In front. **2.** Ahead of time. **—ad·vance'ment** *n.*

ad·vanced (ăd-vănst') *adj.* **1.** Highly developed : complex <*advanced* technology> **2.** At a higher level <*advanced* studies> **3.** Progressive <*advanced* ideas> **4.** Far along in course or age <an *advanced* illness><*advanced* years>

ad·van·tage (ăd-văn'tĭj) *n.* **1.** A factor conducive to success. **2.** Profit or benefit : gain. **3.** The 1st point scored in tennis after deuce. **—take advantage of. 1.** To put to good use. **2.** To exploit. **—ad'van·ta'geous** *adj.* **—ad'van·ta'geous·ly** *adv.* **—ad'van·ta'geous·ness** *n.*

ad·vent (ăd'vĕnt') *n.* **1.** Arrival, esp. of something momentous. **2. Advent. a.** The coming or birth of Christ. **b.** The period of 4 Sundays before Christmas.

ad·ven·ti·tious (ăd'vĕn-tĭsh'əs) *adj.* Acquired by accident : not inherent. **—ad'ven·ti'tious·ly** *adv.* **—ad'ven·ti'tious·ness** *n.*

ad·ven·ture (ăd-vĕn'chər) *n.* **1.** A hazardous undertaking. **2.** An unusual and suspenseful experience. ☆**syns:** EMPRISE, ENTERPRISE, VENTURE *—v.* **-tured, -tur·ing.** To take risks : dare. **—ad·ven'ture·some** *adj.* **—ad·ven'tur·ous** *adj.* **—ad·ven'tur·ous·ly** *adv.* **—ad·ven'tur·ous·ness** *n.*

ad·ven·tur·er (ăd-vĕn'chər-ər) *n.* **1.** One who adventures. **2.** A soldier of fortune. **3.** One who unscrupulously seeks wealth and social position. **—ad·ven'tur·ess** *n.*

ad·verb (ăd'vûrb') *n.* A word used to modify a verb, an adjective, or another adverb. **—ad·ver'bi·al** *adj.* **—ad·ver'bi·al·ly** *adv.*

ad·ver·sar·y (ăd'vər-sĕr'ē) *n., pl.* **-ies.** One who opposes, esp. with animosity.

ad·ver·sa·tive (ăd-vûr'sə-tĭv) *adj.* Expressing antithesis or opposition <the *adversative* conjunction "but"> **—ad·ver'sa·tive** *n.* **—ad·ver'sa·tive·ly** *adv.*

ad·verse (ăd-vûrs', ăd'vûrs') *adj.* **1.** Actively opposed : antagonistic. **2.** Unfavorable : unpropitious. **—ad·verse'ly** *adv.*

ad·ver·si·ty (ăd-vûr'sĭ-tē) *n., pl.* **-ties. 1.** Great affliction or hardship. **2.** A misfortune.

ad·vert (ăd-vûrt') *v.* To allude or refer.

ad·ver·tise (ăd'vər-tīz') *v.* **-tised, -tis·ing. 1.** To call public attention to, esp. to increase sales <*advertise* a new product> **2.** To make gen. known. **—ad'ver·tis'er** *n.*

ad·ver·tise·ment (ăd'vər-tīz'mənt, ădvûr'tĭs-mənt, -tĭz-) *n.* A notice designed to advertise something.

ad·ver·tis·ing (ăd'vər-tī'zĭng) *n.* **1.** The business of the preparation and distribution of advertisements. **2.** Advertisements as a whole.

ad·vice (ăd-vīs') *n.* Counsel about a course of action : guidance.

ad·vis·a·ble (ăd-vī'zə-bəl) *adj.* Prudent : expedient. **—ad·vis'a·bil'i·ty** *n.* **—ad·vis'a·bly** *adv.*

ad·vise (ăd-vīz') *v.* **-vised, -vis·ing. 1.** To offer advice to. **2.** To suggest or recommend. **3.** To inform or notify. **—ad·vi'see** *n.* **—ad·vis'er, ad·vi'sor** *n.*

ad·vis·ed·ly (ăd-vī'zĭd-lē) *adv.* With consideration : deliberately.

ad·vise·ment (ăd-vīz'mənt) *n.* Careful consideration.

ad·vi·so·ry (ăd-vī'zə-rē) *adj.* **1.** Empowered to advise <an *advisory* council> **2.** Of or containing advice <an *advisory* memo> **—ad·vi'so·ry** *n.*

ad·vo·cate (ăd'və-kāt') *v.* **-cat·ed, -cat·ing.** To recommend. *—n.* (ăd'və-kĭt, -kāt'). **1.** One who supports or defends a cause. **2.** One who pleads on behalf of another. **—ad'vo·ca·cy** *n.* **—ad'vo·ca'tor** *n.*

adz or **adze** (ădz) *n.* A cutting tool with the blade at right angles to the handle, used for dressing wood.

ad·zu·ki bean (ăd-zōō'kē) *n.* A plant, *Phaseolus angularis,* widely cultivated in the Orient for its edible seeds.

a·e·des (ā-ē'dēz) *n., pl.* **aedes.** A mosquito, *Aëdes aegypti,* that transmits yellow fever and dengue.

Ae·ge·an Sea (ĭ-jē'ən). Arm of the Mediterranean between Greece and Turkey.

ae·gis (ē'jĭs) *n.* **1.** Protection. **2.** Sponsorship.

Ae·ne·as (ĭ-nē'əs) *n.* The Trojan hero of Virgil's *Aeneid.*

Ae·o·li·an harp (ē-ō'lē-ən, ē-ōl'yən) *n.* A boxlike instrument with stretched strings that sound musically when wind passes over them.

ae·on (ē'ŏn', ē'ən) *n. var. of* EON.

aer·ate (âr'āt') *v.* **-at·ed, -at·ing. 1.** To combine or charge (liquid) with a gas, esp. carbon dioxide. **2.** To purify by exposure to air. **3.** To oxygenate (blood). **—aer·a'tion** *n.* **—aer'a'tor** *n.*

aer·i·al (âr'ē-əl, ā-ĭr'ē-əl) *adj.* **1.** Of, in, or by the air. **2.** Lofty. **3.** Imaginary : unsubstantial. **4.** Of or pertaining to aircraft. **5.** *Bot.* Growing in air rather than soil or water. *—n.* (âr'ē-əl). An antenna.

aer·i·al·ist (âr'ē-ə-lĭst) *n.* An acrobat who performs high above the ground, as on a tightrope or trapeze.

aer·ie *also* **aer·y** (âr'ē, ăr'ē, ĭr'ē) *n., pl.* **-ies.** The nest of a predatory bird, as an eagle, built on a high place.

aer·o·bat·ics (âr'ə-băt'ĭks) *n. (sing. or pl. in number).* Stunt flying.

aer·o·bic (â-rō'bĭk) *adj.* **1.** Living or occurring only in the presence of oxygen <an *aerobic* bacterium> **2.** Of or relating to aerobics. **—aer'obe'** *n.*

aer·o·bics (â-rō'bĭks) *n. (sing. or pl. in number).* Exercises designed to strengthen the cardiopulmonary system.

aer·o·drome (âr'ə-drōm') *n. esp. Brit. var. of* AIRDROME.

aer·o·dy·nam·ics (âr'ō-dī-năm'ĭks) *n. (sing. in number).* The dynamics of gases, esp. of the atmospheric forces exerted on moving objects. **—aer'o·dy·nam'ic** *adj.*

aer·o·nau·tics (âr'ə-nô'tĭks) *n. (sing. in number).* **1.** Design and construction of aircraft. **2.** Aircraft navigation. **—aer'o·naut'** *n.* **—aer'o·nau'tic, aer'o·nau'ti·cal** *adj.* **—aer'o·nau'ti·cal·ly** *adv.*

aer·o·pause (âr'ə-pôz') *n.* The level of the atmosphere above which aircraft cannot fly.

aer·o·plane (âr'ə-plān') *n. esp. Brit. var. of* AIRPLANE.

aer·o·shell (âr'ə-shĕl') *n.* A protective shell for a spacecraft reentering the atmosphere at high speeds.

aer·o·sol (âr'ə-sôl', -sŏl', -sōl') *n.* **1.** A gaseous suspension of fine particles. **2.** A substance, as an insecticide or detergent, packaged under pressure in a dispenser.

aer·o·space (âr'ə-spās') *adj.* **1.** Of or designating the earth's atmosphere and the space beyond. **2.** Of or relating to the science or technology of flight.

Aes·chy·lus (ĕs'kə-ləs, ēs'-). 525–456 B.C. Greek dramatist. **—Aes'chy·le'an** *adj.*

Ae·sop (ē'səp, ē'sŏp'). 6th cent. Greek fabulist. **—Ae·so'pi·an** (ē-sō'pē-ən), **Ae·sop'ic** (ē-sŏp'ĭk) *adj.*

aes·thete or **es·thete** (ĕs'thēt') *n.* One who has or affects a superior appreciation of the beautiful.

aes·thet·ic or **es·thet·ic** (ĕs-thĕt'ĭk) *adj.* **1.** Of aesthetics. **2.** Of or relating to the sense of the beautiful. **3.** Having a love of beauty. **—aes·thet'i·cal·ly** *adv.*

aes·thet·ics or **es·thet·ics** (ĕs-thĕt'ĭks) *n. (sing. in number).* The philosophy of beauty and the fine arts.

A.F. or **AF** *abbr.* **1.** air force. **2.** audio frequency.

a·far (ə-fär') *adv.* Far away : far off.

†**a·feard** *also* **a·feared** (ə-fîrd') *adj. Regional & Archaic.* Afraid.

af·fa·ble (ăf'ə-bəl) *adj.* **1.** Amiable : good-natured. **2.** Gracious : gentle. **—af'fa·bil'i·ty** *n.* **—af'fa·bly** *adv.*

af·fair (ə-fâr') *n.* **1.** A matter or concern. **2. affairs.** Matters of business or public concern. **3.** An occurrence, event, or procedure. **4.** A private matter. **5.** A love affair. **6.** A social gathering.

af·fect[1] (ə-fĕkt') *v.* **1.** To influence. **2.** To move emotionally. ☆**syns:** IMPACT, IMPRESS, INFLUENCE, MOVE, STRIKE, SWAY, TOUCH

af·fect[2] (ə-fĕkt') *v.* **1.** To simulate or imitate in order to impress : pretend. **2.** To like : prefer <*affects* flashy clothes> ☆**syns:** ASSUME, COUNTERFEIT, FAKE, FEIGN, PRETEND, SIMULATE **—af·fect'er** *n.*

af·fec·ta·tion (ăf'ĕk-tā'shən) *n.* Artificial behavior designed to give a desired impression.

af·fect·ed (ə-fĕk'tĭd) *adj.* Behaving unnaturally to make a particular impression. **—af·fect'ed·ly** *adv.* **—af·fect'ed·ness** *n.*

af•fect•ing (ə-fĕk′tĭng) *adj.* Touching : moving <an *affecting* scene of farewell> **—af•fect′ing•ly** *adv.*
af•fec•tion (ə-fĕk′shən) *n.* A fond or tender feeling toward another. **—af•fec′tion•ate** *adj.* **—af•fec′tion•ate•ly** *adv.*
af•fen•pin•scher (ăf′ən-pĭn′chər) *n.* A small dog of European origin, having dark, wiry, shaggy hair and a tufted muzzle.

affenpinscher

af•fer•ent (ăf′ər-ənt) *adj.* Directed toward a central section or organ.
af•fi•ance (ə-fī′əns) *v.* **-anced, -anc•ing.** To betroth.
af•fi•da•vit (ăf′ĭ-dā′vĭt) *n.* A written statement made under oath before an official.
af•fil•i•ate (ə-fĭl′ē-āt′) *v.* **-at•ed, -at•ing.** To associate, join, or connect (with). *—n.* (ə-fĭl′ē-ĭt, -āt′). An associate. **—af•fil′i•a′tion** *n.*
af•fin•i•ty (ə-fĭn′ĭ-tē) *n., pl.* **-ties. 1.** A natural attraction : liking <an *affinity* for politics> **2.** Relationship : kinship.
af•firm (ə-fûrm′) *v.* **1.** To declare positively. **2.** To confirm : ratify. **—af•firm′a•ble** *adj.* **—af•fir′mant** *adj.* & *n.* **—af′fir•ma′tion** *n.*
af•fir•ma•tive (ə-fûr′mə-tĭv) *adj.* Affirming that something is true. *—n.* **1.** An affirmative word or phrase. **2.** The side in a debate that supports the proposition being debated. **—af•fir′ma•tive•ly** *adv.*
affirmative action *n.* Action taken to provide equal opportunity for minority groups and women.
af•fix (ə-fĭks′) *v.* **1.** To attach. **2.** To append. *—n.* (ăf′ĭks′). **1.** Something affixed. **2.** A word element, such as a prefix or suffix, that is attached to a base, stem, or root.
af•fla•tus (ə-flā′təs) *n.* Inspiration.
af•flict (ə-flĭkt′) *v.* To inflict physical or mental suffering on. ☆***syns:*** AGONIZE, CURSE, PLAGUE, RACK, SCOURGE, STRIKE, TORMENT, TORTURE **—af•flic′tion** *n.* **—af•flic′tive** *adj.*
af•flu•ence (ăf′lo͞o-əns) *also* **af•flu•en•cy** (-ən-sē) *n.* **1.** Wealth. **2.** Abundance. **—af′flu•ent** *adj.* **—af′flu•ent•ly** *adv.*
af•ford (ə-fôrd′, ə-fōrd′) *v.* **1.** To be able to pay for. **2.** To be able to spare <could *afford* 2 days for traveling> **3.** To provide <a tree that *affords* shelter><a book that *affords* pleasure> **—af•ford′a•ble** *adj.*
af•for•est (ə-fôr′ĭst, ə-fŏr′-) *v.* **-est•ed, -est•ing, -ests.** To convert (open land) into forest. **—af•for′es•ta′tion** *n.*
af•fray (ə-frā′) *n.* A noisy fight : brawl.
af•front (ə-frŭnt′) *v.* **1.** To insult. **2.** To confront. *—n.* A deliberate insult.
af•ghan (ăf′găn′, -gən) *n.* **1.** A coverlet knitted or crocheted in colorful geometric designs. **2. Afghan.** A native of Afghanistan.
Afghan hound *n.* A large dog with long, thick hair, a pointed snout, and drooping ears.
af•ghan•i (ăf-găn′ē, -gä′nē) *n.* See CURRENCY TABLE.
Af•ghan•i•stan (ăf-găn′ə-stăn′). Country of SC Asia. *Cap.* Kabul. *Pop.* 18,294,000. **—Af′ghan′** *adj.* & *n.*
a•fi•ci•o•na•do (ə-fĭsh′ə-nä′dō, ə-fĭs′ē-, ə-fē′sē-) *n., pl.* **-dos.** An enthusiastic admirer : fan.
a•field (ə-fēld′) *adv.* **1.** To or on a field. **2.** Off the usual path or way : astray. **3.** Away from one's environment : abroad.
a•fire (ə-fīr′) *adj.* & *adv.* Burning.
AFL-CIO or **A.F.L.-C.I.O.** *abbr.* American Federation of Labor and Congress of Industrial Organizations.
a•flame (ə-flām′) *adj.* & *adv.* Flaming.
a•float (ə-flōt′) *adj.* & *adv.* **1.** Floating. **2.** At sea. **3.** Flooded. **4.** In circulation.
a•flut•ter (ə-flŭt′ər) *adj.* Filled with nervous excitement.
a•foot (ə-fo͝ot′) *adj.* & *adv.* **1.** On foot. **2.** In the process of happening : astir.
a•fore•men•tioned (ə-fôr′mĕn′shənd, ə-fōr′-) *adj.* Mentioned earlier.
a•fore•said (ə-fôr′sĕd′, ə-fōr′-) *adj.* Spoken of before.
a•fore•thought (ə-fôr′thôt′, ə-fōr′-) *adj.* Planned beforehand : premeditated.
a•foul of (ə-foul′) *prep.* In a snarl : tangled. **—run** (or **fall**) **afoul of.** To have trouble with : come in conflict with.
a•fraid (ə-frād′) *adj.* **1.** Fearful : frightened. **2.** Reluctant : hesitant <Are you *afraid* of hard work?> **3.** Regretful <I'm *afraid* I have bad news.> ☆***syns:*** APPREHENSIVE, FEARFUL, FRIGHTENED, PETRIFIED, SCARED
A-frame (ā′frām) *n.* A structure, as a house, with a steeply angled roof that reaches to the ground.
a•fresh (ə-frĕsh′) *adv.* Once more : again.
Af•ri•ca (ăf′rĭ-kə). 2nd-largest continent, S of Europe between the Atlantic and Indian oceans. **—Af′ri•can** *adj.* & *n.*
African violet *n.* A plant of the genus *Saintpaulia,* native to Africa, widely cultivated as a house plant and bearing purple, white, or pink flowers.
Af•ri•kaans (ăf′rĭ-käns′, -känz′) *n.* An official language of the Republic of South Africa that developed from 17th-cent. Dutch.
Af•ri•kan•er (ăf′rĭ-kä′nər) *n.* An Afrikaans-speaking descendant of the Dutch who settled South Africa.
Af•ro (ăf′rō′) *n., pl.* **-ros.** A rounded, bushy hair style. *—adj.* **1.** Of or for an Afro hair style. **2.** African in style.
Af•ro-A•mer•i•can (ăf′rō-ə-mĕr′ĭ-kən) *adj.* Of or relating to American blacks of African ancestry, their history, or their culture. **—Af′ro-A•mer′i•can** *n.*
aft (ăft) *adv.* & *adj.* At, toward, in, or close to the stern of a vessel or rear of an aircraft.
af•ter (ăf′tər) *prep.* **1.** Behind in a place or position. **2.** In quest or pursuit of <seek *after* fame> **3.** Concerning <asked *after* the patient> **4.** At a later time than. **5.** With the same name as. *—conj.* Following the time that. *—adv.* **1.** Afterward <forever *after*> **2.** Behind. *—adj.* **1.** Later. **2.** Nearer the rear, esp. of a ship.
af•ter•birth (ăf′tər-bûrth′) *n.* The placenta and membranes ejected from the uterus shortly after childbirth.
af•ter•burn•er (ăf′tər-bûr′nər) *n.* A device that augments the power of a jet engine by injecting extra fuel into the hot exhaust gases.
af•ter•damp (ăf′tər-dămp′) *n.* An asphyxiating mixture of gases in a mine after an explosion.
af•ter•deck (ăf′tər-dĕk′) *n. Naut.* The part of a ship's deck aft amidships.
af•ter•ef•fect (ăf′tər-ĭ-fĕkt′) *n.* A delayed bodily or mental response to a stimulus.
af•ter•glow (ăf′tər-glō′) *n.* The light that is emitted or remains after removal of an illumination source.
af•ter•im•age (ăf′tər-ĭm′ĭj) *n.* An image that continues to be seen after a visual stimulus is no longer present.
af•ter•life (ăf′tər-līf′) *n.* A life held to follow after death.
af•ter•math (ăf′tər-măth′) *n.* **1.** A consequence, esp. of a misfortune or disaster. **2.** A 2nd crop in the same season, esp. of hay.
af•ter•noon (ăf′tər-no͞on′) *n.* The day from noon until sunset.
af•ter-shave (ăf′tər-shāve′) *n.* A usu. fragrant lotion for the face after shaving.
af•ter•taste (ăf′tər-tāst′) *n.* A taste or feeling that remains after the original stimulus is no longer present.
af•ter•thought (ăf′tər-thôt′) *n.* An idea or response that occurs to a person after an event, decision, etc.
af•ter•ward (ăf′tər-wərd) *also* **af•ter•wards** (-wərdz) *adv.* Subsequently.
Ag *symbol for* SILVER.
a•ga *also* **a•gha** (ä′gə, ăg′a) *n.* An important official of the Ottoman Empire.
a•gain (ə-gĕn′) *adv.* **1.** Once more : afresh. **2.** To a previous place or position. **3.** Furthermore. **4.** From another standpoint.
a•gainst (ə-gĕnst′) *prep.* **1.** In a direction opposite to <swam *against* the current> **2.** So as to hit or touch. **3.** In hostile opposition to <struggle *against* fate> **4.** Contrary to <*against* my wishes>
a•gape[1] (ə-găp′, ə-găp′) *adj.* & *adv.* **1.** With wonder and amazement. **2.** Wide open.
a•ga•pe[2] (ä-gä′pā, ä′gə-pā′) *n.* **1.** Christian love. **2.** Love that is spiritual, not sexual.
a•gar (ā′gär′, ä′gär′) *also* **a•gar-a•gar** (ā′gär-ā′gär′, ä′gär-ä′-) *n.* A gelatinous material extracted from certain marine algae, used for gelling foods and as a culture medium.
ag•a•ric (ăg′-ər-ĭk, ə-găr′ĭk) *n.* A fungus of the family Agaricaceae, including the common cultivated mushroom, *Agaricus campestris.*
ag•ate (ăg′ĭt) *n.* **1.** A type of quartz with bands of color. **2.** A playing marble of agate or glass.
a•ga•ve (ə-gä′vē, ə-gā′-) *n.* Any of various fleshy-leaved desert plants of the genus *Agave,* including the century plant.
age (āj) *n.* **1.** The period of existence. **2.** A lifetime. **3.** The time in life when one assumes adult rights and responsibilities : legal age. **4.** A distinctive period of life. **5.** The condition of being old. **6.** A geological or historical period. **7.** *Informal.* A long time. ☆***syns:*** DAY, EPOCH, ERA, PERIOD, TIME *—v.* **aged, ag•ing. 1.** To

grow or cause to grow older. 2. To mature : ripen <wine *aging* in casks>

-age *suff.* 1. Collectively : in general <leaf*age*> 2. Condition : state <bond*age*> 3. Act or result <spoil*age*> 4. Residence or place of <parson*age*> 5. Charge or fee <post*age*>

ag·ed (ā′jĭd) *adj.* 1. Old. 2. (ājd). Of the age of. 3. Mature : ripened. **–ag′ed·ly** *adv.* **–ag′ed·ness** *n.*

age·ing (ā′jĭng) *n. esp. Brit. var. of* AGING.

age·ism (ā′jĭz′əm) *n.* Discrimination against the elderly. **–age′ist** *n.*

age·less (āj′lĭs) *adj.* 1. Not showing the effects of age. 2. Eternal : timeless. **–age′less·ly** *adv.* **–age′less·ness** *n.*

a·gen·cy (ā′jən-sē) *n., pl.* **-cies.** 1. Action : power. 2. A method of action : means. 3. A business that represents or acts on behalf of others. 4. A governmental department.

a·gen·da (ə-jĕn′də) *n. (sing. in number).* A list of things to do : program.

a·gent (ā′jənt) *n.* 1. One that acts. 2. One that represents another. 3. A means by which something is done or caused : instrument. 4. A representative of a governmental department <a CIA *agent*> 5. A spy.

ag·er·a·tum (ăj′ə-rā′təm) *n.* Any of various plants of the genus *Argeratum,* esp. *A. houstonianum,* bearing violet-blue flower clusters.

ag·gior·na·men·to (ə-jôr′nə-mĕn′tō) *n. pl.* **-tos.** The process of updating an institution or organization.

ag·glom·er·ate (ə-glŏm′ə-rāt′) *v.* **-at·ed, -at·ing.** To gather into a rounded mass. *–n.* (ə-glŏm′ər-ĭt). A mass of things clustered together. **–ag·glom′er·a′tion** *n.*

ag·glu·ti·nate (ə-glo͞ot′n-āt′) *v.* **-nat·ed, -nat·ing.** 1. To join by adhesion. 2. To combine (word elements) into a compound. 3. To cause (e.g., red blood cells) to clump. **–ag·glu′ti·na′tion** *n.* **–ag·glu′ti·na′tive** *adj.*

ag·gran·dize (ə-grăn′dīz′, ăg′rən-) *v.* **-dized, -diz·ing.** 1. To increase the scope of. 2. To make greater in power, influence, etc. **–ag·gran′dize·ment** *n.* **–ag·gran′diz′er** *n.*

ag·gra·vate (ăg′rə-vāt′) *v.* **-vat·ed, -vat·ing.** 1. To make worse. 2. *Informal.* To annoy. **–ag′gra·vat′ing·ly** *adv.* **–ag′gra·va′tion** *n.* **–ag′gra·va′tor** *n.*

ag·gre·gate (ăg′rə-gĭt′, -gāt′) *adj.* Gathered into a whole : total. *–n.* (ăg′rə-gĭt). A whole considered with reference to its constituent parts. **–ag′gre·gate′** (-gāt′) *v.* **–ag′gre·gate·ly** *adv.* **–ag′gre·ga′tion** *n.* **–ag′gre·ga′tive** *adj.* **–ag′gre·ga′tor** *n.*

ag·gres·sion (ə-grĕsh′ən) *n.* 1. Initiation of usu. hostile action against another : attack. 2. The practice of attacking. 3. *Psychoanal.* Hostile behavior. **–ag·gres′sor** (-grĕs′ər) *n.*

ag·gres·sive (ə-grĕs′ĭv) *adj.* 1. Hostile : combative. 2. Energetic and enterprising : bold. **–ag·gres′sive·ly** *adv.* **–ag·gres′sive·ness** *n.*

ag·grieve (ə-grēv′) *v.* **-grieved, -griev·ing.** 1. To distress. 2. To treat unjustly.

a·gha (ä′gə, ăg′ə) *n. var. of* AGA.

a·ghast (ə-găst′) *adj.* Stricken with horror : appalled.

ag·ile (ăj′əl, ăj′īl′) *adj.* Moving or able to move with ease and speed : nimble. **–ag′ile·ly** *adv.* **–a·gil′i·ty** (ə-jĭl′ĭ-tē), **ag′ile·ness** *n.*

†a·gin (ə-gĭn′) *prep. Regional.* Against.

ag·ing (ā′jĭng) *n.* The process of becoming old or mature.

ag·i·tate (ăj′ĭ-tāt′) *v.* **-tat·ed, -tat·ing.** 1. To move with sudden force or violence. 2. To upset emotionally. 3. To try to stir up public interest in a cause. **–ag′i·tat′ed·ly** *adv.* **–ag′i·ta′tion** *n.* **–ag′i·ta′tor** *n.*

ag·it·prop (ăj′ĭt-prŏp′) *n.* Communist-oriented political propaganda disseminated esp. through the arts.

a·gleam (ə-glēm′) *adj. & adv.* Gleaming.

a·glim·mer (ə-glĭm′ər) *adj. & adv.* Glimmering.

a·glit·ter (ə-glĭt′ər) *adj. & adv.* Glittering.

a·glow (ə-glō′) *adj. & adv.* Glowing.

ag·nos·tic (ăg-nŏs′tĭk) *n.* One who disclaims any knowledge of God but does not deny the possibility of His existence. **–ag·nos′tic** *adj.* **–ag·nos′ti·cal·ly** *adv.* **–ag·nos′ti·cism** *n.*

a·go (ə-gō′) *adj. & adv.* Earlier than the present time : past.

a·gog (ə-gŏg′) *adj.* In a state of excited anticipation. **–a·gog′** *adv.*

ag·o·nize (ăg′ə-nīz′) *v.* **-nized, -niz·ing.** To suffer great distress <*agonize* over a decision> **–ag′o·niz′ing·ly** *adv.*

ag·o·ny (ăg′ə-nē) *n., pl.* **-nies.** 1. Intense physical or emotional pain. 2. A sudden intense emotion <an *agony* of doubt>

ag·o·ra (ä′gə-rä′) *n., pl.* **-rot** (-rōt′) *or* **-roth** (-rōt′). See *shekel* at CURRENCY TABLE.

ag·o·ra·pho·bi·a (ăg′ə-rə-fō′bē-ə) *n.* Abnormal fear of open, esp. public, spaces. **–ag′o·ra·pho′bic** *adj.*

a·gou·ti (ə-go͞o′tē) *n., pl.* **-tis** *or* **-ties.** A tropical American burrowing rodent of the genus *Dasyprocta,* with grizzled brownish or dark-gray fur.

agr. *abbr.* agriculture; agricultural.

a·grar·i·an (ə-grâr′ē-ən) *adj.* 1. Pertaining to land and its ownership. 2. Pertaining to farming : agricultural. *–n.* One who favors equitable land distribution. **–a·grar′i·an·ism** *n.* **–a·grar′i·an·ly** *adv.*

a·gree (ə-grē′) *v.* **a·greed, a·gree·ing.** 1. To grant consent : assent. 2. To be in accord : match. 3. To come to an understanding or to terms. 4. To be appropriate or beneficial. 5. To correspond in gender, number, case, or person.

a·gree·a·ble (ə-grē′ə-bəl) *adj.* 1. To one's liking : pleasing. 2. In accord : suitable. 3. Ready to consent : willing. 4. Pleasant and friendly. **–a·gree′a·ble·ness** *n.* **–a·gree′a·bly** *adv.*

a·gree·ment (ə-grē′mənt) *n.* 1. Harmony of opinion : accord. 2. A covenant : treaty. 3. Correspondence in gender, number, case, or person.

ag·ri·busi·ness (ăg′rə-bĭz′nĭs) *n.* Farming engaged in as big business, including the producing, processing, and distributing of farm products.

ag·ri·cul·ture (ăg′rĭ-kŭl′chər) *n.* The science, art, and business of soil cultivation, crop production, and the raising of livestock. **–ag′ri·cul′tur·al** *adj.* **–ag′ri·cul′tur·al·ly** *adv.* **–ag′ri·cul′tur·ist** *n.*

a·gron·o·my (ə-grŏn′ə-mē) *also* **ag·ro·nom·ics** (ăg′rə-nŏm′iks) *n.* The application of the various soil and plant sciences to soil management and crop production. **–ag′ro·nom′ic** (ăg′rə-nŏm′ĭk), **ag′ro·nom′i·cal** *adj.* **–a·gron′o·mist** *n.*

a·ground (ə-ground′) *adv. & adj.* Stranded on a reef, shoal, or in shallow water.

agt. *abbr.* 1. agent. 2. agreement.

a·gue (ā′gyo͞o) *n.* A fever accompanied by chills or shivering.

ah (ä) *interj.* Used to express surprise, pain, etc.

a·ha (ä-hä′) *interj.* Used to express surprise or triumph.

a·head (ə-hĕd′) *adv.* 1. At or to the front. 2. In advance : before. 3. Onward. **–be ahead.** *Informal.* 1. To be gaining or winning. 2. To have more than one needs. **–get ahead.** To achieve success.

a·hem (ə-hĕm′) *interj.* Used to attract attention, express doubt, or as a warning.

a·hoy (ə-hoi′) *interj. Naut.* Used to hail a ship or attract attention.

aid (ād) *v.* To give help or assistance (to). *–n.* 1. Assistance. 2. *also* **aide.** An assistant. **–aid′er** *n.*

aide-de-camp (ād′də-kămp′) *n., pl.* **aides-de-camp.** A naval or military officer who acts as a secretary and confidential assistant to a superior officer.

AIDS (ādz) *n.* A disease of no known etiology in which the body's immunological system is destroyed.

ai·grette *or* **ai·gret** (ā-grĕt′, ā′grĕt′) *n.* A decorative tuft of plumes, esp. of egret feathers.

ail (āl) *v.* 1. To feel ill. 2. To make ill or uneasy <What *ails* you?>

ai·lan·thus (ā-lăn′thəs) *n.* A deciduous tree, *Ailanthus altissima,* with compound leaves and malodorous flower clusters.

ai·ler·on (ā′lə-rŏn′) *n.* A movable control flap on the trailing edge of an airplane wing.

ail·ment (āl′mənt) *n.* A usu. mild illness.

aim (ām) *v.* 1. To direct (e.g., a weapon or remark). 2. To direct a weapon. 3. To direct one's effort or purpose <*aim* at eliminating racism> *–n.* 1. The act of aiming. 2. The direction of something aimed. 3. Purpose : intention.

aim·less (ām′lĭs) *adj.* Lacking purpose. **–aim′less·ly** *adv.* **–aim′less·ness** *n.*

ain't (ānt). *Nonstandard.* 1. Am not. 2. Used also as a contraction of *is not, are not, has not,* and *have not.*

Ai·nu (ī′no͞o) *n., pl.* **Ainu** *or* **-nus.** A member of an aboriginal Caucasian people of Japan.

ai·o·li (ī-ō′lē) *n.* A rich garlic-flavored mayonnaise.

air (âr) *n.* 1. The gaseous mixture, mainly nitrogen (approx. 78%) and oxygen (approx. 21%), enveloping the earth. 2. The sky. 3. A breeze. 4. A characteristic impression : appearance <an *air* of superiority> <a house with an *air* of neglect> 5. **airs.** Affectation. 6. *Mus.* A melody : tune. 7. The airwaves. 8. The medium through which aircraft travel. ***syns:** AMBIANCE, ATMOSPHERE, AURA, FEEL, FEELING, MOOD, SMELL, TONE *–v.* 1. To expose to the air : ventilate. 2. To publicly circulate. **–in the air.** Prevalent. **–on (***or* **off) the air.** Being (or not being) broadcast on radio or television. **–up in the air.** 1. Not decided : uncertain. 2. Excited : agitated. **–walk on air.** To feel elated. **–air′less** *adj.* **–air′less·ness** *n.*

air bag *n.* A baglike automotive safety device that inflates upon collision and prevents passengers from pitching forward.

air·boat (âr′bōt′) *n.* A swamp boat.

air•borne (âr′bôrn′, -bōrn′) *adj.* **1.** Carried by or through the air <*airborne* viruses> **2.** In flight.
air brake *n.* A brake operated by the power of compressed air.
air•brush *also* **air brush** (âr′brŭsh′) *n.* An atomizer using compressed air to spray liquids, as paint, on a surface. —*v.* To spray with an airbrush.
air•bus (âr′bŭs′) *n.* A usu. short-range large subsonic jet passenger airplane.
air conditioner *n.* An apparatus for regulating, esp. lowering, the temperature and humidity of an enclosed area. **—air′-con•di′tion** *v.* **—air conditioning** *n.*
air•craft (âr′krăft′) *n., pl.* **aircraft.** A machine or device, such as an airplane, helicopter, glider, or dirigible, that is capable of atmospheric flight.
aircraft carrier *n.* A large warship carrying aircraft.
air•drome (âr′drōm′) *n.* An airport.
air•drop (âr′drŏp′) *n.* A delivery, as of supplies, by parachute from airborne aircraft. **—air′drop′** *v.*
air-dry (âr′drī′) *v.* To dry by exposure to the air.
Aire•dale (âr′dāl′) *n.* A large terrier with a wiry tan coat marked with black.
air•field (âr′fēld′) *n.* **1.** An airport having paved runways. **2.** A landing strip.
air•foil (âr′foil′) *n.* An aircraft control part or surface, such as a wing, propeller blade, or rudder, that controls stability, lift, thrust, etc.
air force *n.* The aviation branch of a country's armed forces.
air gun *n.* A gun that is operated by compressed air.
air lane *n.* An established route of travel for aircraft.
air•lift (âr′lĭft′) *n.* Delivery of troops or supplies by aircraft when surface routes are blocked. **—air′lift′** *v.*
air•line (âr′līn′) *n.* **1.** A business organization providing scheduled transport of passengers and freight by air. **2.** The shortest distance between 2 points.
air•lin•er (âr′lī′nər) *n.* A large passenger airplane operated by an airline.
air lock *n.* An airtight chamber between regions of unequal pressure in which air pressure can be regulated.
air mail *also* **air•mail** (âr′māl′) *n.* **1.** The system of transporting mail by air. **2.** Mail transported by air. **—air′mail′** *v.* & *adj.*
air•man (âr′mən) *n.* **1.** An enlisted person in the U.S. Air Force. **2.** An aviator.
airman basic *n.* An enlisted person of the lowest rank in the U.S. Air Force.
air mass *n.* A large body of air that has approx. the same temperature, pressure, and moisture throughout.
air mile *n.* A unit of distance in air navigation.
air piracy *n.* The hijacking of an airplane in flight. **—air pirate** *n.*
air•plane (âr′plān′) *n.* A vehicle capable of flight, gen. heavier than air, and driven by jet engines or propellers.
air pocket *n.* A downward air current that causes an aircraft to lose altitude abruptly.
air•port (âr′pôrt′, -pōrt′) *n.* A permanent facility that provides space for aircraft to take off and land with a control tower, hangars, and accommodations for passengers and cargo.
air raid *n.* An attack by enemy aircraft.
air•ship (âr′shĭp′) *n.* A dirigible.
air•sick•ness (âr′sĭk′nĭs) *n.* Nausea resulting from flight in an aircraft. **—air′sick′** *adj.*
air•space (âr′spās′) *n.* The section of the atmosphere above a particular land area, esp. that of a nation.
air speed *n.* The speed of an aircraft relative to the air.
air•strip (âr′strĭp′) *n.* A cleared area serving as a landing strip.
air•tight (âr′tīt′) *adj.* **1.** Impermeable by air or gas <an *airtight* seal> **2.** Unassailable <an *airtight* alibi>
air-to-air missile (âr′tə-âr′) *n.* A guided missile designed to be fired from aircraft at aircraft.
air-to-sur•face missile (âr′tə-sûr′fĭs) *n.* A guided missile designed to be fired from aircraft at targets on the ground.
air•waves (âr′wāvz′) *pl.n.* The medium used to transmit radio and television signals.
air•way (âr′wā′) *n.* An air lane.
air•wor•thy (âr′wûr′thē) *adj.* Fit to fly <*airworthy* jets> **—air′wor′thi•ness** *n.*
air•y (âr′ē) *adj.* **-i•er, -i•est. 1.** Of or like the air. **2.** Open to the air : breezy. **3.** Light as air : delicate. **4.** Insubstantial : imaginative <*airy* speculations> **5.** Nonchalant <an *airy* disregard for rules> **—air′i•ly** *adv.* **—air′i•ness** *n.*
aisle (īl) *n.* A passageway between rows of seats, as in a church or theater.
aitch (āch) *n.* The letter *h.*
aitch•bone (āch′bōn′) *n.* **1.** The rump bone in cattle. **2.** The cut of beef containing the aitchbone.
▲word history: *Aitchbone* is a good example of a folk etymology, which is the refashioning of a word so that it resembles a more familiar, but unrelated, word. The incorrect division between the article and the noun in *a nachebon* resulted in a new noun whose 1st syllable was unrecognizable. This element was variously interpreted as *each, ash, ice,* and *aitch,* all familiar English words. The bone itself has no physical resemblance to the letter H.
a•jar[1] (ə-jär′) *adv.* & *adj.* Partially opened.
a•jar[2] (ə-jär′) *adv.* & *adj.* Not in harmony : jarring.
AK *abbr.* Alaska (with Zip Code).
A•khe•na•ton *or* **A•khe•na•ten** (ä′kə-nä′tn, äk′-nä′-). Egyptian pharaoh (1375–58 B.C.) and religious reformer.
a•kim•bo (ə-kĭm′bō) *adj.* & *adv.* With hands on hips and elbows bowed outward.
a•kin (ə-kĭn′) *adj.* **1.** Related by blood. **2.** Similar in quality or character. **3.** Linguistically cognate.
Ak•ron (ăk′rən). Industrial city of NE Ohio. *Pop.* 237,177.
Al *symbol for* ALUMINUM.
AL *abbr.* Alabama (with Zip Code).
-al[1] *suff.* Of, pertaining to, or marked by <parent*al*>
-al[2] *suff.* Act : process <retriev*al*>
à la *also* **a la** (ä′lä, ä′lə, ăl′ə) *prep.* **1.** In the manner or style of <a story *à la* Poe> **2.** According to <*à la* carte>
Ala. *abbr.* Alabama.
Al•a•bam•a (ăl′ə-băm′ə). State of S U.S. *Cap.* Montgomery. *Pop.* 3,890,061. **—Al′a•bam′i•an, Al′a•bam′an** *adj.* & *n.*
al•a•bas•ter (ăl′ə-băs′tər) *n.* A dense, translucent, white or tinted fine-grained gypsum.
à la carte (ä′ lä kärt′, ä′lə, ăl′ə) *adv.* & *adj.* With a separate price for each item on the menu.
a•lac•ri•ty (ə-lăk′rĭ-tē) *n.* **1.** Cheerful eagerness. **2.** Speed : quickness. **—a•lac′ri•tous** *adj.*
à la king (ä′lə kĭng′, ăl′ə) *adj.* Cooked in a cream sauce with green pepper or pimiento and mushrooms <turkey *à la king*>
†al•a•me•da (ăl′ə-mē′də, -mā′-) *n.* *SW U.S.* A promenade or walk, esp. one shaded by alamos.
†al•a•mo (ăl′ə-mō′) *n., pl.* **-mos** *SW U.S.* A poplar tree, esp. a cottonwood.
à la mode (ä′ lä mōd′, ä′lə, ăl′ə) *adj.* **1.** Fashionable. **2.** Served with ice cream.
Al•a•ric (ăl′ə-rĭk). 370?–410. Visigoth king and conqueror of Rome (410).
a•larm (ə-lärm′) *n.* **1.** A sudden feeling of fear. **2.** A warning of imminent danger. **3.** A device that sounds a warning by a sound or signal. **4.** The sounding mechanism of a clock. **5.** A call to arms. ☆*syns:* ALERT, TOCSIN, WARNING —*v.* To fill with alarm : frighten. **—a•larm′a•ble** *adj.*
a•larm•ing (ə-lär′mĭng) *adj.* Frightening. **—a•larm′ing•ly** *adv.*
a•larm•ist (ə-lär′mĭst) *n.* A person who needlessly alarms others. **—a•larm′ism** *n.*
a•las (ə-lăs′) *interj.* Used to express sadness, regret, or anxiety.
Alas. *abbr.* Alaska.
A•las•ka (ə-lăs′kə). State of the U.S., in extreme NW North America. *Cap.* Juneau. *Pop.* 400,481. **—A•las′kan** *adj.* & *n.*
alb (ălb) *n.* A long, white linen robe worn as a liturgical vestment.
al•ba•core (ăl′bə-kôr′, -kōr′) *n.* A large marine fish, *Thunnus alalunga,* whose edible flesh is a major source of canned tuna.
Al•ba•ni•a (ăl-bā′nē-ə, -bān′yə). Country of SE Europe. *Cap.* Tirane. *Pop.* 2,725,000. **—Al•ba′ni•an** *adj.* & *n.*
Al•ba•ny (ôl′bə-nē). Cap. of N.Y., on the W bank of the Hudson. *Pop.* 101,727.
al•ba•tross (ăl′bə-trôs′, -trŏs′) *n.* A large, web-footed, long-winged sea bird of the family Diomedeidae, related to the petrel.
al•be•it (ôl-bē′ĭt, ăl-) *conj.* Although.
Al•ber•ta (ăl-bûr′tə). Province of W Canada. *Cap.* Edmonton. *Pop.* 1,838,037. **—Al•ber′tan** *adj.* & *n.*
al•bi•no (ăl-bī′nō) *n., pl.* **-nos.** An organism lacking normal pigmentation, as a person having inordinately pale skin, very light hair, and lacking normal eye coloring. **—al′bi•nism** *n.*
al•bum (ăl′bəm) *n.* **1.** A book or binder with blank pages for mounting a collection, as of stamps or photographs. **2.** A set of phonograph records stored in one binding.
al•bu•men (ăl-byo͞o′mən) *n.* **1.** The white of an egg. **2.** Albumin.
al•bu•min (ăl-byo͞o′mən) *n.* A simple, water-soluble protein found in egg white, blood serum, milk, and many animal and plant tissues.
al•bu•min•ous (ăl-byo͞o′mə-nəs) *adj.* Of, resembling, or relating to albumin or albumen.
Al•bu•quer•que (ăl′bə-kûr′kē). City of C N. Mex. *Pop.* 331,767.

al•cai•de (ăl-kī′dē) *n.* The commander of a fortress in Spain or Portugal.
al•cal•de (ăl-käl′dē) *n.* The chief governing or judicial official of a Spanish or Spanish-American town.
al•caz•ar (ăl-kăz′ər, ăl′kə-zär′) *n.* A Spanish fortress or palace.
al•che•my (ăl′kə-mē) *n.* **1.** A medieval chemical philosophy whose chief aim was the conversion of base metals into gold. **2.** An apparently magical power. **—al•chem′i•cal, al•chem′ic** *adj.* **—al•chem′i•cal•ly** *adv.* **—al′che•mist** *n.*
al•co•hol (ăl′kə-hôl′) *n.* **1.** Any of a series of hydroxyl compounds that include ethanol and methanol. **2.** Intoxicating liquor containing alcohol.
al•co•hol•ic (ăl′kə-hô′lĭk, -hŏl′ĭk) *adj.* **1.** Of, relating to, or resulting from alcohol. **2.** Containing or preserved in alcohol. **3.** Suffering from alcoholism. —*n.* A sufferer from alcoholism.
al•co•hol•ism (ăl′kə-hô-lĭz′əm) *n.* **1.** Excessive consumption of and psychophysiological dependence on alcoholic beverages. **2.** A pathological condition caused by this.
al•cove (ăl′kōv′) *n.* A recess or partly enclosed extension of a room : nook.
al•de•hyde (ăl′də-hīd′) *n.* Any of a class of highly reactive organic chemical compounds obtained by oxidation of primary alcohols.
al den•te (äl dĕn′tē) *adj. & adv.* Cooked enough to be firm but not soft.
al•der (ôl′dər) *n.* Any of various deciduous shrubs or trees of the genus *Alnus,* growing in cool, moist places.
al•der•man (ôl′dər-mən) *n.* A member of a municipal legislature.
Al•der•ney (ôl′dər-nē) *n., pl.* **-neys.** One of a breed of small dairy cattle orig. raised in the Channel Islands.
ale (āl) *n.* A fermented alcoholic beverage similar to but heavier than beer.
a•le•a•to•ry (ā′lē-ə-tôr′ē, -tōr′ē) *adj.* Dependent on chance or luck.
a•lee (ə-lē′) *adv. Naut.* Away from the wind.
a•lem•bic (ə-lĕm′bĭk) *n.* A container formerly used for distilling.

alembic

a•lert (ə-lûrt′) *adj.* **1.** Vigilantly attentive : observant. **2.** Mentally perceptive and responsive : quick. **3.** Lively or brisk. ☆***syns:*** OBSERVANT, OPEN-EYED, VIGILANT, WAKEFUL, WARY, WATCHFUL, WIDE-AWAKE —*n.* **1.** A warning signal of danger or attack. **2.** The time period during which an alert is in effect. —*v.* **1.** To warn. **2.** To inform. **—a•lert′ly** *adv.* **—a•lert′ness** *n.*
A•leu•tian Islands (ə-lo͞o′shən). Chain of volcanic islands in the N Pacific.
Al•ex•an•der III (ăl′ĭg-zăn′dər, -zän′-). "the Great." 356–323 B.C. King of Macedonia (336–323). **—Al′ex•an′dri•an** *adj.*
Al•ex•an•dri•a (ăl′ĭg-zăn′drē-ə). City of Egypt, on the Mediterranean. *Pop.* 2,409,000. **—Al′ex•an′dri•an** *adj. & n.*
al•ex•an•drine *also* **Al•ex•an•drine** (ăl′ĭg-zăn′drĭn) *n.* A line of verse in iambic hexameter. **—al′ex•an•drine** *adj.*
al•fal•fa (ăl-făl′fə) *n.* A cloverlike plant, *Medicago sativa,* with purple flowers, widely grown for forage.
al•fres•co (ăl-frĕs′kō) *adv. & adj.* In the fresh air : outdoors.
†**al•for•ja** (ăl-fôr′-wä) *n. W U.S.* A leather or canvas saddlebag.
Al•fred (ăl′frĭd). "the Great." 849–99. West Saxon king (871–99) and lawmaker.
al•ga (ăl′gə) *n., pl.* **-gae** (-jē). Any of various aquatic, 1-celled or multicellular plants without true stems, roots, and leaves but containing chlorophyll. **—al′gal** *adj.*
al•ge•bra (ăl′jə-brə) *n.* A mathematical generalization of a set of numbers, a set of sets, a set of statements, etc., and the operations that can be performed on them.
Al•ge•ri•a (ăl-jîr′ē-ə). Country of NW Africa, on the Mediterranean. *Cap.* Algiers. *Pop.* 20,050,000. **—Al•ge′ri•an** *adj. & n.*
Al•giers (ăl-jîrz′). Cap. of Algeria, in the N on the Mediterranean. *Pop.* 1,503,270.
AL•GOL or **Al•gol** (ăl′gŏl′, -gôl′) *n.* A computer language used esp. for scientific problems.
al•go•rism (ăl′gə-rĭz′əm) *n.* The Arabic system of numeration.
al•go•ris•tic (ăl′gə-rĭs′tĭk) *adj.* Yielding a precise answer, as a computational system guaranteeing accurate solution.
al•go•rithm (ăl′gə-rĭth′əm) *n. Math.* A mathematical rule or procedure for solving a problem. **—al′go•rith′mic** *adj.*
▲word history: *Algorithm* originated as a variant spelling of *algorism.* The spelling was prob. influenced by the word *arithmetic* or its Greek source *arithm,* "number." With the development of sophisticated mechanical computing devices in the 20th cent., however, *algorithm* was adopted as a convenient word for a recursive mathematical procedure, the computer's stock in trade. *Algorithm* has ceased to be used as a variant form of the older word.
algorithmic language *n.* A computer language presenting numerical procedures in standard form.
a•li•as (ā′lē-əs, āl′yəs) *n., pl.* **-as•es.** An assumed name. —*adv.* Otherwise named : also known as <Smith, *alias* Jones>
al•i•bi (ăl′ə-bī′) *n., pl.* **-bis.** *Law.* **1.** A form of defense by which a defendant attempts to prove that he or she was elsewhere when the crime in question was committed. **2.** *Informal.* An excuse. **—al′i•bi′** *v.*
a•li•en (ā′lē-ən, āl′yən) *adj.* **1.** Owing political allegiance to another country or government : foreign. **2.** Not one's own : unfamiliar <*alien* culture> **3.** Opposed in character <Stealing is *alien* to my nature.> —*n.* **1.** An unnaturalized resident of a country. **2.** A member of another people, family, region, etc. **3.** An outsider. **4.** *Slang.* A creature from outer space.
al•ien•a•ble (āl′yə-nə-bəl, ā′lē-ə-) *adj. Law.* Capable of being transferred to a new owner. **—al′ien•a•bil′i•ty** *n.*
al•ien•ate (āl′yə-nāt′, ā′lē-ə-) *v.* **-at•ed, -at•ing. 1.** To cause to become indifferent or hostile : estrange. **2.** *Law.* To transfer (property) to a new owner. **—al′ien•a′tion** *n.* **—al′ien•a′tor** *n.*
al•ien•ist (āl′yə-nĭst, ā′lē-ə-) *n. Law.* A psychiatrist.
a•light[1] (ə-līt′) *v.* **a•light•ed** or **a•lit** (ə-lĭt′), **a•light•ing. 1.** To descend and settle, as after flight : land. **2.** To dismount.
a•light[2] (ə-līt′) *adj. & adv.* **1.** Burning. **2.** Illuminated.
a•lign *also* **a•line** (ə-līn′) *v.* **1.** To place in a line. **2.** To ally (oneself) with one side of a cause, dispute, government, etc. **3.** To adjust (e.g., parts of a mechanism) to produce a proper condition or relationship. **—a•lign′er** *n.* **—a•lign′ment** *n.*
a•like (ə-līk′) *adj.* Having close resemblance : similar. —*adv.* In the same manner or degree. **—a•like′ness** *n.*
al•i•ment (ăl′ə-mənt) *n.* Nourishment : food. **—al′i•men′tal** *adj.* **—al′i•men′ta•ry** *adj.* **—al′i•men•ta′tion** *n.*
alimentary canal *n.* The tube of the digestive system extending from the mouth to the anus and including the pharynx, esophagus, stomach, and intestines.
al•i•mo•ny (ăl′ə-mō′nē) *n., pl.* **-nies.** *Law.* A court-ordered allowance for support, usu. given by a man to his former wife after a divorce or legal separation.
a•line (ə-līn) *v. var. of* ALIGN.
A-line (ā′līn′) *adj.* Having a fitted top and a flared bottom <an *A-line* gown>
al•i•phat•ic (ăl′ə-făt′ĭk) *adj.* Relating to organic chemical compounds in which the carbon atoms are linked in open chains.
a•lit (ə-lĭt′) *v. var. p.t. & p.p. of* ALIGHT[1].
a•live (ə-līv′) *adj.* **1.** Having life : living. **2.** In existence or effect <keep a dream *alive*> **3.** Full of life : lively. ☆***syns:*** ANIMATE, LIVE, LIVING, VITAL **—alive to.** Sensitive to <*alive to* the dangers of drugs> **—alive with.** Full of <a room *alive with* chatter>. **—a•live′ness** *n.*
a•li•yah (ä-lē′yä, ə-lē′yə) *n.* Immigration of Jewish people into Israel.
a•liz•a•rin (ə-lĭz′ə-rĭn) *also* **a•liz•a•rine** (-ĭn, -ə-rēn′) *n.* An orange-red compound used in dyes.
al•ka•li (ăl′kə-lī′) *n., pl.* **-lis** or **-lies. 1.** A carbonate or hydroxide of an alkali metal, whose aqueous solution is bitter, slippery, caustic, and basic in reactions. **2.** Any of various soluble mineral salts present in natural water and arid soils.
al•ka•line (ăl′kə-lĭn, -līn′) *adj.* **1.** Of, relating to, or containing an alkali. **2.** Basic. **—al′ka•lin′i•ty** *n.*
al•ka•lize (ăl′kə-līz′) *also* **al•ka•lin•ize** (-lə-nīz′) *v.* **-lized, -liz•ing** *also* **-ized, -iz•ing.** To make alkaline. **—al′ka•li•za′tion** or **al′ka•lin′i•za′tion** *n.*
al•ka•loid (ăl′kə-loid′) *n.* Any of various nitrogen-containing organic bases obtained from plants, including nicotine, quinine, atropine, cocaine, and morphine. **—al′ka•loi′dal** *adj.*
al•ka•lo•sis (ăl′kə-lō′sĭs) *n.* Abnormally high alkali content in the blood and tissues.
al•kyd or **al•kyd resin** (ăl′kĭd) *n.* A durable synthetic resin used in paints.
all (ôl) *adj.* **1.** The total entity or extent of <*all* the west><*all* women> **2.** Being the whole number, amount, or quantity of

<*all* the guests> **3.** Being the utmost possible <in *all* honesty> **4.** Every <*all* manner of trouble> **5.** Any whatsoever <beyond *all* question> **6.** Nothing but : only <*all* work and no play> —*pron.* Each and every one <10 cars raced and *all* crashed.> —*n.* Everything one has <gave our *all* to the cause> —*adv.* **1.** Wholly : entirely <*all* confused> **2.** Each : apiece <The score was 6 *all.*> **3.** Exclusively <The mail is *all* for me.> **—all but.** Almost. **—all in.** Exhausted. **—all in all.** Everything being taken into account. **—and all.** And everything else <learning to drive *and all*> **—at all. 1.** In any and every way. **2.** To any extent. **—for all.** In spite of.

Al•lah (ăl′ə, ä′lə) *n.* The Moslem supreme being.

all-A•mer•i•can (ôl′ə-mĕr′ĭ-kən) *adj.* **1.** Representative of the best or typical of its kind in the U.S. **2.** Selected as the best amateur in the U.S. at a particular sports position or event. **—all′-A•mer′i•can** *n.*

all-a•round (ôl′ə-round′) *adj. var. of* ALL-ROUND.

al•lay (ə-lā′) *v.* **1.** To relieve or lessen (e.g., grief or pain). **2.** To calm <*allay* one's fears> **—al•lay′er** *n.*

all clear *n.* **1.** A signal indicating that an air raid is over. **2.** An expression used to signify the absence of immediate obstacles or danger.

al•lege (ə-lĕj′) *v.* **-leged, -leg•ing. 1.** To state to be true : claim. **2.** To assert without proof. **3.** To cite as an excuse. **—al′le•ga′tion** (ăl′ĭ-gā′shən) *n.* **—al•leg′ed•ly** *adv.* **—al•leg′er** *n.*

Al•le•ghe•ny Mountains (ăl′ə-gā′nē) *also* **Al•le•ghe•nies** (-nēz). W part of the Appalachian Mts., extending from N Pa. to SW Va.

al•le•giance (ə-lē′jəns) *n.* Loyalty owed to a sovereign, nation, or cause : fidelity.

al•le•go•ry (ăl′ĭ-gôr′ē, -gōr′ē) *n., pl.* **-ries.** A literary, dramatic, or pictorial device in which each character, object, and event symbolically illustrates a moral or religious principle. **—al′le•gor′ic, al′le•gor′i•cal** *adj.* **—al′le•gor′i•cal•ly** *adv.* **—al′le•go′rist** *n.*

al•le•gret•to (ăl′ĭ-grĕt′ō) *adv. Mus.* Faster than andante but slower than allegro. Used as a direction. **—al′le•gret′to** *adj.* & *n.*

al•le•gro (ə-lĕg′rō, ə-lā′-grō) *adv. Mus.* Faster than allegretto but slower than presto. Used as a direction. **—al•le′gro** *adj.* & *n.*

al•lele (ə-lēl′) *n.* Any of a group of possible mutational forms of a gene. **—al•le′lic** (ə-lē′lĭk, ə-lĕl′ĭk) *adj.* **—al•le′lism** *n.*

al•le•lo•morph (ə-lē′lə-môrf′, ə-lĕl′ə-) *n.* An allele. **—al•le′lo•mor′phic** *adj.* **—al•le′lo•mor′phism** *n.*

al•le•lu•ia (ăl′ə-lo͞o′yə) *interj.* Hallelujah.

al•ler•gen (ăl′ər-jən) *n.* Something that causes an allergy. **—al′ler•gen′ic** *adj.*

al•ler•gist (ăl′ər-jĭst) *n.* A physician specializing in treating allergies.

al•ler•gy (ăl′ər-jē) *n., pl.* **-gies. 1.** Abnormal or pathological reaction to environmental substances, as pollens, foods, dust, or microorganisms. **2.** *Informal.* An adverse feeling : antipathy. **—al•ler′gic** *adj.*

al•le•vi•ate (ə-lē′vē-āt′) *v.* **-at•ed, -at•ing.** To make less severe : ease. **—al•le′vi•a′tion** *n.* **—al•le′vi•a′tive** *adj.* **—al•le′vi•a′tor** *n.*

al•ley (ăl′ē) *n., pl.* **-leys. 1.** A narrow street or passage between or behind buildings. **2.** A bowling alley.

al•ley•way (ăl′ē-wā′) *n.* ALLEY 1.

al•li•ance (ə-lī′əns) *n.* **1. a.** A pact of confederation between nations. **b.** The nations so united. **2.** A union or relationship by kinship, marriage, friendship, etc.

al•li•ga•tor (ăl′ĭ-gā′tər) *n.* Either of 2 large amphibious reptiles, *Alligator mississipiensis* of the SE U.S. or *A. sinensis* of China, with sharp teeth and strong jaws, closely related to the crocodile.

alligator pear *n.* The avocado.

all-im•por•tant (ôl′ĭm-pôr′tnt) *adj.* Very important.

al•lit•er•a•tion (ə-lĭt′ə-rā′shən) *n.* The occurrence in a phrase or line of speech or writing of 2 or more words having the same initial sound, e.g. <"all summer in the sound of the sea" Whitman> **—al•lit′er•a′tive** *adj.* **—al•lit′er•a′tive•ly** *adv.*

al•lo•cate (ăl′ə-kāt′) *v.* **-cat•ed, -cat•ing.** To allot : assign. **—al′lo•ca′tion** *n.*

al•lot (ə-lŏt′) *v.* **-lot•ted, -lot•ting.** To distribute or set aside as a share. ☆**syns:** ADMEASURE, ALLOCATE, ALLOW, APPORTION, ASSIGN, GIVE, LOT, PORTION **—al•lot′ment** *n.* **—al•lot′ter** *n.*

all out *adv.* With every possible effort or resource <went *all out*> **—all′-out′** *adj.*

all over *adv.* Over the entire area. **—all′o′ver** *adj.*

al•low (ə-lou′) *v.* **1.** To permit. **2.** To permit to have. **3.** To make a provision for <*allow* time for a shower> **4.** To sanction the presence of : let in. **5.** To provide (the needed amount). **6.** To admit : concede. **7.** To grant as a discount. **—al•low′a•ble** *adj.* **—al•low′a•bly** *adv.* **—al•low′ed•ly** *adv.*

al•low•ance (ə-lou′əns) *n.* **1.** The act of allowing. **2.** A regular provision of money, food, etc. **3.** A price discount. **4.** Consideration for modifying circumstances <made an *allowance* for mistakes>

al•loy (ăl′oi′, ə-loi′) *n.* **1.** A homogeneous mixture, usu. of 2 or more metals. **2.** Something added that reduces purity or value. **—al•loy′** *v.*

all right *adv.* **1.** Satisfactory <For an old car, it's *all right.*> **2.** Correct <Your conclusions are *all right.*> **3.** Unhurt. **4.** Very well : yes. **5.** Certainly <It's a genuine antique, *all right*>

all-right (ôl′rīt′) *adj. Slang.* **1.** Of sound character : dependable. **2.** Good <an *all-right* concert>

all-round (ôl′round′) *also* **all-a•round** (ôl′ə-round′) *adj.* **1.** Including all aspects. **2.** Versatile.

all•spice (ôl′spīs′) *n.* A tropical American tree, *Pimenta officianalis,* bearing aromatic berries that are used as a spice.

all-star (ôl′stär′) *adj.* Composed entirely of star performers. **—all′-star′** *n.*

all-time (ôl′tīm′) *adj. Informal.* Of all time <an *all-time* attendance record>

all told *adv.* With everything taken into account.

al•lude (ə-lo͞od′) *v.* **-lud•ed, -lud•ing.** To refer to something indirectly. **—al•lu′sion** *n.* **—al•lu′sive** *adj.* **—al•lu′sive•ly** *adv.*

al•lure (ə-lo͝or′) *v.* **-lured, -lur•ing.** To tempt : entice. —*n.* The power of attracting. **—al•lure′ment** *n.* **—al•lur′er** *n.* **—al•lur′ing•ly** *adv.*

al•lu•vi•um (ə-lo͞o′vē-əm) *n., pl.* **-vi•ums** *or* **-vi•a** (-vē-ə). Sedimentary material deposited by flowing water, as in a delta or riverbed. **—al•lu′vi•al** *adj.*

al•ly (ə-lī′, ăl′ī′) *v.* **-lied, -ly•ing.** To enter into or unite in a formal relationship, as by a treaty. —*n.* (ăl′ī′, ə-lī′), *pl.* **-lies.** One allied with another.

al•ma ma•ter *also* **Al•ma Ma•ter** (ăl′mə mä′tər, äl′mə) *n.* **1.** The school, college, or university one has attended. **2.** The anthem of such an institution.

al•ma•nac (ôl′mə-năk′, ăl′-) *n.* An annual publication including calendars, weather forecasts, astronomical information, and other useful related tabular information.

Al Ma•nam•ah (ăl mə-năm′ə). Cap. of Bahrain, on the Persian Gulf. *Pop.* 89,112.

al•man•dine (ăl′mən-dēn′) *also* **al•man•dite** (-dīt′) *n.* A deep violet-red garnet used as a gemstone.

al•might•y (ôl-mī′tē) *adj.* Having absolute power : omnipotent. —*n.* **the Almighty.** God.

al•mond (ä′mənd, ăm′ənd) *n.* A small tree, *Prunus amygdalus,* bearing pink flowers and oval, edible nuts with soft, light-brown shells.

al•most (ôl′mōst′, ôl-mōst′) *adv.* Very nearly <*almost* finished>

alms (ämz) *pl.n.* Money or goods given in charity.

alms•house (ämz′hous′) *n.* A poorhouse.

al•ni•co (ăl′nĭ-kō′) *n.* A hard, strong alloy of aluminum, cobalt, copper, iron, nickel, and sometimes niobium or tantalum, used to make permanent magnets.

al•oe (ăl′ō) *n.* Any of various fleshy-leaved plants of the genus *Aloe,* native to S Africa.

a•loft (ə-lôft′, ə-lŏft′) *adv.* **1.** In or into a high place. **2.** In or toward a ship's upper rigging.

a•lo•ha (ä-lō′hä′) *interj.* Used as a greeting or farewell.

a•lone (ə-lōn′) *adj.* **1.** Apart from anything or anyone else : solitary. **2.** Excluding anyone else : only. **3.** With nothing else added. **4.** Without equal : unique. ☆**syns:** LONE, LONELY, LONESOME, SOLITARY **—a•lone′** *adv.* **—a•lone′ness** *n.*

a•long (ə-lông′, ə-lŏng′) *adv.* **1.** In a line with : following the course of. **2.** With a forward motion <move *along*> **3.** Together <disease *along* with poverty> **4.** As a companion or company <brought the dog *along*> **5.** *Informal.* Advanced to some degree <well *along* in the day> —*prep.* Over, through, or by the course of.

a•long•shore (ə-lông′shôr′, -shōr′, ə-lŏng′-) *adv.* Along the shore.

a•long•side (ə-lông′sīd′, ə-lŏng′-) *adv.* Along, at, or to the side. —*prep.* Side by side with.

a•loof (ə-lo͞of′) *adj.* Distant or reserved in manner or social relations. **—a•loof′ly** *adv.* **—a•loof′ness** *n.*

al•o•pe•cia (ăl′ə-pē′shə, -shē-ə) *n.* Loss of hair. **—al′o•pe′cic** (-pē′sĭk) *adj.*

a•loud (ə-loud′) *adv.* With the voice : orally.

alp (ălp) *n.* A high mountain.

al•pac•a (ăl-păk′ə) *n., pl.* **alpaca** *or* **-as. 1.** A domesticated South American mammal, *Lama pacos,* related to the llama, with fine, long, fleecy wool. **2. a.** Its wool. **b.** Cloth made from this wool.

al·pes·trine (ăl-pĕs′trĭn) *adj.* Growing at high altitudes.

al·pha·bet (ăl′fə-bĕt′, -bĭt) *n.* **1.** The letters of a given language, arranged in a traditional order. **2.** Basic or elementary principles.

al·pha·bet·i·cal (ăl′fə-bĕt′ĭ-kəl) *also* **al·pha·bet·ic** (-bĕt′ĭk) *adj.* **1.** Arranged in the traditional order of the letters of a language. **2.** Of or using an alphabet. **—al′pha·bet′i·cal·ly** *adv.*

al·pha·bet·ize (ăl′fə-bĭ-tīz′) *v.* **-ized, -iz·ing.** To put in alphabetical order. **—al′pha·bet′i·za′tion** (-bĕt′ĭ-zā′shən) *n.* **—al′pha·bet·iz′er** *n.*

alpha decay *n.* The radioactive decay of an atomic nucleus by emission of an alpha particle.

alpha helix *n.* A common structure of proteins, characterized by a single chain of amino acids stabilized by hydrogen bonds.

al·pha·nu·mer·ic (ăl′fə-no͞o-mĕr′ĭk, -nyo͞o-) *adj.* Consisting of both alphabetic and numerical symbols.

alpha particle *n.* A positively charged composite particle, identical with a helium atom nucleus and having 2 protons and 2 neutrons.

alpha ray *n.* A stream of alpha particles.

alpha rhythm *also* **alpha wave** *n.* The most common waveform of the adult human brain, recorded by electroencephalograph, usu. 8 to 12 oscillations per second in subjects at rest.

al·pine (ăl′pīn′, -pĭn) *adj.* **1.** Of or relating to high mountains. **2.** *Biol.* Living or growing above the timberline.

al·pin·ist *also* **Al·pin·ist** (ăl′pə-nĭst) *n.* A mountain climber : mountaineer.

Alps (ălps). Mountain system of SC Europe, rising to 15,771 ft (4.810.2 m).

al·read·y (ôl-rĕd′ē) *adv.* Before a specified time : previously.

Al·sace-Lor·raine (ăl′săs-lō-rān′, -lô-, -săs-). Region of NE France, annexed by Germany in 1871 and recovered by France in 1919.

al·so (ôl′sō) *adv.* In addition : likewise. *—conj.* And in addition.

al·so-ran (ôl′sō-răn′) *n. Informal.* One defeated in an election, race, etc.

Alta. *abbr.* Alberta.

al·tar (ôl′tər) *n.* An elevated place or structure before which religious ceremonies may be held or sacrifices offered.

al·ter (ôl′tər) *v.* **1.** To make or become different : change. **2.** To tailor (a garment) for a better fit. **3.** *Informal.* To spay or castrate. **—al′ter·a·ble** *adj.* **—al′ter·a·bly** *adv.* **—al′ter·a′tion** *n.*

al·ter·cate (ôl′tər-kāt′) *v.* **-cat·ed, -cat·ing.** To argue vehemently. **—al′ter·ca′tion** *n.*

al·ter e·go (ôl′tər ē′gō) *n.* **1.** Another aspect of one's personality. **2.** A constant companion or intimate friend.

al·ter·nate (ôl′tər-nāt′, ăl′-) *v.* **-nat·ed, -nat·ing. 1.** To happen in successive turns <Day *alternates* with night.> **2.** To change from one condition, action, or place to another regularly <*alternates* between pitcher and catcher> *—adj.* (-nĭt). **1.** Happening successively. **2.** Designating every other one of a series. **3.** Taking the place of another : substitute <an *alternate* method> *—n.* (-nĭt). One who acts in place of another. **—al′ter·nate·ly** *adv.* **—al′ter·na′tion** *n.*

alternating current *n.* An electric current that reverses direction in a circuit at regular intervals.

al·ter·na·tive (ôl-tûr′nə-tĭv, ăl-) *n.* **1.** The choice between possibilities. **2.** One of the possibilities to be chosen. *—adj.* Allowing a choice. **—al·ter′na·tive·ly** *adv.*

al·ter·na·tor (ôl′tər-nā′tər, ăl′-) *n.* A generator producing alternating current.

al·though *also* **al·tho** (ôl-*th*ō′) *conj.* Even though.

al·tim·e·ter (ăl-tĭm′ĭ-tər) *n.* An instrument for measuring and indicating altitude, as of an aircraft. **—al·tim′e·try** *n.*

al·ti·tude (ăl′tĭ-to͞od′, -tyo͞od′) *n.* **1.** The elevation of an object above a reference level, esp. above sea level or the earth's surface. **2.** *Astron.* The angular distance of a celestial object above the horizon. **3.** *Geom.* **a.** A line segment perpendicular to the base of a figure and extending from the base to the opposite vertex, side, or surface. **b.** The measure of the segment. **—al′ti·tu′di·nal** *adj.*

al·to (ăl′tō) *n., pl.* **-tos.** *Mus.* **1.** The lowest female singing voice : contralto. **2.** A countertenor. **3.** The range between soprano and tenor. **4.** A singer whose voice is within the alto range. **5.** A part written for an alto voice or instrument. **6.** An instrument that is within the alto range.

▲word history: *Alto* in Italian means "high." It is applied to the lowest female singing voice because the range of the female alto is the same as that of the highest male singing voice, orig. called the alto.

al·to·geth·er (ôl′tə-gĕ*th*′ər, ôl′tə-gĕ*th*′ər) *adv.* **1.** Completely : entirely. **2.** In all <*Altogether* a dozen gifts arrived.> **3.** As a whole. **—in the altogether.** *Informal.* Nude.

al·tru·ism (ăl′tro͞o-ĭz′əm) *n.* Selfless regard for the well-being of others. **—al′tru·ist** *n.* **—al′tru·is′tic** *adj.* **—al′tru·is′ti·cal·ly** *adv.*

al·um (ăl′əm) *n.* **1.** Any of various sulfates in which a trivalent metal, such as aluminum, chromium, or iron, is combined with a univalent metal, such as potassium or sodium. **2.** Aluminum potassium sulfate, a compound of this type, used medicinally to stop bleeding.

a·lu·mi·na (ə-lo͞o′mə-nə) *n.* Any of several forms of aluminum oxide that occur naturally as corundum, in bauxite, and with various impurities as ruby, sapphire, and emery.

al·u·min·i·um (ăl′yə-mĭn′ē-əm) *n. esp. Brit. var. of* ALUMINUM.

a·lu·mi·nize (ə-lo͞o′mə-nīz′) *v.* **-nized, -niz·ing.** To cover, coat, or treat with aluminum or aluminum paint.

a·lu·mi·nous (ə-lo͞o′mə-nəs) *adj.* Of, relating to, or having aluminum or alum.

a·lu·mi·num (ə-lo͞o′mə-nəm) *n. Symbol* **Al** A lightweight, silvery-white, malleable metallic element used for many hard, light, corrosion-resistant alloys.

a·lum·na (ə-lŭm′nə) *n., pl.* **-nae** (-nē′). A woman graduate or former student of a school, college, or university.

a·lum·nus (ə-lŭm′nəs) *n., pl.* **-ni** (-nī′). A graduate or former student of a school, college, or university.

al·ve·o·late (ăl-vē′ə-lĭt) *adj.* Having alveoli : honeycombed.

al·ve·o·lus (ăl-vē′ə-ləs) *n., pl.* **-li** (-lī′) **1.** A small pit or cavity, as an individual cell of a honeycomb. **2.** A tooth socket. **3.** An air sac of the lungs at the termination of a bronchiole. **—al·ve′o·lar** *adj.*

al·ways (ôl′wāz, -wēz, -wĭz) *adv.* **1.** At every instance. **2.** For all time : forever. **3.** At any time.

a·lys·sum (ə-lĭs′əm) *n.* **1.** A plant of the genus *Alyssum,* with dense yellow or white flower clusters. **2.** Sweet alyssum.

am (ăm; *when unstressed* əm) *v. 1st person sing. present tense of* BE.

Am *symbol for* AMERICIUM.

a.m. or **A.M.** *abbr. Lat.* ante meridiem (before noon); usu. small capitals A.M.

Am. or **Amer.** *abbr.* America; American.

a·mah *also* **a·ma** (ä′mə, ä′mä) *n.* An oriental maidservant, esp. a wet nurse.

a·mal·gam (ə-măl′gəm) *n.* **1.** An alloy of mercury with other metals, as tin or silver. **2.** A mixture.

a·mal·ga·mate (ə-măl′gə-māt′) *v.* **-mat·ed, -mat·ing.** To mix so as to make a unified whole : blend. **—a·mal′ga·ma′tion** *n.* **—a·mal′ga·ma′tor** *n.*

a·man·dine (ä′mən-dēn′, ăm′ən-) *adj.* Made or garnished with almonds.

am·a·ni·ta (ăm′ə-nī′tə, -nē′-) *n.* Any of various mushrooms of the genus *Amanita,* most of which are highly toxic.

a·man·u·en·sis (ə-măn′yo͞o-ĕn′sĭs) *n., pl.* **-ses** (-sēz′). A secretary.

am·a·ranth (ăm′ə-rănth′) *n.* **1.** A weedy plant of the genus *Amaranthus,* with small greenish or purplish flower clusters. **2.** An imaginary flower that does not fade or die. **—am′a·ran′thine** *adj.*

am·a·ret·to (ăm′ə-rĕt′ō) *n.* An almond-flavored liqueur.

Am·a·ril·lo (ăm′ə-rĭl′ō). City of N Tex., in the Panhandle. *Pop.* 149,230.

am·a·ryl·lis (ăm′ə-rĭl′ĭs) *n.* A bulbous, tropical plant, *Amaryllis belladonna,* native to S Africa, bearing large, lilylike flowers.

a·mass (ə-măs′) *v.* To accumulate : collect. **—a·mass′a·ble** *adj.* **—a·mass′er** *n.* **—a·mass′ment** *n.*

am·a·teur (ăm′ə-cho͝or′, -ə-tər, -ə-tyo͝or′) *n.* **1.** One who engages in an art, science, or sport for enjoyment rather than money. **2.** One who lacks professional skill. **—am′a·teur′ish** *adj.* **—am′a·teur′ish·ly** *adv.* **—am′a·teur′ism** *n.*

am·a·to·ry (ăm′ə-tôr′ē, -tōr′ē) *adj.* Of, promoting, or expressing love, esp. sexual love.

a·maze (ə-māz′) *v.* **a·mazed, a·maz·ing.** To affect with great surprise or wonder : astonish. **—a·maz′ed·ly** *adv.* **—a·maze′ment** *n.* **—a·maz′ing·ly** *adv.*

Am·a·zon[1] (ăm′ə-zŏn′, -zən) *n.* **1.** *Gk. Myth.* A member of a race of female warriors alleged to have lived in Scythia. **2. amazon.** A tall, athletic woman. **—Am′a·zo′ni·an** (-zō′nē-ən) *adj.*

▲word history: The Greeks themselves devised what is probably a folk etymology for *Amazon.* According to Greek legends the Amazons cut off their right breasts to be able to use a bow more easily. The word thus appears to be formed in Greek of the prefix *a-*, "not," and *mazos*, "breast," in reference to the Amazons' mutilated condition. However, it is more likely that the word *Amazon* is a Greek spelling of a non-Greek tribal name.

Am•a•zon[2] (ăm'ə-zŏn', -zən). River of South America, flowing c. 3,900 mi (6,275 km) from Peru N and E through N Brazil to the Atlantic.

am•a•zon•ite (ăm'ə-zə-nīt') *n.* A green variety of microcline, often used as a semiprecious gemstone.

am•bas•sa•dor (ăm-băs'ə-dər) *n.* A diplomat of the highest rank accredited by government as representative in residence to another. **—am•bas'sa•do'ri•al** *adj.* **—am•bas'sa•dor•ship'** *n.*

am•ber (ăm'bər) *n.* A translucent yellow, orange, or brownish-yellow fossil resin, used for making decorative objects, esp. jewelry. **—am'ber** *adj.*

am•ber•gris (ăm'bər-grĭs, -grēs') *n.* A waxy grayish substance formed in the intestines of sperm whales and used in perfumes as a fixative.

am•ber•jack (ăm'bər-jăk') *n, pl.* **-jack** or **-jacks.** A food and game fish of the genus *Seriola,* of temperate and tropical marine waters.

am•bi•ance (ăm'bē-əns) *also* **am•bi•ence** *n.* The distinctive atmosphere of an environment or setting.

am•bi•dex•trous (ăm'bĭ-dĕk'strəs) *adj.* Using both hands with equal facility. **—am'bi•dex•ter'i•ty** *n.* **—am'bi•dex'trous•ly** *adv.*

am•bi•ent (ăm'bē-ənt) *adj.* Surrounding.

am•big•u•ous (ăm-bĭg'yo͞o-əs) *adj.* **1.** Liable to more than one interpretation. **2.** Uncertain or indefinite <paper of an *ambiguous* hue> ☆**syns:** CLOUDY, EQUIVOCAL, NEBULOUS, OBSCURE, SIBYLLINE, UNCERTAIN, UNCLEAR, UNEXPLICIT. **—am'bi•gu'i•ty, am•big'u•ous•ness** *n.* **—am•big'u•ous•ly** *adv.*

am•bi•tion (ăm-bĭsh'ən) *n.* **1.** An eager or strong desire to achieve something. **2.** The goal so desired. ☆**syns:** DRIVE, ENTERPRISE, INITIATIVE, PUSH

am•bi•tious (ăm-bĭsh'əs) *adj.* **1.** Marked by ambition. **2.** Requiring much effort : challenging. **—am•bi'tious•ly** *adv.*

am•biv•a•lence (ăm-bĭv'ə-ləns) *n.* The existence of mutually conflicting emotions or thoughts about a person, object, or idea. **—am•biv'a•lent** *adj.* **—am•biv'a•lent•ly** *adv.*

am•ble (ăm'bəl) *v.* **-bled, -bling.** To move at a leisurely pace : saunter. **—am'ble** *n.* **—am'bler** *n.*

am•bro•sia (ăm-brō'zhə) *n.* **1.** *Gk. & Rom. Myth.* The food of the gods. **2.** Something with an esp. delightful flavor or fragrance. **—am•bro'sial, am•bro'sian** *adj.*

am•bu•lance (ăm'byə-ləns) *n.* A vehicle equipped for carrying the sick or injured.

am•bu•late (ăm'byə-lāt') *v.* **-lat•ed, -lat•ing.** To walk or move about. **—am'bu•lant** *adj.* **—am'bu•la•to'ry** *adj.*

am•bus•cade (ăm'bə-skăd', ăm'bə-skăd') *n.* An ambush. **—am'bus•cade** *v.* **—am'bus•cad'er** *n.*

am•bush (ăm'bo͝osh') *n.* **1.** A surprise attack made from a hiding place. **2.** The hiding place from which an ambush is made. **—am'bush** *v.*

a•me•ba (ə-mē'bə) *n. var. of* AMOEBA.

a•meer (ī-mîr', ā-mîr') *n. var. of* EMIR.

a•me•lio•rate (ə-mēl'yə-rāt') *v.* **-rat•ed, -rat•ing.** To make or become better : improve. **—a•me'lio•ra'tion** *n.*

a•men (ā-mĕn', ä-) *interj.* Used at the end of a prayer or a statement to express agreement or approval.

a•me•na•ble (ə-mē'nə-bəl, ə-mĕn'ə-) *adj.* **1.** Obedient : tractable. **2.** Responsible to authority : accountable. **—a•me'na•bly** *adv.*

a•mend (ə-mĕnd') *v.* **1.** To improve. **2.** To correct. **3.** To revise (e.g., a legislative measure) formally by adding, deleting, or rephrasing. **—a•mend'a•ble** *adj.*

a•mend•ment (ə-mĕnd'mənt) *n.* **1.** Improvement. **2.** A correction. **3. a.** A revision. **b.** A formal statement of such a revision.

a•mends (ə-mĕndz') *pl.n.* Reparation for insult, injury, or loss <make *amends*>

a•men•i•ty (ə-mĕn'ĭ-tē, ə-mē'nĭ-) *n., pl.* **-ties. 1.** Pleasantness : agreeableness. **2.** Something that increases physical or material comfort. **3. amenities.** Social courtesies : civilities.

a•men•or•rhe•a or **a•men•or•rhoe•a** (ā-mĕn'ə-rē'ə) *n.* Abnormal suppression or absence of menstruation. **—a•men'or•rhe'ic** *adj.*

am•ent[1] (ăm'ənt, ā'mənt) *n.* A catkin.

a•ment[2] (ā'mĕnt', ā'mənt) *n.* A mentally deficient person.

a•men•tia (ā-mĕn'shə, -shē-ə) *n.* Subnormal mental development.

Am•er•a•sian (ăm'ə-rā'zhən, -shən) *n.* A person of American and Asian descent. **—Am'er•a'sian** *adj.*

a•merce (ə-mûrs') *v.* **a•merced, a•merc•ing.** To punish, esp. by a fine imposed arbitrarily by a court.

A•mer•i•ca (ə-mĕr'ĭ-kə) *n.* **1.** The U.S. **2.** *also* **the Americas.** North America, Central America, and South America.

A•mer•i•can (ə-mĕr'ĭ-kən) *n.* A native or inhabitant of the U.S. or the Americas. **—A•mer'i•can** *adj.* **—A•mer'i•can•i•za'tion** *n.* **—A•mer'i•can•ize'** *v.* **—A•mer'i•can•ness** *n.*

A•mer•i•ca•na (ə-mĕr'ĭ-kä'nə, -kăn'ə, -kā'nə) *pl.n.* A collection of materials relating to American history, geography, or folklore.

American eagle *n.* The bald eagle.

A•mer•i•can•ism (ə-mĕr'ĭ-kə-nĭz'əm) *n.* A custom, language usage, trait, or tradition peculiar to the U.S.

American plan *n.* A hotel plan whereby a guest is charged a fixed daily rate for room, meals, and service.

American Sa•mo•a (sə-mō'ə). U.S. territory in the S Pacific. *Cap.* Pago Pago. *Pop.* 32,297.

am•er•i•ci•um (ăm'ə-rĭsh'ē-əm) *n. Symbol* **Am** A white metallic transuranic element of the actinide series.

Am•er•ind (ăm'ə-rĭnd') *also* **Am•er•in•di•an** (ăm'ə-rĭn'dē-ən) *n.* An American Indian or an Eskimo. **—Am'er•in'di•an, Am'er•in'dic** *adj. & n.*

am•e•thyst (ăm'ə-thĭst) *n.* A purple or violet form of transparent quartz or corundum used as a gemstone. **—am'e•thys'tine** *adj.*

a•mi•a•ble (ā'mē-ə-bəl) *adj.* Pleasant and friendly <an *amiable* companion> ☆**syns:** AFFABLE, AGREEABLE, COMPLAISANT, CORDIAL, EASY, EASYGOING, GENIAL, GOOD-NATURED **—a'mi•a•bil'i•ty, a'mi•a•ble•ness** *n.* **—a'mi•a•bly** *adv.*

am•i•ca•ble (ăm'ĭ-kə-bəl) *adj.* **1.** Friendly. **2.** Harmonious. **—am'i•ca•bil'i•ty, am'i•ca•ble•ness** *n.* **—am'i•ca•bly** *adv.*

a•mid (ə-mĭd') *also* **a•midst** (ə-mĭdst') *prep.* In the middle of : surrounded by.

a•mid•ships (ə-mĭd'shĭps') *also* **a•mid•ship** (-shĭp') *adv. Naut.* Halfway between the bow and the stern.

a•mi•go (ə-mē'gō) *n., pl.* **-gos.** A friend.

a•mi•no acid (ə-mē'nō, ăm'ə-nō') *n.* Any of a class of nitrogenous organic compounds that are essential components of proteins.

A•mish (ä'mĭsh, ăm'ĭsh) *pl.n.* A sect of Mennonites that settled primarily in SE Pa. in the late 1600's. **—A'mish** *adj.*

a•miss (ə-mĭs') *adj.* Out of proper order or place. *—adv.* In a wrong or improper way.

am•i•ty (ăm'ĭ-tē) *n., pl.* **-ties.** Peaceful relations : friendship.

Am•man (ä'män). Cap. of Jordan, in the N. *Pop.* 648,587.

am•me•ter (ăm'mē'tər) *n.* A device for measuring electric current.

am•mo (ăm'ō) *n.* Ammunition.

am•mo•nia (ə-mōn'yə, ə-mō'nē-ə) *n.* **1.** A colorless, pungent gas widely used to make fertilizers and nitrogen-containing compounds. **2.** A solution of ammonia gas dissolved in water.

am•mo•nite (ăm'ə-nīt') *also* **am•mo•noid** (-noid') *n.* The chambered shell of any of various extinct mollusks of the class *Cephalopoda,* found as fossils.

am•mu•ni•tion (ăm'yə-nĭsh'ən) *n.* **1. a.** Projectiles that can be propelled or discharged from guns. **b.** Nuclear, biological, chemical, or explosive material used as a weapon. **2.** A means of offense or defense.

am•ne•sia (ăm-nē'zhə) *n.* Partial or total loss of memory. **—am•ne'si•ac'** (-zē ăk', -zhē ăk'), **am•ne'sic** (-zĭk, -sĭk) *n. & adj.*

am•nes•ty (ăm'nĭ-stē) *n., pl.* **-ties.** A governmental pardon granted to a number of offenders, esp. for political offenses. **—am'nes•ty** *v.*

am•ni•o•cen•te•sis (ăm'nē-ō-sĕn-tē'sĭs) *n., pl.* **-ses** (-sēz'). The surgical removal of an amniotic fluid sample from a pregnant woman, esp. for determining any genetic disorder of the fetus.

am•ni•on (ăm'nē-ən, -ŏn') *n., pl.* **-ni•ons** or **-ni•a** (-nē-ə). A membranous sac of watery fluid containing the embryo of a mammal, bird, or reptile. **—am'ni•ot'ic** (-ŏt'ĭk), **am'ni•on'ic** (-ŏn'ĭk) *adj.*

a•moe•ba *also* **a•me•ba** (ə-mē'bə) *n., pl.* **-bas** or **-bae** (-bē). Any of various protozoans of the genus *Amoeba* and related genera, found in water, soil, and as internal animal parasites, having an indefinite, changeable form and moving by pseudopodia. **—a•moe'bic** *adj.*

a•mok (ə-mŭk', ə-mŏk') *adv. & adj. var. of* AMUCK.

a•mong (ə-mŭng') *also* **a•mongst** (ə-mŭngst') *prep.* **1.** Surrounded by : amid. **2.** In the group, number, or class of. **3.** In the company of <living *among* the poor> **4.** With shares to each of <Divide this *among* you.> **5.** With one another.

a•mon•til•la•do (ə-mŏn'tə-lä'dō) *n., pl.* **-dos.** A pale dry sherry.

a•mor•al (ā-môr'əl, ā-mŏr'əl) *adj.* **1.** Not admitting of moral distinctions or judgments : neither moral nor immoral. **2.** Lacking moral judgment. **—a'mo•ral'i•ty** *n.* **—a•mor'al•ly** *adv.*

am·o·ret·to (ăm′ə-rĕ′ō, ä′mə-) *n., pl.* **-ti** (-tē) *or* **-tos.** A cupid.
am·o·rous (ăm′ər-əs) *adj.* **1.** Feeling or expressing love. **2.** In love. **—am′or·ous·ly** *adv.* **—am′or·ous·ness** *n.*
a·mor·phous (ə-môr′fəs) *adj.* **1.** Lacking definite form : shapeless. **2.** General : vague. **3.** *Chem.* Without distinct crystalline structure. **—a·mor′phous·ness** *n.*
am·or·tize (ăm′ər-tīz′, ə-môr′tīz′) *v.* **-tized, -tiz·ing.** To liquidate (a debt) by installment payments. **—am′or·ti·za′tion, a·mor′tize·ment** *n.*
A·mos (ā′məs) *n.* **1.** 8th cent. B.C. Hebrew prophet. **2.** See BIBLE TABLE.
a·mount (ə-mount′) *n.* **1.** The total of 2 or more quantities : aggregate. **2.** A principal plus its interest. *—v.* **1.** To total in number or quantity. **2.** To be equal or tantamount <silence *amounting* to approval>
a·mour (ə-mo͝or′) *n.* A usu. illicit love affair.
a·mour·pro·pre (ə-mo͝or′ prôp′rə) *n.* Self-respect.
AMP (ā′em-pē′) *n.* A mononucleotide found in animal cells, that is reversibly convertible to ADP and ATP.
am·per·age (ăm′pər-ĭj, ăm′pîr′ĭj) *n.* The strength of an electric current as measured in amperes.
am·pere (ăm′pîr′) *n.* A unit of electric current equal to a flow of 1 coulomb per second.
am·per·sand (ăm′pər-sănd′) *n.* The character or sign (&) that represents *and.*
am·phet·a·mine (ăm-fĕt′ə-mēn′, -mĭn) *n.* A colorless volatile liquid used primarily as a central nervous system stimulant.
am·phib·i·an (ăm-fĭb′ē-ən) *n.* **1.** Any of various cold-blooded, smooth-skinned vertebrate of the class Amphibia, as a frog, that as aquatic larvae breathe by means of gills and metamorphose to an adult form with air-breathing lungs. **2.** An amphibious aircraft or vehicle.
am·phib·i·ous (ăm-fĭb′ē-əs) *adj.* **1.** Capable of living on land and in water. **2.** Capable of operating on land and water, as specially designed military vehicles.
am·phi·bole (ăm′fə-bōl′) *n.* Any of a large group of double silicate minerals, as hornblende, having mixtures of sodium, calcium, magnesium, iron, and aluminum. **—am′phi·bol′ic** (-bŏl′ĭk) *adj.*
am·phi·the·a·ter (ăm′fə-thē′ə-tər) *n.* A round or oval structure with rows of seats rising gradually outward from a central open space.
am·phi·the·a·tre (ăm′fə-thē′ə-tər) *n. esp. Brit. var. of* AMPHITHEATER.
am·pho·ra (ăm′fər-ə) *n., pl.* **-rae** (-fə-rē′) *or* **-ras.** A 2-handled jar with a narrow neck used by the ancient Greeks and Romans.
am·pi·cil·lin (ăm′pə-sĭl′ən) *n.* An antibiotic related to penicillin.
am·ple (ăm′pəl) *adj.* **-pler, -plest. 1.** Of large size, extent, or capacity. **2.** Generous or abundant. **3.** Sufficient. **—am′ple·ness** *n.* **—am′ply** *adv.*
am·pli·fy (ăm′plə-fī′) *v.* **-fied, -fy·ing. 1.** To make larger, louder, or more powerful. **2.** To expand, as by adding details. **—am′pli·fi·ca′tion** *n.* **—am′pli·fi′er** *n.*
am·pli·tude (ăm′plĭ-to͞od′, -tyo͞od′) *n.* **1.** Greatness of size. **2.** Fullness : plenitude. **3.** Breadth or range, as of intelligence. **4.** *Physics.* The highest value of a periodically varying quantity.
amplitude modulation *n.* The encoding of a carrier wave by variation of its amplitude in accordance with an input signal.
am·poule *also* **am·pule** *or* **am·pul** (ăm′po͞ol′, -pyo͞ol′) *n.* A small sealed glass container used for a hypodermic injection.
am·pul·la (ăm-po͝ol′ə, -pŭl′ə) *n., pl.* **-pul·lae** (-po͝ol′ē, -pŭl′ē). A nearly round, 2-handled bottle used by the ancient Romans for wine, oil, or perfume.
am·pu·tate (ăm′pyo͞o-tāt′) *v.* **-tat·ed, -tat·ing.** To cut off (e.g., a limb), esp. by surgery. **—am′pu·tee′** *n.* **—am′pu·ta′tion** *n.* **—am′pu·ta′tor** *n.*
am·ri·ta (ŭm-rē′tə) *n.* **1.** The ambrosia prepared by the Hindu gods that confers immortality. **2.** The immortality conferred.
Am·ster·dam (ăm′stər-dăm′). Constitutional cap. of the Netherlands. *Pop.* 716,919.
amt. *abbr.* amount.
a·muck (ə-mŭk′) *also* **a·mok** (ə-mŭk′, ə-mŏk′) *adv.* In a murderous frenzy <rioters running *amuck*> **2.** In an uncontrolled manner <The disease had run *amuck.*>
am·u·let (ăm′yə-lĭt) *n.* A charm worn as a talisman against evil or injury.
a·muse (ə-myo͞oz′) *v.* **a·mused, a·mus·ing.** To occupy in an agreeable pleasing way. ☆**syns:** DISTRACT, DIVERT, ENTERTAIN **—a·mus′a·ble** *adj.* **—a·muse′ment** *n.* **—a·mus′er** *n.*
a·myg·da·line (ə-mĭg′də-lĭn, -līn′) *adj.* Of, relating to, or similar to an almond.
am·y·lase (ăm′ə-lās′, -lāz′) *n.* An enzyme that converts starch to sugar.
an (ən; ăn *when stressed*) *indef. art.* A form of *a.* Used before words beginning with a vowel or with an unpronounced *h* <*an* emerald><*an* honor>
-an *suff.* **1.** Of, relating to, or like <Americ*an*> **2.** Believing in or following <Confuci*an*>
an·a·bat·ic (ăn′ə-băt′ĭk) *adj.* Of or relating to rising wind currents.
an·a·bol·ic steroid (ăn′ə-bŏl′ĭk) *n.* A synthetic hormone often used to increase muscle size and strength.
a·nach·ro·nism (ə-năk′rə-nĭz′əm) *n.* **1.** The placement of something as existing or occurring at other than its historical time. **2.** Anything out of its proper place. **—a·nach′ro·nis′tic, a·nach′ro·nous** *adj.* **—a·nach′ro·nis′ti·cal·ly, a·nach′ro·nous·ly** *adv.*
an·a·co·lu·thon (ăn′ə-kə-lo͞o′thŏn′) *n., pl.* **-thons** *or* **-tha** (-thə) An abrupt change within a sentence to a 2nd grammatical construction inconsistent with the 1st; e.g., *I warned you that if you continue to smoke, what will become of you?* **—an′a·co·lu′thic** *adj.*
an·a·con·da (ăn′ə-kŏn′də) *n.* A large, nonpoisonous arboreal snake, *Eunectes murinus,* of tropical South America, that suffocates its prey in its coils.
an·a·dem (ăn′ə-dĕm′) *n. Archaic.* A garland or wreath for the head.
a·nad·ro·mous (ə-năd′rə-məs) *adj.* Migrating up rivers from the sea to breed in fresh water, as salmon do.
a·nae·mi·a (ə-nē′mē-ə) *n. var. of* ANEMIA.
an·aer·obe (ăn′ə-rōb′, ăn-âr′ōb′) *n.* A microorganism, as a bacterium, able to live in the absence of free oxygen. **—an′aer·o′bic** (ăn′ə-rō′bĭk, -âr-ō′bĭk) *adj.* **—an′aer·o′bic·al·ly** *adv.*
an·aes·the·sia (ăn′ĭs-thē′zhə) *n. var. of* ANESTHESIA.
an·a·gram (ăn′ə-grăm′) *n.* A word or phrase formed by rearranging the letters of another word or phrase.
An·a·heim (ăn′ə-hīm′). City of S Calif. *Pop.* 221,847.
a·nal (ā′nəl) *adj.* Of, relating to, or near the anus.
anal. *abbr.* **1.** analogous; analogy. **2.** analysis; analytic.
an·a·lects (ăn′ə-lĕkts′) *also* **an·a·lec·ta** (ăn′ə-lĕk′tə) *pl.n.* Collected excerpts from literary works. **—an′a·lec′tic** *adj.*
an·al·ge·si·a (ăn′əl-jē′zē-ə, -zhə) *n.* Inability to feel pain although conscious. **—an′al·ge′sic** *n. & adj.*
analog computer *also* **analogue computer** *n.* A computer in which numerical data are represented by measurable quantities such as lengths, electrical signals, or voltage.
a·nal·o·gous (ə-năl′ə-gəs) *adj.* **1.** Corresponding in certain ways. **2.** *Biol.* Similar in function but not in evolutionary origin.
an·a·logue *also* **an·a·log** (ăn′ə-lôg′, -lŏg′) *n.* **1.** One that is analogous. **2.** *Biol.* An analogous organ or structure.
a·nal·o·gy (ə-năl′ə-jē) *n., pl.* **-gies. 1.** Correspondence in some respects between otherwise unlike things. **2.** A logical inference based on the assumption that if 2 things are known to be alike in some respects, then they must be alike in other respects. **3.** *Biol.* Correspondence in function or position between organs of dissimilar evolutionary origin. **—an′a·log′i·cal** *adj.* **—an′a·log′i·cal·ly** *adv.*
a·nal·y·sand (ə-năl′ĭ-sănd′) *n.* One who is being psychoanalyzed.
an·a·lyse (ăn′ə-līz′) *v. esp. Brit. var. of* ANALYZE.
a·nal·y·sis (ə-năl′ĭ-sĭs) *n., pl.* **-ses** (-sēz′). **1.** Separation of an intellectual or substantial whole into its parts for individual study. **2.** *Chem.* **a.** Separation of a substance into its elements to determine their nature (qualitative analysis) or their proportions (quantitative analysis). **b.** A statement of the results of such a study. **3.** Psychoanalysis. **—an′a·lyst** *n.* **—an′a·lyt′ic, an′a·lyt′i·cal** *adj.*
an·a·lyze (ăn′ə-līz′) *v.* **-lyzed, -lyz·ing. 1.** To make a chemical analysis of. **2.** To psychoanalyze. ☆**syns:** ANATOMIZE, BREAK DOWN, DISSECT **—an′a·lyz′a·ble** *adj.* **—an′a·ly·za′tion** *n.* **—an′a·lyz′er** *n.*
an·a·pest *also* **an·a·paest** (ăn′ə-pĕst′) *n.* A metrical foot made up of 2 short syllables followed by 1 long one, as in *unaligned.* **—an′a·pes′tic** *adj.*
an·ar·chic (ăn-är′kĭk) *or* **an·ar·chi·cal** (-kĭ-kəl) *adj.* **1.** Of, like, or promoting anarchy. **2.** Lawless. **—an·ar′chi·cal·ly** *adv.*
an·ar·chism (ăn′ər-kĭz′əm) *n.* **1.** The doctrine of the abolishment of all forms of government because they are oppressive and undesirable. **2.** Lawlessness. **—an′ar·chist** *n.* **—an′ar·chis′tic** *adj.*
an·ar·chy (ăn′ər-kē) *n., pl.* **-chies. 1.** Lack of any political authority. **2.** Disorder and confusion. **3.** Absence of any common purpose or standard.
a·nas·to·mo·sis (ə-năs′tə-mō′sĭs) *n., pl.* **-ses** (-sēz′). The union or connection of branches as of rivers, leaf veins, or blood vessels. **—a·nas′to·mot′ic** (-mŏt′ĭk) *adj.*

a·nas·tro·phe (ə-năs′trə-fē) *n.* Inversion of the normal syntactic order of words; e.g., *To church went we.*

a·nath·e·ma (ə-năth′ə-mə) *n., pl.* **-mas. 1.** An ecclesiastical ban, curse, or excommunication. **2.** One that is detested. **—a·nath′e·ma·tize′** *v.*

a·nat·o·mize (ə-năt′ə-mīz′) *v.* **-mized, -miz·ing. 1.** *Biol.* To dissect. **2.** To examine in minute detail : analyze.

a·nat·o·my (ə-năt′ə-mē) *n., pl.* **-mies. 1.** The structure of a plant or animal. **2.** The science dealing with the structure of organisms and their elements. **3.** The constituent structure of something. **4.** A detailed analysis. ☆***syns:*** ARCHITECTURE, CONSTITUTION, FABRIC, MAKE-UP **—an′a·tom′i·cal** (ăn′ə-tŏm′ĭ-kəl) *adj.* **—an′a·tom′i·cal·ly** *adv.* **—a·nat′o·mist** *n.*

-ance *suff.* **1.** State or condition <resembl*ance*> **2.** Action <continu*ance*>

an·ces·tor (ăn′sĕs′tər) *n.* **1.** Someone from whom one is descended : forefather. **2.** *Biol.* The organism or type of organism from which later organisms evolved. **3.** A forerunner or predecessor. ☆***syns:*** ANTECEDENT, ASCENDANT, FOREBEAR, FOREFATHER, PROGENITOR. **—an·ces′tral** *adj.* **—an·ces′tral·ly** *adv.*

an·ces·try (ăn′sĕs′trē) *n., pl.* **-tries. 1.** Ancestral descent. **2.** Ancestors as a group.

an·chor (ăng′kər) *n.* **1.** A heavy object attached to a vessel by a rope or cable and cast overboard to hold the vessel in place either by weight or by flukes. **2.** Something that gives security. **3.** An anchorman or anchorwoman. **—an′chor** *v.*

an·chor·age (ăng′kər-ĭj) *n.* **1.** A place for anchoring. **2.** A fee charged for anchoring. **3.** An anchoring or being anchored.

An·chor·age (ăng′kər-ĭj). City of S Alas. *Pop.* 173,992.

an·cho·rite (ăng′kə-rīt′) *also* **an·cho·ret** (-rĕt′) *n.* A hermit who has retired into seclusion for religious reasons. **—an′cho·ress** *n.*

an·chor·man (ăng′kər-măn′) *n.* **1.** *Sports.* The last runner in a relay race. **2.** The narrator or coordinator of a newscast in which several correspondents give reports.

an·chor·wom·an (ăng′kər-wŏŏm′ən) *n.* A woman who narrates or coordinates a newscast in which several correspondents give reports.

an·cho·vy (ăn′chō′vē, ăn-chō′vē) *n., pl.* **-vy** or **-vies.** A small herringlike marine fish.

an·cient (ăn′shənt) *adj.* **1.** Very old. **2.** Of or happening in remote times, esp. before the fall of the Western Roman Empire. *—n.* **1.** A very old person. **2. ancients.** The Greeks and Romans of ancient times. **—an′cient·ly** *adv.* **—an′cient·ness** *n.*

an·cil·lar·y (ăn′sə-lĕr′ē) *adj.* **1.** Subordinate. **2.** Auxiliary : supplementary. **—an′cil·lar′y** *n.*

-ancy *suff.* -ANCE.

and (ənd, ən; ănd *when stressed*) *conj.* **1.** Together or along with : as well as. **2.** Added to : plus. **3.** As a result : in consequence <They invited me *and* here I am.> **4.** Used between two verbs <go *and* find it><come *and* see>

an·dan·te (än-dän′tā, ăn-dăn′tē) *adv. Mus.* Moderate in tempo. Used as a direction. **—an·dan′te** *adj.* & *n.*

an·dan·ti·no (än′dän-tē′nō, ăn′dăn-tē′nō) *adv. Mus.* Slightly faster than andante. **—an′dan·ti′no** *adj.* & *n.*

An·der·sen (ăn′dər-sən), **Hans Christian.** 1805–75. Danish author.

An·des (ăn′dēz). Mountain chain extending the length of W South America and rising to 22,835 ft (6,964.7 m).

and·i·ron (ănd′ī′ərn) *n.* One of a pair of supports for fireplace logs.

and/or *conj.* Used to indicate that either *and* or *or* may be used for connecting words, phrases, or clauses depending upon the meaning intended.

An·dor·ra (ăn-dôr′ə, -dŏr′ə). Country of SW Europe, in the E Pyrenees, between France and Spain. *Cap.* Andorra la Vella. *Pop.* 32,700. **—An·dor′ran** *adj.* & *n.*

an·dro·gen (ăn′drə-jən) *n.* A steroid hormone instrumental in the development and maintenance of masculine characteristics. **—an′dro·gen′ic** *adj.*

an·drog·e·nous (ăn-drŏj′ə-nəs) *adj.* Of or relating to production of male offspring.

an·drog·y·nous (ăn-drŏj′ə-nəs) *adj.* Having both female and male characteristics : hermaphroditic. **—an·drog′y·ny** *n.*

an·droid (ăn′droid′) *adj.* Having human features. *—n.* A synthetic person artificially created from biological materials.

an·ec·dote (ăn′ĭk-dōt′) *n.* A short interesting or humorous account of a real or fictitious incident. ☆***syns:*** FABLE, STORY, TALE, YARN **—an′ec·do′tal** *adj.*

an·e·cho·ic (ăn′ĭ-kō′ĭk) *adj.* Not having or producing echoes.

a·ne·mi·a *also* **a·nae·mi·a** (ə-nē′mē-ə) *n.* Pathological deficiency in the oxygen-carrying material of the blood. **—a·ne′mic** *adj.*

an·e·mom·e·ter (ăn′ə-mŏm′ĭ-tər) *n.* An instrument for measuring wind force and speed. **—an′e·mo·met′ric** (-mō-mĕt′rĭk) *adj.* **—an′e·mom′e·try** *n.*

a·nem·o·ne (ə-nĕm′ə-nē) *n.* **1.** A plant of the genus *Anemone* of the N Temperate Zone, with white, purple, or red flowers. **2.** The sea anemone.

†a·nent (ə-nĕnt′) *prep.* **1.** Regarding : concerning. **2.** *Regional.* Close to : opposite.

aneroid barometer *n.* A barometer in which atmospheric pressure is indicated by the relative bulges of an elastic metal disk covering a chamber in which there is a partial vacuum.

an·es·the·sia *also* **an·aes·the·sia** (ăn′ĭs-thē′zhə) *n.* Complete or partial loss of physical sensation caused by disease or an anesthetic.

an·es·the·si·ol·o·gy *also* **an·aes·the·si·ol·o·gy** (ăn′ĭs-thē′zē-ŏl′ə-jē) *n.* The medical science of anesthetics, their effects, and use. **—an′es·the′si·ol′o·gist** *n.*

an·es·thet·ic *also* **an·aes·thet·ic** (ăn′ĭs-thĕt′ĭk) *adj.* Inducing anesthesia. *—n.* A substance, as a gas or drug, that induces anesthesia. **—a·nes′the·tist** (ə-nĕs′thĭ-tĭst) *n.* **—a·nes′the·ti·za′tion** *n.* **—a·nes′the·tize′** *v.*

a·new (ə-no͞o′, ə-nyo͞o′) *adv.* **1.** Once more : again. **2.** In a new and different manner or form.

an·gel (ān′jəl) *n.* **1.** One of the immortal beings attendant upon God. **2.** A kind and lovable person. **3.** A financial backer of an enterprise, esp. a dramatic production. **—an·gel′ic** (-jĕl′ĭk), **an·gel′i·cal** *adj.* **—an·gel′i·cal·ly** *adv.*

angel dust *n. Slang.* Phencyclidine.

An·ge·le·no (ăn′jə-lē′nō) *n., pl.* **-nos.** A native or inhabitant of Los Angeles.

an·gel·fish (ān′jəl-fĭsh′) *n.* Any of several brightly colored fishes of the family Chaetodontidae of warm seas, with a laterally compressed body.

angel food cake *also* **angel cake** *n.* A white sponge cake made of egg whites, sugar, and flour.

an·gel·i·ca (ăn-jĕl′ĭ-kə) *n.* A plant, *Angelica archangelica,* with aromatic seeds, leaves, stems, and roots that are used medicinally and as flavoring.

an·gel·ol·o·gy (ān′jəl-ŏl′ə-jē) *n.* The branch of theology concerning angels.

angel shark *n.* A shark of the genus *Squatina,* with a broad flat head and body.

an·ger (ăng′gər) *n.* A feeling of great displeasure or hostility : wrath. **—an′ger** *v.*

an·gi·na (ăn-jī′nə) *n.* **1.** A disease, as croup or diphtheria, marked by painful, choking spasms. **2.** Angina pectoris.

angina pec·to·ris (pĕk′tə-rĭs) *n.* Severe paroxysmal chest pain associated with an insufficient supply of blood to the heart.

an·gle[1] (ăng′gəl) *v.* **-gled, -gling. 1.** To fish with a hook and line. **2.** To attempt to get something, esp. by trickery or scheming. **—an′gler** *n.*

an·gle[2] (ăng′gəl) *n.* **1. a.** A flat geometric figure formed by a pair of rays that diverge from a common point. **b.** The rotation required to superimpose either of 2 such lines or angles on the other. **2. a.** The place, position, or direction from which something is presented to view. **b.** A point of view : aspect. **3.** *Slang.* A scheme. *—v.* **-gled, -gling. 1.** To move or turn at an angle. **2.** To hit at an angle <*angled* the puck into the goal>

An·gle (ăng′gəl) *n.* A member of a Germanic people who migrated to England in the 5th cent. A.D..

angle iron *n.* A length of steel or iron bent at a right angle along its long dimension, used as a support or structural framework.

an·gle·worm (ăng′gəl-wûrm′) *n.* A worm, as an earthworm, used as fishing bait.

An·gli·can (ăng′glĭ-kən) *adj.* **1.** Of or typical of the Church of England. **2.** Of or relating to England or the English. **—An′gli·can** *n.* **—An′gli·can·ism** *n.*

Anglican Church *n.* The Church of England and its related churches in other nations, esp. the Protestant Episcopal Church.

An·gli·ce (ăng′glĭ-sē′) *adv.* In English <Venezia, *Anglice* Venice>

An·gli·cize (ăng′glĭ-sīz′) *v.* **-cized, -ciz·ing.** To make or become English in form, idiom, style, or character. **—An′gli·ci·za′tion** *n.*

An·glo (ăng′glō′) *n., pl.* **-glos.** *Informal.* A Caucasian inhabitant of the U.S. who is not of Latin descent. **—An′glo′** *adj.*

An·glo·phile (ăng′glə-fīl′) *n.* One who admires England, the English, and English things.

An·glo·phobe (ăng′glə-fōb′) *n.* One who fears or dislikes England, the English, or English things.

An·glo·phone (ăng′lə-fōn′) *n.* An English-speaking person, esp. in a country where 2 or more languages are spoken.

An·glo-Sax·on (ăng′glō-săk′sən) *n.* **1.** A member of one of the Germanic peoples (Angles, Saxons, and Jutes) who came to Brit-

ain in the 5th and 6th cent. A.D. **2.** Old English. **3.** A person of English ancestry. **—An′glo-Sax′on** *adj.*
An•go•la (ăng-gō′lə). Country of SW Africa. *Cap.* Luanda. *Pop.* 7,000,000. **—An•go′lan** *adj.* & *n.*
An•go•ra (ăng-gôr′ə, -gōr′ə) *n.* **1.** A rabbit, cat, or goat that has long, silky hair. **2. angora.** A yarn made from the hair of an Angora rabbit or goat.

Angora
Angora goat

an•gos•tu•ra bark (ăng′gə-sto͝or′ə, -tyo͝or′ə) *n.* The bitter, aromatic bark of either of 2 Brazilian trees, *Galipea officinalis* or *Cusparia trifoliata*, used as a tonic and a flavoring agent.
an•gry (ăng′grē) *adj.* **-gri•er, -gri•est. 1.** Feeling or showing anger. **2.** Having a threatening aspect <an *angry* sky> **3.** Inflamed, as a sore. ☆**syns:** CHOLERIC, ENRAGED, FURIOUS, INDIGNANT, IRATE, MAD, SEETHING, SORE, WRATHFUL **—an′gri•ly** (-grə-lē) *adv.*
angst (ängkst) *n.* A state of anxiety.
ang•strom *or* **Ång•ström** (ăng′strəm) *n.* A unit of length equal to 1 hundred-millionth (10^{-8}) of a centimeter.
an•guish (ăng′gwĭsh) *n.* An agonizing pain of the body or mind : torment. *—v.* To suffer or cause to suffer anguish. **—an′guished** *adj.*
an•gu•lar (ăng′gyə-lər) *adj.* **1.** Having or forming an angle or angles. **2.** Measured by an angle or degrees of an arc. **3.** Gaunt. **—an′gu•lar′i•ty** (-lăr′ĭ-tē), **an′gu•lar•ness** *n.* **—an′gu•lar•ly** *adv.*
an•hy•drous (ăn-hī′drəs) *adj.* Without water.
an•il (ăn′ĭl) *n.* The indigo plant or a blue dye obtained from it.
an•ile (ăn′īl′, ā′nīl′) *adj.* Of, resembling, or similar to an old woman. **—a•nil′i•ty** *n.*
an•i•line *also* **an•i•lin** (ăn′ə-lĭn) *n.* A colorless, oily, poisonous liquid used to make rubber, dyes, pharmaceuticals, rocket fuels, and other products.
an•i•ma (ăn′ə-mə) *n.* The inner self : soul.
an•i•mad•vert (ăn′ə-măd-vûrt′) *v.* To remark or comment critically, usu. with disapproval. **—an′i•mad•ver′sion** *n.*
an•i•mal (ăn′ə-məl) *n.* **1.** An organism of the kingdom Animalia, distinguished from plants by such characteristics as the power of locomotion and nonphotosynthetic metabolism. **2.** An animal organism other than a human being. **3.** A bestial or brutish person. **4.** Animality. *—adj.* **1.** Of or relating to animals. **2.** Relating to the physical as distinct from the spiritual nature of humans.
an•i•mal•cule (ăn′ə-măl′kyo͞ol′) *n.* A very small or microscopic organism.
an•i•mal•i•ty (ăn′ə-măl′ĭ-tē) *n.* The animal as distinct from the spiritual nature of humans.
animal spirits *pl.n.* Vigorous buoyancy of good health.
an•i•mate (ăn′ə-māt′) *v.* **-mat•ed, -mat•ing. 1.** To give life to. **2.** To give interest or zest to. **3.** To design or produce (a cartoon) creating the illusion of motion. *—adj.* (ăn′ə-mĭt). **1.** Having life : alive. **2.** Of or relating to animal life as distinguished from plant life. **—an′i•mat′ed** *adj.* **—an′i•mat′ed•ly** *adv.* **—an′i•ma′tion** *n.* **—an′i•ma′tor, an′i•mat′er** *n.*
a•ni•ma•to (ä′nə-mä′tō) *adv. Mus.* In an animated or lively manner. Used as a direction. **—a′ni•ma′to** *adj.*
an•i•mism (ăn′ə-mĭz′əm) *n.* A belief among primitive tribes that natural objects and forces have souls. **—an′i•mist** *n.* **—an′i•mis′tic** *adj.*
an•i•mos•i•ty (ăn′ə-mŏs′ĭ-tē) *n., pl.* **-ties.** Deep-seated hostility : enmity.
an•i•mus (ăn′ə-məs) *n.* Ill will : animosity.
an•i•on (ăn′ī′ən) *n.* An ion with a negative charge that is attracted to an anode, as in electrolysis.
an•ise (ăn′ĭs) *n.* **1.** A plant, *Pimpinella anisum*, with yellowish-white flower clusters and licorice-flavored seeds. **2.** Aniseed.
an•i•seed (ăn′ĭ-sēd′) *n.* The seed of the anise used medicinally and for flavoring.
an•i•sette (ăn′ə-sĕt′, -zĕt′) *n.* An anise-flavored liqueur.
An•ka•ra (ăng′kər-ə). Cap. of Turkey. *Pop.* 2,203,729.
ankh (ăngk) *n.* An ansate cross.
an•kle (ăng′kəl) *n.* **1.** The joint that connects the foot with the leg. **2.** The slender part of the leg above this joint.
an•kle•bone (ăng′kəl-bōn′) *n.* The talus.
an•klet (ăng′klĭt) *n.* **1.** An ornament for the ankle. **2.** A sock reaching just above the ankle.
an•lace (ăn′lĭs) *n.* A 2-edged medieval dagger.
an•nals (ăn′əlz) *pl.n.* **1.** A record of events in the order of their occurrence. **2.** A descriptive account. **—an′nal•ist** *n.*
An•nap•o•lis (ə-năp′ə-lĭs). Cap. of Md., on Chesapeake Bay. *Pop.* 31,740.
an•neal (ə-nēl′) *v.* **1.** To subject (glass or metal) to heat and slow cooling to toughen and reduce brittleness. **2.** To temper.
an•ne•lid (ăn′ə-lĭd) *also* **an•nel•i•dan** (ə-nĕl′ĭ-dən) *adj.* Of or belonging to the phylum Annelida, which includes worms having cylindrical segmented bodies, as the earthworms. *—n.* An annelid worm.
an•nex (ə-nĕks′) *v.* **1.** To append or attach, esp. to a larger entity. **2.** To incorporate (territory) into another country or state. *—n.* (ăn′ĕks′). A structure added on to a larger one or placed near a main one. **—an′nex•a′tion** *n.*
An•nie Oak•ley (ăn′ē ōk′lē) *n. Slang.* A complimentary admission ticket.
▲word history: Annie Oakley was a sharpshooter with Buffalo Bill's show, *The Wild West*, who sometimes used playing cards as targets. Free passes that were punched to prevent their being sold were thought to resemble Annie Oakley's handiwork.
an•ni•hi•late (ə-nī′ə-lāt′) *v.* **-lat•ed, -lat•ing.** To destroy all traces of : obliterate. **—an•ni′hi•la′tion** *n.* **—an•ni′hi•la′tor** *n.*
an•ni•ver•sa•ry (ăn′ə-vûr′sə-rē) *n., pl.* **-ries.** The yearly return of the date of an event that happened in an earlier year.
an•no Dom•i•ni (ăn′ō dŏm′ə-nī′, dŏm′ə-nē) *adv.* In a specified year of the Christian era. Used chiefly in the abbreviated form <A.D. 495>
an•no•tate (ăn′ō-tāt′) *v.* **-tat•ed, -tat•ing.** To furnish (a text) with critical commentary or explanatory notes. **—an′no•ta′tion** *n.*
an•nounce (ə-nouns′) *v.* **-nounced, -nounc•ing. 1.** To make known publicly. **2.** To proclaim the presence or arrival of. **3.** To act as an announcer. **—an•nounce′ment** *n.*
an•nounc•er (ə-noun′sər) *n.* One who announces, as on a television program or over a public-address system.
an•noy (ə-noi′) *v.* To bother or irritate. ☆**syns:** AGGRAVATE, BOTHER, BUG, FRET, GALL, IRK, IRRITATE, PEEVE, PROVOKE, RUFFLE, VEX **—an•noy′ing** *adj.* **—an•noy′ing•ly** *adv.*
an•noy•ance (ə-noi′əns) *n.* **1.** The act of annoying. **2.** A nuisance. **3.** Vexation : irritation.
an•nu•al (ăn′yo͞o-əl) *adj.* **1.** Recurring, done, or performed every year : yearly <an *annual* checkup> **2.** Determined by a year's time <*annual* precipitation> **3.** *Bot.* Having a life cycle that is completed in a year or season. *—n.* **1.** A yearbook. **2.** An annual plant. **—an′nu•al•ly** *adv.*
annual ring *n.* A concentric layer of wood, esp. of a tree trunk, indicating a year's growth.
an•nu•i•ty (ə-no͞o′ĭ-tē, ə-nyo͞o′-) *n., pl.* **-ties. 1.** The annual payment of an allowance or income. **2.** An investment from which one receives an income for a lifetime or a specified number of years. **—an•nu′i•tant** *n.*
an•nul (ə-nŭl′) *v.* **-nulled, -nul•ling.** To declare void or invalid, as a marriage or a law : nullify. **—an•nul′ment** *n.*
an•nu•lar (ăn′yə-lər) *adj.* Shaped like or forming a ring.
an•nun•ci•ate (ə-nŭn′sē-āt′) *v.* **-at•ed, -at•ing.** To announce, esp. officially.
an•nun•ci•a•tion (ə-nŭn′sē-ā′shən) *n.* **1.** The act of announcing. **2.** An announcement. **3. Annunciation. a.** The angel Gabriel's announcement of the Incarnation. **b.** The festival, on Mar. 25, that honors this.
an•nus mi•rab•i•lis (ăn′əs mĭ-răb′ə-lĭs) *n.* An extraordinary year.
an•ode (ăn′ōd′) *n.* A positively charged electrode, as of an electron tube.
an•o•dize (ăn′ə-dīz′) *v.* **-dized, -diz•ing.** To coat (a metallic surface) electrolytically with a protective oxide.
an•o•dyne (ăn′ə-dīn′) *adj.* **1.** Capable of relieving pain. **2.** Soothing or comforting <*anodyne* hobbies> **—an′o•dyne′** *n.*
a•noint (ə-noint′) *v.* To apply oil, esp. in a religious ceremony.
a•nom•a•ly (ə-nŏm′ə-lē) *n., pl.* **-lies. 1.** Departure from the normal form, order, or rule. **2.** Something irregular or abnormal. **—a•nom′a•lis′tic** *adj.* **—a•nom′a•lis′ti•cal•ly** *adv.* **—a•nom′a•lous** *adj.*
a•non (ə-nŏn′) *adv.* **1.** At another time : again. **2.** *Archaic.* Soon.
an•o•nym (ăn′ə-nĭm′) *n.* **1.** An anonymous person. **2.** A pseudonym.

a•non•y•mous (ə-nŏn′ə-məs) *adj.* **1.** Nameless or unnamed. **2.** Of unknown source. **—an′o•nym′i•ty** (ăn′ə-nĭm′ĭ-tē) *n.* **—a•non′y•mous•ly** *adv.* **—a•non′y•mous•ness** *n.*
a•noph•e•les (ə-nŏf′ə-lēz′) *n.* Any of various mosquitoes of the genus *Anopheles,* many of which carry the malaria parasite and transmit the disease to humans.
an•o•rak (ăn′ə-răk′) *n.* A heavy, hooded jacket : parka.
an•o•rec•tic (ăn′ə-rĕk′tĭk) or **an•o•ret•ic** (-rĕt′ĭk) *also* **an•o•rex•ic** (-rĕk′sĭk) *adj.* **1.** Characterized by loss of appetite. **2.** Causing loss of or suppressing appetite. **—an′o•rec′tic** *n.*
an•o•rex•i•a (ăn′ə-rĕk′sē-ə) *n.* Loss of appetite, usu. as a result of disease or a psychological disorder.
anorexia nerv•o•sa (nûr-vō′sə) *n.* A pathological condition that occurs mainly in young women, marked by aversion to food, believed to have a psychological origin, and sometimes fatal.
an•oth•er (ə-nŭth′ər) *adj.* **1.** One more : additional <*another* scoop of ice cream> **2.** Distinctly different from the first <tried *another* hair style> **3.** Some other <can do it *another* time> *—pron.* **1.** An additional one. **2.** A different one. **3.** One of an undetermined number or group <by one method or *another*>
ans. *abbr.* answer.
an•sate cross (ăn′sāt′) *n.* A cross shaped like a T with a loop at the top : ankh.
an•swer (ăn′sər) *n.* **1.** A reply, as to a question or demand. **2. a.** A solution or result, as to a puzzle or problem. **b.** The correct solution or response. *—v.* **1.** To respond in words or actions (to). **2.** To respond correctly to. **3.** To serve (e.g., a purpose). **4.** To be liable or accountable. ☆***syns:*** REJOIN, REPLY, RESPOND, RETORT, RETURN **—an′swer•a•bil′i•ty, an′swer•a•ble•ness** *n.* **—an′swer•a•ble** *adj.* **—an′swer•a•bly** *adv.*
ant (ănt) *n.* Any of various insects of the family Formicidae, typically having wings only in the males and fertile females and living in highly organized social colonies.
ant– *pref. var. of* ANTI-.
–ant *suff.* **1. a.** Performing, promoting, or causing a specified action <accept*ant*> **b.** Being in a specified state or condition <flipp*ant*> **2. a.** One that performs, promotes, or causes a specified action <deodor*ant*> **b.** One that undergoes a specified action <inhal*ant*>
ant•ac•id (ănt-ăs′ĭd) *adj.* Neutralizing acids. **—ant•ac′id** *n.*
an•tag•o•nism (ăn-tăg′ə-nĭz′əm) *n.* Mutual enmity : hostility. **—an•tag′o•nist** *n.* **—an•tag′o•nis′tic** *adj.* **—an•tag′o•nis′ti•cal•ly** *adv.*
an•tag•o•nize (ăn-tăg′ə-nīz′) *v.* **-nized, -niz•ing.** To incur the antagonism of.
Ant•arc•tic (ănt-ärk′tĭk, -är′tĭk) *adj.* Of or relating to the regions around the South Pole.
Ant•arc•ti•ca (ănt-ärk′tĭ-kə, -är′tĭ-). Continent chiefly within the Antarctic Circle.
Antarctic Circle *n.* A parallel latitude 66° 33′ S, that marks the limit of the S Frigid Zone.
Ant•arc•tic Ocean (ănt-ärk′tĭk, -är′tĭk). Waters surrounding Antarctica.
An•tar•es (ăn-târ′ēz′) *n.* The brightest star in the southern sky, approx. in Scorpius.
▲word history: The Greek name *Antares* can be interpreted in more than one way: "against Mars," "opposite Mars," or "instead of Mars." Since the planet Mars, which the Greeks called Ares, moves through the sky, it is not always opposite Antares in position. The name *Antares* more likely refers to the star's pronounced red color, which sometimes causes the star to be mistaken for the planet.
ant cow *n.* An aphid from which ants acquire honeydew.
an•te (ăn′tē) *n.* **1.** The stake that each poker player must put into the pool before receiving new cards. **2.** *Slang.* A share paid : price. **—an′te** *v.*
ant•eat•er (ănt′ē′tər) *n.* A tropical American mammal, *Myrmecophaga tridactyla,* with a long snout and long sticky tongue, that feeds on ants and termites.
an•te•bel•lum (ăn′tē-bĕl′əm) *adj.* Of or belonging to the period prior to the U.S. Civil War.
an•te•cede (ăn′tĭ-sēd′) *v.* **-ced•ed, -ced•ing, -cedes.** To precede.
an•te•ce•dent (ăn′tĭ-sēd′nt) *adj.* Going before : preceding. *—n.* **1.** One that precedes. **2.** An occurrence or event preceding another. **3. antecedents.** One's ancestry. **4.** The word, phrase, or clause to which a pronoun refers, esp. a relative pronoun. **—an′te•ce′dence** *n.* **—an′te•ce′dent•ly** *adv.*
an•te•cham•ber (ăn′tē-chām′bər) *n.* A room serving as an entryway into a larger room.
an•te•date (ăn′tĭ-dāt′) *v.* **-dat•ed, -dat•ing. 1.** To be of an earlier date than. **2.** To date prior to the true date.
an•te•di•lu•vi•an (ăn′tĭ-də-lo͞o′vē-ən) *adj.* **1.** Of or occurring in the era before the Biblical Flood. **2.** Very old : antiquated. **—an′te•di•lu′vi•an** *n.*
an•te•lope (ăn′tə-lōp′) *n., pl.* **-lope** or **-lopes. 1.** A slender, swift-running, long-horned ruminant of the family Bovidae of Africa and Asia. **2.** An animal, as the pronghorn, similar to a true antelope.
an•te•me•rid•i•an (ăn′tē-mə-rĭd′ē-ən) *adj.* Of or occurring in the morning.
an•te me•rid•i•em (ăn′tē mə-rĭd′ē-əm) *adv. & adj.* Before noon. Used chiefly in the abbreviated form <10:30 A.M.>
an•te•na•tal (ăn′tē-nāt′l) *adj.* Before birth : prenatal.
an•ten•na (ăn-tĕn′ə) *n.* **1.** *pl.* **-ten•nae** (-tĕn′ē). One of the pair of sensory organs on the head of an insect, crustacean, etc. **2.** *pl.* **-nas.** A metallic apparatus for sending and receiving radio waves : aerial. **—an•ten′nal** *adj.*
▲word history: The classical Latin word *antenna* meant only "sail yard." The word was used in medieval writings for the sensory organs of insects because medieval naturalists thought that these organs resembled the parts of the yard that project beyond the sail.
an•te•pe•nult (ăn′tē-pē′nŭlt′, -pĭ-nŭlt′) *n.* The 3rd syllable from the end in a word, as *te* in *antepenult.* **—an′te•pe•nul′ti•mate** *adj. & n.*
an•te•ri•or (ăn-tîr′ē-ər) *adj.* **1.** Located in front. **2.** Prior in time : earlier. **—an•te′ri•or•ly** *adv.*
an•te•room (ăn′tē-ro͞om′, -ro͝om′) *n.* **1.** An antechamber. **2.** A waiting room.
an•them (ăn′thəm) *n.* **1.** A hymn of praise or allegiance. **2.** A devotional composition set to words from the Bible.
an•ther (ăn′thər) *n.* The pollen-bearing organ at the end of a stamen that secretes pollen.
ant•hill (ănt′hĭl′) *n.* A mound formed by ants or termites in building a nest.
an•thol•o•gy (ăn-thŏl′ə-jē) *n., pl.* **-gies.** A collection of literary works. **—an•thol′o•gist** *n.* **—an•thol′o•gize′** *v.*
an•thra•cite (ăn′thrə-sīt′) *n.* A hard, clean-burning coal.
an•thrax (ăn′thrăks′) *n.* An infectious, usu. fatal disease of cattle, sheep, and other warm-blooded animals, characterized esp. by malignant ulcers.
an•thro•po•cen•tric (ăn′thrə-pō-sĕn′trĭk) *adj.* Regarding the human being as the central fact or final aim of the universe.
an•thro•poid (ăn′thrə-poid′) *adj.* Resembling a human being, as the apes of the family Pongidae. *—n.* An anthropoid ape, as a gorilla, chimpanzee, or orangutan. **—an′thro•poid′al** *adj.*
an•thro•pol•o•gy (ăn′thrə-pŏl′ə-jē) *n.* The study of the origin and physical, social, and cultural development and behavior of humans. **—an′thro•po•log′ic** (-pə-lŏj′ĭk), **an′thro•po•log′i•cal** *adj.* **—an′thro•po•log′i•cal•ly** *adv.* **—an′thro•pol′o•gist** *n.*
an•thro•po•mor•phism (ăn′thrə-pə-môr′fĭz′əm) *n.* The ascribing of human motivation and characteristics to inanimate objects, animals, or natural phenomena. **—an′thro•po•mor′phic** *adj.* **—an′thro•po•mor′phi•cal•ly** *adv.*
an•thro•po•mor•phous (ăn′thrə-pə-môr′fəs) *adj.* **1.** Having or suggesting human form and appearance. **2.** Anthropomorphic.
an•ti (ăn′tī′, -tē) *n., pl.* **-tis.** *Informal.* One who is opposed or against.
anti– or **ant–** *pref.* **1. a.** In opposition to : against <*anti*clerical> **b.** Counteracting : neutralizing <*anti*body> **2.** Reciprocal <*anti*logarithm>
an•ti•a•bor•tion (ăn′tē-ə-bôr′shən) *adj.* Opposed to abortion. **—an′ti•a•bor′tion•ist** *n.*
an•ti•bal•lis•tic missile (ăn′tĭ-bə-lĭs′tĭk) *n.* A missile designed to destroy a ballistic missile in flight.

antiaircraft
anti-American
antibacterial
anticancer
anticapitalist
anti-Catholic
anticlerical
anticolonialism
anti-Communist
antidemocratic
antidepressant
antiestablishment
antifascist
antifeminism
antifeminist
anti-imperialism
anti-imperialist
anti-intellectual
antilabor
antimalarial
antimicrobial
antipollution
antipoverty
antireligious
antislavery
antispasmodic
antisubmarine
antitank
antitrust
antivivisection
antivivisectionist
antiwar

an·ti·bi·ot·ic (ăn′tē-bī-ŏt′ĭk) *n.* A substance, as penicillin or streptomycin, produced by organisms such as fungi and bacteria, effective in the suppression or destruction of microorganisms and widely used for prevention and treatment of diseases. **—an′ti·bi·ot′ic** *adj.* **—an′ti·bi·ot′i·cal·ly** *adv.*

an·ti·bod·y (ăn′tĭ-bŏd′ē) *n.* A protein generated in the blood in reaction to foreign proteins or polysaccharides, capable of neutralizing them and producing immunity to certain disease-producing microorganisms.

an·tic (ăn′tĭk) *n.* Often **antics.** A mischievous act or gesture : caper. *—adj.* Ludicrous : far-fetched.

▲word history: The source of *antic* is Italian *antico,* which means "ancient." The Italians used *antico* to refer to the grotesque designs found on some ancient Roman artifacts. *Antico* is derived from *antiquus,* the same Latin word that is the source of *antique,* which came into English from French. The 2 words are separate borrowings and the English words *antic* and *antique* do not share any meanings.

an·ti·christ (ăn′tĭ-krīst′) *n.* **1.** An enemy of Christ. **2.** A false Christ.

an·tic·i·pate (ăn-tĭs′ə-pāt′) *v.* **-pat·ed, -pat·ing. 1.** To foresee. **2.** To look forward to : expect. **3.** To act in advance so as to prevent : forestall. **—an·tic′i·pa′tion** *n.* **—an·tic′i·pa′tor** *n.* **—an·tic′i·pa·to′ry** (-pə-tôr′ē, -tōr′ē) *adj.*

an·ti·cli·max (ăn′tē-klī′măks′) *n.* **1.** A decline or letdown viewed in disappointing contrast to what has gone before. **2.** A commonplace event that follows a series of significant events. **—an′ti·cli·mac′tic** *adj.* **—an′ti·cli·mac′ti·cal·ly** *adv.*

an·ti·cline (ăn′-tĭ-klīn′) *n. Geol.* A fold with layers sloping downward on both sides from a common crest. **—an′ti·cli′nal** *adj.*

an·ti·co·ag·u·lant (ăn′tē-kō-ăg′yə-lənt) *n.* A substance that delays or counteracts blood coagulation.

an·ti·cy·clone (ăn′tē-sī′klōn′) *n.* A system of winds spiraling outward from a high-pressure center, circling clockwise in the N Hemisphere and counterclockwise in the S Hemisphere. **—an′ti·cy·clon′ic** (-klŏn′ĭk) *adj.*

an·ti·dote (ăn′tĭ-dōt′) *n.* **1.** A substance that counteracts the effects of a poison. **2.** Something that counteracts an injurious effect. **—an′ti·dot′al** *adj.*

an·ti·e·lec·tron (ăn′tē-ĭ-lĕk′trŏn′) *n.* A positron.

an·ti·freeze (ăn′tĭ-frēz′) *n.* A substance, as ethylene glycol, mixed with liquid, esp. water, to lower its freezing point.

an·ti·gen (ăn′tĭ-jən) *n.* A substance that stimulates the production of antibodies. **—an′ti·gen′ic** *adj.* **—an′ti·gen′i·cal·ly** *adv.* **—an′ti·ge·nic′i·ty** *n.*

an·ti·he·ro (ăn′tĭ-hîr′ō) *n.* A fictional protagonist lacking traditional heroic virtues and qualities.

an·ti·his·ta·mine (ăn′tē-hĭs′tə-mēn′, -mĭn) *n.* A drug used to relieve symptoms of allergies and colds by interfering with the production of histamines. **—an′ti·his′ta·min′ic** *adj.*

an·ti·knock (ăn′tĭ-nŏk′) *n.* A substance added to gasoline that prevents too rapid combustion and reduces engine knock.

An·til·les (ăn-tĭl′ēz). The West Indies except for the Bahamas.

an·ti·log (ăn′tē-lôg′, -lŏg′) *n.* An antilogarithm.

an·ti·log·a·rithm (ăn′tē-lô′gə-rĭth′əm, -lŏg′ə-) *n.* The number for which a given logarithm stands; e.g., if $y = \log x$, then $x = \text{antilog}\ y$.

an·ti·ma·cas·sar (ăn′tē-mə-kăs′ər) *n.* A protective covering for the backs or arms of chairs and sofas.

an·ti·mat·ter (ăn′tĭ-măt′ər) *n.* Antiparticle matter having positron-surrounded nuclei composed of antiprotons and antineutrons.

an·ti·mis·sile missile (ăn′tē-mĭs′əl) *n.* A missile that can intercept and destroy another missile in flight.

an·ti·mo·ny (ăn′tə-mō′nē) *n. Symbol* **Sb** A brittle, blue-white metallic element used in many alloys.

an·ti·neu·tri·no (ăn′tē-no͞o-trē′nō, -nyo͞o-) *n., pl.* **-nos.** The antiparticle of the neutrino.

an·ti·neu·tron (ăn′tē-no͞o′trŏn′, -nyo͞o′-) *n.* The antiparticle of the neutron.

an·tin·o·my (ăn-tĭn′ə-mē) *n., pl.* **-mies.** A contradiction, opposition, or conflict.

an·ti·ox·i·dant (ăn′tē-ŏk′sĭ-dənt) *n.* A chemical substance that inhibits oxidation.

an·ti·par·ti·cle (ăn′tē-pär′tĭ-kəl) *n.* Either of a pair of atomic particles, such as a positron and electron, that are identical in mass but exactly opposite in electric charge, magnetic properties, and spin.

an·ti·pas·to (ăn′tĭ-pä′stō, -păs′tō) *n., pl.* **-tos** *or* **-ti** (-tē). An appetizer usu. including cheese, smoked meats, fish, and vegetables, served with oil and vinegar.

an·tip·a·thy (ăn-tĭp′ə-thē) *n., pl.* **-thies. 1.** A feeling of aversion, repugnance, or opposition. **2.** An object of aversion. **—an·tip′a·thet′ic, an·tip′a·thet′i·cal** *adj.* **—an·tip′a·thet′i·cal·ly** *adv.*

an·ti·per·son·nel (ăn′tē-pûr′sə-nĕl′) *adj.* Designed to injure or kill the military personnel or civilians of an enemy country.

an·ti·per·spi·rant (ăn′tē-pûr′spər-ənt) *n.* A preparation applied to the underarm to reduce excessive perspiration.

an·tiph·o·ny (ăn-tĭf′ə-nē) *n., pl.* **-nies. 1.** Responsive singing or chanting. **2.** One that echoes or answers another. **—an·tiph′o·nal** *adj.* **—an·tiph′o·nal·ly** *adv.*

an·ti·pode (ăn′tĭ-pōd′) *n.* A direct opposite. **—an·tip′o·dal** *adj.*

an·tip·o·des (ăn-tĭp′ə-dēz′) *pl.n.* **1.** Two places or regions on opposite sides of the earth. **2.** (*sing. or pl. in number*). Any exact opposite of another.

an·ti·pope (ăn′tĭ-pōp′) *n.* One claiming to be the pope in opposition to the one chosen canonically.

an·ti·pro·ton (ăn′tē-prō′tŏn′) *n.* The antiparticle of the proton.

an·ti·py·ret·ic (ăn′tē-pī-rĕt′ĭk) *adj.* Reducing fever. *—n.* An antipyretic medication.

an·ti·quar·y (ăn′tĭ-kwĕr′ē) *n., pl.* **-ies.** A student or collector of antiquities.

an·ti·quat·ed (ăn′tĭ-kwā′tĭd) *adj.* Out-of-date : obsolete.

an·tique (ăn-tēk′) *adj.* **1.** Of ancient times. **2.** Of or typical of an earlier period. **3.** Old-fashioned. *—n.* An object made in an earlier period. *—v.* **-tiqued, -tiqu·ing.** To give the appearance of an antique to. **—an·tique′ly** *adv.* **—an·tique′ness** *n.*

an·tiq·ui·ty (ăn-tĭk′wĭ-tē) *n., pl.* **-ties. 1.** Ancient times. **2.** The quality of being ancient. **3. antiquities.** Something, as statues, from ancient times.

an·ti-Sem·ite (ăn′tē-sĕm′īt′) *n.* A person hostile toward Jews. **—an′ti-Se·mit′ic** (-sə-mĭt′ĭk) *adj.* **—an′ti-Sem′i·tism** (-sĕm′ĭ-tĭz′əm) *n.*

an·ti·sep·tic (ăn′tĭ-sĕp′tĭk) *adj.* **1.** Destroying or capable of destroying microorganisms that cause disease or decay. **2.** Entirely clean. **—an′ti·sep′tic** *n.* **—an′ti·sep′ti·cal·ly** *adv.*

an·ti·so·cial (ăn′tē-sō′shəl) *adj.* **1.** Not sociable. **2.** Harmful or contrary to the welfare of society <Drug abuse is *antisocial.*>

an·tith·e·sis (ăn-tĭth′ĭ-sĭs) *n., pl.* **-ses** (-sēz′). **1.** Direct contrast : opposition. **2.** The direct opposite. **—an′ti·thet′i·cal** (ăn′tĭ-thĕt′ĭ-kəl), **an′ti·thet′ic** (-thĕt′-ĭk) *adj.* **—an′ti·thet′i·cal·ly** *adv.*

an·ti·tox·in (ăn′tē-tŏk′sĭn) *n.* **1.** An antibody formed in response to and capable of neutralizing a biological poison. **2.** An animal serum containing antitoxin.

ant·ler (ănt′lər) *n.* One of the paired, often branched bony growths on the head of a deer. **—ant′lered** *adj.*

ant lion *n.* An insect of the family Myrmeleontidae whose larva digs holes to trap insects, as ants, for food.

an·to·nym (ăn′tə-nĭm′) *n.* A word having a sense opposite to that of another word. **—an·ton′y·mous** (ăn-tŏn′ə-məs) *adj.* **—an·ton′y·my** *n.*

Ant·werp (ănt′wərp). Port city of N Belgium. *Pop.* 194,073.

A·nu·bis (ə-no͞o′bĭs) *n. Egypt Myth.* A jackal-headed god who conducted the dead to judgment.

Anubis

a·nus (ā′nəs) *n.* The excretory opening of the alimentary canal.

an·vil (ăn′vĭl) *n.* **1.** A heavy iron block on which metals are shaped, esp. by hammering. **2.** *Anat.* The incus.

anx·i·e·ty (ăng-zī′ĭ-tē) *n., pl.* **-ties. 1.** A state of uneasiness : worry. **2.** *Psychiat.* Abnormal fear that lacks a specific cause. ☆**syns:** CARE, CONCERN, DISQUIET, DISQUIETUDE, WORRY **n.**

anx·ious (ăngk′shəs) *adj.* **1.** Uneasy : worried. **2.** Eagerly or earnestly desirous. **—anx′ious·ly** *adv.*

an·y (ĕn′ē) *adj.* **1.** One or some, regardless of kind or quantity <Did I get *any* letters?> **2.** Of whatever number or amount <Is there *any* cake left?> *—pron.* **1.** Any one or ones <Ask *any* of your friends.> **2.** Any quantity or part <If *any* of the salad is left, throw it out.> *—adv.* To any degree or extent : at all <I can't eat *any* more.>

an·y·bod·y (ĕn′ē-bŏd′ē, -bŭd′ē) *pron.* Any person : anyone.

an·y·how (ĕn′ē-hou′) *adv.* **1.** In any case. **2.** In any way or by any means.
†**an·y·more** (ĕn′ē-môr′, -mōr′) *adv.* **1.** At present : now. **2.** *Regional.* Nowadays.
an·y·one (ĕn′ē-wŭn′, -wən) *pron.* Any person : anybody.
an·y·place (ĕn′ē-plās′) *adv.* Anywhere.
an·y·thing (ĕn′ē-thĭng′) *pron.* Any object, occurrence, or matter whatever.
an·y·time (ĕn′ē-tīm′) *adv.* At any time whatever.
an·y·way (ĕn′ē-wā′) *adv.* **1.** In any case : anyhow. **2.** Just the same : nevertheless.
an·y·where (ĕn′ē-hwâr′, -wâr′) *adv.* **1.** To, in, or at any place. **2.** To any extent or degree.
A-O·K *also* **A·O-kay** (ā′ō-kā′) *adj.* & *adv. Informal.* Perfectly o.k.
A-one *also* **A-1** (ā′wŭn′) *adj. Informal.* Excellent : splendid.
a·or·ta (ā-ôr′tə) *n., pl.* **-tas** *or* **-tae** (-tē). The main trunk of the systemic arteries, carrying blood to all bodily organs except the lungs. **—a·or′tal, a·or′tic** *adj.*
a·pace (ə-pās′) *adv.* At a swift pace : rapidly.
†**ap·a·re·jo** (ăp′ə-rā′hō, -rā′ō) *n., pl.* **-jos.** *SW U.S.* A packsaddle made of a stuffed leather pad.
a·part (ə-pärt′) *adv.* **1.** To or in pieces. **2.** Separately in time, place, or position. **3.** To one side : aside.
a·part·heid (ə-pärt′hīt′, -hāt′) *n.* An official policy of racial segregation practiced in the Republic of South Africa.
a·part·ment (ə-pärt′mənt) *n.* A room or suite of rooms designed to live in.
ap·a·thy (ăp′ə-thē) *n.* **1.** Lack of emotion. **2.** Lack of interest : indifference. **—ap′a·thet′ic** (-thĕt′ĭk) *adj.* **—ap′a·thet′i·cal·ly** *adv.*
ape (āp) *n.* **1.** A large tailless primate such as a chimpanzee or gorilla. **2.** A monkey. **3.** A mimic : imitator. **4.** A coarse person. —*v.* **aped, ap·ing.** To mimic : imitate.
ape·man (āp′măn′) *n.* An extinct primate held to be intermediate between apes and modern human beings.
Ap·en·nines (ăp′ə-nīnz′). Mountain range of C Italy.
a·pé·ri·tif (ä-pĕr′ĭ-tēf′) *n.* An alcoholic drink taken before a meal.
ap·er·ture (ăp′ər-chər) *n.* An opening, as a hole : orifice.
a·pex (ā′pĕks′) *n., pl.* **apexes** *or* **a·pi·ces** (ā′pĭ-sēz′, ăp′ĭ-). The highest point : peak.
a·pha·sia (ə-fā′zhə) *n.* Loss of the ability to speak or understand speech. **—a·pha′sic** (-zĭk, -sĭk) *adj.* & *n.*
a·phe·li·on (ə-fē′lē-ən, ə-fēl′yən) *n., pl.* **-li·a** (-lē-ə). The point on a planetary orbit farthest from the sun.
a·phid (ā′fĭd, ăf′ĭd) *n.* A small, soft-bodied insect of the family Aphididae that feeds by sucking sap from plants.
aph·o·rism (ăf′ə-rĭz′əm) *n.* A brief statement of a truth : adage. **—aph′o·ris′tic** (ăf′ə-rĭs′tĭk) *adj.*
aph·ro·dis·i·ac (ăf′rə-dĭz′ē-ăk′) *adj.* Stimulating sexual desire. **—aph′ro·dis′i·ac′** *n.*
A·pi·a (ä-pē′ä). Cap. of Western Samoa, on N Upolu Is. *Pop.* 32,099.
a·pi·ar·y (ā′pē-ĕr′ē) *n., pl.* **-ies.** A place for keeping bees and beehives. **—a′pi·a·rist** (ā′pē-ə-rĭst) *n.*
a·pi·ces (ā′pĭ-sēz′, ăp′ĭ-) *n. var. pl. of* APEX.
a·piece (ə-pēs′) *adv.* To or for each one.
ap·ish (ā′pĭsh) *adj.* **1.** Resembling an ape. **2.** Slavishly or foolishly imitative.
a·plomb (ə-plŏm′, ə-plŭm′) *n.* Self-confidence : assurance.
A·poc·a·lypse (ə-pŏk′ə-lĭps′) *n.* **1.** See BIBLE TABLE. **2. apocalypse.** A prophetic revelation. **—a·poc′a·lyp′tic, a·poc′a·lyp′ti·cal** *adj.*
A·poc·ry·pha (ə-pŏk′rə-fə) *n. (sing. or pl. in number).* **1.** The 14 Biblical books not included in the Old Testament by Protestants as being of doubtful authorship; 11 are accepted by the Roman Catholic Church. See BIBLE TABLE. **2. apocrypha.** Writings of questionable authenticity.
a·poc·ry·phal (ə-pŏk′rə-fəl) *adj.* **1.** Of questionable authenticity. **2. Apocryphal.** Of or relating to the Apocrypha. **—a·poc′ry·phal·ly** *adv.*
ap·o·gee (ăp′ə-jē) *n.* The point most distant from the earth in a satellite's orbit.
a·po·lit·i·cal (a′pə-lĭt′ĭ-kəl) *adj.* **1.** Having no involvement or interest in politics. **2.** Having no political significance. **—a′po·lit′i·cal·ly** *adv.*
A·pol·lo (ə-pŏl′ō) *n.* **1.** *Gk. Myth.* The god of the sun, prophecy, music, medicine, and poetry. **2. apollo.** A very handsome young man.
a·pol·o·get·ic (ə-pŏl′ə-jĕt′ĭk) *adj.* Making or expressing an apology. **—a·pol′o·get′i·cal·ly** *adv.*
a·pol·o·gize (ə-pŏl′ə-jīz′) *v.* **-gized, -giz·ing.** To make an apology. **—a·pol′o·gist** (-jĭst) *n.*
a·pol·o·gy (ə-pŏl′ə-jē) *n., pl.* **-gies. 1.** An expression of regret for an offense or fault. **2.** A formal defense : justification.
ap·o·plex·y (ăp′ə-plĕk′sē) *n.* Sudden loss of consciousness resulting from rupture or blockage of a blood vessel in the brain. **—ap′o·plec′tic** (-plĕk′tĭk) *adj.*
a·port (ə-pôrt′, ə-pōrt) *adv. Naut.* Toward or on the port side of a ship.
a·pos·ta·sy (ə-pŏs′tə-sē) *n., pl.* **-sies.** Abandonment of a former allegiance, as to one's religious faith. **—a·pos′tate′** (-tāt′, -tĭt) *n.* & *adj.*
a pos·te·ri·o·ri (ä′ pŏ-stîr′ē-ôr′ē, -ōr′ē, -ôr′ī′, -ōr′ī′, ā′) *adj.* Denoting reasoning from facts to general principles : inductive.
a·pos·tle (ə-pŏs′əl) *n.* **1. Apostle.** One of the 12 disciples of Christ. **2.** A leader or advocate of a new cause.
ap·os·tol·ic (ăp′ə-stŏl′ĭk) *adj.* **1.** Of or relating to the 12 Apostles or their faith, teachings, or practice. **2.** Papal.
a·pos·tro·phe[1] (ə-pŏs′trə-fē) *n.* The superscript sign (′) used to indicate the omission of 1 or more letters from a word, the possessive case, and certain plurals, esp. of numbers and letters.
a·pos·tro·phe[2] (ə-pŏs′trə-fē) *n.* The addressing in rhetoric of an absent or imaginary person. **—a·pos′tro·phize′** (-fīz′) *v.*
apothecaries' weight *n.* A system of weights used in pharmacy and based on 1 oz equal to 480 g and 1 lb equal to 12 oz.
a·poth·e·car·y (ə-pŏth′ĭ-kĕr′ē) *n., pl.* **-ries.** A druggist.
ap·o·thegm (ăp′ə-thĕm′) *n.* A proverb : maxim.
a·poth·e·o·sis (ə-pŏth′ē-ō′sĭs, ăp′ə-thē′ə-sĭs) *n., pl.* **-ses** (-sēz′). **1.** Elevation to divine stature : deification. **2.** An ideal example.
Ap·pa·la·chi·a (ăp′ə-lā′chē-ə, -chə). Region of E U.S.
Ap·pa·la·chi·an Mountains (ăp′ə-lā′chē-ən, -chən). Mountain system of E North America, from S Que., Canada, to C Ala.
ap·pall (ə-pôl′) *v.* To fill with dismay : horrify. **—ap·pall′ing·ly** *adv.*
ap·pa·loo·sa (ăp′ə-lo͞o′sə) *n.* A saddle horse with a spotted rump.
ap·pa·ra·tus (ăp′ə-rā′təs, -răt′əs) *n., pl.* **-tus** *or* **-tus·es. 1.** Equipment or materials for a specified function or task. **2. a.** A machine. **b.** A group of machines. **3.** A political organization.
ap·par·el (ə-păr′əl) *n.* Clothing : attire. —*v.* **-eled, -el·ing** *or* **-elled, -el·ling.** To dress : clothe.
ap·par·ent (ə-păr′ənt, ə-pâr′-) *adj.* **1.** Easily seen : visible. **2.** Easily perceived : obvious. **3.** Appearing to be true or real : ostensible. **—ap·par′ent·ly** *adv.*
ap·pa·ri·tion (ăp′ə-rĭsh′ən) *n.* A spectral figure : ghost.
ap·peal (ə-pēl′) *n.* **1.** An earnest entreaty : plea. **2.** An application, as to a higher authority, for help or a decision. **3.** The power of arousing interest : attraction. **4.** *Law.* The transfer of a case from a lower to a higher court for a new hearing. —*v.* **1.** To make an appeal, as for help. **2.** To have the power of attracting. **3.** *Law.* To transfer or apply to transfer (a case) to a higher court for a new hearing. **—ap·peal′a·ble** *adj.* **—ap·peal′ing·ly** *adv.*
ap·pear (ə-pîr′) *v.* **1.** To come into view. **2.** To look or seem to be. **3.** To be presented or published. **4.** *Law.* To present oneself formally before a court.
ap·pear·ance (ə-pîr′əns) *n.* **1.** The act of appearing. **2.** The way something looks : outward aspect. **3.** A false show : pretense.
ap·pease (ə-pēz′) *v.* **-peased, -peas·ing.** To calm or pacify, esp. by granting demands : placate. **—ap·pease′ment** *n.* **—ap·peas′er** *n.*
ap·pel·lant (ə-pĕl′ənt) *n.* One who appeals a court decision. —*adj.* Appellate.
ap·pel·late (ə-pĕl′ĭt) *adj.* Empowered to hear and review decisions of lower courts.
ap·pel·la·tion (ăp′ə-lā′shən) *n.* A name or title.
ap·pend (ə-pĕnd′) *v.* **1.** To add, esp. as a supplement. **2.** To fix to : attach.
ap·pend·age (ə-pĕn′dĭj) *n.* **1.** Something appended. **2.** *Biol.* A part or organ joined to an axis or trunk.
ap·pen·dec·to·my (ăp′ən-dĕk′tə-mē) *n., pl.* **-mies.** Surgical excision of the vermiform appendix.
ap·pen·di·ci·tis (ə-pĕn′dĭ-sī′tĭs) *n.* Inflammation of the vermiform appendix.
ap·pen·dix (ə-pĕn′dĭks) *n., pl.* **-dix·es** *or* **-di·ces** (-dĭ-sēz′). **1.** Supplementary material, usu. at the end of a written book. **2.** The vermiform appendix.
ap·per·tain (ăp′ər-tān′) *v.* To belong as a function or part : pertain.
ap·pe·stat (ăp′ĭ-stăt′) *n.* The mechanism in the central nervous system that controls food intake.
ap·pe·tite (ăp′ĭ-tīt′) *n.* **1.** A desire for food. **2.** A craving : desire.
ap·pe·tiz·er (ăp′ĭ-tī′zər) *n.* Food or drink served before a meal to whet the appetite.

ap·pe·tiz·ing (ăp′ĭ-tī′zĭng) *adj.* Appealing to the appetite. **—ap′pe·tiz′ing·ly** *adv.*
ap·plaud (ə-plôd′) *v.* To express approval (of), esp. by clapping. **—ap·plaud′er** *n.*
ap·plause (ə-plôz′) *n.* **1.** Approval expressed esp. by clapping. **2.** Commendation : praise.
ap·ple (ăp′əl) *n.* **1.** A tree, *Pyrus malus,* that bears fragrant flowers and edible fruit. **2.** The firm, rounded fruit of the apple tree.
ap·ple·jack (ăp′əl-jăk′) *n.* Liquor distilled from hard cider.
ap·ple·sauce (ăp′əl-sôs′) *n.* **1.** Apples stewed to a pulp and sweetened. **2.** *Slang.* Nonsense.
ap·pli·ance (ə-plī′əns) *n.* A device, esp. an item of household equipment that is operated by electricity or gas.
ap·pli·ca·ble (ăp′lĭ-kə-bəl, ə-plĭk′ə-) *adj.* Able to be applied : appropriate. **—ap′pli·ca·bil′i·ty** *n.*
ap·pli·cant (ăp′lĭ-kənt) *n.* One who applies, as for a job or admission.
ap·pli·ca·tion (ăp′lĭ-kā′shən) *n.* **1.** The act of applying. **2.** Something applied, esp. to a surface. **3.** A particular use to which something is put. **4.** Usablilty : relevance. **5.** Careful attention : assiduity. **6. a.** A request, as for aid, employment, or admission. **b.** A form used in making such a request.
ap·pli·ca·tor (ăp′lĭ-kā′tər) *n.* An instrument for applying a substance, as medicine.
ap·plied (ə-plīd′) *adj.* Put into practice : used.
ap·pli·qué (ăp′lĭ-kā′) *n.* A cloth ornament cut out from one material and sewn to a larger piece of another. **—ap′pli·qué′** *v.*
ap·ply (ə-plī′) *v.* **-plied, -ply·ing. 1.** To bring into contact : spread or put on. **2.** To put to a special use. **3.** To give (oneself or one's efforts) to something. **4.** To be relevant. **5.** To submit a request, as for employment. **—ap·pli′er** *n.*
ap·point (ə-point′) *v.* **1.** To name officially for an office or position. **2.** To set or fix by authority. **3.** To furnish : equip <a well-*appointed* office> **—ap·point′ee′** *n.*
ap·point·ive (ə-poin′tĭv) *adj.* Relating to or able to be filled by appointment.
ap·point·ment (ə-point′mənt) *n.* **1.** The act of appointing. **2.** An appointive office or position. **3.** An engagement for a meeting. **4. appointments.** Equipment : furnishings.
ap·por·tion (ə-pôr′shən, ə-pōr′-) *v.* To divide according to a proportion or plan : allot. **—ap·por′tion·ment** *n.*
ap·po·site (ăp′ə-zĭt) *adj.* Appropriate : apt. **—ap′po·site·ly** *adv.* **—ap′po·site·ness** *n.*
ap·po·si·tion (ăp′ə-zĭsh′ən) *n.* A grammatical construction in which a noun or noun phrase is followed by another that is an explanatory equivalent, as *the composer* and *Bach* in *a portrait of the composer Bach.* **—ap′po·si′tion·al** *adj.*
ap·pos·i·tive (ə-pŏz′ĭ-tĭv) *adj.* Of, relating to, or being in apposition. **—ap·pos′i·tive** *n.* **—ap·pos′i·tive·ly** *adv.*
ap·praise (ə-prāz′) *v.* **-praised, -prais·ing.** To assign a value to. **—ap·prais′er** *n.*
ap·pre·cia·ble (ə-prē′shə-bəl) *adj.* Capable of being noticed, estimated, or perceptible. **—ap·pre′cia·bly** *adv.*
ap·pre·ci·ate (ə-prē′shē-āt′) *v.* **-at·ed, -at·ing. 1.** To recognize the value or quality of. **2.** To value highly. **3.** To be aware of : realize. **4.** To feel gratitude for. **5.** To increase in value or price. ☆***syns:*** CHERISH, ESTEEM, PRIZE, RESPECT, SAVOR, TREASURE, VALUE **—ap·pre′ci·a′tion** *n.* **—ap·pre′ci·a′tor** *n.*
ap·pre·cia·tive (ə-prē′shə-tĭv, -shē-ā′tĭv) *adj.* Capable of or showing appreciation. **—ap·pre′cia·tive·ly** *adv.*
ap·pre·hend (ăp′rĭ-hĕnd′) *v.* **1.** To arrest. **2.** To understand. **3.** To anticipate fearfully. **—ap′pre·hen′sion** *n.*
ap·pre·hen·sive (ăp′rĭ-hĕn′sĭv) *adj.* Fearful or uneasy about the future : anxious. **—ap′pre·hen′sive·ly** *adv.* **—ap′pre·hen′sive·ness** *n.*
ap·pren·tice (ə-prĕn′tĭs) *n.* **1.** One who is learning a trade or occupation under a skilled worker. **2.** A beginner. *—v.* **-ticed, -tic·ing.** To place as an apprentice. **—ap·pren′tice·ship′** *n.*
ap·prise (ə-prīz′) *v.* **-prised, -pris·ing.** To give notice to : inform.
ap·prize (ə-prīz′) *v. esp. Brit. var. of* APPRISE.
ap·proach (ə-prōch′) *v.* **1.** To come near or nearer (to), as in space or time. **2.** To be close to, as in appearance : approximate. **3.** To begin to deal with. *—n.* **1.** The act of approaching. **2.** A means of reaching something : access. **3.** A way of dealing with or accomplishing something. **—ap·proach′a·bil′i·ty** *n.* **—ap·proach′a·ble** *adj.*
ap·pro·ba·tion (ăp′rə-bā′shən) *n.* The act of approving, esp. formally : approval.
ap·pro·pri·ate (ə-prō′prē-ĭt) *adj.* Suitable for a particular occasion or use : fitting. *—v.* (-āt′) **-at·ed, -at·ing. 1.** To set apart for a particular use. **2.** To take or use, often without permission. **—ap·pro′pri·ate·ly** *adv.* **—ap·pro′pri·ate·ness** *n.*
ap·pro·pri·a·tion (ə-prō′prē-ā′shən) *n.* Money that has been set apart by official action for a particular use.
ap·prov·al (ə-pro͞o′vəl) *n.* The act of approving : sanction. **—on approval.** Subject to acceptance or rejection by a prospective buyer.
ap·prove (ə-pro͞ov′) *v.* **-proved, -prov·ing. 1.** To regard with favor. **2.** To confirm officially : ratify. **—ap·prov′ing·ly** *adv.*
approx. *abbr.* approximate; approximately.
ap·prox·i·mate (ə-prŏk′sə-mĭt) *adj.* Almost exact or accurate. *—v.* (-māt′) **-mat·ed, -mat·ing.** To be nearly the same as : approach. **—ap·prox′i·mate·ly** *adv.* **—ap·prox′i·ma′tion** *n.*
appt. *abbr.* appoint; appointed.
ap·pur·te·nance (ə-pûr′tn-əns) *n.* Something that belongs with or to another more important thing : accessory. **—ap·pur′te·nant** *adj.*
Apr. *abbr.* April.
ap·ri·cot (ăp′rĭ-kŏt′, ā′prĭ-) *n.* A tree, *Prunus armeniaca,* widely cultivated for its edible yellow-orange peachlike fruit.
A·pril (ā′prəl) *n.* The 4th month of the year, having 30 days.
a pri·o·ri (ä′ prē-ôr′ē, -ōr′ē, ā′ prī-ôr′ī′, -ōr′ī′) *adj.* **1.** From a cause to an effect : deductive. **2.** Based on a hypothesis or theory rather than on experience.
a·pron (ā′prən) *n.* **1.** A garment worn over the front of the body to protect the clothes. **2.** The paved strip around an airport hangar and terminal building.
▲word history: *An apron* was orig. *a napron. Apron* is one of the numerous English words that have either lost or gained an initial *n* because of an incorrect division between the indefinite article and the noun. *Apron* is thus closely related to *napkin* and *napery.*
ap·ro·pos (ăp′rə-pō′) *adj.* Relevant : pertinent. *—adv.* **1.** Relevantly : pertinently. **2.** By the way : incidentally. *—prep.* In the matter of : regarding.
apropos of *prep.* With reference to.
apse (ăps) *n.* A semicircular or polygonal building projection, as of a church.
apt (ăpt) *adj.* **1.** Particularly suitable : appropriate. **2.** Having a tendency : likely. **3.** Quick to understand or learn. **—apt′ly** *adv.* **—apt′ness** *n.*
ap·ti·tude (ăp′tĭ-to͞od′, -tyo͞od′) *n.* **1.** A natural ability or talent. **2.** Quickness in understanding or learning. **3.** The quality of being suitable : appropriateness.
aq·ua (ăk′wə, ä′kwə) *n., pl.* **aq·uae** (ăk′wē, ä′kwī′) *or* **aq·uas. 1.** Water. **2.** An aqueous solution. **3.** A light bluish green to greenish blue. **—aq′ua** *adj.*
Aqua Lung. A trademark for an underwater breathing apparatus.
aq·ua·ma·rine (ăk′wə-mə-rēn′, ä′kwə-) *n.* **1.** A transparent blue-green gemstone. **2.** A pale blue to light greenish blue.
aq·ua·naut (ăk′wə-nôt′, ä′kwə-) *n.* One who is trained to live in underwater installations and work in scientific research.
aq·ua·plane (ăk′wə-plān′, ä′kwə-) *n.* A board towed by a motorboat and ridden by a person standing on it. **—aq′ua·plane′** *v.*
aqua re·gia (rē′jə, -jē-ə) *n.* A mixture of hydrochloric and nitric acids that can dissolve platinum and gold.
a·quar·i·um (ə-kwâr′ē-əm) *n., pl.* **-i·ums** or **-i·a** (-ē-ə). **1.** A water-filled container in which to keep and raise aquatic animals and plants. **2.** A place in which aquatic animals and plants are kept for public display.
A·quar·i·us (ə-kwâr′ē-əs) *n.* **1.** A constellation in the S Hemisphere. **2. a.** The 11th sign of the zodiac. **b.** One born under this sign.
a·quat·ic (ə-kwŏt′ĭk, ə-kwăt′-) *adj.* **1.** Living in or on the water. **2.** Occurring in or on the water, as sports. **—a·quat′ic** *n.*
a·qua·vit (ä′kwə-vēt′) *n.* A Scandinavian liquor flavored with caraway seed.
aqua vi·tae (vī′tē) *n.* **1.** Alcohol. **2.** Strong liquor such as whiskey.
aq·ue·duct (ăk′wĭ-dŭkt′) *n.* **1.** A conduit for carrying water from a remote source. **2.** A bridgelike structure supporting a conduit or canal over a river or low ground.
a·que·ous (ā′kwē-əs, ăk′wē-) *adj.* Of, like, containing, or dissolved in water : watery.
aqueous humor *n.* A clear fluid in the chamber of the eye between the cornea and lens.
aq·ui·fer (ăk′wə-fər, ä′kwə-) *n.* A layer of underground sand, gravel, or spongy rock in which water collects.
aq·ui·line (ăk′wə-līn′, -lĭn) *adj.* **1.** Of or like an eagle. **2.** Curved or hooked like the beak of an eagle <an *aquiline* nose>
A·qui·nas (ə-kwī′nəs), Saint **Thomas.** 1225?–74. Italian theologian and philosopher.
ar (är) *n. var. of* ARE[2].

-ar *suff.* Of, relating to, or resembling <pol*ar*>
Ar *symbol for* ARGON.
AR *abbr.* **1.** *also* **A/R** accounts receivable. **2.** Arkansas (with Zip Code).
Ar•ab (ăr′əb) *n.* **1.** A native or resident of Arabia. **2.** A member of a Semitic people of the Middle East and North Africa. **3.** A swift, intelligent graceful horse native to Arabia. **–Ar′ab** *adj.*
ar•a•besque (ăr′ə-bĕsk′) *n.* An intricate design of interwoven leaves, flowers, and geometric forms.
A•ra•bi•a (ə-rā′bē-ə). Peninsula of SW Asia, between the Red Sea and Persian Gulf. **–A•ra′bi•an** (ə-rā′bē-ən) *adj.* & *n.*
Arabian Sea. NW part of the Indian O.
Ar•a•bic (ăr′ə-bĭk) *adj.* Of or relating to Arabs, their language, or their culture. *–n.* The Semitic language of the Arabs.
Arabic numeral *n.* One of the numerical symbols 1, 2, 3, 4, 5, 6, 7, 8, 9, and 0.
ar•a•ble (ăr′ə-bəl) *adj.* Suitable for cultivation by plowing.
a•rach•nid (ə-răk′nĭd) *n.* Any of various arthropods of the class Arachnida, having 4 pairs of legs and including the spiders, scorpions, ticks, and mites.
Ar•a•ma•ic (ăr′ə-mā′ĭk) *n.* A Semitic language used in SW Asia 600 B.C.–A.D. 600.
ar•ba•lest *also* **ar•be•lest** (är′bə-lĭst) *n.* A medieval crossbow.

arbalest

ar•bi•ter (är′bĭ-tər) *n.* One who has the authority to decide.
ar•bit•ra•ment (är-bĭt′rə-mənt) *n.* **1.** The act of arbitrating. **2.** The judgment of an arbitrator.
ar•bi•trar•y (är′bĭ-trĕr′ē) *adj.* **1.** Based on impulse or whim. **2.** Dictatorial. **–ar′bi•trar′i•ly** *adv.* **–ar′bi•trar′i•ness** *n.*
ar•bi•trate (är′bĭ-trāt′) *v.* **-trat•ed, -trat•ing. 1.** To decide as an arbitrator. **2.** To submit (a dispute) to an arbitrator. **3.** To serve as an arbitrator. **–ar′bi•tra′tion** *n.*
ar•bi•tra•tor (är′bĭ-trā′tər) *n.* One chosen to settle the issue between parties engaged in a dispute or controversy.
ar•bor (är′bər) *n.* A shady garden shelter covered with or formed of climbing plants.
ar•bo•re•al (är-bôr′ē-əl, -bōr′-) *adj.* **1.** Of or resembling a tree. **2.** Living in trees.
ar•bo•re•tum (är′bə-rē′təm) *n., pl.* **-tums** *or* **-ta** (-tə). A place for studying and exhibiting growing trees.
ar•bor•vi•tae (är′bər-vī′tē) *n.* Any of several evergreen shrubs and trees of the genus *Thuja* with small, scalelike leaves.
ar•bu•tus (är-byo͞o′təs) *n.* Trailing arbutus.
arc (ärk) *n.* **1.** Something with the shape of an arch or curve. **2.** *Geom.* A segment of a curve. **3.** A luminous discharge of electric current across a gap between 2 electrodes. *–v.* **arced, arc•ing** *or* **arcked, arck•ing.** To form an arc.
ar•cade (är-kād′) *n.* **1.** A row of arches supported by columns. **2.** A roofed passageway, esp. one lined with shops.
ar•cane (är-kān′) *adj.* Mysterious : secret.
arch[1] (ärch) *n.* **1.** A curved structure that spans an open space and supports a load, as a bridge. **2.** Something that is similar to an arch in form or function. *–v.* **1.** To provide with an arch. **2.** To form or cause to form an arch.
arch[2] (ärch) *adj.* **1.** Principal : chief. **2.** Mischievous : roguish. **–arch′ly** *adv.* **–arch′ness** *n.*
ar•chae•ol•o•gy *or* **ar•che•ol•o•gy** (är′kē-ŏl′ə-jē) *n.* The scientific study of material evidence, as buildings and tools, remaining from past human life and culture. **–ar′chae•o•log′i•cal, ar′chae•o•log′ic** *adj.* **–ar′chae•ol′o•gist** *n.*
ar•cha•ic (är-kā′ĭk) *adj.* **1.** Belonging to an earlier time : ancient. **2.** Characteristic of language that was once common but is now used chiefly to suggest an earlier style. **–ar•cha′i•cal•ly** *adv.*
ar•cha•ism (är′kē-ĭz′əm, -kā-) *n.* An archaic word or expression.
arch•an•gel (ärk′ān′jəl) *n.* A member of the highest order of angels.
arch•bish•op (ärch-bĭsh′əp) *n.* A bishop of the highest rank. **–arch•bish′op•ric** *n.*
arch•dea•con (ärch-dē′kən) *n.* A church official, chiefly of the Anglican Church, with powers delegated from the bishop.
arch•di•o•cese (ärch-dī′ə-sĭs, -sēs′, -sēz′) *n.* A diocese under jurisdiction of an archbishop. **–arch′di•oc′e•san** (-ŏs′ĭ-sən) *adj.*
arch•duch•ess (ärch-dŭch′ĭs) *n.* **1.** The wife or widow of an archduke. **2.** A royal princess, esp. of imperial Austria.
arch•duke (ärch-do͞ok′, -dyo͞ok′) *n.* A royal prince, esp. of imperial Austria.
arch•en•e•my (ärch′ĕn′ə-mē) *n., pl.* **-mies.** A chief enemy.
ar•che•ol•o•gy (är′kē-ŏl′ə-jē) *n. var. of* ARCHAEOLOGY.
ar•cher•y (är′chə-rē) *n.* The sport or practice of shooting with a bow and arrow. **–ar′cher** *n.*
ar•che•type (är′kĭ-tīp′) *n.* An original model on which similar things are patterned : prototype. **–ar′che•typ′al, ar′che•typ′ic** (-tĭp′ĭk), **ar′che•typ′i•cal** *adj.*
arch•fiend (ärch-fēnd′) *n.* **1.** A principal fiend. **2.** Satan.
ar•chi•e•pis•co•pal (är′kē-ĭ-pĭs′kə-pəl) *adj.* Relating to an archbishop.
ar•chi•man•drite (är′kə-măn′drīt′) *n.* A cleric in the Greek Orthodox Church ranking below a bishop.
Ar•chi•me•des (är′kə-mē′dēz). 287?–212 B.C. Greek mathematician and physicist. **–Ar′chi•me′de•an** *adj.*
ar•chi•pel•a•go (är′kə-pĕl′ə-gō′) *n., pl.* **-goes** *or* **-gos. 1.** A group of islands. **2.** A sea with a large group of islands.
ar•chi•tect (är′kĭ-tĕkt′) *n.* One who designs and supervises the construction of large structures such as buildings.
ar•chi•tec•ton•ics (är′kĭ-tĕk-tŏn′ĭks) *n. (sing. in number).* **1.** The science of architecture. **2.** The structural design of something, as of a musical composition. **–ar′chi•tec•ton′ic** *adj.*
ar•chi•tec•ture (är′kĭ-tĕk′chər) *n.* **1.** The science or art of designing and erecting structures. **2.** A style or method of construction. **–ar′chi•tec′tur•al** *adj.* **–ar′chi•tec′tur•al•ly** *adv.*
ar•chi•trave (är′kĭ-trāv′) *n.* A horizontal piece supported by the columns of a building in classical architecture.

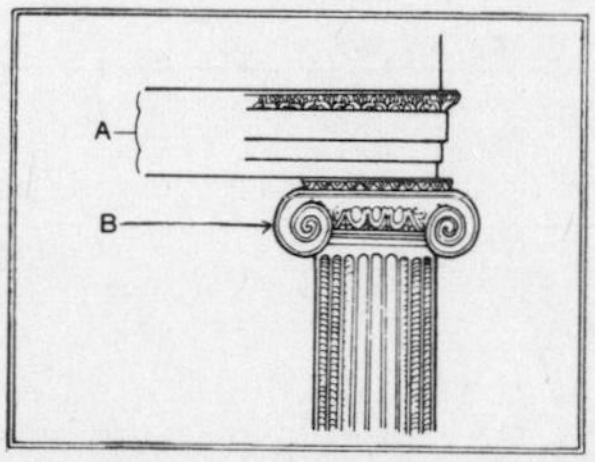

architrave
A column showing
A. the architrave and
B. the volute

ar•chive (är′kīv′) *n. often* **archives. 1.** Public records or documents. **2.** A place where archives are kept. **–ar•chi′val** *adj.* **–ar′chi•vist** (-kə-vĭst, -kī-) *n.*
arch•way (ärch′wā′) *n.* **1.** A passageway under an arch. **2.** An arch over an entrance or passageway.
arcked (ärkt) *v. var. p.t.* & *p.p. of* ARC.
arck•ing (ärk′ĭng) *v. var. pr.p. of* ARC.
arc lamp *n.* An electric lamp in which a current traverses a gas between 2 incandescent electrodes.
arc•tic (ärk′tĭk, är′tĭk) *adj.* **1.** Exceedingly cold : frigid. **2. Arc•tic.** Of or relating to the region N of the Arctic Circle.
Arctic Circle *n.* The parallel of latitude 66° 33′ N marking the limit of the N Frigid Zone.
arctic fox *n.* A fox, *Alopex lagopus,* of arctic regions, with fur that is white or light gray in winter and brown or blue-gray in summer.
Arc•tic Ocean (ärk′tĭk, är′tĭk). Waters surrounding the North Pole between North America and Eurasia.
-ard *or* **-art** *suff.* One who habitually or excessively is in a specified condition or performs a specified action <drunk*ard*> <bragg*art*>
ar•dent (är′dnt) *adj.* **1.** Marked by warmth of emotion : passionate. **2.** Shining : glowing. **3.** Hot as fire : burning. **–ar′dent•ly** *adv.*
ar•dor (är′dər) *n.* **1.** Warmth of emotion : passion. **2.** Intense heat.
ar•du•ous (är′jo͞o-əs) *adj.* Demanding much effort : difficult. **–ar′du•ous•ly** *adv.* **–ar′du•ous•ness** *n.*
are[1] (är) *v. 2nd person sing.* & *1st, 2nd,* & *3rd person pl. present tense of* BE.
are[2] (âr, är) *also* **ar** (är) *n.* See MEASUREMENT TABLE.
ar•e•a (âr′ē-ə) *n.* **1.** A flat space or surface. **2.** A region, as of land. **3.** Range or scope <the *area* of adult education> **4.** The measure of a planar region or of the surface of a solid.

area code *n.* A 3-digit number given to each telephone area in a country, as in the U.S., used to call another area.

ar•e•a•way (âr'ē-ə-wā') *n.* A sunken area affording access, light, and air to a basement.

a•re•ca (ə-rē'kə, ăr'ĭ-kə) *n.* Any of various tall palms of the genus *Areca* of SE Asia, bearing white flowers and red or orange egg-shaped nuts.

a•re•na (ə-rē'nə) *n.* **1.** An enclosed space for public entertainment. **2.** A field of interest or activity : sphere.

aren't (ärnt, är'ənt). Are not.

ar•gent (är'jənt) *n. Archaic.* Silver.

Ar•gen•ti•na (är'jən-tē'nə). Country of SE South America. *Cap.* Buenos Aires. *Pop.* 27,860,000. **—Ar'gen•tine** *adj.* **—Ar'gen•tin'e•an** (-tĭn'ē-ən) *adj.* & *n.*

ar•gen•tite (är'jən-tīt') *n.* A valuable silver ore that is a lustrous lead-gray color.

ar•gil•la•ceous (är'jə-lā'shəs) *adj.* Of, containing, or resembling clay : clayey.

ar•gon (är'gŏn') *n. Symbol* **Ar** An inert gaseous element constituting approx. 1% of the earth's atmosphere and used in electric lamps and vacuum tubes.

ar•go•sy (är'gə-sē) *n., pl.* **-sies. 1.** A large merchant ship. **2.** A fleet of ships.

ar•got (är'gō', -gət) *n.* The specialized vocabulary of a particular group, esp. of the underworld.

ar•gu•a•ble (är'gyōō-ə-bəl) *adj.* Open to argument. **—ar'gu•a•bly** *adv.*

ar•gue (är'gyōō) *v.* **-gued, -gu•ing. 1.** To offer reasons for or against : debate. **2.** To try to prove by reasoning : maintain. **3.** To engage in a quarrel : dispute. **4.** To influence or persuade <*argued* us into staying> ☆*syns:* BICKER, CONTEND, DISPUTE, FIGHT, QUARREL, SQUABBLE, WRANGLE **—ar'gu•ment** *n.* **—ar'gu•er** *n.*

†**ar•gu•fy** (är'gyə-fī') *v.* **-fied, -fy•ing.** *Regional.* To argue (over) : wrangle.

ar•gu•men•ta•tion (är'gyə-mĕn-tā'shən) *n.* The art or process of arguing : debate.

ar•gu•men•ta•tive (är'gyə-mĕn'tə-tĭv) *adj.* Given to arguing : contentious. **—ar'gu•men'ta•tive•ness** *n.*

ar•gus pheasant (är'gəs) *n.* A large bird, *Argusianus argus,* of S Asia, bearing long tail feathers with brilliantly colored eyelike spots.

argus pheasant

ar•gyle *also* **ar•gyll** (är'gīl') *n.* **1.** A knitting pattern of varicolored diamond-shaped areas. **2.** A sock knit in an argyle pattern.

a•ri•a (är'ē-ə) *n.* A solo vocal piece with accompaniment, as in an opera.

ar•id (ăr'ĭd) *adj.* **1.** Lacking in rainfall : dry. **2.** Lacking feeling or interest : dull. **—a•rid'i•ty** (ə-rĭd'ĭ-tē) *n.*

Ar•ies (âr'ēz', âr'ē-ēz') *n.* **1.** A constellation in the N Hemisphere. **2. a.** The 1st sign of the zodiac. **b.** One born under this sign.

a•right (ə-rīt') *adv.* Rightly : correctly.

a•rise (ə-rīz') *v.* **a•rose** (ə-rōz'), **a•ris•en** (ə-rĭz'ən), **a•ris•ing. 1.** To get up. **2.** To move upward : ascend. **3.** To come into existence : originate.

ar•is•toc•ra•cy (ăr'ĭ-stŏk'rə-sē) *n., pl.* **-cies. 1.** A hereditary privileged ruling class or nobility. **2.** Government by the nobility or by a privileged upper class. **3.** A group or class viewed as superior. **—a•ris'to•crat'** *n.* **—a•ris'to•crat'ic** *adj.* **—a•ris'to•crat'i•cal•ly** *adv.*

Ar•is•toph•a•nes (ăr'ĭ-stŏf'ə-nēz'). 448?–380? B.C. Athenian dramatist.

Ar•is•tot•le (ăr'ĭ-stŏt'l). 384–322 B.C. Greek philosopher. **—Ar'is•to•te'li•an** (ăr'ĭs-tə-tē'lē-ən, -tēl'yən) *adj.* & *n.*

a•rith•me•tic (ə-rĭth'mə-tĭk) *n.* The mathematics of integers under addition, subtraction, multiplication, division, involution, and evolution. **—ar'ith•met'ic** (ăr'ĭth-mĕt'ĭk), **ar'ith•met'i•cal** (-ĭ-kəl) *adj.* **—ar'ith•met'i•cal•ly** *adv.* **—a•rith'me•ti'cian** (-tĭsh'ən) *n.*

ar•ith•met•ic mean (ăr'ĭth-mĕt'ĭk) *n.* The number obtained by dividing the sum of a set of quantities by the number of quantities in the set.

Ar•i•zo•na (ăr'ə-zō'nə). State of SW U.S. *Cap.* Phoenix. *Pop.* 2,717,866. **—Ar'i•zo'nan, Ar'i•zo'ni•an** *adj.* & *n.*

ark (ärk) *n.* **1.** The chest containing the Ten Commandments on stone tablets that was carried by the ancient Jews. **2.** The ship that God commanded Noah to build for survival during the Flood.

Ar•kan•sas (är'kən-sô). State of SC U.S. *Cap.* Little Rock. *Pop.* 2,285,513. **—Ar•kan'san** (-kăn'zən) *adj.* & *n.*

arm¹ (ärm) *n.* **1.** One of the upper limbs of the human body. **2.** An armlike part. **3.** Force : power <the *arm* of the law>

arm² (ärm) *n.* **1.** A weapon. **2.** A branch, as the infantry, of a military force. **3. arms** Heraldic bearings. *—v.* **1.** To equip with weapons. **2.** To prepare for or as if for war. **—armed** *adj.*

ar•ma•da (är-mä'də, -mā'-) *n.* A fleet of warships.

ar•ma•dil•lo (är'mə-dĭl'ō) *n., pl.* **-los.** A burrowing mammal of the family Dasypodidae, with an armorlike covering of jointed, bony plates.

Ar•ma•ged•don (är'mə-gĕd'n) *n.* **1.** A final battle between the forces of good and evil. **2.** The time or place of Armageddon.

ar•ma•ment (är'mə-mənt) *n.* **1.** Military weapons and supplies. **2.** *often* **armaments.** The entire military forces and equipment of a country. **3.** The process of arming in preparation for war.

ar•ma•ture (är'mə-chŏŏr', -chər) *n.* **1. a.** The principal moving part of an electric machine or device, as the rotating part of a dynamo or the vibrating part of a buzzer. **b.** A piece of soft iron connecting the poles of a magnet. **2.** Armor.

arm•chair (ärm'châr') *n.* A chair that has supports for the arms.

armed forces (ärmd) *pl.n.* The total military forces of a country.

Ar•me•ni•a (är-mē'nē-ə, -nyə). Ancient country of W Asia. **—Ar•me'ni•an** *adj.* & *n.*

arm•ful (ärm'fŏŏl') *n., pl.* **-fuls.** The amount that an arm can hold.

arm•hole (ärm'hōl') *n.* An opening in a garment for the arm.

ar•mi•stice (är'mĭ-stĭs) *n.* A temporary cessation of combat by mutual consent : truce.

arm•let (ärm'lĭt) *n.* A band worn on the upper arm, as for ornament.

ar•mor (är'mər) *n.* **1.** A defensive covering, as chain mail, worn to protect the body. **2.** The armored vehicles of an army. **—ar'mored** *adj.*

ar•mo•ri•al (är-môr'ē-əl, -mōr'-) *adj.* Of, relating to, or bearing coats of arms.

ar•mor•y (är'mə-rē) *n., pl.* **-ies. 1.** A storehouse for weapons. **2.** A weapons factory.

arm•pit (ärm'pĭt') *n.* The hollow under the arm where it joins the shoulder.

arm•rest (ärm'rĕst') *n.* A support for the arm, as on a chair.

ar•my (är'mē) *n., pl.* **-mies. 1.** A body of troops organized for warfare. **2.** *often* **Army.** The total military land forces of a country. **3.** A group of people who organize for a specific cause. **4.** A large number, as of people or animals.

army ant *n.* Any of various ants of the subfamily Dorylinae, which form large nomadic colonies.

ar•ni•ca (är'nĭ-kə) *n.* A plant of the genus *Arnica* with yellow flowers from which a tincture is made that is used for sprains and bruises.

Ar•nold (är'nəld) **Benedict.** 1741–1801. Amer. Revolutionary general and traitor.

a•ro•ma (ə-rō'mə) *n.* **1.** A distinctive usu. pleasant odor : fragrance. **2.** An aura. **—ar'o•mat'ic** (ăr'ə-măt'ĭk) *adj.*

a•rose (ə-rōz') *v. p.t.* of ARISE.

a•round (ə-round') *adv.* **1.** On or to all sides. **2.** In a circle or circular motion. **3.** In or toward an opposite direction. **4.** From one place to another : here and there. **5.** Close at hand : nearby. *—prep.* **1.** On all sides of <roses *around* the fountain> **2.** About the circumference of so as to encircle <rode *around* the island in a boat> **3.** Close by : near <the surburbs *around* the city> **4.** On or to the farther side of <a store just *around* the corner> **5.** *Informal.* At approximately : near <came *around* 7 o'clock>

a•rouse (ə-rouz') *v.* **a•roused, a•rous•ing. 1.** To wake up from or as if from sleep. **2.** To stir up : excite. **—a•rous'al** *n.*

ar•peg•gi•o (är-pĕj'ē-ō', -pĕj'ō) *n., pl.* **-os.** A chord whose tones are sounded in quick succession rather than simultaneously.

ar•raign (ə-rān') *v.* **1.** *Law.* To call before a court to answer an indictment. **2.** To accuse : charge. **—ar•raign'ment** *n.*

ar•range (ə-rānj') *v.* **-ranged, -rang•ing. 1.** To put in a deliberate order : dispose. **2.** To plan or prepare (for). **3.** To agree about : settle. **4.** To reset (music) for instruments or voices different from those for which it was orig. composed. **—ar·range′ment** *n.* **—ar·rang′er** *n.*

ar·rant (ăr′ənt) *adj.* Being completely such : out-and-out <an *arrant* liar>

ar·ras (ăr′əs) *n.* **1.** A tapestry. **2.** A wall hanging of tapestry.

ar·ray (ə-rā′) *v.* **1.** To arrange or draw up, as troops in battle order. **2.** To dress or decorate in finery : adorn. —*n.* **1.** An arraying, as of troops. **2.** An impressive group. **3.** Magnificent attire : finery.

ar·rears (ə-rîrz′) *pl.n.* **1.** Debts that are overdue. **2.** The condition of not having fulfilled contracted obligations on time <rent in *arrears*> **—ar·rear′age** *n.*

ar·rest (ə-rĕst′) *v.* **1.** To check or stop the motion or growth of. **2.** To seize and hold legally. —*n.* **1.** The act of arresting. **2.** The condition of being arrested. ☆***syns:*** APPREHEND, BUST, COLLAR, DETAIN, NAB, PICK UP, PINCH, RUN IN, SEIZE

ar·rest·ing (ə-rĕs′tĭng) *adj.* Attracting and holding the attention : striking.

ar·ri·ère-pen·sée (ăr′ē-âr′päN-sā′) *n.* An ulterior motive.

ar·ri·val (ə-rī′vəl) *n.* **1.** The act of arriving. **2.** One that arrives.

ar·rive (ə-rīv′) *v.* **-rived, -riv·ing. 1.** To get to a destination. **2.** To take place <The day of victory has *arrived.*> **3.** To attain recognition or success.

ar·ro·gant (ăr′ə-gənt) *adj.* Overbearing and self-important : haughty. ☆***syns:*** DISDAINFUL, HAUGHTY, INSOLENT, LOFTY, LORDLY, OVERBEARING, OVERWEENING, PRESUMPTUOUS, PROUD, SUPERCILIOUS, SUPERIOR **—ar′ro·gance** *n.* **—ar′ro·gant·ly** *adv.*

ar·ro·gate (ăr′ə-gāt′) *v.* **-gat·ed, -gat·ing.** To claim, take, or assume for oneself without right. **—ar′ro·ga′tion** *n.*

ar·row (ăr′ō) *n.* **1.** A straight, thin shaft for shooting from a bow, usu. with a pointed head at the tip end and feathers at the other end. **2.** A sign or symbol with the shape of an arrow for indicating direction.

ar·row·head (ăr′ō-hĕd′) *n.* The pointed tip of an arrow.

ar·row·root (ăr′ō-ro͞ot′, -ro͝ot′) *n.* A tropical American plant, *Maranta arundinacea,* with roots from which an edible starch is derived.

ar·roy·o (ə-roi′ō) *n., pl.* **-os.** A channel or gully eroded by a stream.

ar·se·nal (är′sə-nəl) *n.* **1.** A place for storing and manufacturing arms and ammunition. **2.** A supply or stock.

ar·se·nic (är′sə-nĭk) *n. Symbol* **As** A highly poisonous metallic element used in insecticides, weed killers, etc. **—ar·sen′i·cal** (-sĕn′ĭ-kəl) *adj.* & *n.* **—ar·se′ni·ous** (-sē′nē-əs) *adj.*

ar·son (är′sən) *n.* The crime of maliciously setting fire to property. **—ar′son·ist** *n.*

art[1] (ärt) *n.* **1. a.** The activity of using imagination and skill to create beautiful things. **b.** Works, as paintings, that result from this creativity. **2.** A field or category of artistic activity, as literature, music, or ballet. **3.** A nonscientific branch of learning, esp. one of the humanities. **4.** A trade or craft and the methods employed in it. **5.** A practical skill : knack. **6.** The quality of being cunning : artfulness.

art[2] (ərt; ärt *when stressed*) *v. archaic 2nd person sing. present tense of* BE.

-art *suff. var. of* -ARD.

art dec·o (ärt dĕk′ō, är) *n.* A style of decorative art of the 1920's and 1930's marked by the use of geometric designs and bright colors.

ar·te·ri·ole (är-tîr′ē-ōl′) *n.* A small terminal branch of an artery, esp. one that unites with a capillary. **—ar·te′ri·o′lar** *adj.*

ar·te·ri·o·scle·ro·sis (är-tîr′ē-ō-sklə-rō′sĭs) *n.* A chronic circulatory disease in which the walls of the arteries thicken and harden. **—ar·te′ri·o·scle·rot′ic** (-rŏt′ĭk) *adj.*

ar·ter·y (är′tə-rē) *n., pl.* **-ies. 1.** A blood vessel that carries blood away from the heart. **2.** A major transportation route from which local routes branch. **—ar·te′ri·al** (-tîr′ē-əl) *adj.*

ar·te·sian well (är-tē′zhən) *n.* A well drilled deep enough to reach water that rises to the surface by internal pressure without pumping.

art·ful (ärt′fəl) *adj.* **1.** Clever : ingenious. **2.** Cunning : crafty. **—art′ful·ly** *adv.* **—art′ful·ness** *n.*

ar·thri·tis (är-thrī′tĭs) *n.* Inflammation of a joint or joints. **—ar·thrit′ic** (-thrĭt′ĭk) *adj.* **—ar·thrit′i·cal·ly** *adv.*

ar·thro·pod (är′thrə-pŏd′) *n.* Any of numerous invertebrates of the phylum Arthropoda including insects, crustaceans, arachnids, and myriapods.

Ar·thur (är′thər). **1.** A legendary British hero, reputedly the king of the Britons in the 6th cent. A.D. **2. Chester Alan.** 1830–86. 21st U.S. President (1881–85).

ar·ti·choke (är′tĭ-chōk′) *n.* A thistlelike plant *Cynara scolymus,* bearing an edible flower head with fleshy scalelike bracts.

ar·ti·cle (är′tĭ-kəl) *n.* **1.** An individual thing : item. **2.** A separate section of a written document. **3.** A nonfictional composition in a publication. **4.** A word, as *a* or *the,* that is used to signal nouns and to specify their applications.

ar·tic·u·lar (är-tĭk′yə-lər) *adj.* Of or relating to an anatomical joint.

ar·tic·u·late (är-tĭk′yə-lĭt) *adj.* **1.** Endowed with the power of speech. **2.** Spoken clearly and distinctly. **3.** Capable of, speaking in, or characterized by clear, effective language. **4.** *Biol.* Jointed : segmented. —*v.* (-lāt′) **-lat·ed, -lat·ing. 1.** To utter clearly. **2.** To express in words. **3.** To connect by a joint. **—ar·tic′u·late·ly** *adv.* **—ar·tic′u·late·ness** *n.* **—ar·tic′u·la′tion** *n.* **—ar·tic′u·la·to′ry** *adj.*

ar·ti·fact (är′tə-făkt′) *n.* An object, as a simple tool, produced by human workmanship, esp. one of historical interest.

ar·ti·fice (är′tə-fĭs) *n.* **1.** A crafty stratagem : trick. **2.** Deception : trickery. **3.** Cleverness : ingenuity.

ar·tif·i·cer (är-tĭf′ĭ-sər) *n.* **1.** A skilled craftsman. **2.** An inventor.

ar·ti·fi·cial (är′tə-fĭsh′əl) *adj.* **1.** Made by man, often in imitation of something natural, rather than occurring in nature. **2.** Not natural or genuine : pretended. ☆***syns:*** ERSATZ, MANMADE, SYNTHETIC **—ar′ti·fi′ci·al′i·ty** (-ē-ăl′ĭ-tē) *n.* **—ar′ti·fi′cial·ly** *adv.*

artificial respiration *n.* A method used to restore normal breathing in an asphyxiated person by rhythmically forcing air into and out of the lungs.

ar·til·ler·y (är-tĭl′ə-rē) *n.* **1.** Large-caliber mounted firing weapons, as howitzers. **2.** The army branch specializing in the use of artillery.

ar·ti·san (är′tĭ-zən, -sən) *n.* A manually skilled worker.

art·ist (är′tĭst) *n.* **1.** A practitioner of the fine arts, esp. a painter, sculptor, or musician. **2.** One, esp. a public performer, whose work shows great skill.

ar·tis·tic (är-tĭs′tĭk) *adj.* Showing great skill and artistry. **—ar·tis′ti·cal·ly** *adv.*

art·ist·ry (är′tĭ-strē) *n.* Artistic ability, quality, or workmanship.

art·less (ärt′lĭs) *adj.* **1.** Without guile or deceit : ingenuous. **2.** Free of artificiality : natural. **3.** Lacking skill or art : crude. **—art′less·ly** *adv.* **—art′less·ness** *n.*

art nou·veau (är′no͞o-vō′, ärt′) *n.* A style of decorative art of the late 19th and early 20th cent., characterized by the use of flowing, sinuous lines.

art·y (är′tē) *adj.* **-i·er, -i·est.** Affectedly or showily artistic. **—art′i·ly** *adv.* **—art′i·ness** *n.*

ar·um (âr′əm, ăr′-) *n.* A plant of the genus *Arum* bearing small flowers on a clublike spike surrounded by a leaflike part.

-ary *suff.* **1.** Of or pertaining to <bacill*ary*> **2.** One that pertains to or is connected with <bound*ary*>

Ar·y·an (âr′ē-ən, ăr′-) *n.* A member of the prehistoric people that spoke Indo-European. **—Ar′y·an** *adj.*

†**as** (ăz; əz *when unstressed*) *adv.* **1.** To the same degree or extent : equally <*as* soft as silk> **2.** For example <fragrant flowers, *as* roses> —*conj.* **1.** To the same degree or extent that <soft *as* silk> **2.** In the same way that <Do *as* I say.> **3.** At the same time that : while <The phone rang *as* I sat down to eat.> **4.** Because : since <*As* I was sad, I cried.> **5.** That the consequence is <so ambitious *as* to be ruthless> **6.** Though <Stupid *as* he is, he got the job.> —*pron.* **1.** That which : who <asked the same question *as* you> **2.** A fact that <He's ashamed, *as* you can see.> **3.** *Regional.* Who or which <Those *as* are willing can help clean up.> —*prep.* In the role, capacity, or function of <This will serve *as* a warning.>

As *symbol for* ARSENIC.

as·a·fet·i·da (ăs′ə-fĕt′ĭ-də) *n.* A malodorous plant resin formerly used medicinally.

as·bes·tos (ăs-bĕs′təs, ăz-) *n.* An incombustible fibrous mineral form of magnesium silicate, used esp. for fireproofing.

as·bes·to·sis (ăs′bĕs-tō′sĭs, ăz′-) *n.* Chronic lung inflammation caused by prolonged inhalation of asbestos particles.

as·cend (ə-sĕnd′) *v.* **1.** To move upward (along) : climb. **2.** To succeed to <*ascended* the throne>

as·cen·dant *also* **as·cen·dent** (ə-sĕn′dənt) *adj.* **1.** Moving upward : climbing. **2.** Dominant. —*n.* The condition of being dominant. **—as·cen′dan·cy** *n.*

as·cen·sion (ə-sĕn′shən) *n.* **1.** The act of ascending. **2. Ascension.** The 40th day after Easter, celebrating the ascent of Christ into heaven.

as·cent (ə-sĕnt′) *n.* **1.** The act of moving upward : climb. **2.** An upward slope.

as·cer·tain (ăs′ər-tān′) *v.* To learn by investigating or examining. **—as′cer·tain′a·ble** *adj.* **—as′cer·tain′ment** *n.*

as·cet·ic (ə-sĕt′ĭk) *n.* One who practices rigid self-denial, esp. as a religious act. **—as·cet′ic** *adj.* **—as·cet′i·cism** *n.*

a·scor·bic acid (ə-skôr′bĭk) *n.* Vitamin C.

as•cot (ăs′kət, -kŏt′) *n.* A wide tie or scarf whose ends are laid flat one over the other.
as•cribe (ə-skrīb′) *v.* **-cribed, -crib•ing.** To explain as arising from a particular cause, source, or origin : attribute. **—as•crib′a•ble** *adj.* **—as•crip′tion** (ə-skrĭp′shən) *n.*
a•sep•tic (ə-sĕp′tĭk, ā-) *adj.* Free of pathogenic organisms. **—a•sep′sis** *n.*
a•sex•u•al (ā-sĕk′shōō-əl) *adj.* **1.** Having no sex or sex organs : sexless. **2.** Of or relating to reproduction without the union of male and female gametes. **—a•sex′u•al′i•ty** (-ăl′ĭ-tē) *n.*
as for *prep.* With respect to : regarding.
ash[1] (ăsh) *n.* **1.** The solid material remaining when something is burned. **2.** Pulverized particulate matter from a volcano. **3. ashes.** Human remains.
ash[2] (ăsh) *n.* Any of various trees of the genus *Fraxinus*, having compound leaves and yielding strong, durable wood.
a•shamed (ə-shāmd′) *adj.* **1.** Feeling shame. **2.** Reluctant through fear of shame <*ashamed* to admit the truth> **—a•sham′ed•ly** *adv.*
ash•en (ăsh′ən) *adj.* Resembling the color of ashes : pale.
ash•lar (ăsh′lər) *n.* **1.** A squared building stone. **2.** Masonry of ashlar.
a•shore (ə-shôr′, ə-shōr′) *adv.* To or on the shore.
ash•ram (äsh′rəm) *n.* A religious retreat, esp. of a Hindu philosopher.
ash•tray (ăsh′trā′) *n.* A receptacle for tobacco ashes.
Ash Wednesday *n.* The 1st day of Lent.
ash•y (ăsh′ē) *adj.* **-i•er, -i•est. 1.** Of or pertaining to ashes. **2.** Of the color of ashes : ashen.
A•sia (ā′zhə, ā′shə). Largest of the earth's continents, occupying the E part of the Eurasian land mass and adjacent islands. **—A′sian, A′si•at′ic** *adj.* & *n.*
Asia Minor. W peninsula of Asia, between the Black and Mediterranean seas.
a•side (ə-sīd′) *adv.* **1.** To or toward one side. **2.** Apart. **3.** In reserve : away. —*n.* A line spoken by an actor that other actors on stage are not supposed to hear.
aside from *prep.* **1.** Except for : excluding. **2.** In addition to : besides.
as if *conj.* **1.** Just as it would be if <It was *as if* he had said nothing.> **2.** That <seemed *as if* we should eat>
as•i•nine (ăs′ə-nīn′) *adj.* Stupid or silly : foolish. **—as′i•nin′i•ty** (-nĭn′ĭ-tē) *n.*
ask (ăsk, äsk) *v.* **1.** To put a question to. **2.** To inquire (about). **3.** To request (of). **4.** To demand. **5.** To invite.
a•skance (ə-skăns′) *adv.* **1.** With a sidelong look. **2.** With suspicion or distrust.
a•skew (ə-skyōō′) *adv.* & *adj.* To one side : awry.
a•slant (ə-slănt′) *adv.* & *adj.* At a slant.
a•sleep (ə-slēp′) *adj.* **1.** In or into a condition of sleep. **2.** Inactive. **3.** Numb. **—a•sleep′** *adv.*
a•so•cial (ā-sō′shəl) *adj.* **1.** Shunning the society of others. **2.** Incapable of interacting adequately with others.
as of *prep.* On : at : from <at home *as of* Dec. 1>
asp (ăsp) *n.* Any of several small venomous African snakes, as the horned viper.
as•par•a•gus (ə-spăr′ə-gəs) *n.* A plant, *Asparagus officinalis*, with scales or needlelike branchlets rather than true leaves and succulent, edible young stalks.
as•pect (ăs′pĕkt′) *n.* **1.** Look : appearance. **2.** Phase : facet. **3.** A position or side facing a given direction.
as•pen (ăs′pən) *n.* Any of several trees of the genus *Populus* with leaves that flutter in even a light breeze.
as•per•i•ty (ă-spĕr′ĭ-tē) *n.* **1.** Roughness. **2.** Ill temper : irritability.
as•perse (ə-spûrs′) *v.* **-persed, -pers•ing.** To make false charges or insinuations against : malign. **—as•per′sion** *n.*
as•phalt (ăs′fôlt′) *n.* A thick, sticky brownish-black mixture of petroleum tars used in paving and roofing.
as•pho•del (ăs′fə-dəl′) *n.* Any of several Mediterranean plants of the genera *Asphodeline* and *Asphodelus*, bearing white or yellow flower clusters.
as•phyx•i•a (ăs-fĭk′sē-ə) *n.* Unconsciousness or death caused by a lack of oxygen or an increase of carbon dioxide in the blood. **—as•phyx′i•ant** *n.*
as•phyx•i•ate (ăs-fĭk′sē-āt′) *v.* **-at•ed, -at•ing.** To suffocate. **—as•phyx′i•a′tion** *n.*
as•pic (ăs′pĭk) *n.* A jelly made from meat, fish, or vegetable juices.
as•pi•rant (ăs′pər-ənt, ə-spīr′-) *n.* One who aspires. **—as′pi•rant** *adj.*
as•pi•rate (ăs′pər-ĭt) *n.* **1.** The speech sound represented by the *h* in *happy.* **2.** A speech sound followed by a puff of breath. **—as′pi•rate′** (-pə-rāt′) *v.*
as•pi•ra•tion (ăs′pə-rā′shən) *n.* **1. a.** A strong desire for high achievement or the realization of an ideal. **b.** An object of this desire : goal. **2. a.** The pronunciation of an aspirate. **b.** An aspirate. **3.** The removal of a liquid or gas with an aspirator.
as•pi•ra•tor (ăs′pə-rā′tər) *n.* A device that removes liquids or gases from a space by suction.
as•pire (ə-spīr′) *v.* **-pired, -pir•ing.** To have ambition. **—as•pir′ing•ly** *adv.*
as•pi•rin (ăs′pər-ĭn, -prĭn) *n.* **1.** A white crystalline compound of acetylsalicylic acid used for the relief of pain and reduction of fever. **2.** A tablet of aspirin.
ass (ăs) *n.* **1.** A hoofed mammal of the genus *Equus* that resembles and is related to the horse, esp. the domesticated donkey. **2.** A foolish or stupid person.
as•sail (ə-sāl′) *v.* **1.** To attack with violence. **2.** To attack verbally. **—as•sail′a•ble** *adj.* **—as•sail′ant** *n.* **—as•sail′er** *n.*
as•sas•sin (ə-săs′ĭn) *n.* A murderer, esp. of a prominent person.
as•sas•si•nate (ə-săs′ə-nāt′) *v.* **-nat•ed, -nat•ing.** To murder, esp. for political reasons. **—as•sas′si•na′tion** *n.*
as•sault (ə-sôlt′) *n.* **1.** A violent verbal or physical attack. **2.** *Law.* An unlawful attempt or threat to do physical injury to another. **—as•sault′** *v.* **—as•sault′er** *n.*
as•say (ăs′ā′, ă-sā′) *n.* Chemical analysis of a substance, esp. of an ore or drug. —*v.* (ă-sā′, ăs′ā′). **1.** To subject to a chemical analysis. **2.** To assess : evaluate. **3.** To attempt : try. **—as•say′er** *n.*
as•sem•blage (ə-sĕm′blĭj) *n.* **1.** The act of assembling. **2.** A collection of people or things. **3.** A sculpture made from miscellaneous objects, as metal scraps, pieces of cloth, string, etc.
as•sem•ble (ə-sĕm′bəl) *v.* **-bled, -bling. 1.** To bring or come together as a group. **2.** To put together the parts of. **—as•sem′bler** *n.*
as•sem•bly (ə-sĕm′blē) *n., pl.* **-blies. 1.** A group of persons gathered together : meeting. **2. Assembly.** A lower legislative house. **3. a.** The putting together of parts, as of a machine. **b.** The assembled set of parts. **4.** A signal calling troops to form ranks.
assembly language *n. Computer Sci.* A programming language that is a close approximation of machine code.
assembly line *n.* An arrangement of workers and equipment in which work passes successively from operation to operation to make a completed product.
as•sem•bly•man (ə-sĕm′blē-mən) *n.* A man who is a member of an Assembly.
as•sem•bly•wom•an (ə-sĕm′blē-wŏŏm′ən) *n.* A woman who is a member of an Assembly.
as•sent (ə-sĕnt′) *v.* To express agreement : acquiesce. **—as•sent′** *n.*
as•sert (ə-sûrt′) *v.* **1.** To declare positively : avow. **2.** To defend : maintain. ☆***syns:*** AFFIRM, AVER, AVOUCH, AVOW, DECLARE, HOLD, MAINTAIN, STATE **—as•ser′tion** *n.* **—as•ser′tive** *adj.* **—as•ser′tive•ly** *adv.* **—as•ser′tive•ness** *n.*
as•sess (ə-sĕs′) *v.* **1.** To assign a value to, esp. for taxation. **2.** To fix the amount of (e.g., a tax). **3.** To subject to a special payment, as a tax. **—as•sess′ment** *n.* **—as•ses′sor** *n.* **—as′ses•so′ri•al** *adj.*
as•set (ăs′ĕt′) *n.* **1.** A valuable possession or quality : resource. **2. assets.** All the property of a person or a business that can be applied to cover liabilities.
as•sev•er•ate (ə-sĕv′ə-rāt′) *v.* **-at•ed, -at•ing.** To state seriously and positively : affirm. **—as•sev′er•a′tion** *n.*
as•sid•u•ous (ə-sĭj′ōō-əs) *adj.* Constantly attentive : diligent. **—as′si•du′i•ty** (ăs′ĭ-dōō′ĭ-tē, -dyōō′-) *n.* **—as•sid′u•ous•ly** *adv.* **—as•sid′u•ous•ness** *n.*
as•sign (ə-sīn′) *v.* **1.** To fix : designate <*assign* a day for the test> **2.** To appoint, as to a duty. **3.** To give out : allot. **4.** To attribute : ascribe. **5.** *Law.* To transfer (e.g., property). **—as•sign′a•ble** *adj.* **—as•sign′er** *n.*
as•sig•na•tion (ăs′ĭg-nā′shən) *n.* An arrangement for a tryst between lovers.
as•sign•ment (ə-sīn′mənt) *n.* **1.** The act of assigning. **2.** Something assigned.
as•sim•i•late (ə-sĭm′ə-lāt′) *v.* **-lat•ed, -lat•ing. 1.** *Physiol.* To consume and incorporate into the body : digest. **2.** To take into the mind : understand. **3.** To make or become similar. **4.** To absorb (e.g., a culturally distinct group) into the prevailing culture. **—as•sim′i•la′tion** *n.*
as•sist (ə-sĭst′) *v.* To help : aid. —*n.* **1.** An act of assisting. **2.** A player's maneuver enabling a teammate to put out an opponent, as in baseball, or score a goal, as in hockey or basketball. **—as•sis′tance** *n.* **—as•sis′tant** *n.*
as•size (ə-sīz′) *n.* **1.** A judicial inquest. **2. assizes.** A court session held periodically in English and Welsh counties.
assoc. *abbr.* **1.** associate. **2.** *also* **assn.** association.
as•so•ci•ate (ə-sō′shē-āt′, -sē-) *v.* **-at•ed, -at•ing. 1.** To join in

a relationship. **2.** To link in the imagination or mind. —*n.* (-ĭt). **1.** A colleague or partner. **2.** A companion : comrade. **—as·so'ci·ate** (-ĭt, -āt') *adj.*

as·so·ci·a·tion (ə-sō'sē-ā'shən, -shē-) *n.* **1.** The act of associating. **2.** An organized body of persons : society.

association football *n. esp. Brit.* Soccer.

as·so·ci·a·tive (ə-sō'shē-ā'tĭv, -sē-, -shə-tĭv) *adj.* Of, relating to, or marked by association.

as·so·nance (ăs'ə-nəns) *n.* Repetition of vowel sounds, esp. in poetry.

as·sort (ə-sôrt') *v.* To separate into groups of a like kind : classify.

as·sort·ed (ə-sôr'tĭd) *adj.* Consisting of different kinds : various.

as·sort·ment (ə-sôrt'mənt) *n.* A collection of various persons or things : variety.

asst. *abbr.* assistant.

as·suage (ə-swāj') *v.* **-suaged, -suag·ing.** **1.** To make less intense : ease. **2.** To satisfy.

as·sume (ə-so͞om') *v.* **-sumed, -sum·ing.** **1.** To take upon oneself : undertake <*assume* the payments> **2.** To affect : feign <*assumed* an attitude of indifference> **3.** To take for granted without proof : suppose. **—as·sum'a·ble** *adj.* **—as·sum'a·bly** *adv.* **—as·sum'ed·ly** *adv.*

as·sump·tion (ə-sŭmp'shən) *n.* **1.** The act of assuming. **2.** An idea or statement assumed to be true without proof : supposition. **3. Assumption.** The ascent of the Virgin Mary into heaven after her death, celebrated Aug. 15.

as·sur·ance (ə-sho͝or'əns) *n.* **1.** A statement intended to inspire confidence : guarantee. **2. a.** Certainty. **b.** Self-confidence. **3.** Audacity : boldness.

as·sure (ə-sho͝or') *v.* **-sured, -sur·ing.** **1.** To inform confidently. **2.** To cause to feel confident : convince. **3.** To make sure the realization of : ensure.

As·syr·i·a (ə-sĭr'ē-ə). Ancient empire of W Asia. **—As·syr'i·an** *adj.* & *n.*

as·ta·tine (ăs'tə-tēn', -tĭn) *n. Symbol* **At** A highly unstable radioactive element.

as·ter (ăs'tər) *n.* A plant of the genus *Aster,* with white to bluish, purple, or pink daisylike flowers.

as·ter·isk (ăs'tə-rĭsk') *n.* A character (*) used to indicate an omission of letters or words or a reference to a footnote.

a·stern (ə-stûrn') *adv.* & *adj.* **1.** Behind a ship or vessel. **2.** Toward the rear of a ship or aircraft.

as·ter·oid (ăs'tə-roid') *n.* Any of numerous small planets with orbits lying mainly between Mars and Jupiter. **—as'ter·oid'al** *adj.*

asth·ma (ăz'mə) *n.* An often allergic respiratory disease marked by labored breathing, chest constriction, and coughing. **—asth·mat'ic** (-măt'ĭk) *n.* & *adj.*

as though *conj.* As if.

a·stig·ma·tism (ə-stĭg'mə-tĭz'əm) *n.* A defect of a lens, esp. of a lens of the eye, that causes faulty focusing. **—as'tig·mat'ic** (ăs'tĭg-măt'ĭk) *adj.*

a·stir (ə-stûr') *adj.* **1.** Being in motion. **2.** Out of bed : awake.

as to *prep.* **1.** Concerning : about <no idea *as to* what he meant> **2.** According to : by <rewarded *as to* talent>

as·ton·ish (ə-stŏn'ĭsh) *v.* To fill with sudden wonder : surprise greatly. **—as·ton'ish·ing·ly** *adv.* **—as·ton'ish·ment** *n.*

as·tound (ə-stound') *v.* To strike with confused wonder.

a·strad·dle (ə-străd'l) *adv.* & *prep.* In a straddling position : astride.

as·tra·khan (ăs'trə-kăn', -kən) *n.* The curly fur of a young lamb from the region of Astrakhan in the SE USSR on the Volga River.

as·tral (ăs'trəl) *adj.* Of, relating to, emanating from, or resembling the stars.

a·stray (ə-strā') *adv.* **1.** Away from the right direction or path. **2.** Away from the morally right or good.

a·stride (ə-strīd') *prep.* With a leg on each side of. **—a·stride'** *adv.*

as·trin·gent (ə-strĭn'jənt) *adj.* Capable of drawing together or constricting tissue : styptic. —*n.* An astringent agent. **—as·trin'gen·cy** *n.*

as·tro·bi·ol·o·gy (ăs'trō-bī-ŏl'ə-jē) *n.* Exobiology.

as·tro·dome (ăs'trə-dōm') *n.* A stadium covered by a dome.

as·tro·dy·nam·ics (ăs'trō-dī-năm'ĭks) *n. (sing. in number).* The dynamics of celestial bodies.

as·tro·labe (ăs'trə-lāb') *n.* An instrument formerly used by mariners to determine the altitude of a celestial body.

as·trol·o·gy (ə-strŏl'ə-jē) *n.* The study of the supposed influence of planets and stars on the course of human affairs. **—as·trol'o·ger** *n.* **—as'tro·log'ic** (ăs'trə-lŏj'ĭk), **as'tro·log'i·cal** *adj.*

as·tro·naut (ăs'trə-nôt') *n.* Someone, esp. a crew member, who travels in a spacecraft.

as·tro·nau·tics (ăs'trə-nô'tĭks) *n. (sing. in number).* The science and technology of the design, construction, and operation of spacecraft. **—as'tro·nau'tic, as'tro·nau'ti·cal** *adj.* **—as'tro·nau'ti·cal·ly** *adv.*

as·tro·nom·i·cal (ăs'trə-nŏm'ĭ-kəl) *or* **as·tro·nom·ic** (-nŏm'ĭk) *adj.* **1.** Of or relating to astronomy. **2.** Unimaginably large : immense. **—as'tro·nom'i·cal·ly** *adv.*

astronomical unit *n.* A unit of distance equal to the average distance between the earth and the sun, about 150 million km or 93 million mi.

as·tron·o·my (ə-strŏn'ə-mē) *n.* The science of the universe beyond the earth, esp. the observation, calculation, and interpretation of the positions, distribution, motion, and composition of celestial bodies. **—as·tron'o·mer** *n.*

as·tro·phys·ics (ăs'trə-fĭz'ĭks) *n. (sing. in number).* The physics of stellar phenomena. **—as'tro·phys'i·cal** *adj.* **—as'tro·phys'i·cist** (-fĭz'ĭ-sĭst) *n.*

As·tro·turf (ăs'trō-tûrf'). A trademark for an artificial grasslike ground covering.

as·tute (ə-sto͞ot', ə-styo͞ot') *adj.* Keen in discernment : shrewd. **—as·tute'ly** *adv.* **—as·tute'ness** *n.*

A·sun·ción (ä'so͞on-syôn'). Cap. of Paraguay, in the S. *Pop.* 462,776.

a·sun·der (ə-sŭn'dər) *adv.* **1.** Into separate parts. **2.** Apart from each other in position.

a·sy·lum (ə-sī'ləm) *n.* **1.** An institution for the care of the sick or needy. **2.** A place of sanctuary. **3.** Governmental protection granted to a foreign political refugee.

a·sym·met·ric (ā'sĭ-mĕt'rĭk) *or* **a·sym·met·ri·cal** (-rĭ-kəl) *adj.* Not symmetrical. **—a·sym'me·try** (ā-sĭm'ĭ-trē) *n.*

as·ymp·tote (ăs'ĭm-tōt', -ĭmp-) *n.* A straight line that is approached but never met by a point on a curve as the point moves an infinite distance from the origin. **—as'ymp·tot'ic** (-tŏt'ĭk), **as'ymp·tot'i·cal** *adj.* **—as'ymp·tot'i·cal·ly** *adv.*

at[1] (ăt; ət *when unstressed*) *prep.* **1.** Used to indicate position, location, or condition <*at* school><*at* peace> **2.** Used to indicate direction or aim <smiled *at* him> **3.** Used to indicate a point in time <*at* dawn> **4.** Used to indicate manner, means, or reason <angry *at* his arrogance>

at[2] (ät) *n., pl.* **at.** See *kip* at CURRENCY TABLE.

At *symbol for* ASTATINE.

At·a·brine (ăt'ə-brĭn, -brēn'). A trademark for a preparation used in treating malaria.

at all *adv.* In any way whatever <can't hear it *at all*>

at·a·vism (ăt'ə-vĭz'əm) *n.* The reappearance in an organism of a hereditary characteristic absent for several generations. **—at'a·vis'tic** (-vĭs'tĭk) *adj.*

ate (āt) *v. p.t. of* EAT.

at·el·ier (ăt'l-yā') *n.* **1.** A workshop. **2.** The studio of an artist.

a·the·ism (ā'thē-ĭz'əm) *n.* Denial of or disbelief in the existence of God. **—a'the·ist** *n.* **—a'the·is'tic** *adj.*

A·the·na (ə-thē'nə) *also* **A·the·ne** (-nē) *n. Gk. Myth.* The goddess of wisdom.

ath·e·nae·um *also* **ath·e·ne·um** (ăth'ə-nē'əm) *n.* A library.

Ath·ens (ăth'ənz). Cap. of Greece, in the E central part. *Pop.* 867,023. **—A·the'ni·an** (ə-thē'nē-ən) *adj.* & *n.*

ath·er·o·scle·ro·sis (ăth'ə-rō-sklə-rō'sĭs) *n.* Arteriosclerosis marked by the deposit of pulpy, lipid-containing materials in arterial walls.

a·thirst (ə-thûrst') *adj.* Eager : desirous.

ath·lete (ăth'lēt') *n.* One who participates in competitive sports.

ath·lete's foot *n.* A contagious skin infection caused by a fungus and affecting esp. the feet.

ath·let·ic (ăth-lĕt'ĭk) *adj.* **1.** Of, relating to, or for athletics or athletes. **2.** Physically strong : sturdy. **—ath·let'i·cal·ly** *adv.*

ath·let·ics (ăth-lĕt'ĭks) *n. (sing. or pl. in number).* Activities and exercises that require physical endurance, skill, and strength, esp. competitive sports.

a·thwart (ə-thwôrt') *adv.* From side to side : across. —*prep.* **1.** From one side to the other of : across. **2.** In conflict with : against.

a·tilt (ə-tĭlt') *adj.* & *adv.* Tilted or inclined upward.

-ation *suff.* **1.** Action : process <strangul*ation*> **2.** The result of an action or process <accultur*ation*>

-ative *suff.* Of, relating to, or associated with <talk*ative*>

At·lan·ta (ăt-lăn'tə). Cap. of Ga., in the N part. *Pop.* 525,022.

Atlantic Ocean. 2nd largest of the earth's oceans, extending from the Arctic in the N to the Antarctic in the S and from the Americas in the W to Europe and Africa in the E.

at·las (ăt'ləs) *n.* A book of maps.

at·mos·phere (ăt'mə-sfîr') *n.* **1.** The gaseous mass surrounding a celestial body, esp. the earth. 2. Environment : surroundings. 3. *Physics.* A unit of pressure equal to 1.01325 × 10^5 newtons per sq m. 4. A predominant feeling : mood. **—at'mos·pher'ic** (-sfĕr'ĭk, -sfîr'-) *adj.* **—at'mos·pher'i·cal·ly** *adv.*

at·mos·pher·ics (ăt'mə-sfĕr'ĭks, -sfîr'-) *n. (sing. in number).* 1. Electromagnetic radiation produced by natural phenomena such as lightning. 2. Radio interference caused by this radiation.

at·oll (ăt'ôl', -ōl', ā'tôl', ā'tŏl') *n.* A coral island that forms a ring and partially or totally encloses a lagoon.

at·om (ăt'əm) *n.* 1. A very small particle : bit. 2. *Physics & Chem.* The smallest unit of an element, typically indivisible in chemical reactions except for some removal or exchange of particular electrons.

atom bomb *n.* An atomic bomb.

a·tom·ic (ə-tŏm'ĭk) *adj.* 1. Of or relating to an atom, atomic bombs, or atomic energy. 2. Extremely small : infinitesimal.

atomic bomb *n.* A bomb whose great destructive power is from the energy released in the fission of heavy atomic nuclei, as of uranium 235.

atomic clock *n.* A device that keeps precise time by counting the occurrences of something that happens in an atomic or molecular system at regular intervals.

atomic energy *n.* Energy released as a result of reactions involving atomic nuclei.

atomic number *n.* The number of protons in an atomic nucleus of an element.

atomic pile *n.* A nuclear reactor.

atomic weight *n.* The average weight of an atom of an element.

at·om·ize (ăt'ə-mīz') *v.* **-ized, -iz·ing.** To separate into tiny particles.

at·om·iz·er (ăt'ə-mī'zər) *n.* A device for producing a fine spray, as of medicine or perfume.

atom smasher *n. Physics.* An atomic particle accelerator.

a·ton·al (ā-tō'nəl) *adj. Mus.* Characterized by deliberate avoidance of a traditional key or tonal center. **—a'to·nal'i·ty** *n.* **—a·ton'al·ly** *adv.*

a·tone (ə-tōn') *v.* **a·toned, a·ton·ing.** To make amends (for).
▲word history: The derivation of *atone,* from *at* and *one,* has been obscured somewhat by the fairly recent change in the pronunciation of *one. One* used to be pronounced like *own,* but since the 17th cent. it has been pronounced like *won,* the past tense of *win.* The older pronunciation survives in *alone, lone, lonely,* and *only* in addition to *atone* and its derivatives; the new pronunciation occurs in *once.*

a·tone·ment (ə-tōn'mənt) *n.* 1. Amends for a wrong or injury. 2. *Theol.* The redemption of man through Christ's death.

a·top (ə-tŏp') *prep.* On top of.

-ator *suff.* One that acts in a particular manner <radi*ator*>

-atory *suff.* 1. a. Of or pertaining to <perspir*atory*> b. Tending to <amend*atory*> 2. One connected to or with <reform*atory*>

ATP (ā'tē-pē') *n.* A nucleotide obtained from adenosine that supplies energy to cells through its conversion to ADP.

a·tri·um (ā'trē-əm) *n., pl.* **a·tri·a** (ā'trē-ə) or **a·tri·ums.** 1. The central court of an ancient Roman house. 2. A bodily cavity, esp. one of the chambers of the heart.

a·tro·cious (ə-trō'shəs) *adj.* 1. Exceedingly evil or cruel. 2. Extremely bad : abominable. **—a·tro'cious·ly** *adv.* **—a·tro'cious·ness** *n.*

a·troc·i·ty (ə-trŏs'ĭ-tē) *n., pl.* **-ties.** 1. The state or condition of being atrocious. 2. An atrocious object or act.

at·ro·phy (ăt'rə-fē) *n., pl.* **-phies.** The wasting away of bodily tissues or organs. *—v.* **-phied, -phy·ing.** To undergo or cause to undergo atrophy : wither. **—a·tro'phic** (ā-trō'fĭk) *adj.*

at·ro·pine (ăt'rə-pēn', -pĭn) *n.* A poisonous alkaloid derived from belladonna and related plants and having various medicinal uses, as dilating the pupil of the eye.

at·tach (ə-tăch') *v.* 1. To fasten or become fastened : affix. 2. To bind by personal ties, as of loyalty or affection. 3. *Law.* To seize (property) by legal writ. ☆***syns:*** AFFIX, CLIP, CONNECT, COUPLE, FASTEN, FIX, SECURE **—at·tach'a·ble** *adj.* **—at·tach'er** *n.*

at·ta·ché (ăt'ə-shā', ă-tă'shā') *n.* An expert in a particular area assigned to the staff of an embassy <a cultural *attaché*>

attaché case *n.* A briefcase that has hinges and flat sides and is similar to a small suitcase.

at·tach·ment (ə-tăch'mənt) *n.* 1. Something that fastens one thing to another. 2. A tie of loyalty or affection. 3. A supplementary part, as of an appliance : acessory. 4. The seizure of property by legal writ.

at·tack (ə-tăk') *v.* 1. To set upon with violent physical or verbal force : assail. 2. To begin work on, esp. with vigor. ☆***syns:*** ASSAIL, ASSAULT, BESET, STRIKE *—n.* 1. The act of attacking : assault. 2. The onset of disease, esp. when sudden. **—at·tack'er** *n.*

at·tain (ə-tān') *v.* 1. To achieve, esp. by effort : accomplish. 2. To arrive at, as in time. **—at·tain'a·bil'i·ty** *n.* **—at·tain'a·ble** *adj.*

at·tain·der (ə-tān'dər) *n. Law.* The loss of all civil rights by a person who has been sentenced to death or outlawry, esp. for treason.

at·tain·ment (ə-tān'mənt) *n.* 1. The act of attaining. 2. Something attained.

at·taint (ə-tānt') *v. Law.* To condemn by a sentence of attainder.

at·tar (ăt'ər) *n.* A fragrant essential oil obtained from flowers.

at·tempt (ə-tĕmpt') *v.* To make an effort : try. **—at·tempt'** *n.*

at·tend (ə-tĕnd') *v.* 1. To be present (at). 2. To go with : accompany. 3. To look after : care for. 4. To pay attention : heed. 5. To direct or apply oneself.

at·ten·dance (ə-tĕn'dəns) *n.* 1. The act of attending. 2. Those that attend a function.

at·ten·dant (ə-tĕn'dənt) *n.* One who attends another to provide a service. *—adj.* Following or accompanying as a result : concomitant <flu and *attendant* miseries>

at·ten·tion (ə-tĕn'shən) *n.* 1. Mental concentration. 2. Observation : notice. 3. **attentions.** Acts of courtesy, consideration, or gallantry. 4. A military posture with arms at the side, heels together, and eyes to the front. **—at·ten'tive** *adj.* **—at·ten'tive·ly** *adv.* **—at·ten'tive·ness** *n.*

at·ten·u·ate (ə-tĕn'yo͞o-āt') *v.* **-at·ed, -at·ing.** 1. To make or become fine or thin. 2. To weaken. **—at·ten'u·a'tion** *n.*

at·test (ə-tĕst') *v.* 1. To affirm to be genuine by signing one's name as a witness. 2. To be evidence of. 3. To give testimony. **—at'tes·ta'tion** *n.*

at·tic (ăt'ĭk) *n.* The room or space directly below the roof of a building.

At·ti·la (ăt'ə-lə, ə-tĭl'ə). 406?–53. King of the Huns (433?–53).

at·tire (ə-tīr') *v.* **-tired, -tir·ing.** To dress : clothe. *—n.* Dress : clothing.

at·ti·tude (ăt'ĭ-to͞od', -tyo͞od') *n.* 1. A position of the body or manner of carrying oneself : posture. 2. A state of feeling or mind about a person or situation. 3. The orientation of a spacecraft or aircraft relative to a point of reference, as the horizon.

at·ti·tu·di·nize (ăt'-to͞od'n-īz', -tyo͞od'-) *v.* **-nized, -niz·ing.** To assume an attitude for effect : posture.

attn. *abbr.* attention.

at·tor·ney (ə-tûr'nē) *n., pl.* **-neys.** A person, esp. a lawyer, legally appointed to act as agent for another.

attorney general *n., pl.* **attorneys general.** The chief law officer and legal counsel of a state or nation.

at·tract (ə-trăkt') *v.* 1. To cause to draw near. 2. To draw to oneself by an appealing quality. 3. To allure or be alluring. ☆***syns:*** ALLURE, APPEAL, DRAW, LURE, MAGNETIZE, PULL **—at·trac'tive** *adj.* **—at·trac'tive·ly** *adv.* **—at·trac'tive·ness** *n.*

at·trac·tion (ə-trăk'shən) *n.* 1. The act or capability of attracting. 2. An attractive feature or characteristic. 3. Something that attracts, as a public entertainment.

at·trib·ute (ə-trĭb'yət) *v.* **-ut·ed, -ut·ing.** To regard or explain as arising or resulting from a source or cause. *—n.* (ăt'rə-byo͞ot'). 1. A characteristic of a person or thing. 2. An adjective or term used as an adjective. **—at·trib'ut·a·ble** *adj.* **—at'tri·bu'tion** (at'rə-byo͞o'shən) *n.*

at·trib·u·tive (ə-trĭb'yə-tĭv) *adj.* 1. Placed directly adjacent to a modified noun without a linking verb <"White" in "white house" is an *attributive* adjective.> 2. Of or having the nature of an attribution or attribute. **—at·trib'u·tive** *n.* **—at·trib'u·tive·ly** *adv.*

at·tri·tion (ə-trĭsh'ən) *n.* 1. An eroding by or as if by friction. 2. A gradual natural reduction, as in membership or personnel, through retirement, resignation, or death.

at·tune (ə-to͞on', ə-tyo͞on') *v.* **-tuned, -tun·ing.** To bring into accord : harmonize.

atty. *or* **att.** *abbr.* attorney.

a·twit·ter (ə-twĭt'ər) *adj.* Excited.

a·typ·i·cal (ā-tĭp'ĭ-kəl) *adj.* Not typical : uncharacteristic. **—a·typ'i·cal·ly** *adv.*

Au *symbol for* GOLD.

au·burn (ô'bərn) *n.* A reddish brown color. **—au'burn** *adj.*

au cou·rant (ō' ko͞o-räɴ') *adj.* Informed on current affairs : up-to-date.

auc·tion (ôk'shən) *n.* A public sale of items to the highest bidder. *—v.* To sell at auction. **—auc'tion·eer'** *n.*

auction bridge *n.* A variety of the game of bridge in which tricks made in excess of the contract are scored toward game.

auc·to·ri·al (ôk-tôr'ē-əl, -tōr') *adj.* Of or relating to an author.

au·da·cious (ô-dā'shəs) *adj.* 1. Bold : daring. 2. Arrogantly impudent : insolent. **—au·da'cious·ly** *adv.* **—au·dac'i·ty** (ô-dăs'ĭ-tē) *n.*

au·di·ble (ô′də-bəl) *adj.* Able to be heard. **—au′di·bil′i·ty** *n.* **—au′di·bly** *adv.*
au·di·ence (ô′dē-əns) *n.* **1.** A body of listeners or spectators. **2.** A formal conference or hearing. **3.** An opportunity to express one's views.
au·di·o (ô′dē-ō′) *adj.* Of or relating to sound or sound reproduction. *—n.* **1.** The sound part of television or motion-picture equipment. **2.** The broadcasting or reception of sound.
au·di·ol·o·gy (ô′dē-ŏl′ə-jē) *n.* The science and treatment of hearing defects. **—au′di·o·log′i·cal** (-ə-lŏj′ĭ-kəl) *adj.* **—au′di·ol′o·gist** *n.*
au·di·om·e·ter (ô′dē-ŏm′ĭ-tər) *n.* An instrument for measuring hearing thresholds for pure tones of normally audible frequencies. **—au′di·o·met′ric** (-ə-mĕt′rĭk) **—au′di·om′e·try** *n.*
au·di·o·vis·u·al (ô′dē-ō-vĭzh′o͞o-əl) *adj.* Of, relating to, or involving both hearing and sight.
au·di·o·vis·u·als (ô′dē-ō-vĭzh′o͞o-əlz) *pl.n.* Audiovisual educational materials.
au·dit (ô′dĭt) *n.* An examination or verification of financial records or accounts. *—v.* **1.** To conduct an audit of. **2.** To attend (an academic course) without receiving credit.
au·di·tion (ô-dĭsh′ən) *n.* A hearing, esp. a performance given by an entertainer to demonstrate merit. *—v.* To give or submit to an audition.
au·di·tor (ô′dĭ-tər) *n.* **1.** A listener. **2.** One who audits.
au·di·to·ri·um (ô′dĭ-tôr′ē-əm, -tōr′-) *n.* **1.** A room, as in a school, to accommodate an audience. **2.** A building used for public meetings, artistic performances, etc.
au·di·to·ry (ô′dĭ-tôr′ē, -tōr′ē) *adj.* Of or relating to the sense, the organs, or the experience of hearing.
auf Wie·der·seh·en (ouf vē′dər-zān′) *interj.* Used to express farewell.
Aug. *abbr.* August.
au·ger (ô′gər) *n.* A tool used for boring.
▲word history: *An auger* was orig. *a nauger.* It is one of the numerous English words that have lost an initial *n* as a result of the incorrect division between the indefinite article and the noun. The Old English word from which *auger* is derived, *nafogār,* is actually a compound word made up of *nafu,* "wheel hub" (related to *navel),* and *gār,* "spear." An *auger* is thus a tool for piercing and boring holes.
aught (ôt) *n.* A zero : cipher.
aug·ment (ôg-mĕnt′) *v.* To make or become greater. **—aug′men·ta′tion** *n.*
au gra·tin (ō grät′n, grăt′n) *adj.* Covered with bread crumbs or grated cheese and oven-browned.
au·gur (ô′gər) *n.* A soothsayer : seer. *—v.* **1.** To predict, esp. from signs : foretell. **2.** To be an omen of : presage.
au·gu·ry (ô′gyə-rē) *n., pl.* **-ries. 1.** The practice of auguring. **2.** An omen : sign.
au·gust (ô-gŭst′) *adj.* Inspiring admiration or awe : majestic. **—au·gust′ly** *adv.*
Au·gust (ô′gəst) *n.* The 8th month of the year, having 31 days.
Au·gus·ta (ô-gŭs′tə, ə-gŭs′-). Cap. of Me., in the SW. *Pop.* 21,819.
Au·gus·tine (ô′gə-stēn′, ô-gŭs′tĭn), Saint. 354–430. Church father and philosopher. **—Au′gus·tin′i·an** (ô′gə-stĭn′ē-ən) *adj.* & *n.*
Au·gus·tus (ô-gŭs′təs). "Octavian." 63 B.C.–A.D. 14. 1st Roman emperor. **—Au·gus′tan** *adj.*
au jus (ō zhü′) *adj.* Served with the natural juices that accumulate during roasting.
auk (ôk) *n.* Any of several sea birds of the family Alcidae of arctic regions with a stocky body and short wings.
aunt (ănt, änt) *n.* **1.** A sister of one's father or mother. **2.** The wife of one's uncle.
au·ra (ôr′ə) *n.* **1.** An emanation. **2.** A distinctive air or quality <a city with an *aura* of romance>
au·ral (ôr′əl) *adj.* Of, relating to, or received through the ear.
au·re·ate (ôr′ē-ĭt) *adj.* **1.** Gold in color. **2.** Marked by an affected and pompous literary style.
au·re·ole (ôr′ē-ōl′) *also* **au·re·o·la** (ô-rē′ə-lə) *n.* A halo.
Au·re·o·my·cin (ôr′ē-ō-mī′sĭn). A trademark for chlortetracycline.
au re·voir (ō′ rə-vwär′) *interj.* Used to express farewell.
au·ri·cle (ôr′ĭ-kəl) *n.* **1.** *Anat.* **a.** The outer part of the ear. **b.** An atrium of the heart. **2.** *Biol.* An earlike process, part, or appendage.

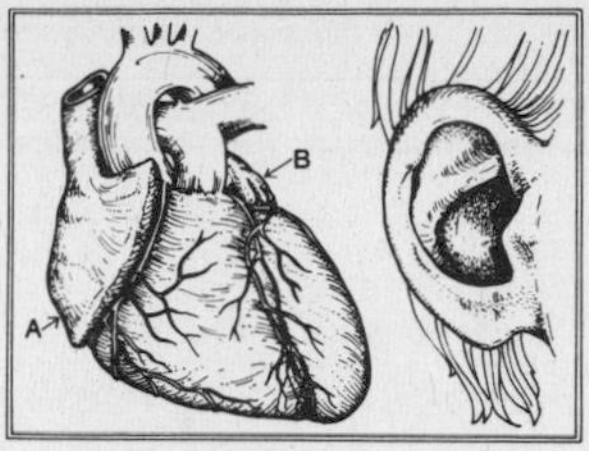

auricle
(Left) *of the heart showing A. right auricle and B. left auricle, and* (right) *of the ear*

au·ric·u·lar (ô-rĭk′yə-lər) *adj.* **1.** Aural. **2.** Of or relating to an auricle.
au·rif·er·ous (ô-rĭf′ər-əs) *adj.* Containing gold : gold-bearing.
au·ro·ra (ə-rôr′ə, ə-rōr′ə) *n.* **1.** A brilliant display of flashing and moving lights visible in the night sky, chiefly in polar regions, believed to result from electrically charged particles. **2.** Dawn. **—au·ro′ral** *adj.*
aurora aus·tra·lis (ô-strā′lĭs) *n.* The aurora of the S Hemisphere.
aurora bo·re·al·is (bôr′ē-ăl′ĭs, bōr′-) *n.* The aurora of the N Hemisphere.
aus·cul·ta·tion (ô′skəl-tā′shən) *n.* The act of monitoring sounds originating in bodily organs as an aid to diagnosis.
aus·pice (ô′spĭs) *n., pl.* **aus·pic·es** (ô′spĭ-sēz′, -sĭz). **1. auspices.** Protection and support : patronage. **2.** An omen : portent.
aus·pi·cious (ô-spĭsh′əs) *adj.* **1.** Affording signs of a successful result : favorable. **2.** Prosperous : successful. **—aus·pi′cious·ly** *adv.* **—aus·pi′cious·ness** *n.*
Aus·ten (ôs′tən), **Jane.** 1775–1817. English novelist.
aus·tere (ô-stîr′) *adj.* **1.** Stern, as in manner : severe. **2.** Marked by abstemiousness : ascetic. **3.** Without ornamentation : simple. **—aus·tere′ly** *adv.* **—aus·ter′i·ty** *n.*
Aus·tin (ô′stən). Cap. of Tex., in the SC part. *Pop.* 345,496.
aus·tral (ô′strəl) *adj.* Southern.
Aus·tra·lia (ô-strāl′yə). **1.** Continent lying SE of Asia between the Pacific and Indian oceans. **2.** Country comprising the continent of Australia, the island of Tasmania, 2 territories, and other dependencies. *Cap.* Canberra. *Pop.* 14,423,500. **—Aus·tra′lian** *adj.* & *n.*
Aus·tri·a (ôs′trē-ə). Country of central Europe. *Cap.* Vienna. *Pop.* 7,456,745. **—Aus′tri·an** *adj.* & *n.*
au·then·tic (ô-thĕn′tĭk) *adj.* Real : genuine. **—au·then′ti·cal·ly** *adv.* **—au′then·tic′i·ty** (-tĭs′ĭ-tē) *n.*
au·then·ti·cate (ô-thĕn′tĭ-kāt′) *v.* **-cat·ed, -cat·ing.** To prove or be proof of the authenticity of. **—au·then′ti·ca′tion** *n.*
au·thor (ô′thər) *n.* **1.** Someone who writes a literary work. **2.** Someone who creates or originates anything. **—au′thor** *v.* **—au′thor·ship′** *n.*
au·thor·i·tar·i·an (ə-thôr′ĭ-târ′ē-ən, ə-thŏr′-, ô-) *adj.* Favoring or marked by absolute and unquestioning obedience to authority. **—au·thor′i·tar′i·an** *n.* **—au·thor′i·tar′i·an·ism** *n.*
au·thor·i·ta·tive (ə-thôr′ĭ-tā′tĭv, ə-thŏr′-, ô-) *adj.* Being, having, or arising from an authority. **—au·thor′i·ta′tive·ly** *adv.* **—au·thor′i·ta′tive·ness** *n.*
au·thor·i·ty (ə-thôr′ĭ-tē, ə-thŏr′-, ô-) *n., pl.* **-ties. 1. a.** The power to command, determine, influence, or judge. **b.** A person or group with this power. **c. authorities.** Government. **2.** Authorization : right. **3. a.** An accepted source of definitive information. **b.** A quotation or citation from such a source. **4.** An expert in a specific field.
au·thor·ize (ô′thə-rīz′) *v.* **-ized, -iz·ing. 1.** To grant legal authority to. **2.** To approve : sanction. **3.** To justify. **—au′thor·i·za′tion** *n.*
au·tism (ô′tĭz′əm) *n.* Engrossment in abnormal mental activity, as hallucinations and fantasies, together with withdrawal from external reality. **—au·tis′tic** *adj.*
au·to (ô′tō) *n., pl.* **-tos.** An automobile.
au·to·bahn (ou′tō-bän′, ô′tō-) *n.* A superhighway in Germany.
au·to·bi·og·ra·phy (ô′tō-bī-ŏg′rə-fē, -bē-) *n., pl.* **-phies.** The biography of a person written by that person. **—au′to·bi′o·graph′ic, au′to·bi′o·graph′i·cal** *adj.*
au·toch·tho·nous (ô-tŏk′thə-nəs) *adj.* Native to a particular place : indigenous.
au·toc·ra·cy (ô-tŏk′rə-sē) *n., pl.* **-cies.** Government by one person with unlimited power. **—au′to·crat′** (ô′tə-krăt′) *n.* **—au′to·crat′ic** *adj.* **—au′to·crat′i·cal·ly** *adv.*
au·to·di·dact (ô′tō-dī′dăkt′) *n.* A self-taught person. **—au′to·di·dac′tic** *adj.*
au·to·gi·ro *also* **au·to·gy·ro** (ô′tō-jī′rō) *n., pl.* **-ros.** An air-

craft powered by a conventional propeller and provided with lift by a freewheeling horizontal rotor.

au·to·graph (ô′tə-grăf′) *n.* **1.** A person's handwritten signature. **2.** A manuscript in the author's handwriting. *—v.* To write one's signature on.

au·to·in·tox·i·ca·tion (ô′tō-ĭn-tŏk′sĭ-kā′shən) *n.* Self-poisoning caused by endogenous microorganisms, metabolic wastes, or other toxins in the body.

au·to·mate (ô′tə-māt′) *v.* **-mat·ed, -mat·ing.** To operate by or convert to automation.

au·to·mat·ic (ô′tə-măt′ĭk) *adj.* **1.** Operating or able to operate with little or no external control : self-operating or self-regulating. **2.** Involuntary : reflex. *—n.* A machine or device, esp. a firearm, that is automatic. **—au′to·mat′i·cal·ly** *adv.*

automatic pilot *n.* An automatic steering mechanism, as on an aircraft.

au·to·ma·tion (ô′tə-mā′shən) *n.* **1.** Automatic operation of equipment, a process, or a system. **2.** The techniques and equipment used to achieve automation. **3.** The state of being automatically operated.

au·tom·a·tize (ô-tŏm′ə-tīz′) *v.* **-tized, -tiz·ing. 1.** To make automatic. **2.** To automate. **—au·tom′a·ti·za′tion** *n.*

au·tom·a·ton (ô-tŏm′ə-tən, -tŏn′) *n., pl.* **-tons** *or* **-ta** (-tə). **1.** A robot. **2.** Someone who behaves mechanically.

au·to·mo·bile (ô′tə-mō-bēl′, -mō′bēl′) *n.* A self-propelled usu. 4-wheeled passenger vehicle.

au·to·mo·tive (ô′tə-mō′tĭv) *adj.* **1.** Self-propelling. **2.** Of or relating to self-propelled land vehicles, esp. automobiles.

au·to·nom·ic nervous system (ô′tə-nŏm′ĭk) *n.* The part of the vertebrate nervous system that regulates involuntary action, as of the glands, and comprises the sympathetic nervous system and the parasympathetic nervous system.

au·ton·o·mous (ô-tŏn′ə-məs) *adj.* Independent, as of another government : self-governing. **—au·ton′o·mous·ly** *adv.* **—au·ton′o·my** *n.*

au·to·pi·lot (ô′tō-pī′lət) *n.* An automatic pilot.

au·top·sy (ô′tŏp′sē, ô′təp-) *n., pl.* **-sies.** Examination of a body after death to determine the cause of death. **—au′top′sy** *v.*

au·to·stra·da (ou′tō-strä′də, ô′tō-) *n.* An expressway in Italy.

au·tumn (ô′təm) *n.* The season between summer and winter. **—au·tum′nal** (ô-tŭm′nəl) *adj.*

aux·il·ia·ry (ôg-zĭl′yə-rē, -zĭl′ə-) *adj.* **1.** Providing assistance : helping. **2.** Acting in a subsidiary capacity. *—n., pl.* **-ries. 1.** One that acts in an auxiliary capacity. **2.** An auxiliary verb.

auxiliary verb *n.* A verb, as *have, can,* or *will,* that accompanies a main verb and expresses the tense, mood, or voice.

aux·in (ôk′sĭn) *n.* A plant hormone that stimulates growth.

av. *or* **ave.** *abbr.* avenue.

a·vail (ə-vāl′) *v.* To be of advantage or use (to). *—n.* Advantage or use <complained to no *avail*>

a·vail·a·ble (ə-vā′lə-bəl) *adj.* **1.** Capable of being obtained. **2.** Accessible for use : at hand. **—a·vail′a·bil′i·ty** *n.* **—a·vail′a·bly** *adv.*

av·a·lanche (ăv′ə-lănch′) *n.* A mass of material, as snow or rock, that slides down a mountainside.

a·vant-garde (ä′vänt-gärd′) *n.* The leaders in inventing and applying new styles and new techniques in a given field, esp. in the arts. **—a′vant-garde′** *adj.*

av·a·rice (ăv′ər-ĭs) *n.* Greedy desire for wealth : cupidity. **—av′a·ri′cious** *adj.*

a·vast (ə-văst′) *interj. Naut.* Used as a command to cease or stop.

av·a·tar (ăv′ə-tär′) *n.* An incarnation.

a·vaunt (ə-vônt′) *interj. Archaic.* Used as a command to go away.

a·venge (ə-vĕnj′) *v.* **a·venged, a·veng·ing.** To take revenge for. ☆***syns:*** REDRESS, REPAY, REQUITE, VINDICATE. **—a·veng′er** *n.* **—a·veng′ing·ly** *adv.*

av·e·nue (ăv′ə-no͞o′, -nyo͞o′) *n.* **1.** A wide street, esp. a thoroughfare lined with trees. **2.** A way of achieving something.

a·ver (ə-vûr′) *v.* **a·verred, a·ver·ring.** To state positively : assert. **—a·ver′ment** *n.*

av·er·age (ăv′ər-ĭj, ăv′rĭj) *n.* **1.** An arithmetic mean. **2.** A usual or typical degree. *—adj.* **1.** Of, relating to, or being a mathematical average. **2.** Typical : usual. **3.** Not exceptional : common. *—v.* **-aged, -ag·ing. 1.** To compute, obtain, or be the average of. **2.** To be, do, have, or get typically <a temperature *averaging* 70°>

a·verse (ə-vûrs′) *adj.* Having a feeling of distaste or reluctance <*averse* to discussing personal problems>

a·ver·sion (ə-vûr′zhən, -shən) *n.* **1.** A strong dislike. **2.** A feeling of distaste for and desire to keep clear of something.

a·vert (ə-vûrt′) *v.* **1.** To turn away or aside <*averted* his eyes> **2.** To keep from happening : prevent.

avg. *or* **av.** *abbr.* average.

a·vi·an (ā′vē-ən) *adj.* Of, relating to, or typical of birds.

a·vi·ar·y (ā′vē-ĕr′ē) *n., pl.* **-ies.** A place, as at a zoo, for keeping and usu. exhibiting live birds. **—a′vi·a·rist** *n.*

a·vi·a·tion (ā′vē-ā′shən, ăv′ē-) *n.* **1.** The operation of aircraft. **2.** The design, development, and production of aircraft.

a·vi·a·tor (ā′vē-ā′tər, ăv′ē-) *n.* The pilot of an aircraft. **—a′vi·a′trix** *n.*

a·vi·a·trix (ā′vē-ā′trĭks, ăv′ē-) *n.* A woman who pilots an aircraft.

av·id (ăv′ĭd) *adj.* **1.** Eagerly desirous : greedy. **2.** Enthusiastic : ardent. **—a·vid′i·ty** (ə-vĭd′ĭ-tē, ă-vĭd′-) *n.* **—av′id·ly** *adv.*

a·vi·on·ics (ā′vē-ŏn′ĭks, ăv′ē-) *n. (sing. in number).* The science and technology of electronics in conjunction with aeronautics and astronautics. **—a′vi·on′ic** *adj.*

a·vi·ta·min·o·sis (ā-vī′tə-mĭ-nō′sĭs) *n.* A disease, as scurvy, caused by a vitamin deficiency. **—a·vi′ta·min·ot′ic** (-nŏt′ĭk) *adj.*

a·vo (ä′vo͞o) *n., pl.* **a·vos.** See *pataca* at CURRENCY TABLE.

av·o·ca·do (ăv′ə-kä′dō, ä′və-) *n., pl.* **-dos. 1.** A tropical American tree, *Persea americana,* grown for its edible fruit. **2.** The pear-shaped fruit of the avocado, having a large seed and greenish-yellow pulp.

av·o·ca·tion (ăv′ə-kā′shən) *n.* A usu. pleasurable activity in addition to one's regular work : hobby.

av·o·cet (ăv′ə-sĕt′) *n.* A shore bird of the genus *Recurvirostra,* having long legs and a slender, upturned beak.

a·void (ə-void′) *v.* **1.** To stay clear of : shun. **2.** To keep from happening : prevent. **3.** To refrain from. ☆***syns:*** BY-PASS, DODGE, DUCK, ELUDE, ESCAPE, ESCHEW, EVADE, SHUN **—a·void′a·ble** *adj.* **—a·void′a·bly** *adv.* **—a·void′ance** *n.*

av·oir·du·pois (ăv′ər-də-poiz′) *n.* **1.** Avoirdupois weight. **2.** *Informal.* Weight or heaviness, esp. personal weight.

av·oir·du·pois weight (ăv′ər-də-poiz′) *n.* A system of weights and measures based on 1 lb of 16 oz, 7,000 gr or 453.59 g.

a·vouch (ə-vouch′) *v.* **1.** To guarantee. **2.** To assert : affirm.

a·vow (ə-vou′) *v.* To state openly. **—a·vow′al** *n.* **—a·vow′ed·ly** *adv.*

a·vun·cu·lar (ə-vŭng′kyə-lər) *adj.* Of, relating to, or suggestive of an uncle.

a·wait (ə-wāt′) *v.* **1.** To wait (for). **2.** To be in store for.

a·wake (ə-wāk′) *v.* **a·woke** (ə-wōk′), **a·waked, a·wak·ing. 1.** To rouse or emerge from sleep : wake up. **2.** To stir up : arouse. *—adj.* **1.** Not asleep. **2.** Alert : watchful.

a·wak·en (ə-wā′kən) *v.* To awake.

a·ward (ə-wôrd′) *v.* **1.** To grant as legally due. **2.** To bestow for performance or quality. *—n.* **1.** A decision, as one made by a judge. **2.** Something awarded.

a·ware (ə-wâr′) *adj.* Being mindful or conscious. ☆***syns:*** COGNIZANT, CONVERSANT, KNOWING, MINDFUL **—a·ware′ness** *n.*

a·wash (ə-wŏsh′, ə-wôsh′) *adj.* & *adv.* **1.** Washed by waves. **2.** Flooded. **3.** Afloat.

a·way (ə-wā′) *adv.* **1.** At or to a long distance <far *away*> **2.** In or to another place or direction <ran *away*> **3.** From one's possession <gave *away* his record collection> **4.** Out of existence <snow melting *away*> **5.** Continuously <dogs barking *away*> **6.** Without delay <fire *away*> *—adj.* **1.** Absent <He's *away* from the office this morning.> **2.** At a distance <10 feet *away*>

awe (ô) *n.* A feeling of reverence and dread mingled with wonder. *—v.* **awed, aw·ing.** To fill with awe.

a·wea·ry (ə-wîr′ē) *adj.* Weary : tired.

a·weigh (ə-wā′) *adj. Naut.* Hanging just clear of the bottom, as a ship's anchor.

awe·some (ô′səm) *adj.* Marked by or inspiring awe. **—awe′some·ly** *adv.* **—awe′some·ness** *n.*

awe·struck (ô′strŭk′) *also* **awe·strick·en** (ô′strĭk′ən) *adj.* Full of awe.

aw·ful (ô′fəl) *adj.* **1.** Inspiring awe. **2.** Very unpleasant : dreadful. **3.** Great <an *awful* lot of work> **—aw′ful·ly** *adv.*

a·while (ə-hwīl′, ə-wīl′) *adv.* For a while.

a·whirl (ə-hwûrl, ə-wûrl′) *adj.* In a whirl : spinning.

awk·ward (ôk′wərd) *adj.* **1.** Marked by a lack of dexterity and grace : clumsy. **2.** Causing embarrassment and distress. **3.** Difficult to manage or handle : unwieldy. ☆***syns:*** GAWKY, GRACELESS, INEPT, UNGAINLY **—awk′ward·ly** *adv.* **—awk′ward·ness** *n.*

awl (ôl) *n.* A pointed tool used to make holes, as in leather.

awn (ôn) *n.* One of the slender bristles of the spikelet in many grasses.

awn·ing (ô′nĭng) *n.* A rooflike structure, esp. of canvas, that serves as a shelter, as over a window.

a·woke (ə-wōk′) *v. p.t. of* AWAKE.

AWOL (ā′wôl′) *adj.* Absent without leave, esp. from military service. **—AWOL** *n.*

a•wry (ə-rī′) *adv.* **1.** Askew. **2.** Away from the correct course : amiss.
ax or **axe** (ăks) *n.* A tool with a bladed head, used to fell or split lumber.
ax•i•al (ăk′sē-əl) *adj.* Of, relating to, on, around, or along an axis.
ax•i•om (ăk′sē-əm) *n.* **1.** A statement universally recognized as true : maxim. **2.** A proposition assumed to be true without proof. **—ax′i•o•mat′ic** *adj.* **—ax′i•o•mat′i•cal•ly** *adv.*
ax•is (ăk′sĭs) *n., pl.* **ax•es** (-sēz′). **1.** A straight line around which an object or body rotates or may be thought to rotate. **2.** A line, ray, or line segment serving to orient a space or geometric object, about which the object is symmetrical. **3.** A reference line in a system of coordinates. **4.** *Bot.* The main stem or central part about which plant parts such as leaves are arranged.

axis deer

axis deer *n.* A deer, *Axis axis,* of C Asia, with a white-spotted brown coat.
ax•le (ăk′səl) *n.* A shaft or spindle on which a wheel or pair of wheels revolves.
ax•le•tree (ăk′səl-trē′) *n.* A crossbar or rod having terminal spindles on which the wheels revolve.
Ax•min•ster (ăks′mĭn′stər) *n.* A carpet with stiff jute backing and long, soft cut-wool pile.
ax•o•lotl (ăk′sə-lŏt′l) *n.* Any of several W North American and Mexican salamanders of the genus *Ambystoma.*
ax•on (ăk′sŏn′) *also* **ax•one** (-sōn′) *n.* The core of a nerve fiber that usu. conducts impulses away from the body of a nerve cell.
a•yah (ä′yə, ā′ə, ī′ə) *n.* A native maid or nursemaid in India.
aye[1] *also* **ay** (ī) *n.* An affirmative vote or voter. *—adv.* Yes.
aye[2] *also* **ay** (ā) *adv.* Ever : always.
AZ *abbr.* Arizona (with Zip Code).
a•zal•ea (ə-zāl′yə) *n.* Any of a group of deciduous or evergreen shrubs of the genus *Rhodendron* grown for their variously colored flowers.
az•i•muth (ăz′ə-məth) *n.* **1.** The horizontal angular distance from a fixed reference direction to a position, object, or object referent, from a point due S, usu. measured clockwise along the horizon. **2.** The lateral deviation of a projectile or bomb. **—az′i•muth′al** *adj.*
A•zores (ā′zôrz, ə-zôrz′). Three Portuguese island groups in the N Atlantic.
Az•tec (ăz′tĕk′) *n.* A member of an Indian people of C Mexico whose empire was invaded by Cortés in 1519. **—Az′tec•an** *adj.*
az•ure (ăzh′ər) *n.* A light purplish blue. **—az′ure** *adj.*

Bb

b or **B** (bē) *n., pl.* **b's** or **B's. 1.** The 2nd letter of the English alphabet. **2.** A speech sound represented by the letter *b.* **3.** The 7th tone in the scale of C major. **4.** The 2nd-highest grade or rank. **5. B** A human blood type of the ABO group.
b. or **B.** *abbr.* **1.** base. **2.** bay. **3.** book.
B *symbol for* BORON.
B. *abbr.* **1.** bachelor. **2.** Baume scale. **3.** British. **4.** Bible.
Ba *symbol for* BARIUM.
B.A. *abbr.* Bachelor of Arts.
Bab•bitt metal (băb′ĭt) *n.* A soft alloy, esp. one of tin, copper, and antimony, used to line bearings.
bab•ble (băb′əl) *v.* **-bled, -bling. 1.** To utter indistinct, meaningless sounds. **2.** To talk idly or foolishly : chatter. **—bab′ble** *n.* **—bab′bler** *n.*
babe (bāb) *n.* An infant : baby.
Ba•bel (bā′bəl, băb′əl) *n.* **1.** The site of a tower in the Old Testament where construction was interrupted by a confusion of tongues. **2. babel.** A confusion of voices or sounds.
ba•boon (bă-bo͞on′) *n.* A large African monkey of the genus *Papio* or related genera, with a long, doglike muzzle.
ba•bush•ka (bə-bo͝osh′kə) *n.* A woman's head kerchief, usu. folded triangularly.
ba•by (bā′bē) *n., pl.* **-bies. 1.** A very young child : infant. **2.** The smallest or youngest member of a group. **3.** An immature person. *—v.* **-bied, -by•ing.** To treat tenderly and often oversolicitously. ☆***syns:*** CODDLE, COSSET, INDULGE, MOLLYCODDLE, PAMPER, SPOIL **—ba′by•hood′** *n.* **—ba′by•ish** *adj.*
baby carriage *n.* A small 4-wheeled carriage for an infant.
baby grand *n.* A small grand piano approx. 5 ft long.
Bab•y•lo•ni•a (băb′ə-lō′nē-ə). Ancient empire of SW Asia. *Cap.* Babylon. **—Bab′y•lo′ni•an** *adj.* & *n.*
ba•by's-breath *also* **ba•bies'-breath** (bā′bēz-brĕth′) *n.* A plant of the genus *Gypsophilos,* bearing numerous small white flowers.
ba•by-sit (bā′bē-sĭt′) *v.* To care for children whose parents are not at home. **—baby sitter** *n.*
bac•ca•lau•re•ate (băk′ə-lôr′ē-ĭt) *n.* **1.** The degree of bachelor conferred by colleges and universities. **2.** A commencement address.
bac•ca•rat (bä′kə-rä′, băk′ə-) *n.* A gambling game played with cards.
bac•cha•nal (băk′ə-năl′, bä′kə-näl′, băk′ə-nəl) *n.* **1.** A riotous or drunken festivity. **2.** A participant in a bacchanal : reveler.
bac•cha•na•lia (băk′ə-nāl′yə) *n.* A drunken or riotous celebration : orgy. **—bac′cha•na′lian** *adj.*
bach•e•lor (băch′ə-lər, băch′lər) *n.* **1.** A man who is not married. **2.** A person who holds a college degree signifying completion of undergraduate studies.
bach•e•lor's-but•ton (băch′ə-lərz-bŭt′n, băch′lərz-) *n.* The cornflower.
ba•cil•lus (bə-sĭl′əs) *n., pl.* **-cil•li** (-sĭl′ī′). Any of various rod-shaped, aerobic bacteria. **—bac′il•lar′y** (băs′ə-lĕr′ē) *adj.*
back (băk) *n.* **1. a.** The part of the vertebrate body nearest the spine. **b.** The analogous part in invertebrates. **2.** The part opposite the front : the rear. **3.** *Football.* A player positioned in the backfield. *—v.* **1.** To move or cause to move backward or in reverse. **2.** To uphold : support. **3.** To form the back of. *—adj.* **1.** In or at the back. **2.** Distant : remote. **3.** Of or for a past time or date. **4.** Operating or moving backward. *—adv.* **1.** At, to, or toward the rear. **2.** To, in, or toward a former state, place, or time. **3.** In concealment, reserve, or check. **4.** In reply or return. **—back′less** *adj.*
back•ache (băk′āk′) *n.* A back pain.
back•bite (băk′bīt′) *v.* To speak spitefully or nastily about someone who is not present. **—back′bit′er** *n.*
back•board (băk′bôrd′, -bōrd′) *n.* A board placed under or behind something to give support.
back•bone (băk′bōn′) *n.* **1.** The spine or spinal column of vertebrates. **2.** A main support : mainstay. **3.** Strength and determination of character.
back•drop (băk′drŏp′) *n.* A painted curtain hung across the back of a stage set.
back•er (băk′ər) *n.* One who gives aid or support.
back•field (băk′fēld′) *n. Football.* **1.** The players who are positioned behind the line of scrimmage. **2.** The area in which the backfield lines up.
back•fire (băk′fīr′) *n.* An explosion of prematurely ignited fuel or unburned exhaust gases in an internal-combustion engine. *—v.* **1.** To explode in a backfire. **2.** To have a result opposite to that intended.
back•gam•mon (băk′găm′ən) *n.* A board game for 2 persons, played with counters and dice.
back•ground (băk′ground′) *n.* **1.** The surface or area against which objects are seen or represented. **2.** Events or conditions surrounding or leading up to something. **3.** A position of relative inconspicuousness. **4.** A person's total experience, education, and knowledge.
back•hand (băk′hănd′) *n.* A stroke, as of a tennis racket, made with the back of the hand facing outward and the arm moving forward. *—adj.* Backhanded. **—back′hand′** *v.*
back•hand•ed (băk′hăn′dĭd) *adj.* **1.** Made with or using a backhand. **2.** Indirect : roundabout.
back•ing (băk′ĭng) *n.* **1.** Something that forms a back. **2. a.** Aid : support. **b.** Those who provide support.
back•lash (băk′lăsh′) *n.* **1.** A sudden violent backward whipping motion. **2.** A strong hostile reaction.

back•log (băk′lôg′, -lŏg′) *n.* **1.** A reserve supply. **2.** An accumulation, esp. of unfilled orders or unfinished work.
back•pack (băk′păk′) *n.* A container for camping supplies mounted on a lightweight frame and worn on the back. *—v.* To hike with a backpack. **—back′pack′er** *n.*
back•ped•al (băk′pĕd′l) *v.* To move backward : retreat or withdraw.
back•rest (băk′rĕst′) *n.* A rest for the back.
back•side (băk′sīd′) *n.* The buttocks.
back•slide (băk′slīd′) *v.* To revert to a former, less desirable condition, esp. in religious practice. **—back′slid′er** *n.*
back•spin (băk′spĭn′) *n.* A spin that tends to retard, arrest, or reverse the linear motion of an object, esp. of a ball.
back•stage (băk′stāj′) *adj.* **1.** Of or occurring in the area behind the performing area in a theater. **2.** Not known to the public : private. **—back′stage′** *adv.*
back•stop (băk′stŏp′) *n.* A screen or fence used to prevent a ball from being hit out of a playing area.
back•stretch (băk′strĕch′) *n.* The part of a racecourse opposite the homestretch.
back•stroke (băk′strōk′) *n.* A swimming stroke executed with the swimmer on his or her back.
back•swept (băk′swĕpt′) *adj.* Swept or angled backward.
back talk *n.* An insolent retort.
back•track (băk′trăk′) *v.* **1.** To retrace one's steps. **2.** To reverse a policy.
back-up (băk′ŭp′) *n.* A reserve or substitute.
back•ward (băk′wərd) *adv.* **1.** At, to, or toward the back. **2.** With the back leading. **3.** In a reverse manner or order. **4.** Toward a worse condition. **5.** To or toward the past. *—adj.* **1.** Reversed. **2.** Shy : bashful. **3.** Behind others or retarded in development. **—back′ward•ness** *n.* **—back′wards** *adv.*
back•wash (băk′wŏsh′, -wôsh′) *n.* A backward motion or flow, as of water or air.
back•wa•ter (băk′wô′tər, -wŏt′ər) *n.* A place or situation considered to be backward or stagnant.
back•woods (băk′wo͝odz′, -wo͝odz′) *pl.n.* Heavily wooded, sparsely populated areas. **—back′woods′man** *n.*
ba•con (bā′kən) *n.* The back and sides of a pig salted and smoked.
Ba•con (bā′kən), **Francis.** 1561–1626. English philosopher, statesman, and essayist. **—Ba•co′ni•an** *adj.* & *n.*
bac•te•ri•cide (băk-tîr′ĭ-sīd′) *n.* A substance that destroys bacteria. **—bac•te′ri•cid′al** *adj.*
bac•te•ri•ol•o•gy (băk-tîr′ē-ŏl′ə-jē) *n.* The scientific study of bacteria. **—bac•te′ri•o•log′ic** (-ə-lŏj′ĭk), **bac•te′ri•o•log′i•cal** *adj.* **—bac•te′ri•ol′o•gist** *n.*
bac•te•ri•o•phage (băk-tîr′ē-ə-fāj′) *n.* A viral organism that destroys bacteria.
bac•te•ri•um (băk-tîr′ē-əm) *n., pl.* **-ri•a** (-ē-ə). Any of numerous unicellular microorganisms of various forms that often cause disease. **—bac•te′ri•al** *adj.*
bad[1] (băd) *adj.* **worse** (wûrs), **worst** (wûrst). **1.** Poor : inferior. **2. a.** Evil. **b.** Disobedient or naughty. **3.** Unfavorable <a *bad* review> **4.** Decayed : spoiled <a *bad* apple> **5.** Intense : severe <a *bad* headache> **6.** Invalid <a *bad* check> *—n.* Something bad. *—adv. Informal.* **1.** In a bad manner : badly. **2.** Greatly. **—bad′ly** *adv.* **—bad′ness** *n.*
bad[2] (băd) *v. archaic p.t. of* BID.
bade (băd, bād) *v. var. p.t. of* BID.
badge (băj) *n.* An emblem usu. worn as a sign of rank, office, membership, or honor.
badg•er (băj′ər) *n.* A burrowing animal of the family Mustelidae, with long claws on the front feet and a thick, grizzled coat. *—v.* To trouble or harry persistently.
bad•i•nage (băd′n-äzh′) *n.* Playful banter.
bad•lands (băd′lăndz′) *pl.n.* An area with eroded ridges, peaks, and mesas and sparse vegetation.
Bad•lands (băd′lănz). Extensive barren region of SW S.Dak. and NW Nebr.
bad•min•ton (băd′mĭn′tən) *n.* A court game played with a shuttlecock and light, long-handled rackets.
baf•fle (băf′əl) *v.* **-fled, -fling. 1.** To perplex : puzzle. **2.** To frustrate : stymie. *—n.* A device or partition that stops, alters, or regulates flow, as of a gas, sound, or liquid. **—baf′fle•ment** *n.*
bag (băg) *n.* **1.** A usu. flexible container, as of paper or leather, that can be closed and is used for carrying or storing something. **2.** An amount of game taken at a time. **3.** *Slang.* An area of skill or interest. *—v.* **bagged, bag•ging. 1.** To put into a bag. **2. a.** To bulge or cause to bulge. **b.** To hang loosely. **3.** To gain possesion of, esp. to capture as game. **—bag′ful′** *n.*
ba•gasse (bə-găs′) *n.* The residue of a plant, as sugar cane, after the juice has been extracted.
bag•a•telle (băg′ə-tĕl′) *n.* A trifle.
ba•gel (bā′gəl) *n.* A glazed ring-shaped roll having a chewy texture.
bag•gage (băg′ĭj) *n.* The bags and belongings of a traveler : luggage.
bag•gy (băg′ē) *adj.* **-gi•er, -gi•est.** Hanging loosely : bulging. **—bag′gi•ly** *adv.* **—bag′gi•ness** *n.*
Bagh•dad *also* **Bag•dad** (băg′dăd′). Cap. of Iraq, on the Tigris. *Pop.* 1,300,000.
bag•man (băg′mən) *n. Slang.* A person who receives and collects illicit payments, as for racketeers.
ba•gnio (băn′yō) *n., pl.* **-gnios.** A brothel.
▲word history: Public bathhouses, at least in England, at one time had such an unsavory reputation as places for illicit sexual encounters that *bagnio,* which was borrowed from Italian with the meaning "bath," eventually lost that meaning and acquired the sense "brothel."
bag•pipe (băg′pīp′) *n. often* **bagpipes.** A musical instrument with an inflatable bag, a tube with valves, and melody and drone pipes. **—bag′pip′er** *n.*
ba•guette (bă-gĕt′) *n.* A gem cut in the shape of a narrow rectangle.
Ba•ha•ma Islands (bə-hä′mə) *also* **Ba•ha•mas** (-məz). Island country in the Atlantic SE of Fla. *Cap.* Nassau. *Pop.* 168,812. **—Ba•ha′mi•an** (-ha′mē-ən, -hä′-), **Ba•ha′man** *adj.* & *n.*
Bah•rain *also* **Bah•rein** (bä-rān′). Sheikdom and archipelago in the Persian Gulf. *Cap.* Al Manamah. *Pop.* 350,000.
baht (bät) *n., pl.* **bahts** or **baht.** See CURRENCY TABLE.
bail[1] (bāl) *n.* **1.** Money given to guarantee the appearance for trial of an arrested person. **2.** Temporary release secured by bail. **3.** One that provides bail. *—v.* **1.** To secure the release of by providing bail. **2.** To release (someone) for whom bail has been paid. **3.** *Informal.* To extricate from a difficult situation. **—bail′a•ble** *adj.* **—bail′or, bail′er** *n.*
bail[2] (bāl) *v.* To empty a boat of water by dipping, filling, and emptying a container. **—bail′er** *n.*
bail[3] (bāl) *n.* The arched handle of a container, as a kettle or pail.
bail•iff (bā′lĭf) *n.* **1.** An official who guards prisoners and keeps order in a courtroom. **2.** An assistant to a British sheriff who executes writs and arrests. **3.** An overseer of an estate, esp. in Britain : steward.
bail•i•wick (bā′lə-wĭk′) *n.* **1.** The district or office of a bailiff. **2.** One's special sphere or province.
bails•man (bālz′mən) *n.* One who posts bail for another.
Bai•ri•ki (bī-rē′kē). Cap. of Kiribati, in the WC Pacific. *Pop.* 17,100.
bairn (bârn) *n. Scot.* A child.
bait (bāt) *n.* **1.** A lure, as food, used to trap animals or catch fish. **2.** A lure : enticement. *—v.* **1.** To provide (e.g., a hook) with bait. **2.** To lure : entice. **3.** To set dogs upon (a captive animal), usu. for sport. **4.** To torment with persistent attacks. ☆***syns:*** BADGER, HECKLE, HECTOR, HOUND, NEEDLE, RIDE, TAUNT **—bait′er** *n.*
bai•za (bī′zä) *n.* See *riyal-omani* at CURRENCY TABLE.
baize (bāz) *n.* A coarse feltlike material.
bake (bāk) *v.* **baked, bak•ing. 1.** To cook, esp. in an oven, with dry heat. **2.** To harden and dry in or as if in an oven <*bake* pottery> *—n.* A social gathering at which baked food is served. **—bak′er** *n.*
baker's dozen *n.* A group of 13.
bak•e•ry (bā′kə-rē) *n., pl.* **-ries.** A place where goods such as bread and pastries are prepared or sold.
bake•shop (bāk′shŏp′) *n.* A bakery.
baking powder *n.* A powder of baking soda, starch, and an acidic compound used as a leavening agent.
baking soda *n.* Sodium bicarbonate.
bak•sheesh (băk′shēsh′, băk-shēsh′) *n.* A gratuity : tip.
bal. *abbr.* balance.
bal•a•lai•ka (băl′ə-lī′kə) *n.* A 3-stringed musical instrument with a triangular body.

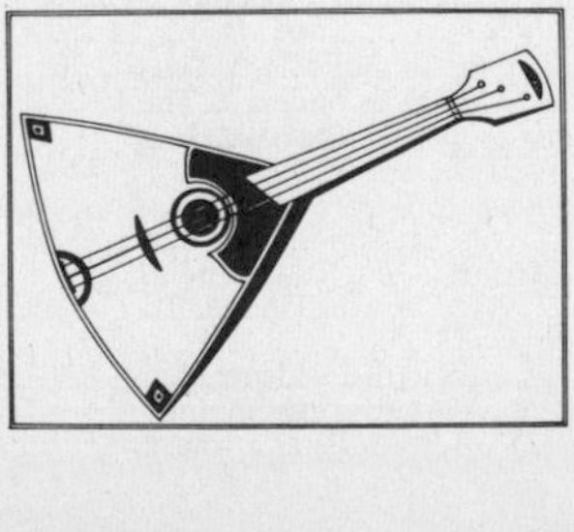

balalaika

bal•ance (băl'əns) *n.* **1.** A device for weighing : scale. **2.** Equilibrium. **3.** A force or influence that tends to produce equilibrium. **4. a.** Agreement of totals in the debit and credit sides of an account. **b.** A difference between these totals. **5.** Something that remains : remainder. ☆***syns:*** COUNTERPOISE, EQUILIBRIUM, EQUIPOISE, STASIS —*v.* **-anced, -anc•ing. 1.** To weigh in or as if in a balance. **2.** To bring or come into equilibrium. **3.** To counterbalance. **4.** To compute the balance of (an account).

balance wheel *n.* A wheel that regulates rate of movement in a mechanism, as a watch.

bal•bo•a (băl-bō'ə) *n.* See CURRENCY TABLE.

Bal•bo•a (băl-bō'ə), **Vasco Núñez de.** 1475–1517. Spanish explorer; discovered the Pacific (1513).

bal•brig•gan (băl-brĭg'ən) *n.* A knitted cotton material.

bal•co•ny (băl'kə-nē) *n., pl.* **-nies. 1.** A platform projecting from the wall of a building and surrounded by a railing or parapet. **2.** A gallery projecting over the main floor in a theater or auditorium.

bald (bôld) *adj.* **1.** Lacking hair on the head. **2.** Not having the usual or natural covering. **3.** Undisguised : outright <a *bald* lie> **—bald'ly** *adv.* **—bald'ness** *n.*

bal•da•chin (bôl'də-kĭn, băl'-) *also* **bal•da•chi•no** (băl'də-kē'nō) *n.* A canopy of fabric carried in processions or placed over an altar, throne, or dais.

bald eagle *n.* A North American eagle, *Haliaeetus leucocephalus,* with a dark body and a white head and tail.

bal•der•dash (bôl'dər-dăsh') *n.* Nonsense.

bald•ing (bôl'dĭng) *adj.* Becoming bald.

bal•dric (bôl'drĭk) *n.* A belt worn across the chest to carry a sword or bugle.

bale (bāl) *n.* A large bound bundle or package. —*v.* **baled, bal•ing.** To wrap in a bale. **—bal'er** *n.*

ba•leen (bə-lēn') *n.* Whalebone.

bale•ful (bāl'fəl) *adj.* **1.** Causing harm : harmful. **2.** Ominous. **—bale'ful•ly** *adv.* **—bale'ful•ness** *n.*

Ba•li (bä'lē). Island of Indonesia, off E Java. **—Ba'li•nese'** (-nēz', -nēs') *adj.* & *n.*

balk (bôk) *v.* **1.** To stop short and refuse to go on. **2.** To check : thwart. **3.** *Baseball.* To make an illegal motion before pitching. —*n.* **1.** A check, hindrance, or defeat. **2.** *Baseball.* An illegal motion made by a pitcher.

Bal•kan (bôl'kən). **1. Mountains** *also* **Bal•kans** (-kənz). Range of mountains extending across N Bulgaria from the Black Sea to the border of Yugoslavia. **2.** Peninsula of SE Europe. **3. the Balkans.** Albania, Bulgaria, continental Greece, SE Rumania, European Turkey, and most of Yugoslavia.

balk•y (bô'kē) *adj.* **-i•er, -i•est.** Tending to balk : obstinate. **—balk'i•ness** *n.*

ball[1] (bôl) *n.* **1.** A round or almost round body or mass. **2. a.** A ball used in a game. **b.** A game played with a ball. **3.** A pitched baseball that does not pass through the strike zone and the batter does not swing at. —*v.* To form into a ball.

ball[2] (bôl) *n.* **1.** A formal dance. **2.** *Slang.* A very enjoyable time.

bal•lad (băl'əd) *n.* **1.** A narrative poem, often of folk origin and intended to be sung. **2.** The music for a ballad. **3.** A popular, esp. romantic song. **—bal'lad•eer'** *n.* **—bal'lad•ry** *n.*

bal•last (băl'əst) *n.* **1.** Heavy material put in a vehicle to provide weight and stability. **2.** Coarse gravel or crushed rock that forms a foundation or roadbed. —*v.* To stabilize with ballast.

ball bearing *n.* **1.** A bearing that reduces friction, in which the moving and stationary parts are kept apart by a track containing freely revolving hard balls. **2.** A ball in a ball bearing.

bal•le•ri•na (băl'ə-rē'nə) *n.* A principal ballet dancer in a company.

bal•let (bă-lā', băl'ā') *n.* **1.** An artistic dance form characterized chiefly by a highly formalized technique. **2.** A choreographic presentation, usu. with music, on a narrative or abstract theme. **3.** A company that performs ballet. **—bal•let'ic** *adj.*

bal•let•o•mane (bă-lĕt'ə-măn') *n.* An ardent ballet enthusiast.

ballistic missile *n.* A self-powered projectile that is guided during ascent and assumes a free-falling trajectory during descent.

bal•lis•tics (bə-lĭs'tĭks) *n. (sing. in number).* **1.** The scientific study of the dynamics of projectiles, as bullets. **2.** The study of the flight characteristics of projectiles. **—bal•lis'tic** *adj.*

ball of fire *n.* A highly energetic person.

bal•loon (bə-lo͞on') *n.* **1.** A bag inflated with a gas, as helium, that causes it to rise and float in the atmosphere. **2.** A toy consisting of an inflatable rubber bag. —*v.* **1.** To expand or cause to expand like a balloon. **2.** To ride in a balloon. **3.** To increase quickly. **—bal•loon'ist** *n.*

balloon tire *n.* A pneumatic tire with a wide tread, inflated to low pressure and designed for maximum cushioning.

bal•lot (băl'ət) *n.* **1.** A paper used to register a vote. **2.** The act or a method of voting. **3.** A list of candidates for office. **4.** The total of votes cast. **5.** The right to vote. —*v.* To cast a ballot : vote.

ball•park (bôl'pärk') *n.* A baseball stadium.

ball-point pen (bôl'point') *n.* A pen with a small self-inking ball bearing as its writing point.

ball•room (bôl'ro͞om', -ro͝om') *n.* A large room for dancing.

bal•ly•hoo (băl'ē-ho͞o') *n. Informal.* **1.** Sensational or exaggerated advertising. **2.** Noisy talk or uproar. **—bal'ly•hoo'** *v.*

balm (bäm) *n.* **1.** A fragrant oil or ointment used medicinally. **2.** Something that soothes, heals, or comforts.

balm•y (bä'mē) *adj.* **-i•er, -i•est. 1.** Having the quality of balm : mild and soothing. **2.** *Slang.* Insane : crazy. **—balm'i•ly** *adv.* **—balm'i•ness** *n.*

ba•lo•ney (bə-lō'nē) *n.* **1.** *informal var. of* BOLOGNA. **2.** *Slang.* Nonsense.

bal•sa (bôl'sə) *n.* A tropical American tree, *Ochroma lagopus,* with extremely light, buoyant wood.

bal•sam (bôl'səm) *n.* **1.** A fragrant resin or ointment obtained from various trees. **2.** A tree that yields balsam, esp. the balsam fir. **3.** A plant of the genus *Impatiens* cultivated for its colorful flowers.

balsam fir *n.* An American evergreen tree, *Abies balsamea,* often used as a Christmas tree.

Bal•tic Sea (bôl'tĭk). Arm of the Atlantic in N Europe.

Bal•ti•more (bôl'tə-môr', -mōr'). City of Md., on upper Chesapeake Bay. *Pop.* 786,775. **—Bal'ti•mo're•an** *adj.* & *n.*

Bal•ti•more oriole (bôl'tə-môr', -mōr') *n.* An American songbird, *Icterus galbula,* the male of which has brilliant orange, black, and white plumage.

bal•us•ter (băl'ə-stər) *n.* One of the upright posts supporting a handrail.

bal•us•trade (băl'ə-strād') *n.* A handrail and the balusters that support it.

Bal•zac (bôl'zăk', băl'-), **Honoré de.** 1799–1850. French author.

Ba•ma•ko (băm'ə-kō'). Cap. of Mali, in the SW on the Niger R. *Pop.* 404,022.

bam•boo (băm-bo͞o') *n.* A tall tropical grass of the genus *Bambusa* with hollow, jointed stems.

bam•boo•zle (băm-bo͞o'zəl) *v.* **-zled, -zling.** *Informal.* To deceive : trick.

ban[1] (băn) *v.* **banned, ban•ning.** To forbid : prohibit. —*n.* An official prohibition.

ban[2] (bän) *n., pl.* **ba•ni** (bä'nē). See *leu* at CURRENCY TABLE.

ba•nal (bə-näl', -năl', bā'nəl) *adj.* Lacking freshness : trite. **—ba•nal'i•ty** *n.*

ba•nan•a (bə-năn'ə) *n.* A treelike tropical or subtropical plant of the genus *Musa,* esp. *M. sapientum,* with hanging clusters of crescent-shaped edible pulpy fruit.

band[1] (bănd) *n.* **1. a.** A strip used to encircle or bind. **b.** A strip used to trim, finish, or reinforce. **2.** A range of radio wavelengths. —*v.* To encircle, bind, or identify with a band.

band[2] (bănd) *n.* **1.** A group of persons or animals. **2.** A group of musicians who play in an ensemble. —*v.* To form, assemble, or unite in a group.

ban•dage (băn'dĭj) *n.* A strip of material used to dress a wound. —*v.* **-daged, -dag•ing.** To put a bandage on.

ban•dan•na *or* **ban•dan•a** (băn-dăn'ə) *n.* A large brightly colored, usu. patterned handkerchief.

Ban•dar Se•ri Be•ga•wan (bŭn'dər sĕr'ē bə-gä'wən). Cap. of Brunei. *Pop.* 37,000.

band•box (bănd'bŏks') *n.* A cylindrical box for carrying articles of apparel.

ban•deau (băn-dō') *n., pl.* **-deaux** (-dōz') *or* **-deaus. 1.** A narrow band, esp. for the hair. **2.** A brassiere.

ban•de•role *or* **ban•de•rol** (băn'də-rōl') *n.* A narrow forked streamer or flag.

ban•dit (băn'dĭt) *n.* **1.** A robber. **2.** A gangster. **—ban'dit•ry** *n.*

ban•do•leer *or* **ban•do•lier** (băn'də-lîr') *n.* A belt, esp. for cartridges, that is worn over the shoulder.

band saw *n.* A power saw in the form of a continuous toothed metal band driven around 2 wheels.

band•stand (bănd'stănd') *n.* An often roofed platform for a band or orchestra.

band•wag•on (bănd'wăg'ən) *n.* **1.** A wagon used to carry musicians in a parade. **2.** *Informal.* A cause or party that gathers increasing approval or support.

ban•dy (băn'dē) *v.* **-died, -dy•ing. 1.** To toss back and forth. **2.** To exchange casually or frivolously. —*adj.* Curved outward <*bandy* legs>

bane (bān) *n.* **1.** A cause of harm or ruin. **2.** A poison. **—bane'ful** *adj.*

bang[1] (băng) *n.* **1.** A sudden loud noise. **2.** *Slang.* A thrill. —*v.* **1.**

To hit or move with a loud noise. **2.** To bump <*banged* her elbow> *—adv.* Exactly : precisely.
bang[2] (băng) *n. often* **bangs.** A fringe of hair cut short, esp. across the forehead.
Bang•kok (băng'kŏk', băng-kŏk'). Cap. of Thailand, in the SW. *Pop.* 4,178,000.
Ban•gla•desh (băng'glə-dĕsh). Country of S Asia. *Cap.* Dacca. *Pop.* 88,700,000.
ban•gle (băng'gəl) *n.* **1.** A rigid bracelet or anklet, esp. one with no clasp. **2.** An ornament that hangs from a necklace.
Ban•gui (băng-gē'). Cap. of Central African Republic. *Pop.* 187,000.
bang-up (băng'ŭp') *adj. Informal.* Excellent <a *bang-up* party>
ban•ish (băn'ĭsh) *v.* **1.** To oblige to leave a country : exile. **2.** To drive away : expel. ☆***syns:*** DEPORT, EXILE, EXPATRIATE, EXPEL, OSTRACIZE **—ban'ish•ment** *n.*
ban•is•ter *also* **ban•nis•ter** (băn'ĭ-stər) *n.* **1.** A baluster. **2.** The handrail of a staircase.
ban•jo (băn'jō) *n., pl.* **-jos** or **-joes.** A fretted stringed instrument with a narrow neck, a hollow circular body, and often 5 strings. **—ban'jo•ist** *n.*
Ban•jul (băn-jo͞o', bän'jo͞ol). Cap. of Gambia, at the mouth of the Gambia R.
bank[1] (băngk) *n.* **1.** A piled-up mass, as of earth or snow. **2.** A slope of land adjoining a body of water, as a river. **3.** An elevation of the sea floor. **4.** The sideways slope of a surface on a curve or of a motor vehicle rounding a curve. *—v.* **1.** To border or protect with a bank. **2.** To pile up in a bank. **3.** To cover (a fire) with ashes or fuel for slow burning. **4.** To construct (a curve) with a slope rising to the outside edge. **5.** To tilt (an aircraft) laterally in flight.
bank[2] (băngk) *n.* **1.** An establishment that performs financial transactions such as receiving, investing, and lending money. **2.** A supply of or storage place for something desired or needed <a blood *bank*> *—v.* **1.** To deposit (money) in a bank. **2.** To transact business with a bank. **3.** To operate a bank. **—bank'er** *n.*
bank[3] (băngk) *n.* **1.** A group of things arranged in a row <a *bank* of elevators> **2.** A row of oars.
bank•book (băngk'bo͝ok') *n.* The depositor's book in which a bank enters deposits and withdrawals.
bank note *n.* A note issued by an authorized bank and acceptable as money.
bank•roll (băngk'rōl') *n. Informal.* A person's ready cash : funds.
bank•rupt (băngk'rŭpt', -rəpt) *n.* A debtor who is judged legally insolvent and whose remaining property is administered for or divided among the creditors. *—adj.* **1.** Financially ruined, esp. legally declared bankrupt. **2.** Depleted or destitute <*bankrupt* of compassion> **—bank'rupt'** *v.* **—bank'rupt'cy** *n.*
ban•ner (băn'ər) *n.* **1.** A piece of cloth attached to a staff and used as a standard by a monarch or commander. **2.** A flag. *—adj.* Unusually good : outstanding.
ban•nock (băn'ək) *n.* A usu. unleavened griddlecake made of oatmeal or barley.
banns (bănz) *pl.n.* An announcement, esp. in church, of a forthcoming marriage.
ban•quet (băng'kwĭt) *n.* **1.** An elaborate feast. **2.** A ceremonial dinner. *—v.* To entertain at or partake of a banquet.
†**ban•quette** (băng-kĕt') *n.* **1.** A platform lining a trench or parapet wall for guns or gunners. **2.** *S U.S.* A sidewalk. **3.** A long upholstered seat against or built into a wall.
ban•shee (băn'shē) *n.* A female spirit in Gaelic folklore whose wailing warns of a death in a family.
ban•tam (băn'təm) *n.* **1.** One of a breed of small domestic fowl. **2.** A small but aggressive person. **—ban'tam** *adj.*
ban•ter (băn'tər) *n.* Good-humored, teasing conversation. *—v.* To engage or indulge in banter.
bant•ling (bănt'lĭng) *n.* A young child.
ban•yan (băn'yən) *n.* A tropical tree, *Ficus benghalensis,* with many aerial roots that grow downward to form additional trunks.
ban•zai (bän-zī') *n.* A Japanese battle cry or cheer.
ba•o•bab (bā'ə-băb', bou'-) *n.* A tree, *Adansonia digitata,* of tropical Africa, with a trunk up to 30 ft in diameter and hard-shelled fleshy fruit.
bap•tism (băp'tĭz'əm) *n.* **1.** A Christian sacrament of spiritual rebirth symbolized by the ritual application of water. **2.** An ordeal by which one is initiated. **—bap•tis'mal** *adj.*
Bap•tist (băp'tĭst) *n.* A member of a Protestant denomination that practices baptism by immersion.
bap•tis•ter•y *also* **bap•tis•try** (băp'tĭ-strē) *n., pl.* **-ies** *also* **-tries.** A place, esp. a part of a church, where the ceremony of baptism is performed.
bap•tize (băp-tīz', băp'tīz') *v.* **-tized, -tiz•ing. 1.** To sprinkle with or immerse in water during baptism. **2.** To initiate. **3.** To christen. **—bap•tiz'er** *n.*
bar (bär) *n.* **1.** A rather long, rigid piece of solid material used esp. as a fastener or support. **2.** A solid block of a substance <a *bar* of soap> **3.** An obstacle : barrier. **4.** A long, narrow marking, as a stripe. **5. a.** The railing in a courtroom enclosing the area where the lawyers and defendants sit. **b.** A system of law courts. **c.** The legal profession. **6.** *Mus.* A vertical line that divides a staff into equal measures. **7. a.** A counter where drinks are served. **b.** A place with such a counter. *—v.* **barred, bar•ring. 1.** To fasten with or as if with bars. **2.** To prohibit : forbid. **3.** To keep out : exclude. *—prep.* Except for : excluding.
bar. *abbr.* **1.** barometer; barometric. **2.** barrel.
barb (bärb) *n.* **1.** A sharp backward-pointing projection, as on an arrow. **2.** A cutting remark. **3.** *Bot.* A hooked bristle or hairlike projection. **—barbed** *adj.*
Bar•ba•dos (bär-bā'dōz, -dōs'). Island country of E West Indies. *Cap.* Bridgetown. *Pop.* 238,141. **—Bar•ba'di•an** *adj.* & *n.*
bar•bar•i•an (bär-bâr'ē-ən) *n.* **1.** A member of a people or culture thought of as being primitive, uncivilized, or savage. **2.** A fierce or cruel person. **3.** A person lacking in culture : boor. **—bar•bar'i•an** *adj.* **—bar•bar'i•an•ism** *n.*
bar•bar•ic (bär-băr'ĭk) *adj.* **1.** Of, relating to, or characteristic of barbarians. **2.** Crude in taste, style, or behavior.
bar•ba•rism (bär'bə-rĭz'əm) *n.* **1.** An act, custom, or trait marked by coarseness or brutality. **2.** A word or form felt to be nonstandard or incorrect in a language.
bar•ba•rous (bär'bər-əs) *adj.* **1.** Uncivilized : primitive. **2.** Cruel : savage. **3.** Uncultured or unrefined, esp. in the use of linguistic forms. **—bar•bar'i•ty** (bär-băr'ĭ-tē) *n.* **—bar'ba•rous•ly** *adv.*
Bar•ba•ry (bär'bə-rē). Region of N Africa on the **Barbary Coast,** stretching from Egypt's W border to the Atlantic.
bar•be•cue (bär'bĭ-kyo͞o') *n.* **1.** A pit or outdoor fireplace for broiling or roasting meat. **2. a.** A whole animal roasted over a fire. **b.** A usu. outdoor social gathering at which food is prepared in this way. *—v.* **-cued, -cu•ing.** To roast (meat) over live coals or an open fire.
barbed wire *n.* Fence wire with barbs at regular intervals.
bar•bel (bär'bəl) *n.* One of the slender, whiskerlike sensory organs on the head of certain fishes, as catfish.
bar•bell (bär'bĕl') *n.* A bar with weights at each end, lifted for exercise.
bar•ber (bär'bər) *n.* One who cuts hair and shaves or trims beards as an occupation. **—bar'ber** *v.*
bar•ber•ry (bär'bĕr'ē) *n.* A spiny shrub of the genus *Berberis* with small orange or red berries.
bar•ber•shop (bär'bər-shŏp') *n.* A barber's place of business. *—adj.* Of, consisting of, or relating to the performance of sentimental songs in 4-part harmony.
bar•bi•can (bär'bĭ-kən) *n.* An outdoor defensive fortification.
bar•bi•tal (bär'bĭ-tôl') *n.* An addictive crystalline compound used as a sedative.
bar•bi•tu•rate (bär-bĭch'ər-ĭt, -ə-rāt') *n.* A barbituric acid derivative used as a sedative or hypnotic.
bar•bi•tu•ric acid (bär'bĭ-to͝or'ĭk, -tyo͝or'-) *n.* An organic acid used in making barbiturates and some plastics.
bar•ca•role *also* **bar•ca•rolle** (bär'kə-rōl') *n.* A song of a Venetian gondolier.
Bar•ce•lo•na (bär'sə-lō'nə). City of NE Spain. *Pop.* 1,902,713.
bard (bärd) *n.* An exalted national poet. **—bard'ic** *adj.*
bare (bâr) *adj.* **bar•er, bar•est. 1.** Without clothing : naked. **2.** Exposed to view : unconcealed. **3.** Without addition or decoration : plain. **4.** Just sufficient : mere. ☆***syns:*** BALD, NAKED, NUDE *—v.* **bared, bar•ing.** To reveal. **—bare'ness** *n.*
bare•back (bâr'băk') *adv.* & *adj.* On an animal, as a horse, without a saddle.
bare•faced (bâr'fāst') *adj.* **1.** Having no covering, esp. no beard, on the face. **2.** Open and brazen <a *barefaced* lie>
bare•foot (bâr'fo͝ot') *also* **bare•foot•ed** (-fo͝ot'ĭd) *adj.* & *adv.* Without covering on the feet.
bare•hand•ed (bâr'hăn'dĭd) *adj.* & *adv.* **1.** Without covering on the hands. **2.** Without the aid of tools or weapons.
bare•head•ed (bâr'hĕd'ĭd) *adj.* & *adv.* With no covering on the head.
bare•leg•ged (bâr'lĕg'ĭd, -lĕgd') *adj.* & *adv.* With no covering over the legs.
bare•ly (bâr'lē) *adv.* **1.** By a very little : scarcely <*barely* enough to eat> **2.** In a scanty manner : sparsely.
barf (bärf) *Slang.* To vomit.
bar•gain (bär'gĭn) *n.* **1.** An agreement or contract, esp. one pertaining to the sale and purchase of goods or services. **2.** Something acquired at a price advantageous to the buyer. *—v.* **1.** To

negotiate the terms of an agreement. **2.** To reach an agreement. **3.** To exchange : barter.

barge (bärj) *n.* **1.** A flat-bottomed boat towed along a canal or river by other craft and used for transporting freight. **2.** A large pleasure boat. **3.** A power boat used by a flag officer. —*v.* **barged, barg•ing. 1.** To transport by barge. **2.** To move clumsily. **3.** To intrude rudely and abruptly.

bar•i•tone (băr'ĭ-tōn') *n.* **1.** A male voice of a range between bass and tenor. **2.** A singer with a baritone voice.

bar•i•um (bâr'ē-əm, băr'-) *n. Symbol* **Ba** A silvery-white metallic element used for deoxidizing copper and in various alloys and rat poison.

bark[1] (bärk) *n.* The harsh, abrupt sound made by a dog. —*v.* **1.** To utter a bark. **2.** To speak gruffly : snap.

bark[2] (bärk) *n.* The outer covering of the stems, roots, and main trunks of trees and other woody plants. —*v.* **1.** To remove bark from. **2.** To rub off the skin from.

bark[3] *also* **barque** (bärk) *n.* A sailing ship with 3 to 5 masts with the after mast fore-and-aft rigged.

bar•keep•er (bär'kē'pər) *also* **bar•keep** (-kēp') *n.* An owner or manager of a bar selling liquor.

bark•er (bär'kər) *n.* One who stands before the entrance to a show and solicits customers with a loud, colorful sales pitch.

bar•ley (bär'lē) *n.* A cereal grass, *Hordeun vulgare,* bearing seeds used for food and making beer and whiskey.

bar mitz•vah (bär mĭts'və) *n.* **1.** A 13-year-old Jewish boy who assumes the moral and religious duties of an adult. **2.** The ceremony recognizing a bar mitzvah.

barn (bärn) *n.* A building used esp. to store farm products and shelter livestock.

bar•na•cle (bär'nə-kəl) *n.* Any of various marine crustaceans of the order Cirripedia with a hard shell that remain attached to a submerged surface. **—bar'na•cled** *adj.*

barn•storm (bärn'stôrm') *v.* To travel around, esp. in rural areas, giving dramatic presentations, lecturing, or making political speeches. **—barn'storm'er** *n.*

barn swallow *n.* A widely distributed bird, *Hirundo rustica,* with a deeply forked tail, a dark-blue back, and tan underparts.

barn•yard (bärn'yärd') *n.* The often fenced yard around a barn.

bar•o•graph (băr'ə-grăf') *n.* A recording barometer. **—bar'o•graph'ic** *adj.*

ba•rom•e•ter (bə-rŏm'ĭ-tər) *n.* An instrument for measuring atmospheric pressure, used in forecasting the weather. **—bar'o•met'ric** (băr'ə-mĕt'rĭk), **bar'o•met'ri•cal** *adj.* **—ba•rom'e•try** *n.*

bar•on (băr'ən) *n.* A member of the lowest rank of nobility in Great Britain. **—bar'on•age** *n.* **—ba•ro'ni•al** (bə-rō'nē-əl) *adj.* **—bar'o•ny** *n.*

bar•on•ess (băr'ə-nĭs) *n.* **1.** The wife or widow of a baron. **2.** A woman who holds the rank of baron in her own right.

bar•on•et (băr'ə-nĭt, băr'ə-nĕt') *n.* A man who holds a hereditary title of honor next below a baron. **—bar'on•et•cy** *n.*

ba•roque (bə-rōk') *adj.* **1.** Of an artistic style characterized by elaborate and ornate forms. **2.** Of a musical style characterized by strict form and elaborate ornamentation. **—ba•roque'** *n.*

ba•rouche (bə-ro͞osh') *n.* A 4-wheeled carriage with a seat for the driver outside and a collapsible top.

barque (bärk) *n. var. of* BARK[3].

bar•racks (băr'əks) *n.(sing. or pl. in number).* A building or group of buildings for housing soldiers.

bar•ra•cu•da (băr'ə-ko͞o'də) *n., pl.* **-da** or **-das.** A large, narrow-bodied, chiefly tropical marine fish of the genus *Sphyraena* with very sharp teeth.

barracuda

bar•rage (bə-räzh') *n.* **1.** A heavy, concentrated discharge of missiles as from small arms. **2.** A concentrated outpouring <*a barrage* of comments> ☆**syns:** BOMBARDMENT, BURST, CANNONADE, FUSILLADE, SALVO, SHOWER, STORM, VOLLEY —*v.* **-raged, -rag•ing.** To direct a barrage at.

†**bar•ran•ca** (bə-răng'kə) *n. SW U.S.* A deep ravine : gorge.

bar•ra•try (băr'ə-trē) *n., pl.* **-tries. 1.** *Law.* Persistent incitement of lawsuits. **2.** An unlawful breach of duty by a ship's master or crew that results in injury to the owner of the ship. **3.** The selling or buying of positions in the state or church.

barred (bärd) *adj.* Marked with stripes : striped.

bar•rel (băr'əl) *n.* **1.** A large cask with round flat ends of equal size and sides that bulge. **2.** The amount a barrel will hold. **3.** A unit of volume or capacity that varies from approx. 117 to 159 L or 31 to 42 gal, as established by law or usage. **4.** A cylindrical part, as the long tube of a gun. —*v.* **-reled, -rel•ing** or **-relled, -rel•ling. 1.** To pack in a barrel. **2.** *Slang.* To move at high speed.

barrel organ *n.* A portable musical instrument similar to a small organ and operated by a hand crank.

bar•ren (băr'ən) *adj.* **1.** Sterile : infertile. **2.** Lacking vegetation <*barren* fields> **3.** Unproductive of results <*barren* efforts> **4.** Lacking : devoid. **—bar'ren•ly** *adv.* **—bar'ren•ness** *n.*

bar•rette (bə-rĕt', bä-) *n.* A clasp used to hold hair in place.

bar•ri•cade (băr'ĭ-kād', băr'ĭ-kād') *n.* A hastily constructed barrier or fortification. —*v.* **-cad•ed, -cad•ing.** To block, confine, or fortify with a barricade.

bar•ri•er (băr'ē-ər) *n.* **1.** A structure, as a fence, built to bar passage. **2.** Something that hinders or restricts <a *barrier* to understanding>

barrier reef *n.* A coral reef parallel to the shore and separated from it by a lagoon too deep for coral growth.

bar•ring (bär'ĭng) *prep.* Apart from the occurrence of : excepting.

bar•ri•o (bär'ē-ō', băr'-) *n., pl.* **-os.** A chiefly Spanish-speaking neighborhood in a U.S. city.

bar•ris•ter (băr'ĭ-stər) *n.* A British attorney admitted to plead at the bar in the superior courts.

bar•room (bär'ro͞om', -ro͝om') *n.* A room or building where alcoholic beverages are sold at a counter or bar.

bar•row[1] (băr'ō) *n.* **1.** A flat, rectangular frame with handles at each end. **2.** A wheelbarrow.

bar•row[2] (băr'ō) *n.* A mound of earth or stones over an ancient burial site.

bar•row[3] (băr'ō) *n.* A pig castrated before reaching sexual maturity.

bar•tend•er (bär'tĕn'dər) *n.* One who serves alcoholic drinks at a bar.

bar•ter (bär'tər) *v.* To trade (e.g., goods) without the exchange of money. —*n.* **1.** The act of bartering. **2.** Something bartered. **—bar'ter•er** *n.*

Bar•ton (bärt'n), **Clara.** 1821–1912. Founder of the Amer. Red Cross.

ba•sal (bā'səl, -zəl) *adj.* **1.** Relating to, located at, or forming a base. **2.** Basic.

basal metabolism *n.* The lowest energy needed to maintain vital functions in an organism at complete rest measured by the heat given off per unit time.

ba•salt (bə-sôlt', bā'sôlt') *n.* A dark, dense volcanic rock.

base[1] (bās) *n.* **1.** The lowest part : bottom. **2.** A fundamental principle : basis. **3.** A main constituent. **4.** The point at or from which a process is begun. **5.** One of the 4 corners of a baseball infield. **6.** A central place : headquarters. **7.** A line used as a reference for computations or measurement. **8.** Any of a large class of chemical compounds, including the hydroxides and oxides of metals, that have the ability to turn litmus blue and to react with acids to form salts. **9.** The number that is raised to various powers to generate the principal counting units of a number system. —*adj.* Forming or serving as a base. —*v.* **based, bas•ing. 1.** To form or make a base for. **2.** To establish.

base[2] (bās) *adj.* **bas•er, bas•est. 1.** Morally bad : contemptible. **2.** Inferior in quality or value. **3.** Menial : lowly. **—base'ly** *adv.* **—base'ness** *n.*

base•ball (bās'bôl') *n.* **1.** A game played with a bat and ball by 2 teams on a field with 4 bases laid out in a diamond pattern. **2.** The ball used in baseball.

base•board (bās'bôrd', -bōrd') *n.* A molding that covers the joint between a wall and abutting floor.

base•born (bās'bôrn') *adj.* **1.** Of humble birth. **2.** Of illegitimate birth. **3.** Contemptible : ignoble.

base hit *n. Baseball.* A hit by which the batter reaches base safely.

base•less (bās'lĭs) *adj.* Unfounded : groundless.

base line *n.* **1.** A line serving as a base. **2.** An area within which a baseball player must stay when running between bases.

base•man (bās'mən) *n.* A baseball player assigned to 1st, 2nd, or 3rd base.

base•ment (bās'mənt) *n.* The substructure or foundation of a building.

ba•ses (bā'sēz') *n. pl. of* BASIS.

bash (băsh) *v. Informal.* To strike or smash with a heavy blow. —*n.* **1.** *Informal.* A heavy blow. **2.** *Slang.* A party.
bash·ful (băsh′fəl) *adj.* Socially timid : shy <a *bashful* child> **—bash′ful·ly** *adv.* **—bash′ful·ness** *n.*
ba·sic (bā′sĭk) *adj.* **1.** Of, pertaining to, or forming a base : fundamental. **2.** Of, being, or serving as a starting point. **3.** Of, producing, or resulting from a chemical base. **—ba′sic** *n.* **—ba′si·cal·ly** *adv.* **—ba·sic′i·ty** (-sĭs′ĭ-tē) *n.*
BA·SIC (bā′sĭk) *n. Computer Sci.* A common programming language.
bas·il (băz′əl, bā′zəl) *n.* An herb, *Ocimum basilicum,* with aromatic leaves used as seasoning in cooking.
ba·sil·i·ca (bə-sĭl′ĭ-kə, -zĭl′-) *n.* **1.** An oblong church building with a semicircular apse at one end. **2.** A church or cathedral given certain ceremonial rights by the pope.
bas·i·lisk (băs′ə-lĭsk′, băz′-) *n.* **1.** A legendary lizardlike serpent with lethal breath and glance. **2.** A tropical American lizard of the genus *Basiliscus,* with an erectile crest.

basilisk

ba·sin (bā′sĭn) *n.* **1.** A round, open container used esp. for holding liquids. **2.** A washbowl : sink. **3.** A region drained by a river system.
ba·sis (bā′sĭs) *n., pl.* **-ses** (-sēz′). **1.** A supporting element : foundation. **2.** The main part. **3.** An essential principle.
bask (băsk) *v.* **1.** To expose oneself to pleasant warmth. **2.** To thrive or take pleasure <*basking* in his wife's praise>
bas·ket (băs′kĭt) *n.* **1.** A container made of woven material, as rushes or twigs. **2.** An open-ended net suspended from a hoop that serves as a goal in basketball. **—bas′ket·ful′** *n.*
bas·ket·ball (băs′kĭt-bôl′) *n.* **1.** A game played by 2 teams who attempt to throw a ball through an elevated basket on the opponent's side of the basketball court. **2.** The ball used in basketball.
basket weave *n.* A textile weave with a checkered pattern similar to that of a woven basket.
bas mitz·vah (bäs mĭts′və) *n. var. of* BAT MITZVAH.
Basque (băsk) *n.* **1.** One of a people of unknown origin living in the W Pyrenees. **2.** The language of the Basques.
Basque Provinces (băsk). Region of N Spain, on the Bay of Biscay.
bas-re·lief (bä′rĭ-lēf′) *n.* Low relief.
bass[1] (băs) *n.* Any of several freshwater or marine food fishes.
bass[2] (bās) *n.* **1.** A low-pitched tone or sound. **2.** The lowest part in vocal or instrumental part music. **3. a.** A male singing voice of the lowest range. **b.** A singer with a bass voice. **4.** An instrument that sounds within the range of a bass. **—bass** *adj.*
basset hound *n.* A dog orig. bred in France, with short crooked forelegs and long drooping ears.
bas·si·net (băs′ə-nĕt′, băs′ə-nĕt′) *n.* A basket on legs, often with a hood at one end, used as an infant's crib.
bas·so (băs′ō) *n., pl.* **-sos** *or* **-si** (-sē). An operatic bass.
bas·soon (bə-so͞on′, bă-) *n.* A low-pitched woodwind instrument with a long wooden body and a double reed. **—bas·soon′ist** *n.*
bass viol (bās) *n. Mus.* A double bass.
bass·wood (băs′wo͝od′) *n.* **1.** A North American linden tree, esp. *Tilia americana.* **2.** The wood of a basswood.
bast (băst) *n.* Strong plant fiber used to make cordage and textiles.
bas·tard (băs′tərd) *n.* **1.** An illegitimate child. **2.** Something of irregular or inferior origin, kind, or form. **3.** *Slang.* A mean or disagreeable person. **—bas′tard·ly** *adj.* **—bas′tard·y** *n.*
▲word history: In Old French *fils de bast* literally meant "child of a packsaddle." The phrase refers to the unsanctified circumstances in which the child was conceived. Travelers used packsaddles as bedsoften, no doubt, as impromptu marriage beds. The word *bastard* was formed in Old French from *bast,* "packsaddle," and the pejorative suffix *-ard.*
bas·tard·ize (băs′tər-dīz′) *v.* **-ized, -iz·ing.** To lower in quality or value : debase. **—bas′tard·i·za′tion** *n.*
baste[1] (bāst) *v.* **bast·ed, bast·ing.** To sew with loose running stitches so as to hold in place temporarily.
baste[2] (bāst) *v.* **bast·ed, bast·ing.** To moisten (e.g., meat) periodically with liquid while cooking.
baste[3] (bāst) *v.* **bast·ed, bast·ing. 1.** To beat thoroughly : thrash. **2.** To berate.
bas·tille (bă-stēl′) *n.* A prison : jail.
bas·ti·na·do (băs′tə-nā′dō, -nä′-) *also* **bas·ti·nade** (-nād -näd′) *n., pl.* **-does** *also* **-nades. 1.** A beating with a stick, esp on the soles of the feet. **2.** A stick : cudgel.
bas·tion (băs′chən) *n.* **1.** A projecting part of a fortification. **2** A well-fortified position : stronghold.
bat[1] (băt) *n.* **1.** A stout wooden stick : club. **2.** A sharp blow. **3.** A usu. wooden club used to strike a ball, as in baseball or cricket **at bat.** Having a turn at batting in baseball. —*v.* **bat·ted, bat·ting. 1.** To hit with or as if with a bat. **2.** To take a turn at bat
bat[2] (băt) *n.* A nocturnal flying mammal of the order Chiroptera with membranous wings.
bat[3] (băt) *v.* **bat·ted, bat·ting.** To flutter or wink.
batch (băch) *n.* **1.** A quantity, as of baked goods, produced or prepared at one time. **2.** An amount needed for one operation. **3** A group of individuals or objects.
bate (bāt) *v.* **bat·ed, bat·ing.** To lessen the intensity of : moderate.
bath (băth, bäth) *n., pl.* **baths** (băthz, bäthz, băths, bäths). **1. a** The act of washing the body. **b.** The water used for washing the body. **2.** A bathroom. **3.** A bathhouse. **4.** A liquid in which an object is dipped or soaked so as to process it.
bathe (bāth) *v.* **bathed, bath·ing. 1.** To take a bath. **2.** To wash in water. **3.** To go swimming. **4.** To apply a liquid to in order to soothe or heal. **5.** To wet : moisten. **6.** To suffuse **—bath′er** *n.*
bath·house (băth′hous′, bäth′-) *n.* **1.** A building equipped with facilities for bathing. **2.** A building equipped with dressing rooms for swimmers.
bathing suit *n.* A swimsuit.
bath·o·lith (băth′ə-lĭth′) *n.* Igneous rock that has melted and intruded surrounding strata. **—bath′o·lith′ic** *adj.*
ba·thos (bā′thŏs′) *n.* **1.** A ludicrously abrupt shift from an elevated to a commonplace style. **2.** Insincere or overly sentimental pathos. **—ba·thet′ic** (bə-thĕt′ĭk) *adj.*
bath·robe (băth′rōb′, bäth′-) *n.* A loose-fitting robe.
bath·room (băth′ro͞om′, -ro͝om′, bäth′-) *n.* A room with a shower or bathtub and usu. a sink and toilet.
bath·tub (băth′tŭb′, bäth′-) *n.* A tub for bathing.
bath·y·scaph (băth′ĭ-skăf′) *also* **bath·y·scaphe** (-skăf′ -skāf′) *n.* A free-diving, self-contained deep-sea research vessel with a manned observation capsule.

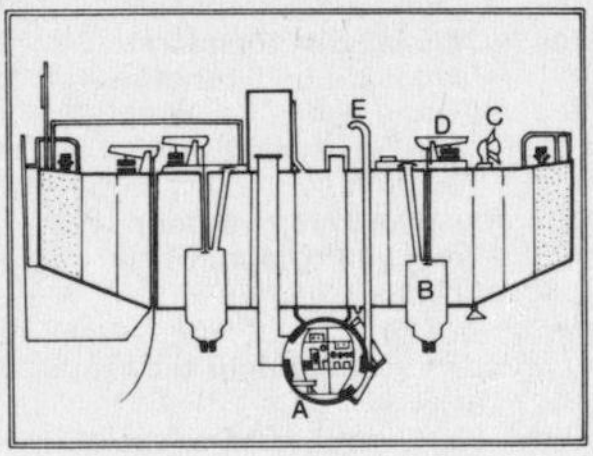

bathyscaph
A. observation gondola, B. pellet ballast hopper, C. propeller, D. release magnet, E. snorkel

bath·y·sphere (băth′ĭ-sfîr′) *n.* A manned deep-diving sphere lowered by cable.
ba·tik (bə-tēk′, băt′ĭk) *n.* **1. a.** A method of dyeing textiles in which the parts not to be dyed are covered with removable wax. **b.** A design created by this method. **2.** Fabric dyed by batik.
ba·tiste (bə-tēst′, bă-) *n.* A fine, sheer fabric used esp. for clothing.
bat mitz·vah (bät mĭts′və) *n. also* **bas mitz·vah** (bäs). **1.** A 12-to-14-year-old Jewish girl who assumes the religious responsibilities of an adult. **2.** The ceremony confirming a bat mitzvah.
ba·ton (bə-tŏn′, băt′n) *n.* A tapered stick, esp. one with which a conductor leads an orchestra or band.
Bat·on Rouge (băt′n ro͞ozh′). Cap. of La., on the Mississippi. *Pop.* 219,486.
ba·tra·chi·an (bə-trā′kē-ən) *adj.* Of or relating to frogs and toads. —*n.* A frog or toad.
bats·man (băts′mən) *n.* A player at bat, esp. in cricket.
bat·tal·ion (bə-tăl′yən) *n.* **1.** A military unit made up of a headquarters company and 4 infantry companies or a headquarters battery and 4 artillery batteries. **2.** A large body of people, esp. of troops.
bat·ten[1] (băt′n) *n.* A flexible wooden strip for sealing cracks or

fastening together parts. —*v.* To secure with or as if with battens.

bat·ten[2] (băt′n) **1.** To become fat. **2.** To thrive and prosper.

bat·ter[1] (băt′ər) *v.* To pound or damage with heavy and repeated blows.

bat·ter[2] (băt′ər) *n.* The baseball or cricket player at bat.

bat·ter[3] (băt′ər) *n.* A thick, beaten mixture, as of flour and liquid, used in cooking.

bat·ter·ing-ram *also* **battering ram** (băt′ər-ĭng-răm′) *n.* An ancient military engine used to batter down walls.

bat·ter·y (băt′ə-rē) *n., pl.* **-ies. 1.** *Law.* The unlawful beating of a person. **2. a.** An artillery emplacement. **b.** A set of heavy guns, as on a warship. **3.** A number of similar things grouped or used together. **4.** The pitcher and catcher on a baseball team. **5.** A device that generates an electric current by chemical reaction.

bat·ting (băt′ĭng) *n.* Rolls or sheets of cotton or wool fiber, as for stuffing mattresses.

bat·tle (băt′l) *n.* **1.** A large-scale military encounter. **2.** An intense competition : struggle. —*v.* **-tled, -tling.** To engage in battle : fight. **—bat′tler** *n.*

bat·tle-ax *or* **bat·tle-axe** (băt′l-ăks′) *n.* A broad-headed ax once used as a weapon.

bat·tle·dore (băt′l-dôr′, -dōr′) *n.* **1.** An early form of badminton played with a flat wooden paddle and a shuttlecock. **2.** The paddle used in battledore.

bat·tle·field (băt′l-fēld′) *n.* A place where a battle is waged.

bat·tle·front (băt′l-frŭnt′) *n.* The area where enemies face one another in battle.

bat·tle·ground (băt′l-ground′) *n.* A battlefield.

bat·tle·ment (băt′l-mənt) *n.* A parapet with indentations that is at the top of a wall and used for defense or decoration.

battle royal *n., pl.* **battles royal. 1.** A battle with more than 2 combatants. **2.** A bitter dispute.

bat·tle·ship (băt′l-shĭp′) *n.* A warship of the largest, most heavily armed and armored class.

bat·ty (băt′ē) *adj.* **-ti·er, -ti·est.** *Slang.* Insane : crazy.

bau·ble (bô′bəl) *n.* A trinket.

baux·ite (bôk′sīt′) *n.* The principal ore of aluminum.

Ba·var·i·a (bə-vâr′ē-ə). Region of S West Germany. **—Ba·var′i·an** *adj.* & *n.*

bawd (bôd) *n.* **1.** A woman who runs a brothel : madam. **2.** A prostitute.

bawd·y (bô′dē) *adj.* **-i·er, -i·est. 1.** Humorously coarse : risqué. **2.** Vulgar : lewd. **—bawd′i·ly** *adv.* **—bawd′i·ness** *n.*

bawl (bôl) *v.* **1.** To cry out loudly : wail. **2.** To shout vehemently.**bawl out.** *Informal.* To scold severely. **—bawl** *n.* **—bawl′er** *n.*

bay[1] (bā) *n.* A wide inlet of a body of water partially enclosed by land.

bay[2] (bā) *n.* **1.** A compartment or main division of a structure. **2.** A compartment projecting from a wall and containing a bay window.

bay[3] (bā) *adj.* Reddish brown. —*n.* **1.** A reddish brown. **2.** A reddish-brown animal, esp. a horse.

bay[4] (bā) *n.* **1.** A deep, prolonged bark, esp. of hounds. **2.** The position of one cornered and forced to turn and fight. —*v.* To utter a bay.

bay[5] (bā) *n.* LAUREL 1.

bay·ber·ry (bā′bĕr′ē) *n.* An aromatic shrub of the genus *Myrica* bearing waxy gray berries.

bay leaf *n.* The dried leaf of the laurel, used as seasoning in cooking.

bay·o·net (bā′ə-nĭt, -nĕt′, bā′ə-nĕt′) *n.* A blade that attaches to the muzzle end of a rifle. —*v.* **-net·ed, -net·ing** or **-net·ted, -net·ting.** To prod or stab with a bayonet.

bay·ou (bī′o͞o, bī′ō) *n.* A marshy, sluggish body of water tributary to a river or lake.

bay rum *n.* An aromatic liquid obtained by distilling the leaves of the bayberry tree, *Pimenta acris,* with rum or synthesized from alcohol, water, and various oils.

bay window *n.* **1.** A large window that projects from the outer wall of a building and forms a bay. **2.** *Slang.* A paunch.

ba·zaar *also* **ba·zar** (bə-zär′) *n.* **1.** An Oriental market consisting of a group of shops and stalls lining a street. **2.** A fair selling articles for charity.

ba·zoo·ka (bə-zo͞o′kə) *n.* A tube-shaped weapon that fires armor-piercing rockets.

BB (bē′bē′) *n.* A shot pellet that measures about .46 cm, or 0.18 in., in diameter.

B.B.A. *abbr.* Bachelor of Business Administration.

B.C. *abbr.* **1.** before Christ. Usu. small capitals <B.C.> **2.** British Columbia.

bd. *abbr.* **1.** board. **2.** bond. **3.** bookbinding. **4.** bound.

B.D. *abbr.* **1.** bank draft. **2.** bills discounted.

bdl. *abbr.* bundle.

be (bē) *v.* **was** (wŏz, wŭz; wəz *when unstressed*) or **were** (wûr), **being** (bē′ĭng), **been** (bĭn) **1.** To exist <I think, therefore I *am.*> **2.** To occupy a particular position <The book *is* on the desk.> **3.** To take place : occur <The party *is* tomorrow.> **4.** To go. Used chiefly in the past and perfect tenses <Have you ever *been* to Europe? **5. a.** To equal in meaning : be identical with <Sunday *is* the first day of the week.> **b.** To symbolize <Food *is* love.> **c.** To belong to a specified class or group <This dog *is* a terrier.> **d.** To have or show a specified quality or characteristic <He *is* intelligent.> **6.** Used with the past participle of a transitive verb to form the passive voice <The house *was* sold.> **7.** Used with the present participle of a verb to express continuing action <She *is* cooking dinner.> **8.** Used with the infinitive of a verb to express intention, obligation, or future action <You *are* to telephone your home immediately>

Be *symbol for* BERYLLIUM.

B/E *abbr.* **1.** bill of entry. **2.** bill of exchange.

beach (bēch) *n.* The often sandy or pebbly shore of a body of water. —*v.* To go or drive ashore.

beach buggy *n.* A dune buggy.

beach·comb·er (bēch′kō′mər) *n.* One who lives on what can be found on beaches.

beach flea *n.* Any of various small, jumping crustaceans of the family Orchestiidae, living on sandy beaches at or near the tide line.

beach·head (bēch′hĕd′) *n.* An area on an enemy shoreline secured by troops in advance of an invading force.

beach plum *n.* A seacoast shrub, *Prunus maritima* of NE North America, with white flowers and edible, plumlike fruit.

bea·con (bē′kən) *n.* **1.** A signal fire. **2.** A coastal signaling or guiding device. **3.** A radio transmitter that emits a signal as a warning or guide.

bead (bēd) *n.* **1.** A small, often round piece of material pierced for threading or stringing. **2. beads. a.** A necklace made of beads. **b.** A rosary. **3.** A small, round mass, as a drop of moisture. **4.** A narrow projecting strip, as of molding. —*v.* **1.** To ornament with beads. **2.** To form into beads. **—bead′ing** *n.* **—bead′y** *adj.*

bea·dle (bēd′l) *n.* A minor parish official, usu. in an English church, whose duties include ushering.

bea·gle (bē′gəl) *n.* A small, short-legged hound with drooping ears and a smooth coat with white, black, and tan markings.

beak (bēk) *n.* **1.** The bill of a bird. **2.** A part or structure resembling a beak.

beak·er (bē′kər) *n.* **1.** A large, wide-mouthed drinking cup. **2.** A cylindrical glass laboratory vessel with a pouring lip.

beam (bēm) *n.* **1.** A large, oblong length of metal or timber used esp. in construction. **2.** The widest part of a ship. **3.** A radio beam. **4.** A ray of light. —*v.* **1. a.** To emit light : shine. **b.** To direct (a radio signal) in a beam. **2.** To smile broadly.

bean (bēn) *n.* **1.** The often edible seed or seed pod of any of various plants of the genus *Phaseolus.* **2.** *Slang.* The head. —*v.* *Slang.* To hit on the head with an object.

bean ball *n.* *Baseball.* A pitched ball aimed at a batter's head.

bean curd *n.* A cheeselike food made from soybeans.

bean·ie (bē′nē) *n.* A small skullcap.

bean sprouts *pl.n.* The tender edible sprouts of bean seeds, esp. soybean seeds.

bear[1] (bâr) *v.* **bore** (bôr, bōr), **borne** (bôrn) or **born, bear·ing. 1.** To support. **2.** To carry. **3.** To endure <couldn't *bear* the tension> **4.** To be equipped with : have <*bore* his uncle's name> **5.** To render as testimony <*bore* witness> **6.** To give birth to. **7.** To yield : produce <a shrub *bearing* fruit> **8.** To exert force <bring pressure to *bear*> **9.** To move in a particular direction <*bore* left at the intersection> **—bear′a·ble** *adj.* **—bear′a·bly** *adv.* **—bear′er** *n.*

bear[2] (bâr) *n.* **1.** Any of various usu. omniverous mammals of the family Ursidae with shaggy fur. **2.** A sullen, ill-mannered person. **3.** One that sells commodities or securities with the expectation of a price fall. **—bear′ish** *adj.* **—bear′ish·ness** *n.*

beard (bîrd) *n.* **1.** The hair on a man's chin, cheeks, and throat. **2.** A hairlike growth, as on a goat's chin or certain plants. —*v.* To confront resolutely and boldly.

bear·ing (bâr′ĭng) *n.* **1.** A manner of conducting oneself : deportment. **2.** A machine part around which another part turns. **3.** A supporting element. **4.** Relationship with something else : connection. **5.** Direction, esp. angular direction as used in navigation. **6. bearings.** Awareness of one's position or situation. **7.** A heraldic emblem.

bear·skin (bâr′skĭn′) *n.* Something, as a tall military headdress, made of the skin of a bear.

beast (bēst) *n.* **1.** An animal, esp. a 4-footed animal. **2.** A vile person.

beast•ly (bēst′lē) *adj.* **-li•er, -li•est. 1.** Of, relating to, or like a beast. **2.** Nasty : disagreeable. **—beast′li•ness** *n.*
beast of burden *n.* A pack animal.
beat (bēt) *v.* **beat, beat•en** (bēt′n) *or* **beat, beat•ing. 1.** To strike repeatedly. **2.** To shape by beating : forge <*beat* silver into a bracelet> **3.** To make by trampling : tread. **4.** To defeat. **5.** To surpass. **6.** To throb : pulsate. **7.** To mix rapidly <*beat* eggs> **8.** To strike so as to produce a signal or music. **9.** *Informal.* To get ahead of <worked hard and *beat* the deadline> *—n.* **1.** A stroke or blow. **2.** A periodic pulsation : throb. **3.** A rhythmic stress, as in music. **4.** A course regularly covered : round. *—adj.* Very tired : exhausted. **—beat′er** *n.*
be•a•tif•ic (bē′ə-tĭf′ĭk) *adj.* Showing or giving extreme joy or bliss.
be•at•i•fy (bē-ăt′ə-fī′) *v.* **-fied, -fy•ing. 1.** To make extremely happy. **2.** *Rom. Cath. Ch.* To proclaim (a deceased person) to be one of the blessed. **—be•at′i•fi•ca′tion** *n.*
be•at•i•tude (bē-ăt′ĭ-to͞od′, -tyo͞od′) *n.* **1.** Supreme blessedness or happiness. **2.** Any of the 9 declarations of blessedness made by Jesus in the Sermon on the Mount.
beat•nik (bēt′nĭk) *n.* A person who acts and dresses unconventionally and disregards established notions of propriety.
beau (bō) *n., pl.* **beaus** *or* **beaux** (bōz). **1.** A suitor. **2.** A dandy : fop.
beau geste (bō zhĕst′) *n, pl.* **beaux gestes** *or* **beau gestes** (bō zhĕst′). A gracious or noble gesture.
beau i•de•al (bō′ ī-dē′əl) *n., pl.* **beau i•de•als.** An idealized model.
Beau•jo•lais (bō′zhō-lā′) *n.* A red table wine of French origin.
beau monde (bō mŏnd′, môɴᴅ′) *n., pl.* **beaux mondes** (bō môɴᴅ′) *or* **beau mondes** (bō mŏndz′). The world of fashionable society.
beau•te•ous (byo͞o′tē-əs, -tyəs) *adj.* Beautiful. **—beau′te•ous•ly** *adv.*
beau•ti•cian (byo͞o-tĭsh′ən) *n.* One who gives cosmetic treatments.
beau•ti•ful (byo͞o′tə-fəl) *adj.* Marked by beauty. ☆***syns:*** BEAUTEOUS, COMELY, FAIR, GOOD-LOOKING, GORGEOUS, LOVELY, PRETTY, RAVISHING **—beau′ti•ful•ly** *adv.*
beau•ti•fy (byo͞o′tə-fī′) *v.* **-fied, -fy•ing.** To make or become beautiful. **—beau′ti•fi•ca′tion** *n.* **—beau′ti•fi′er** *n.*
beau•ty (byo͞o′tē) *n., pl.* **-ties. 1.** A quality or a combination of qualities that delights the senses or appeals to the mind. **2.** One that is beautiful. **3.** An outstanding or conspicuous example.
beauty parlor *n.* An establishment providing hairdressing, manicures, facials, etc.
beauty salon *n.* A beauty parlor.
beauty shop *n.* A beauty parlor.
beaux (bō) *n. var. pl. of* BEAU.
beaux-arts (bō-zär′) *pl.n.* The fine arts.
bea•ver (bē′vər) *n.* **1.** A large aquatic rodent of the genus *Castor* with thick fur, a flat paddlelike tail, and chisellike front teeth. **2.** The fur of a beaver.
be•bop (bē′bŏp′) *n.* BOP[2].
be•calm (bĭ-käm′) *v.* To make (e.g., a ship) motionless for lack of wind.
be•cause (bĭ-kôz′, -kŭz′) *conj.* For the reason that : since.
because of *prep.* On account of.
beck (bĕk) *n.* **1.** A gesture of beckoning. **2.** A summons.
beck•on (bĕk′ən) *v.* **1.** To signal, as by nodding or waving. **2.** To attract.
be•cloud (bĭ-kloud′) *v.* To darken with or as if with clouds : obscure.
be•come (bĭ-kŭm′) *v.* **1.** To grow or come to be. **2.** To be suitable to : suit.
be•com•ing (bĭ-kŭm′ĭng) *adj.* **1.** Suitable : appropriate. **2.** Attractive. **—be•com′ing•ly** *adv.* **—be•com′ing•ness** *n.*
bed (bĕd) *n.* **1.** A piece of furniture for sleeping. **2.** A plot of cultivated or planted ground. **3.** The bottom of a body of water <a river *bed*> **4.** A horizontal layer, as of rock. **5.** A deposit, as of ore. *—v.* **bed•ded, bed•ding. 1.** To put to bed. **2.** To plant in a bed. **3.** To lay flat or in layers.
be•daub (bĭ-dôb′) *v.* To smear.
be•daz•zle (bĭ-dăz′əl) *v.* To bewilder with intense light. **—be•daz′zle•ment** *n.*
bed•bug (bĕd′bŭg′) *n.* A wingless, bloodsucking insect, *Cimex lectularius,* that infests human dwellings and esp. beds.
bed•clothes (bĕd′klōz′, -klōthz′) *pl.n.* Coverings for a bed.
bed•ding (bĕd′ĭng) *n.* **1.** Bedclothes. **2.** A foundation.
be•deck (bĭ-dĕk′) *v.* To deck out : adorn.
be•dev•il (bĭ-dĕv′əl) *v.* **-iled, -il•ing** *or* **-illed, -il•ling. 1.** To torment : plague. **2.** To bewilder : confuse.
be•dew (bĭ-do͞o′, -dyo͞o′) *v.* To moisten with or as if with dew.
bed•fast (bĕd′făst′) *adj.* Bedridden.
bed•fel•low (bĕd′fĕl′ō) *n.* **1.** Someone with whom one shares a bed. **2.** A collaborator, associate, or ally.
be•di•zen (bĭ-dī′zən, -dĭz′ən) *v.* To adorn or dress gaudily.
bed•lam (bĕd′ləm) *n.* **1.** A situation or place of noise and confusion. **2.** *Archaic.* An insane asylum.
Bed•ling•ton terrier (bĕd′lĭng-tən) *n.* A dog orig. bred in England, with a woolly grayish or brownish coat.

Bedlington terrier

bed of roses *n.* A state of idyllic comfort or luxury.
Bed•ou•in (bĕd′o͞o-ĭn, bĕd′wĭn) *n.* A nomadic Arab of the North African, Arabian, or Syrian deserts.
bed•pan (bĕd′păn′) *n.* A receptacle for the excreta of a bedridden person.
bed•post (bĕd′pōst′) *n.* A vertical post of a bed.
be•drag•gled (bĭ-drăg′əld) *adj.* **1.** Wet and limp. **2.** Soiled by or as if by dragging in the mud. **3.** Dilapidated.
bed•rid•den (bĕd′rĭd′n) *adj.* Confined to bed by illness or infirmity.
bed•rock (bĕd′rŏk′) *n.* The solid rock underlying the earth's surface.
bed•roll (bĕd′rōl′) *n.* A roll of bedding that can be carried, as by campers.
bed•room (bĕd′ro͞om′, -ro͝om′) *n.* A room for sleeping.
bed•side (bĕd′sīd′) *n.* The place alongside a bed, esp. of a sick person.
bed•sore (bĕd′sôr′, -sōr′) *n.* A skin ulceration on a bedridden person induced by pressure and chafing.
bed•spread (bĕd′sprĕd′) *n.* A decorative outer covering for a bed.
bed•stead (bĕd′stĕd′) *n.* The framework that supports a bed.
bed•time (bĕd′tīm′) *n.* The time at which one goes to bed.
bee (bē) *n.* **1.** Any of various winged, hairy-bodied insects of the order Hymenoptera, characterized by specialized structures for gathering nectar and pollen from flowers. **2.** A gathering at which people work together or compete <a spelling *bee*> <a quilting *bee*>
beech (bēch) *n.* A tree of the genus *Fagus* with light-colored bark, edible nuts, and strong, heavy wood.
beech•nut (bēch′nŭt′) *n.* The nut of a beech tree.
beef (bēf) *n., pl.* **beeves** (bēvz). **1.** A fattened steer, bull, ox, or cow, esp. one for use as meat. **2.** The flesh of a steer, bull, ox, or cow. **3.** *Informal.* Muscle : brawn. **4.** *pl.* **beefs.** *Slang.* A complaint. *—v. Slang.* To complain. **—beef up.** *Slang.* To make stronger : build up.
beef•cake (bēf′kāk′) *n.* *Informal.* Photographs of minimally clad, muscular men.
beef•eat•er (bēf′ē′tər) *n.* A yeoman of the royal guard in England.
beef•steak (bēf′stāk′) *n.* A slice of beef suitable for broiling or frying.
beef•y (bē′fē) *adj.* **-i•er, -i•est. 1.** Like beef. **2.** Muscular and heavy in build : brawny. **—beef′i•ness** *n.*
bee•hive (bē′hīv′) *n.* A hive for bees.
bee•keep•er (bē′kē′pər) *n.* One who raises and keeps bees. **—bee′keep′ing** *n.*
bee•line (bē′līn′) *n.* A direct straight route.
been (bĭn) *v. p.p. of* BE.
beep (bēp) *n.* A short, usu. high-pitched sound, as from an electronic device, for signaling or warning. **—beep** *v.* **—beep′er** *n.*
beer (bîr) *n.* An alcoholic beverage brewed from malt and hops.
bees•wax (bēz′wăks′) *n.* The wax bees secrete and use to make honeycombs.
beet (bēt) *n.* A cultivated plant of the genus *Beta* with edible leaves and a fleshy root used as a vegetable or sugar source.
Bee•tho•ven (bā′tō-vən), **Ludwig van.** 1770–1827. German composer.
bee•tle[1] (bēt′l) *n.* An insect of the order Coleoptera with modified horny front wings that cover the membranous hind wings when it is not flying.

bee·tle[2] (bēt′l) *adj.* Overhanging : jutting <*beetle* brows> —*v.* **-tled, -tling.** To jut : project.
bee·tle[3] (bēt′l) *n.* A heavy tool for pounding or hammering.
beeves (bēvz) *n. pl. of* BEEF.
be·fall (bĭ-fôl′) *v.* To happen (to).
be·fit (bĭ-fĭt′) *v.* To be appropriate for or suitable to.
be·fog (bĭ-fôg′, -fŏg′) *v.* To obscure with or as if with fog.
be·fore (bĭ-fôr′, -fōr′) *adv.* **1.** In the past : earlier. **2.** In advance : ahead. —*prep.* **1.** Prior to <left *before* dawn> **2.** In front of <stood *before* the judge> **3.** In higher esteem than <put honesty *before* profit> —*conj.* **1.** Prior to the time when < I met you *before*.> **2.** Rather than <would go to jail *before* betraying a fellow soldier>
be·fore·hand (bĭ-fôr′hănd′, -fōr′-) *adv. & adj.* In advance.
be·foul (bĭ-foul′) *v.* To make dirty : sully.
be·friend (bĭ-frĕnd′) *v.* To behave as a friend to.
be·fud·dle (bĭ-fŭd′l) *v.* To confuse.
beg (bĕg) *v.* **begged, beg·ging. 1.** To ask or make a living by asking for charity. **2.** To ask for earnestly : entreat. **3.** To evade <Don't *beg* the question.>
be·gan (bĭ-găn′) *v. p.t. of* BEGIN.
be·get (bĭ-gĕt′) *v.* To father : sire. **—be·get′ter** *n.*
beg·gar (bĕg′ər) *n.* One who begs, esp. for a living. —*v.* To make poor : impoverish. **—beg′gar·y** *n.*
beg·gar·ly (bĕg′ər-lē) *adj.* Of or like a beggar : poor. **—beg′gar·li·ness** *n.*
be·gin (bĭ-gĭn′) *v.* **-gan** (-găn′), **-gun** (-gŭn′), **-gin·ning. 1.** To start doing : commence. **2.** To come into being : arise. **3.** To cause to come into being : originate. ☆**syns:** ARISE, COMMENCE, ORIGINATE, START **—be·gin′ner** *n.*
be·gin·ning (bĭ-gĭn′ĭng) *n.* **1.** The time when or place where something begins or is begun. **2.** The initial part of something : commencement. **3.** A source : origin.
be·gone (bĭ-gôn′, -gŏn′) *interj.* Used as an order of dismissal.
be·go·nia (bĭ-gōn′yə) *n.* Any of various plants of the genus *Begonia* grown for their showy leaves and waxy flowers.
be·grime (bĭ-grīm′) *v.* **-grimed, -grim·ing.** To soil with grime.
be·grudge (bĭ-grŭj′) *v.* **1.** To envy someone the enjoyment or possession of. **2.** To give reluctantly.
be·guile (bĭ-gīl′) *v.* **-guiled, -guil·ing. 1.** To cheat : deceive. **2.** To pass pleasantly : while away. **3.** To charm : delight. **—be·guile′ment** *n.* **—be·guil′er** *n.*
be·guine (bĭ-gēn′) *n.* A ballroom dance based on a native dance of Martinique and St. Lucia.
be·gum (bē′gəm, bā′-) *n.* A Moslem woman of rank.
be·gun (bĭ-gŭn′) *v. p.p. of* BEGIN.
be·half (bĭ-hăf′, -häf′) *n.* Interest, benefit, or support.
be·have (bĭ-hāv′) *v.* **-haved, -hav·ing. 1.** To act, react, or function in a particular manner. **2.** To conduct oneself in a specified and esp. a proper manner.
be·hav·ior (bĭ-hāv′yər) *n.* The way in which someone or something behaves. **—be·hav′ior·al** *adj.*
be·hav·ior·ism (bĭ-hāv′yə-rĭz′əm) *n.* The psychological school holding that observable behavior constitutes the essential or exclusive scientific basis of psychological data and investigation. **—be·hav′ior·ist** *n.* **—be·hav′ior·is′tic** *adj.*
be·head (bĭ-hĕd′) *v.* To decapitate.
be·he·moth (bĭ-hē′məth, bē′ə-) *n.* **1.** An enormous animal described in the Old Testament. **2.** Something of immense size.
be·hest (bĭ-hĕst′) *n.* **1.** An authoritative command. **2.** Insistent prompting.
be·hind (bĭ-hīnd′) *adv.* **1.** In, to, or toward the back. **2.** In the place or condition that is left. **3.** Late. **4.** Slow. —*prep.* **1.** At the back or in the rear of <a garage *behind* the house> **2.** In or to a former place, time, or situation <fears that are now *behind* him> **3.** Later than <*behind* schedule> **4.** Below, as in rank <car sales *behind* last year's> **5.** In support of <Her parents are *behind* her in her efforts.> —*n. Informal.* The buttocks.
be·hind·hand (bĭ-hīnd′hănd′) *adj.* **1.** In arrears. **2.** Behind the times.
be·hold (bĭ-hōld′) *v.* To look at : see. Often used in the imperative.
be·hold·en (bĭ-hōl′dən) *adj.* Indebted : obliged.
be·hoof (bĭ-hōōf′) *n.* Benefit : advantage.
be·hoove (bĭ-hōōv′) *v.* **-hooved, -hoov·ing.** To be proper or necessary for.
beige (bāzh) *n.* A light grayish brown. **—beige** *adj.*
Bei·jing (bā′jyĭng′). Cap. of China, in the NE. *Pop.* 5,400,000.
be·ing (bē′ĭng) *n.* **1.** Existence. **2.** One that lives, esp. a person. **3.** One's basic or essential nature : essence.
Bei·rut (bā-rōōt′). Cap. of Lebanon, on the E Mediterranean. *Pop.* 478,870.
be·la·bor (bĭ-lā′bər) *v.* **1.** To thrash thoroughly. **2.** To harp on.
be·lat·ed (bĭ-lā′tĭd) *adj.* Tardy : late. **—be·lat′ed·ly** *adv.*
be·lay (bĭ-lā′) *v. Naut.* **1.** To secure (e.g., a rope) around a cleat or pin. **2.** To stop <*Belay* there>
bel can·to (bĕl kän′tō) *n.* A style of operatic singing characterized by rich tonal lyricism and brilliant vocal technique.
belch (bĕlch) *v.* **1.** To expel stomach gas noisily through the mouth. **2.** To eject violently. **—belch** *n.*
bel·dam *also* **bel·dame** (bĕl′dəm) *n.* An old woman, esp. an ugly one.
be·lea·guer (bĭ-lē′gər) *v.* **1.** To besiege. **2.** To beset : harass.
Bel·fast (bĕl′făst′, bĕl-făst′). Cap. of Northern Ireland, on the E coast. *Pop.* 357,600.
bel·fry (bĕl′frē) *n., pl.* **-fries. 1.** A bell tower, as on a church. **2.** The part of a belfry where the bells are hung.
Bel·gium (bĕl′jəm). Country of NW Europe. *Cap.* Brussels. *Pop.* 9,855,110. **—Bel′gian** *adj. & n.*
Bel·grade (bĕl′grād′, bĕl-grăd′). Cap. of Yugoslavia, on the Danube. *Pop.* 770,140.
be·lie (bĭ-lī′) *v.* **-lied, -ly·ing. 1.** To give a false picture of : misrepresent. **2.** To demonstrate to be false. **3.** To be inconsistent with : contradict. **—be·li′er** *n.*
be·lief (bĭ-lēf′) *n.* **1.** Trust : confidence. **2.** Something, as a tenet, that is believed : conviction. ☆**syns:** CONVICTION, FEELING, IDEA, NOTION, OPINION, PERSUASION, POSITION, SENTIMENT, VIEW
be·lieve (bĭ-lēv′) *v.* **-lieved, -liev·ing. 1.** To accept as real or true. **2.** To credit with veracity. **3.** To think : suppose. **4.** To hold religious beliefs. **—be·liev′a·ble** *adj.* **—be·liev′er** *n.*
be·lit·tle (bĭ-lĭt′l) *v.* **-tled, -tling.** To speak or think of as small or unimportant : disparage. **—be·lit′tle·ment** *n.*
Be·lize (bə-lēz′). Country of Central America. *Cap.* Belmopan. *Pop.* 127,200.
bell (bĕl) *n.* **1.** A hollow metal instrument that emits a metallic sound when struck. **2.** Something with the flared shape of a bell. **3.** *Naut.* **a.** A stroke on a bell to mark the hour. **b.** The time indicated by the striking of a bell. —*v.* To furnish with a bell.
Bell (bĕl), **Alexander Graham.** 1847–1922. Scottish-born Amer. inventor.
bel·la·don·na (bĕl′ə-dŏn′ə) *n.* **1.** A plant, *Atropa belladonna*, with small poisonous black berries. **2.** Atropine.
bell-bot·toms (bĕl′bŏt′əmz) *pl.n.* Trousers with legs that flare out at the bottom. **—bell′-bot′tom** *adj.*
bell·boy (bĕl′boi′) *n.* A hotel employee who assists guests, as by carrying luggage.
belle (bĕl) *n.* An attractive and much-admired girl or woman.
belles-let·tres (bĕl-lĕt′rə) *pl.n. (sing. in number).* Literature regarded for its artistic rather than informative value.
bel·let·rist (bĕl-lĕt′rĭst) *n.* A writer of belles-lettres.
bell·hop (bĕl′hŏp′) *n.* A bellboy.
bel·li·cose (bĕl′ĭ-kōs′) *adj.* Warlike, as in disposition : pugnacious. **—bel′li·cos′i·ty** (-kŏs′ĭ-tē) *n.*
bel·lig·er·ent (bə-lĭj′ər-ənt) *adj.* **1.** Inclined to be aggressive or hostile. **2.** Waging war. ☆**syns:** BELLICOSE, COMBATIVE, CONTENTIOUS, HOSTILE, PUGNACIOUS, TRUCULENT **—bel·lig′er·ence** *n.* **—bel·lig′er·ent** *n.* **—bel·lig′er·ent·ly** *adv.*
bel·low (bĕl′ō) *v.* **1.** To make the roar characteristic of a bull. **2.** To shout in a deep powerful voice. **—bel′low** *n.*
bel·lows (bĕl′ōz, -əz) *n. (sing. or pl. in number).* A device with a flexible air chamber that contracts a current of air through a nozzle.
bell·weth·er (bĕl′wĕth′ər) *n.* A leader.
bel·ly (bĕl′ē) *n., pl.* **-lies. 1.** The abdomen. **2.** The underside of an animal's body. **3.** The stomach. —*v.* **-lied, -ly·ing.** To bulge or cause to bulge.
bel·ly·ache (bĕl′ē-āk′) *n.* A pain in the stomach or abdomen. —*v. Slang.* To complain.
bel·ly·but·ton (bĕl′ē-bŭt′n) *n. Informal.* The navel.
belly dance *n.* A dance marked by sinuous movements of the belly. **—bel′ly-dance′** *v.* **—belly dancer** *n.*
bel·ly·ful (bĕl′ē-fōōl′) *n. Informal.* An amount exceeding what one can endure.
belly laugh *n.* A deep, jovial laugh.
Bel·mo·pan (bĕl′mə-păn′). Cap. of Belize, in the N central part. *Pop.* 5,000.
be·long (bĭ-lông′, -lŏng′) *v.* **1.** To be the property of. **2.** To be a part of. **3.** To be a member. **4.** To have a suitable or appropriate place.
be·long·ings (bĭ-lông′ĭngz, -lŏng′-) *pl.n.* Personal possessions : effects.
be·lov·ed (bĭ-lŭv′ĭd, -lŭvd′) *adj.* Dearly loved. **—be·lov′ed** *n.*
be·low (bĭ-lō′) *adv.* **1.** In or to a lower place or level. **2.** On earth. —*prep.* **1.** Lower than : under. **2.** Inferior to.
belt (bĕlt) *n.* **1.** A band, as of leather, worn around the waist. **2.** A continuous moving band that transfers motion or conveys material from one wheel or shaft to another. **3.** A geographic region that is distinctive in a specific way. **4.** *Slang.* A powerful

hit : punch. **5.** *Slang.* A drink, esp. of hard liquor. *—v.* **1.** To encircle or attach with a belt. **2.** To hit with or as if with a belt.
belt•way (bĕlt′wā′) *n.* A highway skirting an urban area.
be•lu•ga (bə-lo͞o′gə) *n.* A sturgeon, *Huso huso,* of the Black and Caspian seas, whose roe is used for caviar.
bel•ve•dere (bĕl′vĭ-dîr′) *n.* A structure, as an open roofed gallery, located so as to command a view.
be•moan (bĭ-mōn′) *v.* To lament : mourn.
be•muse (bĭ-myo͞oz′) *v.* **1.** To confuse : bewilder. **2.** To cause to be lost in thought.
bench (bĕnch) *n.* **1.** A long seat for 2 or more persons. **2. a.** The judge's seat in a court of law. **b.** The position or office of a judge. **c.** The judge or judges composing a court. **3.** A craftsman's worktable. *—v.* **1.** To seat on a bench. **2.** To keep out of or remove from a game.
bench mark *also* **bench•mark** (bĕnch′märk′) *n.* **1.** A mark made by a surveyor on a stationary point and used as an elevation reference. **2.** A standard of measurement or evaluation.
bench warrant *n.* A warrant issued by a judge or law court for the arrest of an offender.
bend (bĕnd) *v.* **bent** (bĕnt), **bend•ing. 1.** To bring into tension (e.g., a bow). **2.** To assume or cause to assume a different and esp. a curved shape. **3.** To deflect. **4.** To subdue or coerce. **5.** To apply closely : concentrate. **6.** To fasten. **7.** To submit : yield. *—n.* **1.** The act of bending. **2.** Something bent. **3. bends.** *(sing. or pl. in number).* Caisson disease.
bend•er (bĕn′dər) *n. Slang.* A spree.
be•neath (bĭ-nēth′) *adv.* **1.** In or to a lower position : below. **2.** Underneath. *—prep.* **1.** Under : below. **2.** Unworthy of.
ben•e•dict (bĕn′ĭ-dĭkt′) *n.* A newly married man who was previously considered a confirmed bachelor.
ben•e•dic•tion (bĕn′ĭ-dĭk′shən) *n.* **1.** A blessing. **2.** The invocation of a divine blessing, usu. at the end of a church service. **—ben′e•dic′to•ry** *adj.*
ben•e•fac•tion (bĕn′ə-făk′shən) *n.* A charitable act or gift.
ben•e•fac•tor (bĕn′ə-făk′tər) *n.* One who gives support or financial aid. **—ben′e•fac′tress** *n.*
ben•e•fice (bĕn′ə-fĭs) *n.* A church office endowed with fixed capital assets that provide a living.
be•nef•i•cence (bə-nĕf′ĭ-səns) *n.* **1.** The quality of being charitable or kind. **2.** A charitable act or gift. **—be•nef′i•cent** *adj.*
ben•e•fi•cial (bĕn′ə-fĭsh′əl) *adj.* Bringing benefit : helpful. ☆**syns:** ADVANTAGEOUS, BENIGNANT, FAVORABLE, GOOD, PROPITIOUS, SALUTARY **—ben′e•fi′cial•ly** *adv.*
ben•e•fi•ci•ar•y (bĕn′ə-fĭsh′ē-ĕr′ē, -fĭsh′ə-rē) *n., pl.* **-ies.** The recipient of a benefit, as income from a will or trust fund.
ben•e•fit (bĕn′ə-fĭt) *n.* **1.** An advantage. **2.** Aid : help. **3.** A payment or series of payments to one in need. **4.** A public performance to raise funds. *—v.* **-fit•ed, -fit•ing** or **-fit•ted, -fit•ting. 1.** To be helpful or advantageous to. **2.** To profit.
be•nev•o•lence (bə-nĕv′ə-ləns) *n.* **1.** An inclination to do charitable or kind acts. **2.** A charitable act. **—be•nev′o•lent** *adj.* **—be•nev′o•lent•ly** *adv.*
Ben•gal (bĕn-gôl′, bĕng-). Region of E India and Bangladesh, on the **Bay of Bengal,** arm of the Indian Ocean. **—Ben•gal′i** *adj.* & *n.*
be•night•ed (bĭ-nī′tĭd) *adj.* **1.** Overtaken by night. **2.** In a state of ignorance. **—be•night′ed•ly** *adv.* **—be•night′ed•ness** *n.*
be•nign (bĭ-nīn′) *adj.* **1.** Having a kind disposition : gentle. **2.** Tending to promote well-being : beneficial. **3.** *Pathol.* Not malignant. **—be•nign′ly** *adv.*
be•nig•nant (bĭ-nĭg′nənt) *adj.* **1.** Favorable : beneficial. **2.** Kindly disposed : gracious. **—be•nig′nant•ly** *adv.*
Be•nin (bə-nēn′). Country of W Africa. *Cap.* Porto Novo. *Pop.* 3,469,000.
ben•i•son (bĕn′ĭ-zən) *n.* A benediction : blessing.
ben•ne *or* **ben•ni** (bĕn′ē) *n.* **1.** The sesame plant. **2.** Seeds or oil of the sesame.
ben•ny (bĕn′ē) *n., pl.* **-nies.** *Slang.* An amphetamine tablet.
bent (bĕnt) *adj.* **1.** Not straight : curved or crooked. **2.** Having a fixed purpose : determined. *—n.* A tendency, disposition, or inclination : propensity.
ben•thos (bĕn′thŏs′) *n.* **1.** The bottom of a sea or a lake. **2.** The organisms living there. **—ben′thic, ben•thon′ic** *adj.*
ben•ton•ite (bĕn′tə-nīt′) *n.* Either of 2 principally aluminum silicate clays, used in adhesives and ceramic fillers.
bent•wood (bĕnt′wo͝od′) *n.* Wood that has been steamed until pliable and then bent and shaped. **—bent′wood′** *adj.*
be•numb (bĭ-nŭm′) *v.* **1.** To make numb, esp. by cold. **2.** To make inactive : dull.
Ben•ze•drine (bĕn′zĭ-drēn′). A trademark for a brand of amphetamine.
ben•zene (bĕn′zēn′, bĕn-zēn′) *n.* A colorless, flammable liquid made from petroleum and used in detergents, insecticides, and motor fuels.
ben•zine (bĕn′zēn′, bĕn-zēn′) *also* **ben•zin** (bĕn′zĭn) *n.* **1.** Ligroin. **2.** Benzene.
ben•zo•ate (bĕn′zō-āt′, -ĭt) *n.* An ester or salt of benzoic acid.
ben•zo•caine (bĕn′zə-kān′) *n.* A crystaline ester used as a local anesthetic.
ben•zo•ic acid (bĕn-zō′ĭk) *n.* A white, crystalline, organic acid used to season tobacco and in perfumes, germicides, and dentifrices.
ben•zo•in (bĕn′zō-ĭn, -zoin′) *n.* Any of several resins containing benzoic acid, derived as a gum from trees of the genus *Styrax* and used in ointments, perfumes, and medicine.
ben•zol (bĕn′zôl′, -zōl′) *n.* Benzene.
be•queath (bĭ-kwēth′, -kwēth′) *v.* **1.** *Law.* To leave or give by will. **2.** To pass on : hand down. **—be•queath′al** *n.* **—be•queath′er** *n.* **—be•queath′ment** *n.*
be•quest (bĭ-kwĕst′) *n.* **1.** The act of bequeathing. **2.** Something bequeathed.
be•rate (bĭ-rāt′) *v.* **-rat•ed, -rat•ing.** To scold severely : upbraid.
ber•ceuse (bĕr-sœz′) *n., pl.* **-ceuses** (-sœz′). A lullaby.
be•reave (bĭ-rēv′) *v.* **-reaved** or **-reft** (-rĕft′), **-reav•ing.** To deprive of (something), esp. a loved one by death. **—be•reaved′** *n.* & *adj.* **—be•reave′ment** *n.*
be•ret (bə-rā′, bĕr′ā′) *n.* A soft, round, usu. woolen cap that has no brim.
berg (bûrg) *n.* An iceberg.
ber•ga•mot (bûr′gə-mŏt′) *n.* A small, spiny tree, *Citrus aurantium bergamia,* bearing pear-shaped fruit whose rind yields an aromatic oil that is used in perfumery.
ber•i•ber•i (bĕr′ē-bĕr′ē) *n.* A thiamine-deficiency disease, endemic in E and S Asia and characterized by partial paralysis of the extremities, emaciation, and anemia.
Be•ring Sea (bûr′ĭng, bâr′-). Part of the N Pacific between Siberia and Alas., joined to the Arctic Ocean by the **Bering Strait.**
Berke•ley (bûrk′lē). City and educational center of W Calif. *Pop.* 103,328.
ber•ke•li•um (bər-kē′lē-əm, bûrk′lē-əm) *n. Symbol* **Bk** A synthetic radioactive element.
Ber•lin (bûr-lĭn′). Divided city in East Germany: **East Berlin,** cap. of East Germany (*pop.* 1,128,983); and **West Berlin,** part of West Germany (*pop.* 1,902,250). **—Ber•lin′er** *n.*
Ber•mu•da (bər-myo͞o′də). British island colony in the Atlantic SE of Cape Hateras. **—Ber•mu′di•an** (-dē-ən) *adj.* & *n.*
Bermuda onion *n.* A large, yellow-skinned onion having a mild flavor.
Bermuda shorts *pl.n.* Shorts ending just above the knees.
Bern *also* **Berne** (bûrn, bĕrn). Cap. of Switzerland, in the NW. *Pop.* 141,300.
Ber•ni•ni (bĕr-nē′nē), **Giovanni Lorenzo.** 1598–1680. Italian sculptor, architect, and painter.
ber•ry (bĕr′ē) *n., pl.* **-ries. 1.** A usu. fleshy, edible fruit as the strawberry or raspberry. **2.** *Bot.* A fleshy fruit, as the grape or tomato, that develops from a single ovary but has several or many seeds. **3.** A seed or dried kernel, as that of the coffee plant. *—v.* **-ried, -ry•ing.** To gather berries.
ber•serk (bər-sûrk′, -zûrk′) *adj.* **1.** Destructively or frenziedly violent. **2.** Deranged. **—ber•serk′** *adv.*
berth (bûrth) *n.* **1.** A built-in bed or bunk on a ship or train. **2.** A space at a wharf for a ship to dock. **3.** Sufficient space for a ship to maneuver. **4.** A positon of employment, esp. on a ship. *—v.* **1.** To dock (a ship). **2.** To provide with a berth.
ber•yl (bĕr′əl) *n.* A mineral composed chiefly of beryllium, silicon, and oxygen that occurs in hexagonal prisms, is the major source of beryllium, and is used as a gem. **—ber′yl•line** (-ə-lĭn, -līn′) *adj.*
be•ryl•li•um (bə-rĭl′ē-əm) *n. Symbol* **Be** A lightweight, corrosion-resistant, rigid, steel-gray metallic element.
be•seech (bĭ-sēch′) *v.* **-sought** (-sôt′) or **-seeched, -seech•ing.** To request earnestly : entreat. **—be•seech′er** *n.*
be•seem (bĭ-sēm′) *v. Archaic.* To be suitable for : befit.
be•set (bĭ-sĕt′) *v.* **1.** To attack from all sides : assail. **2.** To trouble persistently : harass <*beset* by doubts>
be•side (bĭ-sīd′) *prep.* **1.** Next to : at the side of. **2.** In comparison with. **3.** Except for. **4.** Wide of : apart from <*beside* the point> *—adv. Archaic.* In addition to.
be•sides (bĭ-sīdz′) *adv.* **1.** In addition : also. **2.** Furthermore : moreover. **3.** Else : otherwise. *—prep.* **1.** In addition to. **2.** Other than : except.
be•siege (bĭ-sēj′) *v.* **1.** To encircle with troops : lay siege to. **2.** To crowd around. **3.** To importune or harass, as with requests. **—be•sieg′er** *n.*
be•smear (bĭ-smîr′) *v.* To smear.
be•smirch (bĭ-smûrch′) *v.* To soil : sully. **—be•smirch′er** *n.* **—be•smirch′ment** *n.*

be·som (bē'zəm) *n.* A bundle of twigs attached to a handle and used as a broom.
be·sot (bĭ-sŏt') *v.* **-sot·ted, -sot·ting.** To stupefy or muddle with or as if with liquor.
be·spat·ter (bĭ-spăt'ər) *v.* To soil by splashing, as with mud.
be·speak (bĭ-spēk') *v.* **1.** To be an indication of : signify. **2.** To reserve. **3.** To foretell.
be·spec·ta·cled (bĭ-spĕk'tə-kəld) *adj.* Wearing eyeglasses.
be·sprin·kle (bĭ-sprĭng'kəl) *v.* To sprinkle.
best (bĕst) *adj.* **1.** Exceeding all others in excellence or quality <the *best* chocolate> **2.** Most satisfactory, suitable, useful, or desirable <the *best* procedure> **3.** Greatest : largest <spent the *best* part of a day studying> *—adv.* **1.** Most advantageously. **2.** To the greatest extent or degree : most. *—n.* **1.** Something that is best. **2.** The best condition, manner, or quality <look your *best*><act your *best*> **3.** One's best efforts <always does her *best*> **4.** One's best clothing. **5.** One's warmest wishes : regards. *—v.* To get the better of : surpass.
bes·tial (bĕs'chəl, bĕst'yəl) *adj.* **1.** Of, relating to, or like an animal. **2.** Having the manners or qualities of a brute : savage. **—bes'ti·al'i·ty** *n.* **—bes'tial·ly** *adv.*
bes·ti·ar·y (bĕs'chē-ĕr'ē, bēs'-) *n., pl.* **-ies.** A medieval collection of allegorical fables about real and imaginary animals, each fable having a moral.
be·stir (bĭ-stûr') *v.* To cause to become active : rouse.
best man *n.* The principal attendant of a bridegroom.
be·stow (bĭ-stō') *v.* To give or present, esp. as an honor : confer. **—be·stow'al** *n.*
be·strew (bĭ-strōō') *v.* To strew.
be·stride (bĭ-strīd') *v.* **1.** To straddle. **2.** To step over. **3.** To tower over.
best seller *n.* A product, as a book, that is among those sold in the greatest numbers. **—best'-sell'ing** *adj.*
bet (bĕt) *n.* **1.** A wager. **2.** The fact, event, or outcome on which a wager is made. **3.** An object or amount risked in a wager : stake. *—v.* **bet** or **bet·ted, bet·ting. 1.** To stake (e.g., an amount) in a bet. **2.** To make a bet on (an outcome or a contestant). **3.** To maintain confidently.
bet. *abbr.* between.
be·take (bĭ-tāk') *v.* To cause (oneself) to go or move.
beta particle *n.* A high-speed electron or positron, usu. emitted by an atomic nucleus undergoing radioactive decay.
beta ray *n.* A stream of beta particles, esp. a stream of electrons.
beta rhythm *also* **beta wave.** *n.* The 2nd most common waveform observed in electroencephalograms of the adult brain, associated with an alert waking state.
be·ta·tron (bā'tə-trŏn', bē'-) *n.* An accelerator capable of raising electrons to energies of up to several hundred million electron volts.
be·tel (bēt'l) *n.* A climbing Asiatic plant, *Piper betle,* whose leaves are wrapped around the betel nut and chewed for a slightly inebriating effect.
betel nut *also* **be·tel·nut** (bēt'l-nŭt') *n.* The seed of the fruit of the betel palm.
bête noire (bĕt nwär') *n.* One particularly disliked or to be avoided.
be·think (bĭ-thĭngk') *v.* To remind (oneself) : remember.
Beth·le·hem (bĕth'lĭ-hĕm, -lē-əm). Town of W Jordan; traditionally, the birthplace of Jesus. *Pop.* 25,000.
be·tide (bĭ-tīd') *v.* To happen to or take place.
be·times (bĭ-tīmz') *adv.* **1.** In good time : early. **2.** *Archaic.* Soon : quickly.
be·to·ken (bĭ-tō'kən) *v.* To be or give a portent or sign of.
be·tray (bĭ-trā') *v.* **1. a.** To be a traitor to or commit treason against. **b.** To be unfaithful or disloyal to. **2.** To make known accidentally. **3.** To reveal : indicate. **4.** To lead astray : deceive. **—be·tray'al** *n.* **—be·tray'er** *n.*
be·troth (bĭ-trōth', -trôth') *v.* To promise to marry. **—be·troth'al** *n.*
be·trothed (bĭ-trōthd', -trôtht') *n.* A person to whom one is engaged to be married.
bet·ter[1] (bĕt'ər) *adj.* **1.** Higher in quality or greater in excellence. **2.** More satisfactory, suitable, useful, or desirable. **3.** Greater : larger. **4.** More healthy than before. *—adv.* **1.** In a more excellent manner. **2.** To a greater degree or extent. **3.** To greater advantage or use. **4.** In excess of : more <*better* than a mile>. *—n.* **1.** Something better. **2.** A superior, as in position, class, or intelligence. *—v.* **1.** To improve. **2.** To surpass : exceed.
bet·ter[2] (bĕt'ər) *n. var. of* BETTOR.
bet·ter·ment (bĕt'ər-mənt) *n.* An improvement.
bet·tor *also* **bet·ter** (bĕt'ər) *n.* One who bets.
be·tween (bĭ-twēn') *prep.* **1.** In the time or position separating. **2. a.** By the combined effect or effort of. **b.** In the combined ownership of <had a controlling interest *between* them> **3.** From one or another of. **—be·tween** *adv.*
be·twixt (bĭ-twĭkst') *prep. & adv. Archaic.* Between.
bev·a·tron (bĕv'ə-trŏn') *n.* An accelerator capable of raising protons to energies of about 1 billion electron volts.
bev·el (bĕv'əl) *n.* **1. a.** The surface formed when 2 planes meet at an angle other than 90°. **b.** The angle at which these planes meet. **2.** *also* **bevel square.** A rule having an adjustable arm, used to draw or measure angles or to fix a surface at an angle. *—v.* **-eled, -el·ing** or **-elled, -el·ling.** To slope or cut to slope at a bevel.
bevel gear *n.* Either of a pair of gears having teeth surfaces cut so that the gear shafts are not parallel.
bev·er·age (bĕv'ər-ĭj, bĕv'rĭj) *n.* A liquid for drinking, usu. other than water.
bev·y (bĕv'ē) *n., pl.* **-ies. 1.** A group of birds or animals, esp. larks or quail : flock. **2.** An assemblage : group.
be·wail (bĭ-wāl') *v.* To express sorrow or regret over. **—be·wail'er** *n.*
be·ware (bĭ-wâr') *v.* **-wared, -war·ing.** To be cautious (of).
be·whis·kered (bĭ-hwĭs'kərd, -wĭs'-) *adj.* Having whiskers.
be·wil·der (bĭ-wĭl'dər) *v.* To befuddle or confuse, esp. with conflicting statements or objects. **—be·wil'dered·ly** *adv.* **—be·wil'der·ment** *n.*
be·witch (bĭ-wĭch') *v.* **1.** To place under one's power by or as if by magic. **2.** To captivate totally : fascinate. **—be·witch'er·y** *n.* **—be·witch'ing** *adj.* **—be·witch'ing·ly** *adv.* **—be·witch'ment** *n.*
bey (bā) *n.* **1.** A provincial governor in the Ottoman Empire. **2.** A ruler of the former kingdom of Tunis. **3.** A Turkish title of honor and respect.
be·yond (bē-ŏnd', bĭ-yŏnd') *prep.* **1.** On or onto the far side of : past. **2.** Outside the scope or reach of. **3.** To a degree or amount greater than. **4.** In addition to : besides. **—be·yond'** *adv.*
bez·el (bĕz'əl) *n.* **1.** A slanting surface or bevel on the edge on a cutting tool. **2.** The upper faceted portion of a cut gem. **3.** A groove or flange that holds a beveled edge, as of a gem or watch crystal.
be·zique (bə-zēk') *n.* A card game similar to pinochle using a deck of 64 cards.
bf *also* **bf.** or **b.f.** *abbr.* boldface.
B/F *abbr. Accounting.* brought forward.
bg. *abbr.* bag.
Bhu·tan (bōō-tăn', -tän'). Country of C Asia, in the E Himalayas. *Cap.* Thimbu. *Pop.* 1,232,000. **—Bhu'tan·ese'** *adj. & n.*
Bi *symbol for* BISMUTH.
bi·a·ly (bē-ä'lē) *n., pl.* **-lys.** A baked roll with onion flakes on top.
bi·an·nu·al (bī-ăn'yōō-əl) *adj.* Taking place twice each year : semiannual. **—bi·an'nu·al·ly** *adv.*
bi·as (bī'əs) *n.* **1.** A line that cuts diagonally across the grain of fabric. **2.** An inclination or preference that interferes with impartial judgment : prejudice. *—adv.* On a diagonal : aslant. *—v.* **-ased, -as·ing** or **-assed, -as·sing.** To cause to have a prejudiced view.
bi·ath·lon (bī-ăth'lən, -lŏn') *n.* An athletic competition that combines events in rifle shooting and cross-country skiing.
bi·ax·i·al (bī-ăk'sē-əl) *adj.* Having 2 axes. **—bi·ax'i·al·ly** *adv.*
bib (bĭb) *n.* A cloth napkin tied under the chin and worn, esp. by children, to protect clothing while eating.
Bib. *abbr.* Bible; Biblical.
bi·be·lot (bē'bə-lō', bē-blō') *n.* A small ornamental object : trinket.
Bi·ble (bī'bəl) *n.* **1. a.** The sacred book of Christianity, including both the Old Testament and the New Testament. **b.** The Old Testament, the sacred book of Judaism. **2. bible** A book held to be authoritative in its field <the *bible* of Japanese cooking> **—Bib'li·cal, bib'li·cal** (bĭb'lĭ-kəl) *adj.* **—Bib'li·cal·ly, bib'li·cal·ly** *adv.*
Bible Belt *n.* Sections of the U.S., esp. in the South and Middle West, where Protestant fundamentalism prevails.
bibliog. *abbr.* bibliographer; bibliography.
bib·li·og·ra·phy (bĭb'lē-ŏg'rə-fē) *n., pl.* **-phies. 1.** A list of the works of an author or publisher. **2.** A list of works or sources of information in print on a particular subject. **3.** A list of works consulted by an author in the preparation of a book or article. **—bib'li·og'ra·pher** *n.* **—bib'li·o·graph'i·cal** (-ə-grăf'ĭ-kəl), **bib'li·o·graph'ic** *adj.* **—bib'li·o·graph'i·cal·ly** *adv.*
bib·li·o·ma·ni·a (bĭb'lē-ə-mā'nē-ə, -mān'yə) *n.* An exaggerated liking for acquiring books. **—bib'li·o·ma'ni·ac'** *n.*
bib·li·o·phile (bĭb'lē-ə-fīl') *also* **bib·li·oph·i·list** (bĭb'lē-ŏf'ə-lĭst) *n.* A book lover or collector.
bib·li·ot·ics (bĭb'lē-ŏt'ĭks) *n. (sing. in number).* Examination of documents to ascertain authorship or authenticity.

BOOKS OF THE BIBLE

HEBREW SCRIPTURES

Genesis	II Samuel	Joel	Haggai	Lamentations
Exodus	I Kings	Amos	Zechariah	Ecclesiastes
Leviticus	II Kings	Obadiah	Malachi	Esther
Numbers	Isaiah	Jonah	Psalms	Daniel
Deuteronomy	Jeremiah	Micah	Proverbs	Ezra
Joshua	Ezekiel	Nahum	Job	Nehemiah
Judges	THE TWELVE	Habakkuk	Song of Songs	I Chronicles
I Samuel	Hosea	Zephaniah	Ruth	II Chronicles

OLD TESTAMENT

Jerusalem Version	King James Version	Jerusalem Version	King James Version
Genesis	Genesis	Song of Solomon	Song of Solomon
Exodus	Exodus	Wisdom	
Leviticus	Leviticus	Ecclesiasticus	
Numbers	Numbers	Isaiah	Isaiah
Deuteronomy	Deuteronomy	Jeremiah	Jeremiah
Joshua	Joshua	Lamentations	Lamentations
Judges	Judges	Baruch	
Ruth	Ruth	Ezekiel	Ezekiel
I Samuel	I Samuel	Daniel	Daniel
II Samuel	II Samuel	Hosea	Hosea
I Kings	I Kings	Joel	Joel
II Kings	II Kings	Amos	Amos
I Chronicles	I Chronicles	Obadiah	Obadiah
II Chronicles	II Chronicles	Jonah	Jonah
Ezra	Ezra	Micah	Micah
Nehemiah	Nehemiah	Nahum	Nahum
Tobit		Habakkuk	Habakkuk
Judith		Zephaniah	Zephaniah
Esther	Esther	Haggai	Haggai
Job	Job	Zechariah	Zechariah
Psalms	Psalms	Malachi	Malachi
Proverbs	Proverbs	I Maccabees	
Ecclesiastes	Ecclesiastes	II Maccabees	

NEW TESTAMENT

Matthew	I Corinthians	II Thessalonians	I Peter
Mark	II Corinthians	I Timothy	II Peter
Luke	Galatians	II Timothy	I John
John	Ephesians	Titus	II John
Acts	Philippians	Philemon	III John
	Colossians	Hebrews	Jude
Romans	I Thessalonians	James	Revelation

bib•u•lous (bĭb′yə-ləs) *adj.* Given to or marked by drinking alcoholic beverages. **–bib′u•lous•ly** *adv.*

bi•cam•er•al (bī-kăm′ər-əl) *adj.* Composed of 2 legislative chambers.

bicarbonate of soda *n.* Sodium bicarbonate.

bi•cen•ten•ni•al (bī′sĕn-tĕn′ē-əl) *also* **bi•cen•ten•a•ry** (bī′sĕn-tĕn′ə-rē, bī-sĕn′tə-nĕr′ē) *adj.* **1.** Happening once very 200 years. **2.** Lasting for 200 years. **3.** Relating to a 200th anniversary or its celebration. **–bi′cen•ten′ni•al** *n.*

bi•ceps (bī′sĕps′) *n.* A muscle with 2 points of origin, esp.: **a.** The large muscle at the front of the upper arm. **b.** The large muscle at the back of the thigh. **–bi•cip′i•tal** (-sĭp′ĭ-tl) *adj.*

bi•chlo•ride (bī-klôr′īd′, -klōr′-) *n.* Dichloride.

bi•chro•mate (bī-krō′māt′, -mĭt) *n.* Dichromate.

bick•er (bĭk′ər) *v.* To engage in petty quarreling : squabble. **–bick′er** *n.*

bi•con•cave (bī′kŏn-kāv′, bī-kŏn′kāv′) *adj.* Concave on 2 surfaces. **–bi′con•cav′i•ty** (-kăv′ĭ-tē) *n.*

bi•con•vex (bī′kŏn-vĕks′, bī-kŏn′vĕks′) *adj.* Convex on 2 surfaces. **–bi′con•vex′i•ty** (-vĕk′sĭ-tē) *n.*

bi•cul•tur•al (bī-kŭl′chər-əl) *adj.* Of or pertaining to 2 distinct cultures in a single nation or geographic region. **–bi•cul′tur•al•ism** *n.*

bi•cus•pid (bī-kŭs′pĭd) *adj.* Having 2 points or cusps, as the crescent moon. *–n.* A bicuspid tooth, esp. a premolar.

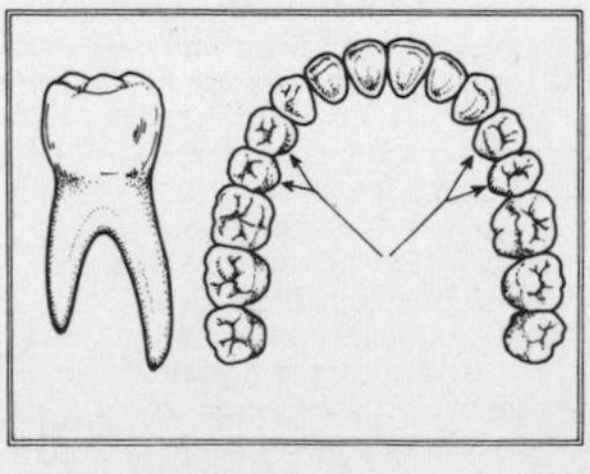

bicuspid

bi•cy•cle (bī′sĭk′əl, -sĭ-kəl) *n.* A lightweight vehicle consisting of a metal frame mounted on 2 spoked wheels and having a seat, handlebars for steering, and 2 pedals. *–v.* **-cled, -cling.** To ride or travel on a bicycle. **–bi′cy•clist** *n.*

bid (bĭd) *v.* **bade** (băd, bād) or **bid, bid•den** (bĭd′n) or **bid, bid•ding. 1.** To command : order. **2.** To utter (a salutation). **3.** To invite or send for. **4.** *p.t.* & *p.p.* **bid.** To state one's intention to take (tricks) in card games. **5.** *p.t.* & *p.p.* **bid.** To offer (an amount) as a price. **6.** *p.t.* & *p.p.* **bid.** To offer to pay or accept a specified price. *—n.* **1. a.** An offer of a specified price. **b.** The amount offered. **2.** An invitation. **3. a.** The act of bidding in card games. **b.** The number and suit of tricks or points declared. **c.** A player's turn to bid. **4.** An effort to attain something. **—bid'der** *n.*

bid·da·ble (bĭd'ə-bəl) *adj.* **1.** Capable of being bid. **2.** Obedient : tractable.

bid·dy[1] (bĭd'ē) *n., pl.* **-dies.** A hen or young chicken.

bid·dy[2] (bĭd'ē) *n., pl.* **-dies.** *Slang.* A woman, esp. a talkative old one.

bide (bīd) *v.* **bid·ed** *or* **bode** (bōd), **bid·ed, bid·ing. 1.** To remain : stay. **2.** To wait : tarry. **3.** To await <*bide* one's time>

bi·det (bē-dā') *n.* A low, basinlike bathroom fixture designed to be straddled for bathing the genital and anal areas.

bi·en·ni·al (bī-ĕn'ē-əl) *adj.* **1.** Living or lasting for 2 years. **2.** Occurring every 2nd year. *—n.* **1.** An event that occurs once every 2 years. **2.** *Bot.* A plant that lives only 2 years. **—bi·en'ni·al·ly** *adv.*

bier (bîr) *n.* A platform on which a coffin is placed before burial.

biff (bĭf) *v. Slang.* To punch. **—biff** *n.*

bi·fo·cal (bī-fō'kəl) *adj.* Having 2 different focal lengths.

bifocals *pl.n.* Lenses that correct for both distant and close vision.

bi·fur·cate (bī'fər-kāt', bī-fûr'-) *v.* **-cat·ed, -cat·ing.** To separate or divide into 2 branches or parts. **—bi'fur·cate'** *adj.* **—bi'fur·ca'tion** *n.*

big (bĭg) *adj.* **big·ger, big·gest. 1.** Of considerable size, intensity, quantity, extent, or magnitude : large. **2.** Grown-up : adult. **3.** Pregnant <*big* with child> **4. a.** Of great significance : momentous. **b.** Having or exercising considerable authority or influence : powerful. **c.** Conspicuous in position or wealth : prominent. **5.** Generous : bountiful. **6.** *Informal.* Boastful : self-important. ☆**syns:** CONSIDERABLE, EXTENSIVE, GOOD, GREAT, HEALTHY, LARGE, SIZABLE, TIDY *—adv.* **1.** A self-important or boastful way <talk *big*> **2.** With much success. **—big'gish** *adj.* **—big'ness** *n.*

big·a·my (bĭg'ə-mē) *n., pl.* **-mies.** *Law.* Entry into marriage with one person while still legally married to another. **—big'a·mous** *adj.* **—big'a·mist** *n.*

big bang theory *n.* A theory that the universe originated billions of years ago from a single violent eruption.

Big Dipper *n.* A cluster of 7 stars in the constellation Ursa Major, 4 forming a bowl and 3 the handle of a dipper.

Big·foot (bĭg'fo͝ot') *n.* The sasquatch.

big·head·ed (bĭg'hĕd'ĭd) *adj.* Conceited : egotistical. **—big'head'ed·ness** *n.*

big-heart·ed (bĭg'här'tĭd) *adj.* Kind : generous. **—big'-heart'ed·ly** *adv.* **—big'-heart'ed·ness** *n.*

big·horn (bĭg'hôrn') *n.* A sheep, *Ovis canadensis,* of W North American mountains, the male having massive horns.

bight (bīt) *n.* **1.** A loop or slack part in a rope. **2. a.** A curve or bend, esp. in a shoreline. **b.** A wide bay formed by such a curve.

big league *n.* **1.** A major league. **2.** *Informal.* Big time. **—big'-league'** *adj.*

big·mouth (bĭg'mouth') *n. Informal.* An indiscreet, gossipy, or loud-mouthed person. **—big'mouthed** *adj.*

big-name (bĭg'nām') *adj.* Well-known and highly popular.

big·ot (bĭg'ət) *n.* One fanatically devoted to one's own group, religion, race, or politics and intolerant of those who differ. **—big'ot·ed** *adj.* **—big'ot·ry** *n.*

big shot *n. Slang.* An influential or important person.

big time *n. Slang.* The most prestigious level of achievement in a competitive profession or field. **—big'-time'** *adj.*

big top *n. Informal.* **1.** The principal tent of a circus. **2.** The circus.

big wheel *n. Slang.* A person of importance or authority.

big·wig (bĭg'wĭg') *n. Slang.* A big wheel.

bike (bīk) *n. Informal.* **1.** A bicycle. **2.** A motorcycle. **—bike** *v.* **—bik'er** *n.*

bi·ki·ni (bĭ-kē'nē) *n.* **1.** A brief 2-piece bathing suit. **2.** Brief underpants that encircle the hips rather than the waist.

bi·lat·er·al (bī-lăt'ər-əl) *adj.* **1.** Relating to or having 2 sides : 2-sided. **2.** Undertaken by or affecting 2 parties : reciprocal <a *bilateral* trade agreement> **—bi·lat'er·al·ism** *n.* **—bi·lat'er·al·ly** *adv.*

bil·ber·ry (bĭl'bĕr'ē) *n.* Any of several shrubby plants of the genus *Vaccinium,* having edible blue or blackish berries.

bile (bīl) *n.* **1.** A bitter alkaline, brownish-yellow or greenish-yellow liquid secreted by the liver that helps digestion by saponifying fats. **2.** Ill temper : irascibility. **—bil'i·ar'y** (bĭl'ē-ĕr'ē) *adj.*

bilge (bĭlj) *n.* **1.** The lowest inner part of the hull of a ship. **2.** Water that seeps into and collects in the bilge. **3.** *Slang.* Nonsense. **—bilg'y** *adj.*

bi·lin·gual (bī-lĭng'gwəl) *adj.* **1.** Able to speak 2 languages with equal facility. **2.** Relating to or expressed in 2 languages. **—bi·lin'gual** *n.* **—bi·lin'gual·ly** *adv.*

bil·ious (bĭl'yəs) *adj.* **1.** Of, relating to, or containing bile. **2.** Relating to, characterized by or undergoing gastric distress caused by sluggishness of the gallbladder or liver. **3.** Irascible. **—bil'ious·ly** *adv.* **—bil'ious·ness** *n.*

bilk (bĭlk) *v.* To defraud, swindle, or cheat. *—n.* A swindle : hoax. **—bilk'er** *n.*

bill[1] (bĭl) *n.* **1.** An itemized list of fees or charges. **2.** A list of items, as a menu. **3.** An advertising poster or public notice. **4.** A piece of legal paper money. **5.** A commercial note, as a bill of exchange. **6.** A draft of a proposed law. **7.** *Law.* A document presented to a court containing a formal statement of a case, petition, or complaint. *—v.* **1.** To present a statement of charges or costs to. **2.** To enter on a statement of fees or charges. **3.** To advertise by public notice. **—bill'er** *n.*

bill[2] (bĭl) *n.* **1.** The horny beak of a bird. **2.** A beaklike mouth part, as of an octopus. **3.** The visor of a cap. *—v.* To touch beaks together. **—billed** *adj.*

bill·board (bĭl'bôrd', -bōrd') *n.* A structure for displaying advertisements.

bil·let (bĭl'ĭt) *n.* **1. a.** Board and lodging for troops, esp. in a civilian building. **b.** A written order directing provision of a billet. **2.** *Informal.* A position of employment : job. *—v.* To lodge or be lodged.

bil·let-doux (bĭl'ā-do͞o') *n., pl.* **bil·lets-doux** (-do͞o', -do͞oz'). A love letter.

bill·fold (bĭl'fōld') *n.* A folding, pocket-sized case for money and personal papers.

bil·liards (bĭl'yərdz) *n. (sing. in number).* A game played on an oblong table with raised, cushioned edges, using a cue to hit 3 small balls. **—bil'liard** *adj.*

bil·lings·gate (bĭl'ĭngz-gāt', -gĭt) *n.* Foul, abusive language.

bil·lion (bĭl'yən) *n.* **1.** The cardinal number equal to 10^9 : a thousand millions. **2.** *Brit.* The cardinal number equal to 10^{12} : a million millions. **—bil'lion** *adj.* & *pron.* **—bil'lionth** *n.* & *adj.* & *adv.*

bil·lion·aire (bĭl'yə-nâr') *n.* A person whose wealth amounts to at least 1 billion, as of dollars or pounds.

bill of exchange *n.* A written order for payment of a specified sum of money to a specified person.

bill of fare *n.* A menu.

bill of lading *n.* A receipt issued by a carrier promising delivery of the merchandise listed.

bill of rights *n.* **1.** A formal summary of the rights and liberties guaranteed to a people. **2. Bill of Rights.** The 1st 10 amendments to the U.S. Constitution.

bil·low (bĭl'ō) *n.* **1.** A large surge or swell of water : wave. **2.** A large surge, as of smoke. *—v.* **1.** To surge in billows. **2.** To swell out. **—bil'low·y** *adj.*

bil·ly club (bĭl'ē) *n.* A short wooden club, used esp. by police officers.

billy goat *n.* A male goat.

bi·lo·bate (bī-lō'bāt') *adj.* Divided into or having 2 lobes.

bil·tong (bĭl'tŏng', -tông') *n. So. Afr.* Narrow strips of meat dried in the sun.

bi·met·al·lism (bī-mĕt'l-ĭz'əm) *n.* The use of 2 metals, esp. gold and silver, as the monetary standard of currency.

bi·mod·al (bī-mŏd'l) *adj.* Having 2 distinct statistical modes. **—bi'mo·dal'i·ty** *n.*

bi·mo·lec·u·lar (bī'mə-lĕk'yə-lər) *adj.* Relating to, consisting of, or affecting 2 molecules. **—bi'mo·lec'u·lar·ly** *adv.*

bi·month·ly (bī-mŭnth'lē) *adj.* **1.** Occurring every 2 months. **2.** Occurring twice a month : semimonthly. *—n., pl.* **-lies.** A bimonthly publication. **—bi·month'ly** *adv.*

bin (bĭn) *n.* A container or enclosed storage space.

bi·na·ry (bī'nə-rē) *adj.* **1.** Composed of 2 different parts or components. **2.** Of or based on the number 2 or the binary numeration system. **3. a.** Consisting of 2 chemical elements. **b.** Containing 2 different kinds of atoms <a *binary* molecule> **—bi'na·ry** *n.*

binary digit *n.* Either of the digits 0 or 1, used to represent numbers in the binary numeration system.

binary numeration system *n.* A system of numeration based on 2, in which numerals are represented as sums of powers of 2 and in which all numerals can be written with the symbols 0 and 1.

binary star *n.* A system composed of 2 stars orbiting a common center of mass.

bi·na·tion·al (bī-năsh'ə-nəl, -năsh'nəl) *adj.* Of or involving 2 nations.

bin·au·ral (bī-nôr'əl) *adj.* **1.** Of or related to hearing with both ears. 2. Of or relating to sound transmission from 2 sources with varying acoustics. **–bin•au'ral•ly** *adv.*

bind (bīnd) *v.* **bound** (bound), **bind•ing.** 1. To secure, as with a rope or belt. 2. To fasten by encircling. 3. To bandage. 4. To restrain with or as if with bonds. 5. To obligate, as with a sense of moral duty. 6. *Law.* To place under legal obligation by contract or oath. 7. To cause to stick together in a mass. 8. To enclose and fasten (pages of a book) between protective covers. 9. To furnish with a border or edge for reinforcement or ornamentation. 10. To be tight and uncomfortable <*binds* across the shoulders> 11. To constipate. **–bind off.** To cast off in knitting. **–bind over.** *Law.* To hold on bail or place under bond. *–n. Informal.* A difficult situation.

bind•er (bīn'dər) *n.* 1. A notebook cover with rings or clamps for holding paper. 2. *Law.* A payment or written statement making an agreement legally binding.

bind•er•y (bīn'də-rē) *n., pl.* **-ies.** A place where books are bound.

bind•ing (bīn'dĭng) *n.* 1. Something that binds or is used as a binder. 2. The cover that holds together the pages of a book. 3. A strip over or along the edge of something for reinforcement or ornamentation. *–adj.* 1. Serving to bind. 2. Uncomfortably tight. 3. Obligatory.

bin•dle•stiff (bĭn'dl-stĭf') *n. Slang.* A hobo or migrant worker.

binge (bĭnj) *n. Slang.* 1. A spree. 2. A period of uncontrolled self-indulgence.

bin•go (bĭng'gō) *n.* A game of chance in which each player puts markers on a card with numbered squares in accordance with the numbers drawn by a caller.

bin•na•cle (bĭn'ə-kəl) *n.* The nonmagnetic stand that holds a ship's compass.

bin•oc•u•lar (bə-nŏk'yə-lər, bī-) *adj.* Relating to, used by, or involving both eyes simultaneously. *–n. often* **binoculars.** An optical device, as field glasses, designed for use by both eyes simultaneously.

bi•no•mi•al (bī-nō'mē-əl) *adj.* Composed of or relating to 2 names or terms. *–n.* 1. *Math.* An expression consisting of 2 terms joined by a plus or minus sign. 2. *Biol.* A taxonomic name. **–bi•no'mi•al•ly** *adv.*

bi•o•chem•is•try (bī'ō-kĕm'ĭ-strē) *n.* The chemistry of biological processes and substances. **–bi'o•chem'i•cal** *adj.* **–bi'o•chem'i•cal•ly** *adv.* **–bi'o•chem'ist** *n.*

bi•o•cide (bī'ə-sīd') *n.* A substance capable of destroying living organisms.

bi•o•de•grad•a•ble (bī'ō-dĭ-grā'də-bəl) *adj.* Able to be decomposed by natural processes.

bi•o•feed•back (bī'ō-fēd'băk') *n.* A technique in which a conscious attempt is made to control bodily functions that are considered involuntary, as heartbeat or blood pressure.

biog. *abbr.* biographer; biographical; biography.

bi•o•ge•og•ra•phy (bī'ō-jē-ŏg'rə-fē) *n.* Biological study of the geographic distribution of animals and plants. **–bi'o•ge'o•graph'ic** (-jē'ə-grăf'ĭk), **bi'o•ge'o•graph'i•cal** *adj.* **–bi'o•ge'o•graph'i•cal•ly** *adv.*

bi•og•ra•phy (bī-ŏg'rə-fē, bē-) *n., pl.* **-phies.** 1. A written account of someone's life. 2. Biographies as a whole. **–bi•og'ra•pher** *n.* **–bi'o•graph'i•cal** (bī'ə-grăf'ĭ-kəl), **bi'o•graph'ic** *adj.* **–bi'o•graph'i•cal•ly** *adv.*

bi•o•haz•ard (bī'ō-hăz'ərd, bī'ō-hăz-) *n.* A biological material, esp. if infective, that threatens humans or their environment.

biol. *abbr.* biological; biologist; biology.

biological clock *n.* An intrinsic biological mechanism responsible for the periodicity of certain classes of behavior in living organisms.

biological warfare *n.* Warfare in which disease-producing microorganisms or organic biocides are used to destroy human life, livestock, or crops.

bi•ol•o•gy (bī-ŏl'ə-jē) *n.* 1. The science of living organisms and life processes, including the study of growth, structure, and reproduction. 2. The life processes or characteristic phenomena of a group or category of living organisms. **–bi'o•log'i•cal** (bī'ə-lŏj'ĭ-kəl), **bi'o•log'ic** *adj.* **–bi'o•log'i•cal•ly** *adv.* **–bi•ol'o•gist** *n.*

bi•ome (bī'ōm') *n.* The entire community of living organisms in a single major ecological region.

bi•o•med•i•cine (bī'ō-mĕd'ĭ-sĭn) *n.* 1. The study of medicine in relationship to all biological systems. 2. The branch of medicine that deals with human response to environmental stress. **–bi'o•med'i•cal** *adj.*

bi•on•ics (bī-ŏn'ĭks) *n. (sing. in number).* The application of biological principles to the design and study of engineering systems, esp. electronic systems. **–bi•on'ic** *adj.* **–bi•on'i•cal•ly** *adv.*

bi•o•phys•ics (bī'ō-fĭz'ĭks) *n. (sing. in number).* The physics of biological processes. **–bi'o•phys'i•cal** *adj.* **–bi'o•phys'i•cal•ly** *adv.* **–bi'o•phys'i•cist** *n.*

bi•op•sy (bī'ŏp'sē) *n., pl.* **-sies.** The examination of tissues taken from a living organism, esp. for the presence of disease.

bi•o•rhythm (bī'ō-rĭth'əm) *n.* 1. An intrinsically patterned cyclical biological function or process. 2. The determining factor in a biorhythm.

bi•o•sphere (bī'ə-sfîr') *n.* The part of the earth, its waters, and atmosphere where organisms can live.

bi•o•ta (bī-ō'tə) *n.* The animal and plant life of a particular region.

bi•ot•ic (bī-ŏt'ĭk) *adj.* Relating to life or specific life conditions.

bi•o•tin (bī'ə-tĭn) *n.* A colorless crystalline vitamin usu. considered a part of the vitamin B complex and found in egg yolk, liver, milk, and yeast.

bi•o•type (bī'ə-tīp') *n.* A group of organisms with identical genetic but varying physical characteristics.

bi•par•ti•san (bī-pär'tĭ-zən, -sən) *adj.* Consisting of or supported by members of 2 political parties. **–bi•par'ti•san•ship'** *n.*

bi•par•tite (bī-pär'tīt') *adj.* 1. Having or being composed of 2 parts. 2. *Bot.* Divided into 2 <*bipartite* leaves>

bi•ped (bī'pĕd') *n.* An animal with 2 feet. **–bi'ped', bi•ped'al** *adj.*

bi•plane (bī'plān') *n.* An aircraft with wings fixed at 2 different levels.

bi•po•lar (bī-pō'lər) *adj.* 1. Relating to or having 2 poles. 2. Involving or concerning the earth's poles. **–bi'po•lar'i•ty** *n.*

bi•ra•cial (bī-rā'shəl) *adj.* Of, for, or composed of members of 2 races.

birch (bûrch) *n.* 1. A deciduous tree of the genus *Betula,* common in the N Hemisphere, with bark separable from the wood in sheets and hard close-grained wood. 2. A rod from a birch, used as a whip. *–v.* To whip with or as if with a birch rod.

bird (bûrd) *n.* 1. A member of the class Aves, which includes warm-blooded, egg-laying, feathered vertebrates having forelimbs modified to form wings. 2. A shuttlecock. 3. *esp. Brit.* A young woman. *–v.* To observe and identify birds in their natural habitat. **–bird'er** *n.*

bird•brain (bûrd'brān') *n. Slang.* A silly person. **–bird'brained'** *adj.*

bird•ie (bûr'dē) *n.* 1. A stroke under par for a hole in golf. 2. A shuttlecock.

bird•lime (bûrd'līm') *n.* A sticky substance smeared on twigs to trap small birds.

bird of paradise *n.* Any of various birds of the family Paradisaeidae, the male of which has brilliant plumage.

bird of passage *n.* A migratory bird.

bird of prey *n.* A predatory carnivorous bird, as the eagle or hawk : raptor.

bird's-eye (bûrdz'ī') *adj.* 1. Dappled or patterned with spots held to resemble birds' eyes. 2. Seen from high above or a great distance <a *bird's-eye* view of the terrain>

bi•reme (bī'rēm') *n.* An ancient galley with 2 tiers of oars on each side.

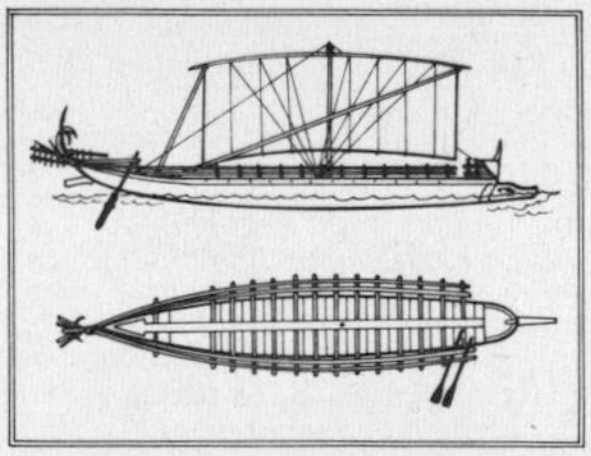

bireme

bi•ret•ta (bə-rĕt'ə) *n.* A square, stiff cap worn by Roman Catholic clergy.

birl•ing (bûr'lĭng) *n.* A game of skill, esp. among lumberjacks, in which 2 competitors try to balance on a floating log while spinning it with their feet. **–birl** *v.*

Bir•ming•ham (bûr'mĭng-hăm', -əm). 1. City of C England. *Pop.* 1,033,900. 2. City of NC Ala. *Pop.* 284,413.

birr (bîr) *n., pl.* **birr** *or* **birrs.** See CURRENCY TABLE.

†**birth** (bûrth) *n.* 1. a. The beginning of existence or the fact of being born. b. A beginning : origin. 2. The act of bearing young : parturition. 3. Ancestry : parentage. *–v. Regional.* To deliver or bear (a baby).

birth control *n.* Control of the number of children conceived, esp. by planned contraceptive techniques.

birth•day (bûrth′dā′) *n.* The day or anniversary of one's birth.
birth•mark (bûrth′märk′) *n.* A blemish or mole on the body since birth : nevus.
birth•place (bûrth′plās′) *n.* A place of birth or origin.
birth•rate (bûrth′rāt′) *n.* The number of births of a specified population per unit of time, esp. per year.
birth•right (bûrth′rīt′) *n.* **1.** A privilege granted to someone by virtue of birth. **2.** A privilege granted to a first-born.
birth•stone (bûrth′stōn′) *n.* A gemstone associated with the month of one's birth.
bis (bĭs) *adv.* Encore : again. Used esp. as a direction in music.
bis•cuit (bĭs′kĭt) *n.* **1.** A small cake of shortened bread leavened with baking powder or soda. **2.** *esp. Brit.* **a.** A cracker. **b.** A cookie.
bi•sect (bī′sĕkt′, bī-sĕkt′) *v.* **1.** To cut into 2 equal parts. **2.** To split into 2 parts : fork. **—bi′sec′tion** *n.* **—bi′sec′tor** *n.*
bi•sex•u•al (bī-sĕk′sho͞o-əl) *adj.* **1.** Of or relating to both sexes. **2.** *Biol.* Having both male and female organs : hermaphroditic. **3.** Having a sexual interest in members of both sexes. **—bi•sex′u•al** *n.* **—bi•sex′u•al′i•ty** *n.* **—bi•sex′u•al•ly** *adv.*
bish•op (bĭsh′əp) *n.* **1.** A Christian cleric of high rank, usu. governing a diocese. **2.** A chess piece that moves diagonally across unoccupied squares of the same color, with no limit as to number of squares.
bish•op•ric (bĭsh′ə-prĭk) *n.* The rank, office, or diocese of a bishop.
Bis•marck (bĭz′märk′). Cap. of N.Dak., in the SC part. *Pop.* 44,485.
Bis•marck (bĭz′märk). Prince **Otto Eduard Leopold von.** 1815–98. 1st chancellor of the German Empire (1871–90).
bis•muth (bĭz′məth) *n. Symbol* **Bi** A brittle, white, crystalline metallic element.
bi•son (bī′sən, -zən) *n.* A bovine mammal, *Bison bison,* of W North America, having a dark-brown coat and short, curved horns.
bisque[1] (bĭsk) *n.* **1.** A thick cream soup made from fish, shellfish, or puréed vegetables. **2.** A dessert of ice cream mixed with nuts or crushed macaroons.
bisque[2] (bĭsk) *n.* Clay that has been fired once, but not glazed.
Bis•sau (bĭ-sou′). Cap. of Guinea-Bissau, on an inlet of the Atlantic. *Pop.* 71,169.
bis•sex•tile (bī-sĕk′stĭl, -stīl′, bĭ-) *adj.* **1.** Of or relating to a leap year. **2.** Of or relating to the extra day falling in a leap year. —*n.* A leap year.
bis•tro (bē′strō, bĭs′trō) *n., pl.* **-tros.** A small nightclub or bar.
bit[1] (bĭt) *n.* **1.** A tiny portion, piece, or amount. **2.** A brief amount of time : moment. **3.** A regularly performed entertainment routine : act. **4.** *Slang.* A particular kind of behavior or activity. **5.** *Informal.* An amount equal to $\frac{1}{8}$ of a dollar. ☆***syns:*** GRAIN, IOTA, JOT, MODICUM, ORT, OUNCE, PARTICLE, SCRAP, SHRED, SMIDGEN, SMITCH, SPECK, TITTLE, WHIT
bit[2] (bĭt) *n.* **1. a.** A threaded, pointed tool designed for drilling and boring. **b.** The sharp part of a tool. **2.** The metal mouthpiece of a horse's bridle.
bit[3] (bĭt) *n. Computer Sci.* **1.** Either of 2 characters, as the binary digits 0 and 1, of a language that has 2 characters only. **2.** A unit of information equivalent to the choice between 2 alternatives having equal likelihood. **3.** A unit of information storage capacity, as of a computer memory.
bitch (bĭch) *n.* **1.** A female canine. **2.** *Slang.* **a.** A mean or spiteful woman. **b.** A lewd woman. **3.** A grievance : complaint. **4.** Something difficult or unpleasant. —*v. Slang.* **1.** To complain. **2.** To botch : bungle. **—bitch′er•y** *n.* **—bitch′i•ly** *adv.* **—bitch′i•ness** *n.* **—bitch′y** *adj.*
bite (bīt) *v.* **bit** (bĭt), **bit•ten** (bĭt′n) *or* **bit, bit•ing. 1.** To tear or cut with or as if with the teeth. **2. a.** To pierce the skin of, esp. with or as if with teeth or fangs. **b.** To cut into with a sharp tool. **3.** To eat into : corrode. **4.** To smart or sting or cause to smart or sting. **5.** To take or swallow bait. —*n.* **1. a.** The act or action of biting. **b.** A wound resulting from this. **2. a.** A smarting or stinging sensation. **b.** A sharp, incisive quality. **3.** An amount of food taken into the mouth at one time : mouthful. **4.** *Informal.* A light meal : snack. **5.** The angle at which the upper and lower teeth meet : occlusion. **—bit′er** *n.*
bit•ing (bī′tĭng) *adj.* **1.** Causing a stinging sensation. **2.** Penetrating : incisive.
bit•stock (bĭt′stŏk′) *n.* A handle or brace in which a boring or drilling bit is secured.
bit•ter (bĭt′ər) *adj.* **1.** Having or being a sharp, unpleasant taste. **2.** Causing or manifesting sharp physical or mental pain or discomfort : harsh. **3.** Caused by or exhibiting strong animosity. **4.** Marked by rancor or disappointment. —*v.* To make or become bitter. —*n.* **bitters.** A bitter, usu. alcoholic liquid made with roots or herbs, used esp. in mixed drinks. **—bit′ter•ly** *adv.* **—bit′ter•ness** *n.*
bit•tern (bĭt′ərn) *n.* A wading bird of the genera *Botaurus* and *Ixobrychus,* with mottled plumage and a deep, resonant call.
bit•ter•sweet (bĭt′ər-swēt′) *n.* A North American woody vine, *Celastrus scandens,* bearing orange or yellowish fruits that split open, exposing seeds enclosed in scarlet arils. —*adj.* **1.** Both bitter and sweet. **2.** Engendering both pain and pleasure.
bi•tu•men (bī-to͞o′mən, -tyo͞o′-, bĭ-) *n.* A mixture of hydrocarbons found in asphalt and tar or distilled from petroleum or coal. **—bi•tu′mi•nous** *adj.*
bituminous coal *n.* A grade of coal that contains a high percentage of bituminous material and burns with a smoky flame.
bi•va•lent (bī-vā′lənt) *adj.* **1.** *Chem.* Having valence 2. **2.** *Biol.* Composed of 2 homologous chromosomes or 2 sets of such chromosomes.
bi•valve (bī′vălv′) *n.* A mollusk, such as an oyster or clam, having a hinged, 2-part shell. **—bi′valve′, bi′valved′** *adj.*
biv•ou•ac (bĭv′o͞o-ăk′, bĭv′wăk′) *n.* A temporary, usu. open-air, military encampment. —*v.* To camp in a bivouac.
bi•week•ly (bī-wēk′lē) *adj.* **1.** Occurring every 2 weeks. **2.** Occurring twice a week : semiweekly. —*n., pl.* **-lies.** A publication issued every 2 weeks. **—bi•week′ly** *adv.*
bi•year•ly (bī-yîr′lē) *adj.* **1.** Occurring every 2 years. **2.** Occurring twice a year : semiyearly. **—bi•year′ly** *adv.*
bi•zarre (bĭ-zär′) *adj.* Extremely unconventional or far-fetched. **—bi•zarre′ly** *adv.* **—bi•zarre′ness** *n.*
Bk *symbol for* BERKELIUM.
bk. *abbr.* **1.** bank. **2.** book.
bkg. *abbr.* banking.
bkpg. *abbr.* bookkeeping.
bkpt. *abbr.* bankrupt.
bl. *abbr.* **1.** barrel. **2.** black. **3.** blue.
B/L *abbr.* bill of lading.
blab (blăb) *v.* **blabbed, blab•bing. 1.** To reveal (secret matters), esp. through indiscreet talk. **2. a.** To chatter indiscreetly. **b.** To gossip. —*n.* **1.** One who blabs. **2.** Lengthy chatter. **—blab′by** *adj.*
blab•ber (blăb′ər) *v.* To blab. —*n.* **1.** Idle chatter. **2.** BLAB 1. **—blab′ber•er** *n.*
blab•ber•mouth (blăb′ər-mouth′) *n. Slang.* An indiscreet, gossipy person.
black (blăk) *adj.* **1.** Being of the darkest achromatic visual value : having no predominant hue. **2.** Of or nearly of the color black. **3.** Having little or no light <a *black* and stormy night> **4.** *often* **Black.** Belonging to an ethnic group with dark skin : Negroid. **5.** Cheerless and depressing. **6.** Wicked : evil <a *black* lie> **7.** Angry : sullen. **8.** Soiled : dirty. ☆***syns:*** EBONY, INKY, JET, JETTY, ONYX, PITCH-BLACK, PITCHY, SABLE, SOOTY —*n.* **1.** An achromatic color value of minimum lightness or maximum darkness. **2.** Absence of light : darkness. **3.** Black clothing, esp. worn for mourning. **4.** *often* **Black.** A member of a Negroid people : Negro. —*v.* To blacken. **—black′ish** *adj.* **—black′ly** *adv.* **—black′ness** *n.*
black-and-blue (blăk′ən-blo͞o′) *adj.* Discolored by bruising.
black•ball (blăk′bôl′) *n.* **1.** A negative vote preventing an applicant's admission to an organization. **2.** A black ball used as a negative ballot. **—black′ball′** *v.*
black belt *n.* **1.** The rank of expert in a martial art, as karate. **2.** A person holding such a rank.
black•ber•ry (blăk′bĕr′ē) *n.* A woody plant of the genus *Rubus,* with usu. thorny stems and black edible berries.
black•bird (blăk′bûrd′) *n.* Any of various New World birds of the family Icteridae, as the grackle, of which the male has black or mostly black plumage.
black•board (blăk′bôrd′, -bōrd′) *n.* A smooth, hard, often dark-colored panel for writing on with chalk : chalkboard.
black•bod•y (blăk′bŏd′ē) *n.* A hypothetical body that would totally absorb all incident radiation.
black box *n.* A device or theoretical construct, esp. an electric circuit, having known or specified performance characteristics but unknown or unspecified constituents and means of operation.
black•en (blăk′ən) *v.* **1.** To make or become dark or black. **2.** To defame or sully. **—black′en•er** *n.*
black eye *n.* A discoloration of the flesh around the eye.
black-eyed Su•san (so͞o′zən) *n.* Any of several North American plants of the genus *Rudbeckia,* esp. *R. hirta,* with hairy stems and leaves and flowers that have orange-yellow petals and dark-brown centers.
black•guard (blăg′ərd, -ärd′) *n.* An unprincipled person : scoundrel.
black•head (blăk′hĕd′) *n.* A small plug of dried fatty matter capped with dust and epithelial debris that clogs a pore.

black-heart•ed (blăk′här′tĭd) *adj.* Wicked : evil.
black hole *n.* A small celestial body with an intense gravitational field believed to be a collapsed star.
black humor *n.* Morbid and absurd humor, esp. in its development as a literary genre. **–black humorist** *n.*
black•jack (blăk′jăk′) *n.* **1.** A leather-covered bludgeon with a short flexible strap or shaft. **2.** A card game in which each player tries to accumulate cards with a combined point count higher than that of the dealer but not greater than 21.
black light *n.* Invisible infrared or ultraviolet electromagnetic radiation.
black•list (blăk′lĭst′) *n.* A list of organizations or persons that are disapproved of or suspected of disloyalty. **–black′list′** *v.*
black magic *n.* Sorcery : witchcraft.
black•mail (blăk′māl′) *n.* **1.** Extortion, esp. of money, by threatening to expose a past criminal or discreditable act. **2.** Something, esp. money, extorted in this way. **–black′mail′** *v.* **–black′mail′er** *n.*

▲word history: *Blackmail* has nothing to do with the post office. *Black* is used in the figurative sense of "evil" or "wicked." *Mail* is a Scottish word meaning "rent" or "tribute." The term *blackmail* originated in Scotland, where Highland chiefs at one time extorted tribute from Lowlanders and Englishmen on the Scottish border in return for protection from being plundered.

Black Ma•ri•a (mə-rī′ə) *n.* A patrol wagon.
black market *n.* The illegal selling or buying of merchandise in violation of such restrictions as rationing or price control. **–black marketer, black marketeer** *n.*
Black Muslim *n.* A member of a black religious group that advocates the establishment of a black nation.
black•out (blăk′out′) *n.* **1.** The concealing or extinguishing of lights that might be seen by enemy aircraft crews during an air raid. **2.** Lack of illumination due to an electrical power failure. **3.** A temporary loss of consciousness or memory. **4.** A suppression or stoppage <a news *blackout*>
Black Power *n.* A movement among black Americans emphasizing social, economic, and political equality.
Black Sea. Inland sea between Europe and Asia Minor.
black sheep *n.* One considered discreditable by a respectable group or family.
black•smith (blăk′smĭth′) *n.* **1.** A person who shapes and forges iron with a hammer and anvil. **2.** A person who makes, repairs, and fits horseshoes.
black•top (blăk′tŏp′) *n.* A bituminous material, esp. asphalt, used to surface roads. **–black′top′** *v.*
black widow *n.* A New World spider, *Latrodectus mactans,* of which the extremely venomous female is black with red markings on the underside.

black widow
Female black widow hanging from web with male attached

blad•der (blăd′ər) *n.* **1.** Any of various expandable, usu. fluid-storing sacs found in most animals, esp. the urinary bladder. **2.** Something resembling a bladder.
blade (blād) *n.* **1. a.** The cutting part of a weapon or tool. **b.** A sword. **2. a.** A thin, flat part or section <the *blade* of a propeller> **b.** The metal part of an ice skate : runner. **3.** *Bot.* The leaf of a grass or similar plant. **4.** A dashing young man.
blah (blä) *Slang. n.* **1.** Nonsense. **2. blahs.** A feeling of dissatisfaction or discomfort. *–adj.* Dull and uninteresting.
Blake (blāk), **William.** 1757–1827. English poet and engraver.
blame (blām) *v.* **blamed, blam•ing. 1.** To hold (someone or something) at fault. **2.** To find fault with : censure. ☆***syns:*** CENSURE, CHARGE, CONDEMN, CRITICIZE, DENOUNCE, FAULT, PAN, RAP *–n.* **1.** Responsibility for a fault or error. **2.** Condemnation : censure. **–blam′a•ble, blame′a•ble** *adj.* **–blame′less** *adj.* **–blame′less•ness** *n.*
blame•wor•thy (blām′wûr′*th*ē) *adj.* Deserving blame. **–blame′wor′thi•ness** *n.*
blanch (blănch) *also* **blench** (blĕnch) *v.* **1.** To take the color from : bleach. **2.** To turn or cause to turn white or pale. **3.** To scald (vegetables).
bland (blănd) *adj.* **1.** Marked by a moderate, undisturbed, or tranquil quality. **2.** Lacking distinctive character : insipid. **–bland′ly** *adv.* **–bland′ness** *n.*
blan•dish (blăn′dĭsh) *v.* To coax by wheedling or flattery : cajole. **–blan′dish•er** *n.* **–blan′dish•ment** *n.*
blank (blăngk) *adj.* **1.** Bearing no markings, writing, or incisions. **2.** Not filled in : incomplete. **3.** Devoid of expression, thought, or feeling : vacant. **4.** Appearing dazed or bewildered. **5.** Absolute : utter. *–n.* **1.** An empty place : void. **2. a.** A space to be filled in on a document. **b.** A document with 1 or more such spaces. **3.** A cartridge containing powder but no bullet. **4.** An unfinished part or object, as a key form. *–v.* **1.** To obscure. **2.** To prevent (an opponent) from scoring in a sports contest. **–blank′ly** *adv.* **–blank′ness** *n.*
blank check *n.* Carte blanche.
blan•ket (blăng′kĭt) *n.* **1.** A piece of usu. woven material used as a covering, esp. on a bed. **2.** A thick covering layer. *–adj.* Covering or applying to a wide variety of requirements or conditions. **–blank′et** *v.*
blank verse *n.* Verse composed of lines that do not rhyme, usu. in iambic meter.
blare (blâr) *v.* **blared, blar•ing.** To sound or cause to sound loudly and stridently. **–blare** *n.*
blar•ney (blär′nē) *n.* **1.** Flattering talk. **2.** Nonsensical or deceptive talk.
bla•sé (blä-zā′, blä′zā) *adj.* **1.** Uninterested because of frequent exposure : bored. **2.** Extremely worldly and sophisticated.
blas•pheme (blăs-fēm′, blăs′fēm′) *v.* **-phemed, -phem•ing.** To speak of or address (something sacred, esp. God) impiously or irreverently. **–blas•phem′er** *n.* **–blas′phe•mous** *adj.* **–blas′phe•mous•ly** *adv.* **–blas′phe•my** *n.*
blast (blăst) *n.* **1.** A strong gust or stream of air or other gas, as steam. **2.** The act of blowing or the sound produced by blowing a wind instrument or whistle. **3.** An explosion or its effect. **4.** A violent verbal assault or outburst. **5.** *Slang.* A wild party or event. *–v.* **1.** To fragment by or as if by an explosion : smash. **2.** To blight : wither. **3.** *Informal.* To attack or criticize vigorously. **4.** *Slang.* To shoot. **–blast off.** To take off, as a space vehicle. **–blast′er** *n.*
blast•off *also* **blast-off** (blăst′ôf′, -ŏf′) *n.* A rocket or space vehicle launch.
blas•tu•la (blăs′chə-lə) *n., pl.* **-las** *or* **-lae** (-lē′). An early embryonic form consisting of a hollow cellular sphere. **–blas′tu•lar** *adj.* **–blas′tu•la′tion** *n.*
bla•tant (blāt′nt) *adj.* **1.** Unpleasantly and often vulgarly loud. **2.** Conspicuous, often offensively so : obvious. **–bla′tan•cy** *n.* **–bla′tant•ly** *adv.*
blath•er (blă*th*′ər) *v.* To talk nonsensically. **–blath′er** *n.* **–blath′er•er** *n.*
blaze[1] (blāz) *n.* **1. a.** A brilliant burst of fire. **b.** A bright, steady light or glare. **2.** A brilliant, striking display. **3.** A sudden outburst <a *blaze* of fury> **4. blazes.** *Slang.* Hell. **–blaze** *v.* **–blaz′ing•ly** *adv.*
blaze[2] (blāz) *n.* **1.** A white or light-colored spot or marking on the face of an animal. **2.** A mark cut or painted on a tree to indicate a trail. *–v.* **blazed, blaz•ing.** To mark (a trail) with blazes.
blaz•er (blā′zər) *n.* A lightweight, informal sports jacket.
bla•zon (blā′zən) *n.* **1.** *Heraldry.* A coat of arms. **2.** An ostentatious display. *–v.* **1.** *Heraldry.* To embellish with or as if with blazons. **2.** To announce : proclaim. **–bla′zon•er** *n.* **–bla′zon•ment** *n.* **–bla′zon•ry** *n.*
bldg. *abbr.* building.
bleach (blēch) *v.* **1.** To remove the color from. **2.** To become or cause to become white or colorless. *–n.* A chemical bleaching agent.
bleach•ers (blē′chərz) *pl.n.* An often unroofed open-air grandstand.
bleak (blēk) *adj.* **1.** Exposed to harsh, natural elements : barren. **2.** Cold and harsh : raw. **3. a.** Gloomy and somber : dreary. **b.** Discouraging : depressing. **–bleak′ly** *adv.* **–bleak′ness** *n.*
blear (blîr) *v.* **1.** To blur (the eyes) with or as if with tears. **2.** To blur : dim. **–blear′i•ly** *adv.* **–blear′i•ness** *n.* **–blear′y** *adj.*
bleat (blēt) *n.* The cry of a goat or sheep or a sound similar to this. **–bleat** *v.* **–bleat′er** *n.* **–bleat′ing•ly** *adv.*
bleed (blēd) *v.* **bled** (blĕd), **bleed•ing. 1.** To extract, emit, or lose blood. **2.** To be wounded. **3.** To feel sympathetic grief. **4.** To extract or exude sap or similar fluid. **5.** *Slang.* To obtain money, esp. by extortion. **6.** To become mixed or run, as dyes. **7.** To draw off (liquid or gaseous contents) from : drain. **–bleed′er** *n.*
bleed•ing-heart (blē′dĭng-härt′) *n.* **1.** Any of several plants of the genus *Dicentra* having nodding pink flowers. **2.** A person regarded as excessively sympathetic toward the underprivileged.

bleep (blēp) *n.* A brief high-pitched sound, as from an electronic device. **–bleep** *v.*
blem·ish (blĕm′ĭsh) *v.* To spoil or impair by a flaw. *–n.* A defect or flaw.
blench¹ (blĕnch) *v.* To recoil out of fear.
blench² (blĕnch) *v. var. of* BLANCH.
blend (blĕnd) *v.* **blend·ed** *or* **blent** (blĕnt), **blend·ing. 1.** To combine so as to make constituent parts indistinguishable. **2.** To mix (differing varieties or grades) thoroughly so as to obtain a new mixture. **3.** To merge or become merged into one : unite. **–blend** *n.* **–blend′er** *n.*
bless (blĕs) *v.* **blessed** *or* **blest** (blĕst), **bless·ing. 1. a.** To make holy : sanctify. **b.** To make the sign of the cross over. **2.** To call for divine favor upon. **3.** To honor as holy : praise. **4.** To confer well-being or prosperity upon.
bless·ed (blĕs′ĭd) *also* **blest** (blĕst) *adj.* **1.** Worthy of being worshiped or held in veneration : revered. **2.** *Rom. Cath. Ch.* Enjoying the eternal happiness of heaven. Used as a title for those who have been beatified. **3.** Enjoying or bringing happiness. **4.** *Slang.* Used as an intensive <without a *blessed* crumb> **–bless′ed·ly** *adv.* **–bless′ed·ness** *n.* **–bless′ing** *n.*
bless·ing (blĕs′ĭng) *n.* **1.** An act of one who blesses. **2.** Something contributing to well-being or prosperity : boon. **3.** Approval. **4.** A short prayer before a meal.
bleth·er (blĕth′ər) *v. & n. var. of* BLATHER.
blew (bloo͞) *v. p.t. of* BLOW.
blight (blīt) *n.* **1.** Any of several plant diseases. **2. a.** An adverse environmental influence or condition, as drought. **b.** An adverse social or psychological influence or condition. **–blight** *v.*
blight·er (blī′tər) *n. esp. Brit.* A worthless fellow.
blimp (blĭmp) *n.* An elongated aircraft with a gas-filled, nonrigid hull.
blind (blīnd) *adj.* **1.** Being without sight. **2.** Of or intended for sightless persons. **3.** Performed by instruments without using sight <*blind* flying> **4.** Unable or unwilling to understand <*blind* to their defects> **5.** Not based on reason or fact <*blind* belief> **6.** Hidden from sight <a *blind* curve><a *blind* seam> **7. a.** Closed at one end <a *blind* passageway> **b.** Without an opening <a *blind* wall> *–n.* **1.** Something that hinders vision or blocks out light. **2.** A shelter for concealment, esp. of hunters. **3.** A subterfuge. *–v.* **1.** To deprive of sight. **2.** To deprive of judgment or perception. **3.** To dazzle. **–blind′ly** *adv.* **–blind′ness** *n.*
blind date *n. Informal.* **1.** A date between 2 strangers, often arranged by a 3rd person. **2.** A person on a blind date.
blind·ers (blīn′dərz) *pl.n.* A pair of flaps attached to the bridle of a horse to restrict lateral vision.
blind·fold (blīnd′fōld′) *v.* To cover the eyes with or as if with a cloth or bandage. *–n.* A bandage covering the eyes to prevent seeing. **–blind′fold′** *adj. & adv.*
bli·ni (blē′nē) *pl.n.* Small pancakes served with caviar, sour cream, and herring.
blink (blĭngk) *v.* **1.** To close and open the eyes rapidly. **2.** To squint. **3.** To twinkle : gleam. *–n.* **1.** The act or action of closing and opening the eyes rapidly. **2.** A quick glimpse. **3.** A flash of light : twinkle. **–on the blink.** Out of order.
blink·er (blĭng′kər) *n.* **1.** A light that signals a message or warning by blinking. **2.** *Slang.* An eye.
blintz (blĭnts) *or* **blin·tze** (blĭn′tsə) *n.* A thin pancake usu. rolled and stuffed with cottage cheese.
blip (blĭp) *v.* **blipped, blip·ping.** To erase or override recorded sounds, as on a videotape. *–n.* **1.** The display of a pulse of information, as a spot of light on a radar screen or oscilloscope. **2.** A brief interruption in a broadcast as a result of blipping.
bliss (blĭs) *n.* **1.** Great happiness : joy. **2.** Ecstasy of salvation : spiritual joy. **–bliss′ful** *adj.* **–bliss′ful·ly** *adv.*
blis·ter (blĭs′tər) *n.* **1.** A thin, rounded swelling of the skin containing watery matter. **2.** An air bubble resembling a blister, as on a painted surface. **–blis′ter** *v.*
blis·ter·ing (blĭs′tər-ĭng) *adj.* **1.** Intensely hot. **2.** Severe : extreme.
blithe (blīth, blīth) *adj.* **blith·er, blith·est. 1.** Filled with gaiety : cheerful. **2.** Carefree : casual. **–blithe′ly** *adv.* **–blithe′ness** *n.* **–blithe′some** *adj.*
blitz (blĭts) *n.* **1.** A blitzkrieg. **2.** An intensive air raid or series of air raids. **3.** An intense campaign. **–blitz** *v.*
blitz·krieg (blĭts′krēg′) *n.* **1.** A sudden, swift military offensive. **2.** A swift, concerted effort.
bliz·zard (blĭz′ərd) *n.* A severe storm accompanied by heavy, driving snow.
blk. *abbr.* **1.** black. **2.** block. **3.** bulk.
bloat (blōt) *v.* **1.** To become or cause to become inflated or swollen. **2.** To puff up, as with vanity.
bloat·er (blō′tər) *n.* A lightly smoked and salted herring or mackerel.
blob (blŏb) *n.* **1.** A soft, amorphous mass. **2.** A shapeless splotch or daub, esp. of color.
bloc (blŏk) *n.* A group united for common action <the Eastern *bloc*><the oil *bloc*>
block (blŏk) *n.* **1.** A solid piece, as of wood, with one or more flat sides. **2.** A stand from which auctioned articles are sold. **3.** A pulley or system of pulleys in a frame. **4.** A set of like items, as shares of stock, sold or handled as a unit. **5. a.** An act of hindering or obstructing. **b.** A hindrance or obstacle. **6. a.** A section of a city or town bounded by 4 intersecting streets. **b.** The part of a street bounded by consecutive streets. **7.** *Can.* A group of townships in an unsurveyed area. **8.** Interruption, esp. obstruction of a neural or digestive process. **9.** *Psychol.* The sudden stopping of a thought process with no immediately seeable cause. *–v.* **1.** To support or keep in place with a block. **2.** To shape with or on a block. **3.** To stop or impede movement through : obstruct. **–on the block.** Up for sale, esp. at an auction. **–block′age** *n.* **–block′er** *n.* **–block′ish** *adj.*
block·ade (blŏ-kād′) *n.* **1.** Closure of an area, as a harbor, to entrance and exit of traffic. **2.** The forces used in a blockade. **–block′ade′** *v.* **–block·ad′er** *n.*
block and tackle *n.* Pulley blocks and ropes or cables used to hoist heavy objects.
block·bust·er (blŏk′bŭs′tər) *n. Informal.* **1.** A bomb having the capacity to destroy an entire city block. **2.** Something notably effective or successful.
block·bust·ing (blŏk′bŭs′tĭng) *n. Informal.* A real estate practice of inducing homeowners to sell by appealing to the fear that property values will decline because minority groups are about to move into the neighborhood.
block·head (blŏk′hĕd′) *n.* A dolt.
block·house (blŏk′hous′) *n.* **1.** A military fortification with small openings for observation and firing weapons. **2.** A strongly reinforced building used for observation of missile and weapons tests.
blond (blŏnd) *adj.* **1.** Having pale-colored hair and skin and usu. light eyes. **2.** Of a flaxen or golden color or of any light shade of auburn or brown. **–blond** *n.* **–blond′ish** *adj.* **–blond′ness** *n.*
blonde (blŏnd) *adj.* Blond. *–n.* A blonde woman or girl.
blood (blŭd) *n.* **1. a.** The fluid that is circulated by the heart through the vertebrate vascular system and carries oxygen and nutrients throughout the body and wastes to excretory channels. **b.** A fluid that has similar functions in an invertebrate. **c.** A fluid resembling blood, as the juice of some plants. **2.** Life : lifeblood. **3.** Bloodshed. **4.** Disposition : temperament. **5.** Kinship. **6.** Racial or national ancestry <of Irish *blood*> **7.** A dashing young man : blade. *–adj.* Purebred <a *blood* mare> **–blood′less** *adj.* **–blood′less·ly** *adv.*
blood bank *n.* A place where plasma or whole blood is typed, processed, and stored for future use.
blood bath *n.* A massacre.
blood count *n.* Determination of the number of red and white corpuscles in a specific volume of blood.
blood·cur·dling (blŭd′kûrd′lĭng) *adj.* Causing great horror : terrifying.
blood·ed (blŭd′ĭd) *adj.* **1.** Having blood or a temperament of a certain kind <Reptiles are cold-*blooded.*><hot-*blooded* youth> **2.** Thoroughbred.
blood group *n.* Any of several immunologically distinct, genetically determined classes of human blood.
blood·hound (blŭd′hound′) *n.* **1.** A hound with a smooth coat, drooping ears, and a keen sense of smell. **2.** *Informal.* One who pursues relentlessly.
blood·let·ting (blŭd′lĕt′ĭng) *n.* **1.** Bleeding of a vein as therapy. **2.** Bloodshed.
blood·line (blŭd′līn′) *n.* Direct line of descent : pedigree.
blood·mo·bile (blŭd′mə-bēl) *n.* A vehicle equipped for collecting blood from donors for blood banks.
blood poisoning *n.* **1.** Toxemia. **2.** Septicemia.
blood pressure *n.* The pressure of the blood against arterial walls.
blood serum *n.* Blood plasma with the fibrin removed.
blood·shed (blŭd′shĕd′) *n.* The shedding of blood, esp. by injuring or killing.
blood·shot (blŭd′shŏt′) *adj.* Red and irritated.
blood·stream *also* **blood stream** (blŭd′strēm′) *n.* The blood circulating in the vascular system of a living body.
blood·suck·er (blŭd′sŭk′ər) *n.* **1.** An animal, as a leech, that sucks blood. **2.** *Informal.* A person who clings to or preys upon another : parasite. **–blood′suck′ing** *adj.*
blood·thirst·y (blŭd′thûr′stē) *adj.* Thirsting for or character-

ized by bloodshed : murderous. **–blood′thirst′i•ly** *adv.* **–blood′thirst′i•ness** *n.*
blood type *n.* Blood group.
blood vessel *n.* A tubular canal through which blood circulates : an artery, vein, or capillary.
blood•y (blŭd′ē) *adj.* **-i•er, -i•est. 1.** Stained with blood. **2.** Of, characteristic of, or containing blood. **3.** Accompanied by or giving rise to bloodshed. **4.** Cruel : bloodthirsty. **5.** Used as an intensive <a *bloody* idiot> *–adv.* Used as an intensive <*bloody* well right> *–v.* **-ied, -y•ing.** To stain with or as if with blood. **–blood′i•ly** *adv.* **–blood′i•ness** *n.*
bloom (blo͞om) *n.* **1.** The blossoms of a plant. **2. a.** The state or time of bearing flowers. **b.** A state or time of vigor, freshness, and beauty : prime. **3.** A healthy, rosy complexion. **4.** *Bot.* A fine, powder layer that coats certain fruits, leaves, and stems. **5.** An excessive planktonic growth in a body of water. *–v.* **1.** To bear flowers. **2.** To shine with health. **3.** To flourish. **☆syns:** BLOSSOM, BURGEON, EFFLORESCE, FLOWER
bloo•mers (blo͞o′mərz) *pl.n.* **1.** Wide, loose trousers gathered at the knee, formerly worn by women and girls for athletics. **2.** Underpants of similar design.
bloop•er (blo͞o′pər) *n.* **1.** *Baseball.* A weak fly ball. **2.** *Informal.* A faux pas.
blos•som (blŏs′əm) *n.* **1.** A flower or mass of flowers, esp. of a plant that bears edible fruit. **2.** The state or time of flowering. *–v.* **1.** To come into flower : bloom. **2.** To develop : flourish.
blot (blŏt) *n.* **1.** A stain : spot. **2.** A moral stigma : disgrace. *–v.* **blot•ted, blot•ting. 1.** To stain or spot. **2.** *Obs.* To disgrace morally. **3.** To cancel or obliterate. **4.** To darken. **5.** To soak up or dry with absorbent material. **6.** To spill or spread in a blot. **7.** To become blotted.
blotch (blŏch) *n.* **1.** A spot : blot. **2.** A discolored area on the skin : blemish. **–blotch** *v.* **–blotch′i•ly** *adv.* **–blotch′i•ness** *n.* **–blotch′y** *adj.*
blot•ter (blŏt′ər) *n.* **1.** A piece or a pad of blotting paper. **2.** A book that contains daily records.
blotting paper *n.* Absorbent paper used to blot up excess ink.
blouse (blous, blouz) *n.* **1.** A loosely fitting shirt extending to or below the waist. **2.** The coat or tunic worn by members of the U.S. Army. *–v.* **bloused, blous•ing.** To hang or cause to hang loose and full.
blow¹ (blō) *v.* **blew** (blo͞o), **blown** (blōn), **blow•ing. 1.** To be in a state of motion, as air. **2.** To move or cause to move by or as if by a current of air. **3. a.** To expel a current of air, as from the mouth. **b.** To expel a current of air, as from a bellows. **4.** To sound or cause to sound by expelling a current of air, as in playing an instrument. **5.** To breathe hard : pant. **6.** To burst or cause to burst. **7.** To burn out or melt, as a fuse. **8.** To spout air and water, as a whale. **9.** To shape or form (e.g., glass) by forcing air or gas through at the end of a pipe. **10.** To free of obstruction by forcing air through. **11.** *Slang.* To spend (money) freely. **12.** *Slang.* To handle ineptly. **13.** *Slang.* To depart in a great hurry <*blew* town> **–blow in.** *Slang.* To arrive. **–blow out. 1.** To extinguish or be extinguished by blowing <*blew out* the candle> **2.** To fail, as an electrical device. **–blow up. 1.** To come into being <A squall *blew up.*> **2.** To fill with air : inflate. **3.** To enlarge (a photographic image or print). **4.** *Slang.* To lose one's temper. *–n.* **1. a.** A blast of air or wind. **b.** A storm. **2.** An act or instance of blowing. **3.** *Slang.* An act of bragging.
blow² (blō) *n.* **1.** A sudden hard hit, as with the fist or a club. **2.** An unexpected shock. **3.** An unexpected attack.
blow³ (blō) *n.* A mass of blossoms. *–v.* **blew** (blo͞o), **blown** (blōn), **blow•ing.** To bloom or cause to bloom.
blow-by-blow (blō′bī-blō′) *adj.* Marked by careful attention to detail.
blow-dry (blō′drī′) *v.* To dry and usu. style with a small, hand-held hair dryer. **–blow′-dry′er** *n.*
blow•er (blō′ər) *n.* **1.** One that blows, esp. a fan. **2.** *esp. Brit.* A telephone.
blow•fly (blō′flī′) *n.* Any of several flies of the family Calliphoridae that deposit their eggs in carrion or in open wounds.
blow•gun (blō′gŭn′) *n.* A long narrow pipe through which pellets or darts are blown.
blow•hard (blō′härd′) *n. Slang.* A braggart.
blow•hole (blō′hōl′) *n.* **1.** A nostril on the head of whales and other cetaceans. **2.** A hole in ice to which aquatic mammals, as dolphins, come to breathe.
blow•out (blō′out′) *n.* **1.** A sudden bursting, as of a tire. **2.** An abrupt escape of confined gas. **3.** *Slang.* A large party : bash.
blow•torch (blō′tôrch′) *n.* A usu. portable gas burner that generates a hot flame used to melt and weld soft metals.
blow•up (blō′ŭp′) *n.* **1.** An explosion. **2.** A violent outburst of temper. **3.** A photographic enlargement.
blow•y (blō′ē) *adj.* **-i•er, -i•est.** Windy.
blow•zy *also* **blow•sy** (blou′zē) *adj.* **-zi•er, -zi•est** *also* **-si•er, -si•est. 1.** Having a coarse bloated appearance. **2.** Disheveled and frowzy : unkempt.
BLT (bē′ĕl-tē′) *n.* A bacon, lettuce, and tomato sandwich.
blub•ber¹ (blŭb′ər) *v.* **1.** To sob noisily. **2.** To utter while sobbing. **–blub′ber•er** *n.* **–blub′ber•ing•ly** *adv.*
blub•ber² (blŭb′ər) *n.* **1.** The thick fat between the skin and muscle layers of whales and other marine mammals. **2.** Excessive body fat. **–blub′ber•y** *adj.*
bludg•eon (blŭj′ən) *n.* A short, heavy, usu. wooden club that has one end loaded or thicker than the other. *–v.* **1.** To strike with or as if with a bludgeon. **2.** To bully or threaten. **–bludg′eon•er** *n.*
blue (blo͞o) *n.* **1.a.** Any of a group of colors whose hue is that of a clear sky : the hue of that portion of the spectrum lying between green and violet. **b.** A pigment of this color. **c.** An object of the color blue. **2.** *often* **Blue.** The Union Army in the Civil War. *–adj.* **blu•er, blu•est. 1.** Of the color blue. **2.** Bluish. **3.** Having a gray or purplish color, as from cold. **4.** *Informal.* Depressed or depressing. **5.** Risqué : indecent. *–v.* **blued, blu•ing.** To make or become blue. **–blue′ly** *adv.* **–blue′ness** *n.* **–blu′ish, blue′ish** *adj.*
blue baby *n.* An infant born with bluish skin caused by inadequate oxygenation of the blood.
blue•bell (blo͞o′bĕl′) *n.* Any of several plants bearing blue, bell-shaped flowers.
blue•ber•ry (blo͞o′bĕr′ē) *n.* A North American shrub of the genus *Vaccinium,* bearing small, edible berries.
blue•bird (blo͞o′bûrd′) *n.* Any of several North American birds of the genus *Sialia,* with blue plumage and in the male of most species a reddish breast.
blue-black (blo͞o′blăk′) *adj.* Very dark blue in color.
blue blood *n.* **1.** Aristocratic descent. **2.** A member of the aristocracy. **–blue′-blood′ed** *adj.*
blue•bot•tle (blo͞o′bŏt′l) *n.* Any of several flies of the genus *Calliphora* that have bright metallic-blue bodies and breed in decaying organic matter.
blue cheese *n.* A semisoft cheese veined with a greenish-blue mold.
blue chip *n.* A stock selling at a high price due to public confidence in its record of consistently steady earnings over the long term. **–blue′-chip′** *adj.*

▲word history: Blue chips in poker are usu. the chips with the highest value. It is from this usage that the term *blue chip* is applied to highly regarded stocks.

blue-col•lar (blo͞o′kŏl′ər) *adj.* Of or relating to wage earners, esp. as a class, whose tasks are performed in work clothes.
blue•fish (blo͞o′fĭsh′) *n.* A voracious food and game fish, *Pomatomus saltatrix,* of temperate and tropical waters of the Atlantic and Indian oceans.
blue•grass (blo͞o′grăs′) *n.* **1.** A grass of the genus *Poa,* esp. *P. pratensis,* native to Eurasia but naturalized throughout North America. **2.** Folk music of the S U.S., usu. played on banjos and guitars in rapid tempos with jazzlike improvisation.
blue-green alga (blo͞o′grēn′) *n.* An alga of the division Cyanophyta or Myxophyceae, one of the simplest plant forms.
blue•ing (blo͞o′ĭng) *n. var. of* BLUING.
blue jay *n.* A North American bird, *Cyanocitta cristata,* having predominantly blue plumage and a crested head.
blue jeans *pl.n.* JEANS 2.
blue law *n.* A law aimed at regulating Sunday commercial activities.
blue•nose (blo͞o′nōz′) *n.* A person who is puritanical.
blue•print (blo͞o′prĭnt′) *n.* **1.** A photographic reproduction, as of architectural plans or technical drawings, with white lines on a blue background. **2.** A carefully designed and usu. detailed plan of action. **–blue′print′** *v.*
blue ribbon *n.* A first prize. **–blue′rib′bon** *adj.*
blues (blo͞oz) *pl.n. (sing. or pl. in number).* **1.** A state of depression. **2.** A style of jazz developed from American Negro secular songs.
blue spruce *n.* An evergreen tree, *Picea pungens,* of the Rocky Mountain region, bearing bluish-green needles.
blue•stock•ing (blo͞o′stŏk′ĭng) *n.* A scholarly or pendantic woman. **–blue′stock′ing** *adj.*

▲word history: The term *bluestocking* orig. signified one who was informally and unfashionably dressed in blue worsted rather than black silk stockings. Such informal wear was common at literary and intellectual gatherings in 18th-cent. London, which were scornfully dubbed "bluestocking" societies, and the term *bluestocking* was transferred, sneer and all, to any woman with aspirations to literature and learning.

blu•ets (blo͞o′ĭts) *n. (sing. or pl. in number).* A low-growing plant, *Houstonia caerulea,* of E North America, having small, light-blue flowers with yellow centers.

blue whale *n.* A very large whale, *Sibbaldus musculus,* with a bluish-gray back.
bluff[1] (blŭf) *v.* **1.** To mislead or deceive. **2.** To impress or intimidate by showing more confidence than the facts support. **3.** To engage in a false display of strength. **–bluff** *n.* **–bluff′a•ble** *adj.* **–bluff′er** *n.*
bluff[2] (blŭf) *n.* A steep headland, promontory, river bank, or cliff. *–adj.* **1.** Having a broad, steep front. **2.** Having a blunt and rough but not unkind manner. **–bluff′ly** *adv.* **–bluff′ness** *n.*
blu•ing *also* **blue•ing** (blo͞o′ĭng) *n.* **1.** A coloring agent for counteracting the yellowing of laundered fabrics. **2.** A rinsing agent for giving a silver tint to graying hair.
blun•der (blŭn′dər) *n.* A mistake usu. caused by ignorance or miscalculation. *–v.* **1.** To move unsteadily or clumsily. **2.** To make a blunder. **–blun′der•er** *n.* **–blun′der•ing•ly** *adv.*
blun•der•buss (blŭn′dər-bŭs′) *n.* A short musket with a flaring muzzle, once used to scatter shot at close range.
blunt (blŭnt) *adj.* **1.** Having a dull edge or end. **2.** Abrupt and frank : brusque. *–v.* **1.** To make or become blunt. **2.** To make less effective : weaken. **–blunt′ly** *adv.* **–blunt′ness** *n.*
blur (blûr) *v.* **blurred, blur•ring. 1.** To make or become hazy and indistinct : obscure. **2.** To smear or stain : smudge. **3.** To lessen the perception of : dim. *–n.* **1.** A smear or blot : smudge. **2.** Something hazy and indistinct. **–blur′ri•ly** *adv.* **–blur′ri•ness** *n.* **–blur′ry** *adj.*
blurb (blûrb) *n.* A brief publicity notice, as on the jacket of a book.
blurt (blûrt) *v.* To speak suddenly and impulsively.
blush (blŭsh) *v.* **1.** To become red in the face esp. from modesty, embarrassment, or shame : flush. **2.** To become red or rosy. **3.** To feel ashamed or embarrassed. **–blush** *n.* **–blush′ful** *adj.* **–blush′ing•ly** *adv.*
blush•er (blŭsh′ər) *n.* **1.** One that blushes. **2.** Make-up for giving a rosy tint to the face and esp. the cheekbones.
blus•ter (blŭs′tər) *v.* **1.** To blow in violent and noisy gusts, as wind in a storm. **2. a.** To act or speak with noisy threats or boasts. **b.** To bully. **–blus′ter** *n.* **–blus′ter•er** *n.* **–blus′ter•y** *adj.*
blvd. *abbr.* boulevard.
b.o. *abbr.* **1.** box office. **2.** branch office. **3.** buyer's option.
bo•a (bō′ə) *n.* **1.** Any of various large, nonvenomous, chiefly tropical snakes of the family Boidae, including the anaconda and boa constrictor, that coil around and suffocate their prey. **2.** A long, fluffy scarf made of soft material such as feathers.
boar (bôr, bōr) *n.* **1.** A male pig. **2.** A wild pig, *Sus scrofa,* of Eurasia and N Africa, that is the ancestor of the domestic hog.
board (bôrd, bōrd) *n.* **1.** A long, flat slab of sawed lumber : plank. **2. a.** A flat piece of rigid material, as wood, adapted for a special use. **b.** A flat surface on which a game is played. **3. a.** A table, esp. one set for serving a meal. **b.** Food or meals as a whole <room and *board*> **4.** A table at which official meetings are held. **5.** An organized body of administrators or investigators <*board* of directors> <*board* of inquiry> **6. boards.** A theater stage. **7.** *Naut.* The side of a ship <lee*board*> <over*board*> **–on board.** Aboard. *–v.* **1.** To close or cover with boards. **2.** To furnish or receive meals or lodging or both, in return for pay. **3.** To enter or go aboard (a vehicle or ship). **4.** To come alongside (a ship).
board•er (bôr′dər, bōr′-) *n.* A person who pays a set amount for regular meals or for meals and lodging.
boarding house *also* **board•ing•house** (bôr′dĭng-hous′, bōr′-) *n.* A house where lodging and meals are provided.
board•walk (bôrd′wôk′, bōrd′-) *n.* A wooden promenade along a waterfront.
boast (bōst) *v.* **1.** To speak with excessive pride, esp. about one's own accomplishments, abilities, or possessions : brag. **2.** To take pride in or be enhanced by the possession of. **3.** To possess <The college *boasts* a new art gallery.> *–n.* **1.** An act of bragging. **2.** A source of pride. **–boast′er** *n.* **–boast•ful** *adj.* **–boast′ful•ly** *adv.* **–boast′ful•ness** *n.*
boat (bōt) *n.* **1.** A rather small, usu. open craft. **2.** A ship. **3.** A boat-shaped dish <a gravy *boat*> **–boat** *v.* **–boat′ing** *n.* **–boat′man** *n.*
boat•er (bō′tər) *n.* **1.** One who boats. **2.** A stiff straw hat with a flat crown.
boat•swain *also* **bo's'n** *or* **bos'n** *or* **bo•sun** (bō′sən) *n.* A petty officer or warrant officer in charge of the deck crew, rigging, cables, and anchors of a ship.
bob[1] (bŏb) *v.* **bobbed, bob•bing. 1.** To move or cause to move up and down. **2.** To curtsey or bow. **3.** To grab for with the teeth <*bob* for apples> **–bob up.** To appear or arise suddenly. *–n.* A quick, jerky movement of the head or body.
bob[2] (bŏb) *n.* **1.** A small, knoblike, hanging object, as a plumb bob. **2.** A fishing float or cork. **3.** A short haircut. *–v.* **bobbed, bob•bing. 1.** To fish with a bob. **2.** To cut short, as hair. **–bob′ber** *n.*
bob[3] (bŏb) *n., pl.* **bob.** *Brit.* A shilling.
bob•bin (bŏb′ĭn) *n.* A spool or reel that holds yarn or thread, as for sewing.
bob•ble (bŏb′əl) *v.* **-bled, -bling. 1.** To bob up and down. **2.** To fumble (e.g., a ball). *–n.* A mistake : blunder.
bob•by (bŏb′ē) *n., pl.* **-bies.** *Brit.* A police officer.
bobby pin *n.* A thin, flat usu. metal hair clip with closely pressed together ends.
bobby socks *also* **bobby sox** *pl.n. Informal.* Ankle socks.
bob•by•sox•er (bŏb′ē-sŏk′sər) *n. Informal.* A teen-aged girl.
bob•cat (bŏb′kăt′) *n.* A North American wildcat, *Lynx rufus,* having spotted reddish-brown fur, tufted ears, and a very short tail.
bob•o•link (bŏb′ə-lĭngk′) *n.* A migratory American songbird, *Dolichonyx oryzivorus,* of which the male has black, white, and yellowish plumage.
bob•sled (bŏb′slĕd′) *n.* **1.** A long racing sled with a steering mechanism to control the front runners. **2. a.** A long sled made of 2 shorter sleds joined in tandem. **b.** Either of these 2 smaller sleds. **–bob′sled′** *v.*
bob•stay (bŏb′stā′) *n.* A rope or chain for steadying a ship's bowsprit.
bob•tail (bŏb′tāl′) *n.* **1.** A short or shortened tail. **2.** An animal, as a horse, having a bobtail. **–bob′tailed′** *adj.*
bob•white (bŏb-hwīt′, -wīt′) *n.* A small North American quail, *Colinus virginianus,* having brown plumage with white markings.
Boc•cac•cio (bō-kä′chē-ō′), **Giovanni.** 1313–75. Italian author.
boc•cie *or* **boc•ci** *or* **boc•ce** (bŏch′ē) *n.* A game originating in Italy that is played with wooden balls on a long narrow court.
bock beer (bŏk) *n.* A dark strong springtime beer.
bode[1] (bōd) *v.* **bod•ed, bod•ing.** To be a sign or omen of : signify.
bode[2] (bōd) *v. p.t. of* BIDE.
bod•ice (bŏd′ĭs) *n.* **1.** The part of a dress extending from the waist to the shoulder. **2.** *Obs.* A corset.
bod•i•less (bŏd′ē-lĭs) *adj.* Having no form or substance.
bod•i•ly (bŏd′l-ē) *adj.* **1.** Of, relating to, situated in, or exhibited by the body. **2.** Physical rather than mental or spiritual. *–adv.* **1.** In the flesh : in person. **2.** As a complete physical entity.
bod•kin (bŏd′kĭn) *n.* **1.** A small, sharply pointed instrument for making holes in leather or fabric. **2.** A blunt needle for pulling ribbon or tape through a series of loops or a hem. **3.** *Archaic.* A dagger : stiletto.
bod•y (bŏd′ē) *n., pl.* **-ies. 1. a.** The entire material structure and substance of an organism. **b.** The physical part of a person as opposed to the mental or spiritual aspect. **c.** A corpse or carcass. **d.** A human being : person. **2.** The torso of a human being or an animal. **3.** A bounded aggregate of matter <a *body* of water> **4.** A number of persons, concepts, or things considered as a whole : group <a legislative *body*> <a *body* of information> **5.** The center or main part of something. **6. a.** Thickness or substantiality <hair with *body*> **b.** Strength or richness, esp. of flavor.
body building *n.* The technique of developing the musculature of the body through exercise and diet.
body English *n.* The tendency of a person to influence the movement of a propelled object, as a ball, by twisting the body toward the goal.
bod•y•guard (bŏd′ē-gärd′) *n.* A usu. armed person or group of persons responsible for the protection of another person.
body language *n.* The postures, gestures, and expressions by which a person communicates nonverbally with others.
body shop *n.* A garage for the repair of automotive vehicular bodies.
body stocking *n.* A tight-fitting, usu. 1-piece garment covering the torso, occas. having sleeves and legs.
bod•y•surf (bŏd′ē-sûrf′) *v.* To ride flat on a wave without a surfboard. **–bod′y•surf′er** *n.* **–bod′y•surf′ing** *n.*
Boer (bōr, bôr, bo͝or) *n.* A South African of Dutch descent. **–Boer** *adj.*
bog (bôg, bŏg) *n.* Soft, waterlogged ground : marsh. *–v.* **bogged, bog•ging.** To sink or cause to sink in or as if in a bog <*bogged* down in regulations> **–bog′gy** *adj.*
bo•gey (bō′gē) *n., pl.* **-geys. 1.** *var. of* BOGY. **2.** One golf stroke over par on a hole. **3.** *Slang.* An unidentified flying aircraft.
bog•ey•man (bo͝og′ē-măn′, bō′gē-, bo͞o′gē-) *n. var. of* BOOGIEMAN.
bog•gle (bŏg′əl) *v.* **-gled, -gling. 1.** To shy away from with or as if with fright or astonishment. **2.** To cause to be overcome, as with fright or astonishment. **3.** To botch.

Bo·go·tá (bō′gə-tä′). Cap. of Colombia, in the C part. *Pop.* 4,067,000.
bo·gus (bō′gəs) *adj.* Counterfeit : fake.
bo·gy *also* **bo·gey** or **bo·gie** (bō′gē) *n., pl.* **-gies** *also* **-geys** or **-gies. 1.** A hobgoblin. **2.** Something causing annoyance.
Bo·he·mi·a (bō-hē′mē-ə). Region of W Czechoslovakia.
Bo·he·mi·an (bō-hē′mē-ən) *n.* **1.** A native or inhabitant of Bohemia. **2.** A Gypsy. **3. bohemian.** One with artistic or literary interests who adopts manners markedly different from those of the majority of society. **–Bo·he′mi·an** *adj.*
▲word history: The nomadic people called *Bohemians* who roamed Europe from late medieval times had in fact come from the borderlands of India and Iran, not from Bohemia. The Europeans gave them such names as *Bohemian* and *Gypsy* (from *Egyptian*) because they did not know their original homelands. The French word *bohémien* was also used of "social gypsies"artists and writers who led unconventional lives. Thackeray introduced this sense of the word into English in *Vanity Fair.*
boil[1] (boil) *v.* **1. a.** To vaporize a liquid by the application of heat. **b.** To reach the boiling point or to undergo boiling. **2.** To cook or clean by boiling. **3.** To be agitated like boiling water : churn. **4.** To be stirred up or greatly excited. **5.** To heat to the boiling point. **6.** To form or separate, as sugar, by the process of boiling. **–boil away.** To evaporate by boiling. **–boil down. 1.** To reduce in size or bulk by boiling. **2.** To condense or become condensed : reduce. **–boil over. 1.** To overflow while boiling. **2.** To lose one's temper. **–boil** *n.*
boil[2] (boil) *n.* A painful, localized pus-filled swelling of the skin caused by an infection of bacterial origin.
boil·er (boi′lər) *n.* **1.** A vessel in which a liquid, usu. water, is heated and often vaporized for heating or power. **2.** A container, as a kettle, for boiling liquids. **3.** A storage tank for hot water.
Boi·se (boi′zē, -sē). Cap. of Idaho, in the SW. *Pop.* 102,145.
bois·ter·ous (boi′stər-əs, -strəs) *adj.* **1.** Stormy and rough : violent. **2.** Loud, noisy, unrestrained, and undisciplined. **–bois′ter·ous·ly** *adv.* **–bois′ter·ous·ness** *n.*
bok choy (bŏk choi′) *n. var. of* PAK CHOI.
bold (bōld) *adj.* **1.** Courageous. **2.** Requiring or showing courage. **3.** Unduly forward : brazen. **4.** Clear and distinct to the eye : conspicuous. **5.** Steep, as a cliff : abrupt. **–bold′ly** *adv.* **–bold′ness** *n.*
bold·face (bōld′fās′) *n.* Type with heavy, thick lines. **–bold′face′** *v.*
bold-faced (bōld′fāst′) *adj.* Impudent.
bole (bōl) *n.* A tree trunk.
bo·le·ro (bō-lâr′ō, bə-) *n., pl.* **-ros. 1.** A very short jacket worn open at the front. **2. a.** A Spanish dance in triple meter. **b.** The music for the bolero.
bo·le·tus (bō-lē′təs) *n., pl.* **-tus·es** or **-ti** (-tī′). A fungus of the genus *Boletus,* with an umbrella-shaped cap, of which some species are poisonous and others edible.
Bol·eyn (bŏŏl′ĭn, bō-lĭn′), **Anne.** 1507–36. 2nd wife of Henry VIII; beheaded.
bo·li·var (bō-lē′vär′, bŏl′ə-vər) *n., pl.* **bo·li·vars** or **bo·li·var·es** (bō′lē-vä′rās′). See CURRENCY TABLE.
Bo·lí·var (bō′lē′vär′), **Simón.** 1783–1830. South American independence leader.
Bo·liv·i·a (bə-lĭv′ē-ə). Country of WC South America. *Cap.* La Paz and Sucre. *Pop.* 4,804,000. **–Bo·liv′i·an** *adj.* & *n.*
boll (bōl) *n.* A rounded seedpod or capsule of a plant, as flax or cotton.
bol·lix (bŏl′ĭks) *v. Slang.* To throw into confusion : botch.
boll weevil *n.* A small, grayish beetle, *Anthonomus grandis,* whose larvae hatch in and damage cotton bolls.
bo·lo (bō′lō) *n., pl.* **-los.** A long and heavy single-edged machete.
bo·lo·gna (bə-lō′nē, -nə, -nyə) *also* **ba·lo·ney** or **bo·lo·ney** (-nē) *n.* A seasoned smoked sausage made of mixed meats.
Bo·lo·gna (bō-lōn′yə, -lō′nyä). City of N Italy. *Pop.* 471,554.
Bol·she·vik (bōl′shə-vĭk′, bŏl′-) *n., pl.* **-viks** or **-vi·ki** (-vē′kē). **1.** A member of the extreme left-wing faction of the Communist Party that seized power in Russia in 1917. **2.** *often* **bolshevik.** An extreme radical. **–Bol′she·vism** *n.* **–Bol′she·vist′** *n.* & *adj.*
bol·ster (bōl′stər) *n.* A long, narrow cushion or pillow. *–v.* **1.** To support or prop up with or as if with a bolster. **2.** To buoy up <*bolstered* morale>
bolt[1] (bōlt) *n.* **1.** A threaded metal pin with a head at one end designed to be used with a nut to hold parts together. **2.** A bar that slides into a socket and is used to fasten doors and gates. **3.** A metal bar or rod in a lock mechanism that is thrown or withdrawn by turning the key. **4.** A sliding metal bar used in a breechloading rifle or other breech mechanism. **5.** A short, thick-headed arrow used with a crossbow. **6.** A flash of lightning : thunderbolt. **7.** A sudden movement to or away. **8.** A large roll of cloth. *–v.* **1.** To lock with or as if with a bolt. **2.** To eat hurriedly and with little chewing : gulp. **3.** To desert or withdraw support from (a political party). **4.** To speak impulsively : blurt out. **5.** To move or run suddenly. **6.** To break away from control and run, esp. as a horse. **–bolt′er** *n.*
bolt[2] (bōlt) *v.* To pass through a sieve : sift. **–bolt′er** *n.*
bo·lus (bō′ləs) *n.* **1.** A small rounded mass, esp. of chewed food. **2.** A large pill.
bomb (bŏm) *n.* **1. a.** An explosive weapon detonated by impact, proximity to target, or timing device, that is hurled at or dropped on a target. **b.** A weapon that releases destructive material, as smoke or gas, upon detonation. **c.** An atomic bomb. **2.** A portable, manually operated container that ejects a spray, gas, or foam under pressure. **3.** *Slang.* A total failure : fiasco. *–v.* **1.** To attack, damage, or destroy with or as if with bombs. **2.** *Slang.* To fail utterly.
bom·bard (bŏm-bärd′) *v.* **1.** To attack with bombs, missiles, or shells. **2.** To attack persistently, as with questions. **3.** To irradiate (an atom). **–bom·bard′er** *n.* **–bom·bard′ment** *n.*
bom·bar·dier[1] (bŏm′bər-dîr′) *n.* **1.** The aircraft crew member operating the bombing equipment. **2.** A noncommissioned British artillery officer.
bom·bar·dier[2] (bŏm′bər-dîr′) *n. Can.* A large enclosed snowmobile.
bom·bast (bŏm′băst′) *n.* Flamboyant, pompous writing or speech. **–bom·bas′tic** *adj.* **–bom·bas′ti·cal·ly** *adv.*
Bom·bay (bŏm-bā′). Port city of WC India. *Pop.* 5,970,575.
bom·ba·zine (bŏm′bə-zēn′) *n.* A twilled fabric of silk and worsted or cotton, often dyed black.
bombed (bŏmd) *adj. Slang.* Drunk.
bomb·er (bŏm′ər) *n.* One that bombs, esp. a military aircraft designed to carry and drop bombs.
bomb·shell (bŏm′shĕl′) *n.* **1.** A bomb. **2.** A shocking surprise.
bo·na fide (bō′nə fīd′, fī′dē, bŏn′ə) *adj.* **1.** Performed or made in good faith : sincere. **2.** Authentic : genuine.
bo·nan·za (bə-năn′zə) *n.* **1.** A rich mine, vein, or pocket of ore. **2.** A source of great prosperity.
bon·bon (bŏn′bŏn′) *n.* A candy coated with chocolate or fondant and having a creamy center.
bond (bŏnd) *n.* **1.** Something, as a cord, that binds or fastens together. **2.** *often* **bonds.** *Archaic.* Captivity : confinement. **3.** A uniting force or tie : link. **4.** A binding agreement : covenant. **5.** The duty, promise, or obligation by which one is bound. **6. a.** An agent that causes objects to cohere <a thermoplastic *bond*> **b.** The union or cohesion brought about by such an agent. **7.** *Law.* **a.** A sum of money paid as bail or surety. **b.** BONDSMAN 2. **8.** A certificate of debt issued by a corporation or government that guarantees payment of the orig. investment plus interest by a specified future date. **9.** The warehousing of taxable goods until the duties or taxes due on them are paid. **10.** An insurance contract in which an agency guarantees payment to an employer in the event of financial loss due to an action of an employee. **11.** A superior grade of white paper, used esp. in business correspondence. *–v.* **1.** To join or hold together securely, as with cement or glue. **2.** To place a guaranteed bond or mortgage on. **3.** To furnish bond or surety for. **4.** To place (e.g., an employee) under bond or guarantee.
bond·age (bŏn′dĭj) *n.* **1.** The condition of a serf or slave : servitude. **2.** The condition of being involuntarily subject to a power, force, or influence.
bond·ser·vant (bŏnd′sûr′vənt) *n.* One obligated to work without wages. **–bond′maid′** *n.* **–bond′wom′an** *n.*
bonds·man (bŏndz′mən) *n.* **1.** *also* **bond·man** (bŏnd′-). A man who is a bondservant. **2.** One who provides surety or bond for another.
bone (bōn) *n.* **1. a.** The dense, semirigid, porous, calcified connective tissue of the skeleton of most vertebrates. **b.** One of the anatomically distinct skeletal structures made of bone. **c.** A piece of bone. **2. bones. a.** The skeleton. **b.** The body. **c.** Mortal remains. **3.** A material, as ivory, resembling bone. **4.** Something made of bone or similar material. *–v.* **boned, bon·ing. 1.** To remove the bones from. **2.** To refresh one's memory. **–bon′i·ness** *n.* **–bon′y** *adj.*
bone-dry (bōn′drī′) *adj.* Without a trace of moisture.
bone·head (bōn′hĕd′) *n. Slang.* A stupid person : dunce. **–bone′head′ed** *adj.* **–bone′head′ed·ness** *n.*
bone meal *n.* Crushed or ground bones used as plant fertilizer and animal feed.
bon·er (bō′nər) *n. Slang.* A blunder.
bon·fire (bŏn′fīr′) *n.* A large outdoor fire.
bong (bŏng, bông) *n.* A deep ringing sound, as of a bell. **–bong** *v.*
bon·go (bŏng′gō, bông′-) *n., pl.* **-gos** or **-goes.** One of a pair of drums played with the hands.

bon·ho·mie (bŏn′ə-mē′) *n.* Geniality.
bo·ni·to (bə-nē′tō) *n., pl.* **-to** *or* **-tos.** One of several marine food and game fishes of the genus *Sarda,* related to the tuna.
bon·kers (bŏng′kərz) *adj. Slang.* Crazy.
bon mot (bôN mō′) *n., pl.* **bons mots** (bôN mō′, mōz′). A clever saying.
Bonn (bŏn). Cap. of West Germany, on the Rhine. *Pop.* 286,184.
bon·net (bŏn′ĭt) *n.* **1.** A hat secured by ribbons tied under the chin. **2.** A feather headdress worn by some American Indians. **3.** *esp. Brit.* HOOD[1] 2.
bon·ny *also* **bon·nie** (bŏn′ē) *adj.* **-ni·er, -ni·est.** *esp. Scot.* Pleasing or attractive : pretty. **—bon′ni·ness** *n.*
bon·sai (bŏn′sī′, bōn′-) *n., pl.* **-sai. 1.** The craft of growing dwarfed, ornamentally shaped shrubs or trees in small, shallow pots. **2.** A shrub or tree grown by bonsai.
bo·nus (bō′nəs) *n.* Something given or paid in addition to the usual.
bon vi·vant (bŏn′ vē-vänt′, bôN′ vē-väN′) *n., pl.* **bons vi·vants** (bŏn′ vē-vänts′, bôN′ vē-väN′). One who has refined tastes and esp. enjoys excellent food and drink.
bon voy·age (bŏn′ voi-äzh′, bôN′ vwȧ-yȧzh′) *n.* Used to wish a departing traveler a pleasant journey.
bonze (bŏnz) *n.* A Buddhist monk.
boo (bo͞o) *n., pl.* **boos.** A vocal sound uttered to show contempt or disapproval. *—interj.* Used to frighten or surprise or to express disapproval. **—boo** *v.*
boob[1] (bo͞ob) *n. Slang.* BOOBY 1.
boob[2] (bo͞ob) *n. Slang.* A woman's breast.
boo-boo (bo͞o′bo͞o) *n., pl.* **-boos.** *Slang.* **1.** A blunder. **2.** A slight physical injury.
boo·by (bo͞o′bē) *n., pl.* **-bies. 1.** *also* **boob** (bo͞ob). A stupid person : dolt. **2.** One of several tropical sea birds of the genus *Sula,* related to the gannets.
booby prize *n.* An insignificant or comical award given to the one with the worst score in a game or contest.
booby trap *n.* A usu. concealed, often explosive device triggered by the movement of an apparently harmless object.
boo·dle (bo͞od′l) *n. Slang.* **1. a.** Money, esp. counterfeit money. **b.** Money taken as a bribe. **2.** Stolen goods : swag.
boog·ie (bo͝og′ē) *v.* **-ied, -ie·ing.** *Slang.* To dance to rock 'n' roll music.
boog·ie·man *also* **boog·y·man** *or* **bog·ey·man** (bo͝og′ē-măn′, bō′gē-, bo͞o′gē-) *n.* A terrifying person or thing : hobgoblin.
boog·ie-woog·ie (bo͝og′ē-wo͝og′ē, bo͞o′gē-wo͞o′gē) *n.* A style of jazz piano marked by a repeated rhythmic and melodic pattern in the bass.
book (bo͝ok) *n.* **1.** A set of pages fastened on 1 side and enclosed between protective covers. **2.** A printed or written literary work. **3.** A main division of a larger printed or written work. **4. Book.** The Bible. **5. a.** A volume for recording financial transactions. **b. books.** Such records as a whole. **6.** A record of bets placed on a race. *—v.* **1.** To record or list in or as if in a book. **2.** To record charges against (a person) on a police blotter. **3.** To arrange for (e.g., tickets) in advance : reserve. **4.** To hire (e.g., entertainers). **—book′ing** *n.*
book·case (bo͝ok′kās′) *n.* A piece of furniture having shelves for holding books.
book·end *also* **book end** (bo͝ok′ĕnd′) *n.* A support at the end of a row of books that serves to keep them upright.
book·ie (bo͝ok′ē) *n. Slang.* BOOKMAKER 2.
book·ish (bo͝ok′ĭsh) *adj.* **1.** Enjoying books : studious. **2.** Pedantic. **—book′ish·ly** *adv.* **—book′ish·ness** *n.*
book·keep·ing (bo͝ok′kē′pĭng) *n.* The art or practice of recording business accounts and transactions. **—book′keep′er** *n.*
book·let (bo͝ok′lĭt) *n.* A pamphlet.
book·mak·er (bo͝ok′mā′kər) *n.* **1.** One who prints, publishes, or binds books. **2.** One who takes and pays off bets. **—book′mak′ing** *n.*
book·mo·bile (bo͝ok′mə-bēl′) *n.* A truck or van equipped to serve as a mobile lending library.
book·plate (bo͝ok′plāt′) *n.* A label usu. pasted on the inside cover of a book that bears the owner's name.
book value *n.* The financial worth of a business in terms of its account books as opposed to its market value.
book·worm (bo͝ok′wûrm′) *n.* **1.** The larva of any of various insects that infest books and feed on the bindings. **2.** One who spends much time studying or reading.
boom[1] (bo͞om) *v.* **1.** To emit a deep, resonant sound. **2.** To grow or develop rapidly : flourish. *—n.* **1.** A booming sound, as of an explosion. **2.** A period of economic prosperity. **3.** A sudden increase, as in wealth.
boom[2] (bo͞om) *n.* **1.** A spar extending from a mast to hold or extend the foot of a sail. **2.** A pole extending upward at an angle from a derrick's mast to support and guide objects being lifted. **3.** A movable arm for maneuvering a microphone.
boo·mer·ang (bo͞o′mə-răng′) *n.* **1.** A flat, curved piece of wood that can be hurled so that it returns to its thrower. **2.** A statement or action that backfires against its originator. **—boo′mer·ang** *v.*
boon[1] (bo͞on) *n.* Something beneficial that is bestowed : favor.
boon[2] (bo͞on) *adj.* Convivial : jolly <a *boon* companion>
boon·docks (bo͞on′dŏks′) *pl.n. Slang.* Rural country.
boon·dog·gle (bo͞on′dô′gəl, -dŏg′əl) *n. Informal.* Pointless, unnecessary work. *—v.* **-gled, -gling.** To waste time or money on boondoggle. **—boon′dog′gler** *n.*
boon·ies (bo͞o′nēz) *pl.n.* BOONDOCKS.
boor (bo͝or) *n.* A crude, rude person. ☆**syns:** BARBARIAN, BOUNDER, CHURL, PHILISTINE, YAHOO **—boor′ish** *adj.* **—boor′ish·ly** *adv.* **—boor′ish·ness** *n.*
boost (bo͞ost) *v.* **1.** To lift by or as if by pushing up from below. **2.** To increase : raise. **3.** To stir up enthusiasm for. **—boost** *n.* **—boost′er** *n.*
boot[1] (bo͞ot) *n.* **1. a.** A protective piece of footgear covering the foot and part or all of the leg. **b.** Any protective sheath or covering. **2.** *esp. Brit.* The trunk of an automotive vehicle. **3.** A marine or naval recruit in basic training. **4. a.** A kick. **b.** *Slang.* A thrill. **5.** A summary dismissal, as from a job. *—v.* **1.** To put boots on. **2.** To kick. **3.** *Slang.* To dismiss : fire.
†**boot[2]** (bo͞ot) *v. Archaic.* To be of help or advantage : avail. *—n.* **1.** *Regional.* Something given in addition. **2.** *Archaic.* Avail : advantage. **—to boot.** In addition.
boot·black (bo͞ot′blăk′) *n.* One who cleans and polishes shoes for a living.
boot·ee *also* **boot·ie** (bo͞o′tē) *n.* A soft, usu. knitted baby shoe.
booth (bo͞oth) *n., pl.* **booths** (bo͞o*th*z, bo͞oths). **1.** A small enclosed compartment, as a toll booth or a phone booth. **2.** A seating area in a restaurant having a table and seats whose backs serve as partitions. **3.** A small stand for the sale of goods.
boot·leg (bo͞ot′lĕg′) *v.* **-legged, -leg·ging.** To make, transport, or sell (e.g., liquor) illegally. **—boot′leg′ger** *n.*
boot·less (bo͞ot′lĭs) *adj.* Useless. **—boot′less·ly** *adv.* **—boot′less·ness** *n.*
boot·lick (bo͞ot′lĭk′) *v.* To treat or behave servilely. **—boot′lick′er** *n.*
boot·strap (bo͞ot′străp′) *n.* **1.** A loop at the side or the top rear of a boot to help in pulling the boot on. **2.** *Computer Sci.* A subroutine used to establish the full routine or another routine. *—v.* To establish (a computer program) with a bootstrap.
boo·ty (bo͞o′tē) *n., pl.* **-ties. 1.** Plunder taken from an enemy in wartime. **2.** Goods stolen or seized. **3.** A valuable prize, award, or gain.
booze (bo͞oz) *Slang. —n.* Alcoholic drink. *—v.* **boozed, booz·ing.** To consume alcoholic drinks excessively. **—booz′er** *n.* **—booz′y** *adj.*
bop[1] (bŏp) *v.* **bopped, bop·ping.** *Informal.* To strike : hit. **—bop** *n.*
bop[2] (bŏp) *n.* Jazz marked by rhythmic, harmonic complexity and innovations.
bo·rate (bôr′āt′, bōr′-) *n.* A boric acid salt.
bo·rax (bôr′ăks′, -əks, bōr′-) *n.* Sodium borate, either in hydrated or anhydrous form.
Bor·deaux[1] (bôr-dō′) *n., pl.* **Bordeaux** (bôr-dōz′). A red or white wine from the region around Bordeaux.
Bor·deaux[2] (bôr-dō′). City of SW France. *Pop.* 223,131.
bor·del·lo (bôr-dĕl′ō) *n., pl.* **-los.** A house of prostitution.
bor·der (bôr′dər) *n.* **1.** A margin or edge. **2.** A decorative strip around an edge. **3.** A geographic or political boundary. *—v.* **1.** To put a border on. **2.** To lie along the border of. **3.** To come near to in character <behavior *bordering on* rudeness>
bor·der·land (bôr′dər-lănd′) *n.* **1.** Land on or near a frontier or border. **2.** An indeterminate area or situation.
bor·der·line (bôr′dər-līn′) *n.* **1.** A line marking a boundary. **2.** An area between 2 conditions or qualities.
bore[1] (bôr, bōr) *v.* **bored, bor·ing. 1.** To make a hole in or through with or as if with a drill. **2.** To make by drilling or digging. *—n.* **1.** A hole or passage made by drilling. **2.** The inside diameter of a hole, tube, or cylinder. **3.** The caliber of a firearm. **4.** A tool for drilling.
bore[2] (bôr, bōr) *v.* **bored, bor·ing.** To tire with dullness or repetition. ☆**syns:** PALL, TIRE, WEARY **—bore** *n.* **—bore′dom** *n.* **—bor′ing·ly** *adv.*
bore[3] (bôr, bōr) *v. p.t. of* BEAR[1].
bo·re·al (bôr′ē-əl, bōr′-) *adj.* Of or located in the north : northern.
boric acid *n.* A crystalline compound used as an antiseptic and a preservative.

born (bôrn) *adj.* **1.** Brought into life or being. **2.** Having a particular talent from birth <a *born* writer> **3.** Derived or resulting from inventions <*born* of necessity>
born-a·gain (bôrn′ə-gĕn′) *adj.* Of, relating to, or being an individual who has made a conversion to Jesus Christ as personal savior <a *born-again* Christian>
borne (bôrn) *v. var. p.p. of* BEAR[1].
Bor·ne·o (bôr′nē-ō′). Island of the Indonesian Archipelago in the W Pacific.
bo·ron (bôr′ŏn′, bōr′-) *n. Symbol* **B** A soft, brown nonmetallic element.
bor·ough (bûr′ō, bŭr′ō) *n.* **1.** A self-governing incorporated town, as in some U.S. states. **2.** One of the 5 administrative units of New York City. **3.** *esp. Brit.* **a.** An incorporated town. **b.** A town that sends 1 or more representatives to Parliament.
bor·row (bŏr′ō, bôr′ō) *v.* **1.** To receive or obtain (something) on loan with the intention of returning it. **2.** To adopt as one's own <*borrowed* another author's ideas>
borscht (bôrsht) *also* **borsch** (bôrsh) *n.* A hot or cold beet soup.
bor·zoi (bôr′zoi′) *n.* A large, slender dog with a silky coat and a narrow head.
bosh (bŏsh) *n. Informal.* Nonsense.
bosk·y (bŏs′kē) *adj.* **-i·er, -i·est.** Thick with trees or bushes : wooded.
bo's'n or **bos'n** (bō′sən) *n. vars. of* BOATSWAIN.
Bos·ni·a (bŏz′nē-ə). Region of WC Yugoslavia. **—Bos′ni·an** *adj.* & *n.*
bos·om (bo͝oz′əm, bo͞o′zəm) *n.* **1.** The human chest, esp. the female breasts. **2.** The part of a garment covering the chest. **3.** The center : heart.
Bos·po·rus (bŏs′pər-əs). Narrow strait linking the Black and Marmara seas.
boss[1] (bôs, bŏs) *n.* **1.** An employer or supervisor. **2.** A politician who controls a party or political machine. *—v.* **1.** To supervise. **2.** To command in a domineering way. **—boss′i·ness** *n. adv.* **—boss′y** *adj.*
boss[2] (bôs, bŏs) *n.* A knoblike circular ornament. *—v.* To decorate with bosses.
Bos·ton (bôs′tən, bŏs′tən). Cap. of Mass. *Pop.* 562,994. **—Bos·to′ni·an** *adj.* & *n.*
Boston cream pie *n.* A cake with custard filling.
Boston terrier *n.* A small dog bred as a cross between a bulldog and a bull terrier.
bo·sun (bō′sən) *n. var. of* BOATSWAIN.
bot·a·ny (bŏt′n-ē) *n.* The science of plants. **—bo·tan′i·cal** (bə-tăn′ĭ-kəl), **bo·tan′ic** *adj.* **—bot′a·nist** *n.*
botch (bŏch) *v.* **1.** To ruin by clumsiness : bungle. **2.** To repair ineptly. ☆***syns:*** BOLLIX, BUNGLE, FUMBLE, MISHANDLE, MISMANAGE, MUDDLE, MUFF, SPOIL **—botch** *n.*
both (bōth) *adj.* Being two in conjunction : one and the other. *—pron.* The one and the other. *—conj.* Used with *and* to indicate that each of two things in a phrase or clause is included <*both* parents and children>
both·er (bŏth′ər) *v.* **1.** To annoy or irritate. **2.** To make nervous : fluster. **3.** To take the trouble : concern oneself. *—n.* An annoyance. *—interj.* Used to express irritation. **—both′er·some** *adj.*
Bot·swa·na (bŏt-swä′nə). Country of SC Africa. *Cap.* Gaborone. *Pop.* 661,000.
Bot·ti·cel·li (bŏt′ĭ-chĕl′ē), **Sandro.** 1444?–1510. Italian painter.
bot·tle (bŏt′l) *n.* **1.** A usu. glass container with a narrow neck. **2.** The quantity that a bottle holds. **3.** Alcoholic drink. *—v.* **-tled, -tling.** To put in or as if in a bottle. **—bot′tler** *n.*
bot·tle-feed (bŏt′l-fēd′) *v.* To feed with a bottle.
bottle green *n.* A dark to grayish green. **—bot′tle-green′** *adj.*
bot·tle·neck (bŏt′l-nĕk′) *n.* **1.** A narrow or obstructed section of a highway or pipeline. **2.** Something that hinders progress or production.
bot·tom (bŏt′əm) *n.* **1.** The deepest or lowest part. **2.** The lowest place or position <at the *bottom* of the class> **3.** The underside. **4.** The supporting part : foundation. **5.** The essence. **6.** The land under a body of water. **7.** *Informal.* The buttocks. *—adj.* Lowest : last. **—bot′tom·less** *adj.*
bottom line *n.* **1.** The lowest line in a financial statement that shows net loss or profit. **2.** The final result : upshot. **3.** The essential point.
bot·u·lism (bŏch′ə-lĭz′əm) *n.* Acute food poisoning caused by bacteria that grow in improperly canned foods.
bou·doir (bo͞o′dwär′, -dwôr′) *n.* A woman's private room.
bouf·fant (bo͞o-fänt′) *adj.* Puffed-out : full <a *bouffant* bridal veil>
bough (bou) *n.* A large tree branch.
bought (bôt) *v. p.t.* & *p.p. of* BUY.
†**bought·en** (bôt′n) *v. regional var. p.p. of* BUY.
bouil·la·baisse (bo͞o′yə-bās′) *n.* A highly seasoned fish stew made with several kinds of fish and shellfish.
bouil·lon (bo͞o′yŏn′, bo͝ol′-, -yən) *n.* A clear, thin broth usu. of beef or chicken.
boul·der (bōl′dər) *n.* A large, rounded rock.
boul·e·vard (bo͝ol′ə-värd′, bo͞o′lə-) *n.* A wide city street.
bounce (bouns) *v.* **bounced, bounc·ing. 1.** To rebound or cause to rebound. **2.** To bound in a lively manner <*bounced* into the room> **3.** To be returned by a bank as worthless <a check that *bounced*> *—n.* **1.** A bound : rebound. **2.** A spring or leap. **3.** Capacity to bounce : spring. **4.** Vivacity : spirit. **—bounc′i·ly** *adv.* **—bounc′i·ness** *n.* **—bounc′y** *adj.*
bounc·er (boun′sər) *n.* One who ejects disorderly persons from a public place.
bounc·ing (boun′sĭng) *adj.* **1.** Healthy : vigorous. **2.** Lively : spirited.
bound[1] (bound) *v.* **1.** To leap forward : spring. **2.** To advance by leaping. **3.** To bounce. **—bound** *n.*
bound[2] (bound) *n.* **1.** *often* **bounds.** A limit <beyond the *bounds* of credibility> **2. bounds.** The territory on or near limiting lines. *—v.* **1.** To limit. **2.** To border on another area : adjoin. **3.** To demarcate.
bound[3] (bound) *adj.* **1.** Confined by bonds. **2.** Under obligation. **3.** Enclosed in a cover or binding. **4.** Certain <We are *bound* to lose.>
bound[4] (bound) *adj.* On the way <*bound* for Berlin>
bound·a·ry (boun′də-rē, -drē) *n., pl.* **-ries.** Something that marks a limit or border.
bound·en (boun′dən) *adj.* **1.** *Archaic.* Under obligation : obliged. **2.** Obligatory : required.
bound·er (boun′dər) *n. esp. Brit.* A vulgar, cocksure person.
bound·less (bound′lĭs) *adj.* Without limits : infinite. **—bound′less·ly** *adv.* **—bound′less·ness** *n.*
boun·te·ous (boun′tē-əs) *adj.* Bountiful. **—boun′te·ous·ly** *adv.*
boun·ti·ful (boun′tə-fəl) *adj.* **1.** Giving liberally. **2.** Copious : plentiful. **—boun′ti·ful·ly** *adv.*
boun·ty (boun′tē) *n., pl.* **-ties. 1.** Liberality in giving. **2.** Something liberally given. **3.** A reward, payment, or inducement, esp. one given by a government for the performance of services beneficial to the state.
bounty hunter *n.* One who hunts predatory animals or outlaws for a bounty.
bou·quet (bō-kā′, bo͞o-) *n.* **1.** Cut flowers fastened in a bunch. **2.** The fragrance typical of a wine.
bou·quet gar·ni (bō-kā′ gär-nē′, bo͞o-) *n., pl.* **bou·quets gar·nis** (bō-kāz′ gär-nē′, bo͞o-). Herbs tied together and immersed in a soup or stew as seasoning.
bour·bon (bûr′bən) *n.* A whiskey distilled from a fermented mash.
bour·geois (bo͝or-zhwä′, bo͝or′zhwä′) *n., pl.* **-geois.** A member of the middle class. **—bour·geois** *adj.*
bour·geoi·sie (bo͝or′zhwä-zē′) *n.* The middle class as opposed to the nobility or the working class.
bour·geon (bûr′jən) *v. var. of* BURGEON.
bourn *also* **bourne** (bôrn, bōrn, bo͝orn) *n. Archaic.* **1.** A goal. **2.** A boundary.
bout (bout) *n.* **1.** A match : contest. **2.** A length of time spent in a particular way <a *bout* of drinking><a *bout* of mumps>
bou·tique (bo͞o-tēk′) *n.* A small shop selling fashionable clothes and accessories.
bou·ton·niere *also* **bou·ton·nière** (bo͞ot′n-îr′, -yâr′) *n.* A flower worn in a buttonhole.
Bou·vier des Flan·dres (bo͞o-vyā′ də flăn′dərz, fläɴ′drə) *n.* A large, rough-coated dog orig. used in Belgium for herding and guarding cattle.
bou·zou·ki (bo͞o-zo͞o′kē, bə-) *n.* A Greek stringed instrument similar to a mandolin.
bo·vine (bō′vīn′, -vēn′) *adj.* **1.** Of or resembling an ox or cow. **2.** Sluggish : dull.
bow[1] (bō) *n.* **1.** A weapon consisting of a curved stave strung taut from end to end and used to launch arrows. **2.** A rod with horsehair drawn tightly between its ends, used to play the violin, viola, and related stringed instruments. **3.** A knot usu. having 2 loops and 2 ends. **4.** A rainbow. *—v.* **1.** To bend into a bow. **2.** To play (a stringed instrument) with a bow.
bow[2] (bou) *v.* **1.** To bend (the head, body, or knee) as an expression of greeting, consent, or courtesy. **2.** To comply : submit. **—bow out.** To withdraw : resign. *—n.* The act or an instance of bowing.
bow[3] (bou) *n.* The forward part of a boat or ship.
bowd·ler·ize (bōd′lə-rīz′, boud′-) *v.* **-ized, -iz·ing.** To expurgate (e.g., a book) prudishly. **—bowd′ler·i·za′tion** *n.*

bow·el (bou′əl, boul) *n.* **1.** An intestine, esp. of a human being. **2.** *often* **bowels.** The digestive tract below the stomach. **3. bowels.** The interior.
bow·er (bou′ər) *n.* A shaded, leafy recess : arbor. **–bow′er·y** *adj.*
bow-front (bō′frŭnt′) *adj.* Having an outward-curving front, as a bureau.
bow·head (bō′hĕd′) *n.* A large-headed whale, *Balaena mysticetus,* of Arctic seas.

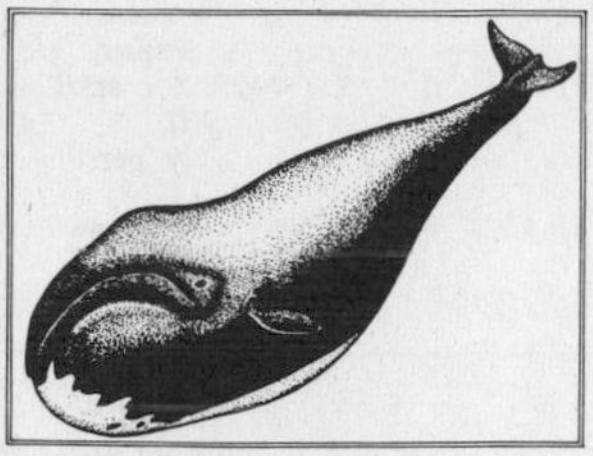

bowhead

bow·ie knife (bō′ē, bo͞o′ē) *n.* A thick-bladed single-edged hunting knife.
bowl¹ (bōl) *n.* **1.** A hemispherical vessel for liquids or food. **2.** A bowl-shaped part, as of a spoon. **3.** A bowl-shaped theater or stadium. **–bowl′ful** *n.*
bowl² (bōl) *n.* **1.** A large wooden ball rolled in certain games. **2.** A roll of the ball, as in bowling. *–v.* **1.** To take part in the game of bowling. **2.** To roll (a ball) in bowling. **–bowl over.** To surprise : astound.
bow·leg (bō′lĕg′) *n.* A leg with outward curvature in the region of the knee. **–bow′leg′ged** *adj.*
bowl·er¹ (bō′lər) *n.* One that bowls.
bowl·er² (bō′lər) *n. esp. Brit.* A derby hat.
bow·line (bō′lĭn, -līn′) *n.* A knot with a loop that won't slip.
bowl·ing (bō′lĭng) *n.* **1.** A game played by rolling a ball down a wooden alley in order to knock down a triangular formation of 10 pins. **2.** A similar game, as skittles.
bowling alley *n.* **1.** A smooth, level lane used for bowling. **2.** A place containing bowling alleys.
bow·man (bō′mən) *n.* An archer.
bow·sprit (bou′sprĭt′, bō′-) *n.* A spar that extends forward from the stem of a ship.
bow·string (bō′strĭng′) *n.* The string of a bow.
bow tie (bō) *n.* A small necktie tied in the shape of a bow.
box¹ (bŏks) *n.* **1.** A usu. rectangular container, typically having a lid. **2.** The amount that a box holds. **3.** A separated compartment in a theater for the seating of a small group. **4.** *Baseball.* A designated area where the batter, pitcher, or coaches stand. **5.** An awkward situation : predicament. *–v.* To put in or as if in a box.
box² (bŏks) *n.* A blow with the hand. *–v.* **1.** To hit with the hand. **2.** To take part in a boxing match (with).
box³ (bŏks) *n., pl.* **box** or **box·es.** An evergreen tree or shrub of the genus *Buxus,* esp. *B. sempervirens,* having hard, yellowish wood and used for hedges.
box·car (bŏks′kär′) *n.* An enclosed railway car used for transporting freight.
box·er¹ (bŏk′sər) *n.* One who boxes, esp. as a profession.
box·er² (bŏk′sər) *n.* A short-haired dog orig. bred in Germany, with a brownish coat and a square muzzle.
box·ing (bŏk′sĭng) *n.* The sport of fighting with the fists, usu. with padded gloves.
box office *n.* A ticket office, as of a stadium or theater.
box spring *n.* A bedspring consisting of a frame enclosed with cloth and containing rows of coil springs.
box·wood (bŏks′wo͝od′) *n.* **1.** The box tree. **2.** The hard wood of the box tree.
boy (boi) *n.* A male child or youth. *–interj.* Used to express mild astonishment, disgust, etc. **–boy′hood′** *n.* **–boy′ish** *adj.* **–boy′ish·ly** *adv.* **–boy′ish·ness** *n.*
boy·cott (boi′kŏt′) *v.* To abstain from buying or using to express protest. **–boy′cott′** *n.*
Boy Scout *n.* A member of a worldwide boys' organization that stresses character development and citizenship training.
boy·sen·ber·ry (boi′zən-bĕr′ē) *n.* A prickly bramble hybridized from the loganberry and various blackberries and raspberries, with large, wine-red, edible berries.
B/P *abbr.* bills payable.
Br *symbol for* BROMINE.
br. *abbr.* **1.** branch. **2.** brief. **3.** bronze. **4.** brother. **5.** brown.
bra (brä) *n.* A brassiere. **–bra′less** *adj.*

brace (brās) *n.* **1.** A clamp. **2.** A device, as a supporting beam, that steadies or supports a weight. **3.** *Med.* An appliance used to support a part of the body. **4.** *often* **braces.** A set of bands and wires fixed to teeth to correct crooked alignment. **5.** One of two symbols, { }, used to connect several lines of text. **6.** A cranklike handle for securing and turning a bit. **7. braces.** *esp. Brit.* Suspenders. **8.** A pair of like things. *–v.* **braced, brac·ing. 1.** To support with or as if with a brace. **2.** To prepare for impact or danger. **3.** To invigorate.
brace·let (brās′lĭt) *n.* An ornamental band encircling the wrist.
brack·en (brăk′ən) *n.* **1.** A fern, *Pteridium aquilinum,* with tough stems. **2.** A growth of bracken.
brack·et (brăk′ĭt) *n.* **1.** An L-shaped fixture, one arm of which is fastened to a vertical surface, the other arm projecting to support a weight, as a shelf. **2.** A small shelf supported by brackets. **3.** Either of a pair of symbols, [ ], used to enclose printed or written material. **4.** A classification or grouping, esp. of taxpayers according to income. *–v.* **1.** To support by means of a bracket. **2.** To set brackets around. **3.** To group together : classify.
brack·ish (brăk′ĭsh) *adj.* Somewhat salty : briny. **–brack′ish·ness** *n.*
bract (brăkt) *n.* A leaflike plant part either on the stalk of a flower cluster or below a flower.
brad (brăd) *n.* A small-headed, tapered nail.
brae (brā) *n. Scot.* A hillside : slope.
brag (brăg) *v.* **bragged, brag·ging.** To talk or assert boastfully. **–brag** *n.* **–brag′ger** *n.*
brag·ga·do·ci·o (brăg′ə-dō′shē-ō′) *n., pl.* **-os. 1.** A braggart. **2. a.** Empty boasting. **b.** An arrogant manner : cockiness.
brag·gart (brăg′ərt) *n.* A boastful person.
Brah·ma (brä′mə) *n.* The member of the Hindu triad who created the universe.
Brah·man (brä′mən) *n.* **1.** *also* **Brah·ma** (-mə). The divine reality of the universe in Hinduism, the eternal spirit from which all being originates and to which all returns. **2.** *also* **Brah·min** (-mĭn). A member of the highest Hindu caste, orig. composed of priests. **3.** *also* **Brah·ma** (-mə) *or* **Brah·min** (-mĭn). One of a breed of cattle developed in the S U.S., with a hump between the shoulders and a pendulous dewlap.
Brah·min (brä′mən) *n.* **1.** A socially and intellectually exclusive person. **2.** *var. of* BRAHMAN 2, 3.
Brahms (brämz), **Johannes.** 1833–97. German composer. **–Brahms′i·an** *adj.*
braid (brād) *v.* **1.** To interweave 3 or more strands of : plait. **2.** To decorate with ornamental braid. **3.** To produce by interweaving. *–n.* **1.** A narrow length of material, as hair, that has been braided. **2.** A thin, woven strip of material used for decorating fabrics. **–braid′er** *n.*
Braille *also* **braille** (brāl) *n.* A system of printing for the blind, in which letters and numerals are represented by raised dots.

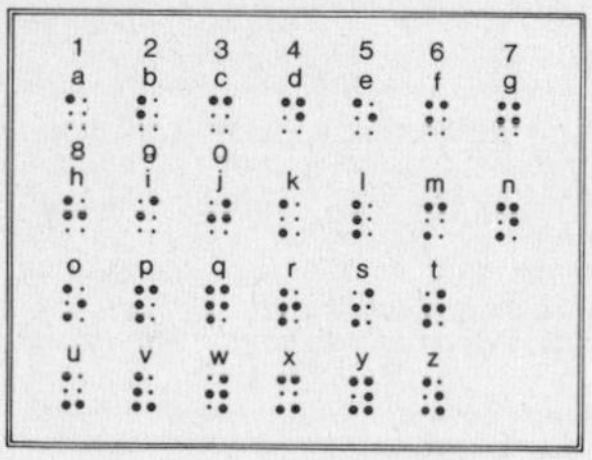

Braille

brain (brān) *n.* **1.** The large mass of gray nerve tissue enclosed in the cranium of a vertebrate that interprets sensory impulses, coordinates and controls bodily functioning, and is the center of emotion and thought. **2. brains.** Intellectual capacity. *–v.* **1.** To smash in the skull of. **2.** *Slang.* To hit on the head. **–brain′i·ness** *n.* **–brain′less** *adj.* **–brain′less·ly** *adv.* **–brain′less·ness** *n.* **–brain′y** *adj.*
brain death *n.* Death as evidenced by the absence of central nervous system activity. **–brain′-dead′** *adj.*
brain·storm (brān′stôrm′) *n.* A sudden clever idea. **–brain′storm′** *v.* **–brain′storm′er** *n.*
brain·storm·ing (brān′stôr′mĭng) *n.* A method of problem solving in which all members of a group spontaneously contribute ideas.
brain·wash (brān′wŏsh′, -wôsh′) *v.* To indoctrinate so as to replace a person's convictions with an opposing set of beliefs.
brain wave *n.* **1.** A rhythmically fluctuating voltage arising from electrical activity in the brain. **2.** A brainstorm.

braise (brāz) *v.* **braised, brais•ing.** To brown (meat or vegetables) in fat and then simmer in a little liquid in a covered pan.
brake[1] (brāk) *n.* A device that slows or stops motion, as of a vehicle. —*v.* **braked, brak•ing. 1.** To slow down with or as if with a brake. **2.** To apply a brake.
brake[2] (brāk) *n.* **1.** A fern, esp. bracken. **2.** An area overgrown with dense bushes : thicket.
brake fluid *n.* Liquid used in a hydraulic brake cylinder.
brake•man (brāk'mən) *n.* A member of a train crew who assists the conductor and inspects the train.
brake shoe *n.* A curved block that presses against and reduces or stops the rotation of a wheel or shaft.
bram•ble (brăm'bəl) *n.* A prickly plant or shrub of the genus *Rubus.*
bran (brăn) *n.* The outer husks of cereals, as wheat, rye, and oats, sifted or bolted from the flour.
branch (brănch) *n.* **1. a.** A secondary woody limb growing out from the trunk of a tree or bush or from another secondary limb. **b.** A similar structure <the *branches* of an antler> **2.** A division of a larger or more complex whole. **3.** A division of a group, as a family or tribe. **4.** A tributary of a river. —*v.* To divide or spread out into or as if into branches.
brand (brănd) *n.* **1. a.** A trademark or distinctive name identifying a product or a manufacturer. **b.** The make of a product thus marked. **2.** A type : kind. **3.** A mark showing identity or ownership, burned on an animal's hide. **4.** A mark once burned on the skin of criminals. **5.** A mark of disgrace : stigma. **6.** Burning or charred wood. —*v.* To mark with or as if with a brand.
bran•dish (brăn'dĭsh) *v.* To wave or flourish threateningly, as a weapon.
brand-new (brănd'no͞o', -nyo͞o') *adj.* Completely new.
bran•dy (brăn'dē) *n., pl.* **-dies.** An alcoholic liquor distilled from fermented fruit juice or wine. **—bran'dy** *v.*
brash (brăsh) *adj.* **1.** Impetuous : rash. **2.** Aggressively self-assertive. **—brash'ly** *adv.* **—brash'ness** *n.*
Bra•sí•lia (brə-zĭl'yə). Cap. of Brazil, in the C plateau. *Pop.* 350,000.
brass (brăs) *n.* **1.** An alloy of copper and zinc. **2.** Utensils or ornaments made of brass. **3.** *often* **brasses** Wind instruments, as the trumpet and trombone, made of brass. **4.** Effrontery : nerve. **—brass'y** *adj.*
bras•se•rie (brăs'ə-rē') *n.* A restaurant serving alcoholic drinks, esp. wine or beer.
brass hat *n. Slang.* A high-ranking military officer or civilian official.
bras•siere or **bras•sière** (brə-zîr') *n.* A woman's undergarment that supports and contours the breasts.
brat (brăt) *n.* An ill-mannered, spoiled child. **—brat'ty** *adj.*
bra•va•do (brə-vä'dō) *n., pl.* **-does** or **-dos. 1.** A pretense of courage. **2.** Defiant, swaggering behavior.
brave (brāv) *adj.* **brav•er, brav•est. 1.** Having or displaying courage : valiant. **2.** Having a fine appearance : splendid. ☆***syns:*** AUDACIOUS, BOLD, COURAGEOUS, DAUNTLESS, FEARLESS, GALLANT, GUTSY, HEROIC, INTREPID, METTLESOME, PLUCKY, STOUTHEARTED, UNAFRAID, UNDAUNTED, VALIANT, VALOROUS —*n.* A North American Indian warrior. —*v.* **braved, brav•ing.** To face or endure courageously. **—brave'ly** *adv.* **—brav'er•y**
bra•vo[1] (brä'vō, brä-vō') *interj.* Used to express approval. **—bra'vo** *n.*
bra•vo[2] *n., pl.* **-voes** or **-voes.** A hired killer.
bra•vu•ra (brə-vo͝or'ə, -vyo͝or'ə) *n.* **1.** *Mus.* Brilliant style or technique in performance. **2.** Showy display.
brawl (brôl) *n.* A noisy fight or argument. **—brawl** *v.* **—brawl'er** *n.*
brawn (brôn) *n.* **1.** Strong muscles. **2.** Muscular strength. **—brawn'i•ness** *n.* **—brawn'y** *adj.*
bray (brā) *n.* The loud, harsh sound made by a donkey. **—bray** *v.*
braze (brāz) *v.* **brazed, braz•ing.** To fuse (metals) together by means of a solder with a high melting point.
bra•zen (brā'zən) *adj.* **1.** Made of or like brass. **2.** Having a loud, resonant sound. **3.** Bold : impudent. —*v.* To face with bold confidence <*brazen* out the crisis> **—bra'zen•ly** *adv.* **—bra'zen•ness** *n.*
bra•zier (brā'zhər) *n.* A metal container that holds burning coals or charcoal.
Bra•zil (brə-zĭl'). Country of E South America. *Cap.* Brasília. *Pop.* 107,145,200. **—Bra•zil'ian** *adj.* & *n.*
Bra•zil nut (brə-zĭl') *n.* A tree, *Bertholletia excelsa,* of South America, that bears pods containing 20 to 30 hard-shelled edible nuts.
Braz•za•ville (brăz'ə-vĭl'). Cap. of Congo, on the N bank of the Congo. *Pop.* 175,000.
breach (brēch) *n.* **1.** A breaking of a law, obligation, or standard. **2.** A gap or rift, esp. in a solid structure. **3.** A disruption of friendly relations : estrangement. ☆***syns:*** BREAK, CLEFT, GAP, HOLE, PERFORATION, RENT, RUPTURE **—breach** *v.*
bread (brĕd) *n.* **1.** A usu. leavened staple food made from a flour or meal mixture that is kneaded and baked. **2.** Food in general. **3.** The necessities of life : livelihood. **4.** *Slang.* Money. —*v.* To cover with bread crumbs, as before cooking.
bread•bas•ket (brĕd'băs'kĭt) *n.* **1.** A region serving as a principal source of grain. **2.** *Slang.* The stomach.
bread•board (brĕd'bôrd', -bōrd') *n.* **1.** A board on which bread is sliced. **2.** *Slang.* An experimental model, as of an electronic circuit : prototype.
bread•fruit (brĕd'fro͞ot') *n.* A tree, *Artocarpus communis* or *A. incisa* of Polynesia, with deeply lobed leaves and edible fruit.
bread•stuff (brĕd'stŭf') *n.* **1.** Bread. **2.** Flour, meal, or grain used to produce bread.
breadth (brĕdth) *n.* **1.** The measurement from side to side : width. **2.** Broad extent or scope. **3.** Freedom from narrowness, as of interests or opinions.
bread•win•ner (brĕd'wĭn'ər) *n.* One whose earnings support a household.
break (brāk) *v.* **broke** (brōk), **bro•ken** (brō'kən), **break•ing. 1.** To reduce to or separate into pieces suddenly : smash. **2.** To crack without separating into pieces. **3.** To make or become unusable or inoperative. **4.** To give way : collapse. **5.** To make or force a way through, into, or out of. **6.** To part the surface of <*break* ground> **7.** To disrupt the order or unity of <*break* ranks> **8.** To come or bring into notice, esp. suddenly. **9.** To begin suddenly <*broke* into laughter> **10.** To change from one tonal register to another. **11.** To overwhelm : overcome. **12.** To destroy : ruin. **13.** To reduce in rank : demote. **14.** To lessen in force <*break* a fall> **15.** *Informal.* To occur. **—break down.** To undergo a breakdown. **—break in. 1.** To train. **2.** To enter forcibly. **3.** To reduce the newness of (e.g., a new product). **—break off. 1.** To stop suddenly, as in speaking. **2.** To discontinue a relationship. **—break out. 1.** To become affected by a skin eruption. **2.** To escape, as from prison. —*n.* **1.** The act of breaking. **2.** The result of breaking : a crack or fracture. **3.** A disruption in regularity. **4.** A beginning <the *break* of day> **5.** *Informal.* A stroke of luck. **—break'a•ble** *n.* & *adj.*
break•age (brā'kĭj) *n.* **1.** The act of breaking. **2. a.** A quantity broken. **b.** An allowance for such a loss.
break•down (brāk'doun') *n.* **1.** The act or process of breaking down or the resulting state. **2.** A collapse in mental or physical health. **3.** An analysis, outline, or summary made up of itemized data. **4.** Decomposition or disintegration into elements.
break•er (brā'kər) *n.* **1.** One that breaks. **2.** A wave that breaks into foam.
break•fast (brĕk'fəst) *n.* The 1st meal of the day. **—break'fast** *v.*
break•front (brāk'frŭnt') *n.* A high, wide cabinet with a central section that projects beyond the end sections.
break-in (brāk'ĭn') *n.* Forcible entry for an illegal purpose, as theft.
break•neck (brāk'nĕk') *adj.* Very fast and dangerous.
break•through (brāk'thro͞o') *n.* **1.** An act of breaking through a restriction or obstacle. **2.** A major achievement or discovery that permits further progress.
break•up (brāk'ŭp') *n.* **1.** A collapse. **2.** Division : dispersion.
break•wa•ter (brāk'wô'tər, -wŏt'ər) *n.* A barrier protecting a shore or harbor from the impact of waves.
bream (brēm) *n., pl.* **bream** or **breams.** A European freshwater fish of the genus *Abramis* with a flat body and silvery scales.
breast (brĕst) *n.* **1.** The mammary gland, esp. of the human female. **2.** The front surface of the body from the neck to the abdomen : chest. **3.** The seat of affection. —*v.* To advance boldly against : confront.
breast•bone (brĕst'bōn') *n.* The sternum.
breast-feed (brĕst'fēd') *v.* To feed (a baby) from the breast : nurse.
breast•plate (brĕst'plāt') *n.* A piece of armor plate for covering the breast.
breast stroke *n.* A swimming stroke performed by lying face down in the water, extending the arms in front of the head, then pulling them both back laterally under the surface of the water while doing a frog kick. **—breast'strok'er** *n.*
breast•work (brĕst'wûrk') *n.* A hastily constructed fortification, usu. breast-high.
breath (brĕth) *n.* **1.** The air inhaled and exhaled in respiration. **2.** The act or process of breathing : respiration. **3.** Capacity to breathe. **4.** A single respiration. **5.** A slight stirring of air. **6.** A trace. **7.** A soft-spoken sound : whisper. **—breath'less** *adj.* **—breath'less•ly** *adv.*
breathe (brēth) *v.* **breathed, breath•ing. 1.** To inhale and exhale air. **2.** To be alive : live. **3.** To pause to rest or regain

breath. **4.** To utter <never *breathed* a word of scandal> **–breath'a·ble** *adj.*

breath·er (brē'*th*ər) *n. Informal.* A short rest period <take a *breather*>

breath·tak·ing (brĕth'tā'kĭng) *adj.* Inspiring awe.

breath·y (brĕth'ē) *adj.* **-i·er, -i·est.** Marked by audible breathing. **–breath'i·ly** *adv.* **–breath'i·ness** *n.*

bred (brĕd) *v. p.t. & p.p.* of BREED.

†**breech** (brēch) *n.* **1.** The buttocks. **2.** The section of a firearm to the rear of the barrel. **3. breech·es** (brĭch'ĭz). **a.** Knee-length trousers. **b.** Trousers. *–v. Archaic & Regional.* To clothe with breeches.

breech delivery *n.* Delivery of a fetus with the feet or buttocks first.

breed (brēd) *v.* **bred** (brĕd), **breed·ing. 1.** To give birth to (offspring). **2.** To bring about : cause. **3.** To raise (animals). **4.** To bring up : rear. *–n.* **1.** A genetic strain, esp. of a domestic animal developed and maintained by humans. **2.** A kind : type. **–breed'er** *n.*

breeder reactor *n.* A nuclear reactor that generates as well as consumes fissionable material, esp. one that generates more fissionable material than it consumes.

breed·ing (brē'dĭng) *n.* **1.** Line of descent. **2.** Training in social conduct.

breeze (brēz) *n.* **1.** A light current of air. **2.** *Informal.* An easily accomplished task. *–v.* **breezed, breez·ing.** *Informal.* To progress swiftly and effortlessly <*breezed* through the interview> **–breez'i·ly** *adv.* **–breez'i·ness** *n.* **–breez'y** *adj.*

breeze·way (brēz'wā') *n.* A roofed, open-sided passageway connecting 2 structures.

Bre·men (brĕm'ən). City of N West Germany, on the Weser R. *Pop.* 556,128.

†**br'er** (brûr, brĕr) *n. S U.S.* BROTHER 1, 2.

breth·ren (brĕ*th*'rən) *n. archaic pl. of* BROTHER.

breve (brĕv, brēv) *n.* **1.** A symbol over a vowel to indicate its short sound. **2.** *Mus.* A single note equivalent to 2 whole notes.

bre·vi·ar·y (brē'vē-ĕr'-ē, brĕv'-ē-) *n., pl.* **-ies.** *Rom. Cath. Ch.* A book containing the daily hymns, offices, and prayers.

brev·i·ty (brĕv'ĭ-tē) *n.* **1.** Brief duration. **2.** Conciseness : terseness.

brew (bro͞o) *v.* **1.** To make (beer or ale) by infusing, boiling, and fermenting malt and hops. **2.** To make (a beverage) by boiling or steeping. **–brew** *n.* **–brew'er** *n.*

brew·er·y (bro͞o'ə-rē, bro͝or'ē) *n., pl.* **-ies.** A place where malt liquors are made.

†**brew·is** (bro͞o'ĭs, bro͞oz) *n. Regional.* A broth.

Brezh·nev (brĕzh'nĕf), **Leonid Ilyich.** 1906–82. Soviet statesman.

bri·ar[1] *also* **bri·er** (brī'ər) *n.* **1.** A shrub, *Erica arborea*, of S Europe with a woody root used to make tobacco pipes. **2.** A pipe made from the root of the briar.

bri·ar[2] (brī'ər) *n. var. of* BRIER[1].

bribe (brīb) *n.* Something, as money, offered or given to influence a person to act dishonestly. ☆*syns:* BOODLE, PAYOFF, PAYOLA *–v.* **bribed, brib·ing.** To corrupt or gain influence over by means of a bribe. **–brib'a·ble** *adj.* **–brib'er·y** *n.*

bric-a-brac (brĭk'ə-brăk') *n.* Small ornamental objects.

brick (brĭk) *n.* A molded rectangular block of clay, baked until hard and used esp. for building. *–v.* To construct or cover with brick.

brick·bat (brĭk'băt') *n.* **1.** A piece of brick, esp. when thrown as a missile. **2.** An uncomplimentary remark.

brick·lay·er (brĭk'lā'ər) *n.* One skilled in building with bricks. **–brick'lay'ing** *n.*

bri·dal (brīd'l) *adj.* Of or relating to a wedding or a bride. *–n.* A wedding.

▲word history: *Bridal* is a compound of 2 Old English words that mean "bride" and "ale." The compound orig. meant "wedding feast," but by late medieval times was used to refer to the ceremony itself. *Bridal* as an adjective prob. arose from the interpretation of *–al* as the common adjectival suffix.

bride (brīd) *n.* A woman recently married or about to be married.

bride·groom (brīd'gro͞om', -gro͝om') *n.* A man recently married or about to be married.

brides·maid (brīdz'mād') *n.* A woman attendant of the bride at a wedding.

bridge[1] (brĭj) *n.* **1.** A structure that spans and provides passage across an obstacle, as a waterway. **2.** The upper bony ridge of the nose. **3.** *Mus.* A thin, upright piece of wood in some stringed instruments supporting the strings above the sounding board. **4.** A removable or fixed replacement for missing natural teeth. **5.** *Naut.* A platform above the main deck of a ship, from which the ship is controlled. *–v.* **bridged, bridg·ing. 1.** To build a bridge over. **2.** To cross by or as if by a bridge. **–bridge'a·ble** *adj.*

bridge[2] (brĭj) *n.* Any of several games derived from whist and played with 1 deck of cards divided equally among 4 people.

bridge·head (brĭj'hĕd') *n.* A military position established in enemy territory.

Bridge·port (brĭj'pôrt', -pōrt'). Industrial city of SW Conn. *Pop.* 142,546.

Bridge·town (brĭj'toun'). Cap. of Barbados, E West Indies. *Pop.* 8,789.

bridge·work (brĭj'wûrk') *n.* A dental bridge.

bri·dle (brīd'l) *n.* **1.** A harness fitted about a horse's head, used to restrain or guide. **2.** A restraint : check. *–v.* **-dled, -dling. 1.** To put a bridle on. **2.** To restrain with or as if with a bridle. **3.** To show scorn or resentment by tossing the head.

brief (brēf) *adj.* **1.** Short in duration or extent. **2.** Condensed : succinct. *–n.* **1.** A short or summarizing statement, esp. of a legal case or argument. **2. briefs.** Short, tight-fitting underpants. *–v.* To give concise instructions to. **–brief'ly** *adv.* **–brief'ness** *n.*

brief·case (brēf'kās') *n.* A portable case used for carrying books and papers.

bri·er[1] *also* **bri·ar** (brī'ər) *n.* A thorny plant or bush. **–bri'er·y** *adj.*

bri·er[2] (brī'ər) *n. var. of* BRIAR[1].

brig (brĭg) *n.* **1.** A 2-masted square-rigged sailing ship. **2.** A ship's prison.

bri·gade (brĭ-gād') *n.* **1.** A military unit consisting of a large number of troops. **2.** A group of people organized for a specific job or purpose.

brig·a·dier general (brĭg'ə-dîr') *n., pl.* **brigadier generals.** An officer who ranks below a major general in the U.S. Army, Air Force, and Marine Corps.

brig·and (brĭg'ənd) *n.* One who plunders and robs : bandit. **–brig'and·age** *n.*

brig·an·tine (brĭg'ən-tēn') *n.* A 2-masted, square-rigged sailing ship with a fore-and-aft mainsail.

bright (brīt) *adj.* **1.** Reflecting or emitting light. **2.** Brilliant : vivid. **3.** Resplendent : splendid. **4.** Intelligent : clever. **5.** Lively : cheerful. ☆*syns:* BRILLIANT, EFFULGENT, INCANDESCENT, LUMINOUS, LUSTROUS, RADIANT, REFULGENT, SHINING *–n.* **brights.** High-beam headlights. *–adv.* In a bright way. **–bright'ly** *adv.* **–bright'ness** *n.*

bright·en (brīt'n) *v.* To make or become bright or brighter.

Brigh·ton (brīt'n). Seaside resort of SE England. *Pop.* 152,700.

bril·liant (brĭl'yənt) *adj.* **1.** Very bright : shining. **2.** Brightly vivid in color. **3.** Exceptionally intelligent. **4.** Splendid : magnificent. *–n.* A precious gem finely cut with numerous facets. **–bril'liance, bril'lian·cy** *n.* **–bril'liant·ly** *adv.*

bril·lian·tine (brĭl'yən-tēn') *n.* An oily, perfumed dressing for the hair.

brim (brĭm) *n.* **1.** The rim of a vessel, as a cup. **2.** A projecting rim <the *brim* of a hat> *–v.* **brimmed, brim·ming.** To fill or be full to the brim. **–brim'ful'** *adj.* **–brim'less** *adj.*

brim·stone (brĭm'stōn') *n.* Sulfur.

brin·dle (brĭn'dl) *also* **brin·dled** (-əld) *adj.* Grayish or tawny with darker flecks.

brine (brīn) *n.* **1.** Water containing large amounts of salt. **2.** The sea. **3.** Salt water for preserving and pickling foods. **–brin'i·ness** *n.* **–brin'y** *adj.*

bring (brĭng) *v.* **brought** (brôt), **bring·ing. 1.** To take with oneself to a place. **2.** To cause <The rains *brought* mud slides.> **3.** To sell for : fetch. **4.** To persuade : induce. **5.** To lead or force into a specified situation or condition. **–bring about.** To cause to happen. **–bring forth.** To produce. **–bring off.** To carry out successfully. **–bring out. 1.** To expose or reveal. **2.** To produce or publish. **–bring to.** To cause to recover consciousness. **–bring up. 1.** To take care of and rear (a child). **2.** To introduce into discussion : mention. **3.** To vomit.

brink (brĭngk) *n.* **1.** The upper edge, as that of a steep slope. **2.** VERGE[1] 2.

brink·man·ship (brĭngk'mən-shĭp') *n.* A perilous course of action that stops just short of the point of no return.

bri·o (brē'ō) *n.* Vivacity : spirit.

bri·oche (brē-ōsh', -ŏsh') *n.* A soft roll made from butter, eggs, flour, and yeast.

bri·quette *also* **bri·quet** (brĭ-kĕt') *n.* A brick-shaped mass of compressed coal dust or charcoal, used for fuel.

bri·sance (brĭ-zäns', -zäNs') *n.* The shattering effect of a sudden release of energy, as in an explosion. **–bri·sant'** *adj.*

Bris·bane (brĭz'bən, -bān'). Seaport of SE Australia. *Pop.* 702,000.

brisk (brĭsk) *adj.* **1.** Vigorous : lively. **2.** Stimulating : invigorating. **–brisk'ly** *adv.* **–brisk'ness** *n.*

bris·ket (brĭs'kĭt) *n.* Meat from the lower chest of an animal.

bris•ling (brĭz'lĭng, brĭs'-) *n.* A small sardine.
bris•tle (brĭs'əl) *n.* A short, stiff, coarse hair. *—v.* **-tled, -tling. 1.** To erect the bristles, as an excited animal. **2.** To react with angry defiance. **3.** To stand on end stiffly. **4.** To be covered or thick with or as if with bristles. **—bris'tly** *adj.*
Bris•tol (brĭs'təl). Port city of SW England. *Pop.* 408,000.
Brit•ain (brĭt'n). **1.** Great Britain. **2.** United Kingdom.
Bri•tan•nic (brĭ-tăn'ĭk) *adj.* British.
britch•es (brĭch'ĭz) *pl.n.* Breeches.
Brit•i•cism (brĭt'ĭ-sĭz-əm) *n.* A word or idiom peculiar to British English.
Brit•ish (brĭt'ĭsh) *n.* **1.** *(pl. in number).* The people of Great Britain. **2.** British English. **—Brit'ish** *adj.*
Brit•ish Co•lum•bi•a (brĭt'ĭsh kə-lŭm'bē-ə). Province of W Canada. *Cap.* Victoria. *Pop.* 2,466,608.
British English *n.* The English language as used in England.
British Isles. Islands off the NW coast of Europe, comprising Great Britain, Ireland, and adjacent smaller islands.
British thermal unit *n.* The quantity of heat required to raise the temperature of 1 lb of water by 1°F.
British Virgin Islands. British colony in the West Indies.
Brit•on (brĭt'n) *n.* **1.** An inhabitant or native of Britain. **2.** One of a Celtic people of Britain prior to the Roman invasion.
Brit•ta•ny (brĭt'n-ē).A region and former province of NW France on a peninsula extending into the Atlantic. **—Bret'on** (brĕt'n) *adj.* & *n.*
brit•tle (brĭt'l) *adj.* Easily broken : fragile. **—brit'tle•ness** *n.*
broach (brōch) *n.* **1.** A tapered tool used for shaping or enlarging a hole. **2.** A tool for tapping a cask. **3.** *var. of* BROOCH. *—v.* **1.** To introduce (a subject) for discussion. **2.** To tap (e.g., a cask) in order to draw off the contents. **—broach'er** *n.*
broad (brôd) *adj.* **1.** Wide. **2.** Large : spacious. **3.** Clear : bright <*broad* daylight> **4.** General in scope <a *broad* restriction> **5.** Main : essential. **6.** Obvious <a *broad* hint> **7.** Coarse : ribald. **—broad'ly** *adv.* **—broad'ness** *n.*
broad•band (brôd'bănd') *adj.* Of, having, or relating to a wide band of electromagnetic frequencies.
broad•cast (brôd'kăst') *v.* **-cast** or **-cast•ed, -cast•ing. 1.** To transmit by television or radio. **2.** To make known widely <*broadcast* gossip> **3.** To throw (seed) about : scatter. *—n.* **1.** Transmission of a radio or television signal. **2.** A radio or television program. **—broad'cast'er** *n.*
broad•cloth (brôd'klôth', -klŏth') *n.* **1.** A densely textured woolen cloth with a lustrous finish. **2.** A closely woven cotton, silk, or synthetic fabric.
broad•en (brôd'n) *v.* To widen.
broad•loom (brôd'lo͞om') *adj.* Woven on a wide loom. *—n.* A broadloom carpet.
broad-mind•ed (brôd'mīn'dĭd) *adj.* Unprejudiced : liberal. **—broad'mind'ed•ly** *adv.* **—broad'-mind'ed•ness** *n.*
broad•side (brôd'sīd') *n.* **1.** The side of a ship above the water line. **2.** Simultaneous discharge of the guns on 1 side of a warship. **3.** A verbal denunciation or attack.
broad-spec•trum (brôd'spĕk'trəm) *adj.* Having wide effectiveness.
broad•sword (brôd'sôrd', -sōrd') *n.* A broad-bladed sword.
bro•cade (brō-kād') *n.* A rich, heavy cloth interwoven with a raised design.
broc•co•li *also* **broc•o•li** (brŏk'ə-lē) *n.* A plant, *Brassica oleracea italica*, with a branched green flower head that is eaten as a vegetable before the buds have opened.
bro•chette (brō-shĕt') *n.* A small skewer.
bro•chure (brō-sho͝or') *n.* A pamphlet.
bro•gan (brō'gən) *n.* A heavy work shoe reaching to the ankle.
brogue (brōg) *n.* **1.** A strong oxford shoe. **2.** A strong dialectal accent, esp. a heavy Irish accent.
broil (broil) *v.* To cook by exposure to direct radiant heat : grill.
broil•er (broi'lər) *n.* **1.** A utensil, as a pan or part of a stove, used for broiling. **2.** A young chicken fit for broiling.
broke (brōk) *adj. Informal.* Completely without money : poor.
bro•ken (brō'kən) *adj.* **1.** Fractured : shattered. **2.** Not upheld : breached <*broken* promises> **3.** Imperfectly spoken. **4.** Subdued : crushed. **5.** Discontinuous : interrupted. **6.** Not functioning : inoperative. **—bro'ken•ly** *adv.*
bro•ken•heart•ed (brō'kən-här'tĭd) *adj.* Crushed by sadness or grief.
bro•ker (brō'kər) *n.* One hired for a fee to negotiate purchases, contracts, or sales.
bro•ker•age (brō'kər-ĭj) *n.* **1.** The business of a broker. **2.** A broker's fee.
bro•mide (brō'mīd') *n.* **1.** A binary compound of bromine. **2.** Potassium bromide. **3. a.** A trite remark : platitude. **b.** A bore. **—bro•mid'ic** *adj.*
▲word history: Several bromine compounds, esp. potassium bromide, have been used medicinally as sedatives. In 1906 Gelett Burgess wrote a book entitled *Are You a Bromide?* in which he used *bromide* to mean a tiresome person of unoriginal thought and trite conversation. *Bromide* was soon after extended to denote the trite remarks made by such persons.
bro•mine (brō'mēn') *n. Symbol* **Br** A heavy, reddish-brown, corrosive, liquid element with irritating fumes.
bron•chi•al (brŏng'kē-əl) *adj.* Of or relating to the bronchi or their extensions.
bron•chi•tis (brŏng-kī'tĭs) *n.* Chronic or acute inflammation of the bronchi. **—bron•chit'ic** (-kĭt'ĭk) *adj.*
bron•chus (brŏng'kəs) *n., pl.* **-chi** (-kī', -kē'). Either of the main branches of the trachea, each leading to a lung.
bron•co (brŏng'kō) *n., pl.* **-cos.** A small semiwild horse of W North America.
bron•co•bust•er (brŏng'kō-bŭs'tər) *n.* A cowboy who tames broncos.
Bron•të (brŏn'tē). English family of novelists, including **Charlotte** (1816–55), **Emily Jane** (1818–48), and **Anne** (1820–49).
bron•to•saur (brŏn'tə-sôr') *also* **bron•to•sau•rus** (-sôr'əs). *n.* A large, herbivorous dinosaur of the genus *Apatosaurus* or *Brontosaurus.*
Bronx or **the Bronx** (brŏngks). Borough of New York City. *Pop.* 1,169,115.
Bronx cheer (brŏngks) *n. Slang.* RASPBERRY 2.
bronze (brŏnz) *n.* **1.** An alloy of tin and copper. **2.** A work of art made in bronze. **3.** A yellowish to olive brown. *—v.* **bronzed, bronz•ing.** To give a bronze appearance to. **—bronze** *adj.* **—bronz'y** *adj.*
Bronze Age *n.* A period of human culture between the Stone Age and the Iron Age, marked by the use of bronze implements and weapons.
brooch *also* **broach** (brōch, bro͞och) *n.* An ornamental clasp or pin.
brood (bro͞od) *n.* A family of young animals or children, esp. a group of birds hatched at the same time. *—v.* **1.** To sit on and hatch (eggs). **2.** To ponder anxiously : worry. ☆**syns:** MOPE, STEW, WORRY
brood•er (bro͞o'dər) *n.* **1.** One that broods. **2.** A heated structure for raising young domestic birds.
brood•mare (bro͞od'mâr') *n.* A mare used for breeding.
brood•y (bro͞o'dē) *adj.* **-i•er, -i•est. 1.** Moody. **2.** Inclined to sit on eggs to hatch them <a *broody* hen> **—brood'i•ness** *n.*
brook[1] (bro͝ok) *n.* A freshwater stream.
brook[2] (bro͝ok) *v.* To tolerate : bear.
brook•let (bro͝ok'lĭt) *n.* A small brook.
Brook•lyn (bro͝ok'lĭn). Borough of New York City, on W Long Is. *Pop.* 2,230,936.
brook trout *n.* A freshwater fish, *Salvelinus fontinalis*, of E North America.
broom (bro͞om, bro͝om) *n.* **1.** A brush made of stiff fibers bound together on a long handle. **2.** A shrub of the genus *Cytisus*, with yellow flowers. **—broom'stick** *n.*
broth (brôth, brŏth) *n., pl.* **broths** (brôths, brŏths, brô*th*z, brŏ*th*z). Stock obtained from boiling meat or vegetables.
broth•el (brŏth'əl, brô'thəl) *n.* A house of prostitution.
broth•er (brŭ*th*'ər) *n.* **1.** A male having 1 or both parents in common with another individual. **2.** A fellow man or a male friend. **3.** A lay member of a men's religious order. **—broth'er•li•ness** *n.* **—broth'er•ly** *adj.* & *adv.*
broth•er•hood (brŭ*th*'ər-ho͝od') *n.* **1.** The state or quality of being brothers. **2.** An association, as a fraternity, united for a common purpose. **3.** The whole body of persons in a profession or trade.
broth•er-in-law (brŭ*th*'ər-ĭn-lô') *n., pl.* **broth•ers-in-law. 1.** The brother of one's spouse. **2.** The husband of one's sister. **3.** The husband of the sister of one's spouse.
brougham (bro͞om, bro͞o'əm, brō'əm) *n.* **1.** A light, closed horse-drawn carriage with the driver's seat outside in front. **2.** An automobile with an open seat for the driver.
brought (brôt) *v. p.t.* & *p.p. of* BRING.
brou•ha•ha (bro͞o'hä-hä') *n.* A noisy wrangle : commotion : uproar.
brow (brou) *n.* **1. a.** The ridge over the eyes. **b.** The forehead. **c.** The eyebrow. **2.** The upper part of a steep place.
brow•beat (brou'bēt') *v.* To intimidate : bully. **—brow'beat'er** *n.*
brown (broun) *n.* One of a group of colors between red and yellow. *—adj.* **1.** Of the color brown. **2.** Of dark or tanned complexion. *—v.* To make or become brown. **—brown'ish** *adj.* **—brown'ness** *n.*
Brown (broun), **John.** 1800–59. Amer. abolitionist.
brown bear *n.* A very large bear, *Ursus arctos*, with brown to yellowish fur.
brown bread *n.* A bread made of a dark whole-wheat flour.
brown•ie (brou'nē) *n.* **1.** A helpful sprite in folklore. **2.**

Brownie. A member of the Girl Scouts from 7 to 9 years of age. **3.** A square or bar of chewy, rich chocolate cake.
Brown·ing (brou′nĭng), **Elizabeth Barrett** (1806–61) and **Robert** (1812–89). English poets.
brown·out (broun′out′) *n.* A curtailment of electrical power.
brown rice *n.* Unpolished rice that retains the germ and the outer layer.
brown·stone (broun′stōn′) *n.* **1.** A reddish-brown sandstone. **2.** A dwelling faced with brownstone.
brown study *n.* A state of reverie.
brown sugar *n.* Sugar whose crystals retain a coating of dark syrup.
browse (brouz) *v.* **browsed, brows·ing. 1.** To casually inspect goods offered for sale. **2.** To skim through a book. **3.** To graze (on). **–browse** *n.* **–brows′er** *n.*
bru·in (bro͞o′ĭn) *n.* A bear.
bruise (bro͞oz) *v.* **bruised, bruis·ing. 1. a.** To injure without rupturing. **b.** To suffer bruising. **2.** To pound into fragments. **3.** To hurt : offend. *–n.* An injury that does not break the skin : contusion.
bruis·er (bro͞o′zər) *n. Slang.* A large, husky man.
bruit (bro͞ot) *v.* To spread news of : report.
brunch (brŭnch) *n.* A meal eaten as a combination of lunch and breakfast.
Bru·nei (bro͞o-nī′). Sultanate on the N coast of Borneo. *Cap.* Bandar Seri Begawan. *Pop.* 136,256.
bru·net (bro͞o-nĕt′) *adj.* **1.** Of a dark complexion. **2.** Having brown or black eyes and hair. *–n.* A person with brown hair.
bru·nette (bro͞o-nĕt′) *adj.* Having brown or dark hair. *–n.* A girl or woman with brown or dark hair.
brunt (brŭnt) *n.* The main shock or impact, esp. of a blow.
brush[1] (brŭsh) *n.* **1.** A device composed of bristles set into a handle, used for cleaning, painting, scrubbing, grooming the hair, etc. **2.** A light touching or grazing. **3.** A brief encounter. **4.** A bushy tail, as of a fox. **5.** A sliding connection completing a circuit between a fixed and a moving conductor. ☆**syns:** FLICK, GLANCE, GRAZE, SKIM *–v.* **1.** To use a brush (on). **2.** To remove or apply with or as if with a brush. **3.** To touch or graze in passing. **–brush up.** To renew one's skill.
brush[2] (brŭsh) *n.* **1.** A thicket of bushes. **2.** Small branches broken from trees. **–brush′wood′** *n.* **–brush′y** *adj.*
brush-off (brŭsh′ôf′, -ŏf′) *n. Slang.* A curt dismissal.
brusque *also* **brusk** (brŭsk) *adj.* Rudely abrupt : blunt. **–brusque′ly** *adv.* **–brusque′ness** *n.*
Brus·sels (brŭs′əlz). Cap. of Belgium, in the NC part. *Pop.* 143,957.
Brus·sels sprouts (brŭs′əlz) *pl.n.* The budlike, edible heads of a cabbage variety, *Brassica oleracea gemmifera.*
bru·tal (bro͞ot′l) *adj.* Savage : harsh. **–bru·tal′i·ty** *n.* **–bru′tal·ly** *adv.*
bru·tal·ize (bro͞ot′l-īz′) *v.* **-ized, -iz·ing. 1.** To make brutal. **2.** To treat in a brutal way. **–bru′tal·i·za′tion** *n.*
brute (bro͞ot) *n.* **1.** A beast. **2.** A brutal person. *–adj.* **1.** Of or pertaining to beasts. **2.** Completely physical or instinctive <*brute* strength> **–brut′ish** *adj.* **–brut′ish·ly** *adv.* **–brut′ish·ness** *n.*
bry·o·phyte (brī′ə-fīt′) *n.* A plant of the division Bryophyta, including the mosses and liverworts.
B.S. *abbr.* **1.** Bachelor of Science. **2.** balance sheet. **3.** bill of sale.
bu. *abbr.* **1.** *also* **bur.** bureau. **2.** bushel.
bub·ble (bŭb′əl) *n.* **1.** A light, thin-walled sphere of liquid holding air or gas. **2.** A small globule of gas, as in a carbonated drink. **3.** A plastic or glass dome. **4.** Something lacking substance or solidity. *–v.* **-bled, -bling.** To form or give off bubbles.
bubble gum *n.* Chewing gum that can be blown into bubbles.
bub·bly (bŭb′lē) *n., pl.* **-blies.** *Informal.* Champagne. *–adj.* **1.** Full of bubbles. **2.** Resembling a bubble.
bu·bo (bo͞o′bō, byo͞o′-) *n., pl.* **-boes.** An inflamed swelling of a lymph gland. **–bu·bon′ic** (-bŏn′ĭk) *adj.*
bubonic plague *n.* A highly contagious, usu. fatal epidemic disease marked by chills, fever, and buboes.
buc·ca·neer (bŭk′ə-nîr′) *n.* A pirate.
Bu·chan·an (byo͞o-kăn′ən, bə-), **James.** 1791–1868. 15th U.S. President (1857–61).
Bu·cha·rest (bo͞o′kə-rĕst′, byo͞o′-). Cap. of Rumania, in the SE. *Pop.* 1,858,418.
buck[1] (bŭk) *n.* **1.** A male animal, as a deer or rabbit. **2.** *Informal.* A bold, high-spirited young man. *–v.* **1.** To leap suddenly forward, as a horse. **2.** To butt (against). **3.** To move forward with sudden jerks. **4.** To throw (e.g., a rider) by bucking. **5.** To resist stubbornly. *–adj.* Of the lowest rank <a *buck* sergeant> **–buck** *adj.*
buck[2] (bŭk) *n. Slang.* A dollar.
buck·a·roo *also* **buck·er·oo** (bŭk′ə-ro͞o′) *n., pl.* **-roos** *also* **-oos.** A cowboy.
buck·board (bŭk′bôrd′, -bōrd′) *n.* An open 4-wheeled carriage with the seat attached to a flexible board extending from the front to the rear axle.

buckboard

buck·et (bŭk′ĭt) *n.* **1.** A cylindrical vessel used for holding or carrying water, coal, sand, etc. : pail. **2.** A similar vessel for holding and conveying material, as the scoop of a steam shovel.
bucket seat *n.* A separate, contoured seat, as in a sports car.
buck·eye (bŭk′ī′) *n.* One of several North American trees of the genus *Aesculus,* with white or reddish flower clusters, compound leaves, and shiny brown nuts.
buck·le[1] (bŭk′əl) *n.* A clasp for fastening ends together. *–v.* **-led, -ling.** To fasten or be fastened with a buckle. **–buckle down.** To apply oneself determinedly.
buck·le[2] (bŭk′əl) *v.* **-led, -ling. 1.** To warp or bend, as under pressure or heat. **2.** To give way : collapse. **–buck′le** *n.*
buck·ler (bŭk′lər) *n.* A small circular shield.
buck·ram (bŭk′rəm) *n.* A coarse, stiffened cloth used esp. for binding books.
buck·saw (bŭk′sô′) *n.* A wood-cutting saw set in a deep, usu. H-shaped frame.
buck·shot (bŭk′shŏt′) *n.* A coarse lead shot used for shooting large game animals.
buck·skin (bŭk′skĭn′) *n.* **1.** A soft, grayish-yellow leather. **2. buckskins.** Clothes made from buckskin.
buck·tooth (bŭk′to͞oth′) *n.* A large projecting upper front tooth. **–buck′toothed′** *adj.*
buck·wheat (bŭk′hwēt′, -wēt′) *n.* **1.** A plant of the genus *Fagopyrum,* native to Asia, with fragrant white flowers and small triangular seeds often used as cereal grain.
bu·col·ic (byo͞o-kŏl′ĭk) *adj.* **1.** Relating to flocks or shepherds : pastoral. **2.** Rural : rustic. *–n.* A pastoral poem.
bud (bŭd) *n.* **1.** *Bot.* A small swelling on a plant from which a leaf or flower grows. **2.** *Biol.* An asexual reproductive structure. **3.** Something that is still undeveloped. *–v.* **bud·ded, bud·ding. 1.** To put forth buds. **2.** To begin to grow from or as if from a bud. **–bud′der** *n.* **–bud′like′** *adj.*
Bu·da·pest (bo͞o′də-pĕst′). Cap. of Hungary, in the NC part. *Pop.* 2,060,000.
Bud·dha (bo͞o′də, bo͝od′ə). 563?–483? B.C. Indian philosopher; founder of Buddhism.
Bud·dhism (bo͞o′dĭz′əm, bo͝od′ĭz′-) *n.* A religion of E and C Asia based on the doctrines and teachings of Buddha. **–Bud′dhist** *n.* **–Bud·dhis′tic** *adj.*
bud·dle·ia (bŭd′lē-ə, bŭd-lē′ə) *n.* One of several shrubs of the genus *Buddleia,* with purplish or white flower clusters.
bud·dy (bŭd′ē) *n., pl.* **-dies.** *Informal.* A friend.
budge (bŭj) *v.* **budged, budg·ing. 1.** To shift or cause to shift slightly. **2.** To change or cause to change an attitude.
budg·er·i·gar (bŭj′ə-rē-gär′) *n.* A small parakeet, *Melopsittacus undulatus,* with blue, green, or yellow plumage.
budg·et (bŭj′ĭt) *n.* **1.** A report of estimated expenditure and income. **2.** The amount of money assigned to a particular purpose. *–v.* **1.** To make a budget. **2.** To allow for in a budget. **–budg′et·ar′y** *adj.*
budg·ie (bŭj′ē) *n. Informal.* A budgerigar.
Bue·nos Ai·res (bwā′nəs ĭr′ēz, âr′-, bō′nəs). Cap. of Argentina. *Pop.* 2,978,000.
buff[1] (bŭf) *n.* **1.** A soft, thick leather made chiefly from buffalo, elk, or oxen skins. **2.** A moderate or light yellow. **3.** *Informal.* The bare skin <swam in the *buff*> *–v.* To polish or shine with a buff.
buff[2] (bŭf) *n. Informal.* An enthusiast.
buf·fa·lo (bŭf′ə-lō′) *n., pl.* **-loes** or **-los** or **-lo. 1.** Any of several oxlike Old World mammals of the family Bovidae. **2.** The bison. *–v.* **-loed, -lo·ing** *Slang.* To baffle or confuse.
Buf·fa·lo (bŭf′ə-lō′). City of W N.Y., at the NE end of Lake Erie. *Pop.* 357,870.
buff·er[1] (bŭf′ər) *n.* One that buffs.
buff·er[2] (bŭf′ər) *n.* **1.** Something that reduces the shock of impact. **2.** *Chem.* A substance that can stabilize the acidity or

alkalinity of a solution by neutralizing, within certain limits, any acid or base that is added. **3.** *Computer Sci.* An area used to store data temporarily.
buf•fet[1] (bə-fā′, bo͞o-) *n.* **1.** A sideboard. **2.** A counter from which food is served. **3.** A meal at which diners serve themselves from dishes displayed on a table.
buf•fet[2] (bŭf′ĭt) *n.* A blow : slap. *—v.* To strike or pound repeatedly : batter.
buf•foon (bə-fo͞on′) *n.* A fool : clown. **—buf•foon′er•y** *n.*
bug (bŭg) *n.* **1.** Any of various sucking insects of the order Hemiptera. **2.** An insect. **3.** *Informal.* A germ or virus. **4.** A defect or problem, as in a machine. **5.** *Slang.* An enthusiast. **6.** A concealed microphone for eavesdropping. *—v.* **bugged, bug•ging. 1.** *Slang.* To bother : annoy. **2.** To hide a microphone in.
bug•a•boo (bŭg′ə-bo͞o′) *n., pl.* **-boos.** A source of concern.
bug•bear (bŭg′bâr′) *n.* An object or source of dread.
bug•eyed (bŭg′īd′) *adj. Slang.* With bulging eyes.
bug•gy (bŭg′ē) *n., pl.* **-gies.** A light, 4-wheeled horse-drawn carriage.
bu•gle (byo͞o′gəl) *n.* A brass wind instrument like a trumpet but without valves. **—bu′gle** *v.* **—bu′gler** *n.*
build (bĭld) *v.* **built** (bĭlt), **build•ing. 1.** To construct. **2.** To give form to : create. **3.** To establish a basis for : found <*built* a case from evidence> *—n.* The physical form of a thing or person. **—build′er** *n.*
build•ing (bĭl′dĭng) *n.* **1.** A usu. roofed and walled structure. **2.** The process or business of constructing buildings.
build-up *also* **build•up** (bĭld′ŭp′) *n.* **1.** Gradual increase. **2.** *Informal.* Widely favorable publicity.
built-in (bĭlt′ĭn′) *adj.* **1.** Made as an integral part of a larger unit. **2.** Inherent.
Bu•jum•bu•ra (bo͞o′jəm-bo͝or′ə, bo͞o-jo͞om′bo͝or′-ə). Cap. of Burundi, on Lake Tanganyika. *Pop.* 157,000.
bulb (bŭlb) *n.* **1.** *Bot.* A rounded, underground bud with roots and a stem, as that of a daffodil or onion. **2.** Any rounded object resembling a bulb. **3.** An incandescent lamp or its glass housing. **—bul′bous** *adj.*
Bul•gar•i•a (bŭl-gâr′ē-ə, bo͝ol-). Country of SE Europe, on the Black Sea. *Cap.* Sofia. *Pop.* 8,846,417. **—Bul•gar′i•an** *adj.* & *n.*
bulge (bŭlj) *n.* A protuberance. *—v.* **bulged, bulg•ing.** To become or cause to become protuberant. **—bulg′i•ness** *n.*
bul•gur (go͝ol-go͝or′, bŭl′gər) *n.* Dried cracked wheat.
bu•lim•i•a (byo͞o-lĭm′ē-ə) *n.* An insatiable craving for food.
bulk (bŭlk) *n.* **1.** Volume, mass, or size, esp. when large. **2.** The greater part. ☆***syns:*** AMPLITUDE, MAGNITUDE, MASS, SIZE, VOLUME **—in bulk. 1.** Not packaged. **2.** In large amounts or volume. *—v.* To have or appear to have massive importance or size. **—bulk′i•ness** *n.* **—bulk′y** *adj.*
bulk•head (bŭlk′hĕd′) *n.* **1.** An upright partition separating compartments in a ship. **2.** A retaining wall, as in a mine.
bull[1] (bo͝ol) *n.* **1.** The adult male of a bovine animal or certain other large animals. **2.** A person who buys commodities or securities expecting their prices to rise. **3.** *Slang.* A police officer. **4.** *Slang.* Nonsense. **—bull′ish** *adj.* **—bull′ish•ness** *n.*
bull[2] (bo͝ol) *n.* A document from the pope.
bull. *abbr.* bulletin.
†bull•dog (bo͝ol′dôg′, -dŏg′) *n.* A short-haired, heavily built dog with large square jaws. *—v. W U.S.* To throw (a steer) by holding its horns and twisting its neck.
bull•doze (bo͝ol′dōz′) *v.* **-dozed, -doz•ing. 1.** To clear using a bulldozer. **2.** *Slang.* To coerce : bully.
bull•doz•er (bo͝ol′dō′zər) *n.* A tractor with a large scoop in front for clearing debris and earth.
bul•let (bo͝ol′ĭt) *n.* A metallic projectile to be shot from a firearm.

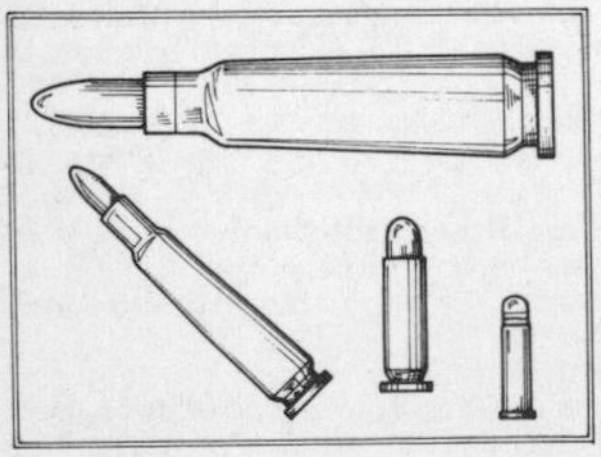

bullet

bul•let•proof (bo͝ol′ĭt-pro͞of′) *adj.* Impenetrable by bullets. **—bul′let•proof′** *v.*
bul•le•tin (bo͝ol′ĭ-tn, -tĭn) *n.* **1.** A brief report on a matter of public interest. **2.** A regular publication of an organization.
bulletin board *n.* A board for displaying notices.
bull•fight (bo͝ol′fīt′) *n.* A spectacle, esp. in Spain and Mexico, in which a bull is provoked and then usu. killed with a sword by a matador. **—bull′fight′er** *n.* **—bull′fight′ing** *n.*
bull•finch (bo͝ol′fĭnch′) *n.* A European songbird, *Pyrrhula pyrrhula,* with a short, thick bill and, in the male, a red breast.
bull•frog (bo͝ol′frôg′, -frŏg′) *n.* A large frog, esp. *Rana catesbeiana,* with a deep, loud croak.
bull•head (bo͝ol′hĕd′) *n.* One of several freshwater catfishes of the genus *Ictalurus.*
bull•head•ed (bo͝ol′hĕd′ĭd) *adj.* Extremely obstinate : headstrong. **—bull′head′ed•ly** *adv.* **—bull′head′ed•ness** *n.*
bul•lion (bo͝ol′yən) *n.* Silver or gold ingots.
bul•lock (bo͝ol′ək) *n.* **1.** A castrated bull : steer. **2.** A young bull.
bull•pen (bo͝ol′pĕn′) *n.* **1.** *Informal.* A temporary detention room for prisoners. **2.** *Baseball.* A practice area for relief pitchers during a game.
bull session *n. Informal.* A rambling, informal group discussion.
bull's-eye *also* **bull's eye** (bo͝olz′ī′) *n.* **1.** The center of a target. **2.** A shot that hits the bull's-eye.
bull terrier *n.* A short-haired dog with a long muzzle and large jaws.
bul•ly (bo͝ol′ē) *n., pl.* **-lies.** One who hurts or intimidates weaker or smaller people. *—v.* **-lied, -ly•ing.** To act like a bully. *—adj. Informal.* First-rate : excellent. *—interj.* Used to express approval.
bul•rush (bo͝ol′rŭsh′) *n.* **1.** A grasslike sedge of the genus *Scirpus* that grows in wet places. **2.** A marsh plant, as a cattail.
bul•wark (bo͝ol′wərk, bŭl′-, -wôrk′) *n.* **1.** A defensive wall or rampart. **2.** Something serving as a principal defense.
bum[1] (bŭm) *n.* **1.** A tramp : vagrant. **2.** One who avoids work and tries to live off others. *—v.* **bummed, bum•ming.** *Informal.* **1.** To live as a bum. **2.** To get by begging. **3.** To loaf. *—adj. Slang.* **1.** Worthless. **2.** Disabled.
bum[2] (bŭm) *n. esp. Brit.* The buttocks.
bum•ble (bŭm′bəl) *v.* **-bled, -bling.** To behave or speak in a clumsy or inept manner. **—bum′bler** *n.*
bum•ble•bee (bŭm′bəl-bē′) *n.* A large, hairy bee of the genus *Bombus.*
bum•mer (bŭm′ər) *n. Slang.* **1.** A bad reaction to a hallucinogenic drug. **2.** An unpleasant person or situation.
bump (bŭmp) *v.* **1.** To collide forcefully (with). **2.** To move with jerks and jolts. **3.** To displace. **—bump into.** To meet by chance. **—bump off.** *Slang.* To kill. *—n.* **1.** A jolt or knock. **2.** A swelling, usu. caused by a blow. **—bump′y** *adj.*
bump•er[1] (bŭm′pər) *n.* A horizontal metal bar at either end of a car for absorbing the shock of a collision.
bump•er[2] (bŭm′pər) *n.* A glass or cup filled to the brim. *—adj.* Exceptionally full or abundant <a *bumper* harvest>
bump•kin (bŭmp′kĭn, bŭm′-) *n.* An awkward or simple country person.
bump•tious (bŭmp′shəs) *adj.* Obtrusively forward and conceited. **—bump′tious•ly** *adv.* **—bump′tious•ness** *n.*
bun (bŭn) *n.* **1.** A small, usu. sweetened bread roll. **2.** Hair worn in a knot at the back of the head.
bunch (bŭnch) *n.* A cluster or group of similar things. **—bunch** *v.*
bun•co *also* **bun•ko** (bŭng′kō) *n., pl.* **-cos** *also* **-kos.** *Informal.* A confidence game. **—bun′co** *v.*
bun•dle (bŭn′dl) *n.* **1.** A group of things fastened together. **2.** *Slang.* A large amount of money. *—v.* **-dled, -dling. 1.** To make into a bundle. **2.** To dress warmly.
bung (bŭng) *n.* A stopper for a bunghole.
bun•ga•low (bŭng′gə-lō′) *n.* A small 1-storied house.
bung•hole (bŭng′hōl′) *n.* The hole for filling or draining a cask or barrel.
bun•gle (bŭng′gəl) *v.* **-gled, -gling.** To do clumsily : botch. **—bun′gler** *n.*
bun•ion (bŭn′yən) *n.* An inflamed swelling on the 1st joint of the big toe.
bunk[1] (bŭngk) *n.* **1.** A narrow bed built against a wall. **2.** *Informal.* A sleeping place. **—bunk** *v.*
bunk[2] (bŭngk) *n. Slang.* Nonsense.
bun•ker (bŭng′kər) *n.* **1.** A container or compartment for storing fuel, as on a ship. **2.** A sandtrap on a golf course. **3.** An underground fortification.
bunk•house (bŭngk′hous′) *n.* Sleeping quarters, as for ranch hands.
bun•kum *also* **bun•combe** (bŭng′kəm) *n.* Empty talk : claptrap.
bun•ny (bŭn′ē) *n., pl.* **-nies.** A rabbit.
buns (bŭnz) *pl.n. Slang.* The buttocks.
Bun•sen burner (bŭn′sən) *n.* A small laboratory burner composed of a vertical metal tube connected to a gas source.

bunt (bŭnt) *v.* **1.** To strike with the head : butt. **2.** *Baseball.* To bat (a pitch) with a half swing so that the ball does not reach beyond the infield. *–n.* **1.** The act of bunting. **2.** A bunted ball.

bunt·ing[1] (bŭn′tĭng) *n.* **1.** A light cloth for making flags. **2.** Decorative flags.

bunt·ing[2] (bŭn′tĭng) *n.* One of various short-billed birds of the family Fringillidae.

Bun·yan (bŭn′yən), **John.** 1628–88. English preacher and author.

buoy (bo͞o′ē, boi) *n.* **1.** *Naut.* A floating object moored in water to mark a channel or to warn of danger. **2.** A ring-shaped life preserver. *–v.* **1.** *Naut.* To mark with or as if with a buoy. **2.** To keep afloat. **3.** To lift the spirits of : hearten.

buoy·an·cy (boi′ən-sē, bo͞o′yən-) *n.* **1.** The ability to float. **2.** The upward force exerted by a fluid on a body in it. **3.** Resilience in recovering from setbacks. **4.** Cheerfulness. **–buoy′ant** *adj.*

bur[1] *also* **burr** (bûr) *n.* **1.** The rough and prickly covering of the seed of certain plants. **2.** *var. of* BURR[1]. *–v. var. of* BURR[1].

bur[2] (bûr) *n.* & *v. var. of* BURR[2].

bur·ble (bûr′bəl) *n.* **1.** A bubbling sound. **2.** Meaningless sounds : babble. *–vi.* **-bled, -bling. 1.** To gurgle. **2.** To babble : gibber.

bur·den[1] (bûr′dn) *n.* **1.** Something carried. **2.** Something difficult to bear physically or emotionally. **3.** The weight of cargo a vessel can carry. *–v.* To put a burden on : oppress. **–bur′den·some** *adj.*

bur·den[2] (bûr′dn) *n.* **1.** *Mus.* A chorus or refrain. **2.** A recurring central idea.

bur·dock (bûr′dŏk′) *n.* One of several coarse, weedy plants of the genus *Arctium,* with purplish flowers surrounded by bristles.

bu·reau (byo͝or′ō) *n., pl.* **-reaus** *or* **bu·reaux** (byo͝or′ōz). **1.** A chest of drawers. **2.** *esp. Brit.* A writing desk with drawers. **3.** A government department. **4.** An agency or business performing a specific service.

bu·reauc·ra·cy (byo͝o-rŏk′rə-sē) *n., pl.* **-cies. 1. a.** Administration of a government through bureaus and their officials. **b.** The departments and their officials collectively. **2.** An administrative system that is unwieldy and inflexible in its operation. **–bu′reau·crat′** *n.* **–bu′reau·crat′ic** *adj.* **–bu′reau·crat′i·cal·ly** *adv.*

bu·rette *also* **bu·ret** (byo͝o-rĕt′) *n.* A graduated glass tube with a small bore used for measuring fluids.

burg (bûrg) *n. Informal.* A town or city.

bur·geon *also* **bour·geon** (bûr′jən) *v.* **1. a.** To put forth fresh growth. **b.** To blossom. **2.** To grow rapidly : flourish.

bur·gess (bûr′jĭs) *n.* A citizen of an English borough.

burgh (bûrg) *n.* A Scottish chartered town or borough.

burgh·er (bûr′gər) *n.* **1.** A citizen of a town. **2.** A prosperous, solid citizen.

bur·gla·ry (bûr′glə-rē) *n., pl.* **-ries.** Breaking and entering a building with intent to steal. **–bur′glar** *n.* **–bur·glar′i·ous** *adj.* **–bur′glar·ize′** *v.* **–bur′glar·proof′** *adj.*

bur·gle (bûr′gəl) *v.* **-gled, -gling.** *Informal.* To commit burglary (on).

bur·go·mas·ter (bûr′gə-măs′tər) *n.* The mayor of some European cities.

Bur·gun·dy[1] (bûr′gən-dē). Region of SE France. **–Bur·gun′di·an** *adj.* & *n.*

Bur·gun·dy[2] (bûr′gən-dē) *n., pl.* **-dies. 1.** A red or white wine orig. produced in Burgundy. **2. burgundy.** A purplish red.

bur·i·al (bĕr′ē-əl) *n.* The act or process of burying a dead body.

burl (bûrl) *n.* **1.** A knot on a tree trunk. **2.** Wood marked with burls, used as veneer.

bur·lap (bûr′lăp′) *n.* A coarse cloth made of jute or hemp used esp. in making bags.

bur·lesque (bər-lĕsk′) *n.* **1.** A witty or mocking literary or dramatic imitation. **2.** Vaudeville entertainment marked by low comedy and striptease acts. *–v.* **-lesqued, -lesqu·ing.** To imitate mockingly.

bur·ly (bûr′lē) *adj.* **-li·er, -li·est.** Strong and muscular : husky. **–bur′li·ness** *n.*

Bur·ma (bûr′mə). Country of SE Asia. *Cap.* Rangoon. *Pop.* 31,512,000. **–Bur·mese′, Bur′man** *adj.* & *n.*

burn (bûrn) *v.* **burned** *or* **burnt** (bûrnt), **burn·ing. 1.** To be or cause to be on fire. **2. a.** To destroy or be destroyed by fire. **b.** To alter or become altered by fire or heat. **c.** *Slang.* To execute, esp. to electrocute. **3.** To make or cause by fire or heat <*burned* a hole in the chair> **4.** To use as a fuel. **5.** To give out light or heat. **6.** To look or feel hot. **7.** To sting : smart. **8.** To be excited. ⋆**syns:** BLAZE, FLAME, FLARE **–burn out. 1.** To stop burning from lack of fuel. **2.** To wear out or become inoperative as a result of friction or heat. **3.** To become exhausted, esp. from stress. *–n.* **1.** An injury produced by heat or fire. **2.** *Aerospace.* A single firing of a rocket.

burn·er (bûr′nər) *n.* **1.** The part of a stove or lamp where the flame is produced. **2.** A device in which matter is burned.

bur·nish (bûr′nĭsh) *v.* To make glossy by or as if by rubbing. *–n.* A smooth, shiny finish. **–bur′nish·er** *n.*

bur·noose (bər-no͞os′) *n.* A hooded cloak worn by Arabs.

burn·out (bûrn′out′) *n.* **1.** A failure in a device attributable to excessive heat. **2.** *Aerospace.* **a.** The cessation of rocket or jet-engine operation when all fuel is burned up. **b.** The point at which this occurs. **3.** Exhaustion from long-term stress.

Burns (bûrnz), **Robert.** 1759–96. Scottish poet.

burnt (bûrnt) *v. var. p.t.* & *p.p. of* BURN.

burp (bûrp) *n.* A belch. **–burp** *v.*

burr[1] *also* **bur** (bûr) *–n.* **1.** A rough edge or area remaining from the cutting of material, esp. metal. **2.** A rotary cutting tool that attaches to a drill. *–v.* **1.** To form a rough edge on. **2.** To remove a rough edge from.

burr[2] *also* **bur** (bûr) *–n.* **1.** The trilling of the letter *r,* as in Scottish speech. **2.** A whir or buzz. *–v.* To speak with a burr.

burr[3] (bûr) *n. var. of* BUR[1].

Burr (bûr), **Aaron.** 1756–1836. Amer. politician; killed Alexander Hamilton.

bur·ri·to (bo͝o-rē′tō, bə-) *n., pl.* **-tos.** A rolled tortilla with a filling, as of beef, beans, or cheese.

bur·ro (bûr′ō, bo͝or′ō, bŭr′ō) *n., pl.* **-ros.** A small donkey.

bur·row (bûr′ō, bŭr′ō) *n.* A hole made in the ground by a small animal, as a rabbit. *–v.* **1.** To dig a burrow (in). **2.** To progress by or as if by digging. **–bur′row·er** *n.*

bur·sa (bûr′sə) *n., pl.* **-sae** (-sē′) *or* **-sas.** A cavity or sac, esp. one between joints.

bur·sar (bûr′sər, -sär′) *n.* An official in charge of finances, as at a college.

bur·si·tis (bər-sī′tĭs) *n.* Inflammation of a bursa.

burst (bûrst) *v.* **burst, burst·ing. 1.** To come open or force apart violently, esp. from internal pressure. **2.** To be full to the point of breaking open. **3.** To come forth suddenly. **4.** To suddenly give vent to <*burst* into tears> **5.** *Computer Sci.* To detach (a continuous printout) into sheets. *–n.* **1.** The result or act of bursting : explosion. **2.** A sudden outburst.

burst·er (bûr′stər) *n. Computer Sci.* An offline device used to burst a printout.

Bu·run·di (bo͝o-ro͞on′dē). Country of EC Africa. *Cap.* Bujumbura. *Pop.* 3,864,000.

bur·y (bĕr′ē) *v.* **-ied, -y·ing. 1.** To conceal by covering with earth. **2.** To place (a corpse) in a grave. **3.** To cover from view : hide. **4.** To absorb. **5.** To put away.

bus (bŭs) *n., pl.* **bus·es** *or* **bus·ses.** A large motor coach that carries passengers. *–v.* **bused, bus·ing** *or* **bussed, bus·sing. 1.** To travel or tansport in a bus. **2.** To work as a bus boy.

bus. *abbr.* business.

bus boy *n.* A waiter's helper.

bus·by (bŭz′bē) *n., pl.* **-bies.** A tall fur hat worn with a full-dress military uniform.

bush (bo͝osh) *n.* **1.** A low, woody plant with spreading branches. **2.** Rough uncleared land. **3.** A shaggy mass. *–v.* To grow like a bush. **–bush′y** *adj.*

bushed (bo͝osht) *adj.* Tired : exhausted.

bush·el (bo͝osh′əl) *n.* See MEASUREMENT TABLE.

bush·ing (bo͝osh′ĭng) *n.* A metal lining for reducing friction on moving parts.

bush-league (bo͝osh′lēg′) *adj. Slang.* Inferior. **–bush′-leagu′er** *n.*

bush·mas·ter (bo͝osh′măs′tər) *n.* A large, poisonous snake, *Lachesis muta,* of tropical America, with brownish markings.

bush·whack (bo͝osh′hwăk′, -wăk′) *v.* **1.** To travel through or live in woods. **2.** To ambush. **–bush′whack′er** *n.*

busi·ness (bĭz′nĭs) *n.* **1.** One's occupation. **2.** Trade : commerce. **3.** A commercial enterprise. **4.** Volume of trade. **5.** Commercial practice or policy. **6.** One's rightful concern. **7.** An affair or matter <a distressing *business* ⋆**syns:** COMMERCE, INDUSTRY, TRADE, TRAFFIC **–bus′i·ness·man** *n.* **–bus′i·ness·wom′an** *n.*

business administration *n.* A college or university course teaching the theories and procedures of business.

bus·ing *also* **bus·sing** (bŭs′ĭng) *n.* The transporting of children by bus to schools outside their neighborhoods, esp. so as to desegregate schools.

bus·kin (bŭs′kĭn) *n.* **1.** A laced halfboot. **2.** Tragic drama.

buss (bŭs) *v.* To kiss. **–buss** *n.*

bust[1] (bŭst) *n.* **1.** A woman's bosom. **2.** A piece of sculpture representing a person's head and torso. **–bust′y** *adj.*

bust[2] (bŭst) *v.* **1.** To break or smash. **2.** To make or become bankrupt. **3.** To reduce the risk of. **4.** To hit. **5.** To arrest. **6.** To break (a horse). —*n.* **1.** A flop. **2.** A financial collapse. **3.** An arrest.

bus·tle[1] (bŭs′əl) *v.* **-tled, -tling.** To hurry busily and briskly. **—bus′tle** *n.*

bus·tle[2] (bŭs′əl) *n.* A pad worn to expand the fullness at the back of a skirt.

bus·y (bĭz′ē) *adj.* **-i·er, -i·est. 1.** Engaged in action : occupied. **2.** Full of activity <a *busy* day> **3.** Prying : nosy. **4.** In use, as a telephone line. **5.** Cluttered with detail to the point of being distracting. —*v.* **-ied, -y·ing.** To make busy. ☆***syns:*** ENGAGE, ENGROSS, OCCUPY **—bus′i·ly** *adv.*

bus·y·bod·y (bĭz′ē-bŏd′ē) *n., pl.* **-ies.** A prying, meddling person.

but (bŭt; *unstressed* bət) *conj.* **1.** On the contrary <caused not success *but* failure> **2.** Contrary to expectation <worked hard *but* accomplished little> **3.** Save : except <everyone *but* me> **4.** Except that. **5.** Without the result that <It never rains *but* it pours.> **6.** Other than <we have no desire *but* to end poverty.> **7.** That. Often used after a negative. **8.** That . . . not. Used after a negative or question. —*prep.* With the exception of : barring. —*n.* An objection or exception <no *buts* about it>

bu·ta·di·ene (byo͞o′tə-dī′ēn′, -dī-ēn′) *n.* A colorless, highly flammable hydrocarbon produced from petroleum.

bu·tane (byo͞o′tān′) *n.* A gas produced from petroleum and used in the manufacture of rubber and as a fuel.

butch·er (bo͝och′ər) *n.* **1.** A person who slaughters animals commercially. **2.** A meat seller. **3.** One who kills brutally. **4.** *Informal.* A bungler. —*v.* **1.** To slaughter or prepare (animals) for market. **2.** To kill barbarously. **3.** To botch. **—butch′er·y** *n.*

but·ler (bŭt′lər) *n.* The head male servant of a household.

butt[1] (bŭt) *v.* To push against with the head or horns. **—butt in** (or **into**). *Informal.* To meddle in another's affairs. —*n.* A blow or push with the head or horns.

butt[2] (bŭt) *v.* To join end to end.

butt[3] (bŭt) *n.* An object of scorn.

butt[4] (bŭt) *n.* **1.** The thicker or larger end. **2.** A stub or stump. **3.** *Slang.* A cigarette. **4.** *Informal.* The buttocks.

butte (byo͞ot) *n.* An isolated, steep hill.

but·ter (bŭt′ər) *n.* **1.** A thick, fatty, yellowish substance produced by churning cream. **2.** A substance resembling butter. —*v.* To put butter on. **—butter up.** To flatter. **—but′ter·y** *adj.*

†butter bean *n.* **1.** The wax bean. **2.** *Regional.* The lima bean.

but·ter·cup (bŭt′ər-kŭp′) *n.* One of various plants of the genus *Ranunculus,* with shiny, bright-yellow flowers.

but·ter·fat (bŭt′ər-făt′) *n.* The natural fat of milk from which butter is made.

but·ter·fin·gers (bŭt′ər-fĭng′gərz) *n. (used with a sing. verb).* A clumsy person who habitually drops things. **—but′ter·fin′gered** *adj.*

but·ter·fish (bŭt′ər-fĭsh′) *n.* A North American marine food fish, *Poronotus triacanthus,* with a flattened body.

but·ter·fly (bŭt′ər-flī′) *n.* **1.** One of various insects of the order Lepidoptera, with slender bodies and broad, usu. colorful wings. **2. butterflies.** Mild nausea due to nervous anticipation.

but·ter·milk (bŭt′ər-mĭlk′) *n.* The thick, sour liquid remaining after butter has been churned.

but·ter·nut (bŭt′ər-nŭt′) *n.* A tree, *Juglans cinerea,* of E North America, bearing egg-shaped edible nuts.

but·ter·scotch (bŭt′ər-skŏch′) *n.* A flavoring, candy, or syrup made from butter and brown sugar.

but·tock (bŭt′ək) *n.* **1.** Either of the 2 rounded fleshy parts of the rump. **2. buttocks.** The rump.

but·ton (bŭt′n) *n.* **1.** A knob-shaped fastener used to join 2 parts of a garment by fitting through a loop or buttonhole. **2.** An object resembling a button. —*v.* To fasten with buttons. **—but′ton·er** *n.*

but·ton·hole (bŭt′n-hōl′) *n.* A slit for a button to pass through. —*v.* **-holed, -hol·ing. 1.** To make a buttonhole (in). **2.** To detain and talk to.

but·ton·hook (bŭt′n-ho͝ok′) *n.* A hook for pulling buttons through buttonholes.

but·tress (bŭt′rĭs) *n.* **1.** A supporting structure built against a wall. **2.** A support : prop. —*v.* To support or prop with or as if with a buttress.

bu·tut (bo͞o′to͞ot′) *n., pl.* **-tut** or **-tuts.** See *dalasi* at CURRENCY TABLE.

bux·om (bŭk′səm) *adj.* Healthily plump and ample of figure, as a large-bosomed woman. **—bux′om·ness** *n.*

buy (bī) *v.* **bought** (bôt), **buy·ing. 1.** To get by paying money. **2.** To be capable of purchasing. **3.** To bribe. **4.** *Slang.* To believe in <wouldn't *buy* their excuses> **—buy up.** To buy all that is available of. —*n.* **1.** A purchase. **2.** *Informal.* A bargain. **—buy′a·ble** *adj.* **—buy′er** *n.*

buzz (bŭz) *v.* **1.** To hum like a bee. **2.** To be filled with sound. **3.** To bustle. **4.** To call with a buzzer. **5.** *Informal.* To make a telephone call to. —*n.* **1.** A droning or vibrating sound. **2.** A low murmur. **3.** *Informal.* A telephone call. **4.** *Slang.* A pleasant stimulation, as from alcohol.

buz·zard (bŭz′ərd) *n.* **1.** Any of various North American vultures. **2.** *esp. Brit.* A hawk of the genus *Butes.*

buzz·er (bŭz′ər) *n.* An electric device that makes a buzzing sound as a signal.

buzz saw *n.* A circular saw.

buzz word *n.* A jargonistic technical word used esp. to impress nonprofessionals.

bx. *abbr.* box.

by (bī) *prep.* **1.** Next to : close to <the light *by* the window> **2.** With the help or use of : through <We came *by* the main road.> **3.** Up to and beyond : past <drove *by* the entrance> **4.** In the period of : during <working *by* night> **5.** Not later than <*by* noon> **6. a.** In the amount of <requests *by* the thousands> **b.** To the extent of <closer *by* a foot> **7. a.** According to. **b.** With respect to. **8.** In the name of <swore *by* my honor> **9.** Through the agency or action of <peace *by* negotiation> **10.** Used to indicate a succession of specified units of measure <filed out one *by* one><Little *by* little they made headway.> **11. a.** Used in multiplication and division <3 *by* 5> **b.** Used with measurements <a section 4 *by* 8 feet> —*adv.* **1.** On hand : nearby <stay *by*> **2.** Aside : away <set it *by* for now> **3.** Up to, alongside, and past <The runner raced *by.*> **4.** Into the past <as time goes *by*>

by-and-by (bī′ən-bī′) *n.* **1.** A time in the future. **2.** The afterlife.

bye *also* **by** (bī) *n.* **1.** A side issue. **2.** The advantage obtained by a competitor who draws no opponent for a round in a tournament thus advancing to the next round.

bye-bye (bī′bī′) *interj. Informal.* Used to express farewell.

by·gone (bī′gôn′, -gŏn′) *adj.* Past. —*n.* A thing of the past.

by·law (bī′lô′) *n.* A rule or law concerning the management of an organization's internal affairs.

by-line *also* **by·line** (bī′līn′) *n.* A line above an article in a newspaper or magazine giving the author's name. **—by′-lin′er** *n.*

by-pass *also* **by·pass** (bī′păs′). —*n.* **1.** A way around an obstruction or a congested area. **2.** *Elect.* A shunt. **3. a.** An alternative passage formed surgically between 2 blood vessels. **b.** The operation itself. —*v.* To go around : avoid.

by-path (bī′păth′, -päth′) *n.* An indirect or minor path.

by-play (bī′plā′) *n.* Secondary action or speech going on aside from the main action, esp. on a theater stage.

by-prod·uct (bī′prŏd′əkt) *n.* **1.** Something produced in the course of making the main product. **2.** A secondary result.

By·ron (bī′rən), **George Gordon.** 1788–1824. English poet.

by·stand·er (bī′stăn′dər) *n.* A witness to an event.

byte (bīt) *n. Computer Sci.* A sequence of adjacent binary digits operated on as a unit.

by·way (bī′wā′) *n.* **1.** A side road. **2.** A secondary aspect or field of study.

by·word (bī′wûrd′) *n.* **1.** A well-known saying. **2.** An object of notoriety.

Byz·an·tine (bĭz′ən-tēn′, -tīn′, bĭ-zăn′tĭn) *adj.* **1.** Of or relating to the ancient city of Byzantium. **2.** Of or designating the architectural style of Byzantium marked by minarets, domes, round arches, and mosaics. **3. a.** Devious. **b.** Intricate. —*n.* A native or inhabitant of Byzantium.

Byzantine Empire. E part of the Roman Empire (395–1453).

By·zan·ti·um (bĭ-zăn′shē-əm, -tē-əm). An ancient Greek city on the site of Constantinople.

Cc

c *or* **C** (sē) *n., pl.* **c's** *or* **C's. 1.** The 3rd letter of the English alphabet. **2.** A speech sound represented by the letter *c*. **3.** *Mus.* The 1st tone in the scale of C major. **4.** The 3rd-highest grade in quality or rank. **5. C** The Roman numeral for 100.

c *abbr.* **1.** carat. **2.** cubic.

C *symbol for* CARBON.

C *abbr.* **1.** Celsius. **2.** centigrade.

c. or **C.** *abbr.* **1.** cape. **2.** cent. **3.** century. **4.** chapter. **5.** *also* **ca** circa. **6.** copy. **7.** copyright.

Ca *symbol for* CALCIUM.

CA *abbr.* California (with Zip Code).

cab (kăb) *n.* **1.** A taxicab. **2.** The covered compartment for the driver or operator of a heavy vehicle.

ca•bal (kə-băl′) *n.* **1.** A group of conspirators. **2.** A secret plot. **–ca•bal′** *v.* **–cab′a•lis′tic** *adj.* **–cab′a•lis′ti•cal•ly** *adv.*

†cab•al•le•ro (kăb′ə-lâr′ō, -əl-yâr′ō) *n., pl.* **-ros. 1.** A Spanish gentleman : cavalier. **2.** *SW U.S.* A skilled equestrian.

ca•ban•a (kə-băn′ə, -băn′yə) *n.* A shelter on a beach or at a swimming pool, used as a bathhouse.

cab•a•ret (kăb′ə-rā′) *n.* A restaurant providing entertainment, as a floor show.

cab•bage (kăb′ĭj) *n.* An edible plant, *Brassica oleracea capitata,* having a large head formed by tightly overlapping leaves.

cab•by or **cab•bie** (kăb′ē) *n., pl.* **-bies.** *Informal.* A driver of a taxicab.

cab•er•net (kăb′ər-nā′) *n.* A dry red wine made from the grape variety *Cabernet sauvignon.*

cab•in (kăb′ĭn) *n.* **1.** A small, roughly constructed house. **2. a.** A compartment on a ship used as living quarters. **b.** An enclosed compartment on an airplane for passengers.

cabin boy *n.* A boy who works as a servant on a ship.

cab•i•net (kăb′ə nĭt) *n.* **1.** An upright cupboardlike repository with shelves, drawers, or compartments, as for the storing or displaying of objects. **2.** *often* **Cabinet.** A body of people appointed by a head of state to act as official advisers and be in charge of the various government departments. **–cab′i•net•ry** *n.*

cab•i•net•mak•er (kăb′ə-nĭt-mā′kər) *n.* A craftsman who makes fine wooden furniture. **–cab′i•net•mak′ing** *n.*

cab•i•net•work (kăb′ə-nĭt-wûrk′) *n.* A cabinetmaker's finished products.

ca•ble (kā′bəl) *n.* **1.** A large-diameter fiber or steel rope. **2.** *Elect.* A bound group of insulated conductors. **3.** A cablegram. **4.** Cable television. *–v.* **-bled, -bling.** To send a cablegram (to).

cable car *n.* A vehicle pulled by an endless cable driven by a stationary engine.

ca•ble•cast (kā′bəl-kăst′) *n.* A cable television telecast. **–ca′ble•cast′** *v.*

ca•ble•gram (kā′bəl-grăm′) *n.* A telegram sent by submarine cable.

cable stitch *n.* A knitting stitch that makes a twisted ropelike pattern.

cable television *also* **cable TV** *n.* A television distribution system in which station signals are picked up by elevated antennas and transmitted via cable to subscribers' receivers.

cab•o•chon (kăb′ə-shŏn′) *n.* A convex-cut, unfaceted gem with a high polish.

ca•boo•dle (kə-bo͞od′l) *n.* *Informal.* The entire lot or group.

ca•boose (kə-bo͞os′) *n.* The last car of a freight train.

cab•ri•o•let (kăb′rē-ə-lā′) *n.* **1.** A light, 2-wheeled 1-horse carriage with 2 seats and a folding top. **2.** A coupé with a folding top.

ca•ca•o (kə-kä′ō, -kā′ō) *n., pl.* **-os.** An evergreen tropical American tree, *Theobroma cacao,* bearing reddish-brown seed pods that are used in making chocolate, cocoa, and cocoa butter.

cach•a•lot (kăsh′ə-lŏt′, -lō′) *n.* The sperm whale.

cache (kăsh) *n.* **1.** A hiding place for storing provisions. **2.** A safe place for concealment, as of valuables. **3.** A store of goods in a cache. **–cache** *v.*

ca•chet (kă-shā′) *n.* **1.** A seal on a document or letter. **2.** A mark of distinction.

cack•le (kăk′əl) *v.* **-led, -ling. 1.** To make the shrill, brittle cry characteristic of a hen. **2.** To talk or laugh in a shrill, broken way. *–n.* **1.** The act or sound of cackling. **2.** Shrill laughter similar to a hen's cackle. **–cack′ler** *n.*

ca•coph•o•ny (kə-kŏf′ə-nē) *n., pl.* **-nies.** Harsh, discordant sound : dissonance. **–ca•coph′o•nous** *adj.* **–ca•coph′o•nous•ly** *adv.*

cac•tus (kăk′təs) *n., pl.* **-ti** (-tī′) *or* **-tus•es.** Any of a large group of leafless plants of the family Cactaceae, of arid regions, having thick, fleshy, often prickly stems.

cad (kăd) *n.* A man whose behavior is ungentlemanly. **–cad′dish** *adj.*

ca•dav•er (kə-dăv′ər) *n.* A dead body : corpse. **–ca•dav′er•ic** *adj.*

ca•dav•er•ous (kə-dăv′ər-əs) *adj.* Pale and gaunt : corpselike.

cad•die *also* **cad•dy** (kăd′ē) *n., pl.* **-dies.** One hired as an attendant to a golfer, esp. to carry the clubs. **–cad′dy** *v.*

cad•dy (kăd′ē) *n., pl.* **-dies.** A small container or chest, esp. for tea.

ca•dence (kād′ns) *also* **ca•den•cy** (kād′n-sē) *n., pl.* **-denc•es** *also* **-den•cies. 1.** Rhythmic, balanced flow or movement as in marching. **2.** Inflection or modulation of the voice. **–ca′denced** *adj.*

ca•den•za (kə-dĕn′zə) *n.* An elaborate virtuosic section for a soloist near the end of a movement of a concerto.

ca•det (kə-dĕt′) *n.* **1.** A student at a military or naval academy. **2.** A younger son or brother. **–ca•det′ship′** *n.*

cadge (kăj) *v.* **cadged, cadg•ing.** *Informal.* To beg or obtain by begging : mooch. **–cadg′er** *n.*

cad•mi•um (kăd′mē-əm) *n.* *Symbol* **Cd** A soft, bluish-white metallic element used in storage batteries, dental amalgams, and solders. **–cad′mic** *adj.*

cad•re (kăd′rē) *n.* **1.** A framework. **2.** A nucleus of trained personnel.

ca•du•ce•us (kə-do͞o′sē-əs, -dyo͞o′-) *n., pl.* **-ce•i** (-sē-ī′). **1.** *Myth.* A winged staff with two serpents entwined around it, carried by Hermes. **2.** An insignia used as the symbol of the medical profession.

cae•cum (sē′kəm) *n.* *var. of* CECUM.

Cae•sar (sē′zər) *n.* **1.** A title of the Roman emperors after Augustus. **2.** *often* **caesar.** A dictator : autocrat.

Caesar, Gaius Julius. 100–44 B.C. Roman statesman and general.

Cae•sar•e•an *also* **Cae•sar•i•an** (sĭ-zâr′ē-ən) *n.* A Caesarean section.

Caesarean section *also* **caesarean section** *n.* Surgical incision through the abdominal and uterine walls to extract a fetus.

caesar salad *n.* A green salad with a dressing of olive oil, lemon juice, and a raw or coddled egg.

cae•si•um (sē′zē-əm) *n.* *var. of* CESIUM.

cae•su•ra (sĭ-zho͝or′ə, -zo͝or′ə) *n., pl.* **-ras** *or* **-su•rae** (-zho͝or′ē, -zo͝or′ē). A pause in a line of verse. **–cae•su′ral, cae•su′ric** *adj.*

ca•fé (kă-fā′, kə-) *n.* A coffeehouse, restaurant, or bar.

café au lait (ō lā′) *n.* Coffee with hot milk.

caf•e•te•ri•a (kăf′ĭ-tîr′ē-ə) *n.* A restaurant in which customers select meals at a counter and carry them on trays to tables.

caf•feine *also* **caf•fein** (kă-fēn′, kăf′ēn′, -ē-ĭn) *n.* A bitter white alkaloid found in coffee, tea, etc., and used as a stimulant.

caf•tan (kăf′tən, kăf-tăn′) *n.* A full-length, often loose-fitting tunic with sleeves, worn chiefly in the Near East.

cage (kāj) *n.* **1. a.** An enclosure with bars or grating for confining birds or animals. **b.** Something resembling a cage. **2.** *Baseball.* **a.** A backstop for batting practice. **b.** A catcher's mask. **3.** *Basketball.* The basket. **4.** The goal in hockey. *–v.* **caged, cag•ing.** To put in or as if in a cage.

ca•gey *also* **ca•gy** (kā′jē) *adj.* **-gi•er, -gi•est. 1.** Wary : careful. **2.** Shrewd. **–ca′gi•ly** *adv.* **–ca′gi•ness** *n.*

ca•hoots (kə-ho͞ots′) *pl.n.* *Informal.* Questionable collaboration <in *cahoots* with a dishonest attorney>

cai•man *also* **cay•man** (kā′mən, kā-măn′, kī-) *n., pl.* **-mans.** A tropical American crocodilian of the genus *Caiman* or related genera, closely related to and resembling the alligator.

Cain (kān) *n.* **1.** Son of Adam and Eve; murderer of Abel. **2.** A murderer.

cairn (kârn) *n.* A mound of stones erected as a marker or memorial.

cairn•gorm (kârn′gôrm′) *n.* A smoky brown or yellow quartz, used as a semiprecious gem.

Cairn terrier *n.* A small dog orig. bred in Scotland, with a rough, shaggy coat.

Cai•ro (kī′rō). Cap. of Egypt, on the Nile. *Pop.* 5,278,000.

cais•son (kā′sŏn′, -sən) *n.* **1.** A watertight structure in which underwater construction is effected. **2.** A device used to raise a sunken vessel. **3. a.** A large box used to hold ammunition. **b.** A horse-drawn vehicle once used to carry ammunition.

caisson disease *n.* A disorder, esp. in divers, caused by release of nitrogen bubbles in the blood upon too rapid a return from high pressure to atmospheric pressure.

ca·jole (kə-jōl′) *v.* **-joled, -jol·ing.** To wheedle : coax. **—ca·jol′er** *n.* **—ca·jol′er·y** *n.* **—ca·jol′ing·ly** *adv.*
Ca·jun (kā′jən) *n.* A native of Louisiana held to be a descendant of the French immigrants from E Canada.
cake (kāk) *n.* **1.** A sweet baked mixture of flour, liquid, and eggs. **2.** A thin baked or fried portion of batter or other food, as a pancake or a fish cake. **3.** A molded piece, as of soap or ice. *—v.* **caked, cak·ing.** To form into a cake : harden.
cal. *abbr.* **1.** calendar. **2.** caliber.
Cal. *abbr.* California.
cal·a·bash (kăl′ə-băsh′) *n.* A large, hard-shelled gourd often used as a utensil.
†cal·a·boose (kăl′ə-bo͞os′) *n. Regional.* A jail.
ca·la·di·um (kə-lā′dē-əm) *n.* Any of various tropical plants of the genus *Caladium*, widely cultivated as potted plants for their showy, variegated foliage.
cal·a·mine (kăl′ə-mīn′, -mĭn) *n.* A zinc oxide powder with a small amount of ferric oxide, used in skin lotions and ointments.
ca·lam·i·ty (kə-lăm′ĭ-tē) *n., pl.* **-ties. 1.** A disaster. **2.** Great distress or misfortune. **—ca·lam′i·tous** *adj.* **—ca·lam′i·tous·ly** *adv.* **—ca·lam′i·tous·ness** *n.*
cal·car·e·ous (kăl-kâr′ē-əs) *adj.* Made up of, having, or characteristic of calcium carbonate, calcium, or limestone : chalky.
cal·ces (kăl′sēz′) *n. var. pl. of* CALX.
cal·cif·er·ous (kăl-sĭf′ər-əs) *adj.* Forming or having calcium or calcium carbonate.
cal·ci·fy (kăl′sə-fī′) *v.* **-fied, -fy·ing.** To make or become stony or chalky. **—cal′ci·fi·ca′tion** *n.*
cal·ci·mine (kăl′sə-mīn′) *n.* A white or tinted liquid containing zinc oxide, water, glue, and coloring, used as a wash for walls and ceilings. **—cal′ci·mine′** *v.*
cal·cine (kăl′sīn′) *v.* **-cined, -cin·ing.** To treat (a substance) by heating to a high temperature without causing it to melt. **—cal′ci·na′tion** (kăl′sə-nā′shən) *n.*
cal·cite (kăl′sīt′) *n.* A common crystalline form of calcium carbonate. **—cal·cit′ic** (-sĭt′ĭk) *adj.*
cal·ci·um (kăl′sē-əm) *n. Symbol* **Ca** A silvery, moderately hard metallic element used in compounds to make plaster, Portland cement, and quicklime.
calcium carbonate *n.* A crystalline compound of calcium, carbon, and oxygen that occurs naturally as chalk, limestone, and marble.
calcium oxide *n.* A white, lumpy powder used in making steel, glass, and insecticides and as an industrial alkali : quicklime.
†cal·cu·late (kăl′kyə-lāt′) *v.* **-lat·ed, -lat·ing. 1.** To compute mathematically : reckon. **2.** To estimate : evaluate. **3.** *Regional.* To intend : plan <I *calculated* on your help.> **—cal′cu·la·ble** *adj.* **—cal′cu·la·bly** *adv.* **—cal′cu·la′tive** *adj.*
cal·cu·lat·ed (kăl′kyə-lā′tĭd) *adj.* Undertaken with careful estimation of the likely outcome <a *calculated* business venture>
cal·cu·lat·ing (kăl′kyə-lā′tĭng) *adj.* Coldly scheming or shrewd.
cal·cu·la·tion (kăl′kyə-lā′shən) *n.* **1.** The act, process, or result of calculating. **2.** Deliberation : foresight.
cal·cu·la·tor (kăl′kyə-lā′tər) *n.* **1.** One who calculates. **2.** A keyboard machine for the automatic performance of mathematical operations.
cal·cu·lus (kăl′kyə-ləs) *n., pl.* **-li** (-lī′) or **-lus·es. 1.** *Pathol.* An abnormal concretion in the body, as a kidney stone, usu. of mineral salts. **2.** The mathematics of differential and integral calculus.
Cal·cut·ta (kăl-kŭt′ə). City of E India, on the Ganges delta. *Metro. Pop.* 9,100,000.
cal·de·ra (kăl-dâr′ə, -dîr′ə, kôl-) *n.* A large crater formed by volcanic explosion or by collapse of a volcanic cone.
cal·dron *also* **caul·dron** (kôl′drən) *n.* A large vessel, as a kettle or vat.

▲word history: The Latin word *caldaria,* "kettle," has 3 descendants in Modern English. *Caldron,* spelled *caudron,* is the earliest form, borrowed from Norman French. The other forms of *caldaria* came from the central French variant of *caudron. Chaldron,* from Old French *chauderon,* was at first used in English as a synonym of *caldron* meaning "kettle." The 3rd form is *chowder,* from the modern French word *chaudiére,* "pot," meaning "fish stew."

cal·en·dar (kăl′ən-dər) *n.* **1.** Any of various systems of showing time divisions by days, weeks, months, and years. **2.** A table showing these divisions, usu. for a specific year. **3.** A usu. chronological list or schedule. *—v.* To enter on a calendar.
cal·en·der (kăl′ən-dər) *n.* A machine in which paper or cloth is made smooth and glossy by pressing between rollers. *—v.* To press in a calender.
cal·ends (kăl′əndz, kā′ləndz) *n., pl.* **-ends.** The 1st day of the new moon and 1st day of the month in the ancient Roman calendar.
ca·len·du·la (kə-lĕn′jə-lə) *n.* A plant of the genus *Calendula,* with orange-yellow flowers.
calf[1] (kăf, käf) *n., pl.* **calves** (kăvz, kävz). **1. a.** A young cow or bull. **b.** The young of certain other mammals, as the elephant or whale. **2.** Calfskin.
calf[2] (kăf, käf) *n., pl.* **calves** (kăvz, kävz). The back part of the leg between the knee and ankle.
calf·skin (kăf′skĭn′, käf′-) *n.* **1.** The hide of a calf. **2.** Leather made from calfskin.
Cal·ga·ry (kăl′gə-rē). City of S Alta., Canada. *Pop.* 560,618.
Calgary Stampede *n. Can.* A rodeo held every year in Calgary, Alta.
cal·i·ber (kăl′ə-bər) *n.* **1. a.** The diameter of the inside of a tube. **b.** The diameter of the bore of a firearm. **c.** The diameter of a shell or bullet. **2.** Degree of worth.
cal·i·brate (kăl′ə-brāt′) *v.* **-brat·ed, -brat·ing. 1.** To check, standardize, or adjust systematically the graduations of (a measuring instrument). **2.** To determine the caliber of (a tube). **—cal′i·bra′tion** *n.* **—cal′i·bra′tor** *n.*
cal·i·bre (căl′ə-bər) *n. esp. Brit. var. of* CALIBER.
cal·i·co (kăl′ĭ-kō′) *n., pl.* **-coes** or **-cos. 1.** A coarse, usu. brightly printed cloth. **2.** An animal, as a cat, having a mottled coat.
Calif. *abbr.* California.
Cal·i·for·nia (kăl′ə-fôrn′yə, -fôr′nē-ə). State of the SW U.S. *Cap.* Sacramento. *Pop.* 23,668,562. **—Cal′i·for′nian** *adj.* & *n.*
California poppy *n.* A plant, *Eschscholtzia californica,* of the North American Pacific Coast, with orange-yellow flowers.
cal·i·for·ni·um (kăl′ə-fôr′nē-əm) *n. Symbol* **Cf** An artificial radioactive element produced in trace quantities by bombarding a curium isotope with helium ions.
cal·i·per *also* **cal·li·per** (kăl′ə-pər) *n. often* **calipers.** An instrument composed of 2 curved hinged legs, used for measuring internal and external dimensions.
ca·liph *also* **ca·lif** (kā′lĭf, kăl′ĭf) *n.* The secular and religious head of a Moslem state. **—ca′liph·ate′** *n.*
cal·is·then·ics (kăl′ĭs-thĕn′ĭks) *n.* (*sing. or pl. in number*). Exercises that develop muscular tone and enhance physical well-being. **—cal′is·then′ic** *adj.*
calk (kôk) *v. var. of* CAULK.
call (kôl) *v.* **1.** To cry out loudly : proclaim. **2. a.** To summon <*called* them to supper> **b.** To convene <*call* a meeting of the board> **3.** To telephone. **4.** To designate : name. **5.** To consider : estimate. **6.** To pay a short visit. **7.** To demand payment of (e.g., a loan). **8.** To stop or postpone (a game) officially. **9.** To demand that an opponent show his or her cards in poker. ☆**syns:** CONVENE, CONVOKE, MUSTER, SUMMON *—n.* **1. a.** A shout. **b.** The characteristic cry of an animal, esp. a bird. **2.** An invitation or summons. **3.** Demand <a big *call* for 10-speed bikes> **4.** A short visit, esp. as a formality. **5.** A communicating by telephone. **—call for. 1.** To go and get. **2.** To be appropriate for : warrant <This *calls for* a celebration.> **—call off. 1.** To cancel or postpone. **2.** To recall : restrain <*called off* the watchdogs> **—call on (or upon). 1.** To pay a visit to. **2.** To appeal to (someone) to do something. **—call out.** To cause to assemble : summon. **—call up. 1.** To summon into military service. **2.** To remember <*call up* old memories> **—on call. 1.** Available whenever summoned. **2.** Payable on demand. **—call′er** *n.*
cal·la *also* **cal·la lily** (kăl′ə) *n.* A plant of the genus *Zantedeschia,* widely cultivated for its showy, white spathe enclosing a clublike flower stalk.
call·back (kôl′băk′) *n.* A recall.
call girl *n.* A prostitute hired by telephone.
cal·lig·ra·phy (kə-lĭg′rə-fē) *n.* **1.** The art of handwriting. **2.** Handwriting : penmanship. **—cal·lig′ra·pher, cal·lig′ra·phist** *n.* **—cal′li·graph′ic** (kăl′ĭ-grăf′ĭk) *adj.*

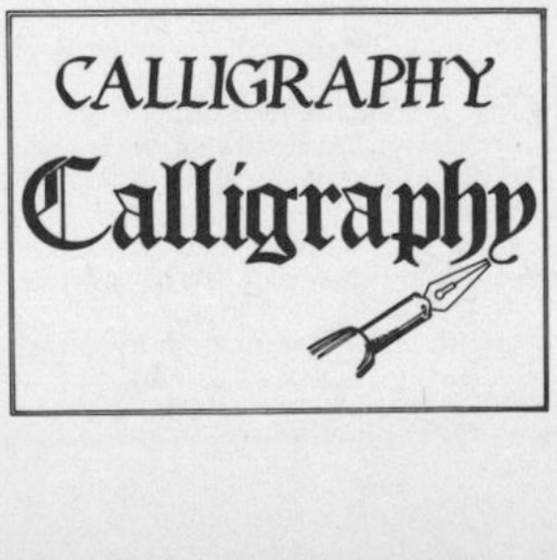

calligraphy

call•ing (kô′lĭng) *n.* **1.** A strong inner urge or impulse. **2.** An occupation : vocation.
cal•li•o•pe (kə-lī′ə-pē′, kăl′ē-ōp′) *n.* A keyboard musical instrument fitted with steam whistles.
cal•li•per (kăl′ə-pər) *n. var. of* CALIPER.
call letters *pl.n.* The identifying code letters of a radio or television station.
call loan *n.* A loan repayable on demand.
call number *n.* A library number used to classify a book and indicate its placement on the shelves.
cal•los•i•ty (kă-lŏs′ĭ-tē, kə-) *n., pl.* **-ties. 1.** The state of being calloused. **2.** Hardheartedness. **3.** A callus.
cal•lous (kăl′əs) *adj.* **1.** Having calluses : toughened. **2.** Insensitive : unfeeling. *—v.* To make or become callous.
cal•low (kăl′ō) *adj.* Immature and inexperienced. **—cal′low•ly** *adv.*
cal•lus (kăl′əs) *n.* A thickening of the horny skin layer. **—cal′lus** *v.*
calm (käm) *adj.* **1.** Almost or utterly motionless : undisturbed <a *calm* ocean> **2.** Not excited or agitated <a *calm* manner> ☆***syns:*** PEACEFUL, PLACID, SERENE, TRANQUIL *—n.* **1.** Absence or cessation of motion. **2.** Serenity : peace. **3.** Little or no wind. *—v.* To make or become calm.
calm•a•tive (kä′mə-tĭv, kăl′mə-) *adj.* Having relaxing or pacifying properties : sedative. **—calm′a•tive** *n.*
cal•o•mel (kăl′ə-mĕl′, -məl) *n.* A white, tasteless compound used as a cathartic.
cal•o•rie (kăl′ə-rē) *n.* **1.** The amount of heat required to raise the temperature of 1 g of water by 1°C at 1 atmosphere pressure : small calorie. **2.** The amount of heat required to raise the temperature of 1 kg of water by 1°C at 1 atmosphere pressure : large calorie. **—ca•lor′ic** (kə-lôr′ĭk, -lŏr′-), **cal′o•rif′ic** *adj.*
cal•o•rim•e•ter (kăl′ə-rĭm′ĭ-tər) *n.* A device for measuring heat. **—ca•lor′i•met′ric** *adj.* **—cal′o•rim′e•try** *n.*
cal•u•met (kăl′yə-mĕt′, kăl′yə-mĕt′) *n.* A long-stemmed pipe used by North American Indians on ceremonial occasions.
ca•lum•ni•ate (kə-lŭm′nē-āt′) *v.* **-at•ed, -at•ing.** To slander. **—ca•lum′ni•a′tion** *n.* **—ca•lum′ni•a′tor** *n.*
cal•um•ny (kăl′əm-nē) *n., pl.* **-nies.** A maliciously false slander. **—ca•lum′ni•ous** *adj.* **—ca•lum′ni•ous•ly** *adv.*
cal•va•dos (kăl′və-dōs′) *n.* A French brandy made from apples.
calve (kăv, käv) *v.* **calved, calv•ing.** To give birth to a calf.
calves (kăvz, kävz) *n. pl. of* CALF.
Cal•vin (kăl′vĭn), **John.** 1509–64. French religious reformer.
Cal•vin•ism (kăl′və-nĭz′əm) *n.* The religious doctrines of John Calvin, emphasizing salvation by God's grace alone. **—Cal′vin•ist** *n.* **—Cal′vin•is′tic** *adj.*
ca•lyp•so (kə-lĭp′sō) *n.* Music that originated in the West Indies and is marked by improvised lyrics on topical subjects.
ca•lyx (kā′lĭks, kăl′ĭks) *n., pl.* **-es** or **ca•ly•ces** (kā′lĭ-sēz′, kăl′ĭ-). The outer protective covering of a flower, composed of usu. green sepals.
cam (kăm) *n.* An eccentric wheel that is mounted on a rotating shaft, used to produce variable or reciprocating motion.
ca•ma•ra•de•rie (kä′mə-rä′də-rē, kăm′ə-răd′ə-) *n.* Rapport and good will between friends.
cam•ber (kăm′bər) *n.* **1.** A slightly arched surface, as of a road or a ship's deck. **2.** A setting of automobile wheels closer together at the bottom than at the top. *—v.* To arch or cause to arch slightly.
cam•bi•um (kăm′bē-əm) *n.* A cell layer in vascular plants that produces phloem and xylem. **—cam′bi•al** *adj.*
Cam•bo•di•a (kăm-bō′dē-ə). Country of SE Asia. *Cap.* Phnom Penh. *Pop.* 8,110,000. **—Cam•bo′di•an** *adj.* & *n.*
cam•bric (kăm′brĭk) *n.* A finely woven linen or cotton fabric.
came (kām) *v. p.t. of* COME.
cam•el (kăm′əl) *n.* A humped long-necked ruminant mammal of the genus *Camelus,* of N Africa and W Asia, domesticated in desert regions as a beast of burden and source of wool, milk, and meat.
ca•mel•lia (kə-mēl′yə, -mē′lē-ə) *n.* A shrub of the genus *Camellia,* esp. *C. japonica,* with shiny evergreen leaves and showy, variously colored flowers.
ca•mel•o•pard (kə-mĕl′ə-pärd) *n. Archaic.* A giraffe.
camel's hair *also* **camel hair** *n.* **1.** The fine hair of a camel or a substitute for it. **2.** A soft, heavy, usu. light tan cloth made mainly of camel's hair.
Cam•em•bert (kăm′əm-bâr′) *n.* A creamy mold-ripened cheese.
cam•e•o (kăm′ē-ō′) *n., pl.* **-os. 1.** A gem with a design engraved in relief, usu. of a different hue. **2.** A brief but dramatic appearance of a prominent performer in a single scene on a television show or in a film.
cam•er•a (kăm′ər-ə, kăm′rə) *n.* **1.** A device for taking photographs, gen. composed of a lightproof enclosure with an aperture having a lens through which an image is recorded on a light-sensitive film or plate. **2.** The part of a television transmitting apparatus that receives the primary image on a light-sensitive cathode tube and transforms it into electrical impulses. **3.** *pl.* **-er•ae** (-ə-rē). A judge's private chamber. **—cam′er•a•man′** *n.*
Cam•e•roon (kăm′ə-rōōn′). Country of WC Africa. *Cap.* Yaoundé. *Pop.* 7,663,246.
†**ca•mi•sa** (kə-mē′sə) *n. SW U.S.* A shirt or chemise.
cam•i•sole (kăm′ĭ-sōl′) *n.* A woman's short, sleeveless undergarment or negligee.
cam•o•mile (kăm′ə-mīl′) *n. var. of* CHAMOMILE.
cam•ou•flage (kăm′ə-fläzh′, -fläj′) *n.* A means of concealment of personnel or materiel esp. one that makes them appear to be part of the natural surroundings. **—cam′ou•flage′** *v.* **—cam′ou•flag′er** *n.*
camp[1] (kămp) *n.* **1.a.** A place where a group of people, as soldiers, are billeted in temporary shelters such as tents. **b.** The shelters in a campsite or the people who use them. **2.** A recreational area with usu. permanent shelters. **3.** A group favorable to a common cause <the liberal *camp*> *—v.* To shelter or lodge in a camp.
camp[2] (kămp) *Slang. —n.* An affectation or appreciation of manners and taste usu. considered outlandish, vulgar, or banal. *—v.* To behave in an affected or vulgar way. **—camp** *adj.* **—camp′y** *adj.*
cam•paign (kăm-pān′) *n.* **1.** A series of military operations launched to accomplish a given objective within a specific area. **2.** An organized operation or activity to achieve a political, social, or commercial goal. **—cam•paign′** *v.* **—cam•paign′er** *n.*
cam•pa•ni•le (kăm′pə-nē′lē) *n.* A bell tower, esp. one close to but unattached to a building.

campanile

cam•pa•nol•o•gy (kăm′pə-nŏl′ə-jē) *n.* The art or study of bell casting and ringing. **—cam′pa•nol′o•gist** *n.*
camp•er (kăm′pər) *n.* **1.** One that camps. **2. a.** A vanlike vehicle equipped as a dwelling for camping or long motor trips. **b.** A portable shelter similar to the top portion of a trailer, made to be set on a pickup truck.
camp•fire (kămp′fīr′) *n.* **1.** An outdoor fire in a camp. **2.** A meeting held around such a campfire.
Camp Fire Girl *n.* A member of the Camp Fire Girls, an organization for girls that develops practical skills and provides recreation.
camp follower *n.* **1.** A civilian follower of an army who sells goods or services to it. **2.** One who follows but does not belong to a main body or group.
camp•ground (kămp′ground′) *n.* An area used for a camp or camp meeting.
cam•phor (kăm′fər) *n.* A volatile crystalline compound used medicinally and as an insect repellent. **—cam′phor•at′ed** *adj.* **—cam•phor′ic** (-fôr′ĭk, -fŏr′-) *adj.*
camphor tree *n.* An evergreen tree, *Cinnamomum camphora,* indigenous to E Asia, having aromatic wood that is a source of camphor.
camp meeting *n.* An evangelistic meeting held outdoors or in a tent.
camp•site (kămp′sīt′) *n.* An area used for camping.
cam•pus (kăm′pəs) *n.* The grounds and buildings of a school, college, or university.
cam•shaft (kăm′shăft′) *n.* An engine shaft fitted with a cam or cams.
can[1] (kăn; kən *when unstressed*) *v. p.t.* **could** (kŏŏd). **1.** Used to indicate: **a.** Mental or physical ability <I *can* see the mountains.> **b.** Possession of a given power, right, or privilege <A citizen *can* vote.> **c.** Possession of a given capacity or skill <They *can* do karate.> **2.** Used to indicate possibility or probability <*Can* you have the wrong address?> **3.** Used to request or grant permission <*Can* I have dinner with you?><Yes, you *can.*>

can[2] (kăn) *n.* **1.** A usu. cylindrical metal container. **2.a.** An airtight container, usu. made of tin-coated iron, in which food is preserved. **b.** The contents of such a container. —*v.* **canned, can•ning. 1.** To preserve in a can or jar. **2.** *Slang.* **a.** To dismiss : fire. **b.** To quit <*can* the chitchat> **—can′ner** *n.*

Ca•naan (kā′nən). Ancient region of Palestine W of the Jordan R. **—Ca′naan•ite′** *adj.* & *n.*

Can•a•da (kăn′ə-də). Country of N North America. *Cap.* Ottawa. *Pop.* 22,992,604. **—Ca•na′di•an** (kə-nā′dē-ən) *adj.* & *n.*

Canada Day *n. Can.* The holiday on July 1 celebrating the anniversary of Canadian Confederation in 1867 : Dominion Day.

Canada goose *n.* A wild goose, *Branta canadensis,* of North America, with a black neck and head and grayish plumage.

Ca•na•di•a•na (kə-nā′dē-ăn′ə) *n. Can.* A collection of things relating to Canadian culture, folklore, or history.

Canadian bacon *n.* Cured rolled bacon from the loin of a hog.

Canadian English *n. Can.* English spoken by Anglophones.

Canadian French *n.* The language of the French-Canadians.

Ca•na•di•an•ize (kə-nā′dē-ə-nīz′) *v.* **-ized, -iz•ing.** *Can.* **1.** To assimilate into Canadian culture. **2.** To become Canadian in spirit or methods.

ca•nal (kə-năl′) *n.* **1.** An artificial waterway. **2.** *Anat.* A tube : duct. **—ca•nal′i•za′tion** *n.* **—ca•nal′ize′** *v.*

can•a•pé (kăn′ə-pā′, -pē) *n.* A cracker or small piece of bread topped with cheese, meat, or relish.

ca•nard (kə-närd′) *n.* A false, unfounded, and misleading story.

ca•nar•y (kə-nâr′ē) *n., pl.* **-ies. 1.** A songbird, *Serinus canaria,* greenish to yellow in color and long bred as a cage bird. **2.** A light to vivid yellow.

Canary Islands. Spanish islands in the Atlantic off the NW coast of Africa.

ca•nas•ta (kə-năs′tə) *n.* A card game for 2 to 6 players, requiring 2 decks of cards and related to rummy.

Can•ber•ra (kăn′bər-ə, -bĕr′ə). Cap. of Australia, in the SE part. *Pop.* 221,000.

canc. *abbr.* Cancel.

can•can (kăn′kăn′) *n.* A dance performed by women and marked by high kicks.

can•cel (kăn′səl) *v.* **-celed, -cel•ing** or **-celled, -cel•ling. 1.** To cross out with markings such as lines : delete. **2.** To annul : invalidate <*cancel* an invitation> **3.** To mark or perforate (e.g., a stamp) to indicate it has been used. **4.** To offset : equalize. **5. a.** To remove a common factor from a fraction. **b.** To remove a common factor from both members of an equation. **—can′cel•a•ble** *adj.* **—can′cel•er** *n.* **—can′cel•la′tion** *n.*

can•cer (kăn′sər) *n.* **1. a.** Any of various malignant neoplasms that manifest invasiveness and a tendency to metastasize. **b.** The pathological condition marked by such growths. **2.** A spreading evil <a *cancer* of bigotry> **3. Cancer.** A constellation in the N Hemisphere. **4. a. Cancer.** The 4th sign of the zodiac. **b.** One born under this sign. **—can′cer•ous** *adj.*

can•de•la•bra (kăn′dl-ä′brə, -ăb′rə, -ā′brə) *n.* A candelabrum.

can•de•la•brum (kăn′dl-ä′brəm, -ăb′rəm, -ā′brəm) *n., pl.* **-bra** (-brə) or **-brums.** A decorative multibranched candlestick.

can•des•cence (kăn-dĕs′əns) *n.* The state of being white hot. **—can•des′cent** *adj.* **—can•des′cent•ly** *adv.*

can•did (kăn′dĭd) *adj.* **1.** Straightforward : frank. **2.** Not posed, as a photograph. **3.** Not prejudiced : impartial. —*n.* An informal photograph. **—can′did•ly** *adv.*

can•di•date (kăn′dĭ-dāt′, -dĭt) *n.* One who seeks an office, prize, etc. **—can′di•da•cy** (-də-sē), **can′di•da•ture′** *n.*

can•dle (kăn′dl) *n.* A solid, usu. cylindrical mass of a fatty substance such as tallow or wax, with an axially embedded wick that is burned for illumination. —*v.* **-dled, -dling.** To examine (an egg) for freshness before a light. **—can′dler** *n.*

can•dle•light (kăn′dl-līt′) *n.* **1.** Illumination from 1 or more candles. **2.** Twilight.

Can•dle•mas (kăn′dl-məs) *n.* A church festival celebrated on Feb. 2 as the feast of the presentation of the infant Christ in the temple.

can•dle•pins (kăn′dl-pĭnz′) *n.* A variation of the game of tenpins using slender bowling pins and a smaller ball.

can•dle•stick (kăn′dl-stĭk′) *n.* A holder for securing a candle.

can•dle•wick (kăn′dl-wĭk′) *n.* The wick of a candle.

can•dor (kăn′dər) *n.* Frankness of expression : straightforwardness.

can•dour (kăn′dər) *n. esp. Brit. var. of* CANDOR.

can•dy (kăn′dē) *n., pl.* **-dies.** A sweet, often rich confection made of sugar or syrup and other ingredients. —*v.* **-died, -dy•ing.** To cook, preserve, saturate, or coat with sugar or syrup.

candy striper *n.* A usu. teen-age volunteer nurse's aide.

can•dy•tuft (kăn′dē-tŭft′) *n.* Any of various plants of the genus *Iberis,* with white, red, or purplish flower clusters.

cane (kān) *n.* **1. a.** A slender, jointed, woody but usu. flexible stem, as of bamboo or rattan. **b.** A plant having such a stem. **c.** Such stems or strips used for wickerwork. **2.** A stick used for walking or for beating. **3.** Sugar cane. —*v.* **caned, can•ing. 1.** To make, supply, or repair with cane. **2.** To beat with a cane. **—can′er** *n.*

cane•brake (kān′brāk′) *n.* A dense cane thicket.

cane sugar *n.* Sucrose.

ca•nine (kā′nīn′) *adj.* **1.** Of or relating to a member of the family Canidae, which includes dogs, wolves, and foxes. **2.** Of or designating 1 of the 4 conical teeth between the incisors and the bicuspids. —*n.* **1.** A canine animal. **2.** A canine tooth.

Ca•nis Ma•jor (kā′nĭs mā′jər, kăn′ĭs) *n.* A constellation in the S Hemisphere.

Canis Mi•nor (mī′nər) *n.* A constellation in the S Hemisphere.

can•is•ter (kăn′ĭ-stər) *n.* **1.** A container for holding dry foods, as flour or tea. **2.** An artillery shell that bursts and scatters the shot it is packed with. **3.** The part of a gas mask that has a filter for removing poison gas from the surrounding air.

can•ker *also* **can•ker sore** (kăng′kər) *n.* An ulcerous sore of the mouth or lips. **—can′ker•ous** *adj.*

can•ker•worm (kăng′kər-wûrm′) *n.* The larva of either of 2 moths, *Paleacrita vernata* or *Alsophila pometaria,* that destroys trees.

can•na (kăn′ə) *n.* Any of various tropical plants of the genus *Canna,* with broad leaves and large yellow or red flowers.

can•na•bis (kăn′ə-bĭs) *n.* The hemp plant.

canned (kănd) *adj.* **1.** Preserved in a can. **2.** *Informal.* Recorded, as laughter, esp. for TV reproduction.

can•ner•y (kăn′ə-rē) *n., pl.* **-ies.** An establishment where foods are canned.

can•ni•bal (kăn′ə-bəl) *n.* **1.** One who eats human flesh. **2.** An animal that feeds on its own kind. **—can′ni•bal•ism** *n.* **—can′ni•bal•is′tic** *adj.*

can•ni•bal•ize (kăn′ə-bə-līz′) *v.* **-ized, -iz•ing.** To take usable parts from (e.g., damaged equipment) for the repair of other equipment. **—can′ni•bal•i•za′tion** *n.*

can•no•li (kə-nō′lē, kă-) *n.* A fried pastry roll with a creamy, usu. sweet filling.

can•non (kăn′ən) *n., pl.* **-non** or **-nons. 1.** A weapon consisting of a heavy metal tube mounted on wheels or a fixed base, used to fire projectiles. **2.** A heavy firearm larger than 0.60 caliber. **—can′non•eer′** *n.*

can•non•ade (kăn′ə-nād′) *v.* **-ad•ed, -ad•ing.** To assault with heavy artillery fire. **—can′non•ade′** *n.*

can•non•ball *also* **can•non ball** (kăn′ən-bôl′) *n.* **1.** A round projectile fired from a cannon. **2.** Something that is fast-moving, as a train. **—can′non•ball′** *v.*

can•not (kăn′ŏt′, kă-nŏt′, kə-) *v.* Can not.

can•ny (kăn′ē) *adj.* **-ni•er, -ni•est.** Careful : shrewd. **—can′ni•ly** *adv.* **—can′ni•ness** *n.*

ca•noe (kə-no͞o′) *n.* A light pointed-ended narrow boat moved by paddling. —*v.* **-noed, -noe•ing.** To carry or travel in a canoe. **—ca•noe′ist** *n.*

can•on[1] (kăn′ən) *n.* **1.** A law or body of laws established by a church. **2.** A basis for judgment : criterion. **3.** The Biblical books officially recognized as the Holy Scripture. **4.** *Rom. Cath. Ch.* **a.** *often* **Canon.** The most important part of the Mass, beginning after the Sanctus. **b.** The calendar of accepted saints.

can•on[2] (kăn′ən) *n.* A priest who serves in a cathedral or collegiate church.

ca•ñon (kăn′yən) *n. var. of* CANYON.

ca•non•i•cal (kə-nŏn′ĭ-kəl) *or* **ca•non•ic** (-nŏn′ĭk) *adj.* **1.** Relating to, required by, or obeying canon law. **2.** Orthodox : authoritative. **—ca•non′i•cal•ly** *adv.* **—can′on•ic′i•ty** (kăn′ə-nĭs′ĭ-tē) *n.*

can•on•ize (kăn′ə-nīz′) *v.* **-ized, -iz•ing. 1.** To declare officially to be a saint. **2.** To glorify. **—can′on•i•za′tion** *n.*

canon law *n.* The body of officially established rules that the members of a Christian church follow.

can•o•py (kăn′ə-pē) *n., pl.* **-pies. 1.** A cloth covering hanging over something or carried over a dignitary. **2.** A rooflike ornamental structure. **3. a.** The transparent enclosure over the cockpit of an aircraft. **b.** The hemispheric surface of a parachute. —*v.* **-pied, -py•ing.** To spread over with or as if with a canopy.

canst (kănst) *v. archaic 2nd person sing. present tense of* CAN[1].

cant[1] (kănt) *n.* **1. a.** Angular deviation from a horizontal or vertical surface or plane. **b.** The tilt caused by such a motion. **2.** A slanted surface or edge. **—cant** *v.*

cant[2] (kănt) *n.* **1.** Whining, affected speech. **2.** Mechanically recited discourse. **3.** Hypocritical and pious language. **4.** The

specialized vocabulary of the members of a group : jargon. —*v.* **1.** To whine or plead. **2.** To moralize. **—cant'ing·ly** *adv.*
can't (kănt, känt). Cannot.
can·ta·bi·le (kän-tä'bē-lā', -bi-, kən-) *adv. Mus.* In a lyrical, flowing style. Used as a direction. **—can·ta'bi·le'** *adj.* & *n.*
can·ta·loupe *also* **can·ta·loup** (kăn'tl-ōp') *n.* A melon, *Cucumis melo cantalupensis,* with a ribbed, rough rind and aromatic orange flesh.
can·tan·ker·ous (kăn-tăng'kər-əs) *adj.* Bad-tempered and argumentative : disagreeable. **—can·tan'ker·ous·ly** *adv.*
can·ta·ta (kən-tä'tə) *n. Mus.* A composition of choruses, solos, and recitatives.
can·teen (kăn-tēn') *n.* **1. a.** A store for on-base military personnel. **b.** *esp. Brit.* A club for soldiers. **2.** An institutional cafeteria or recreation hall. **3.** A temporary eating place, esp. one set up in an emergency <a Red Cross *canteen*> **4.** A flask for carrying drinking water.
can·ter (kăn'tər) *n.* A gait slower than a gallop but faster than a trot. —*v.* To go or cause to go at a canter.
Can·ter·bur·y (kăn'tər-bĕr'ē). Cathedral city of SE England. *Pop.* 117,400.
Canterbury bells *n.* (*sing.* or *pl.* in number). A plant, *Campanula medium,* native to Europe, widely cultivated for its violet-blue bell-shaped flowers.
can·ti·cle (kăn'tĭ-kəl) *n.* A liturgical hymn or chant.
can·ti·le·ver (kăn'tl-ē'vər, -ĕv'ər) *n.* A projecting structure, as a beam, supported only at one end. —*v.* To support by, extend outward, or build as a cantilever.
†can·ti·na (kăn-tē'nə) *n. SW U.S.* A barroom.
can·tle (kăn'təl) *n.* The rear projecting part of a saddle.
can·to (kăn'tō) *n., pl.* **-tos.** A main division of a long poem.
can·ton (kăn'tən, -tŏn') *n.* A small territorial division of a country, esp. one of the Swiss states. —*v.* **1.** To divide into territorial cantons. **2.** To billet (troops). **—can'ton·al** *adj.*
Can·ton (kăn-tŏn', kăn'tŏn'). Guangzhou.
can·ton·ment (kăn-tōn'mənt, -tŏn'-) *n.* **1.** A group of more or less temporary billets for troops. **2.** Assignment of troops to temporary billets.
can·tor (kăn'tər) *n.* The official soloist or chief singer of the liturgy in a synagogue.
can·vas (kăn'vəs) *n.* **1.** A strong, heavy fabric used esp. for making sails and tents. **2.** A piece of canvas used for an oil painting. **3.** Sailcloth. **4.** Sails as a whole. **5.** The floor of a ring for boxing or wrestling.
can·vas·back (kăn'vəs-băk') *n.* A North American duck, *Aythya valisineria,* with a reddish head and a grayish back.
can·vass (kăn'vəs) *v.* **1.** To scrutinize. **2.a.** To go through (e.g., a neighborhood) to solicit votes, subscriptions, etc. **b.** To make a survey : poll. —*n.* **1.** A thorough examination or detailed discussion. **2.** A solicitation of votes, sales orders, opinions, etc. **—can'vass·er** *n.*
can·yon *also* **ca·ñon** (kăn'yən) *n.* A narrow gorge with steep walls.
cap (kăp) *n.* **1.** A usu. soft close-fitting head covering. **2.** An object like a cap in form, use, or position. **3.a.** A percussion cap. **b.** A small explosive charge for use in a cap pistol. —*v.* **capped, cap·ping. 1.** To put a cap on. **2.** To lie over : cover.
ca·pa·ble (kā'pə-bəl) *adj.* **1.** Having ability or capacity : efficient. **2.** Qualified. **3.** Open or susceptible to <a flaw *capable* of correction> **—ca'pa·bil'i·ty, ca'pa·ble·ness** *n.* **—ca'pa·bly** *adv.*
ca·pa·cious (kə-pā'shəs) *adj.* Roomy.
ca·pac·i·tance (kə-păs'ĭ-təns) *n.* **1.** The ratio of charge to potential on an electrically charged, isolated conductor. **2.** The property of a circuit element that permits it to store charge. **—ca·pac'i·tive** *adj.* **—ca·pac'i·tive·ly** *adv.*
ca·pac·i·tor (kə-păs'ĭ-tər) *n. Elect.* A circuit element composed of 2 metallic plates separated by a dielectric, used to store a charge temporarily.
ca·pac·i·ty (kə-păs'ĭ-tē) *n., pl.* **-ties. 1.** The ability to hold, receive, or contain. **2.** The largest amount that can be contained <a room filled to *capacity*> **3.** The most efficient level or maximum of production. **4.** Ability : capability. **5.** Suitability for or receptiveness to specified treatment <the *capacity* of water to freeze> **6.** The role in which a person functions.
cap-a-pie *or* **cap-à-pie** (kăp'ə-pē') *adv.* From head to foot.
ca·par·i·son (kə-păr'ĭ-sən) *n.* **1.** A usu. ornamental covering for a saddle or harness. **2.** Fancy clothing. **—ca·par'i·son** *v.*
cape[1] (kāp) *n.* A sleeveless garment that fastens at the throat and hangs loosely over the shoulders.
cape[2] (kāp) *n.* **1.** A point of land that projects into water. **2.** A Cape Cod cottage.
Cape Cod cottage *n.* A compact house with 1 or $1\frac{1}{2}$ stories, a gabled roof, and a central chimney.
ca·per[1] (kā'pər) *n.* **1.** A playful leap or hop. **2.** An antic : prank. **3.** A criminal undertaking. —*v.* To leap about : frolic.
ca·per[2] (kā'pər) *n.* A pickled bud of a Mediterranean shrub, *Capparis spinosa,* used as a condiment.
Cape Town or **Cape·town** (kāp'toun'). Legislative cap. of South Africa. *Pop.* 697,514.
Cape Verde (vûrd). Island country in the E Atlantic. *Cap.* Praia. *Pop.* 272,071.
cap·il·lar·i·ty (kăp'ə-lăr'ĭ-tē) *n., pl.* **-ties.** The attraction or repulsion between surfaces of a liquid and a solid that prevents the surface of the liquid from being flat.
cap·il·lar·y (kăp'ə-lĕr'ē) *adj.* **1.** Relating to or like a hair. **2.** Having a very small inside diameter, as a tube. **3.** *Anat.* In, of, or relating to the capillaries. **4.** *Physics.* Of or relating to capillarity. —*n., pl.* **-ies. 1.** *Anat.* One of the minute blood vessels that connect arteries and veins. **2.** A tube with a small inside diameter.
cap·i·tal[1] (kăp'ĭ-tl) *n.* **1.** A city or town that is the seat of government in a state or nation. **2.** Material wealth in the form of money or property that is used to produce more wealth. **3.a.** The net worth of a business. **b.** The funds contributed to a business by the owners or stockholders. **4.** Capitalists as a group. **5.** An advantage or asset. **6.** A letter, such as A or B, written or printed in a larger size or different form from its corresponding small letter. —*adj.* **1.** Chief : principal. **2.** Of or relating to a governmental capital. **3.** First-rate <a *capital* idea> **4.** Very serious <a *capital* error> **5.** Involving death or calling for the death penalty <a *capital* felony> **6.** Relating to monetary capital.
cap·i·tal[2] (kăp'ĭ-tl) *n.* The top part of a column or pillar.
capital goods *pl.n.* Goods used in producing commodities.
cap·i·tal-in·ten·sive (kăp'ĭ-tl-ĭn-tĕn'sĭv) *adj.* Requiring or having a large expenditure of capital in comparison to labor.
cap·i·tal·ism (kăp'ĭ-tl-ĭz'əm) *n.* An economic system characterized by open competition in a free market and by private or corporate ownership of the means of production and distribution.
cap·i·tal·ist (kăp'ĭ-tl-ĭst) *n.* **1.** One who invests capital in business. **2.** A supporter of capitalism. **3.** Someone of great wealth. **—cap'i·tal·is'tic** *adj.* **—cap'i·tal·is'ti·cal·ly** *adv.*
cap·i·tal·ize (kăp'ĭ-tl-īz') *v.* **-ized, -iz·ing. 1.** To convert into capital. **2.** To supply with capital. **3.** To profit by : exploit. **4.** To write or print in capital letters. **—cap'i·tal·i·za'tion** *n.*
capital ship *n.* A warship, as a battleship, of the largest class.
cap·i·ta·tion (kăp'ĭ-tā'shən) *n.* A tax of an equal amount per person.
cap·i·tol (kăp'ĭ-tl) *n.* **1.** The building in which a state legislature meets. **2. Capitol.** The building in which the U.S. Congress meets.
ca·pit·u·late (kə-pĭch'ə-lāt') *v.* **-lat·ed, -lat·ing. 1.** To surrender under conditional terms. **2.** To cease resisting. **—ca·pit'u·la'tion** *n.* **—ca·pit'u·la'tor** *n.* **—ca·pit'u·la·to'ry** *adj.*
ca·pon (kā'pŏn', -pən) *n.* A castrated rooster.
cap pistol *n.* A toy pistol with a hammer action that detonates a small charge.
cap·puc·chi·no (kăp'ə-chē'nō, kä'pə-) *n.* Espresso coffee mixed with steamed milk or topped with whipped cream.
ca·price (kə-prēs') *n.* **1.** A change of mind : whim. **2.** A tendency to change one's mind suddenly or impulsively.
ca·pri·cious (kə-prĭsh'əs, -prē'shəs) *adj.* Characterized by or subject to whim. ☆**syns:** CHANGEABLE, ERRATIC, FICKLE, INCONSISTENT, INCONSTANT, MERCURIAL, TEMPERAMENTAL, UNPREDICTABLE, UNSTABLE, UNSTEADY, VARIABLE, VOLATILE, WHIMSICAL **—ca·pri'cious·ly** *adv.*
Cap·ri·corn (kăp'rĭ-kôrn') *n.* **1.** A constellation in the S Hemisphere. **2. a.** The 10th sign of the zodiac. **b.** One born under this sign.
cap·ri·ole (kăp'rē-ōl') *n.* **1.** An upward leap made by a trained horse without forward motion. **2.** A leap : jump. **—cap'ri·ole'** *v.*
cap·size (kăp'sīz', kăp-sīz') *v.* **-sized, -siz·ing.** To overturn, as a boat.
cap·stan (kăp'stən, -stăn') *n.* **1.** *Naut.* A device consisting of a vertical cylinder rotated to hoist weights by winding in a cable. **2.** A small cylindrical pulley that regulates the speed of recorder tape.
cap·su·late (kăp'sə-lāt', -syōō-, -lĭt) *also* **cap·su·lat·ed** (-lā'tĭd) *adj.* In or formed into a capsule.
cap·sule (kăp'səl, -syōōl) *n.* **1.** A soluble, usu. gelatin container for a dose of oral medicine. **2.** A fibrous, membranous, or fatty envelope, as the sac surrounding the kidney, that encloses an organ or part. **3.** A fruit that contains 2 or more seeds and splits open when dry. **4.** A pressurized modular compartment of an

aircraft or spacecraft. **5.** A brief summary. **—cap′su•lar** *adj.* **—cap′sule** *v.*

cap•tain (kăp′tən) *n.* **1.** The leader of a group : chief. **2.** The officer who commands a ship. **3.a.** A commissioned officer in the Army, Air Force, or Marine Corps ranking below a major and above a first lieutenant. **b.** A commissioned officer in the Navy ranking below a rear admiral and above a commander. **4.** A prominent figure. —*v.* To direct or command. **—cap′tain•cy** *n.* **—cap′tain•ship′** *n.*

cap•tion (kăp′shən) *n.* **1.** A title or description accompanying an illustration or picture. **2.** A motion-picture subtitle. **3.** A title, as of a document. **—cap′tion** *v.*

cap•tious (kăp′shəs) *adj.* **1.** Tending to criticize. **2.** Deceptive.

cap•ti•vate (kăp′tĭ-vāt′) *v.* **-vat•ed, -vat•ing.** To fascinate : enrapture. **—cap′ti•va′tion** *n.* **—cap′ti•va′tor** *n.*

cap•tive (kăp′tĭv) *n.* A prisoner. —*adj.* **1.** Held as prisoner. **2.** Subjugated, as a nation. **3.** Enraptured. **4.** Obliged to be present. **—cap•tiv′i•ty** *n.*

cap•tor (kăp′tər, -tôr′) *n.* One that captures.

cap•ture (kăp′chər) *v.* **-tured, -tur•ing. 1.** To take captive. **2.** To win control or possession of, as in a contest. —*n.* **1.** The act of capturing. **2.** One that is captured.

car (kär) *n.* **1.** An automobile. **2.** A conveyance with wheels that runs along tracks, as a railroad car. **3.** A boxlike enclosure for passengers on a conveyance, as an elevator.

▲word history: *Car* was a dying word in English until modern technology revived it. By the middle of the 19th cent. *car* was only a poetic synonym for *chariot*, to which it is related. *Car* sprang to life after the term *motorcar* was adopted late in the 19th cent. for the automobile. *Motorcar* was soon shortened to *car*, which lost all its poetic associations in the brave new era.

Ca•ra•cas (kə-rä′kəs, -răk′əs). Cap. of Venezuela, in the N. *Pop.* 1,662,627.

car•a•cul (kăr′ə-kəl) *n. var. of* KARAKUL.

ca•rafe (kə-răf′, -räf′) *n.* A glass bottle with a flared lip for serving water or wine.

car•a•mel (kăr′ə-məl, -mĕl′, kär′məl) *n.* **1.** A smooth, chewy candy. **2.** Sugar heated to a brown syrup, used for coloring and sweetening foods.

car•a•pace (kăr′ə-pās′) *n. Zool.* A hard bony outer covering, as the fused dorsal plates of a turtle.

car•at (kăr′ət) *n.* **1.** A unit of weight for precious stones, equal to 200 mg. **2.** *var. of* KARAT.

car•a•van (kăr′ə-văn′) *n.* **1.** A group of travelers journeying together, esp. across a desert. **2.** A file of pack animals or vehicles. **3.** A van. **4.** *esp. Brit.* A house trailer.

car•a•van•sa•ry (kăr′ə-văn′sə-rē) *also* **car•a•van•se•rai** (-rī′) *n., pl.* **-ries** *also* **-rais. 1.** An inn with a large courtyard for accommodating caravans in the Near or Far East. **2.** A large inn.

car•a•vel (kăr′ə-vĕl′) *n.* A small, light sailing ship of the 15th and 16th cent.

car•a•way (kăr′ə-wā′) *n.* A Eurasian plant, *Carum carvi*, with pungent aromatic seeds that are used in cooking.

car•bide (kär′bīd′) *n.* A binary carbon compound composed of carbon and a more electropositive element.

car•bine (kär′bīn′, -bēn′) *n.* A light, short-barreled rifle.

car•bo•hy•drate (kär′bō-hī′drāt′, -bə-) *n.* Any of a group of compounds, including sugars, starches, and cellulose, that are composed of carbon, hydrogen, and oxygen.

car•bol•ic acid (kär-bŏl′ĭk) *n.* PHENOL.

car•bon (kär′bən) *n. Symbol* **C 1.** A nonmetallic element occurring as a powdery noncrystalline solid. **2. a.** A sheet of carbon paper. **b.** A copy made with carbon paper. **—car′bon•i•za′tion** *n.* **—car′bon•ize′** *v.* **—car′bon•ous** *adj.*

carbon 14 *n.* A radioactive carbon isotope used in dating ancient objects that contain carbon.

car•bo•na•ceous (kär′bə-nā′shəs) *adj.* Of, containing, or yielding carbon.

car•bon•ate (kär′bə-nāt′) *v.* **-at•ed, -at•ing.** To charge with carbon dioxide gas, as a beverage. **—car′bon•a′tion** *n.*

carbon black *n.* Any of various divided forms of carbon obtained from the incomplete combustion of gas or oil, used chiefly in rubber and ink.

carbon copy *n.* **1.** A copy, as of a letter, made with carbon paper. **2.** *Informal.* A close copy.

carbon dating *n.* Determination of the approx. age, as of a fossil, by use of the radiation rate of carbon 14.

carbon dioxide *n.* A colorless, odorless, nonflammable gas, produced in respiration, combustion, or organic decomposition.

car•bon•ic acid (kär-bŏn′ĭk) *n.* A weak, unstable acid present only in solutions of carbon dioxide and water.

car•bon•if•er•ous (kär′bə-nĭf′ər-əs) *adj.* Of, producing, or containing carbon or coal.

carbon monoxide *n.* A colorless, odorless, extremely poisonous gas formed by incomplete combustion of carbon or any carbonaceous material.

carbon paper *n.* A lightweight paper coated on one side with a waxy pigment that is transferred onto paper by pressure.

carbon tet•ra•chlo•ride (tĕt′rə-klôr′īd′, -klōr′-) *n.* A poisonous, nonflammable, colorless liquid used in fire extinguishers.

car•boy (kär′boi′) *n.* A large bottle usu. in a protective basket or crate and often used for holding corrosive liquids.

car•bun•cle (kär′bŭng′kəl) *n.* A localized, pus-producing painful skin infection. **—car•bun′cu•lar** (-kyə-lər) *adj.*

car•bu•re•tor (kär′bə-rā′tər, -byə-) *n.* A device in gasoline engines that mixes fuel vapor and air for efficient combustion.

car•cass (kär′kəs) *n.* A dead body, esp. of a slaughtered animal.

car•cin•o•gen (kär-sĭn′ə-jən, kär′sə-nə-jĕn′) *n.* A cancer-causing substance or agent. **—car′ci•no•gen′e•sis** (kär′sə-nə-jĕn′ĭ-sĭs) *n.* **—car′cin•o•gen′ic** *adj.* **—car′ci•no•ge•nic′i•ty** (-jə-nĭs′ĭ-tē) *n.*

car•ci•no•ma (kär′sə-nō′mə) *n., pl.* **-mas** *or* **-ma•ta** (-mə-tə). A malignant tumor derived from skin, mucous membrane, or other tissue that covers an organ or structure. **—car′ci•nom′a•tous** (-nŏm′ə-təs, -nō′mə-) *adj.*

car coat *n.* A knee-length coat.

card[1] (kärd) *n.* **1.** A small piece of stiff paper or thin pasteboard, esp.: **a.** A playing card. **b.** A postcard. **c.** A greeting card. **d.** A business card. **2. cards.** *(sing. or pl. in number)* A game played with cards. **3.** A program, esp. for a sports event. **4.** *Informal.* An eccentric or amusing person : character. —*v.* **1.** To attach to or furnish with a card. **2.** To list on a card : catalogue. **3.** *Informal.* To verify the legal age of by checking one's indentification. **—in the cards.** Likely to occur.

card[2] (kärd) *n.* A wire-toothed instrument or machine used to disentangle fibers, as of wool, before spinning or to raise the nap of a fabric. —*v.* To brush or comb out with a card. **—card′er** *n.*

car•da•mom *or* **car•da•mum** (kär′də-məm) *also* **car•da•mon** (-mən) *n.* A tropical Asiatic plant, *Elettaria cardamomum*, having large hairy leaves and capsular fruit with seeds that are used as a spice.

card•board (kärd′bôrd′, -bōrd′) *n.* A thin stiff pasteboard.

card catalog *n.* An alphabetical listing, esp. of books in a library, with a card for each item.

car•di•ac (kär′dē-ăk′) *adj.* Of, near, or relating to the heart <*cardiac* arrest>

cardiac massage *n.* A procedure marked by the rhythmic compression of the chest by an individual in an effort to restore proper circulation and respiration.

Car•diff (kär′dĭf). City of SE Wales. *Pop.* 282,000.

car•di•gan (kär′dĭ-gən) *n.* A sweater or knitted jacket opening down the front.

car•di•nal (kär′dn-əl, kärd′nəl) *adj.* **1.** Being of prime importance. **2.** Of a vivid red color. —*n.* **1.** *Rom. Cath. Ch.* An official appointed by and ranking just below the pope. **2.** Vivid red. **3.** A North American bird, *Richmondena cardinalis*, with a crested head, a short thick bill, and bright-red plumage in the male. **4.** A cardinal number. **—car′di•nal•ly** *adv.*

cardinal number *n.* A number, as 7 or 13 or 946, used to indicate quantity but not order.

car•di•o•gram (kär′dē-ə-grăm′) *n.* The curve recorded by a cardiograph, used in diagnosis of heart defects.

car•di•o•graph (kär′dē-ə-grăf′) *n.* An instrument for recording the mechanical movements of the heart. **—car′di•og′ra•phy** (-ŏg′rə-fē) *n.*

car•di•ol•o•gy (kär′dē-ŏl′ə-jē) *n.* The medical study of the heart, its diseases, and their treatment. **—car′di•ol′o•gist** *n.*

car•di•o•pul•mo•nar•y (kär′dē-ō-po͝ol′mə-nĕr′ē) *adj.* Of or relating to the heart and lungs.

cardiopulmonary resuscitation *n.* A procedure used after cardiac arrest in which cardiac massage, mouth-to-mouth resuscitation, and drugs are used to restore breathing.

car•di•o•vas•cu•lar (kär′dē-ō-văs′kyə-lər) *adj.* Of, relating to, or involving the heart and the blood vessels.

card•sharp (kärd′shärp′) *n.* An expert cheat at cards. **—card′sharp′ing** *n.*

care (kâr) *n.* **1.** Mental distress : worry. **2.** A source of solicitude or attention. **3.** Caution <take *care*> **4.** Supervision : charge <under a doctor's *care*> ☆**syns:** CHARGE, CUSTODY, GUARDIANSHIP, SUPERVISION —*v.* **cared, car•ing. 1.** To be interested or concerned. **2.** To have a liking or inclination. **3.** To give care. **4.** To object : mind.

ca•reen (kə-rēn′) *v.* **1.** To lurch while moving rapidly. **2.** To cause (a ship) to tilt.

ca•reer (kə-rîr′) *n.* **1.** A chosen profession or occupation. **2.** The general progression of one's life, esp. in one's profession. —*v.* To rush headlong.

care•free (kâr′frē′) *adj.* Free from all cares.
care•ful (kâr′fəl) *adj.* **1.** Cautious in thought, speech, or action. **2.** Painstaking : thorough. ☆***syns:*** CAUTIOUS, CHARY, CIRCUMSPECT, PRUDENT **—care′ful•ly** *adv.*
care•less (kâr′lĭs) *adj.* **1.** Inattentive : negligent. **2.** Inconsiderate : thoughtless. **3.** Indifferent to accuracy or neatness. ☆***syns:*** MESSY, SLAPDASH, SLIPSHOD, SLOPPY, SLOVENLY, UNTIDY **—care′less•ly** *adv.*
ca•ress (kə-rĕs′) *n.* A gentle touch or gesture of affection. *—v.* To stroke or touch affectionately. **—ca•ress′er** *n.*
car•et (kăr′ĭt) *n.* A proofreading symbol used to indicate where material is to be inserted in a printed or written line.
care•tak•er (kâr′tā′kər) *n.* One hired to take charge of goods, property, or another person : custodian.
care•worn (kâr′wôrn′, -wōrn′) *adj.* Showing signs of worry or care.
car•fare (kär′fâr′) *n.* Fare charged a passenger, as on a subway or bus.
car•go (kär′gō) *n., pl.* **-goes** *or* **-gos.** The freight carried by a vehicle, vessel, or aircraft.
car•hop (kär′hŏp′) *n.* One who serves customers at a drive-in restaurant.
Car•ib•be•an Sea (kăr′ə-bē′ən, kə-rĭb′ē-ən). Extension of the Atlantic, bounded by the coasts of Central and South America and the West Indies.
car•i•bou (kăr′ə-bo͞o′) *n., pl.* **-bou** *or* **-bous.** A deer, *Rangifer tarandus,* of New World arctic regions.
car•i•ca•ture (kăr′ĭ-kə-cho͝or′, -chər) *n.* **1.** A usu. pictorial representation in which the subject's distinctive features or characteristics are exaggerated for comic or distorted effect. **2.** An absurdly inferior imitation. **—car′i•ca•ture′** *v.* **—car′i•ca•tur′ist** *n.*
car•ies (kâr′ēz′) *n., pl.* **-ies.** Bone or tooth decay.
car•il•lon (kăr′ə-lŏn′, -lən) *n.* A stationary set of tuned bells in a tower, usu. played by means of a keyboard.
†**carl** *or* **carle** (kärl) *n.* **1.** *Archaic.* A peasant or farmer. **2.** *Obs.* A bondman : serf. **3.** *Regional.* A churl.
car•load (kär′lōd′) *n.* The load that a car can carry.
car•mine (kär′mĭn, -mīn′) *n.* A strong to vivid red color.
car•nage (kär′nĭj) *n.* Massive slaughter.
car•nal (kär′nəl) *adj.* **1.** Of sensual desires and appetites. **2.** Not spiritual : temporal. **—car•nal′i•ty** *n.* **—car′nal•ly** *adv.*
car•na•tion (kär-nā′shən) *n.* A plant, *Dianthus caryophyllus,* widely cultivated for its fragrant white, pink, or red flowers.
car•nel•ian (kär-nēl′yən) *n.* A reddish brown variety of clear chalcedony used as a gemstone.
car•ni•val (kär′nə-vəl) *n.* **1.** The season just before Lent, given to feasting and merrymaking. **2.** A traveling show featuring exhibits and rides.
car•ni•vore (kär′nə-vôr′, -vōr′) *n.* An animal of the order Carnivora, including predominantly flesh-eating mammals.
car•niv•o•rous (kär-nĭv′ər-əs) *adj.* **1.** Belonging or relating to the order Carnivora. **2.** Flesh-eating : predatory. **—car•niv′o•rous•ly** *adv.* **—car•niv′o•rous•ness** *n.*
car•ny *also* **car•ney** (kär′nē) *n., pl.* **-nies** *also* **-neys.** *Slang.* **1.** CARNIVAL 2. **2.** A carnival worker.
car•ob (kăr′əb) *n.* **1.** An evergreen tree, *Ceratonia siliqua,* of the Mediterranean region, with compound leaves and edible pods. **2.** The sweet pulp of the carob pod used as a chocolate substitute.
car•ol (kăr′əl) *v.* **-oled, -ol•ing** *or* **-olled, -ol•ling. 1.** To celebrate in song. **2.** To sing joyously. *—n.* A song of joy, esp. for Christmas. **—car′ol•er** *n.*
car•om (kăr′əm) *n.* **1.** A billiards shot in which the cue ball strikes 2 other balls successively. **2.** A collision followed by a rebound, as a ball bouncing off a wall. **—car′om** *v.*
car•o•tene (kăr′ə-tēn′) *also* **car•o•tin** (-tĭn) *n.* An orange-yellow to red hydrocarbon present in many plants as a pigment and converted to vitamin A by the liver.
ca•rot•id (kə-rŏt′ĭd) *n.* Either of the 2 arteries in the neck that supply blood to the head. **—ca•rot′id** *adj.*
ca•rouse (kə-rouz′) *n.* Rowdy, drunken merrymaking. **—ca•rous′al** *n.* **—ca•rouse′** *v.* **—ca•rous′er** *n.*
car•ou•sel *or* **car•rou•sel** (kăr′ə-sĕl′, -zĕl′) *n.* A merry-go-round.
carp[1] (kärp) *v.* To complain and criticize constantly : nag **—carp′er** *n.*
carp[2] (kärp) *n.* An edible freshwater fish, *Cyprinus carpio.*
car•pal (kär′pəl) *adj. Anat.* Of, relating to, or near the carpus. *—n.* A carpus bone.
Car•pa•thi•an Mountains (kär-pā′thē-ən). Mountain system of E Europe.
car•pel (kär′pəl) *n. Bot.* The ovule-bearing female flower organ, composed of a modified leaf that forms 1 or more sections of the pistil. **—car′pel•lar′y** *adj.*
car•pen•ter (kär′pən-tər) *n.* One who builds, finishes, and repairs wooden objects and structures. **—car′pen•ter** *v.* **—car′pen•try** *n.*
car•pet (kär′pĭt) *n.* **1.** A thick, heavy floor covering : rug. **2.** The fabric used for carpets. **3.** A surface like a carpet <a *carpet* of moss> *—v.* To cover with or as if with a carpet. **—on the carpet.** Before a superior for a reprimand.
car•pet•bag (kär′pĭt-băg′) *n.* An old-fashioned traveling bag made of carpet material.
car•pet•bag•ger (kär′pĭt-băg′ər) *n.* A Northerner who was in the South after the Civil War for political or financial gain.
car-pool (kär′po͞ol′) *n.* **1.** An arrangement whereby several commuters share cars and expenses. **2.** A group participating in a car-pool. **—car′-pool′** *v.*
car•port (kär′pôrt′, -pōrt′) *n.* A roof projecting from the side of a building, used to shelter a car.
car•pus (kär′pəs) *n., pl.* **-pi** (-pī′). *Anat.* **1.** The wrist. **2.** The bones in the wrist.
car•rel *also* **car•rell** (kăr′əl) *n.* A nook in a library for private study.
car•riage (kăr′ĭj) *n.* **1.** A 4-wheeled usu. horse-drawn vehicle for passengers. **2.** A baby carriage. **3.** A wheeled support or frame for a heavy object, as a cannon. **4.** A machine part for holding or moving another part. **5. a.** The act or process of carrying or transporting. **b.** (kăr′ē-ĭj). The charge for transporting. **6.** Posture : bearing.
carriage trade *n.* Wealthy patrons, as of a business.
car•ri•er (kăr′ē-ər) *n.* **1.** One that transports or conveys. **2.** One that deals in transporting passengers or goods. **3.** *Med.* One that is immune to a pathogen it transmits to others. **4.** An aircraft carrier.
carrier pigeon *n.* A homing pigeon trained to carry messages.
carrier wave *n.* An electromagnetic wave that can be modulated to transmit speech, music, images, or signals.
car•ri•on (kăr′ē-ən) *n.* Dead, rotting flesh.
car•rot (kăr′ət) *n.* The yellow orange, edible root of a widely cultivated plant, *Daucus carota sativa.*
car•rou•sel (kăr′ə-sĕl′, -zĕl′) *n. var. of* CAROUSEL.
car•ry (kăr′ē) *v.* **-ried, -ry•ing. 1.** To convey : transport <*carry* books><*carry* passengers> **2.** To win over the interest of. **3.** To seize : capture. **4.** To have or keep on one's person. **5.** To involve : imply <The crime *carries* a heavy penalty.> **6.** To behave or conduct (oneself) in a given way. **7.** To sustain : support <Your paycheck *carries* the family.> **8.** To keep in stock : sell. **9.** To cover a range : reach. **10.** To gain support or acceptance for, esp. to secure the adoption of <*carry* a bill> **11.** To win most of the votes of <*carried* the South> **12.** To keep in one's accounts as a debtor. **13.** To place before the public through a mass medium. **—carry away.** To arouse great emotion or enthusiasm in. **—carry on. 1.** To engage in : conduct. **2.** To continue <*carried on* despite difficulties> **3.** To act in an excited, inappropriate, or childish way. *—n., pl.* **-ries. 1.** A portage, as between 2 navigable bodies of water. **2.** The range of a projectile or gun.
car•ry•all (kăr′ē-ôl′) *n.* A large tote bag or pocketbook.
carrying charge *n.* The interest charge on an installment loan.
car•ry•on (kăr′ē-ŏn′) *n.* A piece of luggage compact enough to be carried aboard an airplane.
car•ry•out (kăr′ē-out′) *adj.* Take-out <*carryout* food> **—car′ry•out′** *n.*
car•sick (kär′sĭk′) *adj.* Nauseated from vehicular motion. **—car′sick′ness** *n.*
Car•son City (kär′sən). Cap. of Nev., in the SW. *Pop.* 32,022.
cart (kärt) *n.* **1.** A 2-wheeled vehicle drawn by an animal. **2.** A small, light vehicle moved by hand <a tea *cart*> *—v.* **1. a.** To transport in a cart. **b.** To lug. **2.** To remove or transport by or as if by force. **—cart′a•ble** *adj.* **—cart′er** *n.*
cart•age (kär′tĭj) *n.* **1.** The act of transporting by cart. **2.** The cost of transporting by cart.
carte blanche (kärt′ bläNsh′, blänch′) *n., pl.* **cartes blanches** (bläNsh′, bläN′shĭz, blänch′, blän′chĭz). Unlimited authority.
car•tel (kär-tĕl′) *n.* An association of independent businesses organized to control prices, production, etc.
Car•ter (kâr′tər), **James Earl (Jimmy), Jr.** b. 1924. 39th U.S. President (1977–81).
Car•thage (kär′thĭj). Ancient city and state on the N coast of Africa.
car•ti•lage (kär′tl-ĭj) *n.* A tough elastic connective tissue attached to the surfaces of bones near the joints. **—car′ti•lag′i•nous** (-ăj′ə-nəs) *adj.*
car•tog•ra•phy (kär-tŏg′rə-fē) *n.* The art of making maps. **—car•tog′ra•pher** *n.* **—car′to•graph′ic** (-tə-grăf′ĭk), **car′to•graph′i•cal** *adj.*

car·ton (kär′tn) *n.* A container, esp. one made of cardboard.

car·toon (kär-to͞on′) *n.* **1.** A pictorial satire of a current event, often accompanied by a caption : caricature. **2.** A comic strip. **3.** An animated cartoon. **—car·toon′** *v.* **—car·toon′ist** *n.*

car·tridge (kär′trĭj) *n.* **1.** A tubular metal or metal and cardboard case that contains the primer and powder of small arms ammunition or shotgun shells. **2.** A removable unit of equipment, as a casette, designed to fit into a larger piece of equipment.

cart·wheel (kärt′hwēl′, -wēl′) *n.* **1.** A sideways handspring with the arms and legs spread like the spokes of a wheel. **2.** *Slang.* A silver dollar.

carve (kärv) *v.* **carved, carv·ing. 1.** To slice into pieces. **2.** To disjoint, slice, and serve poultry or meat. **3.** To make or form by or as if by cutting. **—carv′er** *n.*

carv·ing (kär′vĭng) *n.* **1.** The cutting of wood, stone, etc., to form a figure or design. **2.** A figure or design formed by carving.

car wash *n.* A place equipped for washing cars.

car·y·at·id (kăr′ē-ăt′ĭd) *n., pl.* **-ids** or **-at·i·des** (-ăt′ĭ-dēz′). A supporting column sculptured into a woman's figure.

caryatid

ca·sa·ba (kə-sä′bə) *n.* A winter melon having a yellow rind and sweet flesh.

Cas·a·blan·ca (kăs′ə-blăng′kə, kä′sə-bläng′kə). City of NW Morocco, on the Atlantic. *Pop.* 1,371,300.

cas·cade (kă-skād′) *n.* **1.** A waterfall over steep rocks. **2.** Something like to a cascade <a *cascade* of ruffles> *—v.* **-cad·ed, -cad·ing.** To drop in or as if in a cascade.

case[1] (kās) *n.* **1.** An instance of the existence or occurrence of something : example. **2. a.** An occurrence of injury or disease. **b.** A client, as of an attorney or physician. **3.** Circumstances : situation. **4.** A set of arguments, reasons, or supporting facts offered in justification. **5.** A question or problem. **6.** *Law.* **a.** An action or suit. **b.** Grounds for an action. **7.** The syntactic relationship of a noun, pronoun, or adjective to the other words of a sentence, indicated in inflected languages by declensional endings and in noninflected languages by position. *—v.* **cased, cas·ing.** *Slang.* To examine with care before acting <*cased* the bank before robbing it>.

case[2] (kās) *n.* **1.** A container. **2.** A protective covering. **3.** A set or pair, as of pistols. **4.** The frame or framework of a door or window. **5.** A shallow tray for storing printing type. *—v.* **cased, cas·ing.** To cover or protect with a case.

ca·sein (kā′sēn′, -sē-ĭn) *n.* A milk and cheese protein used in foods and in manufacturing plastics and adhesives.

case·ment (kās′mənt) *n.* **1.** A window sash opening outward by hinges. **2.** A casement window.

case·work (kās′wûrk′) *n.* Social work treating the problems of a specific case.

cash (kăsh) *n.* **1.** Money in the form of currency. **2.** Payment in money or by check for goods or services. *—v.* To convert into money <*cash* a check>

cash·ew (kăsh′o͞o, kə-sho͞o′) *n.* A tropical American tree, *Anacardium occidentale,* bearing edible kidney-shaped nuts.

cash·ier[1] (kă-shîr′) *n.* **1.** The officer of a business concern or bank in charge of distributing and receiving money. **2.** An employee who handles cash transactions, as in a supermarket.

ca·shier[2] (kă-shîr′) *v.* To dismiss from a position of command or responsibility.

cash·mere (kăzh′mîr′, kăsh′-) *n.* **1.** Fine wool from the Cashmere goat. **2.** A soft fabric made from cashmere.

Cashmere goat *n.* A goat native to the Himalayan regions of India and Tibet and greatly valued for its wool

cash register *n.* A machine that tabulates and records sales transactions.

cas·ing (kā′sĭng) *n.* An outer cover : case <a shell *casing*>

ca·si·no (kə-sē′nō) *n., pl.* **-nos.** A public room or house, esp. for gambling.

cask (kăsk) *n.* **1.** A barrel. **2.** The quantity a cask will hold.

cas·ket (kăs′kĭt) *n.* **1.** A small chest or case. **2.** A coffin.

Cas·pi·an Sea (kăs′pē-ən). Salt lake between SE Europe and W Asia.

casque (kăsk) *n.* A helmet.

cas·sa·va (kə-sä′və) *n.* A tropical American plant of the genus *Manihot,* with a starchy root used to make tapioca.

cas·se·role (kăs′ə-rōl′) *n.* **1.** A dish in which food is both cooked and served. **2.** Food prepared and served in a casserole.

cas·sette (kə-sĕt′, kă-) *n.* A cartridge for magnetic tape or photographic film.

cas·sia (kăsh′ə) *n.* **1.** Any of various chiefly tropical trees, shrubs, and plants of the genus *Cassia,* with long pods, usu. yellow flowers, and leaves that yield senna. **2.** A tropical Asian tree, *Cinnamomum cassia,* with cinnamonlike bark used as a spice.

cas·sit·er·ite (kə-sĭt′ə-rīt′) *n.* A mineral that is an important tin ore.

cas·sock (kăs′ək) *n.* A long garment worn by members of the clergy.

cast (kăst) *v.* **cast, cast·ing. 1.** To throw forcefully : fling. **2.** To shed <a snake *casting* its skin> **3.** To turn or direct, as a glance. **4.** To deposit (a ballot). **5. a.** To give a certain role to. **b.** To choose theatrical performers for. **6.** To form by pouring into a mold. **7.** To compute. *—n.* **1.** The act of casting : throw. **2.** A throw of dice. **3.** The performers in a theatrical presentation. **4.** A rigid dressing usu. made of gauze and plaster of Paris, as for a broken bone. **5.** An impression formed in a mold. **6.** A slight trace of color. **7.** Outward form or look. **8.** Something shed, as a snake's skin.

cas·ta·nets (kăs′tə-nĕts′) *pl.n.* A rhythm instrument composed of a pair of ivory or hardwood shells held in the palm of the hand and clapped together with the fingers.

cast·a·way (kăst′ə-wā′) *adj.* **1.** Shipwrecked. **2.** Discarded. **—cast′a·way′** *n.*

caste (kăst) *n.* **1.** One of the 4 major hereditary classes of Hindu society. **2.a.** A social class separated from the others by hereditary, professional, or financial differences. **b.** Social status based on caste.

cas·tel·lat·ed (kăs′tə-lā′tĭd) *adj.* Having turrets and battlements.

cast·er *also* **cas·tor** (kăs′tər) *n.* **1.** A small wheel usu. on a swivel fastened to the underside of an object to facilitate moving. **2.** A bottle or cruet for condiments.

cas·ti·gate (kăs′tĭ-gāt′) *v.* **-gat·ed, -gat·ing.** To criticize or punish severely. **—cas′ti·ga′tion** *n.* **—cas′ti·ga′tor** *n.*

cast·ing (kăs′tĭng) *n.* **1.** Something cast out or off. **2.** Something that has been cast in a mold.

cast iron *n.* A hard, brittle nonmalleable alloy of carbon, iron, and silicon.

cas·tle (kăs′əl) *n.* **1.** A fort or fortified cluster of buildings. **2.** A building similar to a castle. **3.** A rook in the game of chess.

cast-off (kăst′ôf′, -ŏf′) *adj.* Discarded : rejected.

cas·tor (kăs′tər) *n. var. of* CASTER.

castor oil *n.* An oil obtained from the seeds of a tropical plant, used as a lubricant and a cathartic.

cas·trate (kăs′trāt′) *v.* **-trat·ed, -trat·ing. 1.** To remove the testicles of : geld. **2.** To remove the ovaries of : spay. **—cas·tra′tion** *n.*

Cas·tro (kăs′trō), **Fidel.** b. 1927. Cuban revolutionary statesman.

ca·su·al (kăzh′o͞o-əl) *adj.* **1.** Occurring by chance. **2.** Nonchalant. **3. a.** Informal. **b.** Suitable for informal use or wear. **4.** Not serious or thorough : superficial. **—ca′su·al·ly** *adv.* **—ca′su·al·ness** *n.*

ca·su·al·ty (kăzh′o͞o-əl-tē) *n., pl.* **-ties. 1.** A calamitous accident. **2.** One who is injured or killed in an accident. **3.** One injured, killed, missing in action, or taken prisoner by an enemy.

ca·su·ist·ry (kăzh′o͞o-ĭ-strē) *n.* Subtle but misleading reasoning, esp. about moral principles. **—ca′su·ist** *n.* **—ca′su·is′tic** *adj.* **—ca′su·is′ti·cal·ly** *adv.*

cat (kăt) *n.* **1. a.** A carnivorous mammal, *Felis catus* or *F. domesticus,* domesticated as a rat catcher and pet. **b.** Any other animal of the family Felidae, including the lion, tiger, leopard, or lynx. **2.** *Slang.* A spiteful woman. **3.** *Slang.* FELLOW 1a.

CAT (kăt) *n.* Computerized axial tomography.

ca·tab·o·lism (kə-tăb′ə-lĭz′əm) *n.* Metabolism of complex molecules into simple molecules. **—cat′a·bol′ic** (kăt′ə-bŏl′ĭk) *adj.* **—ca·tab′o·lize′** *v.*

cat·a·clysm (kăt′ə-klĭz′əm) *n.* A sudden and violent upheaval or disaster. **—cat′a·clys′mic, cat′a·clys′mal** *adj.*

cat·a·combs (kăt′ə-kōmz′) *pl.n.* A series of underground passages with recesses for coffins and graves.

cat·a·falque (kăt′ə-fălk′, -fôlk′) *n.* The raised structure on which a coffin stands during a solemn, state funeral.

cat·a·lep·sy (kăt′l-ĕp′sē) *n.* Muscular rigidity and lack of response to stimuli, associated with epilepsy and schizophrenia. **—cat′a·lep′tic** *adj.*

cat·a·logue *also* **cat·a·log** (kăt′l-ôg′, -ŏg′) *n.* **1. a.** A systemized, usu. descriptive list. **b.** A publication containing such a list <a mail-order *catalogue*> **2.** A card catalog. *—v.* **-logued, -logu·ing** *also* **-loged, -log·ing.** To make a catalogue of. **—cat′a·logu′er, cat′a·log′er** *n.*

ca·tal·pa (kə-tăl′pə, -tôl′-) *n.* A chiefly North American tree of the genus *Catalpa*, with large leaves, whitish flower clusters, and long thin pods.

cat·a·lyst (kăt′l-ĭst) *n.* **1.** *Chem.* A substance that alters and esp. increases the rate at which a chemical reaction takes place. **2.** One that precipitates a process or event. **—ca·tal′y·sis** (kə-tăl′ĭ-sĭs) *n.* **—cat′a·lyt′ic** *adj.* **—cat′a·lyt′i·cal·ly** *adv.*

cat·a·lyze (kăt′l-īz′) *v.* **-lyzed, -lyz·ing.** *Chem.* To act as a catalyst in or for. **—cat′a·lyz′er** *n.*

cat·a·ma·ran (kăt′ə-mə-răn′) *n.* A sailboat with 2 parallel hulls.

cat·a·pult (kăt′ə-pŭlt′, -po͝olt′) *n.* **1.** An ancient military device for hurling stones, spears, or other missiles. **2.** A mechanism for launching aircraft from a ship's deck. **—cat′a·pult′** *v.*

cat·a·ract (kăt′ə-răkt′) *n.* **1.** A huge downpour or waterfall. **2.** *Pathol.* Opacity of the lens or capsule of the eye, causing total or partial blindness.

ca·tarrh (kə-tär′) *n.* Mucous-membrane inflammation, esp. of the nose and throat. **—ca·tarrh′al** *adj.*

ca·tas·tro·phe (kə-tăs′trə-fē) *n.* A sudden and terrible disaster : calamity. **—cat′a·stroph′ic** (kăt′ə-strŏf′ĭk) *adj.* **—cat′a·stroph′i·cal·ly** *adv.*

cat·a·to·ni·a (kăt′ə-tō′nē-ə) *n.* A schizophrenic disorder marked by plastic immobility of the limbs, stupor, negativism, and mutism. **—cat′a·ton′ic** (-tŏn′ĭk) *adj.* & *n.*

cat·bird (kăt′bûrd′) *n.* A North American songbird, *Dumetalla carolinensis*, with chiefly slate-gray plumage.

catbird seat *n.* A powerful position.

cat·call (kăt′kôl′) *n.* A call or whistle of derision or disapproval. **—cat′call′** *v.*

catch (kăch, kĕch) *v.* **caught** (kôt), **catch·ing. 1.** To seize or capture, esp. after a chase. **2.** To trap or snare. **3.** To take by surprise <*caught* me unaware> **4. a.** To overtake. **b.** To reach in time to board <*caught* the train> **5.** To grasp. **6.** To snatch. **7.** To intercept. **8.** To become entangled. **9.** To fasten. **10.** To take fire : kindle. **11.** To become infected by : contract. **12.** *Informal.* To see <*caught* the singer's act> ☆**syns:** CLUTCH, GRAB, NAB, SEIZE, SNATCH **—catch on.** *Informal.* **1.** To understand. **2.** To become popular. *—n.* **1.** The act of catching. **2.** A fastening or stopping device. **3.** Something caught <a *catch* of fish> **4.** *Informal.* One worth catching. **5.** *Informal.* A tricky or unsuspected condition : pitfall. **6.** A game of throwing and catching a ball.

catch·all (kăch′ôl′, kĕch′-) *n.* A container for odds and ends.

catch·er (kăch′ər, kĕch′-) *n.* One that catches, esp. the baseball player whose position is behind home plate.

catch·ing (kăch′ĭng, kĕch′-) *adj.* **1.** Contagious. **2.** Alluring.

Catch-22 (kăch′twĕn-tē-to͞o′, kĕch′-) *n.* A paradox in which seeming alternatives actually cancel each other out, leaving no means of escape from a dilemma.

catch·up (kăch′əp, kĕch′-) *n. var. of* KETCHUP.

catch·y (kăch′ē, kĕch′ē) *adj.* **-i·er, -i·est. 1.** Readily recalled <a *catchy* slogan> **2.** Deceptive : tricky.

cat·e·chism (kăt′ĭ-kĭz′əm) *n.* A short book summarizing the basic tenets of a religion in the form of questions and answers. **—cat′e·chist** *n.* **—cat′e·chize′** *v.*

cat·e·gor·i·cal (kăt′ĭ-gôr′ĭ-kəl, -gŏr′-) *or* **cat·e·gor·ic** (-ĭk) *adj.* **1.** Absolute : certain. **2.** Of, relating to, or included in a category. **—cat′e·gor′i·cal·ly** *adv.*

cat·e·go·rize (kăt′ĭ-gə-rīz′) *v.* **-rized, -riz·ing.** To place in categories : classify. **—cat′e·go·ri·za′tion** *n.*

cat·e·go·ry (kăt′ĭ-gôr′ē, -gōr′ē) *n., pl.* **-ries.** A specifically defined division in a classification system : class.

ca·ter (kā′tər) *v.* **1.** To provide food or food service. **2.** To provide something needed or desired. **—ca′ter·er** *n.*

cat·er·cor·nered (kăt′ər-kôr′nərd, kăt′ē-) *also* **cat·er-cor·ner** (-nər) *or* **cat·ty-cor·nered** (kăt′ē-kôr′nərd) *adj.* Diagonal. **—cat′er-cor′nered** *adv.*

cat·er·pil·lar (kăt′ər-pĭl′ər, kăt′ə-) *n.* The wormlike, often brightly colored, hairy or spiny larva of a butterfly or moth.

cat·er·waul (kăt′ər-wôl′) *v.* To make a harsh cry or shriek. **—cat′er·waul′** *n.*

cat·fish (kăt′fĭsh′) *n.* Any of numerous scaleless, chiefly freshwater fishes of the order Siluriformes, with whiskerlike barbels near the mouth.

cat·gut (kăt′gŭt′) *n.* A tough thin cord or thread made from the dried intestines of certain animals, as sheep.

ca·thar·sis (kə-thär′sĭs) *n., pl.* **-ses** (-sēz′). **1.** Purgation, esp. of the bowels. **2.** Emotional or psychological cleansing.

ca·thar·tic (kə-thär′tĭk) *adj.* Purgative. *—n.* A cathartic agent, as a laxative.

ca·the·dral (kə-thē′drəl) *n.* A large or important church, esp. the main church of a bishop's see.

Cath·e·rine II (kăth′ər-ĭn, kăth′rĭn). "the Great." 1729–96. Empress of Russia (1762–96).

cath·e·ter (kăth′ĭ-tər) *n.* A slender, flexible tube inserted into a bodily duct, as a vein, to expand or maintain an opening. **—cath′e·ter·ize′** *v.*

cath·ode (kăth′ōd′) *n.* **1.** A negatively charged electrode, as of an electron tube. **2.** The positively charged terminal of a primary cell or of a storage battery supplying current. **—ca·thod′ic** (kă-thŏd′ĭk) *adj.*

cath·o·lic (kăth′ə-lĭk, kăth′lĭk) *adj.* **1.** Universal : general <*catholic* appeal> **2. Catholic.** Of the Roman Catholic Church. *—n.* **Catholic.** A member of a Catholic church, esp. a Roman Catholic. **—ca·thol′i·cal·ly** (kə-thŏl′ĭ-klē) *adv.*

Ca·thol·i·cism (kə-thŏl′ə-sĭz′əm) *n.* The faith, doctrine, practice, and organization of the Roman Catholic Church.

cat·i·on (kăt′ī′ən) *n.* A positively charged ion that in electrolytes is attracted to a negative electrode. **—cat′i·on′ic** *adj.*

cat·kin (kăt′kĭn′) *n.* A dense cluster of scalelike flowers, as of a birch.

cat·like (căt′līk′) *adj.* Stealthy.

cat·nap (kăt′năp′) *n.* A short nap.

cat·nip (kăt′nĭp′) *n.* A hairy aromatic plant, *Nepeta cataria*, that attracts cats.

cat-o'-nine-tails (kăt′ə-nīn′tālz′) *n.* A whip having 9 knotted cords fastened to a handle.

CAT scan *n.* A cross-sectional picture produced by a CAT scanner.

CAT scanner *n.* A device that produces cross-sectional x-rays of the body using computerized axial tomography.

cat's cradle *n.* A game in which a looped string is transferred from the hands of one player to the next.

cat's-eye (kăts′ī′) *n.* Any of various semiprecious iridescent gems.

cat's-paw *also* **cats·paw** (kăts′pô′) *n.* One used by another as a dupe.

cat·sup (kăt′səp, kăch′əp, kĕch′-) *n. var. of* KETCHUP.

cat·tail (kăt′tāl′) *n.* A marsh plant of the genus *Typha*, esp. *T. latifolia*, with long straplike leaves and a dense cylindrical head of minute brown flowers.

cat·tle (kăt′l) *pl.n.* Animals of the genus *Bos*, esp. those of the species *B. taurus*, raised for dairy products and meat.

cat·ty (kăt′ē) *adj.* **-ti·er, -ti·est.** Subtly spiteful or malicious. **—cat′ti·ly** *adv.* **—cat′ti·ness** *n.*

cat·ty-cor·nered (kăt′ē-kôr′nərd) *adj.* & *adv. var. of* CATER-CORNERED.

cat·walk (kăt′wôk′) *n.* A narrow elevated pathway, as on the sides of a bridge.

Cau·ca·sian (kô-kā′zhən, -kăzh′ən) *n.* **1.** A native or inhabitant of the Caucasus. **2.** A member of the Caucasoid ethnic division. **—Cau·ca′sian** *adj.*

Cau·ca·soid (kô′kə-soid′) *adj.* Of, relating to, or designating a major ethnic division of the human race with the color of the skin varying from very light to brown. **—Cau′ca·soid′** *n.*

Cau·ca·sus (kô′kə-səs). Region and mountain range of SE European USSR.

cau·cus (kô′kəs) *n., pl.* **-cus·es** *or* **-cus·ses.** A meeting of the members of a political party to make policy decisions and select candidates. **—cau′cus** *v.*

cau·dal (kôd′l) *adj.* Of or near the tail : posterior. **—cau′dal·ly** *adv.*

caught (kôt) *v. p.t.* & *p.p. of* CATCH.

caul·dron (kôl′drən) *n. var. of* CALDRON.

cau·li·flow·er (kô′lĭ-flou′ər, kŏl′ĭ-) *n.* A plant, *Brassica oleracea botrytis*, related to the cabbage and broccoli, with an enlarged edible flower head.

caulk *also* **calk** (kôk) *v.* **1.** To pack the seams of (a boat) with oakum or tar to make it watertight. **2.** To seal (pipes) against leakage. **—caulk′er** *n.*

caus·al (kô′zəl) *adj.* **1.** Relating to or being a cause. **2.** Expressing a cause. **—cau·sal′i·ty** (-zăl′ĭ-tē) *n.* **—caus′al·ly** *adv.*

cau·sa·tion (kô-zā′shən) *n.* **1.** The act or process of causing. **2.** Something that effects a cause.

cause (kôz) *n.* **1.** One that produces an effect, result, or consequence. **2.** A motive. **3.** A reason. **4.** A principle or goal. **5.** *Law.* **a.** Grounds for legal action. **b.** A lawsuit. *—v.* **caused, caus·ing.** To be the cause of : bring about. **—caus′er** *n.*

cause cé·lè·bre (kōz′ sā-lĕb′rə) *n., pl.* **causes cé·lè·bres** (kōz′ sā-lĕb′rə). **1.** A legal case that attracts much attention. **2.** A controversial issue.

cau·se·rie (kōz-rē′) *n.* **1.** A chat. **2.** A short, informal piece of writing.

cause•way (kôz′wā′) *n.* A raised roadway, as across water.
caus•tic (kô′stĭk) *adj.* **1.** Capable of corroding, burning, or dissolving. **2.** Sharp : sarcastic —*n.* A caustic substance or material. **—caus′ti•cal•ly** *adv.*
cau•ter•ize (kô′tə-rīz′) *v.* **-ized, -iz•ing.** To burn or sear with a cautery. **—cau′ter•i•za′tion** *n.*
cau•ter•y (kô′tə-rē) *n., pl.* **-ies.** A caustic agent or a very hot or cold instrument used to destroy aberrant tissue.
cau•tion (kô′shən) *n.* **1.** Careful forethought. **2.** An admonishment : warning. **3.** *Informal.* One that astonishes. ☆***syns:*** CALCULATION, CAREFULNESS, CIRCUMSPECTION, PRECAUTION, WARINESS —*v.* To warn against danger. **—cau′tion•ar′y** *adj.*
cau•tious (kô′shəs) *adj.* Careful : wary.
cav•al•cade (kăv′əl-kād′, kăv′əl-kād′) *n.* **1.** A procession, esp. of riders or horse-drawn carriages. **2.** A colorful display.
cav•a•lier (kăv′ə-lîr′) *n.* **1.** A knight. **2.** A gallant gentleman. **3. Cavalier.** One who supported Charles I of England. —*adj.* **1.** Haughty. **2.** Nonchalant : carefree. **—cav′a•lier′ly** *adv.*
cav•al•ry (kăv′əl-rē) *n., pl.* **-ries.** Troops that fight on horseback or in armored vehicles. **—cav′al•ry•man** *n.*
cave (kāv) *n.* An underground hollow with an opening at the surface. —*v.* **caved, cav•ing.** To hollow out. **—cave in. 1.** To collapse. **2.** *Informal.* To yield.
ca•ve•at (kā′vē-ăt′, kăv′ē-, kä′vē-ăt′) *n.* A warning or caution.
cave-in (kāv′ĭn′) *n.* **1.** An act of caving in. **2.** A place where the ground has caved in.
cave man *n.* **1.** A prehistoric human who lived in caves. **2.** *Informal.* One who is crude or brutal, esp. toward women.
cav•ern (kăv′ərn) *n.* A large cave. **—cav′ern•ous** *adj.*
cav•i•ar *also* **cav•i•are** (kăv′ē-är′) *n.* The roe of a large fish, as a sturgeon, salted and eaten as an appetizer.
cav•il (kăv′əl) *v.* **-iled, -il•ing** or **-illed, -il•ling.** To find fault unnecessarily : quibble. **—cav′il** *n.* **—cav′il•er** *n.*
cav•i•ty (kăv′ĭ-tē) *n., pl.* **-ties. 1.** A hole or hollow. **2.** A pitted area in a tooth caused by decay.
ca•vort (kə-vôrt′) *v.* To prance about.
caw (kô) *n.* The hoarse, raucous cry of a crow or similar bird. **—caw** *v.*
cay (kē, kā) *n.* An islet of sand or coral.
Cay•enne (kī-ĕn′, kā-). Cap. of French Guiana. *Pop.* 30,461.
cayenne pepper *n.* A pungent condiment made from the fruit of a pepper plant, *Capsicum frutescens.*
cay•man (kā′mən, kā-măn′, kī-măn′) *n. var. of* CAIMAN.
†**cay•use** (kī-yo͞os′, kī′yo͞os′) *n. W U.S.* A horse, esp. an Indian pony.
Cb *symbol for* COLUMBIUM.
CB (sē′bē′) *n.* Citizens band. **—CB′er** *n.*
C.B. *abbr.* Cape Breton.
cc *abbr.* cubic centimeter.
cc. *abbr.* chapters.
c.c. or **C.C.** *abbr.* carbon copy.
Cd *symbol for* CADMIUM.
c.d. *abbr.* cash discount.
C.D. *abbr.* civil defense.
Ce *symbol for* CERIUM.
cease (sēs) *v.* **ceased, ceas•ing.** To put or come to an end : stop. **—cease** *n.*
cease-fire (sēs′fīr′) *n.* Suspension of hostilities : truce.
cease•less (sēs′lĭs) *adj.* Continual : endless. **—cease′less•ly** *adv.*
ce•cum *also* **cae•cum** (sē′kəm) *n., pl.* **-ca** (-kə). *Anat.* The blind pouch that forms the start of the large intestine. **—ce′cal** (-kəl) *adj.*
ce•dar (sē′dər) *n.* A coniferous evergreen tree of the genus *Cedrus,* with aromatic, often reddish wood.
cede (sēd) *v.* **ced•ed, ced•ing. 1.** To yield or grant, as by treaty. **2.** To transfer or assign, as a title.
ce•di (sā′dē) *n., pl.* **-di** or **-dis.** —See CURRENCY TABLE.
ce•dil•la (sĭ-dĭl′ə) *n.* A mark placed beneath the letter *c, as in the French word garçon,* to indicate that the *c* is to be pronounced (s).
ceil•ing (sē′lĭng) *n.* **1.** The upper surface of a room. **2.** A vertical boundary, esp. of atmospheric visibility or operable aircraft altitude. **3.** A maximum limit, esp. as prescribed by law <wage and price *ceilings*>
cel•e•brate (sĕl′ə-brāt′) *v.* **-brat•ed, -brat•ing. 1.** To observe (a day or event) with ceremonies of respect, rejoicing, or festivity. **2.** To perform (a religious ceremony) <*celebrate* Mass> **3.** To praise : extol. ☆***syns:*** COMMEMORATE, KEEP, OBSERVE, SOLEMNIZE **—cel′e•brant** *n.* **—cel′e•bra′tion** *n.* **—cel′e•bra′tor** *n.*
cel•e•brat•ed (sĕl′ə-brā′tĭd) *adj.* Well-known : famous.
ce•leb•ri•ty (sə-lĕb′rĭ-tē) *n., pl.* **-ties. 1.** A famous person. **2.** Fame : renown. ☆***syns:*** LUMINARY, NAME, NOTABLE, PERSONAGE
ce•ler•i•ty (sə-lĕr′ĭ-tē) *n.* Speed : swiftness.
cel•er•y (sĕl′ə-rē) *n.* A plant, *Apium graveolens dulce,* grown for its edible stalks.
ce•les•ta (sə-lĕs′tə) *also* **ce•leste** (sə-lĕst′) *n.* A musical instrument with a keyboard and metal plates struck by hammers that produce bell-like tones.
ce•les•tial (sə-lĕs′chəl) *adj.* **1.** Of or relating to the sky. **2.** Heavenly : spiritual.
celestial navigation *n.* Navigation based on the positions of celestial bodies.
celestial sphere *n.* An imaginary sphere of infinite extent with the earth at its center.
cel•i•bate (sĕl′ə-bĭt) *n.* **1.** One who remains unmarried, esp. because of religious vows. **2.** One who is sexually abstinent. **—cel′i•ba•cy** (-bə-sē) *n.* **—cel′i•bate** *adj.*
cell (sĕl) *n.* **1.** A small, confining room, as in a monastery or prison. **2.** The primary organizational unit of a movement <a Communist *cell*> **3.** *Biol.* The smallest unit of an organism that is capable of independent functioning, composed of a membrane enclosing nuclei, cytoplasm, and inanimate matter. **4.** A small, enclosed cavity, as a compartment in a honeycomb. **5.** *Elect.* **a.** A single unit for conversion of chemical energy or heat into electricity, usu. composed of a container with electrodes and an electrolyte. **b.** A solar cell. **6.** *Computer Sci.* A basic storage unit in a computer memory.
cel•lar (sĕl′ər) *n.* **1.** A room for storage, usu. below ground or beneath a building. **2.** A stock of wines.
cel•lo (chĕl′ō) *n., pl.* **-los.** A 4-stringed instrument of the violin family, pitched lower than the viola. **—cel′list** *n.*
cel•lo•phane (sĕl′ə-fān′) *n.* A transparent cellulose material made from wood pulp, used as a moistureproof wrapping.
cel•lu•lar (sĕl′yə-lər) *adj.* **1.** Relating to or resembling a cell. **2.** Made up of cells.
cel•lu•lite (sĕl′yə-līt′) *n.* A fatty deposit, as under the skin around the thighs.
cel•lu•loid (sĕl′yə-loid′) *n.* A flammable plastic material made from cellulose and camphor.
cel•lu•lose (sĕl′yə-lōs′, -lōz′) *n.* An amorphous polymer that is the chief constituent of plant tissues and fibers, used to make paper, cellophane, textiles, and explosives. **—cel′lu•lo′sic** *adj.*
Cel•si•us (sĕl′sē-əs, -shəs) *adj.* Of or relating to a temperature scale on which the freezing point of water is 0° and the boiling point is 100° under normal atmospheric pressure.
Celt (kĕlt, sĕlt) *n.* **1.** One of an ancient people of W and C Europe, including the Britons and the Gauls. **2.** A speaker of a Celtic language.
Celt•ic (kĕl′tĭk, sĕl′-) *n.* A group of Indo-European languages, including Welsh and Gaelic. **—Cel′tic** *adj.*
cem•ba•lo (chĕm′bə-lō′) *n., pl.* **-los.** A harpsichord. **—cem′ba•list** *n.*
ce•ment (sĭ-mĕnt′) *n.* **1.** A construction adhesive of powdered calcined rock and clay materials that form a paste with water and can be molded or poured to set as a solid mass. **2.** A substance that hardens to function as an adhesive : glue. **3.** A binding element. —*v.* **1.** To join or cover with or as if with cement. **2.** To strengthen.
ce•men•tum (sĭ-mĕn′təm) *n.* A bony substance that covers the root of a tooth.
cem•e•ter•y (sĕm′ĭ-tĕr′ē) *n., pl.* **-ies.** A graveyard.
cen•o•taph (sĕn′ə-tăf′) *n.* A monument built in honor of a dead person whose remains are interred elsewhere.
cen•ser (sĕn′sər) *n.* A vessel for incense, used esp. in a religious ceremony.
cen•sor (sĕn′sər) *n.* **1.** One authorized to examine films and printed materials and suppress what is objectionable. **2.** One of 2 Roman officials overseeing the census. —*v.* To subject to a censor's examination. ☆***syns:*** BAN, STIFLE, SUPPRESS **—cen•so′ri•al** (-sôr′ē-əl, -sōr′-) *adj.*
cen•so•ri•ous (sĕn-sôr′ē-əs, -sōr′-) *adj.* Tending to or marked by censure : critical.
cen•sor•ship (sĕn′sər-shĭp′) *n.* **1.** The act or process of censoring. **2.** The office of a Roman censor.
cen•sure (sĕn′shər) *n.* **1.** An expression of strong disapproval or criticism. **2.** An official rebuke. —*v.* **-sured, -sur•ing.** To express strong disapproval of : criticize. **—cen′sur•a•ble** *adj.* **—cen′sur•er** *n.*
cen•sus (sĕn′səs) *n.* An official and usu. periodic enumeration of population.
cent (sĕnt) *n.* See *birr, dollar, guilder, leone, lilangeni, pound, rand, rupee, schilling,* and *shilling* at CURRENCY TABLE.
cen•taur (sĕn′tôr′) *n. Gk. Myth.* One of a race of monsters with a man's head, arms, and trunk and a horse's body and legs.
cen•ta•vo (sĕn-tä′vō) *n., pl.* **-vos.** See *colon, cordoba, cruzeiro, escudo, lempira, peso, quetzal, sol,* and *sucre* at CURRENCY TABLE.
cen•te•nar•i•an (sĕn′tə-nâr′ē-ən) *n.* A person 100 years old or older.

cen·ten·a·ry (sĕn-tĕn′ə-rē, sĕn′tə-nĕr′ē) *n., pl.* **-ries.** A centennial. **—cen·ten′a·ry** *adj.*
cen·ten·ni·al (sĕn-tĕn′ē-əl) *n.* A 100th anniversary or celebration. **—cen·ten′ni·al** *adj.*
cen·ter (sĕn′tər) *n.* **1.** A point equidistant from all points on the outer boundaries of a body or figure : middle. **2.** A point around which something, as an activity, is concentrated : hub. **3.** A place of origin : heart. **4.** A middle part or position. **5.** A group whose political views are midway between liberal and conservative. **6.** A player who occupies a middle position, as in football. ☆**syns:** MIDDLE, MIDPOINT, MIDST —*v.* **1.** To place in or around a center. **2.** To gather at a center : concentrate. **3.** To have a center : focus.
cen·ter·board (sĕn′tər-bôrd′, -bōrd′) *n.* A retractable keellike device, as a flat metal plate, used esp. in sailboats.
cen·ter·piece (sĕn′tər-pēs′) *n.* An ornamental object or arrangement at the center of a table.
cen·tes·i·mal (sĕn-tĕs′ə-məl) *adj.* Relating to or divided into hundredths.
cen·tes·i·mo[1] (sĕn-tĕs′ə-mō′) *n., pl.* **-mos** or **-mi** (-mē). See *lira* at CURRENCY TABLE.
cen·tes·i·mo[2] (sĕn-tĕs′ə-mō′) *n., pl.* **-mos.** See *balboa* and *peso* at CURRENCY TABLE.
cen·ti·grade (sĕn′tĭ-grād′) *adj.* Celsius.
cen·ti·gram (sĕn′tĭ-grăm′) *n.* See MEASUREMENT TABLE.
cen·time (sän′tēm′, sĕn′-) *n.* See *dinar, dirham, franc,* and *gourde* at CURRENCY TABLE.
cen·ti·me·ter (sĕn′tə-mē′tər, sän′-) *n.* See MEASUREMENT TABLE.
cen·ti·mo (sĕn′tə-mō′) *n., pl.* **-mos.** See *bolivar, colon, dobra, ekpwele, guarani,* and *peseta* at CURRENCY TABLE.
cen·ti·pede (sĕn′tə-pēd′) *n.* A flat arthropod of the class Chilopoda with numerous legs and body segments.
cen·tral (sĕn′trəl) *adj.* **1.** At, in, near, or being a center. **2.** Of primary importance : essential. —*n.* **1.** A telephone exchange. **2.** A telephone operator. **—cen′tral·ly** *adv.*
Central African Republic. Country of C Africa. *Cap.* Bangui. *Pop.* 1,637,000.
Central America. Region from S Mexico to N Colombia. **—Central American** *n.* & *adj.*
cen·tral·ize (sĕn′trə-līz′) *v.* **-ized, -iz·ing.** To bring to a center or under a single central authority. **—cen′tral·i·za′tion** *n.*
central nervous system *n.* The part of the vertebrate nervous system consisting of the brain and spinal cord.
cen·tre (sĕn′tər) *n.* & *v. esp. Brit. var. of* CENTER.
cen·trif·u·gal (sĕn-trĭf′yə-gəl, -trĭf′ə-) *adj.* **1.** Directed or moving away from a center or axis. **2.** Operated by centrifugal force.
centrifugal force *n.* The component of force on a body in curvilinear motion that is directed away from the center of curvature or axis of rotation.
cen·tri·fuge (sĕn′trə-fyo͞oj′) *n.* A compartment spun about a central axis to separate materials of different density or simulate gravity with centrifugal force.
cen·trip·e·tal (sĕn-trĭp′ĭ-tl) *adj.* Directed or moving toward a center or axis.
centripetal force *n.* The component of force acting on a body in curvilinear motion that is directed toward the center of curvature or axis of rotation.
cen·trist (sĕn′trĭst) *n.* One whose political views are in the center : moderate.
cen·tu·ri·on (sĕn-to͝or′ē-ən, -tyo͝or′-) *n.* An ancient Roman army officer commanding a century.
cen·tu·ry (sĕn′chə-rē) *n., pl.* **-ries. 1.** A period of 100 years. **2.** A subdivision of a legion in the ancient Roman army.
century plant *n.* A fleshy plant of the genus *Agave,* some species of which bloom only once in 10 to 20 years and then die.
ce·phal·ic (sə-făl′ĭk) *adj.* Of or pertaining to the head or skull.
ce·ram·ic (sə-răm′ĭk) *n.* **1.** Any of various hard, brittle materials made by firing a nonmetallic mineral, as clay. **2. a.** An object made of ceramic. **b. ceramics** *(sing. in number).* The art or technique of making articles of ceramic. **—ce·ram′ist** *n.*
ce·re·al (sîr′ē-əl) *n.* **1.** An edible grain, as wheat or corn. **2.** A grass producing grain. **3.** A food prepared from grain.
cer·e·bel·lum (sĕr′ə-bĕl′əm) *n., pl.* **-bel·lums** or **-bel·la** (-bĕl′ə). The part of the brain that is responsible for the coordination of voluntary muscular movement. **—cer′e·bel′lar** *adj.*
cer·e·bral (sĕr′ə-brəl, sə-rē′-) *adj.* Of or relating to the brain or cerebrum.
cerebral cortex *n.* The extensive outer layer of gray tissue that covers the cerebrum and is largely responsible for higher nervous functions.
cerebral palsy *n.* Impaired muscle control due to brain damage usu. at or prior to birth.
cer·e·brate (sĕr′ə-brāt′) *v.* **-brat·ed, -brat·ing.** To use the power of reason : think. **—cer′e·bra′tion** *n.*
cer·e·brum (sĕr′ə-brəm, sə-rē′-) *n., pl.* **-brums** or **-bra** (-brə). The large rounded brain structure that occupies most of the cranial cavity and is divided into 2 cerebral hemispheres.
cere·cloth (sîr′klôth′, -klŏth′) *n.* Cloth, treated usu. with wax, once used for wrapping corpses.
cere·ment (sîr′mənt) *n.* A cerecloth.
cer·e·mo·ni·al (sĕr′ə-mō′nē-əl) *adj.* Of, relating to, or marked by ceremony. —*n.* **1.** A ceremony. **2.** A set of ceremonies : ritual. **—cer′e·mo′ni·al·ly** *adv.*
cer·e·mo·ni·ous (sĕr′ə-mō′nē-əs) *adj.* **1.** Fond of ceremony and forms. **2.** Marked by ceremony : formal. **3.** Ceremonial. ☆**syns:** COURTLY, FORMAL, POLITE, PUNCTILIOUS **—cer′e·mo′ni·ous·ly** *adv.*
cer·e·mo·ny (sĕr′ə-mō′nē) *n., pl.* **-nies. 1.** A formal act or set of acts performed as prescribed by custom, ritual, or etiquette. **2.** A conventionally polite act. **3.** Strict observance of etiquette or formalities.
ce·re·us (sîr′ē-əs) *n.* A tall tropical American cactus, esp. of the genus *Cereus.*
ce·rise (sə-rēs′, -rēz′) *n.* A deep purplish red.
ce·ri·um (sîr′ē-əm) *n. Symbol* **Ce** A lustrous, iron-gray, malleable metallic element.
cert. *abbr.* certificate; certified.
certif. *abbr.* certificate.
cer·tain (sûr′tn) *adj.* **1.** Without any doubt : indisputable. **2.** Definite : settled. **3.** Sure to happen : inevitable. **4.** Not specified but assumed to be known <a *certain* movie actor> **5.** Appreciable but not specified <a *certain* charm> —*pron.* An indefinite number : some. **—cer′tain·ly** *adv.*
cer·tain·ty (sûr′tn-tē) *n., pl.* **-ties. 1.** Freedom from doubt. **2.** Something, as an established fact, that is certain. ☆**syns:** CERTITUDE, CONFIDENCE, CONVICTION, SURENESS, SURETY
cer·tif·i·cate (sər-tĭf′ĭ-kĭt) *n.* **1.** A document testifying to accuracy or truth. **2.** A document certifying fulfillment of requirements, as of a course of study. **3.** A document certifying ownership.
certificate of deposit *n.* A bank certificate stating the named person has a specified sum of money on deposit.
cer·ti·fi·ca·tion (sûr′tə-fĭ-kā′shən) *n.* **1.** The act of certifying or state of being certified. **2.** A certified statement.
certified check *n.* A check guaranteed by the bank on which it is drawn to be covered by sufficient funds.
certified public accountant *n.* An accountant who has received a certificate stating he or she has met a state's legal requirements to practice.
cer·ti·fy (sûr′tə-fī′) *v.* **-fied, -fy·ing. 1.** To confirm formally : verify. **2.** To guarantee on (a check) that there are sufficient funds on deposit for payment. **3.** To declare legally insane. **—cer′ti·fi′a·ble** *adj.* **—cer′ti·fi′a·bly** *adv.* **—cer′ti·fi′er** *n.*
cer·ti·tude (sûr′tĭ-to͞od′, -tyo͞od′) *n.* Complete assurance.
ce·ru·le·an (sə-ro͞o′lē-ən) *adj.* Azure.
ce·ru·men (sə-ro͞o′mən) *n.* Earwax.
Cer·van·tes (sər-văn′tēz), **Miguel de.** 1547–1616. Spanish author.
cer·vi·cal (sûr′vĭ-kəl) *adj.* Of or relating to the neck or cervix.
cer·vine (sûr′vīn′) *adj.* Relating to, resembling, or typical of a deer.
cer·vix (sûr′vĭks) *n., pl.* **-vix·es** or **-vi·ces** (-vĭ-sēz′, sər-vī′sēz′). **1.** The neck. **2.** A necklike anatomical structure, as the outer end of the uterus.
Ce·sar·e·an or **Ce·sar·i·an** (sĭ-zâr′ē-ən) *adj. vars. of* CAESAREAN.
ce·si·um *also* **cae·si·um** (sē′zē-əm) *n. Symbol* **Cs** A soft, silvery-white metallic element used in photoelectric cells.
ces·sa·tion (sĕ-sā′shən) *n.* The act of ceasing : halt.
ces·sion (sĕsh′ən) *n.* The act of ceding, as of territory, to another.
cess·pool (sĕs′po͞ol′) *n.* A covered hole or underground pit for sewage.
ce·ta·ce·an (sĭ-tā′shən) *adj.* Of or belonging to the order Cetacea, including fishlike aquatic mammals such as the whale and porpoise. —*n.* An aquatic mammal of the order Cetacea.
Cey·lon (sĭ-lŏn′). Sri Lanka. **—Cey′lo·nese′** (-nēz′, -nēs′) *adj.* & *n.*
Cé·zanne (sā-zăn′), **Paul.** 1839–1906. French painter.
Cf *symbol for* CALIFORNIUM.
cf. *abbr.* compare (Lat. *conferre).*
c.f.i. or **C.F.I.** *abbr.* cost, freight, and insurance.
Cha·blis (shă-blē′, shä-, shăb′lē) *n.* A very dry white wine.
Chad (chăd). Country of NC Africa. *Cap.* Ndjamena. *Pop.* 4,030,000.
chafe (chāf) *v.* **chafed, chaf·ing. 1.** To make or become sore

or worn by rubbing. **2.** To irritate. **3.** To warm by rubbing. ☆***syns:*** ABRADE, EXCORIATE, FRET, GALL

cha·fer (chā′fər) *n.* A beetle of the family Scarabaeidae, as the cockchafer.

chaff[1] (chăf) *n.* **1.** Grain husks after being separated from the seed in threshing. **2.** Something trivial or worthless.

chaff[2] (chăf) *v.* To tease good-naturedly. —*n.* Light, good-natured teasing.

chaf·fer (chăf′ər) *v.* To haggle : bargain.

chaf·finch (chăf′ĭnch) *n.* A European songbird, *Fringilla coelebs,* with reddish-brown plumage.

chafing dish *n.* A utensil used for cooking food and keeping it warm at the table.

cha·grin (shə-grĭn′) *n.* Lack of mental ease caused by disappointment, humiliation, or failure. —*v.* To cause to experience chagrin.

chain (chān) *n.* **1.** A series of links, often of metal, connected together. **2. chains. a.** Fetters : bonds. **b.** Captivity : bondage. **3.** A series of related things. **4. a.** A measuring instrument for surveying, composed of 100 linked pieces of iron or steel. **b.** A unit of length equal to 100 links, or approx. 20 m or 66 ft. —*v.* **1.** To bind, fasten, or make fast with a chain. **2.** To bind or fetter.

chain gang *n.* A gang of prisoners chained together.

chain letter *n.* A letter directing the recipient to send out multiple copies so that its circulation increases in a geometric progression.

chain mail *n.* Flexible armor of joined metal rings.

chain reaction *n.* **1.** A series of events each of which induces or otherwise influences its successor. **2.** A multistage nuclear or chemical reaction, esp. a self-sustaining series of reactions. **—chain′-re·act′** *v.*

chain saw *n.* A power saw with teeth set on an endless chain.

chain-smoke (chān′smōk′) *v.* To smoke esp. cigarettes in continuing succession.

chain store *n.* One of several retail stores under the same ownership.

chair (châr) *n.* **1.** A seat with a back intended for one person. **2. a.** A position or office of authority, as that of a chairman. **b.** One who holds such a position or office, esp. a chairman. **3.** *Slang.* The electric chair. **4.** A sedan chair. —*v.* To preside over (a meeting).

chair lift *n.* A chair assembly suspended from cables used to carry people, as skiers, up or down slopes.

chair·man (châr′mən) *n.* The presiding officer of a meeting, committee, board, or other organization. **—chair′man·ship′** *n.* **—chair′per′son** *n.* **—chair′wom′an** *n.*

chaise (shāz) *n.* **1.** A 2-wheeled carriage with a collapsible top. **2.** A post chaise.

chaise longue (shāz lông′) *n., pl.* **chaise longues** or **chaises longues** (shāz lông′). A chair with a long seat that can support the sitter's legs.

cha·lah (KHä′lə) *n. var. of* CHALLAH.

chal·ced·o·ny (kăl-sĕd′n-ē) *n., pl.* **-nies.** A translucent grayish or milky quartz. **—chal′ce·don′ic** (-sĭ-dŏn′ĭk) *adj.*

chal·co·py·rite (kăl′kə-pī′rīt′) *n.* An important copper ore.

Chal·de·a (kăl-dē′ə). Ancient region of S Babylonia. **—Chal·de′an** *adj.* & *n.*

cha·let (shă-lā′) *n.* **1.** A building with balconies and a sloping overhanging roof of the sort that is common in Alpine regions. **2.** A herdsman's hut in the Alps.

chal·ice (chăl′ĭs) *n.* **1.** A drinking goblet. **2.** The cup for the Eucharistic wine.

chalk (chôk) *n.* **1.** A soft mineral derived mainly from fossil seashells. **2.** A piece of chalk used esp. for marking a surface. —*v.* To mark, draw, or write with chalk. **—chalk up.** To credit <*chalked* that *up* to experience> **—chalk′y** *adj.*

chalk·board (chôk′bôrd′, -bōrd′) *n.* A blackboard.

chal·lah *also* **cha·lah** (KHä′lə) *n.* A loaf of yeast-leavened, usu. braided white egg bread traditionally eaten by Jews on the Sabbath and holidays.

chal·lenge (chăl′ənj) *n.* **1.** An invitation to take part in a sports competition. **2.** A demand for an explanation or justification. **3.** A sentry's order to halt and be identified. **4.** *Law.* A formal objection, esp. to the qualifications of a juror or jury. —*v.* **-lenged, -leng·ing. 1.** To invite to take part in a sports competition. **2.** To question the truth of. **3.** To order to halt and be identified. **4.** *Law.* To object formally to (a juror or jury). **—chal′leng·er** *n.*

chal·lis (shăl′ē) *n.* A light, usu. printed clothing material of wool, cotton, or rayon.

cham·ber (chām′bər) *n.* **1.** A room in a house, esp. a bedroom. **2.** *often* **chambers.** A judge's office. **3.** A hall, esp. for meetings of a legislative body. **4.** A legislative, judicial, or deliberative body. **5.** An enclosed space : cavity. **6.** A compartment at the bore of a gun to hold the charge.

chambered nautilus *n.* A mollusk, *Nautilus pompilius,* having a coiled and partitioned shell lined with a pearly layer.

cham·ber·lain (chām′bər-lĭn) *n.* **1.** A treasurer. **2.** A high-ranking official of a royal court.

cham·ber·maid (chām′bər-mād′) *n.* A maid who takes care of bedrooms, as in a hotel.

chamber music *n.* Music composed for performance in a small concert hall by a small group of musicians.

chamber of commerce *n.* An association of merchants and businessmen for the promotion of commercial interests in their community.

cham·bray (shăm′brā′) *n.* A lightweight gingham with white threads across a colored warp.

cha·me·leon (kə-mēl′yən) *n.* An Old World lizard of the family Chamaeleonidae that is able to change color.

cham·fer (chăm′fər) *v.* **1.** To make a bevel on. **2.** To cut a groove in : flute. —*n.* A beveled edge or corner.

cham·ois (shăm′ē) *n., pl.* **cham·ois** (shăm′ēz). **1.** A hoofed mammal, *Rupricapra rupricapra,* of mountainous regions of Europe. **2.** *also* **cham·my** *pl.* **-mies.** Soft leather made from the hide of a chamois, deer, or sheep.

cham·o·mile or **cam·o·mile** (kăm′ə-mīl′) *n.* A plant of the genus *Anthemis,* esp. *A. nobilis,* with white flowers.

champ[1] (chămp) *also* **chomp** (chŏmp) *v.* To chew on noisily.

champ[2] (chămp) *n.* A champion.

cham·pagne (shăm-pān′) *n.* A sparkling white wine.

cham·paign (shăm-pān′) *n.* Level, open country.

cham·pi·gnon (shăm-pĭn′yən) *n.* An edible mushroom, esp. the common species *Agaricus campestris.*

cham·pi·on (chăm′pē-ən) *n.* **1.** A holder of 1st place or winner of 1st prize in a contest. **2.** One who fights for a cause or defends another person. —*v.* To fight for or defend as a champion.

cham·pi·on·ship (chăm′pē-ən-shĭp′) *n.* **1. a.** The title or position of a champion. **b.** A competition or series of competitions held to determine a winner. **2.** Defense or support : advocacy.

chance (chăns) *n.* **1. a.** The unexpected or random element of existence. **b.** This element regarded as a cause of events : luck. **2.** The likelihood of an occurrence : probability. **3.** An opportunity. **4.** A risk : gamble. **5.** A raffle or lottery ticket. **6.** Something that happens unexpectedly or fortuitously. —*v.* **chanced, chanc·ing. 1.** To occur by chance. **2.** To take the risk of. **—chance on** (or **upon**). To come upon unexpectedly.

chan·cel (chăn′səl) *n.* The part of a church that includes the choir and altar.

chan·cel·ler·y (chăn′sə-lə-rē, -slə-rē) *n., pl.* **-ies. 1.** The position or rank of a chancellor. **2.** The staff or office of an embassy or consulate.

chan·cel·lor (chăn′sə-lər, -slər) *n.* **1.** The chief minister of state in certain European countries. **2.** The president of some U.S. universities. **3.** The presiding judge of a court of chancery or equity in certain states of the U.S. **—chan′cel·lor·ship′** *n.*

chan·cer·y (chăn′sə-rē) *n., pl.* **-ies. 1.** A court with jurisdiction in equity. **2.** An office for the collection and safekeeping of official records. **3.** The office of an embassy or consulate.

chan·cre (shăng′kər) *n.* A dull-red, hard, insensitive lesion that is the first manifestation of syphilis.

chan·croid (shăng′kroid′) *n.* A soft, nonsyphilitic, usu. venereal lesion of the genital region.

chanc·y (chăn′sē) *adj.* **-i·er, -i·est.** Hazardous : risky.

chan·de·lier (shăn′də-lîr′) *n.* A branched light fixture suspended from a ceiling.

chan·dler (chănd′lər) *n.* **1.** A maker or seller of candles. **2.** A dealer in specified supplies and equipment <a ship *chandler*> **—chan′dler·y** *n.*

change (chānj) *v.* **changed, chang·ing. 1.** To make or become different : alter. **2.** To take, put, or use in place of another : exchange. **3.** To replace by another. **4.** To give or receive the equivalent of (money) in smaller denominations or foreign currency. **5.** To put fresh coverings or clothes on <*changed* the bed> ☆***syns:*** ALTER, MODIFY, MUTATE, TRANSFORM, TURN, VARY —*n.* **1.** The act or result of changing. **2.** Money of lower denominations exchanged for money of higher denominations. **3.** Coins. **4.** A fresh set of clothing. **5.** *Mus.* A pattern in which bells are rung. **—change′a·ble** *adj.* **—change′a·bly** *adv.* **—change′less** *adj.* **—chang′er** *n.*

change·ling (chānj′lĭng) *n.* An infant secretly exchanged for another.

change of life *n.* The menopause.

change·o·ver (chānj′ō′vər) *n.* A conversion from one thing to another.

change ringing *n.* The ringing of a set of bells with all possible variations.

chan·nel (chăn′əl) *n.* **1.** A streambed. **2.** The deeper navigable part of a river or harbor. 3. A broad strait. 4. A passage, as for liquids : duct. 5. A means of passing, transmitting, or communicating. 6. *Electron.* A band of frequencies for the transmission and reception of electromagnetic signals, as for television. 7. A trench or groove. —*v.* **-neled, -nel•ing** *also* **-nelled, -nel•ling.** 1. To form a channel in or through. 2. To direct or guide along a course. **—chan'nel•i•za'tion** *n.* **—chan'nel•ize'** *v.*

chan•son (shäN-sôN') *n.* A song, esp. one sung in a cabaret.

chant (chănt) *n.* 1. A melody, esp. a liturgical melody, in which a number of words or syllables are sung on the same note. 2. A monotonous rhythmic shout or call. —*v.* 1. To sing a chant. 2. To speak or sing in the manner of a chant. 3. To praise in song.

chan•te•relle (shăn'tə-rĕl', shän'-) *n.* An edible yellow mushroom, *Cantharellus cibarius,* with a pleasant fruity odor.

chan•teuse (shäN-tœz') *n.* A woman cabaret singer.

chan•tey (shăn'tē, chăn'-) *n., pl.* **-teys.** A song that is sung by sailors to the rhythm of their work movements.

chan•ti•cleer (chăn'tĭ-klîr', shăn'-) *n.* A rooster.

chan•try (chăn'trē) *n., pl.* **-tries.** 1. An endowment to cover expenses for the saying of masses and prayers. 2. A chapel endowed for the saying of masses and prayers.

Cha•nu•kah (KHä'nə-kə, hä'-) *n.* An 8-day Jewish festival commemorating the rededication of the Temple in Jerusalem.

cha•os (kā'ŏs') *n.* 1. Total disorder. 2. *often* **Chaos.** The disordered state existing before the creation of the ordered universe. **—cha•ot'ic** *adj.* **—cha•ot'i•cal•ly** *adv.*

chap[1] (chăp) *v.* **chapped, chap•ping.** To dry and split open, esp. from cold and wind.

chap[2] (chăp) *n. Informal.* A man : fellow.

chap. *abbr.* chapter.

†**cha•pa•re•jos** *also* **cha•pa•ra•jos** (shăp'ə-rā'ōs) *pl.n. SW U.S.* Chaps.

chap•ar•ral (shăp'ə-răl') *n.* A dense growth of tangled, often thorny shrubs.

chap•book (chăp'bŏŏk') *n.* A small book containing poems, ballads, stories, or religious tracts.

cha•peau (shă-pō') *n., pl.* **-peaux** *or* **-peaus** (-pōz'). A hat.

chap•el (chăp'əl) *n.* 1. A place of worship subordinate to a church, as in a college or hospital. 2. Religious services held at a chapel. 3. A place of worship for those not affiliated with an established church.

chap•er•on *also* **chap•er•one** (shăp'ə-rōn') *n.* An older person, esp. a woman, who supervises young unmarried people. —*v.* **-oned, -on•ing.** To act as a chaperon to or for. **—chap'er•on'age** *n.*

chap•fall•en (chăp'fô'lən, chŏp'-) *adj.* In low spirits : depressed.

chap•lain (chăp'lən) *n.* A member of the clergy attached to a special group, as a military unit. **—chap'lain•cy** *n.*

chap•let (chăp'lĭt) *n.* 1. A garland for the head. 2. A string of esp. prayer beads.

chaps (chăps, shăps) *pl.n.* Leather trousers without a seat that are worn over trousers by cowboys.

chap•ter (chăp'tər) *n.* 1. A division of a book or other writing. 2. A branch of a group, as a fraternity or religious order.

char[1] (chär) *v.* **charred, char•ring.** 1. To burn partially. 2. To reduce or be reduced to charcoal by incomplete combustion.

char[2] (chär) *n., pl.* **char** *or* **chars.** A fish of the genus *Salvelinus,* related to the trout.

char[3] (chär) *n.* A charwoman. —*v.* **charred, char•ring.** To work as a charwoman.

char. *abbr.* charter.

char•a•banc (shăr'ə-băng') *n. Brit.* A large bus, often used for sightseeing.

char•ac•ter (kăr'ĭk-tər) *n.* 1. A distinguishing feature : characteristic. 2. The group of ethical and mental characteristics that mark a person or group. 3. Moral integrity. 4. Reputation. 5. *Informal.* An eccentric person. 6. A person portrayed in a play or novel. 7. A symbol, as a letter, in a writing system. ☆**syns:** COMPLEXION, DISPOSITION, MAKE-UP, NATURE

char•ac•ter•is•tic (kăr'ĭk-tə-rĭs'tĭk) *adj.* Serving to indicate distinctive character : typical. ☆**syns:** DISTINCTIVE, INDIVIDUAL, PECULIAR, TYPICAL, VINTAGE —*n.* A distinguishing feature or attribute. **—char'ac•ter•is'ti•cal•ly** *adv.*

char•ac•ter•ize (kăr'ĭk-tə-rīz') *v.* **-ized, -iz•ing.** 1. To describe the character or characteristics of. 2. To be a characteristic of. **—char'ac•ter•i•za'tion** *n.*

cha•rade (shə-rād') *n.* 1. **charades** *(sing. or pl. in number).* A game in which the syllables of words to be guessed are acted out. 2. A pretense.

char•broil (chär'broil') *v.* To broil (meat) over charcoal.

char•coal (chär'kōl') *n.* 1. A porous carbonaceous material obtained from the destructive distillation of wood and used as a fuel, filter, and absorbent. 2. A piece of charcoal used for drawing. 3. A dark gray.

chard (chärd) *n.* A variety of beet, *Beta vulgaris cicla,* with large, succulent leaves that are eaten as a vegetable.

charge (chärj) *v.* **charged, charg•ing.** 1. To entrust with a duty or responsibility. 2. To order : command. 3. To accuse. 4. To ask as a price. 5. To hold financially. 6. To record an amount owed against. 7. To rush (at) in or as if in an attack. 8. To load fully : fill. 9. To impregnate. 10. **a.** To cause formation of a net electric charge on or in (a conductor). **b.** To energize (a storage battery). —*n.* 1. Responsibility : care. 2. One entrusted to another's care. 3. A judge's instructions to a jury. 4. An accusation, esp. a formal indictment. 5. Price : cost. 6. A debit to an account. 7. An attack. 8. A burden imposed. 9. A quantity, as of ammunition, needed to fill something. 10. **a.** The intrinsic property of matter responsible for all electric phenomena. **b.** A measure of this property. 11. *Informal.* A pleasant feeling of excitement : thrill. **—charge'a•ble** *adj.*

charge account *n.* A business arrangement by which a customer receives goods or services and pays for them later.

char•gé d'af•faires (shär-zhā' də-fâr') *n., pl.* **char•gés d'af•faires** (-zhā', -zhāz'). A diplomat temporarily in charge of an embassy or legation.

charg•er (chär'jər) *n.* 1. A horse ridden in battle : war-horse. 2. An instrument that recharges electric batteries.

char•i•ot (chăr'ē-ət) *n.* An ancient horse-drawn 2-wheeled vehicle used for war, races, processions, etc. **—char'i•o•teer'** *n.*

cha•ris•ma (kə-rĭz'mə) *n., pl.* **-ma•ta** (-mə-tə). An exceptional ability to secure other people's devotion or loyalty. **—char'is•mat'ic** (kăr'ĭz-măt'ĭk) *adj.*

char•i•ta•ble (chăr'ĭ-tə-bəl) *adj.* 1. Generous in giving to the needy. 2. Lenient in judging others. **—char'i•ta•bly** *adv.*

char•i•ty (chăr'ĭ-tē) *n., pl.* **-ties.** 1. Help or relief given to the poor. 2. A fund or institution that helps the poor. 3. An act or feeling of good will or affection. 4. Tolerance and leniency in judging others. 5. **a.** God's love for mankind. **b.** Brotherly love for others.

cha•ri•va•ri *also* **chiv•a•ree** (shĭv'ə-rē', shĭv'ə-rē') *n., pl.* **-ris** *also* **-rees.** A noisy mock serenade to newlyweds.

char•la•tan (shär'lə-tən) *n.* One who falsely claims to have expert knowledge or skill : quack. **—char'la•tan•ism** *n.*

Char•le•magne (shär'lə-mān'). 742–814. King of the Franks (768–814); emperor of the West (800–14).

Charles I (chärlz). 1600–49. King of England (1625–49); beheaded.

Charles II. 1630–85. King of England following the Restoration (1660–85).

Charles•ton (chärl'stən). Cap. of W.Va., in the W. *Pop.* 63,968.

Charleston *n.* A quick, lively dance popular in the 1920's.

char•ley horse (chär'lē) *n. Informal.* A muscle cramp in an arm or leg.

Char•lotte (shär'lət). City of S N.C. *Pop.* 314,447.

Charlotte A•ma•lie (ə-mäl'yə). Cap. of the U.S. Virgin Islands. *Pop.* 12,220.

Char•lotte•town (shär'lət-toun'). Cap. of P.E.I., Canada, in the S. *Pop.* 19,133.

charm (chärm) *n.* 1. The power or ability to please or delight. 2. A small ornament worn on a chain or bracelet. 3. Something worn for its purported magical effect, as in bringing luck : amulet. 4. An act or formula believed to have magical power. —*v.* 1. To be delightful or pleasing : fascinate. 2. To effect with or as if with magic : bewitch. ☆**syns:** BEWITCH, ENCHANT, ENTHRALL, ENTRANCE, SPELLBIND, WITCH

char•nel *also* **char•nel house** (chär'nəl) *n.* A building or room in which bones or bodies of the dead are placed.

chart (chärt) *n.* 1. A map. 2. Something, as a graph or table, that presents information in an easily viewed form. —*v.* 1. To make a chart of. 2. To plan in detail.

char•ter (chär'tər) *n.* 1. An official document granting certain rights and privileges, as to a bank or college. 2. A document outlining the principles, functions, and organization of a corporate body : constitution. 3. An authorization from a society to create a local chapter. 4. The hiring or leasing of a vehicle, as an aircraft. —*v.* 1. To grant a charter to : establish. 2. To engage the use of for a fee <*charter* a plane>

charter member *n.* An original member or founder of an organization or group.

char•treuse (shär-trōōz', -trōōs', -trœz') *n.* A light greenish yellow.

char•wom•an (chär'wŏŏm'ən) *n.* A woman hired to do cleaning, as of offices.

char•y (châr'ē) *adj.* **-i•er, -i•est.** 1. Cautious : wary. 2. Not wasteful, as of time, money, or resources : sparing. **—char'i•ly** *adv.* **—char'i•ness** *n.*

chase¹ (chās) *v.* **chased, chas•ing. 1.** To follow quickly : pursue. **2.** To hunt. **3.** To cause to leave : drive away. **4.** *Informal.* To hasten : rush. —*n.* **1.** The act of chasing : pursuit. **2.** The sport of hunting. **3.** One that is hunted : quarry.
chase² (chās) *n.* A groove : slot. —*v.* **chased, chas•ing.** To ornament by engraving or embossing.
chas•er (chā'sər) *n.* **1.** One that chases. **2.** *Informal.* A drink, as of beer, taken after undiluted liquor.
chasm (kăz'əm) *n.* A deep opening in the earth's surface : gorge. **—chas'mal** *adj.*
chas•sis (shăs'ē, chăs'ē) *n., pl.* **chas•sis** (-ēz). **1.** The framework that supports the body and engine of an automotive vehicle. **2.** The landing gear of an aircraft. **3.** The structure that supports the functioning parts of electronic equipment such as a radio or television set.
chaste (chāst) *adj.* **chast•er, chast•est. 1.** Pure, as in morals : modest. **2.** Not engaging in sexual intercourse : virtuous. **3.** Celibate. **4.** Not ornate in style : simple. ☆***syns:*** DECENT, MODEST, PURE, VIRTUOUS
chas•ten (chā'sən) *v.* **1.** To punish in order to correct. **2.** To cause to become subdued : restrain. **—chas'ten•er** *n.*
chas•tise (chăs-tīz') *v.* **-tised, -tis•ing. 1.** To punish, esp. by beating. **2.** To scold. **—chas•tis'a•ble** *adj.* **—chas•tise'ment** (chăs-tīz'mənt, chăs'tīz-) *n.*
chas•ti•ty (chăs'tĭ-tē) *n.* The quality or state of being chaste.
chas•u•ble (chăz'ə-bəl, chăs'-) *n.* A vestment without sleeves worn over the alb by the priest officiating at Mass.
chat (chăt) *v.* **chat•ted, chat•ting.** To converse in a relaxed and informal way. —*n.* A relaxed, informal conversation.
cha•teau *or* **châ•teau** (shă-tō') *n., pl.* **-teaux** (-tōz'). **1.** A castle in France. **2.** A large country house.
chat•e•laine (shăt'l-ān') *n.* **1.** The mistress of a castle or chateau. **2.** A clasp or chain for holding keys, a purse, or a watch.
chat•tel (chăt'l) *n.* **1.** An item of personal, movable property. **2.** A slave.
chat•ter (chăt'ər) *v.* **1.** To make short, meaningless sounds <birds *chattering*> **2.** To talk rapidly and inanely : jabber. **3.** To click or rattle repeatedly. **—chat'ter** *n.*
chat•ter•box (chăt'ər-bŏks') *n.* A very loquacious person.
chat•ty (chăt'ē) *adj.* **-ti•er, -ti•est.** Given to chatting : talkative. **—chat'ti•ly** *adv.* **—chat'ti•ness** *n.*
Chau•cer (chô'sər), **Geoffrey.** 1340?–1400. English poet. **—Chau•ce'ri•an** (-sîr'ē-ən) *adj.* & *n.*
chauf•feur (shō'fər, shō-fûr') *n.* A person hired to drive an automobile. **—chauf'feur** *v.*
chau•vin•ism (shō'və-nĭz'əm) *n.* **1.** Blind and fanatical patriotism. **2.** Unreasoning belief in the superiority of one's own group <male *chauvinism*> **—chau'vin•ist** *n.* **—chau'vin•is'tic** *adj.* **—chau'vin•is'ti•cal•ly** *adv.*
†**chaw** (chô) *v. Regional.* To chew. **—chaw** *n.*
cheap (chēp) *adj.* **1.** Low in cost : inexpensive. **2.** Requiring little effort to achieve. **3.** Of little value. **4.** Of poor quality : shoddy. **5.** Not worthy of respect. **6.** Stingy. **—cheap** *adv.* **—cheap'ly** *adv.*
cheap•en (chē'pən) *v.* To make or become cheap or cheaper. **—cheap'en•er** *n.*
cheap shot *n.* An unjust action or statement directed esp. at a vulnerable target.
cheap•skate (chēp'skāt') *n. Slang.* A very stingy person.
cheat (chēt) *v.* **1.** To deprive of by trickery or deceit. **2.** To practice trickery or fraud. **3.** To break rules, as of an examination. ☆***syns:*** BILK, DEFRAUD, GULL, GYP, MULCT, ROOK, SWINDLE, TAKE, VICTIMIZE —*n.* **1.** A fraud or swindle. **2.** One who cheats. **—cheat'er** *n.*
check (chĕk) *n.* **1.** An abrupt stop. **2.** A restraint : control. **3.** A standard for comparing, testing, or verifying. **4.** The act of comparing, testing, or verifying. **5.** A mark to show approval or verification. **6.** A slip or ticket showing identity. **7.** A bill, as at a restaurant. **8.** A written order to a bank to pay money from funds on deposit. **9.a.** A pattern of small squares, as on a chessboard. **b.** A fabric patterned with small squares. **10.** A chess move in which an opponent's king is directly attacked. —*v.* **1.** To arrest the motion of, esp. abruptly : stop. **2.** To hold in restraint : curb. **3.** To test or examine, as for correctness or good condition. **4.** To make a check mark on, as to show that something has been noted. **5.** To deposit for temporary safekeeping <*checked* their luggage> **6.** To correspond item for item : agree. **7.** To mark with a pattern of squares. **—check in.** To register, as at a hotel. **—check out. 1.** To pay for one's lodging and leave, as from a hotel. **2.** To take away after being recorded <*check out* a book from the library>
check•book (chĕk'bo͝ok') *n.* A book that contains blank checks.
check•er (chĕk'ər) *n.* **1. checkers** *(sing. in number).* A game played on a checkerboard by 2 players, each using 12 pieces. **2.** A piece used in the game of checkers. —*v.* **1.** To mark with a pattern of squares. **2.** To cause to undergo frequent changes, as in fortune : vary.
check•er•board (chĕk'ər-bôrd', -bōrd') *n.* A game board divided into 64 squares of 2 alternating colors.
check list *n.* A list in which items can be compared, verified, or identified.
check•mate (chĕk'māt') *v.* **-mat•ed, -mat•ing. 1.** To attack (a chess opponent's king) so that no defense is possible. **2.** To defeat decisively. **—check'mate'** *n.*
check•off (chĕk'ôf', -ŏf') *n.* The authorized deduction of union dues from a member's wages.
check-out (chĕk'out') *n.* **1.** The act, process, or place of checking out, as from a hotel. **2.** A test, as of a machine, for proper functioning.
check•point (chĕk'point') *n.* A place at which vehicular traffic is stopped for inspection, as at a border.
check•room (chĕk'ro͞om', -ro͝om') *n.* A room where items, as clothing or packages, may be left for temporary safekeeping.
check•up (chĕk'ŭp') *n.* A thorough examination, esp. a physical examination.
Ched•dar *also* **ched•dar** (chĕd'ər) *n.* A firm, smooth, usu. yellowish cheese.
cheek (chēk) *n.* **1.** The fleshy part of the face below the eye. **2.** Sauciness.
cheek•bone (chēk'bōn') *n.* A small facial bone below the eye.
cheek•y (chē'kē) *adj.* **-i•er, -i•est.** Impudent. **—cheek'i•ness** *n.*
cheep (chēp) *n.* A faint, high-pitched chirp, as of a young bird. **—cheep'** *v.*
cheer (chîr) *n.* **1.** Good spirits : gaiety. **2.** Something providing happiness or joy. **3.** A shout of encouragement or applause. —*v.* **1.** To give courage to : hearten. **2.** To fill with happiness. **3.** To encourage or applaud with cheers. **4.** To make or become cheerful <quickly *cheered* up> **—cheer'er** *n.*
cheer•ful (chîr'fəl) *adj.* **1.** In good spirits : gay. **2.** Producing a feeling of cheer. ☆***syns:*** BRIGHT, CHEERY, CHIPPER, HAPPY, LIGHTHEARTED, SUNNY **—cheer'ful•ly** *adv.*
cheer•lead•er (chîr'lē'dər) *n.* Someone who directs the cheering of spectators, as at a football game.
cheer•less (chîr'lĭs) *adj.* Devoid of cheer : bleak. **—cheer'less•ly** *adv.*
cheer•y (chîr'ē) *adj.* **-i•er, -i•est.** Bright and cheerful. **—cheer'i•ly** *adv.* **—cheer'i•ness** *n.*
cheese (chēz) *n.* A solid food made from the curd of milk, usu. seasoned, pressed into cakes, and aged.
cheese•burg•er (chēz'bûr'gər) *n.* A hamburger topped with a slice of cheese.
cheese•cake (chēz'kāk') *n.* **1.** A cake made with cream cheese or cottage cheese. **2.** *Slang.* Photographs of pretty girls scantily clothed.
cheese•cloth (chēz'klôth', -klŏth') *n.* A coarse, loosely woven cotton gauze.
cheese-par•ing (chēz'pâr'ĭng) *n.* Stinginess : parsimony. **—cheese'-par'ing** *adj.*
chees•y (chē'zē) *adj.* **-i•er, -i•est. 1.** Containing or resembling cheese. **2.** *Slang.* Shoddy : cheap. **—chees'i•ness** *n.*
chee•tah (chē'tə) *n.* A long-legged, swift-running spotted wildcat, *Acinonyx jubatus,* of Africa and SW Asia.
chef (shĕf) *n.* A cook, esp. a head cook.
chef-d'oeu•vre (shĕ-dœ'vr'ə) *n., pl.* **chefs-d'oeu•vre** (shĕ-). A masterpiece.
Che•khov (chĕk'ôf', -ŏf'), **Anton Pavlovich.** 1860–1904. Russian author.
che•la (kē'lə) *n., pl.* **-lae** (-lē). A pincer-like claw of a crustacean, as a crab.
chem•i•cal (kĕm'ĭ-kəl) *adj.* **1.** Of or relating to chemistry. **2.** Used in or produced by chemistry. —*n.* A substance obtained by or used in a chemical process. **—chem'i•cal•ly** *adv.*
chemical engineering *n.* Engineering that is concerned with the industrial production of chemicals and chemical products. **—chemical engineer** *n.*
chemical warfare *n.* Warfare involving the use of chemicals such as poisons, asphyxiants, and irritants.
che•mise (shə-mēz') *n.* **1.** A woman's loose, shirtlike undergarment. **2.** A loose dress that hangs straight.
chem•ist (kĕm'ĭst) *n.* **1.** A scientist specializing in chemistry. **2.** *esp. Brit.* A pharmacist.
chem•is•try (kĕm'ĭ-strē) *n., pl.* **-tries. 1.** The scientific study of the composition, structure, properties, and reactions of matter. **2.** The composition, structure, properties, and reactions of a substance or a system of substances.
che•mo•ther•a•py (kē'mō-thĕr'ə-pē, kĕm'ō-) *n.* Prevention or treatment of disease with chemicals. **—che'mo•ther'a•peu'tic** (-pyo͞o'tĭk) *adj.*

chem•ur•gy (kĕm'ər-jē, kĕ-mûr'-) *n.* Industrial development of chemical products from organic raw materials, esp. of agricultural origin. **–chem•ur'gic** (kĭ-mûr'jĭk), **chem•ur'gi•cal** *adj.*
che•nille (shə-nēl') *n.* **1.** A soft silk, cotton, or worsted yarn with a thick pile. **2.** Chenille fabric.
cheque (chĕk) *n. esp. Brit. var. of* CHECK 8.
cheq•uer (chĕk'ər) *n. Brit. var. of* CHECKER.
cher•ish (chĕr'ĭsh) *v.* **1.** To hold dear. **2.** To keep fondly in mind.
che•root (shə-ro͞ot', chə-) *n.* A cigar whose ends are square-cut.
cher•ry (chĕr'ē) *n., pl.* **-ries. 1.** Any of several trees of the genus *Prunus* bearing rounded fruit with a small hard stone. **2.** The fruit or wood of a cherry tree. **3.** A deep or purplish red.
cher•ry•stone (chĕr'ē-stōn') *n.* The quahog clam when half-grown.
chert (chûrt) *n.* **1.** Any of various microscopically crystalline mineral varieties of silica. **2.** A siliceous rock of chalcedonic or opaline silica occurring in limestone.
cher•ub (chĕr'əb) *n., pl.* **cher•u•bim** (chĕr'ə-bĭm, -yə-bĭm) **1.** One of the 2nd order of angels. **2.** A representation of a cherub portrayed as a child with a rosy face and wings. **–che•ru'bic** (chə-ro͞o'bĭk) *adj.*
chess (chĕs) *n.* A game for 2 players, each with 16 pieces, played on a chessboard.
chess•board (chĕs'bôrd', -bōrd') *n.* A board with 64 squares of alternate colors, used in playing chess and checkers.
chess•man (chĕs'măn', -mən) *n.* A piece used in chess.
chest (chĕst) *n.* **1.** The part of the body between the neck and abdomen enclosed by the ribs and sternum. **2.** A box with a lid, used esp. for storage. **3.** A piece of furniture with drawers : dresser.
ches•ter•field (chĕs'tər-fēld') *n.* An overcoat with concealed buttons and a velvet collar.
chest•nut (chĕs'nŭt', -nət) *n.* **1.** Any of several trees of the genus *Castanea* bearing edible nuts enclosed in a bur. **2.** The nut or wood of a chestnut tree. **3.** A reddish brown. **4.** A stale old joke or story.
chet•rum (chē'trəm, chĕt'rŭm) *n.* –See *ngultrum* at CURRENCY TABLE.
chev•a•lier (shĕv'ə-lîr') *n.* A member of an order of merit or knighthood, as the French Legion of Honor.
chev•i•ot (shĕv'ē-ət) *n.* A coarse woolen fabric used esp. for suits and overcoats.
chev•ron (shĕv'rən) *n.* A sleeve insignia of stripes meeting at an angle, worn to indicate rank, merit, or length of service, as on a police force.
chew (cho͞o) *v.* To grind and crush with the teeth : masticate. *–n.* **1.** An act of chewing. **2.** Something chewed. **–chew'er** *n.* **–chew'y** *adj.*
chewing gum *n.* A sweet preparation of various flavors for chewing, usu. made from chicle.
chg. *abbr.* **1.** change. **2.** charge.
Chey•enne (shī-ăn', -ĕn'). Cap. of Wyo., in the SE. *Pop.* 47,283.
Chiang Kai-shek (chăng' kī'shek', jē-äng'). 1887–1975. Chinese military and political leader.
Chi•an•ti (kē-än'tē, -ăn'-) *n.* A dry, usu. red table wine.
chi•ao (jē'ou') *n., pl.* **chiao.** –See *renminbi* at CURRENCY TABLE.
chi•a•ro•scu•ro (kē-är'ə-sko͝or'ō, -skyo͝or'ō) *n., pl.* **-ros.** The use of light and shade in pictorial representation. **–chi•a'ro•scu'rist** *n.*
chic (shēk) *adj.* Smartly stylish : fashionable. *–n.* Stylishness. **–chic'ly** *adv.* **–chic'ness** *n.*
Chi•ca•go (shə-kä'gō, -kô'gō, -kä'gə). City of NE Ill., on Lake Michigan. Pop. 3,005,072. **–Chi•ca'go•an** *n.*
Chi•ca•na (chĭ-kä'nə, shĭ-) *n.* A Mexican-American woman. **–Chi•ca'na** *adj.*
chi•can•er•y. (shĭ-kā'nə-rē) *n.* Artful deception : trickery. **–chi•cane'** *n. & v.*
Chi•ca•no (shĭ-kä'nō, chĭ-) *n., pl.* **-nos.** An American of Mexican parentage or ancestry. **–Chi•ca'no** *adj.*
chi•chi (shē'shē) *adj.* Showy.
chick (chĭk) *n.* **1. a.** A young chicken. **b.** A young bird. **2.** *Slang.* A young woman.
chick•a•dee (chĭk'ə-dē') *n.* A small, plump North American bird of the genus *Parus,* with gray plumage and a dark crown.
chick•en (chĭk'ən) *n.* **1.** The common domestic fowl or its young. **2.** The edible flesh of a chicken. *–adj. Slang.* Cowardly. *–v. Slang.* To act in a cowardly way <*chickened* out at the last minute>
chicken feed *n. Slang.* A small sum of money.
chick•en-heart•ed (chĭk'ən-här'tĭd) *adj.* Cowardly : timid.
chicken pox *n.* A contagious viral disease, esp. of children, marked by skin eruptions and fever.
chick•pea (chĭk'pē') *n.* A bushy Old World plant, *Cicer arietenum,* bearing edible pealike seeds.
chick•weed (chĭk'wēd') *n.* A low, weedy plant, *Stellaria media,* with small white flowers.
chic•le (chĭk'əl) *n.* The coagulated milky juice of a tropical American tree, used as the principal ingredient of chewing gum.
chic•o•ry (chĭk'ə-rē) *n., pl.* **-ries 1.** A plant, *Cichorium intybus,* with blue daisylike flowers and leaves used in salad. **2.** The ground, roasted root of the chicory, used usu. as a coffee substitute.
chide (chīd) *v.* **chid•ed** *or* **chid** (chĭd), **chid•ed** *or* **chid** *or* **chid•den** (chĭd'n), **chid•ing.** To scold : reprove. **–chid'er** *n.*
chief (chēf) *n.* One of highest rank or authority : leader. *–adj.* **1.** Highest in rank or authority. **2.** Most important : principal. **–chief'ly** *adv.*
chief of staff *n.* The ranking officer of the U.S. Army, Navy, or Air Force, responsible to the branch secretary and to the President.
chief of state *n.* The formal head of a nation.
chief•tain (chēf'tən) *n.* The leader of a group, esp. a clan or tribe.
chif•fon (shĭ-fŏn', shĭf'ŏn') *n.* A sheer fabric.
chif•fo•nier (shĭf'ə-nîr') *n.* A tall, narrow chest of drawers.
chig•ger (chĭg'ər) *n.* **1.** A mite of the family Trombidiidae that sucks blood and causes intensely irritating itching. **2.** CHIGOE 1.
chi•gnon (shēn'yŏn', shēn-yŏn') *n.* A roll of hair worn at the nape of the neck or the back of the head.
chig•oe (chĭg'ō, chē'gō) *n.* **1.** A small tropical flea, *Tunga penetrans,* that burrows under the skin, causing intense irritation and sores. **2.** CHIGGER 1.
Chi•hua•hua (chĭ-wä'wä, -wə) *n.* A tiny dog, orig. bred in Mexico, with a smooth coat and pointed ears.
chil•blain (chĭl'blān') *n.* An inflammation, as of the hands or feet, caused by exposure to cold. **–chil'blained'** *adj.*
child (chīld) *n., pl.* **chil•dren** (chĭl'drən). **1.** A young person between birth and puberty. **2.** A daughter or son : offspring. **3.** A childish or immature person. **–child'less** *adj.* **–child'less•ness** *n.*

▲word history: The plural of *child* is really a double plural, and neither plural suffix belongs to the original declension of the word. The earliest Old English form *cild* was a neuter noun that formed the plural by adding no suffix, like the Modern English words *sheep* and *deer.* Other neuter nouns, however, formed plurals by suffixing *–ru,* and in later Old English times a new plural, *cildru,* was used for *cild.* This form developed into *childer.* In Old English still another class of nouns formed the plural with the suffix *–an,* which survived in Middle English as *–en. Oxen* and *brethren* are modern plurals that show this suffix. In some dialects of Middle English *–en* was the usual plural suffix, and it was added to *childer* to make it conform to other nouns. *Childeren* was prob. pronounced *children,* which became the modern spelling of the plural of *child.*

child abuse *n.* Physical or sexual maltreatment of a child by a parent, guardian, or other adult.
child•bear•ing (chīld'bâr'ĭng) *n.* Childbirth.
child•birth (chīld'bûrth') *n.* The act or process of giving birth to a child.
child•hood (chīd'ho͝od') *n.* The period or state of being a child.
child•ish (chĭl'dĭsh) *adj.* **1.** Of, relating to, or appropriate for a child. **2.** Marked by or showing lack of maturity : immature. ☆**syns:** BABYISH, IMMATURE, INFANTILE, JUVENILE, PUERILE **–child'ish•ly** *adv.*
child•like (chīld'līk') *adj.* Like a child, as in ingenuousness.
chil•dren (chĭl'drən) *n. pl. of* CHILD.
child's play *n.* Something that is extremely easy to do.
Chil•e (chil'ē). Country of SW South America. *Cap.* Santiago. *Pop.* 10,044,940. **–Chil'e•an** *adj. & n.*
chil•e con car•ne *also* **chil•i con carne** (chĭl'ē kŏn kär'nē) *n.* A spicy dish made of chili powder or chilis, chopped meat, and usu. beans.
chil•i *also* **chil•e** *or* **chil•li** (chĭl'ē) *n., pl.* **-ies** *also* **-es** *or* **-lies. 1. a.** The very pungent fruit of *Capsicum frutescens,* a variety of red pepper. **b.** A powdered condiment made from the dried fruits of the chili. **2.** Chile con carne.
chill (chĭl) *n.* **1.** A moderate cold. **2.** A feeling of coldness, often accompanied by shivering. **3.** A dampening of enthusiasm or joy. *–adj.* Chilly. *–v.* **1.** To make or become chilly or cold. **2.** To dispirit : discourage. **–chill'ness** *n.*
chill•y (chĭl'ē) *adj.* **-i•er, -i•est. 1.** Moderately but penetratingly cold. **2.** Affected with cold : chilled. **3.** Distant : unfriendly <a *chilly* greeting> **–chill'i•ness** *n.*
chime (chīm) *n.* **1.** *often* **chimes.** An instrumental set of bells tuned to the musical scale. **2.** The musical sound produced by

or as if by a set of bells. —*v.* **chimed, chim•ing. 1.** To emit a harmonious sound when struck. **2.** To act or be in harmony : agree. **3.** To make known (e.g., the hour of day) by chiming. **—chime in.** To join in or interrupt a conversation.
chi•me•ra *also* **chi•mae•ra** (kī-mîr′ə, kĭ-) *n.* **1. Chimera.** *Gk. Myth.* A monster with a lion's head, a goat's body, and a serpent's tail. **2.** A foolish fancy.

Chimera

chi•mer•i•cal (kī-mĕr′ĭ-kəl, -mîr′-, kĭ-) *also* **chi•mer•ic** (-mĕr′ĭk, -mîr′-) *adj.* **1.** Imaginary : fantastic. **2.** Given to foolish fancies. **—chi•mer′i•cal•ly** *adv.*
chim•ney (chĭm′nē) *n., pl.* **-neys. 1.** A structural passage for the escape of smoke and gases. **2.** A glass tube that encloses a lamp flame.
chimney swift *n.* A swallowlike bird, *Chaetura pelagica,* that often nests in chimneys.
chimp (chĭmp) *n.* A chimpanzee.
chim•pan•zee (chĭm′păn-zē′, chĭm-păn′zē) *n.* A very intelligent African ape, *Pan troglodytes.*
chin (chĭn) *n.* The central portion of the lower jaw. —*v.* **chinned, chin•ning.** To pull (oneself) up while grasping an overhead horizontal bar until the chin is level with the bar.
chi•na (chī′nə) *n.* Porcelain ware, esp. high-quality ware.
China. 1. Country of E Asia. *Cap.* Beijing. *Pop.* 930,500,000. **2.** Taiwan. **—Chi•nese′** (-nēz′, -nēs′) *adj.* & *n.*
†**chinch** (chĭnch) *n. Regional.* A bedbug.
chinch bug *n.* An insect, *Blissus leucopterus,* destructive to grains and grasses.
chin•chil•la (chĭn-chĭl′ə) *n.* **1.** A South American rodent, *Chinchilla laniger,* widely raised for its soft pale-gray fur. **2.** A thick woolen fabric used esp. for overcoats.
chine (chīn) *n.* **1.** The backbone : spine. **2.** A cut of fish or meat including part of the backbone. **3.** A crest or ridge.
Chinese cabbage *n.* A Chinese plant, *Brassica pekinensis,* bearing a cylindrical head of edible leaves.
Chinese checkers *n.* A game in which players take turns moving marbles from a home point to the opposite point on a board shaped like a 6-pointed star.
chink[1] (chĭngk) *n.* A narrow opening : crack. —*v.* To fill chinks in.
chink[2] (chĭngk) *n.* A short metallic sound. —*v.* To make a chink.
chi•no (chē′nō) *n., pl.* **-nos. 1.** A coarse cotton twill. **2. chinos.** Garments, esp. trousers, of chino.
chintz (chĭnts) *n.* A printed and usu. glazed cotton fabric.
chintz•y (chĭnt′sē) *adj.* **-i•er, -i•est. 1.** Of or like chintz. **2.** Cheap : gaudy.
chip (chĭp) *n.* **1.** A small piece cut or broken off. **2.** A mark left when a chip is broken off. **3.** A disk used as a counter in games, as poker. **4.** A thin, brittle piece of food <a potato *chip*> **5.** *Electron.* A very tiny square of a thin semiconducting material, as silicon, processed to have particular electrical characteristics. —*v.* **chipped, chip•ping. 1.** To break or cut chips from. **2.** To break off in chips. **—chip in.** *Informal.* To contribute.
chip•munk (chĭp′mŭngk′) *n.* A squirrellike rodent, esp. *Tamias striatus,* of E North America, with a striped back.
chipped beef *n.* Very thinly sliced smoked dried beef.
chip•per (chĭp′ər) *adj. Informal.* Pert : cheerful.
chi•rog•ra•phy (kī-rŏg′rə-fē) *n.* Penmanship. **—chi•rog′ra•pher** *n.* **—chi′ro•graph′ic** (kī′rə-grăf′ĭk), **chi′ro•graph′i•cal** *adj.*
chi•ro•man•cy (kīr′ə-măn′sē) *n.* Palmistry. **—chi′ro•man′cer** *n.*
chi•rop•o•dy (kĭ-rŏp′ə-dē, shĭ-) *n.* Podiatry. **—chi•rop′o•dist** *n.*
chi•ro•prac•tic (kī′rə-prăk′tĭk) *n.* A system of therapy in which bodily structures, as the spinal column, are manipulated. **—chi′ro•prac′tor** *n.*
chirp (chûrp) *n.* A high-pitched sound, as that made by a small bird or cricket.
chis•el (chĭz′əl) *n.* A metal tool with a sharp beveled edge used to cut and shape stone, wood, or metal. —*v.* **-eled, el•ing** *or* **-elled, -el•ling. 1.** To use a chisel (on). **2.** *Slang.* **a.** To swindle. **b.** To obtain by swindling. **—chis′el•er** *n.*
chit[1] (chĭt) *n.* A voucher for a small amount owed, as for food or drink.
chit[2] (chĭt) *n.* A pert girl.
chit•chat (chĭt′chăt′) *n.* Trivial or casual conversation : small talk.
chi•tin (kī′tĭn) *n.* A semitransparent horny substance forming the chief component of crustacean shells and insect exoskeletons.
chit•ter•lings *also* **chit•lins** *or* **chit•lings** (chĭt′lĭnz) *pl.n.* Pig intestines prepared as food.
chiv•al•rous (shĭv′əl-rəs) *adj.* **1.** Marked by gallantry and honor. **2.** Of or relating to chivalry. **3.** Marked by courtesy and consideration, esp. toward women.
chiv•al•ry (shĭv′əl-rē) *n., pl.* **-ries. 1.** The qualities, as bravery and courtesy, of the ideal knight. **2.** The institution of knighthood. **3.** A chivalrous act.
chiv•a•ree (shĭv′ə-rē′, shĭv′ə-rē′) *n. var. of* CHARIVARI.
chive (chīv) *n.* A plant, *Allium schoenoprasum,* with purplish flowers and hollow, grasslike leaves used as a seasoning.
chlo•ral (klôr′əl, klōr′-) *n.* A colorless, mobile oily liquid used to make DDT and chloral hydrate.
chloral hydrate *n.* A colorless crystalline compound used medicinally as a sedative and hypnotic.
chlor•dane (klôr′dān′, klōr′-) *also* **chlor•dan** (-dăn′) *n.* An odorless viscous liquid used as an insecticide.
chlo•ride (klôr′īd′, klōr′-) *n.* A binary compound of chlorine.
chlo•ri•nate (klôr′ə-nāt′, klōr′-) *v.* **-nat•ed, -nat•ing.** To treat or combine with chlorine or a chlorine compound. **—chlo′ri•na′tion** *n.* **—chlo′ri•na′tor** *n.*
chlo•rine (klôr′ēn′, klōr′-) *n. Symbol* **Cl** A greenish-yellow, highly irritating gaseous element used to purify water and as a disinfectant and bleach.
chlo•rite (klôr′īt′, klōr′-) *n.* A gen. green or black secondary mineral often formed by metamorphic alteration of primary dark rock minerals.
chlo•ro•form (klôr′ə-fôrm′, klōr′-) *n.* A clear, colorless heavy liquid used in refrigerants and as an anesthetic. —*v.* To use chloroform to anesthetize or kill.
chlo•ro•phyll (klôr′ə-fĭl, klōr′-) *n.* Any of a group of green pigments found in photosynthetic organisms.
chlor•tet•ra•cy•cline (klôr′tĕt-rə-sī′klēn′, klōr′-) *n.* An antibiotic obtained from a soil bacterium.
chock (chŏk) *n.* A wedge placed under something, as a wheel, to keep it from moving or to steady it. **—chock** *v.*
chock-a-block (chŏk′ə-blŏk′) *adj.* Completely full : jammed.
chock-full (chŏk′fo͝ol′, chŭk′-) *adj.* Filled to capacity : stuffed.
choc•o•late (chô′kə-lĭt, chŏk′ə-, chôk′lĭt, chŏk′-) *n.* **1.** Roasted and ground cacao seeds. **2.** A beverage or candy made from chocolate. **3.** A deep brown. **—choc′o•late** *adj.*
choice (chois) *n.* **1.** The act of choosing : selection. **2.** The power, opportunity, or right to choose. **3.** One that is chosen. **4.** A variety or number from which to choose. **5.** The best part. ☆***syns:*** ELECTION, OPTION, PREFERENCE, SELECTION —*adj.* **1.** Of very fine quality. **2.** Chosen with care.
choir (kwīr) *n.* **1.** A group of singers, esp. one performing church music. **2.** The part of a church used by a choir : chancel.
choir•mas•ter (kwīr′măs′tər) *n.* The director of a choir.
choke (chōk) *v.* **choked, chok•ing. 1.** To stop or interfere with breathing, as by constricting the windpipe : suffocate. **2.** To slow or check the action or growth of. **3.** To obstruct : clog. **4.** To reduce the air intake of (a carburetor) to enrich the fuel mixture. —*n.* **1.** The act of choking. **2.** A device used to choke an internal-combustion engine.
chok•er (chō′kər) *n.* A necklace that fits closely around the neck.
chol•er (kŏl′ər, kō′lər) *n.* Disposition to anger : irritability.
chol•er•a (kŏl′ər-ə) *n.* An infectious, often fatal disease marked by watery diarrhea, vomiting, and cramps.
chol•er•ic (kŏl′ə-rĭk, kə-lĕr′ĭk) *adj.* Easily angered : bad-tempered.
cho•les•ter•ol (kə-lĕs′tə-rôl′, -rōl′) *n.* A white, soapy crystalline substance occurring notably in bile, gallstones, the brain, blood cells, plasma, egg yolk, and seeds.
chomp (chŏmp) *v. var. of* CHAMP[1].
chon (chŏn) *n., pl.* **chon.** See *won* at CURRENCY TABLE.
chon•drite (kŏn′drīt′) *n.* A stone of meteoric origin characterized by chondrules. **—chon•drit′ic** (-drĭt′ĭk) *adj.*
chon•drule (kŏn′dro͞ol′) *n.* A small round granule of extraterrestrial origin found embedded in some meteorites.
Chong•qing (cho͝ong′chyĭng′). City of S China on the Yangtze. *Pop.* 2,900,000.

choose (cho͞oz) *v.* **chose** (chōz), **cho•sen** (chō′zən), **choos•ing.** **1.** To pick out : select. **2.** To see fit : desire. ☆*syns:* CULL, ELECT, OPT, PICK, SELECT, SINGLE OUT
choos•y *also* **choos•ey** (cho͞o′zē) *adj.* **-i•er, -i•est.** Difficult to please : particular. **—choos′i•ness** *n.*
chop (chŏp) *v.* **chopped, chop•ping. 1.** To cut by striking repeatedly, as with an ax. **2.** To cut into bits : mince. **3.** To hit (a ball) with a short, swift downward stroke. *—n.* **1.** A short, swift downward blow or stroke. **2.** A cut of meat, often from the rib, containing a bone. **3.** A short, irregular motion, as of waves.
chop•house (chŏp′hous′) *n.* A restaurant usu. specializing in chops and steaks.
Cho•pin (shō′păn′), **Frédéric François.** 1810–49. Polish-born composer.
chop•per (chŏp′ər) *n. Slang.* **1.** A helicopter. **2. choppers.** Teeth, esp. false teeth.
chop•py (chŏp′ē) *adj.* **-pi•er, -pi•est. 1.** Full of short, irregular waves : rough. **2.** Abrupt : jerky. **—chop′pi•ly** *adv.* **—chop′pi•ness** *n.*
chops (chŏps) *pl.n.* The jaws or jowls.
chop•sticks (chŏp′stĭks′) *pl.n.* A pair of sticks used esp. in the Orient as eating utensils.
chop su•ey (chŏp so͞o′ē) *n.* A dish of meat or chicken with bean sprouts and other vegetables, usu. served with rice.
cho•ral (kôr′əl, kōr′-) *adj.* Of, relating to, sung by, or for a chorus or choir. **—cho′ral•ly** *adv.*
cho•rale *also* **cho•ral** (kə-răl′, -räl′) *n.* A Protestant hymn, esp. one that has been harmonized, as for the organ.
chord[1] (kôrd, kōrd) *n.* A combination of musical tones sounded at the same time.
chord[2] (kôrd, kōrd) *n.* **1.** A straight line that joins 2 points on a curve. **2.** A string or cord, esp. a cordlike anatomical structure. **3.** *Archaic.* The string of a musical instrument.
▲word history: The spelling *chord* for *cord* was introduced in the 16th cent. as etymologically more correct by scholars who knew Latin and Greek. The Greek origin of both words is *khordē,* meaning "gut," "string," "musical note," and "sausage." Both instrument strings and sausage casings were made of animal guts. Latin borrowed the Greek word as *chorda* and used it to mean primarily "instrument string" and "cord, rope." English borrowed the word from French, which had preserved the Latin meanings.
chore (chôr, chōr) *n.* **1.** A daily or routine task. **2.** A burdensome or unpleasant task.
cho•re•a (kô-rē′ə, kō-) *n.* A nervous disorder, esp. of children, marked by irregular and uncontrollable muscle movements.
cho•re•og•ra•phy (kôr′ē-ŏg′rə-fē, kōr′-) *n.* The art of creating and arranging dances, esp. ballets. **—cho′re•o•graph′** (-ə-grăf′) *v.* **—cho′re•og′ra•pher** *n.* **—cho′re•o•graph′ic** (-ə-grăf′ĭk) *adj.* **—cho′re•o•graph′i•cal•ly** *adv.*
cho•ris•ter (kôr′ĭ-stər, kōr′-, kŏr′-) *n.* One, esp. a boy, who sings in a choir.
chor•tle (chôr′tl) *v.* **-tled, -tling.** To chuckle throatily, esp. in joy or triumph. **—chort′le** *n.* **—chor′tler** *n.*
cho•rus (kôr′əs, kōr′-) *n., pl.* **-rus•es. 1.** **a.** A group of singers who perform together. **b.** A composition for such a group. **2.** A group of dancers and vocalists who support the soloists, as in a musical comedy. **3.** A group speaking or reciting in unison. **4.** Sounds uttered in concert by many or several. **5.** A repeated part of a song. *—v.* **-rused, -rus•ing** *or* **-russed, -rus•sing.** To utter or sing in chorus. **—cho′ric** *adj.*
chose (chōz) *v. p.t. of* CHOOSE.
cho•sen (chō′zən) *adj.* Selected from or preferred above others.
chow[1] (chou) *n.* A heavy-set dog orig. bred in China, with a blackish tongue and a dense coat.
chow[2] (chou) *n. Slang.* Food.
chow-chow (chou′chou′) *n.* A relish of chopped vegetables pickled in mustard.
chow•der (chou′dər) *n.* A thick soup often made from fish and usu. having a milk base.
chow mein (chou′ mān′) *n.* A stew of diced or shredded meat and cooked vegetables served with fried noodles.
chrism (krĭz′əm) *n.* Consecrated oil used for sacramental anointing.
Christ (krīst) *n.* **1.** The Messiah. **2.** Jesus. **—Christ′like′** *adj.*
chris•ten (krĭs′ən) *v.* **1.** To baptize. **2.** To name at baptism. **3.** To dedicate or name (e.g., a ship) ceremonially. **—chris′ten•er** *n.* **—chris′ten•ing** *n.*
Chris•ten•dom (krĭs′ən-dəm) *n.* **1.** Christians as a whole. **2.** The Christian world.
Chris•tian (krĭs′chən) *n.* A believer in Christianity. *—adj.* **1.** Of, pertaining to, or professing belief in Christianity. **2.** Relating to or derived from Jesus or His teachings. **3.** Relating to Christianity or its adherents.
chris•ti•a•ni•a (krĭs′tē-ăn′ē-ə, krĭs′chē-) *n.* A ski turn at high speed in which the body is swung from a crouching position in order to stop or change direction.

christiania

Chris•ti•an•i•ty (krĭs′chē-ăn′ĭ-tē) *n.* **1.** The religion founded on the teachings of Jesus Christ. **2.** Christendom. **3.** The quality, state, or fact of being a Christian.
Chris•tian•ize (krĭs′chə-nīz′) *v.* **-ized, -iz•ing.** To adopt or convert to Christianity. **—Chris′tian•i•za′tion** *n.*
Christian Science *n.* The church and religious system founded by Mary Baker Eddy, emphasizing healing through spiritual means. **—Christian Scientist** *n.*
Christ•mas (krĭs′məs) *n.* Dec. 25, celebrated by Christians as the anniversary of Christ's birth.
Christ•mas•tide (krĭs′məs-tīd′) *n.* The Christmas season.
chro•mat•ic (krō-măt′ĭk) *adj.* **1.** Of or relating to color. **2.** *Mus.* Proceeding by half steps <a *chromatic* scale> **—chro•mat′i•cal•ly** *adv.* **—chro•mat′i•cism** *n.*
chro•ma•tic•i•ty (krō′mə-tĭs′ĭ-tē) *n.* The aspect of color including consideration of its dominant wavelength and purity.
chro•ma•tog•ra•phy (krō′mə-tŏg′rə-fē) *n.* Separation of complex mixtures by percolation through a selectively adsorbing medium, yielding stratified, sometimes chromatically distinct constituent layers. **—chro•mat′o•graph′ic** (-măt′ə-grăf′ĭk) *adj.* **—chro•mat′o•graph′i•cal•ly** *adv.*
chrome (krōm) *n.* **1.** Chromium. **2.** Something plated with a chromium alloy.
chro•mic (krō′mĭk) *adj.* Of or containing chromium, esp. with valence 3.
chro•mi•um (krō′mē-əm) *n. Symbol* **Cr** A hard, steel-gray metallic element used esp. in steel alloys and stainless steels.
chro•mo•some (krō′mə-sōm′) *n.* A DNA-containing linear body of the cell nuclei that is responsible for determination and transmission of hereditary characteristics. **—chro′mo•so′mal** (-sō′məl) *adj.*
chro•mo•sphere (krō′mə-sfîr′) *n.* **1.** An incandescent, transparent layer of gas that lies above and surrounds the photosphere of the sun. **2.** A similar gaseous layer around a star. **—chro′mo•spher′ic** (-sfîr′ĭk, -sfĕr′-) *adj.*
chron•ic (krŏn′ĭk) *adj.* **1.** Of long duration or frequent recurrence. **2.** Habitual : inveterate. ☆*syns:* CONTINUING, LINGERING, PERSISTENT, PROLONGED, PROTRACTED **—chron′i•cal•ly** *adv.*
chron•i•cle (krŏn′ĭ-kəl) *n.* **1.** A chronological record of events : history. **2. Chronicles** *(sing. in number).* See BIBLE TABLE. *—v.* **-cled, -cling.** To record in or as if in a chronicle. **—chron′i•cler** (-klər) *n.*
chron•o•graph (krŏn′ə-grăf′, krō′nə-) *n.* An instrument that shows or graphically records time intervals. **—chron′o•graph′ic** *adj.* **—chron′o•graph′i•cal•ly** *adv.*
chro•nol•o•gy (krə-nŏl′ə-jē) *n., pl.* **-gies. 1.** The science that deals with determining the dates and sequence of events. **2.** Arrangement of events in time. **3.** A chronological table or list. **—chron′o•log′i•cal** (krŏn′ə-lŏj′ĭ-kəl), **chron′o•log′ic** (-ĭk) *adj.* **—chro•nol′o•gist** *n.*
chro•nom•e•ter (krə-nŏm′ĭ-tər) *n.* An extremely accurate timepiece.
chrys•a•lis (krĭs′ə-lĭs) *n.* The pupa of an insect, esp. a moth or butterfly, enclosed in a firm case.
chry•san•the•mum (krĭ-săn′thə-məm) *n.* A plant of the genus *Chrysanthemum* cultivated esp. for its showy flowers.
chub (chŭb) *n., pl.* **chub** *or* **chubs.** A freshwater fish of the family Cyprinidae, related to the carp and minnow.
chub•by (chŭb′ē) *adj.* **-bi•er, -bi•est.** Plump : chunky. **—chub′bi•ness** *n.*
chuck[1] (chŭk) *v.* **1.** To squeeze or pat affectionately, esp. under the chin. **2.** To toss : throw. **3.** *Informal.* To throw away : discard. **—chuck** *n.*
†chuck[2] (chŭk) *n.* **1.** A cut of beef extending from the neck to the ribs. **2.** *W U.S.* Food. **3.** A device that holds a tool or work in a machine, as a drill or lathe.

†chuck·hole (chŭk′hōl′) *n. Regional.* A rut or pothole in a road.

chuck·le (chŭk′əl) *v.* **-led, -ling.** To laugh quietly or to oneself. **—chuck′le** *n.* **—chuck′ler** *n.*

chuck wagon *n.* A wagon equipped with food and cooking utensils.

chug (chŭg) *n.* The muffled explosive sound made by or as if by a laboring engine. **—chug** *v.*

chuk·ka (chŭk′ə) *n.* An ankle-length usu. suede boot with 2 pairs of eyelets.

chuk·ker *also* **chuk·kar** (chŭk′ər) *n.* A playing period in a polo match.

chum (chŭm) *n.* A close friend : pal. *—v.* **chummed, chum·ming.** To be a close friend.

chum·my (chŭm′ē) *adj.* **-mi·er, -mi·est.** *Informal.* Very friendly : intimate. **—chum′mi·ly** *adv.* **—chum′mi·ness** *n.*

chump (chŭmp) *n.* A foolish person.

chunk (chŭngk) *n.* **1.** A thick piece. **2.** A large amount.

chunk·y (chŭng′kē) *adj.* **-i·er, -i·est. 1.** Short and thick : stocky. **2.** In or containing chunks. **—chunk′i·ness** *n.*

church (chûrch) *n.* **1.** All Christians regarded as a spiritual entity. **2.** A building for public and esp. Christian worship. **3.** A congregation. **4.** A public religious service. **5.** A Christian denomination. **—church′go′er** *n.* **—church′go′ing** *adj.* & *n.*

Church·ill (chûr′chĭl′), Sir **Winston Leonard Spencer.** 1874–1965. British prime minister (1940–45, 1951–55).

church·man (chûrch′mən) *n.* **1.** A clergyman : priest. **2.** A church member.

Church of England *n.* The national church of England.

church·war·den (chûrch′wôr′dn) *n.* An elected lay officer who oversees the secular affairs of an Episcopal church.

church·yard (chûrch′yärd′) *n.* A yard belonging to a church.

churl (chûrl) *n.* **1.** A rude boor. **2.** A miser. **—churl′ish** *adj.* **—churl′ish·ly** *adv.* **—churl′ish·ness** *n.*

churn (chûrn) *n.* A device in which cream or milk is beaten vigorously to make butter. *—v.* **1.** To beat (cream or milk) vigorously in a churn. **2.** To make (butter) by operating a churn. **3.** To move with or produce great agitation. **—churn out.** To produce automatically and in quantity.

chute (sho͞ot) *n.* **1.** An inclined trough, channel, or passage through which something may pass. **2.** *Informal.* A parachute.

chut·ney (chŭt′nē) *n.* A pungent condiment of fruits, spices, and herbs.

chutz·pah (ᴋʜo͝ot′spə) *n. Slang.* Brazenness : nerve.

ciao (chou) *interj.* Used to express greeting or farewell.

ci·ca·da (sĭ-kā′də, -kä′-) *n.* A large insect of the family Cicadidae with a broad head and membranous wings.

cic·a·trix (sĭk′ə-trĭks′) *n., pl.* **-tri·ces** (-trī′sēz′). Scar tissue on a flesh wound.

Cic·e·ro (sĭs′ə-rō′), **Marcus Tullius.** 106–43 B.C. Roman statesman and orator.

cic·e·ro·ne (sĭs′ə-rō′nē, chē′chə-) *n., pl.* **-nes** *or* **-ni** (-nē). A guide for sightseers.

ci·der (sī′dər) *n.* The juice pressed from fruit, esp. apples, used as vinegar or a fermented or unfermented beverage.

ci·gar (sĭ-gär′) *n.* A roll of tobacco leaves used for smoking.

cig·a·rette *also* **cig·a·ret** (sĭg′ə-rĕt′, sĭg′ə-rĕt′) *n.* A small roll of cut tobacco encased in thin paper for smoking.

cig·a·ril·lo (sĭg′ə-rĭl′ō) *n., pl.* **-los.** A small, narrow cigar.

cil·i·ate (sĭl′ē-ĭt, -āt′) *n.* Any of various protozoans of the class Ciliata, having numerous cilia.

cil·i·um (sĭl′ē-əm) *n., pl.* **-i·a** (-ē-ə). **1.** A microscopic hairlike process extending from the surface of a cell and often capable of rhythmical motion. **2.** An eyelash.

cinch (sĭnch) *n.* **1.** A strap for holding a pack or saddle. **2.** *Slang.* **a.** A thing easy to do. **b.** A sure thing : certainty. *—v.* **1.** To tighten a cinch on. **2.** *Slang.* To make certain of : assure.

cin·cho·na (sĭn-kō′nə, sĭng-) *n.* A South American tree of the genus *Cinchona,* whose bark yields quinine.

Cin·cin·nat·i (sĭn′sə-năt′ē, -năt′ə). City of SW Ohio on the Ohio R. *Pop.* 385,457.

cinc·ture (sĭngk′chər) *n.* A girdle : belt. **—cinc′ture** *v.*

cin·der (sĭn′dər) *n.* **1.** A piece of partially burned material, as coal, that cannot be burned further. **2.** A fragment of burned, crustlike lava. **3. cinders.** Ashes.

cinder block *n.* A building block made of coal cinders and cement.

cin·e·ast (sĭn′ē-ăst) *also* **cin·é·aste** (sĭn′ā-ăst′) *n.* A film enthusiast.

cin·e·ma (sĭn′ə-mə) *n.* **1.** A motion picture. **2.** A motion-picture theater. **3.** Motion pictures in general. **—cin′e·mat′ic** *adj.* **—cin′e·mat′i·cal·ly** *adv.*

cin·e·mat·o·graph (sĭn′ə-măt′ə-grăf′) *n.* A movie camera or projector.

cin·e·ma·tog·ra·phy (sĭn′ə-mə-tŏg′rə-fē) *n.* Motion-picture photography. **—cin′e·ma·tog′ra·pher** *n.* **—cin′e·mat′o·graph′ic** (-măt′ə-grăf′ĭk) *adj.*

cin·e·rar·i·a (sĭn′ə-râr′ē-ə) *n.* A tropical plant, *Senecio cruentis,* with flat clusters of variously colored daisylike flowers.

cin·e·rar·i·um (sĭn′ə-râr′ē-əm) *n., pl.* **-i·a** (-ē-ə). A place for keeping the ashes of cremated corpses. **—cin′er·ar′y** (-rĕr′ē) *adj.*

cin·na·bar (sĭn′ə-bär′) *n.* A heavy reddish compound that is the principal source of mercury.

cin·na·mon (sĭn′ə-mən) *n.* **1.** The aromatic bark of a tropical Asian tree that is used as a spice. **2.** A reddish brown.

cinque·foil (sĭngk′foil′, săngk′-) *n.* A plant of the genus *Potentilla,* bearing compound leaves often having 5 lobes.

ci·pher (sī′fər) *n.* **1.** *Math.* The symbol (0) indicating absence of quantity : zero. **2. a.** A system of secret writing : code. **b.** The key to a cipher. *—v.* **1.** To calculate arithmetically. **2.** To put in secret writing.

cir·ca (sûr′kə) *prep.* About <*circa* 1776>

cir·ca·di·an (sər-kā′dē-ən, -kăd′ē-, sûr′kə-dī′ən, -dē′-) *adj. Biol.* Exhibiting approx. 24-hour periodicity.

cir·cle (sûr′kəl) *n.* **1.** A plane curve equidistant from a fixed center within it. **2.** A region of a plane bounded by a circle. **3.** Something shaped like a circle. **4.** A group of people who have in common an interest or activity. **5.** A sphere of influence or interest : domain. *—v.* **-cled, -cling. 1.** To make a circle around : enclose. **2.** To move in a circle (around).

cir·clet (sûr′klĭt) *n.* A small circle <a *circlet* of gold>

cir·cuit (sûr′kĭt) *n.* **1. a.** A closed, usu. circular curve. **b.** The region enclosed by a circuit. **2. a.** *Elect.* A closed path through which an electric current flows or may flow. **b.** A configuration of electrically or electromagnetically connected components or devices. **3.** A regular route, as that followed by a judge, around an assigned area or district. **4.** A chain, as of theaters. *—v.* To make a circuit (of).

circuit breaker *n.* A switch that automatically stops the flow of electric current in an overloaded circuit.

circuit court *n.* The lowest court of record in some U.S. states, occas. holding sessions in different places.

cir·cu·i·tous (sər-kyo͞o′ĭ-təs) *adj.* Indirect : roundabout. **—cir·cu′i·tous·ly** *adv.* **—cir·cu′i·ty, cir·cu′i·tous·ness** *n.*

cir·cuit·ry (sûr′kĭ-trē) *n.* **1.** The plan of an electric circuit. **2.** Electric circuits as a whole.

cir·cu·lar (sûr′kyə-lər) *adj.* **1.** Relating to a circle. **2.** Shaped like a circle : round. **3.** Moving in a circle. **4.** Circuitous. *—n.* A printed notice or advertisement intended for mass distribution. **—cir′cu·lar′i·ty** (-lăr′ĭ-tē) *n.* **—cir′cu·lar·ly** *adv.*

cir·cu·lar·ize (sûr′kyə-lə-rīz′) *v.* **-ized, -iz·ing.** To publicize with or as if with circulars. **—cir′cu·lar·i·za′tion** *n.* **—cir′cu·lar·iz′er** *n.*

cir·cu·late (sûr′kyə-lāt′) *v.* **-lat·ed, -lat·ing. 1.** To move or cause to move in or through a circle or circuit. **2.** To move from person to person or place to place. **3.** To distribute widely : disseminate. **—cir′cu·la′tion** *n.* **—cir′cu·la′tor** *n.* **—cir′cu·la·to′ry** (-lə-tôr′ē, -tōr′ē) *adj.*

cir·cum·cise (sûr′kəm-sīz′) *v.* **-cised, -cis·ing.** To remove the prepuce. **—cir′cum·ci′sion** (-sĭzh′ən) *n.*

cir·cum·fer·ence (sər-kŭm′fər-əns) *n.* **1.** The boundary of a circle : perimeter. **2.** The length of the perimeter of a circle. ☆*syns:* CIRCUIT, COMPASS, PERIMETER **—cir·cum′fer·en′tial** (-fə-rĕn′shəl) *adj.*

cir·cum·flex (sûr′kəm-flĕks′) *n.* A mark (ˆ) used esp. to indicate a vowel quality.

cir·cum·lo·cu·tion (sûr′kəm-lō-kyo͞o′shən) *n.* The use of an excessive number of words to articulate an idea.

cir·cum·lu·nar (sûr′kəm-lo͞o′nər) *adj.* Surrounding or revolving about the moon.

cir·cum·nav·i·gate (sûr′kəm-năv′ĭ-gāt′) *v.* **-gat·ed, -gat·ing.** To travel completely around, esp. by boat. **—cir′cum·nav′i·ga′tion** *n.* **—cir′cum·nav′i·ga′tor** *n.*

cir·cum·po·lar (sûr′kəm-pō′lər) *adj.* **1.** Located in a polar region. **2.** Designating a star that from a given observer's latitude does not go below the horizon.

cir·cum·scribe (sûr′kəm-skrīb′) *v.* **-scribed, -scrib·ing. 1.** To draw a line around. **2.** To confine within bounds. **—cir′cum·scrip′tion** (-skrĭp′shən) *n.*

cir·cum·so·lar (sûr′kəm-sō′lər) *adj.* Surrounding or revolving about the sun.

cir·cum·spect (sûr′kəm-spĕkt′) *adj.* Aware and heedful of consequences : prudent. **—cir′cum·spec′tion** *n.*

cir·cum·stance (sûr′kəm-stăns′) *n.* **1.** A condition or fact attending and having bearing on an event. **2.** A condition or fact that must be considered in determining a course of action. **3. circumstances.** Financial condition or means. **4.** Ceremony : formalities. **5.** Fate : chance.

cir·cum·stan·tial (sûr′kəm-stăn′shəl) *adj.* **1.** Of, relating to,

or dependent on circumstances. **2.** Of no primary significance. **3.** Complete and fully detailed.
circumstantial evidence *n. Law.* Evidence not directly relevant to the facts in dispute but to attendant circumstances from which the occurrence of the facts in dispute might be inferred.
cir•cum•stan•ti•ate (sûr'kəm-stăn'shē-āt') *v.* **-at•ed, -at•ing.** To provide support or circumstantial evidence of.
cir•cum•ter•res•tri•al (sûr'kəm-tə-rĕs'trē-əl) *adj.* Surrounding or revolving about the earth.
cir•cum•vent (sûr'kəm-vĕnt', sûr'kəmvĕnt') *v.* To avoid or overcome, esp. by ingenuity. **—cir'cum•ven'tion** *n.*
cir•cus (sûr'kəs) *n.* **1.** A public entertainment that features acts by acrobats, clowns, and trained animals. **2.** An arena, often circular and covered by a tent, in which a circus performance is presented.
cirque (sûrk) *n.* A deep, steep basin in a mountain valley.
cir•rho•sis (sĭ-rō'sĭs) *n.* A chronic, ultimately fatal liver disease. **—cir•rhot'ic** (sĭ-rŏt'ĭk) *adj.*
cir•rus (sîr'əs) *n., pl.* **cir•ri** (sîr'ī'). A high-altitude cloud composed of thin, gen. white fleecy patches.
cis•lu•nar (sĭs-lo͞o'nər) *adj.* Between the earth and the moon.
cis•tern (sĭs'tərn) *n.* A tank for storing water, esp. rainwater.
cit. *abbr.* **1.** citation. **2.** cited. **3.** citizen.
cit•a•del (sĭt'ə-dəl, -dĕl') *n.* **1.** A fortress overlooking a city. **2.** A stronghold.
cite (sīt) *v.* **cit•ed, cit•ing. 1.** To quote as an authority or example or as proof. **2.** To mention, esp. in commendation, as for meritorious action. **3.** To summon before a court of law. **—ci•ta'tion** *n.*
cit•i•fy (sĭt'ə-fī') *v.* **-fied, -fy•ing.** To urbanize. **—cit'i•fi•ca'tion** *n.*
cit•i•zen (sĭt'ĭ-zən) *n.* **1.** A person who owes loyalty to and is entitled to the protection of a government. **2.** A resident of a city or town. **—cit'i•zen•ship'** *n.*
cit•i•zen•ry (sĭt'ĭ-zən-rē) *n., pl.* **-ries.** Citizens as a group.
citizen's band *n.* A radio-frequency band officially set aside for private use.
cit•ric (sĭt'rĭk) *adj.* Of or derived from citrus fruits.
citric acid *n.* A colorless acid that occurs in lemon, lime, and pineapple juices and is used as a flavoring.
cit•rine (sĭt'rĭn, -rēn') *n.* **1.** A pale-yellow quartz. **2.** A pale yellow. **—cit'rine** *adj.*
cit•ron (sĭt'rən) *n.* **1.** A tree, *Citrus medica,* bearing lemonlike fruit with a thick, aromatic rind. **2.** A variety of watermelon, *Citrullus vulgaris citroides,* bearing fruit with a hard rind that is preserved or candied for use esp. in baking.
cit•ro•nel•la (sĭt'rə-nĕl'ə) *n.* An aromatic oil derived from a tropical grass and used esp. in insect repellents.
cit•rus (sĭt'rəs) *n., pl.* **-rus•es** *or* **-rus.** A tree or shrub of the genus *Citrus,* which includes the orange, lemon, lime, and grapefruit. **—cit'rus** *adj.*
cit•y (sĭt'ē) *n., pl.* **-ies. 1.** A place that is larger or more significant than a town. **2.** A U.S. municipality with legal powers granted by state charter. **3.** The residents of a city.
city hall *n.* **1.** The principal administrative building of a city government. **2.** A municipal bureaucracy.
city manager *n.* An administrator appointed by a city council to manage city affairs.
cit•y-state (sĭt'ē-stāt') *n.* An independent state composed of a city and its surrounding territory.
civ•et (sĭv'ĭt) *n.* Any of various catlike mammals of the family Viverridae that secrete a musky fluid used in prefumes.
civ•ic (sĭv'ĭk) *adj.* Of or relating to a city, a citizen, or citizenship. —*n.* **civics** *(sing. in number).* A social science that deals with civic affairs, esp. the rights and duties of citizenship.
civ•il (sĭv'əl) *adj.* **1.** Of or relating to citizens. **2.** Of or relating to the general public as distinct from the military or ecclesiastical. **3.** Of or relating to legal proceedings concerned with the rights of private individuals. **4.** Courteous. **—civ'il•ly** *adv.*
civil defense *n.* The emergency measures to be taken by civilian volunteers in case of a natural disaster, enemy attack, or invasion.
civil disobedience *n.* Refusal to obey civil laws regarded as unjust, usu. by employing methods of passive resistance.
civil engineer *n.* An engineer trained to design and construct public works. **—civil engineering** *n.*
ci•vil•ian (sĭ-vĭl'yən) *n.* A person not serving in a police, firefighting, or military force.
ci•vil•i•ty (sĭ-vĭl'ĭ-tē) *n., pl.* **-ties. 1.** Courtesy : politeness. **2.** A courteous act or expression.
civ•i•li•za•tion (sĭv'ə-lə-zā'shən) *n.* **1.** A relatively advanced stage of social, political, and cultural development. **2.** The culture of a particular people, place, or epoch.
civ•i•lize (sĭv'ə-līz') *v.* **-lized, -liz•ing. 1.** To bring out of a savage or primitive state. **2.** To educate or enlighten : refine. **—civ'i•liz'a•ble** *adj.* **—civ'i•liz'er** *n.*
civil liberty *n.* Freedom from governmental infringement of such individual rights as freedom of speech and action.
civil rights *pl.n.* Rights guaranteed to an individual by virtue of citizenship.
civil service *n.* The branches of public service that are not legislative, judicial, naval, or military. **—civil servant** *n.*
civil war *n.* A war between opposing factions or regions of the same country.
civ•vies (sĭv'ēz) *pl.n. Slang.* Civilian clothes as opposed to military dress.
ck. *abbr.* check.
cl *abbr.* centiliter.
Cl *symbol for* CHLORINE.
cl. *abbr.* **1.** class; classification. **2.** clause. **3.** clearance. **4.** clerk.
clab•ber (klăb'ər) *n.* Curdled sour milk. —*v.* To curdle.
clack (klăk) *v.* **1.** To make or cause to make an abrupt sound or series of sounds, as of objects being struck together. **2.** To chatter. —*n.* A clacking sound <the *clack* of the machine>
clad (klăd) *v. var. p.t. & p.p. of* CLOTHE.
claim (klām) *v.* **1.** To demand or ask for as one's due or one's own. **2.** To state to be true : assert. **3.** To call for : require. —*n.* **1.** A claiming of something as one's rightful due. **2.** A basis for claiming : title or right. **3.** Something claimed. **4.** A statement that something is true : assertion.
claim•ant (klā'mənt) *n.* Someone making a claim.
clair•voy•ance (klâr-voi'əns) *n.* The power to discern what is beyond the range of the human senses. **—clair•voy'ant** *n. & adj.*
clam (klăm) *n.* **1.** Any of various marine and freshwater bivalve mollusks of the class Pelecypoda, many of them edible. **2.** *Informal.* A close-mouthed person. **—clam** *v.*
clam•bake (klăm'bāk') *n.* A gathering at which foods, as clams and corn, are cooked over hot stones.
clam•ber (klăm'bər) *v.* To climb clumsily, esp. on all fours. **—clam'ber•er** *n.*
clam•my (klăm'ē) *adj.* **-mi•er, -mi•est.** Disagreeably damp, sticky, and usu. cold. **—clam'mi•ly** *adv.* **—clam'mi•ness** *n.*
clam•or (klăm'ər) *n.* **1.** A loud outcry or noise. **2.** A vehement demand or protest. —*v.* To make a clamor. **—clam'or•ous** *adj.* **—clam'or•ous•ly** *adv.*
clamp (klămp) *n.* A device for fastening or holding things together. —*v.* To fasten or hold with or as if with a clamp. **—clamp down.** To become stricter.
clam•shell (klăm'shĕl') *n.* **1.** The shell of a clam. **2.** A dredging bucket consisting of two hinged jaws.
clan (klăn) *n.* **1.** *Sc.* A group of families claiming a common ancestor. **2.** A large group of relatives. **—clan'nish** *adj.* **—clan'nish•ly** *adv.* **—clans'man** *n.* **—clans'wom'an** *n.*
clan•des•tine (klăn-dĕs'tĭn) *adj.* Done in or kept in secrecy.
clang (klăng) *v.* To make or cause to make a loud, resonant metallic sound. **—clang** *n.*
clan•gor (klăng'ər, -gər) *n.* A clang or series of clangs.
clank (klăngk) *n.* A quick, sharp, metallic sound. **—clank** *v.*
clap (klăp) *v.* **clapped, clap•ping. 1.** To strike (the hands) together with a loud sound. **2.** To make a sudden sharp noise. **3.** To applaud. **—clap** *n.*
clap•board (klăb'ərd, klăp'bôrd', -bōrd') *n.* A long board with one edge thicker than the other that is used for surfacing a frame building. **—clap'board** *v.*
clap•per (klăp'ər) *n.* One that claps, esp. the tongue of a bell.
clap•trap (klăp'trăp') *n.* High-flown nonsense.
claque (klăk) *n.* A group of persons hired to applaud at a performance.
clar•et (klăr'ĭt) *n.* A dry red table wine.
clar•i•fy (klăr'ə-fī') *v.* **-fied, -fy•ing.** To make or become clear : elucidate. **—clar'i•fi•ca'tion** *n.*
clar•i•net (klăr'ə-nĕt') *n.* A single-reed woodwind instrument with a cylindrical body and a flaring bell. **—clar'i•net'ist, clar'i•net'tist** *n.*
clar•i•on (klăr'ē-ən) *adj.* Resounding and clear.
clar•i•ty (klăr'ĭ-tē) *n.* The quality or state of being clear.
clash (klăsh) *v.* **1.** To strike together with a harsh, esp. metallic sound. **2.** To be in or come into opposition : conflict. —*n.* **1.** A harsh metallic sound. **2.** A usu. hostile encounter : conflict.
clasp (klăsp) *n.* **1.** A device, as a hook, used to hold parts or objects together. **2. a.** An embrace. **b.** A grip or grasp of the hand. —*v.* **1.** To fasten with a clasp. **2. a.** To embrace. **b.** To grip in or with the hand.
class (klăs) *n.* **1.** A set or group whose members share at least one attribute : kind. **2.** A division based on quality or grade. **3.** A social rank. **4. a.** A group of students graduating at the same time. **b.** A group of students studying the same subject. **5.** *Slang.*

High style or quality. ☆**syns:** CATEGORY, CLASSIFICATION, ORDER —*v.* To classify.

class action *n.* A lawsuit in which the plaintiffs bring suit on their own behalf and on that of others with the same claim.

clas·sic (klăs′ĭk) *adj.* **1.** Serving as a model of excellence : outstanding. **2.** Of or relating to ancient Greek or Roman literature or art. **3.** Of or in accordance with traditional methods and principles. **4.** Of lasting historical or artistic significance or worth. —*n.* **1.** An artist, author, or work of the highest excellence. **2. classics.** The literature or art of ancient Greece and Rome. **3.** A traditional event.

clas·si·cal (klăs′ĭ-kəl) *adj.* **1.** Of, relating to, or in the style of the ancient Greek and Roman classics. **2.** Of, relating to, or concerned with studies of antiquity. **3.** Of or designating European music of the latter half of the 18th cent. **4.** Standard and authoritative. —**clas′si·cal·ly** *adv.*

clas·si·cism (klăs′ĭ-sĭz′əm) *n.* **1.** The rules and ideals, as of form, simplicity, and proportion, that are the basis of the art and literature of ancient Greece and Rome. **2.** Adherence to traditional rules or principles. **3.** Classical scholarship. —**clas′si·cist** (klăs′ĭ-sĭst) *n.*

classified advertisement *n.* A usu. brief advertisement printed, as in a newspaper, with others of the same category.

clas·si·fy (klăs′ə-fī′) *v.* **-fied, -fy·ing. 1.** To assign to or arrange in classes. **2.** To assign to a restricted category for reasons of security. —**clas′si·fi′a·ble** *adj.* —**clas′si·fi·ca′tion** *n.*

class·mate (klăs′māt′) *n.* A member of the same class in a school, college, etc.

class·room (klăs′ro͞om′) *n.* A room, as in a school, in which classes meet.

class·y (klăs′ē) *adj.* **-i·er, -i·est.** *Slang.* Stylish : elegant.

clas·tic (klăs′tĭk) *adj. Geol.* Made up of fragments : fragmental.

clat·ter (klăt′ər) *v.* To make, cause to make, or move with a rattling sound. —**clat′ter** *n.*

clause (klôz) *n.* **1.** A group of words containing its own subject and predicate and forming part of a compound sentence. **2.** A distinct part of a document.

claus·tro·pho·bi·a (klô′strə-fō′bē-ə) *n.* A pathological fear of small spaces. —**claus′tro·pho′bic** *adj.*

clav·i·chord (klăv′ĭ-kôrd′) *n. Mus.* An early keyboard instrument.

clav·i·cle (klăv′ĭ-kəl) *n.* A bone connecting the sternum and the scapula. —**cla·vic′u·lar** (klə-vĭk′yə-lər) *adj.*

cla·vier (klə-vîr′, klā′vē-ər) *n. Mus.* **1.** A keyboard. **2.** An early keyboard instrument, as a harpsichord.

claw (klô) *n.* **1.** A sharp, often curved nail on the toe of an animal. **2.** A clawlike part, as the chela of a lobster. **3.** Something resembling a claw. —*v.* To scratch, grasp, or dig with or as if with claws.

clay (klā) *n.* **1.** A pliable fine-grained earth that hardens when fired, used in making bricks, pottery, and tiles. **2.** Moist earth : mud. **3.** The mortal human body. —**clay′ey** (klā′ē) *adj.*

clay pigeon *n.* A clay disk hurled as a flying target for skeet and trapshooting.

clean (klēn) *adj.* **1.** Free from dirt, impurities, or contamination. **2.** Free from wrongdoing : honorable. **3.** Even : regular <a car with *clean* lines> **4.** Thorough : complete <a *clean* escape> ☆**syns:** ANTISEPTIC, IMMACULATE, SPOTLESS, STAINLESS —*adv.* In a clean manner. —*v.* To make or become clean. —**clean up. 1.** To dispose of : settle. **2.** *Informal.* To make a large profit, esp. in a short time. —**clean′ly** *adv.*

clean-cut (klēn′kŭt′) *adj.* **1.** Clearly outlined or defined. **2.** Trim and neat.

clean·ly (klĕn′lē) *adj.* **-li·er, -li·est.** Habitually clean and neat. —**clean′li·ness** *n.*

clean room *n.* A room that is kept contaminant-free, esp. for the handling of precision parts.

cleanse (klĕnz) *v.* **cleansed, cleans·ing.** To make clean or pure. —**cleans′er** *n.*

clean·up (klēn′ŭp′) *n.* The act, process, or result of cleaning up.

clear (klîr) *adj.* **1.** Free from clouds or precipitation : bright. **2.** Free from impediment, restriction, or hindrance. **3.** Easily perceived by the eye, ear, or mind. **4.** Capable of discerning easily. **5.** Free from confusion or doubt. **6.** Free from impurities. **7.** Transparent. **8.** Free from guilt : innocent. **9.** Freed from burden or obligation. —*v.* **1.** To make or become clear. **2.** To rid of impurities or blemishes. **3.** To become free of obstructions. **4.** To free from blame or guilt. **5.** To pass by, under, or over without contact. **6.** To gain (a given amount) as net earnings or profit. **7.** To pass through a clearing-house, as a check. **8.** To make plain or intelligible : explain. —**clear** *adv.* —**clear′ly** *adv.* —**clear′ness** *n.*

clear·ance (klîr′əns) *n.* **1.** The act of clearing. **2.** The amount or distance by which an object clears another. **3.** Permission to proceed.

clear-cut (klîr′kŭt′) *adj.* **1.** Sharply defined. **2.** Plain : unambiguous.

clear-head·ed (klîr′hĕd′ĭd) *adj.* Having a clear, orderly mind.

clear·ing (klîr′ĭng) *n.* A tract of land from which trees, brush, and other obstructions have been removed.

clear·ing-house *also* **clear·ing·house** (klîr′ĭng-hous′) *n.* An office at which banks settle accounts.

cleat (klēt) *n.* A wood or metal projection that grips, provides support, or prevents slipping.

cleav·age (klē′vĭj) *n.* The act, process, or result of splitting or cleaving.

cleave[1] (klēv) *v.* **cleft** (klĕft) *or* **cleaved** *or* **clove** (klōv), **cleft** *or* **cleaved** *or* **clo·ven** (klō′vən), **cleav·ing. 1.** To split apart : separate. **2.** To penetrate : pierce.

cleave[2] (klēv) *v.* **cleaved, cleav·ing.** To cling fast : adhere.

cleav·er (klē′vər) *n.* A heavy knife used by butchers.

clef (klĕf) *n.* A symbol that indicates which pitch each line and space represents on a musical staff.

cleft (klĕft) *n.* A crack : fissure.

clem·a·tis (klĕm′ə-tĭs, klə-măt′ĭs) *n.* A plant or vine of the genus *Clematis,* bearing white or variously colored flowers.

clem·ent (klĕm′ənt) *adj.* **1.** Merciful : lenient. **2.** Mild, as weather : temperate. —**clem′en·cy** *n.* —**clem′ent·ly** *adv.*

clench (klĕnch) *v.* **1.** To close or set tightly. **2.** To grip or grasp tightly. **3.** To clinch. —**clench** *n.*

Cle·o·pat·ra (klē′ə-păt′rə, -pä′trə, -pā′-). 69–30 B.C. Queen of Egypt (51–49, 48–30).

clere·sto·ry *also* **clear·sto·ry** (klîr′stôr′ē, -stōr′ē) *n.* A wall with windows that rises above an abutting roofed section of a building or room.

cler·gy (klûr′jē) *n.* The body of persons ordained for religious service.

cler·gy·man (klûr′jē-mən) *n.* A member of the clergy.

cler·ic (klĕr′ĭk) *n.* A clergyman.

cler·i·cal (klĕr′ĭ-kəl) *adj.* **1.** Of or pertaining to clerks or office workers. **2.** Of or typical of the clergy or a member of it.

cler·i·cal·ism (klĕr′ĭ-kə-lĭz′əm) *n.* A policy of supporting the political and secular power of the clergy.

clerk (klûrk; *Brit.* klärk) *n.* **1.** An office worker who performs general business tasks. **2.** An official who performs such tasks as keeping records, as for a court or legislative body. **3.** A salesperson in a store. —*v.* To work as a clerk. —**clerk′ship′** *n.*

Cleve·land (klēv′lənd). City of NE Ohio, on Lake Erie. *Pop.* 573,822.

Cleveland, (Stephen) Grover. 1837–1908. 22nd and 24th U.S. President (1885–89, 1893–97).

†**clev·er** (klĕv′ər) *adj.* **1.** Mentally quick and ingenious : quick-witted. **2.** Showing skill : dexterous. **3.** *Regional.* Handy : suitable. ☆**syns:** ALERT, BRIGHT, INTELLIGENT, KEEN, SHARP, SMART —**clev′er·ly** *adv.*

clev·is (klĕv′ĭs) *n.* A U-shaped metal device for attaching parts.

clew (klo͞o) *n.* & *v. var. of* CLUE.

cli·ché (klē-shā′) *n.* A hackneyed expression or idea.

click (klĭk) *n.* A brief, sharp sound. —*v.* **1.** To make or cause to make a click. **2.** *Informal.* **a.** To be successful. **b.** To function or fit well together.

cli·ent (klī′ənt) *n.* **1.** One who secures the professional services of another. **2.** A customer : patron.

cli·en·tele (klī′ən-tĕl′, klē′ən-) *n.* Clients and esp. customers.

cliff (klĭf) *n.* A steep high face of rock.

cliff·hang·er (klĭf′hăng′ər) *n.* **1.** A serial in which each installment ends in suspense. **2.** A closely matched contest whose outcome is doubtful until the very end.

cli·mac·ter·ic (klī-măk′tər-ĭk, klī′măk-tĕr′ĭk) *n.* **1.** A period of life when physiological changes, esp. menopause, take place. **2.** A critical period or stage.

cli·mac·tic (klī-măk′tĭk) *adj.* Of or being a climax. —**cli·mac′ti·cal·ly** *adv.*

cli·mate (klī′mĭt) *n.* **1.** The average weather conditions of a specified region. **2.** A region with particular weather conditions <a tropical *climate*> **3.** A prevailing atmosphere. —**cli·mat′ic** (-măt′ĭk) *adj.* —**cli·mat′i·cal·ly** *adv.*

cli·ma·tol·o·gy (klī′mə-tŏl′ə-jē) *n.* Meteorological study of climate. —**cli′ma·to·log′i·cal** (-tə-lŏj′ĭ-kəl) *adj.* —**cli′ma·tol′o·gist** *n.*

cli·max (klī′măks′) *n.* **1.** The point of greatest intensity or power in a series of events, ideas, or statements. **2.** The stage at which a community of organisms becomes stable and begins to perpetuate itself. ☆**syns:** ACME, APEX, APOGEE, CREST, CROWN, CULMINATION, HEIGHT, PEAK, PINNACLE, SUMMIT, ZENITH —**cli′max** *v.*

climb (klīm) *v.* **1.** To move up or mount, esp. by using the hands and feet : ascend. **2.** To go higher, as in rank or fortune :

rise. **3.** To grow upward. **—climb down.** To descend, esp. by means of the hands and feet. *—n.* **1.** The act of climbing. **2.** A place to be climbed. **—climb'er** *n.*
clime (klīm) *n.* Climate.
clinch (klĭnch) *v.* **1.** To secure or fix, as with a bolt. **2.** To settle definitively <*clinched* the deal> **3.** To hold so as to immobilize. **—clinch** *n.*
clinch•er (klĭn'chər) *n.* One that clinches, esp. a conclusive point, fact, or statement.
cling (klĭng) *v.* **clung** (klŭng), **cling•ing. 1.** To hold tight : adhere. **2.** To be emotionally attached. **—cling'er** *n.*
cling•stone (klĭng'stōn') *n.* A fruit, esp. a peach, with pulp that adheres to the stone.
clin•ic (klĭn'ĭk) *n.* **1.** Medical training in which students observe the examination and treatment of patients. **2.** A facility associated with a hospital that treats chiefly outpatients. **3.** A center offering counsel or instruction <a computer *clinic*>
clin•i•cal (klĭn'ĭ-kəl) *adj.* **1.** Of or relating to a clinic. **2.** Of, related to, or involving direct examination and treatment of patients. **3.** Objective : dispassionate.
cli•ni•cian (klĭ-nĭsh'ən) *n.* A physician or psychologist who specializes in clinical practice rather than research.
clink[1] (klĭngk) *v.* To make or cause to make a light ringing sound. **—clink** *n.*
clink[2] (klĭngk) *n. Slang.* A jail : prison.
clink•er (klĭng'kər) *n.* **1.** Incombustible residue fused into an irregular lump, as that which remains after coal has burned. **2.** *Slang.* An error : mistake.
clip[1] (klĭp) *v.* **clipped, clip•ping. 1.** To cut, cut off, or cut out with shears. **2.** To shorten by cutting. **3.** *Informal.* To strike with a sharp blow. **4.** *Slang.* To cheat or overcharge. *—n.* **1.** Something clipped, as a newspaper item. **2.** *Informal.* A sharp blow. **3.** *Informal.* A brisk pace.
clip[2] (klĭp) *n.* **1.** A device that grips or clasps : fastener. **2.** A holder for rifle cartridges. *—v.* **clipped, clip•ping. 1.** To grip tightly. **2.** To join (one thing) to another. **3.** To block (an opponent in football) illegally.
clip•board (klĭp'bôrd', -bōrd') *n.* A small writing board with a clip at the top for holding papers or a pad.
clip joint *n. Slang.* A place, as a restaurant, where customers are overcharged.
clip•per (klĭp'ər) *n.* **1.** *often* **clippers.** An implement for clipping or shearing. **2.** A very fast sailing vessel.
clip•ping (klĭp'ĭng) *n.* Something, as a newspaper item, that is clipped off or out.
clique (klēk, klĭk) *n.* An exclusive and usu. small group of people. **—clique** *v.* **—cliqu'ey, cliqu'y** *adj.*
clit•o•ris (klĭt'ər-ĭs, klī'tər-) *n.* A small organ at the upper end of the vulva, homologous with the penis. **—clit'o•ral** *adj.*
clk. *abbr.* clerk.
cloak (klōk) *n.* **1.** A loose outer garment. **2.** Something that covers or conceals. *—v.* **1.** To cover with or as if with a cloak. **2.** To hide : conceal.
cloak-and-dag•ger (klōk'ən-dăg'ər) *adj.* Characterized by or suggesting spying and intrigue.
clob•ber (klŏb'ər) *v. Slang.* **1.** To strike violently and repeatedly. **2.** To defeat decisively.
cloche (klōsh) *n.* A woman's close-fitting, bell-shaped hat.
clock[1] (klŏk) *n.* An instrument other than a watch for measuring or indicating time. *—v.* To time the speed of.
clock[2] (klŏk) *n.* A decorative design on a sock or stocking.
clock•wise (klŏk'wīz') *adv.* In the direction in which the hands of a clock rotate. **—clock'wise'** *adj.*
clock•work (klŏk'wûrk') *n.* The delicate and accurate mechanism of a clock.
clod (klŏd) *n.* **1.** A lump of clay or earth. **2.** An ignorant or stupid person : dolt. **—clod'dish** *adj.*
clod•hop•per (klŏd'hŏp'ər) *n.* **1.** A clumsy country fellow : lout. **2.** A large heavy shoe.
clog (klŏg) *n.* **1.** An obstacle or hindrance. **2.** A weight attached, as to the leg of an animal, so as to hinder motion. **3.** A heavy usu. wooden-soled shoe. *—v.* **clogged, clog•ging. 1.** To make or become obstructed. **2.** To hinder with a clog : impede.
cloi•son•né (kloi'zə-nā', klə-wä'-) *n.* Decorative enamelware in which different colors of enamel are poured into areas separated by thin strips of metal.
clois•ter (kloi'stər) *n.* **1.** A covered walk usu. with a colonnade running along the side of a court. **2.** A monastery or convent. *—v.* To confine in or as if in a cloister. **—clois'tral** (-strəl) *adj.*
clomp (klŏmp) *v.* To walk noisily.
clone (klōn) *n.* **1. a.** A group of genetically identical cells descended from a single common ancester. **b.** One or more organisms descended asexually from a single ancestor. **2.** One that is an exact replica of another. *—v.* **cloned, clon•ing.** To duplicate (an organism) asexually. **—clon'al** *adj.*
clop (klŏp) *n.* The sound of a horse's hoofs or a wooden shoe against a pavement. **—clop** *v.*
close (klōs) *adj.* **clos•er, clos•est. 1.** Near, as in time, space, or relation. **2.** With little or no space between elements or parts. **3.** Very short <a *close* haircut> **4.** Nearly even, as a game. **5.** Fitting tightly. **6.** Much like an original : accurate <a *close* copy> **7.** Strict : rigorous <paid *close* attention> **8.** Not open : shut. **9.** Confined in space. **10.** Restricted to specific persons. **11.** Hidden from view : secluded. **12.** Stingy : miserly. **13.** Lacking fresh air : stuffy. *—v.* (klōz) **closed, clos•ing. 1.** To shut or become shut. **2.** To stop or fill up. **3.** To bring or come to an end : terminate. **4.** To bring into contact : join. **5.** To discontinue operations, as of a store. **6.** To reach an agreement. **—close out.** To dispose of, usu. at a reduced price. *—n.* (klōz). An end : conclusion. *—adv.* (klōs). In a close position : near. **—close'ly** (klōs'lē) *adv.* **—close'ness** (klōs'nĭs) *n.*
close call (klōs) *n. Informal.* A narrow escape.
closed circuit *n.* Television with a signal transmitted by wire to a limited number of reception stations.
closed shop *n.* A union shop.
close-fist•ed (klōs'fĭs'tĭd) *adj.* Miserly.
close-knit (klōs'nĭt') *adj.* Closely attached by familial, cultural, or social ties.
close-mouthed (klōs'mouthd', -moutht') *adj.* Discreet and circumspect in speaking.
close-out (klōz'out') *n.* A sale in which all of a business's stock is disposed of at reduced prices.
clos•et (klŏz'ĭt) *n.* **1.** A small compartment, cabinet, or room for storage. **2.** A small private room, as for study. *—v.* To shut up in a private room, as for discussion.
close-up (klōs'ŭp') *n.* **1.** A photograph taken at close range. **2.** A close examination or view.
clo•sure (klō'zhər) *n.* **1.** The act of closing or condition of being closed. **2.** Something that closes. **3.** Cloture.
clot (klŏt) *n.* A thick or solid mass formed from liquid that has thickened and coagulated. **—clot** *v.*
cloth (klôth, klŏth) *n., pl.* **cloths** (klôths, klô*th*z, klŏths, klŏ*th*z). **1.** Material produced by weaving, knitting, or matting natural or synthetic fibers : fabric. **2.** A piece of cloth used for a special purpose, as a tablecloth. **3. a.** Distinctive professional attire, esp. of the clergy. **b.** The clergy.
clothe (klō*th*) *v.* **clothed** *or* **clad** (klăd), **cloth•ing. 1.** To put clothes on or provide clothes for : dress. **2.** To cover as if with clothes : wrap.
clothes (klōz, klō*th*z) *pl.n.* **1.** Wearing apparel : garments. **2.** Bedclothes.
clothes•horse (klōz'hôrs', klō*th*z'-) *n.* One who is excessively concerned with clothing.
clothes•pin (klōz'pĭn, klō*th*z'-) *n.* A clip for fastening clothes to a line.
clothes•press *also* **clothes press** (klōz'prĕs', klō*th*z'-) *n.* A chest, closet, or wardrobe for clothes.
cloth•ier (klō*th*'yər, klō'*th*ē-ər) *n.* A manufacturer or seller of clothing or cloth.
cloth•ing (klō'*th*ĭng) *n.* CLOTHES 1.
clo•ture (klō'chər) *n.* A parliamentary procedure, as calling for an immediate vote, by which debate is limited or ended.
cloud (kloud) *n.* **1. a.** A visible body of fine drops of water or particles of ice in the air. **b.** A similar mass, as of smoke or dust in the air. **2.** A swarm. **3.** Something that looks or seems dark, gloomy, or threatening. *—v.* **1.** To cover or become covered with or as if with clouds. **2.** To tarnish : sully. **—cloud'i•ness** *n.* **—cloud'y** *adj.*
cloud•burst (kloud'bûrst') *n.* A sudden and very heavy rainstorm.
cloud nine *n.* A state of great happiness or elation.
†clout (klout) *n.* **1.** A heavy blow, esp. with the hand. **2.** *Informal.* Influence : pull. **3.** *Archaic & Regional.* A piece of cloth used for mending : patch. *—v.* **1.** To hit heavily, esp. with the hand. **2.** *Archaic & Regional.* To bandage or patch.
clove[1] (klōv) *n.* An evergreen tree, *Eugenia aromatica,* whose aromatic buds are dried for use as a spice.
▲word history: It may seem odd that garlic and the spice called "clove" in English should share the same name, but *clove[1]* and *clove[2]* are not at all related. *Clove[2]*, meaning "bulb section," comes from Old English *clufu,* a noun related to *clēofan,* "to split," the ancestor of *cleave[1]*. *Clove[1]* as a name for the spice is really a misnomer. The full name of the spice in Old French was *clou de girofle,* literally "nail of the clove tree," since the dried flower bud somewhat resembles a small nail. The English gradually shortened the phrase to *clow,* whose modern form is *clove.*
clove[2] (klōv) *n.* A small section of a separable bulb, as that of garlic.
clove[3] (klōv) *v. var. p.t. of* CLEAVE[1].

clo•ven (klō′vən) *v. var. p.p. of* CLEAVE[1].
clo•ver (klō′vər) *n.* A plant of the genus *Trifolium* bearing compound leaves with 3 leaflets and tight flower heads.
clo•ver•leaf (klō′vər-lēf′) *n.* An interchange at which highways cross each other on different levels and have curving access and exit ramps so that vehicles may go in any of 4 directions.
clown (kloun) *n.* **1.** A comedian who entertains, as at a circus. **2.** A coarse, rude person : boor. *–v.* To behave like a clown. **–clown′ish** *adj.* **–clown′ish•ly** *adv.* **–clown′ish•ness** *n.*
cloy (kloi) *v.* To sicken or disgust with too much of something good, esp. of something rich or sweet. **–cloy′ing•ly** *adv.*
club (klŭb) *n.* **1.** A heavy stick of wood used as a weapon. **2.** A stick used to hit a ball in certain games : bat. **3.** One of a suit of playing cards marked with a black figure shaped like a clover leaf. **4.** A group of persons organized together for a common purpose. **5.** The meeting place of a club. *–v.* **clubbed, club•bing. 1.** To hit or beat with a club. **2.** To join or combine for a common purpose.
club•foot (klŭb′fŏŏt′) *n.* **1.** A congenital deformity of the foot in which the front of the foot is twisted out of position. **2.** A foot with clubfoot. **–club′foot′ed** *adj.*
club•house (klŭb′hous′) *n.* **1.** A building occupied by a club. **2.** The locker rooms for an athletic team.
club sandwich *n.* A sandwich usu. made of 3 slices of bread and meat, tomato, lettuce, and dressing.
club soda *n.* Carbonated water.
cluck (klŭk) *n.* The low, short call of a brooding hen. **–cluck** *v.*
clue *also* **clew** (klōō). *–n.* A guide in the solution of a mystery. *–v.* **clued, clue•ing** *or* **clu•ing** *also* **clewed, clew•ing.** To give information <*clued* him in>
clump (klŭmp) *n.* **1.** A thick group, as of trees : cluster. **2.** A heavy dull sound. *–v.* **1.** To walk with a clump. **2.** To form or cause to form clumps.
clum•sy (klŭm′zē) *adj.* **-si•er, -si•est. 1.** Lacking dexterity, coordination, or grace. **2.** Not skillful or tactful : inept. **–clum′si•ly** *adv.* **–clum′si•ness** *n.*
clung (klŭng) *v. p.t. & p.p. of* CLING.
clunk (klŭngk) *n.* **1.** A dull sound : thump. **2.** A hefty blow. **–clunk** *v.*
clunk•er (clŭng′kər) *n.* **1.** A broken-down car. **2.** A flop : failure.
clus•ter (klŭs′tər) *n.* A group : bunch. *–v.* To gather or grow in a cluster.
cluster headache *n.* A severe headache that can occur several times daily.
clutch (klŭch) *v.* To seize or attempt to seize and hold tightly. *–n.* **1.** A hand, claw, talon, or paw in the act of seizing. **2.** *often* **clutches.** Power or control. **3.** A device for connecting and disconnecting 2 sections of a rotating shaft or of a shaft and a driving mechanism. **4.** A crucial or tense situation.
clut•ter (klŭt′ər) *n.* A confused disorder. *–v.* To fill so as to hamper movement or lower efficiency : litter.
Clydes•dale (klīdz′dāl′) *n.* A large, powerful draft horse.
Cm *symbol for* CURIUM.
cm *abbr.* centimeter.
cml. *abbr.* commercial.
co– *pref.* **1.** With : together <*co*exist> **2.** Partner : associate <*co*worker> See below for a list of self-explanatory words formed with the prefix **co–.**
Co *symbol for* COBALT.
CO *abbr.* Colorado (with Zip Code).
co. *abbr.* **1.** company. **2.** county.
c.o. *abbr.* **1.** *also* **c/o** care of. **2.** carried over. **3.** cash order.
coach (kōch) *n.* **1.** A closed 4-wheeled carriage. **2.** A closed automobile usu. with 4 doors. **3.** A bus. **4.** A railroad passenger car. **5.** A trainer of athletes or athletic teams. **6.** A private instructor. *–v.* To teach, train, or act as a coach.
coach•man (kōch′mən) *n.* A man who drives a carriage or coach.
co•ad•ju•tor (kō′ə-jōō′tər, kō-ăj′ə-tər) *n.* An assistant, esp. to a bishop.
co•ag•u•lant (kō-ăg′yə-lənt) *n.* A substance that causes coagulation.
co•ag•u•late (kō-ăg′yə-lāt′) *v.* **-lat•ed, -lat•ing.** To form a soft, semisolid, or solid mass. **–co•ag′u•la•ble** *adj.* **–co•ag′u•la′tion** *n.* **–co•ag′u•la′tor** *n.*
coal (kōl) *n.* **1.** A natural black carbonaceous solid used as a fuel. **2.** An ember. *–v.* To supply with or take on coal.
co•a•lesce (kō′ə-lĕs′) *v.* **-lesced, -lesc•ing.** To grow or come together into one. **–co′a•les′cence** *n.* **–co′a•les′cent** *adj.*
coal gas *n.* A gas distilled from bituminous coal, used as commercial fuel.
co•a•li•tion (kō′ə-lĭsh′ən) *n.* An alliance, esp. a temporary one. **–co′a•li′tion•ist** *n.*
coal tar *n.* Tar distilled from bituminous coal and used esp. in dyes and drugs.
coam•ing (kō′mĭng) *n.* A raised curb or rim around an opening, as in a ship's deck, designed to keep out water.
co–an•chor (kō-ăng′kər) *n.* Either of 2 principle news commentators on a broadcast. **–co–an′chor** *v.*
coarse (kôrs, kōrs) *adj.* **coars•er, coars•est. 1.** Of low or inferior quality. **2.** Lacking refinement. **3.** Consisting of large particles <*coarse* sand> **4.** Harsh. ☆**syns:** BOORISH, CHURLISH, CRASS, CRUDE, GROSS, PHILISTINE, RAW, ROUGH, RUDE, TASTELESS, UNCOUTH, VULGAR
coars•en (kôr′sən, kōr′-) *v.* To make or become coarse.
coast (kōst) *n.* **1.** The seashore. **2.** The act of sliding down a slope. *–v.* To move, as down an incline on a sled, without further acceleration. **–coast′al** *adj.*
coast•er (kō′stər) *n.* **1.** One that coasts. **2.** A small disk used to protect a surface.
coaster brake *n.* A brake and clutch operating on the rear wheel and drive mechanism of a bicycle when pedaling is reversed.
coast guard *n.* The military or naval force patrolling a nation's coast.
coast•line (kōst′līn′) *n.* The shape or outline of a coast.
coat (kōt) *n.* **1.** An outer garment of varying length covering the upper part of the body. **2.** A natural outer covering, as of fur, on an animal. **3.** A layer of covering material. *–v.* To cover with a coat, as of paint. **–coat′ed** *adj.* **–coat′ing** *n.*
coat of arms *n.* Heraldic bearings, as of a family, usu. blazoned on a shield.
coat of mail *n.* An armored garment made of chain mail.
coat•tail (kōt′tāl′) *n.* **1.** The loose back part of a coat below the waist. **2. coattails.** The skirts of a formal or dress coat.
coax (kōks) *v.* **1.** To try to persuade by gentle urging. **2.** To obtain by coaxing : wheedle. ☆**syns:** BLANDISH, CAJOLE, SOFTSOAP, SWEET-TALK, WHEEDLE **–coax′er** *n.*
co•ax•i•al (kō-ăk′sē-əl) *adj.* **1.** Having a common axis. **2.** Of or designating a transmission cable composed of a conducting tube enclosed within another separated by insulation.
cob (kŏb) *n.* **1.** A corncob. **2.** A male swan. **3.** A thickset short-legged horse.
co•balt (kō′bôlt′) *n. Symbol* **Co** A hard, brittle metallic element that resembles nickel and iron.
cob•ble (kŏb′əl) *v.* **-bled, -bling. 1.** To mend or make (boots or shoes). **2.** To make or put together clumsily.
cob•bler[1] (kŏb′lər) *n.* A mender of boots or shoes.
cob•bler[2] (kŏb′lər) *n.* A deep-dish fruit pie with no bottom crust and a thick top crust.
cob•ble•stone (kŏb′əl-stōn′) *n.* A naturally rounded stone once used for paving.
CO•BOL *or* **Co•bol** (kō′bôl′) *n. Computer Sci.* A programming language that is based on English.
co•bra (kō′brə) *n.* A venomous Asian or African snake of the

coadminister
coagency
coagent
coapprove
coarrange
coassist
co-author
coconspirator
cocontributor
codefendant
coderive
codirect
codirector
codiscover
coeditor
coequal
coequality
coequally
coestablish
coexecutor
cofeature
cofinance
cofound
cofounder
coheir
coheiress
cohost
cohostess
coinhabit
coinheritor
coinventor
coinvestigator
coinvolve
cojoin
coleader
co-occupy
co-occur
co-occurrence
co-owner
copartner
copartnership
copayment
coproduce
coproducer
coproduction
copublish
copublisher
corecipient
coresidence
cosovereign
cosponsor
cosponsorship
cotrustee
cowinner
coworker
cowriter

genus *Naja* that is able to expand the skin of the neck into a flattened hood.
cob•web (kŏb′wĕb′) *n.* **1. a.** The web spun by a spider to catch its prey. **b.** A single thread of a spider's web. **2.** Something resembling a cobweb, as in intricacy.
co•caine *also* **co•cain** (kō-kān′, kō′kān′) *n.* A psychologically addictive drug that is extracted from a South American tree and used as a local anesthetic.
coc•cus (kŏk′əs) *n., pl.* **coc•ci** (kŏk′sī′). A bacterium that is spherical in shape.
coc•cyx (kŏk′sĭks) *n., pl.* **coc•cy•ges** (kŏk-sī′jēz, kŏk′sĭ-jēz′). A small bone at the end of the spinal column.
coch•i•neal (kŏch′ə-nēl′) *n.* A brilliant red dye made from the dried pulverized bodies of a tropical American scale insect, *Dactylopius coccus.*
coch•le•a (kŏk′lē-ə) *n., pl.* **-le•ae** (-lē-ē′). A spiral tube of the inner ear resembling a snail shell and having nerve endings necessary for hearing. **—coch′le•ar** (-lē-ər) *adj.*
cock (kŏk) *n.* **1. a.** The adult male of the domestic fowl : rooster. **b.** A male bird. **2.** A faucet or valve for regulating the flow of a liquid. **3. a.** The hammer of a firearm. **b.** The position of the hammer when a firearm is ready for firing. *—v.* **1.** To set the hammer of (a firearm) in firing position. **2.** To tilt or turn, esp. to one side. **3.** To raise in preparation for throwing or hitting.
cock•ade (kŏ-kād′) *n.* An ornament, as a rosette, usu. worn on a hat as a badge.
cock•a•ma•mie *also* **cock•a•ma•my** (kŏk′ə-mā′mē) *adj. Slang.* **1.** Nearly valueless : trifling. **2.** Nonsensical : ludicrous.
cock•a•tiel *also* **cock•a•teel** (kŏk′ə-tēl′) *n.* A crested Australian parrot, *Nymphicus hollandicus,* with gray and yellow plumage.
cock•a•too (kŏk′ə-too͞′) *n.* A crested Australian parrot of the genus *Kakatoe.*
cock•a•trice (kŏk′ə-trĭs, -trīs′) *n.* A mythical serpent with a lethal glance.
cock•chaf•er (kŏk′chā′fər) *n.* An Old World beetle of the family Scarabaeidae, esp. one that is destructive to plants.
cock•crow (kŏk′krō′) *n.* Dawn.
cocked hat *n.* A three-cornered hat.
cock•er•el (kŏk′ər-əl) *n.* A young rooster.
cock•er spaniel (kŏk′ər) *n.* A spaniel with long, drooping ears and a silky coat.
cock•eye (kŏk′ī′) *n.* A squinting eye.
cock•eyed (kŏk′īd′) *adj.* **1.** Cross-eyed. **2.** *Slang.* **a.** Crooked : awry. **b.** Absurd.
cock•fight (kŏk′fīt′) *n.* A fight between gamecocks that are usu. fitted with metal spurs. **—cock′fight′ing** *n.*
cock•le[1] (kŏk′əl) *n.* Any of various bivalve mollusks of the family Cardiidae with shells having radiating ribs.
cock•le[2] (kŏk′əl) *n.* Any of several plants often growing as weeds in grain fields.
cock•le•shell (kŏk′əl-shĕl′) *n.* **1.** The shell of a cockle. **2.** A small, light boat.
cock•ney (kŏk′nē) *n., pl.* **-neys. 1.** *often* **Cockney.** A native of London's East End. **2.** The dialect of the cockneys.
cock•pit (kŏk′pĭt′) *n.* The space in an aircraft for the pilot and crew.
cock•roach (kŏk′rōch′) *n.* A flat-bodied insect of the family Blattidae that is a common household pest.
cocks•comb (kŏks′kōm′) *n.* The fleshy comb on the head of a rooster.
cock•sure (kŏk′sho͝or′) *adj.* **1.** Absolutely sure. **2.** Overconfident.
cock•tail (kŏk′tāl′) *n.* **1.** A mixed alcoholic drink. **2.** An appetizer, as seafood.
cock•y (kŏk′ē) *adj.* **-i•er, -i•est.** Excessively self-confident : conceited. **—cock′i•ly** *adv.* **—cock′i•ness** *n.*
co•co (kō′kō) *n., pl.* **-cos. 1.** The coconut. **2.** The coconut palm.
co•coa (kō′kō) *n.* **1.** A powder made from roasted ground cacao seeds from which much of the fat has been removed. **2.** A hot drink made with cocoa powder, water or milk, and sugar.

▲word history: The confusion of *cocoa* with *coco* can be traced to Samuel Johnson's great dictionary, published in 1755. Johnson himself maintained the distinction between the 2 words in his own writing, but by some editorial or printing error the definitions for *coco* and *cocoa* were printed together under the word *cocoa.* That was unfortunate, because *coco* and *cocoa* are 2 different words that refer to 2 different trees. The cacao tree of tropical America produces both cocoa and chocolate. The name *cacao* comes from Nahuatl (Aztec) *cachuatl* and *chocolate* from Nahuatl *xocolatl. The word cocoa* is simply a variant spelling of *cacao.* The coconut or coco palm originated in the East Indies. Its name is not a native name like *cacao* but comes from Portuguese *coco,* "goblin," referring to the facelike appearance of the three holes at the bottom of the fruit.

cocoa butter *n.* A yellowish-white, waxy solid obtained from cacao seeds and used esp. in pharmaceuticals and soap.
co•co•nut *also* **co•coa•nut** (kō′kə-nŭt′, -nət) *n.* The fruit of the coconut palm, a large hard-shelled seed enclosing edible white meat and a milky fluid.
coconut palm *n.* A tall palm tree, *Cocos nucifera,* bearing coconuts as fruit.
co•coon (kə-ko͞on′) *n.* The protective silk or fiber pupal case spun by insect larvae.
cod[1] (kŏd) *n., pl.* **cod** *or* **cods.** An important food fish, *Gadus morhua* or *G. callarias,* of N Atlantic waters.
†**cod**[2] (kŏd) *n.* **1.** *Regional.* A husk or pod. **2.** *Obs.* A bag. **3.** *Archaic.* The scrotum.
COD *or* **C.O.D.** *abbr.* **1.** cash on delivery. **2.** collect on delivery.
co•da (kō′də) *n.* A section that concludes a musical composition.
cod•dle (kŏd′l) *v.* **-dled, -dling. 1.** To cook in simmering water just below the boiling point. **2.** To treat overindulgently.
code (kōd) *n.* **1.** A comprehensive and systematically arranged body of law. **2.** A system of rules of conduct or procedures <an ethical *code*> **3.** A system of signals used in communication. **4.** An arbitrary system of symbols or letters for transmitting esp. secret messages. **—code** *v.*
co•deine (kō′dēn′, -dē-ĭn) *n.* An alkaloid narcotic obtained from opium or morphine and used esp. to relieve pain.
co•dex (kō′dĕks′) *n., pl.* **co•di•ces** (kō′dĭ-sēz′, kŏd′ĭ-). A manuscript volume, esp. a work of the Scriptures or the classics.
cod•fish (kŏd′fĭsh′) *n.* The cod.
codg•er (kŏj′ər) *n. Informal.* An odd or somewhat eccentric fellow.
cod•i•cil (kŏd′ĭ-səl) *n.* A supplement or appendix that modifies a will. **—cod′i•cil′la•ry** (-sĭl′ə-rē) *adj.*
cod•i•fy (kŏd′ə-fī′, kō′də-) *v.* **-fied, -fy•ing.** To arrange systematically. **—cod′i•fi•ca′tion** *n.*
co•ed (kō′ĕd′) *n. Informal.* A woman student at a coeducational college or university. **—co′ed′** *adj.*
co•ed•u•ca•tion (kō′ĕj-o͞o-kā′shən) *n.* The system of education in which both men and women attend the same institution. **—co′ed•u•ca′tion•al** *adj.*
co•ef•fi•cient (kō′ə-fĭsh′ənt) *n.* **1.** A number by which another number or an algebraic term is multiplied : factor. **2.** A numerical measure of a physical or chemical property that is constant for a system under given conditions.
coe•len•ter•ate (sĭ-lĕn′tə-rāt′, -tər-ĭt) *n.* An invertebrate animal of the phylum Coelenterata, which includes the jellyfishes, hydras, sea anemones, and corals.
co•erce (kō-ûrs′) *v.* **-erced, -erc•ing. 1.** To compel to a course of action or thought. **2.** To dominate or restrain forcibly. **3.** To bring about by threat or force. **—co•er′cion** *n.* **—co•er′cive** *adj.*
co•e•val (kō-ē′vəl) *adj.* Of or originating in the same period of time. **—co•e′val** *n.*
co•ex•ist (kō′ĭg-zĭst′) *v.* **1.** To exist together or at the same time. **2.** To live peaceably with others in spite of differences. **—co′ex•is′tence** *n.*
co•ex•ten•sive (kō′ĭk-stĕn′sĭv) *adj.* Having the same boundaries, limits, or range. **—co′ex•ten′sive•ly** *adv.*
cof•fee (kô′fē, kŏf′ē) *n.* **1.** A beverage prepared from the beanlike seeds of a tropical tree of the genus *Coffea.* **2.** The seeds from which coffee is made.
coffee cake *n.* A cake made of sweetened yeast dough, often shaped into a ring or braid and containing nuts or raisins.
cof•fee•house (kô′fē-hous′, kŏf′ē-) *n.* A restaurant at which coffee and refreshments are sold.
coffee klatch (klăch, kläch) *n.* A gathering for coffee and casual conversation.
cof•fee•pot (kô′fē-pŏt′, kŏf′ē-) *n.* A utensil used for brewing or serving coffee.
coffee shop *n.* A small restaurant serving light meals.
coffee table *n.* A low table that is usu. placed before a sofa.
cof•fer (kô′fər, kŏf′ər) *n.* **1.** A strongbox. **2.** *often* **coffers.** Financial resources.
cof•fer•dam (kô′fər-dăm′, kŏf′ər-) *n.* A temporary enclosure that is pumped dry to expose the bottom of a body of water so that construction may be undertaken.
cof•fin (kô′fĭn, kŏf′ĭn) *n.* A box in which a corpse can be buried.
cog (kŏg) *n.* One of the teeth on the rim of a gear or wheel.
co•gent (kō′jənt) *adj.* Compelling : convincing. **—co′gen•cy** (-jən-sē) *n.*
cog•i•tate (kŏj′ĭ-tāt′) *v.* **-tat•ed, -tat•ing.** To ponder or think carefully about. **—cog′i•ta′tion** *n.* **—cog′i•ta′tive** *adj.*

co·gnac (kōn′yăk′, kŏn′-) *n.* A fine brandy, esp. from the vicinity of Cognac in W France.
cog·nate (kŏg′nāt′) *adj.* **1.** Descended from a common ancestor, esp. linguistically akin. **2.** Similar or identical in nature. **—cog′nate′** *n.* **—cog·na′tion** *n.*
cog·ni·tion (kŏg-nĭsh′ən) *n.* **1.** The mental process or faculty of knowing. **2.** Knowledge. **—cog′ni·tive** (kŏg′nĭ-tĭv) *adj.*
cog·ni·zance (kŏg′nĭ-zəns) *n.* **1.** Conscious recognition : awareness. **2.** Heed : notice. **—cog′ni·zant** *adj.*
cog·no·men (kŏg-nō′mən) *n., pl.* **-mens** or **-nom·i·na** (-nŏm′ə-nə). **1.** A surname. **2.** A nickname.
co·gno·scen·te (kŏn′yə-shĕn′tē, kŏg′nə-) *n., pl.* **-ti** (-tē). A connoisseur.
cog railway *n.* A railway designed to climb steep slopes by means of a cogwheel.
cog·wheel (kŏg′hwēl′, -wēl′) *n.* A wheel with cogs.
co·hab·it (kō-hăb′ĭt) *v.* **1.** To live together as spouses. **2.** To live together as lovers when not married. **—co·hab′i·ta′tion** *n.*
co·here (kō-hîr′) *v.* **-hered, -her·ing.** To hold or stick together.
co·her·ent (kō-hîr′ənt, -hĕr′-) *adj.* **1.** Holding or sticking together : cohering. **2.** Marked by logical consistency. **—co·her′ence** *n.* **—co·her′ent·ly** *adv.*
co·he·sion (kō-hē′zhən) *n.* **1.** The act, process, quality, or state of cohering. **2.** *Physics.* Mutual attraction by which the elements or particles of a body are held together. **—co·he′sive** *adj.* **—co·he′sive·ly** *adv.* **—co·he′sive·ness** *n.*
co·hort (kō′hôrt′) *n.* **1.** A group of people united in an effort or difficulty. **2.** *Informal.* A companion or associate.
co·ho salmon (kō′hō) *n.* A food and game fish, *Oncorhyncus kisutch,* orig. of Pacific waters.
coif (koif) *n.* **1.** A tight-fitting hat. **2.** A coiffure.
coif·feur (kwä-fûr′) *n.* A hairdresser.
coif·feuse (kwä-fûrz′, -fyo͞oz′) *n.* A woman hairdresser.
coif·fure (kwä-fyo͝or′) *n.* A hair style.
coil (koil) *n.* **1.** A series of connected spirals or concentric rings, as of wire. **2.** A spiral or ring. *—v.* To wind in spirals.
coin (koin) *n.* A usu. flat and round piece of metal issued by a government as money. *—v.* **1.** To make (coins) from metal : mint. **2.** To invent (a word or expression).
coin·age (koi′nĭj) *n.* **1.** The act or process of coining. **2.** Metal currency : coins. **3.** A coined word or expression.
co·in·cide (kō′ĭn-sīd′) *v.* **-cid·ed, -cid·ing.** **1.** To be in the same position in space. **2.** To occur at the same time. **3.** To correspond exactly.
co·in·ci·dence (kō-ĭn′sĭ-dəns, -dĕns′) *n.* **1.** Exact correspondence. **2.** A seemingly planned sequence of accidentally occurring events. **—co·in′ci·den′tal, co·in′ci·dent** *adj.* **—co·in′ci·den′tal·ly** *adv.*
co·i·tus (kō′ĭ-təs) *n.* Physical union of male and female sexual organs, leading to orgasm and ejaculation of semen. **—co′i·tal** *adj.*
coitus in·ter·rup·tus (ĭn′tə-rŭp′təs) *n.* Sexual intercourse purposely interrupted by withdrawal of the male prior to ejaculation.
coke (kōk) *n.* The solid carbonaceous residue obtained from bituminous coal after removal of volatile material, used as fuel and in making steel.
col. *abbr.* **1.** collect; collected; collector. **2.** college; collegiate. **3.** column.
co·la[1] (kō′lə) *n.* A carbonated soft drink flavored with an extract from kola nuts.
co·la[2] (kō′lə) *n. var. pl. of* COLON[2].
col·an·der (kŭl′ən-dər, kŏl′-) *n.* A perforated kitchen utensil for draining food.
cold (kōld) *adj.* **1.** Having a low subnormal temperature. **2.** Feeling uncomfortably chilled. **3.** Lacking warmth of emotion. **4.** *Informal.* Unconscious. ☆**syns:** CHILLY, FRIGID, GLADIAL, ICY *—adv.* Totally : thoroughly. *—n.* **1.** A condition of low air temperature. **2.** The sensation of being uncomfortably chilled. **3.** A viral infection of the respiratory passages.
cold-blood·ed (kōld′blŭd′ĭd) *adj.* **1.** Having a body temperature that varies according to the temperature of the surroundings, as reptiles. **2.** Lacking or done without feeling or emotion. **—cold′blood′ed·ly** *adv.*
cold cream *n.* A creamy cosmetic preparation for cleansing and softening the skin.
cold cuts *pl.n.* Assorted sliced cold meats.
cold front *n.* The leading edge of a cold air mass.
cold-heart·ed (kōld′här′tĭd) *adj.* Characterized by lack of sympathy or feeling : callous. **—cold′-heart′ed·ly** *adv.*
cold shoulder *n.* Deliberately cold treatment. **—cold′shoul′der** *v.*
cold sore *n.* A small sore on the lips that is caused by a virus and often accompanies a fever or cold.
cold sweat *n.* Simultaneous chill and perspiration, usu. caused by fear or shock.
cold turkey *n. Informal.* Sudden withdrawal from the use of an addictive drug.
cold war *n.* A conflict between nations that stops short of actual warfare.
cold welding *n.* Welding of two materials under high pressure or vacuum without using heat. **—cold′-weld′** *v.*
cole (kōl) *n.* A plant, as the cabbage or rape, of the genus *Brassica.*
cole·slaw *also* **cole slaw** (kōl′slô′) *n.* A salad made of shredded raw cabbage.
col·ic (kŏl′ĭk) *n.* A sharp, sudden pain in the abdomen. **—col′ick·y** *adj.*
col·i·se·um (kŏl′ĭ-sē′əm) *n.* A large amphitheater used esp. for sports events.
co·li·tis (kō-lī′tĭs, kə-) *n.* Inflammation of the mucous membrane of the colon.
col·lab·o·rate (kə-lăb′ə-rāt′) *v.* **-rat·ed, -rat·ing.** **1.** To work with others. **2.** To cooperate with an enemy that has invaded one's country. **—col·lab′o·ra′tion** *n.* **—col·lab′o·ra′tor** *n.*
col·lage (kō-läzh′, kə-) *n.* An artistic composition consisting of materials, as cloth or paper, pasted on a surface.
col·lapse (kə-lăps′) *v.* **-lapsed, -laps·ing.** **1.** To fall down or in suddenly. **2.** To cease to function, esp. suddenly. **3.** To disintegrate. **4.** To fold together compactly. **—col·lapse′** *n.* **—col·laps′i·ble** *adj.*
col·lar (kŏl′ər) *n.* **1.** The part of a garment that encircles the neck. **2.** A strip or band, as of lace, at the neckline of a garment. **3.** Something that resembles a collar. *—v.* **1.** To seize by or as if by the collar. **2.** *Informal.* To arrest.
col·lar·bone (kŏl′ər-bōn′) *n. Anat.* The clavicle.
col·lard (kŏl′ərd) *n. often* **collards.** A smooth-leaved variety of kale, *Brassica oleracea acephala.*
col·late (kə-lāt′, kō-, kŏl′āt′) *v.* **-lat·ed, -lat·ing.** **1.** To compare (e.g., texts) carefully. **2.** To assemble in correct sequence.
col·lat·er·al (kə-lăt′ər-əl) *adj.* **1.** Side by side. **2.** Serving to corroborate or support. **3.** Secondary : subordinate. **4.** Of or being property used as security for the performance of an obligation. **5.** Descended from a common ancestor but through a different line. *—n.* Property used as security for an obligation, as a loan.
col·la·tion (kə-lā′shən, kŏ-, kō-) *n.* **1.** The act of collating. **2.** A light meal.
col·league (kŏl′ēg′) *n.* A fellow member of a profession, staff, or academic faculty.
col·lect[1] (kə-lĕkt′) *v.* **1.** To bring or gather together in a group : assemble. **2.** To accumulate from a number of sources <*collect* coins> **3.** To obtain payment of. *—adj. & adv.* With payment to be made by the receiver. **—col·lect′i·ble, col·lect′a·ble** *adj.* **—col·lec′tion** *n.* **—col·lec′tor** *n.*
col·lect[2] (kŏl′ĭkt, -ĕkt′) *n.* A brief variable prayer used before the epistle at Mass.
col·lect·ed (kə-lĕk′tĭd) *adj.* Composed : self-possessed.
col·lec·tive (kə-lĕk′tĭv) *adj.* **1.** Made or formed by collecting. **2.** Of or made by a number of individuals acting as a group <a *collective* plan> *—n.* **1.** A cooperative business or undertaking, usu. under government supervision. **2.** A collective noun.
collective bargaining *n.* Negotiation between the representatives of union workers and their employer.
collective noun *n.* A noun denoting a group of persons or things considered as a unit.
col·lec·tiv·ism (kə-lĕk′tə-vĭz′əm) *n.* A system under which ownership and control of the means of producing and distributing goods is in the hands of the people collectively. **—col·lec′tiv·ist** *n.* **—col·lec′tiv·is′tic** *adj.* **—col·lec′tiv·is′ti·cal·ly** *adv.*
col·leen (kō-lēn′, kŏl′ēn′) *n.* An Irish girl.
col·lege (kŏl′ĭj) *n.* **1. a.** A school of higher learning that grants the degree of bachelor. **b.** An undergraduate school or division of a university. **c.** A professional school, often connected with a university <teachers *college*> **d.** The premises of a college. **2.** An assemblage with a common purpose or duties <a *college* of surgeons> **—col·le′giate** (kə-lē′jĭt, -jē-ĭt) *adj.*
col·le·gian (kə-lē′jən, -jē-ən) *n.* A student or recent graduate of college.
col·le·gi·um (kə-lē′jē-əm, -lĕg′ē-) *n., pl.* **-gi·a** (-lē′jē-ə, -lĕg′ē-ə) or **-ums.** An executive council of equally empowered members, esp. one in the Soviet Union.
col·lide (kə-līd′) *v.* **-lid·ed, -lid·ing.** **1.** To come together violently with direct impact. **2.** To be in opposition : clash. **—col·li′sion** (-lĭzh′ən) *n.*

col•lie (kŏl'ē) *n.* A large dog with long hair and a long, narrow muzzle, orig. bred in Scotland to herd sheep.
col•lier (kŏl'yər) *n. esp. Brit.* **1.** A coal miner. **2.** A coal ship.
col•lier•y (kŏl'yə-rē) *n., pl.* **-ies.** *esp. Brit.* A coal mine.
col•lin•e•ar (kə-lĭn'ē-ər, kō-) *adj.* **1.** Being on the same line. **2.** COAXIAL 1.
col•lo•cate (kŏl'ə-kāt') *v.* **-cat•ed, -cat•ing.** To place together in proper order : arrange. **—col'lo•ca'tion** *n.*
col•lo•di•on (kə-lō'dē-ən) *n.* A highly flammable syrupy solution of nitrocellulose in alcohol that hardens and is used for surgical dressings and photographic plates.
col•loid (kŏl'oid') *n.* A suspension of finely divided particles in a continuous medium, as a gaseous, liquid, or solid substance, that do not settle out of the substance and are not readily filtered. **—col•loid'al** *adj.*
col•lo•qui•al (kə-lō'kwē-əl) *adj.* **1.** Characteristic of or appropriate to informal speech and writing. **2.** Relating to conversation. **—col•lo'qui•al•ism** *n.*
col•lo•qui•um (kə-lō'kwē-əm) *n., pl.* **-ums** or **-qui•a** (-kwē-ə). A conference or seminar.
col•lo•quy (kŏl'ə-kwē) *n., pl.* **-quies. 1.** A conversation, esp. a formal one. **2.** A written dialogue.
col•lu•sion (kə-lo͞o'zhən) *n.* A secret agreement between 2 or more persons for a deceitful or illegal purpose. **—col•lu'sive** *adj.* **—col•lu'sive•ly** *adv.*
Colo. *abbr.* Colorado.
co•logne (kə-lōn') *n.* Eau de cologne.
Cologne. City of West Germany on the Rhine. *Pop.* 976,136.
Co•lom•bi•a (kə-lŭm'bē-ə). Country of NW South America. *Cap.* Bogotá. *Pop.* 22,551,811. **—Co•lom'bi•an** *adj.* & *n.*
Co•lom•bo (kə-lŭm'bō). Cap. of Sri Lanka, on the W coast. *Pop.* 1,540,000.
co•lon[1] (kō'lən) *n.* **1.** A punctuation mark (:) used after a word introducing a quotation, example, or series. **2.** The sign (:) used between numbers in expressions of time and ratios <2:30 A.M.><1:2>
co•lon[2] (kō'lən) *n., pl.* **-lons** or **-la** (-lə). The part of the large intestine extending from the cecum to the rectum. **—co•lon'ic** (kə-lŏn'ĭk) *adj.*
co•lon[3] (kō-lōn') *n., pl.* **-lons** or **-lo•nes** (-lō'nās'). See CURRENCY TABLE.
colo•nel (kûr'nəl) *n.* An officer in the U.S. Army, Air Force, or Marine Corps ranking above a lieutenant colonel and below a brigadier general. **—colo'nel•cy, colo'nel•ship'** *n.*
▲word history: The improbable pronunciation "kernel" for the word spelled *colonel* represents the triumph of popular speech over learned tinkering. The French form actually borrowed in the 16th cent. was *coronel,* from the Italian form *colonello.* The substitution of *r* for *l* in the French form is an example of dissimilation. By this process two similar or identical sounds, like the two *l* sounds in *colonello,* become less alike. In English usage *coronel* was respelled as *colonel,* with the original *l* restored, but the pronunciation based on this spelling did not win out over "kernel," which was the pronunciation of the older English form.
co•lo•ni•al (kə-lō'nē-əl) *adj.* **1.** Of, relating to, having, or inhabiting colonies. **2.** *often* **Colonial.** Of or relating to the 13 original American colonies. *—n.* An inhabitant of a colony.
co•lo•ni•al•ism (kə-lō'nē-ə-lĭz'əm) *n.* A governmental policy of controlling foreign dependencies. **—co•lo'ni•al•ist** *n.*
col•o•nist (kŏl'ə-nĭst) *n.* **1.** An original founder or settler of a colony. **2.** An inhabitant of a colony.
col•o•nize (kŏl'ə-nīz') *v.* **-nized, -niz•ing. 1.** To found a colony in. **2.** To settle in a colony. **—col'o•ni•za'tion** *n.*
col•on•nade (kŏl'ə-nād') *n.* A row of columns esp. supporting a roof.
col•o•ny (kŏl'ə-nē) *n., pl.* **-nies. 1.** A group of settlers in a new land who remain subject to the parent nation. **2.** A region ruled by a distant nation. **3.** A group with similar origins or interests or their living area. **4.** A group of similar organisms that live or grow together <an ant *colony*>
col•o•phon (kŏl'ə-fŏn', -fən) *n.* An inscription, usu. at the end of a book, giving publication facts.
col•or (kŭl'ər) *n.* **1.** The aspect of things that is caused by differing qualities of the light emitted or reflected by them. **2.** A substance, as a dye, pigment, or paint, that gives color. **3.** Skin tone : complexion. **4. colors.** A banner or flag, as of a nation or military group. **5.** Outward, often misleading appearance. **6.** Vivid or picturesque detail. *—v.* **1.** To give color to or change the color of. **2.** To give a distinctive quality to. **3.** To distort. **4.** To blush. **—col'or•er** *n.* **—col'or•less** *adj.* **—col'or•less•ly** *adv.*
Col•o•ra•do (kŏl'ə-rä'dō, -răd'ə). **1.** State of the WC U.S. *Cap.* Denver. *Pop.* 2,888,834. **2.** River rising in NC Colo. and flowing 1,450 mi (2,333) km) to the Gulf of California. **—Col'o•ra'dan** *adj.* & *n.*
col•or•a•tion (kŭl'ə-rā'shən) *n.* Arrangement or use of colors.
col•or•a•tu•ra (kŭl'ər-ə-to͝or'ə, -tyo͝or'ə) *n.* **1.** Ornate embellishment in vocal music. **2.** A soprano specializing in coloratura.
color bar *n.* Color line.
col•or•blind (kŭl'ər-blīnd') *adj.* Totally or partially unable to distinguish colors.
col•or•cast (kŭl'ər-kăst') *n.* A television program that is broadcast in color. **—col'or•cast'** *v.*
col•or-code (kŭl'ər-kōd') *v.* To color, as papers or wires, according to a code to facilitate identification.
col•ored (kŭl'ərd) *adj.* **1.** Having color. **2. a.** Of an ethnic group not considered as Caucasian, esp. Negro. **b.** Of mixed racial descent. **3.** Biased or distorted, as by incorrect data. **—col'ored** *n.*
col•or•fast (kŭl'ər-făst') *adj.* Having color that will not fade or run with wear or washing. **—col'or•fast'ness** *n.*
col•or•ful (kŭl'ər-fəl) *adj.* **1.** Full of color. **2.** Richly varied : vivid. ☆*syns:* BRIGHT, GAY, SHOWY, VIVID **—col'or•ful•ly** *adv.*
color line *n.* A social, legal, or economic barrier that separates nonwhite persons from whites.
co•los•sal (kə-lŏs'əl) *adj.* Gigantic in size or degree.
Co•los•sians (kə-lŏsh'ənz, -lŏs'ē-ənz) *pl.n.* (*sing. in number*) See BIBLE TABLE.
co•los•sus (kə-lŏs'əs) *n., pl.* **-los•si** (-lŏs'ī') or **-sus•es. 1.** A gigantic statue. **2.** Something extremely large or important.
co•los•to•my (kə-lŏs'tə-mē) *n., pl.* **-mies.** Surgical construction of an artificial excretory opening from the colon.
col•our (kŭl'ər) *n.* & *v. esp. Brit. var. of* COLOR.
colt (kōlt) *n.* A young male horse : foal. **—colt'ish** *adj.*
Co•lum•bi•a (kə-lŭm'bē-ə). **1.** Cap. of S.C., in the C part. *Pop.* 97,100. **2.** River of SE B.C., Canada, and the NW U.S.
col•um•bine (kŏl'əm-bīn') *n.* A plant of the genus *Aquilegia,* with variously colored flowers having spurred petals.
co•lum•bi•um (kə-lŭm'bē-əm) *n. Symbol* **Cb** Niobium.
Co•lum•bus (kə-lŭm'bəs). Cap. of Ohio, in the C part. *Pop.* 564,871.
Columbus, Christopher. 1451?–1506. Italian navigator; opened New World to exploration. **—Co•lum'bi•an** *adj.*
Columbus Day *n.* Oct. 12, a U.S. holiday celebrated officially on the 2nd Monday in Oct. to honor Columbus.
col•umn (kŏl'əm) *n.* **1.** A supporting or decorative pillar used in building. **2.** Something shaped or used like a pillar. **3.** A vertical section of typed or printed lines on a page. **4.** A feature article that appears regularly, as in a newspaper. **5.** A long row, as of troops. **—co•lum'nar** (kə-lŭm'nər) *adj.*
col•um•nist (kŏl'əm-nĭst, -ə-mĭst) *n.* A writer of a magazine or newspaper column.
com. or **Com.** *abbr.* commissioner.
co•ma (kō'mə) *n., pl.* **-mas.** A deep, prolonged unconsciousness usu. caused by injury, disease, or poison.
co•ma•tose (kō'mə-tōs', kŏm'ə-) *adj.* **1.** Unconscious. **2.** Lethargic.
comb (kōm) *n.* **1.** A thin, toothed strip of material, as plastic, used to arrange or fasten the hair. **2.** Something shaped or used like a comb. **3.** A fleshy crest on the top of the head of a fowl or certain other birds. **4.** A honeycomb. *—v.* **1.** To dress with or as if with a comb. **2.** To card (e.g., wool). **3.** To search thoroughly.
com•bat (kəm-băt', kŏm'băt') *v.* **-bat•ed, -bat•ing** *also* **-bat•ted, -bat•ting. 1.** To fight against in battle. **2.** To oppose or resist vigorously. *—n.* (kŏm'băt'). Fighting, esp. armed conflict : battle. **—com•bat'ant** *n.* **—com•bat'ive** *adj.*
combat fatigue *n.* A nervous disorder induced by combat and involving anxiety, depression, and irritability.
comb•er (kō'mər) *n.* **1.** One that combs. **2.** A long, cresting ocean wave.
com•bi•na•tion (kŏm'bə-nā'shən) *n.* **1.** The act or process of combining or state of being combined. **2.** A result of combining : aggregate. **3.** A sequence of letters or numbers needed to open certain locks.
com•bine (kəm-bīn') *v.* **-bined, -bin•ing. 1.** To make or become united : merge. **2.** *Chem.* To form a compound. *—n.* (kŏm'bīn'). **1.** A harvesting machine that cuts, threshes, and cleans grain. **2.** A group associated for commercial or political gain.
comb•ings (kō'mĭngz) *pl.n.* Material, as hairs or wool, removed with a comb.
combining form *n.* A word element that joins with other word forms to make compounds, e.g., *co-* in *coexist.*
com•bo (kŏm'bō) *n., pl.* **-bos.** A small band of musicians.
com•bus•ti•ble (kəm-bŭs'tə-bəl) *adj.* Capable of igniting and burning. *—n.* A combustible substance. **—com•bus'ti•bil'i•ty** *n.* **—com•bus'ti•bly** *adv.*
com•bus•tion (kəm-bŭs'chən) *n.* **1.** Theprocess of burning. **2.** A rapid chemical change, esp. oxidation, that produces light and heat. **—com•bus'tive** (-tĭv) *adj.*

come (kŭm) *v.* **came** (kām), **come, com•ing. 1.** To approach : advance. **2.** To arrive. **3.** To reach a certain state, position, or result. **4.** To move into view : appear. **5.** To exist at a particular place or point <Spring *comes* before summer.> **6.** To happen <How did you *come* to move here?> **7.** To spring from : originate. **8.** To be available <It *comes* in 3 colors.> **—come about.** To take place : happen. **—come across. 1.** To find or meet accidentally. **2.** *Slang.* To give or do what is wanted. **—come around (***or* **round). 1.** To recover. **2.** To alter one's opinion or standpoint. **—come into.** To inherit. **—come off.** To take place : happen. **—come out. 1.** To be revealed. **2.** To make a debut into society. **—come through. 1.** To succeed. **2.** *Informal.* To do what is expected. **—come to.** To recover consciousness. **—come up with.** *Informal.* To produce.

come•back (kŭm'băk') *n.* **1.** A return to former success or status. **2.** A quick reply.

co•me•di•an (kə-mē'dē-ən) *n.* **1.** A professional entertainer who uses verbal humor or performs comic acts. **2.** An actor in comedy. **3.** A comedy writer. **4.** One who tries to be amusing : clown.

co•me•di•enne (kə-mē'dē-ĕn') *n.* A woman who performs professionally as a comedian.

come•down (kŭm'doun') *n.* **1.** A decline in level or status. **2.** A source or feeling of disappointment or depression.

com•e•dy (kŏm'ĭ-dē) *n., pl.* **-dies. 1.** An amusing entertainment, as a play or motion picture, in which the characters may be humorous and that ends happily. **2.** A literary composition that has a humorous theme or uses the methods of comedy. **3.** A real-life comic occurrence or situation. **—co•me'dic** (kə-mē'dĭk) *adj.*

come•ly (kŭm'lē) *adj.* **-li•er, -li•est.** Good-looking. **—come'li•ness** *n.*

come-on (kŭm'ŏn', -ôn') *n.* Something that entices : inducement.

com•er (kŭm'ər) *n.* One that shows promise of achievement.

co•mes•ti•ble (kə-mĕs'tə-bəl) *adj.* Fit to be eaten. *—n.* Something edible.

com•et (kŏm'ĭt) *n.* A celestial body that orbits the sun and has a solid head surrounded by a brilliant cloud and a long, vaporous tail when the head nears the sun.

come•up•pance *also* **come•up•ance** (kŭm-ŭp'əns) *n. Informal.* Justly deserved punishment.

com•fit (kŭm'fĭt, kŏm'-) *n.* A candy.

com•fort (kŭm'fərt) *v.* To console in time of fear or grief. *—n.* **1.** A state of ease or well-being. **2.** Solace. **3.** Help : assistance <gave *comfort* to the enemy> **4.** One that brings relief or well-being. **5.** Capacity to give physical ease. **—com'fort•ing•ly** *adv.*

com•fort•a•ble (kŭm'fər-tə-bəl, kŭmf'tə-bəl) *adj.* **1.** Affording comfort. **2.** In a state of comfort. **3.** Adequate <a *comfortable* income> **—com'fort•a•bly** *adv.*

com•fort•er (kŭm'fər-tər) *n.* **1.** One that comforts. **2.** A heavy quilt.

comfort station *n.* A public rest room.

com•fy (kŭm'fē) *adj.* **-fi•er, -fi•est.** *Informal.* Comfortable.

com•ic (kŏm'ĭk) *adj.* **1.** Of or characteristic of comedy. **2.** Comical. *—n.* **1.** One who is comical, esp. a comedian. **2. comics.** *Informal.* Comic strips.

com•i•cal (kŏm'ĭ-kəl) *adj.* Humorous : amusing. **—com'i•cal'i•ty, com'i•cal•ness** *n.* **—com'i•cal•ly** *adv.*

comic book *n.* A magazine of comic strips.

comic strip *n.* A narrative series of cartoons.

com•ing (kŭm'ĭng) *adj.* **1.** Approaching. **2.** *Informal.* Showing promise of achievement. *—n.* Advent : arrival.

com•i•ty (kŏm'ĭ-tē) *n., pl.* **-ties.** Social courtesy : civility.

comm. *abbr.* **1.** commerce. **2.** commission; commissioner. **3.** committee. **4.** communication.

com•ma (kŏm'ə) *n.* A punctuation mark (,) used to indicate a separation of elements or ideas in a sentence.

com•mand (kə-mănd') *v.* **1.** To give orders (to). **2.** To rule (over). **3.** To dominate by position : overlook. ☆***syns:*** BID, CHARGE, DIRECT, ENJOIN, INSTRUCT, ORDER, REQUIRE, TELL *—n.* **1.** The act of commanding. **2.** An authoritative order. **3.** A signal that activates a device, as a computer. **4.** Controlling power : mastery. **5. a.** A military unit, post, or district under the control of one officer. **b.** A group of officers authorized to command.

com•man•dant (kŏm'ən-dănt') *n.* A military commander.

com•man•deer (kŏm'ən-dîr') *v.* To confiscate esp. for military or public use.

com•mand•er (kə-măn'dər) *n.* **1.** One who commands : leader. **2.** An officer in the U.S. Navy who ranks above a lieutenant commander and below a captain.

commander in chief *n., pl.* **commanders in chief.** The supreme military commander of a nation's armed forces.

com•mand•ing (kə-măn'dĭng) *adj.* Dominating, as by size or position.

com•mand•ment (kə-mănd'mənt) *n.* **1.** An order : command. **2.** *often* **Commandment.** One of the Ten Commandments.

command module *n.* The part of a spacecraft that houses the astronauts and the controls.

com•man•do (kə-măn'dō) *n., pl.* **-dos** *or* **-does.** A member of a small military force trained to make quick surprise raids.

comme il faut (kŭm' ēl fō') *adj.* In accordance with accepted standards : proper.

com•mem•o•rate (kə-mĕm'ə-rāt') *v.* **-rat•ed, -rat•ing. 1.** To honor the memory of, esp. ceremonially. **2.** To be a memorial to, as a holiday. **—com•mem'o•ra'tion** *n.* **—com•mem'o•ra•tive** (-ər-ə-tĭv, -ə-rā'-) *adj.* & *n.* **—com•mem'o•ra'tor** *n.*

com•mence (kə-mĕns') *v.* **-menced, -menc•ing.** To start : begin.

com•mence•ment (kə-mĕns'mənt) *n.* **1.** A beginning. **2.** A graduation ceremony.

com•mend (kə-mĕnd') *v.* **1.** To praise : applaud. **2.** To recommend. **3.** To entrust to another. **—com•mend'a•ble** *adj.* **—com•mend'a•bly** *adv.* **—com'men•da'tion** (kŏm'ən-dā'shən) *n.*

com•men•da•to•ry (kə-mĕn'də-tôr'ē, -tōr'ē) *adj.* Serving to praise.

com•men•sal (kə-mĕn'səl) *adj.* **1.** Of or relating to those who normally eat at the same table. **2.** *Biol.* Of or marked by commensalism. **—com•men'sal** *n.*

com•men•sal•ism (kə-mĕn'sə-lĭz'əm) *n. Biol.* A relationship in which 2 or more organisms live in close attachment or partnership and in which 1 may benefit but neither is parasitic on the other.

com•men•su•ra•ble (kə-mĕn'sər-ə-bəl, -shər-) *adj.* Measurable by a common standard or unit. **—com•men'su•ra•bil'i•ty** *n.* **—com•men'su•ra•bly** *adv.*

com•men•su•rate (kə-mĕn'sər-ĭt, -shər-) *adj.* **1.** Equal in size, extent, or duration. **2.** Proportionate <a salary *commensurate* with experience> **3.** Commensurable. **—com•men'su•ra'tion** *n.*

com•ment (kŏm'ĕnt') *n.* **1.** A statement of observation, analysis, or criticism. **2.** An expression of opinion. **—com'ment'** *v.*

com•men•tar•y (kŏm'ən-tĕr'ē) *n., pl.* **-ies.** A series of comments that explain or interpret. ☆***syns:*** ANNOTATION, EXEGESIS, INTERPRETATION, NOTE

com•men•tate (kŏm'ən-tāt') *v.* **-tat•ed, -tat•ing.** To comment on or act as a commentator.

com•men•ta•tor (kŏm'ən-tā'tər) *n.* One who reports and analyzes news on radio or television.

com•merce (kŏm'ərs) *n.* The buying and selling of goods : business.

com•mer•cial (kə-mûr'shəl) *adj.* **1.** Of, relating to, or engaged in commerce. **2.** Designed for profit. **3.** Supported by advertising <*commercial* TV> *—n.* An advertisement on television or radio. **—com•mer'cial•ism** *n.* **—com•mer'cial•ist** *n.* **—com•mer'cial•is'tic** *adj.*

commercial bank *n.* A bank whose primary functions are to take demand deposits and negotiate short-term loans.

com•mer•cial•ize (kə-mûr'shə-līz') *v.* **-ized, -iz•ing.** To make commercial, esp. for gain. **—com•mer'cial•i•za'tion** *n.*

com•min•gle (kə-mĭng'gəl) *v.* **-gled, -gling.** To mix together : blend.

com•mis•er•ate (kə-mĭz'ə-rāt') *v.* **-at•ed, -at•ing.** To feel or display sympathy (for). **—com•mis'er•a'tion** *n.* **—com•mis'er•a'tive** *adj.* **—com•mis'er•a'tor** *n.*

com•mis•sar (kŏm'ĭ-sär') *n.* An official of the Communist Party whose duties include political indoctrination and enforcement of party loyalty.

com•mis•sar•i•at (kŏm'ĭ-sâr'ē-ət) *n.* An army department providing food and other supplies.

com•mis•sar•y (kŏm'ĭ-sĕr'ē) *n., pl.* **-ies.** A store for food and supplies, esp. on a military base.

com•mis•sion (kə-mĭsh'ən) *n.* **1. a.** Official permission to carry out a task. **b.** The permission so granted. **c.** The task so consigned. **d.** A document conferring such permission. **2.** A group authorized to carry out certain functions or tasks. **3.** A perpetration <*commission* of a felony> **4.** An allowance to a salesperson or agent for his or her services. **5.** A certificate conferring the rank of a commissioned officer. *—v.* **1.** To give a commission to. **2.** To put in an order for. **—in commission.** In use or in working condition. **—out of commission.** Not in use or in usable condition.

commissioned officer *n.* A military officer who ranks above a warrant officer or an enlisted man or woman.

com•mis•sion•er (kə-mĭsh'ə-nər) *n.* **1.** A member of a commission. **2.** A governmental department official. **3.** An administrative official in a professional sport.

com•mit (kə-mĭt′) *v.* **-mit•ted, -mit•ting. 1.** To be responsible for <*commit* murder> **2.** To entrust : consign. **3.** To place officially in custody or confinement. **4.** To pledge (oneself) to a position. – **–com•mit′ment, com•mit′tal** *n.* **–com•mit′ta•ble** *adj.*

com•mit•tee (kə-mĭt′ē) *n.* A group delegated to perform a particular function or task. **–com•mit′tee•man** *n.* **–com•mit′tee•wom′an** *n.*

com•mix (kə-mĭks′, kō-) *v.* **-mixed, -mix•ing.** To mix or cause to mix together : blend. **–com•mix′ture** *n.*

com•mode (kə-mōd′) *n.* **1.** A low bureau or cabinet. **2.** A movable washstand. **3.** A toilet.

com•mo•di•ous (kə-mō′dē-əs) *adj.* Capacious : roomy.

com•mod•i•ty (kə-mŏd′ĭ-tē) *n., pl.* **-ties. 1.** Something useful. **2.** A transportable item of commerce or trade, esp. a mining or agricultural product.

com•mo•dore (kŏm′ə-dôr′, -dōr′) *n.* **1.** Formerly, a naval officer ranking above a captain and below a rear admiral. **2. a.** The senior captain of a merchant fleet or naval squadron. **b.** The highest-ranking officer of a yacht club.

com•mon (kŏm′ən) *adj.* **1.** Shared by all : mutual. **2.** Relating to the entire community : public. **3.** Widespread : general. **4. a.** Ordinary : usual. **b.** Most widely known. **5.** Standard or average. **6.** Unrefined : vulgar. ☆***syns:*** COMMUNAL, GENERAL, JOINT, MUTUAL, PUBLIC —*n.* **1.** An area of land shared by an entire community. **2. Commons.** The House of Commons. **–com′mon•ly** *adv.*

common carrier *n.* One that transports passengers or goods for a fee.

common denominator *n.* **1.** A number into which all the denominators of a set of fractions may be evenly divided. **2.** A commonly shared characteristic or theme.

com•mon•er (kŏm′ə-nər) *n.* A person not of the nobility.

common fraction *n.* A fraction whose denominator and numerator are both whole numbers.

common law *n.* An unwritten system of law based on judicial decisions, usages, and customs. **–com′mon-law′** *adj.*

common multiple *n.* A number that is a multiple of each of 2 or more given quantities.

com•mon•place (kŏm′ən-plās′) *adj.* Common : ordinary. —*n.* Something ordinary, esp. a trite remark.

common sense *n.* The native ability to make sound judgments.

com•mon•weal (kŏm′ən-wēl′) *n.* **1.** The public good or welfare. **2.** *Archaic.* A commonwealth.

com•mon•wealth (kŏm′ən-wĕlth′) *n.* **1.** The people of a state or nation. **2.** A state or nation governed by the people : republic. **3.** A federation of autonomous states.

Commonwealth Day *n.* Victoria Day.

Commonwealth of Nations. Association including the United Kingdom, its dependencies, and many former colonies.

com•mo•tion (kə-mō′shən) *n.* Turbulent or violent motion : tumult.

com•mu•nal (kə-myōō′nəl, kŏm′yə-nəl) *adj.* **1.** Of or relating to a community or commune. **2.** Public. **–com′mu•nal′i•ty** (-năl′ĭ-tē) *n.* **–com•mu′nal•ly** *adv.*

com•mune[1] (kə-myōōn′) *v.* **-muned, -mun•ing.** To communicate privately <*commune* with nature>

com•mune[2] (kŏm′yōōn′) *n.* **1.** The smallest local political unit of some European countries. **2. a.** Living space shared or owned jointly by a group.**b.** The members of a commune.

com•mu•ni•ca•ble (kə-myōō′nĭ-kə-bəl) *adj.* **1.** Capable of being transmitted. **2.** Talkative. **–com•mu′ni•ca•bil′i•ty** *n.* **–com•mu′ni•ca•bly** *adv.*

com•mu•ni•cant (kə-myōō′nĭ-kənt) *n.* **1.** One who receives Communion. **2.** One who communicates.

com•mu•ni•cate (kə-myōō′nĭ-kāt′) *v.* **-cat•ed, -cat•ing. 1.** To make known : disclose. **2.** To transmit, as a disease. **3.** To have an exchange, as of ideas. **4.** To receive Communion. **–com•mu′ni•ca′tor** *n.*

com•mu•ni•ca•tion (kə-myōō′nĭ-kā′shən) *n.* **1.** The act of communicating. **2.** The exchange of ideas, messages, or information. **3.** A message. **4. communications. a.** A system for communicating. **b.** The art and technology of communicating. **–com•mu′ni•ca′tive** *adj.*

com•mun•ion (kə-myōōn′yən) *n.* **1.** An act or instance of sharing or exchanging, as of feelings or thoughts. **2. a.** A spiritual or religious fellowship. **b.** A Christian denomination. **3. Communion.** The Eucharist or its consecrated elements.

com•mu•ni•qué (kə-myōō′nĭ-kā′, -myōō′nĭ-kā′) *n.* An official message.

com•mu•nism (kŏm′yə-nĭz′əm) *n.* **1.** A system in which production and goods are commonly owned. **2. Communism. a.** The theory of struggle toward communism through revolution. **b.** Socialism as practiced in countries governed by Communist parties. **–com′mu•nist** *n.* **–com′mu•nis′tic** *adj.* **–com′mu•nis′ti•cal•ly** *adv.*

Communist Party *n.* The official state party of the Soviet Union.

com•mu•ni•ty (kə-myōō′nĭ-tē) *n., pl.* **-ties. 1. a.** A group of people residing in the same region and under the same government. **b.** The region in which they reside. **2.** A class or group with common interests. **3.** Likeness or identity. **4.** Society in general.

community college *n.* An often government-funded 2-year college without residential facilities.

community property *n.* Property owned jointly by a married couple.

com•mu•nize (kŏm′yə-nīz′) *v.* **-nized, -niz•ing. 2.** To convert to communistic principles or practices. **–com′mu•ni•za′tion** *n.*

com•mu•ta•tion (kŏm′yə-tā′shən) *n.* **1.** An exchange or substitution. **2.** *Law.* A reduction of a penalty to one less severe. **3.** The travel of a commuter.

com•mu•ta•tive (kŏm′yə-tā′tĭv, kə-myōō′tə-tĭv) *adj.* **1.** Relating to, involving, or marked by substitution or exchange. **2.** Independent of order, as a logical or mathematical operation combining objects 2 at a time. **–com•mu′ta•tiv′i•ty** (kə-myōō′tə-tĭv′ĭ-tē) *n.*

com•mu•ta•tor (kŏm′yə-tā′tər) *n.* A switching device used in electric motors or generators to provide a flow of current in a desired direction through a desired path.

com•mute (kə-myōōt′) *v.* **-mut•ed, -mut•ing. 1.** To substitute : exchange. **2.** To reduce (a penalty or payment) in severity. **3.** To travel as a commuter. —*n. Informal.* The trip made by a commuter.

com•mut•er (kə-myōō′tər) *n.* One who travels regularly between 2 places, as city and suburb.

com•pact[1] (kəm-păkt′, kŏm-, kŏm′păkt′) *adj.* **1.** Solidly united or packed together. **2.** Grouped within a small space. **3.** Expressed concisely. —*v.* (kəm-păkt′). To compress together. —*n.* (kŏm′păkt′). **1.** A small case for cosmetics. **2.** A small automobile. **–com•pact′er** *n.* **–com•pact′ly** *adv.*

com•pact[2] (kŏm′păkt′) *n.* An agreement or covenant.

com•pac•tor (kəm-păk′tər, kŏm′păk′-) *n.* A device for compressing trash into small packages for disposal.

†com•pa•dre (kəm-pä′drā) *n. SW U.S.* A close friend or associate.

com•pan•ion (kəm-păn′yən) *n.* **1.** One who accompanies another. **2.** One hired to live or travel with another. **3.** One of a matched pair or set : mate. **–com•pan′ion•ship′** *n.*

com•pan•ion•a•ble (kəm-păn′yə-nə-bəl) *adj.* Friendly : sociable. **–com•pan′ion•a•bly** *adv.*

com•pan•ion•way (kəm-păn′yən-wā′) *n.* A staircase from a ship's deck to the area or cabins below.

com•pa•ny (kŭm′pə-nē) *n., pl.* **-nies. 1.** A group of people. **2.** People assembled socially. **3.** A guest or guests. **4.** Companionable association. **5.** A commercial enterprise. **6.** A group of theatrical performers. **7.** A subdivision of a batallion or regiment. **8.** A ship's crew and officers.

com•pa•ra•ble (kŏm′pər-ə-bəl) *adj.* **1.** Able to be compared. **2.** Worthy of comparison. **3.** Like or equivalent. **–com′pa•ra•bil′i•ty** *n.* **–com′pa•ra•bly** *adv.*

com•par•a•tive (kəm-păr′ə-tĭv) *adj.* **1.** Of or based on comparison. **2.** Estimated by comparison : relative <*comparative* wealth> **3.** Indicating a degree of comparison of adjectives and adverbs higher than positive and lower than superlative. —*n.* **1.** The comparative degree of an adjective or adverb. **2.** A comparative adjective or adverb. **–com•par′a•tive•ly** *adv.*

com•pare (kəm-pâr′) *v.* **-pared, -par•ing. 1.** To represent as similar or equal : liken. **2.** To examine so as to note the likenesses or differences of. **3.** To form the positive, comparative, or superlative degree of (an adjective or adverb). —*n.* Comparison <cuisine beyond *compare*>

com•par•i•son (kəm-păr′ĭ-sən) *n.* **1.** The act of comparing. **2.** Similarity : likeness. **3.** The modification of an adjective or adverb to indicate the positive, comparative, or superlative degree.

comparison-shop (kəm-păr′ĭ-sən-shŏp′) *v.* To look for bargains by comparing the prices of competing brands or stores.

com•part•ment (kəm-pärt′mənt) *n.* One of the spaces or sections into which an area or container is subdivided. **–com′part•men′tal** (kŏm′pärt-mĕn′tl) *adj.*

com•part•men•tal•ize (kŏm′pärt-mĕn′tl-īz′, kəm-pärt′-) *v.* **-ized, -iz•ing.** To separate into compartments or categories. **–com′part•men′tal•i•za′tion** *n.*

com•pass (kŭm′pəs, kŏm′-) *n.* **1.** A device for determining geographic direction, esp. a magnetic needle mounted or suspended horizontally and free to pivot until aligned with the earth's magnetic field. **2.** *often* **compasses.** A V-shaped device for drawing circles or circular arcs. **3.** An enclosing boundary : circumference. **4.** An enclosed space or area. **5.** A range or scope : extent. —*v.* **1.** To go around : circle. **2.** To shut in on all sides : encircle. **3.** To accomplish or gain. **4.** To plot : scheme.

com•pas•sion (kəm-păsh'ən) *n.* Actively sympathetic concern for the suffering of another : mercy. **—com•pas'sion•ate** *adj.*

com•pat•i•ble (kəm-păt'ə-bəl) *adj.* Capable of living or functioning harmoniously with others. **—com•pat'i•bil'i•ty, com•pat'i•ble•ness** *n.* **—com•pat'i•bly** *adv.*

com•pa•tri•ot (kəm-pā'trē-ət, -ŏt') *n.* A fellow countryman.

com•peer (kəm-pîr', kŏm'pîr') *n.* An equal or peer.

com•pel (kəm-pĕl') *v.* **-pelled, -pel•ling.** To constrain : force.

com•pen•di•um (kəm-pĕn'dē-əm) *n., pl.* **-ums** *or* **-di•a** (-dē-ə). A short, detailed summary.

com•pen•sate (kŏm'pən-sāt') *v.* **-sat•ed, -sat•ing. 1.** To make up for : offset. **2.** To make payment or reparation to : reimburse. **—com'pen•sa'tion** *n.* **—com•pen'sa•to'ry** (kəm-pĕn'sə-tôr'ē, -tōr'ē) *adj.*

com•pete (kəm-pēt') *v.* **-pet•ed, -pet•ing.** To contend with another : vie.

com•pe•tent (kŏm'pĭ-tənt) *adj.* **1.** Qualified : capable. **2.** Adequate for a specified purpose. **3.** *Law.* Legally fit or qualified : admissable. **—com'pe•tence, com'pe•ten•cy** *n.*

com•pe•ti•tion (kŏm'pĭ-tĭsh'ən) *n.* **1.** The act of competing : rivalry. **2.** A test of skill : contest. **—com•pet'i•tive** *adj.*

com•pet•i•tor (kəm-pĕt'ĭ-tər) *n.* One who competes against another, as in business or sports : rival.

com•pile (kəm-pīl') *v.* **-piled, -pil•ing. 1.** To gather into a single book. **2.** To put together from materials gathered from a number of sources. **3.** *Computer Sci.* To convert to machine language. **—com'pi•la'tion** (kŏm'pə-lā'shən) *n.* **—com•pil'er** *n.*

com•pla•cen•cy (kəm-plā'sən-sē) *also* **com•pla•cence** (-səns) *n.* **1.** Gratification. **2.** Smug self-satisfaction. **—com•pla'cent** *adj.* **—com•pla'cent•ly** *adv.*

com•plain (kəm-plān') *v.* **1.** To express feelings of dissatisfaction, pain, or resentment. **2.** To make a formal charge. ☆***syns:*** BEEF, BELLYACHE, GRIPE, GROUSE, KICK, WHINE **—com•plain'er** *n.*

com•plain•ant (kəm-plā'nənt) *n.* One who files a formal charge, as in a court of law : plaintiff.

com•plaint (kəm-plānt') *n.* **1.** An expression of dissatisfaction, pain, or resentment. **2.** A reason or cause for complaining : grievance. **3.** An illness. **4.** *Law.* A plaintiff's formal charge.

com•plai•sance (kəm-plā'səns) *n.* Willingness to comply. **—com•plai'sant** *adj.*

com•pleat (kəm-plēt') *adj.* Of or characterized by a highly developed, wide-ranging proficiency or skill <was the *compleat* chess player>

†**com•plect•ed** (kəm-plĕk'tĭd) *adj. Regional.* Marked by or having a particular facial complexion <dark-*complected*>

com•ple•ment (kŏm'plə-mənt) *n.* **1.** Something that completes, perfects, or makes up a whole. **2.** The number or quantity required to make up a whole. **3.** Either of a pair of angles whose measures add up to 90°. **4.** A word or group of words used to complete a predicate. —*v.* (kŏm'plə-mĕnt'). To make complete or be a complement to. **—com'ple•men'ta•ry** (-tə-rē, -trē) *adj.*

com•plete (kəm-plēt') *adj.* **1.** Having all necessary or normal parts : whole. **2.** At an end : concluded. **3.** Thorough <a *complete* success> ☆***syns:*** ENTIRE, FULL, INTACT, INTEGRAL, PERFECT, WHOLE —*v.* **-plet•ed, -plet•ing. 1.** To make complete. **2.** To end. **—com•ple'tion** *n.*

com•plex (kəm-plĕks', kŏm'plĕks') *adj.* **1.** Consisting of composite parts. **2.** Intricate. ☆***syns:*** BYZANTINE, COMPLICATED, CONVOLUTED, ELABORATE, INTRICATE, INVOLUTE, INVOLVED, KNOTTY, LABYRINTHINE —*n.* (kŏm'plĕks'). **1.** A whole composed of interconnected or intricate parts. **2.** A group of repressed memories, emotions, and desires that influences one's behavior and personality. **—com•plex'i•ty** *n.* **—com•plex'ly** *adv.*

complex fraction *n.* A fraction in which the numerator or denominator is expressed as a fraction.

com•plex•ion (kəm-plĕk'shən) *n.* **1.** The natural color and appearance of the skin, esp. of the face. **2.** General appearance or character. **—com•plex'ioned** *adj.*

complex number *n.* A number of the form $a + bi$, where a and b are real numbers and $i^2 = -1$.

com•pli•ance (kəm-plī'əns) *n. also* **com•pli•an•cy** (-ən-sē) *n.* **1.** Acquiescence to a rule, request, demand, etc. **2.** A tendency or disposition to yield to others. **—com•pli'ant** *adj.* **—com•pli'ant•ly** *adv.*

com•pli•cate (kŏm'plĭ-kāt') *v.* **-cat•ed, -cat•ing.** To make or become complex. **—com'pli•ca'tion** *n.*

com•plic•i•ty (kəm-plĭs'ĭ-tē) *n.* Involvement as an accomplice in a crime or wrongdoing.

com•pli•ment (kŏm'plə-mənt) *n.* **1.** An expression of admiration or praise. **2. compliments.** Good wishes : regards. **—com'pli•ment** *v.*

com•pli•men•ta•ry (kŏm'plə-mĕn'tə-rē, -trē) *adj.* **1.** Expressing a compliment <*complimentary* reviews> **2.** Given free as a favor or courtesy <*complimentary* tickets> **—com'pli•men'ta•ri•ly** *adv.*

com•ply (kəm-plī') *v.* **-plied, -ply•ing.** To agree or yield, as to a wish or command. **—com•pli'er** *n.*

com•po•nent (kəm-pō'nənt) *n.* A constituent element. **—com•po'nent** *adj.*

com•port (kəm-pôrt', -pōrt') *v.* **1.** To conduct (oneself) in a given way. **2.** To be appropriate : harmonize.

com•port•ment (kəm-pôrt'mənt, -pōrt'-) *n.* Deportment : bearing.

com•pose (kəm-pōz') *v.* **-posed, -pos•ing. 1.** To make up : constitute. **2.** To make by combining elements or parts. **3.** To create or produce (e.g., a song or poem). **4.** To make tranquil or calm. **5.** To adjust or settle. **6.** To set or arrange (e.g., type). **—com•pos'ed•ly** *adv.* **—com•pos'er** *n.*

com•pos•ite (kəm-pŏz'ĭt) *adj.* **1.** Made up of distinct components : compound. **2.** Of, belonging to, or typical of the Compositae, a large plant family characterized by flower heads consisting of many small, densely clustered flowers that appear to be a single bloom. —*n.* **1.** A compound. **2.** A composite plant. **—com•pos'ite•ly** *adv.*

com•po•si•tion (kŏm'pə-zĭsh'ən) *n.* **1.** The act or product of composing, esp. an artistic or literary work. **2.** Make-up : constitution. **3.** The unified arrangement of artistic parts. **4.** A short essay, as for school. **5.** The setting of printing type. **—com'po•si'tion•al** *adj.*

com•pos•i•tor (kəm-pŏz'ĭ-tər) *n.* A typesetter.

com•pos men•tis (kŏm'pəs mĕn'tĭs) *adj.* Of sound mind.

com•post (kŏm'pōst') *n.* A fertilizer consisting of decayed organic matter.

com•po•sure (kəm-pō'zhər) *n.* Calm self-possession.

com•pote (kŏm'pōt') *n.* **1.** Fruit cooked or stewed in syrup. **2.** A stemmed dish used for holding fruit, candy, etc.

com•pound[1] (kŏm'pound') *n.* **1.** A combination of 2 or more parts, elements, or ingredients. **2.** A solid or hyphenated word composed of 2 or more words or word elements. **3.** A substance consisting of atoms of 2 or more different elements in definite proportions and usu. having properties unlike those of its constituent elements. —*v.* (kŏm-pound', kəm-). **1.** To combine. **2.** To produce by combining. **3.** To compute (interest) on both the principal and accrued interest. **4.** To increase <Illness *compounded* our woes.> —*adj.* (kŏm'pound', kŏm-pound'). Made up of 2 or more parts. **—com•pound'a•ble** *adj.*

com•pound[2] (kŏm'pound) *n.* A group of buildings enclosed by a wall or fence.

compound eye *n.* The eye of most insects and some crustaceans, composed of many light-sensitive elements, each with its own refractive system that forms a portion of an image.

compound fracture *n.* A fracture in which broken bone lacerates soft tissue.

compound interest *n.* Interest computed on both the principal and accrued unpaid interest.

compound sentence *n.* A sentence formed of 2 or more independent clauses.

com•pre•hend (kŏm'prĭ-hĕnd') *v.* **1.** To perceive or understand. **2.** To include : comprise. **—com'pre•hen'sion** *n.*

com•pre•hen•si•ble (kŏm'prĭ-hĕn'sə-bəl) *adj.* Able to be understood. **—com'pre•hen'si•bil'i•ty** *n.* **—com'pre•hen'si•bly** *adv.*

com•pre•hen•sive (kŏm'prĭ-hĕn'sĭv) *adj.* Broad in scope or content.

com•press (kəm-prĕs') *v.* To press together or condense. —*n.* (kŏm'prĕs'). A soft pad applied to control bleeding or reduce pain or infection. **—com•press'i•bil'i•ty** *n.* **—com•press'i•ble** *adj.* **—com•pres'sion** *n.*

compressed air *n.* Air under greater than atmospheric pressure.

com•pres•sor (kəm-prĕs'ər) *n.* Something that compresses, esp. a machine for compressing gases.

com•prise (kəm-prīz') *v.* **-prised, -pris•ing. 1.** To be made up of : consist of. **2.** To include : contain. **—com•pris'a•ble** *adj.*

com•pro•mise (kŏm'prə-mīz') *n.* **1.** A settlement of differences between opposing sides in which each side makes concessions. **2.** Something combining the qualities of different things. —*v.* **-mised, -mis•ing. 1.** To settle by or accept concessions. **2.** To expose to suspicion, danger, or disrepute. **3.** To make a compromise. **—com'pro•mis'er** *n.*

comp·trol·ler (kən-trō′lər) *n. var. of* CONTROLLER 2.
com·pul·sion (kəm-pŭl′shən) *n.* **1.** The act of compelling or state of being compelled. **2.** An irresistible impulse to act irrationally. **—com·pul′sive** *adj.*
com·pul·so·ry (kəm-pŭl′sə-rē) *adj.* **1.** Using or exerting compulsion : coercive. **2.** Mandatory. ☆***syns:*** IMPERATIVE, MANDATORY, NECESSARY, OBLIGATORY, REQUIRED, REQUISITE **—com·pul′so·ri·ly** *adv.*
com·punc·tion (kəm-pŭngk′shən) *n.* Disquietude caused by a sense of guilt.
com·pute (kəm-pyo͞ot′) *v.* **-put·ed, -put·ing. 1.** To determine by mathematics, esp. by numerical methods. **2.** To determine by or use a computer. **—com·put′a·bil′i·ty** *n.* **—com·put′a·ble** *adj.* **—com′pu·ta′tion** *n.*
com·put·er (kəm-pyo͞o′tər) *n.* One that computes, esp. a high-speed electronic machine that performs mathematical or logical calculations and processes, retrieves, and stores programmed information.
computer graphics *n. (sing. or pl. in number).* Art obtained by programming a computer to create the desired picture.
com·put·er·ize (kəm-pyo͞o′tə-rīz′) *v.* **-ized, -iz·ing. 1.** To process or store (data) with or in a computer or computer system. **2.** To furnish with a computer or computer system. **—com·put′er·i·za′tion** *n.*
computerized axial tomography *n.* Tomography in which computer analysis of a series of cross-sectional scans made along a single axis of a structure is used to construct a three-dimensional image.
computer language *n.* Any of various codes that are used to provide data and instructions to computers.
com·rade (kŏm′răd′, -rəd) *n.* **1.** A companion, friend, or associate. **2.** *often* **Comrade.** A fellow member, esp. of the Communist Party. **—com′rade·ship′** *n.*
Com·sat (kŏm′săt′). A trademark for a communications satellite.
con[1] (kŏn) *adv.* Against <argue pro and *con*> —*n.* An argument or opinion against something.
con[2] (kŏn) *v.* **conned, con·ning.** To examine or study carefully, esp. to memorize.
con[3] (kŏn) *Slang.* —*v.* **conned, con·ning.** To swindle : dupe. —*n.* A swindle.
con[4] (kŏn) *n. Slang.* A convict.
con. *abbr.* **1.** *Law.* conclusion. **2.** consolidate; consolidated.
Con·a·kry (kŏn′ə-krē). Cap. of Guinea, on the Atlantic. *Pop.* 290,000.
con bri·o (kŏn brē′ō, kōn) *adv. Mus.* With vigor. Used as a direction.
con·cat·e·nate (kŏn-kăt′n-āt′, kən-) *v.* **-nat·ed, -nat·ing.** To connect in a series or chain. **—con·cat′e·nate** (-ĭt, -āt′) *adj.* **—con·cat′e·na′tion** *n.*
con·cave (kŏn-kāv′, kŏn′kāv′) *adj.* Curved or rounded inward like the inner surface of a ball. **—con·cav′i·ty** (-kăv′ĭ-tē), **con·cave′ness** *n.*
con·ceal (kən-sēl′) *v.* To keep from sight or disclosure. **—con·ceal′a·ble** *adj.*
con·cede (kən-sēd′) *v.* **-ced·ed, -ced·ing. 1.** To acknowledge as true or real : admit. **2.** To grant, as a privilege. **3.** To yield. **—con·ced′er** *n.*
†con·ceit (kən-sēt′) *n.* **1.** An exaggerated opinion of oneself : vanity. **2.** An imaginative or witty idea. **3.** An elaborate metaphor. —*v. Regional.* To imagine.
†con·ceit·ed (kən-sē′tĭd) *adj.* **1.** Unduly proud of oneself : vain. **2.** *Regional.* Inclined to be whimsical.
con·ceive (kən-sēv′) *v.* **-ceived, -ceiv·ing. 1.** To become pregnant (with). **2.** To create in the mind : devise. **3.** To believe or think. **—con·ceiv′a·bil′i·ty** *n.* **—con·ceiv′a·ble** *adj.* **—con·ceiv′a·bly** *adv.* **—con·ceiv′er** *n.*
con·cen·trate (kŏn′sən-trāt′) *v.* **-trat·ed, -trat·ing. 1.** To draw toward a common center : focus. **2.** *Chem.* To increase the concentration of (a mixture or solution). —*n. Chem.* A product of concentration. **—con′cen·tra′tive** *adj.* **—con′cen·tra′tor** *n.*
con·cen·tra·tion (kŏn′sən-trā′shən) *n.* **1. a.** The act of concentrating, esp. of paying close attention. **b.** The state of being concentrated. **2.** Something concentrated. **3.** *Chem.* The amount of a particular substance in a specified amount of another substance.
concentration camp *n.* A camp for confinement of prisoners of war and political dissidents.
con·cen·tric (kən-sĕn′trĭk) *also* **con·cen·tri·cal** (-trĭ-kəl) *adj.* Having a common center. **—con·cen′tri·cal·ly** *adv.* **—con′cen·tric′i·ty** (-trĭs′ĭ-tē) *n.*
con·cept (kŏn′sĕpt′) *n.* **1.** A general understanding, esp. one derived from particular instances or occurrences. **2.** A thought. **—con·cep′tu·al** *adj.*
con·cep·tion (kən-sĕp′shən) *n.* **1.** The formation of a zygote capable of developing into a new organism. **2.** The ability to form mental concepts. **3.** Something, as a thought or plan, conceived in the mind.
con·cep·tu·al·ize (kən-sĕp′cho͞o-ə-līz′) *v.* **-ized, -iz·ing.** To form concepts (of). **—con·cep′tu·al·i·za′tion** *n.*
con·cern (kən-sûrn′) *v.* **1.** To relate or pertain to : affect. **2.** To engage the attention of. **3.** To cause uneasiness in : trouble. —*n.* **1.** Something interesting or important. **2.** Sincere regard. **3.** Uneasiness : worry. **4.** A business enterprise.
con·cern·ing (kən-sûr′nĭng) *prep.* In regard to : about.
con·cert (kŏn′sûrt′, -sərt) *n.* **1.** A musical performance for an audience. **2.** Agreement in feeling, purpose, or action. —*v.* (kən-sûrt′). **1.** To plan by mutual agreement. **2.** To act together in harmony.
con·cert·ed (kən-sûr′tĭd) *adj.* Achieved or planned together <a *concerted* effort>
con·cer·ti·na (kŏn′sər-tē′nə) *n.* A small accordion with bellows and buttons instead of keys.
con·cert·mas·ter (kŏn′sərt-măs′tər) *n.* The 1st violinist and assistant conductor of a symphony orchestra.
con·cer·to (kən-chĕr′tō) *n., pl.* **-tos** or **-ti** (-tē). An orchestral composition featuring 1 or more solo instruments.
con·ces·sion (kən-sĕsh′ən) *n.* **1.** The act of conceding. **2.** Something conceded. **3.** Something, as a tract of land, granted esp. by a government to be used for a particular purpose. **4.** The privilege of running a subsidiary business on certain premises.
con·ces·sion·aire (kən-sĕsh′ə-nâr′) *n.* The holder or operator of a concession.
con·ces·sive (kən-sĕs′ĭv) *adj.* Like or containing a concession.
conch (kŏngk, kŏnch) *n., pl.* **conchs** (kŏngks) or **conch·es** (kŏn′chĭz). Any of various tropical marine mollusks of the genus *Strombus* and other genera, with large spiral shells and edible flesh.
con·chol·o·gy (kŏng-kŏl′ə-jē) *n.* The study of shells and mollusks. **—con′cho·log′i·cal** (-kə-lŏj′ĭ-kəl) *adj.* **—con·chol′o·gist** *n.*
con·cierge (kôɴ-syârzh′) *n.* A building custodian esp. in France who attends the door and acts as janitor.
con·cil·i·ate (kən-sĭl′ē-āt′) *v.* **-at·ed, -at·ing. 1.** To placate : appease. **2.** To gain the friendship of. **3.** To reconcile. **—con·cil′i·a′tion** *n.* **—con·cil′i·a′tor** *n.* **—con·cil′i·a·to′ry** *adj.*
con·cise (kən-sīs′) *adj.* Short and to the point <a *concise* report>
con·clave (kŏn′klāv′, kŏng′-) *n.* A private or secret meeting, esp. one in which Roman Catholic cardinals elect a new pope.
con·clude (kən-klo͞od′) *v.* **-clud·ed, -clud·ing. 1.** To come or bring to an end : close. **2.** To come to or bring about a settlement or agreement. **3.** To arrive at a decision (about). **4.** To determine : resolve. **—con·clu′sion** *n.*
con·clu·sive (kən-klo͞o′sĭv) *adj.* Serving to end doubt or uncertainty : decisive.
con·coct (kən-kŏkt′) *v.* **1.** To prepare by combining ingredients, as in cookery. **2.** To invent : contrive. **—con·coct′er, con·coc′tor** *n.* **—con·coc′tion** *n.*
con·com·i·tant (kən-kŏm′ĭ-tənt) *adj.* Accompanying. —*n.* Something that accompanies. **—con·com′i·tance** *n.* **—con·com′i·tant·ly** *adv.*
con·cord (kŏn′kôrd′, kŏng′-) *n.* **1.** Harmony : accord. **2.** A formal agreement : treaty.
Con·cord (kŏng′kərd). Cap. of N.H., in the SC part. *Pop.* 30,400.
con·cor·dance (kən-kôr′dns) *n.* **1.** A condition of agreement : harmony. **2.** An alphabetical index of the major words in a text or the works of an author, giving the passages in which they occur.
con·cor·dant (kən-kôr′dnt) *adj.* Harmonious. **—con·cor′dant·ly** *adv.*
con·cor·dat (kən-kôr′dăt′) *n.* A formal agreement : covenant.
con·course (kŏn′kôrs′, -kōrs′, kŏng′-) *n.* **1.** A large crowd. **2. a.** A large open space, as in an airport, for the passage of crowds. **b.** A broad thoroughfare.
con·cres·cence (kən-krĕs′əns) *n.* The growing together of related parts, as of the anatomy.
con·crete (kŏn-krēt′, kŏn′krēt′) *adj.* **1.** Of or pertaining to an actual specific thing or instance <*concrete* facts> **2.** Tangible : real. **3.** Coalesced into one mass : solid. **4.** Made of concrete. —*n.* (kŏn′krēt′, kŏn-krēt′). **1.** A building material made by mixing water with cement, gravel, and sand. **2.** A mass that is formed by the coalescence of particles or elements. —*v.* (kŏn′krēt′, kŏn-krēt′) **-cret·ed, -cret·ing. 1.** To coalesce into a solid mass. **2.** To build or cover with concrete.
con·cre·tion (kən-krē′shən) *n.* **1.** The act or process of con-

creting : coalescence. **2.** A hard, concrete or solid mass. **3.** *Pathol.* CALCULUS 1.

con·cu·bine (kŏng′kyə-bīn′, kŏn′-) *n.* A woman who lives with a man without being legally married to him. **—con·cu′bin·age** (kŏn-kyo͞o′bə-nĭj, kən-) *n.*

con·cu·pis·cence (kŏn-kyo͞o′pĭ-səns) *n.* Strong sexual desire : lust. **—con·cu′pis·cent** *adj.*

con·cur (kən-kûr′) *v.* **-curred, -cur·ring. 1.** To have or express the same opinion : agree. **2.** To cooperate. **3.** To coincide. **—con·cur′rence** *n.*

con·cur·rent (kən-kûr′ənt) *adj.* **1.** Occurring at the same time. **2.** Acting together. **3.** *Law.* Having equal authority.

con·cuss (kən-kŭs′) *v.* To injure by concussion.

con·cus·sion (kən-kŭsh′ən) *n.* **1.** A violent jolt : shock. **2.** An injury of a soft bodily structure, esp. the brain, that results from a severe blow. **—con·cus′sive** (-kŭs′ĭv) *adj.* **—con·cus′sive·ly** *adv.*

con·demn (kən-dĕm′) *v.* **1.** To express strong disapproval of : denounce. **2. a.** To find guilty. **b.** To pronounce judgment against : sentence. **3.** To declare officially unfit for use. **4.** To declare appropriated by law for public use. **—con·demn′a·ble** *adj.* **—con′dem·na′tion** *n.* **—con·dem′na·to′ry** *adj.* **—con·demn′er** *n.*

con·den·sate (kŏn′dən-sāt′, -dĕn-, kən-dĕn′sāt′) *n.* A product of condensation.

con·dense (kən-dĕns′) *v.* **-densed, -dens·ing. 1.** To make or become more compact : concentrate. **2.** To make concise : abridge <*condense* 3 articles into 1> **3.** To form a liquid from (e.g., a vapor). **4.** To undergo condensation. **—con·dens′a·bil′i·ty** *n.* **—con·dens′a·ble, con·dens′i·ble** *adj.* **—con′den·sa′tion** (kŏn′dĕn-sā′shən) *n.* **—con·dens′er** *n.*

condensed milk *n.* Sweetened evaporated milk.

con·de·scend (kŏn′dĭ-sĕnd′) *v.* **1.** To agree to do something one considers beneath one's dignity or rank : deign. **2.** To deal with or treat others in a patronizing way. **—con′de·scend′er** *n.* **—con′de·scend′ing** *adj.* **—con′de·scend′ing·ly** *adv.* **—con′de·scen′sion** *n.*

con·di·ment (kŏn′də-mənt) *n.* A seasoning for food.

con·di·tion (kən-dĭsh′ən) *n.* **1.** Mode or state of being. **2.** A state of health or fitness. **3.** *Informal.* A disease or ailment. **4.** A requirement : prerequisite. **5.** Something that restricts or modifies : qualification. **6.** *often* **conditions.** Existing circumstances <poor sailing *conditions*> ☆**syns:** MODE, POSTURE, SITUATION, STATE, STATUS —*v.* **1.** To make conditional. **2.** To make fit. **3.** To accustom (a person) to : adapt. **4.** *Psychol.* To cause to respond in a given manner to a given stimulus.

con·di·tion·al (kən-dĭsh′ə-nəl) *adj.* **1.** Imposing, based on, or including a condition or conditions. **2.** Stating or implying a grammatical condition. —*n.* A mood, tense, clause, or word expressing a grammatical condition. **—con·di′tion·al′i·ty** (-dĭsh′ə-năl′ĭ-tē) *n.*

con·di·tioned (kən-dĭsh′ənd) *adj.* **1.** Subject to or dependent on conditions. **2.** Prepared for a specific action or process. **3.** *Psychol.* Displaying or trained to display a modified or new response.

con·di·tion·er (kən-dĭsh′ə-nər) *n.* **1.** One that conditions. **2.** An additive or application that improves the quality or usability of a substance.

con·do (kŏn′dō) *n.* *Informal.* CONDOMINIUM 2.

con·dole (kən-dōl′) *v.* **-doled, -dol·ing.** To express sorrow or sympathy. **—con·do′la·to′ry** *adj.* **—con·do′lence** *n.* **—con·dol′er** *n.*

con·dom (kŏm′dəm) *n.* A thin rubber sheath designed to cover the penis during sexual intercourse for contraceptive or antivenereal purposes.

con·do·min·i·um (kŏn′də-mĭn′ē-əm) *n.* **1.** Joint rule or sovereignty. **2. a.** A residential structure, as an apartment building, in which the units are owned individually. **b.** An apartment in such a structure.

con·done (kən-dōn′) *v.* **-doned, -don·ing.** To overlook, disregard, or forgive (an offense). **—con·don′er** *n.*

con·dor (kŏn′dôr′, -dər) *n.* A very large New World vulture, *Vultur gryphus,* of the Andes, or *Gymnogyps californianus,* of the Calif. mountains.

con·duce (kən-do͞os′, -dyo͞os′) *v.* **-duced, -duc·ing.** To lead to a specific result : contribute. **—con·du′cive** *adj.*

con·duct (kən-dŭkt′) *v.* **1.** To direct the course of : control <*conduct* an experiment><*conduct* a meeting> **2.** To guide or lead. **3.** To serve as a medium for conveying : transmit <Some plastics *conduct* light.> **4.** To behave or act in a given way. —*n.* (kŏn′dŭkt′). **1.** The way one behaves. **2.** Management : control. **—con·duct′i·bil′i·ty** *n.* **—con·duct′i·ble** *adj.* **—con·duc′tion** *n.*

con·duc·tance (kən-dŭk′təns) *n.* A measure of a material's capacity for conducting electricity.

con·duc·tive (kən-dŭk′tĭv) *adj.* Exhibiting the power or ability to transmit or conduct. **—con′duc·tiv′i·ty** *n.*

con·duc·tor (kən-dŭk′tər) *n.* **1.** One who conducts, esp: **a.** The person in charge of a public conveyance, as a streetcar or railroad train. **b.** The director of a musical ensemble, as an orchestra. **2.** *Physics.* A substance or medium that conducts heat, light, or sound.

con·duit (kŏn′dĭt, -do͞o-ĭt) *n.* **1.** A channel or pipe for conveying fluids, as water. **2.** A tube or duct through which electric wires or cable pass.

cone (kōn) *n.* **1.** A surface formed by a straight line that passes through a fixed point and moves along the intersection with a fixed curve. **2.** The figure formed by a cone, bound by its vertex and a plane that intersects above or below the vertex. **3.** A scaly cylindrical or rounded structure bearing seeds <a pine *cone*> **4.** A photoreceptor in the retina of the eye. **5.** A cone-shaped wafer for holding ice cream.

co·ney (kō′nē, kŭn′ē) *n. var. of* CONY.

con·fab·u·late (kən-făb′yə-lāt′) *v.* **-lat·ed, -lat·ing.** To converse informally : chat. **—con·fab′u·la′tion** *n.* **—con·fab′u·la′tor** *n.* **—con·fab′u·la·to′ry** *adj.*

con·fec·tion (kən-fĕk′shən) *n.* A sweet preparation, as candy.

con·fec·tion·er (kən-fĕk′shə-nər) *n.* A maker or seller of confections.

con·fec·tion·er·y (kən-fĕk′shə-nĕr′ē) *n., pl.* **-ies. 1.** Candies and confections as a whole. **2.** *also* **con·fec·tion·ar·y.** A confectioner's shop.

con·fed·er·a·cy (kən-fĕd′ər-ə-sē) *n., pl.* **-cies. 1. a.** A political alliance of persons, parties, or states : league. **b.** The 11 S states that seceded from the U.S. during the Civil War. **2.** A conspiracy.

con·fed·er·ate (kən-fĕd′ər-ĭt) *n.* **1.** A member of a confederacy : ally. **2.** An accomplice. **3.** A supporter of the Confederacy. —*v.* (ə-rāt′) **-at·ed, -at·ing.** To join together in a confederacy.

con·fed·er·a·tion (kən-fĕd′ə-rā′shən) *n.* A confederacy.

con·fer (kən-fûr′) *v.* **-ferred, -fer·ring. 1.** To bestow or award. **2.** To hold a conference : consult together. **—con·fer′ment** *n.* **—con·fer′ra·ble** *adj.* **—con·fer′ral** *n.* **—con·fer′rer** *n.*

con·fer·ence (kŏn′fər-əns, -frəns) *n.* **1.** A meeting for discussion. **2.** An association of athletic teams.

con·fess (kən-fĕs′) *v.* **1.** To acknowledge or disclose one's wrongdoing or fault. **2.** To acknowledge belief in. **3.** To disclose (one's sins) to God or a priest for absolution. **—con·fess′ed·ly** (-ĭd-lē) *adv.*

con·fes·sion (kən-fĕsh′ən) *n.* **1.** An act of confessing. **2.** Something confessed. **3.** A formal admission of guilt. **4.** Disclosure of one's sins to a priest for absolution. **5.** A church or religious group adhering to a particular creed.

con·fes·sion·al (kən-fĕsh′ə-nəl) *n.* A small stall in which a priest hears confessions.

con·fes·sor *also* **con·fess·er** (kən-fĕs′ər) *n.* **1.** A priest to whom sins are confessed. **2.** A person who confesses.

con·fet·ti (kən-fĕt′ē) *pl.n.* (*sing. in number*). Small pieces or streamers of colored paper strewn about on festive occasions.

con·fi·dant (kŏn′fĭ-dănt′, -dänt′, kŏn′fĭ-dănt′, -dänt′) *n.* One to whom private matters are confided.

con·fide (kən-fīd′) *v.* **-fid·ed, -fid·ing. 1.** To tell confidentially. **2.** To entrust to another. **—con·fid′er** *n.* **—con·fid′ing** *adj.* **—con·fid′ing·ly** *adv.*

con·fi·dence (kŏn′fĭ-dəns) *n.* **1.** Reliance or trust. **2.** A trusting relationship. **3.** A feeling of self-assurance. **4.** The assurance that someone will keep a secret. **5.** A secret. ☆**syns:** BELIEF, FAITH, RELIANCE, TRUST **—con′fi·dent** *adj.*

confidence game *n.* A swindle brought about by gaining the victim's confidence.

confidence man *n.* One who swindles by using a confidence game.

con·fi·den·tial (kŏn′fĭ-dĕn′shəl) *adj.* **1.** Disclosed in secret. **2.** Entrusted with another's confidence. **—con′fi·den′ti·al′i·ty** *n.* **—con′fi·den′tial·ly** *adv.*

con·fig·u·ra·tion (kən-fĭg′yə-rā′shən) *n.* Arrangement of elements or parts. **—con·fig′u·ra′tion·al·ly** *adv.* **—con·fig′u·ra′tive** (-rā′tĭv), **con·fig′u·ra′tion·al** *adj.*

con·fine (kən-fīn′) *v.* **-fined, -fin·ing. 1.** To keep within bounds : limit or restrict. **2.** To put in prison. —*n.* **confines** (kŏn′fīnz′). The limits of an area : borders. **—con·fin′a·ble, con·fine′a·ble** *adj.* **—con·fine′ment** *n.* **—con·fin′er** *n.*

con·firm (kən-fûrm′) *v.* **1.** To support or establish the validity of : corroborate. **2.** To make stronger : establish. **3.** To ratify formally. **4.** To administer the rite of confirmation to. ☆**syns:** ATTEST, AUTHENTICATE, BACK, BEAR OUT, CORROBORATE, SUBSTANTIATE, VALIDATE, VERIFY, WARRANT **—con·firm′a·ble** *adj.* **—con·fir′ma·to′ry, con·fir′ma·tive** *adj.*

con·fir·ma·tion (kŏn′fər-mā′shən) *n.* **1.** An act of confirm ing. **2.** Something that verifies. **3.** A rite admitting a person to full membership in a church or synagogue.

con•fis•cate (kŏn′fĭ-skāt′) *v.* **-cat•ed, -cat•ing. 1.** To appropriate (private property) for the public treasury. **2.** To appropriate or seize by or as if by authority. **–con′fis•ca′tion** *n.* **–con′fis•ca′tor** *n.*

con•fla•gra•tion (kŏn′flə-grā′shən) *n.* A large, destructive fire.

con•flate (kən-flāt′) *v.* **-flat•ed, -flat•ing.** To combine (e.g., 2 variant texts) into a whole. **–con•fla′tion** *n.*

con•flict (kŏn′flĭkt′) *n.* **1.** Prolonged open warfare. **2.** A state of disharmony : clash. ☆***syns:*** BELLIGERENCY, HOSTILITIES, STRIFE, WAR, WARFARE *–v.* (kən-flĭkt′). To be opposed : differ. **–con•flic′tive** *adj.*

conflict of interest *n.* A conflict between the public obligations and private interests of a public official.

con•flu•ence (kŏn′flo͞o-əns) *n.* **1. a.** A flowing together of 2 or more streams. **b.** The point of juncture of such streams. **2.** An assembly. **–con•flu′ent** *adj.* & *n.*

con•flux (kŏn′flŭks′) *n.* A confluence.

con•form (kən-fôrm′) *v.* **1.** To make or become similar in form or character : correspond. **2.** To act or be in compliance. **3.** To act in accordance with prevailing modes or customs. **–con•form′a•bil′i•ty** *n.* **–con•form′a•ble** *adj.* **–con•form′a•bly** *adv.* **–con•form′er** *n.* **–con•form′ist** *n.*

con•for•mance (kən-fôr′məns) *n.* Conformity.

con•for•ma•tion (kŏn′fər-mā′shən) *n.* The shape, structure, or arrangement of something.

con•for•mi•ty (kən-fôr′mĭ-tē) *n., pl.* **-ties. 1.** Correspondence in form or character : agreement. **2.** Action in agreement with prevailing modes or customs.

con•found (kən-found′, kŏn-) *v.* **1.** To bewilder or perplex. **2.** To mistake (1 thing) for another <*confound* truths and lies> **–con•found′er** *n.*

con•fra•ter•ni•ty (kŏn′frə-tûr′nĭ-tē) *n., pl.* **-ties.** A group united in a common profession or for a common purpose.

con•frere (kŏn′frâr′) *n.* An associate : colleague.

con•front (kən-frŭnt′) *v.* **1.** To come face to face with, esp. with defiance or hostility. **2.** To come up against : encounter. **–con′fron•ta′tion** (kŏn′frən-tā′shən) *n.* **–con′fron•ta′tion•al** *adj.*

Con•fu•cian•ism (kən-fyo͞o′shə-nĭz′əm) *n.* The ethical principles based on the teachings of Confucius. **–Con•fu′cian** *n.* & *adj.* **–Con•fu′cian•ist** *n.*

Con•fu•cius (kən-fyo͞o′shəs). 551–479 B.C. Chinese philosopher.

con•fuse (kən-fyo͞oz′) *v.* **-fused, -fus•ing. 1.** To bewilder : mislead. **2.** To mix up : jumble. **3.** To fail to differentiate from something else <*confuse* wealth with happiness> **4.** To make unclear : blur. ☆***syns:*** DISORDER, JUMBLE, SCRAMBLE, SNARL **–con•fus′ed•ly** (-fyo͞o′zĭd-lē) *adv.* **–con•fus′ing•ly** *adv.* **–con•fu′sion** *n.*

con•fute (kən-fyo͞ot′) *v.* **-fut•ed, -fut•ing.** To disprove decisively : refute. **–con•fut′a•ble** *adj.* **–con′fu•ta′tion** (kŏn′-) *n.* **–con•fu′ta•tive** *adj.*

con•ga (kŏng′gə) *n.* **1.** A dance of Latin-American origin in which the dancers form a long, winding line. **2.** Music for the conga. **–con′ga** *v.*

con game *n. Slang.* A confidence game.

con•geal (kən-jēl′) *v.* **1.** To solidify, as by freezing. **2.** To jell : coagulate. **–con•geal′a•ble** *adj.* **–con•geal′ment** *n.*

con•gen•ial (kən-jēn′yəl) *adj.* **1.** Having the same temperament, habits, or tastes : sympathetic. **2.** Friendly : sociable. **3.** Agreeably suited to one's needs or nature. **–con•ge′ni•al′i•ty** (-jē′nē-ăl′ĭ-tē), **con•gen′ial•ness** *n.* **–con•gen′ial•ly** *adv.*

con•gen•i•tal (kən-jĕn′ĭ-tl) *adj.* **1.** Existing from the time of birth but not hereditary. **2.** Being such as if by nature <a *congenital* liar> **–con•gen′i•tal•ly** *adv.*

con•ger (kŏng′gər) *n.* A large, scaleless marine eel of the family Congridae, esp. *Conger oceanicus*, of Atlantic waters.

con•ge•ries (kŏn′jə-rēz′, kən-jîr′ēz′) *n.* (*sing. in number*). A collection of things.

con•gest (kən-jĕst′) *v.* **1.** To overfill. **2.** *Pathol.* To cause excessive blood accumulation in (an organ or vessel). **–con•ges′tion** *n.* **–con•ges′tive** *adj.*

con•glom•er•ate (kən-glŏm′ə-rāt′) *v.* **-at•ed, -at•ing.** To form or cause to form into a mass of adhering material. *–n.* (-ər-ĭt). **1.** An adhering mass : cluster. **2.** *Geol.* Pebbles and gravel embedded in a cementing material such as hardened clay. **3.** A business enterprise consisting of many widely diversified companies. **–con•glom′er•ate** (-ər-ĭt) *adj.* **–con•glom′er•a′tion** *n.*

Con•go (kŏng′gō). **1.** Country of WC Africa. *Cap.* Brazzaville. *Pop.* 1,405,000. **2.** River of C Africa, flowing to the Atlantic. **–Con′go•lese′** (-lēz′, -lēs′) *adj.* & *n.*

con•grat•u•late (kən-grăch′ə-lāt′) *v.* **-lat•ed, -lat•ing.** To praise or acknowledge the good fortune or achievement of. **–con•grat′u•la′tion** *n.* **–con•grat′u•la′tor** *n.* **–con•grat′u•la•to′ry** (-lə-tôr′ē, -tōr′ē) *adj.*

con•gre•gate (kŏng′grĭ-gāt′) *v.* **-gat•ed, -gat•ing.** To come or bring together in a crowd : assemble. **–con′gre•ga′tor** *n.*

con•gre•ga•tion (kŏng′grĭ-gā′shən) *n.* **1.** An act of congregating. **2.** An assembly. **3.** A group of people gathered for religious worship, esp. on a regular basis.

con•gre•ga•tion•al (kŏng′grĭ-gā′shə-nəl) *adj.* **1.** Of or relating to a congregation. **2. Congregational.** Of or relating to a Protestant denomination in which each individual member church is autonomous. **–con′gre•ga′tion•al•ism** *n.* **–con′gre•ga′tion•al•ist** *n.*

con•gress (kŏng′grĭs) *n.* **1.** A formal meeting or assembly to discuss problems. **2.** The legislature of a nation, esp. of a republic. **3. Congress.** The national legislative body of the U.S., consisting of the Senate and the House of Representatives. **–con•gres′sion•al** *adj.* **–con•gres′sion•al•ly** *adv.*

con•gress•man (kŏng′grĭs-mən) *n.* A member of the U.S. Congress, esp. of the House of Representatives.

con•gress•wom•an (kŏng′grĭs-wo͝om′ən) *n.* A woman member of the U.S. Congress, esp. of the House of Representatives.

con•gru•ent (kŏng′gro͞o-ənt, kən-gro͞o′ənt) *adj.* **1.** Corresponding : congruous. **2.** *Math.* Having the same size and shape <*congruent* triangles> **–con•gru′ence** *n.* **–con′gru•ent•ly** *adv.*

con•gru•ous (kŏng′gro͞o-əs) *adj.* **1.** Corresponding in nature or kind : harmonious. **2.** *Math.* Congruent.

con•ic (kŏn′ĭk) *also* **con•i•cal** (-ĭ-kəl) *adj.* **1.** Shaped like a cone. **2.** Relating to a cone.

con•i•fer (kŏn′ə-fər, kō′nə-) *n.* A usu. evergreen cone-bearing tree, as a fir or pine. **–co•nif′er•ous** (kō-nĭf′ər-əs, kə-) *adj.*

conj. *abbr.* conjunction.

con•jec•ture (kən-jĕk′chər) *n.* Inference based on incomplete or inconclusive evidence. **–con•jec′tur•a•ble** *adj.* **–con•jec′tur•al** *adj.* **–con•jec′ture** *v.*

con•join (kən-join′) *v.* To join or become joined together : unite. **–con•joint′** *adj.*

con•ju•gal (kŏn′jo͝o-gəl, -jə-) *adj.* Of or relating to marriage or the relationship between spouses. **–con′ju•gal•ly** *adv.*

con•ju•gate (kŏn′jə-gāt′) *v.* **-gat•ed, -gat•ing.** To inflect a word, esp. a verb. *–adj.* (-gĭt, -gāt′). Joined together, esp. in pairs : coupled. **–con′ju•gate′ly** *adv.* **–con′ju•ga′tive** *adj.* **–con′ju•ga′tor** *n.*

con•ju•ga•tion (kŏn′jə-gā′shən) *n.* **1.** A verb inflection. **2.** A schematic presentation of the full set of inflected forms of a verb. **–con′ju•ga′tion•al** *adj.*

con•junct (kən-jŭngkt′, kŏn′jŭngkt′) *adj.* Joined together : combined.

con•junc•tion (kən-jŭngk′shən) *n.* **1.** A combination or association. **2.** The simultaneous occurrence of two conditions, events, etc. **3.** A word, as *and* or *but*, that connects other words in a sentence.

con•junc•ti•va (kŏn′jŭngk-tī′və) *n., pl.* **-vas** *or* **-vae** (-vē′). The mucous membrane lining the inner surface of the eyelid and the surface of the eyeball. **–con′junc•ti′val** *adj.*

con•junc•tive (kən-jŭngk′tĭv) *adj.* **1.** Connective : joining. **2.** Joined together : combined. **3.** Of or used as a conjunction. *–n.* A conjunctive word.

con•junc•ti•vi•tis (kən-jŭngk′tə-vī′tĭs) *n. Pathol.* Inflammation of the conjunctiva, often highly contagious.

con•junc•ture (kən-jŭngk′chər) *n.* **1.** A set of circumstances. **2.** A critical set of circumstances : crisis.

con•jure (kŏn′jər, kən-jo͝or′) *v.* **-jured, -jur•ing. 1.** To call on or entreat solemnly, esp. by an oath. **2.** To summon (a spirit) by sorcery. **3.** To cause or effect by or as if by magic. **4.** To call to mind <sights *conjuring* up past Christmases> **–con′ju•ra′tion** *n.* **–con′jur•er, con′ju•ror** *n.*

conk (kŏngk, kôngk) *v. Slang.* **1.** To strike, esp. on the head. **2.** To fail abruptly <The oven *conked* out.> **3.** To fall asleep <*conked* out after dinner>

con man *n. Slang.* A confidence man.

Conn. *abbr.* Connecticut.

con•nect (kə-nĕkt′) *v.* **1.** To join or become joined : unite. **2.** To think of as related : associate. **–con•nect′ed•ly** *adv.* **–con•nec′tor, con•nect′er** *n.*

Con•nect•i•cut (kə-nĕt′ə-kət). State of the NE U.S. *Cap.* Hartford. *Pop.* 3,105,576.

con•nec•tion (kə-nĕk′shən) *n.* **1.** Junction : union. **2.** A link or bond. **3.** An association or relationship. **4.** Logical ordering of words or ideas : coherence. **5.** The relation of a word or idea to its context. **6.** A person with whom one is associated, as by kinship or business. **7.** The meeting of various means of transportation for the transfer of passengers.

con·nec·tive (kə-nĕk′tĭv) *adj.* Serving or tending to connect. —*n.* Something that connects, esp. a connecting word, as a conjunction. **—con′nec·tiv′i·ty** *n.*
connect time *n. Computer Sci.* The elapsed time during which a user of a remote terminal is connected with a timesharing system.
con·nex·ion (kə-nĕk′shən) *n. esp. Brit. var. of* CONNECTION.
conning tower *n.* **1.** The pilothouse of a warship. **2.** An enclosed, raised observation post on a submarine, often used as a means of entrance and exit.
con·nip·tion (kə-nĭp′shən) *n. Informal.* A fit of anger or other violent emotion.
con·nive (kə-nīv′) *v.* **-nived, -niv·ing. 1.** To pretend ignorance of a known wrong, thus implying sanction. **2.** To cooperate secretly. **3.** To conspire. **—con·niv′ance** *n.* **—con·niv′er** *n.* **—con·niv′er·y** *n.*
con·nois·seur (kŏn′ə-sûr′) *n.* An astute judge in matters of art or taste : expert. **—con′nois·seur′ship′** *n.*
con·no·ta·tion (kŏn′ə-tā′shən) *n.* A figurative meaning of a word in addition to the literal meaning. **—con′no·ta′tive** *adj.*
con·note (kə-nōt′) *v.* **-not·ed, -not·ing. 1.** To suggest in addition to literal meaning. **2.** To involve as a condition <Lying often *connotes* guilt.>
con·nu·bi·al (kə-no͞o′bē-əl, -nyo͞o′-) *adj.* Conjugal. **—con·nu′bi·al·ly** *adv.*
con·quer (kŏng′kər) *v.* **1.** To subdue or defeat, esp. by force of arms. **2.** To overcome or surmount. **—con′quer·or** *n.*
con·quest (kŏn′kwĕst′, kŏng′-) *n.* **1.** The act or process of conquering. **2.** Something conquered.
con·quis·ta·dor (kŏn-kwĭs′tə-dôr′, kông-kēs′-) *n., pl.* **-dors** *or* **-do·res** (-dôr′ās, -ēz). A conqueror, esp. one of the 16th-cent. Spanish conquerors of Mexico and Peru.
cons. *abbr.* **1.** consigned; consignment. **2.** constitution; constitutional.
con·san·guin·e·ous (kŏn′săng-gwĭn′ē-əs) *adj.* Having blood relationship. **—con′san·guin′i·ty** *n.*
con·science (kŏn′shəns) *n.* **1.** The faculty of recognizing the difference between right and wrong with regard to one's own behavior. **2.** Conformity to one's own sense of proper conduct.
con·sci·en·tious (kŏn′shē-ĕn′shəs) *adj.* **1.** Honest : scrupulous. **2.** Painstaking.
conscientious objector *n.* One whose religious and moral principles prohibit participation in military service.
con·scious (kŏn′shəs) *adj.* **1. a.** Aware of one's own existence, sensations, and environment. **b.** Capable of thought, will, or perception. **c.** Awake. **2.** Subjectively perceived <*conscious* regret> **3.** Deliberate <a *conscious* affront>
con·script (kŏn′skrĭpt′) *n.* One who is drafted : draftee. —*adj.* Compulsorily enrolled : drafted. —*v.* (kən-skrĭpt′). To draft. **—con·scrip′tion** *n.*
con·se·crate (kŏn′sĭ-krāt′) *v.* **-crat·ed, -crat·ing. 1.** To set apart or declare as holy. **2.** To change (the Eucharistic elements) into the body and blood of Christ. **3.** To induct (a priest) into an order of bishops. **4.** To dedicate to a specific goal. **—con′se·cra′tion** *n.* **—con′se·cra′tor** *n.*
con·sec·u·tive (kən-sĕk′yə-tĭv) *adj.* Successively following without interruption : continuous. **—con·sec′u·tive·ly** *adv.* **—con·sec′u·tive·ness** *n.*
con·sen·sus (kən-sĕn′səs) *n.* **1.** Collective opinion. **2.** General accord.
con·sent (kən-sĕnt′) *v.* To give assent : agree. —*n.* Agreement and acceptance, as to an act. **—con·sent′er** *n.*
con·se·quence (kŏn′sĭ-kwĕns′, -kwəns) *n.* **1.** An effect or result. **2.** Distinction or importance.
con·se·quent (kŏn′sĭ-kwĕnt′, -kwənt) *adj.* Following as a natural effect or result. **—con′se·quent′ly** *adv.*
con·se·quen·tial (kŏn′sĭ-kwĕn′shəl) *adj.* **1.** Of consequence : significant. **2.** Arrogant or self-important : pompous.
con·ser·va·tion (kŏn′sər-vā′shən) *n.* **1.** The act or process of conserving : saving. **2.** Controlled use and protection of natural resources, as forests. **—con′ser·va′tion·al** *adj.* **—con′ser·va′tion·ist** *n.*
con·serv·a·tive (kən-sûr′və-tĭv) *adj.* **1.** Tending to oppose change. **2.** Moderate : cautious. **3.** Traditional in style or manner. **4.** Belonging to a conservative political party. **5.** Tending to conserve : preservative. —*n.* **1.** A conservative person. **2.** A supporter of a conservative political party. **—con·serv′a·tive·ly** *adv.* **—con·serv′a·tive·ness** *n.* **—con·ser′va·tism** *n.*
con·ser·va·tor (kən-sûr′və-tər, kŏn′sər-vā′tər) *n.* **1.** A protector, as against injury. **2.** *Law.* A guardian.
con·serv·a·to·ry (kən-sûr′və-tôr′ē, -tōr′ē) *n., pl.* **-ries. 1.** A greenhouse. **2.** A school of music or dramatic art.
con·serve (kən-sûrv′) *v.* **-served, -serv·ing. 1. a.** To save from loss or depletion. **b.** To avoid wasting. **2.** To preserve (fruits) with sugar. —*n.* (kŏn′sûrv′). A jam of fruits stewed in sugar. **—con·serv′a·ble** *adj.* **—con·serv′er** *n.*
con·sid·er (kən-sĭd′ər) *v.* **1.** To think about seriously. **2.** To regard as : deem. **3.** To judge : believe. **—con·sid′ered** *adj.*
con·sid·er·a·ble (kən-sĭd′ər-ə-bəl) *adj.* **1.** Large in amount, extent, or degree. **2.** Worthy of consideration : important. **—con·sid′er·a·bly** *adv.*
con·sid·er·ate (kən-sĭd′ər-ĭt) *adj.* Mindful of the needs or feelings of others. **—con·sid′er·ate·ly** *adv.*
con·sid·er·a·tion (kən-sĭd′ə-rā′shən) *n.* **1.** Careful deliberation. **2.** Something to be considered in making a decision or judgment. **3.** Mindful regard for others. **4.** Payment : recompense.
con·sid·er·ing (kən-sĭd′ər-ĭng) *prep.* In view of <spry *considering* your age>
con·sign (kən-sīn′) *v.* **1.** To entrust to the care of another. **2.** To deliver (e.g., goods or merchandise) for custody or sale. **—con·sign′a·ble** *adj.* **—con′sign·ee** *n.* **—con·sig′nor, con·sign′er** *n.*
con·sign·ment (kən-sīn′mənt) *n.* **1.** The act of consigning. **2.** Something consigned.
con·sist (kən-sĭst′) *v.* **1.** To be made up or composed <Mud *consists* of soil and water.> **2.** To be inherent : have a basis.
con·sis·ten·cy (kən-sĭs′tən-sē) *n., pl.* **-cies. 1.** Agreement among things or parts. **2.** Compatibility or agreement among successive acts, ideas, or events. **3.** Degree of texture, density, or viscosity. **—con·sis′tent** *adj.* **—con·sis′tent·ly** *adv.*
con·sis·to·ry (kən-sis′tə-rē) *n., pl.* **-ries.** *Rom. Cath. Ch.* A solemn assembly of cardinals with the pope presiding.
con·sole[1] (kən-sōl′) *v.* **-soled, -sol·ing.** To solace : comfort. **—con·sol′a·ble** *adj.* **—con′so·la′tion** *n.* **—con·sol′er** *n.* **—con·sol′ing·ly** *adv.*
con·sole[2] (kŏn′sōl′) *n.* **1.** The desklike section of an organ that contains the keyboard, stops, and pedals. **2.** A radio or television cabinet designed to stand on the floor. **3.** A control panel.

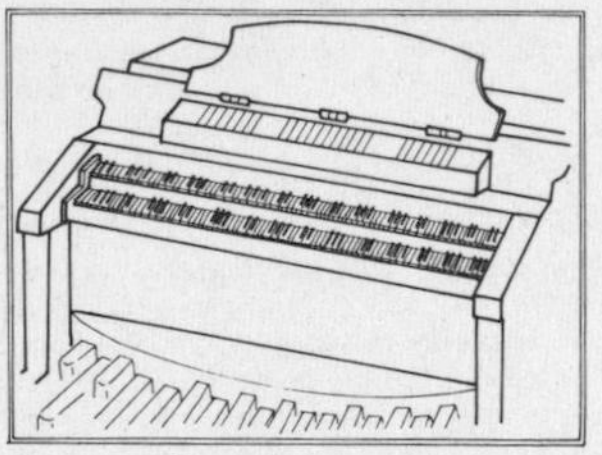

console[2]

con·sol·i·date (kən-sŏl′ĭ-dāt′) *v.* **-dat·ed, -dat·ing. 1.** To form into a compact mass. **2.** To unite or become united into one system or body : combine. **—con·sol′i·da′tion** *n.* **—con·sol′i·da′tor** *n.*
con·som·mé (kŏn′sə-mā′, kŏn′sə-mā′) *n.* A clear soup of meat or vegetable stock.
con·so·nance (kŏn′sə-nəns) *n.* Harmony : agreement.
con·so·nant (kŏn′sə-nənt) *adj.* **1.** Being in agreement or accord. **2.** Corresponding or harmonious in sound. —*n.* **1.** A speech sound produced by partially or completely obstructing the flow of air from the mouth. **2.** A letter of the alphabet representing a consonant, as *b, m, s, t,* etc. **—con′so·nan′tal** *adj.* **—con′so·nan′tal·ly** *adv.* **—con′so·nant·ly** *adv.*
con·sort (kŏn′sôrt′) *n.* A spouse, esp. the spouse of a monarch. —*v.* (kən-sôrt′). **1.** To keep or unite in company : associate. **2.** To be in accord.
con·sor·ti·um (kən-sôr′tē-əm, -shē-) *n., pl.* **-ti·a** (-tē-ə, -shē-ə). An association of financial institutions or capitalists, esp. in international finance.
con·spic·u·ous (kən-spĭk′yo͞o-əs) *adj.* **1.** Obvious : noticeable. **2.** Notable : remarkable. **—con·spic′u·ous·ly** *adv.* **—con·spic′u·ous·ness** *n.*
con·spir·a·cy (kən-spîr′ə-sē) *n., pl.* **-cies. 1.** The act of conspiring. **2.** A group of conspirators.
con·spire (kən-spīr′) *v.* **-spired, -spir·ing. 1.** To plan together in secret to commit a wrongful act. **2.** To act or work together. **—con·spir′a·tor** *n.*
con·sta·ble (kŏn′stə-bəl, kŭn′-) *n.* **1.** A peace officer. **2.** *esp. Brit.* A police officer.
con·stab·u·lar·y (kən-stăb′yə-lĕr′ē) *n., pl.* **-ies. 1.** Constables in general. **2.** An armed police unit organized along military lines.
con·stant (kŏn′stənt) *adj.* **1.** Recurring continually : persistent. **2.** Invariable : uniform. **3.** Steadfast : faithful. —*n.* Some-

thing that is unchanging. **—con'stan·cy** *n.* **—con'stant·ly** *adv.*

Con·stan·tine I (kŏn'stən-tēn'). "the Great." 280?–337. Roman emperor (306–37).

Con·stan·ti·no·ple (kŏn'stăn-tə-nō'pəl). Istanbul.

con·stel·la·tion (kŏn'stə-lā'shən) *n.* Any of 88 stellar groups named after and thought to resemble various mythological characters, inanimate objects, and animals.

con·ster·na·tion (kŏn'stər-nā'shən) *n.* Sudden amazement, confusion, or dismay.

con·sti·pa·tion (kŏn'stə-pā'shən) *n.* Difficult or infrequent evacuation of the bowels. **—con'sti·pate'** *v.*

con·stit·u·en·cy (kən-stĭch'o͞o-ən-sē) *n., pl.* **-cies. 1.** The body of voters represented by an elected legislator. **2.** The district so represented.

con·stit·u·ent (kən-stĭch'o͞o-ənt) *adj.* **1.** Component. **2.** Having power to elect or designate. **3.** Empowered to make or amend a constitution. *—n.* **1.** A member of a group represented by an elected official. **2.** A component part.

con·sti·tute (kŏn'stĭ-to͞ot,' -tyo͞ot') *v.* **-tut·ed, -tut·ing. 1.** To make up : compose. **2.** To set up : establish or enact. **3.** To designate, as for an office : appoint.

con·sti·tu·tion (kŏn'stĭ-to͞o'shən, -tyo͞o'-) *n.* **1. a.** Composition : structure. **b.** A person's physical make-up. **2. a.** The fundamental laws of an institution, as a nation. **b.** The document containing such laws.

con·sti·tu·tion·al (kŏn'stĭ-to͞o'shə-nəl, -tyo͞o'-) *adj.* **1.** Essential : basic <a *constitutional* reluctance to lie> **2.** Consistent with, contained in, or operating under a constitution. *—n.* A regular walk for one's health. **—con'sti·tu'tion·al'i·ty** *n.* **—con'sti·tu'tion·al·ly** *adv.*

con·strain (kən-strān') *v.* **1.** To oblige : compel. **2.** To keep confined. **3.** To check : restrain. **—con·strained'** *adj.* **—con·strain'ed·ly** *adv.*

con·straint (kən-strānt') *n.* **1.** Threat or use of force : compulsion. **2.** A restriction. **3.** The quality or state of being restrained. **4.** Embarrassed reserve.

con·strict (kən-strĭkt') *v.* To contract or compress : squeeze. **—con·stric'tion** *n.* **—con·stric'tive** *adj.* **—con·stric'tive·ly** *adv.*

con·struct (kən-strŭkt') *v.* To make, build, or create. **—con·struct'i·ble** *adj.* **—con·struc'tor, con·struct'er** *n.*

con·struc·tion (kən-strŭk'shən) *n.* **1.** The act, process, or work of building. **2.** Something built. **3.** Arrangement of words in a meaningful clause or sentence. **—con·struc'tion·al** *adj.*

con·struc·tive (kən-strŭk'tĭv) *adj.* **1.** Helpful : useful. **2.** Of or relating to construction. **—con·struc'tive·ly** *adv.* **—con·struc'tive·ness** *n.*

con·strue (kən-stro͞o') *v.* **-strued, -stru·ing. 1.** To analyze the grammatical structure of (e.g., a sentence). **2.** To give a meaning to : interpret. **3.** To translate, esp. aloud.

con·sul (kŏn'səl) *n.* **1.** An official appointed to reside in a foreign city and represent his or her government's citizens and commercial interests there. **2.** A chief magistrate of the ancient Roman Republic. **—con'su·lar** *adj.* **—con'sul·ship'** *n.*

con·sul·ate (kŏn'sə-lĭt) *n.* The premises occupied by a consul.

con·sult (kən-sŭlt') *v.* **1.** To seek information or advice from. **2.** To confer. **—con·sult'ant** *n.* **—con'sul·ta'tion** *n.*

con·sume (kən-so͞om') *v.* **-sumed, -sum·ing. 1.** To eat or drink up : ingest. **2.** To expend (e.g., fuel) : use up. **3.** To squander : waste. **4.** To destroy completely, as by fire. **5.** To engross : absorb. **—con·sum'a·ble** *adj.* & *n.*

con·sum·er (kən-so͞o'mər) *n.* **1.** One that consumes. **2.** A buyer of goods or services.

con·sum·er·ism (kən-so͞o'mə-rĭz'əm) *n.* The protection of the rights of consumers.

con·sum·mate (kŏn'sə-māt') *v.* **-mat·ed, -mat·ing. 1.** To complete : conclude. **2.** To complete (a marriage) with the initial act of sexual intercourse. *—adj.* (kən-sŭm'ĭt). **1.** Perfect. **2.** Highly skilled. **3.** Utter : complete. **—con·sum'mate·ly** *adv.* **—con'sum·ma'tion** *n.*

con·sump·tion (kən-sŭmp'shən) *n.* **1. a.** The act of consuming. **b.** A quantity consumed. **2.** The using of consumer goods and services. **3.** *Pathol.* A wasting of tissue. **4.** Tuberculosis.

con·sump·tive (kən-sŭmp'tĭv) *adj.* **1.** Tending to waste or destroy. **2.** Afflicted with consumption. *—n.* One afflicted with consumption.

cont. *abbr.* **1.** contents. **2.** continent. **3.** continue; continued. **4.** control.

con·tact (kŏn'tăkt') *n.* **1.** The touching of 2 objects or surfaces. **2.** The state of being in communication. **3.** A useful connection. **4.** A connection between 2 electric conductors. **5.** *Informal.* A contact lens. *—v.* **1.** To come or bring into contact. **2.** To communicate with. *—adj.* **1.** Sustaining or making contact. **2.** Caused or transmitted by touching. **—con·tac·tu·al** *adj.*

contact lens *n.* A thin lens worn over the cornea of the eye.

con·ta·gion (kən-tā'jən) *n.* **1. a.** Disease transmission by contact. **b.** A disease transmitted by contact. **2.** The tendency to spread, as of an influence or emotion. **—con·ta'gious** *adj.* **—con·ta'gious·ly** *adv.* **—con·ta'gious·ness** *n.*

con·tain (kən-tān') *v.* **1.** To have within : enclose. **2.** To include : comprise. **3.** To be capable of holding. **4.** To keep back : restrain. **—con·tain'a·ble** *adj.* **—con·tain'ment** *n.*

con·tain·er (kən-tā'nər) *n.* A receptacle for holding or carrying.

con·tain·er·ize (kən-tā'nə-rīz') *v.* **-ized, -iz·ing.** To ship (cargo) in large, standardized containers for ease in handling.

container ship *n.* A ship designed to carry cargo in standardized containers.

con·tam·i·nate (kən-tăm'ə-nāt') *v.* **-nat·ed, -nat·ing.** To pollute by contact or mixture. **—con·tam'i·nant** *n.* **—con·tam'i·na'tion** *n.* **—con·tam'i·na'tive** *adj.* **—con·tam'i·na'tor** *n.*

conte (kôNT) *n., pl.* **contes** (kôNT). An adventure story.

con·temn (kən-tĕm') *v.* To view as contemptible : abhor.

con·tem·plate (kŏn'təm-plāt') *v.* **-plat·ed, -plat·ing. 1.** To look at, ponder, or consider pensively. **2.** To consider as possible : intend. **—con'tem·pla'tion** *n.* **—con·tem'pla·tive** (kən-tĕm'plə-tĭv) *adj.* & *n.* **—con'tem·pla'tor** *n.*

con·tem·po·ra·ne·ous (kən-tĕm'pə-rā'nē-əs) *adj.* Contemporary. **—con·tem'po·ra'ne·ous·ly** *adv.* **—con·tem'po·ra'ne·ous·ness** *n.*

con·tem·po·rar·y (kən-tĕm'pə-rĕr'ē) *adj.* **1.** Belonging to the same period of time. **2.** Modern : current. **—con·tem'po·rar'y** *n.*

con·tempt (kən-tĕmpt') *n.* **1. a.** Bitter scorn or disdain. **b.** The state of being scorned or despised. **2.** *Law.* Willful disobedience or open disrespect.

con·tempt·i·ble (kən-tĕmp'tə-bəl) *adj.* Despicable. **—con·tempt'i·bil'i·ty** *n.* **—con·tempt'i·bly** *adv.*

con·temp·tu·ous (kən-tĕmp'cho͞o-əs) *adj.* Scornful. **—con·temp'tu·ous·ly** *adv.* **—con·temp'tu·ous·ness** *n.*

con·tend (kən-tĕnd') *v.* **1.** To fight, vie, or dispute. **2.** To assert or maintain. **—con·tend'er** *n.*

con·tent[1] (kŏn'tĕnt') *n.* **1.** *often* **contents.** Something contained in a receptacle. **2.** *often* **contents.** Subject matter of a document, book, etc. **3.** Meaning or significance, as of an artistic work. **4.** The proportion of a given substance, as alcohol.

con·tent[2] (kən-tĕnt') *adj.* Contented. *—v.* To make satisfied : gratify. *—n.* Satisfaction : contentment.

con·tent·ed (kən-tĕn'tĭd) *adj.* Satisfied : happy. **—con·tent'ed·ly** *adv.* **—con·tent'ed·ness** *n.*

con·ten·tion (kən-tĕn'shən) *n.* **1.** Controversy. **2.** Rivalry : competition. **3.** An assertion. **—con·ten'tious** *adj.* **—con·ten'tious·ly** *adv.* **—con·ten'tious·ness** *n.*

con·tent·ment (kən-tĕnt'mənt) *n.* Satisfaction : happiness.

con·ter·mi·nous (kən-tûr'mə-nəs) *also* **co·ter·mi·nous** (kō-) *adj.* CONTIGUOUS 1. **—con·ter'mi·nous·ly** *adv.*

con·test (kŏn'tĕst') *n.* **1.** A fight. **2.** A competition. *—v.* (kən-tĕst', kŏn'tĕst'). **1.** To compete or strive (for). **2.** To challenge : dispute <*contest* a will> ☆**syns:** BUCK, CHALLENGE, COMBAT, DISPUTE, FIGHT, OPPOSE, RESIST **—con·test'a·ble** *adj.* **—con·tes'tant** *n.* **—con·test'er** *n.*

con·text (kŏn'tĕkst') *n.* **1.** The explanatory words and ideas surrounding a particular word or statement in a discourse. **2.** The circumstances in which an event occurs. **—con·tex'tu·al** (kən-tĕks'cho͞o-əl) *adj.* **—con·tex'tu·al·ly** *adv.*

con·tig·u·ous (kən-tĭg'yo͞o-əs) *adj.* **1.** Sharing a common boundary. **2.** Adjacent to : nearby. **—con'ti·gu'i·ty** (kŏn'tĭ-gyo͞o'ĭ-tē), **con·tig'u·ous·ness** *n.* **—con·tig'u·ous·ly** *adv.*

con·ti·nence (kŏn'tə-nəns) *n.* **1.** Self-control, esp. with regard to passions and desires. **2.** The ability to control excretory functions. **—con'ti·nent** *adj.*

con·ti·nent (kŏn'tə-nənt) *n.* **1.** One of the 7 principal land masses of the globe. **2. the Continent.** The European mainland.

con·ti·nen·tal (kŏn'tə-nĕn'tl) *adj.* **1.** Of, relating to, or resembling a continent. **2.** *often* **Continental.** Relating to the European mainland. **3. Continental.** Of or relating to the American colonies during and immediately after the Revolutionary War. **—Con'ti·nen'tal** *n.*

continental divide *n.* A divide that separates continental river systems flowing in opposite directions.

con·tin·gen·cy (kən-tĭn'jən-sē) *n., pl.* **-cies.** A possible or fortuitous event.

con·tin·gent (kən-tĭn'jənt) *adj.* **1.** Likely to happen but not certain : possible. **2.** Dependent on condition. **3.** Fortuitous. *—n.* **1.** A share or quota, as of troops. **2.** A representative group.

con·tin·u·a (kən-tĭn'yo͞o-ə) *n. var. pl. of* CONTINUUM.

con·tin·u·al (kən-tĭn′yo͞o-əl) *adj.* **1.** Recurring regularly and frequently. **2.** Continuous in time : incessant <*continual* worry> **—con·tin′u·al·ly** *adv.*
con·tin·u·a·tion (kən-tĭn′yo͞o-ā′shən) *n.* **1.** The act or fact of continuing or the state of being continued. **2.** A supplement or sequel. **3.** Resumption after interruption.
con·tin·ue (kən-tĭn′yo͞o) *v.* **-ued, -u·ing. 1.** To go on : persist. **2.** To last : endure. **3.** To remain in the same state, capacity, or place. **4.** To resume. **5.** To extend. **6.** To cause to remain or last. **7.** *Law.* To adjourn or postpone (a judicial proceeding). **—con·tin′u·ance** *n.* **—con·tin′u·er** *n.*
continuing education *n.* Education courses designed esp. for part-time, adult students.
con·ti·nu·i·ty (kŏn′tə-no͞o′ĭ-tē, -nyo͞o′-) *n., pl.* **-ties. 1.** The quality or state of being continuous. **2.** An uninterrupted succession or unbroken course.
con·tin·u·ous (kən-tĭn′yo͞o-əs) *adj.* Uninterrupted : unbroken. ☆***syns:*** CEASELESS, CONSTANT, CONTINUAL, ENDLESS, ETERNAL, EVERLASTING, INCESSANT, NONSTOP, PERPETUAL, RELENTLESS, ROUND-THE-CLOCK, TIMELESS, UNCEASING, UNREMITTING **—con·tin′u·ous·ly** *adv.* **—con·tin′u·ous·ness** *n.*
con·tin·u·um (kən-tĭn′yo͞o-əm) *n., pl.* **-u·a** (-yo͞o-ə) *or* **-ums.** A continuous extent, succession, or whole no part of which can be distinguished from adjacent parts except by arbitrary partition.
con·tort (kən-tôrt′) *v.* To twist severely out of shape : wrench. **—con·tor′tion** *n.*
con·tor·tion·ist *n.* An acrobat who exhibits extraordinary bodily positions.
con·tour (kŏn′to͝or′) *n.* **1.** The outline of a figure, body, or mass. **2.** *often* **contours.** A surface, esp. of a curving form. *—adj.* Following the contour or form of something <a *contour* seat> **—con′tour′** *v.*
contr. *abbr.* **1.** contract. **2.** contraction.
con·tra·band (kŏn′trə-bănd′) *n.* **1.** Goods barred from import or export. **2.** Smuggling or smuggled goods.
con·tra·bass (kŏn′trə-bās′) *n.* A double bass. **—con′tra·bass′ist** *n.*
con·tra·bas·soon (kŏn′trə-bə-so͞on′, -bă-) *n.* The largest and lowest-pitched of the double-reed wind musical instruments.

contrabassoon

con·tra·cep·tion (kŏn′trə-sĕp′shən) *n.* Prevention of conception. **—con′tra·cep′tive** *adj.* & *n.*
con·tract (kŏn′trăkt′) *n.* A formal agreement between 2 or more parties : covenant. *—v.* (kən-trăkt′, kŏn′trăkt′). **1.** To enter into or settle by contract. **2.** To become afflicted with (a disease). **3.** To draw together : shrink. **4.** To shorten (a word or phrase) by omitting some of the letters or sounds. ☆***syns:*** CATCH, DEVELOP, GET, TAKE **—con·tract′i·bil′i·ty** *n.* **—con·tract′i·ble** *adj.* **—con·trac′tion** *n.* **—con′trac′tor** *n.*
con·trac·tile (kən-trăk′təl, -tīl′) *adj.* Able to contract or causing contraction.
con·trac·tu·al (kən-trăk′cho͞o-əl) *adj.* Of, relating to, or like a contract. **—con·trac′tu·al·ly** *adv.*
con·tra·dict (kŏn′trə-dĭkt′) *v.* **1.** To assert or express the opposite of. **2.** To deny the statement of <*contradicted* the police officer> **3.** To be inconsistent with. **—con′tra·dict′a·ble** *adj.* **—con′tra·dict′er, con′tra·dic′tor** *n.* **—con′tra·dic′tion** *n.* **—con′tra·dic′to·ry** *adj.*
con·trail (kŏn′trāl′) *n.* A visible trail of water droplets or ice crystals produced in the wake of an aircraft at high altitudes.
con·tra·in·di·cate (kŏn′trə-ĭn′dĭ-kāt′) *v.* To indicate the inadvisability of (e.g., use of certain drugs).
con·tral·to (kən-trăl′tō) *n., pl.* **-tos.** *Mus.* **1.** The lowest female voice or singing part. **2.** A woman having a contralto voice.
con·trap·tion (kən-trăp′shən) *n. Informal.* A mechanical contrivance : gadget.
con·tra·pun·tal (kŏn′trə-pŭn′tl) *adj. Mus.* Of, relating to, or incorporating counterpoint. **—con′tra·pun′tal·ly** *adv.*
con·tra·ri·e·ty (kŏn′trə-rī′ĭ-tē) *n., pl.* **-ties. 1.** The quality or state of being contrary. **2.** Something that is contrary.
con·trar·i·wise (kŏn′trĕr′ē-wīz′) *adv.* In a contrary manner or direction.
con·trar·y (kŏn′trĕr′ē) *adj.* **1.** Completely opposite, as in direction or character. **2.** Unfavorable : adverse. **3.** (*also* kən-trâr′ē). Recalcitrant : willful. **4.** Counter : opposed. ☆***syns:*** BALKY, DIFFICULT, FROWARD, IMPOSSIBLE, ORNERY, PERVERSE, WAYWARD *—n., pl.* **-ies.** The opposite. *—adv.* Contrariwise. **—con′trar′i·ly** *adv.* **—con′trar′i·ness** *n.*
con·trast (kən-trăst′) *v.* **1.** To put in opposition in order to point out differences. **2.** To show differences when compared. *—n.* (kŏn′trăst′). **1.** Notable dissimilarity between things compared. **2.** Something markedly dissimilar to something else. **—con·trast′a·ble** *adj.*
con·tra·vene (kŏn′trə-vēn′) *v.* **-vened, -ven·ing. 1.** To act or be contrary to : violate. **2.** To oppose in argument.
con·tre·temps (kŏn′trə-täN′, kôN′trə-täN′) *n., pl.* **-temps** (-täNz′, -täNz′). An embarrassing or inopportune occurrence.
con·trib·ute (kən-trĭb′yo͞ot) *v.* **-ut·ed, -ut·ing. 1.** To give or supply in common with others. **2.** To act as a determining factor. **3.** To submit for publication. **—con′tri·bu′tion** *n.* **—con·trib′u·tive** *adj.* **—con·trib′u·tive·ly** *adv.* **—con·trib′u·tor** *n.* **—con·trib′u·to′ry** *adj.*
con·trite (kən-trīt′, kŏn′trīt′) *adj.* Penitant : repentant. **—con·trite′ly** *adv.* **—con·tri′tion** (-trĭsh′ən) *n.*
con·triv·ance (kən-trī′vəns) *n.* Something that is contrived, as a mechanical device or clever plan.
con·trive (kən-trīv′) *v.* **-trived, -triv·ing. 1.** To plan or devise. **2.** To bring about by artifice : scheme. **3.** To invent or fabricate. **—con·triv′er** *n.*
con·trol (kən-trōl′) *v.* **-trolled, -trol·ling. 1.** To exercise dominating influence or authority over : direct. **2.** To regulate or verify (an experiment) by systematic comparison. *—n.* **1.** Authority or ability to regulate, dominate, or direct. **2.** A check or restraint. **3.** A standard of comparison for checking experimental results. **4.** *often* **controls.** A set of instruments for operating a machine or vehicle. **5.** An organization to direct a space flight. **—con·trol′la·ble** *adj.*
con·trol·ler (kən-trō′lər) *n.* **1.** One that controls, esp. a device that automatically regulates a machine. **2.** *also* **comp·trol·ler.** A business executive or government official who is in charge of financial affairs.
con·tro·ver·sy (kŏn′trə-vûr′sē) *n., pl.* **-sies. 1.** An often public dispute marked by the expression of opposing views. **2.** An argument. **—con′tro·ver′sial** (-vûr′shəl, -sē-əl) *adj.* **—con′tro·ver′sial·ly** *adv.*
con·tro·vert (kŏn′trə-vûrt′) *v.* To deny or contradict. **—con′tro·vert′i·ble** *adj.*
con·tu·ma·cious (kŏn′tə-mā′shəs) *adj.* Obstinately disobedient or insubordinate : recalcitrant. **—con′tu·ma·cy** (-mə-sē) *n.*
con·tu·me·ly (kŏn′to͞o-mə-lē, -tyo͞o-, -təm-lē) *n., pl.* **-lies.** Rude treatment : insolence. **—con′tu·me′li·ous** *adj.*
con·tuse (kən-to͞oz′, -tyo͞oz′) *v.* **-tused, -tus·ing.** To bruise. **—con·tu′sion** *n.*
co·nun·drum (kə-nŭn′drəm) *n.* **1.** A riddle. **2.** A complicated problem.
con·ur·ba·tion (kŏn′ər-bā′shən) *n.* A metropolitan area.
con·va·lesce (kŏn′və-lĕs′) *v.* **-lesced, -lesc·ing.** To return to health after illness : recuperate. **—con′va·les′cence** *n.* **—con′va·les′cent** *adj.* & *n.*
con·vec·tion (kən-vĕk′shən) *n.* Heat transfer by the actual movement of a heated liquid or gas between regions of unequal density. **—con·vec′tion·al** *adj.*
con·vene (kən-vēn′) *v.* **-vened, -ven·ing.** To assemble or convoke formally. **—con·ven′a·ble** *adj.* **—con·ven′er** *n.*
con·ven·ience (kən-vēn′yəns) *n.* **1.** The quality of being suitable or useful. **2.** Material comfort or advantage. **3.** Something that saves time and effort.
con·ven·ient (kən-vēn′yənt) *adj.* **1.** Suited or favorable to a person's needs, comfort, or purpose. **2.** Within easy reach : handy. ☆***syns:*** APPROPRIATE, FIT, GOOD, PROPER, SUITABLE, TAILOR-MADE **—con·ven′ient·ly** *adv.*
con·vent (kŏn′vənt, -vĕnt′) *n.* A community or the premises of a religious order, esp. of nuns. **—con·ven′tu·al** *adj.*
con·ven·ti·cle (kən-vĕn′tĭ-kəl) *n.* A meeting or assembly, esp. a secret one for religious worship.
con·ven·tion (kən-vĕn′shən) *n.* **1. a.** A formal assembly or meeting, as of a political party. **b.** The body of persons at such an assembly. **2.** A compact or agreement, esp. an international one. **3.** General custom or usage. **4.** An accepted or fixed practice.
con·ven·tion·al (kən-vĕn′shə-nəl) *adj.* **1.** Conforming to established practice or custom. **2.** Ordinary : commonplace. **3.** Using means other than nuclear energy <*conventional*

weapons> **—con·ven′tion·al′i·ty** *n.* **—con·ven′tion·al·ly** *adv.*

con·ven·tion·al·ize (kən-vĕn′shə-nə-līz′) *v.* **-ized, -iz·ing.** To make conventional.

con·verge (kən-vûrj′) *v.* **-verged, -verg·ing.** To approach a common point or result : meet. **—con·ver′gence, con·ver′gen·cy** *n.* **—con·ver′gent** *adj.*

con·ver·sant (kən-vûr′-sənt, kŏn′vər-) *adj.* Familiar, as by study <*conversant* with American literature>

con·ver·sa·tion (kŏn′vər-sā′shən) *n.* An informal talk or discussion. **—con′ver·sa′tion·al** *adj.* **—con′ver·sa′tion·al·ist** *n.* **—con′ver·sa′tion·al·ly** *adv.*

con·verse[1] (kən-vûrs′) *v.* **-versed, -vers·ing. 1.** To participate in a conversation. **2.** *Computer Sci.* To interact with a computer on-line. *—n.* (kŏn′vûrs′). Conversation.

con·verse[2] (kən-vûrs′, kŏn′vûrs′) *adj.* Reversed : contrary. *—n.* (kŏn′vûrs′). Reverse : opposite. **—con·verse′ly** *adv.*

con·ver·sion (kən-vûr′zhən, -shən) *n.* **1.** The act of converting or state of being converted. **2.** Adoption of a new religion or belief. **3.** Unlawful appropriation of property. **4.** A score of extra points after a touchdown in football.

con·vert (kən-vûrt′) *v.* **1.** To change into another form, substance, state, or product : transform. **2.** To induce or be induced to adopt a new religion or belief. **3.** To adapt to a new or different use or purpose. **4.** To exchange for something of equal value. **5.** *Law.* To misappropriate (another's property). *—n.* (kŏn′vûrt′). One who has undergone conversion, esp. to a new religion. **—con·vert′er, con·ver′tor** *n.*

con·vert·i·ble (kən-vûr′tə-bəl) *adj.* **1.** Able to be converted. **2.** Having a top that can be folded back or removed, as a car. **—con·vert′i·ble** *n.*

con·vex (kŏn-vĕks′, kŏn′vĕks′) *adj.* Curved or rounded outward like the outer surface of a ball. **—con·vex′i·ty** *n.*

con·vey (kən-vā′) *v.* **1.** To transport : carry. **2.** To transmit : conduct. **3.** To make known : communicate. **—con·vey′a·ble** *adj.* **—con·vey′er, con·vey′or** *n.*

con·vey·ance (kən-vā′əns) *n.* **1.** The act of conveying. **2.** A means of conveying : vehicle. **3.** *Law.* Transfer of title to property or a document effecting it.

con·vict (kən-vĭkt′) *v.* To find or prove (someone) guilty. *—n.* (kŏn′vĭkt′). A convicted person.

con·vic·tion (kən-vĭk′shən) *n.* **1.** The act of convicting or state of being convicted. **2.** A strong opinion or belief.

con·vince (kən-vĭns′) *v.* **-vinced, -vinc·ing.** To cause to believe firmly : persuade. **—con·vinc′ing·ly** *adv.*

con·viv·i·al (kən-vĭv′ē-əl) *adj.* **1.** Sociable. **2.** Festive. **—con·viv′i·al′i·ty** (-ăl′ĭ-tē) *n.* **—con·viv′i·al·ly** *adv.*

con·vo·ca·tion (kŏn′və-kā′shən) *n.* **1.** The act of convoking. **2.** A formal or ceremonial assembly, as of clergy.

con·voke (kən-vōk′) *v.* **-voked, -vok·ing.** To cause to assemble or convene formally. **—con·vok′er** *n.*

con·vo·lut·ed (kŏn′və-lo͞o′tĭd) *adj.* **1.** Coiled : twisted. **2.** Intricate : complex.

con·vo·lu·tion (kŏn′və-lo͞o′shən) *n.* **1.** A convoluted formation or configuration. **2.** A convex fold of the brain's surface.

con·voy (kŏn′voi′, kən-voi′) *v.* To accompany for protection : escort. *—n.* (kŏn′voi′). **1.** A protective armed escort, as for ships or vehicles. **2.** A group, as of vehicles, traveling together.

con·vulse (kən-vŭls′) *v.* **-vulsed, -vuls·ing. 1.** To shake or agitate violently. **2.** To cause to experience convulsions. **—con·vul′sive** *adj.* **—con·vul′sive·ly** *adv.*

con·vul·sion (kən-vŭl′shən) *n.* **1.** An intense paroxysmal involuntary muscular contraction. **2.** A fit, as of uncontrollable laughter. **3.** A violent turmoil.

co·ny *also* **co·ney** (kō′nē, kŭn′ē) *n., pl.* **-nies** *also* **-neys 1. a.** A rabbit, esp. the Old World species *Oryctolagus cuniculus.* **b.** A similar animal. **2.** Rabbit fur.

coo (ko͞o) *n., pl.* **coos. 1.** The soft murmuring sound that a dove or pigeon makes. **2.** A sound resembling a coo. **—coo** *v.*

cook (ko͝ok) *v.* **1.** To apply heat to food before eating. **2.** To prepare or treat by heating. **—cook up.** *Informal.* To fabricate : concoct <*cook up* a scheme> *—n.* One who prepares food.

cook·book (ko͝ok′bo͝ok′) *n.* A book of recipes and directions for cooking.

cook·er (ko͝ok′ər) *n.* One that cooks, esp. a utensil or an appliance for cooking.

cook·er·y (ko͝ok′ə-rē) *n., pl.* **-ies.** The preparation of food.

cook·ie *or* **cook·y** (ko͝ok′ē) *n., pl.* **-ies.** A sweet, usu. small, flat cake.

cook·out (ko͝ok′out′) *n.* A meal cooked and served outdoors.

cool (ko͞ol) *adj.* **1.** Somewhat cold <*cool* fall nights> **2.** Affording or allowing relief from heat. **3.** Controlled : calm. **4.** Indifferent : unenthusiastic <a *cool* handshake> **5.** Impudent : audacious. **6.** *Slang.* Superb : first-rate. *—v.* To make or become cool. *—n.* **1.** Moderate cold or something cool. **2.** *Slang.* Composure <lost my *cool*> **—cool′ly** *adv.* **—cool′ness** *n.*

cool·ant (ko͞o′lənt) *n.* A cooling agent, esp. a fluid that circulates through a machine or bathes some of its parts.

cool·er (ko͞o′lər) *n.* **1.** A container or device for cooling. **2.** *Slang.* A jail.

Coo·lidge (ko͞o′lĭj), **(John) Calvin.** 1872–1933. 30th U.S. President (1923–29).

coo·lie (ko͞o′lē) *n.* An unskilled laborer of the Far East.

coon (ko͞on) *n.* *Informal.* A raccoon.

coon·skin (ko͞on′skĭn′) *n.* **1.** The skin of a raccoon, used as fur. **2.** Something, as a hat, made of coonskin.

coop (ko͞op) *n.* An enclosure or cage. *—v.* To keep in or as if in a coop.

co-op (kō′ŏp′, kō-ŏp′) *n.* A cooperative.

coop. *abbr.* cooperative.

coo·per (ko͞o′pər) *n.* One who makes or repairs barrels. **—coo′per·age** *n.*

co·op·er·ate (kō-ŏp′ə-rāt′) *v.* To act or work together toward a common purpose or end. **—co·op′er·a′tion** *n.* **—co·op′er·a′tor** *n.*

co·op·er·a·tive (kō-ŏp′ər-ə-tĭv, -ŏp′rə-, -ə-rā′tĭv) *adj.* **1.** Done in cooperation with others. **2.** Characterized by willingness to cooperate. **3.** Engaged in joint economic activity. *—n.* An enterprise owned jointly by those who use its facilities or services. **—co·op′er·a·tive·ly** *adv.* **—co·op′er·a·tive·ness** *n.*

co-opt (kō-ŏpt′) *v.* **1.** To elect as a fellow member of a group. **2.** To pre-empt : appropriate. **3.** To take or win over (e.g., a minority group) by assimilating into an established group.

co·or·di·nate (kō-ôr′dn-āt, -ĭt′) *n.* **1.** One that is equal in rank, importance, or degree. **2.** *Math.* Any of a set of numbers that gives the location of a point. *—adj.* (-ĭt, -āt′). **1.** Of equal rank, importance, or degree. **2.** Of or involving coordination. **3.** Of or based on coordinates. *—v.* (-āt′) **-nat·ed, -nat·ing. 1.** To place in proper position or order : adjust. **2.** To work together in a common action or effort. **—co·or′di·nate·ly** *adv.* **—co·or′di·na′tor** *n.*

co·or·di·na·tion (kō-ôr′dn-ā′shən) *n.* **1.** The act of coordinating or state of being coordinate. **2.** Organized muscular action in executing complex movements.

coot (ko͞ot) *n.* **1.** A short-billed, dark-gray aquatic bird of the genus *Fulica.* **2.** *Informal.* A silly old man.

coo·tie (ko͞o′tē) *n.* *Slang.* A body louse.

cop (kŏp) *n.* *Informal.* A police officer. *—v.* **copped, cop·ping.** *Slang.* **1.** To pilfer : steal. **2.** To capture : seize. **—cop out.** *Slang.* **1.** To be noncommittal. **2.** To renege.

cope[1] (kōp) *v.* **coped, cop·ing.** To struggle or contend, esp. successfully.

cope[2] (kōp) *n.* A long capelike ecclesiastical garment.

Co·pen·ha·gen (kō′pən-hā′gən). Cap. of Denmark, in the E part. *Pop.* 1,470,000.

Co·per·ni·cus (kō-pûr′nĭ-kəs), **Nicholaus.** 1473–1543. Polish astronomer.

cop·i·er (kŏp′ē-ər) *n.* One that copies, esp. a machine for making copies.

co·pi·lot (kō′pī′lət) *n.* The associate pilot of an aircraft.

cop·ing (kō′pĭng) *n.* The top part of a wall.

co·pi·ous (kō′pē-əs) *adj.* Large in quantity : abundant. **—co′pi·ous·ly** *adv.*

cop-out (kŏp′out′) *n.* *Slang.* **1.** An act of copping out. **2.** An excuse for copping out.

cop·per (kŏp′ər) *n.* **1.** *Symbol* **Cu** A reddish-brown metallic element that is a very good conductor of heat and electricity. **2.** Something made of copper, as a coin.

cop·per·as (kŏp′ər-əs) *n.* A greenish, crystalline ferrous sulfate used in purifying water and making fertilizers.

cop·per·head (kŏp′ər-hĕd′) *n.* A venomous snake, *Agkistrodon contortrix* or *Ancistron contortrix,* of the E U.S., with reddish-brown markings.

cop·ra (kŏp′rə) *n.* Dried coconut meat from which coconut oil is obtained.

copse (kŏps) *n.* A thicket.

cop·ter (kŏp′tər) *n.* A helicopter.

cop·u·la (kŏp′yə-lə) *n., pl.* **-las.** A linking verb. **—cop′u·la′tive** *adj.*

cop·u·late (kŏp′yə-lāt′) *v.* **-lat·ed, -lat·ing.** To have sexual intercourse. **—cop′u·la′tion** *n.*

cop·y (kŏp′ē) *n., pl.* **-ies. 1.** A reproduction of an original. **2.** One of a number of printed texts having the same contents. **3.** Matter to be set in type. ☆**syns:** DUPLICATE, FACSIMILE, REPLICA, REPRODUCTION *—v.* **-ied, -y·ing. 1.** To make a copy (of). **2.** To imitate. **—cop′y·ist** *n.*

copy desk *n.* The desk where newspaper copy is edited.

cop·y-ed·it (kŏp′ē-ĕd′ĭt) *v.* To correct and edit (e.g., a manuscript) for publication. **—copy editor** *n.*

cop·y·right (kŏp′ē-rīt′) *n.* The sole right to sell, publish, or distribute a literary or artistic work. *—adj.* Protected by copyright. *—v.* To protect by copyright.
cop·y·writ·er (kŏp′ē-rī′tər) *n.* A writer of copy, esp. in advertising.
coq au vin (kōk′ ō văɴ′, kŏk′) *n.* Chicken cooked in wine.
co·quette (kō-kĕt′) *n.* A woman who flirts. **—co·quet′tish** *adj.* **—co·quet′tish·ly** *adv.* **—co·quet′tish·ness** *n.*
cor·a·cle (kôr′ə-kəl, kŏr′-) *n.* A small round boat made of a wicker or wood frame covered with waterproof material.
cor·al (kôr′əl, kŏr′-) *n.* **1.** A hard rocklike material formed by the skeletons of marine polyps and often used for jewelry. **2.** A pinkish orange.
Coral. Sea of the SW Pacific, NE of Australia and SE of New Guinea.
coral reef *n.* A marine ridge or mound made chiefly of compacted coral.
coral snake *n.* A venomous snake of the genus *Micrurus*, of tropical America, brightly banded with red, black, and yellow.
cor·bel (kôr′bəl, -bĕl′) *n.* A bracket, as of stone or brick, projecting from the face of a wall to support an arch or cornice.
cord (kôrd) *n.* **1.** A heavy string of twisted strands. **2.** A thin insulated electric cable used to connect an appliance with an electrical outlet. **3.** A ribbed fabric, as corduroy. **4.** A cubic measure used for cut fuel wood, equal to a stack measuring 4 by 4 by 8 ft. **—cord** *v.* **—cord′er** *n.*
cord·age (kôr′dĭj) *n.* Ropes, esp. ropes in the rigging of a ship.
cor·date (kôr′dāt′) *adj.* With a heart-shaped outline <a *cordate* leaf>
cord·ed (kôr′dĭd) *adj.* **1.** Fastened with cords. **2.** Ribbed, as corduroy. **3.** Stacked in cords, as firewood.
cor·dial (kôr′jəl) *adj.* Warm : heartfelt. *—n.* **1.** A stimulant. **2.** A liqueur. **—cor′dial′i·ty** (-jăl′ĭ-tē, -jē-ăl′-, -dē-ăl′-), **cor′dial·ness** *n.* **—cor′dial·ly** *adv.*
▲word history: *Cordial* had its origin as a medical term, and in early use the word's derivation from Latin *cor*, "heart," was not forgotten. The first recorded use of *cordial* in English is in Chaucer's *Canterbury Tales*, where it indicates a medicine. Such cordials were supposed to achieve a beneficial effect by stimulating the heart. The heart in medieval physiology was also considered the locus of feelings and affections; from this association the adjective *cordial* meaning "hearty" or "heartfelt" arose.
cor·dil·le·ra (kôr′dĭl-yâr′ə, kôr-dĭl′ər-ə) *n.* A mountain chain.
cord·ite (kôr′dīt′) *n.* A smokeless gunpowder.
cord·less (kôrd′lĭs) *adj.* **1.** Without a cord. **2.** Operated by battery.
cor·do·ba (kôr′də-bə, -və) *n.* See CURRENCY TABLE.
cor·don (kôr′dn) *n.* **1.** An encircling line, as of people or ships. **2.** An ornamental braid. *—v.* To encircle with a cordon.
cor·do·van (kôr′də-vən) *n.* A fine, soft leather orig. made in Spain.
cor·du·roy (kôr′də-roi′, kôr′də-roi′) *n.* **1.** A heavy ribbed cotton cloth. **2. corduroys.** Corduroy trousers.
core (kôr, kōr) *n.* **1.** The inedible, seed-bearing central part of certain fruits, as the pear. **2.** The inmost part of something. **3.** *also* **core memory.** *Computer Sci.* A computer memory made up of doughnut-shaped masses of magnetic material. *—v.* **cored, cor·ing.** To remove the core of.
core dump *n. Computer Sci.* A listing of the information stored in a core. **—core′-dump′** *v.*
co·re·spon·dent (kō′rĭ-spŏn′dənt) *n. Law.* A person named as having committed adultery with the defendant in a divorce case.
cor·gi (kôr′gē) *n.* A Welsh corgi.
co·ri·an·der (kôr′ē-ăn′dər, kōr′-) *n.* An herb, *Coriandrum sativum*, cultivated for its aromatic seeds.
Cor·inth (kôr′ĭnth, kŏr′-). City of ancient Greece, in the NE Peloponnesus.
Co·rin·thi·an (kə-rĭn′thē-ən) *adj.* Of or relating to ancient Corinth. *—n.* **1.** A native or inhabitant of Corinth. **2. Corinthians** *(sing. in number).* See BIBLE TABLE.
cork (kôrk) *n.* **1.** The light, elastic bark of the cork oak, used esp. for bottle stoppers. **2.** A stopper made of cork. *—v.* To stop with a cork. **—cork′y** *adj.*
cork·age (kôr′kĭj) *n.* A fee paid at a restaurant for the consumption of a bottle of liquor not bought on the premises.
cork oak *n.* An evergreen oak tree, *Quercus suber*, of S Europe.
cork·screw (kôrk′skroo͞′) *n.* A pointed metal spiral attached to a handle, used for drawing corks from bottles. *—adj.* Like a corkscrew : spiral.
corm (kôrm) *n.* An underground stem, as that of the gladiolus, similar to a bulb.
cor·mo·rant (kôr′mər-ənt) *n.* A large aquatic bird of the genus *Phalacrocorax*, with dark plumage and a hooked bill.
corn[1] (kôrn) *n.* **1. a.** An American cereal plant, *Zea mays*, bearing kernels on large ears. **b.** The kernels of this plant, used for food or fodder. **2.** *esp. Brit.* Grain, esp. wheat. **3.** *Slang.* Something that is corny. *—v.* To pickle in brine.
corn[2] (kôrn) *n.* A hard growth of skin, esp. on or near a toe.
corn·ball (kôrn′bôl′) *adj. Slang.* Corny.
corn bread *also* **corn·bread** (kôrn′brĕd′) *n.* Bread made from cornmeal.
corn chip *n. often* **corn chips.** A crisp snack made from cornmeal batter.
corn·cob (kôrn′kŏb′) *n.* The woody core on which kernels of corn grow.
corn·crib (kôrn′krĭb′) *n.* A structure for drying and storing corn.
cor·ne·a (kôr′nē-ə) *n.* The transparent membrane covering the iris and the pupil of the eyeball. **—cor′ne·al** *adj.*
cor·ner (kôr′nər) *n.* **1. a.** The place where 2 surfaces or lines meet and form an angle. **b.** The angle so formed. **2.** A place where 2 streets come together. **3.** A position from which retreat or escape is impossible. **4.** A region : quarter. **5.** Control of the available supply of a commodity so as to raise its price. *—v.* **1.** To drive into a corner. **2.** To form a corner in (a commodity). **3.** To turn, as at a corner.
cor·ner·back *also* **corner back** (kôr′nər-băk′) *n. Football.* Either of 2 defensive halfbacks stationed a short distance behind the linebackers and near the sidelines.
cor·ner·stone *also* **corner stone** (kôr′nər-stōn′) *n.* **1.** A stone forming part of the corner of a building, esp. one laid with a special ceremony. **2.** The main part : basis.
cor·net (kôr-nĕt′) *n.* A 3-valved brass band instrument resembling a trumpet. **—cor·net′ist, cor·net′tist** *n.*
corn·flow·er (kôrn′flou′ər) *n.* A garden plant, *Centaurea cyanus*, with blue, white, or pink flowers.
cor·nice (kôr′nĭs) *n.* A horizontal projecting part that crowns the wall of a building.
corn·meal *also* **corn meal** (kôrn′mēl′) *n.* Meal made from corn.
†**corn pone** (pōn) *n. S U.S.* Corn bread made without milk or eggs.
corn·row (kôrn′rō′) *v.* To style (hair) by dividing into sections and braiding closely in rows. **—corn′row′** *n.*
corn snow *n.* Coarse granules of snow formed by alternate freezing and melting.
corn·stalk *also* **corn stalk** (kôrn′stôk′) *n.* A stalk of corn.
corn·starch (kôrn′stärch′) *n.* A starch made from corn and used in cooking as a thickener.
corn syrup *n.* A sweet syrup made from cornstarch.
cor·nu·co·pi·a (kôr′nə-kō′pē-ə) *n.* **1.** A goat's horn depicted as overflowing with fruit, flowers, and corn, signifying prosperity. **2.** An abundance.
corn·y (kôr′nē) *adj.* **-i·er, -i·est.** *Slang.* Trite or mawkishly sentimental. **—corn′i·ly** *adv.* **—corn′i·ness** *n.*
co·rol·la (kə-rŏl′ə, -rō′lə) *n. Bot.* The petals of a flower.
cor·ol·lar·y (kôr′ə-lĕr′-ē, kŏr′-) *n., pl.* **-ies. 1.** A deduction from an already proven proposition. **2.** A result : consequence.
co·ro·na (kə-rō′nə) *n., pl.* **-nas** *or* **-nae** (-nē). A colored circle of light around the sun or moon, esp. the halo visible around the sun during a total eclipse.
cor·o·nar·y (kôr′ə-nĕr-ē, kŏr′-) *adj.* Of or designating either of 2 arteries that supply blood to the heart muscle. *—n., pl.* **-ies.** *Informal.* A coronary thrombosis.
coronary thrombosis *n.* Occlusion of a coronary artery by a blood clot, often causing destruction of heart muscle.
cor·o·na·tion (kôr′ə-nā′shən, kŏr′-) *n.* The crowning of a monarch.
cor·o·ner (kôr′ə-nər, kŏr′-) *n.* A public official who determines the cause of deaths not due to natural causes.
cor·o·net (kôr′ə-nĕt′, kŏr′-) *n.* **1.** A small crown worn by nobility. **2.** A headband.
corp. *abbr.* corporation.
cor·po·ra (kôr′pər-ə) *n. pl. of* CORPUS.
cor·po·ral[1] (kôr′pər-əl) *adj.* Of the body : physical. **—cor′po·ral′i·ty** *n.*
cor·po·ral[2] (kôr′pər-əl, -prəl) *n.* A noncommissioned officer ranking above a private first class and below a sergeant.
cor·po·rate (kôr′pər-ĭt, -prĭt) *adj.* **1.** Of or being a corporation. **2.** Combined into one body : joint <*corporate* action>
cor·po·ra·tion (kôr′pə-rā′shən) *n.* A group of persons authorized to act as an entity having privileges and liabilities distinct from those of its members.
cor·po·re·al (kôr-pôr′ē-əl, -pōr′-) *adj.* **1.** Of, relating to, or typical of the body. **2.** Of a material nature : physical.
corps (kôr, kōr) *n., pl.* **corps** (kôrz, kōrz). **1.** A branch or section of the armed forces with a specialized function. **2.** A body

of persons associated under common direction <the press *corps*>
corpse (kôrps) *n.* A dead body.
cor·pu·lence (kôr'pyə-ləns) *n.* Excessive fatness. **—cor'pu·lent** *adj.*
cor·pus (kôr'pəs) *n., pl.* **-po·ra** (-pər-ə). **1.** A body, esp. a corpse. **2.** A body of writings on a specific subject.
Corpus Chris·ti (krĭs'tē). City of SW Tex. *Pop.* 231,999.
cor·pus·cle (kôr'pə-səl, -pŭs'əl) *n.* **1.** A living cell, esp. one, as in blood, capable of free movement in a matrix or fluid. **2.** A minute particle. **—cor·pus'cu·lar** *adj.*
corpus de·lic·ti (də-lĭk'tī') *n.* **1.** *Law.* The material evidence establishing that a crime has been committed. **2.** The body of a murder victim.
corr. *abbr.* correspondence; correspondent.
cor·rade (kə-rād') *v.* **-rad·ed, -rad·ing.** To wear away or be worn away by abrasion. **—cor·ra'sion** *n.* **—cor·ra'sive** *adj.*
cor·ral (kə-răl') *n.* An enclosure for confining or capturing animals. *—v.* **-ralled, -ral·ling. 1.** To drive into or confine in a corral. **2.** *Informal.* To take possession of.
cor·rect (kə-rĕkt') *v.* **1.** To make right. **2.** To mark the errors of. **3.** To reprove or discipline. ☆***syns:*** AMEND, EMEND, MEND, RECTIFY, REMEDY, RIGHT *—adj.* **1.** Free from error : accurate. **2.** Conforming to conventions. **—cor·rect'a·ble, cor·rect'i·ble** *adj.* **—cor·rec'tion** *n.* **—cor·rec'tion·al** *adj.* **—cor·rec'tive** *adj. & n.* **—cor·rect'ly** *adv.* **—cor·rect'ness** *n.*
cor·re·late (kôr'ə-lāt', kŏr'-) *v.* **-lat·ed, -lat·ing.** To connect or be connected by causal, complementary, or parallel relation. **—cor're·late** *n. & adj.* **—cor're·la'tion** *n.* **—cor're·la'tion·al** *adj.*
cor·rel·a·tive (kə-rĕl'ə-tĭv) *adj.* **1.** Reciprocally related. **2.** Indicating a reciprocal grammatical relationship <the *correlative* conjunctions *either . . . or*> **—cor·rel'a·tive** *n.* **—cor·rel'a·tive·ly** *adv.*
cor·re·spond (kôr'ĭ-spŏnd', kŏr'-) *v.* **1.** To be consistent, compatible, or harmonious. **2.** To be equal or similar. **3.** To communicate by letter. **—cor're·spond'ing·ly** *adv.*
cor·re·spon·dence (kôr'ĭ-spŏn'dəns, kŏr'-) *n.* **1.** Agreement between things. **2.** Similarity. **3. a.** Communication by letters. **b.** The letters exchanged.
cor·re·spon·dent (kôr'ĭ-spŏn'dənt, kŏr'-) *n.* **1.** A person who communicates by letter with another. **2.** A reporter, as for a newspaper, who supplies news, often from remote locations. **3.** Something that corresponds. *—adj.* Corresponding.
cor·ri·dor (kôr'ĭ-dər, -dôr', kŏr'-) *n.* **1.** A long, narrow hall, often with rooms opening onto it. **2.** A tract of land forming a passageway through a foreign country.
cor·ri·gen·dum (kôr'ə-jĕn'dəm, kŏr'-) *n., pl.* **-da** (-də). **1.** A typesetting error to be corrected. **2. corrigenda.** A list of errors in a book printed on a separate page with their corrections.
cor·ri·gi·ble (kôr'ĭ-jə-bəl, kŏr'-) *adj.* Capable of being corrected.
cor·rob·o·rate (kə-rŏb'ə-rāt') *v.* **-rat·ed, -rat·ing.** To attest the truth of. **—cor·rob'o·ra'tion** *n.* **—cor·rob'o·ra'tive** *adj.* **—cor·rob'o·ra'tor** *n.*
cor·rode (kə-rōd') *v.* **-rod·ed, -rod·ing.** To eat away or be eaten away gradually, esp. by chemical action. **—cor·rod'i·ble, cor·ro'si·ble** (-rō'sə-bəl) *adj.* **—cor·ro'sion** *n.* **—cor·ro'sive** *adj. & n.*
cor·ru·gate (kôr'ə-gāt', kŏr'-) *v.* **-gat·ed, -gat·ing.** To form into folds or ridges and grooves. **—cor'ru·ga'tion** *n.*
corrugated iron *n.* Sheet iron, usu. galvanized, shaped in parallel grooves and ridges for strength.
cor·rupt (kə-rŭpt') *adj.* **1.** Evil : depraved. **2.** Dishonest : venal <a *corrupt* politician> **3.** Rotting : putrid. ☆***syns:*** CROOKED, DISHONEST, VENAL *—v.* To make or become corrupt. **—cor·rupt'er, cor·rup'tor** *n.* **—cor·rupt'i·bil'i·ty, cor·rupt'i·ble·ness** *n.* **—cor·rupt'i·ble** *adj.* **—cor·rupt'i·bly** *adv.* **—cor·rup'tion** *n.* **—cor·rupt'ly** *adv.* **—cor·rupt'ness** *n.*
cor·sage (kôr-säzh') *n.* A small bunch of flowers worn by a woman.
cor·sair (kôr'sâr') *n.* **1.** A fast-moving pirate ship. **2.** A pirate.
cor·set (kôr'sĭt) *n.* A stiffened undergarment worn on the torso to give shape to the figure. **—cor'se·tière'** *n.*
Cor·si·ca (kôr'sĭ-kə). French island in the N Mediterranean. **—Cor'si·can** *adj. & n.*
cor·tege (kôr-tĕzh', -tāzh') *n.* **1.** A retinue, as for a distinguished person. **2.** A ceremonial procession, esp. a funeral procession.
cor·tex (kôr'tĕks') *n., pl.* **-ti·ces** (-tĭ-sēz') *or* **-tex·es. 1.** *Anat.* The outer layer of an organ or part. **2.** *Bot.* An outer layer of plant tissue. **—cor'ti·cal** (-tĭ-kəl) *adj.*
cor·ti·sone (kôr'tĭ-sōn', -zōn') *n.* A hormone produced by the adrenal cortex and used in the treatment of rheumatoid arthritis, allergies, and gout.
co·run·dum (kə-rŭn'dəm) *n.* A very hard mineral, aluminum oxide, that occurs in gem varieties, as ruby and sapphire, and in a common form used esp. in abrasives.
cor·us·cate (kôr'ə-skāt', kŏr'-) *v.* **-cat·ed, -cat·ing.** To flash : sparkle. **—cor'us·ca'tion** *n.*
cor·vette (kôr-vĕt') *n.* **1.** A lightly armed warship smaller than a destroyer. **2.** An obsolete warship smaller than a frigate.
co·ry (kô'rē, kŏr'ē) *n.* See *syli* at CURRENCY TABLE.
co·ry·za (kə-rī'zə) *n.* An acute inflammation of the upper respiratory tract : head cold.
COS *or* **c.o.s.** *abbr.* cash on shipment.
cosh (kŏsh) *esp. Brit. —n.* A blackjack. *—v.* To hit with a cosh.
co·sign (kō-sīn') *v.* To sign (a document) jointly with another or others.
co·sig·na·to·ry (kō-sĭg'nə-tôr'ē, -tōr'ē) *n., pl.* **-ries.** One who cosigns.
cos lettuce *n.* Romaine.
cos·met·ic (kŏz-mĕt'ĭk) *n.* A preparation, as rouge, designed to beautify the body, esp. the face. *—adj.* **1.** Serving to beautify the body. **2.** Superficial : insignificant. **—cos·met'i·cal·ly** *adv.*
cos·me·tol·o·gy (kŏz'mĭ-tŏl'ə-jē) *n.* The study of cosmetics or the art of their use. **—cos'me·tol'o·gist** *n.*
cos·mic (kŏz'mĭk) *adj.* **1.** Of or relating to the cosmos. **2.** Vast. **—cos'mi·cal·ly** *adv.*
cosmic ray *n.* A stream of radiation of extraterrestrial origin, mainly of protons, alpha particles, and other atomic nuclei, that enters the atmosphere and produces secondary radiation.
cos·mog·o·ny (kŏz-mŏg'ə-nē) *n.* **1.** The origin of the universe. **2.** A theory of the evolution of the universe.
cos·mog·ra·phy (kŏz-mŏg'rə-fē) *n., pl.* **-phies. 1.** The study of the features of nature. **2.** A description of the world.
cos·mol·o·gy (kŏz-mŏl'ə-jē) *n.* The study of the origin and structure of the universe.
cos·mo·naut (kŏz'mə-nôt') *n.* A Soviet astronaut.
cos·mo·pol·i·tan (kŏz'mə-pŏl'ĭ-tn) *adj.* **1.** Common to or representative of many parts of the world. **2.** At home anywhere in the world. *—n.* A cosmopolite.
cos·mop·o·lite (kŏz-mŏp'ə-līt') *n.* A cosmopolitan person.
cos·mos (kŏz'məs, -mōs') *n.* **1.** The universe regarded as a systematically arranged whole. **2.** An orderly harmonious system. **3.** A tall American garden plant of the genus *Cosmos,* esp. *C. bipinnatus,* having variously colored daisylike flowers.
Cos·sack (kŏs'ăk') *n.* A member of a people of the S USSR, famous as horsemen. **—Cos'sack'** *adj.*
cos·set (kŏs'ĭt) *v.* To pamper.
cost (kôst) *n.* **1.** The amount paid or asked for a purchase. **2.** Loss : sacrifice. ☆***syns:*** CHARGE, PRICE, TAB *—v.* To have as a price. **—cost'less** *adj.*
co·star *also* **co-star** (kō'stär') *n.* An actor given equal billing in a play or film. *—v.* To present or act as a costar.
Cos·ta Ri·ca (kŏs'tə rē'kə, kô'stə). Country of Central America. *Cap.* San José. *Pop.* 1,993,800. **—Cos'ta Ri'can** *adj. & n.*
cost-ef·fec·tive (kôst'ĭ-fĕk'tĭv) *adj.* Economical as regards the cost for goods or services received.
cos·tive (kŏs'tĭv) *adj.* Having or causing constipation.
cost·ly (kôst'lē) *adj.* **-li·er, -li·est. 1.** Expensive. **2.** Involving great sacrifice or loss. **—cost'li·ness** *n.*
cost of living *n.* **1.** The average cost of the basic necessities of life, as food, housing, and clothes. **2.** The cost of necessary goods and services as defined by an established standard.
cost-plus (kôst'plŭs', kŏst'-) *n.* The cost of production plus a specified profit margin. **—cost'-plus'** *adj.*
cos·tume (kŏs'to͞om', -tyo͞om') *n.* **1.** Clothes typical of one country or period. **2.** A set of clothes appropriate for a particular season or occasion. **3.** Clothes worn by one playing a part or dressing up in disguise. **—cos'tum·er** *n.*
co·sy (kō'zē) *adj. & n. var. of* COZY.
cot (kŏt) *n.* A small, often collapsible bed.
†**cote** (kōt) *n.* **1.** A small shelter for sheep or birds. **2.** *Regional.* A cottage.
co·te·rie (kō'tə-rē) *n.* A close circle of people who have similar interests.
co·ter·mi·nous (kō-tûr'mə-nəs) *adj. var. of* CONTERMINOUS.
co·til·lion (kō-tĭl'yən, kə-) *n.* **1.** A lively group dance with intricate steps. **2.** A formal ball, esp. one for debutantes.
cot·tage (kŏt'ĭj) *n.* A small house, esp. one in the country. **—cot'tag·er** *n.*
cottage cheese *n.* A soft, white cheese made from soured skim milk.
cottage industry *n.* A small-scale, usu. manufacturing business carried on at home.
cotter pin *n.* A metal pin fastened in place by bending apart its 2 ends after insertion in a hole.
cot·ton (kŏt'n) *n.* **1.** A plant or shrub of the genus *Gossypium,*

grown in warm climates for the fiber surrounding its seeds. **2.** The soft, white, fibrous substance around cottonseeds, used primarily in making textiles. **3.** Cloth or thread made of cotton. —*v. Informal.* To become friendly <doesn't *cotton* to strangers> **—cot′ton·y** *adj.*
cotton candy *n.* Spun sugar.
cot·ton·mouth (kŏt′n-mouth′) *n.* The water moccasin.
cot·ton·seed (kŏt′n-sēd′) *n.* The seed of the cotton plant, yielding oil and meal.
cot·ton·tail (kŏt′n-tāl′) *n.* A New World rabbit of the genus *Sylvilagus,* with a brownish or grayish coat and a tail having a white underside.
cot·ton·wood (kŏt′n-wo͝od′) *n.* A poplar with seeds covered by cottony hair.
cot·y·le·don (kŏt′l-ēd′n) *n. Bot.* A leaf of a plant embryo, one of the first to appear from a sprouting seed. **—cot′y·le′don·al, cot′y·le′do·nous** *adj.*
couch (kouch) *n.* A sofa or bed on which one may recline or sit. —*v.* To phrase in a certain form <*couched* the complaint tactfully>
couch·ant (kou′chənt) *adj. Heraldry.* Lying down with the head up.
cou·gar (ko͞o′gər) *n.* The mountain lion.

cougar

cough (kôf, kŏf) *v.* **1.** To eject air from the lungs suddenly and loudly. **2.** To make a noise similar to that of coughing. **3.** To expel by coughing. **—cough** *n.*
could (ko͝od) *v. p.t. of* CAN.
could·n't (ko͝od′nt). Could not.
†**cou·lee** (ko͞o′lē) *n. W U.S.* A deep gully or ravine formed by rain or melting snow.
cou·lomb (ko͞o′lŏm′, -lōm′) *n.* An electrical charge equal to the electricity transferred by a steady current of 1 amp in 1 sec.
coun·cil (koun′səl) *n.* **1.** A group of people called together for discussion or consultation. **2.** An official legislative or administrative body. **—coun′cil·man** *n.* **—coun′cil·or, coun′cil·lor** *n.* **—coun′cil·wom′an** *n.*
coun·sel (koun′səl) *n.* **1.** Deliberation or consultation. **2.** Advice : guidance. **3.** A plan or action. **4.** A personal opinion <keep one's own *counsel*> **5.** *pl.* **counsel.** A lawyer or group of lawyers, esp. when conducting a case in court. —*v.* **-seled, -sel·ing** *also* **-selled, -sel·ling. 1.** To give counsel (to). **2.** To recommend.
coun·sel·or *also* **coun·sel·lor** (koun′sə-lər, -slər) *n.* **1.** An adviser. **2.** A lawyer.
count[1] (kount) *v.* **1.** To name or indicate one by one in order to find the total number. **2.** To recite numbers in order. **3.** To take account of in a reckoning. **4.** To believe to be : deem. **5.** To have a specified importance. **—count on.** To rely on. —*n.* **1.** The act of counting. **2.** A number obtained by counting. **3.** *Law.* A particular charge in an indictment. **—count′a·ble** *adj.*
count[2] (kount) *n.* A nobleman in certain European countries, corresponding in rank to an English earl.
count·down (kount′doun′) *n.* The act of counting in descending order to indicate the time remaining before an event, as the launching of a rocket.
coun·te·nance (koun′tə-nəns) *n.* **1.** A person's face, esp. the expression of the face. **2.** Approval : favor. —*v.* **-nanced, -nanc·ing.** To condone : approve.
coun·ter[1] (koun′tər) *adj.* In an opposite direction : contrary. —*v.* **1.** To move or act in opposition (to). **2.** To offer in response. **3.** To meet (a blow) with another blow. —*n.* **1.** An opposite. **2.** An answering blow. —*adv.* In an opposing direction or manner.
count·er[2] (koun′tər) *n.* **1.** A level surface on which business is transacted or food served. **2.** A small piece, as of ivory, used for reckoning or for keeping a place in games. **3.** A token or imitation coin.
count·er[3] (koun′tər) *n.* One that counts, esp. an electrical device.
counter– *pref.* **1.** Contrary : opposite <*counter*clockwise> **2.** Retaliatory : in return <*counter*attack> See below for a list of self-explanatory words formed with the prefix **counter–.**
coun·ter·act (koun′tər-ăkt′) *v.* To oppose and make ineffective by contrary action. **—coun′ter·ac′tion** *n.*
coun·ter·at·tack (koun′tər-ə-tăk′) *n.* An attack made in opposition to another attack. **—coun′ter·at·tack′** *v.*
coun·ter·bal·ance (koun′tər-băl′əns) *n.* **1.** A force or influence that balances another. **2.** A weight balancing another. **—coun′ter·bal′ance** *v.*
coun·ter·claim (koun′tər-klām′) *n.* An opposing claim to offset another, esp. in a lawsuit.
coun·ter·clock·wise (koun′tər-klŏk′wīz′) *adj. & adv.* In a direction opposite to that in which the hands of a clock move.
coun·ter·cul·ture (koun′tər-kŭl′chər) *n.* A culture, esp. of the young, with values in opposition to those of traditional society.
coun·ter·es·pi·o·nage (koun′tər-ĕs′pē-ə-näzh′, -nĭj) *n.* Espionage intended to discover and counteract enemy espionage.
coun·ter·feit (koun′tər-fĭt) *v.* **1.** To copy, with the intent to deceive : forge. **2.** To make a show of : feign. —*adj.* **1.** Made in imitation of the genuine so as to deceive : forged. **2.** Pretended : feigned. ☆***syns:*** BOGUS, ERSATZ, FAKE, FALSE, FRAUDULENT, PHONY, SHAM, SPURIOUS **—coun′ter·feit** *n.* **—coun′ter·feit·er** *n.*
coun·ter·foil (koun′tər-foil′) *n.* The portion of a paper, as a check or ticket, kept by the issuer as a record of the transaction.
coun·ter·in·sur·gen·cy (koun′tər-ĭn-sûr′jən-sē) *n.* Military and political activity intended to deal with insurgents.
coun·ter·in·tel·li·gence (koun′tər-ĭn-tĕl′ə-jəns) *n.* An intelligence agency whose duties are to keep valuable information from an enemy, to prevent subversion and sabotage, and to gather political and military data.
coun·ter·ir·ri·tant (koun′tər-îr′ĭ-tənt) *n.* An additional irritation that takes attention away from another.
coun·ter·man (koun′tər-măn′, -mən) *n.* One who serves at a counter.
coun·ter·mand (koun′tər-mănd′) *v.* To reverse (a command) by issuing a contrary order.
coun·ter·of·fen·sive (koun′tər-ə-fĕn′sĭv) *n.* A military offensive undertaken to stop an enemy attack.
coun·ter·pane (koun′tər-pān′) *n.* A coverlet.
coun·ter·part (koun′tər-pärt′) *n.* One that corresponds very closely to another, as in function or appearance.
coun·ter·point (koun′tər-point′) *n.* **1.** *Mus.* The combination of 2 or more melodies into a harmonic relationship while retaining their linear character. **2.** A contrasting but matching element : foil.
coun·ter·poise (koun′tər-poiz′) *n.* **1.** A counterbalancing weight or influence. **2.** The state of being balanced : equilibrium. **—coun′ter·poise′** *v.*
coun·ter·pro·duc·tive (koun′tər-prə-dŭk′tĭv) *adj.* Tending to obstruct rather than aid the achievement of a goal.
coun·ter·rev·o·lu·tion (koun′tər-rĕv′ə-lo͞o′shən) *n.* A movement arising to restore the system overthrown by a revolution.
coun·ter·sign (koun′tər-sīn′) *v.* To add a confirming signature to (a previously signed document). —*n.* **1.** A confirming

counteraccusation
counterassurance
counteragent
counterargument
counterassault
counterbid
counterblockade
counterblow
countercharge
countercheck
countercomplaint
countercoup
countercry
countercurrent
counterdemand
counterdemonstration
counterdeployment
counterevidence
counterfire
counterflow
counterforce
counterfugue
countergovernment
counterinflationary
counterinfluence
counterlegislation
countermarch
countermeasure
countermove
countermovement
counteroffer
counterplan
counterplea
counterplot
counterploy
counterposition
counterpressure
counterpropaganda
counterproposal
counterquestion
counterreaction
counterresolution
counterseal
counterstatement
counterstep
counterstrike
counterstroke
countersuggestion
countersuit
countersurveillance
countertactic(s)
counterterror
counterterrorism
counterthreat
counterthrust
counterviolence

signature added to a previously signed document. **2.** A secret sign or signal given by a person who wishes to pass a guard.
coun·ter·sink (koun′tər-sĭngk′) *n.* **1.** A hole with the top part enlarged so that a screw or bolthead will lie flush with or below the surface. **2.** A tool for making a countersink. **—coun′ter·sink** *v.*
coun·ter·spy (koun′tər-spī′) *n.* A spy engaged in counterespionage.
coun·ter·ten·or (koun′tər-tĕn′ər) *n.* An adult male with a very high voice, higher than a tenor.
coun·ter·vail (koun′tər-vāl′, koun′tər-vāl′) *v.* **-vailed, -vail·ing.** To counteract.
coun·ter·weight (koun′tər-wāt′) *n.* A counterbalance.
count·ess (koun′tĭs) *n.* **1.** The wife or widow of an earl or count. **2.** A woman with either rank in her own right.
count·ing·house *also* **counting house** (koun′tĭng-hous′) *n.* An office in which a firm's bookkeeping and correspondence are carried out.
count·less (kount′lĭs) *adj.* Too many to be counted : infinite.
coun·tri·fied *also* **coun·try·fied** (kŭn′trĭ-fīd′) *adj.* **1.** Typical of country life : rural. **2.** Unsophisticated.
coun·try (kŭn′trē) *n., pl.* **-tries. 1.** An area or region. **2.** An area away from cities and towns. **3. a.** A state or nation. **b.** The territory of a state or nation. **4.** The land of one's origin or citizenship.
country club *n.* A club with facilities for social and sports activities.
coun·try-dance (kŭn′trē-dăns′) *n.* An English folk dance in which dancers face each other, usu. in lines.
coun·try·man (kŭn′trē-mən) *n.* A compatriot. **—coun′try·wom′an** *n.*
country music *n.* Popular music derived from folk music of the rural U.S., esp. the S or SW U.S.
coun·try·side (kŭn′trē-sīd′) *n.* A rural area or its inhabitants.
coun·ty (koun′tē) *n., pl.* **-ties.** An administrative district of a country or state.
coup (ko͞o) *n.* **1.** A brilliant sudden move. **2.** A coup d'état.
coup d'é·tat (ko͞o′ dā-tä′) *n., pl.* **coups d'état** (ko͞o′ dā-tä′). The sudden, violent overthrow of a government.
cou·pé (ko͞o-pā′) *also* **coupe** (ko͞op) *n.* A closed automobile with 2 doors.
cou·ple (kŭp′əl) *n.* **1.** A pair. **2.** Something joining 2 things together. **3.** *(sing. or pl. in number).* Two people closely associated, esp. a man and woman who are married. **4.** A few : some. ☆***syns:*** BRACE, DOUBLET, PAIR *—v.* **-pled, -pling. 1.** To join together. **2.** To form pairs. **3.** To copulate. **—cou′pler** *n.*
cou·plet (kŭp′lĭt) *n.* Two successive rhyming lines of poetry.
cou·pon (ko͞o′pŏn′, kyo͞o′-) *n.* **1.** A detachable certificate on a bond to be presented for payment of interest due. **2.** A certificate that entitles the bearer to a discount, refund, or gift. **3.** Part of an advertisement to be cut out and filled in when sending away for something.
cour·age (kûr′ĭj, kŭr′-) *n.* The ability to face danger without fear. **—cou·ra′geous** *adj.* **—cou·ra′geous·ly** *adv.*
cou·reur de bois (ko͞o-ro͞or′ də bwä′) *n. Can.* A French or Métis woodsman of the Canadian North.
cou·ri·er (ko͝or′ē-ər, kûr′-) *n.* **1.** A messenger, esp. one in the diplomatic service. **2.** A person who assists travelers with their arrangements.
course (kôrs, kōrs) *n.* **1.** Progress or the direction of progress. **2.** The path over which something moves. **3.** Duration <in the *course* of a week> **4.** A way of acting or behaving. **5.** A series : sequence <a *course* of treatment> **6. a.** A complete series of studies. **b.** A unit of such a series. **7.** A portion of a meal served at 1 time <the soup *course*> *—v.* **coursed, cours·ing. 1.** To move rapidly (over or through). **2.** To hunt (game) with dogs. **3.** To flow <tears *coursing* down one's cheeks> **—of course.** Certainly.
cours·er (kôr′sər, kōr′-) *n.* A swift or spirited horse.
court (kôrt, kōrt) *n.* **1.** A courtyard. **2.** A short street, esp. one with buildings on 3 sides. **3.** The residence of a monarch. **4.** The attendants and family of a monarch. **5.** A monarch's council and advisers. **6. a.** A judge or judges whose task it is to try cases of law. **b.** A place where trials are held. **7.** An open area marked off for playing a game. *—v.* **1.** To try to gain the favor of. **2.** To woo. **3.** To behave so as to attract <*court* disaster>
cour·te·ous (kûr′tē-əs) *adj.* Considerate toward others : polite. ☆***syns:*** CIVIL, GENTEEL, MANNERLY, POLITE **—cour′te·ous·ly** *adv.* **—cour′te·ous·ness** *n.*
cour·te·san (kôr′tĭ-zən, kōr′-) *n.* A prostitute, esp. one associating with high-ranking or wealthy men.
cour·te·sy (kûr′tĭ-sē) *n., pl.* **-sies. 1.** Courteous behavior. **2.** A polite remark or gesture.
court·house (kôrt′hous′, kōrt′-) *n.* A building for holding courts of law.
court·i·er (kôr′tē-ər, kōr′-) *n.* An attendant at a royal court.
court·ly (kôrt′lē, kōrt′-) *adj.* **-li·er, -li·est. 1.** Suitable for a royal court. **2.** Dignified in manner : refined. **—court′li·ness** *n.*
court-mar·tial (kôrt′mär′shəl, kōrt′-) *n., pl.* **courts-mar·tial. 1.** A military or naval court for trial of crimes against military or naval law. **2.** A trial by court-martial. **—court′-mar′tial** *v.*
court·room (kôrt′ro͞om′, -ro͝om′, kōrt′-) *n.* A room in which a law court is held.
court·ship (kôrt′shĭp′, kōrt′-) *n.* The time or act of courting.
court·yard (kôrt′yärd′, kōrt′-) *n.* An open space enclosed by walls, within or adjoining a large building.
cous·cous (ko͞os′ko͞os′) *n.* A North African dish of steamed crushed grain.
cous·in (kŭz′ĭn) *n.* **1.** A child of one's uncle or aunt. **2.** A relative. **3.** A member of a culturally similar race or nation <our Canadian *cousins*>
cou·ture (ko͞o-to͝or′) *n.* **1.** The business of a couturier. **2.** Fashion designers as a group.
cou·tu·ri·er (ko͞o-to͝or′ē-ər, -ē-ā′) *n.* One who designs, makes, and sells fashionable women's clothing.
cove (kōv) *n.* A small inlet or bay.
cov·en (kŭv′ən, kō′vən) *n.* A gathering of witches.
cov·e·nant (kŭv′ə-nənt) *n.* A binding agreement : compact. **—cov′e·nant** *v.*
cov·er (kŭv′ər) *v.* **1.** To place something on or over. **2.** To clothe. **3.** To serve as a covering for. **4.** To extend over <a park *covering* many acres> **5.** To conceal : hide. **6.** To insure. **7.** To be sufficient to meet the cost of. **8.** To treat of : include. **9.** To traverse. **10.** To aim a firearm at. **11.** To report the details of <*cover* the election> **12.** *Informal.* To act as a replacement during another's absence. *—n.* **1.** Something that covers. **2.** A position offering protection from attack. **3.** Something that disguises or conceals. **4.** A table setting for 1 person. **5.** A mailing envelope.
cov·er·age (kŭv′ər-ĭj) *n.* **1.** The extent to which something is covered. **2.** All the risks covered by an insurance policy.
cov·er·alls (kŭv′ər-ôlz′) *pl.n.* A 1-piece, protective outer garment.
cover charge *n.* A fixed amount added to the bill, as at a restaurant or nightclub.
cover crop *n.* A crop planted to prevent erosion and provide humus.
cover girl *n.* A model whose picture appears on magazine covers.
cov·er·let (kŭv′ər-lĭt) *n.* A bedspread.
†cov·er·lid (kŭv′ər-lĭd′) *n. Regional.* A coverlet.
cov·ert (kŭv′ərt, kō′vərt) *adj.* **1.** Covered over. **2.** Secret : clandestine. *—n.* **1.** A sheltered place. **2.** A thicket providing cover for game. **—cov′ert·ly** *adv.*
cov·er-up *also* **cov·er·up** (kŭv′ər-ŭp′) *n.* An attempt to conceal scandal or crime.
cov·et (kŭv′ĭt) *v.* **1.** To desire enviously (that which belongs to another). **2.** To crave. **—cov′et·ous** *adj.* **—cov′et·ous·ly** *adv.* **—cov′et·ous·ness** *n.*
cov·ey (kŭv′ē) *n., pl.* **-eys.** A small flock of birds, esp. quail or partridges.
cow[1] (kou) *n.* **1.** The mature female of cattle of the genus *Bos* or of certain other large animals. **2.** A domesticated bovine animal. **3.** *Informal.* An unpleasant woman.
cow[2] (kou) *v.* To intimidate.
cow·ard (kou′ərd) *n.* One who shows ignoble fear in the face of pain or danger. **—cow′ard·ice** *n.*
cow·ard·ly (kou′ərd-lē) *adj.* Ignobly lacking in courage. ☆***syns:*** CHICKEN, CHICKEN-HEARTED, CRAVEN, DASTARDLY, FAINT-HEARTED, GUTLESS, LILY-LIVERED, PUSILLANIMOUS, YELLOW, YELLOW-BELLIED **—cow′ard·li·ness** *n.* **—cow′ard·ly** *adv.*
cow·bird (kou′bûrd′) *n.* A blackbird of the genus *Molothrus* that lays its eggs in the nests of other birds.
cow·boy (kou′boi′) *n.* A ranch hand who rides on horseback tending and herding cattle. **—cow′girl′** *n.*
cow·er (kou′ər) *v.* To cringe from fear.
cow·hand (kou′hănd′) *n.* A cowboy or cowgirl.
cow·herd (kou′hûrd′) *n.* A person who herds cattle.
cow·hide (kou′hīd′) *n.* **1. a.** The hide of a cow. **b.** Leather made from cowhide. **2.** A coarse, heavy usu. braided leather whip.
cowl (koul) *n.* **1.** A monk's hood or the hooded robe. **2.** The top portion at the front of a car to which the windshield and dashboard are attached.
cow·lick (kou′lĭk′) *n.* A tuft of hair that cannot be combed to lie flat.

cowl•ing (kou′lĭng) *n.* A detachable metal covering for an airplane engine.
cow•poke (kou′pōk′) *n. Informal.* A cowhand.
cow•pox (kou′pŏks′) *n.* A mild skin disease of cows caused by a virus that gives humans immunity to smallpox.
cow•punch•er (kou′pŭn′chər) *n. Informal.* A cowhand.
cow•ry *also* **cow•rie** (kou′rē) *n., pl.* **-ries.** Any of numerous mollusks of the family Cypraeidae of tropical waters, with glossy, often brightly colored shells.
cow•slip (kou′slĭp′) *n.* **1.** An Old World primrose, *Primula veris,* with pale-yellow flowers. **2.** The marsh marigold.
cox (kŏks) *Informal.* —*n.* A coxswain. —*v.* To act as coxswain (for).
cox•comb (kŏks′kōm′) *n.* A conceited foolish person : fop.
cox•swain (kŏk′sən, -swān′) *n.* The person who steers a racing shell or boat.
coy (koi) *adj.* Shy or pretending to be shy. **—coy′ly** *adv.* **—coy′ness** *n.*
coy•dog (kī′dôg′, -dŏg′, koi′-) *n.* A predatory animal, prob. a cross between a wolf and a coyote, that now ranges widely throughout the U.S.

coydog

coy•o•te (kī-ō′tē, kī′ōt′) *n.* A wolflike carnivorous animal, *Canis latrans,* native to North America.
coy•pu (koi′po͞o) *n., pl.* **-pus.** A large beaverlike South American rodent, *Myocaster coypu.*
coz•en (kŭz′ən) *v.* To cheat : defraud. **—coz′en•age** *n.*
co•zy *also* **co•sy** (kō′zē) *adj.* **-zi•er, -zi•est** *also* **-si•er, -si•est.** Warm and comfortable : snug. —*n., pl.* **-zies** *also* **-sies.** A covering placed over a teapot to keep the tea hot. **—co′zi•ly** *adv.* **—co′zi•ness** *n.*
C.P.A. *abbr.* certified public accountant
cpd. *abbr.* compound.
CPR (sē′pē-är′) *n.* Cardiopulmonary resuscitation.
cr. *abbr.* credit.
Cr *symbol for* CHROMIUM.
crab[1] (krăb) *n.* **1.** Any of numerous chiefly marine crustaceans with a short, broad shell, 4 pairs of legs, and a pair of pincers. **2.** The crab louse.
crab[2] (krăb) *n. Informal.* A peevish person. **—crab** *v.* **—crab′by** *adj.*
crab apple *n.* Any of several trees of the genus *Pyrus,* with small, sour fruit.
crab•bed (krăb′ĭd) *adj.* **1.** Irritable : morose. **2.** Difficult to read. **—crab′bed•ly** *adv.* **—crab′bed•ness** *n.*
crab•grass (krăb′grăs′) *n.* A coarse, weedy creeping grass of the genus *Digitaria.*
crab louse *n.* A body louse, *Phthirus pubis,* that gen. infests the pubic region.
crack (krăk) *v.* **1.** To break or cause to break apart with a snap. **2.** To break or cause to break without completely separating into parts. **3.** To change sharply in tone. Used of a voice. **4.** To strike with a sudden sharp sound. **5.** To break open <*crack* a safe> **6.** To solve. **7.** *Informal.* To tell (a joke). **8.** To reduce (petroleum) to simpler compounds by heating. **—crack down.** *Informal.* To act to restrain or restrict. **—crack up.** *Informal.* **1.** To damage or wreck. **2.** To have a physical or mental breakdown. **3.** To experience or cause considerable amusement. —*n.* **1.** A sudden sharp noise. **2.** A narrow opening or break : fissure. **3.** A sudden, sharp blow. **4.** A cracking of the voice. **5.** An attempt : try. **6.** A witty remark. —*adj.* Highly proficient : first-rate.
crack•down (krăk′doun′) *n.* An act or example of cracking down.
crack•er (krăk′ər) *n.* **1.** A dry, thin, crisp biscuit or wafer. **2.** A firecracker.
crack•er•jack (krăk′ər-jăk′) *adj. Slang.* Of excellent quality : fine. **—crack′er•jack′** *n.*
crack•le (krăk′əl) *v.* **-led, -ling.** **1.** To make or cause to make a series of sharp snapping sounds. **2.** To become covered with a network of small cracks. **—crack′le** *n.* **—crack′ly** *adj.*
crack•pot (krăk′pŏt′) *n.* A bizarre or eccentric person.
crack•up (krăk′ŭp′) *n. Informal.* **1.** A crash or wreck, as of an aircraft. **2.** A physical or mental breakdown.
cra•dle (krād′l) *n.* **1.** A small, low bed for an infant, often on rockers. **2.** A place of origin. **3.** The support for a telephone receiver. **4.** A frame attached to a scythe for catching grain as it is cut. —*v.* **-dled, -dling.** **1.** To place in or hold in or as if in a cradle. **2.** To take care of in infancy.
craft (krăft) *n.* **1.** A special skill or ability. **2.** Cunning : guile. **3. a.** An occupation, esp. one that demands manual skill. **b.** The members of such an occupation or trade. **4.** *pl.* **craft.** An aircraft, boat, or ship.
crafts•man (krăfts′mən) *n.* A skilled worker : artisan. **—crafts′man•ship′** *n.* **—crafts′wom′an** *n.*
craft•y (krăf′tē) *adj.* **-i•er, -i•est.** Cunning : sly : shrewd. **—craft′i•ly** *adv.* **—craft′i•ness** *n.*
crag (krăg) *n.* A steep cliff or projecting mass of rock. **—crag′gy** *adj.*
cram (krăm) *v.* **crammed, cram•ming.** **1.** To force or stuff. **2.** To pack in tightly. **3.** To eat greedily. **4.** *Informal.* To prepare hastily for an examination.
cramp[1] (krămp) *n.* **1.** A painful involuntary contraction of a muscle usu. resulting from strain or cold. **2. cramps.** Sharp abdominal spasms and pains.
cramp[2] (krămp) *n.* Anything that restrains or compresses, as a clamp. —*v.* **1.** To restrain from free action : hamper. **2.** To turn (the wheels of a car) sharply.
cran•ber•ry (krăn′bĕr′ē) *n.* A trailing North American shrub, *Vaccinium macrocarpon,* growing in damp ground and bearing edible, tart red berries.
crane (krān) *n.* **1.** A large wading bird of the family Cruidae, with very long legs and neck. **2.** A machine for lifting and moving heavy objects. —*v.* **craned, cran•ing.** To strain or stretch (the neck).
cra•ni•um (krā′nē-əm) *n., pl.* **-ums** *or* **-ni•a** (-nē-ə). The skull, esp. the part that encloses the brain. **—cra′ni•al** *adj.*
crank[1] (krăngk) *n.* **1.** A handle attached at right angles to a shaft and turned in order to transmit rotary motion. **2.** *Informal.* An ill-tempered or eccentric person. —*v.* To operate or start by a crank.
†**crank**[2] (krăngk) *adj. Regional.* **1.** Lively. **2.** Overconfident.
crank•case (krăngk′kās′) *n.* The housing of a crankshaft.
crank•shaft (krăngk′shăft′) *n.* A shaft driven by a crank.
crank•y (krăng′kē) *adj.* **-i•er, -i•est.** **1.** Peevish : grouchy. **2.** Eccentric. **—crank′i•ly** *adv.* **—crank′i•ness** *n.*
cran•ny (krăn′ē) *n., pl.* **-nies.** A crevice.
crape (krāp) *n.* Crepe.
craps (krăps) *n. (sing. or pl. in number).* A gambling game played with dice.
crap•shoot•er (krăp′sho͞o′tər) *n.* A person who plays craps.
crash[1] (krăsh) *v.* **1.** To break noisily : smash. **2.** To cause or undergo damage on impact. **3.** To make a sudden loud noise. **4.** To collapse suddenly, as a business. **5.** *Informal.* To get into (e.g., a party) without invitation. —*n.* **1.** A loud, sudden sound. **2.** A collision : wreck. **3.** A sudden failure, esp. of a business. —*adj. Informal.* Intensive <a *crash* diet>
crash[2] (krăsh) *n.* A coarse cotton material used for draperies and towels.
crash helmet *n.* A padded, protective helmet, as worn by motorcyclists.
crash-land (krăsh′lănd′) *v.* To land an aircraft in an emergency, often without the use of the landing gear.
crash pad *n.* Protective padding inside a vehicle, as a tank.
crass (krăs) *adj.* Coarse and unrefined : gross. **—crass′ly** *adv.* **—crass′ness** *n.*
crate (krāt) *n.* A container, as a slatted wooden box. —*v.* **crat•ed, crat•ing.** To pack in a crate.
cra•ter (krā′tər) *n.* **1.** A cavity at the mouth of a volcano. **2.** A hole in the ground made by an explosion or a falling meteorite.
cra•vat (krə-văt′) *n.* A necktie.
crave (krāv) *v.* **craved, crav•ing.** **1.** To desire intensely : long for. **2.** To ask for earnestly : beg.
cra•ven (krā′vən) *adj.* Cowardly. **—cra′ven** *n.* **—cra′ven•ly** *adv.*
crav•ing (krā′vĭng) *n.* An overwhelming longing : yearning.
craw (krô) *n.* **1.** The crop of a bird. **2.** An animal's stomach.
craw•fish (krô′fĭsh′) *n.* A crayfish.
crawl (krôl) *v.* **1.** To move slowly by drawing the body along the ground. **2.** To move on hands and knees. **3.** To feel as if covered with crawling creatures. ☆***syns:*** CREEP, SLIDE, SNAKE, WORM —*n.* **1.** A slow pace. **2.** A swimming stroke performed face down consisting of alternating overarm strokes and a flutterkick.
cray•fish (krā′fĭsh′) *n.* Any of various small, lobsterlike freshwater crustaceans of the genera *Cambarus* and *Astacus.*

cray·on (krā′ŏn′, -ən) *n.* A colored stick, as of wax or charcoal, used for drawing. **—cray′on′** *v.*
craze (krāz) *v.* **crazed, craz·ing.** To make or become insane. *—n.* Something popular for a short time : fad.
cra·zy (krā′zē) *adj.* **-zi·er, -zi·est. 1.** Mad : insane. **2.** *Informal.* Very enthusiastic. **3.** *Informal.* Very impractical. **—cra′zi·ly** *adv.* **—cra′zi·ness** *n.*
crazy bone *n.* The funny bone.
crazy quilt *n.* A patchwork quilt of pieces arranged in no definite pattern.
creak (krēk) *v.* To make a squeaking noise. **—creak** *n.* **—creak′i·ly** *adv.* **—creak′i·ness** *n.* **—creak′y** *adj.*
cream (krēm) *n.* **1.** The yellowish fatty component of unhomogenized milk. **2.** A yellowish white. **3.** A substance resembling or containing cream, as certain cosmetics or foods. **4.** The finest part. *—v.* To beat into a creamy consistency. **—cream′i·ness** *n.* **—cream′y** *adj.*
cream cheese *n.* A soft cheese made from milk enriched with cream.
cream·er (krē′mər) *n.* A small pitcher.
cream·er·y (krē′mə-rē) *n., pl.* **-ies.** A place where dairy products are made or sold.
crease (krēs) *n.* A mark made by folding and pressing. **—crease** *v.*
cre·ate (krē-āt′) *v.* **-at·ed, -at·ing. 1.** To bring into being. **2.** To give rise to.
cre·a·tion (krē-ā′shən) *n.* **1.** The act of creating. **2.** Something that is created. **3.** All things in the world.
cre·a·tive (krē-ā′tĭv) *adj.* Inventive : imaginative. **—cre·a′tive·ly** *adv.* **—cre′a·tiv′i·ty, cre·a′tive·ness** *n.*
cre·a·tor (krē-ā′tər) *n.* **1.** One that creates. **2. Creator.** God.
crea·ture (krē′chər) *n.* **1.** A living being. **2.** A human being.
crèche (krĕsh) *n.* A representation of the stable scene of Jesus' birth.
cre·dence (krēd′ns) *n.* Belief.
cre·den·tial (krĭ-dĕn′shəl) *n.* Something that is a basis for credit or confidence.
cre·den·za (krĭ-dĕn′zə) *n.* A usu. legless cabinet or sideboard.
cred·i·ble (krĕd′ə-bəl) *adj.* **1.** Plausible. **2.** Deserving confidence. **—cred′i·bil′i·ty** *n.* **—cred′i·bly** *adv.*
cred·it (krĕd′ĭt) *n.* **1.** Belief in the truth of something : trust. **2.** A favorable reputation. **3.** A source of distinction. **4.** Praise. **5.** Official certification that a student has completed a course. **6.** Financial trustworthiness. **7.** Time given for payment of goods sold on trust. **8.** An accounting entry of payment received. **9.** The balance of a bank account that is in the holder's favor. *—v.* **1.** To believe in. **2.** To give credit to <*credited* me with the invention.>
cred·it·a·ble (krĕd′ĭ-tə-bəl) *adj.* Meriting praise. **—cred′it·a·bly** *adv.*
credit card *n.* A card authorizing purchases on credit.
cred·i·tor (krĕd′ĭ-tər) *n.* A person to whom money is owed.
credit union *n.* A cooperative organization that makes low-interest loans to its members.
cred·it·wor·thy (krĕd′ĭt-wûr′thē) *adj.* Having a favorable credit rating.
cre·do (krē′dō, krā′-) *n., pl.* **-dos.** Creed.
cred·u·lous (krĕj′ə-ləs) *adj.* Gullible. **—cre·du′li·ty, cred′u·lous·ness** *n.* **—cred′u·lous·ly** *adv.*
creed (krēd) *n.* **1.** A statement of religious belief, esp. one authorized by a church. **2.** A system of principles or opinions.
creek (krēk, krĭk) *n.* A small stream. **—up the creek.** In a difficult position.
creel (krēl) *n.* A wickerwork basket for holding fish.
creep (krēp) *v.* **crept** (krĕpt), **creep·ing. 1.** To move with the body close to the ground : crawl. **2.** To move cautiously or stealthily : sneak. **3.** *Bot.* To grow along a surface, clinging by means of tendrils. **4.** To feel as if covered with creeping creatures. *—n.* **1.** *Slang.* A repulsive person. **2. creeps.** *Informal.* A feeling of fear or repugnance. **—creep′er** *n.* **—creep′y** *adj.*
cre·mate (krē′māt′, krĭ-māt′) *v.* **-mat·ed, -mat·ing.** To incinerate (a corpse). **—cre·ma′tion** *n.*
cre·ma·to·ri·um (krē′mə-tôr′ē-əm, -tōr′-) *n.* A crematory.
cre·ma·to·ry (krē′mə-tôr′ē, -tōr′ē, krĕm′ə-) *n., pl.* **-ries.** A place where corpses are cremated.
crème de la crème (krĕm′ də lä krĕm′) *n.* **1.** The very best. **2.** The social elite.
crème de menthe (krĕm′ də mäNT′) *n.* A green or white mint-flavored liqueur.
cren·el·lat·ed (krĕn′ə-lā′tĭd) *adj.* Having battlements. **—cren′el·la′tion** *n.*
Cre·ole (krē′ōl′) *n.* **1.** A person of European ancestry born in Spanish America or the West Indies. **2. a.** One descended from the orig. French settlers of S U.S. **b.** The French dialect of these people. **3.** A person of mixed Negro and European ancestry.
cre·o·sote (krē′ə-sōt′) *n.* An oily liquid obtained by distilling coal tar and used as a wood preservative.
crepe *also* **crêpe** (krāp) *n.* A thin, soft crinkled fabric of silk or other fiber.
crêpe de Chine (krāp′ də shēn′) *n.* A silk crepe.
crêpe su·zette (krāp′ so͞o-zĕt′) *n.* A thin dessert pancake usu. rolled with orange sauce and often served with a flaming brandy or liqueur sauce.
crept (krĕpt) *v. p.t.* & *p.p.* of CREEP.
cre·pus·cu·lar (krĭ-pŭs′kyə-lər) *adj.* **1.** Of or resembling twilight. **2.** *Zool.* Becoming active at twilight.
cres·cen·do (krə-shĕn′dō, -sĕn′-) *adv. Mus.* Gradually increasing in loudness. **—cres·cen′do** *adj.* & *n.*
cres·cent (krĕs′ənt) *n.* **1.** The shape of the moon in its 1st or 4th quarter with concave and convex edges. **2.** Anything with the shape of a crescent. **—cres′cent** *adj.*
cress (krĕs) *n.* Any of various related plants, as those of the genera *Cardamine* or *Arabis,* with sharp-tasting edible leaves.
crest (krĕst) *n.* **1.** A ridge or tuft on the head of a bird or animal. **2.** *Heraldry.* A device set above the escutcheon on a coat or arms. **3.** The highest point, as of a wave or mountain top. *—v.* **1.** To reach the crest of. **2.** To rise to a crest.
crest·fall·en (krĕst′fô′lən) *adj.* Dispirited : depressed.
Crete (krēt). Greek island in the E Mediterranean. **—Cre′tan** *adj.* & *n.*
cre·tin (krēt′n) *n.* **1.** A person afflicted with myxodema. **2.** An idiot.
cre·tin·ism (krēt′n-ĭz′əm) *n.* Myxodema.
cre·tonne (krĭ-tŏn′, krē′tŏn′) *n.* A strong, colorfully printed cotton or linen cloth.
cre·vasse (krə-văs′) *n.* A deep crack, esp. in a glacier.
crev·ice (krĕv′ĭs) *n.* A narrow crack.
crew[1] (kro͞o) *n.* **1.** A group of people working together. **2.** The persons who man an aircraft, ship, etc. **3.** A team of rowers.
crew[2] (kro͞o) *v. var. p.t.* & *p.p. of* CROW[2].
crew cut *n.* A man's short haircut.
crew·el (kro͞o′əl) *n.* Slackly twisted worsted yarn used in embroidery.
crib (krĭb) *n.* **1.** A small bed with high sides, for a child. **2.** A small building or bin for grain storage. **3.** A trough or rack for fodder : manger. **4.** *Informal.* **a.** Plagiarism. **b.** A petty theft. **c.** PONY 3. *—v.* **cribbed, crib·bing. 1.** To confine. **2.** *Informal.* **a.** To plagiarize. **b.** To steal. **3.** *Informal.* To use a crib for schoolwork. **—crib′ber** *n.*
crib·bage (krĭb′ĭj) *n.* A card game usu. played by 2 players and scored on a board.
crib death *n.* Sudden infant death syndrome.
crick[1] (krĭk) *n.* A painful muscle spasm.
†**crick**[2] (krĭk) *n. Regional.* A creek.
crick·et[1] (krĭk′ĭt) *n.* Any of various leaping insects of the family Gryllidae, the male of the species producing a shrill, chirping sound by rubbing the front wings together.
crick·et[2] (krĭk′ĭt) *n.* An outdoor game played with bats, a ball, and wickets by 2 teams of 11 players each. **—crick′et·er** *n.*

cricket[2]

cri·er (krī′ər) *n.* One who calls out public proclamations.
crime (krīm) *n.* An offense committed against the law.
Cri·me·a (krī-mē′ə). Peninsula of S European USSR, extending into the Black Sea.
crim·i·nal (krĭm′ə-nəl) *adj.* **1.** Of or involving a crime. **2.** Relating to the administration of penal laws. **3.** Guilty of crime. ☆**syns:** ILLEGAL, ILLEGITIMATE, ILLICIT, LAWLESS, UNLAWFUL, WRONGFUL *—n.* A person who has committed a crime. **—crim′i·nal′i·ty** *n.* **—crim′i·nal·ly** *adv.*
criminal law *n.* Law dealing with crime and its punishment.
crim·i·nol·o·gy (krĭm′ə-nŏl′ə-jē) *n.* The scientific study of crime and criminal behavior. **—crim′i·nol′o·gist** *n.*
crimp (krĭmp) *v.* **1.** To cause to become crinkled : corrugate. **2.** To cause (hair) to form tight curls. *—n.* Something, as a hair curl, that has been produced by crimping.

crim•son (krĭm′zən, -sən) *n.* A deep red. —*v.* To make or become crimson.

cringe (krĭnj) *v.* **cringed, cring•ing.** To recoil in fear : cower.

crin•kle (krĭng′kəl) *v.* **-kled, -kling.** To wrinkle. **—crin′kle** *n.* **—crin′kly** *adj.*

crin•o•line (krĭn′ə-lĭn) *n.* A coarse fabric used for lining and stiffening garments.

crip•ple (krĭp′əl) *n.* One who is lame or otherwise disabled. —*v.* **-pled, -pling.** To disable or impair.

cri•sis (krī′sĭs) *n., pl.* **-ses** (-sēz′). **1.** A decisive or crucial moment. **2.** A sudden change for better or worse in the course of an acute illness.

crisp (krĭsp) *adj.* **1.** Easily broken : brittle <*crisp* bacon> **2.** Fresh and firm <*crisp* lettuce> **3.** Brisk : bracing. **4.** Curly. —*n. esp. Brit.* A potato chip. —*v.* To make or become crisp. **—crisp′ly** *adv.* **—crisp′ness** *n.* **—crisp′y** *adj.*

crisp•er (krĭs′pər) *n.* A compartment in a refrigerator used to keep vegetables fresh.

criss•cross (krĭs′krôs′, -krŏs′) *v.* **1.** To mark with crossed lines. **2.** To move back and forth. —*n.* A pattern of crossed lines. **—criss′cross′** *adj. & adv.*

cri•te•ri•on (krī-tîr′ē-ən) *n., pl.* **-te•ri•a** (-tîr′ē-ə) *or* **-ons.** A standard or rule by which something can be judged.

crit•ic (krĭt′ĭk) *n.* **1.** One who forms and expresses judgments of the merits, faults, etc., of a matter. **2.** One who expresses judgments of artistic or literary works. **3.** One inclined to find fault.

crit•i•cal (krĭt′ĭ-kəl) *adj.* **1.** Tending to judge adversely. **2.** Marked by exact and careful judgment and evaluation. **3.** Of or relating to critics or criticism. **4.** Of or forming a crisis : crucial. ☆***syns:*** ACUTE, CRUCIAL, DESPERATE, DIRE **—crit′i•cal•ly** *adv.*

critical mass *n.* The smallest mass of a fissionable material that will sustain a nuclear chain reaction.

crit•i•cism (krĭt′ĭ-sĭz′əm) *n.* **1.** The act of criticizing, esp. adversely : censure. **2. a.** The judgments of a critic. **b.** A review expressing such judgments.

crit•i•cize (krĭt′ĭ-sīz′) *v.* **-cized, -ciz•ing. 1.** To analyze and evaluate. **2.** To judge adversely.

cri•tique (krĭ-tēk′) *n.* A critical analysis or review. **—cri•tique′** *v.*

†crit•ter (krĭt′ər) *n. Regional.* **1.** A domestic animal. **2.** A living creature.

croak (krōk) *n.* A hoarse, rasping cry, as that of a frog. —*v.* **1.** To utter a croak. **2.** *Slang.* To die. **—croak′i•ly** *adv.*

Cro•a•tia (krō-ā′shə). Region of NW Yugoslavia. **—Cro•a′tian** *adj. & n.*

cro•chet (krō-shā′) *n.* Needlework done by looping thread or wool with a hooked needle. —*v.* **-cheted** (-shād′), **-chet•ing** (-shā′ĭng). To make (crochet).

crock (krŏk) *n.* An earthenware pot or jar. **—crock′er•y** *n.*

crocked (krŏkt) *adj. Slang.* Intoxicated.

croc•o•dile (krŏk′ə-dīl′) *n.* Any of various aquatic reptiles of the genus *Crocodylus,* of tropical regions, with thick armorlike skin and long jaws.

crocodile tears *pl.n.* Insincere grief.

croc•o•dil•i•an (krŏk′ə-dĭl′ē-ən, -dĭl′yən) *n.* Any of various reptiles of the order Crocodylia, including the alligators, crocodiles, and caimans. **—croc′o•dil′i•an** *adj.*

cro•cus (krō′kəs) *n., pl.* **-es.** A plant of the genus *Crocus,* widely cultivated in gardens and bearing variously colored flowers.

croft (krôft, krŏft) *n. Brit. & Scot.* A small farm, esp. a tenant farm. **—croft′er** *n.*

crois•sant (krwä-säN′) *n.* A rich crescent-shaped roll, often of puff pastry.

Crom•well (krŏm′wĕl′), **Oliver.** 1599–1658. English military and religious leader.

crone (krōn) *n.* A witchlike old woman.

cro•ny (krō′nē) *n., pl.* **-nies.** A close friend.

crook (kro͝ok) *n.* **1.** A bent or curved object, as a shepherd's staff. **2.** A bend or curve. **3.** *Informal.* A person who lives by dishonest means. —*v.* To bend or curve.

crook•ed (kro͝ok′ĭd) *adj.* **1.** Not straight : bent. **2.** *Informal.* Dishonest. **—crook′ed•ly** *adv.* **—crook′ed•ness** *n.*

crook•neck (kro͝ok′nĕk′) *n.* A squash with a long curved neck and yellow flesh.

croon (kro͞on) *v.* **1.** To sing in a low, soft voice. **2.** To sing popular songs in a sentimental way. **—croon′** *n.* **—croon′er** *n.*

crop (krŏp) *n.* **1. a.** Agricultural produce that can be harvested. **b.** The yield at a harvest. **2.** A short haircut. **3.** A riding whip. **4.** *Zool.* A pouch in a bird's esophagus where food is partially digested. —*v.* **cropped, crop•ping. 1.** To cut off the top of (a plant). **2.** To cut very short : trim. **3.** To harvest. **4.** To appear unexpectedly.

crop-dust•ing (krŏp′dŭs′tĭng) *n.* The spraying of crops with pesticide, usu. from an airplane. **—crop′-dust′** *v.*

crop•per¹ (krŏp′ər) *n.* A sharecropper.

crop•per² (krŏp′ər) *n.* **1.** A heavy fall : tumble. **2.** A fiasco.

cro•quet (krō-kā′) *n.* An outdoor game in which the players drive wooden balls through hoops using long-handled mallets.

cro•quette (krō-kĕt′) *n.* A small patty or roll of minced food fried in deep fat.

cro•sier *also* **cro•zier** (krō′zhər) *n.* A staff carried by bishops and abbots.

cross (krôs, krŏs) *n.* **1.** A structure consisting of an upright post and a crossbar. **2.** A representation of the cross on which Jesus was crucified. **3.** A medal with the shape of a cross. **4.** A mark formed by the intersection of 2 lines. **5.** *Biol.* **a.** A plant or animal produced by crossbreeding. **b.** The process of crossbreeding. —*v.* **1.** To go or pass across. **2.** To intersect. **3.** To make a line across. **4.** To put crosswise. **5.** To interfere with : thwart. **6.** To crossbreed. —*adj.* **1.** Intersecting. **2.** Opposing : contrary. **3.** Ill-tempered : irritable. **4.** Crossbred. **—cross′ly** *adv.* **—cross′ness** *n.*

cross•bar (krôs′bär′, krŏs′-) *n.* A horizontal bar, stripe, or line.

cross•bones (krôs′bōnz′, krŏs′-) *n.* A representation of 2 bones placed crosswise, usu. beneath a skull, symbolizing death or danger.

cross•bow (krôs′bō′, krŏs′-) *n.* A powerful bow fixed crosswise on a wooden stock.

cross•breed (krôs′brēd′, krŏs′-) *v.* To produce (a hybrid) by the mating of individuals of different breeds or varieties. **—cross′breed′** *n.*

cross-coun•try (krôs′kŭn′trē, krŏs′-) *adj.* **1.** Moving across open countryside. **2.** Extending across a country. **—cross′-coun′try** *adv.*

cross•cur•rent (krôs′kûr′ənt, -kŭr′-, krŏs′-) *n.* **1.** A current flowing counter to another. **2.** A conflicting tendency.

cross•cut (krôs′kŭt′, krŏs′-) *v.* To run or cut across or crosswise. —*adj.* **1.** Used or suitable for cutting crosswise. **2.** Cut on the bias or across the grain. —*n.* A cut or course that goes crosswise.

cross-ex•am•ine (krôs′ĭg-zăm′ĭn, krŏs′-) *v.* To question closely, esp. in order to check answers to previous questioning. **—cross′-ex•am′i•na′tion** *n.*

cross-eye (krôs′ī′, krŏs′ī′) *n.* Strabismus in which the eye turns toward the nose. **—cross′-eyed′** *adj.*

cross-file (krôs′fīl′, krŏs′-) *v.* To register as a candidate in the primaries of more than 1 political party. **—cross′-fil′er** *n.*

cross•fire (krôs′fīr′, krŏs′-) *n.* **1.** Crossing lines of gunfire from 2 opposing positions. **2.** A rapid, often acrimonious discussion.

cross•hatch (krôs′hăch′, krŏs′-) *v.* To mark with 2 or more sets of intersecting parallel lines.

cross•ing (krô′sĭng, krŏs′ĭng) *n.* **1.** An intersection, as of 2 streets. **2.** The place for crossing something, as a river or highway.

cross matching *n.* The process in which the compatibility of blood is tested before a blood transfusion.

cross•patch (krôs′păch′, krŏs′-) *n. Informal.* An ill-tempered, grumpy person.

cross•piece (krôs′pēs′, krŏs′-) *n.* A transverse part of a structure.

cross-pur•pose (krôs′pûr′pəs, krŏs′-) *n.* An opposing or conflicting purpose.

cross-re•fer (krôs′rĭ-fûr′, krŏs′-) *v.* To refer from 1 part or passage to another. **—cross′-ref′er•ence** *n.*

cross•road (krôs′rōd′, krŏs′-) *n.* **1.** A road intersecting another. **2.** *often* **crossroads.** An intersection of 2 or more roads.

cross section *n.* **1.** A section cut across an object. **2.** A sample meant to represent the nature of the whole.

cross-town (krôs′toun′, krŏs′-) *adj.* Extending across a town or city <a *cross-town* subway line> **—cross′-town′** *adv.*

cross•walk (krôs′wôk′, krŏs′-) *n.* A lane marked off for pedestrians to use when crossing a street.

cross•wind (krôs′wĭnd′, krŏs′-) *n.* A wind blowing at right angles to one's direction of travel.

cross•wise (krôs′wīz′, krŏs′-) *also* **cross•ways** (-wāz′) *adv.* Across. —*adj.* Crossing.

cross•word puzzle (krôs′wûrd′, krŏs′-) *n.* A puzzle in which a pattern of numbered squares is to be filled with words in answer to correspondingly numbered clues.

crotch (krŏch) *n.* The angle or region of the angle formed by the junction of 2 parts, as legs or branches.

crotch•et (krŏch′ĭt) *n.* A peculiar whim.

crouch (krouch) *v.* **1.** To bend over close to the ground. **2.** To cower. **—crouch** *n.*

croup (kro͞op) *n.* Laryngitis, esp. in children, marked by a harsh cough and difficulty in breathing. **—croup′y** *adj.*

crou•pi•er (kro͞o′pē-ər, -pē-ā′) *n.* One who collects and pays bets at a gaming table.

crou·ton (kro͞o'tŏn', kro͞o-tŏn') *n.* A small crisp piece of fried bread or toast.

crow¹ (krō) *n.* A large, black bird of the genus *Corvus* with a raucous call.

crow² (krō) *v.* **1.** *p.t.* & *p.p.* **crowed** or **crew** (kro͞o). To utter the shrill cry of a rooster. **2.** To exult, esp. over another's misfortune. **3.** To make an inarticulate noise expressing pleasure. —*n.* The shrill cry of a cock.

crow·bar (krō'bär') *n.* A metal bar, usu. with a chisel-shaped end, used as a lever.

crowd (kroud) *n.* **1.** A large number of people or things gathered closely together. **2.** A particular social group. —*v.* **1.** To congregate in numbers. **2.** To press close. **3.** To stuff tightly : cram.

crown (kroun) *n.* **1.** An ornamental circlet or head covering, often made of precious metal and jewels, and worn by royalty. **2.** The power of a sovereign. **3.** A reward or honor for achievement. **4.** Something like a crown. **5. a.** A former British coin. **b.** See CURRENCY TABLE. **6.** The highest part of the head. **7.** The highest point : summit. **8.** The part of a tooth that projects beyond the gum line. —*v.* **1.** To put a crown upon. **2.** To enthrone. **3.** To honor or reward. **4.** To surmount : top. **5.** To put the finishing touch on.

Crown corporation *n. Can.* A government-owned company.

crow's-foot (krōz'fo͝ot') *n., pl.* **-feet.** Any of the wrinkles at the outer corner of the eye.

crow's-nest (krōz'nĕst') *n. Naut.* A small, partly enclosed lookout platform near the top of a ship's mast.

cro·zier (krō'zhər) *n. var. of* CROSIER.

cru·ces (kro͞o'sēz) *n. var. pl. of* CRUX.

cru·cial (kro͞o'shəl) *adj.* **1.** Critical : decisive. **2.** Difficult : severe.

cru·ci·ble (kro͞o'sə-bəl) *n.* A vessel used for melting materials at high temperatures.

cru·ci·fix (kro͞o'sə-fĭks') *n.* A representation of Christ on the cross.

cru·ci·fix·ion (kro͞o'sə-fĭk'shən) *n.* **1.** The act of putting to death on a cross. **2. Crucifixion.** The crucifying of Christ.

cru·ci·form (kro͞o'sə-fôrm') *adj.* In the shape of a cross.

cru·ci·fy (kro͞o'sə-fī') *v.* **-fied, -fy·ing. 1.** To put to death by nailing or binding to a cross. **2.** To treat unfairly or cruelly : torment <was *crucified* by the media>

†**crud** (krŭd) *n.* **1.** *Slang.* **a.** A coating of filth. **b.** One that is disgusting. **2.** *Regional.* A milk curd. **—crud'dy** *adj.*

crude (kro͞od) *adj.* **crud·er, crud·est. 1.** Not refined : raw. **2.** Lacking refinement or tact. **3.** Not carefully made : rough. —*n.* Unrefined petroleum. **—crude'ly** *adv.* **—cru'di·ty, crude'ness** *n.*

crude oil *n.* Petroleum.

cru·di·tés (kro͞o'dĭ-tā') *pl.n.* Raw vegetables, often served with a dip.

cru·el (kro͞o'əl) *adj.* **-el·er, -el·est** or **-el·ler, -el·lest. 1.** Inflicting suffering. **2.** Painful. **—cru'el·ly** *adv.* **—cru'el·ty** *n.*

cru·et (kro͞o'ĭt) *n.* A small, usu. glass bottle for holding oil or vinegar.

cruise (kro͞oz) *v.* **cruised, cruis·ing. 1.** To sail about, as for pleasure. **2.** To move leisurely about the streets. **3.** To travel at a speed providing maximum operating efficiency. **—cruise** *n.*

cruise missile *n.* A medium-range low-flying guided missile that can be launched from land, air, or sea.

cruis·er (kro͞o'zər) *n.* **1.** A fast warship of medium tonnage. **2.** A motorboat equipped with living facilities. **3.** A squad car.

crul·ler (krŭl'ər) *n.* A small, sweet cake fried in deep fat.

crumb (krŭm) *n.* **1.** A small fragment, as of bread. **2.** A small scrap. —*v.* **1.** To crumble. **2.** To cover with crumbs : bread.

crum·ble (krŭm'bəl) *v.* **-bled, -bling.** To break into small pieces. **—crum'bly** *adj.*

crum·my *also* **crumb·y** (krŭm'ē) *adj.* **-mi·er, -mi·est** *also* **-i·er, -i·est.** *Slang.* **1.** Wretched : miserable. **2.** Shabby : worthless.

crum·pet (krŭm'pĭt) *n. esp. Brit.* A light, soft bread similar to a muffin, baked on a griddle and often toasted.

crum·ple (krŭm'pəl) *v.* **-pled, -pling. 1.** To crush together : rumple. **2.** To collapse.

crunch (krŭnch) *v.* **1.** To bite with a crackling noise. **2.** To grind or crush noisily. —*n.* **1.** The sound or act of crunching. **2.** A critical situation. **—crunch'y** *adj.*

cru·sade (kro͞o-sād') *n.* **1.** *often* **Crusade.** Any of the medieval Christian military expeditions to recover the Holy Land from the Moslems. **2.** A vigorous campaign to promote a cause. —*v.* **-sad·ed, -sad·ing.** To take part in a crusade. **—cru·sad'er** *n.*

crush (krŭsh) *v.* **1.** To squeeze between opposing forces so as to damage or injure. **2.** To extract by pressing. **3.** To embrace violently. **4.** To break or grind into small bits. **5.** To put down : suppress. —*n.* **1.** The act of crushing. **2.** A large, closely packed crowd. **3.** *Informal.* An infatuation.

crust (krŭst) *n.* **1.** The hard, outside surface area of bread. **2.** A piece of old dry bread. **3.** A hard surface layer. **4.** The shell of a pie, usu. made of pastry. —*v.* To cover or become covered with a crust.

crus·ta·cean (krŭ-stā'shən) *n.* Any of various chiefly aquatic arthropods of the class *Crustacea,* including lobsters and crabs, with a segmented body and paired, jointed limbs.

crust·y (krŭs'tē) *adj.* **-i·er, -i·est. 1.** Like or with a crust. **2.** Brusk. **—crust'i·ly** *adv.*

crutch (krŭch) *n.* **1.** A support usu. designed to fit under the armpit and used as an aid in walking. **2.** Any support or prop.

crux (krŭks, kro͝oks) *n.* **1.** A crucial or vital moment. **2.** The basic feature. **3.** A difficult problem.

cru·zei·ro (kro͞o-zâr'ō, -ro͞o) *n., pl.* **-ros.** See CURRENCY TABLE.

cry (krī) *v.* **cried, cry·ing. 1.** To shed tears. **2.** To call loudly. **3.** To utter a characteristic call or sound. Used of an animal. **4.** To proclaim publicly. ☆**syns:** BAWL, HOWL, KEEN, SOB, WAIL, WEEP —*n., pl.* **cries. 1.** A loud emotional utterance. **2.** A fit of weeping. **3.** A plea : entreaty. **4.** The characteristic call of an animal.

cry·ba·by (krī'bā'bē) *n.* One who complains or cries often.

crypt (krĭpt) *n.* An underground vault, esp. one used for burying the dead.

cryp·tic (krĭp'tĭk) *adj.* Enigmatic.

cryp·to·gram (krĭp'tə-grăm') *n.* A coded message.

cryp·tog·ra·phy (krĭp-tŏg'rə-fē) *n.* The writing and deciphering of messages in secret code. **—cryp·tog'ra·pher** *n.*

crys·tal (krĭs'təl) *n.* **1. a.** A 3-dimensional structure made up of atoms, molecules, or ions arranged in basic units that are repeated throughout the structure. **b.** The basic unit of such a structure. **c.** Something having such a structure. **2.** A clear, high-quality glass. **—crys'tal·line** *adj.*

crystal ball *n.* A glass globe for foretelling the future.

crystal gazing *n.* Divination by looking into a crystal ball. **—crystal gazer** *n.*

crys·tal·lize (krĭs'tə-līz') *v.* **-lized, -liz·ing. 1.** To assume or cause to assume a crystalline structure. **2.** To assume or cause to assume a definite or fixed shape. **—crys'tal·li·za'tion** *n.*

Cs *symbol for* CESIUM.

CST or **C.S.T.** *abbr.* Central Standard Time.

CT *abbr.* Connecticut (with Zip Code).

C.T. *abbr.* Central Time.

ct. *abbr.* **1.** cent. **2.** court.

ctn. *abbr.* carton.

ctr. *abbr.* center.

Cu *symbol for* COPPER.

cu. or **cu** *abbr.* cubic.

cub (kŭb) *n.* **1.** A young beast of certain animals, as the lion or wolf. **2.** A youth or novice, esp. in newspaper reporting.

Cu·ba (kyo͞o'bə). Island country in the Caribbean. *Cap.* Havana. *Pop.* 8,553,400. **—Cu'ban** *adj.* & *n.*

cub·by·hole (kŭb'ē-hōl') *n.* A small enclosed space, as a cupboard.

cube (kyo͞ob) *n.* **1.** *Math.* A regular solid with 6 congruent square faces. **2.** Something gen. shaped like a cube. **3.** *Math.* The 3rd power of a number <8 is the *cube* of 2> —*v.* **cubed, cub·ing. 1.** To raise (a number) to the 3rd power. **2.** To cut or shape into cubes.

cube root *n.* A number whose cube is equal to a specified number.

cu·bic (kyo͞o'bĭk) *adj.* **1.** Having the form of a cube. **2. a.** Having 3 dimensions. **b.** Having the volume of a cube whose edge is a specified unit <a *cubic* yard>

cu·bi·cle (kyo͞o'bĭ-kəl) *n.* A small, partitioned compartment.

cub·ism (kyo͞o'bĭz'əm) *n.* A style of art in which the subject matter is portrayed by geometric forms, esp. cubes. **—cub'ist** *n.*

cu·bit (kyo͞o'bĭt) *n.* An ancient unit of length equal to approx. 17 to 22 in. or 43 to 56 cm.

Cub Scout *n.* A member of the Boy Scouts aged 8 to 10 years.

cuck·old (kŭk'əld, ko͝ok'-) *n.* A man whose wife is unfaithful. **—cuck'old** *v.*

cuck·oo (ko͞o'ko͞o, ko͝ok'o͞o) *n., pl.* **-oos.** A grayish European bird, *Cuculus canorus,* that lays its eggs in other birds' nests and has a characteristic 2-note call. —*n.* **1.** The characteristic call of the cuckoo. **2.** A fool. —*adj.* Silly.

cuckoo clock *n.* A wall clock with a mechanical cuckoo that indicates intervals of time by a cuckoo call.

cu·cum·ber (kyo͞o'kŭm'bər) *n.* A vine, *Cucumis sativus,* grown for its edible fruit, with a green rind and white flesh.

cud (kŭd) *n.* Food brought up into the mouth of ruminants from the 1st stomach and chewed again.

cud·dle (kŭd'l) *v.* **-dled, -dling. 1.** To hold close and fondle. **2.** To lie close : snuggle. **—cud'dle** *n.* **—cud'dly** *adj.*

cudg·el (kŭj'əl) *n.* A short, thick stick. **—cudg'el** *v.*

cue¹ (kyōō) *n.* A long, tapered rod for propelling the ball in pool and billiards.
cue² (kyōō) *n.* **1.** A word or signal for an actor to enter or begin speaking. **2.** A hint. **—cue** *v.*
cue³ (kyōō) *n.* The letter *q*.
cue ball *n.* A white ball that the player strikes with the cue in pool and billiards.
†**cues·ta** (kwĕs'tə) *n. SW U.S.* A ridge with a cliff on one side and a gentle slope on the other.
cuff¹ (kŭf) *n.* **1.** A lower end of a sleeve. **2.** The turned-up fold of a trouser leg.
cuff² (kŭf) *v.* To slap. **—cuff** *n.*
cuff links *n.* Linked buttons for fastening the cuffs of a shirt.
cui·rass (kwĭ-răs') *n.* Armor for protecting the back and breast.
cui·sine (kwĭ-zēn') *n.* **1.** A characteristic style of cooking or preparing food. **2.** The food prepared.
cul-de-sac (kŭl'dĭ-săk', kōōl'-) *n.* A street closed at one end.
cu·li·nar·y (kyōō'lə-nĕr'ē, kŭl'ə-) *adj.* Of or relating to cookery.
cull (kŭl) *v.* **1.** To select. **2.** To collect : gather. **—cull'er** *n.*
cul·mi·nate (kŭl'mə-nāt') *v.* **-nat·ed, -nat·ing.** To rise to the highest point. **—cul'mi·na'tion** *n.*
cu·lottes (kōō-lŏts', kyōō-) *pl.n.* A woman's full trousers made to look like a skirt.
cul·pa·ble (kŭl'pə-bəl) *adj.* Deserving blame. **—cul'pa·bil'i·ty** *n.*
cul·prit (kŭl'prĭt) *n.* One guilty of a crime.
cult (kŭlt) *n.* **1.** A system of religious worship. **2. a.** Obsessive and faddish devotion to a principle or person. **b.** A group of persons sharing such devotion : sect. **—cult'ic** *adj.* **—cult'ish** *adj.* **—cult'ist** *n.*
cul·ti·vate (kŭl'tə-vāt') *v.* **-vat·ed, -vat·ing. 1.** To prepare and improve (land), as by fertilizing or plowing, for growing crops. **2.** To grow (a plant or crop). **3.** To improve and refine, as by education. **4.** To seek to become familiar with. **—cul'ti·va·ble, cul'ti·vat'a·ble** *adj.* **—cul'ti·va'tion** *n.* **—cul'ti·va'tor** *n.*
cul·ture (kŭl'chər) *n.* **1.** A particular form of civilization, esp. the beliefs, customs, arts, and institutions of a society at a given time. **2.** Refinement in intellectual and artistic taste. **3.** The act of developing the intellectual faculties through education. **4.** Cultivation of soil : tillage. **5.** *Biol.* A growth of microorganisms, as bacteria, in a nutrient medium. **—cul'tur·al** *adj.* **—cul'ture** *v.* **—cul'tured** *adj.*
culture shock *n.* A condition of anxiety and disorientation that can affect someone suddenly exposed to a new culture.
cul·vert (kŭl'vərt) *n.* A sewer or drain crossing under a road or railroad.
cum (kōōm, kŭm) *prep.* Together with : plus <a bedroom-*cum*-study>
cum·ber (kŭm'bər) *v.* To burden. **—cum'ber·some** *adj.* **—cum'ber·some·ly** *adv.* **—cum'brous** *adj.*
cum·in (kŭm'ĭn) *n.* A plant, *Cuminum cyminum*, with aromatic seeds used as a condiment.
cum lau·de (kōōm lou'də, lou'dē, kŭm lô'dē) *adv. & adj.* With honor. Used as a mark of high academic attainment.
cum·mer·bund (kŭm'ər-bŭnd') *n.* A wide sash worn as an accessory to men's formal dress.
cu·mu·la·tive (kyōōm'yə-lā'tĭv, -lə-tĭv) *adj.* Increasing with successive additions. **—cu'mu·la'tive·ly** *adv.*
cu·mu·lo·nim·bus (kyōōm'yə-lō-nĭm'bəs) *n., pl.* **-bus·es** *or* **-bi** (-bī'). A very dense, vertically developed cumulus, usu. producing heavy rains or thunderstorms.
cu·mu·lus (kyōōm'yə-ləs) *n., pl.* **-li** (-lī'). A large white, fluffy cloud with a flat base and rounded outlines on top.
cu·ne·i·form (kyōō'nē-ə-fôrm', kyōō-nē'-) *adj.* Wedge-shaped, as the characters used in ancient Assyrian and Babylonian writing. —*n.* Cuneiform writing.
†**cun·ning** (kŭn'ĭng) *adj.* **1.** Crafty : sly. **2.** Contrived with ingenuity. **3.** *Regional.* Pretty : cute. —*n.* **1.** Craftiness : guile. **2.** Skill : dexterity. **—cun'ning·ly** *adv.*
cup (kŭp) *n.* **1.** A small, bowl-shaped container, usu. having a handle, used for drinking. **2.** The contents of a cup. **3.** A measure of capacity equal to 1/2 pint, 8 oz, 16 tablespoons, or approx. 237 ml. **4.** Something like a cup. —*v.* **cupped, cup·ping.** To shape like a cup. **—cup'ful'** *n.*
cup·board (kŭb'ərd) *n.* A storage closet.
cup·cake (kŭp'kāk') *n.* A small cake baked in a cup-shaped mold.
Cu·pid (kyōō'pĭd) *n.* **1.** *Rom. Myth.* The god of love. **2. cupid.** A representation of a winged boy with a bow and arrow used as a symbol of love.
cu·pid·i·ty (kyōō-pĭd'ĭ-tē) *n.* Excessive desire for material gain : avarice.
cu·po·la (kyōō'pə-lə) *n.* A small structure, usu. a dome, on top of a roof or building.
cu·pro·nick·el (kōō'prō-nĭk'əl, kyōō'-) *n.* An alloy of copper and nickel used in coins.
cur (kûr) *n.* **1.** A dog of mixed bread : mongrel. **2.** A contemptible person.
cur. *abbr.* currency.
cu·rate (kyŏŏr'ĭt) *n.* A member of the clergy who assists a vicar or rector. **—cu'ra·cy** *n.*
cu·ra·tive (kyŏŏr'ə-tĭv) *adj.* Having the ability to cure. **—cu'ra·tive** *n.* **—cur'a·tive·ly** *adv.*
cu·ra·tor (kyŏŏ-rā'tər, kyŏŏr'ā-tər) *n.* One in charge of an institution such as a museum.
curb (kûrb) *n.* **1.** A check or restraint. **2.** A raised stone or concrete edging along the side of a street. **3.** A strap or chain on a bit used to restrain a horse. —*v.* **1.** To control or restrain. **2.** To lead (a dog) into the gutter so that it can excrete waste matter.
curb·ing (kûr'bĭng) *n.* **1.** The material for constructing a curb. **2.** A curb.
curb·stone (kûrb'stōn') *n.* The stone or stones forming a curb.
curd (kûrd) *n.* The coagulated part of milk used for making cheese.
cur·dle (kûr'dl) *v.* **-dled, -dling.** To change into curd.
cure (kyŏŏr) *n.* **1.** Recovery from illness. **2.** A course of medical treatment for restoring health. **3.** A remedy. ☆**syns:** ELIXIR, NOSTRUM, REMEDY —*v.* **cured, cur·ing. 1.** To restore to health. **2.** To rid of (e.g., an ailment). **3.** To process (e.g., meat), as by smoking or salting. **—cur'a·ble** *adj.* **—cure'less** *adj.* **—cur'er** *n.*
cu·ré (kyŏŏ-rā', kyŏŏr'ā') *n.* A parish priest.
cure-all (kyŏŏr'ôl') *n.* A remedy for all evils or diseases.
cu·ret·tage (kyŏŏr'ĭ-täzh') *n.* Surgical scraping and cleaning of a bodily cavity.
cur·few (kûr'fyōō) *n.* **1.** An order enjoining specified segments of the population to leave the streets at a certain hour. **2.** The signal announcing curfew.

▲word history: A *curfew* was orig. a medieval regulation requiring that fires be put out or covered at a certain hour at night. The rule was probably instituted as a public safety measure to minimize the risk of a general conflagration. A bell was rung at the prescribed hour, and the word *curfew* has been extended to denote both the bell and the hour in addition to the regulation.

cu·ri·a *also* **Cu·ri·a** (kyŏŏr'ē-ə) *n.* The official body that governs the Roman Catholic Church.
cu·rie (kyŏŏr'ē, kyŏŏ-rē') *n.* A unit of radioactivity equal to the radioactivity of a sample of an element in which 3.7×10^{10} nuclear disintegrations occur each sec.
cu·ri·o (kyŏŏr'ē-ō') *n., pl.* **-os.** An unusual or strange object.
cu·ri·ous (kyŏŏr'ē-əs) *adj.* **1.** Eager to acquire knowledge. **2.** Inquisitive : prying. **3.** Strange : singular. **—cu'ri·os'i·ty** *n.* **—cu'ri·ous·ly** *adv.* **—cu'ri·ous·ness** *n.*
cu·ri·um (kyŏŏr'ē-əm) *n. Symbol* **Cm** A metallic synthetic radioactive element.
curl (kûrl) *v.* **1.** To form into ringlets. **2.** To curve or coil : wind. **3.** To play the game of curling. —*n.* **1.** Something shaped like a coil. **2.** A ringlet of hair. **—curl'er** *n.* **—curl'i·ness** *n.* **—curl'y** *adj.*
cur·lew (kûrl'yōō, kûr'lōō) *n.* A brownish, long-legged shore bird of the genus *Numenius*, with a downward-curving bill.
curl·i·cue (kûr'lĭ-kyōō') *n.* A fancy flourish or curve.
curl·ing (kûr'lĭng) *n.* A game played on ice, in which 2 4-man teams slide heavy, rounded stones toward a target.
cur·mudg·eon (kər-mŭj'ən) *n.* A quarrelsome and ill-tempered person.
cur·rant (kûr'ənt, kŭr'-) *n.* **1.** Any of various usu. prickly shrubs of the genus *Ribes*, having clusters of black or red fruit used for jellies. **2.** A small seedless raisin.
cur·ren·cy (kûr'ən-sē, kŭr'-) *n., pl.* **-cies. 1.** Money in circulation as a medium of exchange. **2.** General use or acceptance.
cur·rent (kûr'ənt, kŭr'-) *adj.* **1.** Occurring in or belonging to the present. **2.** In widespread or general use. —*n.* **1.** Continuous flow, as of air or water. **2.** The swiftest part of a moving body of gas or liquid. **3. a.** A flow of electric charge. **b.** The rate of electric charge. **—cur'rent·ly** *adv.*
cur·ric·u·lum (kə-rĭk'yə-ləm) *n., pl.* **-la** (-lə) *or* **-lums.** A course of study offered by a school. **—cur·ric'u·lar** *adj.*
cur·ric·u·lum vi·tae (kə-rĭk'yə-ləm vī'tē, kə-rĭk'ə-ləm wē'tī') *n.* A résumé.
cur·ry¹ (kûr'ē, kŭr'ē) *v.* **-ried, -ry·ing. 1.** To groom (a horse) using a currycomb. **2.** To prepare (tanned leather). **—curry favor.** To seek or gain favor by flattery.
cur·ry² (kûr'ē, kŭr'ē) *n., pl.* **-ries. 1.** Curry powder. **2.** A dish or sauce heavily spiced with curry powder and often served with rice. **—cur'ry** *v.*

CURRENCY TABLE

Country	Basic Unit	Subdivision
Afghanistan	afghani	pul
Albania	lek	quintar
Algeria	dinar	centime
Andorra	franc	centime
	peseta	centimo
Angola	kwanza	lwei
Argentina	peso	centavo
Australia	dollar	cent
Austria	schilling	groschen
Bahamas	dollar	cent
Bahrain	dinar	fil
Bangladesh	taka	paisa
Barbados	dollar	cent
Belgium	franc	centime
Belize	dollar	cent
Benin	franc	centime
Bhutan	ngultrum	chetrum
Bolivia	peso	centavo
Botswana	pula	thebe
Brazil	cruzeiro	centavo
Brunei	dollar	cent
Bulgaria	lev	stotinki
Burma	kyat	pya
Burundi	franc	centime
Cambodia	riel	sen
Cameroon	franc	centime
Canada	dollar	cent
Cape Verde	escudo	centavo
Cayman Islands	dollar	cent
Central African Republic	franc	centime
Chad	franc	centime
Chile	peso	centavo
China, People's Republic of	renminbi	chiao
China, Republic of (Taiwan)	yuan	cent
Colombia	peso	centavo
Comoros	franc	centime
Congo	franc	centime
Costa Rica	colon	centimo
Cuba	peso	centavo
Cyprus	pound	mil
Czechoslovakia	crown	haler
Denmark	kroner	öre
Djibouti	franc	centime
Dominica	dollar	cent
Dominican Republic	peso	centavo
Ecuador	sucre	centavo
Egypt	pound	piaster
El Salvador	colon	centavo
Equatorial Guinea	ekpwele	cent
Ethiopia	birr	cent
Fiji	dollar	cent
Finland	markka	penni
France	franc	centime
Gabon	franc	centime
Gambia	dalasi	butut
Germany, East	mark	pfennig
Germany, West	deutsche mark	pfennig
Ghana	cedi	pesewa
Greece	drachma	lepton
Grenada	dollar	cent
Guatemala	quetzal	centavo
Guinea	syli	cory
Guinea-Bissau	peso	centavo
Guyana	dollar	cent
Haiti	gourde	centime
Honduras	lempira	centavo
Hong Kong	dollar	cent
Hungary	forint	fillér
Iceland	krona	eyrir
India	rupee	paisa
Indonesia	rupiah	sen
Iran	rial	dinar
Iraq	dinar	fil
Ireland, Republic of	pound	penny
Israel	shekel	agora
Italy	lira	centesimo
Ivory Coast	franc	centime
Jamaica	dollar	cent
Japan	yen	sen
Jordan	dinar	fil
Kenya	shilling	cent
Korea, North	won	jun
Korea, South	won	chon
Kuwait	dinar	fil
Laos	kip	at
Lebanon	pound	piaster
Lesotho	loti	lisente
Liberia	dollar	cent
Libya	dinar	dirham
Liechtenstein	franc	centime
Luxembourg	franc	centime
Macao	pataca	avo
Madagascar	franc	centime
Malawi	kwacha	tambala
Malaysia	ringgit	sen
Maldives	rupee	laree
Mali	franc	centime
Malta	pound	cent
Mauritania	ouguiya	khoum
Mauritius	rupee	cent
Mexico	peso	centavo
Monaco	franc	centime
Mongolia	tugrik	mongo
Morocco	dirham	centime
Mozambique	metical	centavo
Nauru	dollar	cent
Nepal	rupee	paisa
Netherlands	guilder	cent
Netherlands Antilles	guilder	cent
New Zealand	dollar	cent
Nicaragua	cordoba	centavo
Niger	franc	centime
Nigeria	naira	kobo
Norway	krone	öre
Oman	riyal-omani	baiza
Pakistan	rupee	paisa
Panama	balboa	centesimo
Papua New Guinea	kina	toea
Paraguay	guarani	centimo

CURRENCY *(continued)*

Country	Basic Unit	Subdivision
Peru	sol	centavo
Philippines	peso	centavo
Poland	zloty	grosz
Portugal	escudo	centavo
Qatar	riyal	dirham
Rumania	leu	ban
Rwanda	franc	centime
Saint Lucia	dollar	cent
Saint Vincent	dollar	cent
San Marino	lira	centesimo
São Tomé and Principe	dobra	centimo
Saudi Arabia	riyal	qurush
Senegal	franc	centime
Seychelles	rupee	cent
Sierra Leone	leone	cent
Singapore	dollar	cent
Solomon Islands	dollar	cent
Somalia	schilling	cent
South Africa	rand	cent
Spain	peseta	centimo
Sri Lanka	rupee	cent
Sudan	pound	piaster
Surinam	guilder	cent
Swaziland	lilangeni	cent
Sweden	krona	öre
Switzerland	franc	centime
Syria	pound	piaster
Tanzania	shilling	cent
Thailand	baht	satang
Togo	franc	centime
Tonga	pa'anga	seniti
Trinidad and Tobago	dollar	cent
Tunisia	dinar	millieme
Turkey	pound	kuru
Uganda	shilling	cent
Union of Soviet Socialist Republics	rouble	kopeck
United Arab Emirates	dirham	fil
United Kingdom of Great Britain and Northern Ireland	pound	penny
United States of America	dollar	cent
Upper Volta	franc	centime
Uruguay	peso	centesimo
Vanuatu	franc	centime
Vatican City	lira	centesimo
Venezuela	bolivar	centimo
Vietnam	dong	hao
Western Samoa	tala	sene
Yemen, People's Democratic Republic of (Southern Yemen)	dinar	fil
Yemen Arab Republic (North Yemen)	riyal	fil
Yugoslavia	dinar	para
Zaire	zaire	likuta
Zambia	kwacha	ngwee
Zimbabwe	dollar	cent

cur•ry•comb (kûr′ē-kōm′, kŭr′-) *n.* A metal comb used to groom horses.

curry powder *n.* A powder of blended spices, as coriander, cumin, and turmeric.

curse (kûrs) *n.* **1.** A prayer for harm to befall someone or something. **2.** The harm resulting from an invocation. **3.** A profane oath. **4.** Something bringing or causing harm : scourge. —*v.* **cursed** *or* **curst** (kûrst), **curs•ing. 1.** To call evil down on. **2.** To swear (at). **3.** To bring evil upon.

cur•sive (kûr′sĭv) *adj.* Written with the letters joined together. **—cur′sive•ly** *adv.*

cur•sor (kûr′sər) *n.* A visual indicator on a video display terminal showing the user's position on the screen.

cur•so•ry (kûr′sə-rē) *adj.* Not thorough : hasty. **—cur′so•ri•ly** *adv.*

curt (kûrt) *adj.* Rudely short : abrupt. **—curt′ly** *adv.* **—curt′ness** *n.*

cur•tail (kər-tāl′) *v.* To shorten. **—cur•tail′ment** *n.*

cur•tain (kûr′tn) *n.* Hanging material that can be drawn back, esp. in a window, used to decorate, shade, or screen. **—cur′tain** *v.*

curt•sy (kûrt′sē) *n., pl.* **-sies.** A respectful gesture made by bending the knees with 1 foot forward and lowering the body.

cur•va•ceous (kûr-vā′shəs) *adj.* Voluptuous in figure. **—cur•va′ceous•ness** *n.*

cur•va•ture (kûr′və-cho͝or′, -chər) *n.* An example or measure of curving.

curve (kûrv) *n.* **1.** A bend without angles or straight parts. **2.** Something in the form of a curve. —*v.* **curved, curv•ing.** To form or move in the shape of a curve.

cur•vi•lin•e•ar (kûr′və-lĭn′ē-ər) *adj.* Made up of curved lines.

cush•ion (ko͝osh′ən) *n.* **1.** A pillow or pad with a soft filling. **2.** Something soft and resilent that prevents injury. **3.** The soft, felt rim around a billiard table. —*v.* **1.** To provide a cushion for. **2.** To soften or lessen the shock of.

cush•y (ko͝osh′ē) *adj.* **-i•er, -i•est.** *Slang.* Making few demands : easy <a *cushy* job>

cusp (kŭsp) *n.* A pointed end, as of a tooth.

cus•pid (kŭs′pĭd) *n.* A canine tooth.

cus•pi•dor (kŭs′pĭ-dôr′) *n.* A spittoon.

cuss (kŭs) *v. Informal.* To curse (at). —*n.* **1.** A curse. **2.** A perverse creature.

cuss•ed (kŭs′ĭd) *adj. Informal.* Vexatious : perverse. **—cuss′ed•ness** *n.*

cus•tard (kŭs′tərd) *n.* A sauce or dessert made from milk, eggs, sugar, and flavoring.

cus•to•di•an (kŭ-stō′dē-ən) *n.* **1.** One who has custody or care of something. **2.** A janitor. **—cus•to′di•an•ship′** *n.*

cus•to•dy (kŭs′tə-dē) *n., pl.* **-dies. 1.** The act or right of guarding, esp. as granted by a court. **2.** Detention under guard, esp. by the police. **—cus•to′di•al** *adj.*

cus•tom (kŭs′təm) *n.* **1.** An accepted practice or convention followed by tradition. **2.** A habitual course of action of an individual. **3. customs** *(sing. in number).* Taxes on imported goods. **4.** Business patronage, as of a store. —*adj.* **1.** Made-to-order. **2.** Selling made-to-order goods.

cus•tom•ar•y (kŭs′tə-mĕr′ē) *adj.* **1.** Habitual. **2.** Based on custom or tradition. **—cus′tom•ar′i•ly** *adv.*

cus•tom-built (kŭs′təm-bĭlt′) *adj.* Built to individual order.

cus•tom•er (kŭs′tə-mər) *n.* **1.** A person who buys, esp. on a regular basis. **2.** A person with whom one must deal.

cus•tom•house *also* **cus•tom house** (kŭs′təm-hous′) *n.* An office where customs are paid and ships are cleared for leaving or entering the country.

cut (kŭt) *v.* **cut, cut•ting. 1.** To penetrate with a sharp edge. **2.** To divide into parts using a sharp-edged instrument <*cut* the material> **3.** To leave out as if by cutting : omit. **4.** To sever the outer edges of : shorten. **5.** To reap. **6.** To have (a new tooth) grow through the gums. **7.** *Informal.* To stop <*cut* the foolishness> **8.** To reduce the size, extent, or strength of <*cut* the labor force> **9.** *Informal.* To fail purposely to attend <*cut* classes> ☆***syns:*** GASH, INCISE, PIERCE, SLASH, SLIT **—cut in. 1.** To interrupt. **2.** To interrupt a dancing couple and take 1 of the pair as one's partner. **—cut out. 1.** To put an end to : stop. **2.** *Informal.* To depart suddenly. **—cut up.** *Informal.* To fool around : clown. —*n.* **1.** The act or result of incising or separating. **2.** A part that has been cut from a meat carcass <a *cut* of beef> **3.** A reduction <a budget *cut*> **4.** The manner in which a thing, esp. a piece of clothing, is cut. **5.** A wounding remark. **6.** An excavated passage or channel. **7.** *Informal.* A share, as of

profits. **8.** *Informal.* An unauthorized absence, as from school. **9.a.** An engraved surface for printing. **b.** A print made from such a surface.
cut-and-dried (kŭt′n-drīd′) *adj.* According to a plan or formula.
cu·ta·ne·ous (kyo͞o-tā′nē-əs) *adj.* Of or relating to the skin.
cut·back (kŭt′băk′) *n.* A reduction.
cute (kyo͞ot) *adj.* **cut·er, cut·est. 1.** Delightfully attractive. **2.** Clever : shrewd.
cute·sy (kyo͞ot′sē) *adj.* **-si·er, -si·est.** *Slang.* Obviously contrived to charm.
cut glass *n.* Glassware shaped or decorated using cutting instruments.
cu·ti·cle (kyo͞o′tĭ-kəl) *n.* **1.** The epidermis. **2.** Hardened skin, as at the base of a toenail or fingernail.
cut·lass (kŭt′ləs) *n.* A short, thick, curved sword.
cut·ler·y (kŭt′lə-rē) *n.* **1.** Cutting tools. **2.** Implements used as tableware.
cut·let (kŭt′lĭt) *n.* A thin slice of meat, as lamb or veal.
cut·off (kŭt′ôf′, -ŏf′) *n.* **1.** A short cut or by-pass. **2.** A device for shutting off a flow, as of electricity or water.
cut-offs *also* **cut·offs** (kŭt′ôfs′, -ŏfs′) *pl.n.* Pants, as blue jeans, made into shorts by cutting off part of the legs.
cut·out (kŭt′out′) *n.* Something cut out or prepared for cutting out.
cut-rate (kŭt′rāt′) *adj.* On sale or sold at a lower price.
cut·ter (kŭt′ər) *n.* **1.** One that cuts. **2.** *Naut.* **a.** A ship's boat used to carry pasengers and provisions. **b.** A small, armed Coast Guard powerboat. **3.** A light sleigh.
cut·throat (kŭt′thrōt′) *n.* **1.** A murderer. **2.** A ruthless, unprincipled person. *—adj.* **1.** Murderous : brutal. **2.** Merciless or relentless in competition.
cut·ting (kŭt′ĭng) *adj.* **1.** Sharply penetrating. **2.** Bitterly sarcastic. *—n.* A shoot removed from a plant to form new roots and grow into a new plant.
cut·tle·bone (kŭt′l-bōn′) *n.* The calcareous shell inside the body of the cuttlefish, used as a calcium supplement for caged birds.
cut·tle·fish (kŭt′l-fĭsh′) *n.* A squidlike marine mollusk of the genus *Sepia,* having 10 arms and a calcareous internal shell and secreting a dark, inky fluid.
cut·up (kŭt′ŭp′) *n.* *Informal.* A mischievous person.
c.w.o. *abbr.* **1.** cash with order. **2.** chief warrant officer.
cwt. *abbr.* hundredweight.
-cy *suff.* **1.** State : condition : quality <accura*cy*> **2.** Rank : office <captain*cy*>
cy·a·nide (sī′ə-nīd′) *also* **cy·a·nid** (-nĭd) *n.* Any of a large group of salts and esters, esp. the highly poisonous salts potassium cyanide and sodium cyanide.
cy·ber·net·ics (sī′bər-nĕt′ĭks) *n.* *(sing. in number).* The scientific study of the control processes in mechanical, electronic, and biological systems.
cyc·la·mate (sĭk′lə-māt′, sī′klə-) *n.* A salt of cyclamic acid, having a sweet taste.
cyc·la·men (sĭk′lə-mən, sī′klə-) *n.* Any of several plants of the genus *Cyclaneri,* with pink, white, or red flowers.
cyc·la·mic acid (sĭk′lə-mĭk, sī′klə-). A sour-sweet chemical compound of carbon, hydrogen, oxygen, nitrogen, and sulfur.
cy·cle (sī′kəl) *n.* **1.** A time interval in which an event occurs repeatedly. **2.** A recurring sequence of events. **3.** A series of poems or musical works on a single theme. **4.** A motorcycle or bicycle. *—v.* **-cled, -cling.** To ride a motorcycle or bicycle. **—cy′clic** (sī′klĭk, sĭk′lĭk), **cy′cli·cal** *adj.*
cy·clist (sī′klĭst) *n.* A person who rides a cycle.
cy·clom·e·ter (sī-klŏm′ĭ-tər) *n.* A device that records the revolutions of a wheel for measuring the distance traveled.
cy·clone (sī′klōn′) *n.* *Meteorol.* A storm or system of winds that rotates about a low pressure center and is usu. accompanied by stormy and destructive weather. **—cy·clon′ic** (-klŏn′ĭk) *adj.*

cy·clo·pe·di·a *also* **cy·clo·pae·di·a** (sī′klə-pē′dē-ə) *n.* An encyclopedia.
cy·clo·tron (sī′klə-trŏn′) *n.* An instrument for giving high energy to atomic particles using electric and magnetic forces.

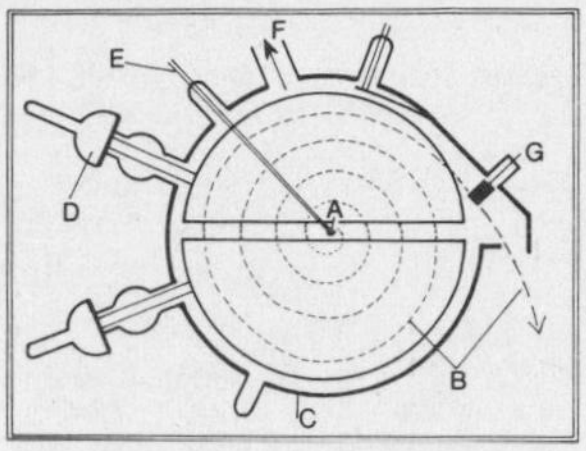

cyclotron
A. source, B. path of ion, C. vacuum chamber, D. high frequency voltage insulator, E. heating wires for ion source, F. pump, G. target

cyg·net (sĭg′nĭt) *n.* A young swan.
cyl·in·der (sĭl′ən-dər) *n.* **1.** *Math.* **a.** A surface that contains all the lines that intersect a given plane curve and that are parallel to a given line. **b.** A solid bounded by a surface of this kind and by 2 parallel planes, esp. when the given curve is a circle and the given line is perpendicular to the plane of the circle. **2.** An object in the shape of a cylinder. **3.** A piston chamber in an engine. **4.** The chamber of a revolver that holds the cartridges. **—cy·lin′dri·cal** (sə-lĭn′drĭ-kəl) *adj.* **—cy·lin′dri·cal·ly** *adv.*
cym·bal (sĭm′bəl) *n.* *Mus.* A concave brass plate sounded by being struck against another or by being hit with a drumstick.
cyn·ic (sĭn′ĭk) *n.* One who believes all human action has selfish motives. **—cyn′i·cal** *adj.* **—cyn′i·cism** *n.*
cy·no·sure (sī′nə-sho͝or′, sĭn′ə-) *n.* A focal point of admiration and interest.
▲word history: A cynosure attracts attention for a compelling reason. The word *cynosure* is derived from Greek *kunosoura,* the Greek name for the constellation now known as Ursa Minor. In ancient times this constellation was used in navigation because it is located near the N celestial pole. *Cynosure* was orig. borrowed into English as the name of the same constellation but was also used figuratively to mean a guide or center of attention.
cy·press (sī′prəs) *n.* An evergreen tree of the genus *Cupressus,* growing in warm climates and bearing small, scalelike needles.
Cy·prus (sī′prəs). Island country in the Mediterranean off S Turkey. *Cap.* Nicosia. *Pop.* 639,000. **—Cyp′ri·an** (sĭp′rē-ən) *adj.* **—Cyp′ri·ot, Cyp′ri·ote** *adj.* & *n.*
cyst (sĭst) *n.* A sac in the body, esp. an abnormal, membranous one containing fluid. **—cys′tic** *adj.*
cystic fibrosis *n.* A congenital disease of mucous glands throughout the body, usu. developing in childhood and resulting in disorders of the pancreas and lungs.
cys·ti·tis (sĭ-stī′tĭs) *n.* Inflammation of the bladder.
cy·tol·o·gy (sī-tŏl′ə-jē) *n.* The scientific study of the structure, formation, and function of cells. **—cy′to·log′i·cal** (-tə-lŏj′ĭ-kəl), **cy′to·log′ic** *adj.* **—cy·tol′o·gist** *n.*
cy·to·plasm (sī′tə-plăz′əm) *n.* The protoplasm outside a cell nucleus. **—cy′to·plas′mic** *adj.*
czar *also* **tsar** *or* **tzar** (zär) *n.* **1.** A former emperor of Russia. **2.** An autocrat. **3.** *Informal.* One having authority.
cza·ri·na (zä-rē′nə) *n.* A czar's wife.
czar·ism (zär′ĭz′əm) *n.* The Russsian system of government under the czars. **—czar′ist** *n.*
Czech·o·slo·va·ki·a (chĕk′ə-slə-vä′kē-ə, -ō-slō-). Country of C Europe. *Cap.* Prague. *Pop.* 15,280,148. **—Czech** *n.* & *adj.* **—Czech′o·slo′vak, Czech′o·slo·va′ki·an** *adj.* & *n.*

Dd

d *or* **D** (dē) *n., pl.* **d's** *or* **D's. 1.** The 4th letter of the English alphabet. **2.** A speech sound represented by the letter *d.* **3.** *Mus.* The 2nd tone in the scale of C major. **4.** The lowest passing academic grade. **5. D** The Roman numeral for 500.
d *abbr.* day.
d. *abbr.* **1.** date. **2.** daughter. **3.** died. **4.** *also* **D.** dose.
D. *abbr.* **1.** December. **2.** *also* **D** democrat; democratic. **3.** Doctor (in academic degrees).
D.A. *abbr.* district attorney.
dab (dăb) *v.* **dabbed, dab·bing. 1.** To apply with light, short strokes. **2.** To touch quickly and lightly : pat. *—n.* **1.** A small amount. **2.** A quick, light pat.
dab·ble (dăb′əl) *v.* **-bled, -bling. 1.** To splatter with or as if with a liquid. **2.** To splash playfully in water. **3.** To work at something casually or without serious purpose. **—dab′bler** *n.*
Dac·ca (dăk′ə). Cap. of Bangladesh. *Pop.* 1,563,517.

dace (dās) *n., pl.* **dace** *or* **dac•es.** A small freshwater fish of the family Cyprinidae, resembling the minnow.
da•cha (dä'chə) *n.* A Russian house in the country.
dachs•hund (däks'ho͝ont', däks'ho͝ond') *n.* A small dog with a long body, very short legs, and drooping ears.
Da•cron (dā'krŏn', dăk'rŏn'). A trademark for a synthetic textile fiber.
dac•tyl (dăk'təl) *n.* A metrical foot of 1 stressed syllable followed by 2 unstressed syllables. **—dac•tyl'ic** (-tĭl'ĭk) *adj.*
dad (dăd) *n. Informal.* Father.
Da•da (dä'dä) *also* **Da•da•ism** (-ĭz'əm) *n.* A literary and artistic movement marked by the abolition of traditional aesthetic and cultural forms and a technique of comic derision. **—Da'da•ist** *n.* **—Da'da•is'tic** *adj.*
dad•dy (dăd'ē) *n., pl.* **-dies.** *Informal.* Father.
daddy long•legs (lông'lĕgz', lŏng'-) *n.* An arachnid of the order Phalangida, with a rounded body and long, thin legs.
daf•fo•dil (dăf'ə-dĭl') *n.* A bulbous plant, *Narcissus pseudonarcissus,* having usu. yellow flowers with a trumpet-shaped center.
daf•fy (dăf'ē) *adj.* **-fi•er, -fi•est.** *Informal.* **1.** Silly. **2.** Crazy.
daft (dăft) *adj.* **1.** Crazy : insane. **2.** Foolish : stupid. **—daft'ly** *adv.* **—daft'ness** *n.*
dag•ger (dăg'ər) *n.* **1.** A short, pointed, sharp-edged weapon used for stabbing. **2.** A reference mark (†) used in printing.
da•guerre•o•type (də-gâr'ə-tīp') *n.* An early photograph with the image produced on a light-sensitive silver-coated plate.
dahl•ia (dăl'yə, däl'-, dāl'-) *n.* A plant of the genus *Dahlia,* with tuberous roots and variously colored flowers.
dai•ly (dā'lē) *adj.* Of, relating to, happening, or published every day. *—adv.* **1.** Every day. **2.** Once a day. *—n., pl.* **-lies.** A daily publication, esp. a newspaper.
daily double *n.* A bet won by selecting the winners of 2 specified races on 1 day.
dain•ty (dān'tē) *adj.* **-ti•er, -ti•est. 1.** Delicately beautiful : exquisite. **2.** Choice : delicious. **3.** Having or showing refined taste : discriminating. **4.** Excessively fastidious. *—n., pl.* **-ties.** A delicacy. **—dain'ti•ly** *adv.* **—dain'ti•ness** *n.*
dai•qui•ri (dī'kə-rē, dăk'ə-) *n., pl.* **-ris.** A drink made with rum and lime juice.
dair•y (dâr'ē) *n., pl.* **-ies. 1.** A commercial establishment for processing and selling milk and milk products. **2.** A dairy farm. **—dair'y•maid'** *n.* **—dair'y•man** *n.*
dairy farm *n.* A farm where milk and milk products are produced.
dair•y•ing (dâr'ē-ĭng) *n.* The business of running a dairy.
da•is (dā'ĭs, dās) *n.* A raised platform, as in a lecture hall, for speakers and guests of honor.
dai•sy (dā'zē) *n., pl.* **-sies. 1.** A plant having rayed flowers, esp. *Chrysanthemum leucanthemum,* with white rays and a yellow center. **2.** A low-growing plant, *Bellis perennis,* having pink or white rayed flowers.
▲word history: The name *daisy,* a compound word meaning "day's eye," was orig. applied to the European plant *Bellis perennis,* which in the U.S. is called the English daisy. The term *day's eye* is particularly appropriate for this plant because it folds its petals at night and opens them in the morning with the sun.
Da•kar (dä-kär'). Cap. of Senegal. *Pop.* 798,792.
da•la•si (dä-lä'sē) *n., pl.* **-si.** See CURRENCY TABLE.
dale (dāl) *n.* A valley.
Dal•las (dăl'əs). City of NE Tex. *Pop.* 904,078.
dal•ly (dăl'ē) *v.* **-lied, -ly•ing. 1.** To flirt. **2.** To waste time : dawdle. **—dal'li•ance** *n.*
Dal•ma•tia (dăl-mā'shə). Region of W Yugoslavia.
Dal•ma•tian (dăl-mā'shən) *n.* **1.** A native or inhabitant of Dalmatia. **2.** A dog having a short, smooth white coat with black spots.
dam¹ (dăm) *n.* A barrier constructed across a waterway for controlling or raising the level of the water. *—v.* **dammed, dam•ming. 1.** To construct a dam across. **2.** To restrain : check.
dam² (dăm) *n.* The female parent of a quadruped.
dam•age (dăm'ĭj) *n.* **1.** Impairment of the worth or usefulness of persons or property : harm. **2. damages.** *Law.* Compensation to be paid for loss or injury. **—dam'age** *v.* **—dam'age•a•ble** *adj.* **—dam'ag•ing•ly** *adv.*
Da•mas•cus (də-măs'kəs). Cap. of Syria. *Pop.* 1,156,000.
dam•ask (dăm'əsk) *n.* **1.** A rich reversible patterned fabric, as of silk or linen. **2.** A fine table linen. **—dam'ask** *adj.*
dame (dām) *n.* **1.** A married woman : matron. **2.** *Slang.* A woman.
damn (dăm) *v.* **1.** To pronounce an adverse judgment on. **2.** To condemn to eternal punishment. **3.** To swear at. *—adj. & adv. Informal.* Used as an intensive <a *damn* fool><*Damn* right I will> *—n. Informal.* A bit : jot <wasn't worth a *damn*> **—dam•na'tion** *n.*
dam•na•ble (dăm'nə-bəl) *adj.* Deserving blame : odious. **—dam'na•bly** *adv.*
damp (dămp) *adj.* Somewhat wet : moist. *—n.* **1.** Humidity : moisture. **2.** A foul or poisonous gas, esp. in a mine. *—v.* **1.** To moisten. **2.** To extinguish (e.g., a fire) by cutting off air. **3.** To check : restrain. **4.** *Physics.* To decrease the amplitude of. **—damp'ish** *adj.* **—damp'ly** *adv.*
damp•en (dăm'pən) *v.* **1.** To moisten. **2.** To depress. **—damp'en•er** *n.*
damp•er (dăm'pər) *n.* **1.** One that depresses or restrains. **2.** An adjustable plate, as in a flue, to control the draft.
dam•sel (dăm'zəl) *n.* A maiden.
dam•sel•fly (dăm'zəl-flī') *n.* A slender-bodied insect of the order Odonata that is related to the dragonfly.
dam•son (dăm'zən) *n.* A Eurasian tree, *Prunus institia,* bearing dark-purple fruit.
dance (dăns) *v.* **danced, danc•ing. 1.** To move rhythmically to music, using improvised or prescribed gestures and steps. **2.** To leap or skip about. **3.** To bob up and down. *—n.* **1.** A series of rhythmic gestures and steps, usu. to music. **2.** A party or gathering for dancing. **3.** A single round of dancing. **4.** The art of dancing. **—danc'er** *n.*
dan•de•li•on (dăn'dl-ī'ən) *n.* A plant, *Taraxacum officinale,* widely naturalized as a weed in North America and having yellow flowers and notched leaves used in salads.
dan•der (dăn'dər) *n. Informal.* Temper.
dan•dle (dăn'dl) *v.* **-dled, -dling.** To move (e.g., a child) up and down on the knees or in the arms. **—dan'dler** *n.*
dan•druff (dăn'drəf) *n.* A scaly scurf formed on and shed from the scalp.
dan•dy (dăn'dē) *n., pl.* **-dies. 1.** One who affects exaggerated elegance. **2.** *Informal.* Something excellent or agreeable. **—dan'di•fy'** *v.* **—dan'dy** *adj.* **—dan'dy•ish** *adj.* **—dan'dy•ism** *n.*
dan•ger (dān'jər) *n.* **1.** Exposure to possible risk, injury, or harm. **2.** A source or instance of risk, injury, or harm. ☆***syns:*** HAZARD, JEOPARDY, PERIL, RISK
dan•ger•ous (dān'jər-əs) *adj.* **1.** Involving or full of danger. **2.** Able or apt to cause harm. **—dan'ger•ous•ly** *adv.* **—dan'ger•ous•ness** *n.*
dan•gle (dăng'gəl) *v.* **-gled, -gling. 1.** To hang or cause to hang loosely and swing back and forth. **2.** To lack clear garmmatical relation in a sentence <a *dangling* participle>
Dan•iel (dăn'yəl) *n.* See BIBLE TABLE.
dank (dăngk) *adj.* Uncomfortably humid and cool. **—dank'ly** *adv.* **—dank'ness** *n.*
dan•seur (däN-sœr') *n., pl.* **-seurs** (-sœr'). A man who is a ballet dancer.
dan•seuse (däN-sœz') *n., pl.* **-seuses** (-sœz'). A woman who is a ballet dancer.
Dan•te A•li•ghie•ri (dän'tē ä'lē-gyârē, -rā). 1265–1321. Italian poet.
Dan•ube (dăn'yo͞ob). River of SE Europe, rising in SW West Germany and flowing E to the Black Sea. **—Dan•u'bi•an** *adj.*
dap•per (dăp'ər) *adj.* **1.** Neatly or stylishly dressed : trim. **2.** Alert and active : jaunty.
dap•ple (dăp'əl) *v.* **-pled, -pling.** To mark with spots of a different color : mottle.
Dar•da•nelles (där'dn-ĕlz'). Strait linking the Sea of Marmara and the Aegean.
dare (dâr) *v.* **dared, dar•ing. 1.** To have the courage necessary for. **2.** To challenge (another) to do something requiring courage. **3.** To confront bravely. ☆***syns:*** BRAVE, CHALLENGE, DEFY, FACE *—n.* A challenge.
dare•dev•il (dâr'dĕv'əl) *n.* One who is daringly bold. **—dare'dev'il** *adj.*
Dar es Sa•laam (där' ĕs sə-läm'). Cap. of Tanzania. *Pop.* 870,000.
dar•ing (dâr'ĭng) *adj.* Fearlessly bold. **—dar'ing** *n.* **—dar'ing•ly** *adv.*
dark (därk) *adj.* **1.** Having little or no light. **2.** Not light in color. **3.** Dismal : gloomy. **4.** Difficult to comprehend : obscure. **5.** Unenlightened : ignorant <a *dark* period in history> **6.** Wicked : sinister. ☆***syns:*** DIM, DUSKY, MURKY, OBSCURE, TENEBROUS *—n.* **1.** Absence of light. **2.** Night or nightfall. **—in the dark. 1.** In secret. **2.** In a state of ignorance. **—dark'ish** *adj.* **—dark'ly** *adv.* **—dark'ness** *n.*
Dark Ages *pl.n.* The early part of the Middle Ages.
dark•en (där'kən) *v.* **1.** To make or become dark or darker. **2.** To make or become sad or gloomy. **3.** To tarnish : stain.
dark horse *n.* A little-known contestant whose chances of winning are uncertain.

dark•room (därk′ro͞om′, -ro͝om′) *n.* A darkened or specially illuminated room for processing photographic materials.
dark star *n.* A star normally obscured or too faint for direct visual observation.
dar•ling (där′lĭng) *n.* **1.** A much-loved person. **2.** A favorite. *—adj.* **1.** Very dear : beloved. **2.** *Informal.* Charming : adorable.
darn (därn) *v.* To mend by weaving stitches across a hole (in). **—darn** *n.*
dar•nel (där′nəl) *n.* An Old World grass of the genus *Lolium.*
darning needle *n.* **1.** A long needle with a large eye. **2.** *Informal.* A dragonfly.
dart (därt) *n.* **1.** A slender, pointed missile either thrown or shot. **2. darts** *(sing. in number).* The game of throwing darts at a target. **3.** Something shaped like a dart. **4.** A sudden, rapid movement. **5.** A tapered tuck to adjust the fit of a garment. *—v.* To move or thrust suddenly.
dart•er (där′tər) *n.* **1.** One that darts. **2.** A small, often brightly colored freshwater fish of the family Percidae, indigenous to E North America.
Dar•win (där′wĭn), **Charles Robert.** 1809–82. English evolutionist. **—Dar•win′i•an** (-wĭn′ē-ən) *adj.* & *n.*
Dar•win•ism (där′wə-nĭz′əm) *n.* A theory of biological evolution that states that species of animals and plants develop through natural selection.
dash (dăsh) *v.* **1.** To break : smash. **2.** To knock, throw, or thrust violently. **3.** To splash. **4.** To perform or finish hastily. **5.** To move quickly : rush. **6.** To destroy : ruin. *—n.* **1.** A swift, harsh blow or stroke. **2.** A splash. **3.** A small amount <a *dash* of pepper> **4.** A sudden movement : rush. **5.** A short race on foot. **6.** Vigor : vitality. **7.** A punctuation mark (—) used in writing or printing. **8.** A dashboard. **—dash′er** *n.*
dash•board (dăsh′bôrd′, -bōrd′) *n.* A panel under the windshield of a motor vehicle where the instruments, dials, and controls are located.
da•shi•ki (də-shē′kē) *n., pl.* **-kis.** A loose-fitting, often brightly colored tunic.
dash•ing (dăsh′ĭng) *adj.* **1.** Audacious and gallant. **2.** Splendidly elegant.
das•tard (dăs′tərd) *n.* A base coward. **—das′tard•li•ness** *n.* **—das′tard•ly** *adj.*
da•ta (dā′tə, dăt′ə, dä′tə) *pl.n. (sing. or pl. in number).* **1.** Information, esp. information organized for analysis. **2.** Numerical information that is used for computer processing. **3.** *pl. of* DATUM.
data bank *n.* A data base.
data base *also* **da•ta•base** (dā′tə-bās′, dăt′ə-) *n.* A collection of data arranged for ease of retrieval, as by a computer.
data processing *n.* **1.** Preparation of information for computer processing. **2.** Storage or processing of raw data by a computer. **—data processor** *n.*
date[1] (dāt) *n.* **1.** Time stated in terms of the day, month, and year. **2.** The day of the month. **3.** A particular point or period in time at which something occurred or existed or is to occur. **4.** Duration of something. **5.** The time or historical period to which something belongs. **6. a.** A social appointment. **b.** A person's companion on a date. *—v.* **dat•ed, dat•ing. 1.** To mark or provide with a date <*date* a letter> **2.** To ascertain the date of. **3.** To reveal the age of. **4.** To have origin in a particular time in the past <a vase *dating* from 400 B.C.> **5.** To go on dates.
date[2] (dāt) *n.* The oblong edible fruit of the date palm.
dat•ed (dā′tĭd) *adj.* **1.** Showing or marked with a date. **2.** Old-fashioned.
date•less (dāt′lĭs) *adj.* **1.** Having no date. **2.** Without limits : endless. **3.** Too old to be dated. **4.** Timeless : eternal.
date•line (dāt′līn′) *n.* A phrase at the beginning of a printed article giving the date and its place of origin.
date palm *n.* A tropical tree, *Phoenix dactylifera,* having featherlike leaves and bearing clusters of dates.
dating bar *n.* A singles bar.
da•tive (dā′tĭv) *adj.* Of, pertaining to, or being a grammatical case in Latin, Russian, and other inflected Indo-European languages that marks the indirect object. *—n.* The dative case.
da•tum (dā′təm, dăt′əm, dä′təm) *n., pl.* **-ta** (-tə). One piece of information : fact.
daub (dôb) *v.* **1.** To cover, coat, or smear with an adhesive substance, as plaster. **2.** To paint unskillfully. *—n.* **1.** A soft adhesive coating material. **2.** A crude painting. **—daub′er** *n.* **—daub′ing•ly** *adv.*
daugh•ter (dô′tər) *n.* **1.** A female offspring. **2.** A female descendant. **3.** A woman considered as being analogous to a daughter <a *daughter* of the nation> **—daugh′ter•ly** *adj.*
daugh•ter-in-law (dô′tər-ĭn-lô′) *n., pl.* **daugh•ters-in-law.** One's son's wife.
daunt (dônt) *v.* **1.** To drain the courage of : intimidate. **2.** To dishearten.
daunt•less (dônt′lĭs) *adj.* Fearless.
dau•phin (dô′fĭn) *n.* The eldest son of a king of France.
dav•en•port (dăv′ən-pôrt′, -pōrt′) *n.* A large couch or sofa.
Da•vis (dā′vĭs), **Jefferson.** 1808–89. President of the Confederate States of America (1861–65).
dav•it (dăv′ĭt, dā′vĭt) *n.* A small crane used esp. for lifting small boats.
daw•dle (dôd′l) *v.* **-dled, -dling. 1.** To take more time than is needed. **2.** To waste time. **—daw′dler** *n.*
dawn (dôn) *n.* **1.** The first appearance of the morning daylight. **2.** A beginning. ☆**syns:** AURORA, COCKCROW, DAYBREAK, MORN, MORNING, SUNRISE, SUNUP *—v.* **1.** To begin to grow light in the morning. **2.** To emerge. **3.** To begin to be understood.
day (dā) *n.* **1.** The period of light between dawn and nightfall. **2.** The 24-hour period of a single rotation of the earth on its axis. **3.** The part of a day set aside for work. **4.** A period of activity or prominence in one's lifetime. **5.** A specified period of time : era <in *days* of old> **6.** The issue at hand <carried the *day*>
day•bed (dā′bĕd′) *n.* A sofa that can be converted into a bed.
day•book (dā′bo͝ok′) *n.* A diary or private journal.
day•break (dā′brāk′) *n.* DAWN 1.
day care *n.* Provision of daytime supervision, training, and medical services, esp. for infants and preschool children.
day•dream (dā′drēm′) *n.* A dreamlike fantasy. **—day′dream** *v.*
day•light (dā′līt′) *n.* **1.** The light of day. **2.** Daybreak. **3.** Daytime. **4.** Understanding or insight into what was once obscure. **5. daylights.** *Slang.* Mental stability : wits.
day•light-sav•ing time (dā′līt-sā′vĭng) *n.* Time that is usu. 1 hour ahead of standard time.
Day of Atonement *n.* Yom Kippur.
days (dāz) *adv.* Regularly or habitually in the daytime <worked *days*>
day•time (dā′tīm′) *n.* The time between dawn and dark : day.
day-to-day (dā′tə-dā′) *adj.* **1.** Happening on a daily or routine basis. **2.** Of or marked by planning or thought only for the present with little regard for the future.
Day•ton (dāt′n). City of SW Ohio. *Pop.* 203,588.
daze (dāz) *v.* **dazed, daz•ing. 1.** To stun, as with a heavy blow or shock : stupefy. **2.** To dazzle, as with intense light. ☆**syns:** BEDAZZLE, BLIND, DAZZLE **—daze** *n.*
daz•zle (dăz′əl) *v.* **-zled, -zling. 1.** To overpower or be overpowered with intense light. **2.** To bewilder or overwhelm with a spectacular display. **—daz′zle** *n.*
dB *abbr.* decibel.
D.B. *abbr.* daybook.
d.b.a. *abbr.* doing business as.
dbl. *abbr.* double.
DC *abbr.* District of Columbia (with Zip Code).
D.C. *abbr.* District of Columbia.
D-day (dē′dā′) *n.* A day on which an operation or military offensive is launched.
D.D.S. *abbr.* Doctor of Dental Science.
DDT (dē′dē-tē′) *n.* A colorless contact insecticide that is toxic to humans and animals when ingested or absorbed.
DE *abbr.* Delaware (with Zip Code).
de– *pref.* **1.** Do or make the opposite of : reverse <*de*criminalize> **2.** Remove or remove from <*de*throne> See below for a list of self-explanatory words formed with the prefix **de–.**
dea•con (dē′kən) *n.* **1.** A clergyman ranking immediately below a priest. **2.** A layperson who assists a minister. **—dea′con•ess** *n.* **—dea′con•ry** *n.*
de•ac•ti•vate (dē-ăk′tə-vāt′) *v.* **1.** To make inactive. **2.** To remove from active military status. **—de•ac′ti•va′tion** *n.*
dead (dĕd) *adj.* **1.** No longer living. **2.** Having no capacity to live : inanimate. **3.** Lacking feeling or sensitivity. **4. a.** No longer in use or existence <a *dead* language> **b.** Dormant <a *dead* volcano> **5.** Unproductive <*dead* capital> **6.** Quiet : dull. **7.**

de-aerate	**dechlorinate**	**decongestion**	**delead**
de-aeration	**decolor**	**decongestive**	**delime**
de-Americanization	**decoloration**	**deconsecrate**	**delouse**
de-Americanize	**decommission**	**de-emphasize**	**deluster**
deassimilation	**decompensate**	**de-energize**	**demast**
decertification	**decompound**	**dehorn**	**dematerialization**
decertify	**decondition**	**dehull**	**dematerialize**

Worn-out : weary. **8.** No longer having significance or relevance <a *dead* issue> **9.** Having the physical look of death. **10.** Exact : unerring. **11.** Drained of electric charge, as a battery. **12.** Lacking bounce or elasticity. **13.** Not circulating : stagnant. **14. a.** Sudden : abrupt <a *dead* stop> **b.** Complete <*dead* silence> *—n.* The period of greatest intensity, as of cold or darkness. *—adv.* **1.** Altogether : absolutely. **2.** Directly <*dead* ahead> **—dead′ness** *n.*

dead•beat (dĕd′bēt′) *n. Slang.* A person who does not pay incurred debts.

dead•en (dĕd′n) *v.* **1.** To make less intense, sensitive, or vigorous. **2.** To make soundproof. **—dead′en•er** *n.*

dead end *n.* **1.** An end of a passage that affords no outlet. **2.** A point beyond which no progress can be made : impasse. **—dead′-end′** *adj.*

dead•eye (dĕd′ī′) *n.* **1.** *Naut.* A flat disk through which lanyards are passed to fasten the shrouds. **2.** *Slang.* A sharpshooter.

deadeye

dead heat *n.* A contest in which 2 or more entrants finish at the same time : tie.

dead•line (dĕd′līn′) *n.* A time limit before which something must be finished.

dead•lock (dĕd′lŏk′) *n.* A stoppage resulting from the uncompromising positions of opposing forces. **—dead′lock′** *v.*

dead•ly (dĕd′lē) *adj.* **-li•er, -li•est. 1.** Causing or tending to cause death. **2.** Like death. **3.** Implacable <*deadly* enemies> **4.** Destructive in effect <gave the play a *deadly* review> **5.** Utter <*deadly* earnestness> **6.** Extreme <under *deadly* strain> **7.** *Informal.* Dull and boring. ☆**syns:** FATAL, LETHAL, MORTAL *—adv.* **1.** So as to resemble death. **2.** To an extreme <I'm *deadly* serious.> **—dead′li•ness** *n.*

dead•pan (dĕd′păn′) *adj.* & *adv. Informal.* With an expressionless face or manner.

dead reckoning *n.* The determination of the position of an aircraft or ship without astronomical observations, as by computations of the course and distance traveled from a known position.

Dead Sea (dĕd). Salt lake between Israel and Jordan.

dead•wood (dĕd′wo͝od′) *n.* **1.** Dead wood on a tree. **2.** One that is burdensome or superfluous.

deaf (dĕf) *adj.* **1.** Partially or totally incapable of hearing. **2.** Unwilling or refusing to listen : heedless. **—deaf′ness** *n.*

deaf•en (dĕf′ən) *v.* To make deaf.

deaf-mute (dĕf′myo͞ot′) *n.* A person who cannot speak or hear.

deal[1] (dēl) *v.* **dealt** (dĕlt), **deal•ing. 1.** To apportion : distribute. **2.** To administer : deliver <*dealt* a blow to the chin> **3.** To give out (playing cards) among players of a game. **4.** To be concerned <a report *dealing* with poverty> **5.** To behave in a particular manner toward another or others. **6.** To take action in response to something <*dealt* with all complaints> **7.** To conduct business : trade. *—n.* **1.** The act of apportioning or distributing. **2. a.** Cards distributed in a card game : hand. **b.** The turn or right of a player to deal cards. **3.** An undetermined quantity, extent, or degree <spent a great *deal* of time> **4.** *Informal.* **a.** A business transaction. **b.** A favorable bargain or sale. **5.** *Informal.* Treatment received <a raw *deal*> **—deal′er** *n.*

deal[2] (dēl) *n.* Pine or fir wood or boards.

deal•er•ship (dē′lər-shĭp′) *n.* A franchise to sell an item in a certain area.

deal•ing (dē′lĭng) *n.* **1. dealings.** Transactions with others, usu. in business. **2.** A way of acting in relation to others.

dean (dēn) *n.* **1.** An administrator in a college, university, or high school. **2.** The head of the body of canons governing a cathedral or collegiate church. **3.** The senior member of a body or group : doyen.

dear (dîr) *adj.* **1. a.** Loved and cherished <my *dear* parents> **b.** Greatly valued : precious. **2.** High-priced : costly. *—n.* A greatly loved person. *—adv.* **1.** Fondly or affectionately. **2.** At a high price. **—dear′ly** *adv.*

dearth (dûrth) *n.* Scarcity : lack.

death (dĕth) *n.* **1.** The cessation of life. **2.** The state of being dead. **3.** Termination or extinction <the *death* of slavery> **4.** The cause of dying. **5.** A manner of dying <a martyr's *death*> **6. a.** Bloodshed. **b.** Execution. **—death′like′** *adj.*

death•bed (dĕth′bĕd′) *n.* **1.** The bed on which a person dies. **2.** The last hours before death.

death•blow (dĕth′blō′) *n.* A blow or event that is fatal.

death cup *n.* A poisonous mushroom, *Amanita phalloides.*

death•less (dĕth′lĭs) *adj.* Not subject to death : immortal.

death•ly (dĕth′lē) *adj.* **1.** Of, resembling, or typical of death. **2.** Causing death : fatal. *—adv.* **1.** In the manner of death. **2.** Very : extremely <*deathly* pale>

death point *n.* An environmental limit, as of temperature or radiation, beyond which a specified life form cannot survive.

death rate *n.* The ratio of deaths to population in a specified community.

death's-head (dĕths′hĕd′) *n.* The human skull symbolizing mortality or death.

death•trap (dĕth′trăp′) *n.* **1.** An unsafe structure. **2.** A perilous situation.

Death Valley. Desert basin in E Calif. and W Nev.

death•watch (dĕth′wŏch′) *n.* A watch kept with a dying or dead person.

deb (dĕb) *n. Informal.* A debutante.

deb. *abbr.* debenture.

de•ba•cle (dĭ-bä′kəl, -băk′əl) *n.* A sudden, calamitous downfall, collapse, or failure.

de•bar (dē-bär′) *v.* To forbid, shut out, or bar. **—de•bar′ment** *n.*

de•bark (dĭ-bärk′) *v.* To disembark.

de•base (dĭ-bās′) *v.* To lower in quality, character, or value : demean. **—de•base′ment** *n.* **—de•bas′er** *n.*

de•bate (dĭ-bāt′) *v.* **-bat•ed, -bat•ing. 1.** To consider : deliberate <*debating* whether to go> **2.** To argue opposing points. **3.** To discuss or argue (e.g., a question) formally. **—de•bate′** *n.* **—de•bat′a•ble** *adj.* **—de•bat′a•bly** *adv.* **—de•bat′er** *n.*

de•bauch (dĭ-bôch′) *v.* To lead away from virtue : corrupt. **—de•bauch′er•y** *n.*

de•ben•ture (dĭ-bĕn′chər) *n.* A certificate or voucher acknowledging a debt.

de•bil•i•tate (dĭ-bĭl′ĭ-tāt′) *v.* **-tat•ed, -tat•ing.** To make weak or feeble. **—de•bil′i•ta′tion** *n.* **—de•bil′i•ta′tive** *adj.*

de•bil•i•ty (dĭ-bĭl′ĭ-tē) *n.* Abnormal bodily weakness.

deb•it (dĕb′ĭt) *n.* An item of debt as recorded in an account. *—v.* **1.** To enter in a ledger as a debit. **2.** To charge with a debt.

deb•o•nair (dĕb′ə-nâr′) *adj.* **1.** Suave : urbane. **2.** Affable : genial. **3.** Jaunty : nonchalant. **—deb′o•nair′ly** *adv.*

de•bouch (dĭ-bouch′, -bo͞osh′) *v.* To march or issue into the open.

de•brief (dē-brēf′) *v.* To interrogate in order to obtain intelligence gathered, esp. on a military mission.

de•bris *also* **dé•bris** (də-brē′, dā′brē′) *n.* **1.** Scattered remains : ruins. **2.** Discarded waste : litter.

debt (dĕt) *n.* **1.** Something owed, as money or goods. **2.** The condition of indebtedness.

▲word history: The pronunciation of *debt* represents the orig. pronunciation of the word, which was borrowed from French *dette.* Medieval writers knew that *dette* was derived from Latin *debitum,* and in the 15th cent. the spelling *debt* first appeared. This form was promoted as more correct by the language reformers of the 16th cent. and is now the only acceptable spelling.

debt•or (dĕt′ər) *n.* One who owes a debt to another.

de•bug (dē-bŭg′) *v.* **1.** To remove insects from. **2.** To find and remove a concealed electronic listening device from. **3.** To correct malfunctioning elements in (e.g., a computer program).

de•bunk (dē-bŭngk′) *v. Informal.* To expose the fallacy or fraudulence of.

de•but *also* **dé•but** (dā-byo͞o′, dĭ-, dā′byo͞o′) *n.* **1.** A 1st public

demesmerize
demount
denationalization
denationalize
denitrate
depasture
depolish
depressurize
deration
derequisition
derestrict
desalt
desanctify
desaturate
descale
descramble
desilver
desize
desocialize
desoil
desugar
devow
dewool
deworm

appearance. **2.** The formal presentation of a young woman to society. **3.** The beginning of a course of action, as a career. **—de·but′** *v.*
deb·u·tante *also* **dé·bu·tante** (dĕb′yo͝o-tänt′, dā′byo͞o-) *n.* A young woman who is making her debut.
dec. *abbr.* **1.** deceased. **2.** decrease.
Dec. *abbr.* December.
dec·ade (dĕk′ād′, dĕ-kād′) *n.* A period of 10 years.
dec·a·dence (dĕk′ə-dəns, dĭ-kād′ns) *n.* A process, period, or condition of decline or deterioration, as in art or morals. **—dec′a·dent** *adj.* **—dec′a·dent·ly** *adv.*
de·caf·fein·at·ed (dē-căf′ə-nā′tĭd) *adj.* Having the caffeine removed.
dec·a·gon (dĕk′ə-gŏn′) *n.* A polygon with 10 angles and 10 sides.
dec·a·gram (dĕk′ə-grăm′) *n.* See MEASUREMENT TABLE.
de·cal (dē′kăl′, dĭ-kăl′) *n.* A picture or design transferred by decalcomania.
de·cal·co·ma·ni·a (dē-kăl′kə-mā′nē-ə) *n.* **1.** The process of transferring designs or pictures printed on special paper to material such as glass or metal. **2.** Decal.
dec·a·li·ter dĕk′ə-lē′tər) *n.* See MEASUREMENT TABLE.
Dec·a·logue or **Dec·a·log** (dĕk′ə-lôg′, -lŏg′) *n.* The Ten Commandments.
dec·a·me·ter (dĕk′ə-mē′tər) *n.* See MEASUREMENT TABLE.
dec·a·me·tre (dĕk′ə-mē′tər) *n. esp. Brit. var. of* DECAMETER.
de·camp (dĭ-kămp′) *v.* **1.** To leave a camping ground. **2.** To depart suddenly.
de·cant (dĭ-kănt′) *v.* To pour off (e.g., wine) without disturbing the sediment.
de·cant·er (dĭ-kăn′tər) *n.* An ornamental bottle for serving liquids, as wine.
de·cap·i·tate (dĭ-kăp′ĭ-tāt′) *v.* **-tat·ed, -tat·ing.** To cut off the head of : behead. **—de·cap′i·ta′tion** *n.* **—de·cap′i·ta′tor** *n.*
dec·a·stere (dĕk′ə-stîr′) *n.* See MEASUREMENT TABLE.
de·cath·lon (dĭ-kăth′lən, -lŏn′) *n.* An athletic contest with 10 different track and field events.
de·cay (dĭ-kā′) *v.* **1.** To rot. **2.** To decline in quality or quantity : deteriorate. **3.** *Physics.* To disintegrate or diminish by radioactive decomposition. ☆***syns:*** DECOMPOSE, DETERIORATE, MOLDER, PUTREFY, ROT, SPOIL, TURN **—de·cay′** *n.*
de·cease (dĭ-sēs′) *v.* **-ceased, -ceas·ing.** To die. **—de·cease′** *n.* **—de·ceased′** *n.*
de·ce·dent (dĭ-sēd′nt) *n.* A deceased person.
de·ceit (dĭ-sēt′) *n.* **1.** Deception. **2.** A trick : stratagem. **—de·ceit′ful** *adj.* **—de·ceit′ful·ly** *adv.* **—de·ceit′ful·ness** *n.*
de·ceive (dĭ-sēv′) *v.* **-ceived, -ceiv·ing.** To mislead or delude. ☆***syns:*** DELUDE, DUPE, FOOL, HOODWINK, MISLEAD **—de·ceiv′a·ble** *adj.* **—de·ceiv′er** *n.*
de·cel·er·ate (dē-sĕl′ə-rāt′) *v.* **-at·ed, -at·ing.** To decrease in velocity. **—de·cel′er·a′tion** *n.* **—de·cel′er·a′tor** *n.*
De·cem·ber (dĭ-sĕm′bər) *n.* The 12th month of the year, having 31 days.
de·cen·ni·al (dĭ-sĕn′ē-əl) *adj.* **1.** Lasting for 10 years. **2.** Happening once every 10 years. **—de·cen′ni·al** *n.*
de·cent (dē′sənt) *adj.* **1.** Marked by conformity to recognized standards of propriety or morality. **2.** Meeting accepted standards : adequate <a *decent* income> **3.** Kind or obliging. **4.** Properly or modestly clothed. **—de′cen·cy** *n.* **—de′cent·ly** *adv.*
de·cen·tral·ize (dē-sĕn′trə-līz′) *v.* **-ized, -iz·ing.** **1.** To distribute the administrative functions of (a central authority) among several local authorities. **2.** To redistribute a concentration of (e.g., population) over a wider area. **—de·cen′tral·i·za′tion** *n.*
de·cep·tion (dĭ-sĕp′shən) *n.* **1.** The use of deceit. **2.** The state or fact of being deceived. **3.** A ruse.
de·cep·tive (dĭ-sĕp′tĭv) *adj.* Intended or tending to mislead or deceive. **—de·cep′tive·ly** *adv.* **—de·cep′tive·ness** *n.*
dec·i·bel (dĕs′ə-bəl, -bĕl′) *n.* A unit for expressing relative difference in sounds.
de·cide (dĭ-sīd′) *v.* **-cid·ed, -cid·ing.** **1.** To settle or conclude. **2.** To determine or influence the settlement of. **3.** To make up or cause to make up one's mind. ☆***syns:*** CONCLUDE, DETERMINE, RESOLVE, SETTLE **—de·cid′a·ble** *adj.* **—de·cid′er** *n.*
de·cid·ed (dĭ-sī′dĭd) *adj.* **1.** Definite : unquestionable. **2.** Resolute. **—de·cid′ed·ly** *adv.* **—de·cid′ed·ness** *n.*
de·cid·u·ous (dĭ-sĭj′o͞o-əs) *adj.* **1.** Falling off or shed usu. at the end of a particular season or stage of growth. **2.** Shedding leaves at the end of the growing season.
dec·i·gram (dĕs′ĭ-grăm′) *n.* See MEASUREMENT TABLE.
dec·i·liter (dĕs′ə-lē′tər) *n.* See MEASUREMENT TABLE.
dec·i·li·tre (dĕs′ə-lē′tər) *n. esp. Brit. var. of* DECILITER.
de·cil·lion (dĭ-sĭl′yən) *n.* **1.** The cardinal number equal to 10^{33}. **2.** *esp. Brit.* The cardinal number equal to 10^{60}. **—de·cil′lionth** *adj.* & *n.*
dec·i·mal (dĕs′ə-məl) *n.* **1.** A linear group of natural numbers that represents a fraction, every decimal place indicating a multiple of a power of 10, e.g., .3 = 3/10, .03 = 3/100, .003 = 3/1000. **2.** A number with a decimal point. *—adj.* **1.** Expressed or capable of being expressed as a decimal. **2. a.** Based on 10. **b.** Ordered or numbered by 10's. **—dec′i·mal·ly** *adv.*
decimal point *n.* A period placed to the left of a decimal.
dec·i·mate (dĕs′ə-māt′) *v.* **-mat·ed, -mat·ing.** **1.** To destroy or kill a large proportion of. **2.** To select by lot and kill 1 in every 10 of. **—dec′i·ma′tion** *n.*
dec·i·me·ter (dĕs′ə-mē′tər) *n.* See MEASUREMENT TABLE.
dec·i·me·tre (dĕs′ə-mē′tər) *n. esp. Brit. var. of* DECIMETER.
de·ci·pher (dĭ-sī′fər) *v.* **1.** To decode. **2.** To interpret or read (something ambiguous or indistinct). **—de·ci′pher·a·ble** *adj.*
de·ci·sion (dĭ-sĭzh′ən) *n.* **1.** A final choice : judgment. **2.** Resoluteness.
de·ci·sive (dĭ-sī′sĭv) *adj.* **1.** Conclusive. **2.** Marked by firm determination : resolute. **3.** Unquestionable <a *decisive* victory> **—de·ci′sive·ly** *adv.* **—de·ci′sive·ness** *n.*
dec·i·stere (dĕs′ĭ-stîr′) *n.* See MEASUREMENT TABLE.
deck[1] (dĕk) *n.* **1. a.** A horizontal platform that extends between the sides of a ship. **b.** A platform similar to a ship's deck. **2.** A set of playing cards. *—v.* **1.** To furnish with a deck. **2.** To knock down, as by punching.
deck[2] (dĕk) *v.* To array or adorn.
deck hand *n.* A member of a ship's crew assigned to work on deck.
de·claim (dĭ-klām′) *v.* To speak or deliver loudly or dramatically. **—dec′la·ma′tion** (dĕk′lə-mā′shən) *n.* **—de·clam′a·to′ry** (-klăm′ə-tôr′ē, -tōr′ē) *adj.*
de·clare (dĭ-klâr′) *v.* **-clared, -clar·ing.** **1.** To state formally or officially. **2.** To state emphatically : affirm. **3.** To reveal : show. **4.** To make a full statement of (e.g., dutiable goods). **—dec′la·ra′tion** *n.* **—de·clar′a·tive** *adj.* **—de·clar′er** *n.*
de·clas·si·fy (dē-klăs′ə-fī′) *v.* To remove the security classification of (a document). **—de·clas′si·fi·ca′tion** *n.*
de·clen·sion (dĭ-klĕn′shən) *n.* **1.** Inflection of nouns, pronouns, and adjectives. **2.** A slope : descent. **3.** A decrease or decline : deterioration. **—de·clen′sion·al** *adj.*
de·cline (dĭ-klīn′) *v.* **-clined, -clin·ing.** **1.** To refuse or reject (something). **2.** To slope downward : descend. **3.** To deteriorate little by little, as from disease. **4.** To wane. **5.** To give the inflected forms of. **—de·clin′a·ble** *adj.* **—dec′li·na′tion** *n.* **—dec′li·na′tion·al** *adj.* **—de·cline′** *n.* **—de·clin′er** *n.*
de·cliv·i·ty (dĭ-klĭv′ĭ-tē) *n., pl.* **-ties.** A steep descending slope.
de·code (dē-kōd′) *v.* To convert (a coded message) into plain text. **—de·cod′er** *n.*
dé·colle·tage (dā′kôl-täzh′) *n.* A low or plunging neckline on a garment.
dé·colle·té (dā′kôl-tā′) *adj.* Having a low or plunging neckline.
de·com·pose (dē′kəm-pōz′) *v.* **1.** To separate or break down into component parts. **2.** To decay or cause to decay. **—de′com·pos′a·ble** *adj.* **—de′com·pos′er** *n.* **—de·com′po·si′tion** (dē-kŏm′pə-zĭsh′ən) *n.*
de·com·press (dē′kəm-prĕs′) *v.* **1.** To relieve of pressure. **2.** To bring (a person working in compressed air) back to normal air pressure. **—de′com·pres′sion** *n.*
de·con·ges·tant (dē′kən-jĕs′tənt) *n.* An agent that alleviates congestion, as of the sinuses.
de·con·tam·i·nate (dē′kən-tăm′ə-nāt′) *v.* To free of contamination.
de·con·trol (dē′kən-trōl′) *v.* To free from control, esp. from governmental control.
dé·cor or **de·cor** (dā′kôr′, dā-kôr′) *n.* An interior decorative arrangement.
dec·o·rate (dĕk′ə-rāt′) *v.* **-rat·ed, -rat·ing.** **1.** To furnish or adorn with fashionable or beautiful things. **2.** To bestow an emblem of honor on.
dec·o·ra·tion (dĕk′ə-rā′shən) *n.* **1.** The act or art of decorating. **2.** An ornament. **3.** An emblem of honor, as a medal.
dec·o·ra·tive (dĕk′ər-ə-tĭv, -ə-rā′-) *adj.* Serving to decorate : ornamental.
dec·o·ra·tor (dĕk′ə-rā′tər) *n.* One who decorates, esp. an interior decorator.
dec·o·rous (dĕk′ər-əs, dĭ-kôr′-, -kōr′-) *adj.* Marked by decorum : seemly.
de·co·rum (dĭ-kôr′əm, -kōr′-) *n.* Conformity to accepted conventions of behavior : propriety.
de·cou·page *also* **dé·cou·page** (dā′ko͞o-päzh′) *n.* The technique of decorating a surface with cutouts, as of paper.
de·coy (dē′koi′, dĭ-koi′) *n.* **1.** An artificial animal used to lure

game. **2.** A means to trap, mislead, or lure into danger. **—de·coy′** *v.* **—de·coy′er** *n.*

de·crease (dĭ-krēs′) *v.* **-creased, -creas·ing.** To grow or cause to grow gradually less : reduce. ☆*syns:* ABATE, DIMINISH, DWINDLE, LESSEN, REDUCE, TAPER —*n.* (dē′krēs′). The act or process of decreasing or the resulting state : decline.

de·cree (dĭ-krē′) *n.* **1.** An authoritative order having legal force. **2.** A judicial judgment. —*v.* **-creed, -cree·ing.** To establish, ordain, or decide by decree.

dec·re·ment (dĕk′rə-mənt) *n.* **1.** A gradual decrease. **2.** The amount lost by gradual waste or diminution. **—dec′re·ment′al** *adj.*

de·crep·it (dĭ-krĕp′ĭt) *adj.* Broken down or worn out, as from long use or old age. **—de·crep′it·ly** *adv.* **—de·crep′i·tude′** *n.*

de·cre·scen·do (dē′krə-shĕn′dō, dā′-) *adv. Mus.* Gradually decreasing in force or loudness. **—de′cre·scen′do** *n.* & *adj.*

de·crim·i·nal·ize (dē-krĭm′ə-nə-līz′) *v.* **-ized, -iz·ing.** To remove the criminal classification of.

de·cry (dĭ-krī′) *v.* To belittle or disparage openly : denounce. **—de·cri′er** *n.*

ded·i·cate (dĕd′ĭ-kāt′) *v.* **-cat·ed, -cat·ing. 1.** To set apart for a special use. **2.** To commit (oneself) to a particular course of action. **3.** To address or inscribe (e.g., a literary work) to someone. **—ded′i·ca′tion** *n.* **—ded′i·ca·to′ry** (-kə-tôr′ē, -tōr′ē) *adj.*

de·duce (dĭ-do͞os′, -dyo͞os′) *v.* **-duced, -duc·ing.** To come to (a conclusion) by reasoning. **—de·duc′i·ble** *adj.*

▲word history: *Deduce* and *deduct* were both borrowed in the early 16th cent. from Latin *deducere,* "to lead or bring away." *Deducere* also meant "to subtract" in classical Latin and developed the sense "to derive a logical conclusion from" in Medieval Latin. In English *deduce* and *deduct* were at first used interchangeably with both meanings of the Latin word, but gradually *deduce* was restricted to "derive" and *deduct* was used primarily to mean "subtract." *Deduction,* however, still serves as the noun for both.

de·duct (dĭ-dŭkt′) *v.* To subtract. **—de·duct′i·ble** *adj.*

de·duc·tion (dĭ-dŭk′shən) *n.* **1.** Subtraction. **2.** An amount that is or may be deducted. **3. a.** The act or process of deducing. **b.** A conclusion arrived at by this process. **—de·duc′tive** *adj.* **—de·duc′tive·ly** *adv.*

deed (dēd) *n.* **1.** Something performed : act. **2.** An exploit : feat. **3.** Performance or action in general. **4.** A legal document, esp. one relating to the transference of property. —*v.* To transfer or convey by deed.

deem (dēm) *v.* To consider or judge.

deep (dēp) *adj.* **1.** Extending far downward below a surface. **2.** Extending far backward from front to rear or far inward from an outer surface. **3.** Coming from or penetrating to a depth. **4.** Far distant in time or space. **5.** Very learned : wise. **6.** Hard to understand : recondite. **7.** Extreme : intense. **8.** Rich and vivid in shade <*deep* green> **9.** Low in pitch : resonant. ☆*syns:* ABSTRUSE, ESOTERIC, HEAVY, PROFOUND, RECONDITE —*n.* **1.** A deep place in land or in a body of water, esp. in the ocean. **2.** The most extreme or intense part, as of the night or winter. **3.** The ocean. —*adv.* **1.** To a great depth : deeply <feelings ran *deep*> **2.** Advanced in time : late. **—deep′ly** *adv.* **—deep′ness** *n.*

deep·en (dē′pən) *v.* To make or become deep or deeper.

deep-freeze (dēp′frēz′) *v.* To quick-freeze.

deep-fry (dēp′frī′) *v.* To fry in a deep pan.

deep-root·ed (dēp′ro͞o′tĭd, -ro͝ot′ĭd) *adj.* Firmly implanted.

deep-sea (dēp′sē′) *adj.* Of, pertaining to, or occurring in deep parts of the sea.

deep-seat·ed (dēp′sē′tĭd) *adj.* Deeply rooted : ingrained.

deep-six (dēp′sĭks′) *v. Slang.* **1.** To throw overboard. **2.** To toss out : get rid of.

deer (dîr) *n., pl.* **deer.** A hoofed ruminant mammal of the family Cervidae, the males of which have deciduous antlers.

deer fly *n.* Any of various blood-sucking flies of the genus *Chrysops.*

deer·skin (dîr′skĭn′) *n.* Leather made from the hide of a deer.

de-es·ca·late (dē-ĕs′kə-lāt′) *v.* To decrease the scope or intensity of (e.g., a war).

def. *abbr.* **1.** definite. **2.** definition.

de·face (dĭ-fās′) *v.* To mar or spoil the surface or appearance of : disfigure.

de fac·to (dĭ făk′tō, dā) *adv.* In actuality or fact : really. —*adj.* **1.** Actual. **2.** Actually exercising authority.

de·fal·cate (dĭ-făl′kāt′, -fôl′-, dĕf′əl-kāt′) *v.* **-cat·ed, -cat·ing.** To misuse funds : embezzle. **—de′fal·ca′tor** *n.*

de·fame (dĭ-fām′) *v.* **-famed, -fam·ing.** To libel or slander. **—def′a·ma′tion** (dĕf′ə-mā′shən) *n.* **—de·fam′a·to′ry** (dĭ-făm′ə-tôr′ē, -tōr′ē) *adj.* **—de·fam′er** *n.*

de·fault (dĭ-fôlt′) *n.* **1.** Failure to fulfill an obligation or perform a task. **2.** Failure to make a required appearance in court. **3.** Failure to complete or participate in a competition. **—de·fault′** *v.* **—de·fault′er** *n.*

de·feat (dĭ-fēt′) *v.* **1.** To win a victory over : beat. **2.** To thwart the success of <*defeated* our plans> ☆*syns:* BEAT, BEST, CLOBBER, CONQUER, DRUB, LICK, OVERCOME, ROUT, SHELLAC, SUBDUE, THRASH, TRIM, TRIUMPH, TROUNCE, VANQUISH, WHIP, WORST —*n.* The act of defeating or state of being defeated. **—de·feat′er** *n.*

de·feat·ism (dĭ-fē′tĭz′əm) *n.* Expectation or acceptance of defeat. **—de·feat′ist** *n.*

def·e·cate (dĕf′ĭ-kāt′) *v.* **-cat·ed, -cat·ing.** To void feces from the bowels. **—def′e·ca′tion** *n.* **—def′e·ca′tor** *n.*

de·fect (dē′fĕkt′, dĭ-fĕkt′) *n.* **1.** A lack of something desirable or necessary. **2.** A fault or imperfection. ☆*syns:* BLEMISH, FAULT, FLAW, IMPERFECTION —*v.* (dĭ-fĕkt′). To desert a country, party, or previously espoused cause. **—de·fec′tion** *n.* **—de·fec′tor** *n.*

de·fec·tive (dĭ-fĕk′tĭv) *adj.* Having a defect : faulty. **—de·fec′tive** *n.*

de·fence (dĭ-fĕns′) *n. esp. Brit. var. of* DEFENSE.

de·fend (dĭ-fĕnd′) *v.* **1.** To protect from danger, attack, or harm. **2.** To maintain or support : justify. **3. a.** To act as a lawyer for (a defendant) in a criminal or civil case. **b.** To oppose (a legal action or claim). ☆*syns:* GUARD, PROTECT, SAFEGUARD, SECURE, SHIELD **—de·fend′a·ble** *adj.* **—de·fend′er** *n.*

de·fen·dant (dĭ-fĕn′dənt) *n.* A person against whom a legal action is brought.

de·fense (dĭ-fĕns′) *n.* **1.** The act of defending : protection. **2.** Something that protects or defends. **3.** An argument that supports or justifies. **4.** A sports team or group of players attempting to keep the opposition from scoring. **5.** A defendant with his or her legal counsel. **—de·fense′less** *adj.* **—de·fen′si·ble** *adj.* **—de·fen′sive** *adj.* & *n.*

defense mechanism *n. Psychoanal.* A usu. unconscious mental mechanism that protects a person from shame, anxiety, or loss of self-esteem.

de·fer[1] (dĭ-fûr′) *v.* **-ferred, -fer·ring.** To put off until a future time : postpone. **—de·fer′ment, de·fer′ral** *n.* **—de·fer′ra·ble** *adj.* **—de·fer′rer** *n.*

de·fer[2] (dĭ-fûr′) *v.* **-ferred, -fer·ring.** To comply with or submit to the wishes, opinion, or decision of another. **—de·fer′rer** *n.*

def·er·ence (dĕf′ər-əns) *n.* Courteous respect for another's opinion, wishes, or judgment. **—def′er·en′tial** *adj.*

de·fi·ance (dĭ-fī′əns) *n.* **1.** Bold resistance to an opposing force or authority. **2.** Deliberately provocative behavior.

de·fi·ant (dĭ-fī′ənt) *adj.* Marked by defiance. **—de·fi′ant·ly** *adv.*

deficiency disease *n.* A disease, as scurvy, caused by a diet lacking in specific vitamins and minerals.

de·fi·cient (dĭ-fĭsh′ənt) *adj.* **1.** Lacking an essential quality or element. **2.** Inadequate in amount or degree : insufficient. **—de·fi′cien·cy** *n.* **—de·fi′cient·ly** *adv.*

def·i·cit (dĕf′ĭ-sĭt) *n.* The amount by which a sum of a money is short of the necessary or expected amount.

de·file[1] (dĭ-fīl′) *v.* **-filed, -fil·ing. 1.** To make dirty : pollute. **2.** To corrupt. **3.** To profane or sully (e.g., a reputation). **4.** To desecrate. **5.** To violate the chastity of : ravish. **—de·file′ment** *n.* **—de·fil′er** *n.*

de·file[2] (dĭ-fīl′) *v.* **-filed, -fil·ing.** To march in single file or in columns. —*n.* A narrow gorge or pass.

de·fine (dĭ-fīn′) *v.* **-fined, -fin·ing. 1.** To state the specific meaning of (a word). **2.** To describe the nature of : explain. **3.** To delineate. **4.** To specify. **—de·fin′a·ble** *adj.* **—de·fin′er** *n.* **—def′i·ni′tion** (dĕf′ə-nĭsh′ən) *n.*

def·i·nite (dĕf′ə-nĭt) *adj.* **1.** Having specified bounds. **2.** Certain : sure <a *definite* success> **3.** Precise and explicit. **4.** Serving to designate a person or thing that is or can be immediately identified <"The" is the *definite* article.> ☆*syns:* CATEGORICAL, CLEAR-CUT, DECIDED, EXPLICIT, EXPRESS, POSITIVE, PRECISE, SPECIFIC, UNAMBIGUOUS, UNEQUIVOCAL **—def′i·nite·ly** *adv.*

de·fin·i·tive (dĭ-fĭn′ĭ-tĭv) *adj.* **1.** Precisely outlining or defining. **2.** Determining finally : decisive. **3.** Being complete and authoritative, as a biographical work.

de·flate (dĭ-flāt′) *v.* **-flat·ed, -flat·ing. 1. a.** To release contained gas or air from. **b.** To collapse through the release of contained gas or air. **2.** To reduce or lessen in importance or magnitude. **3.** To reduce (currency) in value or amount, effecting a decline in prices. **—de·fla′tion** *n.* **—de·fla′tion·ar′y** *adj.*

de·flect (dĭ-flĕkt′) *v.* To turn aside or cause to turn aside : swerve. **—de·flect′a·ble** *adj.* **—de·flec′tion** *n.* **—de·flec′tive** *adj.* **—de·flec′tor** *n.*

de·flow·er (dē-flou′ər) *v.* To destroy the virginity of : ravish.

De·foe (dĭ-fō′), **Daniel.** 1660?–1731. English novelist.

de·fog (dē-fôg′, -fŏg′) *v.* To remove fog from. **—de·fog′ger** *n.*

de•fo•li•ant (dē-fō′lē-ənt) *n.* A chemical dusted or sprayed on plants or trees to cause the leaves to fall off.

de•fo•li•ate (dē-fō′lē-āt′) *v.* **-at•ed, -at•ing.** To strip of leaves, esp. by the use of a defoliant. **—de•fo′li•a′tion** *n.*

de•for•est (dē-fôr′ĭst, -fŏr′-) *v.* To clear of trees or forests. **—de•for′es•ta′tion** *n.*

de•form (dĭ-fôrm′) *v.* **1.** To spoil the natural form of : misshape. **2.** To mar the appearance of : disfigure <a face *deformed* by anger> **—de•form′a•ble** *adj.* **—de′for•ma′tion** (dē′fôr-mā′shən, dĕf′ər-) *n.*

de•for•mi•ty (dĭ-fôr′mĭ-tē) *n., pl.* **-ties. 1.** The state of being deformed. **2.** A bodily malformation.

de•fraud (dĭ-frôd′) *v.* To swindle : cheat. **—de•fraud′er** *n.*

de•fray (dĭ-frā′) *v.* To pay or provide for payment of <*defray* expenses> **—de•fray′a•ble** *adj.* **—de•fray′al** *n.*

de•frost (dē-frôst′, -frŏst′) *v.* **1.** To free or become free from ice or frost. **2.** To cause to thaw out. **—de•frost′er** *n.*

deft (dĕft) *adj.* Dexterous : skillful. **—deft′ly** *adv.* **—deft′ness** *n.*

de•funct (dĭ-fŭngkt′) *adj.* Having ceased to live or exist. **—de•func′tive** *adj.* **—de•funct′ness** *n.*

de•fuse (dē-fyōōz′) *v.* **1.** To remove the fuse or detonator from. **2.** To make less dangerous, tense, or hostile.

de•fy (dĭ-fī′) *v.* **-fied, -fy•ing. 1.** To face up to : challenge. **2.** To withstand or resist successfully. **3.** To dare or challenge to perform something thought to be impossible. **—de•fi′er** *n.*

deg or **deg.** *abbr.* degree (thermometric).

dé•ga•gé (dā′gä-zhā′) *adj.* **1.** Nonchalant. **2.** Casual <a *dégagé* atmosphere>

de•gas (dē-găs′) *v.* To remove gas from.

De Gaulle (də gōl′, gôl′), **Charles.** 1890–1970. French general and statesman.

de•gauss (dē-gous′) *v.* To neutralize the magnetic field of.

de•gen•er•ate (dĭ-jĕn′ə-rāt′) *v.* To decline in value, quality, or desirability : deteriorate. *—adj.* (-ər-ĭt). Morally depraved or sexually deviant. *—n.* (-ər-ĭt). A degenerate person : pervert. **—de•gen′er•a•cy** *n.* **—de•gen′er•ate•ly** *adv.* **—de•gen′er•a′tion** *n.* **—de•gen′er•a•tive** *adj.*

de•grade (dĭ-grād′) *v.* **1.** To reduce in grade, rank, or status : demote. **2.** To corrupt : debase. **—de•grad′able** *adj.* **—deg′ra•da′tion** (dĕg′rə-dā′shən) *n.*

de•gree (dĭ-grē′) *n.* **1.** One of a series of stages or steps. **2.** Relative rank, dignity, or position. **3.** Relative amount or intensity <a high *degree* of competence> **4.** Relative extent or condition <improved to a great *degree*> **5.** A unit on a temperature scale. **6.** A unit of arc or angular measure equal to 1/360 of a complete revolution. **7.** An academic title awarded to a person who has completed a given course of study or conferred as an honor. **8.** A classification according to seriousness, as of a crime. **9.** One of the grammatical forms used in the comparison of adjectives and adverbs. **10.** *Mus.* A note or tone of a musical scale.

de•horn (dē-hôrn′) *v.* To remove the horns from (an animal).

de•hu•man•ize (dē-hyōō′mə-nīz′) *v.* To deprive of human qualities, esp. to make routine and mechanical.

de•hu•mid•i•fy (dē′hyōō-mĭd′ə-fī′) *v.* To remove atmospheric moisture from. **—de′hu•mid′i•fi′er** *n.*

de•hy•drate (dē-hī′drāt′) *v.* To lose or cause to lose water or moisture.

de•ice (dē-īs′) *v.* To rid or keep free of ice. **—de•ic′er** *n.*

de•i•fy (dē′ə-fī′) *v.* **-fied, -fy•ing. 1.** To raise to divine rank. **2.** To worship or revere as a god. **—de′i•fi•ca′tion** *n.*

deign (dān) *v.* To deem barely worthy of one's dignity : condescend.

de•in•sti•tu•tion•al•ize (dē-ĭn′stĭ-tōō′shə-nə-līz′, -tyōō′-) *v.* **1.** To remove the institutional nature from. **2.** To release (e.g., one who is developmentally handicapped or mentally ill) from an institution.

de•ism (dē′ĭz′əm) *n.* A system of thought that affirms the existence of God but denies the validity of revelation. **—de′ist** *n.*

de•i•ty (dē′ĭ-tē) *n., pl.* **-ties. 1.** A god or goddess. **2.** The nature or state of a god. **3. Deity.** God.

de•ject (dĭ-jĕkt′) *v.* To lower the spirits of : dishearten. **—de•jec′tion** *n.* **—de•ject′ed•ly** *adv.* **—de•ject′ed•ness** *n.*

de ju•re (dē jŏŏr′ē, dā yŏŏr′ā) *adv. & adj.* By law : by right.

dek•a•gram (dĕk′ə-grăm′) *n. var. of* DECAGRAM.

dek•a•li•ter (dĕk′ə-lē′tər) *n. var. of* DECALITER.

dek•a•me•ter (dĕk′ə-mē′tər) *n. var. of* DECAMETER.

dek•a•stere (dĕk′ə-stîr′) *n. var. of* DECASTERE.

deke (dēk) *v.* **deked, dek•ing.** *Hockey.* To fake a movement or shot in order to outmaneuver an opposing player.

del. *abbr.* **1.** delegate; delegation. **2.** delete.

Del. *abbr.* Delaware.

Del•a•ware (dĕl′ə-wâr′) State of the E U.S., on the Atlantic. *Cap.* Dover. *Pop.* 595,225.

de•lay (dĭ-lā′) *v.* **1.** To postpone until a later time : defer. **2.** To cause to be detained or late. **3.** To waste time : procrastinate. ☆**syns:** DETAIN, RETARD, SLOW *—n.* **1.** The act of delaying or the state of being delayed. **2.** The time period in which someone is delayed. **—de•lay′er** *n.*

de•le (dē′lē) *n.* A mark indicating that something is to be deleted from typeset material. **—de′le** *v.*

de•lec•ta•ble (dĭ-lĕk′tə-bəl) *adj.* **1.** Exceedingly pleasant : delightful. **2.** Savory : delicious. **—de•lec′ta•bil′i•ty** *n.*

de•lec•ta•tion (dē′lĕk-tā′shən) *n.* Pleasure : enjoyment.

del•e•gate (dĕl′ĭ-gāt′, -gĭt) *n.* **1.** A person empowered to act as representative for another : agent or deputy. **2.** A member of the lower legislative house of Md., Va., and W.Va. *—v.* (-gāt′) **-gat•ed, -gat•ing. 1.** To empower and send as one's delegate. **2.** To commit or entrust to another.

del•e•ga•tion (dĕl′ĭ-gā′shən) *n.* **1.** The act of delegating or state of being delegated. **2.** A person or group of persons empowered to represent another or others.

de•lete (dĭ-lēt′) *v.* **-let•ed, -let•ing.** To remove or cancel : omit. **—de•le′tion** *n.*

del•e•te•ri•ous (dĕl′ĭ-tîr′ē-əs) *adj.* Having an injurious effect : harmful. **—del′e•te′ri•ous•ly** *adv.* **—del′e•te′ri•ous•ness** *n.*

delft (dĕlft) *n.* **1.** A style of glazed, usu. blue and white earthenware. **2.** A piece of pottery that resembles delft.

delft•ware (dĕlft′wâr′) *n.* Delft.

Del•hi (dĕl′ē). City of NC India. *Pop.* 3,706,558.

del•i (dĕl′ē) *n.* A delicatessen.

de•lib•er•ate (dĭ-lĭb′ər-ĭt) *adj.* **1. a.** Planned in advance : premeditated. **b.** Said or done intentionally. **2.** Careful and thorough in deciding or determining. **3.** Leisurely or slow in motion or manner. *—v.* (-ə-rāt′) **-at•ed, -at•ing.** To consider carefully, as by weighing alternatives. **—de•lib′er•ate•ly** *adv.* **—de•lib′er•ate•ness** *n.* **—de•lib′er•a′tion** *n.* **—de•lib′er•a•tive** *adj.* **—de•lib′er•a•tive•ly** *adv.*

del•i•ca•cy (dĕl′ĭ-kə-sē) *n., pl.* **-cies. 1.** The state or quality of being delicate. **2.** A select or choice food.

del•i•cate (dĕl′ĭ-kĭt) *adj.* **1.** Pleasing to the senses, esp. in a subtle way <a *delicate* fragrance> **2.** Exquisitely fine <*delicate* embroidery> **3.** Frail in constitution. **4.** Easily damaged or broken. **5.** Marked by sensitivity or discrimination. **6. a.** Considerate. **b.** Concerned with propriety. **c.** Squeamish or fastidious. **7.** Requiring tactful treatment. **8.** Fine or soft in touch or skill. **9.** Keenly accurate in response or reaction. **10.** Very subtle in difference. ☆**syns:** CHOICE, DAINTY, ELEGANT, EXQUISITE, FINE **—del′i•cate•ly** *adv.*

del•i•ca•tes•sen (dĕl′ĭ-kə-tĕs′ən) *n.* A store that sells cooked or prepared foods.

de•li•cious (dĭ-lĭsh′əs) *adj.* **1.** Highly pleasing to the senses, esp. of taste. **2.** Very pleasant : delightful. ☆**syns:** DELECTABLE, HEAVENLY, LUSCIOUS, SAVORY, SCRUMPTIOUS, TASTY, TOOTHSOME, YUMMY **—de•li′cious•ly** *adv.* **—de•li′cious•ness** *n.*

de•light (dĭ-līt′) *n.* **1.** Great joy or pleasure. **2.** Something that affords delight. *—v.* To take or give great pleasure or joy. **—de•light′ful** *adj.* **—de•light′ful•ly** *adv.*

de•light•ed (dĭ-lī′tĭd) *adj.* Greatly pleased. **—de•light′ed•ly** *adv.* **—de•light′ed•ness** *n.*

de•lim•it (dĭ-lĭm′ĭt) *v.* To fix the limits of : demarcate.

de•lin•e•ate (dĭ-lĭn′ē-āt′) *v.* **-at•ed, -at•ing. 1.** To draw or trace the outline of : sketch. **2.** To represent in words or gestures : portray. **—de•lin′e•a′tion** *n.*

de•lin•quent (dĭ-lĭng′kwənt) *adj.* **1.** Failing to do what is required by law or obligation. **2.** Being behind in payment. **—de•lin′quen•cy** *n.* **—de•lin′quent** *n.* **—de•lin′quent•ly** *adv.*

del•i•quesce (dĕl′ĭ-kwĕs′) *v.* **-quesced, -quesc•ing. 1.** *Chem.* To become liquid by absorbing atmospheric moisture. **2.** To melt. **—del′i•ques′cent** *adj.*

de•lir•i•um (dĭ-lîr′ē-əm) *n.* **1.** A temporary mental disturbance resulting from high fever, intoxication, or shock and marked by confusion, tremors, hallucinations, and incoherent speech. **2.** Uncontrolled emotion, esp. excitement. **—de•lir′i•ous** *adj.* **—de•lir′i•ous•ly** *adv.* **—de•lir′i•ous•ness** *n.*

delirium tre•mens (trē′mənz, trĕm′ənz) *n.* An acute delirium caused by chronic and excessive use of alcohol.

de•liv•er (dĭ-lĭv′ər) *v.* **1.** To set free : liberate. **2.** To assist in the birth of. **3.** To surrender to another : hand over. **4.** To take to the intended recipient <*deliver* mail> **5.** To send to an intended goal or target. **6.** To give or utter. **7.** To do what is desired or expected <*deliver* on a pledge> **—de•liv′er•a•ble** *adj.* **—de•liv′er•ance** *n.* **—de•liv′er•er** *n.*

de•liv•er•y (dĭ-lĭv′ə-rē) *n., pl.* **-ies. 1.** The act of delivering or conveying. **2.** Something delivered. **3.** The act or process of giving birth : parturition. **4. a.** A way of speaking or singing. **b.** Utterance. **5.** The manner or act of throwing.

dell (dĕl) *n.* A small, secluded, usu. wooded valley.

Del•phi (dĕl′fī′). Ancient town of C Greece, near Mt. Parnassus.
del•phin•i•um (dĕl-fĭn′ē-əm) *n.* A plant of the genus *Delphinium*, bearing spikes of variously colored spurred flowers.
del•ta (dĕl′tə) *n.* A usu. triangular alluvial deposit at the mouth of a river.
delta ray *n.* An electron ejected from matter by ionizing radiation.
delta wing *n.* An aircraft with swept-back wings.

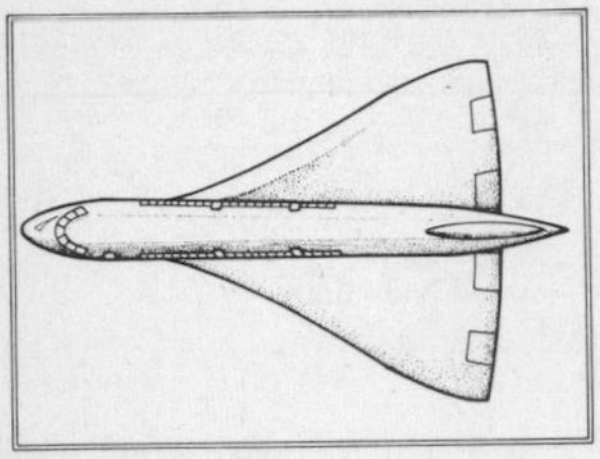

delta wing

de•lude (dĭ-lo͞od′) *v.* **-lud•ed, -lud•ing.** To cause to be deceived.
del•uge (dĕl′yo͞oj) *n.* **1. a.** A great flood. **b.** A heavy downpour. **2.** Something overwhelming. *—v.* **-uged, -ug•ing.** To swamp with or as if with water.
de•lu•sion (dĭ-lo͞o′zhən) *n.* **1. a.** The act or process of deluding. **b.** The state of being deluded. **2.** A false conviction held contrary to invalidating facts, characteristic of some mental disorders. **—de•lu′sion•al** *adj.* **—de•lu′sive** *adj.*
de luxe *also* **de•luxe** (dĭ-lo͝oks′, lŭks′) *adj.* Highly luxurious or elegant.
delve (dĕlv) *v.* **delved, delv•ing.** To search carefully and laboriously.
Dem. *abbr.* Democrat; Democratic.
de•mag•net•ize (dē-măg′nĭ-tīz′) *v.* To rid of magnetic properties. **—de•mag′net•i•za′tion** *n.*
dem•a•gogue *also* **dem•a•gog** (dĕm′ə-gôg′, -gŏg′) *n.* A leader who comes to power by appealing to the prejudices and emotions of the people. **—dem′a•gogu′er•y, dem′a•gog′y** *n.*
de•mand (dĭ-mănd′) *v.* **1.** To ask for firmly : command. **2.** To claim or assert as due or just. **3.** To require : need. *—n.* **1.** The act of demanding. **2.** Something demanded. **3. a.** The state of being desired or sought after. **b.** An urgent requirement, claim, or need. **4. a.** The ability and desire to purchase something. **b.** The quantity of goods wanted at a given price.
de•mand•ing (dĭ-măn′dĭng) *adj.* Needing constant attention or effort.
de•mar•cate (dĭ-mär′kāt′, dē′mär-kāt′) *v.* **-cat•ed, -cat•ing. 1.** To set the boundaries of : delimit. **2.** To separate as if by boundaries. **—de′mar•ca′tion** *n.*
de•mean[1] (dĭ-mēn′) *v.* To conduct or behave (oneself) in a particular manner.
de•mean[2] (dĭ-mēn′) *v.* **1.** To debase or degrade. **2.** To humble (oneself).
de•mean•or (dĭ-mē′nər) *n.* One's conduct toward others : deportment.
de•ment•ed (dĭ-mĕn′tĭd) *adj.* Insane.
de•men•tia (dĭ-mĕn′shə) *n.* Irreversible deterioration of intellectual faculties.
de•mer•it (dĭ-mĕr′ĭt) *n.* **1.** A defect : fault. **2.** A mark against one's record, esp. for bad conduct.
de•mesne (dĭ-mān′, -mēn′) *n.* **1.** The grounds of an estate. **2.** A large piece of landed property : estate. **3.** A region or territory. **4.** A domain : realm.
dem•i•god (dĕm′ē-gŏd′) *n.* A mythological semidivine being, esp. the offspring of a god and a mortal.
dem•i•john (dĕm′ē-jŏn′) *n.* A large, narrow-necked glass or earthenware bottle usu. enclosed in a wicker case.
de•mil•i•ta•rize (dē-mĭl′ĭ-tə-rīz′) *v.* To free from military control, forces, or installations. **—de•mil′i•ta•ri•za′tion** *n.*
dem•i•mon•daine (dĕm′ē-mŏn-dān′) *n.* A woman who belongs to the demimonde.
dem•i•monde (dĕm′ē-mŏnd′) *n.* **1.** A class comprising women who are supported by wealthy lovers or protectors. **2.** A group living on the edge of respectability.
de•mise (dĭ-mīz′) *n.* **1.** Death. **2.** The transfer of an estate by will or lease.
dem•i•tasse (dĕm′ē-tăs′, -täs′) *n.* **1.** A small cup of strong coffee. **2.** The cup used to serve demitasse.
dem•o (dĕm′ō) *n., pl.* **-os.** *Informal.* **1.** A demonstration. **2.** A product used for demonstration purposes.
de•mo•bi•lize (dē-mō′bə-līz′) *v.* **1.** To release from military service. **2.** To disband.
de•moc•ra•cy (dĭ-mŏk′rə-sē) *n., pl.* **-cies. 1.** Government exercised either directly by the people or through elected representatives. **2.** A political or social unit based on democratic rule. **3.** Rule by the majority. **4.** The principles of social equality and respect for the individual within a community.
dem•o•crat (dĕm′ə-krăt′) *n.* **1.** One who advocates democracy. **2. Democrat.** One belonging to the Democratic Party.
dem•o•crat•ic (dĕm′ə-krăt′ĭk) *adj.* **1.** Of, marked by, or advocating democracy. **2.** Relating to, encompassing, or promoting the people's interests. **3.** Believing in or practicing social equality. **4. Democratic.** Of or relating to the Democratic Party. **—dem′o•crat′i•cal•ly** *adv.* **—de•moc′ra•tize′** *v.*
Democratic Party *n.* One of the 2 major political parties in the U.S.
dé•mo•dé (dā′mō-dā′) *adj.* Out-of-date.
de•mog•ra•phy (dĭ-mŏg′rə-fē) *n.* The study of the characteristics of human population, as size, growth, and vital statistics. **—dem′o•graph′ic** (dĕm′ə-grăf′ĭk) *adj.* **—dem′o•graph′i•cal•ly** *adv.*
de•mol•ish (dĭ-mŏl′ĭsh) *v.* **1.** To tear down : raze. **2.** To do away with : end.
dem•o•li•tion (dĕm′ə-lĭsh′ən) *n.* The act or process of demolishing, esp. destruction by the use of explosives.
de•mon (dē′mən) *n.* **1.** An evil being : devil. **2.** A persistently vexatious person, force, or drive. **3.** One who zealously undertakes an activity <a *demon* for work> **—de•mon′ic** (dĭ-mŏn′ĭk) *adj.* **—de•mon′i•cal•ly** *adv.*
de•mon•e•tize (dĭ-mŏn′ĭ-tīz′, -mŭn′-) *v.* **1.** To divest (e.g., a unit of currency) of monetary value. **2.** To stop using (a metal) as a monetary standard.
de•mo•ni•ac (dĭ-mō′nē-ăk′) *also* **de•mo•ni•a•cal** (dē′mə-nī′ə-kəl) *adj.* **1.** Arising or appearing to arise from possession by a demon. **2.** Of, resembling, or suggestive of a demon : fiendish.
de•mon•ol•o•gy (dē′mə-nŏl′ə-jē) *n.* The study of or belief in demons.
de•mon•stra•ble (dĭ-mŏn′strə-bəl) *adj.* **1.** Capable of being demonstrated. **2.** Obvious or apparent. **—de•mon′stra•bil′i•ty** *n.* **—de•mon′stra•bly** *adv.*
dem•on•strate (dĕm′ən-strāt′) *v.* **-strat•ed, -strat•ing. 1.** To prove or show by evidence or reasoning. **2.** To show or reveal <*demonstrates* talent> **3.** To explain, esp. by using examples. **4.** To make a public protest <students *demonstrating* against nuclear weapons> **—dem′on•stra′tion** *n.* **—dem′on•stra′tor** *n.*
de•mon•stra•tive (dĭ-mŏn′strə-tĭv) *adj.* **1.** Serving to manifest or prove. **2.** Involving or marked by demonstration. **3.** Given to or marked by the open expression of emotion, esp. affection. **4.** Specifying the person or thing referred to <a *demonstrative* pronoun> *—n.* A demonstrative adjective or pronoun. **—de•mon′stra•tive•ly** *adv.* **—de•mon′stra•tive•ness** *n.*
de•mor•al•ize (dĭ-môr′ə-līz′, -mŏr′-) *v.* **1.** To undermine the confidence or morale of : discourage. **2.** To corrupt : degrade. **—de•mor′al•i•za′tion** *n.* **—de•mor′al•iz′er** *n.*
De•mos•the•nes (dĭ-mŏs′thə-nēz′). 385?–322 B.C. Greek orator.
de•mote (dĭ-mōt′) *v.* **-mot•ed, -mot•ing.** To reduce in grade, rank, or position. **—de•mo′tion** *n.*
de•mul•cent (dĭ-mŭl′sənt) *adj.* Soothing. *—n.* A soothing ointment used esp. on irritated mucous surfaces.
de•mur (dĭ-mûr′) *v.* **-murred, -mur•ring.** To take issue : object. **—de•mur′ral** *n.*
de•mure (dĭ-myo͝or′) *adj.* **-mur•er, -mur•est. 1.** Modest and reserved. **2.** Feigning modesty : coy. **—de•mure′ly** *adv.*
de•mur•rer (dĭ-mûr′ər, -mŭr′-) *n. Law.* A plea to dismiss a lawsuit on the grounds that the plaintiff's statements are insufficient to sustain the claim.
den (dĕn) *n.* **1.** A wild animal's shelter : lair. **2.** A small and esp. squalid abode. **3.** A small, private room for relaxation or study. **4.** A place in which a secret or illicit activity is carried on <an opium *den*>
de•na•ture (dē-nā′chər) *v.* **-tured, -tur•ing.** To change the nature or natural qualities of, esp. to make unfit for consumption. **—de•na′tur•ant** *n.* **—de•na′tur•a′tion** *n.*
den•drite (dĕn′drīt′) *n.* The branching portion of a nerve cell that carries impulses toward the cell body.
den•drol•o•gy (dĕn-drŏl′ə-jē) *n.* The botanical study of trees.
den•gue (dĕng′gē, -gā′) *n.* An infectious tropical disease transmitted by mosquitoes, characterized by fever and severe joint pains.
de•ni•al (dĭ-nī′əl) *n.* **1.** A refusal to comply with a request. **2.** A refusal to acknowledge the truth of a statement. **3.** A repudiation : disavowal. **4.** Self-denial : abstinence.

den·ier (dĕn′yər) *n.* A measure of fineness for nylon, rayon, and silk yarns.

den·i·grate (dĕn′ĭ-grāt′) *v.* **-grat·ed, -grat·ing.** To defame : slander.

den·im (dĕn′əm) *n.* **1.** A coarse twilled cloth used for jeans, overalls, and work clothes. **2. denims.** Denim garments.

den·i·zen (dĕn′ĭ-zən) *n.* **1.** An inhabitant. **2.** A habitué.

Den·mark (dĕn′märk′). Country of N Europe, consisting of a peninsula and an archipelago between the North and Baltic seas. *Cap.* Copenhagen. *Pop.* 5,122,065. **–Dane** *n.* **–Dan′ish** (dā′nĭsh) *adj.* & *n.*

de·nom·i·nate (dĭ-nŏm′ə-nāt′) *v.* To give a name to : designate.

de·nom·i·na·tion (dĭ-nŏm′ə-nā′shən) *n.* **1.** The act of naming. **2.** The name of a class or group : classification. **3.** A class of units having specified values, as in a system of currency or weights. **4.** An organized body of similar religious congregations. **–de·nom′i·na′tion·al** *adj.*

de·nom·i·na·tor (dĭ-nŏm′ə-nā′tər) *n.* **1.** The numeral below the line in a fraction. **2.** A common trait or characteristic.

de·note (dĭ-nōt′) *v.* **-not·ed, -not·ing. 1.** To indicate or reveal : mark. **2.** To serve as a name or symbol for : signify. **3.** To refer to specifically : mean explicitly. **–de′no·ta′tion** *n.* **–de·no′ta·tive** *adj.*

dé·noue·ment *also* **de·noue·ment** (dā′no͞o-mäɴ′) *n.* The outcome of the plot of a literary work, as a play or novel.

de·nounce (dĭ-nouns′) *v.* **-nounced, -nounc·ing. 1.** To condemn openly, esp. as evil : censure. **2.** To accuse officially or formally. **3.** To announce formally the ending of (e.g., a treaty). **–de·nounc′er** *n.*

dense (dĕns) *adj.* **dens·er, dens·est. 1.** Crowded closely together : compact. **2.** Thick or impenetrable <*dense* smoke> **3.** Slow to understand : stupid. **–dense′ly** *adv.* **–dense′ness** *n.*

den·si·ty (dĕn′sĭ-tē) *n., pl.* **-ties. 1.** The quality or state of being dense. **2.** The amount or quantity of something per unit measure, as of length, area, or volume.

dent (dĕnt) *n.* **1.** A small surface depression made by pressure or a blow. **2.** Meaningful progress : headway. **–dent** *v.*

den·tal (dĕn′tl) *adj.* Of or relating to the teeth or to dentistry.

dental floss *n.* A strong thread used to clean between teeth.

dental hygienist *n.* A licensed dental professional who provides preventive dental services, as cleaning.

den·ti·frice (dĕn′tə-frĭs) *n.* A paste or power for cleaning the teeth.

den·tine (dĕn′tēn′, dĕn-tēn′) *also* **den·tin** (dĕn′tĭn) *n.* The calcareous part of a tooth, beneath the enamel, containing the pulp chamber and root canals.

den·tist (dĕn′tĭst) *n.* Someone whose profession is the diagnosis, treatment, and prevention of diseases of the teeth and gums. **–den′tist·ry** *n.*

den·ti·tion (dĕn-tĭsh′ən) *n.* The kind, number, and arrangement of teeth, as in a human being.

den·ture (dĕn′chər) *n.* A set of artificial teeth.

de·nude (dĭ-no͞od′, -nyo͞od′) *v.* **-nud·ed, -nud·ing.** To remove all covering from. **–den′u·da′tion** (dĕn′yo͝o-dā′shən) *n.*

de·nun·ci·a·tion (dĭ-nŭn′sē-ā′shən, -shē-) *n.* The act of denouncing, esp. a public censure.

Den·ver (dĕn′vər). Cap. of Colo. *Pop.* 491,396.

de·ny (dĭ-nī′) *v.* **-nied, -ny·ing. 1.** To contradict or declare untrue. **2.** To reject as untrue. **3.** To refuse to acknowledge or recognize. **4.** To refuse to grant : withhold.

de·o·dor·ant (dē-ō′dər-ənt) *n.* A substance used to prevent, mask, or destroy unpleasant odors.

de·o·dor·ize (dē-ō′də-rīz′) *v.* **-ized, -iz·ing.** To disguise or absorb the odor of. **–de·o′dor·iz′er** *n.*

de·ox·y·ri·bo·nu·cle·ic acid (dē-ŏk′sē-rī′bō-no͞o-klē′ĭk, -nyo͞o-) *n.* DNA.

dep. *abbr.* **1.** depart; departure. **2.** deposit. **3.** deputy.

de·part (dĭ-pärt′) *v.* **1.** To go away (from) : leave. **2.** To deviate. **3.** To die.

de·part·ment (dĭ-pärt′mənt) *n.* **1.** A specialized division of a large organization, as a government, business, or college. **2.** *Informal.* A sphere of special knowledge or activity. **–de′part·men′tal** *adj.*

de·part·men·tal·ize (dē′pärt-mĕn′tl-īz′) *v.* **-ized, -iz·ing.** To organize into departments. **–de′part·men′tal·i·za′tion** *n.*

department store *n.* A retail store organized into departments and offering a wide variety of goods.

de·par·ture (dĭ-pär′chər) *n.* **1.** The act of going away. **2.** The act of starting out, as on a trip or a new course of action. **3.** A divergence : deviation.

de·pend (dĭ-pĕnd′) *v.* **1.** To place trust : rely. **2.** To be determined, contingent, or dependent. **3.** To hang down.

de·pend·a·ble (dĭ-pĕn′də-bəl) *adj.* Capable of being depended on : reliable. **–de·pend′a·bil′i·ty** *n.*

de·pend·ence *also* **de·pend·ance** (dĭ pĕn′dəns) *n.* **1.** The state or quality of being dependent. **2.** The state of being influenced, determined, or controlled by something else. **3.** Trust : reliance.

de·pend·en·cy *also* **de·pend·an·cy** (dĭ-pĕn′dən-sē) *n., pl.* **-cies. 1.** Dependence. **2.** A territory under the authority and control of another country from which it is geographically separated.

de·pend·ent *also* **de·pend·ant** (dĭ-pĕn′dənt) *adj.* **1.** Determined by or contingent on something or someone else. **2.** Subordinate. **3.** Depending on or needing the aid of another for support. **4.** Hanging down. *–n.* One, as a child, who relies on another for support. **–de·pend′ent·ly** *adv.*

de·pict (dĭ-pĭkt′) *v.* **1.** To represent in a picture or sculpture. **2.** To represent in words : describe. **–de·pic′tion** *n.*

de·pil·a·to·ry (dĭ-pĭl′ə-tôr′ē, -tōr′ē) *n., pl.* **-ries.** A cream or liquid used to remove unwanted body hair.

de·plane (dē-plān′) *v.* To disembark from an aircraft.

de·plete (dĭ-plēt′) *v.* **-plet·ed, -plet·ing.** To use up, empty, or exhaust. **–de·ple′tion** *n.*

de·plor·a·ble (dĭ-plôr′ə-bəl, -plōr′-) *adj.* **1.** Grievous : lamentable. **2.** Very bad : wretched. **–de·plor′a·bly** *adv.*

de·plore (dĭ-plôr′, -plōr′) *v.* **-plored, -plor·ing. 1.** To express or feel great disapproval of : censure. **2.** To express or feel great regret about.

de·ploy (dĭ-ploi′) *v.* To spread out (e.g., troops) to form an extended front. **–de·ploy′ment** *n.*

de·po·lar·ize (dē-pō′lə-rīz′) *v.* To counteract or eliminate the polarization of.

de·po·lit·i·cize (dē′pə-lĭt′ĭ-sīz′) *v.* To remove the political aspect or status from.

de·po·nent (dĭ-pō′nənt) *n.* A person who testifies under oath, esp. in writing.

de·pop·u·late (dē-pŏp′yə-lāt′) *v.* To lower greatly the population of, as by disease or massacre. **–de·pop′u·la′tion** *n.*

de·port (dĭ-pôrt′, -pōrt′) *v.* **1.** To banish from a country. **2.** To behave or conduct (oneself) in a specified manner. **–de′por·ta′tion** *n.* **–de′port·ee′** *n.*

de·port·ment (dĭ-pôrt′mənt, -pōrt′-) *n.* Behavior : demeanor.

de·pose (dĭ-pōz′) *v.* **-posed, -posing. 1.** To remove from office or a powerful position. **2.** To testify under oath, esp. in writing. **–de·pos′a·ble** *adj.* **–de·pos′al** *n.*

de·pos·it (dĭ-pŏz′ĭt) *v.* **1.** To entrust (money) to a bank. **2.** To set or lay down : place. **3.** To put down (e.g., layers of sediment) by a natural process. **4.** To give as partial payment or security. **–de·pos′it** *n.* **–de·pos′i·tor** *n.*

dep·o·si·tion (dĕp′ə-zĭsh′ən) *n.* **1.** The act of deposing, as from office. **2.** The act of depositing. **3.** Testimony given under oath, esp. in writing. **4.** A deposit.

de·pos·i·to·ry (dĭ-pŏz′ĭ-tôr′ē, -tōr′ē) *n., pl.* **-ries.** A place where something is deposited for safekeeping : repository.

de·pot (dē′pō) *n.* **1.** A station. **2.** A warehouse. **3.** A place where military materials are stored or troops are assembled.

de·prave (dĭ-prāv′) *v.* **-praved, -prav·ing.** To debase morally : corrupt. **–de·praved′** *adj.* **–de·prav′i·ty** (-prăv′ĭ-tē) *n.*

dep·re·cate (dĕp′rĭ-kāt′) *v.* **-cat·ed, -cat·ing. 1.** To show disapproval of. **2.** To belittle : depreciate. **–dep′re·ca′tion** *n.* **–dep′re·ca′tor** *n.* **–dep′re·ca·to′ry** *adj.*

de·pre·ci·ate (dĭ-prē′shē-āt′) *v.* **-at·ed, -at·ing. 1.** To diminish or become diminished in value or price. **2.** To disparage. ☆**syns:** CHEAPEN, DEVALUATE, DEVALUE, DOWNGRADE, LOWER **–de·pre′ci·a′tion** *n.* **–de·pre′cia·to′ry** *adj.*

dep·re·da·tion (dĕp′rĭ-dā′shən) *n.* The act of destroying or marauding.

de·press (dĭ-prĕs′) *v.* **1.** To lower in spirits : sadden. **2.** To press down : lower. **3.** To diminish in price or value. **4.** To diminish the activity or force of. **–de·pres′sor** *n.*

de·pres·sant (dĭ-prĕs′ənt) *adj.* Serving to lower the rate of vital activities. *–n.* A depressant agent : sedative.

de·pressed (dĭ-prĕst′) *adj.* **1.** Low in spirits : dejected. **2.** Suffering from social and economic hardship. ☆**syns:** BACKWARD, DISADVANTAGED, IMPOVERISHED, UNDERPRIVILEGED.

de·pres·sion (dĭ-prĕsh′ən) *n.* **1.** The act of depressing or state of being depressed. **2.** An emotional disorder characterized by an inability to concentrate, insomnia, and feelings of guilt and dejection. **3.** A sunken or depressed area : hollow. **4.** A period of severe economic decline. **–de·pres′sive** *adj.*

de·prive (dĭ-prīv′) *v.* **-prived, -priv·ing. 1.** To take something away from. **2.** To keep from possessing or enjoying : deny. **–dep′ri·va′tion** (dĕp′rə-vā′shən) *n.*

dept. *abbr.* department.

depth (dĕpth) *n.* **1.** The quality or state of being deep. **2.** The extent, measurement, or dimension downward, inward, or backward. **3.** *often* **depths.** A deep part or place. **4.** The most profound or extreme stage or part. **5.** Mental complexity : profundity. **6.** The range of one's comprehension.

depth charge *n.* An explosive device designed to detonate underwater.

dep•u•ta•tion (dĕp′yə-tā′shən) *n.* **1.** DELEGATION 2. **2.** The act of deputing or the state of being deputed.

de•pute (dĭ-pyo͞ot′) *v.* **-put•ed, -put•ing.** To delegate.

dep•u•tize (dĕp′yə-tīz′) *v.* **-tized, -tiz•ing.** To appoint as a deputy.

dep•u•ty (dĕp′yə-tē) *n., pl.* **-ties. 1.** A person designated or authorized to act for or assist another. **2.** A representative in a legislative body in certain countries.

de•rail (dē-rāl′) *v.* To run or cause to run off the rails. **—de•rail′ment** *n.*

de•range (dĭ-rānj′) *v.* **-ranged, -rang•ing. 1.** To disturb the arrangement or normal condition of : disarrange. **2.** To make insane. **—de•range′ment** *n.*

der•by (dûr′bē; *Brit.* där′-) *n., pl.* **-bies. 1.** One of various annual horse races, esp. for 3-year-olds. **2.** A race open to all contestants. **3.** A stiff felt hat with a round crown and narrow, curved brim.

der•e•lict (dĕr′ə-lĭkt) *adj.* **1.** Negligent : remiss. **2.** Abandoned by an owner or guardian. *—n.* **1.** Abandoned property, esp. a ship abandoned at sea. **2.** A vagrant.

der•e•lic•tion (dĕr′ə-lĭk′shən) *n.* **1.** Willful neglect, as of responsibility. **2.** Abandonment.

de•ride (dĭ-rīd′) *v.* **-rid•ed, -rid•ing.** To laugh at or ridicule contemptuously. **—de•ri′sion** (-rĭzh′ən) *n.* **—de•ri′sive** *adj.* **—de•ri′sive•ly** *adv.* **—di•ri′so•ry** *adj.*

de ri•gueur (də rē-gûr′) *adj.* Required or prescribed by custom, manners, or fashion : socially obligatory.

der•i•va•tion (dĕr′ə-vā′shən) *n.* **1.** The act or process of deriving. **2.** The source of something : origin. **3.** Etymology. **4.** The process by which new words are formed from existing words, chiefly by the addition of affixes to roots, stems, or words.

de•riv•a•tive (dĭ-rĭv′ə-tĭv) *adj.* Obtained by derivation. *—n.* **1.** Something derived. **2.** A word formed by derivation.

de•rive (dĭ-rīv′) *v.* **-rived, -riv•ing. 1.** To obtain or receive from a source. **2.** To arrive at by reasoning : deduce. **3.** To trace the development or origin of (e.g., a word). **4.** To produce (a compound) from other substances by chemical reaction.

der•mal (dûr′məl) *also* **der•mic** (-mĭk) *adj.* Of or relating to the skin.

der•ma•ti•tis (dûr′mə-tī′tĭs) *n.* Skin inflammation.

der•ma•tol•o•gy (dûr′mə-tŏl′ə-jē) *n.* The medical study of skin physiology and pathology. **—der′ma•tol′o•gist** *n.*

der•o•gate (dĕr′ə-gāt′) *v.* **-gat•ed, -gat•ing. 1.** To take away : detract. **2.** To disparage. **—der′o•ga′tion** *n.*

de•rog•a•to•ry (dĭ-rŏg′ə-tôr′ē, -tōr′ē) *adj.* **1.** Tending to belittle : disparaging. **2.** Detracting. **—de•rog′a•to′ri•ly** *adv.*

der•rick (dĕr′ĭk) *n.* **1.** A machine for lifting and moving heavy objects : crane. **2.** A framework over a drilled hole, as an oil well, used to support boring equipment.

der•ri•ère *also* **der•ri•ere** (dĕr′ē-âr′) *n.* The buttocks.

der•ring-do (dĕr′ĭng-do͞o′) *n.* Daring action or spirit : daring.

der•rin•ger (dĕr′ĭn-jər) *n.* A short-barreled, pocket-sized pistol.

der•vish (dûr′vĭsh) *n.* A member of a Moslem religious order that engages in whirling dances.

DES (dē′ē-ĕs′) *n.* Diethylstilbestrol.

de•sal•i•nate (dē-săl′ə-nāt′) *v.* **-nat•ed, -nat•ing.** To desalinize.

de•sal•i•nize (dē-săl′ə-nīz′) *v.* **-nized, -niz•ing.** To remove (salt) from sea or saline water. **—de•sal′i•ni•za′tion** *n.*

de•salt (dē-sôlt′) *v.* To desalinize.

des•cant (dĕs′kănt′) *v.* **1.** To discourse at length. **2.** To play or sing part music.

Des•cartes (dā-kärt′), **René.** 1596–1650. French philosopher and mathematician.

de•scend (dĭ-sĕnd′) *v.* **1.** To move, come, or go from a higher to a lower level. **2.** To slope. **3. a.** To come down from a source : derive. **b.** To pass through inheritance. **4.** To arrive or attack suddenly.

de•scen•dant (dĭ-sĕn′dənt) *n.* **1.** An individual descended from another. **2.** Something derived from an earlier form or prototype. ☆***syns:*** CHILD, OFFSPRING, SCION *—adj. var. of* DESCENDENT.

de•scen•dent *also* **de•scen•dant** (dĭ-sĕn′dənt) *adj.* **1.** Moving downward : descending. **2.** Descending from an ancestor.

de•scent (dĭ-sĕnt′) *n.* **1.** The act or an instance of descending. **2.** A slope. **3.** Ancestry. **4.** A lowering or decline, as in status or level. **5.** A sudden onslaught.

de•scribe (dĭ-skrīb′) *v.* **-scribed, -scrib•ing. 1.** To give an account of in words. **2.** To trace or draw the outline of, (e.g., a circle). ☆***syns:*** NARRATE, RECITE, RECOUNT, RELATE, REPORT **—de•scrib′a•ble** *adj.* **—de•scrib′er** *n.*

de•scrip•tion (dĭ-skrĭp′shən) *n.* **1.** The act, process, or technique of describing. **2.** A statement or account that describes. **3.** A kind : type. **—de•scrip′tive** *adj.*

de•scry (dĭ-skrī′) *v.* **-scried, -scry•ing. 1.** To catch sight of : discern. **2.** To discover by investigation or close observation. **—de•scri′er** *n.*

des•e•crate (dĕs′ĭ-krāt′) *v.* **-crat•ed, -crat•ing.** To violate the sanctity of : profane. **—des′e•cra′tion** *n.*

de•seg•re•gate (dē-sĕg′rĭ-gāt′) *v.* To abolish segregation, esp. racial segregation, in. **—de•seg′re•ga′tion** *n.*

de•sen•si•tize (dē-sĕn′sĭ-tīz′) *v.* To make insensitive or less sensitive, as to pain. **—de•sen′si•tiz′er** *n.*

des•ert[1] (dĕz′ərt) *n.* A dry, barren region that can support little or no vegetation.

de•sert[2] (dĭ-zûrt′) *n.* **1.** *often* **deserts.** Something, esp. a punishment, that is warranted or merited. **2.** The fact or state of deserving reward or punishment.

de•sert[3] (dĭ-zûrt′) *v.* **1.** To abandon, esp. when most needed. **2.** To abandon (e.g., a military post) in violation of orders. **—de•sert′er** *n.* **—de•ser′tion** *n.*

de•serve (dĭ-zûrv′) *v.* **-served, -serv•ing.** To be worthy of : merit.

des•ic•cant (dĕs′ĭ-kənt) *n.* An agent, as silica gel, used to absorb moisture.

des•ic•cate (dĕs′ĭ-kāt′) *v.* **-cat•ed, -cat•ing.** To dry out completely : dehydrate. **—des′ic•ca′tion** *n.* **—des′ic•ca′tive** *adj.*

de•sid•er•a•tum (dĭ-sĭd′ə-rä′təm, -rā′-) *n., pl.* **-ta** (-tə). A necessary and desired thing.

de•sign (dĭ-zīn′) *v.* **1.** To think up : invent. **2.** To form a plan for <*design* a new marketing strategy> **3.** To have as a goal or intention. **4.** To plan by making preliminary sketches or outlines. *—n.* **1.** A drawing or sketch. **2.** The order or arrangement of the components and details of something in accordance with a plan. **3. a.** A decorative or artistic work. **b.** The art of creating designs. **4.** A plan : project. **5.** A well-thought-out purpose : intention. ☆***syns:*** BLUEPRINT, IDEA, LAYOUT, PLAN, SCHEMA, SCHEME, STRATEGY **—de•sign′ed•ly** *adv.* **—de•sign′er** *n.*

des•ig•nate (dĕz′ĭg-nāt′) *v.* **-nat•ed, -nat•ing. 1.** To point out : specify. **2.** To give a name or title to : characterize. **3.** To appoint or select, as for an office. **—des′ig•nate** (-nĭt) *adj.* **—des′ig•na′tion** *n.*

de•sign•ing (dĭ-zī′nĭng) *adj.* Crafty : conniving. **—de•sign′ing•ly** *adv.*

de•sir•a•ble (dĭ-zīr′ə-bəl) *adj.* **1.** Attractive, pleasing, or valuable. **2.** Worth wanting : advisable <a *desirable* tax reform> **—de•sir′a•bil′i•ty, de•sir′a•ble•ness** *n.*

de•sire (dĭ-zīr′) *v.* **-sired, -sir•ing. 1.** To hope or wish for ardently : crave. **2.** To ask for : request. ☆***syns:*** ACHE, CRAVE, HANKER, LONG, WISH, YEARN *—n.* **1.** A strong wish or longing : craving. **2.** A request or petition. **3.** Something desired. **4.** Sexual appetite : passion. **—de•sir′er** *n.*

de•sir•ous (dĭ-zīr′əs) *adj.* Desiring.

de•sist (dĭ-zĭst′, -sĭst′) *v.* To cease doing something : stop.

desk (dĕsk) *n.* **1.** A piece of furniture usu. with drawers or compartments and a level top for writing. **2.** A table, counter, or booth where specified services are performed. **3.** A department of a large organization in charge of a specified operation.

Des Moines (də moin′). Cap. of Iowa. *Pop.* 191,003.

des•o•late (dĕs′ə-lĭt) *adj.* **1.** Having no inhabitants : deserted. **2.** Made uninhabitable or useless. **3.** Dismal : dreary. **4.** Forlorn : forsaken. *—v.* (-lāt′) **-lat•ed, -lat•ing.** To make desolate. **—des′o•late•ly** *adv.*

des•o•la•tion (dĕs′ə-lā′shən) *n.* **1.** The act of desolating. **2.** The state of being desolate : devastation. **3.** A wasteland. **4.** Loneliness or sadness : misery.

de•spair (dĭ-spâr′) *n.* **1.** Complete absence of hope. **2.** Something destroying all hope. *—v.* To abandon all purpose or hope.

des•patch (dĭ-spăch′) *n. & v. var. of* DISPATCH.

des•per•a•do (dĕs′pə-rä′dō, -rā′-) *n., pl.* **-does** *or* **-dos.** A brazen, dangerous outlaw or criminal.

des•per•ate (dĕs′pər-ĭt, -prĭt) *adj.* **1.** Rash or violent out of despair. **2.** Almost hopeless : grave. **3.** Overpowering : intense.

des•per•a•tion (dĕs′pə-rā′shən) *n.* **1.** The state of being desperate. **2.** Rashness arising out of despair.

des•pi•ca•ble (dĕs′pĭ-kə-bəl, dĭ-spĭk′ə-) *adj.* Deserving scorn or contempt : vile. **—des′pi•ca•bly** *adv.*

de•spise (dĭ-spīz′) *v.* **-spised, -spis•ing. 1.** To regard with scorn or contempt : disdain. **2.** To regard as trivial or worthless. ☆***syns:*** ABHOR, CONTEMN, DISDAIN, SCORN

de•spite (dĭ-spīt′) *prep.* In spite of : notwithstanding.

de•spoil (dĭ-spoil′) *v.* To strip of property or possessions by force : pillage. **—de•spoil′er** *n.* **—de•spoil′ment** *n.*

de·spo·li·a·tion (dĭ-spō'lē-ā'shən) *n.* The act of despoiling or the state of being despoiled.
de·spond (dĭ-spŏnd') *v.* To become discouraged. *—n.* A state of despondency.
de·spon·den·cy (dĭ-spŏn'dən-sē) *n.* Depression of spirits from loss of hope. **—de·spon'dent** *adj.*
des·pot (dĕs'pət) *n.* **1.** An absolute ruler. **2.** A person who wields power oppressively. **—des·pot'ic** (dĭ-spŏt'ĭk) *adj.* **—des·pot'i·cal·ly** *adv.* **—des'pot·ism** *n.*
des·sert (dĭ-zûrt') *n.* A usu. sweet food, as pastry, served as the final course of a meal.
des·ti·na·tion (dĕs'tə-nā'shən) *n.* **1.** The place to which someone is going or something is sent. **2.** The purpose for which something is created or intended.
des·tine (dĕs'tĭn) *v.* **-tined, -tin·ing. 1.** To determine in advance : preordain. **2.** To assign for a specific end, use, or purpose. **3.** To be bound for a specified destination.
des·ti·ny (dĕs'tə-nē) *n., pl.* **-nies. 1.** The inevitable lot to which a person or thing is destined : fate. **2.** A predetermined or inevitable course of events.
des·ti·tute (dĕs'tĭ-to͞ot', -tyo͞ot') *adj.* **1.** Utterly devoid. **2.** Utterly impoverished : indigent. **—des'ti·tu'tion** *n.*
de·stroy (dĭ-stroi') *v.* **1.** To ruin thoroughly : spoil. **2.** To tear down or break up : raze. **3.** To kill.
de·stroy·er (dĭ-stroi'ər) *n.* **1.** One that destroys. **2.** A small, highly maneuverable warship.
de·struct (dĭ-strŭkt') *n.* The deliberate destruction of a space vehicle, missile, or rocket after launching.
de·struc·ti·ble (dĭ-strŭk'tə-bəl) *adj.* Capable of being destroyed.
de·struc·tion (dĭ-strŭk'shən) *n.* **1.** The act of destroying or the state of being destroyed. **2.** A cause or means of destroying. **—de·struc'tive** *adj.* **—de·struc'tive·ly** *adv.* **—de·struc'tive·ness** *n.*
des·ue·tude (dĕs'wĭ-to͞od', -tyo͞od') *n.* A state of disuse.
des·ul·to·ry (dĕs'əl-tôr'ē, -tōr'ē) *adj.* **1.** Marked by lack of continuity : disconnected. **2.** Aimless.
de·tach (dĭ-tăch') *v.* **1.** To disconnect : separate. **2.** To extricate oneself : withdraw. ✩***syns:*** DISCONNECT, DISENGAGE, UNCOUPLE, UNFASTEN **—de·tach'a·ble** *adj.*
de·tached (dĭ-tăcht') *adj.* **1.** Standing apart : separate. **2.** Not emotionally involved : indifferent. **3.** Impartial.
de·tach·ment (dĭ-tăch'mənt) *n.* **1. a.** The act or process of separating. **b.** The state of being separate. **2.** Indifference : aloofness. **3.** Impartiality. **4. a.** The dispatch of military personnel or equipment from a larger unit for special duty. **b.** A permanent military unit, usu. smaller than a platoon, organized for special duties.
de·tail (dĭ-tāl', dē'tāl') *n.* **1.** An individual part : particular. **2.** Particulars considered separately and in relation to a whole. **3.** Military personnel selected for a particular duty. *—v.* **1.** To report in detail. **2.** To name or state explicitly. **3.** To select and dispatch for a particular duty.
de·tain (dĭ-tān') *v.* **1.** To hold back : delay. **2.** To hold in custody : confine.
de·tect (dĭ-tĕkt') *v.* To find out or discover the nature, existence, or fact of. **—de·tect'a·ble, de·tect'i·ble** *adj.* **—de·tec'tion** *n.* **—de·tec'tor** *n.*
de·tec·tive (dĭ-tĕk'tĭv) *n.* A person, often a police officer, whose work is investigating and trying to solve crimes.
de·tent (dĭ-tĕnt') *n.* A pawl.
dé·tente (dā-täNt', -tänt') *n.* A relaxation or reduction of tension, as between nations.
de·ten·tion (dĭ-tĕn'shən) *n.* **1.** The act of detaining or state of being detained. **2.** A period of temporary custody that precedes disposition by a court. **3.** A forced delay.
de·ter (dĭ-tûr') *v.* **-terred, -ter·ring.** To discourage or prevent from acting, as by intimidation. **—de·ter'ment** *n.*
de·ter·gent (dĭ-tûr'jənt) *n.* Any of various usu. synthetic cleaning agents that are chemically different from soap.
de·te·ri·o·rate (dĭ-tîr'ē-ə-rāt') *v.* **-rat·ed, -rat·ing.** To worsen : degenerate.
de·ter·mi·nant (dĭ-tûr'mə-nənt) *n.* Something that influences or determines.
de·ter·mi·nate (dĭ-tûr'mə-nĭt) *adj.* Conclusively.
de·ter·mine (dĭ-tûr'mĭn) *v.* **-mined, -min·ing. 1.** To decide or settle authoritatively or conclusively. **2.** To limit in scope or extent : fix the limits of. **3.** To be the determinant of : regulate <Need will *determine* expenditures.> **4.** To reach a decision, as after consideration or calculation. **5.** To ascertain the extent, position, quality, or nature of something. ✩***syns:*** BOUND, DELIMIT, DEMARCATE, LIMIT **—de·ter'mi·na·ble** *adj.* **—de·ter'mi·na·bly** *adv.* **—de·ter'mi·na'tion** *n.*
de·ter·mined (dĭ-tûr'mĭnd) *adj.* **1.** Firm : resolute. **2.** Decided or resolved. **—de·ter'mined·ly** *adv.*
de·ter·rent (dĭ-tûr'ənt, -tŭr'-) *n.* Something that deters. *—adj.* Serving to deter. **—de·ter'rence** *n.*
de·test (dĭ-tĕst') *v.* To dislike strongly : abhor. **—de·test'a·ble** *adj.* **—de·test'a·bly** *adv.* **—de'tes·ta'tion** *n.*
de·throne (dē-thrōn') *v.* **-throned, -thron·ing.** To depose (e.g., a king).
det·o·nate (dĕt'n-āt') *v.* **-nat·ed, -nat·ing.** To explode violently.
det·o·na·tor (dĕt'n-ā'tər) *n.* A device, as a fuse or percussion cap, used to detonate an explosive.
de·tour (dē'to͝or', dĭ-to͝or') *n.* **1.** A road used temporarily instead of a main road. **2.** A deviation from a direct course of action. *—v.* To take or cause to take a detour.
de·tox·i·fy (dē-tŏk'sə-fī') *v.* **-fied, -fy·ing. 1.** To remove the effects of a toxic substance from (e.g., an alcoholic). **2.** To free from dependence on (e.g., drugs). **—de·tox'i·fi·ca'tion** *n.*
de·tract (dĭ-trăkt') *v.* **1.** To take away : diminish. **2.** To distract. **—de·trac'tion** *n.* **—de·trac'tive** *adj.* **—de·trac'tor** *n.*
de·train (dē-trān') *v.* To leave or cause to leave a railroad train.
det·ri·ment (dĕt'rə-mənt) *n.* **1.** Damage, injury, or loss. **2.** Something that causes damage, injury, or loss. **—det'ri·men'tal** *adj.* **—det'ri·men'tal·ly** *adv.*
de·tri·tus (dĭ-trī'təs) *n.* **1.** Loose fragments, esp. those formed by the disintegration of rocks. **2.** Debris.
De·troit (dĭ-troit'). City of SE Mich. *Pop.* 1,203,339.
deuce[1] (do͞os, dyo͞os) *n.* **1.** A playing card or side of a die with 2 figures or spots. **2.** A tie in which each side has 40 points.
deuce[2] (do͞os, dyo͞os) *n.* The devil. Used as a mild oath.
de·us ex ma·chi·na (dā'əs ĕks mä'kə-nə, -nä', măk'ə-nə) *n.* A character, device, or event suddenly introduced into a literary work to resolve a difficulty.
deu·te·ri·um (do͞o-tîr'ē-əm, dyo͞o-) *n.* An isotope of hydrogen that contains 1 more neutron in its nucleus than hydrogen does.
Deu·ter·on·o·my (do͞o'tə-rŏn'ə-mē, dyo͞o'-) *n.* See BIBLE TABLE.
deut·sche mark (doi'chə märk') *n.* See CURRENCY table.
de·val·u·ate (dē-văl'yo͞o-āt') *v.* **-at·ed, -at·ing. 1.** To lessen or annul the value of. **2.** To lower the exchange value of (currency) by lowering its gold equivalency. **—de·val'u·a'tion** *n.*
de·val·ue (dē-văl'yo͞o) *v.* To devaluate.
dev·as·tate (dĕv'ə-stāt') *v.* **-tat·ed, -tat·ing. 1.** To destroy : ruin. **2.** To overwhelm : overpower. **—dev'as·ta'tion** *n.*
de·vel·op (dĭ-vĕl'əp) *v.* **1.** To realize the possibilities of. **2.** To grow, unfold, or expand gradually. **3.** To make more available or effective. **4.** To elaborate or enlarge. **5.** To acquire gradually. **6.** To process (a photosensitive material) to make the latent image visible. **7.** To progress from earlier to later stages of maturation. **—de·vel'op·er** *n.* **—de·vel'op·ment** *n.* **—de·vel'op·men'tal** *adj.*
de·vi·ant (dē'vē-ənt) *adj.* Deviating from a norm, esp. from an accepted standard. **—de'vi·ance** *n.* **—de'vi·ant** *n.*
de·vi·ate (dē'vē-āt') *v.* **-at·ed, -at·ing.** To turn or cause to turn away from a specified course or prescribed behavior. *—n.* (-ĭt). A deviant person. **—de'vi·a'tion** *n.*
de·vice (dĭ-vīs') *n.* **1.** Something constructed for a specific purpose, esp. a machine. **2.** A plan or scheme : stratagem. **3.** An emblem or motto, esp. in heraldry.
dev·il (dĕv'əl) *n.* **1.** *often* **Devil.** The major spirit of evil, ruler of Hell, and foe of God : Satan. **2.** A subordinate evil spirit : demon. **3.** A wicked or malevolent person. **4.** A person : individual <you lucky *devil*> **5.** An energetic, daring, or clever person. **6.** A printer's apprentice. *—v.* **-iled, -il·ing** *or* **-illed, -il·ling. 1.** To annoy, torment, or harass. **2.** To season (food) highly.
dev·il·ish (dĕv'ə-lĭsh) *adj.* **1.** Of, resembling, or characteristic of a devil : fiendish. **2.** *Informal.* Extreme : excessive.
dev·il-may-care (dĕv'əl-mā-kâr') *adj.* **1.** Reckless. **2.** Rakish and carefree.
dev·il·ment (dĕv'əl-mənt) *n.* Mischief.
devil's advocate *n.* A person who opposes an argument with which he or she may not disagree, as for the sake of argument or to determine its validity.
dev·il·try (dĕv'əl-trē) *also* **dev·il·ry** (-əl-rē) *n., pl.* **-tries** *also* **-ries.** Wanton or reckless mischief.
de·vi·ous (dē'vē-əs) *adj.* **1.** Wandering from a direct or straight course. **2.** Straying from a proper way : erring. **3.** Not straightforward : shifty. **—de'vi·ous·ness** *n.*
de·vise (dĭ-vīz') *v.* **-vised, -vis·ing. 1.** To form or arrange mentally : contrive <*devise* a plan> **2.** *Law.* To give or transmit (real property) by will. *—n. Law.* **1.** The act of giving or transmitting real property by will. **2.** A will or clause in a will that devises real property.

de·vi·tal·ize (dē-vīt′l-īz′) *v.* To reduce or destroy the vitality of.
de·void (dĭ-void′) *adj.* Utterly lacking.
de·voir (dəv-wär′, dĕv′wär′) *n.* **1.** *often* **devoirs.** An act or expression of respect or courtesy : civility. **2.** Responsibility or duty.
de·volve (dĭ-vŏlv′) *v.* **-volved, -volv·ing.** To hand down or delegate to another.
de·vote (dĭ-vōt′) *v.* **-vot·ed, -vot·ing. 1.** To give or apply (one's time, attention, or self) completely. **2.** To consecrate : hallow. **3.** To set aside for a special use <money *devoted* to research>
de·vot·ed (dĭ-vō′tĭd) *adj.* **1.** Showing ardent attachment or loyalty. **2.** Affectionate. **—de·vot′ed·ly** *adv.*
dev·o·tee (dĕv′ə-tē′, -tā′) *n.* A zealous enthusiast or supporter.
de·vo·tion (dĭ-vō′shən) *n.* **1.** Ardent attachment or loyalty. **2.** Religious zeal : piety. **3.** *often* **devotions.** An act of religious observance, esp. private prayer.
de·vour (dĭ-vour′) *v.* **1.** To eat up ravenously. **2.** To destroy or waste. **3.** To take in enthusiastically <*devour* a spy novel> **4.** To engulf. **—de·vour′er** *n.*
de·vout (dĭ-vout′) *adj.* **1.** Extremely religious : pious. **2.** Displaying piety or reverence. **3.** Showing sincerity : earnest. **—de·vout′ly** *adv.* **—de·vout′ness** *n.*
dew (do͞o, dyo͞o) *n.* **1.** Moisture condensed from the atmosphere onto cool surfaces, usu. at night. **2.** Something moist, refreshing, or pure. **—dew′y** *adj.*
DEW *abbr.* distant early warning.
dew·ber·ry (do͞o′bĕr′ē, dyo͞o′-) *n.* A trailing form of the blackberry.
dew·claw (do͞o′klô′, dyo͞o′-) *n.* A vestigial digit on the foot of some mammals.
dew·lap (do͞o′lăp′, dyo͞o′-) *n.* A loose fold of skin that hangs from the neck of certain animals, as cattle.
dew point *n.* The temperature at which dew condenses from the air.
dex·ter·i·ty (dĕk-stĕr′ĭ-tē) *n.* **1.** Proficiency in using the body or hands : adroitness. **2.** Mental agility : cleverness.
dex·ter·ous (dĕk′stər-əs, -strəs) *also* **dex·trous** (-strəs) *adj.* **1.** Skillful or adroit in using the hands, body, or mind. **2.** Performed with dexterity. ☆***syns:*** ADROIT, DEFT, FACILE, NIMBLE, SLICK **—dex′ter·ous·ly** *adv.* **—dex′ter·ous·ness** *n.*
dex·trose (dĕk′strōs′) *n.* A sugar found in plant and animal tissue and derived synthetically from starch.
dia. *abbr.* diameter.
di·a·be·tes (dī′ə-bē′tĭs, -tēz) *n.* A metabolic disorder characterized by excess sugar in the blood and urine, persistent thirst, and excessive discharge of urine. **—di′a·bet′ic** (-bĕt′ĭk) *adj.* & *n.*
di·a·bol·ic (dī′ə-bŏl′ĭk) *also* **di·a·bol·i·cal** (-ĭ-kəl) *adj.* Exceedingly wicked : fiendish. **—di′a·bol′i·cal·ly** *adv.*
di·a·crit·ic (dī′ə-krĭt′ĭk) *n.* A mark, as a circumflex, added to a letter to indicate a special phonetic value or to distinguish words otherwise graphically identical. **—di′a·crit′i·cal, di′a·crit′ic** *adj.*
di·a·dem (dī′ə-dĕm′) *n.* A headband or crown worn esp. as an emblem of royalty.
di·aer·e·sis (dī-ĕr′ĭ-sĭs) *n. var. of* DIERESIS.
di·ag·no·sis (dī′əg-nō′sĭs) *n., pl.* **-ses** (-sēz′). **1.** Identification, as of a disease, by analysis and examination. **2.** The result of diagnosis. **—di′ag·nose′** *v.* **—di′ag·nos′tic** (-nŏs′tĭk) *adj.* **—di′ag·nos·ti′cian** *n.*
di·ag·o·nal (dī-ăg′ə-nəl) *adj.* **1.** *Math.* Joining 2 opposite corners of a polygon that are not adjacent. **2.** Slanting. *—n.* A diagonal plane or line. **—di·ag′o·nal·ly** *adv.*
di·a·gram (dī′ə-grăm′) *n.* A plan, sketch, drawing, or outline designed to explain, demonstrate, or clarify the relationship among parts of a whole or to illustrate how something works. **—di′a·gram′** *v.* **—di′a·gram·mat′ic** (-grə-măt′ĭk), **di′a·gram·mat′i·cal** *adj.* **—di′a·gram·mat′i·cal·ly** *adv.*
di·al (dī′əl) *n.* **1.** A graduated, usu. circular face on which a measurement, as speed, is indicated by a moving pointer. **2. a.** A rotatable disk with numbers and letters that electronically establishes a connection with the number to which a telephone call is made. **b.** The control that selects the station to which a radio or television receiver is tuned. **3. a.** A clockface. **b.** A sundial. *—v.* **-aled, -al·ing** *or* **-alled, -al·ling. 1.** To select or indicate by manipulating a dial. **2.** To call on a telephone.
di·a·lect (dī′ə-lĕkt′) *n.* A regional form of a language. **—di′a·lec′tal** *adj.*
di·a·lec·tic (dī′ə-lĕk′tĭk) *n.* *often* **dialectics** (*sing. in number*). A system of argument or exposition in which the conflict between contradictory facts or ideas is resolved. **—di′a·lec′ti·cal, di′a·lec′tic** *adj.*
di·a·logue *also* **di·a·log** (dī′ə-lôg′, -lŏg′) *n.* **1.** A conversation between 2 or more persons. **2.** A conversational passage in a literary work.
di·al·y·sis (dī-ăl′ĭ-sĭs) *n., pl.* **-ses** (-sēz′). Separation of smaller substances from larger molecules or crystalloid from colloidal particles in a solution by diffusion through semipermeable membranes.
di·am·e·ter (dī-ăm′ĭ-tər) *n.* **1. a.** *Math.* A straight line segment that passes through the center of a circle or sphere with both of its ends on the boundary. **b.** The measure of a diameter. **2.** Thickness or width.
di·a·met·ri·cal (dī′ə-mĕt′rĭ-kəl) *also* **di·a·met·ric** (-rĭk) *adj.* **1.** Of, relating to, or along a diameter. **2.** Being exactly opposite : contrary. **—di′a·met′ri·cal·ly** *adv.*
dia·mond (dī′mənd, dī′ə-) *n.* **1.** A very hard, highly refractive colorless or white crystalline of carbon used as a gemstone and as an industrial abrasive. **2.** A lozenge or rhombus. **3. a.** A playing card with a red, lozenge-shaped figure. **b. diamonds** (*sing. or pl. in number*). The suit comprising cards marked with this figure. **4.** *Baseball.* **a.** An infield. **b.** The entire playing field.
dia·mond·back (dī′mənd-băk′, dī′ə-) *n.* A large, venomous rattlesnake of the genus *Crotalus,* of the S and W U.S. and Mexico.
di·an·thus (dī-ăn′thəs) *n.* A plant of the genus *Dianthus,* including carnations and pinks.
di·a·pa·son (dī′ə-pā′zən, -sən) *n.* **1.** The full range of an instrument or voice. **2.** Either of 2 principal stops on a pipe organ that form the tonal basis for the entire scale.
di·a·per (dī′ə-pər, dī′pər) *n.* A folded piece of absorbent material placed between a baby's legs and fastened at the waist. *—v.* To put a diaper on.
di·aph·a·nous (dī-ăf′ə-nəs) *adj.* **1.** Of such fine texture as to be transparent or translucent. **2.** Delicate in form. **3.** Vague or insubstantial <*diaphanous* fantasies> **—di·aph′a·nous·ly** *adv.*
di·a·phragm (dī′ə-frăm′) *n.* **1. a.** *Anat.* A muscular membranous partition separating the abdominal and thoracic cavities. **b.** A membranous part that separates or divides. **2.** A thin disk, esp. in a microphone, whose vibrations transform sound waves into electric signals or electric signals into sound waves. **3.** A contraceptive device consisting of a usu. rubber disklike cap that covers the uterine cervix.
di·ar·rhe·a *also* **di·ar·rhoe·a** (dī′ə-rē′ə) *n.* Excessively frequent, loose bowel movements.
di·a·ry (dī′ə-rē) *n., pl.* **-ries. 1.** A daily record, esp. a personal record of events, experiences, and observations : journal. **2.** A book for keeping a diary. **—di′a·rist** *n.*
di·as·to·le (dī-ăs′tə-lē) *n. Physiol.* Normal rhythmic dilatation and relaxation of the heart cavities during which they are filled with blood. **—di′a·stol′ic** (-ə-stŏl′ĭk) *adj.*
di·as·tro·phism (dī-ăs′trə-fĭz′əm) *n.* The process by which the major features of the earth's crust, as mountains and continents, are formed.
di·a·ther·my (dī′ə-thûr′mē) *n.* The therapeutic induction of heat in bodily tissues by high-frequency electromagnetic waves. **—di′a·ther′mic** *adj.*
di·a·tom (dī′ə-tŏm′) *n.* Any of various tiny planktonic algae of the class Bacillariophyceae, with siliceous cell walls consisting of 2 overlapping symmetrical parts.
di·a·tom·ic (dī′ə-tŏm′ĭk) *adj.* Having 2 atoms in a molecule.
di·a·ton·ic (dī′ə-tŏn′ĭk) *adj.* Of or relating to a standard major or minor musical scale with 8 tones and no chromatic deviations.
di·a·tribe (dī′ə-trīb′) *n.* A bitter, often abusive criticism or denunciation.
dib·ble (dĭb′əl) *n.* A pointed garden tool used to make holes in soil, esp. for planting seedlings or bulbs. **—dib′ble** *v.*
dice (dīs) *n., pl.* **dice. 1. a.** *pl. of* DIE[2] 2. **b.** A game of chance using dice. **2.** *pl. also* **dic·es.** A small cube, as of food. *—v.* **diced, dic·ing. 1.** To play or gamble with dice. **2.** To cut (food) into small cubes.
di·chlo·ride (dī-klôr′īd′, -klōr′-) *n.* A binary chemical compound containing 2 chloride atoms per molecule.
di·chot·o·my (dī-kŏt′ə-mē) *n., pl.* **-mies.** Division into 2 usu. contradictory parts or opinions. **—di·chot′o·mous** *adj.*
di·chro·mate (dī-krō′māt′, dī′krō-) *n.* A chemical compound with 2 chromium atoms per anion.
dick (dĭk) *n. Slang.* A detective.
Dick·ens (dĭk′ənz), **Charles John Huffam.** 1812–70. English novelist. **—Dick·en′si·an** (dĭ-kĕn′zē-ən) *adj.*
dick·er (dĭk′ər) *v.* To haggle or bargain.
dick·ey *also* **dick·ie** *or* **dick·y** (dĭk′ē) *n., pl.* **-eys** *also* **-ies. 1.** A woman's blouse front worn under a suit jacket or low-necked garment. **2.** A man's detachable shirt front. **3.** A small bird.
di·cot·y·le·don (dī-kŏt′l-ēd′n) *n.* A plant of the subclass

Dicotyledonae, marked by a pair of seed leaves appearing at germination. **—di•cot'y•le'don•ous** *adj.*

dic•tate (dĭk'tāt', dĭk-tāt') *v.* **-tat•ed, -tat•ing. 1.** To speak or read aloud for another to transcribe or record. **2.** To issue or command authoritatively. *—n.* (dĭk'tāt'). A directive, command, or guiding principle. **—dic•ta'tion** *n.*

dic•ta•tor (dĭk'tā'tər, dĭk-tā'-) *n.* **1. a.** A ruler with absolute authority and supreme governmental jurisdiction. **b.** A tyrant. **2.** One who dictates. **—dic•ta'tor•ship'** *n.*

dic•ta•to•ri•al (dĭk'tə-tôr'ē-əl, -tōr-) *adj.* **1.** Tending to dictate : domineering. **2.** Relating to or characteristic of a dictator : autocratic. ☆**syns:** BOSSY, DOGMATIC, IMPERIOUS, MASTERFUL, OVERBEARING, PEREMPTORY **—dic'ta•to'ri•al•ly** *adv.*

dic•tion (dĭk'shən) *n.* **1.** Selection and usage of words in writing or speaking. **2.** Enunciation.

dic•tion•ar•y (dĭk'shə-nĕr'ē) *n., pl.* **-ies.** A reference book containing an explanatory alphabetical list of words with definitions, pronunciations, and often other information, such as synonym lists.

dic•tum (dĭk'təm) *n., pl.* **-ta** (tə) *or* **-tums. 1.** A dogmatic and authoritative statement. **2.** A popular saying : maxim.

did (dĭd) *v. p.t. of* DO.

di•dac•tic (dī-dăk'tĭk) *also* **di•dac•ti•cal** (-tĭ-kəl) *adj.* **1.** Intended to instruct. **2.** Morally instructive. **3.** Inclined to teach or moralize excessively.

did•dle (dĭd'l) *v.* **-dled, -dling. 1.** To swindle : cheat. **2.** To waste time.

did•n't (dĭd'nt). Did not.

di•do (dī'dō) *n., pl.* **-dos** *or* **-does.** *Informal.* A mischievous antic : caper.

die[1] (dī) *v.* **died, dy•ing. 1.** To stop living : expire. **2.** To lose vitality or force : subside. **3.** To cease existing, esp. by degrees : fade. **4.** *Informal.* To desire intensely <*dying* to buy a house> **5.** To cease operation : stop <The engine suddenly *died.*> ☆**syns:** CROAK, DECEASE, DEPART, EXPIRE, GO, PASS, PERISH, SUCCUMB

die[2] (dī) *n.* **1.** *pl.* **dies.** A device used to shape material by stamping or punching. **2.** *pl.* **dice** (dīs). A small cube marked on each side with from 1 to 6 dots, usu. used in pairs in games.

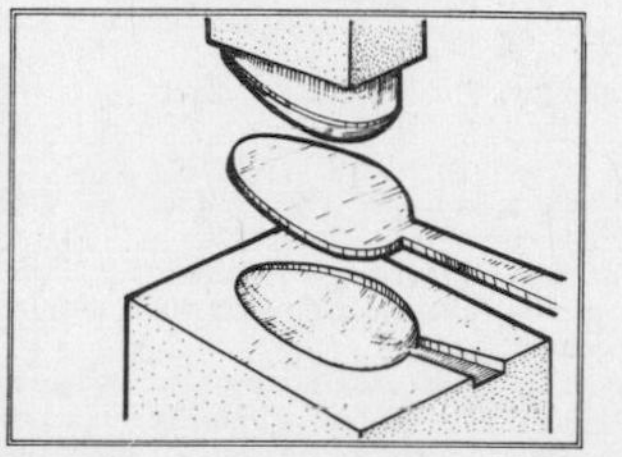

die[2]

die•hard (dī'härd') *n.* One who tenaciously resists change or refuses to abandon a position. **—die'hard'** *adj.*

diel•drin (dēl'drĭn) *n.* A persistent and highly toxic insecticide.

di•e•lec•tric (dī'ĭ-lĕk'trĭk) *n.* A nonconductor of electricity.

di•er•e•sis *also* **di•aer•e•sis** (dī-ĕr'ĭ-sĭs) *n., pl.* **-ses** (-sēz'). A mark (¨) over a vowel to indicate that it is to be pronounced in a separate syllable.

die•sel (dē'zəl, -səl) *n.* **1.** A diesel engine. **2.** A vehicle driven by a diesel engine.

diesel engine *n.* An internal-combustion engine in which an air-fuel mixture is ignited by heat generated from high compression in the cylinder.

di•et[1] (dī'ĭt) *n.* **1.** Food and drink usu. or habitually consumed. **2.** A regulated selection of foods, esp. as medically prescribed. **3.** Something taken or provided regularly <a *diet* of horror movies> *—v.* To eat or cause to eat according to a prescribed regimen. **—di'e•tar'y** *adj.* **—di'et•er** *n.*

di•et[2] (dī'ĭt) *n.* A legislature : assembly.

di•e•tet•ics (dī'ĭ-tĕt'ĭks) *n. (sing. in number).* The study of diet and its relationship to health and hygiene. **—di'e•tet'ic** *adj.* **—di'e•ti'tian, di'e•ti'cian** *n.*

di•eth•yl•stil•bes•trol (dī-ĕth'əl-stĭl-bĕs'trōl', -trôl') *n.* A synthetic estrogen used esp. to treat menstrual disorders.

dif•fer (dĭf'ər) *v.* **1.** To be dissimilar. **2.** To have a different opinion : disagree.

dif•fer•ence (dĭf'ər-əns, dĭf'rəns) *n.* **1.** The quality, state, or degree of being different. **2.** A disagreement or controversy or the cause of one. **3.** *Math.* The amount by which a number or quantity is greater or less than another.

dif•fer•ent (dĭf'ər-ənt, dĭf'rənt) *adj.* **1.** Having dissimilarities : unlike. **2.** Separate, distinct, or varied. **3.** Differing from others : unusual. ☆**syns:** DISPARATE, DISSIMILAR, UNLIKE **—dif'fer•ent•ly** *adv.*

dif•fer•en•tial (dĭf'ə-rĕn'shəl) *adj.* Of, relating to, or showing a difference. *—n.* **1.** The degree or amount to which similar things differ. **2.** A differential gear.

differential calculus *n. Math.* The variation of a function with respect to changes in independent variables.

differential gear *n.* An arrangement of gears used on the powered axle of automotive vehicles to allow different rates of wheel rotation, as on curves.

dif•fer•en•ti•ate (dĭf'ə-rĕn'shē-āt') *v.* **-at•ed, -at•ing. 1.** To distinguish, state, or show the difference. **2.** To make or become different. **—dif'fer•en'ti•a'tion** *n.*

dif•fi•cult (dĭf'ĭ-kŭlt', -kəlt) *adj.* **1.** Hard to do, achieve, understand, or master. **2.** Hard to please or satisfy. ☆**syns:** HARD, KNOTTY, TOUGH

dif•fi•cul•ty (dĭf'ĭ-kŭl'tē, -kəl-tē) *n., pl.* **-ties. 1.** The state or quality of being difficult. **2.** Something requiring great effort. **3.** A cause of trouble or worry. **4.** Conflicts or problems <emotional *difficulties*><financial *difficulties*>

dif•fi•dent (dĭf'ĭ-dənt) *adj.* Shy : timid. **—dif'fi•dence** *n.* **—dif'fi•dent•ly** *adv.*

dif•frac•tion (dĭ-frăk'shən) *n.* The deflection of radiation, esp. a beam of light as it passes an obstacle or aperture.

dif•fuse (dĭ-fyōōz') *v.* **-fused, -fus•ing.** To pour out and cause to spread freely. *—adj.* (-fyōōs'). **1.** Widely scattered. **2.** Wordy : verbose. **—dif•fu'sion** *n.*

dig (dĭg) *v.* **dug** (dŭg), **dig•ging. 1.** To turn over, break up, or remove (e.g., earth), as with a shovel. **2.** To make (a hole) by or as if by digging. **3.** To learn by investigation or research <*dug* up the facts> **4.** To prod against <*dug* me in the back> **5.** *Slang.* To understand, appreciate, or enjoy. *—n.* **1.** A poke : nudge. **2.** A gibe or taunt. **3.** An archaeological excavation. **—dig in. 1.** *Informal.* **a.** To begin to work intensively. **b.** To begin to eat. **2.** To entrench oneself.

di•gest (dĭ-jĕst', dī-) *v.* **1.** To transform (food) into an assimilable state, as by chemical and muscular action in the alimentary canal. **2.** To assimilate mentally. **3.** To organize, usu. by classifying or summarizing. *—n.* (dī'jĕst'). A systematic arrangement of condensed material : synopsis. **—di•gest'i•bil'i•ty** *n.* **—di•gest'i•ble** *adj.* **—di•ges'tion** *n.* **—di•ges'tive** *adj.*

dig•it (dĭj'ĭt) *n.* **1.** A finger or toe. **2.** Any of the Arabic numerals 0 through 9.

dig•i•tal (dĭj'ĭ-təl) *adj.* **1.** Of, like, or involving a digit, esp. a finger. **2.** Expressed in digits, esp. for computer use. **3.** Giving a reading in digits <a *digital* watch>

digital computer *n.* A computer that uses data represented as digits to perform operations.

dig•i•tal•is (dĭj'ĭ-tăl'ĭs) *n.* **1.** A plant of the genus *Digitalis,* which includes the foxgloves. **2.** A drug prepared from digitalis, used as a cardiac stimulant.

dig•ni•fied (dĭg'nə-fīd') *adj.* Possessing or showing dignity : poised.

dig•ni•fy (dĭg'nə-fī') *v.* **-fied, -fy•ing.** To give dignity or distinction to.

dig•ni•tar•y (dĭg'nĭ-tĕr'ē) *n., pl.* **-ies.** A high-ranking, influential person : notable. ☆**syns:** BIG SHOT, BIG WHEEL, BIGWIG, EMINENCE, LEADER, LION, LUMINARY, NABOB, NOTABILITY, NOTABLE, PERSONAGE, PERSONALITY, SOMEBODY, SOMEONE, VIP

dig•ni•ty (dĭg'nĭ-tē) *n., pl.* **-ties. 1.** The state of being esteemed or honored. **2.** Poise or formal reserve in appearance and demeanor. **3.** A high rank or office.

di•graph (dī'grăf') *n.* A pair of letters, as the *ea* in *seat,* that represents a single sound. **—di•graph'ic** *adj.*

di•gress (dĭ-grĕs', dī-) *v.* To wander or turn away from the main subject in a discourse. **—di•gres'sion** *n.* **—di•gres'sive** *adj.* **—di•gres'sive•ly** *adv.*

dik-dik (dĭk'dĭk') *n.* A very small African antelope of the genus *Madoqua.*

dike (dīk) *n.* An embankment, esp. of earth, built to control flood waters : levee.

di•lap•i•dat•ed (dĭ-lăp'ĭ-dā'tĭd) *adj.* In a state of disrepair or decay. **—di•lap'i•da'tion** *n.*

di•late (dī-lāt', dī'lāt') *v.* **-lat•ed, -lat•ing.** To make or become enlarged : expand. **—di•lat'a•ble** *adj.* **—di•la'tion, dil'a•ta'tion** (dĭl'ə-tā'shən) *n.* **—di•la'tor** *n.*

dil•a•to•ry (dĭl'ə-tôr'ē, -tōr'ē) *adj.* **1.** Tending to cause or causing delay. **2.** Marked by procrastination. **—dil'a•to'ri•ly** *adv.*

di•lem•ma (dĭ-lĕm'ə) *n.* **1.** A choice between evenly balanced alternatives. **2.** A predicament defying satisfactory solution.

dil•et•tante (dĭl'ĭ-tänt', -tän'tē, -tănt', -tăn'tē, dĭl'ĭ-tänt') *n., pl.* **-tantes** *or* **-tan•ti** (-tän'tē, -tăn'-). One whose interest in something, as art, is superficial and amateurish. **—dil'et•tan'tism** *n.*

dil•i•gent (dĭl′ə-jənt) *adj.* Marked by persevering, painstaking effort : assiduous. **–dil′i•gence** *n.* **–dil′i•gent•ly** *adv.*
dill (dĭl) *n.* An aromatic herb, *Anethum graveolens,* bearing aromatic leaves and seeds used as seasoning.
dil•ly (dĭl′ē) *n., pl.* **-lies.** *Slang.* One that is extraordinary.
dil•ly•dal•ly (dĭl′ē-dăl′ē) *v.* **-lied, -ly•ing.** To waste time by dawdling or hesitating.
di•lute (dĭ-lo͞ot′, dī-) *v.* **-lut•ed, -lut•ing.** To thin or reduce the concentration or strength of by or as if by admixture. ☆**syns:** CUT, THIN, WEAKEN *–adj.* Reduced in strength : diluted. **–di•lu′tion** *n.*
dim (dĭm) *adj.* **dim•mer, dim•mest. 1.** Minimally lighted. **2.** Faint : indistinct. **3.** Dull. **4.** Lacking sharp perception or clarity of understanding. **5.** Negative or pessimistic. *–v.* **dimmed, dim•ming. 1.** To make or become dim. **2.** To reduce the light of. **–dim′ly** *adv.* **–dim′ness** *n.*
dim. *abbr.* dimension.
dime (dīm) *n.* A U.S. coin worth 10 cents.
di•men•sion (dĭ-mĕn′shən) *n.* **1.** A measure of extension, esp. height, width, or length. **2.** *often* **dimensions.** Scope or magnitude : extent. **–di•men′sion•al** *adj.* **–di•men′sion•al′i•ty** (-shə-năl′ĭ-tē) *n.*
di•min•ish (dĭ-mĭn′ĭsh) *v.* **1.** To make or become less or smaller. **2.** To detract from the prestige of : belittle. **3.** To taper. **–di•min′ish•a•ble** *adj.* **–di•min′ish•ment** *n.* **–dim′i•nu′tion** *n.*
di•min•u•en•do (dĭ-mĭn′yo͞o-ĕn′dō) *adv.* Decrescendo. **–di•min′u•en′do** *adj.* & *n.*
di•min•u•tive (dĭ-mĭn′yə-tĭv) *adj.* **1.** Very small : tiny. **2.** Designating certain suffixes that denote smallness of size, familiarity, youth, or affection, as *-ling* in *duckling.* **–di•min′u•tive** *n.*
dim•i•ty (dĭm′ĭ-tē) *n., pl.* **-ties.** A thin, usu. corded cotton fabric.
dim•mer (dĭm′ər) *n.* A device that reduces the intensity of an electric light.
dim•ple (dĭm′pəl) *n.* **1.** A small depression in the flesh, as in the cheek. **2.** A slight surface depression. *–v.* **-pled, -pling.** To form or produce dimples (in).
dim•wit (dĭm′wĭt′) *n. Slang.* A stupid person. **–dim′wit′ted** *adj.* **–dim′wit′ted•ly** *adv.* **–dim′wit′ted•ness** *n.*
din (dĭn) *n.* Loud, confused, continuous, and harsh noise.
di•nar (dĭ-när′) *n.* **1.** See CURRENCY TABLE. **2.** See *rial* at CURRENCY TABLE.
dine (dīn) *v.* **dined, din•ing. 1.** To eat dinner. **2.** To give dinner to.
din•er (dī′nər) *n.* **1.** One that dines. **2.** A dining car on a train. **3.** A restaurant usu. shaped like a railroad car.
di•nette (dī-nĕt′) *n.* A nook or small room for informal meals.
ding-a-ling (dĭng′ə-lĭng′) *n. Informal.* A silly person : nitwit.
din•ghy (dĭng′ē) *n., pl.* **-ghies. 1.** A small rowboat. **2.** An inflatable rubber life raft.
din•gle (dĭng′gəl) *n.* A dell.
din•go (dĭng′gō) *n., pl.* **-goes.** A wild dog, *Canis dingo,* of Australia.
din•gus (dĭng′əs) *n. Slang.* An object whose name is forgotten or unknown.
din•gy (dĭn′jē) *adj.* **-gi•er, -gi•est. 1.** Dirty and discolored, as from smoke : grimy. **2.** Squalid : dreary. **3.** Shabby or worn. **–din′gi•ly** *adv.* **–din′gi•ness** *n.*
din•ky (dĭng′kē) *adj.* **-ki•er, -ki•est.** *Informal.* Small or insignificant.
din•ner (dĭn′ər) *n.* **1.** The main meal of the day. **2.** A formal meal or banquet.
din•ner•ware (dĭn′ər-wâr′) *n.* **1.** Tableware other than cutlery and flatware used in serving a meal. **2.** A set of dishes.
di•no•saur (dī′nə-sôr′) *n.* Any of various extinct, often gigantic reptiles of the orders Saurischia and Ornithischia.
dint (dĭnt) *n.* **1.** Effort : force <won by *dint* of sheer perseverance> **2.** A dent.
di•o•cese (dī′ə-sĭs, -sēs′, -sēz′) *n.* The district or territory under the jurisdiction of a bishop. **–di•oc′e•san** (-ŏs′ĭ-sən) *adj.* & *n.*
di•ode (dī′ōd′) *n.* **1.** A vacuum tube having 2 electrodes, a cathode, and an anode. **2.** A 2-terminal semiconductor device used mainly as a rectifier.
Di•og•e•nes (dī-ŏj′ə-nēz′). 412?–323 B.C. Greek philosopher.
di•o•ram•a (dī′ə-răm′ə, -rä′mə) *n.* A 3-dimensional scene in miniature.
di•ox•in (dī-ŏk′sĭn) *n.* Any of several carcinogenic or teratogenic hydrocarbons that occur as impurities in petroleum-derived herbicides.
dip (dĭp) *v.* **dipped, dip•ping. 1.** To plunge briefly into a liquid. **2.** To scoop up : ladle. **3.** To lower and then immediately raise (e.g., a flag) in salute. **4.** To lower or drop suddenly : duck. **5.** To appear to sink <The sun *dipped* below the horizon.> **6.** To incline downward : slope. **7.** To investigate a subject superficially : dabble. **8.** To make inroads for money <*dipped* into their savings account> *–n.* **1.** An act of dipping, esp. a brief plunge into water. **2.** A liquid into which something is dipped. **3.** A quantity obtained by dipping. **4.** A downward course : drop <a *dip* in sales> **5.** *Slang.* A silly person.
diph•the•ri•a (dĭf-thîr′ē-ə, dĭp-) *n.* An acute febrile contagious disease caused by a bacillus and characterized by formation of false membranes in the throat and other air passages, causing respiratory difficulty.
diph•thong (dĭf′thông′, -thŏng′, dĭp′-) *n.* A single speech sound that begins with one vowel sound and moves to another in the same syllable, as *oi* in the word *oil.*
di•plo•ma (dĭ-plō′mə) *n.* A document issued by an educational institution showing that a person has earned a degree or finished a course of study.
di•plo•ma•cy (dĭ-plō′mə-sē) *n.* **1.** The practice or art of conducting international negotiations. **2.** Tact and skill in dealing with people.
dip•lo•mat (dĭp′lə-măt′) *n.* A person adroit at or employed in diplomacy. **–dip′lo•mat′ic** *adj.*
dip•per (dĭp′ər) *n.* **1.** One that dips. **2.** A container for dipping, esp. a long-handled cup for dipping water. **3. Dipper. a.** The Big Dipper. **b.** The Little Dipper.
dip•py (dĭp′ē) *adj.* **-pi•er, -pi•est.** Silly.
dip•so•ma•ni•a (dĭp′sə-mā′nē-ə, -mān′yə) *n.* An insatiable craving for alcohol. **–dip′so•ma′ni•ac′** (-mā′nē-ăk′) *n.* & *adj.*
dip•tych (dĭp′tĭk) *n.* A pair of carved or painted panels hinged together.

diptych

dir. *abbr.* director.
dire (dīr) *adj.* **dir•er, dir•est. 1.** Having or warning of terrible consequences : disastrous. **2.** Requiring urgent remedial action. **–dire′ful** *adj.* **–dire′ful•ly** *adv.*
di•rect (dĭ-rĕkt′, dī-) *v.* **1.** To regulate the affairs of : manage. **2.** To take authoritative charge of : control. **3.** To order : command. **4. a.** To guide (someone) toward a goal. **b.** To show the way to. **5.** To cause to move in a direct course. **6.** To address (e.g., a letter) to a destination. **7.** To instruct or supervise the performance of a work. *–adj.* **1.** Moving or lying in a straight line. **2.** Forthright : straightforward <a *direct* question> **3.** With nothing intervening : immediate <*direct* contact> **4.** By action of voters rather than through representatives or delegates. **5.** Without compromise : absolute <*direct* opposites> **6.** Of unbroken descent : lineal. **7.** Consisting of a person's exact words <a *direct* quote> *–adv.* Directly. **–di•rect′ness** *n.*
direct current *n.* An electric current that flows only in 1 direction.
di•rec•tion (dĭ-rĕk′shən, dī-) *n.* **1.** The act of directing. **2.** *often* **directions.** Instructions for doing something. **3.** An order or command. **4.** The line or path along which something travels, lies, or points. **5.** A trend. **–di•rec′tion•al** *adj.*
di•rec•tive (dĭ-rĕk′tĭv, dī-) *n.* An authoritative order or instruction.
di•rect•ly (dĭ-rĕkt′lē, dī-) *adv.* **1.** In a direct line. **2.** At once : immediately.
di•rec•tor (dĭ-rĕk′tər, dī-) *n.* **1.** One that directs : manager. **2.** One who guides or supervises the performers in a theatrical production. **3.** One of a group of persons who supervise the affairs of an institution or corporation. **–di•rec′tor•ship′** *n.*
di•rec•tor•ate (dĭ-rĕk′tər-ĭt, dī-) *n.* **1.** The position or office of a director. **2.** A body of directors.
di•rec•to•ry (dĭ-rĕk′tə-rē, dī-) *n., pl.* **-ries.** A book that lists data, as names and addresses, concerning a specific group of persons or organizations.
dirge (dûrj) *n.* A slow, mournful musical composition.
dir•ham (də-răm′) *n.* **1.** See CURRENCY table. **2.** See *riyal* at CURRENCY TABLE.
dir•i•gi•ble (dîr′ə-jə-bəl, dĭ-rĭj′ə-) *n.* An airship.
dirk (dûrk) *n.* A dagger.

dirn·dl (dûrn′dəl) *n.* A full-skirted dress with a gathered waistband.
dirt (dûrt) *n.* **1.** Earth or soil. **2.** A soiling substance, as grime. **3.** Profane or obscene language. **4.** Hateful or scandalous gossip.
dirt bike *n.* A lightweight motorbike for use on rough surfaces, as dirt roads or trails.
dirt-cheap (dûrt′chēp′) *adj. & adv.* Extremely cheap.
dirt·y (dûr′tē) *adj.* **-i·er, -i·est. 1.** Not clean : grimy. **2.** Lackluster in color. **3.** Menacing : hostile <gave me a *dirty* look> **4.** Rough or stormy, as weather. **5.** Unsportsmanlike. **6.** Indecent, obscene, or scandalous. ☆***syns:*** BLACK, FILTHY, GRIMY, GRUBBY, SOILED, UNCLEAN —*v.* **-ied, -y·ing.** To make or become soiled. **—dirt′i·ness** *n.*
dirty tricks *pl.n. Informal.* **1.** Covert intelligence operations. **2.** Unethical behavior, esp. in politics.
dis– *pref.* **1.** Not <*dis*similar> **2. a.** Absence of <*dis*interest> **b.** Opposite of <*dis*favor> See below for a list of self-explanatory words formed with the prefix **dis–.**
dis·a·ble (dĭs-ā′bəl) *v.* **-bled, -bling. 1.** To incapacitate or make powerless. **2.** To disqualify legally. ☆***syns:*** CRIPPLE, IMMOBILIZE, INCAPACITATE, KNOCK OUT, PARALYZE **—dis′a·bil′i·ty** (-ə-bĭl′ĭ-tē) *n.*
dis·a·buse (dĭs′ə-byo͞oz′) *v.* To free from a misconception or delusion.
dis·ad·van·tage (dĭs′əd-văn′tĭj) *n.* **1. a.** A handicap. **b.** An unfavorable circumstance. **2.** Damage or loss : detriment. **—dis·ad′van·ta′geous** (-ăd′vən-tā′jəs) *adj.*
dis·ad·van·taged (dĭs′əd-văn′tĭjd) *adj.* Suffering socioeconomic disadvantage.
dis·af·fect (dĭs′ə-fĕkt′) *v.* To cause to be discontented, disloyal, or resentful : estrange. **—dis′af·fect′ed** *adj.* **—dis′af·fect′ed·ly** *adv.* **—dis′af·fec′tion** *n.*
dis·a·gree (dĭs′ə-grē′) *v.* **1.** To fail to agree. **2.** To have a different opinion. **3.** To argue : quarrel. **4.** To cause adverse effects. **—dis′a·gree′ment** *n.*
dis·a·gree·a·ble (dĭs′ə-grē′ə-bəl) *adj.* **1.** Unpleasant or offensive. **2.** Quarrelsome : belligerent. **—dis′a·gree′a·ble·ness** *n.* **—dis′a·gree′a·bly** *adv.*
dis·al·low (dĭs′ə-lou′) *v.* To reject or refuse to allow. **—dis′al·low′ance** *n.*
dis·ap·pear (dĭs′ə-pîr′) *v.* **1.** To drop from sight : vanish. **2.** To cease to exist. **—dis′ap·pear′ance** *n.*
dis·ap·point (dĭs′ə-point′) *v.* To fail to satisfy the expectations, desires, or hopes of. **—dis′ap·point′ment** *n.*
dis·ap·pro·ba·tion (dĭs-ăp′rə-bā′shən) *n.* Moral disapproval : condemnation.
dis·ap·prove (dĭs′ə-pro͞ov′) *v.* **1.** To condemn. **2.** To refuse to approve : reject. **—dis′ap·prov′al** *n.*
dis·arm (dĭs-ärm′) *v.* **1.** To divest of weapons. **2.** To make harmless. **3.** To win the trust of. **4.** To reduce or abolish armed forces. **—dis·arm′a·ment** *n.*
dis·ar·range (dĭs′ə-rānj′) *v.* To disturb the order of. **—dis′ar·range′ment** *n.*
dis·ar·ray (dĭs′ə-rā′) *n.* **1.** A state of disorder or confusion. **2.** Disorderly dress. —*v.* To upset or throw into turmoil.
dis·as·sem·ble (dĭs′ə-sĕm′bəl) *v.* To take apart.
dis·as·so·ci·ate (dĭs′ə-sō′shē-āt′, -sē-) *v.* To dissociate. **—dis′as·so′ci·a′tion** *n.*
dis·as·ter (dĭ-zăs′tər) *n.* A grave occurrence having ruinous results. ☆***syns:*** CALAMITY, CATACLYSM, CATASTROPHE, TRAGEDY **—dis·as′trous** *adj.* **—dis·as′trous·ly** *adv.*
dis·a·vow (dĭs′ə-vou′) *v.* To deny or disclaim any knowledge of or responsibility for. **—dis′a·vow′al** *n.*
dis·band (dĭs-bănd′) *v.* To break up : disperse. **—dis·band′ment** *n.*
dis·bar (dĭs-bär′) *v.* To prohibit (a lawyer) from practicing law. **—dis·bar′ment** *n.*
dis·be·lieve (dĭs′bĭ-lēv′) *v.* To refuse to believe (in) : reject or deny. **—dis′be·lief′** *n.* **—dis′be·liev′er** *n.*
dis·burse (dĭs-bûrs′) *v.* **-bursed, -burs·ing.** To pay out. **—dis·burse′ment, dis·bur′sal** *n.* **—dis·burs′er** *n.*
disc (dĭsk) *n.* **1.** *also* **disk.** *Informal.* A phonograph record. **2.** *var. of* DISK.
disc. *abbr.* discount.
dis·card (dĭs-kärd′) *v.* **1.** To get rid of : junk. **2. a.** To throw out (a playing card) from one's hand. **b.** To play (a card other than a trump) from a suit unlike the card led. —*n.* (dĭs′kärd′). **1.** The act of discarding. **2.** One that is discarded.
disc brake *also* **disk brake** *n.* A brake whose retarding friction is generated between stationary pads and a rotating disk.
dis·cern (dĭ-sûrn′, -zûrn′) *v.* **1.** To perceive (something hidden or obscure) : detect. **2.** To perceive as separate and distinct : discriminate. **3.** To comprehend mentally. **—dis·cern′er** *n.* **—dis·cern′i·ble** *adj.* **—dis·cern′ment** *n.*
dis·cern·ing (dĭ-sûr′nĭng, -zûr′-) *adj.* Showing insight and judgment : perceptive. **—dis·cern′ing·ly** *adv.*
dis·charge (dĭs-chärj′) *v.* **1.** To relieve of a burden, load, or contents : unload. **2. a.** To release, as from confinement or duty. **b.** To dismiss from employment. **3.** To send or pour forth. **4.** To shoot or fire. **5.** To perform the obligations or requirements of (e.g., an office). **6.** To comply with the terms of (e.g., a promise or debt). **7.** To undergo or cause electrical discharge. —*n.* (dĭs′chärj′, dĭs-chärj′). **1.** The act of discharging or condition of being discharged. **2.** Something discharging or discharged.
dis·ci·ple (dĭ-sī′pəl) *n.* **1.** A person who believes in and helps dissseminate the teachings of a master. **2.** *often* **Disciple.** One of Christ's followers.
dis·ci·pli·nar·i·an (dĭs′ə-plə-nâr′ē-ən) *n.* A believer in or enforcer of stern discipline.
dis·ci·pline (dĭs′ə-plĭn) *n.* **1. a.** Training intended to elict a specified pattern of behavior or character. **b.** Behavior that results from such training. **2.** A condition of order based on obedience to authority. **3.** Punishment meant to correct or train. **4.** A set of methods or rules of conduct. **5.** A specific branch of knowledge or of teaching. —*v.* **-plined, -plin·ing. 1.** To train or develop by teaching and control. **2.** To penalize. **3.** To impose order on. **—dis′ci·pli·na′ry** *adj.*
disc jockey *n.* A radio announcer whose chief purpose is presenting and playing phonograph records.
dis·claim (dĭs-klām′) *v.* To deny a claim to or association with : disavow. **—dis·claim′er** *n.*
dis·close (dĭs-klōz′) *v.* To make known or open to view : expose. **—dis·clo′sure** *n.*
dis·co (dĭs′kō′) *n., pl.* **-cos.** A discotheque.
dis·col·or (dĭs-kŭl′ər) *v.* To make or become different in color.
dis·com·fit (dĭs-kŭm′fĭt) *v.* **1.** To thwart. **2.** To make upset or uneasy : disconcert. **—dis·com′fi·ture′** *n.*
dis·com·fort (dĭs-kŭm′fərt) *n.* **1.** Physical or mental distress. **2.** An annoyance or inconvenience. —*v.* To make uncomfortable.
dis·com·mode (dĭs′kə-mōd′) *v.* **-mod·ed, -mod·ing.** To inconvenience.

disaccommodate
disaccredit
disacidify
disacknowledge
disacknowledgment
disacquaintance
disacquainted
disamenity
disanchor
disannex
disanoint
disbalance
discommend
discommendable
discommodity
disconfirm
disconfirmation
discongruity
discongruous
disconsider
disconsonant
discrown
diseconomy
disedge
disedify
disembalm
disembellish
disembellishment
disembroil
disembroilment
disemploy
disemployment
disenable
disencourage
disencouragement
disendow
disendowment
disenjoy
disenjoyment
disenroll
disenrollment
disenthrall
disenthrallment
disentitle
disentomb
disentombment
disentrance
disentwine
disequilibrium
disfellowship
disforest
disgarrison
dishallow
dishorn
disimagine
disimpassioned
disimprison
disimprisonment
disimprove
disimprovement
disincarnate
disincarnation
disincorporate
disincorporation
disinflate
disinhibitory
disinvest
disinvite
disinvolve
disluster
disobligingly
disoccupation
dispauperize
dispeace
dispersonify
dispetal
dispope
disprivilege
disrelate
disrelation
disrespectable
disroof
disroot
disthrone
disunification
disuniform
disweapon
disyoke

dis•com•pose (dĭs′kəm-pōz′) *v.* **1.** To disrupt the composure or tranquillity of. **2.** To disorder. **—dis′com•po′sure** *n.*

dis•con•cert (dĭs′kən-sûrt′) *v.* To upset : discompose. **—dis′con•cert′ing•ly** *adv.*

dis•con•nect (dĭs′kə-nĕkt′) *v.* To interrupt or break the connection of or between. **—dis′con•nec′tion** *n.*

dis•con•nect•ed (dĭs′kə-nĕk′tĭd) *adj.* **1.** Not connected. **2.** Incoherent.

dis•con•so•late (dĭs-kŏn′sə-lĭt) *adj.* **1.** Beyond consolation : utterly dejected. **2.** Cheerless : gloomy <a *disconsolate* landscape> **—dis•con′so•late•ly** *adv.*

dis•con•tent (dĭs′kən-tĕnt′) *n.* Lack of contentment : dissatisfaction. **—dis′con•tent′ed** *adj.* **—dis′con•tent′ed•ly** *adv.*

dis•con•tin•ue (dĭs′kən-tĭn′yo͞o) *v.* **1.** To bring or come to an end : terminate. **2.** To stop trying, taking, or using : abandon. **—dis′con•tin′u•ance, dis′con•tin′u•a′tion** *n.*

dis•con•tin•u•ous (dĭs′kən-tĭn′yo͞o-əs) *adj.* Marked by gaps or interruptions. **—dis•con′ti•nu′i•ty** *n.*

dis•cord (dĭs′kôrd′) *n.* **1.** Lack of accord or harmony : dissension. **2.** A harsh or confused mingling of sounds. **3.** An unpleasant combination of musical sounds : dissonance. **—dis•cor′dant** *adj.*

dis•co•theque *also* **dis•co•thèque** (dĭs′kə-tĕk′, dĭs′kə-tĕk′) *n.* A nightclub featuring dancing to recorded or sometimes live music.

dis•count (dĭs′kount′, dĭs-kount′) *v.* **1.** To subtract or deduct, as from a price. **2.** To purchase, sell, or loan money on (a commercial paper, as a bill or note) after deducting the interest. **3.** To disregard or doubt (e.g., a rumor) as being unreliable or exaggerated. **4.** To make allowance for. **5.** To underestimate the significance of : minimize. *—n.* (dĭs′kount′). **1.** A reduction from a standard price or the full amount of a debt. **2.** The rate of interest discounted. **3.** The act or an example of discounting a commercial paper. **—dis′count′a•ble** *adj.*

dis•coun•te•nance (dĭs-koun′tə-nəns) *v.* **1.** To treat or regard with disfavor. **2.** To make uneasy : disconcert.

discount store *n.* A store that sells goods below the manufacturer's suggested retail price.

dis•cour•age (dĭ-skûr′ĭj, -skŭr′-) *v.* **-aged, -ag•ing. 1.** To deprive of enthusiasm : dishearten. **2.** To deter : dissuade. **3.** To try to prevent by expressing doubts or objections. ☆***syns:*** DISHEARTEN, DISPIRIT **—dis•cour′age•ment** *n.* **—dis•cour′ag•ing•ly** *adv.*

dis•course (dĭs′kôrs′, -kōrs′) *n.* **1.** Spoken or written expression. **2.** A conversation. **3.** A formal and lengthy written or spoken discussion of a subject. *—v.* (dĭ-skôrs′, -skōrs′) **-coursed, -cours•ing. 1.** To write or speak formally and extensively. **2.** To converse : talk. **—dis•cours′er** *n.*

dis•cour•te•ous (dĭs-kûr′tē-əs) *adj.* Lacking courteous manners : rude. **—dis•cour′te•ous•ly** *adv.* **—dis•cour′te•sy** *n.*

dis•cov•er (dĭ-skŭv′ər) *v.* **1.** To gain knowledge of through observation or study. **2.** To find, learn of, or observe for the first time. **—dis•cov′er•a•ble** *adj.* **—dis•cov′er•er** *n.* **—dis•cov′er•y** *n.*

dis•cred•it (dĭs-krĕd′ĭt) *v.* **1.** To mar the reputation of : disgrace. **2.** To cause to be doubted. **3.** To refuse to believe. *—n.* **1.** Tarnish to or loss of one's reputation. **2.** Loss of credibility : doubt. **—dis•cred′it•a•ble** *adj.* **—dis•cred′it•a•bly** *adv.*

dis•creet (dĭ-skrēt′) *adj.* **1.** Having or displaying caution and self-restraint : prudent. **2.** Not ostentatious : modest. **—dis•creet′ly** *adv.* **—dis•creet′ness** *n.*

dis•crep•an•cy (dĭ-skrĕp′ən-sē) *also* **dis•crep•ance** (-əns) *n., pl.* **-cies** *also* **-anc•es. 1.** Disagreement, as between facts : inconsistency. **2.** An instance of discrepancy. **—dis•crep′ant** *adj.*

dis•crete (dĭ-skrēt′) *adj.* **1.** Constituting a separate thing : distinct. **2.** Made up of unconnected distinct parts.

dis•cre•tion (dĭ-skrĕsh′ən) *n.* **1.** The quality of being discreet : circumspection. **2.** Freedom or power to act or judge on one's own. **—dis•cre′tion•ar′y** *adj.*

dis•crim•i•nate (dĭ-skrĭm′ə-nāt′) *v.* **-nat•ed, -nat•ing. 1.** To distinguish between things : differentiate. **2.** To act prejudicially. **—dis•crim′i•nate•ly** *adv.* **—dis•crim′i•na′tion** *n.* **—dis•crim′i•na′tive** *adj.*

dis•crim•i•nat•ing (dĭ-skrĭm′ə-nā′tĭng) *adj.* **1.** Recognizing or making fine distinctions : perceptive. **2.** Fussy.

dis•crim•i•na•to•ry (dĭ-skrĭm′ə-nə-tôr′ē, -tōr′ē) *adj.* **1.** Displaying or marked by prejudice : biased. **2.** Discriminating. **—dis•crim′i•na•to′ri•ly** *adv.*

dis•cur•sive (dĭ-skûr′sĭv) *adj.* Covering a wide field of subjects : digressive. **—dis•cur′sive•ly** *adv.* **—dis•cur′sive•ness** *n.*

dis•cus (dĭs′kəs) *n.* **1.** A disk, typically wooden, that is hurled for distance in athletic competitions. **2.** A small, brilliantly colored disk-shaped South American freshwater fish, *Symphysodon discus.*

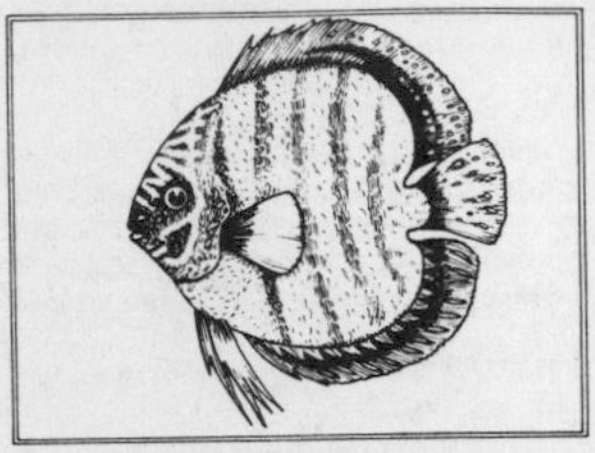

discus
Symphysodon discus

dis•cuss (dĭ-skŭs′) *v.* **1.** To talk over : speak about. **2.** To consider or examine (a subject) through discourse. **—dis•cuss′i•ble** *adj.* **—dis•cus′sion** *n.*

dis•cus•sant (dĭ-skŭs′ənt) *n.* A participant in a discussion.

dis•dain (dĭs-dān′) *v.* **1.** To treat contemptuously : despise. **2.** To reject scornfully. *—n.* Scornful aloofness. **—dis•dain′ful** *adj.* **—dis•dain′ful•ly** *adv.*

dis•ease (dĭ-zēz′) *n.* A condition of an organism that impairs normal physiological functioning. **—dis•eased′** *adj.*

dis•em•bark (dĭs′ĕm-bärk′) *v.* To go or cause to go ashore from a ship.

dis•em•bod•y (dĭs′ĕm-bŏd′ē) *v.* To free (the soul or spirit) from the body.

dis•em•bow•el (dĭs′ĕm-bou′əl) *v.* To eviscerate. **—dis′em•bow′el•ment** *n.*

dis•en•chant (dĭs′ĕn-chănt′) *v.* To divest of illusions or false beliefs.

dis•en•cum•ber (dĭs′ĕn-kŭm′bər) *v.* To relieve of burdens or hardships.

dis•en•fran•chise (dĭs′ĕn-frăn′chīz′) *v.* To disfranchise.

dis•en•gage (dĭs′ĕn-gāj′) *v.* To release from something that holds fast, joins, or entangles. **—dis′en•gage′ment** *n.*

dis•en•tan•gle (dĭs′ĕn-tăng′gəl) *v.* To untangle. **—dis′en•tan′gle•ment** *n.*

dis•es•teem (dĭs′ĭ-stēm′) *v.* To regard with disfavor. *—n.* Lack of esteem.

dis•fa•vor (dĭs-fā′vər) *n.* **1.** Disapproval. **2.** The state of being regarded with disapproval. **—dis•fa′vor** *v.*

dis•fig•ure (dĭs-fĭg′yər) *v.* To mar or ruin the shape or appearance of : deform. **—dis•fig′ure•ment** *n.*

dis•fran•chise (dĭs-frăn′chīz′) *v.* To deprive of a legal right, franchise, or privilege, esp. of the right to vote.

dis•gorge (dĭs-gôrj′) *v.* **1.** To regurgitate : vomit. **2.** To spew forth violently.

dis•grace (dĭs-grās′) *n.* **1.** The state of being strongly and generally disapproved : shame. **2.** Something that brings dishonor, disrespect, or disfavor. ☆***syns:*** DISCREDIT, DISHONOR, DISREPUTE, IGNOMINY, OBLOQUY, OPPROBRIUM, SHAME **—dis•grace′** *v.* **—dis•grace′ful** *adj.* **—dis•grace′ful•ly** *adv.* **—dis•grace′ful•ness** *n.*

dis•grun•tle (dĭs-grŭn′tl) *v.* **-tled, -tling.** To make irritable or upset.

dis•guise (dĭs-gīz′) *v.* **-guised, -guis•ing. 1.** To change the appearance or character of to prevent recognition. **2.** To hide or obscure by dissembling : misrepresent. *—n.* **1.** Clothes and often make-up worn to prevent recognition. **2.** A pretense that conceals the truth.

dis•gust (dĭs-gŭst′) *v.* **1.** To arouse nausea in : sicken. **2.** To offend the moral sense of : repel. **3.** To cause to become impatient or annoyed. *—n.* Profound aversion or repugnance. **—dis•gust′ed•ly** *adv.* **—dis•gust′ing•ly** *adv.*

dish (dĭsh) *n.* **1. a.** An open, gen. shallow container for holding or serving food. **b.** The amount a dish holds. **2. a.** The food served in a dish. **b.** A particular variety or way of preparing food. **3.** Something that resembles a dish, esp. in being concave in shape. *—v.* **1.** To serve (food) in or as if in a dish. **2.** To hollow out : make concave.

dis•ha•bille (dĭs′ə-bēl′) *n.* The state of being casually or carelessly dressed.

dis•har•mo•ny (dĭs-här′mə-nē) *n.* Lack of harmony : discord.

dish•cloth (dĭsh′klôth′, -klŏth′) *n.* A cloth used for washing dishes.

dis•heart•en (dĭs-här′tn) *v.* To discourage, demoralize, or dispirit.

di•shev•el (dĭ-shĕv′əl) *v.* **-eled, -el•ing** or **-elled, -el•ling.** To disorder or disarrange (e.g., the hair). **—di•shev′el•ment** *n.*

dis•hon•est (dĭs-ŏn′ĭst) *adj.* **1.** Tending to lie, cheat, or deceive. **2.** Arising from, gained by, or showing falseness or fraud. **–dis•hon′est•ly** *adv.* **–dis•hon′es•ty** *n.*

dis•hon•or (dĭs-ŏn′ər) *n.* **1.** Loss of honor : disgrace. **2.** Something that causes loss of honor. **3.** Failure to pay a commercial obligation, as a bill or note. –*v.* **1.** To bring shame or disgrace on. **2.** To fail to pay (e.g., a note). **–dis•hon′or•a•ble** *adj.*

dish•rag (dĭsh′răg′) *n.* A dishcloth.

dish•ware (dĭsh′wâr′) *n.* Dishes in which food is served.

dish•wash•er (dĭsh′wŏsh′ər, -wô′shər) *n.* One that washes dishes.

dis•il•lu•sion (dĭs′ĭ-lo͞o′zhən) *v.* To disenchant. **–dis′il•lu′sion** *n.*

dis•in•cline (dĭs′ĭn-klīn′) *v.* To be or cause to be reluctant or unwilling.

dis•in•fect (dĭs′ĭn-fĕkt′) *v.* To cleanse of harmful microorganisms. **–dis′in•fec′tant** *n.* & *adj.* **–dis′in•fec′tion** *n.*

dis•in•gen•u•ous (dĭs′ĭn-jĕn′yo͞o-əs) *adj.* Not candid : crafty. **–dis′in•gen′u•ous•ly** *adv.* **–dis′in•gen′u•ous•ness** *n.*

dis•in•her•it (dĭs′ĭn-hĕr′ĭt) *v.* To exclude or prevent from inheritance.

dis•in•te•grate (dĭs-ĭn′tĭ-grāt′) *v.* **1.** To separate into components : fragment. **2.** To undergo a change in structure, as an atomic nucleus. **–dis•in′te•gra′tion** *n.* **–dis•in′te•gra′tor** *n.*

dis•in•ter (dĭs′ĭn-tûr′) *v.* **1.** To exhume (a corpse). **2.** To disclose, uncover, or expose.

dis•in•ter•est•ed (dĭs-ĭn′trĭ-stĭd, -tə-rĕs′tĭd) *adj.* **1.** Unbiased : impartial. **2.** Not interested : indifferent. **–dis•in′ter•est** *n.* **–dis•in′ter•est•ed•ly** *adv.*

dis•join (dĭs-join′) *v.* To disconnect.

dis•joint (dĭs-joint′) *v.* **1.** To disconnect or separate at the joints. **2.** To destroy the orderly arrangement of.

dis•joint•ed (dĭs-join′tĭd) *adj.* **1.** Separated at the joints. **2.** Lacking unity or order : incoherent <a *disjointed* lecture> **–dis•joint′ed•ly** *adv.*

disk *also* **disc** (dĭsk) *n.* **1.** A thin, flat, round plate. **2.** Something resembling a disk. **3.** *var. of* DISC 1. **4.** *Computer Sci.* A round, flat plate coated with a magnetic substance for storing data.

disk pack *n.* A computer storage device consisting of several magnetic disks that can be used and stored as a unit.

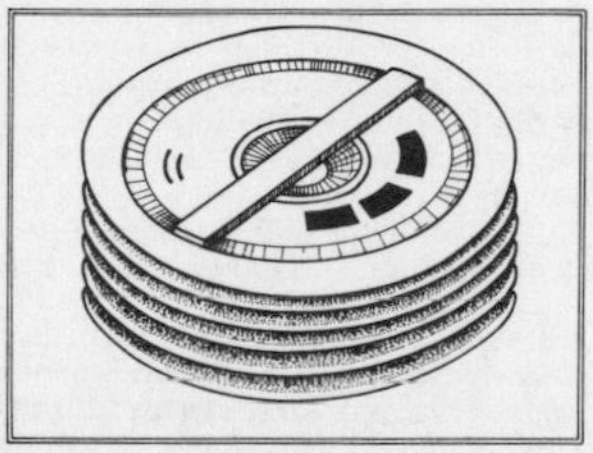

disk pack

dis•like (dĭs-līk′) *v.* To regard with disapproval or distaste. **–dis•like′** *n.*

dis•lo•cate (dĭs′lō-kāt′, dĭs-lō′kāt′) *v.* **1.** To put out of normal position, esp. to displace (a bone) from a socket or joint. **2.** To throw into disorder : disrupt.

dis•lodge (dĭs-lŏj′) *v.* To remove or drive out from a dwelling or position.

dis•loy•al (dĭs-loi′əl) *adj.* Being untrue to duty or obligation : faithless. **–dis•loy′al•ly** *adv.* **–dis•loy′al•ty** *n.*

dis•mal (dĭz′məl) *adj.* **1.** Causing gloom or depression : dreary <*dismal* rain and fog> **2.** Characterized by a lack of hope : dejected. **3.** Causing dread or dismay : dire. **4.** Without substance or interest. **–dis′mal•ly** *adv.* **–dis′mal•ness** *n.*

▲word history: The word *dismal* was orig. a noun phrase –*dis mal*–meaning "evil days," from Latin *dies mali.* In the medieval calendar 2 days each month were considered unlucky. A *dismal day* was one of these unlucky days. By the 16th cent. the phrase *dismal day* had become so common that *dismal* was interpreted as an adjective and came to mean "unlucky" and "causing dread." In more recent times these senses have been weakened to "depressing" and "gloomy."

dis•man•tle (dĭs-măn′tl) *v.* **-tled, -tling. 1.** To divest of equipment or furnishings. **2.** To tear down or take apart. **–dis•man′tle•ment** *n.*

dis•may (dĭs-mā′) *v.* **1.** To cause fear or apprehension in : daunt. **2.** To discourage or trouble greatly. **–dis•may′** *n.*

dis•mem•ber (dĭs-mĕm′bər) *v.* **1.** To cut or tear off the limbs of. **2.** To separate into parts. **–dis•mem′ber•ment** *n.*

dis•miss (dĭs-mĭs′) *v.* **1.** To discharge, as from a job. **2.** To permit or direct to leave. **3.** To rid one's mind of : dispel. **4.** To refuse to accept : repudiate. **5.** *Law.* To disallow or reject further judicial hearing on (a claim or action). **–dis•miss′al** *n.* **–dis•miss′i•ble** *adj.*

dis•mount (dĭs-mount′) *v.* **1.** To get down from (e.g., a horse). **2.** To unseat (a rider) from a horse. **3.** To remove from a mounting, setting, or support. **4.** To take apart : disassemble. **–dis′mount′** *n.*

dis•o•bey (dĭs′ə-bā′) *v.* To fail or refuse to obey. **–dis′o•be′di•ence** (-bē′dē-əns) *n.* **–dis′o•be′di•ent** *adj.*

dis•o•blige (dĭs′ə-blīj′) *v.* **1.** To neglect or refuse to act in accord with the wishes of. **2.** To offend, as by slighting. **3.** To inconvenience. **–dis′o•blig′ing•ly** *adv.*

dis•or•der (dĭs-ôr′dər) *n.* **1.** Lack of order : confusion. **2.** A breach of civil peace : public disturbance. **3.** An ailment. –*v.* To throw into confusion.

dis•or•der•ly (dĭs-ôr′dər-lē) *adj.* **1.** Lacking regular order : untidy. **2.** Not disciplined : unruly. **3.** Disturbing the public peace or decorum. ☆**syns:** RIOTOUS, ROWDY, UNRULY **–dis•or′der•li•ness** *n.*

dis•or•gan•ize (dĭs-ôr′gə-nīz′) *v.* To break up the organization, structure, or unity of.

dis•o•ri•ent (dĭs-ôr′ē-ĕnt′, -ōr′-) *v.* To cause to lose a sense of direction, location, or awareness : confuse.

dis•own (dĭs-ōn′) *v.* To disclaim as one's own : repudiate.

dis•par•age (dĭ-spăr′ĭj) *v.* **-aged, -ag•ing. 1.** To speak of in a belittling manner : decry. **2.** To reduce in rank or esteem. **–dis•par′age•ment** *n.* **–dis•par′ag•ing•ly** *adv.*

dis•pa•rate (dĭs′pər-ĭt, dĭ-spăr′-) *adj.* Completely distinct in kind or quality. **–dis′pa•rate•ly** *adv.* **–dis•par′i•ty** *n.*

dis•pas•sion•ate (dĭs-păsh′ə-nĭt) *adj.* Unaffected by emotion or bias. **–dis•pas′sion** *n.* **–dis•pas′sion•ate•ly** *adv.*

dis•patch *also* **des•patch** (dĭ-spăch′) *v.* **1.** To send off to a particular destination or on specific business. **2.** To deal with promptly. **3.** To kill summarily. –*n.* **1.** The act of dispatching. **2.** Speed in movement or performance. **3.** A message. **4.** An item sent to a news organization, as by a correspondent. **–dis•patch′er** *n.*

dis•pel (dĭ-spĕl′) *v.* **-pelled, -pel•ling. 1.** To rid one's mind of <*dispel* all fears> **2.** To cause to separate : scatter.

dis•pen•sa•ble (dĭ-spĕn′sə-bəl) *adj.* Capable of being dispensed with.

dis•pen•sa•ry (dĭ-spĕn′sə-rē) *n., pl.* **-ries.** A place where medical supplies and preparations are dispensed.

dis•pen•sa•tion (dĭs′pən-sā′shən, -pĕn-) *n.* **1.** The act of dispensing. **2.** Something dispensed. **3.** A system by which something is dispensed. **4.** Exemption or release from rule or obligation. **5.** Divine ordering of worldly affairs. **6.** A religious system or code of commands.

dis•pense (dĭ-spĕns′) *v.* **-pensed, -pens•ing. 1.** To distribute in portions. **2.** To prepare and give out (medicines). **3.** To administer (e.g., laws). **4.** To release or exempt. **–dispense with. 1.** To forgo. **2.** To get rid of. **–dis•pen′ser** *n.*

dis•perse (dĭ-spûrs′) *v.* **-persed, -pers•ing. 1.** To break up : scatter. **2.** To vanish or cause to vanish : dispel. **3.** To disseminate (e.g., knowledge). **–dis•pers′i•ble** *adj.* **–dis•per′sion, dis•per′sal** *n.*

di•spir•it (dĭ-spĭr′ĭt) *v.* To deprive of spirit : discourage. **–di•spir′it•ed•ly** *adv.*

dis•place (dĭs-plās′) *v.* **1.** To change the place or position of : remove. **2.** To take the place of. **3.** To discharge from an office. **4.** To cause a physical displacement of.

displaced person *n.* One who has been driven from his or her homeland by war.

dis•place•ment (dĭs-plās′mənt) *n.* **1.** The act of displacing or the state of being displaced. **2. a.** The volume or weight of fluid displaced by a floating body. **b.** The measure of the distance that a body has been moved through space.

dis•play (dĭ-splā′) *v.* **1.** To put forth for viewing : exhibit. **2.** To make noticeable <*displayed* their fear> **3.** To spread out : unfurl. –*n.* **1.** The act of displaying. **2.** Something displayed. **3.** *Computer Sci.* A device that gives information in a visual form, as on a cathode-ray tube.

dis•please (dĭs-plēz′) *v.* To incur the disapproval or dislike of : offend. **–dis•pleas′ing•ly** *adv.* **–dis•plea′sure** *n.*

dis•port (dĭ-spôrt′, -spōrt′) *v.* To entertain (oneself) : play.

dis•pos•al (dĭs-pō′zəl) *n.* **1.** Order : arrangement. **2.** The act of getting rid of or throwing away. **3.** An apparatus or device for disposing of something. **4.** Management : administration. **5.** The transference of something by gift or sale. **6.** The freedom to use something.

dis•pose (dĭ-spōz′) *v.* **-posed, -pos•ing. 1.** To arrange. **2.** To make willing or receptive : incline. **–dispose of. 1.** To attend to : settle. **2.** To transfer or part with, as by selling. **3.** To get rid of. **–dis•pos′a•ble** *adj.*

dis·po·si·tion (dĭs′pə-zĭsh′ən) *n.* **1.** Temperament. **2.** Habitual inclination or tendency. **3.** Distribution or arrangement. **4.** A final settlement, as of property. **5.** An act of disposing.
dis·pos·sess (dĭs′pə-zĕs′) *v.* To deprive of the ownership or occupancy of land, possessions, or property. **—dis′pos·ses′sion** *n.*
dis·praise (dĭs-prāz′) *v.* To disparage. *—n.* Strong disapproval.
dis·pro·por·tion (dĭs′prə-pôr′shən, -pōr′-) *n.* Absence of proper proportion : disparity. **—dis′pro·por′tion·al, dis′pro·por′tion·ate** *adj.*
dis·prove (dĭs-pro͞ov′) *v.* To show to be false, invalid, or erroneous. ☆***syns:*** BELIE, CONFUTE, DISCREDIT, REBUT, REFUTE **—dis·proof′** *n.*
dis·pu·ta·tion (dĭs′pyo͝o-tā′shən) *n.* **1.** A debate : argument. **2.** A dispute.
dis·pu·ta·tious (dĭs′pyo͝o-tā′shəs) *adj.* Argumentative. **—dis′pu·ta′tious·ly** *adv.*
dis·pute (dĭ-spyo͞ot′) *v.* **-put·ed, -put·ing. 1.** To debate : argue. **2.** To question the validity or truth of. **3.** To strive against : resist. **4.** To quarrel. *—n.* **1.** A verbal controversy. **2.** A quarrel. **—dis·put′a·ble** *adj.* **—dis·put′a·bly** *adv.* **—dis·pu′tant, dis·put′er** *n.*
dis·qual·i·fy (dĭs-kwŏl′ə-fī′) *v.* **1.** To make unqualified, unfit, or ineligible. **2.** To declare unqualified, unfit, or ineligible. **—dis·qual′i·fi·ca′tion** *n.*
dis·qui·et (dĭs-kwī′ĭt) *v.* To trouble : disturb. *—n.* Disquietude. **—dis·qui′et·ing** *adj.* **—dis·qui′et·ing·ly** *adv.*
dis·qui·e·tude (dĭs-kwī′ĭ-to͞od′, -tyo͞od′) *n.* A state of uneasiness : anxiety.
dis·qui·si·tion (dĭs′kwĭ-zĭsh′ən) *n.* A formal, often written discourse.
dis·re·gard (dĭs′rĭ-gärd′) *v.* **1.** To ignore. **2.** To treat without proper attention : neglect. **—dis′re·gard** *n.* **—dis′re·gard′ful** *adj.*
†**dis·re·mem·ber** (dĭs′rĭ-mĕm′bər) *v. Regional.* To fail to remember : forget.
dis·re·pair (dĭs′rĭ-pâr′) *n.* The state of being neglected or in need of repair.
dis·rep·u·ta·ble (dĭs-rĕp′yə-tə-bəl) *adj.* Not respectable. **—dis·rep′u·ta·bly** *adv.*
dis·re·pute (dĭs′rĭ-pyo͞ot′) *n.* Loss of reputation : disgrace.
dis·re·spect (dĭs′rĭ-spĕkt′) *n.* Lack of respect or courteous regard. **—dis′re·spect′ful** *adj.* **—dis′re·spect′ful·ly** *adv.*
dis·robe (dĭs-rōb′) *v.* To undress.
dis·rupt (dĭs-rŭpt′) *v.* **1.** To throw into disorder or confusion. **2.** To break up : interrupt. **—dis·rup′tion** *n.* **—dis·rup′tive** *adj.*
dis·sat·is·fy (dĭs-săt′ĭs-fī′) *v.* To fail to satisfy : disappoint. **—dis·sat′is·fac′tion** *n.* **—dis·sat′is·fied′** *adj.*
dis·sect (dĭ-sĕkt′, dī-, dī′sĕkt′) *v.* **1.** To cut apart (tissue) for study or examination. **2.** To analyze closely or thoroughly. **—dis·sec′tion** *n.*
dis·sect·ed (dĭ-sĕk′tĭd, dī-) *adj. Bot.* Divided into numerous narrow segments or lobes.

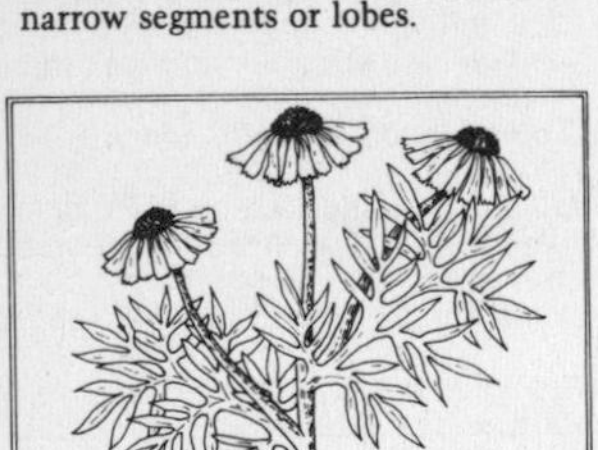

dissected
Dissected leaves

dis·sem·ble (dĭ-sĕm′bəl) *v.* **-bled, -bling. 1.** To conceal the true nature of. **2.** To make a pretense of : simulate.
dis·sem·i·nate (dĭ-sĕm′ə-nāt′) *v.* **-nat·ed, -nat·ing.** To scatter or spread widely <*disseminate* rumors> **—dis·sem′i·na′tion** *n.* **—dis·sem′i·na′tor** *n.*
dis·sen·sion (dĭ-sĕn′shən) *n.* Difference of opinion : discord.
dis·sent (dĭ-sĕnt′) *v.* **1.** To differ in opinion : disagree. **2.** To withhold approval or assent. *—n.* **1.** Disagreement. **2.** Religious nonconformity. **—dis·sent′er** *n.*
dis·ser·ta·tion (dĭs′ər-tā′shən) *n.* A formal discourse, esp. a doctoral thesis.
dis·serv·ice (dĭs-sûr′vĭs) *n.* Injury : harm.
dis·sev·er (dĭ-sĕv′ər) *v.* To sever.
dis·si·dent (dĭs′ĭ-dənt) *adj.* Strongly and openly dissenting, esp. in opinion or belief. **—dis′si·dence** *n.* **—dis′si·dent** *n.*
dis·sim·i·lar (dĭ-sĭm′ə-lər) *adj.* Different. **—dis·sim′i·lar′i·ty** *n.*
dis·si·mil·i·tude (dĭs′ə-mĭl′ĭ-to͞od′, -tyo͞od′) *n.* Lack of resemblance.
dis·sim·u·late (dĭ-sĭm′yə-lāt′) *v.* To dissemble.
dis·si·pate (dĭs′ə-pāt′) *v.* **-pat·ed, -pat·ing. 1.** To drive away or dispel : scatter. **2.** To squander or waste. **3.** To vanish by dispersion. **4.** To indulge in pleasure recklessly : carouse. **5.** To lose (e.g., heat) irreversibly. **—dis′si·pa′tion** *n.*
dis·so·ci·ate (dĭ-sō′shē-āt′, -sē-) *v.* **-at·ed, -at·ing.** To separate or become separated from association with another : disconnect. **—dis·so′ci·a′tion** *n.*
dis·so·lute (dĭs′ə-lo͞ot′) *adj.* Lacking moral restraint : profligate. **—dis′so·lute′ly** *adv.* **—dis′so·lute′ness** *n.*
dis·so·lu·tion (dĭs′ə-lo͞o′shən) *n.* **1.** Disintegration into component parts : decomposition. **2.** Death. **3.** *Law.* Annulment or termination of a legal bond, tie, or contract. **4.** Formal adjournment or dismissal of a legislature or assembly.
dis·solve (dĭ-zŏlv′) *v.* **-solved, -solv·ing. 1.** To pass or cause to pass into solution <*dissolve* sugar in water> **2.** To melt. **3.** To cause to disappear : dispel. **4.** To separate into component parts : disintegrate. **5.** To bring to an end : terminate. **6.** To break down emotionally. **—dis·solv′a·ble** *adj.*
dis·so·nance (dĭs′ə-nəns) *n.* **1.** A harsh or unpleasant combination of sounds : discord. **2.** Lack of agreement : conflict. **—dis′so·nant** *adj.* **—dis′so·nant·ly** *adv.*
dis·suade (dĭ-swād′) *v.* **-suad·ed, -suad·ing.** To sway or try to sway from a course of action by persuasion. **—dis·sua′sion** *n.* **—dis·sua′sive** *adj.*
dis·taff (dĭs′tăf′) *n.* **1.** A stick holding flax or wool from which thread is drawn and spun by hand. **2.** Women as a group.
dis·tal (dĭs′təl) *adj. Anat.* Located far from the place of origin or attachment.
dis·tance (dĭs′təns) *n.* **1.** Spatial or chronological separation. **2.** The length of a path, esp. a straight line segment, that joins 2 points. **3.** The space that separates any 2 specified instants in time. **4. a.** The degree of difference separating 2 things in relationship. **b.** The degree of progress between 2 points in a course. **5.** Aloofness. **6.** The whole way <went the *distance*> *—v.* **-tanced, -tanc·ing.** To outdo.
dis·tant (dĭs′tənt) *adj.* **1.** Apart or separate in time or space. **2.** Far removed <the *distant* past> **3.** Coming from, located at, or going to a distance. **4.** Remotely related. **5.** Reserved : aloof. **—dis′tant·ly** *adv.*
dis·taste (dĭs-tāst′) *n.* Aversion : dislike. **—dis·taste′ful** *adj.* **—dis·taste′ful·ly** *adv.* **—dis·taste′ful·ness** *n.*
dis·tem·per (dĭs-tĕm′pər) *n.* An infectious, often fatal virus disease of certain mammals, as dogs and cats.
dis·tend (dĭ-stĕnd′) *v.* To expand by or as if by internal pressure : swell. **—dis·ten′si·ble** *adj.* **—dis·ten′tion, dis·ten′sion** *n.*
dis·til (dĭ-stĭl′) *v. esp. Brit. var. of* DISTILL.
dis·till (dĭ-stĭl′) *v.* **1.** To subject to or obtain by distillation. **2.** To separate from. **3.** To give off in drops. **—dis·till′er** *n.* **—dis·till′er·y** *n.*
dis·til·late (dĭs′tə-lāt′, -lĭt, dĭ-stĭl′ĭt) *n.* The substance condensed from vapor in distillation.
dis·til·la·tion (dĭs′tə-lā′shən) *n.* Any of various heat-dependent processes used to purify or separate a fraction of a relatively complex mixture or substance, esp. the vaporization of a liquid mixture with subsequent cooling to condensation.
dis·tinct (dĭ-stĭngkt′) *adj.* **1.** Distinguished from all others : individual. **2.** Easily recognized : clear. **3.** Unquestionable : decided. **—dis·tinct′ly** *adv.* **—dis·tinct′ness** *n.*
dis·tinc·tion (dĭ-stĭngk′shən) *n.* **1.** The act of distinguishing. **2.** A difference. **3.** A distinguishing attribute or factor. **4.** Excellence or eminence : virtue. **5.** Honor.
dis·tinc·tive (dĭ-stĭngk′tĭv) *adj.* **1.** Serving to identify or set apart : distinguishing. **2.** Typical : characteristic. **—dis·tinc′tive·ly** *adv.* **—dis·tinc′tive·ness** *n.*
dis·tin·guish (dĭ-stĭng′gwĭsh) *v.* **1.** To recognize as being different. **2.** To perceive clearly : discern. **3.** To discriminate. **4.** To make noticeable or different : set apart. **5.** To make well known. **—dis·tin′guish·a·ble** *adj.* **—dis·tin′guish·a·bly** *adv.*
dis·tin·guished (dĭ-stĭng′gwĭsht) *adj.* **1.** Marked by excellence : eminent. **2.** Dignified in appearance or deportment.
dis·tort (dĭ-stôrt′) *v.* **1.** To twist out of proper shape or condition : contort. **2.** To give an inaccurate and misleading account of : misrepresent. **3.** To reproduce inaccurately. **—dis·tor′tion** *n.*
dis·tract (dĭ-străkt′) *v.* **1.** To cause to turn away from a focus of attention : divert. **2.** To cause to feel conflicting emotions : disturb. **—dis·trac′tion** *n.*
dis·trait (dĭ-strā′) *adj.* Absent-minded or inattentive, esp. because of anxiety.

dis•traught (dĭ-strôt′) *adj.* **1.** Anxious : worried. **2.** Crazed : insane.
dis•tress (dĭ-strĕs′) *v.* To cause anxiety or misery to : trouble greatly. —*n.* **1.** Anxiety or suffering. **2.** Severe mental or physical strain. **3.** The state of needing immediate help. ☆***syns:*** AFFLICTION, AGONY, ANGUISH, HURT, MISERY, PAIN, WOE **—dis•tress′ing•ly** *adv.*
dis•trib•ute (dĭ-strĭb′yo͞ot) *v.* **-ut•ed, -ut•ing. 1.** To divide and dispense in portions. **2.** To deliver or give out. **3.** To supply (goods) to retailers. **4.** To classify. **—dis′tri•bu′tion** *n.* **—dis•trib′u•tive** *adj.*
dis•trib•u•tor (dĭ-strĭb′yə-tər) *n.* **1.** One that distributes, esp. a wholesaler. **2.** A device that directs electric current to the spark plugs of a gasoline engine.
dis•trict (dĭs′trĭkt) *n.* **1.** An administrative or political division of a territory. **2.** A distinctive area <the theater *district*>
district attorney *n.* The prosecuting officer of a designated judicial district.
District of Co•lum•bi•a (kə-lŭm′bē-ə). Federal district of E U.S., coextensive with the city of Washington.
dis•trust (dĭs-trŭst′) *n.* Lack of trust. ☆***syns:*** DOUBT, DOUBTFULNESS, MISTRUST, SUSPICION —*v.* To doubt : suspect. **—dis•trust′ful** *adj.* **—dis•trust′ful•ly** *adv.*
dis•turb (dĭ-stûrb′) *v.* **1.** To trouble or upset the tranquillity of. **2.** To unsettle mentally or emotionally. **3.** To interfere with : interrupt. **4.** To disarrange. **—dis•tur′bance** *n.* **—dis•turb′er** *n.*
dis•u•nite (dĭs′yo͞o-nīt′) *v.* To make or become separate or divided.
dis•u•ni•ty (dĭs-yo͞o′nĭ-tē) *n.* Discord.
dis•use (dĭs-yo͞os′) *n.* The state of being no longer in use : desuetude.
ditch (dĭch) *n.* A trench or furrow dug in the ground. —*v.* **1.** To dig or make a ditch in. **2.** To surround with a ditch. **3.** *Slang.* To throw away : discard. **4.** To bring (a disabled aircraft) down on water.
dith•er (dĭth′ər) *n.* A state of indecision or nervousness.
dit•to (dĭt′ō) *n., pl.* **-tos. 1.** The same as stated above or before. Used to avoid repetition of a word. **2.** One of a pair of marks (″) used as a substitute for the word *ditto.* **3.** A copy or duplicate. —*adv.* As before.
dit•ty (dĭt′ē) *n., pl.* **-ties.** A simple song.
di•u•ret•ic (dī′ə-rĕt′ĭk) *adj.* Causing an increased urine discharge. **—di′u•ret′ic** *n.*
di•ur•nal (dī-ûr′nəl) *adj.* **1.** Relating to or happening in a day or each day : daily. **2.** Active or occurring during the daytime.
div. *abbr.* **1.** divided; division. **2.** dividend.
di•va (dē′və) *n., pl.* **-vas** *or* **-ve** (-vā′). A prima donna.
di•van (dĭ′văn′, dĭ-văn′) *n.* A long backless and armless couch.
dive (dīv) *v.* **dived** *or* **dove** (dōv), **dived, div•ing. 1.** To plunge headfirst into water, esp. as a sport. **2.** To go or cause to go underwater : submerge. **3.** To fall sharply : plummet. **4.** To rush headlong <*dove* into the crowd> **5.** To plunge, as into an activity. —*n.* **1.** An act or instance of diving. **2.** A sudden drop or fall. **3.** *Slang.* A cheap, disreputable bar. **—div′er** *n.*
di•verge (dĭ-vûrj′, dī-) *v.* **-verged, -verg•ing. 1.** To go or move in different directions from a common point : branch out. **2.** To differ, as in opinion or manner. **3.** To turn aside from a set course or norm : deviate. **—di•ver′gence** *n.* **—di•ver′gent** *adj.*
di•vers (dī′vərz) *adj.* Various : several.
di•verse (dĭ-vûrs′, dī-, dī′vûrs′) *adj.* **1.** Unlike in kind : distinct. **2.** Having diversity in form : varied. **—di•verse′ness** *n.*
di•ver•si•fy (dĭ-vûr′sə-fī′, dī-) *v.* **-fied, -fy•ing. 1.** To give variety to : vary. **2.** To spread out over a wide range of types or classes. **—di•ver′si•fi•ca′tion** *n.*
di•ver•sion (dĭ-vûr′zhən, -shən, dī-) *n.* **1.** The act of diverting : deviation. **2.** Something that relaxes or entertains : recreation. **—di•ver′sion•ar′y** *adj.*
di•ver•si•ty (dĭ-vûr′sĭ-tē, dī-) *n., pl.* **-ties. 1.** Difference. **2.** Variety.
di•vert (dĭ-vûrt′, dī-) *v.* **1.** To turn away from a purpose or direction : deflect. **2.** To distract. **3.** To entertain.
di•vest (dĭ-vĕst′, dī-) *v.* **1.** To strip, as of clothing. **2.** To deprive, as of property.
di•vide (dĭ-vīd′) *v.* **-vid•ed, -vid•ing. 1.** To separate or become separated into parts : split. **2.** To classify : group. **3.** To separate into opposing factions : disunite. **4.** To cause to be cut off : keep apart <a wall *dividing* a city> **5.** To apportion among a number : distribute. **6.** *Math.* To perform the operation of division on (a number). **7.** To branch out, as a river. —*n.* A watershed. **—di•vid′a•ble** *adj.*
div•i•dend (dĭv′ĭ-dĕnd′) *n.* **1.** *Math.* A number that is to be divided. **2.** A share of profits paid to a stockholder. **3.** *Informal.* A share of a surplus : bonus.
di•vid•er (dĭ-vī′dər) *n.* **1.** One that divides. **2. dividers.** COMPASS 2.
div•i•na•tion (dĭv′ə-nā′shən) *n.* **1.** The art of foretelling the future or the unknown through supernatural means. **2.** A presentiment.
di•vine[1] (dĭ-vīn′) *adj.* **-vin•er, -vin•est. 1.** Of, relating to, or being a deity. **2.** Emanating from or devoted to a deity. **3.** *Informal.* Supremely pleasing. —*n.* A clergyman. **—di•vine′ly** *adv.* **—di•vine′ness** *n.*
di•vine[2] (dĭ-vīn′) *v.* **-vined, -vin•ing. 1.** To foretell : prophesy. **2.** To infer : guess.
divining rod *n.* A forked branch or stick that allegedly indicates the location of subterranean water or minerals by bending downward when held over a source.
di•vin•i•ty (dĭ-vĭn′ĭ-tē) *n., pl.* **-ties. 1.** The condition or quality of being divine. **2. Divinity.** God. **3.** Theology.
di•vis•i•ble (dĭ-vĭz′ə-bəl) *adj.* Capable of being divided, esp. of being divided evenly with no remainder. **—di•vis′i•bil′i•ty** *n.*
di•vi•sion (dĭ-vĭzh′ən) *n.* **1.** The act of dividing or state of being divided. **2.** Something that serves to separate or divide. **3.** A group or section into which something is divided. **4.** A self-contained tactical military unit capable of independent combat operations. **5.** *Math.* The process of determining how many times 1 quantity is contained in another. **—di•vi′sion•al** *adj.*
di•vi•sive (dĭ-vī′sĭv) *adj.* Creating dissension or disunity. **—di•vi′sive•ness** *n.*
di•vi•sor (dĭ-vī′zər) *n. Math.* The number by which a dividend is to be divided.
di•vorce (dĭ-vôrs′, -vōrs′) *n.* **1.** The legal termination of a marriage. **2.** The complete separation of things. **—di•vorce′** *v.* **—di•vor•cé** *n.* **—di•vor•cée** *n.*
div•ot (dĭv′ət) *n.* A piece of turf torn up by a golf club in hitting the ball.
di•vulge (dĭ-vŭlj′) *v.* **-vulged, -vulg•ing.** To reveal or make known : disclose.
diz•zy (dĭz′ē) *adj.* **-zi•er, -zi•est. 1.** Experiencing a whirling sensation. **2.** Producing or tending to produce giddiness or vertigo. **3.** *Informal.* Silly : foolish. **—diz′zi•ly** *adv.* **—diz′zi•ness** *n.* **—diz′zy** *v.*
Dja•kar•ta (jə-kär′tə). Cap. of Indonesia, on the NW coast of Java. *Pop.* 6,400,000.
Dji•bou•ti (jĭ-bo͞o′tē). **1.** Country of E Africa, on the Gulf of Aden. *Pop.* 150,000. **2.** Cap. of Djibouti, in the SE part. *Pop.* 40,000.
dlvy. *abbr.* delivery.
DMZ *abbr.* demilitarized zone.
DNA (dē′ĕn-ā′) *n.* A nucleic acid having a very complicated structure and forming the main constituent of the chromosomes of living cells : deoxyribonucleic acid.
Dnie•per (nē′pər). River of W European USSR, flowing to the Black Sea.
do (do͞o) *v.* **did** (dĭd), **done** (dŭn), **do•ing, does** (dŭz). **1.** To perform : accomplish. **2.** To carry out the requirements of : fulfill. **3.** To create, compose, or make. **4.** To bring about : effect <The treatment *did* some good.> **5.** To put forth : exert <*did* our best to help> **6.** To attend to : deal with <have to *do* the marketing> **7.** To render or give <*do* honor to the war dead> **8.** To work at for a living <What do you *do*?> **9.** To work out the details of : solve <*did* the puzzle quickly> **10. a.** To present or perform (e.g., a play) : stage. **b.** To have the role of : play. **11.** To tour. **12.** To be sufficient or convenient : suffice. **13.** *Informal.* To serve in prison <*did* time> **14.** *Slang.* To swindle : cheat <*did* them out of their savings> **15.** To behave or conduct oneself : act. **16.** To set or style (the hair). **17.** To get by : fare <not *doing* well> **18.** *Slang.* To partake of : use <didn't *do* drugs> **19.** Used as a substitute for an antecedent verb <earned as much as you *did*> **20.** Used as an auxiliary: **a.** With a simple infinitive to indicate the tense in questions, negative statements, and inverted phrases <*Do* you hear it?><I *did* not play well.> **b.** As a means of emphasis <I *do* want you to come.><*Do* be quick> **—do away with. 1.** To make an end of : eliminate. **2. a.** To destroy. **b.** To kill. **—do in.** *Slang.* **1.** To tire completely : exhaust. **2.** To kill. **—do up. 1.** To adorn or dress lavishly. **2.** To wrap and tie (a package). —*n., pl.* **do's** *or* **dos. 1.** Commotion : ado. **2.** An entertainment : party. **3.** A statement of what should be done <*do*'s and don'ts> **—do′a•ble** *adj.*
do. *abbr.* ditto.
Do•ber•man pin•scher (dō′bər-mən pĭn′shər) *n.* A medium-sized, short-haired dog. orig. bred in Germany.
do•bra (dō′brə) *n.* See CURRENCY TABLE.
dob•son fly (dŏb′sən) *n.* An insect, *Corydalus cornutus,* with 4 many-veined wings.
doc (dŏk) *n. Informal.* Doctor.

do·cent (dō′sənt, dō-sĕnt′) *n.* A teacher or lecturer at certain universities.
doc·ile (dŏs′əl, -īl′) *adj.* Easily taught, trained, or controlled : tractable. **—do·cil′i·ty** (dŏ-sĭl′ĭ-tē, dō-) *n.*
dock[1] (dŏk) *n.* **1. a.** A landing pier for ships or boats. **b.** A loading platform for trucks or trains. **2.** A pier or wharf. —*v.* **1.** To maneuver or come into a dock. **2.** *Aerospace.* To couple (e.g., 2 or more spacecraft) in space.
dock[2] (dŏk) *v.* **1.** To clip or cut off (e.g., an animal's tail). **2.** To deduct or withhold a part of (a salary).
dock[3] (dŏk) *n.* An enclosure where the defendant sits or stands in a criminal court.
dock[4] (dŏk) *n.* A weedy plant of the genus *Rumex,* with small flower clusters.
dock·age (dŏk′ĭj) *n.* **1.** A charge for docking privileges. **2.** Facilities for docking.
dock·et (dŏk′ĭt) *n.* **1.** A calender of cases awaiting adjudication. **2.** An agenda. **—dock′et** *v.*
dock·yard (dŏk′yärd′) *n.* A shipyard.
doc·tor (dŏk′tər) *n.* **1.** A person trained and licensed to practice the healing arts, as medicine or surgery. **2.** A person holding the highest degree given by a university. —*v.* **1. a.** To administer medical treatment to. **b.** To practice medicine. **2.** To repair, esp. in a haphazard way. **3.** To tamper with so as to deceive <*doctored* the coroner's report> **4.** To modify or alter for a desired end. **—doc′tor·al** *adj.*
doc·tor·ate (dŏk′tər-ĭt) *n.* The degree, status, or title of a doctor.
doc·tri·naire (dŏk′trə-nâr′) *n.* One dogmatically attached to a theory or practice.
doc·trine (dŏk′trĭn) *n.* **1.** Something taught as a body of principles. **2.** A dogma. **—doc′trin·al** *adj.*
doc·u·ment (dŏk′yə-mənt) *n.* An official paper that can be used to furnish evidence or information. —*v.* (-mĕnt′). To prove with, support by, or provide by documents. **—doc′u·men·ta′tion** *n.*
doc·u·men·ta·ry (dŏk′yə-mĕn′tə-rē) *adj.* **1.** Of, relating to, or based on documents. **2.** Presented in factual but artistic form. **—doc′u·men′ta·ry** *n.*
dod·der[1] (dŏd′ər) *v.* To tremble or move unsteadily, as from age : totter.
dod·der[2] (dŏd′ər) *n.* A parasitic twining vine of the genus *Cuscuta.*
dodge (dŏj) *v.* **dodged, dodg·ing. 1.** To avoid (e.g., a blow) by moving quickly out of the way. **2.** To evade, esp. by stratagem. **3.** To shift suddenly. **—dodge** *n.*
†**dodg·er** (dŏj′ər) *n.* **1.** One who dodges or evades. **2.** A dishonest or shifty person : trickster. **3.** A small printed handbill. **4.** *U.S.* A corndodger.
Dodg·son (dŏj′sən), **Charles Lutwidge.** "Lewis Carroll." 1832–98. English mathematician and author.
do·do (dō′dō) *n., pl.* **-does** *or* **-dos. 1.** An extinct flightless bird, *Raphus cucullatus,* once found on the island of Mauritius. **2.** *Informal.* One who is entirely out-of-date : fogy. **3.** *Informal.* A stupid person.
doe (dō) *n., pl.* **does** *or* **doe. 1.** A mature female deer. **2.** A female of various mammals, as the hare or kangaroo.
do·er (do͞o′ər) *n.* A person, esp. an energetic person, who does something.
does (dŭz) *v. 3rd person sing. present tense of* DO.
doe·skin (dō′skĭn′) *n.* **1.** Leather made from the skin of a doe, deer, or goat. **2.** A fine, soft, smooth woolen fabric.
does·n't (dŭz′ənt). Does not.
doff (dôf, dŏf) *v.* **1.** To take off (clothing). **2.** To tip or remove (one's hat) in greeting. **3.** To throw away : discard.
dog (dôg, dŏg) *n.* **1.** A domesticated carnivorous mammal, *Canis familiaris,* raised in a wide variety of breeds and held to have orig. derived from several wild species. **2.** Any of various animals of the family Canidae, as the dingo. **3.** *Informal.* A fellow <you witty *dog*> **4.** *Slang.* **a.** An uninteresting or unattractive person. **b.** A hopelessly inferior product or creation. **c.** A contemptible person. **5. dogs.** *Slang.* The feet. **6.** Any of various hooked or U-shaped metallic devices used for gripping or holding heavy objects. —*adv.* Completely <*dog*-weary> —*v.* **dogged, dog·ging. 1.** To track or trail relentlessly. **2.** To hold or fasten with a mechanical dog.
dog·cart (dôg′kärt′, dŏg′-) *n.* A vehicle drawn by 1 horse and accommodating 2 persons seated back to back.
dog days *pl.n.* The hot, sultry period between mid-July and Sept.
doge (dōj) *n.* The chief magistrate of the former republics of Venice and Genoa.
dog-ear (dôg′îr′, dŏg′-) *n.* The turned-down corner of a page of a book. **—dog′-ear** *v.* **—dog′-eared′** *adj.*
dog-eat-dog (dôg′ēt-dôg′, dŏg′ēt-dŏg′) *adj.* Ruthlessly acquisitive or competitive.
dog·fight (dôg′fīt′, dŏg′-) *n.* An aerial battle between fighter planes.
dog·fish (dôg′fĭsh′, dŏg′-) *n.* A small shark, chiefly of the family Squalidae of Atlantic and Pacific coastal waters.
dog·ged (dô′gĭd, dŏg′ĭd) *adj.* Stubbornly unyielding : tenacious. **—dog′ged·ly** *adv.* **—dog′ged·ness** *n.*
dog·ger·el (dô′gər-əl, dŏg′ər-) *n.* Loose, irregular verse, esp. of an inferior nature.
dog·gy *or* **dog·gie** (dô′gē, dŏg′ē) *n., pl.* **-gies.** A dog, esp. a small one.
doggy bag *or* **doggie bag** *n.* A bag for leftover food taken home from a restaurant.
dog·house (dôg′hous′, dŏg′-) *n.* A dog shelter.
†**do·gie** (dō′gē) *n. W U.S.* A stray or motherless calf.
dog·leg (dôg′lĕg′, dŏg′-) *n.* **1.** A sharp bend, esp. in a road. **2.** A golf hole with a sharply angled fairway. **—dog′leg′** *v.*
dog·ma (dôg′mə, dŏg′-) *n.* **1.** A system of doctrines proclaimed true by a religious sect. **2.** A principle, belief, or idea, esp. one considered to be absolute truth.
dog·mat·ic (dôg-măt′ĭk, dŏg-) *adj.* Characterized by an authoritative assertion of unproved or unprovable principles. **—dog·mat′i·cal·ly** *adv.*
dog·ma·tism (dôg′mə-tĭz′əm, dŏg′-) *n.* Dogmatic assertion of belief or opinion.
dog·nap (dôg′năp′) *v.* **-naped, -nap·ing** *or* **-napped, -nap·ping.** To steal (a dog), esp. for sale to a research laboratory. **—dog′nap′er, dog′nap′per** *n.*
do-good·er (do͞o′go͝od′ər) *n. Informal.* An earnest but naive supporter of philanthropic or humanitarian reforms.
dog paddle *n.* A swimming stroke in which the arms paddle and the legs kick up and down. **—dog′-pad′dle** *v.*
dogtooth violet *n.* A plant, *Erythronium americanum,* of North America, bearing lilylike yellow flowers.
†**dog·trot** (dôg′trŏt′, dŏg′-) *n.* **1.** An easy, steady trot. **2.** *Regional.* A roofed passage between 2 parts of a structure.
dog·wood (dôg′wo͝od′, dŏg′-) *n.* A tree, *Cornus florida* of E North America, bearing small greenish flowers surrounded by petallike white or pink bracts.
Do·ha (dō′hə, -hä′). Cap. of Qatar, on the Persian Gulf. *Pop.* 95,000.
doi·ly (doi′lē) *n., pl.* **-lies.** A small, usu. ornamental mat.
do·ings (do͞o′ĭngz) *pl.n.* Events or activities, esp. social activities.
do-it-your·self (do͞o′ĭt-yər-sĕlf′) *adj. Informal.* Designed to be done or used without professional help.
do·jo (dō′jō) *n.* A school for training in Japanese arts of self-defense.
dol. *abbr.* dollar.
dol·ce vi·ta (dōl′chā vē′tä) *n.* A sensual and self-indulgent life.
dol·drums (dōl′drəmz′, dôl′-, dŏl′-) *pl.n.* **1.** The ocean regions near the equator where there is little or no wind. **2.** A period or condition of depression or inactivity.
dole (dōl) *n.* **1. a.** The distribution of goods, esp. of money, food, or clothing, as charity. **b.** Something so distributed. **2.** *esp. Brit.* The governmental distribution of relief payments to the unemployed. —*v.* **doled, dol·ing. 1.** To distribute or dispense as charity. **2.** To distribute sparingly <*dole* out food>
dole·ful (dōl′fəl) *adj.* Filled with or expressing grief : sad. **—dole′ful·ly** *adv.* **—dole′ful·ness** *n.*
doll (dŏl) *n.* **1.** A child's toy representing a human being. **2.** *Slang.* **a.** An attractive person. **b.** A woman. —*v. Slang.* To dress elegantly, as for a special occasion.
dol·lar (dŏl′ər) *n.* See CURRENCY TABLE.
dol·lop (dŏl′əp) *n.* A lump, portion, or helping <a *dollop* of whipped cream>
dol·ly (dŏl′ē) *n., pl.* **-lies. 1.** A doll. **2.** A low platform that moves on small wheels or rollers, used for moving heavy loads. **3.** A wheeled apparatus for moving a motion-picture or television camera about the set.
dol·men (dōl′mən, dŏl′-) *n.* A prehistoric structure made up of 2 or more upright stones supporting a horizontal stone.
do·lo·mite (dō′lə-mīt′, dŏl′ə-) *n.* A gray, pink, or white mineral consisting mainly of calcium and magnesium.
do·lor·ous (dō′lə-rəs, dŏl′-) *adj.* Marked by or expressive of grief or pain. **—do′lor·ous·ly** *adv.* **—do′lor·ous·ness** *n.*
dol·phin (dŏl′fĭn, dôl′-) *n.* **1.** Any of various marine mammals, chiefly of the family Delphinidae, that are related to the whales but are gen. smaller and have a beaklike snout. **2.** Either of 2 iridescently colored marine fishes, *Coryphaena hippurus* or *C. equisetis.*
dolt (dōlt) *n.* A dull, stupid person : clod.
-dom *suff.* **1.** State : condition <star*dom*> **2. a.** Domain : posi-

tion : rank <duke*dom*> **b.** A group having a specified position, office, or character <official*dom*>
do·main (dō-mān′) *n.* **1.** A territory over which rule or control is exercised. **2.** A sphere of activity or interest : field.
dome (dōm) *n.* **1.** A hemispherical vault or roof. **2.** Something suggesting a dome.
do·mes·tic (də-mĕs′tĭk) *adj.* **1.** Of or relating to a home, household, or family life. **2.** Enjoying or interested in home life and household affairs. **3.** Tame : domesticated <*domestic* animals> **4.** Of or relating to the policies or affairs within a country. **5.** Indigenous to or produced in a particular country. —*n.* A household servant. **—do·mes′ti·cal·ly** *adv.* **—do′mes·tic′i·ty** *n.*
do·mes·ti·cate (də-mĕs′tĭ-kāt′) *v.* **-cat·ed, -cat·ing.** To train or adapt to live with and be of use to human beings. **—do·mes′ti·ca′tion** *n.*
dom·i·cile (dŏm′ĭ-sīl′, -səl, dō′mĭ-) *n.* A dwelling place : home. **—dom′i·cile′** *v.* **—dom′i·cil′i·ar′y** (-sĭl′ē-ĕr′ē) *adj.*
dom·i·nant (dŏm′ə-nənt) *adj.* **1.** Having the most control or influence. **2.** Most prominent. **3.** *Genetics* Producing a typical effect even when paired with an unlike gene for the same characteristic. **—dom′i·nance** *n.* **—dom′i·nant·ly** *adv.*
dom·i·nate (dŏm′ə-nāt′) *v.* **-nat·ed, -nat·ing. 1.** To influence, control, or rule by superior power or authority. **2.** To occupy the most prominent position in or over. **—dom′i·na′tion** *n.* **—dom′i·na′tor** *n.*
dom·i·neer (dŏm′ə-nîr′) *v.* **1.** To rule over arbitrarily or arrogantly : tyrannize. **2.** To be bossy or overbearing.
Dom·i·ni·ca (dŏm′ə-nē′kə, də-mĭn′ĭ-kə). Island republic in the E Caribbean. *Cap.* Roseau. *Pop.* 83,100.
Do·min·i·can Republic (də-mĭn′ĭ-kən). Country occupying the E part of Hispaniola. *Cap.* Santo Domingo. *Pop.* 5,660,000.
do·min·ion (də-mĭn′yən) *n.* **1.** Supreme authority or control : sovereignty. **2.** A territory or sphere of control or influence : realm.
Dominion Day *n. Can.* Canada Day.
dom·i·no[1] (dŏm′ə-nō′) *n., pl.* **-noes** or **-nos. 1. a.** A masquerade costume consisting of a cloak with a hood and a mask worn over the top half of the face. **b.** The mask itself. **2.** A person wearing a domino.
dom·i·no[2] (dŏm′ə-nō′) *n., pl.* **-noes** or **-nos. 1.** A small, rectangular block whose face is divided into halves, each half being blank or marked from 1 to 6 dots. **2. dominoes** or **dominos** *(sing. in number).* A game played with a set of gen. 28 dominoes.
don[1] (dŏn) *n.* **1. Don.** Sir. Used as a courtesy title with a man's given name in Spanish-speaking countries. **2.** A Spanish gentleman. **3.** A head, tutor, or fellow at an English university. **4.** A Mafia leader.
don[2] (dŏn) *v.* **donned, don·ning.** To put on : dress in <*donned* a new suit>
Don (dŏn). River of S European USSR.
do·ña (dōn′yə) *n.* **1. Doña.** Lady. Used as a courtesy title with a woman's given name in Spanish-speaking countries. **2.** A Spanish gentlewoman.
do·nate (dō′nāt′, dō-nāt′) *v.* **-nat·ed, -nat·ing.** To present as a gift to a fund or cause. **—do·na′tion** *n.* **—do′na′tor** *n.*
done (dŭn) *adj.* **1.** Completely finished : through. **2.** Cooked adequately. **3.** Socially acceptable <not *done* in public>
dong (dông, dŏng) *n.* See CURRENCY TABLE.
Don Juan (dŏn wŏn′, jo͞o′ən) *n.* A man obsessed with seducing women : libertine.
don·key (dŏng′kē, dŭng′-, dông′-) *n., pl.* **-keys. 1.** The domesticated ass, prob. descended from the wild ass *Equus asinus.* **2.** *Informal.* A stubborn or stupid person.
Donne (dŭn), **John.** 1572?–1631. English poet and theologian.
don·nish (dŏn′ĭsh) *adj.* Of, resembling, or characteristic of a university don : pedantic.
don·ny·brook (dŏn′ē-bro͝ok′) *n.* A brawl.
do·nor (dō′nər) *n.* A person who gives, donates, or contributes, as to a fund or cause.
Don Qui·xo·te (dŏn′ kē-hō′tē, kwĭk′sət) *n.* An impractical idealist.
don't (dōnt). Do not.
do·nut (dō′nŭt′, -nət) *n. var. of* DOUGHNUT.
doo·dad (do͞o′dăd′) *n. Informal.* A nameless or unnamed gadget or article.
doo·dle (do͞od′l) *v.* **-dled, -dling.** To scribble aimlessly, esp. when preoccupied. **—doo′dle** *n.*
doom (do͞om) *n.* **1.** A decision or judgment, esp. an official condemnation to a severe penalty. **2.** Destiny or fate, esp. a ruinous or tragic fate. **3.** Inevitable destruction or ruin : annihilation. —*v.* **1.** To condemn. **2.** To destine, esp. to an unhappy end.

▲word history: The semantics of *doom* illustrates the process of pejoration, by which a word of a good or neutral connotation acquires an evil one. *Doom* is related to the verb *do* and basically means "something set up" and specif. "a law, statute." Even by Old English times, however, *doom* meant "judgment," esp. an adverse judgment, condemnation, or punishment.
dooms·day (do͞omz′dā′) *n.* **1.** Judgment Day. **2.** A dreaded day of judgment or reckoning.
door (dôr, dōr) *n.* **1.** A movable panel for closing off an entrance. **2.** An entrance or passage. **3.** A means of access.
door·bell (dôr′bĕl′, dōr′-) *n.* A bell rung at an outer door as a signal.
door·jamb (dôr′jăm′, dōr′-) *n.* Either of the 2 vertical pieces that frame a doorway and support the lintel.
door·knob (dôr′nŏb′, dōr′-) *n.* A knob that when turned opens a door.
door·man (dôr′măn′, -mən, dōr′-) *n.* An attendant at the entrance of a building.
door·mat (dôr′măt′, dōr′-) *n.* A mat outside a door, used to wipe wet or dirty shoes.
door·step (dôr′stĕp′, dōr′-) *n.* A step that leads to a door.
door·way (dôr′wā′, dōr′-) *n.* An entrance to a room or building.
door·yard (dôr′yärd′, dōr′-) *n.* A yard adjacent to the door of a house.
do·pa (dō′pə) *n.* An amino acid that is used to treat Parkinson's disease.
dope (dōp) *n.* **1.** One of various chiefly liquid preparations added to produce desired properties : additive. **2.** *Informal.* A narcotic, esp. one that is addictive. **3.** *Slang.* A stupid person. **4.** *Slang.* Facts and details : information. —*v.* **doped, dop·ing. 1.** To treat with an additive. **2.** *Informal.* To administer a drug to, esp. in secret : drug. **3.** *Informal.* To figure out.
dope·ster (dōp′stər) *n.* One who analyzes and predicts future events, esp. in sports.
dop·ey *also* **dop·y** (dō′pē) *adj.* **-i·er, -i·est.** *Slang.* **1.** Dazed or sluggish as if drugged. **2.** Stupid or foolish.
dorm (dôrm) *n. Informal.* A dormitory.
dor·mant (dôr′mənt) *adj.* **1.** Asleep or inactive. **2.** *Biol.* Being in a relatively inactive or resting condition in which some processes are slowed down or suspended. **—dor′man·cy** *n.*
dor·mer (dôr′mər) *n.* A window set in a small gable projecting from a roof.
dor·mi·to·ry (dôr′mĭ-tôr′ē, -tōr′ē) *n., pl.* **-ries. 1.** A large room providing sleeping quarters for a number of people. **2.** A building for housing a number of people.
dor·mouse (dôr′mous′) *n.* Any of various squirrellike rodents of the family Gliridae.
†dor·nick (dôr′nĭk) *n. Regional.* A small chunk of rock : stone.
dor·sal (dôr′səl) *adj. Anat.* Of, relating to, or located on or near the back.
do·ry (dôr′ē, dōr′ē) *n., pl.* **-ries.** A small, narrow, flat-bottomed fishing boat with high sides and a sharp prow.
dose (dōs) *n.* **1.** A specified amount of a therapeutic agent prescribed to be taken at 1 time or at stated intervals. **2.** *Med.* The amount of radiation administered to a certain bodily part. **—dos′age** *n.* **—dose** *v.*
do·sim·e·ter (dō-sĭm′ĭ-tər) *n.* A device that measures and indicates the amount of x-rays or radioactivity absorbed.
dos·si·er (dŏs′ē-ā′, dô′sē-ā′) *n.* A collection of documents or papers giving detailed information about a person or subject.
Dos·to·ev·ski *or* **Dos·to·yev·sky** (dôs′tə-yĕf′skē), **Feodor Mikhailovich.** 1821–81. Russian novelist.
dot (dŏt) *n.* **1.** A small speck : spot. **2.** A small round mark made by or as if by a writing implement. **3.** A precise moment in time. —*v.* **dot·ted, dot·ting.** To mark or cover with or as if with dots.
dot·age (dō′tĭj) *n.* Senility.
dot·ard (dō′tərd) *n.* A senile person.
dote (dōt) *v.* **dot·ed, dot·ing. 1.** To show excessive fondness or love. **2.** To show mental deterioration, esp. as a result of senility. **—dot′er** *n.*
dou·ble (dŭb′əl) *adj.* **1.** Twice as much in size, power, quantity, or amount. **2.** Composed of 2 like parts <*double* doors> **3.** Composed of 2 unlike parts : dual <a *double* meaning> **4.** Accommodating or designed for 2. **5. a.** Acting 2 parts. **b.** Marked by duplicity : deceitful. **6.** *Bot.* Having more than the usual number of petals. —*adv.* **1.** Two together <riding *double*> **2.** In 2 <bent *double*> —*n.* **1.** Something or someone that resembles another : duplicate. **2.** An understudy. **3.** A sharp turn in running : reversal. **4. doubles.** A match between 2 pairs of players, as in tennis. **5.** *Baseball* A hit in which the batter reaches 2nd base. **6.** A bid doubling one's opponent's bid in bridge. —*v.* **-bled, -bling. 1.** To make or become twice as great.

2. To fold in 2 <*double* the blanket> 3. *Baseball.* To hit a double. 4. To challenge (an opponent's bid) with a double in bridge. 5. To reverse direction <*double* back over the trail> 6. To serve an additional purpose <My bed *doubles* as a couch.> **—dou′bly** *adv.*

double agent *n.* A spy who pretends to work for a government while actually working for another.

double bass *n.* The largest and lowest-pitched member of the violin family.

dou·ble-breast·ed (dŭb′əl-brĕs′tĭd) *adj.* Fastened by lapping 1 half over the other and usu. having a double row of buttons with a single row of buttonholes.

dou·ble-cross (dŭb′əl-krôs′, -krŏs′) *v. Slang.* To betray. **—dou′ble-cross′** *n.*

dou·ble-deal·ing (dŭb′əl-dē′lĭng) *adj.* Marked by duplicity : treacherous. *—n.* Deceit. **—dou′ble-deal′er** *n.*

dou·ble-deck·er (dŭb′əl-dĕk′ər) *n.* 1. A vehicle, as a bus, with 2 decks for passengers. 2. Two beds built 1 above the other. 3. A sandwich with 3 slices of bread and 2 layers of filling.

double dipping *n.* The practice of holding a salaried governmental position while receiving a pension from another.

dou·ble-en·ten·dre (dŭb′əl-än-tän′drə, do͞o′bläN-täN′drə) *n.* A word or expression having a double meaning, esp. when the 2nd meaning is risqué.

dou·ble-head·er (dŭb′əl-hĕd′ər) *n.* Two games played consecutively on the same day.

dou·ble-joint·ed (dŭb′l-join′tĭd) *adj.* Having flexible joints permitting connected parts to be bent at unusual angles.

double knit *n.* A jerseylike knitted fabric having a double thickness and interlocking stitches.

double play *n. Baseball.* A play in which 2 players are put out.

dou·ble·speak (dŭb′əl-spēk′) *n.* DOUBLE TALK 2.

dou·blet (dŭb′lĭt) *n.* 1. A close-fitting jacket worn by men between the 15th and 17th cent. 2. a. A pair of similar things. b. One of a pair.

double take *n.* A delayed reaction to something unusual.

double talk *n.* 1. Meaningless speech consisting of nonsense syllables mixed with intelligible words : gibberish. 2. Evasive or ambiguous language.

dou·ble·think (dŭb′əl-thĭngk′) *n.* Simultaneous belief in 2 contradictory ideas or points of view.

▲word history: *Doublethink* was coined by George Orwell in his novel *Nineteen Eighty-four,* published in 1949. It is rare that an invented word gains sufficient currency to be included in a dictionary.

dou·bloon (dŭ-blo͞on′) *n.* An obsolete Spanish gold coin.

doubt (dout) *v.* 1. To be uncertain or unsure about. 2. To tend to distrust : disbelieve. *—n.* 1. A lack of certainty or conviction. 2. An uncertain state of affairs. ☆**syns:** DOUBTFULNESS, DUBIETY, QUESTION, SKEPTICISM, UNCERTAINTY **—doubt′er** *n.*

doubt·ful (dout′fəl) *adj.* 1. Not sure : uncertain. 2. Experiencing or exhibiting doubt <*doubtful* about the future> 3. Of uncertain outcome : undecided. 4. Equivocal in nature or character : questionable <a *doubtful* past> **—doubt′ful·ly** *adv.* **—doubt′ful·ness** *n.*

doubt·less (dout′lĭs) *adj.* Assured : positive. *—adv.* 1. Certainly. 2. Probably. **—doubt′less·ly** *adv.*

douche (do͞osh) *n.* 1. A stream of liquid or air applied to a part or cavity of the body in order to cleanse or medicate. 2. A device for application of a douche. **—douche** *v.*

dough (dō) *n.* 1. A thick, soft mixture of flour or meal, liquids, and other ingredients that is baked, esp. to make bread or pastry. 2. A doughlike pasty mass. 3. *Slang.* Money. **—dough′y** *adj.*

dough·boy (dō′boi′) *n.* An American infantryman in World War I.

dough·nut *also* **do·nut** (dō′nŭt′, -nət) *n.* A small, usu. ring-shaped cake made of rich, light dough that is deep-fried.

dough·ty (dou′tē) *adj.* **-ti·er, -ti·est.** Marked by valor : courageous.

Doug·las fir (dŭg′ləs) *n.* An evergreen timber tree, *Pseudotsuga taxifolia,* of NW North America.

dour (do͝or, dour) *adj.* 1. Stern and forbiding. 2. Morose and gloomy : ill-humored.

douse (dous) *v.* **doused, dous·ing.** 1. To plunge into liquid : immerse. 2. To drench. 3. To extinguish.

dove¹ (dŭv) *n.* 1. Any of various birds of the family Columbidae, which includes the pigeons. 2. An advocate of peace and conciliatory measures as opposed to armed conflict. **—dov′ish** *adj.*

dove² (dōv) *v. var. p.t. of* DIVE.

Do·ver (dō′vər). 1. Strait at E end of the English Channel between SE England and N France. 2. Cap. of Del. *Pop.* 23,512.

dove·tail (dŭv′tāl′) *n.* A fan-shaped tenon that when fitted into a corresponding mortise forms a tight interlocking joint. *—v.* 1. To cut into or join by means of dovetails. 2. To connect or combine precisely and harmoniously.

dow·a·ger (dou′ə-jər) *n.* 1. A widow who holds a title or property from her dead husband. 2. An elderly woman of high social position.

dow·dy (dou′dē) *adj.* **-di·er, -di·est.** 1. Not neat : shabby. 2. Old-fashioned.

dow·el (dou′əl) *n.* A round wooden pin that fits tightly into a corresponding hole to fasten together 2 pieces. **—dow′el** *v.*

dow·er (dou′ər) *n.* 1. The part of or interest in a deceased man's real estate allotted by law to his widow for her lifetime. 2. A dowry. *—v.* To give a dower to : endow.

down¹ (doun) *adv.* 1. a. From a higher to a lower place <climb *down*> b. From an upright position to a horizontal position <knocked all the pins *down*> 2. In or to a lower position, point, or state <sit *down*> 3. From earlier times or people. 4. In partial payment at the time of purchase. 5. Earnestly or energetically. 6. In writing. 7. To the source <tracked the gossip *down*> *—adj.* 1. a. Directed or moving downward <the *down* staircase> b. In a low or lower position <The blinds are *down.*> 2. a. Sick <*down* with the flu> b. Low in spirits : dejected. 3. Completed : finished <5 *down,* 5 to go> *—prep.* In a descending direction along, into, upon, or through. *—n.* 1. A movement downward : descent. 2. *Football.* Any of a series of plays during which a team must advance at least 10 yds. to retain possession of the ball. *—v.* 1. To bring, strike, put, or throw down. 2. To gulp.

down² (doun) *n.* 1. Fine, soft, fluffy feathers, as on a young bird. 2. A soft, fine substance like down <peach *down*>

down³ (doun) *n. often* **downs.** An expanse of grassy upland used for grazing.

down·beat (doun′bēt′) *n.* The downward hand movement made by a conductor to indicate the 1st beat of a musical measure.

down·cast (doun′kăst′) *adj.* 1. Directed downward <*downcast* eyes> 2. Low in spirits : dejected.

down·er (dou′nər) *n. Slang.* 1. A depressant or sedative drug, as a barbiturate or tranquilizer. 2. One that is depressing.

down·fall (doun′fôl′) *n.* 1. a. A sudden loss of wealth, position, or happiness : ruin. b. Something that causes a downfall. 2. A fall of rain or snow, esp. when heavy or unexpected. **—down′fall′en** *adj.*

down·grade (doun′grād′) *n.* 1. A downward slope or grade, as in a road. 2. A downward turn or trend. *—v.* To lower in rank, reputation, or importance.

down·heart·ed (doun′här′tĭd) *adj.* Low in spirits : downcast.

down·hill (doun′hĭl′) *adv.* Toward the bottom of a hill. **—down′hill′** *adj.*

down-home (doun′hōm′) *adj.* Of, pertaining to, or typical of the rural S U.S. or its people, as in naturalness or informality.

down payment *n.* A partial payment made at the time of purchase.

down·play (doun′plā′) *v.* To minimize the significance of.

down·pour (doun′pôr′, -pōr′) *n.* A heavy rainfall.

down·right (doun′rīt′) *adj.* 1. Out-and-out : complete. 2. Straightforward : candid. *—adv.* Thoroughly.

down·shift (doun′shĭft′) *v.* To shift into a lower automotive gear.

down·size (doun′sīz′) *v.* To make in a smaller size.

down·stage (doun′stāj′) *adv. & adj.* Toward or at the front of a theater stage.

down·stairs (doun′stârz′) *adv.* 1. Down the stairs. 2. To or on a lower floor. *—n.* (-stârz′) *(sing. in number).* The lower or main floor. **—down′stairs′** *adj.*

down·stream (doun′strēm′) *adv. & adj.* In the direction of a stream's current.

down·swing (doun′swĭng′) *n.* 1. A swing downward. 2. A downward trend.

down·time (doun′tīm′) *n.* A period of time when something, as a machine or a factory, is inactive.

down-to-earth (doun′tə-ûrth′) *adj.* Sensible : practical.

down·town (doun′toun′) *n.* The lower part and esp. the business center of a city or town. *—adv.* (-toun′). To, toward, or in the downtown. **—down′town′** *adj.*

down·trod·den (doun′trŏd′n) *adj.* Subjected to oppression.

down·turn (doun′tûrn′) *n.* A decline, esp. in business or financial affairs.

down under *n. Informal.* Australia or New Zealand.

down·ward (doun′wərd) *also* **down·wards** (-wərdz) *adv.* From a higher to a lower place, point, level, or condition. **—down′ward** *adj.*

down·wind (doun′wĭnd′) *adv. & adj.* In the direction toward which the wind blows : leeward.

dow·ry (dou′rē) *n., pl.* **-ries.** Money or property brought by a bride to her husband at marriage.

dowse (douz) *v.* **dowsed, dows•ing.** To use a divining rod to find underground water or minerals. **–dows'er** *n.*
dox•ol•o•gy (dŏk-sŏl'ə-jē) *n., pl.* **-gies.** A hymn or verse in praise of God.
doy•en (doi-ĕn', doi'ən, dwä-yăN') *n.* The eldest or senior male member of a group.
doy•enne (doi-ĕn', dwä-yĕn') *n.* The eldest or senior female member of a group.
doz. *abbr.* dozen.
doze (dōz) *v.* **dozed, doz•ing.** To sleep lightly : nap. **–doze** *n.*
doz•en (dŭz'ən) *n.* **1.** *pl.* **dozen.** A set of 12. **2.** *pl.* **dozens.** An indefinite number. **–doz'en** *adj.* **–doz'enth** *adj.*
dr *abbr.* dram.
dr. *abbr.* **1.** debit. **2.** debtor.
Dr. *abbr.* **1.** doctor. **2.** drive (in street names).
drab (drăb) *adj.* **drab•ber, drab•best. 1. a.** Of a light, dull brown color. **b.** Of an olive brown : khaki-colored. **2.** Commonplace : dull. **–drab'ness** *n.*
drach•ma (drăk'mə) *n., pl.* **-mas** *or* **-mae** (-mē). **1.** See CURRENCY TABLE. **2.** A silver coin of ancient Greece.
draft (drăft, dräft) *n.* **1. a.** A current of air. **b.** A device in a flue that controls the circulation of air. **2.** The act of pulling or drawing a load. **3.** A preliminary sketch, outline, or version. **4. a.** Compulsory assignment to military service. **b.** The group of people assigned. **5. a.** A gulp, drink, or inhalation of something. **b.** The amount taken in. **6.** A document for the transfer of money. **7.** The depth of a ship's keel below the water line, esp. when loaded. *–v.* **1. a.** To select for a specific duty. **b.** To conscript for military service. **2.** To work up a tentative plan for or sketch of. *–adj.* **1.** Used for drawing heavy loads <*draft* horses> **2.** Drawn from a keg or tap <*draft* beer> **–draft•ee'** *n.*
drafts•man (drăfts'mən, dräfts'-) *n.* A person who draws designs or plans, as of machinery. **–drafts'man•ship'** *n.*
draft•y (drăf'tē, dräf'-) *adj.* **-i•er, -i•est.** Being exposed to or having drafts of air. **–draft'i•ness** *n.*
drag (drăg) *v.* **dragged, drag•ging. 1.** To draw along, pull, or haul by force. **2.** To trail or cause to trail along the ground. **3.** To search or dredge the bottom of (a body of water), as with a hook or net. **4.** To move or cause to move with great reluctance or difficulty. **5.** To pass or proceed slowly <Time *dragged.*> **6.** To prolong boringly <*dragged* out the lecture> **7.** *Slang.* To draw on a cigarette, pipe, or cigar : puff. *–n.* **1.** The act of dragging. **2.** Something, as a harrow, dragged along on the ground. **3.** Something that slows or stops motion, as a brake on a fishing reel. **4.** The retarding force exerted on a moving body by a fluid medium, as air or water. **5.** *Slang.* Someone or something esp. bothersome. **6.** *Slang.* A puff on a cigarette, pipe, or cigar. **7.** *Slang.* A street. **8.** *Slang.* Clothing of either sex worn by a member of the opposite sex. **–drag'ger** *n.*
drag•net (drăg'nĕt') *n.* **1.** A trawling net. **2.** A system of search in which all available resources are used.
drag•o•man (drăg'ə-mən) *n., pl.* **-mans** or **-men.** An interpreter in countries where Arabic, Turkish, or Persian is spoken.
drag•on (drăg'ən) *n.* An imaginary giant reptile of story and legend usu. represented as a winged, fire-breathing monster.
drag•on•fly (drăg'ən-flī') *n.* Any of various large insects of the order Odonata, with 2 pairs of narrow, net-veined wings and a long, slender body.
dra•goon (drə-go͞on', dră-) *n.* A heavily armed mounted soldier of the 17th and 18th cent. *–v.* To coerce.
drain (drān) *v.* **1.** To draw off (a liquid) gradually <*drained* water from the pool> **2. a.** To cause liquid to go out from : empty <*drained* the pool> **b.** To draw off the surface water of. **3.** To use up completely : exhaust. *–n.* **1.** A means, as a pipe or channel, of draining liquid. **2.** The act or process of draining. **3.** Something that drains or exhausts. **–drain'er** *n.*
drain•age (drā'nĭj) *n.* **1.** The act, process, or a way of draining. **2.** A natural or artificial system of drains. **3.** Something that is drained off.
drain•pipe (drān'pīp') *n.* A pipe for carrying off rainwater or sewage.
drake (drāk) *n.* A male duck.
dram (drăm) *n.* **1.** See MEASUREMENT TABLE. **2. a.** A small drink, as of a liqueur. **b.** A small amount : bit.
dra•ma (drä'mə, drăm'ə) *n.* **1.** A play in prose or verse, esp. one recounting a serious story. **2.** Dramatic art of a particular kind or period <Shakespearean *drama*> **3.** A succession of events with the dramatic progression or emotional content typical of a play. **–dra•mat'ic** (drə-măt'ĭk) *adj.* **–dra•mat'i•cal•ly** *adv.* **–dram'a•tist** *n.*
dram•a•tize (drăm'ə-tīz', drä'mə-) *v.* **-tized, -tiz•ing. 1.** To adapt for presentation as a drama. **2.** To present or regard in a dramatic or melodramatic manner. **–dram'a•ti•za'tion** *n.*
drank (drăngk) *v. p.t. of* DRINK.
drape (drāp) *v.* **draped, drap•ing. 1.** To cover or hang with cloth in loose folds <*draped* the sculpture> **2.** To arrange or hang in loose, graceful folds. **3.** To stretch or cause to stretch out loosely <*draped* my arms over the railing> *–n.* **1.** *often* **drapes.** A drapery : curtain. **2.** The manner in which cloth hangs or falls.
drap•er (drā'pər) *n. esp. Brit.* One who deals in dry goods and cloth.
drap•er•y (drā'pə-rē) *n., pl.* **-ies. 1.** Cloth or clothing gracefully arranged in loose folds. **2.** *often* **draperies.** Curtains, usu. of heavy fabric, that hang straight in loose folds. **3.** *esp. Brit.* The business of a draper.
dras•tic (drăs'tĭk) *adj.* Extremely harsh or severe. **–dras'ti•cal•ly** *adv.*
draught (drăft) *n., v., & adj. esp. Brit. var. of* DRAFT.
draughts (drăfts, dräfts) *n. (sing. in number). esp. Brit.* The game of checkers.
draw (drô) *v.* **drew** (dro͞o), **drawn** (drôn), **draw•ing. 1. a.** To move or cause to move in a specified direction or to a specified position, as by leading <*drew* us into the dining room> **b.** To pull or move so as to cover or uncover <*draw* the curtains> **2.** To pull or take out (e.g., a weapon) for use <*draw* a gun> **3. a.** To earn or bring in <savings *drawing* interest> **b.** To withdraw (money). **4.** To take in (air) : inhale. **5.** To describe (a line or figure), as with a pen : sketch. **6.** To elicit in response : evoke <*drew* applause from the audience> **7.** To receive in return for services or efforts <*drew* daily wages> **8.** To get by chance or in a chance drawing. **9.** To attract. **10.** To devise or formulate from evidence at hand <*drew* the wrong conclusion> **11.** To eviscerate. **12.** To displace (a given depth of water) in floating. **13.** To provoke <*drawing* enemy fire> **14.** To end (a contest) undecided or tied. **15.** To compose or write in a set form <*draw up* a legal document> **16.** To change the shape of. **17.** To take (cards) from a dealer or central stack. **18.** To move or cause to move steadily <The holiday was *drawing* near.> *–n.* **1.** The act or result of drawing. **2.** A tied contest. **3.** Something that attracts interest or attendance. **–draw on** (*or* **upon**). To use as a source. **–draw out. 1.** To cause to converse freely and easily. **2.** To prolong.
draw•back (drô'băk') *n.* An undesirable feature : disadvantage.
draw•bridge (drô'brĭj') *n.* A bridge that can be lowered, raised, or turned aside.
draw•er (drô'ər) *n.* **1.** One who draws. **2.** (*also* drôr). A sliding boxlike compartment in furniture. **3. drawers.** Underpants.
draw•ing (drô'ĭng) *n.* **1.** The act of one that draws. **2.** A selection of lots, as at a raffle. **3. a.** The art of representing forms and figures on a surface by means of lines. **b.** A portrayal or representation made by drawing.
drawing card *n.* One that attracts interest or attendance.
drawing room *n.* A living room or parlor in a private house.
drawl (drôl) *v.* To speak with drawn-out vowels. **–drawl** *n.*
drawn (drôn) *v. p.p.* of DRAW.
draw•string (drô'strĭng') *n.* A cord or string run through a casing or hem and pulled to close or tighten an opening.
dray (drā) *n.* A low, heavy cart without sides, used for haulage.
dread (drĕd) *n.* **1.** Great fear : terror. **2.** Nervous or fearful anticipation. *–v.* **1.** To be in great fear of. **2.** To anticipate with alarm, anxiety, or reluctance. *–adj.* **1.** Causing fear : terrifying. **2.** Inspiring awe.
dread•ful (drĕd'fəl) *adj.* **1. a.** Causing fear or dread. **b.** Inspiring awe. **2.** Extremely disagreeable or distasteful. **–dread'ful•ly** *adv.* **–dread'ful•ness** *n.*
dread•locks (drĕd'lŏks') *pl.n.* Hair that has formed long matted clumps due to lack of washing and combing.

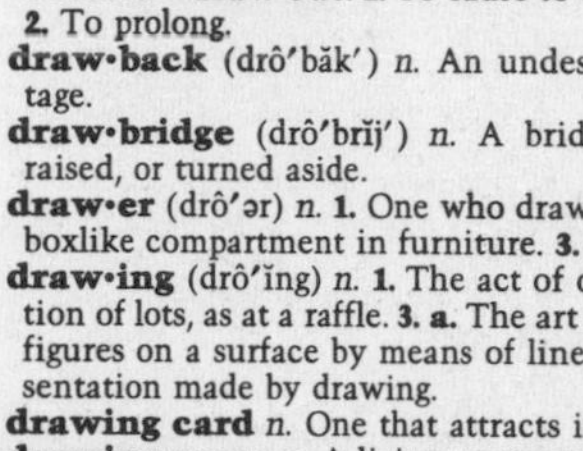

dreadlocks

dread•nought (drĕd'nôt') *n.* A heavily armed battleship.
dream (drēm) *n.* **1.** A series of mental images, thoughts, and emotions occurring in certain stages of sleep. **2.** A daydream. **3.** A state of abstraction : trance. **4.** A hope or aspiration. **5.** One that is esp. lovely or pleasant. *–v.* **dreamed** *or* **dreamt**

(drĕmt), **dream•ing. 1.** To have a dream (of). **2.** To daydream. **3.** To consider possible. **–dream•er** *n.* **–dream'y** *adj.*
dream•world (drēm'wûrld') *n.* A realm of illusion or fantasy.
drear (drîr) *adj.* Dreary.
drea•ry (drîr'ē) *adj.* **-ri•er, -ri•est. 1.** Bleak and gloomy <*dreary* weather> **2.** Monotonous : dull <*dreary* chores> **–drear'i•ly** *adv.* **–drear'i•ness** *n.*
dredge[1] (drĕj) *n.* **1.** A machine used to remove sand or mud, esp. from the bottom of a body of water. **2.** A boat or barge equipped with a dredge. *–v.* **dredged, dredg•ing. 1.** To clean, deepen, or widen with a dredge. **2.** To bring up : unearth <*dredged* up old regrets> **–dredg'er** *n.*
dredge[2] (drĕj) *v.* **dredged, dredg•ing.** To coat (food) by sprinkling with a powder, as flour or sugar.
dregs (drĕgz) *pl.n.* **1.** The sediment of a liquid. **2.** The least desirable part.
drench (drĕnch) *v.* To wet completely.
dress (drĕs) *n.* **1.** A one-piece, outer garment for women and girls. **2.** Clothing. *–v.* **1.** To put clothes on <*dress* the baby> **2.** To decorate or arrange a display in <*dress* a store window> **3.** To groom (the hair). **4.** To apply healing materials to (a wound). **5.** To prepare for use <*dress* lumber> **6.** To make ready for sale or cooking. **7.** To wear formal clothes. **–dress down.** To reprimand.
dres•sage (drə-säzh', drĕ-) *n.* Guidance of a horse through a series of intricate maneuvers by almost imperceptible movements of the hands, legs, and weight.
dress•er[1] (drĕs'ər) *n.* One that dresses.
dress•er[2] (drĕs'ər) *n.* A chest of drawers for clothing, usu. with a mirror above it.
dress•ing (drĕs'ĭng) *n.* **1.** Medicine or bandages applied to a wound. **2.** A sauce, as for salads. **3.** A stuffing, as for fowl.
dressing gown *n.* A lounging robe.
dress•mak•er (drĕs'mā'kər) *n.* A maker of women's dresses. **–dress'mak'ing** *n.*
dress rehearsal *n.* A final rehearsal.
dress•y (drĕs'ē) *adj.* **-i•er, -i•est. 1.** Elegant or showy in dress or appearance. **2.** Smart or stylish : chic. **–dress'i•ness** *n.*
drew (dro͞o) *v.* *p.t. of* DRAW.
drib•ble (drĭb'əl) *v.* **-bled, -bling. 1.** To drip or cause to drip : trickle. **2.** To slobber : drool. **3.** To move (a ball) by bouncing or kicking repeatedly, as in basketball or soccer. *–n.* **1.** A trickle or drip. **2.** A small quantity. **3.** The act of dribbling a ball.
drib•let (drĭb'lĭt) *n.* **1.** A tiny falling drop of liquid. **2.** A very small amount.
dri•er[1] (drī'ər) *n.* **1.** A substance added to varnish, paint, or ink to expedite drying. **2.** *var. of* DRYER.
dri•er[2] (drī'ər) *adj.* *compar. of* DRY.
dri•est (drī'ĭst) *adj.* *superl. of* DRY.
†drift (drĭft) *v.* **1.** To be or cause to be borne along by or as if by currents of air or water. **2.** To move about aimlessly : wander. **3.** To accumulate or cause to accumulate in piles <wind *drifting* the snow> **4.** *W U.S.* To drive (livestock) slowly or far afield, esp. for grazing. *–n.* **1.** The act or state of drifting. **2.** Something moving along on a current of air or water. **3.** A mass of material, as sand or snow, deposited by air or water currents. **4.** A general meaning or direction. **–drift'er** *n.*
drift•wood (drĭft'wo͝od') *n.* Wood floating in or washed ashore by water.
drill[1] (drĭl) *n.* **1.** Any of several tools used for boring. **2.** Ordered and repetitive instruction as a means of teaching or training. **3.** A specific exercise meant to develop a skill or familiarize someone with a procedure <a fire *drill*> *–v.* **1.** To make (a hole) with a drill. **2.** To train by continuous repetition.
drill[2] (drĭl) *n.* **1.** A furrow in which seeds are planted. **2.** An implement or machine for planting seeds in holes or furrows.
drill[3] (drĭl) *n.* Long-wearing cotton or linen twill, gen. used for work clothes.
drillmas•ter (drĭl'măs'tər) *n.* A noncommissioned officer who instructs recruits in military drill.
drink (drĭngk) *v.* **drank** (drăngk), **drunk** (drŭngk), **drink•ing. 1.** To take in and swallow (liquid). **2.** To absorb (moisture or liquid). **3.** To make or join in a toast <*drank* to success> **4.** To take in through the intellect or senses. **5.** To use alcoholic beverages, esp. immoderately. *–n.* **1.** A liquid suitable for drinking : beverage. **2.** An alcoholic beverage. **3.** An amount of liquid swallowed <a *drink* of water> **–drink'a•ble** *adj.* **–drink'er** *n.*
drip (drĭp) *v.* **dripped, drip•ping. 1.** To fall or let fall in drops. **2.** To shed drops. *–n.* **1.** The process of dripping. **2.** Liquid or moisture that falls in drops. **3.** *Slang.* A boring or dull person.
drip-dry (drĭp'drī') *adj.* Made of a fabric that will not wrinkle when hung dripping wet. **–drip'-dry'** *v.*
drive (drīv) *v.* **drove** (drōv), **driv•en** (drĭv'ən), **driv•ing. 1.** To propel, push, force, or press onward. **2.** To repulse by authority or force. **3.** To force into a particular act or state. **4.** To penetrate or force to penetrate. **5. a.** To control, guide, and direct (a vehicle). **b.** To operate or be conveyed in a vehicle. **6.** To supply the motivating force to : spur. **7.** To impress or project energetically and convincingly. **8.** To hit (a ball) hard in a game. **9.** To rush, dash, or advance violently <a *driving* sleet> *–n.* **1.** The act of driving. **2.** A road for vehicles. **3.** A trip in a vehicle. **4.** The means or apparatus by which motion is transmitted to a machine. **5.** An organized movement or campaign to accomplish something. **6.** Initiative, energy, or aggressiveness. **7.** *Psychoanal.* A driving tendency or instinct, esp. of sexual or aggressive origin. **8.** A full-scale military offensive. **9.** A hard-hit ball in a game. **10.** The act of rounding up and driving cattle, as to new pastures.
drive-in (drīv'ĭn') *adj.* Permitting customers to remain in their vehicles while being served. **–drive'-in'** *n.*
driv•el (drĭv'əl) *v.* **-eled, -el•ing** or **-elled, -el•ling. 1.** To drool : slobber. **2.** To talk nonsensically. **–driv'el** *n.*
driv•er (drī'vər) *n.* **1.** One that drives, esp. a chauffeur. **2.** A wooden-headed golf club used for making long shots from the tee.
drive-up (drīv'ŭp') *adj.* Drive-in.
drive•way (drīv'wā') *n.* A private road connecting a building, as a house or garage, with the street.
driz•zle (drĭz'əl) *v.* **-zled, -zling.** To rain gently in fine drops. **–driz'zle** *n.* **–driz'zly** *adj.*
drogue (drōg) *n.* **1.** A sea anchor. **2.** A funnel- or cone-shaped device towed behind an aircraft as a target. **3.** A parachute used to decelerate a fast-moving object, as a spacecraft, or to pull a larger parachute from its storage pack.
droll (drōl) *adj.* Whimsically comical or amusingly odd. **–droll'er•y** *n.*
drom•e•dar•y (drŏm'ĭ-dĕr'ē, drŭm'-) *n.*, *pl.* **-ies.** A 1-humped camel, *Camelus dromedarius,* widely used in N Africa and W Asia as a beast of burden.
drone[1] (drōn) *n.* **1.** A male bee, esp. a honey bee, that is stingless, performs no work, and produces no honey. **2.** A person who lives off others. **3.** An unmanned aircraft operated by remote control.
drone[2] (drōn) *v.* **droned, dron•ing. 1.** To make a low, dull, continuous humming sound. **2.** To speak boringly and monotonously. **–drone** *n.*
drool (dro͞ol) *v.* **1.** To let saliva dribble from the mouth. **2.** *Informal.* To make an exaggerated show of desire. **3.** *Informal* To speak nonsensically. **–drool** *n.*
droop (dro͞op) *v.* **1.** To hang or bend downward : sag. **2.** To become weak or depressed <Our spirits *drooped.*> **–droop** *n.* **–droop'i•ness** *n.* **–droop'y** *adj.*
drop (drŏp) *n.* **1.** A tiny rounded or pear-shaped mass of liquid. **2.** A minute quantity of a substance. **3. drops.** Liquid medicine administered in drops. **4.** A small amount : bit <not a *drop* of compassion> **5.** Something, as an earring, shaped or hanging like a drop. **6.** The act of falling : descent. **7.** A swift decrease or decline, as in quality, quantity, or intensity. **8. a.** The vertical distance from a higher to a lower level. **b.** The distance through which something drops or falls. **9.** A sheer incline, as the face of a cliff. **10.** A delivery by parachute. **11.** Something arranged to fall or be lowered. **12.** A slot through which something is deposited in a receptacle. **13.** A central place where something, as mail, is brought and subsequently distributed. *–v.* **dropped, drop•ping. 1.** To fall or allow to fall <a petal *dropping* from the flower><*dropped* her handkerchief> **2.** To become or cause to become less, as in number, intensity, or volume. **3.** To descend from 1 level to another. **4.** To fall into a state of exhaustion or death. **5.** To pass into a given state or condition <*dropped* into a light sleep> **6.** To bring down <*dropped* the deer with a single shot> **7.** To mention casually. **8.** To write (e.g., a note) at one's leisure. **9.** To cease consideration or treatment of <*dropped* the charges for lack of evidence> **10.** To terminate an association or relationship with. **11.** To leave unfinished <*dropped* what we were doing to help them> **12.** To leave out (e.g., a letter) in speaking or writing. **13.** To leave at a particular place : deposit. **–drop behind.** To fall behind. **–drop by** (or **in**). To stop in for an informal visit. **–drop out. 1.** To withdraw from school without graduating. **2.** To withdraw from conventional society, esp. because of disillusionment with its values.
drop kick *n.* A kick made by dropping a football to the ground and kicking it when it starts to rebound. **–drop'-kick'** *v.*
drop•let (drŏp'lĭt) *n.* A small drop.
drop-off (drŏp'ôf', -ŏf') *n.* **1.** A steep slope. **2.** A noticeable decrease, as in attendance or sales.
drop•out (drŏp'out') *n.* One who drops out, as from shcool.
drop•per (drŏp'ər) *n.* A short, thin tube with a suction bulb at 1 end for drawing in and releasing liquid in drops.

drop•sy (drŏp'sē) *n.* A diseased condition in which abnormally large amounts of fluid collect in body tissues and cavities.
dross (drôs, drŏs) *n.* **1.** The impurity that forms on the surface of molten metal. **2.** Inferior, trivial, or worthless matter.
drought (drout) *also* **drouth** (drouth) *n.* **1.** A long period with no rain. **2.** A shortage.
drove[1] (drōv) *v. p.t. of* DRIVE.
drove[2] (drōv) *n.* **1.** A flock or herd being driven in a body. **2.** A crowd : throng.
drov•er (drō'vər) *n.* One who drives cattle or sheep.
drown (droun) *v.* **1.** To kill or die by submerging and suffocating in a liquid. **2.** To drench with or as if with a liquid. **3.** To deaden one's awareness of as if by immersion. **4.** To cause (a sound) to be overpowered by making a louder sound.
drowse (drouz) *v.* **drowsed, drows•ing.** To doze. **—drowse** *n.*
drows•y (drou'zē) *adj.* **-i•er, -i•est. 1.** Sleepy. **2.** Inducing sleepiness. **—drows'i•ly** *adv.* **—drows'i•ness** *n.*
drub (drŭb) *v.* **drubbed, drub•bing. 1.** To hit harshly with or as if with a stick : thrash. **2.** To defeat completely : trounce.
drudge (drŭj) *n.* A person who does hard, tiresome, or menial tasks. **—drudge** *v.* **—drudg'er•y** *n.*
drug (drŭg) *n.* **1.** A substance used therapeutically in the treatment of disease or illness. **2.** A narcotic, esp. one that is addictive. *—v.* **drugged, drug•ging. 1.** To administer a drug to. **2.** To mix or poison (food or drink) with drugs. **3.** To make dull or sleepy with or as if with a drug.
drug•gist (drŭg'ĭst) *n.* A pharmacist.
drug•store (drŭg'stôr', -stōr') *n.* A store where drugs, medical supplies, and other articles are sold.
dru•id *also* **Dru•id** (drōō'ĭd) *n.* A member of a priesthood of the Celtic religion of ancient Britain and Gaul.
drum (drŭm) *n.* **1.** A musical percussion instrument consisting of a hollow cylinder with a membrane stretched across 1 or both ends that is played by beating with the hands or with sticks. **2.** The sound made by striking a drum. **3.** Something, as a large oil container, shaped like a drum. *—v.* **drummed, drum•ming. 1.** To play a drum. **2.** To tap or thump rhythmically or incessantly. **3.** To instill by continual repetition : inculcate. **4.** To dismiss or expel in disgrace. **—drum up. 1.** To bring about through persistent effort. **2.** To invent : devise.
drum•beat (drŭm'bēt') *n.* The sound produced by striking a drum.
drum•lin (drŭm'lĭn) *n.* A rounded hill of glacial drift.
drum major *n.* A male leader of a marching band.
drum ma•jor•ette (mā'jə-rĕt') *n.* A female leader of a marching band.
drum•mer (drŭm'ər) *n.* **1.** A person who plays a drum, as in a band. **2.** A traveling sales representative.
drum•stick (drŭm'stĭk') *n.* **1.** A stick for playing a drum. **2.** The lower part of a fowl's leg.
drunk (drŭngk) *adj.* **1.** Intoxicated with alcohol to the point of impairment of physical and mental faculties. **2.** Caused or influenced by intoxication. **3.** Overwhelmed by strong feeling or emotion. *—n.* **1.** A drunkard. **2.** A drinking spree.
drunk•ard (drŭng'kərd) *n.* A person who is drunk habitually.
drunk•en (drŭng'kən) *adj.* **1.** DRUNK 1. **2.** Habitually drunk. **3.** Of, relating to, or caused by intoxication. **—drunk'en•ly** *adv.* **—drunk'en•ness** *n.*
drupe (drōōp) *n.* A fleshy fruit, as the plum, usu. having a single hard stone.
dry (drī) *adj.* **dri•er, dri•est** *also* **dry•er, dry•est. 1.** Free from moisture or liquid. **2.** Having or marked by little or no rain <*dry* desert regions> **3.** Not under water. **4.** Not liquid : solid <*dry* foods> **5.** Requiring or desiring drink : thirsty. **6.** Marked by the absence of natural or normal moisture. **7.** Eaten without garnish, as butter or jelly. **8.** Humorous or sarcastic in a shrewd, impersonal way. **9.** Wearisome and dull. **10.** Not sweet. Used of wines. **11.** *Informal.* Prohibiting or opposed to the sale or consumption of alcoholic beverages. *—v.* **dried, dry•ing.** To make or become dry. **—dry'ly** *adv.* **—dry'ness** *n.*
dry•ad (drī'əd, -ăd') *n.* A wood nymph.
dry cell *n.* A sealed electric cell having a paste electrolyte.
dry-clean (drī'klēn') *v.* To cleanse (clothing or fabrics) with chemical solvents rather than water. **—dry cleaning** *n.*
Dry•den (drīd'n), **John.** 1631–1700. English poet, dramatist, and critic.
dry dock *n.* A basin-shaped dock from which water can be emptied, used for building and repairing ships.
dry•er *also* **dri•er** (drī'ər) *n.* An appliance for removing moisture, as by heating.
dry goods *pl.n.* Clothing, sewing articles, and textiles as distinguished esp. from foodstuffs and hardware.
dry ice *n.* Solidified carbon dioxide.
dry measure *n.* A system of units for measuring solids such as grains, fruits, and vegetables by volume.
dry rot *n.* A fungous disease of timber that causes it to become brittle and crumble.
dry run *n.* A trial exercise : rehearsal.
DST or **D.S.T.** *abbr.* daylight-saving time.
D.T.'s (dē-tēz') *pl.n.* Delirium tremens.
du•al (dōō'əl, dyōō'-) *adj.* **1.** Made up of 2 parts : double <*dual* carburetors> **2.** Having a double purpose or character. **—du'al•ism, du•al'i•ty** (-ăl'ĭ-tē) *n.*
dub[1] (dŭb) *v.* **dubbed, dub•bing. 1.** To confer knighthood on. **2.** To nickname.
dub[2] (dŭb) *v.* **dubbed, dub•bing. 1.** To insert a new sound track, often a synchronized translation of the original dialogue, into (a film). **2.** To insert (sound) into a film or tape. **—dub** *n.* **—dub'ber** *n.*
du•bi•e•ty (dōō-bī'ĭ-tē, dyōō-) *n., pl.* **-ties. 1.** The quality or state of being dubious. **2.** An uncertainty.
du•bi•ous (dōō'bē-əs, dyōō'-) *adj.* **1.** Causing doubt : equivocal. **2.** Reluctant to agree : skeptical. **3. a.** Questionable as to quality or validity. **b.** Verging on impropriety. **4.** Not yet decided. **—du'bi•ous•ly** *adv.*
Dub•lin (dŭb'lĭn). Cap. of Ireland, on the Irish Sea. *Pop.* 544,586. **—Dub'lin•er** *n.*
du•cal (dōō'kəl, dyōō'-) *adj.* Of or relating to a duke or dukedom.
duc•at (dŭk'ət) *n.* Any of various gold coins formerly used in Europe.
duch•ess (dŭch'ĭs) *n.* **1.** The wife of a duke. **2.** A woman holding title to a duchy in her own right.
duch•y (dŭch'ē) *n., pl.* **-ies.** The rank or domain of a duke or duchess.
duck[1] (dŭk) *n.* **1.** Any of various wild or domesticated aquatic birds of the family Anatidae, with a broad, flat bill, short legs, and webbed feet. **2.** The flesh of a duck used as food. **3.** *Slang.* A person.
duck[2] (dŭk) *v.* **1.** To lower (the head and body) quickly, esp. to avoid being hit or observed. **2.** To evade (e.g., one's obligations) : shirk. **3.** To push suddenly under water.
duck[3] (dŭk) *n.* **1.** A strong cotton or linen cloth, lighter than canvas. **2. ducks.** Clothing made of duck, esp. white trousers.
duck•bill (dŭk'bĭl') *n.* The platypus.
duck•ling (dŭk'lĭng) *n.* A young duck.
duck•pin (dŭk'pĭn') *n.* **1.** A bowling pin shorter and fatter than a tenpin. **2. duckpins** *(sing. in number).* A bowling game played with duckpins and small balls.
duck soup *n. Slang.* Something easy to accomplish.
duck•y (dŭk'ē) *adj.* **-i•er, -i•est.** *Slang.* Satisfactory : fine.
duct (dŭkt) *n.* **1.** A tube through which something flows. **2.** A bodily passage, esp. one carrying a secretion. **3.** *Elect.* A pipe or tube for carrying wires or cables.
duc•tile (dŭk'tĭl) *adj.* **1.** Able to be drawn into a fine strand or wire <a *ductile* metal> **2.** Easily influenced or persuaded : docile. **—duc•til'i•ty** (-tĭl'ĭ-tē) *n.*
duct•less gland (dŭkt'lĭs) *n.* An endocrine gland.
dud (dŭd) *n. Informal.* **1.** A bomb, shell, or explosive round that fails to detonate. **2.** One that turns out to be a failure. **3. duds. a.** Clothing. **b.** Personal belongings.
dude (dōōd, dyōōd) *n.* **1.** *Informal.* A city person who vacations on a ranch. **2.** *Informal.* A man who is a very stylish dresser. **3.** *Slang.* A guy : fellow.
dude ranch *n.* A vacation resort modeled after a western ranch.
dudg•eon (dŭj'ən) *n.* A sullen, angry, or indignant mood <high *dudgeon*>
due (dōō, dyōō) *adj.* **1.** Payable at once or on demand. **2.** Owing <$40 still *due*> **3.** Proper : fitting <*due* respect> **4.** Meeting special requirements : sufficient. **5.** Scheduled or expected to occur <*due* at noon> *—n.* **1.** Something that is deserved or owed. **2. dues.** A fee or charge for membership, as in a club. *—adv.* Directly <*due* north>
du•el (dōō'əl, dyōō'-) *n.* **1.** A formal combat between 2 people, usu. fought to resolve a point of honor. **2.** A struggle that resembles a duel. **—du'el** *v.* **—du'el•ist** *n.*
du•en•de (dōō-ĕn'dā) *n.* Unusual power to attract or charm.
due process *n.* An established course esp. of judicial proceedings designed to protect the legal rights of the individual.
du•et (dōō-ĕt', dyōō-) *n.* A musical composition for 2 instruments or voices.
due to *prep.* Because of.
duf•fel bag (dŭf'əl) *n.* A large canvas or duck bag for carrying personal belongings.
duf•fer (dŭf'ər) *n. Informal.* An inept, incompetent, or stupid person.
dug (dŭg) *v. p.t. & p.p. of* DIG.

dug•out (dŭg′out′) *n.* **1.** A boat made by hollowing out a log. **2.** A rough shelter dug into the ground, used esp. in combat for protection from artillery. **3.** *Baseball.* Either of 2 usu. sunken shelters at the side of a field for the players.

duke (do͞ok, dyo͞ok) *n.* **1.** A member of the highest level of the British peerage, ranking above a marquis. **2.** A ruler of an independent European duchy. **3. dukes.** *Slang.* The fists. **—duke′dom** *n.*

dul•cet (dŭl′sĭt) *adj.* **1.** Melodious. **2.** Having an agreeable soothing quality.

dul•ci•mer (dŭl′sə-mər) *n.* A musical instrument with wire strings played with 2 small hammers or by plucking.

dull (dŭl) *adj.* **1.** Stupid. **2.** Insensitive. **3.** Dispirited : dejected. **4.** Not brisk or rapid : sluggish. **5.** Having a blunt edge or point : not sharp. **6.** Not intensely or acutely felt. **7.** Arousing no interest or curiosity : unexciting. **8.** Not vivid or bright : drab. **9.** Overcast : cloudy. **10.** Not clear or resonant. ☆**syns:** COLORLESS, DRAB, DRY, FLAT, LACKLUSTER, LIFELESS, PEDESTRIAN, PROSAIC, UNINSPIRED —*v.* To make or become dull. **—dull′ish** *adj.* **—dull′ness** *n.* **—dul′ly** *adv.*

dull•ard (dŭl′ərd) *n.* One who is mentally dull or slow.

Du•luth (də-lo͞oth′). City of Minn., at the W end of Lake Superior. *Pop.* 92,811.

du•ly (do͞o′lē, dyo͞o′-) *adv.* **1.** In a proper manner : rightfully. **2.** Punctually.

Du•mas (do͞o′mä′, dü-mä′). **Alexandre.** "Dumas père." 1802–70. French author.

dumb (dŭm) *adj.* **1.** Unable to speak : mute. **2.** Temporarily speechless, as from shock. **3.** *Informal.* Stupid. **—dumb′ly** *adv.* **—dumb′ness** *n.*

dumb•bell (dŭm′bĕl′) *n.* **1.** A weight consisting of a short bar with a metal ball or disk at each end that is lifted for exercise. **2.** *Slang.* DUMMY 2.

dumb•wait•er (dŭm′wā′tər) *n.* A small elevator used to convey goods, as food or dishes, from 1 floor to another.

dum•dum (dum′dum′) *n.* A soft-nosed bullet designed to expand on contact.

dum•found or **dumb•found** (dŭm′found′) *v.* To confound with amazement.

dum•my (dŭm′ē) *n., pl.* **-mies. 1.** A model of a real object, as a human figure, used as a practical substitute. **2.** A stupid person : dullard. **3.** A person or agency secretly in the service of another. **4. a.** The partner who exposes his or her hand to be played by the declarer in bridge. **b.** The hand thus exposed.

dump (dŭmp) *v.* **1.** To release, throw down, or discard in a mass. **2. a.** To empty (material) out of a container or vehicle. **b.** To empty out (a container or vehicle). **3.** To get rid of by or as if by dumping. **4.** To place (goods) on the market, esp. in a foreign country, in large quantities and at a low price. **5.** *Computer Sci.* To reproduce (data stored internally) onto an external storage medium, as a printout. —*n.* **1.** A place where garbage or trash is dumped. **2.** A military storage place. **3.** *Slang.* A disreputable place.

dump•ling (dŭmp′lĭng) *n.* **1.** A small ball of dough cooked in soup or stew. **2.** Sweetened dough wrapped around fruit, as an apple, baked and served as dessert.

dumps (dŭmps) *pl.n. Informal.* Low, gloomy spirits : depression.

dump truck *n.* A heavy-duty truck with a bed that tilts to dump loose material.

dump•y (dŭm′pē) *adj.* **-i•er, -i•est. 1.** Short and plump : squat. **2.** Run-down : shabby. **—dump′i•ness** *n.*

dun¹ (dŭn) *v.* **dunned, dun•ning.** To ask (a debtor) persistently for payment.

dun² (dŭn) *n.* A brownish gray to dull grayish brown. **—dun** *adj.*

dunce (dŭns) *n.* A slow-witted or stupid person.

▲word history: The word *dunce* comes from the name of John *Duns* Scotus, an eminent 13th-cent. scholastic theologian. In the early 16th cent. the humanist scholars of classical Greek and Latin and the religious reformers criticized the *Dunses,* or followers of Scotus, for their resistance to the new learning and theology. By the end of the 16th cent. *dunse* or *dunce* acquired its meaning of "a stupid person."

dune (do͞on, dyo͞on) *n.* A ridge or hill of sand blown or drifted by the wind.

dune buggy *n.* A small, light, 4-wheeled vehicle equipped with oversized tires for driving on sand dunes.

dung (dŭng) *n.* The excrement of animals : manure.

dun•ga•ree (dŭng′gə-rē′) *n.* **1.** A sturdy, coarse denim fabric, esp. blue denim. **2. dungarees.** Pants or overalls made from dungaree.

dun•geon (dŭn′jən) *n.* A dark, underground prison chamber.

dung•hill (dŭng′hĭl′) *n.* A pile of dung.

dunk (dŭngk) *v.* **1.** To dip (e.g., a doughnut) into a liquid before eating. **2.** To submerge (someone) playfully, as in a swimming pool.

du•o (do͞o′ō, dyo͞o′ō) *n., pl.* **-os. 1.** A duet. **2.** Two people or objects in close association : pair.

du•o•de•num (do͞o′ə-dē′nəm, dyo͞o′-, do͞o-ŏd′n-əm, dyo͞o-) *n., pl.* **-de•na** (-dē′nə) or **-de•nums.** The beginning portion of the small intestine, extending from the lower end of the stomach to the jejunum. **—du′o•de′nal** *adj.*

dup. *abbr.* duplicate.

dupe (do͞op, dyo͞op) *n.* **1.** A person who is easily manipulated or deceived. **2.** One who is the tool of another person or power. —*v.* **duped, dup•ing.** To deceive or trick.

du•ple (do͞o′pəl, dyo͞o′-) *adj. Mus.* Having 2 or a multiple of 2 beats to the measure.

du•plex (do͞o′plĕks′, dyo͞o′-) *adj.* Double. —*n.* **1.** An apartment with rooms on 2 adjoining floors. **2.** A 2-family house.

du•pli•cate (do͞o′plĭ-kĭt, dyo͞o′-) *adj.* **1.** Being identical with another. **2.** Existing in or consisting of 2 corresponding parts. —*n.* **1.** Either of 2 things that are identical. **2.** An exact copy of an original. —*v.* (-kāt′) **-cat•ed, -cat•ing. 1.** To make an exact copy of <*duplicate* a key> **2.** To do or perform again : repeat. **—du′pli•ca′tion** *n.*

du•pli•ca•tor (do͞o′plĭ-kā′tər, dyo͞o′-) *n.* A machine that makes copies of written or printed material.

du•plic•i•ty (do͞o-plĭs′ĭ-tē, dyo͞o-) *n., pl.* **-ties.** Deliberate deception.

du•ra•ble (do͝or′ə-bəl, dyo͝or′-) *adj.* Capable of withstanding wear or decay <a *durable* fabric> **—du′ra•bil′i•ty** *n.*

du•rance (do͝or′əns, dyo͝or′-) *n.* Imprisonment, esp. for a long time.

du•ra•tion (do͝o-rā′shən, dyo͝o-) *n.* The period of time during which something exists or lasts.

du•ress (do͝o-rĕs′, dyo͝o-) *n.* **1.** Compulsion by threat. **2.** *Law.* **a.** Coercion illegally applied. **b.** Forced restraint.

dur•ing (do͝or′ĭng, dyo͝or′-) *prep.* **1.** Throughout the course or duration of. **2.** Within the time of.

dusk (dŭsk) *n.* The time of evening immediately before darkness.

dusk•y (dŭs′kē) *adj.* **-i•er, -i•est. 1.** Marked by dim or inadequate light : shadowy. **2.** Somewhat dark in color, as skin. **—dusk′i•ness** *n.*

Düs•sel•dorf (do͝os′-əl-dôrf′). City of W West Germany, N of Cologne. *Pop.* 594,770.

dust (dŭst) *n.* **1.** Fine, dry particles of matter. **2. a.** Earth, esp. when considered as a place of interment. **b.** The surface of the ground. **3.** Something worthless. **4.** A debased or scorned condition. —*v.* **1.** To remove dust from by wiping, brushing, or beating. **2.** To sprinkle or cover with powdered material. **—dust′y** *adj.*

dust bowl *n.* A region marked by insufficient rainfall and dust storms.

dust•er (dŭs′tər) *n.* **1.** One that dusts. **2.** A brush or cloth used for removing dust. **3.** A loose, lightweight coat or smock.

dust•pan (dŭst′păn′) *n.* A short-handled pan for swept-up refuse.

dust storm *n.* A severe windstorm that sweeps clouds of dust across an arid region.

Dutch (dŭch) *n.* **1.** The people of the Netherlands. **2.** The language of the Netherlands. **—Dutch** *adj.* **—Dutch′man** *n.*

Dutch door *n.* A door divided in half horizontally so that either part can be opened or closed.

Dutch•man's-breech•es (dŭch′mənz-brĭch′ĭz) *n.* A woodland plant, *Dicentra cucullaria,* of E North America, bearing yellowish-white 2-spurred flowers.

Dutchman's-breeches

Dutch oven *n.* A large, usu. cast-iron pot or kettle with a tight lid.

Dutch treat *n. Informal.* An outing for which each person pays his or her own way.

du•te•ous (do͞o′tē-əs, dyo͞o′-) *adj.* Dutiful or obedient. **—du′te•ous•ly** *adv.*

du·ti·a·ble (dōō′tē-ə-bəl, dyōō′-) *adj.* Subject to import tax.
du·ti·ful (dōō′tĭ-fəl, dyōō′-) *adj.* **1.** Careful to perform duties. **2.** Imbued with or expressing a sense of duty. **–du′ti·ful·ly** *adv.* **–du′ti·ful·ness** *n.*
du·ty (dōō′tē, dyōō′-) *n., pl.* **-ties. 1.** Something that a person ought to or must do. **2.** Moral obligation. **3.** A service, action, or task assigned to one, esp. in military service. **4.** A government tax, esp. on imports.
D.V.M. *abbr.* Doctor of Veterinary Medicine.
dwarf (dwôrf) *n., pl.* **dwarfs** *or* **dwarves** (dwôrvz). A person, animal, or plant whose size is very much smaller than normal. *–v.* **1.** To stunt the natural growth of. **2.** To cause to seem small by comparison. **–dwarf′ish** *adj.*
dwell (dwĕl) *v.* **dwelt** (dwĕlt) *or* **dwelled, dwell·ing. 1.** To live as an inhabitant : reside. **2.** To continue in a given place or condition. **3. a.** To focus one's attention. **b.** To treat of at length : expatiate. **–dwell′er** *n.*
dwell·ing (dwĕl′ĭng) *n.* A residence.
dwin·dle (dwĭn′dəl) *v.* **-dled, -dling.** To waste away : diminish.
dwt. *abbr.* pennyweight.
Dy *symbol for* DYSPROSIUM.
dyb·buk (dĭb′ək) *n.* A wandering soul believed in Jewish folklore to enter and control the body of a living person.
dye (dī) *n.* **1.** An agent used to color or stain materials. **2.** A color imparted by a dye. *–v.* **dyed, dye·ing.** To color with or become colored by a dye. **–dy′er** *n.*
dyed-in-the-wool (dīd′ĭn-*thə*-wŏŏl′) *adj.* Thoroughgoing : out-and-out.
dye·stuff (dī′stŭf′) *n.* DYE 1.
dy·ing (dī′ĭng) *adj.* **1.** About to die. **2.** Drawing to an end <a *dying* day> **3.** Uttered or done immediately before death.
dyke (dīk) *n. var. of* DIKE.
dy·nam·ic (dī-năm′ĭk) *adj.* **1.** Energetic : vigorous <a *dynamic* leader> **2.** Marked by or tending to produce progress <*dynamic* social reforms> **3.** Of energy, motion, or force in relation to force. **–dy·nam′i·cal·ly** *adv.*
dy·nam·ics (dī-năm′ĭks) *n.* The branch of physics that deals with force, energy, and motion and the relationship between them.
dy·na·mite (dī′nə-mīt′) *n.* A powerful explosive composed of nitroglycerin or ammonium nitrate combined with an absorbent material and usu. packaged in sticks. *–v.* **-mit·ed, -mit·ing.** To blow up with or as if with dynamite.
dy·na·mo (dī′nə-mō′) *n., pl.* **-mos. 1.** An electric generator, esp. one that produces direct current. **2.** *Informal.* A highly energetic and enthusiastic person.
dy·na·mom·e·ter (dī′nə-mŏm′ĭ-tər) *n.* An instrument for measuring mechanical power or force.
dy·nas·ty (dī′nə-stē) *n., pl.* **-ties. 1.** A succession of rulers from the same line or family. **2.** A family or group that maintains great power, wealth, or position for many years. **–dy·nas′tic** (dī-năs′tĭk) *adj.*
dys·en·ter·y (dĭs′ən-tĕr′ē) *n.* An infection of the lower intestines that produces pain, fever, and severe diarrhea.
dys·lex·i·a (dĭs-lĕk′sē-ə) *n.* Impairment of the ability to read. **–dys·lex′ic** *adj.*
dys·pep·sia (dĭs-pĕp′shə, -sē-ə) *n.* Indigestion. **–dys·pep′tic** *adj.*
dys·pro·si·um (dĭs-prō′zē-əm) *n. Symbol* **Dy** A soft, silvery metallic element used in nuclear research.
dys·tro·phy (dĭs′trə-fē) *n.* Atrophy of muscle tissue, esp. muscular dystrophy.

Ee

e *or* **E** (ē) *n., pl.* **e's** *or* **E's. 1.** The 5th letter of the English alphabet. **2.** A speech sound represented by the letter *e.* **3.** Something shaped like the letter E. **4.** *Mus.* The 3rd tone in the scale of C major. **5.** A grade indicating that a student's work is failing.
e *abbr.* **1.** electron. **2.** *also* **E** *or* **e.** *or* **E.** east; eastern.
E *abbr.* Earth.
E. *abbr.* **1.** *also* **e.** engineer; engineering. **2.** *also* **E** English.
ea. *abbr.* each.
each (ēch) *adj.* Being 1 of 2 or more considered separately : every. *–pron.* Every 1 of 2 or more : each one. *–adv.* For or to each 1 : apiece.
each other *pron.* Each the other. Used to indicate a reciprocal relationship or action <looking out for *each other*>
ea·ger (ē′gər) *adj.* Marked by enthusiastic interest or desire <*eager* to start> ☆**syns:** AGOG, ANXIOUS, ARDENT, ATHIRST, AVID, IMPATIENT, KEEN, RARING, THIRSTY **–ea′ger·ly** *adv.* **–ea′ger·ness** *n.*
ea·gle (ē′gəl) *n.* **1.** A large bird of prey of the family Accipitridae, having a powerful bill, broad strong wings, and soaring flight. **2.** A former U.S. gold coin worth $10. **3.** A score of 2 under par on a hole in golf.
ea·gle-eyed (ē′gəl-īd′) *adj.* Having exceptionally keen vision.
ea·glet (ē′glĭt) *n.* A young eagle.
-ean *suff. var. of* -IAN.
ear[1] (îr) *n.* **1.** The hearing organ in vertebrates, esp. the outer part. **2.** The sense of hearing. **3.** Keenness of hearing. **4.** Attention : heed <give *ear* to these appeals> **5.** Something resembling the external ear <the *ears* of a vase> **–all ears.** Listening closely. **–by ear.** Without reference to a musical score. **–ear′less** *adj.*
ear[2] (îr) *n.* The spike of a cereal plant, as corn, that bears the seeds.
ear·ache (îr′āk′) *n.* An ache in the ear.
ear·drum (îr′drŭm′) *n. Anat.* The tympanic membrane.
eared (îrd) *adj.* **1.** Having ears or earlike projections. **2.** Having a specified kind or number of ears <floppy-*eared*>
eared seal *n.* Any of various seals of the family Otariidae, including the fur seals and sea lions, having external ears and hind flippers that can be turned forward for walking on land.
ear·ful (îr′fŏŏl′) *n.* **1.** A flow of gossip or information. **2.** A scolding.
earl (ûrl) *n.* A British nobleman who ranks above a viscount and below a marquis. **–earl′dom** *n.*
earless seal *n.* Any of various seals of the family Phocidae, including the hair seals, marked by short fore flippers, reduced hind flippers specialized for swimming, and the absence of external ears.
ear·lobe (îr′lōb′) *n.* The fleshy tissue at the lower part of the external ear.
ear·ly (ûr′lē) *adj.* **-li·er, -li·est. 1.** Of, pertaining to, or occurring near the beginning of a series, time period, or course of events. **2.** Belonging to a remote time period : primitive <*early* mammals> **3.** Taking place or appearing before the usual or expected time <an *early* frost> **4.** Taking place in the near future. *–adv.* **-li·er, -li·est. 1.** Near the beginning of a series, time period, or course of events. **2.** Far back in time. **3.** Before the usual or expected time. **–ear′li·ness** *n.*
early bird *n.* **1.** An early riser. **2.** One who arrives early.
early on *adv.* At or during an early stage.
ear·mark (îr′märk′) *n.* An identifying mark or characteristic. *–v.* **1.** To put an identifying mark on <*earmark* cattle> **2.** To reserve for a certain purpose : designate <*earmark* funds for research>
ear·muff (îr′mŭf′) *n.* Either of a pair of ear coverings connected by an adjustable band and worn to protect against the cold.
earn (ûrn) *v.* **1.** To receive in return for work or services. **2.** To acquire as a result of one's efforts <*earn* high marks> **3.** To produce as a profit or return <investments that *earn* interest> ☆**syns:** DESERVE, GAIN, GET, MERIT, RATE, WIN **–earn′er** *n.*
ear·nest[1] (ûr′nĭst) *adj.* **1.** Characterized by or showing deep sincerity : serious. **2.** Important : grave. **–in earnest.** With serious intent. **–ear′nest·ly** *adv.* **–ear′nest·ness** *n.*
ear·nest[2] (ûr′nĭst) *n.* **1.** Money paid in advance to bind an agreement. **2.** A token : promise.
earn·ings (ûr′nĭngz) *pl.n.* Something earned, as salary or profits.
ear·phone (îr′fōn′) *n.* A device that converts electric signals, as from a radio, to audible sound and fits over the ear.
ear·ring (îr′rĭng, îr′ĭng) *n.* A piece of jewelry worn on the lobe of the ear.
ear·shot (îr′shŏt′) *n.* The distance within which sound can be heard.
ear·split·ting (îr′splĭt′ĭng) *adj.* So loud and shrill as to hurt the ears.
earth (ûrth) *n.* **1. Earth.** The planet 3rd in order from the sun,

on which human beings live. **2.** The land surface of the world : ground. **3.** Soil : dirt. **—down to earth.** Realistic : sensible.

earth·en (ûr′thən, -*th*ən) *adj.* **1.** Made of earth. **2.** Worldly.

earth·en·ware (ûr′thən-wâr′, -*th*ən-) *n.* Ware, as dishes or pots, made from porous baked clay.

earth·ling (ûrth′lĭng) *n.* An inhabitant of the earth : human being.

earth·ly (ûrth′lē) *adj.* **1.** Of or pertaining to this earth. **2. a.** Not heavenly or divine : secular. **b.** Terrestrial. **3.** Possible : conceivable <no *earthly* excuse> ☆***syns:*** MUNDANE, SECULAR, TEMPORAL, TERRESTRIAL, WORLDLY **—earth′li·ness** *n.*

earth·quake (ûrth′kwāk′) *n.* A series of waves in the crust of the earth, resulting in movements in the earth's surface.

earth science *n.* Any of several geologic sciences concerned with the origin, structure, and physical phenomena of the earth.

earth·shak·ing (ûrth′shā′kĭng) *adj.* Of enormous importance.

earth station *n.* An on-ground terminal linked to a spacecraft or satellite by an antenna and associated electronic equipment for the purpose of transmitting or receiving messages, tracking, or control.

earth·ward (ûrth′wərd) *adj.* & *adv.* To or toward the earth. **—earth′wards** *adv.*

earth·work (ûrth′wûrk′) *n.* An earthen embankment or military fortification.

earth·worm (ûrth′wûrm′) *n.* Any of various annelid worms of the class Oligochaeta that burrow into soil.

earth·y (ûr′thē) *adj.* **-i·er, -i·est. 1.** Consisting of or like earth or soil. **2.** Crude and natural : unrefined <*earthy* humor> **—earth′i·ness** *n.*

ear·wax (îr′wăks′) *n.* The waxy secretion from the external-ear canal.

ear·wig (îr′wĭg′) *n.* Any of various insects of the order Dermaptera, with pincerlike appendages at the rear of the body.

ease (ēz) *n.* **1.** Freedom from worry, pain, or agitation. **2.** Freedom from embarrassment or awkwardness : naturalness. **3.** Freedom from difficulty or great effort. *—v.* **eased, eas·ing. 1.** To free or become free from pain, worry, or trouble. **2.** To make or become less troublesome or difficult. **3.** To lessen the strain, pressure, or tension of : loosen. **4.** To move into place carefully <*eased* the boat into the slip>

ea·sel (ē′zəl) *n.* A frame to support an artist's canvas or a picture.

east (ēst) *n.* **1. a.** The direction of the earth's axial rotation. **b.** The mariner's compass point 90° clockwise from north. **2.** *often* **East. a.** Asia and the nearby islands of the Indian and Pacific oceans : the Orient. **b.** The E part of the U.S. **c.** The E part of Canada, usu. Ont., Que., and the Atlantic Provinces. *—adj.* **1.** To, toward, of, or in the east. **2.** Coming from the east. *—adv.* In, from, or toward the east. **—east′er·ly** *adj.* & *adv.* **—east′ward** *adj.* & *adv.* **—east′wards** *adv.*

East Ber·lin (bûr-lĭn′). See BERLIN.

Eas·ter (ē′stər) *n.* A Christian festival celebrating Christ's resurrection.

▲word history: The word *Easter,* although the name of a Christian festival, had its origins in pagan times. *Eastre* or *Eostre,* the Old English spelling of *Easter,* was orig. the name of a Germanic goddess who was worshiped at a festival at the spring equinox. Her name is closely related to Latin *aurora* and Greek *ēōs,* both of which mean "dawn."

east·ern (ē′stərn) *adj.* **1.** Of, in, or toward the east. **2.** Coming from the east. **3. Eastern. a.** Of, relating to, or characteristic of E regions or the Orient. **b.** Of, relating to, or designating the Christian church of the Byzantine (or Eastern Roman) Empire or a modern church derived from it. **—east′ern·er, East′ern·er** *n.*

East Ger·ma·ny (jûr′mə-nē). See GERMANY.

East In·dies (ĭn′dēz). **1.** The Malay Archipelago. **2.** The islands of Indonesia.

eas·y (ē′zē) *adj.* **-i·er, -i·est. 1.** Capable of being accomplished with ease : not difficult. **2.** Free from worry, anxiety, or pain. **3.** Relaxed : easygoing. **4.** Not strict : lenient. **5.** Not hurried or forced : moderate. **6.** Readily obtainable <*easy* loans> ☆***syns:*** EFFORTLESS, FACILE, READY, SIMPLE, SMOOTH *—adv. Informal.* In an easy manner : easily. **—eas′i·ly** *adv.* **—eas′i·ness** *n.*

eas·y·go·ing (ē′zē-gō′ĭng) *adj.* Without worry, concern, or haste : carefree.

eat (ēt) *v.* **ate** (āt), **eat·en** (ēt′n), **eat·ing. 1.** To take (food) into the mouth and swallow. **2.** To consume or destroy as if by eating. **3.** To erode or corrode. **—eat (one's) words.** To take back something one has said. **—eat′a·ble** *adj.* **—eat′er** *n.*

eat·er·y (ē′tə-rē) *n., pl.* **-ies.** *Informal.* A restaurant.

eau de co·logne (ō′ də kə-lōn′) *n.* A scented liquid consisting of alcohol and various fragrant oils.

eaves (ēvz) *pl.n.* The overhanging lower edge of a roof.

eaves·drop (ēvz′drŏp′) *v.* To listen secretly to a private conversation. **—eaves′drop′per** *n.*

▲word history: The *eavesdrop* of a building is the space of ground where water falls from the eaves. An *eavesdropper* was orig. someone who stood in the eavesdrop in order to overhear private conversations taking place inside. The noun *eavesdrop* did not survive Old English times, but *eavesdropper* and *eavesdropping,* which was a legal offense, were preserved in legal texts. The modern verb *eavesdrop* is prob. derived from *eavesdropper.*

ebb (ĕb) *n.* **1.** Ebb tide. **2.** A time of decline. *—v.* **1.** To recede, as the tide does. **2.** To decline : diminish.

ebb tide *n.* The period of a tide between high water and a succeeding low water.

eb·o·nite (ĕb′ə-nīt′) *n.* A hard, usu. black rubber.

eb·o·ny (ĕb′ə-nē) *n., pl.* **-nies.** The hard, dark-colored wood of a tropical Asian tree, *Diospyros ebenum.* *—adj.* **1.** Resembling ebony. **2.** Black.

e·bul·lient (ĭ-bo͝ol′yənt, ĭ-bŭl′-) *adj.* **1.** Filled with excitement or lively enthusiasm : exuberant. **2.** Boiling : bubbling. **—e·bul′lience** *n.* **—e·bul′lient·ly** *adv.*

eb·ul·li·tion (ĕb′ə-lĭsh′ən) *n.* **1.** The process or state of boiling or bubbling. **2.** A sudden outpouring, as of emotion.

ec·cen·tric (ĭk-sĕn′trĭk) *adj.* **1.** Departing from an established pattern, as of behavior : unconventional. **2.** Deviating from a circular path or form. **3.** Not at or in the geometric center. **4.** Having different centers <*eccentric* circles> *—n.* **1.** An odd or unconventional person. **2.** A disk or wheel with its axis of revolution displaced from its center so that it is able to impart reciprocating motion. **—ec·cen′tri·cal·ly** *adv.* **—ec′cen·tric′i·ty** (ĕk′sĕn-trĭs′ĭ-tē) *n.*

Ec·cle·si·as·tes (ĭ-klē′zē-ăs′tēz′) *pl.n. (sing. in number)* See BIBLE TABLE.

ec·cle·si·as·tic (ĭ-klē′zē-ăs′tĭk) *adj.* Ecclesiastical. *—n.* A clergyman : cleric.

ec·cle·si·as·ti·cal (ĭ-klē′zē-ăs′tĭ-kəl) *adj.* Of or relating to a church, esp. as an institution. **—ec·cle′si·as′ti·cal·ly** *adv.*

ech·e·lon (ĕsh′ə-lŏn′) *n.* **1.** A steplike formation, as of military aircraft or naval vessels. **2.** A level of command or authority, as in a hierarchy.

ech·o (ĕk′ō) *n., pl.* **-oes. 1. a.** Repetition of a sound caused by sound waves reflecting from a surface. **b.** A sound made in this way. **2.** A repetition or imitation. **3.** *Electron.* A reflected wave that is received by radio or radar. ☆***syns:*** REPERCUSSION, REVERBERATION *—v.* **-oed, -o·ing. 1.** To repeat or be repeated by or as if by an echo. **2.** To repeat or imitate <*echoing* the accepted opinion>

é·clair (ā-klâr′, ā′klâr′) *n.* A light, tube-shaped pastry filled with cream or custard and often iced with chocolate.

é·clat (ā-klä′) *n.* **1.** Great brilliance, as of performance or achievement. **2.** Conspicuous success or acclaim.

ec·lec·tic (ĭ-klĕk′tĭk) *adj.* Consisting of components from diverse sources or styles. **—ec·lec′tic** *n.* **—e·clec′ti·cal·ly** *adv.*

e·clipse (ĭ-klĭps′) *n.* **1.** The complete or partial blocking of a celestial body by another. **2.** A fall into obscurity : decline. *—v.* **e·clipsed, e·clips·ing. 1.** To cause an eclipse of. **2.** To surpass : outshine.

e·clip·tic (ĭ-klĭp′tĭk) *n.* The circle formed by the intersection of the plane of the earth's orbit and the celestial sphere.

ec·logue (ĕk′lôg′, -lŏg′) *n.* A pastoral poem in the form of a dialogue.

ec·o·cide (ek′ō-sīd′, ē′kō-) *n.* Deliberate destruction of the natural environment, as by pollutants.

e·col·o·gy (ĭ-kŏl′ə-jē) *n.* **1.** The science of the interaction and relationships between living organisms and their environments. **2.** The interaction between living organisms and their environment. **—ec′o·log′i·cal** (ĕk′ə-lŏj′ĭ-kəl, ē′kə-), **ec′o·log′ic** *adj.* **—ec′o·log′i·cal·ly** *adv.* **—e·col′o·gist** *n.*

econ. *abbr.* economics; economist; economy.

ec·o·nom·ic (ĕk′ə-nŏm′ĭk, ē′kə-) *adj.* **1.** Of or relating to the development, production, and management of material wealth. **2.** Of or relating to the necessities of life : utilitarian.

ec·o·nom·i·cal (ĕk′ə-nŏm′ĭ-kəl, ē′kə-) *adj.* **1.** Not wasteful in managing funds or resources : frugal. **2.** Operating efficiently. **—ec′o·nom′i·cal·ly** *adv.*

ec·o·nom·ics (ĕk′ə-nŏm′ĭks, ē′kə-) *n. (sing. in number).* The science dealing with the production, distribution, and consumption of commodities. **—e·con′o·mist** (ĭ-kŏn′ə-mĭst) *n.*

e·con·o·mize (ĭ-kŏn′ə-mīz′) *v.* **-mized, -miz·ing.** To reduce expenses : be thrifty. **—e·con′o·miz′er** *n.*

e·con·o·my (ĭ-kŏn′ə-mē) *n., pl.* **-mies. 1.** Careful or thrifty management of resources. **2.** A reduction in expenses. **3.** A system for the management of resources and production of goods and services <a farm-based *economy*>

ec•o•sys•tem (ĕk′ō-sĭs′təm) *n.* An ecological community and its environment interacting and functioning as a unit.
ec•ru (ĕk′ro͞o, ā′kro͞o) *n.* A light yellowish brown.
ec•sta•sy (ĕk′stə-sē) *n.*, *pl.* **-sies.** Intense joy or delight : rapture. **—ec•stat′ic** (ĕk-stăt′ĭk) *adj.* **—ec•stat′i•cal•ly** *adv.*
Ec•ua•dor (ĕk′wə-dôr′). Country of NW South America. *Cap.* Quito. *Pop.* 7,810,000. **—Ec′ua•dor′i•an** *adj.* & *n.*
ec•u•men•i•cal (ĕk′yə-mĕn′ĭ-kəl) *adj.* **1.** Worldwide : universal. **2.** Of or providing unity among Christian churches or religions. **—ec′u•men′i•cal•ly** *adv.* **—ec′u•me•nism** (-mə-nĭz′əm) *n.*
ec•ze•ma (ĕk′sə-mə, ĭg-zē′-) *n.* A noncontagious skin inflammation marked by itching and scaly patches. **—ec•zem′a•tous** (ĕg-zĕm′ə-təs, -zē′mə-) *adj.*
ed. *abbr.* edition; editor.
-ed *suff.* **1.** Used to form the past tense and past participle of regular verbs <lift*ed*> **2.** Characterized by : having <kind-heart*ed*>
E•dam (ē′dəm, ē′dăm′) *n.* A mild, yellow Dutch cheese usu. pressed into balls.
ed•dy (ĕd′ē) *n.*, *pl.* **-dies.** A current, as of air or water, moving against the direction of the main current, esp. in a circular motion. **—ed′dy** *v.*
Ed•dy (ĕd′ē), **Mary Baker.** 1821–1910. Amer. founder of Christian Science.
e•del•weiss (ā′dəl-vīs′, -wīs′) *n.* An Alpine plant, *Leontopodium alpinum*, with whitish, downy leaves and small flowers.
e•de•ma (ĭ-dē′mə) *n.* An abnormal accumulation of serous fluid in the tissues. **—e•dem′a•tous** (ĭ-dĕm′ə-təs) *adj.*
E•den (ēd′n) *n.* **1.** The 1st home of Adam and Eve. **2.** A place or state of ultimate happiness : paradise.
edge (ĕj) *n.* **1.** The usu. thin, sharpened side of a cutting blade. **2.** Keenness : zest. **3.** The line or area where something begins or ends <the *edge* of a table> <at the *edge* of despair> **4.** An advantage. *—v.* **edged, edg•ing. 1.** To put an edge or border on. **2.** To sharpen. **3.** To move gradually <*edged* away from the snarling dog> **—on edge.** Highly tense or nervous.
edge•wise (ĕj′wīz′) *also* **edge•ways** (-wāz′) *adv.* With the edge foremost.
edg•ing (ĕj′ĭng) *n.* Something forming or serving as an edge or border.
edg•y (ĕj′ē) *adj.* **-i•er, -i•est. 1.** Feeling or showing nervous tension. **2.** Having a sharp edge. ☆***syns:*** FIDGETY, JITTERY, JUMPY, NERVOUS, RESTIVE, RESTLESS, SKITTISH, TENSE, UNEASY, UPTIGHT **—edg′i•ness** *n.*
ed•i•ble (ĕd′ə-bəl) *adj.* Safe or fit to be eaten. **—ed′i•bil′i•ty** *n.* **—ed′i•ble** *n.*
e•dict (ē′dĭkt′) *n.* A formal proclamation, command, or decree.
ed•i•fice (ĕd′ə-fĭs) *n.* A building, esp. a large one.
ed•i•fy (ĕd′ə-fī′) *v.* **-fied, -fy•ing.** To instruct so as to promote intellectual or esp. moral improvement : enlighten. **—ed′i•fi•ca′tion** *n.* **—ed′i•fi′er** *n.*
Ed•in•burgh (ĕd′n-bûr′ə). Cap. of Scotland, in the E. *Pop.* 455,126.
Ed•i•son (ĕd′ə-sən), **Thomas Alva.** 1847–1931. Amer. inventor.
ed•it (ĕd′ĭt) *v.* **1.** To prepare for publication, as by adapting or correcting. **2.** To prepare an edition of <*edit* a collection of letters> **3.** To put together the parts of (e.g, a film) by cutting, combining, and splicing. **4.** To delete <*edit* out a dull passage> **—ed′i•tor** *n.* **—ed′i•tor•ship′** *n.*
▲word history: The verb *edit* was derived in English from the noun *editor* and not vice versa as one would expect. The process by which *edit* was formed is called back-formation. By this process a syllable thought to be an affix is removed from what is incorrectly considered to be a base word, and the base becomes a new word in its own right. *Editor* can thus be analyzed as a verb, *edit*, plus the noun suffix *-or*. The English word *editor*, however, was borrowed from Latin *editor* and is recorded 150 years earlier than the verb *edit*.
e•di•tion (ĭ-dĭsh′ən) *n.* **1.** The form in which a book is published. **2.** The entire number of copies, as of a book, printed at one time. **3.** A single copy of a publication. **4.** One similar to an original : version.
ed•i•to•ri•al (ĕd′ĭ-tôr′ē-əl, -tōr′-) *n.* An article in a publication expressing the opinion of a publisher or an editor. *—adj.* **1.** Of or relating to an editor or an editor's work. **2.** Of, expressed in, or being an editorial. **—ed′i•to′ri•al•ly** *adv.*
ed•i•to•ri•al•ize (ĕd′ĭ-tôr′ē-ə-līz′, -tōr′-) *v.* **-ized, -iz•ing. 1.** To express an opinion in or as if in an editorial. **2.** To present opinion as if it were factual reporting. **—ed′i•to′ri•al•iz′er** *n.*
Ed•mon•ton (ĕd′mən-tən). Cap. of Alta., Canada, in the C part. *Pop.* 503,773.
E.D.T. *abbr.* Eastern Daylight Time.
educ. *abbr.* education; educational.
ed•u•ca•ble (ĕj′ə-kə-bəl) *adj.* Capable of being educated.
ed•u•cate (ĕj′ə-kāt′) *v.* **-cat•ed, -cat•ing. 1.** To provide with training or schooling : teach. **2.** To promote or supervise the mental or moral growth of. **—ed′u•ca′tor** *n.*
ed•u•ca•tion (ĕj′ə-kā′shən) *n.* **1.** The process of educating or of being educated. **2.** The knowledge obtained through learning. **3.** The field of teaching and learning : pedagogy. **—ed′u•ca′tion•al** *adj.* **—ed′u•ca′tion•al•ly** *adv.*
e•duce (ĭ-do͞os′, ĭ-dyo͞os′) *v.* **e•duced, e•duc•ing. 1.** To evoke : elicit. **2.** To conclude from given facts : deduce.
-ee *suff.* **1..** One that receives or benefits from a specified action <address*ee*> **b.** One that possesses a specified thing <mortgag*ee*> **2.** One that performs a specified action <absent*ee*>
EEG *abbr.* electroencephalogram; electroencephalograph.
eel (ēl) *n.*, *pl.* **eel** or **eels.** Any of various smooth-skinned, snakelike marine or freshwater fishes of the order Anguilliformes or Apodes.
-eer *suff.* One engaged in or concerned with <ballad*eer*>
e'er (âr) *adv.* Ever.
ee•rie or **ee•ry** (îr′ē) *adj.* **-ri•er, -ri•est.** Suggesting the supernatural or ghostly : uncanny <an *eerie* wailing sound> **—ee′ri•ly** *adv.* **—ee′ri•ness** *n.*
ef•face (ĭ-fās′) *v.* **-faced, -fac•ing.** To remove or obscure by or as if by rubbing out. **—ef•face′ment** *n.* **—ef•fac′er** *n.*
ef•fect (ĭ-fĕkt′) *n.* **1.** Something brought about by a cause : result. **2.** The power or capacity to obtain a desired result : influence. **3.** The way in which something acts on an object <the drying *effect* of strong sunlight> **4.** Something that produces an intended impression <vivid lighting *effects*> **5.** The state of being in force <laws now in *effect*> **6.** Basic meaning : purport <words to that *effect*> **7. effects.** Belongings : possessions. ☆***syns:*** CONSEQUENCE, FRUIT, ISSUE, OUTCOME, RESULT, SEQUEL, UPSHOT *—v.* **1.** To bring into existence. **2.** To bring about. **—take effect.** To become operative. **—ef•fect′er** *n.*
ef•fec•tive (ĭ-fĕk′tĭv) *adj.* **1.** Producing an expected effect. **2.** Producing or designed to produce a desired effect. **3.** In effect : operative. ☆***syns:*** EFFECTUAL, EFFICACIOUS, EFFICIENT, PRODUCTIVE **—ef•fec′tive•ly** *adv.* **—ef•fec′tive•ness** *n.*
ef•fec•tu•al (ĭ-fĕk′cho͞o-əl) *adj.* Producing a desired effect. **—ef•fec′tu•al•ly** *adv.*
ef•fec•tu•ate (ĭ-fĕk′cho͞o-āt′) *v.* **-at•ed, -at•ing.** To bring about : effect.
ef•fem•i•nate (ĭ-fĕm′ə-nĭt) *adj.* Having qualities more often associated with women than with men : unmanly. **—ef•fem′i•na•cy** *n.* **—ef•fem′i•nate•ly** *adv.*
ef•fer•ent (ĕf′ər-ənt) *adj.* Directed outward from a central organ or part. **—ef′fer•ent** *n.* **—ef′fer•ent•ly** *adv.*
ef•fer•vesce (ĕf′ər-vĕs′) *v.* **-vesced, -vesc•ing. 1.** To give off small bubbles as gas comes out of a liquid. **2.** To show high spirits. **—ef′fer•ves′cence** *n.* **—ef′fer•ves′cent** *adj.* **—ef′fer•ves′cent•ly** *adv.*
ef•fete (ĭ-fēt′) *adj.* **1.** Exhausted of force or effectiveness : worn-out. **2.** Decadent. **—ef•fete′ly** *adv.* **—ef•fete′ness** *n.*
ef•fi•ca•cious (ĕf′ĭ-kā′shəs) *adj.* Producing a desired effect <an *efficacious* drug> **—ef′fi•ca′cious•ly** *adv.*
ef•fi•cient (ĭ-fĭsh′ənt) *adj.* **1.** Acting effectively with a minimum of waste or effort. **2.** Exhibiting a high ratio of output to input. **—ef•fi′cien•cy** *n.*
ef•fi•gy (ĕf′ə-jē) *n.*, *pl.* **-gies.** A sculptured or painted representation, esp. a crude image or dummy of a hated person.
ef•flo•resce (ĕf′lə-rĕs′) *v.* **-resced, -resc•ing.** To bloom : blossom.
ef•flo•res•cence (ĕf′lə-rĕs′əns) *n.* **1.** A time or condition of flowering. **2.** A gradual process of development. **3.** The highest point. **—ef′flo•res′cent** *adj.*
ef•flu•ence (ĕf′lo͞o-əns) *n.* **1.** An act or instance of flowing out. **2.** Something that flows out or forth : emanation. **—ef′flu•ent** *adj.* & *n.*
ef•flu•vi•um (ĭ-flo͞o′vē-əm) *n.*, *pl.* **-vi•a** (-vē-ə) or **-vi•ums.** An often foul-smelling outflow or vapor. **—ef•flu′vi•al** *adj.*
ef•fort (ĕf′ərt) *n.* **1.** Exertion of physical or mental energy. **2.** A difficult exertion. **3.** A usu. earnest attempt. **4.** Something done through exertion : achievement. **5.** *Physics.* Force applied against inertia. ☆***syns:*** EXERTION, PAINS, STRAIN, STRUGGLE, TROUBLE **—ef′fort•ful** *adj.* **—ef′fort•less** *adj.*
ef•fron•ter•y (ĭ-frŭn′tə-rē) *n.*, *pl.* **-ies.** Shameless boldness : audacity.
ef•ful•gent (ĭ-fo͝ol′jənt, ĭ-fŭl′-) *adj.* Shining brilliantly. **—ef•ful′gence** *n.*
ef•fu•sion (ĭ-fyo͞o′zhən) *n.* **1.** An act or instance of pouring forth. **2.** An excessive or unrestrained outpouring of feeling, as in speech. **—ef•fuse′** (ĭ-fyo͞oz′) *v.* **—ef•fu′sive** *adj.* **—ef•fu′sive•ly** *adv.*
eft (ĕft) *n.* A newt.

e.g. *abbr.* for example (Lat. *exempli gratia).*
e•gal•i•tar•i•an (ĭ-găl′ĭ-târ′ē-ən) *adj.* Advocating equal rights for all human beings. **—e•gal′i•tar′i•an** *n.* **—e•gal′i•tar′i•an•ism** *n.*
egg[1] (ĕg) *n.* **1.** A female gamete : ovum. **2.** The hard-shelled ovum of a bird, esp. one produced by a chicken, used as food.
egg[2] (ĕg) *v.* To urge or incite to action <Some onlookers *egged* the fighters on.>
egg-and-dart (ĕg′ən-därt′) *n.* A decorative molding alternating egg-shaped figures with anchor, dart, or tongue-shaped figures.

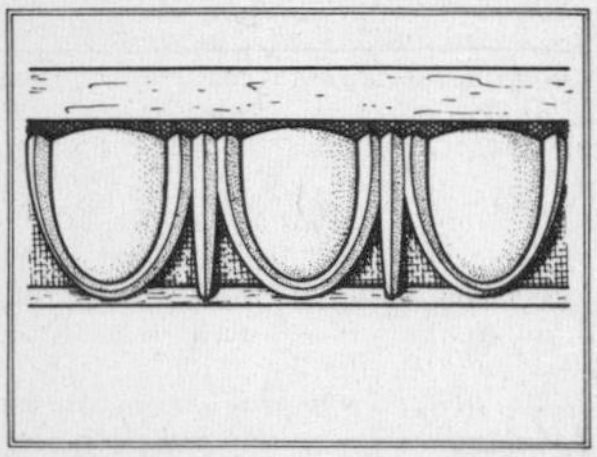

egg-and-dart

egg•beat•er (ĕg′bē′tər) *n.* A kitchen device with rotating blades for whipping, beating, or mixing.
egg•head (ĕg′hĕd′) *n. Slang.* An intellectual.
egg•nog (ĕg′nŏg′) *n.* A drink of beaten eggs, sugar, and milk or cream, often mixed with liquor.
egg•plant (ĕg′plănt′) *n.* A tropical Old World plant, *Solanum melongena,* cultivated for its purple-skinned, ovoid, edible fruit.
egg roll *n.* A cylindrical case made of egg dough filled with minced vegetables and sometimes meat or seafood and fried.
egg•shell (ĕg′shĕl′) *n.* The thin, brittle outer covering of a bird's egg.
e•gis (ē′jĭs) *n. var. of* AEGIS.
eg•lan•tine (ĕg′lən-tīn′, -tēn′) *n.* The sweetbrier.
e•go (ē′gō, ĕg′ō) *n.* **1.** The self, esp. as distinct from the external world. **2.** *Psychoanal.* The conscious personality component that most directly controls behavior and is most in touch with reality. **3.** Self-love : egotism.
e•go•cen•tric (ē′gō-sĕn′trĭk, ĕg′ō-) *adj.* **1.** Thinking, observing, or judging things in relation to the self. **2.** Self-centered : selfish. **—e′go•cen′tric** *n.* **—e′go•cen•tric′i•ty** (-trĭs′ĭ-tē) *n.*
e•go•ism (ē′gō-ĭz′əm, ĕg′ō-) *n.* **1.** The ethical doctrine that self-interest is the proper motive for all human conduct. **2.** Egotism : conceit. **—e′go•ist** *n.* **—e′go•is′tic, e′go•is′ti•cal** *adj.* **—e′go•is′ti•cal•ly** *adv.*
e•go•ma•ni•a (ē′gō-mā′nē-ə, -mān′yə, ĕg′ō-) *n.* Obsession with the self. **—e′go•ma′ni•ac′** (-nē-ăk′) *n.* **—e′go•ma•ni′a•cal** (-mə-nī′ə-kəl) *adj.*
e•go•tism (ē′gə-tĭz′əm, ĕg′ə-) *n.* **1.** The tendency to refer to oneself excessively or boastfully. **2.** Self-importance : conceit. **—e′go•tist** *n.* **—e′go•tis′tic, e′go•tis′ti•cal** *adj.* **—e′go•tis′ti•cal•ly** *adv.*
ego trip *n. Slang.* Something that gratifies the ego. **—e′go-trip′** *v.*
e•gre•gious (ĭ-grē′jəs, -jē-əs) *adj.* Outstandingly bad : flagrant. **—e•gre′gious•ly** *adv.* **—e•gre′gious•ness** *n.*
e•gress (ē′grĕs′) *n.* **1.** The act of going out : emergence. **2.** A means of going out : exit.
e•gret (ē′grĭt, ĕg′rĭt) *n.* Any of several usu. white wading birds, esp. *Casmerodius alba,* having long, drooping plumes.
E•gypt (ē′jĭpt). Country of NE Africa and SW Asia. *Cap.* Cairo. *Pop.* 40,980,000. **—E•gyp′tian** *adj. & n.*
ei•der (ī′dər) *n.* A sea duck of the genus *Somateria,* of N regions, having soft, commercially valuable down.
ei•der•down (ī′dər-doun′) *n.* **1.** The down of the eider duck. **2.** A quilt stuffed with eiderdown.
eight (āt) *n.* **1.** The cardinal number equal to 7 + 1. **2.** The 8th in a set or sequence. **—eight** *adj. & pron.* **—eighth** *n. & adj. & adv.*
eight ball *n.* The black pool ball with the number 8. **—behind the eight ball.** *Slang.* In a disadvantageous position.
eight•een (ā-tēn′) *n.* **1.** The cardinal number equal to 17 + 1. **2.** The 18th in a set or sequence. **—eight•een′** *adj. & pron.* **—eight•eenth′** *n. & adj. & adv.*
eight•y (ā′tē) *n.* The cardinal number equal to 8 × 10. **—eight′i•eth** *n. & adj. & adv.* **—eight′y** *adj. & pron.*
Ein•stein (īn′stīn′), **Albert.** 1879–1955. German-born Amer. physicist.
ein•stein•i•um (īn-stī′nē-əm) *n. Symbol* **Es** A metallic element produced by nuclear bombardment.
Ei•sen•how•er (ī′zən-hou′ər), **Dwight David.** 1890–1969. 34th U.S. President (1953–61).
ei•ther (ē′*th*ər, ī′*th*ər) *pron.* One or the other. *—conj.* Used before the 1st of 2 or more alternatives linked by or <*Either* we go now or we stay here all day.> *—adj.* **1.** One or the other <Use *either* tool.> **2.** One and the other : each <repairs on *either* side of the road> *—adv.* Also : likewise <If you don't diet, I won't *either.*>
e•jac•u•late (ĭ-jăk′yə-lāt′) *v.* **-lat•ed, -lat•ing. 1.** To discharge (e.g., semen) abruptly. **2.** To utter suddenly and energetically : exclaim. **—e•jac′u•la′tion** *n.* **—e•jac′u•la•to′ry** (-lə-tôr′ē, -tōr′ē) *adj.*
e•ject (ĭ-jĕkt′) *v.* To drive or throw off or out forcefully : expel. **—e•jec′tion** *n.* **—e•jec′tor** *n.*
e•jec•ta (ĭ-jĕk′tə) *pl.n.* Ejected matter.
eke (ēk) *v.* **eked, ek•ing.** To earn or supplement with great effort <*eke* out an income with night work>
EKG *abbr.* electrocardiogram; electrocardiograph.
e•kis•tics (ĭ-kĭs′tĭks) *n. (sing. in number).* The science that deals with human settlements, including community design and planning. **—e•kis′tic** *adj.*
ek•pwe•le (ĕk-pwē′lē) *n.* See CURRENCY TABLE.
e•lab•o•rate (ĭ-lăb′ər-ĭt) *adj.* **1.** Planned or done with attention to numerous details or parts. **2.** Very complex : intricate. *—v.* (-ə-rāt′) **-rat•ed, -rat•ing. 1.** To work out with careful detail. **2.** To express in greater detail : provide further information. **—e•lab′o•rate•ly** *adv.* **—e•lab′o•rate•ness** *n.* **—e•lab′o•ra′tion** (-ə-rā′shən) *n.*
é•lan (ā-läɴ′, ā-län′) *n.* **1.** Enthusiasm : vigor. **2.** Spirit and style : flair.
e•land (ē′lənd, ē′lănd′) *n.* A large African antelope, *Taurotragus oryx* or *T. derbianus,* with a tan coat and spirally twisted horns.
e•lapse (ĭ-lăps′) *v.* **e•lapsed, e•laps•ing.** To pass <Much time has *elapsed.*>
e•las•tic (ĭ-lăs′tĭk) *adj.* **1.** *Physics.* Returning to an initial or prior state or form after deformation. **2.** Adapting to changing circumstances : flexible. **3.** Resilient : springy. *—n.* **1.** Something made of elastic. **2.** A rubber band. **—e•las′ti•cal•ly** *adv.* **—e•las•tic′i•ty** (ĭ-lă-stĭs′ĭ-tē, ē′lă-) *n.*
e•late (ĭ-lāt′) *v.* **e•lat•ed, e•lat•ing.** To raise the spirits of. ☆*syns:* BUOY, ELEVATE, EXALT, EXHILARATE, INSPIRE, INSPIRIT, UPLIFT **—e•lat′ed•ly** *adv.* **—e•lat′ed•ness** *n.* **—e•la′tion** *n.*
El•be (ĕl′bə, ĕlb). River of Czechoslovakia, East Germany, and West Germany, flowing to the North Sea.
el•bow (ĕl′bō′) *n.* **1.** The joint of the arm between the upper arm and forearm. **2.** Something with a bend resembling an elbow. *—v.* **1.** To jostle or shove aside with the elbow. **2.** To make (one's way) by pushing with the elbow or elbows.
el•bow•room (ĕl′bō-ro͞om′, -ro͝om′) *n.* Ample room to move about or function in.
eld•er[1] (ĕl′dər) *adj.* Older. *—n.* **1.** An older person, esp. one who is an influential member of a family, community, or tribe. **2.** A governing official of a church. **—el′der•ship′** *n.*
el•der[2] (ĕl′dər) *n.* Any of various shrubs of the genus *Sambucus,* bearing small white flower clusters and red or blackish berries.
el•der•ber•ry (ĕl′dər-bĕr′ē) *n.* The edible fruit of an elder used to make wine or jelly.
eld•er•ly (ĕl′dər-lē) *adj.* Rather old. **—el′der•li•ness** *n.*
eld•est (ĕl′dĭst) *adj.* Greatest in age.
El Do•ra•do (ĕl′ də-rä′dō) *n.* A legendary place of great wealth or opportunity.
elec. *abbr.* electric; electrical; electricity.
e•lect (ĭ-lĕkt′) *v.* **1.** To choose by vote, as for an office. **2.** To choose : pick. **3.** To decide <*elected* to sell the property> *—adj.* **1.** Singled out on purpose. **2.** Elected but not yet installed <the mayor-*elect*> *—n.* **1.** One chosen or selected, esp. for spiritual salvation. **2.** *(pl. in number).* An exclusive or privileged group.
e•lec•tion (ĭ-lĕk′shən) *n.* **1.** The act or power of electing. **2.** The fact of being elected. **3.** Predestined salvation.
e•lec•tion•eer (ĭ-lĕk′shə-nîr′) *v.* To work actively for a political candidate.
e•lec•tive (ĭ-lĕk′tĭv) *adj.* **1.** Filled or selected by election <an *elective* post> **2.** Empowered to elect. **3.** Optional <*elective* courses> *—n.* An optional academic course. **—e•lec′tive•ly** *adv.*
e•lec•tor (ĭ-lĕk′tər) *n.* **1.** A qualified voter. **2.** A member of the U.S. electoral college. **—e•lec′tor•al** *adj.*
electoral college *n.* A group of electors chosen to elect the U.S. President and Vice President.
e•lec•tor•ate (ĭ-lĕk′tər-ĭt) *n.* A body of qualified voters.

e·lec·tric (ĭ-lĕk′trĭk) or **e·lec·tri·cal** (-trĭ-kəl) *adj.* **1.** Of, relating to, or operated by electricity. **2.** Emotionally exciting : thrilling. **3.** Charged with emotion : tense. **—e·lec′tri·cal·ly** *adv.*

electrical storm *n.* A thunderstorm.

electric chair *n.* A chair for electrocuting condemned prisoners.

electric eye *n.* A photoelectric cell.

electric field *n.* A region of space marked by the presence of a detectable electric intensity at every point.

e·lec·tri·cian (ĭ-lĕk-trĭsh′ən, ē′lĕk-) *n.* One whose work is the installation or maintenance of electric equipment.

e·lec·tric·i·ty (ĭ-lĕk-trĭs′ĭ-tē, ē′lĕk-) *n.* **1.** A property of matter that causes bodies to attract or repel each other and is responsible for such phenomena as lightning. **2.** Electric current as a power source. **3.** Emotional excitement or tension.

▲word history: The effects of electricity have been observed since ancient times, when it was noticed that amber when rubbed attracts small bits of straw and wood. When this electromagnetic effect was 1st examined in the early 17th cent., the words *electric* and *electricity* were coined from Greek *ēlektron,* "amber."

e·lec·tri·fy (ĭ-lĕk′trə-fī′) *v.* **-fied, -fy·ing. 1.** To give an electric charge to. **2.** To equip (e.g., a building) for the use of electricity. **3.** To excite greatly : thrill. **—e·lec′tri·fi·ca′tion** *n.* **—e·lec′tri·fi′er** *n.*

e·lec·tro·car·di·o·gram (ĭ-lĕk′trō-kär′dē-ə-grăm′) *n.* The tracing made by an electrocardiograph.

e·lec·tro·car·di·o·graph (ĭ-lĕk′trō-kär′dē-ə-grăf′) *n.* An instrument that records the electrical activity of the heart. **—e·lec′tro·car′di·o·graph′ic** (-grăf′ĭk) *adj.* **—e·lec′tro·car′di·og′ra·phy** (-ŏg′rə-fē) *n.*

e·lec·tro·chem·is·try (ĭ-lĕk′trō-kĕm′ĭ-strē) *n.* The study of phenomena that involve electricity and chemistry. **—e·lec′tro·chem′i·cal** (-ĭ-kəl) *adj.*

e·lec·tro·cute (ĭ-lĕk′trə-kyōōt′) *v.* **-cut·ed, -cut·ing. 1.** To kill with electricity. **2.** To execute (a condemned prisoner) by electricity. **—e·lec′tro·cu′tion** *n.*

e·lec·trode (ĭ-lĕk′trōd′) *n.* A conductor that transfers electric charges into or out of another conducting medium or that influences the flow of current in another conducting medium.

e·lec·tro·dy·nam·ics (ĭ-lĕk′trō-dī-năm′ĭks) *n.* *(sing. in number).* The physics of the interactions of electric, magnetic, and mechanical phenomena. **—e·lec′tro·dy·nam′ic** *adj.*

e·lec·tro·en·ceph·a·lo·gram (ĭ-lĕk′trō-ĕn-sĕf′ə-lə-grăm′) *n.* A tracing of the electrical activity of the brain made by an electroencephalograph.

e·lec·tro·en·ceph·a·lo·graph (ĭ-lĕk′trō-ĕn-sĕf′ə-lə-grăf′) *n.* An instrument for recording the electrical activity of the brain. **—e·lec′tro·en·ceph′a·log′ra·phy** (-lŏg′rə-fē) *n.*

e·lec·trol·o·gist (ĭ-lĕk-trŏl′ə-jĭst, ē′lĕk-) *n.* One who removes hair or blemishes from the body by the use of an electric current.

e·lec·trol·y·sis (ĭ-lĕk-trŏl′ĭ-sĭs, ē′lĕk-) *n.* **1.** A chemical change produced in an electrolyte by an electric current. **2.** Destruction of tissue, esp. hair roots, by an electric current.

e·lec·tro·lyte (ĭ-lĕk′trə-līt′) *n.* A substance that breaks apart into ions when dissolved or melted, thus becoming electrically conductive. **—e·lec′tro·lyt′ic** (-lĭt′ĭk) *adj.* **—e·lec′tro·lyt′i·cal·ly** *adv.*

e·lec·tro·mag·net (ĭ-lĕk′trō-măg′nĭt) *n.* A magnet made of a soft-iron core wound with a coil of wire that magnetizes the core when a current passes through it.

e·lec·tro·mag·net·ic (ĭ-lĕk′trō-măg-nĕt′ĭk) *adj.* Of, caused by, or relating to electromagnetism. **—e·lec′tro·mag·net′i·cal·ly** *adv.*

e·lec·tro·mag·net·ism (ĭ-lĕk′trō-măg′nĭ-tĭz′əm) *n.* **1.** Magnetism arising from electric charge in motion. **2.** The physics of electricity and magnetism.

e·lec·trom·e·ter (ĭ-lĕk-trŏm′ĭ-tər, ē′lĕk-) *n.* An instrument for detecting or measuring electric charge and potential differences.

e·lec·tro·mo·tive (ĭ-lĕk′trō-mō′tĭv) *adj.* Of, relating to, or tending to produce electric current.

electromotive force *n.* **1.** A force that tends to produce an electric current. **2.** The energy per unit of charge that is converted into electrical form by a device such as a battery or generator.

e·lec·tron (ĭ-lĕk′trŏn′) *n.* A subatomic particle with a negative electric charge.

e·lec·tron·ic (ĭ-lĕk-trŏn′ĭk, ē′lĕk-) *adj.* **1.** Of or involving electrons. **2.** Of, based on, or operated by the controlled flow of charge carriers, esp. electrons. **3.** Of or relating to electronics. **—e·lec·tron′i·cal·ly** *adv.*

e·lec·tron·ics (ĭ-lĕk-trŏn′ĭks, ē′lĕk-) *n.* *(sing. in number).* The science and technology of electronic phenomena and devices.

electron microscope *n.* A microscope that uses an electron beam to produce magnified images, esp. of very small objects.

electron tube *n.* A sealed enclosure, either highly evacuated or containing a controlled quantity of gas, in which electrons act as the principal carriers of current between at least 2 electrodes.

e·lec·tro·plate (ĭ-lĕk′trə-plāt′) *v.* To coat with a thin layer of metal by electrolysis.

e·lec·tro·stat·ic (ĭ-lĕk′trō-stăt′ĭk) *adj.* **1.** Of or relating to static electric charges. **2.** Of or relating to electrostatics.

e·lec·tro·stat·ics (ĭ-lĕk′trō-stăt′ĭks) *n.* *(sing. in number).* The physics of static electric charges.

e·lec·tro·type (ĭ-lĕk′trə-tīp′) *n.* A duplicate metal plate used in printing, made by electroplating a mold of the original plate. **—e·lec′tro·type′** *v.*

el·ee·mos·y·nar·y (ĕl′ə-mŏs′ə-nĕr′ē, ĕl′ē-ə-) *adj.* Of, relating to, or contributed as charity.

el·e·gance (ĕl′ĭ-gəns) *n.* **1.** Grace and refinement in appearance, movement, or manners. **2.** Tasteful richness in decoration or presentation. **3.** Something refined and graceful. **—el′e·gant** *adj.*

el·e·gi·ac (ĕl′ə-jī′ək, ĭ-lē′jē-ăk′) *adj.* **1.** Of or relating to an elegy. **2.** Expressing sorrow : mournful. **—el′e·gi′ac·al·ly** *adv.*

el·e·gy (ĕl′ə-jē) *n., pl.* **-gies.** A poem expressing sorrow for one who is dead.

el·e·ment (ĕl′ə-mənt) *n.* **1.** A fundamental part. **2. elements.** The basic principles <the *elements* of biology> **3.** *Math.* A member of a set. **4.** *Chem.* & *Physics.* A substance not separable into less complex substances by chemical means. **5. elements.** The forces of the weather <exposed to the *elements*> **6.** A native or congenial environment. ☆***syns:*** COMPONENT, CONSTITUENT, FACTOR, INGREDIENT, PART

el·e·men·tal (ĕl′ə-mĕn′tl) *adj.* **1.** Of, relating to, or being an element. **2.** Fundamental : essential. **3.** Constituting or like a force of nature in power or effect.

el·e·men·ta·ry (ĕl′ə-mĕn′tə-rē, -trē) *adj.* **1.** Fundamental, essential, or irreducible. **2.** Of or introducing fundamental principles <an *elementary* textbook>

elementary particle *n.* A particle of matter or energy that is thought not to be divisible into smaller particles.

elementary school *n.* A school for the first 6 to 8 grades.

el·e·phant (ĕl′ə-fənt) *n.* Either of 2 very large mammals, *Elephas maximus,* of SC Asia, or *Loxodonta africana,* of Africa, with a long, flexible trunk and curved tusks.

el·e·phan·ti·a·sis (ĕl′ə-fən-tī′ə-sĭs) *n.* Enlargement and hardening of tissues, esp. of the lower body, resulting from the blockage of lymph ducts by parasitic worms.

el·e·phan·tine (ĕl′ə-făn′tēn′, -tīn′, ĕl′ə-fən-) *adj.* **1.** Enormous in size : gigantic. **2.** Heavy-footed : ponderous.

el·e·vate (ĕl′ə-vāt′) *v.* **-vat·ed, -vat·ing. 1.** To lift up : raise. **2.** To promote to a higher rank. **3.** To raise to a higher moral, cultural, or intellectual level. **4.** To lift the spirits of : elate. ☆***syns:*** BOOST, HOIST, LIFT, PICK UP, RAISE, UPLIFT

el·e·va·tion (ĕl′ə-vā′shən) *n.* **1.** The act of elevating or state of being elevated. **2.** An elevated place or position. **3.** The height to which something is elevated, as above sea level.

el·e·va·tor (ĕl′ə-vā′tər) *n.* **1.** A platform or enclosure raised and lowered to carry freight or people. **2.** A building for storing and discharging grain. **3.** A movable surface on an aircraft that produces upward or downward motion.

e·lev·en (ĭ-lĕv′ən) *n.* **1.** The cardinal number equal to 10 + 1. **2.** The 11th in a set or sequence. **3.** Something, esp. a football team, with 11 members. **—e·lev′en** *adj.* & *pron.* **—e·lev′enth** *n.* & *adj.* & *adv.*

elf (ĕlf) *n., pl.* **elves** (ĕlvz). A small, often mischievous imaginary creature. **—elf′in** *adj.* **—elf′ish** *adj.*

e·lic·it (ĭ-lĭs′ĭt) *v.* To bring out or call forth : evoke.

e·lide (ĭ-līd′) *v.* **e·lid·ed, e·lid·ing.** To omit, esp. to slur over (a speech sound) in pronunciation. **—e·li′sion** (ĭ-lĭzh′ən) *n.*

el·i·gi·ble (ĕl′ĭ-jə-bəl) *adj.* **1.** Qualified, as for an office. **2.** Desirable and suited to be chosen, esp. for marriage. **—el′i·gi·bil′i·ty** *n.* **—el′i·gi·ble** *n.*

e·lim·i·nate (ĭ-lĭm′ə-nāt′) *v.* **-nat·ed, -nat·ing. 1.** To get rid of : remove <*eliminate* an injustice> **2.** To leave out : omit. **3.** *Physiol.* To excrete as waste. ☆***syns:*** ERADICATE, LIQUIDATE, PURGE, REMOVE **—e·lim′i·na′tion** *n.* **—e·lim′i·na′tive, e·lim′i·na·to′ry** (-nə-tôr′ē, -tōr′ē) *adj.* **—e·lim′i·na′tor** *n.*

El·i·ot (ĕl′ē-ət). **George.** Mary Ann Evans. 1819–80. English novelist.

e·lite or **é·lite** (ĭ-lēt′, ā-lēt′) *n.* **1.** *(pl. in number).* **a.** The best or most skilled members of a group. **b.** A small but powerful group. **2.** A typewriter type size providing 12 characters to the inch. **—e·lite′** *adj.*

e·lit·ism or **é·lit·ism** (ĭ-lē′tĭz′əm, ā-lē′-) *n.* Rule or domination by or belief in an elite. **—e·lit′ist** *n.*
e·lix·ir (ĭ-lĭk′sər) *n.* **1.** A sweetened aromatic solution of alcohol and water used as a vehicle for medicine. **2.** A medicine regarded as a cure-all : panacea.
E·liz·a·beth I (ĭ-lĭz′ə-bəth). 1533–1603. Queen of England and Ireland (1558–1603). **—E·liz′a·be′than** (-bē′thən) *adj. & n.*
elk (ĕlk) *n., pl.* **elks** or **elk. 1.** The wapiti. **2.** A large deer, *Alces alces,* of N Eurasia.
elk·hound (ĕlk′hound′) *n.* A hunting dog, orig. bred in Scandinavia, with grayish fur and a tail curled up over the back.
ell[1] (ĕl) *n.* A wing of a building at right angles to the main structure.
ell[2] (ĕl) *n.* A former English linear measure, esp. for cloth, equal to 45 in.
el·lipse (ĭ-lĭps′) *n.* A closed plane curve that is oval in shape.

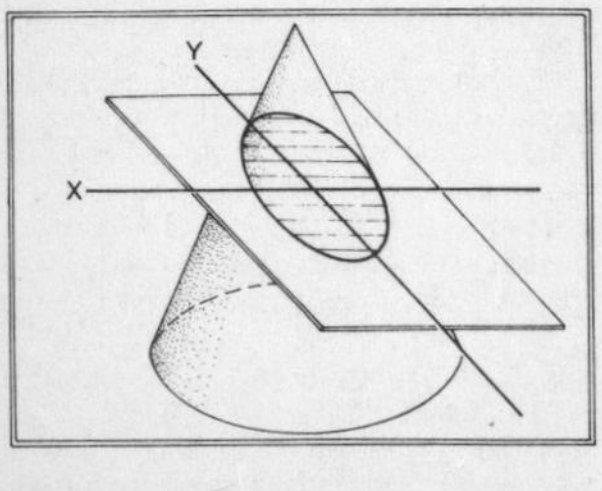

ellipse

el·lip·sis (ĭ-lĭp′sĭs) *n., pl.* **-ses** (-sēz′). **1.** The omission of a word or phrase implied by the context. **2.** A series of marks (e.g., . . . or ***) indicating an omission.
el·lip·tic (ĭ-lĭp′tĭk) or **el·lip·ti·cal** (-tĭ-kəl) *adj.* **1.** Of, relating to, or shaped like an ellipse. **2.** Of, relating to, or marked by ellipsis.
elm (ĕlm) *n.* Any of various deciduous shade trees of the genus *Ulmus,* with arching branches.
el·o·cu·tion (ĕl′ə-kyōō′shən) *n.* The art of public speaking. **—el′o·cu′tion·ar′y** (-shə-nĕr′ē) *adj.* **—el′o·cu′tion·ist** *n.*
e·lon·gate (ĭ-lông′gāt′, ĭ-lŏng′-) *v.* **-gat·ed, -gat·ing.** To make or become longer : lengthen. **—e·lon′ga′tion** *n.*
e·lope (ĭ-lōp′) *v.* **e·loped, e·lop·ing.** To run away, esp. in order to get married. **—e·lope′ment** *n.* **—e·lop′er** *n.*
el·o·quent (ĕl′ə-kwənt) *adj.* **1.** Speaking or spoken fluently and persuasively. **2.** Vividly or movingly expressive <an *eloquent* gesture> **—el′o·quence** *n.* **—el′o·quent·ly** *adv.*
El Sal·va·dor (ĕl săl′və-dôr′). Country of Central America, on the Pacific. *Cap.* San Salvador. *Pop.* 4,360,000.
else (ĕls) *adj.* **1.** Different : other <anybody *else*> **2.** More : additional <Do you need anything *else*?> *—adv.* **1.** Differently : besides <How *else* could I have answered?> **2.** Otherwise <Step high, or *else* you will trip.>
else·where (ĕls′hwâr′, -wâr′) *adv.* To or in another or different place.
e·lu·ci·date (ĭ-lōō′sĭ-dāt′) *v.* **-dat·ed, -dat·ing.** To make clear : clarify. **—e·lu′ci·da′tion** *n.* **—e·lu′ci·da′tor** *n.*
e·lude (ĭ-lōōd′) *v.* **e·lud·ed, e·lud·ing. 1.** To avoid being captured by : evade. **2.** To escape the understanding of.
e·lu·sive (ĭ-lōō′sĭv, -zĭv) *adj.* Tending to elude. **—e·lu′sive·ly** *adv.* **—e·lu′sive·ness** *n.*
el·ver (ĕl′vər) *n.* A young eel.
elves (ĕlvz) *n. pl. of* ELF.
E·ly·si·um (ĭ-lĭz′ē-əm, ĭ-lĭzh′-) *n.* A place of ideal happiness : paradise. **—E·ly′sian** (ĭ-lĭzh′ən) *adj.*
em (ĕm) *n.* A unit of measure for printed matter that is equal to the width of the letter M.
′em (əm) *pron. Informal.* Them.
e·ma·ci·ate (ĭ-mā′shē-āt′) *v.* **-at·ed, -at·ing.** To become or cause to become abnormally thin. **—e·ma′ci·a′tion** *n.*
em·a·nate (ĕm′ə-nāt′) *v.* **-nat·ed, -nat·ing.** To come or send forth, as from a source : issue or emit. **—em′a·na′tion** *n.*
e·man·ci·pate (ĭ-măn′sə-pāt′) *v.* **-pat·ed, -pat·ing.** To set free : liberate. **—e·man′ci·pa′tion** *n.* **—e·man′ci·pa′tor** *n.*
e·mas·cu·late (ĭ-măs′kyə-lāt′) *v.* **-lat·ed, -lat·ing. 1.** To castrate. **2.** To deprive of vigor : enervate. **—e·mas′cu·la′tion** *n.* **—e·mas′cu·la′tor** *n.*
em·balm (ĕm-bäm′) *v.* To treat (a corpse) with preservatives in order to prevent decay. **—em·balm′er** *n.*
em·bank (ĕm-băngk′) *v.* To support or protect with a bank of earth or stone. **—em·bank′ment** *n.*
em·bar·go (ĕm-bär′gō) *n., pl.* **-goes.** A prohibition on trade, esp. a government order forbidding the entry or departure of merchant ships. **—em·bar′go** *v.*
em·bark (ĕm-bärk′) *v.* **1.** To board or cause to board a vessel or aircraft. **2.** To set out on a venture. **—em′bar·ka′tion** *n.*
em·bar·rass (ĕm-băr′əs) *v.* **1.** To cause to feel self-consciously distressed. **2.** To burden with financial difficulties. **3.** To impede : hinder. ☆***syns:*** ABASH, CONFUSE, DISCOMFORT, DISCONCERT, FAZE, MORTIFY **—em·bar′rass·ing·ly** *adv.* **—em·bar′rass·ment** *n.*
em·bas·sy (ĕm′bə-sē) *n., pl.* **-sies. 1.** The position or function of an ambassador. **2.** A mission led by an ambassador. **3.** An ambassador and his or her staff. **4.** The headquarters of an ambassador.
em·bat·tle (ĕm-băt′l) *v.* To prepare for battle.
em·bed (ĕm-bĕd′) *v.* To fix or become fixed tightly in a surrounding mass.
em·bel·lish (ĕm-bĕl′ĭsh) *v.* **1.** To make beautiful by ornamentation : adorn. **2.** To add fanciful details to <*embellished* the account> **—em·bel′lish·ment** *n.*
em·ber (ĕm′bər) *n.* **1.** A piece of glowing coal or wood, as in a dying fire. **2. embers.** The smoldering ashes of a dying fire.
em·bez·zle (ĕm-bĕz′əl) *v.* **-zled, -zling.** To take (e.g., money) fraudulently in violation of a trust. **—em·bez′zle·ment** *n.* **—em·bez′zler** *n.*
em·bit·ter (ĕm-bĭt′ər) *v.* **1.** To make bitter. **2.** To arouse bitter feelings in. **—em·bit′ter·ment** *n.*
em·bla·zon (ĕm-blā′zən) *v.* **1.** To ornament brightly or colorfully. **2.** To make illustrious : extol.
em·blem (ĕm′bləm) *n.* **1.** Something that represents or suggests something else : symbol. **2.** A distinctive design or device. **—em′blem·at′ic** (-blə-măt′ĭk), **em′blem·at′i·cal** *adj.*
em·bod·y (ĕm-bŏd′ē) *v.* **-ied, -y·ing. 1.** To give bodily form to (e.g., an abstraction). **2.** To personify. **3.** To make part of a system or whole. ☆***syns:*** INCARNATE, MANIFEST, PERSONIFY **—em·bod′i·ment** *n.*
em·bold·en (ĕm-bōl′dən) *v.* To impart courage to : encourage.
em·bo·lism (ĕm′bə-lĭz′əm) *n.* The obstruction of a blood vessel, as by an air bubble or a detached clot.
em·bon·point (äN′bôN-pwăN′) *n.* Plumpness : corpulence.
em·boss (ĕm-bôs′, -bŏs′) *v.* **1.** To shape or decorate in relief. **2.** To raise the surface of <*emboss* type>
em·bou·chure (äm′bōō-shōōr′) *n.* **1.** The mouthpiece of a wind instrument. **2.** The way in which the lips are applied to an embouchure to produce a musical tone.
em·bow·er (ĕm-bou′ər) *v.* To enclose in or as if in a bower.
em·brace (ĕm-brās′) *v.* **-braced, -brac·ing. 1.** To clasp in the arms : hug. **2.** To encircle. **3.** To include : encompass. **4.** To take up willingly <*embraced* the cause> *—n.* The act of embracing : hug.
em·bra·sure (ĕm-brā′zhər) *n.* A usu. flared opening in a wall for a door, window, or gun.
em·bro·cate (ĕm′brə-kāt′) *v.* **-cat·ed, -cat·ing.** To moisten and rub with a liquid medicine. **—em′bro·ca′tion** *n.*
em·broi·der (ĕm-broi′dər) *v.* **1.** To decorate (fabric) with needlework. **2.** To add fictitious details (to). **—em·broi′der·er** *n.*
em·broi·der·y (ĕm-broi′də-rē) *n., pl.* **-ies. 1.** The act or art of embroidering. **2.** Embroidered fabric. **3.** Fanciful details.
em·broil (ĕm-broil′) *v.* **1.** To involve in contention or hostile actions. **2.** To throw into confusion. **—em·broil′ment** *n.*
em·bry·o (ĕm′brē-ō′) *n., pl.* **-os. 1.** An organism in its early developmental stage, esp. before birth or germination. **2.** A rudimentary stage <talent in *embryo*> **—em′bry·on′ic** (-ŏn′ĭk) *adj.*
em·bry·ol·o·gy (ĕm′brē-ŏl′ə-jē) *n.* The science concerned with the formation and growth of embryos. **—em′bry·o·log′ic** (-ə-lŏj′ĭk), **em′bry·o·log′i·cal** *adj.* **—em′bry·ol′o·gist** *n.*
em·cee (ĕm′sē′) *n. Informal.* A master of ceremonies. **—em′cee′** *v.*
e·mend (ĭ-mĕnd′) *v.* To correct and improve by textual editing. **—e′men·da′tion** *n.* **—e·mend′er** *n.*
em·er·ald (ĕm′ər-əld, ĕm′rəld) *n.* **1.** A bright-green transparent form of beryl used as a gemstone. **2.** A bright green.
e·merge (ĭ-mûrj′) *v.* **e·merged, e·merg·ing. 1.** To rise or come into view : appear. **2.** To come into existence. **3.** To become evident. **—e·mer′gence** *n.* **—e·mer′gent** *adj.*
e·mer·gen·cy (ĭ-mûr′jən-sē) *n., pl.* **-cies.** An unexpected situation that requires prompt action.
e·mer·i·ta (ĭ-mĕr′ĭ-tə) *adj.* Emeritus. Used of a woman. **—e·mer′i·ta** *n.*
e·mer·i·tus (ĭ-mĕr′ĭ-təs) *adj.* Retired but retaining the title held immediately before retirement <president *emeritus*> **—e·mer′i·tus** *n.*
Em·er·son (ĕm′ər-sən), **Ralph Waldo.** 1803–82. Amer. essayist and poet. **—Em′er·so′ni·an** (-sō′nē-ən) *adj.*
em·er·y (ĕm′ə-rē, ĕm′rē) *n.* A grainy, impure corundum used for polishing and grinding.
e·met·ic (ĭ-mĕt′ĭk) *adj.* Inducing vomiting. **—e·met′ic** *n.*

em·i·grate (ĕm'ĭ-grāt') *v.* **-grat·ed, -grat·ing.** To leave a native country or region to settle elsewhere. **—em'i·grant** *n.* **—em'i·gra'tion** *n.*

é·mi·gré (ĕm'ĭ-grā') *n.* One who emigrates, esp. for political reasons.

em·i·nence (ĕm'ə-nəns) *n.* **1.** Great distinction or superiority. **2.** A high-ranking person. **3.** A rise of ground : hill.

em·i·nent (ĕm'ə-nənt) *adj.* **1.** Standing out : prominent. **2.** Outstanding, as in attainments : distinguished <an *eminent* scientist> **—em'i·nent·ly** *adv.*

eminent domain *n. Law.* The right of a government to take private property for public use.

e·mir (ĕ-mîr') *n.* A prince, chieftain, or governor in some parts of the Middle East and Africa.

em·is·sar·y (ĕm'ĭ-sĕr'ē) *n., pl.* **-ies.** A messenger or agent.

e·mit (ĭ-mĭt') *v.* **e·mit·ted, e·mit·ting. 1.** To send or give out <*emit* radiation> **2.** To express : utter. **3.** To put (e.g., money) into circulation. **—e·mis'sion** *n.*

e·mol·lient (ĭ-mŏl'yənt) *adj.* Soothing and softening, esp. to the skin. **—e·mol'lient** *n.*

e·mol·u·ment (ĭ-mŏl'yə-mənt) *n.* Compensation, as a salary, from a post of employment.

e·mote (ĭ-mōt') *v.* **e·mot·ed, e·mot·ing.** To express emotion theatrically.

e·mo·tion (ĭ-mō'shən) *n.* **1.** Strong feeling. **2.** A particular feeling, as love or hate.

e·mo·tion·al (ĭ-mō'shə-nəl) *adj.* **1.** Of or relating to emotion. **2.** Easily stirred by emotion. **3.** Marked by or stirring the emotions. **—e·mo'tion·al'i·ty** (-năl'ĭ-tē) *n.* **—e·mo'tion·al·ly** *adv.*

em·pa·thize (ĕm'pə-thīz') *v.* **-thized, -thiz·ing.** To feel empathy.

em·pa·thy (ĕm'pə-thē) *n.* Identification with and understanding of the thoughts or feelings of another. **—em'pa·thet'ic** (-thĕt'ĭk), **em·path'ic** (-păth'ĭk) *adj.*

em·pen·nage (ĕm'pə-nĭj) *n.* The tail of an aircraft.

em·per·or (ĕm'pər-ər) *n.* The ruler of an empire.

em·pha·sis (ĕm'fə-sĭs) *n., pl.* **-ses** (-sēz'). **1.** Special weight or significance <an *emphasis* on promptness> **2.** Stress given, as to a syllable or word.

em·pha·size (ĕm'fə-sīz') *v.* **-sized, -siz·ing.** To place emphasis on : stress.

em·phat·ic (ĕm-făt'ĭk) *adj.* Expressed or carried out with emphasis. **—em·phat'i·cal·ly** *adv.*

em·phy·se·ma (ĕm'fĭ-sē'mə) *n.* A pulmonary disease in which the lungs lose their elasticity, resulting in labored breathing and susceptibility to infection.

em·pire (ĕm'pīr') *n.* **1.** A group of territories or nations ruled by a single supreme authority. **2.** Imperial dominion.

em·pir·i·cal (ĕm-pîr'ĭ-kəl) *also* **em·pir·ic** (-pîr'ĭk) *adj.* Relying on or gained from observation or experiment rather than theory <*empirical* knowledge> **—em·pir'i·cal·ly** *adv.*

em·pir·i·cism (ĕm-pîr'ĭ-sĭz'əm) *n.* **1.** The belief that experience, esp. of the senses, is the single source of knowledge. **2.** The use of empirical methods in science. **—em·pir'i·cist** *n.*

em·place·ment (ĕm-plās'mənt) *n.* **1.** A platform or mounting for guns or military equipment. **2.** Placement.

em·ploy (ĕm-ploi') *v.* **1.** To put to service or use. **2.** To apply or devote (e.g., time) to an activity. **3.** To provide with gainful work. *—n.* Employment. **—em·ploy'a·ble** *adj.* **—em·ploy'er** *n.*

em·ploy·ee *also* **em·ploy·e** (ĕm-ploi'ē, ĕm'ploi-ē') *n.* A person who works for another for compensation.

em·ploy·ment (ĕm-ploi'mənt) *n.* **1.** The act of employing or state of being employed. **2.** An occupation or activity.

em·po·ri·um (ĕm-pôr'ē-əm, -pōr'-) *n., pl.* **-ri·ums** *or* **-ri·a** (-ē-ə) A large store carrying a great variety of goods.

em·pow·er (ĕm-pou'ər) *v.* To authorize.

em·press (ĕm'prĭs) *n.* **1.** A woman who rules an empire. **2.** An emperor's wife or widow.

emp·ty (ĕmp'tē) *adj.* **-ti·er, -ti·est. 1.** Containing nothing. **2.** Without occupants : vacant. **3.** Lacking force or substance <*empty* promises> *—v.* **-tied, -ty·ing. 1.** To make or become empty. **2.** To flow or pour out : discharge. *—n., pl.* **-ties.** An empty container. **—emp'ti·ly** *adv.* **—emp'ti·ness** *n.*

emp·ty-hand·ed (ĕmp'tē-hăn'dĭd) *adj.* Bringing or taking away nothing.

em·py·re·an (ĕm'pī-rē'ən) *n.* **1.** The highest part of heaven. **2.** The sky.

e·mu (ē'myōō) *n.* A large, flightless Australian bird, *Dromiceius novaehollandia*, related and similar to the ostrich.

em·u·late (ĕm'yə-lāt') *v.* **-lat·ed, -lat·ing.** To strive to equal or better, esp. by imitating. **—em'u·la'tion** *n.* **—em'u·lous** (-ləs) *adj.*

e·mul·si·fy (ĭ-mŭl'sə-fī') *v.* **-fied, -fy·ing.** To become or cause to become an emulsion. **—e·mul'si·fi·ca'tion** *n.* **—e·mul'si·fi'er** *n.*

e·mul·sion (ĭ-mŭl'shən) *n.* **1.** *Chem.* A suspension of small droplets of 1 liquid in a 2nd liquid with which the 1st will not mix. **2.** A light-sensitive coating on photographic film, paper, or glass. **—e·mul'sive** *adj.*

en (ĕn) *n.* A space equal to half the width of an em.

-en[1] *suff.* **1.** To make or become <deaf*en*><short*en*> **2.** To cause or come to have <strength*en*>

-en[2] *suff.* Of or resembling <earth*en*>

en·a·ble (ĕn-ā'bəl) *v.* **-bled, -bling. 1.** To supply with the means, knowledge, or opportunity. **2.** To give legal power to.

en·act (ĕn-ăkt') *v.* **1.** To make (e.g., a legislative bill) into law. **2.** To act out <*enact* a drama> **—en·act'ment** *n.*

e·nam·el (ĭ-năm'əl) *n.* **1.** A decorative or protective vitreous, usu. opaque coating baked on a surface, as of pottery. **2.** A paint that forms a hard, glossy surface. **3.** The hard, calcareous covering on the exposed portion of a tooth. *—v.* **-eled, -el·ing** or **-elled, -el·ling.** To coat, inlay, or decorate with enamel.

e·nam·el·ware (ĭ-năm'əl-wâr') *n.* Utensils, esp. kitchen utensils, made of metal coated with enamel.

en·am·or (ĭ-năm'ər) *v.* To imbue with love : captivate.

en·am·our (ĭ-năm'ər) *v. esp. Brit. var. of* ENAMOR.

en bloc (äɴ blŏk') *adv.* As a unit.

enc. *or* **encl.** *abbr.* enclosed; enclosure.

en·camp (ĕn-kămp') *v.* To set up or stay in a camp. **—en·camp'ment** *n.*

en·cap·su·late (ĕn-kăp'sə-lāt') *v.* **-lat·ed, -lat·ing.** To enclose or become enclosed in or as if in a capsule. **—en·cap'su·la'tion** *n.*

en·case (ĕn-kās') *v.* To enclose in or as if in a case. **—en·case'ment** *n.*

-ence *or* **-ency** *suff.* **1.** Condition or quality <depend*ence*> **2.** Action <emerg*ence*><insurg*ency*>

en·ceph·a·li·tis (ĕn-sĕf'ə-lī'tĭs) *n.* Inflammation of the brain. **—en·ceph'a·lit'ic** (-lĭt'ĭk) *adj.*

en·chain (ĕn-chān') *v.* To put in chains.

en·chant (ĕn-chănt') *v.* **1.** To cast a spell over : bewitch. **2.** To delight greatly : enrapture. **—en·chant'ment** *n.*

en·chi·la·da (ĕn'chə-lä'də) *n.* A rolled tortilla filled with meat or cheese and served with chili sauce.

en·ci·pher (ĕn-sī'fər) *v.* To encode. **—en·ci'pher·er** *n.* **—en·ci'pher·ment** *n.*

en·cir·cle (ĕn-sûr'kəl) *v.* **1.** To make a circle around : surround. **2.** To move or go around. **—en·cir'cle·ment** *n.*

en·clave (ĕn'klāv', ŏn'-) *n.* **1.** A country or part of a country lying inside the boundaries of another. **2.** A cultural group living within a larger group.

en·close (ĕn-klōz') *v.* **1.** To surround on all sides. **2.** To insert in the same envelope or package with something else. **—en·clo'sure** *n.*

en·code (ĕn-kōd') *v.* **-cod·ed, -cod·ing.** To put (e.g., a message) into code. **—en·cod'er** *n.*

en·co·mi·um (ĕn-kō'mē-əm) *n., pl.* **-mi·ums** *or* **-mi·a** (-mē-ə). High praise.

en·com·pass (ĕn-kŭm'pəs, -kŏm'-) *v.* **1.** To surround. **2.** To envelop : enclose. **3.** To include : comprise.

en·core (ŏn'kôr', -kōr') *n.* **1.** An audience's demand for an additional performance. **2.** A performance in response to an encore. *—v.* **-cored, -cor·ing.** To demand an encore of.

en·coun·ter (ĕn-koun'tər) *n.* **1.** An unplanned or unexpected meeting. **2.** A hostile or violent meeting : clash. *—v.* **1.** To meet or come upon, esp. unexpectedly. **2.** To confront in a hostile situation.

encounter group *n.* A usu. unstructured therapy group in which individuals try to increase their sensitivity and responsiveness, reveal their feelings, and relate to others openly and intimately, as by touching or speaking freely.

en·cour·age (ĕn-kûr'ĭj, -kŭr'-) *v.* **-aged, -ag·ing. 1.** To inspire with courage or hope. **2.** To support : foster. **—en·cour'age·ment** *n.* **—en·cour'ag·ing·ly** *adv.*

en·croach (ĕn-krōch') *v.* To intrude gradually upon the rights or possessions of another <trees that *encroached* upon his neighbor's land> **—en·croach'er** *n.* **—en·croach'ment** *n.*

en·crust (ĕn-krŭst') *v.* To cover or top with crust. **—en'crust·a'tion** (ĕn'krŭ-stā'shən) *n.*

en·cum·ber (ĕn-kŭm'bər) *v.* **1.** To weigh down unduly : burden. **2.** To hinder : impede. **—en·cum'brance** (-brəns) *n.*

-ency *suff. var. of* -ENCE.

en·cyc·li·cal (ĕn-sĭk'lĭ-kəl) *n.* A papal letter to the church bishops.

en·cy·clo·pe·di·a *or* **en·cy·clo·pae·di·a** (ĕn-sī'klə-pē'dē-ə) *n.* A comprehensive reference work with articles on a broad range of subjects. **—en·cy'clo·pe'dic** *adj.*

en·cyst (ĕn-sĭst′) *v.* To enclose in or as if in a cyst. **—en·cyst′ment** *n.*
end (ĕnd) *n.* **1.** A part lying at a boundary : extremity. **2.** The point at which something ceases : conclusion. **3.** A result : outcome. **4.** An ultimate extent : limit <at the *end* of her patience> **5.** A goal : purpose. **6.** A share of responsibility <your *end* of the job> **7.** A remnant : remainder. **8.** *Football.* Either of the players in the outermost position on the line of scrimmage. —*v.* **1.** To come or bring to an end : finish. **2.** To form the end of. **3.** To ruin : destroy. ☆***syns:*** CLOSE, COMPLETE, CONCLUDE, FINISH, TERMINATE
en·dan·ger (ĕn-dān′jər) *v.* To expose to danger : imperil. **—en·dan′ger·ment** *n.*
en·dan·gered (ĕn-dān′jərd) *adj.* Threatened with extinction <an *endangered* species of salmon>
en·dear (ĕn-dîr′) *v.* To make beloved. **—en·dear′ing·ly** *adv.*
en·dear·ment (ĕn-dîr′mənt) *n.* An expression of affection.
en·deav·or (ĕn-dĕv′ər) *n.* A concerted effort : try. **—en·deav′or** *v.*
en·deav·our (ĕn-dĕv′ər) *n.* & *v. esp. Brit. var. of* ENDEAVOR.
en·dem·ic (ĕn-dĕm′ĭk) *adj.* Widespread in or peculiar to a particular area or people.
end·ing (ĕn′dĭng) *n.* **1.** A conclusion : termination. **2.** A suffix.
en·dive (ĕn′dīv′, ŏn′dēv′) *n.* **1.** A plant, *Cichorium endivia,* with crisp succulent leaves used in salads. **2.** A plant, *Cichorium intybus,* related to the endive and bearing a pointed cluster of whitish leaves used in salads.
end·less (ĕnd′lĭs) *adj.* **1.** Having or appearing to have no end : infinite. **2.** Interminable : incessant <an *endless* sermon> **3.** Having the ends joined : continuous <an *endless* belt> **—end′less·ly** *adv.* **—end′less·ness** *n.*
end·most (ĕnd′mōst′) *adj.* At or closest to the end.
en·do·crine (ĕn′də-krĭn, -krēn′, -krīn′) *adj.* Of or relating to a ductless gland, as the thyroid or adrenal, whose internal secretions go directly into the bloodstream. **—en′do·crine** *n.*
en·do·cri·nol·o·gy (ĕn′də-krə-nŏl′ə-jē) *n.* The physiology or study of the endocrine glands. **—en′do·cri·nol′o·gist** *n.*
en·dog·e·nous (ĕn-dŏj′ə-nəs) *adj.* Originating or produced from within.
en·dor·phin (ĕn-dôr′fĭn) *n.* Any of a group of hormones with tranquilizing and pain-killing capabilities that are secreted by the brain.
en·dorse (ĕn-dôrs′) *v.* **-dorsed, -dors·ing. 1.** To write one's signature on the back of (e.g., a check) as evidence that ownership has been legally transferred. **2.** To approve of publicly : support. **—en′dor·see′** *n.* **—en·dorse′ment** *n.*
en·do·scope (ĕn′də-skōp′) *n.* An instrument for examining a bodily canal or hollow organ. **—en′do·scop′ic** (-skŏp′ĭk) *adj.* **—en·dos′co·py** (-dŏs′kə-pē) *n.*
en·do·ther·mic (ĕn′də-thûr′mĭk) *also* **en·do·ther·mal** (-məl) *adj.* Marked by or causing heat absorption.
en·dow (ĕn-dou′) *v.* **1.** To supply with income or income-producing property. **2.** To equip with a quality or talent. **—en·dow′ment** *n.*
en·due (ĕn-do͞o′, -dyo͞o′) *v.* **-dued, -du·ing.** To provide with a quality or power.
en·dur·ance (ĕn-do͝or′əns, -dyo͝or′-) *n.* **1.** The capacity to withstand stress. **2.** Perseverance.
en·dure (ĕn-do͝or′, -dyo͝or′) *v.* **-dured, -dur·ing. 1.** To carry on through : undergo successfully. **2.** To tolerate : bear. **3.** To continue in existence. **—en·dur′a·ble** *adj.*
end·wise (ĕnd′wīz′) *also* **end·ways** (-wāz′) *adv.* **1.** On end. **2.** With the end forward. **3.** Lengthwise.
en·e·ma (ĕn′ə-mə) *n.* **1.** The injection of a liquid into the rectum, esp. for cleansing. **2.** The liquid injected as an enema.
en·e·my (ĕn′ə-mē) *n., pl.* **-mies. 1.** One who seeks to harm another : foe. **2.** A hostile force or power.
en·er·get·ic (ĕn′ər-jĕt′ĭk) *adj.* Possessing or exhibiting energy. ☆***syns:*** DYNAMIC, FORCEFUL, KINETIC, PEPPY, SPRIGHTLY, VIGOROUS **—en′er·get′i·cal·ly** *adv.*
en·er·gize (ĕn′ər-jīz′) *v.* **-gized, -giz·ing.** To give energy to. **—en′er·giz′er** *n.*
en·er·gy (ĕn′ər-jē) *n., pl.* **-gies. 1.** Capacity for working or acting : vigor. **2.** Strength : force. **3.** Vitality of expression. **4.** *Physics.* The work that a physical system is capable of doing. **5.** Usable heat or electric power.
en·er·vate (ĕn′ər-vāt′) *v.* **-vat·ed, -vat·ing.** To deprive of vitality : weaken. **—en′er·va′tion** *n.*
en·fant ter·ri·ble (äN-fäN′ tĕ-rē′blə) *n., pl.* **en·fants ter·ri·bles** (äN-fäN′ tĕ-rē′blə). One whose unconventional behavior and ideas cause embarrassment or dismay.
en·fee·ble (ĕn-fē′bəl) *v.* **-bled, -bling.** To weaken. **—en·fee′ble·ment** *n.*
en·fi·lade (ĕn′fə-lād′, -läd′) *n.* The firing of guns so as to sweep the length of an enemy target.
en·fold (ĕn-fōld′) *v.* **1.** To envelop. **2.** To enclose. **3.** To embrace.
en·force (ĕn-fôrs′, -fōrs′) *v.* **1.** To compel observance of <*enforce* traffic laws> **2.** To bring about by force or firmness <*enforce* silence> **—en·force′a·ble** *adj.* **—en·force′ment** *n.* **—en·forc′er** *n.*
en·fran·chise (ĕn-frăn′chīz′) *v.* **1.** To endow with civil rights, esp. the right to vote. **2.** To free : emancipate. **3.** To give a franchise to. **—en·fran′chise′ment** *n.*
eng. *abbr.* engineer.
en·gage (ĕn-gāj′) *v.* **-gaged, -gag·ing. 1.** To employ : hire. **2.** To secure and hold : engross <*engaged* her interest> **3.** To pledge or promise, esp. to marry. **4.** To enter into conflict (with) <We have *engaged* the enemy.> **5.** To interlock : mesh. **6.** To participate or induce to participate <*engage* in a discussion>
en·gage·ment (ĕn-gāj′mənt) *n.* **1.** Betrothal. **2.** A promise, esp. to meet someone : appointment. **3.** Employment. **4.** A battle.
en·gag·ing (ĕn-gā′jĭng) *adj.* Attractive : charming. **—en·gag′ing·ly** *adv.*
en·gen·der (ĕn-jĕn′dər) *v.* **1.** To give rise to. **2.** To procreate : propagate.
en·gine (ĕn′jən) *n.* **1.** A machine that turns energy into mechanical motion. **2.** A mechanical device or instrument <*engines* of destruction> **3.** A locomotive.
en·gi·neer (ĕn′jə-nîr′) *n.* **1.** One trained or engaged in a branch of engineering. **2.** One who operates an engine, esp. a locomotive. —*v.* **1.** To plan and manage as an engineer. **2.** To plan or accomplish with skill.
en·gi·neer·ing (ĕn′jə-nîr′ĭng) *n.* **1.** The application of scientific principles to practical ends. **2.** The design and construction of large-scale or complex structures such as bridges, roads, and tunnels.
Eng·land (ĭng′glənd). Part of the United Kingdom, in S Great Britain. *Cap.* London. *Pop.* 46,396,100.
Eng·lish (ĭng′glĭsh) *adj.* Of, relating to, or characteristic of England, its people, or their language. —*n.* **1.** The people of England. **2.** The Germanic language of England, the U.S., and other countries that are or were formerly under English control. **—Eng′lish·man** *n.* **—Eng′lish·wom′an** *n.*
English Canada *n.* The part of Canada where English is the predominant language.
English Canadian *n.* A Canadian whose 1st language is English.
English Channel. Arm of the Atlantic separating England and France.
English horn *n.* A woodwind instrument larger than an oboe and pitched lower.
en·gorge (ĕn-gôrj′) *v.* **1.** To devour greedily. **2.** To gorge : glut. **3.** To fill to excess, as with blood. **—en·gorge′ment** *n.*
en·graft (ĕn-grăft′) *v.* To graft (a scion) onto or into another plant.
en·grave (ĕn-grāv′) *v.* **-graved, -grav·ing. 1.** To carve or cut into a surface <*engrave* words on a tombstone> **2. a.** To carve, cut, or etch (e.g., a design) into a printing surface. **b.** To print from a surface made by such a process. **—en·grav′er** *n.*
en·grav·ing (ĕn-grā′vĭng) *n.* **1.** The art or technique of one that engraves. **2.** An engraved printing plate. **3.** A print made from an engraved plate.
en·gross (ĕn-grōs′) *v.* **1.** To occupy the full attention of : absorb. **2.** To copy in a large, clear hand. **—en·gross′ing·ly** *adv.*
en·gulf (ĕn-gŭlf′) *v.* **1.** To enclose completely. **2.** To swallow up by or as if by flowing over.
en·hance (ĕn-hăns′) *v.* **-hanced, -hanc·ing.** To make greater, as in beauty or value : heighten. **—en·hance′ment** *n.*
e·nig·ma (ĭ-nĭg′mə) *n.* One that baffles the understanding.
en·ig·mat·ic (ĕn′ĭg-măt′ĭk) *adj.* Being an enigma. **—en′ig·mat′i·cal·ly** *adv.*
en·jamb·ment *or* **en·jambe·ment** (ĕn-jăm′mənt) *n.* Continuation of a sentence from 1 line or couplet of a poem to the next so that closely related words fall on different lines.
en·join (ĕn-join′) *v.* **1.** To direct with emphasis and authority : command. **2.** To forbid, esp. by legal action. **—en·join′der** *n.*
en·joy (ĕn-joi′) *v.* **1.** To get pleasure from : relish <*enjoyed* the puppet show> **2.** To have the benefit or use of <*enjoying* a successful career> **—en·joy′a·ble** *adj.* **—en·joy′a·bly** *adv.* **—en·joy′ment** *n.*
en·large (ĕn-lärj′) *v.* **-larged, -larg·ing. 1.** To make or become larger <*enlarged* the photograph> **2.** To speak or write in greater detail <*enlarged* on the topic> **—en·large′ment** *n.* **—en·larg′er** *n.*
en·light·en (ĕn-līt′n) *v.* **1.** To provide with spiritual or intellectual understanding. **2.** To inform. **—en·light′en·ment** *n.* **—en·light′en·er** *n.*
en·list (ĕn-lĭst′) *v.* **1.** To enroll for service in the armed forces.

2. To secure the help of <*enlist* the guests for dishwashing> **—en·list′ment** *n.*

enlisted man *n.* A man who has enlisted in the armed forces without an officer's commission or warrant. **—enlisted woman** *n.*

en·liv·en (ĕn-lī′vən) *v.* To make livelier : animate. **—en·liv′en·ment** *n.*

en masse (ŏn măs′) *adv.* All together.

en·mesh (ĕn-mĕsh′) *v.* To catch in or as if in a mesh : entangle.

en·mi·ty (ĕn′mĭ-tē) *n., pl.* **-ties.** Deep hatred, as between enemies.

en·no·ble (ĕn-nō′bəl) *v.* **-bled, -bling. 1.** To make noble : exalt. **2.** To raise in rank to the nobility. **—en·no′ble·ment** *n.*

en·nui (ŏn-wē′, ŏn′wē) *n.* Boredom.

e·nor·mi·ty (ĭ-nôr′mĭ-tē) *n., pl.* **-ties. 1.** Excessive wickedness. **2.** A monstrous offense or crime : outrage.

e·nor·mous (ĭ-nôr′məs) *adj.* Very great in size or degree : immense. **—e·nor′mous·ly** *adv.* **—e·nor′mous·ness** *n.*

e·nough (ĭ-nŭf′) *adj.* Sufficient to satisfy need or desire. *—pron.* An adequate quantity <*enough* for everyone> *—adv.* **1.** To a satisfactory degree. **2.** Tolerably : rather <felt well *enough*>

en·plane (ĕn-plān′) *v.* To board an aircraft.

en·quire (ĕn-kwīr′) *v. var. of* INQUIRE.

en·rage (ĕn-rāj′) *v.* To put into a rage.

en·rap·ture (ĕn-răp′chər) *v.* **-tured, -tur·ing.** To fill with rapture : delight.

en·rich (ĕn-rĭch′) *v.* **1.** To make rich or richer. **2.** To make fuller or more meaningful <metaphors that *enrich* the poem> **—en·rich′ment** *n.*

en·roll *also* **en·rol** (ĕn-rōl′) *v.* **-rolled, -roll·ing. 1.** To enter the name of on a roll, register, or record. **2.** To place one's name on a roll, register, or record. **—en·roll′ment, en·rol′ment** *n.*

en route (ŏn ro͞ot′, ĕn) *adv. & adj.* On the way.

en·sconce (ĕn-skŏns′) *v.* **-sconced, -sconc·ing. 1.** To settle (oneself) securely. **2.** To put in a safe or concealed place.

en·sem·ble (ŏn-sŏm′bəl) *n.* A group of complementary parts contributing to a single effect, esp.: **a.** A coordinated outfit of clothing. **b.** A group of persons, as musicians, performing together. **c.** Music for 2 or more performers.

en·shrine (ĕn-shrīn′) *v.* **-shrined, -shrin·ing. 1.** To place in or as if in a shrine. **2.** To hold sacred : cherish. **—en·shrine′ment** *n.*

en·shroud (ĕn-shroud′) *v.* To cover with or as if with a shroud : obscure.

en·sign (ĕn′sən) *n.* **1.** (*also* ĕn′sīn′). A flag or banner, esp. one displayed on a ship or aircraft. **2.** A commissioned officer of the lowest rank in the U.S. Navy or Coast Guard. **3.** (*also* ĕn′sīn′). A badge or token.

en·si·lage (ĕn′sə-lĭj) *n.* **1.** The process of storing and fermenting green fodder in a silo. **2.** Fodder that has been stored : silage. **—en·sile′** (ĕn-sīl′) *v.*

en·slave (ĕn-slāv′) *v.* To make a slave of : subjugate. **—en·slave′ment** *n.*

en·snare (ĕn-snâr′) *v.* To catch in or as if in a snare : trap.

en·sue (ĕn-so͞o′) *v.* **-sued, -su·ing.** To follow as a result or consequence.

en·sure (ĕn-sho͝or′) *v.* **-sured, -sur·ing.** To make certain of : insure.

-ent *suff.* **1. a.** Performing or causing a specified action <absorb*ent*> **b.** Being in a specified state <bival*ent*> **2.** One that performs or causes a specified action <refer*ent*>

en·tail (ĕn-tāl′) *v.* **1.** To have or require as a necessary accompaniment or result. **2.** To limit the inheritance of (property) to a certain line of heirs. **—en·tail′ment** *n.*

en·tan·gle (ĕn-tăng′gəl) *v.* **1.** To tangle : snarl. **2.** To complicate : confuse. **—en·tan′gle·ment** *n.*

en·tente (ŏn-tŏnt′) *n.* **1.** An agreement between governments for cooperative action. **2.** The parties to an entente.

en·ter (ĕn′tər) *v.* **1.** To go or come into. **2.** To pierce : penetrate. **3.** To start : begin. **4.** To become a member (of) or participant (in). **5.** To enroll or inscribe. **6.** *Law.* **a.** To place formally on record. **b.** To go upon or into in order to take possession.

en·ter·i·tis (ĕn′tə-rī′tĭs) *n.* Intestinal inflammation.

en·ter·prise (ĕn′tər-prīz′) *n.* **1.** An undertaking, esp. a large or risky one. **2.** A business organization. **3.** Readiness to venture : initiative.

en·ter·pris·ing (ĕn′tər-prī′zĭng) *adj.* Exhibiting initiative, imagination, and readiness to venture. **—en′ter·pris′ing·ly** *adv.*

en·ter·tain (ĕn′tər-tān′) *v.* **1.** To hold the attention of : amuse. **2.** To receive as a guest : offer hospitality (to). **3.** To hold in mind : consider. **—en′ter·tain′er** *n.* **—en′ter·tain′ment** *n.*

en·thrall (ĕn-thrôl′) *v.* **1.** To enslave. **2.** To fascinate : captivate. **—en·thrall′ment** *n.*

en·throne (ĕn-thrōn′) *v.* **-throned, -thron·ing. 1.** To seat on a throne. **2.** To raise to a high position : exalt. **—en·throne′ment** *n.*

en·thuse (ĕn-tho͞oz′) *v.* **-thused, -thus·ing.** *Informal.* To make or become enthusiastic.

en·thu·si·asm (ĕn-tho͞o′zē-ăz′əm) *n.* **1. a.** Intense feeling for a subject or cause. **b.** Eagerness : zeal. **2.** Something inspiring. **—en·thu′si·ast′** *n.* **—en·thu′si·as′tic** *adj.* **—en·thu′si·as′ti·cal·ly** *adv.*

en·tice (ĕn-tīs′) *v.* **-ticed, -tic·ing.** To attract by arousing desire or hope : lure. **—en·tice′ment** *n.* **—en·tic′er** *n.* **—en·tic′ing·ly** *adv.*

en·tire (ĕn-tīr′) *adj.* **1.** Having no part left out : whole. **2.** Unlimited : complete <my *entire* attention> **—en·tire′ly** *adv.*

en·tire·ty (ĕn-tī′rə-tē) *n., pl.* **-ties. 1.** The state of being entire : completeness. **2.** The entire amount.

en·ti·tle (ĕn-tīt′l) *v.* **1.** To give a name or title to. **2.** To furnish with a right <a ticket *entitling* the bearer to admission> **—en·ti′tle·ment** *n.*

en·ti·ty (ĕn′tĭ-tē) *n., pl.* **-ties. 1.** The fact of existence. **2.** Something that exists separately : thing.

en·tomb (ĕn-to͞om′) *v.* To place in or as if in a tomb : bury. **—en·tomb′ment** *n.*

en·to·mol·o·gy (ĕn′tə-mŏl′ə-jē) *n.* The scientific study of insects. **—en′to·mo·log′ic** (-mə-lŏj′ĭk), **en′to·mo·log′i·cal** *adj.* **—en′to·mol′o·gist** *n.*

en·tou·rage (ŏn′to͞o-räzh′) *n.* A group of attendants or associates : retinue.

en·tr'acte (ŏn′trăkt′, äN-träkt′) *n.* **1.** An interval between 2 acts of a play. **2.** An entertainment offered during an entr'acte.

en·trails (ĕn′trālz′, -trəlz) *pl.n.* Internal organs : viscera.

en·train (ĕn-trān′) *v.* To put or go on board a train. **—en·train′ment** *n.*

en·trance¹ (ĕn′trəns) *n.* **1.** The act of entering. **2.** A place or means for entering. **3.** The right to enter : admission.

en·trance² (ĕn-trăns′) *v.* **-tranced, -tranc·ing.** To fascinate : enchant. **—en·trance′ment** *n.* **—en·tranc′ing·ly** *adv.*

en·trant (ĕn′trənt) *n.* One who enters a competition.

en·trap (ĕn-trăp′) *v.* To catch in or as if in a trap. **—en·trap′ment** *n.*

en·treat (ĕn-trēt′) *v.* To make an earnest request (of) : implore.

en·treat·y (ĕn-trē′tē) *n., pl.* **-ies.** An earnest request : plea.

en·tre·chat (ŏn′trə-shä′) *n.* A leap during which a ballet dancer crosses the feet repeatedly.

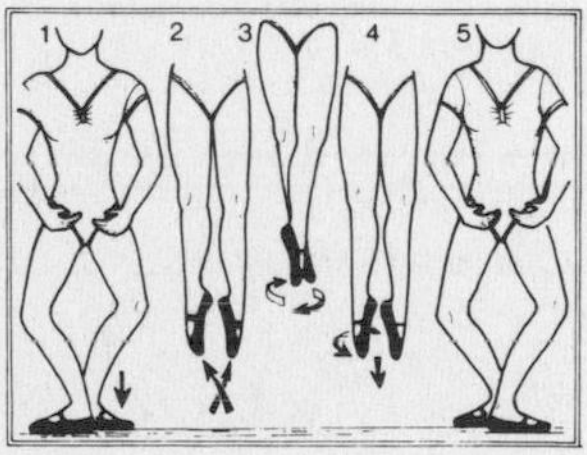

entrechat

en·trée *or* **en·tree** (ŏn′trā′, ŏn-trā′) *n.* **1. a.** The right to enter. **b.** Permission to enter. **2.** The main course of a meal.

en·trench (ĕn-trĕnch′) *v.* **1.** To provide with or dig a trench, as for defense. **2.** To fix or seat firmly. **3.** To encroach. **—en·trench′ment** *n.*

en·tre·pre·neur (ŏn′trə-prə-nûr′) *n.* One who launches or manages a business venture, often assuming risks. **—en′tre·pre·neu′ri·al** (-no͝or′ē-əl, -nyo͝or′-, -nûr′-) *adj.*

en·tro·py (ĕn′trə-pē) *n.* **1.** A measure of a system's capacity to undergo spontaneous change. **2.** A measure of the disorder or randomness in a system.

en·trust (ĕn-trŭst′) *v.* **1.** To give over to another for care or performance <*entrusted* the task to an aide> **2.** To give as a trust to (someone).

en·try (ĕn′trē) *n., pl.* **-tries. 1.** An act or the right of entering. **2.** A place for entering. **3. a.** The act of entering an item, as in a record, list, or reference work. **b.** The item entered <a dictionary *entry*> **4.** One entered in a competition.

en·twine (ĕn-twīn′) *v.* To twine around or together.

e·nu·mer·ate (ĭ-no͞o′mə-rāt′, ĭ-nyo͞o′-) *v.* **1.** To name or count of one by one : list. **2.** To count. **—e·nu′mer·a′tion** *n.* **—e·nu′mer·a′tor** *n.*

e·nun·ci·ate (ĭ-nŭn′sē-āt′, -shē-) *v.* **-at·ed, -at·ing. 1.** To pro-

nounce, esp. with clarity. 2. To announce : proclaim. **—e·nun′ci·a′tion** *n.*
en·u·re·sis (ĕn′yə-rē′sĭs) *n.* Involuntary urination.
en·vel·op (ĕn-vĕl′əp) *v.* To enclose entirely with or as if with a covering. **—en·vel′op·ment** *n.*
en·ve·lope (ĕn′və-lōp′, ŏn′-) *n.* **1.** Something that covers or encloses. **2.** A flat paper container, esp. for a letter. **3.** The gas-filled bag of a balloon.
en·ven·om (ĕn-vĕn′əm) *v.* **1.** To make poisonous. **2.** To embitter.
en·vi·a·ble (ĕn′vē-ə-bəl) *adj.* Highly desirable. **—en′vi·a·bly** *adv.*
en·vi·ous (ĕn′vē-əs) *adj.* Feeling, showing, or marked by envy. **—en′vi·ous·ly** *adv.* **—en′vi·ous·ness** *n.*
en·vi·ron·ment (ĕn-vī′rən-mənt) *n.* **1.** Surroundings. **2.** The combination of external physical conditions affecting the growth and development of organisms. **—en·vi′ron·men′tal** *adj.* **—en·vi′ron·men′tal·ly** *adv.*
en·vi·ron·men·tal·ist (ĕn-vī′rən-mĕn′tl-ĭst) *n.* One who seeks to preserve the natural environment. **—en·vi′ron·men′tal·ism** *n.*
en·vi·rons (ĕn-vī′rənz) *pl.n.* A surrounding area, esp. of a city.
en·vis·age (ĕn-vĭz′ĭj) *v.* **-aged, -ag·ing.** To have or form a mental image of.
en·voi *also* **en·voy** (ĕn′voi′, ŏn′-) *n.* A short closing passage of a poem or book.
en·voy (ĕn′voi′, ŏn′-) *n.* **1.** A messenger or agent. **2.** A governmental representative dispatched on a special diplomatic mission.
en·vy (ĕn′vē) *n.*, *pl.* **-vies. 1.** Discontented desire for someone else's possessions or advantages. **2.** An object of envy. ☆***syns:*** COVETOUSNESS, ENVIOUSNESS, JEALOUSY —*v.* **-vied, -vy·ing.** To feel envy because of or toward.
en·zyme (ĕn′zīm′) *n.* Any of numerous proteins produced by living organisms and functioning as biochemical catalysts in animals and plants. **—en′zy·mat′ic** (ĕn′zə-măt′ĭk) *adj.*
e·o·li·an (ē-ō′lē-ən) *adj.* Of, caused by, or transmitted by the wind.
e·on (ē′ŏn′, ē′ən) *n.* An indefinitely long period of time : age.
-eous *suff.* Having the nature of : resembling <gas*eous*>
ep·au·let *also* **ep·au·lette** (ĕp′ə-lĕt′, ĕp′ə-lĕt′) *n.* A shoulder ornament, as on a military uniform.
é·pée *also* **e·pee** (ā-pā′) *n.* A fencing sword with a bowl-shaped guard and a long blade lacking a cutting edge.
e·pergne (ĭ-pûrn′, ā-pûrn′) *n.* A centerpiece with extended arms or branches supporting holders, as for flowers or fruit, used esp. on a dinner table.
e·phed·rine (ĭ-fĕd′rĭn) *n.* A white, odorless crystalline alkaloid used to treat allergies and asthma.
e·phem·er·al (ĭ-fĕm′ər-əl) *adj.* Lasting but a short time. **—e·phem′er·al·ly** *adv.*
ep·ic (ĕp′ĭk) *n.* **1.** A long narrative poem celebrating the feats of heroes. **2.** A long narrative work, as a novel, that resembles an epic. **—ep′ic** *adj.*
ep·i·can·thic fold (ĕp′ĭ-kăn′thĭk) *n.* A fold of skin of the upper eyelid tending to cover the inner corner of the eye.
ep·i·cen·ter (ĕp′ĭ-sĕn′tər) *n.* The part of the earth's surface directly above the origin of an earthquake.
ep·i·cure (ĕp′ĭ-kyŏŏr′) *n.* One with refined tastes, esp. in food and wine.
ep·i·cu·re·an (ĕp′ĭ-kyŏŏ-rē′ən) *adj.* **1.** Devoted to pleasure. **2.** Suited to the tastes of an epicure <an *epicurean* banquet> **—ep′i·cu·re′an** *n.*
Ep·i·cu·rus (ĕp′ĭ-kyŏŏr′əs). 342?–270. B.C. Greek philosopher.
ep·i·dem·ic (ĕp′ĭ-dĕm′ĭk) *adj.* **1.** Affecting many individuals at the same time <Cholera was *epidemic*.> **2.** Widely prevalent <*epidemic* anxiety> —*n.* **1.** An epidemic outbreak of contagious disease. **2.** A rapid spread or increase in occurrence <an *epidemic* of robberies>
ep·i·der·mis (ĕp′ĭ-dûr′mĭs) *n.* The protective outer layer of the skin. **—ep′i·der′mal** *adj.*
ep·i·glot·tis (ĕp′ĭ-glŏt′ĭs) *n.* The elastic cartilage at the base of the tongue that folds over the glottis to protect the trachea during the act of swallowing. **—ep′i·glot′tal** (-glŏt′l) *adj.*
ep·i·gram (ĕp′ĭ-grăm′) *n.* A terse witty poem or saying. **—ep′i·gram·mat′ic** (-grə-măt′ĭk) *adj.*
ep·i·graph (ĕp′ĭ-grăf′) *n.* **1.** An inscription. **2.** A quotation placed at the beginning of a literary work.
e·pig·ra·phy (ĭ-pĭg′rə-fē) *n.* The study of inscriptions. **—e·pig′ra·pher** *n.*
ep·i·lep·sy (ĕp′ə-lĕp′sē) *n.* A nervous disorder marked by usu. recurring attacks of convulsions and loss of consciousness. **—ep′i·lep′tic** *n.* & *adj.*
ep·i·logue *also* **ep·i·log** (ĕp′ə-lôg′, -lŏg′) *n.* **1.** A speech given by an actor to the audience at the end of a play. **2.** An additional chapter placed at the end of a novel.
ep·i·neph·rine *also* **ep·i·neph·rin** (ĕp′ə-nĕf′rĭn) *n.* An adrenal hormone that raises the blood pressure and quickens the pulse, used in synthesized form as a cardiovascular stimulant.
E·piph·a·ny (ĭ-pĭf′ə-nē) *n.*, *pl.* **-nies.** A Christian festival held on Jan. 6, celebrating the revealing of Christ to the Gentiles as represented by the Magi.
ep·i·phyte (ĕp′ə-fīt′) *n.* A plant that grows on another plant on which it depends for mechanical support but not for nutrients.
e·pis·co·pa·cy (ĭ-pĭs′kə-pə-sē) *n.*, *pl.* **-cies. 1.** An episcopate. **2.** Church government by bishops.
e·pis·co·pal (ĭ-pĭs′kə-pəl) *adj.* **1.** Of or relating to a bishop. **2.** Governed by bishops. **3. Episcopal.** Of or relating to the Protestant Episcopal Church.
E·pis·co·pa·li·an (ĭ-pĭs′kə-pā′lē-ən, -pāl′yən) *n.* A member of the Protestant Episcopal Church. **—E·pis′co·pa′li·an** *n.*
e·pis·co·pate (ĭ-pĭs′kə-pĭt, -pāt′) *n.* **1.** The position, term, or rank of a bishop. **2.** The jurisdiction of a bishop : diocese. **3.** Bishops as a group.
ep·i·sode (ĕp′ĭ-sōd′) *n.* **1.** An incident : occurrence. **2.** A part of a narrative that forms a unit and often a coherent story in itself. **—ep′i·sod′ic** (-sŏd′ĭk) *adj.*
e·pis·tle (ĭ-pĭs′əl) *n.* **1.** A letter. **2. Epistle.** One of the letters in the New Testament. **—e·pis′to·lar′y** (-tə-lĕr′ē) *adj.*
ep·i·taph (ĕp′ĭ-tăf′) *n.* An inscription, as on a gravestone, in memory of a deceased person.
ep·i·the·li·um (ĕp′ə-thē′lē-əm) *n.*, *pl.* **-li·ums** *or* **-li·a** (-lē-ə). The thin membranous tissue forming the covering of the outer bodily surface and most of the internal surfaces and organs. **—ep′i·the′li·al, ep′i·the′li·oid′** *adj.*
ep·i·thet (ĕp′ə-thĕt′) *n.* **1.** A term used to characterize a person or thing. **2.** An abusive word or phrase.
e·pit·o·me (ĭ-pĭt′ə-mē) *n.* **1.** A summary, as of a book. **2.** A perfect example.
e·pit·o·mize (ĭ-pĭt′ə-mīz′) *v.* **-mized, -miz·ing. 1.** To make an epitome of : sum up. **2.** To be a perfect example of : embody.
ep·och (ĕp′ək, ĕp′ŏk′) *n.* **1.** A historical period : era. **2.** An event marking the beginning of a new era. **—ep′och·al** *adj.* **—ep′och·al·ly** *adv.*
ep·ox·y (ĕp′ŏk′sē, ĭ-pŏk′-) *n.*, *pl.* **-ies.** A durable, corrosion-resistant resin used esp. in surface coatings and glues. **—ep′ox′y** *v.*
Ep·som salts (ĕp′səm) *pl.n.* Hydrated magnesium sulfate, used as a cathartic.
eq·ua·ble (ĕk′wə-bəl, ē′kwə-) *adj.* **1. a.** Steady : unvarying. **b.** Free from extremes. **2.** Not easily disturbed : serene <an *equable* temperament> **—eq′ua·bil′i·ty, eq′ua·ble·ness** *n.* **—eq′ua·bly** *adv.*
e·qual (ē′kwəl) *adj.* **1.** Of the same measure, quantity, or value as another. **2.** Possessing the same privileges or rights <*equal* before the law> **3.** Having the necessary strength or ability <*equal* to the task> —*n.* One equal to another. —*v.* **e·qualed, e·qual·ing** *or* **e·qualled, e·qual·ling. 1.** To be equal to. **2.** To do or achieve something equal to : match. **—e·qual′i·ty** (ĭ-kwŏl′ĭ-tē) *n.* **—e′qual·ly** *adv.*
e·qual·ize (ē′kwə-līz′) *v.* **-ized, -iz·ing.** To make or become equal or uniform. **—e′qual·i·za′tion** *n.* **—e′qual·iz′er** *n.*
e·qua·nim·i·ty (ē′kwə-nĭm′ĭ-tē, ĕk′wə-) *n.* Calmness : composure.
e·quate (ĭ-kwāt′) *v.* **e·quat·ed, e·quat·ing.** To make or consider as equal.
e·qua·tion (ĭ-kwā′zhən, -shən) *n.* **1.** The act of equating or state of being equated. **2.** A mathematical statement that 2 expressions are equal. **—e·qua′tion·al** *adj.*
e·qua·tor (ĭ-kwā′tər) *n.* An imaginary great circle around the earth, the plane of which is perpendicular to the axis of rotation and that is everywhere equidistant from the poles. **—e′qua·to′ri·al** (ē′kwə-tôr′ē-əl, -tōr′-, ĕk′wə-) *adj.*
Equatorial Guin·ea (gĭn′ē). Country of W Africa. *Cap.* Malabo. *Pop.* 320,000.
eq·uer·ry (ĕk′wə-rē) *n.*, *pl.* **-ries. 1.** An officer charged with the supervision of the horses belonging to a royal or noble household. **2.** A personal attendant to a member of the British royal family.
e·ques·tri·an (ĭ-kwĕs′trē-ən) *adj.* **1.** Of or relating to horsemanship. **2.** Representing a subject on horseback. —*n.* One who rides or performs on a horse. **—e·ques′tri·enne′** (-trē-ĕn′) *n.*
e·qui·an·gu·lar (ē′kwē-ăng′gyə-lər, ĕk′wē-) *adj.* Having all angles equal.
e·qui·dis·tant (ē′kwə-dĭs′tənt, ĕk′wə-) *adj.* Equally distant. **—e′qui·dis′tance** *n.*
e·qui·lat·er·al (ē′kwə-lăt′ər-əl, ĕk′wə-) *adj.* Having all sides or faces equal. **—e′qui·lat′er·al** *n.*

e•qui•lib•ri•um (ē′kwə-lĭb′rē-əm, ĕk′wə-) *n.* Balance between opposing forces or influences.
e•quine (ē′kwīn′, ĕk′wīn′) *adj.* Of, relating to, or typical of a horse. **—e′quine′** *n.*
e•qui•nox (ē′kwə-nŏks′, ĕk′wə-) *n.* Either of the 2 times a year when the sun crosses the celestial equator and day and night are approx. the same in length. **—e′qui•noc′tial** (-nŏk′shəl) *adj.*
e•quip (ĭ-kwĭp′) *v.* **e•quipped, e•quip•ping.** To furnish with what is needed <*equipped* themselves for a long hike>
eq•ui•page (ĕk′wə-pĭj) *n.* A carriage equipped with horses and attendants.
e•quip•ment (ĭ-kwĭp′mənt) *n.* **1.** The act of equipping or state of being equipped. **2.** Things with which one is equipped.
e•qui•poise (ē′kwə-poiz′, ĕk′wə-) *n.* **1.** Equilibrium : balance. **2.** A counterbalance.
eq•ui•ta•ble (ĕk′wĭ-tə-bəl) *adj.* Impartial in judgment or treatment : just. **—eq′ui•ta•ble•ness** *n.* **—eq′ui•ta•bly** *adv.*
eq•ui•ta•tion (ĕk′wĭ-tā′shən) *n.* The act or art of riding horses.
eq•ui•ty (ĕk′wĭ-tē) *n., pl.* **-ties. 1.** The quality of being just or impartial : fairness. **2.** The value of property beyond a mortgage or liability. **3.** *Law.* **a.** A system of jurisprudence supplementing the common law. **b.** Justice applied in circumstances not covered by law.
e•quiv•a•lent (ĭ-kwĭv′ə-lənt) *adj.* Equal or virtually equal, as in meaning or effect. **—e•quiv′a•lence, e•quiv′a•len•cy** *n.* **—e•quiv′a•lent** *n.* **—e•quiv′a•lent•ly** *adv.*
e•quiv•o•cal (ĭ-kwĭv′ə-kəl) *adj.* **1.** Deliberately ambiguous or misleading. **2.** Questionable : dubious. **—e•quiv′o•cal•ly** *adv.*
e•quiv•o•cate (ĭ-kwĭv′ə-kāt′) *v.* **-cat•ed, -cat•ing.** To use vague or intentionally evasive language. ☆**syns:** HEDGE, PUSSYFOOT, WAFFLE **—e•quiv′o•ca′tion** *n.* **—e•quiv′o•ca′tor** *n.*
Er *symbol for* ERBIUM.
-er[1] *suff.* **1. a.** One that does something specified <build*er*> **b.** One that undergoes something specified <broil*er*> **c.** One that has or contains <six-foot*er*> **2. a.** One associated with <bank*er*> **b.** One living in or coming from <London*er*>
-er[2] *suff.* Used to form the comparative degree of adjectives and adverbs <old*er*><quick*er*>
e•ra (îr′ə, ĕr′ə) *n.* **1.** A time period reckoned from a specific date. **2.** A time period distinguished by a certain characteristic <the gaslight *era*>
e•rad•i•cate (ĭ-răd′ĭ-kāt′) *v.* **-cat•ed, -cat•ing.** To remove by or as if by uprooting : eliminate. **—e•rad′i•ca•ble** *adj.* **—e•rad′i•ca′tion** *n.* **—e•rad′i•ca′tor** *n.*
e•rase (ĭ-rās′) *v.* **e•rased, e•ras•ing. 1.** To remove (e.g., something written) by or as if by rubbing or scraping. **2.** To obliterate. **—e•ras′a•ble** *adj.* **—e•ras′er** *n.* **—e•ra′sure** *n.*
E•ras•mus (ĭ-răz′məs), **Desiderius.** 1466?–1536. Dutch theologian and scholar.
er•bi•um (ûr′bē-əm) *n. Symbol* **Er** A soft, malleable silvery rare-earth element.
ere (âr) *prep.* Previous to : before. *—conj.* **1.** Before. **2.** Rather than.
e•rect (ĭ-rĕkt′) *adj.* Directed upward : upright. *—v.* **1.** To construct : build. **2.** To raise upright <*erect* a tent pole> **3.** To set up : establish. **—e•rect′ly** *adv.* **—e•rect′ness** *n.* **—e•rec′tor** *n.*
e•rec•tile (ĭ-rĕk′təl, -tīl′) *adj.* Of, relating to, or being vascular tissue capable of filling with blood and becoming rigid. **—e•rec•til′i•ty** (-tĭl′ĭ-tē) *n.*
e•rec•tion (ĭ-rĕk′shən) *n.* **1.** The act of erecting : construction. **2.** The state of erectile tissue when filled with blood.
ere•long (âr-lông′, -lŏng′) *adv.* Before long.
er•e•mite (ĕr′ə-mīt′) *n.* A hermit.
erg (ûrg) *n.* A unit of energy or work.
er•go (ûr′gō, âr′-) *conj. & adv.* Therefore : consequently.
er•gos•ter•ol (ûr-gŏs′tə-sôl′, -rōl′) *n.* A steroid alcohol synthesized by yeast from sugars and converted under ultraviolet radiation to vitamin D.
er•got (ûr′gət, -gŏt′) *n.* **1. a.** A disease of rye and other cereal plants. **b.** Any of various fungi of the genus *Claviceps* that cause this disease. **2.** A drug or medicine made from dried ergot fungi.
E•rie (îr′ē) One of the Great Lakes, between S Ont. and W N.Y., NW Pa., N Ohio, and SE Mich.
er•mine (ûr′mĭn) *n.* **1.** A weasel, *Mustela erminea,* with brownish fur that becomes white in its winter phase. **2.** The white fur of the ermine.
e•rode (ĭ-rōd′) *v.* **e•rod•ed, e•rod•ing. 1.** To wear away or become worn away by or as if by rubbing or abrading <a river *eroding* its banks> **2.** To eat away : corrode.
e•rog•e•nous (ĭ-rŏj′ə-nəs) *adj.* Responsive to sexual stimulation.
e•ro•sion (ĭ-rō′zhən) *n.* The process of eroding or state of being eroded. **—e•ro′sion•al** *adj.*
e•ro•sive (ĭ-rō′sĭv) *adj.* Tending to cause erosion. **—e•ro′sive•ness** *n.*
e•rot•ic (ĭ-rŏt′ĭk) *adj.* Of or promoting sexual desire : amatory. **—e•rot′i•cal•ly** *adv.* **—e•rot′i•cism** *n.*
e•rot•i•ca (ĭ-rŏt′ĭ-kə) *pl.n. (sing. or pl. in number).* Literature or art with an erotic quality or theme.
err (ûr, ĕr) *v.* **1.** To make a mistake. **2.** To sin.
er•rand (ĕr′ənd) *n.* A short trip undertaken to perform a specified task, usu. for another.
er•rant (ĕr′ənt) *adj.* **1.** Traveling about, esp. in search of adventure. **2.** Straying from the proper or customary. **3.** Moving aimlessly. **—er′rant** *n.* **—er′rant•ry** *n.*
er•rat•ic (ĭ-răt′ĭk) *adj.* **1.** Lacking a fixed course : wandering. **2.** Irregular : inconsistent. **3.** Eccentric. **—er•rat′i•cal•ly** *adv.*
er•ra•tum (ĭ-rä′təm, ĭ-rā′-) *n., pl.* **-ta** (-tə). An error in printing or writing.
er•ro•ne•ous (ĭ-rō′nē-əs) *adj.* Containing an error : mistaken. **—er•ro′ne•ous•ly** *adv.* **—er•ro′ne•ous•ness** *n.*
er•ror (ĕr′ər) *n.* **1.** Something that unintentionally deviates from what is correct or true : mistake. **2.** The state of being mistaken or wrong. **3.** *Baseball.* A misplay in fielding or throwing.
er•satz (ĕr′zäts′, ĕr-zäts′) *adj.* Being a usu. inferior substitute : artificial.
erst (ûrst) *adv. Archaic.* Formerly.
erst•while (ûrst′hwīl′, -wīl′) *adj.* Former. **—erst′while′** *adv.*
e•ruct (ĭ-rŭkt′) *v.* To belch. **—e•ruc′ta′tion** *n.*
er•u•dite (ĕr′yə-dīt′, ĕr′ə-) *adj.* Deeply learned : scholarly.
er•u•di•tion (ĕr′yə-dĭsh′ən, ĕr′ə-) *n.* Deep learning : scholarship.
e•rupt (ĭ-rŭpt′) *v.* **1.** To emerge or force out violently from limits : explode <Lava *erupted* from the volcano.> **2.** To become suddenly and violently active. **3.** To break out in a skin rash. **—e•rup′tion** *n.* **—e•rup′tive** *adj.*
-ery *suff.* **1.** A place for <bak*ery*> **2.** A collection <fin*ery*> **3.** A condition <slav*ery*> **4.** Act : practice <brib*ery*> **5.** Characteristics or qualities of <snobb*ery*>
er•y•sip•e•las (ĕr′ĭ-sĭp′ə-ləs, îr′-) *n.* An acute, inflammatory skin disease caused by a streptococcus.
e•ryth•ro•cyte (ĭ-rĭth′rə-sīt′) *n.* One of the disk-shaped blood cells that contains hemoglobin and is responsible for the red color of blood.
Es *symbol for* EINSTEINIUM.
-es[1] *suff. var. of* -s[1].
-es[2] *suff. var. of* -s[2].
es•ca•late (ĕs′kə-lāt′) *v.* **-lat•ed, -lat•ing.** To enlarge, increase, or intensify <*escalate* a conflict> **—es′ca•la′tion** *n.*
es•ca•la•tor (ĕs′kə-lā′tər) *n.* A moving stairway consisting of steps attached to an endless belt.
es•cal•lop (ĭ-skŏl′əp, ĭ-skăl′-) *n. & v. var. of* SCALLOP.
es•ca•pade (ĕs′kə-pād′) *n.* A playful or reckless adventure.
es•cape (ĭ-skāp′) *v.* **-caped, -cap•ing. 1.** To break free (from). **2.** To avoid capture or harm. **3.** To succeed in avoiding <*escape* punishment> **4.** To elude the memory of. **5.** To issue involuntarily (from) : leak out. *—n.* **1.** An act, instance, or means of escaping. **2.** Leakage. **3.** Temporary freedom from unpleasant realities : diversion. **—es•cap′ee′** *n.* **—es•cap′er** *n.*
es•cape•ment (ĭ-skāp′mənt) *n.* **1.** A mechanism used esp. in timepieces to control the wheel movement and provide energy impulses to a pendulum or balance. **2.** A mechanism, as in a typewriter, that controls the lateral movement of the carriage. **3.** An escape or means of escape.

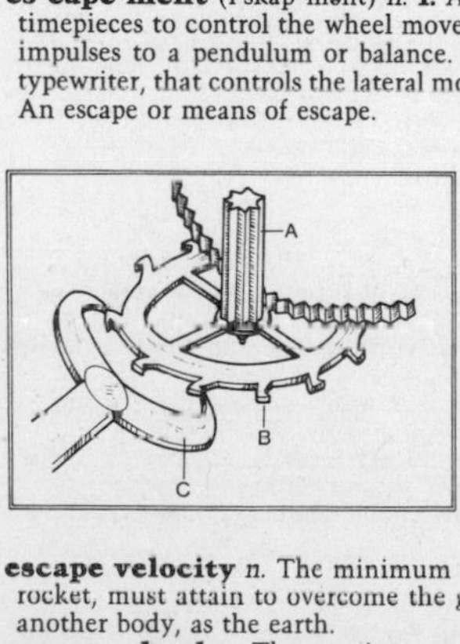

escapement
A. escape wheel spindle, B. escape wheel, C. lever

escape velocity *n.* The minimum velocity that a body, as a rocket, must attain to overcome the gravitational attraction of another body, as the earth.
escape wheel *n.* The rotating notched wheel in an escapement.

es•cap•ism (ĭ-skā'pĭz'əm) *n.* The avoidance of unpleasant realities in fantasy or entertainment. **—es•cap'ist** *n.* & *adj.*
es•ca•role (ĕs'kə-rōl') *n.* Endive.
es•carp•ment (ĭ-skärp'mənt) *n.* **1.** A steep slope or long cliff formed by erosion or faulting. **2.** A steep slope in front of a fortification.
-escence *suff.* The process of giving off light in a specified way <fluor*escence*>
-escent *suff.* **1.** Giving off light in a specified way <phosphor*escent*> **2.** Beginning to be : becoming <sen*escent*>
es•chew (ĕs-cho͞o') *v.* To avoid <*eschew* evil> **—es•chew'al** *n.*
es•cort (ĕs'kôrt') *n.* **1.** One or more persons or vehicles accompanying another to guide, protect, or pay honor. **2.** A man who accompanies a woman. *—v.* (ĭ-skôrt'). To go with as an escort.
es•cri•toire (ĕs'krĭ-twär') *n.* A writing desk.
es•crow (ĕs'krō', ĭ-skrō') *n.* Money or property put into the custody of a 3rd party until specified conditions are met.
es•cu•do (ĭ-sko͞o'dō) *n., pl.* **-dos.** See CURRENCY TABLE.
es•cutch•eon (ĭ-skŭch'ən) *n.* **1.** A shield with an emblem bearing a coat of arms. **2.** A protective plate, as for a keyhole.
-ese *suff.* **1.** Of, characteristic of, or originating in a specified place <Vietnam*ese*> **2.** Native or inhabitant of <Taiwan*ese*> **3.** Language or style of <Chin*ese*><journal*ese*>
Es•ki•mo (ĕs'kə-mō') *n., pl.* **-mo** or **-mos.** A member of a people native to Arctic North America, Greenland, and NE Siberia. **—Es'ki•mo'** *adj.*
Eskimo dog *n.* A large dog orig. bred in Greenland and Labrador with a thick coat and bushy tail.
e•soph•a•gus (ĭ-sŏf'ə-gəs) *n., pl.* **-gi** (-jī'). A muscular, membranous tube for the passage of food from the pharynx to the stomach. **—e•soph'a•ge'al** (ĭ-sŏf'ə-jē'əl) *adj.*
es•o•ter•ic (ĕs'ə-tĕr'ĭk) *adj.* **1.** Meant for or understood only by a particular and often small group <*esoteric* poetry> **2.** Private : confidential. **—es'o•ter'i•cal•ly** *adv.*
ESP (ē'ĕs-pē') *n.* Extrasensory perception.
esp. *abbr.* especially.
es•pa•drille (ĕs'pə-drĭl') *n.* A shoe with a canvas upper and a flexible sole.
es•pal•ier (ĭ-spăl'yər, -yā') *n.* A tree or shrub trained to grow in a flat plane against a surface. **—es•pal'ier** *v.*
es•pe•cial (ĭ-spĕsh'əl) *adj.* Being above or apart from others : exceptional. **—es•pe'cial•ly** *adv.*
Es•pe•ran•to (ĕs'pə-rän'tō, -răn'-) *n.* An artificial language with a vocabulary based on words that are the same in many European languages.
es•pi•o•nage (ĕs'pē-ə-näzh', -nĭj) *n.* The act or practice of spying to obtain secret intelligence.
es•pla•nade (ĕs'plə-näd', -nād') *n.* A flat, open area, esp. along a shoreline.
es•pou•sal (ĭ-spou'zəl) *n.* **1.** The act of supporting <his *espousal* of the immigrants' cause> **2.** A wedding.
es•pouse (ĭ-spouz') *v.* **-poused, -pous•ing.** **1.** To marry. **2.** To give support to.
es•pres•so (ĕ-sprĕs'ō) *n., pl.* **-sos.** Strong coffee made by forcing steam through darkly roasted, powdered coffee beans.
es•prit (ĕ-sprē') *n.* **1.** Mental liveliness : wit. **2.** Spirit.
es•prit de corps (ĕ-sprē' də kôr') *n.* A spirit of enthusiasm and devotion to a common cause among a group.
es•py (ĭ-spī') *v.* **-pied, -py•ing.** To catch a view of : glimpse.
Esq. *abbr.* Esquire (title).
-esque *suff.* Resembling <Lincoln*esque*>
es•quire (ĕs'kwīr', ĭ-skwīr') *n.* **1.** A candidate for knighthood who served as the attendant of a knight. **2.** A member of the English gentry ranking below a knight. **3. Esquire.** Used as a title of courtesy usu. after the full name of a person, esp. an attorney <John Doe, *Esq.*>
-ess *suff.* Female <lion*ess*>
es•say (ĕ-sā', ĕs'ā') *v.* To make an attempt at : try. *—n.* **1.** An attempt : endeavor. **2.** (ĕs'ā'). A short literary composition expressing the author's viewpoint on a subject. **—es•say'er** *n.* **—es'say'ist** *n.*
Es•sen (ĕs'ən). City of W West Germany, on the Ruhr R. *Pop.* 652,501.
es•sence (ĕs'əns) *n.* **1.** The properties of a thing that make it what it is : fundamental nature. **2.** The most important element. **3.** A concentrate of a substance. **4.** A perfume. ☆***syns:*** BEING, ESSENTIALITY, NATURE, PITH, QUINTESSENCE, TEXTURE
Es•sene (ĕs'ēn', ĭ-sēn') *n.* A member of an ascetic Jewish sect of ancient Palestine.
es•sen•tial (ĭ-sĕn'shəl) *adj.* **1.** Of, containing, or being an essence. **2.** Indispensable : necessary. **—es•sen'tial** *n.* **—es•sen'ti•al'i•ty** (-shē-ăl'ĭ-tē), **es•sen'tial•ness** *n.* **—es•sen'tial•ly** *adv.*
est. *abbr.* **1.** established. **2.** *Law.* estate. **3.** estimate.
EST or **E.S.T.** *abbr.* Eastern Standard Time.
-est[1] *suff.* Used to form the superlative degree of adjectives and adverbs <old*est*><quick*est*>
-est[2] *suff.* Used to form the archaic 2nd person present sing. of verbs <know*est*>
es•tab•lish (ĭ-stăb'lĭsh) *v.* **1.** To set in a secure position. **2.** To found : create. **3.** To cause to be recognized or accepted <*establish* a reputation> **4.** To prove.
es•tab•lish•ment (ĭ-stăb'lĭsh-mənt) *n.* **1. a.** The act or process of establishing. **b.** The state of being established. **2.** A place of business or residence, including its staff and possessions. **3.** An organized group. **4.** A group of people who control a field of activity or rule a society or government.
es•tate (ĭ-stāt') *n.* **1.** An extensive tract of land containing a large house. **2.** All of a person's possessions, esp. those left after death. **3.** A stage or condition of life <a pauper's *estate*>
es•teem (ĭ-stēm') *v.* **1.** To regard with respect : prize. **2.** To regard as : consider. *—n.* High regard : respect.
es•ter (ĕs'tər) *n.* Any of a large group of organic compounds formed when an acid and an alcohol interact.
es•thete (ĕs'thēt') *n. var. of* AESTHETE.
es•thet•ic (ĕs-thĕt'ĭk) *adj. var. of* AESTHETIC.
es•thet•ics (ĕs-thĕt'ĭks) *n. var. of* AESTHETICS.
es•ti•ma•ble (ĕs'tə-mə-bəl) *adj.* Deserving of esteem : admirable.
es•ti•mate (ĕs'tə-māt') *v.* **-mat•ed, -mat•ing.** **1.** To calculate the approx. amount or extent of. **2.** To evaluate. *—n.* (-mĭt). **1.** A rough or preliminary calculation, as of work to be done. **2.** An opinion : judgment.
Es•to•ni•a (ĕ-stō'nē-ə). Region and former country of W European USSR. **—Es•to'ni•an** *adj.* & *n.*
es•trange (ĭ-strānj') *v.* **-tranged, -trang•ing.** To make unfriendly, unsympathetic, or distant. ☆***syns:*** ALIENATE, DISAFFECT **—es•trange'ment** *n.*
es•tro•gen (ĕs'trə-jən) *n.* Any of several steroid hormones that regulate female reproductive functions and secondary sex characteristics. **—es'tro•gen'ic** (-jĕn'ĭk) *adj.* **—es'tro•gen'i•cal•ly** *adv.*
es•tu•ar•y (ĕs'cho͞o-ĕr'ē) *n., pl.* **-ies.** The wide lower course of a river into which the tides flow.
E.T. *abbr.* Eastern Time.
é•ta•gère *also* **e•ta•gere** (ā'tä-zhâr') *n.* A piece of furniture with open shelves for ornaments : whatnot.

étagère

et al. *abbr.* and others (Lat. *et alii*).
etc. *abbr.* and so forth (Lat. *et. cetera*).
et cet•er•a *also* **et•cet•er•a** (ĕt sĕt'ər-ə, -sĕt'rə)' And other things of the same kind : and so forth.
etch (ĕch) *v.* **1. a.** To cut into the surface of (e.g., glass) by the action of acid. **b.** To produce (e.g., a pattern) by etching. **2.** To impress deeply <words *etched* in my memory> **—etch'er** *n.*
etch•ing (ĕch'ĭng) *n.* **1.** The process or art of etching. **2. a.** A design etched on a plate. **3.** An impression made from such a plate.
e•ter•nal (ĭ-tûr'nəl) *adj.* **1.** Without beginning or end : everlasting. **2.** Meant to last indefinitely <an *eternal* flame> **3.** Seemingly endless or unvarying. **—e'ter•nal** *n.* **—e'ter•nal'i•ty** (ē'tər-năl'ĭ-tē), **e•ter'nal•ness** *n.* **—e•ter'nal•ly** *adv.*
e•ter•ni•ty (ĭ-tûr'nĭ-tē) *n., pl.* **-ties.** **1.** All time without beginning or end. **2.** The quality of being eternal. **3.** Immortality. **4.** A seemingly endless time.
-eth[1] *suff.* Used to form the archaic 3rd person present sing. of verbs <know*eth*>
-eth[2] *suff. var. of* -TH[2].
eth•ane (ĕth'ān') *n.* A colorless, odorless gas that occurs as a constituent of natural gas and is used for fuel and refrigeration.
eth•a•nol (ĕth'ə-nôl', -nōl') *n.* Alcohol 1.
e•ther (ē'thər) *n.* **1.** A volatile, highly flammable liquid compound used as a solvent and an anesthetic. **2.** The heavens. **3.** A massless substance once thought to fill space.
e•the•re•al (ĭ-thîr'ē-əl) *adj.* **1.** Light and insubstantial. **2.** High-

ly refined : delicate. **3.** Heavenly. **—e·the′re·al·ly** *adv.* **—e·the′re·al·ness** *n.*

eth·ic (ĕth′ĭk) *n.* **1.** A principle of right or good conduct. **2.** A system of moral values. **3. ethics** *(sing. in number).* The branch of philosophy dealing with the rules of right conduct.

eth·i·cal (ĕth′ĭ-kəl) *adj.* **1.** Of or relating to ethics. **2.** Conforming to accepted principles of right and wrong, esp. those governing the conduct of a profession, as medicine. **—eth′i·cal·ly** *adv.*

E·thi·o·pi·a (ē′thē-ō′pē-ə). Country of NE Africa. *Cap.* Addis Ababa. *Pop.* 30,400,000. **—E′thi·o′pi·an** *adj.* & *n.*

eth·nic (ĕth′nĭk) *adj.* Of or relating to a racial, national, or cultural group. *—n. Informal.* A member of an ethnic group, esp. within a larger community. **—eth·nic′i·ty** (-nĭs′ĭ-tē) *n.*

eth·nol·o·gy (ĕth-nŏl′ə-jē) *n.* The anthropological study of the origins and characteristics of racial and cultural groups. **—eth′no·log′ic** (-nə-lŏj′ĭk), **eth′no·log′i·cal** *adj.* **—eth·nol′o·gist** *n.*

e·thol·o·gy (ē-thŏl′ə-jē) *n.* The scientific study of animal behavior. **—e′tho·log′i·cal** (ē′thə-lŏj′ĭ-kəl, ĕth′ə-) *adj.* **—e·thol′o·gist** *n.*

e·thos (ē′thŏs′) *n.* The character, system of values, and attitudes peculiar to a people or culture.

eth·yl (ĕth′əl) *n.* An organic radical occurring in ether and alcohol.

ethyl alcohol *n.* Alcohol 1.

eth·yl·ene (ĕth′ə-lēn′) *n.* A colorless, flammable gas obtained from natural gas and petroleum and used as a fuel.

ethylene glycol *n.* A colorless syrupy alcohol used as an antifreeze.

e·ti·ol·o·gy (ē′tē-ŏl′ə-jē) *n.* **1.** The study of causes or origins. **2.** The cause, esp. of a disease. **—e′ti·o·log′ic** (-ə-lŏj′ĭk), **e′ti·o·log′i·cal** *adj.* **—e′ti·o·log′i·cal·ly** *adv.* **—e′ti·ol′o·gist** *n.*

et·i·quette (ĕt′ĭ-kĕt′, -kĭt) *n.* The prescribed forms and practices of correct behavior.

E·trus·can (ĭ-trŭs′kən) *n.* **1.** An inhabitant of Etruria, an ancient country in WC Italy. **2.** The language of the Etruscans. **—E·trus′can** *adj.*

Et·na (ĕt′nə), **Mount.** Active volcano in E Sicily.

-ette *suff.* **1.** Small <din*ette*> **2.** Female <usher*ette*>

é·tude *also* **e·tude** (ā′to͞od′, ā′-tyo͞od′) *n.* A musical piece for the development of a player's technique.

et·y·mol·o·gy (ĕt′ə-mŏl′ə-jē) *n., pl.* **-gies. 1.** The history of a word as shown by determining its earliest use and recording its changes in form and meaning. **2.** The branch of linguistics that deals with etymologies. **—et′y·mo·log′i·cal** (-mə-lŏj′ĭ-kəl) *adj.* **—et′y·mol′o·gist** *n.*

et·y·mon (ĕt′ə-mŏn′) *n., pl.* **-mons** or **-ma** (-mə) **1.** An earlier form of a word in the same language or in an ancestor language. **2.** A foreign word from which a particular loan-word is derived.

Eu *symbol for* EUROPIUM.

eu·ca·lyp·tus (yo͞o′kə-lĭp′təs) *n., pl.* **-tus·es** or **-ti** (-tī′) A tall native Australian tree of the genus *Eucalyptus,* with aromatic leaves that yield an oil used medicinally.

Eu·cha·rist (yo͞o′kər-ĭst) *n.* **1.** The Christian sacrament of Communion. **2.** The consecrated bread and wine of the Eucharist. **—Eu′cha·ris′tic** *adj.*

eu·chre (yo͞o′kər) *n.* A card game in which the winning side must take 3 of 5 tricks. *—v.* **-chred, -chring.** *Informal.* To cheat : trick.

Eu·clid (yo͞o′klĭd). 3rd cent. B.C. Greek mathematician. **—Eu·clid′e·an, Eu·clid′i·an** *adj.*

eu·gen·ics (yo͞o-jĕn′ĭks) *n. (sing. in number).* The study of and methods for improving a species genetically. **—eu·gen′ic** *adj.* **—eu·gen′i·cist** (-ĭ-sĭst) *n.*

eu·lo·gize (yo͞o′lə-jīz′) *v.* **-gized, -giz·ing.** To write or deliver a eulogy for. **—eu′lo·gist, eu′lo·giz′er** *n.*

eu·lo·gy (yo͞o′lə-jē) *n., pl.* **-gies. 1.** A speech honoring a person or thing. **2.** High praise. **—eu′lo·gis′tic** *adj.*

eu·nuch (yo͞o′nək) *n.* A castrated man.

eu·phe·mism (yo͞o′fə-mĭz′əm) *n.* A less direct term used in place of one considered offensive. **—eu′phe·mis′tic** *adj.* **—eu′phe·mis′ti·cal·ly** *adv.*

eu·pho·ny (yo͞o′fə-nē) *n., pl.* **-nies.** Agreeable sound, esp. of spoken words. **—eu·pho′ni·ous** (-fō′nē-əs) *adj.* **—eu·pho′ni·ous·ly** *adv.*

eu·pho·ri·a (yo͞o-fôr′ē-ə, -fōr′-) *n.* A strong feeling of elation or well-being. **—eu·phor′ic** (-fôr′ĭk, -fōr′-) *adj.*

Eu·phra·tes (yo͞o-frā′tēz). River of SW Asia, flowing c. 1,700 mi (2,735 km) from EC Turkey to the Persian Gulf.

Eur. *abbr.* Europe; European.

Eur·a·sia (yo͝o-rā′zhə). Land mass comprising the continents of Europe and Asia. **—Eur·a′sian** *adj.* & *n.*

eu·re·ka (yo͝o-rē′kə) *interj.* Used to express triumph upon a discovery.

Eu·rip·i·des (yo͝o-rĭp′ə-dēz′). 480?–406 B.C Greek dramatist.

Eu·ro·dol·lar (yo͝or′ō-dŏl′ər) *n.* A U.S. dollar deposited in a foreign bank, esp. in Europe.

Eu·rope (yo͝or′əp). Continent consisting of the section of the Eurasian land mass that extends W from the Dardanelles, the Black Sea, and the Ural Mts. **—Eu′ro·pe′an** (yo͝or′ə-pē′ən) *adj.* & *n.*

European plan *n.* A hotel plan in which rates cover only the cost of the room.

eu·ro·pi·um (yo͝o-rō′pē-əm) *n. Symbol* **Eu** A soft, silvery-white rare-earth element used in nuclear research.

Eu·sta·chian tube (yo͞o-stā′shən, -shē-ən, -stā′kē-ən) *n.* A narrow tube between the middle ear and the pharynx that equalizes air pressure on both sides of the eardrum.

eu·tha·na·sia (yo͞o′thə-nā′zhə, -shə) *n.* The act or practice of killing a suffering individual, esp. painlessly, for reasons considered merciful.

eu·then·ics (yo͞o-thĕn′ĭks) *n. (sing. in number).* The study of ways to improve human functioning and well-being by changes in the environment. **—eu·then′ist** *n.*

e·vac·u·ate (ĭ-văk′yo͞o-āt′) *v.* **-at·ed, -at·ing. 1. a.** To remove the contents of : empty. **b.** To create a vacuum in (a container). **2.** To expel waste matter from (the bowels). **3.** To depart from (e.g., a threatened place) : vacate. **—e·vac′u·a′tion** *n.* **—e·vac′u·a′tor** *n.*

e·vac·u·ee (ĭ-văk′yo͞o-ē′) *n.* One evacuated from a hazardous place.

e·vade (ĭ-vād′) *v.* **e·vad·ed, e·vad·ing.** To elude or avoid by cunning. **—e·vad′er** *n.*

e·val·u·ate (ĭ-văl′yo͞o-āt′) *v.* **-at·ed, -at·ing. 1.** To determine the value of. **2.** To examine carefully : appraise. **—e·val′u·a′tion** *n.* **—e·val′u·a′tor** *n.*

ev·a·nesce (ĕv′ə-nĕs′) *v.* **-nesced, -nesc·ing.** To disappear like vapor : fade away.

ev·a·nes·cent (ĕv′ə-nĕs′ənt) *adj.* Vanishing or passing quickly : fleeting. **—ev′a·nes′cence** *n.* **—ev′a·nes′cent·ly** *adv.*

e·van·gel·i·cal (ē′văn-jĕl′ĭ-kəl) *also* **e·van·gel·ic** (-jĕl′ĭk) *adj.* **1.** Of, relating to, or according to the Christian gospel, esp. the 4 Gospels of the New Testament. **2.** Of or being a Protestant group that stresses the authority of the gospel and salvation by faith in Christ. **3.** Zealous in preaching or proselytizing. **—e′van·gel′i·cal·ism** *n.* **—e′van·gel′i·cal·ly** *adv.*

e·van·gel·ism (ĭ-văn′jə-lĭz′əm) *n.* **1.** Zealous preaching and spreading of the gospel. **2.** Zeal for a cause.

e·van·gel·ist (ĭ-văn′jə-lĭst) *n.* **1.** *often* **Evangelist.** An author of 1 of the 4 New Testament Gospels. **2.** A zealous Protestant preacher or missionary. **—e·van′gel·is′tic** *adj.* **—e·van′gel·is′ti·cal·ly** *adv.*

e·van·gel·ize (ĭ-văn′jə-līz′) *v.* **-ized, -iz·ing. 1.** To preach the gospel (to). **2.** To convert to Christianity.

e·vap·o·rate (ĭ-văp′ə-rāt′) *v.* **-rat·ed, -rat·ing. 1.** To change into vapor. **2.** To concentrate (e.g., milk) by removing moisture. **3.** To disappear : vanish. **—e·vap′o·ra′tion** *n.* **—e·vap′o·ra′tive** *adj.* **—e·vap′o·ra′tor** *n.*

e·va·sion (ĭ-vā′zhən) *n.* An act or means of evading.

e·va·sive (ĭ-vā′sĭv) *adj.* **1.** Marked by evasion <*evasive* action> **2.** Intentionally vague : equivocal. **—e·va′sive·ly** *adv.* **—e·va′sive·ness** *n.*

eve (ēv) *n.* **1.** The evening or day preceding a special day. **2.** The period just before a certain event. **3.** Evening.

Eve (ēv). The wife of Adam.

e·ven (ē′vən) *adj.* **1.** Having a horizontal surface : flat <an *even* road> **2.** Having no irregularities : smooth. **3.** On the same plane or line : level. **4.** Equally matched : balanced <an *even* contest> **5.** Equal in amount or extent. **6.** Neither owing nor being owed. **7.** Fully revenged <getting *even*> **8.** Exactly divisible by 2. **9.** Exact <an *even* dozen> *—adv.* **1.** To a higher extent or degree. Used as an intensive <an *even* worse insult> **2.** At that time : just. **3.** Notwithstanding <*Even* with his bad knee, he walks quickly.> **4.** Indeed. Used as an intensive <looked sad, *even* depressed> *—v.* To make or become even. **—e′ven·ly** *adv.* **—e′ven·ness** *n.*

e·ven·hand·ed (ē′vən-hăn′dĭd) *adj.* Fair : impartial. **—e′ven·hand′ed·ly** *adv.* **—e′ven·hand′ed·ness** *n.*

eve·ning (ēv′nĭng) *n.* The period between sunset and bedtime.

evening star *n.* A bright planet, esp. Venus, seen in the W shortly after sunset.

e·ven·song (ē′vən-sông′, -sŏng′) *n.* **1.** A vesper service. **2.** Evening prayer.

e·vent (ĭ-vĕnt′) *n.* **1.** An occurrence, esp. a significant one <a literary *event*> **2.** An item in a sports program. **3.** A final result : outcome. **—e·vent′ful** *adj.* **—e·vent′ful·ly** *adv.* **—e·vent′ful·ness** *n.*

e·ven·tide (ē′vən-tīd′) *n.* Evening.

e·ven·tu·al (ĭ-vĕn′cho͞o-əl) *adj.* Happening or expected to

happen at an unspecified future time : ultimate <his *eventual* return> **—e·ven′tu·al·ly** *adv.*
e·ven·tu·al·i·ty (ĭ-vĕn′cho͞o-ăl′ĭ-tē) *n., pl.* **-ties.** Something that may take place : possibility.
e·ven·tu·ate (ĭ-vĕn′cho͞o-āt′) *v.* **-at·ed, -at·ing.** To result eventually.
ev·er (ĕv′ər) *adv.* **1.** At all times : always <*ever* attentive> **2.** At any time <Have you *ever* traveled abroad?> **3.** In any possible way or case.
Ev·er·est (ĕv′ər-ĭst, ĕv′rĭst), **Mount.** Mountain, 29,028 ft (8,853.5 m), of the Himalayas between Tibet and Nepal.
ev·er·glade (ĕv′ər-glād′) *n.* A tract of low, swampy land.
ev·er·green (ĕv′ər-grēn′) *adj.* Having green foliage throughout the year. *—n.* An evergreen tree or plant.
ev·er·last·ing (ĕv′ər-lăs′tĭng) *adj.* Lasting forever or for a long time : eternal. *—n.* **1.** Eternity. **2.** A plant, esp. a strawflower, that keeps its form and color long after it is dry. **—ev′er·last′ing·ly** *adv.*
ev·er·more (ĕv′ər-môr′, -mōr′) *adv. Archaic.* Forever.
eve·ry (ĕv′rē) *adj.* **1.** Each with no exception <*every* day of the week> **2.** Each of a particular succession of objects or intervals <*every* 3 hours> **3.** All possible : utmost <given *every* opportunity>
eve·ry·bod·y (ĕv′rē-bŏd′ē) *pron.* Every person : everyone.
eve·ry·day (ĕv′rē-dā′) *adj.* **1.** Suitable for routine occasions. **2.** Common : ordinary.
eve·ry·one (ĕv′rē-wŭn′) *pron.* Every person : everybody.
eve·ry·place (ĕv′rē-plās′) *adv.* Everywhere.
eve·ry·thing (ĕv′rē-thĭng′) *pron.* All factors or things that exist or are pertinent.
eve·ry·where (ĕv′rē-hwâr′, -wâr′) *adv.* In all places.
e·vict (ĭ-vĭkt′) *v.* To put (e.g., a tenant) out by legal process. **—e·vic′tion** *n.* **—e·vic′tor** *n.*
ev·i·dence (ĕv′ĭ-dəns) *n.* **1.** Facts or signs on which a conclusion can be based <fossil *evidence* of climatic change> **2.** An indication. *—v.* **-denced, -denc·ing.** To indicate clearly. **—in evidence.** Clearly present : evident.
ev·i·dent (ĕv′ĭ-dənt) *adj.* Easily seen or understood : obvious. **—ev′i·dent·ly** *adv.*
e·vil (ē′vəl) *adj.* **1.** Morally wrong or bad : wicked. **2.** Causing harm : injurious. *—n.* **1.** Something morally bad : wickedness. **2.** A cause of suffering or injury <social *evils*> **—e′vil·ly** *adv.* **—e′vil·ness** *n.*
▲word history: The word *evil* is ult. related to the words *up* and *over* and to the prefix *hypo–*, "under, beneath." The basic sense of *evil*, which is now lost, was therefore probably "exceeding proper bounds" or "overreaching," and the word did not signify merely the absence of good.
e·vil·do·er (ē′vəl-do͞o′ər) *n.* A perpetrator of evil. **—e′vil·do′ing** *n.*
e·vil·mind·ed (ē′vəl-mīn′dĭd) *adj.* Having evil thoughts or intentions. **—e′vil-mind′ed·ly** *adv.* **—e′vil-mind′ed·ness** *n.*
e·vince (ĭ-vĭns′) *v.* **e·vinced, e·vinc·ing.** To demonstrate : manifest.
e·vis·cer·ate (ĭ-vĭs′ə-rāt′) *v.* **-at·ed, -at·ing.** **1.** To remove the entrails of. **2.** To remove a critical or vital part of. **—e·vis′cer·a′tion** *n.*
e·voke (ĭ-vōk′) *v.* **e·voked, e·vok·ing.** **1.** To call forth : summon <*evoked* dark spirits> **2.** To call to mind <*evoke* childhood memories> **—ev′o·ca′tion** (ĕv′ə-kā′shən) *n.* **—e·voc′a·tive** (ĭ-vŏk′ə-tĭv) *adj.* **—e·voc′a·tive·ly** *adv.*
ev·o·lu·tion (ĕv′ə-lo͞o′shən) *n.* **1.** A gradual process of change or development. **2.** *Biol.* The theory that existing species of plants and animals have developed from previously existing species through a process of gradual change. **—ev′o·lu′tion·ar′y** (-shə-nĕr′ē) *adj.* **—ev′o·lu′tion·ism** *n.* **—ev′o·lu′tion·ist** *n.*
e·volve (ĭ-vŏlv′) *v.* **e·volved, e·volv·ing.** **1.** To change or develop gradually. **2.** *Biol.* To develop by evolutionary processes. **3.** To work out : develop <*evolve* a system> **—e·volve′ment** *n.*
ewe (yo͞o) *n.* A female sheep.
ew·er (yo͞o′ər) *n.* A wide-mouthed jug or pitcher.

ewer

ex[1] (ĕks) *n.* The letter x.
ex[2] (ĕks) *n. Slang.* A former spouse.
ex– *pref.* Former <ex-governor>
ex. *abbr.* **1.** example. **2.** exchange. **3.** *also* **exam.** examination.
ex·ac·er·bate (ĭg-zăs′ər-bāt′, ĭk-săs′-) *v.* **-bat·ed, -bat·ing.** To make worse or more severe : aggravate <*exacerbate* tensions> **—ex·ac′er·bat′ing·ly** *adv.* **—ex·ac′er·ba′tion** *n.*
ex·act (ĭg-zăkt′) *adj.* Strictly accurate and precise : correct. *—v.* **1.** To demand and obtain by or as if by force : extort. **2.** To call for or require <*exact* a great effort> **—ex·ac′tion** *n.* **—ex·act′ly** *adv.* **—ex·act′ness** *n.*
ex·act·ing (ĭg-zăk′tĭng) *adj.* **1.** Making severe demands. **2.** Requiring much care and accuracy. **—ex·act′ing·ly** *adv.*
ex·act·i·tude (ĭg-zăk′tĭ-to͞od′, -tyo͞od′) *n.* The quality of being exact.
ex·ag·ger·ate (ĭg-zăj′ə-rāt′) *v.* **-at·ed, -at·ing.** To represent as greater than is actually the case : overstate. **—ex·ag′ger·a′tion** *n.* **—ex·ag′ger·a′tive, ex·ag′ger·a·to′ry** (-ər-ə-tôr′ē, -tōr′ē) *adj.* **—ex·ag′ger·a′tor** *n.*
ex·alt (ĭg-zôlt′) *v.* **1.** To raise to a high rank or position : elevate. **2.** To praise highly : glorify. **3.** To fill with pride or joy : elate. **—ex′al·ta′tion** *n.*
ex·am (ĭg-zăm′) *n.* An examination.
ex·am·i·na·tion (ĭg-zăm′ə-nā′shən) *n.* **1.** The act of examining or state of being examined. **2.** A test of knowledge or skill.
ex·am·ine (ĭg-zăm′ĭn) *v.* **-ined, -in·ing.** **1.** To inspect closely : observe carefully. **2.** To determine the knowledge or skills of by questioning. **3.** To question formally. **—ex·am′in·ee′** *n.* **—ex·am′in·er** *n.*
ex·am·ple (ĭg-zăm′pəl) *n.* **1.** One that is representative of a group : sample. **2.** One worthy of imitation : model. **3.** A case or punishment serving as a precedent or warning. **4.** An illustrative problem or exercise.
ex·as·per·ate (ĭg-zăs′pə-rāt′) *v.* **-at·ed, -at·ing.** To make angry or frustrated : irritate. **—ex·as′per·at′ing·ly** *adv.* **—ex·as′per·a′tion** *n.*
ex·ca·vate (ĕk′skə-vāt′) *v.* **-vat·ed, -vat·ing.** **1.** To hollow out : dig out. **2.** To remove (e.g., soil) by digging out. **3.** To expose by digging. **—ex′ca·va′tion** *n.* **—ex′ca·va′tor** *n.*
ex·ceed (ĭk-sēd′) *v.* **1.** To surpass. **2.** To go beyond the limits of.
ex·ceed·ing·ly (ĭk-sē′dĭng-lē) *adv.* To an extraordinary degree : extremely <*exceedingly* careful>
ex·cel (ĭk-sĕl′) *v.* **-celled, -cel·ling.** To be greater or do better than (others) : surpass.
ex·cel·lence (ĕk′sə-ləns) *n.* **1.** The quality of being excellent : superiority. **2.** An excellent quality or capacity. **3. Excellence.** Excellency.
Ex·cel·len·cy (ĕk′sə-lən-sē) *n., pl.* **-cies.** Used as a form of address or title for high officials, as ambassadors or bishops.
ex·cel·lent (ĕk′sə-lənt) *adj.* Exceptionally good : fine. ☆***syns:*** CAPITAL, DANDY, FINE, FIRST-CLASS, FIRST-RATE, GREAT, SPLENDID, SUPER, SUPERB, SUPERIOR, TERRIFIC **—ex′cel·lent·ly** *adv.*
ex·cel·si·or (ĭk-sĕl′sē-ər) *n.* Fine curved wood shavings used esp. for packing.
ex·cept (ĭk-sĕpt′) *prep.* Not including : but. *—conj.* **1.** Were it not that : only. **2.** Otherwise than. **3.** *Archaic.* Unless. *—v.* **1.** To leave out : exclude. **2.** To object.
ex·cept·ing (ĭk-sĕp′tĭng) *prep.* Except.
ex·cep·tion (ĭk-sĕp′shən) *n.* **1.** The act of excepting. **2.** One that is excepted, esp. a case not conforming to a rule. **3.** A criticism or objection.
ex·cep·tion·a·ble (ĭk-sĕp′shə-nə-bəl) *adj.* Open to objection. **—ex·cep′tion·a·bil′i·ty** *n.* **—ex·cep′tion·a·bly** *adv.*
ex·cep·tion·al (ĭk-sĕp′shə-nəl) *adj.* **1.** Being an exception : unusual. **2.** Well above average. **—ex·cep′tion·al·ly** *adv.*
ex·cerpt (ĕk′sûrpt′) *n.* A passage, as from a book : extract. *—v.* (ĭk-sûrpt′, ĭg-zûrpt′) To select and take out an excerpt from.
ex·cess (ĭk-sĕs′, ĕk′sĕs′) *n.* **1.** An amount beyond what is required or appropriate. **2.** The state of exceeding what is required or appropriate <talking to *excess*> **3.** Overindulgence : intemperance. ☆***syns:*** GLUT, OVERAGE, OVERSTOCK, OVERSUPPLY, SUPERFLUITY, SURPLUS *—adj.* Exceeding what is required or appropriate.
ex·ces·sive (ĭk-sĕs′ĭv) *adj.* Exceding what is necessary, usual, or proper. **—ex·ces′sive·ly** *adv.* **—ex·cess′ive·ness** *n.*
exch. *abbr.* exchange.
ex·change (ĭks-chānj′) *v.* **-changed, -chang·ing.** **1.** To give in return for something else : trade <*exchange* recipes> **2.** To turn in (merchandise) for a replacement. *—n.* **1.** An act of exchanging. **2.** A place where things are exchanged, esp. a marketplace for securities or commodities. **3.** A central office that makes connections between individual telephones. **—ex·change′a·ble** *adj.*
ex·cheq·uer (ĭks-chĕk′ər, ĕks′chĕk′ər) *n.* **1. Exchequer.**

The British governmental department charged with the collection and care of the national revenue. **2.** A treasury, esp. of a nation or organization. **3.** Financial resources : funds.

▲word history: The Exchequer got its name from the checkered cloth, resembling a chessboard, that covered the counting tables of the Norman and Angevin kings of England. The word *exchequer* is derived from the Old French word *eschequier*, "chessboard." The *x* in *exchequer* is an etymological phantom. Many Old French words beginning with *es–* come from Latin words beginning with *ex–*, but *eschequier* is derived from Latin *scaccus*, "check in chess," which is ult. from Persian *shāh*, "king," the king being the most important piece in chess. When other English words like *exchange* (from Old French *eschangier* and Vulgar Latin *excambiare*) were respelled to reflect their Latin origins, *exchequer* was erroneously altered in the same manner.

ex•cise¹ (ĕk'sīz') *n.* An internal tax on the production, sale, or consumption of a commodity, as tobacco, within a country.

ex•cise² (ĭk-sīz') *v.* **-cised, -cis•ing.** To remove by or as if by cutting, esp. surgically. **—ex•ci'sion** (-sĭzh'ən) *n.*

ex•cit•a•ble (ĭk-sī'tə-bəl) *adj.* Easily excited. **—ex•cit'a•bil'i•ty, ex•cit'a•ble•ness** *n.* **—ex•cit'a•bly** *adv.*

ex•cite (ĭk-sīt') *v.* **-cit•ed, -cit•ing. 1.** To rouse to action or motion : stimulate. **2.** To stir up strong feeling in : provoke. **3.** To elicit : induce <*excited* their interest> **—ex'ci•ta'tion** (ĕk'sī-tā'shən) *n.* **—ex•cit'ed•ly** *adv.* **—ex•cite'ment** *n.* **—ex•cit'ing•ly** *adv.*

ex•claim (ĭk-sklām') *v.* To cry out or utter suddenly, as from emotion.

ex•cla•ma•tion (ĕks'klə-mā'shən) *n.* A sudden, forceful utterance. **—ex•clam'a•to'ry** (ĭk-sklăm'ə-tôr'ē, -tōr'ē) *adj.*

exclamation point *n.* A punctuation mark (!) used after an exclamation or interjection.

ex•clude (ĭk-sklōōd') *v.* **-clud•ed, -clud•ing. 1.** To keep out : bar. **2.** To omit from consideration : disregard. **3.** To put out : expel. **—ex•clu'sion** *n.*

ex•clu•sive (ĭk-sklōō'sĭv) *adj.* **1.** Not shared with others <*exclusive* control> **2.** Excluding certain or most people, as from membership. **3.** For the wealthy : expensive <*exclusive* shops> **4.** Complete : undivided. **—ex•clu'sive•ly** *adv.* **—ex•clu'sive•ness, ex'clu•siv'i•ty** *n.*

exclusive of *prep.* Not including : besides.

ex•com•mu•ni•cate (ĕks'kə-myōō'nĭ-kāt') *v.* To deprive of the right of church membership by ecclesiastical authority. **—ex'com•mu'ni•ca'tion** *n.*

ex•co•ri•ate (ĭk-skôr'ē-āt', -skōr'-) *v.* **-at•ed, -at•ing. 1.** To wear off or tear the skin of : abrade. **2.** To censure harshly : upbraid. **—ex•co'ri•a'tion** *n.*

ex•cre•ment (ĕk'skrə-mənt) *n.* Bodily waste, esp. feces. **—ex'cre•men'tal** *adj.*

ex•cres•cence (ĭk-skrĕs'əns) *n.* An abnormal outgrowth, esp. on the body. **—ex•cres'cent** *adj.*

ex•cre•ta (ĭk-skrē'tə) *pl.n.* Expelled waste matter, as sweat, urine, or feces.

ex•crete (ĭk-skrēt') *v.* **-cret•ed, -cret•ing.** To eliminate (waste matter) from the body. **—ex•cre'tion** *n.* **—ex'cre•to'ry** (ĕk'skrĭ-tôr'ē, -tōr'ē) *adj.*

ex•cru•ci•at•ing (ĭk-skrōō'shē-ā'tĭng) *adj.* Intensely painful : agonizing. **—ex•cru'ci•at'ing•ly** *adv.*

ex•cul•pate (ĕk'skəl-pāt', ĭk-skŭl'-) *v.* **-pat•ed, -pat•ing.** To clear of wrongdoing. **—ex'cul•pa'tion** *n.* **—ex•cul'pa•to'ry** (ĭk-skŭl'pə-tôr'ē, -tōr'ē) *adj.*

ex•cur•sion (ĭk-skûr'zhən) *n.* **1.** A usu. short journey made for pleasure : outing. **2.** A trip at a special reduced fare. **3.** A digression. **—ex•cur'sion•ist** *n.*

ex•cur•sive (ĭk-skûr'sĭv) *adj.* Given to or marked by digression : rambling. **—ex•cur'sive•ly** *adv.* **—ex•cur'sive•ness** *n.*

ex•cuse (ĭk-skyōōz') *v.* **-cused, -cus•ing. 1.** To forgive : pardon. **2.** To make allowance for : overlook. **3.** To apologize for. **4.** To justify. **5.** To release from a duty : exempt. **6.** To allow to leave : release. *—n.* (-skyōōs') **1.** An explanation to elicit forgiveness. **2.** A ground or reason for being excused. **3.** *Informal.* An inferior example <a poor *excuse* for a sailboat> **—ex•cus'a•ble** *adj.* **—ex•cus'a•bly** *adv.*

exec. *abbr.* **1.** executive. **2.** executor.

ex•e•cra•ble (ĕk'sĭ-krə-bəl) *adj.* **1.** Deserving execration : detestable. **2.** Very bad : vile. **—ex'e•cra•bly** *adv.*

ex•e•crate (ĕk'sĭ-krāt') *v.* **-crat•ed, -crat•ing.** To feel or express detestation for : abhor. **—ex'e•cra'tion** *n.* **—ex'e•cra'tor** *n.*

ex•e•cute (ĕk'sĭ-kyōōt') *v.* **-cut•ed, -cut•ing. 1.** To put into effect : carry out. **2.** To make valid, as by signing <*execute* a deed> **3.** To carry out what is called for in <*execute* a will> **4.** To put to death by legal authority. **—ex'e•cu'tion** *n.*

ex•e•cu•tion•er (ĕk'sĭ-kyōō'shə-nər) *n.* One who puts others to death by legal authority.

ex•ec•u•tive (ĭg-zĕk'yə-tĭv) *n.* **1.** An administrator or manager in an organization. **2.** The branch of government responsible for putting the laws of a country into effect. *—adj.* **1.** Of or responsible for the carrying out of plans or policies. **2.** Of or relating to the branch of government that puts laws into effect.

Executive Council *n. Can.* The cabinet of a provincial government.

ex•ec•u•tor (ĭg-zĕk'yə-tər) *n.* A person appointed to carry out a will. **—ex•ec'u•trix'** (-trĭks') *n.*

ex•e•ge•sis (ĕk'sə-jē'sĭs) *n., pl.* **-ses** (-sēz'). Explanation or interpretation of a text. **—ex'e•get'ic** (-jĕt'ĭk), **ex'•e•get'i•cal** *adj.*

ex•em•plar (ĭg-zĕm'plär', -plər) *n.* **1.** One worthy of imitation : model. **2.** A typical example.

ex•em•pla•ry (ĭg-zĕm'plə-rē) *adj.* **1.** Serving as a model. **2.** Worthy of imitation : commendable.

ex•em•pli•fy (ĭg-zĕm'plə-fī') *v.* **-fied, -fy•ing. 1.** To illustrate by giving examples. **2.** To be an example of. **—ex•em'pli•fi•ca'tion** *n.*

ex•empt (ĭg-zĕmpt') *v.* To release from an obligation or duty to which others are subject. **—ex•empt'** *adj.* **—ex•empt'i•ble** *adj.* **—ex•emp'tion** *n.*

ex•er•cise (ĕk'sər-sīz') *n.* **1.** An act of using <the *exercise* of caution> **2.** Physical or mental activity that develops fitness. **3.** Something done to maintain or increase a skill <a piano *exercise*> **4. exercises.** A public ceremony <commencement *exercises*> *—v.* **-cised, -cis•ing. 1.** To put into operation : use. **2.** To bring to bear : exert. **3.** To subject to physical or mental activity so as to develop fitness. **4.** To worry or upset. **—ex'er•cis'er** *n.*

ex•ert (ĭg-zûrt') *v.* **1.** To bring to bear : exercise. **2.** To put (oneself) to a strenuous effort. **—ex•er'tion** *n.*

ex•hale (ĕks-hāl', ĕk-sāl') *v.* **-haled, -hal•ing. 1.** To breathe out. **2.** To emit (e.g., vapor). **—ex'ha•la'tion** (ĕks'hə-lā'shən, ĕk'sə-) *n.*

ex•haust (ĭg-zôst') *v.* **1.** To let out or release (a liquid or gas). **2.** To use up : consume <*exhausted* the food supply> **3.** To use up the energy of : wear out. **4.** To develop or consider completely <*exhaust* a subject> *—n.* **1. a.** The escape of gases, as from an engine. **b.** The gases released. **2.** A device that releases or expels waste gases. **—ex•haust'i•bil'i•ty** *n.* **—ex•haust'i•ble** *adj.* **—ex•haus'tion** (-zôs'chən) *n.*

ex•haus•tive (ĭg-zô'stĭv) *adj.* **1.** Tending to exhaust. **2.** Thorough : comprehensive <an *exhaustive* analysis> **—ex•haus'tive•ly** *adv.* **—ex•haus'tive•ness** *n.*

ex•hib•it (ĭg-zĭb'ĭt) *v.* **1.** To display, esp. for public view. **2.** To introduce (documents or evidence) in a court of law. *—n.* **1.** An act of exhibiting. **2.** Something exhibited. **—ex'hi•bi'tion** (ĕk'sə-bĭsh'ən) *n.* **—ex•hib'i•tor** *n.*

ex•hi•bi•tion•ism (ĕk'sə-bĭsh'ə-nĭz'əm) *n.* The practice of deliberately attracting undue attention to oneself. **—ex'hi•bi'tion•ist** *n.* **—ex'hi•bi'tion•is'tic** *adj.*

ex•hil•a•rate (ĭg-zĭl'ə-rāt') *v.* **-rat•ed, -rat•ing. 1.** To make cheerful : : elate. **2.** To refresh : invigorate. **—ex•hil'a•ra'tion** *n.* **—ex•hil'a•ra'tive** *adj.*

ex•hort (ĭg-zôrt') *v.* To urge or incite by strong appeal, advice, or argument. **—ex'hor•ta'tion** (ĕk'sôr-tā'shən, ĕg'zôr-) *n.* **—ex•hor'ta•tive** *adj.*

ex•hume (ĭg-zyōōm', ĕks-hyōōm') *v.* **-humed, -hum•ing.** To remove from a grave : disinter. **—ex'hu•ma'tion** (ĕks'hyōō-mā'shən) *n.*

ex•i•gen•cy (ĕk'sə-jən-sē, ĕg'zə-) *n., pl.* **-cies. 1.** The quality of requiring immediate attention or effort : urgency. **2.** An emergency. **3.** *often* **exigencies.** Pressing needs. **—ex'i•gence** *n.* **—ex'i•gent** *adj.*

ex•ig•u•ous (ĭg-zĭg'yōō-əs, ĭk-sĭg'-) *adj.* Extremely meager : scanty. **—ex'i•gu'i•ty** (ĕk'sĭ-gyōō'ĭ-tē) *n.* **—ex•ig'u•ous•ly** *adv.*

ex•ile (ĕg'zīl', ĕk'sīl') *n.* **1.** Forced or self-imposed removal from one's native country : banishment. **2.** One who has left or been driven from his or her country. *—v.* **-iled, -il•ing.** To send into exile : banish.

ex•ist (ĭg-zĭst') *v.* **1.** To have being or actuality. **2.** To have life : live. **3.** To occur.

ex•is•tence (ĭg-zĭs'təns) *n.* **1.** The fact or state of existing, living, or occurring. **2.** Manner of existing <a day-to-day *existence*> **—ex•is'tent** *adj.*

ex•is•ten•tial (ĕg'zĭ-stĕn'shəl, ĕk'sĭ-) *adj.* **1.** Of or relating to existence. **2.** Based on experience. **3.** Of or relating to existentialism. **—ex'is•ten'tial•ly** *adv.*

ex•is•ten•tial•ism (ĕg'zĭ-stĕn'shə-lĭz'əm, ĕk'sĭ-) *n.* A philosophy that emphasizes the absence of supernatural authority and the freedom and responsibility of the individual in a universe that lacks essential meaning. **—ex′is·ten′tial·ist** *n.*

ex·it (ĕg′zĭt, ĕk′sĭt) *n.* **1.** The act of going away or out. **2.** A passage or way out. **3.** A departure from the stage, as in a play. **—ex′it** *v.*

ex·o·bi·ol·o·gy (ĕk′sō-bī-ŏl′ə-jē) *n.* The search for and study of extraterrestrial life. **—ex′o·bi·ol′o·gist** *n.*

ex·o·dus (ĕk′sə-dəs) *n.* **1.** A departure of a large number of people. **2. Exodus.** See BIBLE TABLE.

ex of·fi·ci·o (ĕks′ ə-fĭsh′ē-ō′) *adj.* & *adv.* Because of office or position.

ex·og·e·nous (ĕk-sŏj′ə-nəs) *n. Biol.* Derived from external causes.

ex·on·er·ate (ĭg-zŏn′ə-rāt′) *v.* **-at·ed, -at·ing.** To clear of blame. **—ex·on′er·a′tion** *n.* **—ex·on′er·a′tor** *n.*

ex·or·bi·tant (ĭg-zôr′bĭ-tənt) *adj.* Exceeding appropriate or usual limits or bounds : immoderate. **—ex·or′bi·tance** *n.* **—ex·or′bi·tant·ly** *adv.*

ex·or·cise (ĕk′sôr-sīz′, -sər-) *v.* **-cised, -cis·ing. 1.** To expel (an evil spirit) by or as if by enacting a ritual. **2.** To free from evil spirits. **—ex′or·cis′er** *n.* **—ex′or·cism** *n.* **—ex′or·cist** *n.*

ex·o·ther·mic (ĕk′sō-thûr′mĭk) *also* **ex·o·ther·mal** (-məl) *adj.* Releasing rather than absorbing heat.

ex·ot·ic (ĭg-zŏt′ĭk) *adj.* **1.** Of or from another part of the world : foreign. **2.** Intriguingly different. **—ex·ot′ic** *n.* **—ex·ot′i·cal·ly** *adv.*

exp. *abbr.* **1.** expenses. **2.** export. **3.** express.

ex·pand (ĭk-spănd′) *v.* **1.** To make or become greater in size, scope, or range. **2.** To open up or out : unfold. **3.** To speak or write at greater length : enlarge. **—ex·pand′a·ble** *adj.* **—ex·pand′er** *n.*

ex·panse (ĭk-spăns′) *n.* A wide, open extent <the *expanse* of sky>

ex·pan·sion (ĭk-spăn′shən) *n.* **1.** The act or process of expanding or state of being expanded. **2.** An expanded part.

ex·pan·sive (ĭk-spăn′sĭv) *adj.* **1.** Capable of expanding or inclined to expand. **2.** Comprehensive : broad. **3.** Open and generous : outgoing. **—ex·pan′sive·ly** *adv.* **—ex·pan′sive·ness** *n.*

ex par·te (ĕks pär′tē) *adj.* & *adv. Law.* From only 1 side or point of view.

ex·pa·ti·ate (ĭk-spā′shē-āt′) *v.* **-at·ed, -at·ing.** To talk or write at length : elaborate. **—ex·pa′ti·a′tion** *n.*

ex·pa·tri·ate (ĕks-pā′trē-āt′) *v.* **-at·ed, -at·ing. 1.** To send into exile. **2.** To leave one's country and reside in another. *—n.* (-ĭt, -āt′). An expatriated person. **—ex·pa′tri·a′tion** *n.*

ex·pect (ĭk-spĕkt′) *v.* **1.** To look forward to : believe to be probable <*expecting* rain> **2.** To consider due <*expect* civility> **3.** *Informal.* To presume : suppose. **—ex·pect′er** *n.*

ex·pec·tan·cy (ĭk-spĕk′tən-sē) *n., pl.* **-cies. 1.** Expectation. **2.** An expected amount <a life *expectancy* of 76 years>

ex·pec·tant (ĭk-spĕk′tənt) *adj.* **1.** Expecting. **2.** Pregnant. **—ex·pec′tant·ly** *adv.*

ex·pec·ta·tion (ĕk′spĕk-tā′shən) *n.* **1.** The act or state of expecting. **2.** Eager anticipation for something coming. **3. a. expectations.** Something expected. **b.** Future prospects.

ex·pec·to·rant (ĭk-spĕk′tər-ənt) *adj.* Promoting expulsion of mucus from the respiratory tract. *—n.* An expectorant medication.

ex·pec·to·rate (ĭk-spĕk′tə-rāt′) *v.* **-rat·ed, -rat·ing.** To spit. **—ex·pec′to·ra′tion** *n.*

ex·pe·di·ence (ĭk-spē′dē-əns) *n.* Expediency.

ex·pe·di·en·cy (ĭk-spē′dē-ən-sē) *n., pl.* **-cies. 1.** Suitableness : fitness. **2.** The use of self-serving means. **3.** An expedient.

ex·pe·di·ent (ĭk-spē′dē-ənt) *adj.* **1.** Appropriate to a given purpose. **2.** Promoting narrow or selfish interests. *—n.* A means to an end, esp. one disregarding the welfare of others. **—ex·pe′di·ent·ly** *adv.*

ex·pe·dite (ĕk′spĭ-dīt′) *v.* **-dit·ed, -dit·ing. 1.** To speed up : facilitate. **2.** To perform efficiently. **—ex′pe·dit′er, ex′pe·di′tor** *n.*

ex·pe·di·tion (ĕk′spĭ-dĭsh′ən) *n.* **1. a.** A journey of some length or difficulty for a definite purpose. **b.** The group undertaking such a journey. **2.** Speed in performing : promptness.

ex·pe·di·tion·ar·y (ĕk′spĭ-dĭsh′ə-nĕr′ē) *adj.* Of, relating to, or being an expedition, esp. a military one.

ex·pe·di·tious (ĕk′spĭ-dĭsh′əs) *adj.* Acting or done with efficiency and promptness. **—ex′pe·di′tious·ly** *adv.* **—ex′pe·di′tious·ness** *n.*

ex·pel (ĭk-spĕl′) *v.* **-pelled, -pel·ling. 1.** To drive or force out. **2.** To dismiss, as from a school. **—ex·pel′la·ble** *adj.* **—ex·pel′ler** *n.*

ex·pend (ĭk-spĕnd′) *v.* **1.** To spend. **2.** To use up : consume.

ex·pend·a·ble (ĭk-spĕn′də-bəl) *adj.* Subject to being used up or sacrificed if needed : nonessential.

ex·pen·di·ture (ĭk-spĕn′də-chər) *n.* **1.** The act or process of expending. **2.** An amount spent.

ex·pense (ĭk-spĕns′) *n.* **1. a.** Something paid out or given up to attain an end. **b.** Sacrifice <at the *expense* of his pride> **2. expenses. a.** Charges incurred by an employee while at work. **b.** *Informal.* Reimbursement for such charges. **3.** Something necessitating the spending of money.

ex·pen·sive (ĭk-spĕn′sĭv) *adj.* High-priced. ☆***syns:*** COSTLY, DEAR, HIGH

ex·pe·ri·ence (ĭk-spîr′ē-əns) *n.* **1.** Something done, seen, or taken part in <her *experiences* as a nurse> **2.** The events lived through by an individual or group. **3. a.** Participation or observation leading to knowledge or skill. **b.** The knowledge or skill acquired <a worker with extensive *experience*> *—v.* **-enced, -enc·ing.** To participate in personally : undergo.

ex·pe·ri·enced (ĭk-spîr′ē-ənst) *adj.* Knowledgeable through experience.

ex·per·i·ment (ĭk-spĕr′ə-mənt) *n.* A test performed to demonstrate a truth, examine a hypothesis, or learn about something not yet known. *—v.* (-mĕnt′) To conduct an experiment. **—ex·per′i·men′tal** *adj.* **—ex·per′i·men′tal·ly** *adv.* **—ex·per′i·men·ta′tion** *n.* **—ex·per′i·ment′er** *n.*

ex·pert (ĕk′spûrt′) *n.* A person with great knowledge, skill, or experience in a specific subject. *—adj.* (ĭk-spûrt′, ĕk′spûrt′). Having or showing great skill or knowledge. **—ex·pert′ly** *adv.* **—ex·pert′ness** *n.*

ex·per·tise (ĕk′spər-tēz′) *n.* Specialized knowledge, skill, or ability.

ex·pi·ate (ĕk′spē-āt′) *v.* **-at·ed, -at·ing.** To make amends for : atone. **—ex′pi·a′tion** *n.* **—ex′pi·a′tor** *n.* **—ex′pi·a·to′ry** (-ə-tôr′ē, -tōr′ē) *adj.*

ex·pire (ĭk-spīr′) *v.* **-pired, -pir·ing. 1.** To come to an end. **2.** To die. **3.** To breathe out : exhale. **—ex′pi·ra′tion** *n.*

ex·plain (ĭk-splān′) *v.* **1.** To make understandable : clarify. **2.** To give the reason for : account for. **—ex·plain′a·ble** *adj.* **—ex·plain′er** *n.* **—ex′pla·na′tion** (ĕk′splə-nā′shən) *n.* **—ex·plan′a·to·ry** (-splăn′ə-tôr′ē, -tōr′ē) *adj.*

ex·ple·tive (ĕks′plĭ-tĭv) *n.* An often profane or obscene exclamation.

ex·pli·ca·ble (ĕk′splĭ-kə-bəl, ĭk-splĭk′ə-) *adj.* Capable of being explained.

ex·pli·cate (ĕk′splĭ-kāt′) *v.* **-cat·ed, -cat·ing.** To make clearer the meaning of : explain in detail. **—ex′pli·ca′tion** *n.* **—ex′pli·ca′tive** *adj.* **—ex′pli·ca′tor** *n.*

ex·plic·it (ĭk-splĭs′ĭt) *adj.* Clearly expressed or defined : specific <*explicit* instructions> **—ex·plic′it·ly** *adv.* **—ex·plic′it·ness** *n.*

ex·plode (ĭk-splōd′) *v.* **-plod·ed, -plod·ing. 1.** To release or cause to release energy violently and suddenly : burst. **2.** To break out suddenly : burst forth. **3.** To increase rapidly and without control. **4.** To show to be false : refute. **—ex·plod′er** *n.*

ex·ploit (ĕk′sploit′) *n.* A notable deed or act. *—v.* (ĭk-sploit′). **1.** To use to best advantage. **2.** To make use of selfishly or unethically <*exploiting* low-paid farm workers> **—ex·ploit′a·ble** *adj.* **—ex′ploi·ta′tion** *n.* **—ex·ploit′a·tive** *adj.* **—ex·ploit′er** *n.*

ex·plore (ĭk-splôr′, -splōr′) *v.* **-plored, -plor·ing. 1.** To investigate in a systematic way : examine. **2.** To search into or range over for the purpose of discovery. **—ex′plo·ra′tion** (ĕk′splə-rā′shən) *n.* **—ex·plor′a·to′ry** (-ə-tôr′ē, -tōr′ē) *adj.* **—ex·plor′er** *n.*

ex·plo·sion (ĭk-splō′zhən) *n.* **1. a.** A sudden, violent release of energy. **b.** A loud, sharp sound made by this. **2.** A sudden outburst, as of emotion. **3.** A rapid, uncontrolled increase.

ex·plo·sive (ĭk-splō′sĭv) *adj.* **1.** Of or relating to an explosion. **2.** Likely to explode. *—n.* A substance, esp. a chemical preparation, that explodes. **—ex·plo′sive·ly** *adv.* **—ex·plo′sive·ness** *n.*

ex·po·nent (ĭk-spō′nənt) *n.* **1.** One who represents, advocates, or speaks for a cause or group. **2.** *Math.* A number or symbol, as 4 in $(x + y)^4$, that indicates the number of times an expression is used as a factor. **—ex′po·nen′tial** (ĕk′spə-nĕn′shəl) *adj.* **—ex′po·nen′tial·ly** *adv.*

ex·port (ĭk-spôrt′, -spōrt′, ĕk′spôrt′, -spōrt′) *v.* To send or transport abroad for sale or trade. *—n.* (ĕk′spôrt′, -spōrt′). **1.** An act of exporting. **2.** A commodity exported. **—ex·port′a·ble** *adj.* **—ex′por·ta′tion** *n.* **—ex·port′er** *n.*

ex·pose (ĭk-spōz′) *v.* **-posed, -pos·ing. 1.** To lay bare : uncover. **2.** To lay open, as to something harmful <*exposed* himself to a lawsuit> **3.** To make known : reveal. **4.** To subject (e.g., a photographic film) to light. **—ex·pos′er** *n.*

ex·po·sé (ĕk′spō-zā′) *n.* An exposure of something discreditable.

ex·po·si·tion (ĕk′spə-zĭsh′ən) *n.* **1.** A statement of meaning or intent. **2.** Writing or speech that explains or gives information. **3.** A public exhibition. **—ex·pos'i·tor** (ĭk-spŏz'ĭ-tər) *n.* **—ex·pos'i·to'ry** (-tôr'ē, -tōr'ē) *adj.*

ex post fac·to (ĕks' pōst făk'tō) *adj.* Enacted, formulated, or done after the fact : retroactive <*ex post facto* laws>

ex·pos·tu·late (ĭk-spŏs'chə-lāt') *v.* **-lat·ed, -lat·ing.** To reason earnestly in an effort to dissuade or correct someone. **—ex·pos'tu·la'tion** *n.* **—ex·pos'tu·la'tor** *n.* **—ex·pos'tu·la·to'ry** (-lə-tôr'ē, -tōr'ē) *adj.*

ex·po·sure (ĭk-spō'zhər) *n.* **1.** An act of exposing or the state of being exposed. **2.** A position with respect to direction <a northern *exposure*> **3. a.** The act of exposing a sensitized photographic film or plate. **b.** The film or plate exposed.

ex·pound (ĭk-spound') *v.* **1.** To present a detailed statement (of). **2.** To explain at length. **—ex·pound'er** *n.*

ex·press (ĭk-sprĕs') *v.* **1.** To make known in words <*express* an opinion> **2.** To communicate, as by gesture : show. **3.** To represent : symbolize. **4.** To press out, as juice from fruit. **5.** To send by fast transportation. *—adj.* **1.** Clearly stated : explicit. **2.** Sent rapidly and directly <an *express* parcel> **3.** Direct and with few or no local stops <an *express* bus> *—adv.* By express transport. *—n.* An express vehicle or transport system. **—ex·press'i·ble** *adj.* **—ex·press'ly** *adv.*

ex·pres·sion (ĭk-sprĕsh'ən) *n.* **1.** An act of expressing. **2.** Communication, esp. in words : utterance. **3.** Something that expresses. **4.** A particular phrase or word <a regional *expression* like "you-all"> **5.** A manner of expressing oneself, esp. in speech or performance. **6.** A facial aspect or look conveying feeling <an astonished *expression*> **7.** *Math.* A symbol or group of symbols. **—ex·pres'sion·less** *adj.*

ex·pres·sion·ism (ĭk-sprĕsh'ə-nĭz'əm) *n.* A movement in the fine arts that emphasizes subjective expression of the artist's inner experiences. **—ex·pres'sion·ist** *n.* **—ex·pres'sion·is'tic** *adj.*

ex·pres·sive (ĭk-sprĕs'ĭv) *adj.* **1.** Of or relating to expression <*expressive* power> **2.** Serving or tending to express <a tone *expressive* of regret> **3.** Full of expression : significant. **—ex·pres'sive·ly** *adv.* **—ex·pres'sive·ness** *n.*

ex·press·way (ĭk-sprĕs'wā') *n.* A multilane highway designed for high-speed travel.

ex·pro·pri·ate (ĕk-sprō'prē-āt') *v.* **-at·ed, -at·ing.** **1.** To take (another's property), esp. for public use. **2.** To deprive of possession. **—ex·pro'pri·a'tion** *n.* **—ex·pro'pri·a'tor** *n.*

ex·pul·sion (ĭk-spŭl'shən) *n.* The act of expelling or state of being expelled.

ex·punge (ĭk-spŭnj') *v.* **-punged, -pung·ing.** To remove or delete : erase. **—ex·pung'er** *n.*

ex·pur·gate (ĕk'spər-gāt') *v.* **-gat·ed, -gat·ing.** To remove objectionable material from, esp. before publication. **—ex'pur·ga'tion** *n.* **—ex'pur·ga'tor** *n.*

ex·qui·site (ĕk'skwĭ-zĭt, ĭk-skwĭz'ĭt) *adj.* **1.** Intricately or delicately beautiful in design or execution <an *exquisite* miniature portrait> **2.** Acutely perceptive or appreciative <*exquisite* taste> **3.** Intense : keen. **—ex'qui·site·ly** *adv.* **—ex'qui·site·ness** *n.*

ex·tant (ĕk'stənt, ĭk-stănt') *adj.* Still in existence : not lost or destroyed <*extant* writings>

ex·tem·po·ra·ne·ous (ĭk-stĕm'pə-rā'nē-əs) *adj.* Acting or done without preparation or practice beforehand : impromptu. **—ex·tem'po·ra'ne·ous·ly** *adv.* **—ex·tem'po·ra'ne·ous·ness** *n.*

ex·tem·po·re (ĭk-stĕm'pə-rē) *adj.* Extemporaneous. *—adv.* Extemporaneously.

ex·tem·po·rize (ĭk-stĕm'pə-rīz') *v.* **-rized, -riz·ing.** To perform extemporaneously : improvise. **—ex·tem'po·ri·za'tion** *n.* **—ex·tem'po·riz'er** *n.*

ex·tend (ĭk-stĕnd') *v.* **1.** To stretch to full length : spread out. **2.** To make longer, wider, or broader <*extend* boundaries><*extending* individual rights> **3.** To reach : stretch <Her property *extends* to the river.> **4.** To prolong <*extend* a deadline> **5.** To exert to full capacity. **6.** To offer <*extend* congratulations> **—ex·tend'i·bil'i·ty, ex·ten'si·bil'i·ty** *n.* **—ex·tend'i·ble, ex·ten'si·ble** *adj.*

extended family *n.* A family unit making up 1 household that consists of parents, children, and other close relatives.

ex·tend·er (ĕk-stĕn'dər) *n.* A substance added to another to modify, dilute, or adulterate.

ex·ten·sion (ĭk-stĕn'shən) *n.* **1.** The act of extending or state of being extended. **2.** An added part.

ex·ten·sive (ĭk-stĕn'sĭv) *adj.* Great in extent : large or broad. **—ex·ten'sive·ly** *adv.* **—ex·ten'sive·ness** *n.*

ex·tent (ĭk-stĕnt') *n.* **1.** The area over or length to which a thing extends : size. **2.** The degree to which a thing extends. **3.** An expanse.

ex·ten·u·ate (ĭk-stĕn'yo͞o-āt') *v.* **-at·ed, -at·ing.** To minimize or try to minimize the seriousness of : excuse. **—ex·ten'u·a'tion** *n.* **—ex·ten'u·a'tor** *n.*

ex·te·ri·or (ĭk-stîr'ē-ər) *adj.* External : outer. *—n.* An exterior surface or part.

ex·ter·mi·nate (ĭk-stûr'mə-nāt') *v.* **-nat·ed, -nat·ing.** To destroy completely : annihilate. **—ex·ter'mi·na'tion** *n.* **—ex·ter'mi·na'tor** *n.*

ex·tern *or* **ex·terne** (ĕk'stûrn') *n.* A person associated with but not officially residing in an institution, as a hospital.

ex·ter·nal (ĭk-stûr'nəl) *adj.* **1.** Of, for, or on the outside : exterior. **2.** Acting or coming from the outside <*external* influences on a country> **3.** Apparent from outside. **4.** Of or relating to foreign countries. *—n.* **externals.** External circumstances or appearances. **—ex·ter'nal·ly** *adv.*

ex·tinct (ĭk-stĭngkt') *adj.* **1.** No longer existing <*extinct* reptiles> **2.** Not active <an *extinct* volcano> **3.** Extinguished. **—ex·tinc'tion** *n.*

ex·tin·guish (ĭk-stĭng'gwĭsh) *v.* **1.** To put out (e.g., a fire). **2.** To put an end to : destroy. ☆**syns:** DOUSE, QUENCH, SNUFF **—ex·tin'guish·a·ble** *adj.* **—ex·tin'guish·er** *n.*

ex·tir·pate (ĕk'stər-pāt') *v.* **-pat·ed, -pat·ing.** **1.** To root out : uproot. **2.** To destroy : exterminate. **—ex'tir·pa'tion** *n.* **—ex'tir·pa'tive** *adj.* **—ex'tir·pa'tor** *n.*

ex·tol *also* **ex·toll** (ĭk-stōl') *v.* **-tolled, -tol·ling.** To praise highly. **—ex·tol'ler** *n.* **—ex·tol'ment** *n.*

ex·tort (ĭk-stôrt') *v.* To obtain by coercive means, as threats or intimidation. **—ex·tor'tion** *n.* **—ex·tor'tion·ate** (-shə-nĭt) *adj.* **—ex·tor'tion·ist** *n.*

ex·tra (ĕk'strə) *adj.* Being beyond what is expected or usual : additional. *—adv.* Exceptionally : unusually. *—n.* **1.** Something additional : accessory. **2.** An extra edition of a newspaper. **3.** A performer hired to play a minor film part.

ex·tract (ĭk-străkt') *v.* **1.** To draw out, esp. forcibly <*extract* a tooth> **2.** To obtain in spite of resistance <*extract* a confession> **3.** To obtain by chemical or mechanical action. **4.** To remove for separate consideration : excerpt. **5.** *Math.* To determine (a root). *—n.* (ĕk'străkt'). **1.** A passage taken from a longer work : excerpt. **2.** A concentrated substance : essence <maple *extract*> **—ex·tract'a·ble, ex·tract'i·ble** *adj.* **—ex·trac'tor** *n.*

ex·trac·tion (ĭk-străk'shən) *n.* **1.** The act or process of extracting. **2.** Something obtained by extracting : extract. **3.** Origin : ancestry <of German *extraction*>

ex·tra·cur·ric·u·lar (ĕk'strə-kə-rĭk'yə-lər) *adj.* **1.** Outside a school's curriculum. **2.** Outside the usual duties of a job.

ex·tra·dite (ĕk'strə-dīt') *v.* **-dit·ed, -dit·ing.** To surrender to or obtain by extradition. **—ex'tra·dit'a·ble** *adj.*

ex·tra·di·tion (ĕk'strə-dĭsh'ən) *n.* Legal surrender of an alleged criminal to the jurisdiction of another state, country, or government for trial.

ex·tra·dos (ĕk'strə-dŏs', -dō', -dŏs') *n., pl.* **-dos** (-dōz') *or* **-dos·es.** The upper or exterior curve of an arch.

ex·tra·ga·lac·tic (ĕk'strə-gə-lăk'tĭk) *adj.* Situated or coming from beyond the galaxy.

ex·tra·mar·i·tal (ĕk'strə-măr'ĭ-tl) *adj.* Adulterous.

ex·tra·mu·ral (ĕk'strə-myo͝or'əl) *adj.* **1.** Occurring outside the walls or boundaries, as of a community. **2.** Involving teams from different schools.

ex·tra·ne·ous (ĭk-strā'nē-əs) *adj.* **1.** Coming from the outside : foreign. **2.** Not vital or essential. **—ex·tra'ne·ous·ly** *adv.* **—ex·tra'ne·ous·ness** *n.*

ex·traor·di·nar·y (ĭk-strôr'dn-ĕr'ē, ĕk'strə-ôr'-) *adj.* Beyond what is common or usual : remarkable. **—ex·traor'di·nar'i·ly** (-nâr'ə-lē) *adv.*

ex·trap·o·late (ĭk-străp'ə-lāt') *v.* **-lat·ed, -lat·ing.** To infer (unknown information) by projecting or extending known information. **—ex·trap'o·la'tion** *n.* **—ex·trap'o·la'tive** *adj.* **—ex·trap'o·la'tor** *n.*

ex·tra·sen·so·ry (ĕk'strə-sĕn'sə-rē) *adj.* Being beyond the range of the known senses.

ex·tra·ter·res·tri·al (ĕk'strə-tə-rĕs'trē-əl) *adj.* Originating or occurring outside the earth or its atmosphere. **—ex'tra·ter·res'tri·al** *n.*

ex·tra·ter·ri·to·ri·al (ĕk'strə-tĕr'ĭ-tôr'ē-əl, -tōr'-) *adj.* **1.** Situated outside territorial limits. **2.** Of or pertaining to extraterritoriality.

ex·tra·ter·ri·to·ri·al·i·ty (ĕk'strə-tĕr'ĭ-tôr'ē-ăl'ĭ-tē, -tōr-) *n.* Exemption from local legal jurisdiction, as that extended to foreign diplomats.

ex·trav·a·gant (ĭk-străv'ə-gənt) *adj.* **1.** Given to imprudent or lavish spending : wasteful. **2.** Excessive : unrestrained <*extravagant* requests> **—ex·trav'a·gance** *n.* **—ex·trav'a·gant·ly** *adv.*

ex·trav·a·gan·za (ĭk-străv'ə-găn'zə) *n.* A lavish, showy entertainment.

ex•tra•ve•hic•u•lar (ĕk'strə-vē-hĭk'yə-lər) *adj.* Done or occurring outside a vehicle, esp. a spacecraft in flight <*extravehicular* activity>
ex•treme (ĭk-strēm') *adj.* **1.** Farthest from a center : outermost <the *extreme* edge of the continent> **2.** Final : last. **3.** Of the highest or utmost degree <*extreme* poverty><an *extreme* nationalist> **4.** Severe : drastic. —*n.* **1.** The highest or utmost degree. **2.** Either of the 2 ends of a scale or range <the *extremes* of flood and drought> **3.** An extreme condition. **4.** A drastic measure. **—ex•treme'ly** *adv.* **—ex•treme'ness** *n.*
ex•trem•ist (ĭk-strē'mĭst) *n.* One who advocates or resorts to extreme measures, esp. in politics. **—ex•trem'ism** *n.*
ex•trem•i•ty (ĭk-strĕm'ĭ-tē) *n., pl.* **-ties. 1.** The farthest point or portion. **2.** The utmost degree. **3.** Extreme distress or peril. **4.** An extreme measure. **5.** A bodily limb or appendage.
ex•tri•cate (ĕk'strĭ-kāt') *v.* **-cat•ed, -cat•ing.** To free from difficulty or entanglement : disengage. **—ex'tri•ca'tion** *n.*
ex•trin•sic (ĭk-strĭn'sĭk, -zĭk) *adj.* **1.** Not inherent : extraneous. **2.** Coming from the outside : external. **—ex•trin'si•cal•ly** *adv.*
ex•tro•vert *also* **ex•tra•vert** (ĕk'strə-vûrt') *n.* One who is more interested in people and things outside the self than in private thoughts and feelings. **—ex'tro•ver'sion** *n.*
ex•trude (ĭk-strōōd') *v.* **-trud•ed, -trud•ing. 1.** To thrust or push out <A spider *extrudes* filaments.> **2.** To shape (e.g., plastic) by forcing through a die. **3.** To project or protrude. **—ex•tru'sion** *n.* **—ex•tru'sive** *adj.*
ex•u•ber•ant (ĭg-zōō'bər-ənt) *adj.* **1.** Full of unrestrained high spirits : ebullient. **2.** Plentiful : abundant. **—ex•u'ber•ance** *n.* **—ex•u'ber•ant•ly** *adv.*
ex•ude (ĭg-zōōd') *v.* **-ud•ed, -ud•ing. 1.** To ooze forth. **2.** To give off : radiate <*exuding* charm> **—ex'u•da'tion** (ĕks'yōō-dā'shən) *n.* **—ex'u•date'** *n.*
ex•ult (ĭg-zŭlt') *v.* To rejoice greatly : be jubilant. **—ex•ul'tant** *adj.* **—ex•ul'tant•ly** *adv.* **—ex'ul•ta'tion** (ĕk'səl-tā'shən, ĕg'zəl-) *n.*
ex•ur•bi•a (ĕk-sûr'bē-ə, ĕg-zûr'-) *n.* An often wealthy residential area outside the suburbs of a city. **—ex•ur'ban•ite'** *n.*
-ey *suff. var. of* -Y[1].
eye (ī) *n.* **1.** An organ of sight or of light sensitivity. **2.** The faculty of seeing : vision. **3.** A look : gaze. **4.** The ability to perceive, judge, or discriminate. **5.** A point of view. **6.** Something suggesting an eye <the *eye* of a needle> —*v.* **eyed, eye•ing** or **ey•ing.** To watch closely : look at. **—see eye to eye.** To be in complete agreement.
eye•ball (ī'bôl') *n.* The part of the eye enclosed by the socket and eyelids and connected at the rear to the optic nerve.
eye•brow (ī'brou') *n.* **1.** The bony ridge over the eye. **2.** The short hairs covering the eyebrow.
eye•drop•per (ī'drŏp'pər) *n.* A dropper for administering liquid eye medicines.
eye•ful (ī'fōōl') *n.* **1.** A complete or satisfying view. **2.** An impressive sight.
eye•glass (ī'glăs') *n.* **1.** A lens, as a monocle, used to improve vision. **2. eyeglasses.** Corrective lenses set in a frame.
eye•lash (ī'lăsh') *n.* **1.** A row of hairs fringing the eyelid. **2.** A single hair of an eyelash.
eye•let (ī'lĭt) *n.* **1.** A small hole or perforation for a cord or hook to fit through in closing a fastening. **2.** A metal ring reinforcing an eyelet.
eye•lid (ī'lĭd') *n.* Either of 2 folds of skin and muscle that open and close over an eye.
eye•lin•er (ī'lī'nər) *n.* Make-up used to outline the eyes.
eye opener *n.* A startling revelation.
eye•piece (ī'pēs') *n.* The lens or lens group of an optical instrument closest to the eye : ocular.
eye shadow *n.* A colored cosmetic applied to the eyelids.
eye•sight (ī'sīt') *n.* **1.** The faculty of sight : vision. **2.** Range of vision.
eye•sore (ī'sôr', ī'sōr') *n.* Something ugly.
eye•strain (ī'strān') *n.* Fatigue in an eye muscle, marked by symptoms such as pain and headache.
eye•tooth (ī'tōōth') *n.* A canine of the upper jaw.
eye•wash (ī'wŏsh', ī'wôsh') *n.* **1.** A medicated liquid used for washing the eyes. **2.** Meaningless or deceptive language.
eye•wit•ness (ī'wĭt'nəs) *n.* A person who has personally seen something and can testify to it firsthand.
ey•rir (ā'rîr') *n., pl.* **au•rar** (ou'rär', œ'-). See CURRENCY TABLE.
E•ze•ki•el (ĭ-zē'kē-əl). See BIBLE TABLE.

Ff

f or **F** (ĕf) *n., pl.* **f's** or **F's. 1.** The 6th letter of the English alphabet. **2.** A speech sound represented by the letter *f.* **3.** *Mus.* The 4th tone in the scale of C major. **4.** A failing grade.
F *symbol for* FLUORINE.
F *abbr.* Fahrenheit.
f. *abbr.* **1.** *also* **F.** or **f** or **F** female; feminine. **2.** *also* **F.** folio. **3.** franc.
fa•ble (fā'bəl) *n.* **1.** A fictitious story making a moral point and often using animal characters. **2.** A legend. **3.** A falsehood : lie. **—fab'u•list** (făb'yə-lĭst) *n.*
fa•bled (fā'bəld) *adj.* **1.** Renowned through fables : legendary. **2.** Fictitious.
fab•ric (făb'rĭk) *n.* **1.** A complex underlying structure <the *fabric* of civilization> **2.** Cloth produced esp. by knitting, weaving, or felting fibers.
fab•ri•cate (făb'rĭ-kāt') *v.* **-cat•ed, -cat•ing. 1.** To construct by combining or assembling : make. **2.** To make up in order to deceive <*fabricate* excuses> **—fab'ri•ca'tion** *n.* **—fab'ri•ca'tor** *n.*
fab•u•lous (făb'yə-ləs) *adj.* **1.** Like a fable or myth : legendary. **2.** Told of or celebrated in fables. **3.** Hardly believable : astonishing. **4.** *Informal.* Very pleasing or successful. ☆**syns:** AMAZING, ASTONISHING, FANTASTIC, INCREDIBLE, MARVELOUS, MIRACULOUS, PHENOMENAL, PRODIGIOUS, STUPENDOUS, UNBELIEVABLE, WONDERFUL, WONDROUS **—fab'u•lous•ly** *adv.* **—fab'u•lous•ness** *n.*
fa•çade *also* **fa•cade** (fə-säd') *n.* **1.** The face of a building. **2.** An artificial or deceptive outward appearance. ☆**syns:** CLOAK, FACE, FRONT, GUISE, MASK, PRETENSE, PUT-ON, SHOW, VENEER, WINDOW-DRESSING
face (fās) *n.* **1.** The surface of the front of the head from ear to ear and from forehead to chin. **2.** The expression of the features of the countenance. **3.** A contorted facial expression : grimace. **4.** Outward appearance. **5.** Standing in the eyes of others : prestige. **6.** Impudence : effrontery. **7.** The most significant or prominent surface of an object. **8. a.** A planar surface bounding a solid. **b.** Any of the surfaces of a rock or crystal. **9.** Appearance and geologic surface features of an area of land : topography. —*v.* **faced, fac•ing. 1.** To occupy a position with the face forward. **2.** To front on. **3. a.** To confront with awareness. **b.** To overcome by confronting boldly or bravely. **4.** To be certain to encounter <An unskilled youth *faces* a tough life.> **5. a.** To furnish with a cover or surface of a different material. **b.** To line or trim the edge of, esp. with contrasting material. **—face off.** To start play, as in hockey or lacrosse, by releasing the puck or ball between 2 opponents. **—face up to.** To recognize the existence of and confront bravely. **—face'less** *adj.*
face card *n.* A king, queen, or jack of a deck of playing cards.
face•lift•ing (fās'lĭf'tĭng) *also* **face-lift** (-lĭft') *n.* **1.** Plastic surgery for tightening facial tissues and improving facial appearance. **2.** Modernization. **—face'-lift'** *v.*
face-off (fās'ôf', -ŏf') *n.* **1.** The act or action of facing off in hockey, lacrosse, etc. **2.** A confrontation.
face-sav•er (fās'sā'vər) *n.* Something that preserves one's dignity or self-esteem. **—face'-sav'ing** *n.* & *adj.*
fac•et (făs'ĭt) *n.* **1.** One of the flat polished surfaces cut on a gemstone. **2.** A small smooth surface on a tooth or bone. **3.** An aspect : phase <several *facets* to the problem> **—fac'et•ed, fac'et•ted** *adj.*
fa•ce•tious (fə-sē'shəs) *adj.* Playfully jocular : humorous. **—fa•ce'tious•ly** *adv.* **—fa•ce'tious•ness** *n.*
face value *n.* **1.** The value printed or written on the face, as of a bill or bond. **2.** Apparent significance.
fa•cial (fā'shəl) *adj.* Of or having to do with the face. —*n.* A cosmetic treatment for the face. **—fa'cial•ly** *adv.*
fac•ile (făs'əl) *adj.* **1.** Carried out with little effort : easy. **2.** Working, performing, or speaking effortlessly : fluent. **3.** Arrived at without due care, effort, or examination : superficial. **—fac'ile•ly** *adv.*
fa•cil•i•tate (fə-sĭl'ĭ-tāt') *v.* **-tat•ed, -tat•ing.** To make easier. **—fa•cil'i•ta'tion** *n.* **—fa•cil'i•ta'tor** *n.*

fa·cil·i·ty (fə-sĭl′ĭ-tē) *n., pl.* **-ties. 1.** Ease in moving, performing, or doing : aptitude. **2.** *often* **facilities.** Something that facilitates an action or process. **3.** Something created to serve a particular function <a new health *facility*>

fac·ing (fā′sĭng) *n.* **1.** A piece of cloth sewn to a garment as decoration or lining. **2.** An outer protective or decorative layer applied to a surface.

fac·sim·i·le (făk-sĭm′ə-lē) *n.* **1.** An exact copy, as of a document. **2. a.** An electronic method of transmitting images or printed matter. **b.** An image so transmitted.

fact (făkt) *n.* **1. a.** Something put forth as objectively real. **b.** Something objectively verified. **2.** Something with real, demonstrable existence : actuality. **3.** A crime <an accessory before the *fact*>

fac·tion (făk′shən) *n.* **1.** A group of persons forming a cohesive, usu. contentious minority within a larger group. **2.** Conflict within an organization or state : discord. **—fac′tion·al** *adj.* **—fac′tion·al·ism** *n.*

fac·tious (făk′shəs) *adj.* **1.** Produced or marked by faction. **2.** Creating faction : divisive. **—fac′tious·ly** *adv.*

fac·ti·tious (făk-tĭsh′əs) *adj.* **1.** Produced artificially. **2.** Lacking authenticity or genuineness : sham. **—fac·ti′tious·ly** *adv.*

fac·tor (făk′tər) *n.* **1.** One who acts for someone else : agent. **2.** One that actively contributes to an accomplishment, result, or process. **3.** *Math.* One of 2 or more quantities that when multiplied together yield a given product <2 and 8 are *factors* of 16.> **4.** A gene. *—v. Math.* To determine or indicate explicitly the factors of.

fac·to·ry (făk′tə-rē) *n., pl.* **-ries.** A place where goods are manufactured : plant.

fac·to·tum (făk-tō′təm) *n.* An employee or assistant who performs a wide range of functions.

fac·tu·al (făk′cho͞o-əl) *adj.* **1.** Of the nature of fact : real. **2.** Containing facts.

fac·ul·ty (făk′əl-tē) *n., pl.* **-ties. 1.** An inborn ability or power. **2.** Any of the powers or capacities of the human mind. **3.** The ability to act. **4. a.** A division or branch of learning at a college or university <the *faculty* of medicine> **b.** The instructors within a faculty. **c.** A body of instructors as distinguished from their students.

fad (făd) *n.* A transitory fashion adopted with wide enthusiasm. **—fad′dish** *adj.* **—fad′dish·ness** *n.* **—fad′dist** *n.*

fade (fād) *v.* **fad·ed, fad·ing. 1.** To lose or cause to lose brightness, brilliance, or loudness gradually : dim. **2.** To lose freshness : wither. **3.** To lose vitality or strength : wane. **4.** To disappear gradually : vanish. ☆***syns:*** DECLINE, DETERIORATE, FAIL, FLAG, LANGUISH, WANE, WEAKEN **—fade′less** *adj.* **—fade′less·ly** *adv.*

fa·er·ie *also* **fa·er·y** (fā′ə-rē, fâr′ē) *n., pl.* **-ies.** *Archaic.* **1.** A fairy. **2.** The land of the fairies. **—fa′er·ie** *adj.*

fag[1] (făg) *n.* **1.** A drudge : menial. **2.** *esp. Brit.* A public school student who is required to perform menial tasks for an upperclassman. *—v.* **fagged, fag·ging. 1.** To work to the point of exhaustion. **2.** *esp. Brit.* To serve as a fag.

fag[2] (făg) *n. Slang.* A cigarette.

fag end *n.* **1.** The frayed end of a cloth or rope. **2. a.** A remnant. **b.** The last part.

fag·ot *also* **fag·got** (făg′ət) *n.* A bundle of twigs, sticks, or branches tied together.

fag·ot·ing *also* **fag·goting** (făg′ə-tĭng) *n.* A method of decorating cloth by pulling out horizontal threads and tying the remaining vertical threads into hourglass-shaped bunches.

Fahr·en·heit (făr′ən-hīt′) *adj.* Of or relating to a temperature scale that registers the freezing point of water as 32° F and the boiling point of water as 212° F under normal atmospheric pressure.

fa·ience *also* **fa·ïence** (fī-äns′, -äɴs′, fā-) *n.* Earthenware decorated with colorful opaque glazes.

fail (fāl) *v.* **1.** To prove so deficient as to be totally ineffective. **2.** To be unsuccessful. **3.** To give or receive an academic grade below the acceptable minimum. **4.** To weaken, decline, or cease to function properly. **5.** To disappoint or prove undependable. **6.** To omit or neglect.

fail·ing (fā′lĭng) *n.* A minor fault or defect. *—prep.* In the absence of : without.

faille (fīl) *n.* A ribbed fabric of silk, cotton, or rayon.

fail-safe (fāl′sāf′) *adj.* **1.** Able to compensate automatically for a mechanical failure. **2.** Acting according to predetermined conditions to stop a military attack. **3.** Guaranteed not to fail. **—fail′-safe′** *v. & n.*

fail·ure (fāl′yər) *n.* **1.** The state or fact of failing. **2.** One that has failed.

fain (fān) *Archaic. —adv.* Happily : gladly. *—adj.* **1.** Ready : willing. **2.** Pleased : happy. **3.** Required by circumstances.

faint (fānt) *adj.* **1.** Having little strength or vigor : feeble. **2.** Lacking clarity or brightness : dim. **3.** Likely to swoon <felt *faint*> *—n.* A sudden, usu. brief loss of consciousness. *—v.* To fall into a swoon. **—faint′ly** *adv.* **—faint′ness** *n.*

faint-heart·ed (fānt′här′tĭd) *adj.* Lacking courage or conviction : timid or cowardly. **—faint-heart′ed·ness** *n.*

†**fair**[1] (fâr) *adj.* **1.** Visually pleasing : lovely. **2.** Of light color, as hair or skin. **3.** Sunny and clear. **4.** Free of blemishes : : pure. **5.** Favorable : promising. **6. a.** Impartial <a *fair* judge> **b.** Just <a *fair* decision> **7.** In accordance with rules or standards <*fair* tactics> **8.** Moderately good. ☆***syns:*** DISPASSIONATE, EQUITABLE, FAIR-MINDED, IMPARTIAL, JUST, OBJECTIVE, UNBIASED, UNPREJUDICED *—adv.* **1.** In a proper or legal way <played *fair*> **2.** Directly : straight. *—v.* **1.** To join so as to be smooth or regular. **2.** *Regional.* To become clear. **—fair′ly** *adv.* **—fair′ness** *n.*

fair[2] (fâr) *n.* **1.** A gathering for the buying and selling of goods and merchandise : market. **2.** A competitive exhibition, as of farm products or manufactured goods. **3.** A fund-raising event, as for a charity.

fair-haired (fâr′hârd′) *adj.* **1.** Having light-colored hair. **2.** Favorite.

fair-mind·ed (fâr′mīn′dĭd) *adj.* Just and impartial. **—fair′-mind′ed·ness** *n.*

fair-trade agreement (fâr′trād′) *n.* A commercial agreement under which distributors sell a product at no less than a minimum price set by the manufacturer.

fair·way (fâr′wā′) *n.* The part of a golf course covered with short grass and extending from the tee to the putting green.

fair·y (fâr′ē) *n., pl.* **-ies.** A tiny imaginary being in human form depicted as being mischievous and having magical powers.

fair·y·land (fâr′ē-lănd′) *n.* **1.** The land of the fairies. **2.** An enchanting place.

fairy tale *n.* **1.** A fictitious tale of fanciful creatures, usu. for children. **2.** A fictitious, highly fanciful explanation or story.

fait ac·com·pli (fā′tä-kôɴ-plē′, fĕt′ä-) *pl.* **faits ac·com·plis** (fā′tä-kôɴ-plē′, -plēz′, fĕt′ä-). An accomplished and presumably irreversible deed or fact.

faith (fāth) *n.* **1.** Belief in the truth, value, or trustworthiness of someone or something. **2.** Loyalty or allegiance. **3. a.** Belief and trust in God. **b.** Religious conviction. **c.** A system of religious beliefs.

faith·ful (fāth′fəl) *adj.* **1.** Supportive : loyal. **2.** Worthy of trust or belief. **3.** Consistent with fact. ☆***syns:*** CONSTANT, FAST, FIRM, LOYAL, RESOLUTE, STAUNCH, STEADFAST, STEADY, TRUE **—faith′ful·ly** *adv.* **—faith′ful·ness** *n.*

faith·less (fāth′lĭs) *adj.* **1.** Not true to duty or obligation : DISLOYAL. **2.** Lacking religious faith. **3.** Unworthy of trust or belief. ☆***syns:*** DISLOYAL, FALSE, FALSE-HEARTED, PERFIDIOUS, TRAITOROUS, TREACHEROUS, UNFAITHFUL, UNTRUE **—faith′less·ly** *adv.* **—faith′less·ness** *n.*

fake (fāk) *adj.* Having a false or misleading appearance : fraudulent. *—n.* **1.** One that is not genuine or authentic : sham. **2.** A brief feint intended to mislead one's opponent in certain sports. *—v.* **faked, fak·ing. 1.** To fabricate and present as genuine : counterfeit. **2.** To feign : simulate. **3.** To perform a fake in certain sports. **—fak′er** *n.* **—fak′er·y** *n.*

fa·kir (fə-kîr′) *n.* A Hindu or Moslem religious beggar, esp. one performing feats of endurance or magic.

fal·con (făl′kən, fôl′-, fō′kən) *n.* A bird of prey of the family Falconidae, having powerful wings adapted for swift flight. **—fal′con·er** *n.* **—fal′con·ry** *n.*

fall (fôl) *v.* **fell** (fĕl), **fall·en** (fô′lən), **fall·ing. 1.** To drop down freely under the influence of gravity. **2.** To come down from an erect position, esp. suddenly : collapse. **3.** To be severely wounded or killed in battle. **4.** To hang down, as hair. **5.** To assume an expression of disquiet or disappointment <The child's face *fell.*> **6. a.** To be overthrown or conquered. **b.** To suffer ruin or failure. **7.** To slope downward. **8.** To lessen or diminish. **9.** To decline in rank, status, or importance. **10.** To act immorally : err or sin. **11.** To pass into a specific state or situation <*fall* silent><*fall* in love> **12.** To come as if by descending <Night *fell* quickly.> **13.** To happen at a given time or place. **14.** To be allotted or assigned <The worst job *fell* to me.> **15.** To be within the scope or range of something. **16.** To come to rest by chance <My gaze *fell* on the tree. ☆***syns:*** DROP, PITCH, PLUNGE, SPILL, SPRAWL, TOPPLE, TUMBLE **—fall back.** To give ground : retreat. **—fall back on** (or **upon**). To resort to. **—fall for.** *Informal.* **1.** To fall in love with. **2.** To be deceived by. **—fall in.** To take one's place in a military formation. **—fall off.** To become less : decrease. **—fall on** (or **upon**). To attack without warning. **—fall out.** To quarrel. **—fall through.** To collapse or fail. *—n.* **1.** An act of falling. **2.** Something that has fallen <a *fall* of snow> **3. a.** An amount that has fallen. **b.** The distance that something falls. **4.** *often* **Fall.** Autumn. **5. falls** *(sing. or pl. in number).* A waterfall. **6.** A woman's hair piece with long hair. **7.** An overthrow : collapse <the *fall* of a monarchy> **8.** A reduction or decline. **9.** A moral lapse or loss of innocence.

fal·la·cious (fə-lā′shəs) *adj.* **1.** Containing or based on fundamental errors in reasoning. **2.** Misleading : deceptive.
fal·la·cy (făl′ə-sē) *n., pl.* **-cies. 1.** A false notion. **2.** A statement or argument based on a false or invalid inference.
fall·back (fôl′băk′) *n.* **1.** A mechanism for carrying out programmed instructions despite malfunction or failure of the primary device. **2.** Something to which one can retreat or resort.
fall guy *n. Slang.* **1.** A scapegoat. **2.** A gullible victim : dupe.
fal·li·ble (făl′ə-bəl) *adj.* **1.** Capable of making an error. **2.** Apt to be erroneous. **–fal′li·bil′i·ty** *n.* **–fal′li·bly** *adv.*
fall·ing-out (fô′lĭng-out′) *n., pl.* **fall·ings-out** *or* **fall·ing-outs.** A disagreement : quarrel.
falling star *n.* An object, as a meteoroid, often visible as a result of being ignited by atmospheric friction.
fall·off (fôl′ôf′, -ŏf′) *n.* A decrease.
Fal·lo·pi·an tube (fə-lō′pē-ən) *n.* Either of 2 slender ducts connecting the uterus to the region of each of the ovaries in females of higher vertebrates.
fall·out (fôl′out′) *n.* **1. a.** Slow descent through the atmosphere of minute particles of radioactive debris after a nuclear explosion. **b.** The radioactive debris itself. **2.** An incidental result or side effect.
fal·low (făl′ō) *adj.* **1.** Plowed but left unsown during a growing season. **2.** Marked by inactivity <talents lying *fallow*> **–fal′low** *n.* & *v.* **–fal′low·ness** *n.*
fallow deer *n.* Either of 2 Eurasian deer, *Dama dama* or *D. mesopotamica,* having a yellowish coat spotted with white in summer and broad antlers in the male.
false (fôls) *adj.* **fals·er, fals·est. 1.** Being contrary to truth or fact. **2.** Deliberately untrue or deceptive. **3.** Unfaithful : treacherous. **4.** Not real or natural : artificial. **5.** *Mus.* Of incorrect pitch. *–adv.* In a faithless manner. **–false′ly** *adv.* **–false′ness** *n.* **–fal′si·ty** *n.*
false-heart·ed (fôls′här′tĭd) *adj.* Deceitful or disloyal.
false·hood (fôls′ho͝od′) *n.* **1.** Inaccuracy. **2.** The act of lying. **3.** A lie.
fal·set·to (fôl-sĕt′ō) *n., pl.* **-tos. 1.** A male singing voice marked by artificially produced tones in an upper register. **2.** A man who sings falsetto. **–fal·set′to** *adv.*
fal·si·fy (fôl′sə-fī′) *v.* **-fied, -fy·ing. 1.** To give an untruthful account of. **2. a.** To make false by altering or adding to. **b.** To counterfeit : forge. **–fal′si·fi·ca′tion** *n.* **–fal′si·fi′er** *n.*
fal·ter (fôl′tər) *v.* **1.** To waver : hesitate. **2.** To speak hesitatingly : stammer. **3.** To move, operate, or perform ineptly or unsteadily. *–n.* **1.** Unsteadiness in action or speech. **2.** A faltering sound. **–fal′ter·er** *n.* **–fal′ter·ing·ly** *adv.*
fame (fām) *n.* **1.** Great renown. **2.** Public esteem. **–famed** *adj.*
fa·mil·iar (fə-mĭl′yər) *adj.* **1.** Encountered frequently : common. **2.** Having good knowledge of something. **3.** Of established friendship : intimate. **4.** Informal <lectured in a *familiar* style> **5.** Taking undue liberties : presumptuous. *–n.* **1.** A close friend or associate. **2.** A spirit, often taking animal form, believed to serve esp. a witch. **–fa·mil′iar·ly′** *adv.*
fa·mil·i·ar·i·ty (fə-mĭl′ē-ăr′ĭ-tē) *n., pl.* **-ties. 1.** Acquaintance with or knowledge of something. **2.** Established friendship. **3.** Undue liberty : impropriety.
fa·mil·iar·ize (fə-mĭl′yə-rīz′) *v.* **-ized, -iz·ing. 1.** To make familiar, known, or recognized. **2.** To make acquainted with. **–fa·mil′iar·i·za′tion** *n.*
fam·i·ly (făm′ə-lē, făm′lē) *n., pl.* **-lies. 1.** A social unit consisting esp. of a man and woman and their offspring. **2.** A group of people sharing common ancestry. **3.** All the members of a household. **4.** A group of like things : class. **5.** *Biol.* A taxonomic category below an order and above a genus. **–fa·mil′ial** (fə-mĭl′yəl) *adj.*
family tree *n.* **1.** A genealogical diagram of a family. **2.** The ancestors and descendants of a family.
fam·ine (făm′ĭn) *n.* **1.** A drastic, wide-ranging food shortage. **2.** A drastic shortage : dearth. **3.** Severe hunger : starvation.
fam·ish (făm′ĭsh) *v.* To starve or cause to starve. **–fam′ished** *adj.*
fa·mous (fā′məs) *adj.* **1.** Well-known. **2.** *Informal.* Excellent. ☆**syns:** CELEBRATED, DISTINGUISHED, EMINENT, FAMED, ILLUSTRIOUS, NOTED, PRE-EMINENT, PROMINENT, RENOWNED **–fa′mous·ly** *adv.*
fan[1] (făn) *n.* **1.** A device for creating a current of air, as a handheld usu. wedge-shaped, lightweight implement or a machine that rotates thin, rigid vanes. **2.** Something that is similar to an open fan. *–v.* **fanned, fan·ning. 1.** To direct movement of a current of air upon. **2.** To stir up by or as if by fanning. **3.** To spread like a fan. **4.** *Baseball.* To strike out.
fan[2] (făn) *n. Informal.* An ardent devotee.
fa·nat·ic (fə-năt′ĭk) *n.* One having excessive zeal for and irrational attachment to a cause or position. **–fa·nat′ic, fa·nat′i·cal** *adj.* **–fa·nat′i·cism** *n.*
fan·ci·er (făn′sē-ər) *n.* One having a special enthusiasm for or interest in something, esp. breeding a certain plant or animal <a rose *fancier*><a cat *fancier*>
fan·ci·ful (făn′sĭ-fəl) *adj.* **1.** Created in the fancy : unreal. **2.** Tending to indulge in fancy. **3.** Exhibiting invention or whimsy in design : imaginative. **–fan′ci·ful·ly** *adv.* **–fan′ci·ful·ness** *n.*
fan·cy (făn′sē) *n., pl.* **-cies. 1. a.** Imagination, esp. of a fantastic or whimsical nature. **b.** An image created by the mind. **2.** A capricious notion. **3.** Capricious inclination or liking. **4.** Critical sensibility : taste. ☆**syns:** CAPRICE, CONCEIT, HUMOR, IMPULSE, NOTION, VAGARY, WHIM, WHIMSY *–adj.* **-ci·er, -ci·est. 1.** Highly decorated. **2.** Arising in the fancy : capricous. **3.** Skillfully executed. **4.** Of superior grade : fine. **5.** Excessive : exorbitant. *–v.* **-cied, -cy·ing. 1.** To visualize : imagine. **2.** To take a fancy to : like. **3.** To suppose : guess. *–interj.* Used to express surprise. **–fan′ci·ly** *adv.* **–fan′ci·ness** *n.*
fancy dress *n.* A masquerade costume. **–fan′cy-dress′** *adj.*
fan·cy-free (făn′sē-frē′) *adj.* **1.** Carefree. **2.** Not in love : unattached.
fan·cy·work (făn′sē-wûrk′) *n.* Decorative needlework.
fan·dan·go (făn-dăng′gō) *n., pl.* **-gos. 1.** An animated Spanish or Spanish-American dance. **2.** Music for a fandango.
fan·fare (făn′fâr′) *n.* **1.** A loud trumpet flourish. **2.** A spectacular public display.
fang (făng) *n.* **1.** One of the hollow, grooved teeth with which a poisonous snake injects its venom. **2.** A long, pointed tooth of a carnivore. **–fanged** *adj.*

fang
(Left) *of a cat and* (right) *of a snake*

fan·jet (făn′jĕt′) *n.* An aircraft equipped with turbojet engines.
fan mail *n.* Mail sent to a public figure by admirers.
fan·tail (făn′tāl′) *n.* **1.** A fanlike tail or end. **2.** Something, as a bird or fish, having a fanlike tail. **–fan′tailed′** *adj.*
fan·ta·sia (făn-tā′zhə, -zhē-ə, făn′tə-zē′ə) *n. Mus.* A composition structured according to the composer's fancy.
fan·ta·size (făn′tə-sīz′) *v.* **-sized, -siz·ing.** To imagine or indulge in fantasies.
fan·tas·tic (făn-tăs′tĭk) *adj.* **1.** Existing only in the fancy : unreal. **2. a.** Extravagant. **b.** Bizarre. **3.** Capricious or fancifully eccentric. **4.** *Informal.* Superb : wonderful. **–fan·tas′ti·cal·ly** *adv.*
fan·ta·sy (făn′tə-sē, -zē) *n., pl.* **-sies. 1.** Creative imagination. **2.** A creation of the fancy. **3.** A capricious or fantastic idea : conceit. **4.** Fiction marked by highly fanciful or supernatural elements. **5.** *Psychol.* An imagined event fulfilling a wish. **6.** *Mus.* A fantasia.
far (fär) *adv.* **1. a.** To, at, or from a considerable distance. **b.** To a considerable degree : much. **2.** To or at a specific distance, degree, or position. **3.** Not at all : anything but. **4.** To an advanced point or stage <a student who will go *far*> *–adj.* **1.** At considerable distance. **2.** More distant. **3.** Extensive or lengthy. **4.** Of an extreme nature <the *far* right> ☆**syns:** DISTANT, FARAWAY, FAR-OFF, REMOTE, REMOVED **–by far.** To a considerable degree. **–far and away.** By a great margin. **–far and wide.** Everywhere. **–so far. 1.** Up to the present moment. **2.** To a limited degree.
far·ad (făr′əd, -ăd′) *n.* A unit of capacitance equal to the capacitance of a capacitor having a charge of 1 coulomb on each plate and a potential difference of 1 volt between the plates.
far·a·way (făr′ə-wā′) *adj.* **1.** Very distant : remote. **2.** Dreamy <a *faraway* look>
farce (färs) *n.* **1.** A theater piece marked by humorous characterizations and improbable plots. **2.** A ludicrous show : mockery. **3.** A seasoned stuffing. **–far′ci·cal** *adj.*
fare (fâr) *v.* **fared, far·ing. 1.** To get along. **2.** To turn out : go. **3.** To feed on : eat. *–n.* **1.** A transportation charge, as for a bus. **2.** A passenger transported for a fee. **3.** Food and drink : diet <peasant *fare*> **–far′er** *n.*
Far East. SE Asia and the Malay archipelago. **–Far Eastern** *adj.* & *n.*

fare-thee-well (fâr′thē-wĕl′) *n.* **1.** Perfection. **2.** The most extreme degree.
fare·well (fâr-wĕl′) *interj.* Used to say good-by. —*n.* **1.** A good-by. **2.** A departure. **—fare′well′** *adj.*
far-fetched (fär′fĕcht′) *adj.* Highly improbable.
far-flung (fär′flŭng′) *adj.* **1.** Widely distributed. **2.** Distant : remote.
fa·ri·na (fə-rē′nə) *n.* Fine meal prepared from cereal grain or other plant products, used as a cooked cereal or in puddings.
far·i·na·ceous (făr′ə-nā′shəs) *adj.* **1.** Made from, rich in, or composed of starch. **2.** Powdery or mealy in texture.
farm (färm) *n.* **1.** Land cultivated for agricultural production. **2. a.** Land used for the breeding and raising of domestic animals. **b.** An area of water used for the breeding and raising of a particular type of aquatic animals <a trout *farm*> **3.** *Baseball.* A minor-league team affiliated with a major-league team for training recruits and maintaining temporarily unneeded players. —*v.* **1.** To raise livestock or crops as a business. **2.** To use (land or a body of water) for this purpose. **—farm out. 1.** To send (work) from a central point to be done elsewhere. **2.** *Baseball.* To assign (a player) to a minor-league team. **—farm′er** *n.*
farmer cheese *n.* A cheese like cottage cheese but drier and firmer in texture.
farm·house (färm′hous′) *n.* A farm dwelling.
farm·land (färm′lănd′, -lənd) *n.* Land suitable for agricultural production.
farm·stead (färm′stĕd′) *n.* A farm, including its land and buildings.
farm team *n.* *Baseball.* A minor-league team.
farm·yard (färm′yärd′) *n.* An area surrounded by or near farm buildings.
far-off (fär′ôf′, -ŏf′) *adj.* Remote : distant.
far-out (fär′out′) *adj.* *Slang.* Very unconventional.
far·ra·go (fə-rä′gō, -rā′-) *n., pl.* **-goes.** A medley : conglomeration.
far-reach·ing (fär′rē′chĭng) *adj.* Having a wide range, influence, or effect.
far·row (făr′ō) *n.* A litter of pigs. —*v.* To produce a farrow.
far·see·ing (fär′sē′ĭng) *adj.* **1.** FAR-SIGHTED 2. **2.** Keen-sighted.
far·sight·ed (fär′sī′tĭd) *adj.* **1.** Able to see objects at a distance better than those that are nearby. **2.** Planning prudently for the future : foresighted. **—far-sight′ed·ly** *adv.* **—far-sight′ed·ness** *n.*
far·ther (fär′thər) *adv.* **1.** To or at a greater distance. **2.** In addition. **3.** To a greater extent or degree. —*adj.* **1.** More distant or remote. **2.** Additional.
far·ther·most (fär′thər-mōst′) *adj.* Farthest.
far·thest (fär′thĭst) *adj.* Most distant. —*adv.* To or at the most distant point in space or time.
far·thing (fär′thĭng) *n.* **1.** A former British coin worth ¼ of a penny. **2.** Something of little worth.
far·thin·gale (fär′thĭng-gāl′) *n.* A support, as a hoop, worn by 16th- and 17th-cent. women to make skirts swell out.

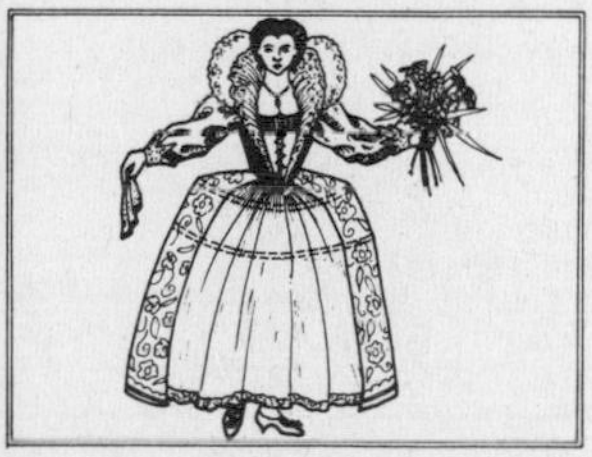

farthingale

fas·ci·nate (făs′ə-nāt′) *v.* **-nat·ed, -nat·ing. 1.** To attract intensely and irresistibly. **2.** To hold motionless : spellbind. **—fas′ci·nat′ing·ly** *adv.* **—fas′ci·na′tion** *n.* **—fas′ci·na′tor** *n.*
fas·cism (făsh′ĭz′əm) *n.* A governmental system marked by a centralized dictatorship, stringent socioeconomic controls, and often belligerent nationalism. **—fas′cist** *n.* **—fas·cis′tic** (fə-shĭs′tĭk) *adj.*
fash·ion (făsh′ən) *n.* **1.** The aspect or configuration of something. **2.** Kind : variety. **3.** Manner of performing : way. **4.** Current style or custom. **5.** A piece of clothing in the current style. —*v.* **1.** To make into a given form or shape. **2.** To make fitting : adapt. **—fash′ion·a·ble** *adj.* **—fash′ion·a·ble·ness** *n.* **—fash′ion·a·bly** *adv.*
fast[1] (făst) *adj.* **1.** Rapid : swift. **2.** Performed quickly. **3.** Ahead of the actual time <a *fast* watch> **4.** Suited to rapid travel, as an expressway lane. **5. a.** Dissipated : wild. **b.** Flouting conventional sexual standards. **6.** Resistant <acid-*fast*> **7.** Securely fixed or fastened. **8.** Tightly shut : secure. **9.** Constant and loyal, as friends. **10.** Resistant to fading <*fast* dyes> **11.** Deep and undisturbed <in a *fast* sleep> **12.** Designed for or compatible with a short exposure time <*fast* camera film> —*adv.* **1.** Securely : tightly. **2.** Deeply : soundly <*fast* asleep> **3.** Quickly : rapidly. **4.** In a dissipated, immoderate way <living *fast*> **—fast′ness** *n.*
fast[2] (făst) *v.* To eat sparingly or abstain from all or certain foods. **—fast** *n.*
fast·back (făst′băk′) *n.* A car with a downward curving slope from roof to rear.
fast-breed·er reactor (făst′brē′dər) *n.* A breeder reactor that requires high-energy neutrons to produce fissionable material.

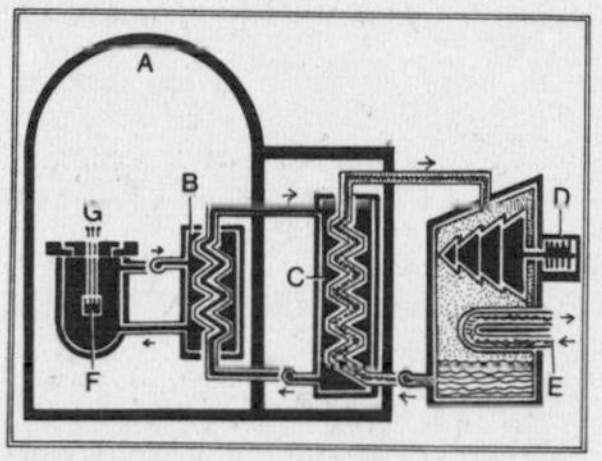

fast-breeder reactor
A. containment structure, B. heat exchange, C. steam generator, D. turbine generator, E. cooling water, F. core, G. control rods

fas·ten (făs′ən) *v.* **1.** To join or become joined to something else : connect. **2. a.** To fix securely. **b.** To close or shut. **3.** To focus steadily. **—fas′ten·er** *n.*
fast-food (făst′fo͞od′) *adj.* Specializing in foods prepared and served quickly.
fas·tid·i·ous (fă-stĭd′ē-əs, fə-) *adj.* **1.** Meticulously attentive to details. **2.** Difficult to please : exacting. **—fas·tid′i·ous·ly** *adv.* **—fas·tid′i·ous·ness** *n.*
fast-talk (făst′tôk′) *v.* To affect or influence, esp. by glib, deceptive talk. **—fast′-talk′er** *n.*
fast-track (făst-trăk) *adj.* High-powered and aggressive <a *fast-track* career>
fat (făt) *n.* **1. a.** Any of various soft solid or semisolid organic compounds that are energy-rich and occur widely in animal tissue and in the nuts, seeds, and fruits of plants. **b.** The tissue that contains a high proportion of such substances. **2.** Obesity : corpulence. **3.** The most desirable part. —*adj.* **fat·ter, fat·test. 1.** Having much or too much flesh or fat. **2.** Greasy : oily. **3.** Abounding in desirable elements. **4.** Fertile or productive : rich. **5.** Abundant : ample <a *fat* paycheck> **6.** Thick : large. ☆**syns:** CORPULENT, FLESHY, GROSS, OBESE, OVERWEIGHT, PORCINE, PORTLY, STOUT, WEIGHTY —*v.* **fat·ted, fat·ting.** To make or become fat. **—fat′ness** *n.* **—fat′ti·ness** *n.* **—fat′ty** *adj.*
fa·tal (fāt′l) *adj.* **1.** Causing death : deadly. **2.** Causing ruin : disastrous. **3.** Decisively important : fateful. **4.** Affecting one's destiny. **—fa·tal′ly** *adv.*

▲word history: The Latin adjective *fatalis,* the source of English *fatal,* meant primarily "destined by fate," but in later Latin it also took on the malign senses of the noun *fatum,* "fate," from which it is derived, and meant "deadly, destructive." English adopted *fatal* with its neutral Latin meaning, though the pejorative sense, "causing ruin or death," has now supplanted the more neutral sense "destined."

fa·tal·ism (făt′l-ĭz′əm) *n.* The belief that events are predetermined by fate and cannot be altered. **—fa′tal·ist** *n.* **—fa′tal·is′tic** *adj.* **—fa′tal·is′ti·cal·ly** *adv.*
fa·tal·i·ty (fă-tăl′ĭ-tē, fə-) *n., pl.* **-ties. 1.** Death by accident or disaster. **2.** A deadly effect : deadliness. **3.** The quality or state of being doomed to disaster.
fat·back (făt′băk′) *n.* The strip of salt-cured fat taken from the upper part of a pork side.
fat cat *n.* *Slang.* **1.** A wealthy, powerful person. **2.** A rich person who contributes heavily to a political campaign.
fate (fāt) *n.* **1.** The power or force held to predetermine events. **2.** Fortune : lot. **3.** A final result. **4.** Unfortunate destiny : doom. ☆**syns:** DESTINY, KISMET, LOT, PORTION, PREDESTINATION
fat·ed (fā′tĭd) **1.** Controlled by fate. **2.** Doomed.
fate·ful (fāt′fəl) *adj.* **1.** Decisively significant. **2.** Governed by fate. **3.** Portentous : ominous. **4.** Bringing disaster or death. **—fate′ful·ly** *adv.* **—fate′ful·ness** *n.*
fa·ther (fä′thər) *n.* **1. a.** A male parent. **b.** A child's male ancestor : forefather. **2.** An originator. **3. Father.** GOD 3. **4. Father.** A priest. Used esp. as a title. **5.** *often* **Father.** One of the authoritative early Christian writers who formulated doctrines and codified observances. **6.** A venerable elderly man. **7.** A promi-

nent citizen <the city *fathers*> —*v.* **1.** To beget. **2.** To act or serve as a father (to). **—fa'ther·hood'** *n.* **—fa'ther·less** *adj.* **—fa'ther·li·ness** *n.* **—fa'ther·ly** *adj.*

fa·ther-in-law (fä'thər-ĭn-lô') *n., pl.* **fa·thers-in-law.** The father of one's spouse.

fa·ther·land (fä'thər-lănd') *n.* **1.** One's native land. **2.** The native land of one's ancestors.

fath·om (făth'əm) *n., pl.* **-oms** *or* **-om.** A unit of length equal to 6 ft or approx. 1.83 m, used chiefly in measuring marine depths. —*v.* **1.** To determine the depth of : sound. **2.** To understand fully. **—fath'om·a·ble** *adj.*

fath·om·less (făth'əm-lĭs) *adj.* **1.** Too deep to be measured. **2.** Too difficult to understand.

fa·tigue (fə-tēg') *n.* **1.** Extreme weariness from prolonged exertion or stress. **2.** Manual labor assigned to military personnel. **3. fatigues.** Military clothes for heavy work and field duty. —*v.* **-tigued, -tigu·ing.** To make or become tired out : exhaust. **—fat'i·ga·ble** (făt'ĭ-gə-bəl) *adj.*

fat·ten (făt'n) *v.* **1.** To make or become fat. **2.** To increase the amount of.

fatty acid *n.* Any of a class of organic acids obtained from decomposing fat, esp. those of a commercially valuable subgroup derived from animals and plants.

fa·tu·i·ty (fə-to͞o'ĭ-tē, -tyo͞o'-) *n.* Stupidity : absurdity.

fat·u·ous (făch'o͞o-əs) *adj.* Complacently foolish : silly. **—fat'u·ous·ly** *adv.* **—fat'u·ous·ness** *n.*

fau·bourg (fō'bo͝org', fō-bo͝or') *n.* **1.** A suburb, esp. of a French city. **2.** An inner city district or quarter.

fau·cet (fô'sĭt) *n.* A fixture for drawing liquid, as from a pipe or cask.

Faulk·ner (fôk'nər), **William.** 1897–1962. Amer. author.

fault (fôlt) *n.* **1.** A defect or impairment : weakness. **2.** A mistake or minor offense. **3.** Responsibility for a mistake or offense : culpability. **4.** *Geol.* A break in the earth's crust in which adjoining surfaces are shifted in a direction parallel to the crack. **5.** A bad service, as in tennis. —*v.* **1.** To criticize. **2.** To produce a geologic fault (in). **3.** To commit a fault or error. **—fault'i·ly** *adv.* **—fault'less** *adj.* **—fault'less·ly** *adv.* **—fault'y** *adj.*

fault·find·er (fôlt'fīn'dər) *n.* A petty critic. **—fault'find'ing** *n.* & *adj.*

faun (fôn) *n. Rom. Myth.* A rural deity represented as part goat and part man.

fau·na (fô'nə) *n., pl.* **-nas** *or* **-nae** (-nē'). Animals as a group, esp. of a given time or region. **—fau'nal** *adj.*

Faust (foust) *n.* A legendary German magician who sold his soul to the devil for power and worldly experience.

fau·vism (fō'vĭz'əm) *n.* An art movement marked by the use of flamboyant colors and bold, often distorted forms.

faux pas (fō pä') *n.,pl.* **faux pas** (fō päz'). A social blunder.

fa·vor (fā'vər) *n.* **1.** A kind or friendly attitude. **2.** A kind act. **3.** An indulgence : privilege. **4. a.** Friendly regard and approval shown esp. by a superior : partiality. **b.** The condition of being held in this regard. **5.** Approval or support : sanction. **6. favors.** Sexual privileges, esp. as granted by a woman. **7.** A token of love or remembrance. **8.** A small gift given to guests at a party. **9.** Advantage : benefit <decided in our *favor*> —*v.* **1.** To oblige kindly. **2.** To like or prefer. **3.** To approve or support. **4.** To facilitate or help. **5.** To look like : resemble. **6.** To treat carefully <*favor* a sore leg> **—fa'vor·er** *n.* **—fa'vor·ing·ly** *adv.*

fa·vor·a·ble (fā'vər-ə-bəl, fāv'rə-) *adj.* **1.** Advantageous : beneficial. **2.** Promising : encouraging. **3.** Approving. **—fa'vor·a·ble·ness** *n.* **—fa'vor·a·bly** *adv.*

fa·vor·ite (fā'vər-ĭt, fāv'rĭt) *n.* **1.** One that is preferred above all others. **2.** One esp. indulged by a superior. **3.** A contestant considered to be the most likely winner. **—fa'vor·ite** *adj.*

favorite son *n.* One favored by his own state delegates for nomination at a national political convention.

fa·vor·it·ism (fā'vər-ĭ-tĭz'əm, fāv'rə-) *n.* A display of often unjust partiality : bias.

fa·vour (fā'vər) *n.* & *v. esp. Brit. var. of* FAVOR.

fawn[1] (fôn) *n.* **1.** A young deer less than a year old. **2.** A light grayish brown.

fawn[2] (fôn) *v.* **1.** To display slavish affection. **2.** To seek favor by servile groveling. **—fawn'er** *n.* **—fawn'ing·ly** *adv.*

fay (fā) *n.* A fairy or elf.

faze (fāz) *v.* **fazed, faz·ing.** To disconcert : discompose.

F.B. *abbr.* freight bill.

FBI *also* **F.B.I.** *abbr.* Federal Bureau of Investigation.

Fe *symbol for* IRON.

fe·al·ty (fē'əl-tē) *n., pl.* **-ties. 1.** Loyalty and allegiance owed to a feudal lord. **2.** Faithfulness.

fear (fîr) *n.* **1. a.** Alarm and agitation caused by expectation or realization of danger. **b.** An example of this feeling. **2.** Reverence : awe. **3.** A state of dread or apprehension <living in fear> —*v.* **1.** To be frightened (of). **2.** To be apprehensive (about). **3.** To be in awe of : revere <*fear* God> **4.** To suspect <I *fear* you are mistaken.> **—fear'er** *n.* **—fear'ful** *adj.* **—fear'ful·ly** *adv.* **—fear'ful·ness** *n.* **—fear'less** *adj.* **—fear'less·ly** *adv.* **—fear'less·ness** *n.*

fear·some (fîr'səm) *adj.* **1.** Causing or able to cause fear. **2.** Timid. **—fear'some·ly** *adv.* **—fear'some·ness** *n.*

fea·si·ble (fē'zə-bəl) *adj.* **1.** Able to be accomplished : possible. **2.** Appropriate : suitable. **3.** Likely. **—fea'si·bil'i·ty, fea'si·ble·ness** *n.* **—fea'si·bly** *adv.*

feast (fēst) *n.* **1.** A periodic religious festival. **2.** A large elaborate meal, usu. for many people : banquet. —*v.* **1.** To give a feast for. **2.** To provide with pleasure : delight. **3.** To eat heartily or with pleasure. **—feast'er** *n.*

feat (fēt) *n.* A notable achievement or exploit. ☆**syns:** ACHIEVEMENT, EXPLOIT, GEST, MASTERSTROKE, STUNT, TOUR DE FORCE

feath·er (fĕth'ər) *n.* **1.** One of the light hollow-shafted structures that form the external covering of birds. **2. feathers.** Plumage. **3. feathers.** Clothing, esp. finery. **4.** Character : nature. —*v.* **1.** To cover, adorn, or line with feathers. **2.** To fit (an arrow) with a feather. **3.** To turn (an oar blade) horizontal to the surface of the water between strokes. **4.** To alter the pitch of (a propeller) so the blades are parallel with the line of flight. **—a feather in (one's) cap.** A creditable achievement. **—in fine feather.** In an excellent mood or condition. **—feath'er·i·ness** *n.* **—feath'er·less** *adj.* **—feath'er·y** *n.*

feather bed *n.* **1.** A mattress stuffed with feathers. **2.** A bed with a feather mattress.

feath·er·bed·ding (fĕth'ər-bĕd'ĭng) *n.* The practice of requiring an employer to limit production or employ more workers than needed because of safety regulations or union rules. **—feath'er·bed'** *v.*

feath·er·edge (fĕth'ər-ĕj') *n.* A thin fragile edge, esp. of a board.

feath·er·stitch (fĕth'ər-stĭch') *n.* An embroidery stitch that produces a decorative zigzag line. **—feath'er·stitch'** *v.*

feath·er·weight (fĕth'ər-wāt') *n.* **1.** A boxer whose weight is between 188 and 127 lb or approx. 54 and 57 kg. **2.** One of little weight, size, or significance.

fea·ture (fē'chər) *n.* **1. a.** The shape or appearance of the face. **b. features.** The face or its parts. **2.** A conspicuous or distinctive characteristic. **3.** The main presentation at a movie theater. **4.** A prominent article in a newspaper or magazine. **5.** A special sales attraction or inducement. —*v.* **-tured, -tur·ing. 1.** To give special attention to : publicize. **2.** To have as a characteristic. **3.** To depict the features of.

Feb. *abbr.* February.

feb·ri·fuge (fĕb'rə-fyo͞oj') *n.* A fever-reducing agent.

feb·rile (fĕb'rəl, fē'brəl) *adj.* Of or marked by a fever : feverish.

Feb·ru·ar·y (fĕb'ro͞o-ĕr'ē, fĕb'yo͞o-) *n., pl.* **-ies** *or* **-ys.** The 2nd month of the year, having 28 days, 29 in leap years.

fe·ces (fē'sēz) *pl.n.* Bodily waste excreted from the bowels : excrement. **—fe'cal** (-kəl) *adj.*

feck·less (fĕk'lĭs) *adj.* **1.** Ineffective : weak. **2.** Careless and irresponsible. **—feck'less·ly** *adv.* **—feck'less·ness** *n.*

fe·cund (fē'kənd, fĕk'ənd) *adj.* Productive or fruitful. **—fe·cun'di·ty** *n.*

fe·cun·date (fē'kən-dāt', fĕk'ən-) *v.* **-dat·ed, -dat·ing.** To fertilize.

fed (fĕd) *v. p.t.* & *p.p. of* FEED.

fed. *abbr.* federal; federated; federation.

fed·er·al (fĕd'ər-əl) *adj.* **1.** Of or designating government in which individual states retain certain controlling powers and are united under a central authority. **2. a.** *often* **Federal.** Of or pertaining to the U.S. central government. **b. Federal.** *Can.* Of or pertaining to the central government of Canada. **3. Federal.** Of or supporting the Union in the American Civil War. —*n.* **Federal.** A soldier or supporter of the Union during the American Civil War. **—fed'er·al·ly** *adv.*

fed·er·al·ism (fĕd'ər-ə-lĭz'əm) *n.* **1.** The doctrine or organizational system of federal government. **2.** Advocacy of this system. **—fed'er·al·ist** *n.*

fed·er·al·ize (fĕd'ər-ə-līz') *v.* **-ized, -iz·ing. 1.** To join in a federal union. **2.** To put under the control of a federal government. **—fed'er·al·i·za'tion** *n.*

fed·er·ate (fĕd'ə-rāt') *v.* **-at·ed, -at·ing.** To unite or join, as in a league or federal union. **—fed'e·ra'tion** *n.*

fe·do·ra (fĭ-dôr'ə, -dōr'ə) *n.* A felt hat with a low crown creased lengthwise and a brim that can be turned up or down.

fed up *adj.* Extremely annoyed or disgusted.

fee (fē) *n.* **1.** A fixed charge <tuition *fees*> **2.** A charge for professional service <a lawyer's *fee*> **3.** *Law.* An inherited estate in land. **4.** A fief.

fee·ble (fē'bəl) *adj.* **-bler, -blest. 1.** Without strength : weak.

2. Lacking force : ineffective or inadequate. **–fee'ble·ness** *n.* **–fee'bly** *adv.*
fee·ble-mind·ed (fē'bəl-mīn'dĭd) *adj.* Intellectually subnormal. **–fee'ble-mind'ed·ness** *n.*
feed (fēd) *v.* **fed** (fĕd), **feed·ing. 1.** To supply with food or provide as food. **2.** To consume food. **3.** To supply for consumption or use. *–n.* **1.** Food for animals : fodder. **2.** *Informal.* A meal. **3. a.** Material fed into a machine. **b.** A device that supplies such material <a paper *feed*> **–feed'er** *n.*
feed·back (fēd'băk') *n.* **1.** Return of a portion of the output of a process or system to the input. **2. a.** Return of data about the result of a process, esp. for correction or control. **b.** The data so returned.
feed·lot (fēd'lŏt') *n.* A place where livestock are fattened for market.
feed·stock (fēd'stŏk') *n.* The raw materials required for an industrial process.
feed·stuff (fēd'stŭf') *n.* FEED 1.
feel (fēl) *v.* **felt** (fĕlt), **feel·ing. 1. a.** To perceive through the sense of touch. **b.** To perceive as a physical sensation <*feel* a dull pain> <*feel* the heat> **2. a.** To touch. **b.** To examine by touching. **3. a.** To undergo the experience of. **b.** To be aware of a sense. **c.** To suffer from emotionally. **4.** To believe : consider. **5.** To have compassion or pity. *–n.* **1.** Perception by touching <the *feel* of velvet> **2.** The sense of touch. **3.** The nature, state, or quality of something perceived through or as if through touch <the *feel* of a new sports car>
feel·er (fē'lər) *n.* **1.** An exploratory remark or suggestion. **2.** A sensory or tactile organ, as an antenna, tentacle, or barbel.
feel·ing (fē'lĭng) *n.* **1. a.** The sensation involving tactile perception. **b.** A sensation perceived by touch. **c.** A physical sensation. **2. a.** Emotion, esp. compassion or sympathy. **b. feelings.** Sensibilities <You hurt my *feelings.*> **3. a.** A mental awareness. **b.** A distinct mood or impression. **4. a.** Opinion : belief. **b.** Sentiment. **5.** Intuitive cognition : hunch. **6.** Emotional and intuitive awareness. **7.** An aptitude : bent. *–adj.* **1. a.** Exhibiting emotional sensitivity. **b.** Easily moved emotionally. **2.** Expressing sympathy. **–feel'ing·ly** *adv.*
feet (fēt) *n. pl. of* FOOT.
feign (fān) *v.* **1.** To give a false appearance (of). **2.** To dissemble : pretend.
feint (fānt) *n.* A misleading movement intended to draw defensive action away from the real target. **–feint** *v.*
†**feist** (fīst) *n. Regional.* A small mongrel dog.
†**feist·y** (fī'stē) *adj.* **-i·er, -i·est. 1.** *Regional.* Touchy : quarrelsome. **2.** Spirited : plucky.
feld·spar (fĕld'spär', fĕl'-) *n.* Any of a large group of minerals consisting largely of silicates that occur principally in igneus, plutonic, and some metamorphic rocks.
fe·lic·i·tate (fĭ-lĭs'ĭ-tāt') *v.* **-tat·ed, -tat·ing.** To wish happiness to : congratulate. **–fe·lic'i·ta'tion** *n.* **–fe·lic'i·ta'tor** *n.*
fe·lic·i·tous (fĭ-lĭs'ĭ-təs) *adj.* **1.** Well-chosen : apt. **2.** Agreeable in manner or style. **–fe·lic'i·tous·ly** *adv.* **–fe·lic'i·tous·ness** *n.*
fe·lic·i·ty (fĭ-lĭs'ĭ-tē) *n., pl.* **-ties. 1.** Blissful happiness. **2.** A cause of bliss. **3.** An apt style or manner of expression or an instance of it.
fe·line (fē'līn') *adj.* **1.** Of or relating to the family Felidae, including wild and domestic cats and related animals such as lions and tigers. **2.** Like a cat, as in stealth or agility. **–fe'line'** *n.* **–fe'line'ly** *adv.* **–fe'line'ness, fe·lin'i·ty** (fĭ-lĭn'ĭ-tē) *n.*
fell[1] (fĕl) *v.* **1.** To cut or knock down. **2.** To kill. **3.** To sew or finish (a seam) with the raw edges turned under and stitched down. **–fell'a·ble** *adj.* **–fell'er** *n.*
fell[2] (fĕl) *adj.* **1.** Fierce and cruel. **2.** Lethal. **–fell'ness** *n.*
fell[3] (fĕl) *n.* An animal's hide : pelt.
fell[4] (fĕl) *v. p.t. of* FALL.
fel·lah (fĕl'ə) *n., pl.* **-lahs** *or* **fel·la·hin** (fĕl'ə-hēn') *or* **-la·heen.** An Arab peasant or agricultural worker.
fel·low (fĕl'ō) *n.* **1.** A man or boy. **2.** *Informal.* A boyfriend. **3.** A comrade : associate. **4.** An equal : peer. **5.** One of a pair : counterpart. **6.** A member of a scientific or literary society. **7.** A recipient of a stipend for graduate study. *–adj.* Sharing certain characteristics, interests, or pursuits.
fel·low·ship (fĕl'ō-shĭp') *n.* **1.** Friendly relationship : companionship. **2.** A union of peers or friends : fraternity. **3. a.** A graduate scholarship or grant. **b.** A foundation awarding such scholarships or grants.
fel·on[1] (fĕl'ən) *n.* A perpetrator of a felony.
fel·on[2] (fĕl'ən) *n.* A festering inflammation near the end of a finger or toe.
fel·o·ny (fĕl'ə-nē) *n., pl.* **-nies.** A serious crime, as murder, rape, or burglary, punishable by a severe sentence. **–fe·lo'ni·ous** *adj.* **–fe·lo'ni·ous·ly** *adv.* **–fe·lo'ni·ous·ness** *n.*
felt[1] (fĕlt) *n.* **1.** A fabric made of matted, pressed animal fibers, as fur or wool. **2.** A fabric or material resembling felt. *–v.* **1.** To make into or become like felt. **2.** To press or mat together.
felt[2] (fĕlt) *v. p.t. & p.p. of* FEEL.
fem. *abbr.* female; feminine.
fe·male (fē'māl') *adj.* **1. a.** Of, relating to, typical of, or designating the sex that produces ova or bears young. **b.** Consisting of members of the female sex. **c.** Suitable to the female sex : feminine. **2.** *Bot.* **a.** Relating to or designating an organ, as a pistil, that produces seeds or spores after fertilization. **b.** Having pistils but not stamens. **3.** Having a hollow part designed to receive a projecting part, as a plug or prong. **–fe'male'** *n.* **–fe'male'ness** *n.*

▲word history: The word *female* is unrelated to the word *male. Female* is a respelling of *femelle,* which is ult. from Latin *femella,* a diminutive of *femina,* "woman." After its adoption into English from French in the 15th cent., *femelle* was used primarily as an adjective. This circumstance led to the respelling of the word as *femal,* where *–al* was regarded as the adjectival suffix. The spelling *femal,* as well as the word's obvious correlation with the word *male,* suggested an etymological association with the word *male.* This error has been preserved in the now standard modern spelling *female.*

fem·i·nine (fĕm'ə-nĭn) *adj.* **1.** Of or designating the female sex. **2.** Characterized by or possessing qualities gen. attributed to women. **3.** Of or designating the class of words or grammatical forms referring chiefly to females. *–n.* **1.** The feminine gender. **2.** A word or form of the feminine gender. **–fem'i·nine·ly** *adv.* **–fem'i·nin'i·ty** *n.*
fem·i·nism (fĕm'ə-nĭz'əm) *n.* **1.** Advocacy of the political and socioeconomic equality of men and women. **2.** The movement supporting feminism. **–fem'i·nist** *n.* **–fem'i·nis'tic** *adj.*
femme fa·tale (fĕm' fə-tăl', -täl', făm') *n., pl.* **femmes fa·tales** (fĕm' fə-tăl', -tălz', -täl', -tälz', făm'). A charming or seductive woman.
fe·mur (fē'mər) *n., pl.* **-murs** *or* **fem·o·ra** (fĕm'ər-ə). **1.** The bone of the vertebrate lower or hind limb, located between the pelvis and knee in humans. **2.** The human thigh. **–fem'o·ral** (fĕm'ər-əl) *adj.*
fen (fĕn) *n.* Low, marshy land : bog.
fence (fĕns) *n.* **1.** A structure that functions as a boundary or barrier, usu. constructed of posts, boards, wire, or rails. **2.** *Slang.* **a.** A recipient and seller of stolen goods. **b.** A place where such goods are sold. *–v.* **fenced, fenc·ing. 1.** To surround, close in, or separate by or as if by a fence. **2.** To engage in fencing. **3.** To be evasive : hedge. **4.** *Slang.* To receive and sell stolen goods. **–on the fence.** *Informal.* Undecided or neutral. **–fenc'er** *n.*
fenc·ing (fĕn'sĭng) *n.* **1.** The art or sport of using a foil, épée, or saber. **2.** Material used in building fences.
fend (fĕnd) *v.* **1.** To keep or ward off. **2.** To manage without help.
fend·er (fĕn'dər) *n.* A protective device, as a guard over the wheel of a vehicle or a fireplace screen.
fen·es·tra·tion (fĕn'ə-strā'shən) *n.* Design and position of windows and doors in a building.
fen·nel (fĕn'əl) *n.* A native Eurasian plant, *Foeniculum vulgare,* with an edible stalk and aromatic seeds used as flavoring.
fe·ral (fîr'əl, fĕr'-) *adj.* **1. a.** Existing in an untamed state. **b.** Having returned to a wild state from domestication. **2.** Of or like a wild animal : savage.
fer-de-lance (fĕr'də-läns') *n.* A venomous tropical American snake, *Bothrops atrox,* with brown and gray markings.
fer·ment (fûr'mĕnt') *n.* **1.** Something, as a yeast, mold, or enzyme, that causes fermentation. **2.** Great agitation or unrest. *–v.* (fər-mĕnt'). **1.** To undergo or subject to fermentation. **3.** To agitate : excite. **–fer·ment'a·bil'i·ty** *n.* **–fer·ment'a·ble** *adj.* **–fer·ment'er** *n.*
fer·men·ta·tion (fûr'mĕn-tā'shən) *n.* **1.** Chemical decomposition of complex organic compounds into simpler substances, esp. the process by which yeasts convert sugar to carbon dioxide and alcohol in the absence of oxygen. **2.** Great agitation : commotion.
fer·mi·um (fûr'mē-əm) *n. Symbol* **Fm** A synthetic metallic radioactive element.
fern (fûrn) *n.* Any of numerous flowerless and seedless plants of the class Filicinae that have fronds with divided leaflets and reproduce by spores. **–fern'y** *adj.*
fe·ro·cious (fə-rō'shəs) *adj.* **1.** Very fierce and cruel, as a wild animal. **2.** Extremely intense <a *ferocious* storm> **–fe·ro'cious·ly** *adv.* **–fe·ro'cious·ness, fe·roc'i·ty** (fə-rŏs'ĭ-tē) *n.*
fer·ret (fĕr'ĭt) *n.* **1.** A domesticated, usu. albino form of the Old World polecat, often trained to hunt rodents or rabbits. **2.** A related North American mammal, *Mustela nigripes,* with yellowish fur. *–v.* **1.** To hunt with ferrets. **2.** To drive out : expel. **3.**

To uncover and bring forward by searching, as a secret. **4.** To search intensively. **–fer'ret·er** *n.* **–fer'ret·y** *adj.*
fer·ric (fĕr'ĭk) *adj.* Of, pertaining to, or containing iron, esp. with valence 3.
ferric oxide *n.* A dark compound occurring as hematite ore and rust.
Fer·ris wheel *also* **fer·ris wheel** (fĕr'ĭs) *n.* A large upright, power-driven wheel with suspended compartments in which passengers ride for amusement.
fer·ro·mag·net·ic (fĕr'ō-măg-nĕt'ĭk) *adj.* Relating to or typical of substances, as iron and nickel, that are readily magnetized. **–fer'ro·mag'ne·tism** *n.*
fer·rous (fĕr'əs) *adj.* Of, pertaining to, or containing iron, esp. with valence 2.
fer·rule (fĕr'əl, -o͞ol') *n.* A ring or cap at or near the end of a wooden handle or cane to reinforce it or prevent splitting.

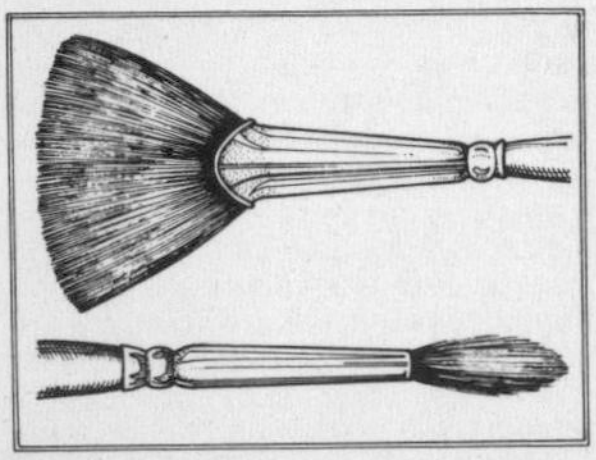

ferrule

fer·ry (fĕr'ē) *v.* **-ried, -ry·ing. 1.** To move or carry by boat across a body of water. **2.** To cross on or as if on a ferry. **3.** To carry from one point to another, esp by aircraft. *–n., pl.* **-ries. 1.** A ferryboat. **2.** The embarkation point for a ferryboat. **3.** The transporting of something, esp. an aircraft, under its own power to its end user.
fer·ry·boat (fĕr'ē-bōt') *n.* A boat used to transport passengers or goods.
fer·tile (fûr'tl) *adj.* **1.** *Biol.* **a.** Able to reproduce. **b.** Able to initiate, sustain, or support reproduction. **2.** Rich in material required to maintain plant growth <*fertile* farm land> **3.** Characterized by great productivity : prolific <a *fertile* intellect> ☆**syns:** FECUND, FRUITFUL, PRODUCTIVE, PROLIFIC, RICH **–fer'tile·ly** *adv.* **–fer·til'i·ty, fer'tile·ness** *n.*
fer·til·ize (fûr'tl-īz') *v.* **-ized, -iz·ing. 1.** To begin biological reproduction esp. by supplying with sperm or pollen. **2.** To make fertile, as by adding fertilizer. **–fer'til·iz'a·ble** *adj.* **–fer'til·i·za'tion** *n.*
fer·til·iz·er (fûr'tl-ī'zər) *n.* One that fertilizes, esp. a material such as manure, compost, or a chemical compound added to increase soil fertility.
fer·ule (fĕr'əl, -o͞ol') *n.* A baton, stick, or cane used to punish children.
fer·vent (fûr'vənt) *adj.* **1.** Ardent : passionate. **2.** Very hot. **–fer'ven·cy, fer'vent·ness** *n.* **–fer'vent·ly** *adv.*
fer·vid (fûr'vĭd) *adj.* **1.** Intensely fervent : impassioned. **2.** Very hot. **–fer'vid·ly** *adv.* **–fer'vid·ness** *n.*
fer·vor (fûr'vər) *n.* **1.** Emotional intensity : ardor. **2.** Intense heat.
fer·vour (fûr'vər) *n. esp. Brit. var. of* FERVOR.
fes·cue (fĕs'kyo͞o) *n.* Any of various grasses of the genus *Festuca,* often cultivated as pasturage.
fes·tal (fĕs'təl) *adj.* FESTIVE 1. **–fes'tal·ly** *adv.*
fes·ter (fĕs'tər) *v.* **1.** To generate pus : suppurate. **2.** To be or become a source of resentment or irritation : rankle.
fes·ti·val (fĕs'tə-vəl) *n.* **1.** A regularly recurring occasion of religious feasting or special ceremonies. **2.** A season or series of related cultural events <an art *festival*> **3.** Conviviality : revelry.
fes·tive (fĕs'tĭv) *adj.* **1.** Of, relating, or appropriate to a feast or festival. **2.** Merry : joyous. **–fes'tive·ly** *adv.* **–fes'tive·ness** *n.*
fes·tiv·i·ty (fĕ-stĭv'ĭ-tē) *n., pl.* **-ties. 1.** A joyous celebration : festival. **2. festivities.** The proceedings or events of a festival. **3.** The gaiety of a festival.
fes·toon (fĕ-sto͞on') *n.* **1.** A string or garland hung in a loop between 2 points. **2.** An ornamental festoon, as in sculpture. *–v.* **1.** To decorate with or as if with festoons. **2.** To make festoons. **–fes·toon'er·y** *n.*
fet·a (fĕt'ə, fē'tə) A white Greek cheese made usu. of goat's or ewe's milk and preserved in brine.
fe·tal *also* **foe·tal** (fēt'l) *adj.* Of, relating to, or like a fetus.
fetal position *n.* A bodily position at rest in which the spine is curved, the head is bowed forward, and the arms and legs are drawn in toward the chest.
fetch (fĕch) *v.* **1.** To go or come after and return with. **2.** To cause to come forth, as tears. **3.** To bring as a price : sell for. **4.** To strike (a blow). **–fetch'er** *n.*
fetch·ing (fĕch'ĭng) *adj. Informal.* Very attractive. **–fetch'ing·ly** *adv.*
fete *also* **fête** (fāt, fĕt) *n.* **1.** A feast or festival. **2.** An elaborate outdoor entertainment. *–v.* **fet·ed, fet·ing.** To honor with a fete.
fet·id (fĕt'ĭd, fē'tĭd) *adj.* Malodorous. **–fet'id·ly** *adv.* **–fet'id·ness** *n.*
fet·ish (fĕt'ĭsh) *n.* **1.** An object believed to have magical powers, esp. of protection. **2.** An object of unreasonably obsessive attention or regard <made a *fetish* of cleanliness> **3.** A nonsexual object that arouses or gratifies sexual desire. **–fet'ish·ism** *n.* **–fet'ish·ist** *n.* **–fet'ish·is'tic** *adj.*
fet·lock (fĕt'lŏk') *n.* A projection above and behind the hoof of a horse or related animal marked by a tuft of hair.
fe·tol·o·gy (fē-tŏl'ə-jē) *n.* Medical study of a fetus. **–fe·tol'o·gist** *n.*
fe·tos·co·py (fē-tŏs'kə-pē) *n.* Examination of a fetus in the uterus by insertion of a fiber-optic device into the amniotic cavity. **–fe'to·scope'** (fē'tə-skōp') *n.*
fet·ter (fĕt'ər) *n.* **1.** A shackle or chain attached to the ankles, used as a restraint. **2. fetters.** A restriction : restraint. *–v.* **1.** To put fetters on : shackle. **2.** To restrict the freedom of.
fet·tle (fĕt'l) *n.* Condition : state <in fine *fettle*>
fet·tuc·ci·ne (fĕt'ə-chē'nē) *n.* Narrow strips of pasta.
fe·tus *also* **foe·tus** (fē'təs) *n.* The unborn young of a mammal from the time the major features of its body have appeared; esp. in humans, the unborn young after the 8th week of development.
feud (fyo͞od) *n.* A bitter, prolonged quarrel, as between families. **–feud** *v.*
feu·dal (fyo͞od'l) *adj.* Of, relating to, or characteristic of feudalism. **–feu'dal·ize'** *v.* **–feu'dal·ly** *adv.*
feu·dal·ism (fyo͞od'l-ĭz'əm) *n.* A medieval European political and economic system based on vassalage. **–feu'dal·ist** *n.* **–feu'dal·is'tic** *adj.*
feu·da·to·ry (fyo͞o'də-tôr'ē, -tōr'ē) *n., pl.* **-ries. 1.** One who holds a feudal fee : vassal. **2.** A feudal fee. *–adj.* Owing feudal homage or allegiance.
fe·ver (fē'vər) *n.* **1.** Abnormally high body temperature. **2.** A disease characterized by an abnormally high body temperature. **3.** Heightened activity or emotion. **4.** A craze. **–fe'ver·ish** *adj.* **–fe'ver·ish·ly** *adv.* **–fe'ver·ish·ness** *n.*
fever blister *n.* A cold sore.
few (fyo͞o) *adj.* Amounting to or made up of a small number. *–n. (pl. in number).* **1.** An indefinitely small number <Only a *few* remained.> **2.** A select or limited group <the discerning *few*> *–pron. (pl. in number).* A small number.
fey (fā) *adj.* **1.** Having visionary power : clairvoyant. **2.** Seemingly spellbound.
fez (fĕz) *n., pl.* **fez·zes.** A usu. red felt black-tasseled hat shaped like a flat-topped cone, worn mainly by men in the E Mediterranean region.
fi·an·cé (fē'än-sā', fē-än'sā') *n.* A man engaged to be married.
fi·an·cée (fē'än-sā', fē-än'sā') *n.* A woman engaged to be married.
fi·as·co (fē-ăs'kō, -äs'-) *n., pl.* **-coes** or **-cos.** A total failure.
fi·at (fē'ät', fī'ăt', -ət) *n.* An authoritative and often arbitrary decree.
fib (fĭb) *n.* A trivial lie. *–v.* **fibbed, fib·bing.** To tell a fib. **–fib'ber** *n.*
fi·ber (fī'bər) *n.* **1.** A slender, elongated structure, as of plant or animal tissue or of synthetic material. **2.** A group of fibers that form a single substance, as muscle or flax. **3.** Internal strength : character. **–fi'brous** (fī'brəs) *adj.*
fi·ber·board (fī'bər-bôrd', -bōrd') *n.* A building material made of plant fibers, as wood, compressed into rigid sheets.
Fi·ber·fil (fī'bər-fĭl'). A trademark for a synthetic resin used as quilt filling.
Fi·ber·glas (fī'bər-glăs'). A trademark for a type of fiber glass.
fiber glass *n.* A material composed of glass fibers in resin.
fiber optics *n. (sing. in number).* The optics of light transmission through very fine, flexible glass rods by internal reflection. **–fi'ber-op'tic** *adj.*
fi·ber·scope (fī'bər-skōp') *n.* A flexible fiber-optic instrument used to view otherwise inaccessible objects.
fi·bre (fī'bər *n. esp. Brit. var. of* FIBER.
fi·bril (fī'brəl, fĭb'rəl) *n.* A small, slender fiber. **–fi'bril·lar** *adj.*
fib·ril·la·tion (fĭb'rə-lā'shən, fī'brə-) *n.* Rapid irregular contractions of the muscle fibers of the cardiac ventricles.

fi·brin (fī′brĭn) *n.* An elastic, insoluble protein formed from fibrinogen in blood clotting.
fi·brin·o·gen (fī-brĭn′ə-jən) *n.* A soluble blood plasma protein that is converted to fibrin in blood clotting.
fi·broid (fī′broid′) *adj.* Resembling or made up of fibrous tissue. —*n.* A benign neoplasm of smooth muscle.
fi·bro·vas·cu·lar (fī′brō-văs′kyə-lər) *adj.* Having both fibrous and vascular tissue, as in the woody tissue of plants.
fib·u·la (fĭb′yə-lə) *n., pl.* **-lae** (-lē′) or **-las.** The smaller outer vertebrate bone of the lower limb or hind leg, in humans between the knee and ankle.
-fic *suff.* Causing : making <sopori*fic*>
-fication *suff.* Production : making <grati*fication*>
fiche (fēsh) *n.* A microfiche.
fi·chu (fĭsh′o͞o, fē′sho͞o) *n.* A woman's lightweight triangular scarf, worn over the shoulders and fastened loosely in front.
fick·le (fĭk′əl) *adj.* Erratically changeable : capricious. **—fick′le·ness** *n.*
fic·tion (fĭk′shən) *n.* **1.** A creation of the imagination. **2. a.** A literary work whose content is produced by the imagination and is not necessarily based on fact. **b.** The category of literature comprising works of this kind, including novels, short stories, and plays. **—fic′tion·al** *adj.*
fic·ti·tious (fĭk-tĭsh′əs) *adj.* **1.** Imaginary : nonexistent. **2.** Deliberately deceptive : false <a *fictitious* address> **—fic·ti′tious·ly** *adv.* **—fic·ti′tious·ness** *n.*
fid·dle (fĭd′l) *n. Informal.* A violin. —*v.* **-dled, -dling. 1.** *Informal.* To play the violin. **2. a.** To fidget. **b.** To putter. **3.** To tinker or tamper with. **—fid′dler** *n.*
fiddler crab *n.* A burrowing crab of the genus *Uca,* the male having a greatly enlarged anterior claw.
fid·dle·sticks (fĭd′l-stĭks′) *interj.* Used to express mild annoyance.
fi·del·i·ty (fĭ-dĕl′ĭ-tē, fī-) *n., pl.* **-ties. 1.** Loyalty : faithfulness. **2.** Exact correspondence to truth or fact : accuracy. **3.** The degree to which an electronic system reproduces distortion-free sound.
fidg·et (fĭj′ĭt) *v.* To move or cause to move nervously or restlessly. —*n.* **fidgets.** Nervousness or restlessness. **—fidg′et·er** *n.* **—fidg′et·i·ness** *n.* **—fidg′et·y** *adj.*
fi·du·ci·ar·y (fĭ-do͞o′shē-ĕr′ē, -dyo͞o′-, fī-) *adj.* **1.** Relating to or involving the holding of something in trust. **2.** Held in trust. —*n., pl.* **-ies.** A fiduciary agent : trustee.
fie (fī) *interj.* Used to express disgust or unpleasant surprise.
fief (fēf) *n.* A feudal estate in land : fee.
field (fēld) *n.* **1.** A broad, level, open expanse of land. **2.** A cultivated expanse of land devoted to the growing of a given crop. **3.** A formation of land that contains a specified natural resource <a natural gas *field*> **4.** An airport or airfield. **5.** A background area, as on a flag or painting. **6. a.** An area in which a sports event takes place : stadium. **b.** All the contestants or participants in an event. **7. a.** An area of activity, knowledge, or interest. **b.** One's profession or employment. **c.** A setting of practical activity or application. **8.** A battle or battlefield. **9.** *Physics.* A region of space marked by a physical property, as electromagnetic force, with a determinable value at each point in the region. —*v.* **1.** To retrieve (a ball) and perform the required maneuver, esp. in baseball. **2.** To place (a sports team) in a contest. **3.** To respond to <*fielded* some tough questions> **—field′er** *n.*
field day *n.* **1.** A day for a given outdoor activity, as athletic competition, nature study, etc. **2.** *Informal.* An opportunity for expressing or asserting oneself with the greatest pleasure or success.
field event *n.* A throwing and jumping event of a track meet.
field glass *n. often* **field glasses.** A portable binocular instrument for viewing distant objects.
field hockey *n.* HOCKEY 2.
field magnet *n.* A magnet that supplies a magnetic field in an electrical device such as a generator or motor.
field marshal *n.* A European army officer usu. ranking just below the commander in chief.
field mouse *n.* A small mouse, as of the genera *Apodemus* or *Microtus,* inhabiting fields and meadows.
field of force *n.* A spatial region throughout which the force of a single agent, as an electric current, is operative.
field·test (fēld′tĕst′) *v.* To test in natural operating conditions. **—field test** *n.*
field trip *n.* A group excursion for firsthand observation, as to a museum, woods, or historical place.
fiend (fēnd) *n.* **1.** An evil spirit : demon. **2.** A diabolically evil person. **3.** *Informal.* An addict <a dope *fiend*> **4.** One totally engrossed in something <a sports *fiend*> **—fiend′ish** *adj.* **—fiend′ish·ly** *adv.* **—fiend′ish·ness** *n.*
fierce (fîrs) *adj.* **fierc·er, fierc·est. 1.** Savage and violent in nature : ferocious. **2.** Extremely severe : terrible <a *fierce* hurricane> **3.** Very ardent or intense <*fierce* dedication> **4.** *Informal.* Very difficult or disagreeable <a *fierce* exam> **—fierce′ly** *adv.* **—fierce′ness** *n.*
fier·y (fīr′ē, fī′ə-rē) *adj.* **-i·er, -i·est. 1. a.** Consisting of or containing fire. **b.** Blazing or glowing. **2.** Hot and inflamed <a *fiery* sunburn> **3. a.** Full of spirit or intense emotion. **b.** Volatile : tempestuous <a *fiery* temper> **—fier′i·ness** *n.*
fi·es·ta (fē-ĕs′tə) *n.* A festival or religious holiday.
fife (fīf) *n.* A small musical instrument like a flute but having a higher range.
fif·teen (fĭf-tēn′) *n.* **1.** The cardinal number equal to 14 + 1. **2.** The 15th in a set or sequence. **—fif·teen′** *adj. & pron.* **—fif·teenth′** *n. & adj. & adv.*
fifth (fĭfth) *n.* **1.** The ordinal number matching the number 5 in a series. **2.** One of 5 equal parts. **3.** ⅕ of a gallon or 4/5 of a quart of liquor. **4. Fifth.** The Fifth Amendment. **—fifth** *adj. & adv.*
Fifth Amendment *n.* An amendment to the U.S. Constitution, ratified in 1791, stating that no one may be forced to testify as a witness against himself or herself.
fifth column *n.* A clandestine subversive organization that operates inside a country to further an enemy's military and political aims. **—fifth columnist** *n.*
fifth wheel *n.* One that is superfluous.
fif·ty (fĭf′tē) *n.* The cardinal number equal to 5 × 10. **—fif′ti·eth** *n. & adj. & adv.* **—fif′ty** *adj. & pron.*
fif·ty-fif·ty (fĭf′tē-fĭf′tē) *adj. Informal.* Divided in 2 equal portions <a *fifty-fifty* split> **—fif′ty-fif′ty** *adv.*
fig (fĭg) *n.* **1.** A tree or shrub of the genus *Ficus,* native to the Mediterranean region, bearing sweet pear-shaped, edible fruit. **2.** A trivial amount <didn't care a *fig*>
fight (fīt) *v.* **fought** (fôt), **fight·ing. 1.** To take part in combat. **2.** To contend (with) : struggle. **3.** To argue : quarrel. **4.** To participate in boxing or wrestling (against). **5.** To try to prevent or oppose (e.g., a cold). **6.** To wage (a battle). **7.** To make (one's way) by or as if by combat. —*n.* **1.** A battle. **2.** A conflict or struggle. **3.** A boxing or wrestling match. **4.** Tendency or power to fight.
fight·er (fī′tər) *n.* **1.** One that fights. **2.** A boxer or wrestler. **3.** A fast, maneuverable aircraft used in combat.
fig·ment (fĭg′mənt) *n.* An invention or fabrication.
fig·u·ra·tive (fĭg′yər-ə-tĭv) *adj.* **1.** Based on or using a figure of speech : metaphorical. **2.** Represented by a figure or symbol : emblematic. **—fig′ur·a·tive·ly** *adv.*
fig·ure (fĭg′yər) *n.* **1.** A written or printed symbol representing something other than a letter, esp. a numeral. **2. figures.** Mathematical calculations. **3.** An amount shown in numbers. **4.** Outline, form, or silhouette. **5.** Human shape or form. **6.** An individual, esp. a famous person. **7.** The impression a person makes <a pathetic *figure*> **8. a.** A diagram. **b.** A design or pattern. **9.** A group of dance steps. **10.** A figure of speech. —*v.* **-ured, -ur·ing. 1.** To compute. **2.** To represent : depict. **3.** To ornament with a design. **4.** *Informal.* **a.** To believe <didn't *figure* that it would happen> **b.** To interpret or regard <*figured* them for cheats> **5.** To be a part of or have importance.
figure eight *n.* A figure, as an ice-skating maneuver, shaped like an 8.
fig·ure·head (fĭg′yər-hĕd′) *n.* **1.** One in a position of nominal head but having no real authority. **2.** A carved figure on a ship's prow.
figure of speech *n.* An expression, as a metaphor or hyperbole, in which words are used in a nonliteral way for a forceful, dramatic, or illuminating effect.
fig·u·rine (fĭg′yə-rēn′) *n.* A small molded or sculptured figure : statuette.
Fi·ji (fē′jē). Island country of the SW Pacific. *Cap.* Suva. *Pop.* 618,979. **—Fi′ji·an** *adj. & n.*
fil (fĭl) *n.* See *dinar, dirham,* and *riyal* at CURRENCY TABLE.
fil·a·ment (fĭl′ə-mənt) *n.* **1.** A thin, finely spun thread, fiber, or wire. **2.** A fine wire enclosed in an electric lamp bulb and heated electrically to incandescence. **—fil′a·men′ta·ry** *adj.* **—fil′a·men′tous** *adj.*
fil·bert (fĭl′bərt) *n.* The edible nut of a Eurasian hazel, *Corylus maxima.*
filch (fĭlch) *v.* To steal. **—filch′er** *n.*
file[1] (fīl) *n.* **1.** A receptacle that keeps loose objects, esp. papers, in proper order. **2.** A collection of objects arranged in or as if in a file. **3.** A line of persons, animals, or things each behind the other. —*v.* **filed, fil·ing. 1.** To arrange or keep in order. **2.** To enter (e.g., a document) on public official record. **3.** To send (copy) to a publication. **4.** To move in a line.

▲word history: The various senses of the noun *file[1]* are derived from 2 different French words that ult. have the same etymology. French *file,* "line of soldiers," is the source of English *file* meaning "line." French *fil*, "thread," is the source of English *file* meaning "a receptacle for papers or documents." This sense developed in English from the practice of keeping papers in order by threading them on string or wire. The word has been extended to various filing systems of all kinds. Both French words, *fil* and *file*, are derived from Latin *filum*, "thread."

file[2] (fīl) *n.* A steel tool with hardened ridged surfaces, used in smoothing, polishing, boring, or grinding down. —*v.* **filed, fil•ing.** To smooth, polish, grind, or remove with or as if with a file.

file clerk *n.* An employee who maintains the files and records of an office.

fi•let[1] (fĭ-lā′, fĭl′ā′) *n.* Net or lace with a pattern of squares.

fi•let[2] (fĭ-lā′, fĭl′ā′) *n.* & *v. var. of* FILLET 2.

fi•let mi•gnon (fĭl′ā mēn-yôN′, fĭ-lā′) *n.* A small, tender cut of beef from the loin.

fil•i•al (fĭl′ē-əl) *adj.* Of, relating to, or appropriate for a son or daughter.

fil•i•bus•ter (fĭl′ə-bŭs′tər) *n.* Use of obstructionist tactics, as prolonged speechmaking, to prevent or hinder legislative action. **—fil′i•bus′ter** *v.* **—fil′i•bus′ter•er** *n.*

fil•i•gree (fĭl′ə-grē′) *n.* Intricate lacelike ornamental work from silver or gold fine twisted wire. **—fil′i•gree′** *v.* & *adj.*

fil•ing (fī′lĭng) *n. often* **filings.** A shaving scraped off with a file.

Fil•i•pi•no (fĭl′ə-pē′nō) *n., pl.* **-nos.** A native or inhabitant of the Philippines. **—Fil′i•pi′no** *adj.*

fill (fĭl) *v.* **1.** To put into or hold as much as possible. **2.** To stop up (e.g., an opening). **3.** To satisfy completely : fulfill <*fill* all requirements> **4.** To supply the materials for <*fill* a prescription> **5.** To supply (an empty space) with material, as writing. **6.** To put someone into (e.g., a vacant position). **7.** To hold or discharge the duties of (e.g., a position). **—fill in.** To act as a substitute. —*n.* **1.** A full amount <ate my *fill*> **2.** A built-up piece of land or the material, as earth or gravel, used for it.

fill•er (fĭl′ər) *n.* **1.** Something added to augment size or weight or to fill space. **2.** A material used to fill pores, cracks, or holes in a surface before it is finished.

fil•lér (fĭl′âr′) *n.* See *forint* at CURRENCY TABLE.

fil•let (fĭl′ĭt) *n.* **1.** A narrow strip of material, as ribbon. **2.** *also* **fi•let** (fĭ-lā′, fĭl′ā′).A boneless piece of fish or meat. —*v.* **1.** To bind or ornament with or as if with a fillet. **2.** *also* **fi•let** (fĭ-lā′, fĭl′ā′). To slice, bone, or make into fillets.

fill•ing (fĭl′ĭng) *n.* **1.** Something used to fill a space, container, or cavity. **2.** An edible mixture used to fill sandwiches, cakes, or pastries. **3.** The horizontal threads crossing the warp in weaving : weft.

filling station *n.* A retail establishment at which vehicles are serviced, esp. with gasoline, oil, air, and water.

fil•lip (fĭl′əp) *n.* **1.** A light blow or gesture made with a snap of the fingers. **2.** Something that arouses or excites : stimulus. **—fil′lip** *v.*

Fill•more (fĭl′môr′, -mōr′), **Millard.** 1800–74. 13th U.S. President (1850–53).

fil•ly (fĭl′ē) *n., pl.* **-lies.** A young female horse.

film (fĭlm) *n.* **1.** A thin skin or membranous coating. **2.** A thin coating <a *film* of dust> **3.** A photosensitive strip or sheet of flexible cellulose material used to make photographic negatives or transparencies. **4. a.** A movie. **b.** Movies as a whole. —*v.* **1.** To cover with or as if with a film. **2.** To make a movie of. **—film′y** *adj.*

film•dom (fĭlm′dəm) *n.* The movie industry.

film•go•er (fĭlm′gō′ər) *n.* One who frequently goes to see movies.

fil•mog•ra•phy (fĭl-mŏg′rə-fē) *n., pl.* **-phies.** Writings, as lists or books, about films or film figures.

film•strip (fĭlm′strĭp′) *n.* A strip of film with graphic matter, as photographs, for still projection on a screen.

fil•ter (fĭl′tər) *n.* **1.** A device containing a porous substance through which a liquid or gas can be passed to separate out suspended matter. **2.** A device for passing waves or oscillations of certain frequencies while blocking others. —*v.* **1.** To put (liquid or gas) through a filter. **2.** To remove by putting through a filter. **—fil′ter•a•bil′i•ty** *n.* **—fil′ter•a•ble, fil′tra•ble** *adj.*

filth (fĭlth) *n.* **1.** Dirty or foul matter or refuse. **2.** Foulness : corruption. **3.** Something considered offensive, esp. obscenity.

filth•y (fĭl′thē) *adj.* **-i•er, -i•est. 1.** Covered with or full of filth. **2.** Obscene. **3.** So objectionable as to elicit despisal. ☆***syns:*** ABHORRENT, CONTEMPTIBLE, DESPICABLE, DISGUSTING, FOUL, LOATHSOME, MEAN, NASTY, ODIOUS, REPUGNANT, ROTTEN, SHABBY, SORRY, VILE, WRETCHED **—filth′i•ly** *adv.* **—filth′i•ness** *n.*

fil•trate (fĭl′trāt′) *v.* **-trat•ed, -trat•ing.** To pass or cause to pass through a filter. —*n.* The portion of matter that passes through the filter. **—fil•tra′tion** *n.*

fin[1] (fĭn) *n.* **1.** A thin, membranous appendage that extends from the body of a fish or other aquatic animal, used esp for swimming and balancing. **2.** Something like a fin. **3.** FLIPPER 2.

fin[2] (fĭn) *n. Slang.* A 5–dollar bill.

fi•na•gle (fĭ-nā′gəl) *v.* **-gled, -gling.** *Informal.* To obtain or achieve by questionable or wily methods : wangle. **—fi•na′gler** *n.*

fi•nal (fī′nəl) *adj.* **1.** Occurring at or forming the end : concluding. **2.** Of, relating to, or constituting the last element in a series, process, etc. **3.** Definitive and decisive : unalterable. —*n.* **1.** The last or one of the last of a series of athletic contests. **2.** A final academic examination. **—fi•nal′i•ty** (fī-năl′ə-tē, fĭ-) *n.* **—fi′nal•ly** *adv.*

fi•na•le (fĭ-năl′ē, -nä′lē) *n.* The concluding part, esp. of a musical composition.

fi•nal•ist (fī′nə-lĭst) *n.* A competitor in the final part of a contest.

fi•nal•ize (fī′nə-līz′) *v.* **-ized, -iz•ing.** To put into final form : complete. **—fi′nal•i•za′tion** *n.* **—fi′nal•iz′er** *n.*

fi•nance (fĭ-năns′, fī-, fī′năns′) *n.* **1.** The management of monetary affairs. **2. finances.** Monetary resources : funds. —*v.* **-nanced, -nanc•ing. 1.** To supply the funds or capital for. **2.** To supply funds to. **3.** To sell or provide on credit. **—fi•nan′cial** *adj.* **—fi•nan′cial•ly** *adv.*

fin•an•cier (fĭn′ən-sîr′, fĭ-năn′-, fī′nən-) *n.* An expert in large-scale financial affairs.

finch (fĭnch) *n.* A relatively small bird of the family Fringillidae, as a goldfinch, grosbeak, or canary, having a short stout bill.

find (fīnd) *v.* **found** (found), **find•ing. 1.** To come upon, as after a search or often by accident. **2.** To attain : achieve. **3.** To ascertain : determine. **4.** To regard : consider <*found* the house charming> **5.** To regain : recover. **6.** To assert as a conclusion or verdict. ☆***syns:*** LOCATE, PINPOINT, SPOT —*n.* **1.** An act of finding. **2.** Something found, esp. a valuable discovery.

find•er (fīn′dər) *n.* **1.** One that finds. **2.** A device on a camera that indicates what will be in the photograph.

fin de siè•cle (făN′ də sē-ĕk′lə) *adj.* Of or typical of the artistic climate of the latter part of the 19th cent.

find•ing (fīn′dĭng) *n.* **1.** Something found or discovered. **2.** *often* **findings.** The conclusion reached after investigation or examination.

fine[1] (fīn) *adj.* **fin•er, fin•est. 1.** Superior, as in quality or skill <*fine* porcelain><a *fine* musician> **2.** Very pleasant and enjoyable. **3.** Very sharp, as a knife edge. **4. a.** Consisting of tiny particles <*fine* dust> **b.** Very thin in texture or diameter. **5.** Subtle <a *fine* distinction> **6.** Marked by refined manners : elegant. **7.** Clear and unclouded. **8.** *Informal.* Being in good health. —*adv. Informal.* Very well <The children are doing *fine.*> **—fine′ly** *adv.* **—fine′ness** *n.*

fine[2] (fīn) *n.* Something, esp. a sum of money, levied as a penalty for an offense. **—fine** *v.*

fine art *n.* Art, as music, painting, and sculpture, created for aesthetic pleasure.

fin•er•y (fī′nə-rē) *n., pl.* **-ies.** Elaborate clothes and jewels.

fi•nesse (fĭ-nĕs′) *n.* **1.** Fineness and delicacy of performance or workmanship. **2.** Skillful handling of a situation.

fin•ger (fĭng′gər) *n.* **1.** Any of the 5 digits of the hand. **2.** A glove part covering a finger. **3.** Something, as a peninsula, that resembles a finger. —*v.* **1.** To touch with the fingers : handle. **2.** *Mus.* To use the fingers in playing an instrument.

fin•ger•board (fĭng′gər-bôrd′, -bōrd′) *n.* A strip of wood on the neck of a stringed instrument against which the strings are pressed by the fingers in playing.

finger bowl *n.* A small bowl of water used for rinsing the fingers at the table.

fin•ger•ing (fĭng′gər-ĭng) *n. Mus.* **1.** The act or technique of using the fingers in playing an instrument. **2.** Marking that indicates which fingers are to be used.

fin•ger•ling (fĭng′gər-lĭng) *n.* A young fish.

fin•ger•nail (fĭng′gər-nāl′) *n.* The thin, transparent plate covering the dorsal surface of the tip of each finger.

fin•ger•print (fĭng′gər-prĭnt′) *n.* A pattern formed by the ridges of the skin on the tips of the fingers and thumbs, used esp. as a means of identification. **—fin′ger•print′** *v.*

finger tip *also* **fin•ger•tip** (fĭng′gər-tĭp′) *n.* The extreme end of a finger.

fin•i•al (fĭn′ē-əl) *n.* An ornamental projecting or terminating part, as on a lamp.

fin•ick•y (fĭn′ĭ-kē) *adj.* Hard to please : choosy. **—fin′ick•i•ness** *n.*

fi•nis (fĭn′ĭs, fī′nĭs) *n.* The end.

fin•ish (fĭn′ĭsh) *v.* **1.** To reach the end (of) <*finish* a road race> **2.** To bring to an end : conclude. **3.** To consume all of : use up <*finish* a cake> **4. a.** To destroy or kill. **b.** To wear out completely. **5.** To give (a surface) a particular texture. —*n.* **1.** The final part : end <a close *finish* in the horse race> **2.** Surface treatment or texture. **3.** Smoothness of execution : perfection. **4.** Refinement in speech, manners, or behavior. **—fin'ish•er** *n.*

fi•nite (fī'nīt') *adj.* **1.** Having limits or bounds. **2.** Being neither infinite nor infinitesimal. **—fi'nite•ly** *adv.* **—fi'nite•ness** *n.*

fink (fĭngk) *n. Slang.* **1.** A hired strikebreaker. **2.** An informer. **3.** An undesirable person. **—fink** *v.*

Fin•land (fĭn'lənd). Country of N Europe. *Cap.* Helsinki. *Pop.* 4,758,008. **—Finn** *n.* **—Fin'nish** *adj.* & *n.*

fin•nan had•die (fĭn'ən hăd'ē) *n.* Smoked haddock.

fin•ny (fĭn'ē) *adj.* **-ni•er, -ni•est. 1.** Having or suggesting fins. **2.** Of, relating to, or typical of fish.

fiord (fyôrd, fyōrd) *n. var. of* FJORD.

fir (fûr) *n.* **1.** An evergreen tree of the genus *Abies*, having flat needles and erect cones. **2.** The wood of a fir.

fire (fīr) *n.* **1. a.** A chemical reaction, esp. the burning of a combustible substance with oxygen that releases heat and light. **b.** A fire distinguished by magnitude, destructive power, or utility <a field *fire*><a stove *fire*> **2.** Great enthusiasm : fervor. **3.** Discharge of firearms. —*v.* **fired, fir•ing. 1.** To cause to ignite or become ignited. **2.** To maintain or tend a fire (in). **3.** To bake in a kiln <*fire* a vase> **4.** To arouse the emotions of. **5.** To discharge (a firearm, explosive, or projectile). **6.** *Informal.* To project or throw suddenly and forcefully. **7.** To let go from a job : dismiss. **—fire'less** *adj.* **—fire'proof'** *adj.* & *v.*

fire alarm *n.* A device used to signal the outbreak of a fire.

fire•arm (fīr'ärm') *n.* A weapon for firing a missile, esp. a pistol or rifle using an explosive charge.

fire•ball (fīr'bôl') *n.* **1.** A ball of fire. **2.** A particularly bright meteor. **3.** A very bright, intensely hot ball-shaped cloud of dust, gas, and vapor caused by a nuclear explosion. **4.** A very energetic person.

fire•box (fīr'bŏks') *n.* **1.** A box containing a fire alarm. **2.** A chamber, as a steam locomotive furnace, in which fuel is burned.

fire•brand (fīr'brănd') *n.* **1.** A piece of burning wood. **2.** One who agitates or stirs up trouble or conflict.

fire•break (fīr'brāk') *n.* A strip of land that is cleared to stop a fire spreading.

fire•brick (fīr'brĭk') *n.* A highly heat-resistant brick esp. of fire clay, used to line fireplaces and furnaces.

fire•bug (fīr'bŭg') *n. Informal.* A pyromaniac : arsonist.

fire clay *n.* The heat-resistant clay used esp. for firebricks.

fire•crack•er (fīr'krăk'ər) *n.* A cylinder of heavy paper containing a small explosive that is set off to make noise, as at a party.

fire•damp (fīr'dămp') *n.* A gas, mainly methane, occurring naturally in coal mines and forming explosive mixtures with air.

fire•dog (fīr'dôg', -dŏg') *n.* An andiron.

fire engine *n.* A large motor vehicle that carries firefighters and extinguishing equipment to a fire.

fire escape *n.* A structure or device for emergency exit from a building.

fire•fight•er (fīr'fī'tər) *n.* One who fights fires as an occupation.

fire•fly (fīr'flī') *n.* A night-flying beetle of the family Lampyridae, having an abdominal organ that gives off a flashing light.

fire•house (fīr'hous') *n.* A fire station.

fire irons *pl.n.* Equipment, including tongs, a shovel, and a poker, used to tend a fire.

fire•light (fīr'līt') *n.* The light from a fire, as in a fireplace.

fire•man (fīr'mən) *n.* **1.** A firefighter. **2.** One who tends fires : stoker.

fire•place (fīr'plās') *n.* An open recess at the base of a chimney for a fire : hearth.

fire•plug (fīr'plŭg') *n.* A hydrant.

fire•pow•er (fīr'pou'ər) *n.* The capacity, as of a weapon, military unit, or ship, for discharging fire.

fire•side (fīr'sīd') *n.* **1.** The area around a fireplace or hearth. **2.** HOME 1.

fire station *n.* A building housing fire equipment and firefighters.

fire tower *n.* A tower where a lookout for forest fires is stationed.

fire•trap (fīr'trăp') *n.* A building susceptible to fire or hard to escape from if there is a fire.

fire wall *n.* A fireproof wall used as a barrier to forestall the spread of a fire in buildings and machinery.

fire•wood (fīr'wo͝od') *n.* Wood burned in a fireplace or for fuel.

fire•works (fīr'wûrks') *pl.n.* Explosives and combustibles used to generate colored lights, smoke, and noise for entertainment.

firing line *n.* **1.** The line of gunfire directed against a target. **2.** The often vulnerable forefront of an activity or pursuit.

firm[1] (fûrm) *adj.* **1.** Not yielding to pressure : solid. **2.** Marked by the tone and resiliency of healthy tissue <*firm* muscles> **3.** Securely fastened or fixed in place. **4.** Indicating resolution or determination. **5.** Constant and steadfast. **6. a.** Fixed : definite <a *firm* deal> **b.** Unfluctuating : steady <*firm* prices> **7.** Strong and sure <a *firm* grip> —*adv.* Unwaveringly : resolutely. —*v.* To make or become firm. **—firm'ly** *adv.* **—firm'ness** *n.*

firm[2] (fûrm) *n.* A business partnership of 2 or more persons.

fir•ma•ment (fûr'mə-mənt) *n.* The expanse of the heavens : sky.

firn (fîrn) *n.* Snow partially consolidated by thawing and freezing but not yet converted to glacial ice.

first (fûrst) *adj.* **1.** Corresponding in order to the number 1. **2.** Coming before all others. **3.** Taking place or acting prior to all others : earliest. **4.** Ranking above all others in importance or quality : foremost. —*adv.* **1.** Before or above all others in time, order, rank, or importance. **2.** For the 1st time. **3.** Preferably : rather. —*n.* **1.** The ordinal number matching the number 1 in a series : 1st. **2.** The 1st in a set or sequence. **3.** The one coming, taking place, or ranking before or above all others. **4.** The beginning <from the *first*><*at first*> **5.** The transmission gear producing the lowest drive speeds in an automotive vehicle. **—first'ly** *adv.*

first aid *n.* Emergency care given to sick or injured persons.

first-born (fûrst'bôrn') *adj.* First in order of birth : eldest. **—first'-born'** *n.*

first class *n.* **1.** The highest or best of a particular group. **2.** A class of mail including letters, postcards, and packages sealed against inspection. **—first'-class'** *adj.* & *adv.*

first-de•gree burn (fûrst'dĭ-grē') *n.* A mild burn causing redness of the skin.

first•hand (fûrst'hănd') *adj.* Coming or received from the original source <*firsthand* information> **—first'hand'** *adv.*

first lady *n.* **1.** *often* **First Lady.** The wife or hostess of the chief executive of a country, state, or city. **2.** The foremost woman of a specified profession or art.

first lieutenant *n.* A military officer who ranks above a 2nd lieutenant and below a captain.

first mate *n.* A ship's officer who ranks just below the captain.

first person *n.* A category of linguistic forms, as verbs or pronouns, indicating the speaker or writer of the sentence in which they are used.

first-rate (fûrst'rāt') *adj.* Foremost in quality, rank, or importance. **—first'rate'** *adv.*

first-string (fûrst'strĭng') *adj.* Being a regular member, as of a team, rather than a substitute.

firth (fûrth) *n. esp. Scot.* A narrow inlet of the sea : fjord.

fis•cal (fĭs'kəl) *adj.* **1.** Of or relating to the treasury or finances of a nation or branch of government. **2.** Of or relating to finances. **—fis'cal•ly** *adv.*

fish (fĭsh) *n., pl.* **fish** *or* **fish•es. 1.** Any of numerous cold-blooded aquatic vertebrates of the superclass Pisces, having fins, gills for breathing, and usu. scales. **2.** The flesh of a fish used as food. —*v.* **1.** To try to catch fish. **2.** To seek by feeling one's way : grope. **3.** To try to get something slyly or indirectly. **4.** To pull or draw forth. **—fish'ing** *n.*

fish and chips *pl.n.* Fried fillets of fish and French-fried potatoes.

fish•bowl (fĭsh'bōl') *n.* **1.** A usu. transparent bowl for keeping live fish. **2.** Lack of privacy.

fish•er•man (fĭsh'ər-mən) *n.* **1.** One who fishes commercially or for sport. **2.** A commercial fishing vessel.

fish•er•y (fĭsh'ə-rē) *n., pl.* **-ies. 1.** The business or occupation of catching, processing, or selling fish. **2.** A place for catching fish. **3.** A fish hatchery.

fish•hook (fĭsh'ho͝ok') *n.* A usu. barbed metal hook used to catch fish.

fishing rod *n.* A rod of wood, steel, or fiber glass with a line and often a reel, used to catch fish.

fish•meal (fĭsh'mēl') *n.* Pulverized dried fish or fish parts used as fertilizer and animal feed.

fish story *n. Informal.* An exaggerated, boastful story that is probably not true.

fish•tail (fĭsh'tāl') *v.* To swing the tail of an aircraft or the rear end of a motor vehicle from side to side while moving forward.

fish•wife (fĭsh'wīf') *n.* A coarse, shrewish woman.

fish•y (fĭsh'ē) *adj.* **-i•er, -i•est. 1.** Resembling fish, as in taste or odor. **2.** Inspiring suspicion <a *fishy* excuse> **—fish'i•ly** *adv.* **—fish'i•ness** *n.*

fis·sile (fĭs′əl, -īl′) *adj.* **1.** Capable of being split. **2.** *Physics.* Fissionable. **–fis·sil′i·ty** (fĭ-sĭl′ĭ-tē) *n.*
fis·sion (fĭsh′ən) *n.* **1.** The act or process of splitting into parts. **2.** *Physics.* A reaction in which an atomic nucleus splits into fragments whose mass does not quite equal the mass of the original nucleus and hundreds of millions of electron volts of energy are generated. **–fis′sion·a·ble** *adj.*
fis·sure (fĭsh′ər) *n.* A narrow crack or opening, as in a rock face. **–fis′sure** *v.*
fist (fĭst) *n.* **1.** A tightly closed hand with the fingers bent into the palm. **2.** INDEX 3.
fist·fight (fĭst′fīt′) *n.* A fight using the fists.
fist·ful (fĭst′fo͝ol′) *n.* A handful.
fist·i·cuffs (fĭs′tĭ-kŭfs′) *pl.n.* **1.** A fight involving use of the fists. **2.** Boxing.
fis·tu·la (fĭs′cho͞o-lə, -chə-) *n., pl.* **-las** *or* **-lae** (-lē′). An abnormal passage leading from an abscess, cavity, or hollow organ to the body surface or to another hollow organ. **–fis′tu·lous** *adj.*
fit[1] (fĭt) *v.* **fit·ted** *or* **fit, fit·ting. 1.** To be the correct size and shape (for). **2.** To be appropriate (to). **3.** To be or make suitable. **4.** To equip or outfit, as a vessel. **5.** To provide a place or time for <The dentist can *fit* you in at 2:00 p.m.> **6.** To belong. *–adj.* **fit·ter, fit·test. 1.** Suited, adapted, or adequate for a particular circumstance or purpose. **2.** Appropriate : proper. **3.** Physically healthy. *–n.* **1.** The quality, state, or way of being fitted. **2.** The way in which a garment fits. **–fit′ly** *adv.* **–fit′ness** *n.* **–fit′ter** *n.*
fit[2] (fĭt) *n.* **1.** *Med.* **a.** A sudden, violent appearance of a disease <a *fit* of malaria> **b.** A convulsion. **2.** A sudden emotional outburst. **3.** A sudden period of activity.
fitch (fĭch) *n.* The fur of the Old World polecat.
fit·ful (fĭt′fəl) *adj.* Irregular : intermittent <*fitful* sleep> **–fit′ful·ly** *adv.* **–fit′ful·ness** *n.*
fit·ting (fĭt′ĭng) *adj.* Suitable to the circumstances. *–n.* **1.** The act of trying on clothes for alteration. **2.** A detachable part for a machine or apparatus. **–fit′ting·ly** *adv.* **–fit′ting·ness** *n.*
Fitz·ger·ald (fĭts-jĕr′əld), **F(rancis) Scott (Key).** 1896–1940. Amer. author.
five (fīv) *n.* **1.** The cardinal number equal to 4 + 1. **2.** The 5th in a set or sequence. **3.** Something having 5 parts, units, or members. **–five** *adj.* & *pron.*
five-pins (fīv′pĭnz′) *n. Can.* A bowling game in which the ball is rolled down an alley in order to knock down the 5 pins at the end of the alley.
†**fix** (fĭks) *v.* **1.** To fasten or place securely. **2.** *Chem.* To make a substance nonvolatile or solid. **3.** *Biol.* To convert (nitrogen) into stable compounds that can be assimilated. **4.** To treat (a photographic image) with a chemical preservative. **5.** To direct steadily <*fixed* her eyes on the screen> **6.** To specify <*fix* a time to meet> **7.** To ascribe : assign <*fixed* the blame on us> **8.** To set right : adjust. **9.** To repair. **10.** To make ready : prepare <*fix* dinner> **11.** *Informal.* To get even with. **12.** To influence or arrange the outcome of illegally. **13.** To spay or castrate (an animal). **14.** *Regional.* To intend <was *fixing* to go home> *–n.* **1.** A difficult or embarrassing situation or position. **2.** The position of a ship, aircraft, etc., as determined by observations or radio. **3.** An example of connivance to prearrange a result. **4.** *Slang.* An injection of a narcotic. **–fix′a·ble** *adj.* **–fix′er** *n.*
fix·a·tion (fĭk-sā′shən) *n.* A strong, often unhealthy attachment or preoccupation. **–fix′ate′** *v.*
fix·a·tive (fĭk′sə-tĭv) *n.* Something used to fix, protect, preserve, or stabilize.
fixed (fĭkst) *adj.* **1.** Set firmly in position : stationary. **2.** Not changing or varying : constant. **3.** Firmly, often dogmatically held in the mind <*fixed* notions> **4.** *Chem.* **a.** Nonvolatile, as certain oils. **b.** Being in a stable combined form. **5.** Prearranged illegally as to outcome. **–fix′ed·ly** *adv.* **–fix′ed·ness** *n.*
fix·ings (fĭk′sĭngz) *pl.n. Informal.* Accessories : trimmings.
fix·i·ty (fĭk′sĭ-tē) *n., pl.* **-ties.** The quality or state of being fixed : stability.
fix·ture (fĭks′chər) *n.* **1.** Something fixed or installed as a part of a larger system <plumbing *fixtures*> **2.** One regarded as permanently established or fixed, as in a certain place <a *fixture* of Paris society>
fizz (fĭz) *v.* To make a hissing or bubbling sound. *–n.* **1.** A fizzing sound. **2.** Tiny gas bubbles : effervescence.
fiz·zle (fĭz′əl) *v.* **-zled, -zling. 1.** To make a hiss or sputter, esp. when going out. **2.** To fail or die out, esp. after a positive beginning. *–n.* A fiasco.
fjord *or* **fiord** (fyôrd, fyōrd) *n.* A long, narrow, often deep inlet from the sea with steep cliffs on either side.
FL *abbr.* Florida (with Zip Code).
fl. *abbr.* flourished (Lat. *floruit*).
Fla. *abbr.* Florida.
flab (flăb) *n.* Loose, flaccid body tissue.
flab·ber·gast (flăb′ər-găst′) *v.* To amaze : astound.
flab·by (flăb′ē) *adj.* **-bi·er, -bi·est. 1.** Flaccid. **2.** Lacking force or vitality : ineffectual. **–flab′bi·ness** *n.*
flac·cid (flăk′sĭd, flăs′ĭd) *adj.* Lacking firmness or resilience. **–flac·cid′i·ty** *n.* **–flac′cid·ly** *adv.*
flack (flăk) *n.* A press agent. **–flack** *v.* **–flack′er·y** *n.*
flac·on (flăk′ən, -ŏn′) *n.* A small stoppered often decorative bottle.
flag[1] (flăg) *n.* **1.** A piece of cloth having a distinctive size, color, and design, used for a symbol, standard, signal, etc. **2.** Something suggestive of a flag in appearance or function. *–v.* **flagged, flag·ging. 1.** To mark with a flag for identification or ornamentation. **2.** To signal with or as if with a flag.
flag[2] (flăg) *n.* A plant, as an iris or cattail, with long blade-shaped leaves.
flag[3] (flăg) *v.* **flagged, flag·ging. 1.** To hang limply : droop. **2.** To lessen in strength or vigor : weaken.
flag[4] (flăg) *n.* Flagstone or a slab of flagstone. **–flag** *v.*
flag·el·late (flăj′ə-lāt′) *v.* **-lat·ed, -lat·ing.** To punish by flogging : scourge. **–flag′el·la′tion** *n.*
flag officer *n.* A U.S. Navy or Coast Guard officer holding the rank of rear admiral, vice admiral, or admiral.
flag·on (flăg′ən) *n.* A container with a handle, and often a lid, used for holding wines or liquors.
flag·pole (flăg′pōl′) *n.* A pole from which a flag is flown.
fla·grant (flā′grənt) *adj.* Conspicuously bad or offensive : outrageous. **–fla′gran·cy, fla′grance** *n.* **–fla′grant·ly** *adv.*
flag·ship (flăg′shĭp′) *n.* **1.** A ship that carries a fleet or squadron commander and his flag. **2.** The chief one of a related group.
flag·staff (flăg′stăf′) *n.* A flagpole.
flag·stone (flăg′stōn′) *n.* A flat, fine-grained, hard, evenly layered stone split into slabs for paving.
flail (flāl) *n.* A device for threshing grain by hand. *–v.* **1.** To beat or strike with or as if with a flail. **2.** To thrash about.
flair (flâr) *n.* **1.** Talent or aptitude : knack. **2.** Distinctive style.
flak (flăk) *n.* **1. a.** Antiaircraft artillery. **b.** The bursting shells fired from such artillery. **2.** *Informal.* **a.** Excessive or abusive criticism. **b.** Dissension.
flake (flāk) *n.* **1.** A flat, thin piece or layer. **2.** *Slang.* An eccentric : oddball. *–v.* **flaked, flak·ing.** To form into or separate in flakes. **–flak′i·ly** *adv.* **–flak′i·ness** *n.* **–flak′y** *adj.*
flam·boy·ant (flăm-boi′ənt) *adj.* **1.** Elaborately showy : ornate. **2.** Rich and vivid in color. **–flam·boy′ance, flam·boy′an·cy** *n.* **–flam·boy′ant·ly** *adv.*
flame (flām) *n.* **1.** The often bright, tongue-shaped zone of burning gases and fine suspended matter that forms in combustion. **2.** Active, blazing combustion. **3.** Something resembling a flame in appearance, motion, or intensity. **4.** Violent passion. **5.** A sweetheart. **–flame** *v.*
fla·men·co (flə-mĕng′kō) *n.* **1.** A dance of the Andalusian Gypsies marked by strong, often improvised rhythms. **2.** Music for the flamenco.
flame·out (flām′out′) *n.* In-flight combustion failure of a jet aircraft engine.
flame thrower *n.* A weapon that shoots ignited incendiary fuel, as napalm.
fla·min·go (flə-mĭng′gō) *n., pl.* **-gos** *or* **-goes.** A large tropical wading bird of the family Phoenicopteridae, having pinkish plumage, long legs, and a long neck.
flam·ma·ble (flăm′ə-bəl) *adj.* Igniting easily and burning rapidly : inflammable. **–flam′ma·bil′i·ty** *n.* **–flam′ma·ble** *n.*
Flan·ders (flăn′dərz). Region of NW Europe, including part of N France and W Belgium. **–Flem′ish** (flĕm′ĭsh) *adj.* & *n.*
flange (flănj) *n.* A projecting rim or edge used to strengthen or guide an object or attach it to another object.
flank (flăngk) *n.* **1. a.** The fleshy part of the body between the last rib and the hip. **b.** A cut of meat from this part of an animal. **2.** A lateral part <the *flank* of a mountain> **3.** The right or left side of a military formation or bastion. *–v.* **1.** To guard the flank of. **2.** To attack or menace the flank of (enemy troops). **3.** To be situated at the flank of. **4.** To put something on each side of. **–flank′er** *n.*
flan·nel (flăn′əl) *n.* **1.** A woven fabric with a nap, made of wool or a wool and cotton or synthetic blend. **2. flannels.** Trousers or undergarments made of flannel. **–flan′nel·ly** *adj.*
flan·nel·ette (flăn′ə-lĕt′) *n.* Cotton flannel.
flap (flăp) *n.* **1.** A loose, flat piece affixed at only 1 side, as on an envelope. **2.** The act or sound of waving or fluttering. **3.** A control section of the rear edge of an aircraft wing that increases lift or drag. **4.** A striking with something flat : slap. **5.** *Slang.* Agitation : commotion. *–v.* **flapped, flap·ping. 1.** To move up and down, as arms or wings. **2.** To move or sway loosely : flutter. **3.** To hit with something flat.
flap·doo·dle (flăp′do͞od′l) *n. Slang.* Nonsense.
flap·jack (flăp′jăk′) *n.* A pancake.

flap·pa·ble (flăp'ə-bəl) *adj. Slang.* Easily excited or upset.
flap·per (flăp'ər) *n.* **1.** One that flaps. **2.** *Informal.* A young woman of the 1920's whose dress and behavior were ostentatiously unconventional.
flare (flâr) *v.* **flared, flar·ing. 1.** To flame up or burn with a bright light. **2.** To erupt or intensify suddenly, as an emotion or activity. **3.** To spread or open outward <a *flared* skirt> —*n.* **1.** A sudden, brief, intense blaze of light. **2.** A signaling or illuminating device that produces a bright light. **3.** An eruption of emotion or activity. **4.** An expanding outward.
flare-up (flâr'ŭp') *n.* An outburst or eruption, as of flame or strong emotion.
flash (flăsh) *v.* **1.** To burst or cause to burst into or as if into flame. **2.** To appear or occur briefly or suddenly. **3.** To emit light intermittently : sparkle. **4.** To cause (light) to burst forth intermittently. **5.** To proceed rapidly. **6.** To signal with beams of light. **7.** To communicate or display (information) very quickly. **8.** To flaunt. —*n.* **1.** A short, sudden burst of light. **2.** A sudden perception <a *flash* of insight> **3.** An instant <did it in a *flash*> **4.** A short, important news transmission or dispatch. **5.** A device, as a flash bulb, that produces instantaneous illumination.
flash·back (flăsh'băk') *n.* The interruption of a story, motion picture, etc., to show or tell about an earlier incident.
flash bulb *n.* A glass bulb full of shredded magnesium or aluminum foil that when electrically ignited produces a very brief flash of light for photography.
flash card *n.* A card printed with words or numbers and briefly displayed as part of a learning drill.
flash·cube (flăsh'kyo͞ob') *n.* A rotating cube containing 4 flash bulbs.
flash flood *n.* A sudden, violent flood after a heavy rain.
flash gun *n.* A portable photographic device that holds and electrically triggers a flash bulb.
flash lamp *n.* An electric lamp used in photography to produce a very brief high-intensity light.
flash·light (flăsh'līt') *n.* A small, portable lamp usu. powered by batteries.
flash point *n.* **1.** The lowest temperature at which the vapor of a combustible liquid will ignite. **2.** The brink of crisis.
flash·y (flăsh'ē) *adj.* **-i·er, -i·est. 1.** Superficially or briefly brilliant. **2.** Tastelessly showy : gaudy. **—flash'i·ly** *adv.* **—flash'i·ness** *n.*
flask (flăsk) *n.* **1.** A small, flat, bottlelike container usu. with a cap. **2.** A long-necked bottle used in laboratories.
flat[1] (flăt) *adj.* **flat·ter, flat·test. 1. a.** Having a horizontal surface with no curvature or tilt. **b.** Having a smooth, even surface, as a board. **2.** Low and shallow, as a box. **3.** Lying prostrate : prone. **4.** Absolute : unequivocal <a *flat* denial> **5.** Unvarying, as a fixed rate or fee. **6.** Uninteresting : dull. **7.** Lacking flavor or zest. **8.** Deflated <a *flat* tire> **9.** *Mus.* **a.** Being below the correct pitch. **b.** Being a semitone lower than the corresponding natural key. —*adv.* **1.** Level with the ground : horizontally. **2.** So as to be flat. **3.** Directly : completely <went *flat* against the rules> **4.** *Mus.* Below the correct pitch. —*n.* **1.** A flat surface or part. **2.** *often* **flats.** A stretch of level land. **3.** A shallow container for a number of seeds or immature plants. **4.** A flat tire. **5.** A shoe with a flat heel. **6.** *Mus.* **a.** A sign (♭) attached to a note to indicate that its pitch is a semitone lower than usual. **b.** A note lowered a semitone. —*v.* **flat·ted, flat·ting. 1.** To make flat. **2.** *Mus.* **a.** To lower (a note) a semitone. **b.** To sing or play below the correct pitch. **—flat'ly** *adv.* **—flat'ness** *n.*
flat[2] (flăt) *n.* An apartment entirely on 1 floor of a building.
flat·bed (flăt'bĕd') *n.* A truck that has a shallow rear platform without sides.
flat·boat (flăt'bōt') *n.* A boat with a flat bottom and square ends for the transport of freight on inland waterways.
flat·car (flăt'kär') *n.* A roofless, sideless railroad freight car.
flat·fish (flăt'fĭsh') *n.* A chiefly marine fish of the order Pleuronectiformes or Heterosomata, as a flounder or sole, having a compressed body with both eyes on the upper side.
flat·foot (flăt'fo͝ot') *n.* **1.** *pl.* **-feet** (-fēt'). A condition in which the arch of the foot is broken down so that all of the sole touches the ground. **2.** *pl.* **-foots.** *Slang.* A police officer. **—flat'-foot'ed** *adj.*
flat·i·ron (flăt'ī'ərn) *n.* An externally heated device used to press clothes.
flat out *adv.* **1.** In a direct, blunt way. **2.** At top speed.
flat-out (flăt'out') *adj.* Thoroughgoing : out-and-out.
flat·ten (flăt'n) *v.* **1.** To make or become flat. **2.** To knock down. **—flat'ten·er** *n.*
flat·ter (flăt'ər) *v.* **1.** To compliment (someone) extravagantly, esp. to win favor. **2.** To gratify the vanity of. **3. a.** To portray favorably. **b.** To show off to advantage. ☆**syns:** ADULATE, BLANDISH, SOFT-SOAP, SWEET-TALK. **—flat'ter·er** *n.* **—flat'ter·ing** *adj.* **—flat'ter·ing·ly** *adv.*
flat·ter·y (flăt'ə-rē) *n.* Excessive often insincere praise.
flat·top (flăt'tŏp') *n.* **1.** An aircraft carrier. **2.** A very short haircut with a flattish, brushlike crown.
flat·u·lent (flăch'ə-lənt) *adj.* **1.** Causing or having excessive gas in the digestive tract. **2.** Pompous : self-important. **—flat'u·lence** *n.* **—flat'u·lent·ly** *adv.*
flat·ware (flăt'wâr') *n.* **1.** Tableware that is relatively flat and fashioned usu. of a single piece, as plates. **2.** Table utensils, as knives, forks, and spoons.
Flau·bert (flō-bâr'), **Gustave.** 1821–80. French novelist. **—Flau·ber'ti·an** *adj.*
flaunt (flônt) *v.* To display ostentatiously : show off <*flaunting* her diamonds> **—flaunt'er** *n.* **—flaunt'ing·ly** *adv.*
flau·tist (flô'tĭst, flou'-) *n.* A flutist.
fla·vor (flā'vər) *n.* **1.** Distinctive taste. **2.** A distinctive, characteristic quality <the *flavor* of Paris> **3.** A flavoring. —*v.* To impart flavor to. **—fla'vor·ful** *adj.* **—fla'vor·less** *adj.* **—fla'vor·some** *adj.*
fla·vor·ing (flā'vər-ĭng) *n.* A substance, as an extract or spice, that imparts flavor.
fla·vour (flā'vər) *n. esp. Brit. var. of* FLAVOR.
flaw (flô) *n.* **1.** An imperfect or defective part, as a crack or blemish. **2.** An intangible defect <a character *flaw*> **—flaw** *v.* **—flaw'less** *adj.* **—flaw'less·ly** *adv.* **—flaw'less·ness** *n.*
flax (flăks) *n.* A plant of the genus *Linum*, with blue flowers, seeds that yield linseed oil, and slender stems from which a fine textile fiber is derived.
flax·en (flăk'sən) *adj.* **1.** Made of or suggesting flax. **2.** Pale yellow, as flax fiber.
flay (flā) *v.* **1.** To strip off the skin of (e.g., an animal). **2.** To scold or criticize harshly.
flea (flē) *n.* A small, wingless, bloodsucking jumping insect of the order Siphonaptera, parasitic on warm-blooded animals.
flea-bit·ten (flē'bĭt'n) *adj.* **1.** Covered with fleas or their bites. **2.** *Informal.* Shabby <a *flea-bitten* hotel>
flea market *n.* A market where antiques and used household goods are sold.
fleck (flĕk) *n.* **1.** A tiny spot or mark. **2.** A small flake or bit. —*v.* To mark with flecks : spot : speckle.
fledg·ling *also* **fledge·ling** (flĕj'lĭng) *n.* **1.** A young bird with newly acquired flight feathers. **2.** A person who is young and inexperienced.
flee (flē) *v.* **fled** (flĕd), **flee·ing. 1.** To run away (from). **2.** To pass swiftly away : vanish. **—fle'er** *n.*
fleece (flēs) *n.* **1.** A coat of wool, as of a sheep or alpaca. **2.** A soft, woolly covering or mass. —*v.* **fleeced, fleec·ing. 1.** To shear the fleece from. **2.** To defraud : swindle. **3.** To cover with or as if with fleece. **—fleec'er** *n.* **—fleec'i·ly** *adv.* **—fleec'i·ness** *n.* **—fleec'y** *adj.*
fleet[1] (flēt) *n.* **1.** A number of warships operating together under a single command. **2.** A number of vehicles, as taxicabs or fishing boats, operated as a unit.
fleet[2] (flēt) *adj.* Moving rapidly or nimbly. **—fleet'ly** *adv.* **—fleet'ness** *n.*
flesh (flĕsh) *n.* **1.** Soft bodily tissue, esp. skeletal muscle. **2.** The meat of animals as distinguished from the edible tissue of fish or fowl. **3.** The pulpy part of a fruit or vegetable. **4.** The carnal body as distinguished from the mind or soul. **5.** Humanity in general. **6.** One's family : kin. —*v.* To fill out (a framework or structure).
flesh and blood *n.* **1.** Human nature or physical existence, together with its weaknesses. **2.** FLESH 6.
flesh·ly (flĕsh'lē) *adj.* **-li·er, -li·est. 1.** Of or relating to the body : corporeal. **2.** Of or relating to carnal desires : sensual. **3.** Not spiritual : worldly. **—flesh'li·ness** *n.*
flesh·pot (flĕsh'pŏt') *n.* **1.** A place in which physical gratification is obtained. **2.** Physical well-being and gratification.
flesh·y (flĕsh'ē) *adj.* **-i·er, -i·est. 1.** Of, relating to, or suggestive of flesh. **2.** Corpulent : plump. **3.** Juicy and pulpy, as fruit. **—flesh'i·ness** *n.*
fleur-de-lis (flûr'də-lē', flo͝or'-) *n., pl.* **fleurs-de-lis** (flûr'də-lēz', flo͝or'-). **1.** A heraldic emblem and artistic design consisting of a stylized 3-petaled iris, once used as the armorial emblem of French sovereigns. **2.** *Can.* The emblem of Quebec Province.
flew (flo͞o) *v. p.t. of* FLY[1].
flex (flĕks) *v.* **1.** To bend, esp. repeatedly. **2.** To contract (a muscle).
flex·i·ble (flĕk'sə-bəl) *adj.* **1.** Able to be bent or flexed : pliable. **2.** Responsive or adaptable to change. **3.** Easily persuaded. **—flex'i·bil'i·ty** *n.* **—flex'i·bly** *adv.*
flex·time (flĕks'tīm') *n.* A plan that allows employees to set their own work schedules within a wide range of hours.

flex·ure (flĕk′shər) *n.* **1.** A bend or turn. **2.** An act of bending.

flick[1] (flĭk) *n.* A light, quick blow, jerk, or touch or the sound accompanying it. —*v.* **1.** To touch or hit with a flick. **2.** To cause to move with a light snap <*flicked* the light switch off>

flick[2] (flĭk) *n. Informal.* A movie.

flick·er[1] (flĭk′ər) *v.* **1.** To flutter <shadows *flickering* on the wall> **2.** To burn unsteadily, as a candle : gutter. —*n.* **1.** A wavering light. **2.** A brief sensation <a *flicker* of understanding>

flick·er[2] (flĭk′ər) *n.* A large North American woodpecker of the genus *Colaptes,* with a brownish back and a spotted breast.

flied (flīd) *v. p.t. & p.p. of* FLY[1] 7.

fli·er *also* **fly·er** (flī′ər) *n.* **1.** One that flies, esp. an aircraft pilot. **2.** A daring or speculative venture. **3.** A printed advertisement for mass distribution.

flight[1] (flīt) *n.* **1.** The act or process of flying. **2.** A scheduled airline run or trip. **3.** A group flying together. **4.** Rapid passage or movement, as of time. **5.** An extraordinary effort or display. **6.** A series of stairs leading from 1 floor to another.

flight[2] (flīt) *n.* An act or an instance of fleeing <unlawful *flight* to escape arrest>

flight attendant *n.* One employed to assist passengers in an aircraft.

flight bag *n.* A lightweight, flexible piece of luggage with zippered outside pockets.

flight·less (flīt′lĭs) *adj.* Incapable of flying <*flightless* birds>

flight·y (flī′tē) *adj.* **-i·er, -i·est. 1.** Inclined to act capriciously : fickle. **2.** Marked by irresponsible behavior. **3.** Easily excited : skittish. **—flight′i·ness** *n.*

flim·flam (flĭm′flăm′) *n. Informal.* **1.** Nonsense. **2.** A swindle. **—flim′flam′** *v.*

flim·sy (flĭm′zē) *adj.* **-si·er, -si·est. 1.** Lacking substance or strength <*flimsy* lace><a *flimsy* chair> **2.** Unconvincing : implausible <a *flimsy* excuse> **—flim′si·ly** *adv.* **—flim′si·ness** *n.*

flinch (flĭnch) *v.* **1.** To wince, as from pain. **2.** To draw away : retreat. **—flinch** *n.* **—flinch′er** *n.*

fling (flĭng) *v.* **flung** (flŭng), **fling·ing. 1.** To throw violently. **2.** To throw (oneself) into an activity energetically. **3.** To toss aside : discard <*fling* caution to the winds> —*n.* **1.** An act of flinging : throw. **2.** A spree. **3.** *Informal.* A brief attempt or effort <took a *fling* at skiing>

flint (flĭnt) *n.* **1.** A hard quartz that sparks when struck with steel. **2.** A spark-producing alloy used in cigarette lighters to ignite the fuel. **—flint′y** *adj.*

flint·lock (flĭnt′lŏk′) *n.* **1.** A gunlock in which a flint strikes a metal plate, thus producing sparks that ignite the charge. **2.** An obsolete firearm equipped with a flintlock.

flip (flĭp) *v.* **flipped, flip·ping. 1.** To turn or toss suddenly or jerkily <*flip* a coin> **2.** To strike or snap quickly or lightly. **3.** *Slang.* **a.** To go crazy. **b.** To react in a strong usu. enthusiastic manner. —*adj.* **flip·per, flip·pest.** *Informal.* **1.** Disrespectful : impudent. **2.** Unconcerned : indifferent. **—flip** *n.*

flip chart *n.* A chart with sheets that can be flipped over to present information sequentially.

flip-flop (flĭp′flŏp′) *n.* **1.** The movement or sound of repeated flapping <the *flip-flop* of sandals on a stone floor> **2.** A backward somersault. **3.** *Informal.* A reversal, as of opinion. **—flip′-flop′** *v.*

flip·pant (flĭp′ənt) *adj.* Marked by disrespect, impudence, or indifference. **—flip′pan·cy** *n.* **—flip′pant·ly** *adv.*

flip·per (flĭp′ər) *n.* **1.** A wide, flat limb, as of a seal, adapted esp. for swimming. **2.** A paddlelike rubber shoe used in swimming and skin diving.

flip side *n.* The reverse side.

flirt (flûrt) *v.* **1.** To make playfully romantic or sexual overtures. **2.** To act so as to attract or provoke : trifle <*flirt* with death> **3.** To move abruptly : jerk. —*n.* **1.** One who flirts. **2.** An abrupt, jerky movement. **—flir·ta′tion** *n.* **—flir·ta′tious** *adj.* **—flir·ta′tious·ness** *n.*

flit (flĭt) *v.* **flit·ted, flit·ting.** To move quickly or abruptly : dart. **—flit′ter** *n.*

flitch (flĭch) *n.* A salted and cured side of bacon.

flit·ter (flĭt′ər) *v.* To flutter.

fliv·ver (flĭv′ər) *n.* An old or cheap car.

float (flōt) *v.* **1. a.** To be or cause to be suspended within or on the surface of a fluid. **b.** To be or cause to be suspended in or move through the air as if supported by water. **2.** To drift randomly from place to place. **3.** To move lightly and easily. **4.** To offer (a security) for sale. **5.** To arrange for (e.g., a loan). —*n.* **1.** Something that floats, as a raft. **2.** A floating object, as a cork, on a fishing line. **3.** A large, flat vehicle carrying a parade exhibit. **4.** A milkshake with ice cream floating in it. **—float′a·ble** *adj.* **—float′er** *n.*

floating rib *n.* One of the 4 lower ribs that, unlike the other ribs, are not attached at the front.

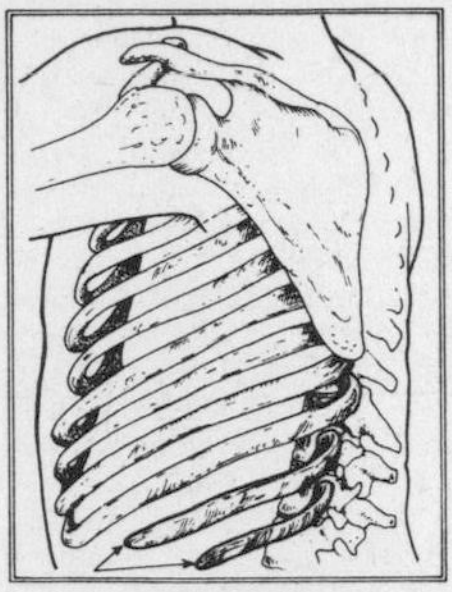

floating rib

flock (flŏk) *n.* **1.** A group of animals living, traveling, or feeding together. **2.** A group led by a single person, esp. the members of a church. **3.** A large number. —*v.* To travel or gather in or as if in a flock.

floe (flō) *n.* A flat mass of floating ice or a segment separated from it.

flog (flŏg, flôg) *v.* **flogged, flog·ging.** To beat with a whip or stick. **—flog′ger** *n.*

flood (flŭd) *n.* **1.** An overflow of water onto land that is normally dry. **2.** A large outpouring <a *flood* of mail> **3. Flood.** The great deluge described in the Old Testament. —*v.* **1.** To inundate with or as if with a flood. **2.** To fill abundantly or excessively <*flood* the market>

flood·gate (flŭd′gāt′) *n.* A gate for controlling the flow from a large body of water.

flood·light (flŭd′līt′) *n.* An electric lamp that produces a broad and intensely bright beam of light. **—flood′light′** *v.*

flood tide *n.* **1.** The incoming tide. **2.** A high point : climax.

floor (flôr, flōr) *n.* **1.** The lower surface of a room on which one stands. **2.** The ground surface <the ocean *floor*><the *floor* of a forest> **3.** The lower part of a room, used for conducting business <the *floor* of the senate> **4.** The right to speak to a meeting or assembly, as granted under parliamentary rules. **5. a.** A story of a building. **b.** The occupants of such a story. —*v.* **1.** To provide or furnish with a floor. **2.** To knock down. **3.** To overwhelm : stun.

floor exercise *n.* A competitive gymnastics event consisting of tumbling maneuvers performed on a mat.

floor show *n.* A series of nightclub acts.

floor·walk·er (flôr′wô′kər, flōr′-) *n.* A department store employee who is in charge of salespeople and aids customers.

flop (flŏp) *v.* **flopped, flop·ping. 1.** To fall down or cause to fall down heavily : plop. **2.** To move about in a clumsy or relaxed way. **3.** *Informal.* To fail completely. **4.** *Slang.* To go to bed. **—flop** *n.*

flop·house (flŏp′hous′) *n.* A cheap hotel.

flop·py (flŏp′ē) *adj.* **-pi·er, -pi·est.** Loose and flexible <a *floppy* hat> **—flop′pi·ly** *adv.* **—flop′pi·ness** *n.*

floppy disk *n. Computer Sci.* A flexible plastic disk coated with magnetic material used to store computer data.

flo·ra (flôr′ə, flōr′ə) *n., pl.* **-ras** *or* **flo·rae** (flôr′ē′, flōr′ē′). Plants as a whole, esp. those of a specific region or season.

flo·ral (flôr′əl, flōr′-) *adj.* Of or relating to flowers. **—flo′ral·ly** *adv.*

Flor·ence (flôr′əns, flōr′-). City on the Arno R. in C Italy. *Pop.* 462,690. **—Flor′en·tine′** (flôr′ən-tēn′, flōr′-) *adj. & n.*

flo·res·cence (flô-rĕs′əns, flə-) *n.* A state or time of blossoming. **—flo·res′cent** *adj.*

flor·id (flôr′ĭd, flōr′-) *adj.* **1.** Flushed with rosy color. **2.** Ornate. **—flo·rid′i·ty, flor′id·ness** *n.* **—flor′id·ly** *adv.*

Flor·i·da (flôr′ə-də, flōr′-). State of the SE U.S. *Cap.* Tallahassee. *Pop.* 9,739,992.

flo·rin (flôr′ĭn, flōr′-) *n.* **1.** A guilder. **2.** A former British coin worth 2 shillings.

flo·rist (flôr′ĭst, flōr′-, flŏr′-) *n.* One whose business is the cultivation or sale of flowers and ornamental plants.

floss (flôs, flŏs) *n.* **1.** Short or waste silk fibers. **2.** A soft, loosely twisted embroidery thread. **3.** A soft, silky, fibrous substance, as the tassel on corn. **4.** Dental floss. —*v.* **1.** To clean between (teeth) with dental floss. **2.** To use dental floss.

floss·y (flô′sē, flŏs′ē) *adj.* **-i·er, -i·est. 1.** Made of or resembling floss. **2.** *Slang.* Ostentatiously stylish. **—floss′i·ness** *n.*

flo·ta·tion (flō-tā′shən) *n.* The act or state of floating.

flo·til·la (flō-tĭl′ə) *n.* **1.** A fleet of small ships. **2.** A group resembling a small fleet.

flot·sam (flŏt′səm) *n.* Wreckage remaining afloat after a ship has sunk.
flounce[1] (flouns) *n.* A strip of gathered material attached along the upper edge to another surface, as on a garment or curtain.
flounce[2] (flouns) *v.* **flounced, flounc·ing.** To move with exaggerated, jerky movements <*flounced* out of the house angrily> **—flounce** *n.*
floun·der[1] (floun′dər) *v.* **1.** To struggle clumsily, as to obtain footing. **2.** To act or speak in a clumsy, confused way.
floun·der[2] (floun′dər) *n.* Any of various edible marine flatfishes of the families Bothidae and Pleuronectidae.
flour (flour) *n.* **1.** A soft, fine, powderlike substance produced by grinding grain, esp. wheat. **2.** A soft, fine powder like flour. *—v.* To coat with flour. **—flour′y** *adj.*
▲word history: The word *flour* is simply a specialized use of the word *flower* in its medieval spelling. The *flower* of wheat or any other grain is the finest part of the meal that is left after the bran has been sifted out. The distinction in spelling between *flour* and *flower* did not become standard until the 19th cent.
flour·ish (flûr′ĭsh, flŭr′-) *v.* **1.** To grow abundantly : thrive. **2.** To do well : succeed and prosper. **3.** To brandish. *—n.* **1.** An added decorative touch, esp. in handwriting : embellishment. **2.** A dramatic act or gesture. **3.** A musical fanfare.
flout (flout) *v.* To have or show contempt for : scorn. **—flout′ing·ly** *adv.*
flow (flō) *v.* **1.** To move or come forth freely like a fluid. **2.** To circulate, as blood. **3.** To move or proceed steadily and easily. **4.** To rise. Used of the tide. **5.** To derive. **6.** To be plentiful : abound. **7.** To hang in a loose, graceful way. **—flow** *n.*
flow chart *n.* A chart or diagram of the sequence and progress of a series of operations for a specific project.
flow·er (flou′ər) *n.* **1.** The part of a seed-bearing plant that contains specialized male and female organs, as stamens and a pistil, and produces seeds and usu. colorful blossoms. **2.** A plant cultivated for its blossoms. **3.** The period of highest development : peak. **4.** The best example or representative. *—v.* **1.** To produce flowers. **2.** To develop fully. **—flow′er·less** *adj.*
flow·er·pot (flou′ər-pŏt′) *n.* A pot, often of earthenware, in which plants are grown.
flow·er·y (flou′ə-rē) *adj.* **-i·er, -i·est. 1.** Full of, covered with, or suggestive of flowers. **2.** Full of high-sounding, ornate expressions. **—flow′er·i·ness** *n.*
flown (flōn) *v. p.p. of* FLY[1].
fl oz *abbr.* fluid ounce.
flu (flo͞o) *n. Informal.* Influenza.
flub (flŭb) *v.* **flubbed, flub·bing.** To bungle : botch. **—flub** *n.*
fluc·tu·ate (flŭk′cho͞o-āt′) *v.* **-at·ed, -at·ing. 1.** To shift irregularly : waver. **2.** To undulate. **—fluc′tu·a′tion** *n.*
flue (flo͞o) *n.* A conduit or passage through which air, gas, steam, or smoke can flow <a chimney *flue*>
flu·ent (flo͞o′ənt) *adj.* **1.** Having facility in language use. **2.** Flowing smoothly and naturally : polished <*fluent* verse> **3.** Flowing or capable of flowing : fluid. **—flu′en·cy** *n.* **—flu′ent·ly** *adv.*
fluff (flŭf) *n.* **1.** Light down : nap. **2.** Something that resembles fluff in consistency or appearance. **3.** Something unimportant. **4.** *Informal.* A mistake or memory lapse, esp. by an actor or announcer. *—v.* **1.** To make or become fluffy. **2.** *Informal.* To misread or forget (one's lines).
fluff·y (flŭf′ē) *adj.* **-i·er, -i·est. 1.** Of, like, or covered with fluff. **2.** Light and airy : soft. **—fluff′i·ly** *adv.* **fluff′i·ness** *n.*
flu·id (flo͞o′ĭd) *n.* A substance, as water or air, that flows readily and tends to assume the shape of its container. *—adj.* **1.** Flowing readily, as a liquid. **2.** Smooth and effortless. **3.** Easily changed or tending to change : adaptable. **4.** Convertible into cash <*fluid* assets> **—flu·id′i·ty, flu′id·ness** *n.* **—flu′id·ly** *adv.*
fluid ounce *n.* See MEASUREMENT TABLE.
fluke[1] (flo͝ok) *n.* A flatfish, esp. a flounder of the genus *Paralichthys.*
fluke[2] (flo͝ok) *n.* **1.** The triangular fastening blade of an anchor. **2.** A barb or barbed head, as on an arrow or harpoon. **3.** One of the 2 lobes of a whale's tail.
fluke[3] (flo͞ok) *n.* An unexpected stroke of good fortune. **—fluk′y** *adj.*
flume (flo͞om) *n.* **1.** A narrow gorge, usu. with a stream running through it. **2.** An artificial channel to carry a stream of water.
flung (flŭng) *v. p.t. & p.p. of* FLING.
flunk (flŭngk) *v. Informal.* **1.** To fail, esp. in an examination or course. **2.** To give a failing grade to.
flun·ky *also* **flun·key** (flŭng′kē) *n., pl.* **-kies** *also* **-keys. 1.** An obsequious person : toady. **2.** One who does menial work.
flu·o·res·cence (flo͞o′ə-rĕs′əns, flo͝o-rĕs′-) *n.* **1.** Emission of electromagnetic radiation, esp. of visible light, caused by absorption of incident radiation and persisting only as long as the stimulating radiation continues. **2.** The radiation emitted. **—flu′o·resce′** *v.* **—flu′o·res′cent** *adj.*
fluorescent lamp *n.* A tubular electric lamp whose inner wall is coated with a material that generates fluorescence by means of secondary radiation.
fluor·i·date (flo͝or′ĭ-dāt′, flôr′-, flōr′-) *v.* **-dat·ed, -dat·ing.** To add a fluorine compound to (e.g., a water supply) to prevent tooth decay. **—fluor′i·da′tion** *n.*
flu·o·ride (flo͞o′ə-rīd′, flo͝or′īd′, flôr′-, flōr′-) *n.* A binary compound of fluorine with another element or a radical.
flu·o·rine (flo͞o′ə-rēn′, -rĭn, flo͝or′ēn′, -ĭn, flôr′-, flōr′-) *n. Symbol* **F** A pale-yellow, corrosive, poisonous gaseous element.
fluor·o·scope (flo͝or′ə-skōp′, flôr′-, flōr′-, flo͞o′ər-ə-) *n.* A fluorescent screen on which the inner structure of an optically opaque object, as the human body, may be viewed by transmission of x-rays through the object. **—fluor′o·scope′** *v.* **—fluor′o·scop′ic** (-skŏp′ĭk) *adj.* **—fluo·ros′co·py** (flo͝o-rŏs′kə-pē) *n.*
flur·ry (flûr′ē, flŭr′ē) *n., pl.* **-ries. 1.** A sudden gust of wind. **2.** A brief, light fall of snow. **3.** A sudden burst of activity or excitement. **—flur′ry** *v.*
flush[1] (flŭsh) *v.* **1.** To flow and spread out suddenly and abundantly. **2.** To blush or cause to blush. **3.** To glow, esp. with a reddish color. **4.** To clean or wash out with a brief, rapid gush of water. **5.** To excite or elate, as with pride. *—n.* **1.** A brief, copious flow, as of water. **2.** A reddish tinge or glow : blush. **3.** Animation or exhilaration. **4.** Freshness or vigor <the *flush* of youth> *—adj.* **1.** Having a reddish color. **2.** Abundant : plentiful. **3.** Affluent : prosperous. **4. a.** Having surfaces in the same plane : even. **b.** Arranged with adjacent sides, surfaces, or edges close together. **c.** Having margins aligned with no indentations. **5.** Direct and accurate, as a blow. *—adv.* **1.** So as to be in one plane, even, or aligned with a margin. **2.** Squarely : solidly.
flush[2] (flŭsh) *n.* A hand in certain card games, as poker, in which all the cards are of the same suit.
flush[3] (flŭsh) *v.* To cause (e.g., a game bird) to fly from cover.
flus·ter (flŭs′tər) *v.* To make or become nervous or upset. **—flus′ter** *n.*
flute (flo͞ot) *n.* **1.** A high-pitched tubular woodwind instrument with finger holes and keys. **2.** One of the long, parallel decorative grooves on the shaft of a column. **3.** A grooved pleat, as in cloth. **—flut′ed** *adj.* **—flut′ing** *n.*
flut·ist (flo͞o′tĭst) *n.* A flute player.
flut·ter (flŭt′ər) *v.* **1.** To flap or wave rapidly and irregularly. **2.** To fly with a light, quick beating of the wings. **3.** To beat rapidly or erratically, as one's heart. **4.** To move about in a restless or excited way. **—flut′ter** *n.* **—flut′ter·y** *adj.*
flux (flŭks) *n.* **1. a.** An act of flowing. **b.** A continued flow : flood. **2.** A state of constant change or fluctuation. **3.** A substance applied in soldering to facilitate flowing and prevent oxide formation. *—v.* **1.** To fuse : melt. **2.** To apply a flux to.
fly[1] (flī) *v.* **flew** (flo͞o), **flown** (flōn), **fly·ing. 1. a.** To move through the air by means of wings or winglike parts. **b.** To travel by air. **c.** To pilot (an aircraft). **2.** To rise, float, or cause to float in the air <pennants *flying*> **3.** To try to escape : flee. **4.** To rush : hasten. **5.** To pass by swiftly. **6.** To react explosively <*flew* into a rage> **7.** *p.t. & p.p.* **flied.** To hit a fly ball. *—n., pl.* **flies. 1.** A fold of cloth covering the fastening on a garment, esp. trousers. **2.** A cloth flap covering an entrance, as of a tent. **3.** A fly ball. **4. flies.** The area directly over the stage of a theater, used esp. for lighting equipment. **—on the fly. 1.** In a great hurry. **2.** In the air. **—fly′a·ble** *adj.*
fly[2] (flī) *n., pl.* **flies. 1.** Any of numerous winged insects of the order Diptera, esp. one of the family Muscidae, which includes the housefly and the tsetse. **2.** A fishing lure simulating a fly.
fly ball *n.* A baseball batted in a high arc.
fly·blown (flī′blōn′) *adj.* Contaminated : spoiled.
fly-by-night (flī′bī-nīt′) *adj.* **1.** Unstable : unreliable. **2.** Temporary : transitory.
fly·catch·er (flī′kăch′ər, -kĕch′-) *n.* Any of various birds of the New World family Tyrannidae or the Old World family Muscicapidae that catch flying insects.
fly·er (flī′ər) *n. var. of* FLIER.
flying boat *n.* A seaplane that is kept afloat by its hull rather than by pontoons.
flying buttress *n.* A projecting arched structure that braces part of a main wall.
flying fish *n.* A marine fish of the family Exocoetidae, having winglike fins that sustain short, gliding flights over the water.
flying saucer *n.* An unidentified flying object usu. reported and described as a luminous disk in the sky.
flying squirrel *n.* A squirrel of the genera *Pteromys, Glaucomys,* and related genera, with membranes between the forelegs and hind legs enabling it to glide through the air.

fly·leaf (flī'lēf') *n.* A blank leaf at the beginning or end of a book.
fly·pa·per (flī'pā'pər) *n.* Paper that is coated with a sticky, occas. poisonous substance to catch flies.
fly·speck (flī'spĕk') *n.* **1.** A tiny, dark speck or stain made by fly excrement. **2.** Something minute or insignificant.
fly·weight (flī'wāt') *n.* A boxer weighing 112 lb. or less.
fly·wheel (flī'hwēl', -wēl') *n.* A rotating wheel with a heavy rim that regulates the speed of a machine shaft.
Fm *symbol for* FERMIUM.
foal (fōl) *n.* The young of an equine animal, as a horse, esp. one under a year old. *—v.* To give birth to a foal.
foam (fōm) *n.* **1.** A mass of bubbles formed in or on the surface of a liquid : froth. **2.** A light, firm, spongy material, as rubber, used esp. for insulation and upholstery. *—v.* To form or cause to form foam. **—foam'i·ness** *n.* **—foam'y** *adj.*
fob¹ (fŏb) *n.* **1.** A short ribbon or chain attached to a pocket watch. **2.** An ornament or seal worn on a fob.
fob² (fŏb) *v.* **1.** To dispose of by fraud or deceit. **2.** To put off by evasion or excuse.
focal length *n.* The distance of a focus from a lens or mirror.
fo'c's'le (fōk'səl) *n. var. of* FORECASTLE.
fo·cus (fō'kəs) *n., pl.* **-cus·es** *or* **-ci** (-sī'). **1.** A point in an optical system to which something converges or from which it appears to diverge. **2. a.** Focal length. **b.** The distinctness or clarity with which an optical system renders an image. **c.** Adjustment for distinctness or clarity. **3.** A center of interest or activity. *—v.* **-cused, -cus·ing** *or* **-cussed, -cus·sing. 1. a.** To produce a clear image of (e.g., photographed material). **b.** To adjust (a lens) to produce a clear image. **2.** To concentrate : direct. **3.** To converge at a point of focus. **—fo'cal** *adj.* **—fo'cal·ly** *adv.*
fod·der (fŏd'ər) *n.* Coarse feed for livestock, as chopped stalks of corn and hay.
foe (fō) *n.* **1.** An enemy, esp. in wartime. **2.** An opponent : adversary.
foe·tal (fēt'l) *adj. var. of* FETAL.
foe·tus (fē'təs) *n. var. of* FETUS.
fog (fôg, fŏg) *n.* **1.** Cloudlike masses of condensed water vapor lying close to the ground and obscuring visibility. **2.** Mental confusion or bewilderment. *—v.* **fogged, fog·ging.** To obscure or be obscured with or as if with fog. **—fog'gi·ly** *adv.* **—fog'gi·ness** *n.* **—fog'gy** *adj.*
fog·horn (fôg'hôrn', fŏg'-) *n.* A warning horn sounded in a fog or in darkness.
fo·gy *also* **fo·gey** (fō'gē) *n., pl.* **-gies** *also* **-geys.** A person with old-fashioned attitudes. **—fo'gy·ish** *adj.*
foi·ble (foi'bəl) *n.* A minor character weakness or failing.
foil¹ (foil) *v.* To keep from being successful : defeat : thwart.
foil² (foil) *n.* **1.** A thin, flexible sheet of metal. **2.** One that by strong contrast intensifies another's characteristics.
foil³ (foil) *n.* A fencing sword with a light, thin, flexible blade and a blunt point.
foist (foist) *v.* To pass off (something inferior or false) as valuable or genuine.
fold¹ (fōld) *v.* **1.** To double or become doubled so that one part lies on another <*fold* paper> **2.** To bring (e.g., wings) from an extended to a closed position. **3.** To place together and intertwine <*fold* one's arms> **4.** To clasp, envelop, or wrap. **5.** To mix in (a cooking ingredient) by very gently turning one part over another. **6.** *Informal.* **a.** To give in : yield. **b.** To fail financially. *—n.* **1.** A part, as a line, layer, pleat, or crease, formed by folding. **2.** A folded piece or edge. **—fold'a·ble** *adj.*
fold² (fōld) *n.* **1. a.** An enclosure for domestic animals <a sheep*fold*> **b.** A flock of sheep. **2. a.** A group of people united by common aims and beliefs. **b.** A church and its members.
fold·er (fōl'dər) *n.* **1.** One that folds. **2.** A printed booklet or circular consisting of 1 or several folded sheets of paper. **3.** A folded sheet of heavy paper or cardboard used for loose papers.
fol·de·rol (fŏl'də-rŏl') *n.* **1.** Nonsense. **2.** A pretty but useless trinket.
fo·li·age (fō'lē-ĭj) *n.* The leaves of growing plants and trees.
fo·li·o (fō'lē-ō') *n., pl.* **-os. 1.** A large sheet of paper folded once in the middle, making 2 leaves or 4 pages of a book or manuscript. **2.** A book consisting of folios. **3.** A page number in a book.
folk (fōk) *n., pl.* **folk** *or* **folks. 1.** An ethnic group, as a tribe or nation. **2.** People of a specified kind or group <rich *folk*> **3. folks.** *Informal.* One's relatives or family. **4. folks.** *Informal.* People in general. *—adj.* Of, pertaining to, or originating among the common people <a *folk* story>
folk etymology *n.* A change in form of a word or phrase so that it resembles a more familiar term mistakenly taken to be analogous, as *sparrowgrass* for *asparagus.*
folk·lore (fōk'lôr', -lōr') *n.* The traditional beliefs, practices, and legends of a people handed down orally. **—folk'lor'ist** *n.*
folk music *n.* Music that originates among the common people of a nation or region, traditionally transmitted orally.
folk singer *n.* One who sings folk songs. **—folk singing** *n.*
folk song *n.* A song that is part of the folk music of a people or region and that is marked by simplicity and directness of the feelings expressed.
folk·sy (fōk'sē) *adj.* **-si·er, -si·est.** *Informal.* **1.** Marked by informality of manner or style. **2.** Congenial : friendly. **—folk'si·ly** *adv.* **—folk'si·ness** *n.*
folk·way (fōk'wā') *n.* A traditional way of acting or thinking shared by the members of a cultural group.
fol·li·cle (fŏl'ĭ-kəl) *n.* **1.** A tiny anatomical cavity or sac <a hair *follicle*> **2.** A structure in an ovary containing ova.
fol·low (fŏl'ō) *v.* **1.** To come or go after. **2.** To chase : pursue. **3.** To attend : accompany. **4.** To go along the course of. **5.** To comply with : obey. **6.** To come after in time, order, or position. **7.** To engage in (e.g., a trade). **8.** To ensue : result. **9.** To pay attention to. **10.** To grasp the meaning or logic of : understand.
fol·low·er (fŏl'ō-ər) *n.* **1.** One that follows, esp. a pursuer. **2. a.** An attendant. **b.** A subordinate. **3.** An adherent of the methods or teachings of another.
fol·low·ing (fŏl'ō-ĭng) *adj.* **1.** Coming next, as in time : succeeding. **2.** Listed or mentioned next. *—n.* A group of admirers, disciples, or attendants.
fol·low-up (fŏl'ō-ŭp') *n.* The act of repeating or supplementing previous action, as by a letter or visit.
fol·ly (fŏl'ē) *n., pl.* **-lies. 1.** Lack of good sense and judgment. **2.** An act or instance of foolishness. **3.** An inordinately costly and often unprofitable undertaking.
fo·ment (fō-mĕnt') *v.* **1.** To stir up : incite. **2.** To treat therapeutically with heat and moisture. **—fo·ment'** *n.* **—fo'men·ta'tion** *n.* **—fo·ment'er** *n.*
fond (fŏnd) *adj.* **1.** Affectionate : loving <a *fond* smile> **2.** Having a liking or affection <*fond* of music> **3.** Immoderately affectionate : doting. **4.** Deeply felt : cherished <*fond* memories> **—fond'ly** *adv.* **—fond'ness** *n.*

▲word history: *Fond* is an example of a word that has undergone *melioration,* or a shift in connotation from bad to neutral or good. *Fond* was originally *fonned,* meaning "insipid or tasteless" and "foolish." It later meant "foolishly affectionate, doting" but even the mild reproach conveyed by this sense was lost, and *fond* now means only "having a strong liking for." The verb *fon,* of which *fond* was orig. a past participle, is very likely the same word as the word *fun.*

fon·dant (fŏn'dənt) *n.* **1.** A sweet, creamy sugar paste used in candies and icings. **2.** A candy containing fondant.
fon·dle (fŏn'dl) *v.* **-dled, -dling.** To stroke, handle, or caress affectionately.
fon·due (fŏn-dōō') *n.* A hot dish of melted cheese usu. flavored with wine.
font¹ (fŏnt) *n.* **1.** A basin in a church that holds baptismal or holy water. **2.** A source of abundance : fount.
font² (fŏnt) *n.* A full set of printing type of the same size and face.
food (fōōd) *n.* **1.** A substance, usu. of plant or animal origin, taken in and assimilated by an organism to maintain life and growth : nourishment. **2.** A specified kind of nourishment <dog *food*><breakfast *food*> **3.** Nourishment in solid form <hearty *food* and drink> **4.** Something that sustains, nourishes, or provides <*food* for thought>
food chain *n.* An ecological community of plants and animals in which each kind uses the kind usu. next below it as food.
food poisoning *n.* Poisoning marked by vomiting, diarrhea, and prostration and caused by eating food contaminated by natural toxins or bacteria.
food processor *n.* An appliance with interchangeable blades that processes food, as by slicing or shredding, at high speed.
food stamp *n.* A stamp issued by the government and sold or given to low-income persons to be redeemed for food.
food·stuff (fōōd'stŭf') *n.* Something that can be used as food.
food web *n.* A complex of interrelated food chains in an ecological community.
fool (fōōl) *n.* **1.** One deficient in good sense or judgment. **2.** A court jester. **3.** One who can easily be tricked : dupe. *—v.* **1.** To dupe. **2.** To take by surprise. **3.** To speak or act in jest : joke. **4.** *Informal.* To amuse oneself : play <just *fooling* around> **5.** To toy or tamper with.
fool·er·y (fōō'lə-rē) *n., pl.* **-ies.** Foolish speech or behavior : nonsense.
fool·har·dy (fōōl'här'dē) *adj.* **-di·er, -di·est.** Unwisely daring : rash. **—fool'har'di·ly** *adv.* **—fool'har'di·ness** *n.*
fool·ish (fōō'lĭsh) *adj.* **1.** Lacking or resulting from a lack of

good sense or judgment : unwise. **2.** Ridiculous : absurd. **—fool'ish·ly** *adv.* **—fool'ish·ness** *n.*

fool·proof (fo͞ol'pro͞of') *adj.* Affording no opportunity for misuse, error, or failure.

fools·cap (fo͞olz'kăp') *n.* A sheet of paper approx. 13 x 16 in.

foot (fo͝ot) *n., pl.* **feet** (fēt). **1.** The lower extremity of the vertebrate leg that is in direct contact with the ground. **2.** Something like a foot in function or position <the *foot* of a hill> **3.** A basic metrical unit that consists of a group of syllables. **4.** See MEASUREMENT TABLE. **5.** The end, as of a bed, that is opposite the head. **6.** The lowest rank or part. *—v.* **1.** To go on foot : walk. **2.** To dance. **3.** To add up <*foot* up the bill> **4.** *Informal.* To pay <*foot the bill*> **—on foot.** Walking rather than riding. **—foot'less** *adj.*

foot·age (fo͝ot'ĭj) *n.* **1.** Length or extent expressed in feet. **2.** A segment of motion-picture film or videotape <news *footage*>

foot·ball (fo͝ot'bôl') *n.* **1. a.** A game played by 2 11-member teams on a long rectangular field with goals at either end. **b.** *Can.* A similar game played by 2 12-member teams. **c.** The inflated oval ball used in either of these games. **2.** *esp. Brit.* Rugby or soccer.

foot·board (fo͝ot'bôrd', -bōrd') *n.* **1.** A board or small platform on which to rest or support the feet. **2.** An upright board that forms the foot of a bedstead.

foot·bridge (fo͝ot'brĭj') *n.* A bridge for pedestrians.

foot·ed (fo͝ot'ĭd) *adj.* **1.** Having a foot or feet <a *footed* vase><a *footed* animal> **2.** Having a particular kind or number of feet <web-*footed*>

foot·fall (fo͝ot'fôl') *n.* **1.** A footstep. **2.** The sound of a footstep.

foot·hill (fo͝ot'hĭl') *n.* A low hill at or near the foot of a mountain.

foot·hold (fo͝ot'hōld') *n.* **1.** A place that provides support for the foot, as in climbing. **2.** A position providing a base for advancement.

foot·ing (fo͝ot'ĭng) *n.* **1.** Secure placement of the feet. **2. a.** A basis : foundation. **b.** A basis for social or business dealings with others : standing.

foot·lights (fo͝ot'līts') *pl.n.* **1.** Lights in a row along the front of a stage floor. **2.** The theater regarded as a profession.

foot·lock·er (fo͝ot'lŏk'ər) *n.* A small trunk for personal belongings kept esp. at the foot of a bed.

foot·loose (fo͝ot'lo͞os') *adj.* Free to do as one pleases.

foot·man (fo͝ot'mən) *n.* A male household servant who attends the door, waits on table, and runs errands.

foot·note (fo͝ot'nōt') *n.* **1.** A note of reference, explanation, or comment usu. at the bottom of a page. **2.** A commentary. **—foot'note'** *v.*

foot·path (fo͝ot'păth', -päth') *n.* A usu. narrow path for persons on foot.

foot·print (fo͝ot'prĭnt') *n.* An outline of the foot on a surface.

foot·sore (fo͝ot'sôr', -sōr') *adj.* Having tired or sore feet, as from walking.

foot·step (fo͝ot'stĕp') *n.* **1.** A step with the foot. **2.** The distance covered by a footstep <a *footstep* away> **3.** The sound of a footstep. **4.** A footprint. **5.** A step up or down.

foot·stool (fo͝ot'sto͞ol') *n.* A low stool for the feet.

foot·wear (fo͝ot'wâr') *n.* Coverings, as shoes or boots, for the feet.

foot·work (fo͝ot'wûrk') *n.* The way in which one uses the feet, as in boxing.

fop (fŏp) *n.* A man preoccupied with his clothes : dandy. **—fop'per·y** *n.* **—fop'pish** *adj.* **—fop'pish·ness** *n.*

for (fôr; fər *when unstressed*) *prep.* **1.** Used to indicate the object, recipient, or aim of an act or activity <studied *for* the exam><a gift *for* you><ran *for* President> **2.** Used to indicate a destination <headed *for* town> **3.** As a result of <jump *for* joy> **4.** Used to indicate amount, extent, or duration <a check *for* $10><walked *for* miles> **5.** Considering the usual nature or character of <cold *for* July> **6.** In spite of <unhappy *for* all their wealth> **7. a.** On behalf of <spoke *for* everyone> **b.** In favor of <Are you *for* or against the plan?> **8.** As equal to <paid $30 *for* the fare> **9.** As against <ounce *for* ounce> **10.** As being <took it *for* granted> **11.** Used to indicate appropriateness or responsibility <It's not *for* me to say.> *—conj.* Because; since.

for·age (fôr'ĭj, fŏr'-) *n.* **1.** Food for domestic animals, esp. that gathered by grazing. **2.** A search for provisions or food. *—v.* **-aged, -ag·ing. 1.** To search for provisions or food. **2.** To make a raid : plunder. **3.** To wander or rummage through, esp. in search of provisions. **—for'ag·er** *n.*

for·ay (fôr'ā', fŏr'ā') *n.* **1.** A raid. **2.** A 1st attempt or venture. **—for'ay'** *v.*

for·bear[1] (fôr-bâr') *v.* **-bore** (-bôr', -bōr'), **-borne** (-bôrn', -bōrn'), **-bear·ing. 1.** To desist or refrain from. **2.** To be patient or tolerant. **—for·bear'ance** *n.*

for·bear[2] (fôr'bâr', fōr'-) *n. var. of* FOREBEAR.

for·bid (fər-bĭd', fôr-) *v.* **-bade** (-băd', -bād') *or* **-bad** (-băd'), **-bid·den** (-bĭd'n) *or* **-bid, -bid·ding. 1.** To order (someone) not to do something. **2.** To prohibit, esp. by law. **3.** To prevent : preclude. ☆**syns:** BAN, DISALLOW, ENJOIN, INTERDICT, OUTLAW, PROHIBIT, PROSCRIBE

for·bid·ding (fər-bĭd'ĭng, fôr-) *adj.* Tending to discourage or repel.

force (fôrs, fōrs) *n.* **1. a.** Energy or strength : power. **b.** The use of such power. **2.** Intellectual vigor or influence. **3.** A group organized or available for a certain purpose. **4.** *Physics.* A vector quantity that tends to produce an acceleration of a body in the direction of its application. *—v.* **forced, forc·ing. 1.** To compel to act. **2.** To get by coercion. **3.** To produce with effort <*force* a smile> **4.** To move (something) against resistance : push. **5.** To open or break down by force. **6.** To inflict or impose, as one's will. **7.** To cause rapid growth by artificial means <*force* lilies> **—in force. 1.** In large numbers. **2.** In effect. **—force'a·ble** *adj.* **—force'ful** *adj.* **—force'ful·ly** *adv.* **—forc'er** *n.*

force·meat (fôrs'mēt', fōrs'-) *n.* Finely ground meat, fish, or poultry usu. used in stuffing.

for·ceps (fôr'səps) *n. (pl. in number).* An instrument that resembles a pair of tongs and is used for grasping, manipulating, or extracting, esp. in surgery.

forc·i·ble (fôr'sə-bəl, fōr'-) *adj.* **1.** Achieved or accomplished by force. **2.** Marked by force. **—forc'i·bly** *adv.*

ford (fôrd, fōrd) *n.* A shallow part of a body of water where a crossing can be made without a boat. *—v.* To cross at a ford.

Ford. 1. Henry. 1863–1947. Amer. automobile manufacturer. **2. Gerald Rudolph.** b. 1913. 38th U.S. President (1974–77).

fore (fôr, fōr) *adj.* & *adv.* In, at, or toward the front : forward. *—n.* The front. *—interj.* Used by a golfer to warn others that a ball is about to be hit their way.

fore-and-aft (fôr'ən-ăft', fōr'-) *adj.* Parallel with a ship's keel.

fore·arm[1] (fôr-ärm', fōr-) *v.* To arm or prepare in advance, as for a conflict.

fore·arm[2] (fôr'ärm', fōr'-) *n.* The arm between the wrist and elbow.

fore·bear *also* **for·bear** (fôr'bâr', fōr'-) *n.* An ancestor.

fore·bode (fôr-bōd', fōr-) *v.* **1.** To give an indication or warning of. **2.** To have a premonition of (future bad fortune). **—fore·bod'ing** *n.* **—fore·bod'ing·ly** *adv.*

fore·cast (fôr'kăst', fōr'-) *v.* **1.** To estimate in advance, esp. to predict (the weather). **2.** To be an indication of : foreshadow. **—fore'cast'** *n.* **—fore'cast'er** *n.*

fore·cas·tle (fōk'səl, fôr'kăs'əl, fōr'-) *also* **fo'c's'le** (fōk'səl) *n.* **1.** The section of a ship's upper deck situated forward of the foremast. **2.** Housing for the crew at the bow of a merchant ship.

fore·check (for'chek', for'-) *v. Hockey.* To check an opponent in his zone.

fore·close (fôr-klōz', fōr-) *v.* **1.** To terminate (a mortgage) and take legal possession of the mortgaged property. **2.** To exclude : debar. **—fore·clo'sure** *n.*

fore·fa·ther (fôr'fä'*th*ər, fōr'-) *n.* An ancestor.

fore·fin·ger (fôr'fĭng'gər, fōr'-) *n.* The finger next to the thumb.

fore·foot (fôr'fo͝ot', fōr'-) *n.* A front foot of an animal.

fore·front (fôr'frŭnt', fōr'-) *n.* The foremost part : vanguard.

fore·go[1] (fôr-gō', fōr-) *v.* To go before : precede.

fore·go[2] (fôr-gō', fōr-) *v. var. of* FORGO.

fore·go·ing (fôr-gō'ĭng, fōr-, fôr'gō'ĭng, fōr'-) *adj.* Just before : previous.

fore·gone (fôr'gôn', -gŏn', fōr'-) *adj.* Known in advance : inevitable.

fore·ground (fôr'ground', fōr'-) *n.* **1.** The part of a picture or view depicted as nearest to the viewer. **2.** The forefront.

fore·hand (fôr'hănd', fōr'-) *n.* A stroke, as in tennis, made with the hand moving palm forward. **—fore'hand'** *adj.* & *adv.*

fore·head (fôr'ĭd, fōr'-, fôr'hĕd', fōr'-) *n.* The part of the head or face above the eyes.

for·eign (fôr'ĭn, fōr'-) *adj.* **1.** Situated outside one's native country <*foreign* cities> **2.** Of, from, by, or for a country other than one's own <*foreign* languages> **3.** Carried on or involved with other nations <*foreign* espionage> **4.** Occurring in an abnormal place in the body. **5.** Not relevant : extraneous. **—for'eign·ness** *n.*

for·eign·er (fôr'ə-nər, fōr'-) *n.* Someone from a foreign country : alien.

fore·knowl·edge (fôr-nŏl'ĭj, fōr-) *n.* Prior knowledge of something : prescience.

fore·leg (fôr'lĕg', fōr'-) *n.* One of an animal's front legs.

fore·limb (fôr'lĭm', fōr'-) *n.* A front appendage, as an arm, wing, foreleg, or flipper.

fore·lock (fôr′lŏk′, fōr′-) *n.* A lock of hair growing from the forehead.
fore·man (fôr′mən, fōr′-) *n.* **1.** One who supervises a group of workers. **2.** The spokesperson for a jury. **–fore′wom′an** *n.*
fore·mast (fôr′məst, -măst′, fōr′-) *n. Naut.* The forward mast of a sailing vessel.
fore·most (fôr′mōst′, fōr′-) *adj.* & *adv.* First in time, rank, or position.
fore·noon (fôr′no͞on′, fōr′-) *n.* The time between sunrise and noon.
fo·ren·sic (fə-rĕn′sĭk, -zĭk) *adj.* Of, relating to, or used in legal proceedings or formal debate. **–fo·ren′si·cal·ly** *adv.*
fore·or·dain (fôr′ôr-dān′, fōr′-) *v.* To decree or ordain beforehand : predestine.
fore·part (fôr′pärt′, fōr′-) *n.* **1.** The first or earliest part. **2.** An anterior part.
fore·quar·ter (fôr′kwôr′tər, fōr′-) *n.* The section including the foreleg and shoulder of an animal or side of meat.
fore·run·ner (fôr′rŭn′ər, fōr′-) *n.* **1.** One that precedes. **2.** One that indicates the approach of others : harbinger.
fore·sail (fôr′səl, -sāl′, fōr′-) *n. Naut.* The principal square sail on the foremast of a square-rigged vessel.
fore·see (fôr-sē′, fōr-) *v.* To know or see beforehand <*foresaw* the outcome> **–fore·see′a·ble** *adj.* **–fore·se′er** *n.*
fore·shad·ow (fôr-shăd′ō, fōr-) *v.* To indicate or warn of beforehand.
fore·shore (fôr′shôr′, fōr′shōr′) *n.* The part of a shore covered at high tide.
fore·short·en (fôr-shôr′tn, fōr-) *v.* To shorten certain lines in (e.g., a figure or design) in order to give the illusion of depth.
fore·sight (fôr′sīt′, fōr′-) *n.* **1.** The act or power of foreseeing. **2.** The act of looking forward. **3.** Concern for the future : prudence. **–fore′sight′ed** *adj.* **–fore′sight′ed·ness** *n.*
fore·skin (fôr′skĭn′, fōr′-) *n.* The prepuce.
for·est (fôr′ĭst, fōr′-) *n.* **1.** A large, thick growth of trees. **2.** Something resembling a forest, as in density or quantity. **–for′est·ed** *adj.* **–for′est·land′** *n.*
fore·stall (fôr-stôl′, fōr-) *v.* To delay or prevent by taking measures against in advance. **–fore·stall′er** *n.*
forest ranger *n.* An officer in charge of managing or protecting a public forest or section of a public forest.
for·est·ry (fôr′ĭ-strē, fōr′-) *n.* The science of developing, maintaining, and managing forestland. **–for′est·er** *n.*
fore·taste (fôr′tāst′, fōr′-) *n.* An advance sample or indication. **–fore·taste′** *v.*
fore·tell (fôr-tĕl′, fōr-) *v.* To tell of beforehand : predict. **–fore·tell′er** *n.*
fore·thought (fôr′thôt′, fōr′-) *n.* Prior thought, preparation, or planning.
fore·to·ken (fôr-tō′kən, fōr-) *v.* To indicate beforehand. **–fore′to′ken** *n.*
for·ev·er (fôr-ĕv′ər, fər-) *adv.* **1.** For eternity. **2.** Without cease : incessantly.
for·ev·er·more (fôr-ĕv′ər-môr′, -mōr′, fər-) *adv.* Forever.
fore·warn (fôr-wôrn′, fōr-) *v.* To warn ahead of time.
fore·word (fôr′wûrd′, -wərd, fōr′-) *n.* An introductory statement, esp. in a book.
for·feit (fôr′fĭt) *n.* **1.** Something given up as punishment : penalty. **2.** Something that is placed in escrow and redeemed after the payment of a fine. **3.** A forfeiture. *–v.* To lose or give up as a forfeit. **–for′feit·a·ble** *adj.* **–for′feit·er** *n.*
for·fei·ture (fôr′fĭ-cho͝or′, -chər) *n.* **1.** The act of forfeiting. **2.** Something forfeited : penalty.
for·gath·er (fôr-găth′ər, fōr-) *v.* To come together : convene.
forge[1] (fôrj, fōrj) *n.* A hearth or furnace where metals are heated and wrought : smithy. *–v.* **forged, forg·ing. 1.** To shape (metal) by heating and beating or hammering. **2.** To give shape to <*forge* a peace treaty> **3.** To make or reproduce esp. for deceptive purposes <*forge* a signature> **–forg′er** *n.* **–for′ger·y** *n.*
forge[2] (fôrj, fōrj) *v.* **forged, forg·ing. 1.** To advance slowly but surely. **2.** To advance quickly and abruptly.
for·get (fər-gĕt′, fôr-) *v.* **-got** (-gŏt′), **-got·ten** (-gŏt′n) *or* **-got, -get·ting. 1.** To be unable to remember. **2.** To fail to attend to : neglect. **3.** To fail to become aware of at the right time <*forgot* about the rent> **–forget (oneself).** To lose one's reserve or self-restraint. **–for·get′ful** *adj.* **–for·get′ful·ly** *adv.* **–for·get′ful·ness** *n.* **–for·get′ta·ble** *adj.*
for·get-me-not (fər-gĕt′mē-nŏt′, fôr-) *n.* A low-growing plant of the genus *Myosotis,* with small blue flower clusters.
for·give (fər-gĭv′, fôr-) *v.* **-gave** (-gāv′), **-giv·en** (-gĭv′ən), **-giv·ing. 1.** To pardon or absolve. **2.** To stop being angry about or resentful against. **3.** To relieve from payment of. **–for·giv′a·ble** *adj.* **–for·give′ness** *n.* **–for·giv′er** *n.*
for·go *also* **fore·go** (fôr-gō′, fōr-) *v.* **-went** (-wĕnt′), **-gone** (-gôn′, -gŏn′), **-go·ing.** To give up or let go : relinquish. **–for·go′er** *n.*
fo·rint (fôr′ĭnt′) *n.* See CURRENCY TABLE.
fork (fôrk) *n.* **1.** A utensil with 2 or more tines for serving or eating food. **2.** A pronged implement used esp. for digging. **3. a.** A separation into 2 or more parts or branches. **b.** The place where this occurs <a *fork* in the road> **c.** Any of the branches <the left *fork*> *–v.* **1.** To lift or carry with a fork. **2.** To give the shape of a fork to. **3.** To divide into 2 or more branches. **4.** *Informal.* To hand over : pay.
forked (fôrkt, fôr′kĭd) *adj.* Shaped like or having a fork.
fork lift *n.* An industrial vehicle with a pronged platform that lifts and carries heavy loads.
for·lorn (fôr-lôrn′, fər-) *adj.* **1.** Abandoned : deserted. **2.** Pitiful. **3.** Almost hopeless. **–for·lorn′ly** *adv.* **–for·lorn′ness** *n.*
form (fôrm) *n.* **1.** The shape and structure of something. **2.** A body, esp. of a person : figure. **3.** The basic nature of something. **4.** The mode in which something exists : variety <a *form* of plant life> **5.** Procedure as established by custom or regulation. **6.** Manners as determined by etiquette or custom. **7.** Performance according to established criteria. **8.** Fitness, as of an animal, with regard to training or health. **9.** A fixed order of words, as in a ceremony : formula. **10.** A document with blanks into which required information is to be inserted. **11.** Manner or style in musical or literary composition. **12.** The design or structure of a work of art <symphonic *form*> **13.** A model from which a mold can be made. **14.** A grade in a British school or in some U.S. private schools. *–v.* **1.** To shape or become shaped. **2.** To assume or shape into a given form. **3.** To develop by instruction. **4.** To come to have. **5.** To constitute or be a part of. **6.** To conceive in the mind <*form* an opinion> **7.** To put in order : arrange.
-form *suff.* Having the form of <cruci*form*>
for·mal (fôr′məl) *adj.* **1.** Of or relating to the outward aspect of something. **2.** Relating to the essential form of something <a *formal* precept> **3.** Following or based on accepted conventions. **4.** Marked by strict observation of forms. **5.** Stiff or cold <a *formal* demeanor> **6.** Outwardly correct but lacking in substance <a purely *formal* leave-taking> **–for′mal·ly** *adv.*
for·mal·de·hyde (fôr-măl′də-hīd′) *n.* A colorless gaseous compound used in water solution as a preservative and disinfectant.
for·mal·ism (fôr′mə-lĭz′əm) *n.* FORMALITY 2. **–for′mal·ist** *n.*
for·mal·i·ty (fôr-măl′ĭ-tē) *n., pl.* **-ties. 1.** The quality or state of being formal. **2.** Rigorous observance of established forms or rules. **3.** An established form or rule.
for·mal·ize (fôr′mə-līz′) *v.* **-ized, -iz·ing. 1.** To give a definite structure or shape to. **2.** To make formal. **3.** To give formal approval to. **–for′mal·i·za′tion** *n.*
for·mat (fôr′măt′) *n.* **1.** A general plan of organization and arrangement. **2.** The form or layout of a publication. *–v.* **-matted, -mat·ting.** *Computer Sci.* To produce (e.g., data) in a specified form.
for·ma·tion (fôr-mā′shən) *n.* **1.** The act or process of forming. **2.** Something formed. **3.** The way in which something is formed : shape. **4.** A given arrangement, as of troops.
for·ma·tive (fôr′mə-tĭv) *adj.* **1.** Forming or capable of forming. **2.** Of or pertaining to formation, growth, or development.
for·mer (fôr′mər) *adj.* **1.** Taking place earlier in time. **2.** Preceding in order or place. **3.** Being the 1st mentioned of 2.
for·mer·ly (fôr′mər-lē) *adv.* Previously.
form·fit·ting (fôrm′fĭt′ĭng) *adj.* Conforming closely to the contours of the body.
For·mi·ca (fôr-mī′kə). A trademark for any of various high-pressure laminated plastic materials, used esp. for chemical- and heat-resistant surfaces.
for·mi·da·ble (fôr′mĭ-də-bəl, fôr-mĭd′ə-bəl) *adj.* **1.** Inspiring dread, fear, or awe. **2.** Difficult to undertake or overcome. **–for′mi·da·bly** *adv.*
form·less (fôrm′lĭs) *adj.* Lacking definite form or shape. **–form′less·ly** *adv.* **–form′less·ness** *n.*
form letter *n.* A usu. impersonal letter in a standardized format, sent to different people or to large numbers of people.
For·mo·sa (fôr-mō′sə). Taiwan.
for·mu·la (fôr′myə-lə) *n., pl.* **-las** *or* **-lae** (-lē′). **1.** An established form of words or rules for use in a ceremony or procedure. **2.** *Chem.* A symbolic representation of the composition or composition and structure of a chemical compound. **3.** *Math.* A statement, esp. an equation, of a logical relation. **4.** A recipe. **5.** A nutritious liquid food for an infant. **–for′mu·la′ic** (-lā′ĭk) *adj.*
for·mu·late (fôr′myə-lāt′) *v.* **-lat·ed, -lat·ing. 1.** To state as a formula. **2.** To express in an orderly and systematic way. **3.** To devise : invent. **4.** To prepare according to a particular formula. **–for′mu·la′tion** *n.* **–form′u·la′tor** *n.*

for•ni•ca•tion (fôr′nĭ-kā′shən) *n.* Sexual intercourse between a man and woman not married to each other. **–for′ni•cate′** *v.* **–for′ni•ca′tor** *n.*

for•sake (fôr-sāk′, fər-) *v.* **-sook** (-sŏŏk′), **-sak•en** (-sā′kən), **-sak•ing. 1.** To give up : forswear. **2.** To abandon or desert.

for•sooth (fôr-sōōth′, fər-) *adv. Archaic.* In truth : certainly.

for•swear (fôr-swâr′, fōr-) *v.* **-swore** (-swôr′, -swōr′), **-sworn** (-swôrn′, -swōrn′), **-swear•ing. 1.** To renounce : forsake. **2.** To swear falsely : perjure oneself.

for•syth•i•a (fôr-sĭth′ē-ə, fər-) *n.* An Asian shrub of the genus *Forsythia,* widely cultivated for its early-blooming yellow flowers.

fort (fôrt, fōrt) *n.* A fortified structure or area, esp. a permanent army post.

Fort-de-France (fōr-də-fräɴs′). Cap. of Martinique. *Pop.* 98,807.

for•te[1] (fôr′tā′, fôrt, fōrt) *n.* An activity in which one excels.

for•te[2] (fôr′tā′) *adv. Mus.* Loudly. Used as a direction. **–for′te′** *adj.*

forth (fôrth, fōrth) *adv.* **1.** Out into plain sight <come *forth*> **2.** Onward or forward <from this time *forth*>

Forth, Firth of. Inlet of the North Sea in SE Scotland.

forth•com•ing (fôrth-kŭm′ĭng, fōrth-) *adj.* **1.** About to appear or occur. **2.** Readily available.

forth•right (fôrth′rīt′, fōrth′-) *adj.* Straightforward : direct. **–forth′right′ly** *adv.* **–forth′right′ness** *n.*

forth•with (fôrth-wĭth′, -wĭth′, fōrth-) *adv.* At once : promptly.

for•ti•fy (fôr′tə-fī′) *v.* **-fied, -fy•ing. 1.** To strengthen and secure with military fortifications. **2.** To give physical strength to : invigorate. **3.** To strengthen morally or mentally : encourage. **4.** To enrich (a substance), as by adding vitamins. **–for′ti•fi•ca′tion** *n.* **–for′ti•fi′er** *n.*

for•tis•si•mo (fôr-tĭs′ə-mō′) *adv. Mus.* Very loudly. Used as a direction. **–for•tis′si•mo′** *adj.*

for•ti•tude (fôr′tĭ-tōōd′, -tyōōd′) *n.* Strength of mind allowing a person to withstand pain or adversity courageously.

fort•night (fôrt′nīt′) *n.* 2 weeks. **–fort′night′ly** *adj.* & *adv.*

FOR•TRAN (fôr′trăn′) *n. Computer Sci.* A programming language for problems expressible in algebraic terms.

for•tress (fôr′trĭs) *n.* A fort.

for•tu•i•tous (fôr-tōō′ĭ-təs, -tyōō′-) *adj.* Occurring by accident or chance : not planned. **–for•tu′i•tous•ly** *adv.*

for•tu•i•ty (fôr-tōō′ĭ-tē, -tyōō′-) *n., pl.* **-ties. 1.** A fortuitous occurrence. **2.** The quality or state of being fortuitous.

for•tu•nate (fôr′chə-nĭt) *adj.* **1.** Bringing or brought by good fortune : auspicious. **2.** Having good fortune ☆***syns:*** HAPPY, LUCKY, PROVIDENTIAL **–for′tu•nate•ly** *adv.*

for•tune (fôr′chən) *n.* **1.** A hypothetical force that controls the events of life : chance. **2.** Good or bad luck : fate. **3.** Success, esp. when resulting from luck. **4. a.** Wealth. **b.** A large amount of money.

fortune hunter *n.* One who seeks wealth, esp. through marriage.

for•tune•tell•er (fôr′chən-tĕl′ər) *n.* One who claims to be able to predict the future. **–for′tune•tell′ing** *n.* & *adj.*

Fort Worth (wûrth). City of NE Tex. *Pop.* 385,141.

for•ty (fôr′tē) *n., pl.* **-ties.** The cardinal number equal to 4 x 10. **–for′ti•eth** *n.* & *adj.* & *adv.* **–for′ty** *adj.* & *pron.*

for•ty-five (fôr′tē-fīv′) *n.* **1.** A .45-caliber pistol. **2.** A phonograph record played at 45 revolutions a minute.

for•ty-nin•er (fôr′tē-nī′nər) *n.* A person in the 1849 California gold rush.

forty winks *n. (sing. or pl. in number). Informal.* A brief nap.

fo•rum (fôr′əm, fōr′-) *n., pl.* **-rums** *or* **fo•ra** (fôr′ə, fōr′ə). **1.** A public square or marketplace in ancient Rome. **2.** A public meeting place or medium for open discussion. **3.** A court of law : tribunal. **4.** A public program involving panel discussion and audience participation.

for•ward (fôr′wərd) *adj.* **1.** At, in, near, belonging to, or situated in the front. **2.** Going, tending to go, or moving frontward. **3.** Lacking restraint : presumptuous. **4.** Well developed, esp. technologically, economically, or politically. **5.** Intellectually or socially advanced : precocious. *–adv.* **1.** *also* **for•wards** (-wərdz). To or toward the front : frontward. **2.** In, into, or toward the future <looking *forward* to the weekend> **3.** Out into view : forth. *–n.* A player in the front line of offense or defense, as in basketball. *–v.* **1.** To send forward to a subsequent destination or address. **2.** To help to advance. **–for′ward•ly** *adv.* **–for′ward•ness** *n.*

for•ward•er (fôr′wər-dər) *n.* One that forwards, esp. an agent who facilitates the passage of received goods to their destination.

for•went (fôr-wĕnt′, fōr-) *v. p.t. of* FORGO.

fos•sil (fŏs′əl) *n.* **1.** The remains or a trace of an animal or plant of a past geologic age embedded in the earth's crust. **2.** One that is outdated or antiquated. **–fos′sil•i•za′tion** *n.* **–fos′si•lize′** *v.*

fos•ter (fô′stər, fŏs′tər) *v.* **1.** To bring up : nurture. **2.** To cultivate and encourage. *–adj.* Giving or receiving parental care though not related through blood or legal ties <*foster* parents><a *foster* child>

foul (foul) *adj.* **1.** Offensive to the senses, esp. to the sense of smell : repulsive. **2.** Rotten, as spoiled meat. **3.** Very dirty : filthy. **4.** Morally detestable. **5.** Vulgar or obscene. **6.** Unpleasant <*foul* weather> **7.** Not fair : dishonorable. **8. a.** Designating the limiting lines of a playing area. **b.** Contrary to the rules of a sport or game. **9.** Entangled or twisted, as an anchor or rope. *–n.* **1. a.** A batted baseball that touches the ground outside fair territory. **b.** An infraction of the rules of play in a sport or game. **2.** A collision or entanglement. *–adv.* In a foul way. *–v.* **1.** To make or become foul : dirty. **2.** To dishonor. **3.** To obstruct : clog. **4.** To entangle or become entangled. **5.** To make or hit a foul. **–foul up.** *Slang.* To blunder or cause to blunder. **–foul′ly** *adv.* **–foul′ness** *n.*

fou•lard (fōō-lärd′) *n.* A lightweight silk or silk and cotton twill or plain-woven fabric usu. having a small printed design.

foul-mouthed (foul′mouthd′, -moutht′) *adj.* Using vulgar or obscene language.

foul play *n.* Unfair or treacherous behavior, esp. when it involves violence.

foul-up (foul′ŭp′) *n. Informal.* **1.** Confusion due to mismanagement. **2.** A mechanical problem.

found[1] (found) *v.* **1.** To establish (e.g., a college), often with funds to permit continuation and maintenance. **2.** To establish the basis of. **–found′er** *n.*

found[2] (found) *v.* **1.** To melt (metal) and pour into a mold. **2.** To make by founding metal. **–found′er** *n.*

found[3] (found) *v. p.t. & p.p. of* FIND.

foun•da•tion (foun-dā′shən) *n.* **1.** The act of founding or state of being founded. **2.** The basis on which something stands or is supported. **3. a.** An endowment fund. **b.** An institution supported by an endowment. **4.** A cosmetic base for make-up. **5.** A corset. **–foun•da′tion•al** *adj.*

foun•der (foun′dər) *v.* **1.** To go or cause to go lame. Used of a horse. **2.** To break down : fail. **3.** *Naut.* To sink, as a ship.

found•ling (found′lĭng) *n.* An abandoned child of unknown parents.

foun•dry (foun′drē) *n., pl.* **-dries.** An establishment where metal is founded.

fount (fount) *n.* **1.** A fountain. **2.** An abundant source.

foun•tain (foun′tən) *n.* **1.** A natural spring of water. **2. a.** An artificially created stream of water. **b.** The device or structure from which such a stream springs. **3.** A point of origin : source. **4.** A soda fountain.

foun•tain•head (foun′tən-hĕd′) *n.* **1.** A spring that is the source of a stream. **2.** A main origin or source.

fountain pen *n.* A pen with a reservoir of ink that feeds the writing point.

four (fôr, fōr) *n.* **1.** The cardinal number equal to 3 + 1. **2.** The 4th in a set or sequence. **3.** Something having 4 parts, units, or members. **–four** *adj.* & *pron.*

four-flush (fôr′flŭsh′, fōr′-) *v. Slang.* To bluff. **–four′-flush′er** *n.*

four•fold (fôr′fōld′, fōr′-) *adj.* **1.** Having 4 parts or aspects. **2.** Being 4 times as many or as much. **–four′fold′** *adv.*

Four-H Club (fôr′āch′, fōr′-) *n.* A youth organization that offers instruction in modern agriculture.

four-in-hand (fôr′ĭn-hănd′, fōr′-) *n.* **1.** A team of 4 horses. **2.** A horse-drawn vehicle driven by 1 person. **3.** A necktie that is tied in a slipknot, the ends being left hanging and overlapping.

four-o'clock (fôr′ə-klŏk′, fōr′-) *n.* A plant of the genus *Mirabilis,* esp. *M. jalapa,* widely cultivated for its tubular flowers that open in the late afternoon.

four-post•er (fôr′pō′stər, fōr′-) *n.* A bed having tall corner posts orig. intended to support a canopy or curtains.

four•score (fôr′skôr′, fōr′skōr′) *adj.* Being 4 times 20 : 80.

four•some (fôr′səm, fōr′-) *n.* **1.** A group of 4 persons, esp. of 2 couples. **2.** The players in a golf match played by 4 persons.

four•square (fôr′skwâr′, fōr′-) *adj.* **1.** Having a square shape. **2.** Unwavering : firm. **3.** Forthright. **–four′square′** *adv.*

four•teen (fôr′tēn′, fōr′-) *n.* **1.** The cardinal number equal to 13 + 1. **2.** The 14th in a set or sequence. **3.** Something having 14 parts, units, or members. **–four•teen′** *adj.* & *pron.* **–four•teenth** *n.* & *adj.* & *adv.*

fourth (fôrth, fōrth) *n.* **1.** The ordinal number matching the number 4 in a series. **2.** One of 4 equal parts. **3.** The 4th forward gear of a motor vehicle. **–fourth** *adj.* & *adv.*

fourth estate *n.* The public press.

Fourth of July *n.* Independence Day.

Fourth World *n.* The least-developed or poorest countries of the Third World.
four-wheel (fôr′hwēl′, -wēl′, fōr′-) *adj.* Of or designating an automotive drive mechanism in which all 4 wheels are linked to the source of driving power.
fowl (foul) *n., pl.* **fowl** *or* **fowls. 1.** A bird of the order Galliformes, used as food or hunted as game, esp. the common domesticated chicken, *Gallus gallus.* **2.** The edible flesh of a fowl. *—v.* To hunt or trap wild fowl. **—fowl′er** *n.*
fox (fŏks) *n.* **1.** A carnivorous mammal of the genus *Vulpes* or related genera, having a pointed snout, upright ears, and a long, bushy tail. **2.** The fur of a fox. **3.** A sly or crafty person. *—v.* To outwit : trick.
foxed (fŏkst) *adj.* Stained with yellowish-brown spots, as an old book or print.
fox•glove (fŏks′glŭv′) *n.* A native European plant of the genus *Digitalis,* esp. *D. purpurea,* having a tall spike of tubular, pinkish-purple flowers and leaves that are the source of digitalis.
fox•hole (fŏks′hōl′) *n.* A shallow pit dug by a soldier for refuge against enemy fire.
fox•hound (fŏks′hound′) *n.* A dog bred and developed for fox hunting.
fox terrier *n.* A small dog, orig. bred in England, having a wiry or smooth white coat with dark markings.
fox trot *n.* **1.** A ballroom dance in 4/4 or 2/4 time. **2.** The music for a foxtrot. **—fox′-trot′** *v.*
fox•y (fŏk′sē) *adj.* **-i•er, -i•est.** Like a fox, as in slyness or cleverness. **—fox′i•ly** *adv.* **—fox′i•ness** *n.*
foy•er (foi′ər, foi′ā′) *n.* **1.** The lobby of a public building, as a hotel. **2.** A vestibule or entrance hall.
fpm or **f.p.m.** *abbr.* feet per minute.
fps or **f.p.s.** *abbr.* feet per second.
fr. *abbr.* **1.** franc. **2.** from.
Fr *symbol for* FRANCIUM.
Fr. *abbr.* father (clergyman).
fra•cas (frā′kəs) *n.* A disorderly uproar.
frac•tion (frăk′shən) *n.* **1.** A small part : bit. **2.** A disconnected piece : fragment. **3.** *Math.* An indicated quotient of 2 quantities. **4.** *Chem.* A component of a compound, separated by distillation or crystallization. **—frac′tion•al** *adj.*
frac•tious (frăk′shəs) *adj.* **1.** Apt to cause trouble : unruly. **2.** Irritable. **—frac′tious•ly** *adv.* **—frac′tious•ness** *n.*
frac•ture (frăk′chər) *n.* **1. a.** The act or process of breaking. **b.** The state of being broken. **2.** A break or crack, as in bone. **—frac′ture** *v.*
frag•ile (frăj′əl, -īl′) *adj.* **1.** Easily damaged or broken. **2.** Tenuous : flimsy <a *fragile* claim to the estate> **—frag′ile•ly** *adv.* **—fra•gil′i•ty** (frə-jĭl′ĭ-tē) *n.*
frag•ment (frăg′mənt) *n.* **1.** A part detached or broken off. **2.** Something unfinished or incomplete <knew *fragments* of the plan> *—v.* (frăg′mĕnt′). To break into fragments. **—frag′men•ta′tion** *n.*
frag•men•tar•y (frăg′mən-tĕr′ē) *adj.* In pieces. **—frag′men•tar′i•ly** (-târ′ə-lē) *adv.* **—frag′men•tar′i•ness** *n.*
fra•grant (frā′grənt) *adj.* Having a pleasant, esp. sweet odor. **—fra′grance** *n.* **—fra′grant•ly** *adv.*
frail (frāl) *adj.* **1.** Delicate <a *frail* child> **2.** Easily damaged. **—frail′ly** *adv.* **—frail′ness** *n.*
frail•ty (frāl′tē) *n., pl.* **-ties. 1.** The quality or state of being frail. **2.** A fault caused by moral weakness.
frak•tur (fräk-to͝or′) *n.* A style of letter formerly used in German manuscripts and printing.

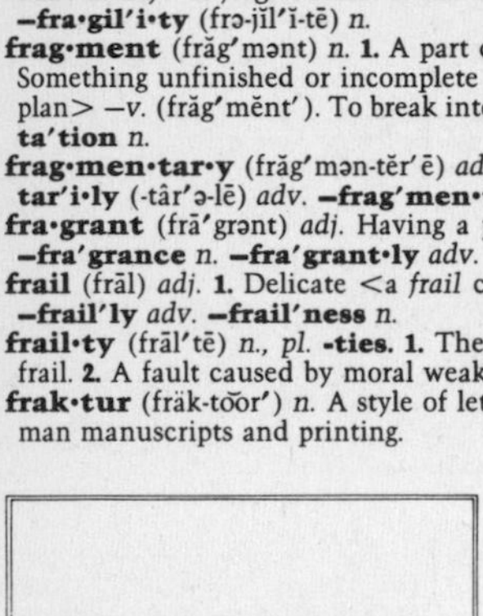

fraktur

frame (frām) *v.* **framed, fram•ing. 1.** To construct from various parts : build. **2.** To conceive or design. **3.** To adjust or arrange for a given purpose <a question *framed* to draw a negative response> **4.** To put into words. **5.** To provide with or as if with a frame : enclose. **6.** *Slang.* To rig events or evidence so as to make (a person) seem guilty. *—n.* **1.** Something made up of parts fitted and joined together, as: **a.** A skeletal structure <the *frame* of a building> **b.** An open structure <a picture *frame*> **c.** A machine built on or using a frame. **d.** The human body. **3.** General structure : system <the *frame* of national government> **4.** One exposure on a roll of movie film. **5.** *Slang.* A frame-up. **—fram′er** *n.*
frame-up (frām′ŭp′) *n. Slang.* A scheme to incriminate an innocent person.
frame•work (frām′wûrk′) *n.* **1.** A supporting or enclosing structure. **2.** A basic system or arrangement, as of ideas.
franc (frăngk) *n.* See CURRENCY TABLE.
France (frăns, fräns). Country of W Europe. *Cap.* Paris. *Pop.* 53,589,000. **—French** (frĕnch) *adj.* & *n.*
fran•chise (frăn′chīz′) *n.* **1.** A privilege granted to a person or group by a government. **2.** Constitutional or statutory right to vote. **3.** Authorization to sell a manufacturer's products. **4.** The limit or territory within which a privilege or immunity is authorized. **—fran′chise′** *v.* **—fran′chi•see′** *n.* **—fran′chis′er** *n.*
fran•ci•um (frăn′sē-əm) *n. Symbol* **Fr** An unstable radioactive metallic element.
Fran•co (frăng′kō, frăng′-), **Francisco.** 1892–1975. Spanish dictator (1939–75).
Fran•co-A•mer•i•can (frăng′kō-ə-mĕr′ĭ-kən) *n.* An American of French descent, esp. a French-Canadian. **—Fran′co-A•mer′i•can** *adj.*
fran•gi•ble (frăn′jə-bəl) *adj.* Breakable. **—fran′gi•bil′i•ty, fran′gi•ble•ness** *n.*
frank (frăngk) *adj.* Sincere and open : straightforward <a *frank* discussion about finances> *—v.* **1.** To mark (mail) officially so that it can be sent free of postage. **2.** To send (mail) without charge. *—n.* **1.** A signature or mark on mail indicating that it can be sent without charge. **2.** The right of sending mail free. **—frank′ly** *adv.* **—frank′ness** *n.*
Frank•en•stein (frăng′kən-stīn′) *n.* **1.** A creation or agency that destroys its creator. **2.** A monster resembling a man.
Frank•fort (frăngk′fərt). Cap. of Ky., in the NC part. *Pop.* 25,973.
Frank•furt (frängk′fo͝ort′). City of C West Germany. *Metro. pop.* 1,880,000.
frank•furt•er (frăngk′fər-tər) *n.* A smoked sausage, as of beef or beef and pork.
frank•in•cense (frăng′kĭn-sĕns′) *n.* An aromatic gum resin obtained from African and Asian trees of the genus *Boswellia* and burned as incense.
Frank•lin (frăngk′lĭn), **Benjamin.** 1706–90. Amer. statesman and scientist.
Franklin stove *n.* A cast-iron stove shaped like a fireplace but utilizing metal baffles to increase its energy efficiency.
fran•tic (frăn′tĭk) *adj.* Emotionally distraught, as from worry or fear. **—fran′ti•cal•ly, fran′tic•ly** *adv.*
frap•pé (fră-pā′, frăp) *n.* **1.** A frozen, often fruit-flavored mixture that is similar to sherbet. **2.** A beverage, as a liqueur, poured over shaved ice. **3.** A milk shake containing ice cream.
fra•ter•nal (frə-tûr′nəl) *adj.* **1. a.** Of or relating to brothers. **b.** Exhibiting comradeship. **2.** Of or being a fraternity. **3.** *Biol.* Of or relating to a twin or twins that developed from separately fertilized ova. **—fra•ter′nal•ism** *n.* **—fra•ter′nal•ly** *adv.*
fra•ter•ni•ty (frə-tûr′nĭ-tē) *n., pl.* **-ties. 1.** A group of persons united by similar interests, backgrounds, or occupations. **2.** A social organization of male college students, usu. designated by Greek letters. **3.** The quality or state of being brothers.
frat•er•nize (frăt′ər-nīz′) *v.* **-nized, -niz•ing. 1.** To associate with others in a friendly or brotherly way. **2.** To associate with the enemy, often in violation of military law. **—frat′er•ni•za′tion** *n.* **—frat′er•niz′er** *n.*
frat•ri•cide (frăt′rĭ-sīd′) *n.* **1.** The act of murdering one's brother or sister. **2.** One who has murdered his brother or sister. **—frat′ri•cid′al** *adj.*
fraud (frôd) *n.* **1.** A deliberate deception perpetrated for unlawful or unfair gain. **2.** A trick or swindle. **3. a.** One who defrauds : cheat. **b.** An impostor.
fraud•u•lent (frô′jə-lənt) *adj.* Marked by, being, or done by fraud. **—fraud′u•lence** *n.* **—fraud′u•lent•ly** *adv.*
fraught (frôt) *adj.* Filled or charged <a mission *fraught* with danger>
fray[1] (frā) *n.* **1.** A scuffle or brawl. **2.** A heated contest or dispute.
fray[2] (frā) *v.* **1.** To wear away, unravel, or tatter (fabric edges) by rubbing. **2.** To irritate or strain (e.g., one's nerves).
fraz•zle (frăz′əl) *v.* **-zled, -zling.** *Informal.* **1.** To tatter or wear out : fray. **2.** To fatigue completely. **—fraz′zle** *n.*
freak (frēk) *n.* **1.** A person, animal, thing, or occurrence that is markedly abnormal or unusual. **2.** A sudden whim : caprice. **3.** *Slang.* **a.** A drug user or addict. **b.** A fan or enthusiast <a jogging *freak*> **—freak out.** *Slang.* **1.** To experience or cause to experience hallucinations or paranoia induced by a drug. **2.** To

make or become highly agitated or excited. **–freak'i•ly** *adv.* **–freak'ish** *adj.* **–freak'ish•ly** *adv.* **–freak'ish•ness** *n.* **–freak'y** *adj.*

freck•le (frĕk'əl) *n.* A small, often sun-induced precipitation of pigment in the skin. **–freck'le** *v.* **–freck'ly** *adj.*

Fred•er•ick II (frĕd'rĭk). "the Great." 1712–86. King of Prussia (1740–86).

free (frē) *adj.* **fre•er, fre•est. 1.** Not imprisoned or constrained. **2.** Not under necessity or obligation. **3. a.** Politically independent <a *free* nation> **b.** Possessing political and civil liberties <a *free* citizenry> **4. a.** Not affected by a specified circumstance or condition. **b.** Exempt <tax-*free*> **5.** Not literal <a *free* translation from the French> **6.** Costing nothing. **7. a.** Not being occupied or used. **b.** Unobstructed : clear <a *free* lane> **8.** Frank : open. **9.** Too familiar : forward. **10.** Lavish or liberal, as with money. *–adv.* **1.** In a free way. **2.** Without charge. *–v.* **freed, free•ing. 1.** To set at liberty. **2.** To release or rid <*freed* from tyranny> **3.** To untangle or clear. **☆syns:** EMANCIPATE, LIBERATE, MANUMIT, RELEASE **–free'ly** *adv.* **–free'ness** *n.*

free•bie *also* **free•bee** (frē'bē) *n. Slang.* Something given or received without cost.

free•board (frē'bôrd', -bōrd') *n. Naut.* The vertical distance between the water line and the uppermost full deck.

free•boot•er (frē'bo͞o'tər) *n.* One who plunders, esp. a pirate.

free•born (frē'bôrn') *adj.* **1.** Born as a free person and not a slave. **2.** Of or appropriate to a freeborn person.

freed•man (frēd'mən) *n.* A man freed from slavery. **–freed'wom'an** *n.*

free•dom (frē'dəm) *n.* **1.** The state of being free of constraints. **2. a.** Political independence. **b.** Possession of political and civil rights. **3.** Free will. **4.** Facility as of movement. **5.** Frankness or boldness of expression. **6.** Unrestricted access or use.

Free•dom•ite (frē'də-mīt') *n. Can.* A member of the Doukhobor sect, the Sons of Freedom.

free-for-all (frē'fər-ôl') *n.* A competition or brawl in which many participate.

free•hand (frē'hănd') *adj.* Done or drawn without mechanical aids <*freehand* sketches> **–free'hand'** *adv.*

free•hold (frē'hōld') *n.* **1.** An estate held in fee or for life. **2.** The tenure by which a freehold is held. **–free'hold'er** *n.*

free lance *n.* One, esp. a writer or artist, who sells his or her services to employers without a long-term commitment. **–free'lance'** *v.* & *adj.*

free•load (frē'lōd') *v. Slang.* To take advantage of the hospitality or generosity of others : sponge. **–free'load'er** *n.*

free love *n.* The practice of living in a sexual relationship without marriage or formal obligations.

free•man (frē'mən) *n.* **1.** A person not in slavery or bondage. **2.** One possessing all the rights and privileges of a citizen.

Free•ma•son (frē'mā'sən) *n.* A member of an international secret fraternity officially called Free and Accepted Masons. **–Free'ma'son•ry** *n.*

fre•er (frē'ər) *adj. compar. of* FREE.

fre•est (frē'ĭst) *adj. superl. of* FREE.

free•stand•ing (frē'stăn'dĭng) *adj.* Standing unsupported or without attachment.

free•stone (frē'stōn') *n.* **1.** A stone, as limestone, that can be cut without splitting or shattering. **2.** A fruit, as a peach, with a stone that does not cling to the pulp.

free•think•er (frē'thĭng'kər) *n.* One who has rejected dogma and authority, esp. in his or her religious thinking. **–free'think'ing** *adj.* & *n.*

Free•town (frē'toun'). Cap. of Sierra Leone, in the W. *Pop.* 274,400.

free trade *n.* Tariff-free trade between nations or states.

free verse *n.* Verse marked by an unconventional metrical or stanzaic pattern and either an irregular rhyme or no rhyme.

free•way (frē'wā') *n.* A multilane highway : expressway.

free•will (frē'wĭl') *adj.* Done voluntarily.

free will *n.* **1.** The ability or discretion to choose freely. **2.** The belief that a human being's choices are or can be made freely, without external constraint.

freeze (frēz) *v.* **froze** (frōz), **fro•zen** (frō'zən), **freez•ing. 1. a.** To change or cause to change from liquid to solid by losing heat. **b.** To acquire a surface of ice from cold. **2.** To preserve (e.g., food) by cooling to an extremely low temperature. **3.** To make or become nonfunctional through the formation of ice or frost. **4.** To injure or be injured by cold. **5. a.** To be at the temperature at which ice forms. **b.** To feel uncomfortably cold. **6.** To make or become rigid : solidify. **7.** To become incapable of acting through shyness or fear. **8.** To be or become icily formal. **9.** To fix (wages or prices) at a given level. **10.** To prohibit further use or manufacture of. *–n.* **1.** An act of freezing or the state of being frozen. **2.** A cold snap.

freeze-dry (frēz'drī') *v.* To preserve (foodstuffs) by freezing and then drying in a vacuum. **–freeze'-dried'** *adj.*

freez•er (frē'zər) *n.* One that freezes, esp. a thermally insulated room or cabinet for freezing and storing perishable food.

freight (frāt) *n.* **1.** Goods transported by a vehicle or vessel : cargo. **2. a.** Commercial transportation of goods. **b.** The fee for such transportation. **3.** A train transporting goods only. *–v.* **1.** To carry as cargo. **2.** To load with cargo.

freight•er (frā'tər) *n.* A vehicle, esp. a ship, that carries freight.

French (frĕnch) *n.* **1.** The language of France. **2.** (*pl. in number*). The people of France. **–French** *adj.* **–French'man** *n.* **–French'wom'an** *n.*

French Canada *n.* The part of Canada where French is the predominant language.

French Canadian *n.* A Canadian whose 1st language is French.

French dressing *n.* **1.** A seasoned oil and vinegar salad dressing. **2.** A commercially prepared creamy dressing, usu. pinkish or orange and often sweet.

French fries *pl.n.* Thin strips of potatoes that are French-fried.

French-fry (frĕnch'frī') *v.* To fry (e.g., potato strips) in deep fat.

French Gui•an•a (gē-ăn'ə, -ä'nə). French overseas department of NE South America. *Cap.* Cayenne. *Pop.* 55,125.

French horn *n.* A brass wind instrument that flares from a narrow mouthpiece to a wide bell.

French Pol•y•ne•sia (pŏl'ə-nē'zhə, -shə). French overseas territory in the SC Pacific. *Cap.* Papeete. *Pop.* 144,000.

fre•net•ic (frə-nĕt'ĭk) *adj.* Wildly excited : frenzied. **–fre•net'i•cal•ly** *adv.*

fren•zy (frĕn'zē) *n., pl.* **-zies. 1.** A state of wild excitement or violent agitation.. **2.** Temporary insanity or delirium. **–fren'zied** *adj.* **–fren'zied•ly** *adv.*

freq. *abbr.* **1.** frequency. **2.** frequently.

fre•quen•cy (frē'kwən-sē) *n., pl.* **-cies. 1.** The number of times a given event occurs within a specific interval, esp.: **a.** The number of complete cycles of a wave occuring per unit of time. **b.** The number of complete vibrations or oscillations that a body undergoes in a unit of time. **2.** The fact or state of occurring frequently.

frequency modulation *n.* Variation of a transmitting radio wave's frequency in accordance with an input signal.

fre•quent (frē'kwənt) *adj.* Happening or appearing often or at close intervals. *–v.* (frē-kwĕnt', frē'kwənt). To visit (a place) often. **–fre•quent'er** *n.* **–fre'quent•ly** *adv.* **–fre'quent•ness** *n.*

fres•co (frĕs'kō) *n., pl.* **-coes** *or* **-cos. 1.** The art of painting on fresh plaster with water-based paint. **2.** A painting executed in fresco.

fresh (frĕsh) *adj.* **1.** Recently produced, made, or harvested. **2.** Not preserved, as by freezing. **3.** Not saline <*fresh* water> **4.** New : additional <*fresh* evidence> **5.** Different <a *fresh* approach to the problem> **6.** Not soiled <*fresh* linen> **7.** Clear <still *fresh* in my mind> **8.** Having just arrived <*fresh* from the country> **9.** Refreshed : revived. **10.** Invigorating <*fresh* mountain air> **11.** Brisk <a *fresh* breeze> **12.** *Informal.* Impudent. **–fresh'ly** *adv.* **–fresh'ness** *n.*

fresh•en (frĕsh'ən) *v.* **1.** To make or become fresh. **2.** To increase in strength. Used of the wind. **–fresh'en•er** *n.*

fresh•et (frĕsh'ĭt) *n.* The overflow of a stream as a result of heavy rain or a thaw.

fresh•man (frĕsh'mən) *n.* **1.** A student in the 1st year of high school or college. **2.** A beginner : novice.

fresh•wa•ter (frĕsh'wô'tər, -wŏt'ər) *adj.* **1.** Of, relating to, living in, or consisting of water that is not saline. **2.** Accustomed to navigating inland waters only <a *freshwater* sailor>

fret[1] (frĕt) *v.* **fret•ted, fret•ting. 1.** To be or cause to be anxious or irritated. **2.** To wear or be worn away : erode. **3.** To make by erosion. **4.** To ripple (water). *–n.* **1.** Agitation : worry. **2.** Erosion.

fret[2] (frĕt) *n.* A ridge set across the fingerboard of a stringed instrument, as a guitar.

fret[3] (frĕt) *n.* An ornamental design, as within a border, composed of repeated symmetric figures. **–fret** *v.*

fret•ful (frĕt'fəl) *adj.* Irritable. **–fret'ful•ly** *adv.* **–fret'ful•ness** *n.*

fret saw *n.* A long, narrow-bladed saw with fine teeth, used in making ornamental work in thin wood or metal.

fret•work (frĕt'wûrk') *n.* **1.** Decorative work consisting of frets. **2.** Ornamental openwork or 3-dimensional fretwork.

Freud (froid), **Sigmund.** 1856–1939. Austrian pioneer psychoanalyst. **–Freud'i•an** *adj.* & *n.*

Fri. *abbr.* Friday.

fri•a•ble (frī'ə-bəl) *adj.* Easily crumbled : brittle. **–fri'a•bil'i•ty, fri'a•ble•ness** *n.*
fri•ar (frī'ər) *n.* A member of a usu. mendicant Roman Catholic order.
fri•ar•y (frī'ə-rē) *n., pl.* **-ies.** A monastery of friars.
fric•as•see (frĭk'ə-sē', frĭk'ə-sē') *n.* Pieces of meat or poultry stewed in gravy. **–fric'as•see'** *v.*
fric•tion (frĭk'shən) *n.* **1.** The rubbing of a surface or object against another. **2.** A conflict : clash. **3.** *Physics.* A force that retards or resists the relative motion of 2 touching objects. **–fric'tion•al** *adj.* **–fric'tion•less** *adj.*
friction match *n.* A match that ignites when struck on an abrasive surface.
friction tape *n.* A strong adhesive tape used esp. to insulate electrical conductors.
Fri•day (frī'dē, -dā') *n.* The 6th day of the week.
friend (frĕnd) *n.* **1.** Someone whom one knows and likes. **2.** A supporter or patron of a cause or group. **3. Friend.** A member of the Society of Friends : Quaker. **–friend'less** *adj.* **–friend'ship'** *n.*
friend•ly (frĕnd'lē) *adj.* **-li•er, -li•est. 1.** Of, relating to, or appropriate to a friend. **2.** Likely to support, favor, or help. **3.** Comforting : warm. ☆***syns:*** AMIABLE, AMICABLE, CHUMMY, CONGENIAL, CONVIVIAL, WARMHEARTED **–friend'li•ness** *n.*
fri•er (frī'ər) *n. var. of* FRYER.
frieze (frēz) *n.* A decorative, often sculptured horizontal band along the upper part of a building or a wall in a room.
frig•ate (frĭg'ĭt) *n.* **1.** A square-rigged warship of the 17th to mid-19th cent. **2.** A medium-sized U.S. warship.
fright (frīt) *n.* **1.** Sudden and intense fear : alarm. **2.** *Informal.* Something very unsightly or strange.
fright•en (frīt'n) *v.* **1.** To fill with fear. **2.** To force or drive by arousing fear <was *frightened* into telling the truth> ☆***syns:*** ALARM, PANIC, SCARE, STARTLE, TERRIFY, TERRORIZE **–fright'en•ing•ly** *adv.*
fright•ful (frīt'fəl) *adj.* **1.** Causing shock or disgust. **2.** Producing or causing fright : terrifying. **3.** *Informal.* **a.** Awful : extreme. **b.** Disagreeable : unpleasant. **–fright'ful•ly** *adv.* **–fright'ful•ness** *n.*
frig•id (frĭj'ĭd) *adj.* **1.** Very cold. **2.** Lacking emotional warmth. **3.** Sexually unresponsive. **–fri•gid'i•ty, frig'id•ness** *n.* **–frig'id•ly** *adv.*
†**fri•jol** (frē-hōl', frē'hōl') *also* **fri•jo•le** (frē-hō'lē) *n., pl.* **fri•jo•les** (frē-hō'lēz, frē'hō'-) *SW U.S.* A cultivated bean used for food.
frill (frĭl) *n.* **1.** A decorative ruffled, pleated, or gathered border or edging. **2.** *Informal.* A superfluous item. **–frill'y** *adj.*
fringe (frĭnj) *n.* **1.** A border or edging that consists of hanging threads, cords, strips, or loops. **2.** Something like a fringe. **3.** A peripheral part <on the *fringes* of the crowd> **–fringe** *v.*
fringe benefit *n.* A benefit, as medical insurance, given an employee in addition to salary or wages.
frip•per•y (frĭp'ə-rē) *n., pl.* **-ies. 1.** Showy and often cheap finery. **2.** An ostentatious or pretentious display.
Fris•bee (frĭz'bē). A trademark for a disk-shaped plastic toy that players throw and catch.
frisk (frĭsk) *v.* **1.** To skip or leap about : frolic. **2.** To search (a person) by running the hands quickly over clothing.
frisk•y (frĭs'kē) *adj.* **-i•er, -i•est.** Lively and playful : frolicsome. **–frisk'i•ly** *adv.* **–frisk'i•ness** *n.*
frit•ter[1] (frĭt'ər) *v.* To squander or reduce (e.g.,money or time) bit by bit.
frit•ter[2] (frĭt'ər) *n.* A small fried cake of batter often containing fruit, vegetables, or fish.
friv•o•lous (frĭv'ə-ləs) *adj.* **1.** Trivial : insignificant. **2.** Devoid of seriousness : silly. **–fri•vol'i•ty** (-vŏl'ĭ-tē), **friv'o•lous•ness** *n.* **–friv'o•lous•ly** *adv.*
frizz (frĭz) *v.* To form or be formed into small, tight curls. **–frizz** *n.* **–friz'zi•ly** *adv.* **–friz'zi•ness** *n.* **–friz'zy** *adj.*
friz•zle[1] (frĭz'əl) *v.* **-zled, -zling. 1.** To fry until curled and crisp. **2.** To fry with a sizzling noise.
friz•zle[2] (frĭz'əl) *v.* **-zled, -zling.** To frizz or cause to frizz. **–friz'zle** *n.*
fro (frō) *adv.* Away : back <running to and *fro*>
frock (frŏk) *n.* **1.** A girl's or woman's dress. **2.** A smock <an artist's *frock*> **3.** A robe worn by monks, friars, and clerics.
frock coat *n.* A man's dress coat with knee-length skirts.
frog (frôg, frŏg) *n.* **1.** A tailless, mainly aquatic amphibian of the order Salientia, and esp. of the family Ranidae, with a smooth, moist skin, webbed feet, and long hind legs adapted for jumping. **2.** A decorative loop of braid or cord for fastening the front of a garment. **3.** An arrangement of intersecting railroad tracks that allows wheels to cross the junction. **4.** A spiked or perforated holder for flower stems. **5.** *Informal.* Hoarseness in the throat.
frog•man (frôg'măn', -mən, frŏg'-) *n.* A swimmer supplied with equipment, as breathing apparatus, that permits the performance of underwater maneuvers, esp. military observation and demolition.
frol•ic (frŏl'ĭk) *n.* **1.** Merriment : gaiety. **2.** Playful, carefree activity. *–v.* **-icked, -ick•ing. 1.** To romp about playfully. **2.** To make merry : have fun. **–frol'ick•er** *n.* **–frol'ic•some** *adj.*
from (frŭm, frŏm; frəm *when unstressed*) *prep.* **1. a.** Used to indicate a particular time or place as a starting point <*from* 7 o'clock on><ran home *from* the store> **b.** Used to indicate a specific point as the 1st of 2 limits <*from* grades 6 to 8> **2.** Used to indicate a source, cause, agent, or instrument <a letter *from* home><take a book *from* the library> **3.** Used to indicate separation, removal, or exclusion <keep me *from* making an error><freedom *from* want> **4.** Used to indicate differentiation <know right *from* wrong>
frond (frŏnd) *n.* A leaf, as of a fern, usu. divided into smaller leaflets.
front (frŭnt) *n.* **1.** The forward surface or part, as of a structure. **2.** The area or position directly before or ahead. **3.** A position of leadership or superiority. **4.** The forehead. **5.** Bearing : demeanor <put up a brave *front*> **6.** A feigned manner or appearance. **7.** Land bordering a body of water or a street. **8.** An area of major combat. **9.** A field of activity <the economic *front*> **10.** *Meteorol.* The boundary between 2 air masses of different temperatures. **11.** An apparently respectable person, group, or business used as a cover for illegal or secret activities. *–adj.* In, of, or facing the front. *–v.* **1.** To look out on : face. **2.** To serve as a front for. **3.** To oppose. **–fron'tal** *adj.* **–fron'tal•ly** *adv.*
front•age (frŭn'tĭj) *n.* **1. a.** The front part of a piece of property, as a building or lot. **b.** The measured extent of such frontage. **2.** Land adjacent to a building, street, etc.
fron•tier (frŭn-tîr', frŏn-) *n.* **1.** An international border or the area adjacent to it. **2.** A region that marks the point of farthest settlement in a territory. **3.** An undeveloped field for research or discovery. **–fron•tiers'man** *n.*
▲word history: *Frontier* and *front* are both derived from Latin *frons,* "forehead, front, façade." *Frontier* was borrowed into English from French in the 15th cent. with the meaning "borderland," the region of a country that fronts on another country. The use of *frontier* to mean "a region at the edge of a settled area" is a special American development. The edge of the settled country was where unlimited cheap land was available to pioneers willing to live the hard but independent life there. This sense of *frontier* has also been extended to other areas of achievement and conquest.
fron•tis•piece (frŭn'tĭ-spēs') *n.* An illustration usu. facing or immediately preceding the title page of a book or periodical.
front-run•ner (frŭnt'rŭn'ər) *n.* A leading contender in a competition, as a race.
front•ward (frŭnt'wərd) *adj.* & *adv.* At or toward the front. **–front'wards** *adv.*
frost (frôst, frŏst) *n.* **1.** A deposit of tiny ice crystals formed from frozen water vapor. **2.** The atmospheric conditions when the temperature is below the freezing point. *–v.* **1.** To cover or become covered with or as if with frost. **2.** To kill or injure by frost. **3.** To cover (glass or metal) with a rough or speckled surface. **4.** To decorate (e.g., a cake) with icing. **–frost'i•ly** *adv.* **–frost'i•ness** *n.* **–frost'y** *adj.*
Frost (frôst, frŏst), **Robert Lee.** 1874–1963. Amer. poet.
frost•bite (frôst'bīt', frŏst'-) *n.* Local bodily tissue destruction resulting from freezing. **–frost'bite'** *v.*
frost heave *n.* An uplifting of a surface caused by freezing beneath the surface.
frost•ing (frô'stĭng, frŏs'tĭng) *n.* **1.** Icing. **2.** A frosted surface on glass or metal.
froth (frôth, frŏth) *n.* **1.** A mass of bubbles on or in a liquid : foam. **2.** A salivary foam, as of an animal, resulting from exhaustion or disease. **3.** Something insubstantial or trivial. *–v.* To expel or exude froth. **–froth'i•ly** *adv.* **–froth'i•ness** *n.* **–froth'y** *adj.*
frou-frou (fro͞o'fro͞o) *n.* **1.** A rustling sound, as of a silk skirt. **2.** Fussy or frilly dress or decoration.
fro•ward (frō'wərd, frō'ərd) *adj.* Obstinate. **–fro'ward•ness** *n.*
frown (froun) *v.* **1.** To wrinkle the brow, as in displeasure or thought. **2.** To regard with distaste or disapproval. **–frown** *n.* **–frown'ing•ly** *adv.*
frow•zy *also* **frow•sy** (frou'zē) *adj.* **-zi•er, -zi•est** *also* **-si•er, -si•est** Appearing unkempt or slovenly. **–frow'zi•ly** *adv.* **–frow'zi•ness** *n.*
froze (frōz) *v. p.t. of* FREEZE.
fro•zen (frō'zən) *adj.* **1.** Covered with, surrounded by, or made into ice. **2.** Extremely cold. **3.** Preserved by freezing. **4.**

Immobilized, as by fear. **5.** Coldly reserved : unfriendly. **6. a.** Kept at a fixed level, as wages. **b.** Not available for withdrawal, sale, or liquidation.
frt. *abbr.* freight.
fruc·ti·fy (frŭk'tə-fī', fro͝ok'-) *v.* **-fied, -fy·ing. 1.** To bear fruit. **2.** To make fruitful. **–fruc'ti·fi·ca'tion** *n.*
fruc·tose (frŭk'tōs', fro͞ok'-, fro͝ok'-) *n.* A very sweet sugar occurring in honey and many fruits.
fru·gal (fro͞o'gəl) *adj.* Economical : thrifty. **–fru·gal'i·ty** (-găl'ĭ-tē), **fru'gal·ness** *n.* **–fru'gal·ly** *adv.*
fruit (fro͞ot) *n., pl.* **fruit** *or* **fruits. 1. a.** The ripened, seed-bearing part of a flowering plant, as a pod or berry. **b.** A fleshy and edible plant part of this kind, as an apple or plum. **2.** The fertile, often spore-bearing structure of a plant that does not bear seeds. **3.** Outcome : result <the *fruit* of our labors> *–v.* To produce or cause to produce fruit. **–fruit'age** *n.* **–fruit'ful** *adj.* **–fruit'less** *adj.*
fruit bat *n.* Any of various tropical and subtropical Old World fruit-eating bats of the family Pteropodidae.

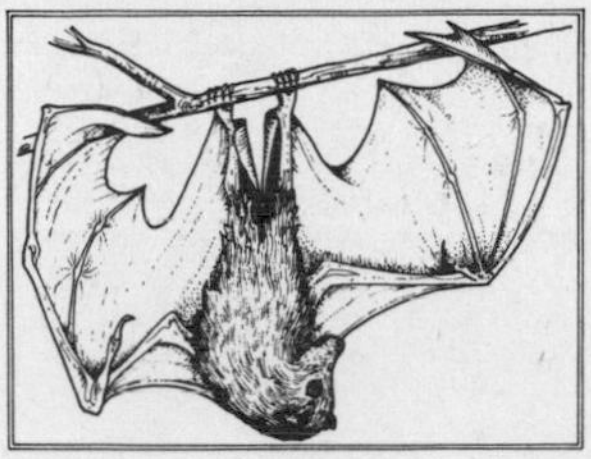

fruit bat

fruit·cake (fro͞ot'kāk') *n.* **1.** A heavy, spiced cake containing nuts and candied or dried fruits. **2.** *Slang.* An insane person.
fruit fly *n.* A small fly of the family Drosophilidae, with larvae that feed on ripening or fermenting fruit.
fru·i·tion (fro͞o-ĭsh'ən) *n.* **1.** Achievement of something worked for or desired : accomplishment. **2.** The state of bearing fruit.
fruit·y (fro͞o'tē) *adj.* **-i·er, -i·est. 1.** Tasting of fruit. **2.** Overly sweet or sentimental. **–fruit'i·ness** *n.*
frump·y (frŭmpē) *adj.* **-i·er, -i·est. 1.** Unfashionable : dowdy. **2.** Dull : staid. **–frump** *n.* **–frump'i·ness** *n.*
frus·trate (frŭs'trāt') *v.* **-trat·ed, -trat·ing. 1.** To prevent from attaining a goal or fulfilling a desire : thwart. **2.** To prevent the fruition of : nullify. **–frus'trat'ing·ly** *adv.* **–frus·tra'tion** *n.*
fry[1] (frī) *v.* **fried, fry·ing.** To cook over direct heat, esp. in hot fat or oil. *–n., pl.* **fries. 1.** A dish of fried food. **2.** A social gathering at which fried food is served.
fry[2] (frī) *n., pl.* **fry. 1.** A small fish, esp. a recently hatched one. **2.** Members of a class or group <the young *fry*>
fry·er *also* **fri·er** (frī'ər) *n.* **1.** One that fries. **2.** A fairly small young chicken suitable for frying.
ft *abbr.* foot.
ft–lb *abbr.* foot-pound.
fuch·sia (fyo͞o'shə) *n.* **1.** A chiefly tropical plant of the genus *Fuchsia,* widely grown for its drooping purplish, reddish, or white flowers. **2.** A strong, vivid purplish red. **–fuch'sia** *adj.*
fud·dle (fŭd'l) *v.* **-dled, -dling.** To make confused : befuddle.
fud·dy-dud·dy (fŭd'ē-dŭd'ē) *n., pl.* **-dies.** A fussy or old-fashioned person.
fudge (fŭj) *n.* **1.** A soft, rich candy containing sugar, butter, and flavoring, as chocolate. **2.** Nonsense. *–v.* **fudged, fudg·ing. 1.** To falsify. **2.** To avoid taking a stand : evade.
fu·el (fyo͞o'əl) *n.* Matter consumed to generate energy, esp.: **a.** A material such as wood, coal, or oil burned to generate heat. **b.** A fissionable substance used in a nuclear reactor. *–v.* **-eled, -el·ing** *or* **-elled, -el·ling. 1.** To take in or provide with fuel. **2.** To stimulate <comments that *fuel* an argument> **–fu'el·er** *n.*
fuel cell *n.* A device in which the chemical energy of a fuel is continuously converted to electricity.
fu·gi·tive (fyo͞o'jĭ-tĭv) *adj.* **1.** Running or trying to run away or escape, as from the law. **2.** Vanishing quickly : fleeting <a *fugitive* hope> *–n.* One who flees.
fugue (fyo͞og) *n.* **1.** *Mus.* A musical composition in which the theme is elaborately repeated by different voices or instruments. **2.** A psychological disturbance in which actions are not remembered after return to a normal state.
Fu·ji (fo͞o'jē) *also* **Fu·ji·ya·ma** (fo͞o'jē-yä'mə). Highest peak (12,389 ft/3,778.6 m) in Japan, in SC Honshu.
-ful *suff.* **1. a.** Full of <event*ful*> **b.** Characterized by <boast*ful*> **c.** Tending, given, or able to <mourn*ful*> **2.** A quantity that fills <cup*ful*>
ful·crum (fo͝ol'krəm, fŭl'-) *n., pl.* **-crums** *or* **-cra** (-krə). The point or support on which a lever turns.
ful·fill *also* **ful·fil** (fo͝ol-fĭl') *v.* **-filled, -fill·ing. 1.** To convert into actuality : effect. **2.** To carry out (e.g., an order). **3.** To satisfy (e.g., requirements). **–ful·fill'er** *n.* **–ful·fill'ment, ful·fil'ment** *n.*
full[1] (fo͝ol) *adj.* **1.** Containing all that is possible or normal : filled. **2.** Complete in every detail <a *full* account> **3.** Of maximum degree <*full* speed> **4.** Having many or a great deal <*full* of flaws> **5.** Completely qualified, empowered, or accepted <a *full* member> **6. a.** Rounded in shape <a *full* figure> **b.** Having much fabric : wide <a *full* skirt> **7.** Satiated, esp. with food or drink. **8.** Having body and depth : rich. **9.** Completely preoccupied, as with thoughts. *–adv.* **1.** Entirely <*full*-grown> **2.** Directly <a blow *full* on the chin> *–n.* The complete or maximum size, amount, or state of development. **–full'ness, ful'ness** *n.*
full[2] (fo͝ol) *v.* To increase the bulk and weight of (woolen cloth) by shrinking and beating or pressing. **–full'er** *n.*
full·back (fo͝ol'băk') *n.* A backfield player stationed behind the halfbacks in football, field hockey, soccer, and rugby.
full-blood·ed (fo͝ol'blŭd'ĭd) *adj.* **1.** Of unmixed blood : purebred. **2.** Vigorous.
full-blown (fo͝ol'blōn') *adj.* **1.** In full bloom. **2.** Fully developed : mature.
full-bod·ied (fo͝ol'bŏd'ēd) *adj.* Having richness and intensity of flavor, as a wine.
full dress *n.* Attire appropriate for ceremonial or formal occasions.
full-fledged (fo͝ol'flĕjd') *adj.* **1.** With developed adult plumage. **2.** Having full rank or status <a *full-fledged* member>
full moon *n.* The phase of the moon when visible as a fully illuminated disk.
full-scale (fo͝ol'skāl') *adj.* **1.** Of the actual size. **2.** Utilizing all resources.
full tilt *adv.* At high or top speed.
ful·ly (fo͝ol'ē) *adv.* **1.** Completely or totally <*fully* satisfied> **2.** At least <*Fully* half the team were sick.>
ful·mi·nate (fo͝ol'mə-nāt', fŭl'-) *v.* **-nat·ed, -nat·ing. 1.** To condemn or denounce severely. **2.** To explode. **–ful'mi·na'tion** *n.* **–ful'mi·na'tor** *n.*
ful·some (fo͝ol'səm) *adj.* Offensively insincere or excessive <*fulsome* flattery> **–ful'some·ly** *adv.* **–ful'some·ness** *n.*
fum·ble (fŭm'bəl) *v.* **-bled, -bling. 1.** To handle idly or nervously. **2.** To grope clumsily or uncertainly : blunder. **3.** To drop or mishandle a baseball or football. *–n.* **1.** The act or an instance of fumbling. **2.** A fumbled ball. **–fum'bler** *n.*
fume (fyo͞om) *n. often* **fumes.** A usu. irritating or disagreeable smoke, gas, or vapor. *–v.* **fumed, fum·ing. 1.** To treat with or subject to fumes. **2.** To emit fumes. **3.** To feel or show anger or distress.
fu·mi·gate (fyo͞o'mĭ-gāt') *v.* **-gat·ed, -gat·ing.** To subject to fumes, usu. so as to exterminate vermin or insects. **–fu'mi·ga'tion** *n.* **–fu'mi·ga'tor** *n.*
fun (fŭn) *n.* **1.** Enjoyment or amusement : pleasure. **2.** Playful, often noisy activity.
func·tion (fŭngk'shən) *n.* **1. a.** The characteristic or proper activity of a person or thing. **b.** The special purpose for which something exists. **2.** Specific duty, occupation, or role. **3.** An official ceremony or formal social occasion. **4.** Something closely related to or dependent on something else. **5.** *Math.* A rule of correspondence between 2 sets such that there is a unique element in 1 set assigned to each element in the other. *–v.* To serve or perform a function. **–func'tion·less** *adj.*
func·tion·al (fŭngk'shə-nəl) *adj.* **1.** Of or relating to a function. **2.** Designed for a particular function or use : practical. **3.** Able to perform : operative. **4.** *Pathol.* Affecting function but not the structure of an organism. **–func'tion·al·ly** *adv.*
functional illiterate *n.* One with some education but below minimum literacy standard.
func·tion·ar·y (fŭngk'shə-nĕr'ē) *n., pl.* **-ies.** One, esp. an official, who performs a certain function.
function word *n.* A word, as a preposition or conjunction, primarily indicating grammatical function.
fund (fŭnd) *n.* **1.** A source of supply : stock. **2. a.** A sum of money put aside for a particular purpose. **b. funds.** Available money. *–v.* **1.** To make long-term arrangements for paying off (a debt). **2.** To furnish a fund for.
fun·da·men·tal (fŭn'də-mĕn'tl) *adj.* **1. a.** Essential : basic. **b.** Of major significance : central. **2.** Serving as the primary origin. **–fun'da·men'tal** *n.* **–fun'da·men'tal·ly** *adv.*
fun·da·men·tal·ism (fŭn'də-mĕn'tl-ĭz'əm) *n.* A Protestant religious movement that emphasizes a belief in the literal truth

of the Bible. **–fun′da•men′tal•ist** *n.* **–fun′da•men′tal•ist′ic** *adj.*
fund raiser *n.* **1.** One who raises funds, as for an organization or a campaign. **2.** A social function, as a dinner, for raising funds. **–fund′-rais′ing** *adj.*
fu•ner•al (fyo͞o′nər-əl) *n.* The service or ceremonies held in conjunction with the burial or cremation of a dead person.
fu•ner•ar•y (fyo͞o′nə-rĕr′ē) *adj.* Of or appropriate for a funeral or burial.
fu•ne•re•al (fyo͞o-nîr′ē-əl) *adj.* **1.** Of or befitting a funeral. **2.** Sorrowful : mournful. **–fu•ne′re•al•ly** *adv.*
fun•gi•cide (fŭn′jĭ-sīd′, fŭng′gĭ-) *n.* A substance that kills or inhibits fungi.
fun•gus (fŭng′gəs) *n., pl.* **fun•gi** (fŭn′jī′) *or* **-gus•es.** Any of numerous spore-bearing plants, including the yeasts, molds, mildews, and mushrooms, that have no chlorophyll. **–fun′gous, fun′gal** *adj.*
fu•nic•u•lar (fyo͞o-nĭk′yə-lər, fə-) *n.* A cable railway on a mountain, esp. one with ascending and descending cars that counterbalance one another.
funk (fŭngk) *n.* **1.** Cowardly fright or panic. **2.** A state of depression.
funk•y (fŭng′kē) *adj.* **-i•er, -i•est.** *Slang.* **1.** Having an earthy quality that is characteristic of the blues <*funky* jazz> **2.** Outlandishly and often humorously vulgar <*funky* clothes> **–funk′i•ness** *n.*
fun•nel (fŭn′əl) *n.* **1.** A cone-shaped utensil with a tube used to channel a substance into a container. **2.** A flue or shaft for ventilation or smoke. *–v.* **-neled, -nel•ing** *or* **-nelled, -nel•ling** To pass or cause to pass through or as if through a funnel.
fun•ny (fŭn′ē) *adj.* **-ni•er, -ni•est. 1.** Evoking amusement or laughter. **2.** Odd : strange <something *funny* going on> *–n., pl.* **-nies.** *Informal.* **1.** A joke. **2. funnies.** Comic strips. **–fun′ni•ly** *adv.* **–fun′ni•ness** *n.*
funny bone *n. Informal.* The point near the elbow where pressure on a nerve may produce a tingling sensation.
fur (fûr) *n.* **1. a.** The thick coat of soft hair covering the body of a mammal, as a fox or beaver. **b.** The dressed pelts of fur-bearing animals used esp. for apparel. **2.** A coating suggestive of fur. **–furred** *adj.* **–fur′ri•ness** *n.* **–fur′ry** *adj.*
fur•be•low (fûr′bə-lō′) *n.* **1.** A ruffle on clothing. **2.** A piece of showy trimming or ornamentation.
fur•bish (fûr′bĭsh) *v.* **1.** To brighten, as by rubbing : polish. **2.** To renovate.
fu•ri•ous (fyo͝or′ē-əs) *adj.* **1.** Full of, showing, or marked by rage. **2.** Marked by violent activity <worked at a *furious* pace> **–fu′ri•ous•ly** *adv.*
furl (fûrl) *v.* **1.** To fold or roll up and secure (a flag or sail) to something, as a pole or mast. **2.** To curl or fold. **–furl** *n.*
fur•long (fûr′lông′, -lŏng′) *n.* A unit of distance or length equal to approx. 201 m or 220 yd.
▲word history: Since Old English times the word *furlong* has been used to indicate a unit of length, literally "a furrow's length." A *furlong* was orig. defined as the length of a furrow in a square field of 10 acres, but as the size of an acre varied during medieval times so did the length of a furrow. *Furlong* was also used to denote 1/8 of both a Roman and an English mile. A *furlong way,* first recorded in Chaucer's poetry, was a measure of timethe length of time it took to walk 1/8 of a mile.
fur•lough (fûr′lō) *n.* A leave of absence from duty granted esp. to personnel of the armed forces. **–fur′lough** *v.*
fur•nace (fûr′nĭs) *n.* An enclosure in which a fuel is consumed, usu. by burning, to produce heat.
fur•nish (fûr′nĭsh) *v.* **1.** To outfit or equip. **2.** To give : supply <*furnish* an example> **–fur′nish•er** *n.*
fur•nish•ings (fûr′nĭ-shĭngz) *pl.n.* **1.** Furniture and other movable equipment, as for a home. **2.** Apparel and accessories.
fur•ni•ture (fûr′nə-chər) *n.* Movable articles, as chairs and tables, that are necessary or useful esp. for a room.
fu•ror (fyo͝or′ôr′, -ōr′) *n.* **1.** Violent anger : rage. **2.** Great excitement. **3.** An uproar.
fur•ri•er (fûr′ē-ər) *n.* One who dresses, designs, sells, or repairs furs. **–fur′ri•er•y** *n.*
fur•ring (fûr′ĭng) *n.* Wood or metal strips applied to a wall or floor to make a level surface or air space.
fur•row (fûr′ō, fŭr′ō) *n.* **1.** A long, narrow trench made in the earth by a plow or other tool. **2.** A deep wrinkle in the skin, esp. of the forehead. **–fur′row** *v.*
fur•ther (fûr′*th*ər) *adj.* **1.** More distant in degree, time, or space <was *further* from the truth><the *further* street light> **2.** Additional. *–adv.* **1.** To a greater extent : more. **2.** In addition : furthermore. **3.** At or to a more distant point in time or space. *–v.* To help forward : advance. **–fur′ther•ance** *n.* **–fur′ther•er** *n.*
fur•ther•more (fûr′*th*ər-môr′, -mōr′) *adv.* In addition : besides.
fur•ther•most (fûr′*th*ər-mōst′) *adj.* Being most distant : farthest.
fur•thest (fûr′*th*ĭst) *adj.* Most distant in degree, time, or space. *–adv.* **1.** To the greatest degree or extent. **2.** At or to the most distant point in time or space.
fur•tive (fûr′tĭv) *adj.* **1.** Stealthy : surreptitious. **2.** Shifty : sly. **–fur′tive•ly** *adv.* **–fur′tive•ness** *n.*
fu•ry (fyo͝or′ē) *n., pl.* **-ries. 1.** Violent anger. **2.** Turbulence. **3.** An angry or spiteful woman. ☆***syns:*** IRE, RAGE, WRATH
furze (fûrz) *n.* Gorse.
fuse[1] (fyo͞oz) *n.* **1.** A length of readily combustible material that can be ignited to carry a flame to detonate an explosive. **2.** *var. of* FUZE.
fuse[2] (fyo͞oz) *v.* **fused, fus•ing. 1.** To reduce to a liquid or plastic state by heating : melt. **2.** To blend or bring together by or as if by melting : mix. *–n.* An electrical circuit safety device that melts when the circuit is overloaded and thus opens the circuit. **–fu′si•bil′i•ty** *n.* **–fus′i•ble** *adj.*
fu•see *also* **fu•zee** (fyo͞o-zē′) *n.* **1.** A large-headed friction match that is difficult to blow out. **2.** A colored signal flare.
fu•se•lage (fyo͞o′sə-läzh′, -zə-) *n.* The central section of an aircraft, to which the wings and tail assembly are joined.
fu•sil•lade (fyo͞o′sə-lăd′, -läd′, -zə-) *n.* A rapid or simultaneous discharge of a number of firearms.
fu•sion (fyo͞o′zhən) *n.* **1.** The act or procedure of liquefying by heat. **2.** A blend or mixture produced by fusion. **3.** A nuclear reaction in which nuclei combine to form more massive nuclei, with the release of huge amounts of energy.
fuss (fŭs) *n.* **1.** Unnecessarily nervous or futile activity : commotion. **2.** Unnecessary worry or concern. **3.** A complaint : objection. **4.** A quarrel. **–fuss** *v.* **–fuss′er** *n.*
fuss-budg•et (fŭs′bŭj′ĭt) *n.* One who fusses over trifles.
fuss•y (fŭs′ē) *adj.* **-i•er, -i•est. 1.** Easily upset. **2.** Frequently complaining. **3. a.** Hard to please : fastidious. **b.** Meticulous. **4. a.** Requiring careful attention <*fussy* work> **b.** Unnecessarily detailed <a *fussy* dress> **–fuss′i•ly** *adv.* **–fuss′i•ness** *n.*
fus•tian (fŭs′chən) *n.* **1.** A sturdy cotton cloth. **2.** Pompous, pretentious language.
fus•ty (fŭs′tē) *adj.* **-ti•er, -ti•est. 1.** Smelling of mold or decay. **2.** Old-fashioned. **–fus′ti•ly** *adv.* **–fus′ti•ness** *n.*
fut. *abbr.* future.
fu•tile (fyo͞ot′l, fyo͞o′tīl′) *adj.* Without useful result : ineffectual. ☆***syns:*** FRUITLESS, UNAVAILING, USELESS, VAIN **–fu′tile•ly** *adv.* **–fu•til′i•ty** *n.*
fu•ture (fyo͞o′chər) *n.* **1.** The time yet to come. **2.** Something that will take place in time yet to be. **3.** A prospective condition, esp. with regard to advancement or success. **4.** The future tense or a verb form in the future tense. *–adj.* That is to be.
future tense *n.* A verb tense expressing future time.
fu•tur•ism (fyo͞o′chə-rĭz′əm) *n.* An artistic movement marked by the depiction of the energetic and dynamic quality of contemporary life. **–fu′tur•ist** *n.* **–fu′tur•is′tic** *adj.*
fu•tu•ri•ty (fyo͞o-to͝or′ĭ-tē, -tyo͝or′-, -cho͝or′-) *n., pl.* **-ties. 1.** FUTURE 1. **2.** The state or quality of being of or in the future. **3.** A future possibility or event.
fuze *also* **fuse** (fyo͞oz) *n.* A mechanical, electrical, or electronic device for detonating an explosive, as a grenade or bomb.
fu•zee (fyo͞o-zē′) *n. var. of* FUSEE.
fuzz[1] (fŭz) *n.* A mass of fine, light fibers, particles, or hairs : down <peach *fuzz*>
fuzz[2] (fŭz) *n. Slang.* The police.
fuzz•y (fŭz′ē) *adj.* **-i•er, -i•est. 1.** Covered with fuzz. **2.** Of or like fuzz. **3. a.** Blurred : indistinct. **b.** Not clearly worked out : confused. **–fuzz′i•ly** *adv.* **–fuzz′i•ness** *n.*
fwd. *abbr.* forward.
FY *abbr.* fiscal year.
-fy *suff.* Cause to become <paci*fy*>
FYI *abbr.* for your information.

Gg

g or **G** (jē) *n., pl.* **g's** or **G's. 1.** The 7th letter of the English alphabet. **2.** A speech sound represented by the letter *g.* **3.** *Mus.* The 5th tone in the scale of C major. **4.** *Slang.* $1,000. **5. G.** A unit of force equal to the gravity exerted on a body at rest.
g *abbr.* **1.** gravity. **2.** gram.
Ga *symbol for* GALLIUM.
GA *abbr.* Georgia (with Zip Code).
Ga. *abbr.* Georgia.
gab (găb) *v.* **gabbed, gab•bing.** *Informal.* To chat idly. **–gab** *n.* **–gab'ber** *n.*
gab•ar•dine (găb'ər-dēn') *n.* **1.** A firm cotton, wool, or rayon twill with a smooth surface and slanting ribs. **2.** GABERDINE 1, 2.
gab•ble (găb'əl) *v.* **-bled, -bling.** To speak or utter incoherently or rapidly : jabber. **–gab'ble** *n.*
gab•bro (găb'rō) *n., pl.* **-bros.** A usu. coarse-grained igneous rock made up of calcic plagioclase and pyroxene. **–gab•bro'ic** (gă-brō'ĭk) *adj.*
gab•by (găb'ē) *adj.* **-bi•er, -bi•est.** *Informal.* Inclined to talk too much : garrulous. **–gab'bi•ness** *n.*
gab•er•dine (găb'ər-dēn') *n.* **1.** A long, coarse cloak or frock worn esp. by Jews in the Middle Ages. **2.** *esp. Brit.* A loose smock worn by laborers. **3.** GABARDINE 1.
gab•fest (găb'fĕst') *n. Slang.* An informal gathering during which news and gossip are exchanged.
ga•ble (gā'bəl) *n.* The triangular wall section formed by the two slopes of a roof. **–ga'bled** *adj.*
Ga•bon (gä-bôN'). Country of WC Africa. *Cap.* Libreville. *Pop.* 550,000.
Gab•o•ro•ne (găb'ə-rō'nə). Cap. of Botswana. *Pop.* 54,000.
Ga•bri•el (gā'brē-əl) *n.* An archangel described in the Bible who acts as God's messenger.
gad (găd) *v.* **gad•ded, gad•ding.** To wander about restlessly and with little or no purpose : rove. **–gad'der** *n.*
gad•a•bout (găd'ə-bout') *n.* Someone who goes about seeking fun or excitement.
gad•fly (găd'flī') *n.* **1.** A fly, esp. of the family Tabanidae, that bites or annoys livestock. **2.** A critical but often constructively provocative person.
gadg•et (găj'ĭt) *n. Informal.* A usu. small mechanical device : contrivance. ☆**syns:** CONTRAPTION, CONTRIVANCE, DOODAD, GIMMICK **–gadg'et•ry** *n.*
gad•o•lin•i•um (găd'l-ĭn'ē-əm) *n. Symbol* **Gd** A silvery-white, malleable, ductile metallic element.
Gael (gāl) *n.* A Celt of Scotland, Ireland, or the Isle of Man.
Gael•ic (gā'lĭk) *n.* A branch of the Celtic languages. **–Gael'ic** *adj.*
gaff (găf) *n.* **1.** An iron hook used for landing large fish. **2.** A spar on the top edge of a fore-and-aft sail. **3.** *Slang.* Harsh treatment : abuse. **–gaff** *v.*

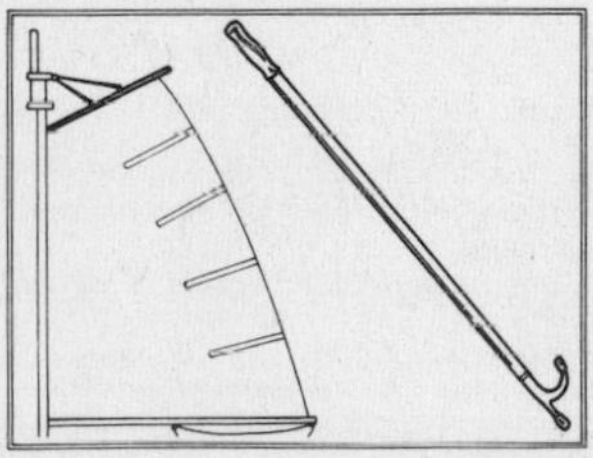

gaff
(Left) *a sail gaff and* (right) *a fishing gaff*

gaffe (găf) *n.* A clumsy social blunder.
†**gaf•fer** (găf'ər) *n.* **1.** *Regional.* **a.** An old man. **b.** A rustic. **2.** A lighting electrician on a film or television set.
gag (găg) *n.* **1.** Something forced into or over the mouth esp. to prevent speech or outcry. **2.** An obstacle to free speech. **3. a.** A practical joke. **b.** A humorous remark : joke. *–v.* **gagged, gag•ging. 1.** To prevent from speaking or crying out by using a gag. **2.** To prevent from speaking out. **3.** To block off : obstruct. **4.** To retch or cause to retch. **5.** To make jokes.
ga•ga (gä'gä') *adj. Slang.* **1.** Silly : crazy. **2.** Totally ethusiastic or infatuated.
gage[1] (gāj) *n.* **1.** Something deposited as security against an obligation : pledge. **2.** Something, as a glove, thrown down as a challenge to fight.
gage[2] (gāj) *n. var. of* GAUGE.
gag•gle (găg'əl) *n.* **1.** A flock of geese. **2.** A cluster : group.
gai•e•ty (gā'ĭ-tē) *n., pl.* **-ties. 1.** A state of joyful exuberance : merriment. **2.** Festive activity. ☆**syns:** FESTIVITY, FUN, MERRYMAKING, REVEL, REVELRY
gai•ly (gā'lē) *adv.* In a gay manner.
gain (gān) *v.* **1.** To acquire possession of : earn. **2.** To win, as in a competition <*gained* 1st prize in the race> **3.** To develop an increase in <*gained* speed> **4.** To come to : reach <*gained* the top of the hill> **5.** To secure as profit. **6.** To improve : progress. *–n.* **1.** Advantage : profit. **2.** An increase. **3.** An acquisition. **–gain'er** *n.*
gain•ful (gān'fəl) *adj.* Producing gain : profitable. **–gain'ful•ly** *adv.*
gain•say (gān-sā') *v.* To dispute : deny. **–gain•say'er** *n.*
gait (gāt) *n.* **1.** A way of moving on foot. **2.** The order of foot movements, as a canter or gallop, by which a horse can move.
gai•ter (gā'tər) *n.* **1.** A leg covering that extends from the knee to the instep. **2.** A spat. **3.** An ankle-high shoe with elastic sides. **4.** An overshoe with a fabric top.
gal (găl) *n. Informal.* A girl.
gal or **gal.** *abbr.* gallon.
ga•la (gā'lə, găl'ə, gä'lə) *n.* A festive celebration. **–ga'la** *adj.*
ga•lac•tose (gə-lăk'tōs') *n.* A simple sugar typically occurring in lactose.
Ga•la•tians (gə-lā'shənz) *n. (sing. in number).* See BIBLE TABLE.
gal•ax•y (găl'ək-sē) *n., pl.* **-ies. 1. a.** Any of numerous large-scale aggregates of stars, gas, and dust that constitute the universe. **b.** *often* **Galaxy.** The Milky Way. **2.** A brilliant or distinguished assembly. **–ga•lac'tic** (gə-lăk'tĭk) *adj.*
gale (gāl) *n.* **1.** A very powerful wind. **2.** An outburst, as of hilarity.
Ga•len (gā'lən). 130?–201? Greek anatomist and physician.
ga•le•na (gə-lē'nə) *n.* A gray mineral that is the principal ore of lead.
Gal•i•lee (găl'ə-lē'), **Sea of.** Freshwater lake bordered by Israel, Syria, and Jordan.
Gal•i•le•o (găl'ə-lē'ō, -lā'ō). 1564–1642. Italian astronomer and philosopher.
gall[1] (gôl) *n.* **1. a.** Liver bile. **b.** The gallbladder. **2.** Bitterness of feeling : animosity. **3.** Something bitter to undergo. **4.** Impudence : brazenness.
gall[2] (gôl) *n.* A skin sore caused by chafing. *–v.* **1.** To make or become sore by chafing. **2.** To irritate : annoy. **–gall'ing** *adj.* **–gall'ing•ly** *adv.*
gall[3] (gôl) *n.* An abnormal swelling of plant tissue caused by insects or disease organisms.
gal•lant (găl'ənt) *adj.* **1.** Showy in appearance or dress : dashing. **2.** Stately : majestic. **3.** Spirited and courageous. **4.** (*also* gə-lănt', -länt'). Courteous and attentive to women : chivalrous. *–n.* (gə-lănt', -länt', găl'ənt). **1.** A fashionable young man. **2.** A man who is courteous and attentive to women. **–gal'lant•ly** *adv.*
gal•lant•ry (găl'ən-trē) *n., pl.* **-ries. 1.** Noteworthy courage. **2.** Courteous attentiveness to women. **3.** A gallant act.
gall•blad•der *also* **gall bladder** (gôl'blăd'ər) *n.* A small sac under the right lobe of the liver in which bile is stored.
gal•le•on (găl'ē-ən, găl'yən) *n.* A large 3-masted sailing ship used for trading and warfare in the 15th and 16th cent.
†**gal•ler•y** (găl'ə-rē, găl'rē) *n., pl.* **-ies. 1.** A long outdoor balcony, esp. one with a roof. **2.** A long narrow passageway, as a corridor. **3.** *Regional.* A porch : verandah. **4.** The balcony of an auditorium, theater, or church. **5.** A group of spectators, as at a golf tournament. **6. a.** A building or room in which works of art are displayed. **b.** An organization that sells works of art. **7.** An underground passageway.
gal•ley (găl'ē) *n., pl.* **-leys. 1.** A medieval ship propelled by sails and oars. **2.** The kitchen of a ship or airliner. **3. a.** A long tray used by printers to hold set type. **b.** A printer's proof taken from composed type in order to detect and correct errors.

galley

Gal·lic (găl′ĭk) *adj.* Of or pertaining to Gaul or France.

†**gal·li·gas·kins** (găl′ĭ-găs′kĭnz) *pl.n.* **1.** Full-length, loosely fitting hose or breeches worn in the 16th and 17th cent. **2.** Loose breeches. **3.** *Regional.* Leggings.

gal·li·mau·fry (găl′ə-mô′frē) *n., pl.* **-fries.** A hodgepodge.

gal·li·nule (găl′ə-no͞ol′, -nyo͞ol′) *n.* A wading bird of the genera *Gallinula, Porphyrio,* or *Porphyrula,* with dark iridescent plumage.

gal·li·um (găl′ē-əm) *n. Symbol* **Ga** A rare silvery metallic element used in semiconductor technology and as a component of various low-melting alloys.

gal·li·vant (găl′ə-vănt′) *v.* To wander about in search of amusement or pleasure.

gal·lon (găl′ən) *n.* See MEASUREMENT TABLE.

gal·lop (găl′əp) *n.* **1.** A horse's 3-beat gait that is faster than a canter. **2.** A fast running pace. **–gal′lop** *v.*

gal·lows (găl′ōz) *n., pl.* **-lows** or **-lows·es. 1.** A framework usu. with 2 upright beams and a crossbeam from which condemned persons are hanged. **2.** Execution on a gallows or by hanging.

gall·stone (gôl′stōn′) *n.* A small, hard concretion of chloresterol crystals that forms in the gallbladder or in a bile duct.

gal·lus·es (găl′ə-sĭz) *pl.n. Informal.* Suspenders for trousers.

ga·lore (gə-lôr′, -lōr′) *adj. Informal.* In abundance : plentiful.

ga·losh (gə-lŏsh′) *n.* A high waterproof overshoe.

gal·va·nism (găl′və-nĭz′əm) *n.* Direct-current electricity, esp. when produced chemically. **–gal·van′ic** (-văn′ĭk) *adj.*

gal·va·nize (găl′və-nīz′) *v.* **-nized, -niz·ing. 1.** To stimulate or shock with or as if with an electric current. **2.** To arouse to awareness or action : provoke. **3.** To coat (iron or steel) with rust-resistant zinc. **–gal′va·ni·za′tion** *n.* **–gal′va·niz′er** *n.*

gal·va·nom·e·ter (găl′və-nŏm′ĭ-tər) *n.* A device for detecting or measuring small electric currents. **–gal′va·no·met′ric** (-nō-mĕt′rĭk) *adj.*

Ga·ma (găm′ə), **Vasco da.** 1469–1524. Portuguese explorer.

Gam·bi·a (găm′bē-ə). Country of W Africa, on the Atlantic. *Cap.* Banjul. *Pop.* 610,000. **–Gam′bi·an** *adj.* & *n.*

gam·bit (găm′bĭt) *n.* **1.** A chess opening in which a piece is sacrificed for a favorable position. **2.** A carefully planned maneuver.

gam·ble (găm′bəl) *v.* **-bled, -bling. 1. a.** To bet (e.g., money) on an uncertain outcome, as of a contest. **b.** To play a game of chance. **2.** To take a chance : speculate. **3.** To expose to risk : venture. *–n.* **1.** A bet : wager. **2.** An undertaking of uncertain outcome. **–gam′bler** *n.*

gam·bol (găm′bəl) *v.* **-boled, bol·ing** or **-bolled, -bol·ling.** To frisk about : frolic. **–gam′bol** *n.*

gam·brel roof (găm′brəl) *n.* A roof with 2 slopes on each side, the lower slope steeper than the upper.

game[1] (gām) *n.* **1.** A way of diverting oneself : amusement. **2. a.** A competitive activity governed by specific rules. **b.** A single contest of a game. **c.** The number of points required to win a game. **3.** A calculated way of doing something : scheme. **4.** Animals, birds, or fish hunted for food or sport. **5.** An object of ridicule or scorn. **6.** *Informal.* A way of earning a living : occupation. *–v.* **gamed, gam·ing.** To gamble. *–adj.* **gam·er, gam·est.** Courageous : plucky. **–game′ly** *adv.* **–game′ness** *n.*

game[2] (gām) *adj.* **gam·er, gam·est.** Lame <a *game* knee>

game·cock (gām′kŏk′) *n.* A rooster bred and trained for cockfighting.

game·keep·er (gām′kē′pər) *n.* Someone in charge of protecting and maintaining wildlife on a private preserve.

game plan *n.* **1.** The strategy devised before or used during a sports event. **2.** A strategy for reaching an objective.

games·man·ship (gāmz′mən-shĭp′) *n.* Skill at winning games by dubious means but without breaking the rules.

game·some (gām′səm) *adj.* Frolicsome : playful. **–game′some·ly** *adv.* **–game′some·ness** *n.*

game·ster (gām′stər) *n.* A gambler, esp. a habitual one.

gam·ete (găm′ēt′, gə-mēt′) *n.* A germ cell, esp. a mature sperm or egg.

game theory *n.* Mathematical analysis of abstract models of strategic competition aimed at determining the best strategy.

gam·in (găm′ĭn) *n.* An often impudent boy who roams the streets : urchin.

ga·mine (gă-mēn′) *n.* **1.** A girl who roams about the streets : urchin. **2.** A girl with impish appeal.

gam·ma globulin (găm′ə) *n.* A globulin fraction of blood serum associated with immune bodies and used to treat infectious diseases.

gamma ray *n.* Electromagnetic radiation emitted by radioactive decay and having energy greater than several hundred thousand electron volts.

†**gam·mer** (găm′ər) *n. Regional.* An elderly woman.

gam·mon[1] (găm′ən) *n. esp. Brit.* Misleading talk : hocus-pocus. **–gam′mon** *v.*

gam·mon[2] (găm′ən) *n.* **1.** A cured ham. **2.** The lower part of a side of bacon.

gam·ut (găm′ət) *n.* The complete range or extent.

gam·y (gā′mē) *adj.* **-i·er, -i·est. 1.** Having the strong flavor of game, esp. when slightly spoiled. **2.** Showing resolute spirit : plucky. **3. a.** Disreputable. **b.** Scandalous. **–gam′i·ness** *n.*

gan·der (găn′dər) *n.* **1.** A male goose. **2.** *Slang.* A quick look : glance.

Gan·dhi (găn′dē, găn′-) **Mohandas Karamchand.** "Mahatma." 1869–1948. Hindu leader; assassinated.

gang (găng) *n.* **1.** A group of persons who work together or socialize regularly. **2.** A group of criminals or adolescent hoodlums. **3.** A set, as of matched tools. *–v.* To group together in or as a gang. **–gang up on.** *Informal.* To attack as a group.

Gan·ges (găn′jēz). River of N India and Bangladesh, flowing SE from the Himalayas to the Bay of Bengal.

gang·land (găng′lănd′) *n.* Organized crime.

gan·gling (găng′glĭng) *adj.* Tall and thin : lanky.

gan·gli·on (găng′glē-ən) *n., pl.* **-gli·a** (-glē-ə) or **-ons.** A compact group of nerve cells located outside the brain or spinal cord. **–gan′gli·on′ic** (-ŏn′ĭk) *adj.*

gang·plank (găng′plăngk′) *n.* A movable board or ramp used to board or leave a ship.

▲word history: The element *gang–* in *gangplank* and *gangway* is the same as the word *gang,* but it preserves an older meaning of that word. *Gang* in Old and Middle English denoted the action of walking, with specific applications such as "way, passage," and "journey." A *gangplank* thus provides passage between a ship and a landing place. *Gangway* denotes a gangplank as well as various other kinds of passageways, such as aisles. *Gang* is related to the Old English verb *gangan,* "to walk, go," which has now been replaced by the verb *go.*

gang·plow (găng′plou′) *n.* A plow equipped with several blades that make parallel furrows.

gan·grene (găng′grēn′, găng-grēn′) *n.* Death and decay of bodily tissue caused esp. by failure of blood supply. **–gan′grene** *v.* **–gan′gre·nous** (-grə-nəs) *adj.*

gang·ster (găng′stər) *n.* A member of a criminal gang : racketeer.

gang·way (găng′wā′) *n.* **1.** A passageway, as through an obstructed area. **2.** A gangplank.

gan·net (găn′ĭt) *n.* A large sea bird, *Morus bassanus,* of rocky coastal regions, with white plumage and black wing tips.

gant·let (gônt′lĭt, gănt′-) *n. var. of* GAUNTLET.

gan·try (găn′trē) *n., pl.* **-tries.** A framelike support, esp. a movable vertical structure with platforms used in assembling or servicing rockets before they are launched.

gaol (jāl) *n.* & *v. esp. Brit. var. of* JAIL.

gap (găp) *n.* **1.** An opening, as in a wall : cleft. **2.** A pass through mountains. **3.** An empty space. **–gap** *v.*

gape (gāp, găp) *v.* **gaped, gap·ing. 1. a.** To open the mouth wide. **b.** To yawn. **2.** To stare in amazement with the mouth open. **3.** To become widely opened or separated. **–gape** *n.* **–gap′er** *n.*

gar (gär) *n.* A fish of the genus *Lepisosteus,* having a long snout and an elongated body covered with bony plates.

ga·rage (gə-räzh′, -räj′) *n.* **1.** A structure in which motor vehicles can be parked. **2.** A business place where motor vehicles are repaired and serviced. **–ga·rage′** *v.*

garage sale *n.* A sale of clothing or used household goods held at the seller's home.

garb (gärb) *n.* **1.** Clothing. **2.** A particular way of dressing. *–v.* To clothe : dress.

gar·bage (gär′bĭj) *n.* **1.** Food wastes. **2.** Unwanted or worthless material : trash.

gar·ban·zo (gär-bän′zō) *n., pl.* **-zos.** The chickpea.

gar·ble (gär′bəl) *v.* **-bled, -bling.** To distort or scramble so as to be unintelligible <*garbles* his words><*garbled* the message> **–gar′ble** *n.* **–gar′bler** *n.*

gar·çon (gär-sôN′) *n., pl.* **-çons** (-sôN′). A waiter in a restaurant.

gar·den (gär′dn) *n.* **1.** A plot of land for growing flowers, vegetables, or fruit. **2.** A parklike public area, esp. one with flowers, plants, or animals on display. **3.** A fertile, well-cultivated region. *–v.* To work in or make into a garden. **–gar′den·er** *n.*

gar·de·nia (gär-dĕn′yə) *n.* A shrub, *Gardenia jasminoides,* with glossy evergreen leaves and fragrant white flowers.

gar·den-va·ri·e·ty (gär′dn-və-rī′ĭ-tē) *adj.* Commonplace : familiar.

Gar·field (gär′fēld′), **James Abram.** 1831–81. 20th U.S. President (1881); assassinated.

gar·gan·tu·an *also* **Gar·gan·tu·an** (gär-găn′cho͞o-ən) *adj.* Of immense size : enormous.

gar•gle (gär′gəl) *v.* **-gled, -gling.** To force exhaled air through a liquid held in the back of the mouth so as to cleanse or medicate the mouth or throat. **–gar′gle** *n.*

gar•goyle (gär′goil′) *n.* A projecting roof spout carved to represent a grotesque human or animal figure.

Gar•i•bal•di (găr′ə-bôl′dē), **Giuseppe.** 1807–82. Italian patriot.

gar•ish (gâr′ĭsh) *adj.* Too bright and showy : gaudy. **–gar′ish•ly** *adv.* **–gar′ish•ness** *n.*

gar•land (gär′lənd) *n.* A chain, wreath, or crown of flowers or leaves. *–v.* To embellish with or form into a garland.

gar•lic (gär′lĭk) *n.* A plant, *Allium sativum,* related to the onion, having a bulb with a strong odor and flavor used as a seasoning. **–gar′lick•y** *adj.*

gar•ment (gär′mənt) *n.* An article of clothing. **–gar′ment** *v.*

gar•ner (gär′nər) *v.* **1.** To gather and store. **2.** To amass : accumulate.

gar•net (gar′nĭt) *n.* **1.** A usu. dark-red silicate mineral used as a gemstone and abrasive. **2.** A dark red.

gar•nish (gär′nĭsh) *v.* **1.** To embellish : decorate. **2.** To add decorative or flavorful touches to (food or drink). **–gar′nish** *n.*

gar•nish•ee (gär′nĭ-shē′) *v.* **-eed, -ee•ing.** *Law.* To attach (e.g., a debtor's pay) by garnishment. **–gar′nish•ee′** *n.*

gar•nish•ment (gär′nĭsh-mənt) *n.* A legal proceeding in which property belonging to a debtor is turned over to a creditor.

gar•ni•ture (gär′nĭ-chər) *n.* Something that garnishes : embellishment.

gar•ret (găr′ĭt) *n.* An attic.

gar•ri•son (găr′ĭ-sən) *n.* **1.** A military installation, esp. a permanent one. **2.** The troops stationed at a garrison. *–v.* To assign to or occupy as a garrison.

gar•rote *or* **gar•rotte** (gə-rŏt′, -rōt′) *n.* **1. a.** A method of execution by strangulation with an iron collar. **b.** The collar used. **2.** Strangulation, esp. so as to commit robbery. **–gar•rote′** *v.* **–gar•rot′er** *n.*

gar•ru•lous (găr′ə-ləs, -yə-) *adj.* Talkative, esp. excessively so : chatty. **–gar•ru′li•ty** (gə-ro͞o′lĭ-tē), **gar′ru•lous•ness** *n.*

gar•ter (gär′tər) *n.* A strap or band worn to hold up hose.

garter snake *n.* A nonvenomous North American snake of the genus *Thamnophis,* with longitudinal stripes.

Gar•y (gâr′ē). City of NW Ind., on Lake Michigan. *Pop.* 151,953.

gas (găs) *n., pl.* **gas•es** *or* **gas•ses. 1.** A substance capable of expanding to fill a container completely and taking on the shape of the container. **2.** A gas used as fuel. **3.** Gasoline. **4.** A gas that is used to produce a poisonous, irritating, or asphyxiating atmosphere. **–gas** *v.* **–gas′e•ous** (găs′ē-əs, găsh′əs) *adj.* **–gas′sy** *adj.*

gash (găsh) *n.* A long, deep cut. **–gash** *v.*

gas•ket (găs′kĭt) *n.* A seal, as of rubber, used between matched machine parts or around pipe joints to prevent the escape of a gas or fluid.

gas•kin (găs′kĭn) *n.* The part of the hind leg of a horse or related animal between the stifle and the hock.

gaskin

gas•light (găs′līt′) *n.* **1.** Light produced by burning illuminating gas. **2.** A gas burner or lamp.

gas mask *n.* A respirator covering the face and having a chemical air filter to protect against poisonous gases.

gas•o•hol (găs′ə-hôl) *n.* A fuel blended from ethanol and unleaded gasoline.

gas•o•line *also* **gas•o•lene** (găs′ə-lēn′, găs′ə-lēn′) *n.* A highly flammable mixture of liquid hydrocarbons derived chiefly from crude petroleum and used esp. as a fuel and a solvent.

gasp (găsp) *v.* **1.** To inhale sharply with emotion, as shock. **2.** To make violent or labored attempts to breathe. **–gasp** *n.*

gas•tric (găs′trĭk) *adj.* Of or relating to the stomach.

gastric juice *n.* The acidic digestive fluid secreted by the stomach glands.

gas•tri•tis (gă-strī′tĭs) *n.* Inflammation of the stomach.

gas•tro•en•ter•ol•o•gy (găs′trō-ĕn′tə-rŏl′ə-jē) *n.* Medical study of the stomach and intestines. **–gas′tro•en′ter•ol′o•gist** *n.*

gas•tro•in•tes•ti•nal (găs′trō-ĭn-tĕs′tə-nəl) *adj.* Of or relating to the stomach and intestines.

gas•tron•o•my (gă-strŏn′ə-mē) *n.* The art of good eating. **–gas′tro•nome′** (găs′trə-nōm′) *n.* **–gas′tro•nom′ic** (-nŏm′ĭk), **gas′tro•nom′i•cal** *adj.*

gas•tro•pod (găs′trə-pŏd′) *n.* A mollusk of the class Gastropoda, as a snail, slug, or limpet, with a single shell and a broad, muscular organ of locomotion.

gas•works (găs′wûrks′) *n.* (*sing. or pl. in number*). A factory where gas is manufactured.

gate[1] (gāt) *n.* **1. a.** An opening in a wall or fence. **b.** An often hinged structure that closes or blocks a gate. **2.** A device for controlling the passage of water or gas through a dam or conduit. **3.** The total admission receipts or number in attendance at a public performance.

†**gate**[2] (gāt) *n. Regional.* A particular way of acting or doing : manner.

gate•crash•er (gāt′krăsh′ər) *n. Slang.* One who gains admittance without invitation or enters without paying.

gate•fold (gāt′fōld′) *n.* A folded insert in a publication whose full size exceeds that of the regular page.

gate•keep•er (gāt′kē′pər) *n.* One in charge of a gate.

gate•post (gāt′pōst′) *n.* An upright post on or against which a gate is hung or closed.

gate•way (gāt′wā′) *n.* **1.** An opening, as in a fence, for a gate. **2.** A way of access.

gath•er (găth′ər) *v.* **1.** To come or bring together. **2.** To accumulate : amass. **3.** To harvest : pick. **4.** To increase gradually <*gather* velocity> **5.** To pull (cloth) along a thread into small folds. **6.** To summon up : muster <*gathered* his wits> **7.** To draw about or close to something. **8.** To conclude : infer. ☆***syns:*** CALL, CONVENE, CONVOKE, MUSTER, SUMMON *–n.* A small fold or pucker made in cloth by gathering. **–gath′er•er** *n.* **–gath′er•ing** *n.*

gauche (gōsh) *adj.* Socially awkward. **–gauche′ly** *adv.* **–gauche′ness** *n.*

gau•che•rie (gō′shə-rē′) *n.* A gauche act.

gau•cho (gou′chō) *n., pl.* **-chos.** A South American cowboy.

gaud (gôd) *n.* A gaudy ornament.

gaud•y (gô′dē) *adj.* **-i•er, -i•est.** Too highly ornamented to be in good taste. ☆***syns:*** CHINTZY, FLASHY, GARISH, GLARING, LOUD, MERETRICIOUS, TACKY, TAWDRY. **–gaud′i•ly** *adv.* **–gaud′i•ness** *n.*

gauge *also* **gage** (gāj) *n.* **1. a.** A standard, system, or scale of measurement. **b.** A standard dimension, quantity, or capacity. **2.** An instrument for measuring, registering, or testing. **3.** A means of estimating or evaluating. **4.** The distance between the 2 rails of a railroad. **5.** The diameter of a shotgun barrel. *–v.* **gauged, gaug•ing** *also* **gaged, gag•ing. 1.** To measure. **2.** To ascertain the capacity, volume, or contents of. **3.** To evaluate : estimate. **–gaug′er** *n.*

Gau•guin (gō-găɴ′), **(Eugène Henri) Paul.** 1848–1903. French painter.

Gaul (gôl). Ancient region in Europe comprising approx. modern France and Belgium.

†**gaum** (gôm) *v. Regional.* To smudge or smear.

gaunt (gônt) *adj.* **1.** Thin and bony : haggard. **2.** Desolate : bleak. **–gaunt′ly** *adv.* **–gaunt′ness** *n.*

gaunt•let[1] *also* **gant•let** (gônt′lĭt, gänt′-) *n.* **1.** A glove that protects the hand. **2.** A challenge to fight.

gaunt•let[2] *also* **gant•let** (gônt′lĭt, gänt′-) *n.* **1.** A double line of men armed with clubs with which to beat a person who is forced to run between them. **2.** A severe trial : ordeal.

gauze (gôz) *n.* A loosely woven, often transparent fabric used esp. for surgical bandages and curtains. **–gauz′i•ly** *adv.* **–gauz′i•ness** *n.* **–gauz′y** *adj.*

ga•vage (gə-väzh′) *n.* Introduction of material into the stomach via a tube.

gave (gāv) *v. p.t. of* GIVE.

gav•el (găv′əl) *n.* The mallet used by a presiding officer or auctioneer. **–gav′el** *v.*

ga•votte (gə-vŏt′) *n.* A French peasant dance similar to the minuet.

gawk (gôk) *v.* To stare stupidly : gape.

gawk•y (gô′kē) *adj.* **-i•er, -i•est.** Clumsy : awkward. **–gawk′i•ness** *n.*

gay (gā) *adj.* **1.** Merry. **2.** Bright and lively, esp. in color. **3.** Inclined to social pleasures. **4.** Homosexual. *–n.* A homosexual.

gaze (gāz) *v.* **gazed, gaz•ing.** To look intently or steadily. ☆***syns:*** GAPE, GAWK, GOGGLE, OGLE, PEER, STARE **–gaze** *n.* **–gaz′er** *n.*

ga•ze•bo (gə-zē′bō, -zā′-) *n., pl.* **-bos.** A summerhouse.
ga•zelle (gə-zĕl′) *n.* A slender, graceful, swift-running horned mammal of the genus *Gazella* or related genera.
ga•zette (gə-zĕt′) *n.* **1.** A newspaper. **2.** An official journal. *—v. esp. Brit.* To announce or publish in a gazette.
gaz•et•teer (găz′ĭ-tîr′) *n.* A dictionary or index of geographic terms.
gaz•pa•cho (gə-spä′cho, gəz-pä′-) *n.* A chilled soup of uncooked tomatoes, onions, green peppers, and herbs.
Gd *symbol for* GADOLINIUM.
gds. *abbr.* goods.
Ge *symbol for* GERMANIUM.
ge•an•ti•cline (jē-ăn′tĭ-klīn′) *n.* A large upward fold of the earth's crust. **—ge•an′ti•cli′nal** *adj.*
gear (gîr) *n.* **1.a.** A toothed wheel that meshes with another toothed part to transmit motion. **b.** A transmission configuration for a given ratio of engine to axle torque in a motor vehicle. **2.** An assembly of parts that performs a particular function <landing *gear*> **3.** Equipment <tennis *gear*> *—v.* **1..** To provide with or connect by gears. **b.** To put into gear. **2.** To adjust or adapt.
gear•box (gîr′bŏks′) *n.* The transmission of a motor vehicle.
gear•shift (gîr′shĭft′) *n.* A mechanism used to shift from 1 transmission gear to another.
gear•wheel (gîr′hwēl′, -wēl′) *n.* A wheel configured with a toothed rim.
geck•o (gĕk′ō) *n., pl.* **-os** *or* **-oes.** Any of various usu. small lizards of the family Gekkonidae, of warm regions, having toes with adhesive pads enabling them to climb on vertical surfaces.

gecko

geese (gēs) *n. pl. of* GOOSE.
gee•zer (gē′zər) *n. Slang.* An old man.
ge•fil•te fish (gĕ-fĭl′tə) *n.* Chopped fish mixed with crumbs, eggs, and seasoning, cooked in a broth and served chilled in balls or oval-shaped cakes.
Gei•ger counter (gī′gər) *n.* An instrument used to detect, measure, and record nuclear radiation and cosmic rays.
gei•sha (gā′shə) *n., pl.* **-sha** *or* **-shas.** A Japanese girl trained to entertain men, as by singing, dancing, or talking amusingly.
gel (jĕl) *n.* A jellylike mixture formed when the particles of a colloid become relatively large.
gel•a•tin *also* **gel•a•tine** (jĕl′ə-tən) *n.* **1.** A transparent, brittle protein derived from boiled animal tissues and used in foods, drugs, and photographic film. **2.** A jelly made with gelatin, used esp. as a salad base or dessert. **—ge•lat′i•nous** (jə-lăt′n-əs) *adj.*
geld (gĕld) *v.* To castrate (e.g., a horse).
geld•ing (gĕl′dĭng) *n.* A gelded animal, esp. a horse.
gel•id (jĕl′ĭd) *adj.* Very cold : frigid. **—ge•lid′i•ty** (jə-lĭd′ĭ-tē) *n.*
gel•ig•nite (jĕl′ĭg-nīt′) *n.* An explosive mixture of nitroglycerin, guncotton, wood pulp, and potassium nitrate.
gem (jĕm) *n.* **1.** A precious or semiprecious stone, esp. one that has been cut and polished. **2.** One that is highly valued.
Gem•i•ni (jĕm′ə-nī′, -nē′) *n.* **1.** *Astron.* A constellation in the N Hemisphere. **2. a.** The 3rd sign of the zodiac. **b.** One born under this sign.
gem•ol•o•gy *or* **gem•mol•o•gy** (jĕ-mŏl′ə-jē) *n.* The study of gems. **—gem′o•log′i•cal** *adj.* **—gem•ol′o•gist** *n.*
gem•stone (jĕm′stōn′) *n.* A precious or semiprecious stone that can be used in jewelry after being cut and polished.
ge•müt•lich (gə-müt′lĭKH) *adj.* Congenial : friendly.
gen. *abbr.* **1.** gender. **2.** general; generally. **3.** genitive.
gen•darme (zhän′därm′) *n.* A policeman in France.
gen•dar•me•rie *also* **gen•dar•mer•y** (zhän-där′mə-rē) *n.* A group of gendarmes.
gen•der (jĕn′dər) *n.* **1.** Any of 2 or more grammatical categories, as masculine or feminine, into which words are divided and that determine agreement with and selection of modifiers or grammatical forms. **2.** Sex classification.
gene (jēn) *n.* A functional hereditary unit located at a particular point on a chromosome that controls or acts in the transmission of hereditary characteristics.
ge•ne•al•o•gy (jē′nē-ŏl′ə-jē, -ăl′-, jĕn′ē-) *n., pl.* **-gies. 1.** A record or account of the descent of a family, group, or person from an ancestor. **2.** Direct descent from a progenitor : pedigree. **3.** The study of ancestry. **—ge′ne•a•log′i•cal** (-ə-lŏj′ĭ-kəl) *adj.* **—ge′ne•a•log′i•cal•ly** *adv.* **—ge′ne•al′o•gist** *n.*
gen•er•a (jĕn′ər-ə) *n. pl. of* GENUS.
gen•er•al (jĕn′ər-əl) *adj.* **1.** Of, relating to, or involving the whole or every member of a group or class. **2.** Affecting or typical of most : prevalent. **3.** Not specialized or restricted. **4.** Being usu. the case. **5.** Not detailed or precise. **6.** Not limited : diversified. **7.** Being superior in rank <a *general* manager> ☆**syns:** BROAD, COMPREHENSIVE, EXPANSIVE, EXTENSIVE, INCLUSIVE, OVERALL, SWEEPING, WIDESPREAD. *—n.* An officer in the U.S. Army, Air Force, or Marine Corps ranking above a colonel. **—gen′er•al•ly** *adv.*

▲word history: The Latin adjective *generalis,* the ult. ancestor of the English word *general,* meant literally "pertaining to the whole genus (kind or class)." The English noun *general* meaning "a military officer" preserves something of the Latin sense. It orig. designated a general officer, the commander of the general, or entire, army. Since such an officer was of a very high rank, the term *general* was also prefixed to the titles of other officers to indicate superiority of rank and command.

general assembly *n.* **1.** A legislative body. **2. General Assembly.** The chief deliberative body of the United Nations.
gen•er•al•is•si•mo (jĕn′ər-ə-lĭs′ə-mō′) *n., pl.* **-mos.** A commander in chief in certain countries.
gen•er•al•i•ty (jĕn′ə-răl′ĭ-tē) *n., pl.* **-ties. 1.** The quality or state of being general. **2.** An inexact, inadequate, or vague statement or idea. **3.** The greatest portion : majority.
gen•er•al•ize (jĕn′ər-ə-līz′) *v.* **-ized, -iz•ing. 1.** To make general rather than specific. **2.** To form a general conclusion (from). **3.** To think or speak in generalities. **—gen′er•al•i•za′tion** *n.*
general practitioner *n.* A physician who treats a variety of medical problems rather than specializing.
general relativity *n.* The theory of gravitation propounded by Albert Einstein, extending the special theory of relativity to accelerated frames of reference and introducing the principle that gravitational forces cannot be distinguished from those caused by inertia.
gen•er•al•ship (jĕn′ər-əl-shĭp′) *n.* **1.** The office or rank of a general. **2.** Leadership or skill displayed by a military commander of high rank. **3.** Skillful management.
general staff *n.* A group of officers charged with assisting the commander of a division or larger unit in planning and supervising military operations.
general store *n.* A retail store that sells a wide variety of merchandise but is not subdivided into departments.
gen•er•ate (jĕn′ə-rāt′) *v.* **-at•ed, -at•ing.** To bring into existence, esp. by a physical or chemical process : create. **—gen′er•a′tive** (-ər-ā′tĭv, -ə-rə-tĭv) *adj.*
gen•er•a•tion (jĕn′ə-rā′shən) *n.* **1.** The act or process of generating : production. **2.** A group of individuals having a common ancestor and constituting a single stage of descent. **3.** The average time interval between the birth of parents and the birth of their offspring. **—gen′er•a′tion•al** *adj.*
gen•er•a•tor (jĕn′ə-rā′tər) *n.* One that generates, esp. a machine to change mechanical energy into electrical energy.
ge•ner•ic (jĭ-nĕr′ĭk) *adj.* **1.** Of, relating to, or indicating an entire class or group : general. **2.** Of or relating to a biological genus. **3.** Not bearing a trademark or trade name. **—ge•ner′i•cal•ly** *adv.*
gen•er•ous (jĕn′ər-əs) *adj.* **1.** Having or showing willingness to give or share freely. **2.** Lacking pettiness or meanness : magnanimous. **3.** Abundant : copious. ☆**syns:** BIG, MAGNANIMOUS, UNSELFISH **—gen′er•os′i•ty** (-ə-rŏs′ĭ-tē) *n.* **—gen′er•ous•ly** *adv.*
gen•e•sis (jĕn′ĭ-sĭs) *n., pl.* **-ses** (-sēz′). **1.** A coming into existence : origin. **2. Genesis.** See BIBLE TABLE.
ge•net•ic (jə-nĕt′ĭk) *adj.* **1.** Of or relating to origin or development. **2.** Of or relating to genetics. **—ge•net′i•cal•ly** *adv.*
genetic code *n.* The information coded within the nucleotide sequences of RNA and DNA that specifies the amino acid sequence in the synthesis of proteins and on which heredity is based. **—genetic coding** *n.*
ge•net•ics (jə-nĕt′ĭks) *n.* (*sing. in number*). The biological study of heredity, esp. the study of hereditary transmission and variation. **—ge•net′i•cist** (-ĭ-sĭst) *n.*
Ge•ne•va (jə-nē′və). City of SW Switzerland. *Metro pop.* 425,000.
Gen•ghis Khan (jĕng′gĭs kän′, gĕng′-). 1162?–1227. Mongol conqueror.
gen•ial (jēn′yəl) *adj.* **1.** Cheerful, friendly, and good-humored :

gracious. **2.** Favorable to health or growth. **—ge'ni•al'i•ty** (jē'nē-ăl'ĭ-tē) *n.* **—gen'ial•ly** *adv.*
ge•nie (jē'nē) *n.* A supernatural creature capable of assuming human form.
gen•i•tal (jĕn'ĭ-təl) *adj.* **1.** Of or pertaining to biological reproduction. **2.** Of the genitalia. *—n.* **genitals.** The genitalia.
gen•i•ta•lia (jĕn'ĭ-tāl'yə) *pl.n.* The reproductive organs, esp. the external sex organs.
gen•i•tive (jĕn'ĭ-tĭv) *adj.* Of, relating to, or designating a grammatical case that marks possession or source. *—n.* The genitive case. **—gen'i•ti'val** (-tī'vəl) *adj.*
gen•i•to•u•ri•nar•y (jĕn'ĭ-tō-yo͝or'ə-nĕr'ē) *adj.* Relating to the genital and urinary organs or their functions.
gen•ius (jēn'yəs) *n.* **1.** Exceptional intellectual ability or creative power. **2.** A person of genius. **3.** A strong inclination or natural talent. **4.** A distinctive or prevailing spirit, as of a place, person, or time. **5.** A person with influence over another. **6.** *pl.* **ge•ni•i** (jē'nē-ī'). The guardian spirit of a person or place.
Gen•o•a (jĕn'ō-ə). City of NW Italy. *Pop.* 782,486.
gen•o•cide (jĕn'ə-sīd') *n.* The systematic annihilation of a political, racial, or cultural group. **—gen'o•cid'al** *adj.*
gen•re (zhän'rə) *n.* **1.** A style of painting in which scenes of everyday life are depicted. **2.** A particular type or category, esp. of literary work.
gens (jĕnz) *n., pl.* **gen•tes** (jĕn'tēz') A Roman clan that includes families of the same name that have descended through the male line.
gent (jĕnt) *n. Informal.* A man : fellow.
gen•teel (jĕn-tēl') *adj.* **1.** Refined : polite. **2.** Elegant : fashionable. **3.** Artificially or prudishly refined. **—gen•teel'ly** *adv.* **—gen•teel'ness** *n.*
gen•tian (jĕn'shən) *n.* A plant of the genus *Gentiana,* with deep-blue flowers.
gen•tile (jĕn'tīl') *n.* **1. Gentile.** Someone, esp. a Christian, who is not a Jew. **2.** A pagan : heathen.
gen•til•i•ty (jĕn-tĭl'ĭ-tē) *n.* **1.** The quality of being genteel. **2.** Gentle birth. **3.** The gentry.
gen•tle (jĕn'tl) *adj.* **-tler, -tlest. 1.** Amiable : kindly. **2.** Not harsh, severe, or violent. **3.** Easily handled or managed : docile. **4.** Not steep or sudden : gradual. **5.** Of or from a family of high social standing : well-born. ☆***syns:*** MILD, SOFT, SOFTHEARTED, TENDER, TENDERHEARTED. **—gen'tle** *v.* **—gen'tle•ness** *n.* **—gen'tly** *adv.*
gen•tle•folk (jĕn'tl-fōk') *also* **gen•tle•folks** (-fōks') *pl.n.* Well-bred persons of good family background.
gen•tle•man (jĕn'tl-mən) *n.* **1.** A man of gentle or noble birth. **2.** A well-bred or polite man. **3.** A man spoken of in a polite way. **—gen'tle•man•ly** *adj.*
gen•tle•wom•an (jĕn'tl-wo͝om'ən) *n.* **1.** A woman of gentle or noble birth. **2.** A well-bred or polite woman. **3.** A woman attendant to a lady of rank.
gen•try (jĕn'trē) *n.* **1.** People of gentle birth and high social standing : aristocracy. **2.** An English social class next below the nobility in rank.
gen•u•flect (jĕn'yə-flĕkt') *v.* To bend one knee, as in worship. **—gen'u•flec'tion** *n.*
gen•u•ine (jĕn'yo͞o-ĭn) *adj.* **1.** Real : authentic. **2.** Not hypocritical : sincere. **—gen'u•ine•ly** *adv.* **—gen'u•ine•ness** *n.*
ge•nus (jē'nəs) *n., pl.* **gen•er•a** (jĕn'ər-ə). **1.** A category of related plants or animals usu. including several species. **2.** A kind or class having common attributes.
ge•o•cen•tric (jē'ō-sĕn'trĭk) *adj.* **1.** Of, relating to, or measured from the center of the earth. **2.** Having the earth as a center. **—ge'o•cen'tri•cal•ly** *adv.*
ge•o•chro•nol•o•gy (jē'ō-krə-nŏl'ə-jē) *n.* The chronology of the earth's history as governed by geologic data. **—ge'o•chron'o•log'ic** (-krŏn'ə-lŏj'ĭk), **ge'o•chron'o•log'i•cal** (-ĭ-kəl) *adj.*
ge•ode (jē'ōd') *n.* A hollow, usu. spheroidal rock with crystals lining the cavity.
ge•o•des•ic (jē'ə-dĕs'ĭk) *adj.* Made of lightweight straight elements that form interlocking polygons <a *geodesic* dome>
ge•od•e•sy (jē-ŏd'ĭ-sē) *n.* The geologic science of the size and shape of the earth. **—ge•od'e•sist** (-sĭst) *n.* **—ge'o•det'ic** (jē'ə-dĕt'ĭk) *adj.*
geog. *abbr.* geographer; geographic; geography.
ge•og•ra•phy (jē-ŏg'rə-fē) *n., pl.* **-phies. 1.** The science dealing with the earth's natural features, climate, resources, and population. **2.** The natural features of an area. **3.** A book on geography. **—ge•og'ra•pher** *n.* **—ge'o•graph'ic** (-ə-grăf'ĭk), **ge'o•graph'i•cal** *adj.* **—ge'o•graph'i•cal•ly** *adv.*
geol. *abbr.* geologic; geologist; geology.
ge•ol•o•gy (jē-ŏl'ə-jē) *n., pl.* **-gies. 1.** The science dealing with the origin, history, and structure of the earth. **2.** The structure of a particular area of the earth's surface. **—ge'o•log'ic** (jē'ə-lŏj'ĭk), **ge'o•log'i•cal** *adj.* **—ge'o•log'i•cal•ly** *adv.* **—ge•ol'o•gist** *n.*
geom. *abbr.* geometric; geometry.
ge•o•mag•ne•tism (jē'ō-măg'nĭ-tĭz'əm) *n.* The magnetism of the earth. **—ge'o•mag•net'ic** (-măg-nĕt'ĭk) *adj.*
geometric progression *n.* A sequence of numbers, as 5, 25, 125, 625, in which each term is the product of a constant factor and the preceding term.
ge•om•e•try (jē-ŏm'ĭ-trē) *n., pl.* **-tries.** The mathematical study of the properties, measurement, and relationships of points, lines, angles, surfaces, and solids. **—ge'o•met'ric** (-ə-mĕt'rĭk), **ge'o•met'ri•cal** *adj.*
ge•o•mor•phol•o•gy (jē'ō-môr-fŏl'ə-jē) *n.* The geologic study of the configuration and evolution of land forms. **—ge'o•mor'pho•log'ic** (-môr'fə-lŏj'ĭk), **ge'e•mor'pho•log'i•cal** *adj.* **—ge'o•mor'pho•log'i•cal•ly** *adv.* **—ge'o•mor•phol'o•gist** *n.*
ge•o•phys•ics (jē'ō-fĭz'ĭks) *n. (sing. in number).* The physics of geologic phenomena. **—ge'o•phys'i•cal** *adj.* **—ge'o•phys'i•cist** *n.*
ge•o•pol•i•tics (jē'ō-pŏl'ĭ-tĭks) *n. (sing. in number).* The study of the relationship between geography and politics. **—ge'o•po•lit'i•cal** (-pə-lĭt'ĭ-kəl) *adj.*
George III (jôrj). 1738–1820. King of Great Britain (1760–1820).
George•town (jôrj'toun'). Cap. of Guyana, on the Atlantic. *Pop.* 72,049.
Geor•gia (jôr'jə). **1.** State of the SE U.S. *Cap.* Atlanta. *Pop.* 5,464,265. **2.** Region of SE European USSR. **—Geor'gian** *n.*
ge•o•sci•ence (jē'ō-sī'əns) *n.* A science, as geology or geochemistry, that deals with the earth.
ge•o•syn•cline (jē'ō-sĭn'klīn') *n.* An extensive depression in the earth's crust in which a succession of sedimentary strata has accumulated. **—ge'o•syn•cli'nal** *adj.*
ge•o•ther•mal (jē'ō-thûr'məl) *also* **ge•o•ther•mic** (-mĭk) *adj.* Of or relating to the internal heat of the earth.
ger. *abbr.* gerund.
ge•ra•ni•um (jĭ-rā'nē-əm) *n.* **1.** A widely cultivated plant of the genus *Geranium,* with rounded leaves and clusters of red, pink, or white flowers. **2.** A plant of the genus *Pelargonium,* with divided leaves and pink or purplish flowers.
▲word history: The word *geranium* refers to plants of 2 different but related genera. One genus is called *Geranium,* which is ult. from Greek *geranos,* "crane." The genus is so named because the fruits of the plants that belong to it are similar in shape to the bill of the crane. The popular name for these plants is *cranesbill.* The plant commonly called the *geranium* in English belongs to the genus *Pelargonium,* from *pelargos,* the Greek word for "stork." The name for this genus also alludes to the shape of its fruit, which resembles the bill of a stork.
ger•bil (jûr'bĭl) *n.* A mouselike rodent of the genus *Gerbillus* or related genera, of desert regions of Africa and Asia Minor, having long hind legs and a long tail.
ger•i•at•rics (jĕr'ē-ăt'rĭks) *n. (sing. in number).* The medical study of the physiology and pathology of old age. **—ger'i•at'ric** *adj.* **—ger'i•a•tri'cian** (-ə-trĭsh'ən) *n.*
germ (jûrm) *n.* **1.** A small organic structure or cell from which a new organism may develop. **2.** An origin from which something larger or more complex may develop. **3.** A microorganism, esp. a pathogen.
Ger•man (jûr'mən) *n.* **1.** A native or inhabitant of Germany. **2.** The language of Germany. **—Ger'man** *adj.*
ger•mane (jər-mān') *adj.* Relevant.
Ger•man•ic (jûr-măn'ĭk) *n.* A branch of the Indo-European language family that comprises English, German, Dutch, Afrikaans, Flemish, the Scandinavian languages, etc. **—Ger•man'ic** *adj.*
ger•ma•ni•um (jər-mā'nē-əm) *n. Symbol* **Ge** A brittle, crystalline, gray-white element widely used as a semiconductor and alloying agent.
German measles *n.* A contagious viral disease capable of causing defects in infants born to mothers infected during the 1st trimester of pregnancy.
German shepherd *n.* A large dog often trained to help the police and the blind.
Ger•ma•ny (jûr'mə-nē). Former state of NC Europe, divided in 1949 into the **German Democratic Republic** (East Germany), *cap.* East Berlin, *pop.* 16,715,000; and the **German Federal Republic** (West Germany), *cap.* Bonn, *pop.* 61,690,000.
germ cell *n.* A cell, as an egg or sperm cell, having reproduction as its primary function.
ger•mi•cide (jûr'mĭ-sīd') *n.* A germ-killing agent. **—ger'mi•ci'dal** *adj.*

ger·mi·nal (jûr′mə-nəl) *adj.* **1.** Of or relating to a germ cell. **2.** Of or in the earliest stage of development.
ger·mi·nate (jûr′mə-nāt′) *v.* **-nat·ed, -nat·ing.** To begin to grow : sprout. **–ger′mi·na′tion** *n.*
germ plasm *n.* **1.** The cytoplasm of a germ cell. **2.** Germ cells as a whole. **3.** Hereditary material : genes.
ger·on·tol·o·gy (jĕr′ən-tŏl′ə-jē) *n.* The study of the physiological and pathological phenomena associated with aging. **–ge·ron′to·log′i·cal** (jə-rŏn′tl-ŏj′ĭ-kəl), **ge·ron′to·log′ic** *adj.* **–ger′on·tol′o·gist** *n.*
ger·ry·man·der (jĕr′ē-măn′dər, gĕr′-) *v.* To divide (an area) into voting districts in order to give an unfair advantage to 1 political party. **–ger′ry·man′der** *n.*
ger·und (jĕr′ənd) *n.* A verbal form that functions as a noun.
gest (jĕst) *n.* A notable feat.
Ge·sta·po (gə-stä′pō, -shtä′-) *n.* The secret police of Nazi Germany.
ges·ta·tion (jĕ-stā′shən) *n.* The carrying of developing offspring in the uterus : pregnancy. **–ges′tate** (jĕs′tāt′) *v.* **–ges·ta′tion·al** *adj.*
ges·tic·u·late (jĕ-stĭk′yə-lāt′) *v.* **-lat·ed, -lat·ing.** To make gestures, esp. while talking. **–ges·tic′u·la′tion** *n.*
ges·ture (jĕs′chər) *n.* **1.** A motion of the limbs or body to express or emphasize a thought or feeling. **2.** The use of gestures. **3.** Something said or done as an often formal sign of attitude or intent. **–ges′ture** *v.* **–ges′tur·er** *n.*
Ge·sund·heit (gə-zo͝ont′hīt′) *interj.* Used to wish good health to a person who has just sneezed.
get (gĕt) *v.* **got** (gŏt), **got** *or* **got·ten** (gŏt′n), **get·ting. 1.** To come into possession of, as by earning, receiving, winning, or buying : acquire or obtain. **2.** To go after and obtain : fetch. **3.** To make contact with, as by telephone. **4.** To acquire involuntarily : catch <got a cold> **5.** To ascertain by calculation. **6.** To have <She's got a large house.> **7.** To understand. **8.** To perceive by hearing : hear. **9.** To cause to be in a particular position or condition <tried to *get* the door open> **10.** To cause to come or go. **11.** To prevail upon : persuade <got her to consent> **12.** To seize : capture. **13.** To kill, esp. in revenge. **14.** To hit : strike. **15.** To elicit an emotional response from. **16.** To annoy : irritate. **17.** To have as an obligation <He has got to be reasonable.> **18.** To become <He got mad when he heard the news.> **19.** To come or go <*got* home early><had to *get* out of town> **20.** To leave immediately. **21.** To be able <never got to go to Europe> **22.** To receive as retribution : incur. **–get along. 1.** To be on friendly terms. **2.** To manage with reasonable success. **–get by. 1.** To survive : manage. **2.** To be successful with the minimum possible effort. **–get over.** To recover from. **–get′ter** *n.*
get·a·way (gĕt′ə-wā′) *n.* **1.** The act or an instance of escaping. **2.** A start, as of a race.
get-to·geth·er (gĕt′tə-gĕth′ər) *n. Informal.* A small party.
get-up (gĕt′ŭp′) *n.* A costume : outfit.
gew·gaw (gyo͞o′gô′) *n.* A bauble : trinket.
gey·ser (gī′zər) *n.* A natural hot spring that intermittently ejects steam and hot water.
Gha·na (gä′nə). Country of W Africa. *Cap.* Accra. *Pop.* 11,835,000. **–Gha′na·ian, Gha′ni·an** *adj.* & *n.*
ghast·ly (găst′lē) *adj.* **-li·er, -li·est. 1.** Shocking : dreadful. **2.** Suggestive of a ghost : deathly pale. **3.** Very unpleasant. ☆***syns:*** GRIM, GRISLY, GRUESOME, HIDEOUS, HORRIBLE, HORRID, MACABRE **–ghast′li·ness** *n.*
▲word history: The words *ghastly* and *ghost* are related, but the former is not derived from the latter. *Ghastly* is formed from the Middle English verb *gasten,* which meant "to frighten, terrify." *Ghost* is the modern descendent of Old English *gāst,* which meant "spirit, soul, spiritual being." Both *ghastly* and *ghost* are derived from a prehistoric Germanic root, *gaist–.* The presence of the *h* in the modern spelling of both words is a relatively recent development. It was introduced into *ghost* in the 15th cent., perhaps from the influence of Flemish *gheest,* "ghost," and appeared in *ghastly* in the 16th cent., prob. as a result of the semantic association of the 2 English words.
ghat (gôt, gät) *n.* A broad flight of steps down to the bank of a river.
gher·kin (gûr′kĭn) *n.* A small cucumber, esp. one suitable for pickling.
ghet·to (gĕt′ō) *n., pl.* **-tos** *or* **-toes.** A section of a city in which a minority group lives because of poverty or social pressure.
ghost (gōst) *n.* **1.** The spirit of a dead person, believed to appear to or haunt living persons : specter. **2.** A slight trace : suggestion <a *ghost* of a frown on his face> **3.** A false, usu. faint, secondary telvision or photographic image. **4.** *Informal.* A ghostwriter. *–v.* To write as a ghostwriter. **–ghost′ly** *adj.*
ghost·writ·er (gōst′rī′tər) *n.* A person hired to write for and give credit of authorship to another. **–ghost′write′** *v.*
ghoul (go͞ol) *n.* A legendary evil spirit that plunders graves and feeds on corpses. **–ghoul′ish** *adj.* **–ghoul′ish·ly** *adv.* **–ghoul′ish·ness** *n.*
GI (jē′ī′) *n., pl.* **GIs** *or* **GI's.** An enlisted person in the U.S. armed forces. *–adj.* **1.** Of, relating to, or characteristic of a GI. **2.** In conformity with military procedures or regulations. **3.** Issued by an official U.S. military supply department.
GI *abbr.* **1.** general issue. **2.** *also* **G.I.** government issue.
gi·ant (jī′ənt) *n.* **1.** An enormous legendary manlike being of extraordinary strength. **2.** One of great power, size, or importance. *–adj.* Huge : enormous. ☆***syns:*** COLOSSAL, ELEPHANTINE, ENORMOUS, GARGANTUAN, GIGANTIC, HERCULEAN, HUGE, IMMENSE, JUMBO, MAMMOTH, MASSIVE, MIGHTY, MONSTROUS, MONUMENTAL, MOUNTAINOUS, STUPENDOUS, TITANIC, TREMENDOUS, VAST **–gi′ant·ess** *n.*
gib·ber (jĭb′ər) *v.* To chatter unintelligibly. **–gib′ber** *n.*
gib·ber·ish (jĭb′ər-ĭsh) *n.* Unintelligible or meaningless speech.
gib·bet (jĭb′ĭt) *n.* A gallows. *–v.* **-bet·ed, -bet·ing** *or* **-bet·ted, -bet·ting.** To hang or execute by hanging on a gibbet.
gib·bon (gĭb′ən) *n.* A tropical Asian ape of the genera *Hylobates* or *Symphalangus,* with a slender body and long arms.
gib·bous (gĭb′əs) *adj.* More than half but not entirely illuminated. Used of the moon or a planet. **–gib′bous·ly** *adv.* **–gib′bous·ness** *n.*
gibe (jīb) *v.* **gibed, gib·ing.** To make taunting remarks : ridicule. **–gibe** *n.* **–gib′er** *n.*
gib·let (jĭb′lĭt) *n. often* **giblets.** The heart, liver, or gizzard of a fowl.
Gib·ral·tar (jĭ-brôl′tər). British colony at the NW end of the **Rock of Gibraltar,** a peninsula on the SC coast of Spain in the **Strait of Gibraltar,** connecting the Atlantic and the Mediterranean. *Pop.* 30,000.
Gib·son (gĭb′sən) *n.* A dry martini with a small pickled onion.
gid·dy (gĭd′ē) *adj.* **-di·er, -di·est. 1. a.** Dizzy. **b.** Causing or capable of causing dizziness. **2.** Frivolous and silly : flighty. ☆***syns:*** BIRDBRAINED, DIZZY, FLIGHTY, FRIVOLOUS, GAGA, HAREBRAINED, LIGHTHEADED, SCATTERBRAINED, SILLY, SKITTISH **–gid′di·ly** *adv.* **–gid′di·ness** *n.*
gift (gĭft) *n.* **1.** Something that is given : present. **2.** The power or act of giving. **3.** A special aptitude or ability : talent.
gift·ed (gĭf′tĭd) *adj.* Endowed with a special aptitude or ability : talented.
gig[1] (gĭg) *n.* **1.** A light 2-wheeled carriage. **2.** A long, light ship's boat.
gig[2] (gĭg) *n.* A spear with prongs used for fishing. **–gig** *v.*
gig[3] (gĭg) *n. Slang.* A job, esp. an engagement for a jazz musician.
gig[4] (gĭg) *n. Slang.* A demerit, esp. one assigned as punishment to military personnel. **–gig** *v.*
gi·gan·tic (jī-găn′tĭk) *adj.* Of extraordinary size : huge. **–gi·gan′ti·cal·ly** *adv.*
gig·gle (gĭg′əl) *v.* **-gled, -gling.** To laugh with repeated short sounds. **–gig′gle** *n.* **–gig′gler** *n.* **–gig′gly** *adj.*
gig·o·lo (jĭg′ə-lō′, zhĭg′-) *n., pl.* **-los.** A man who is supported by a woman, esp. one who is paid to be an escort or dancing partner.
Gi·la monster (hē′lə) *n.* A venomous lizard, *Heloderma suspectum,* of the SW U.S.
gild (gĭld) *v.* **gild·ed** *or* **gilt** (gĭlt), **gild·ing. 1.** To coat with or as if with a thin layer of gold. **2.** To make deceptively attractive : embellish. **–gild′er** *n.*
gill[1] (gĭl) *n.* An organ, as of fishes and various aquatic invertebrates, for taking oxygen from water.
gill[2] (jĭl) *n.* A U.S. Customary System unit of volume or capacity used in liquid measure and equal to 4 fl oz, ¼ pt, or 28.423 ml.
gilt (gĭlt) *adj.* Covered with or of the color of gold. *–n.* A thin layer of gold or a gold-colored substance applied to a surface.
gilt-edged (gĭlt′ĕjd′) *adj.* Of the best quality or highest value.
gim·bal (gĭm′bəl, jĭm′-) *n. often* **gimbals.** A device that keeps an object supported on it, as a ship's compass, level.
gim·crack (jĭm′krăk′) *n.* A cheap and showy object of little or no value.
gim·let (gĭm′lĭt) *n.* A small hand boring tool with a screw tip and a cross handle.
gim·mick (gĭm′ĭk) *n. Informal.* **1.** A tricky device, esp. when used dishonestly or secretly. **2.** A significant feature that is obscured or misrepresented. **3.** A clever new stratagem. **4.** A gadget : contrivance. **–gim′mick·ry** *n.* **–gim′mick·y** *adj.*
gimp (gĭmp) *n. Slang.* A limping walk. **–gimp** *v.* **–gimp′y** *adj.*
gin[1] (jĭn) *n.* A clear alcoholic liquor that is distilled from grain and flavored with juniper berries.

gin[2] (jĭn) *n.* **1.** A machine that separates seeds from cotton fibers. **2.** A snare : trap. *—v.* **ginned, gin•ning.** To remove the seeds from (cotton) with a gin.
gin•ger (jĭn'jər) *n.* **1.** A tropical Asian plant, *Zingiber officinale,* with a pungent aromatic rootstock used esp. as a spice. **2.** *Informal.* Vigor : vivacity. **—gin'ger•y** *adj.*
ginger ale *n.* A sweet carbonated soft drink flavored with ginger.
gin•ger•bread (jĭn'jər-brĕd') *n.* **1.** A molasses cake or cookie flavored with ginger. **2.** Lavish or superfluous ornamentation, esp. in architecture.
gin•ger•ly (jĭn'jər-lē) *adv.* Cautiously. **—gin'ger•li•ness** *n.* **—gin'ger•ly** *adj.*
gin•ger•snap (jĭn'jər-snăp') *n.* A brittle molasses cookie spiced with ginger.
ging•ham (gĭng'əm) *n.* A cotton fabric with a woven pattern.
gin•gi•vi•tis (jĭn'jə-vī'tĭs) *n.* Inflammation of the gums.
gink•go *also* **ging•ko** (gĭng'kō) *n., pl.* **-goes** *also* **-koes.** A widely planted Chinese shade tree, *Ginkgo biloba,* with fan-shaped leaves and yellowish fruit.
gin rummy *n.* A variety of the game rummy.
gin•seng (jĭn'sĕng') *n.* A Chinese herb, *Panax schinseng,* with an aromatic root believed to have medicinal properties.
Giot•to (jôt'ō). 1266?–1337. Florentine painter and sculptor.
Gip•sy (jĭp'sē) *n.* & *adj. var. of* GYPSY.
gi•raffe (jĭ-răf') *n.* An African mammal, *Giraffa camelopardis,* with an extremely long neck and legs.
gir•an•dole (jĭr'ən-dōl') *n.* A branched candleholder, sometimes backed by a mirror.

girandole

gird (gûrd) *v.* **gird•ed** *or* **girt** (gûrt), **gird•ing. 1.** To encircle or attach with or as if with a belt. **2.** To surround. **3.** To prepare, as for action : brace.
gird•er (gûr'dər) *n.* A strong horizontal beam that is a main support in building.
gir•dle (gûr'dl) *n.* **1.** Something, as a belt or sash, that is worn around the waist. **2.** A supporting undergarment worn by women over the waist and hips. **—gir'dle** *v.*
girl (gûrl) *n.* **1.** A female child. **2.** A young unmarried woman. **3.** A sweetheart. **4.** A female employee or servant. **—girl'hood'** *n.* **—girl'ish** *adj.* **—girl'ish•ly** *adv.* **—girl'ish•ness** *n.*
▲word history: In Modern English *girl* is the ordinary word denoting a female child. In Middle English times, however, from the 13th to the 15th cent., *girl* indicated a child or youth of either sex. Nothing is known of the history of *girl* before its appearance in English, and it appears that no related forms exist in any other language.
girl Friday *n.* A woman employee who is responsible for a great variety of tasks.
girl•friend *also* **girl friend** (gûrl'frĕnd') *n.* **1.** A female friend. **2.** *Informal.* A close female companion of a man or boy.
Girl Scout *n.* A member of the Girl Scouts, an organization for girls between 7 and 17.
girt (gûrt) *v. var. p.t.* & *p.p. of* GIRD.
girth (gûrth) *n.* **1.** Distance around something : circumference. **2.** A strap encircling an animal's body to secure something, as a saddle, on its back.
gis•mo *also* **giz•mo** (gĭz'mō) *n., pl.* **-mos.** *Slang.* A device or part whose name is forgotten or unknown : gadget.
gist (jĭst) *n.* The central idea of a matter : essence.
give (gĭv) *v.* **gave** (gāv), **giv•en** (gĭv'ən), **giv•ing. 1.a.** To make a present of. **b.** To deliver in exchange : pay. **2.** To place in the keeping or possession of. **3.** To convey <*Give* her my love.> **4.** To bestow, esp. formally : grant. **5.** To cause to have or be subject to. **6.** To bring forth : produce. **7.** To furnish : provide. **8.** To administer. **9.** To accord or relinquish to another : yield. **10.** To donate : contribute. **11.** To submit for consideration or acceptance : proffer. **12.** To cause to take place, esp. for entertainment. **13.** To apply : devote. **14.** To yield, as to pressure : collapse. **—give away. 1.** To present (a bride) to the bridegroom at a wedding ceremony. **2.** To betray. **—give in.** To surrender : submit. **—give out. 1.** To break down. **2.** To become used up : run out. **—give up. 1.** To surrender. **2.** To leave off : stop. **3.** To part with : relinquish. **4.** To abandon hope for. *—n. Informal.* The quality or state of being resilient : elasticity. **—giv'er** *n.*
give-and-take (gĭv'ən-tāk') *n.* A lively exchange, as of conversation or opinions.
give•a•way (gĭv'ə-wā') *n. Informal.* **1.** Something, as a premium, that is given away free. **2.** Something that betrays, esp. unintentionally.
giv•en (gĭv'ən) *adj.* **1.** Specified <on a *given* day> **2.** Granted as a supposition. **3.** Tending : inclined <*given* to lying> **—giv'en** *n.*
given name *n.* A name given at birth or baptism.
Gi•za (gē'zə). City of NE Egypt; site of the Great Pyramids. *Pop.* 1,246,713.
giz•mo (gĭz'mō) *n. var. of* GISMO.
giz•zard (gĭz'ərd) *n.* A muscular enlargement of the digestive tract of a bird.
gla•brous (glā'brəs) *adj.* Having no hair or down : smooth. **—gla'brous•ness** *n.*
gla•cé (glă-sā') *adj.* **1.** Having a glazed surface. **2.** Coated with a sugar glaze. *—v.* **1.** To glaze. **2.** To candy.
gla•cial (glā'shəl) *adj.* **1.** Of or pertaining to glaciers. **2.** Of, relating to, or being a period in the past when glaciers covered much of the earth's surface. **3.** Extremely cold. **—gla'cial•ly** *adv.*
gla•ci•ate (glā'shē-āt', -sē-) *v.* **-at•ed, -at•ing. 1.** To subject to the action of glaciers. **2.** To freeze. **—gla'ci•a'tion** *n.*
gla•cier (glā'shər) *n.* A very large mass of ice formed from compacted snow and slowly moving down a slope.
gla•ci•ol•o•gy (glā'shē-ŏl'ə-jē, -sē-) *n.* The scientific study of glaciers.
glad[1] (glăd) *adj.* **glad•der, glad•dest. 1.** Experiencing, displaying, or affording joy and pleasure : happy. **2.** Willing <*glad* to help> **3.** Grateful <*glad* for his help> ☆**syns:** CHEERFUL, CHEERY, FESTIVE, GAY, JOYFUL, JOYOUS **—glad'ly** *adv.* **—glad'ness** *n.*
glad[2] (glăd) *n. Informal.* A gladiolus.
glad•den (glăd'n) *v.* To make glad.
glade (glād) *n.* A clearing in a forest.
glad hand *n.* A hearty, effusive, often insincere greeting. **—glad'-hand'** *v.*
glad•i•a•tor (glăd'ē-ā'tər) *n.* **1.** A man who entertained the public by fighting to the death in ancient Rome. **2.** A person engaged in an intense controversy or struggle. **—glad'i•a•to'ri•al** (-ə-tôr'ē-əl, -tōr'-) *adj.*
glad•i•o•lus (glăd'ē-ō'ləs) *n., pl.* **-li** (-lī', -lē') *or* **-lus•es.** A plant of the genus *Gladiolus* that is widely cultivated for its spike of variously colored flowers.
glad•some (glăd'səm) *adj.* Showing or giving cheer : joyful. **—glad'some•ly** *adv.* **—glad'some•ness** *n.*
Glad•stone (glăd'stōn', -stən), **William Ewart.** 1809–98. British statesman.
Gladstone bag *n.* A piece of hand luggage composed of 2 hinged compartments.
glam•or•ize *also* **glam•our•ize** (glăm'ə-rīz') *v.* **-ized, -iz•ing. 1.** To make glamorous. **2.** To treat or portray in a romantic way : idealize.
glam•our *also* **glam•or** (glăm'ər) *n.* A compellingly romantic and exciting attractiveness. **—glam'or•ous, glam'our•ous** *adj.*
glance (glăns) *v.* **glanced, glanc•ing. 1.** To give a brief or hasty look. **2.** To strike a surface at an angle and be deflected. **3.** To shine : glitter. *—n.* **1.** A brief or hasty look. **2.** A light, brief touch : brush. **3.** A gleam.
gland (glănd) *n.* An organ or structure that secretes a substance, esp. one that extracts specific substances from the blood and alters them for subsequent secretion. **—glan'du•lar** (glăn'jə-lər) *adj.*
glans (glănz) *n.* A small mass of erectile tissue at the tip of the penis or clitoris.
glare (glâr) *v.* **glared, glar•ing. 1.** To stare angrily or fiercely. **2.** To shine intensely and dazzlingly. *—n.* **1.** An angry or fierce stare. **2.** An intense and dazzling light.
glar•ing (glâr'ĭng) *adj.* **1.** Staring angrily or fiercely. **2.** Intensely bright : dazzling. **3.** Gaudy : garish **4.** Obtrusively conspicuous : fragrant. **—glar'ing•ly** *adv.*
Glas•gow (glăs'kō, -gō, glăs'-). City of SW Scotland, on the Firth of Clyde. *Pop.* 794,316.
glass (glăs) *n.* **1.** Any of a large class of gen. transparent or translucent materials that harden from the molten state without crystallizing and becoming true solids. **2.** Something, as a container for drinking, made of glass. **3. glasses.** A device with a pair of lenses used as an aid to vision. **4.** A glassful. **5.** Glassware. **—glass** *adj.* **—glass'y** *adj.*

glass blowing *n.* The process or art of shaping objects from molten glass by blowing air into them through a tube. **–glass blower** *n.*
glass·ful (glăs′fo͝ol′) *n.* The amount a glass will hold.
glass·ware (glăs′wâr′) *n.* Objects made of glass.
glau·co·ma (glou-kō′mə, glô-) *n.* An eye disease characterized by abnormally high pressure within the eyeball and partial or complete loss of vision.
glaze (glāz) *n.* **1.** A thin, smooth coating, as on ceramics. **2.** A thin, glassy coating of ice. –*v.* **glazed, glaz·ing. 1.** To fit with glass <*glaze* a window> **2.** To apply glaze to. **3.** To become glassy. **–glaz′er** *n.*
gla·zier (glā′zhər) *n.* Someone who fits glass, esp. in windows.
gleam (glēm) *n.* **1.** A brief beam of light. **2.** A subdued glow of light. **3.** A faint indication : trace <a *gleam* of comprehension in her eyes> –*v.* **1.** To appear briefly : flash. **2.** To glow in a subdued or faint way.
glean (glēn) *v.* **1.** To gather (grain left behind by reapers). **2.** To collect bit by bit. **–glean′er** *n.* **–glean′ings** *pl.n.*
glee (glē) *n.* **1.** Boisterous merriment : joy. **2.** An unaccompanied song for 3 or more usu. male voices. **–glee′ful** *adj.* **–glee′ful·ly** *adv.*
glee club *n.* A singing group that performs usu. short pieces of choral music.
glen (glĕn) *n.* A valley.
Glen·gar·ry (glĕn-găr′ē) *n., pl.* **-ries.** A Scottish woolen cap creased lengthwise with short ribbons at the back.
glib (glĭb) *adj.* **glib·ber, glib·best.** Speaking or spoken easily and fluently but often superficially or insincerely. **–glib′ly** *adv.* **–glib′ness** *n.*
glide (glīd) *v.* **glid·ed, glid·ing. 1.** To move or pass smoothly and with little effort. **2.** To move silently and furtively. **3.** To fly without propelling power. –*n.* **1.** A smooth, effortless motion. **2.** An act of flying without propelling power.
glid·er (glī′dər) *n.* **1.** One that glides. **2.** A light aircraft without an engine that is designed to glide after being towed aloft. **3.** A swinging couch that is suspended in a vertical frame.
glim·mer (glĭm′ər) *n.* **1.** A dim unsteady light. **2.** A faint indication : suggestion. –*v.* **1.** To give off a dim unsteady light. **2.** To appear faintly.
glimpse (glĭmps) *n.* A hurried momentary look. –*v.* **glimpsed, glimps·ing.** To get a glimpse of.
glint (glĭnt) *n.* A brief flash of light : sparkle. **–glint** *v.*
glis·sade (glĭ-säd′, -sād′) *n.* **1.** A gliding ballet step. **2.** A controlled slide, in either a standing or a sitting position, used in descending a steep icy or snowy incline. **–glis·sade′** *v.* **–glis·sad′er** *n.*

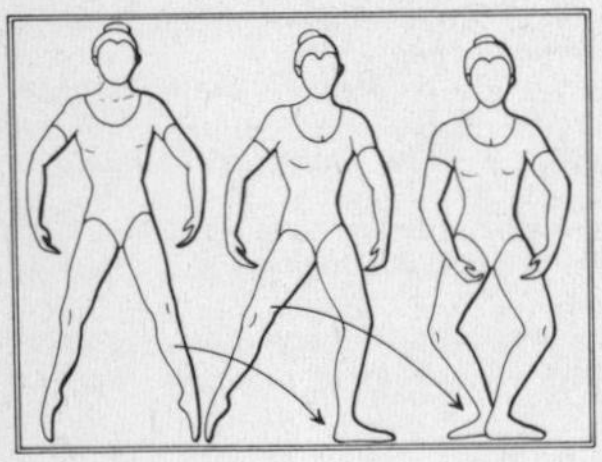

glissade

glis·san·do (glĭ-sän′dō) *n., pl.* **-di** (-dē) *or* **-dos.** A rapid slide through a series of consecutive musical tones.
glis·ten (glĭs′ən) *v.* To shine softly with reflected light. **–glis′ten** *n.*
glis·ter (glĭs′tər) *v.* To glisten. –*n.* Glitter : brilliance.
glitch (glĭch) *n.* **1.** A minor malfunction or mishap. **2.** *Electron.* A false signal caused by an unwanted surge of power.
glit·ter (glĭt′ər) *n.* **1.** Sparkling light. **2.** Showy or brilliant attractiveness. **3.** Small bits of light-reflecting material used for decoration. –*v.* **1.** To sparkle brilliantly. **2.** To be brilliantly but often deceptively attractive. **–glit′ter·y** *adj.*
glitz (glĭts) *n. Slang.* Excessive showiness : flashiness. **–glitz′y** *adj.*
gloam·ing (glō′mĭng) *n.* Twilight.
gloat (glōt) *v.* To feel, express, or observe with great, often malicious pleasure or self-satisfaction. **–gloat′er** *n.*
glob (glŏb) *n.* **1.** A drop. **2.** A large rounded mass.
glob·al (glō′bəl) *adj.* **1.** Spherical. **2.** Worldwide. **3.** Comprehensive. **–glob′al·ize** *v.* **–glob′al·ly** *adv.*
globe (glōb) *n.* **1.** A spherical object, as a representation of the earth. **2.** The earth. **3.** Something, as a fishbowl, shaped like a globe.
globe·trot·ter (glōb′trŏt′ər) *n.* One who travels extensively. **–globe′trot′ting** *n.*
glob·ule (glŏb′yo͞ol) *n.* A tiny, spherical mass. **–glob′u·lar** (-yə-lər) *adj.*
glob·u·lin (glŏb′yə-lĭn) *n.* Any of a class of simple proteins found widely in blood, milk, muscle, tissue, and plant seeds.
glock·en·spiel (glŏk′ən-spēl′, -shpēl′) *n.* A musical percussion instrument consisting of a series of metal bars tuned to the chromatic scale and played with 2 light hammers.
gloom (glo͞om) *n.* **1.** Partial or total darkness. **2.** An atmosphere of depression. **3.** Depression or melancholy. **–gloom′i·ly** *adv.* **–gloom′i·ness** *n.* **–gloom′y** *adj.*
glop (glŏp) *n. Slang.* **1.** A messy mixture, as of food. **2.** Something considered worthless <wrote terrible *glop*>
glo·ri·fy (glôr′ə-fī′, glōr′-) *v.* **-fied, -fy·ing. 1.** To give glory to, as through worship : exalt. **2.** To make glorious by exaggerating the excellence of. **3.** To give high praise to : extol. **–glo′ri·fi·ca′tion** *n.*
glo·ri·ous (glôr′ē-əs, glōr′-) *adj.* **1.** Having or deserving glory : illustrious. **2.** Bringing glory. **3.** Magnificent : resplendent. **4.** *Informal.* Delightful. **–glo′ri·ous·ly** *adv.*
glo·ry (glôr′ē, glōr′ē) *n., pl.* **-ries. 1. a.** Great distinction : renown. **b.** Something that brings glory. **2.** Adoration and praise offered in worship. **3.** Magnificence : splendor. **4.** A wonderful asset. **5.** The height of achievement, triumph, or prosperity. –*v.* **-ried, -ry·ing.** To rejoice jubilantly : exult.
gloss[1] (glôs, glŏs) *n.* **1.** A shine on a surface : luster. **2.** A superficially or deceptively attractive appearance. –*v.* To treat superficially in an attempt to excuse or ignore <tried to *gloss* over the hostility between them>
gloss[2] (glôs, glŏs) *n.* **1.** A note that explains or translates a difficult expression. **2.** A commentary that accompanies a text. **3.** A glossary. –*v.* To provide with glosses.
glos·sa·ry (glô′sə-rē, glŏs′ə-) *n., pl.* **-ries.** A list of words with their definitions.
glos·so·la·li·a (glô′sə-lā′lē-ə, glŏs′ə-) *n.* Fabricated and nonsensical speech, esp. the speech associated with certain schizophrenic syndromes.
gloss·y (glô′sē, glŏs′ē) *adj.* **-i·er, -i·est. 1.** Having a smooth, shiny, lustrous surface. **2.** Superficially attractive : showy. –*n., pl.* **-ies.** A photographic print on smooth, shiny paper. **–gloss′i·ly** *adv.* **–gloss′i·ness** *n.*
glot·tis (glŏt′ĭs) *n., pl.* **-tis·es** *or* **-ti·des** (-ĭ-dēz′). The opening between the vocal cords at the upper part of the larynx. **–glot′tal** (glŏt′l) *adj.*
glove (glŭv) *n.* **1.** A covering for the hand with a separate section for each finger. **2.** An oversized padded leather covering for the hand, as that used in baseball, boxing, or hockey. **–gloved** *adj.*
glow (glō) *v.* **1.** To shine hotly and steadily, esp. without a flame. **2.** To have a bright, warm ruddy color. **3.** To blush. **4.** To be elated or exuberant <*glowing* with parental pride> –*n.* **1.** A light produced by a heated substance. **2.** Warmth or brilliance of color, esp. redness. **3.** A warm feeling of emotion. **4.** A feeling of warmth. **–glow′ing·ly** *adv.*
glow·er (glou′ər) *v.* To look angrily or sullenly : glare. **–glow′er** *n.* **–glow′er·ing·ly** *adv.*
glow·worm (glō′wûrm′) *n.* The luminous larva or grublike female of an insect, esp. a firefly.
glox·in·i·a (glŏk-sĭn′ē-ə) *n.* A tropical South America plant of the genus *Sinningia*, esp. *S. speciosa*, cultivated as a house plant for its variously colored flowers.
gloze (glōz) *v.* **glozed, gloz·ing.** To underplay or minimize : gloss.
glu·cose (glo͞o′kōs′) *n.* **1.** Dextrose. **2.** A colorless to yellowish syrupy mixture of dextrose, maltose, and dextrins with approx. 20% water, used esp. in confectionery.
glue (glo͞o) *n.* Any of various adhesive substances used to stick things together. –*v.* **glued, glu·ing.** To stick or fasten with or as if with glue. **–glu′ey** *adj.* **–glu′i·ness** *n.*
glum (glŭm) *adj.* **glum·mer, glum·mest.** Moody and sullen : morose. **–glum′ly** *adv.* **–glum′ness** *n.*
glut (glŭt) *v.* **glut·ted, glut·ting. 1.** To fill beyond capacity, esp. with food : satiate. **2.** To provide with a supply that exceeds demand. –*n.* An oversupply.
glu·ten (glo͞ot′n) *n.* A mixture of plant proteins used as an adhesive and as a substitute for flour. **–glu′ten·ous** *adj.*
glu·ti·nous (glo͞ot′n-əs) *adj.* Resembling glue : sticky.
glut·ton (glŭt′n) *n.* Someone who eats immoderately. **–glut′ton·ous** *adj.* **–glut′ton·ous·ly** *adv.* **–glut′ton·y** *n.*
glyc·er·in (glĭs′ər-ĭn) *n.* Glycerol.
glyc·er·ol (glĭs′ə-rôl′, -rōl′, -rŏl′) *n.* A sweet, syrupy liquid, derived from fats and oils and used as a solvent, antifreeze, lubricant, and sweetener.

gly·co·gen (glī'kə-jən) *n.* A white powder that is the principal animal storage carbohydrate, chiefly in the liver.
gly·co·side (glī'kə-sīd') *n.* Any of a group of organic compounds, occurring abundantly in plants, that produce sugars and related substances on hydrolysis. **–gly'co·sid'ic** (-sĭd'ĭk) *adj.*
G-man (jē'măn') *n.* An FBI agent.
gnarl (närl) *n.* A hard protruding knot on a tree. **–gnarled** *adj.*
gnash (năsh) *v.* To strike or grind (the teeth) together, as in pain or rage.
gnat (năt) *n.* A small, winged insect, esp. one that bites.
gnaw (nô) *v.* **1.** To bite or chew persistently (on). **2.** To wear away, consume, or produce by gnawing. **3.** To afflict or trouble, as if by gnawing. **–gnaw'er** *n.*
gneiss (nīs) *n.* A banded, granitelike metamorphic rock with the minerals arranged in layers.
gnome (nōm) *n.* A dwarflike creature who lives underground and guards treasure or precious metals. **–gnom'ish** *adj.*
GNP (jē'ĕn-pē') *n.* Gross national product.
gnu (no͞o, nyo͞o) *n.* Either of 2 large bearded African antelopes, *Connochaetes gnou* or *C. taurinus,* with curved horns.
go (gō) *v.* **went** (wĕnt), **gone** (gôn, gŏn), **go·ing. 1.** To move along : proceed <*going* too fast> **2.** To move away from : leave. **3.** To be expecting, intending, or about to do something <is *going* to eat out tonight> **4.** To follow a particular course of action <*go* swimming> **5.** To function correctly <The car won't *go.*> **6.** To be, come to be, or continue in a certain state or condition <*goes* barefoot at home><*go* crazy> **7.** To belong <clothes that *go* in the closet> **8.** To extend <bookcases *going* from floor to ceiling> **9.** To lead <a path that *goes* to town> **10.** To be allotted. **11.** To serve <It *goes* to show that practice makes perfect.> **12.** To be compatible : harmonize. **13.** To die. **14.** To come apart, as under pressure : break. **15.** To fail <His hearing is *going.*> **16.** To be used up <Our money *went* fast.> **17.** To be abolished or discarded <Luxuries will have to *go.*> **18.** To pass, as time : elapse. **19.** To turn out : fare <How is your job *going*?> **20.** To hold out : endure <*go* without food> **21.** To pass as a result of being sold <*went* at a low price> **22.** To be as a general rule <quiet, as children *go*> **23.** To be capable of entering or being held <a sweater that won't *go* in the drawer> **24.** To wager : bid. **25.** To furnish : provide <*went* bail for his client> **26.** To participate to the extent of <*went* halves> **27.** To pass to someone, as by will <furniture that *went* to relatives> *–n., pl.* **goes.** *Informal.* **1.** An attempt : try. **2.** A turn, as in a game. **3.** Vitality : energy. *–adj. Informal.* Functioning properly and ready for action. **–go back on. 1.** To abandon. **2.** To betray. **3.** To fail to keep. **–go for. 1.** To try to obtain. **2.** *Informal.* To having a liking for : enjoy. **–go in for.** *Informal.* To enjoy participating in or partaking of. **–go off. 1.** To take place : happen. **2.** To explode. **–go on. 1.** To proceed. **2.** To continue to exist. **3.** To take place : happen. **–go out.** To become extinguished. **–go over.** To gain acceptance or approval : succeed. **–go places.** To be on the road to success. **–go (someone) one better.** To surpass : outdo. **–go under.** To suffer destruction or defeat : fail.
goad (gōd) *n.* **1.** A pointed stick for prodding an animal. **2.** Something that urges : stimulus. **–goad** *v.*
go-a·head (gō'ə-hĕd') *n. Informal.* Permission to proceed.
goal (gōl) *n.* **1.** A purpose : objective. **2.** The finish line of a race. **3. a.** A structure or area into which participants in certain sports must direct play in order to score. **b.** The score awarded for this.
goal·ie (gō'lē) *n.* A goalkeeper.
goal·keep·er (gōl'kē'pər) *n.* The player who defends the goal, as in soccer and hockey.
goal post *also* **goal·post** (gōl'pōst') *n.* One of a pair of posts with or without a crossbar forming the goal in various games.
goat (gōt) *n.* **1.** A horned, bearded ruminant mammal of the genus *Capra,* orig. of mountainous regions and now widely domesticated. **2.** A lecher. **3.** A scapegoat. **–goat'ish** *adj.*
goat·ee (gō-tē') *n.* A pointed chin beard.
goat·herd (gōt'hûrd') *n.* One who herds and tends goats.
goat·skin (gōt'skĭn') *n.* **1.** The skin of a goat used for leather. **2.** Something, as a container for wine, made from goatskin.
gob[1] (gŏb) *n.* A mass : lump.
gob[2] (gŏb) *n. Slang.* A sailor.
gob·bet (gŏb'ĭt) *n.* **1.** A chunk or piece, esp. of raw meat. **2.** A lump : mass.
gob·ble[1] (gŏb'əl) *v.* **-bled, -bling. 1.** To eat up greedily. **2.** To take greedily : grab.
gob·ble[2] (gŏb'əl) *v.* **-bled, -bling.** To make the guttural, chortling sound of a male turkey. **–gob'ble** *n.*
gob·ble·dy·gook *also* **gob·ble·de·gook** (gŏb'əl-dē-go͝ok') *n.* Wordy and often unintelligible jargon.
gob·bler (gŏb'lər) *n.* A male turkey.
Go·be·lin (gō'bə-lĭn) *n.* A tapestry noted for rich pictorial design.
go-be·tween (gō'bĭ-twēn') *n.* Someone who acts as an intermediary between 2 parties.
Go·bi (gō'bē). Desert of C Asia, mostly in Mongolia.
gob·let (gŏb'lĭt) *n.* A drinking glass with a stem and base.
gob·lin (gŏb'lĭn) *n.* An ugly, grotesque creature said to be mischievous and often maliciously evil.
go-by (gō'bī') *n. Informal.* An intentional slight : snub.
god (gŏd) *n.* **1. God.** A being worshiped by monotheists as the perfect, omnipotent, omniscient originator and ruler of the universe. **2.** A being of supernatural powers and attributes that is worshiped by a people. **3.** Someone or something considered to be extremely valuable or important. **–god'like'** *adj.*
god·child (gŏd'chīld') *n.* A person for whom another serves as sponsor at baptism.
god·daugh·ter (gŏd'dô'tər) *n.* A female godchild.
god·dess (gŏd'ĭs) *n.* **1.** A female deity. **2.** A woman of exceptional beauty, charm, or grace.
god·fa·ther (gŏd'fä'*th*ər) *n.* A man who sponsors a person at baptism.
god·head (gŏd'hĕd') *n.* **1.** Divinity : godhood. **2. Godhead. a.** God. **b.** The divine and essential nature of God.
god·hood (gŏd'ho͝od') *n.* The quality or state of being a god : divinity.
god·less (gŏd'lĭs) *adj.* Not recognizing a god. **–god'less·ness** *n.*
god·ly (gŏd'lē) *adj.* **-li·er, -li·est. 1.** Devout : pious. **2.** Divine. **–god'li·ness** *n.*
god·moth·er (gŏd'mŭ*th*'ər) *n.* A woman who sponsors a person at baptism.
god·par·ent (gŏd'pâr'ənt, -păr'-) *n.* A godfather or godmother.
god·send (gŏd'sĕnd') *n.* Something needed or wanted that comes unexpectedly, as if from God.
god·son (gŏd'sŭn') *n.* A male godchild.
God·win Aus·ten (gŏd'wĭn ô'stĭn). 2nd-highest mountain in the world (28,250 ft/8,616.2 m), in N Pakistan.
Goe·the (gœ'tə), **Johann Wolfgang von.** 1749–1832. German author.
go-get·ter (gō'gĕt'ər) *n. Informal.* An enterprising, energetic person.
gog·gle (gŏg'əl) *v.* **-gled, -gling.** To stare or gaze with bulging eyes. *–n.* **1.** A stare or leer. **2. goggles.** A pair of usu. tinted protective eyeglasses that fit close against the face.
go-go (gō'gō') *adj.* **1.** Of, for, or employed to perform in a discotheque <a go-go dancer> **2.** Very enterprising.
go·ing (gō'ĭng) *n.* **1.** Departure. **2.** The condition of the ground, as for walking. **3.** *Informal.* Progress toward an objective. *–adj.* **1.** Working : running. **2.** Flourishing. **3.** Prevailing : current.
go·ings-on (gō'ĭngz-ŏn') *pl.n. Informal.* Behavior or proceedings, esp. when looked upon with disapproval.
goi·ter (goi'tər) *n.* An abnormal enlargement of the thyroid gland, visible as a swelling at the front of the neck.
gold (gōld) *n.* **1.** *Symbol* **Au** A soft, yellow, highly malleable and ductile metallic element that is used esp. in coins and jewelry. **2.** Coins made of gold. **3.** Money. **4.** A moderate to vivid yellow. **–gold** *adj.*
gold·brick (gōld'brĭk') *also* **gold·brick·er** (-brĭk'ər) *n. Slang.* Someone who avoids work : shirker. **–gold'brick'** *v.*
gold digger *n. Slang.* A woman who seeks money and gifts from men.
gold·en (gōl'dən) *adj.* **1.** Made of, relating to, or containing gold. **2.** Having the color of gold. **3.** Blond. **4.** Rich : splendid <a *golden* voice> **5.** Lustrous : shining <the *golden* sun> **6.** Marked by prosperity : flourishing. **7.** Advantageous : favorable <a *golden* opportunity> **8.** Having a promising future <*golden* youth>
golden ager *n.* An elderly person.
Gold·en Gate (gōl'dn). Strait in W Calif. connecting the Pacific and San Francisco Bay.
gold·en·rod (gōl'dən-rŏd') *n.* A North American plant of the genus *Solidago* with branching clusters of small yellow flowers.
gold·eye (gōld'ī') *n.* A food and game fish, *Amphiodon alosoides,* found in NW Canada.
gold-filled (gōld'fĭld') *adj.* Made of a hard base metal with an outer layer of gold.
gold·finch (gōld'fĭnch') *n.* A small New World bird of the genus *Spinus,* esp. *S. tristis,* the male of which has yellow plumage with a black forehead, wings, and tail.
gold·fish (gōld'fĭsh') *n.* A reddish or brass-colored freshwater fish, *Carassius auratus,* often kept in aquariums and ornamental pools.
gold leaf *n.* Gold beaten into extremely thin sheets used esp. for gilding.

gold•smith (gōld′smĭth′) *n.* One who fashions or deals in objects made of gold.
golf (gŏlf, gôlf) *n.* A game played with a small hard ball and various clubs on a course with 9 or 18 holes. **—golf** *v.* **—golf′er** *n.*
Go•li•ath (gə-lī′əth) *—n.* **1.** Philistine giant killed by David in the Bible. **2.** One of colossal power or achievement.
go•nad (gō′năd′) *n.* An organ that produces gametes : testis or ovary. **—go•nad′al, go•nad′ic** *adj.*
go•nad•o•trop•ic (gō-năd′ə-trŏp′ĭk, -trō′pĭk) *also* **go•nad•o•troph•ic** (-trŏf′ĭk, trō′fĭk) *adj.* Acting on or stimulating the gonads, as a hormone.
go•nad•o•tro•pin (gō-năd′ə-trō′pĭn, -trŏp′ĭn) *also* **go•nad•o•tro•phin** (-trō′fĭn, -trō′pĭn) *n.* A gonadotropic substance.
gon•do•la (gŏn′dl-ə, gŏn-dō′lə) *n.* **1.** A long, narrow boat propelled with a single oar and used on the canals of Venice. **2.** A railroad freight car with low sides. **3.** A cabin suspended under a balloon or dirigible. **4.** An enclosed car suspended from a cable used for transporting passengers, as up and down a ski slope.

gondola
(Left) *Venetian gondola and* (right) *a cable gondola*

gon•do•lier (gŏn′dl-îr′) *n.* Someone who propels a gondola.
gone (gôn, gŏn) *adj.* **1.** Bygone : past. **2.** Dead. **3.** Ruined : lost. **4.** Engrossed : absorbed. **5.** Used up : exhausted. **6.** *Slang.* Infatuated.
gon•er (gô′nər, gŏn′ər) *n. Slang.* One that is doomed or ruined.
gon•fa•lon (gŏn′fə-lŏn′, -lən) *n.* A banner hung from a crosspiece.
gong (gông, gŏng) *n.* A metal disk that produces a loud, sonorous tone. **—gong** *v.*
gon•o•coc•cus (gŏn′ə-kŏk′əs) *n., pl.* **-coc•ci** (-kŏk′sī′, -kŏk′ī′). A bacterium, *Neisseria gonorrhoeae,* causing gonorrhea. **—gon′o•coc′cal** (-kŏk′əl), **gon′o•coc′cic** (-kŏk′ĭk, -kŏk′sĭk) *adj.*
gon•or•rhe•a (gŏn′ə-rē′ə) *n.* An infectious bacterial disease of the genitourinary tract that is transmitted chiefly by sexual intercourse. **—gon′or•rhe′al** *adj.*
goo (gōō) *n. Informal.* **1.** A sticky substance. **2.** Sentimental drivel. **—goo′ey** *adj.*
†**goo•ber** (gōō′bər) *n. Regional.* A peanut.
good (go͝od) *adj.* **bet•ter** (bĕt′ər), **best** (bĕst). **1.** Having desirable or favorable qualities. **2. a.** Suitable : appropriate. **b.** Convenient. **3.** Whole : sound. **4.** Superior to the average : satisfactory <*good* treatment> **5.** Discriminating <has very *good* taste> **6.** Salutary : beneficial <*good* restful sleep> **7.** Competent : skilled <a *good* musician> **8. a.** Sure : safe <a *good* investment> **b.** Valid or sound <a *good* excuse> **c.** Genuine : real. **9. a.** Ample : considerable <a *good* hem> **b.** Bountiful <*good* farmland> **10.** Full <a *good* 10 miles> **11.** Pleasant : enjoyable <a *good* time> **12. a.** Virtuous : upright. **b.** Benevolent : cheerful. **c.** Loyal : staunch. **13 a.** Well-behaved <Try to be *good.*> **b.** Socially correct : proper. *—n.* **1.** Something that is good. **2.** Welfare : benefit <for his own *good*> **3.** Goodness. **4. goods. a.** Wares : merchandise. **b.** Personal belongings. **5. goods.** Fabric : cloth. *—adv. Informal.* Well. **—as good as.** Nearly : almost. **—for good.** Permanently : forever.
good-by or **good-bye** (go͝od-bī′) *interj.* Used to express farewell. *—n., pl.* **-bys** *or* **-byes.** An expression of farewell.
good-for-noth•ing (go͝od′fər-nŭth′ĭng) *n.* One of little worth or usefulness. **—good′-for-noth′ing** *adj.*
Good Friday *n.* The Friday before Easter, commemorating Christ's crucifixion.
good•heart•ed (go͝od′här′tĭd) *adj.* Having a kind, generous disposition. **—good′heart′ed•ness** *n.*
Good Hope (go͝od hōp′), **Cape of.** Promontory on the SW coast of South Africa.
good-hu•mored (go͝od′hyōō′mərd) *adj.* Showing or marked by good humor : amiable. **—good′-hu′mored•ly** *adv.* **—good′-hu′mored•ness** *n.*
good-look•ing (go͝od′lo͝ok′ĭng) *adj.* Of pleasing appearance : handsome.
good•ly (go͝od′lē) *adj.* **-li•er, -li•est. 1.** Pleasing in appearance. **2.** Rather large : considerable.
good-na•tured (go͝od′nā′chərd) *adj.* Easygoing, cheerful, and affable in nature. **—good′na′tured•ly** *adv.* **—good′-na′tured•ness** *n.*
good•ness (go͝od′nĭs) *n.* The condition or quality of being good : virtue, benevolence, or excellence.
good will *also* **good•will** (go͝od′wĭl′) *n.* **1.** Benevolence. **2.** Cheerful willingness. **3.** The value of the relationship between a business enterprise and its customers.
good•y (go͝od′ē) *n., pl.* **-ies.** *Informal.* Something attractive or desirable, esp. something good to eat. *—interj.* Used to express delight.
good•y-good•y (go͝od′ē-go͝od′ē) *adj.* Affectedly good : prudish. **—good′y-good′y** *n.*
goof (gōōf) *Slang. n.* **1.** A stupid or foolish person. **2.** A mistake : blunder. *—v.* **1.** To blunder. **2.** To spend time doing trivial things <*goofed* off all afternoon>
goof-off (gōōf′ôf′, -ŏf) *n.* One who shuns work or responsibility : shirker.
goof•y (gōō′fē) *adj.* **-i•er, -i•est.** *Slang.* Silly : ridiculous. **—goof′i•ly** *adv.* **—goof′i•ness** *n.*
gook (go͝ok) *n. Slang.* A dirty, sludgy, or slimy substance.
goon (gōōn) *n. Slang.* **1.** A thug hired to intimidate or injure opponents. **2.** A stupid person.
goose (gōōs) *n., pl.* **geese** (gēs). **1.** A large water bird of the family Anatidae that is related to the ducks and swans. **2.** A female goose. **3.** *Informal.* A silly person.
goose•ber•ry (gōōs′bĕr′ē, gōōz′-) *n.* The edible greenish berry of a spiny shrub, *Ribers grossularia.*
goose bumps *pl.n.* Goose flesh.
goose flesh *n.* Momentary roughness of skin caused esp. by fear or cold.
goose pimples *pl.n.* Goose flesh.
go•pher (gō′fər) *n.* A burrowing North American rodent of the family Geomyidae, having pocketlike cheek pouches.
gore[1] (gôr, gōr) *v.* **gored, gor•ing.** To stab or pierce with a horn or tusk.
gore[2] (gôr, gōr) *n.* A tapering piece of cloth, as in a skirt or sail. **—gore** *v.*
gore[3] (gôr, gōr) *n.* Blood.
gorge (gôrj) *n.* **1.** A deep, narrow ravine. **2.** The throat. **3.** A mass that obstructs a passage. *—v.* **gorged, gorg•ing. 1.** To devour greedily. **2.** To fill to capacity : satiate. **—gorg′er** *n.*
gor•geous (gôr′jəs) *adj.* Dazzlingly beautiful : magnificent. **—gor′geous•ly** *adv.* **—gor′geous•ness** *n.*
Gor•gon•zo•la (gôr′gən-zō′lə) *n.* A pungent, blue-veined Italian cheese.
go•ril•la (gə-rĭl′ə) *n.* A large African ape, *Gorilla gorilla,* with a stocky body and dark, coarse hair.
Gor•ki or **Gor•ky** (gôr′kē). City of E European USSR, on the Volga. *Pop.* 1,358,000.
Gor•ki (gôr′kē), **Maksim.** 1868–1936. Russian author.
gor•man•dize (gôr′mən-dīz′) *v.* **-dized, -diz•ing.** To eat greedily : gorge. **—gor′man•diz′er** *n.*
gorse (gôrs) *n.* A spiny shrub, *Ulex europaeus,* bearing fragrant yellow flowers.
gor•y (gôr′ē, gōr′ē) *adj.* **-i•er, -i•est. 1.** Covered or stained with blood : bloody. **2.** Marked by much bloodshed or violence.
gos•hawk (gŏs′hôk′) *n.* A large hawk, *Accipiter gentilis,* with broad, rounded wings.
gos•ling (gŏz′lĭng) *n.* A young goose.
gos•pel (gŏs′pəl) *n.* **1.** *often* **Gospel.** The teachings of Christ and the Apostles. **2. Gospel.** Any of the 1st 4 books of the New Testament. **3.** Something accepted as absolute truth. **4.** Gospel music.

▲word history: The ancestor of *gospel* is the Old English compound *gōdspel,* literally "good tidings." It originated as a loan translation of Latin *evangelium,* a borrowing of Greek *euangelion,* which in Christian contexts meant "good tidings," specifically the good news of the kingdom of God brought by Jesus.

gospel music *n.* American religious music associated with evangelism and based on simple folk melodies blended with rhythmic and melodic elements of spirituals and jazz.
gos•sa•mer (gŏs′ə-mər) *n.* **1.** A fine film of cobwebs floating in the air. **2.** A sheer, gauzy fabric. **3.** Something delicate, light, or flimsy. **—gos′sa•mer** *adj.*
gos•sip (gŏs′əp) *n.* **1.** Rumor or talk of a personal or sensational nature. **2.** Someone who habitually spreads sensational or intimate facts. *—v.* To engage in or spread gossip. **—gos′sip•er** *n.* **—gos′sip•y** *adj.*

▲word history: *Gossip* was orig. a compound of *god* and *sib,* meaning "godparent." At first denoting only the relationship of godparent to godchild, *gossip* was later used to indicate the relationship of godparent to parent and the relationship between the godparents of the same child. *Gossip* thus designated a relationship among peers as much as one between generations, and from the extended senses the meaning "friend" evolved. The derogatory use of *gossip* to mean a person who engages in idle chatter and rumor-spreading appeared in the 16th cent., but the use of *gossip* to mean the conversation of a gossip is not recorded until the early 18th cent.

got (gŏt) *v. p.t.* & *p.p. of* GET.

Goth (gŏth) *n.* A member of a Germanic people that invaded the Roman Empire early in the Christian era.

Goth•ic (gŏth'ĭk) *adj.* **1.** Of or pertaining to the Goths. **2.** Of or relating to an architectural style prevalent in W Europe from the 12th through the 15th cent. **3.** *often* **gothic.** Of or relating to a style of fiction emphasizing the grotesque, mysterious, and desolate. —*n.* **1.** The extinct Germanic language of the Goths. **2.** Gothic architecture.

got•ten (gŏt'n) *v. var. p.p. of* GET.

Gou•da (gou'də, gōō'-) *n.* A mild, close-textured cheese made from milk.

gouge (gouj) *n.* **1.** A chisel with a rounded, scooplike blade. **2.** A groove or hole made with or as if with a gouge. —*v.* **gouged, goug•ing. 1.** To make a groove or hole in with or as if with a gouge. **2.** To exact exorbitant prices from. **—goug'er** *n.*

gou•lash (gōō'läsh, -lăsh) *n.* A beef or veal stew seasoned chiefly with paprika.

gou•ra•mi (gŏŏ-rä'mē, gŏŏr'ə-) *n., pl.* **-mis.** Any of various freshwater fishes of the family Anabantidae of SE Asia, many species of which are popular in home aquariums.

gourd (gôrd, gōrd, gŏŏrd) *n.* **1.** A vine of the family Cucurbitaceae that is related to the pumpkin, squash, and cucumber and bears inedible fruit with a hard rind. **2.** The dried, hollowed-out shell of a gourd, used esp. as a drinking utensil.

gourde (gŏŏrd) *n.* See CURRENCY TABLE.

gour•mand (gŏŏr'mənd, -mänd') *n.* A person who enjoys eating well and heartily and often to excess.

gour•met (gŏŏr-mā', gŏŏr'mā') *n.* Someone who understands and appreciates fine food and drink : epicure.

gout (gout) *n.* A disturbance of the uricacid metabolism marked by painful inflammation of the joints. **—gout'y** *adj.*

gov. *abbr.* **1.** government. **2.** or **Gov.** governor.

gov•ern (gŭv'ərn) *v.* **1.** To guide : control. **2.** To direct or manage the public policy and affairs of : rule. **3.** To regulate : determine. **4.** To restrain. **—gov'ern•a•ble** *adj.* **—gov'er•nance** *n.*

gov•ern•ess (gŭv'ər-nĭs) *n.* A woman who educates and trains a child, esp. in a private household.

gov•ern•ment (gŭv'ərn-mənt) *n.* **1.** The administration of the public policy and affairs of an area : rule. **2.** A system or policy by which a political unit is governed. **3.** A governing organization : body. **4.** The agency or organization through which a governing body exercises authority and performs its functions. **—gov'ern•men'tal** *adj.* **—gov'ern•men'tal•ly** *adv.*

gov•er•nor (gŭv'ər-nər) *n.* **1.** One who governs, as the chief executive of a U.S. state or an official appointed to exercise political authority over a territory. **2.** A device that automatically regulates the speed of a machine. **—gov'er•nor•ship'** *n.*

govt. *abbr.* government.

gown (goun) *n.* **1.** A loose, flowing garment, as a nightgown. **2.** A woman's dress, esp. a formal one. **3.** A distinctive official robe, esp. one worn by a scholar, judge, or clergyman.

Go•ya (goi'ə), **Francisco José de.** 1746–1828. Spanish artist.

G.P. or **GP** *abbr.* general practitioner.

GPO *abbr.* **1.** general post office. **2.** Government Printing Office.

gr or **gr.** *abbr.* **1. gr.** grade. **2.** grain. **3.** gross.

grab (grăb) *v.* **grabbed, grab•bing. 1.** To take suddenly : snatch. **2.** *Slang.* To capture the attention of. **—grab** *n.* **—grab'ber** *n.* **—grab'by** *adj.*

grab bag *n.* **1.** A container full of articles, as party favors, to be drawn sight unseen. **2.** A miscellaneous assortment.

gra•ben (gra'bən) *n.* A depression of the earth's crust between 2 parallel faults.

grace (grās) *n.* **1.** Seemingly effortless beauty, ease, and charm of movement, form, or proportion. **2.** A charming or pleasing quality or characteristic. **3.** Skill at avoiding an improper, inept, or clumsy course. **4.** Good will : favor. **5.** A temporary exemption, as from paying a debt : reprieve. **6. a.** Divine love and protection given to mankind by God. **b.** A virtue granted by God. **7.** A short prayer said at mealtime. **8.** Used as a title of courtesy for a duke, duchess, or archbishop. —*v.* **graced, grac•ing. 1.** To favor : honor. **2.** To embellish. **—grace'ful** *adj.* **—grace'ful•ly** *adv.* **—grace'ful•ness** *n.* **—grace'less** *adj.* **—grace'less•ly** *adv.* **—grace'less•ness** *n.*

gra•cious (grā'shəs) *adj.* **1.** Marked by courtesy and kindness. **2.** Compassionate : merciful. **3.** Marked by good taste and elegance. ☆**syns:** AFFABLE, CONGENIAL, CORDIAL, GENIAL, SOCIABLE **—gra'cious•ly** *adv.* **—gra'cious•ness** *n.*

grack•le (grăk'əl) *n.* Any of several New World blackbirds of the family Icteridae with iridescent blackish plumage.

grad (grăd) *n. Informal.* A graduate.

grad. *abbr.* graduate; graduated.

gra•da•tion (grā-dā'shən) *n.* **1. a.** A series of successive steps or stages. **b.** A step or stage in such a series. **c.** Advancement by such a series. **2.** The act of grading. **—gra•da'tion•al** *adj.*

grade (grād) *n.* **1.** A stage or degree in a process or series. **2.** A position in a scale, as of quality. **3.** A group of persons or things falling in the same specified position or rank : class. **4.** A class at an elementary school. **5.** A mark indicating the quality of a student's work. **6.** A military, naval, or civil-service rank. **7.** The degree to which something, as a road, slopes. **8.** A slope. —*v.* **grad•ed, grad•ing. 1.** To arrange in grades : rank or sort. **2.** To evaluate. **3.** To give an academic grade to. **4.** To level to a desired gradient <*grade* a road>

gra•di•ent (grā'dē-ənt) *n.* A slope or degree of slope.

grad•u•al (grăj'ōō-əl) *adj.* Occurring or progressing in degrees or even, continuous stages. **—grad'u•al•ly** *adv.* **—grad'u•al•ness** *n.*

grad•u•al•ism (grăj'ōō-ə-lĭz'əm) *n.* The policy of or belief in advancing toward a goal by gradual, often slow stages.

grad•u•ate (grăj'ōō-āt') *v.* **-at•ed, -at•ing. 1.** To grant or be granted an academic degree or diploma. **2.** To divide into steps, categories, or grades. **3.** To mark with intervals for use in measurement. —*n.* (-ĭt). **1.** One who has received an academic degree or diploma. **2.** A container marked with lines for measuring contents. —*adj.* (-ĭt). **1.** Possessing an academic degree or diploma. **2.** Of or relating to studies beyond a bachelor's degree.

grad•u•a•tion (grăj'ōō-ā'shən) *n.* **1.** The award or receipt of an academic degree or diploma. **2.** A commencement ceremony. **3.** A mark on a graduated scale.

graf•fi•to (grə-fē'tō) *n., pl.* **-ti** (-tē). A drawing or inscription, as one made on a wall in a public place.

graft¹ (grăft) *v.* **1.** To insert (a shoot from one plant) into another living plant so that the 2 grow together as a single plant. **2.** To transplant or implant (tissue) into a bodily part. —*n.* **1. a.** A shoot grafted onto another living plant. **b.** The point of union of such plant parts. **2.** Material, esp. tissue or an organ, used in surgical grafting. **—graft'er** *n.*

graft² (grăft) *n.* **1.** The act of using one's public position unscrupulously for money or advantage. **2.** Money or advantage gained by graft. **—graft** *v.* **—graft'er** *n.*

gra•ham (grā'əm) *n.* Whole-wheat flour.

Grail (grāl) *n.* The legendary cup or chalice used by Christ at the Last Supper and later searched for by knights.

grain (grān) *n.* **1. a.** A small, hard seed or fruit of a cereal grass, as wheat. **b.** The seeds or fruits of such plants as a group. **2.** Cereal grasses as a group. **3.** A small hard particle <a *grain* of sand> **4.** A very small amount. **5.** See MEASUREMENT TABLE. **6.** The arrangement or pattern of the constituents of material such as wood and leather. **7.** Texture. **8.** Basic nature : disposition.

grain alcohol *n.* Ethanol.

grain•field (grān'fēld') *n.* A field in which grain is grown.

grain•y (grā'nē) *adj.* **-i•er, -i•est. 1.** Made of or like grain : granular. **2.** Resembling the grain of wood. **—grain'i•ness** *n.*

gram (grăm) *n.* See MEASUREMENT TABLE.

gram. *abbr.* grammar.

gram•mar (grăm'ər) *n.* **1.** The study of the classes of words, their relations to each other, and their arrangement into sentences. **2.** The system of rules implicit in a language, regarded as a mechanism for generating sentences. **3. a.** The syntactic and inflectional rules of a language. **b.** Writing or speech evaluated with reference to conformity to such rules. **—gram•mar'i•an** (grə-mâr'ē-ən) *n.* **—gram•mat'i•cal** (-măt'ĭ-kəl) *adj.* **—gram•mat'i•cal•ly** *adv.*

grammar school *n.* **1.** An elementary school. **2.** *esp. Brit.* A secondary or preparatory school.

gram•o•phone (grăm'ə-fōn') *n.* A phonograph.

Gra•na•da (grə-nä'də). City of S Spain. *Pop.* 229,108.

gran•a•ry (grăn'ə-rē, grā'nə-) *n., pl.* **-ries.** A building in which grain is stored.

grand (grănd) *adj.* **1.** Large in size, scope, or extent. **2.** Splendid : magnificent. **3.** Of higher rank or greater importance : chief. **4.** Stately : regal. **5.** Lofty : admirable. **6.** Complete : inclusive <the *grand* total> ☆**syns:** BARONIAL, GRANDIOSE, IMPOSING, LORDLY, MAGNIFICENT, MAJESTIC, NOBLE, PRINCELY, REGAL, ROYAL, STATELY —*n.* **1.** A grand piano. **2.** *Slang.* $1,000. **—grand'ly** *adv.* **—grand'ness** *n.*

gran•dam (grăn'dăm') *also* **gran•dame** (-dām') *n.* An old woman.

Grand Canyon. Gorge of the Colorado R. in NW Ariz.

grand•child (grănd′chīld′, grăn′-) *n.* A child of one's son or daughter.
grand•daugh•ter (grăn′dô′tər) *n.* A daughter of one's son or daughter.
grande dame (grän′ däm′, gräN däm′) *n.* A usu. elderly woman of high social position or majestic manner.
gran•dee (grăn-dē′) *n.* A nobleman of the highest rank in Portugal or Spain.
gran•deur (grăn′jər, -jo͝or′) *n.* The condition or quality of being grand : splendor.
grand•fa•ther (grănd′fä′*th*ər, grăn′-) *n.* **1.** The father of one's mother or father. **2.** An ancestor.
grandfather clock *n.* A pendulum clock in a tall narrow cabinet.
gran•dil•o•quence (grăn-dĭl′ə-kwəns) *n.* Pompous or bombastic speech or expression. **–gran•dil′o•quent** *adj.*
gran•di•ose (grăn′dē-ōs′, grăn′dē-ōs′) *adj.* **1.** Grand and impressive. **2.** Affectedly splendid or grand : pompous. **–gran′di•ose′ly** *adv.* **–gran′di•os′i•ty** (-ŏs′ĭ-tē) *n.*
grand mal (grănd′ mäl′, grän′, grän mäl′) *n.* A form of epilepsy marked by severe seizures.
grand•moth•er (grănd′mŭ*th*′ər, grăn′-) *n.* **1.** The mother of one's father or mother. **2.** A female ancestor.
grand opera *n.* A drama with the complete text set to music.
grand•par•ent (grănd′pâr′ənt, -păr′-, grăn′-) *n.* A parent of one's mother or father.
grand piano *n.* A piano with the strings strung in a horizontal frame.
Grand Prix (gräN′ prē′) *n., pl.* **Grand Prix** (prēz′, prē′) Any of several competitive international road races for sports cars of specific engine size.
grand slam *n.* **1.** The taking of all the tricks in the game of bridge. **2.** *Baseball.* A home run hit when 3 runners are on base.
grand•son (grănd′sŭn′, grăn′-) *n.* A son of one's son or daughter.
grand•stand (grănd′stănd′, grăn′-) *n.* A usu. roofed stand for spectators, as at a sports event.
grange (grānj) *n.* **1. Grange.** An association of farmers in the U.S. **2.** *esp. Brit.* A farm with its residence and other buildings.
gran•ite (grăn′ĭt) *n.* A coarse-grained, hard igneous rock that consists chiefly of quartz, orthoclase, and mica and is used for building. **–gra•nit′ic** (grə-nĭt′ĭk) *adj.*
gran•ite•ware (grăn′ĭt-wâr′) *n.* Enameled iron utensils.
†**gran•ny** or **gran•nie** (grăn′ē) *n., pl.* **-nies. 1.** A grandmother. **2.** A fussy person. **3.** *S U.S.* A midwife.
granny knot *n.* An insecure knot resembling a square knot but with the second tie crossed incorrectly.

granny knot

gra•no•la (grə-nō′lə) *n.* Rolled oats mixed, as with dried fruit and seeds, and eaten esp. as a snack.
grant (grănt) *v.* **1.** To consent to : allow. **2.** To bestow : give. **3.** To admit as being true : acknowledge. *–n.* **1.** The act of granting. **2.** Something granted. **3.** *Law.* **a.** A transfer of property by deed. **b.** The instrument by which property is transferred. **c.** Property thus transferred. **–grant•ee′** *n.* **–grant′er, gran′tor** *n.*
Grant (grănt), **Ulysses Simpson.** 1822–85. 18th U.S. President (1869–77).
grants•man•ship (grănts′mən-shĭp′) *n.* The technique of obtaining grants, as to subsidize research.
gran•u•lar (grăn′yə-lər) *adj.* **1.** Composed or seeming to be composed of granules. **2.** Grainy. **–gran′u•lar′i•ty** *n.*
gran•u•late (grăn′yə-lāt′) *v.* **-lat•ed, -lat•ing. 1.** To form into granules or crystals. **2.** To make or become rough and grainy. **–gran′u•la′tion** *n.*
gran•ule (grăn′yo͞ol) *n.* A small grain or particle : pellet.
grape (grāp) *n.* Any of numerous woody vines of the genus *Vitis,* bearing clusters of fleshy, smooth-skinned, purple, red, or green fruit, eaten raw or dried and widely used in winemaking.
grape•fruit (grāp′fro͞ot′) *n.* A tropical or semitropical tree, *Citrus paradisi,* cultivated for its large round edible fruit, with a yellow rind and juicy, acidic pulp.
grape hyacinth *n.* Any of various plants of the genus *Muscari,* with narrow leaves and rounded, usu. blue flowers in dense terminal clusters.
grape•shot (grāp′shŏt′) *n.* A cluster of small iron balls formerly used to charge a cannon.
grape sugar *n.* Dextrose.
grape•vine (grāp′vīn′) *n.* **1.** A vine that produces grapes. **2.** An informal means of transmitting rumor or information.
graph (grăf) *n.* A drawing or diagram that shows a relationship between sets of things. **–graph** *v.*
graph•ic (grăf′ĭk) *also* **graph•i•cal** (-ĭ-kəl) *adj.* **1.** Written, drawn, printed, or engraved. **2.** Vividly set forth or described. **3.** Of or relating to the graphic arts. **–graph′i•cal•ly** *adv.*
graphic arts *pl.n.* The arts, as painting, drawing, and engraving, of representation, writing, or printing on 2-dimensional surfaces.
graph•ics (grăf′ĭks) *n. (sing. or pl. in number).* **1.** The making of drawings or blueprints, as in engineering or architecture, in accordance with the rules of mathematics. **2.** The graphic arts.
graph•ite (grăf′īt′) *n.* A soft form of carbon used in lead pencils, lubricants, paints, and coatings. **–gra•phit′ic** (gră-fĭt′ĭk) *adj.*
graph•ol•o•gy (gră-fŏl′ə-jē) *n.* The study of handwriting, esp. for the purpose of analyzing personality or character. **–graph•ol′o•gist** *n.*
grap•nel (grăp′nəl) *n.* A small anchor with 3 or more flukes.
grap•ple (grăp′əl) *n.* **1.** An implement with hooks used to hold an enemy ship alongside for boarding. **2.** A grapnel. **3.** Hand-to-hand combat. *–v.* **-pled, -pling. 1.** To seize, fasten, or drag with or as if with a grapple. **2.** To seize firmly with the hands. **3.** To try to come to grips : struggle. **4.** To wrestle. **–grap′pler** *n.*
grappling iron *also* **grappling hook** *n.* GRAPPLE 1.
grasp (grăsp) *v.* **1. a.** To seize and grip tightly. **b.** To make a motion of grasping : clutch. **2.** To comprehend : understand. *–n.* **1.** A firm hold : grip. **2.** The power to seize and hold. **3.** Comprehension. **4.** An embrace.
grasp•ing (grăs′pĭng) *adj.* Excessively eager to acquire material possessions : greedy. **–grasp′ing•ly** *adv.* **–grasp′ing•ness** *n.*
grass (grăs) *n.* **1. a.** Any of numerous plants of the family Graminae with narrow leaves and jointed stems. **b.** These plants as a group. **2.** Ground, as a lawn, covered with grass. **3.** *Slang.* Marijuana. **–grass′i•ness** *n.* **–grass′like′** *adj.* **–grass′y** *adj.*
grass•hop•per (grăs′hŏp′ər) *n.* Any of various related jumping insects of the families Locustidae (or Acrididae) and Tettigoniidae with long hind legs.
grass•land (grăs′lănd′) *n.* An area, such as a prairie, that is covered with grass or grasslike vegetation.
grass•roots (grăs′ro͞ots′, -ro͝ots′) *pl.n. (sing. or pl. in number).* Society in local, outlying, or rural levels as opposed to major centers of political leadership. **–grass′roots′** *adj.*
grass widow *n.* A woman who is separated or divorced from her husband.
grate¹ (grāt) *v.* **grat•ed, grat•ing. 1.** To fragment, shred, or pulverize by rubbing against a rough surface. **2.** To make or cause to make a rasping sound. **3.** To annoy : irritate. *–n.* A rasping noise. **–grat′er** *n.* **–grat′ing** *adj.* **–grat′ing•ly** *adv.*
grate² (grāt) *n.* **1.** A framework of bars used to block an opening. **2.** An iron frame similar to a grate that is used to hold burning fuel, as in a fireplace.
grate•ful (grāt′fəl) *adj.* **1.** Thankful : appreciative. **2.** Expressing gratitude. **–grate′ful•ly** *adv.* **–grate′ful•ness** *n.*
grat•i•fy (grăt′ə-fī′) *v.* **-fied, -fy•ing. 1.** To give or be a source of pleasure to. **2.** To fulfill the desires of : indulge. **–grat′i•fi•ca′tion** *n.* **–grat′i•fi′er** *n.*
grat•ing (grā′tĭng) *n.* GRATE² 1.
grat•is (grăt′ĭs, grā′tĭs) *adv. & adj.* Without charge : free.
grat•i•tude (grăt′ĭ-to͞od′, -tyo͞od′) *n.* The state of being grateful : thankfulness.
gra•tu•i•tous (grə-to͞o′ĭ-təs, -tyo͞o′-) *adj.* **1.** Given or done without payment : free. **2.** Unjustified : unwarranted. **–gra•tu′i•tous•ly** *adv.* **–gra•tu′i•tous•ness** *n.*
gra•tu•i•ty (grə-to͞o′ĭ-tē, -tyo͞o′-) *n., pl.* **-ties.** A tip.
grau•pel (grou′pəl) *n.* Precipitation consisting of snow pellets.
gra•va•men (grə-vā′mən) *n., pl.* **-mens** or **-vam•i•na** (-văm′ə-nə). *Law.* The part of a charge or accusation that weighs most heavily against the accused.
grave¹ (grāv) *n.* **1.** An excavation in the ground for the burial of a corpse. **2.** A place of burial <a watery *grave*>
grave² (grāv) *adj.* **grav•er, grav•est. 1.** Very serious : important. **2.** Bringing or threatening great danger or harm : critical. **3.** Solemn : dignified. **4.** Somber. **5.** (*also* gräv). Of, being, or writ-

ten with the mark +s, as the è in *Sèvres*. **–grave'ly** *adv.* **–grave'ness** *n.*

grave³ (grāv) *v.* **graved, grav•en** (grā'vən) *or* **graved, grav•ing.** To carve or sculpt : engrave. **–grav'er** *n.*

grav•el (grăv'əl) *n.* Loose rock fragments.

grav•el•ly (grăv'ə-lē) *adj.* **1.** Of, full of, or covered with gravel. **2.** Having a harsh rasping sound <a *gravelly* voice>

grave•stone (grāv'stōn') *n.* A stone marker on a grave : tombstone.

grave•yard (grāv'yärd') *n.* An area set aside as a burial ground : cemetery.

graveyard shift *n.* **1.** A work shift that begins late at night, as at midnight. **2.** The workers on a graveyard shift.

grav•id (grăv'ĭd) *adj.* Pregnant.

gra•vim•e•ter (gră-vĭm'ĭ-tər, grā'və-mē'-) *n.* An instrument for determining specific gravity. **–gra•vim'e•try** (-vĭm'ĭ-trē) *n.*

grav•i•tate (grăv'ĭ-tāt') *v.* **-tat•ed, -tat•ing. 1.** To move under the force of gravity. **2.** To be drawn as if by an irresistible force.

grav•i•ta•tion (grăv'ĭ-tā'shən) *n.* The attraction or force of attraction that tends to draw material objects together. **–grav'i•ta'tion•al** *adj.* **–grav'i•ta'tion•al•ly** *adv.* **–grav'i•ta'tive** *adj.*

grav•i•ty (grăv'ĭ-tē) *n.* **1.** The attractive central gravitational force exerted by a celestial body such as the earth. **2.** Weight. **3.** Seriousness. **4.** Importance.

gra•vure (grə-vyŏŏr') *n.* **1.** A method of printing from photomechanically prepared plates or cylinders. **2.** Photogravure.

gra•vy (grā'vē) *n., pl.* **-vies. 1. a.** The juices from cooked meat. **b.** A sauce made by seasoning and thickening these juices. **2.** *Slang.* Something desirable, as money, that is unexpectedly or easily gained.

gray *also* **grey** (grā) *adj.* **1.** Of or relating to a neutral color shading between black and white. **2.** Dismal : gloomy. **3.** Having gray hair. *–n.* **1.** A neutral color shading between black and white. **2.** An object or animal of the color gray. **–gray'ish** *adj.* **–gray'ness** *n.*

gray•beard (grā'bîrd') *n.* An old man.

gray•ling (grā'lĭng) *n., pl.* **-ling** *or* **-lings.** Any of several freshwater food and game fishes of the genus *Thymallus,* with a small mouth and a large dorsal fin.

gray matter *n.* The brownish-gray nerve tissue of the brain and spinal cord, consisting principally of nerve cells and fibers.

graze¹ (grāz) *v.* **grazed, graz•ing. 1.** To feed on growing grasses and herbage. **2.** To put (livestock) out to graze. **–graz'er** *n.*

graze² (grāz) *v.* **grazed, graz•ing. 1.** To touch lightly in passing. **2.** To scratch slightly : abrade. **–graze** *n.*

gra•zier (grā'zhər) *n.* One who grazes cattle.

grease (grēs) *n.* **1.** Melted or soft animal fat. **2.** An oily substance, esp. lubricant. *–v.* (grēs, grēz) **greased, greas•ing.** To coat, smear, or lubricate with grease. **–greas'i•ness** *n.* **–greas'y** *adj.*

grease paint *also* **grease•paint** (grēs'pānt') *n.* Theatrical make-up.

great (grāt) *adj.* **1.** Large in size : big. **2.** Superior : outstanding <a *great* painting> **3.** Large in quantity or number : numerous. **4.** Eminent : renowned <a *great* novelist> **5.** *Informal.* Very good : first-rate <a *great* performance> **6.** Being a generation removed from the relative specified <a *great*-uncle> *–n.* One that is great. **–great'ly** *adv.* **–great'ness** *n.*

Great Brit•ain (brĭt'n). **1.** Island off the W coast of Europe, comprising England, Scotland, and Wales. **2.** United Kingdom.

great•coat (grāt'kōt') *n.* An overcoat.

Great Dane *n.* A massive and powerful dog with a smooth, short coat.

great•heart•ed (grāt'här'tĭd) *adj.* **1.** Noble or courageous. **2.** Magnanimous : generous. **–great'heart'ed•ly** *adv.* **–great'heart'ed•ness** *n.*

Great Lakes. Group of 5 freshwater lakes of C North America on either side of the U.S.–Canadian boundary.

Great Plains. High grassland region of C North America.

Great Power *n.* A nation with great influence in international affairs.

Great Salt Lake. Saline lake of NW Utah.

grebe (grēb) *n.* Any of various diving birds of the family Podicipedidae with lobed, fleshy membranes along each toe and a pointed bill.

Gre•co (grĕk'ō), **El.** 1541?–1614? Greek-born Spanish artist.

Greece (grēs). Country of SE Europe, in the S Balkan Peninsula. *Cap.* Athens. *Pop.* 8,768,641. **–Gre'cian** *adj.* & *n.*

greed (grēd) *n.* A desire to acquire more than one needs or deserves : avarice.

greed•y (grē'dē) *adj.* **-i•er, -i•est. 1.** Excessively eager to acquire or possess something, esp. in quantity. ☆***syns:*** ACQUISITIVE, AVARICIOUS, AVID, COVETOUS, DESIROUS, GRABBY, GRASPING, HUNGRY, RAPACIOUS **2.** Wanting to eat or drink more than one can reasonably consume. ☆***syns:*** GLUTTONOUS, HOGGISH, PIGGISH, RAVENOUS, VORACIOUS **3.** Extremely desirous. **–greed'i•ly** *adv.* **–greed'i•ness** *n.*

Greek (grēk) *n.* **1.** A native or inhabitant of Greece. **2.** The ancient or modern language of Greece. **–Greek** *adj.*

green (grēn) *n.* **1.** The color of growing grass. **2. greens.** Leafy plants or plant parts. **3.** A grassy lawn or plot, esp. the closely mowed area of grass at the end of a golf fairway. *–adj.* **1.** Of the color green. **2.** Covered with green foliage or growth. **3.** Made with green or leafy vegetables <a *green* salad> **4.** Not ripe : immature. **5.** Lacking experience. *–v.* To become green. **–green'ish** *adj.* **–green'ness** *n.*

green•back (grēn'băk') *n.* A U.S. legal-tender currency note.

green bean *n.* The string bean.

green•belt (grēn'bĕlt') *n.* An area of recreational parks, farmland, or uncultivated land surrounding a community.

green•er•y (grē'nə-rē) *n., pl.* **-ies.** Green plants or foliage.

green-eyed (grēn'īd') *adj.* Jealous.

green•gro•cer (grēn'grō'sər) *n. esp. Brit.* A retailer of fresh fruit and vegetables. **–green'gro'cer•y** *n.*

green•horn (grēn'hôrn') *n.* An inexperienced person, esp. one easily fooled.

green•house (grēn'hous') *n.* A glass-enclosed structure in which plants requiring an even temperature can be cultivated.

Green•land (grēn'lənd, -lănd'). Danish island in the North Atlantic off NE Canada.

green manure *n.* A growing crop, as a clover or grass, plowed under the soil to enhance fertility.

green pepper *n.* The unripened green fruit of various pepper plants.

green•room (grēn'rōōm', -rŏŏm') *n.* A room or lounge in a theater or concert hall for performers to use when off stage.

green•sward (grēn'swôrd') *n.* Turf that is covered with green grass.

green thumb *n.* An unusual skill at growing plants.

Green•wich time (grĭn'ĭj, -ĭch, grĕn'-) *n.* The time at the meridian at Greenwich, England (0° longitude), used to calculate standard time in most of the world.

green•wood (grēn'wŏŏd') *n.* A forest when the foliage is green.

greet (grēt) *v.* **1.** To address in a friendly way : welcome. **2.** To receive with a specified reaction. **3.** To be perceived by <A fascinating spectacle *greeted* his eyes.> **–greet'er** *n.*

greet•ing (grē'tĭng) *n.* A gesture or word of salutation on meeting.

greeting card *n.* A card imprinted with a greeting and suitable illustration for use on a special occasion or holiday.

gre•gar•i•ous (grĭ-gâr'ē-əs) *adj.* **1.** Tending to form or move in groups. **2.** Enjoying the company of others : sociable. **–gre•gar'i•ous•ly** *adv.* **–gre•gar'i•ous•ness** *n.*

Gre•go•ri•an calendar (grĭ-gôr'ē-ən, -gōr'-) *n.* The calendar, sponsored (1582) by Pope Gregory XIII, that is in use in most of the world.

grem•lin (grĕm'lĭn) *n.* A mischievous elf to whom mechanical malfunctions, esp. in aircrafts, are attributed.

Gre•na•da (grə-nā'də). Island in the West Indies, part of the country of **Grenada.** *Cap.* St. George's. *Pop.* 109,609.

gre•nade (grə-nād') *n.* A small bomb detonated by a fuse and thrown by hand or fired from a rifle equipped with a launcher.

gren•a•dier (grĕn'ə-dîr') *n.* A member of a regiment formerly armed with grenades.

gren•a•dine (grĕn'ə-dēn', grĕn'ə-dēn') *n.* A syrup made from pomegranates or red currants and used esp. in mixed drinks.

grew (grōō) *v. p.t. of* GROW.

grey (grā) *n.* & *adj. var. of* GRAY.

grey•hound (grā'hound') *n.* A slender, swift-running dog with long legs.

grid (grĭd) *n.* **1.** A framework of bars : grate. **2.** A pattern of lines forming squares, used as a reference for locating points on a map, chart, aerial photograph, etc. **3.** A conducting plate in a storage battery. **4.** A network or coil of fine wires located between the plate and filament in an electron tube. **5.** A football field.

grid•dle (grĭd'l) *n.* A flat metal surface used for cooking.

grid•dle•cake (grĭd'l-kāk') *n.* A pancake.

grid•i•ron (grĭd'ī'ərn) *n.* **1.** A flat framework of metal bars used for broiling. **2.** A framework or network suggestive of a gridiron. **3.** A football field.

grief (grēf) *n.* **1.** Deep sadness, as that caused by bereavement : sorrow. **2.** A cause of grief.

griev•ance (grē'vəns) *n.* **1.** Something considered to afford just cause for complaint or protest. **2.** A complaint of unfair treatment, esp. by an employee.

grieve (grēv) *v.* **grieved, griev•ing.** To feel or cause to feel grief.

griev•ous (grē′vəs) *adj.* **1.** Causing grief, anguish, or pain. **2.** Grave : dire. **–griev′ous•ly** *adv.* **–griev′ous•ness** *n.*

grif•fin *also* **grif•fon** or **gryph•on** (grĭf′ĭn) *n.* A fabulous beast with a lion's body and an eagle's head and wings.

griffin

gri•gri *also* **gris-gris** (grē′grē) *n.* An African charm, fetish, or amulet.

grill (grĭl) *n.* **1.** A cooking utensil with parallel metal bars : gridiron. **2.** Food cooked on a grill. **3.** A restaurant, as in a hotel, where grilled foods are a specialty. **4.** *var. of* GRILLE. *–v.* **1.** To broil on a grill. **2.** *Informal.* To question closely and relentlessly.

grille *also* **grill** (grĭl) *n.* A metal grating used as a screen, divider, or barrier.

grim (grĭm) *adj.* **grim•mer, grim•mest. 1.** Unyielding : relentless. **2.** Forbidding in appearance. **3.** Grisly : ghastly. **4.** Gloomy : dismal. **–grim′ly** *adv.* **–grim′ness** *n.*

grim•ace (grĭm′əs, grĭ-mās′) *n.* A facial expression of pain, disapproval, or disgust. **–grim′ace** *v.*

grime (grīm) *n.* Black dirt or soot, usu. clinging to or ingrained in a surface. **–grim′i•ness** *n.* **–grim′y** *adj.*

Grimm (grĭm), **Jakob.** (1785–1863) and **Wilhelm** (1786–1859). German philologists and folklorists.

grin (grĭn) *v.* **grinned, grin•ning.** To smile broadly. **–grin** *n.*

grind (grīnd) *v.* **ground** (ground), **grind•ing. 1.** To reduce to fine particles. **2.** To sharpen, shape, or refine by friction <*grind* a knife> **3.** To press or rub together : gnash <*grinds* his teeth> **4.** To move with noisy friction <a car *grinding* to a halt> **5.** To bear down on harshly : oppress. **6.** To produce or operate by or as if by turning a crank <*ground* out a book a year> **7.** *Informal.* To study or work hard : drudge. *–n.* **1.** *Informal.* Laborious work, routine, or study. **2.** Someone who studies or works excessively. **–grind′ing•ly** *adv.*

grind•er (grīn′dər) *n.* **1.** One that grinds. **2.** A molar. **3. grinders.** *Informal.* The teeth. **4.** HERO 4.

grind•stone (grīnd′stōn′) *n.* A stone disk that revolves on an axle for grinding, polishing, or sharpening.

grip (grĭp) *n.* **1. a.** A firm hold : grasp. **b.** Power and strength in holding firmly. **2.** Understanding : mastery. **3.** A device to be grasped and held : handle. **4.** A suitcase. *–v.* **gripped, grip•ping. 1.** To grasp and keep a firm hold on. **2.** To attract and keep the attention or interest of. **–grip′ping•ly** *adv.*

gripe (grīp) *v.* **griped, grip•ing. 1.** To suffer or cause to suffer sharp bowel pains. **2.** *Informal.* To annoy : vex. **3.** *Informal.* To complain petulantly : grumble. *–n.* **1.** *Informal.* A complaint. **2.** *often* **gripes.** A sharp, repeated bowel pain.

grippe (grĭp) *n.* Influenza. **–grip′py** *adj.*

gris-gris (grē′grē) *n. var. of* GRIGRI.

gris•ly (grĭz′lē) *adj.* **-li•er, -li•est.** Ghastly : gruesome.

grist (grĭst) *n.* **1.** Grain ready to be ground. **2.** Ground grain.

gris•tle (grĭs′əl) *n.* Cartilage. **–gris′tly** *adj.*

grist•mill (grĭst′mĭl′) *n.* A mill for grinding grain.

grit (grĭt) *n.* **1.** Tiny rough granules, as of sand. **2.** *Informal.* Great courage and fortitude. **3. Grit.** *Can.* A member of the Liberal Party of Canada. *–v.* **grit•ted, grit•ting.** To clamp (the teeth) together. **–grit′ty** *adj.*

grits (grĭts) *pl.n.* Coarsely ground grain.

griz•zly (grĭz′lē) *adj.* **-zli•er, -zli•est.** Flecked or mixed with gray. *–n., pl.* **-zlies.** A grizzly bear.

grizzly bear *n.* A large grayish bear, *Ursus horribilis,* of W North America.

groan (grōn) *v.* To utter a deep, prolonged sound indicative of pain, grief, or vexation. **–groan** *n.* **–groan′ing•ly** *adv.*

groat (grōt) *n.* A British coin worth 4 pence, used from the 14th to the 17th cent.

gro•cer (grō′sər) *n.* A storekeeper who sells groceries.

gro•cer•y (grō′sə-rē) *n., pl.* **-ies. 1.** A store in which food and household staples are sold. **2. groceries.** The goods sold in a grocery.

grog (grŏg) *n.* Alcoholic liquor, esp. rum, diluted with water.

grog•gy (grŏg′ē) *adj.* **-gi•er, -gi•est.** Weak, unsteady on the feet, and dazed. **–grog′gi•ly** *adv.* **–grog′gi•ness** *n.*

groin (groin) *n.* **1. a.** The crease where the thigh meets the abdomen. **b.** The area of this crease. **2.** The curved edge of a building formed by 2 intersecting vaults.

grom•met (grŏm′ĭt) *n.* A reinforced eyelet through which something, as a fastener, may be passed.

groom (gro͞om, gro͝om) *n.* **1.** A male servant, esp. one who takes care of horses. **2.** A bridegroom. *–v.* **1.** To make trim and neat. **2.** To clean and brush (an animal). **3.** To prepare for a particular position.

grooms•man (gro͞omz′mən, gro͝omz′-) *n.* A bridegroom's attendant at his wedding.

groove (gro͞ov) *n.* **1.** A long, narrow channel or furrow. **2.** A humdrum, fixed routine. **–groove** *v.*

groov•y (gro͞o′vē) *adj.* **-i•er, -i•est.** *Slang.* Delightful : wonderful.

grope (grōp) *v.* **groped, grop•ing. 1.** To reach or feel about uncertainly in or as if in search. **2.** To look for uncertainly or blindly <*grope* for a reason> **–grope** *n.* **–grop′ing•ly** *adv.*

gros•beak (grōs′bēk′) *n.* Any of several often colorful birds of the genera *Hesperiphona, Pinicola,* and related genera, with a thick, rounded bill.

gro•schen (grō′shən) *n., pl.* **-schen.** See *schilling* at CURRENCY TABLE.

gros•grain (grō′grān′) *n.* A heavy, horizontally ribbed silk or rayon fabric.

gross (grōs) *adj.* **1.** Exclusive of deductions : total <*gross* yearly profits> **2.** Glaringly obvious : egregious. **3.** Lacking refinement or delicacy : coarse. **4.** Obscene : vulgar. **5.** Overweight : corpulent. **6.** General : broad. *–n.* **1.** *pl.* **gross•es.** An entire amount exclusive of deductions : total. **2.** *pl.* **gross.** A group of 12 dozen or 144 items. *–v.* To earn as a total before deductions. **–gross′ly** *adv.* **–gross′ness** *n.*

gross national product *n.* The total market value of all the goods and services produced by a nation during a year.

grosz (grôsh) *n., pl.* **gro•szy** (grô′shē). See *zloty* at CURRENCY TABLE.

gro•tesque (grō-tĕsk′) *adj.* **1.** Ludicrously incongruous or distorted. **2.** Outlandish : bizarre. **–gro•tesque′** *n.* **–gro•tesque′ly** *adv.* **–gro•tesque′ness** *n.*

gro•tes•que•ry *also* **gro•tes•que•rie** (grō-tĕs′kə-rē) *n., pl.* **-ries. 1.** The state of being grotesque. **2.** Something grotesque.

grot•to (grŏt′ō) *n., pl.* **-toes** *or* **-tos. 1.** A cave. **2.** A cavelike excavation or structure.

grouch (grouch) *n.* **1.** A spell of grumbling or sulking. **2.** A habitually irritable or complaining person. **–grouch** *v.* **–grouch′i•ly** *adv.* **–grouch′i•ness** *n.* **–grouch′y** *adj.*

ground[1] (ground) *n.* **1.** The surface of the earth. **2.** Earth : soil. **3.** An area of land set aside for a particular purpose. **4. grounds.** The land surrounding a building. **5.** A basis for an argument, belief, or action. **6.** A background. **7. grounds.** Sediment at the bottom of a liquid, esp. coffee : dregs. **8.** A conducting body, as the earth, used as a return for electric currents and as an arbitrary zero of potential. *–v.* **1.** To place or set on the ground. **2.** To provide a basis or reason for. **3.** To instruct in basic principles. **4.** To prevent (an aircraft, pilot, or crew) from flying. **5.** To connect (an electric current) to a ground. **6.** To run or cause to run aground. **–ground′less** *adj.* **–ground′less•ly** *adv.* **–ground′less•ness** *n.*

ground[2] (ground) *v. p.t. & p.p. of* GRIND.

ground cloth *n.* A ground sheet.

ground cover *n.* Low-growing plants that form a dense, extensive growth and tend to prevent soil erosion.

ground crew *n.* A team of technicians and mechanics who maintain and service aircraft or spacecraft on the ground.

ground-ef•fect machine (ground′ĭ-fĕkt′) *n.* A vehicle designed for traveling over land or water by means of an air cushion.

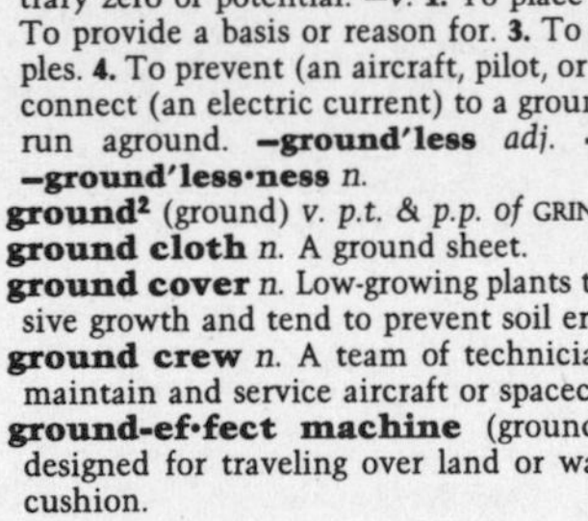

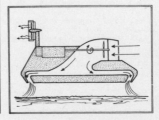

ground-effect machine

ground•er (groun′dər) *n.* A batted baseball that bounces or rolls along the ground.

ground glass *n.* Glass that has been ground or etched to create a roughened, nontransparent surface.

ground hog *also* **ground•hog** (ground′hôg′, -hŏg′) *n.* A woodchuck.

ground•ling (ground′lĭng) *n.* **1.** One with uncultivated tastes. **2.** A spectator in the cheaper part of an Elizabethan theater.

ground•mass (ground′măs′) *n.* The fine-grained crystalline base of porphyritic rock in which larger crystals are embedded.

ground rule *n.* **1.** A rule in sports that modifies play on a particular field, course, or court. **2.** A basic rule.

ground sheet *also* **ground•sheet** (ground′shēt′) *n.* **1.** A waterproof cover for protecting an area of ground, as a baseball field. **2.** A waterproof sheet laid under camp bedding to protect against dampness.

ground squirrel *n.* A rodent of the genus *Citellus* (or *Spermophilus*), related to and resembling the chipmunk.

ground swell *n.* **1.** A deep broad swell in the ocean often caused by a distant earthquake. **2.** A strong, rapid growth : surge.

ground water *also* **ground•wa•ter** (ground′wô′tər, -wŏt′ər) *n.* Water under the surface of the earth that feeds springs and wells.

ground•work (ground′wûrk′) *n.* A basis : foundation.

group (gro͞op) *n.* A number of individuals or objects collected, situated, or classified together. —*v.* To place or be in a group.

grou•per (gro͞o′pər) *n.* A large fish of the genera *Epinephelus, Mycteroperca,* or related genera, indigenous to warm seas.

group•ie (gro͞o′pē) *n. Slang.* A female fan and follower of a rock group esp. when it is touring.

group therapy *n.* Psychotherapy involving sessions guided by a therapist and attended by several patients who discuss their emotional problems with each other.

grouse[1] (grous) *n., pl.* **grouse.** Any of various plump game birds of the family Tetraonidae with brownish plumage.

grouse[2] (grous) *v.* **groused, grous•ing.** To grumble : complain. **—grouse** *n.*

grout (grout) *n.* A material, as mortar, used to fill cracks in masonry or spaces between tiles. **—grout** *v.* **—grout′er** *n.*

grove (grōv) *n.* A small stand of trees usu. lacking undergrowth.

grov•el (grŭv′əl, grŏv′-) *v.* **-eled, el•ing** or **-elled, -el•ling. 1.** To lie or creep in a prostrate position, as from fear. **2.** To behave in a servile way : cringe. **—grov′el•er** *n.* **—grov′el•ing•ly** *adv.*

grow (grō) *v.* **grew** (gro͞o), **grown** (grōn), **grow•ing. 1.** To spring up, develop, and reach maturity. **2.** To be capable of developing : flourish. **3.** To expand : increase. **4.** To come into existence : spring forth. **5.** To come together by or as if by growth. **6.** To become. **7.** To raise : cultivate. **—grow up.** To become an adult. **—grow′er** *n.*

growl (groul) *n.* A deep guttural, threatening sound, as of a dog. **—growl** *v.* **—growl′er** *n.*

grown-up (grōn′ŭp′) *adj.* Of or characteristic of adults : mature. **—grown′-up′** *n.*

growth (grōth) *n.* **1. a.** The process of growing. **b.** A stage attained in the process of growing. **2.** An increase, as in size or amount. **3.** Something that has increased or developed <a *growth of weeds*> **4.** An abnormal formation of bodily tissue, as a tumor.

grub (grŭb) *v.* **grubbed, grub•bing. 1.** To clear of roots by digging. **2.** To dig up by the roots. **3. a.** To search laboriously as if by digging : rummage. **b.** To work hard : drudge. —*n.* **1.** The thick, wormlike larva of certain insects, as beetles. **2.** *Slang.* Food. **3.** A drudge. **—grub′ber** *n.*

grub•by (grŭb′ē) *adj.* **-bi•er, -bi•est.** Unkempt : sloppy **—grub′bi•ly** *adv.* **—grub′bi•ness** *n*

grub•stake (grŭb′stāk′) *n.* Funds or materials supplied to a mining prospector or business entrepreneur for a share of future profits. **—grub′stake′** *v.*

grudge (grŭj) *v.* **grudged, grudg•ing.** To give or allow reluctantly : begrudge. —*n.* A feeling of ill will or deep resentment. **—grudg′er** *n.* **—grudg′ing•ly** *adv.*

gru•el (gro͞o′əl) *n.* A thin porridge.

gru•el•ing *also* **gru•el•ling** (gro͞o′ə-lĭng) *adj.* Extremely tiring : exhausting. **—gru′el•ing•ly** *adv.*

grue•some (gro͞o′səm) *adj.* Causing horror or repugnance : grisly. **—grue′some•ly** *adv.* **—grue′some•ness** *n.*

gruff (grŭf) *adj.* **1.** Brusque and unfriendly in manner. **2.** Harsh in sound : hoarse. ☆***syns:*** BLUFF, BLUNT, BRUSQUE, CURT. **—gruff′ly** *adv.* **—gruff′ness** *n.*

grum•ble (grŭm′bəl) *v.* **-bled, -bling.** To mutter discontentedly. **—grum′ble** *n.* **—grum′bler** *n.* **—grum′bly** *adj.*

grump•y (grŭm′pē) *adj.* **-i•er, -i•est.** Irritable and moody : cranky. **—grump′i•ly!** *adv.* **—grump′i•ness** *n.*

grun•gy (grŭn′jē) *adj.* **-gi•er, -gi•est.** *Slang.* Being in a dirty, run-down, or inferior condition.

grun•ion (grŭn′yən) *n.* A small fish, *Leuresthes tenuis,* of Calif. coastal waters that spawns inshore at approx. full moon.

grunt (grŭnt) *n.* A low, guttural sound, as of a pig. **—grunt** *v.*

G-suit (jē′so͞ot′) *n.* A flight garment designed to counteract the effects of high acceleration by exerting pressure on parts of the body below the chest.

gtd. *abbr.* guaranteed.

GU *abbr.* Guam (with Zip Code).

Gua•da•la•ja•ra (gwŏd′l-ə-hä′rə). City of SW Mexico. *Pop.* 1,813,100.

Gua•de•loupe (gwŏd′l-o͞op′). Overseas department of France, in the West Indies. *Cap.* Basse-Terre. *Pop.* 324,530.

Guam (gwŏm). Largest of the Mariana Is., in the W Pacific; unincorporated U.S. territory. *Cap.* Agana. *Pop.* 107,000.

Guang•zhou (gwäng′jō). City of S China, on a delta near the South China Sea. *Pop.* 2,300,000.

gua•nine (gwä′nēn′) *n.* A purine that is a constituent of both ribonucleic and deoxyribonucleic acids.

gua•no (gwä′nō) *n.* A substance that consists mainly of the excrement of sea birds and is used as a fertilizer.

guar. *abbr.* guaranteed.

gua•ra•ni (gwä′rə-nē′) *n., pl.* **-ni** or **-nis.** See CURRENCY TABLE.

guar•an•tee (găr′ən-tē′) *n.* **1.** A promise or assurance, esp. as to the durability or quality of a product. **2.** GUARANTY 1. **3.** A guarantor. **4.** Something held or given as security : pledge. —*v.* **-teed, -tee•ing. 1.** To assume responsibility for the default or debt of. **2.** To undertake to accomplish, continue, or perform. **3.** To furnish security for. **4.** To give a guarantee for.

guar•an•tor (găr′ən-tər, -tôr′) *n.* One who gives a guarantee or guaranty.

guar•an•ty (găr′ən-tē) *n., pl.* **-ties. 1.** An undertaking to pay another's debts or fulfill another's obligations in the event of default. **2.** Something that guarantees. **3.** A guarantor.

guard (gärd) *v.* **1.** To shield from danger or harm : protect. **2.** To watch over or keep watch at, esp. to prevent escape, violence, or indiscretion. **3.** To take precautions <*guard* against error> —*n.* **1.** A person or group on sentinel duty. **2.** The duty or act of protecting : watchful care. **3.** A defensive position, as in fencing. **4.** One of the 2 football players on either side of the center. **5.** One of the 2 basketball players stationed near the middle of the court. **6.** An apparatus or device that protects against damage, harm, or loss.

guard•house (gärd′hous′) *n.* **1.** A building that serves as headquarters for a military guard. **2.** A military jail.

guard•i•an (gär′dē-ən) *n.* **1.** One that guards, protects, or defends. **2.** One who is legally responsible for the person or property of another. **—guard′i•an•ship′** *n.*

guard•rail (gärd′rāl′) *n.* A protective rail, as on a highway.

guard•room (gärd′ro͞om′, -ro͝om′) *n.* **1.** A room used by guards on duty. **2.** A room for confining military prisoners.

guards•man (gärdz′mən) *n.* **1.** A member of the U.S. National Guard. **2.** *esp. Brit.* A soldier in a household guard regiment.

Gua•te•ma•la (gwä′tə-mä′lə). **1.** Country of N Central America. *Pop.* 7,685,000. **2.** *also* **Guatemala City.** Cap. of Guatemala, in the SC part. *Pop.* 793,336. **—Gua′te•ma′lan** *adj.* & *n.*

gua•va (gwä′və) *n.* A tropical American tree, *Psidium guajava,* bearing edible yellow-skinned fruit.

gu•ber•na•to•ri•al (go͞o′bər-nə-tôr′ē-əl, -tōr′-, gyo͞o′-) *adj.* Of a governor.

gue•non (gə-nōn′) *n.* Any of various African monkeys of the genus *Cercopithecus,* with long hind legs and a long tail.

guenon

guer•don (gûr′dn) *n.* A reward : requital.

Guern•sey (gûrn′zē) *n., pl.* **-seys.** One of a breed of brown-and-white dairy cattle.

guer•ril•la or **gue•ril•la** (gə-rĭl′ə) *n.* A member of an irregular military force that is capable of great speed and mobility.

guess (gĕs) *v.* **1.** To make a judgment (about) on the basis of insufficient evidence. **2.** To come to a correct conclusion about, esp. by chance. **3.** To suppose : believe. **–guess** *n.* **–guess'er** *n.*

guess•work (gĕs'wûrk') *n.* An answer or result obtained by guessing.

guest (gĕst) *n.* **1.** The recipient of hospitality at the table or home of another. **2.** A customer at a commercial establishment, as a hotel or restaurant. **3.** A visiting participant in a program or presentation.

guf•faw (gə-fô') *n.* A loud or coarse burst of laughter. **–guf•faw'** *v.*

guid•ance (gīd'ns) *n.* **1.** An act or instance of guiding. **2.** Counseling, as on emotional difficulties : advice.

guide (gīd) *n.* **1.** One who directs or leads another, as in a course of action. **2.** Someone employed to indicate and explain points of interest, as in a foreign city. **3.** Something, as a sign or mark, that serves to indicate or direct. **4.** A device on a machine that acts as an indicator or regulator. *–v.* **guid•ed, guid•ing. 1.** To show the way to : conduct. **2.** To manage the course of : direct. ☆***syns:*** CONDUCT, DIRECT, ESCORT, LEAD, PILOT, SHEPHERD, SHOW, STEER, USHER **–guid'a•ble** *adj.* **–guid'er** *n.*

guide•book (gīd'bo͝ok') *n.* A handbook of information, esp. for travelers.

guided missile *n.* A missile whose course can be controlled while in flight.

guide•line (gīd'līn') *n.* A statement or outline of procedure or policy.

guide•post (gīd'pōst') *n.* A signpost.

guide•word (gīd'wûrd') *n.* A word or term at the top of a page of a reference book, as a dictionary, indicating the first or last entry on the page.

gui•don (gī'dŏn', gīd'n) *n.* A standard, as a small flag, carried by a military unit.

guild (gĭld) *n.* An association of persons of the same occupation or trade, esp. a medieval society of artisans or merchants.

guil•der (gĭl'dər) *n.* See CURRENCY TABLE.

guile (gīl) *n.* Crafty cunning : deceitfulness. **–guile'ful** *adj.* **–guile'ful•ly** *adv.* **–guile'ful•ness** *n.* **–guile'less** *adj.* **–guile'less•ly** *adv.* **–guile'less•ness** *n.*

guil•lo•tine (gĭl'ə-tēn', gē'ə-) *n.* A machine for beheading condemned prisoners. **–guil'lo•tine'** *v.*

guilt (gĭlt) *n.* **1.** The fact of being responsible for wrongdoing or a crime. **2.** A feeling of responsibility for having done something wrong. **–guilt'less** *adj.* **–guilt'less•ly** *adv.* **–guilt'less•ness** *n.*

guilt•y (gĭl'tē) *adj.* **-i•er, -i•est. 1.** Responsible for or chargeable with a reprehensible act. **2.** Burdened with, prompted by, or showing a feeling of guilt. **–guilt'i•ly** *adv.* **–guilt'i•ness** *n.*

guin•ea (gĭn'ē) *n.* **1.** A former British gold coin worth 1 pound and 5 pence. **2.** The sum of 1 pound and 5 pence.

Guin•ea (gĭn'ē). Country of WC Africa, on the Atlantic. *Cap.* Conakry. *Pop.* 5,070,000. **–Guin'e•an** *adj.* & *n.*

Guin•ea-Bis•sau (gĭn'ē-bĭ-sou'). Country of W Africa. *Cap.* Bissau. *Pop.* 805,000.

guinea fowl *n.* A widely domesticated pheasantlike bird, *Numida meleagris,* having blackish plumage spotted with white.

guinea hen *n.* **1.** A female guinea fowl. **2.** A guinea fowl.

guinea pig *n.* Any of various almost tailless rodents of the genus *Cavia* that are often used for biological experimentation.

guise (gīz) *n.* **1.** Outward and esp. false appearance : semblance. **2.** A mode or form of dress : garb.

gui•tar (gĭ-tär') *n.* A musical instrument usu. with 6 strings that is played by strumming or plucking. **–gui•tar'ist** *n.*

gulch (gŭlch) *n.* A gully : ravine.

gul•den (go͞ol'dən, go͝ol'-) *n., pl.* **-dens** *or* **-den.** A guilder.

gulf (gŭlf) *n.* **1.** A large area of an ocean or sea partially enclosed by land. **2.** A chasm : abyss. **3.** A separation : gap.

gulf•weed (gŭlf'wēd') *n.* Any of several brownish seaweeds of the genus *Sargassum* of tropical Atlantic waters that have rounded air bladders and often form dense floating masses.

gull[1] (gŭl) *n.* Any of various usu. gray and white aquatic birds of the subfamily Larinae with long wings and webbed feet.

gull[2] (gŭl) *n.* A gullible person : dupe. *–v.* To dupe : cheat.

gul•let (gŭl'ĭt) *n.* **1.** The esophagus. **2.** The throat.

gul•li•ble (gŭl'ə-bəl) *adj.* Easily cheated, deceived, or duped. **–gul'li•bil'i•ty** *n.* **–gul'li•bly** *adv.*

gul•ly (gŭl'ē) *n., pl.* **-lies.** A channel or ditch cut in the earth by running water, esp. after a downpour.

gulp (gŭlp) *v.* **1.** To swallow rapidly or greedily. **2.** To gasp or choke, as in nervousness. **3.** To stifle by or as if by swallowing. *–n.* **1.** An act of gulping. **2.** A large mouthful <a *gulp* of hot tea> **3.** *Computer Sci.* A small group of bytes that may be either data or instruction.

gum[1] (gŭm) *n.* **1.** Any of various viscous plant substances that dry into water-soluble, noncrystalline, brittle solids. **2.** A tree that yields gum. **3.** Chewing gum. *–v.* **gummed, gum•ming.** To cover, smear, seal, clog, or fix in place with or as if with gum. **–gum'my** *adj.*

gum[2] (gŭm) *n.* The firm connective tissue surrounding the bases of the teeth.

gum arabic *n.* A gum exuded by various African trees and used esp. in the preparation of pills, emulsions, mucilage, and candies.

gum•bo (gŭm'bō) *n., pl.* **-bos.** A stew or soup containing okra.

gum•boil (gŭm'boil') *n.* A boil or abscess on the gum.

gum•drop (gŭm'drŏp') *n.* A firm jellylike sugar-coated candy made with gum arabic or gelatin.

gump•tion (gŭmp'shən) *n. Informal.* Initiative : enterprise.

gum•shoe (gŭm'sho͞o') *n. Slang.* A detective. **–gum'shoe'** *v.*

gun (gŭn) *n.* **1.** A weapon made of a metal tube that fires a projectile at high velocity. **2.** A cannon. **3.** A portable firearm. **4. a.** A device that sprays forcibly. **b.** A device that shoots a projectile <a dart *gun*> **5.** A discharge of a gun. **6.** A throttle. *–v.* **gunned, gun•ning. 1.** To shoot. **2.** To open the throttle of in order to accelerate. **–gun for.** To try to catch, ruin, or acquire.

gun•boat (gŭn'bōt') *n.* A small lightly armed vessel.

gun•cot•ton (gŭn'kŏt'n) *n.* Nitrocellulose.

gun•fight (gŭn'fīt') *n.* A battle with guns. **–gun'fight'er** *n.*

gun•fire (gŭn'fīr') *n.* The firing of guns.

gung ho (gŭng' hō') *adj. Slang.* Extremely enthusiastic.

gunk (gŭngk) *n. Informal.* A filthy, slimy, or greasy substance. **–gunk'y** *adj.*

gun•lock (gŭn'lŏk') *n.* A device for igniting the charge in a firearm.

gun•man (gŭn'mən) *n.* A man, esp. a criminal, who is armed with a gun.

gun•met•al (gŭn'mĕt'l) *n.* **1.** An alloy of copper with 10% tin. **2.** Metal used for guns. **3.** A dark gray.

gun•nel (gŭn'əl) *n. var. of* GUNWALE.

gun•ner (gŭn'ər) *n.* **1.** A soldier, sailor, or airman who aims or fires a gun. **2.** Someone who hunts with a gun.

gun•ner•y (gŭn'ə-rē) *n.* **1.** The science of the construction and operation of guns. **2.** The use of guns.

gunnery sergeant *n.* A noncommissioned U.S. Marine officer ranking above a staff sergeant and below a master sergeant.

gun•ny (gŭn'ē) *n.* A coarse fabric made of jute or hemp used esp. for making sacks.

gunny sack *n.* A sack made of gunny.

gun•pow•der (gŭn'pou'dər) *n.* An explosive powder used in blasting and in guns.

gun•shot (gŭn'shŏt') *n.* **1.** Shot or a shot fired from a gun. **2.** The range of a gun.

gun-shy (gŭn'shī') *adj.* **1.** Afraid of loud noises, as gunfire. **2.** Very wary : distrustful.

gun•sling•er (gŭn'slĭng'ər) *n.* A gunman.

gun•smith (gŭn'smĭth') *n.* Someone who makes or repairs firearms.

gun•wale *also* **gun•nel** (gŭn'əl) *n.* The upper edge of a ship's side.

gup•py (gŭp'ē) *n., pl.* **-pies.** A small tropical freshwater fish, *Poecilia reticulata* or *Lebistes reticulatus,* popular in home aquariums.

gur•gle (gûr'gəl) *v.* **-gled, -gling. 1.** To flow in a broken, uneven current making low sounds. **2.** To make a sound resembling that of gurgling water. **–gur'gle** *n.* **–gur'gling•ly** *adv.*

Gur•kha (go͝or'kə) *n.* A soldier from Nepal serving in the British or Indian armies.

gu•ru (go͞o'ro͞o', go͞o-ro͞o') *n.* **1.** A spiritual teacher in Hinduism. **2.** A mentor.

gush (gŭsh) *v.* **1.** To flow forth plentifully or violently : spout. **2.** To be overly sentimental or enthusiastic. **–gush** *n.* **–gush'y** *adj.*

gush•er (gŭsh'ər) *n.* **1.** One that gushes. **2.** An oil well with a plentiful natural flow.

gus•set (gŭs'ĭt) *n.* A triangular insert, as in a sleeve, for strengthening or enlarging.

gus•sy (gŭs'ē) *v.* **-sied, -sy•ing.** To dress up : decorate.

gust (gŭst) *n.* **1.** A violent, abrupt rush of wind. **2.** A sudden outburst, as of emotion. *–v.* To blow in gusts. **–gust'i•ly** *adv.* **–gust'i•ness** *n.* **–gust'y** *adj.*

gus•ta•to•ry (gŭs'tə-tôr'ē, -tōr'ē) *adj.* Of, pertaining to, or associated with the sense of taste.

gus•to (gŭs'tō) *n.* Hearty enjoyment : zest.

gut (gŭt) *n.* **1. a.** The alimentary canal. **b.** One of its parts, as the intestines. **2. guts.** The bowels : entrails. **3. guts.** The essential inner parts of something. **4. guts.** *Informal.* Fortitude : courage. *–v.* **gut•ted, gut•ting. 1.** To disembowel : eviscerate. **2.** To destroy the interior of.

Gu•ten•berg (go͞ot′n-bûrg′), **Johann.** 1400?–68? German inventor of movable type.
gut•less (gŭt′lĭs) *adj. Informal.* Lacking courage : cowardly. **–gut′less•ness** *n.*
guts•y (gŭt′sē) *adj.* **-i•er, -i•est.** *Informal.* Courageous.
gut•ter (gŭt′ər) *n.* A channel for draining off water. *–v.* **1.** To melt away rapidly. Used of a candle. **2.** To flicker.
gut•ter•snipe (gŭt′ər-snīp′) *n.* **1.** A street urchin. **2.** One who is of the lowest class.
gut•tur•al (gŭt′ər-əl) *adj.* Of, relating to, produced in, or sounded in the throat. **–gut′tur•al** *n.* **–gut′tur•al•ly** *adv.*
guy[1] (gī) *n.* A rope, cord, or cable fastened to something to steady, guide, or hold it. *–v.* To steady, guide, or hold with a guy.
guy[2] (gī) *n. Informal.* A man : fellow. *–v.* To make fun of : mock.
Guy•a•na (gī-ăn′ə). Country of NE South America. *Cap.* Georgetown. *Pop.* 921,000.
guz•zle (gŭz′əl) *v.* **-zled, -zling.** To drink greedily, excessively, and esp. habitually. **–guz′zler** *n.*
gym (jĭm) *n. Informal.* A gymnasium.
gym•na•si•um (jĭm-nā′zē-əm) *n., pl.* **-ums** or **-si•a** (-zē-ə, -zhə). **1.** A room or building equipped for indoor sports, as gymnastics. **2.** (gĭm-nä′zē-o͝om′). A high school in various C European countries that prepares students to enter the university.
gym•nas•tics (jĭm-năs′tĭks) *n. (sing. or pl. in number).* Body-building exercises, esp. those performed with special apparatus in a gymnasium. **–gym′nast′** *n.* **–gym•nas′tic** *adj.*
gym•no•sperm (jĭm′nə-spûrm′) *n.* A plant of the class Gymnospermae, including the coniferous trees and other plants bearing seeds not enclosed within an ovary.
gy•ne•col•o•gy (gī′nĭ-kŏl′ə-jē, jĭn′ĭ-) *n.* The branch of medicine dealing with the diseases, reproductive physiology, and endocrinology of women. **–gy′ne•co•log′i•cal** (-kə-lŏj′ĭ-kəl), **gy′ne•co•log′ic** *adj.* **–gy′ne•col′o•gist** *n.*
gyp (jĭp) *Informal. –v.* **gypped, gyp•ping.** To cheat, swindle, or defraud. *–n.* **1.** A swindle. **2.** A swindler. **–gyp′per** *n.*
gyp•sum (jĭp′səm) *n.* A white mineral that is used to make plaster of Paris, gypsum plaster, and plasterboard.
Gyp•sy *also* **Gip•sy** (jĭp′sē) *n., pl.* **-sies. 1.** One of a nomadic Caucasoid people orig. from India and now living mainly in Europe and the U.S. **2. gypsy.** One held to resemble a Gypsy in appearance or behavior.
gypsy moth *n.* A moth, *Pothetria dispar,* whose hairy caterpillars are very destructive to trees.
gy•rate (jī′rāt′) *v.* **-rat•ed, -rat•ing. 1.** To revolve around a center or axis. **2.** To move in a circular or spiral path. **–gy•ra′tion** *n.* **–gy′ra′tor** *n.* **–gy′ra•to′ry** *adj.*
gyr•fal•con (jûr′făl′kən, -fôl′-, -fô′kən) *n.* A falcon, *Falco rusticolus,* of N regions, with color phases ranging from black to white.
gy•ro (jī′rō) *n., pl.* **-ros. 1.** A gyroscope. **2.** A gyrocompass.
gy•ro•com•pass (jī′rō-kŭm′pəs, -kŏm′-) *n.* A navigational instrument in which a gyroscope maintains a pointer's N–S orientation.

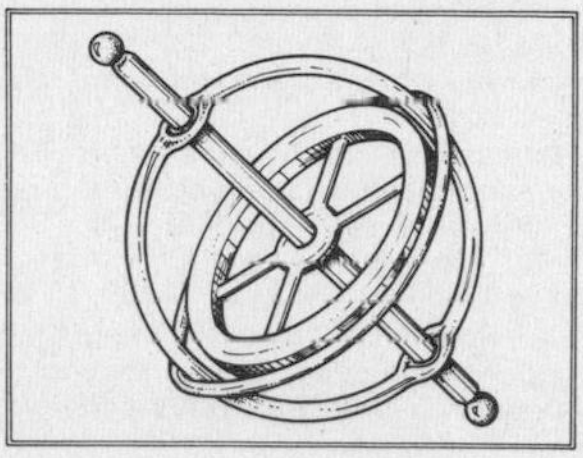

gyroscope

gy•ro•scope (jī′rə-skōp′) *n.* A spinning disk or wheel whose spin axis maintains its angular orientation when not subjected to external torques. **–gy′ro•scop′ic** (-skŏp′ĭk) *adj.*
gyve (jīv) *n. Archaic.* A fetter or shackle, esp. for the leg.

Hh

h or **H** (āch) *n., pl.* **h's** or **H's. 1.** The 8th letter of the English alphabet. **2.** A speech sound represented by the letter *h.* **3.** Something with the shape of the letter H.
H *symbol for* HYDROGEN.
h *abbr.* hour.
h. *also* **H.** *abbr.* height.
ha *abbr.* hectare.
Ha•bak•kuk (hăb′ə-kŭk′, hə-băk′ək) *n.* See BIBLE TABLE.
ha•be•as cor•pus (hā′bē-əs kôr′pəs) *n. Law.* A writ issued to bring a person before a judge or court in order to release that person from unlawful detention or restraint.
hab•er•dash•er (hăb′ər-dăsh′ər) *n.* One who deals in men's furnishings, as shirts and socks.
hab•er•dash•er•y (hăb′ər-dăsh′ə-rē) *n., pl.* **-ies. 1.** Goods sold by a haberdasher. **2.** The shop of a haberdasher.
ha•bil•i•ment (hə-bĭl′ə-mənt) *n.* **1.** *often* **habiliments.** Attire, esp. that characteristic of an office, rank, or occasion. **2. habiliments.** Equipment : trappings.
hab•it (hăb′ĭt) *n.* **1.** An often involuntary pattern of behavior acquired by frequent repetition. **2.** Usual practice or manner. **3.** An addiction. **4.** Distinctive dress or costume <a monk's *habit*> <a riding *habit*> ☆**syns:** CHARACTERISTIC, PATTERN, TRAIT
hab•it•a•ble (hăb′ĭ-tə-bəl) *adj.* Fit for use as a dwelling place. **–hab′it•a•bil′i•ty, hab′it•a•ble•ness** *n.* **–hab′it•a•bly** *adv.*
hab•i•tat (hăb′ĭ-tăt′) *n.* **1.** The environment in which an animal or plant lives or grows. **2.** The place where one can usually be found.
hab•i•ta•tion (hăb′ĭ-tā′shən) *n.* **1.** The act of inhabiting or state of being inhabited. **2. a.** Natural surroundings or region. **b.** A place to live in.
hab•it-form•ing (hăb′ĭt-fôr′mĭng) *adj.* **1.** Tending to cause physiological addiction. **2.** Tending to become habitual.
ha•bit•u•al (hə-bĭch′o͞o-əl) *adj.* **1.** Practiced by or acting according to habit. **2.** Persisting in an ingrained habit : inveterate. **3.** Usual : customary. **–ha•bit′u•al•ly** *adv.* **–ha•bit′u•al•ness** *n.*
ha•bit•u•ate (hə-bĭch′o͞o-āt′) *v.* **-at•ed, -at•ing.** To accustom by frequent exposure or repetition. **–ha•bit′u•a′tion** *n.*
hab•i•tude (hăb′ĭ-to͞od′, -tyo͞od′) *n.* A person's habitual manner or behavior.
ha•bit•u•é (hə-bĭch′o͞o-ā′, hə-bĭch′o͞o-ā′) *n.* One who frequents a particular place.
ha•ci•en•da (hä′sē-ĕn′də, ä′sē-) *n.* **1.** A large estate, plantation, or ranch in Spanish-speaking countries. **2.** The main house of a hacienda.
hack[1] (hăk) *v.* **1.** To cut or chop with irregular, heavy blows. **2.** To cough harshly. **3.** *Informal.* To manage successfully. *–n.* **1.** A blow or notch made by hacking. **2.** A tool, as a hoe, used for hacking. **3.** A rough, dry cough. **–hack′er** *n.*
hack[2] (hăk) *n.* **1.** HACKNEY 1. **2.** A decrepit or overworked horse. **3.** A vehicle, as a coach or carriage, for hire. **4.** One hired to do routine work, esp. writing by formula. **5. a.** A taxicab. **b.** A taxicab driver. *–v.* **1.** To drive a taxicab. **2.** To do routine writing for hire. *–adj.* **1.** By or for a hack. **2.** Hackneyed.
hack•ie (hăk′ē) *n. Slang.* A taxi driver.
hack•le (hăk′əl) *n.* **1.** One of the long, slender, often glossy feathers on the neck of a bird, esp. of a rooster. **2. hackles. a.** The hairs at the back of the neck, esp. of a dog, that can rise and bristle with anger or fear. **b.** Temper : dander.
hack•ney (hăk′nē) *n., pl.* **-neys. 1.** A horse for ordinary driving or riding. **2.** A carriage or coach available for hire. *–v.* To overuse to the point of triteness.
hack•neyed (hăk′nēd) *adj.* Grown stale through overuse : banal.
hack•saw (hăk′sô′) *n.* A fine toothed saw in a frame, used for cutting metal.
had (hăd) *v. p.t. & p.p. of* HAVE.
had•dock (hăd′ək) *n., pl.* **-dock** or **-docks.** A food fish, *Melanogrammus aeglefinus,* of N Atlantic waters.
Ha•des (hā′dēz) *n.* **1.** *Gk. Myth.* The abode of the dead. **2.** *often* **hades.** Hell.
hadj (hăj) *n. var. of* HAJ.
had•n't (hăd′nt). Had not.
Hadri•an (hā′drē-ən). A.D. 76–138. Roman emperor (117–138).

haf•ni•um (hăf′nē-əm) *n. Symbol* **Hf** A silvery metallic element used esp. in nuclear reactor control rods.
haft (hăft) *n.* A hilt or handle, as of a weapon or tool.
hag (hăg) *n.* **1.** A repulsively ugly old woman. **2.** A witch. **–hag′gish** *adj.*
Hag•ga•dah (hə-gä′də, -gô′-) *n., pl.* **-doth** (-dōt′, -dôth′). Traditional Jewish literature, esp. the nonlegal part of the Talmud.
Hag•ga•i (hăg′ē-ī′, hăg′ī′) *n.* See BIBLE TABLE.
hag•gard (hăg′ərd) *adj.* Worn-out and exhausted : gaunt. ☆**syns:** CAREWORN, GAUNT, WAN, WORN **–hag′gard•ly** *adv.* **–hag′gard•ness** *n.*
hag•gle (hăg′əl) *v.* **-gled, -gling.** To argue in an attempt to bargain or come to terms. **–hag′gle** *n.* **–hag′gler** *n.*
hag•i•og•ra•phy (hăg′ē-ŏg′rə-fē, hā′jē-) *n., pl.* **-phies. 1.** Biography of saints or revered persons. **2.** An idealizing biography. **–hag′i•og′ra•pher** *n.* **–hag′i•o•graph′ic** (-ə-grăf′ĭk), **hag′i•o•graph′i•cal** *adj.*
Hague (hāg), **The.** De facto cap. of the Netherlands, in the W near the North Sea. *Pop.* 456,886.
Hai•fa (hī′fə). City and port of NW Israel. *Pop.* 229,300.
hai•ku (hī′ko͞o) *n., pl.* **-ku.** An unrhymed Japanese lyric poem having a fixed 3-line 17-syllable form.
hail[1] (hāl) *n.* **1. a.** Precipitation of small, hard pellets of ice and snow. **b.** A hailstone. **2.** Something giving the effect of hail. *–v.* **1.** To fall as hail. **2.** To pour down or forth like hail.
hail[2] (hāl) *v.* **1. a.** To call to in greeting or welcome. **b.** To acclaim with enthusiasm. **2.** To signal in order to catch the attention of <*hail* a taxi> **–hail from.** To come or originate from. *–n.* **1.** A greeting or expression of approval or acclaim. **2.** Earshot. *–interj.* Used to express a greeting or commendation. **–hail′er** *n.*
Hai•le Se•las•sie (hī′lē sə-lăs′ē, -lä′sē). 1892–1975. Emperor of Ethiopia (1930–36, 1941–74); deposed.
hail•stone (hāl′stōn′) *n.* A hard pellet of snow and ice that forms hail.
hail•storm (hāl′stôrm′) *n.* A storm in which there is precipitation of hail.
hair (hâr) *n.* **1. a.** One of the fine, threadlike strands that grow from the skin of mammals or on a plant or insect. **b.** A covering of such strands, as on an animal or the human head. **2.** A very small distance or slender margin. **–haired** *adj.* **–hair′less** *adj.*
hair•breadth (hâr′brĕdth′) *adj.* Extremely close or narrow <a *hairbreadth* getaway> *–n. var. of* HAIRSBREADTH.
hair•brush (hâr′brŭsh′) *n.* A brush for the hair.
hair•cloth (hâr′klôth′, -klŏth′) *n.* A wiry fabric made esp. from horsehair.
hair•cut (hâr′kŭt′) *n.* **1.** A shortening, trimming, or shaping of the hair by cutting. **2.** The style in which hair is cut.
hair•do (hâr′do͞o′) *n., pl.* **-dos.** A coiffure.
hair•dress•er (hâr′drĕs′ər) *n.* One who cuts or styles hair. **–hair′dress′ing** *n.*
hair•line (hâr′līn′) *n.* **1.** The outline of hair growing on the head, esp. at the forehead. **2.** A very slender line.
hair piece *also* **hair•piece** (hâr′pēs′) *n.* A covering or bunch of human or artificial hair used to conceal baldness or shape or supplement a hairdo.
hair•pin (hâr′pĭn′) *n.* A slender, U-shaped pin for holding the hair in place. *–adj.* Doubled back in a U <a *hairpin* curve>
hair-rais•ing (hâr′rā′zĭng) *adj.* Very exciting or horrifying. **–hair′-rais′er** *n.*
hairs•breadth (hârz′brĕdth′) *also* **hair•breadth** (hâr′brĕdth′) *n.* A small space, extent, or margin.
hair•split•ting (hâr′splĭt′ĭng) *n.* The act or process of making petty distinctions. **–hair′split′ter** *n.*
hair•spring (hâr′sprĭng′) *n.* A fine coiled spring alternately wound and unwound by the balance wheel of a timepiece.
hair•style (hâr′stīl′) *n.* A way of wearing the hair : hairdo. **–hair′styl′ing** *n.* **–hair′styl′ist** *n.*
hair trigger *n.* A gun trigger set to react to the slightest pressure.
hair-trig•ger (hâr′trĭg′ər) *adj.* Reacting immediately to the smallest provocation.
hair•y (hâr′ē) *adj.* **-i•er, -i•est. 1.** Covered with or as if with hair. **2.** Of or suggestive of hair. **3.** *Slang.* Causing anxiety, as from difficulty or danger. **–hair′i•ness** *n.*
Hai•ti (hā′tē). Country of the West Indies, on the W part of Hispaniola. *Cap.* Port-au-Prince. *Pop.* 5,040,000. **–Hai′tian** *adj.* & *n.*
haj *or* **hajj** *also* **hadj** (hăj) *n.* A pilgrimage to Mecca made during Ramadan.
hake (hāk) *n., pl.* **hake** *or* **hakes.** A marine food fish of the genera *Merluccius* and *Urophycis,* resembling the cod.
hal•berd (hăl′bərd) *n.* A medieval weapon consisting of both an axlike blade and a steel spike on the end of a long pole.
hal•cy•on (hăl′sē-ən) *adj.* **1.** Calm and tranquil. **2.** Prosperous.
hale[1] (hāl) *adj.* **hal•er, hal•est.** Not infirm : healthy and robust. **–hale′ness** *n.*
hale[2] (hāl) *v.* **haled, hal•ing.** To force to go <*haled* us into court>
Hale (hāl). **Nathan.** 1755–76. Amer. army officer; hanged by the British.
ha•ler (hä′lər, -lĕr′) *n., pl.* **-lers** *or* **-le•ru** (-lə-ro͞o′). See *crown* at CURRENCY TABLE.
half (hăf, häf) *n., pl.* **halves** (hăvz, hävz). **1.** Either of 2 equal parts composing a whole. **2.** A part of something approx. equivalent to what remains. **3.** Either of the 2 playing periods that make up a game, as in football. *–adj.* **1.** Being one of 2 equal parts composing a whole. **2.** Being nearly a half. **3.** Being partial or incomplete <a *half* smile> **–half** *adv.*
half•back (hăf′băk′, häf′-) *n.* **1.** *Football.* Either of the 2 players who, along with the fullback and quarterback, make up the offensive backfield. **2.** A player positioned behind the front line in various sports.
half-baked (hăf′bākt′, häf′-) *adj.* **1.** Not fully baked. **2.** *Informal.* **a.** Not sufficiently thought out. **b.** Lacking common sense.
half boot *n.* A low boot whose top comes to just above the ankle.
half-breed (hăf′brēd′, häf′-) *n.* One having parents of different racial groups. **–half′-breed′** *adj.*
half brother *n.* A brother related through only 1 parent.
half-caste (hăf′kăst′, häf′-) *n.* A person of mixed racial descent : half-breed. **–half′-caste′** *adj.*
half•cocked (hăf′kŏkt′, häf′-) *adj. Informal.* Not well thought out : ill-conceived. **–half′-cocked′** *adv.*
half•heart•ed (hăf′här′tĭd, häf′-) *adj.* Lacking interest, spirit, or enthusiasm. **–half′heart′ed•ly** *adv.* **–half′heart′ed•ness** *n.*
half-life (hăf′līf′, häf′-) *n. Physics.* The time required for half of something to undergo a specific process, esp. for half the nuclei in a sample of radioactive material to undergo decay.
half-mast (hăf′măst′, häf′-) *n.* The position approx. halfway up a pole at which a flag is flown to symbolize mourning or to signal distress. **–half′-mast′** *v.*
half-moon (hăf′mo͞on′, häf′-) *n.* **1.** The moon with just half its disk visibly lighted. **2.** Something crescent-shaped. **–half′moon′** *adj.*
half•pen•ny (hā′pə-nē, hāp′nē) *n., pl.* **half•pence** (hā′pəns) *or* **half•pen•nies.** A British coin worth one half of a penny.
half sister *n.* A sister related through only 1 parent.
half sole *n.* A shoe or boot sole extending from the arch to the toe.
half step *n. Mus.* A semitone.
half-track (hăf′trăk′, häf′-) *n.* A lightly armored military vehicle propelled by continuous rear treads.
half-truth (hăf′tro͞oth′, häf′-) *n.* A statement usu. meant to deceive by mixing truth and falsehood.
half•way (hăf′wā′, häf′-) *adj.* **1.** In the middle between 2 points or states. **2.** Partial. **–half′way′** *adv.*
halfway house *n.* **1.** A stopping place, as an inn, at the midpoint of a journey. **2.** A rehabilitation center where people who have left an institution are helped to readjust to the outside world.
half-wit (hăf′wĭt′, häf′-) *n.* **1.** A mentally deficient person. **2.** A stupid or silly person. **–half′-wit′ted** *adj.* **–half′-wit′ted•ly** *adv.* **–half′-wit′ted•ness** *n.*
hal•i•but (hăl′ə-bət, hŏl′-) *n., pl.* **-but** *or* **-buts.** Any of several large, edible flatfishes of the genus *Hippoglossus* and related genera, of N Atlantic or Pacific waters.
Hal•i•fax (hăl′ə-făks′). Cap. of N.S., Canada, on the S coast. *Pop.* 117,882.
hal•ite (hăl′īt′, hā′līt′) *n.* Salt in large crystals or masses : rock salt.
hal•i•to•sis (hăl′ĭ-tō′sĭs) *n.* A condition marked by bad-smelling breath.
hall (hôl) *n.* **1. a.** A corridor : passageway. **b.** A large vestibule or lobby. **2. a.** A large public building used esp. for meetings and entertainment. **b.** A large room for such events. **3.** A school, college, or university building. **4. a.** The main residence on a large estate. **b.** The main dwelling of a medieval king or nobleman.
hal•lah (KHä′lə, hä′-) *n. var. of* CHALLAH.
hal•le•lu•jah (hăl′ə-lo͞o′yə) *interj.* Used to express praise, joy, or thanksgiving. *–n.* The exclamation of "hallelujah."
hall•mark (hôl′märk′) *n.* **1.** A mark stamped on an article, esp. of gold or silver, to indicate purity, quality, or origin. **2.** An indication of quality or superiority. **3.** A distinctive characteristic.
hal•low (hăl′ō) *v.* **1.** To sanctify : consecrate. **2.** To honor : revere.

Hal•low•een *also* **Hal•low•e'en** (hăl'ō-ēn', hŏl'-) *n.* Oct. 31, the eve of All Saints' Day, celebrated esp. by children.
hal•lu•ci•na•tion (hə-lo͞o'sə-nā'shən) *n.* **1. a.** An illusion of perceiving something that is nonexistent. **b.** Something, as an image or vision, perceived in a hallucination. **2.** A delusion. **–hal•lu'ci•nate'** *v.* **–hal•lu'ci•na'tion•al** *adj.* **–hal•lu'ci•na'tive** *adj.* **–hal•lu'ci•na•to'ry** (-nə-tôr'ē, -tōr'ē) *adj.*
hal•lu•ci•no•gen (hə-lo͞o'sə-nə-jən) *n.* An agent or substance, esp. a drug, that causes hallucination. **–hal•lu'ci•no•gen'ic** *adj.*
hall•way (hôl'wā') *n.* HALL 1.
ha•lo (hā'lō) *n., pl.* **-los** or **-loes. 1.** A circular band of colored light around a shining body, as the sun or moon. **2.** A circle of light around the head, as in a depiction of a saint. **3.** An aura of glory. **–ha'lo** *v.*
hal•o•gen (hăl'ə-jən) *n.* One of a set of 5 physically and chemically similar nonmetallic elements including fluorine, chlorine, bromine, iodine, and astatine. **–ha•log'e•nous** (hə-lŏj'ə-nəs) *adj.*
halt¹ (hôlt) *n.* **1.** An esp. temporary suspension of movement or progress. **2.** A stop. *–v.* To come or bring to a halt.
halt² (hôlt) *v.* **1.** To hesitate. **2.** To walk with a limp. *–adj. Archaic.* Lame.
hal•ter (hôl'tər) *n.* **1.** A rope or leather strap fitted around the neck or head of an animal, as a horse, to hitch or lead it. **2.** A noose for hanging a condemned person. **3.** A woman's bodice tied behind the neck and across the back. *–v.* **1.** To fit (an animal) with a halter. **2.** To control with or as if with a halter : restrain.
halt•ing (hôl'tĭng) *adj.* **1.** Lame : hobbling. **2.** Defective. **3.** Hesitant.
halve (hăv, häv) *v.* **halved, halv•ing. 1.** To divide into 2 equal portions. **2.** To decrease by half. **3.** *Informal.* To apportion or share equally.
halves (hăvz, hävz) *n. pl. of* HALF.
hal•yard (hăl'yərd) *n.* A rope for hoisting or lowering a sail, flag, or yard.
ham (hăm) *n.* **1.** A cut of meat from the thigh of a hog. **2.** The back of the knee or thigh. **3.** *Slang.* A performer who acts with unnecessary exaggeration. **4.** *Informal.* An amateur radio operator. *–v.* **hammed, ham•ming.** To overact or exaggerate.
ham•a•dry•ad (hăm'ə-drī'əd) *n., pl.* **-ads** or **-a•des** (-ə-dēz'). *Gk. & Rom. Myth.* A wood nymph : dryad.
Ham•burg (hăm'bûrg'). City of N West Germany, on the Elbe. *Pop.* 1,653,043.
ham•burg•er (hăm'bûr'gər) *also* **ham•burg** (-bûrg') *n.* **1. a.** Ground beef. **b.** A cooked patty of ground beef. **2.** A roll or bun containing a hamburger.
Ham•il•ton (hăm'əl-tən). City of SE Ont., Canada, at the W end of Lake Ontario. *Pop.* 305,538.
Hamilton, Alexander. 1755–1804. Amer. Revolutionary statesman.
ham•let (hăm'lĭt) *n.* A small usu. rural village or town.
ham•mer (hăm'ər) *n.* **1.** A hand tool with a heavy head, used to strike or pound forcibly. **2.** A tool or device like a hammer in function or shape, esp.: **a.** The part of a gun that strikes the firing pin or percussion cap, causing it to go off. **b.** Any of the padded wooden pieces that strike the strings of a piano. *–v.* **1.** To strike or pound forcibly. **2.** To flatten or shape with or as if with a hammer. **–ham'mer•er** *n.*
ham•mer•head (hăm'ər-hĕd') *n.* **1.** The heavy striking head of a hammer. **2.** A large, predatory shark of the genus *Sphyrna,* whose eyes are set in long, fleshy projections at the sides of the head.
hammer lock *also* **ham•mer•lock** (hăm'ər-lŏk') *n.* A wrestling hold in which the opponent's arm is twisted upward behind his back.
ham•mer•toe (hăm'ər-tō') *n.* A malformed toe that is bent downward.
ham•mock (hăm'ək) *n.* A hanging bed or couch of strong fabric or heavy netting suspended between 2 supports, as trees.
Ham•mu•ra•bi (hä'mo͞o-rä'bē). 18th cent. B.C. Babylonian king and lawgiver.
ham•per¹ (hăm'pər) *v.* To restrict or impede the movement or progress of.
ham•per² (hăm'pər) *n.* A large, usu. covered receptacle.
ham•ster (hăm'stər) *n.* Any of several rodents of the family Cricetidae, esp. *Mesocricetus auratus,* with large cheek pouches and a short tail, often kept as a pet.
ham•string (hăm'strĭng') *n.* **1.** Either of 2 large tendons at the back of the human knee. **2.** The large tendon at the back of the hind leg of a 4-footed animal. *–v.* **1.** To cripple by severing the hamstring. **2.** To make ineffectual : frustrate.
hand (hănd) *n.* **1.** The part of the arm below the wrist, consisting of the palm, 4 fingers, and an opposable thumb and used esp. for grasping. **2.** A unit of length equal to 4 in., or 10.16 cm, used esp. to indicate the height of a horse. **3.** Something shaped or functioning like the human hand. **4.** A pointer on a circular dial, as of a clock, meter, or gauge. **5.** Lateral direction <at your left *hand*> **6.** A style or sample of handwriting. **7.** A burst of applause. **8.** Assistance : aid. **9. a.** The cards dealt to or held by a player. **b.** A round of play <a *hand* of bridge> **10.** A laborer, worker, or employee. **11.** A member of a group or crew, as of a ship. **12. a.** A participant. **b.** A specialist in a given activity. **13.** Ability : skill. **14.** *often* **hands. a.** Possession : keeping. **b.** Control : dominion. **15.** A source, esp. of information <got the story at first *hand*> **16.** A promise, esp. to marry. *–v.* **1.** To give or convey with or as if with the hand. **2.** To help or direct with the hands. **–hand down. 1.** To pass on, as from parent to offspring. **2.** To deliver (a verdict) officially. **–hand out. 1.** To give out : distribute. **2.** To administer (e.g., punishment). **–hands down. 1.** With ease : effortlessly. **2.** Without any dispute.
hand•bag (hănd'băg') *n.* A small bag for carrying money and small personal articles : pocketbook.
hand•ball (hănd'bôl') *n.* **1.** A court game in which the players hit a small rubber ball against a wall with their hands. **2.** The ball used in handball.
hand•bar•row (hănd'băr'ō) *n.* A flat framework or litter with carrying poles at each end.
hand•bill (hănd'bĭl') *n.* A hand-distributed printed sheet or leaflet.
hand•book (hănd'bo͝ok') *n.* A reference book or manual giving information or instruction on a specific subject.
hand•car (hănd'kär') *n.* A small open railroad car propelled either by a small motor or by hand.
hand•clasp (hănd'klăsp') *n.* A handshake.
hand•craft (hănd'krăft') *v.* To fashion by hand. *–n. var. of* HANDICRAFT.
hand•cuff (hănd'kŭf') *n. often* **handcuffs.** A pair of circular metal shackles chained together that can be fastened around the wrists. *–v.* **1.** To shackle with handcuffs. **2.** To make ineffective.
hand•ed (hăn'dĭd) *adj.* **1.** Using or designed for 1 hand in preference to the other <right-*handed*> **2.** Requiring a certain number of people, as certain card games.
Han•del (hăn'dl), **George Frederick.** 1685–1759. German-born English composer.
hand•ful (hănd'fo͝ol') *n., pl.* **-fuls. 1.** The amount or number that can be held in the hand. **2.** A small, undesignated amount or number. **3.** *Informal.* One hard to control or manage easily.
hand•gun (hănd'gŭn') *n.* A gun that can be grasped and fired with 1 hand : pistol.
hand•i•cap (hăn'dē-kăp') *n.* **1. a.** A competition in which advantages or penalties are given to individual contestants to equalize the odds. **b.** Such an advantage or penalty. **2.** A physiological or mental disability that increases the difficulty of normal achievement. **3.** An impediment : obstacle. *–v.* **-capped, -cap•ping. 1.** To give a handicap to (e.g., a competitor). **2.** To hinder : impede.
hand•i•craft (hăn'dē-krăft') *also* **hand•craft** (hănd'krăft') *n.* **1.** Skill with the hands. **2. a.** A trade, craft, or occupation requiring manual skillfulness. **b.** Skilled work produced by hand.
hand•i•work (hăn'dē-wûrk') *n.* **1.** Work accomplished by hand. **2.** Work performed by a single individual. **3.** The result of one's actions or efforts.
hand•ker•chief (hăng'kər-chĭf, -chēf') *n.* **1.** A small piece of usu. square cloth used esp. to wipe the face or blow the nose. **2.** A kerchief or scarf.
han•dle (hăn'dl) *v.* **-dled, -dling. 1.** To touch, pick up, manipulate, or hold with the hands. **2.** To administer to or represent : manage <*handle* a prizefighter> **3.** To sell or deal in. ☆***syns:*** MANIPULATE, PLY, WIELD *–n.* **1.** A part that is held or controlled with the hand. **2.** *Slang.* One's name. **–han'dler** *n.*
han•dle•bar (hăn'dl-bär') *n. often* **handlebars.** A curved bar for steering, as on a bicycle, with a handle at either end.
hand•made (hănd'mād') *adj.* Made or prepared by hand or a hand operation.
hand•maid (hănd'mād') *also* **hand•maid•en** (-mād'n) *n.* A woman attendant or servant.
hand-me-down (hănd'mē-doun') *n.* Something, as clothing, used by a person after being outgrown or discarded by another. **–hand'-me-down'** *adj.*
hand•out (hănd'out') *n.* **1.** Food, clothing, or cash given to the needy. **2.** A leaflet or folder distributed free of charge : flyer. **3.** A press release, esp. for publicity.
hand-pick (hănd'pĭk') *v.* To select personally and with care.

hand•rail (hănd′rāl′) *n.* A narrow supportive rail gripped with the hand.
hand•set (hănd′sĕt′) *n.* A telephone transmitter and receiver combined in a single unit.
hand•shake (hănd′shāk′) *n.* The clasping of hands by 2 people, as in greeting, farewell, or agreement.
hands-off (hăndz′ôf′, -ŏf′) *adj.* Characterized by noninterference.
hand•some (hăn′səm) *adj.* **-som•er, -som•est. 1.** Very attractive and often striking in appearance. **2.** Liberal : generous <a *handsome* salary> **—hand′some•ly** *adv.* **—hand′some•ness** *n.*
hands-on (hăndz′ŏn′, -ôn′) *adj.* Not theoretical : applied <*hands-on* learning>
hand•spring (hănd′sprĭng′) *n.* An acrobatic feat in which the body flips entirely forward or backward, landing first on the hands, then on the feet.
hand•stand (hănd′stănd′) *n.* The act of supporting the body on the hands with the feet balanced in the air.
hand-to-hand (hănd′tə-hănd′) *adj.* At close quarters, as in fighting.
hand-to-mouth (hănd′tə-mouth′) *adj.* Having or providing barely enough for subsistence.
hand•work (hănd′wûrk′) *n.* Work accomplished by hand.
hand•writ•ing (hănd′rī′tĭng) *n.* **1.** Writing performed with the hand. **2.** The style of writing of an individual.
hand•y (hăn′dē) *adj.* **-i•er, -i•est. 1.** Manually adept. **2.** Easy to reach : accessible. **3. a.** Easy to use. **b.** Useful. **—hand′i•ly** *adv.* **—hand′i•ness** *n.*
hand•y•man (hăn′dē-măn′) *n.* One who does various odd jobs.
hang (hăng) *v.* **hung** (hŭng), **hang•ing. 1.** To attach or be attached from above, unsupported from below. **2.** To suspend or be fastened so as to swing freely on the point of suspension <*hang* a door> **3.** *p.t.* & *p.p.* **hanged** *or* **hung.** To put to death or die by suspension by the neck. **4.** To remain stationary in space : hover. **5. a.** To furnish or decorate by suspending hangings about <*hung* the mantelpiece with holly> **b.** To fasten or attach to a wall <*hang* a picture> **6. a.** To let droop downward <*hang* one's head> **b.** To fit the body in easy lines. **7.** To cause (a jury) to be deadlocked. **—hang around.** *Informal.* **1.** To linger or loiter aimlessly. **2.** To associate. **—hang in.** *Informal.* To persevere. **—hang on. 1.** To cling firmly to something. **2.** To persist : persevere. **3.** To keep a telephone connection open. **—hang out.** *Slang.* To spend one's time in a particular place. **—hang up. 1.** To hamper : impepe. **2.** To complete a telephone conversation by replacing the receiver on its cradle. —*n.* **1.** The manner in which something hangs. **2.** Particular meaning or import. **3.** *Informal.* The proper way of using or doing something.
han•gar (hăng′ər) *n.* A building for sheltering and repairing aircraft.
hang•dog (hăng′dôg′, -dŏg′) *adj.* **1.** Disgraced or guilty. **2.** Downcast : abject.
hang•er (hăng′ər) *n.* **1.** A person who hangs something. **2.** A frame, hook, or strap on which something can be hung or to which something hangs.
hang•er-on (hăng′ər-ŏn′, -ôn′) *n., pl.* **hang•ers-on.** A sycophant : parasite.
hang glider *n.* A kite-shaped device from which a rider hangs suspended in a harness while gliding through the air. **—hang gliding** *n.*

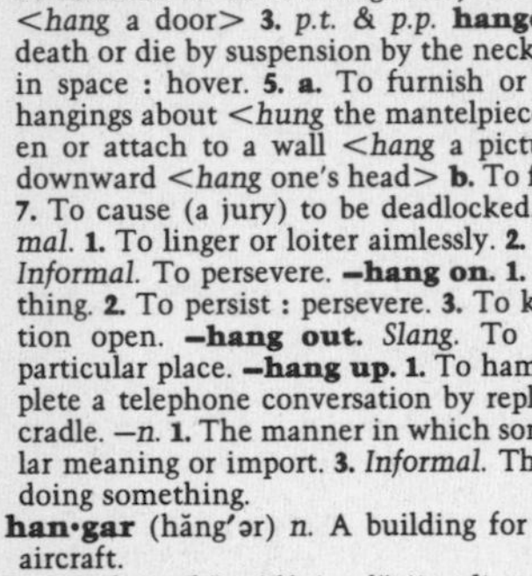

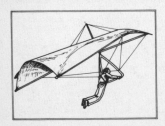

hang glider

hang•ing (hăng′ĭng) *n.* **1.** Execution by suspending by the neck, esp. on a gallows. **2.** *often* **hangings.** Something hung, as curtains or tapestries.
hang•man (hăng′mən) *n.* One employed to execute condemned persons by hanging.
hang•nail (hăng′nāl′) *n.* A small bit of dead skin hanging loose at the side or bottom of a fingernail.
hang•out (hăng′out′) *n.* A frequently visited place : haunt.
hang•o•ver (hăng′ō′vər) *n.* **1.** Disagreeable aftereffects of excessive alcohol consumption. **2.** One that remains from an earlier time : vestige.
hang-up (hăng′ŭp′) *n. Informal.* **1.** An emotional or psychological problem or inhibition. **2.** An impediment or obstacle.
hank (hăngk) *n.* A coil or loop, as of hair or yarn.
han•ker (hăng′kər) *v.* To have a craving : yearn. **—han′ker•er** *n.* **—han′ker•ing** *n.*
han•ky-pan•ky (hăng′kē-păng′kē) *n. Slang.* **1.** Devious or dubious activity. **2.** Foolish talk or action.
Han•ni•bal (hăn′ə-bəl). 247?–183 B.C. Carthaginian general.
Han•no•ver (hä-nō′vər, -fər) *or* **Han•o•ver** (hăn′ō′vər). City of N West Germany, SE of Bremen. *Pop.* 535,854.
Ha•noi (hä-noi′, hă-). Cap. of Vietnam, in the NE. *Pop.* 2,000,000.
han•som (hăn′səm) *n.* A 2-wheeled horse-drawn carriage with the driver's seat elevated in back.
Ha•nuk•kah *or* **Ha•nu•kah** (KHä′nə-kə, hä′-) *n. vars. of* CHANUKAH.
hao (hou) *n., pl.* **hao.** See *dong* at CURRENCY TABLE.
hao•le (hou′lē, -lā) *n.* A person, esp. a Caucasian, who is not a native Hawaiian.
hap (hăp) *n.* **1.** Luck : chance. **2.** An event : happening.
hap•haz•ard (hăp-hăz′ərd) *adj.* Marked by chance : hit-or-miss. **—hap•haz′ard•ly** *adv.* **—hap•haz′ard•ness** *n.*
hap•less (hăp′lĭs) *adj.* Unlucky : unfortunate. **—hap′less•ly** *adv.* **—hap′less•ness** *n.*
hap•loid (hăp′loid′) *adj.* With the number of chromosomes in the normal germ cell equal to half the number in the normal body cell. **—hap′loid′** *n.*
hap•ly (hăp′lē) *adv.* By chance.
hap•pen (hăp′ən) *v.* **1.** To come to pass : occur. **2.** To occur by chance. **3.** To discover something by chance. **4.** To appear or turn up by chance.
hap•pen•ing (hăp′ə-nĭng) *n.* **1.** An event, esp. an important one. **2.** An often spontaneously staged event or performance.
hap•pen•stance (hăp′ən-stăns′) *n.* A chance event.
hap•py (hăp′ē) *adj.* **-pi•er, -pi•est. 1.** Fortunate. **2.** Having, displaying, or marked by pleasure or joy. **3.** Fitting : appropriate. **4.** Pleased and willing. **5.** Unduly enthusiastic or concerned <money-*happy*> **—hap′pi•ly** *adv.* **—hap′pi•ness** *n.*
hap•py-go-luck•y (hăp′ē-gō-lŭk′ē) *adj.* Carefree.
happy hour *n.* The part of the day when a bar offers drinks at lower prices.
ha•ra-ki•ri (hä′rə-kîr′ē, hăr′ə-) *n.* Ritual suicide by disembowelment.
ha•rangue (hə-răng′) *n.* **1.** A long, bombastic speech. **2.** A tirade. **—ha•rangue′** *v.* **—ha•rangu′er** *n.*
ha•rass (hə-răs′, hăr′əs) *v.* **1.** To annoy or disturb persistently. **2.** To make exhausted. **3.** To wear out (an enemy) by frequent attacks. **—ha•rass′er** *n.* **—ha•rass′ment** *n.*
Har•bin (här′bĭn). City of NE China, in Manchuria. *Pop.* 2,400,000.
har•bin•ger (här′bən-jər) *n.* A precursor : herald.
har•bor (här′bər) *n.* **1.** A sheltered anchorage for ships. **2.** A place of shelter : refuge. —*v.* **1.** To provide with shelter. **2.** To entertain (a thought or feeling). **—har′bor•age** *n.* **—har′bor•er** *n.*
hard (härd) *adj.* **1.** Firmly resistant to pressure <a *hard* shell> **2.** Physically or mentally strong : toughened. **3.** Difficult to perform, comprehend, or endure. **4.** Forceful : intense <a *hard* punch in the nose> **5.** Energetic : diligent. **6.** Severe : harsh. **7.** Callous : unsympathetic. **8.** Oppressive : unjust. **9.** Real : factual. **10.** High in alcoholic content. **11.** Containing salts that hinder the lathering of soap <*hard* water> **12.** Backed by bullion : stable <*hard* currency> **13.** Physically addictive and detrimental <Heroin is a *hard* drug.> **—hard up.** *Informal.* Short of cash. **—hard** *adv.* **—hard′ness** *n.*
hard•back (härd′băk′) *adj.* Bound between hard rather than paper covers. **—hard′back′** *n.*
hard•ball (härd′bôl′) *n.* Baseball.
hard-bit•ten (härd′bĭt′n) *adj.* Seasoned or toughened by hard experience.
hard-boiled (härd′boild′) *adj.* **1.** Cooked solid by boiling in the shell. **2.** *Informal.* Callous : unsympathetic.
hard•bound (härd′bound′) *adj.* Hardback.
hard copy *n.* Readable printed copy of the output of a computer.
hard-core *also* **hard•core** (härd′kôr′) *adj.* **1.** Obstinately resistant to change : inveterate <a *hard-core* offender> **2.** Regarded as constituting a stubborn social problem <*hard-core* unemployment> **3.** Extremely explicit. Used of pornography.
hard•cov•er (härd′kŭv′ər) *adj.* Hardback.
hard•en (här′dn) *v.* **1.** To make or become hard or harder. **2.** To make or become physically or mentally tough. **3.** To make or

become callous or unsympathetic. ☆**syns:** CAKE, CONCRETE, CONGEAL, DRY, PETRIFY, SET, SOLIDIFY **–hard′en·er** *n.*
hard hat *n.* **1. a.** A rigid head covering worn for protection by construction workers. **b.** *Informal.* A construction worker. **2.** *Informal.* An ultraconservative person. **–hard′hat′** *adj.*
hard·head·ed (härd′hĕd′ĭd) *adj.* **1.** Willfully stubborn. **2.** Coldly practical or realistic. **–hard′head′ed·ly** *adv.* **–hard′head′ed·ness** *n.*
hard·heart·ed (härd′här′tĭd) *adj.* Unfeeling : heartless. **–hard′heart′ed·ly** *adv.* **–hard′heart′ed·ness** *n.*
har·di·hood (här′dē-ho͝od′) *n.* **1. a.** Unwavering courage. **b.** Audacious boldness. **2.** Vitality : vigor.
Har·ding (här′dĭng), **Warren Gamaliel.** 1865–1923. 29th U.S. President (1921–23); died in office.
hard landing *n.* A landing by impact of a spacecraft lacking devices, as retrorockets, to slow it down.
hard line *n.* An inflexible position, as on an issue. **–hard′-line′, hard′line′** *adj.* **–hard′-lin′er** *n.*
hard·ly (härd′lē) *adv.* **1.** By a very little : just. **2.** Almost certainly not.
hard news *n.* News dealing with significant or serious topics and events.
hard-nosed (härd′nōzd′) *adj.* Stubborn : hard-headed.
hard palate *n.* The fairly hard, bony forward part of the palate forming the roof of the mouth.
hard·pan (härd′păn′) *n.* A compact layer of hard clay or subsoil.
hard rock *n.* Rock music that features harsh, amplified sound and electronic distortion, modulations, and feedback.
hard sell *n.* *Informal.* A sales or advertising method involving aggressive, high-pressure promotion.
hard-shell (härd′shĕl′) *also* **hard-shelled** (-shĕld′) *adj.* **1.** Having a thick or hardened shell. **2.** Uncompromising : inflexible.
hard·ship (härd′shĭp′) *n.* **1.** Extreme privation : suffering. **2.** A source of privation or suffering.
hard·tack (härd′tăk′) *n.* A hard biscuit made with flour and water.
hard·top (härd′tŏp′) *n.* A car with a rigid top designed to suggest a convertible.
hard·ware (härd′wâr′) *n.* **1.** Metal ware, as machine parts, tools, and utensils. **2. a.** The mechanical and electronic components of a computer or spacecraft. **b.** The machines and physical apparatus involved in an industrial, technological, or military operation or system.
hard·wood (härd′wo͝od′) *n.* **1.** The wood of a broad-leaved flowering tree as distinguished from that of a tree with needles and cones. **2.** The tree itself.
har·dy (här′dē) *adj.* **-di·er, -di·est. 1.** Stalwart and robust. **2.** Able to survive very unfavorable conditions, as cold weather <*hardy* perennial plants> **3.** Courageous : intrepid. **4.** Boldly daring : audacious. **–har′di·ly** *adv.* **–har′di·ness** *n.*
Har·dy (här′dē), **Thomas.** 1840–1928. English novelist.
hare (hâr) *n.* Any of various mammals of the family Leporidae, esp. of the genus *Lepus,* related to the rabbits but with longer ears and legs.
hare·brained (hâr′brānd′) *adj.* Silly : foolish <a *harebrained* notion>
hare·lip (hâr′lĭp′) *n.* A congenital condition in which the upper lip is split. **–hare′lipped′** *adj.*
har·em (hâr′əm, hăr′-) *n.* **1.** A house or rooms for the women of a Moslem household. **2.** The women living in a harem.
hark (härk) *v.* To listen closely. **–hark back.** To return to an earlier subject or circumstance.
har·le·quin (här′lə-kwĭn, -kĭn) *n.* A clown : jester. *–adj.* Patterned with vividly colored diamond shapes.
har·lot (här′lət) *n.* A prostitute. **–har′lot·ry** (-lə-trē) *n.*
harm (härm) *n.* **1.** Physical or emotional injury or damage. **2.** Hurt : wickedness. *–v.* To cause harm to : hurt. ☆**syns:** DAMAGE, DETRIMENT, HURT, INJURY **–harm′ful** *adj.* **–harm′ful·ly** *adv.* **–harm′ful·ness** *n.* **–harm′less** *adj.* **–harm′less·ly** *adv.* **–harm′less·ness** *n.*
har·mon·ic (här-mŏn′ĭk) *adj.* **1.** Of or relating to musical harmony or harmonics. **2.** Marked by musical harmony : harmonious. *–n.* **1.** A higher tone in a complex musical tone. **2. harmonics** (*sing. in number*). The study of the physical characteristics of musical sound. **–har·mon′i·cal·ly** *adv.*
har·mon·i·ca (här-mŏn′ĭ-kə) *n.* A small, rectangular musical instrument consisting of a series of tuned metal reeds vibrated by the player's breath.
har·mo·ni·ous (här-mō′nē-əs) *adj.* **1.** Characterized by accord and agreement. **2.** Having components agreeably combined. **3.** Pleasing to the ear : melodious. **–har·mo′ni·ous·ly** *adv.*
har·mo·ni·um (här-mō′nē-əm) *n.* A keyboard wind instrument with free metal reeds actuated by a bellows.
har·mo·ny (här′mə-nē) *n., pl.* **-nies. 1.** Accord or agreement, as of feeling or opinion. **2.** An agreeable combination of component parts. **3.** The combination of musical tones into chords and progressions of chords. ☆**syns:** CONCORD, RAPPORT, UNITY **–har′mo·ni·za′tion** *n.* **–har′mo·nize′** *v.* **–har′mo·niz′er** *n.*
har·ness (här′nĭs) *n.* **1.** The straps and tackle other than a yoke by which a draft animal pulls an implement or vehicle. **2.** Something resembling a harness. *–v.* **1.** To equip (e.g., a draft animal) with a harness. **2.** To control and utilize <*harness* water power> **–har′ness·er** *n.*
harp (härp) *n.* A musical instrument consisting of a triangular upright frame with strings plucked with the fingers. *–v.* To play a harp. **–harp on (***or* **upon).** To write or talk about excessively and tiresomely. **–harp′ist** *n.*
har·poon (här-po͞on′) *n.* A spear with a barbed head used in hunting whales and large fish. **–har·poon′** *v.*
harp·si·chord (härp′sĭ-kôrd′) *n.* A pianolike keyboard instrument whose strings are plucked by means of quills or leather plectrums. **–harp′si·chord′ist** *n.*
har·py (här′pē) *n., pl.* **-pies. 1.** A shrewish or vicious woman. **2.** A predatory person.
har·ri·dan (hăr′ĭ-dn) *n.* A mean, scolding old woman : shrew.
har·ri·er[1] (hăr′ē-ər) *n.* **1.** One that harries. **2.** A slender, narrow-winged hawk of the genus *Circus* that preys on small animals.
har·ri·er[2] (hăr′ē-ər) *n.* **1.** One of a breed of small hounds orig. trained to hunt rabbits. **2.** A cross-country runner.
Har·ri·son (hăr′ĭ-sən). **1. William Henry.** 1773–1841. 9th U.S. President (1841); died in office. **2. Benjamin.** 1833–1901. 23rd U.S. President (1889–93).
har·row (hăr′ō) *n.* An implement with sharp teeth or upright disks for breaking up and smoothing soil. *–v.* **1.** To pulverize (soil) with a harrow. **2.** To distress greatly.
har·ry (hăr′ē) *v.* **-ried, -ry·ing. 1.** To raid : pillage. **2.** To harass.
harsh (härsh) *adj.* **1.** Disagreeable, esp. to the ear. **2.** Extremely severe. **–harsh′ly** *adv.* **–harsh′ness** *n.*
hart (härt) *n., pl.* **harts** *or* **hart.** A fully grown male deer.
Hart·ford (härt′fərd). Cap. of Conn., in the NC part. *Pop.* 136,392.
har·um-scar·um (hâr′əm-skâr′əm, hăr′əm-skăr′əm) *adj.* Irresponsible : reckless. **–har′um-scar′um** *adv.*
har·vest (här′vĭst) *n.* **1.** The act or process of gathering a crop. **2. a.** A ripe crop. **b.** The season for gathering crops. **3.** The result of an action. *–v.* **1.** To reap (a crop). **2.** To acquire as if by gathering. **–har′vest·er** *n.*
has (hăz) *v. 3rd person sing. present tense of* HAVE.
has-been (hăz′bĭn′) *n.* *Informal.* A person who is no longer successful, useful, effective, or popular.
hash[1] (hăsh) *n.* **1.** A usu. fried or baked mixture of chopped meat and potatoes. **2.** A haphazard mixture : hodgepodge. *–v.* **1.** To chop up into small pieces. **2.** *Informal.* To make a mess of. **b.** To discuss carefully : review.
hash[2] (hăsh) *n.* *Slang.* Hashish.
hash·ish (hăsh′ēsh′, -ĭsh) *n.* A dry, resinous extract prepared from the hemp plant and used as a mild narcotic.
has·n't (hăz′ənt). Has not.
hasp (hăsp) *n.* A hinged fastener for a door that is passed over a staple and secured by a pin, bolt, or padlock.
Has·sid (KHä′sĭd) *n. var. of* CHASSID.
has·sle (hăs′əl) *n.* *Slang.* **1.** An argument or trivial quarrel. **2.** Bother : nuisance. **–has′sle** *v.*
has·sock (hăs′ək) *n.* A thick, firm cushion used esp. as a footstool.
haste (hāst) *n.* **1.** Swiftness of motion or action. **2.** Excessive eagerness to act. **3.** Rash or precipitate action. **–make haste.** To hurry : hasten.
has·ten (hā′sən) *v.* To move or cause to move rapidly.
hast·y (hā′stē) *adj.* **-i·er, -i·est. 1.** Swift : rapid. **2.** Made or done too quickly and impulsively. **–hast′i·ly** *adv.* **–hast′i·ness** *n.*
hat (hăt) *n.* A covering for the head, esp. one with a crown and brim.
hat·box (hăt′bŏks′) *n.* A usu. round box for storing or carrying a hat.
hatch[1] (hăch) *n.* **1.** A small door or opening, as in a ship's deck or the roof or floor of a building. **2.** A hatchway.
hatch[2] (hăch) *v.* **1.** To come or cause to come forth from an egg. **2.** To cause (an egg) to produce young by incubation. **3.** To devise or contrive (e.g., a secret plot). **–hatch** *n.* **–hatch′er·y** *n.*
hatch[3] (hăch) *v.* To give an effect of shading by etching or drawing fine crossed or parallel lines on. **–hatch** *n.*

hatch•back (hăch′băk′) *n.* An automobile with a sloping back and an upward-opening rear hatch.
hatch•et (hăch′ĭt) *n.* **1.** A small ax with a short handle. **2.** A tomahawk.
hatchet job *n. Slang.* A usu. malicious verbal attack.
hatchet man *n. Slang.* **1.** One hired to kill. **2.** One hired to carry out a disagreeable task or unscrupulous order.
hatch•way (hăch′wā′) *n.* A hatch leading to a hold, compartment, or cellar.
hate (hāt) *v.* **hat•ed, hat•ing. 1.** To feel animosity or hostility toward : detest. **2.** To have distaste for <*hates* waiting in line> ☆***syns:*** ABOMINATE, DESPISE, DETEST, EXECRATE, LOATHE —*n.* **1.** Intense hatred. **2.** An object or target of hatred. **—hate′ful** *adj.* **—hate′ful•ly** *adv.* **—hate′ful•ness** *n.* **—hat′er** *n.*
ha•tred (hā′trĭd) *n.* Deep-seated antagonism or enmity : violent ill will.
hat•ter (hăt′ər) *n.* One who makes, sells, or repairs hats.
hau•berk (hô′bərk) *n.* A long coat of mail.
haugh•ty (hô′tē) *adj.* **-ti•er, -ti•est.** Arrogantly proud : lordly. **—haugh′ti•ly** *adv.* **—haugh′ti•ness** *n.*
haul (hôl) *v.* **1.** To pull, drag, or carry. **2.** To cart or truck. —*n.* **1.** The act of hauling. **2.** The distance over which someone travels or something is transported. **3.** Something hauled. **4.** An amount acquired or collected at 1 time <a *haul* of sardines>
haul•age (hô′lĭj) *n.* **1.** The act or process of hauling. **2.** A charge for hauling.
haunch (hônch, hŏnch) *n.* **1.** The human and animal hip, buttock, and upper thigh. **2.** The loin and leg of a 4-footed animal : hindquarters.
†**haunt** (hônt, hŏnt) *v.* **1.** To appear to or visit in the form of an apparition, as a ghost. **2.** To visit frequently. **3.** To linger in the mind : obsess. —*n.* **1.** A place often visited. **2.** (hănt). *Regional.* A supernatural being, esp. a ghost. **—haunt′ing** *adj.*
haut•boy *or* **haut•bois** (hō′boi′, ō′boi) *n., pl.* **-boys** *or* **-bois** (-boiz′). An oboe.
haute cou•ture (ōt′ ko͞o-to͝or′) *n.* **1.** The designers who create exclusive fashions for women. **2.** The high-fashion clothing created by these designers.
haute cui•sine (ōt′ kwĭ-zēn′) *n.* Artfully prepared, often elaborate cuisine.
hau•teur (hô-tûr′, hō-) *n.* Disdainful arrogance : haughtiness.
Ha•van•a (hə-văn′ə). Cap. of Cuba, in the W. *Pop.* 1,961,674.
have (hăv) *v.* **had, hav•ing, has. 1.** To own as a material possession or as a characteristic, quality, or function. **2.** To maintain a relation to. **3.** To be obliged : must. **4.** To entertain in one's mind. **5. a.** To gain an advantage over. **b.** *Informal.* To deceive or trick. **6.** To engage in sexual relations with. **7.** To store in a given place. **8.** To choose or accept. **9.** To take a portion of. **10.** To contain, consist of, or be made of. **11.** To show or exercise <*have* compassion> **12.** To permit to take place. **13. a.** To cause to be. **b.** To cause to be done. **c.** To persuade or compel. **14.** To undergo the experience of. **15.** To beget or bear (offspring). **16.** To possess competence in. **17.** To welcome as a guest. **18.** Used with a past participle to form the following tenses indicating completed action: **a.** Present perfect <*has* left> **b.** Past perfect <*had* left> **c.** Future perfect <will *have* left> —*n.* One having material wealth. **—have at.** To make an attack on. **—have had it.** To have tolerated all one can. **—have it in for.** To have a grudge against. **—have it out.** To settle, esp. by dispute. **—have to do with.** To associate, deal, or be concerned with.
ha•ven (hā′vən) *n.* **1.** A harbor or anchorage : port. **2.** A place of refuge : sanctuary.
have-not (hăv′nŏt′) *n.* One who is poor or has very limited material wealth.
have•n't (hăv′ənt). Have not.
hav•er•sack (hăv′ər-săk′) *n.* A soldier's or hiker's sack for supplies, carried over the shoulder.
hav•oc (hăv′ək) *n.* **1.** Widespread destruction. **2.** Confusion : chaos. **—cry havoc.** To sound an alarm.
haw[1] (hô) *n.* An utterance used by a speaker who is groping for words. —*v.* To hesitate in speaking.
haw[2] (hô) *n.* **1.** A hawthorn tree or shrub. **2.** The fruit of a hawthorn.
Ha•wai•i (hə-wä′ē, -wä′yə) *also* **Ha•wai•ian Islands** (-wä′yən). State and island group of the U.S., in the C Pacific. *Cap.* Honolulu. *Pop.* 965,000. **—Ha•wai′ian** (-wä′yən) *adj.* & *n.*
Hawaiian guitar *n.* An electric guitar with a long sounding board and 6 to 8 steel strings that are plucked while being pressed with a steel bar.
hawk[1] (hôk) *n.* **1.** Any of various predatory birds of the order Falconiformes and esp. of the genera *Accipiter* and *Buteo,* with a short, hooked bill and strong claws for seizing small prey. **2. a.** One who advocates a warlike foreign policy. **b.** One with an aggressive or pugnacious attitude. **—hawk′ish** *adj.* **—hawk′ish•ly** *adv.* **—hawk′ish•ness** *n.*
hawk[2] (hôk) *v.* To peddle (goods) by calling out. **—hawk′er** *n.*
hawk-eyed (hôk′īd′) *adj.* Having keen eyesight.
haw•ser (hô′zər) *n.* A heavy rope or cable for towing or mooring a ship.
haw•thorn (hô′thôrn′) *n.* A thorny tree or shrub of the genus *Crataegus,* bearing white or pink flowers and red fruit.
Haw•thorne (hô′thôrn′), **Nathaniel.** 1804-64. Amer. author.
hay (hā) *n.* Forage plants, as grass or alfalfa, cut and dried for animal food. —*v.* To prepare herbage for hay.
hay•cock (hā′kŏk′) *n. esp. Brit.* A conical mound of hay.
Hay•dn (hīd′n), **(Franz) Joseph.** 1732–1809. Austrian composer.
Hayes (hāz), **Rutherford Birchard.** 1822–93. 19th U.S. President (1877–81).
hay fever *n.* An acute, severe irritation of the upper respiratory tract and the eyes, caused by an allergy to certain airborne pollens, esp. of ragweed.
hay•fork (hā′fôrk′) *n.* A hand- or machine-powered fork for moving hay.
hay•loft (hā′lôft′,-lŏft′) *n.* A loft in a barn or stable for storing hay.
hay•mow (hā′mou′). **1.** A hayloft. **2.** The hay stored in a haymow.
hay•seed (hā′sēd′) *n.* **1.** Grass seed or bits of chaff that fall from hay. **2.** *Slang.* A yokel : hick.
hay•stack (hā′stăk′) *n.* A large stack of hay stored outdoors.
hay•wire (hā′wīr′) *adj. Informal.* **1.** Not functioning properly : out of order. **2.** Emotionally upset or out of control.
haz•ard (hăz′ərd) *n.* **1.** A chance event : accident. **2.** A chance or source of danger : risk. **3.** An obstacle, as a sand trap or pond, on a golf course. —*v.* To take a chance on : venture. **—haz′ard•ous** *adj.*
haze[1] (hāz) *n.* **1.** A foglike mixture of dust, smoke, and vapor suspended in the air. **2.** A vague or confused state of mind.
†**haze**[2] (hāz) *v.* **hazed, haz•ing. 1.** To harass with silly, disagreeable, or demeaning tasks. **2.** *Regional.* To drive (e.g., cattle) with saddle horses. **—haz′er** *n.*
ha•zel (hā′zəl) *n.* **1.** A shrub or small tree of the genus *Corylus,* bearing edible brown nuts with smooth shells. **2.** A yellowish or light brown. **—ha′zel** *adj.*
ha•zel•nut (hā′zəl-nŭt′) *n.* The edible nut of a hazel.
haz•y (hā′zē) *adj.* **-i•er, -i•est. 1.** Marked by haze or mist. **2.** Not clear : vague. **—haz′i•ly** *adv.* **—haz′i•ness** *n.*
hdqrs. *abbr.* headquarters.
H-bomb (āch′bŏm′) *n.* A hydrogen bomb.
he (hē) *pron.* **1.** The male that is neither the speaker nor the hearer. **2.** Used to refer to a person whose sex is not specified <*He* who laughs last, laughs best.>
He *symbol for* HELIUM.
head (hĕd) *n.* **1.** The uppermost or forwardmost bodily extremity, containing the brain, the principal nerve centers, and the eyes, ears, nose, and mouth. **2 a.** Mind, intellect, or intelligence. **b.** Ability or aptitude. **3.** Calmness : self-control. **4.** Complete freedom to act or choose. **5.** *often* **heads** *(sing. in number).* The obverse side of a coin. **6. a.** An individual : person. **b.** *pl.* **head.** One animal, as within a herd. **7.** One in charge of something : leader. **8.** The first or foremost position. **9.** A critical point : crisis. **10.** A projecting or striking part of something, as a weapon. **11. a.** The higher or upper part of something. **b.** The most important end <the *head* of the table> **12.** Either of 2 interchangeable ends, as of a drum. **13.** Pressure, as of a gas or liquid. **14.** A rounded, compact mass of leaves, as of lettuce, or flowers, as of a daisy or clover. **15.** *Slang.* One who uses drugs habitually. —*adj.* **1.** Of chief importance. **2.** At the front or top. **3.** Coming from in front <a *head* wind> —*v.* **1.** To be in charge of. **2.** To be in the first or foremost position of. **3.** To aim or turn in a given direction. **4.** To set out or proceed. **—over (one's) head. 1.** Beyond one's power to manage or comprehend. **2.** To one of higher rank <went *over my head* to the boss> **—head′ed** *adj.* **—head′less** *adj.*
head•ache (hĕd′āk′) *n.* **1.** An ache in the head. **2.** *Informal.* An annoying or bothersome problem. **—head′ach′y** *adj.*
head•band (hĕd′bănd′) *n.* A band worn on or around the head.
head•board (hĕd′bôrd′, -bōrd′) *n.* A board, frame, or panel that stands at the head of a bed.
head cold *n.* Coryza.
head•dress (hĕd′drĕs′) *n.* An ornamental covering for the head.
head•first (hĕd′fûrst′) *adv.* **1.** With the head foremost : headlong. **2.** Impetuously : recklessly. **—head′first′** *adj.*

head·gear (hĕd′gîr′) *n.* A decorative or protective covering, as a hat or helmet, for the head.
head-hunt·ing (hĕd′hŭn′tĭng) *n.* **1.** The custom of severing and preserving human heads as trophies. **2.** *Slang.* The effort to seek out and engage executive personnel for a company or corporation. **—head′-hunt′er** *n.*
head·ing (hĕd′ĭng) *n.* **1.** Something, as a title, that stands at the head, as of a page or chapter. **2.** The direction in which a ship or aircraft is moving : course.
head·land (hĕd′lənd, -lănd′) *n.* A high ridge of land or rock jutting out into a body of water.
head·light (hĕd′līt′) *n.* A light mounted on the front of an automotive vehicle.
head·line (hĕd′līn′) *n.* The caption or title of a newspaper article or story printed in large type. *—v.* **-lined, -lin·ing. 1.** To provide (e.g., a newspaper article) with a headline. **2.** To serve or present as the star performer. **—head′lin′er** *n.*
head·lock (hĕd′lŏk′) *n.* A wrestling hold in which the head of a wrestler is locked under the arm of another.

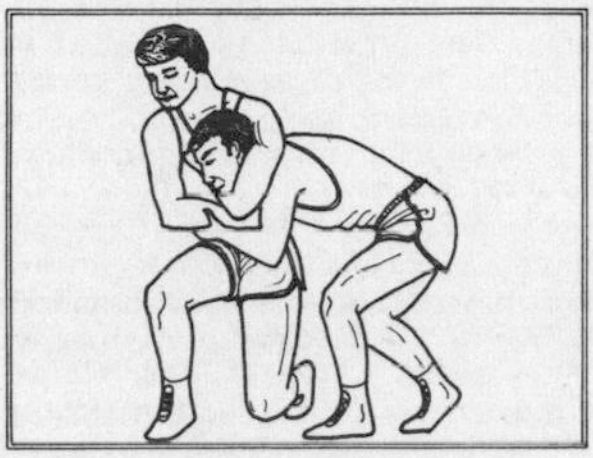

headlock

head·long (hĕd′lông′, -lŏng′) *adv.* **1.** With the head foremost : headfirst. **2. a.** At breakneck speed. **b.** Rashly : impetuously. **—head′long′** *adj.*
head·mas·ter (hĕd′măs′tər) *n.* A man who is a school principal, esp. of a private school.
head·mis·tress (hĕd′mĭs′trĭs) *n.* A woman who is a school principal, esp. of a private school.
head-on (hĕd′ŏn′, -ôn′) *adj.* **1.** Having the front end first in position or contact <a *head-on* collision> **2.** Unwavering : direct. **—head′-on′** *adv.*
head·phone (hĕd′fōn′) *n.* An earphone held over the ear by a headband.
head·piece (hĕd′pēs′) *n.* **1.** A helmet or cap that protects the head. **2.** A headset.
head pin *n.* The central bowling pin in a triangle of tenpins.
head·quar·ters (hĕd′kwôr′tərz) *pl.n.* *(sing. or pl. in number).* **1.** The official center of command, as of a military unit. **2.** An administrative center.
head·rest (hĕd′rĕst′) *n.* **1.** A support for the head, as on a chair back. **2.** A padded cushion at the top of the back of an automobile seat, esp. to prevent whiplash injury.
head·set (hĕd′sĕt′) *n.* A pair of headphones on a headband.
head·stall (hĕd′stôl′) *n.* The part of a horse's bridle that fits over the head.
head·stand (hĕd′stănd′) *n.* The act of supporting the body on the top of the head esp. with the help of the forearms.
head start *n.* An early start that gives an advantage, as to competitors in a race.
head·stone (hĕd′stōn′) *n.* A memorial stone marker at the head of a grave.
head·strong (hĕd′strông′, -strŏng′) *adj.* Rashly willful : obstinate.
head·wait·er (hĕd′wā′tər) *n.* A waiter in charge of a restaurant or hotel dining-room staff.
head·wa·ters (hĕd′wô′tərz, -wŏt′ərz) *pl.n.* The waters that form the source of a river.
head·way (hĕd′wā′) *n.* **1.** Forward movement. **2.** Progress toward a goal. **3.** Clearance beneath an arch or ceiling.
head wind *n.* A wind blowing in the direction directly opposite to the course of an aircraft or ship.
head·work (hĕd′wûrk′) *n.* Work involving mental effort. **—head′work′er** *n.*
head·y (hĕd′ē) *adj.* **-i·er, -i·est. 1.** Tending to intoxicate. **2.** Headstrong. **—head′i·ly** *adv.* **—head′i·ness** *n.*
heal (hēl) *v.* **1.** To restore to sound health. **2.** To set right : remedy. **—heal′a·ble** *adj.* **—heal′er** *n.*
health (hĕlth) *n.* **1.** The overall condition or functioning of an organism at a particular time. **2.** Optimal mental and physical soundness and well-being. **3.** A desire for someone's well-being, often expressed as a toast. **—health′ful** *adj.* **—health′ful·ly** *adv.* **—health′ful·ness** *n.*
health food *n.* A food considered to be very beneficial to a person's health.
health insurance *n.* Insurance against expenses incurred through illness.
health·y (hĕl′thē) *adj.* **-i·er, -i·est. 1.** In a state of good health. **2.** Promoting good health. **3.** Characteristic of good health. **4.** Quite large. **—health′i·ly** *adv.* **—health′i·ness** *n.*
heap (hēp) *n.* **1.** A disorderly or haphazard assortment of things : pile. **2.** *often* **heaps.** *Informal.* A great many. *—v.* **1.** To put, pile, or rise in a heap. **2.** To fill to excess. **3.** To bestow lavishly.
hear (hîr) *v.* **heard** (hûrd), **hear·ing. 1.** To perceive by the ear. **2.** To listen to with careful attention. **3.** To get as information by hearing. **4.** To listen to in order to examine officially or formally, as in a court of law. **—hear′er** *n.*
hear·ing (hîr′ĭng) *n.* **1.** The sense by which sound is detected and perceived. **2.** Range within which sounds can be perceived. **3.** An opportunity to be heard. **4.** *Law.* **a.** A preliminary examination of an accused person. **b.** A usu. investigatory session for listening to argument or testimony.
hearing aid *n.* A small electronic amplifying device used to enhance the hearing of partially deaf persons.
heark·en (här′kən) *v.* To listen closely.
hear·say (hîr′sā′) *n.* Information heard from another person : rumor.
hearse (hûrs) *n.* A vehicle for taking a dead body to a church or graveyard.
heart (härt) *n.* **1.** The hollow, muscular organ in vertebrates that receives blood from the veins and pumps it into the arteries by regular, rhythmic contraction. **2.** The heart considered as an emotional center, as: **a.** Mood or disposition. **b.** Compassion : concern. **c.** Affection : love. **d.** Resolute courage. **3.** The most central and essential part : basis <the *heart* of the controversy> **4. a.** Any of a suit of playing cards marked with a conventionalized red heart-shaped design. **b. hearts** *(sing. in number).* A card game in which the object is either to avoid hearts when taking tricks or to take all the hearts. ☆***syns:*** CORE, ESSENCE, GIST, KERNEL, MARROW, MEAT, NITTY-GRITTY, NUB, PITH, QUINTESSENCE, ROOT, SOUL, STUFF **—by heart.** By memory <learned it *by heart*> **—with all (one's) heart. 1.** With great sincerity or devotion. **2.** Very willingly.
heart·ache (härt′āk′) *n.* Emotional sorrow or grief.
heart attack *n.* An acute episode of impaired or interrupted heart functioning.
heart·beat (härt′bēt′) *n.* **1.** A single complete cycle of contraction and relaxation of the heart. **2.** Vital force.
heart·break (härt′brāk′) *n.* Great sorrow or disappointment. **—heart′break′ing** *adj.* **—heart′break′ing·ly** *adv.*
heart·bro·ken (härt′brō′kən) *adj.* Suffering from or indicating heartbreak. **—heart′bro′ken·ly** *adv.*
heart·burn (härt′bûrn′) *n.* A feeling of burning in the stomach and esophagus, usu. caused by excess acid in the stomach.
heart·en (här′tn) *v.* To impart courage to : encourage.
heart·felt (härt′fĕlt′) *adj.* Deeply felt : earnest and sincere.
hearth (härth) *n.* **1. a.** The floor of a fireplace. **b.** The paved area in front of a fireplace. **2.** The fireside as a symbol of family life or the home. **3.** *Metallurgy.* The lowest part of a refinery furnace, in which a metal or ore is treated by exposure to heat.
hearth·stone (härth′stōn′) *n.* **1.** Stone used in building a hearth. **2.** The home : domestic life.
heart·land (härt′lănd′) *n.* An important central region, esp. one regarded as vital to a nation's economy or defense.
heart·less (härt′lĭs) *adj.* Lacking compassion : pitiless. **—heart′less·ly** *adv.* **—heart′less·ness** *n.*
heart-rend·ing (härt′rĕn′dĭng) *adj.* **1.** Causing great distress or suffering. **2.** Evoking deep sympathy.
heart·sick (härt′sĭk′) *adj.* Profoundly dejected. **—heart′sick′ness** *n.*
heart·strings (härt′strĭngz′) *pl.n.* The deepest feelings, as of pity or affection.
heart·throb (härt′thrŏb′) *n.* **1.** A pulsation of the heart. **2. a.** Tender emotion. **b.** A loved one : sweetheart.
heart-to-heart (härt′tə-härt′) *adj.* Forthright : frank.
heart·warm·ing (härt′wôr′mĭng) *adj.* Eliciting feelings of warm sympathy.
heart·wood (härt′wo͝od′) *n.* The inner, older, no longer active central wood of a tree or woody plant.
heart·y (här′tē) *adj.* **-i·er, -i·est. 1.** Expressed with or marked by exuberant warmth. **2.** Thorough : unequivocal. **3.** Full of health and vigor. **4.** Nourishing : substantial. **—heart′i·ly** *adv.* **—heart′i·ness** *n.*
heat (hēt) *n.* **1.** A form of energy that can be transmitted through a solid or fluid medium by conduction, through a fluid medium by convection, and through space as infrared radiation. **2.** The physiological sensation of being warm. **3. a.** Warmth provided for a building or room. **b.** Intense or excessive warmth.

4. A recurrent condition of readiness to mate in female mammals. 5. Intensity of emotion. 6. *Slang.* a. Pressure : stress. b. Heightening of police activity in pursuing criminals. c. The police. 7. a. One of several rounds in a competition. b. A preliminary race to determine final contenders. —*v.* 1. To make or become warm or hot. 2. To make or become excited. **—heat'er** *n.*

heat exhaustion *n.* A reaction to intense heat, marked by weakness, nausea, dizziness, and profuse sweating.

heath (hēth) *n.* 1. An open, uncultivated stretch of land covered with low-growing shrubs and plants. 2. An Old World, usu. low-growing shrub of the genus *Erica,* with small evergreen leaves and small flowers.

hea•then (hē'*th*ən) *n., pl.* **-thens** or **-then.** 1. A member of a people or nation that does not recognize the God of Judaism, Christianity, or Islam. 2. An uncivilized, unenlightened, or irreligious person. **—hea'then** *adj.* **—hea'then•dom** *n.* **—hea'then•ish** *adj.* **—hea'then•ism** *n.*

heath•er (hĕ*th*'ər) *n.* 1. A low-growing Eurasian shrub, *Calluna vulgaris,* that grows in dense masses and has small evergreen leaves and small pinkish-purple flower clusters. 2. HEATH 2. **—heath'er** *adj.* **—heath'er•y** *adj.*

heat lightning *n.* Sporadic flashes of light unaccompanied by thunder.

heat stroke *n.* Illness caused by prolonged exposure to intense heat and marked by hot, dry skin, high fever, rapid pulse, and in severe cases collapse.

heave (hēv) *v.* **heaved, heav•ing.** 1. To raise or lift, esp. forcibly. 2. To throw : hurl. 3. *p.t. & p.p.* **hove** (hōv). *Naut.* a. To pull, push, or haul, as by a rope. b. To pull into or come to be in a specified position <The barge *hove* alongside.> 4. To utter (e.g., a sigh) with effort. 5. To rise or be forced upward : bulge. 6. *Informal.* To retch or vomit. —*n.* 1. The act or effort of heaving. 2. *Informal.* An act of throwing. 3. **heaves** *(sing. or pl. in number).* A disease of horses affecting the lungs and marked by coughing and difficult breathing. **—heav'er** *n.*

heav•en (hĕv'ən) *n.* 1. *often* **heavens.** The sky as it appears from the earth. 2. The realm of God, the angels, and the blessed souls of the dead. 3. **Heaven.** Divine Providence : God. 4. A place or state of blissful happiness. **—heav'en•li•ness** *n.* **—heav'en•ly** *adj.* **—heav'en•ward** *adv. & adj.* **—heav'en•wards** *adv.*

heav•y (hĕv'ē) *adj.* **-i•er, -i•est.** 1. Having great weight. 2. Having high density or specific gravity. 3. a. Large, as in number or quantity <*heavy* snowfall><*heavy* traffic> b. Intense or concentrated <*heavy* fighting> 4. Very thick or dense <*heavy* jungle growth> 5. a. Forceful : powerful <a *heavy* blow> b. Rough and violent, as stormy weather. 6. Partaking or involved to a great or excessive degree <a *heavy* smoker><a *heavy* gambler> 7. a. Of great seriousness or significance : grave. b. Sorrowful or painful, as bad news. 8. a. Hard to do : arduous. b. Hard to bear : oppressive <*heavy* taxation> 9. a. Substantial : hearty. b. Not rapidly or easily digested. 10. Having large or coarse facial or bodily features. 11. Burdened with care or sadness <a *heavy* heart> 12. Lacking vivacity or grace : clumsy or dull. 13. a. Loaded down <trees *heavy* with fruit> b. Indicating weariness or sleepiness <*heavy* eyelids> 14. Involving large-scale manufacturing, esp. of basic products such as steel. 15. Bearing weighty arms or armor, as cavalry. 16. *Slang.* Of great profundity. —*adv.* In a heavy manner. —*n., pl.* **-vies.** 1. A villain in a novel or drama. 2. A wicked person. 3. *Slang.* An important or influential person. **—heav'i•ly** *adv.* **—heav'i•ness** *n.*

heav•y-du•ty (hĕv'ē-do͞o'tē, -dyo͞o'-) *adj.* Designed for hard use or wear.

heav•y-hand•ed (hĕv'ē-hăn'dĭd) *adj.* 1. Ungainly : clumsy. 2. Tyrannical. 3. Not tactful. **—heav'y-hand'ed•ly** *adv.* **—heav'y-hand'ed•ness** *n.*

heav•y-heart•ed (hĕv'ē-här'tĭd) *adj.* Melancholy : depressed. **—heav'y-heart'ed•ly** *adv.* **—heav'y-heart'ed•ness** *n.*

heav•y•set (hĕv'ē-sĕt') *adj.* Having a heavy, thickset build.

heavy water *n.* An isotopic variety of water, esp. deuterium oxide, used as a moderator in certain nuclear reactors.

heav•y•weight (hĕv'ē-wāt') *n.* 1. One of above average weight. 2. A competitor in the heaviest class, esp. a boxer weighing more than 175 lb. or 81 kg. 3. *Informal.* One of great power or importance : VIP.

heb•e•tude (hĕb'ĭ-to͞od', -tyo͞od') *n.* Mental lethargy. **—heb'e•tu'di•nous** *adj.*

He•bra•ic (hĭ-brā'ĭk) *also* **He•bra•i•cal** (-ĭ-kəl) *adj.* Of, pertaining to, or characteristic of the Hebrews or their language or culture. **—He'bra'ist** (hē'brā'ĭst) *n.*

He•brew (hē'bro͞o) *n.* 1. A member of a Semitic people descended from Abraham, Isaac, and Jacob. 2. The ancient and modern forms of the language of the Hebrews. 3. **Hebrews.** *(sing. in number).* See BIBLE TABLE. **—He'brew** *adj.*

Heb•ri•des (hĕb'rə-dēz). Island group in the Atlantic off the W coast of Scotland.

heck•le (hĕk'əl) *v.* **-led, -ling.** To badger persistently, as with questions, comments, or gibes. **—heck'ler** *n.*

hec•tare (hĕk'târ') *n.* See MEASUREMENT TABLE.

hec•tic (hĕk'tĭk) *adj.* 1. Intensely active, rushed, or chaotic. 2. a. Marked by a persistent and fluctuating fever, as in tuberculosis. b. Feverish : flushed.

hec•to•gram (hĕk'tə-grăm') *n.* See MEASUREMENT TABLE.

hec•to•li•ter (hĕk'tə-lē'tər) *n.* See MEASUREMENT TABLE.

hec•to•li•tre (hĕk'tə-lē'tər) *n. esp. Brit. var. of* HECTOLITER.

hec•to•me•ter (hĕk'tə-mē'tər, hĕk-tŏm'ĭ-tər) *n.* See MEASUREMENT TABLE.

hec•to•me•tre (hĕk'tə-mē'tər) *n. esp. Brit. var. of* HECTOMETER.

hec•tor (hĕk'tər) *n.* A bully. —*v.* 1. To frighten or bully : intimidate. 2. To swagger.

▲word history: The word *hector,* which is both a noun meaning "a bully" and a verb meaning "to intimidate," is derived from *Hector,* the name of the Trojan hero who figures so largely in the *Iliad.* In the 17th cent. the name of this hero was used as a generic term for a swaggering braggart or bully. The behavior of such persons is denoted by the verb *hector,* which appeared at the same time as the noun.

he'd (hēd). 1. He had. 2. He would.

hedge (hĕj) *n.* 1. A boundary or fence of shrubs or low-growing trees. 2. A means of protection, esp. against financial loss. 3. A deliberately ambiguous statement. —*v.* **hedged, hedg•ing.** 1. To bound or fence with or as if with a hedge. 2. To hinder or encumber. 3. To limit financial risk by a counterbalancing transaction <*hedge* a bet> 4. To equivocate. **—hedg'er** *n.*

▲word history: Hedges have been used in England for hundreds of years as fences. They also provide shelter for birds and small animals and will, in a pinch, provide the same for human beings. This property of hedges probably gave rise to the sense "a means of defense or protection," which has been current since the 14th cent. In the 17th cent. that meaning of *hedge* was applied to the case of financial loss, esp. in the areas of investment and gambling.

hedge•hog (hĕj'hôg', -hŏg') *n.* 1. Any of several small Old World mammals of the family Erinaceidae, bearing dense, erectile spines on the back and rolling into a ball in self-defense. 2. A porcupine.

hedge•hop (hĕj'hŏp') *v.* To fly an airplane close to the ground, as in spraying crops. **—hedge'hop'per** *n.*

hedge•row (hĕj'rō') *n.* A row of bushes, shrubs, or trees forming a hedge.

he•don•ism (hēd'n-ĭz'əm) *n.* 1. A way of life devoted to the pursuit of pleasure. 2. The philosophy that pleasure is the principal good in life. **—he'don•ist** *n.* **—he'don•is'tic** *adj.*

heed (hēd) *v.* To pay close attention (to). —*n.* Close attention. **—heed'ful** *adj.* **—heed'ful•ly** *adv.* **—heed'ful•ness** *n.* **—heed'less** *adj.* **—heed'less•ly** *adv.* **—heed'less•ness** *n.*

hee•haw (hē'hô') *n.* 1. The braying sound made by a donkey. 2. A noisy laugh : guffaw. **—hee'haw'** *v.*

heel[1] (hēl) *n.* 1. a. The rounded back part of the human foot under and behind the ankle. b. An analogous part in other vertebrates. 2. The part, as of a shoe, covering or supporting the heel. 3. A lower, rearward, or bottom part. 4. Either end of a loaf of bread. 5. A cad. —*v.* 1. To provide with a heel. 2. *Slang.* To supply esp. with money. 3. To follow along at one's heels. **—on** (or **upon**) **the heels of.** Directly following in time or space. **—heel'less** *adj.*

heel[2] (hēl) *v.* To list or cause to list to one side : tilt. **—heel** *n.*

heft (hĕft) *n. Informal.* Weight : bulk. —*v.* 1. To find or estimate the weight of by lifting. 2. To lift up : hoist.

heft•y (hĕf'tē) *adj.* **-i•er, -i•est.** 1. Heavy : bulky. 2. Powerful : robust. 3. Sizable.

He•gel hā'gəl), **Georg Wilhelm Friedrich.** 1770–1831. German philosopher. **—He•ge'li•an** (hā-gā'lē-ən) *adj. & n.*

he•gem•o•ny (hĭ-jĕm'ə-nē, hĕj'ə-mō'nē) *n.* Dominance, esp. of 1 nation over others.

he•gi•ra (hĭ-jī'rə, hĕj'ər-ə) *n.* A journey esp. to flee danger or privation.

Hei•del•berg (hīd'l-bûrg'). City of SW West Germany. *Pop.* 128,773.

heif•er (hĕf'ər) *n.* A young cow, esp. one that has not had a calf.

height (hīt) *n.* 1. The highest point : summit. 2. a. The highest degree : zenith. b. The point of greatest intensity. 3. a. The distance from the base to the apex of something upright. b. Elevation above a specified level : altitude. 4. Measurement from head to foot. 5. An elevation of ground.

height·en (hīt'n) *v.* **1.** To increase in quantity or degree. **2.** To raise or be raised.

Heim·lich maneuver (hīm'lĭKH', -lĭk') *n.* A maneuver for dislodging food from a choking person's trachea in which the closed fist is placed below the rib cage to force air from the lungs upward.

hei·nous (hā'nəs) *adj.* Abominably wicked. **–hei'nous·ly** *adv.* **–hei'nous·ness** *n.*

heir (âr) *n.* One who inherits or is entitled to inherit another's property or title.

heir apparent *n., pl.* **heirs apparent.** An heir who is legally assured of his right to inherit if he outlives his ancestor.

heir·ess (âr'ĭs) *n.* A woman who is an heir, esp. to a fortune.

heir·loom (âr'lo͞om') *n.* **1.** A valued family possession handed on from generation to generation. **2.** An item of personal property acquired by legal inheritance.

heir presumptive *n., pl.* **heirs presumptive.** An heir who could lose the right to inherit through the birth of a closer relative.

heist (hīst) *Slang.* –*v.* To steal or steal from. –*n.* A theft.

held (hĕld) *v. p.t.* & *p.p. of* HOLD.

Hel·e·na (hĕl'ə-nə). Cap. of Mont., in the W part. *Pop.* 23,938.

hel·i·cal (hĕl'ĭ-kəl) *adj.* Of or having the shape of a helix. **–hel'i·cal·ly** *adv.*

hel·i·ces (hĕl'ĭ-sēz', hē'lĭ-) *n. var. pl. of* HELIX.

hel·i·con (hĕl'ĭ-kŏn', -kən) *n.* A large tuba that encircles the player's shoulder.

helicon

hel·i·cop·ter (hĕl'ĭ-kŏp'tər) *n.* An aircraft supported in the air by horizontal rotors turning on an approx. vertical central axis.

he·li·o·cen·tric (hē'lē-ō-sĕn'trĭk) *also* **he·li·o·cen·tri·cal** (-trĭ-kəl) *adj.* Pertaining to or having the sun as a center. **–he'li·o·cen·tric'i·ty** (-trĭs'ĭ-tē) *n.*

he·li·o·gram (hē'lē-ə-grăm') *n.* A message sent by heliograph.

he·li·o·graph (hē'lē-ə-grăf') *n.* A signaling device using sunlight reflected from a movable mirror to transmit code. **–he'li·o·graph'** *v.* **–he'li·o·graph'ic** *adj.*

he·li·o·trope (hē'lē-ə-trōp', hēl'yə-) *n.* A cultivated American plant of the genus *Heliotropium*, esp. *H. arborescens*, with small, very fragrant purplish or white flowers.

hel·i·port (hĕl'ə-pôrt', -pōrt') *n.* A level area where helicopters land and take off.

he·li·um (hē'lē-əm) *n. Symbol* **He** An extremely light, nonflammable, inert gaseous element.

he·lix (hē'lĭks) *n., pl.* **he·lix·es** *or* **hel·i·ces** (hĕl'ĭ-sēz', hē'lĭ-). **1.** A curve drawn on a cylinder or cone so that it cuts each element of the figure at the same angle. **2.** A spiral shape or structure.

hell (hĕl) *n.* **1.** The underworld abode of the dead. **2.** *often* **Hell.** The abode of the devil and souls condemned to eternal punishment. **3.** A place or condition of evil, torment or destruction. **4. a.** Great distress : anguish. **b.** A cause of trouble or misery. **–hell'ish** *adj.* **–hell'ish·ly** *adv.*

he'll (hēl). **1.** He will. **2.** He shall.

hell-bent (hĕl'bĕnt') *adj.* Obstinately determined. **–hell'-bent'** *adv.*

hell·cat (hĕl'kăt') *n.* **1.** A shrewish, malevolent woman. **2.** A fiendish person.

hel·le·bore (hĕl'ə-bôr', -bōr') *n.* Any of various North American plants of the genus *Veratrum*, esp. *V. viride*, bearing white or greenish flowers and yielding a toxic alkaloid used in medicine.

Hel·lene (hĕl'ēn') *also* **Hel·le·ni·an** (hə-lē'nē-ən) *n.* A Greek.

Hel·len·ic (hə-lĕn'ĭk) *adj.* Of or pertaining to the ancient Greeks or their culture.

Hel·le·nism (hĕl'ə-nĭz'əm) *n.* **1.** Ancient Greek civilization and culture. **2.** Devotion to or adoption of Greek thought, style, or cultural customs. **–Hel'le·nist** *n.* **–Hel'le·nis'tic** *adj.*

†**hell·er** (hĕl'ər) *n. Regional.* One who behaves wildly or rashly.

hell-for-leath·er (hĕl'fər-lĕth'ər) *adv. & adj. Informal.* At breakneck speed.

hell·gram·mite (hĕl'grə-mīt') *n.* The brownish aquatic larva of the dobson fly, used esp. as fishing bait.

hell·hole (hĕl'hōl') *n.* A place of extreme squalor or wretchedness.

hel·lion (hĕl'yən) *n. Informal.* A devilish or vexatious person.

hel·lo (hĕ-lō', hə-) *also* **hul·lo** (hə-). –*interj.* Used esp. as a greeting or to answer the telephone. –*n., pl.* **-loes.** A greeting or call of "hello."

helm (hĕlm) *n.* **1.** A tiller or wheel for steering a ship. **2.** A position of control or command.

hel·met (hĕl'mĭt) *n.* A protective metal, leather, or plastic covering for the head.

helms·man (hĕlmz'mən) *n.* One at the helm of a ship.

hel·ot (hĕl'ət, hē'lət) *n.* A serf : slave. **–hel'ot·ry** *n.*

help (hĕlp) *v.* **1.** To give aid (to) : assist. **2.** To contribute to the progress of : advance. **3.** To give relief to : alleviate. **4.** To benefit (someone) by making improvements. **5.** To have the power to change or prevent. **6.** To keep from : escape. **7.** To wait on, as in a store. –*n.* **1.** Assistance. **2.** Relief. **3.** One that assists. **4. a.** One hired to help. **b.** Such workers in general. **–help'er** *n.* **–help'ful** *adj.* **–help'ful·ly** *adv.* **–help'ful·ness** *n.* **–help'less** *adj.* **–help'less·ly** *adv.* **–help'less·ness** *n.*

help·ing (hĕl'pĭng) *n.* A single serving of food.

help·mate (hĕlp'māt') *n.* A helper and companion, esp. a spouse.

help·meet (hĕlp'mēt') *n.* A helpmate.

▲word history: The word *helpmeet* owes its existence to a misreading of a passage in the King James Bible. In Genesis 2:18 God promises Adam to "make him an help meet for him," that is, a helper suitable for him. The words *help meet* were even in the 17th cent. misread as 1 word, and since the "help" turned out to be Eve, the new compound was interpreted as meaning "spouse." *Helpmate* is an alteration of *helpmeet* that substitutes *mate*, "spouse," for the now unintelligible *meet* of *helpmeet*.

Hel·sin·ki (hĕl'sĭng'kē). Cap. of Finland, in the S. *Pop.* 484,879.

hel·ter-skel·ter (hĕl'tər-skĕl'tər) *adv.* **1.** In confused or disorderly haste. **2.** In an aimless, haphazard way. –*adj.* **1.** Rushed and confused. **2.** Aimless : haphazard. –*n.* Great confusion.

helve (hĕlv) *n.* A handle of a tool such as an ax, chisel, or hammer.

Hel·ve·tian (hĕl-vē'shən) *adj.* & *n.* Swiss.

hem¹ (hĕm) *n.* An edge of cloth folded under and stitched down. –*v.* **hemmed, hem·ming. 1.** To fold under and stitch down the edge of. **2.** To surround and confine. **–hem'mer** *n.*

hem² (hĕm) *n.* A short sound made in clearing the throat used esp. to attract attention or fill a pause in speech. –*v.* **hemmed, hem·ming.** To utter a hem.

he-man (hē'măn') *n. Informal.* A man marked by strength and virility.

hem·a·tite (hĕm'ə-tīt', hē'mə-) *n.* A reddish mineral that is the main ore of iron and consists of a compound of iron and oxygen.

he·ma·tol·o·gy (hē'mə-tŏl'ə-jē) *n.* The biological science that deals with the blood and blood-generating organs. **–he'ma·tol'o·gist** *n.*

heme (hēm) *n.* The iron-containing deep-red pigment of hemoglobin.

Hem·ing·way (hĕm'ĭng-wā'), **Ernest Miller.** 1899–1961. Amer. novelist.

hem·i·sphere (hĕm'ĭ-sfîr') *n.* **1. a.** Either half of a sphere that is divided by a plane passing through its center. **b.** Either symmetrical half of an approx. spherical shape. **2.** Either the N or S half of the earth divided by the equator or the E or W half divided by a geographic meridian. **–hem'i·spher'ic, hem'i·spher'i·cal** *adj.*

hem·lock (hĕm'lŏk') *n.* **1. a.** An evergreen tree of the genus *Tsuga*, of North America and E Asia, having flat needles and small cones. **b.** The wood of a hemlock. **2. a.** Any of several poisonous plants of the genera *Conium* and *Cicuta*, with compound leaves and small whitish flowers. **b.** A poison obtained from the hemlock plant.

he·mo·glo·bin (hē'mə-glō'bĭn) *n.* A protein in the red blood cells of vertebrates that contains iron and carries oxygen to bodily tissues.

he·mo·phil·i·a (hē'mə-fĭl'ē-ə) *n.* An inherited blood disease marked by severe, protracted, sometimes spontaneous bleeding. **–he'mo·phil'i·ac'** *n.*

hem·or·rhage (hĕm'ər-ĭj) *n.* Bleeding, esp. abnormally severe or copious bleeding. **–hem'or·rhage** *v.*

hem•or•rhoid (hĕm′ə-roid′) *n.* **1.** A painful mass of dilated veins in swollen anal tissue. **2. hemorrhoids.** The pathological condition in which hemorrhoids occur.
he•mo•stat (hē′mə-stăt′) *n.* **1.** An agent, as a chemical, that stops bleeding. **2.** A clamplike surgical instrument for preventing or reducing bleeding.
hemp (hĕmp) *n.* **1.** A tall Asian plant, *Cannabis sativa,* whose stems yield a fiber used to make cordage. **2.** The fiber of the hemp. **3.** A narcotic, as hashish, derived from hemp. **–hemp′en** *adj.*
hem•stitch (hĕm′stĭch′) *n.* A decorative stitch, made by pulling out several parallel threads and tying the remaining threads together in even bunches to form designs. **–hem′stitch′** *v.*
hen (hĕn) *n.* A female bird, esp. a full-grown female domestic fowl.
hence (hĕns) *adv.* **1.** For this reason : consequently. **2.** From now <3 days *hence*> **3.** Away from this place.
hence•forth (hĕns′fôrth′) *also* **hence•for•ward** (hĕns-fôr′wərd) *adv.* From this time or point on.
hench•man (hĕnch′mən) *n.* **1.** A loyal follower. **2.** One who supports a political figure chiefly for personal gain.
hen•na (hĕn′ə) *n.* **1. a.** An Asian and N African tree or shrub, *Lawsonia inermis,* bearing fragrant white or reddish flowers. **b.** A brownish-red dyestuff derived from henna leaves and used esp. as a cosmetic dye. **2.** A strong reddish brown. *–v.* To treat or dye (e.g., hair) with henna.
hen•peck (hĕn′pĕk′) *v. Informal.* To subject (one's husband) to chronic nagging.
Hen•ry (hĕn′rē), **Patrick.** 1736–99. Amer. Revolutionary leader.
Henry VII. "Henry Tudor." 1457–1509. King of England (1485–1509).
Henry VIII. 1491–1547. King of England (1509–47).
hep (hĕp) *adj. var. of* HIP[2].
hep•a•rin (hĕp′ər-ĭn) *n.* An organic compound found esp. in liver tissue that is used medically to slow or prevent blood clotting.
he•pat•ic (hĭ-păt′ĭk) *adj.* Of, like, acting on, or affecting the liver.
he•pat•i•ca (hĭ-păt′ĭ-kə) *n.* A forest plant of the genus *Hepatica,* esp. *H. americana,* of E North America, with 3-lobed leaves and white or lavender flowers.
hep•a•ti•tis (hĕp′ə-tī′tĭs) *n.* Inflammation of the liver marked by jaundice and caused by infectious or toxic agents.
her (hûr; hər, ər *when unstressed*) *pron. objective case of* SHE. Used: **1.** As the direct object of a verb <We saw *her* at the park.> **2.** As the indirect object of a verb <We mailed *her* the records.> **3.** As the object of a preposition <That car belongs to *her.*> *–adj.* Used as a modifier before a noun <*her* hat><*her* achievements><*her* lifestyle>
Her•a•cli•tus (hĕr′ə-klī′təs). 6th cent. B.C. Greek philosopher.
her•ald (hĕr′əld) *n.* **1.** A messenger who announces important news. **2.** One that comes before as a sign of what is to follow : harbinger. **3.** An official whose duty it once was to make royal proclamations. *–v.* To announce : proclaim.
he•ral•dic (hə-răl′dĭk) *adj.* Of or pertaining to heralds or heraldry.
her•ald•ry (hĕr′əl-drē) *n., pl.* **-ries. 1.** The art or practice of tracing genealogies and devising and granting coats of arms. **2.** An armorial badge, emblem, or device. **3.** Heraldic pageantry.
herb (ûrb, hûrb) *n.* **1.** A soft-stemmed plant that usu. withers and dies each year. **2.** An often pleasant-smelling plant used in medicine or cooking. **–herb′al** *adj.* & *n.*
her•ba•ceous (ûr-bā′shəs, hûr-) *adj.* **1.** Of, like, or consisting of herbs. **2.** Green and leaflike.
herb•age (ûr′bĭj, hûr′-) *n.* **1.** Grass or leafy vegetation used esp. for grazing. **2.** The fleshy, often edible parts of plants.
herb•al•ist (ûr′bə-lĭst, hûr′-) *n.* One who gathers, grows, or uses herbs, esp. medicinal herbs.
her•bar•i•um (ûr-bâr′ē-əm, hûr-) *n., pl.* **-i•ums** *or* **-i•a** (-ē-ə). **1.** A collection of dried plant specimens esp. for scientific study. **2.** A place housing a herbarium.
her•bi•cide (ûr′bĭ-sīd′, hûr′-) *n.* A chemical agent used to kill plants, esp. weeds. **–her′bi•cid′al** *adj.*
her•bi•vore (ûr′bə-vôr′, -vōr′, hûr-) *n.* A herbivorous animal.
her•biv•o•rous (ûr-bĭv′ər-əs, hûr-) *adj.* Feeding chiefly on plants. **–her•biv′o•rous•ly** *adv.*
her•cu•le•an (hûr′kyə-lē′ən, hûr-kyōō′lē-) *adj.* Of unusual size, force, or difficulty.
herd (hûrd) *n.* **1.** A number of animals of the same kind kept or staying together as a group. **2.** A large crowd of people. *–v.* **1.** To assemble in a herd. **2.** To gather, keep, drive, or lead in or as if in a herd. **–herd′er** *n.* **–herds′man** *n.*
here (hîr) *adv.* **1.** In or at this place <Let's skate *here.*> **2.** At the present time : now <Let's take a vote *here.*> **3.** At or on this point or detail <*Here* we disagree.> **4.** To or toward this place <Bring it *here.*>
here•a•bout (hîr′ə-bout′) *also* **here•a•bouts** (-bouts′) *adv.* Near or around here.
here•af•ter (hîr-ăf′tər) *adv.* **1.** From now on. **2.** In the future or the afterlife. *–n.* Existence after death : afterlife.
here•by (hîr-bī′, hîr′bī′) *adv.* By means of this.
he•red•i•tar•y (hə-rĕd′ĭ-tĕr′ē) *adj.* **1. a.** Passing from an ancestor to a legal heir. **b.** Having an inherited title or possession. **2.** Transmitted or transmissible by genetic inheritance. **3.** Of long-standing tradition. **–he•red′i•tar′i•ly** *adv.*
he•red•i•ty (hə-rĕd′ĭ-tē) *n.* **1.** The genetic passage of physical traits from parent to offspring. **2.** The set of physical traits passed to an organism through heredity.
here•in (hîr-ĭn′) *adv.* In or into this.
here•of (hîr-ŭv′, -ŏv′) *adv.* Relating to or concerning this.
here•on (hîr-ŏn′, -ôn′) *adv.* Hereupon.
her•e•sy (hĕr′ĭ-sē) *n., pl.* **-sies. 1.** An opinion or doctrine in conflict with orthodox religious beliefs. **2. a.** Dissent from accepted or dominant opinion, doctrine, or theory. **b.** Adherence to such dissent.
her•e•tic (hĕr′ĭ-tĭk) *n.* A dissenter from orthodox beliefs, esp. religious beliefs. **–he•ret′i•cal** (hə-rĕt′ĭ-kəl) *adj.*
here•to (hîr-tōō′) *adv.* To this document, matter, or proposition.
here•to•fore (hîr′tə-fôr′, -fōr′) *adv.* Up to the present time.
here•un•to (hîr-ŭn′tōō, hîr′ŭn-tōō′) *adv.* Hereto.
here•up•on (hîr′ə-pŏn′, -pôn′) *adv.* Immediately following this.
here•with (hîr-wĭth′, -wĭ*th*′) *adv.* **1.** Together with this. **2.** Hereby.
her•i•ta•ble (hĕr′ĭ-tə-bəl) *adj.* Capable of being inherited.
her•i•tage (hĕr′ĭ-tĭj) *n.* **1.** Property passed down by inheritance. **2.** Something handed on from past generations : legacy.
her•maph•ro•dite (hər-măf′rə-dīt′) *n.* A person, animal, or plant that has both male and female reproductive organs. **–her•maph′ro•dit′ic** (-dĭt′ĭk) *adj.*
her•met•ic (hər-mĕt′ĭk) *also* **her•met•i•cal** (-ĭ-kəl) *adj.* **1.** Tightly sealed so that air cannot enter or escape : airtight. **2.** Resistant to or proof against outside influences. **–her•met′i•cal•ly** *adv.*

▲word history: An airtight seal is called a *hermetic* seal by a roundabout chain of circumstances. *Hermetic* is an adjective derived from the name *Hermes* Trismegistus, the Greek name for the Egyptian god Thoth, who was regarded as the originator of the science of alchemy. The adjective *hermetic,* beginning in the 17th cent., meant "pertaining to alchemy" and the occult sciences in general. Alchemy, and later chemistry, was itself variously known as the *hermetic* art, philosophy, or science. A *hermetic* seal was a kind of seal used by alchemists that involved melting closed an opening in a glass vessel. Since the resulting seal was airtight, any airtight seal has come to be called *hermetic.*

her•mit (hûr′mĭt) *n.* One who lives as a recluse, esp. for religious reasons.
her•mit•age (hûr′mĭ-tĭj) *n.* **1.** The dwelling place of a hermit. **2.** A secluded retreat : hideaway.
†**hern** (hûrn) *n. Regional.* A heron.
her•ni•a (hûr′nē-ə) *n., pl.* **-ni•as** *or* **-ni•ae** (-nē-ē′). Protrusion of a bodily part, as the intestine, through the abnormally weakened wall that usu. contains it : rupture. **–her′ni•al** *adj.*
he•ro (hîr′ō) *n., pl.* **-roes. 1.** A figure in mythology and legend renowned for great strength, courage, and daring. **2.** A man celebrated for special achievements and attributes. **3.** The leading male character in a story or play. **4.** *Slang.* A long split sandwich roll containing a variety of fillings. **–he•ro′ic** *adj.* **–he•ro′i•cal•ly** *adv.*
Her•od (hĕr′əd). "the Great." 73?–4 B.C. King of Judea (37–4).
Herod An•ti•pas (ăn′tĭ-păs′). Roman tetrarch of Galilee (4 B.C.–A.D. 40).
He•rod•o•tus (hĭ-rŏd′ə-təs). 5th cent. B.C. Greek historian.
heroic couplet *n.* A rhymed couplet in iambic pentameter.
her•o•in (hĕr′ō-ĭn) *n.* A highly addictive narcotic obtained from morphine.
her•o•ine (hĕr′ō-ĭn) *n.* **1.** A woman renowned for her courage and daring. **2.** A woman celebrated for her special achievements and attributes. **3.** The leading female character in a story or play.
her•o•ism (hĕr′ō-ĭz′əm) *n.* **1.** Heroic behavior. **2.** Heroic attributes, esp. courage.
her•on (hĕr′ən) *n.* A bird of the family Ardeidae, with a long pointed bill, long legs, and a long neck.
her•pes (hûr′pēz′) *n.* A viral disease that causes small blisters on the skin or mucous membrane. **–her•pet′ic** (-pĕt′ĭk) *adj.*
her•pe•tol•o•gy (hûr′pĭ-tŏl′ə-jē) *n.* The scientific study of

reptiles and amphibians. **–her'pe·to·log'ic** (-tə-lŏj'ĭk), **her'pe·to·log'i·cal** *adj.* **–her'pe·to·log'i·cal·ly** *adv.* **–her'pe·tol'o·gist** *n.*

Herr (hĕr) *n., pl.* **Her·ren** (hĕr'ən). A courtesy title prefixed to the name or professional title of a German, equivalent to *Mister.*

her·ring (hĕr'ĭng) *n., pl.* **-ring** or **-rings.** A valuable food fish of the family Clupeidae, esp. *Clupea harengus,* of Atlantic and Pacific waters.

her·ring·bone (hĕr'ĭng-bōn') *n.* **1.** A pattern consisting of rows of short slanted parallel lines with adjacent rows slanting in opposite directions. **2.** A fabric with a herringbone pattern.

hers (hûrz) *pron.* Used to indicate the one or ones belonging to her <If your car won't start, take *hers.*>

her·self (hər-sĕlf') *pron.* **1.** That one identical with her. Used: **a.** Reflexively as the direct or indirect object of a verb or as the object of a preposition <She burned *herself.*> **b.** For emphasis <She *herself* couldn't be sure.> **c.** In an absolute construction <In debt *herself,* she was unable to contribute.> **2.** Her normal condition or state <She isn't *herself* today.>

hertz (hûrts) *n.* A unit of frequency equal to 1 cycle per sec.

he's (hēz). **1.** He has. **2.** He is.

hes·i·tant (hĕz'ĭ-tənt) *adj.* Given to hesitating. **–hes'i·tan·cy** *n.*

hes·i·tate (hĕz'ĭ-tāt') *v.* **-tat·ed, -tat·ing. 1.** To pause in doubt before acting, speaking, or deciding : waver. **2.** To be unwilling <Don't *hesitate* to ask for money.> **3.** To falter in speech. ☆***syns:*** FALTER, HALT, PAUSE, SHILLY-SHALLY, STAGGER, VACILLATE, WAVER **–hes'i·tat'ing·ly** *adv.* **–hes'i·ta'tion** *n.*

het·er·o·dox (hĕt'ər-ə-dŏks') *adj.* **1.** Not in accord with established beliefs, esp. at variance with religious doctrine. **2.** Holding unorthodox or unconventional opinions. **–het'er·o·dox'y** *n.*

het·er·o·ge·ne·ous (hĕt'ər-ə-jē'nē-əs, -jēn'yəs) *also* **het·er·og·e·nous** (-ə-rŏj'ə-nəs) *adj.* Consisting of dissimilar parts, elements, or ingredients. **–het'er·o·ge·ne'i·ty** (-rō-jə-nē'ĭ-tē) *n.* **–het'er·o·ge'ne·ous·ly** *adv.*

het·er·o·sex·u·al (hĕt'ə-rō-sĕk'shōō-əl) *adj.* **1.** Of, relating to, or marked by sexual attraction to the opposite sex. **2.** Involving different sexes. **–het'er·o·sex'u·al** *n.* **–het'er·o·sex'u·al'i·ty** (-ăl'ĭ-tē) *n.*

hew (hyōō) *v.* **hewed, hewn** (hyōōn) or **hewed, hew·ing. 1.** To make or give shape to with or as if with an ax. **2.** To fell with an ax. **3.** To adhere strictly <*hew* to the rule> **–hew'er** *n.*

hex (hĕks) *n.* **1.** A malevolent curse. **2.** One held to bring bad luck : jinx. *–v.* **1.** To put under an evil spell. **2.** To jinx.

hex·a·gon (hĕk'sə-gŏn') *n.* A 6-sided polygon. **–hex·ag'o·nal** (-săg'ə-nəl) *adj.* **–hex·ag'o·nal·ly** *adv.*

hex·am·e·ter (hĕk-săm'ĭ-tər) *n.* A line of verse with 6 metrical feet.

hey·day (hā'dā') *n.* A time of maximum power, prosperity, or popularity : peak.

hf *abbr.* high frequency.

Hf *symbol for* HAFNIUM.

Hg *symbol for* MERCURY.

HI *abbr.* Hawaii (with Zip Code).

hi·a·tus (hī-ā'təs) *n.* A slight break or lapse in space, time, or continuity : break.

hi·ba·chi (hĭ-bä'chē) *n., pl.* **-chis.** A portable charcoal brazier used esp. for grilling food.

hi·ber·nate (hī'bər-nāt') *v.* **-nat·ed, -nat·ing.** To spend the winter in an inactive sleeplike state. **–hi'ber·na'tion** *n.* **–hi'ber·na'tor** *n.*

▲word history: The English word *hibernate* is ult. derived from Latin *hibernus,* "wintry." *Hibernus* descends from the Indo-European root *ghiem–,* from which the Sanskrit word *himā–,* "snow," is also derived. The name *Himalaya* is a Sanskrit compound of *himā–,* "snow," and *ālaya,* "abode, place," and means "the place of snow."

hi·bis·cus (hī-bĭs'kəs, hĭ-) *n.* A chiefly tropical plant, shrub, or tree of the genus *Hibiscus,* bearing large, colorful flowers.

hic·cup *also* **hic·cough** (hĭk'ŭp) *n.* **1.** A spasm of the diaphragm that occurs on inhalation and closes the glottis, producing a short, sharp sound. **2. hiccups.** An attack of hiccups. **–hic'cup** *v.*

hick (hĭk) *n. Informal.* An awkward, unsophisticated country person.

hick·o·ry (hĭk'ə-rē) *n., pl.* **-ries.** A chiefly North American deciduous tree of the genus *Carya,* having smooth or shaggy bark, hard edible nuts, and heavy, tough wood.

hi·dal·go (hĭ-dăl'gō) *n., pl.* **-goes.** A member of the lesser nobility in Spain.

hide¹ (hīd) *v.* **hid** (hĭd), **hid·den** (hĭd'n) or **hid, hid·ing. 1.** To put, keep, or remain out of sight. **2.** To keep from being disclosed. **3.** To obscure from sight. **4.** To seek shelter or protection. ☆***syns:*** BURY, CACHE, CONCEAL, ENSCONCE, PLANT, SECRETE, STASH **–hid'er** *n.*

hide² (hīd) *n.* The skin of an animal.

hide-and-seek (hīd'n-sēk') *n.* A game in which 1 player tries to find and catch others who are hiding.

hide·a·way (hīd'ə-wā') *n.* **1.** A place of concealment. **2.** An isolated retreat.

hide·bound (hīd'bound') *adj.* Obstinately narrow-minded or inflexible.

hid·e·ous (hĭd'ē-əs) *adj.* **1.** Physically repulsive. **2.** Morally offensive. **–hid'e·ous·ly** *adv.* **–hid'e·ous·ness** *n.*

hide-out (hīd'out') *n.* HIDEAWAY 1.

hie (hī) *v.* **hied, hie·ing** or **hy·ing.** To make haste : hurry.

hi·er·ar·chy (hī'ə-rär'kē, hī'rär'-) *n., pl.* **-chies. 1.** An authoritative body, esp. of clergy, organized according to rank. **2.** A graded or ranked series of persons or things. **–hi'er·ar'chi·cal, hi'er·ar'chic** *adj.* **–hi'er·ar'chi·cal·ly** *adv.*

hi·er·o·glyph·ic (hī'ər-ə-glĭf'ĭk, hī'rə-) *n.* **1.** A pictorial symbol used in a writing system, esp. that of ancient Egypt. **2. hieroglyphics.** Symbols or writing difficult to decipher. **–hi'er·o·glyph'i·cal·ly** *adv.*

hi-fi (hī'fī') *n., pl.* **-fis. 1.** High fidelity. **2.** Electronic equipment for reproducing high-fidelity sound.

hig·gle·dy-pig·gle·dy (hĭg'əl-dē-pĭg'əl-dē) *adv.* In total confusion.

high (hī) *adj.* **1.** Extending relatively far upward : tall or lofty. **2.** Being at or near a peak or climax <*high* noon> **3.** Long past in time. **4.** Having a shrill or piercing tone. **5.** Far from the equator <*high* latitudes> **6.** Very important or serious. **7.** Having an exalted or noble quality or character. **8.** Above average, as in quantity, magnitude, or degree. **9.** Expensive. **10.** Elated. **11.** *Informal.* Intoxicated, as by alcohol or drugs. **12.** Advanced in development or complexity. *–n.* **1.** A high place, level, or degree. **2.** The transmission gear of a motor vehicle producing the greatest speed. **3.** A center of high barometric pressure. **4.** *Informal.* **a.** Intoxication. **b.** Great elation. *–adv.* **1.** At, in, or to a high position or degree. **2.** In luxury <living *high*> **–high'ly** *adv.*

high·ball (hī'bôl') *n.* A mixed drink usu. served in a tall glass.

high beam *n.* A high-intensity headlight on a vehicle.

high·born (hī'bôrn') *adj.* Of noble or aristocratic birth.

high·boy (hī'boi') *n.* A tall chest of drawers mounted on a base with 4 legs.

high·bred (hī'brĕd') *adj.* **1.** Highborn. **2.** Of or from superior breeding stock.

high·brow (hī'brou') *n. Informal.* One of superior knowledge or culture. **–high'brow', high'browed'** *adj.*

high·er-up (hī'ər-ŭp', hī'ər-ŭp') *n. Informal.* A superior in rank or status.

high·fa·lu·tin (hī'fə-lōōt'n) *adj. Informal.* Pretentious or grandiose.

high fashion *n.* **1.** Haute couture. **2.** The newest in fashion or design.

high fidelity *n.* Minimally distorted electronic sound reproduction, as on records or tape. **–high'-fi·del'i·ty** *adj.*

high-flown (hī'flōn') *adj.* **1.** Exalted. **2.** Pretentious.

high frequency *n.* A radio frequency between 3 and 30 megacycles per sec.

high-hand·ed (hī'hăn'dĭd) *adj.* Overbearing in manner. **–high'hand'ed·ly** *adv.* **–high'hand'ed·ness** *n.*

high-hat (hī'hăt') *adj. Slang.* Supercilious : patronizing. **–high'-hat'** *v.* & *n.*

high jump *n.* A jump for height in a track and field contest.

high jump

high·land (hī'lənd) *n.* **1.** Land elevated above a surrounding area. **2. highlands.** A hilly or mountainous region.

high·light (hī'līt') *n.* A significant event or detail. *–v.* **1.** To emphasize. **2.** To be the major event or detail of.

high-mind·ed (hī'mīn'dĭd) *adj.* Characterized by noble principles or behavior. **–high'-mind'ed·ness** *n.*

high•ness (hī′nĭs) *n.* **1.** The quality or state of being high or tall. **2. Highness.** A title used for royalty.
high-pres•sure (hī′prĕsh′ər) *Informal.* —*adj.* Using or involving aggressive and insistent sales methods. —*v.* To try to persuade by using high-pressure techniques.
high relief *n.* Sculptural relief with modeled forms that project from the background by at least half their depth.
high-rise (hī′rīz′) *n.* An elevator-equipped multistory building.
high•road (hī′rōd′) *n.* **1.** *esp. Brit.* A main road. **2.** A direct or guaranteed way.
high school *n.* A secondary school of grades 9 or 10 through 12. **—high′-school′er** *n.*
high seas *pl.n.* The waters of an ocean or sea beyond the limits of a nation's territorial jurisdiction.
high-sound•ing (hī′soun′dĭng) *adj.* Pompous : bombastic.
high-spir•it•ed (hī′spĭr′ĭ-tĭd) *adj.* **1.** Unbroken in spirit : proud. **2.** Exuberant. **—high′-spir′it•ed•ly** *adv.*
high•stick•ing (hī′stĭk′ĭng) *n. Hockey.* An offense in which a player carries the stick above the shoulders.
high-strung (hī′strŭng′) *adj.* Highly nervous and excitable : temperamental.
high•tail (hī′tāl′) *v. Slang.* To withdraw hastily.
high tech (tĕk) *n.* **1.** A style of interior design incorporating industrial materials or motifs. **2.** High technology.
high technology *n.* Technology involving highly advanced or specialized systems or devices.
high-ten•sion (hī′tĕn′shən) *adj.* Having or using high voltage.
high-test (hī′tĕst′) *adj.* Of or relating to gasoline with a high octane number.
high tide *n.* The highest level reached by the tide.
high-toned (hī′tōnd′) *adj.* **1.** Of superior intellectual, moral, or social quality. **2.** *Informal.* Pretentious.
high•way (hī′wā′) *n.* A main public road, esp. one connecting towns and cities.
high•way•man (hī′wā′mən) *n.* A robber who waylays travelers on a road.
hi•jack (hī′jăk′) *v. Informal.* **1.** To steal (goods) by stopping a vehicle along the road. **2.** To commandeer (a vehicle, esp. an airplane in flight). **—hi′jack′er** *n.*
hike (hīk) *v.* **hiked, hik•ing. 1.** To take a lengthy walk. **2.** To raise in amount. **3. a.** To go up, esp. to be caught up. **b.** To pull up (e.g., clothing) with a sudden motion. **—hike** *n.* **—hik′er** *n.*
hi•lar•i•ous (hĭ-lâr′ē-əs, -lăr′-) *adj.* Provoking or marked by boisterous laughter. **—hi•lar′i•ous•ly** *adv.* **—hi•lar′i•ty** *n.*
hill (hĭl) *n.* **1.** A usu. rounded natural land elevation smaller than a mountain. **2.** A small pile or mound, as of soil. **—hill′i•ness** *n.* **—hill′y** *adj.*
hill•bil•ly (hĭl′bĭl′ē) *n., pl.* **-lies.** *Informal.* One from an isolated rural region.
hill•ock (hĭl′ək) *n.* A low or small hill.
hill•side (hĭl′sīd′) *n.* The side or slope of a hill.
hill•top (hĭl′tŏp′) *n.* The top or summit of a hill.
hilt (hĭlt) *n.* A handle, esp. of a sword or dagger. **—to the hilt.** Fully : completely.
him (hĭm) *pron. objective case of* HE. Used: **1.** As the direct object of a verb <We saw *him* at the park.> **2.** As the indirect object of a verb <We mailed *him* the records.> **3.** As the object of a preposition <That car belongs to *him.*>
Hi•ma•la•yas (hĭm′ə-lā′əz, hĭ-mäl′yəz). Mountain range of SC Asia.
him•self (hĭm-sĕlf′) *pron.* **1.** That one identical with him. Used: **a.** Reflexively as the direct or indirect object of a verb or as the object of a preposition <He burned *himself.*> **b.** For emphasis <He *himself* couldn't be sure.> **c.** In an absolute construction <In debt *himself,* he was unable to contribute.> **2.** His normal condition or state <He isn't *himself* today.>
hind[1] (hīnd) *adj.* Rear or posterior <a dog's *hind* legs>
hind[2] (hīnd) *n.* The female of the European red deer.
hin•der (hĭn′dər) *v.* **1.** To interfere with the action of. **2.** To obstruct the progress of. **—hin′der•er** *n.*
Hin•di (hĭn′dē) *n.* The literary and official language of N India. **—Hin′di** *adj.*
hind•most (hīnd′mōst′) *adj.* Farthest to the back or rear.
hind•quar•ter (hīnd′kwôr′tər) *n.* **1.** The hind part of a side of meat. **2.** *often* **hindquarters.** The rump or haunches of a quadruped.
hin•drance (hĭn′drəns) *n.* **1.** The action of hindering or state of being hindered. **2.** An obstacle : impediment.
hind•sight (hīnd′sīt′) *n.* Comprehension of the meaning of an event that was lacking when it happened.
Hin•du (hĭn′do͞o) *n.* **1.** One of the native peoples of India, esp. N India. **2.** A believer in Hinduism. **—Hin′du** *adj.*
Hin•du•ism (hĭn′do͞o-ĭz′əm) *n.* A complex body of religious, philosophical, and cultural beliefs and practices of India.
hinge (hĭnj) *n.* **1.** A jointed device that permits a part, as a door or gate, to turn or swing on a stationary frame. **2.** A part or structure similar to a hinge. —*v.* **hinged, hing•ing. 1.** To affix by or provide with a hinge. **2.** To be contingent.
hint (hĭnt) *n.* **1.** A slight or indirect indication : clue. **2.** A very small amount : trace. —*v.* **1.** To make known by a hint. **2.** To offer a hint. **—hint′er** *n.*
hin•ter•land (hĭn′tər-lănd′) *n.* **1.** An inland area. **2.** A region far from cities.
hip[1] (hĭp) *n.* **1.** The part of the body between the waist and thigh that projects outward over the hipbone. **2.** The hip joint.
hip[2] (hĭp) *also* **hep** (hĕp) *adj.* **hip•per, hip•pest** *also* **hep•per, hep•pest.** *Slang.* **1.** Informed and up-to-date. **2.** Aware : alert.
hip[3] (hĭp) *n.* The berrylike, often bright-red seed case of a rose.
hip•bone (hĭp′bōn′) *n.* A large, flat bone forming a lateral half of the pelvis.
hip joint *n.* The joint between the hipbone and the thighbone.
hip•pie *also* **hip•py** (hĭp′ē) *n., pl.* **-pies.** *Informal.* A usu. young person who adopts unconventional beliefs or practices.
Hip•poc•ra•tes (hĭ-pŏk′rə-tēz′). 460?–377? B.C. Greek physician. **—Hip′po•crat′ic** (hĭp′ə-krăt′ĭk) *adj.*
hip•po•drome (hĭp′ə-drōm′) *n.* An arena used esp. for horse shows.
hip•po•pot•a•mus (hĭp′ə-pŏt′ə-məs) *n., pl.* **mus•es** or **-mi** (-mī′). A large, thick-skinned, short-legged African aquatic mammal, *Hippopotamus amphibius,* with a broad wide-mouthed muzzle.
hire (hīr) *v.* **hired, hir•ing.** To pay for the services or use of. —*n.* **1.** Money paid for services or for the use of something. **2.** The act of hiring or the state or fact of being hired. **—hir′er** *n.*
hire•ling (hīr′lĭng) *n.* A hired person motivated solely by the pay.
Hi•ro•hi•to (hîr′ō-hē′tō). b. 1901. Emperor of Japan (since 1926).
Hi•ro•shi•ma (hîr′ə-shē′mə, hĭ-rō′shĭ-mə). City of SW Honshu, Japan. *Pop.* 899,394.
hir•sute (hûr′so͞ot′, hîr′-) *adj.* Covered with hair : hairy. **—hir′sute′ness** *n.*
his (hĭz) *adj.* Used to indicate that the male previously referred to is the possessor or the agent or recipient of an action <*his* hat><*his* accomplishments><*his* first romance> —*pron.* *(sing. or pl. in number).* That or those belonging to him <The idea for the fund raiser was *his.*><The cats are *his.*>
His•pan•ic (hĭ-spăn′ĭk) *adj.* Of or relating to the language, people, or culture of Spain or Latin America. —*n.* An American of Spanish or Latin-American origin or descent.
His•pan•io•la (hĭs′pən-yō′lə). Island of the West Indies E of Cuba, divided between Haiti and the Dominican Republic.
hiss (hĭs) *n.* **1.** A sound resembling a sustained *s.* **2.** Disapproval or contempt expressed by a hiss. —*v.* **1.** To emit a hiss. **2.** To denounce by hissing. **—hiss′er** *n.*
his•ta•mine (hĭs′tə-mēn′, -mĭn) *n.* A white crystalline compound that occurs in plant and animal tissue and is believed to cause allergic reactions. **—his′ta•min′ic** (-mĭn′ĭk) *adj.*
his•tol•o•gy (hĭ-stŏl′ə-jē) *n.* The scientific study of the minute structure of animal and plant tissues as seen through a microscope. **—his′to•log′i•cal** (hĭs′tə-lŏj′ĭ-kəl) *adj.* **—his•tol′o•gist** *n.*
his•to•ri•an (hĭ-stôr′ē-ən, -stŏr′-) *n.* A specialist in the writing or study of history.
his•tor•ic (hĭ-stôr′ĭk, -stŏr′-) *adj.* **1.** Significant or renowned in history. **2.** Historical.
his•tor•i•cal (hĭ-stôr′ĭ-kəl, -stŏr′-) *adj.* **1.** Of, relating to, or taking place in history. **2.** Relating to, concerned with, or based on past events. **3.** Historic. **—his•tor′i•cal•ly** *adv.* **—his•tor′i•cal•ness** *n.*
his•to•ric•i•ty (hĭs′tə-rĭs′ĭ-tē) *n.* Historical authenticity.
his•to•ri•og•ra•phy (hĭ-stôr′ē-ŏg′rə-fē, -stŏr′-) *n.* **1.** The principles or techniques of historical research. **2.** The usu. official writing of history. **3.** Literature dealing with history. **—his•to′ri•og′ra•pher** *n.* **—his•to′ri•o•graph′ic** (-ē-ə-grăf′ĭk), **his•to′ri•o•graph′i•cal** *adj.*
his•to•ry (hĭs′tə-rē) *n., pl.* **-ries. 1.** A narrative of events : story. **2.** A chronological record of events, as of the life of a people. **3.** The branch of knowledge concerned with the recording and explanation of historical events. **4.** The recorded events of the past. **5.** A past of particular interest.
his•tri•on•ic (hĭs′trē-ŏn′ĭk) *adj.* **1.** Of or having to do with actors or acting. **2.** Unduly dramatic or emotional : affected. **—his′tri•on′i•cal•ly** *adv.*
his•tri•on•ics (hĭs′trē-ŏn′ĭks) *n.* **1.** *(sing. in number).* Theatri-

cal arts. **2.** *(pl. in number).* Unduly dramatic emotional display calculated for effect.

hit (hĭt) *v.* **hit, hit•ting. 1. a.** To deal a blow (to) : strike. **b.** To come or cause to come against forcefully. **2.** To have an adverse effect on. **3.** To arrive at : reach. **4.** To come upon : discover. **5.** To make an appeal to <*hit* her for a loan> **6.** To drive (e.g., a ball) with a blow. **7.** *Baseball.* To bat successfully. ☆***syns:*** BASH, BELT, BOP, CLIP, CLOBBER, CLOUT, KNOCK, PASTE, SLAM, SLOG, SLUG, SMACK, SMASH, SMITE, SOCK, STRIKE, SWAT, WALLOP, WHACK, WHAM —*n.* **1. a.** A blow. **b.** A collision. **2.** A shot, blow, or throw that succeeds. **3.** A great success. **4.** *Baseball.* A base hit. **—hit it off.** To get along well together. **—hit the road.** To set out : depart. **—hit′ter** *n.*

hit-and-run (hĭt′n-rŭn′) *adj.* Of or indicating a driver who fails to stop after hitting a pedestrian or another vehicle.

hitch (hĭch) *v.* **1.** To catch or tie, esp. with a hook or knot. **2.** To connect : attach. **3.** *Informal.* To unite in marriage. **4.** To lift up by tugging or jerking. **5.** *Informal.* To hitchhike. —*n.* **1.** A temporary knot for fastening. **2.** A short tug : jerk. **3.** A difficulty or delay. **4.** A period of service, esp. military service.

hitch•hike (hĭch′hīk′) *v.* To travel by obtaining rides from passing drivers. **—hitch′hik′er** *n.*

hith•er (hĭth′ər) *adv.* To this place : here. —*adj.* Being on the near side : nearer.

hith•er•to (hĭth′ər-to͞o′) *adv.* Up to now.

Hit•ler (hĭt′lər), **Adolf.** 1889–1945. Austrian-born Nazi dictator.

hit-or-miss (hĭt′ər-mĭs′) *adj.* Having no definite pattern or purpose : random.

hive (hīv) *n.* **1.** A natural or manmade structure in which bees, esp. honeybees, live. **2.** A colony of bees housed in a hive. **3.** A crowded place full of busy people.

hives (hīvz) *pl.n. (sing. or pl. in number).* An allergic condition marked by itching welts.

Ho *symbol for* HOLMIUM.

ho. *abbr.* house.

hoa•gie (hō′gē) *n.* HERO 4.

hoar (hôr, hōr) *adj.* Hoary. —*n.* Hoarfrost.

hoard (hôrd, hōrd) *n.* A hidden stockpile : cache. —*v.* To amass a hoard (of). ☆***syns:*** LAY UP, SQUIRREL, STASH, STOCKPILE **—hoard′er** *n.*

hoar•frost (hôr′frôst′, -frŏst′, hōr′-) *n.* A deposit of ice crystals forming on a cold surface exposed to moist air.

hoarse (hôrs, hōrs) *adj.* **hoars•er, hoars•est. 1.** Having a harsh, grating sound. **2.** Having a grating voice. **—hoarse′ly** *adv.* **—hoarse′ness** *n.*

hoar•y (hôr′ē, hōr′ē) *adj.* **-i•er, -i•est. 1.** Grayish or white <a *hoary* beard> **2.** Very old : aged. **—hoar′i•ness** *n.*

hoax (hōks) *n.* A trick or fraud intended to deceive. **—hoax** *v.* **—hoax′er** *n.*

hob¹ (hŏb) *n.* A projection at the side or back of the inside of a fireplace, used for keeping things warm.

hob² (hŏb) *n.* An elf or hobgoblin.

hob•ble (hŏb′əl) *v.* **-bled, -bling. 1.** To limp or cause to limp along. **2.** To fetter (an animal). **3.** To hinder : impede. —*n.* **1.** A hobbling walk or gait. **2.** A device, as a rope or strap, for hobbling an animal. **—hob′bler** *n.*

hob•by (hŏb′ē) *n., pl.* **-bies.** An activity engaged in primarily for pleasure : pastime. **—hob′by•ist** *n.*

▲word history: *Hobby* is a shortened form of *hobbyhorse,* which orig. denoted a small horse. *Hobbyhorse* developed other senses denoting representations of horses, such as a toy horse for children to ride. It is this last sense that led to the development of the modern meaning of the word *hobby.* A person with a hobby was thought to pursue a favorite pastime or obsession with the single-minded zeal of a child riding a hobbyhorse.

hob•by•horse (hŏb′ē-hôrs′) *n.* **1.** A child's toy consisting of a long stick, usu. with an imitation horse's head at 1 end. **2.** A rocking horse. **3.** A favorite subject or topic.

hob•gob•lin (hŏb′gŏb′lĭn) *n.* **1.** A goblin or elf. **2.** A bugbear : bugaboo.

hob•nail (hŏb′nāl′) *n.* A short, broad-headed nail used on shoe or boot soles for traction or to prevent wear.

hob•nob (hŏb′nŏb′) *v.* **-nobbed, -nob•bing.** To be on familiar terms <*hobnobs* with the jet set>

ho•bo (hō′bō) *n., pl.* **-boes** *or* **-bos.** A vagrant who travels aimlessly about : tramp.

Ho Chi Minh City (hō′ chē′ mĭn′). City of S Vietnam, on the Saigon R. *Pop.* 3,500,000.

hock¹ (hŏk) *n.* The joint or area in the hind leg of a quadruped, as a horse or hog, that corresponds to the human ankle.

hock² (hŏk) *Informal.* —*v.* To pawn. —*n.* The state of being pawned.

hock•ey (hŏk′ē) *n.* **1.** A game played on ice by 2 teams of skaters whose object is to drive a puck into the opponents' goal with curved sticks. **2.** A kind of hockey played on a field with a ball rather than a puck.

ho•cus-po•cus (hō′kəs-pō′kəs) *n.* **1.** Nonsense words or phrases used by sorcerers. **2.** A sleight-of-hand trick. **3.** Chicanery.

hod (hŏd) *n.* **1.** A V-shaped, long-handled trough held over the shoulder for carrying loads, as bricks or mortar. **2.** A pail for carrying coal.

hodge•podge (hŏj′pŏj′) *n.* A jumbled or random mixture.

hoe (hō) *n.* A long-handled tool with a flat blade, used to weed, cultivate, and loosen the soil. **—hoe** *v.* **—ho′er** *n.*

hoe•cake (hō′kāk′) *n.* A thin cake made of cornmeal.

hoe-down (hō′doun′) *n.* **1.** A square dance. **2.** A party featuring hoe-downs.

hog (hôg, hŏg) *n.* **1.** Any of various mammals of the family Suidae, which includes both the domesticated pig and wild species, as the boar and the wart hog. **2.** A greedy, selfish, or dirty person. —*v.* **hogged, hog•ging.** To take selfishly. **—hog′gish** *adj.* **—hog′gish•ly** *adv.* **—hog′gish•ness** *n.*

ho•gan (hō′gän′, -gən) *n.* A North American Indian dwelling usu. built of logs and mud.

hogs•head (hôgz′hĕd′, hŏgz′-) *n.* **1.** A large barrel or cask, esp. one that holds from 63 to 140 gal or from approx. 238 to 530 L. **2.** Any of several U.S. measures of liquid volume or capacity, esp. one equal to 63 gal or approx. 238 L.

hog-tie *also* **hog•tie** (hôg′tī′, hŏg′-) *v.* **1.** To tie together the feet or legs of. **2.** To hamper : impede.

hog•wash (hôg′wŏsh′, -wôsh′, hŏg′-) *n.* **1.** Swill fed to hogs. **2.** False or ridiculous talk or writing.

hoi pol•loi (hoi′ pə-loi′) *n.* The common people : masses.

hoist (hoist) *v.* To raise or haul up : lift. —*n.* **1.** An apparatus, as a crane or winch, for hoisting. **2.** The act of hoisting : pull or lift. **—hoist′er** *n.*

hoke (hōk) *v.* **hoked, hok•ing.** *Slang.* To give a false or misleading quality to.

hold¹ (hōld) *v.* **held** (hĕld), **hold•ing. 1.** To take or have and keep in or as if in one's grasp : possess. **2.** To bear : support. **3.** To keep or put in a particular place, position, or relationship. **4.** To receive or be able to receive as contents : contain. **5.** To have or keep in one's possession : own. **6.** To keep back : control or restrain. **7.** To capture the interest or attention of. **8.** To retain or defend by force. **9.** To stop or delay the movement or progress of. **10.** To occupy (a position, as political office). **11.** To bind : obligate <*held* him to his word> **12.** To keep in the memory. **13. a.** To believe : judge. **b.** To state positively : affirm. **14.** To cause to take place <*hold* a meeting><*hold* a party> **15.** To maintain a grasp or grip. **16.** To remain unyielding or securely fixed <The rope *held.*> **17.** To be valid <Our theory *holds.*> —*n.* **1.** The act or a means of holding : grasp or grip. **2.** A strong influence or power : control. **3.** Something held or used for support. **4.** A cell for prisoners. **5.** *Archaic.* A stronghold. **6.** A temporary halt or delay. **—hold forth.** To talk at great length. **—hold out. 1.** To last. **2.** To continue to work or resist. **3.** To refuse to reach or satisfy an agreement. **—hold over. 1.** To put off : postpone. **2.** To cause to continue longer than planned. **—hold up. 1.** To last : endure. **2.** To rob, esp. at gunpoint. **—hold with.** To be in accord with. **—hold′er** *n.*

hold² (hōld) *n.* The cargo storage area inside an aircraft or ship.

hold•ing (hōl′dĭng) *n.* **1.** Rented or leased land. **2.** *often* **holdings.** Property, as land, money, or stocks, that is legally owned.

holding pattern *n.* A usu. circular course flown by an aircraft awaiting clearance to land at an airport.

hold•out (hōld′out′) *n.* One who refuses to agree or cooperate.

hold•o•ver (hōld′ō′vər) *n.* One that remains from an earlier time, as an officeholder.

hold•up (hōld′ŭp′) *n.* **1.** A delay. **2.** A robbery, esp. at gun point.

hole (hōl) *n.* **1.** An opening in a solid : space or gap. **2.** A hollow place, as a depression or cave. **3.** An animal's habitation : burrow. **4.** An ugly, wretched place. **5.** A fault, error, or omission <*holes* in one's thinking> **6.** A troublesome situation. **7. a.** The small, cup-lined depression into which the ball must be hit in golf. **b.** One of the divisions of a golf course, from the tee to the hole. **—hole up.** To hide, take shelter, or seclude oneself in or as if in a hole. **—hole** *v.*

hol•i•day (hŏl′ĭ-dā′) *n.* **1.** A day free from work, esp. one set aside by law to commemorate a special person or event. **2.** A day set aside for religious observance. **3.** *esp. Brit.* A vacation.

ho•li•ness (hō′lē-nĭs) *n.* **1.** Sanctity : sacredness. **2. Holiness.** Used as a title of address for the pope.

Hol•land (hŏl′ənd). The Netherlands.

hol•lan•daise sauce (hŏl′ən-dāz′) *n.* A rich, creamy sauce of butter, egg yolks, and lemon juice or vinegar.

hol•ler¹ (hŏl′ər) *v.* To shout : yell. **—hol′ler** *n.*

†hol•ler² (hŏl′ər) *adj. & n. & v. Regional. var. of* HOLLOW.

hol·low (hŏl'ō) *adj.* **1.** Having a space or cavity within. **2.** Rounded like the inside of a bowl : concave or sunken. **3.** Lacking substance or significance. **4.** Deep-toned and echoing. *—n.* **1.** An opening, space, or cavity within something. **2.** A small valley. **3.** An emptiness : void. *—v.* To make or become hollow. **—hol'low·ly** *adv.* **—hol'low·ness** *n.*

hol·ly (hŏl'ē) *n., pl.* **-lies.** A tree or shrub of the genus *Ilex*, typically bearing glossy, spiny-edged leaves and bright-red berries.

hol·ly·hock (hŏl'ē-hŏk') *n.* A plant, *Althaea rosea*, widely cultivated for its tall spikes of large, variously colored flowers.

Hol·ly·wood (hŏl'ē-wŏŏd'). District of Los Angeles, Calif.; center of U.S. motion-picture industry.

hol·mi·um (hōl'mē-əm) *n. Symbol* **Ho** A malleable rare-earth element.

hol·o·caust (hŏl'ə-kôst', hō'lə-) *n.* Widespread or complete destruction, esp. by fire.

hol·o·gram (hŏl'ə-grăm', hō'lə-) *n.* A photographic image in 3 dimensions made without the use of a camera lens by a reflected laser beam of light on photographic film.

hol·o·graph (hŏl'ə-grăf', hō'lə-) *n.* A document, as a letter or will, handwritten by the person who signed it. **—hol'o·graph'ic, hol'o·graph'i·cal** *adj.*

ho·log·ra·phy (hō-lŏg'rə-fē) *n.* The process of producing or using a hologram. **—ho'lo·graph'** (hō'lə-grăf') *v.* **—ho·log'ra·pher** *n.* **—ho'lo·graph'ic** *adj.*

Hol·stein (hōl'stīn') *n.* One of a breed of black-and-white dairy cattle.

hol·ster (hōl'stər) *n.* A leather case shaped to hold a pistol. **—hol'stered** *adj.*

ho·ly (hō'lē) *adj.* **-li·er, -li·est. 1.** Belonging to, derived from, or associated with a divine power : sacred. **2.** Regarded with or deserving of worship or veneration : revered. **3.** Spiritually perfect : saintly. ☆**syns:** BLESSED, HALLOWED, SACRED, SACROSANCT, SANCTIFIED

Holy Communion *n.* COMMUNION 3.

Holy Ghost *n.* The 3rd member of the Christian Trinity.

Holy Ro·man Empire (rō'mən). Empire (962–1806) consisting largely of Germanic states in C and W Europe.

Holy Spirit *n.* The Holy Ghost.

ho·ly·stone (hō'lē-stōn') *n.* A piece of soft sandstone for scouring the wooden decks of a ship.

hom·age (ŏm'ĭj, hŏm'-) *n.* Great respect or honor, esp. when shown or expressed publicly.

hom·burg (hŏm'bûrg') *n.* A felt hat with a high, dented crown and a stiff, slightly rolled brim.

home (hōm) *n.* **1. a.** A place where one lives : residence. **b.** An apartment or house. **2.** A household. **3.** A place of origin. **4.** A habitat, as of an animal or plant. **5.** The goal in a game, as baseball. **6.** An institution for those who need help or care. ☆**syns:** ABODE, DIGS, DWELLING, HABITATION, HOUSE, LODGINGS, PAD, PLACE *—adv.* **1.** At or toward home. **2.** At the center of a target. **3.** To the heart or center. *—v.* **homed, hom·ing. 1.** To return home. **2.** To be guided to a target electronically. **—home'less** *adj.*

home·bod·y (hōm'bŏd'ē) *n.* A person whose life is centered around the home.

home·com·ing (hōm'kŭm'ĭng) *n.* **1.** A return to one's home. **2.** A yearly celebration for visiting college alumni.

home economics *n.* The principles and practice of managing a household.

home·land (hōm'lănd') *n.* One's native land.

home·ly (hōm'lē) *adj.* **-li·er, -li·est. 1.** Peculiar to the home or everyday life. **2.** Not pretentious or complex <*homely* proverbs> **3.** Physically unattractive : plain. **—home'li·ness** *n.*

home·made (hōm'mād') *adj.* Made in the home or by one's own hands.

home·mak·er (hōm'mā'kər) *n.* One who runs a household, esp. as a wife and mother. **—home'mak'ing** *n.* & *adj.*

ho·me·op·a·thy (hō'mē-ŏp'ə-thē) *n.* A system of medical treatment based on the use of small quantities of drugs that in large amounts produce symptoms resembling the disease being treated. **—ho'me·o·path'** (-ə-păth') *n.* **—ho'me·o·path'ic** *adj.*

ho·me·o·sta·sis (hō'mē-ō-stā'sĭs) *n.* A state of equilibrium between different but interrelated functions or elements, as in an organism or group. **—ho'me·o·stat'ic** (-stăt'ĭk) *adj.*

home plate *n. Baseball.* A slab at one of the corners of a diamond that a base runner must touch in order to score.

hom·er (hō'mər) *n.* A home run.

Ho·mer Hō'mər). fl. 850? B.C. Greek epic poet. **—Ho·mer'ic** (hō-mĕr'ĭk) *adj.*

home run *n. Baseball.* A hit that enables the batter to make a complete circuit of the bases and score a run.

home·sick (hōm'sĭk') *adj.* Yearning for home and family. **—home'sick'ness** *n.*

home·spun (hōm'spŭn') *adj.* **1.** Spun or woven at home. **2.** Made of a loosely woven, coarse woolen cloth. **3.** Simple and plain : homely <*homespun* wisdom>

home·stead (hōm'stĕd') *n.* **1.** A family's house, esp. a farmhouse, with adjacent buildings and land. **2.** A tract of land granted, as under the Homestead Act, to a settler who cleared, cultivated, and lived on it. **—home'stead'** *v.*

Homestead Act *n.* **1.** An act passed by the U.S. Congress in 1872 under which W settlers became homesteaders. **2.** *Can.* A similar act of Parliament passed in 1862.

home·stead·er (hōm'stĕd'ər) *n.* **1.** A person who has settled land as a homestead. **2.** *Can.* A person who has been given a federal grant of a homestead.

home·stretch (hōm'strĕch') *n.* **1.** The section of a racecourse between the last turn and the finish line. **2.** The final stages of a venture.

home·ward (hōm'wərd) *adj.* & *adv.* To or toward home. **—home'wards** *adv.*

home·work (hōm'wûrk') *n.* **1.** Work, as school assignments, to be done at home. **2.** Preparatory work.

home·y *also* **hom·y** (hō'mē) *adj.* **-i·er, -i·est.** Suggestive of home, as in coziness or intimacy. **—hom'ey·ness** *n.*

hom·i·cide (hŏm'ĭ-sīd', hō'mĭ-) *n.* **1.** A killing of 1 person by another. **2.** A person who kills another. **—hom'i·cid'al** *adj.*

hom·i·let·ics (hŏm'ə-lĕt'ĭks) *n. (sing. in number).* The art of preaching sermons. **—hom'i·let'ic** *adj.*

hom·i·ly (hŏm'ə-lē) *n., pl.* **-lies. 1.** A sermon delivered to a congregation. **2.** A tiresomely moralizing lecture or reprimand.

homing pigeon *n.* A pigeon trained to fly back to its home roost.

hom·i·ny (hŏm'ə-nē) *n.* Hulled and dried kernels of corn, often ground into a coarse white meal and boiled.

ho·mo·ge·ne·ous (hō'mə-jē'nē-əs, -jēn'yəs) *adj.* **1.** Of the same or similar nature or kind. **2.** Of uniform make-up or structure. **—ho'mo·ge·ne'i·ty** (-jə-nē'ĭ-tē) *n.* **—ho'mo·ge'ne·ous·ly** *adv.* **—ho'mo·ge'ne·ous·ness** *n.*

ho·mog·e·nize (hō-mŏj'ə-nīz', hə-) *v.* **-nized, -niz·ing. 1.** To make homogeneous. **2. a.** To disperse particles evenly throughout a fluid. **b.** To make uniform in consistency, esp. to make (milk) homogeneous by emulsifying the fat content. **—ho·mog'e·ni·za'tion** *n.* **—ho·mog'e·niz'er** *n.*

hom·o·graph (hŏm'ə-grăf', hō'mə-) *n.* One of 2 or more words having the same spelling but differing in origin, meaning, and sometimes pronunciation.

ho·mol·o·gous (hō-mŏl'ə-gəs, hə-) *adj.* Similar and related in structure, function, or evolutionary origin. **—hom'o·logue'** (hŏm'ə-lôg', hō'mə-), **hom'o·log'** *n.* **—ho·mol'o·gy** *n.*

hom·o·nym (hŏm'ə-nĭm', hō'mə-) *n.* One of 2 or more words having the same sound and often the same spelling but differing in meaning and origin.

hom·o·phone (hŏm'ə-fōn', hō'mə-) *n.* One of 2 or more words having the same sound but differing in spelling, origin, and meaning.

Ho·mo sa·pi·ens (hō'mō sā'pē-ĕnz', -ənz) *n.* The human race.

ho·mo·sex·u·al (hō'mə-sĕk'shōō-əl, -mō-) *adj.* Of or relating to sexual attraction toward others of the same sex. **—ho'mo·sex'u·al** *n.* **—ho'mo·sex'u·al'i·ty** *n.*

hom·y (hō'mē) *adj. var. of* HOMEY.

Hon. *abbr.* **1.** Honorable (title). **2.** *also* **hon.** honorary.

hon·cho (hŏn'chō) *n., pl.* **-chos.** *Slang.* One who is in charge : boss or manager.

Hon·du·ras (hŏn-dŏŏr'əs, -dyŏŏr'-). Country of NE Central America, mainly on the Caribbean. *Cap.* Tegucigalpa. *Pop.* 3,750,000. **—Hon·dur'an** *adj.* & *n.*

hone (hōn) *n.* A fine-grained stone for sharpening cutting tools, as knives or razors. *—v.* **honed, hon·ing. 1.** To sharpen on a hone. **2.** To perfect.

hon·est (ŏn'ĭst) *adj.* **1.** Not deceptive : truthful. **2.** Not fraudulent : genuine. **3.** Of good repute. **4.** Frank : sincere. **5.** Without affectation. **—hon'est·ly** *adv.*

hon·es·ty (ŏn'ĭ-stē) *n.* The quality or state of being honest. ☆**syns:** INCORRUPTIBILITY, INCORRUPTIBLENESS, INTEGRITY, RECTITUDE, UPRIGHTNESS

hon·ey (hŭn'ē) *n., pl.* **-eys. 1.** A sweet, sticky substance made by honeybees from the nectar of flowers and used as food. **2.** Sweetness. **3.** *Informal.* Darling : dear. **—hon'eyed, hon'ied** *adj.*

hon·ey·bee (hŭn'ē-bē') *n.* Any of various bees of the genus *Apis*, esp. *A. mellifera*, living in highly organized colonies and producing honey.

hon·ey·comb (hŭn'ē-kōm') *n.* A wax structure with many small, hexagonal cells fabricated by honeybees to hold honey

and eggs. —*v.* To fill with openings or spaces like those in a honeycomb.
hon•ey•dew (hŭn′ē-do͞o′, -dyo͞o′) *n.* A sweetish, sticky substance deposited on plant leaves by certain insects, esp. aphids.
honeydew melon *n.* A smooth-skinned, whitish melon, *Cucumis melo,* with sweet green flesh.
hon•ey•moon (hŭn′ē-mo͞on′) *n.* **1.** A trip or holiday taken by a newly married couple. **2.** An early period of harmony, as in a relationship. **—hon′ey•moon′** *v.* **—hon′ey•moon′er** *n.*
hon•ey•suck•le (hŭn′ē-sŭk′əl) *n.* A shrub or vine of the genus *Lonicera,* bearing tubular, often highly fragrant flowers.
Hong Kong *also* **Hong•Kong** (hŏng′ kŏng′, hông′ kông′). British crown colony on SE coast of China, including **Hong Kong Is.** *Cap.* Victoria. *Pop.* 5,265,000.
honk (hôngk, hŏngk) *n.* **1.** The loud, harsh, resonant cry of a goose. **2.** A sound resembling a honk, as that of an automobile horn. **—honk** *v.* **—honk′er** *n.*
hon•ky-tonk (hông′kē-tôngk′, hŏng′kē-tŏngk′) *n.* A cheap, noisy bar or nightclub.
Hon•o•lu•lu (hŏn′ə-lo͞o′lo͞o). Cap. of Hawaii, on the S coast of Oahu. *Pop.* 365,048.
hon•or (ŏn′ər) *n.* **1.** Esteem : respect. **2. a.** Recognition or distinction. **b.** A symbol or gesture of recognition or distinction. **3.** Privilege. **4. a.** Reputation. **b.** A source or cause of credit. **5. Honor.** A person of superior status. Used esp. as a title for mayors and judges. **6.** Personal integrity. **7.** A woman's chastity : purity. —*v.* **1.** To hold in or treat with honor. **2.** To confer honor or distinction upon. **3.** To accept as valid <*honor* a credit card> **—hon′or•er** *n.*
hon•or•a•ble (ŏn′ər-ə-bəl) *adj.* **1.** Deserving honor. **2.** Conferring or accompanied by honor. **3.** Marked by integrity. **4.** Illustrious. **5. Honorable.** Used as a title of respect for a high-ranking person. **—hon′or•a•ble•ness** *n.* **—hon′or•a•bly** *adv.*
hon•o•rar•i•um (ŏn′ə-râr′ē-əm) *n., pl.* **-i•ums** *or* **-i•a** (-ē-ə). A payment made for services for which a fee is not required by law or custom.
hon•or•ar•y (ŏn′ə-rĕr′ē) *adj.* **1.** Conferred or held as an honor without the usual prerequisites <an *honorary* doctorate> **2.** Unpaid : voluntary <*honorary* chairman>
hon•or•if•ic (ŏn′ə-rĭf′ĭk) *adj.* Giving or conveying respect or honor.
hon•our (ŏn′ər) *n.* & *v. esp. Brit. var. of* HONOR.
Hon•shu (hŏn′sho͞o). Largest island of Japan, in the C part.
hood[1] (ho͝od) *n.* **1.** A covering for the head and neck, often attached to a garment. **2.** Something shaped or functioning like a hood, as the hinged metal covering of an automobile engine. **—hood′ed** *adj.*
hood[2] (ho͝od) *n. Slang.* A hoodlum.
-hood *suff.* **1.** Quality or state <child*hood*> **2.** A group sharing a given quality or state <brother*hood*>
hood•lum (ho͞od′ləm, ho͝od′-) *n.* **1.** A ruffian or gangster. **2.** A tough, wild, or destructive young fellow.
hoo•doo (ho͞o′do͞o) *n.* **1.** Voodoo. **2. a.** Misfortune. **b.** One thought to bring misfortune. **—hoo′doo** *v.*
hood•wink (ho͝od′wĭngk′) *v.* To deceive by trickery.
hoo•ey (ho͞o′ē) *n. Slang.* Nonsense.
hoof (ho͝of, ho͞of) *n., pl.* **hooves** (ho͝ovz, ho͞ovz) *or* **hoofs. 1.** The horny covering of the toes or lower part of the foot of a mammal of the orders Perissodactyla and Artiodactyla, as a horse, ox, or deer. **2.** The foot of a hoofed mammal, esp. of a horse. —*v. Slang.* **1.** To dance. **2.** To walk. **—hoofed** (ho͝oft, ho͞oft) *adj.*
hook (ho͝ok) *n.* **1.** A curved or bent object or part, often of metal, used to catch, drag, suspend, attach, or fasten something. **2.** Something shaped like a hook. **3.** A thrown or struck ball, as in golf, that moves in a curving direction. **4.** A short, swinging punch delivered with the arm bent and rigid. —*v.* **1.** To catch or make fast with or as if with a hook. **2.** *Slang.* To cause to become dependent or addicted. **3.** *Slang.* To steal. **4.** To bend like a hook : curve. **—hook up. 1.** To connect (an electric or electronic device) to a source of power. **2.** To form a tie or association.
hoo•kah (ho͝ok′ə) *n.* A smoking pipe with a long tube passing through a container of water that cools the smoke as it is drawn through.
hook•er (ho͝ok′ər) *n. Slang.* A prostitute.
hook•up (ho͝ok′ŭp′) *n.* An arrangement or linkage of parts or devices acting as a unit, as in an electronic system.
hook•worm (ho͝ok′wûrm′) *n.* A parasitic intestinal worm of the family Ancylostomatidae, with hooked mouth parts.
hoo•li•gan (ho͞o′lĭ-gən) *n. Informal.* A hoodlum.
hoop (ho͞op, ho͝op) *n.* **1.** A circular piece of wood or metal used esp. to hold together the staves of a cask or barrel. **2.** A circular or ringlike object. **3.** A circle of pliable material for expanding a skirt. **4.** *Basketball. Informal.* The basket.
hoop•la (ho͞op′lä′, ho͝op′-) *n. Slang.* **1.** Noisy commotion. **2.** Exaggerated or misleading publicity.
hoose•gow (ho͞os′gou′) *n. Slang.* A jail.
Hoo•sier (ho͞o′zhər) *n. Informal.* A native or resident of Indiana.
hoot (ho͞ot) *v.* **1.** To make the deep, hollow cry of an owl. **2.** To make a loud cry, esp. in derision. **—hoot** *n.* **—hoot′er** *n.*
hoo•te•nan•ny (ho͞ot′n-ăn′ē) *n., pl.* **-nies.** An informal gathering at which folk singers perform.
Hoo•ver (ho͞o′vər). **Herbert Clark.** 1874–1964. 31st U.S. President (1929–33).
hooves (ho͝ovz, ho͞ovz) *n. var. pl. of* HOOF.
hop[1] (hŏp) *v.* **hopped, hop•ping. 1.** To move with a light springing motion. **2.** To make a short quick leap on 1 foot. **3.** To move as if by hopping <*hop* aboard> —*n.* **1.** A light, springy leap. **2.** *Informal.* A dance. **3.** A quick trip, esp. by air.
hop[2] (hŏp) *n.* **1.** A vine of the genus *Humulus,* esp. *H. lupulus,* with lobed leaves and green flowers resembling pine cones. **2. hops.** The dried flowers of the hop plant, yielding an oil used in brewing beer.
hope (hōp) *v.* **hoped, hop•ing.** To want or wish for with a feeling of confident expectation. —*n.* **1.** A wish or desire accompanied by expectation of its fulfillment. **2.** Something wished. **3.** One that gives cause for hope. **—hope′ful** *adj.* & *n.* **—hope′ful•ly** *adv.* **—hope′ful•ness** *n.* **—hope′less** *adj.* **—hope′less•ly** *adv.* **—hope′less•ness** *n.*
hop•per (hŏp′ər) *n.* **1.** One that hops, esp. a hopping insect. **2.** A receptacle in which materials, as coal, grain, or ashes, are held in readiness for unloading or dispensing.
hop•scotch (hŏp′skŏch′) *n.* A child's game in which a player throws an object, as a stone, into areas of a figure drawn on the ground and then hops through the areas to retrieve the object.
hor. *abbr.* horizontal.
Hor•ace (hôr′ĭs, hŏr′-). 65–8 B.C. Roman poet.
horde (hôrd, hōrd) *n.* A large crowd.
hore•hound (hôr′hound′, hōr′-) *n.* An aromatic Eurasian plant, *Marrubium vulgare,* with leaves that yield a bitter extract used as flavoring esp. in candy.
ho•ri•zon (hə-rī′zən) *n.* **1.** The line along which the earth and sky appear to meet. **2.** Range or limit of knowledge, experience, or interest.
hor•i•zon•tal (hôr′ĭ-zŏn′tl, hŏr′-) *adj.* Parallel to the horizon. **—hor′i•zon′tal** *n.* **—hor′i•zon′tal•ly** *adv.*
hor•mone (hôr′mōn′) *n.* A product of living cells that is carried, as by the bloodstream, to other cells, which it stimulates by chemical action. **—hor•mon′al** *adj.*
horn (hôrn) *n.* **1.** One of the bony, curved, usu. permanent projections on the heads of certain hoofed mammals, as cattle or antelopes. **2.** Something that resembles a horn. **3.** The hard, smooth substance forming the outer covering of the horns, as of cattle. **4.** A brass wind instrument, esp. a French horn. **5.** A usu. electric device that produces a loud sound. **—horn in.** To join in without being invited : intrude. **—horn′less** *adj.* **—horn′y** *adj.*
Horn, Cape. Headland on an island of Tierra del Fuego, Chile; southernmost point of South America.
horned toad *n.* A short-tailed lizard of the genus *Phrynosoma,* of W North America and Central America, with hornlike projections on the head and a flattened, spiny body.
hor•net (hôr′nĭt) *n.* Any of various large stinging wasps, esp. of the genera *Vespa* and *Vespula,* that build large, papery nests.
horn of plenty *n.* A cornucopia.
horn•pipe (hôrn′pīp′) *n.* An animated, vigorous British folk dance.
horn•pout (hôrn′pout′) *n.* A freshwater catfish, *Ictalurus nebulosus* or *Ameiurus nebulosus,* with a large head bearing barbels.

hornpout

†**horn•swog•gle** (hôrn′swŏg′əl) *v.* **-gled, -gling.** *Regional.* To bamboozle : deceive.
ho•rol•o•gy (hə-rŏl′ə-jē) *n.* **1.** The science of measuring time.

2. The art of making timepieces. **–hor′o·log′i·cal** (hôr′ə-lŏj′ĭ-kəl, hŏr′-) *adj.* **–ho·rol′o·gist** *n.*
hor·o·scope (hôr′ə-skōp′, hŏr′-) *n.* **1.** A chart of the relative positions of the planets and signs of the zodiac at a given moment, as that of a person's birth, used by astrologers esp. to foretell future events. **2.** A forecast based on a horoscope.
hor·ren·dous (hô-rĕn′dəs, hə-) *adj.* Dreadful. **–hor·ren′dous·ly** *adv.*
hor·ri·ble (hôr′ə-bəl, hŏr′-) *adj.* **1.** Arousing or marked by horror. **2.** Extremely disagreeable. **–hor′ri·bly** *adv.*
hor·rid (hôr′ĭd, hŏr′-) *adj.* **1.** HORRIBLE 1. **2.** HORRIBLE 2. **–hor′rid·ly** *adv.*
hor·ri·fy (hôr′ə-fī′, hŏr′-) *v.* **-fied, -fy·ing. 1.** To cause to experience a feeling of horror. **2.** To shock or dismay.
hor·ror (hôr′ər, hŏr′-) *n.* **1.** An intense and painful feeling of revulsion, terror, or dread. **2.** Intense dislike : loathing. **3.** One that causes a feeling of horror. **4.** *Informal.* Something unpleasant or ugly.
hors de com·bat (ôr′ də kôɴ-bä′) *adj.* & *adv.* Out of action : incapacitated.
hors d'oeuvre (ôr dûrv′) *n., pl.* **hors d'oeuvres** (ôr dûrvz′) or **hors d'oeuvre.** An appetizer served with cocktails or before a meal.
horse (hôrs) *n.* **1.** A large, hoofed quadruped mammal, *Equus caballus*, with a long mane and tail, used for riding and for pulling vehicles or carrying loads. **2.** A supporting frame or device consisting of a crossbar and 4 legs. **3.** A piece of gymnastic equipment used esp. for vaulting.
horse·back (hôrs′băk′) *adv.* On the back of a horse <ride *horseback*>
horse chestnut *n.* Any of several Eurasian trees of the genus *Aesculus*, esp. *A. hippocastanum*, with spikes of white flowers and shiny nuts enclosed in a spiny bur.
horse·flesh (hôrs′flĕsh′) *n.* Horses as a group, esp. for driving, riding, or racing.
horse·fly (hôrs′flī′) *n.* A large fly of the family Tabanidae, the female of which sucks the blood of various mammals.
horse·hair (hôrs′hâr′) *n.* **1.** The hair from a horse's mane or tail. **2.** Stiff cloth made of horsehair.
horse·hide (hôrs′hīd′) *n.* **1.** The hide of a horse. **2.** *Informal.* A baseball.
horse·laugh (hôrs′lăf′, -läf′) *n.* A loud, raucous laugh.
horse·man (hôrs′mən) *n.* **1.** One who rides horseback. **2.** One who is skilled at riding horses. **3.** One who breeds or raises horses. **–horse′man·ship′** *n.*
horse·play (hôrs′plā′) *n.* Rowdy, boisterous play.
horse·pow·er (hôrs′pou′ər) *n.* A unit of power equal to 745.7 w or 33,000 ft-lb per min.
horse·rad·ish (hôrs′răd′ĭsh) *n.* A Eurasian plant, *Armoracia rusticana* or *A. lapathifolia*, with a pungent white root used as a condiment.
horse sense *n. Informal.* Native good judgment : common sense.
horse·shoe (hôrs′shōō′, hôrsh′-) *n.* **1.** A protective U-shaped iron plate nailed to the rim of a horse's hoof. **2. horseshoes** *(sing. in number).* A game whose object is to encircle a stake with tossed horseshoes.
horseshoe crab *n.* A marine arthropod of the class Merostomata, of E North America, with a rounded body and a stiff pointed tail.
horse·tail (hôrs′tāl′) *n.* A nonflowering, narrow-leaved plant of the genus *Equisetum*, having a jointed, hollow stem.
horse·whip (hôrs′hwĭp′, -wĭp′) *n.* A whip for controlling a horse. **–horse′whip′** *v.*
hors·y *also* **hors·ey** (hôr′sē) *adj.* **-i·er, -i·est. 1.** Of or resembling a horse. **2.** Relating to or interested in horses and racing.
hor·ta·to·ry (hôr′tə-tôr′ē, -tōr′ē) *adj.* Marked by or given to exhortation.
hor·ti·cul·ture (hôr′tĭ-kŭl′chər) *n.* The science or art of raising and tending plants, esp. garden plants. **–hor′ti·cul′tur·al** *adj.* **–hor′ti·cul′tur·ist** *n.*
ho·san·na (hō-zăn′ə) *interj.* Used to praise or glorify God.
hose (hōz) *n.* **1.** *pl.* **hose.** Stockings and socks. **2.** *pl.* **hos·es.** A flexible tube for carrying fluids or gases under pressure. *–v.* **hosed, hos·ing.** To water, wash, or squirt with a hose.
Ho·se·a (hō-zē′ə, -zā′ə) *n.* See BIBLE TABLE.
ho·sier·y (hō′zhə-rē) *n.* Stockings and socks.
hosp. *abbr.* hospital.
hos·pice (hŏs′pĭs) *n.* **1.** A shelter or lodging for travelers or the needy. **2.** An establishment caring for the physical and emotional needs of terminally ill patients.
hos·pi·ta·ble (hŏs′pĭ-tə-bəl, hŏ-spĭt′ə-bəl) *adj.* **1.** Treating guests with warmth and generosity. **2.** Not narrow-minded : receptive. **–hos′pi·ta·bly** *adv.*
hos·pi·tal (hŏs′pĭ-təl, -pĭt′l) *n.* An institution where the sick and injured receive medical, surgical, and emergency care.
hos·pi·tal·i·ty (hŏs′pĭ-tăl′ĭ-tē) *n., pl.* **-ties.** Hospitable reception, treatment, or inclination.
hos·pi·tal·ize (hŏs′pĭt′l-īz′) *v.* **-ized, -iz·ing.** To admit to a hospital for care or treatment. **–hos′pi·tal·i·za′tion** *n.*
host[1] (hōst) *n.* **1.** One who receives and entertains guests. **2.** *Biol.* A living organism, as an animal or plant, on or in which a parasite lives. **–host** *v.*
host[2] (hōst) *n.* **1.** An army. **2.** A large number : multitude.
host[3] *also* **Host** (hōst) *n.* The consecrated bread of the Eucharist.
hos·tage (hŏs′tĭj) *n.* A person held as security pending the fulfillment of certain terms.
hos·tel (hŏs′təl) *n.* **1.** A supervised, low-priced lodging esp. for young travelers. **2.** An inn or hotel. **–hos′tel·er** *n.*
hos·tel·ry (hŏs′təl-rē) *n., pl.* **-ries.** A lodging, as an inn or hotel.
host·ess (hōs′tĭs) *n.* **1.** A woman who receives and entertains guests. **2.** A woman who greets patrons, as in a restaurant.
hos·tile (hŏs′təl, -tīl′) *adj.* **1.** Of or relating to an enemy. **2.** Experiencing or expressing antagonism. **–hos′tile·ly** *adv.*
hos·til·i·ty (hŏ-stĭl′ĭ-tē) *n., pl.* **-ties. 1.** Deep-seated hatred or oppositon : antagonism. **2. a.** A hostile act or incident. **b. hostilities.** Open warfare.
hos·tler (hŏs′lər) *n.* One who stables and cares for horses, as at an inn.
hot (hŏt) *adj.* **hot·ter, hot·test. 1.** Marked by or giving off great heat. **b.** Being at or marked by a high temperature. **2.** Abnormally, uncomfortably, or undesirably warm. **3.** Very pungent. **4. a.** Electrically charged <a *hot* wire> **b.** Radioactive, esp. to a hazardous degree. **5.** Marked by emotional warmth : ardent. **6.** *Slang.* Recently and unlawfully acquired <a *hot* car> **7.** *Informal.* **a.** Newly produced or obtained <*hot* news> **b.** Arousing intense interest <a *hot* topic> **8.** *Slang.* Having or marked by exceptional skill. **–hot** *adv.* **–hot′ly** *adv.* **–hot′ness** *n.*
hot air *n. Slang.* Vain or idle talk.
hot·bed (hŏt′bĕd′) *n.* **1.** A glass-covered, heated bed of soil used esp. for raising seedlings. **2.** An environment conducive to rapid and excessive growth, esp. of something negative.
hot-blood·ed (hŏt′blŭd′ĭd) *adj.* Easily excited : passionate. **–hot′-blood′ed·ly** *adv.* **–hot′-blood′ed·ness** *n.*
hot·box (hŏt′bŏks′) *n.* An overheated axle or journal bearing, as on a railway car.
hot cake *n.* A pancake.
hot dog *n.* A heated frankfurter usu. served in a long roll.
ho·tel (hō-tĕl′) *n.* A public establishment providing lodging and often meals, entertainment, and other services.
hot flash *n.* A transient vasomotor symptom of menopause involving dilation of the skin capillaries and the sensation of heat.
hot·foot (hŏt′fo͝ot′) *v.* To hasten.
hot·head·ed (hŏt′hĕd′ĭd) *adj.* **1.** Having a fiery temper. **2.** Recklessly impulsive. **–hot′head′** *n.* **–hot′head′ed·ly** *adv.* **–hot′head′ed·ness** *n.*
hot·house (hŏt′hous′) *n.* A heated greenhouse for raising plants.
hot line *n.* A direct communications line for use in a crisis.
hot plate *n.* A portable, often electric appliance for heating or cooking food.
hot potato *n.* An issue or problem that entails embarrassing or unpleasant consequences for anyone handling it.
hot rod *n.* An automobile rebuilt or modified for greater power and speed. **–hot rodder** *n.*
hot seat *n. Slang.* **1.** The electric chair. **2.** A position of difficulty or stress.
hot·shot (hŏt′shŏt′) *n. Slang.* One who ostentatiously displays expertise.
hound (hound) *n.* **1.** Any of several kinds of long-eared dogs orig. bred and used for hunting. **2.** A devotee. *–v.* **1.** To pursue without letup. **2.** To nag constantly.
hour (our) *n.* **1.** One of the 24 parts of a day. **2.** The time of day as indicated on a timepiece. **3. a.** A customary time <lunch *hour*> **b. hours.** A specific period of time <office *hours*>
hour·glass (our′glăs′) *n.* A 2-chambered glass instrument with a narrow connecting neck that measures the passage of an hour by the trickling of sand or mercury from 1 chamber to the other.
hou·ri (ho͝or′ē) *n., pl.* **-ris.** One of the beautiful young maidens of the Moslem paradise.
hour·ly (our′lē) *adj.* **1. a.** Done or occurring every hour. **b.** Recurring frequently. **2.** By the hour <*hourly* wages> **–hour′ly** *adv.*
house (hous) *n., pl.* **hous·es** (hou′zĭz). **1. a.** A residential

building occupied by 1 or more families. **b.** A household. **2. a.** A building used for a given purpose, as entertainment. **b.** The audience or patrons of such a place. **3.** A business firm. **4.** A legislative body. *—v.* (houz) **housed, hous•ing. 1.** To provide with lodgings or work space. **2.** To shelter or store. **3.** To serve as shelter for : contain.

house•boat (hous'bōt') *n.* A barge, equipped for use as a home.

house•break•ing (hous'brā'kĭng) *n.* The act of breaking into another's house for the purpose of committing a felony. **—house'break'er** *n.*

house•bro•ken (hous'brō'kən) *adj.* Trained, as a dog, in habits of excretion appropriate to indoor living.

house•coat (hous'kōt') *n.* A woman's often long-skirted robe for wear at home.

house•fly (hous'flī') *n.* A common fly, *Musca domestica,* that is found in and around human dwellings and is a carrier of a wide variety of diseases.

house•hold (hous'hōld') *n.* A unit comprising a family and others who share the same living space. *—adj.* **1.** Domestic. **2.** Commonplace. **—house'hold'er** *n.*

house•hus•band (hous'hŭz'bənd) *n.* A husband who manages the household while his wife earns the family income.

house•keep•er (hous'kē'pər) *n.* One employed to do household tasks. **—house'keep'ing** *n.*

house•maid (hous'mād') *n.* A woman employed to do housework.

house•moth•er (hous'mŭ*th*'ər) *n.* A woman who supervises a residence, as a dormitory, for young people.

House of Assembly *n. Can.* The provincial legislature of Newf.

house•warm•ing (hous'wôr'mĭng) *n.* A party to celebrate the recent occupancy of a residence.

house•wife (hous'wīf') *n.* **1.** A married woman who manages the affairs of a household. **2.** (hŭz'ĭf) A small container for sewing equipment, as needles and thread. **—house'wife'li•ness** *n.* **—house'wife'ly** *adj.* **—house'wif'er•y** *n.*

house•work (hous'wûrk') *n.* Household tasks, esp. cleaning.

hous•ing (hou'zĭng) *n.* **1.** Habitations for people. **2.** A dwelling place. **3.** Something that covers, protects, or supports.

Hous•ton (hyōō'stən). Port city of Tex., in the SE. *Pop.* 1,594,086.

hove (hōv) *v. Naut. p.t. & p.p. of* HEAVE.

hov•el (hŭv'əl, hŏv'-) *n.* A small, wretchedly squalid dwelling : hut.

hov•er (hŭv'ər, hŏv'-) *v.* **1.** To fly, soar, or float suspended in the air. **2.** To remain or linger close by. **3.** To waver : vacillate. **—hov'er•er** *n.* **—hov'er•ing•ly** *adv.*

how (hou) *adv.* **1.** In what manner or way <*How* do you spell it?> **2.** In what condition or state <*How* is your mother?> **3.** To what extent, degree, or amount <*How* efficient is she?> **4.** For what reason <*How* can you be so sad?> **5.** With what meaning <*How* should we interpret that remark?> *—conj.* **1.** In what manner or state <don't know *how* they did it> **2.** In whatever way : however <do it *how* you like> **—how come.** *Informal.* For what reason : why <*How come* we can't go?>

how•be•it (hou-bē'ĭt) *Archaic. —adv.* Nonetheless. *—conj.* Although.

how•dah (hou'də) *n.* A usu. canopied seat on the back of an elephant or camel.

†**how•dy** (hou'dē) *interj. Regional.* Used to express greeting.

how•ev•er (hou-ev'ər) *adv.* **1.** By whatever manner or means. **2.** To whatever extent or degree. *—conj.* Nevertheless.

how•it•zer (hou'ĭt-sər) *n.* A short cannon that fires shells at a high angle.

howl (houl) *v.* **1.** To utter a long, loud, plaintive sound characteristic of wolves. **2.** To cry loudly : wail. **—howl** *n.*

howl•er (hou'lər) *n.* **1.** One that howls. **2.** An absurd or amusing mistake.

how•so•ev•er (hou'sō-ev'ər) *adv.* **1.** To whatever extent or degree. **2.** By whatever means.

hoy•den (hoid'n) *n.* A lively, boisterous girl or young woman : tomboy.

hp *abbr.* horsepower.

hr *abbr.* hour.

h.s. or **H.S.** *abbr.* high school.

ht *abbr.* height.

hua•ra•che (wə-rä'chē, hə-) *n.* A flat-heeled sandal with woven leather strips on the upper part.

hub (hŭb) *n.* **1. a.** The center of a wheel. **b.** The center of a fan or propeller. **2.** A focus of activity.

hub•bub (hŭb'ŭb') *n.* Noisy uproar or confusion : tumult.

hub•cap (hŭb'kăp') *n.* A removable metal cap fitting over the hub of an automobile wheel.

hu•bris (hyōō'brĭs) *n.* Excessive self-confidence : arrogance. **—hu•bris'tic** *adj.*

huck•le•ber•ry (hŭk'əl-bĕr'ē) *n.* A New World shrub of the genus *Gaylussacia,* related to the blueberries and bearing glossy, blackish, many-seeded edible berries.

huck•ster (hŭk'stər) *n.* **1.** One that peddles goods : hawker. **2.** *Slang.* An advertising copywriter.

hud•dle (hŭd'l) *n.* **1.** A closely packed group or crowd. **2.** *Football.* A brief gathering of teammates to prepare signals for the next play. **3.** A private meeting or conference. *—v.* **-dled, -dling. 1.** To crowd or nestle together. **2.** To consult : confer.

Hud•son (hŭd'sən). **1.** Bay of the Atlantic in EC Canada. **2.** River of E N.Y.

hue (hyōō) *n.* **1.** The characteristic of color that allows it to be categorized on a scale running from red through yellow, green, and blue to violet. **2.** A particular color : shade. **3.** Color <sunset *hues*> **—hued** *adj.*

hue and cry *n.* A vehement public outcry or protest.

huff (hŭf) *n.* A fit of ill temper or resentment. *—v.* To breathe heavily, as from exertion. **—huff'i•ly** *adv.* **—huff'i•ness** *n.* **—huf'fy** *adj.*

hug (hŭg) *v.* **hugged, hug•ging. 1.** To clasp closely : embrace. **2.** To cling, keep, or stay close to. **—hug** *n.* **—hug'ga•ble** *adj.* **—hug'ger** *n.*

huge (hyōōj) *adj.* **hug•er, hug•est.** Of great size, quantity, or extent : immense. **—huge'ly** *adv.* **—huge'ness** *n.*

Hu•go (hyōō'gō), **Victor Marie.** 1802–85. French author.

Hu•gue•not (hyōō'gə-nŏt') *n.* A French Protestant of the 16th and 17th cent.

hu•la (hōō'lə) *n.* A Hawaiian dance marked by undulating movements of the hips, arms, and hands.

hulk (hŭlk) *n.* **1.** A heavy, bulky ship. **2.** An old, dilapidated ship. **3.** One that is massive, unwieldy, or awkward. *—v.* To bulk : loom.

hulk•ing (hŭl'kĭng) *adj.* Unwieldy or bulky : massive.

hull (hŭl) *n.* **1. a.** The cluster of leaflets at the stem end of certain fruits. **b.** The outer husk or pod of certain seeds, nuts, and fruits. **2.** The framework of a ship. **3.** The external casing of a rocket, guided missile, or spaceship. *—v.* To remove the hulls from <*hull* strawberries>

hul•la•ba•loo (hŭl'ə-bə-lōō') *n.* Great uproar or noisy excitement.

hul•lo (hə-lō') *interj. & n. var. of* HELLO.

hum (hŭm) *v.* **hummed, hum•ming. 1.** To emit or produce a continuous low-pitched sound : drone. **2.** To be full of or alive with activity. **3.** To sing with the lips closed. **—hum** *n.* **—hum'mer** *n.*

hu•man (hyōō'mən) *adj.* **1.** Of, relating to, or typical of humankind. **2.** Having or manifesting human qualities or form. **3.** Composed of people <made a *human* blockade> *—n.* An individual person. **—hu'man•ly** *adv.* **—hu'man•ness** *n.*

hu•mane (hyōō-mān') *adj.* **1.** Compassionate : merciful. **2.** Emphasizing human values and concerns. **—hu•mane'ly** *adv.* **—hu•mane'ness** *n.*

hu•man•ism (hyōō'mə-nĭz'əm) *n.* **1.** A philosophy or attitude centered chiefly on the values, interests, and potential of human beings. **2.** *often* **Humanism.** The shift to secular concerns that resulted from the study of the Greek and Roman classics during the Renaissance. **—hu'man•ist** *n.* **—hu'man•is'tic** *adj.*

hu•man•i•tar•i•an (hyōō-măn'ĭ-târ'ē-ən) *n.* One promoting human welfare, esp. through philanthropy. **—hu•man'i•tar'i•an** *adj.* **—hu•man'i•tar'i•an•ism** *n.*

hu•man•i•ty (hyōō-măn'ĭ-tē) *n., pl.* **-ties. 1.** Human beings as a group : humankind. **2.** The quality, state, or fact of being human. **3.** The quality of being humane : kindness. **4. humanities.** The cultural as distinguished from the scientific branches of learning.

hu•man•ize (hyōō'mə-nīz') *v.* **-ized, -iz•ing. 1.** To endow with human form or qualities. **2.** To make humane. **—hu'man•i•za'tion** *n.*

hu•man•kind (hyōō'mən-kīnd') *n.* The human race.

hu•man•oid (hyōō'mə-noid') *adj.* Nearly human, as in appearance. *—n.* An android.

hum•ble (hŭm'bəl) *adj.* **-bler, -blest. 1.** Marked by modesty or meekness. **2.** Respectfully deferential. **3.** Lowly and unpretentious. *—v.* **-bled, -bling. 1.** To make humble. **2.** To lower in status or condition. **—hum'ble•ness** *n.* **—hum'bler** *n.* **—hum'bly** *adv.*

hum•bug (hŭm'bŭg') *n.* **1.** A fraud : hoax. **2.** Foolish talk. *—v.* **-bugged, -bug•ging.** To deceive. **—hum'bug'ger•y** *n.*

hum•din•ger (hŭm'dĭng'ər) *n. Slang.* One that is markedly superior.

hum•drum (hŭm'drŭm') *adj.* Monotonous : boring.

hu·mer·us (hyōō′mər-əs) *n., pl.* **-mer·i** (-mə-rī′). The long bone of the upper arm in humans. **–hu′mer·al** *adj.*
hu·mid (hyōō′mĭd) *adj.* Marked by a large amount of moisture : damp.
hu·mid·i·fy (hyōō-mĭd′ə-fī′) *v.* **-fied, -fy·ing.** To make humid. **–hu·mid′i·fi′er** *n.*
hu·mid·i·ty (hyōō-mĭd′ĭ-tē) *n.* **1.** Dampness. **2.** The amount of moisture in the atmosphere.
hu·mi·dor (hyōō′mĭ-dôr′) *n.* A container for cigars in which the air is kept humidified by a special device.
hu·mil·i·ate (hyōō-mĭl′ē-āt′) *v.* **-at·ed, -at·ing.** To injure the dignity or pride of : humble. **–hu·mil′i·at′ing·ly** *adv.* **–hu·mil′i·a′tion** *n.*
hu·mil·i·ty (hyōō-mĭl′ĭ-tē) *n.* The quality or state of being humble.
hum·ming·bird (hŭm′ĭng-bûrd′) *n.* A very small New World bird of the family Trochilidae, with brilliant plumage and a long, slender bill.
hum·mock (hŭm′ək) *n.* A low, rounded hill or mound, as of earth or snow. **–hum′mock·y** *adj.*
hu·mor (hyōō′mər) *n.* **1.** The quality of being funny or comical. **2.** The ability to perceive, enjoy, or express what is funny or comical. **3. a.** A state of mind or feeling : mood. **b.** Characteristic disposition : temperament. **4.** A sudden whim : caprice. **5.** *Physiol.* A bodily fluid, as blood or lymph. *–v.* To indulge the wishes or mood of. **–hu′mor·ist** *n.* **–hu′mor·less** *adj.* **–hu′mor·less·ly** *adv.* **–hu′mor·less·ness** *n.* **–hu′mor·ous** *adj.* **–hu′mor·ous·ly** *adv.* **–hu′mor·ous·ness** *n.*
hu·mour (hyōō′mər) *n. & v. esp. Brit. var. of* HUMOR.
hump (hŭmp) *n.* **1.** A rounded lump or protuberance, as on the back of a camel. **2.** HUMPBACK 1. **–over the hump.** Past the critical or most difficult stage.
hump·back (hŭmp′băk′) *n.* **1.** An abnormal condition in which the back has a hump or curvature. **2.** A person with a humpback. **–hump′backed′** *adj.*
hu·mus (hyōō′məs) *n.* The dark-colored organic part of soil consisting of decayed plant and animal matter.
Hun (hŭn) *n.* One of a fierce, barbaric race of Asian nomads who invaded Europe in the 5th cent. A.D.
hunch (hŭnch) *n.* An intuitive feeling. *–v.* **1.** To bend or draw up into a hump. **2.** To push or thrust oneself forward.
hunch·back (hŭnch′băk′) *n.* A person with a hunched back. **–hunch′backed′** *adj.*
hun·dred (hŭn′drĭd) *n., pl.* **-dreds** *or* **-dred.** The cardinal number equal to 10 × 10 or 10^2. **–hun′dred** *adj. & pron.* **–hun′dredth** *n. & adj. & adv.*
hun·dred·weight (hŭn′drĭd-wāt′) *n., pl.* **-weight** *or* **-weights. 1.** A unit of weight equal to approx. 45.6 kg or 100 lb. **2.** *esp. Brit.* A unit of weight equal to approx. 50.8 kg or 112 lb.
hung (hŭng) *v. p.t. & p.p. of* HANG.
Hun·ga·ry (hŭng′gə-rē). Country of C Europe. *Cap.* Budapest. *Pop.* 10,945,000. **–Hun·gar′i·an** (hŭng-gâr′ē-ən) *adj. & n.*
hun·ger (hŭng′gər) *n.* **1.** A strong need or desire for food. **2.** A strong craving <a *hunger* for praise> **–hun′ger** *v.* **–hun′gri·ly** *adv.* **–hun′gry** *adj.*
hunk (hŭngk) *n. Informal.* A large piece.
†**hun·ker** (hŭng′kər) *v.* To crouch close to the ground : squat. *–n.* **hunkers.** *Regional.* The haunches.
hun·ky-do·ry (hŭng′kē-dôr′ē, -dōr′ē) *adj. Slang.* Generally satisfactory : fine.
hunt (hŭnt) *v.* **1. a.** To pursue (game) for food or sport. **b.** To make a search (for) : seek. **2.** To chase and try to capture (e.g., a criminal). **3.** To travel over or through in search of prey. *–n.* **1.** The act or sport of hunting. **2. a.** A hunting expedition. **b.** The participants in a hunting expedition. **–hunt′er** *n.* **–hunt′ress** *n.*
hunts·man (hŭnts′mən) *n.* One who hunts, esp. one who has charge of the hounds for a hunt.
hur·dle (hûr′dl) *n.* **1.** A movable barrier to be jumped over in a race. **2.** An obstacle to be overcome. *–v.* **-dled, -dling. 1.** To leap over (a barrier). **2.** To surmount (an obstacle). **–hur′dler** *n.*
hur·dy-gur·dy (hûr′dē-gûr′dē, hûr′dē-gûr′-) *n., pl.* **-dies.** A musical instrument, as a barrel organ, played by turning a crank.
hurl (hûrl) *v.* **1.** To throw forcefully : fling. **2.** To utter with intensity. **3.** *Baseball.* To pitch. **4.** To move very rapidly : hurtle. **–hurl** *n.* **–hurl′er** *n.*
hur·ly-bur·ly (hûr′lē-bûr′lē) *n., pl.* **-lies.** Uproar : turmoil.
Hu·ron (hyŏŏr′ən, -ŏn′), **Lake.** 2nd largest of the Great Lakes.
hur·rah (hŏŏ-rä′, -rô′) *interj.* Used to express pleasure, approval, or exultation. **–hur·rah′** *n. & v.*
hur·ri·cane (hûr′ĭ-kān′, hŭr′-) *n.* A severe tropical cyclone with winds exceeding 75 mph.
hur·ry (hûr′ē, hŭr′ē) *v.* **-ried, -ry·ing. 1.** To move or cause to move speedily or hastily. **2.** To act or urge to act with excessive haste : rush. *–n., pl.* **-ries. 1.** The act of hurrying. **2.** A condition of urgency : rush. **–hur′ried·ly** *adv.* **–hur′ried·ness** *n.*
hurt (hûrt) *v.* **hurt, hurt·ing. 1.** To experience or cause to experience physical pain or emotional distress. **2.** To cause harm to : damage. **3.** To offend. *–n.* **1.** A bodily pain or injury. **2.** Mental suffering. **3.** Damage : harm. **–hurt′ful** *adj.*
hur·tle (hûr′tl) *v.* **-tled, -tling. 1.** To move very swiftly, esp. with a rushing sound. **2.** To hurl or fling forcefully.
hus·band (hŭz′bənd) *n.* A man who is married. *–v.* To use or manage wisely.
hus·band·man (hŭz′bənd-mən) *n.* One engaged in farming : farmer.
hus·band·ry (hŭz′bən-drē) *n.* **1.** Agriculture. **2.** Wise management of resources.
hush (hŭsh) *v.* **1.** To make or become quiet. **2.** To make or become calm. **3.** To keep secret : suppress. *–n.* Silence.
hush-hush (hŭsh′hŭsh′) *adj. Informal.* Confidential : secret.
hush·pup·py (hŭsh′pŭp′ē) *n.* A fritter of cornmeal.
husk (hŭsk) *n.* **1.** The dry or leaflike outer envelope of certain vegetables, fruits, and seeds. **2.** An often worthless external layer or shell. *–v.* To remove the husk from <*husk* corn> **–husk′er** *n.*
husk·y[1] (hŭs′kē) *adj.* **-i·er, -i·est.** Having a hoarse or grating sound. **–husk′i·ly** *adv.* **–husk′i·ness** *n.*
husk·y[2] (hŭs′kē) *adj.* **-i·er, -i·est.** Strong and ruggedly built. **–husk′i·ness** *n.*
hus·ky[3] (hŭs′kē) *n., pl.* **-kies.** A thick-coated Arctic dog used esp. to pull sleds.
hus·sar (hŏŏ-zär′, -sär′) *n.* A member of the light cavalry in some European armies.
hus·sy (hŭz′ē, hŭs′ē) *n., pl.* **-sies. 1.** An impertinent or mischievous girl. **2.** A woman of doubtful morals.
hus·tings (hŭs′tĭngz) *pl.n. (sing. or pl. in number).* **1.** A political campaign. **2.** A place for political campaign speeches.
hus·tle (hŭs′əl) *v.* **-tled, -tling. 1.** To push roughly : jostle. **2.** To move or urge hurriedly along. **3.** To work quickly and busily. **4.** *Slang.* To make energetic efforts to solicit business or make money. **–hus′tle** *n.* **–hus′tler** *n.*
hut (hŭt) *n.* A small, often crudely built and temporary dwelling : shack.
hutch (hŭch) *n.* **1.** A pen for small animals. **2.** A low cupboard usu. with open shelving over it. **3.** A shack : hut.
huz·za *also* **huz·zah** (hə-zä′) *Archaic. interj.* Used to express joy, approval, or exultation. **–huz·za′** *n.*
hwy. *abbr.* highway.
hy·a·cinth (hī′ə-sĭnth) *n.* A bulbous plant of the genus *Hyacinthus,* bearing a cluster of variously colored, highly fragrant bell-shaped flowers.
hy·brid (hī′brĭd) *n.* **1.** An offspring of genetically dissimilar animals or plants, as members of different varieties, species, or breeds. **2.** Something of mixed origin or make-up. **–hy′brid** *adj.*
hy·brid·ize (hī′brĭ-dīz′) *v.* **-ized, -iz·ing.** To produce or cause to produce hybrids : crossbreed. **–hy′brid·i·za′tion** *n.*
Hy·der·a·bad (hī′dər-ə-bäd′, -băd′). City of C India, ESE of Bombay. *Pop.* 1,607,400.
hy·dra (hī′drə) *n., pl.* **-dras** *or* **-drae** (-drē). Any of various small freshwater polyps of the genus *Hydra,* with a tubular body and at 1 end an oral opening surrounded by tentacles.

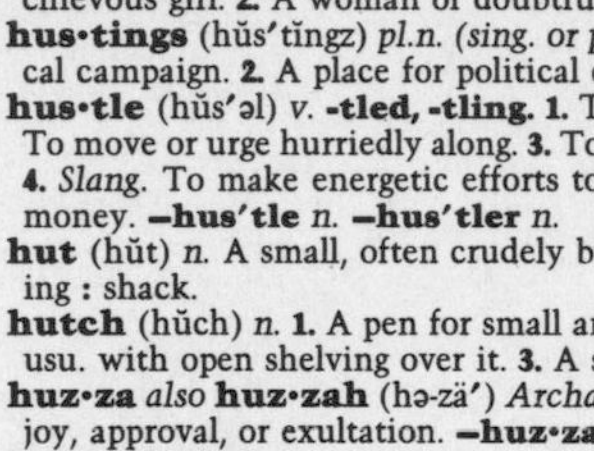

hydra

hy·dran·gea (hī-drān′jə, -drăn′-) *n.* A shrub or tree of the genus *Hydrangea,* bearing large, flat-topped or rounded white, pink, or blue flower clusters.
hy·drant (hī′drənt) *n.* A standing pipe with a valve and spout for drawing water from a water main : fireplug.
hy·drate (hī′drāt′) *n.* A chemical compound formed by the combination of water with another substance in definite proportions. *–v.* **-drat·ed, -drat·ing.** To form a hydrate. **–hy·dra′tion** *n.*

hy·drau·lic (hī-drô′lĭk) *adj.* **1.** Of, involving, moved by, or operated by a pressurized liquid, esp. water. **2.** Of or pertaining to hydraulics. **3.** Hardening under water, as Portland cement.
hy·drau·lics (hī-drô′lĭks) *n. (sing. in number).* The scientific study and technological application of the behavior of fluids.
hy·dro·car·bon (hī′drə-kär′bən) *n.* An organic compound, as methane, that contains only hydrogen and carbon.
hy·dro·ceph·a·lus (hī′drō-sĕf′ə-ləs) *also* **hy·dro·ceph·a·ly** (-lē) *n.* An abnormal accumulation of fluid in the cerebral ventricles that causes skull enlargement and brain atrophy. **—hy′dro·ce·phal′ic** (-sə-făl′ĭk) *adj.*
hy·dro·chlo·ric acid (hī′drə-klôr′ĭk, -klōr′-) *n.* A colorless, fuming, poisonous solution of hydrogen chloride in water.
hy·dro·dy·nam·ics (hī′drō-dī-năm′ĭks) *n. (sing. in number).* The science of the characteristics of fluids in motion, esp. fluids that cannot be compressed.
hy·dro·e·lec·tric (hī′drō-ĭ-lĕk′trĭk) *adj.* Of, pertaining to, or using electricity produced by the power of running water. **—hy′dro·e·lec·tric′i·ty** (-trĭs′ĭ-tē) *n.*
hy·dro·foil (hī′drə-foil′) *n.* **1.** A winglike blade attached to the hull of a boat below the water line to raise it clear of the water for fuel-efficient operation at high speed. **2.** A boat having hydrofoils.
hy·dro·gen (hī′drə-jən) *n. Symbol* **H** A colorless, highly flammable gas that is the lightest of the chemical elements. **—hy·drog′e·nous** (-drŏj′ə-nəs) *adj.*
hy·dro·gen·ate (hī′drə-jə-nāt′, hī-drŏj′ə-) *v.* **-at·ed, -at·ing. 1.** To treat or combine chemically with hydrogen. **2.** To treat (a liquid vegetable oil) with hydrogen and convert it to a solid fat. **—hy′dro·gen·a′tion** *n.*
hydrogen bomb *n.* An extremely destructive bomb whose explosive power is obtained from the rapid release of atomic energy in the fusion of hydrogen and lithium nuclei.
hydrogen peroxide *n.* A colorless, unstable, strongly oxidizing liquid compound used esp. in solution as an antiseptic.
hy·drol·y·sis (hī-drŏl′ĭ-sĭs) *n.* Decomposition of a chemical compound by reaction with the elements of water. **—hy′dro·lize′** (hī′drə-līz′) *v.* **—hy′dro·lyt′ic** (-lĭt′ĭk) *adj.*
hy·drom·e·ter (hī-drŏm′ĭ-tər) *n.* An instrument for measuring the specific gravity of a fluid.
hy·dro·pho·bi·a (hī′drə-fō′bē-ə) *n.* **1.** Pathological fear of water. **2.** Rabies. **—hy′dro·pho′bic** *adj.*
hy·dro·plane (hī′drə-plān′) *n.* **1.** A seaplane. **2.** A speedboat designed so that the prow and much of the hull lift out of the water and skim the surface at high speeds.
hy·dro·pon·ics (hī′drə-pŏn′ĭks) *n. (sing. in number).* The cultivation of plants in a water and mineral solution. **—hy′dro·pon′ic** *adj.* **—hy′dro·pon′i·cal·ly** *adv.*
hy·dro·stat·ics (hī′drə-stăt′ĭks) *n. (sing. in number).* The science of the characteristics of fluids at rest, esp. fluids that cannot be compressed. **—hy′dro·stat′ic, hy′dro·stat′i·cal** *adj.*
hy·dro·ther·a·py (hī′drə-thĕr′ə-pē) *n.* The use of water in the treatment of disease or disability.
hy·drous (hī′drəs) *adj.* Containing water, esp. when chemically combined.
hy·drox·ide (hī-drŏk′sīd′) *n.* A chemical compound of an element or radical joined to an oxygen-and-hydrogen group.
hy·e·na (hī-ē′nə) *n.* Any of several carnivorous mammals of the genera *Hyaena* or *Crocuta,* of Africa and Asia, with coarse hair and powerful jaws.
hy·giene (hī′jēn′) *n.* **1.** The science concerned with maintenance of sound health and prevention of disease. **2.** Conditions and practices that contribute to disease prevention. **—hy′gi·en′ic** (-jē-ĕn′ĭk) *adj.* **—hy′gi·en′i·cal·ly** *adv.* **—hy·gien′ist** *n.*
hy·grom·e·ter (hī-grŏm′ĭ-tər) *n.* An instrument that measures the amount of moisture in the air. **—hy·grom′e·try** *n.*
hy·ing (hī′ĭng) *v. var. pres. p. of* HIE.
hy·men (hī′mən) *n.* A thin membrane partly closing the external vaginal orifice.
hy·me·ne·al (hī′mə-nē′əl) *adj.* Of or relating to a nuptial ceremony or marriage.
hymn (hĭm) *n.* A song of praise or thanksgiving, esp. to God. **—hymn** *v.*
hym·nal (hĭm′nəl) *n.* A book of hymns.
hyp. *abbr.* hypothesis.
hype (hīp) *n. Slang.* **1.** Something intended to deceive. **2.** Exaggerated advertising or promotion. **—hype** *v.*
hyper– *pref.* **1.** Over : above. **2.** Excessive : excessively. See below for a list of self-explanatory words formed with the prefix **hyper–.**
hy·per·ac·tive (hī′pər-ăk′tĭv) *adj.* Excessively or abnormally active. **—hy′per·ac·tiv′i·ty** *n.*
hy·per·bo·la (hī-pûr′bə-lə) *n.* A plane curve that has 2 branches and is composed of the set of all points such that the difference of their distances from the 2 fixed points is a constant.
hy·per·bo·le (hī-pûr′bə-lē) *n.* Exaggeration used as a figure of speech.
hy·per·bol·ic (hī′pər-bŏl′ĭk) *or* **hy·per·bol·i·cal** (-ĭ-kəl) *adj.* **1.** Of or marked by hyperbole. **2.** Of or shaped like a hyperbola.
hy·per·bo·re·an (hī′pər-bôr′ē-ən, -bōr′-, -bə-rē′ən) *adj.* **1.** Of or relating to the far north : arctic. **2.** Very cold : frigid.
hy·per·crit·i·cal (hī′pər-krĭt′ĭ-kəl) *adj.* Overcritical. **—hy′per·crit′i·cal·ly** *adv.*
hy·per·sen·si·tive (hī′pər-sĕn′sĭ-tĭv) *adj.* Abnormally or excessively sensitive. **—hy′per·sen′si·tive·ness, hy′per·sen′si·tiv′i·ty** *n.*
hy·per·ten·sion (hī′pər-tĕn′shən) *n.* A condition of abnormally high blood pressure. **—hy′per·ten′sive** *adj.* & *n.*
hy·per·thy·roid·ism (hī′pər-thī′roi-dĭz′əm) *n.* Abnormally excessive activity of the thyroid gland or the resulting physical condition.

hyperaccuracy
hyperaccurate
hyperacuity
hyperacute
hyperaesthete
hyperaesthetic
hyperaggressive
hyperalert
hyperaltruism
hyperarid
hyperaware
hyperawareness
hyperbarbarism
hyperbarbarous
hypercautious
hypercivilized
hyperconcentration
hyperconfidence
hyperconfident
hyperconformist
hyperconformity
hyperconscientious
hyperconscientiousness
hyperconservative
hyperdeveloped
hyperdevelopment
hyperdiabolical
hyperdistention
hyperelegancy
hyperelegant
hyperemotive
hyperenergetic
hyperenergetically
hyperenthusiasm
hyperenthusiastic
hyperenthusiastically
hyperexcitability
hyperexcitable
hyperexcited
hyperexcitement
hyperexcretion
hyperfastidious
hyperfeminine
hyperflexion
hyperfunctional
hyperfunctioning
hyperimmunize
hyperinflation
hyperinflationary
hyperintellectual
hyperintelligence
hyperintelligent
hypermanic
hypermasculine
hypermetabolic
hypermetabolism
hypermilitant
hypermodern
hypermodernist
hypermodernity
hypermotile
hypermotility
hypermutable
hyperneurotic
hypernutrition
hypernutritive
hyperorthodox
hyperoxygenate
hyperpatriotic
hyperphysical
hyperphysically
hyperpigmentation
hyperpigmented
hyperproducer
hyperproduction
hyperpure
hyperpurist
hyperradical
hyperrational
hyperreactive
hyperreactivity
hyperreactor
hyperrealism
hyperrealist
hyperrealistic
hyperresonance
hyperresonant
hyperresponsive
hyperromantic
hypersaline
hypersalinity
hypersalivation
hyperscrupulous
hypersecretion
hypersensibility
hypersensitize
hypersensual
hypersensuality
hypersensuous
hypersensuousness
hypersentimental
hypersomnolence
hypersophisticated
hyperspeculative
hyperstatic
hypersuggestibility
hypersusceptible
hypersuspicious
hypertechnical
hypertense
hyperthermal
hypertorrid
hypertoxic
hypertoxicity
hypertragic
hypertypical
hypervariability
hypervariable
hypervascularity
hypervigilance
hypervigilant
hypervirulent
hyperviscosity
hyperviscous

hy·per·tro·phy (hī-pûr′trə-fē) *n.* Abnormal overdevelopment of tissue or a bodily organ. **—hy′per·troph′ic** (-trŏf′ĭk) *adj.* **—hy·per′tro·phy** *v.*

hy·phen (hī′fən) *n.* A punctuation mark (-) used to connect or divide words or syllables. **—hy′phen** *v.*

hy·phen·ate (hī′fə-nāt′) *v.* **-at·ed, -at·ing.** To join or separate with a hyphen. **—hy′phen·a′tion** *n.*

hyp·no·sis (hĭp-nō′sĭs) *n., pl.* **-ses** (-sēz′). An induced sleeplike state in which the subject readily accepts the hypnotist's suggestions.

hyp·not·ic (hĭp-nŏt′ĭk) *adj.* **1.** Of or pertaining to hypnosis or hypnotism. **2.** Inducing or tending to induce sleep or a sleeplike state. *—n.* An agent, esp. a drug, that induces sleep. **—hyp·not′i·cal·ly** *adv.*

hyp·no·tism (hĭp′nə-tĭz′əm) *n.* **1.** The theory or practice of inducing hypnosis. **2.** Hypnosis. **—hyp′no·tist** *n.*

hyp·no·tize (hĭp′nə-tīz′) *v.* **-tized, -tiz·ing.** **1.** To practice hypnotism on. **2.** To fascinate : mesmerize. **—hyp′no·tiz′a·ble** *adj.* **—hyp′no·ti·za′tion** *n.*

hy·po (hī′pō) *n., pl.* **-pos.** *Informal.* A hypodermic needle, syringe, or injection.

hy·po·chon·dri·a (hī′pə-kŏn′drē-ə) *n.* Mental depression accompanied by an abnormal preoccupation with imaginary physical ailments. **—hy′po·chon′dri·ac′** (-ăk′) *n.* & *adj.* **—hy′po·chon·dri′a·cal** (-kən-drī′ə-kəl) *adj.*

hy·poc·ri·sy (hĭ-pŏk′rĭ-sē) *n., pl.* **-sies.** The feigning of qualities and beliefs that one does not actually possess or hold, esp. a pretense of piety or moral superiority. **—hyp′o·crite′** (hĭp′ə-krĭt′) *n.* **—hyp′o·crit′i·cal** *adj.* **—hyp′o·crit′i·cal·ly** *adv.*

hy·po·der·mic (hī′pə-dûr′mĭk) *adj.* Injected or used for injection under the skin. *—n.* **1.** A hypodermic injection. **2.** A hypodermic syringe or needle.

hypodermic needle *n.* **1.** A slender, hollow needle for use with a hypodermic syringe. **2.** A hypodermic syringe.

hypodermic syringe *n.* A syringe fitted with a hypodermic needle and used for injecting a substance, as a drug, under the skin.

hy·po·gly·ce·mi·a (hī′pō-glī-sē′mē-ə) *n.* An abnormally low level of glucose in the blood. **—hy′po·gly·ce′mic** *adj.*

hy·pot·e·nuse (hī-pŏt′n-o͞os′, -yo͞os′) *n.* The longest side of a triangle that contains a right angle.

hypoth. *abbr.* hypothesis.

hy·poth·e·sis (hī-pŏth′ĭ-sĭs) *n., pl.* **-ses** (-sēz′). **1.** A theory that explains a set of facts and can be tested by further investigation. **2.** An assumption used as a basis for investigation or argument. **—hy′po·thet′i·cal** (hī′pə-thĕt′ĭ-kəl) *adj.* **—hy′po·thet′i·cal·ly** *adv.*

hy·poth·e·size (hī-pŏth′ĭ-sīz′) *v.* **-sized, -siz·ing.** To set forth as a hypothesis.

hy·po·thy·roid·ism (hī′pō-thī′roi-dĭz′əm) *n.* Abnormally deficient activity of the thyroid gland or the resulting pathological condition.

hys·sop (hĭs′əp) *n.* A woody Asian plant, *Hyssopus officinalis,* bearing spikes of small blue flowers and aromatic leaves used as a condiment and in perfumery.

hys·ter·ec·to·my (hĭs′tə-rĕk′tə-mē) *n., pl.* **-mies.** Partial or complete surgical removal of the uterus.

hys·ter·i·a (hĭ-stĕr′ē-ə, -stîr′-) *n.* **1.** A neurosis marked by physical symptoms, as paralysis, without apparent organic cause. **2.** Excessive or uncontrollable emotion.

hys·ter·ic (hĭ-stĕr′ĭk) *n.* **1.** One suffering from hysteria. **2.** **hysterics** *(sing. or pl. in number).* **a.** A fit of uncontrollable laughing and crying. **b.** An attack of hysteria.

hys·ter·i·cal (hĭ-stĕr′ĭ-kəl) *adj.* **1.** Of, marked by, or caused by hysteria. **2.** Having or tending to have hysterics. **—hys·ter′i·cal·ly** *adv.*

Ii

i or **I** (ī) *n., pl.* **i's** or **I's.** **1.** The 9th letter of the English alphabet. **2.** A speech sound represented by the letter *i.* **3.** Something with the shape of the letter I. **4.** The Roman numeral for 1.

I[1] (ī) *pron.* The one who is speaking or writing. *—n., pl.* **I's.** The self : ego.

I[2] *symbol for* IODINE.

i. or **I.** *abbr.* island; isle.

IA *abbr.* Iowa (with Zip Code).

-ial *suff.* Of or marked by <baron*ial*>

i·amb (ī′ămb′) *also* **i·am·bus** (ī-ăm′bəs) *n.* A metrical foot made up of a short or unstressed syllable followed by a long or stressed syllable. **—i·am′bic** *adj.* & *n.*

-ian *suff.* **1.** Of, belonging to, or like <Washington*ian*> **2.** One skilled in, belonging to, or like <politic*ian*>

i·at·ro·gen·ic (ī-ăt′rə-jĕn′ĭk) *adj.* Induced by a physician's actions or words. Used of a disease. **—i·at′ro·gen′i·cal·ly** *adv.*

ib. or **ibid.** *abbr. Lat.* ibidem (in the same place).

I·ba·dan (ē-bä′dän). City of SW Nigeria. *Pop.* 847,000.

I·be·ri·an (ī-bîr′ē-ən). Peninsula of SW Europe occupied by Spain and Portugal. **—I·be′ri·an** *adj.* & *n.*

i·bex (ī′bĕks′) *n.* An Old World mountain goat, *Capra ibex,* with long, curving horns.

-ibility *suff. var. of* -ABILITY.

i·bis (ī′bĭs) *n.* A long-billed wading bird of the family Threskiornithidae.

-ible *suff. var. of* -ABLE.

Ib·sen (ĭb′sən), **Henrik.** 1828–1906. Norwegian dramatist.

-ic *suff.* **1.** Of, relating to, or marked by <Gael*ic*> **2.** Having a relatively high valence <sulfur*ic* acid>

ice (īs) *n.* **1.** Water that has frozen solid. **2.** A dessert of flavored and sweetened crushed ice. **3.** *Informal.* Extreme coldness of manner. *—v.* **iced, ic·ing.** **1.** To form ice : freeze. **2.** To coat with ice. **3.** To cool or chill. **4.** To cover or decorate (e.g., a cake) with icing. **—ic′i·ly** *adv.* **—ic′i·ness** *n.* **—ic′y** *adj.*

ice age *n.* A cold period characterized by extensive glaciation.

ice bag *n.* A small waterproof bag used as an ice pack.

ice·berg (īs′bûrg′) *n.* A mass of floating ice broken away from a glacier.

ice·boat (īs′bōt′) *n.* **1.** A vehicle with runners and usu. a sail, for use on ice. **2.** An icebreaker.

ice·bound (īs′bound′) *adj.* Locked in or covered by ice.

ice·box (īs′bŏks′) *n.* A refrigerator.

ice·break·er (īs′brā′kər) *n.* **1.** A sturdy ship for breaking a way through icebound waters. **2.** A pier or dock apron forming a buffer against floating ice.

ice cap *n.* An extensive, perennial, usu. level cover of ice and snow.

ice cream *n.* A smooth, sweet, cold food made of milk products and flavorings.

ice hockey *n.* HOCKEY 1.

ice·house (īs′hous′) *n.* A place where ice is stored.

Ice·land (īs′lənd). Island country in the North Atlantic near the Arctic Circle. *Cap.* Reykjavik. *Pop.* 229,000. **—Ice′land·er** *n.* **—Ice·land′ic** *adj.*

ice milk *n.* A food similar to ice cream but containing less butterfat.

ice pack *n.* **1.** A floating mass of compacted ice. **2.** A folded cloth or bag filled with ice and applied to sore body parts.

ice pick *n.* A pointed tool for chipping or breaking ice.

ice skate *n.* A shoe with a runner fixed to it for skating on ice. **—ice′-skate′** *v.*

ice storm *n.* A storm in which precipitation freezes on contact.

ice water *n.* Iced or chilled water.

ich·thy·ol·o·gy (ĭk′thē-ŏl′ə-jē) *n.* The zoological study of fishes. **—ich′thy·o·log′ic** (-ə-lŏj′ĭk), **ich′thy·o·log′i·cal** *adj.* **—ich′thy·ol′o·gist** *n.*

i·ci·cle (ī′sĭ-kəl) *n.* A hanging spike of ice made by dripping water that freezes.

ic·ing (ī′sĭng) *n.* A sweet glaze for coating cakes and cookies.

i·con *also* **i·kon** (ī′kŏn′) *n.* An image, esp. a picture of a sacred Christian personage painted on a wooden panel.

i·con·o·clast (ī-kŏn′ə-klăst′) *n.* **1.** One who destroys or opposes the use of sacred images. **2.** One who attacks traditional beliefs or institutions. **—i·con′o·clasm** *n.* **—i·con′o·clas′tic** *adj.*

-ics *suff.* **1.** Science : art : study : knowledge : skill <aerodynam*ics*> **2.** Activities or practices of <mechan*ics*>

id (ĭd) *n. Psychoanal.* The part of the psyche associated with instinctual needs and drives and providing psychic energy.

I'd (īd). **1.** I had. **2.** I should. **3.** I would.

ID *abbr.* **1.** Idaho (with Zip Code). **2.** *also* **I.D.** identification.

I·da·ho (ī′də-hō′). State of the NW U.S. *Cap.* Boise. *Pop.* 943,935. **—I′da·ho′an** *n.*

i·de·a (ī-dē′ə) *n.* **1.** Something existing in the mind, such as an image or thought. **2.** An opinion : belief. **3.** A plan : design. **4.** Meaning : purport.

i·de·al (ī-dē′əl, ī-dēl′) *n.* **1.** A conception or standard of perfection. **2.** One considered a perfect model. **3.** An ultimate objective : goal. **4.** An honorable principle or motive. ☆***syns:*** EXAMPLE, EXEMPLAR, MODEL, STANDARD —*adj.* **1.** Embodying an ideal : perfect. **2.** Existing only in the mind : imaginary. **—i·de′al·ly** *adv.*

i·de·al·ism (ī-dē′ə-lĭz′əm) *n.* **1.** The practice of seeing things in ideal form. **2.** Pursuit of high-minded or worthy goals. **3.** A philosophical system holding that reality consists of ideas or perceptions. **—i·de′al·ist** *n.* **—i′de·al·is′tic** *adj.*

i·de·al·ize (ī-dē′ə-līz′) *v.* **-ized, -iz·ing.** To envision or represent as ideal. **—i·de′al·i·za′tion** *n.*

i·dem (ī′dĕm′) *pron.* Used to indicate a previously mentioned reference.

i·den·ti·cal (ī-dĕn′tĭ-kəl) *adj.* **1.** Being the same. **2.** Exactly equal and alike. **3.** Of or designating a twin or twins developed from the same ovum. **—i·den′ti·cal·ly** *adv.*

i·den·ti·fi·ca·tion (ī-dĕn′tə-fĭ-kā′shən) *n.* **1.** The act of identifying or state of being identified. **2.** Proof of identity.

i·den·ti·fy (ī-dĕn′tə-fī′) *v.* **-fied, -fy·ing. 1.** To find out the identity of. **2.** To regard as the same or similar : equate. **3.** To associate (oneself) closely with an individual or group. **—i·den′ti·fi′a·ble** *adj.*

i·den·ti·ty (ī-dĕn′tĭ-tē) *n., pl.* **-ties. 1.** The condition or fact of being a certain person or thing and recognizable as such. **2.** The condition or fact of being the same as something else : sameness.

id·e·o·gram (ĭd′ē-ə-grăm′, ī′dē-) *also* **id·e·o·graph** (-grăf) *n.* **1.** A symbol used in a writing system to represent an idea or thing without expressing a particular word or phrase for it, as Chinese characters. **2.** A graphic symbol, as $ or %.

i·de·ol·o·gy (ī′dē-ŏl′ə-jē, ĭd′ē-) *n., pl.* **-gies.** A body of ideas characteristic of a person, group, culture, or political party. **—i′de·o·log′i·cal** (-ə-lŏj′ĭ-kəl) *adj.*

ides (īds) *n. (sing. in number).* The 15th day of Mar., May, Jul., or Oct. or the 13th day of the other months in the ancient Roman calendar.

id·i·o·cy (ĭd′ē-ə-sē) *n., pl.* **-cies. 1.** A condition of subnormal intellectual ability in the lowest measurable range. **2.** Something extremely foolish or stupid.

id·i·om (ĭd′ē-əm) *n.* **1.** An expression having a meaning that cannot be understood from the individual meanings of its component words. **2.** The way of speaking or putting words together peculiar to a language. **3.** A kind of language or vocabulary. **—id′i·o·mat′ic** (-ə-măt′ĭk) *adj.* **—id′i·o·mat′i·cal·ly** *adv.*

▲word history: *Idiom,* like *idiot,* is derived ult. from Greek *idios,* "private." Greek *idiōma* meant basically any peculiarity or unique feature, but esp. a peculiarity of language or literary style. In English the word *idiom* was used to mean "language" in general, then "dialect," and finally to denote a peculiarity of expression, phrase, or grammatical construction in a particular language.

id·i·op·a·thy (ĭd′ē-ŏp′ə-thē) *n.* A disease without a known cause. **—id′i·o·path′ic** (-ə-păth′ĭk) *adj.*

id·i·o·syn·cra·sy (ĭd′ē-ō-sĭng′krə-sē) *n., pl.* **-sies.** A peculiarity, esp. in behavior : eccentricity. **—id′i·o·syn·crat′ic** (-sĭn-krăt′ĭk) *adj.* **—id′i·o·syn·crat′i·cal·ly** *adv.*

id·i·ot (ĭd′ē-ət) *n.* **1.** A mentally deficient person with intelligence in the lowest measurable range. **2.** A stupid person. **—id′i·ot′ic** (-ŏt′ĭk) *adj.* **—id′i·ot′i·cal·ly** *adv.*

▲word history: The development of the pejorative senses of *idiot* occurred in ancient Greek, although the meaning "a mentally deficient person" is a more modern refinement. Greek *idiōtēs,* the source of *idiot,* is derived from *idios,* "private," and orig. meant a private citizen in contrast to a public official. The use of *idiōtēs* was extended to other pairs of opposites such as layman/professional, layman/priest, common person/distinguished person, and unskilled worker/craftsman. A person of no special status, knowledge, or skill was *idiōtēs,* and the term became one of abuse.

i·dle (īd′l) *adj.* **i·dler, i·dlest. 1.** Doing nothing : unoccupied. **2.** Not working : unemployed. **3.** Lazy. **4.** Unfounded : groundless <*idle* talk> —*v.* **i·dled, i·dling. 1.** To pass time unproductively. **2.** To move lazily. **3.** To run at a slow speed or out of gear. **4.** To render unemployed or inactive. **—i′dle·ness** *n.* **—i′dler** *n.* **—i′dly** *adv.*

i·dol (īd′l) *n.* **1.** An image that is worshiped. **2.** One that is blindly adored.

i·dol·a·try (ī-dŏl′ə-trē) *n.* **1.** The worship of idols. **2.** Blind adoration. **—i·dol′a·ter** *n.* **—i·dol′a·trous** *adj.*

i·dol·ize (īd′l-īz′) *v.* **-ized, -iz·ing. 1.** To regard with excessive admiration or devotion. **2.** To worship as an idol. **—i′dol·i·za′tion** *n.* **—i′dol·iz′er** *n.*

i·dyll *also* **i·dyl** (īd′l) *n.* **1.** A poem about country life. **2.** A scene, event, or condition of rural simplicity and happiness. **3.** A romantic interlude. **—i·dyl′lic** (ī-dĭl′ĭk) *adj.* **—i·dyl′li·cal·ly** *adv.*

-ie *suff. var. of* -Y³.

i.e. *abbr.* that is (Lat. *id est*).

if (ĭf) *conj.* **1.** In the event that <*If* the cat's hungry, feed it.> **2.** On condition that <They will work only *if* they are paid in advance.> **3.** Although possibly <a funny *if* tactless reply> **4.** Whether <I wonder *if* she could be right?>

if·fy (ĭf′ē) *adj. Informal.* Marked by doubt, uncertainty, or chance.

ig·loo (ĭg′lo͞o) *n.* A dome-shaped Eskimo dwelling built of blocks of ice.

ig·ne·ous (ĭg′nē-əs) *adj.* **1.** Of fire. **2.** Formed by solidification from a molten state <*igneous* rock>

ig·nite (ĭg-nīt′) *v.* **-nit·ed, -nit·ing.** To start or cause to start to burn.

ig·ni·tion (ĭg-nĭsh′ən) *n.* **1.** An act of igniting. **2.** A system or device for igniting the fuel mixture in an engine.

ig·no·ble (ĭg-nō′bəl) *adj.* **1.** Dishonorable in character or purpose : base. **2.** Not belonging to the nobility. **—ig·no′bly** *adv.*

ig·no·min·i·ous (ĭg′nə-mĭn′ē-əs) *adj.* **1.** Marked by or deserving shame or disgrace : dishonorable. **2.** Deeply embarrassing : humiliating. **—ig′no·min′y** *n.*

ig·no·ra·mus (ĭg′nə-rā′məs) *n.* An ignorant person.

ig·no·rant (ĭg′nər-ənt) *adj.* **1.** Lacking or displaying a lack of education or knowledge. **2.** Not aware : uninformed. ☆***syns:*** OBLIVIOUS, UNAWARE, UNCONSCIOUS, UNWITTING **—ig′no·rance** *n.*

ig·nore (ĭg-nôr′, -nōr′) *v.* **-nored, -nor·ing.** To pay no attention to : disregard. **—ig·nor′a·ble** *adj.*

i·gua·na (ĭ-gwä′nə) *n.* A large tropical American lizard of the family Iguanidae.

i·kon (ī′kŏn′) *n. var. of* ICON.

IL *abbr.* Illinois (with Zip Code).

il·e·i·tis (ĭl′ē-ī′tĭs) *n.* Inflammation of the ileum.

il·e·um (ĭl′ē-əm) *n., pl.* **-e·a** (-ē-ə). The lower part of the small intestine between the jejunum and the cecum.

ilk (ĭlk) *n.* Sort : kind.

ill (ĭl) *adj.* **worse** (wûrs), **worst** (wûrst). **1.** Not healthy : sick. **2.** Unsound : bad <*ill* health> **3.** Hostile : unfriendly. **4.** Not favorable <*ill* omens> **5.** Not up to standards <*ill* treatment> —*adv.* **worse, worst. 1.** In an ill manner : not well. **2.** With difficulty : scarcely. —*n.* **1.** Evil. **2.** Trouble or harm. **3.** Something causing suffering <persistent social *ills*>

I'll (īl). **1.** I will. **2.** I shall.

Ill. *abbr.* Illinois.

ill-ad·vised (ĭl′əd-vīzd′) *adj.* Done without careful thought or good advice.

ill-bred (ĭl′brĕd′) *adj.* Badly brought up : ill-mannered.

il·le·gal (ĭ-lē′gəl) *adj.* Forbidden by law or official rules. ☆***syns:*** ILLICIT, UNLAWFUL **—il′le·gal′i·ty** *n.* **—il·le′gal·ly** *adv.*

il·leg·i·ble (ĭ-lĕj′ə-bəl) *adj.* Not legible. **—il·leg′i·bil′i·ty** *n.* **—il·leg′i·bly** *adv.*

il·le·git·i·mate (ĭl′ə-jĭt′ə-mĭt) *adj.* **1.** Against the law : illegal. **2.** Born out of wedlock. **3.** Illogical. **—il′le·git′i·ma·cy** *n.* **—il′le·git′i·mate·ly** *adv.*

ill-fat·ed (ĭl′fā′tĭd) *adj.* **1.** Destined for misfortune. **2.** Unlucky.

ill-fa·vored (ĭl′fā′vərd) *adj.* **1.** Unattractive : ugly. **2.** Objectionable : offensive.

ill-got·ten (ĭl′gŏt′n) *adj.* Obtained in a dishonest way.

ill-hu·mored (ĭl′hyo͞o′mərd) *adj.* Irritable : surly. **—ill′-hu′mored·ly** *adv.*

il·lib·er·al (ĭ-lĭb′ər-əl) *adj.* Narrow-minded : prejudiced.

il·lic·it (ĭ-lĭs′ĭt) *adj.* Forbidden by custom or law : unlawful. **—il·lic′it·ly** *adv.*

Il·li·nois (ĭl′ə-noi′, -noiz′). State of NC U.S. *Cap.* Springfield. *Pop.* 11,418,461. **—Il′li·nois′an** *adj. & n.*

il·lit·er·ate (ĭ-lĭt′ər-ĭt) *adj.* **1.** Unable to read and write. **2.** Not educated. **—il·lit′er·a·cy** (-ə-sē) *n.* **—il·lit′er·ate** *n.*

ill-man·nered (ĭl′măn′ərd) *adj.* Lacking or showing a lack of good manners : rude.

ill-na·tured (ĭl′nā′chərd) *adj.* Disagreeable in disposition : surly.

ill·ness (ĭl′nĭs) *n.* A sickness.

il·log·i·cal (ĭ-lŏj′ĭ-kəl) *adj.* Contrary to the principles of logic. **—il·log′i·cal′i·ty** (-kăl′ĭ-tē) *n.* **—il·log′i·cal·ly** *adv.*

ill-starred (ĭl′stärd′) *adj.* Ill-fated.

ill-tem·pered (ĭl′tĕm′pərd) *adj.* Having or showing a bad temper.

ill-treat (ĭl′trēt′) *v.* To maltreat. **—ill′-treat′ment** *n.*

il·lu·mi·nate (ĭ-lo͞o′mə-nāt′) *v.* **-nat·ed, -nat·ing. 1.** To supply or brighten with light. **2.** To make understandable : clarify. **3.** To provide with understanding : enlighten. **4.** To decorate

(e.g., a manuscript) with pictures or designs. **—il•lu′mi•na′tion** *n.* **—il•lu′mi•na′tor** *n.*
il•lu•mine (ĭ-lo͞o′mĭn) *v.* **-mined, -min•ing.** To illuminate.
ill-use (ĭl′yo͞oz′) *v.* To maltreat.
il•lu•sion (ĭ-lo͞o′zhən) *n.* **1.** A mistaken perception of reality. **2.** A false belief : misconception. **—il•lu′sive, il•lu′so•ry** *adj.*
il•lus•trate (ĭl′ə-strāt′, ĭ-lŭs′trāt′) *v.* **-trat•ed, -trat•ing. 1.a.** To clarify, esp. by the use of examples. **b.** To clarify by serving as an example or comparison. **2.** To provide (a publication) with explanatory or decorative features. **—il′lus•tra′tor** *n.*
il•lus•tra•tion (ĭl′ə-strā′shən) *n.* **1.** The act of illustrating or state of being illustrated. **2.** An example used to illustrate. **3.** A picture, diagram, or chart in a text.
il•lus•tra•tive (ĭ-lŭs′trə-tĭv, ĭl′ə-strā′tĭv) *adj.* Serving to illustrate.
il•lus•tri•ous (ĭ-lŭs′trē-əs) *adj.* Celebrated : renowned. **—il•lus′tri•ous•ness** *n.*
ill will *n.* Unfriendly feeling : enmity.
I'm (īm). I am.
im•age (ĭm′ĭj) *n.* **1.** A reproduction of the form of someone or something, esp. a sculptured likeness. **2.** An optically formed representation of an object, esp. one made by a mirror or lens. **3. a.** A mental picture of something absent or imaginary. **b.** A figure of speech. **4.** One closely resembling another <the *image* of her mother> **5.** A personification. **6.** The impression made on the public, as by a famous person : reputation. *—v.* **-aged, -ag•ing. 1.** To make a likeness of. **2.** To reflect. **3.** To picture in the mind : imagine. **4.** To describe or depict vividly.
im•age•ry (ĭm′ĭj-rē) *n., pl.* **-ries. 1.** Mental pictures. **2.** Vivid figures of speech conveying mental pictures.
i•mag•in•a•ble (ĭ-măj′ə-nə-bəl) *adj.* Capable of being conceived of by the imagination. **—i•mag′in•a•bly** *adv.*
i•mag•i•nar•y (ĭ-măj′ə-nĕr′ē) *adj.* Existing only in the imagination.
imaginary number *n.* A number whose square is negative.
imaginary unit *n.* The positive square root of –1.
i•mag•i•na•tion (ĭ-măj′ə-nā′shən) *n.* **1.** The mental power of forming images of unreal or absent objects. **2.** Such power used creatively. **3.** Resourcefulness. **—i•mag′i•na•tive** *adj.* **—i•mag′i•na•tive•ly** *adv.*
i•mag•ine (ĭ-măj′ĭn) *v.* **-ined, -in•ing. 1.** To form a mental picture of. **2.** To suppose : think <I *imagine* it's late.>
i•ma•go (ĭ-mā′gō, ĭ-mä′-) *n., pl.* **-goes** *or* **-gi•nes** (gə-nēz′) An insect in its sexually mature adult stage.
i•mam (ĭ-mäm′) *n.* A prayer leader of Islam.
im•bal•ance (ĭm-băl′əns) *n.* A lack of balance, as in proportion.
im•be•cile (ĭm′bə-sĭl, -səl) *n.* **1.** A feeble-minded person. **2.** A stupid person. **—im′be•cile, im′be•cil′ic** (-sĭl′ĭk) *adj.* **—im′be•cil′i•ty** (-sĭl′ĭ-tē) *n.*
im•bed (ĭm-bĕd′) *v. var. of* EMBED.
im•bibe (ĭm-bīb′) *v.* **-bibed, -bib•ing. 1.** To drink. **2.** To take in : absorb. **—im•bib′er** *n.*
im•bri•cate (ĭm′brĭ-kāt′) *adj.* With edges overlapping in a regular arrangement, as roof tiles or fish scales.

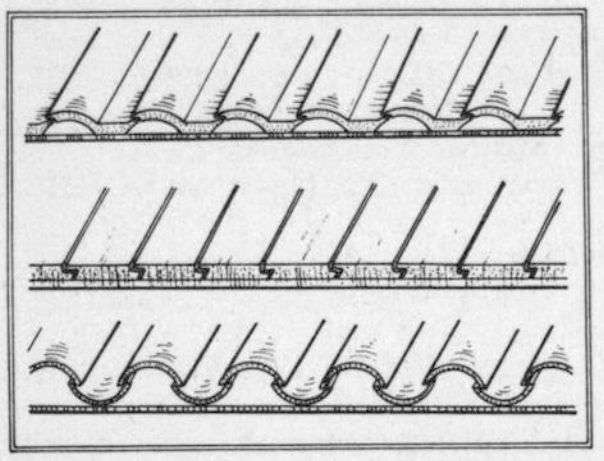

imbricate
Three styles of imbricate roofing, (top) *Spanish,* (middle) *English,* (bottom) *mission*

im•bro•glio (ĭm-brōl′yō) *n., pl.* **-glios. 1.** A complicated situation or disagreement. **2.** A confused heap : tangle.
im•bue (ĭm-byo͞o′) *v.* **-bued, -bu•ing. 1.** To saturate, as with a stain or dye. **2.** To permeate or pervade : instill.
im•i•ta•ble (ĭm′ĭ-tə-bəl) *adj.* Capable or worthy of imitation.
im•i•tate (ĭm′ĭ-tāt′) *v.* **-tat•ed, -tat•ing. 1.!a.** To copy the actions or appearance of (another). **b.** To adopt the style of : model oneself after. **2.** To duplicate : reproduce. **3.** To appear like : resemble. ☆***syns:*** APE, BURLESQUE, MIMIC, MOCK, PARODY **—im′i•ta′tor** *n.*
im•i•ta•tion (ĭm′ĭ-tā′shən) *n.* **1.** An act of imitating. **2.** Something copied from an original.
im•i•ta•tive (ĭm′ĭ-tā′tĭv) *adj.* **1.** Of, marked by, or inclined to imitation. **2.** Not original : derivative.
im•mac•u•late (ĭ-măk′yə-lĭt) *adj.* **1.** Free from sin, stain, or fault : pure. **2.** Impeccably clean. **—im•mac′u•late•ly** *adv.*
im•ma•nent (ĭm′ə-nənt) *adj.* **1.** Existing within : inherent. **2.** Restricted to the mind : subjective. **—im′ma•nence, im′ma•nen•cy** *n.* **—im′ma•nent•ly** *adv.*
im•ma•te•ri•al (ĭm′ə-tîr′ē-əl) *adj.* **1.** Lacking material body or form. **2.** Of no importance or relevance. **—im′ma•te′ri•al•ly** *adv.* **—im′ma•te′ri•al•ness** *n.*
im•ma•ture (ĭm′ə-tyo͝or′, -to͝or′, -cho͝or′) *adj.* **1.** Not fully grown : undeveloped. **2.** Suggesting a lack of maturity. **—im′ma•ture′ly** *adv.* **—im′ma•tur′i•ty** *n.*
im•meas•ur•a•ble (ĭ-mĕzh′ər-ə-bəl) *adj.* **1.** Not capable of being measured. **2.** Very large or great. **—im•meas′ur•a•bly** *adv.*
im•me•di•a•cy (ĭ-mē′dē-ə-sē) *n., pl.* **-cies. 1.** The quality of being immediate : directness. **2.** Something of urgent importance.
im•me•di•ate (ĭ-mē′dē-ĭt) *adj.* **1.** Acting or happening without an intervening object, agent, or cause. **2.** Directly perceived. **3.** Occurring at once : instant. **4.** Close in time, location, or relation <our *immediate* surroundings> **5.** Present <*immediate* needs> **—im•me′di•ate•ly** *adv.*
im•me•mo•ri•al (ĭm′ə-môr′ē-əl, -mōr′-) *adj.* Beyond the limits of memory, tradition, or records.
im•mense (ĭ-mĕns′) *adj.* Exceptionally large : huge. **—im•mense′ly** *adv.* **—im•men′si•ty** *n.*
im•merse (ĭ-mûrs′) *v.* **-mersed, -mers•ing. 1.** To put into a liquid : submerge. **2.** To baptize by submerging in water. **3.** To engross : absorb. **—im•mers′i•ble** *adj.* **—im•mer′sion** *n.*
im•mesh (ĭ-mĕsh′) *v. var. of* ENMESH.
im•mi•grant (ĭm′ĭ-grənt) *n.* One who leaves 1 country to settle in another.
im•mi•grate (ĭm′ĭ-grāt′) *v.* **-grat•ed, -grat•ing.** To leave 1 country and settle in another. **—im′mi•gra′tion** *n.*
im•mi•nent (ĭm′ə-nənt) *adj.* About to happen : impending. **—im′mi•nence** *n.*
im•mo•bile (ĭ-mō′bəl, -bēl′, -bīl′) *adj.* **1.** Not moving : motionless. **2.** Not capable of moving : fixed. **—im′mo•bil′i•ty** *n.*
im•mo•bi•lize (ĭ-mō′bə-līz′) *v.* **-lized, -liz•ing.** To render immobile. **—im•mo′bi•li•za′tion** *n.*
im•mod•er•ate (ĭ-mŏd′ər-ĭt) *adj.* Exceeding normal bounds : extreme. **—im•mod′er•ate•ly** *adv.*
im•mod•est (ĭ-mŏd′ĭst) *adj.* **1.** Lacking modesty : indecent. **2.** Boastful. **—im•mod′est•ly** *adv.* **—im•mod′es•ty** *n.*
im•mo•late (ĭm′ə-lāt′) *v.* **-lat•ed, -lat•ing. 1.** To kill as a sacrifice. **2.** To destroy completely. **—im′mo•la′tion** *n.* **—im′mo•la′tor** *n.*
im•mor•al (ĭ-môr′əl, ĭ-mŏr′-) *adj.* Not moral. **—im•mor′al•ly** *adv.*
im•mo•ral•i•ty (ĭm′ô-răl′ĭ-tē, ĭm′ə-) *n., pl.* **-ties. 1.** Lack of morality. **2.** An immoral act or practice.
im•mor•tal (ĭ-môr′tl) *adj.* **1.** Exempt from death. **2.** Lasting forever, as in fame. *—n.* **1.** One not subject to death. **2.** A person of lasting fame. **—im′mor•tal′i•ty** *n.* **—im•mor′tal•ly** *adv.*
im•mor•tal•ize (ĭ-môr′tl-īz′) *v.* **-ized, -iz•ing.** To make immortal.
im•mov•a•ble (ĭ-mo͞o′və-bəl) *adj.* **1.** Not capable of moving or of being moved. **2.** Adhering closely to a position or principle : steadfast. **—im•mov′a•bly** *adv.*
im•mune (ĭ-myo͞on′) *adj.* **1.** Exempt. **2.** Not affected or responsive. **3.** Resistant, as to a disease. **—im•mu′ni•ty** *n.*
im•mu•nize (ĭm′yə-nīz′) *v.* **-nized, -niz•ing.** To make immune. **—im′mu•ni•za′tion** *n.*
im•mu•nol•o•gy (ĭm′yə-nŏl′ə-jē) *n.* The study of immunity to diseases. **—im′mu•no•log′ic** (-nə-lŏj′ĭk), **im′mu•no•log′i•cal** *adj.* **—im′mu•no•log′i•cal•ly** *adv.*
im•mu•no•sup•pres•sive (ĭm′yə-nō-sə-prĕs′ĭv) *adj.* Acting to suppress a natural immune response to an antigen.
im•mure (ĭ-myo͝or′) *v.* **-mured, -mur•ing. 1.** To confine by or as if by walls : jail. **2.** To build into a wall.
im•mu•ta•ble (ĭ-myo͞o′tə-bəl) *adj.* Unchanging or unchangeable. **—im•mu′ta•bil′i•ty** *n.* **—im•mu′ta•bly** *adv.*
imp (ĭmp) *n.* **1.** A mischievous child. **2.** A little demon.
im•pact (ĭm′păkt′) *n.* **1.!a.** A collision. **b.** The impetus or force produced by a collision. **2.** An initial, usu. strong effect. *—v.* (ĭm-păkt′). **1.** To pack firmly together. **2.** To strike or affect forcefully.
im•pact•ed (ĭm-păk′tĭd) *adj.* **1.** Wedged together at the broken ends <an *impacted* bone> **2.** Wedged inside the gum in such a way that normal eruption is prevented <an *impacted* wisdom tooth>
im•pair (ĭm-pâr′) *v.* To diminish in strength, value, quantity, or quality : harm. **—im•pair′ment** *n.*
im•pa•la (ĭm-pä′lə, -păl′ə) *n.* A large African antelope, *Aepyceros melampus,* the male of which has slender curved horns.

im•pale (ĭm-pāl′) *v.* **-paled, -pal•ing. 1.** To pierce with a sharp stake or point. **2.** To kill by thus piercing. **—im•pale′ment** *n.*

im•pal•pa•ble (ĭm-păl′pə-bəl) *adj.* **1.** Not perceptible to touch : intangible. **2.** Not easily distinguished : elusive. **—im•pal′pa•bil′i•ty** *n.* **—im•pal′pa•bly** *adv.*

im•pan•el (ĭm-păn′əl) *v.* **-eled, -el•ing** *or* **-elled, -el•ling.** To enter the names of (a jury) on a panel or list.

im•part (ĭm-pärt′) *v.* **1.** To grant : bestow <*impart* wisdom> **2.** To make known : communicate <*impart* the bad news>

im•par•tial (ĭm-pär′shəl) *adj.* Not partial : unbiased. **—im•par′ti•al′i•ty** (-shē-ăl′ĭ-tē) *n.* **—im•par′tial•ly** *adv.*

im•pass•a•ble (ĭm-păs′ə-bəl) *adj.* Impossible to travel over or across.

im•passe (ĭm′păs′) *n.* **1.** A road or passage having no exit. **2.** A difficult situation with no apparent way out. **3.** A deadlock.

im•pas•sioned (ĭm-păsh′ənd) *adj.* Filled with passion.

im•pas•sive (ĭm-păs′ĭv) *adj.* **1.** Unemotional : stolid. **2.** Showing no emotion : expressionless. **—im•pas′sive•ly** *adv.*

im•pa•tient (ĭm-pā′shənt) *adj.* **1.** Unwilling to wait or tolerate delay : restless. **2.** Expressing or caused by irritation at having to wait <an *impatient* oath> **3.** Restlessly eager <*impatient* to depart> **4.** Intolerant <*impatient* of weakness> **—im•pa′tience** *n.* **—im•pa′tient•ly** *adv.*

im•peach (ĭm-pēch′) *v.* **1.** To charge with misconduct in public office before a proper court of justice. **2.** To make an accusation against : challenge <*impeached* the witness's honesty> **—im•peach′a•ble** *adj.* **—im•peach′er** *n.* **—im•peach′ment** *n.*

im•pec•ca•ble (ĭm-pĕk′ə-bəl) *adj.* **1.** Having no flaws : perfect. **2.** Not capable of sin. **—im•pec′ca•bly** *adv.*

im•pe•cu•ni•ous (ĭm′pĭ-kyo͞o′nē-əs) *adj.* Having no money : penniless. **—im′pe•cu′ni•ous•ness** *n.*

im•ped•ance (ĭm-pēd′ns) *n.* A measure of the total opposition to the flow of an electric current, esp. in an alternating-current circuit.

im•pede (ĭm-pēd′) *v.* **-ped•ed, -ped•ing.** To obstruct or slow down the progress of.

im•ped•i•ment (ĭm-pĕd′ə-mənt) *n.* **1.** One that stands in the way : obstruction. **2.** Something that impedes, esp. an organic speech defect.

im•ped•i•men•ta (ĭm-pĕd′ə-mĕn′tə) *pl.n.* Things that impede or encumber.

im•pel (ĭm-pĕl′) *v.* **-pelled, -pel•ling. 1.** To spur to action : provoke. **2.** To drive forward : propel. **—im•pel′ler** *n.*

im•pend (ĭm-pĕnd′) *v.* **1.** To hover threateningly. **2.** To be about to happen.

im•pen•e•tra•ble (ĭm-pĕn′ĭ-trə-bəl) *adj.* **1.** Not capable of being penetrated. **2.** Not capable of being seen through or understood : unfathomable. **—im•pen′e•tra•bil′i•ty** *n.* **—im•pen′e•tra•bly** *adv.*

im•pen•i•tent (ĭm-pĕn′ĭ-tənt) *adj.* Not sorry : unrepentant. **—im•pen′i•tence** *n.*

im•per•a•tive (ĭm-pĕr′ə-tĭv) *adj.* **1.** Expressing a command or request <an *imperative* verb form> **2.** Empowered to command or control. **3.** Compulsory. **—im•per′a•tive** *n.* **—im•per′a•tive•ly** *adv.*

im•per•cep•ti•ble (ĭm′pər-sĕp′tə-bəl) *adj.* **1.** Not perceptible by the mind or senses. **2.** Extremely small or slight. ☆***syns:*** IMPALPABLE, INDISTINGUISHABLE, INSENSIBLE, INTANGIBLE, UNAPPRECIABLE, UNNOTICEABLE **—im′per•cep′ti•bly** *adv.*

im•per•fect (ĭm-pûr′fĭkt) *adj.* **1.** Not perfect. **2.** Of or being a verb tense that shows an uncompleted or continuous action or condition. ☆***syns:*** DEFECTIVE, FAULTY —*n.* **1.** The imperfect tense. **2.** A verb in the imperfect tense. **—im•per′fect•ly** *adv.*

im•per•fec•tion (ĭm′pər-fĕk′shən) *n.* **1.** The quality or condition of being imperfect. **2.** A defect.

im•pe•ri•al¹ (ĭm-pîr′ē-əl) *adj.* **1.** Of or relating to an empire or emperor. **2.** Designating a nation or government having dependent colonies. **3.** Majestic : regal. **—im•pe′ri•al•ly** *adv.*

im•pe•ri•al² (ĭm-pîr′ē-əl) *n.* A pointed beard on the lower lip and chin.

im•pe•ri•al•ism (ĭm-pîr′ē-ə-lĭz′əm) *n.* The national policy or practice of acquiring foreign territories or establishing dominance over other nations. **—im•pe′ri•al•ist** *n.* **—im•pe′ri•al•is′tic** *adj.*

imperial moth *n.* A large New World moth, *Eacles imperialis,* with yellow wings having purplish or brownish markings.

im•per•il (ĭm-pĕr′əl) *v.* **-iled, -il•ing** *or* **-illed, -il•ling.** To put in peril : endanger.

im•pe•ri•ous (ĭm-pîr′ē-əs) *adj.* **1.** Commanding : domineering. **2.** Urgent. **—im•pe′ri•ous•ly** *adv.* **—im•pe′ri•ous•ness** *n.*

im•per•ish•a•ble (ĭm-pĕr′ĭ-shə-bəl) *adj.* Not perishable. **—im•per′ish•a•bly** *adv.*

im•per•ma•nent (ĭm-pûr′mə-nənt) *adj.* Not permanent : temporary. **—im•per′ma•nence** *n.* **—im•per′ma•nent•ly** *adv.*

im•per•me•a•ble (ĭm-pûr′mē-ə-bəl) *adj.* Not permeable. **—im•per′me•a•bil′i•ty** *n.* **—im•per′me•a•bly** *adv.*

im•per•mis•si•ble (ĭm′pər-mĭs′ə-bəl) *adj.* Not permissible.

im•per•son•al (ĭm-pûr′sə-nəl) *adj.* **1.** Having no personal reference or connection <an *impersonal* comment> **2.** Showing no emotion or personality <an *impersonal* tone> **—im•per′son•al•ly** *adv.*

im•per•son•ate (ĭm-pûr′sə-nāt′) *v.* **-at•ed, -at•ing.** To assume the chararacter or manner of. **—im•per′son•a′tion** *n.* **—im•per′son•a′tor** *n.*

im•per•ti•nent (ĭm-pûr′tn-ənt) *adj.* **1.** Improperly bold or disrespectful : impudent. **2.** Not pertinent : irrelevant. **—im•per′ti•nence** *n.* **—im•per′ti•nent•ly** *adv.*

im•per•turb•a•ble (ĭm′pər-tûr′bə-bəl) *adj.* Unshakably calm. **—im′per•turb′a•bil′i•ty** *n.* **—im′per•turb′a•bly** *adv.*

im•per•vi•ous (ĭm-pûr′vē-əs) *adj.* **1.** Incapable of being penetrated <material *impervious* to water> **2.** Incapable of being affected <*impervious* to our pleas> **—im•per′vi•ous•ly** *adv.* **—im•per′vi•ous•ness** *n.*

im•pe•ti•go (ĭm′pĭ-tī′gō) *n.* A contagious skin disease marked by pustules.

im•pet•u•ous (ĭm-pĕch′o͞o-əs) *adj.* Marked by sudden action or emotion : impulsive <*impetuous* haste> **—im•pet′u•os′i•ty** (-ŏs′ĭ-tē) *n.* **—im•pet′u•ous•ly** *adv.*

im•pe•tus (ĭm′pĭ-təs) *n.* **1. a.** A driving force : impulse. **b.** An incitement : stimulus. **2.** Momentum.

im•pi•e•ty (ĭm-pī′ĭ-tē) *n., pl.* **-ties. 1.** The quality of being impious : irreverence. **2.** An impious act.

im•pinge (ĭm-pĭnj′) *v.* **-pinged, -ping•ing. 1.** To make impact : strike : collide. **2.** To encroach<next-door neighbors *impinging* on our privacy> **—im•pinge′ment** *n.*

im•pi•ous (ĭm′pē-əs, ĭm-pī′-) *adj.* **1.** Not pious : irreverent. **2.** Disrespectful. **—im′pi•ous•ly** *adv.*

imp•ish (ĭm′pĭsh) *adj.* Mischievous. **—imp′ish•ly** *adv.* **—imp′ish•ness** *n.*

im•pla•ca•ble (ĭm-plăk′ə-bəl, -plā′kə-) *adj.* Not capable of being placated or appeased <*implacable* rage> **—im•pla′ca•bil′i•ty** *n.* **—im•pla′ca•bly** *adv.*

im•plant (ĭm-plănt′) *v.* **1.** To set in firmly. **2.** To fix in the mind : instill. **3.** To insert surgically. **—im′plant′** *n.* **—im′plan•ta′tion** *n.*

im•plau•si•ble (ĭm-plô′zə-bəl) *adj.* Difficult to believe : unlikely. **—im•plau′si•bil′i•ty** *n.* **—im•plau′si•bly** *adv.*

im•ple•ment (ĭm′plə-mənt) *n.* A utensil or tool. —*v.* (-mĕnt′). **1.** To put into effect : carry out. **2.** To furnish with implements. **—im′ple•men•ta′tion** *n.*

im•pli•cate (ĭm′plĭ-kāt′) *v.* **-cat•ed, -cat•ing. 1.** To involve, esp. in illegal activity. **2.** To imply.

im•pli•ca•tion (ĭm′plĭ-kā′shən) *n.* **1.** The act of implicating or state of being implicated. **2.** The act of implying : indirect expression. **3.** Something implied.

im•plic•it (ĭm-plĭs′ĭt) *adj.* **1.** Contained in the nature of someone or something but not readily apparent. **2.** Understood but not directly expressed <an *implicit* assumption> **3.** Complete : absolute. ☆***syns:*** IMPLIED, TACIT, UNDERSTOOD, UNSPOKEN **—im•plic′it•ly** *adv.*

im•plode (ĭm-plōd′) *v.* **-plod•ed, -plod•ing.** To collapse violently : burst inward. **—im•plo′sion** *n.*

im•plore (ĭm-plôr′, -plōr′) *v.* **-plored, -plor•ing.** To appeal urgently to : entreat. **—im•plor′er** *n.* **—im•plor′ing•ly** *adv.*

im•ply (ĭm-plī′) *v.* **-plied, -ply•ing. 1.** To involve by logical necessity : entail. **2.** To express indirectly : suggest.

im•po•lite (ĭm′pə-līt′) *adj.* Rude.

im•pol•i•tic (ĭm-pŏl′ĭ-tĭk) *adj.* **1.** Not expedient : imprudent. **2.** Tactless.

im•pon•der•a•ble (ĭm-pŏn′dər-ə-bəl) *adj.* Incapable of being weighed or evaluated precisely. **—im•pon′der•a•ble** *n.*

im•port (ĭm-pôrt′, -pōrt′, ĭm′pôrt′, -pōrt′) *v.* **1.** To bring in (goods) from a foreign country for trade or sale. **2.** To mean : signify. **3.** To be significant. —*n.* (ĭm′pôrt′, -pōrt′). **1.** Something imported. **2.** Meaning. **3.** Significance : importance. **—im•port′er** *n.*

im•por•tance (ĭm-pôr′tns) *n.* The quality of being important : significance.

im•por•tant (ĭm-pôr′tnt) *adj.* **1.** Likely to determine or influence events : significent. **2.** Having fame or authority : prominent <*important* people> ☆***syns:*** BIG, CONSEQUENTIAL, MOMENTOUS, SIGNIFICANT, WEIGHTY **—im•por′tant•ly** *adv.*

im•por•ta•tion (ĭm′pôr-tā′shən, -pōr-) *n.* **1.** The act or business of importing goods. **2.** Something imported.

im•por•tu•nate (ĭm-pôr′chə-nĭt) *adj.* Persistent in pressing demands or requests. **—im•por′tu•nate•ly** *adv.*

im•por•tune (ĭm′pôr-to͞on′, -tyo͞on′, ĭm-pôr′chən) *v.* **-tuned,**

-tun·ing. To press with repeated requests. **—im′por·tun′er** *n.* **—im′por·tu′ni·ty** *n.*

im·pose (ĭm-pōz′) *v.* **-posed, -pos·ing. 1.** To enact or apply as compulsory. **2.** To obtrude or force (e.g., oneself) upon another or others. **3.** To take unfair advantage <*imposed* on her kindness> **4.** To pass off <*impose* a fraud on the public> **—im′po·si′tion** (-pə-zĭsh′ən) *n.*

im·pos·ing (ĭm-pō′zĭng) *adj.* Awesome : impressive. **—im·pos′ing·ly** *adv.*

im·pos·si·ble (ĭm-pŏs′ə-bəl) *adj.* **1.** Not capable of existing or taking place. **2.** Unlikely to happen or be done. **3.** Unacceptable. **4.** Difficult to tolerate or deal with. **—im·pos′si·bil′i·ty** *n.* **—im·pos′si·bly** *adv.*

im·post (ĭm′pōst′) *n.* A tax or duty.

im·pos·tor (ĭm-pŏs′tər) *n.* One who assumes a false identity. ☆***syns:*** CHARLATAN, FAKE, FRAUD, PHONY, PRETENDER, QUACK

im·pos·ture (ĭm-pŏs′chər) *n.* Deception by the assumption of a false identity.

im·po·tent (ĭm′pə-tənt) *adj.* **1.** Without strength or vigor : weak. **2.** Having no power : ineffectual. **3.** Incapable of sexual intercourse. **—im′po·tence, im′po·ten·cy** *n.* **—im′po·tent·ly** *adv.*

im·pound (ĭm-pound′) *v.* **1.** To confine in or as if in a pound <*impound* stray dogs> **2.** To seize and keep in legal custody. **3.** To hold (water) in a reservoir. **—im·pound′ment** *n.*

im·pov·er·ish (ĭm-pŏv′ər-ĭsh, -pŏv′rĭsh) *v.* **1.** To make poor. **2.** To deprive of natural richness or fertility. **—im·pov′er·ish·ment** *n.*

im·prac·ti·ca·ble (ĭm-prăk′tĭ-kə-bəl) *adj.* Incapable of being done or put into practice. **—im·prac′ti·ca·bly** *adv.*

im·prac·ti·cal (ĭm-prăk′tĭ-kəl) *adj.* **1.** Unwise to put into effect : not sensible or prudent. **2.** Unable to deal with practical or financial matters efficiently. **—im·prac′ti·cal′i·ty** *n.*

im·pre·cise (ĭm′prĭ-sīs′) *adj.* Not precise.

im·preg·na·ble (ĭm-prĕg′nə-bəl) *adj.* Incapable of being successfully attacked : unconquerable. **—im·preg′na·bil′i·ty** *n.*

im·preg·nate (ĭm-prĕg′nāt′) *v.* **-nat·ed, -nat·ing. 1.** To make pregnant. **2.** To fertilize (e.g., an ovum). **3.** To fill throughout : saturate. **—im′preg·na′tion** *n.* **—im·preg′na′tor** *n.*

im·pre·sa·ri·o (ĭm′prĭ-sär′ē-ō′, -sâr′-) *n., pl.* **-os.** A theatrical manager or producer, esp. the director of an opera company.

im·press[1] (ĭm-prĕs′) *v.* **1.** To apply or produce with pressure. **2.** To stamp or mark with or as if with pressure. **3.** To fix firmly in the mind. **4.** To affect strongly and usu. favorably. *—n.* (ĭm′prĕs′). **1.** The act of impressing. **2.** A mark made by impressing. **3.** A stamp or seal for impressing. **—im·press′i·ble** *adj.*

im·press[2] (ĭm-prĕs′) *v.* **1.** To force to serve in a military force. **2.** To confiscate (property). **—im·press′ment** *n.*

im·pres·sion (ĭm-prĕsh′ən) *n.* **1.** A mark or design made on a surface by pressure. **2.** An effect or feeling retained in the mind as a result of experience. **3.** An indistinct notion or recollection. **4.** A satiric or humorous imitation of a famous personality done esp. by an entertainer. **5.** The copies of a publication printed at one time.

im·pres·sion·a·ble (ĭm-prĕsh′ə-nə-bəl) *adj.* Easily influenced : suggestible.

im·pres·sion·ism (ĭm-prĕsh′ə-nĭz′əm) *n.* A style of late 19th-cent. painting in which the immediate appearance of scenes is depicted with unmixed primary colors applied in small strokes to simulate reflected light. **—im·pres′sion·ist** *n.* **—im·pres′sion·ist′ic** *adj.*

im·pres·sive (ĭm-prĕs′ĭv) *adj.* Making a strong impression : striking. **—im·pres′sive·ly** *adv.* **—im·pres′sive·ness** *n.*

im·pri·ma·tur (ĭm′prə-mä′to͝or′) *n.* **1.** Official permission to print or publish. **2.** Authorization.

im·print (ĭm-prĭnt′, ĭm′prĭnt′) *v.* **1. a.** To make or impress (a mark or design) on a surface. **b.** To make or stamp a mark on. **2.** To fix firmly in the mind. *—n.* (ĭm′prĭnt′). **1.** A mark or design made by imprinting. **2.** A lasting influence or effect. **3.** A publisher's name, often with the date and place of publication, printed at the bottom of a title page.

im·pris·on (ĭm-prĭz′ən) *v.* To put in prison. **—im·pris′on·ment** *n.*

im·prob·a·ble (ĭm-prŏb′ə-bəl) *adj.* Not likely to occur or be true. **—im·prob′a·bil′i·ty** *n.* **—im·prob′a·bly** *adv.*

im·promp·tu (ĭm-prŏmp′to͞o, -tyo͞o) *adj.* Devised or performed without prior planning or preparation : extemporaneous. **—im·promp′tu** *adv.*

im·prop·er (ĭm-prŏp′ər) *adj.* **1.** Unsuitable. **2.** Indecorous. **3.** Incorrect. **—im·prop′er·ly** *adv.*

improper fraction *n.* A fraction having a numerator larger than or the same as the denominator.

im·pro·pri·e·ty (ĭm′prə-prī′ĭ-tē) *n., pl.* **-ties. 1.** The quality or state of being improper. **2.** An improper act or remark.

im·prove (ĭm pro͞ov′) *v.* **-proved, -prov·ing. 1.** To make or become better. **2.** To increase (e.g., land) in productivity or value. **—im·prov′a·ble** *adj.*

im·prove·ment (ĭm-pro͞ov′mənt) *n.* **1.** The act or process of improving or the condition of being improved. **2.** A change that improves.

im·prov·i·dent (ĭm-prŏv′ĭ-dənt) *adj.* Not providing for the future. **—im·prov′i·dence** *n.* **—im·prov′i·dent·ly** *adv.*

im·pro·vise (ĭm′prə-vīz′) *v.* **-vised, -vis·ing. 1.** To make up, compose, or perform without preparation. **2.** To make from available materials <*improvise* a costume from sheets> **—im·prov′i·sa′tion** (ĭm-prŏv′ĭ-zā′shən, ĭm′prə-vĭ-) *n.* **—im·prov′i·sa·to′ry** *adj.* **—im′pro·vis′er** *n.*

im·pru·dent (ĭm-pro͞od′nt) *adj.* Not prudent : unwise. **—im·pru′dence** *n.* **—im·pru′dent·ly** *adv.*

im·pu·dent (ĭm′pyə-dənt) *adj.* Marked by rude boldness or disrespect. ☆***syns:*** AUDACIOUS, BOLD, BOLD-FACED, BRAZEN, CHEEKY, FORWARD, FRESH, IMPERTINENT, INSOLENT, SASSY, SAUCY **—im′pu·dence** *n.* **—im′pu·dent·ly** *adv.*

im·pugn (ĭm-pyo͞on′) *v.* To attack as false : cast doubt on.

im·pulse (ĭm′pŭls′) *n.* **1.** A driving force or the motion produced by it. **2.** A sudden spontaneous urge. **3.** A motivating force. **4.** A general tendency. **5.** *Physiol.* A transfer of energy from one neuron to another.

im·pul·sive (ĭm-pŭl′sĭv) *adj.* **1.** Acting on impulse rather than thought. **2.** Resulting from impulse : uncalculated <an *impulsive* gesture> **3.** Setting objects in motion. **—im·pul′sive·ly** *adv.* **—im·pul′sive·ness** *n.*

im·pu·ni·ty (ĭm-pyo͞o′nĭ-tē) *n.* Exemption from punishment.

im·pure (ĭm-pyo͝or′) *adj.* **1.** Not pure : unclean. **2.** Unchaste or obscene. **3.** Mixed with another substance : adulterated. **4.** Deriving from more than 1 source or style. **—im·pure′ly** *adv.* **—im·pu′ri·ty** *n.*

im·pute (ĭm-pyo͞ot′) *v.* **-put·ed, -put·ing.** To attribute (e.g., a mistake) to another : charge. **—im′pu·ta′tion** *n.*

in (ĭn) *prep.* **1.** Within the bounds of <walking *in* the park> **2.** Into. **3.** To a condition of <divided *in* 2><*in* love> **4.** Having the activity or function of <*in* business> **5.** During. **6.** Wearing <a man *in* shorts> **7.** Having the arrangement or style of <hanging *in* pleats><a letter *in* verse> **8.** By means of. **9.** With reference to <4 feet *in* height> **10.** Out of <picked 1 *in* 4> *—adv.* **1.** To the inside <walked *in*> **2.** To a goal or place <drove *in* from the country> **3.** So as to be included or contained. **4.** So as to be fashionable. *—adj.* **1.** Incoming <the *in* bus> **2.** Available or at home. **3.** Having power <the *in* party> **4.** Fashionable or fashion-minded <the *in* crowd> *—n.* **1.** One in office or power. **2.** Influence. **—in for.** Guaranteed to get or have.

in *or* **in.** *abbr.* inch.

In *symbol for* INDIUM.

in– *pref.* Not <*in*congruous> See below for a list of self-explanatory words formed with the prefix **in-.**

In *symbol for* INDIUM.

in ab·sen·tia (ĭn′ ăb-sĕn′shə, -shē-ə) *adv.* In absence.

in·ac·ces·si·ble (ĭn′ăk-sĕs′ə-bəl) *adj.* Not accessible : unreachable. **—in′ac·ces′si·bil′i·ty** *n.* **—in′ac·ces′si·bly** *adv.*

in·ac·tion (ĭn-ăk′shən) *n.* Lack of action.

in·ac·ti·vate (ĭn-ăk′tə-vāt′) *v.* **-vat·ed, -vat·ing.** To make inactive. **—in·ac′ti·va′tion** *n.*

in·ac·tive (ĭn-ăk′tĭv) *adj.* **1.** Not active or inclined to be active. **2.** Out of current use or service. ☆***syns:*** DORMANT, IDLE, INERT, INOPERATIVE **—in·ac′tive·ly** *adv.* **—in′ac·tiv′i·ty, in·ac′tive·ness** *n.*

inability
inacceptable
inaccuracy
inaccurate
inaction
inadmissibility
inadmissible
inadvisability
inadvisable
inapplicable
inapposite
inappreciative
inapproachable
inappropriate
inapt
inaptitude
inartistic
inattention
inattentive
inaudible
inaudibly
inauspicious
incapability
incapable
incivility
incommunicable
incomprehensible
incomprehension
inconceivability
inconceivable
inconclusive
inconsecutive
inconsistency
inconsistent
inconsonant
inconversant
incoordination
incorporeal
incorrect
incurable

in•ad•e•quate (ĭn-ăd'ĭ-kwĭt) *adj.* Not adequate. **—in•ad'e•qua•cy** *n.* **—in•ad'e•quate•ly** *adv.*

in•ad•ver•tent (ĭn'əd-vûr'tnt) *adj.* **1.** Unintentional : accidental. **2.** Inattentive. **—in'ad•ver'tence** *n.* **—in'ad•ver'tent•ly** *adv.*

in•al•ien•a•ble (ĭn-āl'yə-nə-bəl) *adj.* Not capable of being given up or transferred <*inalienable* rights> **—in•al'ien•a•bil'i•ty** *n.* **—in•al'ien•a•bly** *adv.*

in•ane (ĭn-ān') *adj.* Without sense or substance : silly <an *inane* comment> **—in•ane'ly** *adv.* **—in•an'i•ty** (ĭn-ăn'ĭ-tē) *n.*

in•an•i•mate (ĭn-ăn'ə-mĭt) *adj.* **1.** Not having the qualities of living organisms. **2.** Unanimated : lifeless. **—in•an'i•mate•ly** *adv.* **—in•an'i•mate•ness** *n.*

in•a•ni•tion (ĭn'ə-nĭsh'ən) *n.* Exhaustion, esp. from malnourishment.

in•ap•pre•cia•ble (ĭn'ə-prē'shə-bəl) *adj.* Too small to be significant : negligible. **—in'ap•pre'cia•bly** *adv.*

in•ar•tic•u•late (ĭn'är-tĭk'yə-lĭt) *adj.* **1.** Not uttering or forming intelligible words or syllables <an *inarticulate* cry> **2.** Unable to speak : speechless. **3.** Unable to speak clearly or effectively. **4.** Unexpressed. **—in'ar•tic'u•late•ly** *adv.* **—in'ar•tic'u•late•ness** *n.*

in•as•much as (ĭn'əz-mŭch') *conj.* Because of the fact that : since.

in•au•gu•ral (ĭn-ô'gyər-əl) *adj.* **1.** Of or for an inauguration. **2.** Initial : opening. *—n.* **1.** An inauguration. **2.** An inaugural speech.

in•au•gu•rate (ĭn-ô'gyə-rāt') *v.* **-rat•ed, -rat•ing. 1.** To put into office with a formal ceremony : install. **2.** To begin officially. **3.** To open or begin use of formally : dedicate. **—in•au'gu•ra'tion** *n.* **—in•au'gu•ra'tor** *n.*

in between *adv.* & *prep.* Between.

in-be•tween (ĭn'bĭ-twēn') *adj.* Intermediate <The president issued a vague *in-between* statement.> *—n.* An intermediate or intermediary.

in•board (ĭn'bôrd', -bōrd') *adj.* **1.** Within a ship's hull. **2.** Close to or near the fuselage of an aircraft <the *inboard* engines> **—in'board'** *adv.*

in•born (ĭn'bôrn') *adj.* **1.** Possessed at birth : natural. **2.** Hereditary.

in•bound (ĭn'bound') *adj.* Incoming.

in•bred (ĭn'brĕd') *adj.* **1.** Produced by inbreeding. **2.** Deep-seated : innate.

in•breed (ĭn'brēd', ĭn-brēd') *v.* To produce by repeatedly breeding closely related individuals.

inc. *abbr.* **1.** income. **2.** incorporated. **3.** increase.

In•ca (ĭng'kə) *n., pl.* **-ca** *or* **-cas.** One of an Indian people who ruled Peru before the Spanish conquest in the 16th cent. **—In'can** *adj.* & *n.*

in•cal•cu•la•ble (ĭn-kăl'kyə-lə-bəl) *adj.* **1.** Not calculable : indeterminate. **2.** Unpredictable. **—in•cal'cu•la•bly** *adv.*

in•can•des•cent (ĭn'kən-dĕs'ənt) *adj.* **1.** Giving off visible light when heated. **2.** Shining brightly. **3.** Ardently emotional or intense. **—in'can•des'cence** *n.*

incandescent lamp *n.* A lamp in which a filament is heated to incandescence by an electric current.

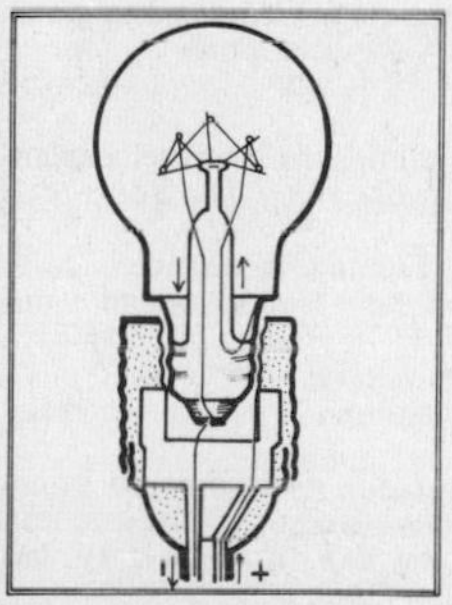

incandescent lamp

in•can•ta•tion (ĭn'kăn-tā'shən) *n.* **1.** A recitation of magic charms or spells. **2.** A magic formula for chanting or reciting.

in•ca•pac•i•tate (ĭn'kə-păs'ĭ-tāt') *v.* **-tat•ed, -tat•ing. 1.** To render incapable : disable. **2.** *Law.* To disqualify. **—in'ca•pac'i•ta'tion** *n.*

in•ca•pac•i•ty (ĭn'kə-păs'ĭ-tē) *n., pl.* **-ties. 1.** Inadequate ability or strength. **2.** A defect : disability. **3.** *Law.* A disqualification.

in•car•cer•ate (ĭn-kär'sə-rāt') *v.* **-at•ed, -at•ing. 1.** To put in jail. **2.** To confine. **—in•car'cer•a'tion** *n.*

in•car•nate (ĭn-kär'nĭt, -nāt') *adj.* **1.** Having a bodily form and nature. **2.** Embodied : personified <beauty *incarnate*> *—v.* (-nāt') **-nat•ed, -nat•ing. 1.** To give bodily form to. **2.** To personify.

in•car•na•tion (ĭn'kär-nā'shən) *n.* **1.** The act of incarnating or state of being incarnated. **2. Incarnation.** The embodiment of God in the human form of Jesus. **3.** One regarded as personifying a given abstract quality or idea.

in•case (ĭn-kās') *v. var. of* ENCASE.

in•cen•di•ar•y (ĭn-sĕn'dē-ĕr'ē) *adj.* **1.** Causing or capable of causing fires <an *incendiary* bomb> **2.** Of or relating to arson. **3.** Tending to inflame : inflammatory. **—in•cen'di•ar•y** *n.*

in•cense[1] (ĭn-sĕns') *v.* **-censed, -cens•ing.** To make angry : infuriate.

in•cense[2] (ĭn'sĕns') *n.* **1.** A substance, as a gum or wood, burned to produce a pleasant odor. **2.** The smoke or odor produced.

in•cen•tive (ĭn-sĕn'tĭv) *n.* Something inciting one to action or effort : stimulus.

in•cep•tion (ĭn-sĕp'shən) *n.* A beginning : origin. **—in•cep'tive** *adj.*

in•cer•ti•tude (ĭn-sûr'tĭ-to͞od', -tyo͞od') *n.* **1.** Uncertainty. **2.** Lack of confidence. **3.** Instability.

in•ces•sant (ĭn-sĕs'ənt) *adj.* Occurring without interruption : continuous. **—in•ces'sant•ly** *adv.*

in•cest (ĭn'sĕst') *n.* Sexual intercourse between persons so closely related that their marriage is forbidden by law or custom. **—in•ces'tu•ous** (ĭn-sĕs'cho͞o-əs) *adj.* **—in•ces'tu•ous•ly** *adv.*

inch (ĭnch) *n.* See MEASUREMENT TABLE. *—v.* To move slowly or by small amounts.

▲word history: The Latin word *uncia,* meaning "a 1/12 part," was borrowed into English twice. *Uncia* was borrowed into Old English as *ynce,* denoting a linear measure of 1/12 of a foot. The word remains in Modern English as *inch. Uncia* also developed into Old French *unce,* a unit of troy weight equal to 1/12 of a pound. It was borrowed into Middle English and survives in Modern English as *ounce.*

in•cho•ate (ĭn-kō'ĭt) *adj.* In an early stage : incipient. **—in•cho'ate•ly** *adv.* **—in•cho'ate•ness** *n.*

inch•worm (ĭnch'wûrm') *n.* A measuring worm.

in•ci•dence (ĭn'sĭ-dəns) *n.* The extent or rate of occurrence <the reduced *incidence* of polio>

in•ci•dent (ĭn'sĭ-dənt) *n.* **1.** A usu. minor event : occurrence. **2.** An event that disrupts normal procedure or causes a crisis. *—adj.* **1.** Tending to occur, esp. along with something else <summer heat and *incident* thunderstorms> **2.** Striking a surface <*incident* radiation>

in•ci•den•tal (ĭn'sĭ-dĕn'tl) *adj.* **1.** Occurring or likely to occur at the same time or as a result. **2.** Subordinate : minor <*incidental* expenses> *—n.* A minor attendant circumstance, item, or expense. **—in'ci•den'tal•ly** *adv.*

in•cin•er•ate (ĭn-sĭn'ə-rāt') *v.* **-at•ed, -at•ing.** To burn up. **—in•cin'er•a'tion** *n.*

in•cin•er•a•tor (ĭn-sĭn'ə-rā'tər) *n.* One that incinerates, esp. a furnace for burning waste.

in•cip•i•ent (ĭn-sĭp'ē-ənt) *adj.* Just beginning to appear or occur. **—in•cip'i•ence** *n.* **—in•cip'i•ent•ly** *adv.*

in•cise (ĭn-sīz') *v.* **-cised, -cis•ing. 1.** To make or cut into with a sharp tool. **2.** To carve (e.g., writing) into a surface : engrave.

in•ci•sion (ĭn-sĭzh'ən) *n.* **1.** The act of incising. **2.** A cut or notch, esp. a surgical cut.

in•ci•sive (ĭn-sī'sĭv) *adj.* **1.** Having or suggesting sharp intellect : penetrating. **2.** Cogent and effective : telling <an *incisive*

indefensible
indefinite
indestructible
indeterminable
indiscernible
indiscoverable
indistinguishable
inductile
inedible
ineducable
ineffective
ineffectual
inefficacious
inefficacy
inelastic
inelasticity
ineligibility
ineligible
inequitable
inequity
ineradicable
inexpedient
inexpensive
inexpressive
inextinguishable
infeasible
infertile
infertility
infrangible
inharmonious
inhospitable
injudicious
inoffensive
insalubrious
insanitary
insensitive
insensitivity
insignificant
insobriety
insuppressible

summary> ☆**syns:** ACUTE, BITING, PENETRATING, PERCEPTIVE, SHARP, SHREWD, TRENCHANT **—in•ci′sive•ly** *adv.* **—in•ci′sive•ness** *n.*

in•ci•sor (ĭn-sī′zər) *n.* A cutting tooth at the front of the mouth.

in•cite (ĭn-sīt′) *v.* **-cit•ed, -cit•ing.** To provoke to action : goad. **—in•cite′ment** *n.* **—in•cit′er** *n.*

in•clem•ent (ĭn-klĕm′ənt) *adj.* **1.** Stormy or rainy <*inclement* weather> **2.** Unmerciful. **—in•clem′en•cy** *n.*

in•cli•na•tion (ĭn′klə-nā′shən) *n.* **1.** An attitude : disposition. **2.** A tendency to act or think in a certain way : propensity. **3.** A preference. **4.** A bow or tilt. **5.** A slope.

in•cline (ĭn-klīn′) *v.* **-clined, -clin•ing. 1.** To deviate or cause to deviate from the horizontal or vertical : slant. **2.** To dispose or be disposed <Experience *inclined* her to be cautious.> **3.** To bow or nod. *—n.* (ĭn′klīn′). An inclined surface.

in•close (ĭn-klōz′) *v. var. of* ENCLOSE.

in•clude (ĭn-klo͞od′) *v.* **-clud•ed, -clud•ing. 1.** To have as a part or member : contain. **2.** To put into a group or total. **—in•clu′sion** *n.* **—in•clu′sive** *adj.* **—in•clu′sive•ly** *adv.*

in•cog•ni•to (ĭn-kŏg′nĭ-tō, ĭn′kŏg-nē′tō) *adv.* & *adj.* With one's identity hidden.

in•co•her•ent (ĭn′kō-hîr′ənt) *adj.* **1.** Lacking order, connection, or harmony. **2.** Unable to think or speak clearly or consecutively. **—in′co•her′ence** *n.* **—in′co•her′ent•ly** *adv.*

in•com•bus•ti•ble (ĭn′kəm-bŭs′tə-bəl) *adj.* Incapable of burning. **—in′com•bus′ti•ble** *n.*

in•come (ĭn′kŭm′) *n.* Money or its equivalent received in return for work, from a business, or as profit from investments.

income tax *n.* A tax on income earned by an individual or business.

in•com•ing (ĭn′kŭm′ĭng) *adj.* Coming in or soon to come in.

in•com•men•su•rate (ĭn′kə-mĕn′sər-ĭt, -shər-) *adj.* **1.** Not commensurate : disproportionate. **2.** Inadequate. **—in′com•men′su•rate•ly** *adv.*

in•com•mode (ĭn′kə-mōd′) *v.* **-mod•ed, -mod•ing.** To inconvenience : disturb.

in•com•mu•ni•ca•do (ĭn′kə-myo͞o′nĭ-kä′dō) *adv.* & *adj.* Without being able to communicate with others.

in•com•pa•ra•ble (ĭn-kŏm′pər-ə-bəl) *adj.* **1.** Incapable of being compared. **2.** Without rival : unique. **—in•com′pa•ra•bly** *adv.*

in•com•pat•i•ble (ĭn′kəm-păt′ə-bəl) *adj.* **1.** Not suited for combination or association <*incompatible* colors><*incompatible* roommates> **2.** Inconsistent. **—in′com•pat′i•bil′i•ty** *n.* **—in′com•pat′i•bly** *adv.*

in•com•pe•tent (ĭn-kŏm′pĭ-tənt) *adj.* Not competent. **—in•com′pe•tence, in•com′pe•ten•cy** *n.* **—in•com′pe•tent** *n.*

in•com•plete (ĭn′kəm-plēt′) *adj.* Not complete. **—in′com•plete′ly** *adv.* **—in′com•plete′ness** *n.*

in•com•press•i•ble (ĭn′kəm-prĕs′ə-bəl) *adj.* Not capable of being compressed. **—in′com•press′i•bil′i•ty** *n.*

in•con•gru•ent (ĭn-kŏng′gro͞o-ənt, ĭn′kŏn-gro͞o′ənt) *adj.* **1.** Not congruent. **2.** Incongruous. **—in′con•gru′ence** *n.* **—in′con•gru′ent•ly** *adv.*

in•con•gru•ous (ĭn-kŏng′gro͞o-əs) *adj.* **1.** Not corresponding : disagreeing. **2.** Made up of diverse or discordant elements. **3.** Unsuited to the surroundings or setting <an *incongruous* costume> **—in′con•gru′i•ty** *n.* **—in•con′gru•ous•ly** *adv.*

in•con•se•quen•tial (ĭn-kŏn′sĭ-kwĕn′shəl) *adj.* Without importance : petty. **—in•con′se•quen′ti•al′i•ty** (-shē-ăl′ĭ-tē) *n.*

in•con•sid•er•a•ble (ĭn′kən-sĭd′ər-ə-bəl) *adj.* Unimportant : trivial. **—in′con•sid′er•a•bly** *adv.*

in•con•sid•er•ate (ĭn′kən-sĭd′ər-ĭt) *adj.* Not considerate : thoughtless. **—in′con•sid′er•ate•ly** *adv.* **—in′con•sid′er•ate•ness** *n.*

in•con•sol•a•ble (ĭn′kən-sō′lə-bəl) *adj.* Incapable of being consoled. **—in′con•sol′a•bly** *adv.*

in•con•spic•u•ous (ĭn′kən-spĭk′yo͞o-əs) *adj.* Not readily seen or noticed. ☆**syns:** OBSCURE, UNNOTICEABLE, UNOBTRUSIVE **—in′con•spic′u•ous•ly** *adv.* **—in′con•spic′u•ous•ness** *n.*

in•con•stant (ĭn-kŏn′stənt) *adj.* **1.** Likely to change : unpredictable. **2.** Faithless : fickle. **—in•con′stan•cy** *n.* **—in•con′stant•ly** *adv.*

in•con•test•a•ble (ĭn′kən-tĕs′tə-bəl) *adj.* Not capable of being challenged or doubted : unquestionable. **—in′con•test′a•bil′i•ty** *n.* **—in′con•test′a•bly** *adv.*

in•con•ti•nent (ĭn-kŏn′tə-nənt) *adj.* **1.** Not restrained : uncontrolled. **2.** Unable to contain or restrain something specified. **3.** Incapable of controlling the excretory functions. **—in•con′ti•nence** *n.* **—in•con′ti•nent•ly** *adv.*

in•con•tro•vert•i•ble (ĭn-kŏn′trə-vûr′tə-bəl) *adj.* Unquestionable : indisputable. **—in•con′tro•vert′i•bly** *adv.*

in•con•ven•ience (ĭn′kən-vēn′yəns) *n.* **1.** The quality or state of being inconvenient. **2.** Something inconvenient. *—v.* **-ienced, -ienc•ing.** To cause inconvenience to : bother.

in•con•ven•ient (ĭn′kən-vēn′yənt) *adj.* Not convenient : causing trouble or difficulty. **—in′con•ven′ient•ly** *adv.*

in•cor•po•rate (ĭn-kôr′pə-rāt′) *v.* **-rat•ed, -rat•ing. 1.** To combine into a unified whole : unite. **2.** To form or cause to form a legal corporation. **3.** To give a physical form to : embody. **—in•cor′po•ra′tion** *n.* **—in•cor′po•ra′tor** *n.*

in•cor•po•re•al (ĭn′kôr-pôr′ē-əl, -pōr′-) *adj.* Without material form or substance. **—in′cor•po′re•al•ly** *adv.*

in•cor•ri•gi•ble (ĭn-kôr′ə-jə-bəl, -kŏr′-) *adj.* Incapable of being reformed or corrected <an *incorrigible* criminal> **—in•cor′ri•gi•bil′i•ty** *n.* **—in•cor′ri•gi•ble** *n.* **—in•cor′ri•gi•bly** *adv.*

in•cor•rupt•i•ble (ĭn′kə-rŭp′tə-bəl) *adj.* **1.** Not capable of being corrupted morally. **2.** Not subject to decay. **—in′cor•rupt′i•bil′i•ty** *n.* **—in′cor•rupt′i•bly** *adv.*

in•crease (ĭn-krēs′) *v.* **-creased, -creas•ing. 1.** To make or become greater or larger. **2.** To have offspring : reproduce. ☆**syns:** AMPLIFY, AUGMENT, ENLARGE, EXPAND, EXTEND, GROW, MAGNIFY, MOUNT, MULTIPLY, SNOWBALL, SWELL *—n.* (ĭn′krēs′). **1.** The act of increasing. **2.** The amount or rate of increasing. **—in•creas′ing•ly** *adv.*

in•cred•i•ble (ĭn-krĕd′ə-bəl) *adj.* **1.** Too unlikely to be believed : unbelievable. **2.** Extraordinary : astonishing. **—in•cred′i•bil′i•ty** *n.* **—in•cred′i•bly** *adv.*

in•cred•u•lous (ĭn-krĕj′ə-ləs) *adj.* **1.** Skeptical : disbelieving. **2.** Expressive of disbelief. **—in′cre•du′li•ty** (ĭn′krĭ-do͞o′lĭ-tē, -dyo͞o′-) *n.* **—in•cred′u•lous•ly** *adv.*

in•cre•ment (ĭn′krə-mənt) *n.* **1.** An increase. **2.** Something gained or added, esp. one of a series of regular additions. **—in′cre•men′tal** *adj.*

in•crim•i•nate (ĭn-krĭm′ə-nāt′) *v.* **-nat•ed, -nat•ing.** To involve in or charge with a wrongful act, as a crime. **—in•crim′i•na′tion** *n.* **—in•crim′i•na•to′ry** (-nə-tôr′ē, -tōr′ē) *adj.*

in•crust (ĭn-krŭst′) *v. var. of* ENCRUST.

in•cu•bate (ĭn′kyə-bāt′, ĭng′-) *v.* **-bat•ed, -bat•ing. 1.** To warm and hatch (eggs), as by bodily heat. **2.** To maintain (e.g., a bacterial culture) in favorable conditions for growth. **—in′cu•ba′tion** *n.*

in•cu•ba•tor (ĭn′kyə-bā′tər, ĭng′-) *n.* **1.** A cabinet in which a desired temperature can be maintained, used for bacterial culture. **2.** An enclosure for maintaining a premature infant in a controlled environment. **3.** A temperature-controlled enclosure for hatching eggs artificially.

in•cu•bus (ĭn′kyə-bəs, ĭng′-) *n., pl.* **-bus•es** or **-bi** (-bī′). **1.** An evil spirit believed to seize or harm sleeping persons. **2.** A nightmare. **3.** A nightmarish burden.

in•cu•des (ĭng-kyo͞o′dēz) *n. pl. of* INCUS.

in•cul•cate (ĭn-kŭl′kāt′) *v.* **-cat•ed, -cat•ing.** To impress on the mind by frequent repetition or instruction. **—in′cul•ca′tion** *n.* **—in•cul′ca′tor** *n.*

in•cul•pate (ĭn-kŭl′pāt′) *v.* **-pat•ed, -pat•ing.** To incriminate.

in•cum•bent (ĭn-kŭm′bənt) *adj.* **1.** Lying or resting on something else. **2.** Imposed as an obligation : obligatory. **3.** Currently in office <the *incumbent* governor> *—n.* One who is currently in office. **—in•cum′ben•cy** *n.* **—in•cum′bent•ly** *adv.*

in•cu•nab•u•lum (ĭn′kyə-năb′yə-ləm, ĭng′-) *n., pl.* **-la** (-lə). A book printed before 1501.

in•cur (ĭn-kûr′) *v.* **-curred, -cur•ring.** To become liable or subject to, esp. because of one's own actions. **—in•cur′rence** *n.*

in•cu•ri•ous (ĭn-kyo͝or′ē-əs) *adj.* Lacking interest : detached.

in•cur•sion (ĭn-kûr′zhən) *n.* A sudden hostile intrusion into another's territory.

in•cus (ĭng′kəs) *n., pl.* **in•cu•des** (ĭng-kyo͞o′dēz). An anvil-shaped bone in the middle ear of mammals.

Ind. *abbr.* Indiana.

in•debt•ed (ĭn-dĕt′ĭd) *adj.* Obligated to another, as for money or a favor : beholden. **—in•debt′ed•ness** *n.*

in•de•cent (ĭn-dē′sənt) *adj.* **1.** Offensive to good taste : improper. **2.** Morally offensive : immodest. **—in•de′cen•cy** *n.* **—in•de′cent•ly** *adv.*

in•de•ci•pher•a•ble (ĭn′dĭ-sī′fər-ə-bəl) *adj.* Not capable of being deciphered or interpreted.

in•de•ci•sion (ĭn′dĭ-sĭzh′ən) *n.* Inability to make up one's mind : irresolution.

in•de•ci•sive (ĭn′dĭ-sī′sĭv) *adj.* **1.** Without a clear-cut result : inconclusive. **2.** Marked by indecision : irresolute. **—in′de•ci′sive•ly** *adv.* **—in′de•ci′sive•ness** *n.*

in•dec•o•rous (ĭn-dĕk′ər-əs) *adj.* Lacking good taste or propriety. **—in•dec′o•rous•ly** *adv.* **—in•dec′o•rous•ness** *n.*

in•deed (ĭn-dēd′) *adv.* **1.** Without doubt : certainly. **2.** In reality

: in fact. **3.** Admittedly. —*interj.* Used to express surprise, irony, or disbelief.

in·de·fat·i·ga·ble (ĭn′dĭ-făt′ĭ-gə-bəl) *adj.* Tireless. **—in·de·fat′i·ga·bly** *adv.*

in·de·fin·a·ble (ĭn′dĭ-fī′nə-bəl) *adj.* Not capable of being defined or precisely described <an *indefinable* charm> **—in′de·fin′a·ble·ness** *n.* **—in′de·fin′a·bly** *adv.*

in·def·i·nite (ĭn-dĕf′ə-nĭt) *adj.* **1.** Not decided or specified <an *indefinite* date> **2.** Vague : unclear. **3.** Lacking fixed limits. ☆**syns:** OPEN, UNCERTAIN, UNDECIDED, UNDETERMINED, UNRESOLVED, UNSETTLED, UNSURE, VAGUE **—in·def′i·nite·ly** *adv.* **—in·def′i·nite·ness** *n.*

in·del·i·ble (ĭn-dĕl′ə-bəl) *adj.* **1.** Not able to be erased or washed away : permanent <an *indelible* memory> **2.** Making marks that are hard to erase or wash away <an *indelible* pen> **—in·del′i·bly** *adv.*

in·del·i·cate (ĭn-dĕl′ĭ-kĭt) *adj.* **1.** Lacking in propriety : coarse. **2.** Lacking sensitivity : tactless. **—in·del′i·ca·cy** *n.* **—in·del′i·cate·ly** *adv.*

in·dem·ni·fy (ĭn-dĕm′nə-fī′) *v.* **-fied, -fy·ing. 1.** To protect against loss or damage : insure. **2.** To make compensation to for loss or damage. **—in·dem′ni·fi·ca′tion** *n.* **—in·dem′ni·fi′er** *n.*

in·dem·ni·ty (ĭn-dĕm′nĭ-tē) *n., pl.* **-ties. 1.** Security against damage or loss : insurance. **2.** A legal exemption from liability for damages. **3.** Compensation for damage or loss.

in·dent¹ (ĭn-dĕnt′) *v.* **1.** To set (e.g., the 1st line of a paragraph) in from the margin. **2.** To make notches in : serrate. —*n.* An indentation.

in·dent² (ĭn-dĕnt′) *v.* **1.** To make a dent or depression in. **2.** To impress : stamp.

in·den·ta·tion (ĭn′dĕn-tā′shən) *n.* **1.** The act of indenting or state of being indented. **2.** The blank space between a margin and the beginning of an indented line. **3.** A recess in a coastline or border. **4.** A notch in an edge.

in·den·ture (ĭn-dĕn′chər) *n.* **1.** A legal deed or contract. **2.** *often* **indentures.** A contract obligating 1 party to work for another for a specified period of time. —*v.* **-tured, -tur·ing.** To bind into the service of another.

in·de·pend·ence (ĭn′dĭ-pĕn′dəns) *n.* The quality or state of being independent.

Independence. City of W Mo. E of Kansas City. *Pop.* 111,806.

Independence Day *n.* July 4, a U.S. legal holiday commemorating the adoption of the Declaration of Independence in 1776.

in·de·pend·ent (ĭn′dĭ-pĕn′dənt) *adj.* **1.** Politically self-governing. **2.** Free from the control of others : self-reliant. **3. a.** Not affiliated with a larger group or system. **b.** Not committed to a political party or faction <an *independent* candidate> **4.** Not relying on others, esp. for financial support. **5.** Providing or being enough income to enable one to live without working. —*n.* One that is independent, esp. a candidate or voter not committed to a political party. **—in′de·pend′ent·ly** *adv.*

in-depth (ĭn′dĕpth′) *adj.* Thorough : detailed <an *in-depth* analysis>

in·de·scrib·a·ble (ĭn′dĭ-skrī′bə-bəl) *adj.* **1.** Incapable of being described. **2.** Exceeding description. **—in′de·scrib′a·bly** *adv.*

in·de·ter·mi·nate (ĭn′dĭ-tûr′mə-nĭt) *adj.* **1.** Not determined. **2.** Incapable of being determined. **3.** Unclear or imprecise : vague. **—in′de·ter′mi·na·cy** *n.* **—in′de·ter′mi·nate·ly** *adv.*

in·dex (ĭn′dĕks′) *n., pl.* **-dex·es** *or* **-di·ces** (-dĭ-sēz′). **1.** A list or catalogue for aiding reference, esp. an alphabetized listing in a printed work that gives the pages on which various names, places, and subjects are mentioned. **2.** Something serving to guide or point out, esp. a printed character calling attention to a paragraph or section. **3.** Something that measures or indicates : sign. **4.** A pointer, as in a scientific instrument. **5. a.** *Math.* A small number just above and to the left of a radical sign indicating what root is to be extracted. **b.** Any number or symbol indicating an operation to be performed on an expression. **6.** A number or scale indicating change in magnitude, as of prices, relative to the magnitude at some specified point usu. taken as 100 <the cost-of-living *index*> —*v.* **1.** To provide with or enter in an index. **2.** To indicate : signal. **3.** To adjust through indexation.

in·dex·a·tion (ĭn′dĕk-sā′shən) *n.* The linkage of economic factors, as wages or prices, to a cost-of-living index so they rise and fall within the rate of inflation.

index finger *n.* The finger next to the thumb.

index of refraction *n.* The quotient of the speed of light in a vacuum divided by the speed of light in a medium under consideration.

In·di·a (ĭn′dē-ə). **1.** Peninsula and subcontinent of S Asia. **2.** Country of S Asia. *Cap.* New Delhi. *Pop.* 669,860,000.

In·di·an (ĭn′dē-ən) *n.* **1.** A native or inhabitant of India. **2.** A member of any of the aboriginal peoples of the Americas. **—In′di·an** *adj.*

Indian Ocean. Ocean extending from S Asia to Antarctica and from E Africa to SE Australia.

In·di·an·a (ĭn′dē-ăn′ə). State of NC U.S. *Cap.* Indianapolis. *Pop.* 5,490,179. **—In′di·an′i·an** *n.* & *adj.*

In·di·an·ap·o·lis (ĭn′dē-ə-năp′ə-lĭs). Cap. of Ind., in the C part. *Pop.* 700,807.

Indian corn *n.* The American corn plant or its ripened ears.

Indian meal *n.* Cornmeal.

Indian pipe *n.* A waxy white woodland plant, *Monotropa uniflora,* with a single nodding flower.

Indian pipe

Indian reserve *n. Can.* A tract of land set aside for Indians by the Federal Government.

Indian summer *n.* A period of mild weather in late autumn.

India paper *n.* **1.** A thin, uncoated, delicate paper used esp. for taking impressions of engravings. **2.** A thin, strong opaque printing paper used esp. for Bibles.

in·di·cate (ĭn′dĭ-kāt′) *v.* **-cat·ed, -cat·ing. 1.** To point out : show <*indicate* the quickest route> **2.** To serve as a sign or symptom : signify. **3.** To suggest the advisability of : call for. **4.** To express briefly. **—in′di·ca′tion** *n.* **—in′di·ca′tor** *n.*

in·dic·a·tive (ĭn-dĭk′ə-tĭv) *adj.* **1.** Serving to indicate. **2.** Of or being a verb mood used to express actions and conditions that are objective facts. —*n.* **1.** The indicative mood. **2.** A verb in the indicative mood.

in·di·ces (ĭn′dĭ-sēz′) *n. var. pl. of* INDEX.

in·dict (ĭn-dīt′) *v.* **1.** To accuse of an offense : charge. **2.** To make a formal accusation against by the findings of a grand jury. **—in·dict′a·ble** *adj.* **—in·dict′er, in·dic′tor** *n.* **—in·dict′ment** *n.*

in·dif·fer·ent (ĭn-dĭf′ər-ənt) *adj.* **1.** Not mattering : unimportant. **2.** Having no marked feeling or preference : impartial. **3.** Uninterested : apathetic. **4.** Neither good nor bad : mediocre. **5.** Neither right nor wrong. **—in·dif′fer·ence** *n.* **—in·dif′fer·ent·ly** *adv.*

in·dig·e·nous (ĭn-dĭj′ə-nəs) *adj.* Living or occurring naturally in an area : native.

in·di·gent (ĭn′də-jənt) *adj.* Impoverished : needy. **—in′di·gence** *n.*

in·di·gest·i·ble (ĭn′dĭ-jĕs′tə-bəl, -dī-) *adj.* Impossible or difficult to digest. **—in′di·gest′i·bil′i·ty** *n.* **—in′di·gest′i·bly** *adv.*

in·di·ges·tion (ĭn′dĭ-jĕs′chən, -dī-) *n.* Difficulty or discomfort in digesting food.

in·dig·nant (ĭn-dĭg′nənt) *adj.* Marked by or filled with indignation. **—in·dig′nant·ly** *adv.*

in·dig·na·tion (ĭn′dĭg-nā′shən) *n.* Anger aroused by injustice or unworthiness.

in·dig·ni·ty (ĭn-dĭg′nĭ-tē) *n., pl.* **-ties. 1.** Humiliating treatment. **2.** Something that offends one's pride : affront.

in·di·go (ĭn′dĭ-gō′) *n., pl.* **-gos** *or* **-goes. 1.** A blue dye obtained from a plant or produced synthetically. **2.** A dark blue.

indigo bunting *n.* A small North American bird, *Passerina cyanea,* the male of which has deep-blue plumage.

indigo snake *n.* A nonvenomous bluish-black snake, *Drymarchon corais,* of the S U.S. and N Mexico.

in·di·rect (ĭn′də-rĕkt′, -dī-) *adj.* **1.** Not taking a direct course : roundabout. **2.** Not straight to the point or forthright : devious. **3.** Not immediate or intended : secondary <*indirect* results> **—in′di·rec′tion** *n.* **—in·di·rect′ly** *adv.*

indirect object *n.* A grammatical object indirectly affected by the action of a verb, as *me* in *sent me a telegram.*

in·dis·creet (ĭn′dĭ-skrēt′) *adj.* Lacking discretion. **—in′dis·creet′ly** *adv.* **—in′dis·cre′tion** (-skrĕsh′ən) *n.*

in·dis·crim·i·nate (ĭn′dĭ-skrĭm′ə-nĭt) *adj.* **1.** Lacking discrimination. **2.** Haphazard : random. **3.** Not sorted out : confused. **—in′dis·crim′i·nate·ly** *adv.*

in·dis·pen·sa·ble (ĭn′dĭ-spĕn′sə-bəl) *adj.* Necessary : essential. **–in′dis·pen′sa·bil′i·ty** *n.* **–in′dis·pen′sa·ble** *n.* **–in′dis·pen′sa·bly** *adv.*

in·dis·posed (ĭn′dĭ-spōzd′) *adj.* **1.** Mildly ill. **2.** Not inclined : averse. **–in·dis′po·si′tion** (-dĭs′pə-zĭsh′ən) *n.*

in·dis·put·a·ble (ĭn′dĭ-spyo͞o′tə-bəl) *adj.* Beyond dispute : undeniable. **–in′dis·put′a·ble·ness** *n.* **–in′dis·put′a·bly** *adv.*

in·dis·sol·u·ble (ĭn′dĭ-sŏl′yə-bəl) *adj.* **1.** Impossible to break or undo. **2.** Incapable of being dissolved or decomposed.

in·dis·tinct (ĭn′dĭ-stĭngkt′) *adj.* **1.** Not clearly outlined : blurred. **2.** Vague, faint, or dim : unclear. **–in′dis·tinct′ly** *adv.* **–in′dis·tinct′ness** *n.*

in·dite (ĭn-dīt′) *v.* **-dit·ed, -dit·ing. 1.** To write : compose. **2.** To put down in writing. **–in·dit′er** *n.*

in·di·um (ĭn′dē-əm) *n. Symbol* **In** A soft, silvery-white metallic element used for mirrors and transistor compounds.

in·di·vid·u·al (ĭn′də-vĭj′o͞o-əl) *adj.* **1.** Of, for, or relating to a single human being. **2.** Existing as a distinct entity : separate. **3.** Having individuality : unlike others <an *individual* style of dancing> *–n.* A single person or organism, as opposed to a group. **–in′di·vid′u·al·ly** *adv.*

in·di·vid·u·al·ism (ĭn′də-vĭj′o͞o-ə-lĭz′əm) *n.* **1.** Individuality. **2.** Assertion of the self. **3. a.** The theory that one should have freedom in one's economic pursuits and should succeed by one's own initiative. **b.** The doctrine that the interests of the individual should have preference over the interests of the state or social group.

in·di·vid·u·al·ist (ĭn′də-vĭj′o͞o-ə-lĭst) *n.* **1.** One who thinks or acts in an independent way. **2.** One advocating individualism. **–in′di·vid′u·al·is′tic** *adj.*

in·di·vid·u·al·i·ty (ĭn′də-vĭj′o͞o-ăl′ĭ-tē) *n.* **1.** The quality of being individual : distinctness. **2.** The aggregate of characteristics that distinguish 1 person from others.

in·di·vid·u·al·ize (ĭn′də-vĭj′o͞o-ə-līz′) *v.* **-ized, -iz·ing. 1.** To give individuality to. **2.** To consider individually. **3.** To modify to suit a specific individual.

in·di·vis·i·ble (ĭn′də-vĭz′ə-bəl) *adj.* Not able to be divided.

In·do·chi·na (ĭn′dō-chī′nə). SE peninsula of Asia.

in·doc·tri·nate (ĭn-dŏk′trə-nāt′) *v.* **-nat·ed, -nat·ing. 1.** To instruct in a doctrine or belief. **2.** To train to accept a system of thought uncritically. **–in·doc′tri·na′tion** *n.*

In·do-Eu·ro·pe·an (ĭn′dō-yo͝or′ə-pē′ən) *n.* A family of languages comprising most of the languages of Europe and parts of S Asia. **–In′do-Eu′ro·pe′an** *adj.*

in·do·lent (ĭn′də-lənt) *adj.* Disinclined to exert oneself : lazy. **–in′do·lence** *n.*

in·dom·i·ta·ble (ĭn-dŏm′ĭ-tə-bəl) *adj.* Incapable of being subdued or defeated. **–in·dom′i·ta·bly** *adv.*

In·do·ne·sia (ĭn′də-nē′zhə, -shə). Country of SE Asia. *Cap.* Djakarta. *Pop.* 153,510,000. **–In′do·ne′sian** *adj.* & *n.*

in·door (ĭn′dôr′, -dōr′) *adj.* Of or within the inside of a building.

in·doors (ĭn-dôrz′, -dōrz′) *adv.* In or into a building.

in·dorse (ĭn-dôrs′) *v. var. of* ENDORSE.

in·du·bi·ta·ble (ĭn-do͞o′bĭ-tə-bəl, -dyo͞o′-) *adj.* Too evident to be doubted : unquestionable. **–in·du′bi·ta·bly** *adv.*

in·duce (ĭn-do͞os′, -dyo͞os′) *v.* **-duced, -duc·ing. 1.** To move by persuasion or influence : prevail upon. **2.** To cause to occur : bring on <*induce* childbirth> **3.** To infer by inductive reasoning. **–in·duc′er** *n.*

in·duce·ment (ĭn-do͞os′mənt, -dyo͞os′-) *n.* **1.** The act of inducing. **2.** Something that induces : motive or incentive.

in·duct (ĭn-dŭkt′) *v.* **1.** To place formally in office : install. **2.** To admit as a new member : initiate. **3.** To summon into military service : draft. **–in′duc·tee′** *n.*

in·duc·tance (ĭn-dŭk′təns) *n.* A circuit element, usu. a conducting coil, in which electromagnetic induction generates electromotive force.

in·duc·tion (ĭn-dŭk′shən) *n.* **1.** The act of inducting or of being inducted. **2.** Reasoning in which conclusions are drawn from particular instances or facts. **3. a.** The generation of electromotive force in a closed circuit by a magnetic field that changes with time. **b.** The production of an electric charge in an uncharged body by bringing a charged body close to it.

in·duc·tive (ĭn-dŭk′tĭv) *adj.* **1.** Of, relating to, or using induction <*inductive* reasoning> **2.** *Elect.* Of or resulting from inductance. **–in·duc′tive·ly** *adv.* **–in·duc′tive·ness** *n.*

in·dulge (ĭn-dŭlj′) *v.* **-dulged, -dulg·ing. 1.** To give in to the desires of, esp. to excess : pamper. **2.** To yield to : gratify <*indulge* a craving> **3.** To allow (oneself) a specialpleasure. **–in·dulg′er** *n.*

in·dul·gence (ĭn-dŭl′jəns) *n.* **1.** The act of indulging or state of being indulgent. **2.** Something indulged in. **3.** Something given as a favor. **4.** Lenient treatment : tolerance. **5.** *Rom. Cath. Ch.* The remission of punishment still due for a sin that has been sacramentally absolved.

in·dul·gent (ĭn-dŭl′jənt) *adj.* Showing, marked by, or inclined to indulgence : lenient. **–in·dul′gent·ly** *adv.*

In·dus (ĭn′dəs). River of SC Asia, rising in SW Tibet and flowing 1,900 mi (3,060 km) to the Arabian Sea.

in·dus·tri·al (ĭn-dŭs′trē-əl) *adj.* **1.** Of, relating to, or used in industry. **2.** Characterized by highly developed industries. **–in·dus′tri·al·ly** *adv.*

in·dus·tri·al·ism (ĭn-dŭs′trē-ə-lĭz′əm) *n.* A system in which industries are dominant. **–in·dus′tri·al·ist** *n.*

in·dus·tri·al·ize (ĭn-dŭs′trē-ə-līz′) *v.* **-ized, -iz·ing.** To become or cause to be industrial. **–in·dus′tri·al·i·za′tion** *n.*

in·dus·tri·ous (ĭn-dŭs′trē-əs) *adj.* Working steadily and hard : diligent. **–in·dus′tri·ous·ly** *adv.* **–in·dus′tri·ous·ness** *n.*

in·dus·try (ĭn′də-strē) *n., pl.* **-tries. 1.** The commercial production and sale of goods and services. **2.** A branch of manufacture and trade <the electronics *industry*> **3.** Industrial management as distinguished from labor. **4.** Diligence.

-ine *suff.* Of or resembling <serpent*ine*>

in·e·bri·ate (ĭn-ē′brē-āt′) *v.* **-at·ed, -at·ing.** To make drunk : intoxicate. *–n.* (-ĭt). An intoxicated person. **–in·e′bri·ant** *adj.* & *n.* **–in·e′bri·a′tion** *n.*

in·ef·fa·ble (ĭn-ĕf′ə-bəl) *adj.* Beyond expression : indescribable or unutterable. **–in·ef′fa·bly** *adv.*

in·ef·face·a·ble (ĭn′ĭ-fā′sə-bəl) *adj.* Not effaceable : indelible.

in·ef·fi·cient (ĭn′ĭ-fĭsh′ənt) *adj.* **1.** Not producing the desired effect. **2.** Wasteful of time, energy, or materials. **–in′ef·fi′cien·cy** *n.* **–in′ef·fi′cient·ly** *adv.*

in·el·e·gant (ĭn-ĕl′ĭ-gənt) *adj.* **1.** Lacking elegance. **2.** Unrefined : crude. **–in·el′e·gance** *n.*

in·e·luc·ta·ble (ĭn′ĭ-lŭk′tə-bəl) *adj.* Not capable of being avoided or overcome : inescapable. **–in′e·luc′ta·bly** *adv.*

in·ept (ĭn-ĕpt′) *adj.* **1.** Not suitable : inappropriate. **2.** Awkward or incompetent : bungling. **–in·ep′ti·tude, in·ept′ness** *n.* **–in·ept′ly** *adv.*

in·e·qual·i·ty (ĭn′ĭ-kwŏl′ĭ-tē) *n., pl.* **-ties. 1.** The condition or an instance of being unequal. **2.** Social or economic disparity. **3.** Lack of regularity : unevenness. **4.** Variability : changeability. **5.** *Math.* An algebraic statement that a quantity is greater than or less than another quantity.

in·eq·ui·ta·ble (ĭn-ĕk′wĭ-tə-bəl) *adj.* Not equitable : unfair. **–in·eq′ui·ta·bly** *adv.*

in·eq·ui·ty (ĭn-ĕk′wĭ-tē) *n., pl.* **-ties. 1.** Injustice : unfairness. **2.** An example of injustice.

in·ert (ĭn-ûrt′) *adj.* **1.** Not able to move or act. **2.** Slow to move or act : sluggish. **3.** Displaying no chemical activity <an *inert* gas> **–in·ert′ly** *adv.* **–in·ert′ness** *n.*

in·er·tia (ĭn-ûr′shə) *n.* **1.** The tendency of a body to remain at rest or to stay in motion unless acted upon by an external force. **2.** Resistance to motion or change. **–in·er′tial** *adj.* **–in·er′tial·ly** *adv.*

in·es·cap·a·ble (ĭn′ĭ-skā′pə-bəl) *adj.* Incapable of being escaped or avoided. **–in′es·cap′a·bly** *adv.*

in·es·ti·ma·ble (ĭn-ĕs′tə-mə-bəl) *adj.* **1.** Incapable of being estimated or calculated. **2.** Of a value too great to be estimated. **–in·es′ti·ma·bly** *adv.*

in·ev·i·ta·ble (ĭn-ĕv′ĭ-tə-bəl) *adj.* Not able to be avoided or prevented. **–in·ev′i·ta·bil′i·ty** *n.* **–in·ev′i·ta·bly** *adv.*

in·ex·act (ĭn′ĭg-zăkt′) *adj.* **1.** Not true, accurate, or precise. **2.** Not rigorous. **–in′ex·act′ly** *adv.*

in·ex·cus·a·ble (ĭn′ĭk-skyo͞o′zə-bəl) *adj.* Not capable of being excused or justified **–in′ex·cus′a·bly** *adv.*

in·ex·haust·i·ble (ĭn′ĭg-zô′stə-bəl) *adj.* **1.** Incapable of being used up. **2.** Tireless. **–in′ex·haust′i·bly** *adv.*

in·ex·o·ra·ble (ĭn-ĕk′sər-ə-bəl) *adj.* Not capable of being moved by entreaty : unyielding. **–in·ex′o·ra·bly** *adv.*

in·ex·pe·ri·ence (ĭn′ĭk-spîr′ē-əns) *n.* Lack of experience.

in·ex·pe·ri·enced (ĭn′ĭk-spîr′ē-ənst) *adj.* Lacking experience. ☆***syns:*** GREEN, RAW, UNPRACTICED, UNSEASONED, UNTRIED

in·ex·pert (ĭn-ĕk′spûrt′) *adj.* Not expert : unskilled. **–in·ex′pert′ly** *adv.*

in·ex·pli·ca·ble (ĭn-ĕk′splĭ-kə-bəl, ĭn′ĭk-splĭk′ə-) *adj.* Not capable of being explained. **–in·ex′pli·ca·bly** *adv.*

in·ex·press·i·ble (ĭn′ĭk-sprĕs′ə-bəl) *adj.* Incapable of being expressed. **–in′ex·press′i·bly** *adv.*

in ex·tre·mis (ĭn′ ĕk-strē′mĭs) *adv.* At the point of death.

in·ex·tri·ca·ble (ĭn-ĕk′strĭ-kə-bəl) *adj.* **1.** Not capable of being untied or untangled. **2.** Too complex to resolve. **–in·ex′tri·ca·bly** *adv.*

in·fal·li·ble (ĭn-făl′ə-bəl) *adj.* **1.** Not capable of making mistakes <an *infallible* leader> **2.** Not capable of failing : certain <an *infallible* method> **–in·fal′li·bil′i·ty** *n.* **–in·fal′li·bly** *adv.*

in·fa·mous (ĭn'fə-məs) *adj.* **1.** Having a bad reputation : notorious. **2.** Shocking or disgraceful. **–in'fa·mous·ly** *adv.*

in·fa·my (ĭn'fə-mē) *n., pl.* **-mies. 1.** Evil notoriety or reputation. **2.** The state of being infamous. **3.** A disgraceful, publicly known act.

in·fan·cy (ĭn'fən-sē) *n., pl.* **-cies. 1.** The condition or time of being an infant. **2.** An early stage of existence. **3.** *Law.* Minority.

in·fant (ĭn'fənt) *n.* **1.** A child in the earliest age : baby. **2.** *Law.* A minor.

in·fan·ti·cide (ĭn-făn'tĭ-sīd') *n.* **1.** The killing of an infant. **2.** One who kills an infant.

in·fan·tile (ĭn'fən-tīl', -tĭl) *adj.* **1.** Of or relating to infants or infancy. **2.** Immature : childish.

infantile paralysis *n.* Poliomyelitis.

in·fan·try (ĭn'fən-trē) *n., pl.* **-tries.** The branch of an army made up of soldiers who are trained to fight on foot. **–in'fan·try·man** *n.*

in·farct (ĭn'färkt', ĭn-färkt') *n.* An area of dead tissue caused by an insufficient supply of blood. **–in·farct'ed** *adj.* **–in·farc'tion** *n.*

in·fat·u·ate (ĭn-făch'o͞o-āt') *v.* **-at·ed, -at·ing.** To arouse an extravagant or foolish love in. **–in·fat'u·at'ed** *adj.* **–in·fat'u·a'tion** *n.*

in·fect (ĭn-fĕkt') *v.* **1.** To contaminate with disease-causing microorganisms. **2.** To transmit a disease to. **3.** To affect as if by contagion <a panic that *infected* the whole town> **–in·fec'tive** *adj.*

in·fec·tion (ĭn-fĕk'shən) *n.* **1.** Invasion of a bodily part by disease-causing microorganisms. **2.** The condition resulting from such an invasion. **3.** An infectious disease.

in·fec·tious (ĭn-fĕk'shəs) *adj.* **1.** Able to cause infection. **2.** Transmitted by infection. **3.** Readily communicated <an *infectious* grin> **–in·fec'tious·ly** *adv.*

in·fe·lic·i·tous (ĭn'fĭ-lĭs'ĭ-təs) *adj.* **1.** Not happy : unfortunate. **2.** Not apt, as in expression. **–in'fe·lic'i·ty** *n.* **–in'fe·lic'i·tous·ly** *adv.*

in·fer (ĭn-fûr') *v.* **-ferred, -fer·ring. 1.** To conclude by reasoning : deduce. **2.** To have as a logical consequence. **3.** To lead to as a result or conclusion. **–in·fer'a·ble** *adj.*

in·fer·ence (ĭn'fər-əns) *n.* **1.** The act or process of inferring <reasoning by *inference*> **2.** Something inferred, as a conclusion. **–in'fer·en'tial** *adj.*

in·fe·ri·or (ĭn-fîr'ē-ər) *adj.* **1.** Located under or below : lower. **2.** Low or lower in order, rank, or quality. **–in·fe'ri·or** *n.* **–in·fe'ri·or'i·ty** (-ôr'ĭ-tē, -ŏr'-) *n.*

in·fer·nal (ĭn-fûr'nəl) *adj.* **1.** Of, like, or relating to hell. **2.** Damnable : abominable. **–in·fer'nal·ly** *adv.*

in·fer·no (ĭn-fûr'nō) *n., pl.* **-nos.** A place or condition suggestive of hell.

in·fest (ĭn-fĕst') *v.* To spread in or over so as to be harmful or offensive. **–in'fes·ta'tion** *n.*

in·fi·del (ĭn'fĭ-dəl, -dĕl') *n.* **1.** One who has no religion. **2.** An unbeliever in a religion, esp. Christianity.

in·fi·del·i·ty (ĭn'fĭ-dĕl'ĭ-tē) *n., pl.* **-ties. 1.** Lack of fidelity : disloyalty. **2.** Lack of religious belief. **3.** Marital unfaithfulness.

in·field (ĭn'fēld') *n.* *Baseball.* The part of a playing field within the base lines. **–in'field'er** *n.*

in·fight·ing (ĭn'fī'tĭng) *n.* **1.** Close-range fighting. **2.** Contention among members of a group. **–in'fight'er** *n.*

in·fil·trate (ĭn-fĭl'trāt', ĭn'fĭl-) *v.* **-trat·ed, -trat·ing. 1.** To pass or cause to pass into something through pores or small openings. **2.** To pass or enter gradually or stealthily <*infiltrate* spies into enemy territory> **–in'fil·tra'tion** *n.*

in·fi·nite (ĭn'fə-nĭt) *adj.* **1.** Without boundaries : limitless <an *infinite* distance><*infinite* caution> **2.** Immeasurably great or large. **3.** *Math.* **a.** Greater in value than any specified number, however large. **b.** Having a measure that is infinite. **–in'fi·nite** *n.* **–in'fi·nite·ly** *adv.*

in·fin·i·tes·i·mal (ĭn-fĭn'ĭ-tĕs'ə-məl) *adj.* Immeasurably small : minute. **–in·fin'i·tes'i·mal·ly** *adv.*

in·fin·i·tive (ĭn-fĭn'ĭ-tĭv) *n.* A verb form that is not inflected and in English is usu. preceded by *to* or an auxiliary verb.

in·fin·i·ty (ĭn-fĭn'ĭ-tē) *n., pl.* **-ties. 1.** The quality or state of being infinite. **2.** Unbounded space, time, or amount. **3.** An indefinitely large number.

in·firm (ĭn-fûrm') *adj.* **1.** Physically weak, esp. from age : feeble. **2.** Not sound or valid.

in·fir·ma·ry (ĭn-fûr'mə-rē) *n., pl.* **-ries.** An institution for the care of the sick or disabled.

in·fir·mi·ty (ĭn-fûr'mĭ-tē) *n., pl.* **-ties. 1.** Physical weakness, esp. from age : feebleness. **2.** A disease : ailment. **3.** A weakness of character : foible.

in·flame (ĭn-flām') *v.* **1.** To set on fire : kindle. **2.** To arouse to strong or excessive feeling. **3.** To intensify. **4.** To produce or affect with inflammation.

in·flam·ma·ble (ĭn-flăm'ə-bəl) *adj.* **1.** Tending to catch fire easily : flammable. **2.** Easily excited

▲word history: Hydrogen was once called the *inflammable* gas not because it does not burn but because it is so easily ignited. *Inflammable* is derived ultimately from the Latin prefix *in-*, "in," and the noun *flamma*, "flame." There is another prefix *in-*, however, which English also borrowed from Latin, that means "not," and the word *inflammable* can be misunderstood as meaning "not capable of burning." In order to eliminate possibly dangerous confusion about the combustibility of various materials, safety officials in the 20th cent. have adopted the word *flammable*, which had a brief life in the early 19th cent. to mean "able to burn." Materials that do not burn are unambiguously labeled *nonflammable*.

in·flam·ma·tion (ĭn'flə-mā'shən) *n.* Localized redness, swelling, heat, and pain in response to an injury or infection.

in·flam·ma·to·ry (ĭn-flăm'ə-tôr'ē, -tōr'ē) *adj.* **1.** Characterized by or causing inflammation. **2.** Arousing strong or uncontrolled feeling <an *inflammatory* harangue>

in·flate (ĭn-flāt') *v.* **-flat·ed, -flat·ing. 1.** To fill and expand with a gas. **2.** To increase unsoundly : puff up <successes that *inflated* our hopes> **3.** To raise (e.g., prices) abnormally. **–in·flat'a·ble** *adj.*

in·fla·tion (ĭn-flā'shən) *n.* **1.** The act of inflating or state of being inflated. **2.** A sharp rise in the prices of goods and services. **–in·fla'tion·ar'y** *adj.*

in·flect (ĭn-flĕkt') *v.* **1.** To turn : veer. **2.** To vary the tone or pitch of (the voice), esp. in speaking. **3.** To change the form of (a word) to indicate number, tense, person, etc. **–in·flec'tive** *adj.*

in·flec·tion (ĭn-flĕk'shən) *n.* **1.** A change in pitch or tone of voice. **2. a.** A change in the form of a word to indicate number, tense, person, etc. **b.** A word derived by such a change <"Gives" and "gave" are *inflections* of "give."> **–in·flec'tion·al** *adj.* **–in·flec'tion·al·ly** *adv.*

in·flex·i·ble (ĭn-flĕk'sə-bəl) *adj.* **1.** Not flexible : rigid. **2.** Not subject to change : unalterable. **3.** Unyielding. ☆**syns:** IMMUTABLE, INVARIABLE, IRONBOUND, IRON CLAD, STIFF, UNCHANGEABLE **–in·flex'i·bil'i·ty** *n.* **–in·flex'i·bly** *adv.*

in·flict (ĭn-flĭkt') *v.* **1.** To cause to be suffered <*inflict* a wound> **2.** To impose. **–in·flict'er, in·flic'tor** *n.* **–in·flic'tion** *n.*

in·flo·res·cence (ĭn'flə-rĕs'əns) *n.* A characteristic arrangement of flowers on a stalk. **–in'flo·res'cent** *adj.*

in·flow (ĭn'flō') *n.* An influx.

in·flu·ence (ĭn'flo͞o-əns) *n.* **1.** The power to produce effects, esp. indirectly or through an intermediary. **2.** The condition of being affected <under the *influence* of drugs> **3.** One exercising indirect power to sway or affect. —*v.* **-enced, -enc·ing. 1.** To exert influence over : affect. **2.** To modify. **–in'flu·en'tial** (-ĕn'shəl) *adj.*

in·flu·en·za (ĭn'flo͞o-ĕn'zə) *n.* An acute infectious viral disease marked by respiratory inflammation, fever, muscular pain, and often intestinal discomfort.

in·flux (ĭn'flŭks') *n.* A stream of people or things coming in.

in·fold (ĭn-fōld') *v.* **1.** To fold inward. **2.** *var. of* ENFOLD.

in·form (ĭn-fôrm') *v.* **1.** To give information to : tell. **2.** To disclose often incriminating information <*inform* against an accomplice> **3.** To give a special quality or character to : imbue.

in·for·mal (ĭn-fôr'məl) *adj.* **1.** Not following a prescribed form or pattern <an *informal* debate> **2.** Characterized by lack of formality. **3.** Of or for ordinary use or communication : casual <*informal* language> ☆**syns:** CASUAL, EASY, EASYGOING, RELAXED **–in'for·mal'i·ty** *n.* **–in·for'mal·ly** *adv.*

in·form·ant (ĭn-fôr'mənt) *n.* One who discloses or furnishes information.

in·for·ma·tion (ĭn'fər-mā'shən) *n.* **1.** The act of informing or state of being informed. **2.** Facts learned, as about current or past events : data. **–in'for·ma'tion·al** *adj.*

in·for·ma·tive (ĭn-fôr'mə-tĭv) *adj.* Providing information : instructive.

in·formed (ĭn-fôrmd') *adj.* Having or based on information.

in·form·er (ĭn-fôr'mər) *n.* **1.** An informant. **2.** One who informs against others.

in·frac·tion (ĭn-frăk'shən) *n.* A violation of a rule.

in·fra·red (ĭn'frə-rĕd') *adj.* Of, being, or using electromagnetic radiation with wavelengths longer than those of visible light and shorter than those of microwaves.

in·fra·son·ic (ĭn'frə-sŏn'ĭk) *adj.* Producing or using waves or vibrations with frequencies below that of audible sound.

in·fra·struc·ture (ĭn'frə-strŭk'chər) *n.* **1.** An underlying base or foundation. **2.** The basic facilities needed for the functioning of a system.

in·fre·quent (ĭn-frē'kwənt) *adj.* **1.** Not frequent : rare. **2.**

Rarely occurring or appearing. ☆**syns:** OCCASIONAL, RARE, SCARCE, SPORADIC **—in•fre'quen•cy** *n.* **—in•fre'quent•ly** *adv.*
in•fringe (ĭn-frĭnj') *v.* **-fringed, -fring•ing. 1.** To break (e.g., a law) : violate. **2.** To encroach : trespass. **—in•fringe'ment** *n.*
in•fu•ri•ate (ĭn-fyo͝or'ē-āt') *v.* **-at•ed, -at•ing.** To make very angry : enrage. **—in•fu'ri•at'ing•ly** *adv.* **—in•fu'ri•a'tion** *n.*
in•fuse (ĭn-fyo͞oz') *v.* **-fused, -fus•ing. 1.** To introduce : inject <*infuse* new enthusiasm into the campaign> **2.** To imbue : fill <*infused* us with pride> **3.** To steep without boiling. **—in•fu'sion** *n.*
in•fus•i•ble (ĭn-fyo͞o'zə-bəl) *adj.* Not able to be fused or melted.
-ing¹ *suff.* Used to form the present participle of verbs and participial adjectives <see*ing*><charm*ing*>
-ing² *suff.* **1.** An action : activity <danc*ing*><berry*ing*> **2.** The result of an action or process <an oil paint*ing*> **3.** Something used in an action or process <stuff*ing*>
in•gen•ious (ĭn-jēn'yəs) *adj.* **1.** Showing great skill in creating or devising : creative. **2.** Original and imaginative <an *ingenious* plan for escape> **—in•gen'ious•ly** *adv.* **—in•gen'ious•ness** *n.*
in•gé•nue (ăn'zhə-no͞o') *n.* **1.** An artless, innocent young woman. **2.** An actress playing such a young woman.
in•ge•nu•i•ty (ĭn'jə-no͞o'ĭ-tē, -nyo͞o'-) *n., pl.* **-ties.** Inventive skill : cleverness.
in•gen•u•ous (ĭn-jĕn'yo͞o-əs) *adj.* **1.** Lacking sophistication : artless. **2.** Straightforward : frank. **—in•gen'u•ous•ly** *adv.* **—in•gen'u•ous•ness** *n.*
in•gest (ĭn-jĕst') *v.* To take in by or as if by swallowing. **—in•ges'tion** *n.*
in•gle•nook (ĭng'gəl-no͝ok') *n.* **1.** A corner or recess beside a fireplace. **2.** A bench in an inglenook.
in•glo•ri•ous (ĭn-glôr'ē-əs, -glōr'-) *adj.* **1.** Not glorious. **2.** Dishonorable : ignominious. **—in•glo'ri•ous•ly** *adv.*
in•got (ĭng'gət) *n.* A mass of metal shaped in a bar or block.
in•grain (ĭn-grān') *v.* To impress or work deeply into the mind or nature : imbue. *—n.* Yarn or fiber dyed before being spun or woven.
in•grained (ĭn-grānd') *adj.* **1.** Worked deeply into the texture or fiber. **2.** Firmly established : deep-seated.
in•grate (ĭn'grāt') *n.* One who is ungrateful.
in•gra•ti•ate (ĭn-grā'shē-āt') *v.* **-at•ed, -at•ing.** To gain favor with deliberately. **—in•gra'ti•at'ing•ly** *adv.* **—in•gra'ti•a'tion** *n.*
in•grat•i•tude (ĭn-grăt'ĭ-to͞od', -tyo͞od') *n.* Lack of gratitude.
in•gre•di•ent (ĭn-grē'dē-ənt) *n.* An element in a mixture or compound.
in•gress (ĭn'grĕs') *n.* **1.** A going in or entering. **2.** Permission to enter.
in•grown (ĭn'grōn') *adj.* Grown abnormally into the flesh.
in•gui•nal (ĭng'gwə-nəl) *adj.* Of or located in the groin.
in•hab•it (ĭn-hăb'ĭt) *v.* To reside in. **—in•hab'it•a•ble** *adj.*
in•hab•i•tant (ĭn-hăb'ĭ-tənt) *n.* A permanent resident.
in•ha•lant (ĭn-hā'lənt) *n.* Something that is inhaled, as a medicine.
in•ha•la•tor (ĭn'hə-lā'tər) *n.* A device that discharges a vapor to ease breathing by inspiration.
in•hale (ĭn-hāl') *v.* **-haled, -hal•ing.** To breathe in or take in by breathing. **—in'ha•la'tion** (-hə-lā'shən) *n.*
in•hal•er (ĭn-hā'lər) *n.* **1.** One that inhales. **2.** An inhalator. **3.** A respirator.
in•here (ĭn-hîr') *v.* **-hered, -her•ing.** To be inherent.
in•her•ent (ĭn-hîr'ənt, -hĕr'-) *adj.* Existing as an essential element or feature : intrinsic. **—in•her'ent•ly** *adv.*
in•her•it (ĭn-hĕr'ĭt) *v.* **1.** To receive (property) from a person by legal succession or will. **2.** *Biol.* To receive genetically from an ancestor. **—in•her'it•a•ble** *adj.* **—in•her'i•tor** *n.*
in•her•i•tance (ĭn-hĕr'ĭ-təns) *n.* **1.** The act of inheriting. **2.** Something inherited or to be inherited. **3.** A heritage.
in•hib•it (ĭn-hĭb'ĭt) *v.* **1.** To hold back : restrain. **2.** To prevent the full expression of : suppress. **3.** To forbid. **—in•hib'it•a•ble** *adj.* **—in•hib'i•tor, in•hib'it•er** *n.* **—in•hib'i•tive, in•hib'i•to'ry** (-tôr'ē, -tōr'ē) *adj.*
in•hi•bi•tion (ĭn'hĭ-bĭsh'ən, ĭn'ĭ-) *n.* **1.** The act of inhibiting or state of being inhibited. **2.** The self-imposed suppression of a feeling, need, or drive.
in-house (ĭn'hous') *adj.* Being or coming from within an organization <an *in-house* publication>
in•hu•man (ĭn-hyo͞o'mən) *adj.* **1.** Lacking kindness, pity, or emotional warmth. **2.** Not suited to human beings <a vast hall of *inhuman* dimensions> **3.** Monstrous. **—in•hu'man•ly** *adv.*
in•hu•mane (ĭn'hyo͞o-mān') *adj.* Lacking pity or compassion : cruel. **—in'hu•mane'ly** *adv.*
in•hu•man•i•ty (ĭn'hyo͞o-măn'ĭ-tē) *n., pl.* **-ties. 1.** Lack of pity or compassion. **2.** An inhumane or cruel act.
in•im•i•cal (ĭn-ĭm'ĭ-kəl) *adj.* **1.** Harmful : injurious <living habits *inimical* to health> **2.** Hostile : malign. **—in•im'i•cal•ly** *adv.*
in•im•i•ta•ble (ĭn-ĭm'ĭ-tə-bəl) *adj.* Incapable of being imitated : matchless. **—in•im'i•ta•bly** *adv.*
in•iq•ui•ty (ĭ-nĭk'wĭ-tē) *n., pl.* **-ties. 1.** Wickedness : sinfulness. **2.** A grossly immoral act : sin. **—in•iq'ui•tous** *adj.*
in•i•tial (ĭ-nĭsh'əl) *adj.* Of, being, or happening at the beginning. *—n.* The 1st letter of a name or a word. *—v.* **-tialed, -tialing** *also* **-tialled, -tial•ling.** To sign or mark with initials. **—in•i'tial•ly** *adv.*
in•i•ti•ate (ĭ-nĭsh'ē-āt') *v.* **-at•ed, -at•ing. 1.** To cause to begin : start or launch. **2.** To introduce (someone) to a new interest or activity. **3.** To admit into membership, as with a ceremony. *—n.* (-ĭt). **1.** One who has been initiated. **2.** A beginner. **—in•i'ti•a'tion** *n.* **—in•i'ti•a'tor** *n.* **—in•i'ti•a•to'ry** (-ə-tôr'ē, -tōr'ē) *adj.*
in•i•ti•a•tive (ĭ-nĭsh'ē-ə-tĭv, ĭ-nĭsh'ə-) *n.* **1.** The ability to originate or follow through with a plan of action or task : enterprise. **2.** The act or role of taking the 1st or leading step <seized the *initiative* and attacked> **3.** A procedure by which citizens propose a law by petition and have it submitted to be voted on by the electorate.
in•ject (ĭn-jĕkt') *v.* **1. a.** To force or drive (a liquid or gas) into something <*inject* fuel into an engine cylinder> **b.** To introduce (liquid medicine, serum, etc.) into the body, as with a hypodermic syringe. **2.** To introduce, as into conversation <*inject* a word of warning. **3.** To put into an orbit, trajectory, or stream. **—in•jec'tion** *n.*
in•junc•tion (ĭn-jŭngk'shən) *n.* **1.** A command or order. **2.** *Law.* A court order forbidding or calling for a certain action. **—in•junc'tive** *adj.*
in•jure (ĭn'jər) *v.* **-jured, -jur•ing. 1.** To cause physical harm to : hurt. **2.** To damage : impair. **3.** To commit an injustice or offense against : wrong.
in•ju•ri•ous (ĭn-jo͝or'ē-əs) *adj.* Causing or apt to cause injury : harmful. **—in•ju'ri•ous•ly** *adv.*
in•ju•ry (ĭn'jə-rē) *n., pl.* **-ries. 1.** An act of injuring or harming. **2.** A wound or other damage suffered. **3.** Injustice.
in•jus•tice (ĭn-jŭs'tĭs) *n.* **1.** Violation of justice or another's rights : unfairness. **2.** An unjust act : wrong.
ink (ĭngk) *n.* A usu. dark-colored liquid or paste used esp. for writing or printing. *—v.* To supply or mark with ink. **—ink'y** *adj.*
ink•horn (ĭngk'hôrn') *n.* A small container made esp. of horn to hold ink.
ink•ling (ĭngk'lĭng) *n.* **1.** A slight suggestion : hint. **2.** A vague notion or idea.
ink•stand (ĭngk'stănd') *n.* **1.** A stand for holding ink and writing implements. **2.** An inkwell.
ink•well (ĭngk'wĕl') *n.* A small reservoir for holding ink.
inky cap *n.* A mushroom of the genus *Coprinus,* with gills that dissolve into a dark liquid on maturing.

inky cap

in•laid (ĭn'lād') *adj.* **1.** Set into a surface in a decorative design. **2.** Ornamented with a pattern set into a surface.
in•land (ĭn'lənd) *adj.* **1.** Of or situated in the interior of a country. **2.** Operating within a country : domestic. *—adv.* In or toward the interior. *—n.* The interior of a country. **—in'land'er** *n.*
in-law (ĭn'lô') *n.* A relative by marriage.
in•lay (ĭn'lā', ĭn-lā') *v.* To set (e.g., wooden pieces)into a surface in a decorative design. *—n.* (ĭn'lā'). **1.** Material or a design set into a surface. **2.** A solid dental filling, as of gold, cemented in place.
in•let (ĭn'lĕt', -lĭt) *n.* **1.** A recess, as a bay or cove, along a coastline. **2.** A narrow passage of water, as between 2 islands. **3.** A drainage passageway.
in•mate (ĭn'māt') *n.* **1.** A resident in a dwelling or building. **2.** One confined to an institution.

in me·mo·ri·am (ĭn' mə-môr'ē-əm, -mōr'-) *prep.* In memory of. Used to honor the dead.

inn (ĭn) *n.* **1.** A lodging house : hotel. **2.** A tavern.

in·nards (ĭn'ərdz) *pl.n. Informal.* **1.** Internal organs : viscera. **2.** The inner parts, as of a structure.

in·nate (ĭ-nāt', ĭn'āt') *adj.* **1.** Having at birth : inborn. **2.** Having as an essential characteristic : inherent <the *innate* strength of steel> **–in·nate'ly** *adv.*

in·ner (ĭn'ər) *adj.* **1.** Situated farther inside <an *inner* compartment> **2.** More hidden : deeper <an *inner* meaning> **3.** Of or relating to the mind or spirit <the *inner* person> **4.** More exclusive or influential <*inner* circles>

in·ner-di·rect·ed (ĭn'ər-dĭ-rĕk'tĭd, -dī-) *adj.* Guided by one's own values rather than by conventional norms.

inner ear *n.* The part of the ear including the semicircular canals, vestibule, and cochlea.

Inner Mongolia. Region of NE China.

in·ner·most (ĭn'ər-mōst') *adj.* **1.** Farthest within. **2.** Most intimate <*innermost* thoughts>

inner tube *n.* An inflatable rubber tube placed inside a tire.

in·ning (ĭn'ĭng) *n.* One of 9 divisions of a regulation baseball game in which each team has a turn at bat.

inn·keep·er (ĭn'kē'pər) *n.* The manager or owner of an inn.

in·no·cent (ĭn'ə-sənt) *adj.* **1.** Free from sin or wrongdoing : sinless. **2.** Not guilty legally of a given crime. **3.** Harmless : innocuous. **4.** Not experienced : naive. **5.** Artless. **–in'no·cence** *n.* **–in'no·cent** *n.* **–in'no·cent·ly** *adv.*

in·noc·u·ous (ĭ-nŏk'yo͞o-əs) *adj.* **1.** Having no ill effect : harmless. **2.** Lacking distinction : insipid. **–in·noc'u·ous·ly** *adv.* **–in·noc'u·ous·ness** *n.*

in·no·vate (ĭn'ə-vāt') *v.* **-vat·ed, -vat·ing.** To begin something new : introduce. **–in'no·va'tive** *adj.* **–in'no·va'tor** *n.*

in·no·va·tion (ĭn'ə-vā'shən) *n.* **1.** The act of innovating. **2.** Something that is new or unusual.

in·nu·en·do (ĭn'yo͞o-ĕn'dō) *n., pl.* **-does.** An indirect, usu. disparaging implication : insinuation.

In·nu·it *also* **In·u·it** (ĭn'yo͞o-ĭt) *n., pl.* **-it** *or* **-its.** An Eskimo of North America and Greenland as distinguished from one of Asia and the Aleutians.

in·nu·mer·a·ble (ĭ-no͞o'mər-ə-bəl, ĭ-nyo͞o'-) *adj.* Countless.

in·oc·u·late (ĭ-nŏk'yə-lāt') *v.* **-lat·ed, -lat·ing.** To introduce a disease virus or other causative agent into so as to immunize, treat, or test. **–in·oc'u·la'tion** *n.*

in·op·er·a·ble (ĭn-ŏp'ər-ə-bəl, -ŏp'rə-) *adj.* **1.** Not operable. **2.** Incapable of being treated by surgery.

in·op·er·a·tive (ĭn-ŏp'ər-ə-tĭv, -ŏp'rə-) *adj.* **1.** Not working. **2.** Not effective.

in·op·por·tune (ĭn-ŏp'ər-to͞on', -tyo͞on') *adj.* Untimely : ill-timed. **–in·op'por·tune'ly** *adv.* **–in·op'por·tune'ness** *n.*

in·or·di·nate (ĭn-ôr'dn-ĭt) *adj.* **1.** Exceeding normal limits. **2.** Not regulated : disorderly. **–in·or'di·nate·ly** *adv.*

in·or·gan·ic (ĭn'ôr-găn'ĭk) *adj.* **1.** Not composed of or involving living organisms or their remains or products. **2.** Mineral.

in·pa·tient (ĭn'pā'shənt) *n.* A patient admitted to a hospital.

in·put (ĭn'po͝ot') *n.* **1.** Something or an amount put in. **2.** Energy or power for driving a machine. **3.** Information put into a data-processing system. **4.** Contribution to a common effort. **–in'put'** *v.*

in·quest (ĭn'kwĕst') *n.* **1.** A judicial inquiry, esp. into the cause of a death. **2.** An investigation : inquiry.

in·quire (ĭn-kwīr') *v.* **-quired, -quir·ing.** **1.** To ask (a question). **2.** To request information <*inquire* about mortgage rates> **3.** To make a study : investigate. **–in·quir'er** *n.* **–in·quir'ing·ly** *adv.*

in·quir·y (ĭn-kwīr'ē, ĭn'kwə-rē) *n., pl.* **-ies.** **1.** The act of inquiring. **2.** A question or request for information. **3.** A close examination : investigation.

in·qui·si·tion (ĭn'kwĭ-zĭsh'ən) *n.* **1.** An official investigation. **2. Inquisition.** *Rom. Cath. Ch.* A tribunal formerly established to seek out and punish heretics. **3.** An investigation or interrogation that violates individual rights. **–in·quis'i·tor** *n.* **–in·quis'i·to'ri·al** *adj.*

in·quis·i·tive (ĭn-kwĭz'ĭ-tĭv) *adj.* **1.** Unduly curious. **2.** Inquiring : probing. **–in·quis'i·tive·ly** *adv.* **–in·quis'i·tive·ness** *n.*

in re (ĭn rā', rē') *prep.* In regard to : concerning.

in·road (ĭn'rōd') *n.* **1.** A hostile intrusion : raid. **2.** An advance, often at the expense of another.

in·rush (ĭn'rŭsh') *n.* A sudden rushing in.

in·sane (ĭn-sān') *adj.* **1.** Afflicted with a serious mental disorder impairing a person's ability to function. **2.** Typical of, used by, or for the insane. **3.** Very foolish or irrational : absurd. ☆**syns:** BATTY, CRAZY, GAGA, LOONY, LUNATIC, MAD, NUTS, SCREWY **–in·sane'ly** *adv.* **–in·san'i·ty** (-săn'ĭ-tē) *n.*

in·sa·tia·ble (ĭn-sā'shə-bəl, -shē-ə-) *adj.* Incapable of being satisfied <an *insatiable* appetite>

in·scribe (ĭn-skrīb') *v.* **-scribed, -scrib·ing.** **1.** To write, print, or cut (letters or words) on a surface. **2.** To mark (a surface) with words or letters. **3.** To enter (a name) in a register : enroll. **4.** To write a short signed message on (a gift). **5.** To enclose (e.g., a polygon) in another geometric figure so that every vertex of the enclosed figure touches the enclosing figure. **–in·scrib'er** *n.* **–in·scrip'tion** (-skrĭp'shən) *n.*

in·scru·ta·ble (ĭn-skro͞o'tə-bəl) *adj.* Difficult to understand or interpret : enigmatic. **–in·scru'ta·bil'i·ty, in·scru'ta·ble·ness** *n.* **–in·scru'ta·bly** *adv.*

in·sect (ĭn'sĕkt') *n.* Any of numerous small, usu. winged invertebrate animals of the class Insecta, with 3 pairs of legs, a segmented body, and usu. 2 pairs of wings.

in·sec·ti·cide (ĭn-sĕk'tĭ-sīd') *n.* A substance for killing insects.

in·sec·tiv·o·rous (ĭn'sĕk-tĭv'ər-əs) *adj.* Feeding on insects.

in·se·cure (ĭn'sĭ-kyo͝or') *adj.* **1.** Not adequately protected or guarded : unsafe. **2.** Unstable <*insecure* footing> **3.** Not self-confident. **–in'se·cure'ly** *adv.* **–in'se·cu'ri·ty** *n.*

in·sem·i·nate (ĭn-sĕm'ə-nāt') *v.* **-nat·ed, -nat·ing.** **1.** To sow seed in. **2.** To introduce semen into the uterus of. **–in·sem'i·na'tion** *n.* **–in·sem'i·na'tor** *n.*

in·sen·sate (ĭn-sĕn'sāt', -sĭt) *adj.* **1.** Inanimate. **2.** Unconscious. **3.** Without sensibility : callous or brutal.

in·sen·si·ble (ĭn-sĕn'sə-bəl) *adj.* **1.** Imperceptible : inappreciable. **2.** Unconscious. **3. a.** Unresponsive : unaffected <*insensible* to heat> **b.** Unaware : unmindful. **–in·sen'si·bil'i·ty** *n.* **–in·sen'si·bly** *adv.*

in·sen·tient (ĭn-sĕn'shənt) *adj.* Without consciousness or sensation. **–in·sen'tience** *n.*

in·sep·a·ra·ble (ĭn-sĕp'ər-ə-bəl) *adj.* Incapable of being separated. **–in·sep'a·ra·bil'i·ty** *n.* **–in·sep'a·ra·bly** *adv.*

in·sert (ĭn-sûrt') *v.* **1.** To put or thrust in <*inserted* the coin in the slot> **2.** To interpolate. *–n.* (ĭn'sûrt'). Something inserted or to be inserted. **–in·ser'tion** *n.*

in·set (ĭn-sĕt', ĭn'sĕt') *v.* To set in : insert. **–in'set'** *n.*

in·shore (ĭn'shôr', -shōr') *adj.* Close to or moving toward a shore. **–in'shore'** *adv.*

in·side (ĭn-sīd', ĭn'sīd') *n.* **1.** An interior part. **2.** An inside side or surface. **3. insides.** *Informal.* The internal organs or parts. **4.** *Slang.* A position of special power or influence. *–adv.* (ĭn-sīd'). Into or in the interior : within. *–prep.* (ĭn-sīd'). **1.** Within <*inside* a box>. **2.** Into <going *inside* the house> **–in'side'** *adj.*

in·sid·er (ĭn-sī'dər) *n.* One who has special knowledge or access to confidential information.

in·sid·i·ous (ĭn-sĭd'ē-əs) *adj.* **1.** Working or spreading harmfully in a stealthy way. **2.** Designed to entrap : treacherous. **3.** Attractive but harmful : seductive. **–in·sid'i·ous·ly** *adv.* **–in·sid'i·ous·ness** *n.*

in·sight (ĭn'sīt') *n.* **1.** The ability to perceive the true or hidden nature of things. **2.** A perceptive observation. **–in'sight'ful** *adj.* **–in'sight'ful·ly** *adv.*

in·sig·ni·a (ĭn-sĭg'nē-ə) *n., pl.* **-nia** *or* **-ni·as.** **1.** A badge of office or rank. **2.** A distinguishing sign.

in·sin·cere (ĭn'sĭn-sîr') *adj.* Hypocritical. **–in'sin·cere'ly** *adv.* **–in'sin·cer'i·ty** *n.*

in·sin·u·ate (ĭn-sĭn'yo͞o-āt') *v.* **-at·ed, -at·ing.** **1. a.** To introduce (e.g., a suspicion) slyly. **b.** To introduce (oneself) by sly and ingenious means. **2.** To hint. **–in·sin'u·at'ing·ly** *adv.* **–in·sin'u·a'tion** *n.*

in·sip·id (ĭn-sĭp'ĭd) *adj.* **1.** Lacking flavor : tasteless. **2.** Lacking interest : dull. **–in·sip'id·ly** *adv.* **–in·sip'id·ness** *n.*

in·sist (ĭn-sĭst') *v.* **1.** To be firm in a course or demand <*insisted* on getting his way> **2.** To assert strongly <*insisted* they were innocent> **–in·sis'tence** *n.* **–in·sis'tent** *adj.* **–in·sis'tent·ly** *adv.*

in si·tu (ĭn sī'to͞o, sĭt'o͞o) *adj. & adv.* In the original place.

in·snare (ĭn-snâr') *v. var. of* ENSNARE.

in·so·far (ĭn'sō-fär') *adv.* To such an extent.

in·sole (ĭn'sōl') *n.* **1.** The inside sole of a shoe. **2.** A strip of material put inside a shoe for protection or comfort.

in·so·lent (ĭn'sə-lənt) *adj.* Disrespectfully or presumptuously arrogant : impertinent. **–in'so·lence** *n.* **–in'so·lent·ly** *adv.*

in·sol·u·ble (ĭn-sŏl'yə-bəl) *adj.* **1.** Not capable of being dissolved. **2.** Not capable of being solved. **–in·sol'u·bil'i·ty, in·sol'u·ble·ness** *n.* **–in·sol'u·bly** *adv.*

in·sol·vent (ĭn-sŏl'vənt) *adj.* Not able to meet debts : bankrupt. **–in·sol'ven·cy** *n.* **–in·sol'vent** *n.*

in·som·ni·a (ĭn-sŏm'nē-ə) *n.* Chronic sleeplessness. **–in·som'ni·ac'** *adj. & n.*

in·so·much as (ĭn'sō-mŭch') *conj.* **1.** To such an extent as. **2.** Inasmuch as : since.

in•sou•ci•ant (ĭn-so͞o′sē-ənt) *adj.* Cheerfully nonchalant. **–in•sou′ci•ance** *n.*

in•spect (ĭn-spĕkt′) *v.* **1.** To examine carefully, esp. for flaws. **2.** To review officially <*inspect* the troops> **–in•spec′tion** *n.* **–in•spec′tor** *n.*

in•spi•ra•tion (ĭn′spə-rā′shən) *n.* **1. a.** Stimulation of the intellect or emotions to a high level. **b.** The condition of being so stimulated. **2.** One that moves the intellect or emotions or prompts action. **3.** A sudden creative idea or act. **4.** Inhalation. **–in′spi•ra′tion•al** *adj.* **–in′spi•ra′tion•al•ly** *adv.*

in•spire (ĭn-spīr′) *v.* **-spired, -spir•ing. 1.** To guide or affect by divine influence. **2.** To fill with high emotion : exalt. **3.** To stimulate to creativity or action. **4.** To elicit : arouse. **5.** To inhale. **–in•spir′er** *n.* **–in•spir′ing•ly** *adv.*

in•spir•it (ĭn-spĭr′ĭt) *v.* To animate.

inst. *abbr.* **1.** instant. **2.** institute; institution. **3.** instrument.

in•sta•bil•i•ty (ĭn′stə-bĭl′ĭ-tē) *n., pl.* **-ties.** Lack of stability.

in•stall *also* **in•stal** (ĭn-stôl′) *v.* **-stalled, stall•ing. 1.** To place in position for use. **2.** To induct into an office or position. **3.** To settle : ensconce. **–in′stal•la′tion** *n.* **–in•stall′er** *n.*

in•stall•ment *also* **in•stal•ment** (ĭn-stôl′mənt) *n.* **1.** One of several successive payments, as of a debt. **2.** A part of something issued at intervals, as a serialized literary work.

in•stance (ĭn′stəns) *n.* **1.** An illustrative case : example. **2.** An occasion <in the first *instance*> **3.** A prompting : request <interceded at the *instance* of a friend> *–v.* **-stanced, -stanc•ing. 1.** To cite as an example. **2.** To illustrate : exemplify.

in•stant (ĭn′stənt) *n.* **1.** A very short time : moment. **2.** A specific point in time. *–adj.* **1.** Immediate. **2.** Designed for quick preparation <*instant* soup> **3.** Urgent.

in•stan•ta•ne•ous (ĭn′stən-tā′nē-əs) *adj.* **1.** Happening or completed instantly or without delay. **2.** Present or happening at a given instant <*instantaneous* velocity> **–in′stan•ta′ne•ous•ly** *adv.*

in•stan•ter (ĭn-stăn′tər) *adv.* Instantly.

in•stant•ly (ĭn′stənt-lē) *adv.* At once : immediately.

in•stead (ĭn-stĕd′) *adv.* In place of that just mentioned <were going to fly, but drove *instead*>

instead of *prep.* In place of : rather than.

in•step (ĭn′stĕp′) *n.* The arched middle portion of the foot.

in•sti•gate (ĭn′stĭ-gāt′) *v.* **-gat•ed, -gat•ing. 1.** To urge forward : goad. **2.** To stir up : foment. **–in′sti•ga′tion** *n.* **–in′sti•ga′tor** *n.*

in•still *also* **in•stil** (ĭn-stĭl′) *v.* **-stilled, -still•ing. 1.** To impart by gradual instruction or effort : implant. **2.** To pour in by drops. **–in′stil•la′tion** *n.* **–in•still′er** *n.*

in•stinct (ĭn′stĭngkt′) *n.* **1.** The innate, complex, and normally adaptive aspect of animal behavior. **2.** A strong impulse or motivation. **3.** A natural talent : aptitude. **–in•stinc′tive** *adj.* **–in•stinc′tive•ly** *adv.* **–in•stinc′tu•al** (-cho͞o-əl) *adj.*

in•sti•tute (ĭn′stĭ-to͞ot′, -tyo͞ot′) *v.* **-tut•ed, -tut•ing. 1.** To establish : found. **2.** To begin : initiate. *–n.* **1.** Something instituted, esp. a law or precept. **2.** An organization established to promote or further a cause. **3.** An educational institution. **4.** A short series of classes : seminar.

in•sti•tu•tion (ĭn′stĭ-to͞o′shən, -tyo͞o′-) *n.* **1.** The act of instituting. **2.** An important cultural or societal custom or practice. **3.** A permanent feature : fixture. **4. a.** An organization, esp. one dedicated to public service. **b.** The buildings of such an organization. **5.** A place of confinement. **–in′sti•tu′tion•al** *adj.* **–in′sti•tu′tion•al•ize′** *v.* **–in′sti•tu′tion•al•ly** *adv.*

in•struct (ĭn-strŭkt′) *v.* **1.** To impart knowledge or skill to : teach. **2.** To direct : order. **–in•struc′tive** *adj.*

in•struc•tion (ĭn-strŭk′shən) *n.* **1.** The act or profession of instructing. **2. a.** Imparted knowledge. **b.** A lesson. **3.** An order or direction. **–in•struc′tion•al** *adj.*

in•struc•tor (ĭn-strŭk′tər) *n.* A person who instructs, esp. a low-ranking college teacher. **–in•struc′tor•ship′** *n.*

in•stru•ment (ĭn′strə-mənt) *n.* **1.** A means by which something is accomplished : agency. **2.** A person controlled by another : dupe. **3.** A mechanical tool or implement. **4.** A device for recording, indicating, or measuring, esp. in a control system. **5.** A device used by a musician in producing music. **6.** A legal document. *–v.* To supply with instruments.

in•stru•men•tal (ĭn′strə-mĕn′tl) *adj.* **1.** Acting as a means. **2.** Performed on or composed for musical instruments. **–in′stru•men′tal•ly** *adv.*

in•stru•men•tal•ist (ĭn′strə-mĕn′tl-ĭst) *n.* A player of a musical instrument.

in•stru•men•tal•i•ty (ĭn′strə-mĕn-tăl′ĭ-tē) *n., pl.* **-ties.** Means : agency.

in•stru•men•ta•tion (ĭn′strə-mĕn-tā′shən) *n.* **1.** The use of instruments. **2.** Instrumentality. **3.** The study and practice of arranging of music for instruments.

in•sub•or•di•nate (ĭn′sə-bôr′dn-ĭt) *adj.* Not obeying orders : disobedient. **–in′sub•or′di•nate•ly** *adv.* **–in′sub•or′di•na′tion** *n.*

in•sub•stan•tial (ĭn′səb-stăn′shəl) *adj.* **1.** Lacking substance : unreal. **2.** Not solid : flimsy. **–in′sub•stan′ti•al′i•ty** *n.*

in•suf•fer•a•ble (ĭn-sŭf′ər-ə-bəl) *adj.* Not able to be endured : intolerable. **–in•suf′fer•a•ble•ness** *n.* **–in•suf′fer•a•bly** *adv.*

in•suf•fi•cient (ĭn′sə-fĭsh′ənt) *adj.* Not enough : inadequate. **–in′suf•fi′cien•cy** *n.* **–in′suf•fi′cient•ly** *adv.*

in•su•lar (ĭn′sə-lər, ĭns′yə-) *adj.* **1.** Of or being an island. **2.** Typical or suggestive of the isolated life of an island. **3.** Narrow-minded. **–in′su•lar′i•ty** *n.*

in•su•late (ĭn′sə-lāt′, ĭns′yə-) *v.* **-lat•ed, -lat•ing. 1.** To set apart : isolate. **2.** To stop the passage of heat, electricity, or sound into or out of, esp. by interposing material that acts as a barrier. **–in′su•la′tion** *n.* **–in′su•la′tor** *n.*

in•su•lin (ĭn′sə-lĭn, ĭns′yə-) *n.* **1.** A hormone in the pancreas that regulates the metabolism of carbohydrates by controlling blood glucose levels. **2.** A preparation derived from the pancreas of the pig or the ox used in the treatment of diabetes.

in•sult (ĭn-sŭlt′) *v.* To speak to or treat insolently or contemptuously : affront. *–n.* (ĭn′sŭlt′). An insolent or contemptuous act or remark.

in•su•per•a•ble (ĭn-so͞o′pər-ə-bəl) *adj.* Not able to be overcome : insurmountable. **–in•su′per•a•bly** *adv.*

in•sup•port•a•ble (ĭn′sə-pôr′tə-bəl, -pōr′-) *adj.* **1.** Unendurable : intolerable. **2.** Unjustifiable <*insupportable* claims>

in•sur•ance (ĭn-sho͝or′əns) *n.* **1.** The act or business of insuring or state of being insured. **2.** A contract binding a company to compensate a party for future specified losses in return for continuing payments. **3.** The total amount to be paid in case of loss <bought $100,000 of life *insurance*> **4.** A protective or compensatory measure.

in•sure (ĭn-sho͝or′) *v.* **-sured, -sur•ing. 1.** To cover with insurance. **2.** To make certain or sure. **–in•sur′a•ble** *adj.* **–in•sur′er** *n.*

in•sured (ĭn-sho͝ord′) *n.* Someone covered by insurance.

in•sur•gent (ĭn-sûr′jənt) *adj.* Rising in insurrection against established authority : rebelling. **–in•sur′gence, in•sur′gen•cy** *n.* **–in•sur′gent** *n.*

in•sur•mount•a•ble (ĭn′sər-moun′tə-bəl) *adj.* Insuperable <*insurmountable* difficulties> **–in′sur•mount′a•bly** *adv.*

in•sur•rec•tion (ĭn′sə-rĕk′shən) *n.* An open revolt against established authority. **–in′sur•rec′tion•ist** *n.*

int. *abbr.* **1.** interest. **2.** interior. **3.** international. **4.** interval.

in•tact (ĭn-tăkt′) *adj.* **1.** Not damaged in any way. **2.** Whole. **–in•tact′ness** *n.*

in•ta•glio (ĭn-tăl′yō, -täl′-) *n., pl.* **-glios.** An engraved figure or design depressed below the surface of hard metal or stone.

in•take (ĭn′tāk′) *n.* **1.** An opening through which a fluid is admitted. **2. a.** The act of taking in. **b.** Something taken in.

in•tan•gi•ble (ĭn-tăn′jə-bəl) *adj.* **1.** Incapable of being touched. **2.** Incapable of being perceived. **3.** Not readily defined or measured <such *intangible* factors as morale> **–in•tan′gi•bil′i•ty, in•tan′gi•ble•ness** *n.* **–in•tan′gi•ble** *n.* **–in•tan′gi•bly** *adv.*

in•te•ger (ĭn′tĭ-jər) *n.* Any member of the set (. . . –2, –1, 0, +1, +2, . . .), including all the positive whole numbers, all the negative whole numbers, and zero.

in•te•gral (ĭn′tĭ-grəl, ĭn-tĕg′rəl) *adj.* **1.** Essential for completeness : constituent. **2.** Entire : whole. **3.** *Math.* Expressed or expressible as integers. *–n.* An entire unit : whole.

integral calculus *n.* The mathematical study of integration, the properties of integrals, and their applications.

in•te•grate (ĭn′tĭ-grāt′) *v.* **-grat•ed, -grat•ing. 1.** To make into a whole by bringing parts together : unify. **2.** To join (e.g., parts) together : unite. **3.** To open to people of all races or ethnic groups. **–in′te•gra′tion** *n.* **–in′te•gra′tive** *adj.*

integrated circuit *n.* A tiny wafer of substrate material on which a complex of electronic components and their interconnections is etched or imprinted. **–integrated circuitry** *n.*

in•teg•ri•ty (ĭn-tĕg′rĭ-tē) *n.* **1.** Strict adherence to a standard of value or conduct. **2.** Personal honesty and independence. **3.** Completeness : unity. **4.** Soundness.

in•teg•u•ment (ĭn-tĕg′yə-mənt) *n.* An outer covering or coat, as an animal's skin, a shell, or a seed coat.

in•tel•lect (ĭn′tl-ĕkt′) *n.* **1. a.** The capacity for understanding and knowledge. **b.** The ability to think abstractly or profoundly. **2.** A person of notable intellect.

in•tel•lec•tu•al (ĭn′tl-ĕk′cho͞o-əl) *adj.* **1.** Of, relating to, or engaging the intellect. **2.** Given to use of the intellect : inclined to rational or creative thought. **–in′tel•lec′tu•al** *n.* **–in′tel•lec′tu•al′i•ty** (-ăl′ĭ-tē) *n.* **–in′tel•lec′tu•al•ly** *adv.*

in•tel•lec•tu•al•ize (ĭn′tl-ĕk′cho͞o-ə-līz′) *v.* **-ized, -iz•ing.**

To examine rationally or objectively, esp. so as to avoid emotional involvement. **–in′tel·lec′tu·al·i·za′tion** *n.* **–in′tel·lec′tu·al·iz′er** *n.*

in·tel·li·gence (ĭn-tĕl′ə-jəns) *n.* **1.** The capacity to learn and to solve problems and difficulties. **2.** Superior mental powers. **3.** News : information. **4. a.** Secret information, esp. about an enemy. **b.** The gathering of this information.

in·tel·li·gent (ĭn-tĕl′ə-jənt) *adj.* Having or showing intelligence. **–in·tel′li·gent·ly** *adv.*

in·tel·li·gent·si·a (ĭn-tĕl′ə-jĕnt′sē-ə, -gĕnt′-) *n.* The intellectual elite of a society.

in·tel·li·gi·ble (ĭn-tĕl′ə-jə-bəl) *adj.* Capable of being understood. **–in·tel′li·gi·bil′i·ty** *n.* **–in·tel′li·gi·bly** *adv.*

in·tem·per·ance (ĭn-tĕm′pər-əns) *n.* Lack of temperance, esp. in drinking alcoholic beverages. **–in·tem′per·ate** *adj.* **–in·tem′per·ate·ly** *adv.*

in·tend (ĭn-tĕnd′) *v.* **1.** To have in mind as a purpose : plan. **2.** To design for a particular use. **3.** To signify : mean.

in·tend·ed (ĭn-tĕn′dĭd) *adj.* **1.** Intentional : deliberate. **2.** Proposed : prospective. *–n. Informal.* One's fiancé or fiancée.

in·tense (ĭn-tĕns′) *adj.* **1.** Extreme in degree, strength, or effect <an *intense* storm> **2.** Marked by great concentration or strain <an *intense* gaze> **3.** Deep : profound. ☆***syns:*** DESPERATE, FIERCE, FURIOUS, TERRIBLE, VEHEMENT, VIOLENT **–in·tense′ly** *adv.* **–in·tense′ness** *n.*

in·ten·si·fy (ĭn-tĕn′sə-fī′) *v.* **-fied, -fy·ing.** To make or become more intense. **–in·ten′si·fi·ca′tion** *n.*

in·ten·si·ty (ĭn-tĕn′sĭ-tē) *n., pl.* **-ties. 1.** Exceptionally great effect, concentration, or force. **2.** Degree : strength.

in·ten·sive (ĭn-tĕn′sĭv) *adj.* **1.** Concentrated and forceful <*intensive* study> **2.** Characterized by a full application of all resources <*intensive* hospital care> **3.** Adding emphasis. *–n.* A linguistic element, as the adverbs *extremely* or *awfully,* that adds emphasis. **–in·ten′sive·ly** *adv.*

in·tent (ĭn-tĕnt′) *n.* **1.** Purpose : aim. **2.** The state of mind with which an act is committed. **3.** Meaning : significance. *–adj.* **1.** Concentrated : intense. **2.** Fixed on a purpose <*intent* on leaving> **–in·tent′ly** *adv.* **–in·tent′ness** *n.*

in·ten·tion (ĭn-tĕn′shən) *n.* **1.** A plan of action : design. **2.** An aim that guides action : object. **3.** Significance : import. ☆***syns:*** AIM, DESIGN, END, GOAL, INTENT, OBJECT, PURPOSE, TARGET, VIEW

in·ten·tion·al (ĭn-tĕn′shə-nəl) *adj.* Deliberately done : intended. **–in·ten′tion·al′i·ty** (-năl′ĭ-tē) *n.* **–in·ten′tion·al·ly** *adv.*

in·ter (ĭn-tûr′) *v.* **-terred, -ter·ring.** To put into a grave : bury. **–in·ter′ment** *n.*

inter– *pref.* **1.** Between or among <*inter*collegiate> **2.** Mutually : together<*inter*relate> See below for a list of self-explanatory words formed with the prefix **inter–**.

in·ter·act (ĭn′tər-ăkt′) *v.* To act on each other. **–in′ter·ac′tion** *n.* **–in′ter·ac′tive** *adj.*

in·ter·breed (ĭn′tər-brēd′) *v.* **1.** To breed with another kind or species. **2.** To inbreed.

in·ter·ca·late (ĭn-tûr′kə-lāt′) *v.* **-lat·ed, -lat·ing** To insert (e.g., an extra day) in a calendar. **–in·ter′ca·lar′y** *adj.* **–in·ter′ca·la′tion** *n.*

in·ter·cede (ĭn′tər-sēd′) *v.* **-ced·ed, -ced·ing. 1.** To argue on another's behalf. **2.** To mediate. **–in′ter·ced′er** *n.*

in·ter·cept (ĭn′tər-sĕpt′) *v.* **1.** To interrupt the course of, esp. by seizing <*intercept* a message><*intercept* a football pass> **2.** To intersect. **3.** *Math.* To cut off or bound part of (e.g., a line). **–in′ter·cept′** *n.* **–in′ter·cep′tion** *n.*

interaffiliation
inter-African
interagency
inter-American
interannual
interassociation
interaxis
interbank
interbasin
interbed
interbehavior
interbelligerent
interborough
interbranch
interbronchial
intercampus
intercapillary
inter-Caribbean
intercaste
intercell
intercellular
intercellularly
intercerebral
interchannel
interchromosomal
interchurch
intercity
intercivic
intercivilization
interclan
interclass
interclub
intercoastal
intercolonial
intercommunal
intercommunity
intercompany
intercompare
intercomparison
intercorporate
intercorpuscular
intercosmic
intercountry
intercounty
intercrater
intercrystalline
intercultural
interculturally
interculture
intercurl
interdealer
interdepend
interdependence
interdependency
interdependent
interdestructive
interdialectal
interdiffuse
interdiffusion
interdistrict
interdivisional
interdominion
interdorsal
interelectrode
interelectronic
interelement
interentanglement
interenvironmental
interepidemic
interethnic
inter-European
interfaculty
interfamily
interfederation
interflow
interfold
interfraternity
intergang
intergenerational
interglandular
interglobular
intergovernmental
intergraft
intergranular
intergroup
interhybridize
interindustry
interinstitutional
interinsular
interisland
interjunction
interlaminar
interlaminate
interlamination
interlap
interlay
interlayer
interlayering
interlend
interlibrary
interloan
interlobular
interlocal
interloop
intermarginal
intermarine
intermelt
intermembrane
intermesh
intermetropolitan
intermigrate
interministerial
intermitotic
intermolar
intermountain
intermunicipal
intermuscular
intermuseum
internasal
internation
internuclear
internucleon
internucleonic
interocean
interoceanic
interoffice
interoperable
interoperative
interoptic
interorbital
interorgan
interownership
interpandemic
interparental
interparenthetic
interparish
interparochial
interparticle
interparty
interpermeate
interpervade
interplanetary
interpollinate
interprofessional
interproportional
interprovincial
interpulmonary
interreflect
interregional
interreligous
interrenal
interrepellent
interrepulsion
interrhyme
interroad
interrow
interrule
intersale
interscience
interscribe
intersectional
intersegment
intersegmental
interseminal
intershock
intersocial
intersocietal
intersoluble
interspheral
interspinal
interstage
interstation
interstimulus
interstrand
interstratification
interstream
interstreet
interstructure
intersystem
intersystematic
intertalk
intertangle
intertarsal
interterm
interterminal
interterritorial
intertextual
intertidal
intertown
intertrade
intertraffic
intertrial
intertribal
intertroop
intertubular
interunion
interunit
interuniversity
intervalley
intervariation
intervarietal
intervarsity
intervascular
intervein
interventricular
interverbal
intervillage
interwed
interweld
interword
interworld
interwrap
interwreathe
interwrought
interzonal
interzone

in•ter•cep•tor *also* **in•ter•cept•er** (ĭn'tər-sĕp'tər) *n.* **1.** One that intercepts. **2.** A fighter plane that intercepts enemy aircraft.

in•ter•ces•sion (ĭn'tər-sĕsh'ən) *n.* **1.** Entreaty in favor of another. **2.** Mediation. **–in'ter•ces'sion•al** *adj.* **–in'ter•ces'sor** *n.* **–in'ter•ces'so•ry** *adj.*

in•ter•change (ĭn'tər-chānj') *v.* **1.** To switch each of (2 things) into the other's place. **2.** To exchange. *–n.* **1.** An exchange. **2.** A highway intersection that allows traffic to move between roads without crossing traffic streams. **–in'ter•change'a•ble** *adj.* **–in'ter•change'a•bly** *adv.* **–in'ter•chang'er** *n.*

in•ter•col•le•giate (ĭn'tər-kə-lē'jĭt, -jē-ĭt) *adj.* Involving or representing 2 or more colleges.

in•ter•com (ĭn'tər-kŏm') *n.* A 2-way communication system, as between parts of a house.

in•ter•com•mu•ni•cate (ĭn'tər-kə-myōō'nĭ-kāt') *v.* **1.** To communicate with each other. **2.** To be connected, as rooms. **–in'ter•com•mu'ni•ca'tion** *n.* **–in'ter•com•mu'ni•ca'tive** *adj.*

in•ter•con•ti•nen•tal (ĭn'tər-kŏn'tə-nĕn'tl) *adj.* Extending or occurring between or among continents.

in•ter•course (ĭn'tər-kôrs', -kōrs') *n.* **1.** Exchange between persons or groups : communication. **2.** Sexual intercourse.

in•ter•dict (ĭn'tər-dĭkt') *v.* To prohibit or forbid, esp. by official decree. *–n.* (ĭn'tər-dĭkt'). A prohibition. **–in'ter•dic'tion** *n.* **–in'ter•dic'tor** *n.* **–in'ter•dic'to•ry** *adj.*

in•ter•est (ĭn'trĭst, -tər-ĭst) *n.* **1. a.** Concern and curiosity about something. **b.** Something that arouses such feelings. **2.** Regard for one's advantage : self-interest. **3.** A claim or legal share in something. **4. a.** A charge for a loan, usu. a percentage of the amount borrowed. **b.** Return on invested capital <*interest* on a bank deposit> *–v.* **1.** To stimulate the curiosity and attention of. **2.** To cause to become concerned or involved with.

in•ter•est•ed (ĭn'trĭ-stĭd, -tər-ĭ-stĭd, -tə-rĕs'tĭd) *adj.* **1.** Feeling or displaying interest <*interested* in architecture> **2.** Having a claim or share. **3.** Influenced by self-interest. **–in'ter•est•ed•ly** *adv.*

in•ter•est•ing (ĭn'trĭ-stĭng, -tər-ĭ-stĭng, -tə-rĕs'tĭng) *adj.* Stimulating interest. **–in'ter•est•ing•ly** *adv.*

in•ter•face (ĭn'tər-fās') *n.* **1.** A surface that forms a common boundary between adjacent areas, strata, or substances. **2. a.** A point at which independent systems interact. **b.** A system by which this is done. **–in'ter•face'** *v.* **–in'ter•fa'cial** *adj.*

in•ter•fere (ĭn'tər-fîr') *v.* **-fered, -fer•ing. 1.** To come between so as to impede : hinder. **2.** To obstruct illegally the movement of an opposing player in some sports. **3.** To intrude in the affairs of others : meddle. **4.** To prevent clear reception of broadcast signals. **–in'ter•fer'ence** *n.*

in•ter•fer•on (ĭn'tər-fîr'ŏn') *n.* A protein produced in cells that acts to prevent duplication of infectious viral forms.

in•ter•ga•lac•tic (ĭn'tər-gə-lăk'tĭk) *adj.* Between galaxies.

in•ter•im (ĭn'tər-ĭm) *n.* An intervening period. *–adj.* Temporary.

in•te•ri•or (ĭn-tîr'ē-ər) *adj.* **1.** Of or in the inside : inner. **2.** Away from a coast or border : inland. *–n.* **1.** The inner part or area : inside. **2.** A person's spiritual or mental being. **3.** A representation of the inside of a room or structure, as in a painting. **4.** The inland part of a country or region.

interior decorator *n.* One who plans the layout, furnishings, and decoration of architectural interiors. **–interior decoration** *n.*

in•ter•ject (ĭn'tər-jĕkt') *v.* To insert between other parts or elements. **–in'ter•jec'tor** *n.* **–in'ter•jec'to•ry** *adj.*

in•ter•jec•tion (ĭn'tər-jĕk'shən) *n.* **1.** An exclamation. **2.** A word used exclamatorily to express emotion that is capable of standing alone grammatically, as *Heavens* or *Oh* **–in'ter•jec'tion•al** *adj.*

in•ter•lace (ĭn'tər-lās') *v.* **-laced, -lac•ing. 1.** To lace together : interweave. **2.** To intersperse.

in•ter•lard (ĭn'tər-lärd') *v.* To insert at intervals : intersperse.

in•ter•lin•e•ar (ĭn'tər-lĭn'ē-ər) *adj.* Inserted between lines of a text <an *interlinear* translation>

in•ter•lock (ĭn'tər-lŏk') *v.* To join closely, as by hooking or overlapping.

in•ter•loc•u•tor (ĭn'tər-lŏk'yə-tər) *n.* One who takes part in a conversation.

in•ter•loc•u•to•ry (ĭn'tər-lŏk'yə-tôr'ē, -tōr'ē) *adj.* Pronounced during a legal action and temporarily in effect <an *interlocutory* decree>

in•ter•lope (ĭn'tər-lōp', ĭn'tər-lōp') *v.* **-loped, -lop•ing. 1.** To violate the rights of others. **2.** To interfere : meddle. **–in'ter•lop'er** *n.*

in•ter•lude (ĭn'tər-lōōd') *n.* **1.** An intervening event or period of time. **2.** An entertainment presented between the acts of a play. **3.** A short musical piece between parts of a longer composition.

in•ter•mar•ry (ĭn'tər-măr'ē) *v.* **1.** To marry a member of another group. **2.** To become connected by the marriages of members <The tribes *intermarried.*> **3.** To marry within one's family, clan, or tribe. **–in'ter•mar'riage** *n.*

in•ter•me•di•ar•y (ĭn'tər-mē'dē-ĕr'ē) *n., pl.* **-ies. 1.** A mediator. **2.** An agent : means. **3.** An intermediate stage. *–adj.* **1.** Acting as a mediator. **2.** Intermediate.

in•ter•me•di•ate (ĭn'tər-mē'dē-ĭt) *adj.* Located or occurring in the middle or between 2 extremes. **–in'ter•me'di•a•cy** *n.* **–in'ter•me'di•ate** *n.* **–in'ter•me'di•ate•ly** *adv.*

in•ter•mez•zo (ĭn'tər-mĕt'sō, -mĕd'zō) *n., pl.* **-zos** *or* **-zi** (-sē, -zē). **1.** *Mus.* A short movement separating sections of a longer composition. **b.** A short instrumental composition. **2.** A brief entr'acte.

in•ter•mi•na•ble (ĭn-tûr'mə-nə-bəl) *adj.* Boringly protracted <an *interminable* lecture> **–in•ter'mi•na•bly** *adv.*

in•ter•min•gle (ĭn'tər-mĭng'gəl) *v.* To blend or become mixed together.

in•ter•mis•sion (ĭn'tər-mĭsh'ən) *n.* A temporary suspension or pause, esp. between the parts of a performance, as of a play.

in•ter•mit•tent (ĭn'tər-mĭt'nt) *adj.* Starting and stopping at intervals. ☆***syns:*** FITFUL, OCCASIONAL, PERIODIC, SPORADIC **–in'ter•mit'tent•ly** *adv.*

in•ter•mix (ĭn'tər-mĭks') *v.* To intermingle. **–in'ter•mix'ture** *n.*

in•tern *also* **in•terne** (ĭn'tûrn') *n.* **1.** An advanced student or recent graduate who undergoes supervised practical training, esp. at a hospital. **2.** One who is interned or confined. *–v.* **1.** To serve as an intern. **2.** (ĭn-tûrn'). To confine, esp. during wartime. **–in•tern'ment** *n.* **–in'tern•ship'** *n.*

in•ter•nal (ĭn-tûr'nəl) *adj.* **1.** Inner : interior. **2.** Coming from or residing within : inherent. **3.** Within the body. **4.** Of or pertaining to a country's domestic affairs. **–in•ter'nal•ly** *adv.*

internal-combustion engine *n.* An engine, as in an automobile, in which fuel is burned inside the engine.

internal medicine *n.* Medical study and treatment of nonsurgical diseases.

in•ter•na•tion•al (ĭn'tər-năsh'ə-nəl) *adj.* Of, pertaining to, or involving 2 or more nations. **–in'ter•na'tion•al•ly** *adv.*

in•ter•na•tion•al•ism (ĭn'tər-năsh'ə-nə-lĭz'əm) *n.* A policy of cooperation among nations, esp. in politics and economy. **–in'ter•na'tion•al•ist** *n.*

in•ter•na•tion•al•ize (ĭn'tər-năsh'ən-ə-līz') *v.* To place under international control. **–in'ter•na'tion•al•i•za'tion** *n.*

international law *n.* A body of rules considered binding between nations.

in•terne (ĭn'tûrn') *n.* & *v. var. of* INTERN.

in•ter•nec•ine (ĭn'tər-nĕs'ēn', -ĭn', -ĭn, -nē'sĭn') *adj.* **1.** Mutually destructive. **2.** Of or pertaining to struggle within a group.

in•tern•ee (ĭn'tûr-nē') *n.* A person who is interned or confined.

in•ter•nist (ĭn'tûr'nĭst, ĭn-tûr'-) *n.* A physician specializing in internal medicine.

in•ter•per•son•al (ĭn'tər-pûr'sə-nəl) *adj.* Between persons <*interpersonal* relationships> **–in'ter•per'son•al•ly** *adv.*

in•ter•plan•e•tar•y (ĭn'tər-plăn'ĭ-tĕr'ē) *adj.* Between planets.

in•ter•play (ĭn'tər-plā') *n.* Action and reaction : interaction. **–in'ter•play'** *v.*

in•ter•po•late (ĭn-tûr'pə-lāt') *v.* **-lat•ed, -lat•ing. 1.** To insert between other things or elements. **2.** To change (a text) by introducing additional material. **–in•ter'po•la'tion** *n.* **–in•ter'po•la'tor** *n.*

in•ter•pose (ĭn'tər-pōz') *v.* **1.** To insert between parts. **2.** To introduce (e.g., a comment) into a conversation or speech. **3.** To put (onself) in : intrude. **4.** To intervene. **–in'ter•pos'er** *n.* **–in'ter•po•si'tion** (-pə-zĭsh'ən) *n.*

in•ter•pret (ĭn-tûr'prĭt) *v.* **1.** To clarify the meaning of by explaining or restating. **2.** To represent or delineate the meaning of, esp. by artistic performance <an actress *interpreting* a role> **3.** To translate. **–in•ter'pret•a•ble** *adj.* **–in•ter'pre•ta'tion** *n.* **–in•ter'pret•er** *n.*

in•ter•pre•ta•tive (ĭn-tûr'prĭ-tā'tĭv) *also* **in•ter•pre•tive** (-prĭ-tĭv) *adj.* Of or based on interpreting : explanatory. **–in•ter'pre•ta'tive•ly** *adv.*

in•ter•ra•cial (ĭn'tər-rā'shəl) *adj.* Between different races.

in•ter•reg•num (ĭn'tər-rĕg'nəm) *n., pl.* **-nums** or **-na** (-nə). **1.** A period of time between 2 successive reigns. **2.** A lapse in continuity. **–in'ter•reg'nal** *adj.*

in•ter•re•late (ĭn'tər-rĭ-lāt') *v.* To put into or have a mutual relationship. **–in'ter•re•la'tion** *n.* **–in'ter•re•la'tion•ship'** *n.*

in•ter•ro•gate (ĭn-tĕr'ə-gāt') *v.* **-gat•ed, -gat•ing. 1.** To question formally. **2.** To send out a signal to (e.g., a computer) for triggering an appropriate response. **—in·ter′ro·ga′tion** *n.* **—in·ter′ro·ga′tor** *n.*

in·ter·rog·a·tive (ĭn′tə-rŏg′ə-tĭv) *adj.* **1.** Being, suggesting, or asking a question. **2.** Used to ask a question <an *interrogative* pronoun> **—in′ter·rog′a·tive** *n.* **—in′ter·rog′a·tive·ly** *adv.*

in·ter·rog·a·to·ry (ĭn′tə-rŏg′ə-tôr′ē, -tōr′ē) *adj.* Interrogative.

in·ter·rupt (ĭn′tə-rŭpt′) *v.* **1.** To break the progress or continuity of. **2.** To impede or stop by breaking in on. **3.** To break in while someone else is speaking or performing. **—in′ter·rupt′er** *n.* **—in′ter·rup′tion** *n.* **—in′ter·rup′tive** *adj.*

in·ter·scho·las·tic (ĭn′tər-skə-lăs′tĭk) *adj.* Occurring or conducted between or among schools.

in·ter·sect (ĭn′tər-sĕkt′) *v.* **1.** To cut through or across. **2.** To form an intersection (with).

in·ter·sec·tion (ĭn′tər-sĕk′shən) *n.* **1.** The act or point of intersecting. **2.** A place where streets or roads intersect. **3.** *Math.* The point or locus of points common to 2 or more geometric elements.

in·ter·sperse (ĭn′tər-spûrs′) *v.* **-spersed, -spers·ing. 1.** To scatter among other things. **2.** To provide with things distributed at intervals. **—in′ter·sper′sion** *n.*

in·ter·state (ĭn′tər-stāt′) *adj.* Between or connecting 2 or more states. —*n.* An interstate highway.

in·ter·stel·lar (ĭn′tər-stĕl′ər) *adj.* Between the stars.

in·ter·stice (ĭn-tûr′stĭs) *n., pl.* **-sti·ces** (-stĭ-sēz′, -sĭz). A small space between things : opening <the *interstices* of a net> **—in′ter·sti′tial** (in′tər-stĭsh′əl) *adj.*

in·ter·twine (ĭn′tər-twīn′) *v.* To twine together. **—in′ter·twine′ment** *n.*

in·ter·ur·ban (ĭn′tər-ûr′bən) *adj.* Situated between or connecting urban areas.

in·ter·val (ĭn′tər-vəl) *n.* **1.** A space between 2 points or objects. **2.** A period of time between 2 events or moments. **3.** The differences in pitch between 2 musical tones. **4.** *Math.* A set containing all the numbers between a pair of given numbers.

†in·ter·vale (ĭn′tər-văl′) *n. Regional.* A tract of low-lying land, esp. along a river.

in·ter·vene (ĭn′tər-vēn′) *v.* **-vened, -ven·ing. 1.** To appear, come, or lie between things, esp. as an unrelated or disruptive circumstance. **2.** To enter or come between so as to modify <The police *intervened* to break up the fight.> **3.** To interfere, often with force, in a foreign dispute or conflict. **—in′ter·ven′tion** (-vĕn′shən) *n.*

in·ter·view (ĭn′tər-vyōō′) *n.* **1.** A formal personal meeting, esp. one arranged for formal discussion or to evaluate an applicant. **2.** A conversation, as one conducted by a reporter, to elicit information. **—in′ter·view′** *v.* **—in′ter·view′er** *n.*

in·ter·weave (ĭn′tər-wēv′) *v.* **1.** To weave together. **2.** To blend together : intertwine.

in·tes·tate (ĭn-tĕs′tāt′, -tĭt) *adj.* **1.** Not having made a legal will. **2.** Not disposed of by a will. **—in·tes′ta·cy** (-tə-sē) *n.*

in·tes·tine (ĭn-tĕs′tĭn) *n. often* **intestines.** The part of the alimentary canal from the stomach to the anus. **—in·tes′ti·nal** *adj.* **—in·tes′ti·nal·ly** *adv.*

in·ti·mate[1] (ĭn′tə-mĭt) *adj.* **1.** Characterized by very close association or familiarity. **2.** Essential : fundamental. **3.** Affording privacy and informality <an *intimate* café> **4.** Very personal. —*n.* An intimate friend. **—in′ti·ma·cy, in′ti·mate·ness** *n.* **—in′ti·mate·ly** *adv.*

in·ti·mate[2] (ĭn′tə-māt′) *v.* **-mat·ed, -mat·ing.** To communicate indirectly : imply artfully. **—in′ti·mat′er** *n.* **—in′ti·ma′tion** *n.*

in·tim·i·date (ĭn-tĭm′ĭ-dāt′) *v.* **-dat·ed, -dat·ing. 1.** To make fearful : frighten. **2.** To discourage, coerce, or suppress by or as if by threatening. **—in·tim′i·da′tion** *n.* **—in·tim′i·da′tor** *n.*

in·to (ĭn′tōō) *prep.* **1.** To the inside of. **2.** To the activity or occupation of <went *into* medicine> **3.** To the condition of. **4.** So as to be in <enter *into* an agreement> **5.** To a point in the course of <lasted *into* the next week> **6.** Against <ran *into* a wall> **7.** *Informal.* Interested in : involved with <*into* yoga>

in·tol·er·a·ble (ĭn-tŏl′ər-ə-bəl) *adj.* **1.** Not tolerable : unbearable. **2.** Inordinate : excessive. **—in·tol′er·a·bly** *adv.*

in·tol·er·ant (ĭn-tŏl′ər-ənt) *adj.* **1.** Not tolerant, as of opposing views : bigoted. **2.** Not able to endure <*intolerant* of hot weather> **—in·tol′er·ance** *n.* **—in·tol′er·ant·ly** *adv.*

in·to·na·tion (ĭn′tō-nā′shən) *n.* **1.** The act of intoning. **2.** A manner of speaking or producing tones. **3.** The ranging of pitch in speech, esp. as an element of meaning.

in·tone (ĭn-tōn′) *v.* **-toned, -ton·ing. 1.** To recite in a chanting voice. **2.** To utter in a monotone. **—in·ton′er** *n.*

in to·to (ĭn tō′tō) *adv.* Totally.

in·tox·i·cate (ĭn-tŏk′sĭ-kāt′) *v.* **-cat·ed, -cat·ing. 1.** To make drunk. **2.** To excite or stimulate. **—in·tox′i·cant** (-kənt) *n.* **—in·tox′i·ca′tion** *n.*

intr. *abbr.* intransitive.

intra– *pref.* Within <*intra*mural>

in·tra·cel·lu·lar (ĭn′trə-sĕl′yə-lər) *adj.* Within a cell or cells.

in·tra·cos·tal (ĭn′trə-kŏs′tl) *adj.* On the inner surface of a rib or ribs.

in·tra·cra·ni·al (ĭn′trə-krā′nē-əl) *adj.* Within the skull.

in·trac·ta·ble (ĭn-trăk′tə-bəl) *adj.* **1.** Hard to manage : obstinate. **2.** Difficult to treat or cure <an *intractable* virus>

in·tra·dos (ĭn′trə-dŏs′, -dō′, -ĭn-trā′dŏs′, -dōs′) *n., pl.* **-dos** (-dōz′) or **-dos·es** (-dŏs′ĭz) The inner curve of an arch.

intrados

in·tra·mu·ral (ĭn′trə-myŏŏr′əl) *adj.* Carried on or being within a school or other institution <*intramural* sports>

in·tra·mus·cu·lar (ĭn′trə-mŭs′kyə-lər) *adj.* Within a muscle.

in·tran·si·gent (ĭn-trăn′sə-jənt) *adj.* Not willing to moderate a position : uncompromising. **—in·tran′si·gence, in·tran′si·gen·cy** *n.* **—in·tran′si·gent** *n.*

in·tran·si·tive (ĭn-trăn′sĭ-tĭv) *adj.* Not needing a direct object to complete its meaning. Used of a verb. —*n.* An intransitive verb or verb construction. **—in·tran′si·tive·ly** *adv.* **—in·tran′si·tive·ness** *n.*

in·tra·oc·u·lar (ĭn′trə-ŏk′yə-lər) *adj.* Within the eyeball.

in·tra·state (ĭn′trə-stāt′) *adj.* Within a state.

in·tra·u·ter·ine (ĭn′trə-yōō′tər-ĭn, -tə-rīn′) *adj.* Within the uterus.

intrauterine device *n.* A metal or plastic loop, ring, or spiral inserted into the uterus as a contraceptive.

in·tra·ve·nous (ĭn′trə-vē′nəs) *adj.* Within a vein. **—in′tra·ve′nous·ly** *adv.*

in·trep·id (ĭn-trĕp′ĭd) *adj.* Outstandingly courageous : fearless. **—in·trep′id·ly** *adv.* **—in·trep′id·ness** *n.*

in·tri·cate (ĭn′trĭ-kĭt) *adj.* **1.** Having many elaborately arranged parts or elements : complex. **2.** Difficult to solve or comprehend. **—in′tri·ca·cy** (-kə-sē) *n.* **—in′tri·cate·ly** *adv.*

in·trigue (ĭn′trēg′, ĭn-trēg′) *n.* **1. a.** A furtive maneuver or plan : plot. **b.** Involvement in such plots. **2.** A clandestine love affair. —*v.* (ĭn-trēg′) **-trigued, -trigu·ing. 1.** To engage in intrigues : plot. **2.** To effect by scheming. **3.** To stimulate the interest or curiosity of. **—in·trigu′er** *n.*

in·trin·sic (ĭn-trĭn′sĭk) *adj.* Of or relating to the fundamental nature of a thing : inherent. **—in·trin′si·cal·ly** *adv.*

in·tro·duce (ĭn′trə-dōōs′, -dyōōs′) *v.* **-duced, -duc·ing. 1.** To present (a person) by name to another : make acquainted. **2.** To bring into use or practice for the first time <*introduce* reforms> **3.** To bring in and establish in a new environment. **4.** To insert or inject. **5.** To bring to another's notice. **6.** To begin : preface. ☆*syns:* INAUGURATE, INITIATE, INSTITUTE, LAUNCH, ORIGINATE **—in′tro·duc′er** *n.* **—in′tro·duc′tion** (-dŭk′shən) *n.* **—in′tro·duc′to·ry** *adj.*

in·tro·it *also* **In·tro·it** (ĭn′trō′ĭt, -troit′, ĭn-trō′ĭt) *n.* **1.** A psalm or hymn sung at the beginning of a service. **2.** *Rom. Cath. Ch.* The beginning of the proper of the Mass.

in·tro·mit (ĭn′trə-mĭt′) *v.* **-mit·ted, -mit·ting.** To cause or allow to enter : admit. **—in′tro·mis′sion** *n.* **—in′tro·mit′tent** *adj.* **—in′tro·mit′ter** *n.*

in·tro·spec·tion (ĭn′trə-spĕk′shən) *n.* Examination of one's thoughts and feelings. **—in′tro·spect′** *v.* **—in′tro·spec′tive** *adj.* **—in′tro·spec′tive·ly** *adv.*

in·tro·vert (ĭn′trə-vûrt′) *n.* One who is chiefly concerned with one's own mental life rather than with friends and social activities. **—in′tro·ver′sion** *n.* **—in′tro·ver′sive** *adj.* **—in′tro·vert′ed** *adj.*

in·trude (ĭn-trōōd′) *v.* **-trud·ed, -trud·ing. 1.** To push or thrust in. **2.** To put or come in without being asked or wanted. **3.** To appear inappropriately. **—in·trud′er** *n.* **—in·tru′sion** *n.* **—in·tru′sive** *adj.* **—in·tru′sive·ly** *adv.*

in·trust (ĭn-trŭst′) *v. var. of* ENTRUST.

in•tu•it (ĭn-to͞o′ĭt, -tyo͞o′-) *v.* To understand or sense through intuition.

in•tu•i•tion (ĭn′to͞o-ĭsh′ən, -tyo͞o-) *n.* **1. a.** The capacity of knowing without the use of rational processes. **b.** Knowledge acquired in this way. **2.** Keen insight. **–in•tu′i•tive** *adj.* **–in•tu′i•tive•ly** *adv.*

In•u•it (ĭn′yo͞o-ĭt) *n. var. of* INNUIT.

in•un•date (ĭn′ən-dāt′) *v.* **-dat•ed, -dat•ing. 1.** To cover with water : overflow. **2.** To overwhelm with or as if with a flood : swamp. **–in′un•da′tion** *n.*

in•ure (ĭn-yo͝or′) *v.* **-ured, -ur•ing.** To make accustomed to something usu. undesirable : harden. **–in•ure′ment** *n.*

inv. *abbr.* **1.** invented; invention. **2.** invoice.

in•vade (ĭn-vād′) *v.* **-vad•ed, -vad•ing. 1.** To go into by force so as to conquer or pillage. **2.** To enter and overrun harmfully. **3.** To encroach upon : violate. **–in•vad′er** *n.*

in•va•lid¹ (ĭn′və-lĭd) *n.* A chronically sick or disabled person. *–adj.* Disabled by disease or injury.

in•val•id² (ĭn-văl′ĭd) *adj.* **1.** Not factually or legally valid. **2.** Falsely reasoned : unsound. **–in′va•lid′i•ty** (-və-lĭd′ĭ-tē) *n.* **–in•val′id•ly** *adv.*

in•val•i•date (ĭn-văl′ĭ-dāt′) *v.* **-dat•ed, -dat•ing.** To make invalid : nullify. **–in•val′i•da′tion** *n.* **–in•val′i•da′tor** *n.*

in•val•u•a•ble (ĭn-văl′yo͞o-ə-bəl) *adj.* **1.** Of great value : priceless. **2.** Of great help or use <his *invaluable* assistance> **–in•val′u•a•ble•ness** *n.* **–in•val′u•a•bly** *adv.*

in•var•i•a•ble (ĭn-vâr′ē-ə-bəl) *adj.* Not changing : constant. **–in•var′i•a•bly** *adv.*

in•va•sion (ĭn-vā′zhən) *n.* The act of invading.

in•va•sive (ĭn-vā′sĭv) *adj.* **1.** Invading. **2.** Tending to spread rapidly and harmfully. **–in•va′sive•ness** *n.*

in•vec•tive (ĭn-vĕk′tĭv) *n.* Vituperative or denunciatory language.

in•veigh (ĭn-vā′) *v.* To protest angrily : rail. **–in•veigh′er** *n.*

in•vei•gle (ĭn-vē′gəl, -vā′-) *v.* **-gled, -gling. 1.** To win over by guile or persuasion. **2.** To obtain by cajolery. **–in•vei′gle•ment** *n.* **–in•vei′gler** *n.*

in•vent (ĭn-vĕnt′) *v.* **1.** To produce or devise first : originate. **2.** To make up : concoct <*invent* an excuse> ☆***syns:*** CONCOCT, CONTRIVE, COOK UP, DEVISE, DREAM UP, FABRICATE, FORMULATE, HATCH, MAKE UP **–in•ven′tor** *n.*

in•ven•tion (ĭn-vĕn′shən) *n.* **1.** The act of inventing. **2.** A new method, process, or device evolved from study and testing. **3.** Something made up, esp. a falsehood. **4.** Skill in inventing : inventiveness.

in•ven•tive (ĭn-vĕn′tĭv) *adj.* **1.** Of or marked by invention. **2.** Having or showing skill in inventing : creative. **–in•ven′tive•ly** *adv.* **–in•ven′tive•ness** *n.*

in•ven•to•ry (ĭn′vən-tôr′ē, -tōr′ē) *n., pl.* **-ries. 1.a.** A list of items, esp. a periodic detailed enumeration of goods or possessions. **b.** The process of making an inventory. **c.** The items listed in an inventory. **2.** A supply : stock. **–in′ven•to′ry** *v.*

in•ver•ness *also* **In•ver•ness** (ĭn′vər-nĕs′) *n.* A loose overcoat with a detachable cape.

in•verse (ĭn-vûrs′, ĭn′vûrs′) *adj.* **1.** Reversed in order or sequence. **2.** Opposite in effects or nature. **3.** Inverted. *–n.* Something opposite : reverse. **–in•verse′ly** *adv.*

in•ver•sion (ĭn-vûr′zhən, -shən) *n.* **1.** The act of inverting or the state of being inverted. **2.** An interchange of position, esp. of adjacent objects in a sequence. **3.** A state in which the temperature of the air increases with increasing altitude and keeps the surface air and pollutants down.

in•vert (ĭn-vûrt′) *v.* **1.** To turn upside down or inside out. **2.** To reverse the position, order, or condition of. **–in•vert′er** *n.* **–in•vert′i•ble** *adj.*

in•ver•tase (ĭn-vûr′tās′, ĭn′vər-tās′, -tāz′) *n.* An enzyme that catalyzes the conversion of sucrose to glucose and fructose.

in•ver•te•brate (ĭn-vûr′tə-brĭt, -brāt′) *adj.* Lacking a backbone or spinal column. **–in•ver′te•brate** *n.*

in•vest (ĭn-vĕst′) *v.* **1.** To put (money) into something, as stocks or property, in order to obtain profit or interest. **2.** To utilize for future benefit <*invested* her time wisely> **3.** To furnish with authority or power. **4.** To place in office : install. **5.** To envelop : shroud. **–in•ves′tor** *n.*

in•ves•ti•gate (ĭn-vĕs′tĭ-gāt′) *v.* **-gat•ed, -gat•ing.** To make a systematic inquiry (into) : examine deeply. **–in•ves′ti•ga′tion** *n.* **–in•ves′ti•ga′tive** *adj.* **–in•ves′ti•ga′tor** *n.*

in•ves•ti•ture (ĭn-vĕs′tə-cho͝or′, -chər) *n.* The act or ceremony of installing someone in a high office.

in•vest•ment (ĭn-vĕst′mənt) *n.* **1.** The act of investing. **2.** An amount invested. **3.** A possession acquired and kept for future benefit. **4.** Investiture.

in•vet•er•ate (ĭn-vĕt′ər-ĭt) *adj.* **1.** Solidly fixed or established : deep-rooted. **2.** Continuing or persisting in a habit <an *inveterate* skeptic> **–in•vet′er•a•cy, in•vet′er•ate•ness** *n.* **–in•vet′er•ate•ly** *adv.*

in•vid•i•ous (ĭn-vĭd′ē-əs) *adj.* Tending to cause animosity or imply a slight <an *invidious* comparison> **–in•vid′i•ous•ly** *adv.* **–in•vid′i•ous•ness** *n.*

in•vig•o•rate (ĭn-vĭg′ə-rāt′) *v.* **-rat•ed, -rat•ing.** To impart strength or vitality to : refresh : animate. **–in•vig′o•rat′ing•ly** *adv.* **–in•vig′o•ra′tion** *n.*

in•vin•ci•ble (ĭn-vĭn′sə-bəl) *adj.* Incapable of being overcome or defeated. ☆***syns:*** IMPREGNABLE, INDOMITABLE, INSUPERABLE, UNCONQUERABLE **–in•vin′ci•bil′i•ty** *n.* **–in•vin′ci•bly** *adv.*

in•vi•o•la•ble (ĭn-vī′ə-lə-bəl) *adj.* **1.** Secure from violation or profanation. **2.** Safe from trespass or assault. **–in•vi′o•la•bil′i•ty** *n.* **–in•vi′o•la•bly** *adv.*

in•vi•o•late (ĭn-vī′ə-lĭt) *adj.* Not violated : intact. **–in•vi′o•late•ly** *adv.* **–in•vi′o•late•ness** *n.*

in•vis•i•ble (ĭn-vĭz′ə-bəl) *adj.* **1.** Not visible. **2.** Not open to view : hidden. **3.** Imperceptible. **–in•vis′i•bil′i•ty** *n.* **–in•vis′i•bly** *adv.*

in•vi•ta•tion (ĭn′vĭ-tā′shən) *n.* **1.** The act of inviting. **2.** A request for someone's presence or participation. **3.** An enticement or attraction.

in•vite (ĭn-vīt′) *v.* **-vit•ed, -vit•ing. 1.** To request the presence or participation of. **2.** To ask formally. **3.** To welcome <*invite* questions from the audience> **4.** To bring on : provoke <only *inviting* trouble> **5.** To tempt : entice. *–n.* (ĭn′vīt′). *Informal.* An invitation.

in•vit•ing (ĭn-vī′tĭng) *adj.* Attractive : tempting. **–in•vit′ing•ly** *adv.* **–in•vit′ing•ness** *n.*

in vi•tro (ĭn vē′trō) *adj. & adv.* In an artificial environment outside the living organism.

in vi•vo *adj. & adv.* Within a living organism.

in•vo•ca•tion (ĭn′və-kā′shən) *n.* **1.** An appeal to a higher power for aid. **2.** A prayer used in invoking, esp. at the opening of a service or ceremony.

in•voice (ĭn′vois′) *n.* **1.** An itemized list of goods shipped or services rendered, detailing the costs : bill. **2.** A consignment of goods. **–in′voice′** *v.*

in•voke (ĭn-vōk′) *v.* **-voked, -vok•ing. 1.** To call on for aid, support, or inspiration <*invoke* the Muse> **2.** To appeal to for justification : cite. **3.** To call for earnestly : solicit. **4.** To conjure. **5.** To resort to : implement <*invoked* martial law> **–in•vok′er** *n.*

in•vol•un•tar•y (ĭn-vŏl′ən-tĕr′ē) *adj.* **1.** Not done willingly or by conscious choice. **2.** Not subject to conscious control <*involuntary* muscles> **–in•vol′un•tar′i•ly** *adv.* **–in•vol′un•tar′i•ness** *n.*

in•vo•lute (ĭn′və-lo͞ot′) *adj.* **1.** Intricate : complex. **2.** Having margins or whorls rolled inward.

in•vo•lu•tion (ĭn′və-lo͞o′shən) *n.* **1.** Complexity : intricacy. **2.** Something complex or intricate, as a complicated grammatical construction.

in•volve (ĭn-vŏlv′) *v.* **-volved, -volv•ing. 1.** To contain as a part. **2.** To have as a consequence : entail. **3.** To make a participant of : draw in. **4.** To engross : absorb. **5.** To make intricate : complicate. **–in•volve′ment** *n.*

in•vul•ner•a•ble (ĭn-vŭl′nər-ə-bəl) *adj.* **1.** Immune to attack : impregnable. **2.** Not able to be damaged or wounded. **–in•vul′ner•a•bil′i•ty** *n.* **–in•vul′ner•a•bly** *adv.*

in•ward (ĭn′wərd) *adj.* **1.** Situated or located inside : inner. **2.** Moving or facing toward the interior. **3.** Of or existing in the mind. *–adv. also* **in•wards** (-wərdz). **1.** Toward the center, inside, or interior. **2.** Toward the mind or the self. **–in′ward•ness** *n.*

in•ward•ly (ĭn′wərd-lē) *adv.* **1.** On or in the inside : within. **2.** To oneself : privately <*inwardly* laughing>

i•o•dide (ī′ə-dīd′) *n.* A chemical compound composed of iodine and another element or radical.

i•o•dine (ī′ə-dīn′, -dĭn, -dēn′) *n.* **1.** *Symbol* **I** A lustrous, gray, corrosive, poisonous element. **2.** A solution of iodine, alcohol, and sodium iodide or potassium iodide, used as an antiseptic.

i•o•dize (ī′ə-dīz′) *v.* **-dized, -diz•ing.** To treat with iodine or an iodide.

i•on (ī′ən, ī′ŏn′) *n.* An atom, group of atoms, or molecule that has acquired a net electric charge by gaining or losing electrons from a neutral configuration.

-ion *suff.* An act, a condition, or the outcome of an act <*creation*><*sedation*>

I•o•ni•a (ī-ō′nē-ə). Region along the Aegean coast of W Asia Minor. **–I•o′ni•an, I•on′ic** (ī-ŏn′ĭk) *adj. & n.*

i•on•ize (ī′ə-nīz′) *v.* **-ized, -iz•ing.** To convert completely or partially into ions. **–i′o•ni•za′tion** *n.*

i•on•o•sphere (ī-ŏn′ə-sfîr′) *n.* An ionized group of layers of the earth's atmosphere that extend from approx. 30 to 250 mi or 50 to 400 km. **–i•on′o•spher′ic** (-sfîr′ĭk, -sfĕr′-) *adj.*

i·o·ta (ī-ō′tə) *n.* A very small amount : bit.
IOU (ī′ō-yo͞o′) *n., pl.* **IOU's** *or* **IOUs.** A promise to pay a debt.
-ious *suff.* Having or full of <*bilious*>
I·o·wa (ī′ə-wə). State of NC U.S. *Cap.* Des Moines. *Pop.* 2,913,387. **–I′o·wan** *n.*
ip·e·cac (ĭp′ĭ-kăk′) *n.* A low-growing South American shrub, *Cephaelis ipecacuanha,* with roots used medicinally.
ip·so fac·to (ĭp′sō făk′tō) *adv.* By that very fact.
IQ *or* **I.Q.** *abbr.* intelligence quotient.
Ir *symbol for* IRIDIUM.
I·ran (ĭ-răn′, ē-rän′). Country of SW Asia. *Cap.* Teheran. *Pop.* 38,940,000. **–I·ra′ni·an** *adj.* & *n.*
I·raq (ĭ-răk′, ē-räk′). Country of SW Asia. Cap. Baghdad. Pop. 13,230,000. **–I·raq′i** *adj.* & *n.*
i·ras·ci·ble (ĭ-răs′ə-bəl, ī-răs′-) *adj.* Easily angered : hot-tempered. **–i·ras′ci·bil′i·ty, i·ras′ci·ble·ness** *n.* **–i·ras′ci·bly** *adv.*
i·rate (ī-rāt′, ī′rāt′) *adj.* Very angry : enraged. **–i·rate′ly** *adv.*
ire (īr) *n.* Anger : rage. **–ire′ful** *adj.* **–ire′ful·ly** *adv.* **–ire′ful·ness** *n.*
Ire·land (īr′lənd). **1.** Island of the British Isles, in the N Atlantic W of Britain. **2.** Country occupying most of Ireland. *Cap.* Dublin. *Pop.* 3,455,000. **3.** Northern Ireland. **–I′rish** (ī′rĭsh) *adj.* & *n.*
i·ren·ic (ī-rĕn′ĭk, ī-rē′nĭk) *adj.* Promoting peace : conciliatory. **–i·ren′i·cal·ly**
ir·i·des·cent (ĭr′ĭ-dĕs′ənt) *adj.* Producing an array of rainbowlike colors. **–ir′i·des′cence** *n.*
i·rid·i·um (ĭ-rĭd′ē-əm, ī-rĭd′-) *n. Symbol* **Ir** A hard, brittle, highly corrosion-resistant, yellow metallic element.
i·ris (ī′rĭs) *n., pl.* **i·ris·es** *or* **i·ri·des** (ī′rĭ-dēz′, ĭr′ĭ-). **1.** The pigmented part of the eye that regulates the size of the pupil by expanding and contracting around it. **2.** A plant of the genus *Iris,* with narrow sword-shaped leaves and showy flowers.
Irish setter *n.* A large, slender dog having a silky reddish-brown coat.
irk (ûrk) *v.* To cause irritation or annoyance : vex. **–irk′some** *adj.* **–irk′some·ly** *adv.* **–irk′some·ness** *n.*
i·ron (ī′ərn) *n.* **1.** *Symbol* **Fe** A hard, gray, brittle metallic element, used alloyed in many important building materials. **2.** Great strength or hardness. **3.** Any of various tools made of iron alloy or similar metal. **4.** A golf club with a metal head. **5.** A device with a weighted flat bottom used when heated for pressing wrinkles from fabric. **6. irons.** Metal restraints for the wrists or ankles : shackles. *–v.* To press with an iron. **–iron out.** To settle through discussion or compromise : work out. **–i′ron·er** *n.* **–i′ron·ing** *n.*
Iron Age *n.* The gen. prehistoric period succeeding the Bronze Age, marked by the introduction of iron metallurgy, in Europe beginning around the 8th cent. B.C..
i·ron·bound (ī′ərn-bound′) *adj.* Rigid : unyielding.
i·ron·clad (ī′ərn-klăd′) *adj.* **1.** Sheathed with protective iron plates. **2.** Rigid : fixed <an *ironclad* law>
Iron Curtain *n.* The political and idealogical barrier between the Soviet bloc and W Europe.
i·ron·ic (ī-rŏn′ĭk) *also* **i·ron·i·cal** (-ĭ-kəl) *adj.* **1.** Marked by or constituting irony. **2.** Given to using irony. **–i·ron′i·cal·ly** *adv.*
iron lung *n.* A tank enclosing the entire body except the head and assisting respiration by alternately increasing and decreasing air pressure.
i·ron·stone (ī′ərn-stōn′) *n.* **1.** An iron ore mixed with silica and clay. **2.** A heavy, hard white pottery.
i·ron·ware (ī′ərn-wâr′) *n.* Products made of iron.
i·ron·work (ī′ərn-wûrk′) *n.* Work in iron, as railings and gates.
i·ron·works (ī′ərn-wûrks′) *n. (sing. or pl. in number).* A place for smelting iron or manufacturing iron products.
i·ro·ny (ī′rə-nē) *n., pl.* **-nies. 1.** The use of words to suggest the opposite of what they literally mean. **2.** Incongruity between what might be expected to happen and what actually happens.
ir·ra·di·ate (ĭ-rā′dē-āt′) *v.* **-at·ed, -at·ing. 1.** To treat with or expose to radiation. **2.** To send forth as if in rays : radiate. **–ir·ra′di·a′tion** *n.* **–ir·ra′di·a′tor** *n.*
ir·ra·tion·al (ĭ-răsh′ə-nəl) *adj.* **1.** Not capable of reasoning. **2.** Having lost mental clarity : incoherent. **3.** Contrary to reason : illogical. **4.** *Math.* Not expressible as an integer or a quotient of integers. **–ir·ra′tion·al′i·ty** *n.* **–ir·ra′tion·al·ly** *adv.*
ir·rec·on·cil·a·ble (ĭ-rĕk′ən-sī′lə-bəl, ĭ-rĕk′ən-sī′-) *adj.* Not capable of being reconciled. **–ir·rec′on·cil′·a·bil′i·ty** *n.* **–ir·rec′on·cil′a·bly** *adv.*
ir·re·cov·er·a·ble (ĭr′ĭ-kŭv′ər-ə-bəl) *adj.* Not capable of being recovered : irreparable. **–ir′re·cov′er·a·ble·ness** *n.* **–ir′re·cov′er·a·bly** *adv.*
ir·re·deem·a·ble (ĭr′ĭ-dē′mə-bəl) *adj.* **1.** Not capable of being bought back or turned in for exchange. **2.** Not convertible into coin. **3.** Not able to be saved or reformed.
ir·re·den·tist (ĭr′ĭ-dĕn′tĭst) *n.* An advocate of the recovery of territory that one's nation has lost. **–ir′re·den′tism** *n.* **–ir′re·den′tist** *adj.*
ir·re·duc·i·ble (ĭr′ĭ-do͞o′sə-bəl, -dyo͞o′-) *adj.* Not capable of being reduced, as to a smaller amount. **–ir′re·duc′i·bil′i·ty** *n.* **–ir′re·duc′i·bly** *adv.*
ir·ref·u·ta·ble (ĭ-rĕf′yə-tə-bəl, ĭr′ĭ-fyo͞o′tə-bəl) *adj.* Not able to be disproved <*irrefutable* evidence> **–ir·ref′u·ta·bil′i·ty** *n.* **–ir·ref′u·ta·bly** *adv.*
ir·reg·u·lar (ĭ-rĕg′yə-lər) *adj.* **1.** Not according to rule or general practice. **2.** Not straight, uniform, or orderly. **3.** Unconventional. **4.** Uneven <an *irregular* pulse> **5.** Not up to standard : imperfect. **6.** Not following a standard pattern of grammatical inflections <The verb "be" is *irregular.*> *–n.* **1.** One that is irregular. **2.** A guerrilla. **–ir·reg′u·lar′i·ty** (-lăr′ĭ-tē) *n.* **–ir·reg′u·lar·ly** *adv.*
ir·rel·e·vant (ĭ-rĕl′ə-vənt) *adj.* Not relating to the subject at hand : not pertinent. ☆**syns:** EXTRANEOUS, IMMATERIAL, INAPPLICABLE. **–ir·rel′e·vance, ir·rel′e·van·cy** *n.* **–ir·rel′e·vant·ly** *adv.*
ir·re·lig·ious (ĭr′ĭ-lĭj′əs) *adj.* Indifferent or opposed to religion. **–ir′re·lig′ious·ly** *adv.* **–ir′re·lig′ious·ness, ir′re·lig′ion** *n.*
ir·re·me·di·a·ble (ĭr′ĭ-mē′dē-ə-bəl) *adj.* Beyond correction or repair : hopeless. **–ir′re·me′di·a·bly** *adv.*
ir·re·mis·si·ble (ĭr′ĭ-mĭs′ə-bəl) *adj.* Not pardonable. **–ir′re·mis′si·bil′i·ty** *n.*
ir·re·mov·a·ble (ĭr′ĭ-mo͞o′və-bəl) *adj.* Not removable. **–ir′re·mov′a·bly** *adv.*
ir·rep·a·ra·ble (ĭ-rĕp′ər-ə-bəl) *adj.* Not able to be repaired or set right again. **–ir·rep′a·ra·bil′i·ty** *n.* **–ir·rep′a·ra·bly** *adv.*
ir·re·place·a·ble (ĭr′ĭ-plā′sə-bəl) *adj.* Not able to be replaced.
ir·re·press·i·ble (ĭr′ĭ-prĕs′ə-bəl) *adj.* Impossible to hold back or restrain. **–ir′re·press′i·bil′i·ty** *n.* **–ir′re·press′i·bly** *adv.*
ir·re·proach·a·ble (ĭr′ĭ-prō′chə-bəl) *adj.* Beyond reproach : impeccable. **–ir′re·proach′a·ble·ness** *n.* **–ir′re·proach′a·bly** *adv.*
ir·re·sist·i·ble (ĭr′ĭ-zĭs′tə-bəl) *adj.* **1.** Impossible to resist. **2.** Highly appealing. **–ir′re·sist′i·bil′i·ty** *n.* **–ir′re·sist′i·bly** *adv.*
ir·res·o·lute (ĭ-rĕz′ə-lo͞ot′) *adj.* Lacking in resolution : indecisive. **–ir·res′o·lute′ly** *adv.* **–ir·res′o·lute′ness** *n.*
ir·re·spec·tive (ĭr′ĭ-spĕk′tĭv) *adj.* Regardless <*irrespective* of race or nationality>
ir·re·spon·si·ble (ĭr′ĭ-spŏn′sə-bəl) *adj.* **1.** Not accountable. **2.** Not fit to assume responsibility. **3.** Showing no sense of responsibility <*irresponsible* behavior> ☆**syns:** FECKLESS, INCAUTIOUS, RECKLESS **–ir′re·spon′si·bil′i·ty** *n.* **–ir′re·spon′si·bly** *adv.*
ir·re·triev·a·ble (ĭr′ĭ-trē′və-bəl) *adj.* Impossible to retrieve or recover.
ir·rev·er·ence (ĭ-rĕv′ər-əns) *n.* **1.** Lack of reverence : disrespect. **2.** A disrespectful action or remark. **–ir·rev′er·ent** *adj.* **–ir·rev′er·ent·ly** *adv.*
ir·re·vers·i·ble (ĭr′ĭ-vûr′sə-bəl) *adj.* Impossible to reverse. **–ir′re·vers′i·bil′i·ty** *n.* **–ir′re·vers′i·bly** *adv.*
ir·rev·o·ca·ble (ĭ-rĕv′ə-kə-bəl) *adj.* Not able to be revoked : irreversible. **–ir·rev′o·ca·bil′i·ty** *n.* **–ir·rev′o·ca·bly** *adv.*
ir·ri·ga·ble (ĭr′ĭ-gə-bəl) *adj.* Able to be irrigated.
ir·ri·gate (ĭr′ĭ-gāt′) *v.* **-gat·ed, -gat·ing. 1.** To supply (land or crops) with water artificially, as with ditches or pipes. **2.** To wash out (e.g., a bodily wound) with water or a medicated fluid. **–ir′ri·ga′tion** *n.* **–ir′ri·ga′tion·al** *adj.* **–ir′ri·ga′tor** *n.*
ir·ri·ta·ble (ĭr′ĭ-tə-bəl) *adj.* **1.** Easily annoyed or irritated. **2.** Ill-tempered. **3.** Abnormally sensitive or responsive to stimuli. ☆**syns:** CANTANKEROUS, CRANKY, CROSS, GROUCHY, GRUMPY, ILL-TEMPERED, IRASCIBLE, PEEVISH, QUERULOUS, SURLY, TESTY **–ir′ri·ta·bil′i·ty, ir′ri·ta·ble·ness** *n.* **–ir′ri·ta·bly** *adv.*
ir·ri·tate (ĭr′ĭ-tāt′) *v.* **-tat·ed, -tat·ing. 1.** To make angry : annoy or bother. **2.** To provoke. **3.** To chafe or inflame. **–ir′ri·tant** *adj.* & *n.* **–ir′ri·tat′ing·ly** *adv.* **–ir′ri·ta′tion** *n.* **–ir′ri·ta′tor** *n.*
ir·rupt (ĭ-rŭpt′) *v.* To rush or burst in : invade. **–ir·rup′tion** *n.* **–ir·rup′tive** *adj.* **–ir·rup′tive·ly** *adv.*
IRS *abbr.* Internal Revenue Service.
is (ĭz) *v. 3rd person sing. present tense of* BE.
is. or **Is.** *abbr.* island; islands.
Is·a·bel·la I (ĭz′ə-bĕl′ə). 1451–1501. Queen of Castile and Aragon.
I·sa·iah (ī-zā′ə, ī-zī′ə) *n.* See BIBLE TABLE.
ISBN *abbr.* International Standard Book Number.

-ish *suff.* **1.** Of or characteristic of <Dan*ish*> **2.** Having the usu. undesirable qualities of <child*ish*> **3.** Somewhat : rather <yellow*ish*> **4.** Approximately <fiv*ish*>

i•sin•glass (ī′zĭng-glăs′, ī′zən-) *n.* A transparent gelatin made from the air bladder of certain fishes.

isl. *abbr.* island.

Is•lam (ĭs′ləm, ĭz′-, ĭ-släm′) *n.* **1.** A Moslem religion based on the teachings of Mohammed. **2.** Moslems, Moslem nations, or Moslem civilization. **–Is•lam′ic** (-lăm′ĭk, -lä′mĭk) *adj.*

Is•lam•a•bad (ĭs-lä′mə-bäd′, ĭz-). Cap. of Pakistan, in the NE. *Pop.* 77,318.

is•land (ī′lənd) *n.* **1.** A land mass, esp. one smaller than a continent, completely surrounded by water. **2.** Something like an island, esp. in being isolated. **–is′land•er** *n.*

isle (īl) *n.* An island, esp. one that is small.

is•let (ī′lĭt) *n.* A little island.

ism (ĭz′əm) *n. Informal.* A particular doctrine or theory.

-ism *suff.* **1.** A practice or policy <terror*ism*> **2.** Typical behavior or quality <hero*ism*> **3.** A condition <pauper*ism*> **4.** A distinctive usage or characteristic <American*ism*> **5.** A system of principles : doctrine <pacif*ism*>

is•n't (ĭz′ənt). Is not.

i•so•bar (ī′sə-bär′) *n.* A line on a map connecting points of equal pressure. **–i′so•bar′ic** (-bär′ĭk, -băr′-) *adj.*

i•so•late (ī′sə-lāt′) *v.* **-lat•ed, -lat•ing. 1.** To set apart from others or the rest : put by itself. **2.** To place in quarantine. **–i′so•la′tion** *n.* **–i′so•la′tor** *n.*

i•so•la•tion•ism (ī′sə-lā′shə-nĭz′əm) *n.* A national policy of avoiding economic or political entanglements with other countries. **–i′so•la′tion•ist** *n.*

i•so•mer (ī′sə-mər) *n.* A compound that has the same kinds and numbers of atoms as another compound but differs in chemical or physical properties because of the arrangement or linkage of the atoms. **–i′so•mer′ic** *adj.*

i•so•met•ric (ī′sə-mĕt′rĭk) *also* **i•so•met•ri•cal** (-rĭ-kəl) *adj.* **1.** Of equal size or dimensions. **2.** *Physiol.* Of or involving muscle contractions occurring when the ends of the muscle are fixed in place so that increases in tension occur without appreciable increases in length <an *isometric* exercise> *–n.* **1.** A line connecting isometric points. **2. isometrics.** *(sing. in number).* Isometric exercise.

i•so•morph (ī′sə-môrf′) *n.* One of 2 or more organisms or objects showing close similarity in form or structure. **–i′so•mor′phic** *adj.* **–i′so•mor′phism** *n.*

i•so•oc•tane (ī′sō-ŏk′tān′) *n.* A highly flammable liquid used to determine the octane numbers of fuels.

i•so•pro•pyl alcohol (ī′sə-prō′pəl) *n.* A clear, colorless, mobile flammable liquid used in antifreeze compounds, solvents, lotions, and cosmetics.

i•sos•ce•les (ī-sŏs′ə-lēz′) *adj.* Having 2 equal sides <an *isosceles* triangle>

i•so•therm (ī′sə-thûrm′) *n.* A line on a map linking points having the same temperature. **–i′so•ther′mal** *adj.*

i•so•tope (ī′sə-tōp′) *n.* One of a set of atoms that contain in their nuclei the same number of protons but different numbers of neutrons. **–i′so•top′ic** (-tŏp′ĭk) *adj.* **–i′so•top′i•cal•ly** *adv.*

i•so•trop•ic (ī′sə-trŏp′ĭk) *adj.* Being the same in all directions. **–i•sot′ro•py** (ī-sŏt′rə-pē), **i•sot′ro•pism** (-pĭz′əm) *n.*

Is•ra•el (ĭz′rē-əl) *n.* **1.** The descendants of Jacob in the Bible. **2.** The Hebrew people. **3.** Country of SW Asia, on the Mediterranean. *Pop.* 3,920,000.

Is•rae•li (ĭz-rā′lē) *adj.* Of or pertaining to the country of Israel or its inhabitants. **–Is•rae′li** *n.*

Is•ra•el•ite (ĭz′rē-ə-līt′) *n.* A Hebrew. **–Is′ra•el•lite′** *adj.*

is•sue (ĭsh′o͞o) *n.* **1.** An act of flowing, going, or giving out. **2.** Something published or offered, as a stamp or a copy of a periodical. **3.** A final result : outcome. **4.** Something proceeding from a source <the *issue* of a creative mind> **5.** Offspring. **6.** A point of debate or discussion or dispute. **7.** A culmination. **8.** An outlet. **9.** *Pathol.* A discharge, as of pus or blood. *–v.* **-sued, -su•ing. 1.** To go or come out. **2.** To come or put forth. **3.** To distribute : give out <*issue* weapons> **4.** To be born or descended. **5.** To result. **6.** To publish or be published. **7.** To circulate. **–take issue.** To disagree. **–is′su•ance** *n.* **–is′su•er** *n.*

-ist *suff.* **1.** One that makes, operates, plays, or is connected with <novel*ist*> **2.** A specialist in <biolog*ist*> **3.** An adherent or advocate of <anarch*ist*> **4.** One characterized by <romantic*ist*>

Is•tan•bul (ĭs′tăn-bo͞ol′, ĭs′tän-). City of NW Turkey. *Pop.* 2,852,539.

isth•mus (ĭs′məs) *n.* A narrow strip of land connecting 2 larger land masses. **–isth′mi•an** *adj.*

it (ĭt) *pron.* **1.** That one previously mentioned. Used to refer to a nonhuman entity, an animal or human being of unknown sex, a group of persons, or an abstraction. **2.** Used as the subject of an impersonal verb <*It* is snowing.> **3.** Used to refer to a general state of affairs <couldn't stand *it*> *–n.* A player in a game who tries to catch or find the others.

ital. *abbr.* italic.

I•tal•ian•ate (ĭ-tăl′yə-nāt′, -nĭt) *adj.* Italian in character.

i•tal•ic (ĭ-tăl′ĭk, ī-tăl′-) *adj.* Of or being a style of printing type in which the letters slant to the right. *–n. often* **italics.** Italic typeface or print.

i•tal•i•cize (ĭ-tăl′ĭ-sīz′, ī-tăl′-) *v.* **-cized, -ciz•ing.** To print in italics. **–i•tal′i•ci•za′tion** *n.*

It•a•ly (ĭt′ə-lē). Country of S Europe, projecting into the Mediterranean. *Cap.* Rome. *Pop.* 57,230,000. **–I•tal′ian** *adj.* & *n.*

itch (ĭch) *n.* **1.** A skin sensation prompting a desire to scratch. **2.** A contagious skin disease characterized by a desire to scratch. **3.** A restless craving. **–itch** *v.* **–itch′i•ness** *n.* **–itch′y** *adj.*

-ite *suff.* **1.** A native or resident of <Manhattan*ite*> **2.** An adherent of <Trotsky*ite*> **3.** A mineral : rock <tekt*ite*> **4.** A commercial product <ebon*ite*>

i•tem (ī′təm) *n.* **1.** A separately specified article or unit in a series or list. **2.** A clause in a document. **3.** A piece of information : detail. **4.** A short article, as in a newspaper or magazine.

i•tem•ize (ī′tə-mīz′) *v.* **-ized, -iz•ing.** To detail item by item : list. **–i′tem•i•za′tion** *n.* **–i′tem•iz′er** *n.*

it•er•ate (ĭt′ə-rāt′) *v.* **-at•ed, -at•ing.** To say or do again : repeat. **–it′er•a′tion** *n.*

i•tin•er•ant (ī-tĭn′ər-ənt, ĭ-tĭn′-) *adj.* Traveling from place to place <an *itinerant* peddler> **–i•tin′er•ant** *n.*

i•tin•er•ar•y (ī-tĭn′ə-rĕr′ē, ĭ-tĭn′-) *n., pl.* **-ies. 1.** A route or scheduled route of a journey. **2.** A travelers' record of a journey. **3.** A guidebook.

it'll (ĭt′l). **1.** It will. **2.** It shall.

its (ĭts) *adj.* Of it. Used to indicate possession or the agent or recipient of an action <a dog wagging *its* tail>

it's (ĭts). **1.** It is. **2.** It has.

it•self (ĭt-sĕlf′) *pron.* The one identical with it. Used reflexively, for emphasis, and in certain idiomatic constructions <turns *itself* off> <in the machine *itself*><acting *itself* again>

-ity *suff.* A condition or quality <abnormal*ity*>

IU *abbr.* international unit.

I•van III (ī′vən). "the Great." 1440–1505. Grand Duke of Muscovy (1462–1505).

Ivan IV. "the Terrible." 1530–84. Czar of Russia (1547–84).

I've (īv). I have.

-ive *suff.* Acting or inclined to act in a specified way <prevent*ive*>

i•vied (ī′vēd) *adj.* Covered with ivy.

i•vo•ry (ī′və-rē, īv′rē) *n., pl.* **-ries. 1.** The hard, smooth, yellowish-white material that forms the tusks of elephants and certain other animals. **2.** A substance similar to ivory. **3.** An object made of ivory. **4.** A yellowish white. **–i′vo•ry** *adj.*

Ivory Coast. Country of W Africa. *Cap.* Abidjan. *Pop.* 8,390,000.

ivory tower *n.* A place or attitude of retreat, esp. preoccupation with remote, lofty, or intellectual considerations rather than mundane affairs.

i•vy (ī′vē) *n., pl.* **i•vies. 1.** A climbing or trailing plant of the genus *Hedera,* esp. *H. helix,* with lobed evergreen leaves. **2.** Any of various similar plants.

-ization *suff.* The action, process, or result of doing something specified <colon*ization*>

-ize *suff.* **1.** To cause to be or to resemble <drama*tize*><human*ize*> **2.** To become <material*ize*> **3.** To treat as <idol*ize*> **4.** To affect with <anesthet*ize*> **5.** To subject to <tyrann*ize*> **6.** To treat according to <pasteur*ize*> **7.** To engage in <botan*ize*>

Jj

j *or* **J** (jā) *n., pl.* **j's** *or* **J's. 1.** The 10th letter of the English alphabet. **2.** A speech sound represented by the letter *j*. **3.** Something with the shape of the letter J.
J *abbr.* joule.
J. *abbr.* **1.** journal. **2.** judge. **3.** justice.
J.A. *abbr.* **1.** joint account. **2.** judge advocate.
jab (jăb) *v.* **jabbed, jab•bing. 1.** To thrust or poke sharply. **2.** To hit with short punches. —*n.* A quick thrust or punch.
jab•ber (jăb′ər) *v.* To speak quickly or unintelligibly. **—jab′ber** *n.*
jab•ber•wock•y (jăb′ər-wŏk′ē) *n.* Nonsensical speech or writing that appears to make sense.
jab•ot (zhă-bō′, jă-) *n.* A decorative frill down the front of a shirt or dress.
jac•a•ran•da (jăk′ə-răn′də) *n.* **1.** A tropical American tree of the genus *Jacaranda,* with compound leaves and pale-purple flower clusters. **2.** The hard, brown wood of the jacaranda tree.

jacaranda

jack (jăk) *n.* **1.** *often* **Jack.** A man : fellow. **2.** A playing card ranking below a queen and bearing a representation of a knave. **3.** A device for lifting heavy objects. **4.** The male of certain animals, esp. the ass. **5. a. jacks** *(sing. or pl. in number).* A game played with a set of 6-pronged metal pieces and a ball. **b.** One of the metal pieces in the game of jacks. **6.** A socket into which a plug is inserted to make an electric circuit. **7.** A small flag on a ship, usu. indicating nationality. —*v.* **1.** To raise by means of a jack. **2.** To raise <*jacked* prices up>
jack•al (jăk′əl, -ôl′) *n.* A doglike mammal of the genus *Canis,* of Asia and Africa.
jack•a•napes (jăk′ə-nāps′) *n.* An impudent person.
jack•ass (jăk′ăs′) *n.* **1.** A male donkey or ass. **2.** A stupid person.
jack•boot (jăk′bo͞ot′) *n.* A stout military boot reaching above the knee.
jack•daw (jăk′dô′) *n.* An Old World bird, *Corvus monedula,* resembling the crow.
jack•et (jăk′ĭt) *n.* **1.** A short coat. **2.** An outer covering, as of a book.
jack•ham•mer (jăk′hăm′ər) *n.* A pneumatic tool for breaking pavement and drilling rock.
jack-in-the-box (jăk′ĭn-thə-bŏks′) *n.* A small box from which a puppet springs up when the lid is released.
jack-in-the-pul•pit (jăk′ĭn-*thə*-po͝ol′pĭt, -pŭl′-) *n.* A plant, *Arisaema triphyllum,* of E North America, with a leaflike spathe enclosing a clublike spadix.
jack•knife (jăk′nīf′) *n.* **1.** A large pocketknife. **2.** A dive executed by bending at the waist in midair and touching the feet with the hands before straightening out. —*v.* To bend or form an acute angle.
jack-of-all-trades (jăk′əv-ôl′trādz′) *n., pl.* **jacks-of-all-trades.** A person who is handy at many kinds of work.
jack-o′-lan•tern (jăk′ə-lăn′tərn) *n.* A hollowed-out pumpkin cut to look like a face and used as a lantern.
jack•pot (jăk′pŏt′) *n.* The cumulative stakes in certain games, as poker.
jack rabbit *n.* A large long-legged hare of the genus *Lepus* of W North America.
jack•screw (jăk′skro͞o′) *n.* A lifting jack operated by a screw.
Jack•son (jăk′sən). Cap. of Miss., in the WC part. *Pop.* 202,895.
Jack•son (jăk′sən), **Andrew.** 1767–1845. 7th U.S. President (1829–37).
Jack•son•ville (jăk′sən-vĭl′). City of NE Fla. *Pop.* 540,898.
Ja•cob (jā′kəb). Hebrew patriarch.
Ja•cob's ladder (jā′kəbz) *n.* A plant of the genus *Polemonium,* with blue flowers and paired ladderlike leaflets.
Ja•cuz•zi (jə-ko͞o′zē, jă-). A trademark for a device that swirls the water in a pool or bath.
jade[1] (jād) *n.* A hard, usu. green gemstone.
jade[2] (jād) *n.* **1.** A worn-out broken-down horse. **2.** A disreputable woman. —*v.* **jad•ed, jad•ing.** To tire or become tired.
jad•ed (jā′dĭd) *adj.* **1.** Worn-out : fatigued. **2.** Made dull by excess : sated. **—jad′ed•ly** *adv.* **—jad′ed•ness** *n.*
jag[1] (jăg) *n.* A sharp projection.
jag[2] (jăg) *n. Slang.* A binge or spree.
jag•ged (jăg′ĭd) *adj.* Having sharp or ragged projections. **—jag′ged•ly** *adv.* **—jag′ged•ness** *n.*
jag•uar (jăg′wär′, -yo͞o-är′) *n.* A large feline mammal, *Panthera onca,* of tropical America, with a tawny coat and black spots.
jai a•lai (hī′lī′, hī′ə-lī′, hī′ə-lī′) *n.* A game like handball in which players catch and propel a ball using a hand-shaped basket strapped to the wrist.
jail (jāl) *n.* A prison, esp. for temporary incarceration. —*v.* To detain in custody. ☆**syns:** IMMURE, IMPRISON, INCARCERATE, INTERN
jail•bird (jāl′bûrd′) *n. Informal.* A prisoner or former prisoner.
jail•break (jāl′brāk′) *n.* An escape from jail, usu. forcibly.
jail•er *also* **jail•or** (jā′lər) *n.* A person in charge of a jail.
†**jakes** (jāks) *n. (sing. in number) Regional.* A privy.
ja•lop•y (jə-lŏp′ē) *n., pl.* **-ies.** An old, run-down vehicle, esp. a car.
ja•lou•sie (jăl′ə-sē) *n.* A blind, window, or door with adjustable horizontal slats.
jam[1] (jăm) *v.* **jammed, jam•ming. 1.** To press or wedge into a tight position. **2.** To apply suddenly, as car brakes. **3.** To lock in an unworkable position. **4.** To crowd into and block. **5.** To clog or block. **6.** To crush. **7.** *Electron.* To make (broadcast signals) unintelligible by electronic means. **8.** *Mus.* To take part in a jazz session. —*n.* **1.** The act of jamming or state of being jammed. **2.** A congestion, as of traffic. **3.** *Informal.* A difficult situation.
jam[2] (jăm) *n.* A preserve of fruit boiled to a pulp with sugar.
Ja•mai•ca (jə-mā′kə). Island country in the Caribbean, S of Cuba. *Cap.* Kingston. *Pop.* 2,137,000. **—Ja•mai′can** *n.* & *adj.*
jamb (jăm) *n.* The vertical side piece of a door or window frame.
jam•ba•lay•a (jŭm′bə-lī′ə) *n.* A Creole dish of oysters, shrimp, and chicken or ham cooked with rice.
jam•bo•ree (jăm′bə-rē′) *n.* **1.** A large, festive gathering. **2.** A large assembly, as of Boy Scouts.
James (jāmz) *n.* See BIBLE TABLE.
James•town (jāmz′toun). Former village of SE Va., 1st permanent English settlement (1607) in the New World.
jam session *n.* Improvisation by a group of jazz musicians.
Jan. *abbr.* January.
jan•gle (jăng′gəl) *v.* **-gled, -gling. 1.** To make or cause to make a harsh, usu. metallic sound. **2.** To jar (the nerves). **—jan′gle** *n.* **—jan′gler** *n.*
jan•i•tor (jăn′ĭ-tər) *n.* A person who attends to cleaning and repairs in a building. **—jan′i•to′ri•al** *adj.*
Jan•u•ar•y (jăn′yo͞o-ĕr′ē) *n., pl.* **-ies.** The 1st month of the year, having 31 days.
ja•pan (jə-păn′) *n.* A black varnish producing a hard, shiny finish. **—ja•pan′** *v.*
Ja•pan (jə-păn′). **1.** Country of Asia, on an archipelago off the NE coast. *Cap.* Tokyo. *Pop.* 117,360,000. **2. Sea of.** Part of the Pacific between Japan and the Asian mainland. **—Jap′a•nese′** (-nēz′, -nēs′) *adj.* & *n.*
Japanese beetle *n.* A brown and green beetle, *Popillia japonica,* that is very damaging to plants.
jape (jāp) *v.* **japed, jap•ing.** To joke. **—jape** *n.* **—jap′er** *n.* **—jap′er•y** *n.*
jar[1] (jär) *n.* A cylindrical vessel with a wide mouth.
jar[2] (jär) *v.* **jarred, jar•ring. 1.** To make a discordant sound. **2.** To have a disturbing effect : grate. **3.** To jolt. **4.** To clash. —*n.* **1.** A jolt. **2.** A harsh sound.
jar•di•nière (jär′dn-îr′, zhär′dē-nyâr′) *n.* An ornamental pot or stand for plants.
jar•gon (jär′gən) *n.* **1.** Unintelligible talk. **2.** The specialized language of a trade or profession <computer *jargon*>
jas•mine (jăz′mĭn) *also* **jes•sa•mine** (jĕs′ə-mĭn) *n.* A vine or shrub, esp. *Jasminum officinalis* of Asia and *Gelsemium sempervirens* of SE U.S., with fragrant white or yellow flowers.
jas•per (jăs′pər) *n.* An opaque variety of quartz, usu. reddish, yellow, or brown.
ja•to (jā′tō) *n.* A takeoff assisted by an auxiliary rocket or jet.
jaun•dice (jôn′dĭs, jän′-) *n. Pathol.* Yellowish staining of the eyes, skin, and bodily fluids by bile pigment.
jaun•diced (jôn′dĭst, jän′-) *adj.* **1.** Affected with jaundice. **2.** Showing prejudice or malice.

jaunt (jônt, jänt) *n.* A short trip for pleasure. **—jaunt** *v.*
jaun·ty (jôn'tē, jän'-) *adj.* **-ti·er, -ti·est. 1.** Stylish. **2.** Buoyantly carefree and self-confident : sprightly. **—jaun'ti·ly** *adv.* **—jaun'ti·ness** *n.*
ja·va (jăv'ə, jä'və) *n. Informal.* Coffee.
Ja·va (jä'və, jăv'ə). Island of Indonesia SE of Sumatra. **—Jav'a·nese'** *adj.* & *n.*
jave·lin (jăv'lən, jăv'ə-) *n.* **1.** A light spear thrown as a weapon. **2.** A spear used in competitions of distance throwing.
jaw (jô) *n.* **1.** Either of 2 bony structures that hold the teeth and frame the mouth. **2.** Either of 2 hinged parts in a mechanical device. *—v. Slang.* To talk, esp. excessively.
jaw·bone (jô'bōn') *n.* A bone of the jaw, esp. the lower jaw. *—v.* To try to persuade by using one's influence.
jaw·break·er (jô'brā'kər) *n.* **1.** A hard piece of candy. **2.** *Slang.* A word that is hard to pronounce.
Jaws of Life. A trademark for a pincerlike metal device used to provide access to persons trapped inside a crushed vehicle.
jay[1] (jā) *n.* The letter j.
jay[2] (jā) *n.* A crested bird of the genera *Garrulus, Cyanocitta,* and *Aphelocoma,* related to the crows and often having a loud, harsh call.
Jay (jā), **John.** 1745–1829. Amer. statesman and jurist.
Jay·cee (jā'sē') *n.* A member of a junior chamber of commerce.
jay·walk (jā'wôk') *v.* To cross a street carelessly without obeying traffic regulations. **—jay'walk'er** *n.*
jazz (jăz) *n.* **1.** A kind of music first played by black musicians in S U.S., having a strong rhythmic structure with frequent syncopation and often involving solo and ensemble improvisations. **2.** *Slang.* **a.** Pretentious talk <all that legal *jazz*> **b.** Nonsense. *—v.* **1.** To play in a jazz style. **2.** *Slang.* To lie or exaggerate (to) <Don't *jazz* me.> **—jazz up.** *Informal.* To make more interesting : enliven. **—jazz'er** *n.* **—jazz'y** *adj.*
jct. *abbr.* junction.
J.D. *abbr.* Doctor of Laws.
jeal·ous (jĕl'əs) *adj.* **1.** Resentful or bitter in rivalry : envious. **2.** Inclined to suspect rivalry. **3.** Vigilant in guarding. **4.** Arising from feelings of envy or bitterness. **5.** Intolerant of infidelity. **—jeal'ous·ly** *adv.* **—jeal'ous·ness, jeal'ous·y** *n.*
jean (jēn) *n.* **1.** A strong, heavy cotton. **2. jeans.** Pants made of jean or denim.
Jeep (jēp) *n.* A trademark for a civilian motor vehicle.
jeer (jîr) *v.* To shout derisively : scoff. **—jeer** *n.* **—jeer'er** *n.* **—jeer'ing·ly** *adv.*
Jef·fer·son (jĕf'ər-sən), **Thomas.** 1743–1826. 3rd U.S. President (1801–9). **—Jef'fer·so'ni·an** (-sō'nē-ən) *adj.* & *n.*
Jef·fer·son City (jĕf'ər-sən). Cap. of Mo., in the C part. *Pop.* 33,619.
Je·ho·vah (jĭ-hō'və) *n.* God, esp in Christian translations of the Old Testament.
je·june (jĭ-jo͞on') *adj.* **1.** Insubstantial. **2.** Lacking interest : dull. **3.** Immature.
je·ju·num (jĭ-jo͞o'nəm) *n., pl.* **-na** (-nə). The part of the small intestine between the duodenum and the ileum.
jell (jĕl) *v.* **1.** To become or cause to become gelatinous. **2.** To take shape or cause to take shape.
jel·ly (jĕl'ē) *n., pl.* **-lies. 1.** A soft, semisolid food with a somewhat elastic consistency, made by the setting of a liquid containing pectin or gelatin. **2.** Something like jelly. **—jel'ly** *v.*
jel·ly·bean (jĕl'ē-bēn') *n.* A small ovoid candy with a hardened sugar coating.
jel·ly·fish (jĕl'ē-fĭsh') *n.* **1.** A usu. free-swimming marine coelenterate of the class Scyphozoa, having a gelatinous, tentacled, often bell-shaped medusoid stage as the dominant or only phase of its life cycle. **2.** *Informal.* A spineless weakling.
jel·ly·roll (jĕl'ē-rōl') *n.* A thin sheet of sponge cake layered with jelly and then rolled up.
jeop·ard·ize (jĕp'ər-dīz') *v.* **-ized, -iz·ing.** To expose to loss or danger.
jeop·ard·y (jĕp'ər-dē) *n.* Exposure to loss or danger : peril.
▲word history: The word *jeopardy* illustrates the human tendency to anticipate the worst in an uncertain situation. The French source of jeopardy, *jeu parti,* literally "divided game," orig. denoted a chess problem, and came to mean a position in any game for which the chances of either winning or losing were even. In English *jeopardy* retained the senses of the French word but extended them to mean "an uncertain or undecided situation." By Chaucer's time, the late 14th cent., *jeopardy* had acquired its modern sense of "peril."
jer·bo·a (jər-bō'ə) *n.* Any of various small, leaping rodents, with long hind legs, of the family Dipodidae, of Asia and Africa.
jer·e·mi·ad (jĕr'ə-mī'əd) *n.* A prolonged complaint or a tale of woe.
Jer·e·mi·ah (jĕr'ĕ-mī'ə) *n.* See BIBLE TABLE.
Jer·i·cho (jĕr'ĭ-kō'). Ancient city of Palestine, near the N end of the Dead Sea.
jerk (jûrk) *v.* **1.** To give a sharp pull or twist to. **2.** To make quick abrupt movements. *—n.* **1.** A sudden movement, as a pull or tug. **2.** A sudden spasmodic, muscular movement. **3.** *Slang.* A foolish or annoying person. ☆*syns:* SNAP, TUG, WRENCH, YANK **—jerk'i·ly** *adv.* **—jerk'i·ness** *n.* **—jerk'y** *adj.*
jer·kin (jûr'kĭn) *n.* A short, close-fitting jacket, usu. sleeveless.
jerk·wa·ter (jûrk'wô'tər, -wŏt'ər) *adj. Informal.* Of little importance.
jer·ry-build (jĕr'ē-bĭld') *v.* To build shoddily and cheaply. **—jer'ry·build'er** *n.*
jer·sey (jûr'zē) *n., pl.* **-seys. 1.** A soft knitted fabric. **2.** A knitted sweater, shirt, or jacket. **3.** *often* **Jersey.** A breed of fawn-colored dairy cattle yielding milk rich in butter fat.
Jersey City. City of NE N.J., on the Hudson. *Pop.* 223,532.
Je·ru·sa·lem (jə-ro͞o'sə-ləm, -zə-ləm). Cap. of Israel, in the EC part. *Pop.* 398,200.
jess (jĕs) *n.* A short strap fastened around the leg of a hawk or falcon, to which a leash may be attached. *—v.* To fasten jesses on. **—jessed** (jĕst) *adj.*
jes·sa·mine (jĕs'ə-mĭn) *n. var. of* JASMINE.
jest (jĕst) *n.* **1.** An act or remark intended to cause laughter. **2.** A playful mood <said only in *jest*> *—v.* **1.** To speak or act playfully. **2.** To make witty remarks.
jest·er (jĕs'tər) *n.* One given to jesting, esp. a fool at a medieval royal court.
Jes·u·it (jĕzh'o͞o-ĭt, jĕz'yo͞o-) *n.* A member of the Society of Jesus, a Roman Catholic order founded by Ignatius Loyola in 1534.
Je·sus (jē'zəs). 4? B.C.–A.D. 29? Founder of Christianity.
jet[1] (jĕt) *n.* **1.** A hard, black mineral that takes a high polish, used in jewelry. **2.** A deep black. **—jet** *adj.* **—jet'ty** *adj.*
jet[2] (jĕt) *n.* **1. a.** A gushing stream of liquid or gas emitted through a narrow opening forcefully. **b.** A nozzle for emitting such a stream. **2.** A jet airplane. *—v.* **jet·ted, jet·ting. 1.** To squirt. **2.** To travel by jet airplane. **3.** To move quickly.
jet airplane *n.* An airplane driven by jet propulsion.
je·té (zhə-tā') *n.* A leap in ballet.
jet engine *n.* **1.** An engine that develops thrust by the ejection of a gaseous jet of combustion products. **2.** An airplane engine equipped to consume atmospheric oxygen.
jet lag *n.* The psychological and physiological disruption of body rhythms resulting from high-speed air travel across several time zones.
jet-pro·pelled (jĕt'prə-pĕld') *adj.* Driven by jet propulsion.
jet propulsion *n.* Propulsion provided by the rearward expulsion of matter in a jet stream, esp. propulsion by jet engines.
jet·sam (jĕt'səm) *n.* **1.** Cargo jettisoned from a vessel in distress. **2.** Discarded cargo and equipment washed ashore.
jet set *n.* An international group of well-to-do people who go from one fashionable place to another for pleasure. **—jet setter** *n.*
jet stream *n.* **1.** A wind near the troposphere, gen. moving from a westerly direction at speeds often exceeding 250 mph or 400 kph. **2.** A high-speed stream : jet.
jet·ti·son (jĕt'ĭ-sən, -zən) *v.* **1.** To throw (cargo) overboard. **2.** To discard as useless or burdensome <*jettisoned* the diet plan>
jet·ty (jĕt'ē) *n., pl.* **-ties. 1.** A wall built out into a body of water to protect a harbor or influence the current. **2.** A pier.
Jew (jo͞o) *n.* **1.** A person whose religion is Judaism. **2.** A descendant of the ancient Hebrew people.
jew·el (jo͞o'əl) *n.* **1.** An expensive ornament for personal adornment made of precious metal set with gems. **2.** A gem. **3.** A small gem or gem substitute used as a bearing in a watch. **4.** One that is highly esteemed or valued. *—v.* **-eled, -el·ing** or **-elled, -el·ling.** To adorn or furnish with jewels. **—jew'el·ry** *n.*
jew·el·er *also* **jew·el·ler** (jo͞o'ə-lər) *n.* A person who makes or deals in jewelry.
Jew·ish (jo͞o'ĭsh) *adj.* Of, relating to, or typical of the Jews, their customs, or their religion. **—Jew'ish·ness** *n.*
Jew·ry (jo͞o'rē) *n.* The Jewish people as a group.
jew's-harp (jo͞oz'härp') *n.* A small musical instrument consisting of a U-shaped frame, held in the mouth, with a springy metal piece attached, that is plucked to produce twanging sounds.
Jez·e·bel (jĕz'ə-bĕl', -bəl) *n.* **1.** 9th cent. B.C. queen of Israel. **2. jezebel.** A scheming, shameless woman.
jib[1] (jĭb) *n. Naut.* A triangular sail set forward of the foremast.
jib[2] (jĭb) *v.* **jibbed, jib·bing.** To stop short : balk.
jibe[1] (jīb) *v.* **jibed, jib·ing.** To shift from one side of a vessel to the other, as a fore-and-aft sail.

jibe[2] (jīb) *v.* **jibed, jib•ing.** *Informal.* To be in accord.
jibe[3] (jīb) *v.* & *n. var. of* GIBE.
jif•fy (jĭf'ē) *also* **jiff** (jĭf) *n., pl.* **-fies** *also* **jiffs.** *Informal.* A very short time.
jig (jĭg) *n.* **1. a.** Any of various lively dances in triple time. **b.** The music for a jig. **2.** A device used to guide a tool. *—v.* **jigged, jig•ging. 1.** To dance a jig. **2.** To jerk up and down. **3.** To operate a jig.
jig•ger (jĭg'ər) *n.* **1.** A small measure for liquor, usu. holding 1½ oz. **2.** A gadget or device whose name eludes one.
jig•gle (jĭg'əl) *v.* **-gled, -gling.** To jerk lightly up and down. **—jig'gle** *n.*
jig•saw (jĭg'sô') *n.* A saw with a narrow, vertical blade, for cutting curves.
jigsaw puzzle *n.* A puzzle consisting of a mass of irregularly shaped pieces that form a picture when fitted together.
ji•had (jĭ-häd') *n.* A Moslem holy war against infidels.
jil•lion (jĭl'yən)*n. Informal.* A large, indeterminate number.
jilt (jĭlt) *v.* To discard (a lover). *—n.* A woman who discards a lover.
Jim Crow *n. Slang.* Discrimination against black people. **—Jim'-Crow'** *adj.* **—Jim'-Crow'ism** *n.*
jim•my (jĭm'ē) *n., pl.* **-mies.** A short crowbar, esp. one used by a burglar. *—v.* **-mied, -my•ing.** To force open with or as if with a jimmy.
jim•son•weed (jĭm'sən-wēd') *n.* A coarse, foul-smelling, poisonous plant, *Datura stramonium,* with large, trumpet-shaped purplish or white flowers.
jin•gle (jĭng'gəl) *v.* **-gled, -gling.** To make or cause to make a metallic clinking noise. *—n.* **1.** A jingling sound. **2.** A short, catchy rhyme or tune.
jin•go•ism (jĭng'gō-ĭz'əm) *n.* Extreme nationalism marked esp. by a belligerent foreign policy. **—jin'go, jin'go•ist** *n.* **—jin'go•is'tic** *adj.*
jin•ni (jĭn'ē, jĭ-nē') *n., pl.* **jinn** (jĭn). A spirit with supernatural powers for good or evil in Moslem legend.
jin•rik•sha (jĭn-rĭk'shô') *n.* A ricksha.
jinx (jĭngks) *n. Informal.* **1.** One thought to bring bad luck. **2.** A period of bad luck. *—v.* To bring bad luck to.
jit•ney (jĭt'nē) *n., pl.* **-neys.** *Informal.* A small bus carrying passengers for a low fare.
jit•ter (jĭt'ər) *v.* **-tered, -ter•ing.** To be nervous : fidget. *—n.* Nervous agitation <Exams give me the *jitters.*> **—jit'ter•y** *adj.*
jit•ter•bug (jĭt'ər-bŭg') *n.* **1.** A lively dance with various 2-step patterns and acrobatic maneuvers. **2.** One who performs this dance. **—jit'ter•bug'** *v.*
jive (jīv) *n. Slang.* **1.** Jazz or swing music. **2.** The specialized speech of jazz musicians and fans. **3.** Foolish or glib talk.
Joan of Arc (jōn'; ärk'), Saint. 1412–31. French heroine and military leader.
job (jŏb) *n.* **1.** A piece of work : task. **2.** Regular work done for payment. **3.** A specific piece of work to be done for a fee <a remodeling *job*> **4.** The position in which one is employed. **5.** A responsibility. *—v.* **jobbed, job•bing. 1.** To do odd jobs or piecework. **2.** To deal in (goods) as a jobber. **3.** To subcontract (work). **—job'less** *adj.* **—job'less•ness** *n.*
Job (jōb) *n.* See BIBLE TABLE.
job action *n.* A workers' strike or slowdown to protest a company decision or to win demands.
job•ber (jŏb'ər) *n.* **1.** One who buys goods in bulk and sells them to retailers. **2.** One who does piecework.
job control language *n. Computer Sci.* A language used for communicating with a computer's operating system.
job•hold•er (jŏb'hōl'dər) *n.* A person with a regular job.
job lot *n.* A miscellaneous assortment of items sold as 1 lot.
job•name (jŏb'nām') *n. Computer Sci.* A code assigned to a specific job instruction in a computer program for user reference.
jock (jŏk) *n. Slang.* A male athlete, esp. in college.
jock•ey (jŏk'ē) *n., pl.* **-eys.** A rider in horse races, esp. a professional. *—v.* **1.** To ride as jockey. **2.** To maneuver for advantage or position.
jo•cose (jō-kōs') *adj.* **1.** Given to joking : playful. **2.** Marked by joking : humorous. **—jo•cose'ly** *adv.* **—jo•cose'ness, jo•cos'i•ty** (-kŏs'ĭ-tē) *n.*
joc•u•lar (jŏk'yə-lər) *adj.* Marked by joking : playful : facetious. **—joc'u•lar'i•ty** (-lăr'ĭ-tē) *n.* **—joc'u•lar•ly** *adv.*
joc•und (jŏk'ənd, jō'kənd) *adj.* Merry : cheerful. **—jo•cun'di•ty** (jō-kŭn'dĭ-tē) *n.* **—joc'und•ly** *adv.*
jodh•purs (jŏd'pərz) *pl.n.* Wide-hipped riding breeches fitting tightly at the knees and ankes.
Jo•el (jō'əl) *n.* See BIBLE TABLE.
jog[1] (jŏg) *v.* **jogged, jog•ging. 1.** To move or shake slightly. **2.** To stir to activity <*jog* one's memory> **3.** To move or ride at a slow steady trot, esp. for sport or exercise. *—n.* **1.** A slight shake or nudge. **2.** A slow steady pace. **—jog'ger** *n.*
jog[2] (jŏg) *n.* **1.** A projecting or indented part in a surface or line. **2.** An abrupt shift in direction.
jog•gle (jŏg'əl) *v.* **-gled, -gling.** To shake slightly. **—jog'gle** *n.*
Jo•han•nes•burg (jō-hăn'ĭs-bûrg', yō-hä'nĭs-). Largest city of South Africa, in the NE part. *Pop.* 1,432,643.
john (jŏn) *n. Slang.* **1.** A toilet. **2.** A prostitute's client.
John[1] (jŏn) *n.* **1.** One of the 12 Apostles. **2.** See BIBLE TABLE.
John[2] 1167?–1216. King of England (1199–1216).
John XXIII. 1881–1963. Pope (1958–63).
John Doe (dō') *n. Law.* A fictitious or unidentified person.
John Han•cock (hăn'kŏk') *n. Informal.* A person's signature.
john•ny•cake (jŏn'ē-kāk') *n.* A thin, flat cornmeal bread.
John•ny-come-late•ly (jŏn'ē-kŭm-lāt'lē) *n., pl.* **-lies.** *Informal.* A latecomer, esp. a recent adherent to a cause or fashion.
John•ny Reb (jŏn'ē rĕb') *n. Informal.* A Confederate soldier.
John•son (jŏn'sən). **1. Samuel.** 1709–84. English lexicographer and author. **2. Andrew.** 1808–75. 17th U.S. President (1865–69). **3. Lyndon Baines.** 1908–73. 36th U.S. President (1963–69). **—John•so'ni•an** (-sō'nē-ən) *adj.*
John the Baptist, Saint. 5 B.C.-A.D. 30. Baptizer of Jesus.
joie de vi•vre (zhwa də vē'vrə) *n.* Lively enjoyment of life.
join (join) *v.* **1.** To put or come together. **2.** To bring or put into close association. **3.** To become a member of. **4.** *Math.* To connect (points), as with a straight line. **5.** To participate. ☆**syns:** CONNECT, LINK, UNITE *—n.* A joint : junction.
join•er (joi'nər) *n.* **1.** *esp. Brit.* A carpenter, esp. a cabinetmaker. **2.** *Informal.* One given to joining clubs and organizations.
joint (joint) *n.* **1.** A place where 2 or more things are joined. **2.** A point of connection between bones. **3.** A cut of meat that can be roasted. **4.** *Slang.* **a.** A shabby or disreputable gathering place. **b.** An establishment <ate at a *fancy* joint> **5.** *Slang.* A marijuana cigarette. *—adj.* **1.** Undertaken or shared by 2 or more <a *joint* tax return> **2.** Marked by cooperation <a *joint* effort> *—v.* **1.** To provide with a joint. **2.** To cut (meat) into joints. **—joint'ly** *adv.*
joint-stock company (joint'stŏk') *n.* a business whose capital is held in transferable shares of stock by its joint owners.
join•ture (join'chər) *n. Law.* **1.** An arrangement by which a husband sets aside property to be used for the support of his wife after his death. **2.** The property itself.
joist (joist) *n.* One of the parallel beams set from wall to wall to support a floor.

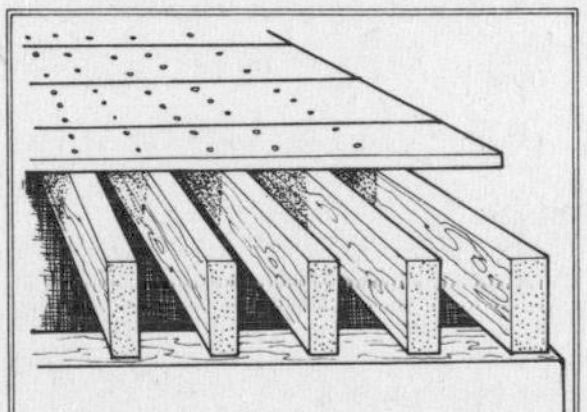

joist

joke (jōk) *n.* **1.** Something said to cause laughter, esp. a brief story with a punch line. **2.** A mischievous trick. **3.** A ridiculous situation. **4.** An object of amusement. ☆**syns:** GAG, JAPE, JEST, QUIP, WITTICISM *—v.* **joked, jok•ing. 1.** To play or tell jokes. **2.** To speak facetiously. **—jok'ing•ly** *adv.*
jok•er (jō'kər) *n.* **1.** One who jokes. **2.** An extra playing card, printed with a jester, used in certain games as a wild card. **3.** A clause in a document or legislative bill that changes or voids its purport. ☆**syns:** CARD, CLOWN, COMEDIAN, COMIC, HUMORIST, JESTER, WAG, WIT, ZANY
jol•li•fi•ca•tion (jŏl'ə-fĭ-kā'shən) *n.* Festivity : revelry.
jol•ly (jŏl'ē) *adj.* **-li•er, -li•est. 1.** Full of good humor : merry. **2.** Enjoyable. *—adv. esp. Brit.* Very <a *jolly* good swimmer> **—jol'li•ty** *n.* **—jol'ly** *v.*
jolt (jōlt) *v.* **1.** To shake or knock about. **2.** To move in a bumpy manner. **3.** To startle. *—n.* **1.** A sudden jarring or jerking. **2.** A sudden shock.
Jo•nah (jō'nə) *n.* See BIBLE TABLE.
Jones (jōnz), **John Paul.** 1747–92. Scottish-born Amer. naval officer.
jon•quil (jŏng'kwĭl, jŏn'-) *n.* A widely grown plant, *Narcissus jonquilla,* with long, narrow leaves and yellow flowers.
Jor•dan (jôrd'n). **1.** Country of SW Asia. *Cap.* Amman. *Pop.* 2,925,000. **2.** River of NE Israel and NW Jordan. **—Jor•da'ni•an** (jôr-dā'nē-ən) *adj.* & *n.*
Jo•seph (jō'zəf, -səf). Husband of Mary, the mother of Jesus.

josh (jŏsh) *v.* **1.** To tease. **2.** To joke.
Josh·u·a (jŏsh'o͞o-ə) *n.* See BIBLE TABLE.
joss (jŏs) *n.* A Chinese idol or image.
joss stick *n.* A stick of incense.
jos·tle (jŏs'əl) *v.* **-tled, -tling. 1.** To come into contact (with). **2.** To make one's way by pushing or shoving. **3.** To contend for a favorable position. **—jos'tle** *n.*
jot (jŏt) *n.* A tiny bit : iota. *—v.* **jot·ted, jot·ting.** To make a brief note of <*jot* down a phone number>
joule (jo͞ol, joul) *n.* A unit of energy equal to the work done by a force of 1 newton acting through a distance of 1 m.
jounce (jouns) *v.* **jounced, jounc·ing.** To bump : jolt. **—jounce** *n.* **—jounc'y** *adj.*
jour. *abbr.* **1.** journal; journalist. **2.** journeyman.
jour·nal (jûr'nəl) *n.* **1.** A personal daily record of experiences and observations : diary. **2.** An official record of daily proceedings, as of a legislative body. **3.** A book in which daily financial transactions are recorded. **4.** A newspaper. **5.** A periodical containing articles of specialized interest <a medical *journal*> **6.** The part of an axle supported by a bearing.
jour·nal·ese (jûr'nə-lēz', -lēs') *n.* The vocabulary and style of writing considered typical of most newspapers.
jour·nal·ism (jûr'nə-lĭz'əm) *n.* **1.** Collection, writing, editing, and dissemination of news through the media. **2.** Material written for publication in the media. **—jour'nal·ist** *n.* **—jour'nal·is'tic** *adj.* **—jour'nal·is'ti·cal·ly** *adv.*
jour·ney (jûr'nē) *n., pl.* **-neys. 1. a.** A trip, esp. one over a long distance. **b.** The distance traveled. **2.** A passage from one stage to another. *—v.* To travel.
jour·ney·man (jûr'nē-mən) *n.* **1.** One who has served an apprenticeship at a trade and works in another's employ. **2.** An experienced, capable worker.
▲word history: A *journeyman*, a skilled craftsman, is not an itinerant worker. *Journeyman* preserves an older sense of the word *journey* that reveals its origins. A *journeyman* was orig. a daily worker, one who worked for another for daily wages. He was distinguished from an apprentice, who was learning the trade, and a master artisan, who was in business for himself. *Journey* is derived from Old French *journee*, which meant "day," "day's work," and "day's travel." *Journee* is descended from Latin *diurnus*, "daily," from *dies*, "day." *Journee* in the sense "day's travel" developed in English into the word *journey*, "a trip."
joust (joust, jŭst, jo͞ost) *n.* A combat with lances between 2 knights on horseback, esp. as part of a medieval tournament. *—v.* To engage in a joust.
Jove (jōv) *interj.* Used to express surprise or emphasis <by *Jove*>
jo·vi·al (jō'vē-əl) *adj.* Good-humored : jolly. **—jo'vi·al'i·ty** (-ăl'ĭ-tē) *n.*
jowl¹ (joul) *n.* **1.** The lower jaw. **2.** The cheek.
jowl² (joul) *n.* **1.** Loose, flabby flesh under the lower jaw. **2.** A similar part, as a dewlap or wattle. **—jowl'y** *adj.*
joy (joi) *n.* **1.** Great happiness : delight. **2.** A source of happiness. **—joy'ful** *adj.* **—joy'ful·ly** *adv.* **—joy'ful·ness** *n.* **—joy'less** *adj.* **—joy'less·ly** *adv.* **—joy'less·ness** *n.*
Joyce (jois), **James.** 1882–1941. Irish novelist.
joy·ous (joi'əs) *adj.* Causing or feeling joy. **—joy'ous·ly** *adv.* **—joy'ous·ness** *n.*
joy ride *n.* A reckless ride at high speed, often in a stolen vehicle.
joy·stick (joi'stĭk') *n. Slang.* The control stick of an airplane.
J.P. *abbr.* justice of the peace.
jr. or **Jr.** *abbr.* junior.
ju·bi·lant (jo͞o'bə-lənt) *adj.* **1.** Exultingly joyful. **2.** Expressing joy. **—ju'bi·lance** *n.* **—ju'bi·lant·ly** *adv.*
ju·bi·la·tion (jo͞o'bə-lā'shən) *n.* **1.** Exultation. **2.** A happy celebration.
ju·bi·lee (jo͞o'bə-lē') *n.* **1.** A special anniversary, such as a 25th or 50th anniversary. **2.** A time of celebration.
Ju·dah (jo͞o'də). Ancient kingdom in S Palestine.
Ju·da·ic (jo͞o-dā'ĭk) *also* **Ju·da·i·cal** (-ĭ-kəl) *adj.* Of or relating to Judaism or Jews. **—Ju·da'i·cal·ly** *adv.*
Ju·da·ism (jo͞o'dē-ĭz'əm) *n.* The monotheistic religion of the Jewish people.
Ju·das (jo͞o'dəs) *n.* **1.** One of the 12 Apostles; betrayer of Jesus. **2.** One who betrays under the appearance of friendship.
Jude (jo͞od) *n.* See BIBLE TABLE.
Ju·de·a (jo͞o-dē'ə). *also* **Ju·dae·a.** Ancient region of S Palestine. **—Ju·de'an, Ju·dae'an** *adj.* & *n.*
judge (jŭj) *v.* **judged, judg·ing. 1.** *Law.* To pass judgment (on) in a court. **2.** To decide authoritatively after deliberation. **3.** To form an evaluation of. **4.** To have as an assumption : suppose. ☆**syns:** ADJUDGE, ADJUDICATE, ARBITRATE, DECIDE, DECREE, DETERMINE, REFEREE, RULE, UMPIRE *—n.* **1.** *Law.* A public official authorized to decide cases brought before a court. **2.** An arbiter designated to decide a competition or contest. **3.** One who can give an authoritative opinion : connoisseur. **4. Judges.** *(sing. in number).* See BIBLE TABLE. **—judge'ship'** *n.*
judg·ment *also* **judge·ment** (jŭj'mənt) *n.* **1.** The ability to make a decision or form an opinion. **2.** An authoritative opinion. **3.** An estimate. **4.** A decision reached after consideration, esp. the decision of an arbiter in a contest. **5.** *Law.* A determination of a court. **—judg·ment'al** *adj.*
ju·di·ca·ture (jo͞o'dĭ-kə-cho͝or', -chər) *n.* **1.** The administration of justice. **2.** Law courts or judges as a whole.
ju·di·cial (jo͞o-dĭsh'əl) *adj.* **1.** Of, relating to, or befitting courts of law or the administration of justice. **2.** Decreed or enforced by a court of law. **—ju·di'cial·ly** *adv.*
ju·di·ci·ar·y (jo͞o-dĭsh'ē-ĕr'ē) *n., pl.* **-ies. 1.** The judicial branch of government. **2. a.** A system of courts of law. **b.** Judges of these courts.
ju·di·cious (jo͞o-dĭsh'əs) *adj.* Having or exercising sound judgment. **—ju·di'cious·ly** *adv.* **—ju·di'cious·ness** *n.*
Ju·dith (jo͞o'dĭth) *n.* See BIBLE TABLE.
ju·do (jo͞o'dō) *n.* A form of self-defense developed from jujitsu that emphasizes principles of balance and leverage, often used as a method of physical training.
jug (jŭg) *n.* **1.** A small pitcher. **2.** A container for liquids with a narrow neck, a handle, and usu. a stopper. **3.** *Slang.* A jail.
jug·ger·naut (jŭg'ər-nôt') *n.* A massive and destructive force or object.
jug·gle (jŭg'əl) *v.* **-gled, -gling. 1.** To keep (several objects) in motion in the air at 1 time by alternately throwing and catching. **2.** To keep (several activities) in progress at 1 time. **3.** To manipulate so as to deceive or cheat <*juggled* the figures> **—jug'gler** *n.*
jug·u·lar (jŭg'yə-lər) *adj.* Of or situated in the region of the neck or throat. *—n.* A jugular vein.
jugular vein *n.* Any of various large veins of the neck.
juice (jo͞os) *n.* **1. a.** A natural fluid in plant or animal tissue. **b.** A bodily secretion. **2.** *Slang.* **a.** Electric current. **b.** Fuel for an engine. *—v.* **juiced, juic·ing.** To extract the juice from. **—juice up.** To add energy, power, or excitement to.
juic·er (jo͞o'sər) *n.* A device for extracting juice from fruit.
juic·y (jo͞o'sē) *adj.* **-i·er, -i·est. 1.** Full of juice. **2. a.** Interesting. **b.** Racy : titillating <*juicy* gossip> **—juic'i·ness** *n.*
ju·jit·su *also* **ju·jut·su** (jo͞o-jĭt'so͞o) *n.* A Japanese martial art using holds, throws, and stunning blows to subdue an opponent.
juke box (jo͞ok) *n.* A coin-operated automatic record player equipped with push buttons for the selection of records.
ju·lep (jo͞o'lĭp) *n.* A mint julep.
Jul·ian calendar (jo͞ol'yən) *n.* A calendar introduced by Julius Caesar in Rome in 46 B.C. that established the 12-month year of 365 days with a leap year every 4 years, eventually replaced by the Gregorian calendar.
ju·li·enne (jo͞o'lē-ĕn') *adj.* Cut into strips. Used of vegetables.
Ju·ly (jo͝o-lī', jo͞o-) *n.* The 7th month of the year, with 31 days.
jum·ble (jŭm'bəl) *v.* **-bled, -bling. 1.** To mix in a confused mass. **2.** To muddle : confuse. **—jum'ble** *n.*
jum·bo (jŭm'bō) *n., pl.* **-bos.** An exceptionally large person, animal, or object. *—adj.* Larger than average <*jumbo* shrimp>
jump (jŭmp) *v.* **1.** To spring into the air by a muscular effort of the legs and feet. **2.** To move suddenly <*jumped* out of the car> **3.** To move involuntarily, as in surprise. **4.** To leap over or cause to leap over. **5.** To spring at with the intent to censure. **6.** To arrive at hastily <*jump* to conclusions> **7.** To react eagerly so as to seize <*jump* at the bargain> **8.** To rise or increase suddenly. **9.** To skip <The typewriter *jumped* a space.> **10.** To take (an opponent's piece) in checkers by moving over it with one's own. **11.** *Computer Sci.* To move from one set of instructions in a program to another further behind or further ahead. **—jump bail.** To forfeit one's bail by absconding. *—n.* **1.** A leap. **2.** A barrier to be jumped. **3.** A sudden, involuntary movement. **4.** A sudden, sharp rise, as in salary.
jump·er¹ (jŭm'pər) *n.* **1.** One that jumps. **2.** A short length of wire used temporarily to by-pass or complete a circuit.
jum·per² (jŭm'pər) *n.* **1.** A sleeveless dress worn usu. over a blouse. **2.** A loose protective garment worn over other clothes. **3.** *often* **jumpers.** A child's pants attached to a biblike bodice.
jumping jack *n.* **1.** A puppet that can be made to dance by pulling on the strings attached to its limbs. **2.** A physical exercise performed by jumping to a position with legs spread wide and hands touching overhead and then back to a standing position with arms at the sides.
jumping mouse *n.* Any of various small rodents of the family Zapodidae, with a long tail and long hind legs.

jumping mouse

jump shot *n. Basketball.* A shot made by a player at the highest point of a jump.

jump-start (jŭmp′stärt′) *v.* To start (an automobile) by connecting a jumper cable from its battery to that of another car or by pushing the automobile and suddenly releasing the clutch. **—jump′-start′** *n.*

jump suit *n.* **1.** A parachutist's uniform. **2.** A 1-piece uniform worn by parachutists.

jump·y (jŭm′pē) *adj.* **-i·er, -i·est.** Jittery : nervous. **—jump′i·ness** *n.*

jun (jŏŏn) *n., pl.* **jun.** See *won* at CURRENCY TABLE.

jun. or **Jun.** *abbr.* junior.

junc. *abbr.* junction.

jun·co (jŭng′kō) *n., pl.* **-cos.** A North American finch of the genus *Junco,* having mainly gray plumage.

junc·tion (jŭngk′shən) *n.* **1.** The process of joining or the state of being joined. **2.** The place where 2 things meet, esp. the place where 2 streets join.

junc·ture (jŭngk′chər) *n.* **1.** The point at which 2 things join. **2.** A point in time, esp. a critical one.

June (jo͞on) *n.* The 6th month of the year, having 30 days.

Ju·neau (jo͞o′nō). Cap. of Alas., in the SE panhandle. *Pop.* 19,528.

June beetle or **June bug** *n.* Any of various North American beetles of the subfamily Melolonthinae, with larvae that live in the soil and often destroy crops.

jun·gle (jŭng′gəl) *n.* **1.** Land covered by dense tropical vegetation. **2.** A dense thicket or growth. **3.** An environment marked by ruthless struggling to survive.

jun·ior (jo͞on′yər) *adj.* **1.** Younger. Used to distinguish the son from the father of the same name. **2.** Intended for or including young people. **3.** Of lower rank or shorter period of tenure <the *junior* partner> **4.** Of or relating to the 3rd year of a U.S. high school or college. *—n.* **1.** One younger than another. **2.** One lower in rank or period of service. **3.** A 3rd-year student in a U.S. high school or college.

junior college *n.* An educational institution offering a 2-year course gen. equivalent to the 1st 2 years of a 4-year undergraduate course.

junior high school *n.* A U.S. school that gen. includes the 7th, 8th, and sometimes 9th grades.

ju·ni·per (jo͞o′nə-pər) *n.* An evergreen tree or shrub of the genus *Juniperus,* having scalelike, often prickly foliage, fragrant wood, and bluish-gray berries.

junk[1] (jŭngk) *n.* **1.** Discarded materials such as glass, paper, rags, and metal that can be used for other purposes. **2.** *Informal.* Something fit to be discarded : trash. **3.** *Informal.* Nonsense. **4.** *Slang.* Heroin. *—v.* To throw away as useless.

junk[2]

junk[2] (jŭngk) *n.* A Chinese flat-bottomed ship with battened sails.

jun·ket (jŭng′kĭt) *n.* **1.** A custardlike dessert of flavored milk set with rennet. **2.** A party, banquet, or outing. **3.** A trip taken by an official and paid for with public funds. **—jun′ket** *v.* **—jun′ket·er** *n.*

▲word history: The transitional stage between the meanings "a food" and "a trip" for *junket* is found in the meaning "picnic." The most recent sense, "a trip taken by a public official at public expense," developed in the U.S. and has acquired decidedly negative connotations.

junk food *n.* Food with little nutritional value in proportion to the number of calories it contains.

junk·ie *also* **junk·y** (jŭng′kē) *n., pl.* **-ies.** *Slang.* **1.** A drug addict, esp. one using heroin. **2.** One with a consuming interest in something <a soap opera *junkie*>

junk mail *n.* Mail of little interest to its recipient, usu. advertisements mailed in bulk.

junk·yard (jŭngk′yärd′) *n.* An area used for storing junk, as scrap metal, that can be resold.

Ju·no·esque (jo͞o′nō-ĕsk′) *adj.* Having a stately bearing and regal beauty.

jun·ta (ho͝on′tə, ho͞on′-, jŭn′-) *n.* A group of persons, esp. military officers, in power following a coup d'état.

Ju·pi·ter (jo͞o′pĭ-tər) *n. Astron.* The 5th planet from the sun and the largest in the solar system, having a diameter of approx. 88,000 mi or 142,000 km.

ju·rid·i·cal (jo͝o-rĭd′ĭ-kəl) *also* **ju·rid·ic** (-ĭk) *adj.* Of or relating to the administration of the law.

ju·ris·dic·tion (jo͝or-ĭs-dĭk′shən) *n.* **1.** The right or power to interpret and apply the law. **2.** Authority or control. **3.** The territorial range over which an authority extends. **—ju′ris·dic′tion·al** *adj.*

ju·ris·pru·dence (jo͝or′ĭs-pro͞od′ns) *n.* **1.** The science or philosophy of law. **2.** A division or department of law.

ju·rist (jo͝or′ĭst) *n.* An expert in the law.

ju·ris·tic (jo͝o-rĭs′tĭk) *also* **ju·ris·ti·cal** (-tĭ-kəl) *adj.* **1.** Of or relating to jurisprudence or a jurist. **2.** Of or relating to legality or law.

ju·ror (jo͝or′ər, -ôr′) *n.* One who serves on a jury.

ju·ry (jo͝or′ē) *n., pl.* **-ries.** **1.** A group of people called by law and sworn to hear evidence in a case and give a verdict. **2.** A committee to select winners in a contest.

just (jŭst) *adj.* **1.** Fair in one's dealings and actions <a *just* king> **2.** Morally right. **3.** Deserved : merited <*just* deserts> **4.** Legitimate. **5.** Proper : fitting <*just* proportions> **6.** Based on sound reason. *—adv.* (jəst, jĭst; jŭst *when stressed).* **1.** Exactly. **2.** A very short time before <*just* left> **3.** By a narrow margin : barely <*just* missed the bus> **4.** Only a little distance <*just* down the street> **5.** Merely : simply <I *just* said it in jest> **6.** Really <*just* lovely> **—just the same.** Nevertheless. **—just′ly** *adv.* **—just′ness** *n.*

jus·tice (jŭs′tĭs) *n.* **1.** The principle of ideal or moral rightness. **2.** The upholding of what is right : fairness. **3.** The administration of law. **4.** A judge.

justice of the peace *n.* A local magistrate empowered to try minor cases, administer oaths, and perform marriages.

jus·ti·fy (jŭs′tə-fī′) *v.* **-fied, -fy·ing.** **1.** To show to be right or valid. **2.** To pronounce free from blame or guilt. **3.** To adjust or space (lines) to the proper length in printing. **—jus′ti·fi′a·ble** *adj.* **—jus′ti·fi′a·bly** *adv.* **—jus′ti·fi·ca′tion** *n.*

Jus·tin·i·an I (jŭ-stĭn′ē-ən). 483–565. Roman emperor of the East (527–65).

jut (jŭt) *v.* **jut·ted, jut·ting.** To protrude : project. **—jut** *n.*

jute (jo͞ot) *n.* Either of 2 Asian plants, *Corchorus capsularis* or *C. olitorius,* yielding a strong, coarse fiber used to make sacking and rope.

Ju·ve·nal (jo͞o′və-nəl). A.D. 60?–140? Roman satirist.

ju·ve·nile (jo͞o′və-nəl, -nīl′) *adj.* **1.** Not yet adult : young. **2.** Childish : immature. **3.** Intended or suitable for children or young people. *—n.* **1.** A young person. **2.** An actor who plays youthful roles. **3.** A children's book. **—ju′ve·nile·ness** *n.*

jux·ta·pose (jŭk′stə-pōz′) *v.* To put side by side. **—jux′ta·posed** *adj.* **—jux′ta·po·si′tion** *n.*

Kk

k or **K** (kā) *n., pl.* **k's** or **K's.** **1.** The 11th letter of the English alphabet. **2.** A speech sound represented by the letter *k.* **3.** *Computer Sci.* A unit of storage capacity equal to 1024 bytes.
k *abbr.* karat.
K *symbol for* POTASSIUM.
K *abbr.* Kelvin.
ka·bob (kə-bŏb′) *n.* Shish kebab.
ka·bu·ki (kä-bo͞o′kē, kə-) *n.* Traditional Japanese drama in which dances and songs are performed in a stylized manner.
Ka·bul (kä′bo͝ol). Cap. of Afghanistan, in the EC part. *Pop.* 318,094.
Kad·dish (kä′dĭsh) *n.* A Jewish prayer recited at the daily service and by mourners after the death of a relative.
kaf·fee klatsch (kô′fē klăch′, kä′fē klăch′) *n. var. of* COFFEE KLATCH.
Kaf·ka (käf′kä), **Franz.** 1883–1924. Austrian novelist. **–Kaf′ka·esque′** *adj.*
kaf·tan (kăf′tən, kăf-tăn′) *n. var. of* CAFTAN.
Kai·ser (kī′zər) *n.* An emperor, esp. a German emperor from 1871–1918.
kale (kāl) *n.* A cabbage, *Brassica oleracea acephala,* with crinkled leaves not forming a tight head.
ka·lei·do·scope (kə-lī′də-skōp′) *n.* **1.** A tubular instrument rotated to produce successive symmetric designs by means of mirrors reflecting the changing patterns made by bits of loose colored glass at the end of the tube. **2.** A series of continuously changing colors. **3.** A series of changing events or phases. **–ka·lei′do·scop′ic** (-skŏp′ĭk), **ka·lei′do·scop′i·cal** *adj.* **–ka·lei′do·scop′i·cal·ly** *adv.*
kal·ends (kăl′əndz, kā′ləndz) *n. var. of* CALENDS.
Kam·chat·ka (kăm-chăt′kə). Peninsula of NE Siberian USSR.
kame (kām) *n.* A short ridge of gravel and sand deposited by melting glacial ice.
ka·mi·ka·ze (kä′mĭ-kä′zē) *n.* **1.** A Japanese pilot in World War II who was trained to make a suicidal crash on a target. **2.** An aircraft loaded with explosives used in a suicide attack.
Kam·pu·che·a (kăm′pə-chē′ə, -po͞o-). Cambodia.
kan·ga·roo (kăng′gə-ro͞o′) *n., pl.* **-roo** or **-roos.** Any of various herbivorous marsupials of the family Macropodidae, of Australia, with short forelegs, large hind limbs adapted for jumping, and a long tail.
kangaroo court *n.* An illegal, self-appointed court, esp. one marked by dishonesty or incompetence.
Kan·sas (kăn′zəs). State of C U.S. *Cap.* Topeka. *Pop.* 2,363,208. **–Kan′san** *n.*
Kansas City. **1.** City of NE Kans., on the Missouri R. *Pop.* 161,087. **2.** City of W Mo., WNW of St. Louis. *Pop.* 448,159.
Kant (kănt, känt), **Immanuel.** 1724–1804. German philosopher. **–Kant′i·an** *adj.*
Kao·hsiung (gou′shē-o͝ong′). Port city of SW Taiwan. *Pop.* 1,172,977.
ka·o·lin *also* **ka·o·line** (kā′ə-lĭn) *n.* A fine clay used in ceramics.
ka·pok (kā′pŏk′) *n.* A silky fiber derived from the fruit of the silk-cotton tree and used for insulation and as padding in mattresses, pillows, and life preservers.
ka·put (kä-po͝ot′) *adj. Informal.* **1.** Destroyed : wrecked. **2.** Out of order.
Ka·ra·chi (kə-rä′chē). City of SE Pakistan, on the Arabian Sea. *Pop.* 3,498,600.
kar·a·kul (kăr′ə-kəl) *n.* One of a breed of C Asian sheep with a pelt that is curly and shiny in the young but coarse and wiry in the adult.
kar·at (kăr′ət) *n.* A unit of measure for the fineness of gold, equal to 1/24 of the total amount of pure gold in an alloy.
ka·ra·te (kə-rä′tē, kä-rä′tā) *n.* A Japanese art of self-defense in which sharp blows and kicks are administered to pressure-sensitive points of an opponent's body.
kar·ma (kär′mə, kûr′mə) *n.* **1.** The total effect of one's conduct, believed in Buddhism and Hinduism to determine one's destiny in a future life. **2.** Fate. **3.** *Informal.* Aura or atmosphere. **–kar′mic** (-mĭk) *adj.*
karst (kärst) *n.* An area of irregular limestone where erosion has produced sinkholes, caverns, and underground streams.
kart (kärt) *n.* A miniature racing car.
Kat·man·du (kät′män-do͞o′). Cap. of Nepal, in the C part. *Pop.* 105,400.
ka·ty·did (kā′tē-dĭd′) *n.* Any of various green insects related to the grasshoppers and the crickets, with specialized organs on the wings of the male that make a shrill sound when rubbed together.
Ka·wa·sa·ki (kä′wə-sä′kē). City of Japan, on Tokyo Bay. *Pop.* 1,040,698.
kay (kā) *n.* The letter *k.*
kay·ak (kī′ăk′) *n.* A watertight Eskimo canoe having a light frame covered with skins except for an opening in the center.
kay·o (kā′ō, kā′ō′) *n., pl.* **-os.** *Slang.* A knockout in boxing. **–kay′o** *v.*
Ka·zakh (kə-zäk′, kä-) *also* **Ka·zakh·stan** (kə-zäk′stän′, zäk′stän′, kä′-). Region of Central Asian USSR, NE of the Caspian Sea.
Ka·zan (kə-zän′). City of E European USSR, on the Volga E of Moscow. *Pop.* 1,002,000.
ka·zoo (kə-zo͞o′) *n., pl.* **-zoos.** A toy musical instrument with a paper membrane that produces buzzing tones when a player hums or sings into the mouthpiece.
kc *abbr.* kilocycle.
Keats (kēts), **John.** 1795–1821. English poet. **–Keats′i·an** *adj.*
ke·bab *also* **ke·bob** (kə-bŏb′) *n.* Shish kebab.
kedge (kĕj) *n.* A small anchor.
keel[1] (kēl) *n.* **1. a.** The main structural member of a ship, running lengthwise along the center line from stern to bow, to which the frames are attached. **b.** A similar structure in an aircraft. **2.** Something that resembles a ship's keel in shape or function, as the breastbone of a bird. *–v.* To capsize. **–keel over.** **1.** To fall over suddenly. **2.** To faint.
†**keel**[2] (kēl) *v. Regional.* To make cool.
keel·haul (kēl′hôl′) *v.* To drag under the keel of a ship as a punishment.
keel·son (kēl′sən, kĕl′-) *n. Naut.* A timber fastened above and parallel to the keel to give additional strength.
keen[1] (kēn) *adj.* **1.** Having a sharp edge or point. **2.** Intellectually acute. **3.** Highly sensitive. **4.** Strong : intense <a *keen* winter wind> **5.** Pungent. **6.** Enthusiastic. **7.** *Slang.* Great : wonderful. **–keen′ly** *adv.* **–keen′ness** *n.*
keen[2] (kēn) *n.* A wailing lament for the dead. **–keen** *v.*
keep (kēp) *v.* **kept** (kĕpt), **keep·ing.** **1.** To retain possession of. **2.** To have as a supply. **3.** To provide with maintenance and support <*kept* a large family on a small income> **4.** To store customarily <*kept* the bread knife in the drawer> **5.** To tend : manage. **6.** To continue or cause to continue in a given state or course of action. **7.** To detain : confine. **8.** To refrain from divulging <*keep* secrets> **9.** To adhere to. **10.** To celebrate. **11.** To remain fresh or unspoiled. ☆***syns:*** RESERVE, RETAIN, WITHHOLD **–keep down.** To prevent from succeeding. **–keep up.** **1.** To maintain in good condition. **2.** To persevere in. **3.** To continue without interruption. *–n.* **1.** Care : custody. **2.** A means of support <earn one's *keep*> **3.** A castle's stronghold. **4.** A jail. **–for keeps.** **1.** Forever : permanently <gave it to me *for keeps*> **–keep at it.** To persevere. **–keep (one's) nose clean.** To keep out of trouble. **–keep′er** *n.*
keep·sake (kēp′sāk′) *n.* A memento.
keg (kĕg) *n.* A small barrel.
keg·ler (kĕg′lər) *n.* A bowler.
Kel·ler (kĕl′ər), **Helen Adams.** 1880–1968. Amer. author and lecturer.
kelp (kĕlp) *n.* Any of various large brown seaweeds of the order Laminariales.
kel·pie[1] *also* **kel·py** (kĕl′pē) *n., pl.* **-pies.** *Scot.* A legendary malevolent water spirit.
kel·pie[2] (kĕl′pē) *n.* A sheep dog orig. bred in Australia.
Kelt (kĕlt) *n. var. of* CELT.
Kelt·ic (kĕl′tĭk) *n.* & *adv. var. of* CELTIC.
Kel·vin (kĕl′vĭn) *adj.* Designating or relating to a temperature scale whose zero point is approx. –273.16°C.
†**ken** (kĕn) *v.* **kenned** or **kent, ken·ning.** **1.** *Scot.* To know (a person or thing). **2.** *Regional.* To recognize. *–n.* **1.** Range of understanding. **2.** Range of vision.
Ken·ne·dy (kĕn′ə-dē), **John Fitzgerald.** 1917–63. 35th U.S. President (1961–63); assassinated.
ken·nel (kĕn′əl) *n.* **1.** A shelter for a dog. **2.** A place where dogs are bred, boarded, or trained. **–ken′nel** *v.*
ke·no (kē′nō) *n.* A game of chance resembling lotto in which balls rather than counters are used.
Ken·tuck·y (kən-tŭk′ē). State of EC U.S. *Cap.* Frankfort. *Pop.* 3,661,433. **–Ken·tuck′i·an** *adj.* & *n.*
Kentucky bluegrass *n.* Bluegrass.
Ken·ya (kĕn′yə, kēn′-). Country of EC Africa. *Cap.* Nairobi. *Pop.* 15,322,000. **–Ken′yan** *adj.* & *n.*
kep·i (kā′pē, kĕp′ē) *n., pl.* **-is.** A military visored cap with a flat round top.
kept (kĕpt) *v. p.t.* & *p.p. of* KEEP.
ker·a·tin (kĕr′ə-tən) *n.* A strong, fibrous protein that is the

basic substance of nails, hair, horns, and hoofs. **–ke•rat'i•nous** (kə-răt'n-əs) *adj.*
kerb (kûrb) *n. esp. Brit. var. of* CURB 2.
ker•chief (kûr'chĭf) *n.* **1.** A piece of cloth worn over the head or around the neck : scarf. **2.** A handkerchief.
ker•nel (kûr'nəl) *n.* **1.** A grain or seed, as of a cereal plant, enclosed in a hard husk. **2.** The inner, usu. edible part of a nut. **3.** The central, most important part.
ker•o•sene *also* **ker•o•sine** (kĕr'ə-sēn', kĕr'ə-sēn') *n.* A thin oil distilled from petroleum and used as a fuel and solvent.
kes•trel (kĕs'trəl) *n.* A small European falcon, *Falco tinnunculus,* with gray and brown plumage.
ketch (kĕch) *n.* A fore-and-aft-rigged sailing vessel with 2 masts.
ketch•up (kĕch'əp, kăch'-) *n.* A spicy, thick, smooth sauce, esp. one made from tomatoes.
ket•tle (kĕt'l) *n.* **1.** A metal pot, usu. with a lid, for boiling or stewing. **2.** A teakettle.
ket•tle•drum (kĕt'l-drŭm') *n.* A large copper or brass hemispherical drum with a parchment head that can be tuned by adjusting the tension.
key[1] (kē) *n., pl.* **keys. 1. a.** A usu. metal notched device for opening or closing a lock. **b.** A device resembling a key, as for winding a clock. **2.** A means of access, control, or possession. **3. a.** A crucial element. **b.** A solution to a test. **c.** A code or table for solving or explaining. **4. a.** A button or lever pressed to operate a machine. **b.** A lever pressed by a finger in playing a musical instrument, as a piano. **5.** *Mus.* A tonal system consisting of 7 tones in fixed relationship to a tonic. **6.** The pitch of a voice. **9.** A characteristic level of intensity or tone. *–v.* **1.** To regulate the musical pitch of. **2.** To bring into harmony : adjust. **3.** To supply an explanatory key for. *–adj.* Of crucial importance. **–key up.** To make nervous.
key[2] (kē) *n., pl.* **keys.** A reef or low island.
Key, Francis Scott. 1779–1843. Amer. lawyer and poet.
key•board (kē'bôrd', -bōrd') *n.* A series of keys, as on a piano, typewriter, or word processor. *–v.* **1.** To set by means of a keyed typesetting machine. **2.** To generate (e.g., documents) by means of a word processor.
key club *n.* A private club serving liquor and offering entertainment.
key•hole (kē'hōl') *n.* A hole into which a key is inserted.
Keynes (kānz), **John Maynard.** 1883–1946. English economist. **–Keynes'i•an** *adj.* & *n.*
key•note (kē'nōt') *n.* **1.** *Mus.* The tonic of a key. **2.** A central idea. *–v.* **1.** To give the keynote of. **2.** To give the keynote address at.
keynote address *n.* An opening speech, as at a political convention, outlining the issues for discussion.
key•punch (kē'pŭnch') *n.* A machine with a keyboard used to punch holes in tapes or cards for data-processing systems. **–key'punch'** *v.* **–key'punch'er** *n.*
key signature *n. Mus.* The group of sharps or flats at the right of the clef on a staff identifying the key.
key•stone (kē'stōn') *n.* **1.** The wedge-shaped stone at the top of an arch that locks its parts together. **2.** A central supporting element.
key•stroke (kē'strōk') *n.* A stroke of a key, as of a typewriter or word processor.
Key West. City of extreme S Fla., on **Key West Is.,** westernmost of the Florida Keys in the Gulf of Mexico. *Pop.* 24,292.
kg *abbr.* kilogram.
khak•i (kăk'ē, kä'kē) *n., pl.* **-is. 1.** A yellowish brown. **2. a.** A sturdy cloth of the color khaki. **b. khakis.** A uniform of khaki cloth. **–khak'i** *adj.*
khan (kän, kăn) *n.* **1.** A chieftain or man of importance in India and some C Asian countries. **2.** A medieval Turkish, Mongolian, or Tartar ruler. **–khan'ate'** *n.*
Khar•kov (kär'kôf', -kôv'). City of SC European USSR, E of Kiev. *Pop.* 1,464,000.
Khar•toum (kär-to͞om'). Cap. of Sudan, in the EC part. *Pop.* 333,921.
khe•dive (kə-dēv') *n.* A Turkish viceroy ruling Egypt from 1867–1914.
khoum (ko͞om, ko͝om) *n.* See *ouguiya* at CURRENCY TABLE.
Khru•shchev (kroosh-chĕf', -chôf'), **Nikita Sergeyevich.** 1894–1971. Soviet statesman.
Khy•ber (kī'bər). Pass through the mountains between Afghanistan and Pakistan.
kib•butz (kĭ-bo͝ots') *n., pl.* **-but•zim** (-bo͝ot'sēm'). An Israeli collective farm.
kib•itz (kĭb'ĭts, kĭ-bĭts) *n. Informal.* To look on and offer unwanted, usu. meddlesome advice to others. **–kib'itz•er** *n.*
ki•bosh (kī'bŏsh') *n.* A check or restraint.
kick (kĭk) *v.* **1.** To strike or strike out with the foot. **2.** *Sports.* **a.** To strike a ball with the foot. **b.** To propel (a ball) by striking it with the foot. **3.** To recoil, as a firearm when fired. **4.** *Informal.* To protest vigorously : object. **–kick around.** *Informal.* **1.** To treat badly. **2.** To move from place to place. **3.** To consider (an idea). **–kick in.** *Slang.* **1.** To contribute (one's share). **2.** To die. **–kick off. 1.** To begin or resume play in a sport with a kickoff. **2.** To begin. *n.* **1. a.** A blow with the foot. **b.** The thrusting motion of the legs in swimming. **2.** The recoil of a firearm. **3.** *Slang.* A complaint. **4.** *Slang.* Pleasurable stimulation. **5.** *Slang.* A temporary enthusiasm. **–kick the bucket.** *Slang.* To die. **–kick upstairs.** *Informal.* To promote to a higher yet less desirable position.
kick•back (kĭk'băk') *n.* **1.** *Slang.* A secret payment to a person who is in a position to influence a source of income. **2.** A very strong reaction : repercussion.
kick•off (kĭk'ôf', -ŏf') *n.* **1.** A kick, as in football or soccer, that begins play. **2.** A beginning.
kick•stand (kĭk'stănd') *n.* A swiveling metal bar for holding a 2-wheeled vehicle upright when not in use.
kick•y (kĭk'ē) *adj.* **-i•er, -i•est.** *Slang.* Providing excitement by being unusual or unconventional.
kid (kĭd) *n.* **1.** A young goat. **2.** Leather made from the skin of a young goat. **3.** *Informal.* A child. *–v.* **kid•ded, kid•ding.** *Informal.* **1.** To mock playfully : tease. **2.** To deceive for fun : fool. **–kid'der** *n.*
kid•dy *also* **kid•die** (kĭd'ē) *n., pl.* **-dies.** *Slang.* A small child.
kid•nap (kĭd'năp') *v.* **-naped, -nap•ing** or **-napped, -nap•ping.** To seize and hold (a person) unlawfully, often for ransom. ☆**syns:** ABDUCT, CARRY OFF, SNATCH, SPIRIT **–kid'nap'er** *n.*
kid•ney (kĭd'nē) *n., pl.* **-neys.** Either of a pair of organs located in the abdominal cavity of vertebrates close to the back that function to keep proper water balance in the body and excrete wastes in the form of urine.
kidney bean *n.* A bean, *Phaseolus vulgaris,* grown for its edible seeds.
kid•vid (kĭd'vĭd') *n. Slang.* Television programs for children.
Kiel (kēl). Seaport of N West Germany.
kiel•ba•sa (kēl-bä'sə, kĭl-, kēl-) *n.* A smoked Polish sausage.
Ki•ev (kē-ĕv', kē'ĕf). City of W European USSR, on the Dnieper. *Pop.* 2,192,000.
Ki•ga•li (kĭ-gä'lē). Cap. of Rwanda, in the C part. *Pop.* 117,700.
Kil•i•man•ja•ro (kĭl'ə-mən-jär'ō). Highest mountain (19,340 ft/5,898.7 m) in Africa, in NE Tanzania.
kill (kĭl) *v.* **1.** To cause the death of. **2.** To pass (time) in aimless activity. **3.** To cause extreme pain to. **4.** To delete. **5.** To thwart passage of <*kill* a legislative bill> ☆**syns:** DESTROY, DISPATCH, FINISH, SLAY, ZAP *–n.* **1.** An act of killing. **2.** An animal killed, esp. in hunting. **–kill'er** *n.*
kill•deer (kĭl'dîr') *n., pl.* **killdeer** or **-deers.** A New World bird, *Charadrius vociferus,* having a distinctive cry.
killer whale *n.* A black and white predatory whale, *Orcinus orca,* inhabiting cold seas.
kill•ing (kĭl'ĭng) *n.* **1.** A murder. **2.** A sudden large profit. *–adj.* **1.** Fatal. **2.** Exhausting. **3.** *Informal.* Extremely funny.
kill•joy (kĭl'joi') *n.* One who spoils the fun of others.
kiln (kĭl, kĭln) *n.* An oven for hardening or drying a substance, esp. one for firing ceramics.
ki•lo (kē'lō) *n., pl.* **-los.** A kilogram.
kil•o•bit (kĭl'ə-bĭt') *n.* 1,000 binary digits.
ki•lo•cy•cle (kĭl'ə-sī'kəl) *n.* **1.** A unit equal to 1,000 cycles. **2.** 1,000 cycles per sec.
kil•o•gram (kĭl'ə-grăm') *n.* See MEASUREMENT TABLE.
kil•o•hertz (kĭl'ə-hûrts') *n.* 1,000 hertz.
kil•o•li•ter (kĭl'ə-lē'tər) *n.* See MEASUREMENT TABLE.
kil•o•me•ter (kĭl'ə-mē'tər, kĭ-lŏm'ĭ-tər) *n.* See MEASUREMENT TABLE. **–kil'o•met'ric** (-mĕt'rĭk) *adj.*
kil•o•ton (kĭl'ə-tŭn') *n.* **1.** 1,000 tons. **2.** An explosive force equal to that of 1,000 tons of TNT.
kil•o•watt (kĭl'ə-wŏt') *n.* 1,000 watts.
kil•o•watt-hour (kĭl'ə-wŏt'our') *n.* A unit of electric power consumption equal to the power of 1 kw acting for 1 hour.
kilt (kĭlt) *n.* A knee-length wool skirt with deep pleats, usu. of tartan, worn esp. by men in the Scottish Highlands.
kil•ter (kĭl'tər) *n.* Good condition <The TV was out of *kilter.*>
Kim•ber•ley (kĭm'bər-lē). Diamond-mining center of C South Africa. *Pop.* 105,258.
ki•mo•no (kə-mō'nə, -nō) *n., pl.* **-nos. 1.** A long, loose, Japanese robe with wide sleeves and a broad sash. **2.** A loose robe worn chiefly by women.
kin (kĭn) *n.* One's relatives.
ki•na (kē'nə) *n., pl.* **-na** or **-nas.** See CURRENCY TABLE.
kind[1] (kīnd) *adj.* Warm-hearted, friendly, or generous in nature. ☆**syns:** BENIGN, GOODHEARTED, KINDHEARTED, KINDLY **–kind'ness** *n.*

▲word history: *Kind*[1] is a word that has undergone *melioration.* By this process a word with neutral connotations develops favorable ones. The Old English ancestor of *kind, gecynde,* meant "natural, inborn, inherent," and was used of such fearsome things as death and thunder. In the 13th cent., however, *kind* was used to mean "well-born," and "of a good nature." These senses have passed from standard English, but the derived sense "possessing all the (good) qualities usu. attributed to those of good birth" underlies the modern meanings of *kind.*

kind[2] (kīnd) *n.* **1.** A category of related individuals. **2.** A specific type. ☆**syns:** BREED, FEATHER, ILK, LOT, SORT, SPECIES, STRIPE, TYPE, VARIETY **–in kind. 1.** With goods or produce rather than money. **2.** In the same manner. **–kind of.** *Informal.* Rather <*kind of* tired.>

kin•der•gar•ten (kĭn′dər-gär′tn) *n.* A school or class for children from 4 to 6 years of age.

kin•der•gart•ner (kĭn′dər-gärt′nər) *n.* **1.** A child who attends kindergarten. **2.** A kindergarten teacher.

kind•heart•ed (kīnd′här′tĭd) *adj.* Having or proceeding from a kind nature. **–kind′heart′ed•ly** *adv.* **–kind′heart′ed•ness** *n.*

kin•dle (kĭnd′l) *v.* **-dled, -dling. 1.** To ignite. **2.** To catch fire. **3.** To stir up : arouse.

kin•dling (kĭnd′lĭng) *n.* Easily ignited material used to start a fire.

kind•ly (kīnd′lē) *adj.* **-li•er, -li•est.** Of a kind or helpful nature. *–adv.* **1.** Out of kindness <*kindly* overlooked their errors> **2.** In a kind way <spoke *kindly* to us> **3.** Pleasantly : agreeably <The sun shone *kindly.*> **4.** In an accommodating way <Would you *kindly* fill in your name?> **–kind′li•ness** *n.*

kin•dred (kĭn′drĭd) *n.* A person's relatives. *–adj.* Having a similar nature. **–kin′dred•ness** *n.*

kine (kīn) *n. archaic var. pl. of* COW[1].

kin•e•mat•ics (kĭn′ə-măt′ĭks) *n. (sing. in number).* The study of motion apart from the effects of mass and force. **–kin′e•mat′ic, kin′e•mat′i•cal** *adj.* **–kin′e•mat′i•cal•ly** *adv.*

kin•e•scope (kĭn′ə-skōp′) *n.* **1.** A cathode-ray tube in a television receiver that translates received electrical signals into a visible picture on a luminescent screen. **2.** A film of a television broadcast.

ki•net•ic (kĭ-nĕt′ĭk) *adj.* Of, pertaining to, or produced by motion.

kinetic energy *n.* Energy associated with motion, equal for a body in pure translational motion at nonrelativistic speeds to ½ the product of its mass and the square of its speed.

ki•net•ics (kĭ-nĕt′ĭks) *n. (sing. in number).* The science that deals with all aspects of motion, encompassing both kinematics and dynamics.

kin•folk (kĭn′fōk′) *also* **kins•folk** (kĭnz′fōk′) *or* **kin•folks** (kĭn′fōks′) *pl.n.* Kindred.

king (kĭng) *n.* **1.** A man who is a monarch. **2.** The most powerful or eminent, as of a group or place. **3.** A playing card with a figure of a king on it. **4. a.** The principal chess piece, capable of being moved 1 square in any direction. **b.** A piece in checkers that has reached the opponent's side of the board. **5. Kings** *(sing. in number).* See BIBLE TABLE. **–king′ship′** *n.*

King, Martin Luther, Jr. 1929–1968. Amer. civil-rights leader; assassinated.

king•bolt (kĭng′bōlt′) *n.* A vertical bolt used to join the body of a vehicle to the front axle and usu. acting as a pivot.

king crab *n.* A large crab, *Paralithodes camtschatica,* inhabiting the coastal waters of Japan, Alaska, and Siberia.

king•dom (kĭng′dəm) *n.* **1.** A land ruled by a king or queen. **2.** An area in which one thing dominates <the *kingdom* of the imagination> **3.** One of the 3 main taxonomic divisions into which natural organisms and objects are classified <the animal **kingdom**>

king•fish•er (kĭng′fĭsh′ər) *n.* Any of various crested birds of the family Alcedinidae that feed on fish.

King James Bible *n.* An Anglican translation of the Bible from Hebrew and Greek published in 1611 under the auspices of James I.

king•ly (kĭng′lē) *adj.* **-li•er, -li•est. 1.** Having the rank or status of king. **2.** Pertaining to or suitable for a king : regal. *–adv.* Royally. **–king′li•ness** *n.*

king•pin (kĭng′pĭn′) *n.* **1.** The foremost pin in an arrangement of bowling pins. **2.** The most important or essential person or thing. **3.** A kingbolt.

king-size (kĭng′sīz′) *also* **king-sized** (-sīzd′) *adj.* Larger than the standard or usual size <a *king-size* bed>

Kings•ton (kĭngz′tən). Cap. of Jamaica, on the SE coast. *Pop.* 665,050.

Kings•town (kĭngz′toun′). Cap. of St. Vincent and the Grenadines, West Indies, on the SW coast of St. Vincent Is. *Pop.* 17,258.

kink (kĭngk) *n.* **1.** A tight twist or curl. **2.** A muscle cramp. **3.** A slight difficulty or flaw. **4.** A mental quirk. *–v.* To form a kink (in).

kink•a•jou (kĭng′kə-jōō′) *n.* A tropical American arboreal mammal, *Potos flavus,* with brown fur and a long prehensile tail.

kink•y (kĭng′kē) *adj.* **1.** Tightly curled : frizzy. **2. a.** Marked by or engaging in a perverted eroticism. **b.** Sexually perverted. **–kink′i•ly** *adv.* **–kink′i•ness** *n.*

kins•folk (kĭnz′fōk′) *pl.n. var. of* KINFOLK.

Kin•sha•sa (kĕn-shä′sə). Cap. of Zaire, in the W part. *Pop.* 2,202,000.

kin•ship (kĭn′shĭp′) *n.* The state or quality of being kin.

kins•man (kĭnz′mən) *n.* **1.** A male relative. **2.** A man sharing the same cultural or national background as another. **–kins′wom′an** *n.*

ki•osk (kē-ŏsk′, kē′ŏsk′) *n.* A small structure used as a refreshment booth or newsstand.

kip[1] (kĭp) *n., pl.* **kip.** See CURRENCY TABLE.

kip[2] (kĭp) *n.* The untanned hide of a young or small animal, as a calf.

Kip•ling (kĭp′lĭng), **Rudyard.** 1865–1936. English author.

kip•per (kĭp′ər) *n.* A salted and smoked herring. *–v.* To cure (fish) by salting and smoking.

Kir•ghiz *also* **Kir•giz** (kîr-gēz′) *or* **Kir•ghiz•stan** (-gē-stän′). Region of SE Central Asian USSR, bordering on NW China.

Ki•ri•ba•ti (kîr′ĭ-băs′, kîr′ĭ-băs′). Island country of the WC Pacific. *Cap.* Bairiki. *Pop.* 56,213.

kirk (kûrk) *n. Scot.* A church.

kirsch (kîrsh) *n.* A colorless brandy made from fermented cherry juice.

kir•tle (kûr′tl) *n.* A woman's long dress or skirt.

kirtle

kis•met (kĭz′mĕt′, -mĭt) *n.* Fate.

kiss (kĭs) *v.* **1.** To touch or caress with the lips as a sign of passion, affection, or greeting. **2.** To touch lightly. *–n.* **1. a.** A touch or caress with the lips. **b.** A light touch. **2.** A small piece of candy.

kiss•er (kĭs′ər) *n.* **1.** One who kisses. **2.** *Slang.* The human mouth. **3.** *Slang.* The human face.

kiss of life *n. esp. Brit.* Mouth-to-mouth resuscitation.

kit (kĭt) *n.* **1.** A set of articles used for a particular purpose <a survival *kit*> **2.** A set of parts to be assembled <a stereo *kit*> **3.** A receptacle, as a box, bag, or knapsack.

kitch•en (kĭch′ən) *n.* A place where food is prepared or cooked.

Kitch•e•ner (kĭch′ə-nər). City of S Ont., Canada, WSW of Toronto. *Pop.* 136,091.

kitch•en•ette (kĭch′ə-nĕt′) *n.* A small kitchen.

kitchen police *n.* **1.** Enlisted military personnel assigned to perform kitchen work. **2.** The work of the kitchen police.

kitch•en•ware (kĭch′ən-wâr′) *n.* Utensils for kitchen use.

kite (kīt) *n.* **1.** A light framework covered with plastic, cloth, or paper designed to fly in a steady breeze at the end of a long string. **2.** Any of various predatory birds of the subfamilies Milvinae and Elaninae, having a long, usu. forked tail.

kith and kin (kĭth) *n.* Friends and neighbors.

kitsch (kĭch) *n.* **1.** Pretentious bad taste, esp. in the arts. **2.** Something that exemplifies kitsch. **–kitsch′y** *adj.*

kit•ten (kĭt′n) *n.* A young cat.

kit•ten•ish (kĭt′n-ĭsh) *adj.* Playful and coy. **–kit′ten•ish•ly** *adv.*

kit•ty[1] (kĭt′ē) *n., pl.* **-ties.** A pool of money.

kit•ty[2] (kĭt′ē) *n., pl.* **-ties.** *Informal.* A cat, esp. a kitten.

kit•ty-cor•nered (kĭt′ē-kôr′nərd) *adj.* Cater-cornered.

ki•wi (kē′wē) *n.* **1.** A flightless bird of the genus *Apteryx,* native to New Zealand, with vestigial wings and a long, slender bill. **2.** A vine, *Actinidia chinensis,* native to Asia, yielding edible fruit with a fuzzy skin.

kl *abbr.* kiloliter.

klep·to·ma·ni·a (klĕp'tə-mā'nē-ə) *n.* Obsessive desire to steal, esp. without economic motive. **—klep'to·ma'ni·ac'** *n.*

klieg light (klēg) *n.* A powerful lamp used esp. in making movies.

Klon·dike (klŏn'dīk'). Region of EC Y.T., Canada; site of abundant gold deposits.

klutz (klŭts) *n. Slang.* A stupid or clumsy person. **—klutz'i·ness** *n.* **—klutz'y** *adj.*

km *abbr.* kilometer.

knack (năk) *n.* **1.** A clever way of doing something. **2.** A natural talent.

knack·wurst *also* **knock·wurst** (nŏk'wûrst', -wo͝orst') *n.* A short, thick, heavily seasoned sausage.

†**knap** (năp) *n. Regional.* The crest of a hill : summit.

knap·sack (năp'săk') *n.* A supply or equipment bag, as of canvas or nylon, worn on the back.

knave (nāv) *n.* **1.** A rogue. **2.** JACK 2. **—knav'er·y** *n.* **—knav'ish** *adj.* **—knav'ish·ly** *adv.* **—knav'ish·ness** *n.*

knead (nēd) *v.* **1.** To work and press into a uniform mass. **2.** To shape by or as if by kneading. **—knead'er** *n.*

knee (nē) *n. Anat.* The joint or region of the human leg that is the articulation for the tibia, fibula, and patella. *—v.* **kneed, knee·ing.** To push or strike with the knee.

knee·cap (nē'kăp') *n.* The patella.

kneel (nēl) *v.* **knelt** (nĕlt) *or* **kneeled, kneel·ing.** To rest or go down on bent knees.

knell (nĕl) *v.* **1.** To sound a bell, esp. for a funeral : toll. **2.** To announce, signal, or summon by or as if by tolling. *—n.* **1.** An act or instance of knelling : toll. **2.** A signal of disaster.

Knes·set (knĕs'ĕt') *n.* The Israeli parliament.

knew (no͞o) *v. p.t. of* KNOW.

knick·ers (nĭk'ərz) *pl.n.* Full breeches gathered and banded below the knee.

knick·knack (nĭk'năk') *n.* A trinket.

knife (nīf) *n., pl.* **knives** (nīvz). **1.** A cutting instrument having a sharp blade and a handle. **2.** A cutting edge : blade. *—v.* **knifed, knif·ing. 1.** To use a knife on, esp. to cut, stab, or wound. **2.** *Informal.* To hurt or betray in an underhand way.

knight (nīt) *n.* **1.** A usu. high-born medieval gentleman-soldier serving a monarch. **2.** The holder of a nonhereditary honor conferred by a monarch in recognition of services to the country. **3.** A member of any of various orders or societies. **4.** A chess piece usu. in the shape of a horse's head. *—v.* To make (a person) a knight. **—knight'hood'** *n.* **—knight'ly** *adj.*

knish (knĭsh) *n.* Dough stuffed with potato, meat, or cheese, and baked or fried.

knit (nĭt) *v.* **knit** *or* **knit·ted, knit·ting. 1.** To make by intertwining thread or yarn in a set of connected loops. **2.** To join securely. **3.** To draw (the brow) together in wrinkles : furrow. **—knit** *n.*

knitting needle *n.* A long, thin, pointed rod for knitting.

knit·wear (nĭt'wâr') *n.* Knitted garments.

knob (nŏb) *n.* **1. a.** A rounded protuberance. **b.** A rounded handle. **2.** A prominent rounded hill. **—knobbed** *adj.* **—knob'by** *adj.*

knock (nŏk) *v.* **1.** To strike with a hard blow. **2.** To produce by hitting. **3.** *Slang.* To criticize : disparage. **4.** To collide. **5.** To make the clanking noise of a defective engine. **—knock around (***or* **about).** *Informal.* **1.** To be rough or brutal with. **2.** To wander from place to place. **3.** To discuss. **—knock back.** *Informal.* To drink quickly. **—knock down. 1.** To declare sold at an auction. **2.** *Informal.* To reduce in price. **—knock off. 1.** *Informal.* To stop. **2.** *Informal.* To make or accomplish hastily. **3.** *Informal.* To deduct. **4.** *Slang.* To kill. **—knock out. 1.** To render unconscious. **2.** *Informal.* To make useless or inoperative. **—knock** *n.*

knock·down (nŏk'doun') *adj.* **1.** Forceful enough to overwhelm <a *knockdown* punch> **2.** Designed to be easily assembled or disassembled <*knockdown* furniture> **—knock'down'** *n.*

knock·er (nŏk'ər) *n.* One that knocks, as a fixture for knocking on a door.

knock-knee (nŏk'nē') *n.* A condition in which 1 or both knees turn inward abnormally. **—knock'-kneed'** *adj.*

knock·out (nŏk'out') *n.* **1.** The act of knocking out or the state of being knocked out. **2.** *Slang.* Something that is exceptionally attractive.

knock·wurst (nŏk'wûrst', -wo͝orst') *n. var. of* KNACKWURST.

knoll (nōl) *n.* A small mound : hillock.

knot (nŏt) *n.* **1. a.** A compact interlacing, as of string or cord. **b.** A fastening made by tying together lengths of material, as string. **2.** A unifying bond, esp. of marriage. **3.** A tight group or cluster. **4.** A difficulty. **5. a.** A hard node on a tree trunk from which a branch grows. **b.** A dark spot in wood marking such a node. **6.** A protuberant growth in living tissue. **7.** *Naut.* A unit of speed, 1 nautical mph, approx. 1.15 statute mph. *—v.* **knot·ted, knot·ting. 1.** To tie in or fasten with a knot. **2.** To entangle. **—knot'ti·ness** *n.* **—knot'ty** *adj.*

knot·hole (nŏt'hōl') *n.* A hole in lumber where a knot used to be.

knout (nout) *n.* A leather scourge for flogging. **—knout** *v.*

know (nō) *v.* **knew** (no͞o, nyo͞o), **known** (nōn), **know·ing. 1.** To perceive directly with the mind or senses. **2.** To believe to be true. **3.** To have understanding or experience of <*know* yacht racing> **4.** To be subjected to <a person who had *known* no pain> **5.** To recognize or be familiar with. ☆**syns:** APPREHEND, COMPREHEND, FATHOM, GRASP, UNDERSTAND *—n.* Knowledge. **—in the know.** Privy to confidential or special information. **—know'a·ble** *adj.*

know-how (nō'hou') *n. Informal.* Special knowledge and skill.

know·ing (nō'ĭng) *adj.* **1.** Having knowledge or comprehension. **2.** Having or exhibiting clever awareness : shrewd. **—know'ing·ly** *adv.* **—know'ing·ness** *n.*

knowl·edge (nŏl'ĭj) *n.* **1.** The fact or state of knowing. **2.** Understanding acquired through experience. **3.** The total or range of what has been perceived or learned. **4.** Erudition : learning. ☆**syns:** EDUCATION, ERUDITION, INSTRUCTION, LEARNING, SCHOLARSHIP **—know'ledge·a·ble** *adj.* **—know'ledge·a·bly** *adv.*

Knox·ville (nŏks'vĭl'). City of E Tenn., NE of Chattanooga. *Pop.* 183,139.

knuck·le (nŭk'əl) *n.* A joint of a finger, esp. 1 connecting a finger to the hand. *—v.* **-led, -ling.** To press or hit with the knuckles. **—knuckle down.** To set to work earnestly. **—knuckle under.** To give in : yield.

knuck·le·bone (nŭk'əl-bōn') *n.* A knobbed bone, as of a joint or knuckle.

knuck·le·head (nŭk'əl-hĕd') *n.* A stupid person.

knurl (nûrl) *n.* **1.** A protuberance, as a knob or knot. **2.** One of a set of small ridges, as along the edge of an object such as a thumbscrew. **—knurl'y** *adj.*

ko·a·la (kō-ä'lə) *n.* An Australian arboreal marsupial, *Phascolarctos cinereus,* with thick grayish fur.

Ko·be (kō'bē, -bā'). City of S Japan, on Osaka Bay in S Honshu. *Pop.* 1,367,392.

ko·bo (kô'bô') *n., pl.* **-bo.** See *naira* at CURRENCY TABLE.

kohl·ra·bi (kōl-rä'bē, -răb'ē) *n., pl.* **-bies.** A plant, *Brassica caulorapa,* with a thickened stem eaten as a vegetable.

kook (ko͞ok) *n. Slang.* An eccentric person. **—kook'i·ness** *n.* **—kook'y** *adj.*

kook·a·bur·ra (ko͝ok'ə-bûr'ə, -bŭr'ə) *n.* A large kingfisher, *Dacelo novaeguineae* or *D. gigas,* native to Australia, with a raucous call similar to laughter.

kookaburra

ko·peck (kō'pĕk') *n.* See *rouble* at CURRENCY TABLE.

Ko·ran (kô-răn', -rän', kō-) *n.* The sacred text of Islam, held to contain the revelations made to Mohammed by Allah. **—Ko·ran'ic** *adj.*

Ko·re·a (kə-rē'ə, kō-). Former country occupying a peninsula of EC Asia, opposite Japan, divided since 1948 into the **People's Democratic Republic of Korea** (unofficially, North Korea), with a *pop.* of 17,072,000 and its *cap.* at Pyongyang; and the **Republic of Korea** (unofficially, South Korea), with a *pop.* of 37,605,000 and its *cap.* at Seoul. **—Ko·re'an** *adj. & n.*

ko·sher (kō'shər) *adj.* **1.** Fit to eat according to Jewish dietary laws. **2.** *Slang.* Permissible : proper.

kow·tow (kou'tou', kō'-) *v.* To show servile deference.

kph *abbr.* kilometers per hour.

Kr *symbol for* KRYPTON.

kraal (kräl) *n. So. Afr.* **1.** A native village. **2.** An enclosure for livestock.

Kra·ków (krăk'ou', krä'kou', krā'kō'). City of S Poland. *Pop.* 719,200.

Krem•lin (krĕm′lən) *n.* **1.** The citadel of Moscow, housing major Soviet offices. **2.** The Soviet government.
Krem•lin•ol•o•gy (krĕm′lə-nŏl′ə-jē) *n.* Study of the policies and strategies of the Soviet government. **–Krem′lin•o•log′i•cal** (-nə-lŏj′ĭ-kəl) *adj.* **–Krem′lin•ol′o•gist** *n.*
Krish•na (krĭsh′nə) *n.* The 8th and principal avatar of Vishnu, often represented as a handsome young man playing a flute.
kro•na[1] (krō′nə) *n., pl.* **-nur** (-nər). See CURRENCY TABLE.
kro•na[2] (krō′nə) *n., pl.* **-nor** (-nôr′, -nər). See CURRENCY TABLE.
kro•ne (krō′nə) *n., pl.* **-ner** (-nər). See CURRENCY TABLE.
kro•ner (krō′nər) *n.* **1.** See CURRENCY TABLE. **2.** *pl. of* KRONE.
kryp•ton (krĭp′tŏn′) *n. Symbol* **Kr** A white, inert gaseous element used mainly in fluorescent lamps.
KS *abbr.* Kansas (with Zip Code).
kt. *abbr.* karat.
Kua•la Lum•pur (kwä′lə lo͝om′po͝or′). Cap. of Malaysia, in the S part of the Malay Peninsula. *Pop.* 451,728.
Ku•blai Khan (ko͞o′blī kän′) *also* **Ku•bla Khan** (-blə). 1216–94. Founder of the Mongol dynasty.
ku•dos (kyo͞o′dŏs′, -dōs′) *n.* Acclaim or prestige resulting from notable achievement or high position.

▲word history: The word *kudos* is etymologically a singular form, a modern borrowing of Greek *kudos*, "glory, renown." In very recent times, however, *kudos* has been reanalyzed as a plural form and consequently a new singular *kudo* sometimes occurs. Certain features of *kudos* predispose it to this kind of treatment. In the first place, it is an unfamiliar word, drawn from the vocabulary of Homer by academic and learned persons. In their usage it did not often occur as the subject of a sentence, where the verb could provide a clue to whether *kudos* was singular or plural. Secondly, *kudos* has no recorded plural in English. A person unfamiliar with Homeric Greek who saw the form *kudos* in an English publication would be likely to interpret it as the regular plural of a noun ending in o, like *typos* for *typo* and *altos* for *alto*. Once *kudos* was treated as a plural, the linguistic pressure to supply a singular would have been very strong. Although the form *kudo* has not achieved general acceptance and the construction "kudos are" is often considered incorrect, the linguistic processes in the development of *kudo/kudos* as the singular and plural forms of an English noun are highly productive and have been going on in English and other languages since prehistoric times. The development of the singular *pea* from the earlier singular form *pease* is an example of the same kind of reanalysis.

kud•zu (ko͝od′zo͞o) *n.* A fast-growing Japanese vine, *Pueraria lobata*, with clusters of reddish-purple flowers, grown for fodder and for containment of erosion.

kudzu

Ku Klux Klan (ko͞o′ klŭks klăn′, kyo͞o′) *n.* A U.S. secret society dedicated to legal and de facto segregation of blacks.
ku•lak (ko͞o-lăk′, -läk′) *n.* A prosperous peasant in czarist Russia.
kum•quat (kŭm′kwŏt′) *n.* A tree or shrub of the genus *Fortunella*, bearing a small edible fruit.
kung fu (ko͝ong′ fo͞o′, go͝ong′-) *n.* A Chinese art of self-defense similar to karate.
ku•ru (ko͞o′ro͞o) *n.* See *pound* at CURRENCY TABLE.
Ku•wait (ko͞o-wāt′, -wīt′). **1.** Country on the Arabian Peninsula at the head of the Persian Gulf. *Pop.* 1,355,827. **2.** Cap. of Kuwait, in the EC part. *Pop.* 181,774. **–Ku•wiat′i** *adj.* & *n.*
kw or **kW** *abbr.* kilowatt.
kwa•cha (kwä′chə) *n.* See CURRENCY TABLE.
kwan•za (kwän′zə) *n., pl.* **-za** or **-zas.** See CURRENCY TABLE.
kwash•i•or•kor (kwäsh′ē-ôr′kôr, kwä′shē-) *n.* Severe malnutrition esp. in children, characterized by anemia, potbelly, depigmentation of the skin, and loss of hair.
kwh or **kWh** *abbr.* kilowatt-hour.
KY *abbr.* Kentucky (with Zip Code).
Ky. *abbr.* Kentucky.
kyat (chät) *n.* See CURRENCY TABLE.
ky•lix (kī′lĭks, kĭl′ĭks) *n., pl.* **ky•li•kes** (-kēz′). A shallow, usu. tall-stemmed ancient Greek drinking cup.
Kyo•to (kō-ō′tō, kyō-). City of S Japan, on S Honshu. *Pop.* 1,472,993.

Ll

l or **L** (ĕl) *n., pl.* **l's** or **L's. 1.** The 12th letter of the English alphabet. **2.** A speech sound represented by the letter *l.* **3.** Something with the shape of the letter L. **4.** The Roman numeral for 50.
l *also* **L** *abbr.* liter.
L. *abbr.* Latin.
l. *abbr.* **1.** *also* **L.** lake. **2.** left. **3.** length. **4.** line. **5.** lira.
†**la** (lä) *interj. Chiefly Regional.* Used to indicate surprise.
La *symbol for* LANTHANUM.
LA *abbr.* Louisiana (with Zip Code).
La. *abbr.* Louisiana.
lab (lăb) *n.* A laboratory.
lab. *abbr.* laboratory.
la•bel (lā′bəl) *n.* **1.** Something, as a slip of paper, that serves to describe or identify. **2.** A descriptive or identifying term. –*v.* **-beled, -bel•ing** or **-belled, -bel•ling. 1.** To affix a label to. **2.** To describe or identify with a label.
la•bi•al (lā′bē-əl) *adj.* Of or pertaining to the lips or labia.
la•bile (lā′bīl′, -bəl) *adj.* **1.** Open to change : adaptable. **2.** Constantly undergoing or likely to undergo chemical change : unstable.
la•bi•um (lā′bē-əm) *n., pl.* **-bi•a** (-bē-ə). Any of the folds of tissue surrounding the vulva.
la•bor (lā′bər) *n.* **1.** Physical or mental exertion : work. **2.** A particular task. **3. a.** Those who do work for wages. **b.** Trade unions or their officials. **4.** The physical efforts involved in childbirth. ☆***syns:*** DRUDGERY, MOIL, SWEAT, TOIL, TRAVAIL, WORK –*v.* **1.** To work. **2.** To strive or treat painstakingly, exhaustively, or laboriously. **3.** To proceed with great effort. **4.** To suffer from a disadvantage or burden <*labored* under a major handicap> **–la′bor•er** *n.*
lab•o•ra•to•ry (lăb′rə-tôr′ē, -tōr′ē) *n., pl.* **-ries. 1.** A place equipped for scientific analysis, experimentation, research, or testing. **2.** A place where chemicals and drugs are produced.
Labor Day *n.* The 1st Monday in Sept., a legal holiday in the U.S. and Canada in recognition of working people.
la•bored (lā′bərd) *adj.* Done without natural ease : strained.
la•bor-in•ten•sive (lā′bər-ĭn-tĕn′sĭv) *adj.* Requiring or marked by a larger expenditure of labor than of capital.
la•bo•ri•ous (lə-bôr′ē-əs, -bōr′-) *adj.* Done, produced with, or requiring much work or effort. **–la•bo′ri•ous•ly** *adv.* **–la•bo′ri•ous•ness** *n.*
la•bor•sav•ing (lā′bər-sā′vĭng) *adj.* Designed to conserve or diminish labor.
la•bour (lā′bər) *n., v., & adj. esp. Brit. var. of* LABOR.
Lab•ra•dor (lăb′rə-dôr′). **1.** Peninsula of NE Canada, between Newf. and Que. **2.** Mainland territory of Newf., Canada.
lab•ra•dor•ite (lăb′rə-dôr′īt′, -dō-rīt′) *n.* A feldspar some specimens of which are marked by brilliant colors.
la•bur•num (lə-bûr′nəm) *n.* A tree or shrub of the genus *Laburnum*, esp. *L. anagyroides*, with drooping yellow flower clusters.
lab•y•rinth (lăb′ə-rĭnth′) *n.* An intricate structure of winding, interconnecting passages : maze. **–lab′y•rin′thine′** (-rĭn′thĭn, -thēn′) *adj.*
lac (lăk) *n.* The resinous secretion of an Asian insect used to make shellac.
lac•co•lith (lăk′ə-lĭth′) *n.* A mass of igneous rock intruded between layers of sedimentary rock, causing uplift.

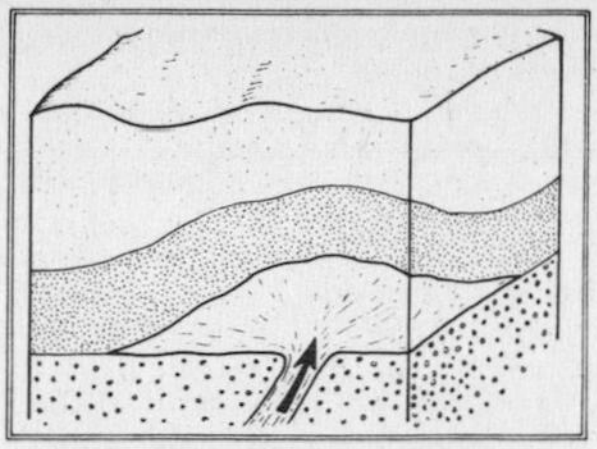

laccolith

lace (lās) *n.* **1.** A string or cord used to pull together 2 edges. **2.** A delicate fabric of fine threads woven in an open weblike pattern. —*v.* **laced, lac•ing. 1.** To tie or be tied with a lace. **2.** To intertwine. **3.** To add a small amount of liquor to. **—lac'y** *adj.*
lac•er•ate (lăs'ə-rāt') *v.* **-at•ed, -at•ing.** To tear or rip. **—lac'er•a'tion** *n.*
lace•wing (lās'wĭng') *n.* Any of various greenish or brownish insects of the families Chrysopidae and Hemerobiidae, with 4 gauzy wings, threadlike antennae, and larvae that feed on insect pests such as aphids.
lach•ry•mal *also* **lac•ri•mal** (lăk'rə-məl) *adj.* Of or relating to tears or the tear-producing glands.
lach•ry•mose (lăk'rə-mōs') *adj.* **1.** Tearful. **2.** Sorrowful. **—lach'ry•mose'ly** *adv.*
lack (lăk) *n.* An absence or deficiency : need. —*v.* **1.** To be without or have little of. **2.** To be deficient (in).
lack•a•dai•si•cal (lăk'ə-dā'zĭ-kəl) *adj.* Lacking spirit, life, or interest. **—lack'a•dai'si•cal•ly** *adv.*
lack•ey (lăk'ē) *n., pl.* **-eys. 1.** A uniformed male servant. **2.** An obsequious follower : toady.
lack•lus•ter (lăk'lŭs'tər) *adj.* Lacking vitality : dull.
la•con•ic (lə-kŏn'ĭk) *adj.* Using few words : terse. **—la•con'i•cal•ly** *adv.*
lac•quer (lăk'ər) *n.* A clear or colored synthetic or resinous surface coating that is dissolved in a solvent and dries to leave a glossy finish. **—lac'quer** *v.*
lac•ri•mal (lăk'rə-məl) *adj. var. of* LACHRYMAL.
la•crosse (lə-krôs', -krŏs') *n.* A game played on a field by 2 teams with long-handled rackets and a hard rubber ball.
lac•tate (lăk'tāt') *v.* **-tat•ed, -tat•ing.** To secrete milk. **—lac•ta'tion** *n.*
lac•te•al (lăk'tē-əl) *n.* Of, producing, or like milk.
lac•tic (lăk'tĭk) *adj.* Of, relating to, or obtained from milk.
lactic acid *n.* A syrupy liquid that is present in sour milk, molasses, various fruits, and wines.
lac•tose (lăk'tōs') *n.* A white crystalline sugar that is found in milk.
la•cu•na (lə-kyōō'nə, -kōō'-) *n., pl.* **-nae** (-nē) *or* **-nas.** A missing part or empty space : gap.
lad (lăd) *n.* **1.** A boy. **2.** A young man.
lad•der (lăd'ər) *n.* A framework of 2 long parallel side pieces crossed by equally spaced rungs for climbing.
lad•die (lăd'ē) *n.* A lad.
lad•en (lād'n) *adj.* **1.** Weighed down with a load : heavy. **2.** Burdened : oppressed.
lad•ing (lā'dĭng) *n.* Freight : cargo.
la•dle (lād'l) *n.* A spoon with a deep bowl and a long handle that is used for taking up and serving liquids. **—la'dle** *v.*
la•dy (lā'dē) *n., pl.* **-dies. 1.** A woman of breeding, cultivation, and often high social position. **2.** The female head of a household. **3.** A woman. **4. Lady.** *Brit.* The general feminine title of rank and esp. of nobility.
▲word history: The word *lady* was not orig. an honorific title, but it did designate a woman of some social importance, at least within her own household. The Old English form of *lady, hlǣfdige,* denoted the mistress of a household, esp. one who had authority over servants and other dependents. The word is ult. a compound of *hlāf,* "bread," and *dīg-,* a root meaning basically "to knead," which is related to *dough* and *diary.* As the "bread kneader" of the household a lady was in a position of some authority and dominance.
la•dy•bug (lā'dē-bŭg') *also* **la•dy•bird** (-bûrd') *n.* Any of numerous small, reddish black-spotted beetles of the family Coccinellidae.
la•dy•fin•ger (lā'dē-fĭng'gər) *n.* A small, oval sponge cake shaped like a finger.
lady in waiting *n., pl.* **ladies in waiting.** A lady appointed to wait on a princess or queen.
la•dy•like (lā'dē-līk') *adj.* **1.** Characteristic of a lady : well-bred. **2.** Appropriate for or becoming to a lady.
la•dy•love (lā'dē-lŭv') *n.* A sweetheart.
la•dy•ship (lā'dē-shĭp') *n. often* **Ladyship.** Used as a form of address for a woman holding the rank of lady.
la•dy's-slip•per (lā'dēz-slĭp'ər) *n.* Any of various orchids of the genus *Cypripedium,* bearing flowers with a pouchlike lip.
La•fay•ette (lä'fē-ĕt', lăf'ē-), Marquis de. 1757–1834. French military and political leader.
lag (lăg) *v.* **lagged, lag•ging. 1.** To fail to keep up : straggle. **2.** To weaken gradually : slacken. —*n.* **1.** The act, process, or state of lagging. **2. a.** The amount or duration of lagging. **b.** An interval, as between events.
la•ger (lä'gər) *n.* A kind of beer that is stored to allow sedimentation.
lag•gard (lăg'ərd) *n.* One that lags.
la•gniappe (lăn-yăp', lăn'yăp') *n.* Something, as a small gift, that is given free or as a bonus.
la•goon (lə-gōōn') *n.* A shallow body of water, esp. one separated from the ocean by sandbars or coral reefs.
La•gos (lä'gŏs', lā'gŏs'). Cap. of Nigeria, in the SW on the Gulf of Guinea. *Pop.* 1,060,800.
La•hore (lə-hôr', -hôr'). City of NE Pakistan. *Pop.* 2,022,577.
la•ic (lā'ĭk) *also* **la•i•cal** (-ĭ-kəl) *adj.* Of or relating to the laity : secular.
laid (lād) *v. p.t.* & *p.p. of* LAY[1].
laid•back (lād'băk') *adj. Informal.* Casual or relaxed in atmosphere or character.
lain (lān) *v. p.p. of* LIE[1].
lair (lâr) *n.* **1.** The dwelling of a wild animal : den. **2.** A refuge or hideaway.
laird (lârd) *n. Scot.* A landed estate owner.
lais•sez faire (lĕs'ā fâr') *n.* An economic doctrine that opposes government regulation of or interference in commerce. **—lais'sez-faire'ism** *n.*
la•i•ty (lā'ĭ-tē) *n.* **1.** Laymen as distinguished from clergy. **2.** Nonprofessionals.
lake (lāk) *n.* **1.** A large inland body of fresh or salt water. **2.** A pool of liquid.
lam (lăm) *Slang.* —*v.* **lammed, lam•ming.** To run away in haste. —*n.* Flight, esp. from the law <on the *lam*>
la•ma (lä'mə) *n.* A Buddhist monk of Tibet or Mongolia.
la•ma•ser•y (lä'mə-sĕr'ē) *n., pl.* **-ies.** A monastery of lamas.
La•maze (lə-mäz') *adj.* Pertaining to or being a method of childbirth in which the mother is prepared physically and psychologically to give birth without using drugs.
lamb (lăm) *n.* **1. a.** A young sheep. **b.** The flesh of a lamb used as meat. **2.** A sweet, gentle person.
lam•baste (lăm-bāst') *v.* **-bast•ed, -bast•ing.** *Slang.* **1.** To beat : thrash. **2.** To berate.
lam•bent (lăm'bənt) *adj.* **1.** Flickering gently. **2.** Radiant : glowing. **3.** Marked by brilliance <*lambent* wit> **—lam'ben•cy** *n.* **—lam'bent•ly** *adv.*
lamb•skin (lăm'skĭn') *n.* A lamb's hide or leather made from it.
lame (lām) *adj.* **lam•er, lam•est. 1.** Disabled in a limb, esp. so as to impair free movement. **2.** Weak : unsatisfactory. —*v.* **lamed, lam•ing.** To make lame. **—lame'ly** *adv.* **—lame'ness** *n.*
la•mé (lă-mā', lä-) *n.* A brocaded fabric with metallic threads in the filling.
lame•brain (lām'brān') *n.* A stupid person : ninny. **—lame'brained'** *adj.*
lame duck *n.* An elected officeholder who has been defeated for re-election but continues in office until the inauguration of his or her successor.
la•mel•la (lə-mĕl'ə) *n., pl.* **-mel•lae** (-mĕl'ē) *or* **-las.** A thin layer, scale, or plate.
la•ment (lə-mĕnt') *v.* **1.** To express sorrow or regret (over) : mourn. **2.** To weep : wail. —*n.* **1.** An expression of sorrow or regret. **2.** An elegy : dirge. **—lam'en•ta•ble** *adj.* **—lam'en•ta•bly** *adv.*
lam•en•ta•tion (lăm'ən-tā'shən) *n.* **1.** An act or instance of lamenting. **2. Lamentations** *(sing. in number).* See BIBLE TABLE.
lam•i•na (lăm'ə-nə) *n., pl.* **-nae** (-nē') *or* **-nas.** A thin plate or layer. **—lam'i•nar, lam'i•nal** *adj.*
lam•i•nate (lăm'ə-nāt') *v.* **-nat•ed, -nat•ing. 1.** To press or form into a thin plate or sheet. **2.** To split into thin layers. **3.** To make by joining several layers. **—lam'i•na'tion** *n.* **—lam'i•nate** (-nĭt, -nāt') *n.* & *adj.* **—lam'i•na'tor** *n.*
lamp (lămp) *n.* **1. a.** A device that generates heat, light, or therapeutic radiation. **b.** A vessel holding oil or alcohol burned through a wick for illumination. **2.** A device similar to a lamp that produces heat.
lamp•black (lămp'blăk') *n.* A black pigment composed of fine soot.
lamp•light•er (lămp'lī'tər) *n.* Someone hired to light gas-burning street lights.

lam•poon (lăm-pōōn′) *n.* A broad satirical piece, esp. one that ridicules a person, group, or institution. **—lam•poon′** *v.* **—lam•poon′er•y** *n.*
lamp•post (lămp′pōst′) *n.* A post to which a street lamp is attached.
lam•prey (lăm′prē) *n., pl.* **-preys.** Any of various primitive eellike fishes of the family Petromyzontidae with a jawless sucking mouth and a rasping tongue.
la•nai (lə-nī′, lä-) *n.* A verandah : porch.
lance (lăns) *n.* **1.** A spear with a sharp metal head. **2.** An implement similar to a lance, esp. a lancet. *—v.* **lanced, lanc•ing. 1.** To pierce with a lance. **2.** To make a surgical incision in.
lance corporal *n.* An enlisted man in the U.S. Marine Corps who ranks above a private first class and below a corporal.
lanc•er (lăn′sər) *n.* A cavalry soldier equipped with a lance.
lan•cet (lăn′sĭt) *n.* A surgical knife with a pointed and usu. double-edged blade.
land (lănd) *n.* **1.** The solid part of the surface of the earth. **2.** A particular region : area. **3.** The people of a nation. **4.** A nation : country. **5.** Real estate : property. *—v.* **1.** To set down or settle on land, esp. after traveling by water or air. **2.** To arrive or cause to arrive at a destination. **3.** To alight or cause to alight. **4.** To catch by or as if by fishing <*landed* a new job>
lan•dau (lăn′dô′, -dou′) *n.* **1.** A 4-wheeled closed carriage with a roof in 2 sections that can be lowered or detached. **2.** A style of automobile with a similar roof.
land•ed (lăn′dĭd) *adj.* Owning land <*landed* gentry>
landed immigrant *n. Can.* A person granted legal status as an immigrant who will eventually be eligible for citizenship.
land•er (lăn′dər) *n.* A space vehicle designed to land on a celestial body.
land•fall (lănd′fôl′) *n.* **1.** The sighting of or reaching land, as after a sea voyage. **2.** The land that is first sighted or reached.
land•fill (lănd′fĭl′) *n.* **1.** A method of waste disposal in which garbage and trash are buried in low-lying ground. **2.** Land built up by landfill.
land grant *n.* A grant of land made by a government esp. for railroads, highways, or state colleges.
land•hold•er (lănd′hōl′dər) *n.* Someone who owns land. **—land′hold′ing** *n.*
land•ing (lăn′dĭng) *n.* **1.** The act of coming to land or rest, esp. after a voyage or flight. **2.** A place for loading and discharging passengers and cargo. **3.** A level area at the top or bottom of a staircase.
landing gear *n.* The structure that supports the weight of an aircraft.
land•locked (lănd′lŏkt′) *adj.* **1.** Completely or almost completely surrounded by land. **2.** Confined to inland waters <*landlocked* salmon>
land•lord (lănd′lôrd′) *n.* **1.** One who owns property and rents or leases it to another. **2.** An innkeeper. **—land′la′dy** *n.*
land•lub•ber (lănd′lŭb′ər) *n.* One not familiar with the sea or seamanship.
land•mark (lănd′märk′) *n.* **1.** A marker that indicates a boundary line. **2.** A prominent feature on land that serves to identify or guide. **3.** A historically significant event, structure, or site.
land•mass (lănd′măs′) *n.* A large land area.
land•own•er (lănd′ō′nər) *n.* A landholder.
land•scape (lănd′skāp′) *n.* **1.** A view or vista of natural scenery on land. **2.** A representation, esp. a painting, that depicts a landscape. *—v.* **-scaped, -scap•ing.** To beautify or improve (a section of ground) by contouring the land and planting flowers, shrubs, or trees. **—land′scap′er** *n.*
land•slide (lănd′slīd′) *n.* **1.** The fall or slide down a steep slope of a mass of earth or rock. **2.** A great victory, esp. in a political contest.
lands•man (lăndz′mən) *n.* One who lives and works on land.
land•ward (lănd′wərd) *adj.* & *adv.* To or toward land. **—land′wards** *adv.*
lane (lān) *n.* **1.** A narrow path or road, often bordered by fences. **2.** A narrow lengthwise division, as of a road : strip <a shipping *lane*>
lan•guage (lăng′gwĭj) *n.* **1.** The sounds, words, and combinations of words that constitute a system for the expression and communication of thoughts and feelings among a number of people, as those with a shared history or set of traditions. **2.** A particular style or form of utterance. ☆***syns:*** DIALECT, SPEECH, TONGUE, VERNACULAR
lan•guid (lăng′gwĭd) *adj.* **1.** Lacking in vitality or energy : weak. **2.** Lacking in spirit : listless. **3.** Sluggish : slow. **—lan′guid•ly** *adv.* **—lan′guid•ness** *n.*
lan•guish (lăng′gwĭsh) *v.* **1.** To become languid : weaken. **2.** To become depressed : pine. **3.** To assume a sad air, esp. in order to gain sympathy. **—lan′guish•er** *n.* **—lan′guish•ment** *n.*
lan•guor (lăng′gər, lăng′ər) *n.* **1.** Lack of energy : weakness. **2.** Languid indolence. **—lan′guor•ous** *adj.*
lank (lăngk) *adj.* **1.** Lean : slender. **2.** Long, straight, and limp <*lank* hair> **—lank′ly** *adv.* **—lank′ness** *n.*
lank•y (lăng′kē) *adj.* **-i•er, -i•est.** Tall, thin, and ungraceful. **—lank′i•ness** *n.*
lan•o•lin (lăn′ə-lĭn) *n.* A fatty substance obtained from sheep's wool and used esp. in soaps and ointments.
Lan•sing (lăn′sĭng). Cap. of Mich., in the SC part. *Pop.* 130,414.
lan•ta•na (lăn-tä′nə, -tăn′ə) *n.* Any of various aromatic, chiefly tropical shrubs of the genus *Lantana,* bearing small variously colored flowers in dense clusters.
lan•tern (lăn′tərn) *n.* **1.** A usu. portable light with transparent or translucent sides. **2.** The chamber in a lighthouse where the light is located.
lan•tha•nide (lăn′thə-nīd′) *n.* A rare-earth element.
lan•tha•num (lăn′thə-nəm) *n. Symbol* **La** A soft, silvery-white metallic element.
lan•yard (lăn′yərd) *n.* **1.** A rope used for securing something on ships. **2.** A cord worn around the neck to hold something, as a knife or whistle.
La•os (lä′ōs′, lā′ōs′, lous). Country of SE Asia. *Cap.* Vientiane. *Pop.* 3,760,000. **—La•o′tian** (lā-ō′shən) *n.* & *adj.*
lap[1] (lăp) *n.* **1.** The front of a seated person from the lower trunk to the knees. **2.** The portion of a garment that covers the lap. **3.** Responsibility : control <dumped her problems in my *lap*>
lap[2] (lăp) *v.* **lapped, lap•ping. 1.** To fold, wind, or wrap over or around something. **2.** To lay or extend so as to overlap. *—n.* **1.** A part that overlaps another. **2.** The amount by which one part overlaps another. **3.** One complete circuit, as around a racetrack. **4.** A single segment, as of a journey.
lap[3] (lăp) *v.* **lapped, lap•ping. 1.** To take up (food or drink) with the tongue. **2.** To wash with a gentle slapping sound <waves *lapping* against the dock> **—lap up.** To take in eagerly : devour <*lapping* up compliments> *—n.* The act, process, or sound of lapping.
La Paz (lə päz′, päz′). Administrative cap. of Bolivia, in the W part. *Pop.* 654,713.
lap•board (lăp′bôrd′, -bōrd′) *n.* A flat board that rests on the lap as a substitute for a table or desk.
lap dog *n.* A small dog that is easily held in the lap.
la•pel (lə-pĕl′) *n.* The part of a garment, esp. a coat, that is an extension of the collar and folds back.
lap•i•dar•y (lăp′ĭ-dĕr′ē) *n., pl.* **-ies.** A cutter and polisher of precious stones. *—adj.* **1.** Of or pertaining to precious stones or the work of a lapidary. **2.** Of, relating to, or suitable for engraving in stone.
lap•in (lăp′ĭn) *n.* Rabbit fur, esp. when sheared and dyed.
lap•is laz•u•li (lăp′ĭs lăz′yə-lē, lăzh′ə-) *n.* An opaque, blue semiprecious stone.
Lap•land (lăp′lănd′, -lənd). Region of N Scandinavia and NW USSR. **—Lapp** *n.*
lap•pet (lăp′ĭt) *n.* A decorative flap or loose fold on a garment or headdress.
lapse (lăps) *v.* **lapsed, laps•ing. 1.** To fall to a less desirable state. **2.** To pass : elapse. **3.** To be no longer in force, as through disuse or the passage of time. *—n.* **1.** A minor failure or error. **2.** A fall to a less desirable state. **3.** An interval of passing time. **4.** The ending of a privilege or right through disuse, neglect, or death.
lap•wing (lăp′wĭng′) *n.* An Old World narrow-crested bird of the genus *Vanellus,* related to the plovers.
lar•board (lär′bərd) *n. Naut.* PORT[2].
lar•ce•ny (lär′sə-nē) *n., pl.* **-nies.** The crime of theft. **—lar′ce•nous** *adj.*
larch (lärch) *n.* A coniferous tree of the genus *Larix,* with deciduous needles and durable wood.
lard (lärd) *n.* The white solid or semisolid rendered fat of a hog. *—v.* **1.** To insert strips of fat into (meat) before cooking. **2.** To enrich (e.g., writing) with additions.
lar•der (lär′dər) *n.* A place, as a room, where foods, as meat, are stored.
lar•ee (lâr′ē) *n.* See *rupee* at CURRENCY TABLE.
lar•es and pe•na•tes (lâr′ēz; pə-nā′tēz, -nä′-) *pl.n.* **1.** Household gods. **2.** Household possessions.
large (lärj) *adj.* **larg•er, larg•est. 1.** Greater than average in size or amount : big. **2.** Greater than average in scope, breadth, or capacity. **—at large. 1.** Not confined : free. **2.** As a whole : generally. **3.** Not representing a particular nation, state, or district. **—large′ly** *adv.* **—large′ness** *n.*
large intestine *n.* The portion of the intestine from the end of the small intestine to the anus.

large-scale (lärj'skāl') *adj.* **1.** Large : extensive. **2.** Drawn to show detail <a *large-scale* map>
lar•gess *also* **lar•gesse** (lär-zhĕs', -jĕs', lär'jĕs') *n.* **1.** Generosity in giving. **2.** A liberal gift.
lar•go (lär'gō) *adv. Mus.* In a slow and solemn manner. Used as a direction. **—lar'go** *adj.* & *n.*
lar•i•at (lăr'ē-ət) *n.* A long rope with a running noose at one end : lasso.
lark[1] (lärk) *n.* **1.** Any of various chiefly Old World birds of the family Alaudidae, having a melodious song. **2.** A bird similar to the lark, as a meadowlark.
lark[2] (lärk) *n.* **1.** A carefree adventure. **2.** A playful prank. *—v.* To engage in fun or playful pranks.
lark•spur (lärk'spûr') *n.* Any of various plants of the genus *Delphinium*, with spurred, often blue or purplish flowers.
†**lar•rup** (lăr'əp) *v. Regional.* To beat : flog. **—lar'rup** *n.*
lar•va (lär'və) *n., pl.* **-vae** (-vē). **1.** The wingless, often wormlike form of a newly hatched insect. **2.** A newly hatched animal, as a tadpole, that differs markedly from the adult. **—lar'val** *adj.*
lar•yn•gi•tis (lăr'ən-jī'tĭs) *n.* Inflammation of the larynx.
lar•ynx (lăr'ĭngks) *n., pl.* **la•ryn•ges** (lə-rĭn'jēz') or **lar•ynx•es.** The upper portion of the respiratory tract between the pharynx and the trachea that contains the vocal cords. **—la•ryn'ge•al** (lə-rĭn'jē-əl, -jəl, lăr'ən-jē'əl) *adj.*
la•sa•gna *also* **la•sa•gne** (lə-zän'yə) *n.* Wide flat noodles, usu. baked with a sauce of meat, tomatoes, and cheese.
las•car (lăs'kər) *n.* An East Indian sailor.
las•civ•i•ous (lə-sĭv'ē-əs) *adj.* Lustful : lewd. **—las•civ'i•ous•ly** *adv.* **—las•civ'i•ous•ness** *n.*
la•ser (lā'zər) *n.* A device that converts incident electromagnetic radiation of mixed frequencies to discrete frequencies of highly amplified and coherent visible radiation.
lash[1] (lăsh) *n.* **1.** A stroke with or as if with a whip. **2.** A whip. **3.** An eyelash. *—v.* **1.** To strike with or as if with a lash : whip. **2.** To move rapidly back and forth. **3.** To attack verbally. **—lash'er** *n.*
lash[2] (lăsh) *v.* To hold securely in place with a cord, rope, or chain.
Las Pal•mas (läs päl'mäs). City of the Canary Is., Spain. *Pop.* 357,158.
lass (lăs) *n.* A young woman : girl.
lass•ie (lăs'ē) *n.* A lass.
las•si•tude (lăs'ĭ-to͞od', -tyo͞od') *n.* Exhaustion, listless weakness, or torpor.
las•so (lăs'ō, lă-so͞o') *n., pl.* **-sos** or **-soes.** A long rope or leather thong with a running noose used esp. to catch horses and cattle. **—las'so** *v.*
last[1] (lăst) *adj.* **1.** Being, coming, or placed after all the rest : final. **2.** Being most recent : latest. **3.** Conclusive : authoritative. **4.** Least likely or expected <the *last* person to criticize> *—adv.* **1.** After all others in chronology or sequence. **2.** Most recently. **3.** At the end : finally. *—n.* **1.** The one that is last. **2.** The end. **—at last.** Finally. **—last'ly** *adv.*
last[2] (lăst) *v.* **1.** To continue to exist or operate. **2.** To be adequate (for).
last[3] (lăst) *n.* A block or form shaped like a human foot on which shoes are made or repaired.
Las Ve•gas (läs vā'gəs). City of SE Nev. *Pop.* 164,674.
lat. *abbr.* latitude.
Lat. *abbr.* Latin.
lat•a•ki•a (lăt'ə-kē'ə) *n.* An aromatic Turkish smoking tobacco.
latch (lăch) *n.* A fastening, as for a gate or door, that usu. consists of a movable bar that fits into a slot or notch. *—v.* To close with or as if with a latch. **—latch on to** (or **onto**). *Informal.* **1.** To cling to. **2.** To get hold of : obtain.
latch•et (lăch'ĭt) *n.* A leather strap or thong for fastening a shoe or sandal.
latch•key (lăch'kē') *n.* A key for opening a latch, esp. one on an outside door or gate.
latch•string (lăch'strĭng') *n.* A cord fastened to a latch and often passed through a hole in the door so that the latch can be lifted from the outside.
late (lāt) *adj.* **lat•er, lat•est. 1.** Coming, happening, or staying after the proper or usual time. **2.** Being or happening toward the end or close. **3.** Of a time just past : recent. **4.** Having recently died <his *late* father> *—adv.* **lat•er, lat•est. 1.** After the proper or usual time. **2.** At or into an advanced point or period of time. **3.** Recently. ☆**syns:** BELATED, OVERDUE, TARDY **—late'ness** *n.*
late•ly (lāt'lē) *adv.* Not long ago : recently.
la•tent (lāt'nt) *adj.* Present but not evident or active. **—la'ten•cy** *n.*
lat•er•al (lăt'ər-əl) *adj.* On, toward, or from the side. *—n. Football.* A usu. underhand pass that is thrown sideways or backward. **—lat'er•al•ly** *adv.*
la•tex (lā'tĕks') *n.* **1.** The usu. milky, viscous sap of certain plants, as the rubber tree. **2.** A water emulsion of rubber or plastic globules used esp. in paints.
lath (lăth) *n., pl.* **laths** (lă*th*z, lăths). **1.** A narrow, thin strip of wood or metal used esp. as a supporting structure for plaster. **2.** A building material, as a sheet of metal mesh, used esp. as a support for plaster.
lathe (lā*th*) *n.* A machine on which a piece of material is held while it is spun and shaped by a tool. **—lathe** *v.*
lath•er (lă*th*'ər) *n.* **1.** A foam or froth, esp. that formed by soap or detergent and water. **2.** Froth formed by sweating, esp. by a horse. **3.** A dither : agitation. *—v.* **1.** To produce lather. **2.** To cover with lather. **—lath'er•er** *n.* **—lath'er•y** *adj.*
Lat•in (lăt'n) *n.* **1.** The language of ancient Rome. **2.** A member of a people speaking a Romance language.
Latin America. Countries of the W Hemisphere S of the U.S. that have Spanish, Portuguese, or French as their official languages. **—Latin American** *n.* **—Lat'in-A•mer'i•can** *adj.*
lat•i•tude (lăt'ĭ-to͞od', -tyo͞od') *n.* **1. a.** The angular distance N or S of the earth's equator measured along a meridian. **b.** A region of the earth indicated by its latitude. **2.** Freedom from limitations. **—lat'i•tu'di•nal** *adj.*
lat•i•tu•di•nar•i•an (lăt'ĭ-to͞od'n-âr'ē-ən, -tyo͞od'-) *adj.* Tolerant, as toward the religious beliefs and behavior of others. **—lat'i•tu'di•nar'i•an** *n.*
la•trine (lə-trēn') *n.* A toilet, as in a barracks.
lat•ter (lăt'ər) *adj.* **1.** Of, pertaining to, or being the second of 2 persons or things mentioned. **2.** Closer to the end. **—lat'ter•ly** *adv.*
lat•ter-day (lăt'ər-dā') *adj.* Of the present time or a time not long past.
lat•tice (lăt'ĭs) *n.* **1.** A framework of interwoven strips, as of wood or metal. **2.** A structure, as a window or gate, that has a lattice.
lat•tice•work (lăt'ĭs-wûrk') *n.* **1.** An object, a structure, or material resembling a lattice. **2.** A structure made of lattices.
Lat•vi•a (lăt'vē-ə). Region and former country of N Europe, on the Baltic. **—Lat'vi•an** *n.* & *adj.*
laud (lôd) *v.* To praise : acclaim. **—laud** *n.* **—laud'a•ble** *adj.* **—laud'a•bly** *adv.*
lau•da•num (lôd'n-əm) *n.* A tincture of opium.
lau•da•to•ry (lô'də-tôr'ē, -tōr'ē) *adj.* Of, pertaining to, or expressing praise.
laugh (lăf, läf) *v.* **1.** To express mirth, joy, or derision with a smile and usu. inarticulate sounds. **2.** To feel or show amusement or derision. *—n.* **1.** The sound or act of laughing. **2.** Something that is amusing or ridiculous : joke. **—laugh'a•ble** *adj.* **—laugh'a•bly** *adj.* **—laugh'ing•ly** *adv.*
laugh•ing•stock (lăf'ĭng-stŏk', lä'fĭng-) *n.* An object of jokes or ridicule : butt.
laugh•ter (lăf'tər, läf'-) *n.* The act of or sound produced by laughing.
launch[1] (lônch) *v.* **1.** To set in motion with force : propel. **2.** To put (a boat) into the water. **3.** To put into operation : initiate. **—launch** *n.* **—launch'er** *n.*
launch[2] (lônch) *n.* **1.** A large ship's boat. **2.** A large open motorboat.
launching pad *also* **launch pad** *n.* A base or platform from which a spacecraft or rocket is launched.
laun•der (lôn'dər) *v.* To wash or wash and iron (e.g., clothes). **—laun'der•er** *n.* **—laun'dress** *n.*
Laun•dro•mat (lôn'drə-măt'). A trademark for a commercial self-service laundry.
laun•dry (lôn'drē) *n., pl.* **-dries. 1.** Clothes or linens that are to be or that have been laundered. **2.** A place where laundering is done. **—laun'dry•man'** *n.*
lau•re•ate (lôr'ē-ĭt, lŏr'-) *n.* One honored for accomplishment, as in science.
lau•rel (lôr'əl, lŏr'-) *n.* **1. a.** A shrub or tree, *Laurus nobilis*, native to the Mediterranean region, with aromatic evergreen leaves and small, blackish berries. **b.** A shrub or tree, as the mountain laurel, that is similar to the laurel. **2.** *often* **laurels. a.** A wreath of laurel leaves. **b.** Glory : honor.
Lau•sanne (lō-zăn', -zän'). City of W Switzerland, on the N shore of the Lake of Geneva. *Pop.* 128,800.
la•va (lä'və, lăv'ə) *n.* **1.** Molten rock from a volcano. **2.** Rock that is formed when lava cools and hardens.
la•va•bo (lə-vā'bō, -vä'-) *n., pl.* **-boes.** A washbowl and water tank with a spout that are fastened to a wall.
la•vage (lə-väzh') *n.* A washing out, esp. of a hollow bodily organ.
La•val (lə-văl'). City of S Que., Canada, near Montreal. *Pop.* 246,243.

lav•a•liere (lăv′ə-lîr′) *also* **la•val•lière** (lä′väl-yâr′) *n.* A pendant that is worn on a chain around the neck.

lav•a•to•ry (lăv′ə-tôr′ē, -tōr′ē) *n., pl.* **-ries. 1.** A permanently installed washbowl with running water. **2.** A bathroom.

lave (lāv) *v.* **laved, lav•ing.** To bathe.

lav•en•der (lăv′ən-dər) *n.* **1.** An aromatic Old World plant of the genus *Lavandula,* bearing small fragrant purplish flower clusters. **2.** A light purple. **–lav′en•der** *adj.*

lav•ish (lăv′ĭsh) *adj.* **1.** Giving or spending profusely. **2.** Marked by or produced with extravagance : luxurious. –*v.* To give or expend unstintingly. **–lav′ish•er** *n.* **–lav′ish•ly** *adv.* **–lav′ish•ness** *n.*

†**law** (lô) *n.* **1. a.** A rule of action or conduct established by authority, society, or custom. **b.** A body of such rules. **c.** The control that ensues when such rules are enforced. **2. a.** The study and science of laws : jurisprudence. **b.** The profession of a lawyer. **3.** The body of precepts that express the divine will as set forth in the Old Testament. **4.** A formulation of a relationship that holds between or among phenomena for all cases in which the specified conditions are met. **5.** A code of ethics or behavior. ☆***syns:*** AXIOM, FUNDAMENTAL, PRINCIPLE, THEOREM –*v. Regional.* To litigate.

law-a•bid•ing (lô′ə-bī′dĭng) *adj.* Acting in accordance with the law.

law•break•er (lô′brā′kər) *n.* Someone who breaks the law.

law•ful (lô′fəl) *adj.* **1.** Allowed by law. **2.** Recognized by law. **–law′ful•ly** *adv.* **–law′ful•ness** *n.*

law•giv•er (lô′gĭv′ər) *n.* A legislator.

law•less (lô′lĭs) *adj.* **1.** Without laws. **2.** Unrestrained by law : disobedient. **–law′less•ly** *adv.* **–law′less•ness** *n.*

law•mak•er (lô′mā′kər) *n.* One who makes laws : legislator. **–law′mak′ing** *n.*

lawn[1] (lôn) *n.* Ground covered with grass that is mowed regularly.

▲word history: The word *lawn*[1], which now denotes a carefully kept ornamental plot of closely mown grass, originated as a variant spelling of *laund,* a word now obsolete that meant "a woodland glade." *Laund* was borrowed from Old French *lande.* It is likely that *lande* entered Old French from a Celtic source, but the ultimate origin of *lande* is Germanic, and the word is cognate withthat is, has the same ancestor asEnglish *land.*

lawn[2] (lôn) *n.* A very fine, thin cotton or linen fabric. **–lawn′y** *adj.*

law•ren•ci•um (lô-rĕn′sē-əm, lō-) *n. Symbol* **Lw** A synthetic radioactive element.

law•suit (lô′so͞ot′) *n.* A case before a court of law.

law•yer (lô′yər, loi′ər) *n.* A person who is trained and qualified to give legal advice to clients and represent them in court.

lax (lăks) *adj.* **1. a.** Careless : negligent. **b.** Not strict : lenient. **2.** Not tense : slack. **–lax′i•ty, lax′ness** *n.* **–lax′ly** *adv.*

lax•a•tive (lăk′sə-tĭv) *n.* A substance, esp. a drug, that stimulates evacuation of the bowels. **–lax′a•tive** *adj.*

lay[1] (lā) *v.* **laid** (lād), **lay•ing. 1.** To place on a surface. **2.** To knock down. **3.** To allay : calm. **4.** To produce and deposit (eggs). **5.** To bet : wager. **6.** To spread over a surface. **7.** To bring to a given condition. **8.** To set or place in position. **9.** To prepare : devise <*lay* plans> **10.** To impose, esp. as a burden or punishment. **11.** To put forth : submit. **–lay away.** To set aside for future delivery or use. **–lay off. 1.** To dismiss (a worker) from a job, esp. temporarily. **2.** *Slang.* To cease : stop. –*n.* The manner, location, or appearance of something relative to something else.

lay[2] (lā) *adj.* **1.** Of, pertaining to, or belonging to the laity. **2.** Nonprofessional.

lay[3] (lā) *n.* A ballad.

lay[4] (lā) *v. p.t. of* LIE[1].

lay•er (lā′ər) *n.* **1.** One that lays. **2.** A single thickness, coating, or sheet that lies over or under another.

lay•er•ing (lā′ər-ĭng) *n.* The process of rooting branches, twigs, or stems still attached to a parent plant, as by placing a specially treated part in moist soil.

lay•ette (lā-ĕt′) *n.* A set of clothing and equipment for a newborn child.

lay•man (lā′mən) *n.* **1.** Someone who is not a member of the clergy. **2.** Someone who does not belong to a particular profession or specialty. **–lay′wom′an** *n.*

lay•off (lā′ôf′, -ŏf′) *n.* **1.** The temporary dismissal of an employee. **2.** A period of temporary suspension, rest, or inactivity.

lay•out (lā′out′) *n.* **1.** An arrangement : plan. **2.** A set, as of tools : outfit.

laze (lāz) *v.* **lazed, laz•ing.** To be lazy : take it easy.

la•zy (lā′zē) *adj.* **-zi•er, -zi•est. 1.** Disposed to be idle. **2.** Moving slowly : sluggish. ☆***syns:*** IDLE, INDOLENT, SHIFTLESS, SLOTHFUL **–la′zi•ly** *adv.* **–la′zi•ness** *n.*

la•zy•bones (lā′zē-bōnz′) *pl.n. (sing. or pl. in number). Slang.* A lazy person.

lazy Su•san (so͞o′zən) *n.* A revolving tray for food or condiments.

lb or **lb.** *abbr.* pound (Lat. *libra*).

l.c. *abbr.* lower-case.

L/C *abbr.* letter of credit.

l.c.d. *abbr.* lowest common denominator.

LDC *abbr.* less-developed country.

lea (lē, lā) *n.* A meadow : grassland.

leach (lēch) *v.* **1.** To pass (a liquid) through a substance so as to remove soluble materials. **2.** To be washed or washed out by leaching. **–leach′a•ble** *adj.*

lead[1] (lēd) *v.* **led** (lĕd), **lead•ing. 1.** To conduct along a way : guide. **2.** To be ahead or at the head of <*led* the procession> **3.** To live : pursue <*lead* a happy life> **4.** To tend toward a given result <practice that *led* to success> **5.** To direct the performance or activity of <*lead* an orchestra> **6.** To make the beginning play, as in a game or contest. **–lead off. 1.** To start : begin. **2.** To be the first player at bat in an inning. **–lead on.** To entice : lure. –*n.* **1.** The front, foremost, or winning position. **2.** A margin of advantage or superiority. **3.** A clue. **4.** Leadership. **5.** An example. **6. a.** A principal role, esp. in a play. **b.** A person playing such a role. **7.** The beginning play in a game. **8. a.** The prerogative of making the initial play in a card game. **b.** The suit or card played. **9.** A leash. **–lead′er** *n.* **–lead′er•ship′** *n.* **–lead′ing** *adj.*

lead[2] (lĕd) *n.* **1.** *Symbol* **Pb** A soft, heavy dull-gray metallic element, used in solder, bullets, and paints. **2.** A plumb bob suspended by a line for making soundings, as in the ocean. **3.** A thin metal strip used in printing to separate lines of type. **4.** A thin usu. graphitic stick used as the writing substance in a pencil. –*v.* **1.** To line, cover, weight, fill, or treat with lead. **2.** To provide space between (lines of printing type) with leads. **3.** To secure (window glass) with lead. **–lead′ing** *n.*

lead•en (lĕd′n) *adj.* **1.** Made of or containing lead. **2.** Of the color of lead : dark gray. **3.** Heavy : oppressive. **4.** Weighted down : burdened. **–lead′en•ness** *n.*

lead•off (lēd′ôf′, -ŏf′) *n.* **1.** An opening move or play. **2.** One that leads off.

lead poisoning *n.* Acute or chronic poisoning caused by the absorption of lead or any of its salts into the system.

lead-time (lēd′tīm′) *n.* The time between the decision to begin a project and its completion.

leaf (lēf) *n., pl.* **leaves** (lēvz). **1.** A usu. green, flat vascular plant structure that is attached to a stem and functions as a main organ of photosynthesis and transpiration. **2.** Something that resembles a leaf, as a page of a book. **3.** Foliage. **4.** A removable or hinged section, as of a table top. –*v.* **1.** To put forth leaves. **2.** To turn the pages of a magazine or book. **–leaf′less** *adj.* **–leaf′y** *adj.*

leaf•age (lē′fĭj) *n.* Leaves : foliage.

leaf•hop•per (lēf′hŏp′ər) *n.* Any of numerous insects of the family Cicadellidae that suck juices from plants.

leaf•let (lēf′lĭt) *n.* **1.** A segment of a compound leaf. **2.** A printed handbill : flier.

leaf mold *n.* Humus or compost made up of organic matter, as of decomposed leaves.

leaf•stalk (lēf′stôk′) *n.* The stalk by which a leaf is attached to a stem : petiole.

league[1] (lēg) *n.* **1.** An association, as of states or persons, for common action : alliance. **2.** *Informal.* A level, as of competition : class. **–league** *v.*

league[2] (lēg) *n.* A unit of distance equal to 3 mi or approx. 4.8 km.

leak (lēk) *v.* **1.** To escape or pass through a breach or flaw. **2.** To allow to escape or pass through a breach or flaw. **3.** To make or become publicly known through a breach of secrecy. –*n.* **1. a.** An opening, as a hole or crack, through which something can escape or pass. **b.** An escape or passage through a leak. **2.** A disclosure of confidential information. **–leak′age** *n.* **–leak′i•ness** *n.* **–leak′y** *adj.*

lean[1] (lēn) *v.* **1.** To bend or slant away from a perpendicular position : incline. **2.** To incline the weight of the body for support. **3.** To rely for help or support. **4.** To have a tendency : be inclined. **–lean** *n.*

lean[2] (lēn) *adj.* **1.** Not fat or fleshy : thin. **2.** Having little or no fat <*lean* beef> **3.** Not productive, plentiful, or satisfying. **–lean′ly** *adv.* **–lean′ness** *n.*

lean•ing (lē′nĭng) *n.* An inclination.

lean-to (lēn′to͞o′) *n., pl.* **-tos. 1.** A structure with a single sloping roof, usu. built against and supported by an outside wall. **2.** A shelter or shed resembling a lean-to.

leap (lēp) *v.* **leaped** *or* **leapt** (lĕpt, lēpt), **leap•ing. 1.** To move from the ground with a spring of the legs : jump. **2.** To jump over. —*n.* A jump. **—leap'er** *n.*

leap•frog (lēp'frôg', -frŏg') *n.* A game in which 1 player leaps over another who is kneeling or bending over. **—leap'frog'** *v.*

leap year *n.* A year in the Gregorian calendar with 366 days, Feb. 29 being the extra day.

learn (lûrn) *v.* **learned** *or* **learnt** (lûrnt), **learn•ing. 1.** To acquire knowledge, understanding, or mastery (of) by study or experience. **2.** To memorize. **3.** To become informed of : discover. **—learn'er** *n.*

learn•ed (lûr'nĭd) *adj.* Erudite : scholarly. **—learn'ed•ly** *adv.* **—learn'ed•ness** *n.*

▲word history: The adjective *learned* is the same word as the past participle of the verb *learn.* Since Old English times *learn* has always meant "to gain knowledge," but in Middle English times it also meant "to teach," although this sense is no longer current in standard Modern English. In Middle English the past participle *learned* has the sense "taught," and it has survived as an adjective, esp. with the meaning "erudite."

learn•ing (lûr'nĭng) *n.* Knowledge and esp. erudition.

lease (lēs) *n.* A contract for the use or occupation of real estate usu. for a given period in exchange for rent. —*v.* **leased, leas•ing. 1.** To grant by lease. **2.** To use or occupy under a lease.

lease•hold (lēs'hōld') *n.* **1.** Possession by lease. **2.** Property held by lease. **—lease'hold'er** *n.*

leash (lēsh) *n.* **1.** A chain, rope, or strap for leading or holding an animal in check. **2.** Control : restraint. **—leash** *v.*

least (lēst) **1.** Lowest in rank or importance. **2.** Smallest in degree or size. —*adv.* In or to the smallest degree. —*n.* One that is least. **—at least.** In any event.

least common denominator *n.* Lowest common denominator.

least common multiple *n.* The smallest quantity exactly divisible by each of 2 or more other numbers; e.g., 12 is the least common multiple of 2, 3, 4, and 6.

†**least•ways** (lēst'wāz') *adv. Regional.* At least.

least•wise (lēst'wīz') *adj. Informal.* At least : anyway.

leath•er (lĕth'ər) *n.* The hide of an animal dressed for use. **—leather** *adj.* **—leath'er•y** *adj.*

leath•er•neck (lĕth'ər-nĕk') *n. Slang.* A U.S. Marine.

leave[1] (lēv) *v.* **left** (lĕft), **leav•ing. 1.** To go away (from). **2. a.** To permit or cause to remain. **b.** To deliver. **3.** To have as a remainder. **4.** To refrain from interfering with. **5.** To bequeath. **6.** To forsake : abandon. **—leave out.** To omit.

leave[2] (lēv) *n.* **1.** Permission. **2.** Official permission for absence from duty. **3.** Formal farewell.

leave[3] (lēv) *v.* **leaved, leav•ing.** To put forth foliage : leaf.

leaved (lēvd) *adj.* **1.** Bearing a leaf or leaves. **2.** Having a given number or kind of leaves <*4-leaved*> <*serrate-leaved*>

leav•en (lĕv'ən) *n.* **1.** A fermenting substance, as yeast, used to cause batters and doughs to rise. **2.** Something that enlivens or lightens. —*v.* **1.** To add a fermenting agent to (dough). **2.** To enliven or lighten.

leav•en•ing (lĕv'ə-nĭng) *n.* An agent that produces fermentation : leaven.

leaves (lēvz) *n. pl. of* LEAF.

leave-tak•ing (lēv'tā'kĭng) *n.* An exchange of good-bys : farewell.

leav•ings (lē'vĭngz) *pl.n.* Bits left over : remnants.

Leb•a•non (lĕb'ə-nən). Country of SW Asia, on the E shore of the Mediterranean. *Cap.* Beirut. *Pop.* 3,205,000. **—Leb'a•nese'** (-nēz', -nēs') *adj. & n.*

lech•er•y (lĕch'ə-rē) *n.* **1.** Excessive indulgence in sexual activity. **2.** Lasciviousness : prurience. **—lech'er** *n.* **—lech'er•ous** *adj.* **—lech'er•ous•ly** *adv.*

lec•i•thin (lĕs'ə-thĭn) *n.* Any of a group of phosphorus-containing compounds found in all plant and animal tissues, derived commercially from egg yolks, soybeans, and corn, and used in the production of foods, pharmaceuticals, cosmetics, and plastics.

lec•tern (lĕk'tərn) *n.* A tall desk, often with a slanted top, that serves as a support for the books or notes of a standing speaker.

lec•tor (lĕk'tər) *n.* One who reads aloud the lessons in a church service.

lec•ture (lĕk'chər) *n.* **1.** A speech delivered before an audience or class, esp. to provide information or instruction. **2.** A reprimand. **—lec'ture** *v.* **—lec'tur•er** *n.*

led (lĕd) *v. p.t. & p.p. of* LEAD[1].

le•der•ho•sen (lā'dər-hō'zən) *pl.n.* Leather shorts worn by men and boys, esp. in Bavaria.

ledge (lĕj) *n* **1.** A horizontal projection forming a shelf, as on a wall or cliff. **2.** An underwater ridge of rock.

ledg•er (lĕj'ər) *n.* A book in which sums of money received and paid out, as by a business, are recorded.

lee (lē) *n.* **1.** The side, as of a ship, that is away from the wind. **2.** Shelter : cover.

Lee (lē), **Robert Edward.** 1807–70. Amer. Confederate commander.

leech (lēch) *n.* **1.** Any of various chiefly aquatic bloodsucking annelid worms of the family Hirudinea, esp. *Hirudo medicinalis,* once used by physicians to bleed their patients. **2.** One who preys on or lives off others : parasite.

Leeds (lēdz). Borough of NC England. *Pop.* 724,300.

leek (lēk) *n.* A plant, *Allium porrum,* related to the onion, with a slender, edible bulb.

leer (lîr) *n.* A sly, suggestive, or cunning look. **—leer** *v.*

leer•y (lîr'ē) *adj.* **-i•er, -i•est.** *Informal.* Distrustful : wary. **—leer'i•ly** *adv.* **—leer'i•ness** *n.*

lees (lēz) *pl.n.* Dregs.

lee•ward (lē'wərd, lōō'ərd) *adj.* Facing or located away from the wind. —*n.* The lee side. **—lee'ward** *adv.*

Leeward. Islands of the West Indies, in the N Lesser Antilles from the Virgin Is. SE to Guadeloupe.

lee•way (lē'wā') *n.* **1.** The drift of a ship or plane away from the correct course. **2.** A permitted margin of variation or freedom.

left[1] (lĕft) *adj.* **1.** Of, at, or located on the side of the body that faces north when the subject is facing east. **2.** *often* **Left.** Of or belonging to the political Left. —*n.* **1. a.** The direction or position that is toward or on the left side. **b.** The left side or hand. **2. Left.** The persons and groups seeking egalitarian political goals through reform or revolution. —*adv.* On or toward the left.

left[2] (lĕft) *v. p.t. & p.p. of* LEAVE[1].

left field *n.* The part of a baseball outfield that is to the left as viewed from home plate. **—left fielder** *n.*

left-hand (lĕft'hănd') *adj.* **1.** Of or located on the left. **2.** Left-handed.

left-hand•ed (lĕft'hăn'dĭd) *adj.* **1.** Using the left hand more easily than the right. **2.** Done with the left hand. **3.** Clumsy : awkward. **4.** Counterclockwise. —*adv.* With the left hand. **—left'-hand'ed•ly** *adv.* **—left'-hand'ed•ness** *n.*

left•ism *also* **Left•ism** (lĕf'tĭz'əm) *n.* The ideology of the Left. **—left'ist** *n.*

left•o•ver (lĕft'ō'vər) *n. often* **leftovers.** An unused portion, esp. of food : remnant.

leg (lĕg) *n.* **1.** A limb or appendage of an animal, used esp. for locomotion and support. **2.** Something that resembles the leg of an animal in shape or function <a piano *leg*> **3.** The part of a garment that covers the leg. **4.** A stage of a trip. —*v.* **legged, leg•ging.** *Informal.* To go on foot.

leg. *abbr.* **1.** legal. **2.** legate. **3.** legislation; legislative; legislature.

leg•a•cy (lĕg'ə-sē) *n., pl.* **-cies. 1.** Something bequeathed by will : bequest. **2.** Something handed down from one who has gone before or from the past.

le•gal (lē'gəl) *adj.* **1.** Of or pertaining to law or lawyers. **2. a.** Based on or authorized by law : lawful. **b.** Established by law : statutory. **—le•gal'i•ty** *n.* **—le'gal•i•za'tion** *n.* **—le'gal•ize'** *v.* **—le'gal•ly** *adv.*

le•gal•ism (lē'gə-lĭz'əm) *n.* Literal and usu. too strict adherence to the letter of the law. **—le'gal•ist** *n.* **—le'gal•is'tic** *adj.*

leg•ate (lĕg'ĭt) *n.* An official envoy, esp. of the pope. **—leg'ate•ship'** *n.*

leg•a•tee (lĕg'ə-tē') *n.* One who inherits a legacy.

le•ga•tion (lĭ-gā'shən) *n.* **1.** A diplomatic mission in a foreign country headed by a minister. **2.** The premises occupied by a minister to a foreign government.

le•ga•to (lĭ-gä'tō) *adv. Mus.* Smoothly and with successive notes connected. Used as a direction. **—le•ga'to** *adj. & n.*

leg•end (lĕj'ənd) *n.* **1.** A story handed down from the past, esp. one that is widely believed but unverifiable. **2.** An inscription or title on an object, as a coin. **3.** An explanatory caption for an illustration.

▲word history: The word *legend* is derived from Latin *legenda,* a participial form derived from the verb *legere,* "to read." In Medieval Latin *legenda* was used to mean "something to be read" and esp. the narrative of a saint's life. These biographies were considered to be important as both historical records and moral examples. The word *legenda* was borrowed into English as *legend* in the 14th cent. It is likely that the utterly incredible exploits and events recounted in some legends led to the development of the sense "unverified popular tale, myth" for the English word.

leg•en•dar•y (lĕj'ən-dĕr'ē) *adj.* Of, based on, or of the nature of a legend.

leg•er•de•main (lĕj'ər-də-mān') *n.* Sleight of hand.

leg•ged (lĕg'ĭd, lĕgd) *adj.* Having a given kind or number of legs <long-*legged*>

leg•gings (lĕg'ĭngz) *pl.n.* A leg covering.

leg•gy (lĕg′ē) *adj.* **-gi•er, -gi•est. 1.** Having very long legs. **2.** Having long, attractive legs. **—leg′gi•ness** *n.*

leg•horn (lĕg′hôrn′, -ərn) *n.* **1.** A hat of finely plaited straw. **2.** *often* **Leghorn.** A domestic fowl orig. bred in Mediterranean regions and raised esp. for producing eggs.

leg•i•ble (lĕj′ə-bəl) *adj.* Capable of being read. **—leg′i•bil′i•ty** *n.* **—leg′i•bly** *adv.*

le•gion (lē′jən) *n.* **1.** A Roman army unit that consisted of from 3,000 to 6,000 infantrymen. **2.** A great number : multitude. *—adj.* Constituting a great number : numerous. **—le′gion•ar′y** (-jə-nĕr′ē) *n.* & *adj.* **—le′gion•naire′** (-jə-nâr′) *n.*

legis. *abbr.* legislation; legislative; legislature.

leg•is•late (lĕj′ĭ-slāt′) *v.* **-lat•ed, -lat•ing. 1.** To pass laws. **2.** To enact into law. **3.** To bring about by or as if by legislating. **—leg′is•la′tor** *n.*

leg•is•la•tion (lĕj′ĭ-slā′shən) *n.* **1.** The act or process of passing laws : lawmaking. **2.** A law or group of laws proposed or enacted by a legislature.

leg•is•la•tive (lĕj′ĭ-slā′tĭv) *adj.* **1.** Of or pertaining to legislation or a legislature. **2.** Having the power to legislate.

Legislative Assembly *n. Can.* The elected governing body in most provinces.

leg•is•la•ture (lĕj′ĭ-slā′chər) *n.* An officially selected body of persons with the power and responsibility to make and change laws.

le•git (lə-jĭt′) *adj. Slang.* Legitimate.

le•git•i•mate (lə-jĭt′ə-mĭt) *adj.* **1.** In accordance with the law : lawful. **2.** In accordance with accepted standards or rules. **3.** Reasonable : sensible. **4.** Genuine : real. **5.** Born of legally married parents. **—le•git′i•ma•cy** *n.* **—le•git′i•mate•ly** *adv.*

leg•man (lĕg′măn′) *n.* **1.** A news reporter whose assignment is to gather information. **2.** An office assistant who runs errands and does routine tasks.

leg•ume (lĕg′yo͞om′, lə-gyo͞om′) *n.* **1.** A plant of the family Leguminosae, as a bean or pea, bearing pods that split when mature. **2.** The pod or seeds of a legume used as food. **—le•gu′mi•nous** *adj.*

leg•work (lĕg′wûrk′) *n. Informal.* A task, as gathering information, that involves physical activity.

Le Ha•vre (lə hä′vrə). City of N France, on the English Channel. *Pop.* 217,881.

lei[1] (lā, lā′ē) *n.* A wreath of flowers, esp. one worn around the neck.

lei[2] (lā) *n. pl. of* LEU.

Leices•ter (lĕs′tər). City of C England. *Pop.* 276,600.

Lei•den *also* **Ley•den** (līd′n). City of SW Netherlands. *Pop.* 103,046.

Leip•zig (līp′sĭg, -sĭk). City of SC East Germany. *Pop.* 563,980.

lei•sure (lē′zhər, lĕzh′ər) *n.* **1.** Time during which one is free from work or duties. **2.** Effortless ease. **—lei′sure•ly** *adj.* & *adv.*

leit•mo•tif *also* **leit•mo•tiv** (līt′mō-tēf′) *n.* Something, as a dominant theme in a novel, that is repeated over and over.

lek (lĕk) *n.* See CURRENCY TABLE.

LEM (lĕm) *n.* A lunar excursion module.

lem•ming (lĕm′ĭng) *n.* A rodent of the genus *Lemmus* and related genera, of N regions, as *L. lemmus,* noted for its mass migrations into the sea.

lem•on (lĕm′ən) *n.* **1.** A tree, *Citrus limonia,* cultivated for its yellow acidic juicy fruit. **2.** *Informal.* Something, as a television set or automobile, that proves to be defective or unsatisfactory.

lem•on•ade (lĕm′ə-nād′) *n.* A sweetened beverage of lemon juice and water.

lem•pi•ra (lĕm-pîr′ə) *n.* See CURRENCY TABLE.

le•mur (lē′mər) *n.* Any of several arboreal primates of the family Lemuridae with soft fur, large eyes, and a long tail.

Le•na (lē′nə). River of E Siberian USSR, flowing c. 2,670 mi (4,295 km) gen. N to the Laptev Sea.

lend (lĕnd) *v.* **lent** (lĕnt), **lend•ing. 1.** To allow the temporary use of. **2.** To give out (money) for temporary use, usu. at interest. **3.** To furnish : provide. **4.** To offer (oneself) : accommodate. **—lend′er** *n.*

length (lĕngkth, lĕngth) *n.* **1.a.** The longest dimension of something. **b.** The measure of something on its longest dimension. **2.** A measured dimension or distance. **3.** Extent or duration. **4.** A measure of something used as a unit to estimate distances <an arm's *length*> **—length′y** *adj.*

length•en (lĕngk′thən, lĕng′-) *v.* To make or become longer.

length•wise (lĕngkth′wīz′, lĕngth′-) *adv.* & *adj.* Of or along the direction of the length : longitudinally.

le•ni•ent (lē′nē-ənt, lēn′yənt) *adj.* **1.** Inclined to be forgiving and mild : merciful. **2.** Not demanding : tolerant. **—le′ni•en•cy, le′ni•ence** *n.* **—le′ni•ent•ly** *adv.*

Le•nin (lĕn′ĭn), **V(ladimir) I(lyich).** 1870–1924. Russian revolutionary leader.

Len•in•grad (lĕn′ĭn-grăd′). City of NW European USSR. *Pop.* 4,119,00.

len•i•tive (lĕn′ĭ-tĭv) *adj.* Capable of easing pain or discomfort. **—len′i•tive** *n.*

lens (lĕnz) *n.* **1.** A curved piece of transparent material, as glass, that is used to refract light rays so that they converge or diverge to form an image. **2.** A combination of 2 or more lenses for forming an image for viewing or photographing. **3.** A transparent structure in the eye that focuses light rays entering through the pupil to form an image on the retina.

lent (lĕnt) *v. p.t.* & *p.p. of* LEND.

Lent (lĕnt) *n.* A 40-day period of fasting and penitence observed by many Christians from Ash Wednesday until Easter. **—Lent′en** *adj.*

▲word history: The word *Lent* is derived from the Old English word *lencten,* which denoted both the season of spring and the ecclesiastical season. *Lencten* is ult. derived from the same root as the adjective *long.* The meaning "spring" probably arose because spring is the time of year when the days grow longer. The ecclesiastical sense developed from the fact that Lent partially coincides with spring.

len•til (lĕn′təl) *n.* A leguminous Old World plant, *Lens esculenta,* bearing pods that contain edible seeds.

Le•o (lē′ō) *n.* **1.** A constellation in the N Hemisphere. **2. a.** The 5th sign of the zodiac. **b.** One born under this sign.

Le•o•nar•do da Vin•ci (lē′ə-när′dō də vĭn′chē). 1452–1519. Florentine artist and engineer.

le•one (lē-ōn′) *n.* See CURRENCY TABLE.

le•o•nine (lē′ə-nīn′) *adj.* Of, pertaining to, or resembling a lion.

leop•ard (lĕp′ərd) *n.* A large feline mammal, *Panthera pardus,* of Africa and Asia, with a tawny coat with dark rosettelike markings.

le•o•tard (lē′ə-tärd′) *n.* A snug-fitting garment worn esp. by dancers.

lep•er (lĕp′ər) *n.* **1.** Someone suffering from leprosy. **2.** An outcast.

lep•re•chaun (lĕp′rĭ-kôn′, -kŏn′) *n.* A mischief-making elf of Irish folklore.

lep•ro•sy (lĕp′rə-sē) *n.* A chronic infectious bacterial disease marked by the progressive destruction of tissue. **—lep′rous** *adj.*

lep•ton (lĕp′tŏn′) *n., pl.* **-ta** (-tə). See *drachma* at CURRENCY TABLE.

les•bi•an (lĕz′bē-ən) *n.* A woman who is a homosexual. **—les′bi•an** *adj.*

lese maj•es•ty *also* **lèse ma•jes•té** (lĕz′ măj′ĭ-stē) *n.* An offense or crime against the ruler or supreme power of a state.

le•sion (lē′zhən) *n.* **1.** A wound : injury. **2.** A well-defined bodily area in which tissue has changed in a way that is characteristic of a disease.

Le•so•tho (lə-sō′tō). Kingdom of S Africa, enclave within EC South Africa. *Cap.* Maseru. *Pop.* 1,360,000.

less (lĕs) *adj.* **1.** Smaller. **2.** Of lower importance, degree, or rank. *—adv.* To a smaller extent, degree, or frequency. *—n.* A smaller amount. *—prep.* Subtracting : minus.

-less *suff.* Without : lacking <blame*less*> <wing*less*>

les•see (lĕ-sē′) *n.* One holding property under a lease.

less•en (lĕs′ən) *v.* To decrease or cause to decrease.

less•er (lĕs′ər) *adj.* Not as great in size or significance <a *lesser* benefit>

Lesser An•til•les (ăn-tĭl′ēz). Island group in the West Indies.

les•son (lĕs′ən) *n.* **1.** Something that is to be or has been learned. **2. a.** A period of instruction : class. **b.** A reading or exercise used to instruct. **3.** An edifying example. **4.** A passage from sacred writings that is read as part of a religious service.

les•sor (lĕs′ôr′, lĕ-sôr′) *n.* One who lets property by a lease.

lest (lĕst) *conj.* For fear that.

let[1] (lĕt) *v.* **let, let•ting. 1.** To give permission to : allow <wouldn't *let* him drive> **2.** To cause to : make <*Let* me hear from you soon.> **3.** To rent : lease. **—let down.** To disappoint. **—let on.** To allow to be known : reveal. **—let up. 1.** To become less : diminish. **2.** To be or become less strict or demanding.

let[2] (lĕt) *n.* **1.** An obstruction : obstacle. **2.** An invalid stroke in a net game, as tennis, that must be replayed.

let•down (lĕt′doun′) *n.* **1.** A decrease, as in effort or energy. **2.** A disappointment.

le•thal (lē′thəl) *adj.* Of, pertaining to, causing, or capable of causing death. **—le′thal•ly** *adv.*

leth•ar•gy (lĕth′ər-jē) *n.* **1.** Drowsiness. **2.** Indifference : apathy. **—le•thar′gic** (lə-thär′jĭk) *adj.* **—le•thar′gi•cal•ly** *adv.*

let's (lĕts). Let us.

Lett (lĕt) *n.* & *adj.* Latvian.

let•ter (lĕt′ər) *n.* **1.** A written symbol that represents a speech sound and constitutes an alphabetical unit. **2.** A printed or written communication sent to a recipient. **3.** The literal sense of something <the *letter* of the law> **4. letters. a.** Literature. **b.** Learning. —*v.* To mark or write with letters : inscribe. **—let'ter·er** *n.*

let·ter·head (lĕt'ər-hĕd') *n.* **1.** A heading on a sheet of letter paper, usu. a name and address. **2.** Stationery printed or engraved with a letterhead.

let·ter-per·fect (lĕt'ər-pûr'fĭkt) *adj.* Absolutely correct.

let·ter·press (lĕt'ər-prĕs') *n.* Printing in which a raised inked surface is pressed directly on paper.

letters patent *pl.n.* A document granting a patentee exclusive right to the enjoyment or possession of an invention.

let·tuce (lĕt'əs) *n.* A plant of the genus *Lactuca,* esp. *L. sativa,* grown for its edible leaves that are used esp. in salads.

let·up (lĕt'ŭp') *n.* **1.** Reduction, as in force or intensity : slowdown. **2.** A pause.

le·u (lĕ'o͞o) *n., pl.* **lei** (lā). See CURRENCY TABLE.

leu·ke·mi·a (lo͞o-kē'mē-ə) *n.* Any of a group of usu. fatal diseases in which white blood cells proliferate in uncontrolled numbers. **—leu·ke'mic** *adj.*

leu·ko·cyte *also* **leu·co·cyte** (lo͞o'kə-sīt') *n.* A white or colorless nucleated blood cell.

lev (lĕf) *n., pl.* **lev·a** (lĕv'ə). See CURRENCY TABLE.

Le·vant (lə-vănt'). Countries bordering on the E Mediterranean.

lev·ee[1] (lĕv'ē) *n.* An embankment built to prevent a body of water, esp. a river, from overflowing.

lev·ee[2] (lĕv'ē, lə-vē', -vā') *n.* **1.** A reception once held by a monarch or other high-ranking personage upon arising from bed. **2.** A formal reception, as at a court.

lev·el (lĕv'əl) *n.* **1.** Relative position, height, or rank on a scale. **2.** A standard elevation from which other heights and depths are measured. **3. a.** A horizontal line or plane at right angles to the plumb. **b.** The position or height of such a line or plane <ankle *level*> **4.** A flat, horizontal surface. **5.** A flat tract of land. **6.** A device for determining whether a surface is horizontal. —*adj.* **1.** Having no irregularities, roughness, or indentations. **2.** Horizontal. **3.** Of the same position, height, or rank as another. **4.** Consistent : uniform. **5.** Steady and reasonable in judgment. —*v.* **-eled, -el·ing** *or* **-elled, -el·ling. 1.** To make or become level or flat. **2.** To tear or knock down : raze. **3.** To equalize. **4.** To direct : aim. **—lev'el·er** *n.* **—lev'el·ly** *adv.* **—lev'el·ness** *n.*

lev·el·head·ed (lĕv'əl-hĕd'ĭd) *adj.* Having or showing common sense and good judgment : sensible. **—lev'el·head'ed·ness** *n.*

lev·er (lĕv'ər, lē'vər) *n.* **1.** A simple machine with a rigid body, usu. a metal bar, pivoted on a fixed fulcrum. **2.** A projecting handle for operating or adjusting a mechanism. **3.** A bar that is used to dislodge or pry something.

lev·er·age (lĕv'ər-ĭj, lē'vər-) *n.* **1. a.** The action of a lever. **b.** The mechanical advantage of a lever. **2.** Power to act effectively.

le·vi·a·than (lə-vī'ə-thən) *n.* **1.** A very large sea creature. **2.** Something of enormous size.

Le·vi's (lē'vīz'). A trademark for heavy denim trousers.

lev·i·tate (lĕv'ĭ-tāt') *v.* **-tat·ed, -tat·ing.** To rise or raise in the air in apparent defiance of gravity. **—lev'i·ta'tion** *n.*

Le·vit·i·cus (lə-vĭt'ĭ-kəs) *n.* See BIBLE TABLE.

lev·i·ty (lĕv'ĭ-tē) *n.* Lack of seriousness : frivolity.

lev·y (lĕv'ē) *v.* **-ied, -y·ing. 1.** To collect or impose (e.g., a tax). **2.** To draft for military service. **3.** To carry on (a war). **4.** To confiscate property to satisfy a legal claim. —*n.* **1.** The act or process of levying. **2.** An amount, as of money or property, levied. **3.** Troops that have been drafted for military service. **—lev'i·er** *n.*

lewd (lo͞od) *adj.* **1.** Preoccupied with sex : lustful. **2.** Indecent : obscene. **—lewd'ly** *adv.* **—lewd'ness** *n.*

▲word history: A thousand years ago it was no disgrace to be a *lewd* person. The word *lewd,* from Old English *lǣwede,* orig. meant "lay, not belonging to the clergy." Each subsequent sense of *lewd* that developed, however, had a worse connotation than the preceding one. During Middle English times the word *lewd* ran the gamut of senses from "lay" through "unlearned," "low-class," "ignorant, ill-mannered," and "wicked" to "lascivious." The last sense is the only one that survives in Modern English.

Lew·is (lo͞o'ĭs). **1. Meriwether.** 1774–1809. Amer. explorer. **2. (Harry) Sinclair.** 1885–1951. Amer. novelist.

lex·i·cog·ra·phy (lĕk'sĭ-kŏg'rə-fē) *n.* The work or process of writing, compiling, or editing dictionaries. **—lex'i·cog'ra·pher** *n.* **—lex'i·co·graph'ic** (-kə-grăf'ĭk), **lex'i·co·graph'i·cal** *adj.*

lex·i·con (lĕk'sĭ-kŏn') *n.* **1.** A dictionary. **2.** A vocabulary, as of an individual or group. **—lex'i·cal** *adj.*

Ley·den (līd'n). Leiden.

lf *abbr.* **1.** lightface. **2.** low frequency.

lg. *or* **lge.** *abbr.* large.

Lha·sa (lä'sə, lăs'ə). City of SW China, traditional cap. of Tibet. *Pop.* 80,000.

Li *symbol for* LITHIUM.

li·a·bil·i·ty (lī'ə-bĭl'ĭ-tē) *n., pl.* **-ties. 1.** The state of being liable. **2.** Something owed to another : debt. **3.** A handicap : disadvantage. **4.** A tendency : likelihood.

li·a·ble (lī'ə-bəl) *adj.* **1.** Legally obligated : responsible. **2.** Subject. **3.** Apt : likely <*liable* to be angry>

li·ai·son (lē'ā-zŏn', lē-ā'zŏn', lē'ə-) *n.* **1.** Communication, as between different units of an organization. **2.** A channel or means of communication. **3.** A close relationship : connection. **4.** An adulterous sexual relationship.

li·ar (lī'ər) *n.* Someone who tells lies.

lib (lĭb) *n. Informal.* Liberation.

lib. *abbr.* **1.** liberal. **2.** librarian; library.

li·ba·tion (lī-bā'shən) *n.* **1. a.** The act of pouring out a liquid as a religious offering. **b.** The liquid poured. **2.** *Informal.* A drink, esp. an alcoholic drink.

li·bel (lī'bəl) *n.* **1.** A written, printed, oral, or pictorial statement that damages by defaming a person's character or reputation. **2.** The act or tort of publishing or uttering a libel. —*v.* **-beled, -bel·ing** *or* **-belled, -bel·ling.** To make or publish a libel about. **—li'bel·ous** *adj.*

lib·er·al (lĭb'ər-əl, lĭb'rəl) *adj.* **1.** Generous. **2.** Abundant : ample. **3.** Not literal : loose. **4.** Of, pertaining to, or based on the liberal arts. **5.** Respectful of the ideas or behavior of others : tolerant. **6.** Favoring democratic reform and the use of governmental resources to effect social progress. **7. Liberal.** Of or belonging to a political party that advocates liberal views, esp. in the U.S., Great Britain, and Canada. —*n.* Someone who holds liberal opinions or ideas. **—lib'er·al·ism** *n.* **—lib'er·al'i·ty** (lĭb'ə-răl'ĭ-tē) *n.* **—lib'er·al·ize'** *v.* **—lib'er·al·ly** *adv.*

liberal arts *pl.n.* Academic disciplines, as languages, history, and philosophy, that provide general cultural information.

lib·er·ate (lĭb'ə-rāt') *v.* **-at·ed, -at·ing.** To set free, as from oppression, confinement, or foreign control. **—lib'er·a'tion** *n.* **—lib'er·a'tor** *n.*

Li·be·ri·a (lī-bîr'ē-ə). Country of W Africa, on the Gulf of Guinea. *Cap.* Monrovia. *Pop.* 1,890,000. **—Li·be'ri·an** *adj.* & *n.*

lib·er·tar·i·an (lĭb'ər-târ'ē-ən) *n.* **1.** A believer in freedom of thought and action. **2.** A believer in free will.

lib·er·tine (lĭb'ər-tēn') *n.* A morally unrestrained, dissolute person. **—lib'er·tin·ism** *n.*

lib·er·ty (lĭb'ər-tē) *n., pl.* **-ties. 1.** The state of being free : freedom. **2.** Permission : authorization. **3.** *often* **liberties.** A disrespectful course of action, esp. unwarranted familiarity. **4.** An authorized leave from naval duty. ☆***syns:*** FREEDOM, LATITUDE, LEEWAY, LICENSE

li·bi·do (lĭ-bē'dō, -bī'-) *n., pl.* **-dos. 1.** Psychic energy that is associated with instinctual biological drives. **2.** Sexual desire. **—li·bid'i·nal** (lə-bĭd'n-əl) *adj.* **—li·bid'i·nous** (-əs) *adj.*

Li·bra (lī'brə, lē'-) *n.* **1.** A constellation in the S Hemisphere. **2. a.** The 7th sign of the zodiac. **b.** One born under this sign.

li·brar·i·an (lī-brâr'ē-ən) *n.* Someone who specializes in library work.

li·brar·y (lī'brĕr'ē) *n., pl.* **-ies. 1.** A place in which literary and artistic materials, as books and periodicals, are kept for reading, reference, or borrowing. **2.** A collection of reading materials.

li·bret·to (lĭ-brĕt'ō) *n., pl.* **-bret·tos** *or* **-bret·ti** (-brĕt'ē). **1.** The text of a dramatic musical work, esp. of an opera. **2.** A book containing a libretto. **—li·bret'tist** *n.*

Li·bre·ville (lē'brə-vēl'). Cap. of Gabon, in the NW. *Pop.* 251,000.

Lib·y·a (lĭb'ē-ə). Country of N Africa. *Cap.* Tripoli. *Pop.* 13,030,000. **—Lib'y·an** *adj.* & *n.*

lice (līs) *n. pl. of* LOUSE.

li·cence (lī'səns) *n. esp. Brit. var. of* LICENSE.

li·cense (lī'səns) *n.* **1. a.** Permission, esp. legal permission to operate or own a specified thing. **b.** Proof, usu. in the form of a document, card, plate, or tag, that a license has been granted. **2.** Latitude of action, esp. when used without restraint. —*v.* **-censed, -cens·ing.** To grant a license to or for. **—li'cens·ee'** *n.* **—li'cens·er** *n.*

li·cen·ti·ate (lī-sĕn'shē-ĭt) *n.* A person who is granted a license by an authorized body to practice a specified profession.

li·cen·tious (lī-sĕn'shəs) *adj.* Lacking in moral restraint : immoral. **—li·cen'tious·ly** *adv.* **—li·cen'tious·ness** *n.*

li·chee (lē'chē) *n. var. of* LITCHI.

li·chen (lī'kən) *n.* Any of numerous plants consisting of a fungus, usu. of the class Ascomycetes, closely combined with certain of the green or blue-green algae to form a crustlike, scaly, or branching growth on rocks and tree trunks. **—li'chened** *adj.* **—li'chen·ous** *adj.*

lic·it (lĭs'ĭt) *adj.* Lawful.

lick (lĭk) *v.* **1.** To pass the tongue along. **2.** To move unsteadily over like a tongue. **3.** *Slang.* **a.** To thrash. **b.** To defeat. —*n.* **1.** An act or process of licking. **2.** A small quantity : bit. **3.** An exposed salt deposit that is licked by animals. **4.** A blow.
lick·e·ty-split (lĭk′ĭ-tē-splĭt′) *adv. Informal.* Very rapidly.
lick·spit·tle (lĭk′spĭt′l) *n.* A fawning underling : toady.
lic·o·rice (lĭk′ər-ĭs, -ĭsh) *n.* **1.** A plant, *Glycyrrhiza glabra,* with blue flowers and a sweet root used esp. to flavor medicines and candy. **2.** A confection made from licorice root.
lid (lĭd) *n.* **1.** A hinged or removable cover for a container. **2.** An eyelid. **3.** *Slang.* A hat. **–lid′ded** *adj.* **–lid′less** *adj.*
lie[1] (lī) *v.* **lay** (lā), **lain** (lān), **ly·ing. 1.** To be in, remain in, or take a horizontal or recumbent position : recline. **2.** To be or stay in a particular condition. **3.** To be located. **4.** To extend. —*n.* The position in which something is located or situated.
lie[2] (lī) *n.* An untrue statement made deliberately : falsehood. ☆***syns:*** CANARD, FALSEHOOD, FALSITY, FIB, PREVARICATION, STORY, TALE, UNTRUTH —*v.* **lied, ly·ing. 1.** To tell a lie. **2.** To give a false impression.
Liech·ten·stein (lĭKH′tən-shtīn, lĭk′tən-stīn′). Principality in C Europe between Austria and Switzerland. *Cap.* Vaduz. *Pop.* 26,000.
lied (lēd, lēt) *n., pl.* **lie·der** (lē′dər). A German art song.
lief (lēf) *adv.* Willingly : readily.
liege (lēj) *n.* **1.** A feudal lord. **2.** A vassal. —*adj.* Faithful : loyal.
Li·ège (lē-ĕzh′, -āzh′). City of E Belgium, on the Meuse. *Pop.* 220,183.
lien (lēn, lē′ən) *n.* The legal right to take and hold or sell the property of another to satisfy an obligation or debt.
lieu (lo͞o) *n. Archaic.* Place : stead. **–in lieu of.** In place of.
lieu·ten·ant (lo͞o-tĕn′ənt) *n.* **1.** An officer in the U.S. Army, Air Force, and Marine Corps ranking below a captain. **2.** An officer in the U.S. Navy ranking above an ensign and below a lieutenant commander. **3.** An officer ranking below a captain in a police or fire department. **4.** Someone authorized to act in place of another : deputy. **–lieu·ten′an·cy** *n.*
lieutenant colonel *n.* An officer in the U.S. Army, Air Force, and Marine Corps ranking above a major and below a colonel.
lieutenant commander *n.* An officer in the U.S. Navy ranking above a lieutenant and below a commander.
lieutenant general *n.* An officer in the U.S. Army, Air Force, and Marine Corps ranking above a major and below a general.
lieutenant governor *n.* **1.** An elected official ranking just below the governor of a U.S. state. **2.** *Can.* The nonelective chief of government of a province.
life (līf) *n., pl.* **lives** (līvz). **1.** The property or quality by which living organisms are distinguished from dead organisms or inanimate matter, esp. as shown in the ability to grow, carry on metabolism, respond to stimuli, and reproduce. **2.** Living organisms as a whole <animal *life*> **3.** A human being. **4.** The period of time between an organism's birth or inception and its death : lifetime. **5.** A biography. **6.** Animate and esp. human activities. **7.** A manner of living. **8.** Animation : vitality. ☆***syns:*** DURATION, EXISTENCE, LIFETIME, TERM **–life′less** *adj.* **–life′like′** *adj.*
life·blood (līf′blŭd′) *n.* An indispensable source of vitality or life.
life·boat (līf′bōt′) *n.* A boat used esp. for rescue at sea.
life·guard (līf′gärd′) *n.* An expert swimmer hired to safeguard other swimmers, as at a beach.
life line *also* **life·line** (līf′līn′) *n.* **1.** A line to which a drowning or falling victim may cling. **2.** A means or route for transporting indispensable supplies. **3.** A source of salvation in a crisis.
life·long (līf′lông′, -lŏng′) *adj.* Continuing throughout a lifetime.
life preserver *n.* A buoyant device, as one in the shape of a ring, used to keep a person afloat in water.
lif·er (lī′fər) *n. Slang.* **1.** A prisoner serving a life sentence. **2.** A career military officer or enlisted person.
life raft *n.* A raft usu. of wood or inflatable material used by people who have been forced into water by emergency.
life·sav·er (līf′sā′vər) *n.* **1.** One that saves a life. **2.** A lifeguard. **3.** A life preserver shaped like a ring. **4.** One that provides help in a crisis or emergency. **–life′sav′ing** *n.* & *adj.*
life·style *also* **life-style** *or* **life style** (līf′stīl′) *n.* A way of life that reflects an individual's preferences.
life·time (līf′tīm′) *n.* The period during which an individual lives or exists.
life·work (līf′wûrk′) *n.* The primary work of a person's lifetime.
lift (lĭft) *v.* **1. a.** To elevate : raise. **b.** To rise : ascend. **2.** To bring to an end : stop. **3.** To repay (a debt). **–lift off.** To begin flight, as a spacecraft. —*n.* **1.** The act or process of lifting. **2.** Force or power available for lifting <the *lift* of a derrick> **3.** A load. **4.** The extent or height to which something is lifted. **5.** An elevation of spirits. **6.** A device or machine designed to pick up, raise, or carry something. **7.** *esp. Brit.* An elevator. **8.** A ride in a vehicle along the way to a destination. **9.** The component of the total aerodynamic force acting on an airfoil or aircraft that is exerted in an upward direction opposing the pull of gravity. **–lift′er** *n.*
lift·off (lĭft′ôf′, -ŏf′) *n.* The vertical takeoff or moment of takeoff of an aircraft and esp. of a rocket.
lig·a·ment (lĭg′ə-mənt) *n.* A band of tough, fibrous tissue joining bones or cartilages or holding a body organ in place. **–lig′a·men′tous** *adj.*
li·gate (lī′gāt′) *v.* **-gat·ed, -gat·ing.** To tie or bind with a ligature.
lig·a·ture (lĭg′ə-cho͝or′, -chər) *n.* **1.** Something, as a cord or wire, that ties or binds. **2.** A thread used in surgery for tying blood vessels. **3.** A printing character, as *fi,* that combines 2 or more letters.
light[1] (līt) *n.* **1.** Electromagnetic radiation that can be perceived by the normal, unaided human eye and has wavelengths between 3,900 and 7,700 angstroms. **2.** Brightness. **3.** A source of light, as an electric lamp. **4.** The illumination from a source of light. **5.** Daylight. **6.** Daybreak : dawn. **7.** A source of fire, as a match. **8.** A way of looking at or considering something. **9.** Enlightenment : understanding. **10.** A prominent person. **11.** A device, esp. a traffic signal, that uses light as a warning. —*adj.* **1.** Not dark : bright. **2.** Mixed with white : pale <a *light* green> —*v.* **light·ed** *or* **lit** (lĭt), **light·ing. 1.** To set or be set on fire : ignite. **2.** To provide with or cause to give out light : illuminate. **–light′ness** *n.*
light[2] (līt) *adj.* **1.** Not heavy. **2.** Of less force, quantity, intensity, or volume than usual or normal <a *light* tap on the arm><*light* snow> **3.** Intended as entertainment : not profound. **4.** Free from worries, cares, or troubles <a *light* spirit> **5.** Frivolous : trivial. **6.** Requiring little exertion or effort <*light* office duties> **7.** Agile : nimble. **8.** Dizzy. —*adv.* **1.** In a light manner : lightly. **2.** With little luggage <traveling *light*> —*v.* **light·ed** *or* **lit** (lĭt), **light·ing. 1.** To come to rest : settle, alight, or land. **2.** To come unexpectedly. **–light out.** To leave hastily. **–light′ly** *adv.* **–light′ness** *n.*
light·en[1] (līt′n) *v.* To make or become light or lighter : brighten. **–light′en·er** *n.*
light·en[2] (līt′n) *v.* **1.** To make or become less heavy. **2.** To make or become less troublesome, oppressive, or severe.
light·er[1] (lī′tər) *n.* A mechanical device used to light a cigarette, cigar, or pipe.
light·er[2] (lī′tər) *n.* A barge used esp. to load and unload a cargo ship.
light·face (līt′fās′) *n.* A typeface with thin, light lines. **–light′faced′** *adj.*
light-fin·gered (līt′fĭng′gərd) *adj.* Skilled at petty thievery.
light·head·ed (līt′hĕd′ĭd) *adj.* **1.** Dizzy. **2.** Not serious : frivolous.
light·heart·ed (līt′här′tĭd) *adj.* Free from trouble, anxiety, or care : cheerful. **–light′heart′ed·ly** *adv.* **–light′heart′ed·ness** *n.*
light·house (līt′hous′) *n.* A structure with a powerful light to guide sailors.
light·ning (līt′nĭng) *n.* The flash of light that accompanies a high-tension natural electric discharge in the atmosphere. —*adj.* Very fast or sudden.
lightning bug *n.* A firefly.
lightning rod *n.* A grounded metal rod positioned high on a structure to protect it from lightning.
light opera *n.* An operetta.
lights (līts) *pl.n.* The lungs, esp. the lungs of an animal used for food.
light·ship (līt′shĭp′) *n.* A ship with a powerful light or horn that is anchored in dangerous waters to warn other vessels.
light show *n.* A display of colored lights in kaleidoscopic patterns, often accompanied by film loops and slides.
light·weight (līt′wāt′) *n.* **1.** One that weighs relatively little. **2.** A boxer or wrestler whose weight is between 127 and 135 lb. **3.** Someone of little consequence. **–light′weight′** *adj.*
light-year *also* **light year** (līt′yîr′) *n.* A measure equal to the distance light travels in a year, approx. 5.878 trillion mi, or 9.458 trillion km.
lig·ne·ous (lĭg′nē-əs) *adj.* WOODY 1, 2.
lig·ni·fy (lĭg′nə-fī′) *v.* **-fied, -fy·ing.** To make or become woody or woodlike.
lig·nite (lĭg′nīt′) *n.* A low-grade, brownish-black soft coal.
lig·ro·in (lĭg′rō-ĭn) *n.* A volatile, flammable fraction of petroleum obtained by distillation and used as a solvent.

lik•a•ble *also* **like•a•ble** (lī′kə-bəl) *adj.* Capable of being liked : pleasing.
†**like**[1] (līk) *v.* **liked, lik•ing. 1.** To find attractive or pleasant : enjoy <*likes* apples> **2.** To want : wish <Do as you *like.*> **3.** To be fond of. **4.** *Regional.* To be pleasing to. ☆***syns:*** ENJOY, RELISH, SAVOR —*n.* Something one enjoys : preference.
like[2] (līk) *prep.* **1.** Similar or similarly to. **2.** Characteristic of. **3.** Disposed to <feels *like* quitting> **4.** Such as <artists *like* painters and sculptors> —*adj.* Being the same or almost the same : similar. ☆***syns:*** ALIKE, ANALOGOUS, COMPARABLE, EQUIVALENT, PARALLEL, UNIFORM —*n.* Something similar or related. —*conj.* In the same way that : as <can't cook *like* she does>
-like *suff.* Resembling : characteristic of <child*like*><shell-*like*>
like•li•hood (līk′lē-ho͝od′) *n.* Probability.
like•ly (līk′lē) *adj.* **-li•er, -li•est. 1.** Probable : apt <*likely* to fail> **2.** Believable : credible <a *likely* explanation> **3.** Apt to succeed or yield a desired result : promising <a *likely* theory> —*adv.* Probably.
like-mind•ed (līk′mīn′dĭd) *adj.* Of the same mind or way of thinking.
lik•en (lī′kən) *v.* To see or describe as being like : compare.
like•ness (līk′nĭs) *n.* **1.** Resemblance. **2.** Appearance : semblance. **3.** A copy : image.
like•wise (līk′wīz′) *adv.* **1.** In a similar way. **2.** As well : also.
lik•ing (lī′kĭng) *n.* **1.** A feeling of approval or fondness. **2.** Preference : taste.
li•ku•ta (lē-ko͞o′tä) *n., pl.* **ma•ku•ta** (mä-). See *zaire* at CURRENCY TABLE.
li•lac (lī′lək, -lŏk′, -lăk′) *n.* **1.** A shrub, *Syringa vulgaris,* widely grown for its large fragrant purplish or white flower clusters. **2.** A pale purple. **–li′lac** *adj.*
li•lan•ge•ni (lĭ-läng′gĕ-nē) *n.* See CURRENCY TABLE.
Lil•li•pu•tian *also* **lil•li•pu•tian** (lĭl′ə-pyo͞o′shən) *n.* A very small being or person. —*adj.* Tiny : diminutive.
Li•long•we (lē lông′wā′). Cap. of Malawi, in the SC part. *Pop.* 102,924.
lilt (lĭlt) *n.* **1.** A light, cheerful tune or song. **2.** A rhythmical way of speaking.
lil•y (lĭl′ē) *n., pl.* **-ies. 1.** Any of various plants of the genus *Lilium,* often bearing trumpet-shaped flowers. **2.** A plant similar or related to the lily, as the water lily.
lil•y-liv•ered (lĭl′ē-lĭv′ərd) *adj.* Timid : cowardly.
lily of the valley *n., pl.* **lilies of the valley.** A widely cultivated plant, *Convallaria majalis,* bearing fragrant, bell-shaped white flowers on a leafless raceme.
Li•ma (lē′mə). Cap. of Peru, in the WC part. *Pop.* 3,158,417.
li•ma bean (lī′mə) *n.* Any of several varieties of a tropical American plant, *Phaseolus limensis,* bearing flat pods with light-green edible seeds.
limb (lĭm) *n.* **1.** A large bough of a tree : branch. **2.** An animal's jointed appendage used for locomotion or grasping, as an arm, leg, wing, or flipper.
lim•ber (lĭm′bər) *adj.* **1.** Bending easily : pliable. **2.** Moving nimbly and easily : agile. —*v.* To make or become limber. **–lim′ber•ly** *adv.* **–lim′ber•ness** *n.*
lim•bo (lĭm′bō) *n., pl.* **-bos. 1.** *often* **Limbo.** The abode of souls kept from entering Heaven by such circumstances as failure to be baptized. **2.** A place or condition of oblivion or neglect.
Lim•burg•er (lĭm′bûr′gər) *n.* A soft white cheese with a very strong odor and flavor.
lime[1] (līm) *n.* A spiny tree, *Citrus aurantifolia,* native to Asia, with evergreen leaves, fragrant white flowers, and edible egg-shaped fruit, with a green rind and acid juice.
lime[2] (līm) *n.* Any of several Old World linden trees.
lime[3] (līm) *n.* **1.** Calcium oxide. **2.** Birdlime. **–lim′y** *adj.*
lime•ade (lī-mād′) *n.* A sweetened beverage of lime juice and water.
lime•kiln (līm′kĭl′, -kĭln′) *n.* A furnace for reducing naturally occurring forms of calcium carbonate to lime.
lime•light (līm′līt′) *n.* **1.** A stage light in which lime is heated to incandescence producing brilliant illumination. **2.** A focus of public attention.
lim•er•ick (lĭm′ər-ĭk) *n.* A humorous verse of 5 lines usu. with the rhyme scheme *aabba.*
lime•stone (līm′stōn′) *n.* A form of sedimentary rock that is composed mainly of calcium carbonate and is used in building and in making lime and cement.
lim•it (lĭm′ĭt) *n.* **1.** The point beyond which something may not or cannot proceed. **2. a.** A boundary. **b. limits.** Bounds. **3.** The greatest or smallest amount or number. —*v.* To place a limit on : confine or restrict. **–lim′i•ta′tion** *n.* **–lim′it•less** *adj.* **–lim′it•less•ly** *adv.*
lim•it•ed (lĭm′ĭ-tĭd) *adj.* **1.** Restricted or confined within limits. **2.** Of or indicating trains or buses that make few stops and provide fast service.
limn (lĭm) *v.* **limned, limn•ing** (lĭm′nĭng). **1.** To describe. **2.** To depict by drawing or painting. **–limn′er** (lĭm′nər) *n.*
li•mo•nite (lī′mə-nīt′) *n.* A yellowish-brown to black natural iron oxide used as an ore of iron.
lim•ou•sine (lĭm′ə-zēn′, lĭm′ə-zēn′) *n.* **1.** A luxurious large automobile, often driven by a chauffeur. **2.** A small bus used to carry passengers esp. to airports and hotels.
limp (lĭmp) *v.* **1.** To walk lamely. **2.** To proceed in an unsteady or unpredictable way. —*n.* A jerky, irregular, or awkward gait. —*adj.* **1.** Lacking or having lost rigidity : flabby. **2.** Not firm or strong : weak. **–limp′ly** *adv.* **–limp′ness** *n.*
lim•pet (lĭm′pĭt) *n.* Any of numerous marine gastropod mollusks, esp. of the families Acmaeidae and Patellidae, that have a conical shell and adhere to tidal rocks.

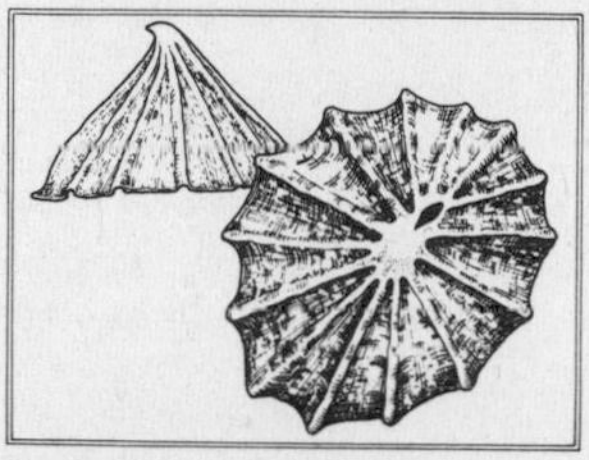
limpet

lim•pid (lĭm′pĭd) *adj.* Transparently clear. **–lim•pid′i•ty** *n.* **–lim′pid•ly** *adv.*
lin•age (lī′nĭj) *n.* The number of lines in a piece of printed or written matter.
linch•pin (lĭnch′pĭn′) *n.* A locking pin inserted through a shaft, as of an axle, to keep a wheel from slipping off.
Lin•coln (lĭng′kən). Cap. of Neb., in the SE. *Pop.* 171,932.
Lincoln, Abraham. 1809–65. 16th U.S. President (1861–65); assassinated.
Lind•bergh (lĭnd′bûrg′, lĭn′-), **Charles Augustus.** 1902–74. Amer. aviator.
lin•den (lĭn′dən) *n.* Any of various shade trees of the genus *Tilia,* having heart-shaped leaves and yellow flowers.
line[1] (līn) *n.* **1.** A path taken by a point that is free to move <a straight *line*> <a *curved* line> **2.** A thin, continuous mark, as that made by a pen applied to a surface. **3. a.** A boundary : border. **b.** A limit. **4.** A contour. **5.** A cable, string, rope, cord, or wire. **6.** An electric cable. **7.** A telephone connection. **8.** A transportation system. **9. a.** A course of action, behavior, or thought. **b.** A course taken by something in motion. **10.** A general manner or method. **11.** Alignment. **12.** An occupation or trade. **13.** A group arranged in a sequence, row, or series. **14.** A horizontal row of written or printed words. **15.** A brief letter : note. **16. lines.** The dialogue of a dramatic work. **17.** *Football.* **a.** A line of scrimmage. **b.** The linemen. ☆***syns:*** COLUMN, FILE, QUEUE, RANK, ROW, STRING —*v.* **lined, lin•ing. 1.** To incise or mark with lines. **2.** To place in or form a line (along). **–line up. 1.** To align. **2.** To secure and make available <*lined up* a group to help>
line[2] (līn) *v.* **lined, lin•ing. 1.** To cover the inner surface of. **2.** To fill generously, as with money or food.
lin•e•age (lĭn′ē-ĭj) *n.* Direct descent from an ancestor : ancestry.
lin•e•al (lĭn′ē-əl) *adj.* **1.** Belonging to, consisting of, or being in a direct line of descent from an ancestor. **2.** Linear.
lin•e•a•ment (lĭn′ē-ə-mənt) *n.* A distinctive contour, shape, or feature of the body and esp. of the face.
lin•e•ar (lĭn′ē-ər) *adj.* **1.** Of, pertaining to, consisting of, or resembling a line. **2.** Long and narrow.
linear perspective *n.* A technique in painting and drawing in which parallel lines converge so as to give the illusion of depth and distance.
line•back•er (līn′băk′ər) *n.* *Football.* One of the defensive players positioned immediately behind the line of scrimmage.
line drive *n.* *Baseball.* A hard-hit ball whose path approximates a straight line nearly parallel with the ground.
line•man (līn′mən) *n.* **1.** Someone who installs or repairs electric power or communication lines. **2.** A player on the forward line of a team, esp. in football.
lin•en (lĭn′ən) *n.* **1.** Thread, yarn, or fabric made of flax. **2.** *often* **linens.** Household articles, as sheets, made of linen or similar fabric. **–lin′en** *adj.*
line of scrimmage *n.* *Football.* An imaginary line across the field where the ball is positioned for each play.

lin•er[1] (lī′nər) *n.* A ship or airplane that carries passengers on a regular route.
lin•er[2] (lī′nər) *n.* One that lines or serves as a lining.
line score *n. Baseball.* A record of the runs, hits, and errors of each inning of a game.
lines•man (līnz′mən) *n.* **1.** *Football.* An official who marks the downs. **2.** An official in a court game, as tennis, who calls shots that fall out of bounds. **3.** LINEMAN 1.
line-up *also* **line•up** (līn′ŭp′) *n.* **1.** A line of persons, esp. suspects, formed for inspection or identification. **2** The members of a team who take part in a game.
ling (lĭng) *n., pl.* **ling** or **lings.** Any of various marine food fishes related to or resembling the cod.
lin•ger (lĭng′gər) *v.* **1.** To stay as if reluctant to leave : tarry. **2.** To persist. **3.** To be slow in acting : procrastinate. **—lin′ger•er** *n.* **—lin′ger•ing•ly** *adv.*
lin•ge•rie (lăn′zhə-rē′, län′zhə-rā′) *n.* Women's underwear.
lin•go (lĭng′gō) *n., pl.* **-goes.** Language that is unfamiliar or unintelligible.
lin•gua fran•ca (lĭng′gwə frăng′kə) *n.* A language used for communication between persons who speak different languages.
lin•guist (lĭng′gwĭst) *n.* **1.** A fluent speaker of several languages. **2.** One who specializes in linguistics.
lin•guis•tics (lĭng-gwĭs′tĭks) *n. (sing. in number).* The study of the nature and structure of human speech. **—lin•guis′tic** *adj.* **—lin•guis′ti•cal•ly** *adv.*
lin•i•ment (lĭn′ə-mənt) *n.* A liquid medicine applied to the skin.
lin•ing (lī′nĭng) *n.* Material used to cover or coat an inside surface.
link (lĭngk) *n.* **1.** One of the rings forming a chain. **2.** Something that is like a link <a sausage *link*>. **3.** A bond : tie. **4.** A cuff link. —*v.* To connect or become connected by or as if by a link or links.
link•age (lĭng′kĭj) *n.* **1. a.** The act or process of linking. **b.** The state of being linked. **2.** A system of connecting structures.
links (lĭngks) *pl.n.* A golf course.
Lin•nae•us (lĭ-nē′əs), **Carolus.** 1707–78. Swedish botanist. **—Lin•nae′an** *adj.*
lin•net (lĭn′ĭt) *n.* A small Old World songbird, *Acanthis cannabina.*
li•no•le•um (lĭ-nō′lē-əm) *n.* A floor and counter-top covering consisting of a surface of hardened linseed oil and a filler, as powdered cork, on a canvas or burlap backing.
lin•seed (lĭn′sēd′) *n.* The seeds of flax, which are the source of an oil used in paints and varnishes.
lin•sey-wool•sey (lĭn′zē-wo͝ol′zē) *n.* A linen or cotton fabric woven with wool.
lint (lĭnt) *n.* **1.** Fine bits of fiber and fluff : fuzz. **2.** Downy material scraped from linen and used to dress wounds.
lin•tel (lĭn′tl) *n.* A horizontal beam across the top of a door or window that supports the weight of the structure above it.
li•on (lī′ən) *n.* **1.** A large carnivorous feline mammal, *Panthera leo,* of Africa and India, with a short tawny coat and a long, heavy mane in the male. **2.** A person of great importance or prestige. **—li′on•ess** *n.*
li•on•heart•ed (lī′ən-här′tĭd) *adj.* Extremely courageous.
li•on•ize (lī′ə-nīz′) *v.* **-ized, -iz•ing.** To treat (a person) as a celebrity.
lip (lĭp) *n.* **1. a.** *Anat.* Either of the 2 fleshy, muscular folds that surround the opening of the mouth. **b.** A part or structure that resembles a lip. **2.** A rim or margin, as of a bell, vessel, or crater. **3.** *Slang.* Impudent talk.
lip reading *n.* A technique for interpreting unheard speech by watching a speaker's lip and facial movements. **—lip′-read′** *v.* **—lip reader** *n.*
lip service *n.* An expression of acquiescence or allegiance that is not acted upon.
lip•stick (lĭp′stĭk′) *n.* A stick of waxy lip coloring enclosed in a cylindrical case.
Lip•tau•er (lĭp′tou′ər) *n.* A soft cheese of Hungarian origin.
liq•ue•fy *also* **liq•ui•fy** (lĭk′wə-fī′) *v.* **-fied, -fy•ing.** To make or become liquid. **—liq′ue•fac′tion** *n.* **—liq′ue•fi′er** *n.*
li•queur (lĭ-kûr′, -kyo͝or′) *n.* A sweet alcoholic beverage flavored with aromatic ingredients : cordial.
liq•uid (lĭk′wĭd) *n.* A substance that flows readily and is difficult to compress. —*adj.* **1.** Of or being a liquid. **2.** Liquefied, esp.: **a.** Melted by heating <*liquid* butter> **b.** Condensed by cooling <*liquid* nitrogen> **3.** Easily converted into or being cash. **4.** Shining and clear <*liquid* eyes> **5.** Flowing readily. **—li•quid′i•ty** *n.*
liq•ui•date (lĭk′wĭ-dāt′) *v.* **-dat•ed, -dat•ing. 1.** To repay (e.g., a debt) : settle. **2.** To close down (e.g., a business firm) by settling accounts and dividing up assets. **3.** To put an end to, esp. to kill. **—liq′ui•da′tion** *n.* **—liq′ui•da′tor** *n.*
liq•uor (lĭk′ər) *n.* **1.** A distilled alcoholic beverage. **2.** A liquid solution or substance.
li•ra (lîr′ə, lē′rə) *n., pl.* **li•re** (lîr′ā, lē′rā) or **li•ras.** See CURRENCY TABLE.
Lis•bon (lĭz′bən). Cap. of Portugal, on the Tagus R. *Pop.* 829,900.
li•sen•te (lē-sĕn′tā) *n., pl.* **-te.** See *loti* at CURRENCY TABLE.
lisle (līl) *n.* A fine, tightly twisted strong cotton thread.
lisp (lĭsp) *n.* A speech defect or mannerism marked by the pronunciation of *s* and *z* as (th) and (*th*). **—lisp** *v.* **—lisp′er** *n.*
lis•some (lĭs′əm) *adj.* **1.** Nimble. **2.** Lithe. **—lis′some•ly** *adv.* **—lis′some•ness** *n.*
list[1] (lĭst) *n.* **1.** A series of numbers or words, as the names of persons. **2.** A catalogue : index. —*v.* **1.** To itemize. **2.** To enter on a list : register.
list[2] (lĭst) *n.* A tilt to 1 side, as of a ship. —*v.* To tilt or cause to tilt.
list[3] (lĭst) *v. Archaic.* To listen or listen to.
lis•ten (lĭs′ən) *v.* **1.** To try to hear. **2.** To pay heed. **—lis′ten•er** *n.*
list•ing (lĭs′tĭng) *n.* **1.** A list. **2.** Something that is entered in a list.
list•less (lĭst′lĭs) *adj.* Lacking energy, spirit, or enthusiasm : lethargic. **—list′less•ly** *adv.* **—list′less•ness** *n.*
list price *n.* An advertised or published price that is often subject to discount.
lists (lĭsts) *pl.n.* **1.** An arena for tournaments, esp. jousting. **2.** A place of combat. **3.** An area of controversy.
Liszt (lĭst), **Franz.** 1811–86. Hungarian composer and pianist.
lit (lĭt) *v. var. p.t. & p.p. of* LIGHT.
lit. *abbr.* literary; literature.
lit•a•ny (lĭt′n-ē) *n., pl.* **-nies.** A prayer in which phrases recited by a leader alternate with answers from a congregation.
li•tchi *also* **li•chee** (lē′chē) *n.* **1.** A Chinese tree, *Litchi chinensis,* bearing edible fruit. **2.** The fruit of the litchi tree.
li•ter (lē′tər) *n.* See MEASUREMENT TABLE.
lit•er•al (lĭt′ər-əl) *adj.* **1.** Conforming to or in accordance with the exact meaning of a word. **2.** Word for word : verbatim. **3.** Concerned primarily with facts : prosaic. **4.** Without embellishment or exaggeration. **—lit′er•al•ly** *adv.* **—lit′er•al•ness** *n.*
lit•er•al•ism (lĭt′ər-ə-lĭz′əm) *n.* **1.** Adherence to the explicit sense of a given doctrine or text. **2.** Literal portrayal : realism. **—lit′er•al•ist** *n.* **—lit′er•al•is′tic** *adj.*
lit•er•ar•y (lĭt′ə-rĕr′ē) *adj.* **1.** Of or pertaining to literature. **2.** Appropriate to or used in literature. **3.** Knowledgeabl_ in literature. **—lit′er•ar′i•ly** *adv.*
lit•er•ate (lĭt′ər-ĭt) *adj.* **1.** Having the ability to read and write. **2.** Having or showing skill in using words. **3.** Knowledgeable : educated. **—lit′er•a•cy** *n.* **—lit′er•ate** *n.*
lit•er•a•ti (lĭt′ə-rä′tē) *pl.n.* The intelligentsia, esp. distinguished writers.
lit•er•a•tim (lĭt′ə-rā′tĭm, -rä′-) *adv.* Letter for letter : literally.
lit•er•a•ture (lĭt′ər-ə-cho͝or′, -chər) *n.* **1.** Writing of lasting value and excellence. **2.** Written works in verse or prose. **3.** Printed matter, as circulars for a political campaign.
lithe (līth, līth) *adj.* **lith•er, lith•est.** Bending easily : resilient : supple. **—lithe′ly** *adv.* **—lithe′ness** *n.*
lithe•some (līth′səm, līth′-) *adj.* Lithe.
lith•i•um (lĭth′ē-əm) *n. Symbol* **Li** A soft, silvery-white metallic element.
li•thog•ra•phy (lĭ-thŏg′rə-fē) *n.* A printing process in which a flat surface, as stone or sheet aluminum, is treated so that the ink adheres only to the portions that are to be printed. **—lith′o•graph′** (lĭth′ə-grăf′) *n.* & *v.* **—li•thog′ra•pher** *n.* **—lith′o•graph′ic, lith′o•graph′i•cal** *adj.*
li•thol•o•gy (lĭ-thŏl′ə-jē) *n.* The microscopic study, description, and classification of rocks. **—li•thol′o•gist** *n.*
lith•o•sphere (lĭth′ə-sfîr′) *n.* The solid outer part of the earth.
Lith•u•a•ni•a (lĭth′o͞o-ā′nē-ə). Region and former country of N Europe, on the Baltic. **—Lith′u•a′ni•an** *adj.* & *n.*
lit•i•gate (lĭt′ĭ-gāt′) *v.* **-gat•ed, -gat•ing.** To engage in or make the subject of legal proceedings. **—lit′i•gant** *n.* **—lit′i•ga′tion** *n.* **—lit′i•ga′tor** *n.*
li•ti•gious (lĭ-tĭj′əs) *adj.* **1.** Of or pertaining to litigation. **2.** Given to engaging in litigation. **—li•ti′gious•ness** *n.*
lit•mus (lĭt′məs) *n.* A blue powder obtained from certain lichens that changes to red with increasing acidity and to blue with increasing alkalinity.
litmus paper *n.* Unsized white paper treated with litmus and used as an acid-base indicator.
li•tre (lī′tər) *n. esp. Brit. var. of* LITER.
lit•ter (lĭt′ər) *n.* **1.** A couch, often with a canopy, that is

mounted on shafts and used to carry a single passenger. **2.** A stretcher for carrying a sick or wounded person. **3.** Material, as straw, that is used as bedding for animals. **4.** The young produced at 1 birth by a multiparous mammal. **5.** An accumulation of waste material : rubbish. *—v.* **1.** To give birth to a litter. **2.** To scatter litter (about). **—lit'ter·er** *n.*

lit·té·ra·teur *also* **lit·ter·a·teur** (lĭt'ər-ə-tûr', lĭt'rə-) *n.* A man of letters.

lit·ter·bug (lĭt'ər-bŭg') *n. Informal.* One who litters a public area, as a park.

lit·tle (lĭt'l) *adj.* **lit·tler** *or* **less** (lĕs), **lit·tlest** *or* **least** (lēst). **1.** Not large : small. **2.** Not very much <*little* time><*little* money> **3.** Not significant : unimportant. **4.** Narrow : petty. ☆***syns:*** BANTAM, PETITE, SMALL *—adv.* **less, least.** Not much : hardly. *—n.* **1.** A small quantity or amount. **2.** A short distance or time. **—lit'tle·ness** *n.*

Little Dipper *n.* Ursa Minor.

Little Rock (rŏk). Cap. of Ark., in the C part. *Pop.* 153,831.

lit·to·ral (lĭt'ər-əl) *adj.* Of, relating to, or existing on a shore. *—n.* A shore.

lit·ur·gy (lĭt'ər-jē) *n., pl.* **-gies.** A prescribed rite for a public religious service : ritual. **—li·tur'gi·cal** (lĭ-tûr'jĭ-kəl) *adj.* **—li·tur'gi·cal·ly** *adv.*

liv·a·ble *also* **live·a·ble** (lĭv'ə-bəl) *adj.* **1.** Suitable to live with or in. **2.** Bearable.

live¹ (lĭv) *v.* **lived, liv·ing. 1.** To be or continue to be alive. **2.** To reside. **3.** To pass (one's life). **4.** To subsist. **5.** To remain in human memory. **—live down.** To live so as to overcome the shame, effect, or remembrance of over time.

live² (līv) *adj.* **1.** Having life : living. **2.** Broadcast during actual performance <a *live* talk show> **3.** Of current interest <a *live* topic> **4.** Burning : glowing <a *live* coal> **5.** Not exploded but capable of exploding <*live* ammunition> **6.** Carrying electric current <a *live* circuit>

live-in (lĭv'ĭn') *adj.* Residing in the place at which one is employed.

live·li·hood (līv'lē-ho͝od') *n.* A means of subsistence or support.

live·long (lĭv'lông', -lŏng') *adj.* Entire : whole <complained the *livelong* day>

live·ly (līv'lē) *adj.* **-li·er, -li·est. 1.** Full of life : vigorous <a *lively* youngster> **2.** Spirited : animated <a *lively* discussion> **3.** Intense : keen <did a *lively* business in clothing> **4.** Bouncing easily on impact : resilient. **—live'li·ness** *n.*

liv·en (lī'vən) *v.* To become or cause to become lively or livelier.

liv·er¹ (lĭv'ər) *n.* A large glandular organ of vertebrates that secretes bile and acts in metabolism and in blood formation.

liv·er² (lĭv'ər) *n.* One with a specified lifestyle <a high *liver*>

liv·er·ish (lĭv'ər-ĭsh) *adj.* **1.** Resembling liver, esp. in color. **2.** Having a liver disorder : bilious. **3.** Having an irritable disposition : peevish.

Liv·er·pool (lĭv'ər-po͞ol'). Borough of NW England, on the Mersey R. *Pop.* 520,200. **—Liv'er·pud'li·an** (-pŭd'lē-ən) *adj.* & *n.*

liv·er·wort (lĭv'ər-wûrt', -wôrt') *n.* One of numerous green nonflowering plants of the class Hepaticae, related to the mosses.

liv·er·wurst (lĭv'ər-wûrst', -wo͝orst') *n.* A kind of sausage made primarily of liver.

liv·er·y (lĭv'ə-rē, lĭv'rē) *n., pl.* **-ies. 1.** A distinctive uniform worn by male household servants. **2. a.** The care and boarding of horses for a fee. **b.** The hiring out of horses and vehicles. **—liv'er·ied** *adj.*

liv·er·y·man (lĭv'ə-rē-mən, lĭv'rē-) *n.* A keeper or employee of a livery stable.

lives (līvz) *n. pl. of* LIFE.

live·stock (līv'stŏk') *n.* Farm animals, as cattle, raised for human use or profit.

live wire (līv) *n. Informal.* An alert, energetic person.

liv·id (lĭv'ĭd) *adj.* **1.** Discolored from a bruise. **2.** Pale : ashen. **3.** Very angry.

liv·ing (lĭv'ĭng) *adj.* **1.** Being alive. **2.** Full of vitality and life. **3.** True to life : natural <the photograph's *living* colors> *—n.* **1.** The condition of maintaining life. **2.** A style of life. **3.** A livelihood. ☆***syns:*** KEEP, LIVELIHOOD, MAINTENANCE, SUBSISTENCE, SUPPORT, SUSTENANCE.

living room *n.* A room in a household for the general use of the occupants.

living wage *n.* A wage sufficient to provide minimally satisfactory living conditions.

Liv·y (lĭv'ē). 59 B.C.-A.D. 17. Roman historian.

liz·ard (lĭz'ərd) *n.* One of numerous reptiles of the suborder Sauria (or Lacertilia) typically with an elongated scaly body, 4 legs, and a tapering tail.

lizard fish *n.* A bottom-dwelling fish of the family Synodontidae of warm seas, with a lizardlike head.

lla·ma (lä'mə) *n.* A South American ruminant, *Lama peruana,* related to the camel and raised for its soft, fleecy wool.

lla·no (lä'nō, lăn'ō) *n., pl.* **-nos.** A grassy plain with few trees, esp. in Latin America.

LL.B. *abbr.* Bachelor of Laws.

LL.D. *abbr.* Doctor of Laws.

lo (lō) *interj.* Used to show surprise or attract attention.

load (lōd) *n.* **1.** A mass or weight that is lifted or supported. **2.** Something conveyed, as by a vehicle, person, or animal. **3.** A share, as of work, that is allotted or required. **4.** Something, as a heavy responsibility, that oppresses : burden. **5.** *often* **loads.** *Informal.* A great amount or number. *—v.* **1.** To place a load in or on. **2.** To take on or receive a load. **3.** To oppress : burden. **4.** To charge with ammunition <*load* a gun> **5.** To insert into (a holder or magazine). **6.** To provide in abundance. **—load'er** *n.* **—load'ing** *n.*

load·ed (lō'dĭd) *adj.* **1.** Intended to trap or trick <a *loaded* question> **2.** *Slang.* Drunk. **3.** *Slang.* Rich : wealthy.

loaf¹ (lōf) *n., pl.* **loaves** (lōvz). A shaped mass of food, esp. bread.

loaf² (lōf) *v.* To spend time idling : laze. **—loaf'er** *n.*

loam (lōm) *n.* Soil that consists chiefly of sand, clay, silt, and decayed plant matter. **—loam'y** *adj.*

loan (lōn) *n.* **1.** Money lent at interest. **2.** Something borrowed for temporary use. *—v.* To lend.

loan shark *n. Informal.* A usurer, esp. one who is financed and supported by gangsters. **—loan'shark'ing** *n.*

loan-word *also* **loan·word** (lōn'wûrd') *n.* A word, as *sombrero,* adopted from one language for use in another.

loath (lōth, lō*th*) *adj.* Averse : reluctant.

loathe (lō*th*) *v.* **loathed, loath·ing.** To dislike intensely : abhor.

loath·ing (lō'*th*ĭng) *n.* Intense dislike : abhorrence.

loath·some (lō*th*'səm, lōth'-) *adj.* Arousing loathing : disgusting. **—loath'some·ly** *adv.* **—loathe'some·ness** *n.*

loaves (lōvz) *n. pl. of* LOAF¹.

lob (lŏb) *v.* **lobbed, lob·bing.** To hit, throw, or propel (a ball) in a high arc. **—lob** *n.* **—lob'ber** *n.*

lob·by (lŏb'ē) *n., pl.* **-bies. 1.** A foyer or waiting room, as in a hotel or theater. **2.** A group of private persons trying to influence legislators. *—v.* **-bied, -by·ing.** To try to influence (legislators), esp. in favor of a special interest. **—lob'by·ist** *n.*

lobe (lōb) *n.* A rounded projecting anatomical part or division, as the fleshy lower part of the ear. **—lo'bar** *adj.* **—lobed** *adj.*

†lob·lol·ly (lŏb'lŏl'ē) *n., pl.* **-lies.** *Regional.* **1.** A mudhole : mire. **2.** A lout.

†lo·bo (lō'bō) *n., pl.* **-bos.** *W U.S.* The gray or timber wolf, *Canis lupus.*

lo·bot·o·my (lō-bŏt'ə-mē, lə-) *n., pl.* **-mies.** Surgical severance of 1 or more cerebral nerve tracts.

lob·ster (lŏb'stər) *n.* **1.** Any of several large, edible marine crustaceans of the genus *Homarus,* with 5 pairs of legs, the 1st pair being large and clawlike. **2.** Any of several crustaceans related to the lobster.

lob·ule (lŏb'yo͞ol) *n.* **1.** A small lobe. **2.** A subdivision or section of a lobe. **—lob'u·lar** (-yə-lər) *adj.*

lo·cal (lō'kəl) *adj.* **1.** Of, pertaining to, being in, or serving a particular area or place. **2.** Making all scheduled stops <a *local* bus> **3.** Confined to a small part of the body <a *local* anesthetic> *—n.* **1.** A local public conveyance, as a train. **2.** A local branch or chapter of an organization, esp. of a labor union. **—lo'cal·ly** *adv.*

lo·cale (lō-kăl', -käl') *n.* **1.** A locality at which a particular event takes place. **2.** The setting or scene, as of a novel.

lo·cal·i·ty (lō-kăl'ĭ-tē) *n., pl.* **-ties.** A specific place, neighborhood, or district.

lo·cal·ize (lō'kə-līz') *v.* **-ized, -iz·ing.** To confine or be confined to a specific locality. **—lo'cal·i·za'tion** *n.*

lo·cate (lō'kāt', lō-kāt') *v.* **-cat·ed, -cat·ing. 1.** To specify or determine the place, position, or boundaries of. **2.** To look for and find. **3.** To establish or become established : settle. **—lo'ca'tor** *n.*

lo·ca·tion (lō-kā'shən) *n.* **1.** An act or process of locating. **2.** A place where something is or can be located. **3.** A site outside a motion-picture or television studio at which a movie is shot.

loc. cit. *abbr.* in the place cited (Lat. *loco citato*).

loch (lŏKH, lŏk) *n. Scot.* **1.** A lake. **2.** An arm of the sea.

lo·ci (lō'sī') *n. pl. of* LOCUS.

lock¹ (lŏk) *n.* **1.** A device that is used, as on a door, to secure or fasten and is operated by a key or combination. **2.** A portion of a waterway closed off with gates to raise or lower boats by changing the level of the water. **3.** A mechanism by which the charge of ammunition in a firearm is exploded. **4.** Any of several wrestling holds. —*v.* **1.** To fasten or be fastened with a lock. **2.** To keep in or out by means of a lock. **3.** To entangle or become entangled : interlock.

lock[2] (lŏk) *n.* **1.** A strand, tuft, or curl of hair. **2. locks.** The hair of the head.

lock•er (lŏk′ər) *n.* **1.** An enclosure, esp. in a public place, that can be locked and is used for storage, as of clothing and valuables. **2.** A flat trunk for storage. **3.** A refrigerated storage compartment.

lock•et (lŏk′ĭt) *n.* A small ornamental case for a picture or keepsake, that is often worn as a pendant on a necklace.

lock•jaw (lŏk′jô′) *n.* **1.** Tetanus. **2.** A symptom of tetanus in which a spasm of the jaw muscles locks the jaws closed.

lock•nut *also* **lock nut** (lŏk′nŭt′) *n.* A usu. thin nut screwed down on another nut to keep it from loosening.

lock•out (lŏk′out′) *n.* The shutdown of a plant by an employer in a labor dispute to force the employees to modify their terms or meet his.

lock•smith (lŏk′smĭth′) *n.* Someone who makes or repairs locks.

lock step *n.* A way of marching in which the marchers follow each other closely.

lock•up (lŏk′ŭp′) *n. Informal.* A jail, esp. one in which accused persons are held prior to court hearings.

lo•co (lō′kō) *adj. Slang.* Insane : crazy.

lo•co•mo•tion (lō′kə-mō′shən) *n.* The act of moving or ability to move from place to place.

lo•co•mo•tive (lō′kə-mō′tĭv) *n.* A self-propelled electric or diesel-powered vehicle that travels on rails and moves railroad cars. —*adj.* **1.** Of or involved in locomotion. **2.** Of or pertaining to a locomotive.

lo•co•mo•tor (lō′kə-mō′tər) *adj.* Of locomotion : LOCOMOTIVE 1.

lo•co•weed (lō′kō-wēd′) *n.* A plant of the genera *Oxytropis* and *Astragalus,* of the W and C U.S., that is poisonous to livestock.

lo•cus (lō′kəs) *n., pl.* **-ci** (-sī′). **1.** A locality : place. **2.** *Geom.* The configuration or set of all points satisfying specified conditions.

lo•cust (lō′kəst) *n.* **1.** Any of numerous grasshoppers of the family Locustidae that often travel in swarms and damage vegetation. **2.** A cicada. **3.** A tree, *Robinia pseudoacacia,* with feathery leaves, fragrant white flower clusters, and hard, durable wood.

lo•cu•tion (lō-kyōō′shən) *n.* **1.** A particular expression or word considered stylistically. **2.** Style of speech : phraseology.

lode (lōd) *n.* A deposit of mineral ore.

lode•star (lōd′stär′) *n.* A star, esp. the North Star, used as a reference point.

lode•stone (lōd′stōn′) *n.* **1.** A magnetized piece of magnetite. **2.** A strong attraction.

lodge (lŏj) *n.* **1.** An often rustic house, as a cabin, used as a temporary or seasonal dwelling or shelter. **2.** An inn. **3.** The den of an animal such as the beaver. **4. a.** A local chapter of a fraternal organization. **b.** The meeting hall of such a chapter. —*v.* **lodged, lodg•ing. 1.** To provide with quarters. **2.** To live in rented accommodations. **3.** To file : register <*lodge* a charge> **4.** To vest (e.g., authority). **5.** To force, fix, or implant. **6.** To be or become embedded.

lodg•er (lŏj′ər) *n.* Someone who rents a room in another's house.

lodg•ing (lŏj′ĭng) *n.* **1.** A place to sleep or live. **2. lodgings.** Rented living quarters.

lodg•ment *also* **lodge•ment** (lŏj′mənt) *n.* **1.** An act of lodging or the state of being lodged. **2.** A place for lodging. **3.** An accumulation or deposit.

lo•ess (lō′əs, lĕs, lōōs) *n.* A fine-grained calcareous clay or silt thought to be deposited as dust blown by the wind.

loft (lôft, lŏft) *n.* **1.** A large, usu. unpartitioned floor of an industrial or commercial building, as a warehouse. **2.** An attic. **3.** A gallery, as in a church <a choir *loft*> —*v.* To throw or strike (a ball) in a high arc.

loft•y (lôf′tē, lŏf′-) *adj.* **-i•er, -i•est. 1.** Imposingly high : towering. **2.** Elevated : noble. **3.** Arrogant : overbearing. **—loft′i•ly** *adv.* **—loft′i•ness** *n.*

log[1] (lôg, lŏg) *n.* **1.** A trunk or section of a trunk of a felled or fallen tree. **2.** A mechanism for determing a ship's speed. **3. a.** A record of a ship's or aircraft's speed or progress. **b.** The book in which this record is kept. —*v.* **logged, log•ging. 1.** To cut down trees for timber. **2. a.** To enter in a log. **b.** To travel (a specified distance or time). **—log′ger** *n.*

log[2] (lôg, lŏg) *n.* Logarithm.

lo•gan•ber•ry (lō′gən-bĕr′ē) *n.* A prickly plant, *Rubus loganobaccus,* cultivated for its edible acidic red fruit.

log•a•rithm (lô′gə-rĭth′əm, lŏg′ə-) *n.* The exponent indicating the power to which a base number must be raised to produce a given number. **—log′a•rith′mic** *adj.*

loge (lōzh) *n.* **1.** A small compartment, esp. a theater box. **2.** The forward rows of a theater mezzanine.

log•ger•head (lô′gər-hĕd′, lŏg′ər-) *n.* A marine turtle, *Caretta caretta,* with a large beaked head. **—at loggerheads.** In a state of contention : at odds.

log•gi•a (lô′jē-ə, lŏj′ē-ə) *n.* **1.** A roofed but open gallery or arcade along the front or side of a building, often at an upper level. **2.** An open balcony in a theater.

log•ic (lŏj′ĭk) *n.* **1.** The scientific study of the principles of reasoning, esp. of the method and validity of deductive reasoning. **2.** Valid reasoning. **3.** A particular system or method of reasoning. **—lo•gi′cian** (lō-jĭsh′ən) *n.*

log•i•cal (lŏj′ĭ-kəl) *adj.* **1.** Of, relating to, or in accordance with logic. **2.** Marked by consistency of reasoning. **3.** Reasonable. **4.** Capable of reasoning rationally. ☆**syns:** CONSEQUENT, INTELLIGENT, RATIONAL, REASONABLE, SENSIBLE **—log′i•cal•ly** *adv.*

lo•gis•tics (lō-jĭs′tĭks) *n. (sing. or pl. in number).* The methods of procuring, distributing, maintaining, and replacing materiel and personnel, as in a military operation. **—lo•gis′tic** *adj.*

log•jam (lôg′jăm′, lŏg′-) *n.* **1.** A mass of floating logs jammed immovably together in a waterway, as a river. **2.** A deadlock.

lo•go (lō′gō, lô′-, lŏg′ō) *n.* A logotype.

lo•go•type (lō′gə-tīp′, lô′-, lŏg′ə-) *n.* A distinctive identifying symbol, as of a company or publication.

log•roll•ing or **log-roll•ing** (lôg′rō′lĭng, lŏg′-) *n.* The exchanging of votes among legislators to assure the success of projects of interest to each one. **—log′roll′er** *n.*

lo•gy (lō′gē) *adj.* **-gi•er, -gi•est.** Marked by sluggishness : lethargic. **—lo′gi•ness** *n.*

loin (loin) *n.* **1. a.** The region of the body between the ribs and pelvis. **b.** A cut of meat from this part of an animal. **2. loins. a.** The area of the thighs and groin. **b.** The reproductive organs.

loin•cloth (loin′klôth′, -klŏth′) *n.* A cloth worn as a garment around the loins.

Loire (lwär). Longest river of France, rising in the SE and flowing c. 630 mi (1,014 km) to the Bay of Biscay.

loi•ter (loi′tər) *v.* **1.** To remain in a place for no apparent reason : linger. **2.** To dawdle : delay. **—loi′ter•er** *n.*

loll (lŏl) *v.* **1.** To move, stand, sit, or rest in an indolent manner. **2.** To droop or hang loosely. **—loll′ing•ly** *adv.*

lol•li•pop *also* **lol•ly•pop** (lŏl′ē-pŏp′) *n.* A piece of hard candy on a stick.

Lo•mé (lō-mā′). Cap. of Togo, in the S on the Gulf of Guinea. *Pop.* 229,400.

Lon•don (lŭn′dən). Cap. of England and of the United Kingdom, on the Thames in SE England. *Pop.* 6,877,100.

lone (lōn) *adj.* **1.** Single : solitary <a *lone* horseman> **2.** Isolated : unfrequented <the *lone* prairie> **3.** Being the only one : sole <the *lone* concert hall in the city>

lone•ly (lōn′lē) *adj.* **-li•er, -li•est. 1.** Being without companions : lone. **2.** Devoid of people : unfrequented. **3. a.** Dejected because of being alone. **b.** Producing such dejection. **—lone′li•ness** *n.*

lon•er (lō′nər) *n. Informal.* Someone who avoids the company of others.

lone•some (lōn′səm) *adj.* **1.** Dejected because of lack of companionship. **2.** Unfrequented : remote. **—lone′some•ly** *adv.* **—lone′some•ness** *n.*

long[1] (lông, lŏng) *adj.* **1. a.** Of considerable length. **b.** Tall. **2..** Of considerable duration. **b.** Too protracted : tedious. **3.** Of a specified length or duration <a foot *long*> <a year *long*> **4.** Far-reaching <a *long* view of the situation> **5.** Having much or too much of something <*long* on optimism> **6.** Being a speech sound or syllable of comparatively great duration. ☆**syns:** EXTENDED, LENGTHY —*adv.* **1.** For or during an extended period of time. **2.** For or throughout a given period <worked all day *long*> —*n.* A long time.

long[2] (lông, lŏng) *v.* To have a strong persistent wish or desire : yearn. **—long′ing** *n.* **—long•ing•ly** *adv.*

long. *abbr.* longitude.

Long Island. Island adjacent to and including sections of New York City.

long•boat (lông′bōt′, lŏng′-) *n.* The longest boat carried by a sailing ship.

long•bow (lông′bō′, lŏng′-) *n.* A wooden bow approx. 5 to 6 ft long.

long distance *n.* Telephone communication with a distant point. **—long′-dis′tance** *adj.* & *adv.*

lon•gev•i•ty (lŏn-jĕv′ĭ-tē) *n.* **1.** Long life. **2.** Long continuance or duration.

Long•fel•low (lông′fĕl′ō, lŏng′-), **Henry Wadsworth.** 1807–82. Amer. poet.

long•hair (lông′hâr′, lŏng′-) *n.* An enthusiast of the arts and esp. of classical music.
long•hand (lông′hănd′, lŏng′-) *n.* Cursive handwriting.
long•horn (lông′hôrn′, lŏng′-) *n.* One of a breed of long-horned cattle formerly raised in the SW U.S.
lon•gi•tu•di•nal (lŏn′jĭ-to͞od′n-əl, -tyo͞od′-) *adj.* **1.** Of or relating to length. **2.** Running or placed lengthwise. **3.** Of or relating to longitude. **–lon′gi•tu′di•nal•ly** *adv.*
lon•gi•tude (lŏn′jĭ-to͞od′, -tyo͞od′) *n.* Angular distance E and W of the prime meridian at Greenwich, England.
long-lived (lông′līvd′, -lĭvd′, lŏng′-) *adj.* Existing or living for a long time.
long-play•ing (lông′plā′ĭng, lŏng′-) *adj.* Pertaining to or being a microgroove phonograph record turning at 33⅓ rpm.
long-range (lông′rānj′, lŏng′-) *adj.* **1.** Involving or requiring an extended time span. **2.** Of, appropriate for, or covering great distances <a *long-range* bomber>
long•shore•man (lông′shôr′mən, -shōr′-, lŏng′-) *n.* A dock laborer who loads and unloads cargo.
long-stand•ing (lông′stăn′dĭng, lŏng′-) *adj.* Having endured for a long time.
long-suf•fer•ing (lông′sŭf′ər-ĭng, lŏng′-) *adj.* Patiently bearing difficulties or wrongs. **–long′-suf′fer•ing•ly** *adv.*
long-term (lông′tûrm′, lŏng′-) *adj.* Involving or in effect for a number of years.
long ton *n.* See MEASUREMENT TABLE.
long-wind•ed (lông′wĭn′dĭd, lŏng′-) *adj.* Tiresomely talkative. **–long′-wind′ed•ly** *adv.* **–long′-wind′ed•ness** *n.*
look (lo͝ok) *v.* **1.** To use the power of sight : see. **2.** To direct one's gaze or attention. **3.** To appear to be : seem <*looks* unhappy> **4.** To face in a certain direction : point. **5.** To have an appearance that accords with <*looks* his age> **–look after.** To take care of. **–look for. 1.** To search for. **2.** To expect. **–look out.** To be on guard : be vigilant. **–look up. 1.** To search for and find, as in a reference book. **2.** To find and make a call on : visit. **3.** *Informal.* To improve. *–n.* **1.** The action of looking : gaze. **2.** Aspect : appearance. **3. looks.** Personal appearance. **–look′er** *n.*
looking glass *n.* A mirror.
look•out (lo͝ok′out′) *n.* **1.** Someone who has been assigned to keep watch, as on a ship. **2.** The act of keeping watch. **3.** A place commanding a wide view for observation. **4.** A matter of worry or concern.
look-see (lo͝ok′sē′) *n. Informal.* A survey.
loom[1] (lo͞om) *v.* **1.** To appear or come into view as a massive or indistinct image. **2.** To seem to be imminent and threatening.
loom[2] (lo͞om) *n.* A machine for interweaving thread or yarn to produce cloth.
loon[1] (lo͞on) *n.* Any of several diving birds of the genus *Gavia*, having a laughlike cry.
loon[2] (lo͞on) *n.* A foolish or crazy person.
loon•y (lo͞o′nē) *adj.* **-i•er, -i•est.** *Informal.* Foolish or crazy. **–loon′y** *n.*
loony bin *n. Informal.* An insane asylum.
loop (lo͞op) *n.* **1.** An approx. circular or oval length of line, as thread, folded over and joined at the ends. **2.** A loop-shaped pattern, figure, or path. *–v.* **1.** To make or form into a loop. **2.** To join, fasten, or encircle with a loop.
loop•hole (lo͞op′hōl′) *n.* **1.** A small hole or slit in a wall through which small arms may be fired. **2.** A means of escape or evasion.
loose (lo͞os) *adj.* **loos•er, loos•est. 1.** Not tightly fastened. **2.** Not confined. **3.** Not taut : slack. **4.** Not tight-fitting. **5.** Not bound, bundled, stapled, or gathered together. **6.** Not exact or strict <a *loose* translation> **7.** Showing a lack of restraint or responsibility. **8.** Not compact or dense in structure. **9.** Sexually unrestrained : immoral. *–adv.* In a loose manner. *–v.* **loosed, loos•ing. 1.** To release. **2.** To make or become loose : undo. **3.** To make less tight or compact : loosen. **4.** To slacken : relax. **5.** To discharge (a missile). **–loose′ly** *adv.* **–loose′ness** *n.*
loos•en (lo͞o′sən) *v.* **1.** To make or become loose or looser. **2.** To allow or cause to become less restrained or strict.
loot (lo͞ot) *n.* **1.** Valuables plundered in time of war. **2.** Goods that have been stolen. *–v.* To plunder : steal. **–loot′er** *n.*
lop (lŏp) *v.* **lopped, lop•ping. 1.** To remove branches or twigs from : trim. **2.** To cut off, esp. with a single blow.
lope (lōp) *v.* **loped, lop•ing.** To run with a steady, easy gait. **–lope** *n.* **–lop′er** *n.*
lop•sid•ed (lŏp′sī′dĭd) *adj.* **1.** Heavier, higher, or larger on 1 side than on the other. **2.** Tilting to 1 side. **–lop′sid′ed•ly** *adv.* **–lop′sid′ed•ness** *n.*
lo•qua•cious (lō-kwā′shəs) *adj.* Too talkative. **–lo•qua′cious•ly** *adv.* **–lo•quac′i•ty** (-kwăs′ĭ-tē) *n.*
lord (lôrd) *n.* **1.** A man with dominion and power over others. **2.** The owner of a feudal estate. **3. Lord.** *esp. Brit.* The general masculine title of rank and esp. of nobility. **4. Lord.** God. *–v.* To behave in a domineering, haughty, or patronizing manner <*lording* it over the new workers>

▲word history: The actual as well as the symbolic importance of bread as a basic foodstuff is exhibited by the word *lord*. *Lord* is derived from a compound formed in very early Old English times from the words *hlāf*, "bread," and *weard*, "ward, guardian." *Lord*, therefore, literally means "guardian of the bread." Since such a position was the dominant one in a household, *lord* came to denote a man of authority and rank in society at large.

lord•ly (lôrd′lē) *adj.* **-li•er, -li•est. 1.** Of, relating to, or typical of a lord. **2.** Noble : grand. **3.** Pretentiously overbearing : haughty. **–lord′li•ness** *n.*
lord•ship (lôrd′shĭp′) *n.* **1.** *often* **Lordship.** Used as a form of address for a man holding the title of lord. **2.** The authority or position of a lord.
Lord's Supper *n.* The Eucharist.
lore (lôr, lōr) *n.* **1.** Traditional fact or belief. **2.** Knowledge, as that gained through experience or education.
lor•gnette (lôrn-yĕt′) *n.* A pair of eyeglasses or opera glasses with a short handle.
lorn (lôrn) *adj.* Forlorn : bereft.
lor•ry (lôr′ē, lŏr′ē) *n., pl.* **-ries.** *esp. Brit.* A motor truck.
Los An•ge•les (lôs ăn′jə-ləs, -lēz′, lōs). City of S Calif. *Pop.* 2,966,763.
lose (lo͞oz) *v.* **lost** (lôst, lŏst), **los•ing. 1.** To fail to find in a customary place : mislay. **2.** To fail to sustain or keep. **3.** To be deprived of <*lost* his job> **4.** To fail to win <afraid they'll *lose* the game> **5.** To fail to use : waste <*lose* an opportunity> **6.** To get rid of <wants to *lose* weight> **7.** To stray from <*lost* her way> **–los′er** *n.*
loss (lôs, lŏs) *n.* **1.** The damage or suffering that is caused by losing. **2.** One that is lost. **3. losses.** Killed, wounded, or captured persons, esp. soldiers : casualties.
loss leader *n.* An article sold at or below cost to attract customers.
lost (lôst, lŏst) *adj.* **1.** Unable to find one's way. **2.** Not won or used. **3.** No longer practiced or possessed : gone. **4.** Unable to function : helpless. **5.** Absorbed.
lot (lŏt) *n.* **1.** An object used in making a choice or determination by chance. **2.** The use of lots for choice or determination. **3.** Fate : fortune. **4.** A group of people or things : set. **5.** A large amount, extent, or number. **6.** A piece of land with designated boundaries : plot.
lo•ti (lō′tē) *n., pl.* **loti.** See CURRENCY TABLE.
lo•tion (lō′shən) *n.* A liquid medicine or cosmetic for external application.
lot•ter•y (lŏt′ə-rē) *n., pl.* **-ies. 1.** A contest in which winners are selected by a chance drawing. **2.** An event or activity whose outcome depends on chance.
lo•tus (lō′təs) *n.* **1. a.** An aquatic plant, *Nelumbo nucifera*, with fragrant pinkish flowers and large leaves. **b.** One of several plants similar or related to the lotus, as certain water lilies. **2.** A fruit described in Homer's *Odyssey* that produced a dreamy, indolent state in those who ate it.
loud (loud) *adj.* **1.** Marked by high volume and intensity of sound. **2.** Producing a loud sound : noisy. **3.** Gaudy, as in color : flashy. **–loud, loud′ly** *adv.* **–loud′ness** *n.*
loud•mouth (loud′mouth′) *n.* Someone who tends to talk loudly, irritatingly, and often indiscreetly. **–loud′mouthed′** (-mouthd′, -moutht′) *adj.*
loud•speak•er (loud′spē′kər) *n.* A device that converts electric signals to audible sound.
Lou•is XIV (lo͞o′ē). "the Sun King." 1638–1715. King of France (1643–1715).
Lou•i•si•an•a (lo͞o-ē′zē-ăn′ə). State of the S U.S. *Cap.* Baton Rouge. *Pop.* 4,203,972.
Lou•is•ville (lo͞o′ē-vĭl′). City of NW Ky., on the Ohio R. *Pop.* 298,451.
lounge (lounj) *v.* **lounged, loung•ing.** To move or act in a relaxed, lazy manner. *–n.* **1.** A waiting room, as in a hotel or theater. **2.** A long couch. **–loung′er** *n.*
lour (lou′ər) *v.* & *n. var. of* LOWER[1].
louse (lous) *n.* **1.** *pl.* **lice** (līs). One of numerous small, flat-bodied, wingless biting or sucking insects of the family Anoplura, many of which live as parasites on various animals, including human beings. **2.** *pl.* **lous•es.** *Slang.* A mean or contemptible person. *–v.* **loused, lous•ing.** *Slang.* To bungle <*loused* up everything>
louse•wort (lous′wûrt′, -wôrt′) *n.* A plant of the genus *Pedicularis*, with irregular, variously colored flower clusters.
lous•y (lou′zē) *adj.* **-i•er, -i•est. 1.** Lice-infested. **2.** *Slang.* **a.** Mean : contemptible. **b.** Inferior : poor. **3.** *Slang.* Abundantly

supplied <*lousy* with jewelry> **–lous'i•ly** *adv.* **–lous'i•ness** *n.*

lout (lout) *n.* An awkward, stupid fellow : oaf. **–lout'ish** *adj.*

lou•ver *also* **lou•vre** (lo͞o'vər) *n.* **1.** A framed opening in a wall fitted with movable slanted slats that let air in but keep precipitation out. **2.** One of the slats used in a louver. **–lou'vered** *adj.*

love (lŭv) *n.* **1.** Intense affection. **2.** A feeling of attraction resulting from sexual desire. **3.** Enthusiasm or fondness <*love* of music> **4.** A beloved person. **5.** A score of zero in tennis. *–v.* **loved, lov•ing. 1.** To feel love for. **2.** To enjoy enthusiastically <*loves* skating> ☆***syns:*** ADORE, CHERISH **–lov'a•ble** *adj.* **–love'less** *adj.*

love•bird (lŭv'bûrd') *n.* Any of various Old World parrots, esp. of the genus *Agapornis,* often kept as a pet.

love•lorn (lŭv'lôrn') *adj.* Bereft of love or a lover. **–love'lorn'ness** *n.*

love•ly (lŭv'lē) *adj.* **-li•er, -li•est. 1.** Beautiful. **2.** Enjoyable. **–love'li•ness** *n.* **–love'ly** *n.*

love•mak•ing (lŭv'mā'kĭng) *n.* **1.** Sexual activity and esp. sexual intercourse. **2.** Courtship.

lov•er (lŭv'ər) *n.* **1.** One who loves another, esp. sexually. **2.** A devotee <an animal *lover*> **3.** A sexual partner.

love seat *n.* A small sofa that seats 2.

love•sick (lŭv'sĭk') *adj.* **1.** Yearning with love. **2.** Showing or expressing a lover's yearning. **–love'sick'ness** *n.*

lov•ing (lŭv'ĭng) *adj.* Feeling or expressing love : affectionate. **–lov'ing•ly** *adv.*

loving cup *n.* A large, ornamental cup with 2 or more handles that is often given as an award or trophy.

low¹ (lō) *adj.* **1.** Not high or tall <a *low* cabinet> **2. a.** Of less than usual depth <*low* water> **b.** Being below a normal surface or level. **3.** Less than average, as in amount, degree, or intensity <a *low* price> **4. a.** *Mus.* Being a sound produced by a relatively small frequency of vibrations <*low* C> **b.** Not loud <a *low* whisper> **5.** Of humble social status. **6.** Morally blameworthy. **7.** Vulgar : coarse. **8.** Sad : dejected. **9.** Near the equator. **10.** Adverse : unfavorable. **11.** Décolleté. *–n.* **1.** A low position, level, or degree. **2.** A region of depressed barometric pressure. **3.** The gear adjustment in an automotive transmission that produces the smallest output speed for a given engine speed. **–low** *adv.* **–low'ness** *n.*

low² (lō) *v.* To moo. **–low** *n.*

low beam *n.* A low-intensity vehicular headlight.

low•brow (lō'brou') *n. Informal.* One who lacks cultivation. **–low'brow'** *adj.*

Low Countries. Belgium, the Netherlands, and Luxembourg.

low•down (lō'doun') *n. Slang.* The full facts : whole truth.

low-down (lō'doun') *adj.* **1.** Despicable : mean. **2.** Emotionally depressed.

low•er¹ *also* **lour** (lou'ər) *v.* **1.** To look angry : frown. **2.** To grow dark or threatening, as the sky. **–low'er** *n.*

low•er² (lō'ər) *adj.* **1.** Being below, as in rank or position. **2.** Being or denoting the larger and usu. more representative house of a bicameral legislature. *–v.* **1.** To let, bring, or move down. **2.** To reduce, as in value, amount, or quality : diminish. ☆***syns:*** CHEAPEN, DOWNGRADE, MARK DOWN, REDUCE

low•er-case (lō'ər-kās') *adj.* Of, relating to, or being small letters as distinguished from capitals. **–lower case** *n.*

lower class *n.* The group in society that ranks below the middle class and is of low social and economic status. **–low'er-class'** *adj.*

lowest common denominator *n.* The least common multiple of the denominators of a set of fractions.

lowest common multiple *n.* Least common multiple.

low frequency *n.* A radio-wave frequency in the range between 30 and 300 kc.

low-key (lō'kē') *also* **low-keyed** (-kēd') *adj.* Restrained : subdued.

low•land (lō'lənd) *n.* Land that is low and usu. level in relation to the surrounding countryside.

low•ly (lō'lē) *adj.* **-li•er, -li•est. 1.** Low in position or rank. **2.** Meek : humble. **–low'li•ness** *n.*

low profile *n.* An unobtrusive mode of behavior or lifestyle.

low relief *n.* Sculptural relief that projects very little from the background.

low-rise (lō'rīz') *adj.* Being 1 or 2 stories high and having no elevators <a *low-rise* apartment building>

low-ten•sion (lō'tĕn'shən) *adj.* **1.** Of or at low potential or voltage. **2.** Operating at low voltage.

low tide *n.* The lowest ebb tide.

lox¹ (lŏks) *n.* Smoked salmon.

lox² (lŏks) *n.* Liquid oxygen.

loy•al (loi'əl) *adj.* **1.** Firm in allegiance to one's country and government. **2.** Faithful to a person, ideal, or cause. **–loy'al•ly** *adv.* **–loy'al•ty** *n.*

loy•al•ist (loi'ə-lĭst) *n.* Someone who is loyal to a government or political party, esp. during a revolt.

loz•enge (lŏz'ənj) *n.* **1.** A figure shaped like a diamond. **2.** A small medicated candy with the shape of a lozenge.

LSD (ĕl'ĕs-dē') *n.* A powerful drug that induces hallucinations.

ltd. or **Ltd.** *abbr.* limited.

Lu *symbol for* LUTETIUM.

Lu•an•da (lo͞o-ăn'də). Cap. of Angola, in the W on the Atlantic. *Pop.* 475,328.

lu•au (lo͞o-ou') *n.* A Hawaiian feast.

lub•ber (lŭb'ər) *n.* **1.** An awkward fellow. **2.** An inexperienced sailor.

lu•bri•cant (lo͞o'brĭ-kənt) *n.* A material, as grease or machine oil, that is applied to moving parts to reduce friction.

lu•bri•cate (lo͞o'brĭ-kāt') *v.* **-cat•ed, -cat•ing.** To apply a lubricant to. **–lu'bri•ca'tion** *n.* **–lu'bri•ca'tor** *n.*

lu•bri•cous (lo͞o'brĭ-kəs) *also* **lu•bri•cious** (lo͞o-brĭsh'əs) *adj.* **1.** Slippery. **2. a.** Lewd : wanton. **b.** Salacious. **3.** Shifty : tricky. **–lu•bric'i•ty** (-brĭs'ĭ-tē) *n.*

Lu•cerne (lo͞o-sûrn'). City of C Switzerland, on Lake Lucerne. *Pop.* 62,400.

lu•cid (lo͞o'sĭd) *adj.* **1.** Readily understood. **2.** Mentally clear : rational. **3.** Translucent. **–lu•cid'i•ty** (-sĭd'ĭ-tē), **lu'cid•ness** *n.* **–lu'cid•ly** *adv.*

Lu•ci•fer (lo͞o'sə-fər) *n.* The devil : Satan.

Lu•cite (lo͞o'sīt'). A trademark for a transparent thermoplastic acrylic resin.

luck (lŭk) *n.* **1.** The random occurrence of good or adverse fortune : chance. **2.** Good fortune. *–v.* To find or attain something advantageous or desirable by chance <*lucked* out when she bought the antique> **–luck'less** *adj.*

Luck•now (lŭk'nou'). City of NC India. *Pop.* 749,239.

luck•y (lŭk'ē) *adj.* **-i•er, -i•est.** Having, believed to bring, or resulting from good luck. **–luck'i•ly** *adv.* **–luck'i•ness** *n.*

lu•cra•tive (lo͞o'krə-tĭv) *adj.* Producing wealth or profits. **–lu'cra•tive•ly** *adv.*

lu•cre (lo͞o'kər) *n.* **1.** Money. **2.** Profit.

lu•cu•brate (lo͞o'kyə-brāt') *v.* **-brat•ed, -brat•ing.** To study laboriously.

lu•di•crous (lo͞o'dĭ-krəs) *adj.* Laughable because of obvious absurdity or incongruousness. **–lu'di•crous•ly** *adv.* **–lu'di•crous•ness** *n.*

luff (lŭf) *v.* To steer a sailing vessel nearer into the wind.

lug¹ (lŭg) *n.* An earlike handle or projection, as on a machine, used as a hold.

lug² (lŭg) *v.* **lugged, lug•ging. 1.** To drag : haul. **2.** To carry with difficulty.

luge (lo͞ozh) *n.* A sled similar to a toboggan that is ridden in a supine position.

luge

lug•gage (lŭg'ĭj) *n.* Baggage, esp. suitcases.

lu•gu•bri•ous (lo͝o-go͞o'brē-əs, -gyo͞o'-) *adj.* Mournful, esp. exaggeratedly so. **–lu•gu'bri•ous•ly** *adv.* **–lu•gu'bri•ous•ness** *n.*

Luke (lo͝ok) *n.* See BIBLE TABLE.

luke•warm (lo͞ok'wôrm') *adj.* **1.** Mildly warm : tepid. **2.** Unenthusiastic : halfhearted. **–luke'warm'ly** *adv.*

lull (lŭl) *v.* **1.** To cause to rest or sleep : soothe. **2.** To cause to have a false sense of safety. *–n.* A temporary period of calm or inactivity.

lul•la•by (lŭl'ə-bī') *n., pl.* **-bies.** A soothing song to lull a child to sleep.

lum•ba•go (lŭm-bā'gō) *n.* Painful inflammatory rheumatism of the muscles and tendons of the lumbar region.

lum•bar (lŭm'bər, -bär') *adj.* Of or situated in the part of the back and sides between the lowest ribs and the pelvis.

lum•ber¹ (lŭm'bər) *n.* **1.** Timber, esp. when sawed into boards and planks. **2.** *esp. Brit.* Miscellaneous stored items. *–v.* To cut and prepare timber for market.

lum•ber[2] (lŭm′bər) *v.* To walk or move clumsily, heavily, or noisily.
lum•ber•jack (lŭm′bər-jăk′) *n.* One who fells trees and prepares them for the sawmill.
lum•ber•yard (lŭm′bər-yärd′) *n.* A commercial establishment where lumber is stored and sold.
lu•mi•nar•y (lo͞o′mə-nĕr′ē) *n., pl.* **-ies. 1.** An object, esp. a celestial body, that is a source of light. **2.** A celebrity.
lu•mi•nes•cence (lo͞o′mə-nĕs′əns) *n.* The production, as in fluorescence, of light without heat. **–lu′mi•nes′cent** *adj.*
lu•mi•nous (lo͞o′mə-nəs) *adj.* **1.** Emitting light. **2.** Lighted : illuminated. **3.** Easily understood : clear. **–lu′mi•nos′i•ty** (-nŏs′ĭ-tē) *n.* **–lu′mi•nous•ly** *adv.*
lum•mox (lŭm′əks) *n.* A clumsy oaf : lout.
lump[1] (lŭmp) *n.* **1.** An irregularly shaped piece or mass. **2.** A small cube, as of sugar. **3.** A swelling or small palpable mass. **4. lumps.** Punishment. *–adj.* Undivided : unbroken <a *lump* sum> *–v.* **1.** To put or consider together indiscriminately. **2.** To form or cause to form lumps. **–lump′i•ness** *n.* **–lump′y** *adj.*
lump[2] (lŭmp) *v. Informal.* To put up with : tolerate <like it or *lump* it>
lu•na•cy (lo͞o′nə-sē) *n., pl.* **-cies. 1.** Insanity. **2.** Great folly.
luna moth *n.* A large, pale-green North American moth, *Actias luna,* with a long projection on each hind wing.
lu•nar (lo͞o′nər) *adj.* Of, relating to, caused by, or affecting the moon.
lunar excursion module *n.* A spacecraft designed to transport astronauts from a command module orbiting the moon to the lunar surface and back.

lunar excursion module

lu•na•tic (lo͞o′nə-tĭk) *adj.* **1.** Insane. **2.** Of or used for the insane. **3.** Wildly foolish. **–lu′na•tic** *n.*
lunch (lŭnch) *n.* **1.** A meal eaten at midday. **2.** Food for lunch. **–lunch** *v.*
lunch•eon (lŭn′chən) *n.* A lunch, esp. a formal one.
lunch•eon•ette (lŭn′chə-nĕt′) *n.* A restaurant at which light lunches are served.
lung (lŭng) *n.* A saclike, usu. paired organ in the chest of most vertebrates that removes carbon dioxide from the blood and provides it with oxygen.
lunge (lŭnj) *n.* **1.** A sudden pass or thrust, as with a fencing foil. **2.** A sudden forward movement : plunge. *–v.* **lunged, lung•ing.** To move with a lunge.
lu•pine (lo͞o′pĭn) *n.* A plant of the genus *Lupinus,* bearing long spikes of variously colored flowers.
lu•pus (lo͞o′pəs) *n.* Any of several diseases of the skin and mucous membranes.
lurch[1] (lûrch) *v.* **1.** To walk with a stagger. **2.** To pitch or roll suddenly or erratically, as a ship. **–lurch** *n.*
lurch[2] (lûrch) *n.* A losing position in cribbage. **–in the lurch.** In a difficult position.
lure (lo͝or) *n.* **1.** Something attractive or appealing : enticement. **2.** An artificial bait to catch fish. *–v.* **lured, lur•ing.** To attract or entice with the prospect of reward or pleasure.
lu•rid (lo͝or′ĭd) *adj.* **1.** Horrifying : gruesome. **2.** Sensational. **3.** Glowing with the glare of fire through a haze. **–lu′rid•ly** *adv.* **–lu′rid•ness** *n.*
lurk (lûrk) *v.* **1.** To lie concealed, as in ambush. **2.** To move furtively.
Lu•sa•ka (lo͞o-sä′kə). Cap. of Zambia, in the SE part. *Pop.* 641,000.
lus•cious (lŭsh′əs) *adj.* **1.** Pleasant to smell or taste : delicious. **2.** Appealing to the senses. **–lus′cious•ly** *adv.* **–lus′cious•ness** *n.*
lush[1] (lŭsh) *adj.* **1.** Covered with luxuriant growth or vegetation <a *lush* green lawn> **2.** Sumptuous : opulent. **–lush′ly** *adv.* **–lush′ness** *n.*
lush[2] (lŭsh) *n. Slang.* An alcoholic.
lust (lŭst) *n.* **1.** Intense and often excessive or unrestrained sexual desire. **2.** An intense desire. **–lust′ful** *adj.* **–lust′ful•ly** *adv.*

▲word history: The noun *lust* preserves the same form it had in Old English, but its meaning is now quite different. It orig. was a word of neutral connotations, meaning simply "pleasure." In theological usage it was used to refer to pleasures and desires, esp. sexual desire, that were considered sinful. In this context *lust* was a term of opprobrium and reproach. This disapproval has carried over to the most recent sense of *lust,* "an overwhelming desire or craving." The meaning "pleasure" is now obsolete.

lus•ter (lŭs′tər) *n.* **1.** A soft and esp. reflected light : sheen or shine. **2.** Brilliance or radiance : brightness. **3.** Splendor : glory. **–lus′trous** (-trəs) *adj.* **–lus′ter•less** *adj.*
lus•tre (lŭs′tər) *n. esp. Brit. var. of* LUSTER.
lust•y (lŭs′tē) *adj.* **-i•er, -i•est. 1.** Full of vitality : vigorous. **2.** *Archaic.* Merry. **–lust′i•ly** *adv.* **–lust′i•ness** *n.*
lute (lo͞ot) *n.* A musical stringed instrument with a fretted fingerboard, a pear-shaped body, and usu. a bent neck.
lu•te•ti•um *also* **lu•te•ci•um** (lo͞o-tē′shē-əm, -shəm) *n. Symbol* **Lu** A silvery rare-earth element.
Lu•ther (lo͞o′thər), **Martin.** 1483–1546. German religious leader.
Lu•ther•an (lo͞o′thər-ən) *n.* A member of a branch of the Protestant Church that adheres to the teachings of Martin Luther. **–Lu′ther•an** *adj.* **–Lu′ther•an•ism** *n.*
Lux•em•bourg (lŭk′səm-bûrg′). **1.** Country and grand duchy of W Europe. *Pop.* 370,000. **2.** *also* **Luxembourg City.** *Cap.* of Luxembourg. *Pop.* 79,300.
lux•u•ri•ant (lŭg-zho͝or′ē-ənt, lŭk-sho͝or′-) *adj.* **1.** Growing or yielding abundantly : lush. **2. a.** Very elaborate : ornate. **b.** Florid. **–lux•u′ri•ance** *n.* **–lux•u′ri•ant•ly** *adv.*
lux•u•ri•ate (lŭg-zho͝or′ē-āt′, lŭk-sho͝or′-) *v.* **-at•ed, -at•ing. 1.** To take pleasure : revel. **2.** To grow abundantly.
lux•u•ri•ous (lŭg-zho͝or′ē-əs, lŭk-sho͝or′-) *adj.* **1.** Fond of or inclined to luxury. **2.** Marked by luxury : sumptuous. ☆***syns:*** LAVISH, LUSH, LUXURIANT, OPULENT, PLUSH, RICH **–lux•u′ri•ous•ly** *adv.*
lux•u•ry (lŭg′zhə-rē, lŭk′shə-) *n., pl.* **-ries. 1.** Something, esp. something that is expensive or hard to obtain, that provides comfort, pleasure, or enjoyment but is not absolutely essential. **2.** Sumptuous surroundings or living.
Lu•zon (lo͞o-zŏn′). Largest island of the Philippines, at the N end of the archipelago.
Lw *symbol for* LAWRENCIUM.
lwei (lwā) *n., pl.* **lwei.** See *kwanza* at CURRENCY TABLE.
–ly[1] *suff.* **1.** Like : resembling : having the characteristics of <fatherly> **2.** Recurring at a specified interval of <hourly>
–ly[2] *suff.* **1.** In a specified manner <gradually> **2.** With respect to <partly>
ly•ce•um (lī-sē′əm) *n.* **1.** A hall in which public programs such as lectures and concerts are presented. **2.** An organization that sponsors public programs such as lectures and concerts.
lye (lī) *n.* **1.** The powerfully alkaline solution yielded by leaching wood ashes. **2.** Potassium hydroxide. **3.** Sodium hydroxide.
ly•ing-in (lī′ĭng-ĭn′) *n.* Confinement of a woman in childbirth.
lymph (lĭmf) *n.* A clear, transparent, watery liquid that contains chiefly white blood cells and some red blood cells and circulates through the system to bathe the tissues, carries fat from the intestines, and supplies lymphocytes to the blood. **–lym•phat′ic** (lĭm-făt′ĭk) *adj.* & *n.*
lymph node *n.* A roundish body of lymphoid tissue that supplies lymphocytes to the heart and blood vessels and purifies the lymph.
lym•pho•cyte (lĭm′fə-sīt′) *n.* A white blood cell formed in lymphoid tissue and constituting 22–28% of all leukocytes.
lym•phoid (lĭm′foid′) *adj.* Of or relating to lymph or lymphatic tissue.
lynch (lĭnch) *v.* To execute, esp. by hanging, without due process of law.
lynx (lĭngks) *n.* A wildcat of the genus *Lynx,* esp. *L. canadensis,* with thick soft fur, a short tail, and tufted ears.
Ly•on (lē-ôN′). City of EC France. *Pop.* 456,716.
lyre (līr) *n.* An ancient stringed instrument related to the harp.
lyr•ic (lĭr′ĭk) *adj.* **1.** Expressing feeling, esp. deep personal emotion, in an affecting and direct way. **2.** Appropriate for singing. *–n.* **1.** A lyric poem. **2.** *often* **lyrics.** The words of a song. **–lyr′i•cal** *adj.* **–lyr′i•cal•ly** *adv.* **–lyr′i•cism** (-sĭz′əm) *n.*
lyr•i•cist (lĭr′ĭ-sĭst) *n.* Someone who writes song lyrics.
ly•ser•gic acid di•eth•yl•am•ide (lĭ-sûr′jĭk, lī-; dī′ĕth-əl-ăm′īd′) *n.* LSD.

Mm

m or **M** (ĕm) *n., pl.* **m's** or **M's. 1.** The 13th letter of the English alphabet. **2.** A speech sound represented by the letter *m.* **3.** Something with the shape of the letter M. **4.** The Roman numeral for 1,000.

m *abbr.* **1.** *also* **M** or **m.** or **M. a.** male. **b.** medium. **2.** meter.

m. *abbr.* mile.

ma (mä, mô) *n. Informal.* Mother.

MA *abbr.* Massachusetts (with Zip Code).

M.A. *abbr.* Master of Arts.

ma'am (măm) *n.* Madam.

ma·ca·bre (mə-kä'brə, -bər) *adj.* Suggestive of the horror of death : gruesome <a *macabre* story of revenge>

mac·ad·am (mə-kăd'əm) *n.* A road pavement consisting of layers of compacted broken stone, now usu. cemented with asphalt or tar. **—mac·ad'am·ize'** *v.*

Ma·cao (mə-kou'). Portuguese colony of SE China. *Cap.* Macao (*pop.* 241,413). *Pop.* 280,000.

ma·caque (mə-kăk', -käk') *n.* A short-tailed monkey of the genus *Macaca* of SE Asia, Japan, Gibraltar, and N Africa.

mac·a·ro·ni (măk'ə-rō'nē) *n.* Dried pasta, usu. in the shape of hollow tubes.

mac·a·roon (măk'ə-ro͞on', măk'ə-ro͞on') *n.* A cookie made with sugar, egg whites, and ground almonds or coconut.

ma·caw (mə-kô') *n.* Any of various tropical American parrots of the genera *Ara* and *Anodorhynchus,* with long tails, powerful curved bills, and usu. brilliant plumage.

Mac·ca·bees (măk'ə-bēz') *pl.n.* (*sing. in number*). See BIBLE TABLE.

mace[1] (mās) *n.* **1.** A heavy club with a flanged or spiked metal head, used in medieval times for crushing armor. **2.** A ceremonial staff carried or displayed as a symbol of authority.

mace[2] (mās) *n.* A spice made from the bright-red covering that partly encloses the nutmeg kernel.

Mac·e·do·ni·a (măs'ĭ-dō'nē-ə). Ancient kingdom N of Greece. **—Mac'e·do'ni·an** *adj.* & *n.*

mac·er·ate (măs'ə-rāt') *v.* **-at·ed, -at·ing. 1.** To make soft so as to separate into constituents by soaking in a liquid. **2.** To cause to become thin, usu. by starvation. **—mac'er·a'tion** *n.*

Mach (mäk) *n.* Mach number.

ma·chet·e (mə-shĕt'ē, -chĕt'ē) *n.* A large heavy knife with a broad blade, used as a weapon and for cutting vegetation.

Mach·i·a·vel·li (măk'ē-ə-vĕl'ē), **Niccolò.** 1469–1527. Italian statesman and political theorist. **—Mach'i·a·vel'li·an** *adj.* & *n.*

Mach·i·a·vel·li·an·ism (măk'ē-ə-vĕl'ē-ə-nĭz'əm, -vĕl'ə-) *n.* The doctrine of Machiavelli that denies the relevance of morality in political affairs.

mach·i·nate (măk'ə-nāt', măsh'-) *v.* **-nat·ed, -nat·ing.** To plot. **—mach'i·na'tion** *n.* **—mach'i·na'tor** *n.*

ma·chine (mə-shēn') *n.* **1. a.** A system or device built to use energy in performing a task <a sewing *machine*> **b.** Any of several simple devices, as an inclined plane, lever, or screw, that act on an applied force so as to change its magnitude or direction or both. **2.** A device or system, as a computer, that performs or helps in performing a human task. **3.** One who acts mechanically or rigidly. **4.** An organized group whose members are under the control of 1 or more leaders. *—v.* **-chined, -chin·ing.** To shape by machine.

machine gun *n.* An automatic rapid-fire gun, often mounted, that uses small-arms ammunition. **—ma·chine'-gun'** *v.* **—machine gunner** *n.*

machine language *n. Computer Sci.* Any of various systems of symbols for coding input data.

ma·chin·er·y (mə-shē'nə-rē, -shēn'rē) *n., pl.* **-ies. 1.** Machines or machine parts as a whole. **2.** The operating parts of a machine. **3.** A system of related elements that functions in a definable way.

ma·chin·ist (mə-shē'nĭst) *n.* A person skilled in the use of machine tools.

ma·chis·mo (mä-chēz'mō) *n.* An exaggerated sense of masculinity stressing aggressiveness, virility, and courage.

Mach number *n.* The ratio of an object's speed to the speed of sound in the surrounding atmosphere.

ma·cho (mä'chō') *adj.* Marked by machismo. *—n., pl.* **-chos. 1.** Machismo. **2.** A man who exhibits machismo.

Mac·ken·zie (mə-kĕn'zē). **1.** District of N.W.T., Canada. **2.** River of NW Canada, c. 1,120 mi (1,800 km) long.

mack·er·el (măk'ər-əl, măk'rəl) *n., pl.* **-el** or **-els.** An Atlantic food fish, *Scomber scombrus,* with dark wavy bars on the back and a silvery belly.

mack·i·naw (măk'ə-nô') *n.* A short double-breasted coat of thick, usu. plaid woolen material.

mack·in·tosh *also* **mac·in·tosh** (măk'ĭn-tŏsh') *n. esp. Brit.* **1.** A raincoat. **2.** A lightweight waterproof fabric orig. of rubberized cotton.

mac·ra·mé (măk'rə-mā') *n.* Lacework made of rough cords or strings woven and knotted into a pattern.

mac·ro·bi·ot·ics (măk'rō-bī-ŏt'ĭks) *n.* (*sing. in number*). A method believed by its adherents to promote longevity, chiefly by means of a diet consisting mainly of whole grains, vegetable, and fish. **—mac'ro·bi·ot'ic** *adj.*

mac·ro·cosm (măk'rō-kŏz'əm) *n.* **1.** The entire world : universe. **2.** A system reflecting on a large scale 1 of its component parts or systems. **—mac'ro·cos'mic** *adj.*

ma·cron (mā'krŏn', -krən) *n.* A diacritical mark, as the (ā) in *take,* placed over a vowel to indicate a long sound or phonetic value in pronunciation.

mac·ro·scop·ic (măk'rə-skŏp'ĭk) *also* **mac·ro·scop·i·cal** (-ĭ-kəl) *adj.* Large enough to be seen with the unaided eye.

mad (măd) *adj.* **mad·der, mad·dest. 1.** Afflicted with a mental disorder : insane. **2.** *Informal.* Very enthusiastic <*mad* about baseball> **3.** Angry : resentful. **4.** Lacking restraint or reason : foolish. **5.** Marked by frantic confusion or excitement <a *mad* dash for the exit> **6.** Boisterously happy : hilarious <a *mad* time at the party> **7.** Rabid. **—mad'ly** *adv.* **—mad'man'** *n.* **—mad'ness** *n.* **—mad'wom'an** *n.*

Mad·a·gas·car (măd'ə-găs'kər). Island country off the SE coast of Africa. *Cap.* Antananarivo. *Pop.* 8,730,000.

Mad·am (măd'əm) *n.* **1.** *pl.* **Mes·dames** (mā-dăm'). **a.** Used as a courtesy title in addressing a woman. **b.** Used formerly as a courtesy title before a given name but now used only before a surname or a title indicating rank or office <*Madam* Justice> **2. madam.** The mistress of a household. **3. madam.** A woman manager of a brothel.

Ma·dame (mə-dăm', măd'əm) *n., pl.* **Mes·dames** (mā-däm') Used as a French courtesy title for a married woman.

mad·cap (măd'kăp') *n.* A rash, impulsive person. *—adj.* Impulsive : wild.

mad·den (măd'n) *v.* **1.** To drive mad : derange. **2.** To make angry : infuriate. **—mad'den·ing·ly** *adv.*

mad·der (măd'ər) *n.* **1. a.** A plant of the genus *Rubia,* esp. *R. tinctoria,* with small yellow flowers and a red fleshy root. **b.** The root of this plant, once an important source of dye. **2.** A red dye derived from the madder root.

mad·ding (măd'ĭng) *adj. Archaic.* Frenzied <the *madding* crowd>

made (mād) *v. p.t.* & *p.p. of* MAKE.

Ma·dei·ra (mə-dîr'ə) *n.* A fortified dessert wine.

Mad·e·moi·selle (măd'ə-mə-zĕl', măd'mwə-zĕl') *n., pl.* **Mad·e·moi·selles** (-zĕlz') or **Mes·de·moi·selles** (măd'mwä-zĕl') **1.** Used as a French courtesy title for a young girl or unmarried woman. **2. mademoiselle.** A French governess.

made-to-or·der (măd'tə-ôr'dər) *adj.* **1.** Custom-made. **2.** Highly suitable.

made-up (măd'ŭp') *adj.* **1.** Invented : fabricated <a *made-up* alibi> **2.** Marked by the application of make-up <*made-up* lips>

mad·house (măd'hous') *n.* **1.** An insane asylum. **2.** *Informal.* A place of great confusion and disorder.

Mad·i·son (măd'ĭ-sən). Cap. of Wis., in the SC part. *Pop.* 170,616.

Madison, James. 1751–1836. 4th U.S. President (1809–17).

Madison Avenue *n.* The American advertising industry.

ma·dras (măd'rəs, mə-drăs', -dräs') *n.* A fine-textured cotton cloth usu. having a striped or plaid design.

Madras. City of SE India, on the Bay of Bengal. *Pop.* 2,469,449.

Ma·drid (mə-drĭd'). Cap. of Spain, in the C part. *Pop.* 3,274,000.

mad·ri·gal (măd'rĭ-gəl) *n.* A musical composition for 2 or more unaccompanied voices that was developed during the early Renaissance.

mael·strom (māl'strəm) *n.* **1.** An extraordinarily violent whirlpool. **2.** A situation resembling a maelstrom in turmoil <a *maelstrom* of scandal>

maes·tro (mīs'trō) *n., pl.* **-tros** or **-tri** (-trē). A master in an art, esp. a famous conductor or composer of music.

Ma·fi·a (mä'fē-ə) *n.* **1.** A secret terrorist organization in Sicily. **2.** An alleged international criminal organization.

Ma·fi·o·so (mä'fē-ō'sō) *n., pl.* **-si** (-sē'). A member of the Mafia.

mag·a·zine (măg'ə-zēn', măg'ə-zēn') *n.* **1.** A place for storage, esp. of ammunition. **2.** A periodical containing written matter, as articles, and usu. illustrations and advertising. **3. a.** A compartment for holding the cartridges in a firearm. **b.** A compartment in a camera for holding rolls or cartridges of film.

▲word history: The use of *magazine* to mean "a periodical publication" is a specialized development of the original, more general meaning "storehouse." *Magazine* was at one time used in book titles to mean a storehouse of information on a special topic, equivalent to the use of *encyclopedia* today. The word was also used in titles of periodical publications that contained a storehouse of miscellaneous literary works, articles on various topics, and other features. From the latter use the word *magazine* became a generic term for all such publications.

Ma•gel•lan (mə-jĕl′ən), **Ferdinand.** 1480?–1521. Portuguese navigator.

Magellan, Strait of. Channel between the S tip of South America and Tierra del Fuego.

ma•gen•ta (mə-jĕn′tə) *n.* A vivid purplish red.

mag•got (măg′ət) *n.* The legless soft-bodied larva of any of various insects of the order Diptera, often found in decaying matter. **—mag′got•y** *adj.*

Ma•gi (mā′jī′) *pl.n.* The 3 wise men of the East who traveled to Bethlehem to worship the infant Jesus.

mag•ic (măj′ĭk) *n.* **1.** The art that purports to control or forecast natural events or forces by invoking the supernatural. **2.** Exercise of sleight of hand or conjuring for entertainment. **3.** A mysterious quality of enchantment <the *magic* of exotic lands> ☆**syns:** CONJURATION, SORCERY, WITCHCRAFT, WITCHING, WIZARDRY **—mag′ic, mag′i•cal** *adj.* **—mag′i•cal•ly** *adv.* **—ma•gi′cian** (mə-jĭsh′ən) *n.*

mag•is•te•ri•al (măj′ĭ-stîr′ē-əl) *adj.* **1.** Of, relating to, or typical of a master or teacher : authoritative. **2.** Overbearing : dogmatic. **3.** Of or relating to a magistrate or his or her official functions.

mag•is•trate (măj′ĭ-strāt′, -strĭt) *n.* **1.** A civil officer empowered to administer and enforce law. **2.** A minor official with limited judicial authority, as a justice of the peace.

mag•ma (măg′mə, mäg′-) *n., pl.* **-ma•ta** (-mä′tə) *or* **-mas.** *Geol.* Molten matter beneath the earth's crust that often cools and hardens to form igneous rock.

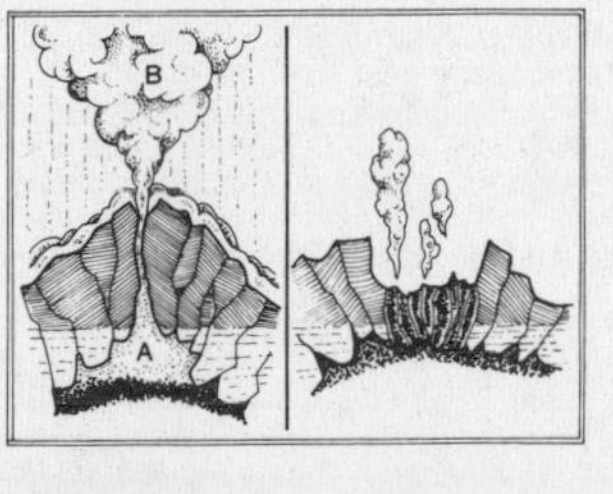

magma
An erupting volcano showing A. magma deposit and B. lava flow

mag•nan•i•mous (măg-năn′ə-məs) *adj.* Noble of heart and mind, esp. generous in forgiving. **—mag′na•nim′i•ty** (-nə-nĭm′ĭ-tē) *n.* **—mag•nan′i•mous•ly** *adv.* **—mag•nan′i•mous•ness** *n.*

mag•nate (măg′nāt′) *n.* A person of influence or power, esp. in business or industry : tycoon <an oil *magnate*>

mag•ne•sia (măg-nē′zhə, -shə) *n.* A white, powdery compound that is an oxide of magnesium and is used esp. as a laxative.

mag•ne•si•um (măg-nē′zē-əm, -zhəm) *n. Symbol* **Mg** A light, moderately hard, silvery metallic element.

mag•net (măg′nĭt) *n.* **1.** A body that attracts certain materials, as iron, by virtue of a surrounding field of force created by the motion of its atomic electrons and the alignment of its atoms. **2.** An electromagnet. **3.** One that exerts attraction. **—mag′net•ism** *n.*

mag•net•ic (măg-nĕt′ĭk) *adj.* **1.** Of or pertaining to magnets or magnetism. **2.** Having the properties of a magnet. **3.** Capable of being magnetized. **4.** Having an unusual ability or power to attract <a *magnetic* personality> **—mag•net′i•cal•ly** *adv.*

magnetic equator *n.* A line joining all points on the earth's surface where there is no magnetic dip.

magnetic field *n.* A condition in a region of space, as that around a magnet, established by the presence of a magnet, or of an electric current, and marked by the existence of a detectable magnetic force at every point in the region.

magnetic north *n.* The direction of the earth's magnetic field to which the N-seeking pole of a magnetic needle points when free from local magnetic influence.

magnetic recording *n.* The recording of a signal, as sound or television images, on a magnetizable surface for storage and subsequent retrieval.

magnetic tape *n.* A plastic tape having a magnetizable coating for use in magnetic recording.

mag•net•ite (măg′nĭ-tīt′) *n.* A mineral form of black iron oxide that is an important iron ore.

mag•net•ize (măg′nĭ-tīz′) *v.* **-ized, -iz•ing. 1.** To make magnetic. **2.** To attract, charm, or influence <a speaker who *magnetized* the audience> **—mag′net•iz′a•ble** *adj.* **—mag′net•i•za′tion** *n.* **—mag′net•iz′er** *n.*

mag•ne•to (măg-nē′tō) *n., pl.* **-tos.** A small alternator that works by means of permanent magnets, used to generate the electricity for the spark in some engines.

mag•ne•tom•e•ter (măg′nĭ-tŏm′ĭ-tər) *n.* An instrument for comparing the intensity and direction of magnetic fields.

mag•ne•to•sphere (măg-nē′tə-sfîr′) *n.* A region surrounding the earth, extending from about 500 to several thousand km above the surface, in which charged particles are trapped and their behavior dominated by the earth's magnetic field.

mag•nif•i•cent (măg-nĭf′ĭ-sənt) *adj.* **1.** Lavish : grand. **2.** Noble in thought or deed : exalted. **3.** Outstanding of its kind : superlative <a *magnificent* painting> **—mag•nif′i•cence** *n.* **—mag•nif′i•cent•ly** *adv.*

mag•ni•fy (măg′nə-fī′) *v.* **-fied, -fy•ing. 1.** To make larger in size : enlarge. **2.** To cause to appear greater or seem more important : exaggerate. **3.** To make (an object) appear larger than it really is, esp. by means of a lens. **4.** To praise or glorify. **—mag′ni•fi•ca′tion** *n.* **—mag′ni•fi′er** *n.*

mag•nil•o•quent (măg-nĭl′ə-kwənt) *adj.* Lofty and extravagant in speech : grandiloquent. **—mag•nil′o•quence** *n.* **—mag•nil′o•quent•ly** *adv.*

mag•ni•tude (măg′nĭ-to͞od′, -tyo͞od′) *n.* **1.** Greatness in size, extent, or significance. **2.** Size : quantity. **3.** *Astron.* The relative brightness of a celestial body expressed on a numerical scale.

mag•no•lia (măg-nōl′yə) *n.* Any of various trees and shrubs of the genus *Magnolia,* many of which are cultivated for their white, pink, purple, or yellow flowers.

mag•num (măg′nəm) *n.* A bottle for wine or liquor holding approx. 2/5 gal.

mag•num o•pus (măg′nəm ō′pəs) *n.* A literary or artistic masterpiece, esp. an artist's, writer's, or composer's greatest single work.

mag•pie (măg′pī′) *n.* Any of various birds of the family Corvidae, found worldwide and noted for their chattering call.

Mag•yar (măg′yär′, mäg′-) *n.* A member of the chief ethnic group of Hungary. **—Mag′yar′** *adj.*

ma•ha•ra•jah *or* **ma•ha•ra•ja** (mä′hə-rä′jə, -zhə) *n.* A king or prince in India ranking above a raja.

ma•ha•ra•ni *or* **ma•ha•ra•nee** (mä′hə-rä′nē) *n.* **1.** The wife of a maharajah. **2.** A princess in India ranking above a rani.

ma•ha•ri•shi (mä′hə-rē′shē, mə-här′ə-shē) *n.* A Hindu teacher of spiritual knowledge.

ma•hat•ma (mə-hät′mə, -hăt′-) *n.* A person venerated in India and Tibet for great knowledge and love of humanity.

ma•hog•a•ny (mə-hŏg′ə-nē) *n., pl.* **-nies. 1.** Any of various tropical American trees of the genus *Swietenia,* prized for their hard, reddish-brown wood. **2.** The wood of a mahogany, esp. of *S. mahogani,* used for making furniture.

ma•hout (mə-hout′) *n.* The keeper and driver of an elephant.

maid (mād) *n.* **1.** A girl or an unmarried woman. **2.** A woman servant.

maid•en (mād′n) *n.* MAID 1. *—adj.* **1.** Of, relating to, or suitable for a maiden. **2.** Being an unmarried woman <a *maiden* aunt> **3.** Earliest or first <a *maiden* flight> **—maid′en•hood′** *n.*

maid•en•hair (mād′n-hâr′) *n.* A fern of the genus *Adiantum,* with dark stems and light-green feathery fronds.

maiden name *n.* A woman's family name before marriage.

maid of honor *n., pl.* **maids of honor.** An unmarried woman who is the chief attendant of a bride.

maid•ser•vant (mād′sûr′vənt) *n.* A woman servant.

mail[1] (māl) *n.* **1. a.** Material, as letters, handled by a postal system. **b.** Mail processed for distribution from a post office at a specified time <the morning *mail*> **2.** *often* **mails.** A nation's system for transporting mail. *—v.* To send by mail. **—mail′er** *n.*

▲word history: The word *mail*[1], which denotes the material handled by the post office, is a survivor of the days when the few letters and dispatches that were exchanged were carried by horsemen in their traveling bags. In Middle English times the word *mail* meant simply "bag," esp. one used by a traveler for provisions. Such bags were used to carry letters, and the word *mail* eventually came to designate the contents rather than the container.

mail[2] (māl) *n.* Armor made of connected metal rings, overlapping scales, or loops of chain. **—mailed** *adj.*

mail•box (māl′bŏks′) *n.* **1.** A public container where mail is deposited for collection. **2.** A private box for incoming mail.

mail drop *n.* **1.** A receptacle or slot for mail delivery. **2.** An address at which one receives mail but does not reside.
mail•man (māl′măn′, -mən) *n.* One who delivers mail.
mail order *n.* An order for goods received and often filled by mail.
maim (mām) *v.* **1.** To disable or disfigure, usu. by depriving of the use of a limb or bodily member : cripple. **2.** To make imperfect or defective : impair.
main (mān) *adj.* Being most important : chief. *—n.* **1.** The principal or most important part or point. **2.** A large pipe, duct, conduit, or conductor used to carry water, oil, gas, or electricity. **3.** Physical power <might and *main*> **—main′ly** *adv.*
Maine (mān) State of the NE U.S. *Cap.* Augusta. *Pop.* 1,124,660.
main•land (mān′lănd′, -lənd) *n.* The chief land mass of a country, territory, or continent.
main•line (mān′līn′) *v. Slang.* To inject a narcotic drug directly into a vein.
main•mast (mān′məst) *n.* The principal mast of a sailing vessel.
main•sail (mān′səl) *n.* The principal sail of a sailing vessel.
main•spring (mān′sprĭng′) *n.* **1.** The principal spring in a mechanism, esp. a clock or watch. **2.** A motivating cause.
main•stay (mān′stā′) *n.* **1.** A strong rope that supports the mainmast of a sailing vessel. **2.** A main support.
main•stream (mān′strēm′) *n.* The chief direction or trend of an action or line of thought. **—main′stream′** *adj.* & *v.*
main street *n.* **1.** The principal street of a small town or city. **2. Main Street.** The smug, materialistic, and provincial culture of a small town.
main•tain (mān-tān′) *v.* **1.** To carry on : continue <*maintain* a sound economy> **2.** To keep in a desirable condition <*maintain* bridges> **3.** To provide for <*maintain* a large family> **4.** To defend, as against attack or danger. **5.** To declare : assert. **—main•tain′a•ble** *adj.* **—main′te•nance** (-tə-nəns) *n.*
maî•tre d′ (mā′trə dē′, mā′tər) *n., pl.* **maî•tre d′s** (dēz′). *Informal.* A maître d'hôtel.
maî•tre d′hô•tel (mā′trə dō-tĕl′) *n., pl.* **maî•tres d′hô•tel** (mā′trə dō-tĕl′). **1.** A headwaiter. **2.** A major-domo.
maize (māz) *n.* Corn.
maj•es•ty (măj′ĭ-stē) *n., pl.* **-ties. 1.** The authority, greatness, and dignity of a sovereign. **2. Majesty.** Used as a title in speaking of or to a sovereign <Your royal *Majesty*> **3.** A quality of stateliness or grandeur. **—ma•jes′tic** (mə-jĕs′tĭk) *adj.* **—ma•jes′ti•cal•ly** *adv.*
ma•jol•i•ca (mə-jŏl′ĭ-kə, -yŏl′-) *n.* Tin-glazed earthenware often richly decorated and colored, esp. an earthenware of this type made in Italy.
ma•jor (mā′jər) *adj.* **1.** Greater in importance, rank, or stature <a *major* breakthrough in virus research> **2.** Demanding great attention : serious <a *major* accident> **3.** *Mus.* Designating a scale or mode with half steps between the 3rd and 4th and the 7th and 8th degrees. *—n.* **1.** An officer in the U.S. Army, Air Force, or Marine Corps ranking above a captain and below a lieutenant colonel. **2. a.** A field or subject selected as an academic specialization. **b.** A student specializing in a particular major. *—v.* To be a student in an academic major.
ma•jor-do•mo (mā′jər-dō′mō) *n., pl.* **-mos. 1.** The chief steward or butler in the household of a sovereign or noble. **2.** A steward or butler.
ma•jor•ette (mā′jə-rĕt′) *n.* A drum majorette.
major general *n.* An officer in the U.S. Army, Air Force, or Marine Corps ranking above a brigadier general and below a lieutenant general.
ma•jor•i•ty (mə-jôr′ĭ-tē, -jŏr′-) *n., pl.* **-ties. 1.** The greater number or part of something. **2.** The excess of a greater number over a smaller number : margin <won by a *majority* of 5,000 votes> **3.** The status of having reached the legal age of responsibility.
ma•jor-med•i•cal (mā′jər-mĕd′ĭ-kəl) *adj.* Of, pertaining to, or being an insurance plan that pays for most of the medical bills incurred during a major illness.
make (māk) *v.* **made** (mād), **mak•ing. 1. a.** To cause to happen or exist. **b.** To bring into being : create or fashion <*make* a blouse> **2. a.** To cause to be or become <*made* our feelings known> **b.** To cause to assume a specified function or role <*made* me boss> **3.** To compel <*made* us go> **4.** To carry out, engage in, or perform <*made* an attempt> **5. a.** To formulate in the mind <*make* plans> **b.** To arrive at <*make* decisions> **6.** To acquire, gain, or earn <*make* friends><*make* money> **7.** To achieve : attain. **8.** To set in order : prepare. **9.** To provide <*make* room> **10. a.** To grow or develop into <*made* a good doctor> **b.** To be capable of being made into <Oak *makes* sturdy furniture.> **11.** To amount to in importance <*makes* a big difference> **12.** To institute or establish : enact <*make* new laws> *—n.* **1.** An act or process of making. **2.** The manner or style in which something is made. **3.** A particular line of manufactured goods : brand <a famous *make* of shoe> **—make believe.** To pretend. **—make do.** To manage with whatever is available. **—make fun of.** To mock : ridicule. **—make good. 1.** To carry out : fulfill <*made good* our vow> **2.** To repay : idemnify <*make good* one's obligations>> **3.** To succeed <*make good* in the leading role> **—make light of.** To treat as unimportant <*made light of* our fears> **—make out. 1.** To see, esp. with difficulty. **2.** To comprehend <couldn't *make out* what he meant> **3.** To fill in (e.g., a document). **4.** *Slang.* To fare <*made out* poorly in politics> **—make up. 1.** To invent : fabricate <*made up* an alibi> **2.** To compensate for a transgression or omission. **3.** To come to a reconciliation after a misunderstanding or argument. **4.** To decide <*make up* your mind.> **5.** To apply cosmetics. **—make way. 1.** To provide room for passage. **2.** To make progress. **—mak′er** *n.*
make-be•lieve (māk′bĭ-lēv′) *n.* Playful pretense. **—make′-be•lieve′** *adj.*
make•shift (māk′shĭft′) *n.* Something used as a temporary substitute. **—make′shift′** *adj.*
make-up *also* **make•up** (māk′ŭp′) *n.* **1.** The manner in which something is put together : construction. **2.** The qualities of temperament constituting a personality. **3.** Cosmetics, as eye shadow or lipstick, applied to the face.
make-work (māk′wûrk′) *n.* Work that consumes time but is not productive.
ma•ku•ta (mä-ko͞o′tä) *n. pl. of* LIKUTA.
Mal•a•bo (măl′ə-bō′). Cap. of Equatorial Guinea, on Bioko Is. in the Gulf of Guinea. *Pop.* 20,000.
Mal•a•chi (măl′ə-kī′). *n.* See BIBLE TABLE.
mal•a•chite (măl′ə-kīt′) *n.* A green mineral carbonate of copper used as an ore of copper and for ornamental stoneware.
mal•ad•just•ed (măl′ə-jŭs′tĭd) *adj.* Poorly adjusted, as to one's environment or circumstances. **—mal′ad•just′ment** *n.*
mal•a•droit (măl′ə-droit′) *adj.* Marked by lack of dexterity : awkward. **—mal′a•droit′ly** *adv.* **—mal′a•droit′ness** *n.*
mal•a•dy (măl′ə-dē) *n., pl.* **-dies.** A disease or disorder : sickness.
Mal•a•gas•y (măl′ə-găs′ē) *n., pl.* **-y** or **-ies.** A native or inhabitant of Madagascar. **—Mal′a•gas′y** *adj.*
mal•aise (mə-lāz′, mă-) *n.* A vague feeling of ill-being.
ma•la•mute (mä′lə-myo͞ot′, măl′ə-) *n.* A powerful dog, orig. bred in Alaska as a sled dog, with a thick gray, black, or white coat and a bushy tail.
mal•a•pert (măl′ə-pûrt′) *adj.* Saucy : impudent. **—mal′a•pert′** *n.*
mal•a•prop•ism (măl′ə-prŏp-ĭz′əm) *n.* Ludicrous misuse of a word.
mal•a•pro•pos (măl′ăp-rə-pō′) *adj.* Inappropriate. **—mal′a•pro•pos′** *adv.*
ma•lar•i•a (mə-lâr′ē-ə) *n.* An infectious disease transmitted by the bite of the infected female anopheles mosquito and marked by cycles of chills, fever, and sweating. **—ma•lar′i•al** *adj.*
ma•lar•key *also* **ma•lar•ky** (mə-lär′kē) *n. Slang.* Nonsense.
Mal•a•thi•on (măl′ə-thī′ŏn′). A trademark for an organic compound used as an insecticide.
Ma•la•wi (mə-lä′wē). Country of SE Africa. *Cap.* Lilongwe. *Pop.* 5,975,000. **—Ma•la′wi•an** *adj.* & *n.*
Ma•lay (mə-lā′, mā′lā′). **1.** Archipelago in the Indian and Pacific oceans, between Australia and SE Asia. **2.** *also* **Ma•la•ya** (mə-lā′ə, mā-). Peninsula of SE Asia. **—Ma•lay′an** *adj.* & *n.*
Ma•lay•sia (mə-lā′zhə, -shə). Country of SE Asia, consisting of the S Malay Peninsula and N Borneo. *Cap.* Kuala Lumpur. *Pop.* 13,650,000. **—Ma•lay′sian** *adj.* & *n.*
mal•con•tent (măl′kən-tĕnt′) *adj.* Unhappy with existing circumstances : discontented. **—mal′con•tent′** *n.*
mal de mer (măl′ də mâr′) *n.* Seasickness.
Mal•dives (môl′dīvz′). Island country in the Indian Ocean SW of Sri Lanka. *Cap.* Male. *Pop.* 136,000. **—Mal•div′i•an** (-dĭv′ē-ən), **Mal•di′van** (-dī′vən) *adj.* & *n.*
male (māl) *adj.* **1.** Of, relating to, or being the sex that has organs to produce spermatozoa for fertilizing ova. **2.** Of, relating to, or typical of the male sex : masculine. **3.** Designed to fit into a matching socket or opening. *—n.* An individual of the male sex. **—male′ness** *n.*
Ma•le (mä′lē). Cap. of the Maldives. *Pop.* 12,000.
mal•e•dic•tion (măl′ĭ-dĭk′shən) *n.* A curse.
mal•e•fac•tor (măl′ə-făk′tər) *n.* **1.** One who has committed a crime : criminal. **2.** An evildoer. **—mal′e•fac′tion** *n.*
ma•lef•ic (mə-lĕf′ĭk) *adj.* **1.** Having a malignant influence : sinister. **2.** Malicious.
ma•lef•i•cence (mə-lĕf′ə-səns) *n.* **1.** Evil or harm. **2.** The quality or state of being malefic. **—ma•lef′i•cent** *adj.*

ma•lev•o•lent (mə-lĕv′ə-lənt) *adj.* **1.** Having or exhibiting ill will or spite : malicious. **2.** Having an evil influence. ☆***syns:*** BITCHY, EVIL, MALICIOUS, MALIGN, MALIGNANT, MEAN, NASTY, POISONOUS, SPITEFUL, VENOMOUS, VICIOUS, WICKED **—ma•lev′o•lence** *n.* **—ma•lev′o•lent•ly** *adv.*

mal•fea•sance (măl-fē′zəns) *n. Law.* Misconduct, esp. by a public official.

mal•for•ma•tion (măl′fôr-mā′shən) *n.* An abnormal form or structure. **—mal•formed′** *adj.*

mal•func•tion (măl-fŭngk′shən) *v.* To fail to function properly. **—mal•func′tion** *n.*

Ma•li (mä′lē). Country of W Africa. *Cap.* Bamako. *Pop.* 6,660,000.

mal•ice (măl′ĭs) *n.* **1.** The desire to harm others : ill will. **2.** *Law.* Intent to commit an unlawful act or injure another without just cause or reason. **—ma•li′cious** (mə-lĭsh′əs) *adj.* **—ma•li′cious•ly** *adv.*

ma•lign (mə-līn′) *v.* To speak evil of. —*adj.* **1.** Evil in nature, intent, or influence. **2.** Strongly suggestive of evil, menace, or harm. ☆***syns:*** BALEFUL, SINISTER **—ma•lign′er** *n.*

ma•lig•nant (mə-lĭg′nənt) *adj.* **1.** Exhibiting intense malevolence. **2.** Extremely harmful : pernicious. **3.** *Pathol.* **a.** Designating an abnormal growth that tends to metastasize. **b.** Life-threatening : virulent. **—ma•lig′nan•cy** *n.* **—ma•lig′nant•ly** *adv.* **—ma•lig′ni•ty** *n.*

ma•lin•ger (mə-lĭng′gər) *v.* To pretend to be ill or injured in order to avoid responsibility or work. **—ma•lin′ger•er** *n.*

mall (môl, măl) *n.* **1.** A shaded public promenade or walk. **2.** **a.** A street lined with shops and closed to vehicles. **b.** A shopping center. **c.** A large concourse affording access to shops, businesses, and restaurants. **3.** A center strip dividing a highway.

mal•lard (măl′ərd) *n., pl.* **mallard** or **-lards.** A wild duck, *Anas platyrhynchos,* the male of which has a green head and neck.

mal•le•a•ble (măl′ē-ə-bəl) *adj.* **1.** Capable of being shaped, bent, or drawn out, as by hammering. **2.** Capable of being altered or influenced : tractable. ☆***syns:*** DUCTILE, FLEXIBLE, MOLDABLE, PLASTIC, PLIABLE, PLIANT, SUPPLE, WORKABLE **—mal′le•a•bil′i•ty, mal′le•a•ble•ness** *n.* **—mal′le•a•bly** *adv.*

mal•let (măl′ĭt) *n.* **1.** **a.** A hammer with a cylindrical wooden head and a short handle. **b.** A tool with a large head for striking a surface without damaging it. **2.** A long-handled implement for striking a ball, as in croquet and polo.

mal•le•us (măl′ē-əs) *n., pl.* **-le•i** (-ē-ī′, -ē-ē′). *Anat.* The largest of 3 small bones in the middle ear.

mal•low (măl′ō) *n.* A plant of the widely distributed genus *Malva,* bearing pink or white flowers.

mal•nour•ished (măl-nûr′ĭsht) *adj.* Improperly nourished.

mal•nu•tri•tion (măl′no͞o-trĭsh′ən, -nyo͞o-) *n.* Faulty and esp. insufficient nutrition.

mal•oc•clu•sion (măl′ə-klo͞o′zhən) *n.* Failure of the upper and lower teeth to meet properly.

mal•o•dor•ous (măl-ō′dər-əs) *adj.* Having a foul odor : smelly. **—mal•o′dor•ous•ly** *adv.* **—mal•o′dor•ous•ness** *n.*

mal•prac•tice (măl-prăk′tĭs) *n.* **1.** Improper or negligent treatment by a physician that results in injury or damage to the patient. **2.** Improper or unethical conduct on the part of one, as a lawyer, rendering professional services.

malt (môlt) *n.* **1.** Grain, usu. barley, that has sprouted, used chiefly in brewing and distilling. **2.** An alcoholic beverage brewed from malt. **—malt′y** *adj.*

Mal•ta (môl′tə). Island nation in the Mediterranean S of Sicily. *Cap.* Valletta. *Pop.* 330,000. **—Mal•tese′** *adj.* & *n.*

malt•ed milk (môl′tĭd) *n.* **1.** A powder consisting of dried milk, a malt extract, and wheat flour. **2.** A drink made of malted milk powder mixed with milk and usu. flavoring and ice cream.

malt liquor *n.* Fermented beer or ale made with malt.

mal•tose (môl′tōs′, -tōz′) *n.* A sugar found in malt.

mal•treat (măl-trēt′) *v.* To treat abusively and harshly. **—mal•treat′ment** *n.*

ma•ma *also* **mam•ma** (mä′mə, mə-mä′) *n.* Mother.

mam•ba (mäm′bə) *n.* A venomous tropical African snake of the genus *Dendraspis,* esp. *D. angusticeps,* a black or green tree snake.

mam•bo (mäm′bō) *n., pl.* **-bos.** A dance of Latin-American origin that resembles the rumba.

mam•mal (măm′əl) *n.* A member of the group of vertebrate animals, including humans, the females of which secrete milk for nourishing their young. **—mam•ma′li•an** (mă-mā′lē-ən) *adj.* & *n.*

mam•ma•ry (măm′ər-ē) *adj.* Of, relating to, or being a mammary gland.

mammary gland *n.* A milk-producing organ in female mammals that consists of clusters of small cavities with ducts terminating in a nipple.

mam•mon (măm′ən) *n. often* **Mammon.** Riches considered as an evil influence or an object of worship.

mam•moth (măm′əth) *n.* An extinct elephant of the genus *Mammuthus,* once found throughout the N Hemisphere. —*adj.* Of great size : enormous.

man (măn) *n., pl.* **men** (mĕn). **1.** A full-grown male human being. **2.** A human being, regardless of sex. **3.** The human race : mankind. **4.** *Informal.* **a.** A husband. **b.** A lover or sweetheart. **5.** A male servant or subordinate. **6.** One of the pieces used in a board game, as chess. **7.** *often* **Man.** *Slang.* **a.** A policeman. **b.** A white man. —*v.* **manned, man•ning. 1.** To supply or furnish with men, as for defense or support. **2.** To be stationed at esp. in order to operate <*man* the guns>

Man. *abbr.* Manitoba.

man•a•cle (măn′ə-kəl) *n.* **1.** One of a pair of handcuffs. **2.** A fetter : restraint. **—man′a•cle** *v.*

man•age (măn′ĭj) *v.* **-aged, -ag•ing. 1.** To direct or control the use of. **2.** **a.** To exert control over. **b.** To make submissive. **3.** To succeed in accomplishing one's purpose : get along. **4.** To direct or administer (e.g., a business). **—man′age•a•bil′i•ty** *n.* **—man′age•a•ble** *adj.* **—man′age•a•bly** *adv.*

man•age•ment (măn′ĭj-mənt) *n.* **1.** The act, practice, or process of managing. **2.** Those who manage an organization. **3.** Executive skill.

man•ag•er (măn′ĭ-jər) *n.* **1.** One who manages a business or enterprise. **2.** One who directs an athlete or team. **—man′a•ge′ri•al** *adj.* **—man′ag•er•ship′** *n.*

Ma•na•gua (mä-nä′gwä). Cap. of Nicaragua, in the W. *Pop.* 375,278.

ma•ña•na (mä-nyä′nä) *adv.* **1.** Tomorrow. **2.** At an indefinite time in the future.

man•a•tee (măn′ə-tē′) *n.* An aquatic mammal of the genus *Trichechus* found in Atlantic coastal waters of the tropical Americas and Africa.

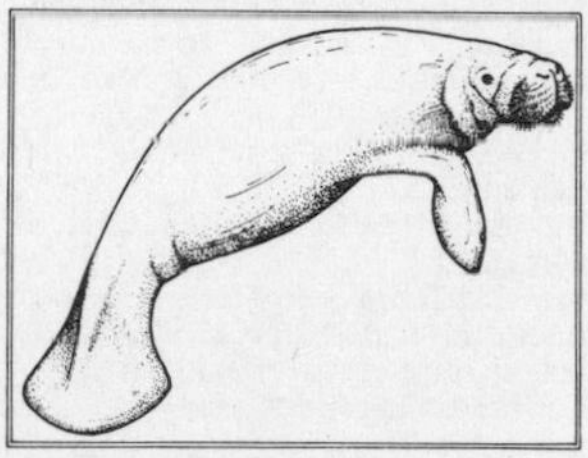

manatee

Man•ches•ter (măn′chĕs′tər, -chĭ-stər). **1.** Borough of NW England. *Pop.* 490,000. **2.** City of SE N.H., S of Concord. *Pop.* 90,936.

Man•chu•ri•a (măn-cho͝or′ē-ə). Region of NE China. **—Man•chu′ri•an** *adj.* & *n.*

man•da•rin (măn′də-rĭn) *n.* A member of 1 of the 9 ranks of high officials in imperial China.

man•date (măn′dāt′) *n.* **1.** An authoritative command. **2.** An instruction given by an electorate to a representative. **3.** **a.** Control over a territory granted by the League of Nations to 1 of its member nations. **b.** A territory under mandate. **—man′date′** *v.*

man•da•to•ry (măn′də-tôr′ē, -tōr′ē) *adj.* **1.** Of, relating to, having the nature of, or containing a mandate. **2.** Obligatory.

man•di•ble (măn′də-bəl) *n.* **1.** A jaw of a vertebrate, esp. a lower jaw. **2.** Either of the parts of a bird's beak. **—man•dib′u•lar** (-dĭb′yə-lər) *adj.*

man•do•lin (măn′dl-ĭn′, măn′dl-ĭn′) *n.* A stringed musical instrument with a pear-shaped body and a fretted neck.

man•drake (măn′drāk′) *n.* A Eurasian plant, *Mandragora officinarum,* bearing purplish flowers and a branched root thought to look like the human body.

man•drel *or* **man•dril** (măn′drəl) *n.* **1.** A spindle or shaft used to hold material that is being shaped on a lathe. **2.** A rotary shaft on which a working tool is mounted.

man•drill (măn′drĭl) *n.* A large fierce baboon, *Mandrillus sphinx,* of W Africa.

mane (mān) *n.* The long hair growing from the neck and head of certain animals, as a horse.

man-eat•er (măn′ē′tər) *n.* **1.** An animal that feeds on human flesh. **2.** A cannibal.

ma•nège *also* **ma•nege** (mă-nĕzh′) *n.* The art and practice of training a horse in classical riding maneuvers and exercises.

ma•nes or **Ma•nes** (mā′nēz′, mä′nās′) *pl.n.* The spirits of the dead, esp. ancestors, deified as minor gods in ancient Rome.

Ma•net (mă-nā′), **Edward.** 1832–83. French painter.

ma•neu•ver (mə-no͞o′vər, -nyo͞o′-) *n.* **1. a.** A tactical or strategic movement, as of troops or warships. **b.** *often* **maneuvers.** A military training exercise simulating combat. **2. a.** A physical movement or way of doing something requiring dexterity and skill. **b.** A controlled change in the course or position of a vehicle, as an aircraft or automobile. **3.** A calculated and skillful move : stratagem. **–ma•neu′ver** *v.* **–ma•neu′ver•a•bil′i•ty** *n.* **–ma•neu′ver•a•ble** *adj.*

man Friday *n.* A devoted man servant, aide, or employee.

man•ful (măn′fəl) *adj.* Manly. **–man′ful•ly** *adv.* **–man′ful•ness** *n.*

man•ga•nese (măng′gə-nēz′, -nēs′) *n. Symbol* **Mn** A gray-white, brittle metallic element used to strengthen steel alloys.

mange (mānj) *n.* A contagious skin disease of mammals marked by itching and hair loss. **–mang′y** *adj.*

man•ger (mān′jər) *n.* A trough holding livestock feed.

man•gle^1 (măng′gəl) *v.* **-gled, -gling. 1.** To disfigure or mutilate by battering, cutting, or tearing. **2.** To spoil or ruin through ineptitude or ignorance <*mangled* the concerto> **–man′gler** *n.*

man•gle^2 (măng′gəl) *n.* A machine that presses laundry by running it between heated rollers.

man•go (măng′gō) *n., pl.* **-goes** *or* **-gos.** A tropical evergreen tree, *Mangifera indica,* cultivated for its sweet, juicy fruit.

man•grove (măn′grōv′, măng′grōv′) *n.* Any of various tropical evergreen trees or shrubs of the genus *Rhizophora,* having stiltlike roots and stems and forming dense thickets along tidal shores.

man•han•dle (măn′hăn′dəl) *v.* To handle roughly.

Man•hat•tan (măn-hăt′n, mən-) *n.* A cocktail of sweet vermouth and whiskey.

Manhattan. Island and borough of New York City. *Pop.* 1,427,533.

man•hole (măn′hōl′) *n.* A hole through which one may enter a sewer, conduit, or drain.

man•hood (măn′ho͝od′) *n.* **1.** The state or condition of being an adult male. **2.** The composite of qualities, as courage, determination, and vigor, often attributed to a man. **3.** Men as a group.

man-hour (măn′our′) *n.* An industrial unit of production equal to the work of 1 person in 1 hr.

man•hunt (măn′hŭnt′) *n.* An extensive organized search for a person, as a criminal fugitive.

ma•ni•a (mā′nē-ə, mān′yə) *n.* **1.** Inordinately intense enthusiasm : craze. **2.** A symptom of manic-depressive psychosis marked by intense excitement and physical overactivity.

-mania *suff.* An intense or unreasonable desire or enthusiasm for <balleto*mania*>

ma•ni•ac (mā′nē-ăk′) *n.* An insane person. **–ma′ni•ac′, ma•ni′a•cal** (mə-nī′ə-kəl) *adj.*

man•ic (măn′ĭk) *adj.* Of, pertaining to, or marked by mania.

man•ic-de•pres•sive (măn′ĭk-dĭ-prĕs′ĭv) *adj.* Characterized by or afflicted with alternating periods of manic excitation and depression. **–man′ic-de•pres′sive** *n.*

man•i•cot•ti (măn′ĭ-kŏt′ē) *n.* Tubular pasta filled with meat or ricotta cheese, usu. served hot with a tomato sauce.

man•i•cure (măn′ĭ-kyo͝or′) *n.* A cosmetic treatment for the hands and fingernails. *–v.* **-cured, -cur•ing. 1.** To shape, clean, and often polish the fingernails of. **2.** To trim or clip evenly or closely. **–man′i•cur′ist** *n.*

man•i•fest (măn′ə-fĕst′) *adj.* Clearly apparent : obvious. *–v.* To reveal : display. *–n.* A list of passengers or cargo. **–man′i•fest•ly** *adv.*

man•i•fes•ta•tion (măn′ə-fĕ-stā′shən) *n.* **1.** The act or process of manifesting : demonstration. **2.** Something that reveals something else.

man•i•fes•to (măn′ə-fĕs′tō) *n., pl.* **-toes** *or* **-tos.** A public declaration of intentions or principles, esp. of a political nature.

man•i•fold (măn′ə-fōld′) *adj.* **1.** Of many kinds : multiple. **2.** Having many parts, forms, or aspects. *–n.* A pipe with several openings for making a number of connections. *–v.* **1.** To make numerous copies of. **2.** To multiply.

man•i•kin *or* **man•ni•kin** (măn′ĭ-kĭn) *n.* **1.** A dwarf. **2.** A mannequin.

Ma•nil•a (mə-nĭl′ə). Cap. of the Philippines, on **Manila Bay,** an inlet of the South China Sea. *Pop.* 1,438,000.

Manila hemp *n.* The fiber of the abaca, used to make rope, paper, and cordage.

Manila paper *n.* Strong, usu. buff-colored paper or thin cardboard orig. manufactured from Manila hemp.

ma•nip•u•late (mə-nĭp′yə-lāt′) *v.* **-lat•ed, -lat•ing. 1.** To control or operate with dexterity : handle. **2.** To manage or influence shrewdly and often deviously <*manipulated* the news> **–ma•nip′u•la′tion** *n.* **–ma•nip′u•la′tive** *adj.* **–ma•nip′u•la′tor** *n.*

Man•i•to•ba (măn′ĭ-tō′bə). Province of SC Canada. *Cap.* Winnipeg. *Pop.* 1,019,000. **–Man′i•to′ban** *adj.* & *n.*

man•kind (măn′kīnd′, -kīnd′) *n.* **1.** The human race. **2.** Men as opposed to women.

man•like (măn′līk′) *adj.* Resembling or typical of a man.

man•ly (măn′lē) *adj.* **-li•er, -li•est. 1.** Having qualities traditionally attributed to a man. **2.** Manlike. *–adv.* In a manly way. **–man′li•ness** *n.*

man-made (măn′mād′) *adj.* Made by human beings.

Mann (măn, män), **Thomas.** 1875–1955. German-born Amer. author.

man•na (măn′ə) *n.* **1.** Food miraculously provided for the Israelites during their flight from Egypt. **2.** Something valuable that one receives unexpectedly.

manned (mănd) *adj.* Conveying or operated by a human being <a *manned* space station>

man•ne•quin (măn′ĭ-kĭn) *n.* **1.** A life-size model of the human body, used to fit or display clothes : dummy. **2.** One who models clothes.

man•ner (măn′ər) *n.* **1. a.** A way of doing something <danced in a graceful manner>. **b.** The way in which a thing is done or takes place. **2.** Characteristic bearing or behavior <a dignified *manner*> **3. manners. a.** Socially correct behavior. **b.** The customs of a society or period, esp. as the subject of a literary work. **4.** Kind : sort. ☆**syns:** MANNERS, DECORUM, ETIQUETTE, PROPRIETIES

man•nered (măn′ərd) *adj.* **1.** Having manners of a specific kind <an ill-*mannered* boor> **2.** Affected or artificial <*mannered* writing>

man•ner•ism (măn′ə-rĭz′əm) *n.* **1.** A distinctive behavioral trait : idiosyncrasy. **2.** Exaggerated or affected style or manner.

man•ner•ly (măn′ər-lē) *adj.* Having good manners : polite. **–man′ner•li•ness** *n.*

man•ni•kin (măn′ĭ-kĭn) *n. var. of* MANIKIN.

man•nish (măn′ĭsh) *adj.* **1.** Of or befitting a man. **2.** Resembling a man. **–man′nish•ly** *adv.* **–man′nish•ness** *n.*

ma•noeu•vre (mə-no͞o′vər, -nyo͞o′-) *n.* & *v. esp. Brit. var. of* MANEUVER.

man-of-war (măn′ə-wôr′) *n., pl.* **men-of-war** (mĕn′-). **1.** A warship. **2.** The Portuguese man-of-war.

ma•nom•e•ter (mə-nŏm′ĭ-tər) *n.* An instrument that measures and indicates the pressure of liquids and gases. **–man′o•met′ric** (măn′ə-mĕt′rĭk) *adj.*

man•or (măn′ər) *n.* **1.** The estate of a medieval lord in W Europe. **2.** A landed estate. **3.** The principal house of an estate. **–ma•no′ri•al** (mă-nôr′ē-əl, -nōr′-) *adj.*

man•pow•er (măn′pou′ər) *n.* **1.** Human physical power. **2.** Power in terms of the workers available to a particular group or needed for a specific task.

man•qué (mäɴ-kā′) *adj.* Frustrated : unfulfilled <a writer *manqué*>

man•sard (măn′särd′) *n.* A roof with 2 slopes on all sides, the lower slope being nearly vertical and the upper nearly horizontal.

manse (măns) *n.* **1.** *esp Scot.* A clergyman's house and land. **2.** A Presbyterian minister's house.

man•ser•vant (măn′sûr′vənt) *n., pl.* **men•ser•vants.** A male servant.

man•sion (măn′shən) *n.* A large, imposing house.

man-sized (măn′sīzd′) *also* **man-size** (-sīz′) *adj. Informal.* Quite large <a *man-sized* sandwich>

man•slaugh•ter (măn′slô′tər) *n. Law.* The unlawful killing of 1 human being by another without express or implied intent to do injury.

man•slay•er (măn′slā′ər) *n.* One who slays a human being.

man•sue•tude (măn′swĭ-to͞od′, -tyo͞od′) *n.* Gentleness : mildness.

man•ta (măn′tə) *n.* **1.** A rough-textured cotton fabric or blanket made and used in Latin America and the SW U.S. **2.** *also* **manta ray.** Any of several fishes of the family Mobulidae, having large, very flat bodies with winglike pectoral fins.

man•teau (măn-tō′) *n.* A loose cloak.

man•tel *also* **man•tle** (măn′təl) *n.* **1.** An ornamental facing surrounding a fireplace. **2.** A shelf over a fireplace.

man•tel•piece (măn′təl-pēs′) *n.* MANTEL 2.

man•til•la (măn-tē′yə, -tē′ə, -tĭl′ə) *n.* A usu. lace scarf worn over the head and shoulders by women esp. in Spain and Latin America.

man•tis (măn′tĭs) *n., pl.* **tis•es** *or* **-tes** (-tēz′). Any of various chiefly tropical insects of the family Mantidae, usu. pale-green and with forelimbs often folded as if in prayer.

man•tis•sa (măn-tĭs′ə) *n. Math.* The fractional part of a logarithm to the base 10.

man•tle (măn′təl) *n.* **1.** A loose sleeveless coat : cloak. **2.** Something that conceals or covers <a *mantel* of snow> **3.** *var. of* MANTEL. **4.** A device in gas lamps consisting of a sheath of

threads that gives off brilliant illumination when heated by a flame. –*v.* **-tled, -tling.** To cover with or as if with a mantle.
man•tra (măn′trə) *n.* A sacred Hindu formula believed to possess magical power.
man•u•al (măn′yo͞o-əl) *adj.* **1.** Of, relating to, or done by the hands <*manual* skill> **2.** Operated by hand <a *manual* gear-shift> **3.** Employing or requiring physical energy <*manual* work> –*n.* **1.** A small reference book, esp. one providing instructions. **2.** An organ keyboard. **3.** Prescribed movements in the handling of a weapon, esp. a rifle. **–man′u•al•ly** *adv.*
man•u•fac•to•ry (măn′yə-făk′tə-rē) *n., pl.* **-ries.** A factory.
man•u•fac•ture (măn′yə-făk′chər) *v.* **-tured, -tur•ing. 1.** To make from raw materials, esp. with the use of industrial machines. **2.** To concoct : fabricate <*manufacture* an alibi> –*n.* **1.** The act, craft, or process of manufacturing. **2.** A manufactured product. **3.** An industry. **–man′u•fac′tur•er** *n.*
man•u•mit (măn′yə-mĭt′) *v.* **-mit•ted, -mit•ting.** To emancipate.
ma•nure (mə-no͝or′, -nyo͝or′) *n.* Fertilizer, esp. animal dung or compost. –*v.* **-nured, -nur•ing.** To apply manure to.
man•u•script (măn′yə-skrĭpt′) *n.* **1.** A typewritten or handwritten composition, as a book or document. **2.** Handwriting.
man•y (mĕn′ē) *adj.* **more** (môr, mōr), **most** (mōst). Amounting to or consisting of a large indefinite number. ☆***syns:*** LEGION, MULTITUDINOUS, MYRIAD, NUMEROUS, VOLUMINOUS –*n. (pl. in number).* A large indefinite number of persons or things. –*pron. (pl. in number).* A large number of persons or things.
man•y•fold (mĕn′ē-fōld′) *adv.* By many times.
Mao•ism (mou′ĭz′əm) *n.* Marxism-Leninism developed in China mainly by Mao Zedong. **–Mao′ist** *n.*
Mao•ri (mou′rē) *n., pl.* **Maori** or **-ris.** A member of an aboriginal people of New Zealand. **–Mao′ri** *adj.*
Mao Ze•dong (mou′ dzŭ′do͝ong′). 1893–1976. Chinese Communist leader.
map (măp) *n.* A usu. plane-surface representation of a region of the earth or sky. –*v.* **mapped, map•ping. 1.** To make a map of. **2.** To plan, esp. in detail : delineate <*mapped* out a new sales technique> **–map′mak′er** *n.* **–map′per** *n.*
ma•ple (mā′pəl) *n.* **1.** A tall deciduous tree or shrub of the genus *Acer,* with lobed leaves and winged seeds borne in pairs. **2.** The hard close-grained wood of a maple, used esp. for furniture and flooring.
maple sugar *n.* Sugar made by boiling down maple syrup.
maple syrup *n.* A sweet syrup made from the sap of the sugar maple.
mar (mär) *v.* **marred, mar•ring. 1.** To deface or damage. **2.** To spoil : ruin.
Mar. *abbr.* March.
mar•a•bou (măr′ə-bo͞o′) *n.* **1.** Any of several large Old World storks of the genus *Leptoptilus.* **2.** The soft down of the marabou, used esp. for trimming women's garments.

marabou

ma•ra•ca (mə-rä′kə) *n.* A percussion instrument having a hollow, gourdlike rattle containing dried beans or pebbles.
mar•a•schi•no (măr′ə-skē′nō, -shē′nō-) *n., pl.* **-nos.** A cherry preserved in a real or imitation cherry cordial.
mar•a•thon (măr′ə-thŏn′) *n.* **1.** A cross-country footrace of 26 mi, 385 yds. **2.** A long-distance race <a swimming *marathon*> **3.** A contest of endurance.
ma•raud (mə-rôd′) *v.* To raid for plunder : pillage. **–ma•raud′er** *n.*
mar•ble (mär′bəl) *n.* **1.** A limestone, often irregularly colored by impurities, used for architectural and ornamental purposes. **2.** A piece or sculpture of marble. **3. a.** A small hard ball, usu. of glass, used in children's games. **b. marbles** (*sing. in number*). Any of various games played with marbles. **4. marbles.** *Slang.* Common sense or sanity <lost their *marbles*> **–mar′ble** *v.* **–mar′bly** *adj.*
mar•bling (mär′bling) *n.* A streaking or veinlike marking of fat in a cut of meat.
march[1] (märch) *v.* **1.** To move or cause to move in or as if in a military formation. **2.** To walk in a determined and forceful manner. **3.** To advance steadily <time *marching* on> –*n.* **1.** The act of marching. **2.** Forward movement : progression <the *march* of history> **3.** A measured pace used in marching. **4.** The distance covered by marching <3 days' *march* from here> **5.** A musical composition with regularly accented rhythm suitable to accompany marching.
march[2] (märch) *n.* The border or boundary of a country or area of land : frontier.
March (märch) *n.* The 3rd month of the year, having 31 days.
mar•chion•ess (mär′shə-nĭs) *n.* **1.** The wife or widow of a marquis. **2.** A peeress holding the rank of marquis in her own right.
Mar•co•ni (mär-kō′nē), Marchese **Guglielmo.** 1874–1937. Italian inventor.
Mar•cus Au•re•li•us An•to•ni•us (mär′kəs ô-rē′lē-əs ăn′tə-nī′nəs). 121–80. Roman emperor and philosopher.
Mar•di gras (mär′dē grä′) *n.* The Tuesday before Ash Wednesday, often celebrated with carnivals and parades of costumed merrymakers.
mare[1] (mâr) *n.* A female of the equine species, esp. a female horse.
ma•re[2] (mä′rā) *n., pl.* **-ri•a** (-rē-ə). *Astron.* One of the large, dark areas on the surface of the moon or Mars.
mar•ga•rine (mär′jər-ĭn) *n.* A butter substitute that is a blend of hydrogenated vegetable oils and other ingredients, as emulsifiers and vitamins.
▲word history: Margarine is a relatively new substance, the product of modern chemistry. Both the substance and its name originated in France in the 19th cent. The substance was orig. made from a combination of animal fats, one of which was called *margaric acid* (*acide margarique* in French). The adjective *margaric* or *margarique* is derived from Greek *margaron,* "pearl," and was applied to the compound in question because its crystals had a pearly sheen. Margarine is naturally white; it is colored yellow in imitation of the natural yellow color of butter.
mar•gin (mär′jən) *n.* **1.** An edge : border. **2.** The blank space bordering the printed or written area on a page. **3.** An amount allowed beyond the necessary <a *margin* for error> **4.** A measure, quantity, or degree of difference <won by a slim *margin*> **–mar′gin•al** *adj.* **–mar′gin•al•ly** *adv.*
mar•gi•na•li•a (mär′jə-nā′lē-ə) *pl.n.* Notes in the margin of a book.
mar•gue•rite (mär′gə-rēt′, -gyə-) *n.* A plant, *Chrysanthemum frutescens,* with white or pale-yellow flowers similar to those of the daisy.
ma•ri•a•chi (mä′rē-ä′chē) *n.* **1.** A Mexican street band. **2. a.** The music performed by a mariachi. **b.** A musician playing in a mariachi.
Ma•rie An•toi•nette (mə-rē′ ăn′twə-nĕt′). 1755–93. Queen of Louis XVI of France (1774–93); executed.
mar•i•gold (măr′ə-gōld′, mâr′-) *n.* Any of various plants of the genus *Tagetes,* native to tropical America, widely cultivated for their orange or yellow flowers.
mar•i•jua•na or **mar•i•hua•na** (măr′ə-wä′nə) *n.* **1.** Hemp. **2.** The dried flower clusters and leaves of the hemp plant, esp. when taken to induce euphoria.
ma•rim•ba (mə-rĭm′bə) *n.* A large xylophone with resonant tubes under the wooden bars.
ma•ri•na (mə-rē′nə) *n.* A boat basin with facilities, as docks, moorings, and supplies, for small boats.
mar•i•nade (măr′ə-nād′) *n.* A liquid mixture, usu. of vinegar or wine and oil with various herbs and spices, for soaking meat, fowl, or fish before cooking.
mar•i•nate (măr′ə-nāt′) *v.* **-nat•ed, -nat•ing.** To soak (e.g., meat) in a marinade.
ma•rine (mə-rēn′) *adj.* **1. a.** Of or pertaining to the sea, sea navigation, or shipping or to maritime affairs. **b.** Native to or formed by the sea <*marine* organisms> **2.** Of or pertaining to marines. –*n.* **1.** The naval or mercantile ships or shipping fleet of a country. **2. a.** A soldier serving on a ship or at a naval installation. **b. Marine.** A member of the Marine Corps.
Marine Corps *n.* A branch of the U.S. armed forces comprising mainly amphibious troops under the authority of the Secretary of the Navy.
mar•i•ner (măr′ə-nər) *n.* A sailor.
mar•i•o•nette (măr′ē-ə-nĕt′) *n.* A jointed wooden figure, as of a person, manipulated from above by attached wires or strings.
mar•i•tal (măr′ĭ-tl) *adj.* Of or pertaining to marriage : conjugal. **–mar′i•tal•ly** *adv.*
mar•i•time (măr′ĭ-tīm′) *adj.* **1.** Located on or close to the sea. **2.** Of or concerned with shipping or navigation.

Maritime Provinces. Canadian provinces of N.S., N.B., and P.E.I.
mar·jo·ram (mär′jər-əm) *n.* **1.** An aromatic plant, *Majorana hortensis,* with leaves used as seasoning. **2.** A plant, *Origanum vulgare,* similar to the marjoram.
mark[1] (märk) *n.* **1.** A visible trace or sign, as a scratch, dent, or stain. **2.** A punctuation mark. **3. a.** An academic grade. **b.** *often* **marks.** An appraisal <got high *marks* for leadership> **4.** Something, as a label or stamp, placed on an article to signify ownership, manufacture, or origin. **5.** A recognized standard of quality : norm. **6.** Importance : significance. **7.** A target. **8.** An objective : goal. **9.** A characteristic <responsibility as a *mark* of maturity> **10.** A lasting impression. **11.** *Slang.* The intended victim of a swindler : dupe <an easy *mark*> **12.** Something used to indicate position. —*v.* **1.** To make a mark (on). **2.** To show by a mark <*marked* my answer in the space provided> **3.** To heed : note <*mark* my words> **4.** To be a feature of : characterize. **5.** To grade (scholastic work). **—mark down.** To mark for sale at a lower price. **—mark up.** To mark for sale at a higher price. **—mark′er** *n.*
mark[2] (märk) *n.* See CURRENCY TABLE.
Mark (märk) *n.* See BIBLE TABLE.
Mark An·to·ny (ăn′tə-nē) *also* **An·tho·ny** (-thə-). 83?–30 B.C. Roman general.
mark·down (märk′doun′) *n.* **1.** A price reduction. **2.** The amount by which a price is reduced.
marked (märkt) *adj.* **1.** Having a clearly defined character : noticeable. **2.** Singled out, as for attack. **—mark′ed·ly** *adv.*
mar·ket (mär′kĭt) *n.* **1. a.** A public gathering for purchasing and selling merchandise. **b.** A place where such a gathering takes place. **2.** A store or shop that sells a particular type of goods <a fish *market*> **3. a.** A geographic region regarded as a place for sales <seafood for the domestic *market*> **b.** A category of a population considered as buyers < the teen *market*> **4.** Demand <no *market* for used stockings> —*v.* **1.** To sell or offer for sale. **2.** To buy food and household supplies. **—mar′ket·a·bil′i·ty** *n.* **—mar′ket·a·ble** *adj.*
mar·ket·place (mär′kĭt-plās′) *n.* **1.** A place, as a public square, where a market is held. **2.** The business world.
mark·ka (mär′kä′) *n., pl.* **-kaa** (-kä′). See CURRENCY TABLE.
marks·man (märks′mən) *n.* One skilled at firing a gun or other weapon. **—marks′wom′an** *n.*
mark·up (märk′ŭp′) *n.* **1.** A price rise. **2.** The difference between the cost of an item and its selling price.
marl (märl) *n.* A mixture of clays, carbonates of calcium and magnesium, and remnants of shells, forming a loam used as fertilizer.
mar·lin (mär′lĭn) *n.* Any of several large marine game fish of the genus *Makaira.*
mar·line·spike (mär′lĭn-spīk′) *also* **mar·ling·spike** (-lĭng-) *n. Naut.* A pointed metal tool used to separate strands of rope in splicing.
mar·ma·lade (mär′mə-lād′) *n.* A preserve made from the pulp and rind of fruits <orange *marmalade*>
mar·mo·re·al (mär-môr′ē-əl, -mōr′-) *also* **mar·mo·re·an** (-ē-ən) *adj.* Like marble, as in smoothness, whiteness, or hardness.
mar·mo·set (mär′mə-sĕt′) *n.* Any of various small tropical American monkeys of the genera *Callithrix, Cebuella, Saguinus,* and *Leontideus,* with soft, dense fur and tufted ears.
mar·mot (mär′mət) *n.* Any of various short-legged rodents of the genus *Marmota,* found throughout the N Hemisphere.

marmot

ma·roon[1] (mə-rōōn′) *v.* **1.** To put (a person) ashore on a deserted island or isolated coast. **2.** To abandon or isolate (a person) with small chance of escape or rescue.
ma·roon[2] (mə-rōōn′) *n.* A dark purplish red.
mar·plot (mär′plŏt′) *n.* A meddler whose interference jeopardizes the success of an undertaking.
mar·quee (mär-kē′) *n.* **1.** A large tent used esp. for outdoor gatherings. **2.** A rooflike structure projecting over an entrance to a building, as a theater.
mar·quess (mär′kwĭs) *n. esp. Brit. var. of* MARQUIS.
mar·que·try (mär′kə-trē) *n.* An inlay, as of wood or ivory, used chiefly for decorating furniture.
mar·quis (mär′kwĭs, mär-kē′) *n.* A nobleman ranking below a duke and above an earl or count.
mar·quise (mär-kēz′) *n., pl.* **-quises** (-kēz′, -kē′zĭz). A marchioness.
mar·qui·sette (mär′kĭ-zĕt′, -kwĭ-) *n.* A fine fabric used for clothing, curtains, and mosquito nets.
mar·riage (măr′ĭj) *n.* **1.** The state of being married : wedlock. **2.** The act of marrying or the ceremony of being married. **3.** Close union <a *marriage* of minds> ☆**syns:** NUPTIALS, WEDDING **—mar′riage·a·bil′i·ty** *n.* **—mar′riage·a·ble** *adj.*
mar·row (măr′ō) *n.* **1.** The soft material that fills bone cavities. **2.** The principal or essential part : core.
mar·ry (măr′ē) *v.* **-ried, -ry·ing. 1.** To take as a husband or wife. **2.** To unite in matrimony. **3.** To become closely united.
Mars (märz) *n.* The 4th planet from the sun.
Mar·seilles (mär-sā′). Seaport of SE France. *Pop.* 908,600.
marsh (märsh) *n.* An area of wet, low-lying land : bog. **—marsh′y** *adj.*
mar·shal (mär′shəl) *n.* **1.** The highest-ranking military officer of some countries. **2. a.** A federal or municipal officer in the U.S. who executes court orders. **b.** The head of a fire or police department in the U.S. **3.** One in charge of a parade or ceremony. **4.** A high official in a royal court. —*v.* **-shaled, -shal·ing** *or* **-shalled, -shal·ling. 1.** To arrange or assemble in methodical order : organize. **2.** To guide (a person) ceremoniously : usher.
marsh·land (märsh′lănd′) *n.* A marshy tract of land.
marsh·mal·low (märsh′mĕl′ō, -măl′ō) *n.* A soft white candy with a spongy texture.
marsh mallow *n.* A plant, *Althaea officinalis,* of E North America, with a mucilaginous root used in confectionery.
marsh marigold *n.* A plant of the genus *Caltha,* esp. *C. palustris,* bearing bright yellow flowers.
mar·su·pi·al (mär-sōō′pē-əl) *n.* A mammal of the order Marsupialia, including the kangaroo, opossum, bandicoot, and wombat, found esp. in Australia.
mart (märt) *n.* A trading center : market.
mar·ten (mär′tn) *n., pl.* **marten** *or* **-tens. 1.** Any of various carnivores of the genus *Martes,* of N wooded areas. **2.** The fur of the marten.
mar·tial (mär′shəl) *adj.* **1.** Of, relating to, or like war. **2.** Of, relating to, or associated with the armed services.
martial art *n.* Any of several Oriental arts of self-defense or combat, as karate or judo, usu. practiced as sport.
martial law *n.* Temporary rule by military authorities imposed on a civilian population esp. in time of war or when civil authority is unable to maintain public safety.
Mar·tian (mär′shən) *adj.* Of or relating to the planet Mars. —*n.* A hypothetical inhabitant of the planet Mars.
mar·tin (märt′n) *n.* A bird that resembles and is closely related to the swallows.
mar·ti·net (mär′tn-ĕt′) *n.* A stern disciplinarian.
mar·ti·ni (mär-tē′nē) *n., pl.* **-nis.** A cocktail of gin or vodka and dry vermouth.
Mar·ti·nique (mär′tĭ-nēk′). Island and overseas department of France, in the West Indies. *Cap.* Fort-de-France. *Pop.* 333,000. **—Mar′ti·ni′can** *adj.* & *n.*
mar·tyr (mär′tər) *n.* **1.** One who chooses to die rather than renounce religious principles. **2.** One who makes great sacrifices to advance a belief, cause, or principle. **3.** One who endures great suffering. **—mar′tyr** *v.* **—mar′tyr·dom** *n.*
mar·vel (mär′vəl) *n.* **1.** One that evokes surprise, admiration, or wonder. **2.** Strong surprise : astonishment. ☆**syns:** MIRACLE, PHENOMENON, PRODIGY, SENSATION, WONDER, WONDERMENT —*v.* **-veled, -vel·ing** *or* **-velled, -vel·ling.** To be filled with wonder or astonishment.
mar·vel·ous (mär′və-ləs) *adj.* **1.** Causing astonishment : wondrous. **2.** Of the highest or best kind : first-rate. **—mar′vel·ous·ly** *adv.* **—mar′vel·ous·ness** *n.*
Marx (märks), **Karl.** 1818–83. German political philosopher and economist. **—Marx′i·an** *n.*
Marx·ism (märk′sĭz′əm) *n.* The system of thought developed by Karl Marx. **—Marx′ist** *n.*
Mar·y (mâr′ē). The mother of Jesus.
Mary I. Mary Tudor. "Bloody Mary." 1516–58. Queen of England and Ireland (1553–58).
Mar·y·land (mâr′ə-lənd, mär′-). State of the EC U.S. *Cap.* Annapolis. *Pop.* 4,216,446. **—Mar′y·land′er** *n.*
Mary Queen of Scots. Mary Stuart. 1542–87. Queen of Scotland; abdicated (1567); beheaded.

mar•zi•pan (mär'zə-pän', märt'sə-pän') *n.* A confection of ground almonds, egg whites, and sugar.
masc. *abbr.* masculine.
mas•car•a (măs-kăr'ə) *n.* A cosmetic for coloring or darkening the eyelashes and eyebrows.
mas•cot (măs'kŏt', -kət) *n.* One that is thought to bring good luck.
mas•cu•line (măs'kyə-lĭn) *adj.* **1.** Of or relating to men or boys : male. **2.** Suggestive or typical of a man. **3.** Of, relating to, or being the gender of nouns classified as male. —*n.* **1.** The masculine gender. **2.** A word or word form belonging to the masculine gender. **—mas'cu•lin'i•ty** *n.*
ma•ser (mā'zər) *n.* Any of several devices that are similar to the laser but operate with microwaves rather than light.
Mas•e•ru (măz'ə-rōō'). Cap. of Lesotho, in the W. *Pop.* 14,700.
mash (măsh) *n.* **1.** A mixture of crushed grain that ferments and is used to distill alcohol or spirits. **2.** A mixture of ground grains for feeding livestock. **3.** A soft pulpy mass. —*v.* **1.** To convert into a soft pulpy mass <*mash* potatoes> **2.** To grind or crush. **—mash'er** *n.*
mask (măsk, mäsk) *n.* **1.** A covering worn over the face to disguise or protect. **2.** A figure of a head worn by actors in Greek and Roman drama to identify a trait. **3.** A mold of a face, esp. one made after death. **4.** The face or facial markings of an animal, as a fox. **5.** A disguise or concealment <a *mask* of concern> —*v.* **1.** To cover for concealment or protection. **2.** To put a mask on for disguise. **3.** To conceal one's true personality, character, or motives.
mas•o•chism (măs'ə-kĭz'əm) *n.* **1.** Abnormal sexual excitement marked by pleasure in being subjected to physical pain or abuse. **2.** Derivation of pleasure from being dominated or mistreated. **—mas'o•chist** *n.* **—mas'o•chis'tic** *adj.*
ma•son (mā'sən) *n.* **1.** A person who works with stone or brick. **2. Mason.** A Freemason.
Ma•son•ic (mə-sŏn'ĭk) *adj.* Of or relating to Freemasons or Freemasonry.
ma•son•ry (mā'sən-rē) *n., pl.* **-ries. 1.** The trade of a mason. **2.** Stonework or brickwork. **3. Masonry.** Freemasonry.
masque (măsk) *n.* **1.** A popular 16th- and early 17th-cent. English dramatic entertainment based on a mythological or allegorical theme. **2.** A masquerade.
mas•quer•ade (măs'kə-rād') *n.* **1. a.** A costume party at which masks are worn. **b.** A costume for such a party. **2.** A disguise or pretense. —*v.* **ad•ed, -ad•ing. 1.** To wear a mask or disguise. **2.** To go about as if in disguise <a spy *masquerading* as a teacher> **—mas'quer•ad'er** *n.*
mass (măs) *n.* **1.** A body or quantity of matter of nonspecific shape. **2.** A large, nonspecific number or amount. **3.** The major part : majority. **4.** Physical bulk or volume. **5.** *Physics.* The measure of a body's resistance to acceleration. **6. masses.** The common people. —*v.* To gather or form into a mass.
Mass or **mass** (măs) *n.* **1.a.** Celebration of the Eucharist in Roman Catholic and some Protestant churches. **b.** A service including this celebration. **2.** A musical setting of certain parts of the Mass.
Mass. *abbr.* Massachusetts.
Mas•sa•chu•setts (măs'ə-chōō'sĭts, -zĭts). State of the NE U.S. *Cap.* Boston. *Pop.* 5,737,037.
mas•sa•cre (măs'ə-kər) *n.* **1.** The savage killing of a considerable number of people. ☆**syns:** BLOOD BATH, BLOODLETTING, BLOODSHED, BUTCHERY, CARNAGE, POGROM, SLAUGHTER **—mas'sa•cre** *v.*
mas•sage (mə-säzh') *n.* A body rub given to improve circulation and relax muscles. **—mas•sage'** *v.*
mas•seur (mă-sûr') *n.* A man whose occupation is giving massages.
mas•seuse (mă-sœz') *n.* A woman whose occupation is giving massages.
mas•sif (mă-sēf') *n.* A large mountain mass or compact group of connected mountains forming a part of a range.
mas•sive (măs'ĭv) *adj.* **1.** Consisting of or constituting a large mass : bulky. **2.** Large or imposing in degree, scope, or intensity <a *massive* project> **—mas'sive•ly** *adv.* **—mas'sive•ness** *n.*
mass medium *n., pl.* **mass media.** A medium, as television, radio, or newspapers, of public communication.
mass-pro•duce (măs'prə-dōōs', -dyōōs') *v.* To manufacture in large quantities. **—mass production** *n.*
mast (măst) *n.* **1.** An upright pole that supports the sails and running rigging of a sailing vessel. **2.** An upright pole.
mas•tec•to•my (mă-stĕk'tə-mē) *n., pl.* **-mies.** Surgical removal of a breast.
mas•ter (măs'tər) *n.* **1.** One with control or authority over another or others. **2.** The captain of a merchant ship. **3.** A male teacher or tutor. **4.** Someone of great learning, skill, or ability : expert. **5.a.** An academic degree signifying completion of at least 1 year of postgraduate study. **b.** One holding such a degree. **6. Master.** Used as a courtesy title in speaking of or to a boy not old enough to be addressed as Mister. **7.** An original from which copies can be made. —*v.* **1.** To make oneself a master of <*mastered* the game> **2.** To overcome (e.g., an addiction) : defeat. **—mas'ter•ship'** *n.*
mas•ter•ful (măs'tər-fəl) *adj.* **1.** Given to playing the master : domineering. **2.** Having or showing mastery : expert <a *masterful* piano technique> **—mas'ter•ful•ly** *adv.*
master key *n.* A key that opens different locks whose keys are not the same.
mas•ter•ly (măs'tər-lē) *adj.* Having or showing the skill of a master. **—mas'ter•li•ness** *n.* **—mas'ter•ly** *adv.*
mas•ter•mind (măs'tər-mīnd') *n.* Someone who plans or directs an undertaking. **—mas'ter•mind'** *v.*
master of ceremonies *n.* The host of a formal event or a program of varied entertainment.
mas•ter•piece (măs'tər-pēs') *n.* An extraordinary and ingenious work. ☆**syns:** CHEF-D'OEUVRE, MAGNUM OPUS, MASTERWORK, TOUR DE FORCE
master plan *n.* A plan giving complete instruction or guidance.
master sergeant *n.* A noncommissioned officer of the next-to-highest rank in the U.S. Army, Air Force, and Marine Corps.
mas•ter•stroke (măs'tər-strōk') *n.* A masterly act, achievement, or action.
mas•ter•work (măs'tər-wûrk') *n.* A masterpiece.
mas•ter•y (măs'tə-rē) *n.* **1.** Consummate skill or knowledge. **2.** The status of a master or ruler <*mastery* of the skies>
mast•head (măst'hĕd') *n.* **1.** The top of a ship's mast. **2.** The listing in a publication, as a newspaper, of its staff and operations.
mas•tic (măs'tĭk) *n.* A pastelike cement.
mas•ti•cate (măs'tĭ-kāt') *v.* **-cat•ed, -cat•ing.** To chew (food). **—mas'ti•ca'tion** *n.*
mas•tiff (măs'tĭf) *n.* A large dog with a short fawn-colored coat.
mas•to•don (măs'tə-dŏn') *n.* Any of several extinct mammals of the genus *Mammut,* resembling the elephant.
mas•toid (măs'toid') *n.* The rear portion of the temporal bone behind the ear. **—mas'toid'** *adj.*
mas•tur•ba•tion (măs'tər-bā'shən) *n.* The act of exciting the genitals, usu. to orgasm, by means, as manual contact, other than sexual intercourse. **—mas'tur•bate'** *v.* **—mas'tur•ba'tor** *n.*
mat[1] (măt) *n.* **1.** A flat, often coarse piece of material, as one used for wiping the feet. **2.** A thick floor pad used in athletic events, as wrestling or tumbling. **3.** A dense or tangled mass. —*v.* **mat•ted, mat•ting.** To form into a dense or tangled mass.
mat[2] (măt) *n.* **1.** A border around a picture serving as a frame or creating a contrast between the picture and a frame. **2.** *also* **matte.** A dull finish. —*adj. also* **matte.** Having a dull finish. **—mat** *v.*
mat•a•dor (măt'ə-dôr') *n.* A bullfighter who performs the final passes and kills the bull.
match[1] (măch) *n.* **1.** One similar or identical to another. **2.** One that harmonizes with another. **3.** An athletic game or contest between 2 or more <a tennis *match*> **4.** A marriage. —*v.* **1.** To be similar or identical. **2.** To harmonize with <a tie that *matches* a shirt> **3.** To place in opposition or competition : pit <*match* wits> **4.** To do as well as or better than : equal. **5.** To provide with an adversary or competitor. **6.** To correspond to <a photograph *matching* the description> **7.** To marry.
match[2] (măch) *n.* A narrow strip, as of wood, that is coated on 1 end with a compound easily ignitable by friction.
match•book (măch'bo͝ok') *n.* A small folder containing rows of safety matches.
match•less (măch'lĭs) *adj.* Without match or equal : peerless. **—match'less•ly** *adv.* **—match'less•ness** *n.*
match•mak•er (măch'mā'kər) *n.* One who arranges marriages.
mate[1] (māt) *n.* **1.** One of a matched pair. **2.** A spouse. **3.** The male or female of a pair of animals or birds. **4.** A companion or associate. **5. a.** An officer on a merchant ship who ranks below the captain. **b.** A U.S. Navy petty officer who is an assistant to a warrant officer. —*v.* **mat•ed, mat•ing. 1.** To join closely or fit together. **2.** To pair or bring together as mates.
mate[2] (māt) *n.* A checkmate. **—mate** *v.*
ma•té (mä'tā') *n.* A beverage, popular in South America, made from the dried leaves of an evergreen tree.
ma•te•ri•al (mə-tîr'ē-əl) *n.* **1.** The substance of which a thing is or can be made. **2.** *often* **materials.** Something, as a tool, needed for making something or carrying out a task. **3.** Fabric : cloth. —*adj.* **1.** Of, relating to, or existing in the form of matter. **2.** Of or relating to the body : bodily <*material* necessities> **3.** Physical as opposed to spiritual or intellectual. **4.** Substantial <a

material difference> **5.** Important : relevant <*material* evidence> **–ma•te′ri•al•ly** *adv.*
ma•te•ri•al•ism (mə-tîr′ē-əl-ĭz′əm) *n.* **1.** *Philos.* The theory that physical matter is the only reality and that everything, including thought, feeling, mind, and will, is explainable in terms of matter. **2.** A great or excessive concern with material as opposed to spiritual or intellectual things. **–ma•te′ri•al•ist** *n.* **–ma•te′ri•al•is′tic** *adj.* **–ma•te′ri•al•is′ti•cal•ly** *adv.*
ma•te•ri•al•ize (mə-tîr′ē-ə-līz′) *v.* **-ized, -iz•ing. 1.** To take or cause to take material form. **2.** To appear as if from nowhere. **–ma•te′ri•al•i•za′tion** *n.*
ma•te•ri•el or **ma•té•ri•el** (mə-tîr′ē-ĕl′) *n.* **1.** The equipment and supplies, as guns and ammunition, of a military force. **2.** An organization's equipment and supplies.
ma•ter•nal (mə-tûr′nəl) *adj.* **1.** Of or relating to a mother or motherhood. **2.** Inherited from or related through a mother <*maternal* grandparents>
ma•ter•ni•ty (mə-tûr′nĭ-tē) *n.* **1.** The state of being a mother. **2.** The feelings associated with motherhood. **3.** A hospital facility for the prenatal and postnatal care of babies and their mothers.
math (măth) *n.* Mathematics.
math. *abbr.* mathematical; mathematician; mathematics.
math•e•mat•ics (măth′ə-măt′ĭks) *n.* (*sing. in number*). The study of numbers, their form, arrangement, and associated relationships, using rigorously defined literal, numerical, and operational symbols. **–math′e•mat′i•cal** *adj.* **–math′e•mat′i•cal•ly** *adv.* **–math′e•ma•ti′cian** (-mə-tĭsh′ən) *n.*
mat•i•nee or **mat•i•née** (măt′n-ā′) *n.* A daytime dramatic or musical performance.
Ma•tisse (mä-tēs′), **Henri.** 1869–1954. French painter.
ma•tri•arch (mā′trē-ärk′) *n.* A woman ruler of a clan, family, or tribe. **–ma′tri•ar′chal** *adj.* **–ma′tri•ar′chy** *n.*
mat•ri•cide (măt′rĭ-sīd′, mā′trĭ-) *n.* **1.** The act of murdering one's own mother. **2.** One who has committed matricide. **–mat′ri•cid′al** (-sīd′l) *adj.*
ma•tric•u•late (mə-trĭk′yə-lāt′) *v.* **-lat•ed, -lat•ing.** To admit or be admitted into a group, esp. into a college or university. **–ma•tric′u•la′tion** *n.*
mat•ri•mo•ny (măt′rə-mō′nē) *n.* Marriage. **–mat′ri•mo′ni•al** *adj.* **–mat′ri•mo′ni•al•ly** *adv.*
ma•trix (mā′trĭks) *n., pl.* **ma•tri•ces** (mā′trĭ-sēz′, măt′rĭ-) or **ma•trix•es. 1.** Something, as a substance, within which something else originates, develops, or is contained. **2.** A die or mold.
ma•tron (mā′trən) *n.* **1.** A married woman, esp. a mature woman of dignity and social position. **2.** A woman supervisor in a public institution, as a prison. **–ma′tron•li•ness** *n.* **–ma′tron•ly** *adj.* & *adv.*
matte (măt) *n.* & *adj. var. of* MAT[2].
mat•ter (măt′ər) *n.* **1. a.** Something that occupies space and displays the properties of inertia and gravitation when at rest as well as in motion. **b.** MATERIAL 1. **2.** A subject of concern, interest, feeling, or action <refused to discuss the *matter*> **3.** Trouble or difficulty <What's the *matter* with her?> **4.** An approximate quantity, amount, or extent <just a *matter* of hours> **5.** Something printed or written. **6.** Something sent by mail. *–v.* To be of significance or importance. **–no matter.** Regardless of <wanted it *no matter* what the cost>
Mat•ter•horn (măt′ər-hôrn′). Mountain, c. 14,685 ft (4,480 m), on the Italian-Swiss border.
mat•ter-of-fact (măt′ər-əv-făkt′) *adj.* Relating to or adhering to facts. **–mat′ter-of-fact′ly** *adv.*
Mat•thew (măth′yo͞o) *n.* See BIBLE TABLE.
mat•tock (măt′ək) *n.* A digging implement with the blade at right angles to the handle.
mat•tress (măt′rĭs) *n.* **1.** A cloth case filled with soft material used on or as a bed. **2.** An inflatable pad used on or as a bed.
mat•u•rate (măch′ə-rāt′) *v.* **-rat•ed, -rat•ing.** To mature. **–mat′u•ra′tion** *n.*
ma•ture (mə-tyo͝or′, -to͝or′, -cho͝or′) *adj.* **-tur•er, -tur•est. 1.** Having attained full growth or development. **2.** Having reached a desired stage, esp. after processing <a *mature* brandy> **3.** Having the characteristics associated with an adult. **4.** Carefully thought out <a *mature* decision> **5.** Due and payable <a *mature* bond> ☆***syns:*** ADULT, BIG, DEVELOPED, FULL-BLOWN, FULL-FLEDGED, FULL-GROWN, GROWN, GROWN-UP, RIPE, RIPENED *–v.* **-tured, -tur•ing.** To make or become mature. **–ma•ture′ly** *adv.* **–ma•tu′ri•ty** *n.*
mat•zo (mät′sə) *n., pl.* **-zoth** (-sōth′, -sōt′, -sōs′) or **-zos** (-səz, -səs, -sōz′). Unleavened bread, eaten esp. during Passover.
matzo ball *n.* A small dumpling made from matzo meal.
maud•lin (môd′lĭn) *adj.* Effusively or tearfully sentimental.
maul (môl) *n.* A heavy hammer with a long handle, used to drive stakes or piles. *–v.* **1.** To injure or damage by or as if by beating or bruising. **2.** To handle roughly.
maun•der (môn′dər) *v.* To speak or wander about in a confused or aimless manner.
Mau•pas•sant (mō′pə-sänt′, mō′pä-säɴ′), **Guy de.** 1850–1893. French author.
Mau•ri•ta•ni•a (môr′ĭ-tā′nē-ə). Country of NW Africa. *Cap.* Nouakchott. *Pop.* 1,640,000. **–Mau′ri•ta′ni•an** *adj.* & *n.*
Mau•ri•tius (mô-rĭsh′əs). Island nation in the SW Indian Ocean. *Cap.* Port Louis. *Pop.* 920,000. **–Mau•ri′tian** *adj.* & *n.*
mau•so•le•um (mô′sə-lē′əm, zə-) *n., pl.* **-le•ums** or **-le•a** (-lē′ə). A large and stately tomb.
mauve (mōv, môv) *n.* A moderate reddish or grayish purple.
ma•ven *also* **ma•vin** (mā′vən) *n.* An expert <a cooking *maven*>
mav•er•ick (măv′ər-ĭk, măv′rĭk) *n.* **1.** An unbranded or orphaned range calf or colt. **2.** A person who refuses to abide by the policies or views of a group.
maw (mô) *n.* **1.** The mouth, gullet, or stomach of a hungry or ferocious animal. **2.** A gaping opening.
mawk•ish (mô′kĭsh) *adj.* Excessively and disgustingly sentimental. **–mawk′ish•ly** *adv.* **–mawk′ish•ness** *n.*
max. *abbr.* maximum.
max•i (măk′sē) *n.* An ankle- or floor-length garment, as a skirt or coat.
max•il•la (măk-sĭl′ə) *n., pl.* **-il•lae** (-sĭl′ē) or **-las.** Either of a pair of bones forming the upper jaw. **–max′il•lar′y** (măk′-sə-lĕr′ē) *adj.*
max•im (măk′sĭm) *n.* A concise saying.
max•i•mal (măk′sə-məl) *adj.* **1.** Of or being a maximum. **2.** Being the greatest or highest possible. **–max′i•mal•ly** *adv.*
max•i•mize (măk′sə-mīz′) *v.* **-mized, -miz•ing. 1.** To increase to the maximum. **2.** To assign the highest importance to.
max•i•mum (măk′sə-məm) *n., pl.* **-mums** or **-ma** (-mə). **1.** The greatest or greatest possible number, measure, quantity, or degree. **2.** An upper limit permitted by authority. **–max′i•mum** *adj.*
may (mā) *v. p.t.* **might** (mīt). **1.** To be allowed or permitted to <You *may* borrow the car.> **2.** Used to indicate a measure of likelihood or possibility <It *may* snow tonight.> **3.** Used to express a desire or wish, purpose, contingency, or result.
May (mā) *n.* The 5th month of the year, having 31 days.
Ma•ya (mä′yə) *n., pl.* **-yas** or **-ya.** A member of an Indian people of S Mexico and Central America. **–Ma′ya** *adj.* **–Ma′yan** *n.* & *adj.*
May apple *n.* A plant, *Podophyllum peltatum,* of E North America, bearing a single nodding white flower, edible yellow fruit, and poisonous roots, leaves, and seeds.
may•be (mā′bē) *adv.* Perhaps.
May Day *n.* May 1, marked by the celebration of spring and in some places as a holiday honoring the labor force.
may•flow•er (mā′flou′ər) *n.* Any of a wide variety of plants, as the trailing arbutus, that blossom in May.
may•hem (mā′hĕm′, mā′əm) *n.* **1.** *Law.* The willfull crippling or maiming of a person. **2.** Wanton violence or damage.
may•n't (mā′ənt, mānt). May not.
may•o (mā′ō) *n. Slang.* Mayonnaise.
may•on•naise (mā′ə-nāz′) *n.* A dressing made of beaten raw egg yolk, oil, lemon juice or vinegar, and seasonings.
may•or (mā′ər, mâr) *n.* The chief magistrate of a town, city, borough, or municipal corporation. **–may′or•al** *adj.* **–may′or•al•ty, may′or•ship′** *n.*
may•pole (mā′pōl′) *n.* A pole hung with streamers around which May Day merrymakers dance.
†**maze** (māz) *n.* A complicated, usu. confusing network of passageways or pathways : labyrinth. *–v.* **mazed, mazing.** *Regional.* To stupefy : daze. **–maz′y** *adj.*
ma•zur•ka (mə-zûr′kə, -zo͝or′-) *n.* **1.** A lively Polish dance similar to the polka. **2.** Music for a mazurka, written in 3/4 or 3/8 time.
M.B.A. *abbr.* Master of Business Administration.
Mba•bane (əm-bä-bän′). Cap. of Swaziland, in the NW. *Pop.* 23,000.
Mc *abbr.* megacycle.
MC (ĕm′sē′) *n.* A master of ceremonies.
m.c. *abbr.* master of ceremonies.
Mc•Kin•ley (mə-kĭn′lē), **Mount.** Highest mountain in North America (20,320 ft/6,197.6 m), in S Alas.
McKin•ley, William. 1843–1901. 25th U.S. President (1897–1901); assassinated.
Md *symbol for* MENDELEVIUM.
MD *abbr.* Maryland (with Zip Code).
Md. *abbr.* Maryland.
M.D. *abbr.* Doctor of Medicine.
mdse. *abbr.* merchandise.
me (mē) *pron. The objective case of* **I.** Used: **1.** As the direct object of a verb <They helped *me.*> **2.** As the indirect object

of a verb <They offered *me* money.> **3.** As the object of a preposition <This memorandum is addressed to *me.*>
ME *abbr.* Maine (with Zip Code).
Me. *abbr.* Maine.
M.E. *abbr.* **1.** mechanical engineer; mechanical engineering. **2.** Middle English.
mead (mēd) *n.* An alcoholic beverage made from fermented honey.
mead•ow (mĕd'ō) *n.* A tract of grassland.
mead•ow•lark (mĕd'ō-lärk') *n.* Any of several songbirds of the genus *Sturnella,* of North America.
meadow mushroom *n.* An edible mushroom, *Agaricus campestris,* that is cultivated for human consumption.
mea•ger *also* **mea•gre** (mē'gər) *adj.* **1.** Lean : thin. **2.** Deficient in quantity <a *meager* income> **3.** Deficient in richness, fertility, or vigor. ☆**syns:** EXIGUOUS, MEASLY, POOR, PUNY, SCANT, SCANTY, SKIMPY, SPARE, SPARSE, STINGY **—mea'ger•ly** *adv.* **—mea'ger•ness** *n.*
meal[1] (mēl) *n.* **1.** The coarsely ground edible seed of a grain. **2.** A granular substance made by grinding. **—meal'y** *adj.*
meal[2] (mēl) *n.* **1.** The food served and eaten at 1 time. **2.** The time or occasion of eating a meal.
meal ticket *n. Slang.* One that is a source of financial support.
meal•time (mēl'tīm') *n.* The usual time set aside for eating a meal.
meal•y•bug (mē'lē-bŭg') *n.* Any of various insects of the genus *Pseudococcus,* some of which are harmful to plants, esp. citrus trees.
meal•y-mouthed (mē'lē-mouthd', -moutht') *adj.* Unwilling to speak simply and directly : evasive.
mean[1] (mēn) *v.* **meant** (mĕnt), **mean•ing. 1. a.** To convey or be intended to convey the sense of : denote. **b.** To be a symbol of : signify. **2.** To have as a purpose : intend. **3.** To be likely to result in <Freezing rain *means* slippery roads.> **4.** To be of a specified significance or importance <Wealth *meant* little to them.>
mean[2] (mēn) *adj.* **1.** Low, as in grade or quality : inferior. **2.** Marked by pettiness and ill will : malicious <a *mean* remark> **3.** Dishonorable : base <a *mean* purpose> **4.** Parsimonious : stingy. **5.** *Slang.* Difficult to cope with <*mean* weather for driving> **—mean'ly** *adv.* **—mean'ness** *n.*
mean[3] (mēn) *n.* **1.** A middle point between 2 extremes. **2.** *Math.* **a.** A number that represents an entire set of numbers, determined for the set in any of several ways : average. **b.** An arithmetic mean. **3. means.** Something, as a method, by which an end is achieved. **4. means.** Wealth, as money or property. *—adj.* Occupying a middle position between 2 extremes.
me•an•der (mē-ăn'dər) *v.* **1.** To take a winding course. **2.** To wander about without fixed direction. **—me•an'der** *n.*
mean•ing (mē'nĭng) *n.* **1. a.** Something signified by a word : denotation or connotation. **b.** Something one wishes to convey, esp. through language. **2.** Something intended : purpose. **3.** Importance : significance. ☆**syns:** ACCEPTION, IMPORT, INTENT, MESSAGE, PURPORT, SENSE, SIGNIFICANCE, SIGNIFICATION, VALUE **—mean'ing•ful** *adj.* **—mean'ing•less** *adj.*
mean•time (mēn'tīm') *n.* The period between occurrences : interval. *—adv.* Meanwhile.
mean•while (mēn'hwīl', -wīl') *n.* Meantime. *—adv.* **1.** During or in the intervening time. **2.** At the same time.
meas. *abbr.* measurable; measure.
mea•sles (mē'zəlz) *n. (sing. in number).* An acute, contagious viral disease, usu. occurring in childhood, characterized by the eruption of red spots.
mea•sly (mēz'lē) *adj.* **-sli•er, -sli•est.** *Slang.* Despicably small : meager.
meas•ure (mĕzh'ər) *n.* **1.** The act, process, or result of determining the dimensions, capacity, or amount of something. **2.** Something, as a ruler, used in determining measures. **3. a.** A unit used in expressing measures. **b.** A system of such units. **4.** A basis for comparison : criterion. **5.** An appropriate or sufficient extent, amount, or degree. **6.** Limit : bounds <wealth knowing no *measure*> **7.** *often* **measures.** An action taken as a means to an end : expedient. **8.** A bill or enactment of a legislature. **9.** The notes and rests between 2 successive bars on a musical staff. *—v.* **-ured, -ur•ing. 1.** To determine the measurements of. **2.** To have a particular measurement. **3.** To estimate by comparison or evaluation : appraise. **4.** To consider carefully <*measure* one's words> **5.** To serve as a measure of <An altimeter *measures* altitude.> **—measure up. 1.** To live up to certain standards. **2.** To be the equal of. **—meas'ur•a•ble** *adj.* **—meas'ura•bly** *adv.* **—meas'ur•er** *n.*
meas•ure•ment (mĕzh'ər-mənt) *n.* **1.** The act or process of measuring. **2.** A dimension, capacity, or amount determined by measuring.
measuring worm *n.* A geometrid caterpillar that moves in alternate contractions and expansions suggestive of measuring.
meat (mēt) *n.* **1.** The flesh of an animal used as food. **2.** The edible, fleshy inner part <pecan *meats*> **3.** The essential part : core. **4.** Nourishment : food. **—meat'i•ness** *n.* **—meat'y** *adj.*
meat•ball (mēt'bôl') *n.* A small ball of often spiced ground or chopped meat.
Mec•ca (mĕk'ə) *n.* **1.** City of W Saudi Arabia; birthplace of Mohammed. *Pop.* 366,801. **2. mecca.** A place that is the center of an activity or interest.
mech. *abbr.* **1.** mechanical; mechanics. **2.** mechanism.
me•chan•ic (mĭ-kăn'ĭk) *n.* A person who is skilled in repairing, building, or using machines or tools.
me•chan•i•cal (mĭ-kăn'ĭ-kəl) *adj.* **1. a.** Of or relating to machines or tools. **b.** Of or relating to mechanics. **2.** Performed, produced, or operated by or as if by a machine. **—me•chan'i•cal•ly** *adv.*
mechanical drawing *n.* **1.** Drafting. **2.** A drawing, as an architect's plans, that is made with instruments.
mechanical engineering *n.* The branch of engineering that encompasses the generation and application of heat and mechanical power and the production, design, and use of machines and tools. **—mechanical engineer** *n.*
me•chan•ics (mĭ-kăn'ĭks) *n. (sing. or pl. in number).* **1.** The scientific study and analysis of the action of forces on matter and systems composed of matter. **2.** The design, operation, construction, and application of machinery or mechanical structures. **3.** The technical side of an activity <the *mechanics* of baseball>
mech•a•nism (mĕk'ə-nĭz'əm) *n.* **1. a.** A mechanical apparatus : machine. **b.** The arrangement of connected machine parts. **2.** A system of interacting parts <the *mechanism* of the brain> **3.** A means or process by which something is done or brought into being.
mech•a•nis•tic (mĕk'ə-nĭs'tĭk) *adj.* **1.** Mechanically determined. **2.** Mechanical. **—mech'a•nis'ti•cal•ly** *adv.*
mech•a•nize (mĕk'ə-nīz') *v.* **-nized, -niz•ing. 1.** To equip with machines or machinery <*mechanize* a factory> **2.** To equip (a military unit) with motor vehicles, as tanks and trucks. **3.** To make mechanical, automatic, or unspontaneous. **—mech'a•ni•za'tion** *n.*
med. *abbr.* **1.** medical. **2.** medieval. **3.** medium.
med•al (mĕd'l) *n.* **1.** A flat piece of metal stamped with a commemorative design or inscription, often presented as an award. **2.** A piece of metal stamped with a religious symbol.
med•al•ist (mĕd'l-ĭst) *n.* **1.** A designer, collector, or maker of medals. **2.** One who is awarded or receives a medal.
me•dal•lion (mə-dăl'yən) *n.* **1.** A large medal. **2.** Something like a large medal.
med•dle (mĕd'l) *v.* **-dled, -dling.** To intrude in other people's business or affairs. **—med'dler** *n.* **—med'dle•some** *adj.*
me•di•a (mē'dē-ə) *n. var. pl. of* MEDIUM.
me•di•ae•val (mē'dē-ē'vəl, mĕ-dē'vəl) *adj. var. of* MEDIEVAL.
me•di•al (mē'dē-əl) *adj.* **1.** Occurring in the middle. **2.** Average or mean : ordinary.
me•di•an (mē'dē-ən) *n.* **1.** Something that lies halfway between 2 extremes. **2.** A number in a set that has the property of having half the other numbers greater than it and half less than it. *—adj.* **1.** Relating to, situated in, or directed toward the middle : medial. **2.** Of, relating to, or constituting the median of a set of numbers.
median strip *n.* A strip dividing opposing highway traffic lanes.
me•di•ate (mē'dē-āt') *v.* **-at•ed, -at•ing. 1.** To help opposing sides in a dispute come to an agreement. **2.** To bring about (e.g., a settlement) by acting as an intermediary. **—me'di•a'tion** *n.* **—me'di•a'tor** *n.*
med•ic (mĕd'ĭk) *n. Informal.* **1.** A surgeon or physician. **2.** A medical student or intern. **3.** A military medical corpsman.
Med•i•caid *also* **med•i•caid** (mĕd'ĭ-kād') *n.* A program jointly funded by the states and the federal government that provides medical aid for people who are unable to pay their own medical expenses.
med•i•cal (mĕd'ĭ-kəl) *adj.* Of or relating to the study or practice of medicine. **—med'i•cal•ly** *adv.*
medical examiner *n.* A physician officially authorized by a governmental unit, as a county, to ascertain the cause of death.
me•dic•a•ment (mĭ-dĭk'ə-mənt, mĕd'ĭ-kə-) *n.* An agent that promotes recovery from injury or illness : medicine.
Med•i•care *also* **med•i•care** (mĕd'ĭ-kâr') *n.* A program under the Social Security Administration that provides medical care, esp. for the elderly.
med•i•cate (mĕd'ĭ-kāt') *v.* **-cat•ed, -cat•ing. 1.** To treat with medicine. **2.** To permeate or tincture with a medicinal substance. **—med'i•ca'tion** *n.*

MEASUREMENT

MEASUREMENT UNITS

Length

U.S. Customary Unit	U.S. Equivalents	Metric Equivalents
inch	0.083 foot	2.540 centimeters
foot	1/3 yard, 12 inches	0.305 meter
yard	3 feet, 36 inches	0.914 meter
rod	5 1/2 yards, 16 1/2 feet	5.029 meters
mile (statute, land)	1,760 yards, 5,280 feet	1.609 kilometers
mile (nautical, international)	1.151 statute miles	1.852 kilometers

Area

U.S. Customary Unit	U.S. Equivalents	Metric Equivalents
square inch	0.007 square foot	6.452 square centimeters
square foot	144 square inches	929.030 square centimeters
square yard	1,296 square inches, 9 square feet	0.836 square meters
acre	43,560 square feet, 4,840 square yards	4,047 square meters
square mile	640 acres	2.590 square kilometers

Weight

U.S. Customary Unit (Avoirdupois)	U.S. Equivalents	Metric Equivalents
grain	0.036 dram, 0.002285 ounce	64.798 milligrams
dram	27.344 grains, 0.0625 ounce	1.772 grams
ounce	16 drams, 437.5 grains	28.350 grams
pound	16 ounces, 7,000 grains	453.592 grams
ton (short)	2,000 pounds	0.907 metric ton (1,000 kilograms)
ton (long)	1.12 short tons, 2,240 pounds	1.016 metric tons

Apothecary Weight Unit	U.S. Customary Equivalents	Metric Equivalents
scruple	20 grains	1.296 grams
dram	60 grains	3.888 grams
ounce	480 grains, 1.097 avoirdupois ounces	31.103 grams
pound	5,760 grains, 0.823 avoirdupois pound	373.242 grams

Volume or Capacity

U.S. Customary Unit	U.S. Equivalents	Metric Equivalents
cubic inch	0.00058 cubic foot	16.387 cubic centimeters
cubic foot	1,728 cubic inches	0.028 cubic meter
cubic yard	27 cubic feet	0.765 cubic meter

U.S. Customary Liquid Measure	U.S. Equivalents	Metric Equivalents
fluid ounce	8 fluid drams, 1.804 cubic inches	29.573 milliliters
pint	16 fluid ounces, 28.875 cubic inches	0.473 liter
quart	2 pints, 57.75 cubic inches	0.946 liter
gallon	4 quarts, 231 cubic inches	3.785 liters
barrel	varies from 31 to 42 gallons, established by law or usage	

U.S. Customary Dry Measure	U.S. Equivalents	Metric Equivalents
pint	1/2 quart, 33.6 cubic inches	0.551 liter
quart	2 pints, 67.2 cubic inches	1.101 liters
peck	8 quarts, 537.605 cubic inches	8.810 liters
bushel	4 pecks, 2,150.420 cubic inches	35.239 liters

British Imperial Liquid and Dry Measure	U.S. Customary Equivalents	Metric Equivalents
fluid ounce	0.961 U.S. fluid ounce, 1.734 cubic inches	28.413 milliliters
pint	1.032 U.S. dry pints, 1.201 U.S. liquid pints, 34.678 cubic inches	568.245 milliliters
quart	1.032 U.S. dry quarts, 1.201 U.S. liquid quarts, 69.354 cubic inches	1.136 liters
gallon	1.201 U.S. gallons, 277.420 cubic inches	4.546 liters
peck	554.84 cubic inches	0.009 cubic meter
bushel	1.032 U.S. bushels, 2,219.36 cubic inches	0.036 cubic meter

THE METRIC SYSTEM

Length

Unit	Number of Meters	Approximate U.S. Equivalent
myriameter	10,000	6.214 miles
kilometer	1,000	0.621 mile
hectometer	100	109.361 yards
decameter	10	32.808 feet
meter	1	39.370 inches
decimeter	0.1	3.937 inches
centimeter	0.01	0.394 inch
millimeter	0.001	0.039 inch

Area

Unit	Number of Square Meters	Approximate U.S. Equivalent
square kilometer	1,000,000	0.386 square mile
hectare	10,000	2.477 acres
are	100	119.599 square yards
deciare	10	11.960 square yards
centare	1	10.764 square feet
square centimeter	0.0001	0.115 square inch

MEASUREMENT *(continued)*

Volume

Unit	Number of Cubic Meters	Approximate U.S. Equivalent	Unit	Number of Cubic Meters	Approximate U.S. Equivalent
decastere	10	13.079 cubic yards	decistere	0.10	3.532 cubic feet
stere	1	1.308 cubic yards	cubic centimeter	0.000001	0.061 cubic inch

Capacity

Unit	Number of Liters	Approximate U.S. Equivalents: Cubic	Dry	Liquid
kiloliter	1,000	1.308 cubic yards		
hectoliter	100	3.532 cubic feet	2.838 bushels	
decaliter	10	0.353 cubic foot	1.135 pecks	2.642 gallons
liter	1	61.024 cubic inches	0.908 quart	1.057 quarts
deciliter	0.10	6.102 cubic inches	0.182 pint	0.211 pint
centiliter	0.01	0.610 cubic inch		0.338 fluid ounce
milliliter	0.001	0.061 cubic inch		0.271 fluid dram

Mass and Weight

Unit	Number of Grams	Approximate U.S. Equivalent	Unit	Number of Grams	Approximate U.S. Equivalent
metric ton	1,000,000	1.102 tons	gram	1	0.035 ounce
quintal	100,000	220.462 pounds	decigram	0.10	1.543 grains
kilogram	1,000	2.205 pounds	centigram	0.01	0.154 grain
hectogram	100	3.527 ounces	milligram	0.001	0.015 grain
decagram	10	0.353 ounce			

METRIC CONVERSION CHART—APPROXIMATIONS

When You Know	Multiply By	To Find
	Length	
millimeters	0.04	inches
centimeters	0.39	inches
meters	3.28	feet
meters	1.09	yards
kilometers	0.62	miles
inches	25.40	millimeters
inches	2.54	centimeters
feet	30.48	centimeters
yards	0.91	meters
miles	1.61	kilometers
	Area	
square centimeters	0.16	square inches
square meters	1.20	square yards
square kilometers	0.39	square miles
hectares (10,000m^2)	2.47	acres
square inches	6.45	square centimeters
square feet	0.09	square meters
square yards	0.84	square meters
square miles	2.60	square kilometers
acres	0.40	hectares
	Mass and Weight	
grams	0.035	ounce
kilograms	2.21	pounds
tons (100kg)	1.10	short tons
ounces	28.35	grams
pounds	0.45	kilograms
short tons (2000 lb)	0.91	tons
	Volume	
milliliters	0.20	teaspoons
milliliters	0.06	tablespoons
milliliters	0.03	fluid ounces
liters	4.23	cups
liters	2.12	pints

When You Know	Multiply By	To Find
	Volume	
liters	1.06	quarts
liters	0.26	gallons
cubic meters	35.32	cubic feet
cubic meters	1.35	cubic yards
teaspoons	4.93	milliliters
tablespoons	14.78	milliliters
fluid ounces	29.57	milliliters
cups	0.24	liters
pints	0.47	liters
quarts	0.95	liters
gallons	3.79	liters
	Volume	
cubic feet	0.03	cubic meters
cubic yards	0.76	cubic meters
	Speed	
miles per hour	1.61	kilometers per hour
kilometers per hour	0.62	miles per hour
	Temperature (exact)	
Celsius temp.	9/5, +32	Fahrenheit temp.
Fahrenheit temp.	−32, 5/9 × remainder	Celsius temp.

Temperatures in degrees Celsius, as in the familiar Fahrenheit system, can only be learned through experience. The following temperatures are ones that are frequently encountered:

0°C	Freezing point of water (32°F)
10°C	A warm winter day (50°F)
20°C	A mild spring day (68°F)
30°C	A hot summer day (86°F)
37°C	Normal body temperature (98.6°F)
40°C	Heat wave conditions (104°F)
100°C	Boiling point of water (212°F)

me·dic·i·nal (mə-dĭs'ə-nəl) *adj.* Of, relating to, or having the properties of medicine.
med·i·cine (mĕd'ĭ-sĭn) *n.* **1.** The science of diagnosing, treating, curing, or preventing disease or damage to the body or mind. **2.** The practice of medicine. **3.** An agent, as a drug, for treating injury or disease.
medicine ball *n.* A large heavy ball used for conditioning exercises.
medicine man *n.* One believed among preliterate peoples to hold supernatural powers, as for healing.
med·i·co (mĕd'ĭ-kō') *n., pl.* **-cos.** *Informal.* **1.** A physician. **2.** A medical student.
me·di·e·val *also* **me·di·ae·val** (mē'dē-ē'vəl, mĕ-dē'vəl) *adj.* Of or relating to the Middle Ages. **—me'di·e'val·ism** *n.* **—me'di·e'val·ist** *n.* **—me'di·e'val·ly** *adv.*
me·di·o·cre (mē'dē-ō'kər) *adj.* Of moderate or low quality : undistinguished. **—me'di·oc'ri·ty** (-ŏk'rĭ-tē) *n.*
med·i·tate (mĕd'ĭ-tāt') *v.* **-tat·ed, -tat·ing. 1.** To think deeply and quietly : ponder. **2.** To consider at length : contemplate. **—med'i·ta'tion** *n.* **—med'i·ta'tive** *adj.*
Med·i·ter·ra·ne·an (mĕd'ĭ-tə-rā'nē-ən). Inland sea bounded by Africa, Asia, and Europe and connecting with the Atlantic through the Strait of Gibraltar.
me·di·um (mē'dē-əm) *n., pl.* **-di·a** (-dē-ə) *or* **-ums. 1. a.** Something that occupies a position midway between extremes. **b.** A middle condition or position. **2.** Something through which energy is transmitted. **3.** A means by which something is accomplished, conveyed, or transferred <money as a *medium* of exchange> **4.** *pl.* **media.** A means of communicating information or ideas, as publishing or television. **5.** *pl.* **mediums.** A person believed to have the power to communicate with the spirits of the dead. **6.** *pl.* **media.** An environment in which something, as a plant or animal, can live or thrive. **7.** An artistic technique or means of expression. **8.** A substance in which something is kept, preserved, or mixed. *—adj.* Intermediate in amount, degree, position, or quality.
med·ley (mĕd'lē) *n., pl.* **-leys. 1.** A jumble mixture. **2.** A piece of music consisting of a series of melodies from various sources.
Mé·doc (mā-dôk', -dŏk') *n.* A red Bordeaux wine.
me·dul·la (mə-dŭl'ə) *n., pl.* **-las** *or* **-dul·lae** (-dŭl'ē) **1.** *Anat.* The core of certain vertebrate structures, as bone marrow. **2.** The medulla oblongata.
medulla ob·lon·ga·ta (ŏb'lông-gä'tə) *n., pl.* **medulla ob·lon·ga·tas** (-təz) *or* **medullae ob·lon·ga·tae** (-tē). A mass of nerve tissue at the base of the brain that controls bodily functions, as breathing and circulation.
me·du·soid (mə-do͞o'soid', -dyo͞o'-) *adj.* Having the shape of a jellyfish. **—me·du'soid'** *n.*
meed (mēd) *n. Archaic.* **1.** A merited wage or reward. **2.** A fitting recompense.
meek (mēk) *adj.* **1.** Showing patience and humility : gentle. **2.** Easily imposed on : submissive. **—meek'ly** *adv.* **—meek'ness** *n.*
meer·schaum (mîr'shəm, -shôm') *n.* A tobacco pipe made of a tough, compact, usu. white mineral.
meet[1] (mēt) *v.* **met** (mĕt), **meet·ing. 1.** To come upon : encounter. **2.** To be present at the arrival of <*met* the bus> **3.** To be introduced to. **4.** To connect (with) : join. **5.** To form a group : assemble. **6.** To come together in order to confer or have a discussion. **7.** To satisfy (e.g., a need) : fulfill <*met* all the conditions> **8.** To perceive through the senses. **9.** To pay : settle. **10.** To deal with : cope. **11.** To come together <Let's *meet* for lunch.> **12.** To fight : oppose. *—n.* A meeting, esp. for athletic competition.
meet[2] (mēt) *adj.* Appropriate : fitting.
meet·ing (mē'tĭng) *n.* **1.** The act or process of coming together : encounter. **2.** An assembly of people.
meg·a·buck (mĕg'ə-bŭk') *n. Slang.* One million dollars.
meg·a·cy·cle (mĕg'ə-sī'kəl) *n. Physics.* **1.** One million cycles. **2.** Megahertz.
me·ga·death (mĕg'ə-dĕth') *n.* One million deaths. Used as a unit in reference to nuclear warfare.
meg·a·hertz (mĕg'ə-hûrtz') *n., pl.* **-hertz.** *Physics.* One million cycles per sec, used esp. as a radio-frequency unit.
meg·a·lith (mĕg'ə-lĭth') *n.* A huge stone used in the building of prehistoric monuments. **—meg'a·lith'ic** *adj.*
meg·a·lo·ma·ni·a (mĕg'ə-lō-mā'nē-ə, -mān'yə) *n.* A psychopathological condition marked by fantasies of power, wealth, or omnipotence. **—meg'a·lo·ma'ni·ac'** (-mā'nē-ăk') *n.* **—meg'a·lo·ma·ni'a·cal** (-mə-nī'ə-kəl) *adj.*
meg·a·lop·o·lis (mĕg'ə-lŏp'ə-lĭs) *n.* An extremely large urban complex.
meg·a·phone (mĕg'ə-fōn') *n.* A funnel-shaped device used to direct and amplify the voice.
meg·a·ton (mĕg'ə-tŭn') *n.* A unit of explosive force equal to that of 1 million t of TNT.
meg·a·watt (mĕg'ə-wŏt') *n.* A unit of electrical power equal to 1 million w.
mei·o·sis (mī-ō'sĭs) *n., pl.* **-ses** (-sēz'). *Biol.* Cell division that reduces the chromosomes of reproductive cells to ½ the normal number. **—mei·ot'ic** (-ŏt'ĭk) *adj.*
Me·kong (mā'kŏng'). River of SE Asia, flowing c. 2,600 mi (4,183 km) to the South China Sea.
mel·an·cho·li·a (mĕl'ən-kō'lē-ə) *n.* A mental disorder marked by feelings of dejection and usu. by withdrawal.
mel·an·chol·ic (mĕl'ən-kŏl'ĭk) *adj.* **1.** Afflicted with or subject to melancholy. **2.** Of or relating to melancholia.
mel·an·chol·y (mĕl'ən-kŏl'ē) *n.* Depression of spirits : gloom. *—adj.* **1.** Sad : depressed. **2.** Tending to cause melancholy.
Mel·a·ne·sia (mĕl'ə-nē'zhə, -shə). Island group in the SW Pacific NE of Australia. **—Mel'a·ne'sian** *adj.* & *n.*
mé·lange *also* **me·lange** (mā-läNzh') *n.* A mixture.
mel·a·nin (mĕl'ə-nĭn) *n.* A dark pigment found in the skin, retina, and hair.
mel·a·nism (mĕl'ə-nĭz'əm) *n.* Abnormally dark pigmentation, as of the skin, resulting esp. from sunburn.
mel·a·no·ma (mĕl'ə-nō'mə) *n., pl.* **-mas** *or* **-ma·ta** (-mə-tə). A dark-colored malignant mole or tumor.
Mel·ba toast (mĕl'bə) *n.* Crisp, thinly sliced toast.
Mel·bourne (mĕl'bərn). Seaport of SE Australia. *Metro. pop.* 2,603,000.
meld[1] (mĕld) *v.* To announce or show (a card or combination of cards) for a score in a card game. *—n.* A card or combination of cards declared for a score.
meld[2] (mĕld) *v.* To merge or cause to merge : blend.
me·lee *also* **mê·lée** (mā'lā', mā-lā') *n.* **1.** Confused hand-to-hand fighting : free-for-all. **2.** A confused and tumultuous mingling, as of a crowd.
mel·io·rate (mēl'yə-rāt', mē'lē-ə-) *v.* **-rat·ed, -rat·ing.** To improve or cause to improve. **—mel'io·ra'tion** *n.* **—mel'io·ra'tive** *adj.* & *n.*
mel·lif·lu·ous (mə-lĭf'lo͞o-əs) *adj.* Flowing smoothly and sweetly. **—mel·lif'lu·ous·ly** *adv.* **—mel·lif'lu·ous·ness** *n.*
mel·low (mĕl'ō) *adj.* **1.** Soft and sweet : fully ripened. **2.** Rich and full-flavored : properly aged <a *mellow* brandy> **3.** Having or showing the gentleness characteristic of maturity. **4.** Relaxed and good-humored : genial. **5.** Soft and resonant <a *mellow* tone> *—v.* To make or become mellow. **—mel'low·ly** *adv.* **—mel'low·ness** *n.*
me·lo·di·ous (mə-lō'dē-əs) *adj.* **1.** Of, pertaining to, or producing melody. **2.** Pleasant to listen to. **—me·lo'di·ous·ly** *adv.*
mel·o·dra·ma (mĕl'ə-drä'mə, -drăm'ə) *n.* **1.** A dramatic presentation marked by suspense, sensational episodes, and romantic sentiment. **2.** Behavior or events having the characteristics of a melodrama. **—mel'o·dra·mat'ic** (-drə-măt'ĭk) *adj.* **—mel'o·dra·mat'i·cal·ly** *adv.*
mel·o·dra·mat·ics (mĕl'ə-drə-măt'ĭks) *n. (sing. or pl. in number).* **1.** A melodrama. **2.** Melodramatic behavior.
mel·o·dy (mĕl'ə-dē) *n., pl.* **-dies. 1.** A succession and esp. a pleasing succession of musical tones : tune. **2.** Musical sounds. **—me·lod'ic** (mə-lŏd'ĭk) *adj.* **—me·lod'i·cal·ly** *adv.*
mel·on (mĕl'ən) *n.* Any of several large fruits, as a cantaloupe or watermelon, that grow on a vine and have a hard rind and juicy flesh.
melt (mĕlt) *v.* **1.** To change or be changed from a solid to a liquid by or as a result of heat or pressure. **2.** To dissolve <sugar *melting* in water> **3.** To disappear : vanish <inhibitions that gradually *melted*> **4.** To pass or merge imperceptibly <*melted* into the crowd> **5.** To make or become gentle or mild : soften.
melt·down (mĕlt'doun') *n.* The melting of a nuclear-reactor core.
melting pot *n.* **1.** A container for melting something. **2.** A place where immigrants of different races or cultures form an integrated society.
Mel·ville (mĕl'vĭl'), **Herman.** 1819–91. Amer. novelist.
mem·ber (mĕm'bər) *n.* **1.** A distinct part of a whole. **2.** A part, as an organ or limb, of a person, animal, or plant. **3.** A person belonging to a group or organization.
mem·ber·ship (mĕm'bər-shĭp') *n.* **1.** The state of being a member. **2.** The total number of members in a group.
mem·brane (mĕm'brān') *n.* A thin pliable layer of tissue covering surfaces or separating or connecting regions, structures, or organs of an animal or plant. **—mem'bra·nous** (-brə-nəs) *adj.*
me·men·to (mə-mĕn'tō) *n., pl.* **-tos** *or* **-toes.** A keepsake : souvenir.
mem·o (mĕm'ō) *n., pl.* **-os.** A memorandum.
mem·oir (mĕm'wär', -wôr') *n.* **1.** An account based on personal experience. **2. a.** *often* **memoirs.** An autobiography. **b.** A biography or biographical sketch. **3. a.** A report, esp. on a schol-

arly or scientific subject. **b. memoirs.** A record of the proceedings of a learned society.
mem·o·ra·bil·i·a (mĕm′ər-ə-bĭl′ē-ə, -bĭl′yə) *pl.n.* Things that are worth remembering or keeping.
mem·o·ra·ble (mĕm′ər-ə-bəl) *adj.* Worth remembering or noting : remarkable. **—mem′o·ra·bly** *adv.*
mem·o·ran·dum (mĕm′ə-răn′dəm) *n., pl.* **-dums** *or* **-da** (-də). **1.** A brief informal note written esp. as a reminder. **2.** A written, informal communication, as from 1 office to another within an organization.
me·mo·ri·al (mə-môr′ē-əl, -mōr′-) *n.* **1.** Something, esp. a monument, designed or established to perpetuate remembrance, as of a person. **2.** A statement of facts addressed to a government or legislature. *—adj.* Serving to perpetuate remembrance. **—me·mo′ri·al·ize′** *v.*
Memorial Day *n.* A U.S. holiday celebrated on the last Monday in May in honor of members of the armed forces killed in war.
mem·o·rize (mĕm′ə-rīz′) *v.* **-rized, -riz·ing.** To commit to memory. **—mem′o·ri·za′tion** *n.* **—mem′o·riz′er** *n.*
mem·o·ry (mĕm′ə-rē) *n., pl.* **-ries. 1.** The mental faculty of storing past experiences and recalling them at will. **2.** The act or an instance of remembering : recollection. **3.** All that a person can remember. **4.** Something remembered. **5.** The time period within which something is remembered. **6.** A unit of a computer that stores data for retrieval.
Mem·phis (mĕm′fĭs). City of SW Tenn., on the Mississippi. *Pop.* 646,356.
men (mĕn) *n. pl. of* MAN.
men·ace (mĕn′ĭs) *n.* **1. a.** A threat <the *menace* of war> **b.** Something that poses a threat : danger. **2.** An annoying person. **—men′ace** *v.* **—men′ac·ing·ly** *adv.*
mé·nage (mā-näzh′) *n.* **1.** A household. **2.** Household management.
me·nag·er·ie (mə-năj′ə-rē, năzh′-) *n.* An exhibition of live wild animals.
me·nar·che (mə-när′kē) *n.* The beginning of menstruation, esp. the 1st occurrence.
mend (mĕnd) *v.* **1.** To repair : fix. **2.** To correct : reform <*mended* their ways> **3.** To get better : heal. *—n.* **1.** The act of mending. **2.** A mended place.
men·da·cious (mĕn-dā′shəs) *adj.* Prone to or marked by lying or deceit : untruthful. **—men·da′cious·ly** *adv.* **—men·dac′i·ty** (-dăs′ĭ-tē) *n.*
Men·del (mĕn′dəl), **Gregor Johann.** 1822–84. Austrian botanist.
men·de·le·vi·um (mĕn′də-lē′vē-əm) *n. Symbol* **Md** A radioactive transuranium element of the actinide series.
Men·dels·sohn (mĕn′dəl-sən), **Felix.** 1809–47. German composer and pianist.
men·di·cant (mĕn′dĭ-kənt) *adj.* Practicing begging. *—n.* **1.** A beggar. **2.** A member of a mendicant order of friars.
men·folk (mĕn′fōk′) or **men·folks** (-fōks′) *pl.n.* **1.** Men as a group. **2.** The male members of a family or community.
men·ha·den (mĕn-hād′n) *n., pl.* **menhaden** *or* **-dens.** An inedible fish, *Brevoortia tyrannus,* of American Atlantic and Gulf waters, used esp. as bait.
me·ni·al (mē′nē-əl, mēn′yəl) *adj.* **1.** Of, relating to, or appropriate to a household servant. **2.** Requiring little skill or responsibility : lowly. *—n.* A servant, esp. a household servant. **—me′ni·al·ly** *adv.*
men·in·gi·tis (mĕn′ĭn-jī′tĭs) *n.* Inflammation of the membranes that enclose the brain and spinal cord.
me·ninx (mē′nĭngks) *n., pl.* **me·nin·ges** (mə-nĭn′jēz′). One of the membranes that enclose the spinal cord and brain. **—men′in·ge′al** (mĕn′ĭn-jē′əl) *adj.*
me·nis·cus (mə-nĭs′kəs) *n., pl.* **-nis·ci** (-nĭs′ī′) *or* **-cus·es. 1.** An object shaped like a crescent. **2.** A concavo-convex lens. **3.** The curved upper surface of a nonturbulent liquid standing in a container.
men·o·pause (mĕn′ə-pôz′) *n.* The time at which menstruation ceases. **—men′o·paus′al** *adj.*
men·ses (mĕn′sēz′) *pl.n.* Blood and dead cell debris discharged from the uterus through the vagina by women who are not pregnant at approx. monthly intervals between puberty and menopause.
men·stru·ate (mĕn′stroo-āt′) *v.* **-at·ed, -at·ing.** To discharge the menses. **—men′stru·al** *adj.* **—men′stru·a′tion** *n.*
men·su·ra·tion (mĕn′sə-rā′shən, -shə-) *n.* The act, process, or art of measuring. **—men′su·ra·ble** *adj.*
-ment *suff.* **1.** Action : process <appease*ment*> **2.** Result of an action or process <advance*ment*> **3.** Means or agent of an action or process <adorn*ment*>
men·tal (mĕn′tl) *adj.* **1.** Of or relating to the mind : intellectual. **2. a.** Of, relating to, or affected by mental disorder. **b.** Intended for the care of the mentally ill <a *mental* ward> **—men′tal·ly** *adv.*
mental age *n.* A measure used in psychological testing that expresses a person's level of mental development relative to the age at which that level is average.
mental deficiency *n.* Subnormal intellectual development marked by deficiencies ranging from impaired learning ability to social incompetence.
men·tal·i·ty (mĕn-tăl′ĭ-tē) *n., pl.* **-ties. 1.** Intellectual capability or power. **2.** A way of thinking : attitude.
mental retardation *n.* Mental deficiency.
men·thol (mĕn′thôl′) *n.* A white organic compound obtained from peppermint oil. **—men′tho·lat′ed** (-thə-lā′tĭd) *adj.*
men·tion (mĕn′shən) *v.* To refer to, esp. casually or incidentally : cite. **—men′tion** *n.* **—men′tion·a·ble** *adj.*
men·tor (mĕn′tôr′, -tər) *n.* A person looked upon for wise advice and guidance.
men·u (mĕn′yōō, mān′-) *n.* **1.** A list of the food and drink available, as at a restaurant. **2.** The dishes available or served at a meal.
me·ow (mē-ou′) *n.* The cry of a cat. **—me·ow′** *v.*
me·phi·tis (mə-fī′tĭs) *n.* **1.** A sickening smell : stench. **2.** An evil-smelling gas emitted from the earth. **—me·phit′ic** *adj.*
mer·can·tile (mûr′kən-tēl′, -tīl′) *adj.* Of or relating to trade or merchants.
mer·ce·nar·y (mûr′sə-nĕr′ē) *adj.* **1.** Concerned only with making money and obtaining material gain. **2.** Paid to serve in a foreign army. **—mer′ce·nar′y** *n.*
mer·cer (mûr′sər) *n. esp. Brit.* A textile dealer.
mer·cer·ize (mûr′sə-rīz′) *v.* **-ized, -iz·ing.** To treat (cotton thread) with sodium hydroxide so as to shrink the fibers and increase color absorption and luster.
mer·chan·dise (mûr′chən-dīz′, -dīs′) *n.* Goods or commodities that may be bought and sold. *—v.* (-dīz′) **-dised, -dis·ing.** To buy and sell (goods or commodities). **—mer′chan·dis′er** *n.*
mer·chant (mûr′chənt) *n.* **1.** One who buys and sells goods for profit. **2.** One who runs a retail business : storekeeper.
mer·chant·man (mûr′chənt-mən) *n.* A commercial ship.
merchant marine *n.* **1.** A nation's commercial ships. **2.** The personnel of the merchant marine.
merchant ship *n.* A merchantman.
mer·cu·ri·al (mər-kyŏŏr′ē-əl) *adj.* **1.** Being rapidly changeable in character <a *mercurial* disposition> **2.** Containing or caused by the action of the element mercury. **—mer·cu′ri·al·ly** *adv.*
mer·cu·ric (mər-kyŏŏr′ĭk) *adj.* Of, relating to, or containing mercury with a valence of +2.
mer·cu·rous (mər-kyŏŏr′əs, mûr′kyə-rəs) *adj. Chem.* Relating to or containing mercury with a valence of +1.
mer·cu·ry (mûr′kyə-rē) *n., pl.* **-ries. 1.** *Symbol* **Hg** A silvery-white liquid metallic element commonly used in thermometers and barometers. **2. Mercury.** The smallest planet in the solar system and the one closest to the sun.
mer·cy (mûr′sē) *n., pl.* **-cies. 1.** Kind and compassionate treatment : clemency. **2.** A disposition to be benevolent and forgiving. **3.** Something to be thankful for <a *mercy* no one was hurt> **—mer′ci·ful** *adj.* **—mer′ci·ful·ly** *adv.* **—mer′ci·less** *adj.* **—mer′ci·less·ly** *adv.*
mere (mîr) *adj. superl.* **mer·est. 1.** Being no more than what is stated <a *mere* whim of mine> **2.** Unadulterated : pure. **—mere′ly** *adv.*
mer·e·tri·cious (mĕr′ĭ-trĭsh′əs) *adj.* **1.** Attractive in a tawdry manner. **2.** Based on error or pretense : spurious. **—mer′e·tri′cious·ly** *adv.* **—mer′e·tri′cious·ness** *n.*
mer·gan·ser (mər-găn′sər) *n.* A duck of the genus *Mergus,* having a narrow, slightly hooked bill and usu. a crested head.
merge (mûrj) *v.* **merged, merg·ing.** To bring or come together so as to form one.
merg·er (mûr′jər) *n.* The union of 2 or more groups, as corporations.
me·rid·i·an (mə-rĭd′ē-ən) *n.* **1. a.** A great circle on the earth's surface passing through the N and S poles. **b.** Either half of such a circle lying between the poles. **2.** The highest point or stage : apex. **—me·rid′i·an** *adj.*
me·ringue (mə-răng′) *n.* A mixture of baked stiffly beaten egg whites and sugar, often used as a topping for cakes or pies.
me·ri·no (mə-rē′nō) *n., pl.* **-nos. 1. a.** A sheep orig. bred in Spain. **b.** The fine wool of the merino. **2.** A soft lightweight fabric orig. made of merino wool.
mer·it (mĕr′ĭt) *n.* **1.** A usu. high level of superiority : worth <a painting of *merit*> **2.** A praiseworthy or blameworthy feature, action, or quality. **3. merits.** The factual substance of a disputed issue and esp. of legal case. ☆**syns:** CALIBER, QUALITY, STATURE, VALUE, VIRTUE, WORTH *—v.* To deserve : earn.

mer·i·toc·ra·cy (mĕr′ĭ-tŏk′rə-sē) *n., pl.* **-cies. 1.** A system in which advancement is based on achievement or ability. **2.** Leadership by talented achievers.
mer·i·to·ri·ous (mĕr′ĭ-tôr′ē-əs, -tōr′-) *adj.* Deserving praise : admirable. **—mer′i·to′ri·ous·ly** *adv.*
mer·maid (mûr′măd′) *n.* A legendary sea creature with the upper body of a woman and the tail of a fish. **—mer′man′** *n.*
mer·ri·ment (mĕr′ĭ-mənt) *n.* **1.** Mirthful delight : amusement. **2.** Lighthearted celebration : festivity.
mer·ry (mĕr′ē) *adj.* **-ri·er, -ri·est. 1.** Full of gaiety : high-spirited. **2.** Marked by or offering festivity. **3.** Delightful : entertaining. **4.** Brisk <a *merry* pace> ☆***syns:*** FESTIVE, GALA, GLAD, GLADSOME, HAPPY, JOYFUL, JOYOUS **—mer′ri·ly** *adv.* **—mer′ri·ness** *n.*
mer·ry-go-round (mĕr′ē-gō-round′) *n.* **1.** A revolving circular platform with seats, often in the form of horses, on which people ride for amusement. **2.** A whirl <a *merry-go-round* of appointments>
mer·ry·mak·ing (mĕr′ē-mā′kĭng) *n.* **1.** Participation in festivity : revelry. **2.** A festivity. **—mer′ry·mak′er** *n.*
me·sa (mā′sə) *n.* A flat-topped hill or small plateau with steep sides.
més·al·liance (mā′zăl-yäɴs′, mā′zə-lī′əns) *n.* A marriage with a person of inferior social position.
mes·cal (mĕ-skăl′) *n.* **1.** A cactus, *Lophophora williamsii,* of Mexico and SW U.S., having buttonlike outgrowths that are dried and chewed as a drug by certain Indian tribes. **2.** A Mexican liquor distilled from the fermented juice of certain species of agave.
mes·ca·line (mĕs′kə-lēn′) *n.* An alkaloid hallucinogenic drug.
Mes·dames (mā-däm′) *n. pl. of* MADAME *or* MADAM.
Mes·de·moi·selles (mā′də-mə-zĕl′, măd′mwə-) *n. pl. of* MADEMOISELLE.
mesh (mĕsh) *n.* **1. a.** One of the open spaces in a thread, cord, or wire network. **b.** *often* **meshes.** The threads, cords, or wires surrounding these spaces. **2.** A network. **3.** A fabric with an open network of interlacing threads. **4.** Something that entraps or snares <the *meshes* of politics> **5. a.** The engagement of gear teeth. **b.** The state of being so engaged. *—v.* **1.** To ensnare : entangle. **2.** To engage or interlock <gears *meshing*> **3.** To fit together effectively : harmonize.
mes·mer·ize (mĕz′mə-rīz′, mĕs′-) *v.* **-ized, -iz·ing. 1.** To hypnotize. **2.** To enthrall. **—mes·mer′ic** (-mĕr′ĭk) *adj.* **—mes′mer·ism** *n.* **—mes′mer·iz′er** *n.*
mes·on (mĕz′ŏn′, mē′zŏn′, mĕs′ŏn′, mē′sŏn′) *n.* One of several subatomic particles.
Mes·o·po·ta·mi·a (mĕs′ə-pə-tā′mē-ə). Ancient country of SW Asia, between the Tigris and Euphrates rivers. **—Mes′o·po·ta′mi·an** *adj. & n.*
mes·o·sphere (mĕz′ə-sfîr′, mĕs′-) *n.* The atmospheric layer above the stratosphere.
mes·quite (mĕ-skēt′, mə-) *n.* A shrub or small tree of the genus *Prosopis,* esp. *P. juliflora,* of the SW U.S. and Mexico, whose pods are used as forage.
mess (mĕs) *n.* **1.** A disorderly accumulation : jumble. **2.** A cluttered, untidy, or dirty state. **3.** A confused, disturbed, or troublesome state : chaos. **4. a.** A serving of food. **b.** A group of persons, usu. in the military, who regularly eat meals together. **c.** A meal eaten by such a group. *—v.* **1.** To make untidy, dirty, or disorderly. **2.** To handle or manage badly : bungle. **3.** *Slang.* To manhandle. **4.** To meddle.
mes·sage (mĕs′ĭj) *n.* **1.** A communication transmitted from 1 person or group to another. **2.** A basic theme or idea <I get the *message.*>
Mes·sei·gneurs (mā′sān-yœr′) *n. pl. of* MONSEIGNEUR.
mes·sen·ger (mĕs′ən-jər) *n.* A person who carries messages or does errands.
messenger RNA *n.* An ribonucleic acid that carries genetic information necessary for protein synthesis in cells.
Mes·si·ah (mə-sī′ə) *n.* **1. a.** The anticipated deliverer and king of the Jews. **b.** Jesus Christ. **2. messiah.** A liberator or deliverer. **—Mes′si·an′ic** (mĕs′ē-ăn′ĭk) *adj.*
Mes·sieurs (mā-syœ′) *n. pl. of* MONSIEUR.
mess·mate (mĕs′māt′) *n.* One with whom one eats regularly.
Messrs. *abbr.* **1.** Messieurs. **2.** *pl. of* MR.
mess·y (mĕs′ē) *adj.* **-i·er, -i·est. 1.** Marked by dirt or disorder. **2.** Lacking precision and neatness. **3.** Unpleasantly difficult to resolve or settle <a *messy* divorce case> ☆***syns:*** DISHEVELED, MUSSY, SLIPSHOD, SLOPPY, SLOVENLY, UNKEMPT, UNTIDY **—mess′i·ly** *adv.* **—mess′i·ness** *n.*
mes·ti·za (mĕ-stē′zə) *n.* A woman of mixed European and American Indian ancestry.
mes·ti·zo (mĕ-stē′zō) *n., pl.* **-zos** *or* **-zoes.** A man of mixed European and American Indian ancestry.
met (mĕt) *v. p.t. & p.p. of* MEET[1].
me·tab·o·lism (mə-tăb′ə-lĭz′əm) *n.* **1.** The complex of chemical and physical processes involved in the maintenance of life. **2.** The use or functioning of a substance or class of substances within a living body. **—met′a·bol′ic** (mĕt′ə-bŏl′ĭk) *adj.* **—me·tab′o·lize′** *v.*
me·tab·o·lite (mə-tăb′ə-līt′) *n.* An organic compound produced by metabolism.
met·a·car·pus (mĕt′ə-kär′pəs) *n.* The part of the hand or forefoot that contains the 5 bones extending from the bones of the fingers or toes to the wrist or ankle.
met·a·gal·ax·y (mĕt′ə-găl′ək-sē) *n.* The universe.
met·al (mĕt′l) *n.* **1.** One of a category of usu. whitish, lustrous electropositive elements that are typically ductile and malleable. **2.** An alloy of 2 or more metallic elements. **3.** Strength of character. **—me·tal′lic** *adj.* **—me·tal′i·cal·ly** *adv.*
met·al·lur·gy (mĕt′l-ûr′jē) *n.* The science and technology of metals and their properties. **—met′al·lur′gic, met′al·lur′gi·cal** *adj.* **—met′al·lur′gist** *n.*
met·a·mor·phism (mĕt′ə-môr′fĭz′əm) *n. Geol.* An alteration in the texture, composition, or structure of rock produced by great heat or pressure. **—met′a·mor′phic** *adj.*
met·a·mor·pho·sis (mĕt′ə-môr′fə-sĭs) *n., pl.* **-ses** (-sēz′). **1.** A transformation, as by supernatural means. **2.** A marked alteration in appearance, condition, character, or function. **3.** *Biol.* Change in the structure and habits of an animal during normal growth, usu. in the postembryonic stage. **—met′a·mor′phose′** (-fōz′, -fōs′) *v.*
met·a·phor (mĕt′ə-fôr′, -fər) *n.* A figure of speech in which a term is transferred from the object it ordinarily designates to an object it may designate only by implicit comparison or analogy, as in the phrase *evening of life.* **—met′a·phor′i·cal** *adj.* **—met′a·phor′i·cal·ly** *adv.*
met·a·phys·ics (mĕt′ə-fĭz′ĭks) *n. (sing. in number).* The branch of philosophy that methodically investigates the nature of 1st principles and problems of ultimate reality. **—met′a·phys′i·cal** *adj.* **—met′a·phy·si′cian** (-fĭ-zĭsh′ən) *n.*
me·tas·ta·sis (mə-tăs′tə-sĭs) *n., pl.* **-ses** (-sēz′). *Pathol.* Transference of a disease-producing agency, as malignant cells, from 1 site to another elsewhere in the body. **—me·tas′ta·size′** *v.* **—met′a·stat′ic** (mĕt′ə-stăt′ĭk) *adj.*
met·a·tar·sus (mĕt′ə-tär′səs) *n., pl.* **-si** (-sī′). **1.** The part of the human foot that forms the instep and consists of the 5 bones between the toes and the ankle. **2.** A part of the hind foot of a 4-legged animal that corresponds to the metatarsus. **—met′a·tar′sal** *adj.*
mete[1] (mēt) *v.* **met·ed, met·ing.** To distribute by or as if by measure : dole.
mete[2] (mēt) *n.* A boundary.
me·te·or (mē′tē-ər, -ôr′) *n.* **1.** The incandescent trail or streak that is seen in the sky when a meteoroid is made luminous by friction with the earth's atmosphere. **2.** A meteoroid.
me·te·or·ic (mē′tē-ôr′ĭk, -ŏr′-) *adj.* **1.** Of, relating to, or produced by a meteor. **2.** Like a meteor in speed, brilliance, or briefness <a *meteoric* career>
me·te·or·ite (mē′tē-ə-rīt′) *n.* The metallic or stony remains of a meteoroid that reaches the earth after burning incompletely in the atmosphere.
me·te·or·oid (mē′tē-ə-roid′) *n.* One of a large number of celestial bodies of various size that appear as meteors when they enter the earth's atmosphere.
me·te·or·ol·o·gy (mē′tē-ə-rŏl′ə-jē) *n.* The science concerned with atmospheric phenomena, esp. weather and weather conditions. **—me′te·or·o·log′i·cal** (-ər-ə-lŏj′ĭkəl), **me′te·or·o·log′ic** *adj.* **—me′te·or·ol′o·gist** *n.*
me·ter[1] (mē′tər) *n.* The measured rhythm typical of verse or music.
me·ter[2] (mē′tər) *n.* See MEASUREMENT TABLE.
me·ter[3] (mē′tər) *n.* **1.** A device for measuring or recording various values, as speed or the rate of flow of a liquid. **2.** A postage meter. **3.** A parking meter. *—v.* To measure or control with a meter.
-meter *suff.* Measuring device <anemo*meter*>
me·ter-kil·o·gram-sec·ond system (mē′tər-kĭl′ə-grăm-sĕk′ənd) *n.* A system of units for mechanics, using the meter, the kilogram, and the second as fundamental units of length, mass, and time.
meter maid *n.* A woman member of a police department who writes tickets for violations of parking regulations.
meth·a·done hydrochloride (mĕth′ə-dōn′) *n.* A synthetic narcotic used in treating heroin addiction.
meth·am·phet·a·mine (mĕth′ăm-fĕt′ə-mēn′, -mĭn) *n.* A derivative of amphetamine used in the form of its crystalline hydrochloride as a stimulant.
meth·ane (mĕth′ān′) *n.* A colorless, odorless, flammable gas

that is the chief component of natural gas and is used esp. as a fuel.
meth•a•nol (mĕth'ə-nôl', -nōl') *n.* A colorless, poisonous, flammable alcohol used as an antifreeze, fuel, general solvent, and denaturant for ethyl alcohol.
meth•a•qua•lone (mĕth'ə-kwā'lān') *n.* A habit-forming sedative and hyponotic drug.
me•thinks (mĭ-thĭngks') *v. p.t.* **me•thought** (-thôt'). *Archaic.* It seems to me.
▲word history: The archaic form *methinks* is strictly speaking not 1 word but 2: the pronoun *me* and the obsolete verb *think*, meaning "to seem." The obsolete verb is related to but not the same as the current verb *think*, meaning "to have in mind." *Methinks* is an impersonal construction, that is, one without an expressed subject. In *methinks, me* is a dative form of the pronoun *I* functioning as the indirect object of *thinks*, and *thinks* is the 3rd person singular form of the verb.
meth•od (mĕth'əd) *n.* **1.** A manner, means, or process for accomplishing something. **2.** Systematic arrangement : order. ☆**syns:** FASHION, MANNER, MODE, SYSTEM, WAY **—me•thod'i•cal** (mə-thŏd'ĭ-kəl), **me•thod'ic** *adj.* **—me•thod'i•cal•ly** *adv.*
Meth•od•ist (mĕth'ə-dĭst) *n.* A member of a Protestant Christian denomination whose theology developed from the teachings of John and Charles Wesley. **—Meth'od•ism** *n.* **—Meth'od•ist** *adj.*
meth•od•ol•o•gy (mĕth'ə-dŏl'ə-jē) *n., pl.* **-gies. 1.** A system of methods and principles used in a specific branch of knowledge. **2.** The branch of logic that deals with the general principles of the formation of knowledge. **—meth'od•o•log'i•cal** (-də-lŏj'ĭ-kəl) *adj.*
Me•thu•se•lah (mə-thōō'zə-lə). Long-lived Biblical patriarch.
meth•yl (mĕth'əl) *n.* An organic radical derived from methane and occurring in many organic compounds.
methyl alcohol *n.* Methanol.
me•tic•u•lous (mə-tĭk'yə-ləs) *adj.* **1.** Very careful : precise. **2.** Excessively concerned with details : nit-picking. **—me•tic'u•lous•ly** *adv.* **—me•tic'u•lous•ness** *n.*
mé•tier (mā-tyā') *n.* A sphere of activity to which one is esp. suited.
Mé•tis *also* **Me•tis** (mā'tē, mā-tē', mā-tēs') *n., pl.* **Métis.** *Can.* A person of mixed white (usu. French) and Indian ancestry. **—Mé'tisse** *n.*
me•tre (mē'tər) *n. esp. Brit. var. of* METER.
met•ric (mĕt'rĭk) *adj.* Of or relating to the metric system.
met•ri•cal (mĕt'rĭ-kəl) *adj.* **1.** Of, relating to, or composed in rhythmic meter. **2.** Of or relating to measurement.
met•ri•ca•tion (mĕt'rĭ-kā'shən) *n.* Conversion to or adoption of the metric system.
metric system *n.* A decimal system of weights and measures based on the meter as a unit of length and the kilogram as a unit of mass.
metric ton *n.* A unit of mass equal to 1,000 kgs.
met•ri•fy (mĕt'rə-fī') *v.* **-fied, -fy•ing.** To convert to or adopt the metric system. **—met'ri•fi•ca'tion** *n.*
met•ro (mĕt'rō) *n., pl.* **-ros. 1.** A subway system. **2.** *also* **Mét•ro.** *Can.* The subway system in Montreal.
met•ro•nome (mĕt'rə-nōm') *n.* A device for marking time by means of a series of clicks at precise intervals. **—met'ro•nom'ic** (mĕt'rə-nŏm'ĭk) *adj.*
me•trop•o•lis (mə-trŏp'ə-lĭs) *n.* **1.** A major city. **2.** A city regarded as the center of a specific activity <a great entertainment *metropolis*> **—met'ro•pol'i•tan** (mĕt'rə-pŏl'ĭ-tn) *adj.*
-metry *suff.* Process or science of measuring <*isometry*>
met•tle (mĕt'l) *n.* **1.** Quality or strength of character. **2.** Courage : spirit. **—met'tle•some** *adj.*
mew[1] (myōō) *n.* **1.** A secret place : hideaway. **2. mews.** A small street with living quarters converted from stables. *—v.* **mewed, mew•ing.** To confine in or as if in a cage.
mew[2] (myōō) *v* To meow. **—mew** *n.*
Mex•i•co (mĕk'sĭ-kō'). **1.** Country of SW North America. *Cap.* Mexico City. *Pop.* 69,381,000. **2. Gulf of.** Inlet of the Atlantic S of North America and surrounded by the U.S., Mexico, and Cuba. **—Mex'i•can** *adj.* & *n.*
Mexico City. Cap. of Mexico, in the C part of the country. *Pop.* 8,591,750.
mez•za•nine (mĕz'ə-nēn', mĕz'ə-nēn') *n.* **1.** A partial story between 2 main stories of a building. **2.** The lowest balcony in a theater, esp. the 1st few rows.
mez•zo-so•pran•o (mĕt'sō-sə-prăn'ō, -prä'nō, mĕd'zō-) *n.* **1.** A woman's voice with a range between soprano and contralto. **2.** A woman with this voice.
mfg. *abbr.* manufacture; manufactured; manufacturing
mfr. *abbr.* manufacture; manufacturer.
Mg *symbol for* MAGNESIUM.
MI *abbr.* Michigan (with Zip Code).
mi. *abbr.* **1.** mile. **2.** mill (monetary unit).
MIA (ĕm'ī-ā') *n.* A serviceman who is reported missing in action whose death cannot be confirmed.
Mi•am•i (mī-ăm'ē, -ăm'ə). Resort city of SE Fla. *Pop.* 346,931.
mi•as•ma (mī-ăz'mə, mē-) *n., pl.* **-mas** *or* **-ma•ta** (-mə-tə). **1.** A poisonous atmosphere once believed to rise from swamps and cause disease. **2.** A harmful influence. **—mi•as'mal, mi•as'mic** *adj.*
mi•ca (mī'kə) *n.* One of a group of silicate minerals that are similar in physical structure and chemical composition and that split easily into thin transparent or translucent sheets. **—mi•ca'ceous** (-kā'shəs) *adj.*
Mi•cah (mī'kə) *n.* See BIBLE TABLE.
mice (mīs) *n. pl. of* MOUSE.
Mich. *abbr.* Michigan.
Mi•chel•an•ge•lo (mī'kə-lăn'jə-lō', mĭk'ə-). 1475–1516. Italian sculptor, painter, architect, and poet.
Mich•i•gan (mĭsh'ĭ-gən). **1.** State of the N U.S. *Cap.* Lansing. *Pop.* 9,258,344. **2. Lake.** 3rd largest of the Great Lakes, between Mich. and Wis.
mi•cra (mī'krə) *n. var. pl. of* MICRON.
mi•crobe (mī'krōb') *n.* A microorganism. **—mi•cro'bi•al, mi•cro'bic** *adj.*
mi•cro•bi•ol•o•gy (mī'krō-bī-ŏl'ə-jē) *n.* The scientific study of microorganisms and their effects on other forms of life. **—mi'cro•bi'o•log'i•cal** (-ə-lŏj'ĭ-kəl) *adj.* **—mi'cro•bi•ol'o•gist** *n.*
mi•cro•bus (mī'krō-bŭs') *n.* A small bus that resembles a station wagon.
mi•cro•ceph•a•ly (mī'krō-sĕf'ə-lē) *n.* Abnormal smallness of the head, often associated with pathological mental conditions. **—mi'cro•ce•phal'ic** (-sə-făl'ĭk) *n.* & *adj.*
mi•cro•cir•cuit (mī'krō-sûr'kĭt) *n.* An electronic circuit that consists of components of very small size. **—mi'cro•cir'cuit•ry** (-kĭ-trē) *n.*
mi•cro•cline (mī'krō-klīn') *n.* A mineral of the feldspar group.
mi•cro•com•put•er (mī'krō-kəm-pyōō'tər) *n.* A computer using a microprocessor.
mi•cro•cosm (mī'krō-kŏz'əm) *n.* A diminutive world, esp. a system that is analogous to a larger one in configuration, constitution, or development. **—mi'cro•cos'mic, mi'cro•cos'mi•cal** *adj.*
mi•cro•e•lec•tron•ics (mī'krō-ĭ-lĕk-trŏn'ĭks) *n. (sing. in number).* A branch of electronics dealing with miniature components. **—mi'cro•e•lec•tron'ic** *adj.*
mi•cro•fiche (mī'krō-fēsh') *n., pl.* **microfiche** *or* **-fich•es.** A microfilm sheet containing rows of written or printed pages in reduced form.
mi•cro•film (mī'krō-fĭlm') *n.* **1.** A film on which printed matter is photographed in greatly reduced size. **2.** A reproduction on microfilm. **—mi'cro•film'** *v.*
mi•cro•groove (mī'krō-grōōv') *n.* A long-playing phonograph record.
mi•crom•e•ter (mī-krŏm'ĭ-tər) *n.* An instrument for measuring minute distances, esp. by the use of a finely threaded screw.
mi•cron (mī'krŏn') *n., pl.* **-crons** *or* **-cra** (-krə). A unit of length equal to one-millionth (10^{-6}) m.
Mi•cro•ne•sia (mī'krō-nē'zhə, -shə). Islands of the W Pacific N of the equator. **—Mi'cro•ne'sian** *adj.* & *n.*
mi•cro•or•gan•ism (mī'krō-ôr'gə-nĭz'əm) *n.* An organism, as a bacterium or a protozoan, too small to be seen without the aid of a microscope.
mi•cro•phone (mī'krə-fōn') *n.* An instrument that converts acoustical waves into electric signals, usu. fed into a recorder, amplifier, or broadcasting transmitter. **—mi'cro•phon'ic** (-fŏn'ĭk) *adj.*
mi•cro•proc•es•sor (mī'krō-prŏs'ĕs-ər) *n. Computer Sci.* A semiconductor processing unit contained on an integrated-circuit chip.
mi•cro•scope (mī'krə-skōp') *n.* An optical instrument that produces magnified images of very small objects, esp. of objects too small to be seen with the unaided eye. **—mi•cros'co•py** (-krŏs'kə-pē) *n.*
mi•cro•scop•ic (mī'krə-skŏp'ĭk) *also* **mi•cro•scop•i•cal** (-ĭ-kəl) *adj.* **1.** Too small to be seen by the unaided eye but large enough to be studied under a microscope. **2.** Of, relating to, or entailing the use of a microscope. **—mi'cro•scop'i•cal•ly** *adv.*
mi•cro•sec•ond (mī'krō-sĕk'ənd) *n.* One-millionth (10^{-6}) sec.
mi•cro•sur•ger•y (mī'krō-sûr'jə-rē) *n.* Surgery on minute living structures, as by means of microscopes and lasers. **—mi'cro•sur'gi•cal** (-jĭ-kəl) *adj.*
mi•cro•wave (mī'krə-wāv') *n.* An electromagnetic wave with a wavelength ranging approx. from 1 mm to 1 m.

microwave oven *n.* An oven in which microwaves heat and cook food.
mid (mĭd) *adj.* Being in the middle or center : central.
mid•air (mĭd-âr′) *n.* A region or point in the air above the surface of the ground.
mid•day (mĭd′dā′) *n.* Noon.
mid•den (mĭd′n) *n.* A dunghill or refuse heap, esp. of a primitive habitation.
mid•dle (mĭd′l) *adj.* **1.** Being equally distant from extremes or limits : central. **2.** Being at neither 1 extreme nor the other. **3. Middle.** Designating or constituting a period, as in the development of a language, between earlier and later stages. —*n.* **1.** An area or point equidistant between extremes : center. **2.** Something intermediate between extremes : mean. **3.** The waist. ☆***syns:*** CENTRAL, INTERMEDIATE, MEAN, MEDIAL, MEDIAN, MID, MIDDLE-OF-THE-ROAD, MIDWAY **—mid′dle•most′** *adj.*
middle age *n.* The period of human life between about 40 and 60. **—mid′dle-aged′** *adj.*
Middle Ages *pl.n.* The period of European history extending approx. from A.D. 476 to 1453.
Middle America *n.* The part of the U.S. middle class that is of average income and education and conservative attitudes and values. **—Middle American** *n.* & *adj.*
mid•dle•brow (mĭd′l-brou′) *n. Informal.* A moderately cultured person. **—mid′dle•brow′** *adj.*
middle class *n.* The social class occupying a socioeconomic position intermediate between the lower and upper classes. **—mid′dle-class′** *adj.*
middle ear *n.* The space between the tympanic membrane and the inner ear through which sound waves are carried by the malleus, incus, and stapes.
Middle East. Area of SW Asia and NE Africa. **—Middle Eastern** *adj.* **—Middle Easterner** *n.*
mid•dle•man (mĭd′l-măn′) *n.* A go-between, esp. one who buys goods from producers for resale at a profit to retailers or consumers.
middle-of-the-road (mĭd′l-əv-thə-rōd′) *adj.* Pursuing or advocating a course of action that avoids extremes, esp. in politics.
middle school *n.* A school that usu. includes grades 5 through 8.
mid•dle•weight (mĭd′l-wāt′) *n.* A boxer weighing between 147 and 160 lbs.
Middle West. Region of NC U.S. extending roughly from Ohio W through Iowa and from the Ohio and Missouri rivers N through the Great Lakes. **—Middle Western** *adj.* **—Middle Westerner** *n.*
†**mid•dling** (mĭd′lĭng) *adj.* **1.** Of medium quality, degree, size, or condition. **2.** Less than excellent : mediocre. —*n. often* **middlings.** *SE U.S.* Pork or bacon cut from between the ham and shoulder of a pig. **—mid′dling** *adv.*
mid•dy (mĭd′ē) *n., pl.* **-dies. 1.** *Informal.* A midshipman. **2.** A loose blouse with a sailor collar worn by women or children.
Mid•east (mĭd′ēst′). The Middle East.
midge (mĭj) *n.* Any of various small, gnatlike flies of the family Chironomidae.
midg•et (mĭj′ĭt) *n.* **1.** An unusually small person. **2.** Something very small of its class.
mid•i (mĭd′ē) *n.* A skirt, dress, or coat extending to the calf.
mid•land (mĭd′lənd) *n.* The middle or interior part of a region or country.
mid•most (mĭd′mōst′) *adj.* **1.** Located in the exact middle : middlemost. **2.** Located nearest the middle. **—mid′most′** *adv.*
mid•night (mĭd′nīt′) *n.* The middle of the night : 12 o'clock.
midnight sun *n.* The sun at midnight during the summer in the Arctic or Antarctic Circle.
mid•point (mĭd′point′) *n.* A point near or at the middle.
mid•riff (mĭd′rĭf′) *n.* **1.** The diaphragm. **2.** The part of the human torso from the chest to the waist.
mid•ship•man (mĭd′shĭp′mən, mĭd-shĭp′mən) *n.* A student training to be a commissioned naval officer.
midst (mĭdst) *n.* **1.** The middle part or position : center. **2.** The condition of being surrounded or enveloped. **3.** A position among others in a group <a guest in our *midst*> —*prep.* Amid : among.
mid•stream (mĭd′strēm′) *n.* The middle of a stream.
mid•sum•mer (mĭd′sŭm′ər) *n.* **1.** The middle of the summer. **2.** The summer solstice.
mid•term (mĭd′tûrm′) *n.* **1.** The middle of a term, esp. an academic term. **2.** An examination given in the middle of an academic term.
mid•town (mĭd′toun′) *n.* A central portion of a city. **—mid′town′** *adj.*
mid•way (mĭd′wā′) *n.* The area of an amusement park, fair, or carnival where amusements, as side shows, are located. —*adv.* & *adj.* In the middle of the distance or way : halfway.
mid•week (mĭd′wēk′) *n.* The middle of the week. **—mid′week′ly** *adj.* & *adv.*
Mid•west (mĭd′wĕst′). The Middle West.
mid•wife (mĭd′wīf′) *n.* A woman who assists other women in childbirth. **—mid′wife′ry** *n.*
mid•win•ter (mĭd′wĭn′tər) *n.* **1.** The middle of the winter. **2.** The winter solstice.
mid•year (mĭd′yîr′) *n.* **1.** The middle of a year. **2.** An examination given in the middle of an academic year. **—mid′year′** *adj.*
mien (mēn) *n.* **1.** A person's bearing or manner : demeanor. **2.** Appearance.
miff (mĭf) *v.* To cause to be displeased.
might[1] (mīt) *n.* **1.** Force : power. **2.** Physical strength.
might[2] (mīt) *v.* Used to indicate a present condition contrary to fact; a possibility or probability weaker than *may*; possibility, probability, or permission in the past; or a greater degree of politeness than *may, should,* or *ought.*
might•y (mī′tē) *adj.* **-i•er, -i•est. 1.** Having or showing great power : strong. **2.** Awesome or imposing : great. —*adv. Informal.* Exceedingly : very. **—might′i•ly** *adv.* **—might′i•ness** *n.*
mi•gnon•ette (mĭn′yə-nĕt′) *n.* A garden plant, *Reseda odorata,* with small, fragrant greenish flowers.
mi•graine (mī′grān′) *n.* Severe, recurrent headache, often accompanied by nausea.
mi•grant (mī′grənt) *n.* One that migrates, esp. from 1 region to another in search of seasonal work. **—mi′grant** *adj.*
mi•grate (mī′grāt′) *v.* **-grat•ed, -grat•ing. 1.** To move from a country or area and settle in another. **2.** To move periodically from 1 climate or region to another. **—mi•gra′tion** *n.* **—mi•gra′tion•al** *adj.* **—mi′gra•to′ry** (-grə-tôr′ē, -tōr′ē) *adj.*
mi•ka•do (mĭ-kä′dō) *n., pl.* **-dos.** An emperor of Japan.
mike (mīk) *n. Informal.* A microphone.
mil[1] (mĭl) *n.* A unit of length equal to one-thousandth (10^{-3}) in.
mil[2] (mĭl) *n.* See *pound* at CURRENCY TABLE.
Mi•lan (mĭ-lăn′, -län′). City of N Italy. *Pop.* 1,724,173. **—Mil′a•nese′** *adj.* & *n.*
milch (mĭlch) *adj.* Giving milk <*milch* cows>
mild (mīld) *adj.* **1.** Gentle in manner, disposition, or behavior. **2.** Not extreme : moderate. **3.** Not sharp, bitter, or strong, as in taste. **—mild′ly** *adv.* **—mild′ness** *n.*
mil•dew (mĭl′do͞o′, -dyo͞o′) *n.* A superficial white or grayish coating formed by fungi on organic materials, as paint, fabric, paper, or leather. **—mil′dew′** *v.* **—mil′dew′y** *adj.*
mile (mīl) *n.* **1.** See MEASUREMENT TABLE. **2.** A nautical mile.
mile•age (mī′lĭj) *n.* **1.** Distance traveled, measured, or expressed in miles. **2.** Service, use, or wear expressed in miles traveled. **3.** Money allowed for travel expenses at a specified rate per mile.
mile•post (mīl′pōst′) *n.* A post that indicates distance in miles to a given place.
mile•stone (mīl′stōn′) *n.* **1.** A stone marker used as a milepost. **2.** An important point in progress or development.
mi•lieu (mēl-yœ′) *n.* Environment.
mil•i•tant (mĭl′ĭ-tənt) *adj.* **1.** Engaged in combat. **2.** Working aggressively for a cause. **—mil′i•tan•cy** *n.* **—mil′i•tant** *n.*
mil•i•ta•rism (mĭl′ĭ-tə-rĭz′əm) *n.* **1.** The predominance of the professional military class in state affairs. **2.** A policy in which military preparedness is of primary importance. **—mil′i•ta•rist** *n.* **—mil′i•ta•ris′tic** *adj.* **—mil′i•ta•ris′ti•cal•ly** *adv.*
mil•i•ta•rize (mĭl′ĭ-tə-rīz′) *v.* **-rized, -riz•ing. 1.** To train or equip for war. **2.** To impart militarism to.
mil•i•tar•y (mĭl′ĭ-tĕr′ē) *adj.* **1.** Of or relating to armed forces, soldiers, or war. **2.** Characteristic of or appropriate to a soldier or the armed forces. —*n.* **1.** The armed forces of a nation. **2.** Members of the military. **—mil′i•tar′i•ly** (-târ′ə-lē) *adv.*
mil•i•tate (mĭl′ĭ-tāt′) *v.* **-tat•ed, -tat•ing.** To have influence or force.
mi•li•tia (mĭ-lĭsh′ə) *n.* A reserve military force that is on call for service only in an emergency. **—mi•li′tia•man** *n.*
milk (mĭlk) *n.* **1.** A whitish liquid produced by the mammary glands of all mature female mammals to feed their young. **2.** A liquid, as the sap of some plants, like milk. —*v.* **1.** To draw the milk from (a female mammal). **2.** To extract as if by milking. **—milk′i•ness** *n.* **—milk′y** *adj.*
milk glass *n.* An opaque or translucent glass orig. of a whitish color.
milk•maid (mĭlk′mād′) *n.* A woman or girl who milks cows.
milk•man (mĭlk′măn′) *n.* A man who delivers or sells milk.
milk of magnesia *n.* A liquid suspension of magnesium hydroxide used as a laxative and antacid.
milk shake *n.* A drink made of milk, flavoring, and usu. ice cream thoroughly shaken or blended.
milk•sop (mĭlk′sŏp′) *n.* A man lacking in manly qualities.

milk tooth *n.* One of the set of temporary 1st teeth of a young mammal.
milk•weed (mĭlk′wēd′) *n.* A plant of the genus *Asclepias,* esp. *A. syriaca,* having milky juice and pointed pods that open to release seeds with downy tufts.
Milky Way *n.* The galaxy in which the solar system is located, visible at night as a luminous band.
mill[1] (mĭl) *n.* **1.** A building with machinery for grinding grain into meal or flour. **2.** A device for crushing or grinding <a pepper *mill*> **3.** A building with machinery for processing materials : factory. —*v.* **1.** To crush or grind in or as if in a mill. **2.** To process or produce in a mill. **3.** To move around in a disorderly or confused mass.
mill[2] (mĭl) *n.* A monetary unit equal to 1/1000 of a U.S. dollar or 1/10 of a cent.
mill•dam (mĭl′dăm′) *n.* A dam constructed to create a millpond.
mil•len•ni•um (mĭ-lĕn′ē-əm) *n., pl.* **-ums** or **-ni•a** (-ē-ə). **1.** A period of 1,000 years. **2.** The 1,000-year reign of Christ on earth mentioned in the New Testament. **3.** A period of prosperity, happiness, justice, and peace. **—mil•len′ni•al** *adj.*
mill•er (mĭl′ər) *n.* **1.** Someone who operates, owns, or works in a mill, esp. a grain mill. **2.** Any of various moths whose wings are covered with a powdery substance.
mil•let (mĭl′ĭt) *n.* A grass, *Panicum miliaceum,* grown for its edible white seeds.
mil•liard (mĭl′yərd, -yärd′, mĭl′ē-ärd′) *n. esp. Brit.* A billion.
mil•lieme (mēl-yĕm′, mē-yĕm′) *n.* See CURRENCY TABLE.
mil•li•gram (mĭl′ĭ-grăm′) *n.* See MEASUREMENT TABLE.
mil•li•li•ter (mĭl′ə-lē′tər) *n.* See MEASUREMENT TABLE.
mil•li•me•ter (mĭl′ə-mē′tər) *n.* See MEASUREMENT TABLE.
mil•li•ner (mĭl′ə-nər) *n.* Someone who makes, designs, or sells women's hats.
mil•li•ner•y (mĭl′ə-nĕr′ē) *n.* **1.** Articles, esp. women's hats, sold by a milliner. **2.** The profession or business of a milliner.
†**mill•ing** (mĭl′ĭng) *n.* **1.** The act or process of grinding, esp. of grinding grain into meal or flour. **2.** The ridged edge of a coin. **3.** *W U.S.* The process of halting a cattle stampede by turning the lead animals in a wide arc so that they form the center of a gradually tightening spiral.
mil•lion (mĭl′yən) *n.* **1.** The cardinal number equal to 1,000 × 1,000 or 10^6. **2.** *often* **millions.** A large unspecified number. **—mil′lion** *adj.* **—mil′lionth** *n.* & *adj.* & *adv.*
mil•lion•aire (mĭl′yə-nâr′) *n.* Someone whose wealth amounts to 1,000,000 or more units of currency, as dollars.
mil•li•pede (mĭl′ə-pēd′) *n.* An arthropod of the class Diplopoda, having a wormlike body with legs attached in double pairs to most body segments.
mil•li•sec•ond (mĭl′ĭ-sĕk′ənd) *n.* A unit of time equal to 1/1000 (10^{-3}) sec.
mill•pond (mĭl′pŏnd′) *n.* A pond created by constructing a dam to produce a waterfall for operating a mill.
mill•race (mĭl′rās′) *n.* **1.** A fast-moving current of water that powers a mill wheel. **2.** A canal in which a millrace flows.
mill•stone (mĭl′stōn′) *n.* One of a pair of large cylindrical stones for grinding grain.
mill•stream (mĭl′strēm′) *n.* **1.** A stream whose flow is used to operate a mill. **2.** A millrace.
milt (mĭlt) *n.* **1.** Fish sperm, including the seminal fluid. **2.** The reproductive glands of male fishes when filled with milt.
Mil•ton (mĭl′tən), **John.** 1608–74. English poet.
Mil•wau•kee (mĭl-wô′kē). City of SE Wis., on Lake Michigan. *Pop.* 636,212.
mime (mīm) *n.* **1. a.** The art of pantomime. **b.** A performer or performance in pantomime. **2.** A mimic. —*v.* **mimed, mim•ing. 1.** To imitate : mimic. **2.** To portray or act in pantomime. **—mim′er** *n.*
mim•e•o•graph (mĭm′ē-ə-grăf′) *n.* A machine that makes duplicates of written, drawn, or typed material from a stencil that is fitted around an inked drum. **—mim′e•o•graph′** *v.*
mi•me•sis (mĭ-mē′sĭs, mī-) *n.* The act or process of mimicking : imitation.
mi•met•ic (mĭ-mĕt′ĭk, mī-) *adj.* Of, relating to, or using mimicry.
mim•ic (mĭm′ĭk) *v.* **-icked, -ick•ing. 1.** To imitate closely, as in speech or behavior : ape. **2.** To imitate so as to ridicule. **3.** To resemble closely : simulate. **—mim′ic** *n.* **—mim′ick•er** *n.*
mim•ic•ry (mĭm′ĭ-krē) *n., pl.* **-ries. 1.** The act, art, or practice of mimicking. **2.** A resemblance of 1 organism to another or to a natural object, as for protection from predators.
mi•mo•sa (mĭ-mō′sə, -zə) *n.* Any of various mostly tropical shrubs or trees of the genus *Mimosa,* with ball-like clusters of small flowers.
min *abbr.* minute (unit of time).
min. *abbr.* minimum.
min•a•ret (mĭn′ə-rĕt′) *n.* A tall, slender tower that is attached to a mosque.
min•a•to•ry (mĭn′ə-tôr′ē, -tōr′ē) *adj.* Conveying a menace : threatening.
mince (mĭns) *v.* **minced, minc•ing. 1.** To chop or cut into small pieces. **2.** To refrain from using, as for the sake of politeness. **—minc′ing•ly** *adv.*
mince•meat (mĭns′mēt′) *n.* Spiced finely chopped raisins, apples, and sometimes meat, used esp. for a pie filling.
†**mind** (mīnd) *n.* **1.** The part of a human being that governs thought, perception, feeling, will, memory, and imagination. **2.** Recollection : memory. **3.** Direction of an individual's thoughts : attention. **4.** Point of view : opinion. **5.** Desire : purpose. **6. a.** Intellectual capacity : intelligence. **b.** A person considered with respect to intellectual ability. **7.** Normal mental or emotional function : sanity. —*v.* **1.** To occupy oneself with <*minding* my own business> **2.** To obey. **3.** To take charge of : tend <*minded* the children> **4.** To be cautious or careful. **5.** To be concerned (about) : object (to). **6.** *Regional.* **a.** To put (a person) in mind of something : remind. **b.** To bring (an object or idea) to mind : remember. **7.** *Regional.* To have in mind as a goal or purpose : intend.
mind-blowing (mīnd′blō′ĭng) *adj. Slang.* **1.** Producing hallucinatory effects : psychedelic. **2.** Affecting the mind or emotions with overwhelming intensity.
mind-bog•gling (mīnd′bŏg′lĭng) *adj. Informal.* Overwhelming.
mind•ed (mīn′dĭd) *adj.* **1.** Disposed : inclined. **2.** Having a specified kind of mind <broad-*minded*>
mind•ful (mīnd′fəl) *adj.* Keeping in mind : heedful. **—mind′ful•ness** *n.*
mind•less (mīnd′lĭs) *adj.* **1.** Lacking intelligence, good sense, or purpose. **2.** Heedless. **—mind′less•ness** *n.*
mine[1] (mīn) *n.* **1.** An underground or in-ground excavation from which minerals, as metals or coal, can be extracted. **2.** A mineral or ore deposit. **3.** A source from which an abundant supply can be obtained. **4. a.** A tunnel dug under an enemy position. **b.** An explosive device, as one floating in the water or buried in the ground, that is detonated by a time fuse or contact. —*v.* **mined, min•ing. 1.** To extract from or as if from a mine. **2.** To dig a mine (in). **3.** To lay explosive mines in. **4.** To undermine : subvert. **—min′er** *n.*
mine[2] (mīn) *pron.* The one or ones belonging to me.
min•er•al (mĭn′ər-əl) *n.* **1.** A natural solid inorganic substance, as silver, quartz, or diamond, having a definite chemical composition and characteristic crystalline structure and being neither animal nor vegetable in origin. **2. a.** A mixture of inorganic compounds, as granite. **b.** An organic derivative, as coal. **3.** An ore. **—min′er•al** *adj.* **—min′er•al•ize′** *v.*
min•er•al•o•gy (mĭn′ə-rŏl′ə-jē, -răl′-) *n.* The scientific study of minerals. **—min′er•a•log′i•cal** (-ər-ə-lŏj′ĭ-kəl) *adj.* **—min′er•al′o•gist** *n.*
mineral oil *n.* A light oil distilled from petroleum, esp. one used as a laxative.
mineral water *n.* Water that contains dissolved minerals or gases.
min•e•stro•ne (mĭn′ĭ-strō′nē) *n.* A thick vegetable soup containing beans and pasta.
mine sweeper *n.* A ship that is designed for the detection, removal, or neutralization of underwater explosive mines.
min•gle (mĭng′gəl) *v.* **-gled, -gling.** To bring or come together in close association : mix. **—min′gler** *n.*
min•i (mĭn′ē) *n.* Something smaller than others of its kind.
min•i•a•ture (mĭn′ē-ə-chŏŏr′, mĭn′ə-, -chər) *n.* **1. a.** A model or copy in greatly reduced size. **b.** Something very small of its class. **2.** A very small painting. —*adj.* On a small or greatly reduced scale.

▲word history: The idea of smallness was not orig. part of the meaning of *miniature. Miniature* is derived from Latin *minium,* "red lead," a compound of lead used as a pigment. In medieval times chapter headings and other important divisions of a text were distinguished by being written in red, while the rest of the book was written in black. The Latin verb *miniare,* derived from *minium,* meant "to color red." *Miniatura,* the past participle, denoted the process of writing in red. Sections of a manuscript were also marked off with large ornate initial capital letters, which often were decorated with small paintings. *Miniatura* was used to denote these paintings as well. Since the paintings were necessarily very small, *miniatura* came to denote a small painting or a small object of any kind.

min•i•a•tur•ize (mĭn′ē-ə-chə-rīz′, mĭn′ə-) *v.* **-ized, -iz•ing.** To plan or make on a greatly reduced scale. **—min′i•a•tur′i•za′tion** *n.*
min•i•bike (mĭn′ē-bīk′) *n.* A small motorcycle for 1 passenger.

min•i•bus (mĭn′ē-bŭs′) *n.* A small bus.
min•i•car (mĭn′ē-kär′) *n.* A small car.
min•i•com•put•er (mĭn′ē-kəm-pyo͞o′tər) *n.* A small computer.
min•im (mĭn′ĭm) *n.* A unit of fluid measure equal to 1/60 fl dr.
min•i•mal (mĭn′ə-məl) *adj.* Of or being a minimum. **—min′i•mal•ly** *adv.*
minimal art *n.* A kind of abstract art that consists mainly of geometric forms and shapes. **—minimal artist** *n.*
min•i•mize (mĭn′ə-mīz′) *v.* **-mized, -miz•ing. 1.** To reduce to a minimum. **2.** To think of or represent as of minimum value or importance.
min•i•mum (mĭn′ə-məm) *n., pl.* **-mums** *or* **-ma** (-mə). **1.** The least possible degree or quantity. **2.** The lowest number, quantity, or degree permitted, reached, or recorded. **—min′i•mum** *adj.*
min•ion (mĭn′yən) *n.* **1.** A usu. servile dependent or follower. **2.** Someone who is much favored. **3.** A subordinate, as in an organization.
min•i•skirt (mĭn′ē-skûrt′) *n.* A very short skirt.
min•is•ter (mĭn′ĭ-stər) *n.* **1.** A pastor of a church, esp. a Protestant church : clergyman. **2.** A high officer of state who heads a governmental division. **3.** A diplomat who ranks next below an ambassador. **4.** An agent for another. *—v.* To attend to the needs of others. **—min′is•te′ri•al** (-stîr′ē-əl) *adj.* **—min′is•trant** (-strənt) *adj. & n.* **—min′is•tra′tion** *n.*
min•is•try (mĭn′ĭ-strē) *n., pl.* **-tries. 1.** The act of serving : ministration. **2. a.** Ministers of religion : clergy. **b.** The position, duties, or term of service of a minister. **3. a.** A department of government headed by a minister. **b.** The position, duties, or term of office of a minister of government. **c.** Governmental ministers as a group.
mink (mĭngk) *n., pl.* **mink** *or* **minks.** A semiaquatic weasel-like carnivore of the genus *Mustela,* esp. *M. vison,* with soft, thick, lustrous fur.
Minn. *abbr.* Minnesota.
Min•ne•ap•o•lis (mĭn′ē-ăp′ə-lĭs). City of SE Minn. *Pop.* 370,951.
Min•ne•so•ta (mĭn′ĭ-sō′tə). State of N U.S. *Cap.* St. Paul. *Pop.* 4,077,148. **—Min′ne•so′tan** *n.*
min•now (mĭn′ō) *n., pl.* **minnow** *or* **-nows.** A small freshwater fish of the family Cyprinidae, often used as bait.
mi•nor (mī′nər) *adj.* **1.** Lesser in amount, size, degree, or importance. **2.** Not legally of age. **3.** *Mus.* **a.** Having a half step between the 2nd and 3rd and 5th and 6th degrees <a *minor* scale> **b.** Based on a minor scale <a *minor* key> *—n.* **1.** One not yet of legal age. **2.** An academic subject secondary in importance to a major. *—v.* To study an academic minor.
mi•nor•i•ty (mĭ-nôr′ĭ-tē, -nŏr′-, mī-) *n., pl.* **-ties. 1.** The smaller in number of 2 groups that form a whole. **2.** A population segment that differs, as in religion, race, or sex, from the larger group to which it belongs. **3.** The state or period of being under legal age.
Minsk (mĭnsk). City of W European USSR. *Pop.* 1,215,000.
min•ster (mĭn′stər) *n.* **1.** A church belonging to a monastery. **2.** A large, important church.
min•strel (mĭn′strəl) *n.* **1.** A medieval traveling musician. **2.** A performer, often made up in imitation of a black, in a variety show featuring songs, jokes, and comic skits.
mint[1] (mĭnt) *n.* **1.** A place where coins are manufactured, esp. by a government. **2.** An enormous amount, esp. of money. *—v.* **1.** To manufacture (coins). **2.** To make up : invent. *—adj.* Undamaged as if newly minted. **—mint′age** *n.*
mint[2] (mĭnt) *n.* A plant of the genus *Mentha,* with aromatic foliage used for flavoring. **—mint′y** *adj.*
mint julep *n.* An iced and sweetened drink made of bourbon and mint leaves.
min•u•end (mĭn′yo͞o-ĕnd′) *n.* A quantity from which another is to be subtracted.
min•u•et (mĭn′yo͞o-ĕt′) *n.* A slow, stately pattern dance or the music for it.
mi•nus (mī′nəs) *prep.* **1.** *Math.* Reduced by the subtraction of : less <9 *minus* 4 equals 5.> **2.** *Informal.* Lacking : without <came *minus* her coat> *—adj.* **1.** *Math.* Less than zero : negative <a *minus* value> **2.** Slightly lower or less than <a mark of A *minus*> *—n.* **1.** The minus sign. **2.** A negative number, quantity, or quality.
min•us•cule (mĭn′ə-skyo͞ol′, mĭ-nŭs′kyo͞ol′) *adj.* Very small : tiny. *—n.* A lower-case letter.
minus sign *n.* A sign (–) used to indicate subtraction or a negative quantity.
min•ute[1] (mĭn′ĭt) *n.* **1. a.** A unit of time equal to 1/60 hour or 60 sec. **b.** A unit of angular measurement equal to 1/60 degree or 60 sec. **2. a.** A short interval of time. **b.** A particular moment in time. **3. minutes.** An official record of transactions or proceedings, esp. of a meeting.
mi•nute[2] (mī-no͞ot′, -nyo͞ot′, mĭ-) *adj.* **-nut•er, -nut•est. 1.** Extremely small : tiny. **2.** Of little significance : trifling. **3.** Characterized by careful examination of details. **—mi•nute′ly** *adv.*
minute hand *n.* The long hand that indicates the minutes on a timepiece.
min•ute•man *or* **Min•ute•man** (mĭn′ĭt-măn′) *n.* A Revolutionary War militiaman pledged to be ready to fight at a minute's notice.
mi•nu•ti•a (mĭ-no͞o′shē-ə, -nyo͞o′-, -shə) *n., pl.* **-ti•ae** (-shē-ē′). A minor detail.
minx (mĭngks) *n.* A high-spirited or impudent girl or woman.
mir•a•cle (mĭr′ə-kəl) *n.* **1.** An event that seems impossible to explain by natural laws and so is regarded as supernatural in origin or as an act of God. **2.** One that excites admiration or awe : wonder. **—mi•rac′u•lous** (mĭ-răk′yə-ləs) *adj.*
mi•rage (mĭ-räzh′) *n.* **1.** An optical illusion, caused by atmospheric conditions, in which nonexistent bodies of water, often with inverted reflections of faraway objects, are seen. **2.** Something illusory and impossible to attain.
mire (mīr) *n.* Deep, heavy mud or soil. *—v.* **mired, mir•ing.** To stick or cause to stick in or as if in mire. **—mir′y** *adj.*
mir•ror (mĭr′ər) *n.* **1.** A surface, as of glass, that reflects undiffused light to form an image of an object. **2.** Something that gives a true representation of something else. *—v.* To reflect in or as if in a mirror.
mirth (mûrth) *n.* Gaiety and merriment expressed by laughter. **—mirth′ful** *adj.* **—mirth′ful•ly** *adv.* **—mirth′ful•ness** *n.* **—mirth′less** *adj.* **—mirth′less•ly** *adv.*
mis– *pref.* **1.** Bad : badly : wrong : wrongly <*mis*conduct> **2.** Failure : lack <*mis*fire> See below for a list of self-explanatory words formed with the prefix **mis–.**
mis•ad•ven•ture (mĭs′əd-vĕn′chər) *n.* A mishap : misfortune.
mis•al•li•ance (mĭs′ə-lī′əns) *n.* An inappropriate alliance, esp. a mésalliance.
mis•an•thrope (mĭs′ən-thrōp′, mĭz′-) *n.* Someone who

misadapt
misadd
misaddress
misadjust
misadminister
misadministration
misadvise
misaim
misalign
misalignment
misallocate
misallocation
misalphabetize
misanalysis
misanalyze
misapplication
misapply
misappraisal
misarticulate
misarticulation
misassemble
misassert
misassertion
misassumption
misattribute
misattribution
misauthorization
misauthorize
misbalance
misbehave
misbehaver
misbehavior
misbelief
misbill
misbound
misbuild
miscalculate
miscalculation
miscatalog
mischannel
mischarge
miscitation
miscite
misclaim
misclassification
misclassify
miscode
miscomprehension
miscomputation
miscompute
misconnect
misconnection
misconstruction
misconstrue
miscopy
miscorrelation
miscut
misdate
misdeclare
misdeem
misdefine
misdeliver
misdelivery
misdescribe
misdescription
misdevelop
misdiagnose
misdiagnosis
misdial
misdistribution
misdivision
misdraw
miseducate
miseducation
misemphasis
misemphasize
misemploy
misemployment
misestimate
misestimation
misevaluate
misevaluation
misfashion
misfield
misfile
misfocus
misform
misformation

scorns or hates humanity. **—mis′an·throp′ic** (-thrŏp′ĭk) *adj.* **—mis·an′thro·py** (-ăn′thrə-pē) *n.*

mis·ap·pre·hend (mĭs-ăp′rĭ-hĕnd′) *v.* To understand incorrectly : misunderstand. **—mis·ap′pre·hen′sion** (-hĕn′shən) *n.*

mis·ap·pro·pri·ate (mĭs′ə-prō′prē-āt′) *v.* **1.** To appropriate wrongly. **2.** To appropriate dishonestly for one's own use. **—mis′ap·pro′pri·a′tion** *n.*

mis·be·got·ten (mĭs′bĭ-gŏt′n) *adj.* Unlawfully begotten, esp. illegitimate.

misc. *abbr.* miscellaneous.

mis·car·riage (mĭs-kăr′ĭj) *n.* **1.** Failure to achieve a proper or desired result. **2.** Premature expulsion of a nonviable fetus from the uterus.

mis·car·ry (mĭs-kăr′ē) *v.* **1.** To go wrong : fail. **2.** To undergo a miscarriage : abort.

mis·cast (mĭs-kăst′) *v.* To cast (e.g., an actor) in an inappropriate role.

mis·ce·ge·na·tion (mĭs′ĭ-jə-nā′shən, mĭ-sĕj′ə-) *n.* Marriage or cohabitation between persons of different races, esp. between white and nonwhite persons.

mis·cel·la·ne·ous (mĭs′ə-lā′nē-əs) *adj.* Consisting of a variety of elements, parts, or characteristics. **—mis′cel·la′ne·ous·ly** *adv.* **—mis′cel·la′ne·ous·ness** *n.*

mis·cel·la·ny (mĭs′ə-lā′nē) *n., pl.* **-nies. 1.** A collection of various elements, items, or ingredients. **2.** A collection of a variety of literary works.

mis·chance (mĭs-chăns′) *n.* **1.** Bad luck. **2.** An unfortunate occurrence : mishap.

mis·chief (mĭs′chĭf) *n.* **1. a.** Behavior that causes annoyance or harm. **b.** A cause of annoyance or harm. **2.** A tendency to misbehave : mischievousness. **3.** Injury caused by a specific human agency.

mis·chie·vous (mĭs′chə-vəs) *adj.* **1.** Tending to behave in a playful way. **2.** Annoying or harmful. **3.** Causing injury. **—mis′chie·vous·ly** *adv.*

mis·ci·ble (mĭs′ə-bəl) *adj. Chem.* Capable of being mixed. **—mis′ci·bil′i·ty** *n.*

mis·con·ceive (mĭs′kən-sēv′) *v.* To mistake the meaning of. **—mis′con·ceiv′er** *n.* **—mis′con·cep′tion** (-sĕp′shən) *n.*

mis·con·duct (mĭs-kŏn′dŭkt′) *n.* **1.** Improper behavior or conduct. **2.** Bad or dishonest management, as by elected officials.

mis·count (mĭs-kount′) *v.* To count incorrectly. —*n.* (mĭs′kount′). An incorrect count.

mis·cre·ant (mĭs′krē-ənt) *n.* Someone who engages in evil or criminal acts. **—mis′cre·ant** *adj.*

mis·cue (mĭs-kyo͞o′) *n.* A mistake : error. **—mis·cue′** *v.*

mis·deed (mĭs-dēd′) *n.* An improper or wrong act.

mis·de·mean·or (mĭs′dĭ-mē′nər) *n.* **1.** A misdeed. **2.** *Law.* An offense less serious than a felony.

mis·di·rect (mĭs′dĭ-rĕkt′, -dī-) *v.* To give an incorrect direction to. **—mis′di·rec′tion** *n.*

mis·do·ing (mĭs-do͞o′ĭng) *n.* Wrongful acts. **—mis·do′er** *n.*

mise en scène (mēz′äɴ sĕn′) *n.* **1.** The arrangement of properties and performers on a stage. **2.** A physical environment.

mi·ser (mī′zər) *n.* A greedy, grasping person, esp. one who hoards money. **—mi′ser·li·ness** *n.* **—mi′ser·ly** *adj.*

mis·er·a·ble (mĭz′ər-ə-bəl, mĭz′rə-) *adj.* **1.** Very unhappy or uncomfortable : wretched. **2.** Causing unhappiness or discomfort. **3.** Very poor : squalid. **4.** Very inadequate : inferior. **—mis′er·a·ble·ness** *n.* **—mis′er·a·bly** *adv.*

mis·er·y (mĭz′ə-rē) *n., pl.* **-ies. 1.** A state of suffering, as that caused by poverty : wretchedness. **2.** A source or cause of suffering : affliction. **3.** Emotional distress.

mis·fea·sance (mĭs-fē′zəns) *n. Law.* Improper and unlawful execution of an act that in itself is lawful and proper.

mis·fire (mĭs-fīr′) *v.* **1.** To fail to fire, explode, or ignite. **2.** To fail to achieve a desired result. **—mis′fire′** *n.*

mis·fit (mĭs′fĭt′, mĭs-fĭt′) *n.* **1.** An improper fit. **2.** Someone who is badly adjusted to his or her environment.

mis·for·tune (mĭs-fôr′chən) *n.* **1.** Bad fortune. **2.** An unfortunate occurrence or condition.

mis·giv·ing (mĭs-gĭv′ĭng) *n. often* **misgivings.** A feeling of concern or doubt.

mis·guide (mĭs-gīd′) *v.* To give mistaken guidance to : misdirect. **—mis·guid′ance** *n.* **—mis·guid′ed·ly** *adv.*

mis·han·dle (mĭs-hăn′dl) *v.* **1.** To handle roughly or clumsily. **2.** To manage badly or inefficiently.

mis·hap (mĭs′hăp′, mĭs-hăp′) *n.* An unfortunate accident.

mish·mash (mĭsh′măsh′) *n.* A random mixture : hodgepodge.

mis·in·ter·pret (mĭs′ĭn-tûr′prĭt) *v.* To understand or explain incorrectly. **—mis′in·ter′pre·ta′tion** *n.*

mis·judge (mĭs-jŭj′) *v.* To err in judging. **—mis·judg′ment** *n.*

mis·lay (mĭs-lā′) *v.* To put in a place one cannot remember : lose.

mis·lead (mĭs-lēd′) *v.* **1.** To lead in a wrong direction. **2.** To lead into wrongdoing or error, often by purposefully deceiving.

mis·like (mĭs-līk′) *v.* To dislike. **—mis·like′** *n.*

mis·name (mĭs-nām′) *v.* To call by an incorrect name.

mis·no·mer (mĭs-nō′mər) *n.* An inappropriate or wrong name.

mi·sog·a·my (mĭ-sŏg′ə-mē) *n.* Hatred of marriage. **—mi·sog′a·mist** *n.*

mi·sog·y·ny (mĭ-sŏj′ə-nē) *n.* Hatred of women. **—mi·sog′y·nist** *n.*

mis·place (mĭs-plās′) *v.* **1. a.** To put in an incorrect place. **b.** To mislay. **2.** To place on a wrong object <*misplaced* confidence> **—mis·place′ment** *n.*

mis·play (mĭs′plā′) *n.* A mistaken or inept play, esp. in a game. **—mis·play′** *v.*

mis·read (mĭs-rēd′) *v.* **1.** To read incorrectly. **2.** To misinterpret.

mis·rep·re·sent (mĭs-rĕp′rĭ-zĕnt′) *v.* To represent falsely, wrongly, or misleadingly. **—mis·rep′re·sen·ta′tion** *n.*

mis·rule (mĭs-ro͞ol′) *v.* To misgovern. **—mis·rule′** *n.*

miss[1] (mĭs) *v.* **1.** To fail to reach, hit, or make contact with. **2.** To fail to understand or perceive. **3.** To fail to accomplish or obtain. **4.** To fail to perform or attend. **5.** To omit. **6.** To avoid. **7.** To feel or regret the absence or loss of. **8.** To misfire. —*n.* **1.** A failure to reach, hit, or succeed. **2.** A misfire.

miss[2] (mĭs) *n.* **1. Miss.** Used as a courtesy title before the name of an unmarried girl or woman. **2.** A young unmarried woman.

Miss. *abbr.* Mississippi.

mis·sal (mĭs′əl) *n. Rom. Cath. Ch.* A book containing the prayers and responses used in the Mass throughout the year.

mis·shape (mĭs-shāp′) *v.* To deform : distort. **—mis·shap′en** *adj.*

mis·sile (mĭs′əl, -īl′) *n.* **1.** An object, as a rock, that is projected

misfunction
misgauge
misgovern
misgovernment
misgrade
mishear
misidentification
misidentify
misinfer
misinference
misinform
misinformation
misinstruct
misinstruction
misjoin
miskick
mislabel
mislearn
mislocate
mislocation
mismake
mismanage
mismanagement
mismark
mismatch
mismate
mismeasure
mismotivate
misnavigate
misnavigation
misnumber
misorder
misorient
misorientation
mispackage
mispage
mispagination
misperceive
misperception
misperform
mispicture
misplan
misposition
misprescribe
misprint
mispronounce
mispronunciation
mispublicized
mispurchase
misquotation
misquote
misrecollection
misreference
misregister
misregistration
misregulate
misrelate
misrely
misremember
misrender
misreport
misreward
misroute
mis-seat
mis-see
misset
misship
misshipment
mis-sing
missort
misspace
missteer
misstrike
misstyle
misteach
misthread
misthrow
mistime
mistitle
mistrain
mistranscribe
mistranscription
mistranslate
mistranslation
mistruth
mistype
misunion
miswire

or thrown at a target : projectile. **2.** A guided missile. **3.** A ballistic missile. **—mis′sile·ry** *n.*
miss·ing (mĭs′ĭng) *adj.* **1.** Absent. **2.** Lost. **3.** Lacking.
mis·sion (mĭsh′ən) *n.* **1. a.** A body of envoys to a foreign country. **b.** A permanent diplomatic office in a foreign country. **2. a.** A body of missionaries sent out by a church. **b.** The place where the ministry of such a body is exercised. **3.** An assignment to be carried out : task. ☆***syns:*** COMMISSION, ERRAND, OFFICE, TASK
mis·sion·ar·y (mĭsh′ə-nĕr′ē) *n., pl.* **-ies.** One sent out to do religious or charitable work. **—mis′sion·ar′y** *adj.*
Mis·sis·sip·pi (mĭs′ĭ-sĭp′ē). **1.** State of S U.S. *Cap.* Jackson. *Pop.* 2,520,638. **2.** River of C U.S., rising in NW Minn. and flowing c. 2,350 mi (3,780 km) SE to the Gulf of Mexico. **—Mis′sis·sip′pi·an** *n.*
mis·sive (mĭs′ĭv) *n.* A written message.
Mis·sou·ri (mĭ-zo͝or′ē, -zo͝or′ə). **1.** State of C U.S. *Cap.* Jefferson City. *Pop.* 4,917,444. **2.** River of the U.S., rising in W Mont. and flowing c. 2,565 mi (4,127 km) to the Mississippi. **—Mis·sou′ri·an** *n.*
mis·spell (mĭs-spĕl′) *v.* To spell incorrectly. **—mis·spell′ing** *n.*
mis·spend (mĭs-spĕnd′) *v.* To squander.
mis·state (mĭs-stāt′) *v.* To state falsely or incorrectly. **—mis·state′ment** *n.*
mis·step (mĭs-stĕp′) *n.* **1.** A wrong step. **2.** A mistake, as in behavior : blunder.
mist (mĭst) *n.* **1.** A mass of tiny water droplets in the air. **2.** Water vapor that condenses on a surface and clouds it. **3.** Something that dims or conceals. *—v.* To be, make, or become misty.
mis·take (mĭ-stāk′) *n.* **1.** A wrong statement, decision, or action : error. **2.** A misunderstanding. **—mis·tak′a·ble** *adj.* **—mis·tak′a·bly** *adv.* **—mis·take′** *v.*
mis·tak·en (mĭ-stā′kən) *adj.* **1.** Having a wrong opinion, perception, or understanding. **2.** Based on error : wrong. **3.** Misunderstood. **—mis·tak′en·ly** *adv.*
Mis·ter (mĭs′tər) *n.* **1.** Used as a title of courtesy before a man's name. **2. mister.** *Informal.* Used as a form of address without a name in speaking to a man.
mis·tle·toe (mĭs′əl-tō′) *n.* A parasitic plant, *Viscum album,* that grows on trees and has evergreen leaves and white berries.
mis·treat (mĭs-trēt′) *v.* To treat wrongly or badly : abuse. **—mis·treat′ment** *n.*
mis·tress (mĭs′trĭs) *n.* **1.** A woman in a position of control, authority, or ownership. **2.** A country enjoying supremacy <*mistress* of the hemisphere> **3.** A woman who cohabits with a man who is not her husband. **4. Mistress.** Used formerly as a title of courtesy when speaking to a woman.
mis·tri·al (mĭs-trī′əl, -trīl′) *n.* A trial that is invalid because of procedural error.
mis·trust (mĭs-trŭst′) *n.* A lack of trust : doubt. *—v.* To have no trust in : doubt or suspect. **—mis·trust′ful** *adj.* **—mis·trust′ful·ly** *adv.*
mist·y (mĭs′tē) *adj.* **-i·er, -i·est. 1.** Consisting of, marked by, or resembling mist. **2.** Clouded or obscured by or as if by mist : dim. **—mist′i·ly** *adv.* **—mist′i·ness** *n.*
mis·un·der·stand (mĭs′ŭn-dər-stănd′) *v.* To fail to understand correctly.
mis·un·der·stand·ing (mĭs′ŭn-dər-stăn′dĭng) *n.* **1.** A misinterpretation. **2.** A quarrel : disagreement.
mis·use (mĭs-yo͞oz′) *v.* **1.** To use improperly or wrongly. **2.** To mistreat : abuse. *—n.* (-yo͞os′). **1.** Improper or wrong use. **2.** Mistreatment : abuse. **—mis·us′age** *n.*
mite[1] (mīt) *n.* Any of various small, often parasitic arachnids.
mite[2] (mīt) *n.* **1.** A very small amount of money. **2. a.** A very small object or creature. **b.** A tiny amount : bit.
mi·ter (mī′tər) *n.* **1.** A tall, pointed headdress worn esp. by bishops. **2.** A joint made by fitting together 2 beveled surfaces to form a right angle. *—v.* To fit together with or meet in a miter joint.
mit·i·gate (mĭt′ĭ-gāt′) *v.* **-gat·ed, -gat·ing.** To make or become less intense, severe, or painful. **—mit′i·ga′tion** *n.* **—mit′i·ga′tive** *adj.* **—mit′i·ga′tor** *n.*
mi·to·sis (mī-tō′sĭs) *n.* **1.** The process in which the chromosomes of a cell duplicate themselves and separate into 2 identical groups just before cell division. **—mi·tot′ic** (-tŏt′ĭk) *adj.*
mitt (mĭt) *n.* **1.** A woman's glove that does not fully cover the fingers. **2.** A baseball glove, as that used by a catcher.
mit·ten (mĭt′n) *n.* A covering for the hand with 1 section for the thumb alone.
mix (mĭks) *v.* **1.** To combine or blend into a single mass. **2.** To make, create, or form by combining constituent parts **3.** To bring or come together : join. **4.** To crossbreed. **5.** To associate. **6.** To confuse <*mixed* up the instructions> **7.** To be or become involved <didn't *mix* in politics> *—n.* Something formed by mixing, esp. a packaged mixture of baking ingredients. **—mix′a·ble** *adj.*
mixed number *n.* A number, as 7½, that represents the sum of an integer and a fraction.
mix·ture (mĭks′chər) *n.* **1.** Something made by mixing. **2.** A combination of diverse qualities or elements. **3. a.** The act or process of mixing. **b.** The state of being mixed. **4.** *Chem.* A composition of substances not bound to each other.
mix-up (mĭks′ŭp′) *n.* A state of confusion : muddle.
miz·zen *also* **miz·en** (mĭz′ən) *n.* **1.** A fore-and-aft sail set on the mizzenmast. **2.** A mizzenmast.
miz·zen·mast *also* **miz·en·mast** (mĭz′ən-məst, -măst′) *n.* The 3rd mast aft on sailing ships with 3 or more masts.
ml *abbr.* milliliter.
mm *abbr.* millimeter.
Mmes. *abbr. pl. of* MRS.
Mn *symbol for* MANGANESE.
MN *abbr.* Minnesota (with Zip Code).
mne·mon·ic (nĭ-mŏn′ĭk) *adj.* Aiding or designed to aid the memory. *—n.* A mnemonic device, as a rhyme or formula.
Mo *symbol for* MOLYBDENUM.
MO *abbr.* Missouri (with Zip Code).
mo. *abbr.* month.
Mo. *abbr.* Missouri.
m.o. or **M.O.** *abbr.* **1.** mail order. **2.** medical officer. **3.** money order.
moan (mōn) *n.* A low, sustained sound, esp. of pain or sorrow. **—moan** *v.*
moat (mōt) *n.* A wide, deep, usu. water-filled ditch surrounding a castle.
mob (mŏb) *n.* **1.** A large, unruly crowd. **2.** The mass of common people : rabble. **3.** *Informal.* A gang of criminals. *—v.* **mobbed, mob·bing. 1.** To crowd around and annoy or jostle. **2.** To crowd into <passengers *mobbing* the railroad station>
▲word history: Every age has its linguistic fads and ephemeral coinages; occasionally some of them survive and become part of the standard vocabulary. In the 17th and 18th cent. the abbreviation of long words or phrases to 1 or 2 syllables had a vogue that was much deplored by the self-appointed literary watchdogs of the day. *Mob* is one such abbreviation that caught on. It is short for *mobile,* which was used in the early 17th cent. to denote "the masses." In this usage *mobile* was itself a shortening of the Latin phrase *mobile vulgus,* "the excitable populace." The note of contempt orig. inherent in English *mob* was also found in the Latin phrase.
mo·bile (mō′bəl, -bēl′, -bīl′) *adj.* **1.** Capable of being moved or of moving. **2.** Changing readily in mood, expression, or appearance. **3.** Enjoying or affording opportunity for a change from 1 social status to another. *—n.* (mō′bēl′). A sculpture consisting of parts that move, esp. in response to air currents. **—mo·bil′i·ty** (-bĭl′ĭ-tē) *n.*
Mo·bile (mō-bēl′). Port city of SW Ala. *Pop.* 200,452.
mobile home *n.* A trailer serving as a permanent home.
mo·bi·lize (mō′bə-līz′) *v.* **-lized, -liz·ing. 1.** To put into motion. **2.** To assemble and prepare for war. **3.** To organize for action or use. ☆***syns:*** MARSHAL, MUSTER, ORGANIZE, RALLY **—mo′bi·li·za′tion** *n.*
mob·ster (mŏb′stər) *n.* A member of a gang of criminals.
moc·ca·sin (mŏk′ə-sĭn) *n.* A soft leather shoe or slipper.
mo·cha (mō′kə) *n.* **1.** A rich coffee of high quality. **2.** A flavoring made of coffee, often with chocolate or cocoa.
mock (mŏk) *v.* **1.** To treat with ridicule or scorn : deride. **2.** To imitate in derision or sport. *—adj.* False : sham. **—mock′er** *n.* **—mock′ing·ly** *adv.*
mock·er·y (mŏk′ə-rē) *n., pl.* **-ies. 1.** Scornful derision or ridicule. **2.** An object of scorn or ridicule. **3.** A false, derisive, or impudent imitation. **4.** Something ludicrously unsuitable or futile. ☆***syns:*** CARICATURE, FARCE, PARODY, SHAM, TRAVESTY
mock-he·ro·ic (mŏk′hĭ-rō′ĭk) *n.* A satirical imitation or burlesque of the heroic manner or style.
mock·ing·bird (mŏk′ĭng-bûrd′) *n.* A songbird, *Mimus polyglottos,* that is common in the S U.S. and often mimics the songs of other birds.
mock orange *n.* Any of several deciduous shrubs of the genus *Philadelphus,* bearing white, usu. fragrant flowers.
mock·up *also* **mock-up** (mŏk′ŭp′) *n.* An often full-sized model of a structure, as an airplane, used for study, demonstration, or testing.
mod (mŏd) *n.* A modern and unconventionally fashionable style of dress. *—adj.* Modern, esp. unconventional in dress.
mode (mōd) *n.* **1. a.** A way or method of doing something : manner. **b.** A particular variety, form, or manner. **2.** The value occurring most frequently in a set of data. **3.** The current or preferred fashion or style in dress. **—mod′al** (mōd′l) *adj.*
mod·el (mŏd′l) *n.* **1.** A miniature representation of an object.

2. A pattern on which something not yet produced will be based. **3.** A design or type. **4.** One serving as an example to be emulated or imitated. **5. a.** One who poses for a photographer or artist. **b.** A fashion mannequin. —*v.* **-eled, -el•ing** or **-elled, -el•ling. 1.** To construct or plan, esp. after a pattern. **2.** To display (clothing) by wearing. **3.** To work as a fashion mannequin. —*adj.* **1.** Serving as or used as a model. **2.** Worthy of imitation <a *model* student> **—mod'el•er** *n.*

mod•er•ate (mŏd'ər-ĭt) *adj.* **1.** Not extreme or excessive. **2.** Temperate. **3. a.** Of average extent or quality. **b.** Mediocre. **4.** Opposed to extreme political measures or views. —*n.* Someone who holds moderate political views or opinions. —*v.* (-ə-rāt') **-at•ed, -at•ing. 1.** To make or become less extreme or intense. **2.** To preside over as a moderator. **—mod'er•a'tion** *n.*

mod•er•a•tor (mŏd'ə-rā'tər) *n.* **1.** One that moderates. **2.** A person who presides over a discussion or meeting.

mod•ern (mŏd'ərn) *adj.* **1.** Of, relating to, or typical of the recent past or the present. **2.** Advanced, as in style : up-to-date. **—mod'ern** *n.* **—mo•der'ni•ty** (mə-dûr'nĭ-tē) *n.* **—mod'ern•ly** *adv.*

mod•ern•ize (mŏd'ər-nīz') *v.* **-ized, -iz•ing.** To make or become modern, as in appearance or style. ☆**syns:** REFURBISH, REJUVENATE, RENOVATE, RESTORE, REVAMP, UPDATE **—mod'ern•i•za'tion** *n.*

mod•ern•ism (mŏd'ər-nĭz'əm) *n.* A theory, practice, or belief characteristic of modern times. **—mod'ern•ist'ic** *adj.*

mod•est (mŏd'ĭst) *adj.* **1.** Having or showing a lack of conceit or vanity. **2.** Retiring or reserved : diffident. **3.** Observing conventional proprieties in behavior, speech, and dress. **4.** Of moderate amount or size. ☆**syns:** DEMURE, DIFFIDENT, SELF-EFFACING, SHY, TIMID **—mod'es•ty** *n.*

mod•i•cum (mŏd'ĭ-kəm) *n.* A small amount.

mod•i•fy (mŏd'ə-fī') *v.* **-fied, -fy•ing. 1.** To alter : change. **2.** To make or become less extreme : moderate. **3.** To limit or qualify the meaning of (e.g., a word or phrase). **—mod'i•fi'a•ble** *adj.* **—mod'i•fi•ca'tion** *n.* **—mod'i•fi'er** *n.*

mod•ish (mō'dĭsh) *adj.* Fashionable : stylish <a *modish* dress> **—mod'ish•ly** *adv.* **—mod'ish•ness** *n.*

mo•diste (mō-dēst') *n.* One who makes, designs, or sells fashionable clothing for women.

mod•u•late (mŏj'ə-lāt', mŏd'yə-) *v.* **-lat•ed, -lat•ing. 1.** To soften : temper. **2.** To vary the tone or intensity of. **3.** *Mus.* To pass from 1 key or tonality to another by a chord progression. **4.** *Electron.* To vary the frequency, amplitude, or phase of (a carrier wave). **—mod'u•la'tion** *n.* **—mod'u•la'tive, mod'u•la•to'ry** (-lə-tôr'ē, -tōr'ē) *adj.* **—mod'u•la'tor** *n.*

mod•ule (mŏj'o͞ol, mŏd'yo͞ol) *n.* **1.** One of a series of standardized units or components that function together in a system. **2.** *Electron.* A self-contained assembly of electronic components and circuitry, as a computer stage. **3.** A self-contained unit of a spacecraft for performing a particular task. **—mod'u•lar** (-ə-lər) *adj.*

mo•dus op•er•an•di (mō'dəs ŏp'ə-răn'dē, -dī') *n.* A method of working or operating.

modus vi•ven•di (vĭ-vĕn'dē, -dī') *n.* A way of life.

Mog•a•dish•o (mŏg'ə-dĭsh'o͞o). Cap. of Somalia, on the Indian Ocean. *Pop.* 230,000.

mo•gul (mō'gəl) *n.* A very powerful or important person.

mo•hair (mō'hâr') *n.* A fabric or yarn made of the silky hair of the Angora goat.

Mo•ham•med (mō-hăm'ĭd, -hä'mĭd). 570?–632. Arab founder of Islam.

Mo•ham•med•an (mō-hăm'ĭ-dən) *adj.* Moslem. **—Mo•ham'med•an** *n.* **—Mo•ham'med•an•ism** *n.*

Mohs scale (mōz) *n.* A scale for classifying the relative hardness of minerals that ranges from 1 for the softest to 15 for the hardest.

moi•e•ty (moi'ĭ-tē) *n.*, *pl.* **-ties. 1.** A half. **2.** A portion : part.

moil (moil) *v.* To toil : drudge. **—moil** *n.*

moi•ré (mwä-rā') *n.* Fabric, esp. silk, with a wavy pattern.

moist (moist) *adj.* Slightly wet : damp. **—moist'ly** *adv.* **—moist'ness** *n.*

mois•ten (moi'sən) To make or become moist. **—mois'ten•er** *n.*

mois•ture (mois'chər) *n.* Dampness, esp. that caused by water present in the air as vapor. **—mois'tur•ize'** *v.* **—mois'tur•iz'er** *n.*

mois•ture•proof (mois'chər-pro͞of') *adj.* Impervious to moisture.

Mo•ja•ve *also* **Mo•ha•ve** (mō-hä'vē). Desert region of S Calif.

mol. *abbr.* molecular; molecule.

mo•lar (mō'lər) *n.* A tooth located behind the bicuspids that has a broad surface for grinding food. **—mo'lar** *adj.*

mo•las•ses (mə-lăs'ĭz) *n.* A dark, thick syrup produced in refining sugar.

mold[1] (mōld) *n.* **1.** A hollow form in which a liquid or plastic substance can be shaped. **2.** A frame around or on which something can be shaped or formed. **3.** Something shaped on or made in a mold. **4.** General shape : form. **5.** Distinctive character or type. —*v.* To shape or form in or as if in a mold. **—mold'a•ble** *adj.*

mold[2] (mōld) *n.* **1.** A growth of fungus often producing disintegration of organic matter. **2.** A fungus that forms mold. —*v.* To become moldy.

mold[3] (mōld) *n.* Loose soil that is rich in decayed plant and animal material.

mold•board (mōld'bôrd', -bōrd') *n.* The curved plate of a plow that turns over the soil.

mold•er (mōl'dər) *v.* To crumble or cause to crumble : disintegrate.

mold•ing (mōl'dĭng) *n.* **1.** Something that is molded. **2.** The act or process of shaping or forming in a mold. **3.** An ornamental strip used to decorate a surface.

mold•y (mōl'dē) *adj.* **-i•er, -i•est. 1.** Of, like, or covered with mold. **2.** Damp or musty, as from decay. **—mold'i•ness** *n.*

mole[1] (mōl) *n.* A small, usu. slightly raised and dark growth on the human skin.

mole[2] (mōl) *n.* A small, burrowing mammal with a narrow snout, minute eyes, and silky fur.

mole[3] (mōl) *n.* A massive stone wall used as a breakwater.

mo•lec•u•lar (mə-lĕk'yə-lər) *adj.* Of, relating to, or caused by molecules.

molecular biology *n.* The branch of biology in which the structure and development of biological systems are studied in terms of their molecular constituents. **—molecular biologist** *n.*

mol•e•cule (mŏl'ĭ-kyo͞ol') *n.* The simplest structural unit that has the characteristic physical and chemical properties of a compound.

mole•hill (mōl'hĭl') *n.* A small mound of earth dug up by a mole.

mole•skin (mōl'skĭn') *n.* **1.** The fur of the mole. **2.** A sturdy napped cotton fabric used esp. to make clothing.

mo•lest (mə-lĕst') *v.* **1.** To bother or annoy. **2.** To accost sexually. **—mo'les•ta'tion** (mō'lĕ-stā'shən) *n.* **—mo•lest'er** *n.*

Mo•lière (mōl-yâr'). Jean Baptiste Poquelin. 1622–73. French playwright and actor.

moll (mŏl) *n.* *Slang.* The girl friend of a gangster.

mol•li•fy (mŏl'ə-fī') *v.* **-fied, -fy•ing. 1.** To soothe the temper of : placate. **2.** To soften. **3.** To make less intense. **—mol'li•fi•ca'tion** *n.*

mol•lusk *also* **mol•lusc** (mŏl'əsk) *n.* Any of various members of the phylum Mollusca, largely marine invertebrates, including the edible shellfish.

mol•ly•cod•dle (mŏl'ē-kŏd'l) *n.* A pampered boy or man. —*v.* To spoil by pampering : coddle.

Mol•o•tov cocktail (mŏl'ə-tôf', mō'lə-) *n.* A makeshift incendiary bomb consisting of a breakable container full of flammable liquid and fitted with a rag wick that is ignited just before the bomb is thrown.

molt (mōlt) *v.* To shed an external covering, as horns, feathers, or skin, which is replaced periodically by new growth. —*n.* The act of molting.

mol•ten (mōl'tn) *adj.* Liquefied by heat : melted and often glowing.

mo•lyb•de•num (mə-lĭb'də-nəm) *n.* *Symbol* **Mo** A hard gray metallic element used to strengthen steel alloys.

mom (mŏm) *n.* *Informal.* Mother.

mo•ment (mō'mənt) *n.* **1.** A brief interval of time : instant. **2.** A particular point in time, esp. the present. **3.** A time of excellence or importance. **4.** Importance. ☆**syns:** FLASH, INSTANT, JIFFY, MINUTE, SECOND, TRICE

mo•men•tar•i•ly (mō'mən-târ'ə-lē) *adv.* **1.** For only a moment. **2.** Very soon. **3.** From moment to moment.

mo•men•tar•y (mō'mən-tĕr'ē) *adj.* **1. a.** Lasting only a moment. **b.** Ephemeral. **2.** Present or occurring at every moment.

mo•men•tous (mō-mĕn'təs) *adj.* Of great importance : significant. **—mo•men'tous•ly** *adv.* **—mo•men'tous•ness** *n.*

mo•men•tum (mō-mĕn'təm) *n.*, *pl.* **-ta** (-tə) *or* **-tums. 1.** The product of a body's mass and linear velocity. **2.** Speed or force of motion : impetus.

Mon. *abbr.* Monday.

Mon•a•co (mŏn'ə-kō', mə-nä'kō). Principality on the Mediterranean coast in the S of France. *Cap.* Monaco-Ville. *Pop.* 30,000. **—Mon'a•can** *adj.* & *n.*

mon•arch (mŏn'ərk, -ärk') *n.* **1.** A usu. hereditary sovereign of a kingdom or empire, as a king or queen. **2.** One of great power or sovereign position. **3.** A very large orange and black butterfly, *Danaus plexippus.* **—mo•nar'chic** (mə-när'kĭk), **mo•nar'chi•cal** *adj.*

mon·ar·chism (mŏn′ər-kĭz′əm) *n.* Belief in or advocacy of monarchic government. **—mon′ar·chist** (-kĭst) *n.* **—mon′ar·chis′tic** *adj.*
mon·ar·chy (mŏn′ər-kē) *n., pl.* **-chies. 1.** Government by a monarch. **2.** A state or nation ruled by a monarch.
mon·as·ter·y (mŏn′ə-stĕr′ē) *n., pl.* **-ies.** A residence of a community of persons under religious vows, esp. monks. **—mon′as·te′ri·al** (-stîr′ē-əl, -stĕr′-) *adj.*
mo·nas·tic (mə-năs′tĭk) *adj.* Of, relating to, or typical of monasteries or monks or life in monasteries.
mo·nas·ti·cism (mə-năs′tĭ-sĭz′əm) *n.* The monastic life or system.
mon·au·ral (mŏn-ôr′əl, mō-nôr′-) *adj.* Of or relating to a system of transmitting, recording, or reproducing sound by techniques in which 1 or more sources are channeled into a single carrier.
Mon·day (mŭn′dē, -dā′) *n.* The 2nd day of the week.
Mo·net (mō-nā′), **Claude.** 1840–1926. French painter.
mon·e·tar·y (mŏn′ĭ-tĕr′ē, mŭn′-) *adj.* Of or relating to money or the means by which it is circulated. **—mon′e·tar′i·ly** *adv.*
mon·ey (mŭn′ē) *n., pl.* **-eys** or **-ies. 1. a.** Something, as paper or metal currency, that is officially established as being exchangeable for goods and services. **b.** Currency officially issued by a government. **2.** Wealth considered in terms of its monetary value.
mon·eyed *also* **mon·ied** (mŭn′ēd) *adj.* **1.** Having ample money : wealthy. **2.** Composed of or arising from money.
mon·ey·lend·er (mŭn′ē-lĕn′dər) *n.* Someone whose business is lending money at interest.
mon·ey·mak·ing (mŭn′ē-mā′kĭng) *n.* The acquisition of money. *—adj.* **1.** Engaged in or successful at moneymaking. **2.** Producing profit : lucrative. **—mon′ey·mak′er** *n.*
money order *n.* An order, usu. issued by a bank or post office, for the payment of a stated amount of money to the payee named on the order.
mon·ger (mŭng′gər, mŏng′-) *n.* **1.** A dealer. **2.** A person who disseminates or stirs up something undesirable.
mon·go (mŏng′gō) *n., pl.* **-go.** See *tugrik* at CURRENCY TABLE.
Mon·gol (mŏng′gəl, -gōl′, mŏn′-) *n.* **1.** A native or inhabitant of Mongolia. **2.** A member of the Mongoloid ethnic division. **—Mon′gol** *adj.*
Mon·go·li·a (mŏng-gō′lē-ə, mŏn-). **1.** Region of EC Asia, extending from Siberia to N China. **2.** Country of NC Asia. *Cap.* Ulan Bator. *Pop.* 1,625,000.
Mon·go·li·an (mŏng-gō′lē-ən, -gōl′yən, mŏn-) *n.* **1.** A native or inhabitant of Mongolia. **2.** A member of the Mongoloid ethnic division. **—Mon·go′li·an** *adj.*
mon·gol·ism (mŏng′gə-lĭz′əm, mŏn′-) *n.* Down's syndrome.
Mon·gol·oid (mŏng′gə-loid′, mŏn′-) *adj.* **1.** Of, relating to, or designating a major ethnic division of the human species whose members characteristically have yellowish-brown to white pigmentation. **2. mongoloid.** Of, affected with, or pertaining to Down's syndrome. **—Mon′gol·oid′** *n.*
mon·goose (mŏng′gōōs′, mŏn′-) *n., pl.* **-goos·es.** A chiefly African or Asian carnivorous mammal, esp. of the genus *Herpestes*, that has the ability to kill venomous snakes.
mon·grel (mŭng′grəl, mŏng′-) *n.* An animal or plant, esp. a dog, that results from interbreeding.
mon·ied (mŭn′ēd) *adj. var. of* MONEYED.
mon·ies (mŭn′ēz) *n. var. pl. of* MONEY.
mon·i·ker or **mon·ick·er** (mŏn′ĭ-kər) *n. Slang.* A person's name.
mo·nism (mō′nĭz′əm, mŏn′ĭz′-) *n.* A metaphysical theory that reality is a unified whole. **—mo′nist** *n.*
mo·ni·tion (mō-nĭsh′ən, mə-) *n.* A caution or warning.
mon·i·tor (mŏn′ĭ-tər) *n.* **1.** A student who is assigned to aid a teacher. **2. a.** A device for recording or controlling an activity or process. **b.** A screen on which the picture being picked up by a television camera is checked or viewed. *—v.* **1.** To check (the transmission quality of a signal) by a receiver. **2.** To test for radiation intensity. **3.** To track by or as if by an electronic device. **4.** To check by means of a receiver for significant content. **5.** To keep watch over : supervise <*monitor* the history test> **—mon′i·to′ri·al** (-tôr′ē-əl, -tōr′-) *adj.*
mon·i·to·ry (mŏn′ĭ-tôr′ē, -tōr′ē) *adj.* Giving a caution or warning.
monk (mŭngk) *n.* A man who belongs to a religious brotherhood and lives in a monastery. **—monk′ish** *adj.* **—monk′ish·ly** *adv.* **—monk′ish·ness** *n.*
mon·key (mŭng′kē) *n., pl.* **-keys.** A member of the order Primates, excluding man, esp. one of the long-tailed smaller species as distinguished from the larger apes. *—v. Informal.* **1.** To play mischievously or idly : fool. **2.** To tamper.
mon·key·shine (mŭng′kē-shīn′) *n. often* **monkeyshines.** *Slang.* A prank.
monkey wrench *n.* A wrench that has 1 adjustable jaw.
monk's cloth *n.* A heavy cotton cloth in a coarse basket weave.
monks·hood (mŭngks′hŏŏd′) *n.* A usu. poisonous plant of the genus *Aconitum*, having variously colored hooded flowers.
mon·o[1] (mŏn′ō) *n.* Mononucleosis.
mon·o[2] (mŏn′ō) *adj.* Monaural.
mon·o·chro·mat·ic (mŏn′ə-krō-măt′ĭk) *adj.* Of, consisting of, or having 1 color. **—mon′o·chro·mat′i·cal·ly** *adv.*
mon·o·cle (mŏn′ə-kəl) *n.* An eyeglass for 1 eye.
mon·o·cot·y·le·don (mŏn′ə-kŏt′l-ēd′n) *n.* Any of various plants of the Monocotyledonae, a major division of angiosperms, marked by a single embryonic seed leaf appearing at germination. **—mon′o·cot′y·le′don·ous** *adj.*
mo·noc·u·lar (mō-nŏk′yə-lər, mə-) *adj.* **1.** Of, relating to, or having 1 eye. **2.** Adapted to the use of only 1 eye.
mon·o·dy (mŏn′ə-dē) *n., pl.* **-dies.** A dirge or elegy. **—mo·nod′ic** (mə-nŏd′ĭk) *adj.* **—mon′o·dist** (-dĭst) *n.*
mo·nog·a·my (mə-nŏg′ə-mē) *n.* Marriage with only 1 person at a time. **—mo·nog′a·mist** *n.* **—mo·nog′a·mous** *adj.*
mon·o·gram (mŏn′ə-grăm′) *n.* A design consisting of 1 or more of the initials of a name. *—v.* **-grammed, -gram·ming** or **-gramed, -gram·ing.** To mark with a monogram.
mon·o·graph (mŏn′ə-grăf′) *n.* A scholarly treatise on a particular and usu. limited subject. **—mon′o·graph′ic** *adj.*
mon·o·lin·gual (mŏn′ə-lĭng′gwəl) *adj.* Using or knowing only 1 language.
mon·o·lith (mŏn′ə-lĭth′) *n.* **1.** A single large stone, as one used in architecture or sculpture. **2.** Something, as a large organization, that constitutes a uniform single unit. **—mon′o·lith′ic** *adj.*
mon·o·logue *also* **mon·o·log** (mŏn′ə-lôg′, -lŏg′) *n.* **1.** A long speech by 1 person that often precludes conversation. **2.** A soliloquy. **3.** A continuous series of jokes and stories delivered by a comedian. **—mo·nol′o·gist** (mə-nŏl′ə-jĭst, mŏn′ə-lô′gĭst, -lŏg′ĭst) *n.*
mon·o·ma·ni·a (mŏn′ə-mā′nē-ə, -mān′yə) *n.* **1.** Pathological obsession with a single idea. **2.** An intense concentration on 1 subject. **—mon′o·ma′ni·ac′** *n.* **—mon′o·ma·ni′a·cal** (-mə-nī′ə-kəl) *adj.*
mon·o·mer (mŏn′ə-mər) *n. Chem.* A molecule that can be chemically bound as a unit of a polymer. **—mon′o·mer′ic** (-mĕr′ĭk) *adj.*
mo·no·mi·al (mō-nō′mē-əl, mə-) *n.* An algebraic expression having only 1 term. **—mo·no′mi·al** *adj.*
mon·o·nu·cle·ar (mŏn′ō-nōō′klē-ər, -nyōō′-) *adj.* Having a single nucleus.
mon·o·nu·cle·o·sis (mŏn′ō-nōō′klē-ō′sĭs, -nyōō′-) *n.* An infectious disease marked by the presence of an abnormally large number of mononuclear leukocytes in the bloodstream.
mon·o·nu·cle·o·tide (mŏn′ō-nōō′klē-ə-tīd′, -nyōō′-) *n.* A nucleotide containing 1 molecule each of a phosphoric acid, a pentose, and either a purine or pyrimidine base.
mon·o·phon·ic (mŏn′ə-fŏn′ĭk) *adj.* Monaural.
mon·o·plane (mŏn′ə-plān′) *n.* An airplane with a single pair of wings.
mo·nop·o·ly (mə-nŏp′ə-lē) *n., pl.* **-lies. 1.** Exclusive control, as of a commodity or service, by 1 group. **2.** A company, person, or group having a monopoly. **3.** A commodity or service controlled by 1 group. **—mo·nop′o·list** *n.* **—mo·nop′o·lis′tic** *adj.* **—mo·nop′o·li·za′tion** *n.* **—mo·nop′o·lize′** *v.*
mon·o·rail (mŏn′ə-rāl′) *n.* **1.** A single rail on which a wheeled vehicle can travel. **2.** A vehicle that travels on a monorail.
mon·o·so·di·um glu·ta·mate (mŏn′ə-sō′dē-əm glōō′tə-māt′) *n.* Sodium glutamate.
mon·o·syl·la·ble (mŏn′ə-sĭl′ə-bəl) *n.* A word consisting of 1 syllable. **—mon′o·syl·lab′ic** (-sĭ-lăb′ĭk) *adj.* **—mon′o·syl·lab′i·cal·ly** *adv.*
mon·o·the·ism (mŏn′ə-thē-ĭz′əm) *n.* The belief or doctrine that there is only 1 God. **—mon′o·the′ist** *n.* **—mon′o·the·is′tic** *adj.*
mon·o·tone (mŏn′ə-tōn′) *n.* A succession of sounds, syllables, or words in a single unvarying tone or pitch.
mo·not·o·nous (mə-nŏt′n-əs) *adj.* **1.** Sounded or uttered in a single unvarying tone or pitch. **2.** Lacking in variety : repetitiously dull. **—mo·not′o·nous·ly** *adv.* **—mo·not′o·ny** *n.*
mon·ox·ide (mə-nŏk′sīd′) *n.* An oxide in which each molecule contains 1 oxygen atom.
Mon·ro·vi·a (mən-rō′vē-ə). Cap. of Liberia, in the NW. *Pop.* 229,300.
Mon·roe (mən-rō′), **James.** 1758–1831. 5th U.S. President (1817–25).
Mon·sei·gneur (mōɴ′sān-yœr′) *n., pl.* **Mes·sei·gneurs**

(mā'săn-yœr'). A French title of honor or respect given to dignitaries, as princes.

Mon•sieur (mə-syœ') *n., pl.* **Mes•sieurs** (mā-syœ'). Used as a courtesy title with the name of a Frenchman.

Mon•si•gnor (mŏn-sēn'yər) *n., pl.* **Mon•si•gnors** *or* **Mon•si•gno•ri** (mŏn'sēn-yôr'ē, -yōr'ē). A title given to certain Roman Catholic prelates.

mon•soon (mŏn-so͞on') *n.* A wind system that affects the climate of a large area and reverses direction seasonally, esp. the one that produces wet and dry seasons in India and S Asia.

mon•ster (mŏn'stər) *n.* **1.** A structurally abnormal or grotesquely deformed animal or plant. **2.** An animal, plant, or object of frightening or strange shape. **3.** An extremely vicious or wicked person. **–mon•stros'i•ty** (-strŏs'ĭ-tē) *n.* **–mon'strous** *adj.* **–mon'strous•ly** *adv.* **–mon'strous•ness** *n.*

mon•strance (mŏn'strəns) *n.* A receptacle in which the consecrated Host is held and displayed.

Mont. *abbr.* Montana.

mon•tage (mŏn-täzh', môN-) *n.* **1.** An artistic composition, esp. a composite photograph, made by combining and arranging several separate or different components. **2.** A rapid sequence of thematically related short scenes or images in a motion picture or television program.

Mon•tan•a (mŏn-tăn'ə). State of NW U.S. *Cap.* Helena. *Pop.* 786,690. **–Mon•tan'an** *n.*

Mon•te Car•lo (mŏn'tē kär'lō). Resort town of Monaco. *Pop.* 9,948.

Mon•te•vi•de•o (mŏn'tə-vĭ-dā'ō). Cap. of Uruguay, in the S. *Pop.* 1,229,700.

Mont•gom•er•y (mŏnt-gŭm'ər-ē, -gŭm'rē). Cap. of Ala., in the C part. *Pop.* 176,860.

month (mŭnth) *n.* **1.** One of the 12 divisions of a year. **2. a.** A period of 4 weeks. **b.** A period of 30 days.

month•ly (mŭnth'lē) *adj.* **1.** Occurring or payable each month. **2.** Continuing for a month. *–n., pl.* **-lies.** A publication issued once a month. **–month'ly** *adv.*

Mont•pe•lier (mŏnt-pēl'yər). Cap. of Vt., in the C part. *Pop.* 8,241.

Mon•tre•al (mŏn'trē-ôl'). City of S Que., Canada, on an island in the St. Lawrence R. *Pop.* 1,080,546.

Montreal canoe *n. Can.* A large canoe used in the early Canadian fur trade.

mon•u•ment (mŏn'yə-mənt) *n.* **1.** A structure, as a statue, built as a memorial to an event or person. **2.** A place, area, or region set aside as public property by a government, as for its historical or aesthetic significance.

mon•u•men•tal (mŏn'yə-mĕn'tl) *adj.* **1.** Of, similar to, or serving as a monument. **2.** Impressively large : massive. **3.** Very important. **4.** Enormous <*monumental* arrogance> **–mon'u•men'tal•ly** *adv.*

moo (mo͞o) *v.* To emit the deep, bellowing sound made by a cow. **–moo** *n.*

mooch (mo͞och) *v. Slang.* To get by wheedling or coaxing : beg. **–mooch'er** *n.*

mood[1] (mo͞od) *n.* **1.** A temporary state of emotion or mind : feeling. **2.** Prevailing spirit : disposition.

mood[2] (mo͞od) *n.* A verb form or set of verb forms inflected to indicate whether the action or state expressed is viewed as fact, possibility, or command.

mood•y (mo͞o'dē) *adj.* **-i•er, -i•est. 1.** Given to moods, esp. of gloom : temperamental. **2.** Morose : gloomy. **–mood'i•ly** *adv.* **–mood'i•ness** *n.*

moon (mo͞on) *n.* **1.** The natural satellite of the earth. **2.** A natural satellite that revolves around a planet. **3.** Moonlight. *–v.* To pass time in romantic reverie.

moon•beam (mo͞on'bēm') *n.* A ray of moonlight.

moon•light (mo͞on'līt') *n.* The light of the moon. *–v. Informal.* To work at a job supplementary to one's regular one. **–moon'light'er** *n.*

moon•lit (mo͞on'lĭt') *adj.* Illuminated by moonlight.

moon•scape (mo͞on'skāp') *n.* **1.** A view or picture of the moon's surface. **2.** A desolate landscape.

moon•shine (mo͞on'shīn') *n.* **1.** Moonlight. **2.** *Informal.* Vacuous or inane talk. **3.** *Slang.* Illegally distilled whiskey.

moon shot *n.* The launching of a spacecraft to the moon.

moon•stone (mo͞on'stōn') *n.* A translucent form of feldspar with a pearly luster that is used as a gem.

moon•struck (mo͞on'strŭk') *adj.* **1.** Mentally unbalanced. **2.** Filled with romantic sentiment.

moon•ward (mo͞on'wərd) *adv.* Toward the moon.

moor[1] (mo͝or) *v.* To make fast by means of lines, cables, or anchors. **–moor'age** *n.*

moor[2] (mo͝or) *n.* A broad expanse of open land, often with boggy areas and patches of low shrubs, as heather.

Moor (mo͝or) *n.* One of a N African people of mixed Berber and Arab descent who invaded and conquered Spain in the 8th cent. **–Moor'ish** *adj.*

moor•ing (mo͝or'ĭng) *n.* **1.** A place where a ship or aircraft can be moored. **2.** *often* **moorings.** A stabilizing element.

moose (mo͞os) *n., pl.* **moose.** A very large North American deer, *Alces americana,* with a broad pendulous muzzle.

moot (mo͞ot) *v.* **1.** To bring up as a subject for debate or discussion. **2.** To debate or discuss. *–adj.* **1.** Open to debate : arguable. **2.** Having no legal significance.

mop (mŏp) *n.* A cleaning implement used esp. for floors and consisting of absorbent material attached to a handle. *–v.* **mopped, mop•ping.** To clean or wash with or as if with a mop. **–mop up.** To complete a task or action.

mope (mōp) *v.* **moped, mop•ing. 1.** To be apathetic or dejected. **2.** To move in a leisurely manner : dawdle. **–mop'er** *n.*

mo•ped (mō'pĕd') *n.* A motorbike that can be pedaled.

mop•pet (mŏp'ĭt) *n.* A child.

mop•up (mŏp'ŭp') *n.* The act or process of completing a task or action.

mo•raine (mə-rān') *n.* Debris, as boulders and stones, deposited by a glacier.

mor•al (môr'əl, mŏr'-) *adj.* **1.** Of or pertaining to the principles of right and wrong. **2.** In accordance with standards of right conduct : virtuous. **3.** Arising from the inner sense of right and wrong. **4.** Psychological rather than physical or concrete <*moral* support> **5.** Likely but not proved <a *moral* certainty> *–n.* **1.** The principle or lesson taught by a story, event, or experience. **2. morals.** Conduct, esp. sexual conduct, with regard to standards of right and wrong. **–mor'al•ly** *adv.*

mo•rale (mə-răl') *n.* **1.** The state of mind of an individual with respect to the tasks he or she is expected to perform. **2.** Esprit de corps.

mor•al•ist (môr'ə-lĭst, mŏr'-) *n.* **1.** Someone who is concerned with moral principles and questions. **2.** Someone who wishes to regulate the morals of others. **–mor'al•ism** *n.* **–mor'a•lis'tic** *adj.* **–mor'al•is'ti•cal•ly** *adv.*

mo•ral•i•ty (mə-răl'ĭ-tē, mô-) *n., pl.* **-ties. 1.** The quality of being virtuous. **2.** Moral behavior : virtue.

mor•al•ize (môr'ə-līz', mŏr'-) *v.* **-ized, -iz•ing.** To think, discuss, or judge in terms of morality. **–mor'al•i•za'tion** *n.* **–mor'al•iz'er** *n.*

mo•rass (mə-răs', mô-) *n.* **1.** A marsh or bog. **2.** Something that hinders, engulfs, or overwhelms.

mor•a•to•ri•um (môr'ə-tôr'ē-əm, -tōr'-, mŏr'-) *n., pl.* **-ums** *or* **-to•ri•a** (-tôr'ē-ə, -tōr'-). A temporary pause in activity.

mo•ray (môr'ā, mə-rā') *n.* Any of various often voracious marine eels of the family Muraenidae, of chiefly tropical waters.

mor•bid (môr'bĭd) *adj.* **1.** Of, pertaining to, or caused by disease. **2.** Preoccupied with unwholesome feelings or matters. **3.** Gruesome : grisly. ☆***syns:*** MACABRE, SICK, SICKLY, UNHEALTHY, UNWHOLESOME **–mor•bid'i•ty** (-bĭd'ĭ-tē), **mor'bid•ness** *n.* **–mor'bid•ly** *adv.*

mor•da•cious (môr-dā'shəs) *adj.* **1.** Prone to biting. **2.** Sarcastic, as in manner : caustic. **–mor•da'cious•ly** *adv.* **–mor•dac'i•ty** (-dăs'ĭ-tē) *n.*

mor•dant (môr'dnt) *adj.* **1.** Biting : caustic. **2.** Incisive : trenchant. **–mor'dan•cy** *n.* **–mor'dant•ly** *adv.*

more (môr, mōr) *adj.* **1.** Greater, as in number, size, or degree. **2.** Additional : supplementary. *–n.* An additional or larger quantity, number, degree, or amount. *–adv.* **1.** In or to a greater extent or degree. **2.** In addition. *–pron.* Additional things or persons <*More* were bought at the same shop.>

mo•rel (mə-rĕl', mô-) *n.* Any of several edible mushrooms, esp. *Morchella esculenta,* with a spongelike cap.

more•o•ver (môr-ō'vər, mōr-, môr'ō'vər, mōr'-) *adv.* Furthermore : besides.

mo•res (môr'āz', mōr'-, -ēz') *pl.n.* **1.** The moral customs and rules of a social group. **2.** Manners : habits.

Mor•gan (môr'gən) *n.* A saddle and trotting horse orig. bred in America.

morgue (môrg) *n.* **1.** A place in which the bodies of persons found dead are kept until claimed or identified. **2.** A file of old issues and reference materials in a newspaper or magazine office.

mor•i•bund (môr'ə-bŭnd', mŏr'-) *adj.* Approaching death. **–mor'i•bun'di•ty** *n.*

Mor•mon (môr'mən) *n.* A member of the Church of Jesus Christ of Latter-day Saints, founded by Joseph Smith in 1830. **–Mor'mon•ism** *n.*

morn (môrn) *n.* Morning.

morn•ing (môr'nĭng) *n.* The early part of the day, from midnight to noon or from sunrise to noon.

morn•ing-glo•ry (môr'nĭng-glôr'ē, -glōr'ē) *n.* A usu. twining

plant of the genus *Ipomoea,* with funnel-shaped flowers that close late in the day.
morning star *n.* A planet, esp. Venus, seen in the E just before or at sunrise.
mo•roc•co (mə-rŏk′ō) *n.* A soft, grainy-textured leather made of goatskin.
Morocco. Kingdom of NW Africa, on the Mediterranan. *Cap.* Rabat. *Pop.* 20,050,000. **–Mo•roc′can** *adj.* & *n.*
mo•ron (môr′ŏn′, mōr′-) *n.* **1.** A mentally retarded person whose intelligence is equal to that of a child between 7 and 12 years of age. **2.** A very stupid person. **–mo•ron′ic** (mə-rŏn′ĭk) *adj.* **–mo•ron′i•cal•ly** *adv.*
mo•rose (mə-rōs′, mô-) *adj.* **1.** Sullen in disposition. **2.** Gloomy. **–mo•rose′ly** *adv.* **–mo•rose′ness** *n.*
mor•pheme (môr′fēm′) *n.* A meaningful linguistic unit that cannot be divided into smaller meaningful parts. **–mor•phem′ic** *adj.* **–mor•phem′i•cal•ly** *adv.*
mor•phi•a (môr′fē-ə) *n.* Morphine.
mor•phine (môr′fēn′) *n.* An addictive narcotic drug derived from opium and used as a sedative and anesthetic.
mor•phol•o•gy (môr-fŏl′ə-jē) *n.* **1.** The study of the form and structure of living organisms. **2.** The study of word formation in a language. **–mor′pho•log′i•cal** (môr′fə-lŏj′ĭ-kəl), **mor′pho•log′ic** *adj.* **–mor•phol′o•gist** *n.*
mor•ris (môr′ĭs, mŏr′-) *n.* An English folk dance performed by costumed dancers.
Morris chair *n.* An easy chair with removable cushions and an adjustable back.
mor•row (môr′ō, mŏr′ō) *n.* The day after a specified day.
Morse (môrs), **Samuel Finley Breese.** 1791–1872. Amer. artist; promoter of the telegraph.
Morse code *n.* A code, used esp. in telegraphy, consisting of short and long sounds or dots and dashes.
mor•sel (môr′səl) *n.* **1.** A small piece, esp. of food. **2.** A tasty delicacy.
†**mor•tal** (môr′tl) *adj.* **1.** Subject to death <Human beings are *mortal.*> **2.** Causing death : fatal. **3.** Of or characteristic of human beings <a *mortal* weakness> **4.** Unrelentingly hostile : implacable <*mortal* enemies> **5.** Extreme : dire <in *mortal* terror> **6.** *Rom. Cath. Ch.* Causing eternal damnation <a *mortal* sin> *–n.* A human being. *–adv. Regional.* Extremely : very. **–mor′tal•ly** *adv.*
mor•tal•i•ty (môr-tăl′ĭ-tē) *n., pl.* **-ties. 1.** The state of being mortal. **2.** Death rate.
mor•tar (môr′tər) *n.* **1.** A vessel in which substances can be crushed or ground with a pestle. **2.** A muzzle-loading cannon for firing shells at short ranges and in high trajectories. **3.** A mix, as of cement with sand and water, that is used in masonry.
mor•tar•board (môr′tər-bôrd′, -bōrd′) *n.* **1.** A square board for holding mortar. **2.** An academic cap topped by a flat square.
mort•gage (môr′gĭj) *n.* **1.** A temporary transfer of property to a creditor as security for the repayment of a debt. **2.** A contract or deed defining the terms of a mortgage. *–v.* **-gaged, -gag•ing.** To pledge or convey by means of a mortgage. **–mort′ga•gee′** *n.* **–mort′ga•gor** *n.*
mor•ti•cian (môr-tĭsh′ən) *n.* An undertaker.
mor•ti•fy (môr′tə-fī′) *v.* **-fied, -fy•ing. 1.** To humiliate. **2.** To discipline (e.g., the body) through pain or self-denial. **3.** To become gangrenous. **–mor′ti•fi•ca′tion** *n.* **–mor′ti•fy′ing•ly** *adv.*
mor•tise (môr′tĭs) *n.* A usu. rectangular hole in a piece of wood that receives a tenon of another piece to form a joint.

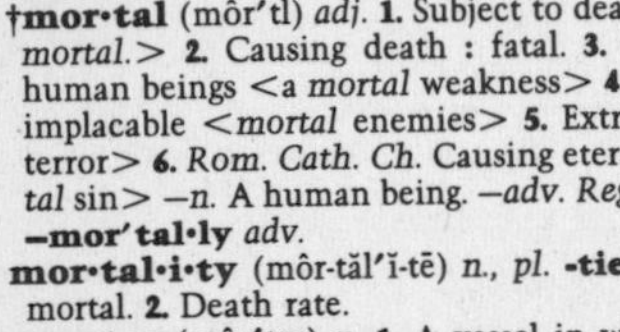

mortise

mor•tu•ar•y (môr′chōō-ĕr′ē) *n., pl.* **-ies.** A place where dead bodies are kept until burial or cremation.
mo•sa•ic (mō-zā′ĭk) *n.* A decorative design on a surface made by inlaying small pieces, as of colored glass or tile, in cement. **–mo•sa′ic** *adj.*
Mos•cow (mŏs′kou′, -kō). Cap. of the USSR, in the WC European part. *Pop.* 8,011,000.
Mos•es (mō′zĭz, -zĭs). Hebrew prophet and lawgiver. **–Mo•sa′ic** *adj.*
mo•sey (mō′zē) *v. Informal.* To move along slowly : amble.
Mos•lem (mŏz′ləm, mŏs′-) *n.* An adherent of Islam. **–Mos′lem** *adj.*
mosque (mŏsk) *n.* A house of worship used by Moslems.
mos•qui•to (mə-skē′tō) *n., pl.* **-toes** or **-tos.** Any of various winged insects of the family Culicidae, of which the females suck the blood of animals.
mosquito net *n.* A fine net or screen for keeping out mosquitoes.
moss (môs, mŏs) *n.* Any of various small green bryophtes of the class Musci that often form a dense, matlike growth. **–moss′i•ness** *n.* **–moss′y** *adj.*
moss•back (môs′băk′, mŏs′-) *n. Slang.* A very conservative or old-fashioned person.
moss rose *n.* A variety of rose, *Rosa centifolia muscosa,* bearing fragrant pink flowers with a mossy flower stalk and calyx.
most (mōst) *adj.* **1.** Greatest <the *most* talent> **2.** The greatest part of <*most* women> *–n.* The greatest amount, quantity, or degree <the *most* I've ever seen> *–pron.* The largest part or number <*Most* left early.> *–adv.* **1.** In or to the highest degree <*most* beautiful><*most* impatiently> **2.** In or to a high degree : very <a *most* meticulous worker>
most•ly (mōst′lē) *adv.* For the most part : mainly.
mot (mō) *n.* A short, witty saying.
mote (mōt) *n.* A particle, as of dust.
mo•tel (mō-tĕl′) *n.* A hotel for motorists, with rooms usu. opening directly onto a parking area.
mo•tet (mō-tĕt′) *n.* A polyphonic choral composition, often based on a religious text and usu. sung without accompaniment.
moth (môth, mŏth) *n., pl.* **moths** (mô*th*z, mŏ*th*z, môths, mŏths). **1.** Any of numerous insects of the order Lepidoptera, gen. distinguished from butterflies by their nocturnal activity, stout bodies, and featherlike antennae. **2.** The clothes moth. **–moth′proof′** *adj.* & *v.*
moth•ball (môth′bôl′, mŏth′-) *n.* **1.** A ball, as of camphor, used to repel moths from clothing. **2. mothballs.** Protective and usu. long-term storage <battleships put into *mothballs*>
moth-eat•en (môth′ēt′n, mŏth′-) *adj.* **1.** Eaten away by moths <a *moth-eaten* blanket> **2. a.** Old-fashioned. **b.** Rundown.
moth•er (mŭ*th*′ər) *n.* **1.** A female parent. **2.** An origin : source. **3.** A woman in a position of responsibility or authority. *–adj.* **1.** Of, pertaining to, or being a mother. **2.** Native <his *mother* country> *–v.* **1.** To give birth to. **2.** To care for like a mother : nourish and protect. **–moth′er•hood′** *n.* **–moth′er•less** *adj.* **–moth′er•li•ness** *n.* **–moth′er•ly** *adj.*
moth•er-in-law (mŭ*th*′ər-ĭn-lô′) *n., pl.* **moth•ers-in-law.** The mother of one's spouse.
moth•er•land (mŭ*th*′ər-lănd′) *n.* **1.** The country of one's birth. **2.** The native country of one's forebears.
moth•er-of-pearl (mŭ*th*′ər-əv-pûrl′) *n.* The pearly internal layer of a mollusk shell.
mo•tif (mō-tēf′) *n.* A thematic element that recurs in a musical, artistic, or literary work.
mo•tile (mōt′l, mō′tīl′) *adj.* Moving or capable of moving spontaneously. **–mo•til′i•ty** (mō-tĭl′ĭ-tē) *n.*
mo•tion (mō′shən) *n.* **1.** The act or process of moving. **2.** A meaningful movement of the body or a bodily part : gesture. **3.** A formal proposal that action be taken, as by a legislative body. *–v.* To signal or direct by making a motion. **–mo′tion•less** *adj.*
motion picture *n.* A series of filmed images projected on a screen so rapidly that the illusion of motion is created. **–mo′tion-pic′ture** *adj.*
motion sickness *n.* Sickness caused by motion and marked by nausea.
mo•ti•vate (mō′tə-vāt′) *v.* **-vat•ed, -vat•ing.** To provide with a motive : actuate. **–mo′ti•va′tion** *n.*
mo•tive (mō′tĭv) *n.* **1.** Something, as a reason or desire, acting as a spur to action. **2.** (*also* mō-tēv′). A musical motif. *–adj.* **1.** Causing or capable of causing motion. **2.** Of, relating to, or being a motive.
mot•ley (mŏt′lē) *adj.* **1.** Made up of a variety of components : heterogeneous. **2.** Multicolored.
mo•tor (mō′tər) *n.* **1.** Something that generates or imparts motion. **2.** A device that converts electrical energy into mechanical energy. **3.** A device that produces mechanical power from fuel : engine. *–adj.* **1.** Imparting or producing motion. **2.** Driven by or equipped with a motor. **3.** Of, relating to, or designed for motor vehicles. **4.** Of or relating to muscular movements. *–v.* To travel in a motor vehicle. **–mo′tor•ist** *n.*
mo•tor•bike (mō′tər-bīk′) *n.* A light motorcycle.

mo·tor·boat (mō′tər-bōt′) *n.* A boat driven by an internal-combustion engine.
mo·tor·cade (mō′tər-kād′) *n.* A procession consisting of motor vehicles.
mo·tor·car (mō′tər-kär′) *n.* An automobile.
motor court *n.* A motel.
mo·tor·cy·cle (mō′tər-sī′kəl) *n.* A 2-wheeled vehicle driven by an internal-combustion engine. **–mo′tor·cy′cle** *v.* **–mo′tor·cy′clist** *n.*
motor home *n.* A motor vehicle built on a truck or bus chassis and equipped to serve as a self-contained home during travel.
mo·tor·ize (mō′tə-rīz′) *v.* **-ized, -iz·ing. 1.** To equip with a motor. **2.** To supply with motor-driven vehicles. **–mo′tor·i·za′tion** *n.*
mo·tor·man (mō′tər-mən) *n.* A driver of a locomotive, streetcar, or subway train.
motor scooter *n.* A small 2-wheeled vehicle resembling a scooter but having a low-powered gasoline engine.
motor vehicle *n.* A self-propelled motor-powered vehicle that does not run on rails but travels on wheels.
†**motte** *also* **mott** (mŏt) *n. W U.S.* A small stand of trees on a prairie.
mot·tle (mŏt′l) *v.* **-tled, -tling.** To mark with spots or streaks of different colors.
mot·to (mŏt′ō) *n., pl.* **-toes** *or* **-tos. 1.** A sentence, phrase, or word inscribed on something, as a coat of arms, to express its purpose or character. **2.** A brief expression of a guiding principle.
moue (mo͞o) *n.* A grimace, as of disapproval : pout.
mould (mōld) *n. & v. esp. Brit. var. of* MOLD.
moult (mōlt) *v. & n. esp. Brit. var. of* MOLT.
mound (mound) *n.* **1.** A pile of earth, gravel, sand, rocks, or debris. **2.** A natural elevation, as a hillock. **3.** The slightly elevated pitcher's area in the center of a baseball diamond.
mount[1] (mount) *v.* **1.** To ascend or rise. **2.** To get up on <*mount* a camel> **3.** To increase in degree, amount, extent, or intensity. **4.** To arrange in an appropriate setting, esp. for display or study. **5. a.** To fix in position <*mount* cannon> **b.** To launch and carry out <*mount* an attack> *–n.* **1.** An animal, esp. a horse, on which to ride. **2.** A support to which something is affixed, as for display, study, or use.
mount[2] (mount) *n.* A lofty hill : mountain.
moun·tain (moun′tən) *n.* A natural elevation of the earth's surface higher than a hill.
mountain ash *n.* Any of various deciduous trees of the genus *Sorbus,* bearing clusters of small white flowers and bright orange-red berries.
moun·tain·eer (moun′tə-nîr′) *n.* **1.** A native or inhabitant of a mountainous area. **2.** Someone who climbs mountains for sport. **–moun′tain·eer′** *v.*
mountain goat *n.* A goatlike mammal, *Oreamnus americanus,* of North America, with short, curved black horns and yellowish-white hair and beard.
mountain laurel *n.* An evergreen shrub, *Kalmia latifolia,* of E North America, with poisonous leaves and clusters of pink or white flowers.
mountain lion *n.* A large, powerful wild cat, *Felis concolor,* of mountainous regions of North and South America.
moun·tain·ous (moun′tə-nəs) *adj.* **1.** Of, relating to, or being a region with many mountains. **2.** Very large : huge.
moun·tain·side (moun′tən-sīd′) *n.* The side of a mountain.
moun·tain·top (moun′tən-tŏp′) *n.* The top of a mountain.
moun·te·bank (moun′tə-băngk′) *n.* A charlatan : quack.
Mount·ie *also* **Mount·y** (moun′tē) *n., pl.* **-ies.** *Can.* A member of the Royal Canadian Mounted Police.
mount·ing (moun′tĭng) *n.* A supporting frame or structure.
mourn (môrn, mōrn) *v.* To express or feel sorrow (for) : grieve. **–mourn′er** *n.*
mourn·ful (môrn′fəl, mōrn′-) *adj.* Feeling, expressing, arousing, or suggesting grief. **–mourn′ful·ly** *adv.* **–mourn′ful·ness** *n.*
mourn·ing (môr′nĭng, mōr′-) *n.* **1.** A sign, as the wearing of black clothing, of grief over a person's death. **2.** The period during which a person's death is mourned.
mourning dove *n.* A North American wild dove, *Zenaidura macroura,* that has a sorrowful call.
mouse (mous) *n., pl.* **mice** (mīs). Any of numerous small rodents of the families Muridae and Cricetidae, usu. having a long, narrow, almost hairless tail.
mous·er (mou′zer) *n.* An animal, esp. a cat, that is skilled at catching mice.
mouse·trap (mous′trăp′) *n.* A trap set to catch mice.
mousse (mo͞os) *n.* A chilled and molded dish, esp. a dessert, made with whipped egg whites or cream and gelatin.
mous·tache (mŭs′tăsh′, mə-stăsh′) *n. var. of* MUSTACHE.
mous·y *also* **mous·ey** (mou′sē, -zē) *adj.* **-i·er, -i·est. 1.** Lacking vividness, as of color. **2.** Timid and fearful. **–mous′i·ness** *n.*
mouth (mouth) *n., pl.* **mouths** (mouthz). **1.** The bodily opening through which an animal takes food in. **2.** Something that resembles the mouth, as the natural opening of a cave or the opening in a container. *–v.* (mouth). **1. a.** To speak : pronounce. **b.** To utter in a declamatory manner. **2.** To articulate or form soundlessly. **–mouth′ful′** *n.*
mouth organ *n.* A harmonica.
mouth·piece (mouth′pēs′) *n.* **1.** A part, as of a musical instrument, that is put in the mouth or with which the mouth makes contact. **2.** *Informal.* A spokesman.
mouth-to-mouth (mouth′tə-mouth′) *adj.* Of, pertaining to, or being a method of artificial resuscitation in which the rescuer's mouth is placed over the victim's to force air into the victim's lungs every few seconds.
mouth·wash (mouth′wŏsh′, -wôsh′) *n.* A usu. flavored antiseptic liquid preparation for cleansing the mouth.
move (mo͞ov) *v.* **moved, mov·ing. 1.** To go or cause to go from 1 place or point to another. **2.** To transfer (a piece in a board game). **3.** To change one's residence or place of business. **4.** To change or cause to change posture or position. **5.** To stir the emotions of. **6.** To initiate or cause to initiate action. **7.** To be busy or active. **8.** To make a formal motion, request, or proposal. **9.** To evacuate the bowels. **–move in.** To occupy as a residence or place of business. *–n.* **1.** The act of moving. **2.** A player's turn to move a piece in a board game. **3.** An action calculated to achieve an end : maneuver. **–mov′a·ble, move′a·ble** *adj.* **–mov′a·bly** *adv.*
move·ment (mo͞ov′mənt) *n.* **1.** The act or process of moving. **2.** The activities of a group toward the achievement of a goal. **3.** A trend : tendency. **4.** Activity : action. **5. a.** An evacuation of the bowels. **b.** Waste matter evacuated from the bowels. **6.** *Mus.* A primary section or division of a musical composition. **7.** A mechanism, as the works of a watch, that produces or transmits motion.
mov·er (mo͞o′vər) *n.* One that moves, esp. a company or person hired to move belongings, as furnishings, from 1 residence or place of business to another.
mov·ie (mo͞o′vē) *n. Informal.* **1.** A motion picture. **2. movies. a.** A showing of a motion picture. **b.** The motion-picture industry. **–mov′ie·go′er** *n.*
mov·ie·mak·er (mo͞o′ve-mā′kər) *n.* One who makes movies as a profession.
moving picture *n.* A motion picture.
mow[1] (mō) *v.* **mowed, mowed** *or* **mown** (mōn), **mow·ing. 1.** To cut down (e.g., grain or grass) with a machine or a scythe. **2.** To cut (e.g., grain or grass) from <*mow* the lawn> **–mow′er** *n.*
mow[2] (mou) *n.* The part of a barn where hay or grain is stored.
Mo·zam·bique (mō′zăm-bēk′). Country of SE Africa. *Cap.* Maputo. *Pop.* 10,460,000.
Mo·zart (mōt′särt′), **Wolfgang Amadeus.** 1756–91. Austrian composer.
†**mo·zo** (mō′zō) *n., pl.* **-zos.** *W U.S.* A man who helps with a pack train or acts as a porter.
moz·za·rel·la (mŏt′sə-rĕl′ə) *n.* A soft smooth white cheese with a mild flavor.
Mp *or* **M.P.** *abbr.* military police.
mpg *or* **m.p.g.** *abbr.* miles per gallon.
mph *or* **m.p.h.** *abbr.* miles per hour.
MPP *abbr. Can.* Member of Provincial Parliament.
Mr. *abbr.* Mister.
Mrs. *abbr.* Mistress.
ms *abbr.* **1.** manuscript. **2.** millisecond.
MS *abbr.* **1.** manuscript. **2.** Mississippi (with Zip Code). **3.** multiple sclerosis.
Ms. *or* **Ms** *abbr.* Used as a courtesy title with a woman's name when her marital status is unknown or irrelevant.
msg. *abbr.* message.
MST *or* **M.S.T.** *abbr.* Mountain Standard Time.
MT *abbr.* Montana (with Zip Code).
mt. *or* **Mt.** *abbr.* mount; mountain.
m.t. *or* **M.T.** *abbr.* **1.** metric ton. **2.** Mountain Time.
mtg. *abbr.* **1.** meeting. **2.** *also* **mtge.** mortgage.
mtn. *abbr.* mountain.
much (mŭch) *adj.* **more** (môr, mōr), **most** (mōst). Great in amount, quantity, degree, or extent <*much* time> *–n.* **1.** A great amount, quantity, degree, or extent. **2.** Something remarkable or important <didn't amount to *much*> *–adv.* **more, most. 1.** To a great degree or extent <*much* prettier> **2.** About : approximately <said *much* the same thing>
mu·ci·lage (myo͞o′sə-lĭj) *n.* A sticky adhesive substance. **–mu′ci·lag′i·nous** (-lăj′ə-nəs) *adj.*

muck (mŭk) *n.* **1. a.** Moist, sticky dirt : filth. **b.** Mud. **2.** Moist animal dung : manure. **3.** Dark, fertile soil containing decayed organic matter. **—muck'y** *adj.*
muck•rake (mŭk'rāk') *v.* To search out and expose real or ostensible corruption on the part of well-known persons. **—muck'rak'er** *n.*
mu•co•sa (myo͞o-kō'zə) *n.* A mucous membrane.
mu•cous (myo͞o'kəs) *adj.* Of, pertaining to, or secreting mucus.
mucous membrane *n.* A membrane covered with mucus-secreting glands that lines bodily channels that communicate with the air.
mu•cus (myo͞o'kəs) *n.* The viscous liquid secreted as a protective coating by glands in the mucous membrane.
mud (mŭd) *n.* **1.** Sticky, soft wet earth. **2.** Slanderous remarks. **—mud'di•ly** *adv.* **—mud'di•ness** *n.* **—mud'dy** *adj.* & *v.*
mud•dle (mŭd'l) *v.* **-dled, -dling. 1.** To make turbid : muddy. **2.** To mix up : jumble. **3.** To confuse, esp. with alcohol. **4.** To make a mess of : bungle. **—mud'dler** *n.*
mud•dle•head•ed (mŭd'l-hĕd'ĭd) *adj.* **1.** Mentally confused. **2.** Inept : stupid. **—mud'dle•head'ed•ness** *n.*
mud•guard (mŭd'gärd') *n.* A shield over a wheel of a vehicle.
mud•sling•er (mŭd'slĭng'ər) *n.* Someone who makes malicious charges, esp. against a political opponent. **—mud'sling'ing** *n.*
Muen•ster or **Mun•ster** (mŭn'stər, mo͝on'-) *n.* A mild, semisoft, creamy fermented cheese.
mu•ez•zin (myo͞o-ĕz'ĭn, mo͞o-) *n.* A Moslem crier who calls the faithful to prayer 5 times a day.
muff[1] (mŭf) *v.* To spoil or ruin through clumsiness or carelessness. **—muff** *n.*
muff[2] (mŭf) *n.* A tubular covering with open ends into which the hands are put for warmth.
muf•fin (mŭf'ĭn) *n.* A small, soft cup-shaped bread that is often served hot.
muf•fle (mŭf'əl) *v.* **-fled, -fling. 1.** To wrap up snugly in order to protect or conceal. **2.** To pad or wrap up in order to deaden the sound of. **3.** To suppress. ☆***syns:*** DAMPEN, DEADEN, MUTE, STIFLE
muf•fler (mŭf'lər) *n.* **1.** A scarf worn around the neck for warmth. **2.** A device that deadens sound, esp. that of an internal-combustion engine.
muf•ti (mŭf'tē) *n.* Civilian clothing.
mug[1] (mŭg) *n.* A cylindrical drinking cup, often with a handle.
mug[2] (mŭg) *n.* **1.** A person's face. **2.** An official photograph of a suspect's face. *—v.* **mugged, mug•ging. 1.** To assault, usu. with the intention of robbing. **2.** To make faces. **—mug'ger** *n.*
mug•gy (mŭg'ē) *adj.* **-gi•er, -gi•est.** Warm, close, and humid. **—mug'gi•ly** *adv.* **—mug'gi•ness** *n.*
mug•wump (mŭg'wŭmp') *n.* One who acts independently, esp. in politics.
Mu•ham•mad (mo͝o-hăm'ĭd, -hä'mĭd). Mohammed.
Mu•ham•mad•an (mō-hăm'ĭ-dən) *n.* A Moslem. **—Mu•ham'mad•an** *adj.* **—Mu•ham'mad•an•ism** *n.*

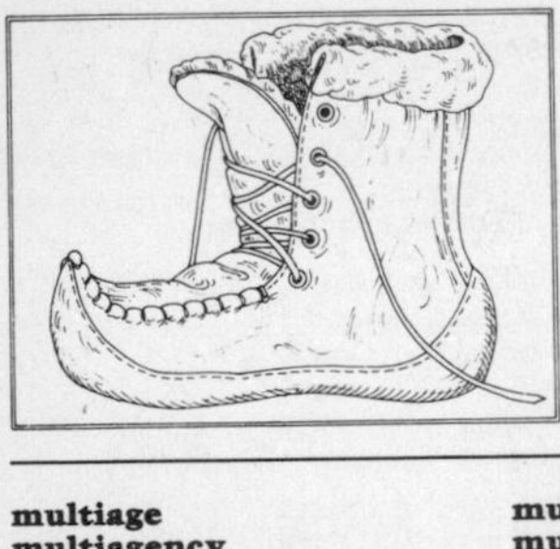
mukluk

muk•luk (mŭk'lŭk') *n.* **1.** A soft Eskimo boot of sealskin or reindeer skin. **2.** A slipper that resembles a mukluk.
mu•lat•to (mo͝o-lăt'ō, -lä'tō, myo͝o-) *n., pl.* **-tos** or **-toes. 1.** A person with 1 white and 1 black parent. **2.** One of mixed black and white ancestry.
mul•ber•ry (mŭl'bĕr'ē) *n.* Any of several trees of the genus *Morus*, bearing edible purplish-red berrylike fruit.
mulch (mŭlch) *n.* A protective covering, as of hay, placed on the earth around growing plants esp. to prevent moisture evaporation, protect roots from freezing, and retard the growth of weeds. **—mulch** *v.*
mulct (mŭlkt) *n.* A penalty, esp. a fine. *—v.* **1.** To penalize, esp. by fining. **2.** To defraud : swindle.
mule[1] (myo͞ol) *n.* **1.** A sterile hybrid animal that is the offspring of a female horse and a male ass. **2.** *Informal.* An extremely stubborn person. **—mul'ish** *adj.* **—mul'ish•ly** *adv.* **—mul'ish•ness** *n.*
mule[2] (myo͞ol) *n.* An open shoe or slipper that leaves the heel bare.
mule deer *n.* A hoofed mammal, *Odocoileus hemionus*, of W North America, with long ears and 2-pronged antlers.
mule•skin•ner (myo͞ol'skĭn'ər) *n. Informal.* A muleteer.
mu•le•teer (myo͞o'lə-tîr') *n.* One who drives mules.
mull[1] (mŭl) *v.* To heat and add sugar and spices to (e.g., wine).
mull[2] (mŭl) *v.* To think about : ponder.
mul•lein (mŭl'ən) *n.* A tall plant of the genus *Verbascum*, esp. *V. thapsus*, with yellow flower clusters and downy leaves.
mul•let (mŭl'ĭt) *n., pl.* **mullet** or **-lets.** Any of various edible marine and freshwater fishes of the family Mugilidae.
mul•li•gan stew (mŭl'ĭ-gən) *n.* A stew of various meats and vegetables.
mul•li•ga•taw•ny (mŭl'ĭ-gə-tô'nē) *n.* A meat soup strongly flavored with curry.
mul•lion (mŭl'yən) *n.* A vertical strip that separates the panes of a window.
multi– *pref.* **1.** Many : much : multiple <*multi*colored> **2. a.** More than 1 <*multi*parous> **b.** More than 2 <*multi*lateral> See below for a list of self-explanatory words formed with the prefix **multi–**.
mul•ti•dis•ci•pli•nar•y (mŭl'tĭ-dĭs'ə-plə-nĕr'ē) *adj.* Of, relating to, or utilizing a combination of academic disciplines.
mul•ti•far•i•ous (mŭl'tə-fâr'ē-əs) *adj.* Having much variety or diversity : diverse. **—mul'ti•far'i•ous•ly** *adv.*
mul•ti•flo•ra rose (mŭl'tə-flôr'ə, -flōr'ə) *n.* A climbing or sprawling Asian shrub, *Rosa multiflora*, bearing small, fragrant flower clusters.
mul•ti•form (mŭl'tə-fôrm') *adj.* Having many shapes, forms, or appearances.
mul•ti•lat•er•al (mŭl'tĭ-lăt'ər-əl) *adj.* **1.** Having many sides. **2.** Of, involving, or participated in by more than 2 governments or parties. **—mul'ti•lat'er•al•ly** *adv.*
mul•ti•lin•gual (mŭl'tə-lĭng'gwəl) *adj.* Using or knowing several languages. **—mul'ti•lin'gual•ism** *n.*
mul•ti•na•tion•al (mŭl'tĭ-năsh'ən-əl, -năsh'nəl) *adj.* **1.** Of, relating to, or involving several countries. **2.** Having subsidiaries or operations in more than 1 country <a *multinational* corporation>
mul•tip•a•rous (mŭl-tĭp'ər-əs) *adj.* Giving birth to more than 1 offspring at a time.
mul•ti•ple (mŭl'tə-pəl) *adj.* Of, having, relating to, or consisting of more than 1 individual, element, or part : manifold. *—n. Math.* A number into which another number can be divided with no remainder.
mul•ti•ple-choice (mŭl'tə-pəl-chois') *adj.* Offering several solutions from which the correct one is to be selected.
multiple sclerosis *n.* A degenerative disease of the central nervous system marked by hardening of tissue in the brain or spinal cord or both.
mul•ti•plex (mŭl'tə-plĕks') *adj.* **1.** Manifold : multiple. **2.** Of,

multiage
multiagency
multiarmed
multiauthor
multiauthored
multiaxial
multiband
multibillion
multibirth
multibladed
multibranched
multibuilding
multicampus
multicar
multicarbon
multicausal
multicell
multicellular
multicenter
multichain
multichambered
multichannel
multicharacter
multicircuit
multicoated
multicolored
multicolumn
multicomponent
multiconductor
multicopy
multicounty
multicrested
multiculturism
multicurrency
multicylinder
multidenominational
multidentate
multidialectal
multidimensional
multidirectional
multidivisional
multidwelling
multielectrode
multielectronic
multielement
multiethnic
multifaced
multifaceted
multifactional
multifamily
multifilament
multiflash
multifluid
multifocal
multifrequency
multifunction
multifunctional
multigrade
multigrid
multigroup

indicating, or being a communications system in which 2 or more messages can be transmitted simultaneously on the same circuit or radio channel. **—mul'ti·plex'** *v.*
mul·ti·pli·cand (mŭl'tə-plĭ-kănd') *n.* A number to be multiplied by another.
mul·ti·pli·ca·tion (mŭl'tə-plĭ-kā'shən) *n.* **1.** The process of multiplying. **2.** The propagation of animals and plants. **3.** Repeated addition in which 1 number indicates how many times another is to be added to itself.
mul·ti·plic·i·ty (mŭl'tə-plĭs'ĭ-tē) *n., pl.* **-ties.** A large variety or number.
mul·ti·pli·er (mŭl'tə-plī'ər) *n.* A number by which another number is or is to be multiplied.
mul·ti·ply (mŭl'tə-plī') *v.* **-plied, -ply·ing. 1.** To increase in number or amount, as by breeding. **2.** To perform the mathematical operation of multiplication (on).
mul·ti·sense (mŭl'tĭ-sĕns') *adj.* Having several meanings.
mul·ti·stage (mŭl'tĭ-stāj') *adj.* Consisting of or performed in successive stages <a *multistage* rocket>
mul·ti·tude (mŭl'tĭ-to͞od', -tyo͞od') *n.* A very large number. **—mul'ti·tu'di·nous** (-to͞od'n-əs, -tyo͞od'-) *adj.*
mul·ti·vi·ta·min (mŭl'tə-vī'tə-mĭn) *adj.* Containing several vitamins. **—mul'ti·vi'ta·min** *n.*
mum¹ (mŭm) *adj.* Not speaking : silent.
mum² (mŭm) *n. Informal.* A chrysanthemum.
mum·ble (mŭm'bəl) *v.* **-bled, -bling.** To utter or speak indistinctly, as by lowering the voice and partially closing the mouth. **—mum'ble** *n.* **—mum'bler** *n.*
mum·ble·ty-peg (mŭm'bəl-tē-pĕg', mŭm'blē-pĕg') *also* **mum·ble-the-peg** (mŭm'bəl-thə-pĕg') *n.* A game in which the players throw a knife from different positions, the object being to stick the blade firmly in the ground.
mum·bo jum·bo (mŭm'bō jŭm'bō) *n.* **1.** An obscure or complicated ritual or incantation. **2.** Complicated and confusing activity or language.
mum·mer (mŭm'ər) *n.* **1.** Someone who acts in a pantomime. **2.** Someone wearing a mask or costume who participates in a celebration, esp. a festival. **—mum'mer·y** *n.*
mum·my (mŭm'ē) *n., pl.* **-mies.** The body of a human being or animal embalmed after death in accordance with the methods of the ancient Egyptians. **—mum'mi·fy'** *v.*
mumps (mŭmps) *pl.n. (sing. or pl. in number).* An acute contagious viral disease characterized by swelling esp. of the salivary glands.
mun. *abbr.* municipal; municipality.
munch (mŭnch) *v.* To chew noisily.
mun·dane (mŭn-dān', mŭn'dān') *adj.* **1.** Of or pertaining to the world : worldly. **2.** Concerned with or characteristic of the ordinary. **—mun·dane'ly** *adv.*
Mu·nich (myo͞o'nĭk). City of S West Germany. *Pop.* 1,293,590.
mu·nic·i·pal (myo͞o-nĭs'ə-pəl) *adj.* **1.** Of, relating to, or typical of a municipality. **2.** Having local self-government. **—mu·nic'i·pal·ly** *adv.*
mu·nic·i·pal·i·ty (myoo-nĭs'ə-păl'ĭ-tē) *n., pl.* **-ties.** A political unit, as a city or town, that is incorporated and self-governing.
mu·nif·i·cent (myo͞o-nĭf'ĭ-sənt) *adj.* Generous in giving : lavish. **—mu·nif'i·cence** *n.* **—mu·nif'i·cent·ly** *adv.*
mu·ni·tions (myo͞o-nĭsh'ənz) *pl.n.* War materiel, esp. guns and ammunition.
Mun·ster (mŭn'stər, mo͝on'-) *n. var. of* MUENSTER.
mu·ral (myo͝or'əl) *n.* A painting applied directly to a wall surface. **—mu'ral·ist** *n.*
mur·der (mûr'dər) *n.* **1.** The crime of unlawfully killing a human being, esp. with malice aforethought. **2.** *Slang.* Something very difficult, dangerous, or uncomfortable. *—v.* **1.** To kill (a human being) unlawfully. **2.** To spoil or mar by ineptness : ruin. **3.** To put an end to : destroy. ☆**syns:** KILL, KNOCK OFF, LIQUIDATE, RUB OUT, SLAY, WASTE, WIPE OUT, ZAP **—mur'der·er** *n.*
mur·der·ous (mûr'dər-əs) *adj.* **1.** Intending or seeming to intend murder. **2.** Marked by or giving rise to murder. **3.** *Informal.* Very difficult, dangerous, or uncomfortable. **—mur'der·ous·ly** *adv.*
murk (mûrk) *n.* Gloom : darkness. **—murk'i·ly** *adv.* **—murk'i·ness** *n.* **—murk'y** *adj.*
mur·mur (mûr'mər) *n.* **1.** An indistinct, low, continuous sound. **2.** An indistinct complaint : mutter. **3.** An abnormal sound, usu. in the thoracic cavity, detectable by a stethoscope. **—mur'mur** *v.*
mur·rain (mûr'ĭn) *n.* A malignant and highly infectious disease of domestic plants or animals, as blight or anthrax.
mus. *abbr.* **1.** museum. **2.** music; musical; musician.
Mus·cat (mŭs'kăt'). Cap. of Oman, on the Gulf of Oman. *Pop.* 15,000.
mus·ca·tel (mŭs'kə-tĕl') *n.* A rich, sweet wine.
mus·cle (mŭs'əl) *n.* **1. a.** Bodily tissue composed of fibers that contract and relax to cause movement or exert force. **b.** A contractile organ of muscle tissue. **2.** Muscular strength. **3.** Force. ☆**syns:** CLOUT, FORCE, POWER, WEIGHT *—v.* **-cled, -cling.** To make one's way by or as if by force.
mus·cle-bound (mŭs'əl-bound') *adj.* Having some muscles that are overdeveloped and lack the capacity to flex fully, usu. from too much exercise.
mus·cu·lar (mŭs'kyə-lər) *adj.* **1.** Of, relating to, or consisting of muscle. **2.** Having well-developed muscles : brawny. **—mus'cu·lar'i·ty** (-lăr'ĭ-tē) *n.*
muscular dystrophy *n.* A chronic noncontagious disease marked by gradual but irreversible muscular deterioration.
mus·cu·la·ture (mŭs'kyə-lə-cho͝or', -chər) *n.* The system of muscles of the body or a bodily part.
muse¹ (myo͞oz) *v.* **mused, mus·ing.** To think about at length. **—mus'er** *n.*
muse² (myo͞oz) *n.* A source of inspiration.
mu·sette (myo͞o-zĕt') *n.* **1.** A small French bagpipe. **2.** A small leather or canvas bag with a shoulder strap.
mu·se·um (myo͞o-zē'əm) *n.* An institution for the acquisition, preservation, and display of works of lasting artistic, historical, and scientific value.
mush (mŭsh) *n.* **1.** Meal, esp. cornmeal, boiled in water. **2.** Soft pulpy matter. **3.** *Informal.* Maudlin sentimentality. **—mush'i·ness** *n.* **—mush'y** *adj.*
mush·room (mŭsh'ro͞om', -ro͝om') *n.* A fleshy fungus of the class Basidiomycetes, characteristically having an umbrella-shaped cap borne on a stalk. *—v.* To multiply, grow, or expand rapidly.
mu·sic (myo͞o'zĭk) *n.* **1.** The art of organizing tones in combinations and sequences that constitute a cohesive, unified, continuous composition. **2.** Vocal or instrumental sounds having melody, rhythm, or harmony. **3. a.** A musical composition. **b.** A body of such compositions. **4.** An aesthetically pleasing or harmonious sound.
mu·si·cal (myo͞o'zĭ-kəl) *adj.* **1.** Of, relating to, or capable of producing music. **2.** Pleasing to the ear, esp. melodious. **3.** Having skill or an interest in music. *—n.* A musical comedy. **—mu'si·cal·ly** *adv.*
musical comedy *n.* A play or motion picture in which spoken dialogue alternates with songs and dances.
mu·si·cale (myo͞o'zĭ-kăl') *n.* A social gathering at which a program of music is performed.
music box *n.* A box enclosing a mechanical device that produces music when activated.
mu·si·cian (myo͞o-zĭsh'ən) *n.* A performer or composer of music. **—mu·si'cian·ly** *adj.* **—mu·si'cian·ship'** *n.*
mu·si·col·o·gy (myo͞o'zĭ-kŏl'ə-jē) *n.* The historical, theoretical, and scientific study of music. **—mus'si·co·log'i·cal** (-kə-lŏj'ĭ-kəl) *adj.* **—mu'si·col'o·gist** *n.*
musk (mŭsk) *n.* A substance with a powerful odor that is secreted by an Asian deer, *Moschus moschiferus,* or produced

multiheaded
multihued
multi-industrial
multi-industry
multilane
multilayer
multilayered
multilevel
multileveled
multilobed
multimanned
multimedia
multimegaton
multimember
multimetallic
multimillion
multimillionaire
multimode
multimolecular
multimotor
multination
multinuclear
multinucleate
multiparameter
multipart
multiparticle
multiparty
multipiston
multiplot
multipower
multiproblem
multiproduct
multipurpose
multiracial
multiramose
multiroomed
multirooted
multiservice
multisided
multiskilled
multisonic
multispeed
multistep
multistoried
multistory
multisyllabic
multisystem
multitalented
multithreaded
multitiered
multitone
multitowered
multitrack
multiunit
multiuse
multivitamin
multivoiced
multiwall
multiwarhead
multiwavelength

synthetically and used in making perfume. **—musk′i•ness** *n.* **—musk′y** *adj.*
mus•keg (mŭs′kĕg′) *n.* A swamp or bog formed by accumulated sphagnum moss, leaves, and decayed matter resembling peat.
mus•kel•lunge (mŭs′kə-lŭnj′) *n., pl.* **muskellunge** or **-lung•es.** A large game fish, *Esox masquinongy,* of cooler fresh waters of North America.
mus•ket (mŭs′kĭt) *n.* A shoulder gun with a long barrel. **—mus′ket•eer′** *n.*
mus•ket•ry (mŭs′kĭ-trē) *n.* **1. a.** Muskets. **b.** The fire of muskets. **2.** Musketeers.
musk•mel•on (mŭsk′mĕl′ən) *n.* A variety of the melon *Cucumis melo,* as the cantaloupe, with a rough rind and usu. juicy edible flesh.
musk ox *n.* A large hoofed mammal, *Ovibos moschatus,* of N Canada and Greenland, with horns and a shaggy coat.
musk•rat (mŭsk′răt′) *n.* An aquatic rodent, *Ondatra zibethica,* of North America, with brown fur.
Mus•lim (mŭz′lĭm, mo͝os′-, mo͝oz′-) *n.* A Moslem. **—Mus′lim** *adj.*
mus•lin (mŭz′lĭn) *n.* A plain-weave coarse or sheer cotton fabric.
†**muss** (mŭs) *v.* To make untidy or messy : disorder. *—n.* **1.** A state of untidiness : disorder. **2.** *Regional.* A squabble : row. **—muss′i•ly** *adv.* **—muss′i•ness** *n.* **—muss′y** *adj.*
mus•sel (mŭs′əl) *n.* **1.** A marine bivalve mollusk, esp. the edible *Mytilus edulis.* **2.** Any of several freshwater bivalve mollusks of the genera *Anodonta* and *Unio,* whose shells are a source of mother-of-pearl.
Mus•so•li•ni (mo͞o′sə-lē′nē), **Benito.** "Il Duce." 1883–1945. Fascist dictator of Italy (1922–43).
Mus•sul•man (mŭs′əl-mən) *n., pl.* **-men** or **-mans.** *Archaic.* A Moslem.
must[1] (mŭst) *v.* Used to indicate necessity or obligation, probability, certainty or inevitability, or insistence. *—n.* **1.** An absolute requirement. **2.** Something that is indispensable.
must[2] (mŭst) *n.* The unfermented or fermenting juice expressed from fruit, esp. grapes.
mus•tache *also* **mous•tache** (mŭs′tăsh′, mə-stăsh′) *n.* The hair that grows on the human upper lip.
mus•tang (mŭs′tăng′) *n.* A wild horse of the W North American plains, descended from Spanish horses.
mus•tard (mŭs′tərd) *n.* **1.** A plant of the genus *Brassica,* with 4-petaled yellow flowers and often pungent seeds. **2.** A condiment or medicinal preparation made from the powdered seeds of mustard.
mustard gas *n.* An oily volatile liquid used in warfare as a blistering agent.
mus•ter (mŭs′tər) *v.* **1.** To bring or come together : convene. **2.** To call or bring forth (e.g., courage). *—n.* **1.** A gathering, esp. of troops, as for review or roll call. **2.** The act of inspecting or examining critically.
must•n't (mŭs′ənt). Must not.
mus•ty (mŭs′tē) *adj.* **-ti•er, -ti•est.** Stale or moldy in taste or odor. **—mus′ti•ly** *adv.* **—mus′ti•ness** *n.*
mu•ta•ble (myo͞o′tə-bəl) *adj.* **1.** Capable of or subject to change. **2.** Apt to change. **—mu′ta•bil′i•ty, mu′ta•ble•ness** *n.*
mu•tant (myo͞ot′nt) *n.* An organism or individual that differs from the parental strain or strains as a result of mutation. **—mu′tant** *adj.*
mu•tate (myo͞o′tāt′, myo͞o-tāt′) *v.* **-tat•ed, -tat•ing.** To undergo or cause to undergo mutation. **—mu′ta′tive** *adj.*
mu•ta•tion (myo͞o-tā′shən) *n.* **1.** A change, as in form. **2.** *Biol.* **a.** A heritable alteration of the genes or chromosomes of an organism. **b.** A mutant.
mute (myo͞ot) *adj.* **mut•er, mut•est. 1.** Unable to speak : dumb. **2.** Not speaking or spoken : silent. *—n.* **1.** One who is incapable of speaking. **2.** One of various devices used for muffling, reducing, or softening the tone of a musical instrument. *—v.* **mut•ed, mut•ing.** To muffle, reduce, or soften the sound of. **—mute′ly** *adv.* **—mute′ness** *n.*
mu•ti•late (myo͞ot′l-āt′) *v.* **-lat•ed, -lat•ing. 1.** To deprive of (an essential part, esp. a limb) : cripple or maim. **2.** To make imperfect by seriously damaging a part. **—mu′ti•la′tion** *n.* **—mu′ti•la′tive** *adj.* **—mu′ti•la′tor** *n.*
mu•ti•ny (myo͞ot′n-ē) *n., pl.* **-nies.** Open rebellion against lawful authority, esp. against superior officers. **—mu′ti•neer′** *n.* **—mu′ti•nous** *adj.* **—mu′ti•ny** *v.*
mutt (mŭt) *n. Slang.* A dog of mixed breed : mongrel.
mut•ter (mŭt′ər) *v.* **1.** To utter or speak indistinctly or in a low voice. **2.** To complain : grumble. **—mut′ter** *n.*
mut•ton (mŭt′n) *n.* The meat of a fully grown sheep.
mutton chops *pl.n.* Whiskers on the sides of the face that are shaped like chops of meat.
mu•tu•al (myo͞o′cho͞o-əl) *adj.* **1.** Having the same relationship each to the other <*mutual* enemies> **2.** Directed and received in equal amount <*mutual* admiration> **3.** Possessed in common <*mutual* avocations> **—mu′tu•al′i•ty** (-ăl′ĭ-tē) *n.*
mutual fund *n.* A company without fixed capitalization that sells its own shares and uses the pooled capital of its shareholders to invest in a variety of securities of other companies.
muu•muu (mo͞o′mo͞o′) *n.* A dress of Hawaiian orig. that hangs loose from the shoulders.

muumuu

muz•zle (mŭz′əl) *n.* **1. a.** The forward, projecting part of the head of certain animals : nose and jaws. **b.** A leather or wire device that fits over the muzzle to prevent biting or eating. **2.** The front end of the barrel of a gun. *—v.* **-zled, -zling. 1.** To put a muzzle on. **2.** To restrain from expressing : silence. **—muz′zler** *n.*
my (mī) *adj.* Used attributively to indicate possession, agency, or reception of an action by the speaker <*my* hat><doing *my* chores><suffered *my* first defeat> *—interj.* Used to express pleasure, surprise, or dismay.
my•ce•li•um (mī-sē′lē-əm) *n., pl.* **-li•a** (-lē-ə). A mass of branching threadlike filaments that form the main growing structure of a fungus. **—my•ce′li•al** *adj.*
my•col•o•gy (mī-kŏl′ə-jē) *n.* The scientific study of fungi. **—my′co•log′i•cal** (-kə-lŏj′ĭ-kəl) *adj.* **—my•col′o•gist** *n.*
my•e•li•tis (mī′ə-lī′tĭs) *n.* Inflammation of the bone marrow or the spinal column.
My•lar (mī′lär′). A trademark for a thin, strong polyester film.
my•na or **my•nah** (mī′nə) *n.* Any of various SE Asian birds of the family Sturnidae, related to the starlings, some of which are known for mimicry of human speech.
my•o•pi•a (mī-ō′pē-ə) *n.* **1.** A visual defect in which distant objects appear fuzzy because their images are focused in front of rather than on the retina. **2.** Failure to think or plan ahead. **—my•op′ic** (mī-ŏp′ĭk, -ō′pĭk) *adj.* **—my•op′i•cal•ly** *adv.*
myr•i•ad (mîr′ē-əd) *adj.* Constituting an extremely large indefinite number : innumerable. **—myr′i•ad** *n.*
myr•i•a•me•ter (mîr′ē-ə-mē′tər) *n.* See MEASUREMENT TABLE.
myr•i•a•pod (mĭr′ē-ə-pŏd′) *n.* An arthropod, as the centipede, having a segmented body and numerous legs.
myr•mi•don (mûr′mĭ-dŏn′, -dən) *n.* A loyal, unquestioning follower.
myrrh (mûr) *n.* An aromatic gum resin yielded by several trees and shrubs of the genus *Commiphora,* of India, Arabia, and E Africa, used in perfumes and incense.
myr•tle (mûr′tl) *n.* **1.** An evergreen shrub of the genus *Myrtus,* esp. *M. communis,* with pink or white flowers and blue-black berries. **2.** PERIWINKLE[2].
my•self (mī-sĕlf′) *pron.* **1.** The one identical with me. Used: **a.** Reflexively <I dressed *myself.*> **b.** For emphasis <I *myself* agreed.> **2.** My normal or healthy condition or state <I have not been *myself* lately.>
mys•te•ri•ous (mĭ-stîr′ē-əs) *adj.* **1.** Of, relating to, or being a mystery <*mysterious* and enduring truths> **2.** Difficult or impossible to comprehend or explain <a *mysterious* phone call> ☆***syns:*** ARCANE, CABALISTIC, MYSTIC, MYSTICAL, MYSTIFYING, UNACCOUNTABLE, UNEXPLAINABLE, UNFATHOMABLE **—mys•te′ri•ous•ly** *adv.* **—mys•te′ri•ous•ness** *n.*
mys•ter•y (mĭs′tə-rē) *n., pl.* **-ies. 1.** Something not fully understood or understandable. **2.** A mysterious quality or character. **3.** A fictional work dealing with a crime and its solution. **4.** A religious truth revealed to the elect.
mys•tic (mĭs′tĭk) *adj.* **1.** Of or relating to mysteries, mystics, or mysticism. **2.** Conveying or containing a sense of mystery : mysterious. *—n.* A person who practices or believes in mysticism.
mys•ti•cal (mĭs′tĭ-kəl) *adj.* **1.** Of, relating to, or stemming from direct communion with God or with ultimate reality. **2.** Spiritually symbolic. **3.** MYSTIC 1. **—mys′ti•cal•ly** *adv.*
mys•ti•cism (mĭs′tĭ-sĭz′əm) *n.* A spiritual discipline aiming at direct union or communion with God or with ultimate reality through trancelike contemplation or deep meditation.

mys•ti•fy (mĭs'tə-fī') *v.* **-fied, -fy•ing. 1.** To bewilder : perplex. **2.** To make mysterious. **—mys'ti•fi•ca'tion** *n.* **—mys'ti•fy'ing•ly** *adv.*

mys•tique (mĭ-stēk') *n.* **1.** A body of attitudes and beliefs associated with a group, person, thing, or idea. **2.** The special quality or skill required in an activity or occupation.

myth (mĭth) *n.* **1.** A traditional story that deals with supernatural beings, ancestors, or heroes that serve as primordial types in a primitive view of the world. **2.** A real or fictional story that appeals to the consciousness of a people by embodying its cultural ideals or by giving expression to deep, commonly felt emotions. **3.** A fictitious or imaginary person, idea, or thing. **—myth'i•cal, myth'ic** *adj.* **—myth'i•cal•ly** *adv.*

myth•mak•er (mĭth'mā'kər) *n.* A creator of myths or mythical situations.

my•thol•o•gy (mĭ-thŏl'ə-jē) *n., pl.* **-gies. 1.** A body of myths, esp. about the ancestors, deities, and heroes of a people. **2.** The systematic collection and study of myths. **—myth'o•log'i•cal** (mĭth'ə-lŏj'ĭ-kəl) *adj.* **—my•thol'o•gist** *n.*

myx•e•de•ma (mĭk'sĭ-dē'mə) *n.* A disease caused by decreased activity of the thyroid gland and marked by mental deterioration and a subnormal metabolic rate.

Nn

n or **N** (ĕn) *n., pl.* **n's** or **N's. 1.** The 14th letter of the English alphabet. **2.** A speech sound represented by the letter *n.* **3.** Something with the shape of the letter N.

N *symbol for* NITROGEN.

N *abbr.* **1.** newton. **2.** *also* **N.** or **n** or **n.** north; northern.

n. *abbr.* **1.** net. **2.** noun. **3.** number.

N. *abbr.* **1.** Norse. **2.** November.

Na *symbol for* SODIUM.

N.A. *abbr.* North America.

nab (năb) *v.* **nabbed, nab•bing.** *Slang.* **1.** To seize (e.g., a fugitive) and arrest. **2.** To grab : snatch.

na•bob (nā'bŏb') *n.* A prominent, wealthy man.

na•celle (nə-sĕl') *n.* A separate streamlined enclosure mounted on an aircraft to house an engine, cargo, or the crew.

na•cho (nä'chō') *n.* A small, often triangular piece of tortilla topped with chili sauce or cheese and broiled.

na•cre (nā'kər) *n.* Mother-of-pearl. **—na'cre•ous** (-krē-əs) *adj.*

na•dir (nā'dər, -dîr') *n.* **1.** A point on the celestial sphere directly opposite the zenith. **2.** The lowest point.

nae (nā) *adv. Scot.* **1.** No. **2.** Not.

nag[1] (năg) *v.* **nagged, nag•ging. 1.** To bother by constant faultfinding, scolding, or complaining. **2.** To torment persistently, as with anxiety. **3.** To find fault, scold, or complain constantly. —*n.* One who nags. **—nag'ger** *n.* **—nag'ging•ly** *adv.*

nag[2] (năg) *n.* An old or worn-out horse.

Na•ga•sa•ki (nä'gə-sä'kē). City of W Kyushu, Japan. *Pop.* 447,091.

Na•hum (nā'həm, nā'əm) *n.* See BIBLE TABLE.

nai•ad (nā'əd, -ăd', nī'-) *n., pl.* **-a•des** (-ə-dēz') or **-ads.** *Gk. Myth.* One of the nymphs living in and presiding over brooks, fountains, and springs.

na•if or **na•ïf** (nä-ēf') *adj.* Naive.

nail (nāl) *n.* **1.** A thin, pointed piece of metal used as a fastener and designed to be hammered in. **2. a.** A fingernail or toenail. **b.** A talon or claw. —*v.* **1.** To fasten or attach with or as if with a nail. **2.** To shut or cover by fastening with nails. **3.** *Slang.* To stop and seize : catch. **4.** *Informal.* To strike : hit. **—nail down.** To establish decisively. **—nail'er** *n.*

nain•sook (nān'so͝ok') *n.* A soft, lightweight cotton fabric.

nai•ra (nī'rə) *n.* See CURRENCY TABLE.

Nai•ro•bi (nī-rō'bē). Cap. of Kenya, in the SC part. *Pop.* 835,000.

na•ive or **na•ïve** (nä-ēv') *adj.* **-iv•er, -iv•est. 1.** Not worldly or sophisticated : artless. **2.** Simple and credulous : ingenuous. **—na•ive'ly** *adv.* **—na•ive'ness** *n.*

na•ive•té or **na•ïve•té** (nä'ēv-tā') *n.* **1.** The quality or state of being naive. **2.** A naive action or statement.

na•ive•ty or **na•ïve•ty** (nä-ēv'tē, -ē'vĭ-tē) *n., pl.* **-ties.** Naiveté.

na•ked (nā'kĭd) *adj.* **1.** Without clothing on the body : nude. **2.** Without covering. **3.** Without disguise or embellishment. **—na'ked•ly** *adv.* **—na'ked•ness** *n.*

naked eye *n.* The eye unaided by an optical instrument, as a telescope.

nam•by-pam•by (năm'bē-păm'bē) *adj.* **1.** Insipid : sentimental. **2.** Indecisive : weak. **—nam'by-pam'by** *n.*

name (nām) *n.* **1.** A word or words by which an entity is called or designated. **2.** A usu. disparaging description or epithet. **3.** Appearance as opposed to reality <equality in *name* only> **4.** Reputation : renown. **5.** *Informal.* One who is famous. ☆**syns:** APPELLATION, COGNOMEN, DENOMINATION, DESIGNATION, HANDLE, MONIKER, TAG —*v.* **named, nam•ing. 1.** To give a name to. **2.** To specify, identify, or cite by name. **3.** To nominate or appoint to an office or honor. **4.** To specify : fix. **—nam'a•ble, name'a•ble** *adj.*

name•less (nām'lĭs) *adj.* **1.** Having no name. **2.** Anonymous. **3.** Inexpressible : indescribable <*nameless* repulsion> **—name'less•ness** *n.*

name•ly (nām'lē) *adv.* Specifically.

name•plate (nām'plāt') *n.* A plate or plaque, as on a door, inscribed with a name.

name•sake (nām'sāk') *n.* One having the same name as another, esp. one named after another.

Na•mi•bia (nə-mĭb'ē-ə). Territory in SW Africa, currently administered by South Africa. **—Na•mib'i•an** *adj. & n.*

Nan•jing (nän'jyĭng') *also* **Nan•king** (năn'kĭng'). City of EC China, on the Yangtze. *Pop.* 1,800,000.

nan•ny (năn'ē) *n., pl.* **-nies.** A children's nurse.

nanny goat *n.* A female goat.

nan•o•sec•ond (năn'ə-sĕk'ənd) *n.* One billionth (10^{-9}) sec.

nap[1] (năp) *n.* A short sleep, often during the day. —*v.* **napped, nap•ping. 1.** To sleep for a short period. **2.** To be unaware of or unprepared.

nap[2] (năp) *n.* A soft or fuzzy surface on fabric or leather. **—nap'less** *adj.*

na•palm (nā'päm') *n.* **1.** An aluminum soap that forms a jelly when mixed with gasoline. **2.** A napalm jelly used in flame throwers and bombs.

nape (nāp) *n.* The back of the neck.

na•per•y (nā'pə-rē) *n.* Household linen, esp. table linen.

naph•tha (năf'thə, năp'-) *n.* A colorless flammable liquid derived from petroleum and used chiefly as a solvent.

naph•tha•lene (năf'thə-lēn', năp'-) *n.* A crystalline compound derived from coal tar and used in dyes, moth repellents, explosives, and solvents.

nap•kin (năp'kĭn) *n.* **1.** A piece of cloth or soft paper, used at meals to protect clothing or wipe the lips and fingers. **2.** A small cloth or towel.

Na•ples (nā'pəlz). Seaport of SC Italy. *Pop.* 1,223,228. **—Ne'a•pol'i•tan** (nē'ə-pŏl'ĭ-tən) *adj. & n.*

na•po•le•on (nə-pō'lē-ən, -pōl'yən) *n.* A pastry of flaky layers filled with custard cream.

Napoleon I. 1769–1821. Emperor of the French (1804–15). **—Na•po'le•on'ic** *adj.*

narc or **nark** (närk) *n. Slang.* A police officer or government agent who deals with narcotics violations.

nar•cis•sism (när'sĭ-sĭz'əm) *n.* Excessive self-admiration or self-love. **—nar'cis•sist** *n.* **—nar'cis•sis'tic** *adj.*

nar•cis•sus (när-sĭs'əs) *n., pl.* **-es** or **-cis•si** (-sĭs'ī', -sĭs'ē). A widely grown plant of the genus *Narcissus,* with narrow grasslike leaves and white or yellow flowers having a cup- or trumpet-shaped crown.

nar•co•sis (när-kō'sĭs) *n., pl.* **-ses** (-sēz'). Deep, drug-induced unconsciousness.

nar•cot•ic (när-kŏt'ĭk) *n.* A habit-forming drug that dulls the senses, relieves pain, and induces sleep. **—nar•cot'ic** *adj.* **—nar•cot'i•cal•ly** *adv.*

nar•co•tize (när'kə-tīz') *v.* **-tized, -tiz•ing. 1.** To subject or treat with a narcotic. **2.** To put to sleep : soothe.

nar•is (nâr'ĭs) *n., pl.* **-es** (-ēz). A nostril.

nar•rate (năr'āt', nă-rāt') *v.* **-rat•ed, -rat•ing. 1.** To give a description or account : relate. **2.** To supply a running commentary for a performance, as of a motion picture. **—nar•ra'tion** *n.* **—nar'ra'tor** *n.*

nar•ra•tive (năr'ə-tĭv) *n.* **1.** A narrated account : story. **2.** The act or an example of narrating. **—nar'ra•tive** *adj.*

†nar•row (năr'ō) *adj.* **-er, -est. 1.** Small or slender in width. **2.**

Limited in area or scope : confined. **3.** Rigid : inflexible. **4.** Barely enough <won by a *narrow* margin> **5.** *Regional.* Miserly : stingy. *—v.* To make or become narrow : contract. *—n.* **narrows.** A narrow body of water between 2 larger ones. **—nar′row•ly** *adv.* **—nar′row•ness** *n.*
nar•row-mind•ed (năr′ō-mīn′dĭd) *adj.* Lacking tolerance or sympathy : petty. **—nar′row-mind′ed•ly** *adv.* **—nar′row-mind′ed•ness** *n.*
nar•whal (när′wəl) *n.* An Arctic aquatic mammal, *Monodon monoceros,* having a long, spirally twisted ivory tusk in the male.

narwhal

†nar•y (nâr′ē) *adj. Regional.* Not one : no.
na•sal (nā′zəl) *adj.* **1.** Of or pertaining to the nose. **2.** Produced while exhaling air through the nose <a *nasal* sound> **—na•sal′i•ty** *n.* **—na′sal•ly** *adv.*
na•sal•ize (nā′zə-līz′) *v.* **-ized, -iz•ing.** To make nasal or produce nasal sounds. **—na′sal•i•za′tion** *n.*
nas•cent (năs′ənt, nā′sənt) *adj.* Coming into existence. **—nas′cence** *n.*
Nash•ville (năsh′vĭl′) *n.* **1.** Cap. of Tenn., in the NC part. *Pop.* 455,651. **2.** The country music industry.
Nas•ser (nä′sər, năs′ər), **Gamal Abdel.** 1918–70. Egyptian soldier and statesman.
Nas•sau (năs′ô′). Cap. of the Bahamas, on New Providence Is. *Pop.* 101,503.
na•stur•tium (nə-stûr′shəm, nă-) *n.* A plant of the genus *Tropaeolum,* with 5-petaled, usu. orange, yellow, or red flowers.
nas•ty (năs′tē) *adj.* **-ti•er, -ti•est. 1.** Disgustingly dirty : filthy. **2.** Morally offensive : obscene. **3.** Malicious : mean. **4.** Unpleasant. **5.** Dangerous or harmful. **—nas′ti•ly** *adv.* **—nas′ti•ness** *n.*
nat. *abbr.* **1.** *also* **natl.** national. **2.** native. **3.** natural.
na•tal (nāt′l) *adj.* Of, pertaining to, or accompanying birth <*natal* trauma>
na•tal•i•ty (nā-tăl′ĭ-tē, nə-) *n., pl.* **-ties.** Birthrate.
na•tion (nā′shən) *n.* **1.** A group of people organized under 1 government. **2.** A tribe or federation, esp. of North American Indians. ☆**syns:** COUNTRY, LAND, STATE
na•tion•al (năsh′ə-nəl, năsh′nəl) *adj.* **1.** Of or belonging to a nation. **2.** Typical of the people of a nation. *—n.* A citizen of a nation. **—na′tion•al•ly** *adv.*
National Guard *n.* The militia reserve unit of a U.S. state, maintained by the state and federal governments and subject to active duty call by either.
na•tion•al•ism (năsh′ə-nə-lĭz′əm, năsh′nə-) *n.* **1.** Concern for or attachment to a particular nation's interests or culture. **2.** Advocacy of national independence. **—na′tion•al•ist** *n.* **—na′tion•al•is′tic** *adj.* **—na′tion•al•is′ti•cal•ly** *adv.*
na•tion•al•i•ty (năsh′ə-năl′ĭ-tē) *n., pl.* **-ties. 1.** The condition of belonging to a particular nation by birth, origin, or naturalization. **2.** A people with common origins or traditions, often forming a nation.
na•tion•al•ize (năsh′ə-nə-līz′, năsh′nə-) *v.* **-ized, -iz•ing. 1.** To change from private to governmental control. **2.** To make national. **—na′tion•al•i•za′tion** *n.*
national monument *n.* A landmark maintained by a national government for public enjoyment or study.
national park *n.* A tract of land maintained by a national government for public recreation and cultural use.
national seashore *n.* A seacoast area maintained by a national government.
na•tion•wide (nā′shən-wīd′) *adj.* Throughout a nation.
na•tive (nā′tĭv) *adj.* **1.** Belonging to one by nature : innate. **2.** Being such by birth or origin. **3.** Belonging to one by birth <my *native* country> **4.** Growing, living, or produced in a particular place : indigenous. *—n.* **1.** One born in or associated with a place by birth. **2. a.** An original inhabitant. **b.** A long-time resident. **3.** Something, as a plant or animal, that originated in a particular place. **—na′tive•ly** *adv.*
Native American *n.* An American Indian.
na•tiv•i•ty (nə-tĭv′ĭ-tē, nā-) *n., pl.* **-ties. 1.** Birth, esp. the place, conditions, or circumstances of being born. **2. Nativity. a.** Jesus' birth. **b.** Christmas.
nat•ty (năt′ē) *adj.* **-ti•er, -ti•est.** *Informal.* Neat and trim : dapper. **—nat′ti•ly** *adv.* **—nat′ti•ness** *n.*
nat•u•ral (năch′ər-əl, năch′rəl) *adj.* **1.** Existing in or produced by nature. **2.** Of or pertaining to nature. **3.** Following the usual or expected course of nature <death from *natural* causes> **4. a.** Not acquired : innate. **b.** Having a particular character by nature <a *natural* athlete> **5.** Free from pretension or artificiality. **6.** Expected and accepted. **7.** *Mus.* Not sharped or flatted. *—n.* **1.** *Informal.* One naturally suited or qualified. **2.** *Mus.* The sign (♮) placed before a note to nullify a preceding sharp or flat. **—nat′u•ral•ness** *n.*
natural childbirth *n.* Childbirth considered as a natural process that involves little stress or pain and requires preparatory training and medical supervision but no anesthesia or surgical aid.
natural gas *n.* A mixture of gaseous hydrocarbons, chiefly methane, found with petroleum deposits and used as a fuel and in manufacturing organic compounds.
natural history *n.* The study of living things and natural objects and their origins and relationships.
nat•u•ral•ism (năch′ər-ə-lĭz′əm, năch′rə-) *n.* **1.** Realistic representation, esp. in art and literature. **2.** The philosophical doctrine that all phenomena can be explained by natural causes and laws. **—nat′u•ral•is′tic** *adj.* **—nat′u•ral•is′ti•cal•ly** *adv.*
nat•u•ral•ist (năch′ər-ə-lĭst, năch′rə-) *n.* **1.** One who studies natural history. **2.** One who advocates naturalism.
nat•u•ral•ize (năch′ər-ə-līz′, năch′rə-) *v.* **-ized, -iz•ing. 1.** To confer full citizenship upon (one of foreign birth). **2.** To adopt into widespread use. **3.** To adapt or become adapted to life in a new environment. **—nat′u•ral•i•za′tion** *n.*
nat•u•ral•ly (năch′ər-ə-lē, năch′rə-) *adv.* **1.** In a natural way. **2.** By nature : innately. **3.** Without a doubt : positively.
natural resource *n.* A necessary or beneficial material source, as of timber or a mineral deposit, occurring in nature.
natural science *n.* A science, as biology, chemistry, or physics, based primarily on quantitative phenomena and hypotheses of the physical world.
natural selection *n.* The principle that in a given environment individuals having characteristics that aid survival will produce more offspring and the proportion of individuals having such characteristics will increase with each succeeding generation.
na•ture (nā′chər) *n.* **1.** The physical world and its phenomena. **2.** The processes and forces producing and controlling the physical world. **3.** The world of living things <the serenity of *nature*> **4.** A primitive state of existence. **5.** Kind : type <an object of that *nature*> **6.** Intrinsic characteristics and qualities <the *nature* of the dilemma> **7.** One's basic character or disposition : temperament <had a kind *nature*> **—na′tured** *adj.*
naught *also* **nought** (nôt) *n.* **1.** Nothing <all for *naught*> **2.** The figure 0 : zero.
naugh•ty (nô′tē) *adj.* **-ti•er, -ti•est. 1.** Unruly : disobedient <a *naughty* schoolboy> **2.** Lacking propriety : indelicate. **—naugh′ti•ly** *adv.* **—naugh′ti•ness** *n.*
Na•u•ru (nä-ōō′rōō). Atoll and country of the C Pacific, S of the equator and W of Kiribati. *Cap.* Yaren. *Pop.* 7,100.
nau•se•a (nô′zē-ə, -zhə, -sē-ə, -shə) *n.* **1.** A stomach disturbance marked by a desire to vomit. **2.** Strong disgust : repugnance.
nau•se•ate (nô′zē-āt′, -zhē-, -sē-, -shē-) *v.* **-at•ed, -at•ing.** To feel or cause to feel nausea. **—nau′se•at′ing•ly** *adv.*
nau•seous (nô′shəs, -zē-əs) *adj.* **1.** Causing nausea. **2.** Affected with nausea. **—nau′seous•ly** *adv.*
nau•ti•cal (nô′tĭ-kəl) *adj.* Of, pertaining to, or typical of ships, shipping, sailors, or navigation. **—nau′ti•cal•ly** *adv.*
nautical mile *n.* An international unit of distance equal to 1,852 m or approx. 6,076 ft.
nau•ti•lus (nôt′l-əs) *n., pl.* **-es** or **-li** (-lī′). A tropical marine mollusk of the genus *Nautilus,* having a spiral shell divided into air-filled chambers.
na•val (nā′vəl) *adj.* Of, relating to, or having a navy.
naval stores *pl.n.* Products, as turpentine or pitch, orig. used to caulk the seams of wooden ships.
nave (nāv) *n.* The central part of a church from the main entrance to the chancel.
na•vel (nā′vəl) *n.* A small mark on the abdomen where the umbilical cord was attached to the fetus.
navel orange *n.* A sweet, usu. seedless orange with a navellike mark at 1 end.
nav•i•ga•ble (năv′ĭ-gə-bəl) *adj.* **1.** Sufficiently wide or deep to allow passage of ships. **2.** Able to be steered. **—nav′i•ga•bil′i•ty, nav′i•ga•ble•ness** *n.*

nav•i•gate (năv'ĭ-gāt') *v.* **-gat•ed, -gat•ing. 1.** To plan and direct the course of a ship or aircraft. **2.** To travel over or through water in a ship : sail. **3.** *Informal.* **a.** To make one's way. **b.** To walk. **—nav'i•ga'tion** *n.* **—nav'i•ga'tion•al** *adj.* **—nav'i•ga'tor** *n.*

na•vy (nā'vē) *n., pl.* **-vies. 1.** A nation's fleet, esp. of warships. **2.** *often* **Navy.** A national organization for naval defense.

navy bean *n.* A variety of the kidney bean, grown for its nutritious white seeds.

navy blue *n.* A dark blue.

nay (nā) *adv.* **1.** No. **2.** And moreover <was good-looking, *nay,* beautiful> *—n.* **1.** A denial or refusal. **2.** A negative vote.

Naz•a•reth (năz'ə-rĭth). Town of N Israel. *Pop.* 40,400.

Na•zi (nät'sē, năt'-) *n., pl.* **-zis.** A member of the fascist party that held power (1933–45) in Germany under Adolf Hitler. **—Na'zi** *adj.* **—Na'zism, Na'zi•ism** *n.*

Nb *symbol for* NIOBIUM.

NB *abbr.* Nebraska (with Zip Code).

n.b. *abbr.* note carefully (Lat. *nota bene*).

N.B. *abbr.* New Brunswick.

NC *abbr.* North Carolina (with Zip Code).

N.C. *abbr.* North Carolina.

Nd *symbol for* NEODYMIUM.

ND *abbr.* North Dakota (with Zip Code).

N.D. *abbr.* North Dakota.

Ndja•me•na (ən-jä'mə-nə). Cap. of Chad, in the SW. Pop. 241,639.

Ne *symbol for* NEON.

NE *abbr.* northeast; northeastern.

N.E. *abbr.* New England.

Ne•an•der•thal (nē-ăn'dər-thôl', -tôl') *adj.* **1.** Of or relating to an extinct primitive Stone Age species or race of man. **2.** Rude or primitive. **—Ne•an'der•thal'** *n.*

neap tide (nēp) *n.* A tide of lowest range, occurring twice a month.

near (nîr) *adv.* **1.** To, at, or within a short distance or time <a house *near* the beach> **2.** Nearly : almost <*near* played out> **3.** In or with a close relationship. *—adj.* **1.** Close in distance, time, or degree <the *near* future> **2.** Closely related by kinship or association : intimate. **3.** Accomplished or missed by a narrow margin <a *near* bull's-eye> **4.** Short and direct. **5. a.** Closer of 2 or more. **b.** On the left side of a vehicle or draft team. ☆***syns:*** CLOSE, IMMEDIATE, NEARBY, NIGH *—prep.* Close to <a motel *near* town> *—v.* To draw near or nearer (to). **—near'ness** *n.*

near beer *n.* A malt liquor not containing enough alcohol to be considered an alcoholic beverage.

near•by (nîr'bī') *adj.* & *adv.* Close at hand : adjacent.

Near East *n.* Region including the countries of the E Mediterranean, the Arabian Peninsula, and, sometimes, NE Africa.

near•ly (nîr'lē) *adv.* **1.** Almost but not quite. **2.** Closely or intimately.

near•sight•ed (nîr'sī'tĭd) *adj.* Afflicted with myopia : shortsighted. **—near'sight'ed•ly** *adv.* **—near'sight'ed•ness** *n.*

neat (nēt) *adj.* **1.** Clean and tidy. **2.** Orderly and precise : systematic. **3.** Skillfully or cleverly done : adroit. **4.** Undiluted <*neat* vodka> **5.** NET[2] 1. **6.** *Slang.* Fine : wonderful. ☆***syns:*** ORDERLY, SHIPSHAPE, SPICK-AND-SPAN, TIDY, TRIM **—neat'ly** *adv.* **—neat'ness** *n.*

▲word history: The adjective *neat* is derived from Old French *net,* which had several meanings. A basic sense of the French word was "free from dirt; clean." Liquor that contained no impurities was called *neat,* a sense that survives in the meaning "undiluted." An amount of money that was not liable to any reduction was also considered *neat.* A variant form of the Old French *net* had the same spelling and meanings but a different pronunciation. It survives in the English word *net,* meaning "remaining after all deductions." A *neat* profit and a *net* profit are in meaning and origin exactly the same.

neath *or* **'neath** (nēth) *prep.* Beneath.

neat's-foot oil (nēts'fo͝ot') *n.* A light yellow oil made from the feet and leg bones of cattle and used primarily to dress leather.

neb (nĕb) *n.* **1. a.** A bird's beak. **b.** A nose or snout. **2.** A sharp point.

Nebr. *also* **Neb.** *abbr.* Nebraska.

Ne•bras•ka (nə-brăs'kə). State of the C U.S. *Cap.* Lincoln. *Pop.* 1,570,006. **—Ne•bras'kan** *n.*

neb•u•la (nĕb'yə-lə) *n., pl.* **-lae** (-lē') or **-las.** A large cloudlike mass of interstellar gas or dust, visible as a bright or dark patch in the sky depending on the way the mass reflects or absorbs light. **—neb'u•lar** *adj.*

neb•u•lize (nĕb'yə-līz') *v.* **-lized, -liz•ing.** To change (a liquid) to a fine spray or mist. **—neb'u•li•za'tion** *n.* **—neb'u•liz'er** *n.*

neb•u•lous (nĕb'yə-ləs) *adj.* **1.** Misty, cloudy, or hazy. **2.** Indefinite in form or limits. **3.** Of or pertaining to a nebula. **—neb'u•los'i•ty** (-lŏs'ĭ-tē) *n.* **—neb'u•lous•ly** *adv.* **—neb'u•lous•ness** *n.*

nec•es•sar•y (nĕs'ĭ-sĕr'ē) *adj.* **1.** Absolutely required : indispensable. **2.** Needed to bring about a certain effect or result. **3. a.** Unavoidably determined by prior circumstances or conditions. **b.** Logically inevitable. ☆***syns:*** ESSENTIAL, INDISPENSABLE, VITAL *—n., pl.* **-ies.** NECESSITY 1b. **—nec'es•sar'i•ly** *adv.*

ne•ces•si•tate (nə-sĕs'ĭ-tāt') *v.* **-tat•ed, -tat•ing. 1.** To make necessary. **2.** To compel or require. **—ne•ces'si•ta'tion** *n.*

ne•ces•si•ty (nə-sĕs'ĭ-tē) *n., pl.* **-ties. 1. a.** The quality or state of being necessary. **b.** Something necessary : requirement. **2.** Something inevitable. **3.** Neediness.

neck (nĕk) *n.* **1.** The bodily part linking the head and the trunk. **2.** The part of a garment that fits the neck. **3.** A somewhat narrow projection or part, as of land, a bottle, or a stringed musical instrument. **4.** A narrow margin <lost by a *neck*> *—v.* *Slang.* To kiss and caress. **—necked** *adj.*

neck•er•chief (nĕk'ər-chĭf) *n.* A scarf worn about the neck.

neck•lace (nĕk'lĭs) *n.* A neck ornament.

neck•line (nĕk'līn') *n.* The edge of a garment at or near the neck.

neck•tie (nĕk'tī') *n.* A narrow strip of material designed to be worn around the neck and tied in front.

ne•crol•o•gy (nə-krŏl'ə-jē, nĕ-) *n., pl.* **-gies. 1.** A list of usu. recently deceased people. **2.** An obituary. **—nec'ro•log'ic** (nĕk'rə-lŏj'ĭk), **nec'ro•log'i•cal**

nec•ro•man•cy (nĕk'rə-măn'sē) *n.* **1.** Communication with the dead in order to foretell the future. **2.** Black magic. **—nec'ro•man'cer** *n.* **—nec'ro•man'tic** *adj.*

ne•crop•o•lis (nə-krŏp'ə-lĭs, nĕ-) *n., pl.* **-lis•es** *or* **-leis** (-lās'). A cemetery, esp. a large elaborate one in an ancient city.

ne•cro•sis (nə-krō'sĭs, nĕ-) *n., pl.* **-ses** (-sēz'). Pathologic death of living plant or animal tissue. **—ne•crot'ic** (-krŏt'ĭk) *adj.*

nec•tar (nĕk'tər) *n.* **1.** The drink of the Greek gods. **2.** A good-tasting drink. **3.** A sweet liquid in various flowers gathered by bees for honey. **—nec'tar•ous** *adj.*

nec•tar•ine (nĕk'tə-rēn') *n.* A type of peach with a smooth glossy skin.

née *also* **nee** (nā) *adj.* Born. Used to indicate the maiden name of a married woman.

need (nēd) *n.* **1.** A lack of something necessary, useful, or desirable. **2.** Obligation or requirement. **3.** Something necessary, useful, or desirable : requisite. **4.** Poverty or misfortune. ☆***syns:*** EXIGENCY, NECESSITY *—v.* **1.** Used as an auxiliary to express obligation or requirement <You *need* not go until tomorrow.> **2.** To require or desire urgently. **3.** To be in need or want.

need•ful (nēd'fəl) *adj.* Required : essential. **—need'ful•ness** *n.*

nee•dle (nēd'l) *n.* **1.a.** A thin, sharp-pointed steel sewing implement, with an eye at 1 end through which thread is passed and held. **b.** A similarly shaped implement, as one used in knitting. **2.** A thin pointed stylus that transmits vibrations from the grooves of a phonograph record. **3.** A thin pointer or indicator, as on a compass or gauge. **4.** A hypodermic needle. **5.** A stiff needle-shaped leaf, as of a fir tree. **6.** A thin, sharp projection, as a spine of a sea urchin or a crystal. *—v.* **-dled, -dling.** *Informal.* **1.** To provoke or prod. **2.** To tease.

nee•dle•point (nēd'l-point') *n.* Decorative stitching on canvas, usu. covering the entire surface of the material.

need•less (nēd'lĭs) *adj.* Unnecessary. **—need'less•ly** *adv.* **—need'less•ness** *n.*

nee•dle•work (nēd'l-wûrk') *n.* Work, as sewing or embroidery, done with a needle. **—nee'dle•work'er** *n.*

need•n't (nēd'nt). Need not.

needs (nēdz) *adv.* Of necessity <I must *needs* stay.>

need•y (nē'dē) *adj.* **-i•er, -i•est.** Being in want : poor. **—need'i•ness** *n.*

ne'er (nâr) *adv.* Never.

ne'er-do-well (nâr'do͞o-wĕl') *n.* An idle, unreliable person. **—ne'er'-do-well'** *adj.*

ne•far•i•ous (nə-fâr'ē-əs) *adj.* Wicked : despicable. **—ne•far'i•ous•ly** *adv.*

Nef•er•ti•ti (nĕf'ər-tē'tē). Queen of Egypt in the early 14th cent. B.C.

neg. *abbr.* negative.

ne•gate (nə-gāt') *v.* **-gat•ed, -gat•ing. 1.** To nullify or make ineffective. **2.** To rule out : deny.

ne•ga•tion (nə-gā'shən) *n.* **1.** The act or process of negating. **2.** A denial, contradiction, or negative statement.

neg•a•tive (nĕg'ə-tĭv) *adj.* **1.** Indicating refusal, denial, contradiction, or disapproval. **2.** Not constructive or helpful. **3.** Not confident : unsure of oneself. **4.** *Math.* **a.** Less than zero. **b.** Of the sign (–) indicating a negative number or one that is to be subtracted. **5.** Of or having an electric charge that tends to repel electrons. **6.** Having light and dark areas opposite to those of the original photographic subject. —*n.* **1.** A negative statement, idea, or action. **2.** A word or part of a word, as *no* or *non-*, that indicates negation. **3.** The side in a debate that opposes or contradicts the question being debated. **4. a.** A negative photographic image. **b.** Photographic material, as a film or plate, having such an image. **5.** *Math.* A negative number. —*v.* **-tived, -tiv·ing. 1.** To refuse to accept or approve. **2.** To contradict or deny. **—neg′a·tive·ly** *adv.* **—neg′a·tive·ness, neg′a·tiv′i·ty** *n.*

neg·a·tiv·ism (nĕg′ə-tĭ-vĭz′əm) *n.* Habitual skepticism or resistance to the ideas, orders, or suggestions of others. **—neg′a·tiv·ist** *n.* **—neg′a·tiv·is′tic** *adj.*

ne·glect (nĭ-glĕkt′) *v.* **1.** To pay no attention to : ignore. **2.** To fail to give proper care or attention to. **3.** To fail to do or accomplish, as through carelessness. —*n.* **1.** An act or instance of neglecting. **2.** The state of being neglected. **3.** Habitual lack of care. **—ne·glect′er, ne·glec′tor** *n.*

ne·glect·ful (nĭ-glĕkt′fəl) *adj.* Careless or unheeding. **—ne·glect′ful·ly** *adv.* **—ne·glect′ful·ness** *n.*

neg·li·gee (nĕg′lĭ-zhā′, nĕg′lĭ-zhā′) *n.* A woman's loose dressing gown, often of fine sheer fabric.

neg·li·gent (nĕg′lĭ-jənt) *adj.* **1.** Marked by or inclined to neglect, esp. habitually. **2.** Extremely heedless. **—neg′li·gence** *n.* **—neg′li·gent·ly** *adv.*

neg·li·gi·ble (nĕg′lĭ-jə-bəl) *adj.* Unworthy of consideration : insignificant.

ne·go·tia·ble (nĭ-gō′shə-bəl, -shē-ə-) *adj.* **1.** Able to be negotiated. **2.** Able to be transferred legally from one to another. **—ne·go′tia·bil′i·ty** *n.* **—ne·go′tia·bly** *adv.*

ne·go·ti·ate (nĭ-gō′shē-āt′) *v.* **-at·ed, -at·ing. 1.** To meet and discuss with another in order to reach an agreement. **2.** To settle by meeting and discussing <*negotiate* a peace treaty> **3.** To transfer title to or ownership of (e.g., notes) to another in exchange for equivalent value. **4.** To accomplish or cope with successfully. **—ne·go′ti·a′tion** *n.* **—ne·go′ti·a′tor** *n.*

Ne·gro (nē′grō) *n., pl.* **-groes.** A Negroid person : black. **—Ne′gro** *adj.*

Ne·groid (nē′groid′) *adj.* Of or pertaining to a major division of the human species whose members characteristically have brown to black pigmentation and often tightly curled hair. **—Ne′groid** *n.*

Ne·he·mi·ah (nē′hə-mī′ə, nē′ə-) *n.* See BIBLE TABLE.

Neh·ru (nā′ro͞o), **Jawaharlal.** 1889–1964. 1st prime minister of India (1947–64).

neigh (nā) *n.* The breathy, high-pitched prolonged cry characteristic of a horse. **—neigh** *v.*

neigh·bor (nā′bər) *n.* **1.** One who lives near or is adjacent to another. **2.** A fellow human being. —*v.* **1.** To live or be located close by. **2.** To border on.

neigh·bor·hood (nā′bər-ho͝od′) *n.* **1.** An area or section having distinguishing characteristics. **2.** The people living in a specific area or section. **3.** Approximate range or amount : vicinity.

neigh·bor·ly (nā′bər-lē) *adj.* Of or like a good neighbor : friendly. **—neigh′bor·li·ness** *n.*

neigh·bour (nā′bər) *n. esp. Brit. var. of* NEIGHBOR.

nei·ther (nē′*th*ər, nī′-) *adj.* Not one nor the other <*Neither* radio works.> —*pron.* Not the one nor the other <*Neither* of them works.> —*conj.* **1.** Used with the correlative conjunction *nor* <*Neither* your house nor mine is big enough for the party.> **2.** Also not : nor <If you won't go, *neither* will I.>

nel·son (nĕl′sən) *n.* A wrestling hold in which pressure is applied with the palm of the hand against the opponent's neck.

Nel·son (nĕl′sən), Viscount **Horatio.** 1758–1805. English admiral.

nem·a·tode (nĕm′ə-tōd′) *n.* An often parasitic threadlike worm of the phylum Nematoda, as the hookworm.

nem·e·sis (nĕm′ĭ-sĭs) *n., pl.* **-ses** (-sēz′). **1.** One that brings about retribution or vengeance. **2.** Just punishment for wrongdoing. **3.** A seemingly unbeatable rival.

ne·o·clas·si·cism (nē′ō-klăs′ĭ-sĭz′əm) *n.* A revival or adaptation of classical forms, esp. in the arts. **—ne′o·clas′sic, ne′o·clas′si·cal** *adj.*

ne·o·dym·i·um (nē′ō-dĭm′ē-əm) *n. Symbol* **Nd** A bright silvery rare-earth element.

ne·ol·o·gism (nē-ŏl′ə-jĭz′əm) *n.* A new word, phrase, or expression or a new meaning for an existing word. **—ne·ol′o·gis′tic, ne·ol′o·gis′ti·cal** *adj.*

ne·on (nē′ŏn′) *n. Symbol* **Ne** An inert gaseous element often used in display lights.

ne·o·nate (nē′ə-nāt′) *n.* A newborn child. **—ne′o·na′tal** *adj.*

ne·o·na·tol·o·gy (nē′ō-nā-tŏl′ə-jē) *n.* The medical study of the first 60 days of an infant's life. **—ne′o·na·tol′o·gist** *n.*

ne·o·phyte (nē′ə-fīt′) *n.* **1.** A new convert. **2.** A novice or beginner.

ne·o·plasm (nē′ə-plăz′əm) *n.* A tumor. **—ne′o·plas′tic** *adj.*

ne·o·prene (nē′ə-prēn′) *n.* A durable synthetic rubber resistant esp. to oil.

Ne·pal (nə-pôl′, -päl′). Kingdom in the Himalayas. *Cap.* Katmandu. *Pop.* 15,155,000. **—Nep′a·lese′** (-lēz′, -lēs′) *adj. & n.*

ne·pen·the (nĭ-pĕn′thē) *n.* Something that eases pain or grief.

neph·ew (nĕf′yo͞o) *n.* The son of one's brother or sister or of one's spouse's brother or sister.

ne·phrit·ic (nə-frĭt′ĭk) *adj.* **1.** Of or relating to the kidneys. **2.** Of, relating to, or afflicted with nephritis.

ne·phri·tis (nə-frī′tĭs) *n.* Inflammation of the kidneys.

nep·o·tism (nĕp′ə-tĭz′əm) *n.* Favoritism shown by those in high office to relatives or friends. **—nep′o·tist** *n.*

Nep·tune (nĕp′to͞on′, -tyo͞on′) *n.* The 8th planet from the sun. **—Nep·tu′ni·an** *adj.*

nep·tu·ni·um (nĕp-to͞o′nē-əm, -tyo͞o′-) *n. Symbol* **Np** A silvery, metallic, naturally radioactive element.

Ne·ro (nîr′ō). A.D. 37–68. Roman emperor (54–68).

nerve (nûrv) *n.* **1.** Any of the bundles of fibers extending from the central nervous system to the various organs and parts of the body and capable of relaying sensory stimuli and motor impulses throughout the body. **2. a.** Calm endurance : patience. **b.** Stamina : fortitude. **c.** Strong will : courage. **d.** *Informal.* Impudent boldness : audacity. **3. nerves.** Agitation brought about by fright, anxiety, or stress. —*v.* **nerved, nerv·ing.** To give strength or courage to.

nerve center *n.* A focal point of influence or control.

nerve·less (nûrv′lĭs) *adj.* **1.** Having little or no strength or energy. **2.** Displaying poise : calm. **—nerve′less·ly** *adv.* **—nerve′less·ness** *n.*

nerve-rack·ing *also* **nerve-wrack·ing** (nûrv′răk′ĭng) *adj.* Extremely irritating or distressing.

nerv·ous (nûr′vəs) *adj.* **1.** Of, affecting, or relating to the nerves or nervous system. **2.** Excitable : jumpy. **3.** Worried : apprehensive. **—nerv′ous·ly** *adv.* **—nerv′ous·ness** *n.*

nervous breakdown *n.* A severe or incapacitating emotional or psychic disorder.

nervous system *n.* A bodily mechanism in all multicellular animals except sponges that coordinates internal functions and responses to stimuli.

nerv·y (nûr′vē) *adj.* **-i·er, -i·est. 1.** Rudely bold or confident. **2.** Showing or requiring fortitude, energy, or stamina. **3.** Nervous.

-ness *suff.* State : condition : quality : degree <dark*ness*>

nest (nĕst) *n.* **1. a.** A shelter or receptacle constructed by a bird to hold its eggs and young. **b.** A similar receptacle that shelters an insect, fish, or animal. **2.** A warm, cozy place. **3.** A group of objects of graduated size that can be stacked together. —*v.* **1.** To construct or live in a nest. **2.** To fit snugly together or inside one another.

nest egg *n.* A sum of money saved for future use.

†nest·er (nĕs′tər) *n.* *W U.S.* A squatter, homesteader, or farmer who settles in cattle-grazing territory.

nes·tle (nĕs′əl) *v.* **-tled, -tling. 1. a.** To settle snugly and comfortably. **b.** To lie in a sheltered location. **2.** To snuggle contentedly. **—nes′tler** *n.*

nest·ling (nĕst′lĭng) *n.* A young bird not yet able to leave the nest.

net¹ (nĕt) *n.* **1.** Openwork fabric made of threads, cords, or ropes woven or knotted together. **2.** Something made of net, esp.: **a.** A device for capturing animals, as fish or butterflies. **b.** A mesh that acts as a barrier <a mosquito *net*> **c.** A mesh for holding the hair in place. **3.** A barrier strung between 2 posts in the center of a tennis, badminton, or volleyball court. **4.** Something that ensnares. —*v.* **net·ted, net·ting.** To catch in, protect, cover, or surround with or as if with a net.

net² (nĕt) *adj.* **1.** Remaining after all additions, subtractions, or adjustments have been made <*net* profits><*net* volume> **2.** Ultimate : final. —*n.* A net amount, as of profit or weight. —*v.* **net·ted, net·ting.** To bring in or yield as profit.

neth·er (nĕ*th*′ər) *adj.* Located beneath or below : lower : under <the *nether* regions>

Neth·er·lands (nĕ*th*′ər-ləndz). Kingdom of NW Europe, on the North Sea. *Constitutional cap.* Amsterdam; *de facto cap.* The Hague. *Pop.* 14,170,000.

Netherlands Antilles. Autonomous territory of the Netherlands, in the West Indies. *Cap.* Willemstad. *Pop.* 225,000.

net·su·ke (nĕt′sə-kē) *n.* A small Japanese toggle, usu. decorated with inlays or carving, used esp. to fasten a purse to a kimono sash.

net·tle (nĕt′l) *n.* A plant of the genus *Urtica,* having toothed leaves covered with hairs that secrete a stinging fluid. —*v.* **-tled, -tling.** To vex : irritate.

net·work (nĕt′wûrk′) *n.* **1.** An openwork fabric or structure in which cords, threads, wires, etc. are interwoven at regular intervals. **2.** Something resembling a net <a *network* of spies> **3.** A group of interconnected broadcasting stations that usu. share a large proportion of their programming.

Neuf•châ•tel (no͞o′shə-tĕl′, nœ′shä-) *n.* A soft cheese made from milk or cream.

neu•ral (no͝or′əl, nyo͝or′-) *adj.* Of or relating to a nerve or the nervous system.

neu•ral•gia (no͝o-răl′jə, nyo͝o-) *n.* Paroxysmal pain along a nerve. **–neu•ral′gic** *adj.*

neu•ras•the•ni•a (no͝or′əs-thē′nē-ə, nyo͝or′-) *n.* A neurotic condition characterized by fatigue, loss of memory, and feelings of anxiety and inadequacy. **–neu′ras•then′ic** (-thĕn′ĭk) *adj.* & *n.* **–neu′ras•then′i•cal•ly** *adv.*

neu•ri•tis (no͝o-rī′tĭs, nyo͝o-) *n.* Inflammation of a nerve, causing pain, loss of reflexes, and muscular atrophy. **–neu•rit′ic** (-rĭt′ĭk) *adj.*

neu•rol•o•gy (no͝o-rŏl′ə-jē, nyo͝o-) *n.* The scientifical and medical study of the nervous system and its disorders. **–neu′ro•log′i•cal** *adj.* **–neu•rol′o•gist** *n.*

neu•ron (no͝or′ŏn′, nyo͝or′-) *also* **neu•rone** (-ōn′) *n.* Any of the cells of nerve tissue consisting of a main portion containing the nucleus and cytoplasmic extensions, the cell body, the dendrites, and axons. **–neu•ron′ic** (-rŏn′ĭk) *adj.*

neu•ro•pa•thol•o•gy (no͝or′ō-pə-thŏl′ə-jē, nyo͝or′-) *n.* Study of diseases of the nervous system. **–neu′ro•path′o•log′ic** (-păth′ə-lŏj′ĭk), **neu′ro•path′o•log′i•cal** *adj.* **–neu′ro•pa•thol′o•gist** *n.*

neu•rop•a•thy (no͝o-rŏp′ə-thē, nyo͝o-) *n.* Disease of the nervous system.

neu•ro•sis (no͝o-rō′sĭs, nyo͝o-) *n., pl.* **-ses** (-sēz′). Any of various functional disorders of the mind or emotions with no obvious physical cause. **–neu•rot•ic** *adj.* & *n.* **–neu•rot′i•cal•ly** *adv.*

neu•ter (no͞o′tər, nyo͞o′-) *adj.* **1.** Neither masculine nor feminine in grammatical gender. **2.** *Biol.* Having no sexual organs. —*n.* **1. a.** The neuter grammatical gender. **b.** A neuter word. **2. a.** A castrated animal. **b.** An animal or plant with undeveloped sex glands or organs, esp. an undeveloped female insect, such as a worker in a colony of ants. **–neu′ter** *v.*

neu•tral (no͞o′trəl, nyo͞o′-) *adj.* **1.** Not supporting or favoring either side in a war, quarrel, or contest. **2.** Belonging to neither side nor party. **3.** *Chem.* Neither acid nor alkaline. **4.** *Physics.* Having a net electric charge of zero. **5.** Of or indicating a color, as gray, black, or white, with no hue : achromatic. —*n.* **1.** One that is neutral. **2.** A neutral color. **3.** A position in which a set of gears is disengaged with no power transmitted. **–neu•tral′i•ty** *n.* **–neu′tral•ly** *adv.*

neu•tral•ism (no͞o′trə-lĭz′əm, nyo͞o′-) *n.* The condition or policy of being neutral, esp. nonparticipation in a war. **–neu′tral•ist** *n.* **–neu′tral•is′tic** *adj.*

neu•tral•ize (no͞o′trə-līz′, nyo͞o′-) *v.* **-ized, -iz•ing. 1.** To make neutral. **2.** To counteract. **–neu′tral•i•za′tion** *n.* **–neu′tral•iz′er** *n.*

neutral spirits *n. (sing. or pl. in number).* Ethyl alcohol distilled at or above 190 proof, frequently used in alcoholic beverage blends.

neu•tri•no (no͞o-trē′nō, nyo͞o-) *n., pl.* **-nos.** A massless, electrically neutral, stable subatomic particle that travels at the speed of light.

neu•tron (no͞o′trŏn′, nyo͞o′-) *n.* An electrically neutral subatomic particle having approx. the mass of a proton. It is stable when bound in an atomic nucleus, contributing to the mass of the nucleus without affecting atomic number or electric charge.

Nev. *abbr.* Nevada.

Ne•vad•a (nə-văd′ə, -vä′də). State of the W U.S. *Cap.* Carson City. *Pop.* 799,184. **–Ne•vad′an** *n.*

né•vé (nā-vā′) *n.* **1.** A snow field at the head of a glacier. **2.** The granular snow typically found in such a field.

nev•er (nĕv′ər) *adv.* **1.** Not ever. **2.** Not at all <*Never* mind.> <*Never* fear.>

nev•er•more (nĕv′ər-môr′, -mōr′) *adv.* Never again.

nev•er-nev•er land (nĕv′ər-nĕv′ər) *n.* An illusory, idyllic, or ideal place.

nev•er•the•less (nĕv′ər-thə-lĕs′) *adv.* Nonetheless.

ne•vus (nē′vəs) *n., pl.* **-vi** (-vī′). A congenital usu. pigmented growth or mark on the skin, as a mole : birthmark.

new (no͞o, nyo͞o) *adj.* **1. a.** Not old : recent <a *new* book> **b.** Never used before. **2.** Just discovered or learned <*new* evidence> **3.** Unfamiliar. **4.** Unaccustomed. **5.** Starting over again in a a cycle <the *new* moon> **6.** Changed for the better : rejuvenated. **7.** Coming after or taking the place of a previous one <a *new* model> **8.** Modern : current <*new* dances> —*adv.* Freshly : recently <*new*-mown hay> **–new′ness** *n.*

new•born (no͞o′bôrn′, nyo͞o′-) *adj.* **1.** Born very recently. **2.** Reborn. —*n.* A neonate.

New Bruns•wick (brŭnz′wĭk). Province of E Canada. *Cap.* Fredericton. *Pop.* 677,250.

New Cal•e•do•ni•a (kăl′ə-dō′nē-ə, -dōn′yə). French overseas territory in the SW Pacific. *Cap.* Nouméa. *Pop.* 133,233.

new•com•er (no͞o′kŭm′ər, nyo͞o′-) *n.* One who has recently arrived.

New Deal *n.* The policies and programs for economic recovery, relief, and social security that President Franklin D. Roosevelt introduced during the 1930's. **–New Dealer** *n.*

New Del•hi (dĕl′ē). Cap. of India, in the NC part. *Pop.* 301,801.

New Democratic Party *n. Can.* One of the 3 major political parties.

new•el (no͞o′əl, nyo͞o′-) *n.* **1.** The vertical support at the center of a circular staircase. **2.** A post that supports a handrail at the bottom or top of a staircase.

New England. Section of the NE U.S., including Me., N.H., Vt., Mass., Conn., and R.I.

new•fan•gled (no͞o′făng′gəld, nyo͞o′-) *adj.* New : novel.

New•found•land (no͞o′fən-lənd, -lănd′, nyo͞o′-). Province of E Canada, including the island of Newfoundland and the mainland area of Labrador. *Cap.* St. John's. *Pop.* 557,725. **–New′found•land•er** *n.*

New Guin•ea (gĭn′ē). Island in the SW Pacific N of Australia; divided between Indonesia and Papua New Guinea. **–New Guin′e•an** *adj.* & *n.*

New Hamp•shire (hămp′shər, -shĭr, hăm′-). State of the NE U.S. *Cap.* Concord. *Pop.* 920,610. **–New Hamp′shir•ite′** *n.*

New Heb•ri•des (hĕb′rə-dēz′). Island group in the S Pacific E of Australia.

New Jer•sey (jûr′zē). State of EC U.S. *Cap.* Trenton. *Pop.* 7,364,158. **–New Jer′sey•ite′** *n.*

new•ly (no͞o′lē, nyo͞o′-) *adv.* **1.** Lately : recently <a *newly* baked pie> **2.** Once more : anew <a *newly* decorated room> **3.** In a new or different way : freshly <an old song *newly* arranged>

new•ly-wed *also* **new•ly•wed** (no͞o′lē-wĕd′, nyo͞o′-) *n.* One recently married.

New Mex•i•co (mĕk′sĭ-kō′). State of the SW U.S. *Cap.* Sante Fe. *Pop.* 1,299,968. **–New Mex′i•can** *n.*

new moon *n.* **1.** The phase of the moon that occurs when it is between the earth and the sun, visible as a thin crescent at sunset. **2.** The crescent moon.

New Or•le•ans (ôr′lē-ənz, ôr′lənz, ôr-lēnz′). City of SE La. *Pop.* 557,482.

news (no͞oz, nyo͞oz) *pl.n. (sing. in number).* **1.** Recent events and happenings, esp. notable or unusual ones. **2. a.** Information about notable recent events, esp. as reported by the media. **b.** A presentation of such information.

news•boy (no͞oz′boi′, nyo͞oz′-) *n.* One who delivers or sells newspapers.

news•cast (no͞oz′kăst′, nyo͞oz′-) *n.* A radio or television broadcast of news. **–news′cast′er** *n.*

news•let•ter (no͞oz′lĕt′ər, nyo͞oz′-) *n.* A printed report, usu. issued at regular intervals, giving news about or information of interest to a particular group.

news•man (no͞oz′măn′, -mən, nyo͞oz′-) *n.* One who gathers, reports, edits, or comments on news.

news•pa•per (no͞oz′pā′pər, nyo͞oz′-) *n.* A usu. daily or weekly publication containing recent news, useful information, editorials, feature articles, and advertisements.

news•pa•per•man (no͞oz′pā′pər-măn′, nyo͞oz′-) *n.* **1.** One who owns or manages a newspaper. **2.** One who works for a newspaper, as a reporter, editor, etc. **–news′pa•per•wom′an** *n.*

news•print (no͞oz′prĭnt′, nyo͞oz′-) *n.* Inexpensive paper made from wood pulp, used chiefly for newspapers.

news•reel (no͞oz′rēl′, nyo͞oz′-) *n.* A short film giving a visual report of recent events.

news•room (no͞oz′ro͞om′, -ro͝om′, nyo͞oz′) A room, as in a newspaper office or a radio or television station, where news is prepared for release.

news•stand (no͞oz′stănd′, nyo͞oz′-) *n.* A booth, shop, or stand where newspapers, magazines, etc. are sold.

news•wor•thy (no͞oz′wûr′thē, nyo͞oz′-) *adj.* Worthy of being reported : interesting or significant. **–news′wor′thi•ness** *n.*

news•y (no͞o′zē, nyo͞o′-) *adj.* **-i•er, -i•est.** *Informal.* Informative.

newt (no͞ot, nyo͞ot) *n.* A small semiaquatic salamander of the genus *Triturus.*

New Testament *n.* The Gospels, Acts, Epistles, and the Book of Revelation, together viewed by Christians as forming the record of the new dispensation belonging to the Church. See BIBLE TABLE.

new·ton (no͞ot′n, nyo͞ot′n) *n. Physics.* The unit of force in the meter-kilogram-second system needed to accelerate a mass of 1 kilogram 1 meter per second per second.

Newton, Sir **Isaac.** 1642–1727. English mathematician, scientist, and philosopher. **–New·ton′i·an** *adj.*

new town *n.* A planned urban community comprising housing, commercial, industrial, and recreational facilities.

New World *n.* The W Hemisphere.

New Year's Day *n.* Jan. 1, the 1st day of the year.

New York (yôrk). **1.** State of the NE U.S. *Cap.* Albany. *Pop.* 17,557,288. **2.** City of SE N.Y., at the mouth of the Hudson R. *Pop.* 7,071,030. **–New York′er** *n.*

New Zea·land (zē′lənd). Island country in the S Pacific SE of Australia. *Cap.* Wellington. *Pop.* 3,125,000.

next (nĕkst) *adj.* **1.** Coming immediately after in time, order, or sequence. **2.** Nearest in position or space. *–adv.* **1.** Following in order immediately after the present or previous thing or action. **2.** On the first occasion after the present or previous one. *–prep.* Adjacent to : nearest.

nex·us (nĕk′səs) *n., pl.* **-us** *or* **-us·es.** A bond or link.

Nfld. *abbr.* Newfoundland.

ngul·trum (ĕn-gŭl′trəm, ĕng-) *n.* See CURRENCY TABLE.

ngwee (ĕn-gwē′) *n., pl.* **ngwee.** See *kwacha* at CURRENCY TABLE.

NH *abbr.* New Hampshire (with Zip Code).

N.H. *abbr.* New Hampshire.

Ni *symbol for* NICKEL.

ni·a·cin (nī′ə-sĭn) *n.* Nicotinic acid.

Ni·ag·a·ra (nī-ăg′rə, -ăg′ər-ə). **1.** River flowing from Lake Erie to Lake Ontario. **2.** Waterfalls of the Niagara R., consisting of the Canadian and the American Falls.

Nia·mey (nyä-mā′). Cap. of Niger, in the SW. *Pop.* 225,300.

nib (nĭb) *n.* **1. a.** A sharp point or tip. **b.** The point of a pen. **2.** A bird's beak.

nib·ble (nĭb′əl) *v.* **-bled, -bling. 1.** To bite (at) with small, gentle bites. **2.** To eat (food) with small, quick bites. **–nib′ble** *n.* **–nib′bler** *n.*

Nic·a·ra·gua (nĭk′ə-rä′gwə). Country of Central America. *Cap.* Managua. *Pop.* 2,610,000. **–Nic′a·ra′guan** *adj.* & *n.*

nice (nīs) *adj.* **nic·er, nic·est. 1.** Enjoyable : pleasant. **2.** Appealing or attractive. **3.** Courteous and polite. **4.** Excessively fussy : fastidious. **5.** Showing discernment and subtlety. **6.** Skillful : deft. **–nice′ly** *adv.* **–nice′ness** *n.*

▲word history: Since its adoption in the 13th cent. the word *nice* has developed from a term of abuse to a term of praise, a process called *melioration. Nice* is derived from Latin *nescius,* "ignorant," and was used in Middle English to mean "foolish; without sense." By the 15th cent. *nice* had acquired the sense "elegant" in conduct and dress, but not in a complimentary sense: *nice* meant "overrefined, overdelicate." This sense survives in the meanings "fastidious" and "precise, subtle." To the extent that delicacy, refinement, and precision have favorable connotations, *nice* developed corresponding senses.

ni·ce·ty (nī′sĭ-tē) *n., pl.* **-ties. 1.** Accuracy : exactness. **2.** A small or subtle detail or distinction. **3.** A dainty or elegant feature.

niche (nĭch, nēsh) *n.* **1.** An alcove or recess in a wall, as for displaying a statue. **2.** Something, as a position or activity, for which one is particularly suited.

nick (nĭk) *n.* A small shallow cut or chip on a surface. *–v.* To make a small shallow cut or chip in. **–in the nick of time.** At the very last moment.

nick·el (nĭk′əl) *n.* **1.** *Symbol* **Ni** A hard, silvery, ductile metallic element often used in alloys. **2.** A U.S. coin worth 5¢, made of a nickel and copper alloy.

nick·el·o·de·on (nĭk′ə-lō′dē-ən) *n.* **1.** An early theater charging 5¢ admission. **2.** A coin-operated musical device, as a juke box.

nickel silver *n.* A hard, silvery alloy of copper, zinc, and nickel.

nick·name (nĭk′nām′) *n.* **1.** A usu. descriptive name added to or replacing the actual name of a person, place, or thing. **2.** A shortened version or familiar form of a proper name. **–nick′name′** *v.*

▲word history: A *nickname* is literally an additional name. The Middle English form of the word *nickname* was *ekename,* from eke, "addition" (related to the verb *eke*), and *name,* "name." *Ekename* acquired an initial *n* from the indefinite article *an,* which frequently preceded it: *an ekename* came to be spelled and pronounced as if it was *a nekename.* In modern times the first syllable *neke-* was respelled *nick-,* and *nickname* has been the usual form ever since.

Nic·o·si·a (nĭk′ə-sē′ə). Cap. of Cyprus, in the NC part. *Pop.* 121,500.

nic·o·tine (nĭk′ə-tēn′) *n.* A poisonous alkaloid found in tobacco and used in medicine and insecticides.

nic·o·tin·ic acid (nĭk′ə-tĭn′ĭk) *n.* A compound of carbon, hydrogen, and nitrogen that is a member of the vitamin B complex and is essential to living cells.

niece (nēs) *n.* A daughter of one's brother or sister or one's spouse's brother or sister.

Nie·tzsche (nē′chə, -chē), **Friedrich Wilhelm.** 1844–1900. German philosopher.

nif·ty (nĭf′tē) *adj.* **-ti·er, -ti·est.** *Slang.* First-rate : excellent.

Ni·ger (nī′jər). **1.** Country of WC Africa. *Cap.* Niamey. *Pop.* 5,380,000. **2.** River of W Africa, flowing c.2,600 mi (4,185 km) to the Gulf of Guinea.

Ni·ge·ri·a (nī-jîr′ē-ə). Country of W Africa. *Cap.* Lagos. *Pop.* 78,135,000. **–Ni·ge′ri·an** *adj.* & *n.*

nig·gard (nĭg′ərd) *n.* A miserly person : cheapskate. **–nig′gard·li·ness** *n.* **–nig·gard·ly** *adj.* & *adv.*

nig·gling (nĭg′lĭng) *adj.* **1.** Fastidious : finicky. **2.** Nagging or petty. **3.** Showing or demanding great care or attention to details. **–nig′gling·ly** *adv.*

†**nigh** (nī) *adv.* **1.** Near in space, time, or relationship. **2.** Nearly : almost. *–adj.* **1.** Being near in space, time, or relationship : close. **2.** *Regional.* Direct : short. *–prep.* Not far from : near.

night (nīt) *n.* **1.** The time between dusk and dawn, esp. the hours of darkness. **2.** Nightfall. **3.** Darkness. **4.** A time of gloom, obscurity, ignorance, or sadness.

night blindness *n.* Lessened ability to see in dim light. **–night′blind′** *adj.*

night·cap (nīt′kăp′) *n.* **1.** A cloth covering for the head worn esp. in bed. **2.** *Informal.* A usu. alcoholic drink taken at the end of an evening's entertainment or just before bedtime.

night·clothes (nīt′klōz′, -klōthz′) *pl.n.* Clothing worn in bed.

night·club (nīt′klŭb′) *n.* An establishment offering food, drink, and entertainment at night.

night crawler *n.* A large earthworm that comes out of the ground at night.

night·dress (nīt′drĕs′) *n.* A nightgown.

night·fall (nīt′fôl′) *n.* The approach of darkness : dusk.

night·gown (nīt′goun′) *n.* A usu. loose garment worn in bed.

night·hawk (nīt′hôk′) *n.* **1.** A nocturnal bird of the genus *Chordeiles,* having tan to black streaked feathers. **2.** A night owl.

night·ie *or* **night·y** (nī′tē) *n., pl.* **-ies.** *Informal.* A nightgown.

night·in·gale (nīt′n-gāl′, nī′tĭng-) *n.* A European songbird, *Luscinia megarhynchos,* having brownish plumage and noted for its nocturnal song.

Nightingale, Florence. 1820–1910. English nursing pioneer.

night·life (nīt′līf′) *n.* Entertainment or social activities available at night.

night·ly (nīt′lē) *adj.* **1.** Of or taking place during the night : nocturnal. **2.** Occurring or done every night. **–night′ly** *adv.*

night·mare (nīt′mâr′) *n.* **1.** A dream causing fear, horror, or distress. **2.** A highly distressing or frightening experience. **–night′mar′ish** *adj.* **–night′mar′ish·ly** *adv.* **–night′mar′ish·ness** *n.*

▲word history: In Old and Middle English *mare* was a word denoting an evil spirit. Although the spirit was imagined to be female, the word *mare* is unrelated to the modern word *mare* meaning "female horse." *Nightmare* is a compound of *night* and the old word *mare;* it denoted an evil spirit thought to afflict sleeping persons by sitting on them and causing a feeling of suffocation. *Nightmare* was also used to denote both the feeling itself and the dream that produced it.

night owl *n.* One who stays up late.

night school *n.* A school offering classes in the evening.

night·shade (nīt′shād′) *n.* Any of several plants of the genus *Solanum,* many of them yielding a poisonous juice.

night·shirt (nīt′shûrt′) *n.* A long, loose shirt worn in bed.

night·stick (nīt′stĭk′) *n.* A heavy club carried by a police officer.

night·time (nīt′tīm′) *n.* The period between dusk and dawn.

ni·hil·ism (nī′ə-lĭz′əm, nī′hə-, nē′-) *n.* The philosophical doctrine that all values and beliefs are unknowable and worthless and that therefore existence is meaningless. **–ni′hil·ist** *n.* **–ni′hil·is′tic** *adj.*

nil (nĭl) *n.* Not anything : zero.

Nile (nīl). Longest river in the world, flowing c. 4,160 mi (6,695 km), through E Africa to the Mediterranean in NE Egypt.

nim·ble (nĭm′bəl) *adj.* **-bler, -blest. 1.** Moving or acting with agility : deft. **2.** Clever in thinking, apprehending, or responding : quick-witted. **–nim′ble·ness** *n.* **–nim′bly** *adv.*

nim·bus (nĭm′bəs) *n., pl.* **-bi** (bī′) *or* **-es. 1.** A halo or bright light depicted about the head, as in a painting. **2.** An atmos-

phere or aura, as of mystery. **3.** A gray rain cloud covering the sky.
nin•com•poop (nĭn'kəm-po͞op', nĭng'-) *n.* A stupid or silly person.
nine (nīn) *n.* **1.** The cardinal number equal to 8 + 1. **2.** The 9th in a set or sequence. **3.** Something having 9 parts, units, or members, as a baseball team. **–nine** *adj. & pron.* **–ninth** *n. & adj. & adv.*
nine days' wonder *n.* One that creates a brief stir.
nine•teen (nīn'tēn') *n.* **1.** The cardinal number equal to 18 + 1. **2.** The 19th in a set or sequence. **–nine'teen'** *adj. & pron.* **–nine'teenth** *n. & adj. & adv.*
nine-to-fiv•er (nīn'tə-fī'vər) *n.* One who works regular daytime hours.
nine•ty (nīn'tē) *n., pl.* **-ties.** The cardinal number equal to 9 × 10. **–nine'ty** *adj. & pron.* **–nine'ti•eth** *n. & adj. & adv.*
nin•ny (nĭn'ē) *n., pl.* **-nies.** A fool : dolt.
ni•o•bi•um (nī-ō'bē-əm) *n. Symbol* **Nb**A soft, silvery, ductile metallic element.
nip[1] (nĭp) *v.* **nipped, nip•ping. 1.** To grab and bite or pinch. **2.** To sever or remove by or as by nipping. **3.** To sting or chill, as with cold. **4.** To halt or retard the further growth or development of. **5.** *Slang.* **a.** To seize hastily. **b.** To steal. *–n.* **1.** A small, sharp bite or pinch. **2.** A small portion. **3.** Intensely sharp cold. **4.** A sharp, biting flavor : tang. **–nip and tuck.** Very close. **–nip'per** *n.* **–nip'ping•ly** *adv.*
nip[2] (nĭp) *n.* A small portion of an alcoholic beverage. *–v.* **nipped, nip•ping.** To drink (liquor) in small portions.
nip•per (nĭp'ər) *n.* **1. nippers.** A pincerlike tool used for grasping or nipping. **2.** A pincerlike part, as the large claw of a crab. **3.** A small boy.
nip•ple (nĭp'əl) *n.* **1.** A small conical projection on the surface of a mammary gland through which the milk passes. **2.** Something like a nipple.
nip•py (nĭp'ē) *adj.* **-pi•er, -pi•est. 1.** Sharp or biting : tangy. **2.** Bitterly cold.
nir•va•na (nîr-vä'nə, nûr-) *n.* **1.** Often **Nirvana.** The state of perfect bliss in Buddhism in which the self is freed from suffering and desire and is united with the creator of the universe. **2.** A time or condition of great peace and joy.
nit (nĭt) *n.* The egg or offspring of a parasitic insect, esp. a louse. **–nit'ty** *adj.*
ni•ter (nī'tər) *n.* A colorless, white, or gray mineral of potassium nitrate, used to make gunpowder.
nit-pick (nĭt'pĭk') *v. Informal.* To be concerned with or critical of trivial details.
ni•trate (nī'trāt') *n.* **1.** A salt or ester of nitric acid. **2.** Fertilizer containing a salt of nitric acid. *–v.* **-trat•ed, -trat•ing.** To treat or combine with nitrate or nitric acid. **–ni•tra'tion** *n.*
ni•tre (nī'tər) *n. esp. Brit. var. of* NITER.
ni•tric (nī'trĭk) *adj.* Of, derived from, or containing nitrogen.
nitric acid *n.* A transparent, colorless, corrosive liquid used esp. to manufacture fertilizers and explosives.
ni•tri•fy (nī'trə-fī') *vt.* **-fied, -fy•ing, -fies. 1.** To oxidize into nitric acid, nitrous acid, or any nitrate or nitrite, as by the action of soil bacteria. **2.** To treat or combine with nitrogen or nitrogen-containing compounds. **–ni'tri•fi•ca'tion** *n.* **–ni'tri•fi'er** *n.*
ni•trite (nī'trīt') *n.* A salt or ester of nitrous acid.
ni•tro•cel•lu•lose (nī'trō-sĕl'yə-lōs') *n.* A pulpy substance formed by nitrating cellulose, used in plastics and explosives.
ni•tro•gen (nī'trə-jən) *n. Symbol* **N** A nonmetallic element occurring as a colorless, odorless, almost inert gas. **–ni•trog'e•nous** (nī-trŏj'ə-nəs) *adj.* **–ni'trous** *adj.*
ni•tro•glyc•er•in *also* **ni•tro•glyc•er•ine** (nī'trō-glĭs'ər-ĭn) *n.* A viscid, light yellow, highly volatile liquid used to make explosives and as a vasodilator.
nitrous acid *n.* An unstable inorganic acid existing only in solution.
nitrous oxide *n.* A colorless, sweet-smelling gas used as an anesthetic.
nit•ty-grit•ty (nĭt'ē-grĭt'ē, nĭt'ē-grĭt'ē) *n. Slang.* The fundamental facts.
nit•wit (nĭt'wĭt') *n. Informal.* A fool.
nix (nĭks) *Slang. –n.* Nothing. *–adv.* No. *–v.* To reject : deny.
Nix•on (nĭk'sən), **Richard Milhous.** b. 1913. 37th U.S. President (1969–74); resigned.
NJ *abbr.* New Jersey (with zip code).
NM *abbr.* New Mexico (with zip code).
N. Mex. *also* **N.M.** *abbr.* New Mexico.
no[1] (nō) *adv.* **1.** Not so. Used to express denial, rejection, or disagreement. **2.** Not at all. Used with a comparative form <*no* worse><*no* less> **3.** Not <like it or *no*> *–n., pl.* **noes.** A denial or rejection.
no[2] (nō) *adj.* **1.** Not one : not any. **2.** Not close to being : not at all.
No *symbol for* NOBELIUM.
no. *or* **No.** *abbr.* **1.** north; northern. **2.** number.
no•bel•i•um (nō-bĕl'ē-əm, -bē'lē-) *n. Symbol* **No** A radioactive element produced synthetically in minute quantities.
No•bel (nō-bĕl'), **Alfred Bernhard.** 1833–96. Swedish chemist, inventor, and philanthropist.
Nobel Prize *n.* Any of the awards made annually by the Nobel Foundation for distinguished achievement in physics, chemistry, medicine or physiology, literature, economics, and the promotion of peace. **–No•bel'ist** *n.*
no•bil•i•ty (nō-bĭl'ĭ-tē) *n., pl.* **-ties. 1.** A social class set apart by high birth or rank. **2.** Noble status or rank. **3.** The quality or state of being noble.
no•ble (nō'bəl) *adj.* **-bler, -blest. 1.** Of or pertaining to the nobility. **2.** Morally good : virtuous. **3. a.** Superior in nature or character : exalted. **b.** Grand and stately <a *noble* vista> *–n.* A person of noble birth or rank. **–no'ble•ness** *n.* **–no'bly** *adv.*
no•ble•man (nō'bəl-mən) *n.* A man of noble birth or rank. **–no'ble•wom'an** *n.*
no•blesse o•blige (nō-blĕs' ō-blēzh') *n.* Honorable and charitable behavior regarded as the responsibility of persons of noble birth or rank.
no•bod•y (nō'bŏd'ē, -bə-dē) *pron.* No person : not anyone. *–n., pl.* **-ies.** One of no significance or influence.
noc•tur•nal (nŏk-tûr'nəl) *adj.* **1.** Of, pertaining to, or happening during the night. **2.** Active at night. **–noc•tur'nal•ly** *adv.*
noc•turne (nŏk'tûrn') *n.* **1.** A painting of a night scene. **2.** A dreamy, romantic musical composition.
nod (nŏd) *v.* **nod•ded, nod•ding. 1.** To lower and raise the head rapidly, as in agreement. **2.** To convey or express by lowering and raising the head. **3.** To let the head droop forward, as in drowsiness. **4.** To be careless, as in a moment of abstraction. **5.** To droop, sway, or bend downward <flowers *nodding* in the wind> **–nod** *n.*
node (nōd) *n.* **1.** A swelling or bulge. **2.** *Bot.* The point on a stem where a leaf, bud, etc., is attached. **3.** *Physics.* A point or region of a vibrating or oscillating system where the amplitude of the vibration or oscillation is minimal. **–nod'al** *adj.*

node
Two examples of nodes: (left) *buckwheat and* (right) *rye grass*

nod•ule (nŏj'o͞ol) *n.* **1.** A small node, as of body tissue. **2.** A small knoblike lump or outgrowth. **–nod'u•lar** *adj.*
No•ël or **No•el** (nō-ĕl') *n.* **1.** Christmas. **2. noël** or **noel.** A Christmas carol.
no-fault (nō'fôlt') *adj.* **1.** Of or designating an automobile insurance plan that compensates accident victims without establishing responsibility or blame. **2.** Of or designating a divorce that is granted without establishing blame.
nog•gin (nŏg'ĭn) *n.* **1.** A small cup or mug. **2.** An amount of liquid equal to ¼ pt. **3.** *Slang.* The head.
no-go (nō'gō') *adj. Slang.* Not in a suitable condition for functioning properly.
no-good (no'go͝od') *adj.* **1.** Having no worth, merit, or use. **2.** Despicable : vile. **–no'-good'** *n.*
no-hit (nō'hĭt') *adj. Baseball.* Of or being a game in which a pitcher allows the opposing team no hits or runs. **–no-hit'ter** *n.*
noise (noiz) *n.* **1.** Sound or a sound that is loud, disagreeable, or unwanted. **2.** Sound or a sound of any sort. **3.** A loud, confused clamor or commotion. **4.** *Physics.* A usu. random, persistent disturbance of a signal. **5.** *Computer Sci.* Meaningless data generated along with desired data. *–v.* **noised, nois•ing.** To spread the report or rumor of. **–noise'less** *adj.* **–noise'less•ly** *adv.*
noise•mak•er (noiz'mā'kər) *n.* One that makes noise, esp. a device for making noise at a celebration.
noise pollution *n.* Annoying or harmful environmental noise.

noi•some (noi′səm) *adj.* **1.** Disgusting : foul. **2.** Harmful or injurious. **–noi′some•ly** *adv.* **–noi′some•ness** *n.*

▲word history: Neither in meaning nor in origin does *noisome* have any connection with the word *noise;* the similarities are purely coincidental. *Noisome* is a compound formed in Middle English from *noy,* an obsolete word meaning "harm" or "annoyance," and the suffix *-some,* which is still current in Modern English where it is used to form adjectives with the gen. sense of "characterized by some quality."

nois•y (noi′zē) *adj.* **-i•er, -i•est. 1.** Producing noise. **2.** Marked by or full of noise. **–nois′i•ly** *adv.* **–nois′i•ness** *n.*

nol•le pros•e•qui (nŏl′ē prŏs′ĭ-kwī′) *n. Law.* A declaration that the plaintiff in a civil case or the prosecutor in a criminal case will drop prosecution of all or part of a suit or indictment.

no•lo con•ten•de•re (nō′lō kən-tĕn′də-rē) *n. Law.* A plea in a criminal prosecution that subjects the defendant to conviction and punishment but allows denial of allegations in other proceedings.

no•mad (nō′măd′) *n.* **1.** A member of a group of people who move about from place to place seeking food, water, and grazing land. **2.** A wanderer.

no•mad•ic (nō-măd′ĭk) *adj.* Wandering from place to place. ☆***syns:*** ITINERANT, PERIPATETIC, ROAMING, ROVING, VAGABOND, VAGRANT, WANDERING **–no•mad′i•cal•ly** *adv.*

no man's land *n.* **1.** An unowned or unclaimed piece of property. **2.** Disputed land, esp. the territory between 2 usu. entrenched armies. **3.** An ambiguous area or circumstance.

nom de guerre (nŏm′ də gâr′) *n.* A pseudonym.

nom de plume (nŏm′ də plo͞om′) *n.* A pen name.

no•men•cla•ture (nō′mən-klā′chər, nō-mĕn′klə-) *n.* An ordered set of names used in a particular art or science.

nom•i•nal (nŏm′ə-nəl) *adj.* **1.** Of, relating to, or like a name or names. **2.** In name but not in fact. **3.** Small : trifling. **4.** Of or pertaining to a noun. **–nom′i•nal•ly** *adv.*

nom•i•nate (nŏm′ə-nāt′) *v.* **-nat•ed, -nat•ing. 1.** To present or select as a candidate, as for elective office. **2.** To designate or appoint to a position, honor, etc. **–nom′i•na′tion** *n.* **–nom′i•na′tor** *n.*

nom•i•na•tive (nŏm′ə-nə-tĭv) *adj.* Of or belonging to a grammatical case that usu. designates the subject of a verb. *–n.* The nominative case.

nom•i•nee (nŏm′ə-nē′) *n.* One who has been nominated for an office, position, etc.

non– *pref.* Not <*non*combatant> See below for a list of self-explanatory words formed with the prefix **non–.**

non•age (nŏn′ĭj, nō′nĭj) *n.* **1.** Legal minority. **2.** A time of youth or immaturity.

non•a•ge•nar•i•an (nŏn′ə-jə-nâr′ē-ən, nō′nə-) *adj.* Between 90 and 100 years old. **–non′a•ge•nar′i•an** *n.*

non•a•ligned (nŏn′ə-līnd′) *adj.* Not in alliance with any power bloc : neutral. **–non′a•lign′ment** *n.*

non•book (nŏn′bo͝ok′) *n.* A book that is usu. a collection, as of photographs or news clippings.

nonce (nŏns) *n.* The present time or occasion <Let's ignore that for the *nonce.*>

nonce word *n.* A word invented, occurring, or used only for a particular occasion.

non•cha•lant (nŏn′shə-länt′) *adj.* Casually unconcerned. **–non′cha•lance′** *n.* **–non′cha•lant′ly** *adv.*

non•com (nŏn′kŏm′) *n. Informal.* A noncommissioned officer.

non•com•bat•ant (nŏn′kəm-băt′nt, nŏn-kŏm′bə-tənt) *n.* **1.** A person serving in the armed forces whose duties do not include combat. **2.** A civilian in wartime, esp. one in a war zone.

non•com•mis•sioned officer (nŏn′kə-mĭsh′ənd) *n.* An enlisted member of the armed forces, as a sergeant, having a rank that confers leadership over others.

non•com•mit•tal (nŏn′kə-mĭt′l) *adj.* Not showing what one thinks or prefers.

non com•pos men•tis (nŏn kŏm′pəs mĕn′tĭs) *adj. Law.* Not of sound mind and hence not responsible.

non•con•duc•tor (nŏn′kən-dŭk′tər) *n.* Something that conducts little or no electricity, heat, sound, etc.

non•con•form•ist (nŏn′kən-fôr′mĭst) *n.* One who does not feel compelled to follow or accept traditional beliefs, customs, or practices. **–non′con•form′i•ty** *n.*

non•cred•it (nŏn-krĕd′ĭt) *adj.* Of or being an academic course that does not offer credit toward a degree.

non•dair•y (nŏn-dâr′ē) *adj.* Not made with dairy products.

non•de•script (nŏn′dĭ-skrĭpt′) *adj.* Difficult to describe : undistinctive. **–non′de•script′** *n.*

non•dis•crim•i•na•tion (nŏn′dĭ-skrĭm′ə-nā′shən) *n.* The policy or practice of refraining from discrimination. **–non′dis•crim′i•na•to′ry** *adj.*

none (nŭn) *pron.* **1.** Not one. **2.** Not any. **3.** No part <*none* of our concern> *–adv.* Not at all <The professor was *none* too pleased with my answer.>

non•en•ti•ty (nŏn-ĕn′tĭ-tē) *n., pl.* **-ties. 1.** Something that does not exist in fact. **2.** One of little or no significance.

none•such (nŭn′sŭch′) *n.* One having no equal. **–none′such′** *adj.*

none•the•less (nŭn′*th*ə-lĕs′) *adv.* However : nevertheless.

non•e•vent (nŏn′ĭ-vĕnt′) *n. Slang.* An event that does not take place or fails to meet one's expectations.

non•ex•ist•ent (nŏn′ĭg-zĭs′tənt) *adj.* Not existing : absent or lacking.

non•fat (nŏn′făt′) *adj.* Lacking fat solids or having fat solids removed.

non•fic•tion (nŏn-fĭk′shən) *n.* Writing based on fact rather than fiction.

non•flam•ma•ble (nŏm-flăm′ə-bəl) *adj.* Not flammable, esp. not readily ignited.

non•he•ro (nŏn-hîr′ō) *n.* An antihero.

no•nil•lion (nō-nĭl′yən) *n.* **1.** The cardinal number equal to 10^{30}. **2.** *esp. Brit.* The cardinal number equal to 10^{54}. **–no•nil′lion** *adj.* **–no•nil′lionth** *n.* & *adj.* & *adv.*

non•in•ter•ven•tion (nŏn′ĭn-tər-vĕn′shən) *n.* Failure to intervene, esp. an official policy of refusing to interfere in another nation's affairs. **–non′in•ter•ven′tion•ist** *n.*

non•met•al (nŏn-mĕt′l) *n.* A chemical element, as nitrogen or oxygen, lacking the characteristic properties of a metal. **–non′me•tal′lic** (nŏn′mə-tăl′ĭk) *adj.*

no-no (nō′nō′) *n. Informal.* Something unacceptable or not permissible.

non•ob•jec•tive (nŏn′əb-jĕk′tĭv) *adj.* Designating a style of graphic art in which objects are not depicted realistically.

no-non•sense (nō-nŏn′sĕns′, -səns) *adj.* Practical : serious.

non•pa•reil (nŏn′pə-rĕl′) *adj.* Without equal : matchless. *–n.* **1.** One having no equal. **2.** A small, usu. flat piece of chocolate covered with white sugar pellets.

non•par•ti•san (nŏn-pär′tĭ-zən) *adj.* Not influenced by or associated with one political party.

non•per•son (nŏn-pûr′sən) *n.* **1.** One whose existence is expunged from public attention, esp. for reasons of ideological deviation. **2.** One who has no legal or social standing.

non•plus (nŏn-plŭs′) *v.* **-plused, -plus•ing** *also* **-plussed, -plus•sing.** To confuse or perplex.

non•prof•it (nŏn-prŏf′ĭt) *adj.* Not intended to yield a profit.

non•pro•lif•er•a•tion (nŏn′prə-lĭf′ə-rā′shən) *adj.* Relating to or advocating the end of proliferation of nuclear weapons.

non•rep•re•sen•ta•tion•al (nŏn-rĕp′rĭ-zən-tā′shə-nəl) *adj.* Nonobjective.

non•res•i•dent (nŏn-rĕz′ĭ-dənt) *adj.* Not residing in a particlar place <a *nonresident* student> **–non•res′i•dent** *n.*

non•re•sis•tance (nŏn′rĭ-zĭs′təns) *n.* Complete obedience to authority even if arbitrary or unjust. **–non′re•sis′tant** *adj.*

non•re•stric•tive (nŏn′rĭ-strĭk′tĭv) *adj.* Indicating a word, clause, or phrase that is descriptive but not required by the meaning of the element it modifies.

non•rig•id (nŏn-rĭj′ĭd) *adj.* Designating a lighter-than-air aircraft that holds its shape by gas pressure.

non•sched•uled (nŏn-skĕj′o͞old) *adj.* Operating without a regular schedule of passenger or cargo flights.

non•sec•tar•i•an (nŏn′sĕk-târ′ē-ən) *adj.* Not restricted to a specific religion.

non•sense (nŏn′sĕns′, -səns) *n.* **1.** Foolish or senseless behavior or language. **2.** Something that is unimportant or of little use. **–non•sen′si•cal** *adj.*

non se•qui•tur (nŏn sĕk′wĭ-tər, -to͝or′) *n.* Something, as a statement, that does not follow as the logical result of what came before it.

non•sex•ist (nŏn-sĕk′sĭst) *adj.* Not discriminating against individuals, esp. women, on the basis of gender.

non•sked (nŏn′skĕd′) *n. Informal.* A nonscheduled airline or cargo plane.

non•skid (nŏn′skĭd′) *adj.* Designed to inhibit or prevent skidding.

non•stan•dard (nŏn-stăn′dərd) *adj.* Designating a word or usage that is usu. avoided by educated speakers and writers.

non•stick (nŏn′stĭk′) *adj.* Facilitating removal of adhered particles, as of food.

non•stop (nŏn′stŏp′) *adj.* **1.** Making no stops. **2.** Unceasing. **–non′stop′** *adv.*

non•sup•port (nŏn′sə-pôrt′, -pōrt′) *n. Law.* Failure to provide for the maintenance of one's dependents.

non•un•ion (nŏn-yo͞on′yən) *adj.* **1.** Not made by or belonging to a labor union. **2.** Not acknowledging a labor union.

non•ver•bal (nŏn-vûr′bəl) *adj.* **1.** Being other than verbal <*nonverbal* expression> **2.** Involving little use of language <a *nonverbal* aptitude test>

non•vi•o•lence (nŏn-vī′ə-ləns) *n.* The principle, policy, or practice of using only peaceful means to gain esp. political objectives. **–non•vi′o•lent** *adj.*
noo•dle[1] (no͝od′l) *n. Slang.* The head.
noo•dle[2] (no͝od′l) *n.* A narrow, flat strip of dried dough, usu. made with eggs.
nook (no͝ok) *n.* **1.** A corner, alcove, or recess, esp. as part of a larger room. **2.** A cozy or secluded place.
noon (no͞on) *n.* The middle of the day : 12 o'clock in the daytime. **–noon** *adj.*
noon•day (no͞on′dā′) *n.* Noon.
no one *pron.* No person : nobody.
noon•time (no͞on′tīm′) *n.* Noon.
noose (no͞os) *n.* A loop of rope secured by a slipknot so that it decreases in size as the rope is pulled.
no-par (nō′pär′) *adj.* Having no face value, as a stock.
nope (nōp) *adv. Slang.* No.
nor (nôr; nər *when unstressed*) *conj.* And not : or not : not either <We have neither time *nor* money for the project.>
Nor•dic (nôr′dĭk) *adj.* Of or pertaining to the subdivision of the Caucasoid ethnic group that is most common in Scandinavia. **–Nor′dic** *n.*
norm (nôrm) *n.* A model or pattern considered typical for a particular group.
nor•mal (nôr′məl) *adj.* **1.** Usual or ordinary : typical. **2. a.** Characterized by average growth or intelligence. **b.** Healthy in mind and body. *–n.* **1.** One that is normal : standard. **2.** The expected or usual condition or amount. **–nor•mal′i•ty, nor′mal•cy** *n.* **–nor′mal•ly** *adv.*
nor•mal•ize (nôr′mə-līz′) *v.* **-ized, -iz•ing.** To make normal or average. **–nor′mal•i•za′tion** *n.* **–nor′mal•iz′er** *n.*
normal school *n.* A school for training esp. elementary-level teachers.
Nor•man (nôr′mən) *n.* **1.** A member of a Scandinavian people who conquered Normandy in the 10th cent. **2.** A member of a people of Norman and French blood who invaded England in 1066. **3.** A native or resident of Normandy. **–Nor′man** *adj.*
Nor•man•dy (nôr′mən-dē). Region and former province of NW France.
nor•ma•tive (nôr′mə-tĭv) *adj.* Pertaining to or imposing a norm or standard. **–nor′ma•tive•ly** *adv.* **–nor′ma•tive•ness** *n.*
Norse (nôrs) *n., pl.* **Norse. 1.** The people of Scandinavia. **2.** The people of W Scandinavia, esp. the Norwegians. **–Norse** *adj.*
Norse•man (nôrs′mən) *n.* A member of an ancient Scandinavian people.
north (nôrth) *n.* **1. a.** The direction 90° counterclockwise from east. **b.** The point on the compass located at 0°. **2.** An area or region to the north of a given point. **3. North.** The N part of the U.S., esp. the states that fought for the Union during the Civil War. *–adj.* To, toward, of, from, facing, or in the north. *–adv.* In, from, or toward the north. **–north′er•ly** *adj. & adv.* **–north′ern** *adj.* **–north′ern•er** *n.* **–north′ern•most′** *adj.* **–north′ward** *adj. & adv.* **–north′wards** *adv.*
North America. N continent of the W Hemisphere, extending from the Colombia-Panama border through Central America, mainland U.S., Canada, and the Arctic Archipelago to the N tip of Greenland. **–North American** *adj. & n.*
North Car•o•li•na (kăr′ə-lī′nə). State of the SE U.S. *Cap.* Raleigh. *Pop.* 5,874,429. **–North Car′o•lin′i•an** (-lĭn′ē-ən) *n.*
North Da•ko•ta (də-kō′tə). State of the NC U.S. *Cap.* Bismark. *Pop.* 652,695. **–North Da•ko′tan** *adj. & n.*
north•east (nôrth-ēst′) *n.* **1.** The direction 45° counterclockwise from east and 45° clockwise from north. **2.** An area or region to the northeast of a given point. **3. Northeast.** Area of the NE U.S. including New England, N.Y., and sometimes Pa. and N.J. **–north•east′** *adj. & adv.* **–north•east′er•ly** *adj. & adv.* **–north•east′ern** *adj.* **–north•east′ward** *adj. & adv.* **–north•east′wards** *adv.*
Northern Ireland. Component of the United Kingdom, in the NE part of the island of Ireland. *Cap.* Belfast. *Pop.* 1,542,200.
North Pole *n.* The northernmost point of the earth.
North Sea. Arm of the Atlantic NW of C Europe and E of Great Britain.
North Star *n.* Polaris.
north•west (nôrth-wĕst′) *n.* **1.** The direction 45° counterclockwise from north and 45° clockwise from west. **2.** An area or region to the northwest of a given point. **–north•west** *adj. & adv.* **–north•west′er•ly** *adj. & adv.* **–north•west′ern** *adj.* **–north•west′ward** *adj. & adv.* **–north•west′wards** *adv.*
Northwest. 1. Formerly, area of the U.S. W of the Mississippi and N of the Missouri R. **2.** U.S. states of Wash., Ore., and Idaho. **3.** Area of Canada N and W of the Great Lakes.
Northwest Territories. Region of NW Canada that includes the Arctic Archipelago, the islands in Hudson Bay, and the mainland N of the Canadian provinces and E of Y.T.
Nor•way (nôr′wā′). Kingdom of N Europe. *Cap.* Oslo. *Pop.* 4,095,000. **–Nor•we′gian** (nôr-wē′jən) *adj. & n.*
nose (nōz) *n.* **1.** The section of the face or forward part of the head containing the nostrils and olfactory organs and forming the opening of the respiratory tract. **2.** The sense of smell. **3.** A capacity for discovering or detecting by or as if by smell. **4.** The forward end of a pointed structure, as an airplane, rocket, submarine, etc. *–v.* **nosed, nos•ing. 1.** To discover by or as if by smell. **2.** To touch or examine with the nose : nuzzle. **3.** To move forward or cause to move forward cautiously. **4.** *Informal.* To pry curiously : snoop.
nose•bleed (nōz′blēd′) *n.* A nasal hemorrhage.
nose cone *n.* The protective forwardmost section of a rocket or missile.
nose dive *n.* **1.** A sudden, steep plunge made by an aircraft. **2.** A swift drop or fall. **–nose′-dive′** *v.*
nose•gay (nōz′gā′) *n.* A small bouquet of flowers.
nos•ey (nō′zē) *adj. var. of* NOSY.
nosh (nŏsh) *n.* A snack. **–nosh** *v.*
no-show (nō′shō′) *n. Slang.* A traveler who reserves space, as on an airplane, but neither claims nor cancels the reservation.
nos•tal•gia (nŏ-stăl′jə, nə-) *n.* A bittersweet yearning for things of the past. **–nos•tal′gic** *adj.*
nos•tril (nŏs′trəl) *n.* Either of the outer openings of the nose.
nos•trum (nŏs′trəm) *n.* **1.** A medicine with doubtful, usu. secret ingredients. **2.** A panacea for problems or evils.
nos•y *also* **nos•ey** (nō′zē) *adj.* **-i•er, -i•est.** *Informal.* Inquisitive : snoopy.
not (nŏt) *adv.* To no degree : in no manner or way. Used to express negation, refusal, or denial.
†no•ta•ble (nō′tə-bəl) *adj.* **1. a.** Deserving notice : remarkable. **b.** Prominent : distinguished. **2.** (*also* nŏt′ə-bəl). *Archaic & Regional.* Diligent and efficient, esp. in household duties. *–n.* A well-known or distinguished person. **–no′ta•bil′i•ty** *n.* **–no′ta•bly** *adv.*
no•ta•rize (nō′tə-rīz′) *v.* **-rized, -riz•ing.** To attest to and certify as a notary public. **–no′ta•ri•za′tion** *n.*
no•ta•ry (nō′tə-rē) *n., pl.* **-ries.** A notary public. **–no•tar′i•al** (nō-târ′ē-əl) *adj.*
notary public *n., pl.* **notaries public.** One legally authorized to witness signatures, certify documents, etc.
no•ta•tion (nō-tā′shən) *n.* **1. a.** A system of figures or symbols used in a specialized field to represent numbers, quantities, tones, or values. **b.** The use of such a system. **2.** A brief record : annotation.
notch (nŏch) *n.* **1.** A V-shaped cut. **2.** A steep-sided gap between mountains. **3.** *Informal.* A step or degree <a *notch* better> *–v.* **1.** To cut a notch in. **2.** To keep track of by or as if by making notches.
note (nōt) *n.* **1.** A brief record written down to aid the memory. **2.** A short, informal message or letter. **3.** A formal official or diplomatic communication. **4.** A comment or explanation, as on a passage in a text. **5.a.** A piece of paper money. **b.** A promissory note. **6.** *Mus.* **a.** A tone of designated pitch. **b.** The symbol for such a tone. **7.** A characteristic call or cry, as of a bird. **8.** A sign or hint of a certain quality <ended the petition on a *note* of despair> **9.** Consequence : distinction. **10.** Observation : heed. *–v.* **not•ed, not•ing. 1.** To perceive : notice. **2.** To write down. **3.** To make mention of : point out.
note•book (nōt′bo͝ok′) *n.* A book with blank pages for writing in.
not•ed (nō′tĭd) *adj.* Famous : eminent.
note•wor•thy (nōt′wûr′thē) *adj.* Significant : notable. **–note′wor′thi•ness** *n.*
noth•ing (nŭth′ĭng) *n.* **1.** Not anything <knows *nothing* about golf> **2.** No portion or part <*Nothing* is left of the cake.> **3.** One of no consequence or interest <The outcome is *nothing* to me.> **4.** Absence of anything perceptible <The music died away into *nothing.*> *–n.* **1.** One having no existence. **2.** One having no quantitative value : zero. **3. a.** Something trivial : trifle. **b.** An inconsequential person : nonentity. *–adv.* In no way or degree.
noth•ing•ness (nŭth′ĭng-nĭs) *n.* **1.** The quality or state of being nothing. **2.** Unoccupied space : emptiness. **3.** Lack of consequence : insignificance.
no•tice (nō′tĭs) *n.* **1.** Perception : observation. **2.** Consideration or polite respect. **3.** A published announcement. **4.** An announcement of purpose, esp. of one's intention to leave a job. **5.** A review, as of a play or book. *v.* **-ticed, -tic•ing. 1.** To become aware of : perceive. **2.** To mention.
no•tice•a•ble (nō′tĭ-sə-bəl) *adj.* **1.** Easily attracting notice. **2.** Worthy of attention : significant. ☆**syns:** ARRESTING, CONSPICU-

OUS, MARKED, OBSERVABLE, OUTSTANDING, POINTED, PROMINENT, REMARKABLE, SALIENT, SIGNAL, STRIKING **—no′tice•a•bly** *adv.*
no•ti•fy (nō′tə-fī′) *v.* **-fied, -fy•ing.** To announce to : give notice to. **—no′ti•fi•ca′tion** *n.* **—no′ti•fi′er** *n.*
no•tion (nō′shən) *n.* **1.** An opinion or belief. **2.** A mental representation : idea. **3.** A whim or fancy. **4. notions.** Small useful articles, as buttons, needles, thread, etc. **—no′tion•al** *adj.*
no•to•ri•ous (nō-tôr′ē-əs, -tōr′-) *adj.* Having a usu. bad reputation : infamous. **—no′to•ri′e•ty** (-tə-rī′ĭ-tē) *n.*
no-trump (nō′trŭmp′) *n.* A declaration to play a hand without a trump suit in card games such as bridge. **—no′-trump′** *adj.*
not•with•stand•ing (nŏt′wĭth-stăn′dĭng, -wĭth-) *prep.* In spite of. *—adv.* All the same : nevertheless. *—conj.* Although.
Nouak•chott (nwäk′shŏt′). Cap. of Mauritania, in the W part. *Pop.* 134,986.
nou•gat (nōō′gət) *n.* A confection made of a sugar or honey paste mixed with nuts.
nought (nôt) *n. var. of* NAUGHT.
Nou•mé•a (nōō-mā′ə). Cap. of New Caledonia. *Pop.* 56,078.
noun (noun) *n.* A word that names a person, place, or thing.
nour•ish (nûr′ĭsh, nŭr′-) *v.* **1.** To provide with the food or other substances needed for life : feed. **2.** To promote the growth or development of. **3.** To keep alive : sustain. **—nour′ish•ing** *adj.* **—nour′ish•ment** *n.*
nou•veau riche (nōō′vō rēsh′) *n., pl.* **nou•veaux riches** (nōō′vō rēsh′). A newly rich person.
nou•velle cuisine (nōō-vĕl) *n.* Cooking that emphasizes the natural flavors of foods and the use of light sauces.
Nov. *abbr.* November.
no•va (nō′və) *n., pl.* **-vae** (-vē) *or* **-vas.** A variable star that suddenly becomes very bright and then gradually dims over a period of time.
Nova Sco•tia (skō′shə). Province and peninsula of SE Canada. *Cap.* Halifax. *Pop.* 828,571. **—Nova Scotian** *adj.* & *n.*
nov•el[1] (nŏv′əl) *n.* A book-length work of fiction. **—nov′el•ist** *n.*
nov•el[2] (nŏv′əl) *adj.* Notably new, different, or unusual. **—nov′el•ly** *adv.*
nov•el•ette (nŏv′ə-lĕt′) *n.* A brief novel.
no•vel•la (nō-vĕl′ə) *n., pl.* **-las** or **-vel•le** (-vĕl′ē). A novelette.
nov•el•ty (nŏv′əl-tē) *n., pl.* **-ties. 1.** The quality of being novel : newness. **2.** Something new or unusual. **3. novelties.** Small inexpensively produced items, as souvenirs or toys.
No•vem•ber (nō-vĕm′bər) *n.* The 11th month of the year, having 30 days.
no•ve•na (nō-vē′nə) *n., pl.* **-nas** or **-nae** (-nē). *Rom. Cath. Ch.* A devotion made on 9 consecutive days.
nov•ice (nŏv′ĭs) *n.* **1.** One new to a field or activity : beginner. **2.** One who has joined a religious order but has not yet taken the final vows.
no•vi•ti•ate (nō-vĭsh′ē-ĭt, -āt′) *n.* **1.** The period of training served by a religious novice. **2.** A place where novices train and live. **3.** NOVICE 2.
No•vo•cain (no′və-kān′). A trademark for the anesthetic procaine hydrochloride.
now (nou) *adv.* **1.** At the present time. **2.** At once : immediately. **3.** In the immediate past : recently. **4.** In the immediate future : soon. **5.** At this stage in the sequence of events : then. **6.** In these circumstances. **7.** Used esp. to express reproof, issue a command, or make a request <*Now* hear this.> *—conj.* Seeing that : since. *—n.* The present. *—adj.* **1.** *Informal.* Of or pertaining to the pesent time. **2.** *Slang.* Trendy <the *now* look in sportswear>
now•a•days (nou′ə-dāz′) *adv.* In the present time.
no•way (nō′wā′) *also* **no•ways** (-wāz′) *adv.* Nowise.
no•where (nō′hwâr′, -wâr′) *adv.* Not anywhere. *—n.* A faraway or unknown place.
no-win (nō′wĭn′) *adj.* Incapable of affording victory or success.
no•wise (nō′wīz′) *adv.* In no way.
nox•ious (nŏk′shəs) *adj.* Harmful to health or morals.
noz•zle (nŏz′əl) *n.* A projecting spout, as at the end of a hose, through which something is discharged.
Np *symbol for* NEPTUNIUM.
N.P. *abbr.* notary public.
N.S. *abbr.* Nova Scotia.
nth (ĕnth) *adj.* **1.** Pertaining to an unspecified or indefinitely large whole number. **2.** Greatest : highest <to the *nth* degree>
nu•ance (nōō-äns′, nyōō-, nōō′äns′, nyōō′-) *n.* **1.** A slight or subtle gradation or variation. **2.** A subtle aspect or quality.
nub (nŭb) *n.* **1.** A protuberance or knob. **2.** Gist : core. **—nub′by** *adj.*
nub•bin (nŭb′ĭn) *n.* **1.** A small, imperfectly developed ear of corn. **2.** A similar small chunk or piece.
nu•bile (nōō′bəl, -bīl′, nyōō′-) *adj.* Of marriageable age or condition.
nu•cle•ar (nōō′klē-ər, nyōō′-) *adj.* **1.** Of, pertaining to, or forming a nucleus or nuclei. **2.** Using or derived from nuclear energy. **3.** Having or using nuclear weapons.
nuclear energy *n.* Energy released by a nuclear reaction.
nuclear reaction *n.* A reaction that changes the structure, composition, or energy of an atomic nucleus.
nuclear reactor *n.* A device in which a nuclear chain reaction is initiated and controlled, thus producing heat used esp. to generate electricity.
nu•cle•ic acid (nōō-klē′ĭk, nyōō-) *n.* A complex chemical compound essential to the functioning of all living cells.
nu•cle•on (nōō′klē-ŏn′, nyōō′-) *n.* A proton or neutron, esp. as a component of an atomic nucleus. **—nu′cle•on′ic** *adj.*
nu•cle•on•ics (nōō′klē-ŏn′ĭks, nyōō′-) *n.* *(sing. in number).* The technology of nuclear energy.
nu•cle•o•side (nōō′klē-ə-sīd′, nyōō′-) *n.* A compound of a sugar and a purine or pyrimidine base.
nu•cle•o•tide (nōō′klē-ə-tīd′, nyōō′-) *n.* Any of various organic compounds composed of a nucleoside combined with phosphoric acid.
nu•cle•us (nōō′klē-əs, nyōō′-) *n., pl.* **-cle•i** (-klē-ī′) *or* **-es. 1.** A central or crucial element around which other elements are grouped. **2.** A basis for future growth or development. **3.** *Biol.* A complex, usu. spherical body within a living cell that controls the metabolism, growth, reproduction, and heredity of the cell. **4.** *Physics.* The positively charged core of an atom, made up of protons and neutrons and containing most of the mass of the atom. **—nu′cle•ate** (-ĭt) *adj.*
nu•clide (nōō′klīd′, nyōō′-) *n.* *Physics.* An atomic nucleus characterized by its atomic number, atomic mass, and energy state. **—nu•clid′ic** (-klĭd′ĭk) *adj.*
nude (nōōd, nyōōd) *adj.* Unclothed : naked. *—n.* **1.** The unclothed human figure or a representation of it. **2.** The state of being nude. **—nude′ness, nu′di•ty** *n.*
nudge (nuj) *v.* **nudged, nudg•ing.** To push or poke gently. **—nudge** *n.*
nud•ism (nōō′dĭz′əm, nyōō′-) *n.* The practice of going nude. **—nud′ist** *n.*
nu•ga•to•ry (nōō′gə-tôr′ē, -tōr′ē, nyōō′-) *adj.* **1.** Unimportant : trifling. **2.** Lacking force : invalid.
nug•get (nŭg′ĭt) *n.* A lump, as of gold.
nui•sance (nōō′səns, nyōō′-) *n.* A source of inconvenience or vexation.
nuke (nōōk, nyōōk) *Slang. —n.* **1.** A nuclear weapon. **2.** A nuclear-powered electric generating plant. *—v.* **nuked, nuk•ing.** To attack with nuclear weapons.
Nu•ku•a•lo•fa (nōō′kōō-ə-lô′fə). Cap. of Tonga, in the SW Pacific. *Pop.* 18,312.
null (nŭl) *adj.* **1.** Devoid of legal or binding force : invalid. **2.** Having no consequence or value : insignificant. **3.** Amounting to nothing. *—n.* Nothing : zero. **—nul′li•ty** *n.*
null and void *adj.* NULL 1.
nul•li•fy (nŭl′ə-fī′) *v.* **-fied, -fy•ing. 1.** To deprive of legal force : annul. **2.** To counteract or negate. **—nul′li•fi•ca′tion** *n.*
numb (nŭm) *adj.* **1.** Lacking the power to feel or move normally. **2.** Stunned or paralyzed, as from shock or strong emotion. **—numb** *v.* **—numb′ness** *n.*
num•ber (nŭm′bər) *n.* **1.** Any of the set of positive integers. **2. numbers.** Arithmetic. **3.** A numeral or series of numerals for reference or identification. **4. a.** A total : sum. **b.** An indeterminate sum. **5.** Quantity of units or individuals. **6.** A multitude. **7.** An item in a group or series. **8. Numbers** *(sing. in number).* See BIBLE TABLE. **9. numbers.** The numbers game. *—v.* **1.** To total in number or amount : add up to. **2.** To count or name one by one. **3.** To include in or belong to a group or category. **4.** To assign a number to. **5.** To restrict in number.
num•ber•less (nŭm′bər-lĭs) *adj.* Too many to be counted.
numbers game *n.* A lottery in which bets are made on an unpredictable number, as a daily stock-exchange figure.
nu•mer•a•ble (nōō′mər-ə-bəl, nyōō′-) *adj.* Countable.
nu•mer•al (nōō′mər-əl, nyōō′-) *n.* A symbol or mark representing a number.
nu•mer•ate (nōō′mə-rāt′, nyōō′-) *v.* **-at•ed, -at•ing.** To enumerate : count. **—nu′mer•a′tion** *n.*
nu•mer•a•tor (nōō′mə-rā′tər, nyōō′-) *n.* The expression above the line in a common fraction.
nu•mer•i•cal (nōō-mĕr′ĭ-kəl, nyōō-) *also* **nu•mer•ic** (-ĭk) *adj.* Of, pertaining to, denoting, or expressed as a number or numbers. **—nu•mer′i•cal•ly** *adv.*
nu•mer•ol•o•gy (nōō′mə-rŏl′ə-jē, nyōō′-) *n.* The occult study of numbers and their supposed influence on human beings. **—nu′mer•ol′o•gist** *n.*

nu•mer•ous (no͞o′mər-əs, nyo͞o′-) *adj.* Made up of many individuals or things. **—nu′mer•ous•ly** *adv.*
nu•mis•mat•ics (no͞o′mĭz-măt′ĭks, -mĭs-, nyo͞o′-) *n.* *(sing. in number).* The study or collection of coins, currency, and often medals. **—nu•mis′ma•tist** *n.*
num•skull (nŭm′skŭl′) *n.* A stupid person : dolt.
nun (nŭn) *n.* A woman member of a religious order.
nun•ci•o (nŭn′sē-ō′, no͝on′-) *n., pl.* **-os.** A high-ranking representative of the pope.
nup•tial (nŭp′shəl, -chəl) *adj.* Of or pertaining to marriage or the wedding ceremony. *—n. often* **nuptials.** A wedding.
nurse (nûrs) *n.* **1.** One specially trained to care for sick or disabled persons. **2.** One hired to care for a child. *—v.* **nursed, nurs•ing. 1.** To feed at the breast : suckle. **2.** To act as a nurse (for). **3.** To try to cure or treat <*nurse* a bad cold> **4.** To keep alive or healthy by constant attention or care : foster. **5.** To keep in the mind : harbor. **6.** To treat carefully : favor <*nursed* a sore foot> **7.** To consume slowly.
nurse•maid (nûrs′mād′) *n.* NURSE 2.
nurs•er•y (nûr′sə-rē, nûrs′rē) *n., pl.* **-ies. 1.** A room or area reserved for babies or children. **2. a.** A nursery school. **b.** A place where children are cared for temporarily. **3.** A place where plants are raised for sale, experimentation, etc.
nursery rhyme *n.* A short poem for children.
nursery school *n.* A school for children who are not old enough for kindergarten.
nurse's aide *n.* One who assists trained nurses, as by giving general patient care.
nursing home *n.* A private hospital for the care of the aged or chronically ill.
nurs•ling (nûrs′lĭng) *n.* **1.** An infant or young animal that is being suckled. **2.** One that is carefully tended.
nur•ture (nûr′chər) *n.* **1.** Sustenance : food. **2.** Upbringing : training. *—v.* **-tured, -tur•ing. 1.** To feed : nourish. **2.** To train or educate. **3.** To help grow or develop : cultivate. **—nur′tur•er** *n.*
nut (nŭt) *n.* **1. a.** A hard-shelled fruit or seed with an inner kernel. **b.** The often edible kernel of such fruits or seeds. **2.** *Slang.* **a.** An eccentric person. **b.** A fan or enthusiast. **3.** A ridge of wood at the end of the fingerboard or neck of stringed instruments over which the strings pass. **4.** A small block of metal or wood with a central, threaded hole designed to fit around and secure a bolt or screw.
nut•crack•er (nŭt′krăk′ər) *n.* A hinged implement for cracking nuts.
nut•hatch (nŭt′hăch′) *n.* A small bird of the family Sittidae, with a long, sharp bill.
nut•meat (nŭt′mēt′) *n.* The edible kernel of a nut.
nut•meg (nŭt′mĕg′) *n.* The hard, aromatic seed of a tropical evergreen tree, *Myristica fragrans,* used as a spice.
nu•tri•a (no͞o′trē-ə, nyo͞o′-) *n.* The coypu or its thick, light-brown fur.
nu•tri•ent (no͞o′trē-ənt, nyo͞o′-) *n.* Something that nourishes. **—nu′tri•ent** *adj.*
nu•tri•ment (no͞o′trə-mənt, nyo͞o′-) *n.* Nourishment : food.
nu•tri•tion (no͞o-trĭsh′ən, nyo͞o-) *n.* The process of nourishing or being nourished, esp. the process by which a living thing ingests and uses food. **—nu•tri′tion•al** *adj.* **—nu•tri′tion•al•ly** *adv.* **—nu•tri′tion•ist** *n.* **—nu′tri•tive** (-trĭ-tĭv) *adj.*
nu•tri•tious (no͞o-trĭsh′əs, nyo͞o-) *adj.* Giving nourishment. ☆***syns:*** NOURISHING, NUTRIENT, NUTRITIVE **—nu•tri′tious•ly** *adv.* **—nu•tri′tious•ness** *n.*
nuts (nŭts) *Slang. —adj.* **1.** Crazy. **2.** Enthusiastic. *—interj.* Used to express refusal, disappointment, or contempt.
nut•shell (nŭt′shĕl′) *n.* The shell enclosing the meat of a nut. **—in a nutshell.** In a few words : concisely.
nut•ty (nŭt′ē) *adj.* **-ti•er, -ti•est. 1.** Containing nuts or having a nutlike flavor. **2.** *Informal.* Eccentric : crazy. **—nut′ti•ly** *adv.* **—nut′ti•ness** *n.*
nux vom•i•ca (nŭks vŏm′ĭ-kə *n.* A tree native to SE Asia, *Strychnos nux-vomica,* bearing poisonous seeds that are the source of strychnine.

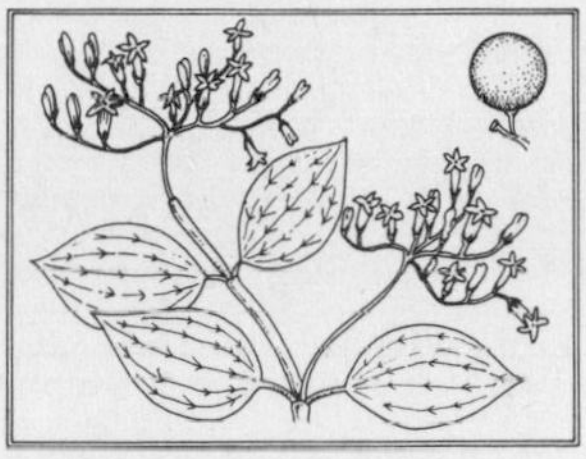

nux vomica

nuz•zle (nŭz′əl) *v.* **-zled, -zling. 1.** To rub or push against gently with or as if with the nose or snout. **2.** To cuddle together.
NV *abbr.* Nevada (with Zip code).
NW *abbr.* northwest; northwestern.
N.W.T. *abbr.* Northwest Territories.
NY *abbr.* New York (with Zip Code).
N.Y. *abbr.* New York.
ny•lon (nī′lŏn′) *n.* **1.** A strong, resilent synthetic material. **2.** Fabric or yarn made from nylon. **3. nylons.** Stockings made of nylon.
nymph (nĭmf) *n.* **1.** *Gk. & Rom. Myth.* A female spirit inhabiting woodlands and waters. **2.** Any of various immature insects that undergo incomplete metamorphosis.

Oo

o *or* **O** (ō) *n., pl.* **o's** *or* **O's. 1.** The 15th letter of the English alphabet. **2.** A speech sound represented by the letter o. **3.** Something with the shape of the letter O. **4.** A zero.
O[1] (ō) *interj.* **1.** Used before a name in formal address <Have mercy, *O Lord.*> **2.** Used as an expression of surprise or strong emotion <O heavens>
O[2] *symbol for* OXYGEN.
O *or* **O.** *abbr.* **1.** ocean. **2.** order.
oaf (ōf) *n.* A clumsy or stupid person. **—oaf′ish** *adj.* **—oaf′ish•ly** *adv.*
O•a•hu (ō-ä′ho͞o). Chief island of Hawaii.
oak (ōk) *n.* A tree or shrub of the genus *Quercus,* bearing acorns as fruit and having hard, durable wood. **—oak′en** *adj.*
Oak•land (ōk′lənd). City of W Calif., opposite San Francisco. *Pop.* 339,288.
oak leaf cluster *n.* A U.S. military decoration of silver or bronze oak leaves and acorns added to various medals to denote an additional decoration.
oa•kum (ō′kəm) *n.* Loose hemp or jute fiber, occas. treated with pitch or tar, used mainly to caulk seams in wooden ships.
oar (ôr, ōr) *n.* **1.** A long, thin, usu. wooden pole with a blade at one end, used to row or occas. to steer a boat. **2.** An oarsman.
oar•lock (ôr′lŏk′, ōr′-) *n.* An often U-shaped device used as a fulcrum to hold an oar in place while rowing.
oars•man (ôrz′mən, ōrz′-) *n.* A rower, esp. in a racing crew.
o•a•sis (ō-ā′sĭs) *n., pl.* **-ses** (-sēz′). A fertile desert area, esp. one with water.
oat (ōt) *n.* **1.** A widely cultivated cereal grass, *Avena sativa.* **2.** *often* **oats** *(sing. or pl. in number).* The seeds of the oat, used as food or fodder. **—oat′en** *adj.*
oath (ōth) *n., pl.* **oaths** (ōthz, ōths). **1.** A solemn promise or declaration, often calling upon God as witness. **2.** A blasphemous use of a sacred name. **3.** A swearword.
oat•meal (ōt′mēl′) *n.* **1.** Meal of rolled or ground oats. **2.** A porridge made from rolled or ground oats.
O•ba•di•ah (ō′bə-dī′ə) *n.* See BIBLE TABLE.
ob•bli•ga•to (ŏb′lĭ-gä′tō) *Mus. adv.* Not to be left out. Used as a direction. **—ob′bli•ga′to** *adj.* & *n.*
ob•du•rate (ŏb′do͞o-rĭt, -dyo͞o-) *adj.* **1.** Hardhearted. **2.** Not yielding to persuasion : obstinate. **—ob′du•ra•cy** *n.*
o•be•di•ent (ō-bē′dē-ənt) *adj.* Obeying or willing to obey, as a command. ☆***syns:*** AMENABLE, BIDDABLE, COMPLIANT, COMPLYING, CONFORMABLE, SUBMISSIVE, TRACTABLE **—o•be′di•ence** *n.*

o•bei•sance (ō-bā′səns, ō-bē′-) *n.* **1.** A gesture or body movement, as a bow, expressing deference. **2.** Deference : homage. **—o•bei′sant** *adj.*

ob•e•lisk (ŏb′ə-lĭsk′) *n.* A 4-sided usu. stone shaft tapering to a pyramidal point.

o•bese (ō-bēs′) *adj.* Extremely fat. **—o•be′si•ty** *n.*

o•bey (ō-bā′) *v.* **1.** To carry out the instructions of. **2.** To carry out (e.g., a command).

ob•fus•cate (ŏb′fə-skāt′, ŏb-fŭs′kāt′) *v.* **-cat•ed, -cat•ing. 1.** To make dark or obscure : cloud. **2.** To confuse. **—ob′fus•ca′tion** *n.* **—ob•fus′ca•to′ry** *adj.*

o•bi (ō′bē) *n.* A wide sash fastened at the back with a bow and worn with a kimono by Japanese women.

O•bie (ō′bē) *n.* An annual award for achievement in off-Broadway theater.

o•bit (ō′bĭt, ō-bĭt′) *n.* An obituary.

o•bi•ter dic•tum (ō′bĭ-tər dĭk′təm) *n., pl.* **obiter dic•ta** (-tə). Something said in passing : incidental observation.

o•bit•u•ar•y (ō-bĭch′o͞o-ĕr′ē) *n., pl.* **-ies.** A published death notice, usu. with a short biography of the deceased.

obj. *abbr.* **1.** object; objective (in grammar). **2.** objection.

ob•ject[1] (əb-jĕkt′) *v.* **1.** To hold or present an opposing view : dissent. **2.** To feel or express disapproval. **—ob•jec′tion** *n.* **—ob•jec′tor** *n.*

ob•ject[2] (ŏb′jĭkt, -jĕkt′) *n.* **1.** Something perceptible, esp. to the sense of touch or vision. **2.** *Philos.* Something intelligible by the mind. **3.** A focus of attention or effort. **4.** The purpose of a specific action. **5. a.** A noun that receives or is affected by the action of a verb. **b.** A noun following and governed by a preposition.

ob•jec•ti•fy (əb-jĕk′tə-fī′) *v.* **-fied, -fy•ing.** To make objective.

ob•jec•tion•a•ble (əb-jĕk′shə-nə-bəl) *adj.* Offensive : disagreeable. **—ob•jec′tion•a•bil′i•ty** *n.* **—ob•jec′tion•a•bly** *adv.*

ob•jec•tive (əb-jĕk′tĭv) *adj.* **1.** Of or pertaining to a material object rather than a mental concept. **2.** Having actual existence. **3.** Not influenced by emotion or personal opinion. **4.** Designating the case of a noun or pronoun that serves as the object of a verb. *—n.* **1.** Something worked toward or aspired to : goal. **2. a.** The objective case. **b.** A word in the objective case. **3.** The lens in a microscope or telescope that is closest to the object. **—ob′jec•tiv′i•ty** *n.*

ob•jet d'art (ôb′zhĕ där′) *n., pl.* **ob•jets d'art** (ôb′zhĕ där′). A small object of artistic value.

ob•jur•gate (ŏb′jər-gāt′, ŏb-jûr′gāt′) *v.* **-gat•ed, -gat•ing.** To reprove sharply : berate. **—ob′jur•ga′tion** *n.*

ob•late (ŏb′lāt′, ŏb-lāt′) *adj.* Flattened at the poles, as the earth. **—ob′late′ly** *adv.*

ob•la•tion (ə-blā′shən, ō-blā′-) *n.* The act or ceremony of offering something in religious worship. **—ob•la′tion•al** *adj.*

ob•li•ga•tion (ŏb′lĭ-gā′shən) *n.* **1.** The act of binding oneself by a moral, social, or legal tie. **2.** A binding responsibility, as a contract or promise. **3.** The binding power of a law, contract, promise, or sense of duty. **4.** Indebtedness to another for a favor. **—ob′li•gate′** *v.*

o•blig•a•to•ry (ə-blĭg′ə-tôr′ē, -tōr′ē, ŏb′lĭ-gə-) *adj.* **1.** Morally or legally binding. **2.** Compulsory. **—o•blig′a•to′ri•ly** *adv.*

o•blige (ə-blīj′) *v.* **o•bliged, o•blig•ing. 1.** To constrain. **2.** To make indebted or grateful. **3.** To perform a service or favor (for). **—o•blig′er** *n.* **—o•blig′ing•ly** *adv.*

o•blique (ō-blēk′, ə-blēk′) *adj.* **1.a.** Slanting or sloping : inclined. **b.** Designating geometric lines or planes that are neither parallel nor perpendicular. **2.** Devious or evasive. **—o•blique′ness, o•bliq′ui•ty** (ō-blĭk′wĭ-tē, ə-blĭk′-) *n.*

o•blit•er•ate (ə-blĭt′ə-rāt′) *v.* **-at•ed, -at•ing. 1.** To eliminate completely. **2.** To make indecipherable : wipe out. **—o•blit′er•a′tion** *n.* **—o•blit′er•a′tive** (-ə-rā′tĭv, -ər-ə-tĭv) *adj.* **—o•blit′er•a′tor** *n.*

o•bliv•i•on (ə-blĭv′ē-ən) *n.* **1.** The state of being utterly forgotten. **2.** An act or instance of forgetting.

o•bliv•i•ous (ə-blĭv′ē-əs) *adj.* **1.** Not mindful : forgetful. **2.** Unaware.

ob•long (ŏb′lông′, -lŏng′) *adj.* **1.** Having a dimension, esp. 1 of 2 perpendicular dimensions, as width or length, greater than the other : rectangular. **2.** *Bot.* Having an elongated form. **—ob′long′** *n.*

ob•lo•quy (ŏb′lə-kwē) *n., pl.* **-quies. 1.** Abusive and defamatory language : calumny. **2.** Damage to one's reputation.

ob•nox•ious (ŏb-nŏk′shəs, əb-) *adj.* Highly disagreeable : repugnant.

o•boe (ō′bō) *n.* A tube-shaped woodwind instrument with keys and holes and a double-reed mouthpiece. **—o′bo•ist** *n.*

obs. *abbr.* **1.** obscure. **2.** obsolete.

ob•scene (ŏb-sēn′, əb-) *adj.* **1.** Offensive to decency. **2.** Designed to incite lustful feelings. **3.** Repulsive : loathsome. ☆***syns:*** COARSE, CRUDE, DIRTY, FILTHY, FOUL, GROSS, INDECENT, LEWD, NASTY, PROFANE, RANK, RAUNCHY, RAW, SCATOLOGICAL, SMUTTY **—ob•scen′i•ty** (-sĕn′ĭ-tē) *n.*

ob•scure (ŏb-skyo͝or′, əb-) *adj.* **-scur•er, -scur•est. 1.** Deficient in light : dark. **2.** Indistinct : faint. **3.** Remote. **4.** Of humble station <an *obscure* civil servant> **5.** Not easily understood. *—v.* **-scured, -scur•ing. 1.** To make dim or indistinct. **2.** To conceal by or as if by covering. **—ob•scure′ly** *adv.* **—ob•scu′ri•ty** *n.*

ob•se•qui•ous (ŏb-sē′kwē-əs, əb-) *adj.* Fawning : servile. **—ob•se′qui•ous•ly** *adv.*

ob•se•quy (ŏb′sĭ-kwē) *n., pl.* **-quies.** *often* **obsequies.** A burial or funeral rite.

ob•ser•vance (əb-zûr′vəns) *n.* **1.** The act or practice of complying with something prescribed, as a law or rule. **2.** The act or custom of celebrating a ritual occasion, as a holiday. **3.** Observation.

ob•ser•va•tion (ŏb′zər-vā′shən) *n.* **1. a.** The act of observing. **b.** The condition of being observed. **2.** The act of noting and recording something as a phenomenon. **3.** A remark : comment. **—ob′ser•va′tion•al** *adj.* **—ob′ser•va′tion•al•ly** *adv.*

ob•ser•va•to•ry (əb-zûr′və-tôr′ē, -tōr′ē) *n., pl.* **-ries.** A building designed for making observations esp. of astronomical or meteorological phenomena.

ob•serve (əb-zûrv′) *v.* **-served, -serv•ing. 1.** To notice : perceive. **2.** To pay special attention to. **3.** To make a scientific observation of. **4.** To say casually : remark. **5.** To adhere to. **6.** To celebrate (e.g., a holiday). **—ob•serv′a•ble** *adj.* **—ob•serv′a•bly** *adv.* **—ob•ser′vant** *adj.* **—ob•serv′er** *n.*

ob•ses•sion (əb-sĕsh′ən, ŏb-) *n.* **1.** A persistent preoccupation with an idea or emotion. **2.** An idea or emotion causing a compulsive preoccupation. **—ob•sess′** *v.* **—ob•ses′sion•al** *adj.* **—ob•ses′sive** *adj.*

ob•sid•i•an (ŏb-sĭd′ē-ən) *n.* A shiny, usu. black or banded glass of volcanic origin.

ob•so•lesce (ŏb′sə-lĕs′) *v.* **-lesced, -lesc•ing.** To become obsolescent.

ob•so•les•cent (ŏb′sə-lĕs′ənt) *adj.* In the process of becoming obsolete. **—ob′so•les′cence** *n.* **—ob′so•les′cent•ly** *adv.*

ob•so•lete (ŏb′sə-lēt′, ŏb′sə-lēt′) *adj.* **1.** No longer in use. **2.** Outmoded in design.

ob•sta•cle (ŏb′stə-kəl) *n.* One that opposes or stands in the way of.

ob•ste•tri•cian (ŏb′stĭ-trĭsh′ən) *n.* A physician who specializes in obstetrics.

ob•stet•rics (ŏb-stĕt′rĭks, əb-) *n.* *(sing. or pl. in number).* The branch of medicine concerned with the care of women during pregnancy, childbirth, and the postpartum period. **—ob•stet′ric, ob•stet′ri•cal** *adj.*

ob•sti•nate (ŏb′stə-nĭt) *adj.* **1.** Stubbornly adhering to an opinion or course of action. **2.** Difficult to manage, control, or subdue. ☆***syns:*** BULLHEADED, DOGGED, HARD-HEADED, HEADSTRONG, INTRACTABLE, INTRANSIGENT, PERTINACIOUS, PERVERSE, PIGHEADED, REFRACTORY, STIFF-NECKED, STUBBORN, TOUGH, WILLFUL **—ob′sti•na•cy** (-nə-sē) *n.* **—ob′sti•nate•ly** *adv.*

ob•strep•er•ous (əb-strĕp′ər-əs, ŏb-) *adj.* Noisy and unruly, esp. in defiance. **—ob•strep′er•ous•ness** *n.*

ob•struct (əb-strŭkt′, ŏb-) *v.* **1.** To stop up (a passage) with obstacles. **2.** To hinder : impede. **3.** To cut off from view. **—ob•struct′er, ob•struc′tor** *n.* **—ob•struc′tion** *n.* **—ob•struc′tive** *adj.*

ob•struc•tion•ist (əb-strŭk′shə-nĭst, ŏb-) *n.* One who systematically hinders progress, esp. one who obstructs legislation. **—ob•struc′tion•ism** *n.*

ob•tain (əb-tān′, ŏb-) *v.* **1.** To gain possession of : acquire. **2.** To be widely accepted. **—ob•tain′a•ble** *adj.* **—ob•tain′er** *n.*

ob•trude (əb-tro͞od′, ŏb-) *v.* **-trud•ed, -trud•ing.** To thrust (oneself or one's ideas) on without invitation. **—ob•trud′er** *n.* **—ob•tru′sion** (-tro͞o′zhən) *n.* **—ob•tru′sive** (-sĭv) *adj.*

ob•tuse (ŏb-to͞os′, -tyo͞os′, əb-) *adj.* **1.** Not sharp : blunt. **2.** Slow in comprehension.

obtuse angle *n.* An angle less than 180° and greater than 90°.

ob•verse (ŏb-vûrs′, əb-, ŏb′vûrs′) *adj.* **1.** Turned toward the observer. **2.** Forming a counterpart. *—n.* (ŏb′vûrs′, ŏb-vûrs′, əb-). **1.** The side of a coin bearing the main stamp or design. **2.** A counterpart.

ob•vi•ate (ŏb′vē-āt′) *v.* **-at•ed, -at•ing.** To anticipate and prevent. **—ob′vi•a′tion** *n.* **—ob′vi•a′tor** *n.*

ob•vi•ous (ŏb′vē-əs) *adj.* Easily seen or discovered. **—ob′vi•ous•ly** *adv.*

oc•a•ri•na (ŏk′ə-rē′nə) *n.* A small simple wind instrument with a mouthpiece and finger holes.

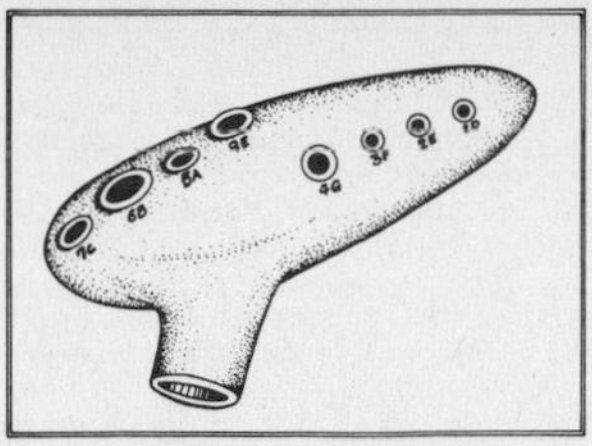

ocarina

oc·ca·sion (ə-kā′zhən) *n.* **1.** An event, esp. a notable event. **2.** The time at which something occurs. **3.** A favorable moment : opportunity. **4.** Something that brings on an event. **5.** A need created by particular circumstances. —*v.* To cause. **—on occasion** From time to time.

oc·ca·sion·al (ə-kā′zhə-nəl) *adj.* **1.** Happening from time to time : intermittent. **2.** Designed for or occurring on a special occasion. **—oc·ca′sion·al·ly** *adv.*

oc·ci·dent (ŏk′sə-dənt, -dĕnt′) *n.* **1.** The west. **2. Occident.** Europe and the W Hemisphere. **—oc′ci·den′tal** *adj.* & *n.*

oc·clude (ə-klōōd′) *v.* **-clud·ed, -clud·ing. 1.** To cause to become closed : obstruct. **2.** *Chem.* To adsorb or absorb. **3.** *Meteorol.* To force (air) upward from the earth's surface. **4.** To close so that the cusps of the teeth come together. **—oc·clu′sion** *n.*

occluded front *n.* The air front established when a warm front is occluded by a cold front.

oc·cult (ə-kŭlt′, ŏ-kŭlt′, ŏk′ŭlt′) *adj.* **1.** Of or pertaining to supernatural phenomena or influences. **2.** Beyond the range of human comprehension. **3.** Available only to the initiate. —*n.* Occult practices or lore. **—oc·cult′ism** *n.* **—oc·cult′ist** *n.*

oc·cu·pan·cy (ŏk′yə-pən-sē) *n.*, *pl.* **-cies. 1. a.** The act of taking or holding possession. **b.** The condition of being occupied. **2.** The period during which land or premises are occupied. **—oc′cu·pant** *n.*

oc·cu·pa·tion (ŏk′yə-pā′shən) *n.* **1.** An activity serving as one's regular employment. **2.** The process of occupying or state of being occupied. **3.** The taking possession of a territory by a foreign military force. **—oc′cu·pa′tion·al** *adj.*

occupational therapy *n.* Creative activity prescribed as a form of therapy. **—occupational therapist** *n.*

oc·cu·py (ŏk′yə-pī′) *v.* **-pied, -py·ing. 1.** To take possession of and retain control over by force. **2.** To fill up (space or time). **3.** To live in. **4.** To hold (e.g., an office). **5.** To keep busy. **—oc′cu·pi′er** *n.*

oc·cur (ə-kûr′) *v.* **-curred, -cur·ring. 1.** To come about. **2.** To be found : appear. **3.** To come to mind. **—oc·cur′rence** *n.* **—oc·cur′rent** *adj.*

o·cean (ō′shən) *n.* **1. a.** The whole body of salt water that covers nearly $\frac{3}{4}$ of the earth's surface. **b.** *often* **Ocean.** Any of the principal divisions of the ocean <the Pacific *Ocean*> **2.** A large quantity <*oceans* of food> **—o′ce·an′ic** *adj.*

O·ce·an·i·a (ō′shē-ăn′ē-ə, -ā′nē-ə). Islands of the C, W, and S Pacific Ocean.

o·cean·ar·i·um (ō′shə-nâr′ē-əm) *n.*, *pl.* **-i·ums** or **-i·a** (-ē-ə). A large aquarium for the exhibition or study of marine life.

o·cean·og·ra·phy (ō′shə-nŏg′rə-fē) *n.* Study and exploration of the ocean and its phenomena. **—o′cean·og′ra·pher** *n.* **—o′cean·o·graph′ic** (-nə-grăf′ĭk), **o′cean·o·graph′i·cal** *adj.*

o·cean·ol·o·gy (ō′shə-nŏl′ə-jē) *n.* Oceanography. **—o′cean·o·log′ic, o′cean·o·log′i·cal** *adj.* **—o′cean·o·log′i·cal·ly** *adv.* **—o′cean·ol′o·gist** *n.*

o·cel·lus (ō-sĕl′əs) *n.*, *pl.* **o·cel·li** (ō-sĕl′ī′) The simple eye of many invertebrates. **—o·cel′lar** *adj.*

oc·e·lot (ŏs′ə-lŏt′, ō′sə-) *n.* A wild cat, *Felis pardalis*, of SW U.S. and Central and South America, with a tawny spotted coat.

o·cher or **o·chre** (ō′kər) *n.* **1.** An earthy iron ore, occurring in brown, yellow, and red and used as a pigment. **2.** A yellowish orange. **—o′cher·ous, o′cher·y** *adj.*

o'clock (ə-klŏk′) *adv.* According to the clock <five *o'clock*>

Oct. *abbr.* October.

oc·ta·gon (ŏk′tə-gŏn′) *n.* A polygon with 8 sides and angles. **—oc·tag′o·nal** (ŏk-tăg′ə-nəl) *adj.* **—oc·tag′o·nal·ly** *adv.*

oc·ta·he·dron (ŏk′tə-hē′drən) *n.*, *pl.* **-drons** or **-dra** (-drə). A polyhedron with 8 plane surfaces.

oc·tal (ŏk′təl) *adj.* Of or being a number expressed in a numbering system of base 8.

oc·tane (ŏk′tān′) *n.* **1.** Any of several hydrocarbon compounds occurring in petroleum. **2.** Octane number.

octane number *n.* A number measuring the antiknock rating of gasoline, based on the percentage of a particular form of octane contained in a sample of gasoline.

octane rating *n.* Octane number.

oc·tant (ŏk′tənt) *n.* 1/8 of a circle or of the circumference of a circle.

oc·tave (ŏk′tĭv, -tāv′) *n.* **1.** *Mus.* **a.** The interval of 8 diatonic degrees between 2 tones. **b.** A tone 8 diatonic degrees above or below another tone. **2.** A group of 8.

oc·ta·vo (ŏk-tā′vō, -tä′-) *n.*, *pl.* **-vos. 1.** A page size (approx. 6 × 9 in.), orig. obtained by folding a printer's sheet into 8 leaves. **2.** A book made up of octavo pages.

oc·tet (ŏk-tĕt′) *n.* **1. a.** A musical composition for 8 voices or instruments. **b.** An ensemble of 8 musicians. **2.** A group of 8. **3.** The first 8 lines of a sonnet.

oc·til·lion (ŏk-tĭl′yən) *n.* **1.** The cardinal number equal to 10^{27}. **2.** *esp. Brit.* The cardinal number equal to 10^{48}.

Oc·to·ber (ŏk-tō′bər) *n.* The 10th month of the year, having 31 days.

▲word history: The Roman year orig. began in March, and October was consequently the 8th month, as its name suggests: *October* is derived from Latin *octo*, "eight." The names of other months are also derived from the Latin names of numbers. *September*, the 7th month, is from *septem*, "seven"; *November*, the 9th month, is from *novem*, "nine"; *December*, the 10th month, is from *decem*, "ten." The months now known as July and August were orig. named *Quintilis*, "5th month," and *Sextilis*, "6th month."

oc·to·ge·nar·i·an (ŏk′tə-jə-nâr′ē-ən) *n.* A person between 80 and 90 years of age.

oc·to·pus (ŏk′tə-pəs) *n.*, *pl.* **-es** or **-pi** (-pī′). A carnivorous nocturnal marine mollusk of the genus *Octopus* or related genera, with a saclike body and 8 tentacles bearing double rows of suckers.

oc·to·roon (ŏk′tə-rōōn′) *n.* A person whose parentage is $\frac{1}{8}$ Negro.

oc·tu·ple (ŏk′tə-pəl, -tōō′pəl, ŏk-tyōō′-) *adj.* **1.** Having 8 parts. **2.** Multiplied by 8. —*v.* **-pled, -pling.** To multiply or be multiplied by 8. **—oc′tu·ple** *n.*

oc·u·lar (ŏk′yə-lər) *adj.* **1.** Of or relating to the eye. **2.** Seen by the eye. —*n.* The eyepiece of an optical instrument.

oc·u·list (ŏk′yə-lĭst) *n.* **1.** An ophthalmologist. **2.** An optometrist.

OD (ō′dē′) *Slang.* —*n.* **1.** An overdose of a narcotic. **2.** One who has taken an overdose. —*v.* **OD'd, OD'ing.** To overdose.

odd (ŏd) *adj.* **1.** Deviating from the customary : unusual. **2. a.** In excess of the indicated number <20-*odd* students> **b.** Being a remainder <a few *odd* tickets still unsold> **3.** Being one of an incomplete set or pair. **4.** *Math.* Designating a number not divisible by 2. **—odd′ly** *adv.*

odd·ball (ŏd′bôl′) *n.* *Informal.* An eccentric person.

Odd Fellow *n.* A member of the Independent Order of Odd Fellows, a benevolent secret society.

odd·i·ty (ŏd′ĭ-tē) *n.*, *pl.* **-ties. 1.** One that is odd. **2.** The state or quality of being odd.

odd·ment (ŏd′mənt) *n.* Something left over : remnant.

odds (ŏdz) *pl.n.* **1.** An advantage assigned to a weaker side in a contest to equalize the chances of winning. **2.** A ratio expressing the probability of an outcome. **3.** The likelihood of something happening. **—at odds.** In conflict.

odds and ends *pl.n.* Miscellaneous items or remnants.

ode (ōd) *n.* A lyric poem usu. in praise of an object or person.

O·des·sa (ō-dĕs′ə). City of SW European USSR. *Pop.* 1,057,000.

o·de·um (ō-dē′əm, ō′dē-) *n.*, *pl.* **o·de·a** (ō-dē′ə, ō′dē-ə) **1.** A small ancient Greek or Roman building used for public performances of poetry and music. **2.** A contemporary theater or music hall.

o·di·ous (ō′dē-əs) *adj.* Arousing hatred or repugnance : abhorrent. **—o′di·ous·ly** *adv.*

o·di·um (ō′dē-əm) *n.* **1.** The quality or state of being odious. **2.** Disgrace resulting from contemptible behavior.

o·dom·e·ter (ō-dŏm′ĭ-tər) *n.* An instrument for measuring distance traveled, as by a vehicle.

o·dor (ō′dər) *n.* **1.** The quality of something that stimulates the sense of smell. **2.** Repute : esteem. **—o′dor·if′er·ous** *adj.* **—o′dor·less** *adj.* **—o′dor·ous** *adj.*

o·dour (ō′dər) *n.* *esp. Brit. var. of* ODOR.

od·ys·sey (ŏd′ĭ-sē) *n.* An extended, adventurous wandering.

Oed·i·pus complex (ĕd′ə-pəs, ē′də-) *n.* *Psychoanal.* Unconscious sexual feelings in a child, esp. a boy, toward the parent of the opposite sex. **—Oed′i·pal** *adj.*

o'er (ôr, ōr) *prep.* & *adv.* Over.

oeu·vre (œ′vrə) *n.*, *pl.* **oeu·vres** (œvrə) **1.** A work of art. **2.** The whole body of an artist's work.

of (ŭv, ŏv; əv *when unstressed*) *prep.* **1.** From. **2.** Caused by <his death *of* cancer> **3.** At a distance from. **4.** So as to be separated from <robbed *of* one's self-respect> **5.** From the total comprising <most *of* the cases> **6.** Made from. **7.** Associated with <a

member *of* your religion> **8.** Belonging or connected to <the rungs *of* a ladder> **9.** Possessing <a person *of* courage> **10.** Containing <a basket *of* peaches> **11.** Specified as <a width *of* 20 feet> **12.** Directed toward <a love *of* dogs> **13.** Produced by. **14.** Marked or identified by <a year *of* discord> **15.** With reference to <speak *of* it tomorrow> **16.** Set aside for <needed a day *of* rest> **17.** Before : until <10 minutes *of* 12> **18.** During or on a specified time.

off (ôf, ŏf) *adv.* **1.** From a place or position <drive *off*> **2.** Distant in space or time. **3.** So as to be no longer on or connected. **4.** So as to be smaller or fewer. **5.** So as to be away from work or duty. *—adj.* **1.** Distant or removed <the *off* side of the pasture> **2.** Not on or connected. **3.** Not operating or operational. **4.** Canceled. **5.** Less or smaller. **6.** Below standard. **7.** In a specified condition <well *off*> **8.** Incorrect. **9.** Away from work or duty. *—prep.* **1.** So as to be removed from <The bird hopped *off* the branch.> **2.** Away from. **3.** By consuming or with the means provided by. **4.** Extending from <an artery *off* the heart> **5.** Not up to the usual standard of. **6.** So as to abstain from <went *off* drugs>

of•fal (ô'fəl, ŏf'əl) *n.* **1.** Waste parts, esp. the entrails and trimmings of a butchered animal. **2.** Refuse : filth.

off•beat (ôf'bēt', ŏf'-) *n. Mus.* An unaccented beat. *—adj.* (ôf'bēt', ŏf'-). *Slang.* Unconventional : eccentric.

off-Broad•way (ôf'brôd'wā', ŏf'-) *adj.* Designating or relating to productions in theaters outside the Broadway entertainment district of New York City.

off-col•or (ôf'kŭl'ər, ŏf'-) *adj.* **1.** Varying from the standard or desired color. **2.** In poor taste : indecent.

of•fence (ə-fĕns') *n. esp. Brit. var. of* OFFENSE.

of•fend (ə-fĕnd') *v.* **1.** To arouse resentment, anger, or vexation in. **2.** To be displeasing (to). **3.** To commit a sin.

of•fense (ə-fĕns') *n.* **1.** The act of offending or the state of being offended. **2. a.** A breach of a social or moral code. **b.** A crime. **3.** (ŏf'ĕns'). The act of attacking. **4.** (ŏf'ĕns'). The side that is attacking in a game or contest. **—of•fen'sive** *adj.* **—of•fen'sive•ly** *adv.* **—of•fen'sive•ness** *n.*

of•fer (ô'fər, ŏf'ər) *v.* **1.** To present for acceptance : tender. **2.** To place on sale. **3.** To propose as payment. **4.** To present as an act of worship. **5.** To provide : furnish. **6.** To present to an audience or to the public. ☆**syns:** EXTEND, PRESENT, PROFFER, TENDER, VOLUNTEER. **—of'fer** *n.* **—of'fer•er, of'fer•or** *n.* **—of'fer•ing** *n.*

of•fer•to•ry (ô'fər-tôr'ē, -tōr'ē, ŏf'ər-) *n., pl.* **-ries.** The presentation of offerings at a religious service.

off•hand (ôf'hănd', ŏf'-) *adv. & adj.* Without preparation : extemporaneously. **—off'hand'ed•ly** *adv.*

off-hour (ôf'our', ŏf'-) *n.* A period of slack activity.

of•fice (ô'fĭs, ŏf'ĭs) *n.* **1. a.** A place in which business or professional activities are conducted. **b.** The personnel working in an office. **2.** A function or duty assigned to someone. **3.** A position of authority, as in a government or institution. **4.** A subdivision of a government. **5.** A public position <was elected to *office*> **6.** *often* **offices.** A favor. **7.** An ecclesiastical ceremony or service, esp. a rite for the dead.

of•fice•hold•er (ô'fĭs-hōl'dər, ŏf'ĭs-) *n.* A person holding a public office.

of•fi•cer (ô'fĭ-sər, ŏf'ĭ-) *n.* **1.** A person holding an office of authority, as in a government or corporation. **2.** A person holding a commission in the armed services. **3.** A licensed master, mate, chief engineer, or assistant engineer in the merchant marine. **4.** A member of a police force.

of•fi•cial (ə-fĭsh'əl) *adj.* **1.** Authorized by a proper authority. **2.** Suitable to a position of authority : formal. *—n.* **1.** One who holds an office or position. **2.** A sports referee or umpire. **—of•fi'cial•dom** *n.*

of•fi•ci•ant (ə-fĭsh'ē-ənt) *n.* One who officiates at a religious service.

of•fi•ci•ate (ə-fĭsh'ē-āt') *v.* **-at•ed, -at•ing.** **1.** To carry out the functions and duties of an office or position. **2.** To preside at a religious service. **3.** To serve as a sports referee or umpire. **—of•fi'ci•a'tor** *n.*

of•fi•cious (ə-fĭsh'əs) *adj.* Excessively inclined to offer one's advice or services to others. **—of•fi'cious•ness** *n.*

off•ing (ô'fĭng, ŏf'ĭng) *n.* The near future <new developments in the *offing*>

off-key (ôf'-kē', ŏf'-) *adj.* **1.** *Mus.* Not in tune : flat or sharp. **2.** At odds with what is considered normal. **—off'-key'** *adv.*

off-limits (ôf-lĭm'ĭts, ŏf-) *adj.* Prohibited to a specific group.

off-line (ôf'līn', ŏf'-) *adj. Computer Sci.* Not controlled directly by a computer.

off-off-Broad•way (ôf'ôf-brôd'wā', ŏf'ŏf-) *n.* A theatrical movement in New York City emphasizing experimental techniques and productions.

off-put•ting (ôf'po͝ot'ĭng, ŏf'-) *adj.* Disconcerting.

off-sea•son (ôf'-sē'zən, ŏf'-) *n.* A period marked by a slackening of activity.

off•set (ôf'sĕt', ŏf'-) *n.* **1.** Something that balances, compensates, or counteracts. **2.** A ledge or recess in a wall. **3.** A bend in a bar or pipe, enabling it to pass around an obstruction. **4.** Offset printing. *—v.* (ôf-sĕt', ŏf-) **1.** To counteract or compensate for. **2.** To print by offset. **3.** To form an offset in (a wall, pipe, or bar). **—off'set'** *adj.*

offset printing *n.* Printing by indirect image transfer.

off•shoot (ôf'sho͞ot', ŏf'-) *n.* One that branches out or develops from a source.

off•shore (ôf'shôr', -shōr', ŏf'-) *adj.* **1.** Moving or directed away from the shore. **2.** Located at a distance from the shore. **—off'shore'** *adv.*

off•side *also* **off side** (ôf'sīd', ŏf'-) *adj.* Illegally forward or in advance of the ball or puck, as in football or hockey.

off•spring (ôf'sprĭng', ŏf'-) *n., pl.* **offspring.** **1.** Progeny. **2.** A product : result.

off-stage (ôf'stāj', ŏf'-) *adj. & adv.* Away from or off the stage of a theater.

off-the-rack (ôf'*th*ə-răk', ŏf'-) *adj.* Ready-made.

off-the-rec•ord (ôf'*th*ə-rĕk'ərd, ŏf'-) *adj. & adv.* Not for publication.

off-the-shelf (ôf'*th*ə-shĕlf', ŏf'-) *adj.* Available as an item carried in stock.

off-the-wall (ôf'*th*ə-wôl', ŏf'-) *adj. Informal.* Unconventional or bizarre.

off-track betting (ôf'trăk', ŏf'-) *n.* A system of gambling in which bets are placed away from a racetrack.

off-white (ôf'hwīt', -wīt', ŏf'-) *n.* A yellowish or grayish white.

off year *n.* **1.** A year in which a major election does not take place. **2.** A year of decreased production or activity.

oft (ôft, ŏft) *adv.* Often.

of•ten (ô'fən, ŏf'ən, ôf'tən, ŏf'-) *adv.* Many times : frequently.

of•ten•times (ô'fən-tīmz', ŏf'ən-, ôf'tən-, ŏf'-) *adv.* Repeatedly : frequently.

o•gee (ō'jē') *n.* **1.** A molding with an S-shaped profile. **2.** An arch formed by 2 curves meeting at a point.

ogee

o•gle (ō'gəl, ô'-gəl) *v.* **o•gled, o•gling.** To stare (at), esp. amorously or impertinently.

o•gre (ō'gər) *n.* **1.** A monster or giant of folklore and legend that eats human beings. **2.** A cruel or dreaded person. **—o'gre•ish** (ō'gər-ĭsh, ō'grĭsh) *adj.* **—o'gress** *n.*

oh (ō) *interj.* **1.** Used to express strong emotion, as fear, surprise, anger, or pain. **2.** Used in direct address <*Oh*, sir You forgot your coat.> **3.** Used to indicate understanding of a statement.

OH *abbr.* Ohio (with Zip Code).

O•hi•o (ō-hī'ō). **1.** State of the N. U.S. *Cap.* Columbus. *Pop.* 10,797,419. **2.** River flowing 981 mi (1,578.4 km) from Pittsburgh, Pa., W and SW to the Mississippi in S Ill. **—O•hi'o•an** *n.*

ohm (ōm) *n.* A unit of electrical resistance equal to the resistance of a conductor through which a 1-amp current flows when a potential difference of 1 volt is applied.

ohm•me•ter (ōm'mē'tər) *n.* An instrument for measuring the resistance of a conductor directly in ohms.

o•ho (ō-hō') *interj.* Used esp. to express surprise or mock astonishment.

-oid *suff.* Like or representing <anthropo*oid*>

oil (oil) *n.* **1.** Any of several mineral and synthetic substances and animal and vegetable fats that are usu. thick, slippery, capable of being burned, liquid or easily melted, and insoluble in water. **2.** Petroleum. **3.** A substance having an oily consistency. **4.** An oil color. **5.** An oil painting. *—v.* To lubricate, coat, or polish with oil.

oil•cloth (oil'klôth', -klŏth') *n.* A cloth made waterproof by being treated with oil, clay, or paint.

oil color *n.* A paint consisting of pigment ground in oil.

oil field *n.* An area containing reserves of recoverable petroleum, esp. one that has been developed for production.

oil paint *n.* A paint in which the vehicle is a drying oil.

oil painting *n.* **1.** A painting in oil colors. **2.** The art of painting with oil colors.

oil•pa•per (oil′pā′pər) *n.* Paper treated with oil to make it transparent and water-repellent.

oil shale *n.* A dark-brown or black shale containing hydrocarbons from which petroleum can be produced by distillation.

oil•skin (oil′skĭn′) *n.* **1.** Cloth treated with oil to make it waterproof. **2.** A protective garment made of oilskin.

oil slick *n.* A thin layer of oil on water.

oil•y (oi′lē) *adj.* **-i•er, -i•est. 1.** Of or like oil. **2.** Greasy. **3.** Excessively suave. **—oil′i•ly** *adv.* **—oil′i•ness** *n.*

oink (oingk) *n.* The characteristic grunting sound of a pig. **—oink** *v.*

oint•ment (oint′mənt) *n.* A viscous substance used on the skin as an emollient, cosmetic, or medicament.

OK *abbr.* Oklahoma (with Zip Code).

O.K. or **OK** or **o•kay** (ō′kā′, ō-kā′) *n., pl.* **O.K.'s** or **OK's** or **o•kays.** Approval : assent. *—v.* **O.K.'d, O.K.'ing** or **OK'd , OK'ing** or **o•kayed, o•kay•ing.** To approve of or consent to : authorize. *—interj.* Used to express assent or approval. *—adj.* Acceptable. *—adv.* Acceptably.

o•ka•pi (ō-kä′pē) *n., pl.* **okapi** or **-pis.** A ruminant mammal, *Okapia johnstoni,* of C Africa, resembling a small giraffe.

O•kie (ō′kē) *n. Slang.* A migrant farm worker, esp. one from Okla. in the 1930's.

Okla. *abbr.* Oklahoma.

O•kla•ho•ma (ō′klə-hō′mə). State of the SW U.S. *Cap.* Oklahoma City. *Pop.* 3,025,266. **—O′kla•ho′man** *n.*

Oklahoma City. Cap. of Okla., in the C part. *Pop.* 403,213.

o•kra (ō′krə) *n.* A tall tropical and semitropical plant, *Hibiscus esculentus,* having mucilaginous green pods used as a vegetable and in soups.

old (ōld) *adj.* **1.** Having existed or lived for a relatively long time. **2.** Made in former times. **3.** Having or exhibiting the characteristics of age. **4.** Having existed for a specified time. **5.** Belonging to or being of an earlier time <my *old* high school> **6.** Known through long acquaintance <an *old* familiar face> **7.** Used as an intensive <any *old* day> *—n.* Former times.

old country *n.* The native country of an immigrant.

old•en (ōl′dən) *adj.* Old : ancient.

Old English *n.* English from the middle of the 5th to the beginning of the 12th cent.

old fashioned *n.* A cocktail made of whiskey, fruit, sugar, and bitters.

old-fash•ioned (ōld′făsh′ənd) *adj.* Of a method or style once in vogue : outdated.

old fogy *also* **old fogey** *n.* One who is excessively conservative or old-fashioned. **—old′fo′gy•ish, old′fo′gey•ish** *adj.*

Old French *n.* French from the 9th to the early 16th cent.

Old Glory *n.* The U.S. flag.

old guard *n. often* **Old Guard.** A conservative, often reactionary element of a particular society, class, or political group.

old hand *n.* One who has long experience.

old hat *adj. Informal.* Old-fashioned.

old•ie (ōl′dē) *n.* Something old or outdated, esp. a song popular in an earlier time.

old lady *n. Slang.* **1.** One's mother. **2. a.** One's wife. **b.** One's girlfriend.

old-line (ōld′līn′) *adj.* **1.** Having conservative or reactionary ideas. **2.** Traditional.

old maid *n.* **1.** *Informal.* A woman, esp. an older woman, who has not married. **2.** *Informal.* A prim and fussy person. **—old′maid′ish** *adj.*

old man *n. Slang.* **1.** One's father. **2. a.** One's husband. **b.** One's boyfriend.

old master *n.* **1.** An eminent European artist of the period from around 1500 to the early 1700's. **2.** A work by an old master.

Old Nick *n.* The devil.

old school *n.* A group that espouses traditional values or practices.

old•ster (ōld′stər) *n. Informal.* An old person.

Old Testament *n.* The 1st of the principal divisions of the Christian Bible. See BIBLE TABLE.

old-tim•er (ōld′tī′mər) *n. Informal.* **1. a.** An oldster. **b.** An old hand. **2.** A very old or antiquated thing.

old wives' tale *n.* A piece of superstitious folklore.

old-world (ōld′wûrld′) *adj.* Antique and picturesque.

Old World *n.* The E Hemisphere, Asia, Africa, and esp. Europe.

o•lé (ō-lā′) *interj.* Used to express excited approval. **—o•lé′** *n.*

o•le•ag•i•nous (ō′lē-ăj′ə-nəs) *adj.* **1.** Of or relating to oil. **2.** Unctuous : oily.

o•le•an•der (ō′lē-ăn′dər, ō′lē-ăn′-) *n.* A poisonous evergreen shrub of the genus *Nerium,* found in warm climates, bearing white, purple, or reddish flower clusters.

o•le•o (ō′lē-ō′) *n., pl.* **-os.** Margarine.

o•le•o•mar•ga•rine (ō′lē-ō-mär′jər-ĭn, -jə-rēn′) *n.* Margarine.

ol•fac•tion (ŏl-făk′shən, ōl-) *n.* **1.** The sense of smell. **2.** An act of smelling.

ol•fac•to•ry (ŏl-făk′tə-rē, -trē, ōl-) *adj.* Of or pertaining to the sense of smell.

ol•i•gar•chy (ŏl′ĭ-gär′kē) *n., pl.* **-chies. 1. a.** Government by a few, esp. by a small group or class. **b.** The persons and families making up such a group. **2.** A state governed by oligarchy. **—ol′i•garch′** *n.* **—ol′i•gar′chic, ol′i•gar′chi•cal** *adj.*

ol•i•gop•o•ly (ŏl′ĭ-gŏp′ə-lē, ō′lĭ-) *n., pl.* **-lies** A market condition in which there are so few sellers that the actions of any one of them can affect price and have a measurable impact on competitors. **—ol′i•gop′o•lis′tic** (-lĭs′tĭk) *adj.*

o•li•o (ō′lē-ō′) *n., pl.* **-os.** A miscellany.

ol•ive (ŏl′ĭv) *n.* **1.** An Old World semitropical evergreen tree, *Olea europaea,* with leathery leaves, yellow flowers, and small oval fruit used as food and a source of oil. **2.** A yellowish green. **—ol′ive** *adj.*

olive branch *n.* **1.** A branch of the olive tree regarded as a symbol of peace. **2.** A peace offering.

olive drab *n.* **1.** A dull brownish or grayish green. **2.** Cloth of an olive-drab color, often used for military uniforms.

olive oil *n.* Oil pressed from olives, used in cooking and as an ingredient of soaps.

ol•i•vine (ŏl′ə-vēn′) *n.* A usu. greenish mineral silicate of iron and magnesium.

O•lym•pi•a (ō-lĭm′pē-ə). Cap. of Wash., in the SW. *Pop.* 27,447.

O•lym•pic games (ō-lĭm′pĭk) *pl. n.* **1.** An ancient Greek festival of athletic games and contests of dance and choral poetry, celebrated every 4 years to honor Zeus. **2.** An international athletic competition held every 4 years.

O•lym•pus (ō-lĭm′pəs). Mountain in N Greece, mythical home of the Greek gods.

O•ma•ha (ō′mə-hô′, -hä′). City of E Neb., on the Missouri R. *Pop.* 311,681.

O•man (ō-män′). Sultanate at the E tip of the Arabian peninsula. *Cap.* Muscat. *Pop.* 900,000.

om•buds•man (ŏm′bŭdz′mən, -bo͝odz′-) *n.* **1.** A government official charged with investigating citizens' complaints against the government. **2.** One who investigates complaints, as from consumers, and helps to achieve settlements.

om•e•let *also* **om•e•lette** (ŏm′ə-lĭt, ŏm′lĭt) *n.* A dish made of eggs beaten with milk and cooked until set.

o•men (ō′mən) *n.* A phenomenon regarded as a portent of future good or evil. ☆***syns:*** AUGURY, FORETOKEN, PORTENT, PRESAGE, PROGNOSTIC, PROGNOSTICATION

om•i•nous (ŏm′ə-nəs) *adj.* **1.** Of or being an omen, esp. an evil one. **2.** Threatening : menacing. **—om′i•nous•ly** *adv.*

o•mit (ō-mĭt′) *v.* **o•mit•ted, o•mit•ting. 1.** To leave out. **2.** To neglect : overlook. **—o•mis′sion** (-mĭsh′ən) *n.*

om•ni•bus (ŏm′nĭ-bŭs′) *n.* A bus. *—adj.* Including or providing for many items at once <an *omnibus* legislative bill>

om•ni•di•rec•tion•al (ŏm′nĭ-dĭ-rĕk′shə-nəl, -dī-) *adj.* Capable of receiving or transmitting signals in all directions.

om•ni•far•i•ous (ŏm′nĭ-fâr′ē-əs) *adj.* Of all kinds. **—om′ni•far′i•ous•ness** *n.*

om•nip•o•tent (ŏm-nĭp′ə-tənt) *adj.* Having absolute power or authority. *—n.* **Omnipotent.** God. **—om•nip′o•tence** *n.*

om•ni•pres•ence (ŏm′nĭ-prĕz′əns) *n.* The fact of being present everywhere. **—om′ni•pres′ent** *adj.*

om•nis•cient (ŏm-nĭsh′ənt) *adj.* Knowing everything. *—n.* **Omniscient.** God. **—om•nis′cience** *n.*

om•ni•vore (ŏm′nə-vôr′, -vōr′) *n.* An omnivorous animal.

om•niv•o•rous (ŏm-nĭv′ər-əs) *adj.* **1.** *Zool.* Eating both vegetable and animal substances. **2.** Eagerly absorbing everything available. **—om•niv′o•rous•ly** *adv.*

on (ŏn, ôn) *prep.* **1.** Used to indicate: **a.** Position upon and in contact with. **b.** Location at or along. **c.** Proximity. **d.** Attachment to or suspension from. **2.** Used to indicate movement or direction toward, against, or onto <jump *on* the platform><a march *on* Washington> **3.** Used to indicate: **a.** Occurrence at a given time <*on* May 1st> **b.** The particular occasion or circumstance <*On* leaving the house, I heard the phone.> **4.** Used to indicate: **a.** The object affected by perceptible action. **b.** The agent or agency of a specified action. **5.** Used to indicate a source or basis <making money *on* the horses> **6.** Used to indicate: **a.** The state or process of <*on* leave><*on* fire> **b.** The purpose of. **c.** A means of conveyance <ride *on* a subway> **d.** Availability by means of <a doctor *on* call> **e.** Association with. **f.** Addition or repetition <opened store *on* store> **7.** Concerning : about. **8.** In the possession of <not a cent *on* me> **9.** At the expense of <Dinner's *on* me.> *—adv.* **1.**

In a position of covering or being in contact with something. **2.** In the direction of. **3.** Forward <moved *on* to a new job> **4.** In a continuous course. **5.** In or into operation or performance.

on•board (ŏn-bôrd′, -bōrd′, ôn-) *adj.* Carried aboard a vehicle.

once (wŭns) *adv.* **1.** 1 time only <*once* a year> **2.** At 1 time in the past. **3.** At any time : ever <Time, *once* gone, will never return.> **4.** By 1 degree of relationship <my 1st cousin, *once* removed> *—n.* 1 time. *—conj.* As soon as. *—adj.* Former <the *once* heavyweight champion>

once-o•ver (wŭns′ō′vər) *n. Informal.* A brief but comprehensive inspection.

on•com•ing (ŏn′kŭm′ĭng, ôn′-) *adj.* Coming nearer.

one (wŭn) *adj.* **1.** Being a single unit or entity <*one* mile> **2.** Characterized by unity. **3.** Occurring or existing as something indefinite <We will meet again *one* day.> **4.** Single in kind. *—n.* **1.** A single individual : unit. **2.** The cardinal number represented by the symbol 1, designating the 1st such unit in a series. *—pron.* An indefinitely specified thing or person.

one-di•men•sion•al (wŭn′dĭ-mĕn′shə-nəl) *adj.* Lacking depth : superficial.

one-horse (wŭn′hôrs′) *adj.* Small and uninteresting <a *one-horse* town>

O'Neill (ō-nēl′), **Eugene Gladstone.** 1888–1953. Amer. dramatist.

one•ness (wŭn′nĭs) *n.* **1.** Singleness. **2.** Sameness of character <the insipid *oneness* of institution food> **3.** Agreement : unity <*oneness* of mind>

one-night stand (wŭn′nīt′) *n.* A musical or dramatic performance given on 1 night only in a place.

on•er•ous (ŏn′ər-əs, ō′nər-) *adj.* Burdensome : oppressive. **—on′er•ous•ly** *adv.*

one•self (wŭn-sĕlf′) *also* **one's self** (wŭn sĕlf′, wŭnz sĕlf′) *pron.* **1.** One's own self <have confidence in *oneself*> **2.** One's normal or healthy condition.

one-shot (wŭn′shŏt′) *adj.* **1.** Effective after a single attempt. **2.** Being the only 1 <a *one-shot* opportunity>

one-sid•ed (wŭn′sī′dĭd) *adj.* **1.** Favoring 1 group : biased <a *one-sided* opinion> **2.** Unequal. **—one′-sid′ed•ness** *n.*

one-step (wŭn′stĕp′) *n.* A ballroom dance consisting of a series of rapid steps in 2/4 time. **—one′-step′** *v.*

one•time (wŭn′tīm′) *adj.* Former <a *onetime* diving champion>

one-time (wŭn′tīm′) *adj.* On only 1 occasion <a *one-time* medalist in 1980>

one-to-one (wŭn′tə-wŭn′) *adj.* **1.** Pairing each member of a class uniquely with a member of another class. **2.** Marked by proportional amounts on both sides.

one-track (wŭn′trăk′) *adj.* Intent on a single goal <a *one-track* mind>

one-up•man•ship (wŭn-ŭp′măn-shĭp′) *n. Informal.* The technique and practice of staying 1 step ahead of one's competitor.

one-way (wŭn′wā′) *adj.* **1.** Moving or allowing movement in only 1 direction. **2.** Relating to travel in only 1 direction.

on•go•ing (ŏn′gō′ĭng, ôn′-) *adj.* Currently taking place or developing.

on•ion (ŭn′yən) *n.* A plant, *Allium cepa*, cultivated worldwide for its rounded bulb having a pungent odor and taste.

▲word history: The Latin source of the English word *onion* is *unio*, which is derived from Latin *unus*, "one." *Unio* had several meanings in Latin, among them "unity" and "union." *Unio* was also used to designate a kind of large pearl, and in rustic speech it designated a kind of onion. The exact reason for calling an onion *unio* is unknown. *Unio* was chosen perhaps because of the onion's single bulb, in contrast to the multisegmented garlic and shallot, both related to the onion. *Unio* could also have been chosen because of some pearllike quality of the bulb, such as roundness.

on•ion•skin (ŭn′yən-skĭn′) *n.* A tough, thin, translucent paper.

on-line (ŏn′līn′, ôn′-) *adj.* **1.** *Computer Sci.* Controlled by a computer. **2.** Being in progress.

on•look•er (ŏn′lo͝ok′ər, ôn′-) *n.* One who looks on : spectator. **—on′look′ing** *adj.*

on•ly (ōn′lē) *adj.* Alone in kind : sole. *—adv.* **1.** Without anything or anyone else. **2. a.** At the very least. **b.** Merely. **3.** Solely : exclusively. *—conj.* But : except.

on•o•mat•o•poe•ia (ŏn′ə-măt′ə-pē′ə) *n.* The use or formation of words, as *hiss* or *cuckoo*, that have a sound imitating what they denote. **—on′o•mat′o•poe′ic** (-pē′ĭk), **on′o•mat′o•po•et′ic** (-pō-ĕt′ĭk) *adj.*

on•rush (ŏn′rŭsh′, ôn′-) *n.* **1.** A forward surge or flow. **2.** An assault.

on•set (ŏn′sĕt′, ôn′-) *n.* **1.** An assault. **2.** A beginning : outset.

on•shore (ŏn′shôr′, -shōr′, ôn′-) *adj.* **1.** Moving or directed toward the shore <an *onshore* breeze> **2.** Based or operating on or along the shore. **3.** Domestic <*onshore* industry> **—on′shore′** *adv.*

on•slaught (ŏn′slôt′, ôn′-) *n.* An attack.

on•stage (ŏn-stāj′, ôn-) *adj.* & *adv.* Toward or on the stage of a theater.

Ont. *abbr.* Ontario.

On•tar•i•o (ŏn-târ′ē-ō′). **1.** Province of EC Canada. *Cap.* Toronto. *Pop.* 8,264,465. **2.** One of the Great Lakes, between SE Ont., Canada, and NW N.Y. **—On•tar′i•an** *n.*

on•to (ŏn′to͞o′, ôn′-, ŏn′tə, ôn′-) *prep.* **1.** To a position on : upon. **2.** *Informal.* Aware of.

o•nus (ō′nəs) *n.* **1.** A burden, esp. an oppressive responsibility. **2.** Blame.

on•ward (ŏn′wərd, ôn′-) *adj.* Moving forward in space or time. *—adv. also* **on•wards** (-wərdz). In an onward direction.

on•yx (ŏn′ĭks) *n.* Chalcedony that occurs in colored bands and is used as a gemstone. *—adj.* Dark : black.

oo•dles (o͞od′lz) *pl.n. Informal.* A large amount : lots.

oo•loo (o͞o′lo͞o′) *n. Can.* An Innuit knife.

oomph (o͝omf) *n. Slang.* **1.** Boundless energy or enthusiasm. **2.** Sex appeal.

ooze[1] (o͞oz) *v.* **oozed, ooz•ing. 1.** To seep or flow out slowly. **2.** To vanish or ebb slowly : drain. ☆***syns:*** BLEED, EXUDE, LEACH, PERCOLATE, SEEP, WEEP **—ooze** *n.* **—ooz′i•ness** *n.* **—ooz′y** *adj.*

ooze[2] (o͞oz) *n.* **1.** Soft, thin mud. **2.** Mudlike sediment covering the floor of lakes and oceans. **—ooz′i•ness** *n.* **—ooz′y** *adj.*

o•pah (ō′pə) *n.* A large brightly colored marine fish, *Lambris regius.*

opah

o•pal (ō′pəl) *n.* A translucent, variously colored mineral composed of a form of silicon, often used as a gem. **—o′pal•ine′** (ō′pə-līn′, -lēn′) *adj.*

o•pal•es•cence (ō′pə-lĕs′əns) *n.* The quality or state of exhibiting a milky iridescence like that of an opal. **—o′pal•esce′** *v.* **—o′pal•es′cent** *adj.*

o•paque (ō-pāk′) *adj.* **1. a.** Impervious to the passage of light. **b.** Not reflecting light : lusterless. **2.** Unperceptive : obtuse. **—o•pac′i•ty** (-păs′ĭ-tē), **o•paque′ness** *n.*

op art *n.* Optical art.

OPEC (ō′pĕk′) *n.* Organization of Petroleum Exporting Countries.

op-ed page (ŏp-ĕd′) *n.* A newspaper section, usu. located opposite the editorial page, featuring articles and columns presenting personal viewpoints.

o•pen (ō′pən) *adj.* **1.** Affording unobstructed entrance and exit. **2.** Not covered or concealed. **3.** Not sealed, fastened, or locked. **4.** Having spaces, gaps, or intervals <an *open* weave> **5.** Accessible to all. **6.** Vulnerable : susceptible. **7.** Available. **8.** Ready to transact business. **9.** Unoccupied. **10. a.** Candid <an *open* manner> **b.** Free from prejudice <an *open* mind> ☆***syns:*** EXPOSED, UNCOVERED, UNPROTECTED *—v.* **1.** To release or become released from a closed position. **2.** To free from obstructions. **3.** To unfold. **4.** To remove the wrapping or cover from. **5.** To begin. **6.** To permit the use of. **7.** To make or become understanding or receptive. **8.** To reveal the secrets of. **9.** To come into view. **—open up. 1.** To begin firing a firearm. **2.** *Informal.* To speak or act freely. *—n.* **1.** The outdoors <camped in the *open*> **2.** An unconcealed state <bring a problem out into the *open*> **3.** A contest for both professionals and amateurs. **—o′pen•er** *n.* **—o′pen•ly** *adv.* **—o′pen•ness** *n.*

o•pen-air (ō′pən-âr′) *adj.* Outdoor.

o•pen-and-shut (ō′pən-ən-shŭt′) *adj.* Easily decided <an *open-and-shut* case>

open classroom *n.* A system of elementary education emphasizing informal individualized methods of teaching.

open door *n.* **1.** An unrestricted opportunity. **2.** Admission or access to all on equal terms. **—o′pen-door′** *adj.*

o•pen-end•ed (ō′pən-ĕn′dĭd) *adj.* **1.** Not restricted by definite limits or structure. **2.** Open to change. **3.** Inconclusive.

open enrollment *n.* A policy permitting admission of students without regard to academic qualifications.

o·pen·hand·ed (ō′pən-hăn′dĭd) *adj.* Generous. **—o′pen·hand′ed·ly** *adv.*

o·pen-heart (ō′pən-härt′) *adj.* Of, relating to, or designating surgery in which the heart is open while its normal functions are performed by external apparatus.

o·pen-hearth (ō′pən-härth′) *adj.* Designating a process of steel production in a furnace with a heat-reflecting roof.

open house *n.* An event to which all are welcome.

o·pen·ing (ō′pə-nĭng) *n.* **1.** An open space : aperture. **2.** An initial stage or period. **3.** A first performance, as of a play. **4.** A series of beginning moves in certain games, esp. chess. **5.** An opportunity. **6.** An unfilled job : vacancy. **7.** The act of becoming open or making open.

open letter *n.* A letter addressed to an individual but intended for general publication or distribution.

open loop *n. Computer Sci.* A control system that cannot correct or alter itself.

o·pen-mind·ed (ō′pən-mīn′dĭd) *adj.* Receptive to new ideas.

open shop *n.* A company employing both union and nonunion workers.

o·pen·work (ō′pən-wûrk′) *n.* Ornamental work, as in cloth or metal, containing openings that form a pattern.

op·er·a¹ (ŏp′ər-ə, ŏp′rə) *n.* A theatrical work consisting of a dramatic performance set to music. **—op′er·at′ic** *adj.*

o·pe·ra² (ō′pər-ə, ŏp′ər-ə) *n. var. pl. of* OPUS.

op·er·a·ble (ŏp′ər-ə-bəl, ŏp′rə-) *adj.* **1.** Able to be used or operated. **2.** Able to be treated surgically.

opera glasses *pl.n.* Small binoculars for use esp. at theatrical performances.

opera house *n.* A theater designed primarily for operas.

op·er·ate (ŏp′ə-rāt′) *v.* **-at·ed, -at·ing. 1.** To run or function effectively. **2.** To have an effect or influence. **3.** To perform surgery. **4.** To direct or control the functioning of. ☆**syns:** HANDLE, RUN, USE, WORK

operating system *n. Computer Sci.* Software designed to complement or support the hardware of a system.

op·er·a·tion (ŏp′ə-rā′shən) *n.* **1.** An act, process, or method of operating. **2.** The condition of being operative. **3.** *Med.* A surgical procedure for remedying an injury or dysfunction in a living body. **4.** *Math.* A procedure performed in a specified sequence and in accordance with specific rules. **5.** *Computer Sci.* An action resulting from a single computer instruction. **6.** A military action or campaign. **—op′er·a′tion·al** *adj.* **—op′er·a′tion·al·ly** *adv.*

op·er·a·tive (ŏp′ər-ə-tĭv, ŏp′rə-, -ə-rā′tĭv) *adj.* **1.** Exerting force or influence. **2.** Efficient. **3.** In effect <*operative* rules> **4.** Of or relating to a surgical operation. *—n.* **1.** A skilled worker, esp. in industry. **2. a.** A secret agent. **b.** A detective.

op·er·a·tor (ŏp′ə-rā′tər) *n.* **1.** One that operates a machine. **2.** The manager or owner of a business. **3.** A symbol, as a multiplication sign, that denotes a mathematical operation. **4.** *Informal.* A shrewd and occas. unscrupulous person.

op·er·et·ta (ŏp′ə-rĕt′ə) *n.* A theatrical production similar to an opera but lighter in subject and style.

oph·thal·mic (ŏf-thăl′mĭk, ŏp-) *adj.* Of or pertaining to the eye.

oph·thal·mol·o·gy (ŏf′thăl-mŏl′ə-jē, ŏp′-, -thəl-) *n.* The medical field encompassing the functions, anatomy, pathology, and treatment of the eye. **—oph′thal·mol′o·gist** *n.*

oph·thal·mo·scope (ŏf-thăl′mə-skōp′, ŏp-) *n.* An instrument consisting of a mirror with a central hole through which the eye is examined.

o·pi·ate (ō′pē-ĭt, -āt′) *n.* **1.** A sedative drug containing opium or an opium derivative. **2.** Any drug. **3.** Something that numbs the senses or the mind.

o·pin·ion (ə-pĭn′yən) *n.* **1.** A belief held with confidence but not substantiated by positive knowledge. **2.** A conclusion based on special knowledge. **3.** A judgment of the value of a person or thing.

o·pin·ion·at·ed (ə-pĭn′yə-nā′tĭd) *adj.* Holding stubbornly and often unreasonably to one's personal opinions.

o·pi·um (ō′pē-əm) *n.* A bitter, yellowish-brown, highly addictive drug prepared from the pods of an Old World poppy and from which alkaloid drugs, as heroin, codeine, and morphine, are derived.

o·pos·sum (ə-pŏs′əm) *n., pl.* **-sum** *or* **-sums.** A nocturnal, arboreal marsupial of the family Didelphidae, esp. *Didelphis marsupialis,* of the W Hemisphere.

op·po·nent (ə-pō′nənt) *n.* One that opposes another or others. ☆**syns:** ADVERSARY, ANTAGONIST, OPPOSITION

op·por·tune (ŏp′ər-to͞on′, -tyo͞on′) *adj.* **1.** Favorable to a particular purpose. **2.** Occurring at an appropriate time.

op·por·tun·ist (ŏp′ər-to͞o′nĭst, -tyo͞o′-) *n.* One who takes advantage of circumstances for self-serving purposes. **—op′por·tun′ism** *n.* **—op′por·tun·is′tic** *adj.*

op·por·tu·ni·ty (ŏp′ər-to͞o′nĭ-tē, -tyo͞o′-) *n., pl.* **-ties. 1.** A favorable combination of circumstances. **2.** A chance for advancement <a job *opportunity*> ☆**syns:** BREAK, CHANCE, OCCASION, OPENING.

op·pose (ə-pōz′) *v.* **-posed, -pos·ing. 1.** To be in conflict or contention with. **2.** To be in disagreement with. **3.** To place in contrasting position to. **—op·pos′a·ble** *adj.* **—op′po·si′tion** (ŏp′ə-zĭsh′ən) *n.*

op·po·site (ŏp′ə-zĭt, -sĭt) *adj.* **1.** Located or placed directly across from. **2.** Moving or tending away from each other. **3.** Sharply contrasting. *—n.* One that is opposite to another. *—adv.* In an opposite position. *—prep.* **1.** Across from or facing. **2.** In a complementary dramatic role.

op·press (ə-prĕs′) *v.* **1.** To persecute or subjugate by force. **2.** To weigh heavily upon. **—op·pres′sion** *n.* **—op·pres′sive** *adj.* **—op·pres′sor** *n.*

op·pro·bri·ous (ə-prō′brē-əs) *adj.* **1.** Expressing contemptuous reproach. **2.** Disgraceful : ignoble.

op·pro·bri·um (ə-prō′brē-əm) *n.* **1.** Disgrace or humiliation resulting from shameful conduct. **2.** Scornful contempt or reproach. **3.** A cause of disgrace.

opt (ŏpt) *v.* To make a choice.

op·tic (ŏp′tĭk) *adj.* Of or pertaining to the eye or to vision.

op·ti·cal (ŏp′tĭ-kəl) *adj.* **1.** Of or pertaining to sight. **2.** Designed to assist vision <*optical* equipment> **3.** Of or pertaining to optics. **—op′ti·cal·ly** *adv.*

optical art *n.* Abstract art employing geometric designs or patterns.

optical illusion *n.* A deceptive visual image.

op·ti·cian (ŏp-tĭsh′ən) *n.* One who makes or sells optical instruments and articles, as lenses and eyeglasses.

optic nerve *n.* Either of 2 sensory nerves connecting the retina with the brain.

op·tics (ŏp′tĭks) *n. (sing. in number). Physics.* Study of light and vision, chiefly of the generation, propagation, and detection of electromagnetic radiation with wavelengths greater than x-rays and shorter than microwaves.

op·ti·mal (ŏp′tə-məl) *adj.* Most favorable or desirable. **—op′ti·mal·ly** *adv.*

op·ti·mism (ŏp′tə-mĭz′əm) *n.* **1.** A disposition to expect the best possible outcome or to emphasize the most positive aspects of a situation. **2.** *Philos.* The doctrine that this world is the best of all possible worlds. **—op′ti·mist** *n.* **—op′ti·mis′tic** *adj.*

op·ti·mize (ŏp′tə-mīz′) *v.* **-mized, -miz·ing. 1.** To improve to the greatest extent possible. **2.** To use most effectively.

op·ti·mum (ŏp′tə-məm) *n., pl.* **-ma** (-mə) *or* **-mums.** The best or most advantageous condition, degree, or amount. *—adj.* Most advantageous : best.

op·tion (ŏp′shən) *n.* **1.** The act of choosing : choice. **2.** A right to buy or sell something at a specified price within a specified time. **3.** Something chosen or available as a choice. **—op′tion·al** *adj.*

op·tom·e·try (ŏp-tŏm′ĭ-trē) *n.* The profession of examining the eyes and treating certain defects by means of corrective lenses. **—op·to·met′ric** (ŏp′tə-mĕt′rĭk) *adj.* **—op·tom′e·trist** *n.*

op·u·lent (ŏp′yə-lənt) *adj.* **1.** Having great wealth. **2.** Extravagant. **—op′u·lence** *n.*

o·pus (ō′pəs) *n., pl.* **o·per·a** (ō′pər-ə, ŏp′ər-ə) *or* **-es.** A creative work, esp. a musical composition.

or (ôr; *unstressed* ər) *conj.* Used to indicate: **1. a.** An alternative, usu. only before the last in a series. **b.** The 2nd of 2 alternatives <I didn't know whether to laugh or cry.> **2.** An equivalent expression <claustrophobia, or fear of enclosed places> **3.** Indefiniteness <3 or 4>

-or¹ *suff.* One that performs an action <percolat*or*>

-or² *suff.* Condition or activity <behavior>

OR *abbr.* Oregon (with Zip Code).

or·a·cle (ôr′ə-kəl, ŏr′-) *n.* **1. a.** A shrine consecrated to a prophetic deity. **b.** One who serves a deity, esp. as a medium for prophecies, at such a shrine. **c.** A divine prophecy, often in the form of an enigmatic statement. **2.** One who gives wise advice. **—o·rac′u·lar** (ô-răk′yə-lər, ō-) *adj.*

o·ral (ôr′əl, ōr′-) *adj.* **1.** Spoken as opposed to written. **2.** Of or relating to the mouth <*oral* surgery> **3.** Used in or administered through the mouth.

oral contraceptive *n.* A pill containing hormones, taken usu. on a monthly schedule to prevent ovulation.

oral history *n.* **1.** Historical information obtained directly, as in interviews, from persons with firsthand knowledge. **2.** A written account based on oral history.

or·ange (ôr′ĭnj, ŏr′-) *n.* **1.** A semitropical evergreen tree of the genus *Citrus,* with white flowers and round, yellowish-red edi-

ble fruit having a sectioned interior and sweet, acid juice. **2.** A yellowish red.
or·ange·ade (ôr′ĭn-jād′, ŏr′-) *n.* A drink made of orange juice, sugar, and plain or carbonated water.
orange pekoe *n.* A grade of black tea.
or·ange·ry (ôr′ĭnj-rē, ŏr′-) *n., pl.* **-ries.** An enclosed place, as a greenhouse, where orange trees are cultivated.
o·rang·u·tan (ō-răng′ə-tăn′, ə-răng′-) *n.* An arboreal anthropoid ape, *Pongo pygmaeus,* of Borneo and Sumatra, with a shaggy coat, very long arms, and no tail.
o·rate (ô-rāt′, ō-rāt′, ôr′āt′, ōr′-) *v.* **o·rat·ed, o·rat·ing.** To speak in a pompous, declamatory manner.
o·ra·tion (ô-rā′shən, ō-rā′-) *n.* A formal speech, esp. one given on a special occasion.
or·a·tor (ôr′ə-tər, ŏr′-) *n.* **1.** A person who delivers an oration. **2.** A person skilled in the art of public speaking.
or·a·to·ri·o (ôr′ə-tôr′ē-ō′, -tōr′-, ŏr′-) *n., pl.* **-os.** A musical composition for voices and instruments, narrating a usu. sacred story without costumes or dramatic action.
or·a·to·ry[1] (ôr′ə-tôr′ē, -tōr′ē, ŏr′-) *n.* **1.** The art of speaking effectively in public. **2.** Rhetorical skill or style. **—or′a·tor′i·cal** *adj.*
or·a·to·ry[2] (ôr′ə-tôr′ē, -tōr′ē, ŏr′-) *n., pl.* **-ries.** A place for prayer, esp. a small private chapel.
orb (ôrb) *n.* **1.** A sphere. **2.** A celestial body. **3.** A jeweled sphere surmounted by a cross, as a symbol of royal power. **—or·bic′u·lar** (-bĭk′yə-lər) *adj.*
or·bit (ôr′bĭt) *n.* **1.** The path of a manmade object or celestial body as it revolves around another body. **2.** The path of a body in a field of force, esp. a path that surrounds another body. **3. a.** A range of activity or experience <one's social *orbit*> **b.** A range of influence <the Soviet *orbit*> —*v.* **1.** To put into an orbit. **2.** To move or revolve in orbit. **—or′bit·al** *adj.*
orc (ôrk) *n.* The killer whale.
or·chard (ôr′chərd) *n.* **1.** Land used for the growing of fruit trees. **2.** The trees cultivated in an orchard.
or·ches·tra (ôr′kĭ-strə, -kĕs′trə) *n.* **1.** A large group of musicians performing together on various instruments. **2.** The area immediately in front of a stage where the musicians sit. **3. a.** The section of seats in a theater nearest the stage. **b.** The entire main floor of a theater. **—or·ches′tral** (-kĕs′trəl) *adj.* **—or·ches′tral·ly** *adv.*
or·ches·trate (ôr′kĭ-strāt′) *v.* **-trat·ed, -trat·ing.** **1.** To arrange or compose (music) for performence by an orchestra. **2.** To organize or manage so as to achieve a desired effect. **—or′ches·tra′tion** *n.* **—or′ches·tra′tor, or′ches·trat′er** *n.*
or·chid (ôr′kĭd) *n.* **1.** A plant of the family Orchidaceae, found worldwide but chiefly in the tropics, with irregularly shaped flowers cultivated esp. for personal adornment. **2.** A pale purple.
or·dain (ôr-dān′) *v.* **1.** To install as a priest, minister, or rabbi. **2.** To order by virtue of established authority. **3.** To prearrange unalterably. **—or·dain′ment** *n.*
or·deal (ôr-dēl′, ôr′dēl′) *n.* A painful or difficult experience.
or·der (ôr′dər) *n.* **1.** A condition of coherent or logical arrangement among the individual elements of a group. **2.** The standard or prescribed state or condition of a thing. **3.** The established organization of a society. **4.** A sequential arrangement in time or space. **5.** The established sequence or procedure. **6.** An authoritative direction : command. **7.** A commission or instruction to buy or sell something. **8.** A meal or portion of food requested by a customer at a restaurant. **9. a.** A grade or rank of the Christian ministry. **b. orders.** The office of an ordained priest or minister. **10.** A group of people living under a religious rule. **11.** An organization of people bound by some common bond or social aim. **12.** A group of persons upon whom a sovereign or government has formally conferred honor <the *Order* of the British Empire> **13.** Degree of importance : rank. **14.** One of a number of styles of classical architecture. **15.** *Biol.* A taxonomic category of animals and plants, above a family and below a class. —*v.* **1.** To give a command (to). **2.** To give a command for. **3.** To request to be supplied with. **4.** To put into a systematic arrangement. **—on the order of.** **1.** Similar to. **2.** Approximately. **—to order.** According to the buyer's specifications.
or·der·ly (ôr′dər-lē) *adj.* **1.** Having a systematic arrangement : neat. **2.** Well-behaved : peaceful. —*n., pl.* **-lies.** **1.** One who performs unskilled work in a hospital. **2.** A soldier assigned to be a messenger or attendant to a superior officer. **—or′der·li·ness** *n.* **—or′der·ly** *adv.*
or·di·nal (ôr′dn-əl) *adj.* Designating a specified position in a numbered series. —*n.* An ordinal number.
ordinal number *n.* A number indicating position in a series, as first (1st) or second (2nd).
or·di·nance (ôr′dn-əns) *n.* **1.** An authoritative order or command. **2.** A municipal regulation or statute.
or·di·nar·i·ly (ôr′dn-âr′ə-lē, ôr′dn-ĕr′-) *adv.* As a general rule.
or·di·nar·y (ôr′dn-ĕr′ē) *adj.* **1.** Usual : normal. **2.** Of no exceptional quality : average. ☆***syns:*** AVERAGE, COMMON, COMMONPLACE, PLAIN, RUN-OF-THE-MILL, UNEXCEPTIONAL **—or′di·nar′i·ness** *n.*
or·di·nate (ôr′dn-ĭt, -āt′) *n. Math.* The coordinate representing the distance from a specified point to the x–axis, measured parallel to the *y*–axis.
or·di·na·tion (ôr′dn-ā′shən) *n.* The act or ordaining or the ceremony of being ordained.
ord·nance (ôrd′nəns) *n.* **1.** Military weapons, ammunition, and equipment. **2.** Heavy guns : artillery.
or·do (ôr′dō) *n., pl.* **-di·nes** (-də-nēz′) or **-dos.** *Rom. Cath. Ch.* A calendar with directions for each day's Mass and office.
or·dure (ôr′jər) *n.* Excrement : dung.
ore (ôr, ōr) *n.* A mineral or rock from which a valuable substance, esp. a metal, can be extracted.
ö·re (œ′rə) *n., pl.* **ö·re.** See *krona, krone,* and *kroner* at CURRENCY TABLE.
Ore. *abbr.* Oregon.
o·re·ad (ôr′ē-ăd′, ōr′-) *n. Gk. Myth.* A mountain nymph.
o·reg·a·no (ə-rĕg′ə-nō′, ô-rĕg′-) *n.* An aromatic plant, *Origanum vulgare,* with pinkish flower spikes and leaves used as seasoning.
Or·e·gon (ôr′ə-gən, -gŏn′, -ŏr′-). State of the NW U.S. *Cap.* Salem. *Pop.* 2,632,663. **—Or′e·go′ni·an** (-gō′nē-ən) *n.*
or·gan (ôr′gən) *n.* **1.** A musical instrument consisting of pipes of varying sizes that sound tones when supplied with air, and a keyboard and pedals that direct the flow of air from the bellows to the pipes. **2.** An instrument, as an electronic organ, that imitates the sound of the organ. **3.** *Biol.* A differentiated part of an organism, adapted for a specific function. **4.** A group or body that is part of a larger organization. **5.** An instrument of communication, esp. a periodical issued by an organization.
or·gan·dy *also* **or·gan·die** (ôr′gən-dē) *n., pl.* **-dies.** A stiff, transparent fabric of silk or cotton.
org. *abbr.* **1.** organic. **2.** organization.
or·gan·ic (ôr-găn′ĭk) *adj.* **1.** Of, pertaining to, or affecting an organ of the body. **2.** Of, pertaining to, or derived from living organisms. **3.** Grown with fertilizers that consist only of plant or natural matter, with no chemical additives. **4.** Like an organism in development or organization. **5.** Constituting a basic part : integral. **6.** *Chem.* Of or designating carbon compounds. **—or·gan′i·cal·ly** *adv.*
organic chemistry *n.* The chemistry of carbon compounds.
or·gan·ism (ôr′gə-nĭz′əm) *n.* **1.** A plant or animal. **2.** A system regarded as analogous to a living body <the social *organism*>
or·gan·ist (ôr′gə-nĭst) *n.* One who plays the organ.
or·gan·i·za·tion (ôr′gə-nĭ-zā′shən) *n.* **1.** An act of organizing or the process of being organized. **2.** The state or manner of being organized. **3.** Something organized or made into an ordered whole. **4.** A number of persons or groups united for a particular purpose. **—or′gan·i·za′tion·al** *adj.*
or·gan·ize (ôr′gə-nīz′) *v.* **-ized, -iz·ing.** **1.** To arrange or assemble into an orderly structured whole. **2.** To give a coherent form to. **3.** To arrange by coordinating and planning. **4.** To form or persuade to form a labor union. **—or′gan·iz′er** *n.*
or·gan·za (ôr-găn′zə) *n.* A sheer, stiff, silk or synthetic fabric.
or·gasm (ôr′găz′əm) *n.* The climax of sexual excitement. **—or·gas′mic, or·gas′tic** (-găs′tĭk) *adj.*
or·gy (ôr′jē) *n., pl.* **-gies.** **1.** A revel involving unrestrained indulgence, esp. sexual activity. **2.** Excessive indulgence in a specific activity. **—or′gi·as′tic** (-ăs′tĭk) *adj.*
o·ri·el (ôr′ē-əl, ōr′-) *n.* A projecting bay window supported from below with a corbel or by brackets.
o·ri·ent (ôr′ē-ənt, -ĕnt′, ōr′-) *n.* **1.** The east. **2. Orient.** The countries of Asia, esp. of E Asia. —*v.* (ôr′ē-ĕnt′, ōr′-). **1.** To place or locate in a specified relation to the points of the compass. **2.** To determine the bearings of. **3.** To make or become familiar or acquainted with a situation. **—o′ri·en·ta′tion** *n.*
o·ri·en·tal (ôr′ē-ĕn′tl, ōr′-) *adj.* **1.** Eastern. **2.** *often* **Oriental.** Of or relating to the Orient. —*n. often* **Oriental.** A native or inhabitant of the Orient.
Oriental rug *n.* A rug made by hand in the Orient.
or·i·en·tate (ôr′ē-ĕn-tāt′, -ən-, ōr′-) *v.* **-tat·ed, -tat·ing.** To orient.
or·i·fice (ôr′ə-fĭs, ŏr′-) *n.* An opening.
or·i·flamme (ôr′ə-flăm′, ŏr′-) *n.* An inspiring symbol or standard.
orig. *abbr.* origin; original; originally.
o·ri·ga·mi (ôr′ĭ-gä′mē) *n.* The Japanese art of folding paper into decorative shapes.
or·i·gin (ôr′ə-jĭn, ŏr′-) *n.* **1.** The cause or source of something.

2. Ancestry : derivation. 3. A coming into being. 4. *Math.* The point of intersection of coordinate axes. ✩**syns:** DERIVATION, FOUNTAIN, PROVENANCE, PROVENIENCE, ROOT, SOURCE, SPRING, WELL

o•rig•i•nal (ə-rĭj′ə-nəl) *adj.* 1. Preceeding all others in time. 2. New and unusual. 3. Inventive. —*n.* 1. A 1st form from which varieties arise or imitations are made. 2. An authentic work of art as opposed to an imitation or reproduction. **—o•rig′i•nal′i•ty** (-năl′ĭ-tē) *n.*

o•rig•i•nate (ə-rĭj′ə-nāt′) *v.* **-nat•ed, -nat•ing.** To bring or come into being. **—o•rig′i•na′tion** *n.* **—o•rig′i•na′tor** *n.*

o•ri•ole (ôr′ē-ōl′, ōr′-) *n.* Any of various songbirds of the families Oriolidae and Icteridae, having bright yellow and black plumage in the males.

or•i•son (ôr′ĭ-sən, -zən, ŏr′-) *n.* A prayer.

Or•lon (ôr′lŏn′). A trademark for a synthetic acrylic fiber.

or•mo•lu (ôr′mə-lo͞o′) *n.* An alloy resembling gold and used for decoration.

or•na•ment (ôr′nə-mənt) *n.* Something that decorates : embellishment. —*v.* (ôr′nə-mĕnt′). To furnish with ornaments. **—or′na•men′tal** *adj.* **—or′na•men′tal•ly** *adv.* **—or′na•men•ta′tion** *n.*

or•nate (ôr nāt′) *adj.* Elaborately or heavily ornamented. **—or•nate′ly** *adv.*

or•ner•y (ôr′nə-rē) *adj.* **-i•er, -i•est.** Stubborn and ill-tempered.

or•ni•thol•o•gy (ôr′nə-thŏl′ə-jē) *n.* The scientific study of birds. **—or′ni•tho•log′i•cal** (-thə-lŏj′ĭ-kəl), **or′ni•tho•log′ic** *adj.* **—or′ni•thol′o•gist** *n.*

or•ni•thop•ter (ôr′nə-thŏp′tər) *n.* A hypothetical aircraft propelled by wing movements.

o•ro•tund (ôr′ə-tŭnd′, ŏr′-, ōr′-) *adj.* 1. Having a full sound : sonorous. 2. Pompous.

or•phan (ôr′fən) *n.* A child whose parents are dead. **—or′phan** *v.*

or•phan•age (ôr′fə-nĭj) *n.* An institution for the care of orphans and other abandoned children.

or•ris (ôr′ĭs, ŏr′-) *n.* Any of several species of iris, esp. *Iris florentina,* with a fragrant root used in cosmetics and perfumes.

ort (ôrt) *n.* 1. A scrap of food remaining after a meal. 2. A bit.

or•tho•don•tia (ôr′thə-dŏn′shə) *also* **or•tho•don•tics** (-tĭks) *n.* The branch of dentistry concerned with correcting abnormally positioned or aligned teeth. **—or′tho•don′tic** *adj.* **—or′tho•don′tist** *n.*

or•tho•dox (ôr′thə-dŏks′) *adj.* 1. Adhering to established or traditional beliefs, esp. in religion. 2. Conforming to accepted standards. 3. **Orthodox. a.** Of or designating any of the Christian churches of the Eastern Orthodox Church. **b.** Of or designating Orthodox Judaism. **—or′tho•dox′y** *n.*

Orthodox Judaism *n.* The branch of the Jewish faith that adheres to the laws of Moses interpreted in the Talmud.

or•thog•o•nal (ôr-thŏg′ə-nəl) *adj. Math.* Pertaining to or composed of right angles.

or•thog•ra•phy (ôr-thŏg′rə-fē) *n., pl.* **-phies.** 1. Correct spelling. 2. The area of language study dealing with systems of spelling. **—or′tho•graph′ic** (-thə-grăf′ĭk) *adj.* **—or•thog′raph•er** *n.*

or•tho•pe•dics *also* **or•tho•pae•dics** (ôr′thə-pē′dĭks) *n.* *(sing. in number).* Surgical or manipulative treatment of disorders of the joints, bones, and associated muscles. **—or′tho•pe′dic** *adj.* **—or′tho•pe′di•cal•ly** *adv.* **—or′tho•pe′dist** *n.*

or•to•lan (ôr′tə-lən) *n.* A small European bird, *Emberiza hortulana,* often eaten as a delicacy.

-ory *suff.* 1. Of, involving, or tending toward <compensatory> 2. A place of or for <reformatory>

Os *symbol for* OSMIUM.

O•sa•ka (ō-sä′kə). Seaport of S Honshu, Japan. *Pop.* 2,648,158.

Os•car (ŏs′kər). A trademark for any of the golden statuettes awarded each year by the Academy of Motion Picture Arts and Sciences for achievement in films.

os•cil•late (ŏs′ə-lāt′) *v.* **-lat•ed, -lat•ing.** 1. To swing back and forth with a regular motion. 2. To waver between 2 or more choices. 3. *Physics.* To vary between alternate extremes, usu. with a definable period. **—os′cil•la′tion** *n.* **—os′cil•la′tor** *n.* **—os′cil•la•to′ry** (-lə-tôr′ē, -tōr′ē) *adj.*

os•cil•lo•scope (ŏ-sĭl′ə-skōp′, ə-sĭl′-) *n.* An instrument producing an instantaneous visual display on a fluorescent screen corresponding to oscillations in an electrical quantity. **—os•cil′lo•scop′ic** *adj.*

os•cu•late (ŏs′kyə-lāt′) *v.* **-lat•ed, -lat•ing.** To kiss. **—os′cu•la′tion** *n.*

-ose *suff.* Having : similar to <grandiose>

o•sier (ō′zhər) *n.* A willow having long, wandlike branches used in basketry, esp. *Salix viminalis* or *S. purpurea.*

Os•lo (ŏz′lō, ŏs′-) Cap. of Norway, in the SE. *Pop.* 454,819.

os•mi•um (ŏz′mē-əm) *n. Symbol* **Os** A hard, bluish-white metallic element, used for pen points and phonograph needles.

os•mo•sis (ŏz-mō′sĭs, ŏs-) *n.* 1. The diffusion of fluid through a semipermeable membrane, as the wall of a living cell. 2. A gradual, often unconscious process of assimilation <learned German by *osmosis*> **—os•mot′ic** (ŏz-mŏt′ĭk, ŏs-) *adj.*

os•prey (ŏs′prē, -prā′) *n., pl.* **-preys.** A large fish-eating hawk, *Pandion haliaetus,* having black and white plumage.

os•si•fy (ŏs′ə-fī′) *v.* **-fied, -fy•ing.** 1. To convert (e.g., cartilage) into bone. 2. To set or become set into a rigidly conventional pattern. **—os′si•fi•ca′tion** *n.*

os•so bu•co (ō′sō bo͞o′kō) *n.* An Italian dish of veal shanks braised in white wine.

os•ten•si•ble (ŏ-stĕn′sə-bəl, ə-stĕn′-) *adj.* Representing or appearing as such : professed. **—os•ten′si•bly** *adv.*

os•ten•ta•tion (ŏs′tĕn-tā′shən, -tən-) *n.* Lavish or pretentious display. **—os′ten•ta′tious** *adj.* **—os′ten•ta′tious•ly** *adv.*

os•te•o•ar•thri•tis (ŏs′tē-ō-är-thrī′tĭs) *n.* A degenerative disease of the joints.

os•te•op•a•thy (ŏs′tē-ŏp′ə-thē) *n.* Medical therapy involving manipulation of the bones for treating disease. **—os′te•o•path′** (ŏs′tē-ə-păth′) *n.* **—os′te•o•path′ic** *adj.*

os•tler (ŏs′lər) *n. var. of* HOSTLER.

os•tra•cize (ŏs′trə-sīz′) *v.* **-cized, -ciz•ing.** To exclude from a group : shun. **—os′tra•cism** *n.*

os•trich (ŏs′trĭch, ô′strĭch) *n.* A large, swift, flightless bird of the genus *Struthio,* with a long bare neck and powerful legs.

oth•er (ŭth′ər) *adj.* **1.a.** Being or designating the remaining one of two or more <the *other* arm> **b.** Being or designating the remaining ones of several <*other* toys in the box> 2. Different from that or those specified. 3. Additional : extra <He has no *other* suit.> 4. Alternate <every *other* year> 5. Of a past or future time. 6. Of the recent past <just the *other* day> —*n.* 1. **a.** The remaining one of two or more. **b. others.** The remaining ones of several. 2. **a.** A different person or thing. **b.** An additional person or thing. —*pron.* A different or additional person or thing. —*adv.* In another way.

oth•er•wise (ŭth′ər-wīz′) *adv.* 1. Differently <believed *otherwise*> 2. Under different circumstances <*Otherwise* I would have called.> 3. In other respects. —*adj.* Different.

oth•er•world•ly (ŭth′ər-wûrld′lē) *adj.* 1. Supernatural. 2. Concerned with spiritual, intellectual, or imaginative matters. **—oth′er•world′li•ness** *n.*

o•ti•ose (ō′shē-ōs′, ō′tē-) *adj.* 1. Idle : lazy. 2. Futile : ineffective.

o•to•lar•yn•gol•o•gy (ō′tō-lăr′ĭng-gŏl′ə-jē) *n.* A branch of medicine dealing with the ear, nose, and throat.

ot•ta•va (ō-tä′və) *adv. Mus.* At an octave lower or higher than written. Used as a direction. **—ot•ta′va** *adj.*

Ot•ta•wa (ŏt′ə-wə, -wä′, -wô′). Cap. of Canada, at the SE tip of Ont. *Pop.* 300,678.

ot•ter (ŏt′ər) *n., pl.* **-ter** *or* **-ters.** Any of several aquatic, carnivorous mammals of the genus *Lutra* and related genera, having webbed feet and thick fur.

ot•to•man (ŏt′ə-mən) *n.* 1. An upholstered sofa without a back or arms. 2. An upholstered or stuffed footstool.

Ottoman Empire. Turkish empire (1299–1919) in SW Asia, NE Africa, and SE Europe.

ou•bli•ette (o͞o′blē-ĕt′) *n.* A dungeon with a trap door in the ceiling as its only means of access.

ouch (ouch) *interj.* Used to express sudden pain or distress.

ought (ôt) *v.* Used to indicate: 1. Duty or obligation <You *ought* to try harder.> 2. Prudence or advisability <They *ought* to have health insurance> 3. Desirability <You *ought* to have been there; it was interesting.> 4. Likelihood or probability <I *ought* to finish soon.>

ou•gui•ya (o͞o-gē′yə) *n.* See CURRENCY TABLE.

ounce (ouns) *n.* 1. See MEASUREMENT TABLE. 2. A tiny bit.

our (our) *adj.* Of or pertaining to us, esp. as possessors, agents, or objects of an action <*our* house><*our* being delayed>

ours (ourz) *pron.* That or those belonging to us <That boat is *ours.*> <*Ours* were the only suggestions adopted.>

our•selves (our-sĕlvz′, är-) *pl. pron.* 1. Those identical with us. Used: **a.** Reflexively as the object of a verb or preposition <We hurt *ourselves.*> **b.** For emphasis <We *ourselves* were not involved.> 2. Our normal state <We have not been *ourselves* since you left.>

-ous *suff.* Full of : having <joyous> <famous> <glorious>

oust (oust) *v.* To force out : eject.

oust•er (ou′stər) *n.* 1. One that ousts. 2. *Law.* Illegal or wrongful dispossession.

out (out) *adv.* 1. In a direction away from the inside or center. 2. Away from a home or business. 3. Outdoors <put the dog *out*> 4. **a.** To depletion, exhaustion, or extinction. 5. To an end or conclusion <serve my time *out*> 6. Into being, availability, circulation, or view <The new cars are *out.*> **7.** Into an unfashionable status <Wide ties have gone *out.*> **8.** *Baseball.* So as to be retired. *—adj.* **1.** Exterior : external. **2.** Not functioning, operating, or flowing. **3.** *Informal.* Not having an amount previously possessed <I am *out* $50.> **4.** Not to be considered. *—prep.* Forth from <fell *out* the window> *—n.* **1.** One that is out, esp. out of power. **2.** A means of evasion or escape. **3.** *Baseball.* A play in which a player is retired. *—v.* To be disclosed <Scandal will *out.*>

out- *pref.* In a way that surpasses, exceeds, or goes beyond <*out*do> See below for a list of self-explanatory words formed with the prefix **out-**.

out•age (ou′tĭj) *n.* A temporary suspension of operation, esp. of electric power.

out-and-out (out′n-out′) *adj.* Utter.

out•back (out′băk′) *n.* The remote, wild part of a country, as of Australia.

out•board (out′bôrd′, -bōrd′) *adj.* **1.** *Naut.* Located outside a vessel's hull. **2.** Located toward the end of the wing of an aircraft. **—out′board′** *adv.*

outboard motor *n.* A detachable engine mounted on the stern of a boat.

out•bound (out′bound′) *adj.* Outward bound : going away.

out•break (out′brāk′) *n.* A sudden occurrence : outburst.

out•build•ing (out′bĭl′dĭng) *n.* A building, as a shed or barn, that is separate from the main building.

out•burst (out′bûrst′) *n.* A sudden eruption, as of emotion or activity.

out•cast (out′kăst′) *n.* One who has been excluded from a group or society.

out•come (out′kŭm′) *n.* A consequence.

out•crop (out′krŏp′) *n.* A stratum or formation, as of bedrock, protruding through the soil level. **—out′crop′** *v.*

out•cry (out′krī′) *n.* **1.** A loud clamor. **2.** A vociferous objection.

out•dat•ed (out-dā′tĭd) *adj.* Old fashioned : antiquated.

out•do (out-dōō′) *v.* To exceed in achievement or performance.

out•door (out′dôr′, -dōr′) *also* **out-of-door** (out′əv-dôr′, -dōr′) *adj.* Done in, located in, or suitable for the open air.

out•doors (out-dôrz′, -dōrz′) *also* **out-of-doors** (out′əv-dôrz′, -dōrz′). *—adv.* In or into the open air. *—n.* The open air.

out•er (ou′tər) *adj.* **1.** Located on the outside. **2.** Farther from the middle or center.

outer ear *n.* The external part of the ear.

out•er•most (ou′tər-mōst′) *adj.* Most distant from the inside or center.

outer space *n.* A region of space beyond the limits of a celestial body or system.

out•face (out-fās′) *v.* **-faced, -fac•ing. 1.** To overcome with a bold look : stare down. **2.** To resist : defy.

out•field (out′fēld′) *n. Baseball.* The playing area extending outward from the infield. **—out′field′er** *n.*

out•fit (out′fĭt′) *n.* **1.** A set of tools, clothes, or equipment for a specialized purpose. **2.** *Informal.* An association of persons, esp. a military unit or business organization. *—v.* To provide with specialized equipment or clothing.

out•flank (out-flăngk′) *v.* To maneuver around and behind the flank of.

out•fox (out-fŏks′) *v.* To outsmart.

out•go (out′gō′) *n., pl.* **-goes.** Something that goes out, esp. money.

out•go•ing (out′gō′ĭng) *adj.* **1. a.** Departing : outbound. **b.** Relinquishing an office. **2.** Sociable : friendly.

out•grow (out-grō′) *v.* **1.** To grow too large for. **2.** To lose in the process of maturing. **3.** To surpass in growth.

out•growth (out′grōth′) *n.* **1.** Something that grows out of something else. **2.** A consequence : result.

out•house (out′hous′) *n.* **1.** An outbuilding. **2.** An outdoor toilet.

out•ing (ou′tĭng) *n.* **1.** A pleasure trip. **2.** A walk outdoors.

out•land•ish (out-lăn′dĭsh) *adj.* Extremely unconventional : bizarre.

out•law (out′lô′) *n.* **1.** A habitual criminal. **2.** One who is excluded from normal legal protection and rights. *—v.* **1.** To declare illegal. **2.** To deprive of legal protection. **—out′law′ry** *n.*

out•lay (out′lā′) *n.* **1.** The spending of money. **2.** An amount spent : expenditure.

out•let (out′lĕt′, -lĭt) *n.* **1.** An exit : vent. **2.** A means of release, as for emotion. **3.** A market for services or goods. **4.** *Elect.* A receptacle, esp. one mounted in a wall, that has a socket for a plug and is connected to a power supply.

out•line (out′līn′) *n.* **1. a.** A line marking the outer edges of a figure or object. **b.** Shape. **2.** Drawing in which objects are delineated in contours without shading. **3.** A general account or description of a subject. ***☆syns:*** CONTOUR, DELINEATION, PROFILE, SILHOUETTE *—v.* **1.** To draw an outline of. **2.** To make a summary of.

out•look (out′lŏŏk′) *n.* **1.** A place that offers a view of something. **2.** A point of view : attitude. **3.** Prospect.

out•ly•ing (out′lī′ĭng) *adj.* Comparatively distant from a center.

out•mod•ed (out-mō′dĭd) *adj.* **1.** No longer fashionable. **2.** Obsolete.

out of *prep.* **1. a.** From within to the outside of <went *out of* the country> **b.** From a given condition <came *out of* the coma> **c.** From a cause or source <made *out of* plastic> **2. a.** In a position beyond the range, sphere, or boundaries of. **b.** In a state different from the usual <*out of* practice> **3.** Because of <did it *out of* jealousy> **4.** From among.

outact
outargue
outbalance
outbargain
outbeg
outbid
outblaze
outbitch
outbluff
outblush
outbluster
outboast
outbox
outbrag
outbrawl
outbrazen
outbuild
outbully
outcatch
outcharge
outcharm
outclass
outclimb
outcoach
outcompete
outcook
outcount
outdance
outdazzle
outdebate
outdeliver
outdesign
outdistance
outdrag
outdress
outdrink
outdrive
outduel
outearn
outeat
outfight
outfigure
outfish
outflatter
outfly
outfumble
outgain
outgallop
outgamble
outglitter
outgrin
outgross
outguess
outhear
outhit
outhomer
outhunt
outhustle
outinfluence
outintrigue
outjump
outkick
outkill
outlast
outlaugh
outleap
outlearn
outlinger
outlive
outman
outmaneuver
outmanipulate
outmarch
outmuscle
outnumber
outorganize
outpass
outperform
outpitch
outplay
outplot
outpolitick
outpoll
outpopulate
outpray
outpreach
outprice
outproduce
outpromise
outpunch
outquote
outrank
outrate
outrival
outroar
outrow
outrun
outsail
outscheme
outscold
outscoop
outscore
outscream
outsell
outshout
outshriek
outsing
outsit
outskate
outsparkle
outspeed
outspend
outspring
outstare
outstay
outstride
outstrive
outswagger
outswear
outswim
outswindle
outtalk
outthrow
outtrade
outtrick
outvalue
outvie
outvote
outwait
outwalk
outwatch
outweep
outwrestle
outwrite
outyell
outyield

out-of-bounds (out'əv-boundz') *adv.* & *adj.* Beyond the established limits.
out-of-date (out'əv-dāt') *adj.* Old-fashioned.
out-of-door (out'əv-dôr', -dōr') *adj. var. of* OUTDOOR.
out-of-doors (out'əv-dôrz', -dōrz') *adv.* &. *n. var. of* OUTDOORS.
out-of-pock·et (out'-əv-pŏk'ĭt) *adj.* Designating expenses entailing the outlay of ready cash.
out-of-the-way (out'əv-*th*ə-wā') *adj.* **1.** Remote : secluded. **2.** Out of the ordinary.
out-of-town·er (out'əv-tou'nər) *n.* A person visiting from another city or town.
out·pa·tient (out'pā'shənt) *n.* A person who receives treatment at a hospital or clinic without being admitted as a patient.
out·port (out'pôrt', -pōrt') *n. Can.* A remote coastal village, esp. in Newf.
out·post (out'pōst') *n.* **1. a.** A detachment of troops stationed away from a main unit. **b.** The station occupied by an outpost. **2.** An outlying settlement.
out·pour·ing (out'pôr'ĭng, -pōr'-) *n.* Something that pours out or is poured out.
out·put (out'pŏŏt') *n.* **1.** An amount produced during a given time. **2. a.** The power, energy, or work produced by a system. **b.** *Computer Sci.* The data produced from a specific input. **—out'put'** *v.*
out·rage (out'rāj') *n.* **1.** An extremely violent or vicious act. **2.** A gross offense to morality or decency. **3.** Anger aroused by such an outrage. *—v.* **-raged, -rag·ing. 1.** To commit an outrage upon. **2.** To rape. **3.** To produce anger in.
out·ra·geous (out-rā'jəs) *adj.* Exceeding the bounds of what is right and proper. ☆**syns:** ATROCIOUS, FLAGRANT, HEINOUS, MONSTROUS, SCANDALOUS, SHOCKING
ou·tré (ōō-trā') *adj.* Highly unconventional : eccentric.
out·reach (out-rēch') *v.* To reach or go beyond. *—n.* An organized effort to extend services beyond usual limits.
out·rig·ger (out'rĭg'ər) *n.* **1.** A narrow float attached to a seagoing canoe by projecting spars for a stabilizing support. **2.** A vessel fitted with an outrigger.
out·right (out'rīt', -rīt') *adv.* **1.** Without reservation. **2.** Utterly. **3.** Straightway. *—adj.* (out'rīt'). **1.** Unqualified. **2.** Complete : thoroughgoing.
out·run (out-rŭn') *v.* **1.** To run faster than. **2.** To go beyond : exceed.
out·set (out'sĕt') *n.* Start : beginning.
out·shine (out-shīn') *v.* **1.** To shine brighter than. **2.** To surpass in beauty or excellence.
out·side (out-sīd', out'sīd') *n.* **1.** The part that faces out. **2.** The space beyond a limit. **3.** An utmost limit <I'll be gone 2 hours at the *outside.*> *—adj.* **1.** Originating or existing at a place beyond certain limits. **2.** Of, restricted to, or situated on the outside of a boundary. **3.** Extreme <an *outside* limit> **4.** Slight : slim <an *outside* chance> *—adv.* On or into the outside. *—prep.* **1.** On or to the outer side of. **2.** Beyond the limits of. **3.** Except for.
outside of *prep.* Outside.
out·sid·er (out-sī'dər) *n.* One who is not part of a particular group.
out·size (out'sīz') *n.* A very large size. **—out'size', out'sized'** *adj.*
out·skirts (out'skûrts') *pl.n.* The parts on the edge of a central area.
out·smart (out-smärt') *v.* To gain the advantage over by cunning or cleverness.
out·spo·ken (out-spō'kən) *adj.* **1.** Said without reserve : candid. **2.** Frank in speech. **—out·spo'ken·ly** *adv.*
out·stand·ing (out-stăn'dĭng, out'stan'-) *adj.* **1.** Projecting outward or upward. **2.** Conspicuous : prominent. **3.** Distinguished. **4.** Not resolved or settled.
out·stretch (out-strĕch') *v.* To extend.
out·strip (out-strĭp') *v.* **1.** To leave behind : outdistance. **2.** To surpass.
out·take (out'tāk') A take or scene of a motion picture that is not included in the final version.
out·ward (out'wərd) *adj.* **1.** Of or moving toward the exterior or outside. **2.** Purely external : superficial. *—adv.* Toward the outside. **—out'wards** *adv.*
out·weigh (out-wā') *v.* To exceed in weight or importance.
out·wit (out-wĭt') *v.* **-wit·ted, -wit·ting.** To outsmart.
ou·zo (ōō'zō) *n., pl.* **-zos.** A colorless Greek liqueur flavored with aniseed.
o·va (ō'və) *n. pl. of* OVUM.
o·val (ō'vəl) *adj.* **1.** Shaped like an egg. **2.** Shaped like an ellipse. **—o'val** *n.*
o·va·ry (ō'və-rē) *n., pl.* **-ries. 1.** The female reproductive gland, typically occurring in pairs, in which ova are produced. **2.** *Bot.* The part of a pistil that contains ovules. **—o·var'i·an** (ō-vâr'ē-ən) *adj.*
o·vate (ō'vāt') *adj.* Oval.
o·va·tion (ō-vā'shən) *n.* An enthusiastic display of approval, usu. in the form of prolonged applause.
ov·en (ŭv'ən) *n.* An enclosed compartment supplied with heat and used for baking or heating food.
ov·en·bird (ŭv'ən-bûrd') *n.* A North American warbler, *Seiurus aurocapillus,* that builds a dome-shaped nest on the ground.
o·ver (ō'vər) *prep.* **1.** Above <a sign *over* the window> **2.** Above and across <a jump *over* the brook> **3.** On the other side of. **4.** Upon. **5.** Throughout : during. **6.** More than in degree, quantity, or extent. **7.** Concerning <an argument *over* technique> *—adv.* **1.** Above the top or surface. **2. a.** Across to the other side. **b.** Across the edge <The milk spilled *over.*> **3. a.** Across a distance in a specific direction. **b.** To another specified place or position <moved the chair *over*> **4.** To a different opinion <won us *over*> **5.** To a different person, state, or title <sign *over* property> **6.** So as to be totally enclosed or covered <The pond froze *over* last night> **7.** Completely : thoroughly. **8. a.** From a horizontal position <The tree fell *over.*> **b.** From an upward to a reversed position <turn a magazine *over*> **9. a.** Again. **b.** In repetition <100 times *over*> **10.** In excess <$5 left *over*> **11.** Used in 2-way radio transmission to indicate the end of a message. *—adj.* **1.** Upper : higher. **2.** External : outer. **3.** In excess.
over– *pref.* Excessive : excessively <*over*expose> See below for a list of self-explanatory words formed with the prefix **over–**.

overanxious
overattached
overcareful
overchill
overcook
overcool
overcourteous
overcritical
overcrowd
overdaring
overdecorate
overdemand
overdevoted
overdevotion
overdiligence
overdiligent
overdiscipline
overdramatic
overdrink
overeager
overearnest
overearnestly
overeasy
overeducate
overelaborate
overelegant
overembellish
overemotional
overemphatic
overenthusiastic
overexcitable
overexcite
overexcitement
overexpand
overexpansion
overexpectant
overexuberant
overfaithful
overfamiliar
overfanciful
overfastidious
overfatten
overfed
overfeed
overfeminine
overfierce
overfill
overfondness
overfrank
overfreely
overfrequent
overfull
overfullness
overfurnish
overgeneralize
overgenerous
overgifted
overglad
overgracious
overgrateful
overgreasy
overhard
overharden
overharsh
overhasty
overheat
overhelpful
overhonest
overidealism
overimaginative
overimpress
overinclined
overinflate
overinflation
overinfluential
overinsistence
overinsistent
overinsure
overintellectual
overintense
overinterest
overinvest
overjealous
overkeen
overkind
overlarge
overlate
overlavish
overlax
overliberal
overlively
overloud
overloyal
overmagnify
overmany
overmature
overmeek
overmerciful
overmighty
overmix
overmodest
overmoist
overmoisten
overmortage
overnear
overneat
overneglect
overnervous

o•ver•act (ō′vər-ăkt′) *v.* To act with unnecessary exaggeration.
o•ver•age[1] (ō′vər-ĭj) *n.* A surplus.
o•ver•age[2] (ō′vər-āj′) *adj.* Over the required or proper age.
o•ver•all *also* **o•ver-all** (ō′vər-ôl′, ō′vər-ôl′) *adj.* **1.** From one end to the other. **2.** Including everything : comprehensive. —*adv.* In general.
o•ver•alls (ō′vər-ôlz′) *pl.n.* Loose-fitting trousers having a bib front and straps over the shoulders.
o•ver•arm (ō′vər-ärm′) *adj.* Done, thrown, or struck with the arm raised above the shoulder.
o•ver•awe (ō′vər-ô′) *v.* To overcome by inspiring awe.
o•ver•bal•ance (ō′vər-băl′əns) *v.* **1.** To outweigh. **2.** To throw off balance.
o•ver•bear (ō′vər-bâr′) *v.* **1.** To crush or bear down on with physical force. **2.** To prevail over : dominate.
o•ver•bear•ing (ō′vər-bâr′ĭng) *adj.* **1.** Overwhelming in power or authority : predominant. **2.** Arrogant.
o•ver•blown (ō′vər-blōn′) *adj.* **1.** Extremely fat. **2.** Inflated : exaggerated.
o•ver•board (ō′vər-bôrd′, -bōrd′) *adv.* Over the side of a ship into the water. **—go overboard.** To exhibit excessive enthusiasm, infatuation, etc.
o•ver•cap•i•tal•ize (ō′vər-kăp′ĭ-tl-īz′) *v.* **1.** To provide (e.g., a business) with excessive capital. **2.** To overestimate the value of (property). **—o′ver•cap′i•tal•i•za′tion** *n.*
o•ver•cast (ō′vər-kăst′, ō′vər-kăst′) *adj.* **1.** Clouded over : obscured. **2.** Gloomy.
o•ver•charge (ō′vər-chärj′) *v.* **1.** To charge an excessive price. **2.** To fill too full : overload. **—o′ver•charge′** *n.*
o•ver•cloud (ō′vər-kloud′) *v.* **1.** To make dark or gloomy. **2.** To become cloudy.
o•ver•coat (ō′vər-kōt′) *n.* A warm, heavy outer coat.
o•ver•come (ō′vər-kŭm′) *v.* **1.** To conquer : defeat. **2.** To prevail over : surmount. **3.** To affect deeply, as with fear or emotion.
o•ver•do (ō′vər-do͞o′) *v.* To do, use, or stress to excess.
o•ver•dose (ō′vər-dōs′) *n.* An excessive dose, esp. of a narcotic. **—o′ver•dose′** *v.*
o•ver•draft (ō′vər-drăft′) *n.* The amount by which a bank account is overdrawn.
o•ver•draw (ō′vər-drô′) *v.* To draw against (a bank account) in excess of credit.
o•ver•dress (ō′vər-drĕs′) *v.* To dress too elaborately or formally.
o•ver•drive (ō′vər-drīv′) *n.* A gear of an automotive engine that transmits to the drive shaft a speed greater than the engine speed.
o•ver•due (ō′vər-do͞o′, -dyo͞o′) *adj.* **1.** Being unpaid after becoming due. **2.** Expected but not yet come.
o•ver•es•ti•mate (ō′vər-ĕs′tə-māt′) *v.* **1.** To set too high an estimate on. **2.** To esteem too highly. **—o′ver•es′ti•mate** (-mĭt) *n.* **—o′ver•es′ti•ma′tion** *n.*
o•ver•ex•pose (ō′vər-ĭk-spōz′) *v.* To expose (a photographic film) too long or with too much light. **—o′ver•ex•po′sure** *n.*
o•ver•flow (ō′vər-flō′) *v.* **1.** To flow or run over the brim, top, or banks (of). **2.** To spread or pour over. —*n.* (ō′vər-flō′). **1.** A flood. **2.** An excess. **3.** An outlet for surplus liquid.
o•ver•grow (ō′vər-grō′) *v.* **1.** To choke or spread over with growth. **2.** To grow beyond usual size. **—o′ver•growth′** *n.*
o•ver•hand (ō′vər-hănd′) *also* **o•ver•hand•ed** (ō′vər-hăn′dĭd) *adj.* Thrown or struck with the hand raised above the shoulder. **—o′ver•hand′** *adv.* & *n.*
o•ver•hang (ō′vər-hăng′) *v.* **1.** To extend or project beyond. **2.** To loom over : menace. **—o′ver•hang′** *n.*
o•ver•haul (ō′vər-hôl′, ō′vər-hôl′) *v.* To examine thoroughly and make needed repairs. **—o′ver•haul′** *n.*
o•ver•head (ō′vər-hĕd′) *n.* The regular operating expenses of a business, including the costs of rent, utilities, upkeep, and taxes. —*adj.* (ō′vər-hĕd′). **1.** Located above the level of the head. **2.** Of or pertaining to overhead expenses. **—o′ver•head′** *adv.*
o•ver•hear (ō′vər-hîr′) *v.* To hear without the speaker's knowledge.
o•ver•joyed (ō′vər-joid′) *adj.* Filled with joy : elated.
o•ver•kill (ō′vər-kĭl′) *n.* **1.** Nuclear destructive capacity beyond what is needed to destroy a target. **2.** An action in excess of what is needed.
o•ver•land (ō′vər-lănd′, -lənd) *adj.* Over or by way of land. **—o′ver•land′** *adv.*
o•ver•lap (ō′vər-lăp′) *v.* **1.** To extend over and cover part of. **2.** To coincide partly with. **—o′ver•lap′** *n.*
o•ver•lay (ō′vər-lā′) *v.* **1.** To spread or lay on or over. **2.** To cover the surface of with a decorative layer <*overlay* silver with gold> **—o′ver•lay′** *n.*
o•ver•look (ō′vər-lo͝ok′) *v.* **1.** To look at from a higher position. **2.** To afford a view over. **3.** To fail to see : miss. **4.** To ignore deliberately : excuse. **5.** To watch over : supervise. **—o′ver•look′** *n.*
o•ver•lord (ō′vər-lôrd′) *n.* A lord with power or authority over other lords.
o•ver•ly (ō′vər-lē) *adv.* To an extreme or excessive degree.
o•ver•much (ō′vər-mŭch′) *adj.* In excess.
o•ver•night (ō′vər-nīt′) *adj.* **1.** Lasting for or remaining during a night. **2.** Immediate : sudden. **—o′ver•night′** *adv.*
o•ver•pass (ō′vər-păs′) *n.* An elevated road or bridge that crosses above a thoroughfare.
o•ver•play (ō′vər-plā′) *v.* **1.** To exaggerate. **2.** To rely too much on the strength of (one's position).
o•ver•pow•er (ō′vər-pou′ər) *v.* **1.** To overcome by superior force. **2.** To overwhelm.
o•ver•reach (ō′vər-rēch′) *v.* To miss or lose by attempting too much.

overoblige
overobsequious
overofficious
overoptimistic
overornate
overparticular
overpassionate
overpassionately
overpatriotic
overpay
overpessimistic
overplain
overpolish
overpopular
overpopulous
overprecise
overpress
overprocrastination
overprolific
overprominent
overprompt
overproud
overprovide
overprovoke
overpublic
overpunish
overpunishment
overquantity
overquick
overquiet
overrational
overready
overrealistic
overreflective
overreliant
overreligious
overreserved
overrestrain
overrich
overrife
overrighteous
overrigid
overrigorous
overrough
overrude
oversad
oversale
oversalt
oversalty
oversaturate
oversaturation
overscented
overscrupulous
overscrupulousness
overseason
overseasoned
oversecure
oversentimental
overserious
oversevere
oversharp
overshort
overshorten
overshrink
oversilent
overskeptical
overslow
oversmall
oversmooth
oversoak
oversoft
oversolemn
oversolicitous
oversophisticated
oversophistication
oversparing
overspecialization
overspecialize
overspeculate
overspeculation
overspeculative
overstimulate
overstimulation
overstrain
overstress
overstretch
overstriving
oversubtle
oversubtlety
oversufficient
oversuperstitious
oversure
oversuspicious
oversuspiciously
oversweet
oversystematic
overtalkative
overtalkativeness
overteach
overtechnical
overtenacious
overtender
overtenderness
overtense
overtension
overthick
overthin
overthoughtful
overthrifty
overtight
overtire
overtruthful
overvaluable
overvariety
overvehement
overventilate
overventurous
overvigorous
overviolent
overwarm
overwarmed
overweak
overwet
overwilling
overwise
overworry
overyoung
overyouthful
overzeal
overzealous
overzealously
overzealousness

o•ver•ride (ō′vər-rīd′) *v.* **1.** To ride across. **2.** To take precedence over. **3.** To declare null and void.
o•ver•rule (ō′vər-ro͞ol′) *v.* **1.** To set aside by virtue of higher authority. **2.** To dominate by strong influence.
o•ver•run (ō′vər-rŭn′) *v.* **1.** To defeat and seize the positions of. **2.** To spread or swarm over destructively : infest. **3.** To extend or run beyond. **4.** To overflow. **—o′ver•run′** *n.*
o•ver•seas (ō′vər-sēz′, ō′vər-sēz′) *adv.* Across the sea : abroad. **—o′ver•seas′** *adj.*
o•ver•see (ō′vər-sē′) *v.* **1.** To direct : supervise. **2.** To inspect. **—o′ver•se′er** *n.*
o•ver•sexed (ō′vər-sĕkst′) *adj.* Having an immoderate sexual drive.
o•ver•shad•ow (ō′vər-shăd′ō) *v.* **1.** To cast a shadow over. **2.** To make insignificant by comparison.
o•ver•shoe (ō′vər-sho͞o′) *n.* A galosh or rubber worn over shoes as protection from water or snow.
o•ver•shoot (ō′vər-sho͞ot′) *v.* **1.** To pass swiftly over or beyond. **2.** To miss by or as if by shooting something too far.
o•ver•sight (ō′vər-sīt′) *n.* **1.** An inadvertent error or omission. **2.** Supervision.
o•ver•size (ō′vər-sīz′) *also* **o•ver•sized** (ō′vər-sīzd′) *adj.* Larger in size than usual.
o•ver•sleep (ō′vər-slēp′) *v.* To sleep beyond the time for waking up.
o•ver•state (ō′vər-stāt′) *v.* To state in exaggerated terms. **—o′ver•state′ment** *n.*
o•ver•stay (ō′vər-stā′) *v.* To stay beyond the set limits or expected duration of.
o•ver•step (ō′vər-stĕp′) *v.* To go beyond (a limit).
o•ver•stock (ō′vər-stŏk′) *v.* To stock too much of. **—o′ver•stock′** *n.*
o•ver•stuff (ō′vər-stŭf′) *v.* **1.** To stuff too much into. **2.** To cover entirely with thickly cushioned upholstery.
o•ver•sub•scribe (ō′vər-səb-skrīb′) *v.* To subscribe to (e.g., a performance series) in excess of the supply available.
o•vert (ō-vûrt′, ō′vûrt′) *adj.* Not hidden or concealed : clearly evident.
o•ver•take (ō′vər-tāk′) *v.* **1.** To catch up with. **2.** To pass after catching up with.
o•ver-the-count•er (ō′vər-*th*ə-koun′tər) *adj.* **1.** Not available on an officially recognized stock exchange. **2.** Available for sale without a prescription.
o•ver•throw (ō′vər-thrō′) *v.* **1.** To overturn. **2.** To bring about the destruction or downfall of, esp. by force. **3.** To throw something over or beyond (a target). ☆***syns:*** OVERTURN, SUBVERT, TOPPLE, TUMBLE **—o′ver•throw′** *n.*
o•ver•time (ō′vər-tīm′) *n.* **1. a.** Working hours in excess of a normal working week. **b.** Payment for additional work beyond the normal working week. **2.** A period of playing time added after the set time for a sports contest. **—o′ver•time′** *adv.*
o•ver•tone (ō′vər-tōn′) *n.* **1.** A harmonic. **2.** An implication : hint.
o•ver•ture (ō′vər-cho͝or′, -chər) *n.* **1.** *Mus.* An instrumental introduction to a dramatic musical work, as an opera. **2.** An opening proposal or offer.
o•ver•turn (ō′vər-tûrn′) *v.* **1.** To cause to turn over : upset. **2.** To defeat.
o•ver•view (ō′vər-vyo͞o′) *n.* A brief comprehensive survey : summary.
o•ver•ween•ing (ō′vər-wē′nĭng) *adj.* **1.** Presumptuously arrogant. **2.** Immoderate.
o•ver•weight (ō′vər-wāt′) *adj.* Above the normal or allowed weight.
o•ver•whelm (ō′vər-hwĕlm′, -wĕlm′) *v.* **1.** To flood over : engulf. **2.** To overcome utterly, as by physical or emotional force. **3.** To turn over : upset.
o•ver•work (ō′vər-wûrk′) *v.* **1.** To work too hard. **2.** To use to excess <*overwork* an analogy>
o•ver•wrought (ō′vər-rôt′) *adj.* **1.** Extremely nervous. **2.** Excessively ornate.
Ov•id (ŏv′ĭd). 43 B.C.–A.D. 17? Roman poet.
o•vi•duct (ō′vĭ-dŭkt′) *n.* A tube through which the ova pass from an ovary to the uterus.
o•void (ō′void′) *also* **o•voi•dal** (ō-void′l) *adj.* Egg-shaped. **—o′void′** *n.*
o•vu•late (ō′vyə-lāt′, ŏv′yə-) *v.* To produce and discharge ova. **—o′vu•la′tion** *n.*
o•vule (ō′vyo͞ol, ŏv′yo͞ol) *n. Bot.* A minute structure from which a plant develops after fertilization. **—o′vu•lar** *adj.*
o•vum (ō′vəm) *n., pl.* **o•va** (ō′və). A female reproductive cell.
owe (ō) *v.* **owed, ow•ing. 1.** To be indebted to the amount of. **2.** To have a moral obligation to offer. **3.** To be in debt to. **4.** To be indebted or obliged for.
owing to *prep.* Because of.
owl (oul) *n.* Any of various often nocturnal birds of prey of the order Strigiformes, having a large head with a short, hooked beak. **—owl′ish** *adj.*
own (ōn) *adj.* Of or belonging to oneself or itself. *—pron. (sing. or pl. in number).* The one or ones belonging to oneself. *—v.* **1.** To have or possess. **2.** To confess : acknowledge. **—own up.** To confess fully. **—own′er** *n.* **—own′er•ship** *n.*
ox (ŏks) *n., pl.* **ox•en** (ŏk′sən). **1.** An adult castrated bull of the genus *Bos,* used as a draft animal. **2.** A bovine mammal.
ox•blood red (ŏks′blŭd′) *n.* A dark brownish red.
ox•bow (ŏks′bō′) *n.* **1.** A U-shaped wooden piece that fits around the neck of an ox and attaches to the yoke. **2. a.** A U-shaped bend in a river. **b.** The land enclosed by an oxbow.
ox•ford (ŏks′fərd) *n.* A sturdy low-cut shoe that is laced and tied over the instep.
ox•i•dant (ŏk′sĭ-dənt) *n.* An oxidizing agent.
ox•i•da•tion (ŏk′sĭ-dā′shən) *n.* **1.** Combination of a substance with oxygen. **2.** A reaction in which an element's valance is increased as a result of losing electrons. **—ox′i•da′tive** *adj.* **—ox′i•da′tive•ly** *adv.*
ox•ide (ŏk′sīd′) *n.* A compound of a radical or element with oxygen. **—ox•id′ic** (ŏk-sĭd′ĭk) *adj.*
ox•i•dize (ŏk′sĭ-dīz′) *v.* **-dized, -diz•ing.** *Chem.* **1.** To combine with oxygen. **2.** To coat with oxide. **—ox′i•diz′er** *n.*
ox•tail (ŏks′tāl′) *n.* The tail of an ox, esp. when used in soup.
ox•y•a•cet•y•lene (ŏk′sē-ə-sĕt′l-ĭn, -ēn′) *adj.* Of or containing a mixture of oxygen and acetylene.
ox•y•gen (ŏk′sĭ-jən) *n. Symbol* **O**A colorless, tasteless, odorless, gaseous element that is essential to life and required for combustion. **—ox′y•gen′ic** *adj.*
▲word history: The word *oxygen* was coined in French by the chemist Antoine Lavoisier in the 18th cent. soon after the element was isolated. The French word *oxygéne* was intended to mean "acid-producing," from Greek *oxus,* "sharp," used in the sense "acid," and the Greek suffix *-genēs,* "born," misinterpreted as "producing." Oxygen was considered at the time to be an essential component of an acid. Although this is not the case, the name *oxygen* has persisted for the element.
ox•y•gen•ate (ŏk′sĭ-jə-nāt′) *v.* **-at•ed, -at•ing.** To combine, treat, or mix with oxygen. **—ox′y•gen•a′tion** *n.*
oxygen tent *n.* An enclosure supplied with oxygen and placed over the head and shoulders of a patient who is having difficulty breathing.
oys•ter (oi′stər) *n.* An edible marine mollusk of the genus *Ostrea,* with a rough, irregularly shaped, double-hinged shell.
oz *also* **oz.** *abbr.* ounce.
o•zone (ō′zōn′) *n.* **1.** A poisonous, blue, unstable gaseous form of oxygen that has 3 atoms per molecule rather than the usual 2. **2.** *Informal.* Pure, clean air.

Pp

p *or* **P** (pē) *n., pl.* **p's** *or* **P's. 1.** The 16th letter of the English alphabet. **2.** A speech sound represented by the letter *p.*
P *symbol for* PHOSPHORUS.
p. *abbr.* **1.** page. **2.** participle. **3.** per. **4.** pint. **5.** population. **6. P.** president.
Pa *symbol for* PROTACTINIUM.
PA *abbr.* **1.** Pennsylvania (with Zip Code). **2.** public-address system.
Pa. *abbr.* Pennsylvania.
P.A. *abbr.* **1.** *also* **P/A** power of attorney. **2.** press agent. **3.** prosecuting attorney.
pa′an•ga (päng′gə) *n.* See CURRENCY TABLE.
pab•u•lum (păb′yə-ləm) *n.* An easily digested and usu. soft food.
Pac. *abbr.* Pacific.
pace (pās) *n.* **1. a.** A step made in walking : stride. **b.** The length of a pace. **2.** Rate of progress or movement. **3.** A gait of a horse in which the feet on 1 side move together. *—v.* **paced, pac•ing. 1.**

To cover or walk at a pace, esp. a slow pace. **2.** To measure by paces. **3.** To regulate or set the pace of. **—pac'er** *n.*

pace•mak•er (pās'mā'kər) *n.* **1.** One that sets the pace, as in a race. **2. a.** Specialized muscle fibers of the heart that regulate the heartbeat. **b.** A surgically implanted electronic device used to stabilize or stimulate the heartbeat.

pach•y•derm (păk'ĭ-dûrm') *n.* A large, hoofed thick-skinned mammal, as the rhinoceros or elephant.

pach•y•san•dra (păk'ĭ-săn'drə) *n.* Any of several plants of the genus *Pachysandra,* with evergreen leaves, grown as a ground cover.

pa•cif•ic (pə-sĭf'ĭk) *adj.* **1.** Tending to reduce conflict. **2.** Peaceful : serene.

Pacific. Earth's largest body of water, extending from the Arctic to the Antarctic and the Americas to Asia and Australia.

Pacific Northwest. Region of the NW U.S., usu. including Wash. and Ore. and sometimes SW B.C., Canada.

pac•i•fi•er (păs'ə-fī'ər) *n.* **1.** One that pacifies. **2.** A device, as an artificial nipple, for a baby to suck or chew on.

pac•i•fism (păs'ə-fĭz'əm) *n.* Opposition to war or violence as a way to resolve disputes. **—pac'i•fist** *n.* **—pac'i•fis'tic** *adj.*

pac•i•fy (păs'ə-fī') *v.* **-fied, -fy•ing. 1.** To alleviate the anger or distress of : calm. **2.** To end war, fighting, or violence in. **—pac'i•fi•ca'tion** *n.*

pack (păk) *n.* **1. a.** A group of items wrapped or tied up : bundle. **b.** A container in which a bundle can be carried, esp. on the back. **2.** A complete set of related items, esp. playing cards. **3.** A large amount or number : heap. **4.** A group of animals or people. **5.** Absorbent material, as gauze, applied to a bodily part. *—v.* **1.** To roll, fold, or combine into a bundle. **2. a.** To put into a container, as for preservation. **b.** To place belongings in boxes or luggage for storing or transporting. **3.** To crowd or be crowded together : cram. **4.** To press or become pressed together : compact. **5.** *Informal.* To carry <*pack* a revolver> **6.** To send without ceremony <*packed* the children off to their aunt's> **7.** To organize the composition of in order to achieve a favorable or hoped-for result <*pack* a jury>

pack•age (păk'ĭj) *n.* **1.** A parcel : bundle. **2.** Something, as an offer, consisting of several items each of which must be accepted <a vacation *package*> *—v.* **-aged, -ag•ing.** To insert in or make into a package.

package store *n.* A store that sells alcoholic beverages in sealed bottles for consumption away from the premises.

pack animal *n.* An animal, as a mule, used to carry loads.

pack•er (păk'ər) *n.* One who packs, esp. one who processes and packs food products, as meats, for transportation and sale.

pack•et (păk'ĭt) *n.* **1.** A small bundle or package. **2.** A regularly scheduled passenger boat that carries cargo and mail.

pack•ing (păk'ĭng) *n.* Material in which something is packed, esp. to prevent seepage or breakage.

packing house *n.* A firm that processes and packs food products, esp. meat.

†pack rat *n.* **1.** A small North American rodent of the genus *Neotoma* that collects in its nest a wide variety of objects. **2.** *W U.S. Slang.* A petty thief. **3.** *Slang.* A collector or hoarder of miscellaneous objects.

pack•sad•dle (păk'săd'l) *n.* A saddle for a pack animal on which loads can be secured.

pact (păkt) *n.* An agreement, as between nations : treaty.

pad[1] (păd) *n.* **1.** Something soft that serves to line, stuff, or cushion. **2.** A drawing or writing tablet. **3.** The broad floating leaf of a water plant. **4.** The cushionlike underpart of the toes and feet of some animals. **5.** *Slang.* A person's living quarters. *—v.* **pad•ded, pad•ding. 1.** To line or stuff with soft material. **2.** To lengthen with extraneous or fraudulent material.

pad[2] (păd) *v.* **pad•ded, pad•ding.** To go on foot, esp. softly and nearly inaudibly.

pad•dle[1] (păd'l) *n.* **1.** A usu. wooden flat-bladed implement used to propel and steer a small boat, as a canoe. **2.** Something resembling a paddle, as: **a.** An implement used for mixing, stirring, or turning. **b.** A small wooden racket used in table tennis. **3.** A board on the circumference of a paddle wheel. *—v.* **-dled, -dling. 1.** To propel through water with or as if with a paddle. **2.** To mix, stir, or beat with a paddle.

pad•dle[2] (păd'l) *v.* **-dled, -dling. 1.** To dabble about in shallow water. **2.** To waddle : toddle.

paddle wheel *n.* A wheel with steam-driven paddles around its circumference, used to propel a ship.

pad•dock (păd'ək) *n.* A usu. enclosed area in which horses are kept, as for being saddled and displayed before a race.

pad•dy (păd'ē) *n., pl.* **-dies.** An irrigated, marshy, or flooded field in which rice is cultivated.

paddy wagon *n.* A police van for conveying suspects.

pad•lock (păd'lŏk') *n.* A detachable lock with a U-shaped piece that can be inserted through the staple of a hasp and then fastened. **—pad'lock'** *v.*

pa•dre (pä'drā, -drē) *n. Informal.* **1.** A priest. **2.** A military chaplain.

pae•an (pē'ən) *n.* A song of thanksgiving, praise, or exultation.

pa•gan (pā'gən) *n.* One who does not acknowledge the god of Christianity, Islam, or Judaism : heathen. **—pa'gan** *adj.*

page[1] (pāj) *n.* Someone hired to run errands or deliver messages, as in a hotel. *—v.* **paged, pag•ing.** To summon or call (a person) by name.

page[2] (pāj) *n.* **1.** A leaf, as of a book. **2.** One side of a page. *—v.* **paged, pag•ing.** To paginate.

pag•eant (păj'ənt) *n.* An elaborate public spectacle, procession, or celebration. **—pag'eant•ry** *n.*

pag•i•nate (păj'ə-nāt') *v.* **-nat•ed, -nat•ing.** To number the pages of.

pa•go•da (pə-gō'də) *n.* A Buddhist tower, esp. one built as a shrine or memorial.

Pa•go Pa•go (päng'gō päng'gō, päng'ō päng'ō). Cap. of American Samoa, on the S coast of Tutuila Is. *Pop.* 2,451.

paid (pād) *v. p.t. & p.p. of* PAY.

pail (pāl) *n.* A usu. cylindrical container with a handle : bucket.

pain (pān) *n.* **1.** Physical or mental suffering or distress, esp. an unpleasant sensation arising from injury or disease. **2. pains.** Effort : trouble. **3.** *Informal.* A nuisance : pest. **4.** Penalty <under *pain* of imprisonment> *—v.* To experience or cause pain. **—pain'ful** *adj.* **—pain'less** *adj.*

Paine (pān), **Thomas.** 1737–1809. English-born Amer. Revolutionary leader.

pain•kill•er (pān'kĭl'ər) *n.* Something, esp. a drug, that alleviates pain. **—pain'kill'ing** *adj.*

pains•tak•ing (pānz'tā'kĭng) *adj.* Diligent and attentive to detail : meticulously careful. **—pains'tak'ing•ly** *adv.*

paint (pānt) *n.* **1. a.** A mixture of a pigment and a liquid that is spread on a surface to form a decorative or protective coating. **b.** The pigment that is used in making paint. **c.** The film that is formed by the application of paint to a surface. **2.** Make-up. *—v.* **1.** To represent in a painting. **2.** To describe vividly in or as if in words. **3.** To decorate or coat with paint. **4.** To use cosmetics (on). **5.** To practice the art of painting pictures. **6.** To cover the surface of with a liquid medicine : swab.

paint•brush (pānt'brŭsh') *n.* A brush with which to apply paint.

paint•er[1] (pān'tər) *n.* One who paints.

pain•ter[2] (pān'tər) *n. Naut.* A rope used for tying up or towing a boat.

†pain•ter[3] (pān'tər) *n. Regional.* A mountain lion or lynx.

paint•ing (pān'tĭng) *n.* **1.** The art, process, or occupation of coating surfaces with paint. **2.** Something, as a picture, produced by the art of painting.

pair (pâr) *n., pl.* **pairs** *or* **pair. 1.** Two things that are similar in function or form. **2.** Something composed of 2 corresponding pieces or parts <a *pair* of scissors> **3.** Two persons or animals <an engaged *pair*><a *pair* of oxen> *—v.* **1.** To arrange in pairs. **2.** To form a pair.

pai•sa (pī-sä') *n., pl.* **-sa** (-sä') *or* **-sas.** See *taka* and *rupee* at CURRENCY TABLE.

pais•ley (pāz'lē) *adj.* Made of a soft wool fabric with colorful abstract swirled or curved shapes.

pa•ja•mas (pə-jä'məz, -jăm'əz) *pl.n.* A loose-fitting 2-piece garment worn for lounging or sleeping.

pak choi (bäk' choi') *n.* A Chinese plant, *Brassica chinensis,* that is similar to the common cabbage and is used as a vegetable.

Pak•i•stan (păk'ĭ-stăn', pä'kĭ-stän'). Country of S Asia. *Cap.* Islamabad. *Pop.* 88,610,000. **—Pak'i•stan'i** *adj. & n.*

pal (păl) *n. Informal.* A good friend : chum.

pal•ace (păl'ĭs) *n.* **1.** The residence of a sovereign. **2.** A splendid house : mansion. **—pa•la'tial** (pə-lā'shəl) *adj.*

pal•a•din (păl'ə-dĭn) *n.* A heroic or knightly champion.

palanquin

pal·an·quin (păl′ən-kēn′) *n.* A covered litter for 1 person that is carried on poles on the shoulders of men.
pal·at·a·ble (păl′ə-tə-bəl) *adj.* Acceptable or agreeable to the taste.
pal·ate (păl′ĭt) *n.* **1.** The roof of the vertebrate mouth, consisting of a hard, bony forward part and a fleshy posterior part. **2.** The sense of taste. **—pal′a·tal** (-ə-təl) *adj.*
pa·lat·i·nate (pə-lăt′n-āt′, -ĭt) *n.* The territory of a palatine.
pal·a·tine (păl′ə-tīn′) *n.* **1.** An administrative official of the late Roman or Byzantine empire. **2.** A feudal lord having sovereign powers within his own domain. *—adj.* **1.** Of or pertaining to a palace. **2.** Of, relating to, or designating a palatine or palatinate.
pa·lav·er (pə-lăv′ər, -lä′vər) *n.* A long talk : parley. **—pa·lav′er** *v.*
pale¹ (pāl) *n.* **1.** A pointed stick, esp. a stake of a fence : picket. **2.** An area enclosed by a fence or boundary. *—v.* **paled, pal·ing.** To enclose with pales.
pale² (pāl) *adj.* **pal·er, pal·est. 1.** Lighter than usual or normal in complexion : pallid <*pale* cheeks> **2.** Of low color intensity : light <*pale* green> **3.** Of a low intensity of light : dim <a *pale* sun> *—v.* **paled, pal·ing.** To become or cause to become pale. **—pale′ness** *n.*
pa·le·og·ra·phy (pā′lē-ŏg′rə-fē) *n.* The study of ancient inscriptions and written documents. **—pa′le·og′ra·pher** *n.*
pa·le·on·tol·o·gy (pā′lē-ŏn-tŏl′ə-jē, -ən-) *n.* The scientific study of fossils. **—pa′le·on·tol′o·gist** *n.*
Pa·ler·mo (pə-lĕr′mō). City of NW Sicily. *Pop.* 693,949.
Pal·es·tine (păl′ĭ-stīn′). Region of SW Asia, on the Mediterranean. **—Pal′es·tin′i·an** (-stĭn′ē-ən) *n.*
pal·ette (păl′ĭt) *n.* **1.** An often oval board, usu. with a hole for the thumb, on which an artist mixes colors. **2.** The range of colors used by an artist.
pal·frey (pôl′frē) *n., pl.* **-freys.** *Archaic.* A saddle horse, esp. one that is suitable for a woman to use.
pal·imp·sest (păl′ĭmp-sĕst′) *n.* Material, as vellum, that is used after having been written upon before and often shows traces of imperfectly erased writing.
pal·in·drome (păl′ĭn-drōm′) *n.* A word, phrase, or sentence, as *Madam I'm Adam,* that reads the same backward or forward.
pal·ing (pā′lĭng) *n.* **1.** A pale, as that used for a fence : picket. **2.** Wood used in making pales. **3.** A fence made of pales.
pal·i·sade (păl′ĭ-sād′) *n.* **1.** A fence of pales, esp. one forming a defense barrier or fortification. **2.** A line of steep cliffs, often along a river.
pall¹ (pôl) *n.* **1.** A heavy cloth covering, as of velvet, for a bier or coffin. **2.** A coffin. **3.** A gloomy atmosphere or effect.
pall² (pôl) *v.* **1.** To be or become dull, boring, or tiresome. **2.** To satiate : jade.
pal·la·di·um (pə-lā′dē-əm) *n. Symbol* **Pd**A soft, white metallic element used in many alloys.
pall·bear·er (pôl′bâr′ər) *n.* Someone who carries or attends the coffin at a funeral.
pal·let¹ (păl′ĭt) *n.* A portable platform on which materials, as cargo or freight, can be stored or moved.
pal·let² (păl′ĭt) *n.* A narrow, hard, often straw-filled bed or mattress.
pal·li·ate (păl′ē-āt′) *v.* **-at·ed, -at·ing. 1.** To try to hide the seriousness of with apologies and excuses. **2.** To ease the pain or force of without curing. **—pal′li·a′tion** *n.* **—pal′li·a′tive** *adj. & n.*
pal·lid (păl′ĭd) *adj.* **1.** Lacking in color : wan. **2.** Lacking in intensity : dull.
pal·lor (păl′ər) *n.* Extreme or abnormal paleness <a deathly *pallor*>
pal·ly (păl′ē) *adj.* **-li·er, -li·est.** *Informal.* Being pals : friendly.
palm¹ (päm) *n.* The inner part of the hand between the wrist and the fingers. *—v.* To hide, pick up, or hold in the palm. **—palm off.** To dispose of or pass off by deception or fraud.
palm² (päm) *n.* **1.** Any of various chiefly tropical trees or shrubs of the family Palmaceae, usu. having an unbranched trunk with a crown of large featherlike or fanlike leaves. **2. a.** An emblem of victory. **b.** Victory : triumph.
pal·mate (păl′māt′, păl′-, pä′māt′) *also* **pal·mat·ed** (-mā′tĭd) *adj.* Resembling a hand with the fingers extended, as coral or antlers.
pal·met·to (păl-mĕt′ō) *n., pl.* **-tos** *or* **-toes.** A small, mostly tropical palm, esp. *Sabal palmetto,* with fan-shaped leaves.
palm·ist·ry (pä′mĭ-strē) *n.* The art or practice of predicting someone's future from the marks and patterns on the palms of his or her hands. **—palm′ist** *n.*
Palm Sunday *n.* The Sunday before Easter, celebrated in commemoration of Christ's entry into Jerusalem.
palm·y (pä′mē) *adj.* **-i·er, -i·est. 1.** Of, relating to, or full of palm trees. **2.** Characterized by success or prosperity : flourishing.
pal·o·mi·no (păl′ə-mē′nō) *n., pl.* **-nos.** A golden or light-tan horse with a lighter tail and mane.
pal·pa·ble (păl′pə-bəl) *adj.* **1.** Capable of being felt or touched : tangible. **2.** Easily perceived : plain. **—pal′pa·bly** *adv.*
pal·pate (păl′pāt′) *v.* **-pat·ed, -pat·ing.** To examine or explore by touch, esp. as an aid in medical diagnosis. **—pal·pa′tion** *n.*
pal·pi·tate (păl′pĭ-tāt′) *v.* **-tat·ed, -tat·ing. 1.** To quiver : flutter. **2.** To beat more quickly than normal : throb. **—pal′pi·tat′ing·ly** *adv.* **—pal′pi·ta′tion** *n.*
pal·sy (pôl′zē) *n., pl.* **-sies. 1.** Paralysis. **2.** A condition characterized by tremor of the body or a bodily part. **—pal′sied** *adj.*
pal·ter (pôl′tər) *v.* **1.** To talk or act deceitfully or insincerely : equivocate. **2.** To quibble, esp. in doing business : haggle.
pal·try (pôl′trē) *adj.* **-tri·er, -tri·est. 1.** Trifling : trivial. **2.** Trashy : shabby. **3.** Contemptible : mean.
pam·pa (păm′pə) *n., pl.* **-pas** (-pəz, -pəs). A large grassland area of South America.
pam·per (păm′pər) *v.* To treat with extreme indulgence : coddle.
pam·phlet (păm′flĭt) *n.* An often short publication with no binding and a paper cover. **—pam′phlet·eer′** *n.*
pan (păn) *n.* **1.** A wide, shallow, open vessel for household use. **2.** Something that resembles a pan. *—v.* **panned, pan·ning. 1.** To wash (gravel or earth) in a pan in search of precious metal, esp. gold. **2.** *Informal.* To criticize unfavorably and harshly. **—pan out.** *Informal.* To be successful.
pan·a·ce·a (păn′ə-sē′ə) *n.* A remedy for all ills, diseases, or difficulties : cure-all.
pa·nache (pə-năsh′, -näsh′) *n.* **1.** An ornamental cluster, as of feathers, esp. on a helmet. **2.** Vividness or dash in manner or action : verve.
Pan·a·ma (păn′ə-mä′). **1.** Country of SW Central America. *Pop.* 2,000,000. **2.** *also* **Panama City.** Cap. of Panama, at the Pacific terminus of the Panama Canal. *Pop.* 467,000. **3. Isthmus of.** Isthmus connecting North and South America and separating the Pacific from the Caribbean. **4.** Ship canal, 51 mi (82 km) long, connecting the Caribbean with the Pacific. **—Pan′a·ma′ni·an** (păn′ə-mā′nē-ən) *adj. & n.*
Panama hat *n.* A hat braided by hand from the leaves of a plant of Central and South America.
Pan-A·mer·i·can (păn′ə-mĕr′ĭ-kən) *adj.* Of or relating to North, South, and Central America as a group.
pan·a·tel·a (păn′ə-tĕl′ə) *n.* A long, slender cigar.
pan·cake (păn′kāk′) *n.* A flat, often thin cake made of batter fried on both sides.
pan·chro·mat·ic (păn′krō-măt′ĭk) *adj.* Sensitive to all colors <*panchromatic* film>
pan·cre·as (păng′krē-əs, păn′-) *n. Anat.* A long, irregularly shaped gland lying behind the stomach that secretes digestive enzymes and produces insulin. **—pan′cre·at′ic** (-ăt′ĭk) *adj.*
pan·da (păn′də) *n.* **1.** A bearlike black and white animal, *Ailuropoda melanoleuca,* of mountainous regions of China and Tibet. **2.** A raccoonlike animal, *Ailurus fulgens,* with reddish fur and a ringed tail.
pan·dem·ic (păn-dĕm′ĭk) *adj.* Occurring or prevalent over a wide geographic area, as a disease : widespread. **—pan·dem′ic** *n.*
pan·de·mo·ni·um (păn′də-mō′nē-əm) *n.* Wild confusion or uproar : tumult.
pan·der (păn′dər) *n.* **1.** A go-between in sexual intrigues. **2.** A pimp. **3.** Someone who profits from exploiting the needs and weaknesses of others. *—v.* To act as a pander (for).
pan·dow·dy (păn-dou′dē) *n., pl.* **-dies.** Sliced fruit, esp. apples, sugared and spiced and baked with a thick top crust.
pane (pān) *n.* A single plate of glass, as in a section of a window or door.
pan·e·gy·ric (păn′ə-jĭr′ĭk, -jī′rĭk) *n.* **1.** A formal speech or written composition of commendation or praise. **2.** Elaborate praise. **—pan′e·gy′ri·cal** *adj.* **—pan′e·gy′rist** *n.*
pan·el (păn′əl) *n.* **1.** A flat, often rectangular piece, esp. of wood, that forms part of a surface or overlays it. **2.** A board on which controls or instruments are mounted. **3. a.** A list of persons selected for jury duty. **b.** A group of people who participate in a discussion or a game show, as on television. *—v.* **-eled, -el·ing** *or* **-elled, -el·ling. 1.** To furnish or decorate with panels. **2.** To impanel (a jury).
pan·el·ing (păn′ə-lĭng) *n.* **1.** A set of ornamental panels. **2.** A paneled wall.
pan·el·ist (păn′ə-lĭst) *n.* A member of a panel.
panel truck *n.* A small truck, as one used to make deliveries, with an enclosed body.
pang (păng) *n.* A sudden, brief, sharp spasm, as of pain.

pan•han•dle[1] (păn′hăn′dl) *v.* **-dled, -dling.** *Informal.* To ask for money or food, esp. on the street. **—pan′han′dler** *n.*
pan•han•dle[2] (păn′hăn′dl) *n.* A narrow strip, as of territory, that projects from a broader area.
pan•ic (păn′ĭk) *n.* A sudden, overpowering fear. *—v.* **-icked, -ick•ing.** To experience or cause to experience panic. **—pan′ick•y** *adj.*
pan•i•cle (păn′ĭ-kəl) *n. Bot.* An irregularly branched flower cluster. **—pan′i•cled** *adj.*
pan•jan•drum (păn-jăn′drəm) *n.* A personage of power and importance.
pan•nier (păn′yər, păn′ē-ər) *n.* A large basket, as one of a pair carried on either side of a pack animal or over a person's shoulders.
pan•o•ply (păn′ə-plē) *n., pl.* **-plies. 1.** A complete array of a warrior's armor and weapons. **2.** A protective covering. **3.** An impressive display : pomp.
pan•o•ram•a (păn′ə-răm′ə, -rä′mə) *n.* **1.** An unlimited view of what is visible in all directions. **2.** A picture or view that unrolls before a spectator. **—pan′o•ram′ic** *adj.*
pan•sy (păn′zē) *n., pl.* **-sies.** A garden plant, *Viola tricolor hortensis,* bearing flowers with rounded, velvety, variously colored petals.
pant (pănt) *v.* **1.** To breathe with difficulty and often in short gasps. **2.** To utter breathlessly or hurriedly. **3.** To feel a longing : yearn. *—n.* A short, labored breath.
pan•ta•loons (păn′tl-o͞onz′) *pl.n.* Trousers, esp. loose, baggy ones.
pan•the•ism (păn′thē-ĭz′əm) *n.* The doctrine that God and the laws and forces of nature are one. **—pan′the•ist** *n.* **—pan′the•is′tic** *adj.*
pan•the•on (păn′thē-ŏn′, -ən) *n.* **1. a.** A temple that is dedicated to the gods. **b.** The gods of a people. **2.** A public building commemorating, honoring, and often serving as a place of burial for the great personages of a nation.
pan•ther (păn′thər) *n.* **1.** The leopard, *Panthera pardus,* esp. in its black, unspotted form. **2.** The mountain lion.
pant•ies (păn′tēz) *pl.n.* Underpants, esp. short ones, for women or girls.
pan•to•mime (păn′tə-mīm′) *n.* **1.** Expressive communication solely by means of facial and bodily movements. **2.** A play in which pantomime is used instead of dialogue. *—v.* **-mimed, -mim•ing.** To express oneself in or represent by pantomime. **—pan′to•mim′ic** (-mĭm′ĭk) *adj.* **—pan′to•mim′ist** (-mī′mĭst, -mĭm′ĭst) *n.*
pan•try (păn′trē) *n., pl.* **-tries.** A closet or room in which food and dishes are stored.
pants (pănts) *pl.n.* **1.** Trousers. **2.** Underpants.
pant•suit *also* **pants suit** (pănt′so͞ot′) *n.* A woman's suit with trousers instead of a skirt.
pant•y•hose (păn′tē-hōz′) *pl.n.* A woman's 1-piece undergarment that consists of stockings and underpants.
pant•y•waist (păn′tē-wāst′) *n.* A sissy.
†**pap[1]** (păp) *n.* **1.** *Regional.* A teat or nipple. **2.** Something resembling a nipple.
pap[2] (păp) *n.* **1.** Soft, easily digested food for invalids or infants. **2.** Something lacking real value or substance.
pa•pa (pä′pə, pə-pä′) *n.* Father.
pa•pa•cy (pā′pə-sē) *n., pl.* **-cies. 1.** The jurisdiction and office of a pope. **2.** The term of office of a pope. **3. Papacy.** *Rom. Cath. Ch.* The system of church government of which the pope is the head.
pa•pa•in (pə-pā′ĭn, -pī-) *n.* A protein-digesting enzyme obtained from the unripe fruit of the papaya and used as a meat tenderizer.
pa•pal (pā′pəl) *adj.* Of or relating to the pope or the papacy.
Papal States. Territories in C Italy ruled by the popes until 1870.
pa•paw *also* **paw•paw** (pô′pô′) *n.* A North American tree, *Asimina triloba,* bearing fleshy, edible fruit.

papaya

pa•pa•ya (pə-pī′ə) *n.* A tropical American tree, *Carica papaya,* bearing large, yellow, edible fruit.
pa•per (pā′pər) *n.* **1. a.** A material made of pulp obtained chiefly from wood and rags and used for printing or writing on, wrapping something in, and covering walls. **b.** A single sheet of paper. **2. a.** A document. **b. papers.** Documents that establish the bearer's identity. **3.** A newspaper. **4.** A written composition, as an essay or report. **5.** Wallpaper. *—v.* To cover with wallpaper. **—pa′per•y** *adj.*
pa•per•back (pā′pər-băk′) *n.* A book that has a flexible paper binding. **—pa′per•backed′** *adj.*
pa•per•board (pā′pər-bôrd′, -bōrd′) *n.* Cardboard.
pa•per•hang•er (pā′pər-hăng′ər) *n.* Someone who applies wallpaper. **—pa′per•hang′ing** *n.*
pa•per•weight (pā′pər-wāt′) *n.* A heavy object used to hold down loose papers.
pa•pier-mâ•ché (pā′pər-mə-shā′, păp′yā-) *n.* A material of waste paper mixed with paste or glue that can be shaped when wet.
pa•pil•la (pə-pĭl′ə) *n., pl.* **-pil•lae** (-pĭl′ē). A small projection from a bodily surface. **—pap′il•lar′y** (păp′ə-lĕr′ē, pə-pĭl′ə-rē) *adj.*
pap•il•lote (pä′pē-yōt′, păp′ē-) *n.* **1.** A frilled paper cover for decorating the bone end of a cooked chop or cutlet. **2.** Oiled parchment in which foods such as meat and fish are baked.
pa•poose (pă-po͞os′, pə-) *n.* A young child of North American Indian parents.
pa•pri•ka (pă-prē′kə, pə-, păp′rĭ-kə) *n.* A mild seasoning made from the ground pods of certain sweet red peppers.
Pap smear (păp) *n.* A Pap test.
Pap test *n.* A test in which a smear of a bodily secretion, esp. from the uterine cervix, is examined for the early detection of cancer.
Pap•u•a New Guin•ea (păp′yo͞o-ə; gĭn′ē). Country occupying the E half of the island of New Guinea. *Cap.* Port Moresby. *Pop.* 2,905,000.
pap•ule (păp′yo͞ol) *n.* A small inflammatory congested spot on the skin : pimple. **—pap′u•lar** (-yə-lər) *adj.*
pa•py•rus (pə-pī′rəs) *n., pl.* **-rus•es** or **-ri** (-rī′). **1.** A tall aquatic sedge, *Cyperus papyrus,* of N Africa. **2.** Paper made from papyrus, used in ancient times as a writing material.
par (pär) *n.* **1.** A normal standard or accepted average. **2.** A common and equal status or level : equality. **3.** The standard number of golf strokes needed by an expert to complete a hole. **4.** Face value, as of a security.
par. *abbr.* **1.** paragraph. **2.** parallel. **3.** parenthesis. **4.** parish.
pa•ra (pä-rä′, pä′rä) *n.* See *dinar* at CURRENCY TABLE.
par•a•ble (păr′ə-bəl) *n.* A story that illustrates a moral lesson.
pa•rab•o•la (pə-răb′ə-lə) *n.* A plane curve formed by: **a.** A conic section taken parallel to an element of the intersected cone. **b.** The locus of points equidistant from a fixed line and a fixed point not on the line. **—par′a•bol′ic** (păr′ə-bŏl′ĭk) *adj.*
par•a•chute (păr′ə-sho͞ot′) *n.* A folding umbrella-shaped apparatus used to retard free fall from an aircraft or the motion of a vehicle. **—par′a•chute′** *v.* **—par′a•chut′ist** *n.*
pa•rade (pə-rād′) *n.* **1.** A public procession, esp. a ceremonial one : march. **2.** A formal review of a body of troops. **3.** A long line : succession. **4.** An ostentatious display <a *parade* of elegant clothes> *—v.* **-rad•ed, -rad•ing. 1.** To take part in or as if in a parade. **2.** To exhibit ostentatiously : show off. **3.** To take a leisurely walk : promenade. **—pa•rad′er** *n.*
par•a•digm (păr′ə-dīm′, -dĭm′) *n.* **1.** A listing of all the inflections of a noun or verb taken as a model for determining the forms of other words like it. **2.** A pattern : model. **—par′a•dig•mat′ic** (-dĭg-măt′ĭk) *adj.*
par•a•dise (păr′ə-dīs′, -dīz′) *n.* **1.** *often* **Paradise.** HEAVEN 2. **2.** A place or state of ideal beauty, loveliness, or rapture. **—par′a•dis′i•ac′** (-dĭz′ē-ăk′), **par′a•di•si′a•cal** (-dĭ-sī′ə-kəl, -zī′-) *adj.*
par•a•dox (păr′ə-dŏks′) *n.* A statement that seems to conflict with common sense or to contradict itself but that may nevertheless be true. **—par′a•dox′i•cal** *adj.* **—par′a•dox′i•cal•ly** *adv.*
par•af•fin (păr′ə-fĭn) *n.* **1.** A waxy white or colorless substance that is used to make candles, lubricants, and sealing materials. **2.** *esp. Brit.* Kerosene. **—par′af•fin** *v.*
par•a•gon (păr′ə-gŏn′, -gən) *n.* A pattern or model of perfection or excellence.
par•a•graph (păr′ə-grăf′) *n.* **1.** A division of a composition that deals with a single aspect or idea and consists of 1 or more sentences. **2.** A mark (¶) used to indicate the beginning of a paragraph. *—v.* To arrange in or divide into paragraphs.
Par•a•guay (păr′ə-gwā′, -gwī′). Country of South America. *Cap.* Asunción. *Pop.* 3,100,000. **—Par′a•guay′an** *adj.* & *n.*
par•a•keet (păr′ə-kēt′) *n.* Any of various small parrots usu. with long, tapering tails.

par•a•le•gal (păr′ə-lē′gəl) *adj.* Of, relating to, or being a person who is trained to assist a lawyer but is not licensed to practice law. **—par′a•le′gal** *n.*

par•al•lax (păr′ə-lăks′) *n.* An apparent change in the position of an object caused by a change in observational position.

par•al•lel (păr′ə-lĕl′, -ləl) *adj.* **1.** Moving or situated in the same direction but always separated by the same distance. **2.** Similar in comparable or corresponding parts : like. ☆***syns:*** CO-EXTENSIVE, COLLATERAL, CONCURRENT —*n.* **1.** A parallel curve, line, or surface. **2.a.** Something that is analogous or similar to something else. **b.** A comparison that indicates analogy or similarity. **3.** One of the imaginary lines that encircles the earth parallel to the equator and represents a specified latitude. —*v.* **-leled, -lel•ing** or **-lelled, -lel•ling. 1.** To extend or be parallel to. **2.** To be analogous or similar to. **—par′al•lel•ism** *n.*

par•al•lel•o•gram (păr′ə-lĕl′ə-grăm′) *n.* A 4-sided plane figure with opposite sides equal and parallel.

pa•ral•y•sis (pə-răl′ĭ-sĭs) *n., pl.* **-ses** (-sēz′). Partial or complete loss of the ability to move or feel sensation. **—par′a•lyt′ic** (păr′ə-lĭt′ĭk) *adj.* & *n.*

par•a•lyze (păr′ə-līz′) *v.* **-lyzed, -lyz•ing. 1.** To affect with paralysis. **2.** To cause to be powerless or inoperative.

Par•a•mar•i•bo (păr′ə-măr′ə-bō′). Cap. of Surinam, on the Atlantic. *Pop.* 102,300.

par•a•me•ci•um (păr′ə-mē′shē-əm, -sē-) *n., pl.* **-ci•a** (-shē-ə, -sē-ə) or **-ums.** Any of various usu. oval-shaped protozoans of the genus *Paramecium* that move by means of cilia.

par•a•med•ic (păr′ə-mĕd′ĭk) *n.* Someone trained to provide emergency medical treatment or to assist physicians. **—par′a•med′i•cal** *adj.*

pa•ram•e•ter (pə-răm′ĭ-tər) *n.* **1.** A constant in a mathematical expression whose values determine the specific form or characteristics of the expression. **2.** *Informal.* A typical element. **—par′a•met′ric** (păr′ə-mĕt′rĭk), **par′a•met′ri•cal** *adj.*

par•a•mil•i•tary (păr′ə-mĭl′ĭ-tĕr-ē) *adj.* Organized on a military pattern and esp. as an auxiliary military force.

par•a•mount (păr′ə-mount′) *adj.* Of highest rank, power, or importance.

par•a•mour (păr′ə-mo͝or′) *n.* A lover, esp. in an adulterous relationship.

par•a•noi•a (păr′ə-noi′ə) *n.* A psychosis marked by delusions of persecution or of grandeur. **—par′a•noid′** (-noid′) *adj.* & *n.*

par•a•pet (păr′ə-pĭt, -pĕt′) *n.* **1.** A low railing or wall, as along the edge of a balcony. **2.** An embankment or rampart to protect soldiers, as in a fort.

par•a•pher•na•lia (păr′ə-fər-nāl′yə, -fə-) *n. (sing. or pl. in number).* **1.** Personal belongings. **2.** The apparatus used in an activity : equipment.

par•a•phrase (păr′ə-frāz′) *v.* **-phrased, -phras•ing.** To restate the meaning of (e.g., a passage or text) in different words. ☆***syns:*** REPHRASE, RESTATE, REWORD, TRANSLATE **—par′a•phrase′** *n.*

par•a•ple•gia (păr′ə-plē′jə, -jē-ə) *n.* Paralysis of the lower half of the body, including both legs. **—par′a•ple′gic** (-jĭk) *adj.* & *n.*

par•a•pro•fes•sion•al (păr′ə-prə-fĕsh′ənəl) *n.* Someone, as a teacher's aide, who is trained to assist a professional person.

par•a•psy•chol•o•gy (păr′ə-sī-kŏl′ə-jē) *n.* The study of phenomena, as telepathy and clairvoyance, that are inexplicable by known natural laws. **—par′a•psy′cho•log′i•cal** *adj.* **—par′a•psy•chol′o•gist** *n.*

par•a•site (păr′ə-sīt′) *n.* **1.** *Biol.* An organism, as a plant, that grows, feeds, and is sheltered on or in a different organism and contributes nothing to its host. **2.** Someone who depends on others, as for support, without providing adequate return. **—par′a•sit′ic** (-sĭt′ĭk) *adj.* **—par′a•sit•ism** (-sĭ-tĭz′əm, -sī-) *n.* **—par′a•sit•ize′** (-sĭ-tīz′) *v.*

par•a•si•tol•o•gy (păr′ə-sĭ-tŏl′ə-jē, -sī-) *n.* The scientific study of parasites, esp. animal parasites. **—par′a•si•tol′o•gist** *n.*

par•a•sol (păr′ə-sôl′, -sŏl′) *n.* A light umbrella used as a sunshade.

par•a•sym•pa•thet•ic nervous system (păr′ə-sĭm′pə-thĕt′ĭk) *n.* The part of the autonomic nervous system tending to dilate blood vessels, stimulate digestive secretions, and slow the heart.

par•a•thi•on (păr′ə-thī′ŏn′) *n.* A highly poisonous yellowish liquid used as an agricultural insecticide.

par•a•thy•roid gland (păr′ə-thī′roid′) *n.* Any of 4 small kidney-shaped glands that are adjacent to the thyroid gland and secrete a hormone necessary for calcium and phosphorus metabolism.

par•a•troops (păr′ə-tro͞ops′) *pl.n.* Troops that are equipped and trained to parachute from an aircraft. **—par′a•troop′er** *n.*

par•a•ty•phoid (păr′ə-tī′foid′) *n.* An acute food poisoning that resembles typhoid fever but is less severe.

par•boil (pär′boil′) *v.* To boil for a brief time.

par•cel (pär′səl) *n.* **1.** A wrapped package : bundle. **2.** A plot or portion of land. **3.** A group, as of things : collection. —*v.* **-celed, -cel•ing** or **-celled, -cel•ling. 1.** To divide into parts and give out. **2.** To make up into a parcel : package.

parcel post *n.* The section of the postalservice that handles parcels.

parch (pärch) *v.* **1.** To make or become very dry, esp. with or from intense heat. **2.** To roast or toast (e.g., corn) with dry heat.

parch•ment (pärch′mənt) *n.* **1.** Sheepskin or goatskin prepared as a material for writing or drawing on. **2.** Something written or drawn on parchment.

par•don (pär′dn) *v.* **1.** To release from disfavor or punishment. **2.** To permit (an offense) to pass without punishment. **3.** To excuse : forgive. —*n.* **1.** *Law.* Exemption of a convicted person from the penalties of a crime or offense. **2.** Forgiveness, as for a fault or rudeness. **—par′don•a•ble** *adj.*

pare (pâr) *v.* **pared, par•ing. 1.** To remove an outer surface of : peel. **2.** To reduce by or as if by paring <*pared* his allowance>

par•e•go•ric (păr′ĭ-gôr′ĭk, -gŏr′-) *n.* A camphorated tincture of opium.

par•ent (pâr′ənt, păr′-) *n.* **1.** A mother or father. **2.** An ancestor : forefather. **3.** An origin : source. **—par′ent•age** (-ən-tĭj) *n.* **—pa•ren′tal** (pə-rĕn′tl) *adj.* **—par′ent•hood′** *n.*

pa•ren•the•sis (pə-rĕn′thĭ-sĭs) *n., pl.* **-ses** (-sēz′). **1.** One of a pair of curved lines, ( ), used in writing and printing to enclose qualifying or explanatory remarks. **2.** A word, phrase, or sentence inserted into a passage by way of qualification or amplification. **—par′en•thet′i•cal** (păr′ən-thĕt′ĭ-kəl), **par′en•thet′ic** (-thĕt′ĭk) *adj.* **—par′en•thet′i•cal•ly** *adv.*

par•ent•ing (pâr′ən-tĭng, păr′-) *n.* The rearing of children by their parents.

pa•re•sis (pə-rē′sĭs, păr′ĭ-) *n.* A partial or slight paralysis.

par ex•cel•lence (pär′ ĕk-sə-läns′) *adj.* Pre-eminent.

par•fait (pär-fā′) *n.* **1.** A sweet dessert of cream, eggs, and flavoring frozen together and served in a tall glass. **2.** A dessert consisting of variously flavored layers of ice cream or ices.

pa•ri•ah (pə-rī′ə) *n.* An outcast.

pa•ri•e•tal (pə-rī′ĭ-tl) *adj.* **1.** Of, relating to, or forming the wall of a hollow anatomical structure. **2.** Of or relating to life or the regulation of life within a college.

par•i•mu•tu•el (păr′ĭ-myo͞o′cho͞o-əl) *n.* A betting system in which the winners divide the total amount bet, after the deduction of management expenses, in proportion to the sums they have wagered.

par•ing (pâr′ĭng) *n.* Something that has been pared off <carrot *parings*>

pa•ri pas•su (păr′ē păs′o͞o) *adv.* With equal pace, speed, or progress.

Par•is (păr′ĭs, pä-rē′). Cap. of France, in the NW on the Seine. *Pop.* 2,050,500. **—Pa•ri′sian** (pə-rē′zhən, -rĭzh′ən) *adj.* & *n.*

Paris green *n.* A poisonous emerald-green powder used as a pigment, wood preservative, and insecticide.

par•ish (păr′ĭsh) *n.* **1. a.** An administrative division of a diocese consisting of an area with its own church. **b.** The members of a parish. **2.** A civil district in the state of Louisiana that corresponds to a county.

pa•rish•ion•er (pə-rĭsh′ə-nər) *n.* A member of a parish.

par•i•ty (păr′ĭ-tē) *n., pl.* **-ties. 1.** Equality, as in value, position, or amount. **2.** The equivalent in value between 2 different kinds of currency.

park (pärk) *n.* **1.** A tract of land reserved for public use, as for recreation. **2.** An enclosed playing field : stadium <a baseball *park*> **3.** A place where vehicles, as cars, are stored or left. —*v.* To put or leave (a vehicle) standing for a time in a particular location.

par•ka (pär′kə) *n.* A warm hooded fur or cloth jacket.

parking meter *n.* A coin-operated device that registers the amount of time purchased for the parking of a motor vehicle.

Par•kin•son's disease (pär′kĭn-sənz) *n.* A progressive nervous disease that is marked by muscular tremor, partial facial paralysis, weakness, and impaired muscular control.

Parkinson's Law *n.* Any of several satirical observations propounded as economic laws, as "work expands to fill the time available for its completion."

park•way (park′wā′) *n.* A wide landscaped highway.

par•lance (pär′ləns) *n.* A particular style of speaking : idiom <scientific *parlance*>

par•lay (pär′lā′) *n.* A series of bets in which the winnings of the 1st and original stake are risked on subsequent wagers. **—par′lay′** *v.*

par•ley (pär′lē) *n., pl.* **-leys.** A discussion, esp. to resolve differences between opponents : conference. **—par′ley** *v.*

par•lia•ment (pär′lə-mənt) *n.* **1. Parliament.** The legislature of various countries, esp. the United Kingdom and Canada. **2.**

An assembly that represents the members of a group. **–par′lia·men′ta·ry** (-mĕn′tə-rē, -mĕn′trē) *adj.*
par·lia·men·tar·i·an (pär′lə-mĕn-târ′ē-ən) *n.* One who is an expert in parliamentary rules, procedure, or debate.
par·lor (pär′lər) *n.* **1.** A room for entertaining visitors or for conversing. **2.** A business establishment <an ice-cream *parlor*>
par·lour (pär′lər) *n. esp. Brit. var. of* PARLOR.
par·lous (pär′ləs) *adj.* Full of peril : dangerous. **–par′lous·ly** *adv.*
Par·me·san (pär′mĭ-zän′, -zăn′, -zən) *n.* A hard, dry, sharp cheese often served grated.
par·mi·gia·na (pär′mĭ-jä′nə) *adj.* Covered with or made of Parmesan <chicken *parmigiana*>
pa·ro·chi·al (pə-rō′kē-əl) *adj.* **1.** Of, relating to, or supported by a church parish. **2.** Limited in range or understanding : provincial. **–pa·ro′chi·al·ly** *adv.*
parochial school *n.* A school that is run and supported by a religious group.
par·o·dy (păr′ə-dē) *n., pl.* **-dies. 1.** A musical or literary work that imitates another work, exaggerating the characteristics of the original to make it seem ridiculous. **2.** A travesty <a *parody* of justice> **–par′o·dist** *n.* **–par′o·dy** *v.*
pa·role (pə-rōl′) *n.* **1.** The conditional release of a prisoner before the expiration of his or her term. **2.** Word of honor : pledge. **–pa·role′** *v.* **–pa·rol′ee′** *n.*
par·ox·ysm (păr′ək-sĭz′əm) *n.* A sudden attack or outburst, as of emotion : spasm. **–par′ox·ys′mal** *adj.*
par·quet (pär-kā′) *n.* **1. a.** The forward part of the main floor of a theater. **b.** The main floor of a theater : orchestra. **2.** A parquetry floor.
par·quet·ry (pär′kĭ-trē) *n., pl.* **-ries.** Woodwork of inlaid pieces fitted together in a pattern.
par·ri·cide (păr′ĭ-sīd′) *n.* **1.** Someone who murders his or her mother or father or a near relative. **2.** The act committed by a parricide. **–par′ri·cid′al** *adj.*
par·rot (păr′ət) *n.* Any of various tropical and semitropical birds of the order Psittaciformes, having short, hooked bills and brightly colored plumage. *–v.* To imitate or repeat mindlessly.
parrot fever *n.* Psittacosis.
par·ry (păr′ē) *v.* **-ried, -ry·ing. 1.** To turn aside (e.g., a weapon) : deflect. **2.** To avoid skillfully or adroitly : evade. **–par′ry** *n.*
parse (pärs) *v.* **parsed, pars·ing.** To identify the part of speech, form, and function of a word or group of words.
par·si·mo·ny (pär′sə-mō′nē) *n.* Extreme reluctance to spend money or use resources : excessive frugality. **–par′si·mo′ni·ous** *adj.* **–par′si·mo′ni·ous·ly** *adv.*
pars·ley (pär′slē) *n.* A cultivated herb, *Petroselinum crispum,* with divided curly leaves used as a garnish and seasoning.
pars·nip (pär′snĭp′) *n.* A plant, *Pastinaca sativa,* cultivated for its long rather strong-tasting edible root.
par·son (pär′sən) *n.* A clergyman, esp. a Protestant clergyman.
par·son·age (pär′sə-nĭj) *n.* The residence provided by a church for its parson.
part (pärt) *n.* **1.** A division, portion, or segment of a whole. **2.** A component of a machine. **3.** The role of an actor, as in a play. **4.** A task or function that must be performed in a common effort : duty. **5. a.** An individual melodic line for a particular instrument or voice. **b.** The score for such a line. **6.** A side in a controversy or dispute. **7.** *often* **parts.** A land, region, or territory. **8.** The line that forms when the hair divides, as from brushing or combing. *–v.* **1.** To divide, split, or break into parts : separate. **2.** To keep or put apart. **3.** To divide (the hair) into a part. **4.** To go away from someone. **5.** To leave : depart. **6.** To give up control or possession <wouldn't *part* with his car> *–adv.* In part : partially.
par·take (pär-tāk′) *v.* **-took** (-to͝ok′), **-tak·en** (-tā′kən), **-tak·ing. 1.** To have or take a share (of) : participate (in). **2.** To take a helping, as of food. **–par·tak′er** *n.*
par·terre (pär-târ′) *n.* **1.** A garden, esp. a flower garden, in which the beds and paths form a pattern. **2.** The section of a theater parquet situated under a rear balcony.
par·the·no·gen·e·sis (pär′thə-nō-jĕn′ĭ-sĭs) *n.* Reproduction without the conjunction of gametes of opposite sexes. **–par′the·no·ge·net′ic** (-jə-nĕt′ĭk) *adj.*
par·tial (pär′shəl) *adj.* **1.** Not total or complete : incomplete. **2.** According preference or favor to 1 side or person over another : biased. **3.** Especially fond <*partial* to classical music> **–par′ti·al′i·ty** (-shē-ăl′ĭ-tē, -shăl′ĭ-) *n.* **–par′tial·ly** *adv.*
par·tic·i·pate (pär-tĭs′ə-pāt′) *v.* **-pat·ed, -pat·ing. 1.** To join with others in something : take part. **2.** To have a share in something. **–par·tic′i·pant** *n.* **–par·tic′i·pa′tion** *n.* **–par·tic′i·pa′tor** *n.* **–par·tic′i·pa·to′ry** *adj.*
par·ti·ci·ple (pär′tĭ-sĭp′əl) *n.* A word that both functions as an adjective and is used with an auxiliary verb to indicate certain tenses. **–par′ti·cip′i·al** *adj.*
par·ti·cle (pär′tĭ-kəl) *n.* **1.** A very small speck of solid matter. **2.** A subatomic particle. **3.** Any of a class of words, as many prepositions and conjunctions, that convey little meaning but help connect, specify, or limit the meanings of other words.
par·ti-col·ored (pär′tē-kŭl′ərd) *adj.* Marked by different tints or colors.
par·tic·u·lar (pər-tĭk′yə-lər) *adj.* **1.** Of, relating to, or associated with a specific person, thing, group, or category. **2.** Separate and distinct : individual. **3.** Special : exceptional. **4. a.** Mindful of details : meticulous. **b.** Difficult to please : fussy. *–n.* An individual fact, item, or detail. **–par·tic′u·lar′i·ty** *n.* **–par·tic′u·lar·ly** *adv.*
par·tic·u·lar·ize (pər-tĭk′yə-lə-rīz′) *v.* **-ized, -iz·ing. 1.** To enumerate, describe, or state in detail : specify. **2.** To give details.
par·tic·u·late (pər-tĭk′yə-lĭt, -lāt′) *adj.* Of or made up of separate particles.
part·ing (pär′tĭng) *n.* **1.** A division : separation. **2.** The act of taking leave. *–adj.* Given, done, or said on departing <a *parting* embrace>
Par·ti Qué·be·cois (par′tē kā-bĕ-kwä′) *n. Can.* A political party of Quebec that advocates independence for the province from the rest of Canada.
par·ti·san (pär′tĭ-zən) *n.* **1.** A supporter of another, as a party or cause. **2.** A guerrilla. **–par′ti·san** *adj.* **–par′ti·san·ship′** *n.*
par·ti·ta (pär-tē′tə) *n. Mus.* A set of related instrumental pieces, as a suite.
par·tite (pär′tīt′) *adj.* Divided into parts.
par·ti·tion (pär-tĭsh′ən) *n.* **1.** The division of something into parts. **2.** Something that separates, esp. an interior structure dividing a larger area. *–v.* **1.** To divide into parts. **2.** To separate by a partition.
part·ly (pärt′lē) *adv.* To some degree or extent : in part.
part·ner (pärt′nər) *n.* **1.** One who is associated with another in a shared activity, esp.: **a.** One of 2 or more persons who jointly own a business. **b.** A husband or wife : spouse. **c.** Either of a pair of persons dancing together. **d.** One of a pair or a team in a game or sport. **2.** An ally. ☆***syns:*** ALLY, ASSOCIATE, COLLEAGUE, CONFEDERATE **–part′ner·ship′** *n.*
part of speech *n.* One of the traditional grammatical classes, as noun or verb, into which words are placed according to their syntactic function.
par·took (pär-to͝ok′) *v. p.t. of* PARTAKE.
par·tridge (pär′trĭj) *n., pl.* **-tridg·es** or **partridge.** Any of several plump-bodied game birds, esp. of the genera *Perdix* and *Alectoris.*
part song *n.* A song with 2 or more voice parts.
part-time (pärt′tīm′) *adj.* During or for fewer than customary hours <*part-time* employment> **–part′-time′** *adv.*
par·tu·ri·tion (pär′cho͞o-rĭsh′ən, -chə-) *n.* Childbirth.
part·way (pärt′wā′) *adv.* In part : partly.
par·ty (pär′tē) *n., pl.* **-ties. 1.** A social gathering, as for entertainment or pleasure. **2.** A group of people participating in a common activity or task <a work *party*> **3.** A group of persons organized to advance its political principles and support its candidates for office. **4.** A group or person involved in a proceeding or affair.
party line *n.* **1.** A telephone circuit shared by 2 or more subscribers within an exchange. **2.** The official policies or principles of a political party.
par·ve·nu (pär′və-no͞o′, -nyo͞o′) *n.* Someone who has suddenly or recently become wealthy or powerful but lacks the background or culture customarily associated with his new status.
pas (pä) *n., pl.* **pas** (pä, päz). A ballet step or series of steps.
Pas·cal (päs-käl′), **Blaise.** 1623–62. French philosopher and mathematician.
PASCAL *n. Computer Sci.* A programming language that processes both numerical and textual data.
pas de deux (pä′ də dœ′) *n., pl.* **pas de deux.** A ballet figure or dance for 2 persons.
pa·sha (pä′shə, păsh′ə) *n.* A former high-ranking military or civil official, esp. in Turkey.
pass (păs) *v.* **1.** To move : proceed. **2.** To move or cause to move over, past, or beyond. **3.** To transfer or be transferred : circulate. **4.** To elapse or let elapse. **5.** To come to an end. **6.** To happen : occur. **7.** To go or be allowed to go without challenge < let the incident *pass*> **8.** To undergo or cause to undergo a trial, test, or course of study with success. **9.** To be accepted or viewed. **10.** To enact or be enacted, as by a legislature. **11.** To pronounce a legal judgment. **12.** To transfer (the puck or ball) to a teammate. **13.** To decline to play or bid, esp. in a card game. **14.** To go through (e.g., an obstacle). **15.** To discharge (bodily wastes).

–pass out. To lose consciousness. **–pass up.** *Informal.* To turn down : decline. *–n.* **1.** The act of passing. **2.** A narrow passage in a mountain range : gap. **3.a.** A written permit or authorization to come or go freely or without charge. **b.** A written leave of absence from duty, esp. military duty. **4.** The act of transferring the puck or ball to a teammate. **5.** An effort : attempt. **6.** A situation : predicament. **7.** A sexual overture or gesture.

pass·a·ble (păs′ə-bəl) *adj.* **1.** Capable of being passed or traversed. **2.** Acceptable but not outstanding. **–pass′a·bly** *adv.*

pas·sage (păs′ĭj) *n.* **1.** The act of passing. **2.** A journey, esp. by air or water. **3.** The permission or right to travel, as on a ship. **4.** Something, as a channel or path, through, over, or along which something may pass. **5.** Enactment, as of a legislative measure. **6.** A selection or portion, as of a musical composition.

pas·sage·way (păs′ĭj-wā′) *n.* A way that permits passage, as a corridor.

pass·book (păs′bo͝ok′) *n.* A bankbook.

pas·sé (pă-sā′) *adj.* **1.** No longer current : out-of-date. **2.** No longer young.

pas·sel (păs′əl) *n. Informal.* A large number or quantity.

pas·sen·ger (păs′ən-jər) *n.* Someone traveling in a vehicle or conveyance, as a car or train.

passe par·tout (păs′ pär-to͞o′) *n.* Something that enables one to go or pass everywhere.

pass·er·by (păs′ər-bī′, păs′ər-bī′) *n., pl.* **pass·ers·by.** Someone who passes by.

pas·ser·ine (păs′ə-rīn′) *adj.* Of or relating to birds of the order Passeriformes, which consists primarily of perching birds and songbirds.

pas·sim (păs′ĭm) *adv.* Here and there : in places throughout.

pass·ing (păs′ĭng) *adj.* **1.** Lasting only a brief time : transitory. **2.** Casual : superficial. *–n.* **1.** The act of one that passes. **2.** A place or means by which one can pass. **3.** Death.

pas·sion (păsh′ən) *n.* **1.** Powerful feeling. **2. a.** Love. **b.** Sexual desire : lust. **c.** The object of such love or desire. **3. a.** Great enthusiasm. **b.** The object of such enthusiasm. **4.** Anger : rage **5. Passion.** Christ's sufferings following the Last Supper to the time of his death. ☆**syns:** ARDOR, ENTHUSIASM, FERVOR, FIRE, ZEAL **–pas′sion·ate** *adj.* **–pas′sion·ate·ly** *adv.* **–pas′sion·less** *adj.*

pas·sion·flow·er (păsh′ən-flou′ər) *n.* A chiefly tropical American vine of the genus *Passiflora,* usu. bearing large, variously colored flowers.

pas·sive (păs′ĭv) *adj.* **1.** Not active but acted upon. **2.** Unresisting : submissive. **3.** Indicating that the grammatical subject of a verb is the recipient or object of the action expressed by the verb. *–n.* **1.** The passive voice of a verb. **2.** A verb form in the passive voice. **–pas′sive·ly** *adv.* **–pas·siv′i·ty** (pă-sĭv′ĭ-tē), **pas′sive·ness** *n.*

pass·key (păs′kē′) *n.* A key that opens more than 1 lock.

Pass·o·ver (păs′ō′vər) *n.* A Jewish holiday that is celebrated in the spring and commemorates the Exodus from Egypt.

pass·port (păs′pôrt′, -pōrt′) *n.* An official document issued by a nation that certifies the identity and citizenship of the holder and grants him or her its protection during travel abroad.

pass·word (păs′wûrd′) *n.* A secret word or phrase that a person must utter in order to pass a guard.

past (păst) *adj.* **1.** Having happened or existed in a time before the present : bygone. **2. a.** Before the present time : ago <12 months *past*> **b.** Just elapsed or gone by <the *past* week> **3.** Of, relating to, or being a verb tense or form used to express time that has gone by. *–n.* **1.** The time before the present. **2. a.** A person's background or history. **b.** A questionable or secret personal past life. **3. a.** The past tense. **b.** A verb form in the past tense. *–adv.* So as to go beyond <The plane flew *past.*> *–prep.* Beyond, as in position or time.

pas·ta (pä′stə) *n.* **1.** A paste, as macaroni, or dough, as ravioli, made of flour and water. **2.** A cooked dish of pasta.

paste (pāst) *n.* **1.** A viscous substance, as a mixture of flour and water, used to stick things together. **2.** Dough, as that used for making pastry. **3.** A food made smooth or creamy by grinding or pounding <tomato *paste*> **4.** A brilliant glass used in artificial gems. *–v.* **past·ed, past·ing. 1.** To cause to stick together by applying paste. **2.** *Slang.* To hit : punch.

paste·board (pāst′bôrd′, -bōrd′) *n.* A firm board that is made of sheets of paper pasted together.

pas·tel (pă-stĕl′) *n.* **1. a.** A paste made of ground pigment. **b.** A crayon made of pastel. **2.** A picture or drawing in pastel. **3.** A light or pale tint.

pas·tern (păs′tərn) *n.* The portion of a horse's foot between the joint at the hoof and the fetlock.

Pas·teur (pă-stûr′), **Louis.** 1822–95. French chemist.

pas·teur·i·za·tion (păs′chə-rĭ-zā′shən) *n.* A process in which a liquid, as milk, is heated to the temperature at which most disease-producing microorganisms are destroyed. **–pas′teur·ize′** (-rīz′) *v.*

pas·tiche (pă-stēsh′, pä-) *n.* **1.** A work, as a musical composition, that is made up of selections from various different works. **2.** A hodgepodge : potpourri.

pas·tille (pă-stēl′) *also* **pas·til** (păs′tĭl) *n.* A medicated or aromatic lozenge.

pas·time (păs′tīm′) *n.* Something that occupies the time pleasantly : diversion.

past master *n.* Someone who is expert in a particular activity or art.

pas·tor (păs′tər) *n.* A Christian clergyman, esp. one who leads a congregation. **–pas′tor·ate** *n.*

pas·tor·al (păs′tər-əl) *adj.* **1.** Of or relating to shepherds or to life in the country. **2.** Of or relating to a pastor or his duties.

pas·to·rale (păs′tə-räl′, -răl′) *n.* A vocal or instrumental composition with a theme that suggests idyllic rural life.

†**pas·to·ri·um** (pă-stôr′ē-əm, -stōr′-) *n. S U.S.* The residence of a pastor : parsonage.

past participle *n.* A participle that expresses action that is completed. Used to form the passive voice and the perfect tenses.

pas·tra·mi (pə-strä′mē) *n.* Highly seasoned smoked beef, usu. prepared from breast or shoulder cuts.

pas·try (pā′strē) *n., pl.* **-tries. 1.** A paste of water, flour, and shortening used for baked crusts, as of pies and tarts. **2.** Baked and esp. sweet goods made with pastry.

pas·tur·age (păs′chər-ĭj) *n.* Pasture.

pas·ture (păs′chər) *n.* **1.** Plants, as grass, on which grazing livestock feed. **2.** A tract of land on which livestock graze. *–v.* **-tured, -tur·ing. 1.** To herd (animals) into a pasture for grazing. **2.** To graze.

past·y[1] (pā′stē) *adj.* **-i·er, -i·est.** Resembling paste, esp. in being pale and unhealthy-looking.

pas·ty[2] (păs′tē) *n., pl.* **-ties.** A pie with a filling of seasoned meat or fish.

▲word history: The noun *pasty*[2], "meat pie," was borrowed from Old French *pastee* in the 13th cent. *Pastee* is derived from Old French *paste,* literally "paste," which orig. referred to an edible dough of flour and liquid. Old French *pastee* is descended from the same word as Italian *pasta.* The modern French form of *pastee* is *pâté,* which was borrowed into English in the 18th cent. as a synonym for *pasty*[2]. *Pâté* in English now denotes the meat alone, without its pastry crust. *Patty* is an anglicized variant of *pâté.*

pat (păt) *v.* **pat·ted, pat·ting. 1. a.** To tap lightly with the open hand or something flat. **b.** To tap softly, esp. with the flat of the hand, as a gesture of affection. **2.** To smooth, flatten, or shape by tapping. *–n.* **1.** A light or gentle tap, esp. with a flat implement or the open hand. **2.** The sound made by a pat. **3.** A small, flat, usu. rectangular mass, as of butter. *–adj.* **1.** Precisely suited to the purpose or occasion. **2.** Learned or memorized exactly. **3.** Glib : facile <a *pat* answer> **4.** Not moving : unyielding. *–adv.* In a pat manner. **–pat′ly** *adv.* **–pat′ness** *n.*

pat. *abbr.* patent.

pa·ta·ca (pə-tä′kə) *n.* See CURRENCY TABLE.

patch (păch) *n.* **1.** A piece of fabric used to cover or reinforce a worn or weakened area in a garment. **2.** A piece of cloth affixed to a garment as an insignia, as of military rank. **3.** A protective pad, dressing, or bandage worn over an injured or missing eye. **4.** A small area that differs from what surrounds it <a *patch* of snow> *–v.* **1.** To cover or reinforce with a patch. **2.** To put together or repair, esp. hastily.

patch test *n.* A test for allergic reaction in which a suspected allergen is applied to the skin with a small surgical pad.

patch·work (păch′wûrk′) *n.* **1.** Something that consists of pieces of various colors, shapes, materials, or sizes. **2.** A miscellany : jumble.

patch·y (păch′ē) *adj.* **-i·er, -i·est. 1.** Consisting of or marked by patches : spotty. **2.** Uneven in quality or performance.

pate (pāt) *n.* The top of the head.

pâ·té (pä-tā′, pă-) *n.* **1.** A paste of seasoned and spiced meat. **2.** A small pastry filled with fish or meat.

pa·tel·la (pə-tĕl′ə) *n., pl.* **-tel·lae** (-tĕl′ē). A flat, triangular bone that forms the front of the knee joint : kneecap.

pat·en (păt′n) *n.* **1.** A plate, esp. one for the Eucharistic bread. **2.** A thin metal disk.

pat·ent (păt′nt) *n.* **1.** A governmental grant assuring an inventor the sole right to his invention for a period of time. **2.** Something that is patented. *–adj.* **1.** (*also* pāt′nt). Obvious : evident. **2.** Protected by a patent. *–v.* **1.** To obtain a patent for. **2.** To grant a patent to. **–pat′ent·ee′** *n.*

patent leather *n.* Leather finished to a smooth, shiny surface.

pa·ter·fa·mil·i·as (pā′tər-fə-mĭl′ē-əs, pä′-) *n., pl.* **pa·tres·**

fa•mil•i•as (pā′trēz-). **1.** The male head of a household. **2.** The father of a family.
pa•ter•nal (pə-tûr′nəl) *adj.* **1.** Of, relating to, or typical of a father : fatherly. **2.** Inherited or received from a father. **3.** Of or relating to a father's side of a family. **–pa•ter′nal•ly** *adv.*
pa•ter•nal•ism (pə-tûr′nə-lĭz′əm) *n.* A practice or policy by which an authority treats or governs those under its jurisdiction in a paternal manner, esp. by filling their needs and regulating their behavior. **–pa•ter′nal•is′tic** *adj.*
pa•ter•ni•ty (pə-tûr′nĭ-tē) *n.* **1.** The state or fact of being a father : fatherhood. **2.** Paternal descent.
path (păth, päth) *n., pl.* **paths** (păthz, päthz, păths, päths). **1.** A way or track made by footsteps. **2.** A course : route. **–path′less** *adj.*
pa•thet•ic (pə-thĕt′ĭk) *adj.* Arousing sympathy, pity, or tenderness. **–pa•thet′i•cal•ly** *adv.*
path•find•er (păth′fīn′dər, päth′-) *n.* One who probes unexplored regions to discover a way : trailblazer.
path•o•gen (păth′ə-jən) *n.* An agent, esp. a microorganism such as a bacterium, that causes disease. **–path′o•gen′ic** (-jĕn′ĭk) *adj.* **–path′o•ge•nic′i•ty** (-jə-nĭs′ĭ-tē) *n.*
pa•thol•o•gy (pə-thŏl′ə-jē, pă-) *n., pl.* **-gies. 1.** The scientific and medical study of the nature of disease. **2.** The functional or anatomic manifestations of disease. **–path′o•log′i•cal** (păth′ə-lŏj′ĭ-kəl) *adj.* **–pa•thol′o•gist** *n.*
pa•thos (pā′thŏs′) *n.* A quality or element that arouses pity, sympathy, or sorrow.
path•way (păth′wā′, päth′-) *n.* A path.
pa•tience (pā′shəns) *n.* **1.** The fact, quality, or habit of being patient. **2.** *esp. Brit.* The game of solitaire.
pa•tient (pā′shənt) *adj.* **1.** Enduring affliction or pain without anger or complaint. **2.** Understanding : tolerant. **3.** Persevering : steadfast. *–n.* Someone receiving medical treatment. **–pa′tient•ly** *adv.*
pat•i•na (păt′n-ə, pə-tē′nə) *n.* A thin film of corrosion, usu. green, that forms on copper and bronze as a result of oxidation.
pat•i•o (păt′ē-ō′) *n., pl.* **-os. 1.** An inner courtyard without a roof. **2.** A recreation area, usu. paved, near a residence.
pat•ois (păt′wä′) *n., pl.* **-ois** (-wäz′). **1.** A regional dialect. **2.** Substandard or illiterate speech. **3.** Jargon.
pa•tri•arch (pā′trē-ärk′) *n.* **1.** A man who is venerated as leader, father, or founder, as of a tribe or family. **2.** An ecclesiastical head, esp. in Eastern churches. **3.** A very old and revered man. **–pa′tri•ar′chal** *adj.* **–pa′tri•ar′chate** (-kĭt, -kāt′) *n.* **–pa′tri•ar′chy** *n.*
pa•tri•cian (pə-trĭsh′ən) *n.* A member of the aristocracy. **–pa•tri′cian** *adj.*
pat•ri•cide (păt′rĭ-sīd′) *n.* **1.** The act of murdering one's own father. **2.** One who has committed patricide. **–pat′ri•cid′al** (-sīd′l) *adj.*
pat•ri•mo•ny (păt′rə-mō′nē) *n., pl.* **-nies.** Something, as property, inherited from one's father. **–pat′ri•mo′ni•al** *adj.*
pa•tri•ot (pā′trē-ət, -ŏt′) *n.* Someone who loves and defends his or her country. **–pa′tri•ot′ic** (-ŏt′ĭk) *adj.* **–pa′tri•ot′i•cal•ly** *adv.* **–pa′tri•ot•ism** *n.*
pa•trol (pə-trōl′) *n.* **1.a.** The action of making a circuit about an area or beat for the purpose of observing or maintaining security. **b.** A person or group carrying out such an action. **2.** A detachment sent out to reconnoiter. *–v.* **-trolled, -trol•ling.** To engage in a patrol (of).
pa•trol•man (pə-trōl′mən) *n.* A policeman assigned to patrol a particular area.
patrol wagon *n.* An enclosed police truck for conveying prisoners.
pa•tron (pā′trən) *n.* **1.** Someone who acts as a special guardian or protector. **2.** Someone who supports or champions an artistically or socially worthwhile cause : sponsor <a *patron* of music> **3.** A regular customer. **–pa′tron•ess** *n.*
pa•tron•age (pā′trə-nĭj, păt′rə-) *n.* **1.** The encouragement or support of a patron. **2. a.** The trade given by customers. **b.** Clientele : customers. **3.** The power to appoint people to governmental or political positions.
pa•tron•ize (pā′trə-nīz′, păt′rə-) *v.* **-ized, -iz•ing. 1. a.** To be a patron to. **b.** To be a regular customer of. **2.** To act in an offensively condescending way toward. **–pa′tron•iz′ing•ly** *adv.*
pat•ro•nym•ic (păt′rə-nĭm′ĭk) *n.* A name that has been derived from that of a paternal ancestor, esp. by the addition of an affix. **–pat′ro•nym′ic** *adj.*
pa•troon (pə-tro͞on′) *n.* A landholder in N.Y. and N.J. with certain feudal powers, esp. under Dutch colonial rule.
pat•sy (păt′sē) *n., pl.* **-sies.** *Slang.* A person who is victimized or cheated.
pat•ter¹ (păt′ər) *v.* To tap or pat quickly, lightly, and repeatedly. **–pat′ter** *n.*
pat•ter² (păt′ər) *v.* To speak glibly, rapidly, or mechanically. *–n.* **1.** The jargon of a specific group : lingo. **2.** Glib, rapid speech, as of a salesman.
▲word history: The word *patter²* is derived from *pater*, a shortened form of *paternoster*, the Latin name for the Lord's Prayer. In medieval times Christian prayers were learned and recited in Latin; they were also often recited rapidly with no regard for the sense of the words. From this practice the name of the prayer became a general word for meaningless chatter. The verb *patter²* is derived from the noun.
pat•tern (păt′ərn) *n.* **1.** A decorative or artistic design. **2.** A model for use in making things. **3.** A combination of elements or characteristics : configuration. **4.** A model worthy of imitation. **5.** A specimen : sample. *–v.* To make, shape, form, or design according to a pattern.
pat•ty (păt′ē) *n., pl.* **-ties. 1.** A small flattened cake, as of chopped meat or minced food. **2.** A small pie.
patty shell *n.* A shell of puff pastry made to hold a filling of creamed meat, seafood, or vegetables.
pau•ci•ty (pô′sĭ-tē) *n.* Smallness of quantity or number : dearth.
paunch (pônch) *n.* A belly, esp. a potbelly. **–paunch′y** *adj.*
pau•per (pô′pər) *n.* A very poor person, esp. one who depends on charity. **–pau′per•ism** *n.* **–pau′per•ize′** *v.*
pause (pôz) *v.* **paused, paus•ing.** To stop, linger, or hesitate for a time. ☆**syns:** BIDE, LINGER, TARRY, WAIT *–n.* **1.** A temporary stop. **2. a.** A hesitation. **b.** A reason for hesitating. **3.** A sign indicating that a musical note or rest is to be held.
pa•vane *also* **pa•van** (pə-vän′, -văn′) *n.* **1.** A slow, stately court dance of the 16th cent. **2.** Music for a pavane.
pave (pāv) *v.* **paved, pav•ing.** To cover (e.g., a street) with a hard, smooth surface, as of concrete, for travel.
pave•ment (pāv′mənt) *n.* **1.** A surface that has been paved. **2.** The material used to make pavement.
pa•vil•ion (pə-vĭl′yən) *n.* **1.** A large, often ornate tent. **2.** A light, often ornamental roofed structure, as in a park, used for shelter or amusement.
pav•ing (pā′vĭng) *n.* Pavement.
paw (pô) *n.* The foot of an animal, as a cat, that has claws. *–v.* **1. a.** To strike or touch with a paw. **b.** To scrape or strike with a hoof. **2.** To handle rudely or clumsily. **3.** To make grabbing motions with the hands.
pawl (pôl) *n.* A hinged or pivoted device that fits into a notch of another machine part to drive it forward or prevent backward motion.
pawn¹ (pôn) *n.* **1.** Something given to another as security for a loan. **2.** The state of being held as a pledge. **3.** A hostage. *–v.* To deposit or give as security for a loan.
pawn² (pôn) *n.* **1.** A chessman of the lowest value. **2.** One used to advance another's purposes.
pawn•bro•ker (pôn′brō′kər) *n.* Someone who lends money on pledged property.
pawn•shop (pôn′shŏp′) *n.* The place where a pawnbroker conducts business.
paw•paw (pô′pô′) *n. var. of* PAPAW.
pay (pā) *v.* **paid** (pād), **pay•ing. 1.** To give to in return for goods purchased or services rendered. **2.** To give the amount required to discharge (a debt or obligation) : settle <*paid* his taxes> **3.** To requite. **4.** To yield as profit : return. **5.** To be worthwhile (to) <It *pays* to study.> **6.** To suffer the consequences of <*paid* the price for lying> **7.** To bestow or give <*paying* close attention> *–adj.* **1.** Functioning only after payment for use has been made <a *pay* phone> **2.** Yielding or containing something valuable, as gold. *–n.* **1.** The fact of being paid, esp. by an employer : employ. **2.** Something paid, as wages. **–pay′a•ble** *adj.* **–pay•ee′** *n.* **–pay′er** *n.*
pay•check (pā′chĕk′) *n.* **1.** A check issued to an employee in payment of wages or salary. **2.** Salary.
P.A.Y.E. *abbr.* **1.** pay as you earn. **2.** pay as you enter.
pay•load (pā′lōd′) *n.* The revenue-producing load, as of cargo, that a vehicle can carry.
pay•mas•ter (pā′măs′tər) *n.* Someone in charge of a payroll.
pay•ment (pā′mənt) *n.* **1.** The act of paying. **2.** Something paid, as an amount.
pay•off (pā′ôf′, -ŏf′) *n.* **1.** Payment, as of a salary or bribe. **2.** *Informal.* The distribution of profits from an undertaking. **3.** *Informal.* The climax of a sequence of events or a narrative.
pay•o•la (pā-ō′lə) *n. Slang.* **1.** Bribery. **2.** A bribe.
pay•roll (pā′rōl′) *n.* **1.** A list of employees who are entitled to receive wages. **2.** The amount of money to be paid to those on a payroll.
Pb *symbol for* LEAD.
P.B. *abbr.* **1.** passbook. **2.** prayer book.
p.c. *also* **pct.** *abbr.* per cent.
p/c or **P/C.** *abbr.* **1.** *also* **p.c.** petty cash. **2.** prices current.

P.C. *abbr. Can.* Progressive Conservative.
Pd *symbol for* PALLADIUM.
pd. *abbr.* paid.
pea (pē) *n.* **1.** A vine, *Pisum sativum*, bearing round edible seeds in green pods. **2.** Any of several plants that are related to or resemble the pea.
peace (pēs) *n.* **1. a.** The absence of hostilities, as war. **b.** A treaty or agreement ending hostilities. **2.** A state of harmony, as between persons : concord. **3.** A state of security under the law <a disturbance of the *peace*> **4.** Freedom from disquieting feelings and thoughts : serenity. **—peace'a•ble** *adj.* **—peace'a•bly** *adv.* **—peace'ful** *adj.* **—peace'ful•ly** *adv.*
peace•keep•ing (pēs'kē'pĭng) *n.* The maintenance of peace, esp. the supervision and enforcement of a truce between hostile nations.
peace•mak•er (pēs'mā'kər) *n.* Someone who makes or tries to make peace.
peace•time (pēs'tīm') *n.* A time without war.
peach (pēch) *n.* A widely cultivated small tree, *Prunus persica*, bearing pink flowers and sweet, juicy edible fruit.
pea•cock (pē'kŏk') *n.* The male peafowl, having a crested head, brilliant blue or green plumage, and long iridescent tail feathers that can be spread like a fan.
pea•fowl (pē'foul') *n.* Either of 2 large Asiatic pheasants, *Pavo cristatus* or *P. muticus.*
pea•hen (pē'hĕn') *n.* The female peafowl.
pea jacket *n.* A short, warm, double-breasted jacket of heavy wool, worn esp. by sailors.
peak (pēk) *n.* **1.** An upward-projecting tapering point. **2. a.** The summit of a mountain or hill. **b.** A mountain. **3.** The visor of a hat or cap. **4.** The point of greatest intensity or development. *—v.* To bring to or achieve a maximum.
peak•ed (pē'kĭd) *adj.* Looking sickly and pale.
peal (pēl) *n.* **1.** The ringing of bells. **2.** A set of bells tuned to each other. **3.** A loud sound or series of sounds <*peals* of laughter> *—v.* To sound in peals : ring.
pea•nut (pē'nŭt', -nət) *n.* **1.** A pealike vine, *Arachis hypogaea*, bearing pods that ripen underground. **2.** The edible nutlike seed of the peanut.
pear (pâr) *n.* **1.** A widely cultivated tree, *Pyrus communis*, bearing white flowers and edible fruit. **2.** The fruit of the pear, spherical at the base and narrow at the stem.
pearl (pûrl) *n.* **1.** A smooth, lustrous, variously colored rounded deposit formed esp. around a grain of sand in the shells of certain mollusks and esteemed as a gem. **2.** Mother-of-pearl. **3.** One that is rare, precious, or fine. **4.** Something resembling a pearl. **5.** A yellowish white. **—pearl'y** *adj.*
peas•ant (pĕz'ənt) *n.* **1.** A member of the class comprising agricultural laborers and small farmers. **2.** An uneducated or ill-bred person. **—peas'ant•ry** *n.*
pea•shoot•er (pē'shōō'tər) *n.* A toy consisting of a small tube through which pellets, esp. dried peas, are blown.
peat (pēt) *n.* Partially carbonized vegetable matter, usu. mosses, obtained in wet ground, as bogs, and used as fertilizer and fuel. **—peat'y** *adj.*
peat moss *n.* **1.** A moss of the genus *Sphagnum*, growing in wet places. **2.** The partly carbonized remains of peat moss, used as a mulch and plant food.
peb•ble (pĕb'əl) *n.* A small, usu. round stone worn smooth by erosion. *—v.* **-bled, -bling.** To produce a rough, crinkled surface on (e.g., leather). **—peb'bly** *adj.*
pe•can (pĭ-kän', -kăn') *n.* A tree, *Carya illinoensis*, of the S U.S. bearing edible nuts.
pec•ca•dil•lo (pĕk'ə-dĭl'ō) *n., pl.* **-loes** or **-los.** A minor fault or offense.
pec•ca•ry (pĕk'ə-rē) *n., pl.* **-ries.** Either of 2 piglike tropical American mammals, *Tayassu tajacu* or *T. pecari*, with long, dark, dense bristles.
peck[1] (pĕk) *v.* **1.** To strike, tap, or pierce with or as if with the beak. **2.** To pick up with or as if with the beak. **3.** To kiss quickly and usu. without enthusiasm. *—n.* **1.** A mark or stroke made by pecking. **2.** A quick, usu. unenthusiastic kiss.
peck[2] (pĕk) *n.* See MEASUREMENT TABLE.
pecking order *n.* **1.** A hierarchic social pattern within poultry flocks in which each member submits to pecking by higher-ranking members and can peck the lower-ranking members without being pecked in return. **2.** A social hierarchy in a human group based on status, authority, etc.
pec•tin (pĕk'tĭn) *n.* Any of various colloidal substances found in ripe fruits and used in making jelly. **—pec'tic** *adj.*
pec•to•ral (pĕk'tər-əl) *adj.* Of or relating to the chest or breast.
pec•u•late (pĕk'yə-lāt') *v.* **-lat•ed, -lat•ing.** To embezzle. **—pec'u•la'tion** *n.*
pe•cu•liar (pĭ-kyōōl'yər) *adj.* **1.** Odd : queer. **2.** Distinctive : typical. **3.** Belonging exclusively to 1 group or person. **—pe•cu'li•ar'i•ty** (-kyōō'lē-ăr'ĭ-tē, -kyōōl-yăr'-) *n.* **—pe•cu'liar•ly** *adv.*
pe•cu•ni•ar•y (pĭ-kyōō'nē-ĕr'ē) *adj.* Of, consisting of, or pertaining to money.
ped•a•gogue *also* **ped•a•gog** (pĕd'ə-gŏg') *n.* A teacher, esp. a schoolteacher.
ped•a•go•gy (pĕd'ə-gō'jē, -gŏj'ē) *n.* The art, profession, or science of teaching. **—ped'a•gog'ic** (-gŏj'ĭk, -gō'jĭk), **ped'a•gog'i•cal** *adj.*
ped•al (pĕd'l) *n.* A lever, as on a musical instrument, that is operated by the foot. *—adj.* Of or pertaining to the foot. *—v.* **-aled, -al•ing** or **-alled, -al•ling. 1.** To operate or use a pedal. **2.** To ride a bicycle.
ped•ant (pĕd'nt) *n.* **1.** Someone, esp. an unimaginative teacher, who emphasizes trivial details of learning. **2.** Someone who makes a great show of learning or scholarship. **—ped'ant•ry** *n.*
pe•dan•tic (pĭ-dăn'tĭk) *adj.* Marked by a narrow, often ostentatious concern for book learning and formal rules. ☆**syns:** ACADEMIC, BOOKISH, DONNISH, FORMALISTIC, SCHOLASTIC **—pe•dan'ti•cal•ly** *adv.*
ped•dle (pĕd'l) *v.* **-dled, -dling.** To offer (goods) for sale while traveling about. **—ped'dler, ped'dlar** *n.*
ped•er•ast (pĕd'ə-răst') *n.* One who engages in anal intercourse, esp. with a boy. **—ped'er•as'ty** *n.*
ped•es•tal (pĕd'ĭ-stəl) *n.* A base or support for an upright structure or part, as a column or statue.
pe•des•tri•an (pĭ-dĕs'trē-ən) *n.* A person who travels on foot. *—adj.* **1.** Traveling on foot. **2.** Commonplace : routine.
pe•di•at•rics (pē'dē-ăt'rĭks) *n. (sing. in number).* The branch of medicine dealing with the diseases and care of infants and children. **—pe'di•at'ric** *adj.* **—pe'di•a•tri'cian** (-ə-trĭsh'ən) *n.*
ped•i•cab (pĕd'ĭ-kăb') *n.* A small 3-wheeled hooded passenger vehicle that is pedaled.
ped•i•cure (pĕd'ĭ-kyŏŏr') *n.* **1.** Care, esp. cosmetic care, of the toenails and feet. **2.** A single treatment of the toenails and feet. **—ped'i•cur'ist** *n.*
ped•i•gree (pĕd'ĭ-grē') *n.* **1.** A line of ancestors : ancestry. **2.** A record of a line of ancestors, as of a purebred animal.
ped•i•ment (pĕd'ə-mənt) *n.* A gablelike triangular decorative or architectural element, as over the door of a building.
pe•dom•e•ter (pĭ-dŏm'ĭ-tər) *n.* An instrument that measures and registers the approx. distance one travels on foot.
pe•dun•cle (pĭ-dŭng'kəl, pē'dŭng'-) *n.* A stalklike supporting structure in some animals and plants.
peek (pēk) *v.* **1.** To look briefly : glance. **2.** To peer or look furtively, as from a hiding place. **—peek** *n.*
peel (pēl) *n.* A rind or skin, esp. of a fruit. *—v.* **1.** To strip the rind, skin, or bark from. **2.** To pull off (an outer covering). **3.** To shed the rind, skin, or bark. **4.** To come off in thin strips or layers. **—peel'er** *n.*
peen (pēn) *n.* The often wedge- or ball-shaped end of a hammerhead opposite the striking surface.
peep[1] (pēp) *v.* To utter a weak, high-pitched sound, as that of a baby bird. *—n.* A weak, high-pitched sound. **—peep'er** *n.*
peep[2] (pēp) *v.* **1.** To look furtively, as through a crack. **2.** To begin to be visible. *—n.* **1.** A quick or furtive look. **2.** The first appearance or glimpse. **—peep'er** *n.*
peep•hole (pēp'hōl') *n.* A hole through which to peep.
peeping Tom *n.* A person who gets pleasure, esp. of a sexual nature, from secretly watching others.
peer[1] (pîr) *v.* **1.** To look searchingly or intently. **2.** To come partially into sight.
peer[2] (pîr) *n.* **1.** One of equal status with another. **2.** A nobleman. **—peer'age** *n.* **—peer'ess** *n.*
peer•less (pîr'lĭs) *adj.* Without equal : matchless. **—peer'less•ly** *adv.*
peeve (pēv) *v.* **peeved, peev•ing.** To cause to feel resentment : vex. *—n.* **1.** A grievance : vexation. **2.** A resentful mood or feeling.
pee•vish (pē'vĭsh) *adj.* Irritable in mood or disposition : petulant. **—pee'vish•ly** *adv.* **—pee'vish•ness** *n.*
pee•wee (pē'wē) *n.* One that is unusually small.
peg (pĕg) *n.* **1.** A small, pointed cylindrical piece, as of wood, used to fasten or pin things down or to fit a hole. **2.** A projecting piece similar to a peg used to mark a boundary or to act as a support. **3.** A degree : step. **4.** A throw, as of a ball. **5.** Something used as a reason, pretext, or occasion. *—v.* **pegged, peg•ging. 1.** To insert a peg into. **2.** To mark with pegs. **3.** To fix (e.g., a price) at a set level. **4.** *Informal.* To categorize. **5.** To throw. **6.** To work with diligence <*pegging* away at the job>
peg•ma•tite (pĕg'mə-tīt') *n.* A coarse-grained granite.
P.E.I. *abbr.* Prince Edward Island.
pei•gnoir (pān-wär', pĕn-) *n.* A woman's dressing gown : negligee.

pe·jo·ra·tive (pĭ-jôr′ə-tĭv, -jŏr-, pĕj′ə-rā′tĭv) *adj.* Tending to make or become worse : derogatory.
Pe·king (pē′kĭng′, bā′jĭng′). Beijing.
Pe·king·ese *also* **Pe·kin·ese** (pē′kĭ-nēz′, -nēs′) *n.* A small, short-legged, flat-nosed, long-haired dog orig. bred in China.
pe·koe (pē′kō) *n.* A black tea made from small leaves.
pel·age (pĕl′ĭj) *n.* The hairy or furry covering of a mammal.
pe·lag·ic (pə-lăj′ĭk) *adj.* Of or relating to the open ocean.
pelf (pĕlf) *n.* Wealth : money.
pel·i·can (pĕl′ĭ-kən) *n.* A large tropical or semitropical web-footed bird of the genus *Pelecanus,* with a large pouch under the lower bill in which it catches and holds fish.
pel·lag·ra (pə-lăg′rə, -lā′grə) *n.* A chronic disease caused by a lack of niacin and characterized by skin eruptions and digestive and nervous disorders. **–pel·lag′rous** *adj.*
pel·let (pĕl′ĭt) *n.* **1.** A small mass or ball, as of medicine. **2. a.** A bullet. **b.** A piece of small shot.
pell-mell *also* **pell·mell** (pĕl′mĕl′) *adv.* **1.** In jumbled confusion. **2.** In disordered haste : headlong.
pel·lu·cid (pə-lo͞o′sĭd) *adj.* Very clear : transparent. **–pel·lu′cid·ly** *adv.*
Pel·o·pon·ne·sus (pĕl′ə-pə-nē′səs). Peninsula forming the S part of Greece. **–Pel′o·pon·ne′sian** *adj.* & *n.*
pelt¹ (pĕlt) *n.* The skin of an animal, esp. with the fur on it.
pelt² (pĕlt) *v.* To strike with a series of missiles or blows.
pel·vis (pĕl′vĭs) *n., pl.* **-vis·es** *or* **-ves** (-vēz′). A basin-shaped structure of the vertebrate skeleton that rests on the lower limbs and supports the spinal column. **–pel′vic** *adj.*
pem·mi·can *also* **pem·i·can** (pĕm′ĭ-kən) *n.* Dried meat that is pounded into paste and mixed with fat.
pen¹ (pĕn) *n.* An instrument, often with a metal point and a supply of ink, used for writing. *–v.* **penned, pen·ning.** To write, esp. with a pen.
pen² (pĕn) *n.* A usu. small enclosure, esp. for animals. *–v.* **penned, pen·ning.** To confine in a pen : enclose.
pen³ (pĕn) *n. Slang.* A penitentiary.
pe·nal (pē′nəl) *adj.* Of or relating to punishment, as for infractions of the law.
pe·nal·ize (pē′nə-līz′, pĕn′ə-) *v.* **-ized, -iz·ing.** To impose a penalty on.
pen·al·ty (pĕn′əl-tē) *n., pl.* **-ties. 1.** A punishment for an offense or crime. **2.** Something that is forfeited when a person fails to meet the terms of an agreement. **3.** A handicap, loss, or disadvantage that results from an action.
pen·ance (pĕn′əns) *n.* **1.** A voluntary act of devotion or self-mortification to show sorrow for a sin or misdeed. **2.** *Eccles.* A sacrament that consists of contrition, confession, acceptance of punishment imposed by the confessor, and absolution.
Pe·na·tes (pĭ-nā′tēz′) *pl.n.* The Roman household gods.
pence (pĕns) *n. esp. Brit. var. pl. of* PENNY.
pen·chant (pĕn′chənt) *n.* A strong and continuous leaning : liking.
pen·cil (pĕn′səl) *n.* **1.** A writing or drawing implement that consists of or contains a thin stick of a marking substance, esp. graphite. **2.** Something resembling a pencil <an eyebrow *pencil*> *–v.* **-ciled, -cil·ing** *or* **-cilled, -cil·ling.** To write, mark, or draw with a pencil.
pen·dant *also* **pen·dent** (pĕn′dənt) *n.* A suspended ornament, as one hanging on a necklace. *–adj. var. of* PENDENT.
pen·dent *also* **pen·dant** (pĕn′dənt) *adj.* Hanging down. *–n. var. of* PENDANT
pend·ing (pĕn′dĭng) *adj.* **1.** Not yet settled or decided. **2.** Impending. *–prep.* **1.** During. **2.** While awaiting : until.
pen·du·lous (pĕn′jə-ləs, pĕnd′yə-) *adj.* Hanging downward loosely : drooping.
pen·du·lum (pĕn′jə-ləm, pĕnd′yə-) *n.* An object hung from a fixed support so that it can swing freely back and forth.
pe·ne·plain *also* **pe·ne·plane** (pē′nə-plān′) *n.* A large, nearly flat eroded land surface.
pen·e·trate (pĕn′ĭ-trāt′) *v.* **-trat·ed, -trat·ing. 1.** To force a way into : pierce. **2.** To permeate. **3.** To grasp the meaning or significance of : understand. **4.** To move profoundly. ☆**syns:** PERFORATE, PIERCE, PUNCTURE **–pen′e·tra·ble** (-trə-bəl) *adj.* **–pen′e·tra′tion** *n.*
pen·e·trat·ing (pĕn′ĭ-trā′tĭng) *adj.* **1.** Having the ability to enter, pierce, or permeate <a *penetrating* scream><*penetrating* cold> **2.** Quick to perceive : discerning <a *penetrating* mind>
pen·guin (pĕng′gwĭn) *n.* Any of various flightless marine birds of the family Spheniscidae, of the S Hemisphere, with webbed feet and flipperlike wings.
pen·i·cil·lin (pĕn′ĭ-sĭl′ĭn) *n.* An antibiotic compound derived from a mold and used to prevent or treat various diseases and infections.
pen·in·su·la (pə-nĭn′sə-lə, -nĭns′yə-) *n.* A long, narrow piece of land that projects into water from a larger land mass. **–pen·in′su·lar** *adj.*
pe·nis (pē′nĭs) *n., pl.* **-nis·es** *or* **-nes** (-nēz′). The male organ of copulation in higher vertebrates and usu. of urination in mammals.
pen·i·tent (pĕn′ĭ-tənt) *adj.* Feeling a sense of sorrow and remorse for sins or misdeeds : repentant. *–n.* Someone who is penitent. **–pen′i·tence** *n.* **–pen′i·ten′tial** (-tĕn′shəl) *adj.*
pen·i·ten·tia·ry (pĕn′ĭ-tĕn′shə-rē) *n., pl.* **-ries.** A federal or state prison for those convicted of serious crimes. *–adj.* Resulting in or punishable by imprisonment in a penitentiary.
pen·knife (pĕn′nīf′) *n.* A small pocketknife.
pen·light (pĕn′līt′) *n.* A flashlight of approx. the size and shape of a fountain pen.
pen·man (pĕn′mən) *n.* **1.** A scribe. **2.** Someone with skill in penmanship. **3.** An author.
pen·man·ship (pĕn′mən-shĭp′) *n.* The art, style, skill, or manner of handwriting.
Penn. *abbr.* Pennsylvania.
pen name *also* **pen·name** (pĕn′nām′) *n.* A pseudonym assumed by an author.
pen·nant (pĕn′ənt) *n.* **1.** A long, tapering nautical flag used for signaling or identification. **2.** A flag that resembles a pennant. **3.** A flag that symbolizes a championship.
pen·ni (pĕn′ē) *n., pl.* **pen·nis** *or* **pen·ni·a** (-ē-ə). See *markka* at CURRENCY TABLE.
pen·ni·less (pĕn′ĭ-lĭs) *adj.* Completely without money.
pen·non (pĕn′ən) *n.* **1.** A banner, esp. a long, narrow flag borne on a lance. **2.** A bird's wing : pinion.
Penn·syl·va·nia (pĕn′səl-vān′yə, -vā′nē-ə). State of the E U.S. *Cap.* Harrisburg. *Pop.* 11,866,728. **–Penn′syl·va′nian** *n.*
pen·ny (pĕn′ē) *n., pl.* **pen·nies** *or* **pence** (pĕns). **1.** See *pound* at CURRENCY TABLE. **2.** A U.S. or Canadian coin worth 1 cent.
penny pincher *n. Informal.* A stingy person : miser. **–pen′ny-pinch′** *v.*
pen·ny·roy·al (pĕn′ē-roi′əl) *n.* A mint, *Mentha pulegium,* with aromatic hairy leaves and small bluish flowers.
pen·ny·weight (pĕn′ē-wāt′) *n.* A unit of troy weight equal to 24 gr, $\frac{1}{20}$ of a troy oz., or approx. 1.555 g.
pen·ny-wise (pĕn′ē-wīz′) *adj.* Wise only in dealing with small matters.
pe·nol·o·gy (pē-nŏl′ə-jē) *n.* The theory and practice of criminal rehabilitation and prison management. **–pe·nol′o·gist** *n.*
pen·sion (pĕn′shən) *n.* An amount of money paid regularly, esp. to a person who has retired. *–v.* To pay or grant a pension to. **–pen′sion·er** *n.*
pen·sive (pĕn′sĭv) *adj.* Deeply thoughtful, often in a melancholy or musing way : reflective. **–pen′sive·ly** *adv.* **–pen′sive·ness** *n.*
pent (pĕnt) *adj.* Closed or shut up.
pen·ta·gon (pĕn′tə-gŏn′) *n.* A polygon having 5 sides and 5 interior angles. **–pen·tag′o·nal** (-tăg′ə-nəl) *adj.*
pen·tam·e·ter (pĕn-tăm′ĭ-tər) *n.* A line of verse that consists of 5 metrical feet.
pen·tath·lon (pĕn-tăth′lən, -lŏn′) *n.* An athletic contest consisting of 5 events for each participant.
Pen·te·cost (pĕn′tĭ-kôst′, -kŏst′) *n.* The 7th Sunday after Easter, celebrated as a Christian festival in commemoration of the descent of the Holy Ghost on the disciples. **–Pen′te·cos′tal** *adj.*
pent·house (pĕnt′hous′) *n.* A dwelling, esp. an apartment, built on the roof of a building.
pent-up (pĕnt′ŭp′) *adj.* Not given expression : repressed <*pent-up* grief>
pe·nul·ti·mate (pĭ-nŭl′tə-mĭt) *adj.* Next to last. **–pe·nul′ti·mate** *n.*
pe·num·bra (pĭ-nŭm′brə) *n., pl.* **-brae** (-brē) *or* **-bras.** A partial shadow, as in an eclipse, between regions of complete shadow and complete illumination.
pe·nu·ri·ous (pĭ-no͝or′ē-əs, -nyo͝or′-) *adj.* **1.** Stingy : miserly. **2.** Characterized by penury : extremely poor.
pen·u·ry (pĕn′yə-rē) *n.* Extreme poverty.
pe·on (pē′ŏn′) *n.* **1.** An unskilled agricultural laborer of Latin America. **2.** A person held in servitude to a creditor until an indebtedness is satisfied. **–pe′on·age** *n.*
pe·o·ny (pē′ə-nē) *n., pl.* **-nies.** A plant of the genus *Paeonia,* cultivated for its large, fragrant pink, red, or white flowers.
peo·ple (pē′pəl) *n., pl.* **people. 1.** Human beings <*People* laughed at him.> **2. a.** The body of persons living under 1 government in the same country : nationality <the French *people*> **b.** Enfranchised citizens : electorate. **3.** *pl.* **peoples.** A group of persons, often related, who share a common culture, language, or inherited condition of life. **4.** The mass of ordinary persons : populace <the *people* asserting their rights> **5.** Persons who constitute a group united by a common interest <sci-

entific *people*> —*v.* **-pled, -pling.** To fill or furnish with people : populate.

pep (pĕp) *Informal.* —*n.* Energy : vigor. —*v.* **pepped, pep·ping.** To imbue with pep : invigorate. **—pep'py** *adj.*

pep·per (pĕp'ər) *n.* **1. a.** A tropical Asian vine, *Piper nigrum,* bearing small berrylike fruit. **b.** The dried fruit of the pepper used to make a pungent condiment. **2.** A bushy plant, *Capsicum frutescens* or *C. annuum,* related to the pepper and cultivated for its mild or pungent fruit, used as a vegetable or condiment. —*v.* **1.** To season or sprinkle with pepper. **2.** To sprinkle liberally <dark hair *peppered* with silver> **3.** To pelt with or as if with small missiles.

pep·per·corn (pĕp'ər-kôrn') *n.* A dried berry of the pepper vine, *Piper nigrum.*

pep·per·mint (pĕp'ər-mĭnt') *n.* **1.** A plant, *Mentha piperita,* having downy leaves that yield a pungent aromatic oil. **2.** A candy flavored with peppermint oil.

pep·per·y (pĕp'ə-rē) *adj.* **1.** Of, resembling, or containing pepper : hot and pungent. **2.** Hot-tempered. **3.** Fiery : scathing <a *peppery* temper>

pep·sin (pĕp'sĭn) *n.* **1.** An enzyme produced in the stomach that acts as a catalyst in the digestion of proteins. **2.** A digestive aid that contains pepsin.

pep·tic (pĕp'tĭk) *adj.* **1.** Pertaining to or aiding digestion. **2.** Caused by or pertaining to the action of digestive secretions.

Pé·quiste (pā-kēst') *n. Can.* A member or supporter of the Parti Québecois.

per (pûr) *prep.* **1.** By the agency of. **2.** For, to, or by each. **3.** According to.

per·ad·ven·ture (pûr'əd-vĕn'chər) *adv. Archaic.* Perhaps : perchance. —*n.* Chance or uncertainty : doubt.

per·am·bu·late (pə-răm'byə-lāt') *v.* **-lat·ed, -lat·ing.** To walk around : stroll. **—per·am'bu·la'tion** *n.*

per·am·bu·la·tor (pə-răm'byə-lā'tər) *n. esp. Brit.* A baby carriage.

per an·num (pər ăn'əm) *adv.* By, for, or in each year : annually.

per·cale (pər-kāl') *n.* A fine, closely woven cotton fabric.

per cap·i·ta (pər kăp'ĭ-tə) *adv. & adj.* Of, by, or for each individual.

per·ceive (pər-sēv') *v.* **-ceived, -ceiv·ing. 1.** To become aware of directly by the senses, esp. to see or hear. **2.** To achieve understanding or awareness of. **—per·ceiv'a·ble** *adj.* **—per·ceiv'a·bly** *adv.*

per cent *also* **per·cent** (pər-sĕnt') —*adv.* Out of each hundred : per hundred. —*n.* **1.** One part in a hundred. **2.** A percentage.

per·cent·age (pər-sĕn'tĭj) *n.* **1.** A fraction or ratio with 100 as its denominator. **2.** A share or proportion in relation to a whole : part. **3.** Probability : odds. **4.** *Informal.* Profit : advantage.

per·cen·tile (pər-sĕn'tīl') *n.* A number that divides the range of a set of data so that a given percentage lies below it.

per·cept (pûr'sĕpt') *n.* A mental impression of something perceived by the senses together with comprehension of what it is.

per·cep·ti·ble (pər-sĕp'tə-bəl) *adj.* Capable of being perceived. **—per·cep'ti·bil'i·ty** *n.* **—per·cep'ti·bly** *adv.*

per·cep·tion (pər-sĕp'shən) *n.* **1.** The act, process, or result of perceiving. **2.** The ability to perceive : understanding or insight.

per·cep·tive (pər-sĕp'tĭv) *adj.* **1.** Of or relating to perception. **2.a.** Having perception. **b.** Marked by perception : discerning. **—per·cep'tive·ly** *adv.*

per·cep·tu·al (pər-sĕp'cho͞o-əl) *adj.* Of, relating to, involving, or based on perception. **—per·cep'tu·al·ly** *adv.*

perch[1] (pûrch) *n.* **1.** Something, as a rod, that serves as a roost for a bird. **2.** A place where one can sit or rest : seat. —*v.* To alight or rest on or as if on a perch.

perch[2] (pûrch) *n., pl.* **perch** or **perch·es. 1.** Either of 2 freshwater food fishes, *Perca flavescens* or *P. fluviatilis.* **2.** Any of various fishes related or similar to the perch.

per·chance (pər-chăns') *adv.* Maybe : perhaps.

per·cip·i·ent (pər-sĭp'ē-ənt) *adj.* Capable of perceiving, esp. perceiving readily and keenly. **—per·cip'i·ence** *n.*

per·co·late (pûr'kə-lāt') *v.* **-lat·ed, -lat·ing. 1.** To filter or trickle through a porous substance. **2.** To force boiling water through (ground coffee) in order to draw out the essence. **—per'co·la'tion** *n.* **—per'co·la'tor** *n.*

per con·tra (pər kŏn'trə) *adv.* **1.** To the contrary. **2.** By way of contrast.

per·cus·sion (pər-kŭsh'ən) *n.* **1. a.** The hitting together of 2 bodies, esp. when noise is created. **b.** A vibration or impact caused by percussion. **2.** Detonation of a cap in a firearm. **3. a.** A musical instrument sounded by striking, as a drum. **b.** Percussion instruments as a group. **—per·cus'sion·ist** *n.*

per di·em (pər dē'əm) *adv.* For or by the day. —*n.* A daily fee or allowance.

per·di·tion (pər-dĭsh'ən) *n.* **1.** Everlasting damnation. **2.** Hell.

per·du·ra·ble (pər-do͝or'ə-bəl, -dyo͝or'-) *adj.* Extremely durable. **—per·du'ra·bil'i·ty** *n.* **—per·du'ra·bly** *adv.*

per·e·gri·nate (pĕr'ə-grə-nāt') *v.* **-nat·ed, -nat·ing.** To travel around from place to place. **—per'e·gri·na'tion** *n.*

per·e·grine falcon (pĕr'ĭ-grĭn, -grēn') *n.* A widely distributed bird of prey, *Falco peregrinus,* once much used in falconry.

per·emp·to·ry (pə-rĕmp'tə-rē) *adj.* **1.** Terminating all debate or action <a *peremptory* decree> **2.** Admitting no refusal or contradiction : imperative. **3.** Expressing or of the nature of a command. **4.** Self-assured, sometimes excessively so : self-confident. **—per·emp'to·ri·ly** *adv.*

per·en·ni·al (pə-rĕn'ē-əl) *adj.* **1.** Lasting from year to year. **2.** Lasting indefinitely : perpetual. **3.** Recurring again and again. —*n.* A plant that lives for several or many years. **—per·en'ni·al·ly** *adv.*

per·fect (pûr'fĭkt) *adj.* **1.** Lacking in no essential : complete. **2.** Being without defect or fault : flawless. **3.** Exact : accurate. **4.** Absolute : utter <a *perfect* fool> **5.** Of, relating to, or constituting a verb form that expresses action completed before a fixed point of reference in time. ☆**syns:** CONSUMMATE, FAULTLESS, FLAWLESS, IMPECCABLE —*n.* **1.** The perfect tense. **2.** A verb or verb form in the perfect tense. —*v.* (pər-fĕkt'). To make perfect. **—per'fect·ly** *adv.* **—per'fect·ness** *n.*

per·fect·i·ble (pər-fĕk'tə-bəl) *adj.* Capable of making progress toward or achieving perfection. **—per·fect'i·bil'i·ty** *n.*

per·fec·tion (pər-fĕk'shən) *n.* **1.** The state or quality of being perfect. **2.** The process or act of perfecting. **3.** A perfect example of excellence.

per·fec·tion·ism (pər-fĕk'shə-nĭz'əm) *n.* A tendency to be dissatisfied with anything less than perfection. **—per·fec'tion·ist** *n.*

per·fec·to (pər-fĕk'tō) *n., pl.* **-tos.** A cigar that is thick in the center and tapers at each end.

per·fi·dy (pûr'fĭ-dē) *n.* Breach of loyalty or faith : treachery. **—per·fid'i·ous** (pər-fĭd'ē-əs) *adj.* **—per·fid'i·ous·ly** *adv.*

per·fo·rate (pûr'fə-rāt') *v.* **-rat·ed, -rat·ing. 1.** To bore or punch a hole in : pierce. **2.** To make rows of holes in for easy separation. **—per'fo·ra'tion** *n.*

per·force (pər-fôrs', -fōrs') *adv.* By force of necessity.

per·form (pər-fôrm') *v.* **1.** To begin and carry out : accomplish. **2.** To fulfill. **3.** To function in a certain way : act. **4.** To give a performance (of). **—per·form'er** *n.*

per·form·ance (pər-fôr'məns) *n.* **1.** The act, process, or manner of performing. **2.** A presentation, as of a musical work, before the public. **3.** An accomplishment : deed.

per·fume (pûr'fyo͞om', pər-fyo͞om') *n.* **1.** A fragrant substance, esp. a liquid, as one distilled from flowers. **2.** A usu. pleasing scent : odor. —*v.* (pər-fyo͞om') **-fumed, -fum·ing.** To fill with or as if with perfume : scent.

per·fum·er·y (pər-fyo͞o'mə-rē) *n., pl.* **-ies. 1.** Perfumes in general. **2.** An establishment at which perfumes are made or sold.

per·func·to·ry (pər-fŭngk'tə-rē) *adj.* Done merely as a matter of routine and with little care or interest. **—per·func'to·ri·ly** *adv.* **—per·func'to·ri·ness** *n.*

per·go·la (pûr'gə-lə) *n.* A structure, as an arbor, with a roof of trelliswork.

per·haps (pər-hăps') *adv.* Maybe but not surely : possibly.

Per·i·cles (pĕr'ə-klēz'). 495?–429 B.C. Athenian statesman.

per·i·gee (pĕr'ə-jē') *n.* The point in the orbit of a satellite of the earth at which it is closest to the earth.

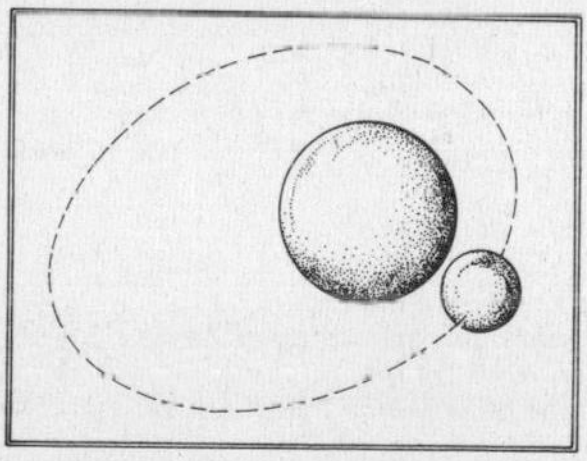

perigee

per·i·he·lion (pĕr'ə-hēl'yən) *n., pl.* **-lia** (-yə). The point in the orbit of a celestial body, as a planet, at which it is closest to the sun.

per·il (pĕr'əl) *n.* **1.** Danger. **2.** Something that is a source of danger. **—per'il·ous** *adj.* **—per'il·ous·ly** *adv.*

pe·rim·e·ter (pə-rĭm'ĭ-tər) *n.* The outer limits or boundary of an area.

pe·ri·od (pîr'ē-əd) *n.* **1. a.** An interval of time. **b.** An interval of time regarded as a phase in development : stage. **2.** An arbitrary temporal unit, as of an academic day. **3.** An occurrence or instance of menstruation. **4.** A point in time at which something ends : completion. **5. a.** The full stop at the end of a sentence. **b.** A punctuation mark (.) used to indicate the end of a sentence or an abbreviation. *—adj.* Of, pertaining to, or representing a particular historical period <a *period* stage setting>

pe·ri·od·ic (pîr′ē-ŏd′ĭk) *adj.* **1.** Having or marked by repeated cycles. **2.** Occurring or appearing at regular intervals. **3.** Happening now and then. **—pe′ri·od′i·cal·ly** *adv.* **—pe′ri·o·dic′i·ty** (-ə-dĭs′ĭ-tē) *n.*

pe·ri·od·i·cal (pîr′ē-ŏd′ĭ-kəl) *adj.* **1.** Periodic. **2. a.** Published at fixed intervals, usu. of more than 1 day. **b.** Of or pertaining to a publication issued at such intervals. *—n.* A periodical publication.

per·i·o·don·tal (pĕr′ē-ō-dŏn′tl) *adj.* Of or constituting tissue and structures that surround and support the teeth. **—per′i·o·don′tal·ly** *adv.* **—per′i·o·don′tist** *n.*

per·i·pa·tet·ic (pĕr′ə-pə-tĕt′ĭk) *adj.* Of, relating to, or carried on while walking or moving around.

pe·riph·er·y (pə-rĭf′ə-rē) *n., pl.* **-ies. 1.** The outermost part within a boundary. **2.** A region just beyond a boundary. **3.** An outer boundary. **—pe·riph′er·al** *adj.*

pe·riph·ra·sis (pə-rĭf′rə-sĭs) *n., pl.* **-ses** (-sēz′). **1.** The use of circumlocution. **2.** A roundabout expression.

per·i·scope (pĕr′ĭ-skōp′) *n.* An optical instrument that permits observation of objects from a position not in a direct line of sight. **—per′i·scop′ic** (-skŏp′ĭk) *adj.*

per·ish (pĕr′ĭsh) *v.* To become ruined, spoiled, or destroyed : die.

per·ish·a·ble (pĕr′ĭ-shə-bəl) *adj.* Apt to spoil or decay easily. *—n.* Something, esp. food, that is perishable.

per·i·stal·sis (pĕr′ĭ-stôl′sĭs, -stăl′-) *n.* Wavelike muscular contractions of the alimentary canal that propel material contained in it onward. **—per′i·stal′tic** (-stôl′tĭk, -stăl′-) *adj.*

per·i·style (pĕr′ĭ-stīl′) *n.* A tier of columns enclosing a court or surrounding a building.

per·i·to·ne·um (pĕr′ĭ-tə-nē′əm) *n., pl.* **-ne·a** (-nē′ə). The membrane that lines the walls of the abdominal cavity and encloses the viscera. **—per′i·to·ne′al** *adj.*

per·i·to·ni·tis (pĕr′ĭ-tə-nī′tĭs) *n.* Inflammation of the peritoneum.

per·i·wig (pĕr′ĭ-wĭg′) *n.* A wig.

▲word history: For more than a cent. (approx. 1660–1780) decorative heads of false hair were almost universally worn by fashionable men and women in Europe. In English such headdresses were called *perukes* or *periwigs.* Both words are derived from Italian *perruca,* which orig. meant "bushy head of hair" and later "wig." *Perruca* was borrowed into French as *perruque,* which developed into 2 forms in English: *peruke* and *periwig,* which are synonymous. *Periwig* was shortened to *wig,* which is the form now in common use.

per·i·win·kle[1] (pĕr′ĭ-wĭng′kəl) *n.* Any of several small edible marine snails, esp. of the genus *Littorina,* with thick cone-shaped shells.

per·i·win·kle[2] (pĕr′ĭ-wĭng′kəl) *n.* A trailing evergreen plant of the genus *Vinca,* esp. *V. minor,* bearing blue flowers.

per·jure (pûr′jər) *v.* **-jured, -jur·ing.** To give false or misleading testimony while under oath. **—per′ju·ry** *n.*

perk[1] (pûrk) *v.* To raise (e.g., the head) pertly. **—perk up. 1.** To regain or cause to regain liveliness or spirit. **2.** To make spruce or trim in appearance : smarten. **—perk′i·ness** *n.* **—perk′y** *adj.*

perk[2] (pûrk) *n. Informal.* A perquisite.

perk[3] (pûrk) *v. Informal.* To percolate.

per·lite (pûr′līt′) *n.* A natural volcanic glass that in a heat-expanded form is used in plaster and concrete and in thermal and acoustic insulation.

perm (pûrm) *n. Informal.* A permanent.

per·ma·frost (pûr′mə-frôst′, -frŏst′) *n.* Permanently frozen subsoil occurring in perennially frigid areas.

per·ma·nent (pûr′mə-nənt) *adj.* Lasting indefinitely : enduring. *—n.* A long-lasting hair wave that is produced by the application of chemicals. **—per′ma·nence, per′ma·nen·cy** *n.* **—per′ma·nent·ly** *adv.*

permanent magnet *n.* A material that retains induced magnetic properties after it is removed from a magnetic field.

permanent press *n.* Durable press.

permanent wave *n.* A permanent.

per·me·a·ble (pûr′mē-ə-bəl) *adj.* Capable of being permeated : penetrable. **—per′me·a·bil′i·ty** *n.* **—per′me·a·bly** *adv.*

per·me·ate (pûr′mē-āt′) *v.* **-at·ed, -at·ing. 1.** To flow or spread through : pervade. **2.** To pass through the openings or pores of. **—per′me·a′tion** *n.*

per·mis·si·ble (pər-mĭs′ə-bəl) *adj.* Admissible : allowable.

per·mis·sion (pər-mĭsh′ən) *n.* Consent, esp. official or formal consent.

per·mis·sive (pər-mĭs′ĭv) *adj.* **1.** Giving permission. **2.** Lenient, often excessively so : indulgent. **—per·mis′sive·ly** *adv.* **—per·mis′sive·ness** *n.*

per·mit (pər-mĭt′) *v.* **-mit·ted, -mit·ting. 1.** To give consent to or for : allow. **2.** To give an opportunity (to). *—n.* (pûr′mĭt′, pər-mĭt′). A document giving permission : license. **—per·mit′ter** *n.*

per·mu·ta·tion (pûr′myo͞o-tā′shən) *n.* **1.** A complete change : transformation. **2.** *Math.* Any of the ordered subsets that can be formed from the elements of a set. **—per′mu·ta′tion·al** *adj.*

per·ni·cious (pər-nĭsh′əs) *adj.* Very harmful or destructive. **—per·ni′cious·ly** *adv.* **—per·ni′cious·ness** *n.*

per·o·ra·tion (pĕr′ə-rā′shən) *n.* The usu. formal concluding part of a speech.

per·ox·ide (pə-rŏk′sīd′) *n.* **1.** Hydrogen peroxide. **2.** An oxygen-containing compound that yields hydrogen peroxide when treated with an acid. *—v.* **-id·ed, -id·ing. 1.** To treat with peroxide. **2.** To bleach (hair) with hydrogen peroxide.

per·pen·dic·u·lar (pûr′pən-dĭk′yə-lər) *adj.* **1.** Forming or intersecting at right angles. **2.** Being at right angles to the plane of the horizon : vertical. **—per′pen·dic′u·lar** *n.* **—per′pen·dic′u·lar′i·ty** (-lăr′ĭ-tē) *n.* **—per′pen·dic′u·lar·ly** *adv.*

per·pe·trate (pûr′pĭ-trāt′) *v.* **-trat·ed, -trat·ing.** To be culpable of : commit. **—per′pe·tra′tion** *n.* **—per′pe·tra′tor** *n.*

per·pet·u·al (pər-pĕch′o͞o-əl) *adj.* **1.** Lasting forever : unceasing. **2.** Continuing without or almost without interruption : constant. **—per·pet′u·al·ly** *adv.*

per·pet·u·ate (pər-pĕch′o͞o-āt′) *v.* **-at·ed, -at·ing.** To cause to be perpetual : keep from dying out. **—per·pet′u·a′tion** *n.*

per·pe·tu·i·ty (pûr′pĭ-to͞o′ĭ-tē, -tyo͞o′-) *n., pl.* **-ties. 1.** The state or quality of being perpetual. **2.** Everlasting time : eternity.

per·plex (pər-plĕks′) *v.* To confuse : bewilder. **—per·plex′ed·ly** (-plĕk′sĭd-lē) *adv.* **—per·plex′i·ty** (-plĕk′sĭ-tē) *n.*

per·qui·site (pûr′kwĭ-zĭt) *n.* Something, as a payment or privilege, received in addition to a regular wage or salary.

per se (pər sā′) *adv.* Of, in, or by itself.

per·se·cute (pûr′sĭ-kyo͞ot′) *v.* **-cut·ed, -cut·ing.** To harass in a way that causes suffering, esp. because of principles or religious belief : oppress. **—per′se·cu′tion** *n.* **—per′se·cu′tor** *n.*

per·se·vere (pûr′sə-vîr′) *v.* **-vered, -ver·ing.** To persist in an idea, purpose, or task despite obstacles. **—per′se·ver′ance** *n.* **—per′se·ver′ing·ly** *adv.*

Per·sia (pûr′zhə). Iran. **—Per′sian** (-zhən) *adj.* & *n.*

Persian cat *n.* A stocky domestic cat with long silky fur.

Persian Gulf. Arm of the Arabian Sea between Arabia and SW Iran.

Persian lamb *n.* The tightly curled, glossy fur of a young karakul lamb.

per·si·flage (pûr′sə-fläzh′) *n.* Light, frivolous, or jesting talk.

per·sim·mon (pər-sĭm′ən) *n.* A tree of the genus *Diospyros,* with hard wood and edible orange-red fruit.

per·sist (pər-sĭst′) *v.* **1.** To continue firmly and steadfastly despite obstacles. **2.** To continue in existence : endure. **—per·sist′ence, per·sist′en·cy** *n.* **—per·sist′ent** *adj.* **—per·sist′ent·ly** *adv.*

per·snick·e·ty (pər-snĭk′ĭ-tē) *adj.* Very fastidious : meticulous.

per·son (pûr′sən) *n.* **1.** A human being. **2.** The physical body of a human being. **3.** The personality of a human being : self. **4.** Reference, as indicated by any of 3 groups of pronouns, to the speaker, the individual addressed, and the individual spoken of.

per·so·na (pər-sō′nə) *n., pl.* **-nae** (-nē). A character in a literary or dramatic work.

per·son·a·ble (pûr′sə-nə-bəl) *adj.* Pleasing in personality : appealing.

per·son·age (pûr′sə-nĭj) *n.* A person of distinction or rank.

per·son·al (pûr′sə-nəl) *adj.* **1.** Of or pertaining to a person : private. **2.** Made or done in person <a *personal* appeal> **3.** Of or relating to the body or physical being <*personal* cleanliness> **4.** Pertaining to an individual, esp. in an objectionable way <disapproves of *personal* remarks> **5.** *Law.* Of or pertaining to movable property <*personal* belongings> **6.** Indicating grammatical person. *—n.* A usu. short item or notice in a newspaper that concerns a person or group or personal affairs. **—per′son·al·ly** *adv.*

per·son·al·i·ty (pûr′sə-năl′ĭ-tē) *n., pl.* **-ties. 1.** The distinctive qualities and traits of an individual. **2. a.** Social and personal traits that make a person appealing. **b.** A person having such traits. **3.** *Informal.* A famous person : celebrity. **4.** An objectionably personal remark <refused to engage in *personalities*>

per•son•al•ize (pûr′sə-nə-līz′) *v.* **-ized, -iz•ing.** To make personal, esp. by marking with one's name or initials.

per•son•al•ty (pûr′sə-nəl-tē) *n., pl.* **-ties.** *Law.* Personal property.

per•so•na non gra•ta (pər-sō′nə nŏn grä′tə, grăt′ə) *n.* One who is unwelcome or unacceptable, esp. to a foreign government.

per•son•i•fy (pər-sŏn′ə-fī′) *v.* **-fied, -fy•ing. 1.** To represent or think of (e.g., an inanimate object) as having human qualities or form. **2.** To be the embodiment of. **—per•son′i•fi•ca′tion** *n.*

per•son•nel (pûr′sə-nĕl′) *n.* The body of persons active in or employed by an organization, business, or service.

per•spec•tive (pər-spĕk′tĭv) *n.* **1.** A drawing or painting technique in which objects represented seem to have distance and depth. **2.** A mental view of the relationship of aspects of a subject to each other and to a whole. **3.** An idea of the relative importance of things.

per•spi•cac•i•ty (pûr′spĭ-kăs′ĭ-tē) *n.* Acuteness of understanding or mental perception. **—per′spi•ca′cious** (-kā′shəs) *adj.* **—per′spi•ca′cious•ly** *adv.*

per•spic•u•ous (pər-spĭk′yo͞o-əs) *adj.* Capable of being easily understood : plain and clear. **—per′spi•cu′i•ty** (pûr′spĭ-kyo͞o′ĭ-tē) *n.* **—per•spic′u•ous•ly** *adv.*

per•spi•ra•tion (pûr′spə-rā′shən) *n.* **1.** The salty moisture secreted by the sweat glands : sweat. **2.** The act of perspiring.

per•spire (pər-spīr′) *v.* **-spired, -spir•ing.** To excrete perspiration.

per•suade (pər-swād′) *v.* **-suad•ed, -suad•ing.** To cause to do or believe by means of reasoning, argument, or entreaty. **—per•suad′er** *n.* **—per•sua′sive** *adj.* **—per•sua′sive•ness** *n.*

per•sua•sion (pər-swā′zhən) *n.* **1.** The act or process of persuading or state of being persuaded. **2.** Belief, esp. religious belief.

pert (pûrt) *adj.* **1.** Impudently forward : saucy. **2.** High-spirited : lively. **3.** Trim and stylish : jaunty. **—pert′ly** *adv.*

per•tain (pər-tān′) *v.* **1.** To refer : relate. **2.** To belong as a feature, adjunct, part, or accessory.

per•ti•na•cious (pûr′tn-ā′shəs) *adj.* **1.** Adhering firmly to a belief, purpose, or opinion. **2.** Stubbornly persistent : tenacious. **—per′ti•na′cious•ly** *adv.* **—per′ti•nac′i•ty** (-ăs′ĭ-tē) *n.*

per•ti•nent (pûr′tn-ənt) *adj.* Relating to the matter being discussed or considered : relevant <a *pertinent* comment> **—per′ti•nence, per′ti•nen•cy** *n.*

per•turb (pər-tûrb′) *v.* To make anxious or uneasy : disquiet greatly. **—per′tur•ba′tion** (pûr′tər-bā′shən) *n.*

Pe•ru (pə-ro͞o′). Country of W South America, on the Pacific. *Cap.* Lima. *Pop.* 17,995,000. **—Pe•ru′vi•an** *adj.* & *n.*

pe•ruke (pə-ro͞ok′) *n.* A wig.

pe•ruse (pə-ro͞oz′) *v.* **-rused, -rus•ing.** To read, esp. with great attention. **—pe•rus′al** *n.* **—pe•rus′er** *n.*

per•vade (pər-vād′) *v.* **-vad•ed, -vad•ing.** To spread or be present in all parts of : permeate. **—per•va′sive** (-vā′sĭv, -zĭv) *adj.* **—per•va′sive•ly** *adv.*

per•verse (pər-vûrs′) *adj.* **1.** Contrary to what is good or right : corrupt. **2.** Obstinately continuing in a fault or error. **—per•verse′ly** *adv.* **—per•verse′ness** *n.* **—per•ver′si•ty** (-vûr′sĭ-tē) *n.*

per•ver•sion (pər-vûr′zhən) *n.* **1.** The act of perverting or state of being perverted. **2.** A deviant form of sexual behavior.

per•vert (pər-vûrt′) *v.* **1.** To lead away from the proper, right, or accepted course : corrupt. **2.** To use wrongly or improperly : misuse. *—n.* (pûr′vûrt′). A person who practices sexual perversion.

pe•se•ta (pə-sā′tə) *n.* See CURRENCY TABLE.

pe•se•wa (pə-sə′wä) *n., pl* **-wa** or **-was.** See *cedi* at CURRENCY TABLE.

pes•ky (pĕs′kē) *adj.* **-ki•er, -ki•est.** Causing irritation or vexation : annoying. **—pes′ki•ly** *adv.* **—pes′ki•ness** *n.*

pe•so (pā′sō) *n., pl.* **-sos.** See CURRENCY TABLE.

pes•si•mism (pĕs′ə-mĭz′əm) *n.* A tendency to take the least hopeful view, as of a situation, or to anticipate the worst. **—pes′si•mist** *n.* **—pes′si•mis′tic** *adj.* **—pes′si•mis′ti•cal•ly** *adv.*

pest (pĕst) *n.* **1.** One that is annoying : nuisance. **2.** A plant or animal that is harmful or injurious to man.

pes•ter (pĕs′tər) *v.* To beset with petty and repeated annoyances : bother.

pes•ti•cide (pĕs′tĭ-sīd′) *n.* A chemical substance used to kill pests, as rodents and insects. **—pes′ti•cid′al** (-sīd′l) *adj.*

pes•tif•er•ous (pĕ-stĭf′ər-əs) *adj.* **1.** Breeding, spreading, or contaminated with an infectious or epidemic disease. **2.** *Informal.* Annoying : irritating.

pes•ti•lence (pĕs′tə-ləns) *n.* A virulent, usu. fatal epidemic disease, esp. bubonic plague.

pes•ti•lent (pĕs′tə-lənt) *also* **pes•ti•len•tial** (pĕs′tə-lĕn′shəl) *adj.* **1.** Tending to destroy life : deadly. **2.** Likely to cause pestilence. **3.** Harmful, as to society : pernicious. **4.** Bothersome : troublesome.

pes•tle (pĕs′əl, pĕs′təl) *n.* A hand tool for crushing substances in a mortar.

pet[1] (pĕt) *n.* **1.** An animal kept for enjoyment or as a companion. **2.** Someone or something of which one is esp. fond : favorite. *—adj.* **1.** Treated or kept as a pet <a *pet* cat> **2.** Particularly liked or indulged. *—v.* **pet•ted, pet•ting. 1.** To stroke or pet gently : caress. **2.** To engage in amorous caressing and fondling.

pet[2] (pĕt) *n.* A fit of bad temper or irritation : pique.

pet•al (pĕt′l) *n.* One of the leaflike segments of a flower corolla.

pe•tard (pə-tärd′) *n.* A bomb once used to break down a gate or blow apart a wall.

pet•cock (pĕt′kŏk′) *n.* A small valve or faucet for draining pipes.

pe•ter (pē′tər) *v.* To lessen gradually and come to an end : run out <The water in the well *petered* out.>

Peter *n.* See BIBLE TABLE.

Peter I. "the Great." 1672–1725. Czar of Russia (1682–1725).

pet•i•ole (pĕt′ē-ōl′) *n. Bot.* A stalk attaching a leaf to a stem.

pe•tite (pə-tēt′) *adj.* Small and slender.

pet•it four (pĕt′ē fôr′, fōr′, fo͝or′, pə-tē′) *n., pl.* **pet•its fours** or **pet•it fours** (pĕt′ē fôrz′, fōrz′, fo͝orz′, pə-tē′). A small, decoratively frosted cake.

pe•ti•tion (pə-tĭsh′ən) *n.* **1.** A solemn request : entreaty. **2.** A formal written petition addressed to a superior. *—v.* To make a petition (to). **—pe•ti′tion•er** *n.*

pet•it point (pĕt′ē point′) *n.* Needlepoint made with a small stitch.

pet•nap (pĕt′năp′) *v.* **-napped, -nap•ping** or **-naped, -nap•ing.** To steal (a pet), usu. for profit. **—pet′nap′per** *n.*

pet•rel (pĕt′rəl) *n.* A small sea bird of the order Procellariiformes.

petrel

pet•ri•fy (pĕt′rə-fī′) *v.* **-fied, -fy•ing. 1.** To change (e.g., wood) into a stony mass. **2.** To immobilize, as with terror. **—pet′ri•fac′tion** (pĕt′rə-făk′shən), **pet′ri•fi•ca′tion** (-fĭ-kā′shən) *n.*

pet•ro•chem•i•cal (pĕt′rō-kĕm′ĭ-kəl) *n.* A chemical obtained from natural gas or petroleum. **—pet′ro•chem′i•cal** *adj.* **—pet′ro•chem′is•try** *n.*

pet•ro•dol•lars (pĕt′rō-dŏl′ərz) *pl.n.* Currency derived by oil-exporting countries from the sale of petroleum abroad.

pe•trog•ra•phy (pə-trŏg′rə-fē) *n.* The scientific classification of rocks. **—pe•trog′ra•pher** *n.* **—pet′ro•graph′ic** (pĕt′rəgrăf′ĭk), **pet′ro•graph′i•cal** *adj.*

pet•rol (pĕt′rəl) *n. esp. Brit.* Gasoline.

pet•ro•la•tum (pĕt′rə-lā′təm) *n.* A usu. colorless semisolid derived from petroleum and used esp. in medicinal ointments.

pe•tro•le•um (pə-trō′lē-əm) *n.* A thick, dark, flammable liquid that occurs naturally below the surface of the earth and is processed into such products as natural gas, gasoline, kerosene, and fuel oils.

petroleum jelly *n.* Petrolatum.

pe•trol•o•gy (pə-trŏl′ə-jē) *n.* The scientific study of the origin, composition, and structure of rocks. **—pet′ro•log′ic** (pĕt′rə-lŏj′ĭk), **pet′ro•log′i•cal** *adj.* **—pet′ro•log′i•cal•ly** *adv.* **—pe•trol′o•gist** *n.*

pet•ti•coat (pĕt′ē-kōt′) *n.* A woman's skirt that is worn as an undergarment. *—adj.* Female : feminine.

pet•ti•fog•ger (pĕt′ē-fô′gər, -fŏg′ər) *n.* **1.** A petty, unscrupulous lawyer : shyster. **2.** Someone who quibbles over unimportant details. **—pet′ti•fog′** *v.*

pet•tish (pĕt′ĭsh) *adj.* Petulant : peevish. **—pet′tish•ly** *adv.*

pet•ty (pĕt′ē) *adj.* **-ti•er, -ti•est. 1.** Insignificant : trivial <a *petty* annoyance> **2.** Contemptibly narrow-minded or mean. **3.** Subordinate in rank. **—pet′ti•ly** *adv.* **—pet′ti•ness** *n.*

petty cash *n.* A small cash fund for incidental expenses, as in an office.
petty officer *n.* A noncommissioned officer in the U.S. Navy or Coast Guard.
pet·u·lant (pĕch′ə-lənt) *adj.* Characterized by fitful ill humor : irritable. **–pet′u·lance** *n.* **–pet′u·lant·ly** *adv.*
pe·tu·nia (pə-to͞on′yə, -tyo͞on′-) *n.* A widely grown plant of the genus *Petunia,* with funnel-shaped flowers.
pew (pyo͞o) *n.* One of the rows of benches for the congregation in a church.
pe·wee (pē′wē) *n.* Any of various small, brownish North American birds of the genus *Contopus.*
pew·ter (pyo͞o′tər) *n.* Any of numerous silver-gray alloys of tin with copper, antimony, and lead used esp. for tableware and kitchen utensils.
pe·yo·te (pā-ō′tē) *n.* **1.** Mescal. **2.** A hallucinatory drug obtained from mescal.
pf. *abbr.* preferred.
Pfc or **Pfc.** *abbr.* private first class.
pfen·nig (fĕn′ĭg) *n., pl.* **-nigs** *or* **pfen·ni·ge** (fĕn′ĭ-gə). See *mark* and *deutsche mark* at CURRENCY TABLE.
pH (pē-āch′) *n. Chem.* A numerical measure of the acidity or alkalinity of a chemical solution.
pha·e·ton (fā′ĭ-tn) *n.* **1.** A light, open 4-wheeled horse-drawn carriage. **2.** A large open automobile for 5 or more passengers.
phage (fāj) *n.* A bacteriophage.
pha·lanx (fā′lăngks′) *n., pl.* **-lanx·es** *or* **pha·lan·ges** (fə-lăn′jēz′, fā-). **1.** A close-knit or compact formation of persons, as troops. **2.** *pl.* **phalanges.** One of the bones of a finger or toe.
phal·a·rope (făl′ə-rōp′) *n.* A small wading bird of the family Phalaropodidae, having lobed toes.
phal·lus (făl′əs) *n., pl.* **phal·li** (făl′ī′) *or* **-lus·es. 1.** The penis. **2.** A representation of the penis. **–phal′lic** *adj.*
phan·tasm (făn′tăz′əm) *n.* **1.** A creation of the imagination : fantasy. **2.** A phantom. **–phan·tas′mal, phan·tas′mic** *adj.*
phan·tas·ma·go·ri·a (făn-tăz′mə-gôr′ē-ə,-gōr′-) *n.* A rapidly shifting sequence of haphazard imagery, as in a dream. **–phan·tas′ma·go′ric** *adj.*
phan·ta·sy (făn′tə-sē) *n. var. of* FANTASY.
phan·tom (făn′təm) *n.* **1.** Something, as a ghost, that is sensed but that has no physical reality : apparition. **2.** An image in the mind. **–phan′tom** *adj.*
phar. or **pharm.** *abbr.* pharmaceutical; pharmacist; pharmacy.
Phar·aoh *also* **phar·aoh** (fâr′ō) *n.* A king of ancient Egypt.
phar·i·see (făr′ĭ-sē) *n.* **1. Pharisee.** A member of an ancient Jewish sect that interpreted and observed the Mosaic law strictly. **2.** A hypocritical or sanctimonious person. **–phar′i·sa′i·cal** (-sā′ĭ-kəl) *adj.*
phar·ma·ceu·ti·cal (fär′mə-so͞o′tĭ-kəl) *or* **phar·ma·ceu·tic** (-tĭk) *adj.* Of or pertaining to pharmacy or pharmacists. **–phar′ma·ceu′ti·cal·ly** *adv.*
phar·ma·cist (fär′mə-sĭst) *n.* Someone trained to practice pharmacy : druggist.
phar·ma·col·o·gy (fär′mə-kŏl′ə-jē) *n.* The scientific study of the composition, uses, and effects of drugs. **–phar′ma·co·log′ic** (-kə-lŏj′ĭk), **phar′ma·co·log′i·cal** *adj.* **–phar′ma·col′o·gist** *n.*
phar·ma·co·poe·ia (fär′mə-kə-pē′ə) *n.* **1.** A book containing a list of medicinal drugs with recommended procedures for their preparation and use. **2.** A stock or collection of drugs.
phar·ma·cy (fär′mə-sē) *n., pl.* **-cies. 1.** The techniques or practice of preparing and dispensing drugs. **2.** A drugstore.
pha·ros (fâr′ŏs′) *n.* A lighthouse.
phar·ynx (făr′ĭngks) *n., pl.* **pha·ryn·ges** (fə-rĭn′jēz′) or **-ynx·es.** The cavity connecting the nasal passages and mouth with the esophagus. **–pha·ryn′ge·al** (fə-rĭn′jē-əl, făr′ĭn-jē′əl) *adj.*
phase (fāz) *n.* **1.** A distinct stage of development. **2.** An aspect, as of a situation : part. **3.** One of the cyclic forms in which the moon or a planet appears. *–v.* **phased, phas·ing.** To carry out or plan systematically in phases. **–phase in (**or **out).** To introduce (or eliminate) in stages.
phase·out (fāz′out′) *n.* Systematic and gradual discontinuation of production or operations.
pheas·ant (fĕz′ənt) *n.* Any of various long-tailed game birds of the family Phasianidae, with colorful plumage.
phen·cy·cli·dine (fĕn-sī′klĭ-dēn′, -dĭn, -sĭk′lĭ-) *n.* A drug used illegally as a hallucinogen.
phe·no·bar·bi·tal (fē′nō-bär′bĭ-tôl′) *n.* A white crystalline compound used as a sedative and hypnotic.
phe·nol (fē′nôl′, -nōl′) *n.* A caustic, poisonous crystalline compound obtained from benzene and used as a disinfectant and in making plastics and drugs.
phe·nom·e·non (fĭ-nŏm′ə-nŏn′) *n., pl.* **-na** (nə) or **-nons. 1. a.** A fact or occurrence that can be perceived or observed. **b.** A rare fact or occurrence. **2.** An extremely outstanding or unusual person or thing : marvel. **–phe·nom′e·nal** *adj.* **–phe·nom′e·nal·ly** *adv.*
pher·o·mone (fĕr′ə-mōn′) *n.* A chemical substance secreted by an animal that influences specific patterns of behavior in other members of the same species.
phi. *or* **philos.** *abbr.* philosopher; philosophical; philosophy.
phi·al (fī′əl) *n.* A vial.
Phil·a·del·phi·a (fĭl′ə-dĕl′fē-ə). City of SE Pa. *Pop.* 1,688,210. **–Phil′a·del′phi·an** *adj.* & *n.*
phi·lan·der (fĭ-lăn′dər) *v.* To make love casually or frivolously : dally.
phi·lan·thro·py (fĭ-lăn′thrə-pē) *n., pl.* **-pies. 1.** The effort to advance human well-being, as through charitable gifts or endowments. **2.** Benevolence toward mankind. **3.** A charitable institution. **–phil′an·throp′ic** (fĭl′ənthrŏp′ĭk), **phil′an·throp′i·cal** *adj.* **–phi·lan′thro·pist** *n.*
phi·lat·e·ly (fĭ-lăt′l-ē) *n.* The collection and study of postage stamps and postmarked materials. **–phil′a·tel′ic** (fĭl′ə-tĕl′ĭk) *adj.* **–phi·lat′e·list** *n.*
Phi·le·mon (fĭ-lē′mən, fī-) *n.* See BIBLE TABLE.
phil·har·mon·ic (fĭl′här-mŏn′ĭk, fĭl′ər-) *adj.* Of or pertaining to a symphony orchestra. **–phil′har·mon′ic** *n.*
Phi·lip·pi·ans (fĭ-lĭp′ē-ənz) *pl.n. (sing. in number).* See BIBLE TABLE.
phi·lip·pic (fĭ-lĭp′ĭk) *n.* An acrimonious verbal attack : tirade.
Phil·ip·pines (fĭl′ə-pēnz′, fĭl′ə-pēnz′). Island country in the W Pacific SE of China. *Cap.* Manila. *Pop.* 48,200,000. **–Phil′ip·pine′** *adj.*
Phil·is·tine (fĭl′ĭ-stēn′, fĭ-lĭs′tĭn, -tēn′) *n.* **1.** A member of an ancient Palestinian people. **2. philistine.** A smug, materialistic person, esp. one who is indifferent to artistic, cultural, or intellectual values.
phil·o·den·dron (fĭl′ə-dĕn′drən) *n., pl.* **-drons** *or* **-dra** (-drə). Any of various climbing tropical American plants of the genus *Philodendron,* often grown as house plants.
▲word history: The name *philodendron* literally means "fond of trees." It was given to a genus of tropical climbing plants because in their native habitat they twine around trees.
phi·lol·o·gy (fĭ-lŏl′ə-jē) *n.* **1.** The study of the chronological development of languages. **2.** The study of literature and of language as it is used in literature. **–phil′o·log′i·cal** (fĭl′ə-lŏj′ĭ-kəl) *adj.* **–phi·lol′o·gist** *n.*
phi·los·o·pher (fĭ-lŏs′ə-fər) *n.* **1.** An expert in or student of philosophy. **2.** Someone who thinks deeply : scholar. **3.** A calm, rational, self-assured person.
philosophers' stone *n.* An imaginary substance believed to have the power of transmuting base metal into gold.
phi·los·o·phize (fĭ-lŏs′ə-fīz′) *v.* **-phized, -phiz·ing.** To speculate or reason like a philosopher.
phi·los·o·phy (fĭ-lŏs′ə-fē) *n., pl.* **-phies. 1. a.** A logical and critical study of the source and nature of human knowledge. **b.** A formal system of ideas based on such study. **2.** The sciences and liberal arts with the exception of law, medicine, and theology <a doctor of *philosophy*> **3.** A basic theory about a particular subject or sphere of activity <the *philosophy* of science> **4.** The set of values, ideas, and opinions of an individual or group. **–phil′o·soph′i·cal** (fĭl′ə-sŏf′ĭ-kəl), **phil′o·soph′ic** *adj.* **–phil′o·soph′i·cal·ly** *adv.*
phil·ter *also* **phil·tre** (fĭl′tər) *n.* **1.** A love potion. **2.** A magic potion or charm.
phle·bi·tis (flĭ-bī′tĭs) *n.* Inflammation of a vein.
phlegm (flĕm) *n.* Thick mucus secreted esp. in the respiratory tract.
phleg·mat·ic (flĕg-măt′ĭk) *adj.* Having or suggesting a stolid, sluggish temperament : unemotional. **–phleg·mat′i·cal·ly** *adv.*
phlo·em (flō′ĕm′) *n.* Vascular plant tissue through which food is conducted from the leaves to plant parts.
phlox (flŏks) *n., pl.* **phlox** *or* **phlox·es.** A plant of the genus *Phlox,* with terminal clusters of white, red, or purple flowers.
Phnom Penh (pə-nôm′ pĕn′). Cap. of Cambodia, in the SW. *Pop.* 393,995.
pho·bi·a (fō′bē-ə) *n.* A persistent illogical fear. **–pho′bic** *adj.*
phoe·be (fē′bē) *n.* A small, dull-colored North American bird of the genus *Sayornis.*
Phoe·ni·cia (fĭ-nĭsh′ə, -nē′shə). Ancient maritime country along the E coast of the Mediterranean. **–Phoe·ni′cian** *adj.* & *n.*
phoe·nix (fē′nĭks) *n.* A bird of legend said to consume itself by fire after centuries and rise renewed from its ashes.
Phoenix Cap. of Ariz., in the SC part. *Pop.* 764,911.
phone (fōn) *Informal –n.* A telephone. *–v.* **phoned, phon·ing.** To call or transmit by telephone.

pho•neme (fō′nēm′) *n.* One of the smallest speech units, as the *m* of *mat* and the *b* of *bat,* that distinguish 1 word or utterance from another. **–pho•ne′mic** (fə-nē′mĭk, fō-) *adj.* **–pho•ne′mics** *n.*

pho•net•ics (fə-nĕt′ĭks) *n. (sing. in number).* The study of the sounds of spoken language. **–pho•net′ic** *adj.* **–pho′ne•ti′cian** (fō′nĭ-tĭsh′ən) *n*

phon•ics (fŏn′ĭks) *n. (sing. in number).* A method of teaching beginning readers through the use of elementary phonetics.

pho•no•graph (fō′nə-grăf′) *n.* An instrument that uses a vibrating needle to reproduce sound from a groove cut into a disc. **–pho′no•graph′ic** *adj.*

pho•nol•o•gy (fə-nŏl′ə-jē, fō-) *n.* The scientific study of the speech sounds of a language, including phonemics and phonetics and often sound changes over time. **–pho′no•log′ic** (fō′nə-lŏj′ĭk), **pho′no•log′i•cal** *adj.* **–pho•nol′o•gist** *n.*

pho•ny *also* **pho•ney** (fō′nē) *adj.* **-ni•er, -ni•est.** *Informal.* Not real or genuine : fake. **–pho′ny** *n.*

phos•phate (fŏs′fāt′) *n.* **1.** *Chem.* A salt or ester of phosphoric acid containing chiefly phosphorus and oxygen. **2.** A fertilizer containing compounds of phosphorus. **–phos•phat′ic** (fŏs-făt′ĭk) *adj.*

phos•phor (fŏs′fər, -fôr′) *n.* A substance capable of emitting light when stimulated by incident radiation.

phos•pho•res•cence (fŏs′fə-rĕs′əns) *n.* **1.** The process or phenomenon of the persistent emission of light by a body after exposure to and removal of radiation. **2.** Organically generated emission of light : bioluminescence. **–phos′pho•resce′** *v.* **–phos′pho•res′cent** *adj.*

phos•phor•ic acid (fŏs-fôr′ĭk, -fŏr′-) *n.* A clear, colorless acid that is used in soaps, fertilizers, and detergents.

phos•pho•rus (fŏs′fər-əs) *n. Symbol* **P** A poisonous nonmetallic element used in safety matches, fertilizers, glass, and steel. **–phos•phor′ic** *adj.* **–phos′pho•rous** *adj.*

pho•to (fō′tō) *n., pl.* **-tos.** *Informal.* A photograph. **–pho′to** *v.*

pho•to•cell (fō′tō-sĕl′) *n.* A photoelectric cell.

pho•to•chem•is•try (fō′tō-kĕm′ĭ-strē) *n.* The chemical action of radiant energy. **–pho′to•chem′i•cal** *adj.*

pho•to•com•po•si•tion (fō′tō-kŏm′pə-zĭsh′ən) *n.* A process by which printed matter is composed for reproduction by photographing type characters on film. **–pho′to•com•pose′** *v.*

pho•to•cop•y (fō′tō-kŏp′ē) *v.* To reproduce (printed matter) by a photographic process such as xerography. **–pho′to•cop′i•er** *n.* **–pho′to•cop′y** *n.*

pho•to•e•lec•tric (fō′tō-ĭ-lĕk′trĭk) *also* **pho•to•e•lec•tri•cal** (-trĭ-kəl) *adj.* Of or relating to electrical effects that result from or depend on the presence of light.

photoelectric cell *n.* An electronic device having an electrical output that varies in response to light.

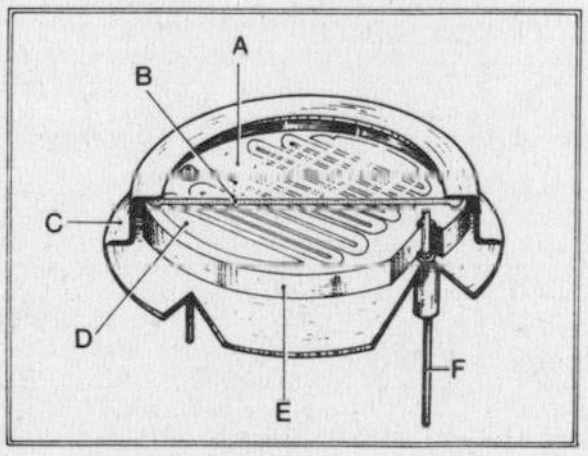

photoelectric cell
A. electrode, B. glass window, C. metal case, D. photoconductive material, E. ceramic substrate, F. base pin

pho•to•e•lec•tron (fō′tō-ĭ-lĕk′trŏn′) *n.* An electron released from a substance in the photoelectric effect.

pho•to•e•mis•sion (fō′tō-ĭ-mĭsh′ən) *n.* The emission of photoelectrons.

pho•to•en•grav•ing (fō′tō-ĕn-grā′vĭng) *n.* **1.** The process of reproducing a drawing or photograph by transferring the image onto a metal plate in etched relief for printing. **2.** A reproduction made by photoengraving. **–pho′to•en•grave′** *v.*

photo finish *n.* A race finish so close that the winner can only be determined from a photograph of the finish.

pho•to•flash (fō′tō-flăsh′) *n.* A flash bulb.

pho•to•gen•ic (fō′tə-jĕn′ĭk) *adj.* Suitable and esp. attractive as a subject for photography. **–pho′to•gen′i•cal•ly** *adv.*

pho•to•graph (fō′tə-grăf′) *n.* An image, esp. a positive print, recorded by a camera and reproduced on a photosensitive surface. **–pho′to•graph′** *v.*

pho•to•graph•ic (fō′tə-grăf′ĭk) *adj.* **1.** Of or used in photography or a photograph. **2.** Suggestive of a photograph, as in detail or accuracy. **–pho′to•graph′i•cal•ly** *adv.*

pho•tog•ra•phy (fə-tŏg′rə-fē) *n.* The process, art, technique, or profession of taking photographs. **–pho•tog′ra•pher** *n.*

pho•to•gra•vure (fō′tə-grə-vyŏŏr′) *n.* The art or process of printing from an intaglio plate etched photographically.

pho•to•jour•nal•ism (fō′tō-jûr′nə-lĭz′əm) *n.* Journalism in which text is less important than pictorial matter, esp. photographs. **–pho′to•jour′nal•ist** *n.*

pho•tom•e•try (fō-tŏm′ĭ-trē) *n.* Measurement of the properties of light, esp. luminous intensity or flux. **–pho′to•met′ric** (fō′tə-mĕt′rĭk) *adj.* **–pho•tom′e•ter** *n.*

pho•ton (fō′tŏn′) *n.* A quantum of electromagnetic energy. **–pho•ton′ic** *adj.*

pho•to-off•set (fō′tō-ôf′sĕt′, -ŏf′-) *n.* Offset printing.

pho•to•play (fō′tō-plā′) *n.* A motion picture.

pho•to•sen•si•tive (fō′tō-sĕn′sĭ-tĭv) *adj.* Sensitive to change as a result of exposure to light. **–pho′to•sen′si•tiv′i•ty** *n.*

pho•to•sphere (fō′tə-sfîr′) *n.* The layer of a star, esp. the sun, that emits directly observable radiation, as light. **–pho′to•spher′ic** (-sfîr′ĭk, -sfĕr′-) *adj.*

Pho•to•stat (fō′tə-stăt′). A trademark for a device that makes photographic copies of graphic material.

pho•to•syn•the•sis (fō′tō-sĭn′thĭ-sĭs) *n.* The chemical process by which chlorophyll-containing plants use light to convert carbon dioxide and water into carbohydrates, releasing oxygen as a by-product. **–pho′to•syn′the•size′** (-sīz′) *v.* **–pho′to•syn•thet′ic** (-thĕt′ĭk) *adj.*

phr. *abbr.* phrase.

phrase (frāz) *n.* **1.** A brief or concise expression. **2.** A sequence of 2 or more words that form a meaningful syntactic unit less completely predicated than a sentence. **3.** A portion of a musical composition that usu. consists of 4 to 8 measures. *–v.* **phrased, phras•ing. 1.** To write or express in words. **2.** To play music in a way that reveals its melodic phrases. **–phras′al** *adj.* **–phras′al•ly** *adv.*

phra•se•ol•o•gy (frā′zē-ŏl′ə-jē) *n., pl.* **-gies.** A style or manner of using words and phrases.

phre•net•ic (frə-nĕt′ĭk) *adj. var. of* FRENETIC.

phren•ic (frĕn′ĭk, frē′nĭk) *adj. Anat.* Of or pertaining to the diaphragm.

phre•nol•o•gy (frĭ-nŏl′ə-jē) *n.* The study of the conformation of the human skull as a means of determining character and intelligence. **–phre•nol′o•gist** *n.*

phy•lac•ter•y (fĭ-lăk′tə-rē) *n., pl.* **-ies.** Either of 2 small leather boxes containing parchment strips inscribed with scriptural quotations that are worn on the forehead and the left arm by Jewish men for morning worship.

phy•log•e•ny (fī-lŏj′ə-nē) *n., pl.* **-nies.** The evolutionary development of a species of animal or plant.

phy•lum (fī′ləm) *n., pl.* **-la** (-lə). A broad category of the animal or plant kingdom into which organisms are divided.

phys•ic (fĭz′ĭk) *n.* A medicine, esp. a cathartic. *–v.* **-icked, -ick•ing.** To administer a physic to : purge.

phys•i•cal (fĭz′ĭ-kəl) *adj.* **1.** Of or relating to the body rather than the emotions or mind. **2.** Material rather than imaginary. **3. a.** Of, pertaining to, or produced by nonliving matter and energy. **b.** Of or pertaining to physics. ☆**syns:** ANIMAL, CARNAL, FLESHLY, SENSUAL *–n.* A medical examination to determine a person's physical condition. **–phys′i•cal•ly** *adv.*

physical education *n.* Instruction in the development, care, and exercise of the human body, including calisthenics, sports, and hygiene.

physical science *n.* A science, as chemistry, physics, or geology, that deals primarily with the properties of energy and nonliving matter.

physical therapy *n.* The treatment of disease or injury by means such as exercise, heat, baths, and massage. **–physical therapist** *n.*

phy•si•cian (fĭ-zĭsh′ən) *n.* A licensed medical doctor.

phys•i•cist (fĭz′ĭ-sĭst) *n.* A scientist specializing in physics.

phys•ics (fĭz′ĭks) *n. (sing. in number).* **1.** The science of matter and energy and of the interactions between them. **2.** Physical interactions, properties, laws, or processes.

phys•i•og•no•my (fĭz′ē-ŏg′nə-mē, -ŏn′ə-) *n., pl.* **-mies.** Facial expression and features, esp. as an indication of character.

phys•i•og•ra•phy (fĭz′ē-ŏg′rə-fē) *n.* The study of the structure and phenomena of the earth's surface. **–phys′i•og′ra•pher** *n.* **–phys′i•o•graph′ic** (-ə-grăf′ĭk) *adj.*

phys•i•ol•o•gy (fĭz′ē-ŏl′ə-jē) *n.* **1.** The scientific study of essential and typical life processes, activities, and functions. **2.** The vital processes and functions of an organism. **–phys′i•o•log′i•cal** (-ə-lŏj′ĭ-kəl), **phys′i•o•log′ic** *adj.* **–phys′i•o•log′i•cal•ly** *adv.* **–phys′i•ol′o•gist** *n.*

phys•i•o•ther•a•py (fĭz′ē-ō-thĕr′ə-pē) *n.* Physical therapy. **–phys′i•o•ther′a•peu′tic** *adj.* **–phys′i•o•ther′a•pist** *n.*

phy•sique (fĭ-zēk′) *n.* The human body with respect to its muscular development, proportions, and appearance : build.

pi[1] (pī) *n., pl.* **pis.** A transcendental number that represents the ratio of the circumference of a circle to its diameter.

pi[2] *also* **pie** (pī) *n., pl.* **pis** *also* **pies.** Jumbled type.

pi•a•nis•si•mo (pē′ə-nĭs′ə-mō′) *adv. Mus.* Very softly. Used as a direction. **—pi′a•nis′si•mo′** *adj.* & *n.*

pi•an•ist (pē-ăn′ĭst, pē′ə-nĭst) *n.* Someone who plays the piano.

pi•an•o[1] (pē-ăn′ō, -ä′nō) *n., pl.* **-os.** A musical instrument with a manual keyboard and felt-covered hammers that strike wire strings.

pi•a•no[2] (pē-ä′nō) *adv. Mus.* Softly. Used as a direction. **—pi•a′no** *adj.* & *n.*

pi•an•o•for•te (pē-ăn′ō-fôr′tā, -tē, -fôrt′, -ä′nō-) *n.* A piano.

pi•as•ter *also* **pi•as•tre** (pē-ăs′tər, -ä′stər) *n.* See *pound* at CURRENCY TABLE.

pi•az•za (pē-ăz′ə, -ä′zə) *n.* **1.** A public square, esp. in an Italian town. **2.** A porch.

pi•broch (pē′brŏKH′) *n.* A series of variations on a traditional dirge or martial theme for the bagpipe.

pic (pĭk) *n., pl.* **pics** or **pix.** *Slang.* **1.** A photograph. **2.** A movie.

pi•ca (pī′kə) *n.* **1.** A printer's type size equal to 12 points or approx. 1/6 in. **2.** A typewriter size with 10 characters an in.

pic•a•dor (pĭk′ə-dôr′) *n., pl.* **-dors** or **-do•res** (-dôr′ēz). A horseman in bullfighting who weakens the bull by lancing its neck muscles.

pic•a•resque (pĭk′ə-rĕsk′, pē′kə-) *adj.* Of, pertaining to, or involving rogues.

Pi•cas•so (pĭ-kä′sō), **Pablo.** 1881–1973. Spanish-born painter and sculptor.

pic•a•yune (pĭk′ē-yo͞on′) *adj.* **1.** Of little importance or value : paltry. **2.** Mean in spirit : petty.

pic•ca•lil•li (pĭk′ə-lĭl′ē) *n.* A spicy relish of chopped and pickled vegetables.

pic•co•lo (pĭk′ə-lō′) *n., pl.* **-los.** A small flute with a hard, brilliant sound that is pitched an octave above an ordinary flute.

pick[1] (pĭk) *v.* **1.** To choose from a group : select. **2.** To gather by or as if by plucking <*pick* cotton> **3. a.** To remove an outer covering from. **b.** To remove, as by tearing off, bit by bit. **4.** To pull at with the fingers. **5.** To break up, detach, or pierce with a pointed or sharp instrument. **6.** To steal the contents of <*picks* pockets> **7.** To open without using a key <*pick* a lock> **8.** To pull gently or dig at. **9.** To cause deliberately : provoke <*pick* a fight> **—pick on.** To tease or harass. **—pick out.** To play the notes of singly or uncertainly <*picked out* the melody on the organ> **—pick up. 1.** To take on (e.g., freight or passengers). **2.** To become better : improve. **3.** To set in order : tidy. **4.** To learn, esp. without great effort. **5.** To arrest. —*n.* **1.** The act or right of choosing : selection. **2.** The choicest or best part. **—pick′er** *n.*

pick[2] (pĭk) *n.* **1.** A tool consisting of a curved bar sharpened at both ends and fitted to a long handle that is used for breaking up hard surfaces. **2.** A small flat piece, as of bone, used to pluck the strings of a musical instrument : plectrum.

pick•a•back (pĭk′ə-băk′) *adv.* & *n. var. of* PIGGYBACK.

pick•ax or **pick•axe** (pĭk′ăks′) *n.* A pick with 1 end of the blade pointed, the other end having a chisellike edge.

†**picked** (pĭkt) *adj. Regional.* Pointed <a *picked* cap>

pick•er•el (pĭk′ər-əl, pĭk′rəl) *n., pl.* **-el** or **-els.** Any of various North American freshwater food and game fishes of the genus *Esox* that are related to but gen. smaller than the pike.

pick•er•el•weed (pĭk′ər-əl-wēd′, pĭk′rəl-) *n.* A North American plant, *Pontederia cordata,* found in freshwater shallows and having heart-shaped leaves and violet-blue flower spikes.

pick•et (pĭk′ĭt) *n.* **1.** A pointed stake, as one driven into the ground to support a fence. **2. a.** A detachment of soldiers on guard duty. **b.** A soldier on guard duty : sentinel. **3.** A person stationed outside a place of employment, esp. during a strike, to discourage entry by nonstriking workers or customers. —*v.* **1.** To secure, enclose, tether, mark out, or fortify with pickets. **2.** To guard with or post as a picket. **3.** To station pickets at <*picketing* a restaurant> **4.** To act as a picket.

picket line *n.* A line of people picketing a place of employment.

pick•ings (pĭk′ĭngz) *pl.n.* **1.** Scraps, esp. of edible food : leftovers. **2. a.** Result or gain from effort exerted <slim *pickings*> **b.** A share of spoils.

pick•le (pĭk′əl) *n.* **1.** A solution of brine or vinegar for flavoring and preserving food. **2.** A food, as a cucumber, preserved in a pickle. **3.** *Informal.* A difficult or troublesome situation : predicament. —*v.* **-led, -ling.** To flavor or preserve in a pickle.

pick•lock (pĭk′lŏk′) **1.** One who picks locks, esp. a thief. **2.** An instrument for picking a lock.

pick-me-up (pĭk′mē-ŭp′) *n. Informal.* Something, esp. an alcoholic drink, that invigorates or stimulates.

pick•pock•et (pĭk′pŏk′ĭt) *n.* Someone who steals from pockets.

pick•up (pĭk′ŭp′) *n.* **1.** The act or process of picking up. **2.** Acceleration. **3.** Renewed activity : improvement. **4.** *Electron.* **a.** A device for converting the oscillations of a phonograph needle into electrical impulses. **b.** The tone arm of a record player. **5. a.** The conversion of light or sound waves into electrical impulses. **b.** A device used for such conversion. **6.** A casual temporary acquaintance. **7.** A small, light truck with low sides and an open body.

pick•y (pĭk′ē) *adj.* **-i•er, -i•est.** *Informal.* Excessively meticulous : fussy.

pic•nic (pĭk′nĭk) *n.* An excursion in which members of a group eat a meal outdoors. —*v.* **-nicked, -nick•ing.** To go on a picnic. **—pic′nick•er** *n.*

▲<u>word history:</u> The word *picnic* is most probably derived from French *pique-nique,* whose origin is not known with absolute certainty. The word seems to have originated in the 18th cent., when it referred to a meal for which each guest contributed a dish to be served. At some point it became common to hold such parties outdoors, and by the 19th cent. *picnic* referred to any open-air meal.

pi•cot (pē′kō′) *n.* One of a series of small loops that form an ornamental edging, as on ribbon.

pic•to•ri•al (pĭk-tôr′ē-əl, -tōr′-) *adj.* Of, pertaining to, or composed of pictures. **—pic•to′ri•al•ly** *adv.*

pic•ture (pĭk′chər) *n.* **1.** A representation that is drawn, painted, or photographed. **2.** A vivid, realistic verbal description. **3.** One that closely resembles another : image. **4.** An embodiment, as of a state of mind <the *picture* of health> **5.** A set of circumstances : situation. **6.** A motion picture. —*v.* **-tured, -tur•ing. 1.** To make a picture of. **2.** To visualize mentally. **3.** To describe vividly in words.

pic•tur•esque (pĭk′chə-rĕsk′) *adj.* **1.** Suggesting or resembling a picture <a *picturesque* colonial village> **2.** Quaintly attractive : charming. **3.** Strikingly expressive : vivid. **—pic′tur•esque′ly** *adv.* **—pic′tur•esque′ness** *n.*

picture window *n.* A large, usu. single-paned window that frames a broad view of the outside.

pid•dling (pĭd′lĭng) *adj.* Trivial : trifling.

pidg•in (pĭj′ĭn) *n.* A simplified medium of speech used for communication between groups who speak different languages.

pie[1] (pī) *n.* A baked pastry crust with a filling, as of fruit or meat.

pie[2] (pī) *n. var. of* PI[2].

pie•bald (pī′bôld′) *adj.* Patched or spotted <a *piebald* horse>

piece (pēs) *n.* **1.** A part, unit, or element of a whole : portion or fragment. **2.** One of a set or group <a *piece* of furniture> **3.** A musical, artistic, or literary work. **4.** An example : specimen. **5.** A coin. **6.** A firearm. —*v.* **pieced, piec•ing. 1.** To complete or mend by adding pieces. **2.** To unite into a whole : join.

pièce de ré•sis•tance (pē-ĕs′ də rā′zē-stäNS′) *n.* **1.** The main dish of a meal. **2.** An outstanding example.

piece•meal (pēs′mēl′) *adv.* Bit by bit : gradually. **—piece′meal′** *adj.*

piece•work (pēs′wûrk′) *n.* Work that is paid for by the piece. **—piece′work′er** *n.*

pied (pīd) *adj.* Of more than 1 color in patches : piebald.

pied-à-terre (pyā′-dä-târ′) *n., pl.* **pieds-à-terre** (pyā-dä-târ′). A 2nd or temporary lodging.

pie•plant (pī′plănt′) *n.* Rhubarb.

pier (pîr) *n.* **1.** A structure that extends into the water and is used to protect, secure, and provide access to vessels. **2.** A structure that supports the spans of a bridge. **3.** A vertical supporting structure.

pierce (pîrs) *v.* **pierced, pierc•ing. 1.** To puncture or pass into or through with or as if with a sharp instrument : stab. **2.** To make a hole in. **3.** To make a way through : penetrate. **—pierc′ing•ly** *adv.*

Pierce, Franklin. 1804–69. 14th U.S. President (1853–57).

Pierre (pîr). Cap. of S.Dak., in the C part. *Pop.* 11,973.

pi•e•ty (pī′ĭ-tē) *n., pl.* **-ties. 1.** Devotion to God : devoutness. **2.** Faithfulness and reverence to parents and family. **3.** A pious thought or act.

pi•e•zo•e•lec•tric•i•ty (pē-ā′zō-ĭ-lĕk-trĭs′ĭ-tē) *n.* The generation of electricity in dielectric crystals subjected to mechanical stress. **—pi•e′zo•e•lec′tric, pi•e′zo•e•lec′tri•cal** *adj.*

pif•fle (pĭf′əl) *n.* Foolish or trivial talk.

pig (pĭg) *n.* **1.** Any of several hoofed mammals with short legs, cloven hoofs, bristly hair, and a cartilaginous snout used for rooting, esp. the domesticated hog, *Sus scrofa,* when young. **2.** A person resembling a pig, as in being greedy or gross. **3.** A block of metal, usu. lead or iron, poured from a smelting furnace into a mold.

pi•geon (pĭj′ən) *n.* Any of several doves of the family Columbidae, with a prominent chest and short legs.

pi•geon•hole (pĭj′ən-hōl′) *n.* A small compartment, as in a desk, for holding letters and papers. —*v.* **1.** To place in a pigeonhole : file. **2.** To categorize : classify. **3.** To put aside indefinitely.

pi•geon-toed (pĭj′ən-tōd′) *adj.* Having toes that turn inward.

pig•gish (pĭg′ĭsh) *adj.* **1.** Like a pig : greedy or dirty. **2.** Pigheaded.

pig•gy•back (pĭg′ē-băk′) *also* **pick•a•back** (pĭk′ə-) *adv.* **1.** On the shoulders and back. **2.** In, on, or by means of truck trailers carried on railroad flatcars. **—pig′gy•back′** *adj.*

pig•head•ed (pĭg′hĕd′ĭd) *adj.* Stubborn.

pig iron *n.* Crude iron as it is drawn from the blast furnace.

pig•let (pĭg′lĭt) *n.* A small young pig.

pig•ment (pĭg′mənt) *n.* **1.** A substance or material used as coloring. **2.** *Biol.* A substance, as hemoglobin or chlorophyll, that imparts a characteristic color to animal or plant tissue.

pig•men•ta•tion (pĭg′mən-tā′shən) *n.* *Biol.* **1.** Coloration of tissues by pigment. **2.** Deposition of pigment by cells.

pig•my (pĭg′mē) *n.* & *adj.* *var. of* PYGMY.

pig•nut (pĭg′nŭt′) *n.* A hickory tree, *Carya glabra* or *C. ovalis,* of the E U.S., bearing edible nuts.

pig•pen (pĭg′pĕn′) *n.* **1.** A pen in which pigs are kept. **2.** A very dirty place.

pig•skin (pĭg′skĭn′) *n.* **1. a.** The skin of a pig. **b.** Leather made from pigskin. **2.** *Informal.* **a.** A football. **b.** A saddle.

pig•sty (pĭg′stī′) *n.* A pigpen.

pig•tail (pĭg′tāl′) *n.* A plait of tightly braided hair.

pike¹ (pīk) *n.* A long spear with a sharp-pointed steel head once used by infantry.

pike² (pīk) *n., pl.* **pike** or **pikes. 1.** A large freshwater food and game fish, *Esox lucius,* having a long snout and a narrow body. **2.** A similar or related fish.

pike³ (pīk) *n.* A turnpike.

pike⁴ (pīk) *n.* A sharp point or spike, as the tip of spear.

pi•ker (pī′kər) *n.* *Slang.* A petty, stingy person.

pi•laf or **pi•laff** (pĭ-läf′, pē′läf′) *n.* A dish made of rice in a seasoned broth with shellfish, meat, or vegetables.

pi•las•ter (pĭ-lăs′tər, pĭ-lăs′-) *n.* A vertical column, often ornamental, that projects slightly from a wall.

pil•chard (pĭl′chərd) *n.* Any of various sardinelike fishes related to the herrings, esp. *Sardina pilchardus,* a commercially important edible species.

pile¹ (pīl) *n.* **1.** A mass of things in a heap. **2.** A large quantity or number. **3.** A funeral pyre. **4.** A very big building. **5.** A nuclear reactor. —*v.* **piled, pil•ing. 1.** To put into or form a pile : stack. **2.** To accumulate into a pile. **3.** To move forward in a group or mass <*pile* into a bus>

pile² (pīl) *n.* A heavy post or column, as of steel, driven into the ground as a foundation or support for a structure.

pile³ (pīl) *n.* **1.** The surface of certain fabrics, as velvet and carpeting, consisting of cut or uncut loops of yarn. **2.** Soft, fine fur, hair, or wool. **—piled** *adj.*

piles (pīlz) *pl.n.* Hemorrhoids.

pil•fer (pĭl′fər) *v.* To steal articles of little value : filch. **—pil′fer•age** *n.*

pil•grim (pĭl′grĭm) *n.* **1.** A person who goes on a pilgrimage. **2.** Someone who travels in foreign countries. **3. Pilgrim.** One of a group of English Puritans who founded the colony of Plymouth in New England in 1620.

pil•grim•age (pĭl′grə-mĭj) *n.* **1.** A journey to a shrine or sacred place. **2.** An extended journey with a purpose.

pill (pĭl) *n.* **1.** A small tablet of medicine to be taken orally. **2. the pill.** *Informal.* An oral contraceptive. **3.** Something that is unpleasant but must be accepted. **4.** *Slang.* A disagreeable or boring person.

pil•lage (pĭl′ĭj) *v.* **-laged, -lag•ing.** To take loot : plunder. **—pil′lag•er** *n.*

pil•lar (pĭl′ər) *n.* A freestanding vertical shaft or column that serves as a support or stands alone as a monument.

pill•box (pĭl′bŏks′) *n.* **1.** A small box for holding pills. **2.** An emplacement of reinforced concrete, esp. for a machine gun.

pil•lion (pĭl′yən) *n.* A cushion for a passenger behind the saddle on a motorcycle or horse.

pil•lo•ry (pĭl′ə-rē) *n., pl.* **-ries.** A wooden frame with holes in which the head and hands were locked as public punishment. —*v.* **-ried, -ry•ing. 1.** To put in a pillory. **2.** To expose to public abuse or ridicule.

pil•low (pĭl′ō) *n.* A cloth case filled with soft material, as down, and used to cushion a person's head during sleep. —*v.* **1.** To rest on or as if on a pillow. **2.** To serve as a pillow for. **—pil′low•y** *adj.*

pil•low•case (pĭl′ō-kās′) *n.* A removable open-ended covering for a pillow.

pi•lot (pī′lət) *n.* **1.** Someone who operates or is licensed to operate an aircraft or spacecraft. **2.** Someone licensed to steer ships into and out of port. **3.** A helmsman. **4.** A leader or guide. **5.** A television program produced as a prototype of a proposed series. —*v.* **1.** To serve as the pilot of. **2.** To control the course of : conduct. —*adj.* Serving as a guide or model for future development or experiment <a *pilot* study>

pi•lot•age (pī′lə-tĭj) *n.* The technique or business of piloting.

pi•lot•house (pī′lət-hous′) *n.* An enclosed area on the bridge or deck of a ship from which it is steered.

pilot light *n.* A small permanent flame used to ignite a gas burner or oven.

pi•men•to (pĭ-mĕn′tō) *also* **pi•mien•to** (pĭ-mĕn′tō, -myĕn′-) *n., pl.* **-tos.** A mild-flavored garden pepper, *Capsicum annuum,* with red fruit.

pimp (pĭmp) *n.* A man who procures clients for a prostitute. **—pimp** *v.*

pim•per•nel (pĭm′pər-nĕl′, -nəl) *n.* A low-growing plant, *Anagallis arvensis,* whose flowers close in wet weather.

pim•ple (pĭm′pəl) *n.* A small swelling on the skin that sometimes contains pus. **—pim′ply** *adj.*

pin (pĭn) *n.* **1.** A small, straight, rigid piece of wire with a sharp point and a blunt head, used esp. for fastening. **2.** Something, as a hairpin, that resembles a pin in shape or use. **3.** An ornament fastened to clothing with a clasp : brooch or badge. **4.** A cylindrical piece of metal or wood used for supporting or fastening. **5.** One of the wooden clubs serving as the target in bowling. **6.** The staff bearing the pennant that marks a hole on a golf course. **7. pins.** *Informal.* The legs. —*v.* **pinned, pin•ning. 1.** To secure or fasten with or as if with a pin. **2.** To make contingent <*pinned* our future on his success> **3.** To hold fast : immobilize. **4.** To establish clearly : define <couldn't *pin* down the source of the trouble> **5.** To assign culpability for <tried to *pin* the theft on the stranger>

pin•a•fore (pĭn′ə-fôr′, -fōr′) *n.* A sleeveless apronlike garment.

pin•ball (pĭn′bôl′) *n.* A game played on a device in which the player manipulates a ball over a slanted surface having obstacles and targets.

pince-nez (păɴs-nā′, păns-) *n., pl.* **pince-nez** (-nāz′, -nā′). Eyeglasses clipped with a spring to the bridge of the nose.

pin•cer (pĭn′sər) *n.* **1. pincers.** A grasping implement with 2 jaws and 2 handles pivoted together to work in opposition. **2.** A jointed, prehensile claw of certain arthropods, as a crab or lobster.

pinch (pĭnch) *v.* **1.** To squeeze between the thumb and forefinger or the jaws of an implement. **2.** To squeeze or compress so as to cause discomfort or pain. **3.** To shrivel : wither. **4.** To be thrifty or miserly. **5.** *Slang.* To steal. **6.** *Slang.* To arrest. —*n.* **1.** The act of pinching. **2.** An amount that can be held between the thumb and forefinger <a *pinch* of salt> **3.** A critical time : emergency. **4.** Strain : stress <felt the *pinch* of poverty> **5.** *Slang.* An arrest.

pinch-hit (pĭnch′hĭt′) *v.* **1.** *Baseball.* To bat in place of another player, esp. when a hit is badly needed. **2.** *Informal.* To act as a substitute for another. **—pinch hitter** *n.*

pin curl *n.* A coiled strand of usu. damp hair secured with a bobby pin or clip and combed into a wave or curl when dry.

pin•cush•ion (pĭn′ko͝osh′ən) *n.* A firm cushion in which pins and needles are stuck when not in use.

pine¹ (pīn) *n.* **1.** An evergreen tree of the genus *Pinus,* bearing cones and clusters of needle-shaped leaves. **2.** The wood of a pine tree. **—pin′y, pine′y** *adj.*

pine² (pīn) *v.* **pined, pin•ing. 1.** To long for something : yearn. **2.** To lose health or vitality from longing or grief.

pin•e•al body (pĭn′ē-əl, pī′nē-) *n.* A small rudimentary glandular body of uncertain function located in the brain.

pine•ap•ple (pīn′ăp′əl) *n.* A tropical American plant, *Ananas comosus,* bearing a large, fleshy, edible fruit.

pin•feath•er (pĭn′fĕth′ər) *n.* A growing feather still enclosed in its horny sheath, esp. one just emerging through the skin.

ping (pĭng) *n.* A high-pitched sound, as of a bullet striking metal. **—ping** *v.*

Ping-Pong (pĭng′pông′, -pŏng′). A trademark for table tennis.

pin•head (pĭn′hĕd′) *n.* **1.** The head of a pin. **2.** A stupid person : fool.

pin•hole (pĭn′hōl′) *n.* A very small hole made by or as if by a pin.

pin•ion¹ (pĭn′yən) *n.* The wing of a bird. —*v.* **1.** To immobilize or restrain (a person) by binding the arms. **2.** To fix in place : hold fast.

pin•ion² (pĭn′yən) *n.* A small cogwheel designed to mesh with a larger cogwheel or a rack.

pink¹ (pĭngk) *n.* **1.** Any of various plants of the genus *Dianthus,* related to the carnation and often cultivated for their fragrant flowers. **2.** A light or pale red. **3.** The highest degree possible <the *pink* of health> —*adj.* **1.** Of the color pink. **2.** Sympathetic with or holding Communist opinions.

pink[2] (pĭngk) *v.* **1.** To stab or pierce lightly with a pointed instrument. **2.** To ornament with a pattern of perforations. **3.** To cut a notched or zigzag edge on, as to prevent raveling.

pink•eye *also* **pink eye** (pĭngk'ī') *n.* Acute contagious conjunctivitis.

pink•ie *also* **pink•y** (pĭng'kē) *n., pl.* **-ies.** The 5th or smallest finger.

†**Pink•ster** *also* **Pinx•ter** (pĭngk'stər) *n. Regional.* Whitsunday.

pin money *n.* Money for incidental expenditures.

pin•nace (pĭn'əs) *n.* **1.** A small sailing boat once used as a tender. **2.** A small ship or ship's boat.

pin•na•cle (pĭn'ə-kəl) *n.* **1.** A small spirelike turret, as on a roof. **2.** A tall, pointed formation, as a mountain peak. **3.** The highest point : summit.

pinnacle

pin•nate (pĭn'āt') *adj.* Having like parts, as leaflets, arranged along each side of a common axis.

pi•noch•le *also* **pi•noc•le** (pē'nŭk'əl, -nŏk'-) *n.* A card game played with a special deck of 48 cards.

pi•ñon *also* **pin•yon** (pĭn'yən, -yōn') *n.* Any of several pine trees bearing edible, nutlike seeds, esp. *Pinus cembroides edulis,* of W North America.

pin•point (pĭn'point') *n.* **1.** The point of a pin. **2.** A very small spot or thing : particle. —*v.* To identify and locate precisely.

pin•prick (pĭn'prĭk') *n.* **1.** A very small puncture made by or as if by a pin. **2.** A small annoyance.

pin•stripe (pĭn'strīp') *n.* A fabric with thin, narrow stripes.

pint (pīnt) *n.* See MEASUREMENT TABLE.

pin•to (pĭn'tō) *n., pl.* **-tos** or **-toes.** A horse with irregular spots.

pint-size (pīnt'sīz') *also* **pint•sized** (-sīzd') *adj. Informal.* Very small.

pin•up (pĭn'ŭp') *n.* **1.** A picture, esp. of an attractive girl, to be pinned up on a wall. **2.** Someone, esp. a girl, considered suitable as the subject of a pinup. **—pin'up'** *adj.*

pin•wheel (pĭn'hwēl', -wēl') *n.* **1.** A toy consisting of a stick to which revolving vanes of paper or plastic are fastened. **2.** A firework in the form of a revolving wheel of colored flames.

pin•worm (pĭn'wûrm') *n.* A small nematode worm, *Enterobius vermicularis,* that infests the human intestines and rectum.

Pinx•ter (pĭngk'stər) *n. var. of* PINKSTER.

Pin•yin or **pin•yin** (pĭn'yĭn', -yĭn') *n.* A system for transliterating Chinese ideograms into the Latin alphabet.

pin•yon (pĭn'yən, -yōn') *n. var. of* PIÑON.

pi•o•neer (pī'ə-nîr') *n.* **1.** An early settler of an unknown or unclaimed territory. **2.** Someone who starts or leads others in the development of something new : innovator. **—pi'o•neer'** *v.*

▲word history: The word *pioneer* is derived from French *pion,* "foot soldier." *Pioneer* orig. denoted a soldier whose task was to prepare the way for the main body of troops marching to a new area. From this use the word was applied to anyone who ventures into an unknown region.

pi•ous (pī'əs) *adj.* **1. a.** Reverently and earnestly religious : devout. **b.** Falsely and ostentatiously devout. **2.** Characterized by solemn hypocrisy. **3.** Of or pertaining to devotion : sacred. **4.** Having or showing a sense of duty : high-minded. **—pi'ous•ly** *adv.* **—pi'ous•ness** *n.*

pip[1] (pĭp) *n.* A small fruit seed, as of an orange.

pip[2] (pĭp) *n.* A dot that indicates numerical value, as on dice or dominoes.

pip[3] (pĭp) *n.* **1.** A disease of birds. **2.** An imaginary or minor human ailment.

pipe (pīp) *n.* **1.** A long hollow cylinder through which a fluid or gas can flow : tube. **2.** A tube with a small bowl at 1 end and a mouthpiece at the other that is used for smoking tobacco. **3. a.** A musical instrument, as a small flute, that consists of a tube. **b.** A bagpipe. —*v.* **piped, pip•ing. 1.** To convey in or as if in pipes. **2.** To play (music) on a pipe. **3.** To speak in a shrill voice. **—pipe down.** *Slang.* To stop talking : be quiet. **—pipe up.** *Slang.* To begin talking : speak up. **—pip'er** *n.*

pipe dream *n.* An unattainable or fantastic idea or hope.

pipe fitter *n.* One who installs and repairs piping systems.

pipe•line (pīp'līn') *n.* **1.** A channel of pipe for conveying fluids, esp. water or petroleum, over great distances. **2.** A direct channel through which information is transmitted. **—pipe'line'** *v.*

pipe organ *n.* ORGAN 1.

pi•pette *also* **pi•pet** (pī-pĕt') *n.* An open-ended and often graduated tube used for transferring small volumes of liquid.

pip•ing (pī'pĭng) *n.* **1.** A system of pipes. **2.** A narrow band or fold of material used to trim seams or edges.

pip•it (pĭp'ĭt) *n.* A widely distributed songbird of the genus *Anthus.*

pip•kin (pĭp'kĭn) *n.* A small earthenware or metal cooking pot.

pip•pin (pĭp'ĭn) *n.* **1.** Any of several varieties of apple. **2.** *Slang.* One that is greatly admired.

pip-squeak (pĭp'skwēk') *n.* A small or unimportant person.

pi•quant (pē'kənt, -känt', pē-känt') *adj.* **1.** Pleasantly pungent in taste or odor : spicy. **2.** Appealingly stimulating or provocative. **—pi'quan•cy** *n.* **—pi'quant•ly** *adv.*

pique (pēk) *n.* A feeling or fit of resentment stemming from wounded vanity or pride. —*v.* **piqued, piqu•ing. 1.** To cause to feel pique. **2.** To arouse <silence that *piqued* our curiosity>

pi•qué (pĭ-kā') *n.* A firm clothing fabric with ribs in various patterns.

pi•ra•nha *also* **pi•ra•ña** (pĭ-rän'yə, -răn'-) *n.* Any of several sharp-toothed tropical American freshwater fishes of the genus *Serrasalmus* that often attack animals.

pi•rate (pī'rĭt) *n.* **1.** Someone who commits robbery on the high seas. **2.** Someone who uses or reproduces the work of another illicitly or without authorization. **—pi'ra•cy** *n.* **—pi'rate** *v.* **—pi•rat'ic** (pī-răt'ĭk), **pi•rat'i•cal** *adj.* **—pi•rat'i•cal•ly** *adv.*

pi•rogue (pĭ-rōg') *n.* A canoe made from a hollowed tree trunk.

pir•ou•ette (pĭr'o͞o-ĕt') *n.* A full turn of the body on the ball of the foot or the tip of the toe. **—pir'ou•ette'** *v.*

pis•ca•to•ri•al (pĭs'kə-tôr'ē-əl, -tōr'-) *adj.* Of or pertaining to fishing.

Pi•sces (pī'sēz') *n.* **1.** A constellation in the N Hemisphere. **2. a.** The 12th sign of the zodiac. **b.** One born under this sign.

pis•mire (pĭs'mīr', pĭz'-) *n.* An ant.

pis•ta•chi•o (pĭ-stăsh'ē-ō', -stä'shē-ō') *n., pl.* **-os.** A tree, *Pistacia vera,* bearing hard-shelled, edible nuts with a green kernel.

pis•til (pĭs'təl) *n.* The seed-bearing female reproductive organ of a flower.

pis•tol (pĭs'təl) *n.* A small firearm that can be held and fired with 1 hand.

pis•tol-whip (pĭs'təl-hwĭp', -wĭp') *v.* To beat with the barrel of a pistol.

pis•ton (pĭs'tən) *n.* A solid cylinder that fits into a larger cylinder and moves back and forth under fluid pressure, as in an engine, or displaces or compresses fluids, as in a pump.

pit[1] (pĭt) *n.* **1.** A natural or manmade hole in the ground. **2.** Hell. **3.** An enclosed space, as that used for cockfighting. **4. a.** A natural depression in the surface of a body, organ, or part. **b.** An indentation in the skin caused by injury or disease. **5.** The section directly in front of a theater stage for the orchestra. **6.** The section of a commodities exchange where trading is carried on. **7.** An area for repair and refueling at an auto racecourse. **8. pits.** *Slang.* The worst <a situation that's the *pits*> —*v.* **pit•ted, pit•ting. 1. a.** To make pits in. **b.** To become marked with pits. **2.** To set into contest or competition.

pit[2] (pĭt) *n.* The single, central kernel of certain fruits, as a cherry or peach. —*v.* **pit•ted, pit•ting.** To extract the pit from.

pi•ta (pē'tə) *n.* Round, flat bread that is hollow inside and forms a pocket when cut.

pit•a•pat (pĭt'ə-păt') *n.* A rapid series of taps, steps, or beats.

pitch[1] (pĭch) *n.* **1.** A thick, dark, sticky substance derived esp. from the distillation residue of coal tar or petroleum. **2.** A resin derived from the sap of a conifer.

pitch[2] (pĭch) *v.* **1.** To throw, often toward a target : toss. **2.** *Baseball.* To throw (the ball) from the mound to the batter. **3.** To set up and fix in position <*pitched* the tent> **4.** To fix at a certain level <*pitched* her hopes too high> **5.** To fall forward : plunge. **6.** *Naut.* To dip bow and stern alternately. **7.** To slope downward. **—pitch in. 1.** To set to work vigorously. **2.** To cooperate with others in working toward a common goal. —*n.* **1.** An act or instance of pitching. **2.** A degree of slant. **3.** A level or degree of a state or quality <enthusiasm at a feverish *pitch*> **4.**

Lowness or highness of a sound, esp. a musical sound. **5. a.** The throw of a baseball by a pitcher to a batter. **b.** The ball so thrown. **6.** *Slang.* A line of talk intended to persuade.

pitch-black (pĭch′blăk′) *adj.* Extremely dark or black.

pitch•blende (pĭch′blĕnd′) *n.* A brownish-black mineral that is the essential ore of uranium.

pitch-dark (pĭch′därk′) *adj.* Extremely dark <a *pitch-dark* night>

pitch•er¹ (pĭch′ər) *n. Baseball.* The player who pitches the ball to the batter.

pitch•er² (pĭch′ər) *n.* A container, usu. with a handle and a lip or spout, for holding and pouring liquids.

pitcher plant *n.* An insectivorous plant of the genera *Sarracenia, Nepenthes,* or *Darlingtonia,* with pitcher-shaped leaves that trap insects.

pitch•fork (pĭch′fôrk′) *n.* A large fork with widely spaced prongs used esp. for pitching hay.

pitch•man (pĭch′mən) *n.* A vender or peddler of small wares, esp. one with a colorful or high-powered sales talk.

pitch pipe *n.* A small pipe sounded to establish the pitch for singing a piece of music or tuning an instrument.

pit•e•ous (pĭt′ē-əs) *adj.* Arousing pity : sad. **—pit′e•ous•ly** *adv.*

pit•fall (pĭt′fôl′) *n.* **1.** A trap, esp. a concealed pit in the ground used for snaring animals. **2.** An unexpected difficulty or hidden danger.

pith (pĭth) *n.* **1.** *Bot.* The soft, spongelike tissue in the center of the stems and branches of many vascular plants. **2.** The central or essential part : essence.

pith•y (pĭth′ē) *adj.* **-i•er, -i•est. 1.** Of or like pith. **2.** Terse, cogent, and meaningful. **—pith′i•ly** *adv.* **—pith′i•ness** *n.*

pit•i•a•ble (pĭt′ē-ə-bəl) *adj.* Pitiful.

pit•i•ful (pĭt′ĭ-fəl) *adj.* **1.** Deserving or arousing pity <a *pitiful* orphan> **2.** Meriting contempt : contemptible <a *pitiful* salary> **—pit′i•ful•ly** *adv.*

pit•i•less (pĭt′ĭ-lĭs) *adj.* Without pity : merciless. **—pit′i•less•ly** *adv.* **—pit′i•less•ness** *n.*

pi•ton (pē′tŏn′) *n.* A metal spike, often with an eye through which a rope can be passed, that can be driven into ice or rock as a support, as in mountain climbing.

pit•tance (pĭt′ns) *n.* A small portion or amount, as of money.

pit•ter-pat•ter (pĭt′ər-păt′ər) *n.* A rapid series of light sounds or taps. **—pit′ter-pat′ter** *v.*

Pitts•burgh (pĭts′bûrg′). City of SW Pa. *Pop.* 423,938.

pi•tu•i•tar•y (pĭ-to͞o′ĭ-tĕr′ē, -tyo͞o′-) *n., pl.* **-ies.** A small, oval endocrine gland situated at the base of the vertebrate brain. **—pi•tu′i•tar′y** *adj.*

pit viper *n.* A venomous snake of the family Crotalidae, as a rattlesnake or copperhead, with a small pit on each side of the head.

pit•y (pĭt′ē) *n., pl.* **-ies. 1.** A feeling of sorrow for another's misfortune : compassion. **2.** A regrettable fact or situation. ☆**syns:** COMMISERATION, COMPASSION, SYMPATHY *—v.* **-ied, -y•ing.** To feel pity for.

piv•ot (pĭv′ət) *n.* **1.** A shaft or rod on which something turns. **2.** One on which the direction, development, or effect of something else depends. *—v.* To swing or turn on or as if on a pivot. **—piv′ot•al** *adj.*

pix¹ (pĭks) *n. var. of* PYX.

pix² (pĭks) *n. var. pl. of* PIC.

pix•y *also* **pix•ie** (pĭk′sē) *n., pl.* **-ies.** An elfin or mischievous creature.

piz•za (pēt′sə) *n.* An open pie consisting of a crust covered usu. with a spiced mixture, as of tomatoes and cheese, and baked.

piz•zazz *also* **pi•zazz** (pĭ-zăz′) *n. Slang.* Zest : flair.

piz•ze•ri•a (pēt′sə-rē′ə) *n.* A place where pizzas are baked and sold.

piz•zi•ca•to (pĭt′sĭ-kä′tō) *adv. Mus.* By plucking rather than bowing. Used as a direction. **—piz′zi•ca′to** *adj.*

pj's (pē′jāz′) *pl.n. Informal.* Pajamas.

pk. *abbr.* **1.** pack. **2.** park. **3.** peak. **4.** *also* **pk** peck.

pkg. or **pkge.** *abbr.* package.

pl. *abbr.* **1.** platoon. **2.** plural.

plac•ard (plăk′ärd′, -ərd) *n.* A notice, esp. a poster for display in a public place. *—v.* **1.** To announce in or as if in a placard. **2.** To post placards on, in, or throughout.

pla•cate (plā′kāt′, plăk′āt′) *v.* **-cat•ed, -cat•ing.** To mollify, esp. by yielding concessions : appease. **—plac′a•ble** *adj.*

place (plās) *n.* **1.** An area : region. **2.** An area, as a building, set aside for a particular use or purpose. **3.** A particular location, as a population center. **4.** A public square in a city or town. **5.** A position of employment : job. **6.** The position occupied by a substitute : stead. **7.** A relative position in a sequence or series : standing. **8. a.** A residence. **b.** A seat <took her *place* at the table> *—v.* **placed, plac•ing. 1.** To put in a particular place or order : set. **2.** To recognize : identify <couldn't *place* his face> **3.** To rank in a sequence or order. **4.** To make : give <*place* an order> **5.** To finish in 2nd place or among the first 3 finishers in a competition, as a race.

pla•ce•bo (plə-sē′bō) *n., pl.* **-bos** *or* **-boes. 1.** A substance having no medication that is administered for its psychological effect on a patient. **2.** An inert substance used as a control in an experiment.

place kick *n. Football.* The kicking, as for a field goal, of a ball that is held or placed in a fixed position on the ground. **—place′-kick′** *v.*

place mat *n.* A mat for a single setting at a meal.

place•ment (plās′mənt) *n.* **1.** The act or an instance of placing. **2.** The business or function of finding positions, as employment, for applicants.

pla•cen•ta (plə-sĕn′tə) *n., pl.* **-tas** *or* **-tae** (-tē). The vascular, membranous structure that supplies a mammalian fetus with nourishment before its birth and to which the fetus is attached by the umbilical cord. **—pla•cen′tal** (-sĕn′tl) *adj.*

plac•er (plăs′ər) *n.* A deposit left by a glacier or river that contains particles of valuable minerals.

plac•id (plăs′ĭd) *adj.* Marked by calm, quiet, or composure : serene. **—pla•cid′i•ty** (plə-sĭd′ĭ-tē) *n.* **—plac′id•ly** *adv.*

plack•et (plăk′ĭt) *n.* A slit in a dress, blouse, or skirt.

pla•gia•rize (plā′jə-rīz′) *v.* **-rized, -riz•ing.** To take and use as one's own the ideas or writings of another. **—pla′gia•rism** *n.* **—pla′gia•rist** *n.*

plague (plāg) *n.* **1.** An affliction : calamity. **2.** A cause of irritation : nuisance. **3.** An infectious and often fatal epidemic disease, esp. bubonic plague. *—v.* **plagued, plagu•ing. 1.** To afflict with or as if with calamity or disease. **2.** To harass : pester.

plaice (plās) *n., pl.* **plaice** *or* **plaic•es. 1.** An edible marine flatfish, *Pleuronectes platessa,* of W European waters. **2.** A related flatfish, *Hippoglossoides platessoides,* of North American Atlantic waters.

plaid (plăd) *n.* **1.** A rectangular piece of wool of a tartan pattern worn esp. over 1 shoulder by Scottish Highlanders. **2.** A fabric, esp. of wool, with a tartan pattern. **3.** A tartan pattern. **—plaid** *adj.*

plain (plān) *adj.* **1.** Free from obstructions : open <in *plain* sight> **2.** Easy to understand : clear. **3.** Not complicated : simple <*plain* food> **4.** Straightforward : candid <*plain* talk> **5.** Common : ordinary <just *plain* folks> **6.** Having little ornamentation : undecorated. **7.** Not beautiful : homely. *—n.* An extensive region of level, treeless land. *—adv.* In a plain manner. **—plain′ly** *adv.* **—plain′ness** *n.*

plain•clothes man (plān′klōz′) *also* **plain•clothes•man** (plān′klōz′mən) *n.* A police officer who wears civilian clothes while on duty.

plain•spo•ken (plān′spō′kən) *adj.* Candid : straightforward.

plaint (plānt) *n.* **1.** A complaint. **2.** An utterance of sorrow or grief : lamentation.

plain•tiff (plān′tĭf) *n.* The party that files a complaint in a lawsuit.

plain•tive (plān′tĭv) *adj.* Expressive of sorrow or melancholy : woeful. **—plain′tive•ly** *adv.* **—plain′tive•ness** *n.*

plait (plāt, plăt) *n.* **1.** A braid, esp. of hair. **2.** A pleat. **—plait** *v.*

plan (plăn) *n.* **1.** A method or scheme for achieving or doing something. **2.** An aim : goal. **3.** A diagram or drawing prepared to scale. *—v.* **planned, plan•ning. 1.** To draw up a plan of : design <*planned* a new shopping mall> **2.** To have in mind : intend. **3.** To formulate a way to achieve or do. **—plan′ner** *n.*

plane¹ (plān) *n.* **1.** A surface containing all the straight lines required to connect any 2 points on it. **2.** A level or flat surface. **3.** A level of development or existence. **4.** An airplane. **5.** A supporting surface of an airplane.

plane² (plān) *n.* A tool for leveling or smoothing a wood surface. *—v.* **planed, plan•ing.** To level or smooth with or as if with a plane. **—plan′er** *n.*

plan•et (plăn′ĭt) *n.* A nonluminous celestial body illuminated by light from a star around which it revolves. **—plan′e•tar′y** (-ĭ-tĕr′ē) *adj.*

plan•e•tar•i•um (plăn′ĭ-târ′ē-əm) *n., pl.* **-ums** *or* **-i•a** (-ē-ə). **1.** A device to project images of celestial bodies in their courses, as onto the inner surface of a dome. **2.** A room or building containing a planetarium.

plane tree *n.* A tree of the genus *Platanus,* with ball-shaped clusters of fruit and outer bark that usu. flakes off in patches.

plan•gent (plăn′jənt) *adj.* **1.** Deep and reverberating in sound. **2.** Plaintive. **—plan′gen•cy** *n.* **—plan′gent•ly** *adv.*

plank (plăngk) *n.* **1.** A long, thick board. **2.** An item in a political platform. *—v.* **1.** To cover with planks. **2.** To cook and serve (meat or fish) on a board. **3.** To set or put down with force.

plank·ing (plăng′kĭng) *n.* **1.** Planks as a whole. **2.** Something made of planks.

plank·ton (plăngk′tən) *n.* Microscopic plant and animal organisms that float or drift in great numbers in bodies of water. **–plank·ton′ic** (-tŏn′ĭk) *adj.*

plant (plănt) *n.* **1.** An organism typically having cellulose cell walls, manufacturing its own food by photosynthesis, and being incapable of locomotion. **2.** A soft-stemmed, herbaceous plant as distinguished from a tree or shrub. **3.** An establishment for industry or manufacturing : factory. **4.** The physical structures, equipment, and fixtures of an institution. *–v.* **1.** To place (e.g., seeds) in the ground for growing. **2.** To set firmly or forcibly in position. **3.** To start : establish. **4.** To instill <*plant* an idea> **5.** To place with intent to spy or deceive.

plan·tain[1] (plăn′tən) *n.* A weedy plant of the genus *Plantago*, esp. *P. major*, with a spike of small greenish flowers.

plan·tain[2] (plăn′tən) *n.* A large tropical plant, *Musa paradisiaca*, resembling the banana and bearing similar fruit.

plan·tar (plăn′tər, -tär′) *adj.* Of, relating to, or located on the sole of the foot.

plan·ta·tion (plăn-tā′shən) *n.* **1.** A sizable group of trees or plants under cultivation. **2.** A large landed estate devoted to crop production, usu. by resident workers.

plant·er (plăn′tər) *n.* **1.** One that plants, esp. a sowing tool or machine. **2.** One who owns or manages a plantation. **3.** An ornamental container for a plant.

plaque (plăk) *n.* **1.** A flat piece often made of metal, ornamented or engraved for mounting, as on a building or memorial. **2.** An ornamental pin : brooch. **3.** A bacteria-containing deposit on a tooth.

plash (plăsh) *n.* **1.** A light splash. **2.** The sound of a plash. **–plash** *v.*

plas·ma (plăz′mə) *n.* **1.** The clear, liquid part of blood, lymph, or intramuscular fluid. **2.** The watery part of milk : whey. **3.** *Physics.* An electrically neutral, usu. hot gas containing ionized and neutral particles. **–plas·mat′ic, plas′mic** *adj.*

plas·ter (plăs′tər) *n.* **1.** A paste that hardens while drying, used for covering walls and ceilings. **2.** Plaster of Paris. **3.** An often medicated pastelike mixture spread on a piece of material and applied to a part of the body. *–v.* To coat or cover with or as if with plaster. **–plas′ter·y** *adj.*

plas·ter·board (plăs′tər-bôrd′, -bōrd′) *n.* A wallboard made up of layers of fiberboard or paper over a plaster core.

plaster of Paris *n.* A quick-setting paste of white gypsum powder and water, used esp. for casts and statuary molds.

plas·tic (plăs′tĭk) *adj.* **1.** Capable of being shaped or molded : malleable. **2.** Of, marked by, or using expressive shaping or modeling <the *plastic* arts> **3.** Marked by artificiality : synthetic <the *plastic* world of advertising> *–n.* A synthetically produced material that can be molded and hardened into objects or formed into films or textile fibers. **–plas·tic′i·ty** (plă-stĭs′ĭ-tē) *n.* **–plas′ti·cize′** *v.*

plastic surgery *n.* Surgery concerned with repairing, restoring, or remodeling bodily parts chiefly by bone or tissue transfer. **–plastic surgeon** *n.*

plate (plāt) *n.* **1.** A flat, thin piece of material, as metal. **2. a.** Forged, rolled, or cast metal in sheet form. **b.** A flat piece of engraved metal. **3. a.** A prepared surface, as of metal or plastic, from which printing is done. **b.** A print from such a surface. **c.** Something printed from an engraving. **4.** A sheet of glass or metal sensitized to light and used in photography. **5.** A part made of metal or plastic that is fitted to the gums to hold false teeth in place. **6.** *Baseball.* Home plate. **7.** A shallow, usu. circular dish. **8.** Food and service for 1 person. **9.** Household articles, as forks and knives, made of or plated with gold or silver. *–v.* **plat·ed, plat·ing. 1.** To cover with a thin layer of metal, esp. gold or silver. **2.** To make a printing surface from or for.

pla·teau (plă-tō′) *n., pl.* **-teaus** or **-teaux** (-tōz′). **1.** A level expanse of elevated land. **2. a.** A stage of development. **b.** A stable period or state.

plate glass *n.* Rolled and polished glass in thick, strong sheets.

plat·en (plăt′n) *n.* **1.** A flat metal plate that holds the paper against the type in a printing press. **2.** The roller in a typewriter against which the keys hit.

plat·form (plăt′fôrm′) *n.* **1.** An elevated horizontal surface, as for speakers or at a railroad station. **2.** A formal statement of principles or policy, as of a political party.

plat·ing (plā′tĭng) *n.* A thin layer, coating, or covering of metal or of metal plates.

plat·i·num (plăt′n-əm) *n. Symbol* **Pt** A silver-white, corrosive-resistant metallic element used esp. in jewelry.

plat·i·tude (plăt′ĭ-to͞od′, -tyo͞od′) *n.* A trite and shallow idea or remark. **–plat′i·tu′di·nize′** *v.* **–plat′i·tu′di·nous** *adj.*

Pla·to (plā′tō). 427?–347 B.C. Greek philosopher. **–Pla·ton′ic** *adj.*

pla·ton·ic (plə-tŏn′ĭk, plā-) *adj.* Transcending sexual desire : purely intellectual or spiritual. **–pla·ton′i·cal·ly** *adv.*

pla·toon (plə-to͞on′) *n.* **1.** A military unit usu. consisting of 2 or more squads. **2.** A group of players, esp. in football, acting as an offensive or defensive body.

plat·ter (plăt′ər) *n.* **1.** A large, shallow plate for serving food. **2.** *Slang.* A phonograph record.

plat·y·pus (plăt′ə-pəs) *n., pl.* **-es.** A semiaquatic, web-footed, egg-laying Australian mammal, *Ornithorhynchus anatinus*, with a snout resembling a duck's bill.

plau·dit (plô′dĭt) *n.* An act or expression of approval or praise.

plau·si·ble (plô′zə-bəl) *adj.* Appearing true, believable, or reasonable. **–plau′si·bil′i·ty** *n.* **–plau′si·bly** *adv.*

play (plā) *v.* **1.** To amuse oneself, as in recreation. **2.** To participate in (a game or sport). **3.** To do in jest <*play* a joke> **4.** To act frivolously or idly : trifle. **5.** To behave in a given way. **6.** To perform (a dramatic role). **7. a.** To perform music on (an instrument). **b.** To perform (music) on an instrument. **8.** To be presented. **9.** To move lightly, rapidly, or sporadically. **10.** To make a pretense of being <*play* dead> **11.** To strive against in a game. **12. a.** To fill (a position) in a game. **b.** To use (e.g., a player or card) in a game. **13.** To perform (a role or part) in a process. **14. a.** To gamble. **b.** To make wagers on. **15.** To cause (e.g., a record or phonograph) to emit sounds. *–n.* **1. a.** A literary composition for the stage. **b.** The performance of a play. **2.** Recreational activity for pleasure, esp. the impulsive activity of children. **3.** Fun : jest. **4.** The act or manner of engaging in a game or sport. **5.** A way of operating. **6.** A maneuver in a game. **7.** Scope or freedom for action or use. **8.** Free motion, as of machinery. **–play ball.** To cooperate. **–play down.** To minimize the importance of. **–play up.** To give emphasis to. **–play′a·ble** *adj.* **–play′er** *n.*

pla·ya (plī′ə) *n.* A level area at the bottom of a desert basin that is at times covered with water.

play-act (plā′ăkt′) *v.* **1.** To perform in a theatrical production. **2.** To make believe : pretend. **3.** To behave in an affected or insincere way. **–play′-act′ing** *n.*

play·back (plā′băk′) *n.* The act or process of replaying a newly made record or tape.

play·bill (plā′bĭl′) *n.* An advertising poster for a play.

play·boy (plā′boi′) *n.* A man devoted to pleasure-seeking.

player piano *n.* A mechanically operated piano using a punched paper roll to activate the keys.

play·ful (plā′fəl) *adj.* **1.** Full of high spirits : lively. **2.** Full of humor : jocular. **–play′ful·ly** *adv.* **–play′ful·ness** *n.*

play·go·er (plā′gō′ər) *n.* One who frequently goes to see plays.

play·ground (plā′ground′) *n.* An area set aside for outdoor play and recreation, esp. for children.

play·house (plā′hous′). **1.** A theater. **2.** A small house for children to play in. **3.** A doll house.

playing card *n.* A card of a specified rank and suit that belongs to a deck and is used in playing card games.

playing field *n.* A field for games such as cricket and soccer.

play·let (plā′lĭt) *n.* A short play.

play·mate (plā′māt′) *n.* A friend in play.

play-off (plā′ôf′, -ŏf′) *n.* A sports contest or series of contests to determine a winner or championship.

play·pen (plā′pĕn′) *n.* A portable enclosure in which a baby or small child can be left to play.

play·thing (plā′thĭng′) *n.* A toy.

play·wright (plā′rīt′) *n.* A dramatist.

pla·za (plä′zə, plăz′ə) *n.* **1.** An open area, esp. a public square, in a town or city. **2.** A shopping center or mall.

plea (plē) *n.* **1.** An appeal or urgent request. **2.** An explanation by way of defense or excuse : pretext. **3.** *Law.* A defendant's answer to a charge or indictment.

plea-bar·gain (plē′bär′gən) *v.* To make a pretrial agreement to plead guilty to a lesser charge if a more serious one is dropped. **–plea′-bar′gain·ing** *n.*

plead (plēd) *v.* **plead·ed** or **pled** (plĕd), **plead·ing. 1.** To appeal fervently : entreat. **2.** To make an argument for or against something, as in a court. **3.** To give as an excuse <*plead* fatigue> **4.** *Law.* To put forward a formal plea of <*plead* not guilty> **5.** To present or argue (a case) before a court. **–plead′a·ble** *adj.*

pleas·ant (plĕz′ənt) *adj.* **1.** Affording pleasure : very agreeable. **2.** Pleasing in manner or appearance. **–pleas′ant·ly** *adv.* **–pleas′ant·ness** *n.*

pleas·ant·ry (plĕz′ən-trē) *n., pl.* **-ries. 1.** An entertaining or humorous act or remark. **2.** An amiable social remark.

please (plēz) *v.* **pleased, pleas·ing. 1.** To make happy or satisfied. **2.** To be the wish or will of <May it *please* the tribunal.> **3.** To be willing or disposed to <*Please* sit down.> **4.** To wish or prefer <We do as we *please.*> **–pleas′er** *n.*

pleas·ur·a·ble (plĕzh′ər-ə-bəl) *adj.* Giving pleasure : agreeable or gratifying. **–pleas′ur·a·bly** *adv.*

pleas·ure (plĕzh′ər) *n.* **1.** A feeling of enjoyment or satisfaction. **2.** Something that gives enjoyment. **3.** One's choice, wish, or preference.

pleat (plēt) *n.* A fold in fabric made by doubling the cloth back and stitching it down. **–pleat** *v.*

plebe (plēb) *n.* A 1st-year student at a military academy.

ple·be·ian (plĭ-bē′ən) *adj.* Vulgar : crude. *–n.* **1.** One of the common people. **2.** One who is considered vulgar or coarse.

pleb·i·scite (plĕb′ĭ-sīt′) *n.* A direct vote by an electorate on an important issue or proposal.

plebs (plĕbz) *n., pl.* **ple·bes** (plē′bēz′). **1.** The commoners of ancient Rome. **2.** The common people : the masses.

plec·trum (plĕk′trəm) *n., pl.* **-trums** *or* **-tra** (-trə). A small, thin piece, as of metal or plastic, used to pluck the strings of an instrument, as a guitar.

pled (plĕd) *v. var. p.t. & p.p. of* PLEAD.

pledge (plĕj) *n.* **1.** A solemn vow or promise. **2.** Something given or held as security for the fulfillment of a debt or an obligation. **3.** One who has promised to join a fraternity. *–v.* **pledged, pledg·ing. 1.** To vow or promise solemnly. **2.** To put under obligation or commitment by or as if by a pledge. **3.** To give as security.

ple·na·ry (plē′nə-rē, plĕn′ə-) *adj.* **1.** Complete : full. **2.** Including all members qualified to attend. **–ple′na·ri·ly** *adv.*

plen·i·po·ten·ti·ar·y (plĕn′ə-pə-tĕn′shē-ĕr′ē, -shə-rē) *n., pl.* **-ies.** A diplomat given full authority to act for a government. **–plen′i·po·ten′ti·ar′y** *adj.*

plen·i·tude (plĕn′ĭ-to͞od′, -tyo͞od′) *n.* The quality or state of being full or abundant.

plen·te·ous (plĕn′tē-əs) *adj.* Plentiful. **–plen′te·ous·ness** *n.*

plen·ti·ful (plĕn′tĭ-fəl) *adj.* **1.** Existing in great abundance. **2.** Having or producing an abundance. **–plen′ti·ful·ly** *adv.* **–plen′ti·ful·ness** *n.*

plen·ty (plĕn′tē) *n.* **1.** An ample amount or supply. **2.** Abundance or prosperity.

ple·num (plē′nəm, plĕn′əm) *n., pl.* **ple·nums** *or* **ple·na** (plē′nə, plĕn′ə). **1.** An enclosure in which the air is at a pressure greater than that outside the enclosure. **2.** An assembly attended by all members.

pleth·o·ra (plĕth′ər-ə) *n.* An excess.

pleu·ra (plo͝or′ə) *n., pl.* **pleu·rae** (plo͝or′ē). Either of 2 membranous sacs lining the thoracic cavity and enveloping the lungs. **–pleu′ral** *adj.*

pleu·ri·sy (plo͝or′ĭ-sē) *n.* Inflammation of the pleura. **–pleu·rit′ic** (-rĭt′ĭk) *adj.*

Plex·i·glas (plĕk′sĭ-glăs′). A trademark for a strong, transparent thermoplastic.

plex·us (plĕk′səs) *n., pl.* **-us** *or* **-us·es.** An intertwining network, as of nerves or blood vessels.

plf. *abbr.* plaintiff.

pli·a·ble (plī′ə-bəl) *adj.* **1.** Flexible : pliant. **2.** Easily influenced by others. **–pli′a·bil′i·ty, pli′a·ble·ness** *n.* **–pli′a·bly** *adv.*

pli·ant (plī′ənt) *adj.* **1.** Flexible : pliable. **2.** Readily adaptable to change. **–pli′an·cy** *n.* **–pli′ant·ly** *adv.*

pli·ers (plī′ərz) *pl.n.* (*sing. or pl. in number*). A pincerslike tool for bending, cutting, or holding.

plight[1] (plīt) *n.* A condition or situation, esp. a distressing one.

plight[2] (plīt) *v.* To bind or promise by a pledge, esp. to promise to marry.

plink (plĭngk) *v.* To make or cause to make a metallic clinking sound.

plinth (plĭnth) *n.* A block or slab at the base of a column.

plod (plŏd) *v.* **plod·ded, plod·ding. 1.** To walk or proceed in or as if in a slow, heavy-footed way. **2.** To work doggedly or laboriously. **–plod′der** *n.* **–plod′ding·ly** *adv.*

plop (plŏp) *v.* **plopped, plop·ping. 1.** To fall or move with a sound resembling that of an object dropping into water. **2.** To drop or allow to drop heavily.

plot (plŏt) *n.* **1.** A small piece of ground <a garden *plot*> **2.** The series of actions or events of a literary work, as a novel. **3.** A secret, esp. illicit plan. ☆***syns:*** COLLUSION, CONSPIRACY, INTRIGUE, MACHINATION, SCHEME *–v.* **plot·ted, plot·ting. 1.** To mark, note, or represent, as on a chart or map. **2.** To plan or scheme secretly : intrigue. **–plot′ter** *n.*

plough (plou) *n. & v. esp. Brit. var. of* PLOW.

plov·er (plŭv′ər, plō′vər) *n., pl.* **-ers** *or* **-er.** Any of various widely distributed wading birds of the family Charadriidae, with rounded bodies, short bills, and short tails.

plow (plou) *n.* **1.** An implement used for breaking up, turning over, and cutting soil. **2.** An implement functioning like a plow, esp. a snowplow. *–v.* **1.** To break up, turn over, and cut (soil) with a plow. **2.** To remove snow (from) with a snowplow. **3.** To move or advance forcefully or laboriously. **–plow back.** To put (earned profits) back into one's business. **–plow′a·ble** *adj.* **–plow′er** *n.*

plow·boy (plou′boi′) *n.* A boy who guides a plow or animals used in plowing.

plow·share (plou′shâr′) *n.* The cutting part of a plow.

ploy (ploi) *n.* A maneuver or scheme to outwit an opponent.

pluck (plŭk) *v.* **1.** To remove by pulling off or out : pick. **2.** To pull (e.g., hair or feathers) from. **3.** To pull at and release (the strings of an instrument) *–n.* **1.** The act of plucking. **2.** Courage and fortitude : spirit. **–pluck′er** *n.*

pluck·y (plŭk′ē) *adj.* **-i·er, -i·est.** Marked by spirit and courage. **–pluck′i·ly** *adv.* **–pluck′i·ness** *n.*

plug (plŭg) *n.* **1.** A device used to close an opening. **2. a.** A fitting, usu. with metal prongs, attached to a cord and used in a socket to make an electrical connection. **b.** A spark plug. **3.** A fireplug. **4.** A cake of chewing tobacco. **5.** *Slang.* An inferior or worn-out horse. **6.** *Informal.* An instance of favorable publicity or free advertising. *–v.* **plugged, plug·ging. 1.** To stop up tightly with or as if with a plug. **2.** To connect or disconnect by means of a plug. **3.** *Slang.* To shoot with a bullet. **4.** *Informal.* To publicize or advertise favorably or insistently. **5.** *Informal.* To work persistently. **–plug′ger** *n.*

plum (plŭm) *n.* **1.** A shrub or small tree of the genus *Prunus,* bearing smooth-skinned, fleshy, edible fruit with a single hard-shelled pit. **2.** Something considered very desirable, as a prestigious job.

plum·age (plo͞o′mĭj) *n.* **1.** The feathers of a bird. **2.** Finery.

plumb (plŭm) *n.* A weight on the end of a line used to measure depth or test vertical alignment. *–adj.* **1.** Precisely vertical. **2.** *Informal.* Thorough : downright. *–adv.* **1.** Straight up and down. **2.** Thoroughly : completely. *–v.* To test the alignment or depth of with or as if with a plumb.

plumb·er (plŭm′ər) *n.* One who fits and repairs plumbing pipes and equipment.

plumb·ing (plŭm′ĭng) *n.* **1.** The equipment, as pipes and fixtures, of a water, gas, or sewage system. **2.** The activities or business of a plumber.

plume (plo͞om) *n.* A feather, esp. a large and showy one used for decoration. *–v.* **plumed, plum·ing. 1.** To adorn with or as if with feathers. **2.** To permit (oneself) to feel or show pride or satisfaction. **–plumed** *adj.* **–plum′y** *adj.*

plum·met (plŭm′ĭt) *v.* To fall or plunge straight downward.

plump[1] (plŭmp) *adj.* Having a full, rounded shape. *–v.* To make or become rounded and full. **–plump′ish** *adj.* **–plump′ly** *adv.* **–plump′ness** *n.*

plump[2] (plŭmp) *v.* **1.** To throw or drop down heavily or suddenly. **2.** To support someone or something strongly. *–n.* **1.** A heavy or sudden fall. **2.** The sound of a plump. *–adv.* **1.** Heavily or abruptly. **2.** Straight down or straight ahead. **3.** Without reservations : wholeheartedly.

plun·der (plŭn′dər) *v.* To deprive of goods or property forcibly and unlawfully : pillage. *–n.* Seized or stolen property or goods. **–plun′der·er** *n.*

plunge (plŭnj) *v.* **plunged, plung·ing. 1. a.** To cast oneself into or as if into water. **b.** To immerse or submerse. **2.** To enter or cause to enter abruptly into a specified state or activity. **3.** To fall or descend steeply or sharply **4.** To move swiftly or forcefully downward or forward. **5.** To gamble rashly. **–plunge** *n.*

plung·er (plŭn′jər) *n.* **1.** A machine part, as a piston, that works with a repeated plunging movement. **2.** A rubber suction cup on a handle that is used to clean out clogged drains and pipes.

plunk (plŭngk) *v. Informal.* **1.** To put down or drop heavily or suddenly. **2.** To make or cause to make a hollow, twanging sound. **–plunk** *n.* **–plunk′er** *n.*

plu·per·fect (plo͞o-pûr′fĭkt) *adj.* Of, relating to, or constituting a verb that designates an action or state completed before a specified or implied time in the past. **–plu·per′fect** *n.*

plu·ral (plo͝or′əl) *adj.* Of, relating to, or constituting a word form that designates more than 1. **–plu′ral** *n.*

plu·ral·i·ty (plo͞o-răl′ĭ-tē) *n., pl.* **-ties. 1.** The condition of being plural. **2.** The number of votes cast for a winning candidate if this number is less than a majority but more than that cast for any other candidate. **3.** The excess of votes cast for a winner over the closest opposing candidate.

plu·ral·ize (plo͝or′ə-līz′) *v.* **ized, -iz·ing.** To make plural. **–plu′ral·i·za′tion** *n.*

plus (plŭs) *prep.* **1.** Increased by <2 *plus* 2 equals 4> **2.** Along with : in addition to <has brains *plus* looks> *–adj.* **1.** Of or relating to addition. **2.** Greater than zero, as on a scale : positive. **3.** Added or extra. **4.** Slightly better than <a grade of C *plus*> *–n.* **1. a.** A symbol (+) designating addition. **b.** A positive number. **2.** Something added. **3.** A favorable factor : advantage.

plush (plŭsh) *n.* A velvetlike fabric with a soft, thick pile.

–adj. Luxurious : elegant. **–plush′i•ly** *adv.* **–plush′i•ness** *n.* **–plush′ly** *adv.* **–plush′y** *adj.*

Plu•tarch (plo͞o′tärk′). A.D. 46?–120? Greek biographer and philosopher.

Plu•to (plo͞o′tō) *n.* The 9th and outermost planet from the sun.

plu•toc•ra•cy (plo͞o-tŏk′rə-sē) *n., pl.* **-cies. 1.** Governmental control by the wealthy. **2.** A governing group of wealthy people. **–plu′to•crat′** (-tə-krăt′) *n.* **–plu′to•crat′ic** *adj.*

plu•ton (plo͞o′tŏn′) *n.* Igneous rock formed beneath the surface of the earth. **–plu•ton′ic** *adj.*

plu•to•ni•um (plo͞o-tō′nē-əm) *n. Symbol* **Pu** A radioactive, silvery metallic element used esp. in nuclear weapons.

plu•vi•al (plo͞o′vē-əl) *adj.* **1.** Of or relating to rain. **2.** Marked by abundant rain.

ply[1] (plī) *v.* **plied, ply•ing. 1.** To mold or twist together. **2.** To fold or double over (e.g., cloth). *–n., pl.* **plies. 1.** A layer or thickness, as of folded cloth or plywood. **2.** One of the twisted strands constituting yarn, rope, or thread.

ply[2] (plī) *v.* **plied, ply•ing. 1.** To use or wield (a tool). **2.** To perform (e.g., a trade) regularly. **3.** To traverse (a route or course) regularly. **4.** To keep supplying or presenting <*plied* us with tidbits>

Plym•outh Rock (plĭm′əth) *n.* An American breed of medium-sized domestic fowl raised for both meat and eggs.

Plymouth Rock

ply•wood (plī′wo͝od′) *n.* A construction material made of thin layers of wood glued and pressed together.

Pm *symbol for* PROMETHIUM.

pm. *abbr.* premium.

p.m. *abbr.* **1.** *also* **P.M.** postmortem. **2.** *also* **P.M.** post meridiem (usu. small capitals P.M.).

P.M. *abbr.* **1.** past master. **2.** *also* **PM** postmaster. **3.** prime minister.

P.M.G. *abbr.* postmaster general.

p.n. or **P/N** *abbr.* promissory note.

pneu•mat•ic (no͞o-măt′ĭk, nyo͞o-) *adj.* **1.** Of or relating to air or another gas. **2.** Filled with or operated by compressed air. **–pneu•mat′i•cal•ly** *adv.*

pneu•mo•co•ni•o•sis (no͞o′mō-kō′nē-ō′sĭs, nyo͞o′-) *n.* A lung disease caused by prolonged inhalation of metallic or mineral dusts.

pneu•mo•nia (no͝o-mōn′yə, nyo͝o-) *n.* An acute or chronic inflammatory disease of the lungs caused by viruses, bacteria, chemicals, or irritation. **–pneu•mon′ic** (-mŏn′ĭk) *adj.*

Po *symbol for* POLONIUM.

P.O. *abbr.* **1.** Personnel Officer. **2.** *also* **p.o.** petty officer. **3.** postal order. **4.** *also* **p.o.** post office.

poach[1] (pōch) *v.* To cook in liquid below or just at the boiling point. **–poach′er** *n.*

poach[2] (pōch) *v.* To hunt or fish unlawfully, esp. by trespassing on private property. **–poach′er** *n.*

pock (pŏk) *n.* **1.** A pus-filled swelling of the skin caused by an eruptive disease, as smallpox. **2.** A pockmark.

pock•et (pŏk′ĭt) *n.* **1.** A pouch with an open top or side stitched into or onto a garment and used esp. for carrying small items. **2.** Something resembling a pocket in appearance or function. **3.** Monetary supply <out of *pocket*> **4.** A small area or group set apart from others. *–adj.* **1.** Of a size that fits in a pocket. **2.** Very small : miniature. *–v.* **1.** To deposit in or as if in a pocket. **2.** To take (e.g., money) illicitly. **–pock′et•ful′** *n.*

pock•et•book (pŏk′ĭt-bo͝ok′) *n.* **1.** A wallet. **2.** A handbag. **3.** Supply of money.

pocket bread *n.* Pita.

pock•et•knife (pŏk′ĭt-nīf′) *n.* A small knife with a folding blade.

pocket veto *n.* An indirect veto of a legislative bill by an executive through retention of the unsigned bill until the legislature has adjourned.

pock•mark (pŏk′märk′) *n.* A scar left on the skin by an eruptive disease, as smallpox. **–pock′marked′** *adj.*

po•co (pō′kō) *adv. Mus.* A little. Used as a direction.

†**po•co•sin** (pə-kō′sĭn) *n. SE U.S.* A swamp in an upland coastal region.

pod (pŏd) *n.* **1.** *Bot.* A seed casing, as of a pea or bean, that splits open to release the enclosed seeds. **2.** An external housing, as for a jet engine or fuel, on an aircraft. **3.** A detachable compartment in a spacecraft for personnel or instruments.

po•di•a•try (pə-dī′ə-trē) *n.* The professional study, care, and treatment of the feet. **–po•di′a•trist** *n.*

po•di•um (pō′dē-əm) *n., pl.* **-di•a** (-dē-ə) or **-ums. 1.** A raised platform for an orchestra conductor. **2.** A reading stand for a lecturer or public speaker.

P.O.E. *abbr.* port of entry.

po•em (pō′əm) *n.* A composition, usu. in verse, marked by language chosen esp. for its sound, beauty, and evocative power.

po•e•sy (pō′ĭ-zē, -sē) *n.* Poetry.

po•et (pō′ĭt) *n.* **1.** A writer of poetry. **2.** One having the power of lyrical expression. **–po′et•ess** *n.*

poet. *abbr.* poetic; poetical; poetry.

po•et•as•ter (pō′ĭ-tăs′tər) *n.* A writer of inferior poems.

po•et•ic (pō-ĕt′ĭk) *or* **po•et•i•cal** (-ĭ-kəl) *adj.* **1.** Of or characteristic of poetry or poets. **2.** Written in verse. **3.** Highly fanciful or idealized. **–po•et′i•cal•ly** *adv.*

poetic justice *n.* An often ironically appropriate outcome in which wrongdoing is punished and virtue rewarded.

poetic license *n.* Artistic deviation from conventional form or fact to achieve a certain effect.

poet laureate *n., pl.* **poets laureate** or **poet laureates.** A poet appointed by the British monarch as chief poet of the kingdom for life.

po•et•ry (pō′ĭ-trē) *n.* **1.** The art or works of a poet. **2.** Writing in metrical verse.

po•grom (pə-grŭm′, -grŏm′, pō′grəm) *n.* An organized persecution or massacre, esp. of Jews.

poi (poi, pō′ē) *n.* A pastelike, often fermented Hawaiian food made from cooked taro root.

poign•ant (poin′yənt) *adj.* **1.** Emotionally painful or distressing. **2.** Deeply affecting : touching. **–poign′ance, poign′an•cy** *n.* **–poign′ant•ly** *adv.*

poin•ci•an•a (poin′sē-ăn′ə, -ä′nə) *n.* An ornamental tropical tree of the genus *Poinciana,* with large red or orange flowers.

poin•set•ti•a (poin-sĕt′ē-ə, -sĕt′ə) *n.* A tropical American shrub, *Euphorbia pulcherrima,* bearing usu. scarlet bracts around small yellow or greenish flowers.

point (point) *n.* **1.** A sharp or tapered end : tip. **2.** A tapering piece of land extending into water. **3.** A geometric object having no dimensions and no property other than location. **4.** A certain place or location. **5.** A given degree, stage, or condition. **6.** A definite moment in time. **7.** An important or essential factor, part, or idea. **8.** A purpose, objective, or reason. **9.** A separate item, element, or detail. **10.** A distinguishing quality or feature. **11.** A single unit, as in counting, measuring, or evaluating. **12. a.** A punctuation mark indicating a full stop. **b.** A decimal point. **13.** One of the 32 direction marks on a compass. *–v.* **1.** To aim : direct. **2.** To call attention to. **3.** To indicate the direction or position of, esp. by using the finger. **4.** To emphasize : stress. **5.** To be turned or directed. **–beside the point.** Not pertinent. **–to the point.** Pertinent.

point•blank (point′blăngk′) *adj.* **1.** Aimed straight at or being close to a mark or target. **2.** Forthright. *–adv.* **1.** With a direct aim. **2.** Without hesitating.

point•ed (poin′tĭd) *adj.* **1.** Having a sharp or tapered end. **2.** To the point : incisive. **3.** Clearly aimed at a particular person or group. **4.** Clearly evident : marked. **–point′ed•ly** *adv.* **–point′ed•ness** *n.*

point•er (poin′tər) *n.* **1.** A marker or device that indicates a number, as on a watch. **2.** A long, slender rod for pointing to a chart or blackboard. **3.** A hunting dog with a short-haired smooth coat. **4.** A helpful hint. **5.** *Computer Sci.* A word that directs the user to a core storage location.

poin•til•lism (point′tl-ĭz′əm, pwăn′-) *n.* A theory or technique of applying small strokes or dots of paint to a canvas so that they blend together when viewed from a distance. **–poin′til•list** *n. & adj.*

point•less (point′lĭs) *adj.* Devoid of meaning or purpose. **–point′less•ly** *adv.*

point of no return *n.* A crucial point, as in an action, beyond which return or reversal is no longer possible.

point of view *n.* **1.** A position from which things are considered. **2.** One's way of viewing things.

poise (poiz) *v.* **poised, pois•ing.** To bring into or be maintained in equilibrium : balance. *–n.* **1.** Balance : equilibrium. **2. a.** Composure. **b.** Bearing : carriage.

poi•son (poi′zən) *n.* A substance that causes injury, illness, or death, esp. by chemical means. *–v.* **1.** To kill or injure with poison. **2.** To put poison on or into. **3.** To have a destructive influence on : corrupt. **—poi'son·er** *n.* **—poi'son·ous** *adj.*

poison ivy *n.* A North American shrub or vine, *Rhus radicans,* bearing greenish flowers, whitish berries, and shiny trifoliate leaflets that cause a skin rash on contact.

poison oak *n.* A North American shrub, *Rhus toxicodendron* or *R. diversiloba,* related to poison ivy and causing a similar skin rash.

poison sumac *n.* A swamp shrub, *Rhus vernix,* of the SE U.S., with greenish-white berries and compound leaves that cause a skin rash similar to that caused by the related poison ivy.

poke (pōk) *v.* **poked, pok·ing. 1.** To push or prod, as with an implement or finger. **2.** To make by or as if by poking. **3.** To thrust forward : stick out. **4.** To snoop or intrude. **5.** To rummage in a leisurely way. **6.** To proceed slowly. *—n.* A quick push, thrust, or jab.

pok·er[1] (pō'kər) *n.* A metal stick or bar for stirring a fire.

pok·er[2] (pō'kər) *n.* A card game played by 2 or more players who bet on the value of their hands in order to win a pool.

poker face *n.* An expressionless face, as that of an expert poker player. **—pok'er·faced'** *adj.*

poke·weed (pōk'wēd') *n.* A North American plant, *Phytolacca americana,* with blackish-red berries, small white flowers, and a poisonous root.

pok·y *also* **poke·y** (pō'kē) *adj.* **-i·er, -i·est.** *Informal.* **1.** Irritatingly slow. **2.** Lacking adequate space.

pol (pŏl) *n. Informal.* A politician.

pol. *abbr.* political; politician; politics.

Po·land (pō'lənd). Country of C Europe. *Cap.* Warsaw. *Pop.* 35,645,000. **—Po'lish** (-lĭsh) *adj.* & *n.*

po·lar (pō'lər) *adj.* **1.** Of or measured in relation to a pole, as of a magnet or sphere. **2.** Of or situated near the North or South Pole. **3.** Completely opposite.

polar bear *n.* A large white-furred bear, *Thalarctos maritimus,* of arctic regions.

Po·lar·is (pō-lăr'ĭs, -lâr'-) *n.* A bright star near the N celestial pole, at the tip of Ursa Minor.

po·lar·i·ty (pō-lăr'ĭ-tē, -lâr'-) *n., pl.* **-ties. 1.** Basic division or separation into opposing or contrary types, esp. of a physical property <magnetic *polarity*> **2.** The demonstration of 2 contrary tendencies. **3.** A designated polar extreme.

po·lar·ize (pō'lə-rīz') *v.* **-ized, -iz·ing. 1.** To cause polarity in. **2.** To set at opposite extremes. **3.** To acquire polarity : become polarized. **4.** To cause (light or radiation waves) to oscillate in a definite way. **—po'lar·i·za'tion** *n.*

pole[1] (pōl) *n.* **1.** Either extremity of an axis through a sphere, as the earth. **2.** Either of the earth's geographic poles. **3.** Either of 2 regions in a magnet at which the magnetism is concentrated. **4.** Either of a pair of oppositely charged electric terminals. **5.** Either of 2 forces in opposition.

pole[2] (pōl) *n.* **1.** A long, slender rod. **2.** An upright post. *—v.* **poled, pol·ing. 1.** To push or move along (e.g., a boat) with a pole. **2.** To use poles in skiing.

pole·ax or **pole·axe** (pōl'ăks') *n.* A medieval battle-ax consisting of an ax and hammer combination on a long pole.

pole·cat (pōl'kăt') *n.* **1.** A carnivorous Old World mammal, *Mustela putorius,* with dark fur. **2.** A skunk.

po·lem·ic (pə-lĕm'ĭk) *n.* **1.** A verbal attack, esp. on opposing doctrines or opinions : controversy. **2. polemics** *(sing. or pl. in number).* The art or practice of controversy or debate. **—po·lem'ic, po·lem'i·cal** *adj.* **—po·lem'i·cist** *n.*

pole·star (pōl'stär') *n.* **1.** The North Star. **2.** A guiding or determining principle.

pole vault *n.* An athletic contest in which each participant uses a long pole to vault over a high crossbar. **—pole'-vault'** *v.* **—pole'-vault'er** *n.*

po·lice (pə-lēs') *n., pl.* **-lice. 1. a.** A division of government organized for maintenance of law and order and the prevention and investigation of crime. **b.** *(pl. in number).* The members of such a governmental division. **2.** An organized group functioning like a police force. **3.** Soldiers detailed to perform a specified task, as cleaning. *—v.* **-liced, -lic·ing. 1.** To guard or patrol, esp. to maintain order or enforce the law. **2.** To make (e.g., a military area) neat or clean.

po·lice·man (pə-lēs'mən) *n.* A member of a police force. **—po·lice'wom'an** *n.*

police state *n.* A repressive totalitarian political state utilizing a secret police force.

pol·i·cy[1] (pŏl'ĭ-sē) *n., pl.* **-cies. 1.** A principle or course of action chosen to guide decision making. **2.** Prudent management.

pol·i·cy[2] (pŏl'ĭ-sē) *n., pl.* **-cies.** A written insurance contract.

pol·i·cy·hold·er (pŏl'ĭ-sē-hōl'dər) *n.* A holder of an insurance policy.

po·li·o (pō'lē-ō') *n.* Poliomyelitis.

po·li·o·my·e·li·tis (pō'lē-ō-mī'ə-lī'tĭs) *n.* A contagious viral disease, esp. of children, that attacks the central nervous system and can result in paralysis.

pol·ish (pŏl'ĭsh) *v.* **1.** To make or become smooth and shiny, as by rubbing or chemical action. **2.** To develop or refine to a high degree. *—n.* **1.** A smooth, shiny surface : sheen. **2.** A substance used for polishing. **3.** Refinement of style or manners. **—polish off.** *Informal.* To finish or get rid of quickly. **—pol'ish·er** *n.*

polit. *abbr.* political; politics.

pol·it·bu·ro (pŏl'ĭt-byŏŏr'ō, pə-lĭt'-) *n.* A Communist Party executive committee that determines policy.

po·lite (pə-līt') *adj.* **-lit·er, -lit·est. 1.** Marked by good manners and tactful behavior : courteous. **2.** Refined : urbane. **—po·lite'ly** *adv.* **—po·lite'ness** *n.*

pol·i·tesse (pŏl'ĭ-tĕs', pô'lĭ-) *n.* Formal courtesy : decorum.

pol·i·tic (pŏl'ĭ-tĭk) *adj.* **1.** Wisely discerning, as in matters of policy. **2.** Shrewdly expedient. **—pol'i·tic·ly** *adv.*

po·lit·i·cal (pə-lĭt'ĭ-kəl) *adj.* **1.** Of or concerning the structure or affairs of government. **2.** Of or concerning politics, political parties, or politicians. **—po·lit'i·cal·ly** *adv.* **—po·lit'i·cize'** (-sīz') *v.*

political science *n.* The study of government and political institutions. **—political scientist** *n.*

pol·i·ti·cian (pŏl'ĭ-tĭsh'ən) *n.* A person active in government or politics, esp. one holding a political office.

pol·i·tick (pŏl'ĭ-tĭk') *v.* To engage in political discussion or campaigning.

po·lit·i·co (pə-lĭt'ĭ-kō') *n., pl.* **-cos.** A politician.

pol·i·tics (pŏl'ĭ-tĭks') *n.* **1.** *(sing. in number).* The art or science of government. **2.** *(sing. in number).* The policies, activities, and methods of a government or political party. **3.** *(pl. in number).* Factional intrigue or competition, as in a company. **4.** *(pl. in number).* One's general political standpoint.

pol·i·ty (pŏl'ĭ-tē) *n., pl.* **-ties. 1.** A political unit, as a nation or state. **2.** The form of government of a polity.

Polk (pōk), **James Knox.** 1795–1849. 11th U.S. President (1845–49).

pol·ka (pōl'kə, pō'kə) *n.* **1.** A spirited dance of C European orig. **2.** Music for the polka. **—pol'ka** *v.*

poll (pōl) *n.* **1. a.** The casting and recording of votes in an election. **b.** The total votes cast or recorded. **c.** *often* **polls.** The place where votes are cast and counted. **2.** A public survey on a given issue. **3.** The head. *—v.* **1. a.** To receive (votes) in an election. **b.** To record the votes of. **2.** To question in a public survey. **3.** To clip a part of (an animal or plant). **—poll'er** *n.*

pol·len (pŏl'ən) *n.* Dustlike, usu. yellow grains containing the male reproductive cells of flowering plants.

pollen count *n.* The average number of pollen grains, esp. of ragweed, in a standard volume of air at a particular time and place.

pol·li·nate (pŏl'ə-nāt') *v.* **-nat·ed, -nat·ing.** To fertilize by carrying pollen to the female part of (a plant). **—pol'li·na'tion** *n.* **—pol'li·na'tor** *n.*

pol·li·wog *also* **pol·ly·wog** (pŏl'ē-wŏg', -wôg') *n.* A tadpole.

pol·lock *also* **pol·lack** (pŏl'ək) *n., pl.* **-lock** or **-locks** *also* **-lack** or **-lacks.** A marine food fish, *Pollachius virens,* of N Atlantic waters.

poll·ster (pōl'stər) *n.* One who takes or analyzes the results of public-opinion polls.

poll tax *n.* A fixed tax levied on persons, esp. as a requirement for voting.

pol·lute (pə-lōōt') *v.* **-lut·ed, -lut·ing.** To contaminate, as with harmful waste substances. **—pol·lut'ant, pol·lut'er** *n.* **—pol·lu'tion** *n.*

po·lo (pō'lō) *n.* A game in which players on horseback try to drive a wooden ball through the opposing team's goal with long-handled mallets. **—po'lo·ist** *n.*

Polo, Marco. 1254?–1324? Venetian traveler in E Asia.

pol·o·naise (pŏl'ə-nāz', pō'lə-) *n.* **1.** A Polish dance in which couples formally promenade in 3/4 time. **2.** Music for or in the style of the polonaise.

po·lo·ni·um (pə-lō'nē-əm) *n. Symbol* **Po** A naturally radioactive metallic element produced by the disintegration of radium.

pol·ter·geist (pōl'tər-gīst') *n.* A mischievous ghost, esp. one that makes mysterious noises.

pol·troon (pŏl-trōōn') *n. Archaic.* An utter coward. **—pol·troon'er·y** *n.*

pol·y·an·dry (pŏl'ē-ăn'drē) *n.* The practice of having more than 1 husband at a time. **—pol'y·an'drous** *adj.*

pol·y·clin·ic (pŏl'ĭ-klĭn'ĭk) *n.* A clinic or hospital for a wide variety of illnesses.

pol·y·es·ter (pŏl'ē-ĕs'tər) *n.* A lightweight, strong, water-resistant synthetic resin used esp. in plastics and fibers.

pol·y·eth·yl·ene (pŏl'ē-ĕth'ə-lēn') *n.* A lightweight, water-resistant thermoplastic resin used esp. in packaging and molded products.

po•lyg•a•my (pə-lĭg′ə-mē) *n.* The practice of having more than 1 husband or wife at a time. **–po•lyg′a•mist** *n.* **–po•lyg′a•mous** *adj.*
pol•y•glot (pŏl′ĭ-glŏt′) *adj.* **1.** Speaking, reading, or writing several languages. **2.** Written in or composed of several languages. **–pol′y•glot′** *n.*
pol•y•gon (pŏl′ĭ-gŏn′) *n.* A flat, closed geometric figure bounded by 3 or more straight lines. **–po•lyg′o•nal** (pə-lĭg′ə-nəl) *adj.*
pol•y•graph (pŏl′ĭ-grăf′) *n.* An instrument that records fluctuations in physiological processes, as heartbeat and blood pressure, used esp. as a lie detector. **–pol′y•graph′ic** *adj.*
po•lyg•y•ny (pə-lĭj′ə-nē) *n.* The practice of having more than 1 wife at a time. **–po•lyg′y•nous** *adj.*
pol•y•he•dron (pŏl′ĭ-hē′drən) *n., pl.* **-drons** *or* **-dra** (-drə). A solid geometric figure bounded by polygons. **–pol′y•he′dral** *adj.*

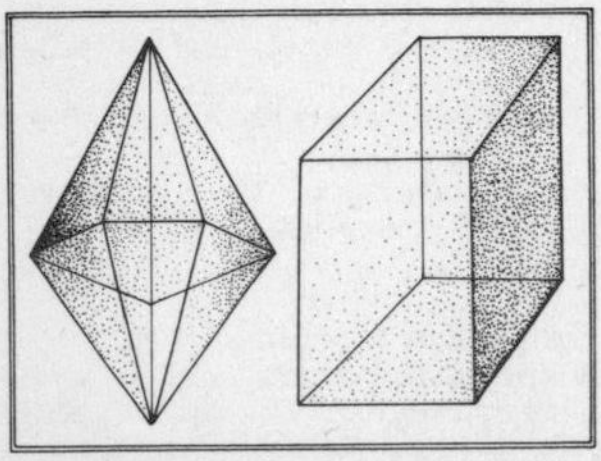

polyhedron

pol•y•math (pŏl′ĭ-măth′) *n.* A person of extensive learning.
pol•y•mer (pŏl′ə-mər) *n.* A natural or synthetic compound consisting of similar molecules linked together. **–pol′y•mer′ic** (-mĕr′ĭk) *adj.*
po•lym•er•ize (pə-lĭm′ə-rīz′, pŏl′ə-mə-) *v.* **-ized, -iz•ing.** To make or combine into a polymer. **–po•lym′er•i•za′tion** *n.*
Pol•y•ne•sia (pŏl′ə-nē′zhə, -shə). Group of islands of the C and S Pacific Ocean. **–Pol′y•ne′sian** *adj.* & *n.*
pol•y•no•mi•al (pŏl′ĭ-nō′mē-əl) *adj.* Of or composed of more than 2 terms. *–n.* **1.** An algebraic function of 2 or more summed terms. **2.** A mathematical expression of 2 or more terms.
pol•yp (pŏl′ĭp) *n.* **1.** A coelenterate, as a hydra or coral, with a hollow, tubular body and a mouth opening usu. with tentacles. **2.** An abnormally projecting growth of mucous membrane. **–pol′yp•oid′** *adj.*
po•lyph•o•ny (pə-lĭf′ə-nē) *n.* Music consisting of several independent but harmonizing melodic parts. **–pol′y•phon′ic** (pŏl′ĭ-fŏn′ĭk) *adj.*
pol•y•sty•rene (pŏl′ĭ-stī′rēn′) *n.* A clear, hard, rigid thermoplastic polymer used esp. as insulation and in molded products.
pol•y•syl•la•ble (pŏl′ĭ-sĭl′ə-bəl) *n.* A word having at least 3 syllables. **–pol′y•syl•lab′ic** (-sĭ-lăb′ĭk) *adj.*
pol•y•tech•nic (pŏl′ĭ-tĕk′nĭk) *adj.* Of, dealing with, or instructing in technical or industrial arts or applied sciences.
pol•y•the•ism (pŏl′ĭ-thē-ĭz′əm) *n.* Belief in a number of gods. **–pol′y•the′ist** *n.* **–pol′y•the•is′tic** *adj.*
pol•y•un•sat•u•rat•ed (pŏl′ē-ŭn-săch′ə-rā′tĭd) *adj.* Of or pertaining to an organic compound, as an oil or fat, that is rich in unsaturated bonds.
pol•y•u•re•thane (pŏl′ē-yŏŏr′ə-thān′) *n.* A thermoplastic or thermosetting resin used esp. in tough, resistant coatings and electrical insulation.
po•made (pə-mād′, -mäd′, pō-) *n.* A scented ointment for the hair. **–po•made′** *v.*
pome•gran•ate (pŏm′grăn′ĭt, pŭm′-) *n.* A semitropical Asian shrub or small tree, *Punica granatum,* widely cultivated for its fruit that has a tough reddish rind and many seeds.
pom•mel (pŭm′əl, pŏm′-) *n.* **1.** A knob on a sword handle. **2.** The raised knoblike front part of a saddle. *–v.* **-meled, -mel•ing** *or* **-melled, -mel•ling.** To beat severely : pummel.
pomp (pŏmp) *n.* **1.** Stately or splendid display. **2.** Pretentious or excessive display.
pom•pa•dour (pŏm′pə-dôr′, -dōr′) *n.* A puffy hairstyle in which the hair is swept straight up from the forehead.
pom•pa•no (pŏm′pə-nō′, pŭm′-) *n., pl.* **-no** *or* **-nos. 1.** A marine food fish of the genus *Trachinotus,* esp. *T. carolinus,* of tropical and temperate Atlantic waters. **2.** A small, edible butterfish, *Palometa simillima,* of American Pacific coastal waters.
Pom•peii (pŏm-pā′). Ancient city of S Italy; destroyed by an eruption of Mt. Vesuvius in A.D. 79. **–Pom•pe′ian** *adj.* & *n.*
pom•pom (pŏm′pŏm′) *also* **pom•pon** (-pŏn′) *n.* **1.** A small, decorative ball or tuft of material used esp. on caps. **2.** A small, buttonlike chrysanthemum or dahlia.
pom•pous (pŏm′pəs) *adj.* **1.** Suggesting ostentatious display. **2.** Marked by pretention or self-importance. **3.** Bombastic : grandiose. **–pom•pos′i•ty** (-pŏs′ĭ-tē) *n.*
pon•cho (pŏn′chō) *n., pl.* **-chos. 1.** A blanketlike loose outer garment having a hole in the middle for the head. **2.** A water-resistant garment resembling a poncho.
pond (pŏnd) *n.* A body of water smaller in size than a lake.
pon•der (pŏn′dər) *v.* **1.** To think about carefully : deliberate. **2.** To engage in contemplation. **–pon′der•er** *n.*
pon•der•o•sa pine (pŏn′də-rō′sə, -zə) *n.* A tall timber tree, *Pinus ponderosa,* of W North America, with dark-green needles.
pon•der•ous (pŏn′dər-əs) *adj.* **1. a.** Very heavy : massive. **b.** Clumsy : unwieldy. **2.** Lacking fluency of style. ☆**syns:** ELEPHANTINE, HEAVY-HANDED, LABORED **–pon′der•os′i•ty** (-də-rŏs′ĭ-tē), **pon′der•ous•ness** *n.* **–pon′der•ous•ly** *adv.*
pon•gee (pŏn-jē′, pŏn′jē′) *n.* A thin, soft, usu. tan silk fabric.
pon•iard (pŏn′yərd) *n.* A dagger.
pon•tiff (pŏn′tĭf) *n.* **1.** A bishop. **2.** A pope.
pon•tif•i•cal (pŏn-tĭf′ĭ-kəl) *adj.* Of or relating to a pontiff. *–n.* **pontificals.** The insignia and ceremonial vestments of a pontiff. **–pon•tif′i•cal•ly** *adv.*
pon•tif•i•cate (pŏn-tĭf′ĭ-kĭt, -kāt′) *n.* The state, office, or term of office of a pontiff. *–v.* (-kāt′) **-cat•ed, -cat•ing. 1.** To perform the duties and functions of a pontiff. **2.** To express oneself pompously or dogmatically. **–pon•tif′i•ca′tion** *n.* **–pon•tif′i•ca′tor** *n.*
pon•toon (pŏn-to͞on′) *n.* **1.** A flat-bottomed boat or supporting structure for a floating bridge. **2.** One of the floats supporting a seaplane.
po•ny (pō′nē) *n., pl.* **-nies. 1.** A horse that is small when full-grown. **2.** A translation used in preparing foreign-language lessons.
po•ny•tail (pō′nē-tāl′) *n.* A hair style in which the hair is gathered and fastened at the back of the head.
pooch (po͞och) *n. Slang.* A dog.
poo•dle (po͞od′l) *n.* A dog with a heavy, curly coat.
pooh-pooh (po͞o′po͞o′, po͞o-po͞o′) *v. Informal.* To regard with contempt : deride.
pool¹ (po͞ol) *n.* **1.** A body of water smaller than a pond. **2.** A puddle.
pool² (po͞ol) *n.* **1.** The total staked by all players in a gambling game. **2.** A mutually shared supply, as of resources. **3.** A business arrangement between competitors for common profit. **4.** Any of several billiards games played on a table with 6 pockets. *–v.* **1.** To combine in a shared fund for mutual use or advantage. **2.** To form or become a member of a pool.
poop¹ (po͞op) *n. Naut.* **1.** A raised structure in the stern of a ship. **2.** A poop deck.
poop² (po͞op) *v. Slang.* To exhaust or become exhausted.
poop³ (po͞op) *n. Slang.* Inside information.
poop deck *n.* A small deck above the rear half of a ship's main deck.
poor (po͝or) *adj.* **1.** Lacking money and possessions. **2.** Lacking in quantity or quality : inadequate or inferior. **3.** Not productive <*poor* soil> **4.** Not favorable or satisfactory <a *poor* attitude> **5.** Deserving pity : unfortunate. ☆**syns:** BROKE, BUSTED, DESTITUTE, IMPOVERISHED, INDIGENT, NEEDY, PENNILESS, PENURIOUS, STRAPPED **–poor′ness** *n.*
poor boy *n.* HERO 4.
poor•house (po͝or′hous′) *n.* A publicly maintained home for destitute people.
†**poor•ly** (po͝or′lē) *adv.* In a poor manner. *–adj. Regional.* In poor health : ill.
poor-mouth (po͝or′mouth′, -mouth′) *v.* **1.** To claim poverty as an excuse or defense. **2.** To complain about lack of money.
pop¹ (pŏp) *v.* **popped, pop•ping. 1.** To make, cause to make, burst, or cause to burst with a sudden sharp, explosive sound. **2.** To go, come, or appear suddenly. **3.** To bulge from the sockets <eyes *popping* with delight> **4.** To thrust or put quickly or suddenly. **5.** To shoot (at). **6.** *Baseball.* To hit a pop fly. *–n.* **1.** A sudden sharp, explosive noise. **2.** A gunshot. **3.** A carbonated soft drink. **–pop′per** *n.*
pop² (pŏp) *n. Informal.* Father.
pop³ (pŏp) *adj. Informal.* **1.** Of, pertaining to, or dealing with popular music. **2.** Of or pertaining to culture produced or influenced by the mass media. **3.** Of or pertaining to pop art.
pop art *n.* A style of art typically centering on commonplace objects that are sometimes physically incorporated into the work itself. **–pop artist** *n.*
pop•corn (pŏp′kôrn′) *n.* **1.** A variety of corn, *Zea mays everta,* with kernels that when heated pop to form small white puffs. **2.** The popped kernels of popcorn.
pope (pōp) *n. often* **Pope.** The head of the Roman Catholic Church.
pop fly *n. Baseball.* A short and high fly ball.

pop·gun (pŏp′gŭn′) *n.* A toy gun that shoots corks or pellets by air compression.
pop·in·jay (pŏp′ĭn-jā′) *n.* A conceited, often talkative person.
pop·lar (pŏp′lər) *n.* Any of several slender trees of the genus *Populus,* with triangular leaves and soft, light-colored wood.
pop·lin (pŏp′lĭn) *n.* A strong fabric with fine crosswise ridges.
pop·o·ver (pŏp′ō′vər) *n.* A light, hollow muffin that puffs up while baking.
pop·py (pŏp′ē) *n., pl.* **-pies.** A plant of the genus *Papaver,* with showy red, orange, or white flowers and milky white juice.
pop·py·cock (pŏp′ē-kŏk′) *n.* Nonsense.
Pop·si·cle (pŏp′sĭ-kəl, -sĭk′əl). A trademark for colored and flavored ice in the shape of a rectangle on 2 flat sticks.
pop·u·lace (pŏp′yə-ləs) *n.* **1.** The general public : masses. **2.** A population.
pop·u·lar (pŏp′yə-lər) *adj.* **1.** Widely liked. **2.** Of, relating to, or representing the general public. **3.** Widespread : prevalent. **4.** Generally affordable. **5.** Readily understandable. **—pop′u·lar′i·ty** (-lăr′ĭ-tē) *n.*
pop·u·lar·ize (pŏp′yə-lə-rīz′) *v.* **-ized, -iz·ing.** To make or become popular. **—pop′u·lar·i·za′tion** *n.* **—pop′u·lar·iz′er** *n.*
pop·u·late (pŏp′yə-lāt′) *v.* **-lat·ed, -lat·ing. 1.** To supply with a population. **2.** To live in : inhabit.
pop·u·la·tion (pŏp′yə-lā′shən) *n.* **1.** The people or total number of people in a given area. **2.** A group or set under statistical study. **3.** *Ecol.* All the plants or animals of the same kind found in a given area.
population explosion *n.* Great and rapid growth of a living population, esp. the enormous increase in the human population resulting from both increased infant survival and adult longevity.
pop·u·lism (pŏp′yə-lĭz′əm) *n.* Belief in or advocacy of the rights, interests, or wisdom of the common people. **—pop′u·list** *n.*
pop·u·lous (pŏp′yə-ləs) *adj.* **1.** Heavily populated. **2.** Filled up : crowded. **—pop′u·lous·ly** *adv.* **—pop′u·lous·ness** *n.*
por·ce·lain (pôr′sə-lĭn, pōr′-, pôrs′lĭn, pōrs′-) *n.* **1.** A hard, translucent ceramic made by firing and glazing a fine clay. **2.** An article made of porcelain.
porch (pôrch, pōrch) *n.* **1.** A roofed platform forming the entrance to a house. **2.** A verandah.
por·cine (pôr′sīn′) *adj.* Of, resembling, or typical of swine.
por·cu·pine (pôr′kyə-pīn′) *n.* Any of various rodents, including members of the Old World genus *Hystrix* and the New World genus *Erethizon,* that are covered with long, sharp quills.
pore¹ (pôr, pōr) *v.* **pored, por·ing. 1.** To read or examine with great care and attention <*pored* over the contract> **2.** To ponder : meditate.
pore² (pôr, pōr) *n.* A very small space or hole, as in the skin or soil.
pork (pôrk, pōrk) *n.* The flesh of swine prepared for use as food.
pork barrel *n. Slang.* A government project or appropriation affording benefits to a specific politician's district.
pork·er (pôr′kər, pōr′-) *n.* A usu. young pig fattened for use as food.
por·no (pôr′nō) *also* **porn** (pôrn) *n. Slang.* Pornography.
por·nog·ra·phy (pôr-nŏg′rə-fē) *n.* Pictures, writing, or films designed to arouse sexual excitement. **—por·nog′ra·pher** *n.* **—por′no·graph′ic** (-nə-grăf′ĭk) *adj.*
po·rous (pôr′əs, pōr′-) *adj.* **1.** Containing pores. **2.** Capable of being permeated by gas or fluid. **—po·ros′i·ty** (pə-rŏs′ĭ-tē) *n.*
por·phy·ry (pôr′fə-rē) *n., pl.* **-ries.** A fine-grained igneous rock with large feldspar or quartz crystals.
por·poise (pôr′pəs) *n.* **1.** A gregarious aquatic mammal of the genus *Phocaena,* usu. with a blunt snout and a triangular dorsal fin. **2.** An aquatic mammal, as the dolphin, that is related to the porpoise.
por·ridge (pôr′ĭj, pŏr′-) *n.* Meal of grains or legumes boiled in water or milk.
por·rin·ger (pôr′ĭn-jər, pŏr′-) *n.* A shallow, 1-handled cup or bowl.
port¹ (pôrt, pōrt) *n.* **1.** A town or city with a harbor. **2.** A harbor. **3.** A port of entry.
port² (pôrt, pōrt) *n.* The left side of a ship or aircraft facing toward the front. *—adj.* Of or on the port side. *—v.* To turn or shift the helm to the port side.
port³ (pôrt, pōrt) *n.* **1.** A porthole. **2.** A vent or opening, as in an engine, for steam or fluid.
port⁴ (pôrt, pōrt) *n.* A sweet fortified dark-red wine.
port·a·ble (pôr′tə-bəl, pōr′-) *adj.* Capable of being carried or moved. **—port′a·bil′i·ty** *n.* **—port′a·ble** *n.*
port·age (pôr′tĭj, pōr′-, pôr-täzh′) *n.* **1.** The carrying of boats and goods overland between 1 waterway and another. **2.** A route for portage. *—v.* **-aged, -ag·ing.** To carry over or make a portage.
por·tal (pôr′tl, pōr′-) *n.* A doorway or entrance, esp. one that is large and impressive.
Port-au-Prince (pôrt′ō-prĭns′, pōrt′-). Cap. of Haiti, in the SW. *Pop.* 745,700.
port·cul·lis (pôrt-kŭl′ĭs, pōrt-) *n.* A grating that can be let down to prevent entrance to a fortified place.
porte-co·chère *or* **porte-co·chere** (pôrt′kō-shâr′, pōrt′-) *n.* A roofed extension of a building over a driveway that shelters passengers getting into and out of vehicles.
por·tend (pôr-tĕnd′, pōr-) *v.* **1.** To give an indication or warning of in advance. **2.** To serve as an indication of.
por·tent (pôr′tĕnt′, pōr′-) *n.* **1.** An augury of a future event. **2.** Ominous significance. **3.** A cause of wonder or amazement.
por·ten·tous (pôr-tĕn′təs, pōr-) *adj.* **1.** Ominous : foreboding. **2.** Extraordinary : amazing. **3.** Marked by pompousness. **—por·ten′tous·ly** *adv.*
por·ter¹ (pôr′tər, pōr′-) *n.* **1.** One hired to carry travelers' baggage. **2.** An attendant in a railway sleeping or parlor car. **3.** One hired to do routine cleaning, as in a public building. **—por′ter·age** *n.*
por·ter² (pôr′tər, pōr′-) *n. esp. Brit.* A doorman or doorkeeper.
por·ter³ (pôr′tər, pōr′-) *n.* A heavy dark beer.
por·ter·house (pôr′tər-hous′, pōr′-) *n.* A choice cut of beef containing a T-bone and a large piece of tenderloin.
port·fo·li·o (pôrt-fō′lē-ō′, pōrt-) *n., pl.* **-os. 1.** A flat carrying case for documents or drawings. **2.** The position and duties of a cabinet member or minister of state. **3.** The securities of an investor.
port·hole (pôrt′hōl′, pōrt′-) *n.* A small round opening in the side of a ship or an aircraft.
por·ti·co (pôr′tĭ-kō′, pōr′-) *n., pl.* **-coes** *or* **-cos.** A walkway or porch with a roof supported by a row of columns.
por·tière *or* **por·tiere** (pôrt-yâr′, pōrt-) *n.* A drapery hanging across a doorway.
por·tion (pôr′shən, pōr′-) *n.* **1.** A section or part of a whole. **2.** One's allotted part or share. **3.** A dowry. **4.** One's destiny : lot. *—v.* **1.** To divide and give out in portions. **2.** To give to as a portion. **—por′tion·a·ble** *adj.* **—por′tion·less** *adj.*
Port·land (pôrt′lənd, pōrt′-). City of NW Ore. on the Columbia R. *Pop.* 366,383.
Portland cement *n.* A hydraulic cement made by roasting and grinding a clay-and-limestone mixture.
Port Lou·is (lo͞o′ĭs, lo͞o′ē, lo͞o-ē′). Cap. of Mauritius, in the NW. *Pop.* 142,853.
port·ly (pôrt′lē, pōrt′-) *adj.* **-li·er, -li·est.** Rather corpulent : stout. **—port′li·ness** *n.*
port·man·teau (pôrt-măn′tō′, pōrt-, pôrt′măn-tō′, pōrt′-) *n., pl.* **-teaus** *or* **-teaux** (-tōz). A large piece of luggage.
portmanteau word *n.* A word, as *smog,* formed by merging the sounds and meanings of different words.
Port Mores·by (môrz′bē, mōrz′-). Cap. of Papua New Guinea, on SE New Guinea Is. *Pop.* 106,600.
port of call *n.* A port where ships dock en route for cargo, overhaul, or supplies.
port of entry *n.* An official place of entrance and exit for foreign goods or travelers.
Port of Spain (spān). Cap. of Trinidad and Tobago, on the NW coast of Trinidad. *Pop.* 42,950.
Por·to-No·vo (pôr′tō-nō′vō, pōr′-). Cap. of Benin, in the SE. *Pop.* 104,000.
por·trait (pôr′trĭt, -trāt′, pōr′-) *n.* An artistic or photographic image of a person, esp. one showing the face.
por·trait·ist (pôr′trə-tĭst, pōr′-) *n.* A maker of portraits, esp. a painter.
por·trai·ture (pôr′trĭ-cho͝or′, -chər, pōr′-) *n.* The art or practice of creating portraits.
por·tray (pôr-trā′, pōr-) *v.* **1.** To show by means of a picture. **2.** To describe verbally. **3.** To enact on the stage or screen. **—por·tray′al** *n.*
Port Sa·lut (pôr′ sä-lo͞o′) *also* **Port du Sa·lut** (pôr′ dü sä-lo͞o′) *n.* A semihard fermented cheese orig. made in France.
Por·tu·gal (pôr′chə-gəl, pōr′-). Country of SW Europe. *Cap.* Lisbon. *Pop.* 9,980,000. **—Por′tu·guese′** (-gēz′, -gēs′) *adj.* & *n.*
Portuguese man-of-war *n.* A chiefly tropical marine invertebrate organism of the genus *Physalia,* with a bluish bladderlike float and long stinging tentacles.
por·tu·lac·a (pôr′chə-lăk′ə, pōr′-) *n.* A plant of the genus *Portulaca,* esp. *P. grandiflora,* bearing fleshy stems and leaves and grown for its colorful flowers.
pos. *abbr.* **1.** position. **2.** positive.
pose (pōz) *v.* **posed, pos·ing. 1.** To assume or place in a certain position, as for a portrait. **2.** To assume a certain manner or attitude, esp. for effect and often to deceive <*posed* as a naval

officer> **3.** To put forth (e.g., a question). –*n.* **1.** A usu. sustained bodily posture, esp. one assumed in modeling. **2.** An affectation or pretense.
pos•er[1] (pō'zər) *n.* A person who poses.
pos•er[2] (pŏ'zər) *n.* A perplexing question.
po•seur (pō-zûr') *n.* One who assumes a pose or attitude, esp. for effect.
posh (pŏsh) *adj.* Fashionable and smart.
pos•it (pŏz'ĭt) *v.* To take for granted without proof : postulate.
po•si•tion (pə-zĭsh'ən) *n.* **1.** The place or location occupied by something. **2.** The right or proper place. **3. a.** A way of being placed or arranged. **b.** A bodily posture <a sitting *position*> **4.** Relative place or situation <not in a *position* to argue> **5.** A viewpoint : attitude. **6.** A post of employment : job. **7.** Social status or official rank. –*v.* To place in proper position. **–po•si'tion•al** *adj.* **–po•si'tion•er** *n.*
pos•i•tive (pŏz'ĭ-tĭv) *adj.* **1. a.** Indicating affirmation, approval, or acceptance. **b.** Constructive : helpful. **2.** Expressed unequivocally <a *positive* denial> **3.** Incapable of being doubted or disproved. **4.** Absolutely certain : very confident. **5.** Existing in reality. **6.** *Math.* **a.** Greater than zero. **b.** Of the sign (+) indicating a positive number or one that is to be added. **7.** Of or having an electric charge that tends to attract electrons. **8.** Having the areas of light and dark in their natural relationship <a *positive* photographic print> **9.** Of or indicating the simple uncompared grammatical degree of an adjective or adverb. –*n.* **1.** A positive photographic image. **2.** A positive word form or the positive degree of an adjective or adverb. **3.** A positive number. **4.** A positive electric charge. **–pos'i•tive•ly** *adv.* **–pos'i•tive•ness** *n.*
pos•i•tron (pŏz'ĭ-trŏn') *n.* The antiparticle that corresponds to the electron.
poss. *abbr.* **1.** possession; possessive. **2.** possible; possibly.
pos•se (pŏs'ē) *n.* A group deputized by a sheriff, as for pursuing a lawbreaker.
pos•sess (pə-zĕs') *v.* **1.** To have or own (e.g., property). **2.** To have as a quality, trait, or skill. **3.** To dominate : control. **–pos•ses'sor** *n.*
pos•sessed (pə-zĕst') *adj.* Controlled by or as if by a supernatural force.
pos•ses•sion (pə-zĕsh'ən) *n.* **1. a.** The act or fact of possessing. **b.** The state of being possessed. **2.** Something owned : property. **3.** Control, as of one's emotions or actions. **4.** The state of being dominated, as by an evil spirit. **5.** A territory ruled by a foreign power.
pos•ses•sive (pə-zĕs'ĭv) *adj.* **1.** Displaying a desire to possess, esp. to control. **2.** Of or being a noun or pronoun case that indicates ownership. –*n.* **1.** The possessive case. **2.** A word or form in the possessive case. **–pos•ses'sive•ness** *n.*
pos•si•ble (pŏs'ə-bəl) *adj.* **1.** Capable of existing or being true. **2.** Capable of happening or being accomplished. **3.** Potential <*possible* hazards> **4.** Capable of being used for a certain purpose. **–pos'si•bil'i•ty** *n.* **–pos'si•bly** *adv.*
pos•sum (pŏs'əm) *n.* An opossum.
post[1] (pōst) *n.* **1.** An upright, usu. wooden or metal support. **2.** A stake set up as a marker or guide. **3.** The starting gate at a racecourse. –*v.* **1.** To put up (e.g., a notice) in a public place. **2.** To announce by or as if by a public notice <*post* test results> **3.** To protect (property) against trespassers by putting up signs. **4.** To enter (a name) on a public list.
post[2] (pōst) *n.* **1.** A base or garrison for military personnel. **2.** A soldier's or sentry's assigned station. **3.** A person's assigned position or duty. **4.** Employment, esp. in public office. **5.** A trading station. –*v.* **1.** To position or station in a particular place. **2.** To put forward (e.g., a bail bond).
post[3] (pōst) *n. esp. Brit.* **1. a.** A governmental system for the transportation and delivery of mail. **b.** A mail delivery. **2.** A post office. –*v.* **1.** To make haste in riding or traveling. **2.** *esp. Brit.* To mail <*posted* the note> **3.** To make aware. **4.** To make entries in (an account book).
post– *pref.* **1.** Subsequent to : after <*post*script> **2.** Posterior to : behind <*post*nasal> See below for a list of self-explanatory words formed with the prefix **post–.**
post•age (pō'stĭj) *n.* The fee for mailing something.
postage meter *n.* A machine used to print the amount of postage required on pieces of mail.
post•al (pō'stəl) *adj.* Of or relating to the post office or mail system.
postal card *n.* A postcard.
post•box *also* **post box** (pōst'bŏks') *n.* A mailbox.
post•card *also* **post card** (pōst'kärd') *n.* A card for a short message that can be mailed without an envelope.
post•date (pōst-dāt') *v.* **1.** To mark with a later date than the actual one <*postdate* a check> **2.** To come after in time.
post•doc•tor•al (pōst-dŏk'tər-əl) *adj.* Of or engaged in academic study beyond a doctor's degree <*postdoctoral* candidates>
post•er (pō'stər) *n.* A publicly posted, often decorative placard or advertisement.
pos•te•ri•or (pŏ-stîr'ē-ər, pō-) *adj.* **1.** Located behind or toward the back. **2.** Subsequent in time. –*n.* The human buttocks.
pos•ter•i•ty (pŏ-stĕr'ĭ-tē) *n.* **1.** Generations or time to come. **2.** The body of descendants from 1 ancestor.
pos•tern (pō'stərn, pŏs'tərn) *n.* A back gate or side entrance.
Post Exchange. A trademark for a general store on a military post for authorized personnel and their families.
post•grad•u•ate (pōst-grăj'ōō-ĭt, -āt') *adj.* Of or engaged in academic study beyond a bachelor's degree. **–post•grad'u•ate** *n.*
post•haste (pōst'hāst') *adv.* As speedily as possible.
post•hu•mous (pŏs'chə-məs) *adj.* **1.** Given or taking place after one's death. **2.** Published after the death of the author. **3.** Born after the father has died. **–post'hu•mous•ly** *adv.*
post•hyp•not•ic (pōst'hĭp-nŏt'ĭk) *adj.* Of, relating to, or intended for the period following hypnosis.
pos•til•ion *also* **pos•til•lion** (pō-stĭl'yən, pə-) *n.* A rider on the left-hand lead horse of a team drawing a carriage.
post•lude (pōst'lōōd') *n.* An organ solo at the conclusion of a church service.
post•man (pōst'mən) *n.* One whose occupation is delivering mail.
post•mark (pōst'märk') *n.* An official postal mark that cancels the stamp on a piece of mail. **–post'mark'** *v.*
post•mas•ter (pōst'măs'tər) *n.* One who officially manages a post office. **–post'mis'tress** *n.*
postmaster general *n., pl.* **postmasters general.** The chief official of a national postal system.

postaccident
postadolescent
postamputation
postarrest
postatomic
postattack
postaudit
postbaccalaureate
postbachelor
postbaptismal
postbase
post-Biblical
postbreakfast
postchlorination
post-Christian
postcivilization
postcoital
postcollege
postcollegiate
postcolonial
post-Columbian
postconception
postconcert
postconquest
postconsonantal
postconvalescent
postconvention
postcoronary
postcoup
postcrisis
postcrystallization
postdeadline
postdebate
postdebutante
postdelivery
postdepression
postdevaluation
postdrug
postediting
posteducational
postelection
postembryonic
postemergency
postexercise
postexperimental
postexplosion
postexposure
postflight
postfracture
post-Freudian
postgame
postglacial
postgraduation
postharvest
postheat
posthibernation
posthospital
postimpact
postimperial
postinaugural
postindependence
postindustrial
postinfection
postinjection
postinoculation
postirradiation
postisolation
postlarval
postlaunch
postliberation
postmarital
postmastectomy
postmating
postmedieval
postmenopausal
postmenstrual
postmidnight
postmortal
postneonatal
postpollination
postprimary
postprison
postpuberty
postpubescent
postrace
postrecession
post-Reformation
post-Renaissance
postretirement
postrevolutionary
postseason
poststimulatory
poststimulus
poststrike
postsurgical
posttreatment
posttrial
postvaccination
post-Victorian
postwar

post me•rid•i•em (pōst′ mə-rĭd′ē-əm) *adj.* After noon.
post•mor•tem (pōst-môr′təm) *adj.* **1.** Taking place or done after death. **2.** Of or relating to a postmortem. —*n.* **1.** A postmortem examination of a dead body, esp. to determine the cause of death : autopsy. **2.** *Informal.* An evaluation or review of a recent event.
post•na•sal (pōst-nā′zəl) *adj.* Of, in, or from the posterior part of the nasal cavity <a *postnasal* drip>
post•na•tal (pōst-nāt′l) *adj.* Following birth.
post office *n.* **1.** A governmental department in charge of the conveyance and delivery of the mails. **2.** A local office where mail is handled.
post•op•er•a•tive (pōst-ŏp′ər-ə-tĭv, -ŏp′rə-, -ŏp′ə-rā′-) *adj.* Following surgery.
post•paid (pōst′pād′) *adj.* Having the postage already paid.
post•par•tum (pōst-pär′təm) *adj.* Subsequent to childbirth.
post•pone (pōst-pōn′, pōs-pōn′) *v.* **-poned, -pon•ing.** To put off to a later time. **—post•pon′a•ble** *adj.* **—post•pone′ment** *n.* **—post•pon′er** *n.*
post•script (pōst′skrĭpt′, pōs′skrĭpt′) *n.* A usu. short message added after a letter has been completed.
post time *n.* The time just before the official start of a race after which no further betting is allowed.
pos•tu•lant (pŏs′chə-lənt) *n.* A candidate for membership in a religious order.
pos•tu•late (pŏs′chə-lāt′) *v.* **-lat•ed, -lat•ing.** To assume to be true. —*n.* (-lĭt, -lāt′). A self-evident or gen. accepted theory or statement : axiom. **—pos′tu•la′tion** *n.*
pos•ture (pŏs′chər) *n.* **1.** A way of carrying or positioning the body. **2.** Mode or status <a country's revolutionary *posture*> **3.** An attitude or tendency. —*v.* **-tured, -tur•ing.** To assume a pose, esp. for effect. **—pos′tur•er** *n.*
po•sy (pō′zē) *n.*, *pl.* **-sies. 1. a.** A flower. **b.** A bouquet. **2.** *Archaic.* A short, usu. sentimental poem or motto.
pot (pŏt) *n.* **1.** A rounded, somewhat deep container used esp. in cooking and for holding plants. **2.** All the money staked in 1 hand of a card game. **3.** *Informal.* A pool of funds shared by all members of a group. **4.** *Slang.* Marijuana. **5.** *Computer Sci.* A section of computer storage for accumulated data. —*v.* **pot•ted, pot•ting. 1.** To put or plant in a pot. **2.** To cook or preserve in a pot. **3.** To shoot (game), esp. for food. **—pot′ful′** *n.*
pot. *abbr.* potential.
po•ta•ble (pō′tə-bəl) *adj.* Fit to drink.
pot•ash (pŏt′ăsh′) *n.* Any of several chemical compounds that contain potassium, esp. a strongly alkaline material obtained from wood ashes and used esp. in fertilizers.
po•tas•si•um (pə-tăs′ē-əm) *n.* *Symbol* **K** A soft, silver-white, highly reactive metallic element used esp. in fertilizers.
potassium bromide *n.* A white crystalline salt used as a sedative and in developing photographs.
potassium carbonate *n.* A white salt used esp. in glass, pigments, and soaps.
potassium hydroxide *n.* A corrosive solid used as a bleach and in detergents.
potassium nitrate *n.* A soluble white crystalline salt used esp. to preserve meat and to make explosives and fertilizers.
po•ta•tion (pō-tā′shən) *n.* A drink, esp. an alcoholic beverage.
po•ta•to (pə-tā′tō) *n.*, *pl.* **-toes.** A plant, *Solanum tuberosum,* widely grown for its starchy, edible tubers.
potato chip *n.* A very thin slice of potato deep-fried until crisp.
pot•bel•ly (pŏt′bĕl′ē) *n.* A sagging or protruding abdomen. **—pot′bel′lied** *adj.*
pot•boil•er (pŏt′boi′lər) *n.* A usu. inferior literary or artistic work produced solely to make a profit.
pot cheese *n.* Cottage cheese.
po•tent (pōt′nt) *adj.* **1.** Strong and powerful. **2.** Highly effective or influential. **3.** Strongly affecting the body or mind, as a drug or poison. **4.** Capable of having sexual intercourse. Used of a male. **—po′ten•cy** *n.* **—po′tent•ly** *adv.*
po•ten•tate (pōt′n-tāt′) *n.* A powerful ruler : monarch.
po•ten•tial (pə-tĕn′shəl) *adj.* **1.** Not yet actual or real : latent <a *potential* problem> **2.** Capable of being developed <a *potential* source of energy> —*n.* **1.** Capacity for realization or development. **2.** The potential energy of a unit electric charge depending on its position in an electric circuit or field. **—po•ten′ti•al′i•ty** (-shē-ăl′ĭ-tē) *n.* **—po•ten′tial•ly** *adv.*
po•ten•ti•ate (pə-tĕn′chē-āt′) *v.* **-at•ed, -at•ing.** To increase the potency of (a drug) by administering a 2nd drug at the same time.
pot•head (pŏt′hĕd′) *n.* *Slang.* A habitual smoker of marijuana.
poth•er (pŏ*th*′ər) *n.* A commotion or fuss.
pot•herb (pŏt′ûrb′, -hûrb′) *n.* A plant whose leaves, stems, or flowers are cooked and eaten or used as seasoning.
†pot•hole (pŏt′hōl′) *n.* **1.** A dent or hole, esp. in a road. **2.** *W U.S.* A place filled with mud or quicksand that is a hazard to cattle.
pot•hook (pŏt′ho͝ok′) *n.* An iron hook for hanging a pot over an open fire.
po•tion (pō′shən) *n.* A drink or dose, esp. of medicine or poison.
pot•luck (pŏt′lŭk′) *n.* The food on hand, esp. when offered to a guest at mealtime.
Po•to•mac (pə-tō′mək). River flowing c. 285 mi (459 km) from NE W.Va. along the Va.–Md. border to Chesapeake Bay.
pot•pie (pŏt′pī′) *n.* Meat or poultry stew covered with a pastry crust and baked in a deep dish.
pot•pour•ri (pō′po͝o-rē′) *n.* **1.** A miscellaneous combination or collection. **2.** A mixture of sweet-smelling dried flower petals and spices.
pot roast *n.* A cut of beef braised in a covered pot.
pot•sherd (pŏt′shûrd′) *n.* A pottery fragment found esp. at a dig.
pot shot *n.* **1.** A shot fired casually or at an easy target. **2.** A critical remark aimed at a vulnerable target.
pot•tage (pŏt′ĭj) *n.* A thick soup or stew.
pot•ter[1] (pŏt′ər) *n.* A maker of pottery.
pot•ter[2] (pŏt′ər) *v.* To putter.
pot•ter•y (pŏt′ə-rē) *n.*, *pl.* **-ies. 1.** Molded and fired clay objects, as pots, bowls, and vases. **2.** The art or work of a potter. **3.** The workshop of a potter.
pouch (pouch) *n.* **1.** A small bag, esp. for carrying tobacco. **2.** A flexible bag, esp. for holding or transporting mail or diplomatic dispatches. **3.** *Zool.* A saclike anatomical structure, as one in which marsupials carry their young. —*v.* To assume the form of a pouch or pouchlike cavity. **—pouch′y** *adj.*
pouil•ly•fuis•sé (po͞o-yē′fwē-sā′) *n.* A dry white Burgundy wine.
poul•ter•er (pōl′tər-ər) *n.* A dealer in poultry or poultry products.
poul•tice (pōl′tĭs) *n.* A soft, usu. warmed and medicated mass applied on cloth to a sore or inflamed body part. **—poul′tice** *v.*
poul•try (pōl′trē) *n.* Domestic fowl raised for meat or eggs.
pounce (pouns) *v.* **pounced, pounc•ing.** To seize by or as if by swooping or springing abruptly. **—pounce** *n.* **—pounc′er** *n.*
pound[1] (pound) *n.*, *pl.* **pounds** or **pound. 1.** See MEASUREMENT TABLE. **2.** See CURRENCY TABLE.
▲word history: The word *pound[1]*, "a unit of currency," is a specialized use of the word *pound* meaning "a unit of weight." The word *pound[1]* is derived from Latin *pondo*, "a measure of weight." The orig. Latin word for "a pound weight" was *libra. Pondo,* which is actually the ablative case of *pondus,* "a weight," developed into a separate noun from the phrase *libra pondo,* "a pound by weight." *Pondo* descended into Old English as *pund,* which had the same meanings as modern *pound[1]*. The monetary unit was orig. the value of a pound weight of silver. The symbol £ still used for the British pound is a stylized *L* that stands for the Latin word *libra.*
pound[2] (pound) *v.* **1.** To strike forcefully or repeatedly. **2.** To pulverize or crush by beating. **3.** To instill by repetition. **4.** To move along or over heavily and loudly. **5.** To beat or throb rapidly and violently.
pound[3] (pound) *n.* A public enclosure for stray dogs and cats.
pound•age (poun′dĭj) *n.* Weight reckoned in pounds.
pound cake *n.* A cake rich in butter, sugar, and eggs.
pound-fool•ish (pound′fo͞o′lĭsh) *adj.* Not prudent in dealing with large amounts of money or weighty matters.
pour (pôr, pōr) *v.* **1.** To flow or cause to flow profusely or in a continuous stream. **2.** To supply abundantly. **3.** To rain hard.
pout (pout) *v.* **1.** To express disapproval or resentment by protruding the lips. **2.** To look sulky or sullen. **—pout** *n.*
pov•er•ty (pŏv′ər-tē) *n.* **1.** A chronic pressing need for money and material goods. **2.** Dearth. **3.** Inferior quality, as of soil.
pov•er•ty-strick•en (pŏv′ər-tē-strĭk′ən) *adj.* Completely impoverished.
POW (pē′ō′dŭb′əl-yo͞o) *n.* A prisoner of war.
pow•der (pou′dər) *n.* **1.** A dry substance composed of very fine particles. **2.** A medicine, cosmetic, or cleaning agent in the form of powder. **3.** An explosive mixture, as gunpowder. **4.** Light, dry snow. —*v.* **1.** To reduce to powder, as by pulverizing. **2.** To cover or dust with or as if with powder. **—pow′der•y** *adj.*
pow•der-puff (pou′dər-pŭf′) *adj.* Of or being a usu. competitive activity for women. —*n.* **powder puff.** PUFF 3.
powder room *n.* A restroom for women.
†pow•er (pou′ər) *n.* **1.** The capacity or ability to do or accomplish something. **2.** *often* **powers.** A particular ability, capability, or skill. **3. a.** Strength, force, or might. **b.** Forceful impact : effectiveness. **4.** The authority or ability to control others. **5.** One having great authority or influence <a world *power*> **6.** Physical force or energy. **7.** The measured rate of time at which

work is done or energy is transferred. **8.** Electrical energy : electricity. **9.** *Math.* The number of times a number or expression is to be multiplied by itself, as indicated by an exponent. **10.** The degree of magnification of an optical lens. **11.** *Regional.* A large number or amount. ☆***syns:*** AUTHORITY, CLOUT, CONTROL —*v.* To supply (e.g., a motor or machine) with power. **—pow'er·less** *adj.*

power broker *n.* One, esp. a politician, who exerts strong influence by virtue of the individuals and votes he or she controls.

†**pow·er·ful** (pou'ər-fəl) *adj.* **1.** Having power, authority, or influence. **2.** *Regional.* Great <a *powerful* lot of harm> —*adv. Regional.* Very <It was *powerful* humid yesterday.> **—pow'er·ful·ly** *adv.*

pow·er·house (pou'ər-hous') *n.* **1.** A place where electrical power is generated. **2.** A forceful, energetic person.

power of attorney *n.* A legal document conferring authority to act as attorney or agent for another.

power plant *n.* **1.** The equipment making up the power source of a self-propelled unit, as a spacecraft. **2.** A powerhouse.

pow·wow (pou'wou') *n.* **1.** A North American Indian prayer ceremony, esp. before hunting or battle. **2.** *Informal.* A meeting or conference for discussion.

pox (pŏks) *n.* An eruptive disease, as smallpox, marked by pustules.

pp. *abbr.* **1.** pages. **2.** past participle.

p.p. or **P.P.** *abbr.* **1.** parcel post. **2.** past participle. **3.** postpaid.

ppd. *abbr.* **1.** postpaid. **2.** prepaid.

P.Q. *abbr.* Parti Québecois.

Pr *symbol for* PRASEODYMIUM.

pr. *abbr.* **1.** pair. **2.** present. **3.** price. **4.** printing. **5.** pronoun.

PR *abbr.* **1.** *also* **P.R.** public relations. **2.** Puerto Rico (with Zip Code).

prac·ti·ca·ble (prăk'tĭ-kə-bəl) *adj.* **1.** Capable of being done or put into effect. **2.** Capable of being used. **—prac'ti·ca·bil'i·ty** *n.* **—prac'ti·ca·bly** *adv.*

prac·ti·cal (prăk'tĭ-kəl) *adj.* **1.** Serving a purpose : useful. **2.** Resulting from or involving experience, practice, or use rather than theory or speculation. **3. a.** Inclined to action : unspeculative. **b.** Down-to-earth : sensible. **4.** Being so in effect : virtual. ☆***syns:*** FUNCTIONAL, HANDY, SERVICEABLE, USEFUL, UTILITARIAN **—prac'ti·cal'i·ty** (-kăl'ĭ-tē) *n.* **—prac'ti·cal·ly** *adv.*

practical joke *n.* A prank played on someone to cause embarrassment. **—practical joker** *n.*

practical nurse *n.* A nurse who is usu. licensed by a state to provide routine patient care.

prac·tice (prăk'tĭs) *n.* **1.** A habit, custom, or method of doing something. **2. a.** Repetition to acquire or perfect a skill. **b.** Skill gained or maintained through repeated exercise. **3.** Actual performance or use <put knowledge into *practice*> **4.** The exercise of a profession. **5.** The business of a professional, as a doctor or lawyer. ☆***syns:*** DRILL, EXERCISE, REHEARSAL, STUDY, TRAINING —*v.* **-ticed, -tic·ing. 1.** To make a habit or custom of <*practice* courteous driving> **2.** To do repeatedly in order to acquire proficiency. **3.** To pursue as a profession <*practice* medicine> **4.** To put into effect : apply.

prac·tise (prăk'tĭs) *n.* & *v. esp. Brit. var. of* PRACTICE.

prac·ti·tio·ner (prăk-tĭsh'ə-nər) *n.* One who practices a profession.

prae·tor (prē'tər) *n.* A magistrate of ancient Rome, ranking below a consul. **—prae·to'ri·an** (-tôr'ē-ən, -tōr'-) *adj.*

prag·mat·ic (prăg-măt'ĭk) *also* **prag·mat·i·cal** (-ĭ-kəl) *adj.* **1.** Concerned with practice rather than theory : practical. **2.** Of or pertaining to the theory or methods of pragmatism. **—prag·mat'i·cal·ly** *adv.*

prag·ma·tism (prăg'mə-tĭz'əm) *n.* **1.** The theory that actions and beliefs must be judged by their practical results. **2.** The use of practical means to solve problems. **—prag'ma·tist** *n.*

Prague (präg). Cap. of Czechoslovakia, in the W. *Pop.* 1,193,345.

prai·rie (prâr'ē) *n.* A wide area of level or rolling grassland, as in the C U.S.

prairie dog *n.* A burrowing rodent of the genus *Cynomys,* of WC North America, with yellowish fur and a barklike call.

prairie schooner *n.* A large canvas-covered wagon used by pioneers in traveling across the North American prairies.

praise (prāz) *v.* **praised, prais·ing. 1.** To express approval of or admiration for. **2.** To extol or glorify (e.g., a deity or hero). ☆***syns:*** ACCLAIM, APPLAUD, COMMEND, LAUD **—praise** *n.* **—praise'wor'thy** *adj.*

pra·line (prä'lēn', prā'-) *n.* A candy of boiled brown sugar or maple sugar in which nut kernels are embedded.

pram (prăm) *n. esp. Brit.* A baby carriage.

prance (prăns) *v.* **pranced, pranc·ing. 1.** To spring forward on the hind legs <*prancing* horses> **2. a.** To caper about. **b.** To swagger or strut. **—pranc'er** *n.* **—pranc'ing·ly** *adv.*

prank (prăngk) *n.* A playful or mischievous act or trick. ☆***syns:*** ANTIC, CAPER, JOKE, LARK, MONKEYSHINE, SHENANIGAN, TOMFOOLERY, TRICK **—prank'ster** *n.*

pra·se·o·dym·i·um (prā'zē-ō-dĭm'ē-əm, -sē-) *n. Symbol* **Pr** A soft silvery rare-earth element used esp. in metallic alloys.

prate (prāt) *v.* **prat·ed, prat·ing.** To chatter idly and volubly.

prat·fall (prăt'fôl') *n.* A fall in which one lands on the buttocks.

pra·tique (pră-tēk') *n. Naut.* Clearance granted to a ship to proceed into a port after compliance with regulations.

prat·tle (prăt'l) *v.* **-tled, -tling. 1.** To prate. **2.** To babble childishly. —*n.* Foolish or childish talk.

prawn (prôn) *n.* An edible crustacean of the genus *Palaemonetes,* closely related to the shrimps.

pray (prā) *v.* **1.** To address God or a deity, esp. with devout petition. **2.** To request something fervently. **3.** To implore.

prayer (prâr) *n.* **1.** An expression, esp. of devout petition, addressed to God or a deity. **2.** A formal set of words used in praying. **3.** *often* **prayers.** A religious service esp. for the saying of prayers. **4.** An earnest entreaty. **5.** A minimal chance or hope.

prayer·ful (prâr'fəl) *adj.* **1.** Deeply religious : devout. **2.** Deeply sincere : earnest. **—prayer'ful·ly** *adv.*

praying mantis *n.* A predatory insect, *Mantis religiosa,* that holds its front legs folded as if in prayer.

pre– *pref.* **1. a.** Prior to : earlier <*pre*natal> **b.** Preparatory : preliminary <*pre*flight> **c.** In advance <*pre*heat> **2.** In front of <*pre*fix> See below for a list of self-explanatory words formed with the prefix **pre–.**

---

preadmission
preadult
preadvise
preagitate
preanesthetic
preannounce
preantepenult
preapprove
prearrange
prearrangement
preassign
preaudit
preballot
prebattle
pre-Biblical
preboil
prebridal
pre-Byzantine
prechill
pre-Christian
precivilization
preclearance
precode
precoital
precollect
precollection
precollege
precolonial
precombustion
precompensate
precompute
preconstruct
preconvention
preconviction
precook
precool
precoronation
precounsel
precoup
precrash
precrease
precut
predawn
predelivery
predemocratic
predeparture
predepletion
predesignate
predesignation
predetect
predetection
predevaluation
predevelopment
prediagnosis
predinner
predischarge
predisclose
prediscovery
predrill
predusk
predynastic
pre-edit
pre-educate
pre-education
pre-election
pre-embargo
pre-employment
pre-endorse
pre-enrollment
pre-erect
pre-establish
pre-experiment
prefade
prefertilize
prefight
prefile
prefinance
prefire
preflame
preformat
preformulate
prefreeze
pregame
preharvest
preheadache
prehiring
pre-Hispanic
preholiday
preimbibe
preimpression
preinaugural
preincorporation
preinduction
preindustrial
preinterview
preinvasion
preinvestigate
preinvestigation
prekindergarten
preknowledge
prelabel
prelaunch
prelaw
prelife
preliteracy
prelunch
preluncheon
premanufacture

preach (prēch) *v.* **1.** To urge or advocate earnestly. **2.** To deliver (a sermon) formally. **3.** To offer moral advice, esp. tediously. **–preach′er** *n.* **–preach′ment** *n.* **–preach′y** *adj.*

pre•ad•o•les•cence (prē′ăd′l-ĕs′əns) *n.* The period between childhood and adolescence. **–pre′ad′o•les′cent** *n.* & *adj.*

pre•am•ble (prē′ăm′bəl) *n.* An introduction, esp. to a formal document.

pre•am•pli•fi•er (prē-ăm′plə-fī′ər) *n.* An electronic amplifier designed to augment very weak signals, as from a phonograph pickup, before they are further amplified.

preb•end (prĕb′ənd) *n.* **1.** An endowment of a cathedral or collegiate church from which a prebendary's stipend is drawn. **2.** The stipend drawn from a prebend.

preb•en•dar•y (prĕb′ən-dĕr′ē) *n.*, *pl.* **-ies.** A clergyman granted a prebend for serving in a church.

pre•can•cer•ous (prē-kăn′sər-əs) *adj.* Tending or likely to become cancerous.

pre•car•i•ous (prĭ-kâr′ē-əs) *adj.* **1.** Perilously unstable. **2.** Dependent on chance : uncertain. **–pre•car′i•ous•ly** *adv.* **–pre•car′i•ous•ness** *n.*

pre•cau•tion (prĭ-kô′shən) *n.* A measure taken in advance to safeguard against harm. **–pre•cau′tion•ar′y** (-shə-nĕr′ē) *adj.*

pre•cede (prĭ-sēd′) *v.* **-ced•ed, -ced•ing.** To come or be before in time, order, position, or rank. **–prec′e•dence** (prĕs′ĭ-dns, prĭ-sēd′ns) *n.*

prec•e•dent (prĕs′ĭ-dnt) *n.* An instance, case, or decision that may serve as an example or justification for a later similar one. *–adj.* **pre•ce•dent** (prĭ-sēd′nt, prĕs′ĭ-dnt). Coming before : prior.

pre•cen•tor (prĭ-sĕn′tər) *n.* One who leads a church choir or congregation in singing.

pre•cept (prē′sĕpt′) *n.* A general rule of conduct or procedure.

pre•cep•tor (prĭ-sĕp′tər, prē′sĕp′-) *n.* A teacher or tutor.

pre•cinct (prē′sĭngkt′) *n.* **1.** An administrative district of a city or town <a police *precinct*> **2.** *often* **precincts.** An area or enclosure with definite boundaries. **3. precincts.** Surrounding areas : environs.

pre•ci•os•i•ty (prĕsh′ē-ŏs′ĭ-tē, prĕs′ē-) *n.*, *pl.* **-ties.** Extreme fastidiousness.

pre•cious (prĕsh′əs) *adj.* **1.** Highly valuable : costly. **2.** Highly esteemed. **3.** Cherished : beloved. **4.** Affectedly refined.

prec•i•pice (prĕs′ə-pĭs) *n.* A very steep crag or cliff.

pre•cip•i•tant (prĭ-sĭp′ĭ-tənt) *adj.* Precipitate. **–pre•cip′i•tance** (-təns), **pre•cip′i•tan•cy** (-tən-sē) *n.*

pre•cip•i•tate (prĭ-sĭp′ĭ-tāt′) *v.* **-tat•ed, -tat•ing. 1.** To cast down from a high place. **2.** To bring on, esp. abruptly or unexpectedly. **3.** To condense and fall as rain, hail, or snow. **4.** *Chem.* To separate (a solid substance) out of a solution. *–adj.* (-tĭt, -tāt′). **1.** Rushing headlong and heedlessly. **2.** Acting impulsively or rashly. **3.** Abrupt or unexpected. *–n.* (-tāt′, -tĭt). *Chem.* A solid separated out from a solution. **–pre•cip′i•tate•ly** *adv.* **–pre•cip′i•tate•ness** *n.* **–pre•cip′i•ta′tor** *n.*

pre•cip•i•ta•tion (prĭ-sĭp′ĭ-tā′shən) *n.* **1.** Impetuous haste. **2. a.** Condensed water vapor that falls as rain, hail, or snow. **b.** The quantity of this water vapor. **3.** *Chem.* The production of a precipitate in a chemical reaction.

pre•cip•i•tous (prĭ-sĭp′ĭ-təs) *adj.* **1. a.** Like a precipice in being very steep. **b.** Having or marked by precipices. **2.** Precipitate. **–pre•cip′i•tous•ly** *adv.* **–pre•cip′i•tous•ness** *n.*

pré•cis (prā-sē′) *n.*, *pl.* **-cis** (-sēz′). A concise summary : abstract. **–pré•cis′** *v.*

pre•cise (prĭ-sīs′) *adj.* **1.** Accurately stated or described : definite. **2.** Highly exact : correct. **3.** Distinct from others : particular <on this *precise* spot> **4.** Strictly observant of established forms and procedures. ☆***syns:*** EXACT, IDENTICAL, VERY **–pre•cise′ly** *adv.* **–pre•cise′ness** *n.*

pre•ci•sion (prĭ-sĭzh′ən) *n.* The state, property, or quality of being precise.

pre•clude (prĭ-klōōd′) *v.* **-clud•ed, -clud•ing.** To make impossible : prevent.

pre•co•cious (prĭ-kō′shəs) *adj.* Marked by the early development of skills and abilities. **–pre•co′cious•ly** *adv.* **–pre•coc′i•ty** (-kŏs′ĭ-tē) *n.*

pre•cog•ni•tion (prē′kŏg-nĭsh′ən) *n.* Clairvoyant knowledge of something prior to its happening. **–pre•cog′ni•tive** *adj.*

pre-Co•lum•bi•an (prē′kə-lŭm′bē-ən) *adj.* Of, pertaining to, or originating in the Americas before the voyages of Columbus <*pre-Columbian* art>

pre•con•ceive (prē′kən-sēv′) *v.* To form an opinion or conception of before knowing all the facts. **–pre′con•cep′tion** (-sĕp′shən) *n.*

pre•con•di•tion (prē′kən-dĭsh′ən) *n.* A prerequisite. *–v.* To put into a certain condition or mental attitude beforehand.

pre•cur•sor (prĭ-kûr′sər, prē′kûr′-) *n.* **1.** An indicator of one to come : forerunner. **2.** A predecessor.

pre•da•cious *or* **pre•da•ceous** (prĭ-dā′shəs) *adj.* Preying on other animals.

pre•date (prē-dāt′) *v.* **1.** To come before in time : antedate. **2.** To mark with a date earlier than the actual one.

pred•a•to•ry (prĕd′ə-tôr′ē, -tōr′ē) *adj.* **1.** Of, relating to, or marked by plunder. **2.** Selfishly exploiting others. **3.** Predacious. **–pred′a•tor** *n.*

pre•de•cease (prē′dĭ-sēs′) *v.* To die before (another).

pred•e•ces•sor (prĕd′ĭ-sĕs′ər, prē′dĭ-) *n.* **1.** One that comes before another, esp. in an office or function. **2.** An ancestor.

pre•des•ti•na•tion (prē-dĕs′tə-nā′shən) *n.* **1.** The act by which God is held to have unalterably predestined all events. **2.** The doctrine that the destiny of each soul has been foreordained by God.

pre•des•tine (prē-dĕs′tĭn) *v.* To destine in advance : foreordain.

pre•de•ter•mine (prē′dĭ-tûr′mĭn) *v.* To determine in advance. **–pre′de•ter′mi•na′tion** *n.* **–pre′de•ter′min•er** *n.*

pred•i•ca•ble (prĕd′ĭ-kə-bəl) *adj.* Capable of being asserted or predicated.

pre•dic•a•ment (prĭ-dĭk′ə-mənt) *n.* A difficult or distressing situation.

pred•i•cate (prĕd′ĭ-kāt′) *v.* **-cat•ed, -cat•ing. 1.** To find a basis for : establish. **2.** To assert to be a quality or characteristic <*predicate* humanity's resilient spirit> *–n.* (-kĭt). The part of a sentence or clause that makes a statement about the subject. **–pred′i•ca′tion** *n.* **–pred′i•ca′tive** *adj.*

pre•dict (prĭ-dĭkt′) *v.* To state in advance. ☆***syns:*** FORECAST, FORETELL, PORTEND, PROGNOSTICATE **–pre•dict′a•bil′i•ty** *n.*

premarket
premarriage
premeal
premeasure
premedicate
premedieval
premenopausal
premenstrual
premerger
premetamorphic
premidnight
premigration
premigratory
premix
premixture
premodern
premodification
premodify
premoisten
premold
premorning
prenegotiation
prenoon
prenotification
prenotify
prenumber
prenuptial
preopening
preoperation
preoperational
preorder
preoutfit
prepaste
preplan
preportion
preprice
preprimary
preprimer
preproduction
preprogram
prepublication
prepupal
prepurchase
prequalify
preracing
prerecession
pre-Reformation
prerehearsal
prerelease
pre-Renaissance
prerental
prerequire
prerequirement
preretirement
prereturn
prereveal
prereview
prerevolution
prerevolutionary
prerinse
preroyalty
presale
preschedule
prescreen
preseason
presentence
presentencing
preservice
preshow
presleep
preslice
presong
presort
prespecify
presplit
prestamp
presterilize
prestorage
presuggest
presummit
presurgery
presurgical
presweeten
pretape
pretaste
pretelevision
pretermination
pretheater
pretournament
pretrain
pretraining
pretravel
pretreat
pretreatment
pretrial
pretrim
pretry
pretype
preuniversity
pre-Victorian
previsit
prevote
prewar
prewash
prewelcome
prework
prewrap
prewrapping

—pre·dict'a·ble *adj.* **—pre·dict'a·bly** *adv.* **—pre·dic'tion** *n.* **—pre·dic'tor** *n.*
pre·di·gest (prē'dĭ-jĕst', -dī-) *v.* To subject to partial digestion, as by enzymatic action. **—pre'di·ges'tion** *n.*
pre·di·lec·tion (prĕd'l-ĕk'shən, prēd'l-) *n.* A natural or habitual preference.
pre·dis·pose (prē'dĭ-spōz') *v.* **1.** To incline or influence beforehand. **2.** To make susceptible. **—pre·dis'po·si'tion** *n.*
pre·dom·i·nant (prĭ-dŏm'ə-nənt) *adj.* **1.** Superior in power or importance : dominant. **2.** Most commonly occurring or existing : prevalent. **—pre·dom'i·nance** *n.* **—pre·dom'i·nant·ly** *adv.*
pre·dom·i·nate (prĭ-dŏm'ə-nāt') *v.* **1.** To be of greater strength, number, importance, or prominence. **2.** To have authority or controlling influence : dominate. **—pre·dom'i·nate·ly** *adv.*
pree·mie (prē'mē) *n. Informal.* A baby born prematurely.
pre-em·i·nent or **pre·em·i·nent** (prē-ĕm'ə-nənt) *adj.* Excelling all others : outstanding. **—pre-em'i·nence** *n.*
pre-empt or **pre·empt** (prē-ĕmpt') *v.* **1.** To gain buying rights to (public land) by settling before others. **2.** To take for oneself before others. **3.** To take the place of (a scheduled program). **—pre-emp'tion** *n.* **—pre-emp'tive** *adj.*
preen (prēn) *v.* **1.** To groom (feathers) with the beak. **2.** To primp. **3.** To take self-satisfied pride in (oneself).
pre-ex·ist or **pre·ex·ist** (prē'ĭg-zĭst') *v.* To exist before something else. **—pre'-ex·ist'ence** *n.* **—pre'-ex·ist'ent** *adj.*
pref. *abbr.* **1.** preface; prefatory. **2.** preference; preferred. **3.** prefix.
pre·fab (prē'făb') *n.* A prefabricated building or structural part.
pre·fab·ri·cate (prē-făb'rĭ-kāt') *v.* To manufacture in standard sections for easy shipping and assembly. **—pre·fab'ri·ca'tion** *n.* **—pre·fab'ri·ca'tor** *n.*
pref·ace (prĕf'ĭs) *n.* An introductory statement or remark : foreword. —*v.* **-aced, -ac·ing.** To introduce or provide with a preface. **—pref'a·to'ry** (-ə-tôr'ē, -tōr'ē) *adj.*
pre·fect (prē'fĕkt') *n.* **1.** A high administrative official or magistrate. **2.** A student monitor, esp. in a private school. **—pre'fec'ture** (-fĕk'chər) *n.*
pre·fer (prĭ-fûr') *v.* **-ferred, -fer·ring. 1.** To select as being more desirable : favor. **2.** To present (e.g., a charge against another) before a legal authority. **—pref'er·a·ble** (prĕf'ər-ə-bəl) *adj.* **—pref'er·a·bly** *adv.*
pref·er·ence (prĕf'ər-əns) *n.* **1.** Choice : option. **2.** Partiality for something over another. **3.** One that is favored or chosen. **—pref'er·en'tial** (-ə-rĕn'shəl) *adj.*
pre·fer·ment (prĭ-fûr'mənt) *n.* Selection for promotion or favored treatment.
pre·fig·ure (prē-fĭg'yər) *v.* **1.** To indicate in advance : foreshadow. **2.** To imagine ahead of time. **—pre·fig'ure·ment** *n.*
pre·fix (prē'fĭks', prē-fĭks') *v.* To put (e.g., a title) before. —*n.* (prē'fĭks'). An affix that occurs at the beginning of a word.
pre·flight (prē'flīt') *adj.* Readying for or taking place before aircraft flight.
preg·na·ble (prĕg'nə-bəl) *adj.* Unprotected against attack or capture, as a fort. **—preg'na·bil'i·ty** *n.*
preg·nant (prĕg'nənt) *adj.* **1.** Carrying an unborn fetus or offspring. **2.** Significant : meaningful. **—preg'nan·cy** *n.*
pre·heat (prē-hēt') *v.* To heat (e.g., an oven) in advance.
pre·hen·sile (prĭ-hĕn'sĭl, -sīl') *adj.* Adapted for seizing or holding, esp. by wrapping around.

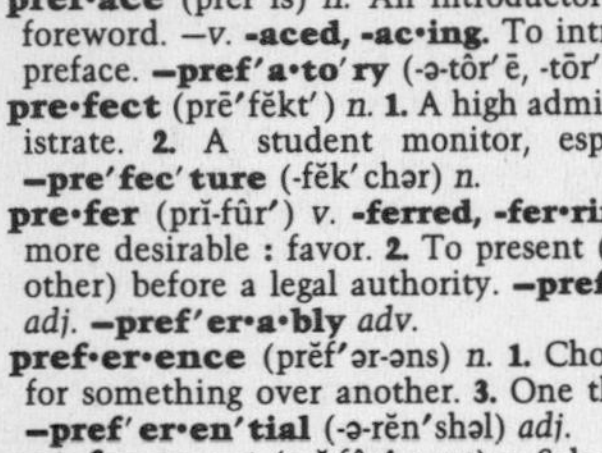

prehensile
Two examples of prehensile tails: (left) *opossum and* (right) *spider monkey*

pre·his·tor·ic (prē'hĭ-stôr'ĭk, -stŏr'-) *also* **pre·his·tor·i·cal** (-ĭ-kəl) *adj.* Of, relating to, or belonging to the period prior to recorded history. **—pre'his·tor'i·cal·ly** *adv.*
pre·ig·ni·tion (prē'ĭg-nĭsh'ən) *n.* Ignition of fuel in an internal-combustion engine before the spark passes through the fuel.
pre·judge (prē-jŭj') *v.* To judge before knowing all the facts. **—pre·judg'er** *n.* **—pre·judg'ment, pre·judge'ment** *n.*
prej·u·dice (prĕj'ə-dĭs) *n.* **1.** A bias for or against something formed without sufficient basis. **2.** Irrational intolerance of or hostility toward members of a certain race, religion, or group. **3.** Detriment, esp. to one's legal rights. —*v.* **-diced, -dic·ing. 1.** To fill with prejudice : bias. **2.** To be detrimental to. **—prej'u·di'cial** (-dĭsh'əl) *adj.*
prel·ate (prĕl'ĭt) *n.* A high-ranking member of the clergy, as a bishop or cardinal. **—prel'a·cy** (-ə-sē) *n.*
pre·lim·i·nar·y (prĭ-lĭm'ə-nĕr'ē) *adj.* Preceding or preparing for the main event or business. —*n., pl.* **-ies.** Something, as a remark, that is preliminary. **—pre·lim'i·nar'i·ly** (-nâr'ə-lē) *adv.*
pre·lit·er·ate (prē-lĭt'ər-ĭt) *adj.* Of or relating to a culture lacking a written language. **—pre·lit'er·ate** *n.*
prel·ude (prĕl'yo͞od', prā'lo͞od') *n.* **1.** An introductory or preliminary action, performance, or event. **2.** *Mus.* **a.** A piece or movement preceding the main theme. **b.** A short composition in free style. **c.** An organ solo played before a church service.
prem. *abbr.* premium.
pre·mar·i·tal (prē-măr'ĭ-tl) *adj.* Existing or happening before marriage.
pre·ma·ture (prē'mə-to͝or', -tyo͝or', -cho͝or') *adj.* Appearing, done, occurring, or born before the usual or correct time : early. **—pre'ma·ture'ly** *adv.*
pre·med (prē'mĕd') *adj. Informal.* Premedical. —*n.* **1.** A premedical student. **2.** Premedical studies.
pre·med·i·cal (prē-mĕd'ĭ-kəl) *adj.* Preparing for or preceding the study of medicine.
pre·med·i·tate (prē-mĕd'ĭ-tāt') *v.* To plan or plot beforehand. **—pre·med'i·tat'ed** *adj.* **—pre·med'i·ta'tion** *n.*
pre·mier (prē'mē-ər, prĭ-mîr') *adj.* **1.** Foremost in importance or rank : chief. **2.** First or earliest in time. —*n.* (prĭ-mîr'). The chief executive or prime minister of a government. **—pre·mier'ship'** *n.*
pre·mière (prĭ-mîr', prĭm-yâr') *n.* An initial public presentation, as of a play or film. —*v.* **-mièred, -mièr·ing.** To present or receive an initial public presentation.
prem·ise (prĕm'ĭs) *n.* **1.** A postulate, assumption, or hypothesis serving as the basis of an argument. **2. premises.** Real estate and the structures on it. —*v.* **-ised, -is·ing.** To make or state as a premise.
pre·mi·um (prē'mē-əm) *n.* **1.** An award or prize. **2.** An additional sum paid esp. as an incentive : bonus. **3.** An additional amount charged above the nominal value. **4.** An exceptionally high value <put a *premium* on honesty> **5.** A payment, often in installments, for an insurance policy.
pre·mo·lar (prē-mō'lər) *n.* One of 8 paired bicuspids situated between the canines and molars. **—pre·mo'lar** *adj.*
pre·mo·ni·tion (prē'mə-nĭsh'ən, prĕm'ə-) *n.* **1.** An advance warning. **2.** A presentiment. **—pre·mon'i·to'ry** (-mŏn'ĭ-tôr'ē, -tōr'ē) *adj.*
pre·na·tal (prē-nāt'l) *adj.* Existing or happening before birth. **—pre·na'tal·ly** *adv.*
pre·oc·cu·py (prē-ŏk'yə-pī') *v.* **1.** To absorb wholly the mind or attention of. **2.** To occupy beforehand or before another. **—pre·oc'cu·pa'tion** (-pā'shən) *n.* **—pre·oc'cu·pied'** *adj.*
pre·op·er·a·tive (prē-ŏp'ər-ə-tĭv, -ŏp'rə-, -ŏp'ə-rā'-) *adj.* Prior to surgery.
pre·or·bit·al (prē-ôr'bĭ-tl) *adj.* Occurring before establishment of an orbit.
pre·or·dain (prē'ôr-dān') *v.* To decree or ordain in advance.
prep (prĕp) *Informal.* —*adj.* Preparatory. —*v.* **prepped, prep·ping. 1.** To study or train for something. **2.** To prepare for medical examination or surgery.
prep. *abbr.* **1.** preparation; preparatory. **2.** preposition.
pre·pack·age (prē-păk'ĭj) *v.* To wrap or package (e.g., food) before selling.
prep·a·ra·tion (prĕp'ə-rā'shən) *n.* **1.** The act or process of preparing. **2.** The state of being prepared. **3.** *often* **preparations.** Preparatory measures. **4.** Something prepared, as a medicinal mixture.
pre·par·a·to·ry (prĭ-păr'ə-tôr'ē, -tōr'ē, -pâr'-) *adj.* Serving to prepare.
preparatory school *n.* A private school preparing students chiefly for college.
pre·pare (prĭ-pâr') *v.* **-pared, -par·ing. 1.** To make or get ready for some purpose, task, or event. **2.** To produce by combining elements or ingredients. **3.** To provide in advance : equip. **4.** To put into writing.
pre·par·ed·ness (prĭ-pâr'ĭd-nĭs) *n.* A state of sufficient preparation, esp. for war.
pre·pay (prē-pā') *v.* To pay or pay for ahead of time. **—pre·pay'ment** *n.*
pre·pon·der·ate (prĭ-pŏn'də-rāt') *v.* **-at·ed, -at·ing.** To be superior in power, weight, number, or importance. **—pre·**

pon′der•ance *n.* **–pre•pon′der•ant** *adj.* **–pre•pon′der•ant•ly** *adv.*
prep•o•si•tion (prĕp′ə-zĭsh′ən) *n.* A word, as *by,* that indicates the relation of a substantive to a verb, adjective, or another substantive. **–prep′o•si′tion•al** *adj.*
pre•pos•sess (prē′pə-zĕs′) *v.* **1.** To influence in advance : bias. **2.** To make a favorable impression on beforehand.
pre•pos•sess•ing (prē′pə-zĕs′ĭng) *adj.* Creating a favorable impression : pleasing.
pre•pos•ter•ous (prĭ-pŏs′tər-əs) *adj.* **1.** Beyond all reason : absurd. **2.** Ridiculous : silly. **–pre•pos′ter•ous•ly** *adv.* **–pre•pos′ter•ous•ness** *n.*
prep•pie or **prep•py** (prĕp′ē) *n., pl.* **-pies.** *Informal.* **1.** A student attending a preparatory school. **2.** A student or young adult who dresses and behaves traditionally and conservatively.
pre•pu•ber•ty (prē-pyo͞o′bər-tē) *n.* The period just before puberty.
pre•pu•bes•cence (prē′pyoo-bĕs′əns) *n.* Prepuberty. **–pre′pu•bes′cent** *adj.*
pre•puce (prē′pyo͞os′) *n.* The foreskin.
pre•re•cord (prē′rĭ-kôrd′) *v.* To record (a radio or television program) ahead of time.
pre•req•ui•site (prē-rĕk′wĭ-zĭt) *adj.* Required as a preliminary condition. **–pre•req′ui•site** *n.*
pre•rog•a•tive (prĭ-rŏg′ə-tĭv) *n.* A special right or privilege, esp. of one holding a certain rank or status.
pres. *abbr.* **1.** present (time). **2.** *also* **Pres.** president.
pres•age (prĕs′ĭj) *n.* **1.** An omen of a future event : portent. **2.** A premonition : foreboding. *–v.* **pre•sage** (prĭ-sāj′, prĕs′ĭj) **-saged, -sag•ing. 1.** To foreshadow : portend. **2.** To foretell : prophesy.
pres•by•o•pi•a (prĕz′bē-ō′pē-ə, prĕs′-) *n.* Inability of the eye, esp. with advancing age, to focus sharply on close objects. **–pres′by•op′ic** (-ŏp′ĭk, -ō′pĭk) *adj.*
pres•by•ter (prĕz′bĭ-tər, prĕs′-) *n.* **1.** An elder in the Presbyterian Church. **2.** A priest or minister.
pres•by•te•ri•an (prĕz′bĭ-tîr′ē-ən, prĕs′-) *adj.* **1.** Of or relating to legislative and judicial church government by presbyters. **2. Presbyterian.** Of or relating to a Presbyterian Church. *–n.* A member of a Presbyterian Church. **–pres′by•te′ri•an•ism** *n.*
Presbyterian Church *n.* Any of various Protestant churches governed by presbyters and traditionally Calvinist in doctrine.
pres•by•ter•y (prĕz′bĭ-tĕr′ē, prĕs′-) *n., pl.* **-ies. 1.** A governmental body in Presbyterian churches composed of the ministers and representative elders of a certain district. **2.** The part of a church set aside for the clergy officiating at a service.
pre•school (prē′sko͞ol′) *adj.* Of or intended for a child too young for kindergarten. **–pre′school′er** *n.*
pre•science (prē′shəns, prē′shē-əns, prĕsh′əns, prĕsh′ē-əns) *n.* Accurate foreknowledge or foresight of future events. **–pre′scient** *adj.* **–pre′sci•ent•ly** *adv.*
pre•scribe (prĭ-skrīb′) *v.* **-scribed, -scrib•ing. 1.** To impose as a rule or guide : direct. **2.** To order or recommend (e.g., a specific drug) in medical treatment. **–pre•scrip′tive** (-skrĭp′tĭv) *adj.*
pre•scrip•tion (prĭ-skrĭp′shən) *n.* **1.** The act or process of prescribing. **2. a.** A physician's written instruction for the preparation and use of a medicine. **b.** A medicine ordered by prescription. **c.** Specifications for corrective lenses.
pres•ence (prĕz′əns) *n.* **1.** The fact or state of being present. **2.** Immediate proximity in time or space. **3.** Someone or something that is present. **4. a.** Carriage or bearing, esp. stately bearing. **b.** Self-assured confidence : poise.
pres•ent¹ (prĕz′ənt) *n.* **1.** The current moment or period : now. **2. a.** The verb tense expressing action, condition, or state in the present. **b.** A verb form in the present tense. **3. presents.** *Law.* The document or instrument under examination. *–adj.* **1.** Currently existing or occurring. **2.** Being in view or at hand. **3.** Of, pertaining to, or being a verb tense or form that indicates the actual or hypothetical present.
pre•sent² (prĭ-zĕnt′) *v.* **1.** To introduce to another, esp. formally. **2.** To offer (e.g., a new play) to the public. **3.** To make a gift or award of or to. **4.** To put forth for consideration. **5.** To aim or salute with (a weapon). **6.** *Law.* To bring (a charge or indictment) before a court. *–n.* **pres•ent** (prĕz′ənt). A gift. **–pre•sent′a•ble** *adj.* **–pres′en•ta′tion** *n.*
pres•ent-day (prĕz′ənt-dā′) *adj.* Currently existing or occurring.
pre•sen•ti•ment (prĭ-zĕn′tə-mənt) *n.* An intuitive feeling that something will soon occur : premonition.
pres•ent•ly (prĕz′ənt-lē) *adv.* **1.** Shortly : soon. **2.** Currently : now.
present participle *n.* A participle that expresses present action, condition, or state and that is formed in English by adding *-ing* to the infinitive.
pre•serve (prĭ-zûrv′) *v.* **-served, -serv•ing. 1.** To protect from harm. **2.** To maintain intact or unchanged. **3.** To prepare or treat in order to prevent spoilage or decay. *–n.* **1.** *often* **preserves.** Fruit preserved with sugar. **2.** An area for the safeguarding of wildlife or natural resources. **–pres′er•va′tion** (prĕz′ər-vā′shən) *n.* **–pre•serv′a•tive** *adj.* & *n.* **–pre•serv′er** *n.*
pre•set (prē′sĕt′) *v.* To set (an automatic device) in advance.
pre•shrunk *also* **pre-shrunk** (prē′shrŭngk′) *adj.* Processed during manufacture to minimize later shrinkage.
pre•side (prĭ-zīd′) *v.* **-sid•ed, -sid•ing. 1.** To be in a position of control, esp. to serve as chairperson. **2.** To have or exercise authority.
pres•i•dent (prĕz′ĭ-dənt, -dĕnt′) *n.* **1.** One selected to preside. **2.** *often* **President.** The chief of state of a republic, esp. the chief political executive of the U.S. **3.** The chief executive official of an organization, as a corporation. **–pres′i•den•cy** *n.* **–pres′i•den′tial** (-dĕn′shəl) *adj.*
pre•soak (prē-sōk′) *v.* To soak before laundering.
press (prĕs) *v.* **1.** To exert steady force or pressure (against). **2.** To squeeze out the juice or contents of (e.g., grapes). **3. a.** To force into a desired shape or smoothness by steady pressure. **b.** To smooth by ironing. **4.** To urge insistently. **5.** To constrain : harass. **6.** To pursue with determination. **7.** To force one's way. **8.** To crowd together. **9.** To weigh heavily, as on the mind. *–n.* **1.** A machine or device for exerting pressure. **2.** A printing press. **3.** An establishment for printing. **4.** The art, process, or business of printing. **5. a.** Printed matter, esp. newspapers and periodicals. **b.** Persons, as reporters, employed in the news media. **c.** Comment and criticism by the news media. **6.** A crowd : throng. **7.** The act of applying pressure or the state of being pressed. **8.** Urgent claim or demand. **9.** The correctly creased state of a pressed garment or fabric. **10.** An upright storage closet. **–press′er** *n.*
press agent *n.* An agent hired to promote favorable publicity for a client.
press•ing (prĕs′ĭng) *adj.* Urgent : critical.
press•man (prĕs′mən, -măn′) *n.* The operator of a printing press.
press•room (prĕs′ro͞om′, -ro͝om′) *n.* **1.** The location of the presses in a printing establishment. **2.** A room for reporters.
pres•sure (prĕsh′ər) *n.* **1.** The act of pressing or the state of being pressed. **2.** The application of steady force by 1 body in direct contact with another. **3.** The amount of force applied per unit of area of a surface. **4.** A compelling or constraining influence. **5.** Urgent requirements. **6.** A distressing or oppressive burden. *–v.* **-sured, -sur•ing.** To force, as by influencing or persuading.
pressure cooker *n.* **1.** An airtight metal pot that uses steam under pressure at high temperature to cook food quickly. **2.** A position of difficulty, stress, or anxiety.
pressure group *n.* A group that exerts pressure, esp. on legislators, in order to advance or safeguard its interests.
pressure suit *n.* An airtight suit worn in high-altitude aircraft or in spacecraft to protect against low-pressure conditions.

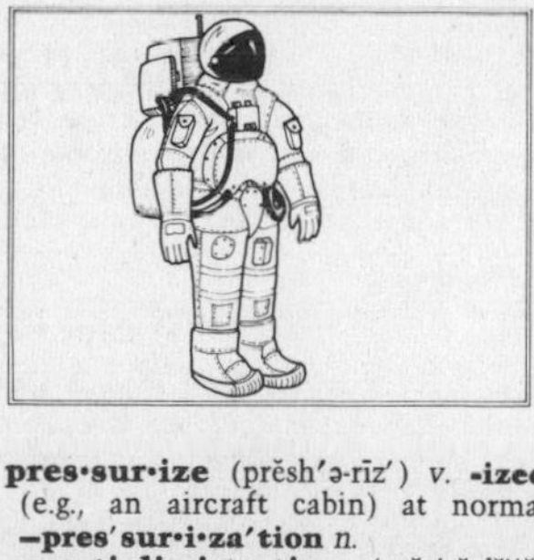

pressure suit

pres•sur•ize (prĕsh′ə-rīz′) *v.* **-ized, -iz•ing.** To maintain (e.g., an aircraft cabin) at normal atmospheric pressure. **–pres′sur•i•za′tion** *n.*
pres•ti•dig•i•ta•tion (prĕs′tĭ-dĭj′ĭ-tā′shən) *n.* Sleight of hand. **–pres′ti•dig′i•ta′tor** *n.*
pres•tige (prĕ-stēzh′, -stēj′) *n.* A person's standing or repute in the opinion of others. **–pres•tig′ious** (-stĭj′əs, -stē′jəs) *adj.*
pres•to (prĕs′tō) *adv.* **1.** *Mus.* Very quickly. Used as a direction. **2.** At once : immediately. **–pres′to** *adj.*
pre•sume (prĭ-zo͞om′) *v.* **-sumed, -sum•ing. 1.** To assume to be true : take for granted. **2.** To act without authority or leave : dare. **3.** To take undue advantage of something <*presumed* on their hospitality> **–pre•sum′a•ble** *adj.* **–pre•sum′a•bly** *adv.* **–pre•sum′er** *n.*
pre•sump•tion (prĭ-zŭmp′shən) *n.* **1.** Audacious behavior or

language : effrontery. **2. a.** An assumption or supposition based on reasonable evidence. **b.** Grounds for accepting or presuming. **—pre·sump′tive** *adj.* **—pre·sump′tive·ly** *adv.*

pre·sump·tu·ous (prĭ-zŭmp′cho͞o-əs) *adj.* Unduly or impertinently bold : forward. **—pre·sump′tu·ous·ness** *n.*

pre·sup·pose (prē′sə-pōz′) *v.* **1.** To suppose beforehand : assume. **2.** To require as a necessary prior condition. **—pre·sup′po·si′tion** (-sŭp′ə-zĭsh′ən) *n.*

pre·teen (prē′tēn′) *n.* A preadolescent child. **—pre′teen′** *adj.*

pre·tence (prē′tĕns′, prĭ-tĕns′) *n. esp. Brit. var. of* PRETENSE.

pre·tend (prĭ-tĕnd′) *v.* **1.** To make believe : feign <*pretended* to be furious> **2.** To claim falsely : profess <didn't *pretend* to be an expert> **3.** To assert a claim, as to a throne. **—pre·tend′er** *n.*

pre·tense (prē′tĕns′, prĭ-tĕns′) *n.* **1.** A false and deceptive appearance or action. **2.** A false purpose : pretext. **3.** An outward show or attempt. **4.** An unsupported claim. **5.** Ostentatious display. **6.** Affectation.

pre·ten·tious (prĭ-tĕn′shəs) *adj.* **1.** Making claims, as to distinction or excellence. **2.** Extravagantly showy : ostentatious. **—pre·ten′sion** *n.* **—pre·ten′tious·ly** *adv.* **—pre·ten′tious·ness** *n.*

pret·er·it *or* **pret·er·ite** (prĕt′ər-ĭt) *adj.* Designating a verb tense used to express past or completed action or condition. **—pret′er·it** *n.*

pre·ter·nat·u·ral (prē′tər-năch′ər-əl, -năch′rəl) *adj.* **1.** Going beyond the ordinary course of nature. **2.** Having no natural explanation or cause. **—pre′ter·nat′u·ral·ly** *adv.* **—pre′ter·nat′u·ral·ness** *n.*

pre·text (prē′tĕkst′) *n.* A professed rather than a real reason.

Pre·to·ri·a (prĭ-tôr′ē-ə, -tōr′-). Administrative cap. of South Africa, in the NE. *Pop.* 545,450.

pret·ti·fy (prĭt′ĭ-fī′) *v.* **-fied, -fy·ing.** To make pretty. **—pret′ti·fi·ca′tion** *n.*

†**pret·ty** (prĭt′ē) *adj.* **-ti·er, -ti·est. 1.** Pleasing or appealing, esp. in a delicate way. **2.** First-rate : fine. Usu. used ironically <a *pretty* job of bungling> **3.** *Informal.* Sizable <a *pretty* sum> *—adv.* **1.** Somewhat : moderately <a *pretty* bad cut> **2.** *Regional.* In a pretty or pleasing way. *—v.* **-tied, -ty·ing.** *Informal.* To make pretty. **—pret′ti·ly** *adv.* **—pret′ti·ness** *n.*

pret·zel (prĕt′səl) *n.* A hard, salted cracker usu. shaped like a loose knot.

pre·vail (prĭ-văl′) *v.* **1.** To win control : triumph. **2.** To be effective : succeed. **3.** To be common or frequent : predominate. **4.** To be in force or use : persist. **—prevail on** (or **upon**). To persuade successfully. **—pre·vail′er** *n.* **—pre·vail′ing·ly** *adv.*

prev·a·lent (prĕv′ə-lənt) *adj.* In widespread existence, occurrence, or use. **—prev′a·lence** *n.* **—prev′a·lent·ly** *adv.*

pre·var·i·cate (prĭ-văr′ĭ-kāt′) *v.* **-cat·ed, -cat·ing. 1.** To speak evasively : equivocate. **2.** To stray from the truth : lie. **—pre·var′i·ca′tion** *n.* **—pre·var′i·ca′tor** *n.*

pre·vent (prĭ-vĕnt′) *v.* **1.** To keep from taking place : ward off. **2.** To keep (someone) from acting. **—pre·vent′a·ble, pre·vent′i·ble** *adj.* **—pre·ven′tion** *n.*

pre·ven·tive (prĭ-vĕn′tĭv) *also* **pre·ven·ta·tive** (-tə-tĭv) *adj.* **1.** Protecting, as against failure : precautionary. **2.** Preventing disease. **—pre·ven′tive** *n.*

pre·view *also* **pre·vue** (prē′vyo͞o′) *—n.* **1.** An advance showing or viewing prior to public presentation. **2.** The presentation of excerpts from a forthcoming motion picture to advertise it. **3.** An advance indication. *—v.* **-viewed, -view·ing** *also* **-vued, -vu·ing.** To view or show beforehand.

pre·vi·ous (prē′vē-əs) *adj.* Existing or occurring earlier. **—pre′vi·ous·ly** *adv.*

previous to *prep.* Prior to : before.

pre·vi·sion (prĭ-vĭzh′ən) *n.* **1.** Foreknowledge : foresight. **2.** A prediction : forecast.

prey (prā) *n.* **1.** An animal hunted or seized for food. **2.** One helpless, as against attack : victim. **3.** The act or habit of preying. *—v.* **1.** To seek or eat as prey. **2.** To take unfair advantage of : victimize. **3.** To have a detrimental effect.

price (prīs) *n.* **1.** The sum of money expected or given for the sale of something. **2.** The cost at which something is obtained. **3.** The cost of bribing someone. *—v.* **priced, pric·ing. 1.** To set a price for. **2.** To ask or discover the price of.

price·less (prīs′lĭs) *adj.* Of incalcuable worth : invaluable.

price war *n.* A period of business competition in which competitors repeatedly undercut each other's prices.

prick (prĭk) *n.* **1. a.** An act or instance of piercing. **b.** The sensation of being pierced. **2.** A tiny mark or hole made by piercing. **3.** Something pointed or sharp, as a thorn. *—v.* **1.** To pierce lightly. **2.** To affect sharply with emotional pain. **3.** To outline by means of small perforations.

prick·le (prĭk′əl) *n.* **1.** A small, sharp spine or thorn, as on a plant. **2.** A slight tingling sensation. *—v.* **-led, -ling. 1.** To prick slightly, as with a thorn. **2.** To feel or cause tingling. **—prick′ly** *adj.*

prickly heat *n.* Inflammation of the sweat glands marked by an itching and tingling skin rash.

prickly pear *n.* A cactus of the genus *Opuntia,* with bristly flattened or cylindrical joints, usu. yellow flowers, and edible ovoid fruit.

pride (prīd) *n.* **1.** Proper respect for one's own dignity and worth. **2.** Pleasure or satisfaction over something done, achieved, or owned. **3.** A source of pride. **4.** Excessive self-esteem : conceit. *—v.* **prid·ed, prid·ing.** To take pride in (oneself). **—pride′ful** *adj.* **—pride′ful·ly** *adv.*

prie·dieu (prē-dyœ′) *n., pl.* **-dieus** *or* **-dieux** (-dyœz′). A low bench for kneeling in prayer, fitted with an elevated shelf for supporting a prayerbook or the elbows.

priest (prēst) *n.* A member of the clergy, esp. in the Roman Catholic, Eastern Orthodox, and Anglican churches, ranking below a bishop. **—priest′ess** *n.* **—priest′hood′** *n.* **—priest′li·ness** *n.* **—priest′ly** *adj.*

prig (prĭg) *n.* A smugly proper or prudish person. **—prig′gish** *adj.*

prim (prĭm) *adj.* **prim·mer, prim·mest.** Affectedly proper or precise : strait-laced. **—prim′ly** *adv.* **—prim′ness** *n.*

prim. *abbr.* **1.** primary. **2.** primitive.

pri·ma·cy (prī′mə-sē) *n., pl.* **-cies. 1.** The state of ranking 1st. **2.** The rank, office, or duties of an ecclesiastical primate.

pri·ma don·na (prē′mə dŏn′ə, prĭm′ə) *n., pl.* **prima don·nas. 1.** The principal female soloist of an opera company. **2.** A self-centered or temperamental person.

pri·ma fa·cie (prī′mə fā′shē, fā′shə) *adj. & adv.* At 1st view : apparent <*prima facie* proof>

pri·mal (prī′məl) *adj.* **1.** 1st in time : primitive. **2.** 1st in importance : chief.

pri·mar·i·ly (prī-mĕr′ə-lē, -mâr′-) *adv.* **1.** In the 1st place. **2.** For the most part.

pri·ma·ry (prī′mĕr′ē, -mə-rē) *adj.* **1. a.** 1st in time or sequence : original. **b.** Serving to prepare. **2.** 1st in degree, quality, or importance : chief. **3.** Not derived from something else : firsthand <a *primary* source> **4.** Fundamental : basic <a *primary* need> ☆***syns:*** CAPITAL, CARDINAL, CHIEF, DOMINANT, FIRST, FOREMOST, MAIN, PARAMOUNT, PRE-EMINENT, PREMIER, PRIME, PRINCIPAL, TOP *—n., pl.* **-ries. 1.** Something that is primary in time, sequence, or importance. **2.** A preliminary election in which party candidates are nominated for office by registered voters.

primary school *n.* **1.** A school that includes the 1st 3 or 4 grades and sometimes kindergarten. **2.** Elementary school.

pri·mate (prī′māt′) *n.* **1.** (*also* -mĭt). The highest-ranking bishop of a province or country. **2.** One of the group of mammals that includes the lemurs, monkeys, apes, and human beings.

prime (prīm) *adj.* **1.** 1st in quality, importance, rank, or time <*prime* beef><his *prime* favorite> **2.** Of or indicating a prime number. *—n.* **1.** The earliest phase of something, esp. dawn or spring. **2.** The most vigorous, flourishing, or successful stage or period. **3.** The best or most select part. **4.** A prime number. *—v.* **primed, prim·ing. 1.** To prepare (a gun or mine) for detonating. **2.** To put (e.g., a pump) in operation by filling with a liquid. **3.** To cover with a preliminary coat before painting. **4.** To teach or train beforehand.

prime meridian *n.* The meridian of 0° longitude at Greenwich, England, from which longitude E and W is measured.

prime minister *n.* **1.** The chief minister of a ruler or government. **2.** The head of the cabinet and often also the chief executive of a parliamentary democracy.

prime number *n.* A positive number that has no factor other than itself and 1.

prim·er[1] (prĭm′ər) *n.* **1.** An elementary textbook for teaching reading to children. **2.** A usu. small book covering the fundamentals of a topic.

prim·er[2] (prī′mər) *n.* **1.** One that primes. **2.** Material for priming a surface. **3.** A device for firing an explosive.

pri·me·val (prī-mē′vəl) *adj.* Of or relating to the earliest ages : primordial.

prim·i·tive (prĭm′ĭ-tĭv) *adj.* **1.** Of or in an early stage of development. **2.** Crude or simple : unsophisticated <*primitive* technology> **3.** Of or pertaining to early human culture. **4.** Having skills acquired by oneself without formal training. *—n.* **1.** A member of a primitive society or culture. **2.** A self-taught artist. **3.** *Computer Sci.* A basic or fundamental unit of machine instruction or translation. **—prim′i·tive·ly** *adv.* **—prim′i·tive·ness** *n.*

prim·i·tiv·ism (prĭm′ĭ-tĭ-vĭz′əm) *n.* The style of art of primitive artists or cultures.

pri·mo·gen·i·tor (prī′mō-jĕn′ĭ-tər) *n.* An earliest ancestor.

pri·mo·gen·i·ture (prī′mō-jĕn′ĭ-cho͝or′, -chər) *n.* **1.** The state

of being the first-born child of a family. **2.** An exclusive right of the eldest child, esp. the eldest son, to inherit a family's estate.
pri•mor•di•al (prī-môr′dē-əl) *adj.* **1.** Existing 1st or in an original state : primeval. **2.** Fundamental : primary.
primp (prĭmp) *v.* To dress or arrange carefully : preen.
prim•rose (prĭm′rōz′) *n.* A plant of the genus *Primula,* bearing tubular, variously colored 5-lobed flowers.
prin. *abbr.* **1.** principal. **2.** principle.
prince (prĭns) *n.* **1.** A male ruler of a principality. **2.** A male member of a royal family, esp. a son of the sovereign. **3.** An illustrious man, as in a group. **—prince′dom** *n.* **—prince′ly** *adj.*
Prince Ed•ward Island (ĕd′wərd). Island and province of SE Canada. *Cap.* Charlottetown. *Pop.* 118,229.
prin•cess (prĭn′sĭs, -sĕs′, prĭn-sĕs′) *n.* **1.** A female ruler of a principality. **2.** A female member of a royal family, esp. a daughter of the sovereign. **3.** The wife of a prince.
prin•ci•pal (prĭn′sə-pəl) *adj.* Most important : chief. *—n.* **1.** The chief official of an elementary, junior high, or high school. **2.** A chief participant. **3.** A leading performer, as in a play. **4. a.** A financial holding as distinguished from its interest or revenue. **b.** A debt on which interest is calculated. **5.** *Law.* **a.** One who authorizes another to act as agent. **b.** One primarily responsible for an obligation. **—prin′ci•pal•ly** *adv.*
prin•ci•pal•i•ty (prĭn′sə-păl′ĭ-tē) *n., pl.* **-ties.** The territory, position, or jurisdiction of a prince.
principal parts *pl.n.* The series of inflected forms of a verb.
prin•ci•ple (prĭn′sə-pəl) *n.* **1.** A fundamental truth, law, or postulate. **2. a.** A rule or code of behavior. **b.** Moral or ethical standards in general : integrity. **3.** An underlying or established rule or policy. **4.** A scientific law underlying the working of natural phenomena or mechanical processes. **5.** A primary or original source.
prin•ci•pled (prĭn′sə-pəld) *adj.* Based on or acting from moral or ethical principles.
prink (prĭngk) *v.* To primp.
print (prĭnt) *n.* **1.** A mark made by pressing on a surface. **2.** Something marked or stamped with an impression. **3. a.** Inked impressions, as of lettering. **b.** Printed matter. **4.** A design or picture transferred from an engraved plate, wood block, or lithographic stone. **5.** The positive image of a photograph. **6. a.** Fabric stamped with a design. **b.** The design itself. *—v.* **1.** To stamp (e.g., a mark or design) on or in a surface. **2.** To mark or stamp (a surface) with a device, as a die. **3.** To produce by means of a printing press. **4.** To offer in printed form : publish. **5.** To write in block letters similar to commonly used printer's type. **6.** To make (a positive picture) on a photographically sensitive surface. **—print out.** To print automatically : produce a printout.
print•a•ble (prĭn′tə-bəl) *adj.* **1.** Capable of being printed or yielding a print. **2.** Suitable for publication.
printed circuit *n.* An electronic circuit made by applying a pattern of conductive metal to an insulating surface.
print•er (prĭn′tər) *n.* **1.** One that prints, esp. one whose occupation is printing. **2.** The part of a computer that produces printed matter.
print•ing (prĭn′tĭng) *n.* **1.** The art, operation, or business of producing printed matter. **2.** Something printed. **3.** All the copies of a publication printed at one time.
printing press *n.* A machine that prints on a surface from inked type or plates.
print•out (prĭnt′out′) *n.* Printed material produced by a computer.
pri•or[1] (prī′ər) *adj.* **1.** Previous in time or order. **2.** Given or taking precedence, esp. in importance or value. **—pri•or′i•ty** (-ôr′ĭ-tē, -ŏr′-) *n.*
pri•or[2] (prī′ər) *n.* The head of a religious house. **—pri′or•ess** *n.*
pri•or•i•tize (prī-ôr′ĭ-tīz′, -ŏr′-) *v.* **-tized, -tiz•ing.** To dispose of or handle in order of importance.
prior to *prep.* Earlier than : before.
pri•or•y (prī′ə-rē) *n., pl.* **-ies.** A religious house governed by a prior or prioress.
prism (prĭz′əm) *n.* **1.** A geometric solid with equal and parallel polygons as ends and parallelograms as sides. **2.** A transparent prism with triangular ends and rectangular sides, used to refract light or disperse it into a spectrum. **3.** A decorative glass pendant, as on a chandelier. **—pris•mat′ic** (-măt′ĭk) *adj.*
pris•on (prĭz′ən) *n.* A place of confinement for accused or convicted persons.
pris•on•er (prĭz′ə-nər, prĭz′nər) *n.* **1.** A person held in confinement, esp. in a prison. **2.** A person not able or allowed to speak or act freely.
pris•sy (prĭs′ē) *adj.* **-si•er, -si•est.** Fussily prim and proper. **—pris′si•ly** *adv.* **—pris′si•ness** *n.*
pris•tine (prĭs′tēn′, prĭ-stēn′) *adj.* **1.** Of the earliest time or condition. **2.** Remaining in a pure, unspoiled state.
prith•ee (prĭth′ē, prĭth′ē) *interj. Archaic.* Used to express a request or wish.
pri•va•cy (prī′və-sē) *n., pl.* **-cies. 1.** Seclusion or isolation from others. **2.** Secrecy.
pri•vate (prī′vĭt) *adj.* **1.** Secluded from others. **2. a.** Of or restricted to a single person : personal. **b.** Intimate : secret. **3.** Not for public use or participation. **4.** Owned or controlled by a person or group rather than the public or government. **5.** Not holding office <a *private* citizen> *—n.* An enlisted person of the lowest rank in the U.S. Army or Marine Corps. **—pri′vate•ly** *adv.*
▲word history: The noun *private,* denoting a soldier of the lowest rank, developed from the adjective *private* in the sense "not holding an official or public position." Just as a private citizen is one who holds no public office, so a private soldier is one who has neither special responsibilities nor the rank that goes with them.
private detective *n.* A privately employed detective.
pri•va•teer (prī′və-tîr′) *n.* **1.** A privately owned vessel commissioned in wartime to seize enemy ships. **2.** The master or a crew member of a privateer. **—pri′va•teer′** *v.*
private eye *n.* A private detective.
private first class *n.* An enlisted person ranking above private and below corporal in the U.S. Army or Marine Corps.
pri•va•tion (prī-vā′shən) *n.* **1.** Lack of basic life necessities or comforts. **2.** An act or instance of deprivation.
priv•et (prĭv′ĭt) *n.* A shrub, *Ligustrum vulgare* or *L. ovalifolium,* with small dark-green pointed leaves and white flower clusters, widely used for hedges.
priv•i•lege (prĭv′ə-lĭj) *n.* A special right or immunity granted to a person or group. **—priv′i•lege** *v.*
priv•i•leged (prĭv′ə-lĭjd) *adj.* **1.** Having or benefiting from a privilege. **2.** Legally exempted from disclosure <a *privileged* communication>
priv•y (prĭv′ē) *adj.* **1.** Made a party to secret information. **2.** Private or personal rather than official. *—n., pl.* **-ies.** A toilet, esp. an outhouse.
prize[1] (prīz) *n.* **1.** Something offered or awarded in a contest or lottery. **2.** Something worth pursuing or attaining. *—adj.* **1.** Offered or awarded as a prize. **2.** Given or deserving a prize. **3.** Outstanding : exceptional. *—v.* **prized, priz•ing.** To place a high value on : esteem.
prize[2] (prīz) *n.* Enemy property, esp. a vessel, captured in wartime.
†**prize[3]** (prīz) *v.* **prized, priz•ing.** To move or force with or as if with a lever : pry. *—n.* **1.** Leverage. **2.** *Regional.* Something used as a lever.
prize•fight (prīz′fīt′) *n.* A match between professional boxers. **—prize′fight′er** *n.* **—prize′fight′ing** *n.*
prize•win•ner (prīz′wĭn′ər) *n.* A winner of a prize. **—prize′win′ning** *adj.*
pro[1] (prō) *n., pl.* **pros. 1.** An argument in support of something. **2.** A person or side in favor of something. *—adv.* In favor. *—adj.* Favoring.
pro[2] (prō) *Informal. —n., pl.* **pros. 1.** A professional, esp. in sports. **2.** An expert in a given field. *—adj.* Professional <*pro* football>
pro-a•bor•tion (prō′ə-bôr′shən) *adj.* Favoring or supporting legalized abortion.
prob. *abbr.* **1.** probable; probably. **2.** problem.
prob•a•bil•i•ty (prŏb′ə-bĭl′ĭ-tē) *n., pl.* **-ties. 1.** The state or quality of being probable. **2.** Something, as a situation, that is probable. **3.** *Math.* A number, esp. a ratio, expressing the likelihood of occurrence of a given event.
prob•a•ble (prŏb′ə-bəl) *adj.* **1.** Likely to be or become a reality. **2.** Plausible but not certain or proved. **—prob′a•bly** *adv.*
pro•bate (prō′bāt′) *n.* Legal determination of the validity of a will. *—v.* **-bat•ed, -bat•ing.** To prove the validity of (a will) by probate.
pro•ba•tion (prō-bā′shən) *n.* **1.** Determination during a trial period of a person's suitability, as for membership in a working or social group. **2.** The supervised release of a convicted offender on the promise of good conduct. **—pro•ba′tion•al, pro•ba′tion•ar′y** (-shə-nĕr′ē) *adj.*
pro•ba•tion•er (prō-bā′shə-nər) *n.* A person undergoing a period of probation.
pro•ba•tive (prō′bə-tĭv) *adj.* **1.** Serving to test or explore. **2.** Serving to prove.
probe (prōb) *n.* **1.** A device for investigating an unknown environment, as outer space. **2.** A slender instrument used esp. for examining a wound or bodily cavity. **3.** A careful examination or investigation with or as if with a probe. *—v.* **probed, prob•ing. 1.** To examine with a probe. **2.** To investigate painstakingly.

pro•bi•ty (prō′bĭ-tē) *n.* Moral uprightness : integrity.

prob•lem (prŏb′ləm) *n.* **1.** A difficult or perplexing question or issue. **2.** One that is troublesome or vexatious. **3.** A question proposed for consideration, discussion, or solution. **–prob′lem** *adj.*

prob•lem•at•ic (prŏb′lə-măt′ĭk) *or* **prob•lem•at•i•cal** (-ĭ-kəl) *adj.* **1.** Posing a problem or question. **2.** Open to doubt : dubious. **–prob′lem•at′i•cal•ly** *adv.*

pro•bos•cis (prō-bŏs′ĭs) *n., pl.* **-cis•es** or **-bos•ci•des** (-bŏs′ĭ-dēz′). **1.** A long, movable snout, as an elephant's trunk. **2.** A long, tubelike mouth part of certain insects.

pro•bus•ing (prō′bŭs′ĭng) *adj.* Favoring or supporting the busing of children to schools outside their neighborhoods as a means of achieving racial integration.

pro•caine hydrochloride (prō′kān′) *n.* A white crystalline compound used as a local anesthetic.

pro•ce•dure (prə-sē′jər) *n.* **1.** A certain way of getting something done. **2.** An established series of steps. **3.** A prescribed or traditional set of forms to be followed. **–pro•ce′dur•al** *adj.*

pro•ceed (prō-sēd′, prə-) *v.* **1.** To continue, esp. after stopping. **2.** To carry on an action or process. **3.** To go forward in an orderly way : advance. **4.** To issue : arise. **5.** To begin legal action.

pro•ceed•ing (prō-sē′dĭng, prə-) *n.* **1.** A course of action. **2.** Something transacted. **3. proceedings. a.** A succession of events : doings. **b.** A record of business conducted in an organization. **c.** Legal action.

pro•ceeds (prō′sēdz′) *pl.n.* The profits from a business or fund-raising venture.

proc•ess (prŏs′ĕs′, prō′sĕs′) *n.* **1.** An orderly or established series of steps or operations toward a desired result or product. **2.** A natural action or function marked by gradual change from 1 state to another. **3.** *Law.* **a.** A mandate to appear in court. **b.** The course of a judicial proceeding. **4.** A projecting part of an organ or organism. *–v.* **1.** To subject to a process. **2.** *Computer Sci.* To perform operations on data.

pro•ces•sion (prə-sĕsh′ən) *n.* A group moving along esp. in an organized and ceremonial way : parade.

pro•ces•sion•al (prə-sĕsh′ə-nəl) *n.* **1.** Music to accompany a procession, esp. a hymn at the beginning of a church service. **2.** A formal procession.

proc•es•sor (prŏs′ĕs′ər) *n.* **1.** One that processes. **2. a.** A computer. **b.** A central processing unit of a computer. **c.** A program that translates another into a form acceptable to the computer being used.

pro-choice (prō′chois′) *adj.* Pro-abortion.

pro•claim (prō-klām′, prə-) *v.* To declare officially and publicly. **–pro•claim′er** *n.* **–proc′la•ma′tion** (prŏk′lə-mā′shən) *n.*

pro•cliv•i•ty (prō-klĭv′ĭ-tē) *n., pl.* **-ties.** A natural inclination or tendency.

pro•con•sul (prō-kŏn′səl) *n.* **1.** The chief adminstrator of an ancient Roman province. **2.** A usu. powerful adminstrator in a modern colonial empire. **–pro•con′su•lar** *adj.* **–pro•con′su•late** *n.*

pro•cras•ti•nate (prə-krăs′tə-nāt′, prō-) *v.* **-nat•ed, -nat•ing.** To put off until a later time : defer. **–pro•cras′ti•na′tion** *n.* **–pro•cras′ti•na′tor** *n.*

pro•cre•ate (prō′krē-āt′) *v.* **-at•ed, -at•ing.** To beget or produce offspring. **–pro′cre•a′tion** *n.* **–pro′cre•a′tive** *adj.* **–pro′cre•a′tor** *n.*

pro•crus•te•an (prō-krŭs′tē-ən) *adj.* Coldly disregarding individual differences or special circumstances.

proc•tor (prŏk′tər) *n.* One appointed to monitor college students, as at an examination. **–proc′tor** *v.* **–proc•to′ri•al** (-tôr′ē-əl, -tōr′-) *adj.*

proc•u•ra•tor (prŏk′yə-rā′tər) *n.* An administrator, esp. an official in charge of an ancient Roman province.

pro•cure (prō-kyŏŏr′, prə-) *v.* **-cured, -cur•ing. 1.** To get : acquire. **2.** To bring about : accomplish. **3.** To obtain (women) for prostitution. **–pro•cur′er** *n.*

prod (prŏd) *v.* **prod•ded, prod•ding. 1.** To goad with a pointed object <*prod* cattle> **2.** To incite to action : urge. **–prod** *n.* **–prod′der** *n.*

prod•i•gal (prŏd′ĭ-gəl) *adj.* **1.** Extravagantly wasteful. **2.** Profuse : abundant. **–prod′i•gal** *n.* **–prod′i•gal′i•ty** (-găl′ĭ-tē) *n.* **–prod′i•gal•ly** *adv.*

pro•di•gious (prə-dĭj′əs) *adj.* **1.** Of very great size, force, or extent : immense. **2.** Extraordinary : wonderful. **–pro•di′gious•ly** *adv.* **–pro•di′gious•ness** *n.*

prod•i•gy (prŏd′ĭ-jē) *n., pl.* **-gies. 1.** An exceptionally talented child. **2.** Something marvelous : wonder.

pro•duce (prə-dōōs′, -dyōōs′, prō-) *v.* **-duced, -duc•ing. 1.** To bring forth by a natural process : yield. **2.** To bring about : create. **3.** To make by a special process : manufacture. **4.** To cause to exist : give rise to. **5.** To present for inspection : show. **6.** To sponsor and present publicly. *–n.* (prŏd′ōōs, -yōōs, prō′dōōs, -dyōōs). Something produced, esp. agricultural products, as fruits and vegetables. **–pro•duc′er** *n.*

prod•uct (prŏd′əkt) *n.* **1.** Something produced by nature or by human or mechanical effort. **2.** *Math.* The number obtained by multiplying.

pro•duc•tion (prə-dŭk′shən, prō-) *n.* **1.** The act or process of producing. **2.** Something produced, as a play or film. **–pro•duc′tive** *adj.* **–pro•duc′tive•ly** *adv.* **–pro′duc•tiv′i•ty** (prō′dŭk-tĭv′ĭ-tē, prŏd′ək-), **pro•duc′tive•ness** *n.*

pro•em (prō′ĕm′) *n.* **1.** A preface. **2.** A prelude.

prof (prŏf) *n. Informal.* A professor.

prof. or **Prof.** *abbr.* professor.

pro•fane (prō-fān′, prə-) *adj.* **1.** Debasing what is sacred : blasphemous. **2.** Not religious in nature or use. **3.** Irreverent or vulgar <*profane* language> ☆**syns:** LAY, SECULAR, TEMPORAL, WORLDLY *–v.* **-faned, -fan•ing. 1.** To desecrate by treating contemptuously or irreverently : blaspheme. **2.** To put to an unworthy or degrading use : misuse. **–prof′a•na′tion** (prŏf′ə-nā′shən) *n.* **–pro•fan′a•to′ry** (-făn′ə-tôr′ē, -tōr′ē) *adj.* **–pro•fane′ly** *adv.* **–pro•fane′ness** *n.*

pro•fan•i•ty (prō-făn′ĭ-tē, prə-) *n., pl.* **-ties. 1.** The quality or state of being profane. **2. a.** Irreverent, abusive, or vulgar language. **b.** The use of profane language.

pro•fess (prə-fĕs′, prō-) *v.* **1.** To admit openly. **2.** To make a false show of. **3. a.** To claim skill or learning in. **b.** To practice (a profession or trade). **4.** To be an adherent of (a religion). **–pro•fess′ed•ly** (-fĕs′ĭd-lē) *adv.*

pro•fes•sion (prə-fĕsh′ən) *n.* **1.** An occupation usu. requiring advanced study and specialized training. **2.** The entire group of persons practicing a profession. **3.** An open declaration, esp. of religious faith.

pro•fes•sion•al (prə-fĕsh′ə-nəl) *adj.* **1.** Of, pertaining to, typical of, or practicing a profession. **2.** Engaged in a specified activity as a career. **3.** Engaging or engaged in for pay : not amateur <*professional* basketball> *–n.* One engaged in a profession. **–pro•fes′sion•al•ly** *adv.*

pro•fes•sion•al•ism (prə-fĕsh′ə-nə-lĭz′əm) *n.* **1.** Professional standing, techniques, attributes, or ethics. **2.** Participation in a profession, as organized athletics, for pay.

pro•fes•sion•al•ize (prə-fĕsh′ə-nə-līz′) *v.* **-ized, -iz•ing.** To make professional in character. **–pro•fes′sion•al•i•za′tion** *n.*

pro•fes•sor (prə-fĕs′ər) *n.* **1.** A faculty member of the highest rank in a college or university. **2.** A teacher, esp. at a college or university. **–pro′fes•so′ri•al** (prō′fĭ-sôr′ē-əl, -sōr′-, prŏf′ĭ-) *adj.*

prof•fer (prŏf′ər) *v.* To offer for acceptance. **–prof′fer** *n.*

pro•fi•cient (prə-fĭsh′ənt) *adj.* Highly competent in an art, skill, or field of knowledge : adept. **–pro•fi′cien•cy** *n.* **–pro•fi′cient•ly** *adv.*

pro•file (prō′fīl′) *n.* **1. a.** A view of something, esp. of a human head, from the side. **b.** A representation of a side view, esp. of a human head. **2.** The outline of something. **3.** A biographical sketch. *–v.* **-filed, -fil•ing. 1.** To depict in profile. **2.** To write a profile of.

prof•it (prŏf′ĭt) *n.* **1.** An advantage gained : benefit. **2.** Financial return after all business expenses have been met. *–v.* **1.** To gain financially. **2.** To gain an advantage : benefit. **–prof′it•less** *asj.*

prof•it•a•ble (prŏf′ĭ-tə-bəl) *adj.* Affording profit. ☆**syns:** ADVANTAGEOUS, FAT, LUCRATIVE, MONEYMAKING, REMUNERATIVE **–prof′it•a•bil′i•ty, prof′it•a•ble•ness** *n.* **–prof′it•a•bly** *adv.*

prof•i•teer (prŏf′ĭ-tîr′) *n.* One who profits unduly, esp. by selling goods in short supply. **–prof′i•teer′** *v.*

prof•li•gate (prŏf′lĭ-gĭt, -gāt′) *adj.* **1.** Heedlessly or extravagantly wasteful. **2.** Completely lacking in self-restraint : dissolute. **–prof′li•ga•cy** (-gə-sē) *n.* **–prof′li•gate** *n.* **–prof′li•gate•ly** *adv.*

pro for•ma (prō fôr′mə) *adj.* For the sake of form.

pro•found (prə-found′, prō-) *adj.* **1.** Of great depth : deep. **2.** Deeply felt or held. **3.** Penetrating : insightful. **4.** Complete : total <*profound* quiet> **–pro•found′ly** *adv.* **–pro•fun′di•ty** (-fŭn′dĭ-tē) *n.*

pro•fuse (prə-fyōōs′, prō-) *adj.* Giving or given in great amount or quantity : abundant. **–pro•fuse′ly** *adv.* **–pro•fu′sion** (-fyōō′zhən), **pro•fuse′ness** *n.*

pro•gen•i•tor (prō-jĕn′ĭ-tər) *n.* **1.** An ancestor in a direct line. **2.** One that originates or sets a pattern for something.

prog•e•ny (prŏj′ə-nē) *n.* Offspring or descendants.

pro•ges•ter•one (prō-jĕs′tə-rōn′) *n.* A female hormone secreted by the ovary.

prog·na·thous (prŏg′nə-thəs) *adj.* Having jaws that jut beyond the upper face.
prog·no·sis (prŏg-nō′sĭs) *n., pl.* **-ses** (-sēz′). A prediction, esp. of the course and outcome of a disease.
prog·nos·tic (prŏg-nŏs′tĭk) *n.* **1.** A sign or omen of a future event. **2.** A prediction. **—prog·nos′tic** *adj.*
prog·nos·ti·cate (prŏg-nŏs′tĭ-kāt′) *v.* **-cat·ed, -cat·ing.** To predict from current indications. **—prog·nos′ti·ca′tion** *n.* **—prog·nos′ti·ca′tor** *n.*
pro·gram (prō′grăm′, -grəm) *n.* **1.** A list of the sequence of events or the subjects treated, as for a public presentation. **2.** A public presentation, performance, or entertainment. **3. a.** An organized plan of procedures : schedule. **b.** An organized effort to achieve a goal by stages. **4. a.** A set of logical steps for solving a problem. **b.** A coded set of instructions for a computer. **5.** Material for programmed instruction. *—v.* **-grammed, -gram·ming** *or* **-gramed, gram·ing. 1.** To include in a program : schedule. **2.** To provide (a computer) with a problem-solving program. **—pro·gram′ma·bil′i·ty** *n.* **—pro′gram′ma·ble** *adj.* **—pro′gram·mat′ic** (prō′grə-măt′ĭk) *adj.* **—pro′gram′mer, pro′gram′er** *n.*
pro·gramme (prō′grăm′, -grəm) *n. & v. esp. Brit. var. of* PROGRAM.
programmed instruction *n.* Instruction in which information is presented in discrete units, each requiring a correct response before the learner goes on to the next unit.
programming *or* **programing** *n.* The designing, scheduling, or planning of a program, esp. one for a computer.
prog·ress (prŏg′rĕs′, -rĭs) *n.* **1.** Onward movement : advance. **2.** Gradual steady improvement. *—v.* **pro·gress** (prə-grĕs′). **1.** To move along : proceed. **2.** To advance toward a higher stage.
pro·gres·sion (prə-grĕsh′ən) *n.* **1.** Movement : progress. **2.** Advancement to a higher or different stage. **3.** A connected series : sequence.
pro·gres·sive (prə-grĕs′ĭv) *adj.* **1.** Moving forward : advancing. **2.** Continuing in steps or by stages or degrees. **3.** Advocating or working for political or social reform : liberal. **4.** Of or being a verb tense or form that expresses an action or condition in progress at the time indicated. *—n.* **1.** One that is progressive. **2.** A proponent of reform, as in politics and education. **—pro·gres′sive·ly** *adv.* **—pro·gres′sive·ness** *n.*
Progressive Conservative Party *n.* A Canadian political party.
pro·hib·it (prō-hĭb′ĭt, prə-) *v.* **1.** To forbid by law. **2.** To prevent : proscribe. **—pro·hib′i·to′ry** (-ĭ-tôr′ē, -tōr′ē) *adj.*
pro·hi·bi·tion (prō′ə-bĭsh′ən) *n.* **1.** The act of prohibiting or the state of being prohibited. **2.** A legal ban on the manufacture and sale of alcoholic beverages. **—pro′hi·bi′tion·ist** *n.*
pro·hib·i·tive (prō-hĭb′ĭ-tĭv, prə-) *adj.* **1.** Tending to prohibit. **2.** Tending to prevent purchase or use. **—pro·hib′i·tive·ly** *adv.*
proj·ect (prŏj′ĕkt′, -ĭkt) *n.* **1.** A particular plan or intention. **2.** A planned or contemplated venture. *—v.* **pro·ject** (prə-jĕkt′). **1.** To protrude or cause to protrude. **2.** To throw forward or upward. **3.** To make (one's voice) clearly audible at a distance. **4.** To plan in the mind. **5.** To cause (light or an image) to fall upon a surface. **—pro·jec′tion** *n.*
pro·jec·tile (prə-jĕk′təl, -tīl′) *n.* **1.** A projected missile, as a stone or bullet. **2.** A self-powered missile, as a rocket.
pro·jec·tion·ist (prə-jĕk′shə-nĭst) *n.* **1.** An operator of a motion-picture projector. **2.** One who makes maps.
pro·jec·tor (prə-jĕk′tər) *n.* A device for projecting images on a screen.
pro·le·gom·e·non (prō′lĭ-gŏm′ə-nŏn′, -nən) *n., pl.* **-na** (-nə). Introductory remarks. **—pro′le·gom′e·nous** *adj.*
pro·le·tar·i·an (prō′lĭ-târ′ē-ən) *adj.* Of, relating to, or characteristic of the proletariate. **—pro′le·tar′i·an** *n.*
pro·le·tar·i·at (prō′lĭ-târ′ē-ət) *n.* The working class, esp. industrial workers who earn their living by selling their labor.
pro-life (prō-līf′) *adj.* Opposed to legalized abortion. **—pro-lif′er** *n.*
pro·lif·er·ate (prə-lĭf′ə-rāt′) *v.* **-at·ed, -at·ing. 1.** To grow or produce by rapid multiplication of parts, as cells. **2.** To increase or spread rapidly. **—pro·lif′er·a′tion** *n.* **—pro·lif′er·a′tive** *adj.*
pro·lif·ic (prə-lĭf′ĭk) *adj.* **1.** Producing offspring or fruit in great numbers. **2.** Abundantly productive <a *prolific* novelist> **—pro·lif′i·cal·ly** *adv.*
pro·lix (prō-lĭks′, prō′lĭks′) *adj.* Long-winded : verbose. **—pro·lix′i·ty** (-lĭk′sĭ-tē) *n.* **—pro·lix′ly** *adv.*
pro·logue *also* **pro·log** (prō′lôg′, -lŏg′) *n.* An introduction, as to a play : preface.
pro·long (prə-lông′, -lŏng′) *v.* To lengthen in time, range, or extent. **—pro′lon·ga′tion** (prō′lông-gā′shən) *n.*
prom (prŏm) *n.* A formal dance usu. given by a class in high school or college.
prom·e·nade (prŏm′ə-nād′, -näd′) *n.* **1.** An unhurried walk : stroll. **2.** A public place for strolling. **3.** A formal march at the beginning of a ball. **—prom′e·nade′** *v.*
pro·me·thi·um (prə-mē′thē-əm) *n. Symbol* **Pm** A radioactive rare-earth metallic element.
prom·i·nence (prŏm′ə-nəns) *n.* **1.** The quality or state of being prominent : importance. **2.** Something that is prominent. **3.** A shining cloud of gas rising from the sun's surface.
prom·i·nent (prŏm′ə-nənt) *adj.* **1.** Jutting or bulging outward : projecting. **2.** Immediately noticeable : conspicuous. **3.** Widely known and esteemed.
pro·mis·cu·ous (prə-mĭs′kyo͞o-əs) *adj.* **1.** Made up of miscellaneous parts or kinds. **2.** Lacking discrimination or selectivity, esp. having a number of sexual partners. **—prom′is·cu′i·ty** (prŏm′ĭ-skyo͞o′ĭ-tē, prō′mĭ-), **pro·mis′cu·ous·ness** *n.* **—pro·mis′cu·ous·ly** *adv.*
prom·ise (prŏm′ĭs) *n.* **1.** An assurance that one will or will not do something specified : pledge. **2.** Something promised. **3.** A sign of what may be expected, esp. future development or success. ☆*syns:* COVENANT, GUARANTEE, PLEDGE, VOW *—v.* **-ised, -is·ing. 1.** To offer a promise (of). **2.** To give reason for expecting <Your future *promises* to be happy.> **3.** To portend <a sky that *promised* snow>
prom·is·ing (prŏm′ĭ-sĭng) *adj.* Giving hope of future excellence, benefit, or success. **—prom′is·ing·ly** *adv.*
prom·is·so·ry (prŏm′ĭ-sôr′ē, -sōr′ē) *adj.* Of, containing, or implying a promise.
pro·mo (prō′mō) *n., pl.* **-mos.** *Informal.* A promotional presentation.
prom·on·to·ry (prŏm′ən-tôr′ē, -tōr′ē) *n., pl.* **-ries.** A high ridge of land or rock projecting into water, esp. into the sea.
pro·mote (prə-mōt′) *v.* **-mot·ed, -mot·ing. 1.** To raise to a higher position, rank, or class. **2.** To further the progress or growth of : advance. **3.** To advocate the adoption or use of. **4.** To try to sell or popularize by publicity. **—pro·mo′tion** *n.* **—pro·mo′tion·al** *adj.*
pro·mot·er (prə mō′tər) *n.* **1.** An active advocate. **2.** A finance and publicity organizer, as of a sports event.
prompt (prŏmpt) *adj.* **1.** Acting or arriving on time : punctual. **2.** Done without delay : immediate. **3.** Ready to act quickly. *—v.* **1.** To incite to action. **2.** To encourage or inspire. **3.** To assist (e.g., a performer) by cueing. **—prompt′er** *n.* **—promp′ti·tude′** (prŏmp′tĭ-to͞od′, -tyo͞od′), **prompt′ness** *n.* **—prompt′ly** *adv.*
prom·ul·gate (prŏm′əl-gāt′, prō-mŭl′-) *v.* **-gat·ed, -gat·ing.** To make known or put into effect (e.g., a decree or law) by public declaration. **—prom′ul·ga′tion** *n.* **—prom′ul·ga′tor** *n.*
pron. *abbr.* **1.** pronominal; pronoun. **2.** pronounced; pronunciation.
prone (prōn) *adj.* **1.** Lying flat or face downward. **2.** Having a tendency : inclined. **—prone′ly** *adv.* **—prone′ness** *n.*
prong (prông, prŏng) *n.* **1.** A sharply pointed end of a tool or utensil, as a fork. **2.** A slender pointed projection, as of a deer's antler.
prong·horn (prông′hôrn′, prŏng′-) *n.* A small antelopelike deer, *Antilocapra americana,* of W North American plains.

pronghorn

pro·noun (prō′noun′) *n.* One of a class of words used as substitutes for nouns and noun phrases.
pro·nounce (prə-nouns′) *v.* **-nounced, -nounc·ing. 1.** To produce or articulate (a word or speech sound). **2.** To declare officially, formally, or as an opinion. **—pro·nounce′a·ble** *adj.* **—pro·nun′ci·a′tion** (-nŭn′sē-ā′shən) *n.*
pro·nounced (prə-nounst′) *adj.* Strongly marked : unmistakable.
pro·nounce·ment (prə-nouns′mənt) *n.* **1.** A formal declaration. **2.** An authoritative statement.
pron·to (prŏn′tō) *adv. Informal.* Right away : immediately.

pro·nun·ci·a·men·to (prə-nŭn′sē-əmĕn′tō) *n., pl.* **-tos.** An edict.
proof (pro͞of) *n.* **1.** Evidence that establishes the truth or validity of something. **2.** Demonstration of the truth of a statement in mathematics or logic. **3.** The act of testing the truth or validity of something by experiment or trial. **4.** A trial impression, as of composed type or an engraved plate. **5.** Alcoholic content of a liquor, expressed as a percentage <100 *proof* whiskey> —*adj.* **1.** Able to withstand, repel, or resist : resistant. **2.** Of standard alcoholic strength or quality. —*v.* **1.** To proofread. **2.** To make resistant.
-proof *suff.* Safe from : resistant to <bullet*proof*>
proof·read (pro͞of′rēd′) *v.* To read and mark corrections in (printed, typed, or written material). **—proof′read′er** *n.*
prop¹ (prŏp) *n.* **1.** A support for keeping something upright. **2.** One depended on for support or aid. **—prop** *v.*
prop² (prŏp) *n.* A property on a stage or motion-picture set.
prop³ (prŏp) *n. Informal.* A propeller.
prop. *abbr.* **1.** proper; properly. **2.** property. **3.** proposition. **4.** proprietor.
prop·a·gan·da (prŏp′ə-găn′də) *n.* **1.** The systematic widespread promotion of a particular doctrine or idea. **2.** Material distributed to win people over to a particular doctrine. **—prop′a·gan′dist** *n.* **—prop′a·gan·dis′tic** *adj.* **—prop′a·gan′dize′** *v.*
prop·a·gate (prŏp′ə-gāt′) *v.* **-gat·ed, -gat·ing. 1.** To reproduce or cause to reproduce (offspring or new growth) : multiply. **2.** *Physics.* To spread or cause to spread through a medium <*propagate* light> **—prop′a·ga′tion** *n.*
pro·pane (prō′pān′) *n.* A gaseous hydrocarbon found in natural gas and petroleum and used as a fuel.
pro·pel (prə-pĕl′) *v.* **-pelled, -pel·ling. 1.** To thrust or drive forcefully onward. **2.** To impel to action : motivate.
pro·pel·lant *also* **pro·pel·lent** (prə-pĕl′ənt) *n.* Something, as an explosive charge or fuel, used to propel. **—pro·pel′lant** *adj.*
pro·pel·ler *also* **pro·pel·lor** (prə-pĕl′ər) *n.* A fanlike, usu. power-driven device for propelling aircraft or boats.
pro·pen·si·ty (prə-pĕn′sĭ-tē) *n., pl.* **-ties.** A natural inclination : bent.
prop·er (prŏp′ər) *adj.* **1.** Suitable : appropriate. **2.** Pertaining exclusively to a person or thing : peculiar. **3.** Correct by rule or convention. **4.** Strictly conforming to social convention. **5.** Strictly so called <the downtown *proper*> **—prop′er·ly** *adv.*
proper noun *n.* A noun that refers to a particular person, place, or thing.
prop·er·tied (prŏp′ər-tēd) *adj.* Owning property, as real estate, esp. as a chief source of income.
prop·er·ty (prŏp′ər-tē) *n., pl.* **-ties. 1.** Something owned, esp. real estate. **2.** A characteristic trait, quality, or attribute. **3.** The exclusive right to own something : ownership. **4.** A movable article other than costumes and scenery that is used in a play or movie. **—prop′er·ty·less** *adj.*
proph·e·cy (prŏf′ĭ-sē) *n., pl.* **-cies. 1.** A forewarning : prediction. **2.** The divinely inspired utterance of a prophet.
proph·e·sy (prŏf′ĭ-sī′) *v.* **-sied, -sy·ing. 1.** To reveal by or as if by divine inspiration. **2.** To foretell. **—proph′e·si′er** *n.*
proph·et (prŏf′ĭt) *n.* **1.** One whose revelations are divinely inspired. **2.** One who foretells the future. **—proph′et·ess** *n.*
pro·phet·ic (prə-fĕt′ĭk) *also* **pro·phet·i·cal** (-ĭ-kəl) *adj.* Of, pertaining to, or characteristic of a prophet or prophecy. **—pro·phet′i·cal·ly** *adv.*
pro·phy·lac·tic (prō′fə-lăk′tĭk, prŏf′ə-) *adj.* Serving to defend against or prevent something, esp. disease. —*n.* A prophylactic measure, drug, or device.
pro·phy·lax·is (prō′fə-lăk′sĭs, prŏf′ə-) *n., pl.* **-lax·es** (-lăk′sēz′). Protective treatment for or prevention of disease.
pro·pin·qui·ty (prə-pĭng′kwĭ-tē) *n.* **1.** Proximity in time or space. **2.** Kinship.
pro·pi·ti·ate (prō-pĭsh′ē-āt′) *v.* **-at·ed, -at·ing.** To win or win back the favor of : placate. **—pro·pi′ti·a′tion** *n.* **—pro·pi′ti·a·to′ry** (-ə-tôr′ē, -tōr′ē) *adj.*
pro·pi·tious (prə-pĭsh′əs) *adj.* Indicating a favorable condition or an auspicious outcome. **—pro·pi′tious·ly** *adv.*
prop-jet (prŏp′jĕt′) *n.* A turboprop.
pro·po·nent (prə-pō′nənt) *n.* A supporter of something : advocate.
pro·por·tion (prə-pôr′shən, -pōr′-) *n.* **1.** The relationship of a part to a whole or to another part as to magnitude, quantity, or degree : ratio. **2.** Harmonious relationship : symmetry or balance. **3.** *often* **proportions.** Dimensions. —*v.* **1.** To bring the size or dimensions of (different things) into proper relationship. **2.** To arrange with harmony and balance. **—pro·por′tion·al** *adj.* **—pro·por′tion·al·ly** *adv.* **—pro·por′tion·ate** *adj.* **—pro·por′tion·ate·ly** *adv.*
pro·pose (prə-pōz′) *v.* **-posed, -pos·ing. 1.** To present for consideration or action. **2.** To suggest (a person) for a position, office, or membership : nominate. **3.** To declare an intention : plan. **4.** To tender an offer, esp. of marriage. ☆***syns:*** OFFER, POSE, PROPOUND, SUBMIT, SUGGEST **—pro·pos′al** *n.* **—pro·pos′er** *n.*
prop·o·si·tion (prŏp′ə-zĭsh′ən) *n.* **1.a.** Something, as a plan, proposed for consideration. **b.** A sexual overture. **2. a.** A statement to be discussed or analyzed. **b.** A statement in mathematics or logic. **3.** *Informal.* An often difficult situation <a sticky *proposition*> —*v. Informal.* To make a proposition to, esp. to make a sexual overture to. **—prop′o·si′tion·al** *adj.*
pro·pound (prə-pound′) *v.* To put forward for consideration or argument.
pro·pri·e·tar·y (prə-prī′ĭ-tĕr′ē) *adj.* **1.** Of, pertaining to, or characteristic of a proprietor. **2.** Owned, made, and sold by one holding a trademark or patent.
pro·pri·e·tor (prə-prī′ĭ-tər) *n.* An owner, as of a building or business. **—pro·pri′e·tor·ship′** *n.* **—pro·pri′e·tress** *n.*
pro·pri·e·ty (prə-prī′ĭ-tē) *n., pl.* **-ties. 1.** The quality or state of being proper. **2.** Conformity to accepted standards of social conduct. **3. proprieties.** The rules and conventions of polite social behavior.
pro·pul·sion (prə-pŭl′shən) *n.* **1.** The act or process of propelling. **2.** A propelling force. **—pro·pul′sive** *adj.*
pro ra·ta (prō ră′tə, răt′ə, rä′tə) *adv.* In due proportion.
pro·rate (prō-rāt′, prō′rāt′) *v.* **-rat·ed, -rat·ing.** To divide, distribute, or assess on the basis of proportion. **—pro·ra′tion** *n.*
pro·rogue (prō-rōg′) *v.* **-rogued, -rogu·ing.** To adjourn or dissolve a session of (a legislature). **—pro′ro·ga′tion** *n.*
pro·sa·ic (prō-zā′ĭk) *adj.* **1.** Literal : matter-of-fact. **2.** Ordinary : commonplace. **3.** Lacking in imagination. **—pro·sa′i·cal·ly** *adv.* **—pro·sa′ic·ness** *n.*
pro·sce·ni·um (prō-sē′nē-əm) *n., pl.* **-ni·ums** or **-ni·a** (-nē-ə). The part of the stage that separates it from the audience.
pro·sciut·to (prō-sho͞o′tō) *n.* An aged, dry-cured, usu. thin-sliced Italian ham.
pro·scribe (prō-skrīb′) *v.* **-scribed, -scrib·ing. 1.** To make unlawful : prohibit. **2.** To banish : outlaw. **—pro·scrip′tion** (-skrĭp′shən) *n.* **—pro·scrip′tive** *adj.*
prose (prōz) *n.* Ordinary speech or writing as distinguished from verse or poetry.
pros·e·cute (prŏs′ĭ-kyo͞ot′) *v.* **-cut·ed, -cut·ing. 1.** To institute or subject to legal proceedings <*prosecute* an embezzler> **2.** To pursue to the end <*prosecute* a war> **—pros′e·cu′tion** *n.* **—pros′e·cu′tor** *n.* **—pros′e·cu·to′ri·al** (-tôr′ē-əl, -tōr′-) *adj.*
pros·e·lyte (prŏs′ə-līt′) *n.* A convert to a religion, doctrine, or party. —*v.* **-lyt·ed, -lyt·ing.** To proselytize.
pros·e·ly·tize (prŏs′ə-lə-tīz′) *v.* **-tized, -tiz·ing.** To convert (someone) from 1 religion, doctrine, or party to another. **—pros′e·ly·tiz′er** *n.*
pros·o·dy (prŏs′ə-dē) *n.* The study of the making of verses and esp. of metrical form. **—pro·sod′ic** (prə-sŏd′ĭk) *adj.*
pros·pect (prŏs′pĕkt′) *n.* **1.** Something anticipated : expectation. **2.** *often* **prospects.** Potential for success. **3. a.** A possible customer. **b.** A likely candidate. **4.** Direction of exposure, as to weather. **5. a.** A place affording an extensive view. **b.** The view itself. **c.** A scene. —*v.* To search about or explore, esp. for mineral deposits. **—pro·spec′tive** (prə-spĕk′tĭv) *adj.* **—pro·spec′tive·ly** *adv.* **—pros′pec′tor** *n.*
pro·spec·tus (prə-spĕk′təs) *n., pl.* **-tus·es.** A description of a proposed enterprise or venture distributed to prospective parties.
pros·per (prŏs′pər) *v.* To achieve success. ☆***syns:*** BOOM, FLOURISH, THRIVE
pros·per·i·ty (prŏ-spĕr′ĭ-tē) *n.* Prosperous condition, esp. financially successful circumstances.
pros·per·ous (prŏs′pər-əs) *adj.* **1.** Successful : flourishing. **2.** Favorable : auspicious. ☆***syns:*** COMFORTABLE, WELL-FIXED, WELL-HEELED, WELL-OFF, WELL-TO-DO
pros·tate (prŏs′tāt′) *n.* A gland at the base of the male urethra. **—pros·tat′ic** (prŏ-stăt′ĭk) *adj.*
pros·the·sis (prŏs-thē′sĭs) *n., pl.* **-ses** (-sēz′). An artificial replacement for a missing bodily part. **—pros·thet′ic** (-thĕt′ĭk) *adj.*
pros·ti·tute (prŏs′tĭ-to͞ot′, -tyo͞ot′) *n.* One hired as a sexual partner. —*v.* **-tut·ed, -tut·ing. 1.** To offer (oneself or another) as a paid sexual partner. **2.** To devote to an unworthy or debasing cause. **—pros′ti·tu′tion** *n.*
pros·trate (prŏs′trāt′) *adj.* **1.** Lying face down, as in submission or adoration. **2.** Lying flat, esp. on the ground <a *prostrate* tree trunk> **3.** In a state of helplessness : overcome <*prostrate* with grief> —*v.* **-trat·ed, -trat·ing. 1.** To put or throw down

into a prostrate position. **2.** To lay low : overcome. **–pros·tra′tion** *n.*

pro·tac·tin·i·um (prō′tăk-tĭn′ē-əm) *n. Symbol* **Pa** A rare radioactive metallic element similar to uranium.

pro·tag·o·nist (prō-tăg′ə-nĭst) *n.* **1.** The leading character in a story or play. **2.** A champion of a cause.

pro·te·an (prō′tē-ən, prō-tē′-) *adj.* Easily taking on different shapes or forms.

▲word history: The word *protean* comes from *Proteus,* the name of a Greek sea god who had the power to change his shape. Proteus had the gift of prophecy, but those who wanted to consult him had to bind him securely first. Proteus would then change into various shapes, as a wild boar, a tiger, a rush of water, and a raging fire. A questioner who could keep Proteus restrained until he returned to his orig. shape would receive an answer.

pro·tect (prə-tĕkt′) *v.* To guard from harm, attack, or injury : shield. **–pro·tec′tive** *adj.* **–pro·tec′tive·ly** *adv.*

pro·tec·tion (prə-tĕk′shən) *n.* **1.** The act of protecting or state of being protected. **2.** One that serves to protect. **3.** A system by which high duties are imposed on foreign competitors to protect domestic producers. **–pro·tec′tion·ism** *n.*

pro·tec·tor (prə-tĕk′tər) *n.* **1.** Someone or something that protects. **2.** One ruling a kingdom as regent. **–pro·tec′tor·ship′** *n.*

pro·tec·tor·ate (prə-tĕk′tər-ĭt) *n.* **1.** A guardian. **2. a.** Partial control by a superior power over a dependent political unit. **b.** A dependent political unit so controlled. **3.** The office or term of a protector.

pro·té·gé (prō′tə-zhā′) *n.* One whose well-being or career is furthered by an influential person. **–pro′té·gée′** *n.*

pro·tein (prō′tēn′, -tē-ĭn) *n.* Any of a very large group of complex organic compounds occurring in all living matter that are composed of amino acids and are essential for tissue growth and repair.

pro tem (prō tĕm′) *adv.* For the present.

pro tem·po·re (prō tĕm′pə-rē) *adv.* For the present : temporarily.

pro·test (prə-tĕst′, prō-) *v.* **1.** To object strongly (to), esp. formally or publicly. **2.** To declare earnestly : affirm. *–n.* (prō′tĕst′). **1.** The act of protesting, esp. disapproval or objection formally expressed. **2.** An individual or organized public demonstration of disapproval. **–prot′es·ta′tion** (prŏt′ĭ-stā′shən) *n.* **–pro·test′er** *n.*

Prot·es·tant (prŏt′ĭ-stənt) *n.* **1.** A member of one of the Christian churches arising from the Reformation. **2. protestant** (*also* prə-tĕs′tənt). One who makes a protest or declaration. **–Prot′es·tant·ism** *n.*

pro·to·col (prō′tə-kôl′, -kōl′, -kŏl′) *n.* **1.** A code of ceremony and etiquette followed by diplomats, heads of state, and the military. **2.** The orig. copy of a formal document, esp. of a treaty before ratification. **3.** A 1st draft or record, as of an agreement.

pro·ton (prō′tŏn′) *n.* A stable subatomic particle having a positive charge equal in magnitude to that of an electron.

pro·to·plasm (prō′tə-plăz′əm) *n.* The complex jellylike colloid that forms the living substance of plant and animal cells. **–pro′to·plas′mic** (-plăz′mĭk) *adj.*

pro·to·type (prō′tə-tīp′) *n.* An original model after which other similar things are patterned. **–pro′to·typ′al** (-tī′pəl), **pro′to·typ′ic** (-tĭp′ĭk), **pro′to·typ′i·cal** *adj.*

pro·to·zo·an (prō′tə-zō′ən) *n., pl.* **-zo·ans** or **-zo·a** (-zō′ə). Any of a very large group of 1-celled, usu. microscopic organisms.

pro·tract (prō-trăkt′, prə-) *v.* To extend in time or space : prolong. **–pro·trac′tion** *n.* **–pro·trac′tive** *adj.*

pro·trac·tor (prō-trăk′tər) *n.* A semicircular graduated device for measuring and drawing angles.

pro·trude (prō-tro͞od′) *v.* **-trud·ed, -trud·ing.** To thrust outward : project. **–pro·tru′sion** *n.* **–pro·tru′sive** *adj.*

pro·tu·ber·ance (prō-to͞o′bər-əns, -tyo͞o′-) *n.* An object or part that bulges or swells outward. **–pro·tu′ber·ant** *adj.*

proud (proud) *adj.* **1.** Feeling greatly pleased or satisfied. **2.** Highly gratifying <my *proudest* possession> **3.** Having proper self-esteem. **4.** Worthy of honor and respect. **5.** Marked by dignity or majesty : stately. **6.** Having too much self-esteem : arrogant. **7.** Spirited. **–proud′ly** *adv.*

prove (pro͞ov) *v.* **proved, proved** or **prov·en** (pro͞o′vən), **prov·ing. 1.** To show to be true or valid by evidence or argument. **2.** To demonstrate convincingly. **3.** To test the quality or worth of. **4.** To turn out to be. **–prov′a·ble** *adj.* **–prov′a·bly** *adv.* **–prov′er** *n.*

prov·e·nance (prŏv′ə-nəns) *n.* An origin or source.

Pro·vence (prō-väns′). Region of SE France, on the Mediterranean. **–Pro′ven·çal′** (prō′vən-säl′) *adj.* & *n.*

prov·en·der (prŏv′ən-dər) *n.* **1.** Dry feed, as hay, for livestock. **2.** Food supplies.

pro·ve·nience (prə-vēn′yəns, -vē′nē-əns) *n.* Provenance.

prov·erb (prŏv′ûrb′) *n.* **1.** A concise saying that illustrates a truth. **2. Proverbs** (*sing. in number*). See BIBLE TABLE **–pro·ver′bi·al** (prə-vûr′bē-əl) *adj.*

pro·vide (prə-vīd′) *v.* **-vid·ed, -vid·ing. 1.** To supply or furnish (something needed or useful). **2.** To have or offer for use. **3.** To stipulate, as in a will. **4.** To take advance measures <*provide* against illness> **5.** To supply means of support <*provide* for one's dependents> **–pro·vid′er** *n.*

pro·vid·ed (prə-vī′dĭd) *conj.* On condition that.

prov·i·dence (prŏv′ĭ-dəns, -dĕns′) *n.* **1.** The state or quality of being provident. **2.a.** Divine protection and guidance. **b. Providence.** God.

Prov·i·dence (prŏv′ĭ-dəns, -dĕns′). Cap. of R.I., in the NE. *Pop.* 156,804.

prov·i·dent (prŏv′ĭ-dənt, -dĕnt′) *adj.* **1.** Showing prudent forethought. **2.** Economical : thrifty. **–prov′i·dent·ly** *adv.*

prov·i·den·tial (prŏv′ĭ-dĕn′shəl) *adj.* **1.** Of, pertaining to, or ordained by Providence. **2.** Highly opportune. **–prov′i·den′tial·ly** *adv.*

pro·vid·ing (prə-vī′dĭng) *conj.* With the proviso that : provided.

prov·ince (prŏv′ĭns) *n.* **1. a.** A political subdivision of a nation. **b.** *Can.* One of 10 such units in Canada. **2. provinces.** Outlying regions of a country away from the population centers or the capital. **3.** A domain, as of knowledge : sphere.

pro·vin·cial (prə-vĭn′shəl) *adj.* **1.** Of or relating to a province. **2.** Limited and narrow in perspective <a *provincial* point of view> **–pro·vin′cial·ism, pro·vin′ci·al′i·ty** (-shē-ăl′ĭ-tē) *n.*

provincial park *n. Can.* A park established by and under the jurisdiction of a province.

provincial parliament *n. Can.* The legislative assembly of a province.

provincial police *n. Can.* A police force maintained by a province.

proving ground *n.* A place for experimentation, as with new weapons or ideas.

pro·vi·sion (prə-vĭzh′ən) *n.* **1.** The act of providing. **2.** Something provided. **3.** *often* **provisions.** A supply of food and needed equipment. **4.** A measure taken in advance. **5.** A stipulation, as in a will. *–v.* To furnish with provisions.

pro·vi·sion·al (prə-vĭzh′ə-nəl) *adj.* Provided temporarily pending permanent arrangements. **–pro·vi′sion·al·ly** *adv.*

pro·vi·so (prə-vī′zō) *n., pl.* **-sos** or **-soes.** A clause with a condition or qualification : stipulation. **–pro·vi′so·ry** *adj.*

pro·voke (prə-vōk′) *v.* **-voked, -vok·ing. 1.** To cause to be irritated or angry. **2.** To incite to action. **3.** To evoke. ☆**syns:** AROUSE, EXCITE, GOAD, IMPEL, INCITE, INFLAME, INSPIRE, INSTIGATE, KINDLE, MOTIVATE, MOVE, ROUSE, SPUR, STIMULATE **–prov′o·ca′tion** (prŏv-ə-kā′shən) *n.* **–pro·voc′a·tive** (prə-vŏk′ə-tĭv) *adj.*

pro·vo·lo·ne (prō′və-lō′nē) *n.* A smooth, hard, often smoked cheese orig. from Italy.

pro·vost (prō′vōst′, prŏv′əst) *n.* A high-ranking administrative official, esp. of a university.

pro·vost marshal (prō′vō) *n.* The head of a military police unit.

prow (prou) *n.* **1.** The front of a ship : bow. **2.** A similar projecting part, as the forward end of a ski.

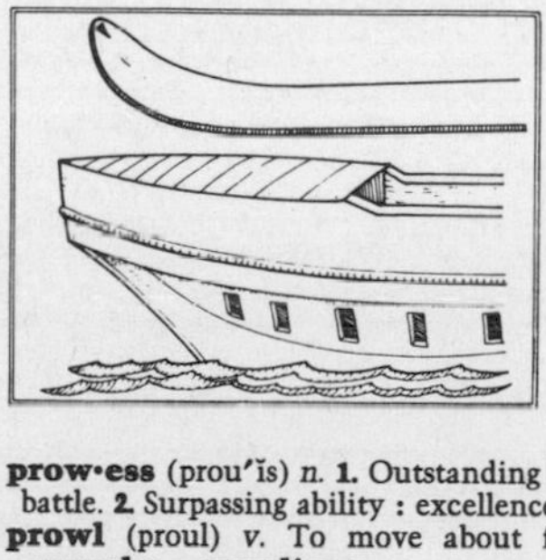

prow
Two types of prows: (above) of a ski and (below) of a boat

prow·ess (prou′ĭs) *n.* **1.** Outstanding bravery and skill, esp. in battle. **2.** Surpassing ability : excellence.

prowl (proul) *v.* To move about furtively or predatorily. **–prowl** *n.* **–prowl′er** *n.*

prowl car *n.* A squad car.

prox·i·mal (prŏk′sə-məl) *adj.* Proximate.

prox·i·mate (prŏk′sə-mĭt) *adj.* **1.** Very near : close. **2.** Immediate : direct.

prox•im•i•ty (prŏk-sĭm′ĭ-tē) *n.* The quality, state, or fact of being near : closeness.
prox•y (prŏk′sē) *n., pl.* **-ies. 1.** An authorized agent for another. **2.** Authority or written authorization to act for another.
prude (pro͞od) *n.* One excessively concerned with propriety or morality. **–prud′er•y** *n.* **–prud′ish** *adj.* **–prud′ish•ly** *adv.* **–prud′ish•ness** *n.*
pru•dent (pro͞od′nt) *adj.* **1.** Handling practical matters judiciously. **2.** Managing carefully : provident. **3.** Behaving circumspectly : discreet. **–pru′dence** *n.* **–pru•den′tial** (pro͞o-dĕn′shəl) *adj.*
prune[1] (pro͞on) *n.* The partially dried fruit of the common plum.
prune[2] (pro͞on) *v.* **pruned, prun•ing. 1.** To cut or trim parts of (a plant or tree). **2.** To remove unnecessary or unwanted parts.
pru•ri•ent (pro͝or′ē-ənt) *adj.* Arousing or experiencing lustful feelings. **–pru′ri•ence** *n.* **–pru′ri•ent•ly** *adv.*
Prus•sia (prŭsh′ə). Region and former state of NC Europe. **–Prus′sian** *adj.* & *n.*
pry[1] (prī) *v.* **pried, pry•ing.** To look inquisitively or furtively : snoop.
pry[2] (prī) *v.* **pried, pry•ing. 1.** To raise, move, or open forcibly with or as if with a lever. **2.** To get with effort or difficulty. *–n., pl.* **pries.** A tool for prying.
P.S. *abbr.* **1.** Police Sergeant. **2.** postscript. **3.** public school.
psalm (säm) *n.* **1.** A sacred song or poem. **2. Psalms.** *(sing. in number).* See BIBLE TABLE. **–psalm′ist** *n.*
Psal•ter *also* **psal•ter** (sôl′tər) *n.* A book containing the Book of Psalms, esp. for use in church services.
p's and q's (pēz′ ən kyo͞oz′) *pl.n. Informal.* Proper conduct : manners.
pseu•do (so͞o′dō) *adj.* False : sham.
pseu•do•nym (so͞od′n-ĭm′) *n.* An assumed name, esp. a pen name. **–pseu•don′y•mous** (so͞o-dŏn′ə-məs) *adj.*
psil•o•cy•bin (sĭl′ə-sī′bĭn, sī′lə-) *n.* A strongly hallucinogenic compound derived from the mushroom *Psilocybe mexicana.*
psit•ta•co•sis (sĭt′ə-kō′sĭs) *n.* A viral disease of parrots and related birds that is transmissible to humans.
pso•ri•a•sis (sə-rī′ə-sĭs) *n.* A chronic inflammatory skin disease marked by white scaly patches.
PST or **P.S.T.** *abbr.* Pacific Standard Time.
psych (sīk) *Informal. –n.* Psychology. *–v.* **1.** To prepare oneself mentally or emotionally. **2.** To intimidate by psychological means. **3.** To outguess or outwit.
psy•che (sī′kē) *n.* **1.** The soul or spirit. **2.** The mind.
psy•che•del•ic (sī′kĭ-dĕl′ĭk) *adj.* Of, producing, or marked by abnormal psychic effects, as hallucinations and perceptual distortions. **–psy′che•del′ic** *n.* **–psy′che•del′i•cal•ly** *adv.*
psy•chi•a•try (sĭ-kī′ə-trē, sī-) *n.* The branch of medicine dealing with the diagnosis and treatment of mental disorders. **–psy′chi•at′ric** (sī′kē-ăt′rĭk) *adj.* **–psy′chi•at′ri•cal•ly** *adv.* **–psy•chi′a•trist** *n.*
psy•chic (sī′kĭk) *also* **psy•chi•cal** (-kĭ-kəl) *adj.* **1.** Of or relating to the psyche. **2.** Of or caused by phenomena unexplainable by known natural laws. **3.** Responsive to supernatural or nonphysical phenomena. *–n.* **1.** One responsive to or influenced by psychic forces. **2.** One held to communicate with the spirit world.
psy•cho (sī′kō) *n. pl.* **-chos.** *Slang.* A psychopath. **–psy′cho** *adj.*
psy•cho•ac•tive (sī′kō-ăk′tĭv) *adj.* Chemically affecting the mind or behavior <a *psychoactive* drug>
psy•cho•a•nal•y•sis (sī′kō-ə-năl′ĭ-sĭs) *n.* A means of treating mental disorder through the analysis of usu. subconscious feelings and conflicts. **–psy′cho•an′a•lyst** (-ăn′ə-lĭst) *n.* **–psy′cho•an′a•lyt′ic** (-ăn′ə-lĭt′ĭk), **psy′cho•an′a•lyt′i•cal** *adj.* **–psy′cho•an′a•lyze′** (-līz′) *v.*
psy•cho•bi•ol•o•gy (sī′kō-bī-ŏl′ə-jē) *n.* The study of the interactions between mental and biological processes. **–psy′cho•bi•ol′o•gist** *n.*
psy•cho•dra•ma (sī′kō-drä′mə, -drăm′ə) *n.* Psychotherapy in which individuals spontaneously act out roles assigned by the therapist.
psy•cho•gen•ic (sī′kō-jĕn′ĭk) *adj.* Arising in the mind or in emotional conflict.
psy•cho•lin•guis•tics (sī′kō-lĭng-gwĭs′tĭks) *n. (sing. in number).* The study of the interaction between psychological factors and linguistic behavior. **–psy′cho•lin′guist** *n.* **–psy′cho•lin•guis′tic** *adj.*
psy•chol•o•gy (sī-kŏl′ə-jē) *n., pl.* **-gies. 1.** The science of mind, emotions, and behavior. **2.** The emotional characteristics and behavior associated with an individual. **–psy′cho•log′i•cal** (-kə-lŏj′ĭ-kəl) *adj.* **–psy•chol′o•gist** *n.*
psy•cho•path (sī′kə-păth′) *n.* A person with a mental disorder manifested esp. in aggressively antisocial behavior. **–psy′cho•path′ic** *adj.*
psy•cho•sis (sī-kō′sĭs) *n., pl.* **-ses** (-sēz′). A severe mental disorder marked by the degeneration of mental and social functioning and withdrawal from reality. **–psy•chot′ic** (-kŏt′ĭk) *adj.* & *n.*
psy•cho•so•mat•ic (sī′kō-sə-măt′ĭk) *adj.* Of, pertaining to, or caused by phenomena that are both physiological and psychological. **–psy′cho•so•mat′ic** *n.*
psy•cho•ther•a•py (sī′kō-thĕr′ə-pē) *n.* Treatment of emotional or mental disorders by psychological methods. **–psy′cho•ther′a•peu′tic** (-pyo͞o′tĭk) *adj.* **–psy′cho•ther′a•pist** *n.*
psy•cho•tro•pic (sī′kə-trō′pĭk, -trŏp′ĭk) *adj.* Having a mind-altering effect.
Pt *symbol for* PLATINUM.
pt. *abbr.* **1.** part. **2.** pint. **3.** point. **4.** port.
P.T. *abbr.* **1.** *also* **PT** Pacific Time. **2.** physical therapy.
PTA or **P.T.A.** *abbr.* Parent-Teachers Association.
ptar•mi•gan (tär′mĭ-gən) *n., pl.* **-gan** or **-gans.** A bird of the genus *Lagopus,* of N regions, with feathered feet.
PT boat (pē-tē′) *n.* A fast, maneuverable boat used to torpedo enemy ships.
ptg. *abbr.* printing.
Ptol•e•my (tŏl′ə-mē). 2nd cent. Greek astronomer, mathematician, and geographer. **–Ptol′e•ma′ic** (tŏl′ə-mā′ĭk) *adj.*
pto•maine *also* **pto•main** (tō′mān′, tōmān′) *n.* Any of various sometimes poisonous nitrogenous products of protein putrefaction and decomposition.
ptomaine poisoning *n.* Food poisoning caused by bacteria or their toxins.
Pu *symbol for* PLUTONIUM.
pub (pŭb) *n.* A public tavern or bar.
pub. *abbr.* **1.** public. **2.** publication; published; publisher.
pu•ber•ty (pyo͞o′bər-tē) *n.* The stage of human physical development in which sexual reproduction can 1st occur. **–pu′ber•tal, pu′ber•al** (-bər-əl) *adj.*
pu•bes•cent (pyo͞o-bĕs′ənt) *adj.* **1.** Covered with short soft hairs. **2.** Reaching or having arrived at puberty. **–pu•bes′cence** *n.*
pu•bic (pyo͞o′bĭk) *adj.* Of, relating to, or in the region of the pubis.
pu•bis (pyo͞o′bĭs) *n., pl.* **-bes** (-bēz′). The anterior part of either of the hipbones, joining to form the anterior pelvic arch.
pub•lic (pŭb′lĭk) *adj.* **1.** Of, pertaining to, or affecting the community or the people as a whole <the *public* good> **2.** For the use of all <a *public* telephone> **3.** Participated in by the people or community <a *public* occasion> **4.** Serving or acting for the people or community <a *public* defender> **5.** Open to the knowledge of all. **6.** Widely known. ☆*syns:* DEMOCRATIC, GENERAL, POPULAR *–n.* **1.** The general populace. **2.** A body of people having a mutual interest. **–pub′lic•ly** *adv.*
pub•lic-ad•dress system (pŭb′lĭkə-drĕs′) *n.* An electronic amplification system for projecting sound.
pub•li•can (pŭb′lĭ-kən) *n.* **1.** *esp. Brit.* The proprieter of a public house. **2.** A tax collector in the ancient Roman Empire.
pub•li•ca•tion (pŭb′lĭ-kā′shən) *n.* **1.** The act or process of publishing. **2.** Something published, as a magazine.
public domain *n.* Land under governmental ownership and control.
public house *n. esp. Brit.* A licensed inn, tavern, or bar.
pub•li•cist (pŭb′lĭ-sĭst) *n.* One who publicizes, esp. a press agent.
pub•lic•i•ty (pŭ-blĭs′ĭ-tē) *n.* **1.** Information issued to attract public attention. **2.** Public attention or notoriety. **3.** The work of a publicist.
pub•li•cize (pŭb′lĭ-sīz′) *v.* **-cized, -ciz•ing.** To bring to public attention.
public relations *pl.n. (sing. or pl. in number).* **1.** Methods and means by which a person or an organization seeks to promote a favorable relationship with the public. **2.** The degree of success in promoting good public relations.
public school *n.* **1.** A tax-supported U.S. school providing free education. **2.** A private secondary boarding school in Great Britain.
pub•lic-spir•i•ted (pŭb′lĭk-spĭr′ĭ-tĭd) *adj.* Dedicated to promoting the well-being of the general public.
public television *n.* Privately supported noncommercial television that provides educational and cultural programs for the public.
pub•lish (pŭb′lĭsh) *v.* **1.** To produce and present (printed and other material) for public distribution or sale. **2.** To publicize : announce. **–pub′lish•a•ble** *adj.* **–pub′lish•er** *n.* **–pub′lish•ment** *n.*
puck[1] (pŭk) *n.* A hard rubber disk used in ice hockey.

puck[2] (pŭk) *n.* A mischievous elf or sprite. **–puck′ish** *adj.*

puck•er (pŭk′ər) *v.* To draw up into wrinkles or folds. *–n.* A small wrinkle or fold.

pud•ding (po͝od′ĭng) *n.* A sweet custardlike or cakelike dessert.

pud•dle (pŭd′l) *n.* A small pool of liquid, esp. of muddy water.

pud•dling (pŭd′lĭng) *n.* The conversion of pig iron into pure iron by heat and agitation in an oxidizing atmosphere.

pu•den•dum (pyo͞o-dĕn′dəm) *n., pl.* **-da** (-də). A woman's external genital organs.

pudg•y (pŭj′ē) *adj.* **-i•er, -i•est.** Short and chubby. **–pudg′i•ness** *n.*

pueb•lo (pwĕb′lō) *n., pl.* **-los.** A community of SW U.S. Indian tribes consisting of adobe or stone houses with flat roofs.

pu•er•ile (pyo͞o′ər-əl, pyo͝or′əl) *adj.* Childishly silly : juvenile. **–pu′er•il′i•ty** (pyo͞o′ə-rĭl′ĭ-tē) *n.*

pu•er•per•al (pyo͞o-ûr′pər-əl) *adj.* Of or relating to childbirth.

Puer•to Ri•co (pwĕr′tō rē′kō, pōr′-). Island of the West Indies, E of Hispaniola; a self-governing U.S. commonwealth. *Cap.* San Juan. *Pop.* 3,187,570. **–Puer′to Ri′can** *adj. & n.*

puff (pŭf) *n.* **1. a.** A brief, usu. forceful discharge, as of smoke or air. **b.** A slight explosive sound made by a puff. **2.** A small swelling <*puffs* of clouds> **3.** A soft, light pad, esp. for applying powder. **4.** A light, flaky pastry. **5.** A highly complimentary review or recommendation. *–v.* **1.** To blow or come forth in puffs. **2.** To breathe heavily : pant. **3.** To give forth puffs, as of smoke. **4.** To swell or appear to swell. **5.** To inflate with pride or conceit. **6.** To praise or advertise extravagantly. **–puff′i•ly** *adv.* **–puff′i•ness** *n.* **–puff′y** *adj.*

puff•ball (pŭf′bôl′) *n.* A rounded, often edible fungus of the genus *Lycoperdon* and related genera that when broken open releases spores in dustlike puffs.

puff•er•y (pŭf′ə-rē) *n.* Favorable and often exaggeratedly flattering publicity.

puf•fin (pŭf′ĭn) *n.* Any of several sea birds of the genera *Fratercula* and *Lunda,* with black and white plumage and a flattened, brightly colored bill.

pug[1] (pŭg) *n.* **1.** A small dog, orig. bred in China, with a snub nose, a wrinkled face, and a curled tail. **2.** A short, upturned, somewhat flattened nose.

pug[2] (pŭg) *n. Slang.* A boxer.

pu•gi•lism (pyo͞o′jə-lĭz′əm) *n.* The sport of fighting with the fists : boxing. **–pu′gi•list** *n.* **–pu′gi•lis′tic** (-lĭs′tĭk) *adj.*

pug•na•cious (pŭg-nā′shəs) *adj.* Disposed to quarrel or fight : combative. **–pug•na′cious•ly** *adv.* **–pug•nac′i•ty** (-năs′ĭ-tē) *n.*

puis•sance (pwĭs′əns, pyo͞o′ĭ-səns) *n.* Power : might. **–puis′sant** *adj.*

puke (pyo͞ok) *v.* **puked, puk•ing.** *Slang.* To vomit.

puk•ka (pŭk′ə) *adj.* **1.** Authentic. **2.** First-rate.

pul (po͞ol) *n., pl.* **puls** or **pu•li** (po͞o′lē). See *afghani* at CURRENCY TABLE.

pul•chri•tude (pŭl′krĭ-to͞od′, -tyo͞od′) *n.* Physical beauty. **–pul′chri•tu′di•nous** (-to͞od′n-əs, -tyo͞od′-) *adj.*

pule (pyo͞ol) *v.* **puled, pul•ing.** To whine or whimper <a *puling* child>

Pu•lit•zer Prize (po͝ol′ĭt-sər, pyo͞o′lĭt-) *n.* Any of several awards conferred annually for accomplishment in various fields, as journalism, music, and literature.

pull (po͝ol) *v.* **1.** To apply force to so as to draw toward the force. **2.** To draw out or forth from a fixed position. **3.** To tug at. **4.** To break or tear apart. **5.** To stretch (e.g., taffy) repeatedly. **6.** To injure (a muscle or tendon) by straining. **7.** To move by automotive means. **8.** *Informal.* To carry out, esp. skillfully. **9.** To draw out (a knife or gun) in readiness for use. **10.** To produce (e.g., a printed proof) from type. **11.** *Informal.* To attract. **12.** To put on (clothing). **–pull off.** To accomplish despite difficulty. **–pull through.** To survive illness or trouble successfully. *–n.* **1.** The act or process of pulling. **2.** Force or effort used in pulling. **3.** A force that attracts or draws. **4.** A device used for pulling. **5.** *Slang.* Special advantage or influence. **–pull (oneself) together.** To regain one's composure.

pull•back (po͝ol′băk′) *n.* An orderly withdrawal of military troops.

pul•let (po͝ol′ĭt) *n.* A young hen.

pul•ley (po͝ol′ē) *n., pl.* **-leys. 1.** A wheel with a grooved rim through which a rope or chain is run for hoisting or changing the direction of a pulling force. **2.** A wheel turned by or driving a belt.

Pull•man (po͝ol′mən) *n.* A railway sleeping car or parlor car.

pull•out (po͝ol′out′) *n.* **1.** A military pullback. **2.** Something, as a magazine insert, to be pulled out.

pull•o•ver (po͝ol′ō′vər) *n.* A garment, esp. a sweater, put on by being pulled down over the head. **–pull′o′ver** *adj.*

pull-up (po͝ol′ŭp′) *n.* The exercise of chinning.

pul•mo•nar•y (po͝ol′mə-nĕr′ē, pŭl′-) *adj.* Of, pertaining to, or affecting the lungs.

pulp (pŭlp) *n.* **1.** A soft, moist substance or mass. **2.** The soft juicy or fleshy part of a fruit or vegetable. **3.** Ground and moistened cellulose material used to make paper. **4.** The soft inner tissue of a tooth. **5.** A magazine printed on cheap paper and often containing lurid subject matter. **–pulp′i•ness** *n.* **–pulp′y** *adj.*

pul•pit (po͝ol′pĭt, pŭl′-) *n.* **1.** An elevated platform with a lectern used in preaching or conducting a church service. **2.** The ministry as a profession.

pulp•wood (pŭlp′wo͝od′) *n.* Soft wood used in papermaking.

pul•sar (pŭl′sär′) *n. Astron.* Any of several celestial objects that emit pulsating radio waves.

pul•sate (pŭl′sāt′) *v.* **-sat•ed, -sat•ing.** To beat or vibrate rhythmically. **–pul•sa′tion** *n.* **–pul′sa′tor** *n.*

pulse (pŭls) *n.* **1.** The rhythmical expansion and contraction of the arteries generated by the regular beating of the heart. **2.** A quick temporary change in electrical or wave energy. *–v.* **pulsed, puls•ing.** To pulsate. **–pulse′less** *adj.*

pul•ver•ize (pŭl′və-rīz′) *v.* **-ized, -iz•ing. 1.** To reduce or be reduced to tiny particles. **2.** To destroy completely : demolish. **–pul′ver•iz′a•ble** *adj.* **–pul′ver•i•za′tion** *n.* **–pul′ver•iz′er** *n.*

pu•ma (pyo͞o′mə) *n.* The mountain lion.

pum•ice (pŭm′ĭs) *n.* A light, porous volcanic rock used esp. as an abrasive.

pum•mel (pŭm′əl) *v.* **-meled, -mel•ing** or **-melled, -mel•ling.** To strike repeatedly : pound.

pump[1] (pŭmp) *n.* A device for moving a gas or liquid from 1 place or container to another. *–v.* **1.** To raise or move (liquid or gas) with a pump. **2.** To fill with air by means of a pump. **3.** To empty of water or air. **4.** To move up and down or back and forth. **5.** To force or propel with or as if with a pump. **6.** To question relentlessly.

pump[2] (pŭmp) *n.* A low shoe without laces or straps.

pum•per•nick•el (pŭm′pər-nĭk′əl) *n.* A coarse, dark, sour rye bread.

pump•kin (pŭmp′kĭn, pŭm′-, pŭng′-) *n.* A trailing vine, *Cucurbita pepo,* widely cultivated for its large pulpy round fruit with a thick, orange-yellow rind and many seeds.

pun (pŭn) *n.* A humorous play on a word that evokes more than 1 interpretation. **–pun** *v.*

punch[1] (pŭnch) *n.* **1.** A tool for piercing, perforating, cutting, or embossing. **2.** A tool for driving a pin, bolt, or nail in or out of a hole. *–v.* To use a punch on.

†punch[2] (pŭnch) *v.* **1.** To hit sharply with the fist. **2.** *W U.S.* To herd (cattle). *–n.* **1.** A blow with or as if with the fist. **2.** Vigor : energy. **–punch in** (or **out**). To check in (or out) formally at a job before (or after) a day's work.

punch[3] (pŭnch) *n.* A beverage of fruit juices often with wine or liquor.

punch card *n.* A computer card punched with a pattern of holes or notches to represent data.

punch-drunk (pŭnch′drŭngk′) *adj.* Dazed or bewildered by or as if by too many blows to the head.

pun•cheon (pŭn′chən) *n.* A large cask for liquids.

punch line *n.* The phrase or sentence making the point of a joke.

punc•til•i•o (pŭngk-tĭl′ē-ō′) *n., pl.* **-os. 1.** A fine detail of formal conduct. **2.** Scrupulous observance of ceremony and etiquette.

punc•til•i•ous (pŭngk-tĭl′ē-əs) *adj.* Characterized by meticulous observance of the forms of conduct and etiquette. **–punc•til′i•ous•ly** *adv.*

punc•tu•al (pŭngk′cho͞o-əl) *adj.* Acting or being habitually on time : prompt. **–punc′tu•al′i•ty** (-ăl′ĭ-tē) *n.*

punc•tu•ate (pŭngk′cho͞o-āt′) *v.* **-at•ed, -at•ing. 1.** To provide (written material) with punctuation. **2.** To interrupt repeatedly. **3.** To give emphasis to.

punc•tu•a•tion (pŭngk′cho͞o-ā′shən) *n.* **1.** The use of standardized marks in written material to separate structural units and clarify meaning. **2.** The marks used in punctuating written material.

punc•ture (pŭngk′chər) *v.* **-tured, -tur•ing. 1.** To pierce with or as if with something sharp. **2.** To cause to collapse by or as if by puncturing. *–n.* **1.** An act or instance of puncturing. **2.** A small hole, as in a tire, made by puncturing.

pun•dit (pŭn′dĭt) *n.* One who is erudite or authoritative.

†pung (pŭng) *n. New England.* A low 1-horse box sleigh.

pun•gent (pŭn′jənt) *adj.* **1.** Sharp or acrid to the taste or smell. **2.** Having a penetrating quality : biting or caustic. ***☆syns:*** PIQUANT, SHARP, SPICY, ZESTY **–pun′gen•cy** (-jən-sē) *n.* **–pun′gent•ly** *adv.*

pun•ish (pŭn′ĭsh) *v.* **1.** To subject to a penalty for wrongdoing.

2. To impose a penalty for. **3.** To treat roughly or injuriously. **–pun′ish•a•ble** *adj.*

pun•ish•ment (pŭn′ĭsh-mənt) *n.* **1.** A penalty for a crime or offense. **2.** Rough or injurious treatment.

pu•ni•tive (pyo͞o′nĭ-tĭv) *adj.* Imposing or aiming to impose punishment. **–pu′ni•tive•ly** *adv.* **–pu′ni•tive•ness** *n.*

punk[1] (pŭngk) *n.* **1.** Easily crumbled decayed wood used as kindling. **2.** A substance that smolders when lighted, used to ignite fireworks.

punk[2] (pŭngk) *Slang. n.* **1.** A young inexperienced or insignificant person. **2.** A young hoodlum or tough. **3.** Punk rock. *–adj.* **1.** Of inferior quality. **2.** In poor health. **3.** Of, relating to, or being a purposefully bizarre style of dress affected by punk rock groups.

†pun•kin (pŭng′kĭn) *n. Regional.* A pumpkin.

punk rock *n.* Hard rock music marked by themes of bitter hostility toward established society. **–punk rocker** *n.*

pun•ster (pŭn′stər) *n.* One giving to making puns.

punt[1] (pŭnt) *n.* A narrow flat-bottomed boat propelled by a long pole. *–v.* To propel (e.g., a punt) with a pole.

punt[2] (pŭnt) *n.* A play in which a football is dropped and kicked before it hits the ground. **–punt** *v.*

pu•ny (pyo͞o′nē) *adj.* **-ni•er, -ni•est.** Small or inferior in size, strength, or worth.

pup (pŭp) *n.* **1.** A puppy. **2.** The young of such animals as the seal and fox.

pu•pa (pyo͞o′pə) *n., pl.* **-pae** (-pē) *or* **-pas.** The inactive stage in the life cycle of many insects between the larval and adult forms. **–pu′pal** *adj.*

pu•pil[1] (pyo͞o′pəl) *n.* A young person being instructed by a teacher.

pu•pil[2] (pyo͞o′pəl) *n.* The dark opening in the center of the iris through which light enters the eye.

pup•pet (pŭp′ĭt) *n.* **1.** A figure of a person or animal manipulated by hand or by strings or wires. **2.** One whose actions are controlled by others. **–pup′pet•eer′** *n.* **–pup′pet•ry** *n.*

pup•py (pŭp′ē) *n., pl.* **-pies.** A young dog.

pup tent *n.* A waterproof shelter tent.

pur•blind (pûr′blīnd′) *adj.* **1.** Partially or nearly blind. **2.** Slow in understanding.

pur•chase (pûr′chĭs) *v.* **-chased, -chas•ing.** To acquire by paying money or its equivalent : buy. *–n.* **1.** Something purchased. **2.** The act or an instance of purchasing. **3.** A secure hold or position. **–pur′chas•a•ble** *adj.* **–pur′chas•er** *n.*

pur•dah (pûr′də) *n.* The Hindu practice of secluding women from public view.

pure (pyo͝or) *adj.* **pur•er, pur•est. 1.** Having a homogeneous composition : unmixed. **2.** Free from impurities or contaminants : clean. **3.** Utter : sheer <*pure* foolishness> **4.** Free from faults : sinless. **5.** Chaste. **6.** Theoretical : abstract. **7.** Containing nothing inappropriate or unnecessary. **8.** Purebred. **–pure′ly** *adv.* **–pure′ness** *n.* **–pur′i•ty** *n.*

pure•bred (pyo͝or′brĕd′) *adj.* Having many generations of ancestors of the same breed or kind. **–pure′bred′** *n.*

pu•rée (pyo͝o-rā′, pyo͝or′ā′) *v.* **-réed, -rée•ing.** To press (cooked food) through a strainer. *–n.* Food or a dish, as soup, prepared by puréeing.

pur•ga•tion (pûr-gā′shən) *n.* An act or result of purging.

pur•ga•tive (pûr′gə-tĭv) *adj.* Tending to purge, esp. causing the bowels to empty. *–n.* A cathartic.

pur•ga•to•ry (pûr′gə-tôr′ē, -tōr′ē) *n., pl.* **-ries. 1.** *Rom. Cath. Ch.* An intermediate state in which the souls of those who have died in grace must atone for their sins before attaining heaven. **2.** A place or state of temporary punishment or suffering. **–pur′ga•to′ri•al** (-tôr′ē-əl, -tōr′-) *adj.*

purge (pûrj) *v.* **purged, purg•ing. 1.** To make clean or pure, esp. to free from sin or guilt. **2.** To rid of what is considered undesirable, esp. to rid of unwanted persons by harsh methods. **3.** To experience or cause emptying of the bowels. *–n.* **1.** The act, process, or result of purging, esp. the harsh elimination of unwanted persons. **2.** Something that purges, esp. a cathartic.

pu•ri•fy (pyo͝or′ə-fī′) *v.* **-fied, -fy•ing.** To make or become clean or pure. **–pu′ri•fi•ca′tion** *n.* **–pu′ri•fi′er** *n.*

Pu•rim (po͝or′ĭm) *n.* A Jewish holiday commemorating the deliverance of the Jews from massacre by Haman.

pu•rine (pyo͝or′ēn′) *n.* **1.** A crystalline base used in organic synthesis and metabolism studies. **2.** A naturally occurring basic compound derived from or related to purine, as uric acid, adenine, and guanine.

pur•ism (pyo͝or′ĭz′əm) *n.* Strict adherence to or demand for precision and correctness, esp. in language. **–pur′ist** *n.*

Pu•ri•tan (pyo͝or′ĭ-tn) *n.* **1.** A member of a 16th- and 17th-cent. Protestant group of England and New England that opposed the elaborate ceremonies of the Church of England. **2. puritan.** An advocate of a very strict moral and religious code. **–pu′ri•tan′i•cal** (-tăn′ĭ-kəl) *adj.* **–pu′ri•tan′i•cal•ly** *adv.* **–pur′i•tan•ism** *n.*

purl[1] (pûrl) *v.* To flow in ripples or with a low murmuring sound. *–n.* The sound made by rippling water.

purl[2] (pûrl) *v.* To knit with a reversed stitch. *–n.* A reversed knitting stitch.

pur•lieu (pûrl′yo͞o, pûr′lo͞o) *n.* **1.** An outlying area, as of a city. **2. purlieus. a.** Outskirts : environs. **b.** Confines : borders.

pur•loin (pər-loin′, pûr′loin′) *v.* To steal.

pur•ple (pûr′pəl) *n.* **1.** A color with a hue between that of violet and red. **2.** Cloth or clothing of the color purple formerly worn as a symbol of royalty or high authority. *–adj.* **1.** Of the color purple. **2.** Showy and ornate <*purple* prose> **3.** Vulgar or profane <*purple* language> *–v.* **-pled, -pling.** To make or become purple. **–pur′plish** *adj.*

pur•port (pər-pôrt′, -pōrt′) *v.* To have or give the appearance of being or intending : profess. *–n.* (pûr′pôrt′, -pōrt′). An apparent meaning or intention. **–pur•port′ed•ly** (-pôr′tĭd-lē, -pōr′-) *adv.*

pur•pose (pûr′pəs) *n.* **1.** An intended or desired result : goal. **2.** Determination : resolve. *–v.* **-posed, -pos•ing.** To intend to do : resolve. **–pur′pose•ful** *adj.* **–pur′pose•less** *adj.* **–pur′pose•ly** *adv.*

purr (pûr) *n.* A low, vibrating murmur characteristic of a contented cat. **–purr** *v.*

purse (pûrs) *n.* **1. a.** A small bag or pouch for money. **b.** A pocketbook or handbag. **2.** Financial resources : wealth. **3.** A sum of money tendered as a gift or prize. *–v.* **pursed, purs•ing.** To pucker or wrinkle.

purs•er (pûr′sər) *n.* A passenger ship's officer charged with keeping accounts.

purs•lane (pûr′slĭn, -slān′) *n.* A trailing weed, *Portulaca oleracea,* with small yellow flowers, reddish stems, and fleshy leaves sometimes used in salads.

pur•su•ance (pər-so͞o′əns) *n.* The act of putting something into effect.

pur•su•ant to (pər-so͞o′ənt) *prep.* In accordance with : in carrying out.

pur•sue (pər-so͞o′) *v.* **-sued, -su•ing. 1.** To follow in order to catch : chase. **2.** To seek to achieve or accomplish. **3.** To proceed along (a course). **4.** To engage in or keep at (an activity). **–pur•su′er** *n.*

pur•suit (pər-so͞ot′) *n.* **1.** The act or an instance of pursuing. **2.** An activity regularly engaged in.

pu•ru•lent (pyo͝or′ə-lənt, pyo͝or′yə-) *adj.* Containing, discharging, or accompanied by pus. **–pu′ru•lence** *n.*

pur•vey (pər-vā′) *v.* To supply or furnish (e.g., provisions), usu. as a service. **–pur•vey′ance** *n.* **–pur•vey′or** *n.*

pur•view (pûr′vyo͞o′) *n.* **1.** Scope or extent of function, ability, or authority. **2.** Range of foresight, understanding, or experience.

pus (pŭs) *n.* A thick, yellowish-white fluid formed in infected tissue that contains bacteria, white blood cells, and tissue debris.

push (po͝osh) *v.* **1.** To press forcefully against in order to move. **2.** To move by exerting force : thrust. **3.** To press or urge forward vigorously. **4.** To pressure insistently. **5.** *Slang.* **a.** To publicize or sell, esp. aggressively. **b.** To sell illicitly <*push* drugs> *–n.* **1.** The act of pushing : thrust or shove. **2.** An energetic or insistent effort. **3.** A stimulus to action. **4.** *Informal.* Energy : drive. **–push around.** *Informal.* To attempt to intimidate.

push button *n.* A small button that when pressed activates something.

push•cart (po͝osh′kärt′) *n.* A light cart pushed by hand.

push•down (po͝osh′doun′) *n. Computer Sci.* A section of stored data from which the most recently stored material must be the first to be used.

push•er (po͝osh′ər) *n.* One that pushes, esp. one who sells narcotics illicitly.

push•o•ver (po͝osh′ō′vər) *n.* **1.** Something easily done. **2.** One easily defeated or deceived.

push•up (po͝osh′ŭp′) *n.* **1.** An exercise performed with the face and hands to the floor that consists of pushing the body up and down with the arms. **2.** *Computer Sci.* A section of stored data from which the earliest stored material must be the first to be utilized.

push•y (po͝osh′ē) *adj.* **-i•er, -i•est.** *Informal.* Objectionably forward or aggressive. **–push′i•ly** *adv.* **–push′i•ness** *n.*

pu•sil•lan•i•mous (pyo͞o′sə-lăn′ə-məs) *adj.* Faint-hearted : cowardly. **–pu′sil•la•nim′i•ty** (-lə-nĭm′ĭ-tē) *n.* **–pu′sil•lan′i•mous•ly** *adv.*

puss[1] (po͝os) *n. Informal.* A cat.

puss[2] (po͝os) *n. Slang.* **1.** The mouth. **2.** The face.

puss•y[1] (po͝os′ē) *n., pl.* **-ies.** *Informal.* A cat.

pus·sy² (pŭs′ē) *adj.* **-si·er, -si·est.** Resembling or filled with pus.
pus·sy·cat (po͝os′ē-kăt′) *n.* A cat.
puss·y·foot (po͝os′ē-fo͝ot′) *v.* **1.** To move with stealth or wariness. **2.** *Slang.* To avoid taking a stand : equivocate.
pussy willow *n.* A North American shrub or small tree, *Salix discolor,* with silky catkins.
pus·tule (pŭs′cho͞ol′, -tyo͞ol′) *n.* A pus-filled blister. **–pus′tu·lar** *adj.*
put (po͝ot) *v.* **put, put·ting. 1.** To cause to be in a given position or location : place. **2.** To cause to be in a given state. **3.** To cause to undergo. **4.** To regard in a given way : attribute. **5.** To estimate : reckon. **6.** To impose or levy (e.g., a tax). **7.** To hurl for distance in the shot-put. **8.** To present for consideration or decision. **9.** To state : express <*putting* it bluntly> **10.** To translate. **11.** To arrange : adapt. **12.** To devote : apply <*put* effort into a project> **13.** To proceed on a particular course <*put* out to sea> **14.** To wager : bet. **–put down. 1.** To suppress : quell. **2.** *Slang.* To criticize, belittle, or humiliate. **–put in. 1.** To interpose : say. **2.** To spend time doing <*put in* 8 hours of typing> **3.** To enter (an offer, request, or application). **–put off. 1.** *Informal.* To repel. **2.** *Informal.* To evade. **3.** To postpone. **–put on. 1.** To don. **2.** To activate. **3.** To pretend to have. **4.** To mislead or tease. **5.** To add (e.g., weight). **–put out. 1.** To irritate or anger. **2.** To inconvenience. **3.** *Baseball.* To retire (a runner). **–put up. 1.** To build. **2.** To contribute. **3.** To offer for sale. **4.** To preserve (food). **5.** To accommodate. **6.** To endure. **–put up with.** To tolerate.
pu·ta·tive (pyo͞o′tə-tĭv) *adj.* Commonly accepted or supposed.
put-down (po͝ot′doun′) *n. Slang.* A critical or belittling remark.
put-on (po͝ot′ŏn′, -ôn′) *adj.* Pretended : assumed. *–n. Slang.* **1.** The act of deliberately misleading someone. **2.** A hoax or joke : spoof.
put·out (po͝ot′out′) *n. Baseball.* A play in which a batter or base runner is retired.
pu·tre·fy (pyo͞o′trə-fī′) *v.* **-fied, -fy·ing.** To decay or cause to decay : rot. **–pu′tre·fac′tion** *n.* **–pu′tre·fac′tive** *adj.*
pu·tres·cent (pyo͞o-trĕs′ənt) *adj.* Becoming rotten : decaying. **–pu·tres′cence** *n.*
pu·trid (pyo͞o′trĭd) *adj.* **1.** Decomposed : rotten. **2.** Morally corrupt : vile. **–pu·trid′i·ty** *n.* **–pu′trid·ly** *adv.*
putsch (po͝och) *n.* A sudden attempt to overthrow a government by a secret plot.
putt (pŭt) *n.* A light golf stroke made on the green to get the ball into the hole. **–putt** *v.*
put·tee (pŭ-tē′, pŭt′ē) *n.* **1.** A strip of cloth wrapped around the lower leg. **2.** A leather gaiter.
putt·er¹ (pŭt′ər) *n.* **1.** A golf club used for putting. **2.** A golfer who is putting.
put·ter² (pŭt′ər) *v.* **1.** To busy oneself without getting much done. **2.** To tinker.
put·ty (pŭt′ē) *n., pl.* **-ties.** A doughlike cement of ground chalk and linseed oil, used esp. to fill cracks and secure panes of glass in sashes. **–put′ty** *v.*
puz·zle (pŭz′əl) *v.* **-zled, -zling. 1.** To confuse or perplex : bewilder. **2.** To be in a state of perplexity. **3.** To ponder laboriously <*puzzle* over an assignment> **4.** To use reasoning or ingenuity in solving. *–n.* **1.** Something that puzzles. **2.** A problem, game, or device that calls for inventive skill or reasoning. **–puz′zler** *n.*
pvt. or **Pvt.** *abbr.* private.
py·a (pē-ä′) *n.* See *kyat* at CURRENCY TABLE.
pyg·my *also* **pig·my** (pĭg′mē) *n., pl.* **-mies. 1.** One of very small size : dwarf. **2. Pygmy.** A member of any of several African and Asian peoples whose height ranges from 4 to 5 ft. **–pyg′my** *adj.*
py·ja·mas (pə-jä′məz, -jăm′əz) *pl.n. esp. Brit. var. of* PAJAMAS.
py·lon (pī′lŏn′) *n.* **1.** A monumental gateway, esp. to an Egyptian temple, consisting of a pair of truncated pyramids. **2.** A tower marking a prescribed turning point in an aircraft race. **3.** A steel tower supporting high-tension electric wires or cables.
Pyong·yang (pyŭng′yăng′). Cap. of North Korea, in the SW. *Pop.* 840,000.
py·or·rhe·a *or* **py·or·rhoe·a** (pī′ə-rē′ə) *n.* Inflammation of the tooth sockets.
pyr·a·mid (pĭr′ə-mĭd) *n.* **1.** A solid geometric figure having a polygon as its base and triangular faces that meet at a common point. **2.** A massive, monumental structure with a rectangular base and 4 triangular faces that meet at the top. *–v.* **1.** To heap up or build in or as if in pyramid form. **2.** To increase with rapidity and on a broadening base. **–py·ram′i·dal** (pĭ-răm′ĭ-dl) *adj.*
pyre (pīr) *n.* A pile of combustible material for burning a corpse as a funeral rite.
Pyr·e·ness (pĭr′ə-nēz′). Mountain range between France and Spain.
py·re·thrum (pī-rē′thrəm) *n.* An Old World plant of the genus *Chrysanthemum* and related genera, with showy flowers.
Py·rex (pī′rĕks′). A trademark for any of several types of heat-resistant and chemical-resistant glassware.
py·rim·i·dine (pī-rĭm′ĭ-dēn′, pĭ-) *n.* **1.** A liquid and crystalline basic organic compound. **2.** One of several basic compounds, as cytosine, that is similar to pyrimidine and is a component of RNA and DNA.
py·rite (pī′rīt′) *n.* A yellowish-brown mineral sulfide containing iron and sulfur. **–py·rit′ic** (-rĭt′ĭk) *adj.*
py·ri·tes (pī-rī′tēz, pī-) *n., pl.* **-tes.** Any of a group of minerals composed chiefly of metallic sulfides, esp. of iron.
py·rol·y·sis (pī-rŏl′ĭ-sĭs) *n.* Chemical change effected by heat. **–py′ro·lyt′ic** (-rə-lĭt′ĭk) *adj.*
py·ro·ma·ni·a (pī′rō-mā′nē-ə, -mān′yə) *n.* An irresistible urge to set fires. **–py′ro·ma′ni·ac′** (-mā′nē-ăk′) *n.*
py·ro·tech·nics (pī′rə-tĕk′nĭks) *n.* **1.** *(sing. in number).* A usu. large display of fireworks. **2.** *(sing. or pl. in number).* An impressively brilliant display, as of rhetoric or wit. **–py′ro·tech′nic, py′ro·tech′ni·cal** *adj.* **–py′ro·tech′ni·cal·ly** *adv.*
Pyr·rhic victory (pĭr′ĭk) *n.* A victory won at a staggering cost.
Py·thag·o·ras (pĭ-thăg′ər-əs). d. 497 B.C. Greek philosopher. **–Py·thag′o·re′an** (-ə-rē′ən) *adj.* & *n.*
py·thon (pī′thŏn′, -thən) *n.* Any of various nonvenomous Old World snakes of the family *Pythonidae* that suffocate their prey by coiling around it.
pyx *also* **pix** (pĭks) *n.* **1.** A container holding supplies of Eucharistic wafers. **2.** A container for taking the Eucharist to the sick.

Qq

q or **Q** (kyo͞o) *n., pl.* **q's** *or* **Q's. 1.** The 17th letter of the English alphabet. **2.** A speech sound represented by the letter *q.*
q or **q.** *abbr.* quintal.
q. *abbr.* **1.** quart. **2.** query. **3.** question.
Qa·tar (kä′tär′). Country of E Arabia, on the Persian Gulf. *Cap.* Doha. *Pop.* 160,000.
qr. *abbr.* quarter; quarterly.
qt or **qt.** *abbr.* quart.
qt. or **qty.** *abbr.* quantity.
q.t. (kyo͞o′tē′) *n. Slang.* Quiet <on the *q.t.*>
qu. *abbr.* **1.** query. **2.** question.
quack¹ (kwăk) *n.* The sound uttered by a duck. **–quack** *v.*
quack² (kwăk) *n.* **1.** A person who pretends to have medical expertise. **2.** A charlatan. **–quack** *v.* **–quack′er·y** *n.*
quad¹ (kwŏd) *n.* QUADRANGLE 2.
quad² (kwŏd) *n.* A quadruplet.
quad·ran·gle (kwŏd′răng′gəl) *n.* **1.** *Math.* A plane figure consisting of 4 points, no 3 of which lie on the same straight line, connected by straight lines. **2.** A rectangular area bordered by buildings.
quad·rant (kwŏd′rənt) *n.* **1.** *Geom.* **a.** A circular arc subtending a central angle of 90° : ¼ of a circle. **b.** The plane area bounded by 2 perpendicular radii and the arc they subtend. **2.** An instrument for determining altitudes.
quad·ra·phon·ic (kwŏd′rə-fŏn′ĭk) *adj.* Of or used in a stereophonic sound system having 2 additional channels.
quad·rat·ic (kwŏ-drăt′ĭk) *adj.* Of, relating to, or possessing mathematical quantities of the 2nd degree or less.
quad·ren·ni·al (kwŏ-drĕn′ē-əl) *adj.* **1.** Occurring once in 4 years. **2.** Lasting for 4 years. **–quad·ren′ni·al·ly** *adv.*
quad·ri·lat·er·al (kwŏd′rə-lăt′ər-əl) *n.* A 4-sided polygon. **–quad′ri·lat′er·al** *adj.*

qua•drille (kwŏ-drĭl′, kwə-, kə-) *n.* **1.** A square dance of 5 figures performed by 4 couples. **2.** Music for the quadrille.
quad•ril•lion (kwŏ-drĭl′yən) *n.* **1.** The cardinal number equal to 10^{15}. **2.** *Brit.* SEPTILLION 1. **–quad•ril′lion** *adj. & pron.* **–quad•ril′lionth** *n. & adj. & adv.*
quad•ri•par•tite (kwŏd′rə-pär′tīt′) *adj.* **1.** Composed of or divided into 4 parts. **2.** Involving 4 participants.
quad•ru•ped (kwŏd′rə-pĕd′) *n.* An animal having 4 feet.
quad•ru•ple (kwŏ-dro͞o′pəl, -drŭp′əl, kwŏd′o͝o-pəl) *adj.* **1.** Consisting of 4 parts. **2.** Multiplied by 4. **3.** *Mus.* Having 4 beats to the measure. **–quad•ru′ple** *n. & v.*
quad•ru•plet (kwŏ-drŭp′lĭt, -dro͞o′plĭt, kwŏd′rə-plĭt) *n.* **1.** One of 4 born at a single birth. **2.** A group or set of 4.
quad•ru•pli•cate (kwŏ-dro͞o′plĭ-kĭt) *adj.* **1.** QUADRUPLE 2. **2.** Reproduced or copied 4 times. *–n.* One of a set of 4 identical things. **–quad•ru′pli•cate′** (-kāt′) *v.* **–quad•ru′pli•ca′tion** *n.*
quaff (kwŏf, kwăf, kwôf) *v.* To drink heartily. *–n.* A hearty draft.
quag•mire (kwăg′mīr′, kwŏg′-) *n.* **1.** Land with a soft, yielding surface. **2.** A difficult or irksome situation.
qua•hog *also* **qua•haug** (kwô′hôg′, -hŏg′, kwō′-, kō′-) *n.* A hard-shelled edible clam of the Atlantic coast of North America.
quail[1] (kwāl) *n., pl.* **quail** *or* **quails. 1.** A small chickenlike game bird of the genus *Coturnix*, having a short tail. **2.** A bird, as the bobwhite, resembling the quail.
quail[2] (kwāl) *v.* To recoil in fear : cower.
quaint (kwānt) *adj.* **1.** Charmingly curious or old-fashioned. **2.** Unusual or unfamiliar : strange. **–quaint′ness** *n.*
quake (kwāk) *v.* **quaked, quak•ing. 1.** To tremble or shake. **2.** To shiver or tremble, as with fright. *–n.* **1.** A quaking. **2.** An earthquake. **–quak′y** *adj.*
Quak•er (kwā′kər) *n. Informal.* FRIEND 3.
qual•i•fi•ca•tion (kwŏl′ə-fĭ-kā′shən) *n.* **1.** An act of qualifying or the state of being qualified. **2.** A quality, ability, or skill that makes one suitable for a given position or task. **3.** A restriction or modification.
qual•i•fied (kwŏl′ə-fīd′) *adj.* **1. a.** Competent. **b.** Having met the requirements for a specific position or task. **2.** Not total or wholehearted. ☆***syns:*** LIMITED, MODIFIED, RESERVED, RESTRICTED
qual•i•fy (kwŏl′ə-fī′) *v.* **-fied, -fy•ing. 1.** To describe by specifying the characteristics of : characterize. **2.** To make competent or eligible for a task or position. **3.** To certify as competent or capable. **4.** To modify or restrict. **5.** To make less intense. **6.** To modify the meaning of (e.g., a noun). **–qual′i•fi′er** *n.*
qual•i•ta•tive (kwŏl′ĭ-tā′tĭv) *adj.* Of, relating to, or concerning quality.
qual•i•ty (kwŏl′ĭ-tē) *n., pl.* **-ties. 1.** Essential character : nature. **2. a.** An inherent or distinguishing attribute : property. **b.** A character trait. **3.** Degree or grade of excellence. **4.** High social standing.
quality control *n.* Maintenance of proper standards in manufactured goods, esp. by regular inspection of the product.
qualm (kwŏm, kwôm) *n.* **1.** A sudden feeling of faintness or nausea. **2.** A sensation of doubt or uneasiness : misgiving. **3.** A conscience pang. ☆***syns:*** COMPUNCTION, MISGIVING, RESERVATION, SCRUPLE
quan•da•ry (kwŏn′də-rē, -drē) *n., pl.* **-ries.** A perplexing situation or state.
quan•ti•ta•tive (kwŏn′tĭ-tā′tĭv) *adj.* Of, relating to, or expressed as a quantity, measure, or amount.
quan•ti•ty (kwŏn′tĭ-tē) *n., pl.* **-ties. 1.** A specified or undetermined number or amount. **2.** A measurable whole. **3.** A large number or amount <bought office supplies in *quantity*> ☆***syns:*** AMOUNT, BODY, BULK, CORPUS, QUANTUM
quan•tum (kwŏn′təm) *n., pl.* **-ta** (-tə). **1.** A quantity or amount. **2.** *Physics.* An indivisible unit of energy, as a photon.
quantum theory *n. Physics.* A theory of dynamic systems in which variables are represented by abstract mathematical operators having properties that specify the behavior of the system.
quar•an•tine (kwôr′ən-tēn′, kwŏr′-) *n.* **1. a.** A period of enforced isolation, as of a person, animal, ship, etc., to prevent the spread of a contagious disease. **b.** A place for such isolation. **2.** A state of enforced isolation or detention. **–quar′an•tine′** *v.*
quark (kwôrk) *n.* Any of a group of hypothetical subatomic particles having electric charges of magnitude $\frac{1}{3}$ or $\frac{2}{3}$ that of the electron, proposed as the fundamental units of matter.
quar•rel (kwôr′əl, kwŏr′-) *n.* **1.** An angry disagreement or dispute. **2.** A cause for complaint or dispute. *–v.* **-reled, -rel•ing** *or* **-relled, -rel•ling. 1.** To take part in a disagreement. **2.** To complain.
quar•ry[1] (kwôr′ē, kwŏr′ē) *n., pl.* **-ries. 1.** An animal hunted for food or sport. **2.** The object of a hunt or chase.
quar•ry[2] (kwôr′ē, kwŏr′ē) *n., pl.* **-ries.** An excavation or pit from which stone is cut or blasted. **–quar′ri•er** *n.* **–quar′ry** *v.*
quart (kwôrt) *n.* See MEASUREMENT TABLE.
quar•ter (kwôr′tər) *n.* **1.** One of 4 equal parts. **2.** A coin valued at $\frac{1}{4}$ of the U.S. or Canadian dollar. **3.** $\frac{1}{4}$ of an hour. **4.** Any of the 4 divisions of the compass as defined by the cardinal points. **5. quarters. a.** A place of lodging or residence. **b.** Barracks. **6.** A section of a city. **7.** *often* **quarters.** An unspecified person or group <praise from all *quarters*> **8.** Mercy or clemency <give the enemy no *quarter*> *–v.* **1.** To cut or divide into 4 equal or equivalent parts. **2.** To dismember (a carcass) into 4 parts. **3.** To provide with shelter or lodgings. *–adj.* Being 1 of 4 equal or equivalent parts.
quar•ter•back (kwôr′tər-băk′) *n. Football.* The offensive backfield player who directs the plays. **–quar′ter•back′** *v.*
quar•ter-deck (kwôr′tər-dĕk′) *n.* The stern portion of the upper deck of a ship.
quarter horse *n.* A strong, muscular saddle horse orig. bred in the W U.S.
quar•ter•ly (kwôr′tər-lē) *adj.* Happening at 3-month intervals. *–n., pl.* **-lies.** A publication issued 4 times a year.
quar•ter•mas•ter (kwôr′tər-măs′tər) *n.* **1.** A military officer in charge of administering provisions and supplies. **2.** A petty officer in charge of the navigation of a ship.
quarter section *n.* A quarter of a sq mi of land or 160 acres.
quar•tet *also* **quar•tette** (kwôr-tĕt′) *n.* **1.** A musical composition for instruments or voices. **2.** A set of 4 persons or things.
quar•to (kwôr′tō) *n., pl.* **-tos. 1.** A page size equal to $\frac{1}{4}$ whole sheet, orig. obtained by folding a sheet into quarters. **2.** A book made up of quarto pages.
quartz (kwôrts) *n.* A clear, hard, transparent mineral occurring abundantly as a component of granite and sandstone or as various pure crystals.
quartz•ite (kwôrt′sīt′) *n.* A metamorphic rock formed by the recrystallization of quartz sandstone.
qua•sar (kwā′zär′, -sär′) *n.* A quasi-stellar object.
quash (kwŏsh, kwôsh) *v.* **1.** *Law.* To set aside or annul, esp. by judicial action. **2.** To crush or forcibly suppress.
qua•si (kwā′zī′, -sī′, kwä′zē, -sē) *adj.* Having a likeness to something : resembling <a *quasi* government>
qua•si-stel•lar object (kwā′zī-stĕl′ər, -sī-, kwä′zē-, -sē-). A starlike object that emits radio waves and visible radiation and apparently has great speed and energy.
quat•rain (kwŏt′rān′, kwŏ-trān′) *n.* A stanza or poem consisting of 4 lines.
quat•re•foil (kăt′ər-foil′, kăt′rə-) *n.* A stylized representation of a 4-petaled flower or a 4-lobed leaf.

quatrefoil

qua•ver (kwā′vər) *v.* **1.** To tremble, as from emotion or weakness. **2.** To speak in a tremulous voice. **–qua′ver** *n.*
quay (kē) *n.* A wharf.
Que. *abbr.* Quebec.
quea•sy (kwē′zē) *adj.* **-si•er, -si•est.** Nauseated. **–quea′si•ness** *n.*
Que•bec (kwĭ-bĕk′) *also* **Qué•bec** (kā-). **1.** Province of E Canada. *Pop.* 6,234,445. **2.** Cap. of Que., Canada, on the St. Lawrence. *Pop.* 177,082.
Que•beck•er *or* **Que•bec•er** (kwə-bĕk′ər) *n. Can.* A native or resident of Quebec.
Qué•be•cois (kā′bĕ-kwä′) *n. Can.* A native of Quebec.
queen (kwēn) *n.* **1.** The wife or widow of a king. **2.** A woman who is a monarch. **3.** A woman regarded as pre-eminent in a given field or domain. **4.** The chess piece with the most power. **5.** A playing card that has the figure of a queen on it. **6.** A fertile female in a colony of social insects, as bees, usu. the only one of its kind in the colony. **–queen′li•ness** *n.* **–queen′ly** *adj.*
queen mother *n.* The mother of a reigning monarch.
Queens (kwēnz). Borough of New York City, on W Long Is. *Pop.* 1,891,325.
queen-size (kwēn′sīz′) *adj.* **1.** Of, for, or being a bed approx. 60 in. by 80 in. <a *queen-size* mattress> **2.** Extra large.

queer (kwîr) *adj.* **1.** Different from the normal or expected : strange. **2.** Eccentric : odd. **3.** Suspicious. —*v. Slang.* **1.** To thwart or ruin. **2.** To put in a bad position.
quell (kwĕl) *v.* **1.** To suppress forcibly : put down. **2.** To pacify : quiet.
quench (kwĕnch) *v.* **1.** To put out (e.g., a fire) : extinguish. **2.** To squelch : dampen <couldn't *quench* our spirits> **3.** To satisfy : slake. **4.** To cool (metal) by immersing in liquid. **—quench'a•ble** *adj.*
que•nelle (kə-nĕl') *n.* A forcemeat dumpling poached in stock or water.
quer•u•lous (kwĕr'ə-ləs, kwĕr'yə-) *adj.* **1.** Constantly complaining or fretting : peevish. **2.** Uttering or expressing complaints or criticism. **—quer'u•lous•ness** *n.*
que•ry (kwîr'ē) *n., pl.* **-ries. 1.** A request for information : question. **2.** A doubt. **3.** A question mark. **—que'ry** *v.*
ques. *abbr.* question.
quest (kwĕst) *n.* **1.** A seeking or inquiring : search. **2.** An adventurous pursuit undertaken by a knight in medieval romance.
ques•tion (kwĕs'chən) *n.* **1.** An expression of inquiry requiring or inviting an answer. **2.** A point or subject open to debate. **3.** An unresolved matter : problem. **4.** A proposition brought up for consideration, as by an assembly. **5.** Uncertainty : doubt. **6.** Possibility : chance <no *question* of turning back now> —*v.* **1.** To put a question to. **2.** To interrogate, as a suspect or witness. **3.** To dispute.
ques•tion•a•ble (kwĕs'chə-nə-bəl) *adj.* **1.** Open to question or doubt : problematical. **2.** Of dubious morality or respectability. **—ques'tion•a•bly** *adv.*
question mark *n.* A punctuation symbol (?) placed at the end of a sentence to indicate a question.
ques•tion•naire (kwĕs'chə-nâr') *n.* A set of related questions, esp. one designed to gather statistical information from a sample population, as for a survey.
quet•zal (kĕt-säl') *n., pl.* **-zals** or **-za•les** (-sä'lās). **1.** A bird, *Pharomacrus mocino*, of Central America, having bronze-green and red plumage and long flowing tail feathers in the male. **2.** See CURRENCY TABLE.

quetzal

queue (kyōō) *n.* **1.** A line, as of people or vehicles, waiting a turn. **2.** *Computer Sci.* A sequence of stored data or programs awaiting processing. —*v.* **queued, queu•ing.** To form or wait in a line <*queued* up at the post office>
quib•ble (kwĭb'əl) *v.* **-bled, -bling.** To raise trivial objections, esp. over minor matters. **—quib'ble** *n.* **—quib'bler** *n.*
quiche (kēsh) *n.* Unsweetened custard baked in a pastry shell often with other ingredients, as vegetables or seafood.
▲word history: A quiche may seem to be a quintessentially French dish, but the word *quiche* is actually a Gallicized German word. Quiche was orig. a specialty of Lorraine, a region in NE France bordering on Germany. The region was claimed by both countries at various times, and both French and German are spoken there. The word *quiche* is a borrowing of Alsatian German *küche*, a diminutive of *kuche*, "cake." The form *quiche* is a French spelling of the German word.
quick (kwĭk) *adj.* **1.** Moving or performing with speed and agility. **2.** Occurring or accomplished in a short time. **3.** Thinking, understanding, or responding rapidly and easily. **4.** Tending to react hastily or impulsively. —*n.* **1.** Raw or sensitive exposed flesh, as under the fingernails. **2.** The most sensitive aspect of one's emotions. **3.** The living <the *quick* and the dead> **—quick'ly** *adv.* **—quick'ness** *n.*
quick•en (kwĭk'ən) *v.* **1.** To make or become more rapid : accelerate. **2.** To vitalize. **3.** To stimulate : stir.
quick-freeze (kwĭk'frēz') *v.* To freeze (food) by a process sufficiently rapid to retain flavor and nutritional value.
quick•lime (kwĭk'līm') *n.* CALCIUM OXIDE.
quick•sand (kwĭk'sănd') *n.* A soft, shifting mass of loose sand mixed with water that yields easily to pressure and in which a heavy object tends to sink.
quick•sil•ver (kwĭk'sĭl'vər) *n.* The element mercury. —*adj.* Unpredictable.
▲word history: The name *quicksilver* for the element mercury is a translation of Latin *argentum vivum*, literally "living silver." Mercury was so called because it is a silvery colored metal that is liquid at ordinary temperatures. In *quicksilver* the word *quick* preserves its original but now archaic sense "living, alive."
quick•step (kwĭk'stĕp') *n.* A march, esp. to accompany military quick time.
quick-tem•pered (kwĭk'tĕm'pərd) *adj.* Easily aroused to anger.
quick time *n.* A military marching pace of 120 steps per minute.
quick-wit•ted (kwĭk'wĭt'ĭd) *adj.* Quick to think and act : mentally alert.
quid¹ (kwĭd) *n.* A cut of something to be chewed, esp. a plug of tobacco.
quid² (kwĭd) *n., pl.* **quid** or **quids.** *esp. Brit.* A pound sterling.
quid pro quo (kwĭd' prō kwō') *n.* An equal exchange or substitution.
qui•es•cent (kwī-ĕs'ənt, kwē-) *adj.* Inactive : still. **—qui•es'cence** *n.*
qui•et (kwī'ĭt) *adj.* **1.** Making little or no sound : silent. **2.** Free of noise : hushed. **3.** Calm and unmoving : still. **4.** Free of agitation and turmoil. **5.** Restful : soothing. **6.** Marked by tranquillity. **7.** Not showy or obtrusive. —*n.* The state or quality of being quiet. —*v.* To make or become quiet. **—qui'et•ly** *adv.*
qui•e•tude (kwī'ĭ-tōōd', -tyōōd') *n.* Quiet tranquillity.
qui•e•tus (kwī-ē'təs) *n.* **1.** Death. **2.** A final discharge, as of an obligation.
quill (kwĭl) *n.* **1.** The hollow stemlike principal shaft of a feather. **2.** A large wing or tail feather. **3.** A writing pen made from a long, stiff feather. **4.** One of the sharp hollow spines of a hedgehog or porcupine.
quilt (kwĭlt) *n.* A padded bed covering. **—quilt** *v.* **—quilt'ing** *n.*
quince (kwĭns) *n.* A tree, *Cydonia oblonga*, bearing white flowers and yellow applelike fruit, edible when cooked.
qui•nine (kwī'nīn') *n.* A bitter, colorless, crystalline powder, obtained from cinchona and used as an antimalarial drug.
quinine water *n.* A carbonated beverage flavored with quinine.
quin•quen•ni•al (kwĭn-kwĕn'ē-əl, kwĭng-) *adj.* **1.** Occurring once every 5 years. **2.** Lasting for 5 years.
quin•sy (kwĭn'zē) *n.* Acute tonsillitis, often accompanied by fever and the formation of an abscess.
quint (kwĭnt) *n.* A quintuplet.
quin•tal (kwĭn'tl) *n.* See MEASUREMENT TABLE.
quin•tar (kēn-tär') *n.* See *lek* at CURRENCY TABLE.
quin•tes•sence (kwĭn-tĕs'əns) *n.* **1.** The pure, undiluted essence of something. **2.** The purest or most characteristic instance. **—quin'tes•sen'tial** (-tĭ-sĕn'shəl) *adj.*
quin•tet *also* **quin•tette** (kwĭn-tĕt') *n.* **1.** A musical composition for 5 voices or instruments. **2.** An ensemble of 5 musicians. **3.** A group of 5.
quin•til•lion (kwĭn-tĭl'yən) *n.* **1.** The cardinal number equal to 10^{18}. **2.** *esp. Brit.* The cardinal number equal to 10^{30}. **—quin•til'lion** *adj.* **—quin•til'lionth** *n.* & *adj.* & *adv.*
quin•tu•ple (kwĭn-tōō'pəl, -tyōō'-, -tŭp'əl, kwĭn'tə-pəl) *adj.* **1.** Consisting of 5 parts. **2.** Multiplied by 5. **—quin•tu'ple** *n.* & *v.*
quin•tu•plet (kwĭn-tŭp'lĭt, -tōō'plĭt, -tyōō'plĭt, kwĭn'tə-plĭt) *n.* **1.** One of 5 born at a single birth. **2.** A group or set of 5.
quin•tu•pli•cate (kwĭn-tōō'plĭ-kĭt, -tyōō'-). *adj.* **1.** QUINTUPLE 2. **2.** Reproduced or copied 5 times. —*n.* One of a set of 5 identical things. **—quin•tu'pli•cate'** (-kāt') *v.*
quip (kwĭp) *n.* A witty, offhand remark. —*v.* **quipped, quip•ping.** To make a quip. **—quip'ster** *n.*
quire (kwīr) *n.* A uniform set of 24 or sometimes 25 sheets of paper : 1/20 ream.
quirk (kwûrk) *n.* **1.** A sudden sharp bend or crook. **2.** A peculiarity : idiosyncracy. **—quirk'i•ness** *n.* **—quirk'y** *adj.*
quirt (kwûrt) *n.* A riding whip with a lash of braided rawhide.
quis•ling (kwĭz'lĭng) *n.* A traitor, esp. one collaborating as the puppet of an occupying enemy force.
quit (kwĭt) *v.* **quit** or **quit•ted, quit•ting. 1.** To depart from : leave. **2.** To give up or withdraw from <*quit* school> **3.** To abandon or put aside. **4.** To cease to perform : stop. **—quit'ter** *n.*
quit•claim (kwĭt'klām') *n.* The transfer of a title, right, or claim to another.
quite (kwīt) *adv.* **1.** To the fullest extent : completely. **2.** Actually : really. **3.** To a degree : rather <*quite* late>
Qui•to (kē'tō). Cap. of Ecuador, on the Andean plateau. *Pop.* 742,858.

quits (kwĭts) *adj.* Being on equal terms, as by payment or requital.
quit·tance (kwĭt′ns) *n.* **1.** Release from a debt, obligation, or penalty. **2.** Something given or done as recompense.
quiv·er[1] (kwĭv′ər) *v.* To shake or cause to shake with a rapid slight motion : tremble. **–quiv′er** *n.*
quiv·er[2] (kwĭv′ər) *n.* A portable case for arrows.
qui vive (kē vēv′) *n.* **1.** A challenge by a sentinel. **2.** Vigilance : alertness.
quix·ot·ic (kwĭk-sŏt′ĭk) *adj.* Idealistic in a romantic or impractical way. **–quix·ot′i·cal·ly** *adv.* **–quix′o·tism** *n.*
quiz (kwĭz) *v.* **1.** To question closely or repeatedly. **2.** To test the knowledge of by posing questions. *–n., pl.* **quiz·zes. 1.** A questioning or inquiry. **2.** A written or oral test. **–quiz′zer** *n.*
quiz·zi·cal (kwĭz′ĭ-kəl) *adj.* **1.** Showing puzzlement : perplexed. **2.** Teasing : mocking. **–quiz′zi·cal·ly** *adv.*
quoin (koin, kwoin) *n.* **1.** An exterior structural angle, as of a masonry wall. **2.** A stone forming a quoin : cornerstone.
quoit (kwoit, koit) *n.* **1. quoits** *(sing. in number).* A game in which iron or rope rings are pitched at a stake. **2.** A ring used in quoits.
quon·dam (kwŏn′dəm, -dăm′) *adj.* That once was : former.
quo·rum (kwôr′əm, kwōr′-) *n.* The minimum number of officers and members of a constituted body necessary for the valid transaction of business.
quot. *abbr.* quotation.
quo·ta (kwō′tə) *n.* **1. a.** A proportional share : allotment. **b.** A production assignment. **2.** The highest number or proportion, esp. of people, permitted admission, as to a nation, group, or institution.
quot·a·ble (kwō′tə-bəl) *adj.* Suitable for or worthy of quoting.
quo·ta·tion mark (kwō-tā′shən) *n.* Either of a pair of punctuation marks (" " *or* ' ') used esp. to designate the beginning and end of a quoted passage.
quote (kwōt) *v.* **quot·ed, quot·ing. 1.** To repeat or copy the words of (another), usu. acknowledging the source. **2.** To cite or refer to for authority or illustration. **3.** To state (a price) for securities, goods, or services. *–n. Informal.* **1.** Something quoted. **2.** A quotation mark. **–quo·ta′tion** *n.*
quoth (kwōth) *v. Archaic.* Uttered : said.
quo·tid·i·an (kwō-tĭd′ē-ən) *adj.* **1.** Recurring daily. **2.** Ordinary : everyday.
quo·tient (kwō′shənt) *n.* The quantity resulting from the division of 1 quantity by another.
qu·rush (ko͞o′rəsh) *n., pl.* **-rush** *or* **-es.** See *riyal* at CURRENCY TABLE.
q.v. *abbr.* which see (Lat. *quod vide).*
qy. *abbr.* query.

Rr

r *or* **R** (är) *n., pl.* **r's** *or* **R's. 1.** The 18th letter of the English alphabet. **2.** A speech sound represented by the letter *r.*
r *or* **R** *abbr.* **1.** radius. **2.** *Elect.* resistance. **3.** roentgen. **4.** revolution.
r. *abbr.* **1.** *or* **R.** railroad; railway. **2.** range. **3.** retired. **4.** *or* **R.** right. **5.** *or* **R.** river. **6.** *or* **R.** road. **7.** rod (unit of length).
R. *abbr.* **1.** Republican. **2.** royal.
Ra *symbol for* RADIUM.
Ra·bat (rä-bät′). Cap. of Morocco, on the Atlantic coast. *Pop.* 367,620.
rab·bet (răb′ĭt) *n.* A groove along the edge of a board cut to fit another piece to form a joint. *–v.* **1.** To cut a rabbet in. **2.** To connect by a rabbet.
rab·bi (răb′ī′) *n., pl.* **-bis. 1.** An ordained spiritual leader of a Jewish congregation. **2.** Formerly, a teacher or interpreter of Jewish law. **–rab·bin′i·cal** (rə-bĭn′ĭ-kəl), **rab·bin′ic** *adj.*
rab·bin·ate (răb′ĭn-at′) *n.* **1.** The office of a rabbi. **2.** Rabbis as a group.
rab·bit (răb′ĭt) *n., pl.* **-bits** *or* **-bit. 1.** A furry, long-eared, burrowing mammal of the family Leporidae. **2.** The fur of a rabbit.
rab·ble (răb′əl) *n.* A tumultuous crowd.
rab·ble-rous·er (răb′əl-rou′zər) *n.* A demagogue.
Rab·e·lais (răb′ə-lā′), **François.** 1494?–1553. French author. **–Rab′e·lai′se·an** (-zē-ən, -zhən) *adj.*
rab·id (răb′ĭd) *adj.* **1.** Afflicted with rabies. **2.** Extreme : fanatical. **3.** Raging : violent <*rabid* hostility> **–rab′id·ly** *adv.*
ra·bies (rā′bēz) *n.* An acute, infectious, often fatal viral disease of the central nervous system transmitted by the bite of an infected animal.
rac·coon (ră-ko͞on′) *n., pl.* **-coons** *or* **-coon. 1.** A North American mammal, *Procyon lotor,* with black, masklike facial markings and a bushy, black-ringed tail. **2.** The fur of a raccoon.
race[1] (rās) *n.* **1.** A division of the human population distinguished by physical characteristics transmitted by genes. **2.** A body of people united by a common history or nationality <the Spanish *race*> **3.** Humanity as a whole. **4.** A subspecies or breed, as of domestic animals. **–ra′cial** *adj.*
race[2] (rās) *n.* **1.** A competition of speed. **2.** A competition, as for an elective office. **3.** A rapid onward movement. **4. a.** A strong flow of water. **b.** The channel of a current of water. *–v.* **raced, rac·ing. 1.** To compete in a race (with). **2.** To move rapidly : rush. **–rac′er** *n.*
race·course (rās′kôrs′) *n.* A racetrack.
race·horse (rās′hôrs′) *n.* A horse bred and used for racing.
ra·ceme (rā-sēm′, rə-) *n.* An inflorescence in which stalked flowers are arranged along a common stem.
race·track (rās′trăk′) *n.* A course designed for racing.
rac·ism (rā′sĭz′əm) *n.* **1.** The belief that some races are inherently superior to others. **2.** Discrimination based on race. **–rac′ist** *n. & adj.*
rack (răk) *n.* **1.** A framework or stand for holding and usu. displaying something. **2.** A toothed metal bar designed to mesh with another toothed machine part. **3.** A frame on which a torture victim's body was stretched. *–v.* **1.** To place in a rack. **2.** To torture on a rack. **3.** To torment <*racked* with pain> **4.** To strain with great effort <*racked* her brain trying to remember>
rack·et[1] *also* **rac·quet** (răk′ĭt) *n.* A light bat with a handle and netting stretched tightly across an open oval frame, used to strike a ball or shuttlecock.
rack·et[2] (răk′ĭt) *n.* **1.** An uproar or din. **2.** A fraudulent or dishonest business.
rack·et·eer (răk′ĭ-tîr′) *n.* One engaged in an illegal business, esp. an extortionist.
rac·on·teur (răk′ŏn-tûr′, -ən-) *n.* An accomplished and witty storyteller.
rac·quet·ball (răk′ĭt-bôl′) *n.* A game played with a short racket and a rubber ball in a 4-walled court.
rac·y (rā′sē) *adj.* **-i·er, -i·est. 1.** Pungent : piquant. **2.** Slightly improper or indelicate. ☆***syns:*** OFF-COLOR, RISQUÉ, SPICY, SUGGESTIVE **–rac′i·ly** *adv.* **–rac′i·ness** *n.*
ra·dar (rā′där′) *n.* A device for detecting the position, velocity, and size of distant objects by analysis of radio waves reflected from their surfaces.
ra·dar·scope (rā′där-skōp′) *n.* The oscilloscope viewing screen of a radar receiver.
ra·di·al (rā′dē-əl) *adj.* **1.** Of or arranged like rays or radii. **2.** Having or marked by radiating parts. **3.** Directed along a radius.
radial tire *n.* A pneumatic tire strengthened by having the cords of its inner fabric laid at right angles to the center line of the tread.
ra·di·ant (rā′dē-ənt) *adj.* **1.** Emitting light or heat. **2.** Being or emitted as radiation. **3.** Filled with a strong, projecting quality <*radiant* with love> **4.** Glowing : brilliant. **–ra′di·ance, ra′di·an·cy** *n.*
ra·di·ate (rā′dē-āt′) *v.* **-at·ed, -at·ing. 1.** To emit rays. **2.** To issue or be transmitted in rays. **3.** To spread out from a center. **4.** To manifest glowingly.
ra·di·a·tion (rā′dē-ā′shən) *n.* **1.** An act or process of radiating. **2.** *Physics.* **a.** Emission of waves or particles. **b.** The propagating waves or particles, as light, sound, or radiant heat, emitted by radioactivity.
radiation sickness *n.* An illness caused by overexposure to radiation, ranging in severity from nausea and diarrhea to hemorrhaging and death.
ra·di·a·tor (rā′dē-ā′tər) *n.* **1.** A framework of pipes that heats the surrounding air by means of a circulation of steam or hot water. **2.** A cooling device, as in an engine.
rad·i·cal (răd′ĭ-kəl) *adj.* **1.** Arising from or reaching a root or source : basic. **2.** Drastic : extreme. **3.** Favoring or effecting basic

changes. —*n.* **1.** A supporter of basic changes, esp. political revolution. **2.** *Math.* **a.** The indicated root of a quantity. **b.** The sign (√) placed before a quantity indicating that its root is to be taken. **3.** *Chem.* An atom or group of atoms that has at least 1 unpaired electron. **—rad′i•cal•ness** *n.*

rad•i•cal•ism (răd′ĭ-kə-lĭz′əm) *n.* The beliefs or methods of political radicals.

ra•di•i (rā′dē-ī′) *n. var. pl. of* RADIUS.

ra•di•o (rā′dē-ō′) *n., pl.* **-os. 1.** The use of electromagnetic waves in the radio frequency range to transmit and receive electric signals without the use of wires. **2.** The equipment used to transmit or receive radio signals. **3.** The broadcast of programmed material to the public by radio. —*v.* **1.** To transmit (a message) by radio. **2.** To communicate (with) by radio.

ra•di•o•ac•tiv•i•ty (rā′dē-ō-ăk-tĭv′ĭ-tē) *n.* Spontaneous emission of radiation from decaying atomic nuclei or as a consequence of a nuclear reaction. **—ra′di•o•ac′tive** *adj.*

radio astronomy *n.* Study of celestial phenomena by observation and analysis of their associated radio-frequency emissions.

radio beam *n.* A focused beam of radio signals used to guide ships or aircraft.

ra•di•o•car•bon (rā′dē-ō-kär′bən) *n.* Radioactive carbon, esp. carbon 14.

radio frequency *n.* An electromagnetic wave frequency used for radio and television transmission, in the range from about 10 kc/sec to about 300,000 Mc/sec.

ra•di•o•gram (rā′dē-ō-grăm′) *n.* A message sent by wireless telegraphy.

ra•di•o•graph (rā′dē-ō-grăf′) *n.* An image produced by radiation other than light, esp. by x-rays. **—ra′di•o•graph′** *v.* **—ra′di•o•graph′ic** *adj.* **—ra′di•o•graph′i•cal•ly** *adv.* **—ra′di•og′ra•phy** (-ŏg′rə-fē) *n.*

ra•di•o•i•so•tope (rā′dē-ō-ī′sə-tōp′) *n.* A radioactive isotope of an element.

ra•di•ol•o•gy (rā′dē-ŏl′ə-jē) *n.* The use of x-rays and other forms of radiation to diagnose and treat diseases. **—ra′di•o•log′i•cal** (-ə-lŏj′ĭ-kəl) *adj.* **—ra′di•ol′o•gist** *n.*

ra•di•om•e•ter (rā′dē-ŏm′ĭ-tər) *n.* A device for detecting and measuring radiation. **—ra′di•o•met′ric** (-ō-mĕt′rĭk) *adj.* **—ra′di•om′e•try** *n.*

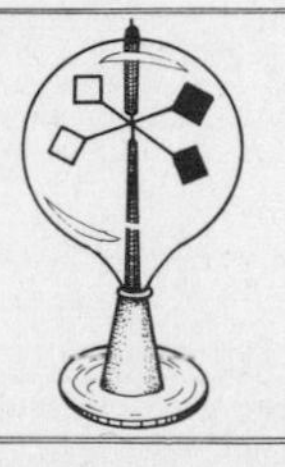

radiometer

ra•di•o•sonde (rā′dē-ō-sŏnd′) *n.* An instrument carried aloft usu. by balloon for transmitting meteorological data.

ra•di•o•te•leg•ra•phy (rā′dē-ō-tə-lĕg′rə-fē) *n.* Wireless telegraphy. **—ra′di•o•tel′e•graph′** (-tĕl′ĭ-grăf′) *n.*

ra•di•o•tel•e•phone (rā′dē-ō-tĕl′ə-fōn′) *n.* A telephone system for 2-way communication by means of radio. **—ra′di•o•te•leph′o•ny** (-tə-lĕf′ə-nē) *n.*

radio telescope *n.* A radio receiver for detecting and analyzing radio waves of extraterrestrial origin.

ra•di•o•ther•a•py (rā′dē-ō-thĕr′ə-pē) *n.* Treatment of disease by radiation.

radio wave *n.* A radio-frequency electromagnetic wave.

rad•ish (răd′ĭsh) *n.* A plant, *Raphanus sativus,* having a sharp-tasting edible root.

ra•di•um (rā′dē-əm) *n. Symbol* **Ra** A rare brilliant-white, highly radioactive metallic element used in radiotherapy.

ra•di•us (rā′dē-əs) *n., pl.* **-di•i** (-dē-ī′) *or* **-us•es. 1. a.** A line segment between the center of a circle and any point on its circumference. **b.** A line segment between the center of a sphere and any point on its surface. **2.** A measure of circular area <every town within a *radius* of 50 miles> **3.** The shorter and thicker of the 2 bones of the forearm.

ra•don (rā′dŏn′) *n. Symbol* **Rn** A colorless, radioactive, heavy gaseous element used in radiotherapy.

raf•fi•a (răf′ē-ə) *n.* A fiber from the leaves of an African palm tree, *Raphia ruffia,* used for mats and baskets.

raff•ish (răf′ĭsh) *adj.* **1.** Showy : flashy. **2.** Jaunty. **—raff′ish•ness** *n.*

raf•fle (răf′əl) *n.* A lottery in which a number of persons buy chances to win a prize. **—raf′fle** *v.*

raft¹ (răft) *n.* A low, floating structure of logs, planks, etc., used for water transport or as a platform. **—raft** *v.*

raft² (răft) *n. Informal.* A great number, amount, or collection.

raft•er (răf′tər) *n.* One of the sloping parallel beams that support a pitched roof.

rag¹ (răg) *n.* A scrap of cloth.

rag² (răg) *v.* **ragged, rag•ging.** *Slang.* **1.** To taunt : tease. **2.** To scold.

rag³ (răg) *n.* A piece of ragtime music.

ra•ga (rä′gə) *n.* A traditional form in Hindu music, usu. having a thematic set of tones and improvised variations.

rag•a•muf•fin (răg′ə-mŭf′ĭn) *n.* A dirty or untidily dressed child.

rage (rāj) *n.* **1. a.** Violent anger. **b.** A fit of anger. **2.** A craze : fad. —*v.* **raged, rag•ing. 1.** To be violently angry. **2.** To move or spread with violent force.

rag•ged (răg′ĭd) *adj.* **1.** Tattered. **2.** Dressed in tattered clothes. **3.** Having rough edges. **4.** Uneven <a *ragged* performance> **—rag′ged•ly** *adv.*

rag•lan (răg′lən) *n.* A loose garment with slanted shoulder seams and sleeves that extend in 1 piece to the neckline.

ra•gout (ră-gōō′) *n.* A thick, spicy stew of meat and vegetables.

rag•time (răg′tīm′) *n.* A jazz style marked by an elaborately syncopated melody and a steadily accented accompaniment.

rag•weed (răg′wēd′) *n.* Any of several weeds of the genus *Ambrosia,* whose airborne pollen is a chief cause of hay fever.

raid (rād) *n.* **1.** A surprise attack, esp. by a small military force. **2.** A sudden and forcible entry. —*v.* To make a raid (on).

rail¹ (rāl) *n.* **1.** A horizontal bar supported at both ends or at intervals by posts, as in fences. **2.** A steel bar usu. used in pairs as a track for wheeled vehicles. **3.** A railroad. —*v.* To enclose or furnish with a rail.

rail² (rāl) *n.* A small brownish marsh bird of the family Rallidae.

rail³ (rāl) *v.* To condemn or complain bitterly or abusively. **—rail′er** *n.*

rail•ing (rā′lĭng) *n.* A fence, balustrade, or barrier made of rails.

rail•ler•y (rā′lə-rē) *n., pl.* **-ies.** Good-natured teasing : banter.

rail•road (rāl′rōd′) *n.* **1.** A road made of parallel steel rails on a bed of ties that provides a track for trains. **2.** A complete system of railroad track, along with stations, rolling stock, and other property. —*v.* **1.** To transport by railroad. **2.** *Informal.* **a.** To push through quickly so as to forestall discussion <*railroad* a bill through the legislature> **b.** To convict hastily or unfairly.

rail•way (rāl′wā′) *n.* **1.** A railroad. **2.** A runway for wheeled vehicles.

rai•ment (rā′mənt) *n.* Clothing.

rain (rān) *n.* **1.** Water condensed from atmospheric vapor, falling to earth in drops. **2.** An abundant outpouring : shower. —*v.* **1.** To fall as or like rain. **2.** To send or pour down abundantly. **—rain out.** To force the postponement of because of rain. **—rain′i•ness** *n.* **—rain′y** *adj.*

rain•bow (rān′bō′) *n.* An arc of spectral colors, esp. one appearing as a result of the refractive dispersion of sunlight in raindrops or mist.

rain check *n.* **1.** The stub of a ticket that entitles a holder to admission at a future date if the scheduled event is posponed because of bad weather. **2.** A postponement of the acceptance or fulfillment of an offer.

rain•coat (rān′kōt′) *n.* A waterproof coat.

rain•fall (rān′fôl′) *n.* **1.** A fall of rain. **2.** *Meteorol.* PRECIPITATION 3b.

rain forest *n.* A dense usu. tropical evergreen forest having an annual rainfall of at least 100 in.

rain•mak•ing (rān′mā′kĭng) *n.* The action or ceremony of producing or trying to bring on rain. **—rain′mak′er** *n.*

rain•storm (rān′stôrm′) *n.* A storm with heavy rain.

rain•wa•ter (rān′wô′tər, -wŏt′ər) *n.* Water that has fallen as rain.

raise (rāz) *v.* **raised, rais•ing. 1.** To cause to move upward : lift. **2.** To build : erect. **3.** To cause to appear <The sting *raised* a bump.> **4.** To increase the quantity, size, or worth of. **5.** To increase the strength, degree, or pitch of. **6.** To increase the rank or status of : promote. **7.** To grow or breed. **8.** To bring up : rear. **9.** To put forward for consideration. **10.** To stir up : arouse. **11.** To amass : collect <*raise* funds> **12.** To cause (dough) to rise. —*n.* An increase, as in amount or pay.

rai•sin (rā′zĭn) *n.* A dried usu. seedless grape.

rai•son d'ê•tre (rā′zôN dĕt′rə) *n.* Reason for existing.

ra•jah *or* **ra•ja** (rä′jə) *n.* A prince in India or the East Indies.

rake¹ (rāk) *n.* A garden tool with a long handle and teeth at the head. —*v.* **raked, rak•ing. 1.** To gather, loosen, or smooth with or as if with a rake. **2.** To gain in abundance <*raking* in the cash> **3.** To bring to light : uncover <*rake* up old scandals> **4.** To examine thoroughly <*rake* over the evidence> **5.** To aim heavy gunfire along the length of. **–rak′er** *n.*

rake[2] (rāk) *n.* A roué : libertine.

rake[3] (rāk) *n.* A slope, as of a ship's mast. *–v.* To slant or incline.

rake-off (rāk′ôf′, -ŏf′) *n. Slang.* A percentage of the profits.

rak•ish[1] (rā′kĭsh) *adj.* **1.** *Naut.* Trim and streamlined. **2.** Jaunty or showy. **–rak′ish•ly** *adv.* **–rak′ish•ness** *n.*

rak•ish[2] (rā′kĭsh) *adj.* Like a rake : dissolute. **–rak′ish•ly** *adv.* **–rak′ish•ness** *n.*

rale *also* **râle** (räl) *n.* An abnormal or pathological respiratory sound.

Ra•leigh (rô′lē). Cap. of N.C., in the EC part. *Pop.* 149,771.

ral•ly (răl′ē) *v.* **-lied, -ly•ing. 1.** To gather or call together for a common purpose : assemble. **2.** To restore to order : reassemble. **3.** To rouse from decline or inactivity. **4.** To recover from a setback or disadvantage. *–n., pl.* **-lies. 1.** An assembly, esp. one intended to inspire enthusiasm. **2.** A sharp improvement or abrupt recovery.

ram (răm) *n.* **1.** A male sheep. **2.** A bar-shaped device used to drive, batter, or crush by impact. *–v.* **rammed, ram•ming. 1.** To strike against heavily : butt. **2.** To force into place. **3.** To stuff : cram.

RAM *abbr. Computer Sci.* random-access memory.

ram•ble (răm′bəl) *v.* **-bled, -bling. 1.** To walk aimlessly. **2.** To digress. **–ram′ble** *n.* **–ram′bling•ly** *adv.*

ram•bler (răm′blər) *n.* **1.** One that rambles. **2.** A climbing rose.

ram•bunc•tious (răm-bŭngk′shəs) *adj.* Unruly : boisterous.

ram•ie (răm′ē) *n.* A flexible fiber derived from the stems of an Asian plant, used in fabrics and cordage.

ram•i•fy (răm′ə-fī′) *v.* **-fied, -fy•ing. 1.** To branch out. **2.** To have branchlike consequences. **–ram′i•fi•ca′tion** *n.*

ramp (rămp) *n.* An inclined passage or roadway connecting different levels.

ram•page (răm′pāj′) *n.* A course of violent, destructive, or unrestrained action. *–v.* (răm-pāj′) **-paged, -pag•ing.** To move about wildly. **–ram•pa′geous** *adj.*

ram•pant (răm′pənt) *adj.* Growing or extending rapidly and without control : rife. **–ram′pan•cy** *n.* **–ram′pant•ly** *adv.*

ram•part (răm′pärt′, -pərt) *n.* A defensive embankment, often with a parapet.

ram•rod (răm′rŏd′) *n.* **1.** A metal rod for plunging the charge into a muzzle-loading firearm. **2.** A rod for cleaning the barrel of a firearm.

ram•shack•le (răm′shăk′əl) *adj.* Falling apart from poor construction or upkeep.

ran (răn) *v. p.t. of* RUN.

ranch (rănch) *n.* **1.** A large farm for raising livestock, as beef cattle, sheep, or horses. **2.** A large farm specializing in a kind of crop or animal <a mink *ranch*> *–v.* To work on or run a ranch.

†**ran•che•ri•a** (răn′chə-rē′ə) *n. SW U.S.* **1.** A Mexican herdsmen's hut. **2.** An Indian village.

†**ran•che•ro** (răn-châr′ō) *n., pl.* **-ros.** *SW U.S.* A rancher.

†**ran•cho** (răn′chō) *n., pl.* **-chos.** *SW U.S.* **1.** A hut or group of huts for housing ranch workers. **2.** A ranch.

ranch house *n.* A 1-story house with a low-pitched roof.

ran•cid (răn′sĭd) *adj.* Having the rank odor or taste of spoiled fats or oils : putrid. **–ran•cid′i•ty, ran′cid•ness** *n.*

ran•cor (răng′kər) *n.* Bitter long-lasting resentment. **–ran′cor•ous** *adj.*

rand (rănd) *n.* See CURRENCY TABLE.

R & D *abbr.* research and development.

ran•dom (răn′dəm) *adj.* **1.** Having no specific pattern or purpose : haphazard. **2.** Selected in such a way that each member of a set has an equal chance of being chosen.

ran•dom-ac•cess (răn′dəm-ăk′sĕs′) *adj. Computer Sci.* Allowing access to stored data without regard to data sequence.

R and R *abbr.* rest and recreation.

rang (răng) *v. p.t. of* RING[2].

range (rānj) *n.* **1.** An extent included or reached, esp. by perception, ability, or knowledge. **2.** An area of activity : sphere. **3.** An extent of variation <the daily temperature *range*> **4.** The maximum effective distance that can be traversed <within mortar *range*> **5.** A place for shooting at targets or testing weaponry. **6.** A tract of open land for grazing livestock. **7.** An act of roaming. **8.** A region in which a plant or animal is to be found. **9.** An extended series or chain, esp. of mountains. **10.** A large cooking stove with an oven and several burners. ☆***syns:*** EXTENT, ORBIT, REACH, REALM, SCOPE, SPHERE *–v.* **ranged, rang•ing. 1.** To arrange in order, esp. in lines or rows. **2.** To classify. **3.** To roam or wander freely. **4.** To explore. **5.** To extend in a particular direction. **6.** To vary within specified limits.

rang•er (rān′jər) *n.* **1.** A rover. **2.** An armed, usu. mounted law officer. **3.** One who patrols and guards a forest or park.

Ran•goon (răng-gōōn′). Cap. of Burma, in the C part. *Pop.* 2,276,000.

rang•y (rān′jē) *adj.* **-i•er, -i•est.** Thin and long-limbed. **–rang′i•ness** *n.*

ra•ni *also* **ra•nee** (rä′nē) *n., pl.* **-nis** *also* **-nees.** The wife of a rajah.

rank[1] (răngk) *n.* **1.** Relative position in an ordered group. **2.** Position or status, as in society. **3.** Eminent position. **4.** An official grade <the *rank* of corporal> **5.** A row, line, or series. **6.** A line of soldiers or vehicles standing side by side in close order. **7. ranks.** Personnel, esp. enlisted military personnel. *–v.* **1.** To place in a row or rows. **2.** To classify. **3.** To hold a specified rank <*ranking* 2nd in the class> **4.** To take precedence over.

rank[2] (răngk) *adj.* **1.** Growing profusely or unmanageably <*rank* weeds> **2.** Strong and offensive in odor or taste. **3.** Indecent. **–rank′ly** *adv.* **–rank′ness** *n.*

rank and file *n.* **1.** The troops of an army. **2.** Ordinary members, as of a group or organization.

ran•kle (răng′kəl) *v.* **-kled, -kling. 1.** To be a source of persistent irritation or resentment. **2.** To become sore or inflamed.

ran•sack (răn′săk′) *v.* **1.** To search or rummage thoroughly. **2.** To pillage.

ran•som (răn′səm) *n.* **1.** The release of a detained person or property in return for payment. **2.** The price demanded or payment made. **–ran′som** *v.*

rant (rănt) *v.* To speak loudly, wildly, and at length : rave. **–rant′er** *n.*

rap[1] (răp) *v.* **rapped, rap•ping. 1.** To hit sharply : strike. **2.** To utter sharply. **3.** To criticize : blame. *–n.* **1.** A quick knock or blow. **2.** A reprimand. **3.** *Slang.* Blame or punishment.

rap[2] (răp) *v.* **rapped, rap•ping.** *Slang.* To converse freely and at length.

ra•pa•cious (rə-pā′shəs) *adj.* **1.** Feeding on live prey. **2.** Ravenous : voracious. **3.** Plundering. **–ra•pa′cious•ly** *adv.* **–ra•pa′cious•ness, ra•pac′i•ty** (rə-păs′ĭ-tē) *n.*

rape[1] (rāp) *n.* **1.** The crime of forcing another person to submit to sexual intercourse. **2.** The act of seizing and carrying off : abduction. **3.** Abusive treatment : violation. **–rape** *v.* **–rap′ist** *n.*

rape[2] (rāp) *n.* A Eurasian plant, *Brassica napus,* cultivated as fodder and for its oil-rich seeds.

Raph•a•el (răf′ē-əl, rā′fē-). 1483–1520. Italian painter and architect.

rap•id (răp′ĭd) *adj.* Very fast : swift. *–n. often* **rapids.** A fast-moving, steeply descending section of a river. **–ra•pid′i•ty** (rə-pĭd′ĭ-tē), **rap′id•ness** *n.*

rapid eye movement *n.* REM.

ra•pi•er (rā′pē-ər, rāp′yər) *n.* A long, slender, 2-edged sword.

rap•ine (răp′ĭn) *n.* Forcible seizure of another's property : plunder.

rap•pel (ră-pĕl′) *n.* The method of descending a sheer face, as of a cliff, by means of a double rope passed under the thigh and over the opposite shoulder. **–rap•pel′** *v.*

rap•port (ră-pôr′, -pōr′, rə-) *n.* A relationship, esp. a trustful or harmonious one.

rap•proche•ment (rä′prôsh-mäN′) *n.* A renewal of cordial relations, as between 2 governments.

rap•scal•lion (răp-skăl′yən) *n.* A rascal.

rapt (răpt) *adj.* **1.** Deeply delighted : enraptured. **2.** Deeply absorbed : engrossed.

rap•tor (răp′tər) *n.* A bird of prey. **–rap•to′ri•al** (-tôr′ē-əl, -tōr′-) *adj.*

rap•ture (răp′chər) *n.* A state or expression of ecstasy. **–rap′tur•ous** *adj.*

ra•ra a•vis (râr′ə ā′vĭs) *n.* One that is rare or unique.

rare[1] (râr) *adj.* **rar•er, rar•est. 1.** Occurring infrequently : uncommon. **2.** Highly valued owing to uncommonness : special. **3.** Thin in density : rarefied. **–rare′ly** *adv.* **–rare′ness** *n.* **–rar′i•ty** *n.*

rare[2] (râr) *adj.* **rar•er, rar•est.** Cooked only a short time <*rare* beef>

▲word history: The adjective *rare[2]* meaning "lightly cooked" referred only to eggs until modern times. Its application to other foods, esp. meats, was considered an Americanism until recently, when it was adopted into British usage.

rare-earth element (râr′ûrth′) *n.* Any of the metallic elements with atomic numbers 57 through 71.

rar•e•fy (râr′ə-fī′, răr′-) *v.* **-fied, -fy•ing. 1.** To make or become thin, light, or less dense. **2.** To refine : purify. **–rar′e•fac′tion** *n.* **–rar′e•fac′tive** *adj.*

rar•ing (râr′ĭng) *adj. Informal.* Full of enthusiasm : eager <*raring* to go>

ras•cal (răs'kəl) *n.* **1.** A dishonest person : rogue. **2.** A playfully mischievous person. **–ras•cal'i•ty** *n.* **–ras'cal•ly** *adj.*

rash[1] (răsh) *adj.* Marked by ill-considered boldness or haste : impetuous.

rash[2] (răsh) *n.* **1.** A skin eruption. **2.** An outbreak of many occurrences <a *rash* of house fires>

rash•er (răsh'ər) *n.* **1.** A thin slice of fried or broiled bacon. **2.** A dish of rashers.

rasp (răsp) *n.* **1.** A coarse file having raised, pointed projections. **2.** A grating, abrasive sound or voice. *–v.* **1.** To scrape or file with or as if with a rasp. **2.** To utter in a grating voice. **3.** To grate upon (e.g., one's nerves). **–rasp'er** *n.* **–rasp'y** *adj.*

rasp•ber•ry (răz'bĕr'ē) *n.* **1.** A shrubby, usu. thorny plant of the genus *Rubus,* as *R. strigosus* of E North America, bearing edible, usu. reddish berries. **2.** *Slang.* A jeering or contemptuous sound made by exhaling so that the protruded tongue vibrates against the lips.

rat (răt) *n.* **1.** A long-tailed rodent similar to but larger than the mouse, esp. one of the genus *Rattus.* **2.** *Slang.* A despicable or treacherous person. *–v.* **rat•ted, rat•ting. 1.** To hunt or catch rats, esp. with dogs. **2.** *Slang.* To betray one's comrades.

ratch•et (răch'ĭt) *n.* A device consisting of a pawl that permits a wheel or bar to move in only 1 direction by engaging its sloping teeth.

rate[1] (rāt) *n.* **1.** A quantity measured with respect to another measured or fixed quantity <a *rate* of speed of 20 mph> **2.** A measure of a part to a whole : proportion <the mortality *rate*> **3.** A charge or payment calculated by means of a proportion or ratio. **4.** A level of quality. *–v.* **rat•ed, rat•ing. 1.** To calculate the value of : appraise. **2.** To assign or be assigned to a rank or class. **3.** *Informal.* To deserve : merit. **4.** *Informal.* To have status. **–at any rate. 1.** In any case. **2.** At least.

rate[2] (rāt) *v.* **rat•ed, rat•ing.** To berate.

rate of exchange *n.* The ratio at which a unit of currency may be exchanged for another.

rath•er (răth'ər, rä'*th*ər) *adv.* **1.** Preferably. **2.** With more reason or justification. **3.** More accurately : exactly. **4.** Somewhat. **5.** On the contrary.

raths•kel•ler (rät'skĕl-ər, răth'-) *n.* A restaurant in the style of a German tavern.

rat•i•fy (răt'ə-fī') *v.* **-fied, -fy•ing.** To approve formally and thereby validate <*ratify* a treaty> **–rat'i•fi•ca'tion** *n.*

rat•ing (rā'tĭng) *n.* **1.** A position assigned on a scale : standing. **2.** An evaluation of financial status <a credit *rating*>

ra•tio (rā'shō, -shē-ō') *n., pl.* **-tios. 1.** The quotient of a pair of numbers, used as a means of comparing them. **2.** A relationship between the amounts or sizes of 2 things, expressed as a quotient : proportion.

ra•ti•oc•i•nate (răsh'ē-ŏs'ə-nāt') *v.* **-nat•ed, -nat•ing.** To think methodically : reason. **–ra'ti•oc'i•na'tion** *n.* **–ra'ti•oc'i•na'tive** *adj.* **–ra'ti•oc'i•na'tor** *n.*

ra•tion (răsh'ən, rā'shən) *n.* **1.** A fixed share or portion, esp. of allotted food. **2. rations.** Food allotted. *–v.* **1.** To provide with rations. **2.** To distribute : allot. **3.** To restrict to limited amounts.

ra•tio•nal (răsh'ə-nəl) *adj.* **1.** Having or exercising the power to reason. **2.** Of or consistent with reason. **3.** Of sound mind : sane. **4.** *Math.* Of or being a number expressible as an integer or a quotient of 2 integers. **–ra'tion•al'i•ty** *n.*

ra•tio•nale (răsh'ə-năl') *n.* **1.** A fundamental reason : rational basis. **2.** An exposition of guiding principles : justification.

ra•tio•nal•ism (răsh'ə-nə-lĭz'əm) *n.* The view that reason constitutes the only valid basis for action, belief, or faith. **–ra'tio•nal•ist** *n.* **–ra'tio•nal•is'tic** *adj.*

ra•tio•nal•ize (răsh'ə-nə-līz') *v.* **-ized, -iz•ing. 1.** To make rational. **2.** To cause to seem rational. **3.** To devise self-satisfying but incorrect explanations for (e.g., one's behavior). **–ra'tio•nal•i•za'tion** *n.*

rat•line *also* **rat•lin** (răt'lĭn) *n.* Any of the small ropes fastened horizontally to the shrouds of a ship.

rat•tan (ră-tăn', rə-) *n.* An Asian climbing palm of the genera *Calamus, Daemonorops,* or *Plectomia,* with strong, pliant stems used to make wickerwork.

rat•tle (răt'l) *v.* **-tled, -tling. 1.** To make or cause to make a quick succession of short, sharp sounds. **2.** To move with such sounds. **3.** To chatter. **4.** *Informal.* To unnerve : fluster. *–n.* **1.** A quick series of short, sharp sounds. **2.** A device, as a toy, that rattles when shaken. **3.** One or all of the dry, horny structures at the end of a rattlesnake's tail.

rat•tler (răt'lər) *n.* A rattlesnake.

rat•tle•snake (răt'l-snāk') *n.* A venomous New World snake of the genera *Crotalus* or *Sistrurus,* having a rattle at the end of the tail.

rat•tling (răt'lĭng) *Informal.* *–adj.* **1.** Animated : brisk. **2.** Very good. *–adv.* Especially <a *rattling* good party>

rat•ty (răt'ē) *adj.* **-ti•er, -ti•est. 1.** Characteristic of or overrun by rats. **2.** *Slang.* Dilapidated : shabby.

rau•cous (rô'kəs) *adj.* **1.** Loud and hoarse : strident. **2.** Boisterous : disorderly.

raun•chy (rôn'chē, rän'-) *adj.* **-chi•er, -chi•est.** *Slang.* **1.** Filthy : grubby. **2.** Obscene : vulgar <*raunchy* jokes> **–raun'chi•ly** *adv.* **–raun'chi•ness** *n.*

rav•age (răv'ĭj) *v.* **-aged, -ag•ing. 1.** To bring heavy destruction on : devastate. **2.** To sack : pillage. *–n.* **1.** The act of ravaging. **2.** Heavy damage. **–rav'ag•er** *n.*

rave (rāv) *v.* **raved, rav•ing. 1.** To speak irrationally or wildly. **2.** To rage : roar. **3.** To be wildly enthusiastic. *–n.* **1.** The act of raving. **2.** *Informal.* An extravagantly enthusiastic review or opinion.

rav•el (răv'əl) *v.* **-eled, -el•ing** *also* **elled, -el•ling. 1.** To separate the fibers or strands of (e.g., rope) : unravel. **2.** To complicate : confuse. *–n.* **1.** A raveled part. **2.** A loose thread. **3.** A tangle. **–rav'el•er** *n.*

rav•el•ing *also* **rav•el•ling** (răv'ə-lĭng) *n.* A thread separated from woven material.

ra•ven (rā'vən) *n.* A large bird, *Corvus corax,* with black plumage and a croaking cry. *–adj.* Black and glossy.

rav•en•ous (răv'ə-nəs) *adj.* **1.** Extremely hungry. **2.** Rapacious. **3.** Greedy. ☆**syns:** FAMISHED, HUNGRY, STARVING

ra•vine (rə-vēn') *n.* A steep, narrow cut in the earth's surface.

rav•i•o•li (răv'ē-ō'lē, rä'vē-) *pl.n.* Small casings of pasta filled with meat or cheese.

rav•ish (răv'ĭsh) *v.* **1.** To seize and carry off by force. **2.** To rape. **3.** To overwhelm with delight. **–rav'ish•ment** *n.*

rav•ish•ing (răv'ĭ-shĭng) *adj.* Alluring.

raw (rô) *adj.* **1.** Uncooked. **2. a.** Not refined or processed. **b.** Not coated or treated <*raw* wood> **3.** Inexperienced <*raw* recruits> **4.** Recently applied : fresh. **5.** Inflamed : sore. **6.** Damp and chilly. **7.** Unfair <a *raw* deal> **8.** Coarse : obscene. **–raw'ly** *adv.* **–raw'ness** *n.*

raw•boned (rô'bōnd') *adj.* Having a lean, gaunt, bony frame.

raw•hide (rô'hīd') *n.* **1.** The untanned hide of cattle. **2.** A whip or thong made of rawhide.

ray[1] (rā) *n.* **1.** A thin line or narrow beam of radiation, esp. visible light. **2.** A small amount : trace. **3. a.** A straight line extending from a point. **b.** A structure having this form, as a bony spine or a daisy petal.

ray[2] (rā) *n.* A marine fish of the order Rajiformes or Batoidei, having a horizontally flattened body and narrow tail.

ray•on (rā'ŏn') *n.* **1.** A synthetic textile fiber produced by forcing a cellulose solution through fine spinnerets. **2.** Fabric knit or woven from rayon.

raze (rāz) *v.* **razed, raz•ing.** To tear down : demolish.

ra•zor (rā'zər) *n.* An implement with a sharp-edged blade, used esp. for shaving.

razz (răz) *v. Slang.* To taunt with loud, scornful noises : heckle.

Rb *symbol for* RUBIDIUM.

rbi or **r.b.i.** *abbr. Baseball.* run (or runs) batted in.

rd *abbr.* rod (unit of length).

RD or **R.D.** *abbr.* rural delivery.

rd. *abbr.* **1.** or **Rd.** road. **2.** round.

re (rē, rā) *prep.* In reference to.

Re *symbol for* RHENIUM.

re– *pref.* **1.** Again : anew <*re*build> **2.** Backwards : back <*re*act> See below for a list of self-explanatory words formed with the prefix **re–.**

reach (rēch) *v.* **1.** To stretch out (a bodily part). **2.** To touch or

reabandon
reabsorb
reabsorption
reaccept
reaccommodate
reaccompany
reacquire
readapt
readdress
readjourn
readjournment
readmission
readmit
readmittance
readopt
readorn
readvance
reanimate
reanimation
reannex
reanoint
reappear
reappearance
reapply
reappoint
reappointment
reargue
reargument
reascend
reascent
reassemble
reassembly
reassert
reassertion
reassign
reassimilate
reassimilation
reassociate
reassume
reassumption
reattach
reattack
reattain
reattempt

try to grasp by stretching <couldn't *reach* the top shelf> **3.** To arrive at <*reach* a verdict> **4.** To succeed in communicating with. **5.** To extend (to). **6.** To amount to : aggregate. —*n.* **1.** The act or ability of stretching or thrusting out. **2.** The distance something can reach. **3.** An unbroken expanse. **4.** The range of one's understanding.

re•act (rē-ăkt′) *v.* **1.** To act in response to a stimulus. **2.** To act in opposition. **3.** *Chem.* To undergo chemical change. **—re•ac′tant** *n.* **—re•ac′tive** *adj.*

re•ac•tance (rē-ăk′təns) *n.* Opposition to alternating electric current flow caused in a circuit by inductance and capacitance.

re•ac•tion (rē-ăk′shən) *n.* **1.** A response to a stimulus or the condition resulting from such a response. **2.** A contrary or opposing action. **3.** A political tendency to oppose progress or favor a return to former conditions. **4.** A chemical transformation or change. **5.** *Physics.* A nuclear reaction.

re•ac•tion•ar•y (rē-ăk′shə-nĕr′ē) *adj.* Opposing progress or favoring a return to former conditions. **—re•ac′tion•ar′y** *n.*

re•ac•tor (rē-ăk′tər) *n.* **1.** One that reacts. **2.** A nuclear reactor.

read (rēd) *v.* **read** (rĕd), **read•ing. 1.** To look through and take in the meaning of (written or printed words or symbols). **2.** To speak aloud the words of (written or printed material). **3.** To interpret the meaning of <*reading* the clues> **4.** To determine the thoughts or intent of <*read* someone's mind> **5.** To predict or foretell. **6.** To receive or comprehend (e.g. a radio message). **7.** To study <*read* philosophy> **8.** To learn by reading. **9.** To indicate or register <The speedometer *read* 60.> **10.** To have a certain wording or literary quality <How does the title *read?*> **—read′a•bil′i•ty, read′a•ble•ness** *n.*

read•ing (rē′dĭng) *n.* **1.** Written or printed matter. **2.** A public recitation of written material. **3.** An interpretation. **4.** A specific form or variation of a text. **5.** Information indicated, as by a gauge.

read•out *also* **read-out** (rēd′out′) *n. Computer Sci.* A presentation of data from storage or calculations.

read•y (rĕd′ē) *adj.* **-i•er, -i•est. 1.** Prepared or available for service or action. **2.** Mentally disposed : willing. **3.** Prompt in understanding or reacting <a *ready* wit> —*v.* **-ied, -y•ing.** To cause to be ready. **—read′i•ly** *adv.* **—read′i•ness** *n.*

read•y-made (rĕd′ē-mād′) *adj.* Already made or prepared <*ready-made* pie crust>

Rea•gan (rā′gən, rē′-), **Ronald Wilson.** b. 1911. 40th U.S. President (since 1981).

re•a•gent (rē-ā′jənt) *n.* A substance used in a chemical reaction to detect, measure, or yield other substances.

re•al (rē′əl, rēl) *adj.* **1.** Not imaginary or pretended : actual. **2.** Authentic or genuine <*real* gold> **3.** Essential : basic. **4.** Serious : substantial. **5.** *Law.* Of or constituting fixed or stationary property, as buildings or land. ☆*syns:* SUBSTANTIAL, SUBSTANTIVE, TANGIBLE —*adv. Informal.* Very.

real estate *n.* Land owned as property, along with its natural resources and permanent buildings.

re•al•ism (rē′ə-lĭz′əm) *n.* **1.** Concern with factual truth and things as they really are : practicality. **2.** Artistic representation intended as an unidealized portrayal of objective reality. **—re′al•ist** *n.* **—re′al•is′tic** *adj.* **—re′al•is′ti•cal•ly** *adv.*

re•al•i•ty (rē-ăl′ĭ-tē) *n., pl.* **-ties. 1.** The quality or state of being actual or true. **2.** One that is real. **3.** The totality of all existing things.

re•al•ize (rē′ə-līz′) *v.* **-ized, -iz•ing. 1.** To comprehend fully or correctly. **2.** To make real : fulfill <*realized* her potential> **3.** To obtain or achieve <*realize* a profit> **—re′al•iz′a•ble** *adj.* **—re′al•i•za′tion** *n.*

re•al•ly (rē′ə-lē, rē′lē) *adv.* **1.** In actual fact. **2.** Truly. **3.** Indeed.

realm (rĕlm) *n.* **1.** A kingdom. **2.** A field or sphere : domain.

real number *n.* A rational or irrational number.

re•al•po•li•tik (rā-äl′pō′lĭ-tēk′) *n.* A diplomatic policy based on the aggressive pursuit of national interests without regard for ethical or philosophical considerations.

real time *n. Computer Sci.* The actual time in which a physical process under computer study or control occurs.

Re•al•tor (rē′əl-tər, -tôr′). A collective mark for a real-estate agent belonging to the National Association of Realtors.

re•al•ty (rē′əl-tē) *n., pl.* **-ties.** Real estate.

ream¹ (rēm) *n.* **1.** A quantity of paper, usu. 500 sheets. **2.** *often* **reams.** A great amount.

ream² (rēm) *v.* **1.** To enlarge or shape (e.g., a hole) with or as if with a reamer. **2.** To squeeze out (material) with a reamer.

ream•er (rē′mər) *n.* **1.** A tool for enlarging or shaping holes. **2.** A juicer with a conical, ridged center.

reap (rēp) *v.* **1.** To cut and gather (e.g., grain), as with a scythe or reaper. **2.** To harvest a crop from <*reap* a wheat field> **3.** To gain as a result of effort.

reap•er (rē′pər) *n.* One that reaps, esp. a machine for harvesting.

rear¹ (rîr) *n.* **1.** A hind part. **2.** A point or area farthest from the front. —*adj.* Of, at, or in the rear. **—rear′most′** *adj.*

rear² (rîr) *v.* **1.** To care for during early life. **2.** To lift upright : raise. **3.** To erect : build. **4.** To tend (plants or animals). **5.** To rise on the hind legs, as a horse.

rear admiral *n.* A naval officer ranking below a vice admiral and above a captain.

rear•ward (rîr′wərd) *adj.* & *adv.* At or toward the rear. **—rear′wards** *adv.*

rea•son (rē′zən) *n.* **1.** The motive or basis for an action, decision, feeling, or belief. **2.** An underlying cause or fact that gives logical justification <no *reason* to delay> **3.** The ability or capacity for rational thought. **4.** Mental balance : sanity. —*v.* **1.** To use reason : think logically. **2.** To talk or discuss logically. **3.** To decide or determine by logical thinking. **—rea′son•ing** *n.*

rea•son•a•ble (rē′zə-nə-bəl) *adj.* **1.** Able to reason : rational. **2.** Consistent with reason : logical. **3.** Not extreme : moderate <*reasonable* rates> **—rea′son•a•bly** *adv.*

re•bate (rē′bāt′) *n.* A deduction from an amount charged or a return of part of a price paid. —*v.* (*also* rĭ-bāt′) **-bat•ed, -bat•ing.** To return (part of an amount) or deduct from (an amount due).

re•bel (rĭ-bĕl′) *v.* **-belled, -bel•ling. 1.** To refuse allegiance to and oppose by force an established authority. **2.** To defy or resist established convention. **3.** To feel strong unwillingness or revulsion. —*n.* **reb•el** (rĕb′əl). One who rebels or is rebellious.

re•bel•lion (rĭ-bĕl′yən) *n.* **1.** An uprising designed to change or overthrow an existing government or authority. **2.** Open defiance toward an authority or convention. ☆*syns:* INSURGENCE, INSURRECTION, MUTINY, REVOLT, UPRISING.

re•bel•lious (rĭ-bĕl′yəs) *adj.* **1.** Taking part in or favoring rebellion. **2.** Resisting direction or control : unruly.

re•birth (rē-bûrth′, rē′bûrth′) *n.* **1.** A reincarnation. **2.** A revival.

re•born (rē-bôrn′) *adj.* Emotionally or spiritually renewed.

re•bound (rē′bound′, rĭ-) *v.* **1.** To bounce or spring back after a collision. **2.** To recover, as from a decline. —*n.* (rē′bound′, rĭ-bound′). **1.** A bouncing or springing back : recoil. **2.** *Sports.* A rebounding basketball or hockey puck.

re•buff (rĭ-bŭf′) *n.* **1.** An abrupt or curt repulse or refusal. **2.** A check or setback. —*v.* **1.** To snub. **2.** To drive back.

re•buke (rĭ-byo͞ok′) *v.* **-buked, -buk•ing.** To reprove : reprimand. **—re•buke′** *n.*

re•bus (rē′bəs) *n.* A message containing pictures that represent words or syllables.

re•but (rĭ-bŭt′) *v.* **-but•ted, -but•ting.** To try to show to be false by presenting opposing arguments : argue against. **—re•but′tal** *n.* **—re•but′ter** *n.*

rec. *abbr.* **1.** receipt. **2.** record; recording. **3.** recreation.

re•cal•ci•trant (rĭ-kăl′sĭ-trənt) *adj.* Stubbornly resistant to guidance : refractory. **—re•cal′ci•trance, re•cal′ci•tran•cy** *n.*

re•call (rĭ-kôl′) *v.* **1.** To ask or order to return. **2.** To recollect : remember. **3.** To cancel : revoke. **4.** To bring back : restore. —*n.*

reavow
reawake
reawaken
rebill
rebloom
reboil
rebury
recarry
recelebrate
rechallenge
recharter
recheck
rechoose
rechristen
recircle
recirculate
reclasp
reclean
reclothe
recoin
recoinage
recolonize
recolor
recombine
recommence
recommission
recommit
recommitment
recondense
reconduct
reconquer
reconquest
reconsecrate
reconsolidate
reconstitution
reconvene
recopy
recoronation
recross
recrown
recrystallization
recrystallize
recultivate
rededication
redefeat
redefine
redemand
redemonstrate
redeny
redeposit
redescend
redescent
redescribe
redetermine
redigest
rediscover

(*also* rē′kôl′). **1.** An act of recalling. **2.** The capacity to remember. **3.** An act of revoking : cancellation. **4.** The removal of an official from public office by popular vote. **5.** A request by the maker of a defective product for its return for repairs.
re·cant (rĭ-kănt′) *v.* To make a formal denial of (e.g. an earlier statement) : retract. **—re′can·ta′tion** *n.* **—re·cant′er** *n.*
re·cap[1] (rē-kăp′) *v.* To restore (a worn tire) by bonding new rubber onto the old casing. *—n.* (rē′kăp′). A recapped tire.
re·cap[2] (rē′kăp′) *v.* **-capped, -cap·ping.** To summarize. *—n.* A summary.
re·ca·pit·u·late (rē′kə-pĭch′ə-lāt′) *v.* **-lat·ed, -lat·ing.** To repeat in shorter form : summarize. **—re′ca·pit′u·la′tion** *n.* **—re·ca·pit′u·la′tive** *adj.*
recd. or **rec'd.** *abbr.* received.
re·cede (rĭ-sēd′) *v.* **-ced·ed, -ced·ing. 1.** To move away or back. **2.** To slope backward. **3.** To become or seem to become farther away. ☆***syns:*** EBB, RETRACT, RETREAT
†**re·ceipt** (rĭ-sēt′) *n.* **1.** The act of receiving something or the fact of being received. **2. receipts.** The amount or quantity received <box office *receipts*> **3.** A written acknowledgment that something has been received. **4.** *Regional.* A recipe. *—v.* **1.** To indicate (a bill) as having been paid. **2.** To give or write a receipt for.
re·ceiv·a·ble (rĭ-sē′və-bəl) *adj.* **1.** Appropriate for being accepted. **2.** Waiting for payment : due <accounts *receivable*>
re·ceive (rĭ-sēv′) *v.* **-ceived, -ceiv·ing. 1.** To take (e.g., something given or sent) : get. **2.** To take into the mind. **3.** To meet with : encounter <*receive* kind treatment> **4.** To greet : welcome <*receive* a caller> **5.** To respond to <*received* the apology with dignity> **6.** *Electron.* To convert incoming electromagnetic waves into pictures or sounds. **7.** To accept as true or correct.
re·ceiv·er (rĭ-sē′vər) *n.* **1.** One that receives. **2.** *Law.* A person appointed to hold the property or funds of others during litigation. **3.** *Electron.* An apparatus, as a part of a radio, television, or telephone, that receives electrical signals and changes them into perceptible form.
re·ceiv·er·ship (rĭ-sē′vər-shĭp′) *n.* *Law.* **1.** The office or tasks of a receiver. **2.** The state of being held by a receiver.
re·cent (rē′sənt) *adj.* **1.** Of, from, or happening at a time just before the present. **2.** Modern : new. **—re′cent·ly** *adv.* **—re′cen·cy, re′cent·ness** *n.*
re·cep·ta·cle (rĭ-sĕp′tə-kəl) *n.* **1.** A container. **2.** *Elect.* An electrical fitting connected to a power supply and designed to take a plug.
re·cep·tion (rĭ-sĕp′shən) *n.* **1.** An act or process of receiving something. **2.** A welcome or acceptance. **3.** A usu. large social gathering. **4.** *Electron.* **a.** The receiving of electromagnetic signals. **b.** The quality of received signals.
re·cep·tion·ist (rĭ-sĕp′shə-nĭst) *n.* An office employee who greets callers, gives information, and answers the telephone.
re·cep·tive (rĭ-sĕp′tĭv) *adj.* **1.** Able to receive. **2.** Ready to consider or listen <*receptive* to our plan> **—re′cep·tiv′i·ty, re·cep′tive·ness** *n.*
re·cep·tor (rĭ-sĕp′tər) *n.* **1.** A specialized nerve ending that senses or receives stimuli. **2.** A sense organ.
re·cess (rē′sĕs′, rĭ-sĕs′) *n.* **1. a.** A temporary halt in usual activities. **b.** The period of such a halt. **2.** *often* **recesses.** A remote, secret, or concealed place. **3.** An indentation, as in a wall. *—v.* **1.** To put in a recess. **2.** To make a recess in. **3.** To halt or pause for a recess.
re·ces·sion (rĭ-sĕsh′ən) *n.* **1.** The act of withdrawing or returning. **2.** The procession of clergy and choir members leaving a church after a service. **3.** A moderate slowdown in economic activity.
re·ces·sion·al (rĭ-sĕsh′ə-nəl) *n.* A hymn sung during the exit of the clergy and choir after a church service.
re·ces·sive (rĭ-sĕs′ĭv) *adj.* **1.** Tending to recede. **2.** *Genetics.* Of or designating a gene that is not manifested in the organism when paired with a dominant gene for the same characteristic. **—re·ces′sive** *n.*
re·cher·ché (rə-shĕr′shā′) *adj.* **1.** Uncommonly rare and exquisite : choice. **2.** Refined and elegant to an extreme.
re·cid·i·vism (rĭ-sĭd′ə-vĭz′əm) *n.* A tendency to slip back into a previous, esp. criminal, behavior pattern. **—re·cid′i·vist** *n.* **—re·cid′i·vis′tic** *adj.*
rec·i·pe (rĕs′ə-pē) *n.* **1.** A set of directions for preparing something, esp. food. **2.** A prescription or formula.
re·cip·i·ent (rĭ-sĭp′ē-ənt) *n.* One that receives.
re·cip·ro·cal (rĭ-sĭp′rə-kəl) *adj.* **1.** Given or felt by each to the other <*reciprocal* pledges><*reciprocal* esteem> **2.** Interchangeable. **3.** Complementary. **4.** *Math.* Of or relating to a quantity divided by 1. *—n.* **1.** One that is reciprocal. **2.** *Math.* The quotient of a quantity divided into 1.
re·cip·ro·cate (rĭ-sĭp′rə-kāt′) *v.* **-cat·ed, -cat·ing. 1.** To give and take mutually : interchange. **2.** To show or feel in response. **3.** To make a return for a gift or favor. **—re·cip′ro·ca′tion** *n.* **—re·cip′ro·ca′tive** *adj.* **—re·cip′ro·ca′tor** *n.*
reciprocating engine *n.* An engine with a crankshaft turned by linearly reciprocating pistons.

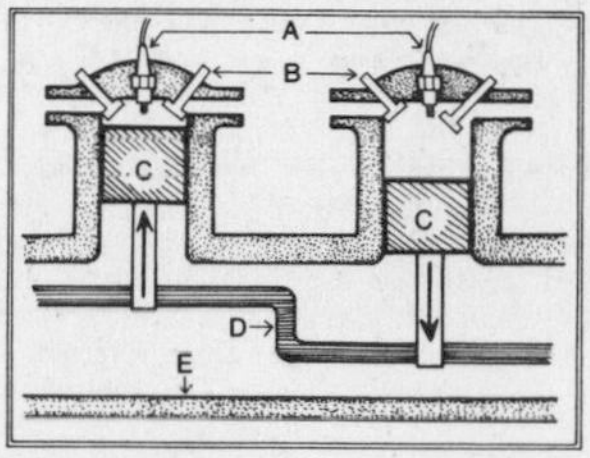

reciprocating engine
A. spark plug, B. valve, C. piston, D. crank, E. crankcase

rec·i·proc·i·ty (rĕs′ə-prŏs′ĭ-tē) *n.* **1.** A reciprocal relationship. **2.** An interchange of favors, esp. the exchange of trading rights between nations.
re·cit·al (rĭ-sīt′l) *n.* **1.** A public reading. **2.** A detailed account or narration. **3.** A music or dance performance, esp. by a soloist.
rec·i·ta·tion (rĕs′ĭ-tā′shən) *n.* **1.** An act of reciting. **2.** A spoken presentation of prepared lessons by a student.
re·cite (rĭ-sīt′) *v.* **-cit·ed, -cit·ing. 1.** To say aloud (e.g., something memorized), esp. with an audience. **2.** To recount in detail. **3.** To enumerate : list. **—re·cit′er** *n.*
reck·less (rĕk′lĭs) *adj.* **1.** Careless. **2.** Heedless of consequences : rash.
reck·on (rĕk′ən) *v.* **1.** To calculate : compute. **2.** To consider : regard <*reckoned* him a fool> **3.** *Informal.* To think or assume <I *reckon* I'll be there.>
reck·on·ing (rĕk′ə-nĭng) *n.* **1.** An act of counting. **2.** An itemized bill. **3.** The determination of a geographic position, as of a ship, by calculation.
re·claim (rĭ-klām′) *v.* **1.** To make fit for growing crops or living on <*reclaiming* marshes> **2.** To extract (useful substances) from wastes. **3.** To reform. **—rec′la·ma′tion** (rĕk′lə-mā′shən) *n.*
re·cline (rĭ-klīn′) *v.* **-clined, -clin·ing.** To assume or cause to assume a prone or leaning position : lie or lay down.
re·cluse (rĭ-klo͞os′, rĭ-klo͞os′) *n.* One who retreats from the world to live in solitude. **—re·clu′sive** (-sĭv, -zĭv) *adj.*
rec·og·ni·tion (rĕk′əg-nĭsh′ən) *n.* **1.** An act of recognizing or the state of being recognized. **2.** An acknowledgment, esp. of the legitimacy of a government. **3.** Favorable notice.
re·cog·ni·zance (rĭ-kŏg′nĭ-zəns, -kŏn′ĭ-) *n.* *Law.* An obligation of record that commits a person to do something, as to make a court appearance. **—re·cog′ni·zant** *adj.*
rec·og·nize (rĕk′əg-nīz′) *v.* **-nized, -niz·ing. 1.** To know to be something perceived or experienced before <*recognize* a

rediscovery
redissolve
redistill
redivide
redivision
redo
redraft
redraw
redrive
redry
redye
re-edit
re-elevate
re-embark
re-embody
re-embrace
re-emerge
re-emergence
re-emigrate
re-encourage
re-encouragement
re-endow
re-engage
re-engagement
re-engrave
re-enlist
re-enlistment
re-enslave
re-erect
re-establish
re-evaluate
re-evaluation
re-exchange
re-exhibit
re-expel
re-experience
re-export
reface
refashion
refasten
refertilize
refire
reflow
reflower
refold
reforge
reformulate
refortification
refortify
reframe
refreeze
refurnish
regather
regear
regerminate
regermination

face> **2.** To acknowledge the validity or reality of <*recognized* the new government> **3.** To be aware or appreciative of. **–rec′og·niz′a·ble** *adj.* **–rec′og·niz′a·bly** *adv.*

re·coil (rĭ-koil′) *v.* **1.** To spring or jerk back, as upon firing. **2.** To shrink back in fear or repulsion. **–re′coil′** (rē′koil′, rĭkoil′) *n.* **–re·coil′er** *n.*

rec·ol·lect (rĕk′ə-lĕkt′) *v.* To recall to one's mind. **–rec′ol·lec′tion** *n.*

re·com·bi·nant DNA (rē-kŏm′bĭ-nənt) *n.* DNA from the genes of different species, divided and spliced together in a laboratory to produce new kinds of cells.

rec·om·mend (rĕk′ə-mĕnd′) *v.* **1.** To represent to another as desirable or worthy : endorse. **2.** To make attractive <Her experience *recommends* her.> **3.** To advise <*recommend* a change of climate> **–rec′om·men·da′tion** *n.*

rec·om·pense (rĕk′əm-pĕns′) *v.* **-pensed, -pens·ing.** To award compensation to or for. *–n.* **1.** Amends made, as for damage or loss. **2.** Payment for services.

rec·on·cile (rĕk′ən-sīl′) *v.* **-ciled, -cil·ing. 1.** To re-establish friendship between. **2.** To settle (e.g., a dispute). **3.** To bring (oneself) to acceptance. **4.** To make consistent or compatible <*reconcile* their opposing views> **–rec′on·cil′a·bil′i·ty** *n.* **–rec′on·cil′a·ble** *adj.* **–rec′on·cile′ment, rec′on·cil′i·a′tion** (-sĭl′ē-ā′shən) *n.* **–rec′on·cil′er** *n.* **–rec′on·cil′i·a·to′ry** (-sĭl′ē-ə-tôr′ē, -tōr′ē) *adj.*

rec·on·dite (rĕk′ən-dīt′, rĭ-kŏn′dīt′) *adj.* **1.** Not easily understood : abstruse. **2.** Concealed : hidden. **–rec′on·dite′ly** *adv.*

re·con·nais·sance (rĭ-kŏn′ə-səns, -zəns) *n.* An exploration of an area, esp. to obtain military information.

re·con·noi·ter (rē′kə-noi′tər, rĕk′ə-) *v.* **1.** To make a preliminary inspection (of). **2.** To make a reconnaissance.

re·con·sid·er (rē′kən-sĭd′ər) *v.* To consider again, esp. with intent to change an earlier decision. **–re′con·sid′er·a′tion** *n.*

re·con·struct (rē′kən-strŭkt′) *v.* To construct again.

re·con·struc·tion (rē′kən-strŭk′shən) *n.* **1.** The act or result of reconstructing. **2. Reconstruction.** The period (1865–77) during which the Confederate states were administered by the federal government before being readmitted to the Union.

re·cord (rĭ-kôrd′) *v.* **1.** To set down for preservation in writing or other permanent form. **2.** To register (sound) in permanent form for reproduction, esp. on a disk or tape. **3.** To register : indicate. *–n.* **–rec·ord** (rĕk′ərd). **1.** An account, as of events, set down to preserve or transmit the truth. **2.** Information on a subject, collected and preserved. **3.** Known history of performance <your school *record*> **4.** The best performance known, as in a sports event. **5.** The highest or lowest statistical mark known. **6.** A disk designed to be played on a phonograph. **–off the record.** Not for publication.

re·cord·er (rĭ-kôr′dər) *n.* **1.** One that records, esp. a tape recorder. **2.** A usu. wooden flute with a mouthpiece like a whistle.

re·cord·ing (rĭ-kôr′dĭng) *n.* Something on which sound or visual images have been recorded.

re·count (rĭ-kount′) *v.* To tell the facts or details of : describe.

re-count (rē-kount′) *v.* To count again. *–n.* (rē′kount′, rē-kount′). An additional count, as of votes cast.

re·coup (rĭ-ko͞op′) *v.* **1.** To get an equivalent for <*recouped* his losses on the next bet> **2.** To reimburse.

re·course (rē′kôrs′, -kōrs′, rĭ-kôrs′, -kōrs′) *n.* **1.** A turning to for help or security. **2.** A source of aid or protection.

re·cov·er (rĭ-kŭv′ər) *v.* **1.** To get back : regain. **2.** To regain normal health, control, or balance. **3.** To win a favorable judgment in a lawsuit. ☆**syns:** RECOUP, REGAIN, RETRIEVE. **–re·cov′er·a·ble** *adj.* **–re·cov′er·y** *n.*

re-cov·er (rē-kŭv′ər) *v.* To cover anew.

rec·re·ant (rĕk′rē-ənt) *adj.* **1.** Unfaithful : disloyal. **2.** Cowardly. **–rec′re·ance** *n.*

rec·re·ate (rĕk′rē-āt′) *v.* **-at·ed, -at·ing.** To relax and divert (oneself).

re-cre·ate (rē′krē-āt′) *v.* To create anew. **–re′-cre·a′tion** *n.*

rec·re·a·tion (rĕk′rē-ā′shən) *n.* Refreshment and relaxation of one's body or mind after work. **–rec′re·a′tion·al** *adj.*

recreational vehicle *n.* A motor vehicle, as a camper or a mobile home, used for traveling and recreational activities.

re·crim·i·nate (rĭ-krĭm′ə-nāt′) *v.* **-nat·ed, -nat·ing.** To accuse (an accuser) in return. **–re·crim′i·na′tion** *n.*

re·cru·desce (rē′kro͞o-dĕs′) *v.* **-desced, -desc·ing.** To break out again after a dormant period. **–re′cru·des′cence** *n.* **–re′cru·des′cent** *adj.*

re·cruit (rĭ-kro͞ot′) *v.* **1.** To seek out and engage (someone) for work or service. **2.** To strengthen or raise (an armed force) by enlistment. **3.** To renew or restore <*recruited* her health> *–n.* A new member, esp. of a military force. **–re·cruit′er** *n.*

rec·ta (rĕk′tə) *n. var. pl. of* RECTUM.

rec·tan·gle (rĕk′tăng′gəl) *n.* A parallelogram with right angles. **–rec·tan′gu·lar** *adj.* **–rec·tan′gu·lar′i·ty** (-lăr′ĭ-tē) *n.*

rec·ti·fy (rĕk′tə-fī′) *v.* **-fied, -fy·ing. 1.** To make right : correct. **2.** To refine : purify. **–rec′ti·fi′a·ble** *adj.* **–rec′ti·fi·ca′tion** *n.* **–rec′ti·fi′er** *n.*

rec·ti·lin·e·ar (rĕk′tə-lĭn′ē-ər) *adj.* Moving in, made up of, or marked by a straight line or lines.

rec·ti·tude (rĕk′tĭ-to͞od′, -tyo͞od′) *n.* **1.** Moral integrity. **2.** Correctness.

rec·to (rĕk′tō) *n., pl.* **-tos.** A right-hand page of a book.

rec·tor (rĕk′tər) *n.* **1.** A member of the clergy in charge of a parish. **2.** *Rom. Cath. Ch.* A priest appointed to be head of a church, seminary, or university. **3.** A school or college principal.

rec·to·ry (rĕk′tə-rē) *n., pl.* **-ries.** A rector's residence.

rec·tum (rĕk′təm) *n., pl.* **-tums** or **-ta** (-tə). The lower portion of the alimentary canal between the colon and the anus. **–rec′tal** *adj.*

re·cum·bent (rĭ-kŭm′bənt) *adj.* Lying down : reclining.

re·cu·per·ate (rĭ-ko͞o′pə-rāt′, -kyo͞o′-) *v.* **-at·ed, -at·ing. 1.** To regain strength or health : recover. **2.** To recover from financial loss. **–re·cu′per·a′tion** *n.* **–re·cu′per·a′tive** (-pə-rā′tĭv, -pər-ə-tĭv) *adj.*

re·cur (rĭ-kûr′) *v.* **-curred, -cur·ring.** To occur or come up again. **–re·cur′rence** *n.* **–re·cur′rent** *adj.*

re·cy·cle (rē-sī′kəl) *v.* **-cled, -cling. 1.** To put through a cycle again. **2.** To recover useful materials from. **3.** To use again instead of discarding <*recycle* glass bottles> **4.** To recondition and adapt to a new use.

red (rĕd) *n.* **1. a.** Any of a group of colors whose hue is like that of blood. **b.** A pigment or dye with a red hue. **2.** *often* **Red.** A Communist. *–adj.* **red·der, red·dest. 1.** With a color like blood. **2.** Ruddy or flushed, esp. in the face <turned *red* with shame> **3.** *often* **Red.** Communist. **–in the red.** In debt.

Red Sea. Sea separating the Arabian Peninsula from Africa.

red blood cell *n.* An erythrocyte.

red-blood·ed (rĕd′blŭd′ĭd) *adj.* Strong and virile. **–red′-blood′ed·ness** *n.*

red·breast (rĕd′brĕst′) *n.* A robin or other bird with a red breast.

red·coat (rĕd′kōt′) *n.* A British soldier esp. in the American Revolution.

†redd (rĕd) *v.* **redd·ed** *or* **redd, redd·ing.** *Regional.* To put in order : tidy <*redded* up the front room>

red·den (rĕd′n) *v.* To make or become red or reddish.

red·dish (rĕd′ĭsh) *adj.* Somewhat red.

†rede (rēd) *v.* **red·ed, red·ing.** *Regional.* To advise : counsel. **–rede** *n.*

re·deem (rĭ-dēm′) *v.* **1.** To regain possession of by paying a specified sum. **2.** To pay off. **3.** To turn in (e.g., coupons) and receive something in exchange. **4.** To rescue or ransom. **5.** To save from sin. **6.** To make up for. **7.** To fulfill **–re·deem′a·ble** *adj.* **–re·deem′er** *n.*

re·demp·tion (rĭ-dĕmp′shən) *n.* An act of redeeming or the state of being redeemed. **–re·demp′tion·al, re·demp′tive, re·demp′to·ry** *adj.*

regild
reglaze
reglue
regrade
regraft
regrant
rehandle
reheat
reheel
rehire
reignite
reimplant
reimport
reimpose
reimposition
reimpregnate
reimpress
reimprison
reimprisonment
reinaugurate
reincite
reincorporate
reincur
reinduce
reinfect
reinflame
reinform
reinfuse
reinhabit
reinoculate
reinoculation
reinscribe
reinsert
reinsertion
reinspect
reinspection
reinspire
reinstall
reinstallation
reinstruct
reinter
reinterrogate
reintroduce
reintroduction
reinvent
reinvestigate
reinvestigation
reinvestment
reinvite
reinvolve
rejudge
rekindle
relabel
relace
relaunch
relearn

red-hand•ed (rĕd'hăn'dĭd) *adv.* & *adj.* In the act of doing something wrong.
red•head (rĕd'hĕd') *n.* A person with red hair.
red herring *n.* Something designed to divert attention from the matter at hand.
red-hot (rĕd'hŏt') *adj.* **1.** Glowing hot. **2.** Very recent <*red-hot* information>
re•dis•trict (rē-dĭs'trĭkt) *v.* To divide again into esp. election districts.
red-let•ter (rĕd'lĕt'ər) *adj.* Memorably happy <a *red-letter* occasion>
red•line (rĕd'līn') *v.* To discriminate against (an area or neighborhood) by refusing to grant fair loans, mortgages, or insurance policies.
red•o•lent (rĕd'l-ənt) *adj.* **1.** Having a pleasant scent : aromatic. **2.** Suggestive : reminiscent. **—red'o•lence** *n.*
re•doubt (rĭ-dout') *n.* A small defensive fortification.
re•doubt•a•ble (rĭ-dou'tə-bəl) *adj.* **1.** Arousing awe or fear : formidable. **2.** Worthy of respect. **—re•doubt'a•bly** *adv.*
re•dound (rĭ-dound') *v.* **1.** To have an effect <achievements that *redound* to one's credit> **2.** To contribute : accrue.
re•dress (rĭ-drĕs') *v.* **1.** To rectify : remedy. **2.** To make amends for or to. —*n.* (rē'drĕs', rĭ-drĕs'). **1.** Satisfaction for wrong done : amends. **2.** Correction.
Red River cart *n. Can.* A 2-wheeled horse-drawn cart formerly used in the Canadian West.
red snapper *n.* A marine food fish of the genus *Lutjanus,* with a reddish body.
red tape *n.* Official forms and bureaucratic procedures.
red tide *n.* Ocean waters discolored by floating masses of reddish, 1-celled plantlike animals in numbers great enough to poison fish.
re•duce (rĭ-do͞os', -dyo͞os') *v.* **-duced, -duc•ing. 1.** To lessen in extent, number, amount, degree, or price : diminish. **2.** To conquer : subject. **3.** To put in order. **4.** To separate into components : analyze. **5.** To bring to a simpler or lower condition <*reduced* the farmers to poverty> **6.** To lose weight, esp. by dieting. **—re•duc'er** *n.* **—re•duc'i•bil'i•ty** *n.* **—re•duc'i•ble** *adj.* **—re•duc'i•bly** *adv.* **—re•duc'tion** (-dŭk'shən) *n.* **—re•duc'tive** *adj.*
re•dun•dant (rĭ-dŭn'dənt) *adj.* **1.** Exceeding what is required or natural. **2.** Unnecessarily repetitive. **—re•dun'dan•cy** *n.*
red-winged blackbird (rĕd'wĭngd') *n.* A North American blackbird, *Agelaius phoeniceus,* the male of which has scarlet patches on the wings.
red•wood (rĕd'wo͝od') *n.* A very tall evergreen tree, *Sequoia sempervirens,* of coastal and N Calif., with soft, reddish wood.
reed (rēd) *n.* **1.** Any of several tall swamp or marsh grasses with jointed, hollow stalks. **2.** A primitive wind instrument made of a hollow reed stalk. **3.** *Mus.* **a.** A flexible strip of cane or metal set into the mouthpiece of certain instruments to create tone by vibrating. **b.** An instrument, as a clarinet, equipped with a reed. **—reed'i•ness** *n.* **—reed'y** *adj.*
reef[1] (rēf) *n.* A ridge of sand, coral, etc., that rises to or close to the water surface.
reef[2] (rēf) *n.* A part of a sail tucked in or rolled and tied down to reduce the amount of sail exposed to the wind. **—reef** *v.*
reef•er (rē'fər) *n. Slang.* Marijuana, esp. a marijuana cigarette.
reek (rēk) *v.* **1.** To smoke or steam : fume. **2.** To give off a stench. **3.** To be strongly and offensively suggestive <an arrangement *reeking* of corruption> —*n.* **1.** A stench. **2.** Vapor : steam.
reel[1] (rēl) *n.* **1.** A device, as a cylinder or spool, that spins on an axis and is used for letting out and winding up rope, tape, or fishing line. **2.** The amount of material wound on a reel. **3.** A fast, lively folk dance. —*v.* **1.** To wind on a reel. **2.** To bring in with a fishing rod and reel.
reel[2] (rēl) *v.* **1.** To fall back or be thrown off balance. **2.** To stagger or lurch. **3.** To feel dizzy or confused.
re-en•ter *or* **re•en•ter** (rē-ĕn'tər) *v.* To come in or enter again. **—re-en'trance** *n.*
re-en•try *or* **re•en•try** (rē-ĕn'trē) *n., pl.* **-tries.** *Aerospace.* Return of a missile or spacecraft to the earth's atmosphere after a space flight.
ref. *abbr.* **1.** reference. **2.** referred. **3.** refining. **4.** reformation; reformed. **5.** refund.
re•fec•to•ry (rĭ-fĕk'tə-rē) *n., pl.* **-ries.** A dining room, esp. in a monastery or college.
re•fer (rĭ-fûr') *v.* **-ferred, -fer•ring. 1.** To direct to a source of information or help. **2.** To attribute : assign. **3.** To submit to an authority. **4.** To direct the attention of. **5.** To make reference : allude. **6.** To turn to, as for information. **—ref'er•a•ble** (rĕf'ər-ə-bəl, rĭ-fûr'-) *adj.* **—re•fer'ral** *n.*
ref•e•ree (rĕf'ə-rē') *n.* **1.** One to whom matters are referred for settlement : arbitrator. **2.** *Sports.* An official who supervises play : umpire. **—ref'e•ree'** *v.*
ref•er•ence (rĕf'ər-əns, rĕf'rəns) *n.* **1.** An act of referring. **2.** Relation : regard <in *reference* to> **3.** An allusion to an event or situation. **4.** A note in a publication guiding the reader to another passage or source. **5.** The consultation of sources of information. **6. a.** One who is in a position to recommend or vouch for another, as for a position. **b.** A statement about someone's character or qualifications. **—ref'er•en'tial** (-ə-rĕn'shəl) *adj.*
ref•er•en•dum (rĕf'ə-rĕn'dəm) *n., pl.* **-dums** *or* **-da** (-də). **1.** The submission of a proposed law or other issue to a popular vote. **2.** The vote itself.
re•fill (rē-fĭl') *v.* To fill again. —*n.* (rē'fĭl'). **1.** A product packaged to replace the contents of a container. **2.** An additional filling. **—re•fill'a•ble** *adj.*
re•fine (rĭ-fīn') *v.* **-fined, -fin•ing. 1.** To remove unwanted material from : purify. **2.** To free from coarseness. **3.** To make more precise or subtle. **4.** To improve : perfect.
re•fined (rĭ-fīnd') *adj.* **1.** Marked by good, well-informed taste and manners : cultivated. **2.** Purified. **3.** Precise or exact.
re•fine•ment (rĭ-fīn'mənt) *n.* **1.** An act or result of refining or the state of being refined. **2.** An improvement or elaboration. **3.** Fineness of thought, manners, or expression. **4.** A subtle or precise phrasing.
re•fin•er•y (rĭ-fī'nə-rē) *n., pl.* **-ies.** An industrial plant where crude substances, esp. petroleum, are purified.
re•fin•ish (rē-fĭn'ĭsh) *v.* To apply a new finish to (furniture). **—re•fin'ish•er** *n.*
re•flect (rĭ-flĕkt') *v.* **1.** To throw or bend back (e.g., light) from a surface. **2.** To mirror or be mirrored. **3.** To manifest : reveal. **4.** To think seriously : meditate. **5.** To bring blame or reproach. **—re•flec'tion** *n.* **—re•flec'tive** *adj.*
re•flec•tor (rĭ-flĕk'tər) *n.* One that reflects, esp. a surface that reflects light.
re•flex (rē'flĕks') *adj.* **1.** Turned, directed, or bent backward. **2.** Involuntary <A sneeze is a *reflex* response.> —*n.* **1.** A reflection. **2.** *Physiol.* Involuntary response to a stimulus. **3.** *Psychol.* An unlearned or instinctive response.
re•flex•ive (rĭ-flĕk'sĭv) *adj. Gram.* **1.** Designating a verb with an identical subject and direct object. **2.** Designating a pronoun used as direct object of a reflexive verb. **—re•flex'ive** *n.* **—re•flex'ive•ly** *adv.*
re•for•est (rē-fôr'ĭst, -fŏr'-) *v.* To replant (an area) with forest trees. **—re•for'es•ta'tion** *n.*
re•form (rĭ-fôrm') *v.* **1.** To improve by removing defects or correcting errors. **2.** To remove abuse or malpractice in. **3.** To give up or cause to give up evil ways. —*n.* **1.** An act of reforming. **2.** A change for the better. **3.** Moral improvement. **4.** Social or political change that seeks to remove corruption or malpractice.
re-form (rē'fôrm') *v.* To form again.
ref•or•ma•tion (rĕf'ər-mā'shən) *n.* **1.** An act of reforming or the state of being reformed. **2. Reformation.** The 16th-cent. movement leading to separation of the Protestant churches from the Roman Catholic Church. **—ref'or•ma'tion•al** *adj.*

relight
reliquidate
reliquidation
reload
reloan
remarry
remeasure
remelt
remerge
remigrate
remigration
remix
remodification
remodify
remold
rename
renavigate
renotify
reobtain
reobtainable
reoccupation
reoccupy
reoccur
reoccurrence
reoppose
reordain
reordination
reorient
repacify
repack
repaint
repaper
repave
repenalize
repledge
replunge
repolish
repopulate
repopulation
repour
reprocess
reproclaim
repurchase
repurify
repursue
reradiate
reread
rerecord
rerise
reroll
reroute
resaddle
resail
resalute
reseal
reseat

re•for•ma•to•ry (rĭ-fôr′mə-tôr′ē, -tōr′ē) *n., pl.* **-ries.** A penal institution for reforming young offenders.
re•frac•tion (rĭ-frăk′shən) *n.* The bending of a wave path, as of light or sound, at the boundary between 2 different mediums. **—re•fract′** *v.* **—re•frac′tive** *adj.* **—re•frac′tive•ly** *adv.* **—re•frac′tive•ness, re′frac•tiv′i•ty** (rē′frăk-tĭv′ĭ-tē) *n.*
re•frac•to•ry (rĭ-frăk′tə-rē) *adj.* **1.** Obstinate : unmanageable. **2.** Difficult to melt or work. **3.** Not responsive to treatment. *—n., pl.* **-ries.** One that is refractory, esp. a heat-resistant material. **—re•frac′to•ri•ly** *adv.* **—re•frac′to•ri•ness** *n.*
re•frain[1] (rĭ-frān′) *v.* To hold oneself back <*refrain* from speaking> ☆*syns:* ABSTAIN, FORBEAR, KEEP, WITHHOLD
re•frain[2] (rĭ-frān′) *n.* A verse or phrase recurring throughout a song or poem.
re•fresh (rĭ-frĕsh′) *v.* **1.** To revive or become revived, as with rest or food. **2.** To make cool or clean : freshen. **3.** To renew by stimulation <*refreshed* her memory>
re•fresh•ment (rĭ-frĕsh′mənt) *n.* **1.** An act of refreshing or the state of being refreshed. **2.** Something that refreshes. **3. refreshments.** An assortment of light foods.
re•frig•er•ant (rĭ-frĭj′ər-ənt) *n.* A substance, as ammonia, water, or carbon dioxide, used for producing refrigeration.
re•frig•er•ate (rĭ-frĭj′ə-rāt′) *v.* **-at•ed, -at•ing. 1.** To chill (a substance) in a refrigerator. **2.** To preserve (food) by chilling. **—re•frig′er•a′tion** *n.*
re•frig•er•a•tor (rĭ-frĭj′ə-rā′tər) *n.* An insulated cabinet or room used for storing food at a low temperature.
ref•uge (rĕf′yo͞oj) *n.* **1.** The state of being protected, as from danger. **2.** A place providing protection : haven. ☆*syns:* ASYLUM, SANCTUARY, SHELTER
ref•u•gee (rĕf′yo͝o-jē′) *n.* One who flees for refuge, esp. from war or oppression.
re•ful•gent (rĭ-fo͝ol′jənt, -fŭl′-) *adj.* Shining radiantly. **—re•ful′gence** *n.*
re•fund (rĭ-fŭnd′, rē′fŭnd′) *v.* To give or pay back. *—n.* (rē′fŭnd′). **1.** A repayment of funds. **2.** The sum repaid.
re•fur•bish (rē-fûr′bĭsh) *v.* To make clean, bright, or new-looking again.
re•fuse[1] (rĭ-fyo͞oz′) *v.* **-fused, -fus•ing.** To decline to do, accept, give, or allow. **—re•fus′al** *n.*
ref•use[2] (rĕf′yo͞os) *n.* Something rejected or discarded as worthless : trash.
re•fute (rĭ-fyo͞ot′) *v.* **-fut•ed, -fut•ing.** To prove to be false or mistaken : disprove. **—re•fut′a•ble** *adj.* **—re•fut′a•bly** *adv.* **—ref•u•ta•tion** (rĕf′yo͝o-tā′shən) *n.*
reg. *abbr.* **1.** regent. **2.** regiment. **3.** region. **4.** register; registered; registry. **5.** registrar. **6.** regular; regularly. **7.** regulation; regulator.
re•gain (rē-gān′) *v.* **1.** To get back : recover. **2.** To reach again.
re•gal (rē′gəl) *adj.* Of or appropriate for a monarch : royal. **—re′gal•ly** *adv.*
re•gale (rĭ-gāl′) *v.* **-galed, -gal•ing. 1.** To give pleasure to. **2.** To entertain lavishly.
re•ga•lia (rĭ-gāl′yə) *n. (sing. or pl. in number).* **1.** Objects that symbolize royalty, as a crown and scepter. **2.** The distinguishing symbols of a rank, office, or group. **3.** Splendid attire : finery.
re•gard (rĭ-gärd′) *v.* **1.** To look at closely : watch. **2.** To look upon : consider <*regarded* his teacher as a friend> **3.** To have great esteem for. **4.** To relate to : concern. *—n.* **1.** A look : gaze. **2.** Careful attention : heed. **3.** Respect, affection, or esteem. **4. regards.** Good wishes : greetings. **5.** Reference : relation. **6.** A specific point or respect <right in that *regard,* but wrong in others> **—re•gard′ful** *adj.*
re•gard•ing (rĭ-gär′dĭng) *prep.* In reference to.
re•gard•less (rĭ-gärd′lĭs) *adj.* Heedless. *—adv.* In spite of everything : anyway.
re•gat•ta (rĭ-gä′tə, -găt′ə) *n.* A gathering of boats for racing.
re•gen•cy (rē′jən-sē) *n., pl.* **-cies. 1.** The office or government of a regent. **2.** The period during which a regent governs. **3.** A regent or group of regents.
re•gen•er•ate (rĭ-jĕn′ə-rāt′) *v.* **-at•ed, -at•ing. 1.** To reform morally or spiritually. **2.** To build, make, or start anew. **3.** *Biol.* To replace (e.g., a lost organ) by formation of new tissue. *—adj.* (-ər-ĭt). **1.** Morally or spiritually reformed. **2.** Restored : renewed. **—re•gen′er•a′tion** *n.* **—re•gen′er•a′tive** *adj.* **—re•gen′er•a′tor** *n.*
re•gent (rē′jənt) *n.* **1.** One who rules during the minority or disability of a monarch. **2.** One who serves on a governing board of an institution.
reg•i•cide (rĕj′ĭ-sīd′) *n.* **1.** The murder of a king. **2.** One who murders a king.
re•gime *also* **ré•gime** (rā-zhēm′, rĭ-) *n.* **1.** The government in power : administration. **2.** A system of management. **3.** A regimen.
reg•i•men (rĕj′ə-mən, -mĕn′) *n.* **1.** Rule : administration. **2.** A system, as of therapy or diet.
reg•i•ment (rĕj′ə-mənt) *n.* A military unit of ground or airborne troops composed of at least 2 battalions. *—v.* (-mĕnt′). **1.** To put into systematic order. **2.** To impose strict uniformity and discipline upon. **—reg′i•men′tal** *adj.* **—reg′i•men′tal•ly** *adv.* **—reg′i•men•ta′tion** *n.*
Re•gi•na (rĭ-jī′nə). Cap. of Sask., Canada, in the S. *Pop.* 149,593.
re•gion (rē′jən) *n.* **1.** A large, usu. continuous portion of a surface or space : area. **2.** An area of the body.
re•gion•al *adj.* **1.** Of, pertaining to, or typical of a geographic region. **2.** Of or limited to a particular region or district : localized.
reg•is•ter (rĕj′ĭ-stər) *n.* **1. a.** An official record of names, items, or statistics. **b.** A book for these entries. **2.** A device that automatically registers an amount or number <a cash *register*> **3.** An adjustable grill through which heated or cooled air is released. **4.** *Mus.* The range of a voice or instrument. *—v.* **1.** To enter in a register. **2.** To enroll formally. **3.** To indicate, as on a scale. **4.** To show (emotion). **5.** To cause (mail) to be handled with special care by payment of a fee. **6.** To place one's name on an official list of eligible voters. **—reg′is•tra•ble** *adj.* **—reg′is•trant** *n.*
registered nurse *n.* A nurse who has passed a test given by a state.
reg•is•trar (rĕj′ĭ-strär′, rĕj′ĭ-strär′) *n.* An officer, as of a college, who keeps records.
reg•is•tra•tion (rĕj′ĭ-strā′shən) *n.* **1.** The act of registering. **2.** The number registered : enrollment. **3.** A document certifying that one has registered.
reg•is•try (rĕj′ĭ-strē) *n., pl.* **-tries. 1.** Registration. **2.** A place or book for official records. **3.** A ship's registered nationality.
re•gress (rĭ-grĕs′) *v.* To go back to a former and usu. worse condition. *—n.* (rē′grĕs′). An act or way of going back : return. **—re•gres′sion** *n.* **—re•gres′sive** *adj.*
re•gret (rĭ-grĕt′) *v.* **-gret•ted, -gret•ting. 1.** To feel sorry or distressed about. **2.** To mourn. *—n.* **1.** A sense of loss for someone or something gone. **2.** Distress over having done the wrong thing. **3.** An expression of disappointment or sorrow. **4. regrets.** A polite declining of an invitation. **—re•gret′ful** *adj.* **—re•gret′ta•ble** *adj.* **—re•gret′ta•bly** *adv.*
reg•u•lar (rĕg′yə-lər) *adj.* **1.** Customary or normal : usual. **2.** Orderly, methodical, or symmetric. **3.** Conforming to a set procedure. **4.** Occurring at fixed intervals : periodic. **5.** Not varying : constant. **6.** Formally correct : proper. **7.** Thorough : out-and-out. **8.** Conforming to a standard mode of grammatical inflection. **9.** *Geom.* Having equal sides and angles. **10.** Of or constituting a nation's permanent army. *—n.* **1.** A loyal, dependable person. **2.** A soldier belonging to a regular army. **—reg′u•lar′i•ty** *n.*
regular army *n.* A nation's permanent standing army.
reg•u•late (rĕg′yə-lāt′) *v.* **-lat•ed, -lat•ing. 1.** To direct or control in agreement with rules or laws. **2.** To adjust the amount, rate, or flow of <*regulate* traffic> **3.** To adjust for proper functioning. **—reg′u•la′tive** *adj.* **—reg′u•la′tor** *n.* **—reg′u•la•to′ry** *adj.*

relight
reliquidate
reliquidation
reload
reloan
remarry
remeasure
remelt
remerge
remigrate
remigration
remix
remodification
remodify
remold
rename
renavigate
renotify
reobtain
reobtainable
reoccupation
reoccupy
reoccur
reoccurrence
reoppose
reordain
reordination
reorient
repacify
repack
repaint
repaper
repave
repenalize
repledge
replunge
repolish
repopulate
repopulation
repour
reprocess
reproclaim
repurchase
repurify
repursue
reradiate
reread
rerecord
rerise
reroll
reroute
resaddle
resail
resalute
reseal
reseat

reg•u•la•tion (rĕg'yə-lā'shən) *n.* **1.** An act of regulating. **2.** A principle, rule, or law for controlling behavior. **3.** A governmental order with the force of law.
re•gur•gi•tate (rē-gûr'jĭ-tāt') *v.* **-tat•ed, -tat•ing.** To cast up (partly digested food) : vomit. **—re•gur'gi•ta'tion** *n.*
re•ha•bil•i•tate (rē'hĭ-bĭl'ĭ-tāt') *v.* **-tat•ed, -tat•ing.** To restore to customary activity by education and therapy. **—re'ha•bil'i•ta'tion** *n.* **—re'ha•bil'i•ta'tive** *adj.*
re•hash (rē-hăsh') *v.* To go over or present (old material) again. **—re'hash'** *n.*
re•hears•al (rĭ-hûr'səl) *n.* **1.** The act or process of practicing for a performance. **2.** An oral repetition or recital.
re•hearse (rĭ-hûrs') *v.* **-hearsed, -hears•ing.** **1.** To practice (e.g., a play or song) in preparation for a performance. **2.** To perfect by repetition. **3.** To recite or retell.
reign (rān) *n.* **1. a.** The exercise of power by a sovereign. **b.** The term during which a sovereign rules. **2.** Widespread influence : dominance <a *reign* of terror> *—v.* **1.** To exercise sovereign power. **2.** To have widespread influence : prevail.
re•im•burse (rē'ĭm-bûrs') *v.* **-bursed, -burs•ing.** To pay back.
rein (rān) *n.* **1.** *often* **reins.** A long, narrow leather strap fastened to a bridle bit and used to control a horse or other animal. **2.** A means of restraint or guidance. *—v.* **1.** To hold back. **2.** To control or guide.
rein•deer (rān'dîr') *n.* A large deer, *Rangifer tarandus,* of arctic regions, having branched antlers.
re•in•force (rē'ĭn-fôrs', -fōrs') *v.* **-forced, -forc•ing.** **1.** To give more strength or support to : strengthen. **2.** To strengthen militarily with troops or equipment. **3.** To encourage to behave in a desired way, as by giving a reward. **—re'in•forc'er** *n.*
re•in•state (rē'ĭn-stāt') *v.* **-stat•ed, -stat•ing.** **1.** To restore to a former condition or place. **2.** To bring back into use or existence. **—re'in•state'ment** *n.*
re•it•er•ate (rē-ĭt'ə-rāt') *v.* To state again : repeat. **—re•it'er•a'tion** *n.* **—re•it'er•a'tive** *adj.*
re•ject (rĭ-jĕkt') *v.* **1.** To refuse to accept or use : repudiate. **2.** To refuse to grant : deny <*rejected* his appeal> **3.** To throw away : discard. *—n.* (rē'jĕkt'). One rejected. **—re•jec'tion** *n.*
re•joice (rĭ-jois') *v.* **-joiced, -joic•ing.** To be joyful. **—re•joic'er** *n.*
re•join (rĭ-join') *v.* To answer : respond.
re-join (rē-join') *v.* To join or come together again.
re•join•der (rĭ-join'dər) *n.* An answer, esp. to a reply.
re•ju•ve•nate (rĭ-jo͞o'və-nāt') *v.* **-nat•ed, -nat•ing.** To restore to youthful vigor or appearance. **—re•ju've•na'tion** *n.* **—re•ju've•na'tor** *n.*
re•lapse (rĭ-lăps') *v.* **-lapsed, -laps•ing.** To revert to an earlier condition, esp. after partial recovery from illness. *—n.* (rē'lăps', rĭ-lăps'). The act of relapsing.
re•late (rĭ-lāt') *v.* **-lat•ed, -lat•ing.** **1.** To narrate : tell. **2.** To have relation or reference. **3.** *Informal.* To interact with other persons in a satisfying way <can't *relate* to strangers> **4.** To respond favorably.
re•lat•ed (rĭ-lā'tĭd) *adj.* **1.** Connected : associated. **2.** Connected by kinship, marriage, or common origin.
re•la•tion (rĭ-lā'shən) *n.* **1.** A natural or logical association between 2 or more things : connection. **2.** The connection of persons by blood or marriage : kinship. **3.** A relative. **4. relations.** Dealings or associations among persons or groups <diplomatic *relations*> **5.** Reference : regard. **6.** An account or narration.
rel•a•tive (rĕl'ə-tĭv) *adj.* **1.** Connected : related. **2.** Considered with respect to others <his *relative* standing in the class> **3.** Referring to or modifying an antecedent <a *relative* pronoun> *—n.* **1.** One related to another by kinship. **2.** One that is relative. **3.** A relative grammatical term.
relative humidity *n.* A measure of the amount of water vapor in the air, expressed as a percentage of the maximum that the air could hold at the current temperature.
rel•a•tiv•i•ty (rĕl'ə-tĭv'ĭ-tē) *n.* **1.** The quality or state of being relative. **2.** *Physics.* A theory leading to the statement that mass and energy are equal and mass, dimension, and time increase with velocity.
re•lax (rĭ-lăks') *v.* **1.** To make or become lax or less tight : loosen. **2.** To make or become less strict or severe. **3.** To relieve from effort : unburden. **4.** To cease working or straining : rest. **5.** To become less tense, formal, or reserved. **—re'lax•a'tion** *n.* **—relax'ed•ly** *adv.*
re•lax•ant (rĭ-lăk'sənt) *n.* Something, as a drug or therapeutic treatment, that relaxes the muscles.
re•lay (rē'lā', rĭ-lā') *n.* **1.** A team or crew that relieves others at work <a *relay* of stagecoach horses> **2.** The act of passing something along. **3.** A relay race. **4.** *Elect.* A device that activates switches or other devices in an electric circuit in response to a small current or voltage charge. *—v.* **1.** To pass or send along by stages <*relay* a letter> **2.** To provide with fresh relays.
re-lay (rē-lā') *v.* To lay again.
relay race *n.* A race between teams in which each member of each team runs a portion of the race and then is relieved by a teammate.
re•lease (rĭ-lēs') *v.* **-leased, -leas•ing.** **1.** To set free from confinement or restraint : liberate. **2.** To relieve from obligation or debt. **3.** To let go of : free. **4.** To permit sale, publication, performance, or circulation of. **5.** To give up (e.g., a claim). *—n.* **1.** The act of releasing. **2.** An authoritative discharge. **3.** A catch for locking and releasing, as on a machine. **4.** Something issued or put into circulation <a news *release*> **—re•leas'a•ble** *adj.*
rel•e•gate (rĕl'ĭ-gāt') *v.* **-gat•ed, -gat•ing.** **1.** To consign to a lower position. **2.** To assign to a given class or category. **3.** To refer (e.g., a task) for performance or decision. **4.** To banish. **—rel'e•ga'tion** *n.*
re•lent (rĭ-lĕnt') *v.* **1.** To become softened in attitude, temper, or resolve : give in. **2.** To slacken : abate.
re•lent•less (rĭ-lĕnt'lĭs) *adj.* **1.** Unyieldingly stern or harsh. **2.** Persistent.
rel•e•vant (rĕl'ə-vənt) *adj.* Related to the matter at hand. ☆***syns:*** APROPOS, GERMANE, MATERIAL, PERTINENT **—rel'e•vance, rel'e•van•cy** *n.*
re•li•a•ble (rĭ-lī'ə-bəl) *adj.* Capable of being relied upon : dependable. **—re•li'a•bil'i•ty, re•li'a•ble•ness** *n.* **—re•li'a•bly** *adv.*
re•li•ance (rĭ-lī'əns) *n.* **1.** The act or condition of relying : dependence. **2.** Confidence : trust. **3.** One that is relied on. **—re•li'ant** *adj.* **—re•li'ant•ly** *adv.*
rel•ic (rĕl'ĭk) *n.* **1.** Something that has survived from a past culture or period. **2.** A keepsake : souvenir. **3.** An object of religious significance. **4. relics.** A corpse.
rel•ict (rĕl'ĭkt, rĭ-lĭkt') *n.* **1.** *Ecol.* An organism or species of an earlier era surviving in a changed environment. **2.** A widow.
re•lief (rĭ-lēf') *n.* **1.** A lessening of pain or discomfort : ease. **2.** Something that reduces pain or discomfort. **3.** Aid, as money or food, given to the needy, aged, or unfortunate. **4.** Release from a job, post, or duty. **5.** Figures or forms that project from a flat background, as in sculpture. **6.** Variations in elevation of a region.

relief
(Top) *low relief and* (bottom) *high relief*

relief map *n.* A map showing variations in elevation of land, as with contour lines.
relief pitcher *n.* *Baseball.* A pitcher replacing another pitcher during a game.
re•lieve (rĭ-lēv') *v.* **-lieved, -liev•ing.** **1.** To lessen the distress of : alleviate. **2.** To free from pain or trouble. **3.** To aid (one in need). **4.** To take away from. **5.** To release from a burden, duty, or task, esp. by acting as a replacement. **6.** To make less unpleasant or tiresome. **7.** To make clear or effective through contrast. **—re•liev'er** *n.*
re•lig•ion (rĭ-lĭj'ən) *n.* **1. a.** Belief in and reverence for a supernatural power accepted as the creator and governor of the universe. **b.** A specific unified system of this expression <the Buddhist *religion*> **2.** A belief, activity, or cause pursued with fervor and devotion. ☆***syns:*** CREED, DENOMINATION, FAITH, PERSUASION, SECT
re•lig•ious (rĭ-lĭj'əs) *adj.* **1.** Of, pertaining to, or teaching religion. **2.** Adhering to or showing religion. **3.** Faithful : conscientious. *—n., pl.* **religious.** One belonging to a religious order. **—re•lig'ious•ly** *adv.*
re•lin•quish (rĭ-lĭng'kwĭsh) *v.* **1.** To retire from. **2.** To give up doing, professing, or intending. **3.** To surrender. **4.** To release.
rel•i•quar•y (rĕl'ĭ-kwĕr'ē) *n., pl.* **-ies.** A receptacle for sacred relics.
rel•ish (rĕl'ĭsh) *n.* **1.** An appetite for something : liking. **2.** Pleasure : zest. **3.** A savory or spicy condiment served with food. **4.** The flavor of an appetizing food. *—v.* **1.** To enjoy. **2.** To give spice or flavor to.

re•live (rē-lĭv′) *v.* To experience again, esp. by using the imagination.
re•luc•tant (rĭ-lŭk′tənt) *adj.* **1.** Unwilling : averse <*reluctant* to go> **2.** Marked by unwillingness <a *reluctant* witness> **—re•luc′tance, re•luc′tan•cy** *n.*
re•ly (rĭ-lī′) *v.* **-lied, -ly•ing.** To trust confidently <*rely* on one's doctor for advice>
rem (rĕm) *n. Physics.* The amount of ionizing radiation needed to produce the same biological effect as 1 roentgen of high-penetration x-rays.
REM (rĕm) *n.* Rapid, periodic, jerky movement of the eyes during phases of the sleep cycle when dreaming occurs.
re•main (rĭ-mān′) *v.* **1.** To continue without change. **2.** To stay after the removal or loss of others. **3.** To be left as still to be dealt with <Repairs *remain* to be completed.> **4.** To persist or endure.
re•main•der (rĭ-mān′dər) *n.* **1.** Something left over : the rest. **2.** *Math.* **a.** The difference between the dividend and the product of the divisor and quotient in division. **b.** The difference in subtraction. **3.** A book remaining with a publisher after sales have dropped, sold at a discount. —*v.* To sell (a book) as a remainder.
re•mains (rĭ-mānz′) *pl.n.* **1.** What is left after other parts have been removed or destroyed. **2.** A corpse.
re•mand (rĭ-mănd′) *v.* **1.** To send or order back. **2.** *Law.* To send back to prison or court for further action.
re•mark (rĭ-märk′) *n.* **1.** A casual or brief expression of opinion : comment. **2.** The act of noticing or mentioning. —*v.* **1.** To make a comment or observation. **2.** To take notice of : observe.
re•mark•a•ble (rĭ-mär′kə-bəl) *adj.* **1.** Worthy of being noticed or commented on. **2.** Extraordinary : uncommon. **—re•mark′a•ble•ness** *n.* **—re•mark′a•bly** *adv.*
Rem•brandt (rĕm′brănt′). 1606–69. Dutch painter.
re•me•di•al (rĭ-mē′dē-əl) *adj.* Meant to correct a deficiency <a *remedial* course in reading> **—re•me′di•al•ly** *adv.*
rem•e•dy (rĕm′ĭ-dē) *n., pl.* **-dies. 1.** Something, as medicine or therapy, that eases pain, treats disease, or corrects a disorder. **2.** Something that corrects a fault or error. —*v.* **-died, -dy•ing. 1.** To relieve or cure. **2.** To set right : rectify.
re•mem•ber (rĭ-mĕm′bər) *v.* **1.** To recall to the mind. **2.** To retain in the mind. **3.** To keep (someone) in one's thoughts or affections. **4.** To transmit greetings from.
re•mem•brance (rĭ-mĕm′brəns) *n.* **1.** An act of remembering or condition of being remembered. **2.** A memorial. **3.** The time spanned by one's memory. **4.** Something remembered : recollection. **5.** A memento : souvenir. **6.** A greeting.
Remembrance Day *n. Can.* Nov. 11, observed in memory of the victims of the World Wars.
re•mind (rĭ-mīnd′) *v.* To cause to remember. **—re•mind′er** *n.*
rem•i•nis•cence (rĕm′ə-nĭs′əns) *n.* **1.** The act or practice of recalling the past. **2.** A memory. **3.** *often* **reminiscences.** An account of bygone experiences. **—rem′i•nisce′** *v.* **—rem′i•nis′cent** *adj.*
re•miss (rĭ-mĭs′) *adj.* Lax in performing duties : negligent.
re•mis•si•ble (rĭ-mĭs′ə-bəl) *adj.* Capable of being remitted <*remissible* sins> **—re•mis′si•bil′i•ty** *n.* **—re•mis′si•bly** *adv.*
re•mis•sion (rĭ-mĭsh′ən) *n.* **1. a.** An act of remitting. **b.** The state or period of being remitted. **2.** A lessening of intensity, as of the symptoms of a disease.
re•mit (rĭ-mĭt′) *v.* **-mit•ted, -mit•ting. 1.** To send (money). **2. a.** To refrain from exacting (e.g., a punishment). **b.** To forgive <*remit* a sin> **3.** To relax : slacken. **4.** To abate : let up. **—re•mit′ta•ble** *adj.* **—re•mit′tal** *n.* **—re•mit′ter** *n.*
re•mit•tance (rĭ-mĭt′ns) *n.* Money or credit remitted.
rem•nant (rĕm′nənt) *n.* **1.** Something left over. **2.** A surviving trace : vestige.
re•mod•el (rē-mŏd′l) *v.* To remake with a new structure : reconstruct.
re•mon•strate (rĭ-mŏn′strāt′, rĕm′ən-) *v.* **-strat•ed, -strat•ing.** To say or speak in protest or reproof. **—re•mon′stra′tion, re•mon′strance** (-strəns) *n.* **—re•mon′stra•tive** (-strə-tĭv) *adj.*
rem•o•ra (rĕm′ər-ə) *n.* A marine fish of the family Echeneidae, with a sucking disk on its head with which it fastens itself to larger sea animals and ship hulls.
re•morse (rĭ-môrs′) *n.* Deep moral anguish and regret for past misdeeds. **—re•morse′ful** *adj.* **—re•morse′less** *adj.*
re•mote (rĭ-mōt′) *adj.* **-mot•er, -mot•est. 1.** Situated far away. **2.** Distant in time. **3.** Barely perceptible : slight <a *remote* chance> **4.** Distant in relation <a *remote* cousin> **5.** Distant in manner : aloof.
remote control *n.* The control of an activity or machine from a distance, as by radioed instructions or coded signals.
re•move (rĭ-mo͞ov′) *v.* **-moved, -mov•ing. 1.** To move from a position occupied <*removed* the dishes> **2.** To take from one's person : doff. **3.** To take away : eliminate. **4.** To dismiss from office. **5.** To change one's residence or place of business : move. —*n.* **1.** An act of removing. **2.** Distance or degree of separation <at a safe *remove* from the blast> **—re•mov′a•ble** *adj.* **—re•mov′a•bly** *adv.* **—re•mov′al** *n.*
re•mu•ner•ate (rĭ-myo͞o′nə-rāt′) *v.* **-at•ed, -at•ing.** To pay (someone) for goods, services, etc. **—re•mu′ner•a′tion** *n.* **—re•mu′ner•a′tive** *n.* **—re•mu′ner•a′tor** *n.*
ren•ais•sance (rĕn′ĭ-säns′, -zäns′, rĭ-nā′səns) *n.* **1.** A revival : rebirth. **2. Renaissance.** The revival of classical art, literature, and learning in Europe during the 14th–16th cent. **3.** *often* **Renaissance.** A period of revived intellectual or artistic activity.
re•nal (rē′nəl) *adj.* Of or relating to the kidneys.
re•nas•cent (rĭ-năs′ənt, -nā′sənt) *adj.* Showing fresh growth or vigor. **—re•nas′cence** *n.*
rend (rĕnd) *v.* **rent** (rĕnt) or **rend•ed, rend•ing. 1.** To tear apart violently : split. **2.** To remove forcibly. **3.** To disturb as if by tearing <A scream *rent* the stillness.> **4.** To distress painfully. **—rend′er** *n.*
ren•der (rĕn′dər) *v.* **1.** To submit <*render* an account> **2.** To give or make available. **3.** To give (what is due). **4.** To surrender : yield. **5.** To represent verbally or artistically : depict. **6.** To translate. **7.** To cause to become : make. **8.** To melt down (e.g., fat) by heating. **—ren′der•er** *n.*
ren•dez•vous (rän′dā-vo͞o′, -də-) *n., pl.* **-vous** (-vo͞oz′). **1.** A meeting place or meeting arranged in advance. **2.** A popular gathering place. —*v.* To meet or bring together at a prearranged time and place.
ren•di•tion (rĕn-dĭsh′ən) *n.* **1.** An act of rendering. **2.** A performance of a musical or dramatic work. **3.** A translation.
ren•e•gade (rĕn′ĭ-gād′) *n.* **1.** One who rejects one's religion, cause, or allegiance for another. **2.** An outlaw. **—ren′e•gade′** *adj.*
re•nege (rĭ-nĭg′, -nĕg′) *v.* **-neged, -neg•ing. 1.** To fail to perform a promise or commitment. **2.** To fail to follow suit in a card game when able and obliged to do so. **—re•neg′er** *n.*
re•new (rĭ-no͞o′, -nyo͞o′) *v.* **1.** To make new or as if new again : restore. **2.** To take up once more : resume. **3.** To arrange for the extension of. **—re•new′al** *n.*
ren•min•bi (rĕn′mĭn-bē′) *n.* See CURRENCY TABLE.
ren•net (rĕn′ĭt) *n.* An extract from a calf's stomach lining used for curdling milk to make cheeses.
ren•nin (rĕn′ĭn) *n.* A milk-coagulating enzyme derived from rennet.
Ren•oir (rĕn′wär′), **Pierre Auguste.** 1841–1919. French painter.
re•nounce (rĭ-nouns′) *v.* **-nounced, -nounc•ing. 1.** To give up, esp. with a formal announcement. **2.** To reject : disown.
ren•o•vate (rĕn′ə-vāt′) *v.* **-vat•ed, -vat•ing.** To restore to good condition. **—ren′o•va′tion** *n.* **—ren′o•va′tor** *n.*
re•nown (rĭ-noun′) *n.* The quality of being widely known and honored : fame. **—re•nowned′** *adj.*
rent[1] (rĕnt) *n.* Periodic payment made by someone in return for the right to occupy or use another's property. —*v.* **1.** To obtain occupancy or use of (another's property) in return for periodic payments. **2.** To grant occupancy or use of (one's own property) in return for rent. **—rent′er** *n.*
rent[2] (rĕnt) *v. var. p.t. & p.p. of* REND. —*n.* **1.** An opening made by rending. **2.** A breach of relations between persons.
rent•al (rĕn′tl) *n.* **1.** An amount paid out or received as rent. **2.** Property rented or available for renting. **3.** An act of renting.
re•nun•ci•a•tion (rĭ-nŭn′sē-ā′shən) *n.* **1.** The act of renouncing. **2.** A declaration renouncing something. **—re•nun′ci•a′tive, re•nun′ci•a•to′ry** (-ə-tôr′ē, -tōr′ē) *adj.*
rep[1] (rĕp) *n.* A ribbed fabric.
rep[2] (rĕp) *n. Informal.* A representative.
rep. *abbr.* **1.** repair. **2.** repetition. **3.** report; reporter. **4.** *or* **Rep.** representative. **5.** reprint. **6.** *or* **Rep.** republic.
Rep. *abbr.* Republican.
re•pair[1] (rĭ-pâr′) *v.* **1.** To bring back to good or usable condition : fix. **2.** To make right : remedy. **3.** To refresh : renew. —*n.* **1.** The act or work of repairing. **2.** Operating condition after use or repairing <a car in good *repair*> **3.** An instance in which repairing is done. **—re•pair′a•ble** *adj.*
re•pair[2] (rĭ-pâr′) *v.* To go <*repair* to the drawing room>
re•pair•man (rĭ-pâr′măn′, -mən) *n.* One whose job is making repairs.
rep•a•ra•ble (rĕp′ər-ə-bəl) *adj.* Able to be repaired.
rep•a•ra•tion (rĕp′ə-rā′shən) *n.* **1.** An act or the process of repairing or making amends. **2.** Something done or paid as amends : compensation. **3. reparations.** Compensation required from a defeated nation for damage inflicted during a war. **—re•par′a•tive, re•par′a•to′ry** *adj.*

rep·ar·tee (rĕp′ər-tē′, -tā′, -är-) *n.* **1.** A quick, witty reply. **2.** Witty, combative conversation.
re·past (rĭ-păst′) *n.* **1.** A meal. **2.** The food eaten or offered at a meal.
re·pa·tri·ate (rē-pā′trē-āt′) *v.* **-at·ed, -at·ing.** To send back to the country of birth or citizenship. **–re·pa′tri·ate** (-ĭt, -āt′) *n.* **–re·pa′tri·a′tion** *n.*
re·pay (rĭ-pā′) *v.* **1.** To pay back (money). **2.** To give in return : requite <*repay* rudeness with rudeness> **–re·pay′ment** *n.*
re·peal (rĭ-pēl′) *v.* To revoke or rescind, esp. by a formal act. **–re·peal′** *n.*
re·peat (rĭ-pēt′) *v.* **1.** To say or do (something) again. **2.** To say in imitation of another. **3.** To manifest or express in the same way. **4.** To recite from memory. *–n.* **1.** The act of repeating. **2.** Something repeated. **–re·peat′a·ble** *adj.*
re·peat·ed (rĭ-pē′tĭd) *adj.* Said, done, or happening over and over. **–re·peat′ed·ly** *adv.*
re·pel (rĭ-pĕl′) *v.* **-pelled, -pel·ling. 1.** To drive back : keep away <*repel* mosquitoes> **2.** To reject : spurn. **3.** To cause distaste or aversion in. **4.** To be unable to absorb or mix with. **5.** To push away or back by a force <Electric charges of like signs *repel* one another. ☆*syns:* DISGUST, NAUSEATE, REPULSE, REVOLT, SICKEN
re·pel·lent (rĭ-pĕl′ənt) *adj.* **1.** Acting or tending to repel. **2.** Arousing strong distaste. **3.** Resistant to a particular substance <a water-*repellent* coat> *–n.* **1.** A substance for repelling insects. **2.** A substance or treatment that makes a surface resistant to something. **–re·pel′lence, re·pel′len·cy** *n.*
re·pent (rĭ-pĕnt′) *v.* **1.** To feel regret or remorse (for). **2.** To resolve to reform oneself morally. **–re·pen′tance** *n.* **–re·pen′tant** *adj.* **–re·pen′tant·ly** *adv.*
re·per·cus·sion (rē′pər-kŭsh′ən, rĕp′ər-) *n.* **1.** An indirect or unforeseen effect of an event or action. **2.** A rebound or recoil. **3.** A reflection, esp. of sound : echo. **–re′per·cus′sive** *adj.*
rep·er·toire (rĕp′ər-twär′) *n.* **1.** All of the songs, plays, etc., that a player or company is prepared to perform. **2.** The skills or accomplishments of a person or group.
rep·er·to·ry (rĕp′ər-tôr′ē, -tōr′ē) *n., pl.* **-ries. 1.** A repertoire. **2.** A theater in which a resident company performs a number of different plays during a season. **3.** A repository. **–rep′er·to′ri·al** *adj.*
rep·e·ti·tion (rĕp′ĭ-tĭsh′ən) *n.* **1.** An act, process, or instance of repeating or the condition of being repeated. **2.** Something repeated. **–rep′e·ti′tious, re·pet′i·tive** (rĭ-pĕt′ĭ-tĭv) *adj.*
re·pine (rĭ-pīn′) *v.* **1.** To be discontented : fret. **2.** To yearn.
re·place (rĭ-plās′) *v.* **1.** To put back in a previous place. **2.** To fill or take the place of. **–re·place′a·ble** *adj.* **–re·place′ment** *n.* **–re·plac′er** *n.*
re·play (rē-plā′) *v.* To play (e.g., a video tape) again. **–re′play′** *n.*
re·plen·ish (rĭ-plĕn′ĭsh) *v.* To add a new supply to. **–re·plen′ish·ment** *n.*
re·plete (rĭ-plēt′) *adj.* **1.** Abounding <a table *replete* with delicacies> **2.** Satiated. **–re·ple′tion, re·plete′ness** *n.*
rep·li·ca (rĕp′lĭ-kə) *n.* A copy or close reproduction, esp. of an art work.
rep·li·cate (rĕp′lĭ-kāt′) *v.* **-cat·ed, -cat·ing.** To duplicate. **–rep′li·ca′tion** *n.*
re·ply (rĭ-plī′) *v.* **-plied, -ply·ing.** To give an answer in writing or speech : respond. *–n., pl.* **-plies.** An answer : response. **–re·pli′er** *n.*
re·port (rĭ-pôrt′, -pōrt′) *n.* **1.** A usu. detailed and formal account. **2.** Common talk : rumor. **3.** Reputation : repute. **4.** An explosive noise : bang. *–v.* **1.** To present an account (of), often formally. **2.** To tell about : relate. **3.** To make known to the proper authorities. **4.** To write or supply an account (of) for publication or broadcast. **5.** To complain about <*reported* the suspicious character to the police> **6.** To present oneself <*report* for work on time>
re·port·age (rĕp′ər-tazh′, rĭ-pôr′tĭj, -pōr′-) *n.* **1.** The reporting of news. **2.** Something reported.
report card *n.* A report of a student'sprogress sent to a parent or guardian.
re·port·ed·ly (rĭ-pôr′tĭd-lē, -pōr′-) *adv.* According to reports.
re·port·er (rĭ-pôr′tər, -pōr′-) *n.* **1.** One who reports. **2.** A writer or broadcaster of news. **–rep′or·to′ri·al** *adj.*
re·pose¹ (rĭ-pōz′) *n.* **1.** An act of resting or the state of being at rest. **2.** Tranquillity. **3.** Poise : composure. *–v.* **-posed, -pos·ing. 1.** To lie or lay at rest. **2.** To lie supported by something. **–re·pose′ful** *adj.*
re·pose² (rĭ-pōz′) *v.* **-posed, -pos·ing.** To place (e.g., trust) <They *reposed* their hopes in their children.>
re·pos·i·to·ry (rĭ-pŏz′ĭ-tôr′ē, -tōr′ē) *n., pl.* **-ries.** A place where things are stored, as for safekeeping.
re·pos·sess (rē′pə-zĕs′) *v.* To regain or reclaim ownership of, esp. for failure to make payments. **–re′pos·ses′sion** *n.*
rep·re·hend (rĕp′rĭ-hĕnd′) *v.* To express disapproval of. **–rep′re·hen′sion** *n.*
rep·re·hen·si·ble (rĕp′rĭ-hĕn′sə-bəl) *adj.* Deserving of censure : blameworthy. **–rep′re·hen′si·bly** *adv.*
rep·re·sent (rĕp′rĭ-zĕnt′) *v.* **1.** To stand for : symbolize. **2.** To portray : depict. **3.** To be an example of. **4.** To act or speak on behalf of. **5.** To describe as having certain characteristics. ☆*syns:* EMBODY, EPITOMIZE, EXEMPLIFY, PERSONIFY, SYMBOLIZE, TYPIFY **–rep′re·sent′a·bil′i·ty** *n.* **–rep′re·sent′a·ble** *adj.*
rep·re·sen·ta·tion (rĕp′rĭ-zĕn-tā′shən, -zən-) *n.* **1.** An act of representing or the state of being represented. **2.** Something that represents. **3.** A statement, as of facts or accusations.
rep·re·sen·ta·tive (rĕp′rĭ-zĕn′tə-tĭv) *n.* **1.** One that exemplifies others of the same class. **2.** A delegate, agent, or spokesperson. **3.** A member of a legislative body, esp. a lower house. *–adj.* **1.** Of or relating to government by representation. **2.** Authorized to act as an agent or delegate. **3.** Typical of others of the same class.
re·press (rĭ-prĕs′) *v.* **1.** To hold back : restrain. **2.** To suppress : put down <*repress* an uprising> **3.** To exclude from the conscious mind. **–re·press′i·ble** *adj.* **–re·pres′sion** *n.* **–re·pres′sive** *adj.*
re·pres·sor (rĭ-prĕs′ər) *n.* **1.** One that represses. **2.** *Biol.* A chemical compound that prevents the synthesis of a protein by interfering with the actions of DNA.
re·prieve (rĭ-prēv′) *v.* **-prieved, -priev·ing. 1.** To delay the punishment of. **2.** To give temporary relief to. **–re·priev′a·ble** *adj.* **–re·prieve′** *n.*
rep·ri·mand (rĕp′rĭ-mănd′) *v.* To rebuke, esp. formally : censure. **–rep′ri·mand′** *n.*
re·print (rē′prĭnt′) *n.* **1.** A new or additional printing, as of a book, exactly like the original. **2.** A separately printed excerpt. **–re·print′** *v.* **–re·print′er** *n.*
re·pri·sal (rĭ-prī′zəl) *n.* An attack or other action intended to inflict injury in return for an injury suffered : retaliation.
re·prise (rĭ-prēz′) *n. Mus.* A repetition of a theme or phrase.
re·proach (rĭ-prōch′) *v.* To rebuke : blame. *–n.* **1.** Rebuke : blame. **2.** Shame : disgrace. **–re·proach′a·ble** *adj.*
rep·ro·bate (rĕp′rə-bāt′) *n.* A morally unprincipled person. *–adj.* Morally unprincipled : profligate. **–rep′ro·ba′tion** *n.*
re·pro·duce (rē′prə-do͞os′, -dyo͞os′) *v.* **-duced, -duc·ing. 1.** To produce an image or copy of. **2.** *Biol.* To generate offspring. **3.** To produce again : re-create. **4.** To undergo copying. **–re′pro·duc′er** *n.* **–re′pro·duc′i·ble** *adj.* **–re′pro·duc′tion** (-dŭk′shən) *n.* **–re′pro·duc′tive** *adj.*
re·proof (rĭ-pro͞of′) *n.* An act or expression of reproving : rebuke.
re·prove (rĭ-pro͞ov′) *v.* **-proved, -prov·ing. 1.** To rebuke : scold. **2.** To find fault with. **–re·prov′ing·ly** *adv.*
rep·tile (rĕp′tĭl, -tīl′) *n.* A cold-blooded, usu. egg-laying vertebrate of the class Reptilia, as a snake or turtle, having an outer covering of scales or horny plates. **–rep·til′i·an** (-tĭl′ē-ən, -tĭl′yən) *adj. & n.*
re·pub·lic (rĭ-pŭb′lĭk) *n.* **1. a.** A political order whose head of state is not a monarch but usu. a president. **b.** A nation with such a political order. **2. a.** A political order in which the power is held by the elected representatives of its citizens. **b.** A nation with such a political order.
re·pub·li·can (rĭ-pŭb′lĭ-kən) *adj.* **1.** Of, pertaining to, or favoring a republic. **2. Republican.** Of or relating to the U.S. Republican Party. *–n.* **1.** One who favors a republican form of government. **2. Republican.** A member of the U.S. Republican Party. **–re·pub′li·can·ism** *n.*
Republican Party *n.* One of the 2 major U.S. political parties, organized in 1854.
re·pu·di·ate (rĭ-pyo͞o′dē-āt′) *v.* **-at·ed, -at·ing. 1.** To reject as invalid or untrue. **2.** To refuse to recognize or pay. **3.** To disown. ☆*syns:* DENY, DISAVOW, DISCLAIM, DISOWN **–re·pu′di·a′tion** *n.*
re·pug·nant (rĭ-pŭg′nənt) *adj.* **1.** Arousing extreme dislike : offensive. **2.** *Logic.* Inconsistent. **–re·pug′nance** *n.*
re·pulse (rĭ-pŭls′) *v.* **-pulsed, -puls·ing. 1.** To drive back : repel. **2.** To reject rudely or coldly <*repulsed* his advances> *–n.* **1.** An act of repulsing or the state of being repulsed. **2.** A rejection. **–re·pul′sion** *n.*
re·pul·sive (rĭ-pŭl′sĭv) *adj.* **1.** Arousing extreme aversion : loathsome. **2.** Tending to drive off. **–re·pul′sive·ly** *adv.*
rep·u·ta·ble (rĕp′yə-tə-bəl) *adj.* Possessing a good reputation. **–rep′u·ta·bly** *adv.*
rep·u·ta·tion (rĕp′yə-tā′shən) *n.* **1.** The general estimation of a person or thing held by the public. **2.** The condition of being highly regarded.
re·pute (rĭ-pyo͞ot′) *n.* **1.** Reputation. **2.** A good reputation. *–v.* **-put·ed, -put·ing.** To regard : suppose.

re•put•ed (rĭ-pyo͞o′tĭd) *adj.* Assumed to be such <a *reputed* gangster> ☆***syns:*** ALLEGED, CONJECTURAL, PUTATIVE, SUPPOSED **—re•put′ed•ly** *adv.*

req. *abbr.* **1.** requirement. **2.** requisition.

re•quest (rĭ-kwĕst′) *v.* **1.** To ask for. **2.** To ask (someone) to do something. *—n.* **1.** The act of asking. **2.** Something asked for. **3.** The fact or condition of being requested <available on *request*>

req•ui•em (rĕk′wē-əm, rē′kwē-) *n.* **1. Requiem.** *Rom. Cath. Ch.* **a.** A mass for a deceased person. **b.** A musical composition for such a mass. **2.** A composition or service commemorating the dead.

re•quire (rĭ-kwīr′) *v.* **-quired, -quir•ing. 1.** To need. **2.** To insist upon : demand. **3.** To oblige : compel. **—re•quire′ment** *n.*

req•ui•site (rĕk′wĭ-zĭt) *adj.* Needed : necessary. *—n.* A necessity.

req•ui•si•tion (rĕk′wĭ-zĭsh′ən) *n.* **1.** A formal written request or demand for something needed. **2.** The state of being needed. **—req′ui•si′tion** *v.*

re•quite (rĭ-kwīt′) *v.* **-quit•ed, -quit•ing. 1.** To make return for <*requite* another's love> **2.** To avenge. **—re•quit′al** *n.*

rer•e•dos (rĕr′ĭ-dŏs′, rîr′-, rîr′dŏs′) *n.* The back of an open hearth of a fireplace.

re•run (rē′rŭn′) *n.* **1.** A repetition. **2.** Another showing of a recorded motion-picture or television program. **—re•run′** *v.*

res. *abbr.* **1.** reserve. **2.** residence; resident. **3.** resolution.

re•scind (rĭ-sĭnd′) *v.* To make void : annul. **—re•scind′a•ble** *adj.* **—re•scind′er** *n.* **—re•scis′sion** (-sĭzh′ən) *n.*

res•cue (rĕs′kyo͞o) *v.* **-cued, -cu•ing.** To free from confinement or danger : save. **—res′cue** *n.* **—res′cu•er** *n.*

re•search (rĭ-sûrch′, rē′sûrch′) *n.* **1.** Scientific or scholarly investigation. **2.** Close, careful study. **—re•search′** *v.*

re•sec•tion (rĭ-sĕk′shən) *n.* The excision of part of an organ or structure by surgery.

re•sem•blance (rĭ-zĕm′bləns) *n.* A similarity in nature, form, or appearance.

re•sem•ble (rĭ-zĕm′bəl) *v.* **-bled, -bling.** To have a similarity to : be like.

re•sent (rĭ-zĕnt′) *v.* To feel angry or indignant about : object to. **—re•sent′ful** *adj.* **—re•sent′ful•ly** *adv.* **—re•sent′ment** *n.*

res•er•va•tion (rĕz′ər-vā′shən) *n.* **1.** The act of reserving or the condition of being reserved. **2.** Something reserved. **3.** A limiting qualification or exception. **4.** Land set apart by a government for a special purpose, esp. an area for the use of an American or Canadian Indian people. **5.** An arrangement by which accommodations are secured ahead of time.

re•serve (rĭ-zûrv′) *v.* **-served, -serv•ing. 1.** To save for future use or a special purpose. **2.** To set apart for a particular person or use. **3.** To keep for oneself : retain. **4.** To defeat : put off. *—n.* **1.** Something saved for future use or a special purpose. **2.** The condition of being reserved <food held in *reserve*> **3.** Reticence. **4.** A reservation of public land. **5.** *often* **reserves.** A fighting force kept inactive until needed.

re•served (rĭ-zûrvd′) *adj.* **1.** Kept back or set aside. **2.** Reticent. **—re•serv′ed•ly** *adv.* **—re•serv′ed•ness** *n.*

res•er•voir (rĕz′ər-vwär′, -vwôr′, -vôr′) *n.* **1.** A body of water collected and stored for future use. **2.** A chamber for storing a fluid. **3.** A large supply : reserve.

re•side (rĭ-zīd′) *v.* **-sid•ed, -sid•ing. 1.** To live in a place : dwell. **2.** To be present : inhere. **—re•sid′er** *n.*

res•i•dence (rĕz′ĭ-dəns) *n.* **1.** The place where one lives. **2.** The act or a period of living somewhere.

res•i•den•cy (rĕz′ĭ-dən-sē, -dĕn′-) *n., pl.* **-cies. 1.** Residence. **2.** The period during which a physician receives specialized clinical training.

res•i•dent (rĕz′ĭ-dənt, -dĕnt′) *n.* **1.** One whose home is in a particular location. **2.** A physician serving a period of residency.

res•i•den•tial (rĕz′ĭ-dĕn′shəl) *adj.* **1.** Of or having residence. **2.** Containing or appropriate for residences.

re•sid•u•al (rĭ-zĭj′o͞o-əl) *adj.* Of, relating to, or left over as a residue. *—n.* **1.** An amount remaining : residue. **2.** A payment made to a performer for each repeat showing of a recorded television show.

res•i•due (rĕz′ĭ-do͞o′, -dyo͞o′) *n.* The remainder of something after treatment or removal of a part.

re•sign (rĭ-zīn′) *v.* **1.** To submit (oneself) to something unavoidable <*resigned* himself to waiting for the next bus> **2.** To give up (a job or position) : quit. **3.** To relinquish (a right, privilege, or claim).

res•ig•na•tion (rĕz′ĭg-nā′shən) *n.* **1.** An act of resigning. **2.** A formal statement that one is quitting a job. **3.** Passive acceptance, as of the unavoidable.

re•signed (rĭ-zīnd′) *adj.* Acquiescent. **—re•sign′ed•ly** *adv.*

re•sil•ience (rĭ-zĭl′yəns) *also* **re•sil•ien•cy** (-yən-sē) *n.* **1.** Ability to recover rapidly, as from misfortune : buoyancy. **2.** The property of a material that enables it to regain its original shape after being bent, stretched, or compressed : elasticity. **—re•sil′ient** *adj.* **—re•sil′ient•ly** *adv.*

res•in (rĕz′ĭn) *n.* **1.** A viscid substance that oozes from certain trees and plants, used in varnishes, synthetic plastics, and for many other purposes. **2.** Any of various artificial substances that have similar properties. **—res′in•ous** *adj.*

res•in•ate (rĕz′ə-nāt′) *v.* **-at•ed, -at•ing.** To impregnate or flavor with resin.

re•sist (rĭ-zĭst′) *v.* **1.** To oppose actively : strive against. **2.** To withstand. **—re•sist′er** *n.* **—re•sist′i•ble** *adj.*

re•sis•tance (rĭ-zĭs′təns) *n.* **1.** The act of resisting or the capacity to resist. **2.** A force that tends to oppose or retard motion. **3.** *Elect.* Opposition to electric current characteristic of a medium, substance, or circuit element. **4.** An underground organization seeking to overthrow a usu. totalitarian government. **—re•sis′tant** *adj.*

re•sis•tor (rĭ-zĭs′tər) *n.* An electric element used for providing resistance in a circuit.

res•o•lute (rĕz′ə-lo͞ot′) *adj.* Marked by firm determination : unwavering.

res•o•lu•tion (rĕz′ə-lo͞o′shən) *n.* **1.** Firm determination. **2. a.** The act of resolving. **b.** Something resolved, esp. a decision or expression of opinion adopted by a deliberative body. **3.** A solving, as of a problem.

re•solve (rĭ-zŏlv′) *v.* **-solved, -solv•ing. 1.** To make or cause to make a firm decision. **2.** To state formally in a resolution. **3.** To separate into component parts. **4.** To find a solution to. **5.** To deal with successfully : settle. **—re•solve** *n.* **—re•solv′a•ble** *adj.*

re•solved (rĭ-zŏlvd′) *adj.* Determined.

res•o•nance (rĕz′ə-nəns) *n.* **1.** The quality or state of being resonant. **2.** *Physics.* Enhancement of the response of a system to a periodic driving force oscillating at the frequency at which the system tends to oscillate naturally. **3.** Intensification of sound by sympathetic vibration.

res•o•nant (rĕz′ə-nənt) *adj.* **1.** Continuing to sound : echoing. **2.** Of or showing resonance. **3.** Having a full, deep, rich sound. **—res′o•nant•ly** *adv.*

res•o•nate (rĕz′ə-nāt′) *v.* **-nat•ed, -nat•ing. 1.** To show or produce resonance. **2.** To resound. **—res′o•na′tion** *n.*

res•o•na•tor (rĕz′ə-nā′tər) *n.* A hollow chamber or cavity that permits internal resonance, as of sound waves.

re•sort (rĭ-zôrt′) *v.* **1.** To have recourse <*resorted* to rationing> **2.** To go commonly or often : repair. *—n.* **1.** A place visited for relaxation or recreation. **2.** Recourse. **3.** One turned to for help or relief.

re•sound (rĭ-zound′) *v.* **1.** To be filled with sound : reverberate. **2.** To make a long, loud sound. **—re•sound′ing•ly** *adv.*

re•source (rē′sôrs′, -sōrs′, -zôrs′, -zōrs′, rĭ-) *n.* **1.** A source of support or aid. **2.** An ability to handle a situation in an effective manner. **3. resources. a.** Means that can be used profitably. **b.** Capital : assets. **4.** A natural resource. **—re•source′ful** *adj.*

re•spect (rĭ-spĕkt′) *v.* **1.** To feel or show deferential regard for : esteem. **2.** To avoid violation of or inteference with. **3.** To relate to : concern. *—n.* **1.** Deferential regard : esteem. **2.** The state of being regarded with deference or esteem. **3.** Willingness to show consideration or appreciation. **4. respects.** Polite expressions of consideration or deference <paid our *respects*> **5.** A specific aspect, feature, or detail. **6.** Relation : reference. **—re•spect′er** *n.* **—re•spect′ful** *adj.* **—re•spect′ful•ly** *adv.*

re•spect•a•ble (rĭ-spĕk′tə-bəl) *adj.* **1.** Deserving respect or esteem : worthy. **2.** Conventional or proper in conduct or appearance. **3.** Reasonably good. **4.** Considerable <a *respectable* amount> **—re•spect′a•bil′i•ty** *n.* **—re•spect′a•bly** *adv.*

re•spect•ing (rĭ-spĕk′tĭng) *prep.* With reference to.

re•spec•tive (rĭ-spĕk′tĭv) *adj.* Separate : particular <took their *respective* seats>

re•spec•tive•ly (rĭ-spĕk′tĭv-lē) *adv.* Singly in the order given.

res•pi•ra•tion (rĕs′pə-rā′shən) *n.* **1.** The act of inhaling and exhaling. **2.** The metabolic process by which an organism assimilates oxygen and releases carbon dioxide and other products of oxidation. **—res′pi•ra•to′ry** (-pər-ə-tôr′ē, -tōr′ē) *adj.*

res•pi•ra•tor (rĕs′pə-rā′tər) *n.* **1.** A device used in administering artificial respiration. **2.** A filtering device worn over the mouth and nose to protect the respiratory tract.

re•spire (rĭ-spīr′) *v.* **-spired, -spir•ing. 1.** To breathe. **2.** To undergo the metabolic process of respiration.

res•pite (rĕs′pĭt) *n.* **1.** A short period of rest or relief. **2.** A temporary suspension.

re•splen•dent (rĭ-splĕn′dənt) *adj.* Full of splendor. **—re•splen′dence** *n.*

re•spond (rĭ-spŏnd′) *v.* **1.** To reply : answer. **2.** To act because or at the prompting of something : react. **3.** To react positively.

re•spon•dent (rĭ-spŏn′dənt) *n.* **1.** One who responds. **2.** *Law.* A defendant in a divorce or equity case.

re•sponse (rĭ-spŏns′) *n.* **1.** An act of responding. **2.** A reply : answer. **3.** A reaction to a stimulus.

re•spon•si•bil•i•ty (rĭ-spŏn′sə-bĭl′ĭ-tē) *n., pl.* **-ties. 1.** The quality, state, or fact of being responsible. **2.** One that a person is responsible for.

re•spon•si•ble (rĭ-spŏn′sə-bəl) *adj.* **1.** Having to account for one's actions : answerable <a government *responsible* to the people> **2.** Having a duty or obligation <*responsible* for washing the dishes tonight> **3.** Being a source or cause. **4.** Dependable. **5.** Involving important duties or obligations. **—re•spon′si•bly** *adv.*

re•spon•sive (rĭ-spŏn′sĭv) *adj.* **1.** Answering : responding. **2.** Promptly reacting to appeals or suggestions.

rest[1] (rĕst) *n.* **1.** A state or period of inactivity, relaxation, or sleep. **2.** Absence of motion. **3.** *Mus.* **a.** An interval of silence equal in duration to a note of the same value. **b.** The symbol indicating such a pause and its duration. **4.** A supporting device. *—v.* **1.** To stop work or motion. **2.** To give rest to. **3.** To lie down. **4.** To be at peace or ease. **5.** To be still or inactive. **6.** To be or cause to be supported. **7.** To depend : rely. **8.** To be placed or imposed <It *rests* with you to carry on.> **—rest′ful** *adj.* **—rest′ful•ly** *adv.*

rest[2] (rĕst) *n.* **1.** The part left over : remainder. **2.** Those remaining <The *rest* are coming later.>

res•tau•rant (rĕs′tər-ənt, -tə-ränt′) *n.* A place for serving meals to the public.

res•tau•ra•teur (rĕs′tər-ə-tûr′) *n.* One who owns or runs a restaurant.

rest home *n.* An establishment where old or sick people are housed and cared for.

res•ti•tu•tion (rĕs′tĭ-to͞o′shən, -tyo͞o′-) *n.* **1.** An act of returning something to its rightful owner. **2.** An act of compensating for loss, damage, or injury.

res•tive (rĕs′tĭv) *adj.* **1.** Impatient under restriction or delay : uneasy. **2.** Hard to control : balky. **—res′tive•ness** *n.*

rest•less (rĕst′lĭs) *adj.* **1.** Without rest or quiet <*restless* sleep> **2. a.** Unable or unwilling to rest or be still. **b.** Nervous : fidgety. **—rest′less•ly** *adv.*

res•to•ra•tion (rĕs′tə-rā′shən) *n.* **1.** The act or an instance of restoring or the state of being restored. **2.** Something that has been restored to a previous condition.

re•stor•a•tive (rĭ-stôr′ə-tĭv, -stōr′-) *adj.* **1.** Of or for restoration. **2.** Tending to restore health or strength. **—re•stor′a•tive** *n.*

re•store (rĭ-stôr′, -stōr′) *v.* **-stored, -stor•ing. 1.** To put back into existence or use. **2.** To bring back to a former or original condition. **3.** To give back : return. ☆**syns:** REINSTATE, RENEW, REVIVE **—re•stor′er** *n.*

re•strain (rĭ-strān′) *v.* **1.** To hold back. **2.** To take away the freedom of. **3.** To limit or restrict. **—re•strain′a•ble** *adj.*

re•straint (rĭ-strānt′) *n.* **1.** An act of restraining or the condition of being restrained. **2.** Loss of freedom. **3.** A limitation. **4.** Something that restrains. **5.** Moderation in action or expression.

re•strict (rĭ-strĭkt′) *v.* To hold within limits : confine. **—re•stric′tion** *n.* **—re•stric′tive** *adj.* **—re•stric′tive•ly** *adv.*

rest room *n.* A public lavatory.

re•sult (rĭ-zŭlt′) *v.* **1.** To happen or exist as a consequence. **2.** To end in a particular way. *—n.* A consequence : outcome. **—re•sul′tant** *adj.* & *n.*

re•sume (rĭ-zo͞om′) *v.* **-sumed, -sum•ing. 1.** To begin or take up again after an interruption. **2.** To occupy or assume again. **—re•sump′tion** (-zŭmp′shən) *n.*

ré•su•mé (rĕz′o͝o-mā′, rĕz′o͝o-mā′) *n.* A summary, esp. of one's personal history and employment experience.

re•sur•gent (rĭ-sûr′jənt) *adj.* Rising or surging again. **—re•sur′gence** *n.*

res•ur•rec•tion (rĕz′ə-rĕk′shən) *n.* **1.** An act of returning or bringing from death to life. **2. Resurrection. a.** The rising again of Christ after the Crucifixion. **b.** The rising again of the dead at the Last Judgment. **3.** A revival. **—res′ur•rect′** *v.*

re•sus•ci•tate (rĭ-sŭs′ĭ-tāt′) *v.* **-tat•ed, -tat•ing.** To return to consciousness or life : revive. **—re•sus′ci•ta′tion** *n.* **—re•sus′ci•ta′tor** *n.*

re•tail (rē′tāl′) *n.* The sale of goods in small quantities to the public. *—v.* **1.** To sell at retail. **2.** To tell and retell. **—re′tail′** *adj.* & *adv.* **—re′tail′er** *n.*

re•tain (rĭ-tān′) *v.* **1.** To keep in one's possession : hold. **2.** To keep or hold in a certain place, condition, or position. **3.** To hold in the memory : remember. **4.** To hire (e.g., an attorney) by paying an initial fee. **—re•tain′a•ble** *adj.* **—re•tain′ment** *n.*

re•tain•er (rĭ-tā′nər) *n.* **1.** One that retains. **2. a.** An attendant in a noble household, as in feudal times. **b.** A domestic servant. **c.** An employee. **3.** The fee paid to engage a professional adviser.

re•take (rē-tāk′) *v.* **1.** To take again. **2.** To photograph again. *—n.* (rē′tāk′). A rephotographed scene, as for a film.

re•tal•i•ate (rĭ-tăl′ē-āt′) *v.* **-at•ed, -at•ing.** To return like for like, esp. evil for evil. **—re•tal′i•a′tion** *n.* **—re•tal′i•a•to′ry** *adj.*

re•tard (rĭ-tärd′) *v.* To slow the progress of : delay. **—re•tar′dant** *adj.* & *n.*

re•tar•da•tion (rē′tär-dā′shən) *n.* **1.** The act of retarding or state of being retarded. **2.** A delay. **3.** Mental deficiency.

re•tard•ed (rĭ-tär′dĭd) *adj.* Abnormally slow in mental or emotional development.

retch (rĕch) *v.* To try to vomit.

re•ten•tion (rĭ-tĕn′shən) *n.* **1.** An act of retaining or the state of being retained. **2.** The ability to retain. **—re•ten′tive** *adj.*

ret•i•cent (rĕt′ĭ-sənt) *adj.* Reluctant to speak freely. **—ret′i•cence** *n.*

ret•i•na (rĕt′n-ə) *n., pl.* **-nas** or **-nae** (-n-ē′). A delicate light-sensitive membrane lining the inner eyeball and connected to the brain by the optic nerve. **—ret′i•nal** *adj.*

ret•i•nue (rĕt′n-o͞o′, -yo͞o′) *n.* A group of attendants accompanying a high-ranking person. ☆**syns:** ENTOURAGE, FOLLOWING, SUITE, TRAIN

re•tire (rĭ-tīr′) *v.* **-tired, -tir•ing. 1.** To withdraw, as for rest or seclusion. **2.** To go to bed. **3.** To give up working or serving, usu. because of advancing age. **4.** To remove from active service. **5.** To withdraw troops : retreat. **6.** To remove from circulation. **7.** *Baseball.* To put out. **—re•tired′** *adj.* **—re•tir′ee′** *n.* **—re•tire′ment** *n.*

re•tir•ing (rĭ-tīr′ĭng) *adj.* Unobtrusive and reserved. **—re•tir′ing•ly** *adv.*

re•tort[1] (rĭ-tôrt′) *v.* **1.** To reply to, esp. in a quick, sharp way. **2.** To retaliate. *—n.* A quick, sharp reply. ☆**syns:** COMEBACK, COUNTER, REPARTEE, RIPOSTE

re•tort[2] (rĭ-tôrt′, rē′tôrt′) *n.* A closed laboratory vessel used for distillation or decomposition by heat.

re•touch (rē-tŭch′) *v.* **1.** To try to improve by adding details or small corrections : touch up. **2.** *Photog.* To change, esp. by taking out defects.

re•trace (rē-trās′) *v.* **1.** To trace again. **2.** To go back over <*retraced* his steps>

re•tract (rĭ-trăkt′) *v.* **1.** To take back : disavow <*retracted* the accusation> **2.** To draw back or in. **—re•tract′a•ble, re•tract′i•ble** *adj.* **—re•trac′tion** *n.*

re•trac•tile (rĭ-trăk′tĭl, -tīl′) *adj.* Able to be drawn back or in <*retractile* claws>

re•tread (rē-trĕd′) *v.* To fit (a worn tire) with a new tread. *—n.* (rē′trĕd′). A retreaded tire.

re•treat (rĭ-trēt′) *n.* **1.** An act of going back or withdrawing, esp from danger or an enemy attack. **2.** A quiet, private place : refuge. **3.** A time of seclusion, esp. for quiet thought, prayer, or study. **4. a.** The signal for a military withdrawal. **b.** A bugle call that signals the lowering of the flag. *—v.* To make a retreat : withdraw.

re•trench (rĭ-trĕnch′) *v.* **1.** To cut down. **2.** To cut back expenses or operations.

ret•ri•bu•tion (rĕt′rə-byo͞o′shən) *n.* A suitable return, esp. punishment, for what one has done. **—re•trib′u•tive** (rĭ-trĭb′yə-tĭv), **re•trib′u•to′ry** (-tôr′ē, -tōr′ē) *adj.*

re•trieve (rĭ-trēv′) *v.* **-trieved, -triev•ing. 1.** To bring or get back : regain. **2.** To find and bring back (e.g., game) : fetch. **3.** To put right : rectify. **—re•triev′a•ble** *adj.* **—re•triev′a•bly** *adv.* **—re•triev′al** *n.*

re•triev•er (rĭ-trē′vər) *n.* **1.** One that retrieves. **2.** A dog trained to retrieve game.

ret•ro•ac•tive (rĕt′rō-ăk′tĭv) *adj.* Applying to a period prior to enactment.

ret•ro•en•gine (rĕt′rō-ĕn′jĭn) *n.* A spacecraft's rocket engine producing thrust in a direction opposite to that of the spacecraft's motion, used to decelerate.

ret•ro•fire (rĕt′rō-fīr′) *v.* **-fired, -fir•ing.** To ignite. Used of a retroengine.

ret•ro•grade (rĕt′rə-grād′) *adj.* **1.** Moving or directed backward. **2.** Reverting to an earlier or inferior condition. *—v.* **1.** To move backward. **2.** To decline : degenerate.

ret•ro•gress (rĕt′rə-grĕs′, rĕt′rə-grĕs′) *v.* To go backward, esp. to an earlier or worse condition. **—ret′ro•gres′sion** *n.* **—ret′ro•gres′sive** *adj.*

ret•ro•rock•et (rĕt′rō-rŏk′ĭt) *n.* A retroengine.

ret•ro•spect (rĕt′rə-spĕkt′) *n.* A consideration or review of past events. **—ret′ro•spec′tion** *n.* **—ret′ro•spec′tive** *adj.* & *n.*

re•turn (rĭ-tûrn′) *v.* **1.** To go or come back. **2.** To give or send back to a former possessor. **3.** To reciprocate. **4.** To reply. **5.** To produce (e.g., profit). **6.** To deliver or submit (e.g., a verdict). **7.** To re-elect. *—n.* **1.** The act of returning or fact of being returned. **2.** Something returned. **3.** A recurrence. **4.** A reply. **5.** A profit : yield. **6.** An official report or document to be submitted. **7.** *Sports.* A ball sent or carried back. *—adj.* **1.** Of or involving a return <a *return* ticket> **2.** Given or done in return. **—re•turn'a•ble** *adj.* **—re•turn'ee'** *n.* **—re•turn'er** *n.*

re•un•ion (rē-yōōn'yən) *n.* **1.** The act or an instance of reuniting. **2.** A gathering of the separated members of a group.

re•u•nite (rē'yōō-nīt') *v.* To come or bring together again.

rev (rĕv) *Informal. —n.* A revolution of a motor. *—v.* **revved, rev•ving.** To increase the speed or pace of <*rev* up an engine><*revving* up factory production>

rev. *abbr.* **1.** revenue. **2.** reverse; reversed. **3.** review; reviewed. **4.** revise; revision. **5.** *or* **Rev.** revolution.

re•vamp (rē-vămp') *v.* **1.** To patch up : restore. **2.** To revise.

re•vanch•ism (rĭ-vănch'ĭz'əm) *n.* A political policy of seeking to win back lost national territory. **—re•vanch'ist** *n.*

re•veal (rĭ-vēl') *v.* **1.** To make known. **2.** To bring to view : show clearly.

rev•eil•le (rĕv'ə-lē) *n.* A signal, as on a bugle, given to awaken soldiers early in the morning.

rev•el (rĕv'əl) *v.* **-eled, -el•ling** *or* **-elled, -el•ling. 1.** To take great pleasure <*reveled* in his triumph> **2.** To make merry : celebrate. *—n. often* **revels.** Merrymaking. **—rev'el•er** *n.* **—rev'el•ry** *n.*

rev•e•la•tion (rĕv'ə-lā'shən) *n.* **1.** An act of revealing. **2.** Something revealed, esp. something dramatic. **3. Revelation.** See BIBLE TABLE. **—rev'e•la•to'ry** *adj.*

re•venge (rĭ-vĕnj') *v.* **-venged, -veng•ing.** To impose or inflict injury in return for (injury or insult) : avenge. *—n.* **1.** The act of revenging. **2.** A desire for revenge. **—re•venge'ful** *adj.* **—re•veng'er** *n.*

rev•e•nue (rĕv'ə-nōō', -nyōō') *n.* **1.** Government income from all sources. **2.** Yield from investments.

re•ver•ber•ate (rĭ-vûr'bə-rāt') *v.* **-at•ed, -at•ing. 1.** To echo : resound. **2.** To rebound or recoil. **—re•ver'ber•a'tion** *n.*

re•vere (rĭ-vîr') *v.* **-vered, -ver•ing.** To regard with great devotion or respect.

rev•er•ence (rĕv'ər-əns) *n.* **1.** A profound feeling of awe and respect. **2.** An expression of respect, as a bow. **3. Reverence.** Used as a title of respect for a cleric. **—rev'er•ence** *v.* **—rev'er•ent** *adj.*

rev•er•end (rĕv'ər-ənd) *adj.* **1.** Worthy of reverence. **2. Reverend.** Used as a title for a cleric. *—n. Informal.* A cleric.

rev•er•en•tial (rĕv'ə-rĕn'shəl) *adj.* Expressing reverence. **—rev'er•en'tial•ly** *adv.*

rev•er•ie (rĕv'ə-rē) *n.* **1.** Abstracted musing. **2.** A daydream.

re•ver•sal (rĭ-vûr'səl) *n.* **1.** An act of reversing or the condition of being reversed. **2.** A change for the worse.

re•verse (rĭ-vûrs') *adj.* **1.** Turned backward in position, order, or direction. **2.** Causing backward movement. *—n.* **1.** The contrary of something. **2.** A back or rear part. **3.** A change in fortune from better to worse. **4.** A mechanism for reversing movement, as a gear in a motor vehicle. *—v.* **-versed, -vers•ing. 1.** To turn to the opposite position or direction. **2.** To turn inside out or upside down. **3.** To transpose. **4.** *Law.* To revoke or annul (a decision or decree). **5.** To put or drive in reverse. **—re•vers'er** *n.* **—re•vers'i•ble** *adj.* & *n.*

re•vert (rĭ-vûrt') *v.* **1.** To return to an earlier state, practice, or belief. **2.** *Law.* To return to a previous owner or the previous owner's heirs. **—re•ver'sion** *n.* **—re•ver'sion•ar'y** *adj.*

re•view (rĭ-vyōō') *v.* **1.** To study or examine again. **2.** To look back on. **3.** To write or give a critical report on (e.g., a new book). **4.** *Law.* To examine (a decision or action) again, as in a higher court. **5.** To subject to a formal inspection <*review* troops> *—n.* **1.** A re-examination : reconsideration. **2.** A summary of previous material or past events. **3.** The act of restudying. **4.** An inspection or examination with the intention of evaluating. **5. a.** A critical report or essay that evaluates a work or performance. **b.** A periodical devoted to such reports. **6.** *Law.* A re-examination of an action or decision. ☆**syns:** COMMENT, COMMENTARY, CRITICISM, CRITIQUE, NOTICE

re•vile (rĭ-vīl') *v.* **-viled, -vil•ing.** To denounce with abusive language. **—re•vile'ment** *n.* **—re•vil'er** *n.*

re•vise (rĭ-vīz') *v.* **-vised, -vis•ing. 1.** To look over (a text) in order to improve or correct. **2.** To change : modify. **—re•vis'er, re•vi'sor** *n.* **—re•vi'sion** (-vĭzh'ən) *n.*

re•vi•tal•ize (rē-vīt'l-īz') *v.* To give new life to. **—re•vi'tal•i•za'tion** *n.*

re•viv•al (rĭ-vī'vəl) *n.* **1.** An act of reviving or the state of being revived. **2.** A new presentation, as of an old film. **3.** An evangelistic meeting or series of meetings to reawaken religious faith.

re•vive (rĭ-vīv') *v.* **-vived, -viv•ing. 1.** To return to life or consciousness. **2.** To impart new health, vigor, or spirit to. **3.** To restore to use or notice. **—re•viv'er** *n.*

re•viv•i•fy (rē-vĭv'ə-fī') *v.* **-fied, -fy•ing.** REVIVE 2. **—re•viv'i•fi•ca'tion** *n.*

re•voke (rĭ-vōk') *v.* **-voked, -vok•ing.** To nullify by canceling or reversing : annul. **—rev'o•ca•ble** (rĕv'ə-kə-bəl) *adj.* **—rev'o•ca'tion** *n.* **—re•vok'er** *n.*

re•volt (rĭ-vōlt') *v.* **1.** To try to overthrow one's rulers : rebel. **2.** To rise in strenuous opposition <*revolt* against new taxes> **3.** To fill with disgust : repel. *—n.* An uprising : rebellion.

re•volt•ing (rĭ-vōl'tĭng) *adj.* Disgustingly offensive. **—re•volt'ing•ly** *adv.*

rev•o•lu•tion (rĕv'ə-lōō'shən) *n.* **1. a.** Orbital motion about a point <Saturn's yearly *revolution* around the sun> **b.** Rotational motion about an axis. **2.** An abrupt overthrow of a government or group of rulers. **3.** A sudden or radical change in a system or state of affairs <a *revolution* in medicine> **—rev'o•lu'tion•ist** *n.*

rev•o•lu•tion•ar•y (rĕv'ə-lōō'shə-nĕr'ē) *adj.* **1.** Of, relating to, or promoting revolution. **2.** Marked by or effecting radical change. **—rev'o•lu'tion•ar'y** *n.*

rev•o•lu•tion•ize (rĕv'ə-lōō'shə-nīz') *v.* **-ized, -iz•ing.** To bring about radical changes in.

re•volve (rĭ-vŏlv') *v.* **-volved, -volv•ing. 1.** To move around a central point : orbit. **2.** To rotate : spin. **3.** To recur periodically. **4.** To consider : ponder. **—re•volv'a•ble** *adj.*

re•volv•er (rĭ-vŏl'vər) *n.* A handgun having a revolving cylinder with several cartridge chambers.

re•vue (rĭ-vyōō') *n.* A usu. satirical musical show with skits, songs, and dances.

re•vul•sion (rĭ-vŭl'shən) *n.* **1.** Sudden, strong disgust or loathing. **2.** Withdrawal from or aversion to something.

re•ward (rĭ-wôrd') *n.* Something given or offered for a special service, as the return of something lost. *—v.* **1.** To give a reward to or for. **2.** To recompense.

re•ward•ing (rĭ•wôrd'ĭng) *adj.* Yielding benefits or a sense of satisfaction.

re•word (rē-wûrd') *v.* To express again in different words.

Rey•kja•vik (rā'kyə-vēk'). Cap. of Iceland, in the SW. *Pop.* 83,536.

RF *abbr.* radio frequency.

RFD *also* **R.F.D.** *abbr.* rural free delivery.

Rh *symbol for* RHODIUM.

rhap•so•dize (răp'sə-dīz') *v.* **-dized, -diz•ing.** To express oneself with extravagant enthusiasm.

rhap•so•dy (răp'sə-dē) *n., pl.* **-dies. 1.** Extravagantly enthusiastic expression of feeling. **2.** A work, esp. a musical composition, marked by an impassioned style. **—rhap•sod'ic** (-sŏd'ĭk) *adj.* **—rhap•sod'i•cal•ly** *adv.* **—rhap'so•dist** *n.*

rhe•a (rē'ə) *n.* A flightless, 3-toed South American bird of the genus *Rhea*, resembling the ostrich.

rhea

rhe•ni•um (rē'nē-əm) *n. Symbol* **Re** A rare, dense, silvery-white metallic element used in electrical contacts and high-temperature thermocouples.

rhe•o•stat (rē'ə-stăt') *n.* A variable electrical resistor used to regulate current. **—rhe'o•stat'ic** *adj.*

rhe•sus monkey (rē'səs) *n.* A brownish monkey, *Macaca mulatta*, of India, often used in biological experiments.

rhet•o•ric (rĕt'ər-ĭk) *n.* **1.** The art of the effective and persuasive use of language. **2.** Public speaking designed to persuade. **3.** Showy, bombastic language. **—rhe•tor'i•cal** (rĭ-tôr'ĭ-kəl, -tŏr-) *adj.* **—rhet'o•ri'cian** (rĕt'ə-rĭsh'ən) *n.*

rhetorical question *n.* A question to which one does not expect an answer.

rheum (rōōm) *n.* A thin watery mucous discharge from the eyes or nose.

rheu•mat•ic (rōō-măt'ĭk) *adj.* Of, relating to, or affected with rheumatism. *—n.* One affected with rheumatism.

rheumatic fever *n.* A severe infectious disease chiefly of children, marked by fever and painful inflammation of the joints and often resulting in permanent heart damage.

rheu•ma•tism (ro͞o′mə-tĭz′əm) *n.* A painful and disabling disorder of the muscles, tendons, joints, bones, or nerves.

rheu•ma•toid arthritis (ro͞o′mə-toid′) *n.* A chronic disease characterized by stiffness and inflammation of the joints.

Rh factor (är′āch′) *n.* Any of several substances in red blood cells that can cause severe antigenic reactions when mixed with blood lacking the factor.

Rhine (rīn). River of W Europe, rising in E Switzerland and flowing to the North Sea.

rhine•stone (rīn′stōn′) *n.* An artificial gem made of paste or glass in imitation of a diamond.

rhi•no (rī′nō) *n., pl.* **-nos.** *Informal.* A rhinoceros.

rhi•noc•er•os (rī-nŏs′ər-əs) *n.* A large, thick-skinned mammal of the family Rhinocerotidae, of Africa and Asia, having 1 or 2 upright horns on the snout.

rhi•nol•o•gy (rī-nŏl′ə-jē) *n.* The anatomy, physiology, and pathology of the nose.

rhi•no•plas•ty (rī′nō-plăs′tē, -nə-) *n.* Plastic surgery of the nose.

rhi•zome (rī′zōm′) *n.* A fleshy plant stem that grows horizontally under or along the ground, sending out roots below and leaves or shoots above.

Rh-neg•a•tive (är′āch-nĕg′ə-tĭv) *adj.* Not having an Rh factor.

Rhode Island (rōd). State of the NE U.S. *Cap.* Providence. *Pop.* 947,154. **—Rhode Islander** *n.*

Rho•de•sia (rō-dē′zhə). Zimbabwe. **—Rho•de′sian** *adj.* & *n.*

rho•di•um (rō′dē-əm) *n. Symbol* **Rh** A hard, durable, silvery-white metallic element used to form high-temperature alloys and corrosion-resistant coatings.

rho•do•den•dron (rō′də-dĕn′drən) *n.* Any of various evergreen shrubs of the genus *Rhododendron,* having variously colored flower clusters.

rhom•boid (rŏm′boid′) *n.* A parallelogram having unequal adjacent sides. **—rhom•boi′dal** *adj.*

rhom•bus (rŏm′bəs) *n., pl.* **-es** or **-bi** (-bī′). An equilateral parallelogram. **—rhom′bic** *adj.*

Rhone *also* **Rhône** (rōn). River of SW Switzerland and SE France.

Rh-pos•i•tive (är′āch-pŏs′ĭ-tĭv) *adj.* Having an Rh factor.

rhu•barb (ro͞o′bärb′) *n.* **1.** A garden plant, *Rheum rhaponticum,* having long, fleshy, edible leafstalks. **2.** *Slang.* A noisy quarrel.

rhyme *also* **rime** (rīm) *—n.* **1. a.** Correspondence in the final sounds of words or lines of verse. **b.** Verse having such correspondence. **2.** A word that corresponds with another in terminal sound <"Forlorn" is a *rhyme* for "outworn."> *—v.* **rhymed, rhym•ing** *also* **rimed, rim•ing. 1.** To be a rhyme. **2.** To compose verse. **3.** To use as a rhyme. **—rhym′er** *n.*

rhythm (rĭth′əm) *n.* **1.** A movement or action marked by regular recurrence of elements <the steady *rhythm* of knitting> **2.** *Mus.* A recurrent pattern formed by notes of differing stress and duration. **3. a.** The rise and fall of the voice in speech or of the mind's voice in reading. **b.** Poetic meter. **—rhyth′mi•cal, rhyth′mic** *adj.*

rhythm and blues *n.* Popular music developed by black Americans that combines elements of blues and jazz.

rhythm method *n.* A birth-control method in which intercourse is avoided during the period of ovulation.

RI *abbr.* Rhode Island (with Zip Code).

R.I. *abbr.* Rhode Island.

ri•al (rē-ôl′, -äl′) *n.* See CURRENCY TABLE.

rib (rĭb) *n.* **1.** One of a series of long, paired, curved bones that extend from the spine toward the sternum and protect the chest cavity in most vertebrates. **2.** A rod that gives shape or support <the *ribs* of an umbrella> **3.** A raised ridge in fabric. *—v.* **ribbed, rib•bing. 1.** To support, shape, or provide with a rib or ribs. **2.** To make with ridges. **3.** *Slang.* To poke fun at.

rib•ald (rĭb′əld) *adj.* Marked by or indulging in coarse humor. **—rib′ald•ry** *n.*

rib•bon (rĭb′ən) *n.* **1.** A narrow strip or band of decorative fabric. **2. ribbons.** Ragged strips. **3.** An inked strip of cloth or polyethylene used in a typewriter, adding machine, etc.

ri•bo•fla•vin (rī′bō-flā′vĭn) *n.* The chief growth-promoting factor of the vitamin B complex, found in leafy vegetables, milk, egg yolks, and meat.

ri•bo•nu•cle•ic acid (rī′bō-no͞o-klē′ĭk, -nyo͞o-) *n.* A compound having a complicated, single-strand structure, found in the nucleus, cytoplasm, and ribosomes of all living cells and functioning in the synthesis of proteins : RNA.

ri•bo•some (rī′bə-sōm′) *n.* A spherical, RNA-containing particle in cytoplasm, active in the synthesis of protein. **—ri′bo•so′mal** *adj.*

rice (rīs) *n.* A cereal grass, *Oryza sativa,* with starchy edible seeds widely grown in warm regions.

†**rice•bird** (rīs′bûrd′) *n. S. U.S.* The bobolink.

rich (rĭch) *adj.* **1.** Having great wealth. **2.** Having great value or abundance <a *rich* harvest> **3.** Magnificent : luxurious. **4.** Abounding <*rich* in mineral resources> **5.** Extremely productive. **6.** Containing much fat or sugar <a *rich* pastry> **7. a.** Full and mellow <a *rich* baritone voice> **b.** Warm and strong in color. ☆**syns:** AFFLUENT, MONEYED, WEALTHY, WELL-TO-DO

rich•es (rĭch′ĭz) *pl.n.* **1.** Abundant wealth. **2.** Valuable possessions.

Rich•mond (rĭch′mənd). Cap. of Va., in the EC part. *Pop.* 219,214.

Rich•ter scale (rĭk′tər) *n.* A logarithmic scale used to express the magnitude of earthquakes.

rick (rĭk) *n.* A stack, as of straw or hay.

rick•ets (rĭk′ĭts) *n. (sing. in number).* A disease of children resulting from a lack of vitamin D and in defective bone growth.

rick•et•y (rĭk′ĭ-tē) *adj.* **-i•er, -i•est. 1.** Apt to fall apart : shaky. **2.** Feeble, with age. **3.** Of or affected with rickets.

rick•sha or **rick•shaw** (rĭk′shô′) *n.* A small 2-wheeled Oriental carriage drawn usu. by 1 man.

ric•o•chet (rĭk′ə-shā′) *v.* **-cheted** (-shād′), **chet•ing** (-shā′ĭng) *also* **-chet•ted** (-shĕt′ĭd), **-chet•ting** (-shĕt′ĭng). To rebound from a surface. **—ric′o•chet′** *n.*

ri•cot•ta (rĭ-kŏt′ə) *n.* A soft, white, Italian cheese resembling cottage cheese.

rid (rĭd) *v.* **rid** or **rid•ded, rid•ding.** To make free : relieve <*rid* the house of vermin> **—rid′dance** *n.*

rid•dle[1] (rĭd′l) *v.* **-dled, -dling. 1.** To pierce with many small holes : perforate. **2.** To spread throughout <a paper *riddled* with spelling mistakes>

rid•dle[2] (rĭd′l) *n.* A puzzling question or situation requiring thought to be solved.

ride (rīd) *v.* **rode** (rōd), **rid•den** (rĭd′n), **rid•ing. 1.** To be conveyed in a vehicle or on an animal. **2.** To travel over a surface <a car that *rides* well> **3.** To float or move on or as if on water. **4.** To sit on and drive <*ride* a bicycle> **5.** To be carried upon <*riding* the waves> **6.** To take part in (e.g., a race) by sitting on and controlling an animal or vehicle. **7.** To cause to leave, esp. on horseback <*rode* him out of town> **8.** *Informal.* To ridicule. *—n.* **1.** An act of riding. **2.** A path for riding. **3.** A device, as at an amusement park, that one rides for pleasure or excitement. **—ride out.** To survive : outlast.

rid•er (rī′dər) *n.* **1.** One that rides. **2.** An addition to a document, esp. a clause added to a legislative bill.

ridge (rĭj) *n.* **1.** A long, narrow upper section or crest. **2.** A long, narrow land elevation. **3.** A line formed where 2 sloping surfaces meet, as on a roof. **4.** A narrow raised strip, as on cloth. **—ridge** *v.*

ridge•pole (rĭj′pōl′) *n.* A horizontal beam at the ridge of a roof, to which the rafters are attached.

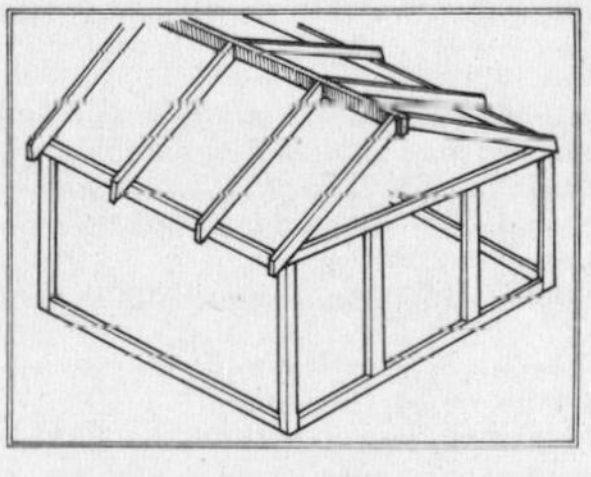

ridgepole

rid•i•cule (rĭd′ĭ-kyo͞ol′) *n.* Words or actions intended to make people laugh scornfully at a person or thing. *—v.* **-culed, -cul•ing.** To make fun of. ☆**syns:** DERIDE, GIBE, MOCK, TAUNT, TWIT

ri•dic•u•lous (rĭ-dĭk′yə-ləs) *adj.* Meriting or inspiring ridicule : ludicrous.

ri•el (rē-ĕl′) *n.* See CURRENCY TABLE.

rife (rīf) *adj.* **rif•er, rif•est. 1.** Common in occurrence : prevalent. **2.** Abounding.

riff (rĭf) *n.* A rhythmic phrase constantly repeated esp. in jazz. **—riff** *v.*

riff•raff (rĭf′răf′) *n.* **1.** Disreputable people. **2.** Trash : rubbish.

ri•fle[1] (rī′fəl) *n.* A firearm having a long barrel containing spiral grooves. *—v.* **-fled, -fling.** To cut spiral grooves within.

ri•fle[2] (rī′fəl) *v.* **-fled, -fling.** To search through disruptively, esp. with intent to steal : ransack. **—ri′fler** *n.*

rift (rĭft) *n.* **1. a.** *Geol.* A fault. **b.** A narrow rock fissure. **2.** A breach in friendly relations. *—v.* To split open : break.

†**rig** (rĭg) *v.* **rigged, rig·ging. 1.** To fit out with harness or equipment. **2.** To equip (a ship) with shrouds, sails, and yards. **3.** *Informal.* To dress : clothe <*rigged* out in her finery> **4.** To make or construct hastily. **5.** To manipulate dishonestly <*rig* the election> *—n.* **1.** The arrangement of masts, sails, and spars on a sailing vessel. **2.** Special equipment or gear. **3.** A carriage with its horses. **4.** *Informal.* An outfit. **5.** An apparatus for drilling oil wells. **6.** *W U.S.* A saddle.
rig·a·ma·role (rĭg′ə-mə-rōl′) *n. var. of* RIGMAROLE.
rig·ging (rĭg′ĭng) *n.* **1.** The system of ropes, chains, and tackle for supporting and maneuvering the masts, sails, and yards of a sailing ship. **2.** Equipment for a particular task, as construction work.
right (rīt) *n.* **1.** The side or direction opposite the left. **2.** That which is ethical, good, just, or proper. **3.** A conservative political group or faction. **4.** Something due to one by force of law or nature. **5.** A just moral or legal claim <the *right* to vote> *—adj.* **1. a.** Of or located on the side opposite the left. **b.** Toward this side <made a *right* turn> **2.** Of or inclined to politically conservative views or policies. **3.** Conforming with law, justice, or morality. **4.** In accord with fact, truth, or reason : correct. **5.** Fitting : appropriate. **6.** Advantageous : desirable. **7.** Made to be placed outward or upward <the *right* side of a sweater> *—adv.* **1.** In a straight line : directly. **2.** Properly : well <doesn't fit *right*> **3.** Precisely : just. **4.** Immediately. **5.** On or toward the right side. **6.** Very <the *Right* Honorable Prime Minister> **7.** Used as an intensive <kept *right* on singing> *—v.* **1.** To restore to an upright or proper position. **2.** To put in order : set right. **3.** To redress <*right* an injustice>
▲word history: The political sense of *right*, meaning "conservative" or "reactionary," goes back to the French Revolution. In the French National Assembly of 1789 the nobles sat on the president's right and the commoners on the left. The nobility as a group tended to be politically more conservative than the commoners. In later assemblies and parliaments seating continued to be assigned on the basis of political views as established in the 1st assembly.
right angle *n.* An angle of 90°, formed by 2 perpendicular line segments.
right away *adv.* Without delay.
right·eous (rī′chəs) *adj.* Meeting the standards of what is right and just. **—right′eous·ness** *n.*
right field *n. Baseball.* The portion of the outfield to the right as seen from home plate. **—right fielder** *n.*
right·ful (rīt′fəl) *adj.* **1.** Proper or right : just. **2.** Having a just claim <the *rightful* owner> **—right′ful·ly** *adv.*
right-hand (rīt′hănd′) *adj.* **1.** On or toward the right side. **2.** Of or done by the right hand. **3.** Helpful and reliable.
right-hand·ed (rīt′hăn′dĭd) *adj.* **1.** Using the right hand more often and skillfully than the left. **2.** Of, for, or done by the right hand. **3.** Clockwise. **—right′-hand′ed, right′-hand′ed·ly** *adv.*
right·ist (rī′tĭst) *n.* A political conservative or reactionary. **—right′ism** *n.*
right·ly (rīt′lē) *adv.* **1.** In a proper way : correctly. **2.** With honesty : justly.
right off *adv.* Straightaway : immediately.
right of way *also* **right-of-way** (rīt′əv-wā′) *n.* **1.** *Law.* **a.** The right to pass over someone else's land. **b.** The path or area on which such passage is made. **2.** The strip of land over which railroads, pipelines, etc., run. **3.** The customary or legal right of a person or vehicle to pass before another.
right on *interj. Slang.* Used as an exclamation of support or approval.
rig·id (rĭj′ĭd) *adj.* **1.** Not bending : stiff. **2.** Not moving : stationary. **3.** Stern : severe. **—ri·gid′i·ty, rig′id·ness** *n.*
rig·ma·role (rĭg′mə-rōl′) *also* **rig·a·ma·role** (-ə-mə-rōl′) *n.* **1.** Incoherent speech. **2.** A needlessly complicated procedure.
rig·or (rĭg′ər) *n.* **1.** Strictness : severity. **2.** A trying circumstance : hardship. **3.** Precision. **4.** A shivering, as from a chill. **—rig′or·ous** *adj.* **—rig′or·ous·ly** *adv.*
rig·or mor·tis (rĭg′ər môr′tĭs) *n.* A temporary muscular stiffening after death.
rile (rīl) *v.* **riled, ril·ing.** To irritate : vex.
rill (rĭl) *n.* A small brook.
rim (rĭm) *n.* **1.** The outer edge of something. **2.** The outside of a wheel around which a tire fits. *—v.* **rimmed, rim·ming.** To provide with a rim.
rime[1] (rīm) *n.* A granular ice coating on plants, rocks, etc. **—rim′y** *adj.*
rime[2] (rīm) *n.* & *v. var. of* RHYME.
rind (rīnd) *n.* A tough outer covering, as the skin of a melon.
ring[1] (rĭng) *n.* **1.** A circular object or form with an empty circular center. **2.** A small circular band worn as an ornament on a finger. **3.** An enclosed area for staging exhibitions or contests. **4.** The sport of boxing. **5.** A group of people acting together, esp. illegally. *—v.* **1.** To surround with a ring : encircle. **2.** To form into a ring.
ring[2] (rĭng) *v.* **rang** (răng), **rung** (rŭng), **ring·ing. 1.** To make or cause to make a clear, resonant sound. **2.** To sound a bell as a summons or signal. **3.** To seem to a listener or observer : sound <a tale that *rings* true> **4.** To resound. **5.** To hear a persistent humming <Our ears *rang* from the explosion.> **6.** To telephone. **—ring up. 1.** To record, as on a cash register. **2.** To telephone. *—n.* **1.** The sound made by or as if by a bell. **2.** A loud, usu. continued or repeated sound. **3.** A telephone call. **4.** A particular sound or quality <a plan with a suspicious *ring*>
ring·er (rĭng′ər) *n.* **1.** One that rings a bell. **2.** *Slang.* A contestant entered fraudulently in a competition. **3.** *Slang.* One that strikingly resembles another.
ring·git (rĭng′gĭt′) *n.* See CURRENCY TABLE.
ring·lead·er (rĭng′lē′dər) *n.* A leader, esp. in unlawful or underhand activities.
ring·let (rĭng′lĭt) *n.* A curled lock of hair.
ring·mas·ter (rĭng′măs′tər) *n.* A person who supervises and usu. introduces the acts in a circus ring.
ring·side (rĭng′sīd′) *n.* A place providing a close view, as of a prizefight.
ring·worm (rĭng′wûrm′) *n.* A contagious skin disease caused by a fungus and marked by ring-shaped itching patches.
rink (rĭngk) *n.* **1.** An area covered with smooth ice for skating. **2.** A smooth floor used for roller-skating.
rinse (rĭns) *v.* **rinsed, rins·ing. 1.** To wash lightly in water. **2.** To remove (e.g., soap) with water. *—n.* **1.** An act of rinsing. **2.** The liquid used for rinsing. **3.** A cosmetic solution used in tinting or conditioning the hair. **—rins′er** *n.*
Ri·o de Ja·nei·ro (rē′ō dā zhə-nâr′ō, jə-). City of SE Brazil. *Pop.* 5,394,900.
Rio Grande (grănd). River rising in S Colo. and flowing c. 1,885 mi (3,033 km) to the Gulf of Mexico.
ri·ot (rī′ət) *n.* **1.** A violent public disturbance. **2.** An uncontrolled outbreak, as of laughter. **3.** A profuse display. **4.** *Slang.* One that is irresistibly funny. *—v.* **1.** To take part in a riot. **2.** To engage in unrestrained revelry. **—ri′ot·ous** *adj.*
rip (rĭp) *v.* **ripped, rip·ping. 1.** To tear or become torn apart forcefully. **2.** To saw or split (wood) along the grain. **3.** To remove by pulling or tearing roughly. **4.** To move rapidly. **5.** To criticize harshly : excoriate. *—n.* A torn place : tear. **—rip off.** *Slang.* **1.** To steal (from). **2.** To swindle : defraud. **—rip′per** *n.*
R.I.P. *abr. Lat.* requiescat in pace (may he rest in peace).
ri·par·i·an (rĭ-pâr′ē-ən) *adj.* Of or on the bank of a natural course of water.
rip·cord (rĭp′kôrd′) *n.* A cord pulled to open a parachute.
ripe (rīp) *adj.* **rip·er, rip·est. 1.** Fully developed : mature. **2.** Fully prepared or aged for use. **3.** Suitable : opportune <The time was *ripe* for action.> **—ripe′ness** *n.*
rip·en (rī′pən) *v.* To make or become ripe.
rip-off (rĭp′ôf′, -ŏf′) *n. Slang.* **1.** A theft. **2.** A deception : swindle.
ri·poste (rĭ-pōst′) *n.* **1.** A quick thrust delivered after parrying a lunge in fencing. **2.** A quick, clever reply : retort. **—ri·poste′** *v.*
rip·ple (rĭp′əl) *v.* **-pled, -pling. 1.** To form or cause to form little waves on the surface. **2.** To waver gently in tone or volume. **—rip′ple** *n.*
rip·saw (rĭp′sô′) *n.* A saw for cutting wood along the grain.
rise (rīz) *v.* **rose** (rōz), **ris·en** (rĭz′ən), **ris·ing. 1.** To go from a lower to a higher position. **2.** To assume a standing position after sitting, lying, or kneeling. **3.** To get out of bed. **4.** To increase in height, volume, or size. **5.** To increase in amount, number, or value. **6.** To increase in intensity or speed <The wind started to *rise.*> **7.** To advance in rank or condition. **8.** To slope upward. **9.** To appear above the horizon. **10.** To come into existence. **11.** To return to life. **12.** To be erected. **13.** To rebel. ☆***syns:*** ASCEND, CLIMB, MOUNT, SOAR *—n.* **1.** An act of going up : ascent. **2.** A slope upward. **3.** The appearance of a celestial body above the horizon. **4.** An increase, as in height, amount, or intensity. **5.** An elevation in rank or condition. **6.** An origin : source **7.** *Informal.* An angry reaction.
ris·er (rī′zər) *n.* **1.** One who rises <an early *riser*> **2.** The vertical part of a step.
ris·i·bil·i·ty (rĭz′ə-bĭl′ĭ-tē) *n., pl.* **-ties. 1.** The capacity or tendency to laugh. **2.** *often* **risibilities.** One's sense of the comic. **3.** Laughter. **—ris′i·ble** *adj.* **—ris′i·bly** *adv.*
risk (rĭsk) *n.* The possibility of suffering harm or loss : danger. *—v.* **1.** To expose to the possibility of loss or damage. **2.** To incur the risk of. **—risk′y** *adj.*
ris·qué (rĭ-skā′) *adj.* Verging on impropriety or indelicacy : racy.

ris·sole (rĭ'sōl, rē-sôl') *n.* A small pastry-enclosed croquette usu. fried in deep fat.
rite (rīt) *n.* **1.** A formal, often religious procedure : ceremony. **2.** The prescribed form for a religious ceremony.
rit·u·al (rĭch'o͞o-əl) *n.* **1.** The form for conducting a ceremony. **2.** A ceremony or body of ceremonies. **3.** A procedure repeated customarily or automatically. **–rit'u·al** *adj.* **–rit'u·al·ism** *n.* **–rit'u·al·is'tic** *adj.* **–rit'u·al·is'ti·cal·ly** *adv.*
ritz·y (rĭt'sē) *adj.* **-i·er, -i·est.** *Slang.* Elegant : swank.
▲word history: The word *ritzy* comes from the name of various celebrated hotels called *Ritz,* such as the *Hôtel Ritz* in Paris and the *Ritz Hotel* in London, which have a reputation for opulent elegance. They were founded by César Ritz, a Swiss hotelier who lived from 1850 to 1918.
ri·val (rī'vəl) *n.* **1.** One competing with another. **2.** One that equals or almost equals another. *—v.* **-valed, -val·ing** *also* **-valled, -val·ling. 1.** To try to equal or surpass. **2.** To be the equal of : match. **–ri'val** *adj.* **–ri'val·ry** *n.*
rive (rīv) *v.* **rived, rived** or **riv·en** (rĭv'ən), **riv·ing. 1.** To tear or be torn apart : rend. **2.** To break into pieces : shatter.
riv·er (rĭv'ər) *n.* A relatively large natural stream of water.
riv·er·bank (rĭv'ər-băngk') *n.* The bank of a river.
riv·er·bed (rĭv'ər-bĕd') *n.* The area between the banks of a river covered or once covered by water.
riv·er·boat (rĭv'ər-bōt') *n.* A boat suitable for use on a river.
riv·er·side (rĭv'ər-sīd') *n.* The bank or side of a river.
riv·et (rĭv'ĭt) *n.* A metal bolt or pin used to join 2 or more objects by inserting it through a hole in each piece and then hammering the narrow end flat to form another head. *—v.* **1.** To fasten with or as if with a rivet. **2.** To engross (e.g., the attention).
Riv·i·er·a (rĭv'ē-âr'ə). Resort area of SE France and NW Italy.
riv·u·let (rĭv'yə-lĭt) *n.* A small stream.
Ri·yadh (rē-yäd'). Cap. of Saudi Arabia, in the C part. *Pop.* 666,840.
ri·yal (rē-ôl', -äl') *n.* See CURRENCY TABLE.
ri·yal-o·man·i (rē-ôl'ō-mä'nē, rē-äl'-) *n.* See CURRENCY TABLE.
rm. *abbr.* **1.** ream. **2.** room.
Rn *symbol for* RADON.
RN or **R.N.** *abbr.* registered nurse.
RNA (är'ĕn-ā') *n.* Ribonucleic acid.
roach¹ (rōch) *n.* A N European freshwater fish, *Rutilus rutilus.*
roach² (rōch) *n.* **1.** The cockroach. **2.** *Slang.* The butt of a marijuana cigarette.
road (rōd) *n.* **1.** An open, gen. public way for moving vehicles, persons, and animals. **2.** A course or path. **3. roads.** An anchorage for ships.
road·bed (rōd'bĕd') *n.* **1.** The foundation on which railroad ties, rails, and ballast are laid. **2.** The foundation of a road.
road·block (rōd'blŏk') *n.* **1.** An obstruction set up on a road to prevent or monitor passage. **2.** An obstacle : hindrance.
road·run·ner (rōd'rŭn'ər) *n.* A swift-running crested bird, *Geococcyx californianus,* of SW North America.
road·stead (rōd'stĕd') *n* *Naut.* A sheltered offshore anchorage area for ships.
road·ster (rōd'stər) *n.* An open car with a single wide seat.
road·way (rōd'wā') *n.* A road, esp. the part used by vehicles.
road·work (rōd'wûrk') *n.* **1.** Road construction or repairs. **2.** Physical training consisting of long outdoor runs.
roam (rōm) *v.* To move or travel aimlessly (through) : wander. **–roam'er** *n.*
roan (rōn) *adj.* Having a dark coat thickly sprinkled with white or gray <a *roan* colt> *—n.* A roan animal.
roar (rôr) *v.* **1.** To utter a long, deep, loud sound, esp. in rage or excitement. **2.** To utter with a long, deep, loud sound. **3.** To laugh loudly. **–roar** *n.* **–roar'er** *n.*
roast (rōst) *v.* **1.** To cook with dry heat. **2.** To expose to great heat. **3.** *Metallurgy.* To heat (ore) in order to purify, dehydrate, or oxidize. **4.** *Informal.* To criticize harshly. *—n.* **1.** A cut of meat suitable for roasting. **2.** An outing at which food is roasted.
rob (rŏb) *v.* **robbed, rob·bing. 1.** To take property unlawfully (from) : steal. **2.** To deprive unjustly <*robbed* me of my peace of mind> ☆**syns:** HEIST, HIT, HOLD UP, KNOCK OFF, RIP OFF, STICK UP. **–rob'ber** *n.* **–rob'ber·y** *n.*
robe (rōb) *n.* **1.** A long, flowing outer garment, esp. one worn on ceremonial occasions. **2.** A dressing gown or bathrobe. **3.** A blanket for the lap and legs. *—v.* **robed, rob·ing.** To dress in or don a robe.
rob·in (rŏb'ĭn) *n.* **1.** A North American songbird, *Turdus migratorius,* with a red breast and dark plumage. **2.** A small Old World bird, *Erithacus rubecula,* having an orange breast and a brown back.
ro·bot (rō'bət, -bŏt') *n.* **1.** A machine that looks like a human being and has the capacity to perform human tasks. **2.** A person who works mechanically. **3.** An automatic or remote-controlled device.
▲word history: The word *robot* was invented by the Czech author Karel Čapek in his play *R.U.R.,* which stands for "Rossum's Universal Robots." The play was written in 1920 and was translated into English a few years later. The word *robot* quickly gained currency in English. Čapek derived the word from Czech *robota,* "forced labor, drudgery."

robot

ro·bust (rō-bŭst', rō'bŭst) *adj.* **1.** Full of health and strength : vigorous. **2.** Rich and full. **–ro·bust'ly** *adv.* **–ro·bust'ness** *n.*
roc (rŏk) An enormous, powerful, legendary bird of prey.
rock¹ (rŏk) *n.* **1. a.** A hard, naturally formed material of mineral origin. **b.** A piece of such material : stone. **2.** *Geol.* A mineral mass constituting a significant part of the earth's crust. **3.** One who is firm or dependable. **4. rocks.** *Slang.* Money. **–on the rocks. 1.** In or close to ruin. **2.** Served over ice cubes.
rock² (rŏk) *v.* **1.** To move back and forth, esp. rhythmically. **2.** To shake or sway violently, as from a blow. *—n.* **1.** A rocking motion. **2.** Rock 'n' roll.
rock-and-roll (rŏk'ən-rōl') *n. var. of* ROCK 'N' ROLL.
rock-bound (rŏk'bound') *adj.* Covered or bordered with rocks.
rock·er (rŏk'ər) *n.* **1.** One that rocks. **2.** A rocking chair. **3.** A curved support on which something, as a rocking chair, rocks.
rock·et (rŏk'ĭt) *n.* **1. a.** A device propelled through the air by a thrust developed by ejection of matter, esp. by the high-speed ejection of gaseous combustion products of solid or liquid fuels. **b.** An engine that produces a thrust in this way. **2.** A rocket-propelled explosive weapon. *—v.* To move rapidly and directly.
rock·et·ry (rŏk'ĭ-trē) *n.* The science and technology of designing, building, and flying rockets.
rock·ing chair (rŏk'ĭng) *n.* A chair mounted on rockers.
rocking horse *n.* A toy horse mounted on rockers.
rock 'n' roll *also* **rock-and-roll** (rŏk'ən-rōl') *n.* Popular music combining elements of blues and country music, marked by a heavily accented beat.
rock-ribbed (rŏk'rĭbd') *adj.* **1.** Rocky. **2.** Unyielding : stern.
rock salt *n.* Common salt in large chunks.
rock·y¹ (rŏk'ē) *adj.* **-i·er, -i·est. 1.** Made of, covered with, or full of rocks. **2.** Like rock, as in hardness. **–rock'i·ness** *n.*
rock·y² (rŏk'ē) *adj.* **-i·er, -i·est. 1.** Inclined or prone to sway unsteadily : shaky. **2.** Weak or dizzy. **–rock'i·ness** *n.*
Rocky Mountains *also* **Rock·ies** (rŏk'ēz). Mountain system extending from NW Alas. to N Mexico.
ro·co·co (rə-kō'kō, rō'kə-kō') *adj.* **1.** Of or designating an artistic style marked by florid, ornate asymmetric ornamentation. **2.** Excessively elaborate. **–ro·co'co** *n.*
rod (rŏd) *n.* **1.** A thin, straight stick or bar. **2. a.** A stick used for whipping. **b.** Punishment. **3.** A fishing rod. **4.** A staff symbolizing rank or office. **5.** A measuring stick. **6.** See MEASUREMENT TABLE.
rode (rōd) *v. p.t.* of RIDE.
ro·dent (rōd'nt) *n.* A mammal of the order Rodentia, as a mouse, rat, or beaver, having large incisors adapted for gnawing.
ro·de·o (rō'dē-ō', rō-dā'ō) *n., pl.* **-os. 1.** A cattle roundup. **2.** A public show featuring cowboy skills and competitions.
roe¹ (rō) *n.* The egg-laden ovary of a fish.
roe² (rō) *n.* The roe deer.
roe deer *n.* A small, delicately formed Eurasian deer, *Capreolus capreolus.*
roent·gen (rĕnt'gən, rŭnt'-) *n.* An obsolete unit of radiation dosage.
rog·er (rŏj'ər) *interj.* Used in radio communications to indicate that a message has been received.
rogue (rōg) *n.* **1.** An unprincipled person : scoundrel. **2.** A playfully mischievous person : scamp. **–rog'uer·y** *n.* **–rog'uish** *adj.* **–rog'uish·ly** *adv.*

roil (roil) *v.* **1.** To make (a liquid) cloudy by stirring up sediment. **2.** To disturb : vex.

role *also* **rôle** (rōl) *n.* **1.** A part played by an actor. **2.** A function or position.

roll (rōl) *v.* **1.** To move on a surface by turning over and over. **2.** To move on wheels or rollers. **3.** To move with steady or increasing momentum. **4.** To go by : pass <The months *rolled* on.> **5.** To recur periodically. **6.** To sway or cause to sway from side to side, as a ship. **7.** To make a deep, prolonged sound, as thunder. **8.** To rotate <*rolled* his eyes in impatience> **9.** To pronounce with a trill <*roll* one's r's> **10.** To wrap (something) round and round upon itself or a center. **11.** To enfold in a covering. **12.** To spread or flatten with a roller <*roll* dough> **13.** To throw (dice). **–roll back.** To reduce to a previous level. *–n.* **1.** An act of rolling. **2.** Something rolled up in a cylinder. **3.** A list of names of members. **4. a.** A small rounded portion of bread. **b.** A food shaped like a tube with a filling <an egg *roll*> **5.** A swaying or rocking motion. **6.** A deep prolonged sound : rumble. **7.** A quick succession of short sounds <a drum *roll*>

roll•back (rōl′băk′) *n.* A reduction, as of prices or wages, to a previous level.

roll call *n.* A reading aloud of a list of names of people to find out who is present.

roll•er (rō′lər) *n.* **1.** A small spokeless wheel, as on a roller skate. **2.** A rod around which something is wound. **3.** A heavy cylinder for leveling or crushing operations. **4.** A cylinder used for applying a liquid, as paint, to a surface. **5.** A heavy wave that breaks on the shore.

roller bearing *n.* A bearing using rollers to reduce friction between machine parts.

roller coaster *n.* A coiled elevated railway with small open cars operated as an amusement-park ride.

roller skate *n.* A skate with 4 wheels for skating on surfaces other than ice. **–roll′er-skate′** *v.* **–roller skater** *n.*

rol•lick (rŏl′ĭk) *v.* To frolic : romp. **–rol′lick** *n.* **–rol′lick•ing** *adj.*

rolling pin *n.* A smooth usu. wood cylinder for rolling dough.

ro•ly-po•ly (rō′lē-pō′lē) *adj.* Short and plump : pudgy.

ro•maine (rō-mān′) *n.* A variety of lettuce, *Lactuca sativa longifolia,* having dark green leaves in a long, narrow head.

Ro•man (rō′mən) *adj.* **1.** Of or relating to Rome and its people, esp. ancient Rome. **2.** Latin. **3.** Of or relating to the Roman Catholic Church. **4. roman.** Of, set, or printed in the most common type style, characterized by upright letters. *–n.* **1.** A native or resident of Rome, esp. ancient Rome. **2.** Latin. **3. roman.** Roman type. **4. Romans.** See BIBLE TABLE.

Roman candle *n.* A firework made of a tube from which balls of fire shoot out.

Roman Catholic *adj.* Of or relating to the Roman Catholic Church. **–Roman Catholic** *n.*

Roman Catholic Church *n.* The Christian church having a hierarchical structure of priests and bishops with the pope at its head.

ro•mance (rō-măns′, rō′măns′) *n.* **1.a.** A medieval narrative of the adventures of chivalric heroes. **b.** A long, fictitious tale of adventure, heroism, or mystery. **c.** A quality or spirit suggestive of such tales. **2.** A story or film about a love affair. **3. a.** A love affair. **b.** Romantic involvement : love. *–adj.* **Romance.** Of, relating to, or designating the languages that developed from Latin, including French, Italian, Portuguese, Rumanian, and Spanish. *–v.* (rō-măns′) **-manced, -manc•ing. 1.** To invent fanciful stories. **2.** To carry on a courtship or love affair with : woo. **–ro•manc′er** *n.*

Roman Empire. Empire (27 B.C.–A.D. 395) stretching from Britain to N Africa to the Persian Gulf.

Ro•man•esque (rō′mə-nĕsk′) *adj.* Of, relating to, or designating a style of architecture that prevailed in Europe from the 9th–12th cent. **–Ro′man•esque′** *n.*

Ro•ma•ni•a (rō-mā′nē-ə, -mān′yə) *n.* Rumania.

Roman numeral *n.* A numeral formed with the characters I, V, X, L, C, D, or M based on the system used by the ancient Romans.

Ro•ma•no (rə-mä′nō, rō-) *n.* A dry, sharp-flavored, hard Italian cheese.

ro•man•tic (rō-măn′tĭk) *adj.* **1.** Of or marked by romance. **2.** Given to thoughts or feelings of adventure, heroism, or love. **3.** Imaginative but impractical : quixotic. **4.** Of love or strong, idealized affection. **5.** Of or characteristic of romanticism in the arts. *–n.* A romantic person.

ro•man•ti•cism (rō-măn′tĭ-sĭz′əm) *n.* An intellectual and artistic movement emphasizing strong emotion, imagination, freer forms, and the opposition of the individual to society. **–ro•man′ti•cist** *n.*

ro•man•ti•cize (rō-măn′tĭ-sīz′) *v.* **-cized, -ciz•ing. 1.** To give a quality of adventure, heroism, or mystery to. **2.** To think or talk in a romantic way.

Rome (rōm). **1.** Cap. of Italy, in the WC part. *Pop.* 2,911,671. **2.** The Roman Empire.

romp (rŏmp) *v.* **1.** To play or frolic boisterously. **2.** *Slang.* To win easily. **–romp** *n.*

romp•er (rŏm′pər) *n.* **1.** One that romps. **2. rompers.** A playsuit with short bloomers worn by small children.

rood (ro͞od) *n.* **1.** A cross or crucifix. **2.** A measure of land area equal to $\frac{1}{4}$ acre.

roof (ro͞of, ro͝of) *n.* **1.** The outside covering of the top of a building. **2.** The top covering of something <the *roof* of a vehicle> **3.** A vaulted inner structure. *–v.* To furnish or cover with a roof. **–roof′er** *n.*

roof•ing (ro͞o′fĭng, ro͝of′ĭng) *n.* Materials used in building a roof.

rook[1] (ro͝ok) *n.* A crowlike Old World bird, *Corvus frugilegus.* *–v. Slang.* To swindle : cheat.

rook[2] (ro͝ok) *n.* A chess piece that may move in a straight line across any number of unoccupied squares in a rank or file.

rook•er•y (ro͝ok′ə-rē) *n., pl.* **-ies. 1.** A place where rooks nest. **2.** A breeding ground of certain other birds and animals.

rook•ie (ro͝ok′ē) *n. Slang.* **1.** An untrained recruit. **2.** A novice player in sports. **3.** An inexperienced person.

room (ro͞om, ro͝om) *n.* **1.** Space that can be or is occupied. **2. a.** A part of a building set off by walls or partitions. **b.** The people within such an area <The whole *room* fell silent.> **3. rooms.** Living quarters. **4.** Opportunity or leeway. *–v.* To occupy a room. **–room′ful′** *n.* **–room′i•ness** *n.* **–room′y** *adj.*

room•er (ro͞o′mər, ro͝om′ər) *n.* A lodger.

room•ette (ro͞o-mĕt′, ro͝om-ĕt′) *n.* A small room in a railroad sleeping car.

room•ing house (ro͞o′mĭng, ro͝om′ĭng) *n.* A house where lodgers can rent rooms.

room•mate (ro͞om′māt′, ro͝om′-) *n.* A person with whom one shares a room or apartment.

Roo•se•velt (rō′zə-vĕlt′, rōz′vĕlt′, ro͞o′zə-). **1. Theodore.** 1858–1919. 26th U.S. President (1901–9). **2. Franklin Delano.** 1882–1945. 32nd U.S. President (1933–45).

roost (ro͞ost) *n.* **1.** A perch on which birds sleep or rest. **2.** A place with perches for fowl or other birds. *–v.* To rest or sleep on or as if on a roost.

roost•er (ro͞o′stər) *n.* An adult male of the domestic fowl : cock.

root[1] (ro͞ot, ro͝ot) *n.* **1. a.** The usu. underground part of a plant that serves as support and draws water and nutrients from the soil. **b.** A similar underground plant part, as a tuber. **2.** The embedded part of a tooth, hair, or other body structure. **3.** A base : foundation. **4.** A source : origin. **5.** The essential part : heart. **6. roots.** Ties to a place or community. **7.** *Ling.* A word or word element from which other words or inflections are formed. **8.** *Math.* A number that when multiplied by itself an indicated number of times forms a product equal to a specified number <2 is a 4th *root* of 16.> *–v.* **1.** To grow a root or roots. **2.** To become or cause to become firmly established. **3.** To remove by or as if by the roots. **–root′less** *adj.* **–root′like′** *adj.*

root[2] (ro͞ot, ro͝ot) *v.* **1.** To dig with or as if with the snout. **2.** To rummage.

root[3] (ro͞ot, ro͝ot) *v.* **1.** To give encouragement to a team or contestant by cheering. **2.** To lend support. **–root′er** *n.*

root beer *n.* A carbonated soft drink flavored with certain plant-root extracts.

root canal *n.* A narrow pulp-filled cavity in a root of a tooth.

rope (rōp) *n.* **1.** A heavy, strong cord of twisted fiber. **2.** A string of items joined in 1 line by twisting, braiding, or beading. **3. ropes.** *Informal.* Specialized procedures or techniques <learned the *ropes*> *–v.* **roped, rop•ing. 1.** To fasten with or as if with rope. **2.** To enclose with a rope <*roped* off the accident scene> **3.** To lasso. **4.** *Informal.* To deceive : trick.

Roque•fort (rōk′fərt). A trademark for a tangy French cheese made from ewes' milk.

Ror•schach test (rôr′shäk′, -shäKH) *n.* A psychological test in which a subject's interpretations of standard inkblot patterns are used to analyze personality and detect emotional disorders.

ro•sa•ry (rō′zə-rē) *n., pl.* **-ries.** *Rom. Cath. Ch.* **1.** A series of prayers. **2.** A string of beads for counting prayers.

rose[1] (rōz) *n.* **1.** A shrub or vine of the genus *Rosa,* having prickly stems and variously colored, usu. fragrant flowers. **2.** A deep pink. **3.** A rosette.

rose[2] (rōz) *v. p.t. of* RISE.

ro•sé (rō-zā′) *n.* A pink, light wine.

ro•se•ate (rō′zē-ĭt, -āt′) *adj.* **1.** Rose-colored. **2.** Highly optimistic : cheerful.

rose•bud (rōz′bŭd′) *n.* A bud of a rose.

rose•bush (rōz′bo͝osh′) *n.* A shrub bearing roses.

rose-col·ored (rōz′kŭl′ərd) *adj.* **1.** Of the color rose. **2.** Overoptimistic.

rose·mar·y (rōz′mâr′ē) *n., pl.* **-ies.** An aromatic evergreen shrub, *Rosmarinus officinalis*, with leaves used esp. in cooking.

ro·sette (rō-zĕt′) *n.* **1.** An ornament of ribbon or silk that is gathered to resemble a rose. **2.** A roselike form or marking.

rose water *n.* A fragrant liquid made from rose petals steeped in water, used in cosmetics and cookery.

rose·wood (rōz′wo͝od′) *n.* The hard, often fragrant wood of any of several tropical trees, used in making furniture.

Rosh Ha·sha·nah (rŏsh′ hə-shä′nə, rōsh′) *n.* The Jewish New Year, a religious holiday celebrated in late Sept. or early Oct.

ros·in (rŏz′ĭn) *n.* A translucent resin obtained from the sap of pine trees, used to increase sliding friction on violin bows and as an ingredient in varnish, solder, and other products. **—ros′in·y** *adj.*

ros·ter (rŏs′tər, rô′stər) *n.* A list of names, esp. of personnel available for duty.

ros·trum (rŏs′trəm, rô′strəm) *n., pl.* **-trums** *or* **-tra** (-trə). A raised platform for public speakers.

ros·y (rō′zē) *adj.* **-i·er, -i·est. 1.** Pink or red in color. **2.** Promising : bright. **—ros′i·ly** *adv.* **—ros′i·ness** *n.*

rot (rŏt) *v.* **rot·ted, rot·ting.** To decompose : decay. *—n.* **1. a.** The process of rotting or condition of being rotten. **b.** Rotten matter. **2.** A plant disease marked by the breakdown of tissue. **3.** *Informal.* Foolish talk or writing.

ro·ta·ry (rō′tə-rē) *adj.* Of or marked by rotation, esp. axial rotation. *—n., pl.* **-ries. 1.** Something that rotates around an axis. **2.** A traffic circle.

ro·tate (rō′tāt′) *v.* **-tat·ed, -tat·ing. 1.** To turn on an axis. **2.** To move among positions in a recurring order. **3.** To plant (crops) in a fixed order of succession. **—ro′tat′a·ble** *adj.* **—ro·ta′tion** *n.* **—ro′ta′tor** *n.* **—ro′ta·to′ry** *adj.*

ROTC *abbr.* Reserve Officers' Training Corps.

rote (rōt) *n.* **1.** Memorization by repetition without full comprehension. **2.** Thoughtless, mechanical repetition.

ro·tis·ser·ie (rō-tĭs′ə-rē) *n.* A cooking device with a rotating spit for roasting food.

ro·to·gra·vure (rō′tə-grə-vyo͝or′) *n.* **1.** An intaglio printing process in which the impression is transferred from an etched copper cylinder in a rotary printing press. **2.** The material printed by rotogravure.

ro·tor (rō′tər) *n.* **1.** A rotating part of an electrical or mechanical device. **2.** The assembly of rotating horizontal blades that supports a helicopter.

rot·ten (rŏt′n) *adj.* **1.** Decayed : decomposed. **2.** Putrid : fetid. **3.** Morally corrupt. **4.** Very bad : wretched <*rotten* luck>

Rot·ter·dam (rŏt′ər-dăm′). City of SW Netherlands. *Pop.* 579,194.

rott·wei·ler (rŏt′wī′lər, rôt′vī′-) *n.* A German breed of dog having a stocky body, short black fur, and tan face markings.

ro·tund (rō-tŭnd′) *adj.* Rounded : plump. **—ro·tun′di·ty** *n.*

ro·tun·da (rō-tŭn′də) *n.* A circular building or hall, esp. one with a dome.

rou·ble *or* **ru·ble** (ro͞o′bəl) *n.* See CURRENCY TABLE.

rou·é (ro͞o-ā′) *n.* A lecherous man : rake.

rouge (ro͞ozh) *n.* **1.** A red or pink cosmetic for coloring the cheeks or lips. **2.** A reddish powder used to polish metal and gems.

rough (rŭf) *adj.* **1.** Having an irregular surface : not smooth **2.** In violent motion : turbulent. **3.** Not gentle : violent or harsh <*rough* handling> **4.** Rude : uncouth. **5.** Difficult : trying. **6.** Harsh : grating. **7.** In a natural state <*rough* gems> **8.** Done hastily or incompletely <a *rough* sketch> *—n.* **1.** Rugged, overgrown ground. **2.** A crude or unfinished condition. **3.** A crude person : boor. *—v.* **1.** To make rough. **2.** To manhandle. **3.** To make or do hastily or incompletely <*rough* out a plan> **—rough′ly** *adv.* **—rough′ness** *n.*

rough·age (rŭf′ĭj) *n.* The coarse, indigestible parts of certain foods, as bran, that stimulate peristalsis.

rough·en (rŭf′ən) *v.* To make or become rough.

rough·hew (rŭf′hyo͞o′) *v.* **1.** To hew (e.g., timber) roughly, without finishing. **2.** To make in rough form.

rough·house (rŭf′hous′) *n.* Rowdy, boisterous play. **—rough′house′** *v.*

rough·neck (rŭf′nĕk′) *n.* A rowdy or uncouth person.

rough·shod (rŭf′shŏd′) *adj.* Marked by brutal force.

rou·lette (ro͞o-lĕt′) *n.* **1.** A gambling game in which players bet on which slot of a rotating disk a small ball will come to rest. **2.** A tool with a rotating toothed disk for making rows of dots or slits.

Rou·ma·ni·a (ro͞o-mā′nē-ə, -mān′yə) *n.* Rumania.

round (round) *adj.* **1.** Ball-shaped : spherical. **2.** Curved. **3.** Circular. **4.** Whole : full. **5.** Expressed as a whole number. **6.** Not exact : approximate. **7.** Full in tone : sonorous. *—n.* **1.** Something round, as a circle, globe, or disk. **2.** The hind leg of beef between the shank and rump. **3.** A recurring course or succession. **4.** *often* **rounds.** A series of customary or prescribed acts or stops <a postman on his *rounds*> **5.** A single distribution among members of a group <a *round* of drinks> **6.** An outburst of cheering or applause. **7.** A single shot or cartridge. **8.** An interval of play or action in various games. **9.** *Mus.* A composition in which each voice enters at a different time with the same melody. *—v.* **1.** To make or become round. **2.** To make or become plump : fill out. **3.** To bring to an end : finish. **4.** To go around. **5.** To surround. **6.** To express as a round number. **—round up.** To bring together. *—adv.* Around. *—prep.* **1.** Around. **2.** Throughout <*round* the year> **—in the round. 1.** Free standing <sculpture *in the round*> **2.** With the stage in the center of the audience.

round·a·bout (round′ə-bout′) *adj.* Not direct : circuitous.

roun·de·lay (roun′də-lā′) *n.* A poem or song with a regularly recurring refrain.

round·house (round′hous′) *n.* **1.** A circular building for storing, servicing, and switching locomotives. **2.** A punch delivered with a sweeping sidearm movement.

round robin *n.* **1.** A tournament in which each contestant plays every other contestant in turn. **2.** A letter circulated among the members of a group.

round-shoul·dered (round′shōl′dərd) *adj.* Having the shoulders and upper back bent forward : stooped.

round table *n.* A discussion or conference with several participants.

round-the-clock (round′*th*ə-klŏk′) *adj.* Throughout a 24-hour day : continuous.

round trip *n.* A trip to a place and back, usu. over the same route.

round·up (round′ŭp′) *n.* **1.** The herding together of cattle, as for shipping. **2.** A gathering up, as of suspects by the police. **3.** A summary.

round·worm (round′wûrm′) *n.* A nematode.

rouse (rouz) *v.* **roused, rous·ing. 1.** To awaken from sleep or unconsciousness : arouse. **2.** To stir up, as to action : excite.

roust·a·bout (rou′stə-bout′) *n.* **1.** An unskilled worker, esp. on a wharf or in an oil field. **2.** A laborer in a circus.

rout[1] (rout) *n.* **1.** A disorderly retreat. **2.** An overwhelming defeat. **—rout** *v.*

rout[2] (rout) *v.* **1.** To drive from a resting or hiding place. **2.** To dig up or gouge out. **3.** To rummage. **—rout′er** *n.*

route (ro͞ot, rout) *n.* **1. a.** A way for traveling : course. **b.** A means of achieving a goal. **2.** A regular course of travel. **3.** A highway. *—v.* **rout·ed, rout·ing. 1.** To send by a certain route. **2.** To assign a route to.

rou·tine (ro͞o-tēn′) *n.* **1.** A series of activities performed regularly. **2.** A regularly performed show or presentation. *—adj.* **1.** According to standard procedure. **2.** Ordinary.

roux (ro͞o) *n.* A mixture of flour and fat cooked together and used as a thickening.

rove (rōv) *v.* **roved, rov·ing.** To wander about, esp. over a wide area : roam. **—rov′er** *n.* **—rov′ing** *adj.*

row[1] (rō) *n.* **1.** A number of persons or objects positioned next to each other, usu. in a straight line. **2.** A continuous line of buildings on a street. **3.** Succession <3 years in a *row*>

row[2] (rō) *v.* **1.** To propel (a boat) with oars. **2.** To carry or travel in a rowboat. *—n.* A trip by rowboat. **—row′er** *n.*

row[3] (rou) *n.* A noisy quarrel. **—row** *v.*

row·boat (rō′bōt′) *n.* A small boat propelled by oars.

row·dy (rou′dē) *adj.* **-di·er, -di·est.** Noisy and disorderly. **—row′di·ness, row′dy·ism** *n.* **—row′dy** *n.*

row·el (rou′əl) *n.* A small toothed wheel inserted into a spur. **—row′el** *v.*

roy·al (roi′əl) *adj.* **1.** Of or relating to a king or queen. **2.** Fit for royalty : grand.

Royal Canadian Mounted Police *n. Can.* The Federal police force.

roy·al·ist (roi′ə-lĭst) *n.* A supporter of government by monarchs. **—roy′al·ism** *n.*

roy·al·ty (roi′əl-tē) *n., pl.* **-ties. 1.** Monarchs and their families as a group. **2.** The authority or status of monarchs. **3.** Royal quality or bearing. **4. a.** A share of the proceeds from the sale or performance of a work paid to the author or composer. **b.** A payment to an inventor or proprietor for the right to use his invention or services.

rpm *or* **r.p.m.** *abbr.* revolutions per minute.

RR *also* **R.R.** *abbr.* **1.** railroad. **2.** rural route.

R.S.V.P. *also* **r.s.v.p.** *abbr.* please reply (French *répondez s'il vous plaît.*

rt. *abbr.* right.

rte. *abbr.* route.

Ru *symbol for* RUTHENIUM.
rub (rŭb) *v.* **rubbed, rub·bing. 1.** To subject (a surface) to pressure and friction. **2.** To cause to move firmly along a surface. **3.** To contact or cause to contact with friction. **4.** To irritate : chafe. **–rub down.** To massage. **–rub out. 1.** To obliterate. **2.** *Slang.* To kill. *–n.* **1.** An act of rubbing. **2.** A massage. **3.** A difficulty : catch.
rub·ber[1] (rŭb′ər) *n.* **1.** A solid, elastic substance, derived from the coagulated and processed sap of various tropical plants or made synthetically. **2.** Something made of rubber, esp.: **a.** A waterproof overshoe. **b.** An eraser. **3.** One that rubs. **–rub′ber·y** *adj.*
▲word history: The noun *rubber[1]*, denoting a substance made from the sap of the rubber tree, is derived from the verb *rub*, since one of the first uses of this substance was rubbing out pencil marks.
rub·ber[2] (rŭb′ər) *n.* **1.** A series of games, as in bridge, of which a majority must be won to end play. **2.** An odd-numbered game that breaks a tie.
rub·ber·ize (rŭb′ə-rīz′) *v.* **-ized, -iz·ing.** To treat or coat with rubber.
rub·ber·neck (rŭb′ər-nĕk′) *v.* To stare wonderingly or inquisitively : gawk.
rub·bing (rŭb′ĭng) *n.* A representation of a raised or incised surface obtained by putting paper over the surface and rubbing with a marking agent.
rub·bish (rŭb′ĭsh) *n.* **1.** Worthless material : trash. **2.** Foolish talk : nonsense.
rub·ble (rŭb′əl) *n.* **1.** Fragments of crumbled rock or masonry. **2.** Irregular pieces of rock used in masonry.
rub·down (rŭb′doun′) *n.* A massage.
rube (ro͞ob) *n. Slang.* An unsophisticated country person : bumpkin.
ru·bel·la (ro͞o-bĕl′ə) *n.* German measles.
Ru·bens (ro͞o′bənz), **Peter Paul.** 1577–1640. Flemish painter. **–Ru′ben·esque′** *adj.*
ru·bi·cund (ro͞o′bĭ-kənd) *adj.* Ruddy. **–ru′bi·cun′di·ty** (-kŭn′dĭ-tē) *n.*
ru·bid·i·um (ro͞o-bĭd′ē-əm) *n. Symbol* **Rb** A soft, silvery, highly reactive element used in photoelectric cells.
ru·ble (ro͞o′bəl) *n. var. of* ROUBLE.
ru·bric (ro͞o′brĭk) *n.* **1.** A title, heading, or initial letter of a manuscript or book, esp. when printed in ornamental red lettering. **2.** The name of a class or category. **3.** A direction in a liturgical book.
ru·by (ro͞o′bē) *n., pl.* **-bies. 1.** A deep-red, translucent corundum, greatly valued as a precious stone. **2.** A deep red. **–ru′by** *adj.*
ruche (ro͞osh) *n.* A ruffle or pleat of fine fabric, as lace, used for trimming.
ruck·sack (rŭk′săk′, ro͝ok′-) *n.* A knapsack.
ruck·us (rŭk′əs) *n. Informal.* A noisy disturbance.
rud·der (rŭd′ər) *n.* A hinged structure attached vertically to the stern of a vessel or aircraft for steering.
rud·dy (rŭd′ē) *adj.* **-di·er, -di·est.** Reddish or rosy, esp. in complexion. **–rud′di·ness** *n.*
rude (ro͞od) *adj.* **rud·er, rud·est. 1.** Primitive : uncivilized. **2.** Lowly : humble. **3.** Ill-mannered : discourteous. **4.** Crude : makeshift. **5.** Abrupt : jarring <a *rude* surprise> ☆**syns:** DISCOURTEOUS, ILL-MANNERED, IMPOLITE, UNMANNERLY **–rude′ness** *n.*
ru·di·ment (ro͞o′də-mənt) *n. often* **rudiments 1.** A fundamental principle, element, or skill. **2.** Something in an undeveloped form : beginning. **3.** *Biol.* Vestigial. **–ru′di·men′ta·ry** (-mĕn′tə-rē) *adj.*
rue[1] (ro͞o) *v.* **rued, ru·ing.** To feel regret or sorrow (for). **–rue′ful** *adj.* **–rue′ful·ly** *adv.* **–rue′ful·ness** *n.*
rue[2] (ro͞o) *n.* An aromatic Eurasian plant, *Ruta graveolens*, with leaves that yield a volatile oil once used medicinally.
ruff (rŭf) *n.* **1.** A stiff, frilled or pleated circular collar worn in the 16th–17th cent. **2.** A collarlike fringe of feathers or fur around the neck of a bird or animal.
ruf·fi·an (rŭf′ē-ən, rŭf′yən) *n.* **1.** A rowdy fellow : tough. **2.** A thug.
ruf·fle (rŭf′əl) *n.* **1.** A decorative band of frilled or pleated fabric. **2.** A ruff. **3.** An annoyance : vexation. **4.** A ripple. *–v.* **-fled, -fling. 1.** To gather (fabric) into a ruffle. **2.** To erect (feathers or fur). **3.** To make or become rough or irregular. **4.** To fluster : discompose.
rug (rŭg) *n.* **1.** A piece of heavy fabric for covering a floor. **2.** *esp. Brit.* A piece of warm fabric or fur for the lap or legs.
rug·by (rŭg′bē) *n.* A kind of football in which players may kick, dribble, or run with the ball.
rug·ged (rŭg′ĭd) *adj.* **1.** Having a rough, irregular surface. **2.** Having strong features and deep wrinkles or furrows. **3.** Stormy : turbulent. **4.** Difficult to do or endure. **5.** Robust : hardy. **–rug′ged·ness** *n.*
rug·ger (rŭg′ər) *n. esp. Brit.* Rugby.
Ruhr (ro͝or). Industrial region of NW West Germany.
ru·in (ro͞o′ĭn) *n.* **1.** Total destruction or collapse. **2.** Total loss or defeat. **3.** The cause of total destruction or loss. **4.** *often* **ruins.** The remains of something destroyed or collapsed. *–v.* **1.** To destroy utterly. **2.** To injure or harm irreparably. **3.** To reduce to poverty : bankrupt. **–ru′in·a′tion** *n.* **–ru′in·ous** *adj.*
rule (ro͞ol) *n.* **1.** The act or power of governing. **2.** An authoritative statement of what may or may not be done : regulation. **3.** A usual or prevailing way of acting. **4.** A statement of what is true in most or all cases. **5.** A standard procedure or method. **6.** A straightedge : ruler. *–v.* **ruled, rul·ing. 1.** To exercise authority (over) : govern. **2.** To dominate by strong influence <*ruled* by his passions> **3.** To determine judicially : decree. **4.** To mark with straight parallel lines. **–rule out.** To exclude.
rul·er (ro͞o′lər) *n.* **1.** One that rules, esp. a sovereign. **2.** A straight rigid strip, as of wood or metal, for measuring lengths or drawing straight lines.
rul·ing (ro͞o′lĭng) *adj.* **1.** Exercising authority : governing. **2.** Predominant. *–n.* An official decision <a judge's *ruling*>
rum (rŭm) *n.* An alcoholic liquor distilled from fermented sugar cane or molasses.
Ru·ma·ni·a (ro͞o-mā′nē-ə, -mān′yə). Country of SE Europe. *Cap.* Bucharest. *Pop.* 22,345,000. **–Ru·ma′ni·an** *adj.* & *n.*
rum·ba (rŭm′bə, ro͞om′-) *n.* A rhythmical dance originating in Cuba or an adaptation of it. **–rum′ba** *v.*
rum·ble (rŭm′bəl) *v.* **-bled, -bling. 1.** To make a long, deep, rolling sound. **2.** To move with a rumbling sound. *–n.* **1.** A long, deep, rolling sound. **2.** Widespread expression of unrest. **3.** *Slang.* A gang fight. **4.** A separate compartment or seat at the rear of a carriage or automobile.
ru·mi·nant (ro͞o′mə-nənt) *n.* Any of various hoofed, cud-chewing mammals of the suborder Ruminantia, as a cow, sheep, deer, or giraffe. *–adj.* **1.** Cud-chewing. **2.** Meditative : reflective.
ru·mi·nate (ro͞o′mə-nāt′) *v.* **-nat·ed, -nat·ing. 1.** To chew cud. **2.** To think or ponder at length. **–ru′mi·na′tion** *n.* **–ru′mi·na′tive** *adj.* **–ru′mi·na′tor** *n.*
rum·mage (rŭm′ĭj) *v.* **-maged, -mag·ing. 1.** To search thoroughly by turning over or disarranging things. **2.** To discover by searching in this way. **–rum′mage** *n.*
rum·my (rŭm′ē) *n.* A card game, the object of which is to procure sets of 3 or more cards of the same suit or rank.
ru·mor (ro͞o′mər) *n.* **1.** Information of uncertain truthfulness, usu. spread by talk. **2.** Hearsay. *–v.* To spread or tell by rumor.
ru·mour (ro͞o′mər) *n.* & *v. esp. Brit. var. of* RUMOR.
rump (rŭmp) *n.* **1. a.** An animal's fleshy hindquarters. **b.** A cut of meat from this part. **2.** The human buttocks. **3.** A small remaining part.
rum·ple (rŭm′pəl) *v.* **-pled, -pling.** To form into untidy folds or creases : wrinkle or muss up. **–rum′ple** *n.* **–rum′ply** *adj.*
rum·pus (rŭm′pəs) *n.* A noisy ruckus.
rumpus room *n.* A family recreation room, often in the basement.
run (rŭn) *v.* **ran** (răn), **run, run·ning. 1.** To move swiftly on foot with both feet leaving the ground during each stride. **2.** To depart rapidly : flee. **3.** To carry at a rapid pace <*ran* the ball 12 yards> **4.** To make a quick trip or visit, esp. on foot or on wheels. **5.** To move about at will. **6.** To swim in large numbers, as migrating fish do. **7.** To turn for help : resort. **8.** To go on a regular route <The ferry *runs* hourly.> **9.** To drive : chase <*ran* him out of town> **10.** To become in the course of time. **11.** To participate or cause to participate in a race. **12.** To compete or present for elective office. **13.** To finish a race or contest in a specified position <*ran* 3rd in the primary> **14.** *Naut.* To sail or steer. **15.** To flow and spread, as dyes do in fabric. **16.** To flow or cause to flow <*run* water over dishes> **17.** To discharge (a liquid). **18.** To move or pass quickly <*ran* his toes through the grass> **19.** To thrust. **20.** To pass through by force <*run* a blockade> **21.** To subject oneself to <*run* a risk> **22.** To extend : stretch. **23.** To spread or climb while growing. **24.** To remain in effect <The contract *runs* for 2 years.> **25.** To vary : range <reactions that *ran* from dismay to delight> **26.** To incline : tend. **27.** To put or be in operation <*run* an engine><a motor that *runs* well> **28.** To manage : direct. **29.** To publish : print. **30.** To tear or unravel along a line <The stocking *ran.*> **31.** To recur <The defect *runs* in the family.> **32.** To accumulate <*run* up a big bill> **–run across.** To find by chance. **–run along.** To leave. **–run down. 1.** To stop for lack of power. **2.** To collide with and knock down. **3.** To chase and capture. **4.** To trace to a source. **–run in.** *Slang.* To arrest. **–run off.** To duplicate : copy. **–run out.** To become used up or exhausted. **–run through.** To present, rehearse, or examine

quickly. —*n.* **1.** A pace faster than a walk. **2. a.** An act or period of running. **b.** A distance covered by running. **3.** A quick trip or visit. **4.** *Baseball.* A score made by advancing around the bases and reaching home plate safely. **5.** A migration of fish. **6.** Unrestricted freedom or use. **7.** A track or slope, as for skiers. **8.** A regular or scheduled route. **9.** A continuous period of operation, as of a printing press. **10.** A movement or flow. **11.** A small fast-flowing brook. **12.** A pipe or channel through which something flows. **13.** A continuous length, extent, series, or sequence <a *run* of bricks> <a *run* of cold winters> **14.** A vein or seam, as of ore. **15.** A direction or tendency <the *run* of the grain in leather> **16.** An enclosure for domestic animals <a chicken *run*> **17.** A length of torn or unraveled stitches in fabric. **18.** A series of unexpected, urgent demands, as by bank depositors. **19.** A sustained condition <a *run* of bad luck> **20.** The average or common kind <the broad *run* of humanity> **—on the run. 1.** Hurrying about busily. **2.** In hiding or retreat.

run•a•bout (rŭn′ə-bout′) *n.* A small, light auto, carriage, or motorboat.

run-a•round (rŭn′ə-round′) *n.* Treatment marked by evasions, delays, or misinformation.

run•a•way (rŭn′ə wā′) *n.* **1.** One that has run away. **2.** *Informal.* An easy victory. —*adj.* **1.** Escaping or having escaped confinement. **2.** Out of control. **3.** Easily won.

run-down (rŭn′doun′) *n.* A point-by-point summary. —*adj.* **1.** Falling apart : dilapidated. **2.** Worn-out : exhausted.

rune (ro͞on) *n.* **1.** One of the letters of an alphabet used by ancient Scandinavians and other Germanic peoples. **2.** A magic charm. **—ru′nic** *adj.*

rung[1] (rŭng) *n.* **1.** A bar that forms a step of a ladder. **2.** A crosspiece between the legs of a chair. **3.** A spoke of a wheel.

rung[2] (rŭng) *v. p.p. of* RING[2].

run-in (rŭn′ĭn′) *n.* A quarrel : argument.

run•ner (rŭn′ər) *n.* **1.** One who runs. **2.** A contestant in a race. **3.** One who performs errands or delivers messages. **4.** A smuggler. **5.** A part that slides, esp.: **a.** The blade of an ice skate. **b.** One of the parallel structures on which a sled or sleigh moves. **6.** A supporting structure or groove in which a drawer or door slides. **7.** A long narrow carpet. **8.** *Bot.* **a.** A slender creeping stem that puts forth roots at intervals along its length. **b.** A plant with such a stem.

run•ner-up (rŭn′ər-ŭp′) *n.* A contestant that takes 2nd place.

run•ning (rŭn′ĭng) *n.* **1.** The sport or activity of one who runs. **2.** Competition <in the *running* for the award> —*adj.* Continuous. —*adv.* Consecutively.

running mate *n.* The candidate or nominee for the lesser of 2 closely associated political offices.

run•ny (rŭn′ē) *adj.* **-ni•er, -ni•est.** Inclined to flow or discharge fluid.

run-off (rŭn′ôf′, -ŏf′) *n.* **1.** Overflow from a container. **2.** An added competition for breaking a tie.

run-of-the-mill (rŭn′əv-*th*ə-mĭl′) *adj.* Not exceptional : ordinary.

runt (rŭnt) *n.* **1.** A small animal, esp. the smallest in a litter. **2.** A very small person. **—runt′i•ness** *n.* **—runt′y** *adj.*

run-through (rŭn′thro͞o′) *n.* A complete but fast review or performance, as of a play.

run•way (rŭn′wā′) *n.* **1.** A path or channel over which something runs. **2.** A narrow platform extending from a stage into an auditorium. **3.** A strip of paved level ground for aircraft to take off and land.

ru•pee (ro͞o-pē′, ro͞o′pē) *n.* See CURRENCY TABLE.

ru•pi•ah (ro͞o-pē′ə) *n., pl.* **-ah** or **-ahs.** See CURRENCY TABLE.

rup•ture (rŭp′chər) *n.* **1.** The act of bursting or breaking open. **2.** A break in friendly or normal relations. **3.** A hernia. **—rup′tur•a•ble** *adj.* **—rup′ture** *v.*

ru•ral (ro͝or′əl) *adj.* Of the country or country life. **—ru•ru•al′i•ty** *n.*

ruse (ro͞os, ro͞oz) *n.* An action meant to confuse or mislead : wily deception.

rush[1] (rŭsh) *v.* **1.** To move or cause to move swiftly. **2.** To attack : charge <*rushed* the fort> **3.** To perform hastily. ☆***syns:*** DASH, HASTEN, HURRY, HUSTLE, RACE, RUN, SCURRY, SPEED —*n.* **1.** A swift forward motion. **2.** Impatient movement toward or from a place. **3.** General haste or busyness. **4.** A sudden attack. **5.** A rapid, often noisy flow. —*adj.* Requiring haste.

rush[2] (rŭsh) *n.* A marsh plant of the family Juncaceae, with pliant hollow or pithy stems used to make baskets and mats.

rusk (rŭsk) *n.* Sweet raised bread baked until browned and dried.

rus•set (rŭs′ĭt) *n.* **1.** A reddish brown. **2.** A type of apple with a rough reddish-brown skin. **—rus′set** *adj.*

Rus•sia (rŭsh′ə). **1.** Union of Soviet Socialist Republics. **2.** The Russian Empire under czarist rule. **—Rus′sian** *adj.* & *n.*

rust (rŭst) *n.* **1.** Any of various scaly or powdery reddish-brown ferric oxides that form a coating on iron and iron-containing materials exposed to oxygen and moisture. **2.** A plant disease caused by various parasitic fungi that make reddish or brownish spots on leaves and stems. **3.** A reddish brown. —*v.* **1.** To form rust (on). **2.** To corrode. **2.** To deteriorate through neglect or inactivity. **—rust′y** *adj.*

rus•tic (rŭs′tĭk) *adj.* **1.** Of or characteristic of country life : rural. **2.** Not sophisticated. **3.** Made of rough tree branches <a *rustic* shelter> —*n.* **1.** A rural person. **2.** A crude or simple person. **—rus′ti•cal•ly** *adv.* **—rus•tic′i•ty** (-tĭs′ĭ-tē) *n.*

rus•ti•cate (rŭs′tĭ-kāt′) *v.* **-cat•ed, -cat•ing.** To go or send to live in the country. **—rus′ti•ca′tion** *n.* **—rus′ti•ca′tor** *n.*

rus•tle (rŭs′əl) *v.* **-tled, -tling. 1.** To move or cause to move with soft crackling or fluttering sounds. **2.** *Informal.* To make or get by acting hastily <*rustle* up some food> **3.** To steal (cattle). **—rus′tle** *n.* **—rus′tler** *n.* **—rus′tling•ly** *adv.*

rut[1] (rŭt) *n.* **1.** A sunken track made by the wheels of passing vehicles. **2.** A fixed, unvarying routine. **—rut′ted** *adj.*

rut[2] (rŭt) *n.* A cyclically recurring condition of sexual excitement and activity, esp. in male deer.

ru•ta•ba•ga (ro͞o′tə-bā′gə) *n.* A Eurasian plant, *Brassica napobrassica,* having a thick, bulbous root used as food and fodder.

Ruth (ro͞oth) *n.* See BIBLE TABLE.

ru•the•ni•um (ro͞o-thē′nē-əm) *n. Symbol* **Ru** A hard, white, acid-resistant metallic element.

ruth•less (ro͞oth′lĭs) *adj.* Lacking compassion : merciless. **—ruth′less•ly** *adv.*

RV (är′vē′) *n.* A recreational vehicle.

Rwan•da (ro͞o-än′də). Country of EC Africa. *Cap.* Kigali. *Pop.* 4,780,000. **—Rwan′dan** *n.* & *adj.*

Rx (är′ĕks′) *n.* **1.** A prescription for medicine or medical appliances. **2.** A cure, remedy, or solution for a problem or a disorder.

▲word history: There is no x in *Rx.* The spelling is an attempt to represent in ordinary letters the symbol ℞, which is merely a capital *R* with a slash through the tail. ℞ is a symbol for *recipe,* which orig. meant "a medicinal prescription" and only later came to mean "a formula used in cooking." *Recipe* is the imperative form of Latin *recipere,* "to take, receive." In Medieval Latin *recipe* often occurred as the 1st word of medicinal prescriptions directing one to take a certain quantity of a preparation.

-ry *suff. var. of* -ERY.

rye (rī) *n.* **1.** A widely cultivated cereal grass, *Secale cereale,* whose seeds are used to make flour and whiskey. **2.** Whiskey distilled from rye.

Ss

s or **S** (ĕs) *n., pl.* **s's** or **S's. 1.** The 19th letter of the English alphabet. **2.** A speech sound represented by the letter *s.* **3. S** A grade indicating that a student's work is satisfactory. **4.** Something with the shape of the letter S.

s *abbr.* **1.** second. **2.** *also* **S, s., S.** south; southern. **3.** stere.

s. *abbr.* **1.** son. **2.** substantive. **3.** shilling.

S *symbol for* SULFUR.

S. *abbr.* **1.** Saturday. **2.** school. **3.** sea. **4.** September. **5.** Sunday.

-s[1] *suff.* Used to form plural nouns <books>

-s[2] *suff.* Used to form the 3rd person sing. present tense of regular and most irregular verbs <walks> <hits>

-s[3] *suff.* Used to form adverbs <caught unawares in the storm>

-'s *suff.* Used to form the possessive case <state's> <women's>

S.A. *abbr.* **1.** South Africa. **2.** South America.

Saar (sär). River, c. 150 mi (240 km), of NE France and W West Germany.

Sab•bath (săb′əth) *n.* **1.** Saturday, the 7th day of the week, set apart as a day of worship by Jews and some Christians. **2.** Sunday, the 1st day of the week, set apart as a day of worship by most Christians.

sab•bat•i•cal year *also* **sabbatical** (sə-băt'ĭ-kəl) *n.* A leave from work, esp. a paid leave of absence granted, as to a professor, usu. every 7th year, for rest, study, etc.

sa•ber (sā'bər) *n.* **1.** A cavalry sword with a single-edged curved blade. **2.** A light double-edged sword used in fencing.

Sa•bin vaccine (sā'bĭn) *n.* A polio vaccine administered orally.

sa•ble (sā'bəl) *n.* **1.** A carnivorous mammal, *Martes zibellina,* of N Europe and Asia, having soft dark fur. **2. a.** The color black, esp. in heraldry. **b. sables.** Black mourning garments. **—sa'ble** *adj.*

sab•o•tage (săb'ə-täzh') *n.* **1.** Destruction of property or obstruction of normal operations, as by enemy agents in a war. **2.** Treacherous action to defeat or hinder an endeavor. **—sab'o•tage'** *v.*

sab•o•teur (săb'ə-tûr') *n.* A person who commits sabotage.

sa•bre (sā'bər) *n. esp. Brit. var. of* SABER.

sac (săk) *n.* A baglike or pouchlike part of an animal or plant.

sac•cha•rin (săk'ər-ĭn) *n.* A very sweet white crystalline powder used as a substitute for sugar.

sac•cha•rine (săk'ər-ĭn) *adj.* **1.** Of or like sugar : sweet. **2.** Insincerely or sickeningly sweet <a *saccharine* smile>

sac•er•do•tal (săs'ər-dōt'l, săk'-) *adj.* Of or relating to priests or the priesthood.

sa•chem (sā'chəm) *n.* The chief of a North American Indian tribe.

sa•chet (să-shā') *n.* A small bag or packet filled with a sweet-smelling substance and used to scent clothes and linens.

sack[1] (săk) *n.* **1. a.** A large bag of strong, coarse material. **b.** A smaller bag, esp. of paper. **2.** *also* **sacque.** A loose-fitting garment for women and children. **3.** *Slang.* Dismissal from a job or position <got the *sack* for being late> **4.** *Slang.* A bed, mattress, or sleeping bag. *—v.* **1.** To put into a sack. **2.** *Slang.* To fire from a job.

sack[2] (săk) *v.* To plunder : loot.

sack[3] *n.* A dry white wine popular in England in the 16th and 17th cent.

sack•cloth (săk'klôth', -klŏth') *n.* **1.** Sacking. **2. a.** A rough cloth of camel's hair, goat's hair, hemp, cotton, or flax. **b.** A garment made of sackcloth and worn as a symbol of sorrow or repentance.

sack•ing (săk'ĭng) *n.* Material, as burlap, used for making sacks.

sa•cra (sā'krə, săk'rə) *n. pl. of* SACRUM.

sac•ra•ment (săk'rə-mənt) *n.* **1.** A formal Christian rite, as baptism or matrimony, esp. one thought to have been instituted by Jesus. **2.** *often* **Sacrament. a.** The Eucharist. **b.** The consecrated elements of the Eucharist. **—sac'ra•men'tal** *adj.*

Sac•ra•men•to (săk'rə-mĕn'tō). Cap. of Calif., in the NC part. *Pop.* 275,741.

sa•cred (sā'krĭd) *adj.* **1.** Dedicated to or reserved for the worship of a deity. **2.** Regarded with religious veneration. **3.** Dedicated to or set apart for a single use, purpose, or person. **4.** Worthy of respect : venerable. **5.** Of or relating to religion. **—sa'cred•ly** *adv.* **—sa'cred•ness** *n.*

sacred cow *n.* One that is immune to attack or criticism.

sac•ri•fice (săk'rə-fīs') *n.* **1. a.** The act of offering something, as an animal's life, to a deity, as in propitiation. **b.** A victim offered in sacrifice. **2. a.** Forfeiture of something valuable for the sake of something else. **b.** Something given up in this way. **3.** A loss <forced to sell at a *sacrifice*> **4.** *Baseball.* **a.** A fly ball enabling a runner to score after it is caught by a fielder. **b.** A bunt allowing a runner to advance a base while the batter is retired. *—v.* **-ficed, -fic•ing. 1.** To offer as a sacrifice. **2.** To give up (something valuable) for the sake of something else. **3.** To sell or give at a loss. **4.** *Baseball.* To make a sacrifice. **—sac'ri•fi'cial** (-fĭsh'əl) *adj.*

sac•ri•lege (săk'rə-lĭj) *n.* Desecration, profanation, or theft of something sacred. **—sac'ri•le'gious** (-lĭj'əs, -lē'jəs) *adj.*

sac•ris•tan (săk'rĭ-stən) *n.* **1.** A person in charge of a sacristy. **2.** A sexton.

sac•ris•ty (săk'rĭ-stē) *n., pl.* **-ties.** A room in a church where vestments and sacred articles are kept : vestry.

sac•ro•il•i•ac (săk'rō-ĭl'ē-ăk') *adj.* Of, relating to, or affecting the sacrum and ilium. *—n.* The sacroiliac region or cartilage.

sac•ro•sanct (săk'rō-săngkt') *adj.* Sacred and inviolable. **—sac'ro•sanc'ti•ty** *n.*

sa•crum (sā'krəm, săk'rəm) *n., pl.* **sa•cra** (sā'krə, săk'rə) A triangular bone consisting of 5 fused vertebrae and forming the posterior section of the pelvis.

sad (săd) *adj.* **sad•der, sad•dest. 1.** Marked by unhappiness or sorrow. **2.** Expressing sorrow or regret. **3.** Causing sorrow or gloom. **4.** Deplorable <a *sad* state of affairs> **—sad'ly** *adv.* **—sad'ness** *n.*

sad•den (săd'n) *v.* To make sad.

sad•dle (săd'l) *n.* **1.** A leather seat for a rider, as of an animal or a bicycle. **2.** A cut of meat including a portion of the backbone and both loins. *—v.* **-dled, -dling. 1.** To put a saddle on. **2.** To load down : encumber <*saddled* with too much work>

sad•dle•bag (săd'l-băg') *n.* One of a pair of pouches that hang across the back of a horse behind the saddle or over the rear wheel of a bicycle or motorcycle.

sad•dle•bow (săd'l-bō') *n.* The arched upper front part of a saddle.

saddle horse *n.* A horse bred or trained for riding.

saddle soap *n.* A mild soap used for cleaning and softening leather.

Sad•du•cee (săj'ə-sē', săd'yə-) *n.* A member of an ancient Jewish sect that retained the older interpretation of the written Mosaic law. **—Sad'du•ce'an** *adj.*

sa•dism (sā'dĭz'əm, săd'ĭz'-) *n.* **1.** Abnormal enjoyment of cruelty. **2.** Extreme cruelty. **—sa'dist** *n.* **—sa•dis'tic** (sə-dĭs'tĭk) *adj.* **—sa•dis'ti•cal•ly** *adv.*

sa•do•mas•o•chism (sā'dō-măs'ə-kĭz'əm, săd'ō-) *n. Psychol.* Derivation of pleasure, esp. sexual gratification, from simultaneous sadism and masochism. **—sa'do•mas'o•chist** *n.* **—sa'do•mas'o•chis'tic** *adj.*

sa•fa•ri (sə-fä'rē) *n., pl.* **-ris. 1.** An expedition for hunting or exploring, esp. in E Africa. **2.** *Informal.* A journey or trip.

safe (sāf) *adj.* **saf•er, saf•est. 1.** Secure from harm, danger, or evil. **2.** Free from injury or danger : unhurt. **3.** Not risky : sure <a *safe* bet> **4.** Giving protection <a *safe* place> **5.** *Baseball.* Having reached a base without being put out. *—n.* A usu. metal container used to store and protect valuables. **—safe'ly** *adv.* **—safe'ness** *n.*

safe-con•duct (sāf'kŏn'dŭkt) *n.* A document permitting safe passage through enemy lands.

safe-de•pos•it box (sāf'dĭ-pŏz'ĭt) *n.* A fireproof metal box, usu. in a bank vault, for storing valuables.

safe•guard (sāf'gärd') *n.* Something, as a device or course of action, that serves as a protection or defense. *—v.* To furnish a safeguard for : protect.

safe•keep•ing (sāf'kē'pĭng) *n.* The act of keeping safe or state of being kept safe.

safe•ty (sāf'tē) *n., pl.* **-ties. 1.** The state of being safe. **2.** A device designed to prevent accidents. **3.** *Football.* **a.** A play in which a member of the offensive team downs the ball behind his own goal line. **b.** One of 2 defensive backs.

safety glass *n.* A shatterproof material consisting of 2 sheets of glass with an intermediate layer of clear plastic.

safety match *n.* A match that can be ignited only when struck on a specially prepared surface.

safety pin *n.* A pin shaped like a clasp, with a guard covering the point.

safety razor *n.* A razor whose blade is held betweeen guards.

safety valve *n.* A valve, as in a steam boiler, that opens automatically when pressure reaches a hazardous level.

saf•flow•er (săf'lou'ər) *n.* A plant, *Carthamus tinctorius,* native to Asia, with orange flowers yielding a dyestuff and seeds that are the source of an oil used in cooking, cosmetics, paints, and medicine.

saf•fron (săf'rən) *n.* **1.** A plant, *Crocus sativus,* having flowers with orange stigmas. **2.** The dried stigmas of the saffron, used to color foods and as a spice.

sag (săg) *v.* **sagged, sag•ging. 1.** To droop, sink, or settle from or as if from pressure or weight. **2.** To lose strength, firmness, or resilience. **3.** To decline in amount or value <profits that *sagged*> **—sag** *n.*

sa•ga (sä'gə) *n.* **1.** A 12th- and 13th-cent. narrative of historical and legendary events and exploits in Iceland. **2.** A modern narrative resembling a saga.

sa•ga•cious (sə-gā'shəs) *adj.* Marked by keen perception : wise. **—sa•ga'cious•ly** *adv.* **—sa•gac'i•ty** (-găs'ĭ-tē) *n.*

sage[1] (sāj) *n.* One renowned for judgment and wisdom. *—adj.* **sag•er, sag•est.** Wise : judicious. **—sage'ly** *adv.* **—sage'ness** *n.*

sage[2] (sāj) *n.* **1.** A plant or shrub of the genus *Salvia,* esp. *S. officinalis,* with aromatic grayish-green leaves used as seasoning. **2.** Sagebrush.

sage•brush (sāj'brŭsh') *n.* A shrub, *Artemisia tridentata,* of arid regions of W North America, with aromatic sagelike leaves.

Sag•it•tar•i•us (săj'ĭ-târ'ē-əs) *n.* **1.** A constellation in the S Hemisphere. **2. a.** The 9th sign of the zodiac. **b.** One born under this sign.

sa•go (sā'gō) *n., pl.* **-gos.** A powdery starch obtained from the pith of a tropical Asian palm.

sa•gua•ro (sə-gwä'rō, sə-wä'-) *n., pl.* **-ros.** A large cactus,

Carnegiea gigantea, of the SW U.S. and N Mexico, with upward-curving branches and edible red fruit.

Sa·har·a (sə-hâr′ə, -hä′rə). Vast arid area of N Africa, extending from the Atlantic coast to the Nile valley and from the Atlas Mts. S to the Sudan.

said (sĕd) *v. p.t. & p.p. of* say.

Sai·gon (sī-gŏn′). Ho Chi Minh City.

sail (sāl) *n.* **1.** A piece of strong fabric that catches the wind and causes a ship to move. **2.** *pl.* **sail** *or* **sails.** A sailing vessel. **3.** A trip in a sailing vessel. **4.** Something that resembles a sail. —*v.* **1.** To travel by sailing ship. **2.** To travel over or across in a ship <*sail* the Atlantic> **3.** To begin a voyage across water. **4.** To operate a sailing vessel, esp. for sport. **5.** To move quickly, smoothly, or effortlessly.

sail·boat (sāl′bōt′) *n.* A boat propelled partly or wholly by sail.

sail·cloth (sāl′klôth′, -klŏth′) *n.* A strong canvas used to make sails or tents.

sail·fish (sāl′fĭsh′) *n.* A large marine fish of the genus *Istiophorus,* with the upper jaw prolonged into a spearlike bone and a large, saillike dorsal fin.

sailfish

sail·ing (sā′lĭng) *n.* The act or sport of operating, racing, or riding in a sailboat.

sail·or (sā′lər) *n.* **1.** One who sails, esp. a member of a ship's crew. **2.** An enlisted man in a navy.

saint (sānt) *n.* **1. a.** One officially recognized, esp. by canonization, as being entitled to public veneration. **b.** One who has died and gone to heaven. **2.** A patient, unselfish, highly virtuous person. **—saint′ed** *adj.* **—saint′hood′** *n.* **—saint′li·ness** *n.* **—saint′ly** *adj.*

Saint Ber·nard (bər-närd′) *n.* A large, strong dog, orig. bred in Switzerland, formerly used to rescue lost travlers.

Saint George's (jôr′jəz) *also* **Saint George** (jôrj). Cap. of Grenada, in the West Indies. *Pop.* 10,000.

Saint John's (jŏnz′). Cap. of Antigua, on the N coast of the island. *Pop.* 21,814.

Saint Kitts-Nevis (kĭts′nē′vĭs, -nĕv′ĭs). Island country in the British West Indies. *Cap.* Basseterre. *Pop.* 47,457.

Saint Law·rence (lôr′əns, lŏr′-). **1. Gulf of.** Arm of the NW Atlantic off SE Canada, between N.B. and Newf. **2.** River of SE Canada, flowing 744 mi (1,197.1 km) NE from Lake Ontario to the Gulf of St. Lawrence. **3.** Waterway, 2,342 mi (3,768.3 km) long, consisting of a system of canals, dams, and locks in the St. Lawrence R. and connecting channels between the Great Lakes.

Saint Lou·is (lo͞o′ĭs, lo͞o′ē). City of E Mo., on the Mississippi. *Pop.* 453,085.

Saint Lu·ci·a (lo͞o′shə, lo͞o-sē′ə). Island nation of the West Indies in the E Caribbean. *Cap.* Castries. *Pop.* 117,500.

Saint Paul (pôl). Cap. of Minn., in the E adjacent to Minneapolis. *Pop.* 270,230.

Saint Pe·ters·burg (pē′tərz-bûrg′). **1.** Leningrad. **2.** City of WC Fla. *Pop.* 236,893.

Saint Vin·cent and the Gren·a·dines (vĭn′sənt; grĕn′ə-dēnz′). Island nation of the West Indies in the E Caribbean. *Cap.* Kingstown. *Pop.* 89,129.

sake[1] (sāk) *n.* **1.** Reason : motive <arguing for the *sake* of arguing> **2.** Benefit : good <for the *sake* of the community>

sa·ke[2] *also* **sa·ki** (sä′kē) *n.* A Japanese alcoholic beverage made from rice.

sa·laam (sə-läm′) *n.* **1.** An obeisance, esp. a low bow performed while placing the right palm on the forehead. **2.** A respectful ceremonial greeting performed esp. in the East. **—sa·laam′** *v.*

sa·la·cious (sə-lā′shəs) *adj.* Lewd : lascivious. **—sa·la′cious·ly** *adv.*

sal·ad (săl′əd) *n.* A usu. cold dish, as of raw vegetables, fruit, or meat, served with dressing.

sal·a·man·der (săl′ə-măn′dər) *n.* A small, lizardlike amphibian of the order Caudata, with porous, scaleless skin.

sa·la·mi (sə-lä′mē) *n.* A heavily spiced sausage made esp. of pork and beef.

sal·a·ry (săl′ə-rē, săl′rē) *n., pl.* **-ries.** Fixed compensation paid on a regular basis for services. **—sal′a·ried** *adj.*

sale (sāl) *n.* **1.** The act of selling. **2.** An opportunity to sell : demand. **3.** A disposal of goods at reduced prices. **4.** An auction. **—sal′a·ble, sale′a·ble** *adj.*

Sa·lem (sā′ləm). Cap. of Ore., in the NW. *Pop.* 89,233.

sales·clerk (sālz′klûrk′) *n.* A person who sells goods in a store.

sales·man (sālz′mən) *n.* A man who sells goods or services. **—sales′man·ship′** *n.*

sales·per·son (sālz′pûr′sən) *n.* A salesclerk.

sales tax *n.* A tax levied on sales.

sales·woman (sālz′wo͝om′ən) *n.* A woman who sells goods or services.

sal·i·cyl·ic acid (săl′ĭ-sĭl′ĭk) *n.* A white crystalline acid used esp. to make aspirin.

sa·li·ent (sā′lē-ənt, sāl′yənt) *adj.* **1.** Projecting beyond a line or surface. **2.** Conspicuous : prominent.

sa·line (sā′lēn′, -līn′) *adj.* Of, relating to, or containing salt : salty. **—sa·lin′i·ty** (sə-lĭn′ĭ-tē) *n.*

Salis·bur·y (sôlz′bĕr′ē, -bə-rē). Cap. of Zimbabwe, in the NE part. *Pop.* 118,500.

sa·li·va (sə-lī′və) *n.* The watery, tasteless liquid secretion discharged into the mouth that aids digestion. **—sal′i·var′y** (săl′ə-vĕr′ē) *adj.*

sal·i·vate (săl′ə-vāt′) *v.* **-vat·ed, -vat·ing.** To secrete saliva. **—sal′i·va′tion** *n.*

Salk vaccine (sôlk) *n.* A vaccine against poliomyelitis administered by injection.

sal·low (săl′ō) *adj.* Of a sickly yellow color <a *sallow* complexion>

sal·ly (săl′ē) *n., pl.* **-lies. 1.** A sudden rush forward, esp. in order to launch an assault : sortie. **2.** A sudden burst of activity : outbreak. **3.** A witticism : quip. **4.** An excursion : jaunt. **—sal·ly** *v.*

salm·on (săm′ən, sä′mən) *n., pl.* **salmon** *or* **-ons. 1.** A large food and game fish of the genera *Salmo* and *Oncorhynchus,* of N waters, having delicate pinkish flesh. **2.** A moderate, light, or strong yellowish pink. **—salm′on** *adj.*

sal·mo·nel·la (săl′mə-nĕl′ə) *n., pl.* **-nel·lae** (-nĕl′ē) *or* **-las** *or* **-la.** Any of various rod-shaped bacteria of the genus *Salmonella,* many of which are pathogenic.

sa·lon (sə-lŏn′, sä-lôN′) *n.* **1.** A large drawing room or reception room. **2.** A periodic gathering of prominent persons, as artists or literary figures. **3.** A fashionable commercial establishment <a beauty *salon*>

sa·loon (sə-lo͞on′) *n.* **1.** A place where alcoholic drinks are sold and drunk : tavern. **2.** A large room, as for receptions or public entertainment, esp. on a passenger ship. **3.** *esp. Brit.* A sedan automobile.

sal soda *n.* A hydrated sodium carbonate used as a general cleanser.

salt (sôlt) *n.* **1.** A white crystalline solid, mainly sodium chloride, used esp. as a preservative and seasoning. **2.** Any of a large class of chemical compounds formed when 1 or more hydrogen ions of an acid are replaced by metallic ions. **3.** *often* **salts.** Any of various salts of inorganic acids used as cathartics. **4.** *Informal.* A sailor. —*adj.* **1.** Of or containing salt : salty. **2.** Preserved in salt or brine. —*v.* To season, sprinkle, or preserve with salt. **—salt away.** To lay aside and save (e.g., money). **—salt′i·ness** *n.* **—salt′y** *adj.*

▲word history: The word *salt* is a native English word; over the centuries it has formed many compounds, most of which have obvious meanings. *Salt* is related to Latin *sal,* "salt," which has many derivatives in English whose origins are not immediately apparent. The word *salary* is perhaps the most notable word derived from *sal.* The Latin source of *salary* is *salarium,* which orig. meant "money given to soldiers to buy salt" but later meant "a stipend, wages." Salt, of course, was put on food, both as a seasoning and as a preservative. *Salad* and *sauce* orig. denoted salted accompaniments to a meal. *Salami* and *sausage* denote preparations of meat preserved with salt.

salt·box (sôlt′bŏks′) *n.* A frame house with 2 stories in front and 1 in the rear and a long sloped roof.

salt·cel·lar (sôlt′sel′ər) *n.* A small dish for holding salt at the table.

sal·tine (sôl-tēn′) *n.* A thin, crisp cracker sprinkled with coarse salt.

Salt Lake City. Cap. of Utah, in the N part. *Pop.* 163,033.

salt lick *n.* A deposit of exposed salt that animals lick.

salt·pe·ter (sôlt′pē′tər) *n.* **1.** Potassium nitrate. **2.** Sodium nitrate. **3.** Niter.

salt·shak·er (sôlt′shā′kər) *n.* A container for salt with a perforated top.

salt·water (sôlt'wô'tər, -wŏt'ər) *adj.* Of consisting of, or living in salt water.
sa·lu·bri·ous (sə-lo͞o'brē-əs) *adj.* Conducive or favorable to health or well-being.
sal·u·tar·y (săl'yə-tĕr'ē) *adj.* **1.** Effecting improvement : remedial. **2.** Promoting health : wholesome.
sal·u·ta·tion (săl'yə-tā'shən) *n.* An expression or gesture of greeting or good will.
sa·lute (sə-lo͞ot') *v.* **-lut·ed, -lut·ing. 1.** To greet with politeness, respect, or honor. **2.** To pay respect to (a superior officer), as by raising the right hand to the forehead or cap. **3.** To honor ceremoniously. *—n.* An act, ceremony, or gesture of saluting.
Sal·va·dor (săl'-və-dôr'). City of E Brazil, on the Atlantic. *Pop.* 1,445,700.
sal·vage (săl'vĭj) *n.* **1. a.** The rescue of a ship, its crew, or its cargo, as from fire or shipwreck. **b.** The ship, crew, or cargo so rescued. **c.** Compensation given to those who aid in such a rescue. **2. a.** The act of saving endangered property from total loss. **b.** The property so saved. *—v.* **-vaged, -vag·ing.** To save from total loss or destruction. **—sal'vage·a·ble** *adj.*
sal·va·tion (săl-vā'shən) *n.* **1. a.** The act of saving or state of being saved, as from danger or destruction. **b.** A means or agent of salvation. **2.** Deliverance from sin or death : redemption.
salve (săv, säv) *n.* **1.** An analgesic or medicinal ointment, as for burns. **2.** Something that soothes or heals : balm. *—v.* **salved, salv·ing.** To soothe with or as if with salve.
sal·ver (săl'vər) *n.* A tray for serving food or drinks.
sal·vo (săl'vō) *n., pl.* **-vos** *or* **-voes. 1.** The firing of a number of weapons at the same time. **2.** A sudden outburst, as of cheers.
sa·mar·i·um (sə-mâr'ē-əm, -mär'-) *n. Symbol* **Sm** A pale-gray or silvery metallic rare-earth element.
same (sām) *adj.* **1.** Being exactly alike : identical. **2.** Alike, as in kind : similar. **3.** Being the one previously mentioned. ☆**syns:** IDENTICAL, SELFSAME, VERY *—adv.* In the same way. *—pron.* The very same one or ones. **—same'ness** *n.*
Sa·mo·a (sə-mō'ə). Island group of the S Pacific ENE of Fiji, divided between American Samoa and Western Samoa. **—Sa·mo'an** *adj.* & *n.*
sam·o·var (săm'ə-vär') *n.* A metal urn with a spigot, used esp. in Russia to boil water for tea.
sam·pan (săm'păn') *n.* A flat-bottomed boat of the Orient, propelled usu. by 2 short oars.
sam·ple (săm'pəl) *n.* A portion, piece, or segment that is representative of a whole : example. *—v.* **-pled, -pling.** To take a sample of, as for study.
sam·pler (săm'plər) *n.* A piece of cloth embroidered with designs or mottoes in various stitches.
sam·u·rai (săm'ə-rī') *n., pl.* **-rai** *or* **-rais. 1.** The feudal military aristocracy of Japan. **2.** A professional warrior belonging to the samurai.
San·a *also* **Sa·n'a** *or* **Sa·naa** (sä-nä'). Cap. of North Yemen. *Pop.* 192,045.
San An·to·ni·o (săn' ăn-tō'nē-ō'). City of SC Tex., SSW of Austin. *Pop.* 785,410.
san·a·to·ri·um (săn'ə-tôr'ē-əm, -tōr'-) *n., pl.* **-ums** *or* **-ri·a** (-ē-ə). An institution for the treatment of chronic diseases or supervision of convalescence.
sanc·ta (săngk'tə) *n. var. pl. of* SANCTUM.
sanc·ti·fy (săngk'tə-fī') *v.* **-fied, -fy·ing. 1.** To make holy or sacred. **2.** To free from sin : purify. **—sanc'ti·fi·ca'tion** *n.*
sanc·ti·mo·ni·ous (săngk'tə-mō'nē-əs) *adj.* Feigning piety or righteousness. **—sanc'ti·mo'ni·ous·ly** *adv.* **—sanc'ti·mo'ni·ous·ness** *n.*
sanc·tion (săngk'shən) *n.* **1.** Authoritative approval or permission. **2.** A measure, as moral pressure or a fine, imposed to ensure compliance or conformity. *—v.* To give approval to : authorize.
sanc·ti·ty (săngk'tĭ-tē) *n., pl.* **-ties. 1.** Saintliness : godliness. **2.** The quality of being sacred : sacredness.
sanc·tu·ar·y (săngk'cho͞o-ĕr'ē) *n., pl.* **-ies. 1.** A sacred place, as a church, temple, or mosque. **2.** A place giving refuge or asylum <a game *sanctuary*>
sanc·tum (săngk'təm) *n., pl.* **-tums** *or* **-ta** (-tə). A private place, as an office, where one is free from intrusion.
sand (sănd) *n.* Loose, fine grains of disintegrated rock. *—v.* **1.** To sprinkle or cover with sand. **2.** To smooth or polish with an abrasive, as sandpaper. **—sand'y** *adj.*
san·dal (săn'dəl) *n.* **1.** A shoe with a sole fastened to the foot by thongs or straps. **2.** A light slipper or low-cut shoe fastened to the foot by an ankle strap.
san·dal·wood (săn'dəl-wo͝od') *n.* An Asian tree of the genus *Santalum*, esp. *S. album*, with aromatic yellowish heartwood used in cabinetmaking and wood carving.
sand·bag (sănd'băg') *n.* A bag filled with sand, often used in protective walls or dikes. **—sand'bag'** *v.*
sand·bank (sănd'băngk') *n.* A large mass of sand, as on a hillside or in a river.
sand·bar (sănd'bär') *n.* An offshore shoal of sand built up by waves or currents.
sand·blast (sănd'blăst') *n.* A high-velocity blast of air or steam carrying sand to etch glass or clean stone or metal surfaces. **—sand'blast'** *v.*
sand·box (sănd'bŏks') *n.* A low box containing sand for children to play in.
sand·hog (sănd'hôg', -hŏg') *n.* A construction worker who builds underwater tunnels.
San Di·e·go (dē-ā'gō). City of S Calif., on the Pacific. *Pop.* 875,504.
sand·lot (sănd'lŏt') *n.* A vacant lot used esp. by children for unorganized sports. **—sand'lot'** *adj.*
sand·man (sănd'măn') *n.* A folklore character who makes children sleepy.
sand·pa·per (sănd'pā'pər) *n.* Paper with a coating of abrasive material on 1 side, used for smoothing or polishing.
sand·pip·er (sănd'pī'pər) *n.* A small wading bird of the family Scolopacidae, usu. having a long, straight bill.
sand·stone (sănd'stōn') *n.* Sedimentary rock formed of grains of quartz cemented together esp. by lime or silica.
sand·storm (sănd'stôrm') *n.* A windstorm that carries clouds of sand.
sand trap *n.* A hazard on a golf course having a depression filled with sand.
sand·wich (sănd'wĭch) *n.* **1.** Two or more slices of bread with a filling, as meat, between them. **2.** Something resembling a sandwich. *—v.* To insert between 2 other things, esp. tightly.
sane (sān) *adj.* **san·er, san·est. 1.** Of sound mind. **2.** Having or showing sound judgment : reasonable. **—sane'ly** *adv.* **—sane'ness, san'i·ty** (săn'ĭ-tē) *n.*
San Fran·cis·co (frən-sĭs'kō). City of W Calif., on an inlet of the Pacific. *Pop.* 678,974. **—San Fran·cis'can** (-kən) *n.*
sang (săng) *v. p.t. of* SING.
sang-froid (säɴ-frwä') *n.* Composure : equanimity.
san·gui·nar·y (săng'gwə-nĕr'ē) *adj.* **1.** Accompanied by bloodshed **2.** Bloody.
san·guine (săng'gwĭn) *adj.* **1. a.** Of the color of blood : red. **b.** Ruddy. **2.** Cheerfully confident : optimistic. **—san·guin'i·ty** *n.* **—san·guin'e·ous** *adj.*
san·i·tar·i·an (săn'ĭ-târ'ē-ən) *n.* A public-health or sanitation expert.
san·i·tar·i·um (săn'ĭ-târ'ē-əm) *n., pl.* **-ums** *or* **-i·a** (-ē-ə). A sanatorium.
san·i·tar·y (săn'ĭ-tĕr'ē) *adj.* **1.** Of or relating to health. **2.** Free from elements, as filth or bacteria, that endanger health.
sanitary napkin *n.* A disposable pad worn to absorb menstrual flow.
san·i·ta·tion (săn'ĭ-tā'shən) *n.* **1.** The application of measures designed to protect public health. **2.** Disposal of sewage.
san·i·tize (săn'ĭ-tīz') *v.* **-tized, -tiz·ing. 1.** To make sanitary. **2.** To make more acceptable by removing potentially offensive elements from.
San Jo·se (hō-zā'). City of W Calif., SE of San Francisco. *Pop.* 636,550.
San Jo·sé (săn' hō-zā'). Cap. of Costa Rica, on the C plateau. *Pop.* 239,800.
San Juan (săn' hwän', wän'). Cap. of Puerto Rico, on the NE coast. *Pop.* 422,701.
sank (săngk) *v. p.t. of* SINK.
San Ma·ri·no (mə-rē'nō). Country within NC Italy, in the Apennines. *Cap.* San Marino (*pop.* 4,628). *Pop.* 20,000.
sans (sănz) *prep.* Without.
San Sal·va·dor (săl'və-dôr'). Cap. of El Salvador, in the WC part. *Pop.* 397,100.
San·skrit (săn'skrĭt') *n.* The ancient language of Hinduism and the classical literary language of India. **—San'skrit'** *adj.*
San·ta An·a (săn'tə ăn'ə). City of SW Calif., E of Long Beach. *Pop.* 203,713.
Santa Claus (klôz) *n.* The personification of Christmas, usu. represented as a fat, white-bearded, red-suited old man.
Santa Fe (fā'). Cap. of N.Mex., in the NC part. *Pop.* 48,899.
San·ti·a·go (săn'tē-ä'gō). Cap. of Chile, in the C part. *Pop.* 3,448,700.
San·to Do·min·go (săn'tō də-mĭng'gō). Cap. of the Dominican Republic, in the S on the Caribbean. *Pop.* 979,608.
São Pau·lo (souɴ pou'lo͞o). City of SE Brazil. *Pop.* 8,407,500.
São To·mé and Prin·ci·pe (to͞o-mā'; prēɴ'sē-pə). Island country in the Gulf of Guinea W of Gabon. *Cap.* São Tomé (*pop.* 17,380). *Pop.* 73,631.
sap¹ (săp) *n.* **1.** The liquid that circulates through plant tissues, carrying food substances. **2.** Vigor : energy. **3.** *Slang.* A gullible person : dupe.

sap[2] (săp) *v.* **sapped, sap·ping. 1.** To weaken gradually. **2.** To undermine.

sa·pi·ent (sā′pē-ənt) *adj.* Wise : sagacious. **—sa′pi·ence** *n.*

sap·ling (săp′lĭng) *n.* A young tree.

sa·pon·i·fy (sə-pŏn′ə-fī′) *v.* To convert (an oil or fat) into soap by treating with an alkali.

sap·phire (săf′īr′) *n.* **1.** A clear, deep-blue form of corundum valued as a gem. **2.** The deep-blue color of a gem sapphire.

sap·py (săp′ē) *adj.* **-pi·er, -pi·est. 1.** Full of sap. **2.** *Slang.* Silly or foolish : fatuous.

sap·ro·phyte (săp′rə-fīt′) *n.* A plant, as a mushroom, that derives its nourishment from decaying organic matter. **—sap′ro·phyt′ic** (-fĭt′ĭk) *adj.*

sap·suck·er (săp′sŭk′ər) *n.* Either of 2 small North American woodpeckers, *Sphyrapicus varius* or *S. thyrsoides.*

sap·wood (săp′wo͝od′) *n.* Newly formed outer wood that lies just inside the cambium of a tree or woody plant.

Sar·a·cen (săr′ə-sən) *n.* A Moslem, esp. during the Crusades.

sa·ran (sə-răn′) *n.* A thermoplastic resin derived from vinyl compounds and used esp. in the manufacture of packaging films.

sar·casm (sär′kăz′əm) *n.* **1.** A taunting or contemptuously ironic remark. **2.** The use of sarcasm. **—sar·cas′tic** (-kăs′tĭk) *adj.* **—sar·cas′ti·cal·ly** *adv.*

sar·co·ma (sär-kō′mə) *n., pl.* **-ma·ta** (-mə-tə) *or* **-mas.** A usu. malignant tumor derived from connective tissue.

sar·coph·a·gus (sär-kŏf′ə-gəs) *n., pl.* **-gi** (-jī′) *or* **-gus·es.** A stone coffin.

sar·dine (sär-dēn′) *n.* A small or half-grown edible herring or related fish of the family Clupeidae, often canned in oil.

Sar·din·i·a (sär-dĭn′ē-ə). Island of Italy, in the Mediterranean S of Corisca. **—Sar·din′i·an** *adj.* & *n.*

sar·don·ic (sär-dŏn′ĭk) *adj.* Mockingly cynical : sarcastic. **—sar·don′i·cal·ly** *adv.*

sarge (särj) *n. Informal.* Sergeant.

sa·ri (sä′rē) *n.* A garment worn by Hindu women that consists of a length of cloth wrapped around the body and over the shoulder.

sa·rong (sə-rông′, -rŏng′) *n.* A length of cloth wrapped about the body like a skirt and worn by both men and women in Malaysia and the Pacific islands.

sar·sa·pa·ril·la (săs′pə-rĭl′ə, särs′-) *n.* **1.** The dried roots of a tropical American plant of the genus *Smilax,* used as a flavoring. **2.** A soft drink flavored with sarsaparilla extract.

sar·to·ri·al (sär-tôr′ē-əl, -tōr′-) *adj.* Of or relating to a tailor, tailoring, or tailored clothing.

sash[1] (săsh) *n.* An ornamental band worn around the waist or over the shoulder.

sash[2] (săsh) *n.* **1.** A frame that holds the glass panes of a window or door. **2.** The sliding section of a window.

sa·shay (să-shā′) *v. Informal.* To move or walk in an ostentatious manner : strut.

sa·shi·mi (sä-shē′mē) *n.* A Japanese dish of raw fish sliced very thin.

Sask. *abbr.* Saskatchewan.

Sas·katch·e·wan (săs-kăch′ə-wän′, -wən). Province of SC Canada. *Cap.* Regina. *Pop.* 921,323.

Sas·quatch (săs′kwăch′) *n.* A large hairy mammal reputed to exist in the Pacific Northwest and W Canada.

sass (săs) *Informal.* —*n.* Impudent, disrespectful speech. —*v.* To talk impudently or disrespectfully to.

sas·sa·fras (săs′ə-frăs′) *n.* **1.** A North American tree, *Sassafras albidum,* with irregularly shaped leaves and aromatic bark. **2.** The dried root bark of the sassafras, used as flavoring and as a source of a volatile oil.

sas·sy (săs′ē) *adj.* **-si·er, -si·est.** Given to back talk : impudent.

sat (săt) *v. p.t. & p.p. of* SIT.

Sat. *abbr.* Saturday.

Sa·tan (sāt′n) *n.* The devil.

sa·tang (sə-tăng′) *n., pl.* **satang.** See *baht* at CURRENCY TABLE.

sa·tan·ic (sə-tăn′ĭk) *or* **sa·tan·i·cal** (-ĭ-kəl) *adj.* **1.** Of, relating to, or suggestive of Satan. **2.** Extremely evil : fiendish.

satch·el (săch′əl) *n.* A small bag for books or clothing, often having a shoulder strap.

sate (sāt) *v.* **sat·ed, sat·ing. 1.** To satisfy fully. **2.** To indulge excessively. ☆**syns:** CLOY, GLUT, GORGE, SATIATE, SURFEIT.

sa·teen (să-tēn′) *n.* A durable cotton fabric with a smooth, glossy, satinlike finish.

sat·el·lite (săt′l-īt′) *n.* **1.** A relatively small celestial body orbiting a larger one. **2.** A manmade object designed to orbit a celestial body. **3.** A subservient follower.

sa·ti·ate (sā′shē-āt′) *v.* **-at·ed, -at·ing.** To sate. **—sa′ti·a′tion** *n.*

sa·ti·e·ty (sə-tī′ĭ-tē) *n.* The state of being excessively full : surfeit.

sat·in (săt′n) *n.* A smooth fabric, as of silk, nylon, or rayon, with a glossy face and dull back. **—sat′in·y** *adj.*

sat·in·wood (săt′n-wo͝od′) *n.* A tree, *Chloroxylon swietenia,* of S Asia, with hard, yellowish, close-grained wood.

sat·ire (săt′īr′) *n.* **1.** Irony, derision, or caustic wit used to attack or expose folly, vice, or stupidity. **2.** A literary work in which satire is used to ridicule or attack human vice or folly. **—sa·tir′i·cal** (sə-tĭr′ĭ-kəl), **sa·tir′ic** *adj.* **—sa·tir′i·cal·ly** *adv.* **—sat′i·rist** *n.* **—sat′i·rize′** *v.*

sat·is·fac·tion (săt′ĭs-făk′shən) *n.* **1. a.** The fulfillment or gratification of a need, desire, or appetite. **b.** Pleasure derived from such fulfillment. **2.** Compensation for injury or loss : reparation. **3.** A source of fulfillment or gratification.

sat·is·fac·to·ry (săt′ĭs-făk′tə-rē) *adj.* Affording satisfaction. **—sat′is·fac′to·ri·ly** *adv.* **—sat′is·fac′to·ri·ness** *n.*

sat·is·fy (săt′ĭs-fī′) *v.* **-fied, -fy·ing. 1.** To fulfill or gratify. **2.** To free from question or doubt : convince. **3. a.** To discharge (e.g., an obligation). **b.** To discharge an obligation to (a creditor). **4.** To comply with the requirements of (a standard or rule). **5.** To make reparation for : redress. **—sat′is·fy′ing·ly** *adv.*

sa·trap (sā′trăp′, săt′răp′) *n.* A petty ruler or official.

sat·u·rate (săch′ə-rāt′) *v.* **-rat·ed, -rat·ing. 1.** To imbue or impregnate thoroughly. **2.** To soak or load to capacity. **—sat′u·ra·ble** *adj.* **—sat′u·ra′tion** *n.*

Sat·ur·day (săt′ər-dē, -dā′) *n.* The 7th day of the week.

Saturday night special *n. Informal.* A cheap, easily obtainable handgun.

Sat·urn (săt′ərn) *n.* The 6th planet from the sun.

sat·ur·nine (săt′ər-nīn′) *adj.* Having a melancholy or surly disposition : sardonic.

sat·yr (săt′ər, sā′tər) *n.* **1.** *Gk. Myth.* A woodland god often having the pointed ears, legs, and short horns of a goat. **2.** A lecherous man.

sauce (sôs) *n.* **1.** A dressing or relish for food. **2.** Stewed, sweetened fruit. **3.** *Informal.* Impertinence. —*v.* **sauced, sauc·ing. 1.** To season or dress with sauce. **2.** To add flavor or piquancy to. **3.** *Informal.* To be impertinent to.

sauce·pan (sôs′păn′) *n.* A deep cooking pan with a handle.

sau·cer (sô′sər) *n.* A small, shallow dish for holding a cup.

sauc·y (sô′sē) *adj.* **-i·er, -i·est. 1.** Impertinent. **2.** Pert <a *saucy* glance> **—sauc′i·ly** *adv.* **—sauc′i·ness** *n.*

Sa·u·di A·ra·bi·a (sä-o͞o′dē ə-rā′bē-ə, sou′dē, sô′-). Kingdom on the Arabian peninsula. *Cap.* Riyadh. *Pop.* 7,012,642. **—Sa·u′di′, Sa·u′di A·ra′bi·an** *adj.* & *n.*

sau·er·bra·ten (sour′brät′n) *n.* Pot-roasted beef marinated before cooking.

sau·er·kraut (sour′krout′) *n.* Salted and fermented chopped or shredded cabbage.

sault (so͞o) *n. Can.* A waterfall or rapids.

sau·na (sou′nə, sô′-) *n.* **1.** A steam bath with steam produced by water poured over heated rocks. **2.** A room or enclosure for a sauna.

saun·ter (sôn′tər) *v.* To walk at a leisurely pace : stroll. **—saun′ter** *n.*

sau·sage (sô′sĭj) *n.* Chopped and usu. highly seasoned meat, as pork, stuffed into a casing and cooked and cured.

sau·té (sō-tā′, sô-) *v.* **-téed, -té·ing.** To fry lightly and quickly in a shallow pan using a small amount of fat or oil.

sau·terne (sō-tûrn′, sô-) *n.* A relatively sweet white wine.

sav·age (săv′ĭj) *adj.* **1.** Wild. **2.** Uncivilized : primitive. **3.** Ferocious. **4.** Cruel or merciless : brutal. ☆**syns:** FERAL, WILD —*n.* **1.** A member of a primitive society. **2.** A fierce, vicious, or crude person. **—sav′age·ly** *adv.* **—sav′age·ry** *n.*

sa·van·na *also* **sa·van·nah** (sə-văn′ə) *n.* A flat, largely treeless grassland.

Savannah. City of E Ga. *Pop.* 141,634.

sa·vant (sə-vänt′) *n.* A scholar.

save[1] (sāv) *v.* **saved, sav·ing. 1.** To rescue from harm, danger, or loss. **2.** To keep in a safe state : safeguard. **3.** To prevent the waste or loss of : conserve. **4.** To keep for future use : store. **5.** To deliver from sin : redeem. **—sav′er** *n.*

save[2] (sāv) *prep.* Except : but. —*conj.* Were it not.

sav·ing (sā′vĭng) *n.* **1.** Preservation from harm, danger, or loss. **2.** Avoidance of overspending : economy. **3. savings.** An amount, as of money, saved.

sav·ior (sāv′yər) *n.* **1.** One who saves. **2. Savior.** Christ.

sav·iour (sāv′yər) *n. esp. Brit. var. of* SAVIOR.

sa·voir-faire (săv′wär-fâr′) *n.* The ability to say and do the correct thing : tact.

sa·vor (sā′vər) *n.* **1.** The taste or smell of something. **2.** A particular quality or flavor. —*v.* **1.** To have a particular taste, smell, or quality. **2.** To taste with enjoyment : relish. **—sa′vor·y** *adj.*

sa•vour (sā'vər) *n.* & *v. esp. Brit. var. of* SAVOR.
sav•vy (săv'ē) *Slang.* –*v.* **-vied, -vy•ing.** To know : comprehend. –*n.* Practical understanding : common sense.
saw[1] (sô) *n.* A tool with a thin, sharp-toothed metal blade used to cut hard materials. –*v.* **sawed, sawed** *or* **sawn** (sôn), **saw•ing. 1.** To cut or divide with or as if with a saw. **2.** To produce or shape with or as if with a saw.
saw[2] (sô) *n.* A trite or banal saying.
▲word history: The noun *saw[2]*, "a saying," is descended from the same Germanic ancestor as the noun *saga*, "a narrative," and both are related to the verb *say*. *Saw* is a native English word whose Old English form was *sagu*. *Saga* was borrowed from Icelandic in the 18th cent. as the name of the historical legends of the Scandinavian peoples. In Old Norse and Old Icelandic *saga* basically meant a story or legend transmitted orally; the narratives now called *sagas* were written down several centuries after the events they recount.
saw[3] (sô) *v. p.t. of* SEE[1].
saw•dust (sô'dŭst') *n.* Small particles, as of wood, produced by sawing.
sawed-off (sôd'ôf', -ŏf') *adj.* **1.** Shortened <a *sawed-off* shotgun> **2.** *Slang.* Short.
saw•horse (sô'hôrs') *n.* A rack used to support something being sawed.
saw•mill (sô'mĭl') *n.* A plant or factory where logs are sawed into boards.
sawn (sôn) *v. var. p.p. of* SAW[1].
sax (săks) *n. Informal.* A saxophone.
sax•i•frage (săk'sə-frĭj, -frāj') *n.* A low-growing plant of the genus *Saxifraga*, with leaves sometimes arranged in a rosette.
Sax•on (săk'sən) *n.* A member of a West Germanic tribe that invaded England in the 5th cent. **–Sax'on** *adj.*
sax•o•phone (săk'sə-fōn') *n.* A keyed wind instrument with a reed mouthpiece and a curved conical metal body. **–sax'o•phon'ist** *n.*
say (sā) *v.* **said** (sĕd), **say•ing. 1.** To utter aloud : pronounce. **2.** To express in words. **3.** To state positively : declare. **4.** To recite. **5.** To report or maintain : allege. **6.** To show : indicate <My watch *says* 2 o'clock.> –*n.* **1.** An assertion. **2.** A turn or opportunity to speak. **3.** The right or power to make a decision : authority.
say•ing (sā'ĭng) *n.* A familiar expression or sentiment : adage.
say-so (sā'sō') *n., pl.* **-sos.** *Informal.* **1.** An authoritative assertion. **2.** The right to make a final decision.
Sb *symbol for* ANTIMONY.
S.B. *abbr.* Bachelor of Science.
Sc *symbol for* SCANDIUM.
SC *abbr.* South Carolina (with Zip Code).
sc. *abbr.* **1.** scene. **2.** scruple (weight). **3.** scilicet.
s.c. *abbr.* small capitals.
S.C. *abbr.* **1.** South Carolina. **2.** Supreme Court.
scab (skăb) *n.* **1.** The crustlike exudate that covers a healing wound. **2.** Any of various plant diseases characterized by crustlike spots. **3. a.** One who works while others are on strike : strikebreaker. **b.** One who is hired to replace a striking worker. –*v.* **scabbed, scab•bing. 1.** To form a scab. **2.** *Informal.* To act or work as a scab. **–scab'by** *adj.*
scab•bard (skăb'ərd) *n.* A sheath or case for the blade of a sword, dagger, or bayonet.
sca•bies (skā'bēz') *n.* A contagious skin disease caused by a mite, *Sarcoptes scabiei*, that is marked by severe itching.
scab•rous (skăb'rəs, skā'brəs) *adj.* **1.** Rough to the touch : scaly or scabby. **2.** Difficult to handle : thorny. **3.** Salacious.
scads (skădz) *pl.n. Informal.* A large amount <*scads* of money>
scaf•fold (skăf'əld, -ōld') *n.* **1.** A raised platform used by workers while constructing, painting, or repairing a structure. **2.** A platform on which condemned prisoners are executed.
scal•a•wag (skăl'ə-wăg') *n. Informal.* A reprobate : rascal.
scald (skôld) *v.* **1.** To injure or burn with or as if with hot liquid or steam. **2.** To heat (a liquid) to a temperature just below the boiling point. –*n.* A bodily injury caused by scalding.
scale[1] (skāl) *n.* **1. a.** A small platelike structure that forms the protective outer covering esp. of fishes and reptiles. **b.** A similar part, as one of the overlapping structures that form the covering on the wings of butterflies and moths. **2.** A thin flake or crust, as of paint, rust, or dandruff. **3.** A plant disease or infestation caused by scale insects. –*v.* **scaled, scal•ing. 1.** To remove the scales of. **2.** To fall or come off in scales : flake. **–scal'y** *adj.*
scale[2] (skāl) *n.* **1. a.** A series of marks at fixed distances, used for measuring. **b.** An instrument having a scale. **2.** The size of a representation in proportion to the size of what it represents. **3. a.** A graduated series <a wage *scale*> **b.** Relative extent <living on a grand *scale*> **4.** A standard by which something can be estimated. **5.** An ascending or descending series of musical tones proceeding in accordance with a specified scheme of intervals. –*v.* **scaled, scal•ing. 1.** To climb up or over : ascend. **2.** To arrange in a particular proportion or scale. **3.** To adjust or regulate according to a standard.
scale[3] (skāl) *n.* **1.** A weighing instrument or machine. **2.** Either of the pans, trays, or dishes of a balance.
scale insect *n.* Any of various small, destructive sucking insects of the family Coccidae, the females of which secrete and are covered by waxy scales on plant tissue.
sca•lene (skā'lēn', skā-lēn') *adj.* Having 3 unequal sides <a *scalene* triangle>
scal•lion (skăl'yən) *n.* A young onion before the enlargement of the bulb.
scal•lop (skŏl'əp, skăl'-) *n.* **1. a.** A marine mollusk of the family Pectinidae, with a fan-shaped, fluted bivalve shell. **b.** The fleshy, edible muscle of a scallop. **2.** One of a series of curves shaped like semicircles that form a border. –*v.* **1.** To border (e.g., cloth) with scallops. **2.** To bake in a sauce, often with bread crumbs.
scalp (skălp) *n.* The skin that covers the top of the human head. –*v.* **1.** To tear or cut the scalp from. **2.** *Informal.* To buy and resell (e.g., tickets) at greatly inflated prices. **–scalp'er** *n.*
scal•pel (skăl'pəl) *n.* A small straight knife with a thin, sharp blade used in surgery and dissection.
scam (skăm) *n. Slang.* A fraudulent scheme : swindle.
scamp (skămp) *n.* **1.** A scheming person : rogue. **2.** A playful, mischievous person.
scam•per (skăm'pər) *v.* To run hurriedly or playfully. **–scam'per** *n.*
scan (skăn) *v.* **scanned, scan•ning. 1.** To examine (something) closely. **2.** To look over rapidly but thoroughly. **3.** To analyze (verse) so as to show rhythmical patterns. **4.** *Electron.* **a.** To move a radar beam over in search of a target. **b.** To search (e.g., a magnetic tape) automatically for specific data. **–scan** *n.* **–scan'ner** *n.*
scan•dal (skăn'dl) *n.* **1.** Something that offends public morality : disgrace. **2.** Malicious talk : gossip. **–scan'dal•ous** *adj.* **–scan'dal•ous•ly** *adv.*
scan•dal•ize (skăn'dl-īz') *v.* **-ized, -iz•ing.** To shock the propriety or moral sense of. **–scan'dal•i•za'tion** *n.*
scandal sheet *n.* A newspaper whose stories are predominantly scandalous.
Scan•di•na•vi•a (skăn'də-nā'vē-ə, -nāv'yə). **1.** Peninsula of N Europe occupied by Norway and Sweden. **2.** Norway, Sweden, and Denmark, and sometimes also Iceland, Finland, and the Faeroe Is. **–Scan'di•na'vi•an** *adj.* & *n.*
scan•di•um (skăn'dē-əm) *n. Symbol* **Sc** A silvery, lightweight metallic element.
scant (skănt) *adj.* **1.** Barely enough in amount or quantity : inadequate. **2.** Being slightly less than a specific measure. –*v.* To provide an inadequate amount of : skimp. **–scant'ly** *adv.* **–scant'ness** *n.*
scant•ling (skănt'lĭng, -lĭn) *n.* A small beam or section of timber, as an upright in a structural frame.
scant•y (skăn'tē) *adj.* **-i•er, -i•est.** Barely adequate or sufficient : meager. **–scant'i•ly** *adv.* **–scant'i•ness** *n.*
scape•goat (skāp'gōt') *n.* One that is made an object of blame for others. ☆**syns:** FALL GUY, GOAT, PATSY, WHIPPING BOY
scape•grace (skāp'grās') *n.* An unscrupulous or incorrigible person : reprobate.
scap•u•la (skăp'yə-lə) *n., pl.* **-lae** (-lē') *or* **-las.** Either of a pair of large, flat, triangular bones that form the back part of the shoulder. **–scap'u•lar** *adj.*
scar (skär) *n.* **1.** A mark that remains after an injury has healed. **2.** A mark or sign of damage. –*v.* **scarred, scar•ring.** To mark with or form a scar.
scar•ab (skăr'əb) *n.* **1.** A large, broad-bodied beetle. **2.** An ornamental representation of a scarab.
scarce (skârs) *adj.* **scarc•er, scarc•est. 1.** Not common : rare. **2.** Insufficient to meet a demand or requirement. **–scar'ci•ty** *n.*
scarce•ly (skârs'lē) *adv.* **1.** By a narrow margin : barely. **2.** Hardly <*scarcely* ever watched television> **3.** Certainly not <could *scarcely* object>
scare (skâr) *v.* **scared, scar•ing.** To startle : frighten. –*n.* A state of alarm or panic. **–scare up.** To find or gather with considerable effort. **–scar'y** *adj.*
scare•crow (skâr'krō') *n.* A roughly fashioned figure of a person used to scare birds away from growing crops.
scarf (skärf) *n., pl.* **scarfs** *or* **scarves** (skärvz). **1.** A piece of cloth worn over the head or around the neck or shoulders. **2.** A long strip of cloth, as for a dresser.
scar•i•fy (skăr'ə-fī') *v.* **-fied, -fy•ing. 1.** To make superficial cuts in : scratch. **2.** To criticize severely : flay.

scar·la·ti·na (skär'lə-tē'nə) *n.* Scarlet fever, esp. in a mild form.
scar·let (skär'lĭt) *n.* A strong or vivid red.
scarlet fever *n.* A severe contagious disease marked by a scarlet-colored rash and high fever.
scat (skăt) *v.* **scat·ted, scat·ting.** *Informal.* To leave hastily.
scath·ing (skā'thĭng) *adj.* Extremely harsh or bitterly severe.
sca·tol·o·gy (skə-tŏl'ə-jē, skă-) *n.* Interest in or preoccupation with obscenity. **—scat'o·log'i·cal** (skăt'l-ŏj'ĭ-kəl) *adj.*
scat·ter (skăt'ər) *v.* **1.** To break or cause to break up and go in many directions : disperse. **2.** To distribute irregularly : strew. ☆***syns:*** DISPEL, DISPERSE, DISSIPATE
scat·ter·brain (skăt'ər-brān') *n.* A disorganized, giddy person. **—scat'ter·brained'** *adj.*
scat·ter-gun (skăt'ər-gŭn') *n.* A shotgun.
scatter rug *n.* A small rug that covers only part of a floor.
scav·enge (skăv'ənj) *v.* **-enged, -eng·ing.** To act as a scavenger.
scav·en·ger (skăv'ən-jər) *n.* **1.** An animal, as a vulture, that feeds on dead or decaying material. **2.** One who searches for something useful in discarded material.
sce·nar·i·o (sĭ-nâr'ē-ō', -när'-) *n., pl.* **-os. 1.** A synopsis of a dramatic or literary plot. **2.** A screenplay.
scene (sēn) *n.* **1.** A view. **2.** The place where an action or event occurs : locale. **3. a.** One of the divisions of an act in a play. **b.** A short section of a motion picture. **4.** The scenery and properties for a dramatic presentation. **5.** A public display of passion or temper. **6.** *Slang.* **a.** A sphere of activity <the bar *scene*> **b.** A situation <a bad *scene*> **—sce'nic** *adj.*
scen·er·y (sē'nə-rē) *n.* **1.** A landscape. **2.** The structures or curtains on the stage of a theater that represent the play's setting.
scent (sĕnt) *n.* **1.** A smell : odor. **2.** A perfume. **3.** An odor left by the passing of an animal. **4.** The course or trail of an animal or fugitive that is being hunted or tracked. *—v.* **1.** To perceive by or as if by smelling. **2.** To fill with odor : perfume.
scep·ter (sĕp'tər) *n.* A rod or staff held by a sovereign as a sign of authority.
scep·tic (skĕp'tĭk) *n. var. of* SKEPTIC.
scep·ti·cism (skĕp'tĭ-sĭz'əm) *n. var. of* SKEPTICISM.
scep·tre (sĕp'tər) *n.* & *v. esp. Brit. var. of* SCEPTER.
sch. *abbr.* school.
sched·ule (skĕj'o͞ol) *n.* **1.** A written or printed list of items. **2.** A program of future events or appointments. **3.** A table of departure and arrival times. **4.** A plan allocating work and specifying deadlines for a project. *—v.* **-uled, -ul·ing. 1.** To place on a schedule. **2.** To set up a schedule for.
schee·lite (shā'līt') *n.* A natural form of calcium tungstate that occurs in igneous rocks and is used as a source of tungsten.
sche·ma (skē'mə) *n., pl.* **-ma·ta** (-mə-tə) *or* **-mas.** A diagrammatic presentation, as an outline.
sche·mat·ic (skē-măt'ĭk) *adj.* Of, relating to or in the form of a diagram or scheme. **—sche·mat'i·cal·ly** *adv.*
scheme (skēm) *n.* **1.** A plan for doing something. **2.** An orderly combination of related or successive parts : system. **3.** An underhand or secret plot : intrigue. *—v.* **schemed, schem·ing.** To plot underhandedly. **—schem'er** *n.*
scher·zo (skĕr'tsō) *n., pl.* **-zos** *or* **-zi** (-tsē). A lively musical movement.
Schick test (shĭk) *n.* A skin test for susceptibility to diphtheria.
schil·ling (shĭl'ĭng) *n.* See CURRENCY TABLE.
schism (sĭz'əm, skĭz'-) *n.* **1.** A separation from or division within a religious body. **2.** Disunity. **—schis·mat'ic** (-măt'ĭk) *adj.*
schist (shĭst) *n.* A metamorphic rock made up of laminated layers of chiefly micaceous minerals. **—schis'tose'** (shĭs'tōs'), **schis'tous** (-təs) *adj.*
schis·to·so·mi·a·sis (shĭs'tō-sə-mī'ə-sĭs) *n.* A severe, gen. tropical disease caused by infestation with parasitic worms.
schiz·o·phre·ni·a (skĭt'sə-frē'nē-ə) *n.* A mental disorder marked by loss of awareness of reality, often with disturbances of behavior and the inability to reason. **—schiz'oid'** (skĭt'soid') *adj.* & *n.* **—schiz'o·phren'ic** (-frĕn'ĭk) *adj.* & *n.*
schle·miel (shlə-mēl') *n. Slang.* A bungler : dolt.
schlock (shlŏk) *n. Slang.* Cheap or inferior merchandise.
schmaltz *also* **schmalz** (shmälts) *n.* Excessively sentimental art or music. **—schmaltz'y** *adj.*
schnapps (shnäps, shnăps) *n.* A strong alcoholic liquor.
schnau·zer (shnou'zər, shnout'sər) *n.* A dog, orig. bred in Germany, having a wiry gray coat and a blunt muzzle.
schnoz·zle (shnŏz'əl) *also* **schnozz** (shnŏz) *n. Slang.* The human nose.
schol·ar (skŏl'ər) *n.* **1. a.** An erudite person. **b.** A person with much knowledge in a particular field. **2.** One who attends school : pupil. **—schol'ar·ly** *adv.*
schol·ar·ship (skŏl'ər-shĭp') *n.* **1.** The methods and achievements of a scholar. **2.** Financial aid awarded to a student.
scho·las·tic (skə-lăs'tĭk) *adj.* Of or relating to schools. **—scho·las'ti·cal·ly** *adv.*
school[1] (sko͞ol) *n.* **1. a.** An institution for teaching and learning. **b.** The group of students attending a school. **2.** Attendance at or the process of being educated at a school. **3.** A group of persons of similar principles, beliefs, or opinions. *—v.* **1.** To instruct : educate. **2.** To discipline : train.
school[2] (sko͞ol) *n.* A large group of aquatic animals, esp. fish, swimming together : shoal.
school·book (sko͞ol'bo͝ok') *n.* A textbook.
school·boy (sko͞ol'boi') *n.* A boy who attends school. **—school'girl'** *n.*
school·house (sko͞ol'hous') *n.* A building used as a school.
school·marm (sko͞ol'märm') *also* **school·ma'am** (-măm') *n. Informal.* A woman who is a teacher, esp. a pedantic or old-fashioned one.
school·mas·ter (sko͞ol'măs'tər) *n.* A man who is a teacher or headmaster.
school·mate (sko͞ol'māt') *n.* A school companion.
school·mis·tress (sko͞ol'mĭs'trĭs) *n.* A woman who is a teacher or headmistress.
school·room (sko͞ol'ro͞om', -ro͝om') *n.* A classroom in a school.
school·teach·er (sko͞ol'tē'chər) *n.* A person who teaches in a school.
school·work (sko͞ol'wûrk') *n.* Lessons done at school or assigned as homework.
schoo·ner (sko͞o'nər) *n.* A fore-and-aft-rigged sailing vessel.
Schu·bert (sho͞o'bərt), **Franz.** 1797–1828. Austrian composer.
Schu·mann (sho͞o'män'), **Robert.** 1810–56. German composer.
schuss (sho͝os) *v.* To make a fast straight run in skiing. *—n.* **1.** A straight downhill course for skiing. **2.** The act of schussing.
schwa (shwä) *n.* **1.** An unstressed vowel, as the *a* in *sofa* or *e* in *linen.* **2.** The symbol (ə) used to represent a schwa.
Schwei·tzer (shwīt'sər, shvīt'-), **Albert.** 1875–1965. French philosopher, missionary physician, and musicologist.
sci. *abbr.* science; scientific.
sci·at·i·ca (sī-ăt'ĭ-kə) *n.* **1.** Neuralgia of the nerve running down the back of the thigh. **2.** Chronic pain in the hip or thigh.
sci·ence (sī'əns) *n.* **1.** The study and theoretical explanation of natural phenomena. **2.** A systematic activity requiring study and method. **3.** Knowledge, esp. that acquired through experience. **—sci'en·tif'ic** (sī'ən-tĭf'ĭc) *adj.* **—sci'en·tif'i·cal·ly** *adv.* **—sci'en·tist** (sī'ən-tĭst) *n.*
science fiction *n.* Fiction in which imaginative scientific possibilities are used in the plot.
sci-fi (sī'fī') *n. Informal.* Science fiction.
scim·i·tar (sĭm'ĭ-tər, -tär') *n.* A short, curved, single-edged sword.
scin·til·la (sĭn-tĭl'ə) *n.* A tiny amount.
scin·til·late (sĭn'tə-lāt') *v.* **-lat·ed, -lat·ing. 1.** To throw off sparks : flash. **2.** To be animated or brilliant. **—scin'til·la'tion** *n.*
sci·on (sī'ən) *n.* **1.** A descendant. **2.** A twig or shoot removed from 1 plant for grafting onto another.
scis·sors (sĭz'ərz) *pl.n. (sing. or pl. in number).* A cutting tool consisting of 2 blades joined and pivoted so that the cutting edges close against each other.
scissors kick *n.* A swimming kick in which the legs are opened and closed like scissors.
scle·ro·sis (sklə-rō'sĭs) *n., pl.* **-ses** (-sēz'). A thickening or hardening of a bodily part, as an artery. **—scle·rot'ic** (-rŏt'ĭk) *adj.*
scoff (skôf, skŏf) *v.* To show derision or mockery. **—scoff'er** *n.*
scoff·law (skŏf'lô', skôf'-) *n.* One who habitually violates the law.
scold (skōld) *v.* To reprove severely : berate. *—n.* One who scolds.
sconce (skŏns) *n.* A decorative wall bracket for candles or electric lights.
scone (skōn, skŏn) *n.* A small biscuitlike pastry or quick bread baked on a griddle.
scoop (sko͞op) *n.* **1.** A shovellike utensil, usu. having a deep, curved bowl and a short handle. **2.** A ladle : dipper. **3.** The bucket of a power shovel or dredge. **4.** A scooping action or movement. **5.** *Slang.* An exclusive news story. *—v.* **1.** To lift out or up with or as if with a scoop. **2.** To hollow out by digging. **3.** *Slang.* To get the better of (a competitor) by getting a news scoop.
scoot (sko͞ot) *v.* To go quickly and suddenly. **—scoot** *n.*
scoot·er (sko͞o'tər) *n.* **1.** A child's vehicle consisting of a long footboard between 2 small end wheels, the forward wheel controlled by an upright steering bar. **2.** A motor scooter.

scope (skōp) *n.* **1.** The range of one's actions or thoughts. **2.** Space or opportunity to operate or function. **3.** The extent of an activity, situation, or subject.

-scope *suff.* An instrument for observing <micro*scope*>

scorch (skôrch) *v.* **1.** To burn slightly so as to change in color or flavor. **2.** To shrivel or parch with heat. **–scorch** *n.*

scorch•er (skôr'chər) *n.* **1.** One that scorches. **2.** *Informal.* A very hot day.

score (skôr, skōr) *n.* **1.** A notch or mark. **2.** A usu. numerical record of points made by competitors, as in a game. **3.** A result of a test or examination. **4. a.** An amount due : debt. **b.** A grievance that requires satisfaction : grudge. **5.** A group of 20 items. **6.** The written form of a musical arrangement or composition with all the orchestral or vocal parts indicated. **7.** *Informal.* **a.** The act or fact of gaining an advantage. **b.** The act of buying illicit drugs. **8.** A motive or reason. *–v.* **scored, scor•ing. 1. a.** To gain (a point or points) in or as if in a competitive event. **b.** To count or be worth as points. **2.** To achieve, win, or gain. **3.** To record the points in a competitive event. **4.** To mark with lines, notches, or cuts. **5.** To correct and assign a grade to. **6.** To arrange or compose a score for. **7.** To gain an advantage : succeed. **–score'less** *adj.* **–scor'er** *n.*

score•board (skôr'bôrd', skōr'bōrd') *n.* A large board for displaying the score of a game.

sco•ri•a (skôr'ē-ə, skōr'-) *n., pl.* **-ri•ae** (-ē-ē') *Geol.* Rough particles of burnt, crustlike lava.

scorn (skôrn) *n.* **1.** Open contempt : disdain. **2.** An expression of scorn : derision. *–v.* To consider or treat with scorn : disdain. **–scorn'ful** *adj.*

Scor•pi•o (skôr'pē-ō') *n.* **1.** A constellation in the S Hemisphere. **2. a.** The 8th sign of the zodiac. **b.** One born under this sign.

scor•pi•on (skôr'pē-ən) *n.* An arachnid of the order Scorpionida, having an erectile tail tipped with a poisonous sting.

Scor•pi•us (skôr'pē-əs) *n.* SCORPIO 1.

Scot (skŏt) *n.* A native or inhabitant of Scotland.

scotch (skŏch) *v.* To put an end to : crush <*scotched* the rumor>

Scotch (skŏch) *n.* **1.** *(pl. in number).* The people of Scotland. **2.** Scots. **3.** A whiskey distilled in Scotland from malted barley. **–Scotch** *adj.* **–Scotch'man** *n.*

scot-free (skŏt'frē') *adj.* Free from harm, punishment, obligation, or penalty.

Scot•land (skŏt'lənd). Constituent country of the United Kingdom, in N Great Britain. *Cap.* Edinburgh. *Pop.* 5,167,000.

Scots (skŏts) *adj.* Scottish. *–n.* The English dialect of Scotland.

Scots•man (skŏts'mən) *n.* A Scot.

Scott (skŏt), Sir **Walter.** 1771–1832. Scottish author.

Scot•tish (skŏt'ĭsh) *adj.* Of, relating to, or characteristic of Scotland, its people, or its language. *–n.* **1.** Scots. **2.** *(pl. in number).* The people of Scotland.

scoun•drel (skoun'drəl) *n.* A wicked, dishonorable person : villain.

scour[1] (skour) *v.* **1.** To clean or polish by harsh rubbing, as with an abrasive agent. **2.** To remove by scrubbing.

scour[2] (skour) *v.* **1.** To range over or about (an area), esp. in a search. **2.** To move quickly : rush.

scourge (skûrj) *n.* **1.** A whip. **2.** A means of inflicting punishment or pain. **3.** A cause of affliction, as pestilence or war. *–v.* **scourged, scourg•ing. 1.** To flog. **2.** To chastise or punish severely.

scout[1] (skout) *v.* **1.** To observe or explore in order to obtain information. **2.** To search <*scout* around for bargains> *–n.* **1.** A person, aircraft, or ship sent out to obtain information. **2. a.** A member of the Boy Scouts. **b.** A member of the Girl Scouts. **3.** A person <a good *scout*>

scout[2] (skout) *v.* To reject contemptuously : scorn.

scout•mas•ter (skout'măs'tər) *n.* The adult leader in charge of a Boy Scout troop.

scow (skou) *n.* A large open barge used to transport freight, as gravel or garbage.

scowl (skoul) *v.* To lower or contract the brow, as in anger or displeasure. **–scowl** *n.* **–scowl'ing•ly** *adv.*

scrab•ble (skrăb'əl) *v.* **-bled, -bling. 1.** To scratch or grope about frantically. **2.** To struggle <*scrabbled* for a living> **3.** To ascend hastily : scramble. **4.** To scribble. **–scrab'ble** *n.* **–scrab'bler** *n.*

scrag•gly (skrăg'lē) *adj.* **-gli•er, -gli•est. 1.** Messy : unkempt. **2.** Irregular : uneven.

scram (skrăm) *v.* **scrammed, scram•ming.** *Slang.* To leave immediately.

scram•ble (skrăm'bəl) *v.* **-bled, -bling. 1.** To move rapidly, esp. on the hands and knees. **2.** To struggle or contend eagerly or urgently. **3.** To mix confusedly : jumble. **4.** To cook (eggs) by mixing and stirring while frying. **5.** *Electron.* To process (a signal) so that it cannot be used or understood without a special receiver. **–scram'ble** *n.* **–scram'bler** *n.*

scrap[1] (skrăp) *n.* **1.** A section or piece : fragment. **2.** Discarded waste material, esp. metal suitable for reprocessing. *–v.* **scrapped, scrap•ping. 1.** To separate into parts for salvage or disposal. **2.** To discard as worthless : junk.

scrap[2] (skrăp) *Slang.* *–v.* **scrapped, scrap•ping.** To fight, often with the fists. *–n.* A fight or scuffle : brawl. **–scrap'per** *n.* **–scrap'pi•ly** *adv.* **–scrap'pi•ness** *n.* **–scrap'py** *adj.*

scrap•book (skrăp'bo͝ok') *n.* A book with blank pages for mounting mementos.

scrape (skrāp) *v.* **scraped, scrap•ing. 1.** To rub (a surface) forcefully, as to clean, smooth, or shape. **2.** To remove by rubbing with a hard edge <*scrape* ice from a window> **3.** To bring or come into sliding, abrasive contact, often with a harsh grating sound. **4.** To injure the surface of by rubbing with something rough or sharp. **5.** To gather or produce with difficulty <*scrape* up new evidence> **6.** To practice small economies : skrimp. *–n.* **1.** The act or an instance of scraping. **2.** Something produced by scraping. **3.** *Slang.* **a.** An embarrassing or difficult situation. **b.** A fight : scuffle. **–scrap'er** *n.*

scratch (skrăch) *v.* **1.** To mark, injure, or scrape with or as if with the nails or claws. **2.** To rub to alleviate itching. **3.** To remove or cancel (e.g., a word) by or as if by drawing a line through. **4.** To make a rough, scraping sound. *–n.* **1.** A line or mark made by scratching. **2.** A harsh, scraping sound. *–adj.* **1.** Used for hasty notes or sketches <*scratch* paper> **2.** Done by chance. **–scratch'y** *adj.*

scratch•pad (skrăch'păd') *n.* A usu. high-speed internal register used for temporary storage in a computer memory.

scrawl (skrôl) *v.* To write quickly and often illegibly. **–scrawl** *n.* **–scrawl'y** *adj.*

scraw•ny (skrô'nē) *adj.* **-ni•er, -ni•est.** Thin and bony. **–scraw'ni•ness** *n.*

scream (skrēm) *v.* To utter a loud, piercing cry, as of pain. *–n.* **1.** A loud, piercing cry. **2.** *Slang.* One that is extremely funny.

scree (skrē) *n.* A mass of small stones or rock debris at the base of an incline or cliff.

screech (skrēch) *v.* **1.** To scream. **2.** To make a shrill, grating sound. **–screech** *n.*

screen (skrēn) *n.* **1.** An often movable frame used to protect, divide, conceal, or decorate <a mesh door *screen*> **2.** Something that serves to conceal <a smoke *screen*> **3.** A sieve used to separate fine particles from larger ones. **4. a.** A surface on which a picture is projected for viewing. **b.** The motion-picture industry. *–v.* **1.** To provide with a screen. **2.** To conceal, protect, guard, shield, or separate with or as if with a screen. **3.** To show or project (e.g., a motion picture) on a screen.

screen•ing (skrē'nĭng) *n.* **1.** Wire or plastic mesh used to make screens. **2.** A presentation, as of a motion picture.

screen•play (skrēn'plā') *n.* A motion-picture script.

screen test *n.* A short film sequence used to judge the talent or suitability of a person for a role in a motion picture. **–screen'-test'** *v.*

screw (skro͞o) *n.* **1.** A metal piece resembling a nail with a helical or spiral groove and slotted head that can be turned by a screwdriver to fasten things together. **2.** A propeller, esp. for a ship or motorboat. *–v.* **1. a.** To fasten, attach, or tighten by or as if by means of a screw. **b.** To attach (e.g., a threaded cap) by twisting into place. **2.** To turn or twist out of shape : contort. **3.** To cheat. **–screw up.** *Slang.* To make a mess of (an undertaking).

screw•ball (skro͞o'bôl') *n.* **1.** *Baseball.* A pitch that curves in the direction opposite that of a curve ball. **2.** *Slang.* An eccentric, whimsical, or irrational person.

screw•driv•er (skro͞o'drī'vər) *n.* **1.** A tool for turning screws. **2.** A mixed drink of vodka and orange juice.

screw•y (skro͞o'ē) *adj.* **-i•er, -i•est.** *Slang.* **1.** Insane : crazy. **2.** Absurdly odd, unusual, or inappropriate.

scrib•ble (skrĭb'əl) *v.* **-bled, -bling.** To write or draw in a hurried, careless manner. **–scrib'ble** *n.* **–scrib'bler** *n.*

scribe (skrīb) *n.* **1. a.** A professional copyist of manuscripts and documents. **b.** A public secretary or clerk. **2.** A writer, esp. a journalist.

scrim (skrĭm) *n.* A durable, loosely woven cotton or linen fabric.

scrim•mage (skrĭm'ĭj) *n.* *Football.* **1.** The play of the ball that follows the snap. **2.** A team's practice session. **–scrim'mage** *v.*

scrimp (skrĭmp) *v.* To economize severely. **–scrimp'y** *adj.*

scrim•shaw (skrĭm'shô') *n.* **1.** The art of carving or incising elaborate designs on whalebone or whale ivory. **2.** A decorative article made by scrimshaw.

scrip[1] (skrĭp) *n.* Paper money issued for temporary use.

scrip[2] (skrĭp) *n.* A certificate entitling the holder to a fractional share, as of stock.

script (skrĭpt) *n.* **1.** Handwriting, esp. a style with cursive characters. **2.** The text of a broadcast, play, or motion picture.
Scrip•ture (skrĭp′chər) *n.* **1. a.** A sacred writing or book. **b.** A passage from such a writing or book. **2.** *often* **Scriptures.** The Bible. **—Scrip′tur•al** *adj.*
scriv•en•er (skrĭv′ə-nər) *n.* A scribe.
scrod (skrŏd) *n.* A young haddock or cod.
scroll (skrōl) *n.* **1.** A roll, as of parchment, used esp. for writing. **2.** An ornament or ornamental design resembling a scroll.
scroll saw *n.* A thin-bladed saw used to cut curved or irregular shapes.
scro•tum (skrō′təm) *n., pl.* **-ta** (-tə) *or* **-tums.** The external sac of skin that encloses the testes in most mammals. **—scro′tal** (skrōt′l) *adj.*
scrounge (skrounj) *v.* **scrounged, scroung•ing.** *Slang.* **1.** To forage or obtain by foraging. **2.** To cadge : mooch. **—scroung′er** *n.*
scrub¹ (skrŭb) *v.* **scrubbed, scrub•bing. 1.** To clean by rubbing, as with a brush. **2.** *Slang.* To cancel : drop <*scrubbed* the project> **—scrub** *n.*
scrub² (skrŭb) *n.* **1. a.** A stunted tree or shrub. **b.** A growth or tract of stunted vegetation. **2.** An undersized or underdeveloped domestic animal. **3.** One who is undersized or insignificant. **4.** A player not on a varsity or first team. **—scrub′by** *adj.*
scrub•wom•an (skrŭb′wo͝om′ən) *n.* A woman hired to clean : charwoman.
scruff (skrŭf) *n.* The back of the neck.
scruf•fy (skrŭf′ē) *adj.* **-fi•er, -fi•est.** Shabby : unkempt.
scrump•tious (skrŭmp′shəs) *adj. Slang.* Delightful : first-rate.
scru•ple (skro͞o′pəl) *n.* **1.** A dictate of conscience or ethical principle that tends to inhibit action. **2.** A tiny part or amount. **3.** See MEASUREMENT TABLE.
scru•pu•lous (skro͞o′pyə-ləs) *adj.* **1.** Having scruples : ethical. **2.** Painstaking : careful. **—scru′pu•lous•ly** *adv.*
scru•ti•nize (skro͞ot′n-īz′) *v.* **-nized, -niz•ing.** To inspect or observe carefully or critically. **—scru′ti•niz′er** *n.*
scru•ti•ny (skro͞ot′n-ē) *n., pl.* **-nies. 1.** Close, careful inspection or study. **2.** Close observation : surveillance.
scu•ba (sko͞o′bə) *n.* An apparatus used by divers for breathing underwater.
scuba diver *n.* One who uses scuba gear in underwater swimming.
scud (skŭd) *v.* **scud•ded, scud•ding.** To move along quickly and easily. *—n.* Wind-driven clouds, snow, mist, or rain.
scuff (skŭf) *v.* **1.** To drag the feet while walking. **2.** To scrape or become scraped and roughened on the surface. *—n.* **1.** A mark or worn spot resulting from scuffing. **2.** A flat-soled, backless house slipper.
scuf•fle (skŭf′əl) *v.* **-fled, -fling. 1.** To fight or struggle in a confused manner at close quarters. **2. a.** To shuffle. **b.** To walk with shuffling steps. **—scuf′fle** *n.*
scull (skŭl) *n.* **1.** A long oar mounted on the stern of a boat and twisted from side to side. **2.** One of a pair of short oars used by a single oarsman. **3.** A light racing boat for 1, 2, or 4 oarsmen. *—v.* To propel (a boat) by using sculls.

scull

scul•ler•y (skŭl′ə-rē) *n., pl.* **-ies.** A room next to the kitchen where kitchen chores, as dishwashing, are done.
scul•lion (skŭl′yən) *n. Archaic.* A servant employed to do menial kitchen tasks.
sculpt (skŭlpt) *v.* To sculpture.
sculp•tor (skŭlp′tər) *n.* A person who produces sculptures.
sculp•tress (skŭlp′trĭs) *n.* A woman who produces sculptures.
sculp•ture (skŭlp′chər) *n.* **1.** The art of making 3-dimensional figures or designs, as by chiseling marble or casting metal. **2. a.** A work of art created by sculpture. **b.** Such works as a group. *—v.* **-tured, -tur•ing.** To fashion into, depict in, or decorate with sculpture. **—sculp′tur•al** *adj.*
scum (skŭm) *n.* **1.** A thin, filmy layer of material on the surface of a liquid. **2.** Worthless matter : refuse. **3.** Vile or despicable people : rabble.
scup•per (skŭp′ər) *n.* An opening in the side of a ship that allows water to run off.
scurf (skûrf) *n.* **1.** Scaly or flaky dry skin, as dandruff. **2.** A scaly crust covering a surface, esp. of a plant. **—scurf′y** *adj.*
scur•ri•lous (skûr′ə-ləs) *adj.* **1.** Tending to use vulgar or abusive language : foul-mouthed. **2.** Expressed in or containing vulgar or abusive language.
scur•ry (skûr′ē) *v.* **-ried, -ry•ing.** To scamper.
scur•vy (skûr′vē) *n.* A disease resulting from a deficiency of vitamin C and marked by spongy and bleeding gums, bleeding under the skin, and extreme weakness. *—adj.* **-vi•er, -vi•est.** Worthless : contemptible.
scutch•eon (skŭch′ən) *n. var. of* ESCUTCHEON.
scut•tle¹ (skŭt′l) *n.* A small opening or hatch with a movable lid, esp. in the deck or hull of a ship. *—v.* **-tled, -tling. 1.** To cut a hole in (a ship's hull) in order to sink. **2.** *Informal.* To throw away : discard.
scut•tle² (skŭt′l) *n.* A metal pail used to carry coal.
scut•tle³ (skŭt′l) *v.* **-tled, -tling.** To move with quick little steps : scurry.
scut•tle•butt (skŭt′l-bŭt′) *n. Slang.* Rumor or gossip.
scythe (sīth) *n.* A tool used for mowing or reaping, having a long, curved single-edged blade with a long, bent handle. **—scythe** *v.*
SD *abbr.* South Dakota (with Zip Code).
S.D. *abbr.* special delivery.
S.Dak. *abbr.* South Dakota.
Se *symbol for* SELENIUM.
SE *abbr.* southeast; southeastern.
sea (sē) *n.* **1. a.** The body of salt water that covers most of the earth's surface. **b.** A relatively large body of salt water. **c.** A relatively large body of fresh water. **2.** The ocean's surface <a calm *sea*> **3.** Something that suggests the sea, as in vastness <a *sea* of humanity> **—at sea.** Confused : perplexed.
sea anemone *n.* A marine coelenterate of the class Anthozoa or Actinozoa, with a flexible, cylindrical body and petallike tentacles surrounding a central mouth.
sea•bed (sē′bĕd′) *n.* The bottom of a sea or ocean.
sea bird *n.* A bird, as an albatross, that frequents the open waters of the ocean.
sea•board (sē′bôrd′, -bōrd′) *n.* **1.** A seacoast. **2.** The land area near the sea.
sea•coast (sē′kōst′) *n.* Land bordering the sea.
sea•far•er (sē′fâr′ər) *n.* A sailor.
sea•far•ing (sē′fâr′ĭng) *n.* A sailor's calling. **—sea′far′ing** *adj.*
sea•food (sē′fo͞od′) *n.* Fish or shellfish, as flounder or lobster, eaten as food.
sea•go•ing (sē′gō′ĭng) *adj.* **1.** Made for ocean voyages or for use on the open sea. **2.** Seafaring.
sea gull *n.* A gull.
sea horse *n.* A small marine fish of the genus *Hippocampus*, swimming erect and having a horselike head.
seal¹ (sēl) *n.* **1. a.** A device with an engraved design used to stamp an impression on soft material, as wax. **b.** The impression made by such a device. **2.** Something, as a commercial hallmark, that serves to authenticate or verify. **3. a.** A fitting or closure that prevents a liquid or gas from entering or escaping. **b.** A material, as rubber, used to make such a fitting or closure. **4.** A small paper sticker used to decorate or fasten an envelope. *—v.* **1.** To affix a seal to, esp. as a mark of authenticity. **2.** To fasten with or as if with a seal. **3.** To fix irrevocably <Their fate was *sealed.*>
seal² (sēl) *n.* **1.** Any of various aquatic mammals of the families Phocidae and Otariidae, with a sleek, streamlined body and limbs modified into paddlelike flippers. **2.** The pelt or fur of a seal, esp. a fur seal. *—v.* To hunt seals. **—seal′er** *n.*
sea-lane (sē′lān′) *n.* An established or frequently used sea route.
seal•ant (sē′lənt) *n.* A sealing agent.
sea legs *pl.n. Informal.* The ability to walk without faltering on board ship.
sea level *n.* The level of the surface of the ocean, used as a standard in determining land elevation or sea depths.
sea lion *n.* An eared seal of the family Otariidae, esp. *Zalophus californianus*, of the N Pacific.
seal•skin (sēl′skĭn′) *n.* **1.** The pelt of a fur seal. **2.** A garment made of sealskin.
seam (sēm) *n.* **1.** The line formed by joining 2 pieces, esp. of material, at the edges, as by sewing. **2.** A crack or wrinkle. **3.** A thin stratum or layer, as of coal. *—v.* **1.** To join with or as if with a seam. **2.** To mark with a seamlike line, as a scar or wrinkle.

sea·man (sē′mən) *n.* **1.** A mariner or sailor. **2.** An enlisted person in the U.S. Navy or Coast Guard ranking above a seaman apprentice and below a petty officer.
seaman apprentice *n.* An enlisted person in the U.S. Navy or Coast Guard ranking above a seaman recruit and below a seaman.
seaman recruit *n.* An enlisted person of the lowest rank in the U.S. Navy or Coast Guard.
sea·man·ship (sē′mən-shĭp′) *n.* The skill or art of handling a ship.
sea·mount (sē′mount′) *n.* A submarine mountain.
seam·stress (sēm′strĭs) *n.* A woman who sews, esp. in order to make living.
seam·y (sē′mē) *adj.* **-i·er, -i·est.** Unpleasant : sordid <the *seamy* side of politics>
sé·ance (sā′äns′) *n.* **1.** A gathering of spiritualists to receive messages from spirits. **2.** A meeting or session.
sea·plane (sē′plān′) *n.* An aircraft capable of taking off from or landing on water.
sea·port (sē′pôrt′, -pōrt′) *n.* A port for seagoing ships.
sear (sîr) *v.* **1.** To make withered or dried up : shrivel. **2.** To scorch, char, or burn the surface of.
search (sûrch) *v.* **1.** To look over carefully in order to find something. **2.** To examine carefully : probe. **3.** To seek <*searching* for an answer> **—search** *n.* **—search′er** *n.*
search·light (sûrch′līt′) *n.* **1. a.** An apparatus for projecting a strong beam of light. **b.** The beam so projected. **2.** A flashlight.
search warrant *n.* A warrant legally authorizing a search.
sea·scape (sē′skāp′) *n.* A view or depiction of the sea.
sea·shell (sē′shĕl′) *n.* The calcareous shell of a marine mollusk.
sea·shore (sē′shôr′, -shōr′) *n.* Land bordering or near the sea.
sea·sick·ness (sē′sĭk′nĭs) *n.* Nausea caused by the pitching and rolling motions of a ship. **—sea′sick′** *adj.*
sea·side (sē′sīd′) *n.* The seashore.
sea·son (sē′zən) *n.* **1.** One of the 4 divisions of the year, spring, summer, autumn, and winter. **2.** A period marked by particular activities, celebrations, or crops <the Christmas *season*> *—v.* **1.** To heighten the flavor of (food) by adding condiments. **2.** To add enjoyment or interest to. **3.** To bring to a suitable condition, as by aging. **4.** To make capable or fit through trial and experience. **—sea′son·al** *adj.*
sea·son·a·ble (sē′zə-nə-bəl) *adj.* **1.** Appropriate to the time or season. **2.** Occurring or performed at the proper time. **—sea′son·a·bly** *adv.*
sea·son·ing (sē′zə-nĭng) *n.* Something, as a spice, used to season : condiment.
season ticket *n.* A ticket that can be used during a specified period of time.
seat (sēt) *n.* **1.** Something, as a bench or chair, to sit on. **2.** A place where one may sit <found her *seat*> **3. a.** The buttocks. **b.** The part of a garment that covers the buttocks. **4.** A capital or center of activity or authority. **5.** Membership in a legislature or stock exchange. *—v.* **1. a.** To place on or in a seat. **b.** To cause or help to sit. **2.** To have or provide seats for.
seat belt *n.* An adjustable strap or harness that holds one securely in a seat, as in an automobile.
seat·ing (sē′tĭng) *n.* **1.** The act of providing with seats. **2.** The arrangement of seats, as in an auditorium.
Se·at·tle (sē-ăt′l). City of W C Wash., on Puget Sound. *Pop.* 493,846.
sea urchin *n.* An echinoderm of the class Echinoidea, having a soft body enclosed in a thin, spiny shell.
sea wall *n.* A wall or embankment designed to prevent erosion of a shoreline.
sea·ward (sē′wərd) *adj.* & *adv.* At or toward the sea. **—sea′wards** *adv.*
sea·way (sē′wā′) *n.* An inland waterway used by oceangoing ships.
sea·weed (sē′wēd′) *n.* Any of numerous marine algae, as the kelp or rockweed.
sea·wor·thy (sē′wûr′*th*ē) *adj.* Fit for a voyage on the sea. Used of a ship.
se·ba·ceous (sĭ-bā′shəs) *adj.* Of, relating to, or secreting fat or sebum.
sec *abbr.* second (unit).
sec. *abbr.* **1.** second; secondary. **2.** secretary. **3.** section. **4.** sector.
se·cede (sĭ-sēd′) *v.* **-ced·ed, -ced·ing.** To withdraw from an association or organization, esp. a political one. **—se·ces′sion** (-sĕsh′ən) *n.* **—se·ces′sion·ist** *n.*
se·clude (sĭ-klōōd′) *v.* **-clud·ed, -clud·ing.** To remove, keep apart, or withdraw from others. **—se·clu′sion** (-klōō′zhən) *n.* **—se·clu′sive** (-sĭv) *adj.*
sec·ond[1] (sĕk′ənd) *n.* **1.** A unit of time equal to $1/60$ of a minute. **2.** *Informal.* A very brief time : instant. **3.** *Math.* A unit equal to $1/60$ of a minute of arc.
sec·ond[2] (sĕk′ənd) *adj.* **1.** Coming next after the 1st. **2.** Another <a *second* chance> **3.** Being inferior or subordinate <*second* to none> *—n.* **1.** The ordinal number matching the number 2 in a series. **2.** One that is second. **3.** An inferior or imperfect article, esp. of merchandise. **4.** The transmission gear in a motor vehicle that produces the next-to-slowest speed. *—v.* **1.** To give support to : assist. **2.** To endorse (e.g., a motion) as a means of bringing it to a vote. **—sec′ond, sec′ond·ly** *adv.*
sec·on·dar·y (sĕk′ən-dĕr′ē) *adj.* **1.** Of the 2nd rank : inferior. **2.** Not primary or original : derivative. **3.** Of or pertaining to a secondary school. **—sec′on·dar′i·ly** *adv.*
secondary school *n.* A school between elementary school and college.
sec·ond-class (sĕk′ənd-klăs′) *adj.* **1.** Of secondary quality or status : inferior. **2.** Of or relating to travel accommodations ranking next below the 1st or highest class. **3.** Of or relating to a class of mail consisting mainly of newspapers and periodicals. **—sec′ond-class′** *adv.*
second generation *n. Computer Sci.* The period of computer technology that utilized solid-state circuitry and offline storage and highly developed software.
sec·ond-guess (sĕk′ənd-gĕs′) *v.* **1.** To be critical of (e.g., a decision) after the event. **2.** To outguess.
sec·ond·hand (sĕk′ənd-hănd′) *adj.* **1.** Not new : worn or used. **2.** Dealing in previously used merchandise. **3.** Obtained, derived, or borrowed from another. **—sec′ond·hand′** *adv.*
second lieutenant *n.* An officer in the U.S. Army, Air Force, or Marine Corps having the lowest commissioned grade.
second nature *n.* Deeply ingrained habits and characteristics.
second person *n.* The form of a pronoun or verb used in referring to the person addressed, as *you* and *may* in *you may go.*
sec·ond-rate (sĕk′ənd-rāt′) *adj.* Inferior or mediocre in quality or value.
sec·ond·sto·ry man (sĕk′ənd-stôr′ē, -stōr′ē) *n.* A burglar who enters through an upstairs window.
sec·ond-string (sĕk′ənd-strĭng′) *adj.* Being a substitute, as on a football team.
second wind *n.* Renewed strength or energy, as during a competition.
se·cre·cy (sē′krĭ-sē) *n.* **1.** The state or quality of being secret. **2.** The practice of keeping secrets.
se·cret (sē′krĭt) *adj.* **1.** Kept from general knowledge or view. **2.** Operating in a hidden or clandestine manner <*secret* police> **3.** Not frequented : secluded. **4.** Beyond common understanding : mysterious. ☆*syns:* CLANDESTINE, COVERT, HUSH-HUSH, UNDERCOVER *—n.* **1.** Something concealed from others. **2.** Something not readily understood : mystery. **3.** A method or formula for accomplishing something. **—se′cret·ly** *adv.*
sec·re·tar·i·at (sĕk′rĭ-târ′ē-ĭt) *n.* **1.** The department managed by a governmental secretary. **2.** The office or position of a governmental secretary. **2.** The headquarters of secretariat.
sec·re·tar·y (sĕk′rĭ-tĕr′ē) *n., pl.* **-ies. 1.** A person hired to do clerical work, as handling correspondence, for a superior. **2.** An officer charged with keeping an organization's records, as minutes or correspondence. **3.** The head of a governmental department. **4.** A writing desk. **—sec′re·tar′i·al** (-târ′ē-əl) *adj.*
se·crete[1] (sĭ-krēt′) *v.* **-cret·ed, -cret·ing.** To produce and separate out (e.g., an oily substance) from cells or bodily fluids. **—se·cre′tion** *n.*
se·crete[2] (sĭ-krēt′) *v.* **-cret·ed, -cret·ing.** To hide away : conceal.
se·cre·tive (sē′krə-tĭv, sĭ-krē′-) *adj.* Practicing or inclined to secrecy. **—se′cre·tive·ness** *n.*
Secret Service *n.* A branch of the U.S. Treasury Department charged with the suppression of counterfeiting and the protection of the President.
sect (sĕkt) *n.* **1.** A group of people, often part of a larger group, who are united by common interests or beliefs. **2.** A religious body, esp. one that has separated from a larger denomination.
sec·tar·i·an (sĕk-târ′ē-ən) *adj.* **1.** Of or relating to a sect. **2.** Narrow-minded : parochial. *—n.* **1.** A member of a sect. **2.** A narrow-minded or bigoted person. **—sec·tar′i·an·ism** *n.*
sec·tion (sĕk′shən) *n.* **1.** A part or piece of something : portion. **2.** A separate part, as of a newspaper. **3.** A view of the internal structure of a solid object as it would appear if cut straight through. *—v.* To divide into sections.
sec·tion·al (sĕk′shə-nəl) *adj.* **1.** Of, relating to, or like a section. **2.** Divided into or made up of sections. **3.** Not general : regional or local. **—sec′tion·al·ism** *n.*
sec·tor (sĕk′tər) *n.* **1.** *Math.* The part of a circle bounded by 2

radii and 1 of the intercepted arcs. **2.** A division of a defensive or offensive area for which 1 military unit is responsible. **3.** A distinct part <the agricultural *sector* of the economy>
sec·u·lar (sĕk'yə-lər) *adj.* **1.** Temporal rather than spiritual : worldly. **2.** Not religious or sacred. **3.** Not bound by monastic restrictions <*secular* clergy>
sec·u·lar·ism (sĕk'yə-lə-rĭz'əm) *n.* The belief that religion and religious considerations should be rejected or ignored. **—sec'u·lar·ist** *n.*
sec·u·lar·ize (sĕk'yə-lə-rīz') *v.* **-ized, -iz·ing. 1.** To change from ecclesiastical to lay or civil use or control. **2.** To make secular. **—sec'u·lar·i·za'tion** *n.*
se·cure (sĭ-kyŏŏr') *adj.* **-cur·er, -cur·est. 1.** Free from harm, risk, or loss : safe. **2.** Free from anxiety or doubt : confident. **3.** Not likely to fail or give way : stable. **4.** Sure : certain. *—v.* **-cured, -cur·ing. 1.** To keep from harm, risk, or loss. **2.** To fasten firmly. **3.** To guarantee : ensure. **4.** To gain possession of : acquire. **—se·cure'ly** *adv.*
se·cu·ri·ty (sĭ-kyŏŏr'ĭ-tē) *n., pl.* **-ties. 1.** Freedom from risk or danger : safety. **2.** Freedom from doubt, anxiety, or fear : confidence. **3.** Something given to assure the fulfillment of an obligation : pledge. **4. securities.** Written evidence of ownership or creditorship, esp. stocks or bonds. **5.** Measures designed to protect, as from theft, attack, or disclosure. **6.** *Computer Sci.* Prevention of the unauthorized use of a program or device.
secy. *abbr.* secretary.
se·dan (sĭ-dăn') *n.* **1.** A closed automobile having a front and rear seat. **2.** An enclosed chair carried on poles by 2 men.
se·date¹ (sĭ-dāt') *adj.* **-dat·er, -dat·est.** Serene and dignified : composed.
se·date² (sĭ-dāt') *v.* **-dat·ed, -dat·ing.** To administer a sedative to. **—se·da'tion** *n.*
sed·a·tive (sĕd'ə-tĭv) *adj.* Having a calming, soothing, or tranquilizing effect. *—n.* A sedative drug or agent.
sed·en·tar·y (sĕd'n-tĕr'ē) *adj.* Requiring or marked by much sitting.
sedge (sĕj) *n.* Any of various plants of the family Cyperaceae, resembling grasses but having solid stems.
sed·i·ment (sĕd'ə-mənt) *n.* **1.** Material that settles to the bottom of a liquid. **2.** Material, as stones, deposited by wind or water. **—sed'i·men'ta·ry** (-mĕn'tə-rē, -mĕnt'rē) *adj.* **—sed'i·men·ta'tion** *n.*
se·di·tion (sĭ-dĭsh'ən) *n.* Behavior or language that brings about rebellion against the established authority of the state. **—se·di'tious** *adj.*
se·duce (sĭ-dōōs', -dyōōs') *v.* **-duced, -duc·ing. 1.** To draw away from duty or proper conduct : corrupt. **2.** To persuade or entice to have sexual intercourse. **3.** To beguile. **—se·duc'er** *n.* **—se·duc'tion** (-dŭk'shən) *n.* **—se·duc'tive** *adj.*
sed·u·lous (sĕj'ə-ləs) *adj.* Assiduous.
see¹ (sē) *v.* **saw** (sô), **seen** (sēn), **see·ing. 1.** To perceive by or have the power of sight. **2.** To comprehend. **3.** To have a mental picture of : visualize <*saw* the town as it once was> **4.** To know through firsthand experience : undergo. **5.** To take note of : heed. **6.** To encounter, esp. regularly. **7.** To visit, esp. for consultation <*seeing* a doctor> **8.** To attend : view <*saw* a movie> **—see through. 1.** To understand the real character or nature of. **2.** To fulfill or finish (a task or obligation).
see² (sē) *n.* The authority, jurisdiction, or position of a bishop.
seed (sēd) *n., pl.* **seeds** *or* **seed. 1.** A fertilized and ripened plant ovule having an embryo capable of germinating to produce a new plant. **2.** A propagative part of a plant, as a bulb, tuber, or spore. **3.** A source : origin. **4.** Offspring : descendants. *—v.* **1.** To plant seeds in : sow. **2.** To remove the seeds from. **—go (**or **run) to seed. 1.** To progress to the seed-bearing stage. **2.** To deteriorate. **—seed'er** *n.*
seed·ling (sēd'lĭng) *n.* A young plant grown from a seed.
seed money *n.* Money required or given to start a new project.
seed·pod (sēd'pŏd') *n.* A pod, as of a pea, that splits open when ripe.
seed·time (sēd'tīm') *n.* A time for sowing seeds.
seed vessel *n. Bot.* A pericarp.
seed·y (sē'dē) *adj.* **-i·er, -i·est. 1.** Having numerous seeds. **2.** Run-down and shabby : unkempt. **3.** Squalid : disreputable.
see·ing (sē'ĭng) *conj.* Considering that.
seek (sēk) *v.* **sought** (sôt), **seek·ing. 1.** To make a search (for). **2.** To try to reach or obtain. **3.** To attempt : try. **—seek'er** *n.*
seem (sēm) *v.* **1.** To appear to be <*seemed* worried> **2.** To appear to oneself. **3.** To appear to exist or be true.
seem·ing (sē'mĭng) *adj.* Apparent : ostensible. **—seem'ing·ly** *adv.*
seem·ly (sēm'lē) *adj.* **-li·er, -li·est.** Proper : appropriate. **—seem'li·ness** *n.*
seen (sēn) *v. p.p. of* SEE¹.
seep (sēp) *v.* To pass slowly through small openings or pores : ooze. **—seep'age** *n.*
seer (sē'ər) *n.* A person supposedly able to visualize and thus predict the future.
seer·suck·er (sîr'sŭk'ər) *n.* A lightweight fabric, gen. of cotton or rayon, having a crinkled surface and usu. a striped pattern.
see·saw (sē'sô') *n.* **1. a.** A game in which 2 children alternate in riding up and down on opposite ends of a long board balanced in the middle. **b.** The board used in seesaw. **2.** An up-and-down or back-and-forth movement. **—see'saw'** *v.*
seethe (sēth) *v.* **seethed, seeth·ing. 1.** To bubble, foam, boil, or churn. **2.** To be greatly agitated.
seg·ment (sĕg'mənt) *n.* **1.** Any of the parts into which something can be divided : section. **2.** *Math.* A section of a figure cut off by a line or plane. **—seg·ment'** (sĕg-mĕnt') *v.* **—seg·ment'al** *adj.* **—seg'men·ta'tion** *n.*
seg·re·gate (sĕg'rĭ-gāt') *v.* **-gat·ed, -gat·ing. 1.** To isolate from others. **2.** To impose racial segregation on.
seg·re·ga·tion (sĕg'rĭ-gā'shən) *n.* **1.** The act or process of segregating or the state of being segregated. **2.** The policy or practice of isolating or separating an ethnic group or race, as in schools, housing, and employment. **—seg're·ga'tion·ist** *n.*
seign·ior (sān-yôr', sān'yôr') *n.* A feudal lord. **—sei·gnio'ri·al** *adj.*
seine (sān) *n.* A large fishing net with weights at the lower edge and floats at the top. *—v.* To fish with a seine.
Seine (sān, sĕn). River of N France, flowing c. 480 mi (772 km) gen. NW to its estuary on the English Channel.
seis·mic (sīz'mĭk) *adj.* Of, relating to, or caused by an earthquake. **—seis·mic'i·ty** (-mĭs'ĭ-tē) *n.*
seis·mo·gram (sīz'mə-grăm') *n.* The record of an earth tremor made by a seismograph.
seis·mo·graph (sīz'mə-grăf') *n.* An instrument for automatically detecting and measuring earthquakes and other ground

self-abasement
self-accusation
self-acting
self-addressed
self-adjusting
self-adminstered
self-admiration
self-advancement
self-advertising
self-aggrandizement
self-aid
self-aligning
self-analysis
self-appointed
self-approved
self-asserting
self-assertion
self-assertive
self-assurance
self-assured
self-authorized
self-awareness
self-betrayal
self-blame
self-charging
self-cleaning
self-closing
self-command
self-complacent
self-conceit
self-concerned
self-condemned
self-conducted
self-confessed
self-confidence
self-confident
self-conflict
self-congratulation
self-congratulatory
self-constituted
self-consuming
self-contempt
self-contradiction
self-contradictory
self-control
self-correcting
self-corruption
self-created
self-criticism
self-cultivation
self-cure
self-deceit
self-deceiving
self-deception
self-defeating
self-defrosting
self-degradation
self-delusion
self-denial
self-denying
self-deprecating
self-depreciation
self-destruction
self-destructive
self-determination
self-direction
self-discipline
self-discovery
self-distrust
self-doubt
self-driven
self-educated
self-employed
self-employment
self-emptying
self-esteem
self-evident
self-examination
self-explaining
self-explanatory
self-expression
self-feeding
self-filling
self-forgetful

vibrations. **—seis·mog′ra·pher** (sīz-mŏg′rə-fər) *n.* **—seis′mo·graph′ic** *adj.* **—seis·mog′ra·phy** *n.*

seis·mol·o·gy (sīz-mŏl′ə-jē) *n.* The science that deals with earthquakes and with the mechanical properties of the earth. **—seis′mo·log′ic** (-mə-lŏj′ĭk), **seis′mo·log′i·cal** *adj.* **—seis·mol′o·gist** *n.*

seize (sēz) *v.* **seized, seiz·ing. 1.** To take possession or hold of quickly and forcibly. **2.** To take prisoner : arrest. **3.** To take eagerly <*seized* the opportunity> **4.** To comprehend. **5.** To affect suddenly : overwhelm. **—sei′zure** (sē′zhər) *n.*

sel·dom (sĕl′dəm) *adv.* Rarely.

se·lect (sĭ-lĕkt′) *v.* To pick out or choose from a number of choices. *—adj.* **1.** Carefully picked or chosen. **2.** Choice <a *select* wine> **3.** Fastidious in selection : discriminating. **—se·lec′tive** *adj.* **—se·lec′tiv′i·ty** (-lĕk′tĭv′ĭ-tē) *n.*

se·lec·tee (sĭ-lĕk′tē′) *n.* One selected for military service.

se·lec·tion (sĭ-lĕk′shən) *n.* **1. a.** The act of selecting. **b.** One selected. **2.** A collection of carefully chosen persons or things. **3.** *Biol.* A process that favors or brings about the survival and perpetuation of 1 kind of organism rather than others.

selective service *n.* A system for drafting individuals for military service.

se·lect·man (sĭ-lĕkt′mən) *n.* One of a board of officers chosen annually in most New England towns to manage local affairs.

sel·e·nite (sĕl′ə-nīt′) *n.* Gypsum in the form of clear colorless crystals.

se·le·ni·um (sĭ-lē′nē-əm) *n. Symbol* **Se** A nonmetallic element with chemical properties similar to sulfur.

sel·e·nog·ra·phy (sĕl′ə-nŏg′rə-fē) *n.* The study of the physical features of the moon.

sel·e·nol·o·gy (sĕl′ə-nŏl′ə-jē) *n.* The astronomical study of the moon.

self (sĕlf) *n., pl.* **selves** (sĕlvz). **1.** The essential being of 1 person as distinct from any other. **2.** A particular aspect of a person. **3.** Personal welfare, interest, or advantage : selfishness.

self– *pref.* **1.** Oneself : itself <*self*-control> **2.** Automatic : automatically <*self*-loading> See below for a self-explanatory list of words formed with the prefix **self–.**

self-a·ban·doned (sĕlf′ə-băn′dənd) *adj.* Abandoned by oneself, esp. having yielded to one's impulses.

self-cen·tered (sĕlf′sĕn′tərd) *adj.* Concerned only with oneself : selfish. **—self′-cen′tered·ness** *n.*

self-com·posed (sĕlf′kəm-pōzd′) *adj.* Having control over one's emotions.

self-con·scious (sĕlf′kŏn′shəs) *adj.* **1.** Uncomfortably aware of one's appearance or manner. **2.** Socially uncomfortable. **—self′-con′scious·ly** *adv.* **—self′-con′scious·ness** *n.*

self-con·tained (sĕlf′kən-tānd′) *adj.* **1.** Complete within itself. **2.** Self-sufficient. **3.** Keeping to oneself : reserved.

self-de·fense (sĕlf′dĭ-fĕns′) *n.* **1.** The act of defending oneself or what belongs to oneself. **2.** *Law.* The right to use whatever means reasonably necessary to protect oneself against violence or threatened violence.

self-de·struct (sĕlf′dĭ-strŭkt′) *v.* To destroy oneself or itself.

self-ef·fac·ing (sĕlf′ĭ-fā′sĭng) *adj.* Humble : modest. **—self′-ef·face′ment** *n.*

self-en·forc·ing (sĕlf′ĕn-fôr′sĭng, -fōr′-) *adj.* Having within itself the means or a guarantee of its enforcement <a *self-enforcing* order>

self-fer·til·i·za·tion (sĕlf′fûr′tl-ĭ-zā′shən) *n.* Fertilization by sperm from the same animal, as in some hermaphrodites, or by pollen from the same flower.

self-flag·el·la·tion (sĕlf′flăj′ə-lā′shən) *n.* Harsh criticism of oneself.

self-ful·fill·ing (sĕlf′fo͝ol-fĭl′ĭng) *adj.* **1.** Attaining one's own expectation or goals. **2.** Occurring largely as a result of having been predicted or expected <a *self-fulfilling* prophecy>

self·ish (sĕl′fĭsh) *adj.* Concerned only or primarily with oneself without regard for others. ☆**syns:** SELF-CENTERED, SELF-SEEKING **—self′ish·ness** *n.*

self·less (sĕlf′lĭs) *adj.* Without thought for oneself : unselfish. **—self′less·ly** *adv.* **—self′less·ness** *n.*

self-load·ing (sĕlf′lō′dĭng) *adj.* Semiautomatic, as a firearm.

self-made (sĕlf′mād′) *adj.* Successful through one's own actions <a *self-made* millionaire>

self-pol·li·na·tion (sĕlf′pŏl′ə-nā′shən) *n.* The transfer of pollen from an anther to a stigma of the same flower.

self-right·eous (sĕlf′rī′chəs) *adj.* Piously or smugly convinced of one's own righteousness. **—self′-right′eous·ly** *adv.*

self·same (sĕlf′sām′) *adj.* Exactly the same : identical. **—self′same′ness** *n.*

self-seal·ing (sĕlf′sē′lĭng) *adj.* Capable of sealing itself, as after a puncture.

self-serv·ing (sĕlf′sûr′vĭng) *adj.* Serving one's own interests, esp. without concern for the needs or interests of others.

self-start·er (sĕlf′stär′tər) *n.* **1.** A device for automatically starting an internal-combustion engine. **2.** An individual having initiative.

self-will (sĕlf′wĭl′) *n.* Willfulness, esp. in satisfying one's own desires : stubbornness. **—self′-willed′** *adj.*

sell (sĕl) *v.* **sold** (sōld), **sell·ing. 1.** To exchange (e.g., goods or services) for money or its equivalent. **2. a.** To offer for sale. **b.** To be sold or on sale. **3.** To promote the sale, acceptance, or adoption of <tried to *sell* the idea to his parents> ☆**syns:** HANDLE, MARKET, MERCHANDISE, RETAIL, VEND **—sell out. 1.** To sell all of one's property. **2.** To betray. **—sell′er** *n.*

selling climax *n.* A sharp decline in stock prices on a heavy volume of trading followed by a rally.

selt·zer (sĕlt′sər) *n.* **1.** Effervescent mineral water. **2.** Artificially carbonated water.

sel·vage *also* **sel·vedge** (sĕl′vĭj) *n.* The edge of a fabric woven so that it will not ravel.

selves (sĕlvz) *n. pl. of* SELF.

se·man·tic (sə-măn′tĭk) *adj.* Of or relating to meaning.

se·man·tics (sə-măn′tĭks) *n. (sing. in number).* **1.** The study of meaning in language, esp. with regard to historical changes. **2.** The study of the relationships between signs and symbols.

sem·a·phore (sĕm′ə-fôr′, -fōr′) *n.* **1.** A visual signaling apparatus with mechanically moving arms. **2.** A system for signaling with flags held in the hand. **—sem′a·phore′** *v.*

sem·blance (sĕm′bləns) *n.* **1.** A representation : likeness. **2.** An outward appearance or superficial show.

se·men (sē′mən) *n.* The thick, whitish secretion of the male reproductive organs.

se·mes·ter (sə-mĕs′tər) *n.* One of the 2 divisions of an academic year.

---

self-giving
self-governing
self-government
self-guidance
self-hardening
self-healing
self-help
self-hypnosis
self-image
self-immolation
self-importance
self-important
self-imposed
self-improvement
self-incrimination
self-induced
self-indulgence
self-indulgent
self-inflicted
self-inking
self-instructed
self-insurance
self-interest
self-lighting
self-limiting
self-locking
self-love
self-lubricating
self-management
self-mastery
self-mockery
self-mocking
self-moving
self-oiling
self-operating
self-ordained
self-perpetuating
self-pity
self-portrait
self-possessed
self-possession
self-praise
self-preservation
self-proclaimed
self-propelled
self-propelling
self-protection
self-realization
self-recording
self-regard
self-registering
self-regulating
self-reliance
self-reliant
self-reproach
self-reproof
self-respect
self-respecting
self-restraint
self-revealing
self-revelation
self-rewarding
self-rule
self-sacrifice
self-sacrificing
self-satisfaction
self-satisfied
self-seeker
self-seeking
self-service
self-starting
self-study
self-styled
self-sufficiency
self-sufficient
self-supporting
self-sustaining
self-taught
self-therapy
self-torment
self-trust
self-vindication
self-winding
self-worship

semi– *pref.* **1.** Half of <*semi*circle> **2.** Partial : partially <*semi*professional> **3.** Occurring 2 times during <*semi*annual> See below for a list of self-explanatory words formed with the prefix **semi–.**

sem·i·an·nu·al (sĕm′ē-ăn′yo͞o-əl) *adj.* Occurring or issued twice a year.

sem·i·au·to·mat·ic (sĕm′ē-ô′tə-măt′ĭk) *adj.* Ejecting the shell and loading the succeeding round of ammunition automatically after each shot has been fired. Used of firearms.

sem·i·cir·cle (sĕm′ĭ-sûr′kəl) *n.* A half of a circle. **–sem′i·cir′cu·lar** (-kyə-lər) *adj.*

sem·i·co·lon (sĕm′ē-kō′lən) *n.* A mark of punctuation (;) that indicates a degree of separation greater than that of a comma but less that that of a period.

sem·i·con·duc·tor (sĕm′ē-kən-dŭk′tər) *n.* A solid crystalline substance, as selenium or silicon, that has electrical conductivity greater than an insulator but less than a conductor.

sem·i·fi·nal (sĕm′ē-fī′nəl) *adj.* Immediately preceding the final, as in a tournament. *–n.* A semifinal match or competition. **–sem′i·fi′nal·ist** *n.*

sem·i·month·ly (sĕm′ē-mŭnth′lē) *adj.* Happening or issued twice a month. *–n., pl.* **-lies.** A semimonthly event or publication. **–sem′i·month′ly** *adv.*

sem·i·nal (sĕm′ə-nəl) *adj.* **1.** Of, pertaining to, or containing semen or seed. **2.** Of, relating to, or possessing the power to originate : creative. **–sem′i·nal·ly** *adv.*

sem·i·nar (sĕm′ə-när′) *n.* **1. a.** A course of study pursued by a group of advanced college or graduate students who do independent research under the guidance of a professor. **b.** A meeting of such a group. **2.** A meeting for an exchange of ideas.

sem·i·nar·y (sĕm′ə-nĕr′ē) *n., pl.* **-ies. 1. a.** A school where priests, ministers, or rabbis are educated and trained. **2.** A secondary school, esp. a private school for girls. **–sem′i·nar′i·an** (-nâr′ē-ən) *n.*

sem·i·per·me·a·ble (sĕm′ē-pûr′mē-ə-bəl) *adj.* **1.** Somewhat permeable. **2.** Permeable to some molecules but not to all. **–sem′i·per′me·a·bil′i·ty** *n.*

sem·i·pre·cious (sĕm′ē-prĕsh′əs) *adj.* Of smaller value than a precious stone.

sem·i·pri·vate (sĕm′ē-prī′vĭt) *adj.* Shared with usu. 1 to 3 other hospital patients <a *semiprivate* room>

sem·i·pro (sĕm′ē-prō′) *adj. Informal.* Semiprofessional. **–sem′i·pro′** *n.*

sem·i·pro·fes·sion·al (sĕm′ē-prə-fĕsh′ə-nəl) *adj.* **1.** Participating in an activity for pay but not as a full-time occupation. **2.** Made up of or engaged in by semiprofessional players. **–sem′i·pro·fes′sion·al** *n.*

Sem·ite (sĕm′īt′) *n.* A member of any of a group of Middle Eastern peoples, esp. Arabs and Jews. **–Se·mit′ic** (sə-mĭt′ĭk) *adj.*

sem·i·tone (sĕm′ē-tōn′) *n. Mus.* An interval of a half tone.

sem·i·trail·er (sĕm′ē-trā′lər) *n.* A trailer with a set or sets of wheels at the rear only, supported in front by a truck tractor or towing vehicle.

sem·i·trop·i·cal (sĕm′ē-trŏp′ĭ-kəl) *adj.* Partly tropical.

sem·i·week·ly (sĕm′ē-wēk′lē) *adj.* Happening or issued twice a week. *–n., pl.* **-lies.** A semiweekly event or publication. **–sem′i·week′ly** *adv.*

sen (sĕn) *n., pl.* **sen.** See *riel, ringgit, rupiah,* and *yen* at CURRENCY TABLE.

sen. or **Sen.** *abbr.* **1.** senate. **2.** senator. **3.** senior.

sen·ate (sĕn′ĭt) *n.* The upper house in a bicameral legislature, as the U.S. Congress.

sen·a·tor (sĕn′ə-tər) *n.* A member of a senate. **–sen′a·to′ri·al** (-tôr′ē-əl, -tōr′-) *adj.* **–sen′a·to′ri·al·ly** *adv.*

send (sĕnd) *v.* **sent** (sĕnt), **send·ing. 1.** To cause to be conveyed or dispatched. **2.** To direct, allow, or enable to go. **3.** To give off (e.g., heat) : emit. **4.** To drive with force : propel. **5.** *Slang.* To transport with pleasure : delight. ☆***syns:*** DISPATCH, FORWARD, ROUTE, SHIP, TRANSMIT **–send′er** *n.*

send·off (sĕnd′ôf′, -ŏf′) *n.* A demonstration of good wishes, as for the start of a new undertaking.

se·ne (sā′nā) *n., pl.* **sene.** See *tala* at CURRENCY TABLE.

Sen·e·gal (sĕn′ĭ-gôl′). Country of W Africa. *Cap.* Dakar. *Pop.* 5,085,388. **–Sen′e·ga·lese′** (-gə-lēz′, -lēs′) *adj.* & *n.*

se·nes·cent (sĭ-nĕs′ənt) *adj.* Growing old : aging. **–se·nes′cence** *n.*

se·nile (sē′nīl′, sĕn′īl′) *adj.* **1.** Of or proceeding from old age. **2.** Exhibiting the mental deterioration often associated with old age. **–se·nil′i·ty** (sə-nĭl′ĭ-tē) *n.*

sen·ior (sēn′yər) *adj.* **1.** Of or being the older of 2 : elder. **2.** Of higher rank or standing than another. **3.** Of or relating to the final year of high school or college. *–n.* **1.** A person who is older or of higher rank than another. **2.** A student in the final year of high school or college.

senior citizen *n.* An elderly, usu. retired person.

senior high school *n.* A school usu. including grades 10, 11, and 12.

sen·ior·i·ty (sēn-yôr′ĭ-tē, -yŏr′-) *n.* **1.** The state or fact of being senior. **2.** Priority over others by reason of service.

sen·i·ti (sĕn′ĭ-tē) *n., pl.* **seniti.** See *pa′anga* at CURRENCY TABLE.

sen·na (sĕn′ə) *n.* A plant of the genus *Cassia,* with compound leaves that are dried and used medicinally as a cathartic.

se·ñor (sān-yôr′) *n., pl.* **se·ñor·es** (sān-yôr′ās). **1.** The Spanish title of courtesy for a man, equivalent to English *Mr.* or *sir.* **2.** A Spanish or Spanish-speaking man.

se·ño·ra (sān-yôr′ə) *n., pl.* **se·ñor·as** (sān-yôr′əs). **1.** The Spanish title of courtesy for a married woman, equivalent to English *Mrs.* or *madam.* **2.** A Spanish or Spanish-speaking woman.

se·ño·ri·ta (sān′yə-rē′tə) *n.* **1.** The Spanish title of courtesy for an unmarried woman or girl, equivalent to English *Miss.* **2.** An unmarried Spanish or Spanish-speaking woman or girl.

sen·sa·tion (sĕn-sā′shən) *n.* **1. a.** An awareness associated with the stimulation of a sense organ <the *sensation* of cold> **b.** The capacity to feel or perceive physically. **2.** A nonspecific feeling <a *sensation* of floating> **3. a.** A condition of strong interest and excitement. **b.** An event or object causing this condition. **–sen·sa′tion·al** *adj.*

sen·sa·tion·al·ism (sĕn-sā′shə-nə-lĭz′əm) *n.* The use of material or methods intended to shock, excite, or arouse curiosity.

sense (sĕns) *n.* **1. a.** One of the functions of sight, hearing, touch, smell, and taste. **b.** The faculty of perceiving by means of these functions. **2.** Ability to estimate, judge, appreciate, or understand <a *sense* of humor> **3.** A vague feeling or impression <a *sense* of doom> **4.** *often* **senses.** The ability to think or reason soundly <Come to your *senses.*> **5.** Significance : meaning. *–v.* **sensed, sens·ing. 1.** To perceive by or as if by the senses. **2.** To detect automatically <*sensed* victory>

sense·less (sĕns′lĭs) *adj.* **1.** Unconscious. **2.** Lacking sense : pointless. **–sense′less·ly** *adv.* **–sense′less·ness** *n.*

sen·si·bil·i·ty (sĕn′sə-bĭl′ĭ-tē) *n., pl.* **-ties. 1.** The capacity to perceive sensation. **2.** Refinement in feeling : sensitivity.

sen·si·ble (sĕn′sə-bəl) *adj.* **1.** Capable of perceiving or being perceived through or as if through the senses. **2.** Capable of : sensitive. **3.** Conscious : aware. **4.** Having or displaying good sense. **–sen′si·bly** *adv.*

sen·si·tive (sĕn′sĭ-tĭv) *adj.* **1.** Sensory. **2.** Responding readily to small changes of condition or environment. **3.** Readily affected, as by the emotions or circumstances of others. **4.** Easily offended, hurt, damaged, or irritated. **–sen′si·tive·ly** *adv.* **–sen′si·tiv′i·ty** (-tĭv′ĭ-tē), **sen′si·tive·ness** *n.*

sen·si·tize (sĕn′sĭ-tīz′) *v.* **-tized, -tiz·ing.** To make or become sensitive. **–sen′si·ti·za′tion** *n.* **–sen′si·tiz′er** *n.*

semiagricultural
semianimated
semiarid
semiattached
semiautonomous
semibald
semibarbaric
semibarren
semibelted
semibiographic
semibleached
semicarved
semicivilized
semiclassical
semicoagulated
semicollapsible
semiconcealed
semiconfident
semiconfinement
semiconscious
semiconservative
semicooperative
semicultivated
semicultured
semidangerous
semidarkness
semideaf
semidecay
semidecayed
semidelirious
semidependent
semideveloped
semidigested
semidiurnal
semidivine
semidocumentary
semidomesticated
semidormant
semidry
semienclosed
semiexpanded
semiexposed
semifailure
semifeudalism
semifictional
semifixed
semiflexed
semifluid
semiformal
semiformed
semiglaze
semiglazed
semigloss
semigod
semi-Gothic
semihard
semihistorical
semihostile
semihumorous
semihysterical
semi-idle
semi-independent
semi-intoxicated
semi-invalid
semi-ironic
semijocular

sen•sor (sĕn′sər, -sôr′) *n.* A device, as a photoelectric cell, that responds to a signal or stimulus.
sen•so•ry (sĕn′sə-rē) *adj.* Of or relating to the senses.
sen•su•al (sĕn′sho͞o-əl) *adj.* **1. a.** Of, relating to, or preoccupied with the gratification of the senses, esp. the sexual appetite. **b.** Suggesting sexuality : voluptuous. **2.** Not spiritual or intellectual : physical. **–sen′su•al•ist** *n.* **–sen′su•al′i•ty** (-ăl′ĭ-te) *n.* **–sen′su•al•ly** *adv.*
sen•su•ous (sĕn′sho͞o-əs) *adj.* **1.** Of or arising from the senses. **2.** Appealing to the senses. **3.** Voluptuous. **–sen′su•ous•ly** *adv.* **–sen′su•ous•ness** *n.*
sent (sĕnt) *v. p.t. & p.p. of* SEND.
sen•tence (sĕn′təns) *n.* **1.** A grammatical construction that contains a finite verb or verb phrase and usu. a subject and its predicate. **2. a.** A judicial decision, esp. one detailing punishment to be inflicted on a convicted person. **b.** The penalty imposed. *–v.* **-tenced, -tenc•ing.** To impose a sentence on (a convicted person). **–sen•ten′tial** (sĕn-tĕn′shəl) *adj.*
sen•ten•tious (sĕn-tĕn′shəs) *adj.* **1.** Given to or marked by the use of aphorisms. **2.** Abounding in or given to smug moralizing.
sen•tient (sĕn′shənt) *adj.* Capable of feeling or perceiving : conscious.
sen•ti•ment (sĕn′tə-mənt) *n.* **1.** A general cast of mind. **2.** An idea, opinion, or attitude based more on feeling than on reason. **3. a.** Susceptibility to emotion. **b.** Emotion, esp. romantic or nostalgic feeling. ☆***syns:*** ATTITUDE, DISPOSITION, FEELING
sen•ti•men•tal (sĕn′tə-mĕn′tl) *adj.* **1.** Marked, swayed, or affected by sentiment. **2.** Arising from, expressive of, or appealing to the sentiments, esp. nostalgic or romantic feelings <*sentimental* pictures> **–sen′ti•men′tal•ism** *n.* **–sen′ti•men′tal•ist** *n.* **–sen′ti•men•tal′i•ty** (-tăl′ĭ-tē) *n.* **–sen′ti•men′tal•ly** *adv.*
sen•ti•men•tal•ize (sĕn′tə-mĕn′tl-īz′) *v.* **-ized, -iz•ing.** To be sentimental (about).
sen•ti•nel (sĕn′tə-nəl) *n.* One that guards or warns of approaching danger.
sen•try (sĕn′trē) *n., pl.* **-tries.** A guard, esp. a military guard : sentinel.
Seoul (sōl). Cap. of South Korea, in the NW part. *Pop.* 8,114,000.
se•pal (sē′pəl) *n.* One of the usu. green segments forming the calyx of a flower.
sep•a•ra•ble (sĕp′ər-ə-bəl, sĕp′rə-) *adj.* Capable of being separated.
sep•a•rate (sĕp′ə-rāt′) *v.* **-rat•ed, -rat•ing. 1.** To put or keep apart : disjoin. **2.** To serve to keep apart, as a barrier does. **3.** To go different ways : part. **4.** To extract <*separate* cream from milk> ☆***syns:*** DIVIDE, PART, PARTITION, SECTION, SEGMENT *–adj.* (sĕp′ər-ĭt, sĕp′rĭt). **1.** Set aside from others. **2.** Distinct from others. **3.** Particular : individual <*separate* directions> *–n.* (sĕp′ər-ĭt, sĕp′rĭt). A garment, as a skirt, designed to be worn in various combinations with other garments. **–sep′a•rate•ly** *adv.*
sep•a•ra•tion (sĕp′ə-rā′shən) *n.* **1.** The act or process of separating or the state of being separated. **2.** A place, line, or point of division. **3.** A space or interval that separates.
sep•a•ra•tist (sĕp′ər-ə-tist, sĕp′rə-, sĕp′ə-rā′-) *n.* A person who advocates separation, as from a political or religious affiliation. **–sep′a•ra•tism** *n.*
sep•a•ra•tor (sĕp′ə-rā′tər) *n.* One that separates, esp. an apparatus that separates cream from milk.
se•pi•a (sē′pē-ə) *n.* A grayish yellowish brown to dark brown.
sep•sis (sĕp′sĭs) *n.* The presence of disease-causing organisms or their toxins in the blood or body tissues.
Sept. *abbr.* September.
Sep•tem•ber (sĕp-tĕm′bər) *n.* The 9th month of the year, having 30 days.
sep•tic (sĕp′tĭk) *adj.* **1.** Of, relating to, or having the nature of sepsis. **2.** Causing sepsis : putrefactive.
sep•ti•ce•mi•a (sĕp′tĭ-sē′mē-ə) *n.* A condition in which disease-causing microorganisms or their toxins are present in the bloodstream.
septic tank *n.* A tank in which sewage is decomposed by bacteria.
sep•tu•a•ge•nar•i•an (sĕp′to͞o-ə-jə-nâr′ē-ən, -tyo͞o-) *n.* One between the ages of 70 and 80. **–sep′tu•a•ge•nar′i•an** *adj.*
Sep•tu•a•gint (sĕp′cho͞o-ə-jĭnt′, sĕp′to͞o-) *n.* A 3rd cent. B.C. Greek translation of the Old Testament.
sep•ul•cher (sĕp′əl-kər) *n.* A burial vault. *–v.* To put in a sepulcher : inter. **–se•pul′chral** (sə-pŭl′krəl) *adj.*
sep•ul•chre (sĕp′əl-kər) *n. & v. esp. Brit. var. of* SEPULCHER.
seq. *abbr.* **1.** sequel. **2.** the following (Lat. *sequens*).
se•quel (sē′kwəl) *n.* **1.** Something that follows or comes after. **2.** A literary work forming the continuation of an earlier work. **3.** A result : outcome.
se•quence (sē′kwəns) *n.* **1.** The following of 1 thing after another. **2.** A number of things or events that follow each other. **3.** The order in which things or events occur or are arranged. **–se•quen′tial** (sĭ-kwĕn′shəl) *adj.* **–se•quen′tial•ly** *adv.*
se•quent (sē′kwənt) *adj.* **1.** Following : subsequent. **2.** Resultant : consequent.
se•ques•ter (sĭ-kwĕs′tər) *v.* **1.** To set apart : segregate. **2.** To withdraw : seclude. **–se′ques•tra′tion** (sē′kwĭ-strā′shən) *n.*
se•quin (sē′kwĭn) *n.* A small, usu. shiny decorative spangle.
se•quoi•a (sĭ-kwoi′ə) *n.* An extremely large evergreen tree of the genus *Sequoia,* which includes the redwood.
ser. *abbr.* **1.** serial. **2.** series. **3.** sermon.
se•ra (sîr′ə) *n. var. pl. of* SERUM.
se•ra•glio (sĭ-răl′yō, -räl′-) *n., pl.* **-glios. 1.** A harem. **2.** The palace of a sultan.
se•ra•pe (sə-rä′pē) *n.* An often brightly colored woolen blanket worn as a cloak or poncho, esp. in certain parts of Mexico.
ser•aph (sĕr′əf) *n., pl.* **-aphs** or **-a•phim** (-ə-fĭm′). An angel of the highest rank in the 9 orders of angels. **–se•raph′ic** (sə-răf′ĭk) *adj.*
Ser•bi•a (sûr′bē-ə). Region and constituent republic of E Yugoslavia. **–Serb** *n.* **–Ser′bi•an** *adj. & n.*
sere (sîr) *adj.* Withered : dry.
ser•e•nade (sĕr′ə-nād′) *n.* Music performed to compliment or express love for someone. *–v.* **-nad•ed, -nad•ing.** To perform a serenade (to).
ser•en•dip•i•ty (sĕr′ən-dĭp′ĭ-tē) *n.* The faculty of discovering desirable or valuable things accidentally or unexpectedly. **–ser′en•dip′i•tous** *adj.*
se•rene (sə-rēn′) *adj.* **1.** Peaceful : calm. **2.** Perfectly clear <a *serene* moonlit sky> **–se•ren′i•ty** (sə-rĕn′ĭ-tē) *n.*
serf (sûrf) *n.* A medieval European peasant who was owned by a lord and bound to the land. **–serf′dom** *n.*
serge (sûrj) *n.* A twilled cloth of worsted or a blend of worsted and wool.
ser•geant (sär′jənt) *n.* **1.** A noncommissioned officer in the U.S. Army, Air Force, or Marine Corps ranking next above a corporal. **2.** A police officer ranking just below a captain or sometimes a lieutentant.
sergeant at arms *n., pl.* **sergeants at arms.** An officer charged with keeping order, as at the meeting of a legislature.
se•ri•al (sîr′ē-əl) *adj.* **1.** Consisting of or arranged in a series. **2.** Presented in installments <a *serial* television drama> *–n.* A serial story or play. **–se′ri•al•i•za′tion** *n.* **–se′ri•al•ize′** *v.* **–se′ri•al•ly** *adv.*
serial number *n.* One of a series of numbers used esp. for identification.

---

semiliberal
semiliquid
semiliterate
semiluxury
semimechanical
semimilitary
semimobile
semimoderate
semimodern
semimute
semimystical
semimythic
semineurotic
seminocturnal
semiparalysis
semipagan
semipastoral
semiperishable
semipermanent
semipetrified
semiplastic
semipolitical
semipreserved
semiprimitive
semiprone
semiprotected
semipublic
semiradical
semiraw
semireactionary
semireligious
semiresolute
semirespectable
semiretired
semiretirement
semiromantic
semirural
semirustic
semisacred
semisatirical
semisavage
semischolastic
semiscientific
semisecrecy
semisentimental
semiserious
semishade
semiskilled
semisoft
semisolid
semispontaneous
semistiff
semistratified
semisuburban
semisuccessful
semisweet
semitailored
semitechnical
semitraditional
semitrained
semitransparent
semitruthful
semivolatile
semivoluntary
semiwild
semiyearly

se·ries (sîr′ēz) *n., pl.* **series.** A number of things or events, esp. of the same kind, occurring in a row or following 1 after the other : succession.

se·ri·ous (sîr′ē-əs) *adj.* **1.** Grave : sober. **2.** Not jesting : earnest. **3.** Not trivial : weighty. **4.** Marked by or demanding thought, effort, or devotion. **5.** Giving cause for worry : dangerous. **—se′ri·ous·ly** *adv.* **—se′ri·ous·ness** *n.*

ser·mon (sûr′mən) *n.* **1.** A discourse delivered by a clergyman during a church service. **2.** An often long-winded lecture on duty or behavior. **—ser′mon·ize′** *v.* **—ser′mon·iz′er** *n.*

se·rol·o·gy (sĭ-rŏl′ə-jē) *n.* The medical science dealing with serums. **—se′ro·log′ic** (sîr′ə-lŏj′ĭk), **se′ro·log′i·cal** *adj.*

ser·pent (sûr′pənt) *n.* A snake.

ser·pen·tine (sûr′pən-tēn′, -tīn′) *adj.* **1.** Of or like a serpent in form or movement : sinuous. **2.** Subtly sly : cunning.

ser·rate (sĕr′āt′) *also* **ser·rat·ed** (-ā′tĭd) *adj.* Having a notched sawlike edge.

ser·ried (sĕr′ēd) *adj.* Pressed or close together : crowded.

se·rum (sîr′əm) *n., pl.* **-rums** *or* **se·ra** (sîr′ə). **1.** The clear fluid obtained when whole blood is separated into its solid and liquid components. **2.** A liquid extracted from the tissues of an immunized animal and used esp. as an antitoxin.

serv. *abbr.* service.

ser·vant (sûr′vənt) *n.* **1.** One employed to perform household services. **2.** One that serves another.

serve (sûrv) *v.* **served, serv·ing. 1.** To be a servant (to). **2.** To prepare and offer <*serve* lunch> **3.** To supply service to : wait on <*serving* the public> **4.** To do a term of duty <*served* in the army > **5.** To put in : spend <*served* 6 years in the senate> **6.** To be of assistance to : benefit <*serving* the national interest> **7.** To meet the requirements of : satisfy <*serve* the purpose> **8.** To act in a specific capacity <*served* as chairman> **9.** To be used profitably by <a port that *serves* a wide region> **10.** To put a ball or shuttlecock into play, as in court games. *—n.* The act, right, or manner of serving a ball or shuttlecock. **—serv′er** *n.*

serv·ice (sûr′vĭs) *n.* **1.** The occupation of a servant. **2.** Employment, esp. for a government <public *service*> **3.** A government branch or department and its personnel <the civil *service*> **4. a.** One of the military forces of a nation. **b.** Duty in one of these forces. **5.** Work or duties performed for others <a house-cleaning *service*> **6.** A facility offering repair or maintenance. **7.** A facility providing the public with a utility, as water or transportation. **8.** A religious ceremony or rite. **9.** Assistance : benefit. **10.** A set of utensils or dishes <a china *service*> **11.** The act, manner, or right of serving, as in tennis : serve. *—v.* **-iced, -ic·ing. 1.** To adjust, repair, or maintain. **2.** To provide or furnish a service to.

serv·ice·a·ble (sûr′vĭ-sə-bəl) *adj.* **1.** Ready or fit for service : useful. **2.** Capable of giving long service : durable.

serv·ice·man (sûr′vĭs-măn′, -mən) *n.* **1.** A member of the military forces of a nation. **2.** A person whose work is the maintenance and repair of equipment.

service mark *n.* A symbol or mark used in the sale or advertising of services to distinguish them from the services of others.

service station *n.* A station where services, esp. repairs, can be obtained for motor vehicles.

ser·vile (sûr′vəl, -vīl′) *adj.* **1.** Slavishly submissive. **2.** Of or suitable to a servant or slave. ☆**syns:** OBSEQUIOUS, SLAVISH, SUBSERVIENT **—ser·vil′i·ty** (sər-vĭl′ĭ-tē) *n.*

serv·ing (sûr′vĭng) *n.* A helping.

ser·vi·tor (sûr′vĭ-tər, -tôr′) *n.* A man servant : attendant.

ser·vi·tude (sûr′vĭ-to͞od′, -tyo͞od′) *n.* The state of being a slave or serf : bondage.

ser·vo (sûr′vō) *n., pl.* **-vos. 1.** A servomotor. **2.** A servomechanism.

ser·vo·mech·a·nism (sûr′vō-mĕk′ə-nĭz′əm) *n.* A feedback system composed of a sensory element, an amplifier, and a servomotor that automatically controls the functions of a mechanical device.

ser·vo·mo·tor (sûr′vō-mō′tər) *n.* An electric motor or hydraulic piston that powers a servomechanism.

ses·a·me (sĕs′ə-mē) *n.* A plant, *Sesamum indicum*, of tropical Asia, yielding small, flat seeds that are a source of oil.

ses·qui·cen·ten·ni·al (sĕs′kwĭ-sĕn-tĕn′ē-əl) *adj.* Occurring every 150 years. *—n.* A 150th anniversary.

ses·qui·pe·da·li·an (sĕs′kwĭ-pĭ-dā′lē-ən, -dāl′yən) *adj.* **1.** Containing many syllables : polysyllabic. **2.** Tending to use polysyllabic words.

ses·sion (sĕsh′ən) *n.* **1.** A meeting or series of meetings, as of a judicial or legislative body. **2.** A meeting devoted to a specific activity. **3.** A period during the day or year when a school holds classes.

ses·tet (sĕ-stĕt′) *n.* A stanza making up the last 6 lines of a sonnet.

†**set**[1] (sĕt) *v.* **set, set·ting. 1.** To put in a particular position : place. **2.** To cause to do or be <*set* me thinking><*set* him free> **3. a.** To place in a firm or secure position : fix. **b.** To become firm, secure, or fixed. **4.** To prepare for proper functioning <*set* a trap> **5.** To adjust : regulate <*set* a timer> **6.** To arrange <*set* the table> **7. a.** To compose (music) to fit a text. **b.** To write (words) to fit a melodic line. **8.** To establish : settle <*set* the date> **9.** To place in a mounting or frame <*set* a jewel><*set* type> **10.** To cause to sit. **11.** To sit on eggs to hatch them. **12.** To make as an estimate of worth <*set* a high value on work> **13.** To sink below the horizon. **14.** To harden or congeal <cement *setting*> **15.** To have a particular course or direction. **16.** *Regional.* To sit. **—set back. 1.** To retard the progress of : hinder. **2.** *Informal.* To cost <That car *set* me *back* $8,000.> **—set forth. 1.** To present for consideration : propose. **2.** To express in words. **—set off. 1. a.** To cause to begin. **b.** To cause to explode. **2.** To call attention to by contrast : accentuate. **—set out. 1.** To undertake. **2.** To begin a journey. **—set up. 1.** To put together and erect. **2.** To establish : found. *—adj.* **1.** Fixed or determined by agreement or convention. **2.** Deliberate : intentional. **3.** Fixed and rigid. **4.** Unwilling to change <*set* in one's ways> **5.** Ready <*set* to go> *—n.* **1.** The act or process of setting. **2.** The way something is held or placed.

set[2] (sĕt) *n.* **1.** A group of persons or things of the same kind or sharing a common characteristic and usu. classed or associated together. **2.** An assemblage of parts that functions as a unit <a television *set*> **3.** A structure representing the place where the action of a play or motion picture takes place. **4.** *Math.* A collection of distinct elements <a *set* of integers> **5.** A group of games, as in tennis, that forms 1 unit or part of a match.

set·back (sĕt′băk′) *n.* An unanticipated delay or reverse in progress.

set·screw (sĕt′skro͞o′) *n.* A screw used to hold 2 parts securely in position or to regulate the tension of a spring.

set·tee (sĕ-tē′) *n.* A small sofa with a back and arms.

set·ter (sĕt′ər) *n.* Any of several breeds of long-haired hunting dogs.

set·ting (sĕt′ĭng) *n.* **1.** The context and environment in which something occurs. **2.** The scenery for a dramatic performance. **3.** A mounting, as for a jewel.

set·tle (sĕt′l) *v.* **-tled, -tling. 1.** To put in order. **2.** To establish residence (in). **3.** To come or cause to come to rest <*settled* back in my chair> **4.** To restore tranquillity to : calm. **5.** To sink or cause to sink and condense. **6.** To end or resolve <*settle* a dispute> **7.** To fix through mutual accord. **8.** To make compensation or payment for (a claim or debt). **9.** To give by formal or legal process. **10.** To establish in a business or way of life. **11.** To become more composed : stabilize. **—set′tler** *n.*

set·tle·ment (sĕt′l-mənt) *n.* **1.** The act orprocess of settling. **2.** A small, relatively new community. **3.** Establishment, as of people in a new area. **4.** An adjustment or accord reached, as in financial matters. **5. a.** Transfer of property to provide for the future needs of a person. **b.** Property thus transferred. **6.** A welfare center offering community services to the needy.

set-to (sĕt′to͞o′) *n., pl.* **-tos.** A brief but usu. angry conflict.

set·up (sĕt′ŭp′) *n.* **1.** *Informal.* The manner in which something is planned or arranged. **2.** *often* **setups.** *Informal.* Ice and nonalcoholic ingredients, as soda water, furnished to customers who add their own liquor. **3.** *Slang.* A competition or undertaking made easy to win or accomplish.

sev·en (sĕv′ən) *n.* **1.** The cardinal number equal to 6 + 1. **2.** The 7th in a set or sequence. **—sev′en** *adj. & pron.* **—sev′enth** *adj. & adv. & n.*

sev·en·teen (sĕv′ən-tēn′) *n.* **1.** The cardinal number equal to 16 + 1. **2.** The 17th in a set or sequence. **—sev′en·teen′** *adj. & pron.* **—sev′en·teenth′** *adj. & adv. & n.*

sev·en·teen-year locust (sĕv′ən-tēn′yîr′) *n.* A cicada, *Magicicada septendecim*, of the E U.S., having a nymphal stage in which it remains underground for 17 or sometimes 13 years.

seventh heaven *n.* A state of extreme happiness and satisfaction.

sev·en·ty (sĕv′ən-tē) *n., pl.* **-ties.** The cardinal number equal to 7 × 10. **—sev′en·ty** *adj. & pron.* **—sev′en·ti·eth** *adj. adv. & n.*

sev·er (sĕv′ər) *v.* To separate forcibly, as by cutting or breaking. **—sev′er·ance** *n.*

sev·er·al (sĕv′ər-əl, sĕv′rəl) *adj.* **1.** Being of a number greater than 2 or 3 but not many. **2.** Single : distinct. *—pron.* Several persons or things. **—sev′er·al·ly** *adv.*

severance pay *n.* A sum of money, usu. based on length of employment, that an employee is eligible for on termination.

se·vere (sə-vîr′) *adj.* **-ver·er, -ver·est. 1.** Harshly unsparing : strict <*severe* terms> **2.** Corresponding strictly and inflexibly to established rule. **3.** Austere : somber. **4.** Extremely plain in style. **5.** Extremely intense <*severe* pain> **–se•vere'ly** *adv.* **–se•ver'i•ty** (-vĕr'ĭ-tē) *n.*

Se•ville (sə-vĭl'). City of SW Spain. *Pop.* 630,329.

sew (sō) *v.* **sewed, sewn** (sōn) *or* **sewed, sew•ing. 1.** To make, close, repair, or attach with stitches made with a needle and thread. **2.** To work with a needle and thread <*sews* for a hobby>

sew•age (so͞o'ĭj) *n.* Liquid and solid waste material that passes through sewers.

sew•er (so͞o'ər) *n.* A channel or conduit to carry off waste material.

sew•er•age (so͞o'ər-ĭj) *n.* **1.** A network of sewers. **2.** Sewage.

sew•ing (sō'ĭng) *n.* **1.** The act or occupation of one who sews. **2.** Something made or being made with needle and thread.

sewing machine *n.* A machine used for sewing.

sewn (sōn) *v. var. p.p. of* SEW.

sex (sĕks) *n.* **1.** One of the 2 divisions, male and female, into which many living things are grouped. **2.** The physiological and functional differences that distinguish the male and female. **3.** Sexual intercourse. **–sex'less** *adj.*

sex•a•ge•nar•i•an (sĕk'sə-jə-nâr'ē-ən) *n.* One who is between the ages of 60 and 70. **–sex'a•ge•nar'i•an** *adj.*

sex appeal *n.* Physical attractiveness that arouses sexual interest in another person.

sex chromosome *n.* One of a pair of chromosomes that in combination determine the sex of an individual in human beings, most animals, and some plants.

sex hormone *n.* An animal hormone, as estrogen or androgen, that affects the growth or function of the reproductive organs and the development of secondary sex characteristics.

sex•ism (sĕk'sĭz'əm) *n.* Prejudice or discrimination based on sex, esp. against women. **–sex'ist** *adj.* & *n.*

sex•tant (sĕk'stənt) *n.* An instrument used in navigation to measure the altitude between the plane of the horizon and a line extending to a celestial body.

sex•tet (sĕk-stĕt') *n.* **1. a.** A musical composition for 6 performers. **b.** A group of 6 musicians who perform a sextet. **2.** A group of 6 persons or things.

sex•ton (sĕk'stən) *n.* One who maintains church property.

sex•u•al (sĕk'sho͞o-əl) *adj.* Of, relating to, or involving sex, the sexes, or the sex organs. **–sex'u•al'i•ty** (-ăl'ĭ-tē) *n.* **–sex'u•al•ly** *adv.*

sexual intercourse *n.* Coitus, esp. between human beings.

sex•y (sĕk'sē) *adj.* **-i•er, -i•est.** *Informal.* Arousing or intended to arouse sexual interest or desire : erotic. **–sex'i•ness** *n.*

Sey•chelles (sā-shĕl', -shĕlz'). Island country in the Indian Ocean E of Tanzania. *Cap.* Victoria. *Pop.* 52,437.

sgd. *abbr.* signed.

sgt. *abbr.* sergeant.

sh. *abbr.* **1.** share (capital stock). **2.** sheet.

shab•by (shăb'ē) *adj.* **-bi•er, -bi•est. 1.** Worn-out : ragged. **2.** Dressed in worn-out, frayed, or threadbare clothes. **3.** Contemptible : nasty. **–shab'bi•ly** *adv.* **–shab'bi•ness** *n.*

shack (shăk) *n.* A small, crude building.

shack•le (shăk'əl) *n.* **1.** A metal ring fastened or locked around the wrist or ankle of a prisoner. **2.** A device used to fasten or couple. **3.** Something that restrains or confines. *–v.* **-led, -ling.** To fasten, restrain, or confine with shackles.

shad (shăd) *n., pl.* **shad** *or* **shads.** A marine food fish of the genus *Alosa* that swims up rivers to spawn.

shade (shād) *n.* **1.** Comparative darkness caused by the interception of light rays. **2.** An area or space of shade. **3.** Shelter from the sun's rays. **4.** A device used to reduce or screen light. **5. shades.** *Slang.* Sunglasses. **6.** Relative obscurity. **7.** Degree of darkness of a color. **8.** A minor variation or difference. **9.** A small amount. **10.** A phantom : ghost. ☆***syns:*** GRADATION, NUANCE *–v.* **shad•ed, shad•ing. 1.** To shield or screen from light or heat. **2.** To obscure : hide. **3.** To mark or draw indications of shade in <*shade* a drawing> **4.** To alter (e.g., meaning) by slight degrees.

shad•ing (shā'dĭng) *n.* **1.** Protection against light or heat. **2.** Marks, as lines, used to represent gradations of colors or darkness. **3.** A slight variation, gradation, or difference.

shad•ow (shăd'ō) *n.* **1.** Partial illumination in an area from which light is blocked by an opaque object. **2.** An image cast on a surface by an object blocking rays of light. **3. a.** Gloom : unhappiness. **b.** Something that causes gloom. **4.** A shaded area in a picture or photograph. **5.** A ghost : phantom. **6.** A slight indication, portion, or amount. *–v.* **1.** To throw a shadow on : shade. **2.** To represent vaguely or mysteriously. **3.** To follow secretly : trail. **–shad'ow•y** *adj.*

shad•ow•box (shăd'ō-bŏks') *v.* To box with an imaginary opponent, as for exercise. **–shad'ow•box'ing** *n.*

shad•y (shā'dē) *adj.* **-i•er, -i•est. 1.** Full of shade. **2.** Of questionable character. ☆***syns:*** DOUBTFUL, DUBIOUS, FISHY, QUESTIONABLE, SUSPECT, SUSPICIOUS **–shad'i•ly** *adv.* **–shad'i•ness** *n.*

shaft (shăft) *n.* **1.** The long narrow body of an arrow or spear. **2.** An arrow or spear. **3.** One of 2 parallel poles by which an animal is harnessed to a vehicle. **4.** A ray or beam of light. **5.** The handle of an implement or tool. **6. a.** A cylindrical bar on which a rotating part turns. **b.** A similar bar that turns and transmits power. **7.** A long, narrow passage beneath the surface of the ground : tunnel. **8.** A vertical passage for an elevator. **9.** An air duct or conduit.

shag (shăg) *n.* **1.** A tangled or matted mass of hair, wool, or fiber. **2.** A coarse long nap, as on woolen cloth.

shag•gy (shăg'ē) *adj.* **-gi•er, -gi•est. 1.** Having or consisting of long, rough hair, wool, or fibers. **2.** Rough and bushy or uneven <*shaggy* hair>

shah (shä) *n.* The title of the former ruler of Iran.

shake (shāk) *v.* **shook** (sho͝ok), **shak•en** (shā'kən), **shak•ing. 1.** To move or cause to move up and down or back and forth with short, quick movements. **2.** To tremble or cause to tremble : quake. **3.** To throw off or displace by or as if by shaking <*shook* the snow from my coat> **4.** To bring or come to a particular condition by or as if by shaking. **5.** To agitate or disturb : disconcert <was *shaken* by the survivors' reports> **6.** To wave or brandish <*shake* one's fist> **7.** To clasp (hands) in greeting, farewell, or agreement. **8.** To make less firm : weaken <*shook* my confidence> *–n.* **1.** An act of shaking. **2. shakes.** *Informal.* Uncontrollable trembling. **3.** *Slang.* Deal : treatment <a fair *shake*> **–shake down.** *Informal.* **1.** To obtain money from by extortion. **2.** To make a complete search of. **3.** To subject to a shakedown test. **–shak'a•ble, shake'a•ble** *adj.*

shake•down (shāk'doun') *n.* **1.** *Informal.* Extortion of money. **2.** *Informal.* A complete search of a person or place. **3.** A test of performance, as of a new aircraft or ship.

shak•er (shā'kər) *n.* **1.** One that shakes <a salt *shaker*><a cocktail *shaker*> **2. Shaker.** A member of a religious sect originating in England in 1747.

Shake•speare (shāk'spîr'), **William.** 1564–1616. English dramatist. **–Shak•spear'e•an, Shake•spear'i•an** *adj.* & *n.*

shake•up (shāk'ŭp') *n.* A complete, often drastic reorganization.

shak•y (shā'kē) *adj.* **-i•er, -i•est. 1.** Tremulous : quaking. **2.** Rickety : unsound. **3.** Unreliable : precarious. **–shak'i•ly** *adv.* **–shak'i•ness** *n.*

shale (shāl) *n.* A rock consisting of claylike particles that split into layers easily.

shale oil *n.* A crude dark oil obtained from oil shale by heating and distillation.

shall (shăl) *v. p.t.* **should** (sho͝od). Used as an auxiliary to indicate simple futurity, determination or promise, inevitability, or command.

shal•lop (shăl'əp) *n.* An open boat having oars or sails or both.

shal•lot (shə-lŏt', shăl'ət) *n.* An onionlike plant, *Allium ascalonicum,* with a mild-flavored edible bulb.

shal•low (shăl'ō) *adj.* **1.** Not deep from bottom to top or surface. **2.** Lacking intellectual or emotional depth. *–n.* A shallow part or place in a body of water.

sham (shăm) *n.* **1.** Something or someone false that purports to be genuine : imitation. **2.** A decorative cover that simulates an article of household linen and is used in its place <a pillow *sham*> *–adj.* Not genuine : false. *–v.* **shammed, sham•ming.** To pretend to have or feel : feign. **–sham'mer** *n.*

sha•man (shä'mən, shā'-) *n.* A priest who uses magic to foretell and control events and to cure the sick. **–sha'man•ism** *n.*

sham•ble (shăm'bəl) *v.* **-bled, -bling.** To walk awkwardly while shuffling the feet. **–sham'ble** *n.*

sham•bles (shăm'bəlz) *pl.n. (sing. in number).* A state or scene of complete disorder or destruction.

shame (shām) *n.* **1.** A painful feeling of guilt, embarrassment, or disgrace. **2.** The capacity to feel shame. **3.** A source of shame. **4.** Dishonor : disgrace. **5.** Something that is unfortunate or regrettable. *–v.* **shamed, sham•ing. 1.** To cause to feel shame. **2.** To bring disgrace upon. **–shame'ful** *adj.* **–shame'ful•ly** *adv.* **–shame'less** *adj.* **–shame'less•ly** *adv.*

shame•faced (shām'fāst') *adj.* **1.** Ashamed. **2.** Bashful. **–shame'fac'ed•ly** (-fā'sĭd-lē) *adv.*

sham•my (shăm'ē) *n. var. of* CHAMOIS 2.

sham•poo (shăm-po͞o') *n., pl.* **-poos. 1.** A preparation, as of soap, used to wash the hair and scalp. **2.** A preparation used to clean rugs or upholstery. **3.** The act or process of washing or cleaning with shampoo. **–sham•poo'** *v.*

sham•rock (shăm'rŏk') *n.* A plant, as a clover, that has 3 leaflets and is regarded as the national emblem of Ireland.

shang•hai (shăng-hī') *v.* **1.** To force to board a ship and serve as a sailor. **2.** To compel to do something, esp. by force.

Shang·hai (shăng-hī′). City of E China, on the Yangtze. *Pop.* 8,100,000.
Shan·gri-la (shăng′grĭ-lä′) *n.* An imaginary paradise on earth : utopia.
shank (shăngk) *n.* **1. a.** The portion of the human leg between the ankle and knee. **b.** A corresponding part in other vertebrates. **2.** A cut of meat, as lamb, from the leg. **3.** The part of an instrument or tool that connects the functioning part and the handle.
shan't (shănt, shänt). Shall not.
shan·tung (shăn-tŭng′) *n.* A fabric, orig. of wild silk, with a nubby surface.
shan·ty (shăn′tē) *n., pl.* **-ties.** A roughly built or dilapidated cabin or shelter : shack.
shape (shāp) *n.* **1.** The outline or surface configuration of something : form. **2.** The contour of a person's body : figure. **3.** Condition, as for effective functioning <a swimmer in good *shape*> **4.** A form in which something may appear or exist. —*v.* **shaped, shap·ing. 1.** To take or cause to take form, esp. a particular form. **2.** To adjust to fit : adapt. **3.** To cause to take a particular course.
shape·less (shāp′lĭs) *adj.* **1.** Lacking definite shape. **2.** Lacking beauty or elegance of shape. **—shape′less·ly** *adv.* **—shape′less·ness** *n.*
shape·ly (shāp′lē) *adj.* **-li·er, -li·est.** Pleasing in shape. **—shape′li·ness** *n.*
shard (shärd) *n.* A piece broken off, esp. from a brittle substance : fragment.
share[1] (shâr) *n.* **1.** A portion belonging to an individual. **2.** One of the equal parts into which the capital stock of a corporation is divided. —*v.* **shared, shar·ing. 1.** To divide and parcel out in shares : apportion. **2.** To participate in, experience, or use in common. **—shar′er** *n.*
share[2] (shâr) *n.* A plowshare.
share·crop·per (shâr′krŏp′ər) *n.* A farmer who gives a share of the crop to the owner of the land he works.
share·hold·er (shâr′hōl′dər) *n.* A stockholder.
shark (shärk) *n.* **1.** Any of various often large and voracious marine fishes of the order Squaliformes, with a cartilaginous skeleton and small, toothlike scales. **2.** A ruthless, greedy person.
shark·skin (shärk′skĭn′) *n.* **1.** The skin of a shark or leather made from it. **2.** A material, as of rayon and acetate, with a smooth, shiny surface.
sharp (shärp) *adj.* **1.** Having a thin, keen edge or a fine point. **2.** Not rounded or smooth <a *sharp* chin> **3.** Not gradual : abrupt <a *sharp* drop> **4.** Distinct : clear <in *sharp* focus> **5.** Astute : shrewd <a *sharp* mind> **6.** Vigorous : energetic. **7.** Alert. **8.** Biting : harsh <*sharp* criticism> **9.** Sudden and shrill <a *sharp* blast of the horn> **10.** Intensely felt : severe <a *sharp* pain> **11.** *Mus.* **a.** Raised in pitch by a semitone. **b.** Above the correct pitch. **12.** *Informal.* Fashionable : stylish <a *sharp* suit> —*adv.* **1.** In a sharp manner. **2.** Precisely : exactly <came at 6 *sharp*> —*n.* **1.** *Mus.* **1.** A sign (♯) indicating that a note is a semitone higher than a given note. **2.** *Informal.* A shrewd cheater, esp. at gambling. **—sharp′ly** *adv.* **—sharp′ness** *n.*
sharp·en (shär′pən) *v.* To make or become sharp or sharper. **—sharp′en·er** *n.*
sharp·shoot·er (shärp′sho͞o′tər) *n.* An expert marksman.
Shas·ta (shăs′tə), **Mount.** Extinct volcano, 14,162 ft (4,319.4 m), in the Cascade Range of N Calif.
shat·ter (shăt′ər) *v.* To smash or burst suddenly into pieces.
shat·ter·proof (shăt′ər-pro͞of′) *adj.* Impervious or resistant to shattering.
shave (shāv) *v.* **shaved, shaved** or **shav·en** (shā′vən), **shav·ing. 1. a.** To remove (bodily hair, esp. the beard) from with a razor. **b.** To cut bodily hair, esp. the beard, close to the surface of the skin. **2. a.** To cut or scrape thin slices of or from. **b.** To cut or scrape into thin slices. **3.** To graze or come close to in passing. —*n.* The act, process, or result of shaving.
shav·er (shā′vər) *n.* **1.** An electrically operated razor. **2.** *Informal.* A young boy.
Shaw (shô), **George Bernard.** 1856–1950. Irish-born English author. **—Sha′vi·an** (shā′vē-ən) *adj.* & *n.*
shawl (shôl) *n.* A square or oblong piece of cloth worn esp. by women as a covering for the head, neck, and shoulders.
shay (shā) *n. Informal.* A chaise.
she (shē) *pron.* **1.** The female last mentioned <*She* left early.> **2.** Something, as a ship, traditionally regarded as feminine.
sheaf (shēf) *n., pl.* **sheaves** (shēvz). **1.** A bundle of stalks, esp. of grain. **2.** A collection of things held or bound together.
shear (shîr) *v.* **sheared, sheared** or **shorn** (shôrn, shōrn), **shear·ing. 1.** To remove (the fleece or hair) from by cutting with a sharp instrument : clip. **2.** To strip of by or as if by clipping. **3.** To cut with shears. **—shear′er** *n.*
shears (shîrz) *pl.n.* **1.** A cutting implement that resembles scissors but is gen. larger. **2.** An implement or machine that cuts with a scissorslike action.
sheath (shēth) *n., pl.* **sheaths** (shē*th*z, shēths). **1.** A case for a blade, as of a sword. **2.** A covering, part, or structure resembling a sheath. **3.** A close-fitting dress.
sheathe (shē*th*) *v.* **sheathed, sheath·ing. 1.** To insert into a sheath. **2.** To provide with a protective covering or structure.
sheath·ing (shē′*th*ĭng) *n.* **1.** A layer of material applied to the outer frame of a building to serve as a base for an exterior covering. **2.** An exterior protective covering on the underwater part of a ship's hull.
she·bang (shə-băng′) *n. Informal.* A situation, contrivance, or collection <mailed the whole *shebang*>
shed[1] (shĕd) *v.* **shed, shed·ding. 1.** To pour or cause to pour forth <*shed* tears><*shed* blood> **2.** To give off : emit <*shed* light> **3.** To throw off without penetration <Glass *sheds* water.> **4.** To cast off, esp. by a natural process <a snake *shedding* its skin>
shed[2] (shĕd) *n.* A small structure for storage or shelter.
she'd (shēd). **1.** She had. **2.** She would.
sheen (shēn) *n.* Luster : brightness.
sheep (shēp) *n., pl.* **sheep. 1.** A hoofed, thick-fleeced mammal of the genus *Ovis*, widely domesticated for wool and meat. **2.** A meek and submissive person.
sheep dog *also* **sheep·dog** (shēp′dôg′, -dŏg′) *n.* A dog that is trained to herd and guard sheep.
sheep·ish (shē′pĭsh) *adj.* **1.** Embarrassed and apologetic. **2.** Timid : shy. **—sheep′ish·ly** *adv.* **—sheep′ish·ness** *n.*
sheep·skin (shēp′skĭn′) *n.* **1. a.** The skin of a sheep either tanned with the fleece left on or in the form of leather. **b.** Parchment. **2.** A diploma.
sheer[1] (shîr) *v.* To swerve from a course.
sheer[2] (shîr) *adj.* **1.** Thin and fine : transparent. **2.** Absolute : utter <*sheer* stupidity> **3.** Almost perpendicular : very steep. **—sheer** *adv.* **—sheer′ness** *n.*
sheet[1] (shēt) *n.* **1.** A large piece of cloth, as cotton, used esp. as a bed covering. **2.** A piece of paper. **3.** A broad, continuous surface <a *sheet* of ice>
sheet[2] (shēt) *n.* **1.** A rope or chain that secures and regulates a sail. **2. sheets.** The spaces at either end of an open boat.
sheet·ing (shē′tĭng) *n.* **1.** Fabric, as plain cotton, made into sheets. **2.** Material, as plastic, manufactured in the form of a continuous sheet.
Sheet·rock (shēt′rŏk′). A trademark for plasterboard.
sheik (shēk, shāk) *n.* The leader of an Arab village, family, or tribe. **—sheik′dom** *n.*
shek·el (shĕk′əl) *n.* See CURRENCY TABLE.
shelf (shĕlf) *n., pl.* **shelves** (shĕlvz). **1.** A flat, usu. narrow and rectangular structure fixed at right angles to a wall to hold or store things. **2.** Something, as a ledge of rock, that resembles a shelf.
shelf life *n.* The length of time during which a material can be stored without deteriorating.
shell (shĕl) *n.* **1. a.** The usu. hard outer covering of certain organisms, as a turtle. **b.** A similar outer covering of a fruit, egg, or nut. **2.** Something resembling a shell <a pastry *shell*> **3.** A long, narrow racing boat propelled by oarsmen. **4. a.** A case containing explosives and fired from a cannon. **b.** A case containing the charge, primer, and shot for smaller guns. —*v.* **1.** To remove from the shell : shuck. **2.** To fire shells at : bombard. **—shell out.** *Informal.* To pay. **—shell′er** *n.* **—shell′-like′** *adj.*
she'll (shēl). **1.** She will. **2.** She shall.
shel·lac (shə-lăk′) *n.* **1.** A purified lac formed into flakes and used esp. in varnishes. **2.** A thin varnish made by dissolving flake shellac in alcohol. —*v.* **-lacked, -lack·ing. 1.** To apply shellac (to). **2.** *Slang.* To defeat roundly.
shell bean *n.* A bean cultivated for its edible seeds rather than for its pods.
Shel·ley (shĕl′ē), **Percy Bysshe.** 1792–1822. English poet.
shell·fire (shĕl′fīr′) *n.* The shooting or firing of shells.
shell·fish (shĕl′fĭsh′) *n.* An aquatic animal, as a clam or lobster, with a shell or shell-like external covering.
shell shock *n.* A nervous disorder originating in trauma suffered under fire in modern warfare. **—shell′-shocked′** *adj.*
shel·ter (shĕl′tər) *n.* **1. a.** Something that provides protection or cover. **b.** A refuge. **2.** The state of being protected or covered. —*v.* To give protection or cover to.
shelve (shĕlv) *v.* **shelved, shelv·ing. 1.** To arrange or store on a shelf. **2.** To put aside or off. **3.** To slope : incline.
shelves (shĕlvz) *n. pl. of* SHELF.
shelv·ing (shĕl′vĭng) *n.* **1.** Shelves as a whole. **2.** Material for shelves.
she·nan·i·gan (shə-năn′ĭ-gən) *n. Informal.* **1.** A devious trick.

2. *often* **shenanigans. a.** Playful activities : mischief. **b.** Shifty or questionable behavior.

shep•herd (shĕp′ərd) *n.* One who takes care of sheep. —*v.* To take care of as or in the manner of a shepherd. **—shep′herd•ess** *n.*

sher•bet (shûr′bĭt) *n.* A sweet, frozen dessert made of fruit juice, water or milk, and gelatin or egg whites.

Sher•i•dan (shĕr′ĭ-dn), **Richard Brinsley.** 1751–1816. English dramatist.

sher•iff (shĕr′ĭf) *n.* A high law-enforcement official of a U.S. county.

sher•ry (shĕr′ē) *n., pl.* **-ries.** A fortified amber-colored wine.

Shet•land pony (shĕt′lənd) *n.* A small, compactly built pony.

shew (shō) *v. archaic var. of* SHOW.

shib•bo•leth (shĭb′ə-ləth) *n.* **1.** A language usage that distinguishes the members of 1 group from another. **2.** A catchword : slogan.

shield (shēld) *n.* **1.** A piece of protective armor carried on the forearm. **2.** Something resembling a shield. **3.** Something that serves to conceal or protect. —*v.* To conceal or protect with or as if with a shield. **—shield′er** *n.*

shield law *n.* A law that protects journalists from being forced to reveal confidential sources of information.

shi•er (shī′ər) *adj. var. compar. of* SHY[1].

shi•est (shī′ĭst) *adj. var. superl. of* SHY[1].

shift (shĭft) *v.* **1.** To change or cause to change place, direction, or position. **2.** To exchange (1 thing for another) : switch. **3.** To change gears in an automobile. **4.** To manage to take care of one's needs : get along. —*n.* **1.** A change from 1 place, direction, or position to another : transfer. **2. a.** A group of workers on duty at the same time. **b.** The working period of such a group. **3.** A gearshift. **4.** A woman's chemise, slip, or loose-fitting dress.

shift•less (shĭft′lĭs) *adj.* Lacking efficiency, ambition, or purpose : inefficient or lazy. **—shift′less•ness** *n.*

shift•y (shĭf′tē) *adj.* **-i•er, -i•est. 1.** Crafty : tricky. **2.** Suggestive of trickiness : furtive. **—shift′i•ly** *adv.* **—shift′i•ness** *n.*

shill (shĭl) *n. Slang.* Someone who works as a decoy, as in a gambling game, by posing as an innocent bystander or a customer.

shil•le•lagh (shə-lā′lē) *n.* A club : cudgel.

shil•ling (shĭl′ĭng) *n.* See CURRENCY TABLE.

shil•ly-shal•ly (shĭl′ē-shăl′ē) *v.* **-lied, -ly•ing.** To be hesitant or indecisive : waver.

shim (shĭm) *n.* A thin wedge of material, as wood, used to fill space, as in leveling a chair on the floor.

shim•mer (shĭm′ər) *v.* To shine with a flickering or wavering light. **—shim′mer** *n.* **—shim′mer•y** *adj.*

†**shim•my** (shĭm′ē) *n., pl.* **-mies. 1.** A dance marked by rapid shaking of the body. **2.** An abnormal vibration or wobble, as in the steering mechanism of an automobile. **3.** *Regional.* A chemise. **—shim′my** *v.*

shin (shĭn) *n.* The front part of the leg below the knee and above the ankle. —*v.* **shinned, shin•ning.** To climb (e.g., a tree) by alternating gripping and pulling with the hands and legs.

shin•bone (shĭn′bōn′) *n.* The tibia.

shin•dig (shĭn′dĭg′) *n. Slang.* A usu. large and festive party.

shine (shīn) *v.* **shone** (shōn) *or* **shined, shin•ing. 1.** To emit or reflect light. **2.** To aim or direct the light of <*shining* the flashlight in the corner> **3.** To distinguish oneself : excel. **4.** To make bright or glossy by polishing. —*n.* **1.** Radiance : brightness. **2.** A polish given to shoes. **3.** Fair weather.

shin•er (shī′nər) *n.* **1.** *Slang.* A black eye. **2.** Any of numerous small, silvery fishes of the family Cyprinidae.

shin•gle[1] (shĭng′gəl) *n.* **1.** A thin rectangular piece of material, as wood or asbestos, laid in overlapping rows to cover the roof or side of a house. **2.** *Informal.* A small signboard. —*v.* **-gled, -gling.** To apply shingles to. **—shin′gler** *n.*

shin•gle[2] (shĭng′gəl) *n.* **1.** Beach gravel consisting of coarse smooth pebbles. **2.** A beach covered with shingle.

shin•gles (shĭng′gəlz) *pl.n. (sing. or pl. in number).* A painful viral infection marked by skin eruptions along a nerve path.

shin•ny (shĭn′ē) *v.* **-nied, -ny•ing.** To climb by shinning.

Shin•to (shĭn′tō′) *n.* The traditional religion of Japan, marked by the worship of nature spirits and ancestors. **—Shin′to•ism** *n.* **—Shin′to•ist** *n.*

shin•y (shī′nē) *adj.* **-i•er, -i•est.** Shining : bright. **—shin′i•ness** *n.*

ship (shĭp) *n.* **1.** A large vessel built for deep-water navigation. **2.** A ship's company. **3.** An airplane, airship, or spacecraft. —*v.* **shipped, ship•ping. 1.** To take or place on board a ship. **2.** To cause to be transported. **3.** To take (water) into a boat. **4.** To enlist for service on a ship.

-ship *suff.* **1.** Quality, state, or condition <scholar*ship*> **2.** Rank, status, or office <professor*ship*> **3.** Art, skill, or craft <penman*ship*>

ship•board (shĭp′bôrd′, -bōrd′) *n.* A ship.

ship•build•ing (shĭp′bĭl′dĭng) *n.* The business of building or designing ships. **—ship′build′er** *n.*

ship•mate (shĭp′māt′) *n.* A fellow sailor.

ship•ment (shĭp′mənt) *n.* **1.** The act or process of shipping goods. **2.** The goods that are shipped.

ship•ping (shĭp′ĭng) *n.* **1.** The act or business of transporting goods. **2.** The body of ships that are in 1 port or belong to 1 country. **—ship′per** *n.*

ship•shape (shĭp′shāp′) *adj.* In good order : tidy. **—ship′shape′** *adv.*

ship•worm (shĭp′wûrm′) *n.* A wormlike marine mollusk of the genera *Teredo* and *Bankia* that bores into wood, often doing extensive damage.

ship•wreck (shĭp′rĕk′) *n.* **1.** The remains of a wrecked ship. **2.** The destruction of a ship. **3.** Total destruction : ruin. —*v.* To suffer or cause to suffer shipwreck.

ship•wright (shĭp′rīt′) *n.* A carpenter employed in ship construction or maintenance.

ship•yard (shĭp′yärd′) *n.* A place where ships are built, repaired, and outfitted.

shire (shīr) *n.* One of the counties of Great Britain.

shirk (shûrk) *v.* To avoid doing (work or duty). **—shirk′er** *n.*

shirr (shûr) *v.* **1.** To make shirring in (fabric). **2.** To bake (eggs) in buttered dishes.

shir•ring (shûr′ĭng) *n.* A decorative gathering of cloth into parallel rows.

shirt (shûrt) *n.* **1.** A garment for the upper body, usu. having a collar, sleeves, and a front opening. **2.** An undershirt.

shirt•ing (shûr′tĭng) *n.* Fabric for making shirts.

shirt•tail (shûrt′tāl′) *n.* The part of a shirt that extends below the waist, esp. in the back.

shirt•waist (shûrt′wāst′) *n.* A woman's dress or blouse styled to resemble a man's shirt.

shish ke•bab (shĭsh′ kə-bŏb′) *n.* Cubes of meat and vegetables, as onions, tomatoes, or green peppers, cooked on skewers.

shiv (shĭv) *n. Slang.* A knife or razor used esp. as a weapon.

shiv•er[1] (shĭv′ər) *v.* To shake from or as if from the cold : tremble. **—shiv′er** *n.* **—shiv′er•y** *adj.*

shiv•er[2] (shĭv′ər) *v.* To break or cause to break into fragments : shatter.

shoal[1] (shōl) *n.* **1.** A shallow place in a body of water. **2.** A sandbar or sandbank.

shoal[2] (shōl) *n.* A large group, esp. of fish.

shoat (shōt) *n.* A young pig.

shock[1] (shŏk) *n.* **1.** A violent impact or collision. **2.** A violent, unexpected disturbance of mental or emotional balance. **3.** An offense to the sense of decency or propriety : outrage. **4.** A physiological reaction to bodily trauma, usu. marked by loss of blood pressure and the lowering of vital signs. **5.** The effect caused by an electric current passing through the body. **6.** Apoplexy. **7.** A shock absorber. —*v.* **1.** To strike with great surprise, agitation, outrage, or disgust. **2.** To subject (an individual) to an electric shock.

shock[2] (shŏk) *n.* **1.** A number of sheaves of grain stacked upright in a field. **2.** A bushy mass <a *shock* of red hair>

shock absorber *n.* Any of various devices for absorbing mechanical shocks, esp. one used in automobiles.

shock•er (shŏk′ər) *n.* Something, as a sensational story or novel, that shocks.

shock•ing (shŏk′ĭng) *adj.* Highly disturbing or distasteful. **—shock′ing•ly** *adv.*

shock therapy *n.* The induction of convulsions by the use of electric current or drugs, as a treatment for mental illness.

shock troops *pl.n.* Military personnel specially trained to lead attacks.

shod•dy (shŏd′ē) *n., pl.* **-dies. 1. a.** Wool fibers obtained by shredding woolen rags or waste. **b.** Yarn or fabric made from shoddy. **2.** Inferior goods. —*adj.* **-di•er, -di•est. 1.** Consisting of or made of shoddy. **2.** Imitative in a cheap way : sham. **3.** Shabby. **—shod′di•ly** *adv.* **—shod′di•ness** *n.*

shoe (sho͞o) *n.* **1.** An outer covering for the human foot. **2.** A horseshoe. **3.** The outer casing of a rubber tire. **4.** The brake part that presses against the wheel or drum to slow or stop its motion. —*v.* **shod** (shŏd), **shoe•ing.** To provide or fit with shoes.

shoe•horn (sho͞o′hôrn′) *n.* A curved tool, as of horn, used for putting on a shoe.

shoe•lace (sho͞o′lās′) *n.* A cord used for lacing shoes.

shoe•mak•er (sho͞o′mā′kər) *n.* One who repairs or makes shoes.

shoe•string (sho͞o′strĭng′) *n.* **1.** A shoelace. **2.** A very small amount of money.

sho·ji (shō'jē) *n.* A translucent screen used as a partition or door in a Japanese house.
shone (shōn) *v. var. p.t. & p.p. of* SHINE.
shoo-in (shōō'ĭn') *n. Informal.* An easy and sure winner.
shook (shŏŏk) *v. p.t. of* SHAKE.
shook-up (shŏŏk-ŭp') *adj. Slang.* Emotionally upset : disturbed.
shoot (shōōt) *v.* **shot** (shŏt), **shoot·ing. 1. a.** To hit, kill, or wound with a missile. **b.** To fire (a missile) from a weapon. **c.** To fire (a weapon). **2.** To send forth swiftly or forcibly <*shot* a rocket into space> **3.** To pass over, along, or through swiftly <*shoot* the rapids> **4.** To record on film : photograph. **5.** To stick or cause to stick out : extend. **6.** To move rapidly : dart. **7. a.** To begin to grow by or as if by germinating : sprout. **b.** To develop : mature. **8.** To propel (e.g., a ball) toward an objective. **—shoot up. 1.** *Informal.* To rise suddenly and rapidly. **2.** *Slang.* To inject (a narcotic) directly into a vein. *—n.* **1. a.** The young growth from a germinating seed : sprout. **b.** A plant part, as a leaf, that has just begun to grow or develop. **2.** A shooting party or match. **—shoot'er** *n.*
shooting iron *n. Informal.* A handgun, esp. a six-shooter.
shooting star *n.* METEOR 1.
shoot-out *also* **shoot·out** (shōōt'out') *n.* An armed confrontation in which opponents shoot firearms at one another.
shop (shŏp) *n.* **1.** A retail store. **2.** A place where goods are manufactured or repaired : factory. **3.** A workshop. *—v.* **shopped, shop·ping.** To visit stores to examine or buy merchandise. **—shop'per** *n.*
shop·keep·er (shŏp'kē'pər) *n.* An operator of a retail shop.
shop·lift·er (shŏp'lĭf'tər) *n.* Someone who steals merchandise on display in stores. **—shop'lift'** *v.* **—shop'lift'ing** *n.*
shop·talk (shŏp'tôk') *n.* Talk about or topics peculiar to a business or occupation.
shop·worn (shŏp'wôrn', -wōrn') *adj.* Tarnished, frayed, or faded from long display or too much handling in a store.
shore[1] (shôr, shōr) *n.* The land along the edge of a body of water, as an ocean.
shore[2] (shôr, shōr) *v.* **shored, shor·ing.** To support, as with an inclined timber : prop up.
shore bird *n.* A bird, as a sandpiper, that frequents coastal or inland shores.
shore patrol *n.* A detail of the U.S. Navy, Marine Corps, or Coast Guard functioning as military police ashore.
shorn (shôrn, shōrn) *v. var. p.p. of* SHEAR.
short (shôrt) *adj.* **1.** Having little length or height. **2.** Of brief duration in time. **3.** Rudely abrupt : curt. **4.** Insufficient : inadequate. **5.** Not very great in distance. **6.** Containing a large amount of shortening : flaky. **7. a.** Not owning the stocks or commodities one is selling. **b.** Relating to or designating a sale of stocks or goods that the seller does not yet own but must produce to meet the terms of a contract. *—adv.* **1.** Suddenly and abruptly. **2.** At a point before a goal, limit, or target. **3.** Without owning what one is selling <sold *short*> *—n.* **1.** Something that is short. **2. shorts.** Trousers or underpants that extend to the knee or above. **3.** A short circuit. *—v.* To have or cause to have a short circuit. **—short'ness** *n.*
short·age (shôr'tĭj) *n.* A deficiency in the amount needed : insufficiency.
short·bread (shôrt'brĕd') *n.* A rich cookie made of flour, sugar, and butter.
short·cake (shôrt'kāk') *n.* A dessert consisting of a rich biscuit split, filled with fruit, and topped with cream.
short·change (shôrt'chānj') *v.* To give less change than is due, esp. intentionally.
short circuit *n. Elect.* A low-resistance connection, often accidentally established, between 2 points in a circuit. **—short'-cir'cuit** *v.*
short·com·ing (shôrt'kŭm'ĭng) *n.* A fault : failing.
short cut *n.* **1.** A shorter, more direct route than the one customarily taken. **2.** A faster method of doing something.
short·en (shôr'tn) *v.* To make or become short or shorter. **—short'en·er** *n.*
short·en·ing (shôr'tn-ĭng, shôrt'nĭng) *n.* A fat, as butter or lard, that makes cake or pastry light and flaky.
short·fall (shôrt'fôl') *n.* **1.** A failure to reach a need, level, or goal : shortage. **2.** The amount of a shortfall.
short·hand (shôrt'hănd') *n.* Any of several systems of rapid handwriting in which symbols and abbreviations represent words, phrases, and letters : stenography.
short-hand·ed (shôrt'hăn'dĭd) *adj.* Lacking the necessary number of workers.
short-horn (shôrt'hôrn') *n.* One of a breed of cattle orig. developed in England and having short curved horns.
short-lived (shôrt'līvd', -lĭvd') *adj.* Living or lasting for a brief time.
short·ly (shôrt'lē) *adv.* **1.** In a short time : soon. **2.** In a few words : succinctly.
short order *n.* Food quickly cooked and served, as at a diner.
short shrift *n.* **1.** A short respite granted a condemned person for confession before execution. **2.** Little sympathy or heed.
short·sight·ed (shôrt'sī'tĭd) *adj.* **1.** Near-sighted : myopic. **2.** Without foresight. **—short'sight'ed·ness** *n.*
short·stop (shôrt'stŏp') *n. Baseball.* **1.** The position between 2nd and 3d bases. **2.** The player who plays shortshop.
short story *n.* A short fictional prose narrative aiming at unity of characterization, theme, and effect.
short subject *n.* A brief film projected with a featured motion picture.
short-tem·pered (shôrt'tĕm'pərd) *adj.* Easily moved to anger : irascible.
short-term (shôrt'tûrm') *adj.* **1.** Involving or occurring over a short time period. **2.** Of or relating to a financial transaction, as a loan, based on a time period usu. of less than 1 year.
short ton *n.* See MEASUREMENT TABLE.
short wave *n.* A radio wave with a wavelength of 80 m or less. **—short'wave'** *adj.*
Shos·ta·ko·vich (shŏs'tə-kō'vĭch), **Dmitri.** 1906–75. Russian composer.
shot[1] (shŏt) *n.* **1.** The discharge of a weapon, as a gun. **2.** *pl.* **shot. a.** A missile, as a bullet, that is fired from a weapon. **b.** A group of pellets to be fired from a shotgun. **3.** A throw, hit, stroke, or drive in any of several games. **4.** A marksman. **5.** Reach : range. **6.** A guess, try, or opportunity. **7.** The metal ball that is thrown for distance in the shot-put. **8. a.** A photograph. **b.** A single photographed scene or take in a motion picture. **9.** A hypodermic injection. **10.** A drink of liquor.
shot[2] (shŏt) *v. p.t. & p.p. of* SHOOT.
shot·gun (shŏt'gŭn') *n.* A gun with a smooth bore that fires a charge of small shot at close range.
shot-put (shŏt'pŏŏt') *n.* An athletic event in which participants throw the shot for distance. **—shot'-put'ter** *n.*
should (shŏŏd) *v. p.t. of* **shall.** Used to express duty, obligation, necessity, probability, expectation, or contingency.
shoul·der (shōl'dər) *n.* **1. a.** The part of the human body between the neck and upper arm. **b.** The joint connecting the arm with the trunk. **c.** The corresponding part of an animal's body. **2.** A sloping or projecting part, as the edge bordering a roadway, that resembles the human shoulder. *—v.* **1.** To carry on or push with the shoulder. **2.** To take on : assume <*shoulder* blame>
shoulder belt *n.* An automobile safety belt that is worn diagonally across the body and over the shoulder.
shoulder blade *n.* The scapula.
should·n't (shŏŏd'nt). Should not.
shout (shout) *n.* A loud cry : yell. **—shout** *v.* **—shout'er** *n.*
shove (shŭv) *v.* **shoved, shov·ing.** To push rudely or forcefully. **—shove** *n.*
shov·el (shŭv'əl) *n.* **1.** A tool with a long handle and a scoop for picking up material such as dirt and snow. **2.** The amount the scoop of a shovel can hold. *—v.* **-eled, -el·ing** *or* **-elled, -el·ling. 1.** To dig into, move, or remove with a shovel. **2.** To make or clear out with a shovel.
show (shō) *v.* **showed, shown** (shōn) *or* **showed, show·ing. 1.** To allow or cause to be seen : display <*show* surprise> **2.** To guide : conduct <*showed* me around town> **3.** To teach : instruct <*showed* her how to cook> **4.** To manifest : reveal <a coat that *showed* signs of wear> **5.** To bestow : confer <*showed* pity> **6.** To be visible <The moon *showed* in the treetops.> **7.** To establish : prove <*shows* that he cares> **8.** To finish 3rd or better in a race. ☆**syns:** DEMONSTRATE, DISPLAY, EVIDENCE, EVINCE, EXHIBIT, MANIFEST **—show off.** To behave or display ostentatiously or conspicuously. **—show up.** To put in an appearance : arrive *—n.* **1.** A demonstration : display. **2.** A false appearance : pretense. **3.** A spectacle. **4.** A public exhibition or theatrical presentation. **5.** *Informal.* An undertaking <tried to run the whole *show*> **6.** 3rd place or better in a race.
show·case (shō'kās') *n.* A case in which objects are displayed, as in a store. *—v.* **-cased, -cas·ing.** To display prominently and advantageously : feature.
show·down (shō'doun') *n.* An action, event, or circumstance that forces the settlement of a disputed issue.
show·er (shou'ər) *n.* **1.** A brief fall of rain, hail, snow, or sleet. **2.** An abundant flow : outflow <a *shower* of criticism> **3.** A party given in honor of someone to whom gifts are presented. **4.** A bath in which water is sprayed on the bather. *—v.* **1.** To spray : sprinkle. **2.** To bestow in abundance. **3.** To fall or pour down in a shower. **4.** To take a shower. **—show'er·y** *adj.*
show·ing (shō'ĭng) *n.* **1.** The act of displaying or presenting. **2.** Performance, as in a competition or test of skill.
show·man (shō'mən) *n.* **1.** A theatrical producer. **2.** Someone

with a flair for visual or dramatic effectiveness. **–show'man•ship'** *n.*
show•off (shō'ôf', -ŏf') *n.* Someone who shows off : exhibitionist.
show place *also* **show•place** (shō'plās') *n.* A place that is shown, admired, or viewed for its beauty or historical interest.
show room *also* **show•room** (shō'ro͞om', -ro͝om') *n.* A room in which merchandise is displayed.
show•y (shō'ē) *adj.* **-i•er, -i•est.** Striking and conspicuous : flashy. **–show'i•ly** *adv.* **–show'i•ness** *n.*
shpt. *abbr.* shipment.
shr. *abbr.* share.
shrank (shrăngk) *v. var. p.t. of* SHRINK
shrap•nel (shrăp'nəl) *n., pl.* **-nel. 1.** An artillery shell containing metal balls that explodes in the air. **2.** Fragments from a high-explosive shell.
shred (shrĕd) *n.* **1.** A long, narrow strip torn or cut off. **2.** A small amount : bit. *–v.* **shred•ded** *or* **shred, shred•ding.** To tear or cut into shreds.
Shreve•port (shrēv'pôrt', -pōrt'). City of NW La., near the Tex. border. *Pop.* 205,815.
shrew (shro͞o) *n.* **1.** Any of several very small mouselike mammals of the family Soricidae, with a narrow, pointed snout. **2.** A scold. **–shrew'ish** *adj.*
shrewd (shro͞od) *adj.* Clever and usu. practical. ☆**syns:** ASTUTE, CAGEY, SLICK **–shrewd'ly** *adv.* **–shrewd'ness** *n.*
shriek (shrēk) *n.* A loud, sharp, shrill cry : scream. **–shriek** *v.*
shrike (shrīk) *n.* Any of various carnivorous birds of the family Laniidae, having a hooked bill and often impaling their prey on sharp-pointed thorns.

shrike

shrill (shrĭl) *adj.* Thin and high-pitched : piercing. *–v.* To make a shrill sound. **–shrill'ness** *n.* **–shril'ly** *adv.*
shrimp (shrĭmp) *n., pl.* **shrimp** *or* **shrimps. 1.** Any of various small, often edible marine crustaceans of the suborder Natantia. **2.** *Slang.* One that is small or unimportant.
shrine (shrīn) *n.* **1.** A receptacle for sacred relics. **2.** The tomb of a venerated person, esp. a saint. **3.** An object or site hallowed for its associations. **–shrine** *v.*
shrink (shrĭngk) *v.* **shrank** (shrăngk) *or* **shrunk** (shrŭngk), **shrunk** *or* **shrunk•en** (shrŭng'kən), **shrink•ing. 1.** To become smaller, as from heat : contract. **2.** To lessen, as in amount : dwindle. **3.** To recoil : flinch. *–n. Slang.* A psychiatrist. **–shrink'a•ble** *adj.* **–shrink'er** *n.*
shrink•age (shrĭng'kĭj) *n.* **1.** The process of shrinking. **2.** A reduction in value : depreciation. **3.** The amount or extent to which something lessens or contracts.
shrinking violet *n. Informal.* A shy or retiring person.
shrive (shrīv) *v.* **shrove** (shrōv) *or* **shrived, shriv•en** (shrĭv'ən) *or* **shrived, shriv•ing.** To hear the confession of and give absolution to.
shriv•el (shrĭv'əl) *v.* **-eled, -el•ing** *or* **-elled, -el•ling.** To shrink or cause to shrink and wrinkle.
shroud (shroud) *n.* **1.** A cloth used to wrap a dead body. **2.** Something that screens, conceals, or protects. **3.** One of a set of ropes stretched from a vessels's masthead to the sides to support the mast. *–v.* To screen from view : conceal.
shrub (shrŭb) *n.* A low, woody plant that gen. has several stems. **–shrub'by** *adj.*
shrub•ber•y (shrŭb'ə-rē) *n., pl.* **-ies. 1.** A group of shrubs. **2.** Shrubs in general.
shrug (shrŭg) *v.* **shrugged, shrug•ging.** To raise (the shoulders), esp. in doubt, indifference, or disdain. **–shrug off. 1.** To minimize. **2.** To rid oneself of. **3.** To wriggle out of (a garment). **–shrug** *n.*
shrunk (shrŭngk) *v. var. p.t. & p.p. of* SHRINK.
shrunk•en (shrŭng'kən) *v. var. p.p. of* SHRINK.
shtg. *abbr.* shortage.
shtick (shtĭk) *n. Slang.* **1.** A characteristic talent, attribute, or trait. **2.** One's method of doing something. **3.** An entertainment routine.
shuck (shŭk) *n.* An outer covering : husk or shell. *–v.* **1.** To remove the shuck from. **2.** To cast off (e.g., clothing).
shud•der (shŭd'ər) *v.* To tremble convulsively, as from aversion or fear : shiver. **–shud'der** *n.*
shuf•fle (shŭf'əl) *v.* **-fled, -fling. 1.** To move with a dragging or shambling gait. **2.** To move (something) from 1 place to another. **3.** To handle or mix together in a haphazard, disorderly fashion. **4.** To change the order of (e.g., playing cards) by mixing together. **–shuf'fle** *n.*
shuf•fle•board (shŭf'əl-bôrd', -bōrd') *n.* A game in which long-handled sticks are used to push disks along a smooth, level surface toward numbered squares.
shun (shŭn) *v.* **shunned, shun•ning.** To keep away from deliberately and esp. consistently : eschew. **–shun'ner** *n.*
shunt (shŭnt) *n.* **1.** The act or process of moving to an alternate course. **2.** A railroad switch. *–v.* **1.** To turn or cause to turn to 1 side. **2.** To shift or switch (a train or car) from 1 track to another.
shut (shŭt) *v.* **shut, shut•ting. 1.** To move (e.g., a door) so as to cover an opening : close. **2.** To block entrance, passage, or access to. **3.** To lock up : confine. **4.** To halt, cease, or suspend operations (in) <*shut* down a factory> **5.** To close by bringing together the parts of <*shut* his book> **–shut out. 1.** To keep out. **2.** To prevent (an opposing player or team) from scoring in a game. **–shut up.** To be, cause to be, or become silent.
shut•down (shŭt'doun') *n.* A temporary stoppage of operations, as in a factory.
shut•eye (shŭt'ī') *n. Slang.* Sleep.
shut-in (shŭt'ĭn') *n.* Someone who has to stay indoors because of illness or disability.
shut•out (shŭt'out') *n.* A game in which 1 side does not score.
shut•ter (shŭt'ər) *n.* **1.** A usu. hinged movable cover for a window or door. **2.** A device on a camera that opens and shuts the lens opening to expose the film.
shut•ter•bug (shŭt'ər-bŭg') *n. Informal.* An amateur photographer.
shut•tle (shŭt'l) *n.* **1.** A device used in weaving that carries the woof threads between the warp threads. **2.** A vehicle, as a train or plane, that travels back and forth over an established, often short route. *–v.* **-tled, -tling.** To move back and forth like a shuttle.
shut•tle•cock (shŭt'l-kŏk') *n.* A light rounded object, as of cork, that has a crown of feathers and is used in badminton.
shy¹ (shī) *adj.* **shi•er** *or* **shy•er, shi•est** *or* **shy•est. 1.** Readily frightened : timid. **2.** Bashfully reserved : diffident. **3.** Cautious : wary. **4.** *Informal.* Lacking : deficient. *–v.* **shied, shy•ing. 1.** To move aside suddenly through fear. **2.** To draw back : recoil. **–shy'ly** *adv.* **–shy'ness** *n.*
shy² (shī) *v.* **shied, shy•ing.** To throw swiftly, esp. with a sideways motion : toss.
shy•lock (shī'lŏk') *n.* An unscrupulous moneylender : shark.
shy•ster (shī'stər) *n. Slang.* An unscrupulous or unethical politician or lawyer.
Si *symbol for* SILICON.
Si•am sī-ăm'). **1. Gulf of.** Arm of the South China Sea between the Malay Peninsula and Indochina. **2.** Thailand. **–Si'a•mese'** (sī'ə-mēz', -mēs') *adj. & n.*
Siamese twin *n.* One of a set of twins born with their bodies joined.
Si•be•ri•a (sī-bîr'ē-ə). Region of N Asian USSR, from the Urals to the Pacific. **–Si•be'ri•an** *adj. & n.*
sib•i•lant (sĭb'ə-lənt) *adj.* Producing, containing, or having a hissing sound. *–n.* A sibilant speech sound, as (s) or (z).
sib•ling (sĭb'lĭng) *n.* One of 2 or more offspring of the same parents.
sib•yl (sĭb'əl) *n.* A female prophet. **–sib'yl•line'** (-ə-līn', -lēn') *adj.*
sic¹ (sĭk, sēk) *adv.* So : thus. Used in written material to indicate that a passage, phrase, or word is as it was in an original <wrote me that her mother was two *sic* busy to receive visitors>
sic² (sĭk) *v.* **sicced, sic•cing** *also* **sicked, sick•ing.** To urge to attack or harry.
Sic•i•ly (sĭs'ə-lē). Island of S Italy, in the Mediterranean. **–Si•cil'ian** *adj. & n.*
sick (sĭk) *adj.* **1. a.** In poor health : ill. **b.** Nauseated. **2.** Of, pertaining to, or for sick persons <*sick* leave> **3.** Unwholesome : morbid. **4. a.** Revolted : disgusted. **b.** Experiencing an aversion from excess : weary <*sick* of working> **c.** Pining : longing. **–sick'ness** *n.*
sick•bay (sĭk'bā') *n.* The hospital and dispensary of a ship.
sick•bed (sĭk'bĕd') *n.* A bed in which a sick person lies.
sick•en (sĭk'ən) *v.* To make or become sick. **–sick'en•ing** *adj.*

sick•le (sĭk′əl) *n.* A semicircular blade attached to a handle used for cutting grain or tall grass.

sickle cell anemia *n.* A hereditary anemia marked by abnormal crescent-shaped red blood cells that are deficient in oxygen.

sick•ly (sĭk′lē) *adj.* **-li•er, -li•est. 1.** Prone to sickness : ailing. **2.** Of, caused by, or associated with sickness <a *sickly* look> **3.** Weak : feeble <a *sickly* smile>

side (sīd) *n.* **1.** A surface or border of an object, esp. the surface joining a bottom and a top. **2.** One of the 2 surfaces of a flat object, as a piece of paper. **3.** The part to the left or right of a vertical axis, as of the body. **4.** The space immediately beside someone or something. **5. a.** Something, as a set of opinions, considered as being opposite to another. **b.** One of the parties to a debate or dispute. **6.** An aspect or quality. *—adj.* **1.** Located to or on a side. **2.** To or from 1 side : oblique. **3.** Incidental <a *side* interest> **4.** Supplementary : additional <a *side* order of salad> *—v.* **sid•ed, sid•ing.** To support the opinion or position of a particular side. **—sid′ed** *adj.*

side•arm (sīd′ärm′) *adj. Baseball.* Performed with a sideways motion of the arm. **—side′arm′** *adv.*

side arm *n.* A weapon, as a pistol, that can be carried at the side or waist.

side•board (sīd′bôrd′, -bōrd′) *n.* A piece of furniture that holds linens and tableware.

side•burns (sīd′bûrnz′) *pl.n.* Whiskers down the sides of a man's face in front of the ears.

side•car (sīd′kär′) *n.* A 1-wheeled car for a passenger at the side of a motorcycle.

side effect *n.* A secondary and usu. untoward effect, esp. of a drug.

side•kick (sīd′kĭk′) *n. Slang.* A close friend : pal.

side•light (sīd′līt′) *n.* Incidental knowledge or information about a subject.

side•line (sīd′līn′) *n.* **1.** A boundary line along either of the 2 sides of a playing court or field. **2.** A subsidiary activity, job, or line of merchandise.

side•long (sīd′lông′, -lŏng′) *adj.* Directed or tending to 1 side : oblique <a *sidelong* glance> **—side′long′** *adv.*

side•man (sīd′măn′) *n.* A jazz musician.

si•de•re•al (sī-dîr′ē-əl) *adj.* Of, relating to, or measured by means of the stars.

side•sad•dle (sīd′săd′l) *n.* A saddle on which a woman may sit with both legs on the same side of the horse. *—adv.* On a sidesaddle.

side•show (sīd′shō′) *n.* **1.** A small show offered in addition to a main attraction, as of a carnival. **2.** A subordinate incident.

side•split•ting (sīd′splĭt′ĭng) *adj.* Extremely funny : hilarious.

side•step (sīd′stĕp′) *v.* **1.** To step out of the way of. **2.** To evade : avoid.

side stroke *n.* A swimming stroke performed on 1 side in which the arms are thrust forward alternately while the legs do a scissors kick.

side•swipe (sīd′swīp′) *v.* To strike along the side in passing. **—side′swipe′** *n.*

side•track (sīd′trăk′) *v.* **1.** To switch from a main railroad track to a siding. **2.** To deviate from a main issue, purpose, or course. *—n.* A railroad siding.

side•walk (sīd′wôk′) *n.* A walk for pedestrians along the side of a street or road.

side wall *n.* One of the side surfaces of an automobile tire.

side•ways (sīd′wāz′) *adv.* **1.** Toward, to, from, or at 1 side. **2.** With 1 side forward. **—side′ways′** *adj.*

side•wind•er (sīd′wīn′dər) *n.* A small rattlesnake, *Crotalus cerastes,* of the SW U.S. and Mexico, that moves by a distinctive lateral, looping bodily motion.

sid•ing (sī′dĭng) *n.* **1.** A short section of railroad track linked to a main track. **2.** Material used for covering the sides of a frame building.

si•dle (sīd′l) *v.* **-dled, -dling.** To move sideways, esp. furtively.

siege (sēj) *n.* **1.** The surrounding of a town or fortress by an army in order to capture it. **2.** A prolonged attack, as of illness.

Si•en•a (sē-ĕn′ə). City of C Italy, S of Florence. *Pop.* 63,961. **—Si′en•ese′** *adj.* & *n.*

si•er•ra (sē-ĕr′ə) *n.* A rugged mountain range whose tops have a serrate outline.

Sierra Le•one (lē-ōn′). Country of NW Africa, on the Atlantic. *Cap.* Freetown. *Pop.* 4,125,000.

Sierra Nevada. Mountain range of E Calif., rising to 14,494 ft (4,420.7 m).

si•es•ta (sē-ĕs′tə) *n.* A rest or nap taken esp. after the midday meal.

sieve (sĭv) *n.* A wire mesh utensil used for straining, sifting, ricing, or puréeing. **—sieve** *v.*

sift (sĭft) *v.* **1.** To pass through or as if through a sieve. **2.** To separate by or as if by using a sieve. **3.** To subject to careful examination. **—sift′er** *n.*

sig. *abbr.* **1.** signal. **2.** signature.

sigh (sī) *v.* **1.** To exhale a long, audible breath, as in sorrow, weariness, or relief. **2.** To experience grief or longing. **—sigh** *n.*

†**sight** (sīt) *n.* **1.** The act, process, or faculty of seeing. **2.** The range of a person's vision. **3.** Something seen : view. **4.** Something worth seeing. **5.** A device, as on a firearm, that guides the eye in aiming. **6.** *Regional.* A large number or quantity. *—v.* **1.** To catch sight of : see. **2.** To take aim.

sight•ed (sī′tĭd) *adj.* Capable of seeing.

sight•less (sīt′lĭs) *adj.* Unable to see : blind.

sight•ly (sīt′lē) *adj.* **-li•er, -li•est.** Pleasant to the sight.

sight-read (sīt′rēd′) *v.* To read or perform (e.g., music) without preparation or prior study. **—sight′-read′er** *n.*

sight•see•ing (sīt′sē′ĭng) *n.* The act of traveling around to see places of interest. **—sight′se′er** *n.*

sign (sīn) *n.* **1.** Something suggesting the presence or existence of a fact, state, or quality : indication. **2.** A gesture that conveys an idea, wish, or command. **3.** A notice displayed publicly as an advertisement, to impart information, or to give guidance. **4.** A symbol. **5.** A portent : omen. **6.** A vestige or trace. **7.** One of the 12 divisions of the zodiac. ☆***syns:*** EVIDENCE, INDICATION, INDICATOR, MANIFESTATION, MARK, SYMPTOM, TOKEN *—v.* **1.** To write one's signature on. **2.** To approve, guarantee, or ratify by affixing a signature or seal. **3.** To transfer or relinquish legally by signature. **4.** To make or mark with a sign : signal. **—sign off.** To stop transmission after identifying the broadcasting station. **—sign on.** To agree to or hire for work. **—sign out.** To record the departure of by signing. **—sign′er** *n.*

sig•nal (sĭg′nəl) *n.* **1.** A sign that serves to communicate a notice or warning. **2.** Something that indicates that action is to begin. **3. a.** *Electron.* An impulse or fluctuating electric quantity, as voltage or current, whose variations represent coded information. **b.** The sound, image, or message transmitted or received in electronic communications, as television. *—adj.* Out of the ordinary : outstanding. *—v.* **-naled, -nal•ing** or **-nalled, -nal•ling. 1.** To give a signal (to). **2.** To communicate or make known by signals. **—sig′nal•ly** *adv.*

sig•nal•ize (sĭg′nə-līz′) *v.* **-ized, -iz•ing. 1.** To make noticeable. **2.** To point out in particular.

sig•na•to•ry (sĭg′nə-tôr′ē, -tōr′ē) *n., pl.* **-ries.** A signer of something, as a treaty.

sig•na•ture (sĭg′nə-cho͝or′, -chər) *n.* **1.** A person's name as written by that person. **2.** Something, as a distinctive mark, that indicates identity. **3.** The symbol on a musical staff that indicates the key or meter.

sign•board (sīn′bôrd′, -bōrd′) *n.* A board that bears a sign.

sig•net (sĭg′nĭt) *n.* A seal, esp. one used to stamp official documents.

sig•nif•i•cance (sĭg-nĭf′ĭ-kəns) *n.* **1.** The state or quality of being significant : importance. **2.** The meaning of something : import. **3.** Implied meaning.

sig•nif•i•cant (sĭg-nĭf′ĭ-kənt) *adj.* **1.** Having or expressing meaning, often hidden meaning : meaningful. **2.** Important : weighty. **—sig•nif′i•cant•ly** *adv.*

sig•ni•fy (sĭg′nə-fī′) *v.* **-fied, -fy•ing. 1.** To be a sign of : betoken. **2.** To make known by a sign : indicate. **3.** To have importance. **—sig′ni•fi•ca′tion** *n.*

sign language *n.* A communication system using hand gestures.

sign•post (sīn′pōst′) *n.* A post that bears a sign.

Sikh (sēk) *n.* A member of a monotheistic Hindu religious sect. **—Sikh′ism** *n.*

Sik•kim (sĭk′ĭm). State and former kingdom of NE India, in the E Himalayas.

si•lage (sī′lĭj) *n.* Fodder prepared for use by being stored and fermented in a silo.

si•lence (sī′ləns) *n.* **1.** The state, fact, or quality of being silent. **2.** The absence of sound : stillness. **3.** Failure or refusal to disclose : secrecy. *—v.* **-lenced, -lenc•ing. 1.** To cause to be silent : still. **2.** To suppress.

si•lenc•er (sī′lən-sər) *n.* A device for deadening the sound of a gunshot.

si•lent (sī′lənt) *adj.* **1.** Making no sound : quiet. **2. a.** Unwilling to speak : taciturn. **b.** Unable to speak : mute. **3.** Unexpressed : tacit. **4.** Unpronounced, as the *g* in *gnome.* ☆***syns:*** HUSHED, NOISELESS, SOUNDLESS, STILL **—si′lent•ly** *adv.*

Si•le•sia (sī-lē′zhə, -shə, sĭ-). Region of C Europe, chiefly in SW Poland.

sil•hou•ette (sĭl′o͞o-ĕt′) *n.* **1.** A representation of the outline of something, as a human profile, filled in with a solid color, esp. black. **2.** The outline of a body or object <the *silhouette* of

a tree> —*v.* **-et•ted, -et•ting.** To represent or cause to be seen as a silhouette.
sil•i•ca (sĭl'ĭ-kə) *n.* A crystalline compound that occurs widely in mineral form, as quartz, sand, and flint.
sil•i•cate (sĭl'ĭ-kāt', -kĭt) *n.* Any of numerous compounds containing silicon, oxygen, and a metallic or organic radical.
si•li•ceous (sĭ-lĭsh'əs) *adj.* Of, pertaining to, containing, or resembling silica.
sil•i•con (sĭl'ĭ-kən, -kŏn') *n.* *Symbol* **Si** A nonmetallic element that occurs in both crystalline and amorphous forms and is used in glass, concrete, and silicones.
sil•i•cone (sĭl'ĭ-kōn') *n.* Any of a group of semi-inorganic polymers used in adhesives, lubricants, paints, and electrical insulation.
sil•i•co•sis (sĭl'ĭ-kō'sĭs) *n.* A disease of the lungs caused by inhalation of silica dust over a long time period.
silk (sĭlk) *n.* **1.** The fine, lustrous fiber produced by the larvae of certain insects, esp. the silkworm. **2.** Fabric or thread made from silk. **—silk'en** *adj.* **—silk'y** *adj.*
silk-cot•ton tree (sĭlk'kŏt'n) *n.* A tropical American tree, *Ceiba pentandra,* cultivated for its fruit containing the silklike fiber kapok.

silk-cotton tree

silk screen *n.* A stencil method in which ink is forced through a screen of fabric, esp. silk, onto a printing surface. **—silk'-screen'** *v.*
silk•worm (sĭlk'wûrm') *n.* A caterpillar that produces a silk cocoon, esp. the larva of an Asian moth, *Bombyx mori,* that spins a cocoon of fine lustrous fiber.
sill (sĭl) *n.* A horizontal supporting member, as of wood, that forms the bottom part of a window or door frame.
sil•ly (sĭl'ē) *adj.* **-li•er, -li•est. 1.** Lacking or showing a lack of good sense : foolish or stupid. **2.** Lacking seriousness or substance : frivolous. **—sil'li•ness** *n.*
si•lo (sī'lō) *n., pl.* **-los. 1.** A pit or tall, cylindrical structure for the storage of fodder. **2.** An underground shelter for a missile.
silt (sĭlt) *n.* A sedimentary material consisting of fine mineral particles found esp. at the bottom of bodies of water. —*v.* To fill, cover, or obstruct with silt.
silt•stone (sĭlt'stōn') *n.* Stone consisting mainly of hardened silt.
sil•ver (sĭl'vər) *n.* **1.** Symbol **Ag** A lustrous, white, ductile, malleable metallic element used in jewelry, tableware, and coinage. **2.** Coins made of silver. **3.** Household articles, esp. tableware, made of or plated with silver. **4.** A medium gray color. —*adj.* **1.** Of the color silver. **2.** Persuasive : eloquent. —*v.* To plate, cover, or decorate with or as if with silver.
silver bromide *n.* A crystalline compound used as the light-sensitive component on photographic plates and films.
sil•ver•fish (sĭl'vər-fĭsh') *n.* A silvery, wingless insect, *Lepisma saccharina,* that causes damage to books and clothing.
silver iodide *n.* A pale-yellow powder used in photography and as an antiseptic.
silver nitrate *n.* A poisonous, colorless crystalline compound used in photography and as an external antiseptic.
sil•ver•smith (sĭl'vər-smĭth') *n.* Someone who makes or repairs articles of silver.
sil•ver•ware (sĭl'vər-wâr') *n.* Tableware, as forks, knives, and spoons, made of or plated with silver.
sim•i•an (sĭm'ē-ən) *adj.* Of, relating to, or resembling an ape or monkey. —*n.* An ape or monkey.
sim•i•lar (sĭm'ə-lər) *adj.* Having resemblance but not identical. **—sim'i•lar'i•ty** *n.* **—sim'i•lar•ly** *adv.*
sim•i•le (sĭm'ə-lē) *n.* A figure of speech in which 2 unlike things are compared, as in "hair like silk."
si•mil•i•tude (sĭ-mĭl'ĭ-to͞od', -tyo͞od') *n.* Resemblance : similarity.
sim•mer (sĭm'ər) *v.* **1.** To cook just below or at the boiling point. **2.** To be nearly at the point of erupting, as with emotion : seethe. **—sim'mer** *n.*
si•mon-pure (sī'mən-pyo͝or') *adj.* **1.** Genuinely pure. **2.** Superficially or hypocritically virtuous.
sim•o•ny (sĭm'ə-nē, sī'mə-) *n.* Purchase or sale of ecclesiastical pardons or offices.
sim•pa•ti•co (sĭm-pä'tĭ-kō', -păt'ĭ-) *adj.* **1.** Compatible : harmonious. **2.** Having pleasing qualities : likable.
sim•per (sĭm'pər) *v.* To smile in an inane manner. **—sim'per** *n.*
sim•ple (sĭm'pəl) *adj.* **-pler, -plest. 1.** Having or composed of a single part or unit. **2.** Not difficult or complicated : easy. **3.** Without additions or qualifications : mere. **4.** Not showy or ornate : unadorned. **5.** Not affected : straightforward and unpretentious. **6.** Lacking or showing a lack of sense, intelligence, or education. **—sim'ple•ness** *n.* **—sim'ply** *adv.*
sim•ple-mind•ed (sĭm'pəl-mīn'dĭd) *adj.* **1.** Not sophisticated : artless. **2.** Stupid or foolish. **3.** Mentally defective.
sim•ple•ton (sĭm'pəl-tən) *n.* A fool.
sim•plic•i•ty (sĭm-plĭs'ĭ-tē) *n.* **1.** Lack of showiness or ornateness : plainness. **2.** Lack of sophistication, affectation, or pretense : artlessness. **3.** Lack of complexity or difficulty. **4.** Foolishness.
sim•pli•fy (sĭm'plə-fī') *v.* **-fied, -fy•ing.** To make simple or simpler. **—sim'pli•fi•ca'tion** *n.* **—sim'pli•fi'er** *n.*
sim•plis•tic (sĭm-plĭs'tĭk) *adj.* Spuriously simple because complexities or complications have been ignored. **—sim•plis'ti•cal•ly** *adv.*
sim•u•late (sĭm'yə-lāt') *v.* **-lat•ed, -lat•ing. 1.** To have or duplicate the appearance, form, effect, or sound of. **2.** To pretend : feign. **—sim'u•la'tion** *n.* **—sim'u•la'tor** *n.*
si•mul•cast (sī'məl-kăst', sĭm'əl-) *v.* To broadcast simultaneously by radio and television. **—si'mul•cast'** *n.*
si•mul•ta•ne•ous (sī'məl-tā'nē-əs, sĭm'əl-) *adj.* Occurring, existing, or carried out at the same time. **—si'mul•ta'ne•ous•ly** *adv.* **—si'mul•ta'ne•ous•ness** *n.*
sin (sĭn) *n.* **1.** The act of breaking a religious or moral law. **2.** An offense, error, or fault. —*v.* **sinned, sin•ning.** To commit a sin. **—sin'less** *adj.* **—sin'ner** *n.*
Si•nai (sī'nī'). Peninsula between the Gulfs of Suez and Aqaba.
since (sĭns) *adv.* **1.** From then until now. **2.** Before now : ago. —*prep.* **1.** During the time after <haven't seen him *since* the party> **2.** Continuously after <has been at home *since* noon> —*conj.* **1.** As a result of the fact that : because. **2.** From the time at which.
sin•cere (sĭn-sîr') *adj.* **-cer•er, -cer•est. 1.** Not deceitful or hypocritical : honest. **2.** Genuine : true. **—sin•cere'ly** *adv.* **—sin•cer'i•ty** (-sĕr'ĭ-tē) *n.*
si•ne•cure (sī'nĭ-kyo͝or', sĭn'ĭ-) *n.* A position that pays a good salary but requires little or no work.
si•ne di•e (sī'nī dī'ē, sĭn'ā dē'ā') *adv.* Without a future time or date being specified : indefinitely.
si•ne qua non (sĭn'ĭ kwä nŏn', nōn') *n.* An essential element.
sin•ew (sĭn'yo͞o) *n.* **1.** A tendon. **2.** Muscular power : strength. **—sin'ew•y** *adj.*
sin•ful (sĭn'fəl) *adj.* Characterized by or full of sin : wicked. **—sin'ful•ly** *adv.* **—sin'ful•ness** *n.*
sing (sĭng) *v.* **sang** (săng) *or* **sung** (sŭng), **sung, sing•ing. 1. a.** To use the voice to produce musical tones. **b.** To utter (e.g., a series of words) in musical tones. **2.** To produce musical sounds <canaries *singing*> **3.** To extol, esp. in verse or song. **4.** To produce a high-pitched, shrill sound <a teakettle *singing*> **5.** *Slang.* To give evidence or information. **—sing'er** *n.*
sing. *abbr.* singular.
Sin•ga•pore (sĭng'gə-pôr', sĭng'ə-). **1.** Country of SE Asia, comprising Singapore Is. and adjacent islands off the S tip of the Malay Peninsula. *Pop.* 2,465,000. **2.** Cap. of Singapore, on the Strait of Singapore.
singe (sĭnj) *v.* **singed, singe•ing. 1.** To burn the surface of slightly : scorch. **2.** To remove the feathers, down, or bristles of with a flame.
sin•gle (sĭng'gəl) *adj.* **1.** Being 1 only : solitary. **2.** Consisting of only 1 form, feature, or part. **3.** Individual : separate. **4.** Designed or intended to accommodate 1 person or family. **5.** Unmarried. ☆**syns:** DISCRETE, INDIVIDUAL, SEPARATE, SINGULAR —*n.* **1.** A separate person or thing : individual. **2.** An accommodation for 1 person or family. **3.** An unmarried person. **4.** A dollar bill. **5.** A hit in baseball that enables the batter to reach 1st base. **6. singles.** A tennis match between 2 players, 1 on each side. —*v.* **-gled, -gling. 1.** To select or distinguish from among a group. **2.** To hit a single in baseball. **—sin'gle•ness** *n.* **—sin'gly** *adv.*
sin•gle-breast•ed (sĭng'gəl-brĕs'tĭd) *adj.* Closing in the center with very little overlap <a *single-breasted* coat>
single file *n.* A line of individuals 1 behind the other. **—single file** *adv.*
sin•gle-hand•ed (sĭng'gəl-hăn'dĭd) *adj.* Working or done

without help from others : unassisted. **—sin′gle-hand′ed·ly** *adv.*
sin·gle-mind·ed (sĭng′gəl-mīn′dĭd) *adj.* Having a single overriding purpose.
sin·gle·ton (sĭng′gəl-tən) *n.* A playing card that is the only one of its suit in a player's hand.
sing·song (sĭng′sông′, -sŏng′) *n.* Monotonous regularity of rhythm or rhyme.
sin·gu·lar (sĭng′gyə-lər) *adj.* **1.** Of, pertaining to, or being a word form that denotes a single person, thing, or unit. **2.** Extraordinary : exceptional. **3.** Very odd : peculiar. **—sin′gu·lar** *n.* **—sin′gu·lar′i·ty** *n.* **—sin′gu·lar·ly** *adv.*
sin·is·ter (sĭn′ĭ-stər) *adj.* **1.** Suggesting evil : wicked. **2.** Threatening or presaging evil or trouble : ominous.
sink (sĭngk) *v.* **sank** (săngk) *or* **sunk** (sŭngk), **sunk** *or* **sunk·en** (sŭng′kən), **sink·ing. 1.** To submerge or cause to submerge beneath a surface. **2.** To descend slowly or bit by bit. **3.** To drive into the ground. **4.** To make (a shaft, hole, or well) in the earth by digging or drilling. **5.** To deteriorate in physical condition or strength. **6.** To become weaker, quieter, or less forceful. **7.** To slope downward : incline. **8.** To penetrate : seep. **9.** To invest. —*n.* **1.** A basin for water fixed to a wall or floor and connected with a drain. **2.** A cesspool. **3.** A sinkhole. **—sink′a·ble** *adj.*
sink·er (sĭng′kər) *n.* A weight used for sinking a fishing net or line.
sink·hole (sĭngk′hōl′) *n.* A natural depression in a land surface, esp. in a limestone region, that communicates with an underground passage, esp. a cavern.
sin·u·ous (sĭn′yo͞o-əs) *adj.* Having many bends or curves : winding. **—sin′u·os′i·ty** (-ŏs′ĭ-tē) *n.* **—sin′u·ous·ly** *adv.*
si·nus (sī′nəs) *n.* **1.** A bodily channel, esp. for the passage of blood. **2.** Any of several air-filled cavities in the cranial bones, esp. one communicating with the nostrils.
si·nus·i·tis (sī′nə-sī′tĭs) *n.* Inflammation of a sinus membrane.
Si·on (sī′ən) *n. var. of* ZION.
sip (sĭp) *v.* **sipped, sip·ping.** To drink in small quantities. **—sip** *n.*
si·phon *also* **sy·phon** (sī′fən) *n.* A bent tube through which liquid can be moved by means of atmospheric pressure up and over the lip of 1 container and down into another situated at a lower level. —*v.* To draw off through or as if through a siphon.
sir (sûr) *n.* **1.** Used as a respectful form of address in place of a man's name. **2. Sir.** Used as an honorific before the given or full name of a baronet or knight.
sire (sīr) *n.* **1. a.** A father. **b.** *Archaic.* A forefather. **2.** The male parent of an animal. **3.** *Archaic.* A form of address for a superior. —*v.* **sired, sir·ing.** To beget.
si·ren (sī′rən) *n.* **1.** A captivating or seductive woman. **2.** An often electrically operated whistle that makes a loud wailing sound as a signal or warning.
sir·loin (sûr′loin′) *n.* A cut of meat, esp. beef, from the upper loin.
si·roc·co (sĭ-rŏk′ō) *n., pl.* **-cos. 1.** A hot wind of S Europe, originating in the Sahara. **2.** A warm or hot southerly wind.
sir·up (sĭr′əp, sûr′-) *n. var. of* SYRUP.
si·sal (sī′zəl, -səl) *n.* A strong, sturdy cordage fiber obtained from the agave.
sis·sy (sĭs′ē) *n., pl.* **-sies. 1.** An effeminate man or boy. **2.** A cowardly or timorous person. **—sis′si·fy′** *v.*
sissy bar *n.* An inverted U-shaped bar rising from behind a motorcycle or bicycle seat to support the driver or a passenger.

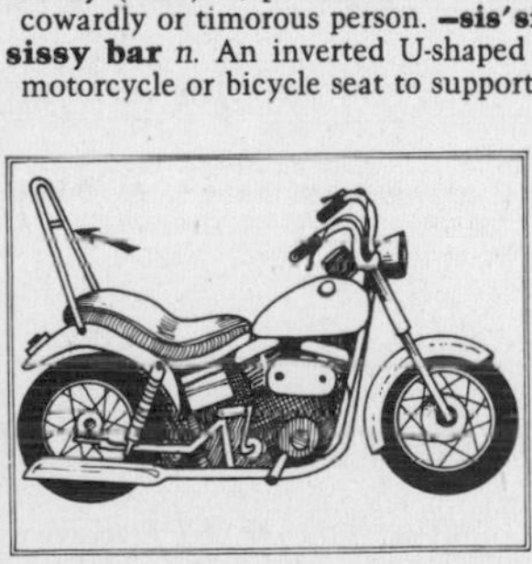

sissy bar

sis·ter (sĭs′tər) *n.* **1.** A woman or girl having the same parents as another. **2.** A fellow member, as of a sorority. **3.** A nun. **4.** *esp. Brit.* A nurse. **—sis′ter·ly** *adj.*
sis·ter·hood (sĭs′tər-ho͝od′) *n.* **1.** The relationship or state of being a sister or sisters. **2.** The quality of being sisterly. **3.** A group, society, or community of sisters.
sis·ter-in-law (sĭs′tər-ĭn-lô′) *n., pl.* **sis·ters-in-law. 1.** The sister of one's spouse. **2.** The wife of one's brother.

sit (sĭt) *v.* **sat** (săt), **sit·ting. 1.** To assume a position with the body resting on the buttocks. **2.** To perch : roost. **3.** To cover eggs for hatching : brood. **4.** To keep one's seat on (a horse). **5.** To be located : lie. **6.** To pose for a photographer or artist. **7.** To be in session. **8.** To remain inactive, unused, or quiet. **9.** To baby-sit. **10. a.** To cause to sit : seat. **b.** To occupy a seat, as in a legislature. **—sit in. 1.** To be present or participate as a visitor. **2.** To take part in a sit-in. **—sit′ter** *n.*
si·tar (sĭ-tär′) *n.* An Indian stringed instrument with a long, fretted neck and usu. 6 or 7 playing strings. **—si·tar′ist** *n.*
sit·com *also* **sit-com** (sĭt′kŏm′) *n. Informal.* A situation comedy.
sit-down (sĭt′doun′) *n.* A work stoppage in which employees remain in their place of work until their demands are met.
site (sīt) *n.* A location. —*v.* **sit·ed, sit·ing.** To locate : situate.
sit-in (sĭt′ĭn′) *n.* A demonstration in which participants sit in seats or on the floor or ground in a public place as a means of protest.
sit·ting (sĭt′ĭng) *n.* **1.** The position or act of one that sits. **2.** A period during which one is seated. **3.** A session or term, as of a legislature.
sitting duck *n. Informal.* An easy target.
sit·u·ate (sĭch′o͞o-āt′) *v.* **-at·ed, -at·ing.** To put in a certain position or place : locate.
sit·u·a·tion (sĭch′o͞o-ā′shən) *n.* **1.** A site : location. **2.** A set of circumstances : state. **3.** A position of employment.
situation comedy *n.* A humorous radio or television series consisting of episodes with the same characters.
sit-up (sĭt′ŭp′) *n.* A form of exercise performed on the back in which the trunk is raised to a sitting position without the support of the arms and then returned to the orig. position.
six (sĭks) *n.* **1.** The cardinal number equal to 5 + 1. **2.** The 6th in a set or sequence. **3.** Something having 6 parts or units, esp. a motor vehicle with 6 cylinders. **—six** *adj. & pron.* **—sixth** *n. & adj. & adv.*
six-pack (sĭks′păk′) *n.* **1.** A pack or container for 6 cans or bottles of a beverage sold together. **2.** The contents of a six-pack.
six-shoot·er (sĭks′sho͞o′tər) *n. Informal.* A revolver with 6 chambers.
six·teen (sĭk′stēn′) *n.* **1.** The cardinal number equal to 15 + 1. **2.** The 16th in a set or sequence. **—six′teen′** *adj. & pron.* **—six′teenth′** *n., adj., & adv.*
six·ty (sĭk′stē) *n., pl.* **-ties.** The cardinal number equal to 6 × 10. **—six′ti·eth** *n. & adj. & adv.* **—six′ty** *adj. & pron.*
siz·a·ble *also* **size·a·ble** (sī′zə-bəl) *adj.* Fairly large. **—siz′a·bly** *adv.*
size[1] (sīz) *n.* **1.** Physical dimension, bulk, or extent : magnitude. **2.** One of a series of graduated dimensions by which manufactured articles are classified. —*v.* **sized, siz·ing.** To arrange or classify according to size. **—size up.** To form a judgment or opinion of.
size[2] (sīz) *n.* A gluey substance used to glaze or fill holes in paper, cloth, or wall surfaces. —*v.* **sized, siz·ing.** To glaze, fill, or coat with size.
siz·ing (sī′zĭng) *n.* SIZE[2].
siz·zle (sĭz′əl) *v.* **-zled, -zling. 1.** To make the hissing sound of frying fat. **2.** To seethe, as with indignation. **—siz′zle** *n.*
skate[1] (skāt) *n.* **1.** An ice skate. **2.** A roller skate. **—skate** *v.* **—skat′er** *n.*
skate[2] (skāt) *n.* Any of several marine fishes of the family Rajidae, with a flattened body and winglike fins.
skate[3] (skāt) *n.* A fellow <a good *skate*>
skate·board (skāt′bôrd′, –bōrd′) *n.* A short, narrow board to which roller-skate wheels are attached. **—skate′board′** *v.* **—skate′board′er** *n.*
ske·dad·dle (skĭ-dăd′l) *v.* **-dled, -dling.** *Informal.* To leave hastily : flee.
skeet (skēt) *n.* A form of trapshooting in which clay targets are thrown to simulate the flight of game birds.
skein (skān) *n.* A loose, long coil of thread or yarn.
skel·e·ton (skĕl′ĭ-tn) *n.* **1.** The internal vertebrate structure composed of bone and cartilage that protects and supports the soft organs and tissues. **2.** A structure that supports : framework. **3.** A brief plan : outline or sketch. **—skel′e·tal** *adj.*
skeleton key *n.* A key that can open more than 1 lock.
skep·tic *also* **scep·tic** (skĕp′tĭk) *n.* **1.** Someone who habitually doubts or questions. **2.** Someone inclined to philosophical or religious skepticism. **—skep′ti·cal** *adj.*
skep·ti·cism *also* **scep·ti·cism** (skĕp′tĭ-sĭz′əm) *n.* **1.** A doubting or questioning attitude. **2.** The philosophical doctrine that the attainment of absolute knowledge is impossible. **3.** Disbelief in religious principles or tenets.
sketch (skĕch) *n.* **1.** An undetailed drawing, esp. one made as a preliminary study. **2.** A rough outline, as of a book not yet completed. **3. a.** A brief or light literary composition. **b.** A short,

often comical act in a revue or variety show. —*v.* To make a sketch (of). **—sketch'y** *adj.*
skew (skyo͞o) *v.* To place or turn at an angle : slant. —*n.* A slant.
skew·er (skyo͞o'ər) *n.* A long pin, as of metal, used to secure food and esp. meat while it cooks. **—skew'er** *v.*
ski (skē) *n., pl.* **skis.** One of a pair of long, flat runners that are fastened 1 on each foot for gliding over snow. —*v.* **skied, ski·ing.** To move or glide on skis. **—ski'er** *n.*
ski·bob (skē'bŏb') *n.* A vehicle for gliding downhill over snow, having a seat for the rider who wears small skis for balance.

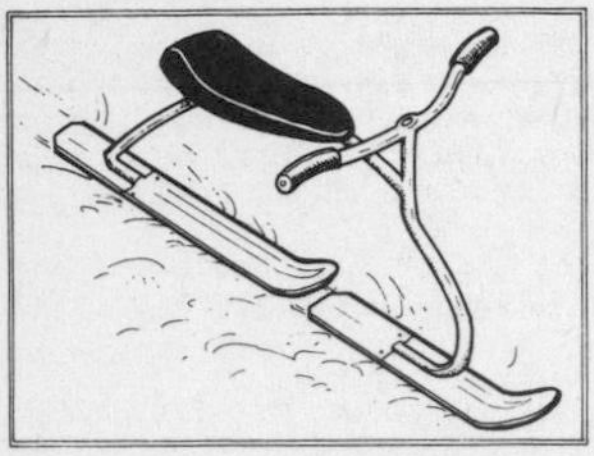

skibob

skid (skĭd) *n.* **1.** The act or process of slipping or sliding sideways over a surface. **2. a.** A plank or log forming a support or track on which something can be slid or rolled. **b.** PALLET[1]. **3.** A runner that forms part of the landing gear of an aircraft, as a helicopter. **4.** A wedge placed under a wheel to keep it from turning. —*v.* **skidded, skid·ding. 1.** To slip or slide sideways over a surface <a truck *skidding* on the icy road> **2.** To slide without revolving <a bicycle wheel *skidding* after the brakes were applied>
ski·doo (skĭ-do͞o') *n. Can.* A motorized toboggan.
skid row *n. Slang.* A squalid urban district with cheap bars that is frequented by derelicts and vagrants.
skiff (skĭf) *n.* A boat with a flat bottom.
skil·ful (skĭl'fəl) *adj. esp. Brit. var. of* SKILLFUL.
ski lift *n.* A motor-driven conveyor for carrying skiers to the top of a mountain, trail, or slope.
skill (skĭl) *n.* **1.** Proficiency or ability : expertise. **2.** An art, trade, or technique, esp. one requiring use of the hands or body. **—skilled** *adj.*
skil·let (skĭl'ĭt) *n.* A frying pan.
skill·ful (skĭl'fəl) *adj.* **1.** Possessing, exercising, or showing skill. **2.** Requiring or done with skill. **—skill'ful·ly** *adv.* **—skill'ful·ness** *n.*
skim (skĭm) *v.* **skimmed, skim·ming. 1. a.** To remove floating matter or scum from (a liquid). **b.** To remove (floating matter) from <*skimmed* the foam from the boiling broth> **2.** To pass lightly and quickly over. **3.** To glance through or read quickly and superficially. **—skim'mer** *n.*
skim milk *n.* Milk from which the cream has been skimmed.
ski·mo·bile (skē'mō-bēl', -mə-) *n.* A snowmobile.
skimp (skĭmp) *v.* **1.** To do without sufficient care or effort or with inferior material. **2.** To be sparing, esp. with money.
skimp·y (skĭm'pē) *adj.* **-i·er, -i·est.** Inadequate in fullness, size, or amount : scanty.
skin (skĭn) *n.* **1.** The tough, membranous tissue that forms the external covering of the animal body. **2.** An animal pelt, esp. when prepared for use, as in a garment. **3.** An outer covering or layer, as the rind of fruit. —*v.* **skinned, skin·ning. 1.** To remove the skin from. **2.** To injure the surface of by scraping. **—skin'less** *adj.*
skin diving *n.* Underwater swimming with a face mask, a snorkel or scuba equipment to permit breathing, and often flippers. **—skin'-dive'** *v.* **—skin diver** *n.*
skin flick *n.* A pornographic movie.
skin·flint (skĭn'flĭnt') *n.* A miser.
skin graft *n.* A surgical graft of skin from 1 part of the body to another or from 1 individual to another.
†**skin·ner** (skĭn'ər) *n.* **1.** One who flays, dresses, or sells animal skins. **2.** *W U.S.* A mule driver.
skin·ny (skĭn'ē) *adj.* **-ni·er, -ni·est.** Very thin. **—skin'ni·ness** *n.*
skin·ny-dip (skĭn'ē-dĭp') *v. Informal.* To swim in the nude. **—skin'ny-dip'ping** *n.*
skin·tight (skĭn'tīt') *adj.* Fitted closely to the body.
skip (skĭp) *v.* **skipped, skip·ping. 1. a.** To move by hopping, jumping, or springing. **b.** To hop, jump, or spring lightly over. **2.** To pass from 1 point to another ignoring what intervenes. **3.** To pass over without considering, mentioning, or noticing : omit. **4.** *Informal.* To leave hastily and esp. furtively <*skip* town> —*n.* **1.** A skipping gait, movement, or step. **2.** An omission.
skip·per (skĭp'ər) *n.* The master of a ship, esp. a small one.
skir·mish (skûr'mĭsh) *n.* A minor encounter in war. **—skir'mish** *v.*
skirt (skûrt) *n.* **1.** The part of a garment, as a dress, that extends down from the waist. **2.** A garment that extends down from the waist. —*v.* **1.** To extend along the edge of : border. **2.** To pass around the edge or border of. **3.** To evade, esp. by circumlocution : avoid.
skit (skĭt) *n.* A short, often comic theatrical sketch.
ski touring *n.* Cross-country skiing engaged in for pleasure.
ski tow *n.* A ski lift.
skit·ter (skĭt'ər) *v.* To skip or glide rapidly or lightly along a surface.
skit·tish (skĭt'ĭsh) *adj.* **1.** Easily excited or frightened : nervous. **2.** Capricious or undependable.
skiv·vy (skĭv'ē) *n., pl.* **-vies.** *Slang. often* **skivvies.** Men's underwear consisting of an undershirt and shorts.
ski·wear (skē'wâr') *n.* Clothing appropriate for skiing.
skulk (skŭlk) *v.* **1.** To lie in concealment : lurk. **2.** To move around stealthily. **—skulk'er** *n.*
skull (skŭl) *n.* The bony framework of the head that protects the brain.
skull·cap (skŭl'kăp') *n.* A close-fitting cap without a brim.
skull·dug·ger·y *also* **skul·dug·ger·y** (skŭl-dŭg'ə-rē) *n.* Crafty or dishonest behavior : trickery.
skunk (skŭngk) *n.* **1.** Any of various New World mammals, esp. of the genus *Mephitis,* that have black and white fur and eject a malodorous secretion if startled. **2.** *Slang.* A despicable person. —*v. Slang.* To defeat overwhelmingly, esp. by preventing from scoring in a game.
skunk cabbage *n.* A North American swamp plant, *Symplocarpus foetidus,* bearing minute unpleasant-smelling flowers.
sky (skī) *n., pl.* **skies. 1.** The upper atmosphere. **2.** The celestial regions : heaven.
sky·cap (skī'kăp') *n.* A porter employed at an airport.
sky·dive (skī'dīv') *v.* To jump from an airplane and perform various maneuvers before opening the parachute. **—sky'div'er** *n.* **—sky'div'ing** *n.*
sky·jack (skī'jăk') *v.* To hijack (an aircraft, esp. one in flight). **—sky'jack'er** *n.* **—sky'jack'ing** *n.*
sky·lark (skī'lärk') *n.* An Old World bird, *Alauda arvensis,* noted for singing while high in flight. —*v.* To frolic.
sky·light (skī'līt') *n.* A window in a ceiling or roof.
sky·line (skī'līn') *n.* **1.** The horizon. **2.** An outline seen against the sky.
sky marshal *n.* An armed federal law-enforcement officer assigned to prevent skyjackings.
sky·rock·et (skī'rŏk'ĭt) *n.* A firework that shoots into the air and explodes brilliantly. —*v.* To rise suddenly and rapidly.
sky·scrap·er (skī'skrā'pər) *n.* An extremely tall building.
sky·ward (skī'wərd) *adv.& adj.* Toward the sky. **—sky'wards** *adv.*
sky·way (skī'wā') *n.* **1.** An airline route : air lane. **2.** An elevated highway.
sky·writ·ing (skī'rī'tĭng) *n.* Writing in the sky formed by the release of a visible vapor from an airplane. **—sky'writ'er** *n.*
slab (slăb) *n.* **1.** A broad, somewhat thick piece or slice. **2.** The outside piece cut from a log in squaring it for lumber.
slack (slăk) *adj.* **1.** Lacking in strength or liveliness : sluggish. **2.** Not active or busy. **3.** Not tense or taut : loose. **4.** Negligent : remiss. —*v.* **1.** To slacken. **2.** To slake (lime). —*n.* **1.** A part of something that is not drawn tight or that hangs loose. **2.** A period of reduced activity : lull. **3. slacks.** Long trousers for informal wear. **—slack'ly** *adv.* **—slack'ness** *n.*
slack·en (slăk'ən) *v.* **1.** To make or become slower. **2.** To loosen.
slack·er (slăk'ər) *n.* Someone who shirks work or evades responsibility.
slag (slăg) *n.* The glassy refuse that remains after the smelting of metallic ore.
slain (slān) *v. p.p. of* SLAY.
slake (slāk) *v.* **slaked, slak·ing. 1.** To allay (e.g., thirst) : quench. **2.** To combine (lime) chemically with water or moist air.
sla·lom (slä'ləm) *n.* Downhill skiing, esp. in a race, along a zigzag course.
slam[1] (slăm) *v.* **slammed, slam·ming. 1.** To shut forcefully and noisily. **2.** To throw, drive, or strike with a loud, forceful impact. —*n.* A loud noise produced by a forceful impact : bang.
slam[2] (slăm) *n.* The winning of all or all but 1 of the tricks in a hand of bridge.
slam·mer (slăm'ər) *n. Slang.* A jail.
slan·der (slăn'dər) *n.* A false and malicious statement injurious to another's reputation. —*v.* To spread or utter slander about : defame. **—slan'der·ous** *adj.*

slang (slăng) *n.* A nonstandard vocabulary used esp. in casual speech and consisting of arbitrary and often ephemeral coinages and figures of speech. **–slang'i·ness** *n.* **–slang'y** *adj.*

slant (slănt) *v.* **1.** To lie or cause to lie in an oblique direction : slope. **2.** To present or interpret so as to conform with a particular outlook. *–n.* **1.** A sloping plane, direction, line, or course. **2.** A particular or personal outlook. **–slant'ing·ly** *adv.* **–slant'wise'** *adv.* & *adj.*

slap (slăp) *n.* **1. a.** A sharp blow with the open hand. **b.** The sound of a slap. **2.** An injury to one's pride, esp. an insult. *–v.* **slapped, slap·ping. 1.** To give a slap to. **2.** To reprimand, insult, or criticize sharply.

slap·dash (slăp'dăsh') *adj.* Careless : slipshod. **–slap'dash'** *adv.*

slap·hap·py (slăp'hăp'ē) *adj. Slang.* Dazed, silly, or incoherent from or as if from blows to the head.

slap·stick (slăp'stĭk') *n.* A type of broad comedy marked by horseplay and farce.

slash (slăsh) *v.* **1.** To cut with forceful sweeping strokes. **2.** To make a slit in (a fabric or garment). **3.** To reduce greatly. *–n.* **1.a.** A forceful sweeping stroke, as with a sharp instrument. **b.** A cut made by slashing : gash. **2.** A virgule. **–slash'er** *n.*

slat (slăt) *n.* A flat, narrow thin strip, as of wood.

slate (slāt) *n.* **1.a.** A fine-grained rock that splits into thin layers with smooth surfaces. **b.** A writing surface or roofing tile made of slate. **2.** A list of political candidates running for office. *–v.* **slat·ed, slat·ing. 1.** To cover with slate. **2.** To schedule.

slath·er (slăth'ər) *v. Informal.* To spread thickly on or with.

slat·tern (slăt'ərn) *n.* An untidy woman. **–slat'tern·ly** *adj.*

slaugh·ter (slô'tər) *n.* **1.** The killing of livestock for food. **2.** The killing of a great number of people, esp. in battle : carnage. *–v.* **1.** To kill (livestock) for food : butcher. **2.** To kill savagely or in great numbers. **–slaugh'ter·er** *n.*

slaugh·ter·house (slô'tər-hous') *n.* A place for butchering animals.

Slav (släv) *n.* A Slavic-speaking person of E Europe.

slave (slāv) *n.* **1.** A person who is bound in servitude as chattel. **2.** A person completely controlled by a dominating influence <a *slave* to his work> *–v.* **slaved, slav·ing.** To work like a slave : labor.

slav·er[1] (slăv'ər, slā'vər) *v.* To slobber : drool. **–slav'er** *n.*

slav·er[2] (slā'vər) *n.* **1.** A ship engaged in slave traffic. **2.** A person who traffics in slaves.

slav·er·y (slā'və-rē, slāv'rē) *n.* **1.** Bondage to a master or household : servitude. **2.** The practice of owning slaves. **3.** Hard work : drudgery.

Slav·ic (slä'vĭk, slăv'ĭk) *adj.* Of or pertaining to the Slavs or their languages. *–n.* A branch of the Indo-European language family that includes Bulgarian, Czech, Polish, and Russian.

slav·ish (slā'vĭsh) *adj.* **1.** Resembling or befitting a slave : submissive. **2.** Showing no originality : imitative. **–slav'ish·ly** *adv.*

slaw (slô) *n.* Coleslaw.

slay (slā) *v.* **slew** (slo͞o), **slain** (slān), **slay·ing.** To kill, esp. by violent means. **–slay'er** *n.*

slea·zy (slē'zē) *adj.* **-zi·er, -zi·est. 1.** Lacking in substance : flimsy. **2.** Of poor quality : shoddy.

sled (slĕd) *n.* A vehicle mounted on runners used for coasting over snow or ice. *–v.* **sled·ded, sled·ding.** To convey or ride on a sled.

sledge[1] (slĕj) *n.* A vehicle on low runners for transporting loads over snow and ice.

sledge[2] (slĕj) *n.* A sledgehammer.

sledge·ham·mer (slĕdj'hăm'ər) *n.* A heavy, large hammer wielded with both hands.

sleek (slēk) *adj.* **1.** Lustrous and smooth : glossy. **2.** Neat and trim in appearance. *–v.* **1.** To make sleek. **2.** To cover up : conceal. **–sleek'ly** *adv.* **–sleek'ness** *n.*

sleep (slēp) *n.* **1.** A natural periodic state of rest marked by the suspension of consciousness. **2.** A state, as coma, that resembles sleep. *–v.* **slept** (slĕpt), **sleep·ing. 1.** To be in a state of sleep. **2.** To be in a state of quiet or inactivity. **3.** To spend in a period of sleep <*slept* away the afternoon> **–sleep'less** *adj.* **–sleep'less·ly** *adv.* **–sleep'less·ness** *n.*

sleep·er (slē'pər) *n.* **1.** One that sleeps. **2.** A sleeping car. **3.** *Informal.* Someone or something that achieves unexpected popularity, recognition, or success.

sleeping bag *n.* A warmly lined bag in which a person can sleep, esp. outdoors.

sleeping car *n.* A railroad car with sleeping accommodations.

sleeping sickness *n.* An often fatal endemic infectious disease of tropical Africa that is transmitted by the tsetse fly and marked by fever and lethargy.

sleep·walk·ing (slēp'wô'kĭng) *n.* Somnambulism. **–sleep'walk'er** *n.*

sleep·y (slē'pē) *adj.* **-i·er, -i·est. 1.** Ready to fall asleep : drowsy. **2.** Quiet, inactive, and often dull <a *sleepy* little town> **–sleep'i·ly** *adv.* **–sleep'i·ness** *n.*

sleet (slēt) *n.* **1.** Partially frozen rain. **2.** A thin coating of ice : glaze. **–sleet** *v.* **–sleet'y** *adj.*

sleeve (slēv) *n.* **1.** The part of a garment that covers the arm. **2.** An encasement into which something fits <a phonograph-record *sleeve*> **–sleeve'less** *adj.*

sleigh (slā) *n.* A light vehicle mounted on runners and used on ice or snow. *–v.* To ride in or drive a sleigh.

sleight (slīt) *n.* **1.** Deftness : dexterity. **2.** A sly trick : stratagem.

sleight of hand *n.* A trick so skillfully performed that its manner of execution cannot be observed.

slen·der (slĕn'dər) *adj.* **1.** Thin or slim. **2.** Inadequate in extent or amount : meager. **–slen'der·ly** *adv.* **–slen'der·ness** *n.*

slen·der·ize (slĕn'də-rīz') *v.* **-ized, -iz·ing.** To make or become slender.

slept (slĕpt) *v. p.t.* & *p.p. of* SLEEP.

sleuth (slo͞oth) *n. Informal.* A detective. **–sleuth** *v.*

slew[1] *also* **slue** (slo͞o) *n. Informal.* A large number or amount.

slew[2] (slo͞o) *v. p.t. of* SLAY.

slew[3] (slo͞o) *v.* & *n. var. of* SLUE[1].

slice (slīs) *n.* **1.** A thin, flat piece cut from something. **2.** A share : portion. **3.** An implement with a broad, flexible blade used esp. for serving food. **4.** A flight of a ball, as in golf, that curves off to the right if the player is right-handed or to the left if the player is left-handed. *–v.* **sliced, slic·ing. 1.** To cut into slices. **2.** To cut a slice from a larger piece. **3.** To hit (a ball) with a stroke causing a slice. **–slic'er** *n.*

slick (slĭk) *adj.* **1.** Smooth and slippery. **2.** Marked by deftness : adroit. **3.** Shrewd : clever. **4.** Superficially polished but without quality or depth. *–n.* **1.** A smooth area of water filmed with oil. **2.** *Informal.* A magazine with popular appeal that is printed on glossy paper. *–v.* To make smooth, glossy, or oily.

slick·er (slĭk'ər) *n.* **1.** A loose, glossy raincoat, often made of yellow oilcloth. **2.** *Informal.* A clever swindler.

slide (slīd) *v.* **slid** (slĭd), **slid·ing. 1.** To move or cause to move smoothly over a surface while keeping continuous contact. **2.** To lose one's balance and fall. **3.** To pass quietly : glide. ☆***syns:*** COAST, DRIFT, GLIDE, SLIP *–n.* **1.** A sliding action or movement. **2.** A smooth surface on which something can slide. **3.** A part, as the bolt in certain locks, that operates by sliding. **4.** A photographic image on a transparent plate for projecting on a screen. **5.** A small glass plate on which specimens to be examined under a microscope can be mounted. **6.** A fall down a slope of a mass of ice, snow, earth, or rocks.

slid·er (slīd'ər) *n.* **1.** One that slides. **2.** A baseball pitch that curves slightly downward at the last moment.

slide rule *n.* A device for performing mathematical operations that consists of 2 logarithmically scaled rules mounted to slide along each other.

sliding scale *n.* A flexible scale in which prices or fees vary in accordance with another factor, as medical charges with a patient's income.

sli·er (slī'ər) *adj. var. compar. of* SLY.

sli·est (slī'ĭst) *adj. var. superl. of* SLY.

slight (slīt) *adj.* **1.** Small in amount or degree. **2.** Insignificant : unimportant. **3. a.** Slender and delicate. **b.** Frail. *–v.* **1.** To treat as insignificant. **2.** To ignore rudely : snub. **3.** To do or perform with negligence. *–n.* A deliberate act of disrespect or discourtesy. **–slight'ly** *adv.*

slim (slĭm) *adj.* **slim·mer, slim·mest. 1.** Slight : slender. **2.** Meager : scanty. *–v.* **slimmed, slim·ming.** To make or become slim. **–slim'ly** *adv.* **–slim'ness** *n.*

slime (slīm) *n.* **1.** Thick, sticky mud. **2.** A viscous, slippery substance, as that secreted by a slug. **–slim'y** *adj.*

sling (slĭng) *n.* **1.** A belt, rope, strap, or chain for securing something, as a load, that is to be hoisted, lowered, secured, or carried. **2.** A weapon consisting of a looped strap from which a stone is thrown. *–v.* **slung** (slŭng), **sling·ing. 1.** To throw forcibly : fling. **2.** To place or carry in a sling. **–sling'er** *n.*

sling·shot (slĭng'shŏt') *n.* A Y-shaped stick with an elastic band used for throwing small stones.

slink (slĭngk) *v.* **slunk** (slŭngk), **slink·ing.** To move furtively or quietly.

slink·y (slĭng'kē) *adj.* **-i·er, -i·est. 1.** Furtive : stealthy. **2.** *Informal.* Sinuous.

slip[1] (slĭp) *v.* **slipped, slip·ping. 1.** To move or cause to move smoothly and quietly : glide. **2.** To lose one's balance or footing. **3.** To escape, esp. without being noticed. **4.** *Informal.* To decline in ability, strength, or performance. **5.** To pass unfinished or unnoticed. **6.** To make an error. *–n.* **1.** The act of slipping. **2.** An accident or mishap. **3.** An error : blunder. **4. a.** A docking place for a ship : pier. **b.** A space for a ship between 2 docks or

wharves. **5.** A woman's undergarment serving as a lining for a dress. **6.** A pillowcase. **—slip'page** *n.*
slip² (slĭp) *n.* **1.** A twig or shoot cut from a plant for propagation. **2.** A strip, esp. of paper <a sales *slip*>
slip·cov·er (slĭp'kŭv'ər) *n.* A fitted, usu. cloth cover for a piece of furniture that can be slipped on and off.
slip·knot (slĭp'nŏt') *n.* A knot that slips along the rope or cord around which it is formed.
slipped disk *n.* A rupture of 1 of the cushioning disks between the spinal vertebrae that results in back pain.
slip·per (slĭp'ər) *n.* A light, low shoe that slips on and off easily.
slip·per·y (slĭp'ə-rē) *adj.* **-i·er, -i·est. 1.** Causing or tending to cause sliding, slipping, or falling. **2.** Untrustworthy : shifty. **—slip'per·i·ly** *adv.* **—slip'per·i·ness** *n.*
slip·shod (slĭp'shŏd') *adj.* Marked by carelessness : sloppy.
slip·stream (slĭp'strēm') *n.* The turbulent flow of air driven backward by the propeller of an aircraft.
slip-up (slĭp'ŭp') *n. Informal.* A mistake.
slit (slĭt) *n.* A straight, narrow tear or incision. *—v.* **slit·ted, slit·ting. 1.** To cut a slit in. **2.** To split.
slith·er (slĭth'ər) *v.* **1.** To slip and slide. **2.** To move in a sinuous manner, as a snake does : glide. **—slith'er·y** *adj.*
sliv·er (slĭv'ər) *n.* A thin, sharp-ended piece : splinter. **—sliv'er** *v.*
slob (slŏb) *n. Informal.* A coarse or slovenly person.
slob·ber (slŏb'ər) *v.* To let saliva dribble from the mouth. **—slob'ber** *n.*
slob ice *n. Can.* Chunks of disintegrating sea ice.
sloe (slō) *n.* The blue-black, plumlike fruit of a thorny Eurasian shrub, *Prunus spinosa.*
sloe-eyed (slō'īd') *adj.* Having slanted eyes.
sloe gin *n.* A liqueur with a gin base flavored with sloes.
slog (slŏg) *v.* **slogged, slog·ging. 1.** To walk slowly and heavily : plod. **2.** To work hard for long hours. **3.** To hit hard.
slo·gan (slō'gən) *n.* A phrase that expresses the nature or aims of an enterprise, cause, or group : motto.
sloop (slo͞op) *n.* A fore-and-aft-rigged sailing boat with 1 mast, a mainsail, and a jib.
slop (slŏp) *n.* **1.** Spilled or splashed liquid. **2.** Soft mud. **3.** Unappetizing, watery food or drink. **4.** *often* **slops.** Waste food used as animal feed : swill. *—v.* **slopped, slop·ping.** To spill or splash carelessly.
slope (slōp) *v.* **sloped, slop·ing.** To incline upward or downward : slant. *—n.* **1.** A stretch of ground forming an incline. **2. a.** An upward or downward incline : slant. **b.** The degree of such an incline.
slop·py (slŏp'ē) *adj.* **-pi·er, -pi·est. 1.** Wet : slushy or muddy. **2.** Messy : untidy.
sloppy joe (jō) *n.* Ground cooked meat in a usu. spicy sauce served on a bun.
slosh (slŏsh) *v.* To splash through a liquid, as water : flounder. **—slosh'y** *adj.*
slot (slŏt) *n.* **1.** A long, narrow groove or aperture. **2.** *Informal.* A position or place, as in a hierarchy : niche.
sloth (slōth, slôth, slŏth) *n.* **1.** Indolence : laziness. **2.** A slow-moving arboreal tropical American mammal of the family Bradypodidae. **—sloth'ful** *adj.*
slot machine *n.* A vending or gambling machine operated by insertion of a coin.
slouch (slouch) *n.* **1.** An awkward, relaxed, or drooping posture or gait. **2.** An inefficient or lazy person. *—v.* To sit, stand, or move with a slouch.
slough¹ (slo͞o, slou) *n.* **1.** A muddy hollow in the ground. **2.** A bog : swamp. **3.** A state of dejection.
slough² (slŭf) *n.* Something, esp. an outer layer or covering, that can be shed. *—v.* To cast off : shed.
Slo·vak·i·a (slō-vä'kē-ə). Region of E Czechoslovakia. **—Slo·vak'i·an** *adj.* & *n.*
slov·en (slŭv'ən) *n.* A habitually untidy or careless person. **—slov'en·ly** *adj.*
slow (slō) *adj.* **1.** Moving or proceeding at a low rate of speed. **2.** Taking or requiring more time than usual. **3.** Indicating a time earlier than the correct time. **4.** Naturally inactive : sluggish. **5.** Lacking in liveliness : boring. **6.** Not quick to comprehend : dull. ☆***syns:*** DILATORY, POKY, TARDY *—adv.* In a slow manner. *—v.* **1.** To make or become slow or slower. **2.** To delay. **—slow'ly** *adv.* **—slow'ness** *n.*
slow burn *n.* A gradual build-up of anger.
slow·down (slō'doun') *n.* A slowing down, esp. in production.
slow motion *n.* A motion-picture technique in which the action as projected appears to be slower than the actual action.
sludge (slŭj) *n.* **1.** Mud, esp. that forming a deposit : ooze. **2.** Slushy matter, as that formed in the treatment of sewage.
slue¹ *also* **slew** (slo͞o) *v.* **slued, slu·ing** *also* **slewed, slew·ing.** To turn to the side : twist. **—slue, slew** *n.*
slue² (slo͞o) *n. var. of* SLEW¹.
slug¹ (slŭg) *n.* **1.** A lump of metal, esp. a bullet. **2.** *Informal.* A small amount, esp. a jigger, of liquor. **3.** A metal disk used in place of a coin.
slug² (slŭg) *n.* A terrestrial gastropod mollusk, esp. of the genus *Limex,* that is related to the snails but has no shell.
slug³ (slŭg) *v.* **slugged, slug·ging.** To strike heavily and hard, esp. with the fist. **—slug** *n.* **—slug'ger** *n.*
slug·gard (slŭg'ərd) *n.* An indolent person. **—slug'gard·ly** *adj.*
slug·gish (slŭg'ĭsh) *adj.* **1.** Slow in performance, response, or movement. **2.** Inactive : stagnant. **3.** Lazy : indolent. **—slug'gish·ly** *adv.* **—slug'gish·ness** *n.*
sluice (slo͞os) *n.* **1. a.** A manmade channel for water with a gate to control the flow. **b.** The gate in a sluice. **2.** A sluiceway. **3.** A sloping trough, as for floating logs. *—v.* **sluiced, sluic·ing. 1.** To flush with running water. **2.** To draw off by means of a sluice. **3.** To send (e.g., logs) through a sluice.
slum (slŭm) *n.* A squalid, heavily populated urban residential area marked by poverty and substandard housing. *—v.* **slummed, slum·ming.** To visit a slum, esp. out of curiosity.
slum·ber (slŭm'bər) *v.* **1. a.** To sleep. **b.** To doze. **2.** To be quiescent or dormant. *—n.* **1.** Sleep. **2.** A condition of quiescence or dormancy. **—slum'ber·er** *n.*
slum·ber·ous (slŭm'bər-əs) *also* **slum·brous** (-brəs) *adj.* **1.** Sleepy or sleeping. **2.** Tranquil : peaceful.
slump (slŭmp) *v.* **1.** To drop or sink suddenly. **2.** To slouch. **—slump** *n.*
slung (slŭng) *v. p.t. & p.p. of* SLING.
slunk (slŭngk) *v. p.t. & p.p. of* SLINK.
slur (slûr) *v.* **slurred, slur·ring. 1.** To pass over lightly or without due consideration. **2.** To pronounce indistinctly. **3.** *Mus.* To perform a succession of notes smoothly and without a break. *—n.* **1.** A derogatory remark : aspersion. **2.** *Mus.* A curved line connecting notes to indicate that they are to be slurred.
slurp (slûrp) *v.* To drink or eat noisily. **—slurp** *n.*
slush (slŭsh) *n.* **1.** Partially melted snow. **2.** Soft mud : mire. **—slush'y** *adj.*
slut (slŭt) *n.* **1.** A slatternly woman. **2.** A prostitute. **—slut'tish** *adj.*
sly (slī) *adj.* **sli·er, sli·est** *also* **sly·er, sly·est. 1.** Artfully clever : cunning. **2.** Stealthy : furtive. **3.** Playfully mischievous : roguish. ☆***syns:*** FURTIVE, SECRETIVE, SURREPTITIOUS **—sly'ly** *adv.* **—sly'ness** *n.*
sm. *abbr.* small.
Sm *symbol for* SAMARIUM.
smack¹ (smăk) *v.* **1.** To press together and open (the lips) with a sharp noise. **2.** To slap or kiss with a sharp noise. *—n.* **1.** The sharp sound made by smacking the lips. **2.** A noisy slap or kiss. *—adv.* Directly and sharply <drove *smack* into a tree>
smack² (smăk) *n.* **1.** A distinctive flavor. **2.** A trace : suggestion. *—v.* **1.** To have a flavor. **2.** To have a trace : suggest.
smack³ (smăk) *n.* A sailing boat used esp. in fishing.
smack⁴ (smăk) *n. Slang.* Heroin.
smack·er (smăk'ər) *n.* **1.** A loud kiss. **2.** A resounding blow. **3.** *Slang.* A dollar.
small (smôl) *adj.* **1.** Little in size, extent, or quantity. **2.** Unimportant : trivial. **3.** Operating with limited resources or funds. **4.** Petty : mean. **5.** Humbled : humiliated. *—n.* A part that is smaller than the rest <the *small* of the back> **—small'ness** *n.*
small arms *pl.n.* Firearms that can be fired while held in the hand.
small·pox (smôl'pŏks') *n.* An acute, highly infectious viral disease marked by high fever and pustular eruptions.
small talk *n.* Casual conversation.
small·time (smôl'tīm') *adj. Informal.* Of little standing : minor. **—small'tim'er** *n.*
smarm·y (smär'mē) *adj.* **-i·er, -i·est.** Marked by an insincere or exaggerated earnestness : unctuous.
smart (smärt) *adj.* **1. a.** Quick-witted : bright. **b.** Amusingly clever : witty. **2.** Fashionable : stylish. *—v.* **1.** To feel or cause to feel a sharp, stinging pain. **2.** To feel mental distress or pain. **—smart'ly** *adv.* **—smart'ness** *n.*
smart al·eck (ăl'ĭk) *n. Informal.* An obnoxiously self-assured person.
smart·en (smär'tn) *v.* To make or become smart or smarter.
smart·y (spär'tē) *n., pl.* **-ies.** A smart aleck.
smash (smăsh) *v.* **1.** To break or be broken into pieces. **2.** To throw or move forward violently so as to crush or shatter. **3.** To strike heavily : hit. **4.** To destroy completely : ruin. *—n.* **1.** The act or sound of smashing. **2.** Complete destruction : ruin. **3.** A collision : crash. **4.** A powerful overhand stroke, esp. in tennis.

5. A resounding success : hit. *—adj. Informal.* Extraordinary : outstanding. **—smash'er** *n.*
smat·ter·ing (smăt'ər-ĭng) *n.* **1.** Slight or surface knowledge. **2.** A small, scattered amount or number.
smear (smîr) *v.* **1.** To cover, spread, or stain with a sticky, oily, or dirty substance. **2.** To soil : smudge. **3.** To injure the reputation of : slander. *—n.* A smudge or spot made by smearing. **—smear'y** *adj.*
smell (smĕl) *v.* **smelled** *or* **smelt** (smĕlt), **smell·ing. 1. a.** To perceive the odor of by means of the olfactory sense organs. **b.** To detect by or as if by use of these organs. **2.** To have or emit an odor. *—n.* **1. a.** The sense by which odors are perceived. **b.** The ability to perceive odors. **2.** The odor of something : scent. **3.** The act or an instance of smelling.
smelling salts *pl.n.* A preparation based on spirits of ammonia that is used esp. to relieve faintness.
smell·y (smĕl'ē) *adj.* **-i·er, -i·est.** Having a bad odor. ☆**syns:** FETID, FOUL, MALODOROUS, REEKING, STINKING.
smelt[1] (smĕlt) *v.* To melt or fuse (ores) in order to extract the metallic constituents.
smelt[2] (smĕlt) *n., pl.* **smelts** *or* **smelt.** Any of various small silvery food fishes of the family Osmeridae.
smelt·er (smĕl'tər) *n.* **1.** An establishment where ores are smelted. **2.** One that smelts.
smidg·en *also* **smidg·in** (smĭj'ən) *n. Informal.* A minute quantity : bit.
smi·lax (smī'lăks') *n.* **1.** A plant of the genus *Smilax,* which includes various climbing vines. **2.** A vine, *Asparagus asparagoides,* with glossy foliage.
smile (smīl) *n.* A facial expression in which the corners of the mouth curve upward to indicate pleasure, amusement, or derision. *—v.* **smiled, smil·ing. 1.** To have, exhibit, or form a smile. **2.** To show approval. **3.** To express with a smile. **—smil'ing·ly** *adv.*
smirch (smûrch) *v.* **1.** To soil, dirty, or stain. **2.** To disgrace. **—smirch** *n.*
smirk (smûrk) *v.* To smile in an obnoxiously conceited manner : simper. **—smirk** *n.* **—smirk'er** *n.*
smite (smīt) *v.* **smote** (smōt), **smit·ten** (smĭt'n) *or* **smote, smit·ing. 1.** To hit hard, esp. with the hand. **2.** To kill by smiting. **3.** To impress powerfully : affect.
smith (smĭth) *n.* A metalworker, esp. a blacksmith.
Smith. 1. John. 1580–1631. English adventurer, colonist in Virginia, and author. **2. Adam.** 1723–90. Scottish political economist. **3. Joseph.** 1805–44. Amer. founder of the Mormon Church.
smith·er·eens (smĭth'ə-rēnz') *pl.n. Informal.* Pieces : fragments.
smith·y (smĭth'ē, smĭth'ē) *n., pl.* **-ies.** The shop of a smith, esp. a blacksmith.
smock (smŏk) *n.* A loose coatlike garment, often worn to protect the clothes while working. *—v.* To gather (fabric) in a decorative honeycomb pattern.
smog (smŏg, smôg) *n.* Fog mixed with smoke. **—smog'gy** *adj.*
smoke (smōk) *n.* **1.** Vapor consisting of small particles of carbonaceous matter from the incomplete combustion of organic materials such as wood. **2.** A cloud of fine particles. **3.** A suspension of particles in a gaseous medium. *—v.* **smoked, smok·ing. 1.** To emit smoke. **2.** To inhale and exhale smoke from (e.g., a cigarette or cigar). **3.** To preserve (e.g., meat) by exposure to smoke. **—smoke'less** *adj.* **—smok'er** *n.* **—smok'y** *adj.*
smoke·house (smōk'hous') *n.* A structure in which meat or fish is smoked.
smoke screen *n.* **1.** A mass of smoke to conceal military operations. **2.** Something intended to conceal, mislead, or confuse.
smoke·stack (smōk'stăk') *n.* A large vertical pipe, as on a ship, through which smoke and combustion gases are emitted.
smol·der *also* **smoul·der** (smōl'dər) *v.* **1.** To burn with little smoke and without flame. **2.** To exist in a barely suppressed state. **—smol'der** *n.*
smooch (smo͞och) *n. Slang.* A kiss. **—smooch** *v.*
smooth (smo͞oth) *adj.* **1.** Not irregular or rough. **2.** Fine in texture or consistency. **3.** Free from jolts or jerks <a *smooth* ride> **4.** Without difficulties or obstructions. **5.** Agreeable and esp. ingratiating in manner. *—v.* **1.** To make or become smooth. **2.** To rid of difficulties or troubles. **—smooth'ly** *adv.* **—smooth'ness** *n.*
smor·gas·bord (smôr'gəs-bôrd', -bōrd') *n.* A buffet meal consisting of a variety of dishes.
smote (smōt) *v. p.t. & var. p.p. of* SMITE.
smoth·er (smŭth'ər) *v.* **1.** To suffocate or be suffocated. **2.** To suppress or conceal. **3.** To cover thickly. **—smoth'er·y** *adj.*
smudge (smŭj) *v.* **smudged, smudg·ing.** To make dirty or blurred, esp. by rubbing : smear. *—n.* **1.** A smear or blotch. **2.** Dense smoke used to protect against frost or repel insects. **—smudg'y** *adj.*
smug (smŭg) *adj.* **smug·ger, smug·gest.** Self-righteous or self-satisfied : complacent. **—smug'ly** *adv.* **—smug'ness** *n.*
smug·gle (smŭg'əl) *v.* **-gled, -gling. 1.** To import or export illegally or without paying customs duties. **2.** To bring in or take out stealthily. **—smug'gler** *n.*
smut (smŭt) *n.* **1. a.** Something, as a particle of dirt, that smudges. **b.** A smudge. **2.** Obscene language or material. **3.** Any of several plant diseases caused by fungi and marked by the formation of black, powdery masses. **4.** Obscenity. **—smut'ty** *adj.*
Sn *symbol for* TIN.
snack (snăk) *n.* **1.** A hurried or light meal. **2.** Food eaten between meals. **—snack** *v.*
snaf·fle (snăf'əl) *n.* A jointed bit used on a horse's bridle.

snaffle

snag (snăg) *n.* **1.** A jagged or sharp protuberance. **2.** A part of a tree, esp. a stump, that protrudes from the surface of a body of water. **3.** An unforeseen obstacle or difficulty. *—v.* **snagged, snag·ging. 1.** To be caught on or as if on a snag. **2.** *Informal.* To catch quickly or unexpectedly : snatch.
snail (snal) *n.* Any of numerous aquatic or terrestrial mollusks of the class Gastropoda, typically with a spiral, coiled shell, a broad retractile foot, and a distinct head.
snake (snāk) *n.* **1.** Any of various scaly, legless, occas. venomous reptiles of the suborder Serpentes, having a long, tapering body. **2.** An untrustworthy or insidious person. *—v.* **snaked, snak·ing.** To move or drag with a snakelike motion. **—snak'i·ly** *adv.* **—snak'y** *adj.*
Snake. River of the NW U.S., flowing 1,038 mi (1,670 km) W from NW Wyo. to the Columbia in SE Wash.
snake·bite (snāk'bīt') *n.* **1.** The bite of a snake. **2.** Poisoning resulting from the bite of a venomous snake.
snap (snăp) *v.* **snapped, snap·ping. 1.** To make, cause to make, or break suddenly with a brisk, sharp cracking noise. **2.** To give way suddenly <His mind *snapped.*> **3.** To seize or snatch at something with or as if with the teeth. **4.** To speak abruptly, angrily, or sharply. **5.** To sparkle : flash <eyes *snapping* with anger> **6.** *Football.* To pass the ball to start a play. *—n.* **1.** The sound or act of snapping. **2.** A fastener or catch that opens and closes with a snap. **3.** A thin, crisp cookie. **4.** Vitality : energy. **5.** A short spell of cold weather. **6.** *Informal.* Something requiring little effort. **7.** *Football.* The passing of the ball that starts a play. **—snap'pish** *adj.* **—snap'py** *adj.*
snap bean *n.* A bean, as the string bean, grown for its crisp, edible pods.
snap·drag·on (snăp'drăg'ən) *n.* A plant, *Antirrhinum majus,* with 2-lipped, variously colored flower clusters.
snap·per (snăp'ər) *n., pl.* **-per** *or* **-pers.** Any of numerous marine food and game fishes of the family Lutjanidae.
snapping turtle *n.* Any of several New World freshwater turtles of the family Chelydridae, with powerful hooked jaws.
snap·shot (snăp'shŏt') *n.* A picture taken with a small hand-held camera.
snare[1] (snâr) *n.* **1.** A device, often consisting of a noose, for trapping small animals and birds. **2.** Something that entangles. **—snare** *v.* **—snar'er** *n.*
snare[2] (snâr) *n.* A string or wire stretched across the lower head of a drum.
snarl[1] (snärl) *v.* **1.** To growl angrily or ominously, esp. while baring the teeth. **2.** To speak in an angry or surly manner. **—snarl** *n.* **—snarl'ing·ly** *adv.*
snarl[2] (snärl) *n.* A tangle. *—v.* To become or cause to become tangled : knot.
snatch (snăch) *v.* **1.** To seize or try to seize something suddenly. **2.** To take suddenly and esp. illicitly : grab. *—n.* **1.** The act of snatching. **2.** A brief period. **3.** A fragment : bit <a *snatch* of an old story>
snaz·zy (snăz'ē) *adj.* **-zi·er, -zi·est.** Attractive in a flashy or showy way.

sneak (snēk) *v.* To move, take, or act in a quiet, stealthy way. ☆*syns:* CREEP, GLIDE, LURK, PROWL, SKULK, SLIDE, SLINK, SLIP, STEAL —*n.* **1.** A person who acts in a stealthy or underhanded way. **2.** An act or example of sneaking. **—sneak'i•ly** *adv.* **—sneak'i•ness** *n.* **—sneak'y** *adj.*

sneak•er (snē'kər) *n.* A usu. canvas sports shoe with a soft rubber sole.

sneer (snîr) *v.* To show contempt by curling the upper lip or by speaking in a derisive or scornful manner. **—sneer** *n.*

sneeze (snēz) *v.* **sneezed, sneez•ing.** To expel air forcibly through the nose and mouth by an involuntary convulsive action. **—sneeze** *n.*

snick•er (snĭk'ər) *n.* A partly stifled laugh. **—snick'er** *v.*

snide (snīd) *adj.* **snid•er, snid•est.** Sneakily derogatory. **—snide'ly** *adv.*

sniff (snĭf) *v.* **1.** To inhale audibly. **2.** To show contempt or disdain. **3.** To detect by or as if by sniffing. **—sniff** *n.*

snif•fle (snĭf'əl) *v.* **-fled, -fling.** To sniff frequently to prevent nasal discharge from running. —*n.* **1.** The act or sound of sniffling. **2. sniffles.** *Informal.* A head cold marked by sniffling. **—snif'fler** *n.*

snif•ter (snĭf'tər) *n.* A pear-shaped goblet used esp. for brandy.

snig•ger (snĭg'ər) *v.* To snicker. **—snig'ger** *n.* **—snig'ger•ing•ly** *adv.*

snip (snĭp) *v.* **snipped, snip•ping.** To cut or cut off with many quick strokes : clip. —*n.* **1.** A stroke made with shears or scissors. **2.** A small piece snipped off.

snipe (snīp) *n., pl.* **snipe** or **snipes.** A long-billed, brownish wading bird of the genus *Capella.* —*v.* **sniped, snip•ing. 1.** To shoot at individuals in the open from a hidden position. **2.** To make malicious attacks or remarks. **—snip'er** *n.*

snip•pet (snĭp'ĭt) *n.* A bit.

snip•py (snĭp'ē) *adj.* **-pi•er, -pi•est.** *Informal.* Impudent : impertinent.

snit (snĭt) *n. Slang.* Agitation : uproar.

snitch (snĭch) *v. Slang.* **1.** To steal : pilfer. **2.** To turn informer. **—snitch** *n.*

sniv•el (snĭv'əl) *v.* **-eled, -el•ing** or **-elled, -el•ling. 1.** To complain or speak tearfully : whine. **2.** To run at the nose. **—sniv'el** *n.* **—sniv'el•er** *n.*

snob (snŏb) *n.* Someone who considers himself socially superior and condescends to those he considers to be his inferiors. **—snob'ber•y** *n.* **—snob'bish** *adj.*

snob•bish (snŏb'ĭsh) *adj.* Characteristic of or resembling a snob. ☆*syns:* ELITIST, HIGH-HAT, SNOOTY, UPPITY. **—snob'bish•ly** *adv.* **—snob'bish•ness** *n.*

snood (sno͞od) *n.* A small netlike cap worn by women to hold the hair in place.

snoop (sno͞op) *Informal.* —*v.* To pry in a sly or intrusive manner. —*n.* One who snoops. **—snoop'y** *adj.*

snoot (sno͞ot) *n. Slang.* **1.** The snout. **2.** The nose. **3.** A snob.

snoot•y (sno͞o'tē) *adj.* **-i•er, -i•est.** *Informal.* Haughty : snobbish.

snooze (sno͞oz) *v.* **snoozed, snooz•ing.** *Informal.* To take a light nap : doze. **—snooze** *n.* **—snooz'er** *n.*

snore (snôr, snōr) *v.* **snored, snor•ing.** To breathe with a hoarse, harsh noise while sleeping. **—snore** *n.* **—snor'er** *n.*

snor•kel (snôr'kəl) *n.* A tube that projects above the surface of water, used by skin divers for breathing with the face submerged. **—snor'kel** *v.* **—snor'kel•er** *n.*

snort (snôrt) *n.* **1.** To force air noisily through the nostrils. **2.** To express scorn, surprise, or anger by snorting. **3.** *Slang.* To inhale a drug. **—snort** *n.* **—snort'er** *n.*

snot (snŏt) *n. Slang.* **1.** Nasal mucus. **2.** A supercilious or contemptible person.

snout (snout) *n.* **1.** The long, projecting nose, jaws, or anterior facial part of an animal's muzzle. **2.** *Slang.* The human nose, esp. when excessively large.

snow (snō) *n.* **1.** Solid precipitation in the form of translucent ice crystals formed from water vapor in the upper atmosphere. **2.** A fall or shower of snow. —*v.* **1.** To fall to the earth as snow. **2.** To isolate or cover with or as if with snow. **3.** *Slang.* To overwhelm or deceive with insincere talk. **—snow'y** *adj.*

snow•ball (snō'bôl') *n.* A mass of snow formed into a ball. —*v.* To develop or accumulate at a rapidly increasing rate.

snow•bank (snō'băngk') *n.* A slope or rounded mass of snow.

snow•bound (snō'bound') *adj.* Confined or blockaded by snow.

snow•drift (snō'drĭft') *n.* Snow piled up by the wind.

snow•drop (snō'drŏp') *n.* Any of several bulbous plants of the genus *Galanthus,* with a nodding white flower that blooms in the early spring.

snow•fall (snō'fôl') *n.* **1.** A fall of snow. **2.** The amount of snow that falls in a particular storm or within a given time.

snow fence *n.* Temporary fencing of thin upright slats used to prevent snow from drifting onto roads and walks.

snow•mo•bile (snō'mō-bēl') *n.* A small automotive vehicle with skilike runners in front and tanklike treads used for driving in or traveling on snow.

snow•plow (snō'plou') *n.* A device or vehicle for removing snow.

snow•shoe (snō'sho͞o') *n.* A racketlike frame strung with leather strips that is attached to the shoe to prevent the foot from sinking into snow. **—snow'shoe'** *v.*

snow•storm (snō'stôrm') *n.* A storm with a heavy snowfall.

snow•suit (snō'so͞ot') *n.* A child's lined winter coveralls.

snow tire *n.* A tire with a deep tread that gives added traction on snow or ice.

snub (snŭb) *v.* **snubbed, snub•bing. 1.** To treat with contempt or scorn : slight. **2.** To check or stop the movement of by turning around a post. **—snub** *n.*

snub-nosed (snŭb'nōzd') *adj.* Having a short, stubby nose.

snuff[1] (snŭf) *v.* **1.** To draw in through the nostrils. **2.** To examine or sense by smell : sniff. —*n.* Finely pulverized tobacco that can be snuffed through the nostrils.

snuff[2] (snŭf) *v.* **1.** To cut off the charred portion of (a candle). **2.** To extinguish.

snuff•box (snŭf'bŏks') *n.* A small box for carrying snuff.

snuf•fle (snŭf'əl) *v.* **-fled, -fling. 1.** To breathe noisily, as through an obstructed nose. **2.** To sniffle. **—snuf'fle** *n.*

snug (snŭg) *adj.* **snug•ger, snug•gest. 1.** Pleasant and comfortable : cozy. **2.** Small but arranged well <a *snug* house> **3.** Close-fitting : tight <a *snug* winter jacket> **—snug, snug'ly** *adv.* **—snug'ness** *n.*

snug•gle (snŭg'əl) *v.* **-gled, -gling.** To lie or hold close : cuddle.

so (sō) *adv.* **1.** In the manner indicated or expressed : thus. **2. a.** To an extent indicated or expressed. **b.** To a great extent : very. **3.** As a result : consequently. **4.** Likewise : also. **5.** In truth : indeed <He did *so* lie.> —*conj.* With the result or consequence that <She didn't eat, *so* she lost weight.> —*pron.* **1.** The same <became a teacher and remained *so*> **2.** About that <needs a yard or *so* of silk for the blouse>

so. *abbr.* south; southern.

s.o. *abbr.* **1.** seller's option. **2.** strikeout.

soak (sōk) *v.* **1.** To make or become thoroughly wet : saturate. **2.** To take in through or as if through pores : absorb. **3.** To be immersed in a liquid. **4.** *Slang.* To overcharge. —*n.* **1.** The act or process of soaking. **2.** *Slang.* A drunkard.

so-and-so (sō'ən-sō') *n., pl.* **-sos. 1.** One that is unnamed or unspecified. **2.** *Informal.* A nasty person : bastard.

soap (sōp) *n.* **1.** A cleansing agent made by the action of an alkali on natural oils and fats. **2.** *Slang.* A soap opera. —*v.* To treat, rub, or cover with soap. **—soap'y** *adj.*

soap•box (sōp'bŏks') *n.* An improvised platform on which a street orator stands.

soap opera *n.* A radio or television serial characterized by sentimentality and melodrama.

soap•stone (sōp'stōn') *n.* Steatite.

soar (sôr, sōr) *v.* **1.** To fly or glide high in the air. **2.** To rise suddenly above the normal level <*soaring* spirits><*soaring* prices>

sob (sŏb) *v.* **sobbed, sob•bing.** To weep with convulsive gasps. **—sob** *n.*

so•ber (sō'bər) *adj.* **1.** Abstemious in the use of liquor : temperate. **2.** Not intoxicated. **3.** Grave or serious : solemn. **4.** Marked by restraint : reasonable. —*v.* To make or become sober. **—so'ber•ly** *adv.* **—so•bri'e•ty, so'ber•ness** *n.*

so•bri•quet (sō'brĭ-kā', -kĕt') *n.* **1.** A nickname. **2.** An assumed name.

soc. *abbr.* **1.** socialist. **2.** society.

so-called (sō'kôld') *adj.* Commonly but often incorrectly named or designated.

soc•cer (sŏk'ər) *n.* A game played on a field by 2 teams who try to kick a round ball into the opposing team's goal.

▲word history: Soccer, which is probably the most popular team sport everywhere except in the U.S., was invented in England. The word *soccer* is derived from *association.* The official name of the game is *Association Football,* that is, football as played under the rules of the Football Association of England, founded in 1863.

so•cia•ble (sō'shə-bəl) *adj.* **1.** Liking the company of others : friendly. **2.** Marked by friendly social relations. **—so'cia•bil'i•ty, so'cia•ble•ness** *n.* **—so'cia•bly** *adv.*

so•cial (sō'shəl) *adj.* **1.** Living in communities or groups. **2.** Of or relating to the life and interrelationships of human beings in society. **3.** Marked by friendly companionship with others. **4. a.** Of, pertaining to, or based on status in a specific society

<wasn't his *social* equal> **b.** Of or pertaining to the upper classes. —*n.* An informal social gathering. **—so'cial·ly** *adv.*
Social Credit Party *n.* A Canadian political party.
social disease *n.* A venereal disease.
so·cial·ism (sō'shə-lĭz'əm) *n.* A social system or theory in which the producers possess political power and the means of producing and distributing goods. **—so'cial·ist** *n.* **—so'cial·is'tic** *adj.*
so·cial·ite (sō'shə-līt') *n.* A member of fashionable society.
so·cial·ize (sō'shə-līz') *v.* **-ized, -iz·ing. 1.** To place under government or group ownership or control. **2.** To adapt to the needs of society. **3.** To participate in social activities. **—so'cial·i·za'tion** *n.*
socialized medicine *n.* Provision of hospital and medical services at nominal cost by means of government regulation of health services and subsidies derived from taxation.
social science *n.* A science, as sociology or anthropology, that studies society and individual relationships in and to society.
social security *n.* A government program of monthly payments to the elderly, the disabled, and the unemployed, financed by taxation of employers and employees.
social work *n.* Activities and services designed to aid the poor and those with social problems. **—social worker** *n.*
so·ci·e·ty (sə-sī'ĭ-tē) *n.*, *pl.* **-ties. 1. a.** The totality of social relationships among human beings. **b.** A group of human beings bound together by shared institutions and culture. **2. a.** The rich, privileged, and fashionable social class. **b.** The socially dominant members of a community. **3.** Companionship : company. **4.** An association of people with mutual aims or interests. **—so·ci'e·tal** *adj.*
so·ci·o·ec·o·nom·ic (sō'sē-ō-ĕk'ə-nŏm'ĭk, -ē'kə-, -shē-) *adj.* Of, pertaining to, or involving both social and economic factors.
so·ci·ol·o·gy (sō'sē-ŏl'ə-jē, -shē-) *n.* The study of the organization, institutions, and development of human society. **—so'ci·o·log'ic** (-ə-lŏj'ĭk), **so'ci·o·log'i·cal** *adj.* **—so'ci·ol'o·gist** *n.*
so·ci·o·path (sō'sē-ə-păth', -shē-) *n.* A person manifesting antisocial behavior patterns or character traits.
sock[1] (sŏk) *n.*, *pl.* **socks** *or* **sox** A stocking extending above the ankle and ending below the knee.
sock[2] (sŏk) *v.* *Slang.* To strike forcefully : punch. **—sock** *n.*
sock·et (sŏk'ĭt) *n.* An opening or cavity into which something fits.
sock·eye salmon (sŏk'ī') *n.* A salmon, *Oncorhynchus nerka*, of N Pacific coastal waters, that is a valuable food fish.
Soc·ra·tes (sŏk'rə-tēz'). 470?–399 B.C. Greek philosopher. **—So·crat'ic** *adj.*
So·cred (sō'krĕd') *n. can.* **1.** The Social Credit Party. **2.** A member of this Party.
sod (sŏd) *n.* The surface of the soil held together by roots of grass : turf. —*v.* **sod·ded, sod·ding.** To cover with sod.
so·da (sō'də) *n.* **1. a.** Any of various forms of sodium carbonate. **b.** Chemically combined sodium. **2. a.** Soda water. **b.** A flavored carbonated soft drink. **c.** A drink made of carbonated water, flavoring, and often ice cream.
soda fountain *n.* A counter equipped for preparing and serving soft drinks, ice-cream dishes, and sandwiches.
so·dal·i·ty (sō-dăl'ĭ-tē) *n.*, *pl.* **-ties. 1.** A society or association, esp. a devotional or charitable society in the Roman Catholic Church. **2.** Fellowship.
soda pop *n.* SODA 2b.
soda water *n.* A mixer or beverage of water charged with carbon dioxide.
sod·den (sŏd'n) *adj.* **1.** Thoroughly soaked : drenched. **2.** Soggy and heavy, as from improper cooking : doughy. **3.** Lacking in vitality or expressiveness : dull.
so·di·um (sō'dē-əm) *n.* Symbol **Na** A soft, light, extremely malleable silver-white metallic element.
sodium bicarbonate *n.* A white crystalline compound used esp. in making effervescent beverages and baking soda.
sodium carbonate *n.* **1.** A white powdery compound used in manufacturing ceramics, detergents, and soap. **2.** Any of various hydrated carbonates of sodium.
sodium chloride *n.* SALT 1.
sodium hydroxide *n.* An alkaline compound used in chemicals and soaps and in petroleum refining.
sodium nitrate *n.* A white crystalline compound used as a fertilizer and in solid rocket propellants and explosives.
Sod·om (sŏd'əm). City of ancient Palestine.
sod·om·y (sŏd'ə-mē) *n.* **1.** Anal copulation of one male with another. **2.** Anal or oral copulation with a member of the opposite sex. **3.** Copulation with an animal.
so·ev·er (sō-ĕv'ər) *adv.* In any way : at all.
so·fa (sō'fə) *n.* An upholstered couch with a back and arms.
sofa bed *n.* A sofa whose seat unfolds to form a bed.
So·fi·a (sō'fē-ə, sō-fē'ə). Cap. of Bulgaria, in the WC part. *Pop.* 1,047,920.
soft (sôft, sŏft) *adj.* **1.** Not hard or firm. **2.** Lacking stamina or robustness : flabby. **3.** Not rough, harsh, loud, or irritating. **4.** Mild : gentle. **5.** Easily swayed or affected emotionally. **6.** Lacking strength of character : weak. **7.** *Informal.* Mentally feeble. **8.** *Informal.* Not requiring much work or effort : easy <a *soft* job> **9.** Likely to fluctuate or devaluate. **10.** Containing relatively little dissolved mineral matter <*soft* water> **—soft, soft'ly** *adv.* **—soft'ness** *n.*
soft·ball (sôft'bôl', sŏft'-) *n.* **1.** A game similar to baseball that is played on a smaller diamond with a larger, softer ball. **2.** The ball used in softball.
soft·bound (sôft'bound', sŏft'-) *adj.* Not bound between hard covers.
soft coal *n.* Bituminous coal.
soft drink *n.* A nonalcoholic beverage.
soft·en (sô'fən, sŏf'ən) *v.* To make or become soft or softer. **—soft'en·er** *n.*
soft·heart·ed (sôft'här'tĭd, sŏft'-) *adj.* Easily moved to tenderness : sympathetic.
soft landing *n.* The landing of a space vehicle at a velocity low enough to prevent damaging or destructive impact.
soft palate *n.* The movable muscular fold suspended from the rear of the hard palate that closes off the nasal cavity from the oral cavity when swallowing.
soft-ped·al (sôft'pĕd'l, sŏft'-) *v.* *Informal.* To make less conspicuous : play down.
soft sell *n.* A method of selling or advertising that relies on subtle persuasion.
soft soap *n.* *Informal.* Sweet words : flattery. **—soft'-soap'** *v.*
soft·ware (sôft'wâr', sŏft'-) *n.* *Computer Sci.* Data, as programs, routines, and symbolic languages, essential to the operation and maintenance of computers.
soft·wood (sôft'wŏŏd', sŏft'-) *n.* **1.** The wood of a coniferous tree. **2.** A tree yielding softwood. **—soft'wood'** *adj.*
soft·y (sôf'tē, sŏf'-) *n.*, *pl.* **-ies.** *Informal.* Someone who finds it difficult to punish or be stict.
sog·gy (sŏg'ē, sô'gē) *adj.* **-gi·er, -gi·est.** Sodden with moisture : saturated. **—sog'gi·ly** *adv.* **—sog'gi·ness** *n.*
soi·gné *also* **soi·gnée** (swän-yā') *adj.* **1.** Fashionable. **2.** Well-groomed : polished.
soil[1] (soil) *n.* **1.** The loose top layer of the earth's surface in which plant life can grow. **2.** Ground : earth. **3.** Land : country.
soil[2] (soil) *v.* **1.** To make or become dirty. **2.** To tarnish : disgrace. **3.** To corrupt morally : defile. —*n.* **1. a.** The state of being soiled. **b.** A stain. **2.** Excrement, esp. human excrement : waste.
soi·ree *or* **soi·rée** (swä-rā') *n.* An evening reception or party.
so·journ (sō'jûrn', sō-jûrn') *v.* To stay in a place for a time. **—so'journ'** *n.* **—so'journ'er** *n.*
sol (sōl, sôl) *n.*, *pl.* **so·les** (sō'lās). See CURRENCY TABLE.
sol·ace (sŏl'əs) *n.* **1.** Comfort in sorrow, misfortune, or distress. **2.** A source of solace. **—sol'ace** *v.* **—sol'ac·er** *n.*
so·lar (sō'lər) *adj.* **1.** Of, relating to, or proceeding from the sun. **2.** Utilizing or operated by means of energy derived from the sun. **3.** Determined or measured with respect to the sun <the *solar* year>
solar battery *n.* A device that converts solar radiation into electrical energy.
solar flare *n.* A temporary outburst of solar gases from the sun's surface, a source of intense radiation.
so·lar·i·um (sō-lâr'ē-əm, -lăr'-) *n.*, *pl.* **-i·a** (-ē-ə) *or* **-i·ums.** A glassed-in room or porch exposed to the sun.
solar plexus *n.* **1.** A network of nerves and nerve tissue situated behind the stomach. **2.** *Informal.* The pit of the stomach.
solar system *n.* The sun together with the celestial bodies that orbit it.
solar wind *n.* Plasma ejected at high speed from the sun's surface.
sold (sōld) *v.* *p.t.* & *p.p.* *of* SELL.
sol·der (sŏd'ər, sô'dər) *n.* Any of various alloys, esp. of tin and lead, used in the melted state to join or repair metal parts. —*v.* To join or repair with or as if with solder. **—sol'der·er** *n.*

▲word history: The letter *l* in the word *solder* has a long history. The ancestor of *solder* is Latin *solidare*, "to make solid, to fasten together." The Latin word descended into Old French as *souder*, meaning "to join with melted metal"; loss of *l* in certain situations was a normal development in Old French. An *l* was reinserted in the Old French word by those who knew its derivation from Latin, and the variant *solder* existed alongside *souder*. These forms were both borrowed into English, as *solder* and *soder*, respectively, each being pronounced as it was spelled. The spelling *soder* eventually was displaced by *solder*. In British English both pronunciations still exist, but in American English the pronunciation without *l* has completely prevailed.

sol·dier (sōl′jər) *n.* **1.** Someone, esp. an enlisted person, who serves in an army. **2.** An active, loyal, and militant follower. *—v.* To serve as a soldier. **—sol′dier·ly** *adj.*

soldier of fortune *n.* One who engages in a military career in any army for money, pleasure, or adventure.

sol·dier·y (sōl′jə-rē) *n., pl.* **-ies. 1.** Soldiers as a group. **2.** A body of soldiers. **3.** The military profession.

sole[1] (sōl) *n.* **1.** The undersurface of the foot. **2.** The undersurface of a boot or shoe. *—v.* **soled, sol·ing.** To put a sole on (e.g., a shoe).

sole[2] (sōl) *adj.* Being the only one : single. **—sole′ly** *adv.*

sole[3] (sōl) *n., pl.* **sole** *or* **soles.** Any of various mainly marine flatfishes of the family Soleidae, valued as food.

sol·e·cism (sŏl′ĭ-sĭz′əm, sō′lĭ-) *n.* **1.** An error in grammar or word usage. **2.** A violation of etiquette. **—sol′e·cist** *n.*

sol·emn (sŏl′əm) *adj.* **1.** Deeply serious : grave. **2.** Performed with or marked by full religious ceremony. **3.** Formal in nature or character : ceremonious. **4.** Somber : gloomy. **—so·lem′ni·ty** (sə-lĕm′nĭ-tē), **sol′emn·ness** *n.* **—sol′emn·ly** *adv.*

sol·em·nize (sŏl′əm-nīz′) *v.* **-nized, -niz·ing. 1.** To celebrate, honor, or observe with formal ceremonies. **2.** To perform (a marriage) with formal religious rites. **—sol′em·ni·za′tion** *n.*

so·le·noid (sō′lə-noid′) *n.* A cylindrical coil of insulated wire in which an axial magnetic field is established by a flow of electric current.

so·lic·it (sə-lĭs′ĭt) *v.* **1.** To try to obtain. **2.** To beg : entreat. **3.** To tempt : entice. **—so·lic′i·ta′tion** *n.*

so·lic·i·tor (sə-lĭs′ĭ-tər) *n.* **1.** One that solicits. **2.** A lawyer, esp. the chief law officer of a city, town, or government department. **3.** *esp. Brit.* A lawyer who is not a barrister.

so·lic·i·tous (sə-lĭs′ĭ-təs) *adj.* **1.** Anxious and concerned : worried. **2.** Eager : desirous.

so·lic·i·tude (sə-lĭs′ĭ-to͞od′, -tyo͞od′) *n.* The state or quality of being solicitous.

sol·id (sŏl′ĭd) *adj.* **1.** Not liquid or gaseous. **2.** Not hollow. **3.** Being of the same character or substance throughout. **4.** Of, having, or involving 3 dimensions. **5.** Of a satisfactory and substantial character <*solid* pleasure> **6.** Written or printed without a space or hyphen. **7.** Upstanding and reliable : dependable. **8.** Sound : valid <a *solid* argument> **9.** Acting together : unanimous. **10.** Without gaps, crevices, or breaks : compact. *—n.* **1.** A solid body or substance. **2.** A geometric figure, as a cube, that has 3 dimensions. **—so·lid′i·fi·ca′tion** *n.* **—so·lid′i·fy′** *v.* **—so·lid′i·ty** (sə-lĭd′ĭ-tē), **sol′id·ness** *n.* **—sol′id·ly** *adv.*

sol·i·dar·i·ty (sŏl′ĭ-dăr′ĭ-tē) *n.* Unity arising from common purpose, sympathy, or interests : fellowship.

solid geometry *n.* The geometry of 3-dimensional figures and surfaces.

sol·id-state (sŏl′ĭd-stāt′) *adj.* **1.** Of, relating to, or concerned with the physical properties of crystalline solids. **2.** Based on or composed principally or entirely of transistors or related semiconductor devices.

so·lil·o·quize (sə-lĭl′ə-kwīz′) *v.* **-quized, -quiz·ing.** To deliver a soliloquy.

so·lil·o·quy (sə-lĭl′ə-kwē) *n., pl.* **-quies. 1.** A dramatic monologue in which a character's thoughts are revealed with no listener present. **2.** The act of speaking to oneself.

sol·i·taire (sŏl′ĭ-târ′) *n.* **1.** A single gemstone, as a diamond, set by itself, esp. in a ring. **2.** A card game played by 1 person.

sol·i·tar·y (sŏl′ĭ-tĕr′ē) *adj.* **1.** Existing, being, or living alone. **2.** Happening, passed, or done alone. **3.** Secluded : remote. **4.** Only : sole. **—sol′i·tar′i·ness** *n.*

sol·i·tude (sŏl′ĭ-to͞od′, -tyo͞od′) *n.* **1.** The state of being alone : isolation. **2.** A secluded or lonely place.

soln. *abbr.* solution.

so·lo (sō′lō) *n., pl.* **-los. 1.** *Mus.* A composition for a single voice or instrument with or without accompaniment. **2.** An action performed by 1 person. *—v.* To perform alone. **—so′lo** *adj.* & *adv.* **—so′lo·ist** *n.*

Sol·o·mon (sŏl′ə-mən). 10th cent. B.C. king of Israel.

Solomon Islands *also* **Solomons. 1.** Islands of the W Pacific E of New Guinea, divided between Papua New Guinea and the independent Solomon Is. **2.** Nation comprising the Solomons SE of Bougainville. *Cap.* Honiara. *Pop.* 225,000.

so·lon (sō′lən) *n.* **1.** A wise lawgiver. **2.** A lawmaker : legislator.

Solon. 638?–559 B.C. Athenian statesman.

sol·stice (sŏl′stĭs, sōl′-) *n.* Either of 2 times of the year, approx. June 22 and Dec. 22, when the sun reaches an extreme northward or southward motion. **—sol·sti′tial** (-stĭsh′əl) *adj.*

sol·u·ble (sŏl′yə-bəl) *adj.* **1.** Able to be dissolved. **2.** Able to be solved or explained. **—sol′u·bil′i·ty** *n.* **—sol′u·bly** *adv.*

sol·ute (sŏl′yo͞ot′, sō′lo͞ot′) *n.* A substance that has been dissolved.

so·lu·tion (sə-lo͞o′shən) *n.* **1.a.** A homogeneous mixture of 2 or more usu. liquid substances. **b.** Formation of such a mixture. **2. a.** The method or process of solving a problem. **b.** The answer to a problem.

solve (sŏlv) *v.* **solved, solv·ing.** To find a solution or answer to. **—solv′a·ble** *adj.*

sol·vent (sŏl′vənt) *adj.* **1.** Capable of meeting financial obligations. **2.** Having the capability to dissolve another substance. *—n.* A liquid that can dissolve another substance. **—sol′ven·cy** *n.*

So·ma·li·a (sō-mä′lē-ə, -mäl′yə). Country of E Africa, on the Indian Ocean. *Cap.* Mogadishu. *Pop.* 4,535,000.

So·ma·li·land (sō-mä′lē-lănd′). Region of E Africa, including Somalia, Djibouti, and parts of Ethiopia.

so·mat·ic (sō-măt′ĭk, sə-) *adj.* Of or relating to the body : physical.

som·ber (sŏm′bər) *adj.* **1.** Gloomy : dark. **2.** Melancholy : dejected.

som·bre (sŏm′bər) *adj. esp. Brit. var. of* SOMBER.

som·bre·ro (sŏm-brâr′ō) *n., pl.* **-ros.** A large, broad-brimmed felt or straw hat worn esp. in Mexico and the SW U.S.

some (sŭm) *adj.* **1.** Being an indefinite or unspecified number or quantity <*some* candy> **2.** Being unknown or unspecified by name <*Some* friend left a message.> **3.** A little or a few <*some* days past> *—pron.* An indefinite or unspecified number or quantity <*Some* of the roses wilted.> *—adv.* **1.** Approximately <*some* 10 books> **2.** *Informal.* Somewhat.

-some[1] *suff.* Marked by a specific quality, condition, or action <bother*some*>

-some[2] *suff.* A group of a specified number of members <two*some*>

some·bod·y (sŭm′bŏd′ē, -bŭd′ē, -bə-dē) *pron.* A person unspecified or unknown. *—n. Informal.* An important person.

some·day (sŭm′dā′) *adv.* At an unspecified future time.

some·how (sŭm′hou′) *adv.* In a way not specified or known.

some·one (sŭm′wŭn′, -wən) *pron.* Somebody. *—n.* An important person.

som·er·sault (sŭm′ər-sôlt′) *n.* The act of rolling the body in a complete circle, with heels over head. **—som′er·sault′** *v.*

some·thing (sŭm′thĭng) *pron.* A thing undetermined or unspecified.

some·time (sŭm′tīm′) *adv.* **1.** At an unstated or indefinite time. **2.** At an indefinite future time.

some·times (sŭm′tīmz′) *adv.* Now and then : occasionally.

some·what (sŭm′hwŏt′, -wŏt′, -hwət, -wət′) *adv.* To some degree or extent.

some·where (sŭm′hwâr′, -wâr′) *adv.* At, in, or to an unspecified or unknown place.

Somme (sôm). River, c. 150 mi (241 km), of N France.

som·nam·bu·lism (sŏm-năm′byə-lĭz′əm) *n.* The act of walking in one's sleep. **—som·nam′bu·list** *n.*

som·no·lent (sŏm′nə-lənt) *adj.* Sleepy : drowsy. **—som′no·lence** *n.*

son (sŭn) *n.* **1.** A male offspring. **2.** A male descendant. **3.** A male associated with a particular place, as a country or school.

so·nance (sō′nəns) *n.* Sound.

so·nar (sō′när′) *n.* A system or apparatus that uses reflected acoustic waves to detect and locate submerged objects.

so·na·ta (sə-nä′tä) *n. Mus.* An instrumental composition, as for the piano, in 3 or 4 movements contrasting in mood and tempo but related in key.

son·a·ti·na (sŏn′ə-tē′nə) *n.* A sonata with shorter movements than the typical sonata.

song (sông, sŏng) *n.* **1.** A usu. brief musical composition meant to be sung. **2.** The act or art of singing. **3.** Poetry. **—for a song.** For a small amount of money.

song·bird (sông′bûrd′, sŏng′-) *n.* A bird with a melodious call.

Song of Solomon *n.* See BIBLE TABLE.

Song of Songs *n.* See BIBLE TABLE.

song·ster (sông′stər, sŏng′-) *n.* A singer.

son·ic (sŏn′ĭk) *adj.* Of or pertaining to sound or the speed of sound.

sonic barrier *n.* The sudden sharp increase in aerodynamic drag experienced by aircraft approaching the speed of sound.

sonic boom *n.* A loud, explosive sound caused by an aircraft traveling at a supersonic speed.

son-in-law (sŭn′ĭn-lô′) *n., pl.* **sons-in-law.** The husband of one's daughter.

son·net (sŏn′ĭt) *n.* A fixed 14-line verse form, usu. in iambic pentameter, with a prescribed rhyme scheme.

so·no·rous (sə-nôr′əs, -nōr′-, sŏn′ər-) *adj.* **1.** Producing sound, esp. full, deep, or rich sound : resonant. **2.** Elevated : lofty. **—so·nor′i·ty** (sə-nôr′ĭ-tē, -nŏr′-) *n.*

soon (so͞on) *adv.* **1.** In the near future. **2.** Early. **3.** Fast : quickly. **4.** Readily : willingly <I'd as *soon* stop right now>

soot (so͝ot, so͞ot, sŭt) *n.* A fine black powder, mainly carbon, generated by the incomplete combustion of fuel, as wood or coal. **–soot'i•ness** *n.* **–soot'y** *adj.*

sooth (so͞oth) *n. Archaic.* Reality : truth.

soothe (so͞oth) *v.* **soothed, sooth•ing. 1.** To calm by showing concern : mollify. **2.** To ease the pain, discomfort, or distress of. **–sooth'er** *n.* **–sooth'ing•ly** *adv.*

sooth•say•er (so͞oth'sā'ər) *n.* One who predicts the future or foretells events.

sop (sŏp) *v.* **sopped, sop•ping. 1.** To soak, dip, or drench in a liquid : saturate. **2.** To take up by absorption. *–n.* Something given or conceded to placate : bribe.

SOP *abbr.* standard operating procedure.

soph. *abbr.* sophomore.

soph•ism (sŏf'ĭz'əm) *n.* **1.** A plausible argument that is actually fallacious. **2.** Sophistry. **–soph'ist** *n.* **–so•phis'tic, so•phis'ti•cal** *adj.*

so•phis•ti•cate (sə-fĭs'tĭ-kĭt) *n.* A sophisticated person.

so•phis•ti•cat•ed (sə-fĭs'tĭ-kā'tĭd) *adj.* **1.** Experienced in the ways of the world : knowing. **2.** Complex : complicated <a *sophisticated* computer> **3.** Appealing to the tastes of a sophisticate <a *sophisticated* novel> ☆***syns:*** COSMOPOLITAN, WORLDLY, WORLDLY-WISE **–so•phis'ti•ca'tion** *n.*

soph•ist•ry (sŏf'ĭ-strē) *n.* Plausible but fallacious argumentation or reasoning.

Soph•o•cles (sŏf'ə-klēz'). 496–406 B.C. Greek dramatist.

soph•o•more (sŏf'ə-môr', -mōr') *n.* A student in the 2nd year of college or high school.

soph•o•mor•ic (sŏf'ə-môr'ĭk, -mōr'-, -mŏr'-) *adj.* **1.** Of, pertaining to, or typical of a sophomore. **2.** Brash and overconfident but immature and ill informed.

sop•o•rif•ic (sŏp'ə-rĭf'ĭk) *adj.* **1.** Inducing drowsiness or sleep. **2.** Drowsy. : sleepy. **–sop'o•rif'ic** *n.*

so•pran•o (sə-prăn'ō, -prä'nō) *n., pl.* **-os. 1.** A singing voice of the highest range. **2. a.** A singer with a soprano. **b.** A part for a soprano.

sor•cer•y (sôr'sə-rē) *n.* The use of supernatural power : witchcraft. **–sor'cer•er** *n.* **–sor'cer•ess** *n.*

sor•did (sôr'dĭd) *adj.* **1.** Dirty : filthy. **2.** Squalid. **3.** Marked by moral degradation : base. **–sor'did•ly** *adv.* **–sor'did•ness** *n.*

sore (sôr, sōr) *adj.* **sor•er, sor•est. 1.** Causing or suffering pain or tenderness. **2.** Painful : sensitive. **3.** Causing sorrow, misery, or distress. **4.** Offended : angry. *–n.* **1.** An open skin lesion, wound, or ulcer. **2.** A source of distress or pain. **–sore'ly** *adv.* **–sore'ness** *n.*

sore•head (sôr'hĕd', sōr'-) *n. Slang.* One easily offended or angered.

sore throat *n.* Inflammation of the tonsils, pharynx, or larynx.

sor•ghum (sôr'gəm) *n.* An Old World grass, *Sorghum vulgare,* grown as grain and forage and as a source of syrup.

so•ror•i•ty (sə-rôr'ĭ-tē, -rŏr'-) *n., pl.* **-ties.** A social club for women, esp. at a college.

sor•rel[1] (sôr'əl, sŏr'-) *n.* Any of several plants of the genus *Rumex,* with sour-tasting leaves.

sor•rel[2] (sôr'əl, sŏr'-) *n.* **1.** A reddish brown color. **2.** A horse of the color sorrel.

sor•row (sŏr'ō, sôr'ō) *n.* **1.** Mental suffering : anguish. **2.** A cause of sadness or grief. **3.** An expression of sadness or grief. **–sor'row•ful** *adj.* **–sor'row•ful•ly** *adv.*

sor•ry (sŏr'ē, sôr'ē) *adj.* **-ri•er, -ri•est. 1.** Feeling or showing sympathy, pity, or regret. **2.** Worthless : wretched. **3.** Sad : dismal. ☆***syns:*** CONTRITE, PENITENT, REGRETFUL, REMORSEFUL, REPENTANT

sort (sôrt) *n.* **1.** A group or number of individuals having common attributes : class. **2.** Character : nature. **3.** Manner : way. *–v.* To arrange according to class, kind, or size : classify. **–out of sorts.** *Informal.* **1.** Somewhat sick. **2.** In a bad mood : grouchy.

sor•tie (sôr'tē, sôr-tē') *n.* **1.** An attack on enemy forces launched from a besieged place. **2.** A combat mission by a warplane. **–sor'tie** *v.*

SOS (ĕs'ō-ĕs') *n.* A call for rescue or help.

so-so (sō'sō') *adj.* Neither very good nor very bad : passable. **–so'-so'** *adv.*

sot (sŏt) *n.* A chronic drunkard.

sot•to vo•ce (sŏt'ō vō'chē) *adv.* In a quiet voice : softly.

sou•brette (so͞o-brĕt') *n.* A saucy, coquettish maid in a comedy or comic opera.

souf•flé (so͞o-flā') *n.* A light, fluffy dish made of egg yolks and stiffly beaten egg whites combined with other ingredients as a main dish or sweetened as a dessert.

sough (sŭf, sou) *v.* To make a soft sighing or rustling sound. **–sough** *n.*

sought (sôt) *v. p.t. & p.p. of* SEEK.

soul (sōl) *n.* **1.** The animating spiritual principle in a human being, often believed to survive death. **2.** A human being <not a *soul* at home> **3.** A central or active part. **4.** Embodiment : personification <the *soul* of honor> **5.** A person's spiritual, emotional, and moral nature. **6.** Intensity of emotion and expression, esp. in music. *–adj. Slang.* Of, relating to, or derived from American blacks and their culture.

soul•ful (sōl'fəl) *adj.* Filled with or expressing deep feeling. **–soul'ful•ly** *adv.*

sound[1] (sound) *n.* **1.a.** A vibratory disturbance in the pressure and density of a fluid, as air, capable of being detected by the organs of hearing. **b.** The sensation produced in the organs of hearing by such a disturbance. **2.** Noise <the *sound* of laughter> **3.** The distance within which something can be heard : earshot. **4.** A mental impression : implication. *–v.* **1.** To make or cause to make a sound. **2.** To seem to be <*sounds* sensible> **3.** To summon, order, or signal by a sound <*sound* a warning> **4.** To examine (e.g., a bodily organ) by causing to emit sound. **–sound'less** *adj.*

sound[2] (sound) *adj.* **1.** Free from defect, damage, flaw, or disease. **2.** Solid. **3.** Strong : secure. **4.** Based on or showing valid reasoning or good judgment. **5.** Thorough <a *sound* defeat> **6.** Deep and undisturbed <*sound* sleep> **7.** Legally valid. ☆***syns:*** FIRM, SECURE, SOLID, STABLE, STURDY, SURE **–sound'ly** *adv.* **–sound'ness** *n.*

sound[3] (sound) *n.* A long, relatively wide body of water larger than a channel or strait that often connects larger bodies of water.

sound[4] (sound) *v.* **1.** To measure the depth of (water), esp. by means of a weighted line. **2.** To attempt to learn the opinions or attitudes of : probe. **3.** To dive suddenly downward, as a whale does.

sound barrier *n.* The sonic barrier.

sounding board *n.* **1.** A thin board used in a musical instrument to increase resonance. **2.** A structure, as over a podium, designed to direct sound toward an audience. **3.** A person or group whose reactions, as to an idea, serve to help in an evaluation.

sound•proof (sound'pro͞of') *adj.* Permitting little or no sound to pass. **–sound'proof'** *v.* **–sound'proof'ing** *n.*

sound•track (sound'trăk') *n.* The strip on a motion-picture film that carries the sound recording.

soup (so͞op) *n.* A liquid food consisting of meat, fish, or vegetable stock, often with various solid ingredients added. **–soup up.** *Slang.* To increase the power or speed of.

soup•çon (so͞op-sôN') *n.* A tiny amount : trace.

soup•y (so͞o'pē) *adj.* **-i•er, -i•est. 1.** Having the appearance or consistency of soup. **2.** Foggy. **3.** *Informal.* Sentimental.

sour (sour) *adj.* **1.** Sharp, tart, or acid in taste. **2.** Rancid : spoiled <a *sour* smell> **3.** Disagreeable : unpleasant <a *sour* face> *–v.* To make or become sour. **–sour'ly** *adv.* **–sour'ness** *n.*

sour•ball (sour'bôl') *n.* A round piece of hard candy with a tart flavor.

source (sôrs, sōrs) *n.* **1.** A point of origin. **2.** The place of origin of a stream of water. **3.** One that supplies information.

Sou•sa (so͞o'zə, -sə), **John Philip.** 1854–1932. Amer. bandmaster and composer.

souse (sous) *v.* **soused, sous•ing. 1.** To immerse in a liquid. **2.** To drench. **3.** To steep in a brine : pickle. **4.** *Slang.* To make drunk. *–n.* **1.** The act or process of sousing. **2. a.** Something, as pork trimmings, steeped in pickle. **b.** Brine. **3.** *Slang.* A drunkard.

▲word history: The orig. meaning of the verb *souse* was "to pickle" and of the noun, "pickled meat." Various liquids can be used to pickle or preserve food, but a common one is brine, which is very heavily salted water. The etymology of *souse* reflects this fact, for the word is ult. derived from the Germanic stem *sult-,* a variant of *salto-,* the direct ancestor of English *salt.* The Germanic stem, or a word derived from it, was borrowed into Old French as *sous,* and this form entered Middle English and became the modern word *souse.*

south (south) *n.* **1. a.** The direction 90° clockwise from east. **b.** The point on the compass 180° clockwise from north. **2.** An area or region to the south of a given point. **3. South.** The S part of the U.S., esp. the states that fought for the Confederacy during the Civil War. *–adj.* To, toward, of, from, facing, or in the south. *–adv.* In, from, or toward the south. **–south'er•ly** (sŭth'ər-lē) *adj. & adv.* **–south'ern** (sŭth'ərn) *adj.* **–south'ern•er** *n.* **–south'ern•most'** *adj.* **–south'ward** *adj. & adv.* **–south'wards** *adv.*

South Africa. Country of S Africa, on the Atlantic and Indian

oceans. *Caps.* Pretoria, Cape Town. *Pop.* 29,645,000. **–South African** *adj.* & *n.*
South America. S continent of the W Hemisphere, lying mostly S of the equator. **–South American** *adj.* & *n.*
South Car·o·li·na (kăr′ə-lī′nə). State of the SE U.S. on the Atlantic. *Cap.* Columbia. *Pop.* 3,119,208. **–South Car′o·lin′i·an** (-lĭn′ē-ən) *n.*
South China Sea. Section of the W Pacific between Southeast Asia and the Philippines.
South Da·ko·ta (də-kō′tə). State of the NC U.S. *Cap.* Pierre. *Pop.* 690,178. **–South Da·ko′tan** *n.*
south·east (south-ēst′, sou-ēst′) *n.* **1.** The direction 45° clockwise from east and 45° clockwise from south. **2.** An area or region to the southeast of a given point. **–south·east′** *adj.* & *adv.* **–south·east′er·ly** *adj.* & *adv.* **–south·east′ern** *adj.* **–south·east′ward** *adj.* & *adv.* **–south·east′wards** *adv.*
Southeast Asia (ā′zhə, ā′shə). Region gen. considered to include the Philippines, Indochina, Malaysia, Singapore, Indonesia, and Brunei.
south·paw (south′pô′) *n.* A left-handed person, esp. a left-handed baseball pitcher. **–south′paw′** *adj.*
South Pole *n.* The southernmost point of the earth.
South Seas. 1. All seas S of the equator. **2.** The S Pacific.
south·west (south-wĕst′, sou-wĕst′) *n.* **1.** The direction 45° clockwise from south and 45° clockwise from west. **2.** An area or region to the southwest of a given point. **–south·west′** *adj.* & *adv.* **–south·west′er·ly** *adj.* & *adv.* **–south·west′ern** *adj.* **–south·west′ward** *adj.* & *adv.* **–south·west′wards** *adv.*
sou·ve·nir (so͞o′və-nîr′) *n.* Something kept as a token of remembrance : memento.
sov·er·eign (sŏv′ər-ən, sŏv′rən) *n.* **1.** The head of state in a monarchy. **2.** A British gold coin worth 1 pound. *–adj.* **1.** Supreme : paramount. **2.** Supreme in power or rank. **3.** Self-governing : independent. **4.** Of fine quality : excellent.
sov·er·eign·ty (sŏv′ər-ən-tē, sŏv′rən-) *n., pl.* **-ties. 1.** Supremacy of rule or authority. **2.** The rank, authority, or power of a sovereign. **3.** Political autonomy.
so·vi·et (sō′vē-ĕt′, -ĭt, sŏv′ē-) *n.* **1.** A popularly elected legislative assembly in the USSR. **2. Soviets.** The people and government of the USSR.
sow[1] (sō) *v.* **sowed, sown** (sōn) *or* **sowed, sow·ing. 1.** To scatter (seed) for growing. **2.** To scatter with or as if with seed. **3.** To stir up : foment. **–sow′er** *n.*
sow[2] (sou) *n.* A fully grown female pig.
sox (sŏks) *n. var. pl. of* SOCK[1].
soy (soi) *n.* **1.** The soybean. **2.** A salty liquid condiment made by fermenting soybeans in brine.
soy·bean (soi′bēn′) *n.* An Asiatic leguminous plant, *Glycine max,* cultivated for forage and for its nutritious, edible seeds.
sp. *abbr.* **1.** special. **2.** species. **3.** spelling.
†spa (spä) *n.* **1.** A mineral spring. **2.** A place, esp. a resort, having mineral springs. **3.** *Regional.* A soda fountain.
space (spās) *n.* **1. a.** A set of points or elements satisfying specified geometric conditions. **b.** The infinite 3-dimensional area within which all material bodies move and exist. **2.** The expanse in which the solar system, stars, and galaxies exist : universe. **3.** An empty area. **4.** A particular place, as a seat on a train. **5.** An interval or period of time. *–v.* **spaced, spac·ing.** To place, arrange, or organize with spaces between. **–spac′er** *n.*
space·craft (spās′krăft′) *n.* A vehicle designed for space travel.
spaced-out (spāst′out′) *adj. Slang.* Stupefied from or as if from a drug : dopey.
space flight *n.* Flight beyond the atmosphere of the earth.
space heater *n.* A small, usu. portable device for heating an enclosed area.
space·man (spās′măn′) *n.* A person who travels in outer space : astronaut.
space·port (spās′pôrt′, -pōrt′) *n.* An installation for testing and launching spacecraft.
space·ship (spās′shĭp′) *n.* A spacecraft.
space shuttle *n.* A spacecraft serving as transportation between the earth and an orbiting space station.
space station *n.* A manned satellite designed for permanent orbit around the earth.
space suit *n.* A pressurized suit designed to permit the wearer relatively free movement in space.
space walk *n.* Activity or movement outside a spacecraft by an astronaut. **–space′-walk′** *v.* **–space walker** *n.*
spa·cious (spā′shəs) *adj.* Affording ample space : roomy. **–spa′cious·ly** *adv.* **–spa′cious·ness** *n.*
spade[1] (spād) *n.* A flat-bladed digging tool with a long handle. *–v.* **spad·ed, spad·ing.** To dig or cut with a spade.
spade[2] (spād) *n.* Any of a suit of playing cards marked with a black figure shaped like an inverted heart with a short stalk at the bottom.

▲word history: The word *spade[1]*, "digging tool," has no etymological relation to *spade[2]*, "suit of playing cards." *Spade[1]* comes directly from Old English *spadu,* and *spade[2]* is from Italian *spada,* "sword." On Italian playing cards a broad-bladed sword was used as the symbol of a suit; this suit was called "spades" in English. Because the word *spade* was confused with the native English word, on English playing cards the symbol was reshaped to resemble a digging tool.

spade·work (spād′wûrk′) *n.* The usu. hard and often uninteresting preliminary work in a project or activity.
spa·dix (spā′dĭks) *n., pl.* **-di·ces** (-dĭ-sēz′). A clublike stalk bearing tiny flowers, often enclosed in a sheathlike spathe.

spadix
A. spadix and B. spathe of a jack-in-the-pulpit

spa·ghet·ti (spə-gĕt′ē) *n.* Pasta in the form of long, thin solid strings.
Spain (spān). Country of SW Europe. *Cap.* Madrid. *Pop.* 37,790,000.
span[1] (spăn) *n.* **1.** The extent of space between 2 points or extremities, as of a bridge. **2.** The section between 2 intermediate supports of a bridge. **3.** Something, as a bridge, that spans. **4.** A unit of measure equal to approx. 9 in. **5.** A time period. *–v.* **spanned, span·ning. 1.** To measure by or as if by the fully extended hand. **2.** To extend across.
span[2] (spăn) *n.* A pair of animals, as oxen, harnessed together.
span·gle (spăng′gəl) *n.* A small disk of shiny material, as metal, used esp. on a dress for decoration. **–span′gle** *v.*
Span·iard (spăn′yərd) *n.* A native or inhabitant of Spain.
span·iel (spăn′yəl) *n.* Any of several dogs of usu. small size with drooping ears, short legs, and silky hair.
Span·ish (spăn′ĭsh) *adj.* Of or relating to Spain, its inhabitants, or their language or culture. *–n.* **1.** The Romance language of Spain and most of Central and South America. **2.** *(pl. in number).* The inhabitants of Spain.
Span·ish-A·mer·i·can (spăn′ĭsh-ə-mĕr′ĭ-kən) *adj.* **1.** Of or relating to the countries or people of Spanish America. **2.** Of or relating to people of Spanish descent residing in the U.S. **–Span′ish-A·mer′i·can** *n.*
Spanish fly *n.* **1.** A European blister beetle, *Lytta vesicatoria,* that secretes a substance capable of blistering the skin. **2.** A preparation made from the crushed, dried body of the Spanish fly and once used medicinally and as an aphrodisiac.
Spanish moss *n.* A plant, *Tillandsia usneoides,* growing in long threadlike masses from trees.
spank (spăngk) *v.* To slap on the buttocks with an object or the open hand. **–spank** *n.* **–spank′er** *n.*
spank·ing (spăng′kĭng) *adj.* Fresh : brisk <a *spanking* breeze>
†span-new (spăn′no͞o′, -nyo͞o′) *adj. Regional.* Brand-new.
spar[1] (spär) *n.* A wooden or metal pole, as a mast or boom, that supports rigging.
spar[2] (spär) *v.* **sparred, spar·ring. 1.** To box without landing a heavy blow, esp. for practice. **2.** To dispute verbally.
spare (spâr) *v.* **spared, spar·ing. 1.** To refrain from destroying or harming : treat mercifully. **2.** To exempt from doing or experiencing something. **3.** To use with thrift or restraint. **4.** To do without : dispense with. *–adj.* **spar·er, spar·est. 1. a.** Kept in reserve <a *spare* bedroom>. **b.** Beyond what is needed <*spare* cash> **2. a.** Not abundant. **b.** Thin or lean. *–n.* **1.** Something, esp. a tire, kept in reserve for future use. **2.** The act of knocking down all 10 pins with 2 successive rolls of a bowling ball. **–spare′ness** *n.*
spare·ribs (spâr′rĭbz′) *pl.n.* A cut of pork ribs with most of the meat trimmed off.
spar·ing (spâr′ĭng) *adj.* Frugal : thrifty. **–spar′ing·ly** *adv.*
spark[1] (spärk) *n.* **1.** An incandescent particle, as one thrown off from burning wood or produced by friction. **2.** A flash of light : sparkle. **3.** A short luminous discharge of electricity. **4.** A factor

or quality with the potential for development : seed. –*v.* **1.** To emit sparks. **2.** To stir up : rouse.
spark² (spärk) *n.* An elegant young man : dandy. –*v.* To woo : court.
spar·kle (spär′kəl) *v.* **-kled, -kling. 1.** To emit or shine with flashes of light : gleam. **2.** To flash with wit. **3.** To effervesce. –*n.* **1.** A gleaming particle : spark. **2.** Vivacity : animation. **–spar′kler** *n.*
spark plug *n.* A device that ignites the fuel mixture in an engine by an electric spark.
spar·row (spăr′ō) *n.* A small singing bird of the family Fringillidae, with grayish or brownish plumage.
†**spar·row·grass** (spăr′ə-grăs′, -grəs) *n. Regional.* Asparagus.
sparrow hawk *n.* A small, predatory North American falcon, *Falco sparverius,* or European hawk, *Accipter nisus.*
sparse (spärs) *adj.* **spars·er, spars·est.** Thinly distributed : meager. **–sparse′ly** *adv.* **–spar′si·ty** (spär′sĭ-tē) *n.*
Spar·ta (spär′tə). City-state of ancient Greece, in the SE Peloponnesus.
spar·tan (spär′tn) *adj.* Marked by self-discipline, frugality, and often stoicism : austere. **–spar′tan** *n.*
spasm (spăz′əm) *n.* **1.** A sudden, involuntary muscular contraction. **2.** A sudden and temporary burst of activity, energy, or emotion. **–spas·mod′ic** (spăz-mŏd′ĭk) *adj.* **–spas·mod′i·cal·ly** *adv.*
spas·tic (spăs′tĭk) *adj.* Of, relating to, marked by, or affected by abnormal muscular spasms. **–spas′tic** *n.*
spat¹ (spăt) *v. var. p.t. & p.p. of* SPIT¹.
spat² (spăt) *n., pl.* **spat** *or* **spats.** A bivalve mollusk, as an oyster, in the larval stage.
spat³ (spăt) *n.* A gaiter covering the ankle and the upper shoe.
spat⁴ (spăt) *n.* A short, petty quarrel : tiff. **–spat** *v.*
spate (spāt) *n.* A sudden flood or outpouring : rush.
spathe (spāth) *n.* A leaflike part that encloses the base of the spadix of certain plants, as the calla.
spa·tial (spā′shəl) *adj.* Of or pertaining to space. **–spa′tial·ly** *adv.*
spat·ter (spăt′ər) *v.* **1.** To scatter, dash, or splash (a liquid) in drops. **2.** To throw off sprinkles or splashes.
spat·u·la (spach′ə-lə) *n.* An implement with a flexible blade used esp. for spreading or mixing soft substances.
spav·in (spăv′ĭn) *n.* A bony deposit on the hock joint of a horse. **–spav′ined** *adj.*
spawn (spôn) *n.* **1.** The eggs of aquatic animals, as oysters, fishes, or frogs. **2.** Offspring, esp. produced in large numbers : brood. –*v.* **1.** To produce eggs. Used of an aquatic animal. **2.** To produce offspring, esp. in large numbers. **3.** To generate.
spay (spā) *v.* To remove the ovaries of (a female animal).
speak (spēk) *v.* **spoke** (spōk), **spo·ken** (spō′kən), **speak·ing. 1.** To utter words : talk. **2.** To express (e.g., one's thoughts) in words. **3.** To deliver a speech or lecture. **4.** To talk or be able to talk in (a language) <*speak* Russian>
speak·eas·y (spēk′ē′zē) *n., pl.* **-ies.** A place where alcoholic beverages are sold illegally.
speak·er (spē′kər) *n.* **1.** One who speaks. **2.** Someone who presides over a legislative assembly. **3.** A loudspeaker.
spear (spîr) *n.* **1.** A weapon for throwing or thrusting that consists of a long shaft with a sharply pointed head. **2.** A shaft with a sharp point and barbs for catching fish. **3.** A spearlike stalk, as of asparagus. –*v.* To pierce, strike, or stab with or as if with a spear.
spear·head (spîr′hĕd′) *n.* **1.** The military force that goes before others in an attack. **2.** A leading force in an endeavor. **–spear′head′** *v.*
spear·mint (spîr′mĭnt′) *n.* A common mint, *Mentha spicata,* that yields an aromatic oil widely used as a flavoring.
spe·cial (spĕsh′əl) *adj.* **1.** Different from what is ordinary or usual : exceptional. **2.** Distinct from others : unique. **3.** Limited to or intended for a particular function, application, or occasion. **4.** Additional : extra. **5.** Regarded with particular favor. **–spe′cial** *n.* **–spe′cial·ly** *adv.*
Special Forces *pl.n.* A division of the U.S. Army composed of soldiers specially trained in guerrilla fighting.
spe·cial·ist (spĕsh′ə-lĭst) *n.* **1.** One, as a physician, who devotes himself to a particular activity or branch of study. **2.** Any of several enlisted ranks in the U.S. Army that correspond to those of corporal through sergeant 1st class.
spe·cial·ize (spĕsh′ə-līz′) *v.* **-ized, -iz·ing. 1.** To focus one's efforts on a particular activity, study, or field. **2.** *Biol.* To adapt to a particular environment or function. **–spe′cial·i·za′tion** *n.*
spe·cial·ty (spĕsh′əl-tē) *n., pl.* **-ties. 1.** A branch of study, occupation, or business in which one specializes. **2.** A product of special distinction <Pecan pie is the baker's *specialty.*> **3.** A special detail or feature.
spe·cie (spē′shē, -sē) *n.* Money in the form of coins.
spe·cies (spē′shēz, -sēz) *n., pl.* **-cies. 1.a.** A taxonomic classification category comprising organisms that are able to interbreed. **b.** An organism in this category. **2.** A kind : sort.
specif. *abbr.* specifically.
spe·cif·ic (spĭ-sĭf′ĭk) *adj.* **1.** Precisely specified : definite. **2.** Of, relating to, characterizing, or constituting a species. **3.** Special, unique, or distinctive, as a trait. **4.** Effective in the treatment and usu. the cure of a particular disease. –*n.* A specific remedy. **–spe·cif′i·cal·ly** *adv.* **–spec′i·fic′i·ty** (spĕs′ə-fĭs′ĭ-tē) *n.*
spec·i·fi·ca·tion (spĕs′ə-fĭ-kā′shən) *n.* **1.** Something that is specified : item. **2.** *often* **specifications.** A statement of particulars, esp. one describing materials, dimensions, and workmanship for the building, installation, or manufacture of something.
specific gravity *n.* **1.** The quotient of the measure of the mass of a solid or liquid divided by the measure of the mass of an equal volume of water at 4°C. **2.** The quotient of the measure of the mass of a gas divided by the measure of an equal volume of air or hydrogen under prescribed conditions of temperature and pressure.
spec·i·fy (spĕs′ə-fī′) *v.* **-fied, -fy·ing.** To state, name, or mention explicitly, exactly, and unambiguously.
spec·i·men (spĕs′ə-mən) *n.* A part or element representative of an entire set or whole : sample.
spe·cious (spē′shəs) *adj.* Apparently attractive, true, or correct but not actually so : deceptive. **–spe′cious·ly** *adv.*
speck (spĕk) *n.* **1.** A small mark, flaw, or spot. **2.** A small particle : bit. –*v.* To mark with specks.
speck·le (spĕk′əl) *n.* A small speck. –*v.* **-led, -ling.** To cover or mark with or as if with speckles.
specs (spĕks) *pl.n. Informal.* **1.** Eyeglasses. **2.** SPECIFICATIONS 2.
spec·ta·cle (spĕk′tə-kəl) *n.* **1.** A public display, esp. on a large scale. **2.** Something exhibited to public view. **3. spectacles.** Eyeglasses. **–spec′ta·cled** *adj.*
spec·tac·u·lar (spĕk-tăk′yə-lər) *adj.* Of the nature of a spectacle : striking. –*n.* A lavish spectacle.
spec·ta·tor (spĕk′tā′tər) *n.* One who is present and watches : onlooker.
spec·ter (spĕk′tər) *n.* **1.** A ghost : apparition. **2.** A haunting or threatening vision <the *specter* of nuclear war>
spec·tral (spĕk′trəl) *adj.* **1.** Of, pertaining to, or resembling a specter. **2.** Of, relating to, or produced by a spectrum.
spec·tre (spĕk′tər) *n. esp. Brit. var. of* SPECTER.
spec·trom·e·ter (spĕk-trŏm′ĭ-tər) *n.* A spectroscope with scales for measuring the positions of spectral lines.
spec·tro·scope (spĕk′trə-skōp′) *n.* An instrument used to resolve radiation into spectra and to make observations or recordings. **–spec′tro·scop′ic** (-skŏp′ĭk), **spec′tro·scop′i·cal** *adj.* **–spec′tro·scop′i·cal·ly** *adv.* **–spec·tros′co·pist** (spĕk-trŏs′kə-pĭst) *n.* **–spec·tros′co·py** *n.*
spec·trum (spĕk′trəm) *n., pl.* **-tra** (-trə) *or* **-trums. 1.** *Physics.* The distribution of a characteristic of a physical system or phenomenon, esp.: **a.** The distribution of energy emitted by a radiant source, as an incandescent body, arranged in order of wavelengths. **b.** A graphic or photographic representation of such a distribution. **2.** A broad range or sequence <a wide *spectrum* of feelings>
spec·u·late (spĕk′yə-lāt′) *v.* **-lat·ed, -lat·ing. 1.** To think deeply : reflect. **2.** To engage in a business venture offering the possibility of a large profit but entailing risk. **–spec′u·la′tion** *n.* **–spec′u·la′tive** *adj.* **–spec′u·la′tor** *n.*
speech (spēch) *n.* **1.** Manner or act of speaking. **2.** The faculty of speaking. **3.** Conversation. **4.** A public address. **5.** A language or dialect. ☆**syns:** DISCOURSE, TALK, UTTERANCE **–speech′less** *adj.*
speed (spēd) *n.* **1.** Rate of motion, action, activity, or performance. **2.** Rapidity : celerity. **3.** A gear in the transmission of a motor vehicle. **4.** *Slang.* An amphetamine drug. **5.** *Archaic.* Success : prosperity. –*v.* **sped** (spĕd) *or* **speed·ed, speed·ing. 1.** To move fast, esp. at a high or illegal rate of speed. **2.** To cause to go at an increased rate of speed : accelerate. **–speed′er** *n.* **–speed′i·ly** *adv.* **–speed′y** *adj.*
speed·boat (spēd′bōt′) *n.* A fast motorboat or launch.
speed·om·e·ter (spē-dŏm′ĭ-tər, spĭ-) *n.* **1.** An instrument that measures and indicates speed. **2.** An odometer.
speed·ster (spēd′stər) *n.* **1.** One that speeds. **2.** A fast car.
speed·up (spēd′ŭp′) *n.* Acceleration, esp. an acceleration in production without an increase in pay.
speed·way (spēd′wā′) *n.* **1.** A racecourse for motorcycles or automobiles. **2.** A road designed for high-speed traffic.
speed·well (spēd′wĕl′) *n.* A low-growing plant of the genus *Veronica,* with clusters of small, usu. blue flowers.
spe·le·ol·o·gy (spē′lē-ŏl′ə-jē) *n.* **1.** The study of the physical,

geologic, and biological aspects of caves. **2.** Cave exploration. **—spe'le·ol'o·gist** *n.*

spell¹ (spĕl) *v.* **spelled** or **spelt** (spĕlt), **spell·ing. 1.** To name or write in order the letters of (a word). **2.** To signify : mean. **—spell out.** To state or explain explicitly.

spell² (spĕl) *n.* **1.** A formula supposed to have magic power : incantation. **2.** A state of bewitchment : trance. **3.** A compelling or dominating influence.

spell³ (spĕl) *n.* **1.** An indefinite, often short period of time. **2.** *Informal.* A period of a particular kind of weather. **3.** One's turn at work : shift. **4.** A period of illness or distress : attack. *—v.* To relieve (another person) for a time by taking a turn.

spell·bind (spĕl'bīnd') *v.* To hold by or as if by a spell : fascinate.

spell·bind·er (spĕl'bīn'dər) *n.* An eloquent public speaker.

spell·bound (spĕl'bound') *adj.* Bound by or as if by a spell : entranced.

spell·er (spĕl'ər) *n.* **1.** One who spells words. **2.** A textbook for teaching spelling.

spe·lun·ker (spĭ-lŭng'kər, spē'lŭng'kər) *n.* A person whose hobby is exploring caves. **—spe·lun'king** *n.*

spend (spĕnd) *v.* **spent** (spĕnt), **spend·ing. 1.** To use up or wear out : exhaust. **2.** To pay out (e.g., money) : expend. **3.** To pass (time). **4.** To use wastefully : squander. **—spend'er** *n.*

spend·thrift (spĕnd'thrĭft') *n.* One who squanders money.

Spen·ser (spĕn'sər), **Edmund.** 1552?–99. English poet. **—Spen·se'ri·an** *adj.*

spent (spĕnt) *adj.* Depleted of energy : exhausted.

sperm (spûrm) *n.* **1.** Spermatozoon. **2.** Semen. **—sper·mat'ic** (spər-măt'ĭk) *adj.*

sper·mat·o·zo·on (spər-măt'ə-zō'ŏn', spûr'mə-tə-, -ən) *n., pl.* **-zo·a** (-zō'ə). A male reproductive cell.

sperm whale *n.* A whale, *Physeter catodon,* with a large head and a long, narrow lower jaw.

spew (spyo͞o) *v.* **1.** To vomit. **2.** To force or come out in a stream.

sphag·num (sfăg'nəm) *n.* A moss of the genus *Sphagnum,* growing in wet areas, as swamps, that decomposes to form peat.

sphere (sfîr) *n.* **1.** *Math.* A 3-dimensional geometric surface having all its points the same distance from a given point. **2.** A sphere-shaped figure or object : ball. **3.** A heavenly body, as a planet or star. **4.** An area, range, or extent of power, action, or influence : domain. **—spher'i·cal** (sfîr'ĭ-kəl, sfĕr'-) *adj.* **—spher'i·cal·ly** *adv.*

sphe·roid (sfîr'oid', sfĕr'-) *n.* An ellipsoid generated by revolving an ellipse on or about 1 of its axes.

sphinc·ter (sfĭngk'tər) *n.* A ringlike muscle that closes a bodily passage or orifice.

sphinx (sfĭnks) *n., pl.* **sphinx·es** or **sphin·ges** (sfĭn'jēz'). **1.** An ancient Egyptian figure with the body of a lion and the head of a man, ram, or hawk. **2.** *Gk. Myth.* A monster having wings, a woman's head, and a lion's body, esp. one that destroyed all passers-by who could not answer the riddle it asked them. **3.** An enigmatic or mysterious person.

spice (spīs) *n.* **1.** A pungently aromatic or pungent vegetable substance, as cinnamon or nutmeg, used to flavor or season food. **2.** Something that adds zest, flavor, and interest. **—spice** *v.* **—spic'y** *adj.*

spick-and-span *also* **spic-and-span** (spĭk'ən-spăn') *adj.* **1.** Immaculately clean : spotless. **2.** Brand-new.

spic·ule (spĭk'yo͞ol) *n.* A small needlelike structure or part.

spi·der (spī'dər) *n.* **1.** Any of numerous 8legged arachnids of the order Araneae that have a body divided into 2 parts and spin webs. **2.** A cast-iron frying pan with a long handle. **—spi'der·y** *adj.*

spiel (spēl) *v.* *Slang.* To talk at length and usu. extravagantly. **—spiel** *n.*

spif·fy (spĭf'ē) *adj.* **-fi·er, -fi·est.** *Slang.* Stylish : smart.

spig·ot (spĭg'ət) *n.* A faucet.

spike¹ (spīk) *n.* **1.** A long, thick heavy nail. **2.** A sharp-pointed projection, as on the sole of a shoe to add traction. *—v.* **spiked, spik·ing. 1.** To secure with spikes. **2.** To impale on, injure with, or pierce with a spike. **3.** To put an end to : suppress <*spike* a rebellion> **4.** *Slang.* To add alcoholic liquor to (a drink).

spike² (spīk) *n.* **1.** An ear of grain. **2.** *Bot.* A long stalkless or almost stalkless flower cluster.

spill (spĭl) *v.* **spilled** or **spilt** (spĭlt), **spill·ing. 1.** To cause or allow inadvertently to run out or flow. **2.** To shed (blood). **3.** To cause to fall, as from a horse. **4.** To run from or as if from a container : overflow. *—n.* **1.** An act of spilling. **2.** An amount spilled. **3.** Something spilled. **4.** A fall, as from a horse. **5.** A spillway.

spill·way (spĭl'wā') *n.* A channel for the overflow of surplus water.

spin (spĭn) *v.* **spun** (spŭn), **spin·ning. 1. a.** To draw out (fibers) and twist into thread. **b.** To form (thread) by spinning. **2. a.** To form thread by extruding viscous filaments from the body. **b.** To construct from such filaments <*spinning* a cocoon> **3.** To tell slowly and esp. imaginatively <*spin* a story> **4.** To revolve or cause to revolve rapidly : twirl. **5.** To reel : whirl. **6.** To move quickly, as in a vehicle. *—n.* **1.** A rapid revolving motion. **2.** *Informal.* A short drive in a vehicle. **—spin'ner** *n.*

spin·ach (spĭn'ĭch) *n.* A widely cultivated plant, *Spinacia oleracea,* having edible leaves.

spi·nal (spī'nəl) *adj.* Of, relating to, or near the spinal column or spinal cord. **—spi'nal·ly** *adv.*

spinal column *n.* The vertebrae enclosing the spinal cord and forming the supporting axis of the body.

spinal cord *n.* The part of the central nervous system extending from the brain along the back in the cavity of the spinal column.

spin·dle (spĭn'dl) *n.* **1.** A thin, rounded, tapering rod or pin holding a bobbin or spool on which thread is wound on a spinning wheel or machine. **2.** A slender rod that rotates or serves as an axis on which other parts rotate.

spin·dly (spĭn'dlē) *adj.* **-dli·er, -dli·est.** Elongated, thin, and usu. weak.

spin·drift (spĭn'drĭft') *n.* Sea spray blown by the wind.

spine (spīn) *n.* **1.** The spinal column. **2.** A sharp-pointed, projecting part on a plant or animal, as a quill. **—spin'y** *adj.*

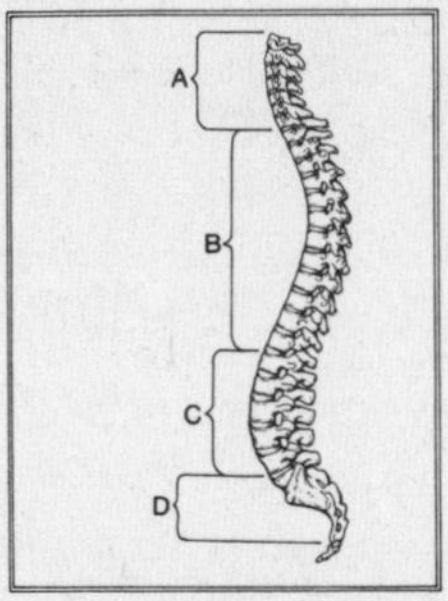

spine
The human spine: A. cervical vertebrae, B. thoracic vertebrae, C. lumbar vertebrae, D. sacral vertebrae.

spi·nel (spĭ-nĕl') *n.* A hard crystalline mineral valued as a gem.

spine·less (spīn'lĭs) *adj.* **1.** Lacking a spinal column. **2.** Lacking courage.

spin·et (spĭn'ĭt) *n.* **1.** A small, compact upright piano. **2.** A harpsichord with a single keyboard.

spin·na·ker (spĭn'ə-kər) *n.* A large triangular sail set opposite the mainsail.

spin·ner·et (spĭn'ə-rĕt') *n.* A posterior structure in spiders and certain insect larvae that contains passages through which silky filaments are secreted.

spinning jenny *n.* An early machine with several spindles for spinning fibers.

spinning wheel *n.* A device for spinning yarn or thread that consists of a large foot- or hand-driven wheel and 1 spindle.

spin-off *also* **spin·off** (spĭn'ôf', -ŏf') *n.* A product, effect, or enterprise that is a byproduct of a larger or more complex one.

spin·ster (spĭn'stər) *n.* An unmarried woman who is beyond the conventional age of marrying. **—spin'ster·hood'** *n.*

spiny lobster *n.* An edible marine crustacean of the family Palinuridae, having a spiny carapace and lacking the large pincers characteristic of true the lobster.

spi·ral (spī'rəl) *n.* **1.** The 2-dimensional locus of a point moving around a fixed center at an increasing or decreasing distance from the center. **2.** A helix. **3.** Something shaped like a spiral <*spirals* of smoke> **4.** A continuously expanding increase or decrease. *—adj.* **1.** Of or being a spiral. **2.** Helical. *—v.* **-raled, -ral·ing** or **-ralled, -ral·ling.** To take or cause to take a spiral shape or course. **—spi'ral·ly** *adv.*

spi·rant (spī'rənt) *n.* A consonant, as *f* or *s,* produced by forcing the breath through a constricted oral passage.

spire (spīr) *n.* **1.** The pointed tip of something that tapers upward. **2.** A formation or structure, as a steeple, that tapers upward to a point. **—spir'y** *adj.*

spi·re·a *also* **spi·rae·a** (spī-rē'ə) *n.* A plant or shrub of the genus *Spiraea,* with small white or pink flower clusters.

spir·it (spĭr'ĭt) *n.* **1.** A vital or animating force : soul. **2.** The part of a human being associated with the feelings and mind. **3.** Real meaning or sense : significance. **4.** A person. **5.** The prevailing tenor : tone <the *spirit* of the times> **6. Spirit.** The Holy

Ghost. 7. A ghost : specter. 8. Mood : disposition. 9. Animation and vigor. 10. Strong loyalty <team *spirit*> 11. *often* **spirits.** A distilled alcoholic liquor. ☆**syns:** BRIO, DASH, ÉLAN, ESPRIT, LIVELINESS, PEP —*v.* To carry away mysteriously or secretly. **—spir'it·less** *adj.*

spir·it·ed (spĭr'ĭ-tĭd) *adj.* 1. Full of or marked by spirit. 2. Courageous.

spir·i·tu·al (spĭr'ĭ-cho͞o-əl) *adj.* 1. Of, relating to, or having the nature of spirit. 2. Of or relating to religion or religious matters : ecclesiastical or sacred. —*n.* A religious song of S black American origin. **—spir'i·tu·al'i·ty** (-ăl'ĭ-tē) *n.* **—spir'i·tu·al·ize'** *v.* **—spir'i·tu·al·ly** *adv.*

spir·i·tu·al·ism (spĭr'ĭ-cho͞o-ə-lĭz'əm) *n.* The belief that the dead are able communicate with the living, usu. through a medium. **—spir'i·tu·al·ist** *n.*

spir·i·tu·ous (spĭr'ĭ-cho͞o-əs) *adj.* Of or containing alcohol.

spi·ro·chete *also* **spi·ro·chaete** (spī'rə-kēt') *n.* Any of several twisted microorganisms of the order Spirochaetales, including those that cause syphilis.

spirt (spûrt) *n.* & *v. esp. Brit. var. of* SPURT.

spit[1] (spĭt) *n.* 1. Expectorated saliva : spittle. 2. The act of spitting. —*v.* **spat** (spăt) *or* **spit, spit·ting.** 1. To expectorate. 2. To send forth as if by spitting. 3. To make a sputtering or hissing sound.

spit[2] (spĭt) *n.* 1. A slender, pointed rod on which meat is skewered for roasting or broiling. 2. A narrow point of land projecting into a body of water. —*v.* **spit·ted, spit·ting.** To skewer on or as if on a spit.

spit·ball (spĭt'bôl') *n.* 1. Paper chewed and shaped into a ball to be thrown as a projectile. 2. *Baseball.* An illegal pitch in which the ball has been moistened on 1 side with saliva.

spite (spīt) *n.* Ill will with an urge to hurt, humiliate, or thwart : malice. —*v.* **spit·ed, spit·ing.** To treat with spite. **—in spite of.** Regardless of : notwithstanding. **—spite'ful** *adj.* **—spite'ful·ly** *adv.* **—spite'ful·ness** *n.*

spit·tle (spĭt'l) *n.* Saliva : spit.

spit·tle·bug (spĭt'l-bŭg') *n.* An insect of the family Cercopidae, whose larvae form frothy masses of liquid on plant stems.

spit·toon (spĭ-to͞on') *n.* A receptacle into which one may spit.

spitz (spĭts) *n.* A dog with a thick, usu. white coat and a tail curled over the back.

splash (splăsh) *v.* 1. To dash (a liquid) about in flying masses. 2. To dash a liquid on. 3. To fall or move with the sound of splashing. **—splash** *n.* **—splash'y** *adj.*

splash·down (splăsh'doun') *n.* The landing of a spacecraft or missile in the ocean.

splat[1] (splăt) *n.* A single slat, as of wood, in a chair back.

splat[2] (splăt) *n.* A slapping noise.

splat·ter (splăt'ər) *v.* To spatter. **—splat'ter** *n.*

splay (splā) *adj.* 1. Turned or spread outward. 2. Clumsy : awkward. —*v.* 1. To spread apart or out. 2. To slope or slant. **—splay** *n.*

splay·foot (splā'fo͝ot') *n.* A deformed foot that is abnormally flat and turned out. **—splay'foot'ed** *adj.*

spleen (splēn) *n.* 1. An organ located below the diaphragm in most vertebrates that functions to filter and store blood. 2. Ill will : malice.

splen·did (splĕn'dĭd) *adj.* 1. Brilliant with color or light : shining. 2. Sumptuous : magnificent. 3. Illustrious : grand. 4. Excellent. **—splen'did·ly** *adv.*

splen·dif·er·ous (splĕn-dĭf'ər-əs) *adj.* Splendid.

splen·dor (splĕn'dər) *n.* 1. Great luster or light : brilliance. 2. Glory : magnificence.

splen·dour (splĕn'dər) *n. esp. Brit. var. of* SPLENDOR.

sple·net·ic (splĭ-nĕt'ĭk) *adj.* 1. Splenic. 2. Marked by ill will, malice, or irritability.

splen·ic (splĕn'ĭk) *adj.* Of, pertaining to, or near the spleen.

splice (splīs) *v.* **spliced, splic·ing.** 1. a. To join (e.g., 2 lengths of film) at the ends. b. To join (e.g., 2 ropes) by weaving together the strands. 2. To join (e.g., 2 pieces of wood) by overlapping and binding together the ends. **—splice** *n.*

splint (splĭnt) *n.* 1. Rigid material or a device used to immobilize an injured body part, as a fractured bone. 2. A flexible wooden strip, as one used in basket making.

splin·ter (splĭn'tər) *n.* A thin, sharp piece of something, as glass, split off lengthwise from a main body. —*v.* To split or cause to split into splinters.

split (splĭt) *v.* **split, split·ting.** 1. To divide, esp. cleanly, sharply, or suddenly, into lengthwise sections. 2. To burst or break apart, esp. with force. 3. To divide and share <*split* the bill> 4. To separate into sections, layers, or parts. 5. *Slang.* To leave, esp. suddenly. —*n.* 1. The act or result of splitting. 2. A breach : rupture.

split-lev·el (splĭt'lĕv'əl) *adj.* Built so that the floor levels of adjoining rooms are separated by approx. a half story.

split personality *n.* A form of hysteria in which 2 relatively distinct identities are manifested.

split·ting (splĭt'ĭng) *adj.* Very acute : severe <a *splitting* headache>

splotch (splŏch) *n.* An irregularly shaped discolored area : blotch. **—splotch** *v.* **—splotch'y** *adj.*

splurge (splûrj) *n.* 1. An extravagant expense or indulgence. 2. An ostentatious display. **—splurge** *v.*

splut·ter (splŭt'ər) *v.* 1. To make a short popping or spitting sound. 2. To speak indistinctly and hastily. **—splut'ter** *n.*

spoil (spoil) *v.* **spoiled** *or* **spoilt** (spoilt), **spoil·ing.** 1. To impair in quality or value : damage. 2. To destroy the perfection of : ruin. 3. a. To harm the character of by overindulging. b. To pamper : coddle. 4. *Archaic.* To rob : plunder. 5. To become decayed : rot. 6. To be very eager <*spoiling* for an argument> —*n.* **spoils.** 1. Loot seized by force : plunder. 2. Political patronage at the disposal of a successful party or candidate. **—spoil'age** *n.* **—spoil'er** *n.*

spoil·sport (spoil'spôrt') *n.* Someone whose behavior and reactions spoil the pleasure of others.

Spo·kane (spō-kăn'). City of NE Wash., near the Idaho border. *Pop.* 171,300.

spoke[1] (spōk) *n.* 1. One of the rods that connect the rim of a wheel to its hub. 2. A rung of a ladder.

spoke[2] (spōk) *v. p.t. of* SPEAK.

spo·ken (spō'kən) *v. p.p. of* SPEAK.

spokes·man (spōks'mən) *n.* One who is authorized to speak on behalf of another or others. **—spokes'wom'an** *n.*

spo·li·a·tion (spō'lē-ā'shən) *n.* The act of plundering, esp. in wartime.

sponge (spŭnj) *n.* 1. Any of numerous primitive marine animals of the phylum Porifera, with a soft, porous skeleton. 2. The absorbent skeleton of a sponge, used for such purposes as bathing, wiping, or cleaning. 3. A substance or mass with spongelike properties. —*v.* **sponged, spong·ing.** 1. To bathe, wipe, or clean with a sponge. 2. To fish for or gather sponges. 3. *Slang.* To live by imposing on the generosity of another. **—spong'er** *n.* **—spong'y** *adj.*

sponge cake *n.* A light cake that contains no shortening.

sponge rubber *n.* A soft, porous rubber that resembles a sponge in texture.

spon·sor (spŏn'sər) *n.* 1. Someone who takes the responsibility for another person or thing. 2. A godparent. 3. A business that finances a radio or television program in return for advertising time. **—spon'sor** *v.* **—spon'sor·ship'** *n.*

spon·ta·ne·ous (spŏn-tā'nē-əs) *adj.* 1. Occurring, acting, or arising without apparent external cause. 2. Produced or done naturally and voluntarily <*spontaneous* laughter> **—spon'ta·ne'i·ty** (-tə-nē'ĭ-tē, -nā'-) *n.* **—spon·ta'ne·ous·ly** *adv.*

spontaneous combustion *n.* Ignition in a thermally isolated substance, as oily rags, caused by heat generated by slow internal oxidation.

spoof (spo͞of) *n.* 1. Nonsense. 2. A hoax. 3. A good-natured satirical imitation : parody. **—spoof** *v.*

spook (spo͞ok) *Informal.* —*n.* A specter : ghost. —*v.* 1. To haunt. 2. To scare : frighten. **—spook'y** *adj.*

spool (spo͞ol) *n.* A cylinder on which thread, ribbon, wire, tape, or film is wound.

spoon (spo͞on) *n.* 1. A cooking or eating utensil that consists of a small, shallow bowl on a handle. 2. A shiny, curved metal fishing lure. —*v.* 1. To scoop up and carry in or as if in a spoon. 2. *Informal.* To kiss or caress. **—spoon'ful'** (-fo͝ol') *n.*

spoon·bill (spo͞on'bĭl') *n.* A wading bird of the subfamily Plataleidae, having a long, flat bill with a spoonlike tip.

spoon·er·ism (spo͞o'nə-rĭz'əm) *n.* An unintentional transposition of esp. initial sounds in 2 or more words, as *sew a sheet* for *show a seat.*

spoon-feed (spo͞on'fēd') *v.* 1. To feed with a spoon. 2. To provide information (to) in such completeness or detail that independent thought or action is precluded.

spoor (spo͝or) *n.* A trail or track of an animal, esp. a wild animal.

spo·rad·ic (spə-răd'ĭk) *adj.* Occurring at irregular intervals. **—spo·rad'i·cal·ly** *adv.*

spore (spôr, spōr) *n.* A usu. single-celled reproductive structure produced by nonflowering plants and certain lower animals.

sport (spôrt, spōrt) *n.* 1. An amusing or interesting pastime : diversion. 2. A physical activity, esp. one with a set form and body of rules. 3. Jest : mockery <made *sport* of his discomfort> 4. One who accepts an outcome, esp. an adverse one, with grace. 5. *Informal.* One who leads a fast, extravagant life. 6. A genetic mutation. —*v.* 1. To have a good time : play. 2. To

show off : display. —*adj.* Of, relating to, or appropriate for sport <a *sport* jacket> **—sport'ive** *adj.* **—sport'y** *adj.*
sport·ing (spôr'tĭng, spōr'-) *adj.* **1.** Appropriate for or used in sports. **2.** Marked by sportsmanship. **3.** Of or relating to gambling. **4.** Offering a reasonable hope of success <a *sporting* chance>
sports car *n.* A low 1- or 2-passenger car designed for high-speed driving.
sports·cast (spôrts'kăst', spōrts'-) *n.* A television or radio broadcast of sports news or a sports event. **—sports'cast'er** *n.*
sports·man (spôrts'mən, spōrts'-) *n.* **1.** Someone who is active in sports. **2.** Someone who observes the rules of play and wins or loses with grace. **—sports'man·ship'** *n.* **—sports'wom'an** *n.*
sports·writ·er (spôrts'rī'tər) *n.* A writer about sports.
spot (spŏt) *n.* **1.** An area that differs sharply, as in color, from the area surrounding it. **2.** A location : position. **3.** *Informal.* A situation, esp. a dangerous or difficult one. —*v.* **spot·ted, spot·ting. 1.** To become or cause to become marked with spots. **2.** To notice : detect. —*adj.* **1.** Paid, made, or delivered immediately <*spot* cash> **2.** Done at random <a *spot* inspection> **—spot'less** *adj.* **—spot'less·ly** *adv.* **—spot'less·ness** *n.*
spot-check (spŏt'chĕk') *v.* To check or test at random. **—spot check** *n.*
spot·light (spŏt'līt') *n.* **1.a.** A beam of strong light used to illuminate a person, group, area, or object, as on a stage. **b.** A lamp that produces this light. **2.** Public attention. **—spot'light'** *v.*
spot·ter (spŏt'ər) *n.* One who watches for and reports something, as the approach of enemy aircraft.
spot·ty (spŏt'ē) *adj.* **-ti·er, -ti·est.** Inconsistent : uneven. **—spot'ti·ly** *adv.* **—spot'ti·ness** *n.*
spou·sal (spou'zəl, -səl) *n. often* **spousals.** Nuptials.
spouse (spous, spouz) *n.* One's wife or husband.
spout (spout) *v.* **1.** To issue forth or discharge copiously and forcibly. **2.** To utter or speak pompously. —*n.* **1.** A tube, hole, or pipe through which liquid spouts. **2.** A continuous stream of liquid.
sprain (sprān) *n.* **1.** A wrenching and laceration of the ligaments of a muscle or joint. **2.** The condition resulting from a sprain. —*v.* To cause a sprain in.
sprang (sprăng) *v. var. p.t. of* SPRING.
sprat (sprăt) *n.* **1.** A small marine food fish, *Clupea sprattus,* of NE Atlantic waters. **2.** A young herring.
sprawl (sprôl) *v.* **1.** To sit or lie with the arms and legs spread out awkwardly. **2.** To spread out or develop haphazardly. **—sprawl** *n.* **—sprawl'er** *n.*
spray¹ (sprā) *n.* **1.** Liquid moving in fine droplets or mist. **2.!a.** A jet of vapor, as that discharged from a pressurized container. **b.** A device, as an atomizer, for discharging such a jet. —*v.* **1.** To disperse (a liquid) in the form of spray. **2.** To apply spray to (a surface). **—spray'er** *n.*
spray² (sprā) *n.* A branch or decorative arrangement of buds, flowers, or berries.
spray gun *n.* A device for applying a liquid in a spray.
spread (sprĕd) *v.* **spread, spread·ing. 1.** To open out fully or more fully. **2.** To push or force apart : stretch. **3.** To distribute over a surface : apply <*spread* paint on a wall> **4.** To distribute or be distributed widely over an area. **5.** To make or become widely known. **6.** To extend in time. **7.** To prepare (a table) for a meal. ☆**syns:** DIFFUSE, DISPERSE, RADIATE, SCATTER —*n.* **1.** The act or process of spreading. **2.** An open area : expanse. **3.** The extent to which something is or can be spread : range. **4.** A cloth cover for a table or bed. **5.** A food to be spread, as on bread. **6.** Printed matter extending across facing pages or adjacent columns. **7.** A difference, as between 2 totals : gap. **—spread'er** *n.*
spree (sprē) *n.* **1.** A drinking bout. **2.** Overindulgence in an activity <a shopping *spree*>
sprig (sprĭg) *n.* A small shoot of a plant : twig.
spright·ly (sprīt'lē) *adj.* **-li·er, -li·est.** Lively : vivacious. **—spright'li·ness** *n.*
spring (sprĭng) *v.* **sprang** (sprăng) or **sprung** (sprŭng), **sprung, spring·ing. 1.** To move forward or upward suddenly : jump. **2.** To break out, esp. suddenly : emerge. **3.** To move suddenly and with resilience. **4.** To come into existence : arise. **5.** To become warped, cracked, or bent, as wood. **6.** To release suddenly from a checked position <*spring* a trap> **7.** To produce unexpectedly and suddenly <*spring* a trick question> —*n.* **1.** An elastic device, esp. a coil of wire, that returns to its original shape when it is released after being compressed, extended, or twisted. **2.** Resilience : elasticity. **3.** The act of springing, esp. a jump or leap. **4.** A natural flow of water from the ground. **5.** An origin or source. **6.** The season between winter and summer. **—spring'y** *adj.*
spring·board (sprĭng'bôrd', -bōrd') *n.* **1.** A flexible board used in gymnastics and diving. **2.** *Informal.* A starting place.
spring·bok (sprĭng'bŏk') *n., pl.* **springbok** or **-boks.** A small white gazelle, *Antidorcas marsupialis,* of S Africa, capable of leaping high into the air.
†**spring·er** (sprĭng'ər) *n. U.S.* A cow about to calve.
spring fever *n.* Feelings of languor or restlessness that people often experience at the beginning of spring.
Spring·field (sprĭng'fēld'). Cap. of Ill., in the C part. *Pop.* 99,367.
spring·time (sprĭng'tīm') *n.* SPRING 6.
sprin·kle (sprĭng'kəl) *v.* **-kled, -kling. 1.** To scatter about or release in small particles or drops. **2.** To rain or fall in small infrequent drops. ☆**syns:** BESPRINKLE, DUST, POWDER —*n.* **1.** An act of sprinkling. **2.** A light rainfall. **3.** A small amount. **—sprin'kler** *n.*
sprin·kling (sprĭng'klĭng) *n.* A small number or quantity.
sprint (sprĭnt) *n.* A short, fast run or race. —*v.* To run or race as fast as possible, usu. for a short distance. **—sprint'er** *n.*
sprite (sprīt) *n.* **1.** A small supernatural being : elf. **2.** A ghost.
sprock·et (sprŏk'ĭt) *n.* A toothlike part that projects from the rim of a sprocket wheel.
sprocket wheel *n.* A wheel rimmed with sprockets and used to engage the links of a chain in a pulley or drive a system.
sprout (sprout) *v.* **1.** To start growing and send out new growth. **2.** To develop or grow rapidly. —*n.* A young plant growth.
spruce¹ (spro͞os) *n.* **1.** A coniferous evergreen trees of the genus *Picea,* with needlelike foliage, drooping cones, and soft wood often used for paper pulp. **2.** Any of various trees similar or related to the spruce.
spruce² (spro͞os) *adj.* **spruc·er, spruc·est.** Tidy, neat, or trim. —*v.* **spruced, spruc·ing.** To make or become spruce.
sprung (sprŭng) *v. p.p. & var. p.t. of* SPRING.
spry (sprī) *adj.* **spri·er, spri·est** or **spry·er, spry·est.** Briskly active.
spud (spŭd) *n.* **1.** A sharp, spadelike digging tool. **2.** *Slang.* A potato.
spume (spyo͞om) *n.* Foam or froth on a liquid.
spu·mo·ne *also* **spu·mo·ni** (spo͝o-mō'nē) *n.* An Italian frozen dessert of ice cream containing fruit, nuts, or candies.
spun (spŭn) *v. p.t. & p.p. of* SPIN.
spun glass *n.* **1.** Fiber glass. **2.** Fine blown glass with a delicate threading or filigree.
spunk (spŭngk) *n.* **1.** Tinder, as punk. **2.** *Informal.* Courage. **—spunk'y** *adj.*
spur (spûr) *n.* **1.** A device with a projecting point or sharp-toothed wheel behind, worn on a rider's boot and used to urge on a horse. **2.** An incentive. **3.** A spurlike attachment or projection, as the spinelike process on the leg of some birds. **4.** A side railroad track that connects with the main line. —*v.* **spurred, spur·ring. 1.** To urge (a horse) on with spurs. **2.** To move to action : prompt. **—spurred** *adj.*
spurge (spûrj) *n.* A chiefly tropical plant of the genus *Euphorbia,* having milky juice and small flowers.
spu·ri·ous (spyo͝or'ē-əs) *adj.* Not authentic or genuine : false.
spurn (spûrn) *v.* To reject scornfully.
spurt (spûrt). *n.* **1.** A sudden, forcible gush. **2.** A sudden outbreak or short burst of effort or activity. —*v.* **1.** To squirt <oil *spurting* into the air> **2.** To show a sudden, brief increase in activity.
sput·nik (spŭt'nĭk, spo͝ot'-) *n.* A manmade earth satellite launched by the U.S.S.R.
sput·ter (spŭt'ər) *v.* **1. a.** To spit out small particles in short bursts. **b.** To make a coughing noise characteristic of sputtering. **2.** To speak hastily or confusedly : stammer. **—sput'ter** *n.*
spu·tum (spyo͞o'təm) *n., pl.* **-ta** (-tə). Matter, as saliva or mucus, that is expectorated : spittle.
spy (spī) *n., pl.* **spies. 1.** A secret agent employed, as by a government, to obtain intelligence. **2.** A person who furtively watches another or others. —*v.* **spied, spy·ing. 1.** To keep under surveillance with hostile intent. **2.** To see <*spied* a bluejay> **3.** To observe secretly <*spying* on the neighbors>
spy·glass (spī'glăs') *n.* **1.** A small telescope. **2. spyglasses.** Binoculars.
squab (skwŏb) *n.* A young, unfledged pigeon, esp. one used as food.
squab·ble (skwŏb'əl) *v.* **-bled, -bling.** To engage in a minor quarrel : bicker. **—squab'ble** *n.* **—squab'bler** *n.*
squad (skwŏd) *n.* **1.** A small organized group of soldiers. **2.** A small group engaged in a common enterprise.
squad car *n.* A police patrol car.
squad·ron (skwŏd'rən) *n.* Any of various military units, as of soldiers, planes, or ships.
squal·id (skwŏl'ĭd) *adj.* **1.** Wretched or unkempt in appearance. **2.** Despicably repulsive : sordid.

squall[1] (skwôl) *n.* A harsh, loud yell or outcry. **–squall** *v.*
squall[2] (skwôl) *n.* A sudden, violent windstorm, often accompanied by rain or snow. **–squall'y** *adj.*
squal•or (skwŏl'ər) *n.* The quality or state of being squalid.
squan•der (skwŏn'dər) *v.* To spend extravagantly or wastefully : dissipate.
square (skwâr) *n.* **1.** A rectangle having 4 sides that are equal in length. **2.** Something having the shape of a square. **3.** A T-shaped or L-shaped instrument used for drawing or testing 90° angles. **4.** The product that results when a number is multiplied by itself. **5.** **a.** An open, often quadrilateral area at the intersection of 2 or more avenues or streets. **b.** A rectangular area bounded by streets : block. **6.** *Slang.* A rigidly conventional or unsophisticated person. *–adj.* **squar•er, squar•est. 1.** Having 4 equal sides and 4 90° angles. **2.** Forming a right angle <a board with *square* corners> **3.** Of, being, or expressed in units that measure area <*square* yards> **4.** Solid : substantial <a *square* meal> **5.** Fair : equitable <finally got a *square* deal> **6.** *Slang.* Stiffly conventional. **7.** Paid up : settled. *–v.* **squared, squar•ing. 1.** To cut a rectangular or square shape. **2.** To settle : adjust <*square* an account> **3.** To bring into harmony or conformity. **4.** To multiply (a quantity or number) by itself. **–square'ly** *adv.* **–square'ness** *n.*
square dance *n.* A dance in which couples in sets of 4 form squares. **–square'-dance'** *v.* **–square'-danc'er** *n.*
square-rigged (skwâr'rĭgd') *adj.* Having square sails set at right angles to the keel. **–square'-rig'ger** *n.*
square root *n.* A number that when taken twice as a factor gives a result that is equal to a given number.
squash[1] (skwŏsh, skwôsh) *n.* A plant of the genus *Cucurbita,* grown in many varieties for its fleshy edible fruit.
squash[2] (skwŏsh, skwôsh) *v.* **1.** To beat, squeeze, or crush to a pulp. **2.** To put down : suppress <*squash* a revolt> *–n.* **1.** The act or sound of squashing. **2.** Something that has been squashed. **3.** A game played in a walled court by players who hit a hard rubber ball with a racket.

squash[2]

squat (skwŏt) *v.* **squat•ted, squat•ting. 1.** To sit on one's heels. **2.** To settle on land without having legal title. **3.** To settle on public land in order to obtain legal title. *–adj.* **squat•ter, squat•test.** Low and broad. *–n.* **1.** A squatting or crouching posture. **2.** The act of squatting or crouching. **–squat'ter** *n.*
squaw (skwô) *n.* A North American Indian woman.
squawk (skwôk) *v.* **1.** To utter a harsh scream : screech. **2.** *Slang.* To make a noisy, angry protest. **–squawk** *n.*
squeak (skwēk) *v.* **1.** To make or utter a thin, shrill cry or sound. **2.** To pass or win by a narrow margin <*squeaked* through the test> **–squeak** *n.* **–squeak'y** *adj.*
squeal (skwēl) *v.* **1.** To make or utter a high, loud, drawn-out cry or sound. **2.** *Slang.* To betray a friend or a secret : snitch. **–squeal** *n.* **–squeal'er** *n.*
squea•mish (skwē'mĭsh) *adj.* **1.** Easily sickened or nauseated. **2.** Easily disgusted or offended : prudish. **3.** Excessively fastidious : oversensitive. **–squea'mish•ness** *n.*
squee•gee (skwē'jē') *n.* A tool having a rubber or leather blade set perpendicular to a handle, used to remove water from a flat surface, as a window. **–squee'gee'** *v.*
squeeze (skwēz) *v.* **squeezed, squeez•ing. 1.** To press hard on or together : compress. **2.** To extract by exerting pressure <*squeeze* juice from an orange> **3.** To extract dishonestly : extort. **4.** To make room or passage for by pressure : cram. *–n.* **1.** An act or instance of squeezing. **2.** An amount squeezed out. **3.** Financial pressure caused by shortages or narrowing economic margins. **–squeez'er** *n.*
squelch (skwĕlch) *v.* To suppress totally : squash. **–squelch** *n.*
squib (skwĭb) *n.* **1.** **a.** A firecracker. **b.** A firecracker that burns but does not explode. **2.** A short, often witty literary piece.
squid (skwĭd) *n., pl.* **squids** *or* **squid.** A marine cephalopod mollusk of the genera *Loligo, Rossia,* or related genera, having a usu. elongated body, 10 arms surrounding the mouth, and a vestigial internal shell.
squig•gle (skwĭg'əl) *n.* A short, scrawlike mark or wavy line. **–squig'gle** *v.* **–squig'gly** *adj.*
squint (skwĭnt) *v.* **1.** To look with partly closed eyes. **2.** To close the eyes partly. **3.** To look to the side. **4.** To suffer from strabismus. **–squint** *n.*
squire (skwīr) *n.* **1.** A young nobleman attendant on and ranking just below a knight. **2.** An English country gentleman. **3.** A local dignitary, as a judge. **4.** A lady's escort. *–v.* **squired, squir•ing.** To accompany as a squire or escort.
squirm (skwûrm) *v.* **1.** To twist about in a writhing motion : wriggle. **2.** To experience or show distress. **–squirm** *n.*
squir•rel (skwûr'əl, skwŭr'-) *n.* A rodent of the genus *Sciurus* or related genera, usu. with gray or reddish-brown fur and a long, flexible, bushy tail.
squirt (skwûrt) *v.* To eject (liquid) quickly in a narrow stream. *–n.* **1.** A device for squirting. **2.** A quantity of liquid squirted. **3.** *Informal.* An impudent person.
sr. *abbr.* senior.
Sr *symbol for* STRONTIUM.
Sr. *abbr.* **1.** senior (after surname). **2.** sister (religious).
Sri Lan•ka (srē läng'kə, shrē). Island country in the Indian Ocean SE of India. *Cap.* Colombo. *Pop.* 15,470,000. **–Sri Lan'kan** *adj. & n.*
sRNA *n.* Transfer RNA.
S.R.O. *abbr.* standing room only.
st. *abbr.* **1.** stanza. **2.** state. **3.** *also* **St.** statute. **4.** stet. **5.** stitch. **6.** stone. **7.** *also* **St.** street. **8.** strophe.
St. *abbr.* **1.** saint. **2.** strait.
–st *suff. var. of* -EST[2].
sta. *abbr.* **1.** station. **2.** stationary.
stab (stăb) *v.* **stabbed, stab•bing. 1.** To wound or puncture with or as if with a pointed weapon. **2.** To thrust or lunge. *–n.* **1.** A thrust or lunge. **2.** A wound caused by stabbing. **3.** An attempt : try.
sta•bi•lize (stā'bə-līz') *v.* **-lized, -liz•ing. 1.** To make or become stable. **2.** To keep in a stable condition. **–sta'bi•li•za'tion** *n.* **–sta'bi•liz'er** *n.*
sta•ble[1] (stā'bəl) *adj.* **-bler, -blest. 1.** Resisting changes of condition or position. **2.** *Physics.* Having no known mode of decay. Used of atomic particles. **3.** Unchanging and permanent : enduring. **4.** *Chem.* Not easily modified chemically. **5.** **a.** Dependable. **b.** Rational <a *stable* person> **–sta•bil'i•ty** (stə-bĭl'ĭ-tē) *n.*
sta•ble[2] (stā'bəl) *n.* **1.** A building for sheltering and feeding domestic animals, esp. horses and cattle. **2.** All of the racehorses belonging to 1 owner. *–v.* **-bled, -bling.** To keep or put in a stable.
stac•ca•to (stə-kä'tō) *adj.* **1.** *Mus.* Crisply detached : disconnected. **2.** Composed of short, distinct parts or sounds. **–stac•ca'to** *n. & adv.*
stack (stăk) *n.* **1.** A large, usu. cone-shaped pile of straw or hay left outdoors for storage. **2.** An orderly mass or pile. **3.** A chimney or vertical exhaust pipe. **4.** **stacks.** The section of a library where most of the books are arranged on shelves. **5.** *Informal.* A large amount. *–v.* **1.** To pile up in a stack. **2.** To fix (e.g., a deck of playing cards) in order to cheat. **–stack up.** To bear comparison.
stack•up (stăk'ŭp') *n.* A number of airplanes awaiting landing instructions and circling at different altitudes.
sta•di•um (stā'dē-əm) *n.* A large, often open structure for holding athletic events.
staff (stăf) *n., pl.* **staffs** *or* **staves** (stāvz). **1.** A rod, pole, or stick, esp.: **a.** A walking stick : cane. **b.** A cudgel : club. **c.** A rod carried as a symbol of authority. **2.** *pl.* **staffs. a.** A group of assistants who aid an executive or director. **b.** A group of military or naval officers who do not participate in combat and who lack the authority to command. **3.** *Mus.* The set of horizontal lines on which notes are written. *–v.* **1.** To furnish with a staff. **2.** To serve on the staff of.
staff•er (stăf'ər) *n. Informal.* A staff member.
stag (stăg) *n.* **1.** The adult male of various deer, esp. the red deer. **2.** A man who attends a social function without a woman. *–adj.* Intended for men only <a *stag* party> *–adv.* Unaccompanied by a woman <went *stag* to the dance>
stage (stāj) *n.* **1.** A scaffold for workers. **2.** **a.** A raised platform on which dramatic performances are presented. **b.** The acting profession. **3.** The setting for an event. **4.** A resting or stopping place on a journey. **5.** A stagecoach. **6.** A level, degree, or period of time in the evolution of a process <a disease in its early *stages*> **7.** Any of a series of rocket propulsion units. *–v.* **staged, stag•ing. 1.** To produce or direct (a theatrical performance). **2.** To set up and put in motion <*staged* an attack>

stage•coach (stāj′kōch′) *n.* A horse-drawn coach once used to transport mail, parcels, and passengers.
stage•craft (stāj′krăft′) *n.* Skill in the use of theatrical techniques or devices.
stage•hand (stāj′hănd′) *n.* One who works backstage in a theater.
stage-struck (stāj′strŭk′) *adj.* Having a passionate desire to become an actor.
stag•ger (stăg′ər) *v.* **1.** To move unsteadily : totter. **2.** To cause to totter or sway. **3.** To lose strength or confidence. **4.** To overwhelm with a severe shock, defeat, or misfortune. **5. a.** To arrange on alternating sides of a median line. **b.** To schedule in overlapping time periods. *—n.* **1.** A staggering gait. **2. staggers** *(sing. in number).* A disease of the nervous system in animals, esp. a cerebrospinal disease of horses marked by loss of coordination.
stag•ger•ing (stăg′ər-ĭng) *adj.* Overwhelming <*staggering* medical bills> ☆***syns:*** MIND-BLOWING, MIND-BOGGLING, OVERWHELMING, SPECTACULAR, STUNNING **—stag′ger•ing•ly** *adv.*
stag•nant (stăg′nənt) *adj.* **1.** Not flowing : still <*stagnant* water> **2.** Foul from standing still : stale <*stagnant* air> **3.** Not changing or growing : inactive <a *stagnant* period for sales>
stag•nate (stăg′nāt′) *v.* **-nat•ed, -nat•ing. 1.** To be or become stagnant. **2.** To fail to progress or develop : remain inactive. **—stag•na′tion** *n.*
staid (stād) *adj.* Sedate and reserved.
stain (stān) *v.* **1.** To discolor or become discolored : soil. **2.** To corrupt : taint. **3.** To color with dye. *—n.* **1.** A discolored spot. **2.** A blemish on one's moral character or reputation. **3.** A substance applied esp. to wood that penetrates the surface and imparts color. **—stain′less** *adj.*
stained glass *n.* Glass that is colored esp. for use in windows.
stainless steel *n.* Steel alloyed with chromium so as to inhibit corrosion, oxidation, or rusting.
stair (stâr) *n.* **1. stairs.** A flight of steps. **2.** One of a series of steps.
stair•case (stâr′kās′) *n.* A flight or series of flights of steps and a supporting structure connecting separate levels.
stair•way (stâr′wā′) *n.* A staircase.
stair•well (stâr′wĕl′) *n.* A vertical shaft containing a staircase.
stake (stāk) *n.* **1.** A sharpened piece, esp. of wood, for driving into the ground as a support or marker. **2. a.** A post to which an offender is bound for execution by burning. **b.** Execution by burning at the stake. **3. a.** Money or property risked in a bet or game of chance. **b.** The prize awarded the winner of a contest or race : purse. **4.** A share in an enterprise. *—v.* **staked, stak•ing. 1.** To indicate the boundaries of with or as if with stakes. **2.** To fasten or support with a stake. **3.** To tie to a stake. **4.** To gamble or risk : hazard. **5.** To provide working capital for. **—stake out. 1.** To assign (a police officer) to conduct surveillance of an area. **2.** To establish a stakeout on.
stake•out (stāk′out′) *n.* Police surveillance, as of a building or area.
sta•lac•tite (stə-lăk′tīt′) *n.* A cylindrical or conical deposit that projects downward from the roof of a cavern.
sta•lag•mite (stə-lăg′mīt′) *n.* A cylindrical or conical deposit that projects upward from the floor of a cavern.
stale (stāl) *adj.* **stal•er, stal•est. 1.** Having lost freshness, effervescence, or taste. **2.** Too old or overused to be effective. **3.** Impaired in efficacy or strength. ☆***syns:*** FLAT, TIRED **—stale** *v.*
stale•mate (stāl′māt′) *n.* **1.** A position in chess in which only the king can move but only into check. **2.** A situation in which no further action can be taken : deadlock. **—stale′mate′** *v.*
Sta•lin (stä′lĭn), **Joseph.** 1879–1953. Soviet revolutionary and political leader.
stalk[1] (stôk) *n.* **1.** A stem or main axis of a plant. **2.** A slender or elongated support.
stalk[2] (stôk) *v.* **1.** To walk in a stiff, arrogant, or angry manner. **2.** To track (game) in a stealthy manner.
stall (stôl) *n.* **1.** An enclosure for a domestic animal in a barn or shed. **2.** An enclosure for selling or displaying merchandise, as at a fair : booth. **3. a.** An enclosed seat in a church chancel. **b.** A church pew. **4.** *esp. Brit.* A theater seat in the front part of the orchestra. **5.** A sudden loss in the power or effectiveness of an engine. *—v.* **1.** To put or lodge in a stall. **2.** To come or bring to a standstill inadvertently. **3.** To try to put off action through delaying tactics.
stal•lion (stăl′yən) *n.* A full-grown male horse that has not been castrated.
stal•wart (stôl′wərt) *adj.* **1.** Strong : robust. **2.** Steadfast : resolute.
sta•men (stā′mən) *n.* One of the pollen-producing reproductive organs of a flower, usu. consisting of a filament and an anther.
stam•i•na (stăm′ə-nə) *n.* Endurance.
stam•i•nate (stăm′ə-nət, -nāt′) *adj. Bot.* **1.** Having stamens. **2.** Bearing stamens but no pistils.
stam•mer (stăm′ər) *v.* **1.** To make involuntary pauses or syllabic repetitions while speaking. **2.** To utter or say with a stammer. **—stam′mer** *n.* **—stam′mer•er** *n.*
stamp (stămp) *v.* **1.** To thrust (the foot) down heavily (on). **2.** To imprint or impress with a mark, design, or message. **3.** To put a gummed marker, as a postage stamp, on. **4.** To shape or cut out by forcing into or against a mold or die. *—n.* **1.** An act of stamping. **2. a.** An implement or device for stamping. **b.** An impression made by stamping. **3.** A mark or impression that indicates a fact, as approval or ownership. **4.** A postage stamp. **5.** A characteristic mark.
stam•pede (stăm-pēd′) *n.* **1.** A sudden, headlong rush, esp. of startled animals. **2.** *Can.* A rodeo with fair amusements, as the Calgary Stampede. *—v.* **-ped•ed, -ped•ing. 1.** To act or cause to act impulsively in or as if in a stampede. **2.** To cause to stampede.
stamping ground *n.* A customary or favorite environment.
stance (stăns) *n.* **1.** The position of a standing person or animal. **2.** An emotional or intellectual attitude.
stanch[1] *also* **staunch** (stônch, stŏnch) *v.* **1.** To stop or check the flow of. **2.** To check the flow of blood from (a wound).
stanch[2] (stônch, stŏnch) *adj. var. of* STAUNCH[1].
stan•chion (stăn′chən) *n.* A vertical pole, post, or support.
stand (stănd) *v.* **stood** (stŏŏd), **stand•ing. 1.** To take, be placed in, or maintain an upright or erect position. **2.** To assume or be in a specified position <*stand* straight> **3.** To remain valid, intact, or unchanged <The temperature *stands* at 32°.> **4.** To be situated or placed. **5.** To be in a specified position or degree : rank <*stood* at the head of the class> **6.** To remain stationary. **7.** To take up or maintain an attitude or conviction <*stand* fast> **8. a.** To resist : withstand <can *stand* high temperatures> **b.** To endure : bear <can't *stand* the suspense> **9.** To undergo <will *stand* trial> **10.** To set on end. *—n.* **1.** The act of standing. **2.** A stop on a performance tour. **3.** A small booth or stall for selling goods. **4.** A position one is prepared to defend <take a *stand*> **5. stands.** The seating area at a stadium or playing field. **6.** A witness stand. **7.** A rack or framework for holding something <a music *stand*> **8.** A growth of plants or trees. **—stand by. 1.** To be loyal to. **2.** To keep : fulfill. **3.** To be ready to act, esp. as a substitute. **—stand for.** To represent : symbolize. **—stand out.** To be prominent or outstanding. **—stand up. 1.** To prove valid, satisfactory, or durable. **2.** *Informal.* To fail to keep an appointment with <My date *stood* me *up.*>
stan•dard (stăn′dərd) *n.* **1.** A flag, as one serving as the emblem of a nation. **2.** Something accepted as a basis for comparison : criterion. **3.** A pedestal on which something is supported. **—stan′dard** *adj.*
stan•dard-bear•er (stăn′dərd-bâr′ər) *n.* **1.** One that bears the colors of a military unit. **2.** One in the forefront of a movement, cause, etc.
stan•dard•ize (stăn′dər-dīz′) *v.* **-ized, -iz•ing.** To cause to conform with a standard. **—stan′dard•i•za′tion** *n.*
standard of living *n.* A measure of the quality and quantity of goods and services enjoyed by a person, group, or nation.
standard time *n.* The time in any of the 24 zones into which the earth is divided longitudinally.
stand•by (stănd′bī′) *n., pl.* **-bys. 1.** One that is dependable. **2.** One kept in readiness to serve as a substitute.
stand•ee (stăn-dē′) *n.* One who stands.
stand-in (stănd′ĭn′) *n.* **1.** One who substitutes for an actor during camera and light adjustments. **2.** A substitute.
stand•ing (stăn′dĭng) *n.* **1 a.** Status with respect to achievement or reputation. **b.** High reputation : esteem. **2.** Length of time : duration. *—adj.* **1.** Remaining upright : erect. **2.** Made or performed from an upright position <*standing* jumps> **3.** Permanent and unchanging <a *standing* order> **4.** Not moving : stationary. **5.** Not flowing or circulating : stagnant.
stand-off (stănd′ôf′, -ŏf′) *n.* A tie, as in a competitive event : draw.
stand•off•ish (stănd-ô′fĭsh, -ŏf′ĭsh) *adj.* Not sociable : distant.
stand•out (stănd′out′) *n.* One that is extraordinary.
stand•point (stănd′point′) *n.* A point of view.
stand•still (stănd′stĭl′) *n.* A stop <production that came to a *standstill*>
stand•up *or* **stand-up** (stănd′ŭp′) *adj.* **1.** Erect : upright. **2.** Of, relating to, or being a performer who works alone and without props <a *standup* comedian>
stank (stănk) *v. var. p.t. of* STINK.
stan•za (stăn′zə) *n.* One of the divisions of a poem, consisting of 2 or more lines. **—stan•za′ic** (-zā′ĭk) *adj.*

sta·pes (stā′pēz′) *n., pl.* **stapes** *or* **sta·pe·des** (stə-pē′dēz′). One of the 3 small bones of the inner ear.
staph·y·lo·coc·cus (stăf′ə-lō-kŏk′əs) *n., pl.* **-coc·ci** (-kŏk′sī′, -kŏk′ī′). Any of various spherical parasitic bacteria of the genus *Staphylococcus,* causing infections such as boils, septicemia, etc. **—staph′y·lo·coc′cal** (-kŏk′əl), **staph′y·lo·coc′cic** (-kŏk′sĭk, -kŏk′ĭk) *adj.*
sta·ple[1] (stā′pəl) *n.* **1.** A major commodity grown or produced in a region. **2.** A major trade item in steady demand. **3.** A major element or feature. **4.** Raw material. **5.** Fiber, as of cotton or wool, graded with respect to length or fineness.
sta·ple[2] (stā′pəl) *n.* **1.** A U-shaped metal fastener with pointed ends designed to be driven into a surface to hold something, as a wire. **2.** A thin U-shaped piece of wire used as a fastening for materials such as paper or cloth. **—sta′ple** *v.* **—sta′pler** *n.*
star (stär) *n.* **1.** *Astron.* A self-luminous, self-containing mass of gas. **2.** Any of the celestial bodies that can be seen at night from the earth as usu. twinkling points of light. **3.** A symbol or graphic design that resembles a star. **4. a.** One who plays the leading role in a dramatic performance. **b.** An outstanding performer. **5.** An asterisk. **6. stars.** The constellations of the zodiac believed to influence personal destiny. **7. stars.** The future : destiny. *—v.* **starred, star·ring. 1.** To decorate with stars. **2.** To mark with an asterisk. **3.** To play or present in the leading role. **4.** To perform in an outstanding manner. **—star′dom** *n.* **—star′less** *adj.* **—star′ry** *adj.*
star·board (stär′bərd) *n.* The right side of a ship or aircraft facing forward. **—star′board** *adj. & adv.*
starch (stärch) *n.* **1.** Any of various nutrient carbohydrates that occur widely in plants, as potatoes or rice. **2.** A purified form of starch occurring chiefly as a white, tasteless powder used esp. for stiffening fabrics. *—v.* To stiffen (fabric) with starch. **—starch′i·ness** *n.* **—starch′y** *adj.*
stare (stâr) *v.* **stared, star·ing.** To look with an intent, direct gaze. **—stare** *n.* **—star′er** *n.*
star·fish (stär′fĭsh′) *n.* A marine echinoderm of the class Asteroidea, having 5 arms extending from a central disk.
stark (stärk) *adj.* **1.** Bare : blunt <the *stark* truth> **2.** Complete : total <*stark* poverty> **3.** Forbidding in appearance : barren <a *stark* wasteland> *—adv.* Completely <*stark* naked> **—stark′ly** *adv.* **—stark′ness** *n.*
star·let (stär′lĭt) *n.* A young motion-picture actress.
star·light (stär′līt′) *n.* The light produced by the stars.
star·ling (stär′lĭng) *n.* An Old World bird of the family Sturnidae, with dark, often iridescent plumage, esp. *Sturnus vulgaris,* widely naturalized in the U.S.
star·lit (stär′lĭt′) *adj.* Illuminated by the light of the stars.
star·quake (stär′kwāk′) *n.* A seismological occurrence on a star.
star·ry-eyed (stär′ē-īd′) *adj.* **1.** Naively enthusiastic. **2.** Marked by idealism.
Stars and Stripes *pl.n. (sing. or pl. in number).* The flag of the U.S.
Star-Span·gled Banner (stär′spăng′gəld) *n.* **1.** The flag of the U.S. **2.** The national anthem of the U.S.
start (stärt) *v.* **1.** To begin to move, go, or act : commence. **2.** To move with a sudden involuntary motion : jerk. **3.** To put into operation, motion, or action. **4.** To introduce : originate. *—n.* **1.** A beginning. **2.** A sudden involuntarily bodily movement. **3.** A time or place at which to begin. **4.** A position of advantage over another : lead. **—start′er** *n.*
star·tle (stär′tl) *v.* **-tled, -tling. 1.** To cause to make a start, as of surprise. **2.** To fill with sudden surprise. ☆*syns:* JOLT, SHOCK **—star′tling·ly** *adv.*
starve (stärv) *v.* **starved, starv·ing. 1.** To suffer or die from hunger. **2.** To cause to starve. **3.** To suffer from deprivation. **4.** To compel or force by withholding. **—star·va′tion** *n.*
starve·ling (stärv′lĭng) *n.* One that is emaciated from or as if from starvation.
stash (stăsh) *v.* To put away or hide in a secret place. *—n.* **1.** A cache of money or valuables. **2.** Something hidden away.
sta·sis (stā′sĭs) *n., pl.* **-ses** (-sēz′). A state of balance, as among opposing forces.
state (stāt) *n.* **1.** A condition or mode of existence. **2.** An emotional or mental condition. **3.** A social position or rank. **4.** A form of government <a fascist *state*> **5.** A body politic, esp. one constituting a nation. **6.** One of the subdivisions of a federal government, as the U.S. *—v.* **stat·ed, stat·ing. 1.** To express verbally. **2.** To establish : fix. **—state′hood′** *n.*
state·craft (stāt′krăft′) *n.* The art of leading a country.
state house *n.* A building in which sessions of a state legislature are held.
state·ly (stāt′lē) *adj.* **-li·er, -li·est. 1.** Marked by grace and dignity. **2.** Impressive : grand. **—state′li·ness** *n.*
state·ment (stāt′mənt) *n.* **1.** The act of stating or declaring. **2.** Something stated : declaration. **3.** An abstract of a financial account : bill. **4.** A monthly report sent to a debtor or bank depositor.
state of the art *n.* The highest level of development, as of a device, technique, or science, achieved at a particular time. **—state′of-the-art′** *adj.*
state·room (stāt′ro͞om′, -ro͝om′) *n.* A private compartment on a train or ship.
state·side (stāt′sīd′) *adj. & adv.* Of, to, or in the continental U.S.
states·man (stāts′mən) *n.* One who shows great skill and wisdom in dealing with governmental affairs and important issues. **—states′man·like′, states′man·ly** *adj.* **—states′man·ship′** *n.*
state·wide (stāt′wīd′) *adj. & adv.* Taking place throughout a state.
stat·ic (stăt′ĭk) *adj.* **1. a.** Not in motion : at rest. **b.** Marked by the absence of motion or progress. **2.** *Elect.* Of, relating to, or creating stationary electric charges. **3.** Of, relating to, or produced by random noise in a radio receiver. *—n.* **1.** Random noise in a radio receiver or visible specks on a television screen caused by atmospheric disturbances. **2.** *Slang.* **a.** Back talk. **b.** Obstruction. **—stat′i·cal·ly** *adv.*
sta·tion (stā′shən) *n.* **1.** The place or position where one stands or is directed to stand : post. **2.** A scheduled stopping place, as on a railroad or bus line : depot. **3.** Social standing : rank. **4.** A place having radio or television transmission equipment. *—v.* To post or place in a station. ☆*syns:* ASSIGN, POST, SET
sta·tion·ar·y (stā′shə-nĕr′ē) *adj.* **1. a.** Not moving. **b.** Not capable of being moved : fixed. **2.** Unchanging.
station break *n.* A pause in a broadcast program to allow for network or station identification.
sta·tion·er (stā′shə-nər) *n.* A person who sells stationery.
sta·tion·er·y (stā′shə-nĕr′ē) *n.* **1.** Writing paper and envelopes. **2.** Writing or typing materials.
station house *n.* **1.** A police station. **2.** A fire station.
sta·tion·mas·ter (stā′shən-măs′tər) *n.* An official in charge of a railroad station.
station wagon *n.* An automobile having a fairly large interior, usu. a tailgate, and a row of folding or removable seats.
sta·tis·tic (stə-tĭs′tĭk) *n.* **1.** An item of numerical data. **2.** An estimate of a variable, as an average or mean, made on the basis of a sample taken from a larger set of data. **—sta·tis′ti·cal** (-tĭ-kəl) *adj.* **—sta·tis′ti·cal·ly** *adv.*
sta·tis·tics (stə-tĭs′tĭks) *n.* **1.** *(sing. in number).* The branch of mathematics that deals with the organization, analysis, collection, and interpretation of statistical data. **2.** *(pl. in number).* A collection or set of numerical data. **—stat′is·ti′cian** (stăt′ĭ-stĭsh′ən) *n.*
stat·u·ar·y (stăch′o͞o-ĕr′ē) *n., pl.* **-ies. 1.** Statues as a group. **2.** The art of making statues.
stat·ue (stăch′o͞o) *n.* A form or likeness sculpted, modeled, carved, or cast in material such as stone, clay, wood, or bronze.
stat·u·esque (stăch′o͞o-ĕsk′) *adj.* Like a statue, esp. in size, grace, or dignity : stately.
stat·u·ette (stăch′o͞o-ĕt′) *n.* A small statue.
stat·ure (stăch′ər) *n.* **1.** Natural height of a human or animal body when upright. **2.** A level of development or achievement.
sta·tus (stā′təs, stăt′əs) *n.* **1.** The state of a person or thing as defined by law, regulations, or customs. **2.** A relative or high position, esp. in a social system. **3.** A state of affairs : situation.
sta·tus quo (stā′təs kwō′, stăt′əs) *n.* The current state of affairs.
stat·ute (stăch′o͞ot) *n.* **1.** A law enacted by the legislative assembly of a nation or state. **2.** A decree or edict.
statute of limitations *n. Law.* A statute setting a time limit on legal action in certain cases.
stat·u·to·ry (stăch′ə-tôr′ē, -tōr′ē) *adj.* **1.** Of or relating to a statute. **2.** Defined by or regulated by statute.
staunch[1] *also* **stanch** (stônch, stŏnch) *adj.* **1.** Firm and steadfast : loyal <a *staunch* ally> **2.** Solidly built or made. **—staunch′ly** *adv.*
staunch[2] (stônch, stŏnch) *v. var. of* STANCH[1].
stave (stāv) *n.* **1.** One of the narrow strips of wood forming part of the sides of a container, as a barrel. **2.** A heavy stick or pole : staff. **3.** A set of verses : stanza. *—v.* **staved** *or* **stove** (stōv), **stav·ing.** To break a hole in by or as if by puncturing staves. **—stave off.** To repel.
staves (stāvs) *n. var. pl. of* STAFF.
stay[1] (stā) *v.* **1.** To remain in 1 place or condition. **2.** To dwell : live. **3.** To pause : wait. **4.** To last : endure. **5.** To stop or halt : check. **6.** To delay (e.g., the carrying out of an order), as by legal action : suspend. **7.** To satisfy temporarily <*stayed* my hunger> **8.** To remain during or through <*stayed* the night> *—n.*

1. A short visit or sojourn. 2. A halt or pause. 3. A postponement, as of an execution.
stay[2] (stā) *v.* To support or brace. —*n.* 1. A part that props up or braces. 2. A strip of rigid material, as bone or metal, used to stiffen a garment. 3. **stays.** A corset.
stay[3] (stā) *n.* A rope or cable that serves as a brace or support for a mast or spar.
staying power *n.* Stamina : endurance.
std. *abbr.* standard.
stead (stĕd) *n.* 1. The place or position of another. 2. Advantage <intelligence that stood him in good *stead*>
stead·fast (stĕd′făst′) *adj.* 1. Not moving : fixed. 2. Unyieldingly firm in purpose, faith, or attachment : loyal. **—stead′fast′ly** *adv.* **—stead′fast′ness** *n.*
stead·y (stĕd′ē) *adj.* **-i·er, -i·est.** 1. Firmly fixed or placed : stable. 2. Not faltering : controlled. 3. Not changing movement, direction, or quality <a *steady* rain> 4. Not easily excited or upset : composed. 5. Dependable : reliable. 6. Regular <a *steady* customer> —*v.* **-ied, -y·ing.** To make or become steady : stabilize. **—stead′i·ly** *adv.* **—stead′i·ness** *n.* **—stead′y** *adv.*
stead·y-state theory (stĕd′ē-stāt′) *n.* A cosmological theory that the expansion of the universe is compensated for by the continuous creation of matter.
steak (stāk) *n.* A piece of fish or meat, esp. beef, cut in a thick slice.
steal (stēl) *v.* **stole** (stōl), **sto·len** (stō′lən), **steal·ing.** 1. To take (the property of another) without permission or right. 2. To take or enjoy secretly or furtively <*steal* a glimpse> 3. To move or pass imperceptibly or secretly. 4. *Baseball.* To gain (a base) without the ball being batted. —*n.* 1. The act of stealing. 2. *Slang.* A bargain.
stealth (stĕlth) *n.* Secret, surreptitious, or clandestine activity : furtiveness.
stealth·y (stĕl′thē) *adj.* **-i·er, -i·est.** Marked by or acting with stealth. **—stealth′i·ly** *adv.* **—stealth′i·ness** *n.*
steam (stēm) *n.* 1. **a.** Water in the gaseous state, esp. when hot. **b.** The mist that forms when hot water vapor cools and condenses. 2. A heating system in which steam generated in a boiler is piped to radiators. 3. Energy : power. —*v.* 1. To generate or emit steam. 2. To turn into or escape as steam. 3. To move by or as if by steam power. **—steam′y** *adj.*
steam·boat (stēm′bōt′) *n.* A steamship.
steam engine *n.* An engine in which the energy of hot steam is converted into mechanical power, esp. one in which the steam expands in a closed cylinder and drives a piston.
steam·er (stē′mər) *n.* 1. A steamship. 2. A container in which something is exposed to or treated with steam.
steam·fit·ter (stēm′fĭt′ər) *n.* A person whose trade is the repair and installation of heating, ventilating, refrigerating, or air-conditioning systems.
steam·roll·er (stēm′rō′lər) *n.* A vehicle equipped with a heavy roller for smoothing road surfaces. —*v.* 1. To smooth or level with a steamroller. 2. To overwhelm as if with a steamroller.
steam·ship (stēm′shĭp′) *n.* A ship powered by steam.
steam shovel *n.* A steam-powered machine for excavating.
ste·a·tite (stē′ə-tīt′) *n.* A solid form of talc used in ceramics and insulation.
steed (stēd) *n.* A spirited horse.
steel (stēl) *n.* 1. Any of various hard, strong alloys of iron and carbon. 2. A hard, unflinching quality. 3. Something, as a sword, made of steel. —*v.* 1. To plate, edge, or tip with steel. 2. To make hard or strong : strengthen. **—steel′y** *adj.*
steel band *n.* A musical band composed chiefly of percussion instruments fashioned from oil drums.
steel guitar *n.* A Hawaiian guitar.
steel-trap (stēl′trăp′) *adj.* Very quick and keen : trenchant <a *steel-trap* mind>
steel wool *n.* Fine fibers of steel used esp. for cleaning or polishing.
steel·yard (stēl′yärd′) *n.* A balance consisting of a scaled arm suspended off center, a hook at the shorter end on which to hang the object being weighed, and a counterbalance at the longer end that can be moved to find the weight.
steep[1] (stēp) *adj.* 1. Sharply inclined : precipitous. 2. Exorbitant. **—steep′ly** *adv.* **—steep′ness** *n.*
steep[2] (stēp) *v.* 1. To soak or saturate in a liquid. 2. To pervade : permeate <*steeped* in tradition>
steep·en (stē′pən) *v.* To make or become steeper.
stee·ple (stē′pəl) *n.* 1. A tall tower, as one surmounting a church, often ending in a spire. 2. A spire.
stee·ple·chase (stē′pəl-chās′) *n.* A race in which horsemen travel across open land or through a course with artificial obstacles. **—stee′ple·chas′er** *n.*
stee·ple·jack (stē′pəl-jăk′) *n.* A person who works on high structures, as steeples.
steer[1] (stîr) *v.* 1. To direct the course of (e.g., a vehicle). 2. To be guided or capable of being guided. 3. To fix and travel on (a course). 4. To direct : guide. **—steer′a·ble** *adj.* **—steers′man** *n.*
steer[2] (stîr) *n.* A young male of domestic cattle, esp. one castrated and raised for beef.
steer·age (stîr′ĭj) *n.* 1. The act of steering. 2. The section of a passenger ship affording the least expensive accommodations.
stein (stīn) *n.* A large mug, esp. for beer.
stel·lar (stĕl′ər) *adj.* 1. Of, relating to, or consisting of stars. 2. Of or befitting a star performer. 3. Outstanding.
stem[1] (stĕm) *n.* 1. **a.** The main ascending axis of a plant : stalk or trunk. **b.** A plant part supporting another part, as a flower. 2. A part resembling a stem <the *stem* of a goblet> 3. A line of genealogical descent. 4. The part of a word to which affixes may be added, as to form inflections. —*v.* **stemmed, stem·ming.** 1. To derive from : originate. 2. To make progress against.
stem[2] (stĕm) *v.* **stemmed, stem·ming.** 1. To plug up : stop. 2. To check the flow or advance of : hold back.
stem·ware (stĕm′wâr′) *n.* Glassware, as goblets, with stems.
stench (stĕnch) *n.* An offensive smell.
sten·cil (stĕn′səl) *n.* A sheet of material, as plastic or cardboard, into which a design or lettering has been cut so that paint or ink applied to the sheet will reproduce the pattern on the surface underneath. **—sten′cil** *v.*
ste·nog·ra·phy (stə-nŏg′rə-fē) *n.* The skill or process of writing in shorthand. **—ste·nog′ra·pher** *n.* **—sten′o·graph′ic** (stĕn′ə-grăf′ĭk) *adj.*
sten·to·ri·an (stĕn-tôr′ē-ən, -tōr′-) *adj.* Very loud.
step (stĕp) *n.* 1. **a.** A single complete movement made by raising 1 foot and putting it down in another spot. **b.** Manner of walking : gait. 2. **a.** A distance traversed in taking a step. **b.** A very short distance. 3. A rest for the foot in ascending or descending. 4. **a.** Any of a series of actions or measures taken to accomplish an end or goal. **b.** A stage in a process or degree in a scale. —*v.* **stepped, step·ping.** 1. **a.** To move by taking steps : walk. **b.** To step in a certain manner <*stepping* lively> 2. To press the foot down or against. 3. To measure by stepping. 4. To make or arrange in or as if in a series of steps. **—step down.** 1. To resign, esp. from a high office. 2. To reduce, esp. by degrees. **—step up.** To increase, esp. by degrees.
step·broth·er (stĕp′brŭth′ər) *n.* The son of one's stepparent by an earlier marriage.
step·child (stĕp′chīld′) *n.* A stepson or stepdaughter.
step·daugh·ter (stĕp′dô′tər) *n.* The daughter of one's spouse by an earlier marriage.
step·fa·ther (stĕp′fä′thər) *n.* The husband of one's mother by a later marriage.
step·lad·der (stĕp′lăd′ər) *n.* A portable hinged ladder with steps.
step·moth·er (stĕp′mŭth′ər) *n.* The wife of one's father by a later marriage.
step·par·ent (stĕp′pâr′ənt, -păr′-) *n.* A stepfather or stepmother.
steppe (stĕp) *n.* A vast arid, grassy plain found esp. in SE Europe and Siberia.
step·ping·stone (stĕp′ĭng-stōn′) *n.* 1. A stone on which to step, as in crossing a brook. 2. A means of advancement.
step·sis·ter (stĕp′sĭs′tər) *n.* The daughter of one's stepparent by an earlier marriage.
step·son (stĕp′sŭn′) *n.* The son of one's spouse by an earlier marriage.
step-up (stĕp′ŭp′) *n.* An increase, as in size, amount, or activity.
-ster *suff.* 1. One that is associated with, creates, or does <song*ster*> 2. One that is <old*ster*>
stere (stîr) *n.* See MEASUREMENT TABLE.
ste·re·o (stĕr′ē-ō′, stîr′-) *n., pl.* **-os.** 1. **a.** A stereophonic sound-reproduction system. **b.** Stereophonic sound. 2. A stereoscopic system or photograph. **—ste′re·o′** *adj.*
ster·e·o·phon·ic (stĕr′ē-ə-fŏn′ĭk, stîr′-) *adj.* Of, being, or used in a system of sound reproduction in which 2 separate channels are utilized in order to produce the effect of 3-dimensional sound distribution. **—ster′e·o·phon′i·cal·ly** *adv.*
ster·e·o·scope (stĕr′ē-ə-skōp′, stîr′-) *n.* An optical device through which 2 slightly different views of a scene are presented, 1 to each eye, giving a 3-dimensional illusion. **—ster′e·o·scop′ic** (-skŏp′ĭk) *adj.* **—ster′e·o·scop′i·cal·ly** *adv.*
ster·e·os·co·py (stĕr′ē-ŏs′kə-pē, stîr′-) *n.* The act of viewing objects in 3 dimensions.
ster·e·o·type (stĕr′ē-ə-tīp′, stîr′-) *n.* 1. A conventional, formulaic, usu. highly simplified opinion, conception, or belief. 2. A metal printing plate cast from a matrix made from a raised

surface, as type. —*v.* **1.** To develop a stereotype about. **2.** To print from a stereotype. **—ster′e·o·typ′ic** (-tĭp′ĭk), **ster′e·o·typ′i·cal** *adj.*

ster·ile (stĕr′əl, -īl′) *adj.* **1.** Not capable of reproducing or producing : infertile or unproductive. **2.** Free from microorganisms, esp. those that cause disease. ☆***syns:*** SANITARY, SANITIZED, STERILIZED **—ste·ril′i·ty** (stə-rĭl′ĭ-tē) *n.*

ster·il·ize (stĕr′ə-līz′) *v.* **-ized, -iz·ing.** To make sterile. **—ster′il·i·za′tion** *n.* **—ster′il·iz′er** *n.*

ster·ling (stûr′lĭng) *n.* **1.** British money. **2. a.** An alloy consisting of 92.5% silver with copper. **b.** Articles, as flatware, made of sterling. —*adj.* **1.** Of, relating to, or expressed in British money. **2.** Made of sterling silver. **3.** First-rate.

stern[1] (stûrn) *adj.* **1.** Rigid : inflexible. **2.** Grim : forbidding. **3.** Harsh : austere. **4.** Firmly maintained. **—stern′ly** *adv.* **—stern′ness** *n.*

stern[2] (stûrn) *n.* The rear section of a ship or boat.

ster·num (stûr′nəm) *n., pl.* **-na** (-nə) *or* **-nums.** A long flat bone articulating with the cartilages of and forming the support of most of the ribs. **—stern′al** *adj.*

ster·oid (stîr′oid′, stĕr′-) *n.* Any of numerous naturally occurring, fat-soluble organic compounds, including many hormones.

steth·o·scope (stĕth′ə-skōp′) *n.* An instrument for listening to internal bodily sounds.

ste·ve·dore (stē′və-dôr′, -dōr′) *n.* A worker who loads or unloads ships.

stew (sto͞o, styo͞o) *v.* **1.** To cook by slowly boiling : simmer. **2.** *Informal.* To be anxious : worry. —*n.* **1.** A dish, esp. of meat and vegetables, cooked by stewing. **2.** *Informal.* A state of anxiety : worry.

stew·ard (sto͞o′ərd, styo͞o′-) *n.* **1.** One who manages another's financial affairs or property. **2.** A person responsible for the household affairs of a large institution, as an estate. **3.** A ship's officer responsible for provisions and dining arrangements. **4.** An attendant on a ship or aircraft. **—stew′ard·ess** *n.* **—stew′ard·ship′** *n.*

stick (stĭk) *n.* **1.** A slender, often long piece of wood, as a twig or branch. **2.** A cane or walking stick. **3.** Something that resembles a stick <a *stick* of dynamite> **4.** : sticks *Informal.* A rural area. **5.** *Informal.* A spiritless or dull person. —*v.* **stuck** (stŭk), **stick·ing. 1.** To pierce or prick with a sharply pointed object. **2. a.** To fasten by pushing in a pointed object. **b.** To impale. **3.** To attach with or as if with an adhesive, as glue. **4. a.** To be or cause to be fixed and unable to move. **b.** To become obstructed or jammed. **5. a.** To remain attached : adhere or cling. **b.** To remain firm, resolute, loyal, or faithful. **6.** To extend, project, or protrude. **—stick up.** To rob, esp. at gunpoint. **—stick up for.** To defend : support.

stick·er (stĭk′ər) *n.* **1.** One that sticks. **2.** An adhesive label. **3.** A thorn or barb.

stick-in-the-mud (stĭk′ĭn-*th*ə-mŭd′) *n. Informal.* One lacking initiative, imagination, or enthusiasm.

stick·le·back (stĭk′əl-băk′) *n.* A small freshwater or marine fish of the family Gasterosteidae, with erectile spines along the back.

stickleback

stick·ler (stĭk′lər) *n.* One who insists on meticulous observance of detail.

stick shift *n.* A manually operated gearshift on an automobile.

stick·up (stĭk′ŭp′) *n. Slang.* A robbery, esp. at gunpoint.

stick·y (stĭk′ē) *adj.* **-i·er, -i·est. 1.** Having the property of sticking : adhesive. **2.** Very damp and warm : muggy. **3.** *Informal.* Unpleasant or difficult. ☆***syns:*** HUMID, MUGGY, SOGGY

stiff (stĭf) *adj.* **1.** Not flexible or pliant. **2.** Not moving or functioning with ease. **3.** Stretched tight : taut. **4.** Rigidly formal. **5.** Not flowing easily : thick <a *stiff* batter> **6.** Strong : powerful <a *stiff* current> **7.** Difficult, laborious, or rigorous. **8.** Harsh : stern. **9.** Excessively high <a *stiff* price> ☆***syns:*** STARCHY, STILTED, WOODEN **—stiff′ly** *adv.* **—stiff′ness** *n.*

stiff·en (stĭf′ən) *v.* To make or become stiff or stiffer. **—stiff′en·er** *n.*

stiff-necked (stĭf′nĕkt′) *adj.* Obstinate.

sti·fle[1] (stī′fəl) *v.* **-fled, -fling. 1.** To smother. **2.** To suffocate. **3.** To put out : extinguish. **4.** To cut off (e.g., the voice). **5.** To keep back : suppress <*stifle* a yawn>

sti·fle[2] (stī′fəl) *n.* A leg joint of certain quadrupeds, as the horse, analogous to the human knee.

stig·ma (stĭg′mə) *n., pl.* **stig·ma·ta** (stĭg-mä′tə, stĭg′mə-) *or* **-mas. 1.** A mark of infamy or disgrace. **2.** *pl.* **-mas.** *Bot.* The apex of the pistil of a flower, on which pollen is deposited at pollination. **3. stigmata.** Marks resembling the crucifixion wounds of Jesus. **—stig·mat′ic** (stĭg-măt′ĭk) *adj.*

stig·ma·tize (stĭg′mə-tīz′) *v.* **-tized, -tiz·ing. 1.** To brand as shameful or dishonorable. **2.** To mark with a stigma.

stile (stīl) *n.* A set of steps for crossing a wall or fence.

sti·let·to (stĭ-lĕt′ō) *n., pl.* **-tos** *or* **-toes.** A small dagger with a slender blade that tapers to a sharp point.

†**still**[1] (stĭl) *adj.* **1.** Quiet : silent. **2.** Devoid of movement : stationary. **3.** Calm : peaceful. **4.** Of, relating to, or being a static photograph rather than a motion picture. —*n.* **1.** Quiet : silence. **2.** A still photograph, esp. one from a scene of a motion picture. —*adv.* **1.** Without motion <stood *still*> **2.** Up to or at the time indicated <*still* alive> **3.** Even or yet <*still* angrier> **4.** All the same : nevertheless. **5.** *Archaic & Regional.* Always : constantly. **—still** *v.* **—still′ness** *n.*

still[2] (stĭl) *n.* **1.** An apparatus for distilling liquids, esp. alcohols. **2.** A distillery.

still·birth (stĭl′bûrth′) *n.* The birth of a dead fetus.

still·born (stĭl′bôrn′) *adj.* Dead at birth.

still life *n., pl.* **still lifes.** A painting or photograph of inanimate objects, as flowers or fruit.

stilt (stĭlt) *n.* **1.** One of a pair of long, slender poles, each with a foot support, used for walking. **2.** A supporting pole for a structure that is raised above the level of the ground or water.

stilt·ed (stĭl′tĭd) *adj.* Stiffly formal.

Stil·ton (stĭl′tən) *n.* A rich, waxy cheese with a blue-green mold.

stim·u·lant (stĭm′yə-lənt) *n.* **1.** An agent that temporarily arouses or accelerates physiological or organic activity. **2.** A stimulus or incentive. **3.** An alcoholic beverage. **—stim′u·lant** *adj.*

stim·u·late (stĭm′yə-lāt′) *v.* **-lat·ed, -lat·ing. 1.** To excite to activity or to heightened action. **2.** To act or serve as a stimulant or stimulus. **—stim′u·la′tion** *n.* **—stim′u·la′tive** *adj.*

stim·u·lus (stĭm′yə-ləs) *n., pl.* **-li** (-lī′). Something that stimulates. ☆***syns:*** CATALYST, IMPETUS, IMPULSE, INCENTIVE, MOTIVATION, SPUR, STIMULANT

sting (stĭng) *v.* **stung** (stŭng), **sting·ing. 1.** To wound or prick painfully with or as if with a sharply pointed part or organ, as that of certain insects. **2.** To feel or cause to feel a sharp, smarting pain. **3.** To cause to suffer in the mind or feelings. ☆***syns:*** BITE, BURN, SMART —*n.* **1.** An act of stinging. **2.** A wound or mark caused by or as if by stinging. **3.** A sharp, piercing organ or part, as of a bee, often ejecting a venomous secretion. **—sting′er** *n.*

sting·ray (stĭng′rā′) *n.* A ray of the family Dasyatidae, having a whiplike tail with a venomous spine capable of inflicting severe injury.

stin·gy (stĭn′jē) *adj.* **-gi·er, -gi·est. 1.** Reluctant to give or spend. **2.** Skimpy : meager. ☆***syns:*** CHEAP, CLOSE, MEAN, MISERLY, NIGGARDLY, PARSIMONIOUS, PENURIOUS, TIGHT, TIGHTFISTED **—stin′gi·ly** *adv.* **—stin′gi·ness** *n.*

stink (stĭngk) *v.* **stank** (stăngk) *or* **stunk** (stŭngk), **stunk, stink·ing. 1.** To give off a foul odor. **2. a.** To be highly offensive. **b.** To be in very bad repute. —*n.* A foul odor : stench **—stink′er** *n.*

stink·bug (stĭngk′bŭg′) *n.* An insect of the family Pentatomidae, having a flattened body and emitting a foul odor.

stint (stĭnt) *v.* **1.** To restrict or limit. **2.** To be sparing in order to economize. ☆***syns:*** PINCH, SCRAPE, SCRIMP, SKIMP —*n.* **1.** An allotted amount of work. **2.** A restriction : limit.

sti·pend (stī′pĕnd′, -pənd) *n.* A regular fixed payment, as a salary or allowance.

stip·ple (stĭp′əl) *v.* **-pled, -pling. 1.** To draw, engrave, or paint in dots or short strokes. **2.** To apply (e.g., paint) in dots or short strokes. **3.** To dot, fleck, or speckle. **—stip′ple** *n.*

stip·u·late (stĭp′yə-lāt′) *v.* **-lat·ed, -lat·ing. 1.** To specify as a condition of an agreement. **2.** To make an agreement. ☆***syns:*** DETAIL, PARTICULARIZE, SPECIFY **—stip′u·la′tion** *n.*

stir[1] (stûr) *v.* **stirred, stir·ring. 1.** To mix by passing an implement through in a repeated circular motion. **2.** To move or cause to move slightly. **3.** To incite, provoke, or agitate. **4.** To excite the emotions of. —*n.* **1.** The act of stirring. **2.** A commotion : fuss. **—stir′rer** *n.*

stir[2] (stûr) *n. Slang.* Prison.

stir-fry (stûr′frī′) *v.* To fry (e.g., vegetables) quickly over high heat in a small amount of oil while stirring continuously.

stir•ring (stûr′ĭng) *adj.* **1.** Exciting : thrilling. **2.** Vigorous : lively.

stir•rup (stûr′əp, stĭr′-) *n.* A flat-based ring or loop hung from a horse's saddle to support the rider's foot.

stitch (stĭch) *n.* **1.** A single loop formed by a threaded needle, as in sewing. **2.** A single loop of yarn or thread around a knitting needle or crochet hook. **3.** A style of arranging the threads in sewing, knitting, or crocheting. **4.** A sudden sharp pain in the side. —*v.* **1.** To fasten or join with or as if with stitches. **2.** To make stitches : sew.

stk. *abbr.* stock.

stoat (stōt) *n., pl.* **stoats** or **stoat.** *esp. Brit.* The ermine, esp. in its brown color phase.

stock (stŏk) *n.* **1.** The supply of goods kept on hand by a merchant or commercial establishment. **2.** *(sing. or pl. in number).* Animals kept or raised on a farm : livestock. **3. a.** A line of descent. **b.** The original from which a group of animals or plants is descended. **4.** The raw material used to make something. **5.** The broth from boiled meat or fish. **6.** A wooden supporting structure, block, or frame, as the part of a rifle to which the barrel is attached. **7.** The shares of a corporation. **8. stocks.** A pillory. **9.** A theatrical stock company. **10. a.** An assessment : estimate <took *stock* of the situation> **b.** Confidence or credence <put no *stock* in the rumor> —*v.* **1.** To provide with stock : supply. **2.** To gather and store a supply of something. —*adj.* **1.** Kept in stock. **2.** Standard <a *stock* response>

stock•ade (stŏ-kād′) *n.* A barrier of upright posts set side by side in the ground for defense or imprisonment.

stock•bro•ker (stŏk′brō′kər) *n.* A broker who buys and sells securities.

stock car *n.* **1.** A car of a standard make specially equipped and modified for racing. **2.** A railroad car for carrying livestock.

stock company *n.* A group of actors and technicians attached to a single theater and performing in repertory.

stock exchange *n.* **1.** A place where securities, as stocks or bonds, are bought and sold. **2.** An association of stockbrokers.

stock•hold•er (stŏk′hōl′dər) *n.* A person who owns stock in a company.

Stock•holm (stŏk′hōlm′). Cap. of Sweden, in the E on the Baltic Sea. *Pop.* 649,384.

stock•ing (stŏk′ĭng) *n.* A close-fitting, usu. knitted covering for the foot and leg.

stock market *n.* **1.** A stock exchange. **2.** The purchase and sale of stocks.

stock•pile (stŏk′pīl′) *n.* A supply stored for future use. **—stock′pile′** *v.*

stock-still (stŏk′stĭl′) *adj.* Motionless.

stock•y (stŏk′ē) *adj.* **-i•er, -i•est. 1.** Built solidly : sturdy. **2.** Plump : chubby.

stock•yard (stŏk′yärd′) *n.* A yard in which livestock is temporarily kept until slaughtered or shipped.

stodg•y (stŏj′ē) *adj.* **-i•er, -i•est. 1.** Dull and commonplace. **2.** Pompous : stuffy.

sto•ic (stō′ĭk) *also* **sto•i•cal** (-ĭ-kəl) *adj.* Apparently indifferent to or unaffected by pleasure or pain : impassive. **—sto′ic** *n.* **—sto′i•cal•ly** *adv.* **—sto′i•cism** *n.*

stoke (stōk) *v.* **stoked, stok•ing. 1.** To stir up and feed a fire. **2.** To feed fuel to and tend (a furnace). **—stok′er** *n.*

stole[1] (stōl) *n.* **1.** A long, narrow strip of linen or silk worn about the neck by priests and bishops. **2.** A long scarf worn about a woman's shoulders.

stole[2] (stōl) *v. p.t. of* STEAL.

sto•len (stō′lən) *v. p.p. of* STEAL.

stol•id (stŏl′ĭd) *adj.* Feeling or exhibiting little emotion : apathetic. **—sto•lid′i•ty** (stə-lĭd′ĭ-tē) *n.* **—stol′id•ly** *adv.*

stom•ach (stŭm′ək) *n.* **1.** The enlarged saclike portion of the alimentary canal into which food passes from the esophagus. **2.** The abdomen. **3.** An appetite for food. **4.** A desire : inclination. —*v.* To tolerate.

stom•ach•ache (stŭm′ək-āk′) *n.* Abdominal pain.

sto•mach•ic (stə-măk′ĭk) *adj.* **1.** Of or relating to the stomach. **2.** Stimulating digestion in the stomach. **—sto•mach′ic** *n.*

stomp (stômp, stŏmp) *v.* To trample heavily (on) : stamp. —*n.* **1.** The act of stomping. **2.** A jazz dance marked by a rhythmical and heavy stamp.

stone (stōn) *n.* **1. a.** Hard or compacted mineral or earthy matter : rock. **b.** A small piece of this material. **2.** A gem. **3.** A seed, as of a cherry or plum, with a hard covering : pit. **4.** A hard mass of mineral matter that collects in a hollow bodily organ, as the kidney. **5.** *pl.* **stone.** A British unit of weight equal to 6.36 kgms or 14 lbs avoirdupois. —*v.* **stoned, ston•ing. 1.** To hurl or kill with stones. **2.** To remove the stones from. **—ston′y** *adj.*

Stone Age *n.* The earliest known period in the history of mankind, marked by the use of stone implements and weapons.

stoned (stōnd) *adj. Slang.* **1.** Drunk. **2.** Being under the influence of a drug.

stone's throw *n.* A short distance.

stone•ware (stōn′wâr′) *n.* Heavy pottery.

stood (stŏŏd) *v. p.t. & p.p. of* STAND.

stooge (stōōj) *n.* **1.** The straight man to a comedian. **2.** Someone whose actions are controlled by another.

stool (stōōl) *n.* **1.** A backless and armless single seat. **2.** A low support on which to rest the feet. **3. a.** A bowel movement. **b.** Fecal matter.

stool pigeon *n. Slang.* **1.** A person functioning as a decoy. **2.** An informer, esp. for the police.

stoop[1] (stōōp) *v.* **1.** To bend forward from the waist. **2.** To lower oneself : condescend. —*n.* **1.** An act of stooping. **2.** A stooping posture.

stoop[2] (stōōp) *n.* A small platform or porch leading to the entrance of a house.

stop (stŏp) *v.* **stopped, stop•ping. 1.** To cease or cause to cease moving, acting, or operating. **2.** To close (an opening) by filling in, covering over, or plugging up. **3.** To obstruct or block. **4.** To desist from what one is doing <*stopped* reading> **5.** To halt for a brief visit or stay. ☆**syns:** CEASE, DESIST, DISCONTINUE, HALT, QUIT —*n.* **1. a.** An act of stopping. **b.** The state of being stopped : cessation. **2.** A point of completion : end. **3.** A stay or visit, as during a trip. **4.** A place stopped at. **5.** Something, as a plug, that obstructs or blocks. **6. a.** A tuned set of organ pipes producing tones similar in timbre. **b.** A knob, key, or pull that regulates such pipes. **—stop′page** *n.*

stop•cock (stŏp′kŏk′) *n.* A valve that regulates the flow of fluid through a pipe.

stop•gap (stŏp′găp′) *n.* An improvised substitute or temporary expedient.

stop•light (stŏp′līt′) *n.* **1.** A traffic signal. **2.** A light on the rear of a vehicle activated when the brakes are applied.

stop•o•ver (stŏp′ō′vər) *n.* **1.** A stop in the course of a journey. **2.** A place visited briefly during a journey.

stop•per (stŏp′ər) *n.* A device, as a cork or plug, for closing an opening.

stop•watch (stŏp′wŏch′) *n.* A watch with a hand that can be instantly started and stopped for exact measurement of time, as during a race.

stor•age (stôr′ĭj, stōr′-) *n.* **1. a.** The act of storing. **b.** The state of being stored. **c.** A space for storing goods. **2.** *Computer Sci.* The part of a computer that stores information for subsequent use or retrieval.

storage battery *n.* A group of rechargeable secondary cells that function as a unit.

store (stôr, stōr) *n.* **1.** An establishment offering goods for sale. **2.** A supply set aside for future use. **3.** A storehouse. **4.** A great number or quantity : abundance. —*v.* **stored, stor•ing. 1.** To set aside or reserve for future use. **2.** To put away for safekeeping, as in a warehouse.

store•front (stôr′frŭnt′, stōr′-) *n.* **1.** The side of a store that faces a street. **2.** A room or suite of rooms on a storefront.

store•house (stôr′hous′, stōr′-) *n.* **1.** A building for the storage of goods : warehouse. **2.** An abundant source or supply.

store•keep•er (stôr′kē′pər, stōr′-) *n.* One who runs a retail store or shop.

store•room (stôr′rōōm′, -rŏŏm′, stōr′-) *n.* A room in which goods or supplies are stored.

sto•rey (stôr′ē, stōr′ē) *n. esp. Brit. var. of* STORY[2].

sto•ried (stôr′ēd, stōr′-) *adj.* Famous in story or history.

stork (stôrk) *n.* A large wading bird of the family Ciconiidae, with long legs and a long straight bill.

storm (stôrm) *n.* **1.** An atmospheric disturbance manifested in strong winds accompanied by rain, snow, hail, or sleet. **2.** *Meteorol.* A wind ranging from 64 to 72 mph. **3.** A strong outburst or violent disturbance. **4.** A sudden, violent attack on a fortified place. —*v.* **1. a.** To blow forcefully. **b.** To rain, snow, hail, or sleet. **2.** To be very angry : rant and rave. **3.** To move tumultuously or angrily. **4.** To capture or try to capture by storm. **—storm′y** *adj.*

storm door *n.* An outer door added for protection against inclement weather.

storm window *n.* An outer window placed over an ordinary window to protect against inclement weather.

sto•ry[1] (stôr′ē, stōr′ē) *n., pl.* **-ries. 1.** A narration of an event or series of events. **2.** The plot of a narrative or dramatic work. **3.** A report, statement, or allegation of facts. **4.** A news article or broadcast. **5.** An anecdote. **6.** A lie.

sto•ry[2] (stôr′ē, stōr′ē) *n., pl.* **-ries.** One of the horizontal divisions of a building.

sto·ry·book (stôr'ē-bŏŏk', stōr'-) *n.* A book containing a collection of stories, usu. for children.
sto·ry·tell·er (stôr'ē-tĕl'ər, stōr'-) *n.* **1.** One who tells or writes stories. **2.** *Informal.* A liar. **–sto'ry·tell'ing** *n.*
sto·tin·ki (stō-tĭng'kē) *n., pl.* **-ki.** See *lev* at CURRENCY TABLE.
stoup (stōōp) *n.* A font for holy water at the entrance of a church.
stout (stout) *adj.* **1.** Determined, bold, or brave. **2.** Physically strong : sturdy. **3.** Solid : substantial. **4.** Corpulent. **5.** Forceful : powerful. **6.** Staunch : firm. *–n.* A heavy, very dark beer or ale. **–stout'ly** *adv.*
stout·heart·ed (stout'här'tĭd) *adj.* Brave : courageous.
stove[1] (stōv) *n.* An apparatus that provides heat for warmth or cooking, using either fuel or electricity as a source of power.
stove[2] (stōv) *v. var. p.t. & p.p. of* STAVE.
stove·pipe (stōv'pīp') *n.* A pipe, usu. of thin sheet iron, used to carry smoke or fumes from a stove to a chimney.
stow (stō) *v.* To put away, esp. in a neat, compact way. **–stow away. 1.** To store so as to be hidden. **2.** To be a stowaway.
stow·a·way (stō'ə-wā') *n.* A person who hides aboard a vehicle, as a ship or aircraft, to avoid paying for passage.
stra·bis·mus (strə-bĭz'məs) *n.* An abnormality of the eyes in which 1 eye cannot focus with the other on an object.
strad·dle (străd'l) *v.* **-dled, -dling. 1.** To stand or sit astride (of). **2.** To appear to be in accord with both sides of an issue. **–strad'dle** *n.* **–strad'dler** *n.*
strafe (strāf) *v.* **strafed, straf·ing.** To attack (e.g., ground troops) with automatic weapon fire from low flying aircraft.
strag·gle (străg'əl) *v.* **-gled, -gling. 1.** To stray from the fixed course. **2.** To proceed or spread out in an irregular group. **–strag'gler** *n.* **–strag'gly** *adj.*
straight (strāt) *adj.* **1.** Being without bends, curves, crooks, or angles. **2.** Not deviating from the proper or correct course <a *straight* thinker> **3.** Being in correct sequence or arrangement. **4.** Upright : honorable. **5.** Not diluted : pure <*straight* vodka> **6.** *Slang.* **a.** Conventional or conservative. **b.** Heterosexual. **c.** SQUARE 6. *–adv.* **1.** In a straight line : directly. **2.** In an erect posture : upright. **3.** Without detour or delay. **4.** Without circumlocution : candidly. *–n.* **1.** A straight line, part, piece, or position. **2.** A numerical sequence of 5 cards of various suits in a poker hand. **–straight'ly** *adv.* **–straight'ness** *n.*
straight angle *n.* An angle of 180°.
straight-arm (strāt'ärm') *v. Football.* To ward off (a tackler) by holding the arm out straight.
straight-a·way (strāt'ə-wā') *n.* A straight course, stretch, or track.
straight·edge (strāt'ĕj') *n.* A rigid strip, as of wood, with a straight edge for testing or drawing straight lines.
straight·en (strāt'n) *v.* To make or become straight.
straight face *n.* A face betraying no emotion. **–straight'faced'** *adj.*
straight·for·ward (strāt-fôr'wərd) *adj.* **1.** Moving in a straight line : direct. **2.** Honest : candid.
straight-jack·et (strāt'jăk'ĭt) *n. var. of* STRAITJACKET.
straight man *n.* An entertainer serving as a foil for a comedian.
straight·way (strāt'wā', -wā') *adv.* At once : immediately.
strain[1] (strān) *v.* **1.** To draw or stretch tight. **2.** To exert to the limit. **3.** To injure by overuse or overexertion : wrench <*strain* a muscle> **4.** To force or stretch beyond the usual or proper limit. **5.** To pass or remove by passing through a strainer : filter. *–n.* **1.** Great tension or exertion, as of the emotions. **2.** An injury resulting from excessive effort or use. **3.** *Physics.* A deformation caused by stress.
strain[2] (strān) *n.* **1. a.** Ancestry : descent. **b.** A group or type having the same ancestry or line of descent. **2. a.** An inborn or inherited characteristic or tendency. **b.** A streak : trace. **3.** A musical tune.
strain·er (strā'nər) *n.* A device for separating liquids from solids.
strait (strāt) *n.* **1.** A narrow passage that connects 2 bodies of water. **2.** *often* **straits.** A situation of difficulty, perplexity, distress, or need. *–adj Archaic.* **1.** Narrow or constricted. **2.** Strict.
strait·en (strāt'n) *v.* **1.** To confine : limit. **2.** To cause to undergo hardship.
strait·jack·et *also* **straight·jack·et** (strāt'jăk'ĭt) *n.* **1.** A jacketlike garment of strong material used to bind the arms tightly against the body as a means of restraining a violent or unmanageable patient or prisoner.
strait-laced (strāt-lāst') *adj.* Strict in matters of behavior or morality.
strand[1] (strănd) *n.* Land bordering a body of water : shore. *–v.* **1.** To drive or be driven ashore. **2.** To put or leave in a helpless or difficult position.
strand[2] (strănd) *n.* **1.** Fibers or filaments twisted together to form a cable, rope, thread, or yarn. **2.** A single filament <a *strand* of hair> **3.** Something, as a string of pearls, that is plaited or twisted into a ropelike length.
strange (strānj) *adj.* **strang·er, strang·est. 1.** Previously unknown : new. **2. a.** Out of the ordinary : unusual. **b.** Peculiar : odd. **3.** Not of one's own kind, environment, or locality : exotic. **4.** Inexperienced : unacquainted. ☆**syns:** ECCENTRIC, ODD, PECULIAR, QUAINT, QUEER, UNUSUAL **–strange'ly** *adv.* **–strange'ness** *n.*
strang·er (strān'jər) *n.* **1.** One who is neither friend nor acquaintance. **2.** A foreigner. **3.** A newcomer.
stran·gle (străng'gəl) *v.* **-gled, -gling. 1. a.** To kill by choking : throttle. **b.** To smother. **2.** To repress, suppress, or stifle. **–stran'gler** *n.*
stran·gle·hold (străng'gəl-hōld') *n.* **1.** An illegal wrestling hold that chokes an opponent. **2.** Something that restricts or suppresses freedom or progress.
stran·gu·late (străng'gyə-lāt') *v.* **-lat·ed, -lat·ing.** *Pathol.* To compress, constrict, or obstruct so as to cut off circulation. **–stran'gu·la'tion** *n.*
strap (străp) *n.* A long, narrow strip of pliant material, as leather, used esp. for holding or fastening objects together. *–v.* **strapped, strap·ping. 1.** To bind or fasten with a strap. **2.** To flog with a strap. **3.** To sharpen (e.g., a razor).
strap·hang·er (străp'hang'ər) *n.* A passenger, as on a bus or subway, who grips a hanging strap for support.
strap·less (străp'lĭs) *adj.* Having no straps and esp. no shoulder straps.
strapped (străpt) *adj. Informal.* Having little or no money.
strap·ping (străp'ĭng) *adj.* Tall and strong.
stra·ta (strā'tə, străt'ə) *n. var. pl. of* STRATUM.
strat·a·gem (străt'ə-jəm) *n.* **1.** A military maneuver intended to surprise or deceive an enemy. **2.** A deception.
strat·e·gy (străt'ə-jē) *n., pl.* **-gies. 1.** The science or art of military command as applied to the general planning and conduct of full-scale combat operations. **2.** A plan of action, esp. for attaining a goal. **–stra·te'gic** (strə-tē'jĭk) *adj.* **–strat'e·gist** *n.*
Strat·ford-on-A·von (stră'fərd-ŏn-ā'vŏn', -ā'vən). Borough of C England; birthplace and burial place of Shakespeare.
strat·i·fy (străt'ə-fī') *v.* **-fied, -fy·ing.** To form or lay down in layers or strata. **–strat'i·fi·ca'tion** *n.*
stra·tig·ra·phy (strə-tĭg'rə-fē) *n.* The study of rock strata. **–strat'i·graph'ic** (străt'ĭ-grăf'ĭk), **strat'i·graph'i·cal** *adj.*
strat·o·sphere (străt'ə-sfîr') *n.* The part of the earth's atmosphere above the troposphere and below the mesophere. **–strat'o·spher'ic** *adj.*
stra·tum (strā'təm, străt'əm) *n., pl.* **-ta** (-tə) or **-tums. 1.** A horizontal layer, as 1 of a number of layers of rock of the same kind. **2.** A social level of persons with similar social, cultural, or economic status.
Strauss (strous, shtrous). Family of Austrian composers, including: **1. Johann.** "the Elder." 1804–49. **2. Johann.** "the Younger," "the Waltz King." 1825–99.
Stra·vin·sky (strə-vĭn'skē), **Igor Fëodorovich.** 1882–1971. Russian-born Amer. composer.
straw (strô) *n.* **1. a.** Stalks of grain, as wheat or oats, after threshing. **b.** A single stalk of straw. **2.** A slender tube for sucking up a liquid. **3.** Something of little value or importance. *–adj.* **1.** Of the color of straw : yellowish. **2.** Made of straw. **3.** Of little value or force : unimportant.
straw·ber·ry (strô'bĕr'ē) *n.* **1.** Any of various low-growing plants of the genus *Fragaria*, with white flowers and red, fleshy fruit. **2.** The edible fruit of the strawberry.
straw boss *n. Informal.* A worker who acts as a boss or assistant foreman in addition to regular duties.
straw·flow·er (strô'flou'ər) *n.* An Australian plant, *Helichrysum bracteatum*, having flowers with variously colored bracts that retain their color when dried.
straw vote *n.* An unofficial poll or vote indicating the trend of political opinion.
stray (strā) *v.* **1.** To wander : roam. **2.** To deviate from a course : go astray. *–n.* A person or animal that has strayed and is lost. *–adj.* **1.** Strayed or having strayed : lost. **2.** Scattered <a few *stray* crumbs> **–stray'er** *n.*
streak (strēk) *n.* **1. a.** A mark, as a line, that differs in color or texture from its surroundings. **b.** A bolt of lightning. **2.** A character trait <a mean *streak*> **3.** *Informal.* A brief stretch : run <a *streak* of good luck> *–v.* **1.** To mark or become marked with streaks. **2.** To move rapidly : rush. **–streak'er** *n.* **–streak'y** *adj.*
stream (strēm) *n.* **1.** A body of water running over the earth's surface in a channel. **2.** A steady flow of a fluid. **3.** A continuous succession or flow. *–v.* **1.** To flow in or as if in a stream. **2.** To pour forth a stream of liquid. **3.** To move like a flowing stream.

4. To wave or float outward <flags that *streamed* in the breeze>

stream•bed (strēm′bĕd′) *n.* The channel through which a natural stream of water runs or once ran.

stream•er (strē′mər) *n.* **1. a.** A long, narrow banner, flag, or pennant. **b.** A long, flowing strip of material. **2.** A shaft or ray of light extending upward from the horizon. **3.** A newspaper headline running entirely across the page.

stream•lined (strēm′līnd′) *adj.* **1.** Designed or configured to offer minimum resistance to fluid flow. **2.** Improved in efficiency or look : simplified or modernized. **–stream′line′** *v.*

stream•lin•er (strēm′lī′nər) *n.* A streamlined passenger train.

street (strēt) *n.* **1.** A public thoroughfare in a city or town. **2.** The people who live, work, etc. in or along a street.

street•car (strēt′cär′) *n.* A car on rails that provides public transportation usu. along the streets.

street•walk•er (strēt′wô′kər) *n.* A prostitute who solicits in the street.

street•wise (strēt′wīz′) *adj.* Capable of surviving in the frequently violent environment of a large city.

strength (strĕngkth, strĕngth) *n.* **1.** The quality, state, or property of being strong : power. **2. a.** The power to resist force, stress, or wear. **b.** The power to resist attack. **3.** Concentration or potency, as of a drug. **4.** Intensity. **5.** Firmness : toughness. **6.** A source of power or force. **7.** Numerical force <a battalion at half *strength*>

strength•en (strĕngk′thən, strĕng′-) *v.* To make or become strong or stronger. **–strength′en•er** *n.*

stren•u•ous (strĕn′yo͞o-əs) *adj.* Requiring or marked by vigorous effort or exertion. **–stren′u•ous•ly** *adv.*

strep throat (strĕp) *n.* A throat infection caused by streptococci and marked by fever and inflammation of the tonsils.

strep•to•coc•cus (strĕp′tə-kŏk′əs) *n., pl.* **-coc•ci** (-kŏk′sī′, -kŏk′ī′). Any of various round to ovoid pathogenic bacteria of the genus *Streptococcus,* occurring in pairs or chains. **–strep′to•coc′cal** *adj.*

strep•to•my•cin (strĕp′tə-mī′sĭn) *n.* An antibiotic produced from mold cultures of bacteria of the genus *Streptomyces* and used esp. in the treatment of tuberculosis.

stress (strĕs) *n.* **1.** Importance or emphasis. **2.** Emphasis placed on a sound or syllable. **3.** A force that tends to strain or deform. **4.** Mental, emotional, or physical tension, strain, or distress. *–v.* **1.** To put emphasis on. **2.** To subject to strain or pressure. **3.** To accent.

stretch (strĕch) *v.* **1. a.** To draw out to the full or a fuller length, breadth, or extent. **b.** To become or be capable of becoming stretched. **2.** To extend or cause to extend, as from 1 place to another. **3.** To put forth : hold out. **4.** To exert to the utmost : strain. **5.** To extend beyond proper or reasonable limits. **–6.** To prolong. *–n.* **1.** The act of stretching or state of being stretched. **2.** The degree to which something can be stretched. **3.** A continuous or unbroken expanse of space or time. **4.** A straight section of a racecourse, esp. the section just before the finish line. **–stretch′a•ble** *adj.* **–stretch′y** *adj.*

stretch•er (strĕch′ər) *n.* **1.** One that stretches. **2.** A litter, usu. of canvas stretched over a frame, for transporting the sick, wounded, or dead.

stretch•er-bear•er (strĕch′ər-bâr′ər) *n.* One who helps carry a stretcher.

strew (stro͞o) *v.* **strewed, strewed** or **strewn** (stro͞on), **strew•ing. 1.** To scatter here and there. **2.** To cover by scattering. **3.** To be or become dispersed.

stri•a (strī′ə) *n., pl.* **stri•ae** (strī′ē′). **1.** A shallow groove or channel. **2.** A thin line or band, esp. 1 of a group that are parallel. **–stri′at′ed** *adj.* **–stri•a′tion** *n.*

strick•en (strĭk′ən) *adj.* **1.** Struck or injured, as by an arrow. **2.** Afflicted with strong emotion, illness, or trouble.

strict (strĭkt) *adj.* **1.** Exact : precise. **2.** Kept within specific and narrow limits. **3. a.** Imposing rigorous standards. **b.** Rigorously maintained or enforced : stringent. **–strict′ly** *adv.* **–strict′ness** *n.*

stric•ture (strĭk′chər) *n.* **1.** An unfavorable remark : adverse criticism. **2.** *Pathol.* An abnormal constriction in a bodily duct or passage.

stride (strīd) *v.* **strode** (strōd), **strid•den** (strĭd′n), **strid•ing.** To walk vigorously with long steps. ☆**syns:** MARCH, STALK *–n.* **1. a.** A long step. **b.** The distance covered in a stride. **2.** *often* **strides.** A step forward : advance. **–strid′er** *n.*

stri•dent (strīd′nt) *adj.* Harsh, grating, and loud : shrill.

strife (strīf) *n.* **1.** Discord : conflict. **2.** A struggle : contention.

strike (strīk) *v.* **struck** (strŭk), **struck** or **strick•en** (strĭk′ən), **strik•ing. 1.a.** To hit with or as if with the hand. **b.** To inflict (a blow). **2. a.** To collide with. **b.** To cause to collide. **3.** To afflict suddenly, as with a disease or disorder. **4.** To indicate by a sound <a clock *striking* the hour> **5.** To produce by stamping, printing, or punching <*strike* a coin> **6.** To ignite (a match) by friction. **7.** To expunge or remove. **8.** To impress, esp. strongly or anew. **9.** To discover <*struck* oil> **10.** To affect deeply with (an emotion). **11.** To make or conclude <*struck* a deal> **12.** To assume (e.g., a pose). **13.** To stop working in protest against something or in support of demands made of an employer. **14.** To start out, esp. in a new direction. *–n.* **1.** An act or instance of striking. **2.** An attack, esp. a military air attack. **3.** A sudden achievement or valuable discovery, as of a precious mineral. **4. a.** *Baseball.* A pitched ball counted against the batter. **b.** The knocking down of all the pins in bowling with the 1st ball. **–strike out.** *Baseball.* To put or be put out with 3 strikes. **–strike up. 1.** To start or cause to start to sing or play. **2.** To initiate. **–strik′er** *n.*

strike•break•er (strīk′brā′kər) *n.* One who works or provides an employer with workers during a strike : scab. **–strike′break′ing** *n.*

strike•out (strīk′out′) *n. Baseball.* An act or instance of striking out.

strik•ing (strī′kĭng) *adj.* Extraordinarily impressive <a *striking* resemblance> **–strik′ing•ly** *adv.* **–strik′ing•ness** *n.*

string (strĭng) *n.* **1.** A cord, as of twisted fibers, for fastening, tying, or lacing. **2.** Something resembling a string. **3.** A set of objects with a cord running through them <a *string* of pearls> **4.** A series of related events, acts, or items arranged or falling in a line <a *string* of defeats> **5.** *Computer Sci.* A set of data arranged in ascending or descending sequence according to a key within the data. **6. a.** A cord stretched across the sounding board of a musical instrument that produces a tone when caused to vibrate. **b. strings.** Musical instruments with strings. **7.** *often* **strings.** Hidden conditions or provisos. **8.** A cord or fiber in a plant. *–v.* **strung** (strŭng), **string•ing. 1.** To furnish, fasten, or tie with strings. **2.** To thread on a string. **3.** To make tense : tighten. **4.** To extend : stretch. **5.** To remove the strings from (vegetables). **–stringed** *adj.* **–string′y** *adj.*

string bean *n.* A bushy or climbing plant, *Phaseolus vulgaris,* cultivated for its narrow, green, edible pods.

strin•gent (strĭn′jənt) *adj.* **1.** Rigorously exacting : strict. **2.** Marked by scarcity, esp. of money. **–strin′gen•cy** *n.*

strip¹ (strĭp) *v.* **stripped, strip•ping. 1.** To remove the covering or clothing from. **2.** To divest, as of rank. **3.** To take or pull off : remove. **4.** To make bare, as by separating leaves from a stalk. **5.** To damage the threads or teeth of (e.g., a gear). **6.** To rob : despoil. **7.** To remove all one's clothes. **–strip′per** *n.*

strip² (strĭp) *n.* **1.** A long, slender piece, usu. of uniform width. **2.** An airstrip.

stripe (strīp) *n.* **1.** A long, narrow band distinguished, as by color, from its background. **2.** A strip of cloth worn on the sleeve of a uniform to show rank or length of service : chevron. **3.** Type : kind. *–v.* **striped, strip•ing.** To mark or provide with stripes.

striped bass *n.* A food and game fish, *Roccus saxatilis,* of North American coastal waters, with dark longitudinal stripes along its sides.

strip•ling (strĭp′lĭng) *n.* A youth.

strip mine *n.* An open mine, esp. a coal mine, whose seams or outcrops run close to ground level and are exposed by the stripping of topsoil. **–strip-mine′** *v.*

strip•tease *also* **strip tease** (strĭp′tēz′) *n.* An entertainment featuring a person who slowly removes clothing usu. to a musical accompaniment. **–strip′teas′er** *n.*

strive (strīv) *v.* **strove** (strōv) *or* **strived, striv•en** (strĭv′ən) or **strived, striv•ing. 1.** To exert strenuous efforts : labor. **2.** To struggle against : contend. **–striv′er** *n.*

strobe (strōb) *n.* **1.** A stroboscope. **2.** A strobe light.

strobe light *n.* A flash lamp that produces high-intensity short-duration light pulses by electric discharge in a gas.

stro•bo•scope (strō′bə-skōp′) *n.* An instrument used to study moving objects by making them appear stationary, esp. with pulsed illumination or devices that intermittently interrupt observation. **–stro′bo•scop′ic** (-skŏp′ĭk) *adj.*

strode (strōd) *v. p.t. of* STRIDE.

stroke (strōk) *n.* **1.** An act of striking : blow. **2.** A sudden process, event, or action having a powerful effect <a *stroke* of luck> **3.** A single complete movement over or through water or air <a swimming *stroke*> **4.** A single movement or mark made by or as if by a pen or brush. **5.** A single complete movement of a machine part, as a piston. **6.** The striking or sound of striking of a clock, bell, or gong. **7.** Apoplexy. *–v.* **stroked, strok•ing.** To move the hand over gently : rub lightly.

stroll (strōl) *v.* To walk around in a leisurely way : amble. **–stroll** *n.*

stroll•er (strō′lər) *n.* **1.** One that strolls. **2.** A chairlike baby carriage.

strong (strông) *adj.* **1.** Physically powerful. **2.** Robust : healthy.

3. Difficult to break : durable. 4. Intense : violent <*strong* feelings> 5. Persuasive or forceful. 6. Drastic : extreme. 7. Having a specified number of members or units <an orchestra 110 *strong*> **—strong'ly** *adv.*
strong-arm (strông'ärm') *adj. Informal.* Excessively forceful : coercive <*strong-arm* tactics> **—strong'-arm'** *v.*
strong•box (strông'bŏks') *n.* A stoutly made safe or box for storing valuables.
strong•hold (strông'hōld') *n.* A fortress.
strong-mind•ed (strông'mīn'dĭd) *adj.* Strong, determined, and independent in mind and will.
stron•ti•um (strŏn'chē-əm, -tē-) *n. Symbol* **Sr** A soft, readily oxidized metallic element used in various alloys.
strop (strŏp) *n.* A flexible strip, as of leather, used esp. to sharpen a razor. *—v.* **stropped, strop•ping.** To sharpen (a razor) on a strop.
stro•phe (strō'fē) *n.* A stanza of a poem.
strove (strōv) *v. var. p.t. of* STRIVE.
struck (strŭk) *adj.* Shut down or affected by a labor strike.
struc•ture (strŭk'chər) *n.* **1.** Something made up of a number of parts assembled in a particular pattern. **2.** The way in which parts are combined or arranged to form a whole. **3.** Something constructed, as a building or bridge. *—v.* **-tured, -tur•ing.** To give structure to. **—struc'tur•al** *adj.*
stru•del (strōōd'l, shtrōōd'l) *n.* A pastry consisting of filling rolled up in a thin sheet of dough and baked.
strug•gle (strŭg'əl) *v.* **-gled, -gling. 1.** To exert strenuous efforts against resistance or opposition : strive. **2.** To progress with effort or difficulty. *—n.* **1.** Strenuous effort : striving. **2.** A battle : contest.
strum (strŭm) *v.* **strummed, strum•ming.** To play (a stringed instrument) by stroking the strings lightly with the fingers.
strum•pet (strŭm'pĭt) *n.* A prostitute.
strung (strŭng) *v. p.t. & p.p. of* STRING.
strung-out (strŭng'out') *adj. Slang.* Emotionally or physically debilitated from or as if from long-term drug use.
strut (strŭt) *v.* **strut•ted, strut•ting.** To walk in an affectedly self-important manner. *—n.* **1.** An affectedly self-important gait. **2.** A rod or bar for bracing against forces applied from the side.
strych•nine (strĭk'nīn', -nĭn, -nēn') *n.* A poisonous substance derived from certain plants and used to kill pests, as rodents, and as a stimulant.
stub (stŭb) *n.* **1.** A short end remaining after something has been used up or snapped off <a pencil *stub*> **2. a.** The part of a check or receipt kept as a record of payment made. **b.** The part of a ticket returned to the purchaser as proof of payment. *—v.* **stubbed, stub•bing.** To strike (e.g., one's toe) against something.
stub•ble (stŭb'əl) *n.* **1.** The short stalks, as of grain, that remain in the soil after a crop has been harvested. **2.** Something resembling stubble. **—stub'bly** *adj.*
stub•born (stŭb'ərn) *adj.* **1.** Unreasonably inflexible : obstinate and willful. **2.** Determined and persistent. **3.** Difficult to control or handle : resistant. **—stub'born•ly** *adv.* **—stub'born•ness** *n.*
stub•by (stŭb'ē) *adj.* **-bi•er, -bi•est.** Resembling a stub : short and thick.
stuc•co (stŭk'ō) *n., pl.* **-coes** *or* **-cos.** Plaster or cement used to coat exterior walls. *—v.* To cover or coat with stucco.
stuck (stŭk) *v. p.t. & p.p. of* STICK.
stuck-up (stŭk'ŭp') *adj. Informal.* Snobbish and supercilious : conceited.
stud[1] (stŭd) *n.* **1.** An upright post in the framework of a building to which sheets of lath, wallboard, or paneling are fastened. **2.** Something, as a knob or nail head, that projects from a surface. **3.** A small removable button used as an ornament or fastener, as on a shirt. *—v.* **stud•ded, stud•ding. 1.** To provide or decorate with studs. **2.** To strew : dot.
stud[2] (stŭd) *n.* A male animal, esp. a stallion, kept for breeding.
stud•book (stŭd'bŏŏk') *n.* A book in which the pedigrees of thoroughbred animals are recorded.
stud•ding (stŭd'ĭng) *n.* **1.** Studs, esp. for walls. **2.** Material used for studs.
stu•dent (stōōd'nt, styōōd'-) *n.* **1.** Someone who studies, esp. at a school or college. **2.** An attentive observer <a *student* of world affairs>
stud•ied (stŭd'ēd) *adj.* Carefully planned : contrived.
stu•di•o (stōō'dē-ō', styōō'-) *n., pl.* **-os. 1.** An artist's place of work. **2.** A place where an art is studied or taught. **3.** A place equipped for the production of motion pictures or television or radio programs.
studio couch *n.* A couch, usu. without a back, that can serve as a bed.
stu•di•ous (stōō'dē-əs, styōō'-) *adj.* **1.** Devoted to study. **2.** Earnestly diligent. **—stu'di•ous•ly** *adv.*
stud•y (stŭd'ē) *n., pl.* **-ies. 1.** The act or process of applying the mind to acquire knowledge. **2.** A close examination. **3.** A branch of knowledge. **4.** A room equipped and used esp. for writing and reading. *—v.* **-ied, -y•ing. 1.** To apply the mind to acquire knowledge or understanding of (a subject). **2.** To think about : ponder. **3.** To examine in detail : scrutinize.
stuff (stŭf) *n.* **1. a.** The material of which something consists or is made : essential substance. **b.** Raw material. **2.** Material of an unspecified nature or kind. **3.** Worthless objects. **4.** Words or ideas of little value. **5.** *esp. Brit.* Woven material, esp. woolens. **6.** Special capability. *—v.* **1. a.** To pack tightly : cram. **b.** To stop up : block. **2.** To fill (e.g., a turkey) with stuffing. **3.** To eat too much : gorge. **—stuff'er** *n.*
stuffed shirt *n. Informal.* A pompous, self-satisfied person.
stuff•ing (stŭf'ĭng) *n.* Material used to stuff, esp. a seasoned mixture used to fill meat, poultry, fish, or vegetables.
stuff•y (stŭf'ē) *adj.* **-i•er, -i•est. 1.** Lacking ventilation : close. **2.** Congested <a *stuffy* nose> **3.** *Informal.* Not very lively or interesting : stodgy.
stul•ti•fy (stŭl'tə-fī') *v.* **-fied, -fy•ing. 1.** To make ineffectual or useless : cripple. **2.** To cause to seem stupid or illogical. **3.** To make torpid or dull.
stum•ble (stŭm'bəl) *v.* **-bled, -bling. 1. a.** To trip and nearly fall. **b.** To move unsteadily : falter. **c.** To act or speak clumsily. **2.** To make an error, esp. a moral mistake : blunder. **3.** To come upon unexpectedly. **—stum'ble** *n.*
stum•ble•bum (stŭm'bəl-bŭm') *n. Slang.* **1.** A blundering or inept person. **2.** An inept or clumsy prizefighter.
stumbling block *n.* An impediment : obstacle.
stump (stŭmp) *n.* **1.** The part of a tree remaining in the ground after the top has fallen or been cut down. **2.** A part, as of a tooth, that is left after the main part has worn away or been cut off. **3.** An occasion or place for political speeches. *—v.* **1.** To clear stumps from (land). **2.** To travel around (an area) making political speeches. **3.** To walk stiffly and heavily. **4.** To puzzle : perplex. **—stump'er** *n.* **—stump'y** *adj.*
stun (stŭn) *v.* **stunned, stun•ning. 1.** To make senseless by or as if by a blow : daze. **2.** To stupefy, as with strong emotion : shock. **—stun** *n.*
stung (stŭng) *v. p.t. & p.p. of* STING.
stunk (stŭngk) *v. var. p.t. & p.p. of* STINK.
stun•ning (stŭn'ĭng) *adj.* Remarkably attractive. **—stun'ning•ly** *adv.*
stunt[1] (stŭnt) *v.* To hinder the growth or development of. **—stunt'ed** *adj.*
stunt[2] (stŭnt) *n.* **1.** A feat showing unusual skill, strength, or daring. **2.** Something unusual done esp. for publicity.
stu•pe•fy (stōō'pə-fī', styōō'-) *v.* **-fied, -fy•ing. 1.** To make physically groggy or dull. **2.** To astound : astonish. **—stu'pe•fac'tion** *n.* **—stu'pe•fi'er** *n.*
stu•pen•dous (stōō-pĕn'dəs, styōō-) *adj.* **1.** Causing amazement : astonishing. **2.** Of enormous size. **—stu•pen'dous•ly** *adv.*
stu•pid (stōō'pĭd, styōō'-) *adj.* **1.** Slow to understand : dull. **2.** Showing or resulting from lack of intelligence. ☆**syns:** DENSE, DUMB, OBTUSE, THICK **—stu•pid'i•ty** *n.* **—stu'pid•ly** *adv.*
stu•por (stōō'pər, styōō'-) *n.* **1.** A condition of reduced feeling or sense : numbness. **2.** A condition of apathy that is often caused by shock or stress : torpor. **—stu'por•ous** *adj.*
stur•dy (stûr'dē) *adj.* **-di•er, -di•est. 1.** Physically robust : strong. **2.** Mentally vigorous : resolute. **—stur'di•ly** *adv.* **—stur'di•ness** *n.*
stur•geon (stûr'jən) *n.* Any of various large freshwater and marine food fishes of the family Acipenseridae, whose roe is a source of caviar.
stut•ter (stŭt'ər) *v.* To speak with involuntary hesitation, prolongation, or repetition of sounds. **—stut'ter** *n.*
Stutt•gart (stŏŏt'gärt', stŭt'-). City of SW West Germany. *Pop.* 581,989.
sty[1] (stī) *n., pl.* **sties. 1.** A pen or enclosure for pigs. **2.** An extremely messy or dirty place.
sty[2] (stī) *n., pl.* **sties.** Inflammation and swelling of a gland on the edge of an eyelid.
style (stīl) *n.* **1.** A way, method, or manner of saying, writing, or performing. **2.** Kind : sort. **3.** Individuality that is reflected in a person's actions and tastes. **4. a.** An elegant mode of life. **b.** Grace, elegance, or excellence in appearance or performance : distinction. **5. a.** The current fashion : vogue. **b.** A particular fashion. **6.** A scheme or custom adhered to in presenting printed material, including punctuation, spelling, capitalization, typography, and arrangement. **7.** A stylus. *—v.* **styled, styl•ing. 1.** To name : designate. **2.** To arrange, fashion, or design in a particular mode or style. **—sty•lis'tic** *adj.*

styl·ish (stī′lĭsh) *adj.* Conforming to the current style : fashionable. **–styl′ish·ly** *adv.* **–styl′ish·ness** *n.*
styl·ist (stī′lĭst) *n.* **1.** A specialist in style, esp. literary style. **2.** A designer of or consultant on style.
styl·ize (stī′līz′) *v.* **-ized, -iz·ing.** To conform to a style rather than representing according to nature.
sty·lus (stī′ləs) *n., pl.* **-lus·es** or **-li** (-lī′). **1.** A pointed instrument used for writing esp. on wax or for engraving. **2.** A phonograph needle.
sty·mie (stī′mē) *v.* **-mied, -mie·ing.** To frustrate : thwart.
styp·tic (stĭp′tĭk) *adj.* **1.** Astringent. **2.** Tending to arrest bleeding.
Sty·ro·foam (stī′rə-fōm′). A trademark for a light, resilient polystyrene plastic.
suave (swäv) *adj.* **suav·er, suav·est.** Smoothly but sometimes superficially gracious : urbane. **–suav′i·ty** *n.*
†**sub¹** (sŭb) *n. Informal.* **1.** A submarine. **2.** *Regional.* HERO 4.
sub² (sŭb) *n. Informal.* A substitute. **–sub** *v.*
sub– *pref.* **1.** Below : under : beneath <*sub*soil> **2.** Subordinate : secondary <*sub*plot> **3.** Less than completely or normally : nearly : almost <*sub*human>
sub. *abbr.* **1.** subaltern. **2.** substitute. **3.** suburb; suburban.
sub·al·tern (sə-bôl′tərn) *n.* **1.** A subordinate. **2.** *esp. Brit.* A military officer holding a rank below captain.
sub·a·tom·ic (sŭb′ə-tŏm′ĭk) *adj.* Of or pertaining to the constituents of the atom.
sub·com·mit·tee (sŭb′kə-mĭt′ē) *n.* A subdivision of a committee.
sub·com·pact (sŭb-kŏm′păkt′) *n.* An automobile smaller in size than a compact.
sub·con·scious (sŭb-kŏn′shəs) *adj.* Existing or occurring below the threshold of consciousness. **–sub·con′scious** *n.* **–sub·con′scious·ly** *adv.* **–sub·con′scious·ness** *n.*
sub·con·ti·nent (sŭb′kŏn′tə-nənt) *n.* A very large land mass that is part of a continent.
sub·con·tract (sŭb-kŏn′trăkt′) *n.* A contract assigning some of the obligations of a contract to a 3rd party. **–sub′con·tract′** (-kən-trăkt′) *v.*
sub·cul·ture (sŭb′kŭl′chər) *n.* A cultural subgroup differentiated from a larger group by such factors as status, ethnic background, and religion.
sub·cu·ta·ne·ous (sŭb′kyo͞o-tā′nē-əs) *adj.* Located, used, or introduced beneath the skin <a *subcutaneous* injection>
sub·di·vide (sŭb′dĭ-vīd′) *v.* **1.** To divide into smaller parts. **2.** To divide (land) into lots. **–sub′di·vi′sion** *n.*
sub·due (səb-do͞o′, -dyo͞o′) *v.* **-dued, -du·ing.** **1.** To subjugate : vanquish. **2.** To bring under control. **3.** To make less intense.
sub·group (sŭb′gro͞op′) *n.* A subordinate group.
sub·head (sŭb′hĕd′) *n.* **1.** A heading of a subdivision of a printed work. **2.** A subordinate title or heading.
subj. *abbr.* **1.** subject. **2.** subjective. **3.** subjunctive.
sub·ject (sŭb′jĭkt) *adj.* **1.** Under the authority, rule, or power of another. **2.** Disposed : prone <*subject* to infections> **3.** Liable <*subject* to misinterpretation> **4.** Dependent : contingent <permission *subject* to further discussion> *–n.* **1.** A person under the rule of another. **2.** The person or thing being dealt with or discussed : topic. **3.** An area or course of study. **4.** An individual as an object of study or experiment. **5.** A word, phrase, or clause about which something is predicated. *–v.* (səb-jĕkt′). **1.** To gain control over : subdue. **2.** To lay open : expose. **3.** To cause to undergo or experience. **–sub·jec′tion** (-jĕk′shən) *n.*
sub·jec·tive (səb-jĕk′tĭv) *adj.* **1.** Of or existing within an individual's mind rather than outside : personal. **2.** Of, pertaining to, or being a subject. **–sub·jec′tive·ly** *adv.* **–sub′jec·tiv′i·ty** *n.*
subject matter *n.* Matter being discussed, considered, or studied.
sub·join (sŭb-join′) *v.* To add on at the end : append.
sub ju·di·ce (sŭb jo͞o′dĭ-sē′, yo͞o′dĭ-kā′) *adv. Law.* Under judicial deliberation.
sub·ju·gate (sŭb′jə-gāt′) *v.* **-gat·ed, -gat·ing.** **1.** To compel to submit : conquer. **2.** To enslave. **–sub′ju·ga′tion** *n.*
▲word history: The word *subjugate* is borrowed from Latin *subjugare,* literally "to bring under the yoke." In accordance with an ancient Latin custom survivors of a defeated army were forced to pass under a symbolic yoke made of 2 upright spears, with a 3rd used as a crossbar. The Romans regarded subjugation as the worst possible humiliation.
sub·junc·tive (sŭb-jŭngk′tĭv) *adj.* Of, pertaining to, or being a verb form or set of forms used to express uncertainty, desire, contingency, or unlikelihood. **–sub·junc′tive** *n.*
sub·let (sŭb-lĕt′) *v.* **1.** To rent (property held by lease) to another. **2.** To subcontract (work). **–sub′let′** *n.*
sub·li·mate (sŭb′lə-māt′) *v.* **-mat·ed, -mat·ing.** **1.** *Chem.* To pass or cause to pass from a solid to a gas or from a gas to a solid without becoming a liquid. **2.** To modify the expression of (e.g., an impulse) so as to be socially acceptable. **–sub′li·ma′tion** *n.*
sub·lime (sə-blīm′) *adj.* **1.** Noble : lofty. **2.** Inspiring awe : awesome. *–v.* **-limed, -lim·ing.** *Chem.* To sublimate. **–su·blim′i·ty** (sə-blĭm′ĭ-tē) *n.*
sub·lim·i·nal (sŭb-lĭm′ə-nəl) *adj.* Not within the area of conscious perception or awareness. **–sub·lim′i·nal·ly** *adv.*
sub·lu·na·ry (sŭb′lo͞o′nə-rē) *adj.* Located beneath the moon.
sub·ma·chine gun (sŭb′mə-shēn′) *n.* An automatic or semiautomatic gun fired from the hip or shoulder.
sub·mar·gin·al (sŭb′mär′jə-nəl) *adj.* Being below a required minimum <*submarginal* living conditions>
sub·ma·rine (sŭb′mə-rēn′, sŭb′mə-rēn′) *adj.* Being or growing beneath the surface of the sea : undersea. *–n.* **1.** A ship that can operate both on the surface of the water and underwater. **2.** HERO 4.
sub·ma·rin·er (sub′mə-rē′nər, -măr′ə-) *n.* A crew member of a submarine.
sub·merge (səb-mûrj′) *v.* **-merged, -merg·ing.** **1.** To place or plunge under the surface of a liquid, esp. water. **2.** To cover with water. **–sub·mer′gi·ble** *adj.* **–sub·mer′gence** *n.*
sub·merse (səb-mûrs′) *v.* **-mersed, -mers·ing.** To submerge. **–sub·mers′i·ble** *adj.* **–sub·mer′sion** *n.*
sub·mi·cro·scop·ic (sŭb′mī′-krə-skŏp′ĭk) *adj.* Too small to be seen with an optical microscope.
sub·min·i·a·ture (sŭb′mĭn′ē-ə-cho͝or′, -chər) *adj.* Extremely small.
sub·mit (səb-mĭt′) *v.* **-mit·ted, -mit·ting.** **1.** To surrender to the authority, discretion, or will of another. **2.** To commit to the decision, consideration, or judgment of another. **3.** To offer as a suggestion or opinion. **4.** To acquiesce. **–sub·mis′sion** *n.* **–sub·mis′sive** *adj.* **–sub·mit′tal** *n.*
sub·nor·mal (sŭb-nôr′məl) *adj.* Being less than normal. **–sub′nor·mal′i·ty** *n.*
sub·or·bit·al (sŭb-ôr′bĭ-tl) *adj.* Of, being, or involving less than 1 orbit.
sub·or·di·nate (sə-bôr′dn-ĭt) *adj.* **1.** Of lower rank or class : inferior. **2.** Subject to the control or authority of another. **3.** Dependent on other elements in a sentence <a *subordinate* clause> *–n.* One that is subordinate. ☆***syns:*** INFERIOR, JUNIOR, SUBALTERN, UNDERLING *–v.* (-nāt′) **-nat·ed, -nat·ing.** **1.** To put in a lower rank or class. **2.** To make subservient. **–sub·or′di·na′tion** *n.* **–sub·or′di·na′tive** *adj.*
sub·orn (sə-bôrn′) *v.* To induce to commit an unlawful act, esp. perjury. **–sub′or·na′tion** *n.* **–sub·orn′er** *n.*
sub·plot (sŭb′plŏt′) *n.* A secondary plot in drama or fiction.
sub·poe·na (sə-pē′nə) *n.* A legal writ requiring the person named in it to appear in court. *–v.* To serve with a subpoena.
sub ro·sa (sŭb rō′zə) *adv.* In secret : covertly <negotiations held *sub rosa*>
subs. *abbr.* subscription.
sub·scribe (səb-scrīb′) *v.* **-scribed, -scrib·ing.** **1.** To sign (one's name) to a document. **2.** To give testimony, attestation, or consent by signing one's name. **3. a.** To pledge to contribute. **b.** To contribute. **4.** To be in agreement <don't *subscribe* to your opinion> **5.** To contract to pay for and receive a periodical at regular intervals. **–sub·scrib′er** *n.*
sub·script (sŭb′skrĭpt′) *n.* A symbol or letter written next to and slightly below another character.
sub·scrip·tion (səb-skrĭp′shən) *n.* **1.** The act of signing one's name : signature. **2.** A purchase by signed order, as for issues of a periodical.
sub·se·quent (sŭb′sĭ-kwənt) *adj.* Following in order or time : succeeding. **–sub′se·quent·ly** *adv.* **–sub′se·quent·ness** *n.*
sub·ser·vi·ent (səb-sûr′vē-ənt) *adj.* **1.** Subordinate, as in condition or function. **2.** Servile : submissive **–sub·ser′vi·ence** *n.* **–sub·ser′vi·ent·ly** *adv.*
sub·set (sŭb′sĕt′) *n.* A mathematical set each of whose members is included within another set.
sub·side (səb-sīd′) *v.* **-sid·ed, -sid·ing.** **1.** To move to a lower level : descend. **2.** To sink to the bottom of a liquid : settle. **3.** To become less agitated or intense : abate. **–sub·sid′ence** *n.*
sub·sid·i·ar·y (səb-sĭd′ē-ĕr′ē) *adj.* **1.** Providing support or assistance. **2.** Secondary, as in importance : subordinate. **3.** Of or pertaining to a subsidy. *–n., pl.* **-ies.** One that is subsidiary, esp. a company owned and controlled by another.
sub·si·dize (sŭb′sĭ-dīz′) *v.* **-dized, -diz·ing.** To provide or aid with a subsidy.
sub·si·dy (sŭb′sĭ-dē) *n., pl.* **-dies.** A financial grant, as that given by a government to a private undertaking or to another country.
sub·sist (səb-sĭst′) *v.* **1.** To exist or continue in existence. **2.** To have or receive what is necessary to maintain life.

sub•sis•tence (səb-sĭs′təns) *n.* **1.** The means necessary to maintain life. **2.** Existence. **–sub•sis′tent** *adj.*

sub•soil (sŭb′soil′) *n.* The layer of earth just beneath the surface soil.

sub•son•ic (sŭb′sŏn′ĭk) *adj.* **1.** Of or having less than audible frequency. **2.** Of, pertaining to, or being a speed less than that of sound in a designated medium.

subst. *abbr.* **1.** substantive. **2.** substitute.

sub•stance (sŭb′stəns) *n.* **1. a.** Matter that occupies space and has mass. **b.** Matter of a particular constitution or kind. **2. a.** Essential character : essence. **b.** The most basic or important quality or part : gist <the *substance* of the sermon> **3.** Actuality : reality <an idea without *substance*> **4.** Material belongings : property.

sub•stan•dard (sŭb′stăn′dərd) *adj.* Being below a standard or norm.

sub•stan•tial (səb-stăn′shəl) *adj.* **1.** Having substance : material. **2.** Not imaginary : real. **3.** Solid and firm : strong. **4.** Providing sustenance : nourishing <a *substantial* breakfast> **5.** Considerable <a *substantial* snowfall> **6.** Moderately wealthy : well-to-do. **–sub•stan′tial•ly** *adv.*

sub•stan•ti•ate (səb-stăn′shē-āt′) *v.* **-at•ed, -at•ing.** To support with proof : verify. **–sub•stan′ti•a′tion** *n.*

sub•stan•tive (sŭb′stən-tĭv) *adj.* **1.** Substantial : real. **2.** Of, relating to, or being the essence of something : essential. *–n.* **1.** A noun. **2.** A group of words functioning as a noun. **–sub′stan•tive•ly** *adv.*

sub•sta•tion (sŭb′stā′shən) *n.* A subsidiary station, as of a post office.

sub•sti•tute (sŭb′stĭ-to͞ot′, -tyo͞ot′) *n.* One that takes the place of another. ☆***syns:*** ALTERNATE, PINCH HITTER, REPLACEMENT, STAND-IN, SUB, SURROGATE *–v.* **-tut•ed, -tut•ing. 1.** To use or put in the place of another. **2.** To act as a substitute. **–sub′sti•tu′tion** *n.*

sub•stra•tum (sŭb′strā′təm, -străt′əm) *n.* **1.** A layer that lies beneath. **2.** Subsoil.

sub•struc•ture (sŭb′strŭk′chər) *n.* An underlying support : foundation.

sub•sume (səb-so͞om′, -syo͞om′) *v.* **-sumed, -sum•ing.** To place in a larger or more comprehensive category.

sub•ten•ant (sŭb′-tĕn′ənt) *n.* One that rents property, as a house, from a tenant.

sub•ter•fuge (sŭb′tər-fyo͞oj′) *n.* A trick or tactic used to escape, evade, or conceal.

sub•ter•ra•ne•an (sŭb′tə-rā′nē-ən) *adj.* **1.** Located, being, or operating underground. **2.** Hidden : secret <*subterranean* plots>

sub•ti•tle (sŭb′tĭt′l) *n.* **1.** A subordinate and often explanatory title, as of a book. **2.** A printed translation of foreign-language dialogue projected at the bottom of a motion-picture screen.

sub•tle (sŭt′l) *adj.* **-tler, -tlest. 1.** Difficult to detect or analyze : barely perceptible. **2.** Marked by or having sharp discernment : keen. **3. a.** Expert : skillful. **b.** Sly : crafty. **–sub′tle•ty** *n.* **–sub′tly** *adv.*

sub•to•tal (sŭb′tōt′l) *n.* The total of part of a series of numbers. **–sub′to′tal** *v.*

sub•tract (səb-trăkt′) *v.* To take away (e.g., 1 number from another) by deducting. **–sub•trac′tion** *n.*

sub•tra•hend (sŭb′trə-hĕnd′) *n.* A quantity to be subtracted from another.

sub•trop•i•cal (sŭb-trŏp′ĭ-kəl) *adj.* Of, pertaining to, or being geographic areas adjacent to the tropics.

sub•urb (sŭb′ûrb′) *n.* **1.** A small, usu. residential community near a city. **2. suburbs.** A residential area in the vicinity of a city. **–sub•ur′ban** (sə-bûr′bən) *adj.*

sub•ur•ban•ite (sə-bûr′bə-nīt′) *n.* Someone who lives in a suburb.

sub•ur•bi•a (sə-bûr′bē-ə) *n.* **1.** Suburbs. **2.** Suburbanites as a cultural class.

sub•ven•tion (səb-vĕn′shən) *n.* A subsidy : endowment.

sub•vert (səb-vûrt′) *v.* **1.** To overthrow. **2.** To corrupt the character or morals of. **–sub•ver′sion** *n.* **–sub•ver′sive** *adj.*

sub•way (sŭb′wā′) *n.* **1.** An underground passage. **2.** An underground railroad, esp. one powered by electricity.

suc•ceed (sək-sēd′) *v.* **1. a.** To come next in order or time : follow. **b.** To replace another in an office or position. **2.** To accomplish or achieve something desired, intended, or attempted.

suc•cès d'es•time (sük-sĕ′ dĕ-stēm′) *n.* An artistic work that receives critical acclaim without achieving popular success.

suc•cès fou (sük-sĕll fo͞o′) *n.* A wild success.

suc•cess (sək-sĕs′) *n.* **1.** The achievement of something desired, intended, or attempted. **2.** The gaining of fame or prosperity. **3.** One that succeeds. **–suc•cess′ful** *adj.* **–suc•cess′ful•ly** *adv.*

suc•ces•sion (sək-sĕsh′ən) *n.* **1.** The process or act of following in order. **2.** A group of persons or things that follow in order : sequence. **3.** The sequence, right, or act of succeeding to a title, throne, or estate.

suc•ces•sive (sək-sĕs′ĭv) *adj.* Following in uninterrupted order : consecutive. **–suc•ces′sive•ly** *adv.* **–suc•ces′sive•ness** *n.*

suc•ces•sor (sək-sĕs′ər) *n.* One that succeeds another, as to a throne.

suc•cinct (sək-sĭngkt′) *adj.* Marked by brevity : concise. **–suc•cinct′ly** *adv.* **–suc•cinct′ness** *n.*

suc•cor (sŭk′ər) *n.* Assistance : aid. **–suc′cor** *v.*

suc•co•tash (sŭk′ə-tăsh′) *n.* A mixture of cooked corn and lima or shell beans.

suc•cour (sŭk′ər) *n. esp. Brit. var. of* SUCCOR.

suc•cu•lent (sŭk′yə-lənt) *adj.* **1.** Full of sap. or juice : juicy. **2.** Having fleshy stems or leaves that conserve moisture. *–n.* A succulent plant, as a cactus. **–suc′cu•lence** *n.* **–suc′cu•lent•ly** *adv.*

suc•cumb (sə-kŭm′) *v.* **1.** To give in, as to something overpowering : yield. **2.** To die.

such (sŭch) *adj.* **1.** Of this or that kind. **2.** Of a quality that has been or is to be specified. *–adv.* To such a degree : so. *–pron.* **1.** Such a person or thing <a joke, if it can be be called *such*> **2.** The like <blouses, dresses, and *such*>

such•like (sŭch′līk′) *adj.* Like : similar. *–pron.* A person or thing of a like kind.

suck (sŭk) *v.* **1. a.** To draw liquid in with the mouth. **b.** To draw liquid from by sucking <*suck* a lemon> **2.** To draw in by or as if by suction. *–n.* The act of sucking : suction.

suck•er (sŭk′ər) *n.* **1.** One that sucks. **2.** *Slang.* A person who is easily duped. **3.** A lollipop. **4.** A freshwater fish of the family Catostomidae, with thick lips adapted for feeding by suction. **5.** A part of an animal's body adapted for clinging by suction. **6.** A shoot growing from the base of a plant.

suck•le (sŭk′əl) *v.* **-led, -ling. 1.** To give or take milk from the breast or udder. **2.** To foster : rear.

suck•ling (sŭk′lĭng) *n.* A young mammal not yet weaned.

su•cre (so͞o′krā) *n.* See CURRENCY TABLE.

Su•cre (so͞o′krä). Constitutional cap. of Bolivia, in the SC part. *Pop.* 62,207.

su•crose (so͞o′krōs′) *n.* A sugar obtained esp. from sugar cane and sugar beet.

suc•tion (sŭk′shən) *n.* **1.** The act or process of sucking. **2.** The act or process of drawing something, as ink, into a space, as the reservoir of a fountain pen, by producing a partial vacuum in the space.

Su•dan (so͞o-dăn′). Country of NE Africa, S of Egypt. *Cap.* Khartoum. *Pop.* 18,630,000. **–Su′da•nese′** *adj.* & *n.*

sud•den (sŭd′n) *adj.* **1.** Coming or happening quickly or without warning <a *sudden* snowstorm> **2.** Abrupt : sharp <a *sudden* drop in the road> **3.** Marked by excessive haste : rash <a *sudden* departure> **4.** Rapid : fast. **–sud′den•ly** *adv.* **–sud′den•ness** *n.*

sudden death *n. Sports.* An extra period of play added to a tied game that ends when 1 team scores.

sudden infant death syndrome *n.* The unexpected death of an apparently healthy infant that usu. occurs during the first 4 months of life while sleeping.

suds (sŭdz) *pl.n.* **1.** Soapy water. **2.** Lather : foam. **–suds′y** *adj.*

sue (so͞o) *v.* **sued, su•ing. 1.** To satisfy a claim or redress a grievance by instituting legal proceedings. **2.** To make a request or appeal : entreat.

suede *also* **suède** (swād) *n.* **1.** Leather with a soft napped surface. **2.** Fabric with a surface resembling that of suede.

su•et (so͞o′ĭt) *n.* The hard fat around the kidneys of cattle and sheep from which tallow is obtained.

Su•ez (so͞o-ĕz′, so͞o′ĕz′). Isthmus of NE Egypt connecting Africa and Asia and traversed by the Suez Canal (107 mi/172 km) from the Mediterranean to the Gulf of Suez, N arm of the Red Sea.

suf. *or* **suff.** *abbr.* **1.** sufficient. **2.** suffix.

suf•fer (sŭf′ər) *v.* **1.** To endure or feel distress or pain. **2.** To sustain damage, injury, or loss. **3.** To be or seem to be at a disadvantage. **4.** To undergo : experience. **5.** To permit : allow. **–suf′fer•er** *n.*

suf•fer•ance (sŭf′ər-əns, sŭf′rəns) *n.* **1.** Endurance : forbearance. **2.** Approval or permission implied by failure to prohibit.

suf•fer•ing (sŭf′ər-ĭng, sŭf′rĭng) *n.* Mental or physical pain : misery.

suf•fice (sə-fīs′) *v.* **-ficed, -fic•ing. 1.** To be adequate or sufficient. **2.** To answer a purpose or meet all requirements.

suf•fi•cient (sə-fĭsh′ənt) *adj.* As much as is needed or desired : enough. **–suf•fi′cien•cy** *n.* **–suf•fi′cient•ly** *adv.*

suf•fix (sŭf′ĭks′) *n.* An affix appended to the end of a word.

suf·fo·cate (sŭf′ə-kāt′) *v.* **-cat·ed, -cat·ing. 1.** To kill by depriving of oxygen. **2.** To die from a lack of oxygen. **3.** To stifle : suppress. **—suf′fo·ca′tion** *n.*
suf·fra·gan (sŭf′rə-gən) *n.* A bishop elected or appointed as an assistant to the bishop of a diocese. **—suf′fra·gan** *adj.* **—suf′fra·gan·ship′** *n.*
suf·frage (sŭf′rĭj) *n.* **1.** A vote. **2.** The right to vote : franchise.
suf·fra·gette (sŭf′rə-jĕt′) *n.* A woman advocate of suffrage for women.
suf·fra·gist (sŭf′rə-jĭst) *n.* An advocate of the extension of suffrage, esp. to women.
suf·fuse (sə-fyo͞oz′) *v.* **-fused, -fus·ing.** To spread through or over with or as if with liquid or light. **—suf·fu′sion** *n.*
sug·ar (sho͝og′ər) *n.* Any of a class of water-soluble crystalline carbohydrates with a characteristically sweet taste. *—v.* **1.** To coat, cover, or sprinkle with sugar. **2.** To make more palatable : sugar-coat.
sugar beet *n.* A beet, *Beta vulgaris,* with white roots from which sugar is obtained.
sugar cane *n.* A tall grass, *Saccharum officinarum,* that grows in warm regions and has thick stems that yield sugar.
sug·ar-coat (sho͝og′ər-kōt′) *v.* To cause to seem more acceptable or appealing <*sugar-coated* the criticism with endearments>
sugar maple *n.* A maple tree, *Acer saccharum,* of E North America, with sap that is the source of maple sugar and syrup.
sug·ar·plum (sho͝og′ər-plŭm′) *n.* A small candy in the shape of a ball.
sug·ar·y (sho͝og′ə-rē) *adj.* **-i·er, -i·est. 1.** Tasting of or containing sugar. **2.** Cloyingly or deceitfully sweet : saccharine.
sug·gest (səg-jĕst′, sə-jĕst′) *v.* **1.** To put forth (e.g., a plan or idea) for action or consideration : propose. **2.** To bring or call to mind by association : evoke. **3.** To make evident indirectly : imply. ☆***syns:*** HINT, IMPLY, INSINUATE, INTIMATE
sug·gest·i·ble (səg-jĕs′tə-bəl, sə-jĕs′-) *adj.* Readily influenced by suggestion.
sug·ges·tion (səg-jĕs′chən, sə-jĕs′-) *n.* **1.** The act of suggesting. **2.** Something suggested. **3.** A slight trace : hint.
sug·ges·tive (səg-jĕs′tĭv, sə-jĕs′-) *adj.* **1.** Tending to suggest something, as ideas or thoughts. **2.** Tending to suggest something indecent or improper. **—sug·ges′tive·ly** *adv.* **—sug·ges′tive·ness** *n.*
su·i·cide (so͞o′ĭ-sīd′) *n.* **1.** The act of killing oneself intentionally. **2.** A person who commits suicide. **—su′i·cid′al** *adj.*
su·i·cid·ol·o·gy (so͞o′ĭ-sī-dŏl′ə-jē) *n.* The study of suicide, suicidal behavior, and suicide prevention. **—su′i·cid·ol′o·gist** *n.*
su·i gen·e·ris (so͞o′ī jĕn′ər-ĭs, so͞o′ē) *adj.* Being unique of its kind.
suit (so͞ot) *n.* **1.** A set of things to be used together <a *suit* of clothes> **2.** One of the 4 sets of playing cards constituting a deck. **3.** A court proceeding to recover a right or claim. **4.** The act of appealing or entreating, esp. courtship. *—v.* **1.** To meet the requirements or desires of : satisfy or please. **2.** To be appropriate or proper. **3.** To be becoming to.
suit·a·ble (so͞o′tə-bəl) *adj.* Appropriate for a particular purpose or occasion : proper. **—suit′a·bil′i·ty** *n.* **—suit′a·bly** *adv.*
suit·case (so͞ot′kās′) *n.* A flat and usu. rectangular piece of luggage.
suite (swēt) *n.* **1.** A staff of attendants, as for a monarch : retinue. **2.** A group of connected rooms used as a unit. **3.** (*also* so͞ot). A set of matched furniture. **4.** *Mus.* An instrumental composition consisting of several movements of varying characters or of material taken from a longer work.
suit·ing (so͞o′tĭng) *n.* Fabric from which suits of clothes are made.
suit·or (so͞o′tər) *n.* **1.** One who petitions or entreats. **2.** A man who courts a woman.
su·ki·ya·ki (so͞o′kē-yä′kē, skē-) *n.* A dish of Japanese orig. that consists of thinly sliced meat and vegetables cooked together, usu. with soy sauce.
sul·fa drug (sŭl′fə) *n.* Any of a group of synthetic organic compounds used to inhibit bacterial growth and activity.
sul·fa·nil·a·mide (sŭl′fə-nĭl′ə-mīd′) *n.* A white, odorless compound used to treat various bacterial infections.
sul·fate (sŭl′fāt′) *n.* A salt or ester of sulfuric acid.
sul·fide (sŭl′fīd′) *n.* A compound of sulfur and another element or radical.
sul·fur *also* **sul·phur** (sŭl′fər) *n.* *Symbol* **S** A pale-yellow nonmetallic element that occurs naturally in both free and combined forms and is used in gunpowder, rubber vulcanization, insecticides, pharmaceuticals, and industrial chemicals.
sulfur dioxide *n.* A colorless, very irritating gas that is used esp. in manufacturing sulfuric acid.
sul·fu·ric (sŭl-fyo͝or′ĭk) *adj.* Of, pertaining to, or containing sulfur.
sulfuric acid *n.* A very corrosive, dense, oily acid used esp. in the manufacture of a wide variety of chemicals.
sul·fur·ous (sŭl′fər-əs, sŭl-fyo͝or′əs) *adj.* **1.** Of, pertaining to, derived from, or containing sulfur. **2.** Emanating from or characteristic of burning sulfur <a *sulfurous* odor>
sulk (sŭlk) *v.* To be sullenly aloof or silent. *—n.* A sulky mood or display.
sulk·y[1] (sŭl′kē) *adj.* **-i·er, -i·est.** Given to sulking : moody. **—sulk′i·ly** *adv.* **—sulk′i·ness** *n.*
sulk·y[2] (sŭl′kē) *n., pl.* **-ies.** A light 2-wheeled 1-horse vehicle for 1 person.
sul·len (sŭl′ən) *adj.* **1.** Ill-humored and surly : morose. **2.** Gloomy or melancholy. **—sul′len·ly** *adv.* **—sul′len·ness** *n.*
sul·ly (sŭl′ē) *v.* **-lied, -ly·ing.** To soil or defile : taint.
sul·phur (sŭl′fər) *n. var. of* SULFUR.
sul·tan (sŭl′tən) *n.* A ruler of a Moslem country. **—sul′tan·ate′** (-tə-nāt′) *n.*
sul·tan·a (sŭl-tăn′ə, -tä′nə) *n.* **1.** The mother, wife, sister, or daughter of a sultan. **2. a.** A seedless, pale yellow grape. **b.** A raisin of the sultana.
sul·try (sŭl′trē) *adj.* **-tri·er, -tri·est. 1.** Hot and humid : muggy. **2.** Extremely hot : torrid. **3.** Voluptuous : sensual.
sum (sŭm) *n.* **1. a.** The result obtained by addition : total. **b.** An arithmetic problem. **2.** The whole quantity, amount, or number : aggregate. **3.** An amount of money. **4.** A summary. *—v.* **summed, sum·ming.** To find the sum of : add. **—sum up.** To recapitulate : summarize.
su·mac *also* **su·mach** (so͞o′măk′, sho͞o′-) *n.* A shrub or small trees of the genus *Rhus,* with compound leaves and clusters of small, usu. red berries.
Su·ma·tra (so͞o-mä′trə). Island of Indonesia, in the Indian Ocean W of Malaysia and Borneo. **—Su·ma′tran** *adj. & n.*
Su·mer (so͞o′mər). Ancient country of Mesopotamia in present-day S Iraq. **—Su·me′ri·an** (-mĕr′ē-ən, -mîr′-) *adj. & n.*
sum·ma·rize (sŭm′ə-rīz′) *v.* **-rized, -riz·ing.** To state in a summary <*summarize* the report> **—sum′ma·ri·za′tion** *n.*
sum·ma·ry (sŭm′ə-rē) *n., pl.* **-ries.** A succinct statement of the principal points. *—adj.* **1.** Covering the principal points concisely : brief. **2.** Done quickly and without ceremony <*summary* dismissal> **—sum·mar′i·ly** (sə-mâr′ə-lē) *adv.*
sum·ma·tion (sə-mā′shən) *n.* A final statement that summarizes the principal points, esp. of the arguments in a trial.
sum·mer (sŭm′ər) *n.* The warmest season of the year, following spring and preceding autumn. *—v.* To pass the summer. **—sum′mer·y** *adj.*
sum·mer·house (sŭm′ər-hous′) *n.* A roofed structure that furnishes a shady refuge in a garden or park.
summer squash *n.* A squash that is eaten shortly after being picked rather than kept for storage.
sum·mer·time (sŭm′ər-tīm′) *n.* Summer.
sum·mit (sŭm′ĭt) *n.* The highest part, point, level, or degree.
sum·mon (sŭm′ən) *v.* **1.** To call together : convene. **2.** To send for : bid to come. **3.** To order to make an appearance in court. **4.** To call forth, esp. with effort : arouse <*summoned* up his nerve>
sum·mons (sŭm′ənz) *n., pl.* **-mons·es. 1.** A command or order to perform a particular duty or appear at a particular place. **2.** *Law.* A notice summoning a defendant, witness, or juror to appear in court.
su·mo (so͞o′mō) *n.* A stylized Japanese form of wrestling.
sump·tu·ous (sŭmp′cho͞o-əs) *adj.* Very rich, expensive, luxurious, or splendid.
sun (sŭn) *n.* **1.** The star around which the earth and the other planets of the solar system orbit and whose heat and light sustain life on the earth. **2.** A star that is the center of a planetary system. **3.** The radiant energy, esp. visible light and heat, emitted by the sun : sunshine. *—v.* **sunned, sun·ning.** To bask in or expose to or as if to the rays of the sun. **—sun′less** *adj.*
Sun. *abbr.* Sunday.
sun·bathe (sŭn′bāth′) *v.* To expose the body to sunlight. **—sun′bath′** (-băth′, -bäth′) *n.* **—sun′bath′er** *n.*
sun·belt *or* **Sun·belt** (sŭn′bĕlt′) *n.* The S and SW states of the U.S.
sun·bon·net (sŭn′bŏn′ĭt) *n.* A bonnet with a wide brim shading the face and neck from the sun.
sun·burn (sŭn′bûrn′) *n.* An inflammation of the skin caused by overexposure to direct sunlight. *—v.* To affect or be affected with sunburn.
sun·burst (sŭn′bûrst′) *n.* A design in the form of a central sunlike disk with radiating rays.
sun·dae (sŭn′dē, -dā′) *n.* A portion of ice cream with a topping, as of syrup or nuts.
Sun·day (sŭn′dē, -dā′) *n.* The 1st day of the week.

sun•der (sŭn′dər) *v.* To break apart.
sun•di•al (sŭn′dī′əl) *n.* An instrument that indicates the time of day from the shadow cast on a calibrated dial by a pointer.
sun•down (sŭn′doun′) *n.* The time at which the sun sets.
sun•dries (sŭn′drēz) *pl.n.* Miscellaneous small items or articles.
sun•dry (sŭn′drē) *adj.* Miscellaneous.
sun•fish (sŭn′fĭsh′) *n.* **1.** Any of various flat-bodied North American freshwater fishes of the family Centrarchidae. **2.** Any of several very large, round-bodied marine fishes of the family Molidae.
sun•flow•er (sŭn′flou′ər) *n.* A plant of the genus *Helianthus*, bearing large yellow-rayed dark-centered flowers with edible seeds rich in oil.
sung (sŭng) *v. p.p. & var. p.t. of* SING.
sun•glass•es (sŭn′glăs′ĭz) *pl.n.* Eyeglasses with tinted or polarized lenses to protect the eyes from the sun.
sunk (sŭngk) *v. p.p. & var. p.t. of* SINK.
sunk•en (sŭng′kən) *adj.* **1.** Fallen in : hollowed <*sunken* cheeks> **2.** Submerged <a *sunken* ship> **3.** Built or lying below a surrounding level <a *sunken* recreation room><a *sunken* pond>
sun lamp *n.* A lamp that emits a wide range of radiation and is used for cosmetic and therapeutic purposes.
sun•light (sŭn′līt′) *n.* Sunshine.
sun•lit (sŭn′lĭt′) *adj.* Illuminated by the light of the sun.
sun•ny (sŭn′ē) *adj.* **-ni•er, -ni•est. 1.** Exposed to or full of sunshine. **2.** Bright and cheerful : merry.
sun•rise (sŭn′rīz′) *n.* **1.** The first appearance of the sun above the horizon. **2.** The time of sunrise.
sun•roof (sŭn′ro͞of′, -ro͝of′) *n.* A car roof with a panel that can be slid back or lifted.
sun•set (sŭn′sĕt′) *n.* **1.** The disappearance of the sun below the horizon. **2.** The time of sunset.
sun•shade (sŭn′shād′) *n.* Something, as a parasol or a billed cap, used as a shield against the sun's rays.
sun•shine (sŭn′shīn′) *n.* **1.** The direct rays of the sun. **2.** A source of cheer or happiness. **—sun′shin′y** *adj.*
sun•spot (sŭn′spŏt′) *n.* A dark spot that appears on the surface of the sun.
sun•stroke (sŭn′strōk′) *n.* Heat stroke caused by exposure to the sun.
sun•tan (sŭn′tăn′) *n.* A darkening of the skin from exposure to the sun. **—sun′tanned′** *adj.*
sun•up (sŭn′ŭp′) *n.* Sunrise.
Sun Yat-sen (so͝on′ yät′sĕn′). 1866–1925. Chinese revolutionary leader.
sup (sŭp) *v.* **supped, sup•ping.** To eat supper.
sup. 1. above (Lat. *supra*). **2.** superior. **3.** superlative. **4.** supplement. **5.** supply.
su•per¹ (so͞o′pər) *n. Informal.* A superintendent, esp. of an apartment building.
su•per² (so͞o′pər) *adj. Slang.* **1.** First-rate : excellent. **2.** Excessive in degree : extreme.
super– *pref.* **1.** Above : over : upon <*super*impose> **2.** Superior in size, quality, number, or degree <*super*power> **3. a.** Exceeding a norm <*super*sonic> **b.** Excessive in degree or intensity <*super*subtle> **4.** More inclusive than a specified category <*super*order> See below for a list of self-explanatory words formed with the prefix **super–.**
super. *abbr.* **1.** superior. **2.** superintendent.
su•per•a•bun•dant (so͞o′pər-ə-bŭn′dənt) *adj.* More than sufficient. **—su′per•a•bun′dance** *n.*
su•per•an•nu•at•ed (so͞o′pər-ăn′yo͞o-ā′tĭd) *adj.* **1.** Retired from active duty because of age or infirmity. **2.** Obsolete.
su•perb (so͝o-pûrb′, sə-) *adj.* **1.** Of supreme quality : first-rate. **2.** Majestic : grand. **—su•perb′ly** *adv.*
su•per•car•go (so͞o′pər-kär′gō) *n.* A merchant marine officer in charge of the cargo.
su•per•charg•er (so͞o′pər-chär′jər) *n.* A device, as a compressor, for supplying air under high pressure to an internal-combustion engine.
su•per•cil•i•ous (so͞o′pər-sĭl′ē-əs) *adj.* Marked by or expressive of haughty scorn : disdainful. **—su′per•cil′i•ous•ly** *adv.*
su•per•class (so͞o′pər-klăs′) *n. Biol.* A taxonomic category ranking between a phylum and a class.
su•per•con•duc•tiv•i•ty (so͞o′pər-kŏn′dŭk-tĭv′ĭ-tē) *n.* The complete loss of electrical resistance in certain metals and alloys at temperatures near absolute zero. **—su′per•con•duc′tive** (-kən-dŭk′tĭv) *adj.* **—su′per•con•duc′tor** *n.*
su•per•e•go (so͞o′pər-ē′gō, -ĕg′ō) *n.* The part of the psyche that reflects the moral standards of the community and the conscience of authority.
su•per•e•rog•a•to•ry (so͞o′pər-ə-rŏg′ə-tôr′ē, -tōr′ē) *adj.* Superfluous.
su•per•fi•cial (so͞o′pər-fĭsh′əl) *adj.* **1.** Of, pertaining to, affecting, or located on a surface. **2.** Concerned only with what is apparent. **3.** Lacking substance or depth. ☆***syns:*** CURSORY, SHALLOW, SKETCHY **—su′per•fi′ci•al′i•ty** (-fĭsh′ē-ăl′ĭ-tē) *n.* **—su′per•fi′cial•ly** *adv.*
su•per•flu•ous (so͝o-pûr′flo͞o-əs) *adj.* Being beyond what is necessary, desirable, or sufficient : surplus. **—su′per•flu′i•ty** (so͞o′pər-flo͞o′ĭ-tē) *n.*
su•per•high•way (so͞o′pər-hī′wā′) *n.* A broad highway, as an expressway, for high-speed traffic.
su•per•hu•man (so͞o′pər-hyo͞o′mən) *adj.* **1.** Being beyond or above the human : divine. **2.** Exceeding ordinary or normal human capability, power, or experience.
su•per•im•pose (so͞o′pər-ĭm-pōz′) *v.* To place (1 thing) on or over something else.
su•per•in•tend (so͞o′pər-ĭn-tĕnd′) *v.* To supervise. **—su′per•in•ten′dence** *n.* **—su′per•in•ten′dent** *n. & adj.*
su•pe•ri•or (so͝o-pîr′ē-ər, sə-) *adj.* **1.** Of higher authority or rank. **2.** Of a higher kind or nature <*superior* knowledge> **3.** Of greater significance or value. **4.** Greater in amount or

superachievement
superachiever
superacid
superactivity
superacute
superadaptable
superaesthetic
superaffluence
superagency
superalkaline
superambitious
superangelic
superarduous
superarrogant
superathletic
superattraction
superattractive
superbad
superbenefit
superbillionaire
superbitch
superblunder
superbold
superbomb
superbrave
superbright
superbureaucrat
superbusy
supercandid
supercapable
supercaution
superceremonious
superchic
supercivilized
superclean
supercolossal
supercomfortable
supercomplex
supercompression
superconfident
superconglomerate
superconservative
supercool
supercordial
supercountry
supercriminal
supercritic
supercritical
supercultivated
supercurious
supercute
supercynical
superdad
superdanger
superdelicate
superdeluxe
superdemand
superdesirous
superdevilish
superdevotion
superdifficult
superdiplomat
superdividend
supereffective
superefficiency
superefficient
superegoist
superelastic
superelegance
superelite
supereloquent
supereminence
supereminent
superemphasis
superendurance
superethical
superexacting
superexalt
superexcellence
superexcellent
superexcited
superexpenditure
superexpress
superexpressive
superexquisite
superfan
superfast
superfeminine
superfervent
superfine
superflack
superfluid
superformal
superformidable
superfriendly
superfund
supergallant
supergenerosity
superglorious
supergovernment
supergroup
supergrowth
superhandsome
superhearty
superheat
superhero
superheroic
superheroine
superhit
superhype
superimportant
superimproved
superincentive
superindignant
superindividualist
superinduce
superinduction
superindulgence
superindustrious
superinfluence
superingenious
superinitiative
superinjustice
superinquisitive
superinsistent
superintellectual
superjock
superjumbo

number. **5.** Haughty : arrogant. **6.** Seemingly indifferent, as to adversity or pain. **7.** Located higher up. *—n.* **1.** One who surpasses another in quality or is above another in rank. **2.** The head of a religious order or house. **—su·pe′ri·or′i·ty** (-pîr′ē-ôr′ĭ-tē, -ŏr′-) *n.*

Superior. One of the Great Lakes between the U.S. and Canada.

superl *abbr.* superlative.

su·per·la·tive (so͝o-pûr′lə-tĭv) *adj.* **1.** Of the highest degree of superiority : supreme. **2.** Of, pertaining to, or being the degree of comparison of an adjective or adverb that indicates the extreme or greatest extent or level. *—n.* **1.** One that is superlative. **2.** The very highest degree : peak. **3. a.** The superlative degree in a language. **b.** The superlative form of an adjective or adverb. **—su·per′la·tive·ly** *adv.*

su·per·mar·ket (so͞o′pər-mär′kĭt) *n.* A large self-service retail store at which food and household goods can be purchased.

su·per·nal (so͝o-pûr′nəl) *adj.* **1.** Heavenly : celestial. **2.** Of or coming from above.

su·per·nat·u·ral (so͞o′pər-năch′ər-əl) *adj.* **1.** Of or pertaining to an order of existence beyond the natural world. **2.** Of, pertaining to, or attributed to a divine agent. **—su′per·nat′u·ral·ly** *adv.*

su·per·no·va (so͞o′pər-nō′və) *n.* A rare and extremely bright nova.

su·per·nu·mer·ar·y (so͞o′pər-no͞o′mə-rĕr′ē, -nyo͞o′-) *adj.* Being in excess of the required, usual, or proper number : extra. *—n., pl.* **-ies. 1.** An extra thing or person. **2.** An actor who plays a nonspeaking part.

su·per·pow·er (so͞o′pər-pou′ər) *n.* An extremely influential and powerful nation.

su·per·sat·u·rate (so͞o′pər-săch′ə-rāt′) *v.* To make (e.g., a chemical solution) more highly concentrated than is normally possible. **—su′per·sat′u·ra′tion** *n.*

su·per·scribe (so͞o′pər-skrīb′) *v.* **-scribed, -scrib·ing.** To write on the upper part or outside. **—su′per·scrip′tion** *n.*

su·per·script (so͞o′pər-skrĭpt′) *n.* A symbol or letter written next to and slightly above another character.

su·per·sede (so͞o′pər-sēd′) *v.* **-sed·ed, -sed·ing. 1.** To take the place of : supplant. **2.** To set aside : displace.

su·per·son·ic (so͞o′pər-sŏn′ĭk) *adj.* Of, relating to, caused by, or moving at a speed greater than that of sound.

su·per·sti·tion (so͞o′pər-stĭsh′ən) *n.* **1.** A belief that is maintained despite evidence that it is unfounded or irrational. **2.** A belief, practice, or rite resulting from faith in chance, magic, or dogma. **—su′per·sti′tious** *adj.* **—su′per·sti′tious·ly** *adv.*

su·per·struc·ture (so͞o′pər-strŭk′chər) *n.* A structure built on top of something else.

su·per·vene (so͞o′pər-vēn′) *v.* **-vened, -ven·ing.** To come or take place as something added, extraneous, or unexpected.

su·per·vise (so͞o′pər-vīz′) *v.* **-vised, -vis·ing.** To direct and inspect the work, actions, or performance of : oversee. **—su′per·vi′sion** (-vĭzh′ən) *n.* **—su′per·vi′sor** *n.* **—su′per·vi′so·ry** (-vī′zə-rē) *adj.*

su·pine (so͞o-pīn′, so͞o′pīn′) *adj.* **1.** Lying on the back with the face upward. **2.** Not disposed to act : lethargic.

sup·per (sŭp′ər) *n.* The evening meal served when dinner is eaten at midday.

supper club *n.* A nightclub.

sup·plant (sə-plănt′) *v.* To take the place of (another), esp. by underhand means or by force : supersede.

sup·ple (sŭp′əl) *adj.* **-pler, -plest. 1.** Readily bent without cracking or breaking : pliant. **2.** Marked by agility : limber. **3.** Yielding readily : compliant.

sup·ple·ment (sŭp′lə-mənt) *n.* **1.** Something that compensates for a deficiency or constitutes an addition. **2.** A part or section, as of a book, giving additional information or correcting errors. *—v.* (-mĕnt′). To be or provide a supplement to. **—sup′ple·men′ta·ry** (-mĕn′tə-rē, -mĕn′trē), **sup′ple·ment′al** (-mĕn′tl) *adj.*

sup·pli·ant (sŭp′lē-ənt) *n.* One who supplicates : pleader.

sup·pli·cant (sŭp′lĭ-kənt) *n.* A suppliant.

sup·pli·cate (sŭp′lĭ-kāt′) *v.* **-cat·ed, -cat·ing. 1.** To ask for humbly and earnestly by or as if by praying to God. **2.** To make an earnest appeal. **—sup′pli·ca′tion** *n.*

sup·ply (sə-plī′) *v.* **-plied, -ply·ing. 1.** To make available for use : furnish. **2.** To provide with what is lacking or needed. **3.** To fill sufficiently : satisfy <*supply* a lack> *—n., pl.* **-plies. 1.** The act of supplying. **2.** An amount or quantity, esp. of a commodity, that is available or needed. **3.** *often* **supplies.** A quantity, as of merchandise, held in reserve and dispensed when needed : provisions. **4.** The commodities available for meeting a demand or for purchase at a given price. **—sup·pli′er** *n.*

sup·port (sə-pôrt′, -pōrt′) *v.* **1.** To bear the weight of and maintain in position : hold up. **2.** To be able to bear : tolerate. **3.** To supply with the necessities of life, as food, shelter, and money : maintain. **4.** To corroborate : substantiate. **5.** To give aid or assistance to : back up. *—n.* **1.** The act of supporting or state of being supported. **2.** One that supports. **—sup·port′a·ble** *adj.* **—sup·port′er** *n.* **—sup·por′tive** *adj.*

sup·pose (sə-pōz′) *v.* **-posed, -pos·ing. 1.** To assume as true, esp. for the sake of argument. **2.** To consider likely or probable <I *suppose* you're right.> **3.** To expect <She's *supposed* to wait.>

sup·posed (sə-pōzd′, -pō′zĭd) *adj.* Accepted as being, often mistakenly. **—sup·pos′ed·ly** (-pō′zĭd-lē) *adv.*

sup·pos·ing (sə-pō′zĭng) *conj.* Assuming that.

sup·po·si·tion (sŭp′ə-zĭsh′ən) *n.* **1.** The act of supposing. **2.** Something supposed.

sup·pos·i·to·ry (sə-pŏz′ĭ-tôr′ē, -tōr′ē) *n., pl.* **-ries.** A solid medication designed for insertion into a bodily cavity, as the rectum, where it melts.

sup·press (sə-prĕs′) *v.* **1.** To put an end to, esp. by force : subdue <*suppress* a rebellion> **2.** To keep from being revealed,

superlaborious
superlarge
superlenient
superlie
superliner
superloyal
superlucky
superluxurious
supermacho
superman
supermarvelous
supermasculine
supermilitant
supermillionaire
supermodern
supermodest
supermoisten
supermom
supermorose
supermundane
supernotable
superobese
superobjectionable
superobstinate
superoffensive
superofficious
superoptimistic
superordinary
superorganic
superorganize
superpatient
superpatriotic
superphysical
superpious
superplane
superpolite
superpositive
superpowerful
superpraise
superprecise
superpressure
superprize
superpro
superproduce
superprosperous
superpure
superrace
superradical
superrational
superrealism
superrealist
superrefined
superrespectable
superresponsible
superreward
superrich
superrighteous
superroad
superromantic
supersacrifice
supersafe
supersalesman
supersarcastic
supersatisfaction
superscale
superscholarly
superschool
superscientific
superscout
supersecrecy
supersecret
supersell
superseller
supersensitive
supersentimental
superserious
supershow
supersimplify
supersize
supersleuth
superslick
supersmart
supersmooth
supersoft
supersolemn
superspecial
superspecialize
superspeed
superspirituality
superspy
superstar
superstate
superstore
superstratum
superstrength
superstrenuous
superstrict
superstrong
superstud
superstylish
supersubtle
supersurgeon
supersurprise
supersweet
supertanker
supertension
superterrific
superthankful
superthick
superthin
superthorough
superthriller
supertight
supertrick
superugly
superurgent
supervigilant
supervigorous
supervirile
supervital
superwave
superweapon
superwide
superwife
superwise
superwoman
superworldly
superzealous

circulated, or published. **3.** To hold back : repress <*suppressed* her laughter> **–sup·pres′sion** *n.* **–sup·pres′sive** *adj.*
sup·pu·rate (sŭp′yə-rāt′) *v.* **-rat·ed, -rat·ing.** To discharge or form pus. **–sup′pu·ra′tion** *n.*
su·pra·na·tion·al (so͞o′prə-năsh′ə-nəl) *adj.* Extending beyond national boundaries or authority.
su·prem·a·cist (so͝o-prĕm′ə-sĭst) *n.* One who advocates the supremacy of a particular group.
su·prem·a·cy (so͝o-prĕm′ə-sē) *n., pl.* **-cies. 1.** The state or quality of being supreme. **2.** Supreme power, authority, or rank.
su·preme (sə-prēm′) *adj.* **1.** Of highest power, authority, or rank. **2.** Of greatest importance or finest quality. **3.** Final : ultimate <the *supreme* moment> **–su·preme′ly** *adv.* **–su·preme′ness** *n.*
Supreme Being *n.* God.
supt. or **Supt.** *abbr.* superintendent.
sur·cease (sûr′sēs′) *n.* Cessation, esp. a temporary end.
sur·charge (sûr′chärj′) *n.* **1.** An extra charge added to a cost or amount. **2.** Something overprinted on a postage stamp to give it a new value or denomination. **3.** An excessive burden : overload. *–v.* **1.** To charge an extra amount. **2.** To overcharge. **3.** To print a surcharge on (a stamp).
sur·cin·gle (sûr′sĭng′gəl) *n.* A girth that binds something, as a saddle or pack, to a horse's body.
sure (sho͝or) *adj.* **sur·er, sur·est. 1.** Impossible to doubt : certain. **2.** Firm and steady <a *sure* foothold> **3.** Feeling certainty : confident. **4.** Bound to happen : inevitable. **5.** Dependable : reliable. *–adv.* In a sure manner : surely. **–sure′ly** *adv.*
sure-fire (sho͝or′fīr′) *adj. Informal.* Certain to be successful.
sure-foot·ed (sho͝or′fo͝ot′ĭd) *adj.* Unlikely to stumble or fall.
sure·ty (sho͝or′ĭ-tē) *n., pl.* **-ties. 1.** The state of being sure : certainty. **2.** Something that secures, as against damage : guarantee. **3.** One who has agreed to be legally responsible for another person.
surf (sûrf) *n.* The waves of the sea as they break on the shoreline. *–v.* To engage in surfing. **–surf′er** *n.*
sur·face (sûr′fəs) *n.* **1.** The topmost or outside boundary of a body or object. **2.** Outward or superficial appearance. *–adj.* **1.** Of or situated on a surface. **2.** Superficial. *–v.* **-faced, -fac·ing. 1.** To provide with a surface. **2.** To rise or come to the surface.
surf·board (sûrf′bôrd′, -bōrd′) *n.* A long, narrow board used in surfing.
sur·feit (sûr′fĭt) *v.* To feed or supply to repletion : satiate. *–n.* **1. a.** Overindulgence, as in food or drink. **b.** Disgust caused by such overindulgence. **2.** An overabundant amount : excess.
surf·ing (sûr′fĭng) *n.* The sport of riding the surf into shore, esp. on a surfboard.
surg. *abbr.* surgeon; surgery; surgical.
surge (sûrj) *v.* **surged, surg·ing. 1.** To move in or as if in billows or waves : swell. **2.** To increase suddenly to a high or excessive level. *–n.* **1.** A large wave of water : swell. **2.** A swelling like that of rolling waves <a *surge* of anger> **3.** A sudden increase <a *surge* of electric current>
sur·geon (sûr′jən) *n.* A physician who specializes in surgery.
sur·ger·y (sûr′jə-rē) *n., pl.* **-ies. 1.** The branch of medicine in which physical injury, deformity, and disease are treated by the cutting and removal or repair of bodily parts. **2.** A surgical operating room or laboratory. **3.** The work of a surgeon.
sur·gi·cal (sûr′jĭ-kəl) *adj.* **1.** Of, relating to, or characteristic of surgeons or surgery. **2.** Used in surgery. **–sur′gi·cal·ly** *adv.*
Su·ri·nam (so͝or′ə-năm′). Country of NE South America, on the Atlantic. *Cap.* Paramaribo. *Pop.* 425,000.
sur·ly (sûr′lē) *adj.* **-li·er, -li·est.** Bad-tempered and rude. **–sur′li·ness** *n.*
sur·mise (sər-mīz′) *v.* **-mised, -mis·ing.** To conjecture : guess. **–sur·mise′** *n.*
sur·mount (sər-mount′) *v.* **1.** To conquer : overcome. **2.** To ascend to or be at the top of. **–sur·mount′a·ble** *adj.*
sur·name (sûr′nām′) *n.* A person's last or family name.
sur·pass (sər-păs′) *v.* **1.** To be beyond the limits, capacity, or powers of. **2.** To be better, greater, or stronger than. ☆***syns:*** EXCEED, EXCEL, OUTDO, OUTSHINE, OUTSTRIP, TRANSCEND **–sur·pass′ing·ly** *adv.*
sur·plice (sûr′plĭs) *n.* A loose-fitting white ecclestiastical vestment with full, flowing sleeves that is worn over a cassock.
sur·plus (sûr′pləs) *n.* An amount or quantity beyond what is used or needed : excess. *–adj.* Being a surplus.
sur·prise (sər-prīz′) *v.* **-prised, -pris·ing. 1.** To catch or take unawares. **2.** To attack without warning. **3.** To cause to feel astonishment : amaze. *–n.* **1.** A feeling of astonishment : amazement. **2.** Something that surprises. **3.** An attack made without warning. **–sur·pris′ing·ly** *adv.*
sur·re·al (sə-rē′əl) *adj.* Having the characteristics and qualities associated with surrealism : grotesque.
sur·re·al·ism (sə-rē′ə-lĭz′əm) *n.* A 20th-cent. literary and artistic movement in which fantastic imagery and incongruous juxtapositions are meant to express the workings of the subconscious. **–sur·re′al·ist** *n.* **–sur·re′al·is′tic** *adj.* **–sur·re′al·is′ti·cal·ly** *adv.*
sur·ren·der (sə-rĕn′dər) *v.* **1.** To give up control or possession of to another on demand or under compulsion. **2.** To give (oneself) over, as to an emotion : yield. *–n.* The act of surrendering.
sur·rep·ti·tious (sûr′əp-tĭsh′əs) *adj.* Made, done, or acting in secret : stealthy. **–sur′rep·ti′tious·ly** *adv.*
sur·rey (sûr′ē, sŭr′ē) *n., pl.* **-reys.** A horse-drawn 4-wheeled carriage with 2 seats.
sur·ro·gate (sûr′ə-gĭt, -gāt′, sŭr′-) *n.* **1.** A substitute. **2.** A judge in some U.S. states with jurisdiction over the probate of wills and settlement of estates.
sur·round (sə-round′) *v.* **1.** To extend around all edges of. **2.** To shut in on all sides so as to prevent escape : confine. ☆***syns:*** CIRCLE, COMPASS, ENCIRCLE, ENCLOSE, GIRD, RING
sur·round·ings (sə-roun′dĭngz) *pl.n.* The conditions that surround one.
sur·tax (sûr′tăks′) *n.* A tax imposed in addition to a normal tax.
sur·veil·lance (sər-vā′ləns) *n.* Close observation, esp. of a person or group under suspicion.
sur·vey (sər-vā′, sûr′vā′) *v.* **1. a.** To look over and examine in detail. **b.** To study or view comprehensively. **2.** To determine the position, boundaries, area, and elevation of a part of the earth's surface by measuring angles and distances. *–n.* (sûr′vā′), *pl.* **-veys. 1.** A detailed examination : inspection. **2.** A comprehensive view <a *survey* of European history> **3. a.** The process of surveying land. **b.** A map or plan of surveyed land. **–sur·vey′or** *n.*
sur·vey·ing (sər-vā′ĭng) *n.* The act, profession, or science of making land surveys.
sur·vive (sər-vīv′) *v.* **-vived, -viv·ing. 1.** To continue to live or exist. **2.** To live longer than : outlive. **–sur·viv′al** *n.* **–sur·vi′vor** *n.*
sus·cep·ti·ble (sə-sĕp′tə-bəl) *adj.* **1.** Easily influenced, moved, or affected : sensitive. **2.** Prone to be subject <*susceptible* to infections> **3.** Capable of accepting or permitting <an argument not *susceptible* of proof> **–sus·cep′ti·bil′i·ty** *n.*
su·shi (so͞o′shē) *n.* A dish of Japanese origin that consists of thin slices of fresh raw fish or seaweed wrapped around a cake of cooked rice.
sus·pect (sə-spĕkt′) *v.* **1.** To believe without being sure : surmise. **2.** To be suspicious about : distrust. **3.** To consider to be guilty without proof. *–n.* (sŭs′pĕkt′). Someone who is suspected, esp. of a crime. *–adj.* (sŭs′pĕkt′). Open to or considered with suspicion.
sus·pend (sə-spĕnd′) *v.* **1.** To bar for a period from an office, privilege, or position. **2.** To cause to stop temporarily : interrupt. **3.a.** To put off for a time : postpone <*suspend* judgment> **b.** To make temporarily ineffective <*suspend* parking regulations> **4.** To hang, esp. so as to allow free movement except at the point of attachment. **5.** To keep from falling or sinking without apparent support <particles of cork *suspended* in wine>
sus·pend·er (sə-spĕn′dər) *n.* One of a pair of straps worn over the shoulders to support a skirt or trousers.
sus·pense (sə-spĕns′) *n.* **1.** Suspension. **2.** Apprehension resulting from uncertainty : anxiety. **3.** A feeling of pleasurable excitement as to a result. **–sus·pense′ful** *adj.*
sus·pen·sion (sə-spĕn′shən) *n.* **1.** The act of suspending or state of being suspended. **2.** A device by which something, as a mechanical part, is suspended. **3.** *Chem.* A noncolloidal dispersion of solid particles in a liquid.
suspension bridge *n.* A bridge whose roadway is hung from cables stretched between supporting towers.
sus·pi·cion (sə-spĭsh′ən) *n.* **1.** The act or an instance of suspecting something, esp. something wrong, without sufficient evidence or proof. **2.** A minute trace : hint.
sus·pi·cious (sə-spĭsh′əs) *adj.* **1.** Arousing or tending to arouse suspicion. **2.** Given to suspicion : distrustful. **3.** Expressing suspicion. **–sus·pi′cious·ly** *adv.*
sus·tain (sə-stān′) *v.* **1.** To hold up : support. **2.** To keep up : maintain <couldn't *sustain* their interest> **3.** To supply with nourishment. **4.** To support the spirits, courage, or resolution of. **5.** To withstand : endure <*sustain* a disappointment> **6.** To undergo : suffer <*sustained* an injury> **7.** To uphold as valid, true, or legal. **8.** To corroborate : confirm. ☆***syns:*** BOLSTER, BUOY, PROP, SUPPORT, UPHOLD
sus·te·nance (sŭs′tə-nəns) *n.* **1.** The act of sustaining or state of being sustained. **2.** Something that nourishes : food. **3.** Something that sustains, strengthens, or supports. **4.** Means of maintaining life : livelihood.
su·ture (so͞o′chər) *n.* **1.** Material or a stitch used to join the

edges of a wound or incision. **2.** A seamlike line of junction, as between 2 bones of the skull. **—su'ture** *v.*

Su·va (so͞o'və). Cap. of Fiji, on the SE coast of Viti Levu. *Pop.* 63,628.

su·ze·rain (so͞o'zər-ən, -zə-rān') *n.* **1.** A feudal lord. **2.** A nation that controls the international affairs of another nation but permits it domestic sovereignty. **—su'ze·rain·ty** *n.*

svelte (sfĕlt) *adj.* **svelt·er, svelt·est.** Slender : willowy.

SW *abbr.* southwest.

swab (swŏb) *n.* **1.** A small mass of absorbent material used esp. for cleaning or applying medicine. **2.** A mop, as that used to clean decks. **3.** *Slang.* A sailor. *—v.* **swabbed, swab·bing.** To clean, treat, or remove with a swab.

swad·dle (swŏd'l) *v.* **-dled, -dling. 1.** To wrap closely : envelop. **2.** To wrap (an infant) in strips of cloth.

swaddling clothes *pl.n.* **1.** Strips of cloth wrapped around a newborn infant to hold its legs and arms still. **2.** Restrictions imposed on the immature.

swag (swăg) *n. Slang.* Stolen money or property : booty.

swage (swāj) *n.* A tool used to shape metal. **—swage** *v.*

swag·ger (swăg'ər) *v.* **1.** To walk with an insolent or conceited air : strut. **2.** To brag : boast. **—swag'ger** *n.*

Swa·hi·li (swä-hē'lē) *n.* A language of E and C Africa that is widely used as a lingua franca.

swain (swān) *n.* **1.** A country youth, esp. a shepherd. **2.** A suitor.

swal·low¹ (swŏl'ō) *v.* **1.** To cause to pass into the stomach through the mouth. **2.** To consume as if by swallowing : engulf. **3.** To accept humbly : bear. **4.** *Slang.* To believe without questioning. **5.** To take back : retract <had to *swallow* his words> *—n.* **1.** The act of swallowing. **2.** The amount that can be swallowed at 1 time.

swal·low² (swŏl'ō) *n.* A bird of the family Hirundinidae, with long wings and a usu. forked tail.

swal·low·tail (swŏl'ō-tāl') *n.* **1.** A deeply forked tail of or like that of a swallow. **2.** A butterfly of the family Papilionidae, with a taillike projection on each hind wing. **3.** A man's black coat worn for formal daytime occasions and having a long rounded and split tail.

swam (swăm) *v. p.t.* of SWIM.

swa·mi (swä'mē) *n.* A Hindu mystic or religious teacher.

swamp (swŏmp, swômp) *n.* A wet lowland region : marsh. *—v.* **1.** To cover with or drench in liquid. **2.** To deluge : overwhelm. **3.** To submerge by filling with water. **—swamp'i·ness** *n.* **—swamp'y** *adj.*

swamp fever *n.* Malaria.

swan (swŏn) *n.* A large aquatic bird, esp. of the genera *Cygnus* or *Olor,* with webbed feet, a long slender neck, and usu. white plumage.

swank (swăngk) *also* **swank·y** (swăng'kē) *adj.* **-i·er, -i·est. 1.** Fashionable and elegant. **2.** Ostentatious : showy. *—n.* **swank. 1.** Elegance. **2.** Ostentation : showiness.

swan's-down (swŏnz'doun') *n.* **1.** The soft down of a swan. **2.** A soft woolen or cotton fabric with a thick nap.

swan song *n.* A farewell or final appearance, declaration, work, or act.

swap (swŏp) *v.* **swapped, swap·ping.** *Informal.* To trade 1 thing for another : exchange. **—swap** *n.*

sward (swôrd) *n.* Grass-covered ground.

swarm (swôrm) *n.* **1.** A large number of bees, together with a queen bee, moving together to start a new colony. **2.** A large number of persons or things, esp. when in motion : crowd. *—v.* **1.** To leave a beehive in a swarm. **2.** To gather in large numbers : throng. **3.** To be filled : teem <*swarming* with mosquitoes>

swart (swôrt) *adj.* Swarthy.

swar·thy (swôr'thē) *adj.* **-thi·er, -thi·est.** Of dark color or complexion.

swash (swŏsh, swôsh) *v.* To move with a splashing sound. **—swash** *n.*

swash·buck·ler (swŏsh'bŭk'lər, swôsh'-) *n.* A flamboyant soldier, adventurer, or daredevil. **—swash'buck'ling** *adj.*

swas·ti·ka (swŏs'tĭ-kə) *n.* A symbol consisting of a Greek cross with the ends of the arms bent at right angles.

swat (swŏt) *v.* **swat·ted, swat·ting.** To hit with a sharp blow : slap. **—swat** *n.* **—swat'ter** *n.*

swatch (swŏch) *n.* A sample strip, as of fabric.

swath (swŏth, swôth) *n.* **1.** The width of a stroke of a scythe or mowing-machine blade. **2. a.** A path made in mowing. **b.** The cut grass or grain lying on a swath.

swathe (swŏ*th,* swôth) *v.* **swathed, swath·ing.** To wrap with or as if with bandages : bind.

sway (swā) *v.* **1.** To move or cause to move from side to side or back and forth. **2.** To bend to 1 side : veer. **3.** To vacillate. **4.** To exert control over or influence on. ☆**syns:** TEETER, TOTTER, WAVER, WEAVE, WOBBLE *—n.* **1.** The act of swinging from side to side or back and forth. **2.** Dominion : power. **3.** Influence.

sway·back (swā'băk') *n.* An abnormal sagging of the spine. **—sway'backed'** *adj.*

Swa·zi·land (swä'zē-lănd'). Country of SE Africa. *Cap.* Mbabane. *Pop.* 565,000.

swear (swâr) *v.* **swore** (swôr, swōr), **sworn** (swôrn, swōrn), **swear·ing. 1.** To declare solemnly under oath. **2.** To vow : promise. **3.** To use profanity : curse. **4.** To declare to be true while calling on God or something held sacred. **5.** To administer a legal oath to. **6.** To bind by or as if by means of an oath. **—swear in.** To administer an oath of office to. **—swear'er** *n.*

swear·word (swâr'wûrd') *n.* An obscene or blasphemous word or phrase.

sweat (swĕt) *v.* **sweat·ed** *or* **sweat, sweat·ing. 1.** To excrete or cause to excrete salty liquid through the pores of the skin : perspire. **2.** To condense and accumulate drops of moisture on the surface. **3.** To work hard enough to sweat. **4.** *Informal.* To cause to work too hard : overwork. **5.** *Informal.* To be anxious : worry. *—n.* **1.** Salty liquid excreted by the sweat glands : perspiration. **2.** Moisture that condenses on a surface in the form of drops. **3.** *Informal.* A state of anxiety. **—sweat'y** *adj.*

sweat·er (swĕt'ər) *n.* A knitted or crocheted outer garment for the upper body.

sweat gland *n.* Any of the numerous small, tubular glands of the skin in most mammals that acts to secrete perspiration externally through pores.

sweat shirt *n.* A loose cotton jersey pullover.

sweat·shop (swĕt'shŏp') *n.* A shop or factory in which employees work long hours under bad conditions at low wages.

Swe·den (swēd'n). Country on the Scandinavian Peninsula in N Europe. *Cap.* Stockholm. *Pop.* 8,315,010. **—Swede** *n.* **—Swe'dish** (swē'dĭsh) *adj.* & *n.*

sweep (swēp) *v.* **swept** (swĕpt), **sweep·ing. 1.** To clean or remove with or as if with a brush. **2.** To touch lightly in passing over : brush. **3.** To move, remove, or convey by wind or rain. **4.** To surge or flow over with speed and sustained force <flood waters *sweeping* over the river bank> **5.** To move majestically or gracefully. **6.** To carry away, destroy, or remove by continuous action <*swept* the papers off the desk> *—n.* **1.** The act or motion of sweeping <the *sweep* of oars> **2.** Scope : range. **3.** An extent : reach <a *sweep* of ice> **4.** A surging or flowing force or movement. **5.** A contour : curve. **6.** A chimney sweep. **7.** The winning of all the stages or prizes in a contest. **—sweep'er** *n.*

sweep·ing (swē'pĭng) *adj.* **1.** Extending over a wide area. **2.** Curving. **3.** Thoroughgoing : extensive <*sweeping* changes> *—n.* **sweepings.** Things that are swept up : debris. **—sweep'ing·ly** *adv.*

sweep·stakes (swēp'stāks') *also* **sweep·stake** (-stāk') *n., pl.* **-stakes. 1.** A lottery in which the participants' contributions form a fund to be awarded as a prize to the winner or winners. **2.** An event or contest, as a horse race, whose result determines the winner of a sweepstakes.

sweet (swēt) *adj.* **1. a.** Having a sugary taste. **b.** Pleasing in taste. **2.** Pleasing to the senses or feelings <the *sweet* fragrance of lilacs> <a *sweet* satisfaction> **3.** Agreeable in disposition. **4.** Not salty or salted <*sweet* butter> **5.** Not spoiled, sour, or stale <*sweet* cream> *—n.* **1.** Something that is sweet. **2.** Candy. **3.** A dear or beloved person. **—sweet'ness** *n.*

sweet alyssum *n.* A widely cultivated plant, *Lobularia maritima,* bearing small, fragrant white or purplish flower clusters.

sweet·bread (swēt'brĕd') *n.* The thymus or pancreas of a young animal, as a calf, used for food.

sweet·bri·er *also* **sweet·bri·ar** (swēt'brī'ər) *n.* A European rose, *Rosa eglanteria,* with prickly stems, fragrant leaves, and pink flowers.

sweet corn *n.* An edible variety of corn, *Zea mays rugosa,* with kernels that are sweet when young.

sweet·en (swēt'n) *v.* To make or become sweet or sweeter. **—sweet'en·er** *n.*

sweet·en·ing (swēt'n-ĭng) *n.* Something used to sweeten.

sweet·heart (swēt'härt') *n.* One who is loved : dear.

sweet·meat (swēt'mēt') *n.* **1.** Candy. **2.** Crystallized or candied fruit.

sweet pea *n.* A climbing plant, *Lathyrus odoratus,* grown for its fragrant, variously colored flowers.

sweet pepper *n.* A pepper plant, *Capsicum frutescens grossum,* raised for its edible, bell-shaped, mild-flavored fruit.

sweet potato *n.* A tropical American vine, *Ipomoea batatas,* raised for its orange-colored edible root.

sweet-talk (swēt'tôk') *v.* To coax with flattery : cajole. **—sweet talk** *n.*

sweet tooth *n. Informal.* A fondness or desire for sweets, as pastry.

sweet Wil·liam (wĭl′yəm) *n.* A widely grown plant, *Dianthus barbatus,* with flat, dense varicolored flower clusters.
swell (swĕl) *v.* **swelled, swelled** or **swol·len** (swō′lən), **swell·ing. 1.** To increase in size, volume, force, number, or intensity. **2. a.** To expand excessively or abnormally, as from internal pressure. **b.** To bulge : protrude. **3.** To fill or be filled with an emotion <*swelled* with self-importance> —*n.* **1.** A long ocean wave that moves continuously without breaking. **2.** A gradual increase, as in size or volume. **3.** *Informal.* One who is fashionably dressed or prominent in fashionable society. —*adj.* **1.** *Informal.* Stylish. **2.** Fine : excellent.
swelled head *n.* An unduly high opinion of oneself : conceit.
swell·head (swĕl′hĕd′) *n.* Someone with a swelled head. **—swell′head′ed** *adj.*
swell·ing (swĕl′ĭng) *n.* **1.** The state of being swollen. **2.** Something that is swollen.
swel·ter (swĕl′tər) *v.* To suffer from oppressive heat.
swept (swĕpt) *v. p.t.* & *p.p.* of SWEEP.
swerve (swûrv) *v.* **swerved, swerv·ing.** To turn aside abruptly from a straight or direct course : veer. **—swerve** *n.*
swift (swĭft) *adj.* **1.** Moving or capable of moving with great speed. **2.** Occurring, coming, or accomplished quickly. —*n.* Any of several dark-colored birds of the family Apodidae, with long, slender wings. **—swift′ly** *adv.* **—swift′ness** *n.*
Swift, Jonathan. "Dean Swift." 1667–1745. English satirist.
swig (swĭg) *Informal.* —*n.* A long draft of a liquid : gulp. **—swig** *v.*
swill (swĭl) *n.* **1.** A mixture of edible garbage and liquid fed to animals. **2.** Refuse : garbage. —*v.* **1.** To drink greedily or to excess. **2.** To feed (animals) with swill.
swim (swĭm) *v.* **swam** (swăm), **swum** (swŭm), **swim·ming. 1.** To propel oneself through water by movements of the body or parts of the body. **2.** To move smoothly as though gliding. **3.** To be flooded or covered with or as if with a liquid. **4.** To feel dizzy : reel. **5.** To cross by swimming. —*n.* The act or a period of swimming. **—in the swim.** *Informal.* Participating or involved in the main current of affairs or activities. **—swim′mer** *n.*
swim·ming·ly (swĭm′ĭng-lē) *adv.* With ease and success.
swim·suit (swĭm′so͞ot′) *n.* A garment worn for swimming.
swin·dle (swĭn′dl) *v.* **-dled, -dling.** To cheat out of money or property : defraud. **—swin′dle** *n.* **—swin′dler** *n.*
swine (swīn) *n., pl.* **swine. 1.** A hoofed mammal of the family Suidae, which includes pigs and hogs. **2.** A despicable person. **—swin′ish** *adj.*
swing (swĭng) *v.* **swung** (swŭng), **swing·ing. 1.** To move or cause to move freely back and forth suspended or as if suspended from above. **2.** To walk or move with a free swaying motion. **3.** To move in a broad arc. **4.** To turn or move in place on a pivot or hinge. **5.** *Slang.* To be executed by hanging. **6.** To manage successfully. **7.** To have a compelling rhythm. **8.** *Slang.* To be up-to-date and spirited. —*n.* **1.** The act of swinging. **2.** The distance through which something travels while swinging. **3.** A seat suspended from above on which to swing for amusement. **4.** Music based on jazz but usu. played by a larger band and marked by simpler harmonic and rhythmic patterns. **—swing′er** *n.*
swing shift *n. Informal.* A factory work shift between the day and night shifts that lasts from approx. 4 P.M. to midnight.
swipe (swīp) *n.* A heavy sweeping blow or stroke. —*v.* **swiped, swip·ing. 1.** To strike with or make a swipe. **2.** *Slang.* To filch : steal.
swirl (swûrl) *v.* To move with a rotating motion like that of a whirlpool : spin. **—swirl** *n.* **—swirl′y** *adj.*
swish (swĭsh) *v.* **1.** To make or move with a hissing sound. **2.** To make or move with a rustling sound. **—swish** *n.*
Swiss (swĭs) *n., pl.* **Swiss.** A native or inhabitant of Switzerland. **—Swiss** *adj.*
Swiss chard *n.* Chard.
Swiss cheese *n.* A hard pale-yellow or white cheese with large holes.
Swiss steak *n.* A round or shoulder steak that is pounded with flour and braised.
switch (swĭch) *n.* **1.** A thin flexible rod, stick, whip, or twig. **2.** A blow administered with a switch. **3.** A device for breaking or opening an electric circuit. **4.** A device for transferring a railroad locomotive or car from 1 track to another. **5.** A shift from 1 thing to another. **6.** A thick strand of hair used to supplement one's own hair in a coiffure. —*v.* **1.** To whip with or as if with a switch : lash. **2.** To swish back and forth : whisk. **3.** To change : exchange. **4.** To connect, disconnect, or transfer by operating a switch.
switch·back (swĭch′băk′) *n.* A road, railroad, or trail that ascends a steep incline in a zigzag course.
switch·blade knife (swĭch′blād′) *n.* A pocket knife with a blade operated by a spring.
switch·board (swĭch′bôrd′, -bōrd′) *n.* A panel on which switches for operating and controlling electric circuits are mounted.
switch hitter *n.* A baseball player who can bat with both the right and the left hand.
switch·man (swĭch′mən) *n.* Someone who operates a railroad switch.
Swit·zer·land (swĭt′sər-lənd). Country of C Europe. *Cap.* Bern. *Pop.* 6,314,200.
swiv·el (swĭv′əl) *n.* A coupling device, as a link or pivot, that permits attached parts to rotate freely. —*v.* **-eled, -el·ing** or **-elled, -el·ling.** To rotate or turn on or as if on a swivel.
swiz·zle stick (swĭz′əl) *n.* A rod for stirring mixed drinks.
swol·len (swō′lən) *v. var. p.p.* of SWELL.
swoon (swo͞on) *v.* To faint. **—swoon** *n.*
swoop (swo͞op) *v.* To pounce swiftly and suddenly like a bird descending on its prey. **—swoop** *n.*
sword (sôrd) *n.* **1.** A weapon consisting of a long, pointed cutting or thrusting blade. **2.** A symbol of martial power or authority. **3.** The use of force, as in war.
sword·fish (sôrd′fĭsh′) *n.* A very large marine game and food fish, *Xiphias gladius,* with the upper jaw projecting in a long, swordlike extension.
sword·play (sôrd′plā′) *n.* The act, skill, or art of using a sword.
swords·man (sôrdz′mən) *n.* Someone skilled in the use of the sword. **—swords′man·ship′** *n.*
sword·tail (sôrd′tāl′) *n.* A small, brightly colored freshwater fish, *Xiphophorus helleri,* of Central America.

swordtail

swore (swôr, swōr) *v. p.t.* of SWEAR.
sworn (swôrn, swōrn) *v. p.p.* of SWEAR.
swum (swŭm) *v. p.p.* of SWIM.
swung (swŭng) *v. p.t.* & *p.p.* of SWING.
syb·a·rite (sĭb′ə-rīt′) *n.* Someone who is devoted to pleasure and luxury. **—syb′a·rit′ic** (-rĭt′ĭk) *adj.*
syc·a·more (sĭk′ə-môr′, -mōr′) *n.* **1.** A North American deciduous tree, *Platanus occidentalis,* with lobed leaves and ball-like seed clusters. **2.** An Old World tree, *Acer pseudoplatanus,* that resembles and is related to the maples.
syc·o·phant (sĭk′ə-fənt, -fănt′) *n.* An obsequious flatterer. **—syc′o·phan·cy** *n.* **—syc′o·phan′tic** (-făn′tĭk) *adj.*
Syd·ney (sĭd′nē). City of SE Australia. *Metro. pop.* 3,193,300.
sy·li (sē′lē) *n.* See CURRENCY TABLE.
syl·la·bar·y (sĭl′ə-bĕr′ē) *n., pl.* **-ies.** A list of syllables, esp. a list or set of written characters, each representing a syllable.
syl·lab·i·cate (sə-lăb′ĭ-kāt′) *v.* **-cat·ed, -cat·ing.** To divide or form into syllables. **—syl·lab′i·ca′tion** *n.*
syl·lab·i·fy (sə-lăb′ə-fī′) *v.* **-fied, -fy·ing.** To syllabicate. **—syl·lab′i·fi·ca′tion** *n.*
syl·la·ble (sĭl′ə-bəl) *n.* **1.** A unit of spoken language that consists of a single uninterrupted sound and forms a whole word, as *cat,* or a division of a word, as *dif-* in *difficult.* **2.** One or more letters or phonetic symbols representing a syllable. **—syl·lab′ic** (sə-lăb′ĭk) *adj.*
syl·la·bus (sĭl′ə-bəs) *n., pl.* **-bus·es** or **-bi** (-bī′). A brief outline of the main points of a book, lecture, or course of study.
syl·lo·gism (sĭl′ə-jĭz′əm) *n.* A formal argument consisting of a major premise and a minor premise and a conclusion that is logically derived from the premises. **—syl′lo·gis′tic** *adj.*
sylph (sĭlf) *n.* **1.** An imaginary being believed to inhabit the air. **2.** A gracefully slim woman.
syl·van (sĭl′vən) *adj.* **1.** Of, relating to, living in, or typical of forest regions. **2.** Abounding in trees : wooded.
sym. *abbr.* **1.** symbol. **2.** symphony.
sym·bi·o·sis (sĭm′bē-ō′sĭs, -bī-) *n. Biol.* The living together in close association of 2 unlike organisms, esp. when mutually advantageous. **—sym′bi·ot′ic** (-ŏt′ĭk) *adj.*
sym·bol (sĭm′bəl) *n.* **1.** Something that represents or stands for something else, as by resemblance or association. **2.** A written or printed character or sign representing an element, operation,

quantity, quality, or relation, as in mathematics, chemistry, or music. **–sym·bol'ic** (-bŏl'ĭk), **sym·bol'i·cal** *adj.* **–sym·bol'i·cal·ly** *adv.*

sym·bol·ism (sĭm'bə-lĭz'əm) *n.* The use of symbols to represent invisible, intangible, or abstract things.

sym·bol·ize (sĭm'bə-līz') *v.* **-ized, -iz·ing. 1.** To serve as or be a symbol of : stand for. **2.** To represent by a symbol. **–sym'bol·i·za'tion** *n.*

sym·me·try (sĭm'ĭ-trē) *n., pl.* **-tries. 1.** Correspondence in form, size, and arrangement of parts on opposite sides of a boundary, as a dividing line or around an axis. **2.** An arrangement characterized by balance and harmonious proportions. **–sym·met'ric** (sĭ-mĕt'rĭk), **sym·met'ri·cal** *adj.* **–sym·met'ri·cal·ly** *adv.*

sym·pa·thet·ic (sĭm'pə-thĕt'ĭk) *adj.* **1.** Of, marked by, feeling, or resulting from sympathy. **2.** Favorably disposed : approving. **–sym'pa·thet'i·cal·ly** *adv.*

sympathetic nervous system *n.* The part of the autonomic nervous system that tends to depress secretion, decrease smooth-muscle tone and contractility, and cause vascular contraction.

sym·pa·thize (sĭm'pə-thīz') *v.* **-thized, -thiz·ing. 1.** To express or feel sympathy. **2.** To share another's feelings. **–sym'pa·thiz'er** *n.*

sym·pa·thy (sĭm'pə-thē) *n., pl.* **-thies. 1. a.** A relationship between individuals in which whatever affects one affects the other in a similar way. **b.** Mutual affection or understanding. **2. a.** The capacity to share another's feelings. **b.** A feeling or expression of sorrow for another's distress or loss. **c.** Pity : compassion. **3.** Favor : accord.

sym·pho·ny (sĭm'fə-nē) *n., pl.* **-nies. 1.** A large and elaborate sonata for orchestra. **2.** A large orchestra with string, wind, and percussion sections. **3.** Harmony, esp. of sound. **–sym·phon'ic** (-fŏn'ĭk) *adj.*

sym·po·si·um (sĭm-pō'zē-əm) *n., pl.* **-si·ums** or **-si·a** (-zē-ə). **1.** A meeting at which a particular topic is discussed by several participants. **2.** A collection of written opinions on a particular topic.

symp·tom (sĭmp'təm) *n.* **1.** A change in bodily sensation, function, or appearance that indicates disorder, abnormality, or disease. **2.** A sign : indication. **–symp'to·mat'ic** (-tə-măt'ĭk) *adj.*

syn. *abbr.* synonymous; synonym; synonymy.

syn·a·gogue *also* **syn·a·gog** (sĭn'ə-gŏg') *n.* **1.** A meeting place for Jewish worship and religious instruction. **2.** A Jewish congregation.

syn·apse (sĭn'ăps') *n.* The point at which a nerve impulse is transmitted from an axon of 1 neuron to the dendrite of another.

sync *also* **synch** (sĭngk) *Informal.* *–n.* Synchronization. *–v.* To synchronize.

syn·chro·nize (sĭng'krə-nīz', sĭn'-) *v.* **-nized, -niz·ing. 1.** To take place or cause to take place at the same moment. **2.** To operate or cause to operate in unison. **3.** To cause to agree precisely in rate or time. **4.** To represent or arrange to indicate coexistence or parallel occurrence. **–syn'chro·ni·za'tion** *n.* **–syn'chro·niz'er** *n.*

syn·chro·nous (sĭng'krə-nəs, sĭn'-) *adj.* **1.** Taking place or existing at the same time. **2.** Moving or operating together at the same rate. **–syn'chro·nous·ly** *adv.*

syn·co·pate (sĭng'kə-pāt', sĭn'-) *v.* **-pat·ed, -pat·ing.** To shift a regular musical accent to a beat that is normally weak. **–syn'co·pa'tion** *n.*

syn·co·pe (sĭng'kə-pē, sĭn'-) *n.* **1.** The shortening of a word by dropping a sound, letter, or syllable from the middle, as in *bo's'n* for *boatswain.* **2.** *Pathol.* A brief loss of consciousness : swoon.

syn·di·cate (sĭn'dĭ-kĭt) *n.* **1.** A group of people who form an association to undertake a project or carry out a business transaction. **2.** An agency that sells materials for simultaneous publication in a number of periodicals or newspapers. *–v.* (-kāt') **-cat·ed, -cat·ing. 1.** To manage as or organize into a syndicate. **2.** To publish through a syndicate. **–syn'di·ca'tion** *n.*

syn·drome (sĭn'drōm') *n.* A set of symptoms that together characterize a disease or disorder.

syn·er·gism (sĭn'ər-jĭz'əm) *also* **syn·er·gy** (-ər-jē) *n.* The combined action of 2 or more substances or agencies to achieve an effect greater than that of which each is individually capable. **–syn·er'gic** (sĭ-nûr'jĭk) *adj.* **–syn'er·gist** *n.* **–syn'er·gis'tic** *adj.* **–syn'er·gis'ti·cal·ly** *adv.*

syn·od (sĭn'əd) *n.* A council or assembly, esp. of churches or church officials. **–syn'od·al** (sĭn'ə-dl), **sy·nod'i·cal** (sĭ-nŏd'ĭ-kəl), **sy·nod'ic** (-ĭk) *adj.*

syn·o·nym (sĭn'ə-nĭm') *n.* A word whose meaning is identical or almost identical to that of another word in the same language. **–syn·on'y·mous** (sĭ-nŏn'ə-məs) *adj.* **–syn·on'y·my** *n.*

syn·op·sis (sĭ-nŏp'sĭs) *n., pl.* **-ses** (-sēz'). A shortened statement or outline, as of a narrative : abstract.

syn·tax (sĭn'tăks') *n.* The way in which words are put together to form sentences, clauses, and phrases. **–syn·tac'tic** (-tăk'tĭk), **syn·tac'ti·cal** *adj.*

syn·the·sis (sĭn'thĭ-sĭs) *n., pl.* **-ses** (-sēz'). The combination of elements, parts, or substances into a whole. **–syn'the·size'** *v.*

syn·the·siz·er (sĭn'thĭ-sī'zər) *n.* An electronic device that duplicates the sounds of musical instruments.

syn·thet·ic (sĭn-thĕt'ĭk) *adj.* **1.** Of, relating to, or involving synthesis. **2. a.** Not genuine. **b.** Manmade. **–syn·thet'ic** *n.* **–syn·thet'i·cal·ly** *adv.*

syph·i·lis (sĭf'ə-lĭs) *n.* A chronic infectious venereal disease caused by a spirochete. **–syph'i·lit'ic** (-lĭt'ĭk) *adj.* & *n.*

sy·phon (sī'fən) *n.* & *v.* *var. of* SIPHON.

Syr·i·a (sîr'ē-ə). Country of SW Asia, on the E Mediterranean. *Cap.* Damascus. *Pop.* 8,401,000. **–Syr'i·an** *adj.* & *n.*

sy·ringe (sə-rĭnj', sîr'ĭnj) *n.* **1.** A medical instrument for injecting fluids into or drawing them from the body. **2.** A hypodermic syringe. **–syr·inge'** *v.*

syr·up *also* **sir·up** (sĭr'əp, sûr'-) *n.* A thick, sweet liquid, esp. that made by boiling sugar and water. **–syr'up·y** *adj.*

sys·tem (sĭs'təm) *n.* **1.** A group of elements that interact and function together as a whole. **2. a.** The human body as a functional unit. **b.** A group of bodily organs that together perform a vital function <the vascular *system*> **3.** A procedure : method. **4.** An orderly pattern or arrangement. **–sys'tem·at'ic** (-tə-măt'ĭk) *adj.* **–sys'tem·at'i·cal·ly** *adv.*

sys·tem·a·tize (sĭs'tə-mə-tīz') *v.* **-tized, -tiz·ing.** To form into or reduce to a system. **–sys'tem·a·ti·za'tion** *n.*

sys·tem·ic (sĭ-stĕm'ĭk) *adj.* Of, pertaining to, or affecting the whole body.

sys·tem·ize (sĭs'tə-mīz') *v.* **-ized, -iz·ing.** To systematize.

systems analysis *n.* The use of mathematical means to study an activity, determine its desired goal, and formulate the most efficient means of attaining it. **–systems analyst** *n.*

sys·to·le (sĭs'tə-lē) *n.* The rhythmic contraction of the heart by means of which blood is driven through the aorta and pulmonary artery. **–sys·tol'ic** (sĭ-stŏl'ĭk) *adj.*

Tt

t or **T** (tē) *n., pl.* **t's** *or* **T's. 1.** The 20th letter of the English alphabet. **2.** A speech sound represented by the letter *t.* **3.** Something with the shape of the letter T. **–to a T.** Perfectly <The job suits me *to a T.*>

t *abbr.* **1.** or **t.** teaspoon; teaspoonful. **2.** ton. **3.** troy.

T *abbr.* **1.** temperature. **2.** or **T.** tablespoon; tablespoonful.

t. *abbr.* **1.** tense (in grammar). **2.** or **T.** territory. **3.** or **T.** time. **4.** or **T.** transit. **5.** transitive (in grammar).

T. *abbr.* Testament.

Ta *symbol for* TANTALUM.

tab (tăb) *n.* **1.** A small projecting loop, tag, etc., to help in opening, handling, or identifying something. **2.** *Informal.* An amount paid or owed, as for a meal. **–keep tabs on.** To keep close watch on.

Ta·bas·co (tə-băs'kō). A trademark for a spicy sauce made from red peppers.

tab·by (tăb'ē) *n., pl.* **-bies. 1.** A domestic cat with darkish striped or mottled fur. **2.** A female cat.

tab·er·na·cle (tăb'ər-năk'əl) *n.* **1.** *often* **Tabernacle.** The temporary sanctuary carried by the Hebrews during the Exodus. **2.** A container on an altar for the consecrated Eucharist. **3.** A temple.

ta•ble (tā'bəl) *n.* **1.** A flat-topped piece of furniture supported by legs. **2.** An orderly arrangement of data. **3.** A brief outline or listing. **4.** A flat usu. inscribed tablet. *—v.* **-bled, -bling. 1.** To place on a table. **2.** To list or record in a table. **3.** To postpone, as legislation.
tab•leau (tăb'lō', tă-blō') *n., pl.* **-leaux** (-lōz', -blōz') or **-leaus. 1.** A vivid depiction. **2.** A stage scene in which costumed actors neither speak nor move.
ta•ble•cloth (tā'bəl-klôth', -klŏth') *n.* A cloth to cover a dining table.
ta•ble d'hôte (tä'bəl dōt') *n., pl.* **ta•bles d'hôte** (tä'bəl dōt'). A full-course restaurant meal offered at a fixed price.
ta•ble•land (tā'bəl-lănd') *n.* A flat elevated region : plateau.
ta•ble•spoon (tā'bəl-spo͞on') *n.* **1.** A large serving spoon. **2.** See MEASUREMENT TABLE. **—ta'ble•spoon'ful'** *n.*
tab•let (tăb'lĭt) *n.* **1.** A flat piece of stone, ivory, etc., fit for or bearing an inscription. **2.** A pad consisting of sheets of writing paper glued at one edge. **3.** Oral medication in the form of a small flat pellet.
table tennis *n.* A game resembling tennis that is played on a table with light wooden paddles and a small plastic ball.
ta•ble•ware (tā'bəl-wâr') *n.* The dishes, glassware, and silverware used in setting a dining table.
tab•loid (tăb'loid') *n.* A small-format illustrated newspaper with short, often sensational news items.
ta•boo *also* **ta•bu** (tə-bo͞o', tă-) *—n., pl.* **-boos** *also* **-bus. 1.** A prohibition against doing, using, or mentioning something because of association with powerful supernatural forces. **2.** A cultural prohibition against some word or act. *—adj.* **1.** Set apart as inviolable. **2.** Banned for social or moral reasons. **—ta•boo'** *v.*
tab•u•lar (tăb'yə-lər) *adj.* **1.** Arranged in a table or list. **2.** Calculated by means of a table. **—tab'u•lar•ly** *adv.*
tab•u•late (tăb'yə-lāt') *v.* **-lat•ed, -lat•ing.** To condense and list, as in a table. **—tab'u•la'tion** *n.* **—tab'u•la'tor** *n.*
ta•chom•e•ter (tə-kŏm'ĭ-tər) *n.* An instrument for determining speed, as of a rotating shaft. **—tach'o•met'ric** (tăk'ə-mĕt'rĭk) *adj.* **—ta•chom'e•try** *n.*
tach•y•car•di•a (tăk'ĭ-kär'dē-ə) *n.* Excessively rapid heartbeat.
tac•it (tăs'ĭt) *adj.* **1.** Expressed nonverbally : unspoken. **2.** Expressed indirectly : implied. **—tac'it•ly** *adv.* **—tac'it•ness** *n.*
tac•i•turn (tăs'ĭ-tûrn') *adj.* Uncommunicative. **—tac'i•tur'ni•ty** (-tûr'nĭ-tē) *n.*
Tac•i•tus (tăs'ĭ-təs), **Publius Cornelius.** A.D. 55?–118? Roman historian and orator.
tack (tăk) *n.* **1.** A small flat-headed nail with a sharp point. **2. a.** The direction of a ship with respect to the trim of its sails. **b.** The act of changing from 1 direction to another. **3.** An approach or course of action. **4.** An alternating course. **5.** A loose, temporary sewing stitch. *—v.* **1.** To secure or attach with a tack. **2.** To append as an extra item. **3.** To change a ship's course. **4.** To sew with loose stitches. **—tack'er** *n.*
tack•le (tăk'əl) *n.* **1.** Equipment or gear for an occupation or sport, esp. fishing. **2.** (*also* tā'kəl). A system of ropes and pulley blocks for hoisting and pulling weights esp. on a ship. **3.** *Football.* **a.** A lineman positioned between guard and end. **b.** The act of stopping an opposing player by seizing and bringing him down. *—v.* **-led, -ling. 1.** To take on : deal with (e.g., a problem). **2.** *Football.* To seize and bring down (an opposing player). **—tack'ler** *n.*
tack•y¹ (tăk'ē) *adj.* **-i•er, -i•est.** Somewhat sticky, as a newly painted surface. **—tack'i•ness** *n.*
tack•y² (tăk'ē) *adj.* **-i•er, -i•est.** *Informal.* **1.** Shabby. **2. a.** Not stylish <*tacky* clothes> **b.** Vulgar : tasteless <*tacky* jokes> **—tack'i•ly** *adv.* **—tack'i•ness** *n.*
ta•co (tä'kō) *n., pl.* **-cos.** A folded tortilla filled with ground meat, cheese, beans, etc.
tac•o•nite (tăk'ə-nīt') *n.* A fine-grained rock containing hematite and mined as a low-grade iron ore.
tact (tăkt) *n.* The ability to do or say the right thing at the right time : diplomacy. **—tact'ful** *adj.* **—tact'less** *adj.*
tac•tic (tăk'tĭk) *n.* **1.** An expedient for achieving an end. **2. tactics** *(sing. in number).* **a.** The science of using strategy to gain military objectives. **b.** Skillful maneuvering to achieve a goal. **—tac'ti•cal** *adj.* **—tac•ti'cian** *n.*
tac•tile (tak'təl, -tīl') *adj.* **1.** Of, perceptible to, or issuing from the sense of touch. **2.** Used for feeling <a *tactile* organ> **—tac•til'i•ty** (-tĭl'ĭ-tē) *n.*
tad (tăd) *n. Informal.* **1.** A small boy. **2.** A small amount or degree.
tad•pole (tăd'pōl') *n.* A frog or toad larva, with a tail and external gills.
taf•fe•ta (tăf'ĭ-tə) *n.* A crisp, glossy fabric esp. of silk, rayon, or nylon.
taf•fy (tăf'ē) *n., pl.* **-fies.** A chewy candy made of molasses or brown sugar.
Taft (tăft), **William Howard.** 1857–1930. 27th U.S. President (1909–13).
tag¹ (tăg) *n.* **1.** A piece of paper, plastic, metal, etc., attached or hung in order to identify, classify, or label. **2.** A hard tip on a shoelace. **3.** A descriptive term or epithet. **4.** A cliché *—v.* **tagged, tag•ging. 1.** To use a tag for labeling or identifying. **2.** To follow along after. **—tag'ger** *n.*
tag² (tăg) *n.* **1.** A children's game in which a player runs after the others and attempts to touch 1 of them. **2.** *Baseball.* The act of making an out by touching a runner with the ball. *—v.* **tagged, tag•ging. 1.** To touch in or as if in a game of tag. **2.** *Baseball.* To touch (a runner) with the ball in order to make an out. **—tag'ger** *n.*
Ta•hi•ti (tə-hē'tē). An island of French Polynesia. **—Ta•hi'tian** *adj.* & *n.*
tai•ga (tī'gə) *n.* The far N forest regions of Siberia, Eurasia, and North America.
tail (tāl) *n.* **1. a.** The hindmost part or an extension beyond the main part of an animal's body. **b.** The hindmost, rear, or lower part of something. **2.** Something that looks, hangs, or trails like an animal's tail. **3. tails.** The reverse side of a coin <Heads I win, *tails* you win.> **4. tails.** Formal evening attire for men. **5.** One who follows or keeps close watch on another. *—v.* To follow <The detective *tailed* the suspect.>
tail•gate (tāl'gāt') *n.* A hinged section at the rear of a truck, wagon, etc. for loading and unloading. *—v.* **-gat•ed, -gat•ing.** To follow too closely behind (another vehicle).
tail•light (tāl'līt') *n.* A warning light at the rear of a vehicle.
tai•lor (tā'lər) *n.* One who makes, mends, and alters clothing. *—v.* **1.** To fashion (a garment). **2.** To make or adapt for a specific purpose.
tai•lor-made (tā'lər-mād') *adj.* **1.** Made to order. **2.** Perfectly suited.
tail pipe *n.* The pipe through which exhaust gases from an engine are discharged.
tail•spin (tāl'spĭn') *n.* **1.** The nose-down spiraling descent of an aircraft. **2.** An abrupt decline. **3.** An emotional collapse.
tail wind *n.* A wind blowing in the same direction as that in which an aircraft, ship, etc. is traveling.
taint (tānt) *v.* **1.** To affect with something objectionable. **2.** To make rotten : spoil. **3.** To corrupt morally. *—n.* **1.** A moral blemish or defect. **2.** A corrupting influence.
Tai•pei (tī'pā'). Cap. of Taiwan, in the N. *Pop.* 2,196,237.
Tai•wan (tī'wän'). Island off the SE coast of China, constituting the Republic of China. *Cap.* Taipei. *Pop.* 18,055,000. **—Tai'wan•ese'** *adj.* & *n.*
ta•ka (tä'kə) *n.* See CURRENCY TABLE.
take (tāk) *v.* **took** (to͝ok), **tak•en** (tā'kən), **tak•ing. 1.** To get possession of. **2.** To grip and hold with the hands. **3.** To carry or cause to go with one to a different place. **4.** To convey or conduct to a different place. **5.** To remove from an occupied position. **6.** To please greatly : charm. **7.** To put into one's body, as air, food, medicine, etc. **8. a.** To assume for oneself. **b.** To commit oneself to : undertake. **9.** To govern grammatically <A transitive verb *takes* a direct object.> **10.** To select : choose. **11.** To use for conveying or traveling. **12.** To make use of : occupy. **13.** To require or need. **14.** To measure or observe in order to determine <*take* a reading> **15.** To record by writing. **16.** To make by a photographic process. **17.** To accept or receive, as money, counsel, etc. **18.** To undergo or endure (e.g., criticism). **19.** To follow or pursue (e.g., a lead). **20.** To engage in : do. **21.** To let in : admit <The cellar *took* water.> **22.** To react to in a given way <*took* us seriously> **23.** To deduct : subtract. **24.** To study <*take* chemistry> **25.** To be effective : work. **26.** To come to be <*took* ill> **27.** To swindle : cheat. **—take after.** To look or act like : resemble. **—take back.** To retract or deny (e.g., a statement). **—take in. 1.** To look at : view. **2.** To include : contain. **3.** To fathom : understand. **4.** To deceive : swindle. **—take off. 1.** To remove. **2.** To leave the ground, as an aircraft. **3.** *Informal.* To go away : depart. **—take on. 1.** To hire. **2.** To compete against. **—take over.** To gain control or management (of). *—n.* **1. a.** The act or process of acquiring. **b.** The quantity acquired, esp. at one time. **2.** The total admission receipts to an event. **3.** The nonstop running of filming or recording equipment. **—tak'er** *n.*
take•off (tāk'ôf', -ŏf') *n.* **1.** The act or process of rising up in flight. **2.** *Informal.* An amusing imitation of someone.
take-out (tāk'out') *n.* Something, as food, that is consumed away from the premises. **—take'-out'** *adj.*
take•o•ver *also* **take-o•ver** (tāk'ō'vər) *n.* The act or process of taking control or management of or responsibility for.
tak•ing (tā'kĭng) *n.* **1.** The act or process of possessing. **2. takings.** Something received, esp. money.

ta·la (tä′lə) *n.* See CURRENCY TABLE.

talc (tălk) *n.* A soft, fine-grained, soapy-textured mineral used esp. in making talcum powder.

tal·cum powder (tăl′kəm) *n.* A fine body powder made from purified talc.

tale (tāl) *n.* **1.** A recital of events <a *tale* of woe> **2.** A usu. fictitious narrative. **3.** A false or malicious story.

tal·ent (tăl′ənt) *n.* **1.** A mental or physical ability : aptitude. **2. a.** Superior natural ability : genius. **b.** A person or people with such ability. **3.** Any of various ancient coins or weights. **–tal′ent·ed** *adj.*

tal·is·man (tăl′ĭs-mən, -ĭz-) *n.* An object held to have magical or protective powers : charm. **–tal′is·man′ic** (-măn′ĭk) *adj.*

talk (tôk) *v.* **1.** To utter words. **2. a.** To communicate by speech. **b.** To discuss <*talk* politics> **3.** To use (a language) in communicating. **4.** To engage in gossip or idle chatter. **5.** To negotiate. **6.** To consult or confer <*talked* with the lawyer> **7.** To influence : persuade. **–talk back.** To make a rude reply. **–talk down.** To speak condescendingly. **–talk over.** To discuss esp. in depth. *–n.* **1.** The act of conversing. **2.** A way of speaking. **3.** An informal address. **4.** Hearsay : rumor. **5.** A subject or topic of conversation. **6.** A conference or negotiation. **–talk′er** *n.*

talk·a·tive (tô′kə-tĭv) *adj.* Tending to talk excessively. **–talk′a·tive·ness** *n.*

talk·ing-to (tô′kĭng-to͞o′) *n., pl.* **-tos.** *Informal.* A reprimand : scolding.

tall (tôl) *adj.* **1.** Of greater than average height. **2.** Of a designated height. **3.** Imaginary : fanciful <a *tall* tale> **4.** Unusually big, long, or difficult. ☆***syns:*** HIGH, LOFTY, TOWERING. *–adv.* Straight, as in pride <walk *tall*> **–tall′ness** *n.*

Tal·la·has·see (tăl′ə-hăs′ē). Cap. of Fla., in the NW. *Pop.* 81,548.

tal·low (tăl′ō) *n.* Hard fat rendered esp. from cattle or sheep and used in candles, soaps, and lubricants. **–tal′low·y** *adj.*

tal·ly (tăl′ē) *n., pl.* **-lies. 1.** A stick that is notched in keeping count. **2.** A reckoning or score. *–v.* **-lied, -ly·ing. 1.** To count, reckon, or score. **2.** To match.

tal·ly·ho (tăl′ē-hō′) *interj.* Used in fox hunting when the fox is sighted.

Tal·mud (täl′mo͝od′, tăl′məd) *n.* The early authoritative religious writings that form the basis of orthodox Judaism. **–Tal·mu′dic, Tal·mu′di·cal** *adj.*

tal·on (tăl′ən) *n.* The claw of a bird or animal that seizes other animals as prey.

ta·ma·le (tə-mä′lē) *n.* Chopped meat, chili, and seasonings wrapped in cornhusks and steamed.

tam·a·rack (tăm′ə-răk′) *n.* A North American larch tree, esp. *Larix laricina,* with short deciduous needles.

tam·a·rind (tăm′ə-rĭnd′) *n.* A tropical tree, *Tamarindus indica,* with red-striped yellow flowers and pulpy fruit.

tam·a·risk (tăm′ə-rĭsk′) *n.* A native Eurasian shrub or small tree of the genus *Tamarix,* with pink flower clusters.

tam·ba·la (täm-bä′lə) *n.* See *kwacha* at CURRENCY TABLE.

tam·bou·rine (tăm′bə-rēn′) *n.* A percussion instrument consisting of a small drumhead with jingling disks in the rim.

tame (tām) *adj.* **tam·er, tam·est. 1.** Brought from a wild to a manageable or domesticated state. **2. a.** Naturally gentle. **b.** Docile or submissive. **3.** Dull. **–tame** *v.* **–tame′ly** *adv.* **–tam′er** *n.*

tam-o′-shan·ter (tăm′ə-shăn′tər) *n.* A Scottish cap with a flat, circular top.

tamp (tămp) *v.* To pack down tightly by repeated light blows.

Tam·pa (tăm′pə). City of WC Fla. *Pop.* 271,523.

tam·per (tăm′pər) *v.* **1.** To handle something idly, ignorantly, or injuriously. **2.** To make clandestine or illicit arrangements <*tamper* with a contract> ☆***syns:*** FOOL, MEDDLE, MESS, MONKEY, TINKER

tam·pon (tăm′pŏn′) *n.* An absorbent plug inserted into a wound or bodily cavity.

tan (tăn) *v.* **tanned, tan·ning. 1.** To make (hide) into leather, esp. by exposure to tannin. **2.** To make or become brown by exposure to sunlight. **3.** *Informal.* To spank hard. *–n.* **1.** A light yellowish brown. **2.** The brownish color of skin exposed to sunlight. **–tan** *adj.*

tan·a·ger (tăn′ə-jər) *n.* A New World bird of the family Thraupidae, often with brightly colored plumage in the male.

tan·bark (tăn′bärk′) *n.* The bark of certain trees, used as a source of tannin.

tan·dem (tăn′dəm) *n.* **1.** A bicycle for 2 or more persons. **2.** An arrangement of 2 or more persons, animals, or things placed 1 behind the other. **3.** A 2-wheeled carriage drawn by horses harnessed in tandem. **–tan′dem** *adj. & adv.*

tang (tăng) *n.* **1.** A distinctively pungent taste or smell. **2.** A projecting part that joins a tool to its handle. **–tang′y** *adj.*

tan·gent (tăn′jənt) *adj.* Touching at a single point or along a line but not intersecting. *–n.* **1.** A line, curve, or surface that is tangent with another. **2.** A sudden change of course : digression. **–tan′gen·cy** (-jən-sē) *n.* **–tan·gen′tial** *adj.*

tan·ger·ine (tăn′jə-rēn′) *n.* A widely cultivated citrus tree, *Citrus nobilis deliciosa,* bearing easily peeled deep-orange fruit.

tan·gi·ble (tăn′jə-bəl) *adj.* **1.** Discernible by touch. **2.** Existing in reality : concrete. *–n.* **1.** Something tangible. **2. tangibles.** Appraisable assets. **–tan′gi·bil′i·ty, tan′gi·ble·ness** *n.* **–tan′gi·bly** *adv.*

tan·gle (tăng′gəl) *v.* **-gled, -gling. 1.** To mix together in a confused mass : snarl. **2.** To be or become complicated or confused : entangle. **3.** *Informal.* To wrestle. *–n.* **1.** An intertwined mass. **2.** A confused or muddled condition. **–tang′ler** *n.*

tan·go (tăng′gō) *n., pl.* **-gos.** A Latin-American ballroom dance marked by long gliding steps. **–tan′go** *v.*

tank (tăngk) *n.* **1.** A large receptacle for fluids or gases. **2.** An enclosed, heavily armored and armed military vehicle that moves on caterpillar treads.

tan·kard (tăng′kərd) *n.* A large drinking cup with a handle and a hinged lid.

tank·er (tăng′kər) *n.* A ship, truck, or plane equipped with tanks for transporting large amounts of liquid, as oil.

tan·ner (tăn′ər) *n.* One who tans hides.

tan·ner·y (tăn′ə-rē) *n., pl.* **-ies.** A place where hides are tanned for leather.

tan·nic acid (tăn′ĭk) *n.* An astringent substance obtained from certain fruits and bark and used esp. in tanning.

tan·nin (tăn′ĭn) *n.* **1.** Tannic acid. **2.** A substance used in tanning hides.

tan·ta·lize (tăn′tl-īz′) *v.* **-lized, -liz·ing.** To tease or harass by showing but keeping out of reach something highly desirable. ☆***syns:*** BAIT, TEASE, TORMENT **–tan′ta·li·za′tion** *n.* **–tan′ta·liz′er** *n.* **–tan′ta·liz′ing·ly** *adv.*

tan·ta·lum (tăn′til-əm) *n. Symbol* **Ta** A very hard corrosion-resistant ductile metallic element.

tan·ta·mount (tăn′tə-mount′) *adj.* Identical in effect or value.

tan·trum (tăn′trəm) *n.* An outburst of anger, rage, etc.

Tan·za·ni·a (tăn′zə-nē′ə, tăn-zā′nē-ə). Country of E Africa. *Cap.* Dar es Salaam. *Pop.* 18,785,000. **–Tan′za·ni′an** *adj. & n.*

Tao·ism (tou′ĭz′əm, dou′-) *n.* A Chinese philosophy and religion influenced by Buddhism and emphasizing simplicity. **–Tao′ist** *n.* **–Tao·is′tic** *adj.*

tap¹ (tăp) *v.* **tapped, tap·ping. 1.** To strike lightly or repeatedly. **2.** To repair or reinforce (shoe heels or toes) by putting on a tap. **3.** To choose, as for membership. *–n.* **1.** A slight, audible blow. **2.** A layer of material or a metal plate applied to the toe or heel of a shoe.

tap² (tăp) *n.* **1.** A valve and spout for regulating fluid flow : faucet or spigot. **2.** An alcoholic beverage drawn from a tap. **3.** A tool to cut threads in an internal screw. **4.** A point at which a connection is made in an electric circuit. **5.** *Med.* Removal of bodily fluid <a spinal *tap*> *–v.* **tapped, tap·ping. 1.** To provide with a spigot or tap. **2.** To make a hole in for drawing off liquid. **3.** To draw (liquid) from a container. **4.** To connect a local outlet with (a main gas or water pipe). **5. a.** To monitor by a wiretap. **b.** To make a connection in (an electric power line). **6.** To cut screw threads in (a collar or socket). **7.** To make use of : draw from.

tap dance *n.* A dance in which the clicking heels and toes of the dancer's shoes sound out the rhythm. **–tap′-dance′** *v.* **–tap dancer** *n.*

tape (tāp) *n.* **1.** A strong, narrow strip of woven fabric. **2.** A long, narrow, flexible strip, as of paper or metal. **3.** Magnetized recording tape. **4.** A string stretched across the finish line of a race. *–v.* **taped, tap·ing. 1.** To fasten, wrap, or support with tape. **2.** To measure with a measuring tape. **3.** To make a tape recording (of).

tape deck *n.* A tape recorder and player having no built-in amplifiers or speakers, used as a component in a high-fidelity sound system.

tape measure *n.* A device for linear measuring, consisting of a tape marked off in a scale.

ta·per (tā′pər) *n.* **1.** A slender candle or long, wax-coated wick. **2.** A gradual lessening in thickness or width. *–v.* **1.** To make or become gradually thinner toward 1 end. **2.** To slacken off.

tape recorder *n.* An instrument capable of recording and usu. playing back sound on magnetic tape. **–tape′-re·cord** *v.* **–tape recording** *n.*

tap·es·try (tăp′ĭ-strē) *n., pl.* **-tries.** A rich, heavy cloth woven with multicolored pictorial designs, used esp. as a wall hanging. **–tap′es·tried** *adj.*

tape·worm (tāp′wûrm′) *n.* A long ribbonlike parasitical worm of the class Cestoda that lives in vertebrate intestines.

tap·i·o·ca (tăp'ē-ō'kə) *n.* A beadlike cassava starch used esp. for puddings.

ta·pir (tā'pər, tə-pîr') *n.* A tropical American or Asian mammal of the genus *Tapirus,* with a heavy body, short legs, and a long, fleshy snout.

tap·room (tăp'ro͞om', -ro͝om') *n.* A bar or barroom.

tap·root (tăp'ro͞ot', -ro͝ot') *n.* The usu. large main root of a plant, growing straight downward from the stem and sending out smaller side roots.

taps (tăps) *pl.n. (sing. in number).* A bugle call sounded at night to signal lights out or a similar one at funerals and memorial services.

tar[1] (tär) *n.* A thick, dark, oily substance distilled esp. from wood, coal, or peat. —*v.* **tarred, tar·ring.** To cover or treat with tar. **—tar'ry** *adj.*

tar[2] (tär) *n. Informal.* A sailor.

tar·an·tel·la (tăr'ən-tĕl'ə) *n.* A spirited, whirling dance of S Italy.

ta·ran·tu·la (tə-răn'chə-lə) *n., pl.* **-las** or **-lae** (-lē'). Any of various large, hairy, chiefly tropical spiders of the family Theraphosidae that can inflict a painful bite.

tar·dy (tär'dē) *adj.* **-di·er, -di·est. 1.a.** Later than expected. **b.** Tending to delay. **2.** Moving slowly : sluggish. **—tar'di·ly** *adv.* **—tar'di·ness** *n.*

tare[1] (târ) *n.* A weed growing esp. in grain fields.

tare[2] (târ) *n.* The weight of a container or wrapper, subtracted from the gross weight to obtain the net weight.

tar·get (tär'gĭt) *n.* **1. a.** A marked surface to shoot at. **b.** Something aimed or shot at. **2.** An object of attack or criticism. **3.** A desired goal. —*v.* To make into a target.

tar·iff (tăr'ĭf) *n.* **1. a.** A list or system of taxes governmentally imposed on imported or exported goods. **b.** A tax of this kind. **2.** A scale of rates or charges.

tar·nish (tär'nĭsh) *v.* **1.** To lose or cause to lose luster. **2.** To spoil or taint. **—tar'nish** *n.* **—tar'nish·a·ble** *adj.*

ta·ro (tär'ō, tăr'ō) *n., pl.* **-ros.** A widely cultivated tropical plant, *Colocasia esculenta,* with broad leaves and a large, starchy, edible root.

tar·ot (tăr'ō) *n.* Any of a set of 22 fortune-telling cards depicting vices, virtues, and elemental forces.

tar·pau·lin (tär-pô'lĭn, tär'pə-) *n.* A sheet of waterproof canvas.

tar·pon (tär'pən) *n., pl.* **-pon** or **-pons.** A large, silvery game fish, *Megalops atlantica,* of Atlantic coastal waters.

tarpon

tar·ra·gon (tăr'ə-gŏn', -gən) *n.* A native Eurasian aromatic herb, *Artemisia dracunculus,* with leaves used as seasoning.

tar·ry (tăr'ē) *v.* **-ried, -ry·ing. 1.** To delay or be late in coming or going : linger. **2.** To stay for a time : sojourn. **—tar'ri·er** *n.*

tar·sus (tär'səs) *n., pl.* **-si** (-sī'). The part of the vertebrate foot between the leg and the metatarsus : the ankle. **—tar'sal** *adj.*

tart[1] (tärt) *adj.* **1.** Pungent or pleasantly sour to the taste. **2.** Sharp in tone or meaning. **—tart'ly** *adv.* **—tart'ness** *n.*

tart[2] (tärt) *n.* **1.** A pastry shell or pie filled with fruit, custard, etc. **2.** A prostitute.

tar·tan (tär'tn) *n.* Any of numerous plaid fabric patterns of Scottish origin consisting of stripes of varying widths and colors crossing at right angles against a solid background. **—tar'tan** *adj.*

tar·tar (tär'tər) *n.* **1.** A reddish crustlike deposit from grapes formed esp. on the sides of wine casks. **2.** A hard deposit on the teeth, composed of food, secretions, and calcium salts. **—tar·tar'ic** *adj.*

Tar·tar (tär'tər) *n.* **1.** A member of any of the Mongolian peoples who invaded W Asia and E Europe in the 13th cent. **2.** A fierce or violent person.

tar·tar sauce *also* **tar·tare sauce** (tär'tər) *n.* A mayonnaise sauce containing chopped onion and pickles.

Tash·kent (täsh-kĕnt'). City of S Central Asian USSR *Pop.* 1,816,000.

task (tăsk) *n.* **1.** A piece of work usu. assigned to be done. **2.** A difficult undertaking. ☆***syns:*** CHORE, DUTY, JOB, STINT —*v.* To overburden.

task force *n.* A temporary grouping to accomplish a goal.

task·mas·ter (tăsk'măs'tər) *n.* One who imposes heavy or burdensome work.

Tas·ma·ni·a (tăz-mā'nē-ə). Island state off SE Australia. **—Tas·ma'ni·an** *adj.* & *n.*

Tasmanian devil *n.* A burrowing carniverous marsupial, *Sarcophilus harrisii,* with a long, almost hairless tail.

tas·sel (tăs'əl) *n.* **1.** An ornamental bunch of threads or cords fastened at 1 end and hung on curtains, clothing, etc. **2.** Something resembling a tassel, as the male flower cluster of a corn plant. —*v.* **-seled, -sel·ing** or **-selled, -sel·ling. 1.** To decorate with tassels. **2.** To put forth tassels.

taste (tāst) *v.* **tast·ed, tast·ing. 1.** To determine the flavor of by putting into the mouth. **2.** To ingest a small amount (of) esp. as a sample. **3.** To partake of : experience. **4.** To have a particular flavor. —*n.* **1.** The sense by which the qualities of sweet, sour, salty, and bitter are perceived in the mouth. **2.** A distinctive sensation produced by or as if by a substance taken into the mouth : flavor. **3.** A small amount tasted or eaten. **4.** A first or limited experience. **5.** A personal liking. **6. a.** Ability to discern what is aesthetically pleasing or appropriate. **b.** A sense of moral or social propriety. **—tast'a·ble** *adj.* **—taste'ful** *adj.* **—taste'less** *adj.* **—tast'er** *n.*

taste bud *n.* Any of the numerous cells on the tongue that are the end organs of the sense of taste.

tast·y (tā'stē) *adj.* **-i·er, -i·est.** Agreeable in flavor : savory. **—tast'i·ly** *adv.* **—tast'i·ness** *n.*

tat (tăt) *v.* **tat·ted, tat·ting.** To do or make by tatting. **—tat'ter** *n.*

tat·ter (tăt'ər) *n.* **1.** A torn and hanging shred. **2. tatters.** Ragged clothing. —*v.* To make or become torn or shredded.

tat·ter·de·ma·lion (tăt'ər-də-māl'yən, -măl'-) *n.* A ragged unkempt person, esp. a child. **—tat'ter·de·ma'lion** *adj.*

tat·ting (tăt'ĭng) *n.* **1.** A delicate lace made by looping and knotting thread on a small hand shuttle. **2.** The art or process of making tatting.

tat·tle (tăt'l) *v.* **-tled, -tling. 1.** To betray the secrets of another by gossiping. **2.** To chatter idly. **—tat'tler** *n.*

tat·tle·tale (tăt'l-tāl') *n.* One who tattles on others : informer.

tat·too[1] (tă-to͞o') *n.* **1.** A military drum or bugle call to quarters at night. **2.** A rhythmic drumming or tapping.

tat·too[2] (tă-to͞o') *n.* A mark or design made on the skin by pricking and ingraining an indelible dye or by raising scars. **—tat·too'** *v.* **—tat·too'er** *n.*

taught (tôt) *v.* *p.t.* & *p.p.* of TEACH.

taunt (tônt) *v.* To jeer at : deride. —*n.* A scornful remark. **—taunt'ing·ly** *adv.*

taupe (tōp) *n.* A brownish gray or a yellowish brown. **—taupe** *adj.*

Tau·rus (tôr'əs) *n.* **1.** A constellation in the N Hemisphere. **2. a.** The 2nd sign of the zodiac. **b.** One born under this sign.

taut (tôt) *adj.* **1.** Pulled or drawn tight. **2.** Emotionally tense. **3.** Kept in tidy shape.

tau·tol·o·gy (tô-tŏl'ə-jē) *n., pl.* **-gies. 1. a.** Needless repetition esp. in speech or writing : redundancy. **b.** An instance of tautology. **2.** A statement that is always true because it includes all logical possibilities. **—tau'to·log'i·cal** (tô'tə-lŏj'ĭ-kəl) *adj.*

tav·ern (tăv'ərn) *n.* **1.** An establishment licensed to sell alcoholic beverages to be consumed on the premises. **2.** An inn where travelers may lodge.

taw·dry (tô'drē) *adj.* **-dri·er, -dri·est.** Cheap and garish : gaudy. **—taw'dri·ly** *adv.* **—taw'dri·ness** *n.*

▲word history: The word *tawdry* is an alteration of the name *Saint Audrey,* an Anglo-Saxon princess who died of a throat ailment. A fair was held annually in her honor at which cloth neckbands, called *tawdry laces,* were sold. These must have been showy but inexpensive souvenirs, because the word *tawdry* became an adjective in its own right meaning "gaudy."

taw·ny (tô'nē) *n.* A light golden brown or brownish orange.

tax (tăks) *n.* **1.** A payment imposed upon persons or groups for governmental support. **2.** A heavy demand : strain. —*v.* **1.** To place a tax on (income, property, or goods). **2.** To require a tax from. **3.** To make excessive demands upon. **4.** To make a charge against : accuse. **—tax'a·ble** *adj.* **—tax·a'tion** *n.* **—tax'er** *n.* **—tax'pay'er** *n.*

tax·i (tăk'sē) *n., pl.* **-is** or **-ies.** A taxicab. —*v.* **-ied, -i·ing. 1.** To transport or go by taxicab. **2.** To move along on the ground or water surface before taking off or after landing.

tax·i·cab (tăk'sē-kăb') *n.* An automobile that transports passengers for a charge.

tax·i·der·my (tăk'sĭ-dûr'mē) *n.* The art of preparing, stuffing, and mounting animal skins. **—tax'i·derm'ist** *n.*

tax•on•o•my (tăk-sŏn'ə-mē) *n.* The science, laws, or principles of classifying living organisms in specially named categories based on shared characteristics and natural relationships. **—tax'o•nom'ic** (-sə-nŏm'ĭk), **tax'o•nom'i•cal** *adj.* **—tax'o•nom'i•cal•ly** *adv.* **—tax•on'o•mist** *n.*

tax shelter *n.* A financial strategy or provision that reduces current taxes.

Tay•lor (tā'lər), **Zachary.** 1784–1850. 12th U.S. President (1849–50).

Tb *symbol for* TERBIUM.

T-bone (tē'bōn') *n.* A small, thick steak tenderloin containing a T-shaped bone.

tbsp *or* **tbsp.** *abbr.* tablespoon; tablespoonful.

Tc *symbol for* TECHNETIUM.

Tchai•kov•sky (chī-kôf'skē, -kŏf'-), **Peter Ilich.** 1840–93. Russian composer.

Te *symbol for* TELLURIUM.

tea (tē) *n.* **1.a.** An Asian shrub, *Thea sinensis* or *Camellia sinensis,* with fragrant white flowers and evergreen leaves. **b.** The dried leaves of this shrub, used to make a drink by steeping in boiling water. **c.** The drink so made. **2.** A drink resembling tea <herbal *tea*> **3.** A light meal or a social gathering at which tea is served.

teach (tēch) *v.* **taught** (tôt), **teach•ing. 1.** To communicate knowledge or skill (to). **2.** To provide instruction in. **3.** To give insight by example or experience. ☆***syns:*** INSTRUCT, TRAIN, TUTOR **—teach'a•bil'i•ty, teach'a•ble•ness** *n.* **—teach'a•ble** *adj.* **—teach'a•bly** *adv.* **—teach'er** *n.*

teach•ing (tē'chĭng) *n.* **1.** The act, practice, or occupation of teachers. **2.** Something taught, esp. a precept or doctrine.

teak (tēk) *n.* A tall, evergreen Asian tree, *Tectona grandis,* with hard, durable, yellowish-brown wood used esp. in shipbuilding and furniture-making. **—teak** *adj.*

tea•ket•tle (tē'kĕt'l) *n.* A covered kettle with a handle and a spout, used esp. for boiling water for tea.

teal (tēl) *n.* Any of several small wild river ducks, esp. one of the genus *Anas,* with brightly marked plumage.

team (tēm) *n.* **1.** Two or more draft animals harnessed to a farm implement or a vehicle. **2.** Two or more players on the same side in a game. **3.** A group working together. *—v.* **1.** To join together (animals) in a team. **2.** To unite in a team. **—team'mate** *n.* **—team'work'** *n.*

team•ster (tēm'stər) *n.* **1.** One who drives a team of draft animals. **2.** One whose occupation is truck driving.

tea•pot (tē'pŏt') *n.* A covered pot with a spout, for preparing and pouring tea.

tear[1] (târ) *v.* **tore** (tôr, tōr), **torn** (tôrn, tōrn), **tear•ing. 1.** To pull apart or become divided into pieces. **2.** To make (a hole) by or as if by ripping. **3.** To lacerate (the skin). **4.** To separate or remove by force. **5.** To divide or disrupt emotionally. **6.** To move with great haste. **—tear down.** To demolish : destroy. *—n.* A hole, rip, or flaw.

tear[2] (tîr) *n.* **1.** A drop of the clear salty fluid that moistens the eye and the inner eyelid. **2. tears.** The act of crying. *—v.* To become full of tears. **—tear'ful** *adj.* **—tear'ful•ness** *n.* **—tear'i•ly** *adv.* **—tear'i•ness** *n.* **—tear'y** *adj.*

tear gas (tîr) *n.* A chemical substance that causes severe eye and respiratory irritation when dispersed.

tear-jerk•er (tîr'jûr'kər) *n. Slang.* An extremely sad story, drama, or performance.

tease (tēz) *v.* **teased, teas•ing. 1.** To vex or annoy by taunting or making fun of. **2.** To try to get by coaxing or begging. **3.** To tantalize. **4.** To comb apart and lay straight the fibers of (wool). **5.** To raise the nap of (cloth) with a teasel. **6.** To give (the hair) a bouffant effect by combing. **—teas'er** *n.*

tea•sel *also* **tea•zel** *or* **tea•zle** (tē'zəl) *n.* **1.** An Old World plant of the genus *Dipsacus,* with thistlelike flowers surrounded by stiff bristles. **2.** The bristly flower head of *D. fullonum,* used to produce a napped surface on fabrics.

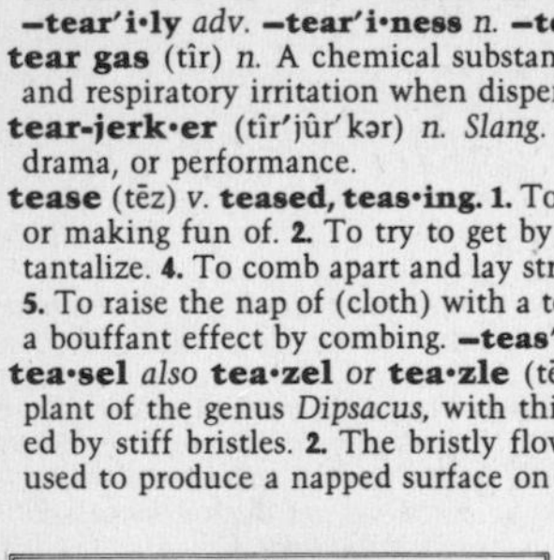

teasel

tea•spoon (tē'spōōn') *n.* **1.** A small spoon used esp. for stirring and for eating desserts. **2.** See MEASUREMENT TABLE.

teat (tēt, tĭt) *n.* A nipple.

tech. *abbr.* technical.

tech•ne•ti•um (tĕk-nē'shē-əm) *n. Symbol* **Tc** A silvery-gray, radioactive, artificially produced metallic element.

tech•ni•cal (tĕk'nĭ-kəl) *adj.* **1.** Of, relating to, or derived from technique. **2.** Of a particular subject : specialized. **3.** Of or using scientific knowledge. **4.** In principle rather than practice. **5.** Of, relating to, or derived from technology. **—tech'ni•cal•ly** *adv.* **—tech'ni•cal•ness** *n.*

tech•ni•cal•i•ty (tĕk'nĭ-kăl'ĭ-tē) *n., pl.* **-ties. 1.** The quality or state of being technical. **2.** A point or detail having meaning only to a specialist.

tech•ni•cian (tĕk-nĭsh'ən) *n.* A person highly skilled in a certain field or process.

Tech•ni•col•or (tĕk'nĭ-kŭl'ər). A trademark for a motion-picture color process.

tech•nique (tĕk-nēk') *n.* **1.** The systematic procedure by which a complex or scientific task is accomplished. **2.** *also* **tech•nic** (tĕk'nĭk). The degree of expertise shown in a procedure or performance.

tech•noc•ra•cy (tĕk-nŏk'rə-sē) *n., pl.* **-cies.** Government by technical experts, esp. scientists and engineers. **—tech'no•crat'** (-nə-krăt') *n.* **—tech'no•crat'ic** *adj.*

technol. *abbr.* technological; technology.

tech•nol•o•gy (tĕk-nŏl'ə-jē) *n., pl.* **-gies. 1.** The application of scientific knowledge, esp. in industry or business. **2.** The methods and materials of applied science. **—tech'no•log'i•cal** (-nə-lŏj'ĭ-kəl) *adj.* **—tech•nol'o•gist** *n.*

tec•ton•ics (tĕk-tŏn'ĭks) *n. (sing. in number).* **1.** The art or science of construction. **2.** The geology of structural changes in the earth's crust. **—tec•ton'ic** *adj.*

ted•dy bear (tĕd'ē) *n.* A stuffed toy bear.

te•di•ous (tē'dē-əs) *adj.* Wearisome : boring. **—te'di•ous•ness** *n.*

te•di•um (tē'dē-əm) *n.* The quality or state of being tedious : boredom.

tee (tē) *n.* **1.** A small peg stuck in the ground for holding a golf ball for a 1st stroke. **2.** The raised area from which a golfer tees off. *—v.* **teed, tee•ing.** To place (a ball) on a golf tee. **—tee off. 1.** To make one's 1st stroke toward a hole from the tee. **2.** *Slang.* To begin. **3.** *Slang.* To make or become annoyed or angry.

teem (tēm) *v.* To be full of : abound.

teen (tēn) *adj.* Teen-age. *—n.* One between 13 and 19 : teenager.

teen-age (tēn'āj') *also* **teen-aged** (-ājd') *adj.* Of, relating to, or descriptive of those aged 13 through 19. **—teen'-ag'er** *n.*

teens (tēnz) *pl.n.* **1.** The numbers 13 through 19. **2.** The span of years between ages 13 and 19.

tee•ny (tē'nē) *adj.* **-ni•er, -ni•est.** *Informal.* Very small : tiny.

tee shirt (tē'shûrt') *n. var. of* T-SHIRT.

tee•ter (tē'tər) *v.* **1.** To walk or move unsteadily. **2.** To vacillate. **—tee'ter** *n.*

teeth (tēth) *n. pl. of* TOOTH.

teethe (tē*th*) *v.* **teethed, teeth•ing.** To cut teeth.

tee•to•tal•er (tē-tōt'l-ər) *n.* One who abstains from alcoholic beverages. **—tee•to'tal•ism** *n.*

▲word history: The word *teetotaler* is derived from the phrase *teetotal abstainer,* which was coined by temperance workers in the 1830's. The syllable *tee-* is simply a spelling of the pronunciation of the letter T, which is the reduplication of the initial letter of *total. Teetotal* was therefore a catchy way of saying "absolutely total."

Tef•lon (tĕf'lŏn'). A trademark for a durable plastic used as a nonstick coating.

Te•gu•ci•gal•pa (tā-gōō'sə-gäl'pä). Cap of Honduras, in the SC part. *Pop.* 316,800.

Te•he•ran (tĕ'ə-răn', -rän', tā'-) *also* **Teh•ran** (tĕ-rän). Cap. of Iran, in the NC part. *Pop.* 4,496,159.

tek•tite (tĕk'tīt') *n.* A usu. small and round, dark brown to green glassy rock that may be of meteoric origin.

tel. *abbr.* **1.** telegram. **2.** telegraph; telegraphic. **3.** telephone.

Tel A•viv–Jaf•fa (tĕl'ə-vēv'jăf'ə, -yä'fə). City of C Israel. *Pop.* 336,300.

tel•e•cast (tĕl'ĭ-kăst') *v.* **-cast** *or* **-cast•ed, -cast•ing.** To broadcast (a program) by television. **—tel'e•cast'** *n.*

tel•e•com•mu•ni•ca•tion (tĕl'ĭ-kəmyōō'nĭ-kā'shən) *n. often* **telecommunications** *(sing. in number).* The science and technology of distance communication by electrical or electronic means.

tel•e•gen•ic (tĕl'ə-jĕn'ĭk, -jē'nĭk) *adj.* Having a pleasing appearance on television.

tel•e•gram (tĕl'ĭ-grăm') *n.* A message or communication transmitted by telegraph.

tel•e•graph (tĕl′ĭ-grăf′) *n.* **1.** A communications system in which a transmission is sent, either by wire or radio, to a receiving station. **2.** A message sent by telegraph : telegram. *—v.* To send or communicate by telegraph. **—te•leg′ra•pher** (tə-lĕg′rə-fər), **te•leg′ra•phist** *n.* **—tel′e•graph′ic** *adj.* **—tel′e•graph′i•cal•ly** *adv.* **—te•leg′ra•phy** *n.*

tel•e•ki•ne•sis (tĕl′ə-kĭ-nē′sĭs, -kī-) *n.* Movement of objects by scientifically inexplicable means. **—tel′e•ki•net′ic** (-nĕt′ĭk) *adj.* **—tel′e•ki•net′i•cal•ly** *adv.*

te•lem•e•try (tə-lĕm′ĭ-trē) *n.* The science and technology of the transmission and measurement of data from a distant source, as a spacecraft. **—tel′e•me′ter** (tĕl′ə-mē′tər) *n.* **—tel′e•met′ric** (tĕl′ə-mĕt′rĭk), **tel′e•met′ri•cal** *adj.*

te•lep•a•thy (tə-lĕp′ə-thē) *n.* Communication between individuals by mental processes rather than ordinary sensory means. **—tel′e•path′ic** (tĕl′ə-păth′ĭk) *adj.* **—tel′e•path′i•cal•ly** *adv.* **—te•lep′a•thist** *n.*

tel•e•phone (tĕl′ə-fōn′) *n.* An electronic device or system for sound reception or reproduction at a distance. *—v.* **-phoned, -phon•ing. 1.** To communicate (with) by telephone. **2.** To transmit by telephone. **—tel′e•phon′er** *n.*

te•leph•o•ny (tə-lĕf′ə-nē) *n.* The science and technology of electrical sound transmission between distant points. **—tel′e•phon′ic** (-fŏn′ĭk) *adj.*

tel•e•pho•to (tĕl′ə-fō′tō) *adj.* Of, relating to, or being a photographic lens or lens system for producing a large image of a distant object. **—tel′e•pho′to•graph′** *n.* & *v.* **—tel′e•pho′to•graph′ic** *adj.* **—tel′e•pho′tog′ra•phy** *n.*

tel•e•play (tĕl′ə-plā′) *n.* A play written or adapted for television.

tel•e•scope (tĕl′ĭ-skōp′) *n.* An arrangement of lenses or mirrors or both that collects light, allowing observation of remote objects, esp. stars and planets. *—v.* **-scoped, -scop•ing. 1.** To slide or cause to slide 1 within another, as the tubular parts of a hand telescope. **2.** To make shorter : condense. **—tel′e•scop′ic** (-skŏp′ĭk) *adj.* **—tel′e•scop′i•cal•ly** *adv.*

tel•e•thon (tĕl′ə-thŏn′) *n.* A long telecast usu. for fund-raising.

Tel•e•type (tĕl′ĭ-tīp′). A trademark for a teletypewriter.

tel•e•type•writ•er (tĕl′ĭ-tīp′rī′tər) *n.* A telegraphlike typewriter that either transmits or receives electrically coded messages.

tel•e•vise (tĕl′ə-vīz′) *v.* **-vised, -vis•ing.** To broadcast by television : telecast.

tel•e•vi•sion (tĕl′ə-vĭzh′ən) *n.* **1.** Transmission and reception of images and usu. sound by electronic means. **2.** A receiving device that reproduces transmitted images on a screen. **3.** The television industry.

tell (tĕl) *v.* **told** (tōld), **tell•ing. 1.** To describe or relate : narrate. **2.** To express in words : say. **3.** To make known. **4.** To direct : command. **5.** To perceive or discern by observation. **6.** To have a marked effect or impact <The strain on the team began to *tell.*> **—tell off.** *Informal.* To scold or criticize. **—tell′a•ble** *adj.*

tell•er (tĕl′ər) *n.* **1.** One who tells or narrates. **2.** A bank employee who handles money paid out and received.

tell•ing (tĕl′ĭng) *adj.* **1.** Effective : forceful. **2.** Meaningful. **—tell′ing•ly** *adv.*

tell•tale (tĕl′tāl′) *n.* One that reveals information or secrets. **—tell′tale′** *adj.*

tel•lu•ri•um (tĕ-lo͝or′ē-əm, tə-) *n. Symbol* **Te** A brittle, silvery-white, sulfurlike metallic element used esp. in alloys.

te•mer•i•ty (tə-mĕr′ĭ-tē) *n.* Audacity.

temp. *abbr.* **1.** temperature. **2.** temporary.

tem•per (tĕm′pər) *v.* **1.** To modify by the addition of something. **2.** To bring to the right degree of texture or firmness, esp. to harden or toughen (a metal), as by gradual heating and cooling. **3.** To tune (a keyboard instrument). *—n.* **1.** A usual state of mind or emotions. **2.** Mental or emotional composure. **3. a.** A tendency to become irritable or angry. **b.** A violent outburst of anger. **4.** The degree of hardness achieved by tempering. **—tem′per•a•ble** *adj.*

tem•per•a (tĕm′pər-ə) *n.* **1.** A type of paint made by mixing pigment with a water-soluble substance such as size or egg yolk. **2.** Painting done with tempera.

tem•per•a•ment (tĕm′pər-ə-mənt, -prəmənt) *n.* **1.** A person's characteristic way of thinking, behaving, and reacting : disposition. **2.** Undue irritability or sensitivity. **—tem′per•a•men′tal** *adj.*

tem•per•ance (tĕm′pər-əns, -prəns) *n.* **1.** Moderation in one's appetites or emotions : self-restraint. **2.** Moderation in or total abstinence from drinking alcoholic beverages.

tem•per•ate (tĕm′pər-ĭt, -prĭt) *adj.* **1.** Practicing moderation and self-restraint. **2.** Not excessive or extreme. **3.** Of or having a mild or moderate climate.

tem•per•a•ture (tĕm′pər-ə-cho͝or′, -chər, tĕm′prə-) *n.* **1.** The relative hotness or coldness of a body or environment as measured on a standard scale. **2.** An abnormally high body temperature usu. as a result of illness.

tem•pered (tĕm′pərd) *adj.* Having a particular disposition <hot-*tempered*>

tem•pest (tĕm′pĭst) *n.* A violent storm often with rain, snow, hail, etc.

tem•pes•tu•ous (tĕm-pĕs′cho͞o-əs) *adj.* Of or resembling a tempest : turbulent. **—tem•pes′tu•ous•ness** *n.*

tem•plate (tĕm′plĭt) *n.* A gauge or pattern, as a thin metal plate, used in making or copying something accurately.

tem•ple¹ (tĕm′pəl) *n.* **1.** A place or house of worship, esp. a synagogue. **2.** A place devoted to a special purpose.

tem•ple² (tĕm′pəl) *n.* The flattened area on either side of the forehead.

tem•po (tĕm′pō) *n., pl.* **-pos** *or* **-pi** (-pē). **1.** The speed at which a musical composition is to be played. **2.** A rate or rhythm of something : pace.

tem•po•ral¹ (tĕm′pər-əl, -prəl) *adj.* **1.** Of, pertaining to, or limited by time. **2.** Of or pertaining to worldly or secular matters.

tem•po•ral² (tĕm′pər-əl, -prəl) *adj.* Of or near the temples or sides of the head.

tem•po•rar•y (tĕm′pə-rĕr′ē) *adj.* Having a limited duration or use : impermanent. *—n., pl.* **-ies.** A temporary worker, as in an office. **—tem′po•rar′i•ly** *adv.*

tem•po•rize (tĕm′pə-rīz′) *v.* **-rized, -riz•ing. 1.** To postpone acting or deciding in order to gain time. **2.** To adapt to circumstances. **—tem′po•ri•za′tion** *n.*

tempt (tĕmpt) *v.* **1.** To draw into a wrong or foolish course of action. **2.** To attract : invite. **3.** To risk provoking, as fate. **4.** To incline strongly <was *tempted* to quit> ☆**syns:** ALLURE, ENTICE, INVEIGLE, LURE, SEDUCE **—temp•ta′tion** *n.* **—tempt′er** *n.* **—tempt′ress** *n.*

tem•pu•ra (tĕm′po͞o-rə, tĕm-po͝or′ə) *n.* A Japanese dish of batter-dipped deep-fried vegetables and seafood.

ten (tĕn) *n.* **1.** The cardinal number equal to 9 + 1. **2.** The 10th in a set or sequence. **3.** A 10-dollar bill. **—ten** *adj.* & *pron.* **—tenth** *n.* & *adj.* & *adv.*

ten•a•ble (tĕn′ə-bəl) *adj.* Capable of being defended or sustained. **—ten′a•bil′i•ty, ten′a•ble•ness** *n.* **—ten′a•bly** *adv.*

te•na•cious (tə-nā′shəs) *adj.* **1.** Holding firmly, stubbornly, or persistently. **2.** Tending to cling or adhere. **3.** Retaining easily and well <a *tenacious* memory> **—te•na′cious•ly** *adv.* **—te•nac′i•ty** (-năs′ə-tē), **te•na′cious•ness** *n.*

ten•an•cy (tĕn′ən-sē) *n., pl.* **-cies. 1.** The possession or occupancy by lease or rent of another's land or building. **2.** The duration of a tenant's occupancy.

ten•ant (tĕn′ənt) *n.* **1.** One who pays rent to occupy another's property. **2.** An inhabitant : dweller.

Ten Commandments *n.* The 10 moral laws given to Moses by God.

tend¹ (tĕnd) *v.* **1.** To be directed, as a course of travel. **2. a.** To be apt or likely <Stress *tends* to cause illness.> **b.** To be inclined <*tends* toward stinginess>

tend² (tĕnd) *v.* **1.** To look after : take care of. **2.** To serve at : manage, as a bar.

ten•den•cy (tĕn′dən-sē) *n., pl.* **-cies. 1.** An inclination to think or behave in a particular way. **2.** A general drift or trend.

ten•den•tious (tĕn-dĕn′shəs) *adj.* Tending toward a certain point of view : biased.

ten•der¹ (tĕn′dər) *adj.* **1.** Easily damaged : fragile. **2.** Young : immature. **3. a.** Easily hurt <*tender* skin> **b.** Painful : sore <a *tender* tooth> **4.** Readily cut or chewed. **5.** Kind : gentle. **6.** Sympathetic. **—ten′der•ly** *adv.* **—ten′der•ness** *n.*

ten•der² (tĕn′dər) *n.* **1.** A formal bid or offer. **2.** Something offered, esp. money <legal *tender*> *—v.* To offer or present formally. **—ten′der•er** *n.*

tend•er³ (tĕn′dər) *n.* **1.** One who tends something. **2.** *Naut.* A small vessel that services larger vessels. **3.** A railroad car carrying fuel and water for the locomotive, to which it is attached.

ten•der•foot (tĕn′dər-fo͝ot′) *n., pl.* **-foots** *or* **-feet. 1.** One not used to rough outdoor life. **2.** A novice.

ten•der•heart•ed (tĕn′dər-här′tĭd) *adj.* Compassionate. **—ten′der•heart′ed•ly** *adv.* **—ten′der•heart′ed•ness** *n.*

ten•der•ize (tĕn′də-rīz′) *v.* **-ized, -iz•ing.** To make (meat) tender, as by pounding or marinating. **—ten′der•iz′er** *n.*

ten•der•loin (tĕn′dər-loin′) *n.* **1.** A tender portion of a beef or pork loin. **2.** A city district notorious for vice and corruption.

ten•don (tĕn′dən) *n.* A band of tough, fibrous tissue connecting a muscle and a bone. **—ten′di•nous** *adj.*

ten•dril (tĕn′drəl) *n.* **1.** A slender coiling stemlike part by which a climbing plant attaches itself to a support. **2.** Something, as a ringlet of hair, resembling a tendril.

ten•e•brous (tĕn′ə-brəs) *adj.* Dark and gloomy.

ten•e•ment (tĕn'ə-mənt) *n.* **1.** A building used as a dwelling. **2.** A low-rent apartment building that is minimally maintained.
ten•et (tĕn'ĭt) *n.* A basic principle, doctrine, or dogma.
ten-gal•lon hat (tĕn'găl'ən) *n.* A wide-brimmed felt hat with a tall crown.
Tenn. *abbr.* Tennessee.
ten•nis (tĕn'ĭs) *n.* A game played with rackets and a light ball by 2 or 4 players on a court divided by a net.
Ten•nes•see (tĕn'ĭ-sē'). State of the SE U.S. *Cap.* Nashville. *Pop.* 4,590,750. **—Ten'nes•se'an** *n.*
Ten•ny•son (tĕn'ĭ-sən), **Alfred.** 1st Baron Tennyson. 1809–92. English poet.
ten•on (tĕn'ən) *n.* A projecting piece, as on wood, designed to fit into a mortise.
ten•or (tĕn'ər) *n.* **1.** General meaning : purport. **2. a.** A male singing voice higher than a baritone. **b.** A singer with a tenor voice. **c.** A part written for a tenor.
ten•pin (tĕn'pĭn') *n.* **1.** A bowling pin grouped in sets of 10 for playing tenpins. **2. tenpins** *(sing. in number).* The game of bowling with tenpins.
tense[1] (tĕns) *adj.* **tens•er, tens•est. 1.** Stretched tightly : taut. **2.** Experiencing emotional tension. **3.** Distressingly suspenseful. *—v.* **tensed, tens•ing.** To make or become tense. **—ten'si•ty** *n.*
tense[2] (tĕns) *n.* Any of the inflected forms of a verb that designate the time of the action or state.
ten•sile (tĕn'səl, -sīl') *adj.* **1.** Of, relating to, or involving tension. **2.** Capable of being stretched. **—ten•sil'i•ty** *n.*
ten•sion (tĕn'shən) *n.* **1.** The act or process of stretching or the state of being stretched. **2.** A force that tends to stretch something. **3. a.** Mental or emotional strain. **b.** A forced often hostile mutual relation. **4.** Voltage or electrical potential.
tent (tĕnt) *n.* A movable shelter consisting of material stretched over a supporting framework. *—v.* To shelter in a tent.
ten•ta•cle (tĕn'tə-kəl) *n.* A long flexible unjointed projection from the bodies of certain invertebrates, as an octopus. **—ten•tac'u•lar** (-tăk'yə-lər) *adj.*
ten•ta•tive (tĕn'tə-tĭv) *adj.* **1.** Experimental or provisional in nature : not definite. **2.** Hesitant : unsure. **—ten'ta•tive•ly** *adv.*
ten•ter•hook (tĕn'tər-ho͝ok') *n.* A hooked nail used to fasten cloth on a framework for drying and stretching. **—on tenterhooks.** Anxious or suspenseful.
ten•u•ous (tĕn'yo͞o-əs) *adj.* **1.** Slender in form : fine. **2.** Rarefied, as high-altitude air. **3.** Lacking substance or significance. ☆***syns:*** FEEBLE, FLIMSY, INSUBSTANTIAL, UNSUBSTANTIAL **—ten'u•ous•ness** *n.*
ten•ure (tĕn'yər, -yo͝or') *n.* **1.** The act, state, right, or period of holding something, as land or an office. **2.** The conditions by which something is held. **3.** Permanence of position. **—ten'ured** *adj.*
te•pee (tē'pē) *n.* A North American Indian tent usu. made of hides or bark and shaped like a cone.
tep•id (tĕp'ĭd) *adj.* **1.** Lukewarm. **2.** Halfhearted. **—tep'id•ly** *adv.*
te•qui•la (tə-kē'lə) *n.* An alcoholic liquor made from a fleshy-leaved Central American agave plant, *Agave tequilana.*
ter•a•to•gen•ic (tĕr'ə-tə-jĕn'ĭk) *adj.* Causing fetal malformations or monstrosities.
ter•bi•um (tûr'bē-əm) *n. Symbol* **Tb** A soft, silvery-gray metallic rare-earth element used as a laser material.
ter•cen•ten•a•ry (tûr'sĕn-tĕn'ə-rē, tərsĕn'tə-nĕr'ē) *n., pl.* **-ries. 1.** A time span of 300 years. **2.** A 300th anniversary or its celebration. **—ter'cen•ten'a•ry** *adj.*
ter•cen•ten•ni•al (tûr'sĕn-tĕn'ē-əl) *n. & adj.* Tercentenary.
term (tûrm) *n.* **1. a.** A limited duration <a school *term*> **b.** A designated period for one to serve. **2. a.** A point of time initiating or terminating a period. **b.** A set date, as for paying money owed. **c.** The end of a normal pregnancy. **3. a.** A word or phrase having a precise meaning <a technical *term*> **b. terms.** Words or manner of expression <spoke in plain *terms*> **4. terms. a.** Conditions or provisions <the *terms* of a treaty> **b.** Mutual relations <on friendly *terms*> **5.** *Math.* **a.** Each of the numbers connected by plus or minus signs in an equation or series. **b.** Either number of a ratio. *—v.* To designate with a term : call.
ter•ma•gant (tûr'mə-gənt) *n.* A scolding, shrewish woman.
ter•mi•nal (tûr'mə-nəl) *adj.* **1.** Of, located at, or forming the boundary or end of something. **2.** In conclusion : final. **3.** Of or taking place in a term or every term. **4.** Resulting in death : fatal. *—n.* **1.** An ending or extreme point, limit, or part. **2.** An electrical connection point in a component. **3.** A station at the end of a railway, bus line, or airline. **4.** *Computer Sci.* An instrument through which data can enter or leave a computer.
ter•mi•nate (tûr'mə-nāt') *v.* **-nat•ed, -nat•ing. 1.** To come or bring to an end : conclude. **2.** To discontinue the employment of : fire. **—ter'mi•na•ble** *adj.* **—ter'mi•na'tion** *n.* **—ter'mi•na'tor** *n.*
ter•mi•nol•o•gy (tûr'mə-nŏl'ə-jē) *n., pl.* **-gies.** The technical vocabulary of a specific trade, science, or art.
ter•mi•nus (tûr'mə-nəs) *n., pl.* **-es** *or* **-ni** (-nī'). **1.** The final point : end. **2.** The terminal of a transportation line.
ter•mite (tûr'mīt') *n.* Any of numerous highy destructive social insects of the order Isoptera that usu. feed on wood.
tern (tûrn) *n.* Any of various sea birds of the genus *Sterna* and related genera, with narrow wings and a forked tail.
terp•si•cho•re•an (tûrp'sĭ-kə-rē'ən, -kôr'ē-ən, -kōr'-) *adj.* Of or pertaining to dancing. *—n.* A dancer.
terr. *abbr.* territory.
ter•race (tĕr'əs) *n.* **1.** An open porch or balcony. **2.** An open area adjoining a house : patio. **3.** A flat-topped mound of earth with vertical or sloping sides. **4.** A row of dwellings built on a raised or sloping site. *—v.* **-raced, -rac•ing.** To make into or supply with a terrace.
ter•ra cot•ta (tĕr'ə kŏt'ə) *n.* **1.** A hard ceramic pottery and building clay. **2.** A brownish orange. **—ter'ra-cot'ta** *adj.*
ter•rain (tə-rān', tĕ-) *n.* A tract of land esp. with respect to its physical features.
ter•ra•pin (tĕr'ə-pĭn) *n.* An aquatic often edible North American turtle of the genus *Malaclemys* and related genera.
ter•rar•i•um (tə-râr'ē-əm, -răr'-) *n., pl.* **-ums** *or* **-i•a** (-ē-ə). A usu. closed glass container for growing small plants or keeping small animals, as turtles or lizards.
ter•res•tri•al (tə-rĕs'trē-əl) *adj.* **1.** Of or pertaining to the earth or its inhabitants. **2.** Living or growing on land <*terrestrial* animals> *—n.* A terrestrial inhabitant. **—ter•res'tri•al•ly** *adv.*
ter•ri•ble (tĕr'ə-bəl) *adj.* **1.** Causing great fear or dread. **2.** Extreme : intense <*terrible* cold> **3.** Very difficult or distressing <a *terrible* dilemma> **4. a.** Unpleasant : disagreeable. **b.** Of inferior quality. **—ter'ri•ble•ness** *n.* **—ter'ri•bly** *adv.*
ter•ri•er (tĕr'ē-ər) *n.* An active small dog orig. bred to dig for burrowing game.
ter•rif•ic (tə-rĭf'ĭk) *adj.* **1.** Causing great fear : terrifying. **2.** *Informal.* Very good : excellent <a *terrific* idea> **3.** Causing awe or amazement. **4.** Very bad or intense <*terrific* pain> **—ter•rif'i•cal•ly** *adv.*
ter•ri•fy (tĕr'ə-fī') *v.* **-fied, -fy•ing.** To fill with fear.
ter•ri•to•ry (tĕr'ĭ-tôr'ē, -tōr'ē) *n., pl.* **-ries. 1.** A usu. sizable geographic area : region. **2.** The land and waters under the jurisdiction of a state, nation, or sovereign. **3. Territory.** A part of a nation not accorded full status. **4.** The area to which one is assigned as an agent or representative. **5.** A field of interest or activity. **—ter'ri•to'ri•al** *adj.* **—ter'ri•to'ri•al•ly** *adv.*
ter•ror (tĕr'ər) *n.* **1.** Overwhelmingly intense fear. **2.** One that causes terror. **3.** Violence by a group to achieve a usu. political objective.
ter•ror•ism (tĕr'ə-rĭz'əm) *n.* Systematic use of terror and intimidation esp. in order to coerce. **—ter'ror•ist** *n.*
ter•ror•ize (tĕr'ə-rīz') *v.* **-ized, -iz•ing. 1.** To fill with great fear : terrify. **2.** To control and dominate by intimidation or violence. **—ter'ror•i•za'tion** *n.* **—ter'ror•iz'er** *n.*
ter•ry cloth (tĕr'ē) *n.* An absorbent pile fabric with uncut loops on both sides.
terse (tûrs) *adj.* **ters•er, ters•est.** Brief : concise. **—terse'ly** *adv.* **—terse'ness** *n.*
tes•sel•late (tĕs'ə-lāt') *v.* **-lat•ed, -lat•ing.** To form into or ornament with a mosaic pattern. **—tes'sel•la'tion** *n.*
test (tĕst) *n.* **1.** A means of examining or evaluating something. **2.** Something devised and administered to determine one's skill, knowledge, intelligence, etc. **3.** A criterion in measuring or examining : standard. **—test** *v.* **—test'er** *n.*
tes•ta•ment (tĕs'tə-mənt) *n.* **1.** The legal disposition of one's personal property by a written will. **2. Testament.** Either of the 2 principal sections of the Bible, the Old Testament and the New Testament. **3.** A statement of belief. **4.** Convincing evidence. **—tes'ta•men'ta•ry** *adj.*
tes•tate (tĕs'tāt') *adj.* Having made a valid will.
tes•ta•tor (tĕs'tā'tər) *n.* One who has made a valid will. **—tes•ta'trix** *n.*
tes•ti•cle (tĕs'tĭ-kəl) *n.* A testis.
tes•ti•fy (tĕs'tə-fī') *v.* **-fied, -fy•ing. 1.** To give evidence under oath. **2.** To serve as evidence or proof. **3.** To affirm publicly. **—tes'ti•fi'er** *n.*
tes•ti•mo•ni•al (tĕs'tə-mō'nē-əl, -mōn'yəl) *n.* **1.** A formal statement attesting to something. **2.** A written statement affirming another's good character or value. **3.** Something given as a formal tribute. **—tes'ti•mo'ni•al** *adj.*
tes•ti•mo•ny (tĕs'tə-mō'nē) *n., pl.* **-nies. 1. a.** A solemn declaration or affirmation made under oath. **b.** The total of such

declarations in a specific legal case. **2.** Supporting evidence : proof. **3.** A public declaration of religious experience.
tes•tis (tĕs'tĭs) *n., pl.* **-tes** (-tēz'). The male sperm-producing gland, one of a pair in a pouchlike enclosure.
tes•tos•ter•one (tĕs-tŏs'tə-rōn') *n.* A male sex hormone.
test tube *n.* A clear glass cylinder usu. closed at one end, used in laboratory experiments.
test-tube baby (tĕst'to͞ob') *n.* A baby conceived outside the womb through fertilization of an egg removed from the mother.
tes•ty (tĕs'tē) *adj.* **-ti•er, -ti•est.** Showing or marked by ill humor : irritable. **—tes'ti•ly** *adv.* **—tes'ti•ness** *n.*
tet•a•nus (tĕt'n-əs) *n.* An often fatal bacterial disease marked by muscular spasms and rigidity esp. of the jaw.
tête-à-tête (tāt'ə-tāt') *n.* A private conversation between 2 persons. **—tête'-à-tête'** *adj. & adv.*
teth•er (tĕth'ər) *n.* **1.** A rope or chain that allows an animal limited freedom to move about. **2.** The limit of one's resources or strength. *—v.* To restrict with or as if with a tether.
tet•ra•cy•cline (tĕt'rə-sī'klēn') *n.* A yellow crystalline compound.
tet•ra•eth•yl lead (tĕt'rə-ĕth'əl) *n.* An oily poisonous lead compound used as an antiknock agent in gasoline.
tet•ra•he•dron (tĕt'rə-hē'drən) *n., pl.* **-drons** *or* **-dra** (-drə). A polyhedron with 4 triangular faces. **—tet'ra•he'dral** *adj.*

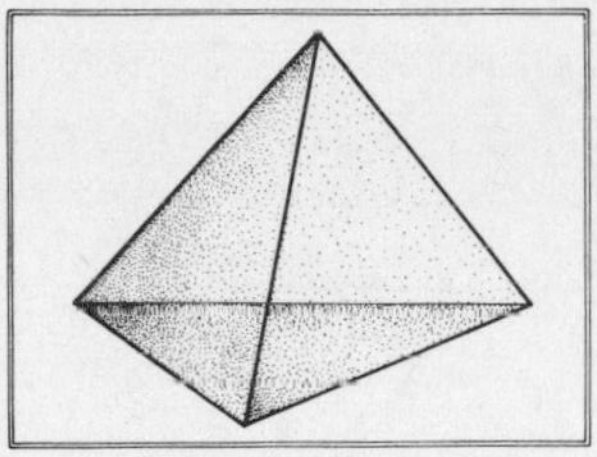

tetrahedron

te•tram•e•ter (tĕ-trăm'ĭ-tər) *n.* A line of verse with 4 metrical feet.
Teu•ton (to͞ot'n, tyo͞ot'n) *n.* **1.** A member of an ancient N European people. **2.** A German. **—Teu•ton'ic** *adj. & n.*
Tex. *abbr.* Texas.
Tex•as (tĕk'səs). State of the SC U.S. *Cap.* Austin. *Pop.* 14,228,383. **—Tex'an** *n.*
text (tĕkst) *n.* **1.** The wording or words of an author's work. **2.** The main body of a printed work. **3.** A Scriptural passage to be treated in a sermon. **4.** The theme of a discourse. **5.** A textbook. **—tex'tu•al** (tĕks'cho͞o-əl) *adj.* **—tex'tu•al•ly** *adv.*
text•book (tĕkst'bo͝ok') *n.* A book used in studying a subject.
tex•tile (tĕk'stīl', -stəl) *n.* **1.** Cloth esp. when knitted or woven. **2.** Fiber or yarn for making cloth. **—tex'tile** *adj.*
tex•ture (tĕks'chər) *n.* **1.** The surface look or feel of something. **2.** The basic make-up or structure of a substance. **3.** Distinctive or identifying character. **—tex'tur•al** *adj.* **—tex'tur•al•ly** *adv.*
-th[1] *suff. var. of* -ETH[1].
-th[2] *suff.* Used to form ordinal numbers <hundred*th*>
Th *symbol for* THORIUM.
Thai•land (tī'lănd'). Country of SE Asia, on the Gulf of Siam. *Cap.* Bangkok. *Pop.* 47,845,000. **—Thai** *adj. & n.*
thal•a•mus (thăl'ə-məs) *n., pl.* **-mi** (-mī'). *Anat.* A large rounded mass of gray nerve tissue at the base of the brain that relays sensory stimuli to the brain cortex. **—tha•lam'ic** (thə-lăm'ĭk) *adj.*

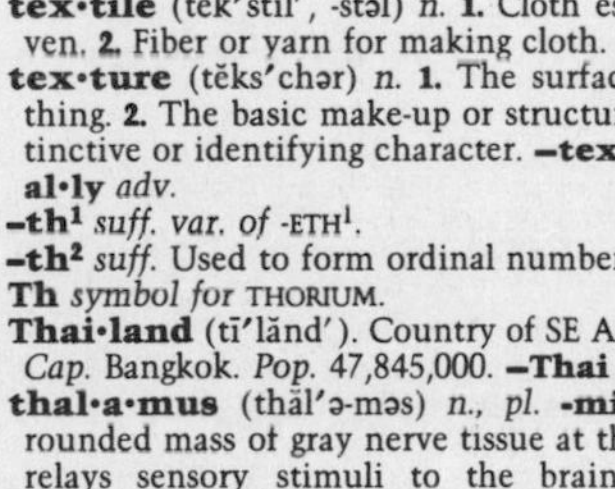

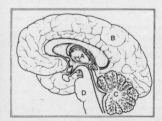

thalamus
A. thalamus, B. cerebrum, C. cerebellum, D. medulla oblongata

tha•lid•o•mide (thə-lĭd'ə-mīd') *n.* A sedative found to cause fetal abnormalities when used by pregnant women.
thal•li•um (thăl'ē-əm) *n. Symbol* **Tl** A soft, malleable, highly toxic metallic element used esp. in rodent and ant poisons.
Thames (tĕmz). River of S England, flowing c. 210 mi (337.8 km) to the North Sea.
than (thăn; thən *when unstressed*) *conj.* **1.** Used to indicate the 2nd element or clause after a comparative adjective or adverb <You are much taller *than* I am.> **2.** Used in statements of preference <would rather walk *than* ride> *—prep.* In comparison with.
thane (thān) *n.* A Scottish feudal lord.
thank (thăngk) *v.* **1.** To express one's thanks to. **2.** To hold responsible : credit.
thank•ful (thăngk'fəl) *adj.* Showing or feeling gratitude : grateful. **—thank'ful•ly** *adv.* **—thank'ful•ness** *n.*
thank•less (thăngk'lĭs) *adj.* **1.** Ungrateful. **2.** Unappreciated. **—thank'less•ly** *adv.* **—thank'less•ness** *n.*
thanks (thăngks) *pl.n.* An expression of appreciation. *—interj.* Used to express gratefulness. **—thanks to.** Because of.
thanks•giv•ing (thăngks-gĭv'ĭng) *n.* An act of expressing gratitude, esp. to God.
Thanksgiving Day *n.* A U.S. holiday celebrated on the 4th Thursday of Nov.
that (thăt; thət *when unstressed) adj., pl.* **those** (thōz). **1.** Being the one present or under discussion <*that* cat> **2.** Being less immediate than or contrasted with another <this room or *that* one> *—pron., pl.* **those. 1.** The one that is present or being discussed <*That* is our car.> **2.** Who, whom, or which <friends *that* are far away><jobs *that* are available> **3.** In, on, by, or with which <the day *that* you were sick> **4.** The one that is less immediate than or contrasted with another <This is mine, *that* is yours.> **5.** Something just mentioned <After *that*, we quit.> *—adv.* To such an extent : so <Are you *that* tired?> *—conj.* **1.** Used to introduce a dependent clause. **2.** Used to introduce an expression of desire.
thatch (thăch) *n.* Plant material, as straw, reeds, or palm fronds, used for roofing. *—v.* To overlay with or as if with thatch.
thaw (thô) *v.* **1.** To change or cause to change from a frozen to a soft or liquid state. **2.** To grow warmer so that snow and ice melt. **3.** To become less formal or reserved : relax. **—thaw** *n.*
the (thē *before a vowel;* thə *before a consonant*) *def. art.* **1.** Used as a determiner before nouns and noun phrases designating particular persons or things. **2.** Used before a singular noun to make it general <*the* human brain> **3.** Used before an adjective functioning as a noun <*the* strong and *the* weak> **4.** Used like a preposition before a noun, meaning *per. —adv.* To that or what extent <*the* quicker *the* better>
the•a•ter *or* **the•a•tre** (thē'ə-tər) *n.* **1.** A building or outdoor structure for presenting dramatic performances or motion pictures. **2.** A usu. large room with tiers of seats, as for lectures. **3.** Dramatic works or production. **4.** A context for dramatic events. **5.** An area of military operations.
the•at•ri•cal (thē-ăt'rĭ-kəl) *adj.* **1.** Of or appropriate for the theater. **2.** Marked by exaggeration. **3.** Extravagant. *—n.* **theatricals.** Performance of theatrical works. **—the•at'ri•cal'i•ty, the•at'ri•cal•ness** *n.* **—the•at'ri•cal•ly** *adv.*
the•at•rics (thē-ăt'rĭks) *pl.n.* **1.** *(sing. in number).* Theatricals. **2.** Behavior contrived for effect.
the•be (thā'bā) *n., pl.* **thebe.** See *pula* at CURRENCY TABLE.
Thebes (thēbz). Ancient religious center of Egypt. **—The'ban** *adj. & n.*
thee (thē) *pron. archaic objective case of* THOU.
theft (thĕft) *n.* The act or an instance of stealing : larceny.
their (thâr; thər *when unstressed) pron. possessive case of* THEY. Used before a noun as a modifier.
theirs (thârz) *pron.* That or those belonging to them.
the•ism (thē'ĭz'əm) *n.* Belief in a god or gods. **—the'ist** *n.* **—the•is'tic** *adj.*
them (thĕm; thəm *when unstressed) pron. objective case of* THEY. Used as the direct or indirect object of a verb or as the object of a preposition.
theme (thēm) *n.* **1.** A subject or topic. **2.** The subject of a work of art. **3.** A short composition written esp. by a student. **4.** The principal melody of a musical composition or movement. **—the•mat'ic** (thĭ-măt'ĭk) *adj.* **—the•mat'i•cal•ly** *adv.*
them•selves (thĕm-sĕlvz', thəm-) *pron.* They or them. Used: **1.** Reflexively as the direct or indirect object of a verb or as the object of a preposition <helped *themselves* to the pie><bought *themselves* a house><billed it to *themselves*> **2.** For emphasis <They *themselves* couldn't be sure.>
then (thĕn) *adv.* **1.** At that past time. **2.** After that : next. **3.** At a future time. **4.** In that case. **5.** Moreover. **6.** However. *—n.* That time or instance. *—adj.* Being or acting so at that time.
thence (thĕns, thĕns) *adv.* **1.** From there on. **2.** From that fact, event, or origin. **3.** From then on.
thence•forth (thĕns-fôrth', thĕns-) *adv.* From that time on.

thence·for·ward (thĕns-fôr′wərd, thĕns-) *also* **thence·for·wards** (-wərdz) *adv.* From then on.
the·oc·ra·cy (thē-ŏk′rə-sē) *n., pl.* **-cies. 1.** Government by officials claiming sanction by a deity. **2.** A state governed by a theocracy. **—the′o·crat′** *n.* **—the′o·crat′ic** *adj.* **—the′o·crat′i·cal·ly** *adv.*
the·ol·o·gy (thē-ŏl′ə-jē) *n., pl.* **-gies. 1.** The study of the nature of God, of religious ideas, beliefs, and practices, and esp. of humankind's relation to God. **2.** An organized body of opinions about such a relationship. **—the′o·lo′gi·an** (thē′ə-lō′jən) *n.* **—the′o·log′i·cal** (-lŏg′ĭ-kəl) *adj.* **—the′o·log′i·cal·ly** *adv.*
the·o·rem (thē′ə-rəm) *n.* **1.** An idea proven or assumed to be true : proposition. **2.** *Math.* A statement whose truth can be proved on the basis of a given set of axioms.
the·o·rize (thē′ə-rīz′) *v.* **-rized, -riz·ing.** To conceptualize or analyze theories. **—the′o·re·ti′cian** *n.* **—the′o·ri·za′tion** *n.* **—the′o·riz′er, the′o·rist** *n.*
the·o·ry (thē′ə-rē) *n., pl.* **-ries. 1.** A general principle formulated to account for certain observable phenomena : hypothesis. **2.** A body of principles governing the study or practice of an art or discipline. **3.** Abstract reasoning. **4.** An assumption or guess. **—the′o·ret′i·cal** (-rĕt′ĭ-kəl) *adj.* **—the′o·ret′i·cal·ly** *adv.*
the·os·o·phy (thē-ŏs′ə-fē) *n., pl.* **-phies.** Religious theory based on mystical insight into the nature of God. **—the′o·soph′ic** (-ə-sŏf′ĭk), **the′o·soph′i·cal** *adj.* **—the′o·soph′i·cal·ly** *adv.* **—the·os′o·phist** *n.*
ther·a·peu·tic (thĕr′ə-pyōō′tĭk) *adj.* Having the power to heal or cure. **—ther′a·peu′ti·cal·ly** *adv.*
ther·a·peu·tics (thĕr′ə-pyōō′tĭks) *n. (sing. in number).* Medical treatment of disease : therapy. **—ther′a·peu′tist** *n.*
ther·a·py (thĕr′ə-pē) *n., pl.* **-pies.** A procedure designed to treat disease, illness, or disability. **—ther′a·pist** *n.*
there (thâr) *adv.* **1.** In or at that place <Let's sit *there.*> **2.** To, into, or toward that place <took the train *there*> **3.** In that matter <I agree with you *there.*> *—n.* That place or point <got out of *there* fast> *—pron.* Used to introduce a sentence or clause.
there·a·bouts (thâr′ə-bouts′) *also* **there·a·bout** (-bout′) *adv.* **1.** Near that number or degree. **2.** Near that place or time.
there·af·ter (thâr-ăf′tər) *adv.* Afterward.
there·at (thâr-ăt′) *adv.* **1.** At that place. **2.** At that time. **3.** By reason of that.
there·by (thâr-bī′) *adv.* **1.** By means of that. **2.** With reference to that.
there·fore (thâr′fôr′, -fōr′) *adv.* For that reason : in consequence.
there·from (thâr-frŭm′, -frŏm′) *adv.* From this or that.
there·in (thâr-ĭn′) *adv.* **1.** In that place. **2.** In that circumstance or respect.
there·in·af·ter (thâr′ĭn-ăf′tər) *adv.* In a later part, as of a book or speech.
there·of (thâr-ŭv′, -ŏv′) *adv.* **1.** Of that or it. **2.** From that origin or cause.
there·on (thâr-ŏn′, -ôn′) *adv.* **1.** On or upon that. **2.** Directly following that.
there·to (thâr-tōō′) *adv.* To that or it.
there·to·fore (thâr′tə-fôr′, -fōr′) *adv.* Before that.
there·un·to (thâr′ŭn-tōō′) *adv.* Thereto.
there·up·on (thâr′ə-pŏn′, -pôn′) *adv.* **1.** On or upon that or it. **2.** Directly following that. **3.** For that reason : therefore.
there·with (thâr-wĭth′, -wĭth′) *adv.* **1.** With that or it. **2.** Directly after that.
ther·mal (thûr′məl) *adj.* **1.** Of, making use of, producing, or caused by heat. **2.** Designed to retain body heat <*thermal* underwear> **—ther′mal·ly** *adv.*
ther·mo·dy·nam·ics (thûr′mō-dī-năm′ĭks) *n. (sing. in number).* Physics involving the relations of heat with mechanical forms of enery. **—ther′mo·dy·nam′ic** *adj.* **—ther′mo·dy·nam′i·cal·ly** *adv.*
ther·mom·e·ter (thər-mŏm′ĭ-tər) *n.* An instrument for measuring temperature, esp. a glass tube in which mercury rises and falls with temperature variations. **—ther′mo·met′ric, ther′mo·met′ri·cal** *adj.*
ther·mo·nu·cle·ar (thûr′mō-nōō′klē-ər) *adj.* **1.** Of or derived from the fusion of atomic nuclei at high temperatures or the energy so produced. **2.** Of atomic weapons based on nuclear fusion.
ther·mo·plas·tic (thûr′mə-plăs′tĭk) *adj.* Soft and pliable when heated but hard when cooled. **—ther′mo·plas′tic** *n.*
Ther·mos bottle (thûr′məs). A trademark for a flask designed to maintain the desired temperature of the contents.
ther·mo·set·ting (thûr′mō-sĕt′ĭng) *adj.* Hardening permanently when heated.
ther·mo·stat (thûr′mə-stăt′) *n.* A device that automatically responds to temperature changes and activates switches controlling equipment such as furnaces, refrigerators, and air conditioners. **—ther′mo·stat′ic** *adj.* **—ther′mo·stat′i·cal·ly** *adv.*
the·sau·rus (thĭ-sôr′əs) *n., pl.* **-es** or **-sau·ri** (-sôr′ī′). **1.** A book of selected words or concepts, as a specialized vocabulary of a given field such as medicine or music. **2.** A book of synonyms.
▲word history: A thesaurus is literally a treasury of words and informaiton, for the word itself comes form Greek *thesauros,* "treasure." The Romans borrowed the Greek word, and Latin *thesaurus* developed into Old French *tresor,* which was borrowed into English as *treasure.* The Latin word *thesaurus* was used in titles of English books in early modern times, but it did not become a generic term for a particular kind of book until the 19th cent.
these (thēz) *pron. pl. of* THIS.
the·sis (thē′sĭs) *n., pl.* **-ses** (-sēz′). **1.** A statement advanced for consideration and maintained by argument. **2.** A formal paper or treatise written, as by a degree candidate, after original academic research.
thes·pi·an *also* **Thes·pi·an** (thĕs′pē-ən) *—adj.* Of or relating to drama. *—n.* A stage performer.
Thes·sa·lo·ni·ans (thĕs′ə-lō′nē-ənz) *pl.n. (sing. in number).* See BIBLE TABLE.
thews (thōōz, thyōōz) *pl.n.* **1.** Sinews or muscles. **2.** Muscular strength or power.
they (thā) *pron.* **1.** The ones just mentioned. Used as the plural of *he, she,* and *it.* **2.** People in general.
they'd (thād). **1.** They had. **2.** They would.
they'll (thāl). They will.
they're (thâr). They are.
they've (thāv). They have.
thi·a·mine (thī′ə-mĭn, -mēn′) *also* **thi·a·min** (-mĭn) *n.* A B-complex vitamin essential for normal metabolic and nerve functioning.
thick (thĭk) *adj.* **1. a.** Having considerable depth or extent from 1 surface or side to the other <a *thick* board> **b.** Determined by measurement <10 in. *thick*> **2.** Heavily or stockily built. **3.** Packed densely or abundantly. **4.** Having a viscous consistency. **5.** Numerous : abounding. **6.** Uttered indistinctly. **7.** Noticeable <a *thick* accent> **8.** Lacking mental quickness. **9.** *Informal.* Friendly. **10.** *Informal.* Excessive. *—n.* **1.** The thickest part of something. **2.** The most active or crowded part. **—thick′ly** *adv.* **—thick′ness** *n.*
thick·en (thĭk′ən) *v.* **1.** To make or become thick. **2.** To make more complex. **—thick′en·er** *n.* **—thick′en·ing** *n.*
thick·et (thĭk′ĭt) *n.* A close-packed growth of shrubs, small trees, etc.
thick·set (thĭk′sĕt′) *adj.* Having a stout, stocky body.
thick-skinned (thĭk′skĭnd′) *adj.* **1.** Having a thick skin. **2.** Not easily offended.
thief (thēf) *n., pl.* **thieves** (thēvz). One that steals, esp. furtively.
thieve (thēv) *v.* **thieved, thiev·ing.** To engage in or take by theft. **—thiev′er·y** *n.*
thigh (thī) *n.* The part of the vertebrate leg between the hip and the knee.
thigh·bone (thī′bōn′) *n.* The femur, extending from the hip to the knee.
thim·ble (thĭm′bəl) *n.* A small, cuplike guard worn to protect the finger in needlework. **—thim′ble·ful′** *n.*
Thim·bu (thĭm′bōō′) *also* **Thim·phu** (-pōō′). Cap. of Bhutan. *Pop.* 8,982.
thin (thĭn) *adj.* **thin·ner, thin·nest. 1.** Having little depth or extent from 1 surface or side to the other <a *thin* board> **2.** Fine in diameter <a *thin* wire> **3.** Slender in build. **4.** Not densely packed or abundant : sparse. **5. a.** Having a fluid consistency. **b.** Rarefied <*thin* air> **6.** Lacking force or substance. **—thin** *v.* **—thin′ly** *adv.* **—thin′ness** *n.*
thine (thīn) *pron. Archaic & Poetic.* That which belongs to thee. Used as a possessive form of *thou.*
thing (thĭng) *n.* **1.** Something that has a separate existence : entity. **2.** A real or material object. **3.** An inanimate object as distinguished from an animate being. **4.** A living being. **5. things. a.** Personal belongings. **b.** General conditions. **6.** A garment <not a *thing* to wear> **7.** An act or deed. **8.** A conception, idea, or utterance. **9.** A matter to be treated : concern. **10.** An incident : happening. **11.** An item or detail. **12.** A mild phobia or fixation. **13.** *Slang.* Something one enjoys or does esp. well.
think (thĭngk) *v.* **thought** (thôt), **think·ing. 1.** To formulate (a thought) in the mind. **2.** To reflect on : ponder. **3.** To exercise the power of reason. **4.** To have a view (about) : believe. **5.** To recall : remember. **6.** To visualize. **7.** To weigh or consider. **8.** To

dispose the mind in a given way <*think* big> **–think up.** To invent. **–think'a·ble** *adj.* **–think'er** *n.*
thin·ner (thĭn'ər) *n.* A liquid, as turpentine, mixed with paint to make it flow more easily.
thin-skinned (thĭn'skĭnd') *adj.* **1.** Having a thin skin or rind. **2.** Easily offended.
third (thûrd) *n.* **1.** The ordinal number that matches the number 3 in a series. **2.** One of 3 equal parts. **3.** The 3rd forward gear in the transmission of a motor vehicle. **–third** *adj.* & *adv.* **–third'ly** *adv.*
third degree *n.* Physical or mental torture to obtain information or a confession from a prisoner.
third-de·gree burn (thûrd'dĭ-grē') *n.* A severe burn marked by destruction of the epidermis and exposure of nerve endings.
third person *n.* The pronouns or verb forms used when making reference to a person or thing other than the speaker or writer or the one spoken to.
Third World *also* **third world** *n.* Underdeveloped or developing countries, esp. those not allied with the Communist or non-Communist blocs.
thirst (thûrst) *n.* **1. a.** A dry feeling in the mouth related to a wish to drink. **b.** The wish to drink. **2.** A fervent wish or craving. *–v.* **1.** To experience thirst. **2.** To have a craving : yearn. **–thirst'i·ly** *adv.* **–thirst'i·ness** *n.* **–thirst'y** *adj.*
thir·teen (thûr'tēn') *n.* **1.** The cardinal number equal to 12 + 1. **2.** The 13th in a set or sequence. **–thir'teen'** *adj.* & *pron.* **–thir'teenth'** *n.* & *adj.* & *adv.*
thir·ty (thûr'tē) *n.*, *pl.* **-ties.** The cardinal number equal to 3 × 10. **–thir'ti·eth** *n.* & *adj.* & *adv.* **–thir'ty** *adj.* & *pron.*
this (thĭs) *pron.*, *pl.* **these** (thēz). **1.** The one that is present or being discussed <*This* is our car.> **2.** Something about to be said <Now hear *this.*> **3.** The one that is more immediate than or contrasted with another <*This* is mine, that is yours.> **4.** The present time : now. *–adj.*, *pl.* **these. 1.** Being present or under discussion. **2.** Being more immediate than or contrasted with another. **3.** Being about to be said. *–adv.* To such an extent.
this·tle (thĭs'əl) *n.* Any of various plants, chiefly of the genera *Cirsium, Carduus,* or *Onopordum,* with usu. purplish flowers and prickly leaves.
this·tle·down (thĭs'əl-doun') *n.* The silky, fluffy material attached to the seeds of a thistle.
thith·er (thĭth'ər, *thĭth'-*) *adv.* To that place : there. *–adj.* Being on the farther or more distant side.
thole pin (thōl) *n.* A peg set in pairs in the gunwale of a boat to hold oars in place.
thong (thông, thŏng) *n.* A narrow strip of material, as leather, used esp. for binding.
tho·rax (thôr'ăks', thōr'-) *n.*, *pl.* **-es** *or* **tho·ra·ces** (thôr'ə-sēz', thōr'-). **1.** The section of the mammalian body between the neck and the abdomen : chest cavity. **2.** The middle section of the 3-part body of an insect. **–tho·rac'ic** (thə-răs'ĭk) *adj.*
tho·ri·um (thôr'ē-əm, thōr'-) *n. Symbol* **Th** A silvery-white radioactive metallic element used in magnesium alloys.
thorn (thôrn) *n.* **1. a.** A sharp, woody projection on a plant stem. **b.** A shrub, tree, or plant bearing such projections. **2.** One that causes irritation or annoyance. **–thorn'i·ness** *n.* **–thorn'y** *adj.*
thor·ough (thûr'ō, thŭr'ō) *adj.* **1.** Intensive : complete. **2.** Very careful or accurate. **3.** Absolute : unqualified. **–thor'ough·ly** *adv.* **–thor'ough·ness** *n.*
thor·ough·bred (thûr'ō-brĕd', thûr'ə-, thŭr'-) *adj.* Of pure breeding stock. *–n.* **1.** An animal bred of pure or pedigreed stock. **2. Thoroughbred.** Any of an English breed of racehorses.
thor·ough·fare (thûr'ō-fâr', thûr'ə-, thŭr'-) *n.* A public street, road, or highway.
thor·ough·go·ing (thûr'ō-gō'ĭng, thûr'ə-, thŭr'-) *adj.* **1.** Complete. **2.** Absolute.
those (thōz) *adj.* & *pron. pl. of* THAT.
thou (thou) *pron. Archaic.* The person spoken to : you.
though (thō) *adv.* None the less : however. *–conj.* **1.** Regardless of the fact that : although. **2.** Supposing that : even if.
thought (thôt) *n.* **1.** The act, process, or power of thinking. **2.** A product of thinking : idea. **3.** A body of ideas, as of a given time or place in history. **4.** Attentive consideration. **5.** An opinion, viewpoint, or belief. **6.** A small amount or degree.
thought·ful (thôt'fəl) *adj.* **1.** Contemplative. **2.** Marked by careful thought. **3.** Considerate. **–thought'ful·ness** *n.*
thought·less (thôt'lĭs) *adj.* **1.** Careless. **2.** Reckless : rash. **3.** Inconsiderate. **–thought'less·ness** *n.*
thou·sand (thou'zənd) *n.* The cardinal number equal to 10 × 100 or 10^3. **–thou'sand** *adj.* & *pron.* **–thou'sandth** *n.* & *adj.* & *adv.*

Thrace (thrās). Ancient country in the SE part of the Balkan Peninsula.
thrall (thrôl) *n.* **1.** A slave or serf. **2.** Bondage : servitude. **–thrall'dom** (-dəm), **thral'dom** *n.*
thrash (thrăsh) *v.* **1.** To strike or beat with or as if with a whip. **2.** To move violently about. **3.** To defeat : vanquish. **4.** To discuss fully <*thrash* out the problem> **5.** To thresh (grain).
thrash·er (thrăsh'ər) *n.* A long-tailed New World songbird of the genus *Toxostoma,* often with a spotted breast.
thread (thrĕd) *n.* **1.** A fine, thin cord made of 2 or more fibrous strands twisted together. **2.** Something resembling a thread <a *thread* of smoke> **3.** A ridge that winds around a screw, nut, or bolt. **4.** A cohesive element. *–v.* **1.** To pass a thread through (e.g., a needle). **2.** To string on a thread. **3.** To make one's way cautiously. **–thread'y** *adj.*
thread·bare (thrĕd'bâr') *adj.* **1.** So worn that the threads show through : shabby. **2.** Hackneyed : trite.
threat (thrĕt) *n.* **1.** An expression of the intent to inflict harm. **2.** A possible source of danger : menace.
threat·en (thrĕt'n) *v.* **1.** To make a threat (against). **2.** To menace. **3.** To give warning signs of : portend. **–threat'en·er** *n.* **–threat'en·ing·ly** *adv.*
three (thrē) *n.* **1.** The cardinal number equal to 3 + 1. **2.** The 3rd in a set or sequence. **3.** Something having 3 parts, units, or members. **–three** *adj.* & *pron.*
three-D *or* **3-D** (thrē'dē') *adj.* Three-dimensional.
three-di·men·sion·al (thrē'dĭ-mĕn'shən-əl) *adj.* **1.** Of or having 3 dimensions. **2.** Producing visual images that give an illusion of depth and perspective.
three-fold (thrē'fōld') *adj.* **1.** Having or consisting of 3 parts. **2.** 3 times as many or as much. **–three'fold'** *adv.*
three·score (thrē'skôr', -skōr') *adj.* Being 3 times 20 : 60. **–three'score'** *n.*
three·some (thrē'səm) *n.* 3 persons or things together.
thren·o·dy (thrĕn'ə-dē) *n.*, *pl.* **-dies.** A song of mourning. **–thren'o·dist** *n.*
thresh (thrĕsh) *v.* **1.** To separate the seeds from (cereal plants) by striking or beating. **2.** To beat severely : thrash.
thresh·old (thrĕsh'ōld', -hōld') *n.* **1.** A horizontal length of wood or stone serving as a doorsill. **2.** An entranceway. **3.** The place or point of beginning. **4.** The point at which a stimulus is perceptible or can produce an effect.
threw (thro͞o) *v. p.t. of* THROW.
thrice (thrīs) *adv.* **1.** Three times. **2.** Threefold in manner or degree.
thrift (thrĭft) *n.* Prudent management of money and other resources. **–thrift'i·ly** *adv.* **–thrift'i·ness** *n.* **–thrift'y** *adj.*
thrill (thrĭl) *v.* **1.** To experience or cause to experience sudden intense excitement, joy, fear, etc. **2.** To quiver : vibrate. **–thrill** *n.* **–thrill'ing·ly** *adv.*
thrive (thrīv) *v.* **throve** (thrōv) *or* **thrived, thrived** *or* **thriven** (thrĭv'ən), **thriving. 1.** To be healthy or do well : flourish. **2.** To be succcessful : prosper.
throat (thrōt) *n.* **1.** The section of the digestive tract forming a passage between the back of the mouth and the esophagus. **2.** The front section of the neck.
throat·y (thrō'tē) *adj.* **-i·er, -i·est.** Sounded or apparently coming from deep in the throat : guttural or husky. **–throat'i·ly** *adv.* **–throat'i·ness** *n.*
throb (thrŏb) *v.* **throbbed, throb·bing. 1.** To beat quickly or forcefully : pound. **2.** To vibrate or sound slowly and rhythmically. **–throb** *n.* **–throb'bing·ly** *adv.*
throe (thrō) *n.* **1.** *often* **throes.** A severe pang or spasm of pain, as in childbirth. **2. throes.** A very painful or effortful struggle.
throm·bo·sis (thrŏm-bō'sĭs) *n.*, *pl.* **-ses** (-sēz'). The development or presence of a thrombus.
throm·bus (thrŏm'bəs) *n.*, *pl.* **-bi** (-bī'). A blood clot occluding a blood vessel or formed in a heart cavity.
throne (thrōn) *n.* **1.** The ceremonial chair of a monarch, bishop, etc. **2.** The rank or power of a monarch.
throng (thrŏng) *n.* A large crowd : multitude. *–v.* **1.** To crowd into or around : fill. **2.** To move in or as if in a crowd.
throt·tle (thrŏt'l) *n.* **1.** An engine valve that regulates the vaporized fuel or steam flow. **2.** A lever or pedal controlling the throttle. *–v.* **-tled, -tling. 1.** To control (an engine speed or fuel) with a throttle. **2.** To choke (a person). **3.** To prevent by force : suppress. **–throt'tler** *n.*
through (thro͞o) *prep.* **1.** In 1 side and out the opposite or another side of <came *through* the tunnel> **2.** In the midst of <flew *through* the clouds> **3.** By way of <got in *through* the cellar> **4.** By means of <found the job *through* an ad> **5.** Around <biked *through* Europe> **6.** For the duration of <slept *through* the movie> **7.** At or to the end of <We're *through* the worst part.> **8.** As a result of <failed *through* carelessness> *–adv.* **1.** In 1 end or side and out the other. **2.**

From start to finish. **3.** Completely <chilled *through*> —*adj.* **1.** Extending from 1 end, side, or surface to another. **2.** Allowing unobstructed passage : direct. **3.** Finished. **4.** No longer effective or valued.

through·out (thro͞o-out′) *prep.* Through the whole extent or duration of. —*adv.* **1.** Everywhere. **2.** From start to finish.

throve (thrōv) *v. var. p.t. of* THRIVE.

throw (thrō) *v.* **threw** (thro͞o), **thrown** (thrōn), **throw·ing.** **1.** To cause to move through the air with a flinging motion of the arm. **2. a.** To hurl forcefully, as in anger. **b.** To cause to fall. **3.** To direct : cast <*threw* a glance my way> **4.** To put on or take off (clothing) hurriedly. **5.** *Informal.* To be the giver of (a party or social affair). **6.** *Informal.* To lose (a contest) by design. **7.** To move (a controlling lever or switch). **8.** To put abruptly into a given state <The threat *threw* us into turmoil.> **—throw up.** To vomit. —*n.* **1.** The act of throwing. **2.** The distance or height to which a projectile is or can be thrown. **3.** A light scarf, shawl, or coverlet.

throw·back (thrō′băk′) *n.* A reversion to an ancestral type or earlier stage : atavism.

thru (thro͞o) *prep.* & *adv.* & *adj. Informal.* Through.

thrum (thrŭm) *v.* **thrummed, thrum·ming.** To play idly on (a stringed instrument). **—thrum** *n.*

thrush (thrŭsh) *n.* A songbird of the family Turdidae, usu. with brownish upper plumage and a spotted breast.

thrush

thrust (thrŭst) *v.* **thrust, thrust·ing.** **1.** To push or shove with force. **2.** To stab, as with a dagger. **3.** To force (oneself or another) into a particular state or situation. **4.** To interject (e.g., comments). —*n.* **1.** A sudden forceful push or shove. **2. a.** A force or pressure that drives an object. **b.** The propelling force produced in a rocket or jet engine by the high-velocity rearward discharge of fuel gases. **3.** A stab with a pointed weapon. **4.** Stress or pressure of 1 part of a structure against another. **5.** General direction or tendency.

thru·way *also* **through·way** (thro͞o′wā′) *n.* A multilane highway : expressway.

Thu·cyd·i·des (tho͞o-sĭd′ə-dēz′). 5th cent. B.C. Greek historian.

thud (thŭd) *n.* **1.** A dull thumping sound. **2.** A blow or fall causing a thud. **—thud** *v.*

thug (thŭg) *n.* A tough or violent ruffian, hoodlum, or gangster. **—thug′ger·y** *n.* **—thug′gish** *adj.*

thu·li·um (tho͞o′lē-əm) *n. Symbol* **Tm** A silvery rare-earth metallic element.

thumb (thŭm) *n.* **1.** The short 1st digit of the hand, capable of touching the other 4 fingers. **2.** The part of a mitten or glove that fits over the thumb. —*v.* **1.** To browse rapidly through (a publication). **2.** To dirty or impair by excess handling. **3.** *Informal.* To hitchhike by signaling with the thumb.

thumb·nail (thŭm′nāl′) *n.* The nail of the thumb. —*adj.* Concise.

thumb·screw (thŭm′skro͞o′) *n.* **1.** A screw that can be turned with the thumb and index finger. **2.** An instrument of torture that crushed the thumb.

thumb·tack (thŭm′tăk′) *n.* A tack with a round, smooth head that can be pressed into place with the thumb.

thump (thŭmp) *n.* **1.** A blow with something blunt or weighty. **2.** The dull or muffled sound made by such a blow : thud. —*v.* **1.** To hit with something blunt or dull so as to make a thump. **2.** To throb : pound.

thun·der (thŭn′dər) *n.* **1.** The explosive or rumbling sound following a discharge of lightning. **2.** A loud rumbling noise similar to thunder. —*v.* **1.** To produce thunder or thunderlike sounds. **2.** To utter loudly. **—thun′der·ous** *adj.*

thun·der·bolt (thŭn′dər-bōlt′) *n.* A discharge of lightning immediately followed by thunder.

thun·der·clap (thŭn′dər-klăp′) *n.* A loud crash of thunder.

thun·der·cloud (thŭn′dər-kloud′) *n.* A large, dark cloud carrying an electric charge and producing thunder and lightning.

thun·der·head (thŭn′dər-hĕd′) *n.* The swollen upper part of a thundercloud.

thun·der·show·er (thŭn′dər-shou′ər) *n.* A brief, sometimes heavy rainstorm with thunder and lightning.

thun·der·storm (thŭn′dər-stôrm′) *n.* A rainstorm with thunder and lightning.

thun·der·struck (thŭn′dər-strŭk′) *adj.* Astounded : amazed.

Thurs. *also* **Thur.** *abbr.* Thursday.

Thurs·day (thûrz′dē, -dā′) *n.* The 5th day of the week.

thus (thŭs) *adv.* **1.** In this or that way. **2.** To such an extent or degree. **3.** Therefore.

thwack (thwăk) *v.* To strike hard with something flat : whack. **—thwack** *n.*

thwart (thwôrt) *v.* To keep from happening : frustrate. —*n.* A seat placed across a boat for an oarsman. —*adj.* Extending across something : transverse. —*adv.* & *prep. Archaic.* Across.

thy (thī) *adj. Archaic.* Of or pertaining to thee or thyself. Used as a possessive form of *thou.*

thyme (tīm) *n.* An aromatic plant of the genus *Thymus,* esp. *T. vulgaris,* of S Europe, with leaves used in cooking.

thy·mine (thī′mēn′) *n.* A pyrimidine base that is an essential constituent of deoxyribonucleic acid.

thy·mus (thī′məs) *n.* **1.** A glandlike structure near the throat that is usu. vestigial in adults. **2.** A similar structure in other vertebrate animals, used esp. as a sweetbread. **—thy′mic** *adj.*

thy·roid (thī′roid′) *adj.* Of or pertaining to the thyroid gland. —*n.* **1.** The thyroid gland. **2.** A medicine prepared from the thyroid gland of certain domestic animals.

thyroid gland *n.* A 2-lobed endocrine gland located at the base of the neck in humans and producing thyroxin.

thy·rox·in (thī-rŏk′sĭn) *also* **thy·rox·ine** (-sēn′, -sĭn) *n.* An iodine-containing hormone produced by the thyroid gland to regulate growth and metabolism and made synthetically to treat thyroid disorders.

thy·self (thī-sĕlf′) *pron. Archaic.* Yourself.

Ti *symbol for* TITANIUM.

ti·ar·a (tē-ăr′ə, -âr′ə, -är′ə) *n.* **1.** An often bejeweled, crownlike ornamental headdress worn by women on formal occasions. **2.** The tall triple crown worn by the pope.

Ti·ber (tī′bər). River of C Italy.

Ti·bet (tĭ-bĕt′). Region and former state of SW Asia. **—Ti·bet′an** *adj.* & *n.*

tib·i·a (tĭb′ē-ə) *n., pl.* **-i·ae** (-ē-ē′) *or* **-as.** The larger inner bone of the vertebrate lower leg. **—tib′i·al** *adj.*

tic (tĭk) *n.* A recurring muscular spasm, usu. in the face or limbs.

tick[1] (tĭk) *n.* **1.** A light rhythmical tapping sound, as made by a clock. **2.** A small check mark used on a list or to call attention to an item. **—tick** *v.*

tick[2] (tĭk) *n.* Any of numerous bloodsucking parasitic arachnids of the family Ixodidae or louselike insects of the family Hippoboscidae, many of which are carriers of disease.

tick[3] (tĭk) *n.* **1.** The sturdy fabric used to cover a mattress or pillow. **2.** Ticking.

tick·er (tĭk′ər) *n.* **1.** A telegraphic printing or display device that automatically receives and records news or stock-market quotations. **2.** *Slang.* The human heart.

ticker tape *n.* The strip of paper on which a telegraphic ticker prints.

tick·et (tĭk′ĭt) *n.* **1.** A paper slip or card entitling its holder to a specified service or privilege. **2.** A certifying document or license. **3.** An identifying or descriptive tag. **4.** A list of political candidates supported by a party or group. **5.** A legal summons for a violation. —*v.* **1.** To supply with a ticket. **2.** To label. **3.** To designate for a certain use. **4.** To serve with a legal summons.

tick·ing (tĭk′ĭng) *n.* A strong, sturdy, often striped fabric used to make casings for pillows and mattresses.

tick·le (tĭk′əl) *v.* **-led, -ling.** **1.** To touch (a bodily part) lightly so as to cause twitching or laughter. **2.** To delight or amuse. **3.** To experience a tingling or twitching sensation. **—tick′le** *n.* **—tick′ler** *n.*

tick·lish (tĭk′lĭsh) *adj.* **1.** Sensitive to being tickled. **2.** Easily upset or offended. **3.** Requiring diplomacy or delicacy.

tick-tack-toe *also* **tic-tac-toe** (tĭk′tăk-tō′) *n.* A game in which each of 2 players tries to make a line of 3 X's or 3 O's inside a 9-space box.

tidal wave *n.* **1.** An unusual rise of water along the seashore esp. as a result of strong winds. **2.** A very large ocean wave caused esp. by an earthquake. **3.** A widespread display, as of opinion or sentiment.

tid·bit (tĭd′bĭt′) *n.* A choice bit, esp. of food or gossip.

tide (tīd) *n.* **1. a.** The periodic rise and fall of the surface level of the oceans, caused by the gravitational pull of the moon and sun. **b.** A particular occurrence of a tide. **c.** The water that moves in a tide. 2. A forceful trend. 3. A time or season. **—tid'al** *adj.*

tide·land (tīd'lănd') *n.* Coastal land that is under water during high tide.

tide·wa·ter (tīd'wô'tər, -wŏt'ər) *n.* **1.** Water that inundates the land when the tide is very high. **2.** River water and streams affected by tides. **3.** Low coastal land.

tid·ings (tī'dĭngz) *pl.n.* News.

ti·dy (tī'dē) *adj.* **-di·er, -di·est. 1.** Neat and clean : orderly. **2.** *Informal.* Substantial <a *tidy* sum of money> *—v.* **-died, -dy·ing.** To make (things) orderly. **—ti'di·ly** *adv.* **—ti'di·ness** *n.*

tie (tī) *v.* **tied, ty·ing. 1.** To bind or secure with a cord, rope, line, etc. **2.** To fasten by bringing together and knotting strings or laces. **3.** To form (a knot or bow). **4.** To make a knot or bow in. **5.** To link : unite. **6.** To match (an opponent or score) in a competition. ☆***syns:*** BIND, KNOT, SECURE *—n.* **1.** A cord, string, rope, etc. by which something is tied. **2.** A necktie. **3.** Something that unites. **4.** An equality of scores, votes, etc. **5.** A beam, rod, etc., that gives structural support. **6.** A timber laid crosswise to support railway tracks.

tie-dye (tī'dī') *n.* A method of dyeing fabric by tying parts of it to prevent absorption of the dye, creating a streaked or mottled pattern. **—tie'-dye'** *v.*

tier (tîr) *n.* A row or layer, esp. 1 of a series of rows arranged 1 above or behind another. **—tiered** *adj.*

tie-up (tī'ŭp') *n.* **1.** A temporary suspension or delay. **2.** A connection.

tiff (tĭf) *n.* **1.** A fit of annoyance. **2.** A petty dispute. **—tiff** *v.*

ti·ger (tī'gər) *n.* A large carnivorous Asian cat, *Panthera tigris,* with a tawny black-striped coat. **—ti'gress** *n.*

ti·ger-eye (tī'gər-ī') *also* **ti·ger's-eye** (tī'gərz-) *n.* A yellow-brown gemstone.

tiger lily *n.* An Asian plant, *Lilium tigrinum,* with black-spotted orange flowers.

†**tight** (tīt) *adj.* **1.** So close in construction or texture that air, water, etc., cannot penetrate. **2.** Fixed firmly in place. **3.** Set closely together : compact. **4.** Stretched taut. **5.** Fitting uncomfortably close <*tight* boots> **6.** Constricted : compressed. **7.** Close-fisted : stingy. **8.** Difficult <was in a *tight* spot> **9.** Evenly matched <a *tight* race> **10.** *Slang.* Intoxicated. **11.** *Regional.* Neat and trim. *—adv.* **1.** In a firm way. **2.** In a deep or sound way. **—tight'ly** *adv.* **—tight'ness** *n.*

tight·en (tīt'n) *v.* To make or become tight. **—tight'en·er** *n.*

tight·fist·ed (tīt'fĭs'tĭd) *adj.* Stingy.

tight·lipped (tīt'lĭpt') *adj.* Reticent.

tight·rope (tīt'rōp') *n.* A tightly stretched rope or wire high above the ground on which acrobats perform.

tights (tīts) *pl.n.* A tight-fitting stretchable garment designed esp. for the lower half of the body.

tight·wad (tīt'wŏd') *n. Slang.* A stingy person : miser.

Ti·gris (tī'grĭs). River of SW Asia, rising in E Turkey and flowing c. 1,150 mi (1,850 km) to the Euphrates in S Iraq.

Ti·jua·na (tē-wä'nə). City of NW Mexico. *Pop.* 535,000.

til·de (tĭl'də) *n.* A diacritical mark (˜) used to indicate certain nasal sounds in Spanish and Portuguese.

tile (tīl) *n.* **1.** A thin slab of baked clay, plastic, concrete, etc., used to cover walls, floors, or roofs. **2.** A short earthenware pipe used in drains, chimneys, etc. **—tile** *v.*

till[1] (tĭl) *v.* To plow, harrow, and fertilize (land) before planting. **—till'a·ble** *adj.*

till[2] (tĭl) *prep.* Until. *—conj.* **1.** Until. **2.** Before or unless.

till[3] (tĭl) *n.* A small drawer for money, esp. in a store or bank.

till·age (tĭl'ĭj) *n.* **1.** The work of cultivating land. **2.** Cultivated land.

till·er[1] (tĭl'ər) *n.* A person or machine that tills land.

till·er[2] (tĭl'ər) *n.* A steering lever used to turn a boat's rudder from side to side.

tilt (tĭlt) *v.* **1.** To tip or cause to tip, as by raising 1 end. **2.** To engage in a joust. *—n.* **1.** A sloping surface or direction. **2.** A joust with lances. **3.** A spirited verbal contest **—at full tilt.** As fast as possible.

tim·ber (tĭm'bər) *n.* **1.** Growing trees or wooded land. **2.** †**a.** Wood used for building : lumber. **b.** A finished piece of wood, esp. a structural beam. **c.** A curved support in a ship's frame. **—tim'bered** *adj.*

tim·ber·line (tĭm'bər-līn') *n.* The height or limit beyond which trees do not grow in mountainous or artic regions.

tim·bre (tĭm'bər, tăm'-) *n.* The quality of a sound that makes it distinct from others of the same pitch and volume.

time (tīm) *n.* **1.a.** A continuous measurable quantity in which events occur in apparently irreversible order. **b.** An interval bounded by 2 points of this quantity : duration. **c.** A numerical measure of this interval, as in years, days, or minutes. **d.** A number representing a given point, as the present, as determined from a given point in the past. **e.** A system of numerical measure for this quantity <standard *time*> **2.** *often* **times.** A particular period in history : era. **3.** An opportune moment. **4.** A fixed or customary moment or period <dinner *time*> **5.** One of a series of instances <tried 3 *times*> **6.** An occasion associated with a certain experience <had a *great time*> **7.** *Informal.* A period in prison. **8.** Rate of speed. **9.** A musical meter. **10. a.** The regular period of work. **b.** The pay received. *—adj.* **1.** Of or pertaining to time. **2.** Set to operate at a certain moment. **3.** Of or pertaining to paying in installments. *—v.* **timed, tim·ing. 1.** To arrange the time for (an event or occasion) : schedule. **2.** To adjust (a timepiece) to keep accurate time. **3.** To adjust or control so that movements or events occur in proper sequence. **4.** To set, maintain, or record the pace or duration of. **—on time. 1.** According to schedule : promptly. **2.** By making successive payments. **—tim'er** *n.*

time clock *n.* An instrument that records the times employees begin and finish work.

time-hon·ored (tīm'ŏn'ərd) *adj.* Respected because of age or long tradition.

time·keep·er (tīm'kē'pər) *n.* **1.** A timepiece. **2.** One who times a contest or contestants or records employee work hours.

time·less (tīm'lĭs) *adj.* **1.** Having no limit or end : eternal. **2.** Unaffected by time : ageless. **—time'less·ness** *n.*

time·ly (tīm'lē) *adj.* **-li·er, -li·est.** Occurring or done at an opportune or appropriate time. **—time'li·ness** *n.*

time-out (tīm'out') *n.* A brief period of rest or consultation during a game.

time·piece (tīm'pēs') *n.* An instrument, as a clock or watch, that measures, records, or indicates time.

times (tīmz) *prep.* Multiplied by.

time-shar·ing (tīm'shâr'ĭng) *n.* **1.** Simultaneous sharing of a computer by many users at different sites. **2.** Joint ownership with individual use of vacation property.

time·ta·ble (tīm'tā'bəl) *n.* A schedule listing the time at which certain events, as arrivals and departures at a transportation station, are expected to take place.

time·worn (tīm'wôrn', -wōrn') *adj.* **1.** Impaired or affected by long wear or use. **2.** Hackneyed : trite.

tim·id (tĭm'ĭd) *adj.* **1.** Fearful. **2.** Lacking in self confidence : shy. **—ti·mid'i·ty, tim'id·ness** *n.* **—tim'id·ly** *adv.*

tim·or·ous (tĭm'ər-əs) *adj.* Easily frightened : timid. **—tim'or·ous·ly** *adv.*

tim·o·thy (tĭm'ə-thē) *n.* A native Eurasian grass, *Phleum pratense,* with narrow, cylindrical flower spikes, grown for hay.

Tim·o·thy (tĭm'ə-thē) *n.* See BIBLE TABLE.

tim·pa·ni *also* **tym·pa·ni** (tĭm'pə-nē) *pl.n.* A set of kettledrums in an orchestra. **—tim'pa·nist** *n.*

tin (tĭn) *n.* **1.** *Symbol* **Sn** A soft silvery malleable metallic element. **2.** A container or box made of or plated with tin. **3.** *esp. Brit.* A can in which food is preserved. *—v.* **tinned, tin·ning. 1.** To coat or plate with tin. **2.** *esp. Brit.* To preserve in tins.

tinc·ture (tĭngk'chər) *n.* **1.** A pigment for dyeing. **2.** A shade of a color : tint. **3.** A slight trace. **4.** An alcohol solution of a medicine that does not change readily into a vapor. *—v.* **-tured, -tur·ing.** To tint.

tin·der (tĭn'dər) *n.* Readily ignited material used for kindling.

tin·der·box (tĭn'dər-bŏks') *n.* **1.** A metal box for holding tinder. **2.** A firetrap. **3.** A highly dangerous or explosive situation.

tine (tīn) *n.* A narrow pointed part, as of a fork or an antler.

tin·foil (tĭn'foil') *n.* A thin pliable sheet of aluminum or a tin alloy.

tinge (tĭnj) *v.* **tinged** (tĭnjd), **tinge·ing** *or* **ting·ing. 1.** To impart a trace of color to : tint. **2.** To affect slightly, as by admixture. *—n.* A slight trace, as of color or flavor.

tin·gle (tĭng'gəl) *v.* **-gled, -gling.** To feel or cause a prickling, stinging sensation. **—tin'gle** *n.* **—tin'gler** *n.* **—tin'gly** *adj.*

tink·er (tĭng'kər) *n.* **1.** One who usu. travels from place to place mending household utensils. **2.** One unskillful at making repairs : bungler. *—v.* **1.** To do a tinker's work. **2.** To toy with machine parts experimentally in an effort to repair.

tin·kle (tĭng'kəl) *v.* **-kled, -kling.** To make or cause to make a series of metallic ringing sounds <bells *tinkling*> **—tin'kle** *n.* **—tin'kly** *adj.*

tin·ny (tĭn'ē) *adj.* **-ni·er, -ni·est. 1.** Of, having, yielding, or suggestive of tin. **2.** Of or producing a thin metallic sound.

tin plate *n.* Thin sheet iron or steel coated with tin. **—tin'-plate'** *v.*

tin·sel (tĭn'səl) *n.* **1.** Very slender strips or threads of a glittering material, as metal foil, used for decoration. **2.** Something showy but worthless. **—tin'sel** *adj.*

tin·smith (tĭn'smĭth') *n.* A person who makes and repairs tin articles.

tint (tĭnt) *n.* **1.** A shade of a color, esp. a pale or faint variation : tinge. **2.** A slight coloration : hue. **3.** A barely detectable degree :

trace. **4.** A dye for the hair. —*v.* To give a tint to or take on a tint.

tin·tin·nab·u·la·tion (tĭn′tĭ-năb′yə-lā′shən) *n.* The ringing of bells.

tin·type (tĭn′tīp′) *n.* A positive photograph made directly on a treated iron plate.

tin·work (tĭn′wûrk′) *n.* **1.** Work in tin. **2. tinworks** *(sing. or pl. in number).* A place where tin is smelted and rolled.

ti·ny (tī′nē) *adj.* **-ni·er, -ni·est.** Very small : minute.

-tion *suff.* Action : process <absorp*tion*>

tip[1] (tĭp) *n.* **1.** The end of something, esp. of something pointed or projecting. **2.** A piece or attachment designed to be fitted to the end of something. —*v.* **tipped, tip·ping. 1.** To provide with a tip. **2.** To cover, ornament, or remove the tip of.

tip[2] (tĭp) *v.* **tipped, tip·ping. 1.** To topple over : upset. **2.** To tilt. **—tip** *n.*

tip[3] (tĭp) **tipped, tip·ping. 1.** To strike softly : tap. **2.** *Baseball.* To hit (the ball) with the side of the bat so that it glances off. —*n.* A light blow : tap.

tip[4] (tĭp) *n.* **1.** A small sum of money given as an acknowledgment of services rendered : gratuity. **2. a.** Advance or inside information given as a guide to action. **b.** A helpful hint. —*v.* **tipped, tip·ping. 1.** To give a gratuity (to). **2.** To provide advance or inside information to. **—tip′per** *n.*

tip-off (tĭp′ôf′, -ŏf′) *n.* **1.** *Informal.* An item of advance or inside information. **2.** *Basketball.* The act or practice of beginning a game or overtime period with a jump ball.

tip·pet (tĭp′ĭt) *n.* **1.** A covering for the shoulders, as of fur, with long ends that hang in front. **2.** A long hanging part, as of a sleeve, hood, or cape.

tip·ple (tĭp′əl) *v.* **-pled, -pling.** To drink alcoholic beverages, esp. to excess. —*n.* Alcoholic liquor. **—tip′pler** *n.*

tip·ster (tĭp′stər) *n. Informal.* A person who sells inside information, as to those who gamble or bet.

tip·sy (tĭp′sē) *adj.* **-si·er, -si·est. 1.** Slightly inebriated. **2.** Likely to tip over. **—tip′si·ly** *adv.* **—tip′si·ness** *n.*

tip·toe (tĭp′tō′) *v.* To walk stealthily on or as if on the tips of one's toes. —*n.* The tip of a toe. —*adj.* **1.** Standing or walking on or as if on the tips of one's toes. **2.** Stealthy : wary. —*adv.* On or as if on tiptoe.

tip·top (tĭp′tŏp′) *n.* **1.** The highest point : apex. **2.** The highest degree of quality or excellence. **—tip′top′** *adj.* & *adv.*

ti·rade (tī′răd′, tī-răd′) *n.* A long angry or violent speech, usu. of a censorious or denunciatory nature. ☆**syns:** DIATRIBE, FULMINATION, HARANGUE, JEREMIAD, OBLOQUY, PHILIPPIC

Ti·ra·në (tĭ-rä′nə). Cap. of Albania, in the C part. *Pop.* 192,300.

tire[1] (tīr) *v.* **tired, tir·ing. 1.** To make or become weary : fatigue. **2.** To make or become uninterested or bored.

tire[2] (tīr) *n.* **1.** A covering for a wheel, usu. made of rubber reinforced with cords of nylon or fiber glass and filled with compressed air. **2.** A hoop, as of rubber or metal, fitted around a wheel.

tired (tīrd) *adj.* **1. a.** Marked by weariness : fatigued. **b.** Not enthusiastic : bored. **2.** Lacking originality : trite <a *tired* joke>

tire·less (tīr′lĭs) *adj.* Not tiring easily : indefatigable. **—tire′less·ly** *adv.*

tire·some (tīr′səm) *adj.* **1.** Causing fatigue : wearisome. **2.** Causing boredom : tedious. **3.** Causing annoyance : bothersome. **—tire′some·ness** *n.*

'tis (tĭz). It is.

tis·sue (tĭsh′o͞o) *n.* **1.** *Biol.* **a.** An aggregation of morphologically and funtionally similar cells. **b.** Cellular matter regarded as a collective entity. **2.** A soft, absorbent piece of paper used as a disposable handkerchief or towel. **3.** *also* **tissue paper.** Thin, nearly translucent paper used for packing, wrapping, or protecting delicate articles. **4.** A light, thin, sheer cloth. **5.** An interrelated number of things <a *tissue* of lies>

tit (tĭt) *n.* **1.** Any of various small European birds of the family Paridae, related to and resembling the American chickadees. **2.** A bird similar or related to the tit.

ti·tan (tīt′n) *n.* One that is great in size, importance, or achievement.

ti·tan·ic (tī-tăn′ĭk) *adj.* **1.** Having great stature or enormous strength : huge. **2.** Enormous in scope, power, or influence.

ti·ta·ni·um (tī-tā′nē-əm, tĭ-) *n. Symbol* **Ti** A strong, shiny white metal element that is highly resistant to corrosion.

tithe (tīth) *n.* **1.** A 10th part of one's annual income, contributed voluntarily for charity or due as a tax for the support of the clergy or church. **2.** A 10th part. **—tithe′** *v.* **—tith′er** *n.*

ti·tian (tĭsh′ən) *n.* Auburn.

tit·il·late (tĭt′ə-lāt′) *v.* **-lat·ed, -lat·ing. 1.** To stimulate by touching or tickling lightly. **2.** To excite pleasingly. **—tit′il·lat′ing·ly** *adv.* **—tit′il·la′tion** *n.*

ti·tle (tīt′l) *n.* **1.** An identifying name given to something, as a book, play, film, etc. **2. a.** Written matter included in a film or television program to give credits. **b.** A subtitle in a film. **3.** *Law.* **a.** The aggregate evidence that gives rise to a legal right of possession or control. **b.** The document that constitutes this evidence, as a deed. **4.** Something that justifies a claim. **5.** A formal appellation attached to a person or family by virtue of office, rank, hereditary privilege, etc. **6.** A descriptive appellation : epithet. **7.** A championship in sports. —*v.* **-tled, -tling.** To provide with a title : confer a name on.

ti·tle·hold·er (tīt′l-hōl′dər) *n.* One that holds a title, esp. for a championship.

tit·mouse (tĭt′mous′) *n.* **1.** Any of several small North American birds of the genus *Parus,* having grayish plumage and a pointed crest. **2.** TIT 1.

tit·ter (tĭt′ər) *v.* To utter a suppressed, nervous giggle. **—tit′ter** *n.*

tit·tle (tĭt′l) *n.* The smallest bit : jot.

tit·tle-tat·tle (tĭt′l-tăt′l) *n.* Petty gossip. —*v.* To engage in gossip.

tit·u·lar (tĭch′o͝o-lər) *adj.* **1.** Of or having a title. **2.** In name only <the *titular* head of the department> **—tit′u·lar·ly** *adv.*

Ti·tus (tī′təs) *n.* See BIBLE TABLE.

tiz·zy (tĭz′ē) *n., pl.* **-zies.** *Slang.* A nervous, excited state of confusion : snit.

tkt. *abbr.* ticket.

Tl *symbol for* THALLIUM.

Tm *symbol for* THULIUM.

TM *abbr.* trademark.

TN *abbr.* Tennessee (with Zip Code).

tn. *abbr.* **1.** town. **2.** train.

TNT (tē′ĕn-tē′) *n.* Trinitrotoluene.

to (to͞o; *unstressed* tə) *prep.* **1.** In a direction toward <went *to* town> <turned *to* us and spoke> **2. a.** Reaching as far as <rotten *to* the core> **b.** To the extent of <beaten *to* death> **c.** With the resultant condition of <torn *to* bits> **3.** Toward a specified state <his rise *to* power> **4.** In contact with <a face pressed *to* the glass> **5.** In front of <stood face *to* face> **6.** Used to indicate possession <I have the belt *to* this coat.> **7.** Concerning <deaf *to* our pleas> **8.** In a given relationship with <at right angles *to* the line> **9.** As an accompaniment of <danced *to* the music> **10.** In respect of <the secret *to* my success> **11.** Composing <4 qts *to* a gal> **12.** In harmony with <not *to* my taste> **13.** In comparison with. **14. a.** Before <The time is 5 minutes *to* 10.> **b.** Until <worked from 8 *to* 4> **15. a.** For the purpose of <went out *to* dinner> **b.** In honor of. **16.** Used before a verb to indicate the infinitive <I'd like *to* rest.> Also used alone when the infinitive is understood <Rest if you want *to.*> **17. a.** Used to indicate the relationship of a verb with its complement <refer *to* a thesaurus><refer me *to* a thesaurus> **b.** Used with a reflexive pronoun to indicate exclusivity or separateness <had the train all *to* ourselves> —*adv.* **1.** In a direction toward <ran *to* and fro> **2.** Into a shut or closed position <pushed the gate *to*> **3.** Into a state of consciousness <The doctor brought the patient *to.*> **4.** Into a state of action <sat down to eat and fell *to*>

toad (tōd) *n.* Any of numerous tailless amphibians chiefly of the family Bufonidae, resembling the frogs but having rougher, drier skin.

toad·stool (tōd′sto͞ol′) *n.* A poisonous or inedible fungus with an umbrella-shaped fruiting body.

toad·y (tō′dē) *n., pl.* **-ies.** One who obsequiously flatters or defers to others in order to gain favor : sycophant. **—toady** *v.*

toast[1] (tōst) *v.* **1.** To heat and brown (e.g., bread) by placing it in a toaster or close to a fire. **2.** To warm thoroughly, as before a fire. —*n.* Sliced bread that has been heated and browned. **—toast′y** *adj.*

toast[2] (tōst) *n.* **1.** The act of drinking to the health of or in honor of another. **2.** The one honored by a toast. **3.** One receiving much attention or acclaim <the *toast* of Hollywood> —*v.* To drink or propose a drink in honor of or the health of.

toast·er (tō′stər) *n.* A device for toasting bread, esp. by electrically heated coils.

toast·mas·ter (tōst′măs′tər) *n.* One who introduces speakers at a banquet. **—toast′mis′tress** *n.*

to·bac·co (tə-băk′ō) *n., pl.* **-cos** or **-coes. 1.** A tropical American plant of the genus *Nicotiana,* esp. *N. tabacum* widely cultivated for its leaves, which are dried and processed for smoking or chewing as snuff. **2.** Products made from tobacco.

to·bac·co·nist (tə-băk′ə-nĭst) *n.* A dealer in tobacco.

To·bit (tō′bĭt) *n.* See BIBLE TABLE.

to·bog·gan (tə-bŏg′ən) *n.* A long, narrow sled without runners, made of thin boards curved upward at the front end. —*v.* **1.** To ride on a toboggan. **2.** To decline sharply <sales that *tobogganed*> **—to·bog′gan·er, to·bog′gan·ist** *n.*

toc·sin (tŏk′sĭn) *n.* **1.** An alarm sounded on a bell. **2.** A warning.

to·day *also* **to-day** (tə-dā′) *adv.* **1.** On or during the present day. **2.** At or during the present time. *—n.* The present time, day, or period.

tod·dle (tŏd′l) *v.* **-dled, -dling.** To walk unsteadily with short steps. **—tod′dler** *n.*

tod·dy (tŏd′ē) *n., pl.* **-dies.** A drink of brandy or other liquor mixed with hot water, sugar, and spices.

to-do (tə-dōō′) *n., pl.* **-dos** (-dōōz′). *Informal.* Commotion : fuss.

toe (tō) *n.* **1.** One of the extensions from the foot, esp. of a vertebrate animal. **2.** The part of a shoe, sock, or boot covering the toes. **3.** Something resembling a toe. *—v.* **toed, toe·ing.** To touch, kick, or reach with the toe. **—on (one's) toes.** Prepared to act : alert.

toe·a (toi′ə) *n., pl.* **toea.** See *kina* at CURRENCY TABLE.

toe·hold (tō′hōld′) *n.* **1.** A small indentation on which the toe can find support in climbing. **2.** A slight advantage.

toe·nail (tō′nāl′) *n.* The nail on a toe.

tof·fee (tŏf′ē, tô′fē) *n.* A hard, chewy candy made of brown sugar and butter.

to·fu (tō′fōō) *n.* Bean curd.

tog (tŏg, tôg) *Informal.* *—n.* **1.** A coat or cloak. **2. togs.** Clothes <jogging *togs*> *—v.* **togged, tog·ging.** To clothe or dress <*togged* themselves out in high boots>

to·ga (tō′gə) *n.* A loosely draped outer garment worn in public by citizens in ancient Rome. **—to′gaed** *adj.*

to·geth·er (tə-gĕth′ər) *adv.* **1.** In or into a single mass, group, or place <gathered *together* for dinner> **2.** Mutually or reciprocally <couldn't get along *together*> **3.** Regarded collectively : jointly. **4.** Simultaneously. **5.** In accord or harmony <stood *together* on the issue> **6.** *Informal.* In an effective, coherent condition <Get yourself *together* and stop complaining.> *—adj. Slang.* **1.** In tune with what is going on : hip <a *together* person> **—to·geth′er·ness** *n.*

tog·gle (tŏg′əl) *n.* An ornamental crosspiece or button, as of wood or bone, inserted into a loop as a fastening.

To·go (tō′gō). Country of W Africa. *Cap.* Lomé. *Pop.* 2,565,000.

toil[1] (toil) *v.* **1.** To work laboriously and continuously. **2.** To advance with difficulty. **—toil′some** *adj.*

toil[2] (toil) *n. often* **toils.** An entanglement <caught up in the *toils* of politics>

toi·let (toi′lĭt) *n.* **1. a.** An apparatus consisting of a porcelain bowl fitted with a hinged seat and a flushing device, used for the disposal of bodily wastes. **b.** A room or stall containing such an apparatus. **2.** TOILETTE 1. **3.** *Archaic.* A dressing table. **4.** Dress : attire.

toi·let·ry (toi′lĭ-trē) *n., pl.* **-ries.** An article or cosmetic for grooming oneself.

toi·lette (twä-lĕt′) *n.* **1.** The act or process of dressing or grooming oneself. **2.** One's dress or style of dress.

toilet water *n.* A scented liquid weaker than perfume and stronger than cologne.

To·kay (tō-kā′) *n.* A sweet, gold-colored dessert wine.

to·ken (tō′kən) *n.* **1.** An indication or representation of a fact, event, or emotion : sign. **2.** A symbol or evidence of authority, validity, or identity. **3.** A keepsake. **4.** A piece of stamped metal used as a substitute for money. *—adj.* **1.** Done as an indication or pledge <a *token* contribution> **2. a.** Perfunctory. **b.** Symbolic.

To·ky·o (tō′kē-ō′). Cap. of Japan, in E Honshu. *Pop.* 8,349,209.

told (tōld) *v. p.t. & p.p. of* TELL.

To·le·do (tə-lē′dō). City of NW Ohio, on Lake Erie. *Pop.* 354,635.

tol·er·a·ble (tŏl′ər-ə-bəl) *adj.* **1.** Able to be tolerated. **2.** Allowable : permissible. **3.** Fair : passable. **—tol′er·a·bil′i·ty, tol′er·a·ble·ness** *n.* **—tol′er·a·bly** *adv.*

tol·er·ance (tŏl′ər-əns) *n.* **1.** Recognition of and respect for the opinions, beliefs, or actions of others. **2. a.** The amount of variation from a standard that is allowed. **b.** The permissible deviation from a specified value of a structural dimension. **3.** Capacity to withstand pain or hardship. **4. a.** Physiological resistance to poison. **b.** Capacity to absorb a drug continuously or in large dosages without adverse effect. **—tol′er·ant** *adj.* **—tol′er·ant·ly** *adv.*

tol·er·ate (tŏl′ə-rāt′) *v.* **-at·ed, -at·ing.** **1.** To allow. **2.** To recognize and respect (the rights, opinions, or practices of others). **3.** To put up with. **4.** *Med.* To have tolerance for (a drug or poison). **—tol′er·a′tion** *n.*

toll[1] (tōl) *n.* **1.** A fixed fee or tax, esp. for passage across a bridge or along a road. **2.** A charge for a service, as a person-to-person telephone call. **3.** The extent or amount of loss or destruction caused by a disaster. ☆*syns:* CHARGE, EXACTION, FEE

toll[2] (tōl) *v.* **1.** To sound (a large bell) in slowly repeated single tones. **2.** To announce or call together by tolling. *—n.* **1.** An act of tolling. **2.** The sound of a bell that is tolled.

toll·booth (tōl′bōōth′) *n.* A booth at a tollgate where a toll is collected.

toll·gate (tōl′gāt′) *n.* A place, often equipped with a gate, at which vehicles must stop and pay a toll to secure passage.

toll·house (tōl′hous′) *n.* A tollbooth.

Tol·stoy (tōl′stoi′, tŏl′-), Count **Leo.** 1828–1910. Russian novelist.

tol·u·ene (tŏl′yōō-ēn′) *n.* A colorless flammable liquid derived from coal tar or petroleum and used in high-octane fuels.

tom (tŏm) *n.* The male of various animals, esp. a male cat or turkey.

tom·a·hawk (tŏm′ə-hôk′) *n.* **1.** A light ax once used as a tool or weapon by North American Indians. **2.** An implement similar to a tomahawk.

to·ma·to (tə-mā′tō, -mä′-) *n., pl.* **-toes.** A plant, *Lycopersicon esculentum,* native to South America, widely cultivated for its edible, fleshy, usu. red fruit.

tomb (tōōm) *n.* **1.** A chamber or vault for burying the dead. **2.** A place of burial. **3.** A monument commemorating the dead.

tom·boy (tŏm′boi′) *n.* A girl whose behavior is like that held to be characteristic of a boy. **—tom′boy′ish** *adj.*

tomb·stone (tōōm′stōn′) *n.* A gravestone.

tom·cat (tŏm′kăt′) *n.* A male cat.

tome (tōm) *n.* A large or scholarly book.

tom·fool (tŏm′fōōl′) A stupid, foolish person : blockhead. *—adj.* Foolish : stupid. **—tom′fool′er·y** *n.*

tom·my·rot (tŏm′ē-rŏt′) *n.* Nonsense.

to·mog·ra·phy (tō-mŏg′rə-fē) *n.* A method for making x-ray pictures of a plane section of an object.

to·mor·row (tə-môr′ō, -mŏr′ō) *n.* **1.** The day immediately following today. **2.** The near future. *—adv.* On or for the day immediately following today.

tom·tit (tŏm′tĭt′) *n.* A small bird, as a tit.

tom-tom (tŏm′tŏm′) *n.* **1.** Any of various drums having small heads that are beaten with the hands. **2.** A monotonous rhythmical drumbeat or similar sound.

ton (tŭn) *n.* **1.** See MEASUREMENT TABLE. **2.** *Informal.* A large amount.

to·nal·i·ty (tō-năl′ə-tē) *n., pl.* **-ties.** *Mus.* The arrangement of the tones and chords of a composition in relation to a tonic.

tone (tōn) *n.* **1.** A sound that has a distinct pitch, duration, loudness, and quality. **2.** *Mus.* The characteristic quality or timbre of a specific instrument or voice. **3.** A style or mode of expression. **4.** General quality, effect, or atmosphere. **5.** A color or shade of color. **6.** *Physiol.* **a.** The tension in muscles at rest. **b.** Normal firmness of body tissues. *—v.* **toned, ton·ing.** **1.** To give a particular inflection or tone to. **2.** To soften or change the color of. **3.** To sound monotonously. **4.** To harmonize in color. **—to′nal** *adj.* **—to′nal·ly** *adv.*

tone arm *n.* The pivoted arm of a record player that holds the cartridge and stylus.

tong (tông, tŏng) *n.* A Chinese association, clan, or fraternity, esp. a secret society in the U.S.

Ton·ga (tŏng′gə). Island nation of the SW Pacific. *Cap.* Nukualofa. *Pop.* 97,000. **—Ton′gan** *adj. & n.*

tongs (tôngz, tŏngz) *pl.n. (sing. or pl. in number).* An implement that consists of 2 arms joined at 1 end by a hinge or pivot, used for holding or grasping something.

tongue (tŭng) *n.* **1.** The fleshy, muscular organ attached in most vertebrates to the bottom of the mouth that is the main organ of taste, moves to facilitate chewing and swallowing, and, in humans, acts in speech. **2.** The tongue of an animal, as a lamb, used as food. **3.** A language or dialect. **4.** Style or quality of utterance <your sharp *tongue*> **5.** The flap of material under the laces or buckles of a shoe. **6.** Something resembling a tongue, as in shape <*tongues* of flames>

tongue-in-cheek (tŭng′ən-chēk′) *adj.* Ironic or facetiously exaggerated.

tongue-lash·ing (tŭng′lăsh′ĭng) *n. Informal.* A harsh scolding.

tongue-tied (tŭng′tīd′) *adj.* Speechless, as from shyness or astonishment.

tongue twister *n.* A word or expression hard to articulate rapidly, usu. due to a succession of similar consonantal sounds.

†**ton·ic** (tŏn′ĭk) *n.* **1.** An invigorating, refreshing, or restorative agent. **2.** *Mus.* The 1st note of a diatonic scale. **3. a.** Quinine water. **b.** *Regional.* A flavored carbonated beverage. *—adj.* **1.** Stimulating mental, physical, or emotional vigor. **2.** *Mus.* Of or based on the tonic.

to·night (tə-nīt′) *adv.* On or during the coming or present night. *—n.* This night or the night of this day.

ton·nage (tŭn′ĭj) *n.* **1.** The number of tons of water a ship will displace when afloat. **2.** The capacity of a merchant ship ex-

pressed in units of 100 cu ft. **3.** A duty or charge per ton on cargo. **4.** The total shipping of a port or country, computed in tons. **5.** Weight measured in tons.
tonne (tŭn) *n. Can.* A metric ton.
ton·sil (tŏn′səl) *n.* A mass of tissue similar to that found in lymph nodes, esp. either of 2 such masses located on both sides of the inner wall of the throat.
ton·sil·lec·to·my (tŏn′sə-lĕk′tə-mē) *n., pl.* **-mies.** The removal of a tonsil or tonsils by means of surgery.
ton·sil·li·tis (tŏn′sə-lī′tĭs) *n.* Inflammation of a tonsil or tonsils.
ton·so·ri·al (tŏn-sôr′ē-əl, -sōr′-) *adj.* Of or pertaining to a barber or to barbering.
ton·sure (tŏn′shər) *n.* **1.** The act of shaving the crown of the head, esp. prior to becoming a priest or a monk. **2.** The part of a head that has been shaved.
To·ny (tō′nē) *n.* An annual award for outstanding theatrical achievement.
too (to͞o) *adv.* **1.** As well : also <I'm coming *too.*> **2.** More than sufficiently <You study *too* much.> **3.** Extremely <They're only *too* willing to help.>
took (to͝ok) *v. p.t. of* TAKE.
tool (to͞ol) *n.* **1.** An implement or machine used to do work or perform a task. **2.** Something regarded as necessary to the performance of one's occupational or professional tasks <Words are the *tools* of my trade.> **3.** One utilized to carry out the designs of another. *—v.* **1.** To work or shape with a tool or tools. **2.** To equip (e.g., a factory) for production by providing tools and machinery. **3.** *Informal.* To travel in a vehicle <*tooled* around town in my new car>
toot (to͞ot) *v.* To sound or cause to sound, esp. in short bursts <*tooted* the car horn> **—toot** *n.* **—toot′er** *n.*
tooth (to͞oth) *n., pl.* **teeth** (tēth). **1. a.** One of a set of hard bonelike structures rooted in sockets in the jaws of most vertebrates, typically composed of a core of soft pulp surrounded by a layer of hard dentine coated with cement or enamel. **b.** A similar structure in invertebrates. **2.** A small, notched, projecting part resembling a tooth, as on a comb, saw, or leaf. **3. teeth. a.** Something destructive in its concentrated force <the *teeth* of the storm> **b.** Effective means of enforcement <regulations with *teeth* to them> **4.** Taste or appetite. **—toothed** *adj.* **—tooth′less** *adj.*

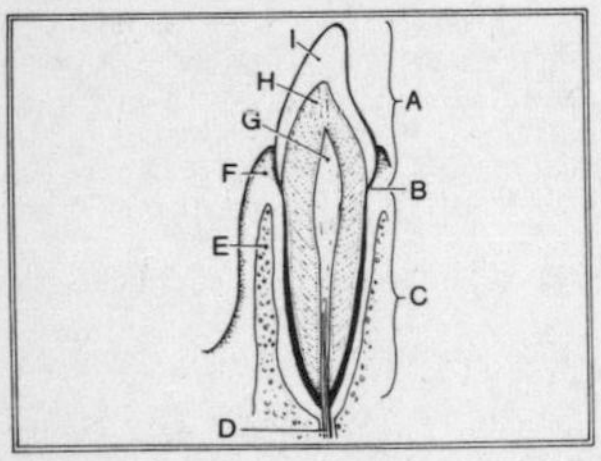

tooth
Cross section of a tooth showing: A. crown, B. neck, C. root, D. root canal, E. bone, F. gum, G. pulp, H. dentine, I. enamel

tooth·ache (to͞oth′āk′) *n.* An aching pain in or near a tooth.
tooth·brush (to͞oth′brŭsh′) *n.* A small brush used to clean the teeth.
tooth·paste (to͞oth′pāst′) *n.* A dentifrice.
tooth·pick (to͞oth′pĭk′) *n.* A small piece of wood or plastic for removing food particles from between the teeth.
tooth·pow·der (to͞oth′pou′dər) *n.* A powder for cleaning teeth.
tooth·some (to͞oth′səm) *adj.* **1.** Delicious <a *toothsome* morsel of cake> **2.** Attractive <a *toothsome* business offer>
tooth·y (to͞o′thē) *adj.* **-i·er, -i·est.** Having prominent teeth. **—tooth′i·ly** *adv.*
top[1] (tŏp) *n.* **1.** The highest part, point, surface, or end. **2.** The crown of the human head. **3.** The part of a plant, as of a rutabaga, above the ground. **4.** A part, as a lid or cap, that covers or forms the uppermost section of something <a box *top*> **5.** The highest degree, pitch, or point. **6.** The highest position or rank. **7.** The earliest part <the *top* of the 8th inning> *—v.* **topped, top·ping. 1.** To provide with, form, or function as a top. **2.** To reach the top of. **3.** To surpass : exceed.
top[2] (tŏp) *n.* A toy consisting of a symmetric rigid body spun on a pointed end about the axis of symmetry.
to·paz (tō′păz′) *n.* **1.** A colorless, blue, yellow, brown, or pink aluminum silicate mineral valued as a gemstone. **2.** A yellow gemstone, esp. a yellow sapphire or corundum. **3.** A light-yellow quartz.
top·coat (tŏp′kōt′) *n.* A light overcoat.
top-dress (tŏp′drĕs′) *v.* To cover (e.g., land) with loose material not worked in, esp. to cover with fertilizer.
To·pe·ka (tə-pē′kə). Cap. of Kans., in the NE. *Pop.* 115,266.
top·er (tō′pər) *n.* A drunkard.
top·flight (tŏp′flīt′) *adj.* First-rate.
top hat *n.* A man's hat having a narrow brim and a tall crown shaped like a cylinder, and usu. made of silk.
top-heav·y (tŏp′hĕv′ē) *adj.* Likely to topple over because of too much weight or bulk at the top.
top·ic (tŏp′ĭk) *n.* **1.** A subject discussed in a speech, essay, thesis, etc. : theme. **2.** A subject of discussion or conversation. **3.** A subdivision of a theme, thesis, or outline.
top·i·cal (tŏp′ĭ-kəl) *adj.* **1.** Of or belonging to a particular location or place : local. **2.** Of current interest : contemporary <*topical* issues> **3.** *Med.* Of or applied to an isolated part of the body. **4.** Of or relating to a particular topic or topics. **—top′i·cal′i·ty** (-kăl′ə-tē) *n.* **—top′i·cal·ly** *adv.*
top·knot (tŏp′nŏt′) *n.* **1.** A crest or knot of hair or feathers on the crown of the head. **2.** An ornamental ribbon or bow worn as a headdress.
top·less (tŏp′lĭs) *adj.* **1.** Having no top <*topless* jars> **2.** So high as to appear to extend out of sight <*topless* towers>
top·most (tŏp′mōst′) *adj.* Being the highest : uppermost.
top·notch (tŏp′nŏch′) *adj. Informal.* First-rate <a *topnotch* writer>
to·pog·ra·phy (tə-pŏg′rə-fē) *n., pl.* **-phies. 1.** Detailed and precise description of a place or region. **2.** The technique of graphically representing the exact physical features of a place or region on a map. **3.** The physical features of a place or region. **4.** The surveying of the features of a region or place. **—to·pog′ra·pher** *n.* **—top′o·graph′ic** (tŏp′ə-grăf′ĭk), **top′o·graph′i·cal** *adj.* **—top′o·graph′i·cal·ly** *adv.*
top·ping (tŏp′ĭng) *n.* A frosting, garnish, or sauce for food.
top·ple (tŏp′əl) *v.* **-pled, -pling. 1.** To overturn. **2.** To overthrow. **3.** To fall.
top round *n.* A cut of meat taken from the inner section of a round of beef.
tops (tŏps) *adj. Slang.* First-rate.
top·sail (tŏp′səl, -sāl′) *n. Naut.* **1.** A square sail set above the lowest sail on the mast of a square-rigged ship. **2.** A triangular or square sail set above the gaff of a lower sail on a fore-and-aft-rigged ship.
top-se·cret (tŏp′sē′krĭt) *adj.* Designating documents or data of the highest level of security classification.
top·side (tŏp′sīd′) *n.* **1.** *often* **topsides.** The upper parts of a ship above the main deck. **2.** The highest position of authority. *—adv. & adj.* **1.** On or to the upper decks of a ship. **2.** In a position of authority.
top·soil (tŏp′soil′) *n.* The usu. fertile layer of soil at the surface of the ground.
top·sy-tur·vy (tŏp′sē-tûr′vē) *adv.* **1.** With the top down and the bottom up. **2.** In complete disarray. *—adj.* In a confused or disordered state. *—n.* Confusion : disorder. **—top′sy-tur′vi·ly** *adv.* **—top′sy-tur′vi·ness** *n.*
toque (tōk) *n.* A small, close-fitting hat with no brim, worn by women.
to·rah *also* **To·rah** (tôr′ə, tōr′ə) *n.* **1.** The complete body of Jewish religious law and learning. **2.** A scroll or scrolls of parchment containing the 1st 5 Old Testament books.
torch (tôrch) *n.* **1.** A portable light consisting of flaming material wound about the end of a stick of wood. **2.** A portable device that burns a fuel, usu. a gas, often with a supply of oxygen, to produce a flame hot enough for welding, brazing, or cutting metal. **3.** Something that illuminates. **4.** *esp. Brit.* A flashlight. *—v. Slang.* To set fire to <*torched* the building>
torch song *n.* A sentimental popular song, esp. one lamenting a lost or unrequited love. **—torch singer** *n.*
tore (tôr, tōr) *v. p.t. of* TEAR[1].
tor·e·a·dor (tôr′ē-ə-dôr′) *n.* A bullfighter.
tor·ment (tôr′mĕnt′) *n.* **1.** Extreme physical pain or mental anguish. **2.** A source of harassment, annoyance, or pain. **3.** Torture inflicted on prisoners being interrogated. *—v.* (tôr-mĕnt′, tôr′mĕnt′). **1.** To cause to undergo great pain or anguish. **2.** To upset or agitate greatly. **3.** To annoy, pester, or harass. **—tor·ment′ing·ly** *adv.* **—tor·men′tor** *n.*
torn (tôrn, tōrn) *v. p.p. of* TEAR[1].
tor·na·do (tôr-nā′dō) *n., pl.* **-does** *or* **-dos. 1.** A rotating column of air usu. accompanied by a funnel-shaped downward extension of a thundercloud and having a vortex several hundred yds in diameter whirling destructively at speeds of up to 300 mph. **2.** A violently destructive whirlwind.
To·ron·to (tə-rŏn′tō). Cap. of Ont., Canada, on Lake Ontario. *Pop.* 635,685.
tor·pe·do (tôr-pē′dō) *n., pl.* **-does.** A self-propelled missile

launched from a ship, submarine, or aircraft and designed to explode near a target or on contact with it. **–tor·pe′do** *v.*

▲word history: The original sense of *torpedo* in English was "electric ray," a fish that produces an electric charge. The word was borrowed from Latin *torpedo,* which also denoted the same fish but which basically meant "numbness." *Torpedo* is related to *torpidus,* "numb," the Latin source of English *torpid.* The word *torpedo* was first applied to drifting underwater mines in the early 19th cent.; self-propelled torpedoes were a later invention.

torpedo boat *n.* A fast boat fitted with torpedo tubes.

tor·pid (tôr′pĭd) *adj.* **1.** Having been deprived of the power of motion or feeling : benumbed. **2.** Dormant : hibernating. **3.** Apathetic : spiritless. **–tor·pid′i·ty** *n.* **–tor′pid·ly** *adv.*

tor·por (tôr′pər) *n.* **1.** Mental or physical inactivity or insensibility : sluggishness. **2.** Apathy : dullness.

torque (tôrk) *n.* **1.** The capability or tendency of a force for producing torsion or rotation about an axis. **2.** A turning or twisting force.

tor·rent (tôr′ənt, tŏr′-) *n.* **1.** A swift, turbulent stream. **2.** A deluge. **3.** An overwhelming flow <*torrents* of criticism> **–tor·ren′tial** (tô-rĕn′shəl, tə-) *adj.*

tor·rid (tôr′ĭd, tŏr′-) *adj.* **1.** Dried by the heat of the sun : parched. **2.** Scorching : burning. **3.** Passionate : ardent <a *torrid* love affair> **–tor·rid′i·ty, tor′rid·ness** *n.* **–tor′rid·ly** *adv.*

Torrid Zone *n.* The region of the earth's surface between the tropics of Cancer and Capricorn.

tor·sion (tôr′shən) *n.* **1.** The act of twisting or turning or the state of being twisted or turned. **2.** Stress produced when one end of an object is twisted out of line with the other. **–tor′sion·al** *adj.*

tor·so (tôr′sō) *n., pl.* **-sos** *or* **-si** (-sē′). **1.** TRUNK 2. **2.** A statue of the trunk of the human body.

tort (tôrt) *n. Law.* A wrongful act, damage, or injury done willfully, negligently, or in circumstances involving strict liability for which a civil suit can be brought.

torte (tôrt, tôr′tə) *n., pl.* **tortes** *or* **tor·ten** (tôr′tn). A rich cake made with many eggs and little flour and usu. containing chopped nuts.

tor·tel·li·ni (tôr′tl-ē′nē) *n.* Small stuffed pasta dumplings.

tor·til·la (tôr-tē′yə) *n.* A thin, round, unleavened bread, usu. made from cornmeal or flour and served hot with toppings of ground meat or cheese.

tor·toise (tôr′təs) *n.* **1.** A terrestrial turtle, esp. one of the family Testudinidae, with thick, scaly limbs. **2.** One that moves or acts slowly.

tor·toise·shell *also* **tor·toise-shell** *or* **tortoise shell** (tôr′təs-shĕl′) *n.* The mottled, horny, translucent brownish covering of the carapace of certain sea turtles, used to make combs, jewelry, etc.

tor·tu·ous (tôr′chōō-əs) *adj.* **1.** Marked by or having repeated turns or bends : twisting. **2.** Not straightforward : devious. **3.** Complex. **–tor′tu·ous·ly** *adv.* **–tor′tu·ous·ness** *n.*

tor·ture (tôr′chər) *n.* **1. a.** Infliction of severe physical pain as punishment or coercion. **b.** The state of being tortured. **2.** Mental anguish. **3.** Something causing pain or anguish. *–v.* **-tured, tur·ing. 1.** To subject (a person or animal) to torture. **2.** To afflict with great physical or mental pain. **3.** To twist or turn abnormally : distort. **–tor′tur·er** *n.* **–tor′tur·ous** *adj.*

To·ry (tôr′ē, tōr′ē) *n., pl.* **-ries. 1.** A member of a British political party, founded in 1689, known as the Conservative Party since about 1832. **2.** An American siding with the English side during the Amer. Revolution. **3.** A member of a Conservative Party, as in Canada. **–To′ry·ism** *n.*

toss (tôs, tŏs) *v.* **1.** To throw or be heaved about continuously <*tossed* by the waves> **2.** To throw lightly with or as if with the hand or hands <*toss* a ball> **3.** *Informal.* To discuss casually. **4.** To move or lift (the head) with a sudden motion. **5.** To throw to the ground. **6.** To flip a coin in order to make a decision. **7.** To mix (a salad) with a dressing. **8.** To move oneself about restlessly <*tossed* in my sleep> ☆**syns:** HEAVE, PITCH, ROCK, ROLL *–n.* **1.** The act of tossing or state of being tossed. **2.** A rapid movement or lift, as of the head.

toss·up (tôs′ŭp′, tŏs′-) *n.* **1.** The flip of a coin to decide an issue. **2.** An even chance.

tot[1] (tŏt) *n.* **1.** A young child. **2.** A small amount, as of liquor <a *tot* of brandy>

tot[2] (tŏt) *v.* **tot·ted, tot·ting.** To total <*totted* up the bill>

to·tal (tōt′l) *n.* **1.** A number or quantity reached by addition : sum. **2.** A whole quantity : entirety. *–adj.* **1.** Being the whole : entire. **2.** Complete : absolute. *–v.* **-taled, -tal·ing** *or* **-talled, -tal·ling. 1.** To find the sum of. **2.** To equal a total of <The number of victims *totals* 200.> **3.** *Slang.* To demolish (a vehicle) completely. **–to′tal·ly** *adv.*

to·tal·i·tar·i·an (tō-tăl′ə-târ′ē-ən) *adj.* Having or exercising complete political control. **–to·tal′i·tar′i·an** *n.* **–to·tal′i·tar′i·an·ism** *n.*

to·tal·i·ty (tō-tăl′ə-tē) *n., pl.* **-ties. 1.** The state of being total. **2.** An aggregate sum.

to·tal·iz·er (tōt′l-ī′zər) *n.* **1.** A pari-mutuel machine. **2.** An adding machine.

tote (tōt) *v.* **tot·ed, tot·ing. 1.** To haul, esp. on the back or in the arms : lug. **2.** To have on one's person. *–n.* **1.** A load : burden. **2.** A tote bag. **–tot′er** *n.*

tote bag *n. Informal.* A large handbag or shopping bag.

to·tem (tō′təm) *n.* **1. a.** An animal, plant, or natural object serving as the emblem of a clan or family by virtue of an asserted ancestral relationship. **b.** A representation of this being. **2.** A venerated symbol.

totem pole *n.* **1.** A post carved and painted with totems and erected in front of a dwelling, as among some Indian peoples of the NW coast of North America. **2.** *Slang.* A hierarchy.

tot·ter (tŏt′ər) *v.* **1. a.** To sway as if about to fall. **b.** To appear about to collapse <a *tottering* government> **2.** To move unsteadily. **3.** To waver : vacillate <*tottered* between capitulation and resistance> **–tot′ter** *n.* **–tot′ter·y** *adj.*

tou·can (tōō′kăn′, -kän′) *n.* Any of various tropical American birds of the family Ramphastidae, having brightly colored plumage and a very large bill.

touch (tŭch) *v.* **1.** To cause or allow a bodily part, esp. the hand or fingers, to come into contact with so as to feel. **2. a.** To bring something into contact with <*touched* the metal plate with a wire> **b.** To bring (one thing) into contact with something else <*touch* a wire to the metal plate> **3.** To tap, press, or strike lightly. **4.** To lay hands on in violence <I never *touched* you> **5.** To eat or drink : taste <You didn't *touch* your dinner.> **6.** To disturb by handling. **7.** To reach <*touch* land> **8.** To measure up to : equal. **9.** To deal with as a subject. **10.** To be relevant to : concern. **11.** To have an effect on : move emotionally. **–touch down.** To land or make contact with a landing surface, as an aircraft or spacecraft. **–touch off. 1.** To cause to explode : fire. **2.** To initiate (e.g., a chain of events) : trigger. **–touch up.** To improve by making small changes or additions. *–n.* **1.** An act or instance of touching. **2.** The physiological sense by which external objects or forces are perceived through contact with the body. **3.** A sensation experienced in touching something with a characteristic texture. **4.** A light tap or shove. **5.** An improving change or addition. **6.** A mild attack <a *touch* of indigestion> **7.** A tiny amount : trace <a *touch* of garlic> **8. a.** A manner or technique of striking the keys of a keyboard instrument, as a piano or typewriter. **b.** The resistance to being struck by the fingers characteristic of a keyboard. **9.** A characteristic way or style of doing things. **10.** The state of being in contact or communication <Let's keep in *touch.*> **–touch′a·ble** *adj.*

touch·back (tŭch′băk′) *n. Football.* A play in which one recovers a ball propelled by an opposing player and touches it to the ground behind one's own goal line.

touch·down (tŭch′doun′) *n.* **1.** *Football.* A play worth 6 points, accomplished by being in possession of the ball when it is declared dead on or behind the opponent's goal line. **2.** The contact or moment of contact of an aircraft or spacecraft with the landing surface.

tou·ché (tōō-shā′) *interj.* Used to express concession to an opponent for a point well made, as in an argument.

touch football *n.* A variety of football played on an improvised field and without protective equipment, involving the substitution of touching for tackling.

touch·ing (tŭch′ĭng) *adj.* Causing a sympathetic reaction : moving.

touch·stone (tŭch′stōn′) *n.* **1.** A hard black stone once used to test the quality of gold or silver. **2.** A criterion.

touch-type (tŭch′tīp′) *v.* To type without having to look at the keyboard.

touch·up (tŭch′ŭp′) *n.* The act or process of finishing or improving by small alterations and additions.

touch·y (tŭch′ē) *adj.* **-i·er, -i·est. 1.** Easily taking offense : oversensitive. **2.** Requiring tact or skill <a *touchy* situation> **–touch′i·ly** *adv.* **–touch′i·ness** *n.*

tough (tŭf) *adj.* **1.** So strong and resilient as to withstand great strain without tearing or breaking. **2.** Difficult to chew or cut <a *tough* steak> **3.** Physically hardy : rugged. **4.** Severe <a *tough* winter> **5.** Vicious : rough <a *tough* hoodlum> **6.** Demanding or troubling : difficult. **7.** Strong-minded : resolute. *–n.* A thug. **–tough′ly** *adv.* **–tough′ness** *n.*

tough·en (tŭf′ən) *v.* To make or become tough. **–tough′en·er** *n.*

tough-mind·ed (tŭf′mīn′dĭd) *adj.* Not sentimental or afraid. **–tough′-mind′ed·ly** *adv.* **–tough′-mind′ed·ness** *n.*

tou•pee (to͞o-pā′) *n.* A partial wig or hair piece worn to cover a bald spot.
tour (to͝or) *n.* **1.** A trip including visits to points of interest. **2.** A group organized for a tour. **3.** A journey to fulfill a schedule of engagements in several places <a concert *tour*> **4.** A shift, as in a factory. **5.** A period of service at a single place or job. —*v.* To go on tour or make a tour of.
tour de force (to͝or′ də fôrs′) *n.* A feat of strength or virtuosity.
tour•ism (to͝or′ĭz′əm) *n.* **1.** Traveling for pleasure. **2.** The business of providing tours and services for tourists.
tour•ist (to͝or′ĭst) *n.* A person who travels for pleasure.
tourist class *n.* Travel accommodations less luxurious than first class or cabin class.
tour•ma•line (to͝or′mə-lĭn, -lēn′) *n.* A complex crystalline silicate used in electronic instrumentation and valued as a gem in certain varieties.
tour•na•ment (to͝or′nə-mənt, tûr′-) *n.* **1.** A contest involving a number of competitors who vie against each other in a series of games or trials. **2.** A medieval sport in which 2 groups of mounted contestants fought with blunted lances or swords.
tour•ne•dos (to͝or′ nə-dō′) *n., pl.* **tour•ne•dos** (-dō′, -dōz′). A fillet of beef cut from the tenderloin.
tour•ney (to͝or′nē, tûr′-) *n., pl.* **-neys.** A tournament.
tour•ni•quet (to͝or′nĭ-kĭt, -kā′, tûr′-) *n.* A device, as a cloth band tightened around a limb, used to temporarily stop the flow of blood through a large artery.

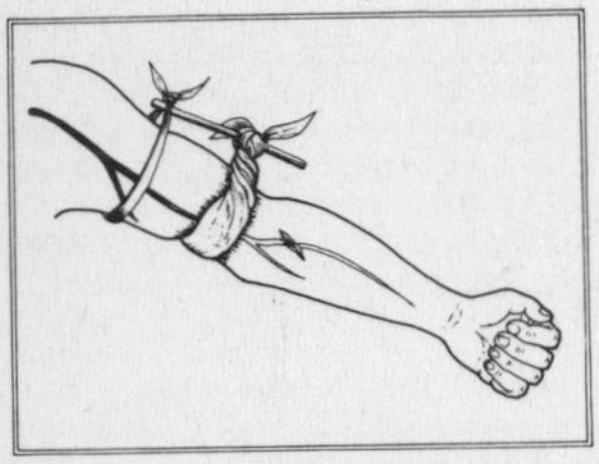

tourniquet

tou•sle (tou′zəl) *v.* **-sled, -sling.** To disarrange : muss.
tout (tout) *v. Informal.* **1.** To obtain or sell information on (e.g., a racehorse) for the guidance of bettors. **2.** To publicize or praise highly. —*n.* One who obtains information on racehorses and sells ito to bettors. **—tout′er** *n.*
tow[1] (tō) *v.* To pull or draw along behind as by a rope or chain. —*n.* **1.** An act of towing or the state of being towed. **2.** Something, as a tugboat, that tows. **3.** A rope or cable used in towing <a ski *tow*> **—tow′age** *n.* **—tow′er** *n.*
tow[2] (tō) *n.* Coarse broken flax or hemp fiber prepared for spinning.
to•ward (tôrd, tōrd, tə-wôrd′) *also* **to•wards** (tôrdz, tōrdz, tə-wôrdz′) *prep.* **1.** In the direction of <driving *toward* them> **2.** In a position facing <had your back *toward* me> **3.** Somewhat before in time : approaching <It began to sleet *toward* morning.> **4.** With regard to <didn't like my attitude *toward* the work> **5.** In furtherance or partial fulfillment of <paid only $20 *toward* the bill> **6.** By way of achieving <efforts *toward* reconciliation>
tow-a•way zone (tō′ə-wā′) *n.* A no-parking zone from which cars may be legally towed.
tow•el (tou′əl) *n.* A piece of absorbent cloth or paper used for wiping or drying. —*v.* **-eled, -el•ing** or **-elled, -el•ling.** To wipe or rub dry with a towel.
tow•el•ette (tou′ə-lĕt′) *n.* A small, usu. moist piece of material used for cleansing, as of the hands or face.
tow•el•ing (tou′əl-ĭng) *n.* A fabric of cotton or linen used for making towels.
tow•er (tou′ər) *n.* **1. a.** A very tall building : skyscraper. **b.** An extremely tall part of a building. **2.** A tall framework or structure for observing, signaling, or pumping. —*v.* To rise to a noticeable height : loom.
tow•er•ing (tou′ər-ĭng) *adj.* **1.** Of impressive height. **2.** Outstanding : pre-eminent <*towering* scientific achievements> **3.** Fiercely intense <a *towering* rage>
tow•head (tō′hĕd′) *n.* **1.** A head of white-blond hair. **2.** One with a towhead. **—tow′head′ed** *adj.*
tow•hee (tō′hē, tō-hē′) *n.* A North American bird of the genera *Pipilo* or *Chlorura,* esp. *P. erythrophthalmus,* with black, white, and rust plumage in the male.
town (toun) *n.* **1.** An often incorporated population center larger than a village and smaller than a city. **2.** *Informal.* A city. **3.** The residents of a town. **—go to town.** *Slang.* To go all out.
town clerk *n.* A public official who keeps the records of a town.
town hall *n.* The building that contains the offices of the public officials of a town and houses the town council and courts.
town house *n.* **1.** A city residence. **2.** One of a row of houses connected by common side walls.
town meeting *n.* A legislative assembly of townspeople.
town•ship (toun′shĭp′) *n.* **1.** A subdivision of a county in many U.S. states. **2.** A unit of land area used in surveying, equal to 36 sections or 36 sq mi.
towns•man (tounz′mən) *n.* **1.** A resident of a town. **2.** A fellow resident of one's town. **—towns′wom′an** *n.*
towns•peo•ple (tounz′pē′pəl) *pl.n.* The residents of a town or city.
tow•path (tō′păth′, -päth′) *n.* A path beside a river or canal used by people or animals towing boats.
tow truck *n.* WRECKER 2a.
tox•e•mi•a (tŏk-sē′mē-ə) *n.* A condition in which the blood contains toxins, either produced by microorganisms that infect the body or by body cells through faulty metabolism or absorbed from an external source. **—tox•e′mic** *adj.*
tox•ic (tŏk′sĭk) *adj.* **1.** Of or relating to a toxin. **2.** Harmful, destructive, or deadly <*toxic* wastes><*toxic* fumes> **—tox′i•cal•ly** *adv.* **—tox•ic′i•ty** (-sĭs′ə-tē) *n.*
tox•i•col•o•gy (tŏk′sĭ-kŏl′ə-jē) *n.* The study of the nature, effects, and detection of poisons and the treatment of poisoning. **—tox′i•co•log′i•cal** (-kə-lŏj′ĭ-kəl) *adj.* **—tox′i•col′o•gist** *n.*
tox•i•co•sis (tŏk′sĭ-kō′sĭs) *n., pl.* **-ses** (-sēz′). A pathological condition resulting from poisoning.
tox•in (tŏk′sĭn) *n.* A poisonous substance, having a protein structure, that is secreted by certain organisms and is capable of causing toxicosis when introduced into the body tissues but is also capable of inducing production of an antitoxin.
toy (toi) *n.* **1.** An object designed or meant for a child to play with. **2.** Something insignificant : trifle. **3.** A small ornament : bauble. **4.** A diminutive thing, as a dog of a very small breed or 1 much smaller than is characteristic of its breed. —*v.* To entertain oneself idly : trifle.
tr. *abbr.* **1.** transitive (in grammar). **2.** transpose; transposition.
trace[1] (trās) *n.* **1.** A visible sign or mark of a person, thing, or event that was once present, but is no longer. **2. a.** A very small amount <a *trace* of smoke> **b.** A constituent, as a chemical compound or element, present in less than standard quantities. ☆***syns:*** RELIC, REMAINS, VESTIGE —*v.* **traced, trac•ing. 1.** To follow the track or trail of. **2.** To follow the successive stages in the development or progress of <*trace* the development of a culture> **3.** To locate or discover (e.g., a cause) by researching evidence. **4.** To sketch (a figure). **5.** To form (e.g., letters) with careful concentration. **6.** To copy by following lines seen through a sheet of transparent paper. **—trace′a•bil′i•ty** *n.* **—trace′a•ble** *adj.* **—trace′a•bly** *adv.* **—trac′er** *n.*
trace[2] (trās) *n.* Either of 2 side straps or chains that connect a harnessed draft animal to the vehicle it pulls.
tracer bullet *n.* A bullet that leaves a luminous or smoky trail.
trac•er•y (trā′sə-rē) *n., pl.* **-ies.** Ornamental work of interlaced, ramefied lines, as the lacy openwork in a Gothic window.
tra•che•a (trā′kē-ə) *n., pl.* **-che•ae** (-kē-ē′) *or* **-as.** A respiratory passage leading from the larynx to the bronchi.
tra•che•ot•o•my (trā′kē-ŏt′ə-mē) *n., pl.* **-mies.** Surgical incision into the trachea via the neck.
track (trăk) *n.* **1.** A mark, as a footprint, wheel rut, etc., or a trail of marks left behind by something <tire *tracks*> **2.** A path or course over which something moves or may move. **3.** A course of action : method. **4. a.** A road or course set up for running or racing. **b.** Athletic competition on such a course. **c.** Track and field. **5.** A rail or set of parallel rails on which a rail vehicle, as a train, runs. —*v.* **1.** To follow the footprints or trail of. **2.** To pursue successfully. **3.** To deposit (e.g., matter carried on the shoes). **—track′a•ble** *adj.* **—track′er** *n.*
track•age (trăk′ĭj) *n.* Railway tracks.
track and field *n.* Athletic events, as the long jump or the shot-put, performed on a running track and associated field.
track meet *n.* A track and field meet.
track•suit (trăk′so͞ot′) *n.* A loose-fitting jacket and pants worn while exercising.
tract[1] (trăkt) *n.* **1.** A stretch of land. **2.** *Anat.* **a.** A system of body organs and tissues that together perform a specialized function <the digestive *tract*> **b.** A bundle of nerve fibers with a common origin, termination, and function.
tract[2] (trăkt) *n.* A paper or pamphlet containing a declaration or appeal, esp. one distributed by a special interest group.

trac•ta•ble (trăk′tə-bəl) *adj.* **1.** Easily managed : obedient. **2.** Easily handled or worked. **—trac′ta•bil′i•ty, trac′ta•ble•ness** *n.* **—trac′ta•bly** *adv.*
tract house *n.* One of numerous houses of similar design constructed on a tract of land. **—tract housing** *n.*
trac•tile (trăk′təl, -tīl′) *adj.* Capable of being drawn out in length : ductile <*tractile* metals> **—trac•til′i•ty** (-tĭl′ĭ-tē) *n.*
trac•tion (trăk′shən) *n.* **1.** The act of pulling, as a load over a surface. **2.** The state of being pulled. **3.** The friction that prevents a wheel from slipping or skidding over the surface on which it runs. **4.** The ability of an apparatus, as a railroad engine, to pull loads. **—trac′tive** *adj.*
trac•tor (trăk′tər) *n.* **1.** A gasoline- or diesel-powered vehicle with large, heavily treaded tires that is used in farming for pulling machinery. **2.** A truck with a cab and no body, used for pulling large vehicles such as trailers.
trade (trād) *n.* **1.** An occupation requiring skilled labor : craft <the *trade* of a plumber> **2.** The business of buying and selling commodities : commerce. **3.** The people working in or associated with a specified industry or business. **4.** The customers of a specified industry or business. **5.** An instance of buying or selling : transaction. **6.** Exchange of 1 thing for another. *—v.* **trad•ed, trad•ing. 1. a.** To engage in buying, selling, or bartering. **b.** To make an exchange of 1 thing for another. **2.** To shop as regular customers. **—trade in.** To give (an old or used item) as partial payment on a new purchase. **—trade on.** To put to advantage : utilize <*traded* on looks and charm> **—trad′a•ble** *adj.* **—trad′er** *n.*
trade-in (trād′ĭn′) *n.* **1.** Merchandise accepted as partial payment for a new purchase. **2.** A transaction involving a trade-in.
trade•mark (trād′märk′) *n.* A device, as a symbol or name, that identifies a product, is officially registered, and is restricted by law to the exclusive use of the owner or manufacturer.
trade•off *also* **trade-off** (trād′ôf′, -ŏf′) *n.* Exchange of 1 thing in return for another, esp. a giving up of something valued or desirable for another thought to be more valuable or desirable.
trade school *n.* A secondary school providing instruction in skilled trades.
trades•man (trādz′mən) *n.* **1.** One engaged in the retail trade, esp. a shopkeeper : dealer. **2.** A skilled worker.
trade union *n.* A labor union, esp. one whose membership is limited to people in the same trade. **—trade unionism** *n.* **—trade unionist** *n.*
trade wind *n.* One of an extremely consistent system of winds occupying most of the tropics, blowing toward the equator, northeasterly in the N Hemisphere and southeasterly in the S Hemisphere.
trading post *n.* A store in a remote and thinly populated area established by traders to barter supplies for local products.
trading stamp *n.* A stamp given by a retailer to a buyer for a purchase of a specified amount and intended to be redeemed in quantity for merchandise.
tra•di•tion (trə-dĭsh′ən) *n.* **1.** Transmittal of elements of a culture from 1 generation to another, esp. by oral communication. **2.** A set of customs and usages transmitted from 1 generation to another and viewed as a coherent body of precedents influencing the present : heritage. **3.** A time-honored practice or set of such practices. **—tra•di′tion•al** *adj.* **—tra•di′tion•al•ist** *n.* **—tra•di′tion•al•ly** *adv.*
tra•duce (trə-do͞os′, -dyo͞os′) *v.* **-duced, -duc•ing. 1.** To speak falsely of : misrepresent. **2.** To betray : violate. **—tra•duce′ment** *n.* **—tra•duc′er** *n.*
traf•fic (trăf′ĭk) *n.* **1. a.** Commercial exchange of goods : commerce <heavy *traffic* in steel> **b.** Illegal or improper commercial activity <drug *traffic*> **2. a.** The business of moving passengers and cargo through a transportation system. **b.** The amount of cargo or number of passengers conveyed in a transportation system. **3. a.** Passage of persons, vehicles, or messages through transportation routes. **b.** The number, as of vehicles, in transit <heavy *traffic* on the expressways> **4.** Dealings between groups or individuals. *—v.* **-ficked, -fick•ing. 1.** To carry on trade in. **2.** To travel over <roads that are heavily *trafficked*> **—traf′fick•er** *n.*
traffic light *n.* A signal that flashes a red, green, or yellow warning light to direct vehicular and pedestrian traffic to stop, go, or proceed with caution.
tra•ge•di•an (trə-jē′dē-ən) *n.* **1.** A writer of tragedies. **2.** A performer of tragic roles.
tra•ge•di•enne (trə-jē′dē-ĕn′) *n.* An actress who performs tragic roles.
trag•e•dy (trăj′ə-dē) *n., pl.* **-dies. 1. a.** A dramatic or literary work that ends with great misfortune or ruin for the main character or characters. **b.** The literary genre of tragic dramatic works. **2.** A dramatic, unhappy, often disastrous event, esp. one of moral significance. **3.** A tragic element or aspect.
trag•ic (trăj′ĭk) *adj.* **1.** Relating to or having the nature of tragedy. **2.** Writing or performing in tragedy. **—trag′i•cal•ly** *adv.*
trail (trāl) *v.* **1. a.** To permit to drag or stream behind. **b.** To be dragged along behind. **2.** To follow the tracks or scent of, as in hunting <dogs *trailing* deer> **3.** To lag behind <*trailing* by 10 points in the 1st half> **4.** To extend, grow, or droop along or over a surface <grape vines *trailing* over an arbor> **5.** To become gradually weaker : dwindle <voices *trailing* off in the distance> *—n.* **1.** Something that hangs loose and long <*trails* of ribbons> **2.** Something that is drawn along or follows behind : train. **3. a.** A mark, trace, course, or path left by a moving body <white jet *trails*> **b.** Scent : track <the *trail* of a wolf> **c.** A beaten track or blazed path. **4.** The act of trailing.
trail bike *n.* A small motorcycle designed for cross-country, off-road riding.
trail•blaz•er (trāl′blā′zər) *n.* **1.** One that blazes a trail. **2.** A pioneer in a specific field of endeavor. **—trail′blaz′ing** *adj.*
trail•er (trā′lər) *n.* **1.** One that trails. **2.** A large transport vehicle designed to be hauled by a heavy-duty vehicle, as a truck or tractor. **3.** A furnished van pulled by a truck or car and used as a house or office.
trailing arbutus *n.* A low-growing plant, *Epigaea repens*, of E North America, with evergreen leaves and fragrant pink or white flower clusters.
train (trān) *n.* **1.** A part of a long gown that trails behind the wearer. **2.** A staff of attendants : retinue. **3.** A long moving line, as of persons or vehicles. **4.** A string of railroad cars coupled together and pulled by a locomotive. **5.** An orderly series of related thoughts or events : sequence. *—v.* **1.** To instruct or condition to some manner of behavior or performance. **2.** To make proficient through special instruction and drill. **3.** To make or become fit for an athletic performance. **4.** To cause (e.g., a plant) to grow in or take on a desired shape or course. **5.** To direct : aim. **—train′a•ble** *adj.* **—train•ee′** *n.* **—train′er** *n.* **—train′ing** *n.*
train•man (trān′mən) *n.* A crew member on a railroad train, esp. the brakeman.
traipse (trāps) *v.* **traipsed, traips•ing.** To walk about aimlessly or intrusively.
trait (trāt) *n.* **1.** A distinguishing feature, as of one's character. **2.** A characteristic that is inherited.
trai•tor (trā′tər) *n.* **1.** One who betrays a cause or another's confidence. **2.** One who commits treason. **—trai′tor•ous** *adj.*
tra•jec•to•ry (trə-jĕk′tə-rē) *n., pl.* **-ries. 1.** The path of a moving object, as a projectile, esp. such a path in 3 dimensions. **2.** *Math.* A curve that cuts all of a given family of curves or surfaces at the same angle.
tram (trăm) *n.* **1.** *esp. Brit.* **a.** A streetcar. **b.** A cable car. **2.** A 4-wheeled, open box-shaped wagon or iron car run on tracks in a coal mine.
tram•mel (trăm′əl) *n.* **1.** A shackle for teaching a horse to amble. **2.** *often* **trammels.** A restriction on free activity or movement. *—v.* **-meled, -mel•ing** *or* **melled, -mel•ling. 1.** To hinder, restrict, or confine. **2.** To ensnare : enmesh.
tramp (trămp) *v.* **1.** To walk with a heavy step : trudge. **2. a.** To go on foot : hike. **b.** To wander about aimlessly. **3.** To trample <*tramp* down snow> *—n.* **1. a.** A heavy footfall. **b.** The sound made by heavy footsteps. **2.** A trip made by walking : hike. **3.** One who travels about aimlessly on foot, doing odd jobs or begging for a living : vagrant. **4. a.** A prostitute. **b.** A promiscuous person. **5.** A cargo ship having no regular schedule but taking on freight wherever it may be found and unloading it wherever required. **—tramp′er** *n.*
tram•ple (trăm′pəl) *v.* **-pled, -pling. 1.** To tread heavily so as to bruise, crush, or destroy. **2.** To treat ruthlessly, as if tramping on. **—tram′ple** *n.* **—tram′pler** *n.*
tram•po•line (trăm′pə-lēn′) *n.* A device for performing acrobatic feats, consisting of a sheet of taut canvas attached with springs to a metal frame. **—tram′po•lin′ist** *n.*
trance (trăns) *n.* **1.** A dreamlike mental condition, as produced by hypnosis or drugs. **2.** The condition of being so lost in thought as to be unaware of one's surroundings. **3.** A dazed state, as between sleeping and waking : stupor. ☆***syns:*** ABSTRACTION, MUSE, REVERIE, STUDY
tran•quil (trăn′kwəl) *adj.* **1.** Free from disturbance : serene. **2.** Steady : even <a *tranquil* flame> **—tran•quil′li•ty, tran•quil′i•ty** *n.* **—tran′quil•ly** *adv.*
tran•quil•ize *also* **tran•quil•lize** (trăn′kwə-līz′) *v.* **-ized, -iz•ing** *also* **-lized, -liz•ing.** To make or become tranquil. **—tran′quil•i•za′tion** *n.*
tran•quil•iz•er (trăn′kwə-lī′zər) *n.* A drug used to calm or pacify.

trans. *abbr.* **1.** transaction. **2.** transitive (in grammar). **3.** translated; translation; translator. **4.** transportation.

trans·act (trăn-săkt′, -zăkt′) *v.* To do, perform, carry out, manage, or conduct (e.g., business). **—trans·ac′tor** *n.*

trans·ac·tion (trăn-săk′shən, -zăk′shən) *n.* **1.** The act of transacting or the fact of being transacted. **2.** Something transacted. **3. transactions.** The proceedings, as of a convention. **—trans·ac′tion·al** *adj.*

trans·at·lan·tic (trăns′ət-lăn′tĭk, trănz′ət-) *adj.* **1.** Situated on the other side of the Atlantic. **2.** Traversing the Atlantic.

trans·ceiv·er (trăn-sē′vər, -zē′-) *n.* A module composed of a radio receiver and transmitter.

tran·scend (trăn-sĕnd′) *v.* **1. a.** To pass beyond (a human limit). **b.** To exist above and independent of (material experience or the universe). **2.** To surpass.

tran·scen·dent (trăn-sĕn′dənt) *adj.* **1.** That surpasses all others of the same kind : pre-eminent. **2.** Above and independent of the material universe. **—tran·scen′dence, tran·scen′den·cy** *n.* **—tran·scen′dent·ly** *adv.*

tran·scen·den·tal (trăn′sĕn-dĕnt′l) *adj.* **1.** Of or relating to transcendentalism. **2.** Rising above common thought or ideas : mystical. **—tran′scen·den′tal·ly** *adv.*

tran·scen·den·tal·ism (trăn′sən-dĕnt′l-ĭz′əm) *n.* The philosophical belief that knowledge of reality comes from intuition rather than from objective experience. **—tran′scen·den′tal·ist** *n.*

transcendental number *n.* An irrational number that cannot occur as a root or solution of any algebraic equation whose coefficients are all rational numbers.

trans·con·ti·nen·tal (trăns′kŏn′tə-nĕn′təl, trănz′-) *adj.* Traversing a continent.

tran·scribe (trăn-skrīb′) *v.* **-scribed, -scrib·ing. 1. a.** To make a copy of by writing out fully, as from shorthand notes or via an electronic medium <*transcribe* a memorandum> **b.** To transfer (information) from 1 recording and storing system to another. **2.** To arrange or adapt (a musical composition) for a voice or instrument other than the original. **3.** To record, usu. on tape, for broadcasting at some later date <*transcribe* a talk show> **—tran·scrib′a·ble** *adj.* **—tran·scrib′er** *n.*

tran·script (trăn′skrĭpt′) *n.* Transcribed matter, esp. a written, typewritten, or printed copy, as of an academic record.

tran·scrip·tion (trăn-skrĭp′shən) *n.* **1.** The act or process of transcribing. **2.** Something transcribed, esp.: **a.** An arrangement of a musical composition other than the original. **b.** A television or radion program that is recorded. **—tran·scrip′tion·al** *adj.* **—tran·scrip′tion·al·ly** *adv.*

trans·cul·tu·ra·tion (trăns′kŭl-chə-rā′shən) *n.* Cultural change brought about by the introduction of elements of a foreign culture.

trans·duc·er (trăns-dōō′sər, -dyōō′-, trănz-) *n.* A substance or device, as a photoelectric cell, that converts input energy of 1 form into output energy of another. **—trans·duce′** *v.*

tran·sept (trăn′sĕpt′) *n.* Either of the 2 lateral arms of a church built in the shape of a cross.

trans·fer (trăns-fûr′, trăns′fər) *v.* **-ferred, -fer·ring. 1.** To carry, remove, or shift from 1 person, position, or place to another. **2.** To convey or make over the possession or legal title of (e.g., property) to another. **3.** To shift (e.g., a design) from one surface to another. **4.** To change from 1 motor carrier to another. —*n.* (trăns′fər). **1.** *also* **trans·fer·al** (trăns-fûr′əl). Conveyance or removal of a thing from 1 person or place to another. **2.** *also* **transferal.** One that has or has been transferred. **3.** A ticket that entitles a passenger to change from 1 motor carrier to another. **4.** *also* **transferal.** *Law.* Conveyance of title or property from 1 party to another. **—trans·fer′a·bil′i·ty** *n.* **—trans·fer′a·ble** *adj.* **—trans·fer′ence** *n.* **—trans·fer′er** *n.*

trans·fer·al *also* **trans·fer·ral** (trăns′fûr-əl) *n.* A transfer.

transfer RNA *n.* A ribonucleic acid that acts as a carrier in the transport of a specific amino acid to the site where a protein molecule is being synthesized.

trans·fig·ure (trăns-fĭg′yər) *v.* **-ured, -ur·ing. 1.** To transform the figure or outward appearance of. **2.** To glorify : exalt. **—trans·fig′u·ra′tion** *n.*

trans·fix (trăns-fĭks′) *v.* **1.** To pierce with or as if with a pointed weapon. **2.** To make motionless, as with terror, amazement, or awe. **—trans·fix′ion** *adj.*

trans·form (trăns-fôrm′) *v.* **1.** To alter markedly the appearance or form of. **2.** To change the nature, function, or condition of : convert <a steam engine *transforming* heat into energy> **—trans·form′a·ble** *adj.* **—trans·form′a·bly** *adv.* **—trans′for·ma′tion** *n.* **—trans·form′er** *n.*

trans·fuse (trăns-fyōōz′) *v.* **-fused, -fus·ing. 1.** To transfer (liquid) by pouring from 1 container into another. **2.** To permeate, imbue, or instill. **3.** *Med.* To inject a liquid, as plasma, into the bloodstream. **—trans·fus′er** *n.* **—trans·fu′sion** *n.*

trans·gress (trăns-grĕs′, trănz-) *v.* **1.** To breach (a boundary or limit). **2.** To act in violation of (e.g., a law). **—trans·gress′i·ble** *adj.* **—trans·gres′sion** *n.* **—trans·gres′sive** *adj.* **—trans·gres′sor** *n.*

tran·sient (trăn′shənt, -zhənt, -zē-ənt) *adj.* **1.** Lasting only a short time : transitory. **2.** Passing through from 1 place to another <*transient* farm laborers> **—tran′sience, tran′sien·cy** *n.* **—tran′sient** *n.* **—tran′sient·ly** *adv.*

tran·sis·tor (trăn-zĭs′tər, trăn-sĭs′-) *n.* **1.** A 3-terminal semiconductor device for amplification, switching, and detection. **2.** A radio fitted with transistors. **—tran·sis′tor·i·za′tion** *n.* **—tran·sis′tor·ize′** *v.*

tran·sit (trăn′sĭt, -zĭt) *n.* **1. a.** Passage over, across, or through. **b.** Conveyance of goods or persons from place to place, esp. on a local system of public transport. **2.** An instrument used in surveying that measures horizontal and vertical angles.

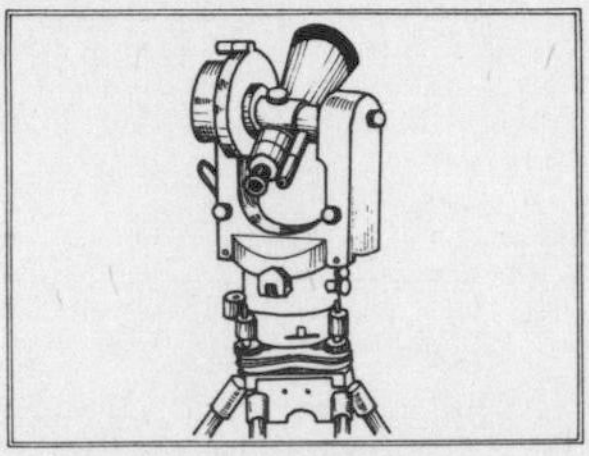

transit

tran·si·tion (trăn-zĭsh′ən, -sĭsh′ən) *n.* **1.** An act, process, or instance of changing from 1 state, form, activity, or place to another. **2.** Passage from 1 subject to another, as in discourse. **—tran·si′tion·al** *adj.* **—tran·si′tion·al·ly** *adv.*

tran·si·tive (trăn′sə-tĭv, trăn′zə-) *adj.* **1.** Expressing an action carried from the subject to the object and requiring a direct object to complete the meaning. Used of a verb or verb construction. **2.** Marked by or effecting transition. —*n.* A transitive verb. **—tran′si·tive·ly** *adv.* **—tran′si·tive·ness, tran′si·tiv′i·ty** *n.*

tran·si·to·ry (trăn′sə-tôr′ē, -tōr′ē, trăn′zə-) *adj.* Lasting only a short time. ☆**syns:** MOMENTARY, PASSING, SHORT-LIVED, TEMPORARY, TRANSIENT **—tran′si·to′ri·ly** *adv.* **—tran′si·to′ri·ness** *n.*

trans·late (trăns-lāt′, trănz-, trăns′lāt′, trănz′-) *v.* **-lat·ed, -lat·ing. 1.** To express in another language while retaining the original sense. **2.** To simplify or explain. **3.** To change from 1 form or style to another : convert <*translate* ideas into reality> **—trans·lat′a·bil′i·ty, trans·lat′a·ble·ness** *n.* **—trans·lat′a·ble** *adj.* **—trans·la′tion** *n.* **—trans·la′tor** *n.*

trans·lit·er·ate (trăns-lĭt′ə-rāt′, trănz-) *v.* **-at·ed, -at·ing.** To write (words or letters) in the corresponding characters of another alphabet. **—trans·lit′er·a′tion** *n.*

trans·lu·cent (trăns-lōō′sənt, trănz-) *adj.* Admitting and diffusing light so that objects beyond cannot be clearly perceived. **—trans·lu′cence, trans·lu′cen·cy** *n.*

trans·mi·grate (trăns-mī′grāt′, trănz-) *v.* To pass into another body after death. Used of the soul. **—trans′mi·gra′tion** *n.* **—trans·mi′gra′tor** *n.* **—trans·mi′gra·to′ry** (-grə-tôr′ē, -tōr′ē) *adj.*

trans·mis·si·ble (trăns-mĭs′ə-bəl, trănz-) *adj.* Capable of undergoing transmission <*transmissible* viruses>

trans·mis·sion (trăns-mĭsh′ən, trănz-) *n.* **1.** The act of transmitting or state of being transmitted. **2.** Something, as a voice or message, that is transmitted. **3.** An automotive assembly of gears and associated parts by which power is transmitted from the engine to a driving axle. **4.** Passage of modulated carrier waves from a transmitter. **—trans·mis′sive** *adj.*

trans·mit (trăns-mĭt′, trănz-) *v.* **-mit·ted, -mit·ting. 1.** To convey or dispatch from 1 person, thing, or place to another. **2.** To cause to spread a contagious disease <*transmit* an infection> **3.** To convey to others by heredity. **4.** *Electron.* To send (a signal) as by wire or radio. **5.** *Physics.* To cause (a disturbance) to propagate through a medium. **—trans·mis′si·ble, trans·mit′ta·ble** *adj.* **—trans·mit′tal** *n.*

trans·mit·ter (trăns-mĭt′ər, trănz-) *n.* One that transmits, as: **a.** A telegraphic sending instrument. **b.** The part of a telephone that converts sounds into electrical impulses. **c.** Electronic equipment that generates and amplifies a carrier wave and sends out the resulting signal.

trans·mog·ri·fy (trăns-mŏg′rə-fī′, trănz-) *v.* **-fied, -fy·ing.** To change into a different, esp. fantastic or bizarre shape or form. **—trans·mog′ri·fi·ca′tion** *n.*

trans·mute (trăns-myōōt′, trănz-) *v.* **-mut·ed, -mut·ing.** To change from 1 nature, form, substance, or state into another.

—**trans•mut'a•bil'i•ty** *n.* —**trans•mut'a•ble** *adj.* —**trans•mut'a•bly** *adv.* —**trans'mu•ta'tion** *n.*

trans•o•ce•an•ic (trăns'ō-shē-ăn'ĭk, trănz'-) *adj.* **1.** Situated on the other side of the ocean. **2.** Traversing the ocean.

tran•som (trăn'səm) *n.* **1. a.** A small, often hinged window above another window or a door. **b.** The horizontal crosspiece to which such a window is hinged. **2.** A horizontal piece of wood or stone in a window that serves to divide it. —**tran'somed** *adj.*

tran•son•ic (trăn-sŏn'ĭk) *adj.* Of or relating to aerodynamic flow or flight conditions at speeds close to the speed of sound.

trans•pa•cif•ic (trăns'pə-sĭf'ĭk) *adj.* **1.** Situated on the other side of the Pacific. **2.** Traversing the Pacific.

trans•par•ent (trăns-pâr'ənt, -păr'ənt) *adj.* **1.** Capable of transmitting light so that objects and images beyond can be clearly perceived. **2.** Permeable to electromagnetic radiation of specified frequencies. **3.** So fine or delicate in texture that objects may be easily seen on the other side : diaphanous. **4. a.** Easily detected : obvious. **b.** Readily understandable. —**trans•par'en•cy** *n.* —**trans•par'ent•ly** *adv.*

tran•spire (trăn-spīr') *v.* **-spired, -spir•ing. 1.** To give off (vapor containing waste products) through animal or plant pores. **2.** To be revealed. **3.** To take place. —**tran'spi•ra'tion** *n.*

trans•plant (trăns-plănt', -plänt') *v.* **1.** To remove (a living plant) from the place where it is growing and plant it in another place. **2.** To relocate. **3.** *Med.* To transfer (an organ or tissue) from 1 body or bodily part to another. —**trans'plant'** *n.* —**trans•plant'a•ble** *adj.* —**trans'plan•ta'tion** *n.*

trans•po•lar (trăns-pō'lər) *adj.* Extending across or crossing over either of the geographic polar regions.

trans•port (trăns-pôrt', -pōrt') *v.* **1.** To convey from 1 place to another. **2.** To affect with strong emotion. **3.** To send across the sea to a penal colony. —*n.* (trăns'pôrt', -pōrt'). **1.** The act or process of transporting. **2.** The state of being carried away by emotion. **3.** A ship or aircraft for transporting troops or military equipment. **4.** A vehicle, as an airplane, for transporting mail, freight, or passengers. —**trans•port'a•bil'i•ty** *n.* —**trans•port'a•ble** *adj.* —**trans'por•ta'tion** *n.* —**trans•port'er** *n.*

trans•pose (trăns-pōz') *v.* **-posed, -pos•ing. 1.** To reverse the order or place of. **2.** To move into a different position or order. **3.** *Mus.* To write or perform (a composition) in a key other than the one in which it was written. —**trans•pos'a•ble** *adj.* —**trans•pos'er** *n.* —**trans'po•si'tion** *n.*

trans•sex•u•al (trăns-sĕk'sho͞o-əl) *n.* **1.** One predisposed to become a member of the opposite sex. **2.** One whose sex has been changed externally by surgery.

trans•ship (trăns-shĭp') *also* **tran•ship** (trăn-) *v.* To transfer (cargo) from 1 vessel or vehicle to another for reshipment. —**trans•ship'ment** *n.*

tran•sub•stan•ti•a•tion (trăn'səb-stăn'shē-ā'shən) *n. Theol.* The doctrine that the bread and wine of the Eucharist are transformed into the true presence of Christ, although their appearance is the same.

trans•u•ran•ic (trăns'yo͝o-răn'ĭk, -rā'nĭk, trănz'-) *adj.* Having an atomic number higher than 92.

trans•ver•sal (trăns-vûr'səl, trănz-) *adj.* Transverse. —*n.* A line intersecting a system of lines. —**trans•ver'sal•ly** *adv.*

trans•verse (trăns-vûrs', trănz-, trăns'vûrs', trănz'-) *adj.* Located or lying across. —*n.* (trăns'vûrs', trănz'). Something, as a part or beam, that is transverse. ☆***syns:*** CROSSING, CROSSWISE, THWART, TRANSVERSAL, TRAVERSE —**trans•verse'ly** *adv.*

trans•ves•tism (trăns-vĕs'tĭz-əm) *n.* The practice of adopting the dress and often the manners or behavior of the other sex. —**trans•ves'tite** (-tīt) *n.* & *adj.*

trap (trăp) *n.* **1.** A device, as a net or a clamplike apparatus that springs shut suddenly, for catching and holding animals. **2.** A stratagem or device used to trick or surprise an unsuspecting victim. **3. a.** A receptacle, as a grease trap, for collecting waste materials. **b.** A device for sealing a passage, as a drainpipe, against the escape of gases. **4.** A device that hurls clay pigeons, balls, or disks into the air to be shot at. **5.** A land hazard, as a sand-filled depression, on a golf course. **6.** A light 2-wheeled carriage with springs. **7.** A trap door. **8. traps.** Percussion instruments. —*v.* **trapped, trap•ping. 1.** To catch in or as if in a trap. **2.** To place in a confining or embarassing position. **3.** To trap animals. —**trap'per** *n.*

trap door *n.* A movable door in a floor, roof, or ceiling.

tra•peze (tră-pēz') *n.* A short horizontal bar suspended from 2 parallel ropes, used for acrobatic stunts or exercise.

trap•e•zoid (trăp'ə-zoid') *n.* **1.** A quadrilateral having 1 pair of parallel sides. **2.** A small bone in the wrist near the base of the index finger. —**trap'e•zoi'dal** *adj.*

trap•ping (trăp'ĭng) *n.* **1.** *often* **trappings.** An ornamental covering or harness for a horse. **2. trappings. a.** Articles of dress or adornment. **b.** Outward signs or indications.

trap•shoot•ing (trăp'sho͞o'tĭng) *n.* The sport of shooting at clay pigeons.

trash (trăsh) *n.* **1.** Worthless, discarded material : junk. **2.** Worthless literary or artistic matter. **3.** One considered ignorant or contemptible. —**trash'y** *adj.*

trau•ma (trou'mə, trô'-) *n., pl.* **-mas** *or* **-ma•ta** (-mə-tə). **1.** *Pathol.* A wound, esp. 1 caused by sudden physical injury. **2.** *Psychiat.* An emotional shock that creates substantial and lasting damage to the psychological development of the individual, gen. leading to neurosis. **3.** Something that severely jars the mind or emotions. ☆***syns:*** BLOW, JOLT, SHOCK —**trau•mat'ic** *adj.* —**trau•mat'i•cal•ly** *adv.* —**trau'ma•tize'** *v.*

tra•vail (trə-vāl', trăv'āl') *n.* **1.** Strenuous physical or mental exertion. **2.** Tribulation : distress. **3.** The labor of childbirth. **4.** *Can.* A travois. —*v.* **1.** To labor strenuously : toil. **2.** To undergo the labor of childbirth.

trav•el (trăv'əl) *v.* **-eled, -el•ing** *or* **-elled, -el•ling. 1.** To move from 1 place to another : journey. **2.** To journey from 1 place to another as a sales representative. **3.** To be transmitted, as sound. **4.** To associate <*travels* in a fast circle> **5.** To admit of being transported <Some perishable goods *travel* poorly.> —*n.* **1.** The act or process of traveling. **2.** *often* **travels. a.** A series of journeys. **b.** A written account of a series of journeys. —**trav'el•er** *n.*

▲word history: The hardships of making a journey in earlier times is reflected in the etymological identity of the words *travel* and *travail.* Both are derived from Old French *travailler,* which orig. meant "to torment, trouble" and later came to mean "to be troubled, be in pain, work hard." *Travailler* was borrowed into English as *travail,* which at 1st had the same meanings as the Old French word but later came to mean "to toil, make a difficult journey," and simply "to journey." *Travel* was orig. a variant of *travail,* but it has now become a separate word used exclusively in the sense "to journey."

travel agency *n.* An agency that arranges for travel itineraries, tickets, and accommodations. —**travel agent** *n.*

travel bureau *n.* A travel agency.

traveler's check *n.* An internationally redeemable draft available in various denominations and valid only with the holder's own endorsement against his or her original signature.

trav•e•logue *also* **trav•e•log** (trăv'ə-lôg', -lŏg') *n.* A lecture illustrated by slides or a narrated film about travels.

tra•verse (trə-vûrs', trăv'ərs) *v.* **-versed, -vers•ing. 1.** To pass across, over, or through. **2.** To move forward and backward over. **3.** To extend across <a bridge *traversing* a gorge> **4.** To go counter to : thwart. —*n.* **1. a.** The act of traversing. **b.** A route or path across. **2.** Something lying across something else, as a transom. —*adj.* Transverse. —**trav'ers•a•ble** *adj.* —**tra•vers'al** *n.* —**tra•vers'er** *n.*

trav•es•ty (trăv'ĭ-stē) *n., pl.* **-ties.** A grotesque imitation with intent to ridicule. —*v.* **-tied, -ty•ing.** To make a travesty of.

tra•vois (trə-voi', trăv'oi') *n., pl.* **tra•vois** (trə-voiz', trăv'oiz') *or* **-es.** *Can.* A primitive Indian sledge consisting of a platform or netting supported by 2 long trailing poles, the forward ends of which are fastened to a dog or horse.

travois

trawl (trôl) *n.* A large tapered and flattened or conical fishing net towed along the sea floor. —**trawl** *v.*

tray (tra) *n.* A flat, shallow container having a raised edge, used for holding, carrying, or displaying something.

treach•er•ous (trĕch'ər-əs) *adj.* **1.** Disloyal : traitorous. **2. a.** Undependable. **b.** Dangerous. —**treach'er•ous•ly** *adv.* —**treach'er•ous•ness** *n.*

treach•er•y (trĕch'ə-rē) *n., pl.* **-ies. 1.** Deliberate betrayal of confidence or trust : perfidy. **2.** An act or instance of betraying confidence or trust.

trea•cle (trē'kəl) *n.* **1.** Cloying sentiment. **2.** *esp. Brit.* Molasses. —**trea'cly** *adj.*

tread (trĕd) *v.* **trod** (trŏd), **trod•den** (trŏd'n) *or* **trod, tread•ing. 1.** To walk over, on, or along. **2.** To stamp or trample. **3.** To execute (e.g., a step or measure) by walking or dancing. —*n.* **1.**

The act, manner, sound, or an instance of treading. **2.** The horizontal section of a step in a staircase. **3.** The portion of a wheel that makes contact with the ground or rails. **4.** The grooved surface of a tire.

tread·le (trĕd′l) *n.* A foot pedal for activating a circular drive, as in a potter's wheel or sewing machine.

tread·mill (trĕd′mĭl′) *n.* **1.** A mechanism activated by walking on the moving steps of a wheel or treading an endless sloping belt. **2.** A monotonous task.

treas. *abbr.* treasurer; treasury.

trea·son (trē′zən) *n.* **1.** Violation of allegiance toward one's country or sovereign, esp. the betrayal of one's own country by waging war against it or by consciously and purposely acting to aid its enemies. **2.** A betrayal of trust or confidence. **—trea′son·a·ble** *adj.* **—trea′son·ous** *adj.*

treas·ure (trĕzh′ər) *n.* **1.** Accumulated or hidden wealth, as jewels or money. **2.** One regarded as esp. valuable. *—v.* **-ured, -ur·ing. 1.** To accumulate and save for future use. **2.** To value greatly : cherish.

treas·ur·er (trĕzh′ər-ər) *n.* A person having charge of funds or revenues, esp. a financial officer for a government, company, or society. **—treas′ur·er·ship′** *n.*

treas·ure-trove (trĕzh′ər-trōv′) *n.* **1.** Unclaimed treasure found hidden. **2.** A valuable discovery : trove.

treas·ur·y (trĕzh′ə-rē) *n., pl.* **-ies. 1.** A place where treasure is kept. **2.** A place where private or public funds are kept and managed. **3.** Public funds or revenues. **4.** A collection of valuable things. **5. Treasury.** The governmental department in charge of the collection, management, and expenditure of public revenue.

treat (trēt) *v.* **1.** To have to do with or behave in a specified manner toward. **2.** To consider or regard in a given manner. **3.** To deal with in speech or writing. **4.** To represent or deal with in a specified style or manner. **5.** To provide food or entertainment for (another) at one's own expense <*treated* me to dinner> **6.** To subject to an action, process, or change <*treat* sick patients><*treat* the garden with compost> *—n.* **1.** The act of treating. **2.** Something, as one's food or entertainment, paid for by another person. **3.** A special delight <A trip to Paris was a real *treat.*> **—treat′a·ble** *adj.* **—treat′er** *n.*

trea·tise (trē′tĭs) *n.* A formal written account treating a subject systematically.

treat·ment (trēt′mənt) *n.* **1.** The act or manner of treating : handling. **2.** Medical application of remedies so as to effect a cure : therapy.

trea·ty (trē′tē) *n., pl.* **-ties.** A formal agreement between 2 or more states or nations. ☆**syns:** ACCORD, AGREEMENT, CONCORD, CONVENTION, PACT

treb·le (trĕb′əl) *adj.* **1.** Triple : threefold. **2.** *Mus.* Of, having, or performing the highest part, voice, or range. **3.** Having a high pitch : shrill. *—n.* **1.** *Mus.* The highest part, voice, instrument, or range : soprano. **2.** A high, shrill voice or sound. *—v.* **-led, -ling.** To increase 3 times : triple. **—treb′le·ness** *n.* **—treb′ly** *adv.*

tree (trē) *n.* **1.** A usu. tall woody plant having comparatively great height and a single trunk. **2.** A plant, as a shrub, resembling a tree in form or size. **3.** Something similar to a tree, as a pole with pegs for hanging clothes. **4.** A diagram with a branching form, as one used to show family descent. *—v.* **treed, tree·ing. 1.** To force to climb a tree in evasion of pursuit. **2.** *Informal.* To force into a difficult position : corner. **—tree′less** *adj.* **—tree′like′** *adj.*

tree farm *n.* Forested land on which trees are grown commercially.

tree frog *n.* A small, arboreal frog of the genus *Hyla* and related genera, with long toes terminating in adhesive disks.

tree line *n.* **1.** The limit of N or S latitude beyond which trees cannot grow except as stunted forms. **2.** A timberline.

tree of heaven *n.* The ailanthus.

tre·foil (trē′foil′, trĕf′oil′) *n.* **1.** Any of various plants of the genera *Trifolium, Lotus,* and related genera, having compound leaves with 3 leaflets. **2.** A stylized representation of a trefoil leaf.

trek (trĕk) *v.* **trekked, trek·king.** To make a slow, arduous journey. *—n.* A journey or leg of a journey, esp. when slow and difficult. **—trek′ker** *n.*

trel·lis (trĕl′ĭs) *n.* A frame supporting open latticework, used for training vines and other climbing plants.

trem·ble (trĕm′bəl) *v.* **-bled, -bling. 1.** To shake involuntarily, as from fear, cold, etc. : shiver. **2.** To feel or express fear or anxiety. **—trem′ble** *n.* **—trem′bler** *n.* **—trem′bly** *adj.*

tre·men·dous (trĭ-mĕn′dəs) *adj.* **1.** Fearful : terrible. **2. a.** Particularly large : enormous. **b.** *Informal.* Marvelous : wonderful. **—tre·men′dous·ly** *adv.*

trem·o·lo (trĕm′ə-lō′) *n., pl.* **-los.** *Mus.* A vibrating effect made by quickly repeating 1 tone or by quickly alternating 2 tones.

trem·or (trĕm′ər) *n.* **1.** A quick vibratory or shaking movement. **2.** Involuntary trembling of the body.

trem·u·lous (trĕm′yə-ləs) *adj.* **1.** Vibrating : quivering : trembling. **2.** Timid. **—trem′u·lous·ly** *adv.*

trench (trĕnch) *n.* **1.** A furrow. **2. a.** A ditch. **b.** A ditch embanked with its own soil used for protection, esp. in warfare. *—v.* **1.** To cut or dig a trench. **2.** To fortify with a trench. **3.** To encroach <*trenched* on my land> **—trench′er** *n.*

trench·ant (trĕn′chənt) *adj.* **1.** Forcefully effective : vigorous. **2.** Very perceptive : incisive. **—trench′an·cy** *n.*

trench coat *n.* A loose-fitting, belted raincoat with numerous pockets and flaps.

trench·er (trĕn′chər) *n.* A wooden cutting or serving board.

trench·er·man (trĕn′chər-mən) *n.* A hearty eater.

trench foot *n.* A condition of the feet resembling frostbite caused by prolonged exposure to damp cold.

trench mouth *n.* Contagious gingivitis.

trend (trĕnd) *n.* **1.** A general inclination or tendency : drift. **2.** A direction of movement : course. *—v.* To have a specified direction or tendency. **—trend′set′ter** *n.*

trend·y (trĕn′dē) *adj.* **-i·er, -i·est.** *Informal.* Of or being in accord with the latest fashion or fad <*trendy* attire> **—trend′i·ly** *adv.* **—trend′i·ness** *n.*

Tren·ton (trĕn′tən). Cap. of N.J., in the WC part. *Pop.* 92,124.

tre·pan (trĭ-păn′) *n.* A trephine. *—v.* **-panned, -pan·ning.** To trephine.

tre·phine (trĭ-fīn′) *n.* A surgical instrument with sawlike edges, used for cutting out disks of bone, usu. from the skull. **—tre·phine** *v.* **—treph′i·na′tion** *n.*

trep·i·da·tion (trĕp′ə-dā′shən) *n.* Great alarm or dread.

tres·pass (trĕs′pəs, -păs′) *n.* **1.** To commit a sin or offense : transgress. **2.** To infringe upon another's privacy, time, or attention. **3.** *Law.* To invade the property, rights, or person of another without consent. *—n.* **1.** A transgression. **2.** *Law.* The act of trespassing. **—tres′pass·er** *n.*

tress (trĕs) *n.* **1.** A lock of hair. **2. tresses.** A woman's long hair.

tres·tle (trĕs′əl) *n.* **1.** A horizontal beam or bar held up by 2 pairs of legs and used as a support, as for a table. **2.** A framework composed of vertical, slanted supports and horizontal crosspieces holding up a bridge.

trey (trā) *n.* A card, die, or domino with 3 pips : three.

tri·a·ble (trī′ə-bəl) *adj.* **1.** Capable of being tried or tested. **2.** *Law.* Subject to judicial examination. **—tri′a·ble·ness** *n.*

tri·ad (trī′ăd′, -əd) *n.* A group of 3 persons or things. **—tri·ad′ic** *adj.*

tri·al (trī′əl, trīl) *n.* **1.** *Law.* Examination and hearing of evidence before a court to decide the issue of specified charges or claims. **2.** The act or process of trying and proving by use and experience : experiment. **3.** An effort or attempt. **4.** A source of vexation or distress that tests patience and endurance. *—adj.* **1.** *Law.* Of or relating to a trial. **2.** Made, done, performed, or used during a test or experiment.

tri·an·gle (trī′ăng′gəl) *n.* **1.** A plane geometric figure with 3 angles and 3 sides. **2.** Something shaped like a triangle. **3.** *Mus.* A percussion instrument composed of a piece of metal formed into a triangle. **—tri·an′gu·lar** *adj.* **—tri·an′gu·lar′i·ty** *n.*

tri·an·gu·late (trī-ăng′gyə-lāt′) *v.* **-lat·ed, -lat·ing. 1.** To divide into triangles. **2.** To measure by trigonometry. **—tri·an′gu·late·ly** *adv.* **—tri·an′gu·la′tion** *n.*

tribe (trīb) *n.* **1.** A system of social organization comprising several villages, districts, bands, lineages, or other groups that share a common ancestry, culture, language, and name. **2.** A group sharing a common occupation, interest, or habit. **—trib′al** *adj.* **—trib′al·ism** *n.* **—trib′al·ly** *adv.*

tribes·man (trībz′mən) *n.* A member of a tribe. **—tribes′wom′an** *n.*

trib·u·la·tion (trĭb′yə-lā′shən) *n.* **1.** Great trial, affliction, or distress. **2.** A cause of great distress.

tri·bu·nal (trī-byo͞o′nəl, trĭ-) *n.* **1.** A court of justice <a military *tribunal*> **2.** One empowered to determine or judge.

trib·une (trĭb′yo͞on′, trĭ-byo͞on′) *n.* **1.** An ancient Roman official chosen by the plebs to protect their rights against the patricians. **2.** A protector or champion of the people. **—trib′u·nar′y** *adj.*

trib·u·tar·y (trĭb′yə-tĕr′ē) *adj.* **1.** Flowing into another. **2.** Contributory. **3.** Of the nature of or paying tribute. *—n., pl.* **-ies. 1.** A river or stream flowing into a larger river or stream. **2.** One that pays tribute.

trib·ute (trĭb′yo͞ot) *n.* **1.** A gift or testimonial expressing gratitude or admiration. **2.** Money or valuables given by a ruler or nation to another in submission or as the price for protection.

trice (trīs) *n.* An extremely short period of time : instant.

tri•ceps (trī'sĕps') *n.* A large 3-headed muscle running along the back of the upper arm and functioning to extend the forearm.

tri•cer•a•tops (trī-sĕr'ə-tŏps') *n.* A horned herbivorous dinosaur of the genus *Triceratops.*

tri•chi•na (trĭ-kī'nə) *n., pl.* **-nae** (-nē) *or* **-nas.** A parasitic nematode worm infesting the intestines of mammals.

trich•i•no•sis (trĭk'ə-nō'sĭs) *n.* A disease caused by trichinae-infested pork that has not been cooked enough and marked by fever, muscular swelling, and pain.

trick (trĭk) *n.* **1.** An indirect, often deceptive or fraudulent means of achieving an end. **2.** A mischievous act : prank. **3.** A stupid, disgraceful, or childish act. **4.** A mannerism. **5.** A special skill : knack. **6.** A feat of magic or legerdemain. **7.** A difficult, dexterous, or clever act designed to amuse or impress. **8.** The cards played in a single round in a card game. *—v.* **1.** To cheat or deceive. **2.** To adorn <*tricked* out in rhinestones> *—adj.* Weak, defective, or likely to fail <a *trick* elbow>

trick•er•y (trĭk'ə-rē) *n., pl.* **-ies.** Deception by stratagem.

trick•le (trĭk'əl) *v.* **-led, -ling. 1.** To fall or flow in drops or droplets or in a thin stream. **2.** To move or advance slowly or bit by bit. **—trick'le** *n.*

trick•ster (trĭk'stər) *n.* One that plays tricks : swindler.

trick•y (trĭk'ē) *adj.* **-i•er, -i•est. 1.** Given to or marked by trickery : wily. **2.** Requiring skill or caution <a *tricky* pastry recipe> **—trick'i•ly** *adv.* **—trick'i•ness** *n.*

tri•col•or (trī'kŭl'ər) *n.* **1.** A flag of 3 colors. **2.** The French flag. **—tri'col'ored** *adj.*

tri•corn *also* **tri•corne** (trī'kôrn') *n.* A hat whose brim is turned up on 3 sides.

tri•cor•nered (trī'kôr'nərd) *adj.* Having 3 corners.

tri•cy•cle (trī'sĭk'əl, -sĭ-kəl) *n.* A vehicle with 3 wheels, usu. pedal-propelled.

tri•dent (trīd'ənt) *n.* A long, 3-pronged fork, weapon, or spear.

tried (trīd) *adj.* Thoroughly tested and proved to be good or reliable.

tri•en•ni•al (trī-ĕn'ē-əl) *adj.* **1.** Occurring every 3rd year. **2.** Lasting 3 years. **—tri•en'ni•al** *n.* **—tri•en'ni•al•ly** *adv.*

Tri•este (trē-ĕst'). Seaport of extreme NE Italy. *Pop.* 260,291.

tri•fle (trī'fəl) *n.* **1.** Something unimportant or of little value. **2.** A small amount : jot. **3.** Cake soaked in wine or brandy and topped with jam. *—v.* **-fled, -fling. 1.** To handle something as if it were of little importance or value. **2.** To toy with something <*trifle* with someone's affections> **3.** To waste (e.g., time). **—tri'fler** *n.*

tri•fling (trī'flĭng) *adj.* **1.** Of little importance : insignificant. **2.** Marked by frivolity. **—tri'fling•ly** *adv.*

tri•fo•cal (trī-fō'kəl) *adj.* Having 3 focal lengths. *—pl.n.* **trifocals.** Eyeglasses with trifocal lenses.

trig[1] (trĭg) *adj.* **1.** Neat and trim : tidy. **2.** Being in good condition. **—trig** *v.* **—trig'ly** *adv.* **—trig'ness** *n.*

trig[2] (trĭg) *n.* Trigonometry.

trig•ger (trĭg'ər) *n.* **1.** The small lever of a firearm that is pressed by the finger to discharge it. **2.** A similar device that releases or activates a mechanism. **3.** Stimulus. *—v.* To set off : activate.

trigonometric function *n.* A function of an angle expressed as a ratio of 2 of the sides of a right triangle that contains the angle.

trig•o•nom•e•try (trĭg'ə-nŏm'ə-trē) *n.* The study of the properties and applications of trigonometric functions. **—trig'o•no•met'ric —trig'o•no•met'ri•cal** *adj.* **—trig'o•no•met'ri•cal•ly** *adv.*

tril•by (trĭl'bē) *n., pl.* **-bies.** *esp. Brit.* A soft felt hat with a deeply creased crown.

trill (trĭl) *n.* **1.** A tremulous sound : warble. **2.** *Mus.* Rapid alternating of 2 tones a whole or a half tone apart. **3. a.** A rapid vibration of 1 speech organ against another. **b.** A sound pronounced with a trill, as Spanish *rr.* *—v.* **1.** *Mus.* To sound, sing, or play with a trill. **2.** To articulate with a trill.

tril•lion (trĭl'yən) *n.* **1.** The cardinal number equal to 10^{12}. **2.** *esp. Brit.* The cardinal number equal to 10^{18}. **—tril'lion** *adj. & pron.* **—tril'lionth** *n. & adj. & adv.*

tril•o•gy (trĭl'ə-jē) *n., pl.* **-gies.** A series of 3 literary works that are related in subject matter or theme.

trim (trĭm) *v.* **trimmed, trim•ming. 1.** To neaten by clipping or pruning. **2.** To remove excess from by cutting <*trimmed* the budget> **3.** To decorate : ornament. **4.** *Informal.* To defeat soundly. **5.** *Naut.* **a.** To adjust (the sails and yards) for proper wind reception. **b.** To balance (a ship) by shifting the contents. **6.** To balance (an aircraft) in flight by regulating the control surfaces and tabs. *—n.* **1.** State of order, arrangement, or appearance : condition <in good *trim*> **2. a.** Exterior ornamentation, as moldings or framework. **b.** Ornamentation, as for clothing. **3.** Rejected or excised material. **4. a.** The readiness of a vessel for sailing. **b.** The balance or position of a ship or aircraft. *—adj.* **trim•mer, trim•mest. 1.** In good order. **2.** Having neat, pleasing forms or lines <a *trim* figure> <a *trim* sailboat> **—trim'ly** *adv.* **—trim'mer** *n.* **—trim'ness** *n.*

tri•mes•ter (trī-mĕs'tər) *n.* A stage or period of 3 months.

trim•ming (trĭm'ĭng) *n.* **1.** Material added as an ornament or decoration. **2. trimmings.** Accessories <turkey and *trimmings*> **3.** *Informal.* A sound defeat.

Trin•i•dad (trĭn'ə-dăd'). Island off Venezuela. **—Trin'i•dad'i•an** *adj. & n.*

Trinidad and To•ba•go (tə-bā'gō). Country of SE West Indies, comprising the islands of Trinidad and Tobago. *Cap.* Port-of-Spain. *Pop.* 920,000.

trin•i•ty (trĭn'ə-tē) *n., pl.* **-ties. 1.** A group of 3 members in union : triad. **2. Trinity.** The union of the Father, Son, and Holy Ghost in a single Godhead.

trin•ket (trĭng'kĭt) *n.* **1.** A small ornament. **2.** A trivial thing : trifle.

tri•ni•tro•tol•u•ene (trī-nī'trō-tŏl'yo͞o-ēn') *n.* A yellow crystalline compound used chiefly as a high explosive.

tri•o (trē'ō) *n., pl.* **-os. 1.** A group or set of 3. **2.** *Mus.* **a.** A composition for 3 performers. **b.** The group performing a trio.

trip (trĭp) *n.* **1.** Travel from one place to another : journey. **2.** *Slang.* **a.** A hallucinatory experience induced by a psychedelic drug. **b.** An exciting experience. **3.** A stumble : fall. **4.a.** A device, as a pawl, for triggering a mechanism. **b.** The action of a trip. *—v.* **tripped, trip•ping. 1.** To stumble or cause to stumble : fall. **2.** To move nimbly with light, rapid steps : skip. **3.** To make a mistake. **4.** To release or be released, as a catch, switch, or trigger.

tri•par•tite (trī-pär'tīt') *adj.* **1.** Made up of or divided into 3 parts. **2.** Pertaining to or carried out by 3 parties.

tripe (trīp) *n.* **1.** The stomach lining of ruminants, esp. oxen, used as food. **2.** *Informal.* Something worthless : rubbish.

tri•ple (trĭp'əl) *adj.* **1.** Having 3 parts. **2.** Multiplied by 3. *—n.* **1.** A number or amount 3 times greater than another. **2.** A group or set of 3. **3.** *Baseball.* A 3-base hit. *—v.* **-pled, -pling. 1.** To make or become 3 times as large in number or amount. **2.** *Baseball.* To hit a triple. **—tri'ply** *adv.*

trip•let (trĭp'lĭt) *n.* **1.** A group or set of 3 of a kind. **2.** One of 3 born at a single birth.

tri•plex (trĭp'lĕks', trī'plĕks') *adj.* Consisting of 3 parts <*triplex* windows> *—n.* Something triplex, as a building containing 3 apartments.

trip•li•cate (trĭp'lĭ-kĭt) *n.* A set of 3 identical things or copies <typed in *triplicate*> *—v.* (trĭp'lĭ-kāt') **-cat•ed, -cat•ing.** To make 3 identical copies of. **—trip'li•cate•ly** *adv.* **—trip'li•ca'tion** *n.*

trip•ping•ly (trĭp'ĭng-lē) *adv.* Lightly and easily : fluently.

tri•pod (trī'pŏd') *n.* A 3-legged object, as a cauldron, stool, or table.

Trip•o•li (trĭp'ə-lē). Cap. of Libya, in the NW. *Pop.* 551,477.

trip•tych (trĭp'tĭk) *n.* A work of art composed of 3 hinged or folding panels.

tri•reme (trī'rēm') *n.* An ancient Greek or Roman galley or warship, with 3 banks of oars on each side.

tri•sect (trī'sĕkt', trī-sĕkt') *v.* To divide into 3 equal parts. **—tri'sec'tion** *n.*

tris•mus (trĭz'məs) *n.* Lockjaw. **—tris'mic** *adj.*

trite (trīt) *adj.* **trit•er, trit•est.** Devoid of freshness or appeal due to overuse. ☆***syns:*** BANAL, COMMONPLACE, HACKNEYED, PLATITUDINOUS, TIMEWORN

trit•i•um (trĭt'ē-əm, trĭsh'ē-) *n.* A rare radioactive hydrogen isotope with atomic mass 3, prepared artificially as a tracer and a constituent of hydrogen bombs.

tri•umph (trī'əmf) *v.* **1.** To be victorious : win. **2.** To be jubilant : exult. *—n.* **1.** An instance or the fact of being victorious : success. **2.** Jubilant exultation. **—tri•um'phal** *adj.* **—tri•um'phant** *adj.* **—tri•um'phant•ly** *adv.* **—tri'umph•er** *n.*

tri•um•vir (trī-ŭm'vər) *n., pl.* **-virs** or **-vi•ri** (-və-rī'). One of a group of 3 men who shared public administration or civil authority, as in ancient Rome. **—tri•um'vi•ral** *adj.* **—tri•um'vi•rate** *n.*

tri•va•lent (trī-vā'lənt) *adj.* Having valence 3. **—tri•va'lence, tri•va'len•cy** *n.*

triv•et (trĭv'ĭt) *n.* **1.** A 3-legged stand. **2.** A metal stand with short feet, used under a hot dish or platter on a table.

triv•i•a (trĭv'ē-ə) *pl.n.* Insignificant or superfluous matters. ☆***syns:*** MINUTIAE, TRIFLES, TRIVIALITY

triv•i•al (trĭv'ē-əl) *adj.* **1.** Relatively insignificant : unimportant. **2.** Commonplace : ordinary. **—triv'i•al'i•ty** *n.*

-trix *suff.* A woman associated with a specified thing <executrix>

tRNA (tē'är-ĕn'ā') *n.* Transfer RNA.

tro•che (trō'kē) *n.* A small, usu. round medicinal lozenge.

tro•chee (trō′kē) *n.* A metrical foot in prosody consisting of a stressed syllable followed by an unstressed syllable. **—tro•cha′ic** (-kā′ĭk) *adj.* & *n.*
trod (trŏd) *v. p.t. & var. p.p. of* TREAD.
trod•den (trŏd′n) *v. p.p. of* TREAD.
troi•ka (troi′kə) *n.* **1.** A small Russian carriage drawn by a team of 3 horses abreast. **2.** A group or association of 3.
Tro•jan (trō′jən) *n.* **1.** A native or resident of ancient Troy. **2.** A courageous, determined, or energetic person. **—Tro′jan** *adj.*
Trojan horse *n.* A subversive group or device placed within enemy ranks.
troll[1] (trōl) *v.* **1.** To fish for by running a baited line behind a slowly moving boat. **2.** To trail (a baited line) in fishing. **3.** To sing the parts of (e.g., a round). **4.** To sing lustily. *—n.* **1.** The act of trolling for fish. **2.** A lure used for trolling. **3.** A musical round. **—troll′er** *n.*
troll[2] (trōl) *n.* A creature of Scandinavian folklore variously portrayed as a dwarf or a giant living in caves or under bridges.
trol•ley *also* **trol•ly** (trŏl′ē) *n., pl.* **-leys** *also* **-lies. 1.** A streetcar. **2.** A wheeled carriage, cage, or basket hung from and traveling on an overhead track. **3.** A device that gathers electric current from an underground conductor, an overhead wire, or a 3rd rail, and transmits it to the motor of an electric vehicle.
trolley bus *n.* A trackless bus that is powered by electricity from an overhead wire.
trolley car *n.* A streetcar.
trol•lop (trŏl′əp) *n.* **1.** A slattern. **2.** A sexually promiscuous woman.
trom•bone (trŏm-bōn′, trəm-, trŏm′bōn′) *n.* A brass musical instrument composed of a long tube bent upon itself twice ending in a bell-shaped mouth. **—trom•bon′ist** *n.*
tromp (trŏmp) *v. Informal.* **1.** To tramp. **2.** To trample underfoot. **3.** To trounce.
trompe l'oeil (trômp′loi′) *n.* **1.** A style of painting that creates an illusion of photographic reality. **2.** A trompe l'oeil effect.
troop (tro͞op) *n.* **1.** A group or company of people or animals. **2. a.** A group of soldiers. **b. troops.** Military units : soldiers. *—v.* To advance or go as a throng.
troop carrier *n.* A transport aircraft for deploying troops.
troop•er (tro͞o′pər) *n.* **1. a.** A cavalry soldier. **b.** A cavalry horse. **2.** A mounted police officer. **3.** A state police officer.
troop•ship (tro͞op′shĭp′) *n.* A ship for transporting troops.
trope (trōp) *n.* Figurative use of a word or expression : figure of speech.
tro•phy (trō′fē) *n., pl.* **-phies.** Something, as a prize or memento won or received as a symbol of achievement or victory.
trop•ic (trŏp′ĭk) *n.* **1.** Either of 2 parallels of latitude that constitute the boundaries of the Torrid Zone. **2. tropics.** The region of the earth's surface lying between these latitudes. *—adj.* Of or pertaining to the tropics : tropical.
trop•i•cal (trŏp′ĭ-kəl) *adj.* **1.** Of, occurring in, or typical of the tropics. **2.** Hot and humid : torrid. **—trop′i•cal•ly** *adv.*
tropic of Cancer *n.* The parallel of latitude 23° 27′ N of the equator and the N boundary of the Torrid Zone.
tropic of Capricorn *n.* The parallel of latitude 23° 27′ S of the equator and the S boundary of the Torrid Zone.
tro•pism (trō′pĭz′əm) *n.* Growth or movement of a plant or animal in response to an external stimulus.
tro•po•sphere (trō′pə-sfîr′, trŏp′ə-) *n.* The lowest region of the atmosphere between the earth's surface and the lower stratosphere, marked by decreasing temperature with increasing altitude.
trot (trŏt) *n.* **1.** A gait of a 4-footed animal between a walk and a run in speed in which the right and left diagonal legs move forward together. **2.** A gait of a person, faster than a walk : jog. **3.** *Informal.* A literal translation of a text, used esp. by students : pony. *—v.* **trot•ted, trot•ting. 1.** To go or advance at a trot. **2.** To hurry. **—trot′ter** *n.*
troth (trôth, trōth, trŏth) *n.* **1.** Good faith : fidelity. **2. a.** One's pledged fidelity. **b.** Betrothal. **—troth** *v.*
trou•ba•dour (tro͞o′bə-dôr′, -dōr′, -do͝or′) *n.* **1.** A 12th- and 13th-cent. lyric poet attached to the courts of Provence and N Italy, who composed songs in complex metrical form. **2.** A strolling minstrel.
trou•ble (trŭb′əl) *n.* **1.** Distress, affliction, danger, or need <in *trouble* with the authorities> **2.** A cause or source of distress, affliction, danger, or need. **3.** Pains : exertion <went to a lot of *trouble* to give us a good time> **4.** Pain, disease, or malfunction <heart *trouble*><car *trouble*> *—v.* **-bled, -bling. 1.** To stir up : agitate. **2.** To afflict with discomfort or pain. **3.** To cause confusion or distress in : perturb. **4.** To inconvenience : bother. **5.** To take pains. **—troub′ler** *n.* **—troub′ling•ly** *adv.*
trou•ble•mak•er (trŭb′əl-mā′kər) *n.* One that makes trouble.
trou•ble-shoot•er (trŭb′əl-sho͞o′tər) *n.* One who pinpoints and gets rid of sources of trouble. **—trou′ble-shoot′** *v.*
trou•ble•some (trŭb′əl-səm) *adj.* **1.** Causing trouble or anxiety. **2.** Difficult to treat, manage, or cope with. ☆***syns:*** MEAN, PESKY, TRYING, VEXATIOUS, WICKED **—trou′ble•some•ly** *adv.* **—trou′ble•some•ness** *n.*
trough (trôf, trŏf) *n.* **1.** A long, shallow receptacle, esp. one to hold food and water for animals. **2.** A gutter below the eaves of a roof. **3.** A long, narrow depression, as between waves. **4.** A low point in a business cycle or on a statistical graph. **5.** *Meteorol.* An elongated region of low atmospheric pressure, often associated with a front.
trounce (trouns) *v.* **trounced, trounc•ing. 1.** To beat : thrash. **2.** To defeat soundly : whip.
troupe (tro͞op) *n.* A company, esp. of theatrical performers. *—v.* **trouped, troup•ing.** To tour with a company of performers. **—troup′er** *n.*
trou•sers (trou′zərz) *pl.n.* An outer garment for covering the body from the waist to the ankles, with sections that fit each leg separately.
trous•seau (tro͞o′sō′, tro͞o-sō′) *n., pl.* **-seaux** (-sōz′, -sōz′) *or* **-seaus.** The wardrobe and household goods, esp. linens, assembled by a bride.
trout (trout) *n., pl.* **trout** *or* **trouts.** A freshwater anadromous food or game fish of the genera *Salvelinus* and *Salmo*, related to the salmon.
trove (trōv) *n.* **1.** Something valuable discovered or found : find. **2.** A collection of usu. valuable objects.
trow (trō) *v. Archaic.* To suppose : think.
trow•el (trou′əl) *n.* **1.** A flat-bladed hand tool for spreading, smoothing, or shaping such substances as cement, plaster, or mortar. **2.** A small scoop-shaped gardening tool. **—trow′el** *v.* **—trow′el•er** *n.*

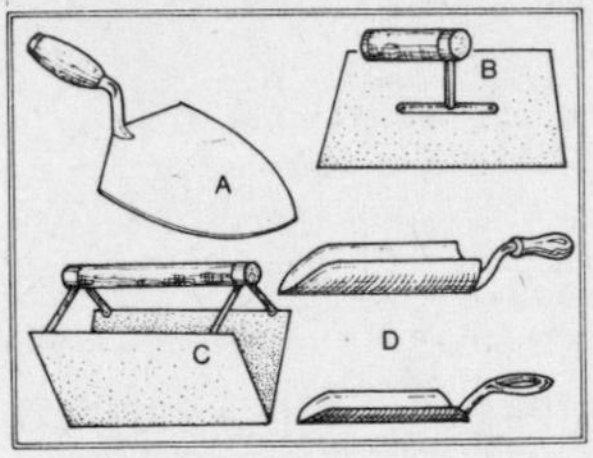

trowel
Four types of trowels: A. brick, B. plaster, C. corner, D. garden

troy (troi) *adj.* Of, pertaining to, or expressed in troy weight.
Troy (troi). Ancient city of NW Asia Minor; site of the Trojan War.
troy weight *n.* A system of units of weight in which the pound consists of 12 oz, 240 dwt, or 5,760 gr.
tru•ant (tro͞o′ənt) *n.* One who avoids doing work or fulfilling a duty, esp. one who is absent from school without permission. **—tru′an•cy** *n.* **—tru′ant** *adj.*
truce (tro͞os) *n.* A temporary cessation of hostilities by mutual agreement : armistice.
truck[1] (trŭk) *n.* **1.** An automotive vehicle designed to carry heavy loads. **2.** A 2-wheeled barrow with a pair of handles at 1 end for moving heavy objects by hand. **3.** A swiveling frame with wheels at each end of a railroad car, locomotive, or streetcar, used to support and guide. *—v.* **1.** To drive a truck. **2.** To carry by truck. **—truck′er** *n.*
truck[2] (trŭk) *v.* **1.** To barter : exchange. **2.** To have dealings or commerce : traffic. *—n.* **1.** Garden produce, esp. vegetables, raised for the market. **2.** Barter : exchange. **3.** *Informal.* Dealings. **—truck′load′** *n.*
truck•age (trŭk′ĭj) *n.* **1.** Transport of goods by truck. **2.** The charge for truckage.
truck farm *n.* A farm raising vegetables for the market. **—truck farmer** *n.* **—truck farming** *n.*
truck•ing (trŭk′ĭng) *n.* TRUCKAGE 1.
truck•le (trŭk′əl) *v.* **-led, -ling.** To yield weakly to another's will : submit.
truc•u•lent (trŭk′yə-lənt) *adj.* **1.** Fierce : savagely cruel. **2.** Belligerent : pugnacious. **—truc′u•lence** *n.* **—truc′u•lent•ly** *adv.*
Tru•deau (tro͞o-dō′), **Pierre Elliott.** b. 1919. Canadian statesman.
trudge (trŭj) *v.* **trudged, trudg•ing.** To walk heavily and laboriously : plod. *—n.* A long, wearying walk.
true (tro͞o) *adj.* **tru•er, tru•est. 1.** Consistent with reality or fact <a *true* statement> **2.** Real : genuine. **3.** Loyal : faithful. **4.** Legitimate : rightful <the *true* successor> **5.** Conforming ex-

actly to an orig. pattern or standard. **6.** Rightfully so called. **7.** Determined with reference to the earth's axis, not the magnetic poles <*true* south> ☆***syns:*** GENUINE, REAL, SINCERE —*adv.* **1.** Truthfully. **2.** Precisely : accurately. **3.** Without deviation from an ancestral type or stock <breed *true*> —*v.* **trued, tru·ing** *or* **true·ing.** To adjust so as to conform with a standard, esp. of accuracy. —*n.* **1.** Truth. **2.** Accurate adjustment or alignment. **—tru'ly** *adv.*

true-blue (tro͞o'blo͞o') *n.* A truly loyal person. **—true'-blue'** *adj.*

true·love (tro͞o'lŭv') *n.* One who is beloved : sweetheart.

truf·fle (trŭf'əl) *n.* Any of various edible underground fungi, esp. of the genus *Tuber,* esteemed as a delicacy.

tru·ism (tro͞o'ĭz'əm) *n.* An obvious or self-evident truth.

Tru·man (tro͞o'mən), **Harry S** 1884–1972. 33rd U.S. President (1945–53).

trump (trŭmp) *n.* **1.** A suit any of whose cards outrank all other cards for the duration of a hand. **2.** A card of a trump. —*v.* To play a trump card. **—trump up.** To concoct, esp. fraudulently : fabricate.

trump·er·y (trŭm'pə-rē) *n.* **1.** Worthless items : junk. **2.** Nonsense.

trum·pet (trŭm'pĭt) *n.* **1.** A brass wind instrument consisting of a long metal tube with a flared bell at 1 end and a mouthpiece at the other. **2.** Something resembling a trumpet in shape or sound. **3.** A horn-shaped instrument for directing sound into the ear of a partially deaf person. —*v.* **1.** To play a trumpet. **2.** To proclaim loudly. **—trum'pet·er** *n.*

trun·cate (trŭng'kāt') *v.* **-cat·ed, -cat·ing.** To shorten by or as if by cutting off. **—trun·ca'tion** *n.*

trun·cheon (trŭn'chən) *n.* A club carried by policemen.

trun·dle (trŭnd'l) *v.* **-dled, -dling.** To push or move on wheels : roll.

trundle bed *n.* A low bed, usu. on casters, that can be slid under another bed.

trunk (trŭngk) *n.* **1.** The principal woody stem of a tree. **2.** The body of a human being excluding the limbs and head. **3.** The main section or part of something. **4.** A box or case in which clothes or belongings can be packed, as for storage or travel. **5.** The covered luggage compartment of an automobile. **6.** The long, prehensile snout of an elephant : proboscis. **7. trunks.** Men's shorts worn esp. for athletics.

trunk line *n.* The main line of a communications or transportation system.

truss (trŭs) *n.* **1.** A device worn to keep a hernia in place. **2.** A framework, as of wood or metal, supporting a structure such as a bridge. —*v.* **1.** To tie securely : bind. **2.** To brace or support with a truss.

trust (trŭst) *n.* **1.** Firm reliance in the honesty, dependability, strength, or character of someone or something. **2.** One in which faith or confidence is placed. **3.** Care : custody. **4. a.** Something given into one's care for the benefit or interest of another : charge. **b.** The state and obligation resulting from this. **5.** Reliance on something in the future : hope. **6.** An interest in property that is held by 1 party for the benefit of another. **7.** A combination of corporations or firms formed esp. for the purpose of reducing competition. **8.** Confidence in a person's willingness and ability to pay : credit. —*v.* **1.** To have or place confidence in : rely. **2.** To be confident : hope. **3.** To assume or expect. **4.** To believe. **5.** To entrust. **6.** To allow to have, use, or care for without misgivings. **7.** To extend financial credit to.

trust company *n.* A commercial bank that manages trusts.

trus·tee (trŭs-tē') *n.* **1.** A person or agent to whom the property of a beneficiary is legally entrusted. **2.** A member of a board that directs the policies and funds of an institution, as a hospital or college. **—trus·tee'ship'** *n.*

trust·ful (trŭst'fəl) *adj.* Full of trust and confidence. **—trust'ful·ly** *adv.*

trust territory *n.* A colony or territory placed under the administration of a country by commission of the United Nations.

trust·wor·thy (trŭst'wûr'thē) *adj.* Worthy of trust : reliable. **—trust'wor'thi·ly** *adv.* **—trust'wor'thi·ness** *n.*

trust·y (trŭs'tē) *adj.* **-i·er, -i·est.** Reliable : trustworthy. —*n., pl.* **-ies.** A trusted person, esp. a convict held worthy of trust and granted special privileges.

truth (tro͞oth) *n., pl.* **truths** (tro͞othz, tro͞oths). **1.** Accordance with knowledge, fact, or actuality. **2.** The real state of affairs : fact. **3.** Actuality : reality. **4.** A statement that is or is accepted as being true. **5.** The state of being truthful : honesty.

truth·ful (tro͞oth'fəl) *adj.* **1.** Telling or inclined to tell the truth : honest. **2.** Corresponding to fact or reality. **—truth'ful·ly** *adv.* **—truth'ful·ness** *n.*

truth serum *n.* Any of various hypnotic drugs believed to cause a subject being interrogated to talk uninhibitedly.

try (trī) *v.* **tried, try·ing. 1.** To subject to trial or test, as to determine strength or effect. **2. a.** To hear or examine by judicial process. **b.** To ascertain the guilt or innocence of (an accused person) in a court of law. **3.** To subject to hardship, affliction, or strain : tax. **4.** To separate impurities from (fat) by melting : render. **5.** To make an effort to do something : attempt. **—try on.** To put on (e.g., a garment) to test appearance and fit. —*n., pl.* **tries.** An attempt.

try·ing (trī'ĭng) *adj.* Causing severe strain, annoyance, or distress. **—try'ing·ly** *adv.*

try·out (trī'out') *n.* A test to determine the qualifications of applicants, as for a role in a play.

tryp·sin (trĭp'sĭn) *n.* One of the enzymes of the pancreatic juice, active in the digestive processes. **—tryp'tic** *adj.*

tryst (trĭst) *n.* **1.** An agreement, esp. between lovers, to meet. **2.** A meeting or meeting place for a tryst.

tsar (zär) *n. var. of* CZAR.

tset·se fly (tsĕt'sē, tsēt'sē) *n.* An African fly of the genus *Glossina* that often carries and transmits the microorganisms that cause sleeping sickness.

T-shirt *also* **tee shirt** (tē'shûrt') *n.* A short-sleeved, collarless men's undershirt. **2.** An outer shirt that resembles a T-shirt.

tsp *or* **tsp.** *abbr.* teaspoon; teaspoonful.

T-square (tē'skwâr') *n.* A ruler with a crosspiece at 1 end for establishing and drawing parallel lines.

tsu·na·mi (tso͞o-nä'mē) *n.* A huge ocean wave caused by an underwater earthquake or volcanic eruption.

tub (tŭb) *n.* **1.** A low, round, flat-bottomed vessel, as one used for washing. **2. a.** A bathtub. **b.** A bath taken in a bathtub.

tu·ba (to͞o'bə, tyo͞o'-) *n.* A large valved brass wind instrument with a low range.

tu·bal (to͞o'bəl, tyo͞o'-) *adj.* Of, relating to, or taking place in a tube, esp. the Fallopian tube <a *tubal* pregnancy>

tu·bate (to͞o'bāt', tyo͞o'-) *ajd.* Forming or having a tube.

tub·by (tŭb'ē) *adj.* **-bi·er, -bi·est.** Short and fat : pudgy.

tube (to͞ob, tyo͞ob) *n.* **1.** A hollow cylinder, esp. one that conveys fluids : channel. **2.** A small, flexible cylindrical container sealed at 1 end from which substances such as pigments and toothpaste can be squeezed. **3. a.** An electron tube. **b.** A vacuum tube. **4.** *esp. Brit.* A subway. **5.** An airtight rubber tube inside a tire that holds air under pressure. **6.** *Informal.* Television. **—tubed** *adj.* **—tube'less** *adj.*

tu·ber (to͞o'bər, tyo͞o'-) *n.* A swollen, usu. underground stem, as that of the potato, bearing buds from which new plants arise.

tu·ber·cle (to͞o'bər-kəl, tyo͞o'-) *n.* **1.** A small, knobby protuberance or excrescence, as on a plant or animal. **2.** *Pathol.* **a.** A tubercular lesion. **b.** A nodule or swelling.

tubercle bacillus *n.* A rod-shaped bacterium, *Mycobacterium tuberculosis,* the cause of tuberculosis.

tu·ber·cu·lar (to͝o-bûr'kyə-lər, tyo͝o-) *adj.* **1.** TUBERCULATE 1. **2.** Of, relating to, or afflicted with tuberculosis.

tu·ber·cu·late (to͝o-bûr'kyə-lĭt, tyo͝o-) *adj.* **1.** Of, pertaining to, or covered with tubercles. **2.** TUBERCULAR 2.

tu·ber·cu·lin (to͝o-bûr'kyə-lĭn, tyo͝o-) *n.* A substance derived from cultures of tubercle bacilli and used in diagnosing and treating tuberculosis.

tu·ber·cu·lo·sis (to͝o-bûr'kyə-lō'sĭs, tyo͝o-) *n.* A communicable disease of humans and animals that is caused by a microorganism and marked by lesions, esp. of the lung. **—tu·ber'cu·lous** *adj.*

tube·rose (to͞ob'rōz', tyo͞ob'-) *n.* A tuberous plant, *Polianthes tuberosa,* native to Mexico, grown for its fragrant flowers.

tu·ber·ous (to͞o'bər-əs, tyo͞o'-) Of, bearing, or being a plant tuber.

tub·ing (to͞o'bĭng, tyo͞o'-) *n.* **1. a.** A system of tubes. **b.** A length of tube. **2.** Fabric in the form of a tube.

tu·bule (to͞o'byo͞ol, tyo͞o'-) *n.* An extremely small tube.

tu·bu·lar (to͞o'byə-lər, tyo͞o'-) *adj.* Consisting of or having the form of a tube.

tuck (tŭk) *n.* A flattened fold in fabric that is stitched in place to decorate or adjust fit. —*v.* **1.** To make tucks in. **2.** To turn under the edge of (e.g., a blanket or shirt) in order to secure. **3.** To cover snugly by tucking in sheets and blankets. **4.** To put in a snug, safe, or concealed place.

tuck·er (tŭk'ər) *v. Informal.* To tire out : exhaust.

Tuc·son (to͞o'sŏn'). City of SE Ariz., SSE of Phoenix. *Pop.* 330,537.

-tude *suff.* A condition, state, or quality <exacti*tude*>

Tues. *abbr.* Tuesday.

Tues·day (to͞oz'dē, tyo͞oz'-, -dā') *n.* The 3rd day of the week.

tu·fa (to͞o'fə, tyo͞o'-) *n.* Calcareous and siliceous rock deposited by springs, streams, or ground water. **—tu·fa'ceous** *adj.*

tuft (tŭft) *n.* **1.** A small cluster of flexible, elongated strands, as of hair, attached or growing close together. **2.** A clump, esp. of

threads fastened at the base and cut off very short, used esp. as decoration. —*v.* To decorate or provide with tufts.
tug (tŭg) *v.* **tugged, tug•ging. 1.** To pull and strain vigorously (at). **2.** To move by pulling vigorously. **3.** To tow by tugboat. —*n.* **1. a.** The act of tugging : a vigorous pull. **b.** A strong pulling force. **2.** A tugboat. **—tug'ger** *n.*
tug•boat (tŭg'bōt') *n.* A powerfully built small boat used for towing larger vessels.
tug of war *n.* **1.** A contest in which 2 teams tug against each other at opposite ends of a rope. **2.** A struggle for supremacy.
tu•grik (to͞o'grĭk) *n.* See CURRENCY TABLE.
tu•i•tion (to͞o-ĭsh'ən, tyo͞o-) *n.* **1.** A payment or fee for instruction, as at a college. **2.** Teaching : instruction.
tu•la•re•mi•a (to͞o'lə-rē'mē-ə, tyo͞o'-) *n.* An infectious bacterial disease transmitted to humans by infected rodents and marked by fever and swelling of the lymph nodes.
tu•lip (to͞o'lĭp, tyo͞o'-) *n.* **1.** Any of various bulb-bearing plants of the genus *Tulipa,* widely grown for their variously colored flowers. **2.** A flower of a tulip.
tulip tree *n.* A tall deciduous tree, *Liriodendron tulipifera,* with large green and orange flowers and yellowish soft wood.
tulle (to͞ol) *n.* A fine starched silk, rayon, or nylon net used esp. for veils, gowns, and ballet tutus.
Tul•sa (tŭl'sə). City of NE Okla. *Pop.* 360,919.
tum•ble (tŭm'bəl) *v.* **-bled, -bling. 1.** To perform acrobatic feats, as rolls, somersaults, and twists. **2.** To roll end over end. **3.** To spill out in confusion, haste, and disorder. **4.** To fall or cause to fall headlong. **5.** To decline, esp. suddenly : collapse. **6.** *Slang.* To come suddenly to understand. —*n.* **1.** An act of tumbling : fall. **2.** A state of disorder or confusion.
tum•ble-down (tŭm'bəl-doun') *adj.* Ramshackle : dilapidated.
tum•bler (tŭm'blər) *n.* **1.** A gymnast or acrobat. **2.** A drinking glass with no handle or stem. **3.** The part in a lock that throws the bolt when a key is used.
tum•ble•weed (tŭm'bəl-wēd') *n.* Any of various plants, esp. of the genus *Amaranthus,* that break off from their roots when withered and are rolled about by the wind.
tum•brel or **tum•bril** (tŭm'brəl) *n.* **1.** A cart, esp. one that can be tilted to discharge a load. **2.** A crude cart that was used to carry condemned prisoners to a place of execution, as during the French Revolution.

tumbrel

tu•mid (to͞o'mĭd, tyo͞o'-) *adj.* **1.** Distended : swollen. **2.** Overblown, esp. in language : bombastic. **—tu•mid'i•ty** *n.*
tum•my (tŭm'ē) *n., pl.* **-mies.** *Informal.* The abdomen : stomach.
tu•mor (to͞o'mər, tyo͞o'-) *n.* A circumscribed noninflammatory growth arising from existing tissue but growing independently of the normal rate or structural development of such tissue and serving no physiological function. **—tu'mor•ous** *adj.*
tu•mult (to͞o'məlt, tyo͞o'-) *n.* **1.** The turmoil of a crowd with its accompanying din and commotion. **2.** A turbulent uprising : riot. **3.** Agitation of the emotions or mind.
tu•mul•tu•ous (to͝o-mŭl'cho͞o-əs, tyo͝o-) *adj.* **1.** Marked by or causing tumult. **2.** Confusedly or violently agitated.
tun (tŭn) *n.* **1.** A large cask. **2.** A measure of liquid capacity, esp. one equivalent to approx. 954 L or 252 gal.
tu•na (to͞o'nə, tyo͞o'-) *n., pl.* **-na** *or* **-nas.** An often large marine food fish of the genus *Thunnus* and related genera, commercially important as a source of canned fish.
tun•dra (tŭn'drə) *n.* A treeless area of arctic regions with a subsoil that is permanently frozen.
tune (to͞on, tyo͞on) *n.* **1.** A melody, esp. a simple and easily remembered one. **2.** Correct musical pitch. **3.** Harmony or agreement <in *tune* with modern times> —*v.* **tuned, tun•ing. 1.** To adjust so as to be in correct musical pitch. **2.** To adjust (e.g., an engine) for most efficient performance. **3.** To adjust a radio or television receiver to receive a broadcast. **—tun'a•ble, tune'a•ble** *adj.* **—tun'a•bly** *adv.* **—tun'er** *n.*
tune•ful (to͞on'fəl, tyo͞on'-) *adj.* **1.** Musical : melodious. **2.** Producing music. **—tune'ful•ly** *adv.* **—tune'ful•ness** *n.*
tune•less (to͞on'lĭs, tyo͞on'-) *adj.* **1.** Not melodious. **2.** Producing no music. **—tune'less•ly** *adv.* **—tune'less•ness** *n.*
tune-up (to͞on'ŭp', tyo͞on'-) *n.* **1.** Adjustment of a motor or engine for maximum efficiency. **2.** An engine warm-up.
tung•sten (tŭng'stən) *n. Symbol* **W** A hard metallic element that is resistant to corrosion and high temperatures.
tu•nic (to͞o'nĭk, tyo͞o'-) *n.* **1.** A loose-fitting garment extending to the knees, worn esp. by ancient Greeks and Romans. **2.** A usu. hip-length jacket or blouse.
tuning fork *n.* A 2-pronged metal device that makes a sound of fixed pitch when struck that is used as a reference, as in tuning musical instruments.
Tu•nis (to͞o'nĭs, tyo͞o'-). Cap. of Tunisia, in the N part. *Pop.* 550,404.
Tu•ni•sia (to͞o-nē'zhə, -shə, -nĭzh'ə, -nĭsh'ə, tyo͞o-). Country of N Africa. *Cap.* Tunis. *Pop.* 6,410,000. **—Tu•ni'sian** *adj.* & *n.*
tun•nel (tŭn'əl) *n.* A passageway under the ground or the water. —*v.* **-neled, -nel•ing** *or* **-nelled, -nel•ling.** To make a tunnel under or through.
tun•ny (tŭn'ē) *n., pl.* **-ny** *or* **-nies.** Tuna.
tur•ban (tûr'bən) *n.* **1.** A headdress that is worn esp. by Moslems and consists of a long scarf wound around the head. **2.** A woman's close-fitting hat like a turban.
tur•bid (tûr'bĭd) *adj.* **1.** Opaque with suspended sediment or foreign particles <a *turbid* lake> **2.** Heavy, dense, or dark, as with smoke. **3.** In turmoil : confused <*turbid* emotions> **—tur'bid•ly** *adv.* **—tur'bid•ness, tur'bid'i•ty** *n.*
tur•bine (tûr'bĭn, -bīn') *n.* A machine in which the kinetic energy of a moving fluid is converted to mechanical power by the reaction of the fluid with a series of buckets, paddles, or blades fitted around the circumference of a wheel or cylinder.
tur•bo•fan (tûr'bō-făn') *n.* **1.** A turbojet engine in which a fan supplements the total thrust by forcing air diverted from the main engine directly into the hot turbine exhaust. **2.** An aircraft with a turbofan.
tur•bo•jet (tûr'bō-jĕt') *n.* **1.** A jet engine having a turbine-driven compressor and developing thrust from the exhaust of hot gases. **2.** An aircraft with a turbojet.
tur•bo•prop (tûr'bō-prŏp') *n.* **1.** A turbojet engine used to drive an external propeller. **2.** An aircraft equipped with a turboprop.
tur•bot (tûr'bət) *n., pl.* **-bot** *or* **-bots.** A European flatfish, *Psetta maxima,* that is a highly regarded food fish.
tur•bu•lent (tûr'byə-lənt) *adj.* **1.** Marked by violent agitation : disturbed. **2.** Causing disturbance or unrest. **—tur'bu•lence** *n.* **—tur'bu•lent•ly** *adv.*
tu•reen (to͝o-rēn', tyo͝o-) *n.* A broad deep dish, often with a cover from which foods, as soups or stews, are served.
turf (tûrf) *n.* **1.a.** The surface layer of earth with its dense growth of grass and matted roots. **b.** A piece of turf. **2.** A piece of peat burned as fuel. **3. a.** A racetrack. **b.** The business or sport of horse racing. —*v.* To cover with turf.
Tur•ge•nev (to͝or-gā'nyəf), **Ivan Sergeevich.** 1818–83. Russian novelist.
tur•gid (tûr'jĭd) *adj.* **1.** Marked by swelling : distended. **2.** Excessively grand in language or style : pompously ornate. **—tur•gid'i•ty, tur'gid•ness** *n.*
Tu•rin (to͞o'rĭn, tyo͞o'-). City of NW Italy. *Pop.* 1,160,686.
tur•key (tûr'kē) *n., pl.* **-keys. 1.** A large, widely domesticated North American bird, *Meleagris gallopavo,* with a bare head and neck with fleshy wattles. **2.** The flesh of a turkey used as food.
Tur•key (tûr'kē). Country of SW Asia, between the Mediterranean and the Black Sea. *Cap.* Ankara. *Pop.* 45,955,000. **—Turk'ish** *adj.* & *n.*
turkey buzzard *n.* A New World vulture, *Cathartes aura,* with dark plumage and a bare red head and neck.
Turkish bath *n.* A steam bath that is followed by a shower and massage.
Turkish towel *n.* A cotton towel with a thick nap.
tur•mer•ic (tûr'mər-ĭk) *n.* **1.** An Indian plant, *Curcuma longa,* with yellow flowers and an aromatic rootstock. **2.** The powdered rootstock of the turmeric used as a spice and as a yellow dye.
tur•moil (tûr'moil) *n.* A state of great confusion or agitation.
turn (tûrn) *v.* **1. a.** To move or cause to move around a center or axis : revolve or rotate <*turned* the doorknob> **b.** To alter or control the functioning of by revolving or rotating. **2.** To shape on a lathe <*turn* a chair leg> **3.** To form or articulate with elegance or distinction <*turn* a phrase> **4. a.** To change or cause to change position so as to show another surface or side. **b.** To change or cause to change position by rotating : pivot. **5.** To injure by twisting : wrench <*turned* her ankle> **6.** To nau-

seate or become nauseated : upset. **7.a.** To set in a particular course or direction <*turning* his head to face the mirror> **b.** To change one's course or direction. **8.** To make a course around or about <*turn* the corner> **9.** To direct (e.g., the attention) toward or away from something <*turn* your thoughts to your work> **10.** To make or become antagonistic. **11.** To send or drive <*turning* the trespasser off his property> **12.** To transform or become transformed : change. **13.** To reach or exceed <has already *turned* 65> **14.** To have recourse : resort. **15.** To be contingent : hinge. **16.** To change or cause to change color. **17.** To spoil or cause to spoil : sour. **18.** To be, seem to be, or become dizzy : whirl. **—turn down.** To refuse to accept : reject. **—turn in. 1.** To give over to another : hand in. **2.** *Informal.* To go to bed. **—turn off. 1.** To stop the flow or operation of. **2.** *Slang.* To affect with dislike, revulsion, or displeasure. **—turn on. 1.** To start the flow or operation of. **2.** *Slang.* **a.** To affect with pleasure or excitement. **b.** To use a drug in order to get high. **—turn out. 1.** To shut off (e.g., a light). **2.** To arrive and assemble. **3.** To produce <*turning out* good work> **4.** To come or prove to be in the end : result. **—turn over. 1.** To think about : ponder. **2.** To transfer to another <*turned over* his paycheck to his mother> **—turn up. 1.** To cause to increase, as in volume. **2.** To find or be found. **3.** To appear : arrive. —*n.* **1.** The act of turning around a center or axis : revolution or rotation. **2.** A change of direction <a sharp *turn* to the right> **3.** A change, as in a trend or course of events <a *turn* for the worse> **4.** An opportunity to do something, esp. in a particular order <your *turn* to play> **5.** Natural inclination, style, or aptitude <a scientific *turn* of mind> **6.** A deed or action that affects another <a good *turn*> **7.** A short excursion or walk <took a *turn* around the park> **8.** A single twist, as of wire around a spool. **9.** An elegant or distinctive fashioning <a pretty *turn* of phrase> **10.** A momentary shock or scare. **—turn'er** *n.*

†turn•a•bout (tûrn'ə-bout') *n.* **1.** A change and esp. a reversal in direction, opinion, allegiance, or policy. **2.** *Regional.* A dance or party to which girls invite boys.

turn•buck•le (tûrn'bŭk'əl) *n.* A metal coupling, used for tightening a rod or wire rope, having an oblong piece internally threaded at both ends into which a threaded rod is screwed.

turn•coat (tûrn'kōt') *n.* One, esp. a traitor, who abandons a side or party to which he has given, owes, or professes allegiance.

turn•down (tûrn'doun') *n.* **1.** A rejection. **2.** Something rejected.

turning point *n.* A point at which a decisive change takes place.

tur•nip (tûr'nĭp) *n.* A cultivated plant, *Brassica rapa*, with a large edible root.

turn•key (tûrn'kē') *n.* The person in charge of the keys in a prison : jailer.

turn•off (tûrn'ôf', -ŏf') *n.* A place for turning off, esp. a highway exit.

turn•on (tûrn'ŏn', -ôn') *n. Slang.* Something that causes pleasurable excitement.

turn•out (tûrn'out') *n.* **1.** The number of people present at a gathering : attendance. **2.** An outfit of clothing. **3.** A widened section in a highway where vehicles can pass.

turn•o•ver (tûrn'ō'vər) *n.* **1.** The act of turning over : upset. **2.** A reversal : change. **3.** A filled pastry with half the crust turned over the other half. **4.** The number of times a stock of goods is purchased, sold, and restocked during a given period. **5.** The volume of business transacted during a given period. **6. a.** The number or workers hired within a given period to replace those who have left. **b.** The ratio of this number to the number of workers employed.

turn•pike (tûrn'pīk') *n.* A highway, esp. a superhighway with tollgates.

turn•stile (tûrn'stīl') *n.* A device permitting the passage of 1 person at a time that consists of horizontal arms set into and revolving around a central post.

turn•ta•ble (tûrn'tā'bəl) *n.* A circular rotating platform, as that used for turning a phonograph record or locomotive.

tur•pen•tine (tûr'pən-tīn') *n.* **1.** A sticky mixture of resin and oil obtained from certain pine trees. **2.** A thin, volatile oil distilled from a turpentine and used esp. as a paint thinner and solvent.

tur•pi•tude (tûr'pə-tōōd', -tyōōd') *n.* Vileness : depravity.

tur•quoise (tûr'kwoiz', -koiz') *n.* **1.** A bluish-green mineral containing aluminum and copper and valued as a gem. **2.** A light bluish green. **—tur'quoise'** *adj.*

tur•ret (tûr'ĭt) *n.* **1.** A small, usu. ornamental tower on a building. **2.** A tower-shaped, usu. rotating armored structure, as on a warship or tank, on which guns are mounted. **3.** A rotating cylindrical block, as on a lathe, for holding various tools for successive use. **—tur'ret•ed** *adj.*

tur•tle¹ (tûrt'l) *n.* Any of various reptiles of the order Chelonia with the body encased in a carapace into which the head, legs, and tail can be retracted.

tur•tle² (tûrt'l) *n. Archaic.* A turtledove.

tur•tle•dove (tûrt'l-dŭv') *n.* A slender European dove, *Streptopelia turtur*, with a soft, purring coo.

tur•tle•neck (tûrt'l-nĕk') *n.* **1.** A high, turned-down collar fitting closely around the neck. **2.** A sweater with a turtleneck.

Tus•ca•ny (tŭs'kə-nē).5713 Region of NW Italy. **—Tus'can** *adj.* & *n.*

tush (tŭsh) *interj.* Used to express mild reproof, disapproval, or admonition.

tusk (tŭsk) *n.* A pointed elongated tooth, as of an elephant or walrus, that projects outside the closed mouth.

tusk•er (tŭs'kər) *n.* An animal, as a wild boar, that has tusks.

tus•sle (tŭs'əl) *v.* **-sled, -sling.** To fight roughly : scuffle. **—tus'sle** *n.*

tus•sock (tŭs'ək) *n.* A thick tuft, esp. of grass : clump. **—tus'sock•y** *adj.*

tu•te•lage (tōō'tə-lĭj, tyōō'-) *n.* **1.** The function or act of being a guardian : guardianship. **2.** Instruction, esp. that provided by a tutor. **3.** The state of being under a guardian or tutor.

tu•te•lar•y (tōōt'l-ĕr'ē, tyōōt'-) *adj.* **1.** Being or serving as a guardian or protector <*tutelary* gods> **2.** Of or pertaining to a guardian or guardianship. **—tu'te•lar'y** *n.*

tu•tor (tōō'tər, tyōō'-) *n.* A person who is responsible for instructing another, esp. one who gives individual or private instruction. —*v.* To act as a tutor (to). **—tu•to'ri•al** (-tôr'ē-əl, -tōr'-) *adj.* **—tu'tor•ship'** *n.*

tut•ti-frut•ti (tōō'tē-frōō'tē) *n.* A confection, esp. ice cream, that contains various chopped candied fruits.

tu•tu (tōō'tōō) *n.* A very short projecting ballet skirt of gathered sheer fabric.

Tu•va•lu (tōō-väl'ōō, -vär'-). Island country of the W Pacific, N of Fiji. *Cap.* Funafuti. *Pop.* 7,500.

tux (tŭks) *n. Informal.* A tuxedo.

tux•e•do (tŭk-sē'dō) *n., pl.* **-dos. 1.** A man's semiformal, usu. black tailless jacket. **2.** A semiformal suit with a tuxedo jacket.

TV (tē-vē') *n.* Television.

twad•dle (twŏd'l) *n.* Trivial, foolish, or idle talk. **—twad'dle** *v.* **—twad'dler** *n.*

twain (twān) *n.* Two.

Twain, Mark. Samuel L. Clemens.

twang (twăng) *n.* **1.** A sharp, ringing sound like that made by the plucked string of a musical instrument. **2.** Nasal resonance or tone of voice. —*v.* **1.** To emit or cause to emit a twang. **2.** To speak in a nasal twang. **—twang'y** *adj.*

'twas (twŭz). It was.

tweak (twēk) *v.* To pinch sharply and twist. **—tweak** *n.*

tweed (twēd) *n.* **1.** A coarse woolen fabric usu. woven in a twill weave, often in several colors. **2. tweeds.** Clothing, esp. a suit, made of tweed.

tweed•y (twē'dē) *adj.* **-i•er, -i•est. 1.** Made of or resembling tweed. **2.** Wearing or fond of wearing tweeds.

tweet (twēt) *v.* To utter a weak chirping sound. **—tweet** *n.*

tweet•er (twē'tər) *n.* A loudspeaker that reproduces high-pitched sounds.

tweez•ers (twē'zərz) *pl.n.* A small, pincerlike device used for grasping or plucking small things.

twelve (twĕlv) *n.* **1.** The cardinal number equal to 11 + 1. **2.** The 12th in a set or sequence. **—twelve** *adj.* & *pron.* **—twelfth** *n.* & *adj.* & *adv.*

twen•ty (twĕn'tē) *n.* The cardinal number equal to 2 x 10. **—twen'ti•eth** *n.* & *adj.* & *adv.* **—twen'ty** *adj.* & *pron.*

twerp *also* **twirp** (twûrp) *n.* A contemptible or unimportant person.

twice (twīs) *adv.* **1.** In 2 cases or on 2 occasions. **2.** In doubled degree or quantity <works *twice* as hard>

twid•dle (twĭd'l) *v.* **-dled, -dling. 1.** To turn around idly or lightly : twirl. **2.** To toy idly with something : trifle.

twig (twĭg) *n.* A small branch or slender shoot. **—twig'gy** *adj.*

twi•light (twī'līt') *n.* **1.** The soft, diffuse light cast by the sun when it is below the horizon, esp. following sunset. **2.** A period or state of decline.

twill (twĭl) *n.* **1.** A textile weave that produces parallel ribs on the surface of a fabric. **2.** A fabric with a twill. **—twilled** *adj.*

twin (twĭn) *n.* **1.** One of 2 born at a single birth. **2.** One of 2 similar or identical persons or things : counterpart. —*adj.* **1.** Being 1 or both of 2 offspring produced at the same birth <a *twin* sister><*twin* boys> **2.** Being 1 of 2 similar or identical persons or things <*twin* houses> **3.** Consisting of 2 similar or identical parts. —*v.* **twinned, twin•ning. 1.** To give birth to twins. **2.** To be paired or coupled.

twine (twīn) *v.* **twined, twin•ing. 1.** To twist together (e.g., threads) : intertwine. **2.** To form by twisting. **3.** To coil about : wind. **4.** To move in a winding manner. *—n.* A strong thread, string, or cord consisting of 2 or more strands twisted together.
twinge (twĭnj) *n.* **1.** A sudden, sharp pain. **2.** An emotional or mental pang. *—v.* **twinged, twing•ing.** To feel or cause to feel a sudden sharp pain.
twin•kle (twĭng′kəl) *v.* **-kled, -kling. 1.** To shine or cause to shine with a sparkling or intermittent light. **2.** To be bright, as with happiness : sparkle. **3.** To wink or blink. *—n.* **1.** An intermittent gleam of light. **2.** A sparkle, as of merriment, in the eye. **3.** A very brief interval : twinkling. **—twin′kler** *n.*
twin•kling (twĭng′klĭng) *n.* An instant.
twirl (twûrl) *v.* To rotate or cause to rotate briskly : whirl. **—twirl** *n.*
twirp (twûrp) *n. var. of* TWERP.
twist (twĭst) *v.* **1.** To wind (2 or more threads) together to make a single strand. **2.** To coil around something : twine. **3. a.** To give a spiral shape to. **b.** To form a spiral shape. **4.** To open or break off by turning. **5.** To wrench and injure <*twisted* his leg> **6.** To change the true form, shape, or meaning of : distort. **7.** To move in a winding course. **8.** To revolve or rotate. *—n.* **1.** Something formed by winding or twisting. **2. a.** The act of twisting. **b.** the state of being twisted. **3. a.** A spin or twirl. **b.** A spiral curve or turn. **4.** Torsional strain or stress. **5.** A wrench, as of a joint. **6.** An unexpected development. **7.** A distortion in form or meaning. **8.** A new or unexpected procedure, system, or approach.
twist•er (twĭs′tər) *n.* **1.** One that twists. **2.** A ball thrown or batted with a twisting, spinning motion. **3.** *Informal.* **a.** A cyclone. **b.** A tornado.
twit (twĭt) *v.* **twit•ted, twit•ting.** To tease or taunt, esp. about a mistake or fault.
†**twitch** (twĭch) *v.* **1.** To move, cause to move, or pull with a jerk. **2.** To move spasmodically. *—n.* **1.** An involuntary muscular jerk. **2.** A sudden pull or tug. **3.** *W U.S.* A looped cord used to restrain a horse by tightening it around the upper lip.
twit•ter (twĭt′ər) *v.* **1.** To make a series of chirping sounds. **2.** To chatter, esp. nervously or excitedly. *—n.* **1.** A series of chirping sounds. **2.** Excitement or agitation : flutter. **—twit′ter•y** *adj.*
twixt *also* **'twixt** (twĭkst) *prep. & adv.* Betwixt : between.
two (to͞o) *n.* **1.** The cardinal number equal to 1 + 1. **2.** The 2nd in a set or sequence. **3.** Something with 2 parts, units, or members. **—two** *adj. & pron.*
two-bit (to͞o′bĭt′) *adj. Slang.* Cheap or insignificant : trifling.
two bits *pl.n. Informal.* **1.** Twenty-five cents. **2.** A petty sum.
two-by-four (to͞o′bī-fôr′, -fōr′, to͞o′bə-) *n.* A length of lumber 15/8′ thick and 33/8′ wide.
two-faced (to͞o′fāst′) *adj.* **1.** Having 2 faces. **2.** Double-dealing or hypocritcal : treacherous. **—two′-fac′ed•ly** *adv.*
two•fold (to͞o′fōld′, -fōld′) *adj.* **1.** Having 2 parts or units. **2.** Being twice as much or as many : double. **—two′fold′** *adv.*
two-ply (to͞o′plī′) *adj.* Consisting of 2 layers, thicknesses, or strands.
two•some (to͞o′səm) *n.* **1.** Two persons or things : pair. **2.** A golf game for 2 players.
two-time (to͞o′tīm′) *v. Slang.* To deceive or be unfaithful to. **—two′-tim′er** *n.*
two-way (to͞o′wā′) *adj.* Affording movement or permitting communication in 2 directions.
TX *abbr.* Texas (with Zip Code).
-ty *suff.* Condition : quality <novel*ty*>
ty•coon (tī-ko͞on′) *n. Informal.* A businessman of power and wealth : magnate.
tyke (tīk) *n.* **1.** A small child. **2.** A mongrel dog : cur.
Ty•ler (tī′lər), **John.** 1790–1862. 10th U.S. President (1841–45).
tym•pa•ni (tĭm′pə-nē) *n. var. of* TIMPANI.
tym•pan•ic membrane (tĭm-păn′ĭk) *n.* The thin, semitransparent, oval membrane separating the middle and external ear.
tym•pa•num (tĭm′pə-nəm) *n., pl.* **-na** (-nə) *or* **-nums. 1.** The middle ear. **2.** The tympanic membrane.
type (tīp) *n.* **1. a.** A group, kind, or class sharing common traits or characteristics : category. **b.** An individual having the characteristics of such a group, kind, or class : variety or sort <a tree of the deciduous *type*> **2.** An example : model. **3.** Small blocks, usu. of metal, with raised characters that leave a printed impression when inked and pressed upon paper. **4.** Printed or typewritten letters or characters : print. *—v.* **typed, typ•ing. 1.** To classify or identify according to type. **2.** To typewrite.
type•cast (tīp′kăst′) *v.* **1.** To cast (an actor) repeatedly in the same kind of role. **2.** To cast (an actor) in a role requiring characteristics typical of the actor in real life.
type•face (tīp′fās′) *n.* A design or style of printing type.
type•script (tīp′skrĭpt′) *n.* Typewritten material, as the manuscript of a book.
type•set•ter (tīp′sĕt′ər) *n.* Someone who sets type : compositor. **—type′set′ting** *n.*
type•write (tīp′rīt′) *v.* To write with or use a typewriter.
type•writ•er (tīp′rī′tər) *n.* A machine for writing letters and characters by means of manually activated keys that strike the paper through an inked ribbon.
ty•phoid (tī′foid′) *n.* An acute, highly infectious bacterial disease transmitted by contaminated water or food marked by high fever and intestinal hemorrhaging. **—ty′phoid′** *adj.*
ty•phoon (tī-fo͞on′) *n.* A tropical hurricane in the W Pacific or the China Sea.
ty•phus (tī′fəs) *n.* A severe infectious disease caused by microorganisms of the genus *Rickettsia,* and marked by severe headache, high fever, delirium, and red rash.
typ•i•cal (tĭp′ĭ-kəl) *also* **typ•ic** (-ĭk) *adj.* **1.** Exhibiting the essential traits and characteristics of a kind, class, or group <a *typical* urban community> **2.** Of or relating to a representative specimen : characteristic. **3.** Conforming to or being a type. **—typ′i•cal•ly** *adv.* **—typ′i•cal•ness** *n.*
typ•i•fy (tĭp′ə-fī′) *v.* **-fied, -fy•ing. 1.** To be a typical or characteristic example of. **2.** To represent by an image, model, or form. **—typ′i•fi•ca′tion** *n.*
typ•ist (tī′pĭst) *n.* An operator of a typewriter.
ty•po (tī′pō) *n., pl.* **-pos.** *Informal.* An error in setting type or in typewriting.
ty•pog•ra•phy (tī-pŏg′rə-fē) *n.* **1.** The act or art of printing with type. **2.** The arrangement and appearance of printed material. **—ty•pog′ra•pher** *n.* **—ty′po•graph′i•cal** (-pə-grăf′ĭ-kəl), **ty′po•graph′ic** *adj.*
ty•ran•ni•cal (tĭ-răn′ĭ-kəl, tī-) *also* **ty•ran•nic** (-răn′ĭk) *adj.* Of, relating to, or characteristic of a tyrant : despotic. **—ty•ran′ni•cal•ly** *adv.*
tyr•an•nize (tĭr′ə-nīz′) *v.* **-nized, -niz•ing. 1.** To rule as a tyrant. **2.** To treat or act as a tyrant might. **—tyr′an•niz′er** *n.*
ty•ran•no•saur (tĭ-răn′ə-sôr′, tī-) *n.* A carnivorous dinosaur of the genus *Tyrannosaurus,* with small forelimbs and a large head.
tyr•an•nous (tĭr′ə-nəs) *adj.* Tyrannical.
tyr•an•ny (tĭr′ə-nē) *n., pl.* **-nies. 1.** A government in which the ruler has absolute power. **2.** The unjust or cruel exercise of power. **3.** A tyrannical act. **4.** A state of severity : rigor.
ty•rant (tī′rənt) *n.* **1.** An absolute ruler, esp. an unjust, oppressive, or cruel one. **2.** Someone who exercises power, control, or authority unfairly or harshly.
tyre (tīr) *n. esp. Brit. var. of* TIRE[2].
ty•ro *also* **ti•ro** (tī′rō) *n., pl.* **-ros.** A beginner : novice.
Ty•rol (tĭ-rōl′, tī′rōl′, tĭr′ōl′). Region of the E Alps in W Austria and N Italy. **—Ty′ro•lese′, Ty•ro′le•an** *adj. & n.*
tzar (zär) *n. var. of* CZAR.

Uu

u *or* **U** (yo͞o) *n., pl.* **u's** *or* **U's. 1.** The 21st letter of the English alphabet. **2.** A speech sound represented by the letter *u*. **3. U.** A grade indicating that a student's work is unsatisfactory. **4.** Something with the shape of the letter U.
U *symbol for* URANIUM.
U. *abbr.* **1.** university. **2.** upper.
u·biq·ui·tous (yo͞o-bĭk'wĭ-təs) *adj.* Being or seeming to be present everywhere. **—u·biq'ui·tous·ly** *adv.* **—u·biq'ui·ty** *n.*
U-boat (yo͞o'bōt') *n.* A German underwater vessel.
ud·der (ŭd'ər) *n.* The large pouchlike mammary gland of a cow, ewe, or goat, having 2 or more teats.
UFO (yo͞o'ĕf-ō') *n., pl.* **UFOs** *or* **UFO's.** An unidentified flying object.
u·fol·o·gy (yo͞o-fŏl'ə-jē) *n.* Study of unidentified flying objects. **—u·fol'o·gist** *n.*
U·gan·da (yo͞o-găn'də, o͞o-găn'dä). Country of EC Africa. *Cap.* Kampala. *Pop.* 12,115,000. **—U·gan'dan** *adj.* & *n.*
ugh (ŭg, ŭk) *interj.* Used to express horror or disgust.
ug·ly (ŭg'lē) *adj.* **-li·er, -li·est. 1.** Unpleasant to look at. **2.** Offensive <*ugly* gossip> **3.** Deserving censure <an *ugly* crime> **4.** Menacing <an *ugly* sky> **5.** Having or showing a bad temper. ☆**syns:** HIDEOUS, UNSIGHTLY **—ug'li·ness** *n.*
uh (ŭ) *interj.* Used to express hesitation or uncertainty.
uhf *or* **UHF** *abbr.* ultrahigh frequency.
uh-huh (ə-hŭ') *interj. Informal.* Used to express the affirmative.
U.K. *abbr.* United Kingdom.
u·kase (yo͞o-kās', -kāz', yo͞o'kās', -kāz') *n.* An official decree : edict.
U·kraine (yo͞o-krān'). Region of SW European USSR. **—U·krai'ni·an** *adj.* & *n.*
u·ku·le·le (yo͞o'kə-lā'lē, o͞o'kə-) *n.* A small 4-stringed Hawaiian guitar.
U·lan Ba·tor (o͞o'län bä'tôr'). Cap. of Mongolia, in the NC part. *Pop.* 287,000.
ul·cer (ŭl'sər) *n.* **1.** An often festering lesion in skin or mucous membrane resulting in destruction of the tissue. **2.** Something that corrupts. **—ul'cer·ous** *adj.*
ul·cer·ate (ŭl'sə-rāt') *v.* **-at·ed, -at·ing.** To make or become affected with or as if with an ulcer. **—ul'cer·a'tion** *n.* **—ul'cer·a'tive** (-sə-rā'tĭv, -sər-ə-tĭv) *adj.*
ul·na (ŭl'nə) *n., pl.* **-nae** (-nē') *or* **-nas.** The inner, larger bone of the forearm. **—ul'nar** *adj.*

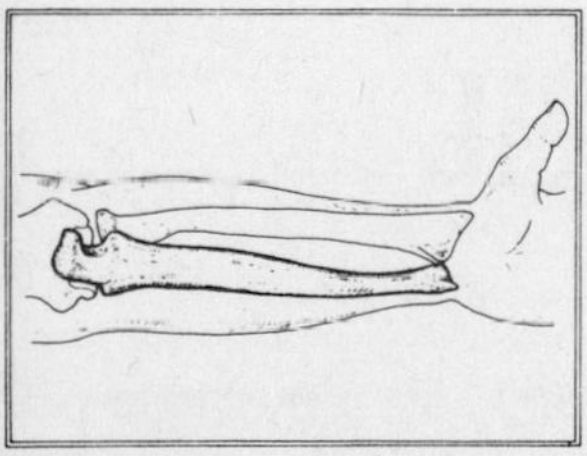

ulna

ul·ster (ŭl'stər) *n.* A long loose overcoat.
ult. *abbr.* ultimate; ultimately.
ul·te·ri·or (ŭl-tîr'ē-ər) *adj.* **1.** Going beyond what is obvious or admitted : concealed. **2.** Lying beyond a particular area or region : farther.
ul·ti·mate (ŭl'tə-mĭt) *adj.* **1.** Final : conclusive <the *ultimate* defeat> **2.** Most extreme : greatest <the *ultimate* crime> **3.** Unable to be further divided or analyzed, as a subatomic particle. **4.** Fundamental : basic <*ultimate* truths> **5.** Most remote in time or space. *—n.* Something that is ultimate. **—ul'ti·mate·ly** *adv.*
ul·ti·ma·tum (ŭl'tə-mā'təm, -mä'-) *n., pl.* **-tums** *or* **-ta** (-tə). A final proposal, demand, or offer, as in negotiating.
ul·ti·mo (ŭl'tə-mō') *adv.* In or of the month just past.
ul·tra (ŭl'trə) *adj.* Exceeding the usual, average, etc. : extreme. *—n.* One with extreme views, esp. in politics.
ultra– *pref.* **1.** Beyond the range, scope, or limit of <*ultra*microscope> **2.** Beyond the usual degree : extreme <*ultra*liberal>
ul·tra·con·ser·va·tive (ŭl'trə-kən-sûr'və-tĭv) *adj.* Conservative to an extreme, esp. in political beliefs : reactionary. **—ul'tra·con·ser'va·tism** *n.* **—ul'tra·con·ser'va·tive** *n.*
ul·tra·high (ŭl'trə-hī') *adj.* Exceedingly high.
ultrahigh frequency *n.* A band of radio frequencies from 300 to 3,000 megacycles per sec.
ul·tra·lib·er·al (ŭl'trə-lĭb'ər-əl, -lĭb'rəl) *adj.* Liberal to an extreme, esp. in political beliefs : radical. **—ul'tra·lib'er·al** *n.* **—ul'tra·lib'er·al·ism** *n.*
ul·tra·ma·rine (ŭl'trə-mə-rēn') *n.* **1.** A blue pigment made esp. from powdered lapis lazuli. **2.** A bright deep blue. *—adj.* **1.** Having a bright deep-blue color. **2.** Of or located beyond the sea.
ul·tra·mi·cro·scope (ŭl'trə-mī'krə-skōp') *n.* A microscope that uses high-intensity light for the study of very minute particles. **—ul'tra·mi·cros'co·py** (-krŏs'kə-pē) *n.*
ul·tra·mi·cro·scop·ic (ŭl'trə-mī'krə-skŏp'ĭk) *adj.* **1.** So small as to be invisible with an ordinary microscope. **2.** Of or pertaining to an ultramicroscope.
ul·tra·mod·ern (ŭl'trə-mŏd'ərn) *adj.* Extremely modern or advanced in ideas or style. **—ul'tra·mod'ern·is'tic** *adj.*
ul·tra·mon·tane (ŭl'trə-mŏn'tān', -mŏntān') *adj.* Of or relating to peoples or countries beyond the mountains, esp. the Alps. **—ul'tra·mon'tane'** *n.*
ul·tra·son·ic (ŭl'trə-sŏn'ĭk) *adj.* Relating to, consisting of, or using sound frequencies inaudible to humans, above approx. 20,000 cycles per sec.
ul·tra·son·ics (ŭl'trə-sŏn'ĭks) *n. (sing. in number).* The scientific study and practical application of ultrasonic sound.
ul·tra·so·nog·ra·phy (ŭl'trə-sə-nŏg'rə-fē) *n.* Diagnostic use of ultrasonic waves to visualize internal body structures. **—ul'tra·son'o·graph'ic** (-sŏn'ə-grăf'ĭk, -sō'nə-) *adj.*
ul·tra·sound (ŭl'trə-sound') *n.* Ultrasonic sound.
ul·tra·vi·o·let (ŭl'trə-vī'ə-lĭt) *adj.* Of, producing, or using radiation with wavelengths just shorter than those of visible light and just longer than those of x-rays. **—ul'tra·vi'o·let** *n.*
ul·u·late (ŭl'yə-lāt') *v.* **-lat·ed, -lat·ing.** To wail or howl loudly. **—ul'u·la'tion** *n.*
um·bel (ŭm'bəl) *n. Bot.* A rounded or flat-topped flower cluster in which the individual flower stalks radiate from approx. the same point on the main stem, as in carrots and parsley. **—um'bel·late'** *adj.*
um·ber (ŭm'bər) *n.* **1.** A natural brown earth containing chiefly iron and manganese oxides and used as pigment. **2.** A dark reddish brown. **—um'ber** *adj.*
um·bil·i·cal (ŭm-bĭl'ĭ-kəl) *adj.* Of, relating to, or near the umbilical cord or navel. *—n.* An umbilical cord.
umbilical cord *n.* **1.** The cordlike structure by which the fetus is joined at the navel to the placenta and which nourishes the fetus and removes its wastes. **2.** A line attached to a spacecraft that supplies an astronaut working outside the vehicle with air and usu. a means of communication.
um·bil·i·cus (ŭm-bĭl'ĭ-kəs, ŭm'bə-lī'kəs) *n., pl.* **-ci** (-sī'). The navel.
um·bra (ŭm'brə) *n., pl.* **-brae** (-brē). **1.** A dark area, esp. the darkest part of a shadow. **2.** The shadow thrown by the moon on a part of the earth during a total solar eclipse.
um·brage (ŭm'brĭj) *n.* **1.** A feeling of resentment or offense <took *umbrage* at the slight> **2.** *Archaic.* Shadow, shade, or a source of shade.
um·brel·la (ŭm-brĕl'ə) *n.* **1.** A collapsible covering mounted on a handle that is used for protection from the rain or sun. **2.** *Zool.* The rounded gelatinous mass composing the body of most jellyfishes.

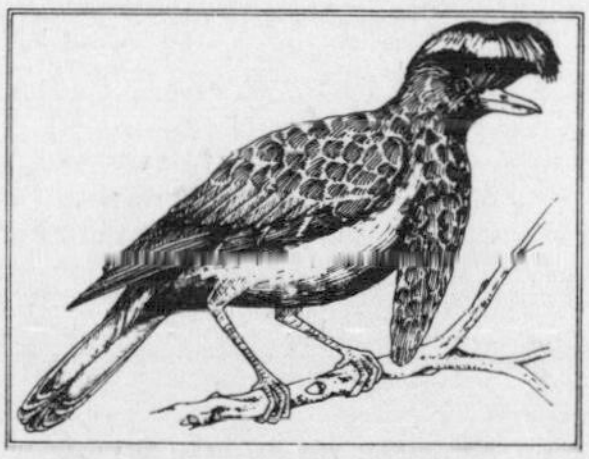

umbrella bird

umbrella bird *n.* A tropical American bird, *Cephalopterus ornatus,* having a retractile crest and a long feathered wattle.
u·mi·ak (o͞o'mē-ăk') *n.* An open Eskimo boat made of wood and covered with skins.
um·laut (o͝om'lout') *n.* **1.** A vowel changed in sound by partial assimilation to a vowel in the next syllable. **2.** The diacritical mark (¨) placed esp. over a German vowel to indicate an umlaut.

um•pire (ŭm′pīr′) *n.* **1.** One who rules on plays, as in baseball. **2.** One empowered to settle a dispute. **—um′pire′** *v.*
ump•teen (ŭmp-tēn′, ŭm-) *adj. Informal.* Of an indefinitely large number. **—ump•teenth′** *adj.*
Um•ta•ta (o͝om-tä′tə). Cap. of the Transkei, in the WC part. *Pop.* 25,216.
UN *also* **U.N.** *abbr.* United Nations.
un-¹ *pref.* Not or opposite <*un*pleasant>
un-² *pref.* **1.** Reversal or cancellation of an action <*un*do> **2.** Release or removal from <*un*fetter> See below for a list of self-explanatory words formed with the prefixes **un-¹** and **un-²**.
un•a•ble (ŭn-ā′bəl) *adj.* **1.** Not able. **2.** Lacking mental capability.
un•ac•com•pa•nied (ŭn′ə-kŭm′pə-nēd) *adj.* **1.** Being without a companion : alone. **2.** *Mus.* Having no accompaniment : solo.
un•ac•count•a•ble (ŭn′ə-koun′tə-bəl) *adj.* **1.** Incapable of being explained. **2.** Not to be held responsible. **—un′ac•count′a•bil′i•ty** *n.* **—un′ac•count′a•bly** *adv.*
un•ac•count•ed (ŭn′ə-koun′tĭd) *adj.* Not explained or understood <The mistake was *unaccounted* for.>
un•ac•cus•tomed (ŭn′ə-kŭs′təmd) *adj.* **1.** Not customary or usual <*unaccustomed* boldness> **2.** Not habituated or used to <*unaccustomed* to hardship>
un•a•dul•ter•at•ed (ŭn′ə-dŭl′tə-rā′tĭd) *adj.* Free from extraneous elements : pure.
un•ad•vised (ŭn′əd-vīzd′) *adj.* **1.** Not informed or counseled. **2.** Not prudent : rash. **—un′ad•vis′ed•ly** *adv.*
un•af•fect•ed (ŭn′ə-fĕk′tĭd) *adj.* **1.** Not affected. **2.** Free from affectation. **—un′af•fect′ed•ness** *n.*
un•al•loyed (ŭn′ə-loid′) *adj.* **1.** Not alloyed, as a metal : pure. **2.** Unqualified : absolute <an *unalloyed* success>
un-A•mer•i•can (ŭn′ə-mĕr′ĭ-kən) *adj.* Considered contrary to the institutions or principles of the U.S.
u•nan•i•mous (yo͞o-năn′ə-məs) *adj.* **1.** Being in complete agreement. **2.** Based on the assent or agreement of all. **—u′na•nim′i•ty** (-nə-nĭm′ĭ-tē) *n.*
un•ap•proach•a•ble (ŭn′ə-prō′chə-bəl) *adj.* **1.** Not friendly. **2.** Not able to be reached. **3.** Without equal : unrivaled.
un•armed (ŭn-ärmd′) *adj.* Lacking means of defense, as weapons.
un•as•sail•a•ble (ŭn′ə-sā′lə-bəl) *adj.* **1.** Not open to doubt : undeniable. **2.** Not open to attack : impregnable. **—un′as•sail′a•bil′i•ty** *n.* **—un′as•sail′a•bly** *adv.*
un•as•sist•ed (ŭn′ə-sĭs′tĭd) *adj.* **1.** Not assisted. **2.** *Baseball.* Designating a play handled without an assist.
un•as•sum•ing (ŭn′ə-so͞o′mĭng) *adj.* Modest : reserved.
un•at•tached (ŭn′ə-tăcht′) *adj.* **1.** Not attached. **2.** Not married or engaged.
un•a•vail•ing (ŭn′ə-vā′lĭng) *adj.* Unsuccessful : futile. **—un′a•vail′ing•ly** *adv.*
un•a•void•a•ble (ŭn′ə-voi′də-bəl) *adj.* Certain to occur : inevitable. **—un′a•void′a•bil′i•ty** *n.* **—un′a•void′a•bly** *adv.*
un•a•ware (ŭn′ə-wâr′) *adj.* Not consciously aware. *—adv.* Unawares.
un•a•wares (ŭn′ə-wârz′) *adv.* **1.** Without warning : by surprise. **2.** Without forethought : unprepared.
un•bal•anced (ŭn-băl′ənst) *adj.* **1.** Not in proper balance. **2. a.** Mentally deranged. **b.** Not of sound judgment. **3.** Not adjusted so that credits are equal to debits.
un•bar (ŭn-bär′) *v.* To open.
un•bear•a•ble (ŭn-bâr′ə-bəl) *adj.* Not endurable : intolerable. **—un•bear′a•bly** *adv.*
un•beat•a•ble (ŭn-bē′tə-bəl) *adj.* Impossible to defeat or outdo.
un•beat•en (ŭn-bēt′n) *adj.* **1.** Never beaten. **2.** Not walked or trampled on. **3.** Not pounded or whipped.
un•be•com•ing (ŭn-bĭ-kŭm′ĭng) *adj.* **1.** Not pleasing : unattractive. **2.** Not proper : indecorous. **—un•be•com′ing•ly** *adv.*
un•be•known (ŭn′bĭ-nōn′) *or* **un•be•knownst** (-nōnst′) *adj.* Without one's knowledge : not known.
un•be•lief (ŭn′bĭ-lēf′) *n.* Lack of belief, esp. religious belief. **—un′be•liev′er** *n.* **—un′be•liev′ing** *adj.*
un•be•liev•a•ble (ŭn′bĭ-lē′və-bəl) *adj.* Not to be believed : incredible. **—un′be•liev′a•bly** *adv.*
un•bend (ŭn-bĕnd′) *v.* **1.** To make or become straight : straighten. **2.** To make or become relaxed : unwind.
un•bend•ing (ŭn-bĕn′dĭng) *adj.* Inflexible : unyielding.
un•bid•den (ŭn-bĭd′n) *also* **un•bid** (-bĭd′) *adj.* Not asked or invited.
un•bind (ŭn-bīnd′) *v.* **1.** To untie. **2.** To set free.
un•blink•ing (ŭn-blĭng′kĭng) *adj.* **1.** Not blinking. **2.** Showing little emotion. **3.** Willing to face reality.
un•blush•ing (ŭn-blŭsh′ĭng) *adj.* **1.** Lacking remorse : shameless. **2.** Not becoming red-faced. **—un•blush′ing•ly** *adv.*
un•bolt (ŭn-bōlt′) *v.* To remove the bolts from : unlock.
un•born (ŭn-bôrn′) *adj.* **1.** Not yet born. **2.** Not yet in existence.
un•bos•om (ŭn-bo͝oz′əm, -bo͞o′zəm) *v.* **1.** To reveal : divulge. **2.** To divulge the thoughts or feelings of (oneself).
un•bound•ed (ŭn-boun′dĭd) *adj.* Having no bounds or limits : unrestrained.
un•bowed (ŭn-boud′) *adj.* **1.** Not bowed or bent. **2.** Not subdued : unyielding.
un•bri•dled (ŭn-brīd′ld) *adj.* **1.** Not wearing a bridle. **2.** Unbounded : unrestrained.
un•bro•ken (ŭn-brō′kən) *adj.* **1.** Not broken : whole. **2.** Not breached or violated. **3.** Continuing without interruption. **4.** Not tamed or subdued.
un•bur•den (ŭn-bûr′dn) *v.* **1.** To free from a burden. **2.** To free (oneself) from fears or cares.
un•but•ton (ŭn-bŭt′n) *v.* **1.** To undo the buttons (of). **2.** To open by or as if by undoing buttons.
un•called-for (ŭn-kôld′fôr′) *adj.* **1.** Not requested. **2.** Unwarranted : gratuitous.
un•can•ny (ŭn-kăn′ē) *adj.* **-ni•er, -ni•est. 1.** Mysterious : strange. **2.** Seemingly supernatural or superhuman. **—un•can′ni•ly** *adv.* **—un•can′ni•ness** *n.*
un•ceas•ing (ŭn-sē′sĭng) *adj.* Never ceasing : incessant. **—un•ceas′ing•ly** *adv.*
un•cer•e•mo•ni•ous (ŭn-sĕr′ə-mō′nē-əs) *adj.* **1.** Marked by informality. **2.** Rudely abrupt. **—un•cer′e•mo′ni•ous•ly** *adv.* **—un•cer′e•mo′ni•ous•ness** *n.*
un•cer•tain (ŭn-sûr′tn) *adj.* **1.** Not sure : doubtful. **2.** Not capable of being known in advance. **3.** Not yet determined or settled. **4.** Likely to change : variable. **—un•cer′tain•ly** *adv.* **—un•cer′tain•ty** *n.*
un•char•i•ta•ble (ŭn-chăr′ĭ-tə-bəl) *adj.* Judging others too harshly. **—un•char′i•ta•ble•ness** *n.* **—un•char′i•ta•bly** *adv.*
un•chart•ed (ŭn-chär′tĭd) *adj.* **1.** Not charted on a map or plan : unexplored. **2.** Not known : unfamiliar.
un•chaste (ŭn-chāst′) *adj.* Morally impure. **—un•chaste′ly** *adv.*
un•chris•tian (ŭn-krĭs′chən) *adj.* **1.** Not of the Christian religion. **2.** Contrary to the Christian spirit.
un•cial (ŭn′shəl, -shē-əl) *adj.* Of or relating to a script with rounded capital letters found esp. in Greek and Latin manuscripts of the 4th to the 8th cent. **—un′cial** *n.*

uncial

un•cir•cum•cised (ŭn-sûr′kəm-sīzd′) *adj.* **1.** Not circumcised. **2.** Heathen.
un•civ•il (ŭn-sĭv′əl) *adj.* **1.** Not civilized. **2.** Discourteous : rude.
un•civ•i•lized (ŭn-sĭv′ə-līzd′) *adj.* Not civilized : barbarous.
un•clad (ŭn-klăd′) *adj.* Naked.
un•clasp (ŭn-klăsp′) *v.* **1.** To loosen the clasp of. **2.** To release from a clasp or hold.
un•cle (ŭng′kəl) *n.* **1.** The brother of one's father or mother. **2.** The spouse of one's aunt. *—interj. Slang.* Used to indicate capitulation, as in a fight.
un•clean (ŭn-klēn′) *adj.* **1.** Not clean : dirty or foul. **2.** Immoral : unchaste. **3.** Ceremonially or religiously unfit.
un•clean•ly (ŭn-klĕn′lē) *adj.* **-li•er, -li•est.** Habitually unclean in mind or body. **—un•clean′li•ness** *n.*
Uncle Sam (săm) *n.* A figure of a tall thin white-bearded man that symbolizes the U.S. or the U.S. government.
Uncle Tom (tŏm) *n.* A black man regarded as being unduly deferential or subservient to whites. **—Uncle Tom′ism** *n.*
un•cloak (ŭn-klōk′) *v.* **1.** To remove a cloak or covering from. **2.** To reveal.
un•close (ŭn-klōz′) *v.* **1.** To open. **2.** To disclose.
un•clothe (ŭn-klōth′) *v.* To undress or uncover.
un•com•fort•a•ble (ŭn-kŭm′fər-tə-bəl, -kŭmf′tə-bəl) *adj.* **1.** Feeling mental or physical discomfort. **2.** Causing discomfort : troubling. **—un•com′fort•a•bly** *adv.*

un•com•mit•ted (ŭn′kə-mĭt′ĭd) *adj.* Not committed to or involved in a particular cause or course of action.

un•com•mon (ŭn kŏm′ən) *adj.* **1.** Not commonly found. **2.** Surpassing the usual. ☆***syns:*** EXCEPTIONAL, EXTRAORDINARY, RARE, REMARKABLE, SINGULAR, UNUSUAL **—un•com′mon•ly** *adv.*

un•com•mu•ni•ca•tive (ŭn′kə-myōō′nĭ-kā′tĭv, -kə-tĭv) *adj.* Not inclined or willing to talk : taciturn.

un•com•pro•mis•ing (ŭn-kŏm′prə-mī′zĭng) *adj.* Unwilling to compromise.

un•con•cern (ŭn′kən-sûrn′) *n.* **1.** Lack of interest : indifference. **2.** Freedom from anxiety or concern.

un•con•cerned (ŭn′kən-sûrnd′) *adj.* **1.** Indifferent. **2.** Free from anxiety or concern. **—un′con•cern′ed•ly** *adv.*

un•con•di•tion•al (ŭn′kən-dĭsh′ə-nəl) *adj.* Not subject to limitations or reservations. **—un′con•di′tion•al•ly** *adv.*

un•con•di•tioned (ŭn′kən-dĭsh′ənd) *adj.* **1.** Unconditional. **2.** *Psychol.* Not acquired by learning or conditioning <an *unconditioned* response>

un•con•quer•a•ble (ŭn-kŏng′kər-ə-bəl) *adj.* Incapable of being conquered or defeated : indomitable.

un•con•scion•a•ble (ŭn-kŏn′shə-nə-bəl) *adj.* **1.** Not guided or restrained by conscience : unscrupulous. **2.** Exceeding reasonable limits : excessive. **—un•con′scion•a•bly** *adv.*

un•con•scious (ŭn-kŏn′shəs) *adj.* **1.** Not available to or observable by the conscious mind <*unconscious* feelings> **2.** Temporarily lacking conscious awareness, as in sleep or a coma. **3.** Not consciously realized or controlled : involuntary. *—n.* The part of the mind inaccessible to conscious awareness or control. **—un•con′scious•ly** *adv.* **—un•con′scious•ness** *n.*

un•con•sti•tu•tion•al (ŭn′kŏn-stĭ-tōō′shə-nəl, -tyōō′-) *adj.* Incompatible with the constitution of a country or organized group. **—un′con•sti•tu′tion•al′i•ty** *n.* **—un′con•sti•tu′tion•al•ly** *adv.*

un•con•trol•la•ble (ŭn′kən-trō′lə-bəl) *adj.* Incapable of being controlled or restrained. **—un′con•trol′la•bly** *adv.*

un•con•ven•tion•al (ŭn′kən-vĕn′shə-nəl) *adj.* Not conforming to convention : unusual. **—un′con•ven′tion•al′i•ty** *n.* **—un′con•ven′tion•al•ly** *adv.*

un•cork (ŭn-kôrk′) *v.* **1.** To pull the cork from. **2.** To free from a sealed or confined condition.

un•cou•ple (ŭn-kŭp′əl) *v.* To disconnect (e.g., railroad cars). **—un•cou′pler** *n.*

un•couth (ŭn-kōōth′) *adj.* **1.** Speaking or acting crudely : unrefined. **2.** Awkward or clumsy : ungainly. **—un•couth′ly** *adv.* **—un•couth′ness** *n.*

un•cov•er (ŭn-kŭv′ər) *v.* **1.** To take the cover from. **2.** To lay bare : disclose. **3.** To remove the hat from in courtesy or respect.

un•cross (ŭn-krôs′, -krŏs′) *v.* To change the crossed position of (e.g., one's legs).

unc•tion (ŭngk′shən) *n.* **1.** The act of anointing, as in a consecration ceremony or ritual of healing. **2.** An ointment, salve, or oil used for anointing. **3.** Something soothing or restorative : balm. **4.** Exaggerated sincerity and desire to please.

unc•tu•ous (ŭngk′chōō-əs) *adj.* **1.** Full of oil or grease. **2.** Unduly ingratiating <an *unctuous* manner> **—unc′tu•ous•ly** *adv.* **—unc′tu•ous•ness** *n.*

un•cut (ŭn-kŭt′) *adj.* **1.** Not sliced, carved, etc. **2.** Not abridged. **3.** Not shaped or polished, as a gemstone. **4.** Not slit or trimmed, as book pages.

un•daunt•ed (ŭn-dôn′tĭd, -dän′-) *adj.* Not discouraged : resolute. **—un•daunt′a•ble** *adj.* **—un•daunt′ed•ly** *adv.*

un•de•ceive (ŭn′dĭ-sēv′) *v.* To free from illusion or misconception.

un•de•cid•ed (ŭn′dĭ-sī′dĭd) *adj.* **1.** Not yet determined : unsettled. **2.** Having arrived at no decision : irresolute.

un•de•mon•stra•tive (ŭn′dĭ-mŏn′strə-tĭv) *adj.* Not inclined to show one's feelings : reserved. **—un′de•mon′stra•tive•ly** *adv.* **—un′de•mon′stra•tive•ness** *n.*

un•de•ni•a•ble (ŭn′dĭ-nī′ə-bəl) *adj.* **1.** Not open to denial or doubt. **2.** Indisputably good or authentic. **—un′de•ni′a•bly** *adv.*

un•der (ŭn′dər) *prep.* **1. a.** Lower than : below <*under* the house> **b.** So as to be covered or concealed by <*under* my coat> **2.** Below the surface of <*under* the ice> **3.** Assuming the disguise of <*under* a pen name> **4.** Less, smaller, or lower than <paid *under* $50 for it> **5.** Less or lower than the requisite amount or degree of <*under* legal age> **6.** Lower in rank or status than. **7.** Subject to the authority or control of <worked *under* the governor> **8.** Acted on or affected by <*under* great stress> **9.** Bound or obligated by <*under* oath> **10.** Within the designation or grouping of <filed *under* expenses> **11.** Subject to : undergoing <*under* dispute> **12.** On account of <*under* the circumstances> *—adv.* **1.** In or into a place lower than or covered by something. **2. a.** Into a state of submission, inferiority, or defeat. **b.** Into an unconscious state. **3.** So as to be covered or submerged. **4.** Lower than a given quantity or level. *—adj.* **1.** Located lower than or beneath something else <the *under* lip> **2.** Subordinate in rank or importance. **3.** Lower or less in amount, caliber, or degree.

under– *pref.* **1.** Location below or beneath <*under*water> **2.** Subordination in rank or importance <*under*graduate> **3.** Degree, rate, or quantity that is lower or less than normal <*under*privileged>

un•der•a•chieve (ŭn′dər-ə-chēv′) *v.* To fail to perform at an expected level of ability, esp. in school. **—un′der•a•chiev′er** *n.*

un•der•age (ŭn′dər-āj′) *adj.* Not having reached the customary or legal age.

un•der•arm (ŭn′dər-ärm′) *adj.* **1. a.** Located or placed under the arm. **b.** Used in the armpit <*underarm* deodorant> **2.** Underhand <an *underarm* pitch> *—adv.* With an underarm movement. *—n.* The hollow under the arm : armpit.

un•der•bel•ly (ŭn′dər-bĕl′ē) *n.* **1.** The underside of an animal's body. **2.** A vulnerable area or part.

un•der•bid (ŭn′dər-bĭd′) *v.* **1.** To bid lower than (a competitor). **2.** To bid too low, as in bridge. **—un′der•bid′** *n.* **—un′der•bid′der** *n.*

un•der•brush (ŭn′dər-brŭsh′) *n.* Small trees, shrubs, etc., growing thickly beneath taller trees.

un•der•car•riage (ŭn′dər-kăr′ĭj) *n.* **1.** A supporting framework or structure, as of a motor vehicle. **2.** The landing mechanism of an aircraft.

un•der•charge (ŭn′dər-chärj′) *v.* To charge (someone) an insufficient amount. **—un′der•charge′** *n.*

un•der•class•man (ŭn′dər-klăs′mən) *n.* A freshman or sophomore at a secondary school or college.

un•der•clothes (ŭn′dər-klōz′, -klō*thz*′) *pl.n.* Underwear.

un•der•cloth•ing (ŭn′der-klō′*th*ĭng) *n.* Underclothes.

un•der•coat (ŭn′dər-kōt′) *n.* **1.** A coat worn beneath another. **2.** A growth of short hair, fur, or feathers partly covered by a longer outer growth. **3. a.** *also* **un•der•coat•ing** (-kō′tĭng). A coat of paint or sealing material applied before a final coat or finish. **b.** A tarlike rust-preventive substance sprayed on the underside of a motor vehicle. *—v.* To apply an undercoat to.

un•der•cov•er (ŭn′dər-kŭv′ər) *adj.* Acting or carried on in secret.

un•der•cur•rent (ŭn′dər-kûr′ənt, -kŭr′-) *n.* **1.** A current, as of water or air, flowing beneath another current or surface. **2.** An underlying tendency or force.

un•der•cut (ŭn′dər-kŭt′) *v.* **1.** To cut into an underlying part. **2.** To undersell or work for less money than. **3.** To hamper or weaken the effectiveness of. **4. a.** To strike (a golf ball or baseball) downward and forward so as to impart backspin. **b.** To cut or slice (e.g., a tennis ball) with an underarm stroke. **—un′der•cut′** *n.*

un•der•de•vel•oped (ŭn′dər-dĭ-vĕl′əpt) *adj.* **1.** Not developed in a full or normal way. **2.** Delayed in economic and industrial development.

un•der•dog (ŭn′dər-dôg′, -dŏg′) *n.* **1.** A loser or expected loser in a contest or struggle. **2.** One in a disadvantageous position.

un•der•done (ŭn′dər-dŭn′) *adj.* Not sufficiently cooked.

un•der•dressed (ŭn′dər-drĕst′) *adj.* **1.** Dressed too informally. **2.** Not wearing enough clothing.

un•der•em•ployed (ŭn′dər-ĕm-ploid′) *adj.* Employed at a low-paying job for which one is overqualified. **—un′der•em•ploy′ment** *n.*

un•der•es•ti•mate (ŭn′dər-ĕs′tə-māt′) *v.* To make too low an estimate of. **—un′der•es′ti•ma′tion** *n.*

un•der•ex•pose (ŭn′dər-ĭk-spōz′) *v.* To expose (film) to light for too short a time to produce normal image contrast. **—un′der•ex•po′sure** *n.*

un•der•foot (ŭn′dər-fŏŏt′) *adv.* **1.** Underneath the feet. **2.** So close to one's feet as to be in the way.

un•der•gar•ment (ŭn′dər-gär′mənt) *n.* A garment worn under others.

un•der•go (ŭn′dər-gō′) *v.* **1.** To be subjected to. **2.** To suffer through : endure.

un•der•grad•u•ate (ŭn′dər-grăj′ōō-ĭt) *n.* A college or university student who is studying for a bachelor's degree.

un•der•ground (ŭn′dər-ground′) *adj.* **1.** Below the earth's surface. **2.** Acting or conducted in secret. **3.** Of or relating to an avant-garde movement or its films, publications, etc. *—n.* **1.** A secret political organization, esp. one seeking to overthrow a government. **2.** *esp. Brit.* An underground railway : subway. **3.** An avant-garde or nonestablishment movement or group. *—adv.* (ŭn′dər-ground′). **1.** Below the ground. **2.** In secret : clandestinely.

un•der•growth (ŭn′dər-grōth′) *n.* Low-growing underbrush esp. in a forest.

un•der•hand (ŭn′dər-hănd′) *adj.* **1.** Done secretly and deceitfully. **2.** Done with the hand kept below shoulder level <an *underhand* pitch> —*adv.* **1.** With an underhand action. **2.** In an underhand way.

un•der•hand•ed (ŭn′dər-hăn′dĭd) *adj.* & *adv.* Underhand. **—un′der•hand′ed•ly** *adv.* **—un′der•hand′ed•ness** *n.*

un•der•lie (ŭn′dər-lī′) *v.* **1.** To be situated under or below. **2.** To be the basis for.

un•der•line (ŭn′dər-līn′, ŭn′dər-līn′) *v.* **1.** To draw a line under. **2.** To place emphasis on. **—un′der•line′** *n.*

un•der•ling (ŭn′dər-lĭng) *n.* One in a subordinate position.

un•der•ly•ing (ŭn′dər-lī′ĭng) *adj.* **1.** Located under or below. **2.** Fundamental <*underlying* truths> **3.** Implicit <an *underlying* meaning>

un•der•mine (ŭn′dər-mīn′) *v.* **1.** To excavate a mine or tunnel underneath. **2.** To weaken or impair gradually.

un•der•most (ŭn′dər-mōst′) *adj.* & *adv.* Lowest in position, rank, or place.

un•der•neath (ŭn′dər-nēth′) *adv.* **1.** In a place below or beneath. **2.** On the underside or lower side. —*prep.* **1.** Below : beneath. **2.** Under the controlling authority of. —*n.* The underside.

un•der•nour•ished (ŭn′dər-nûr′ĭsht) *adj.* Lacking sufficient nourishment for proper health and growth. **—un′der•nour′ish•ment** *n.*

un•der•pants (ŭn′dər-pănts′) *pl.n.* Pants or shorts worn under outer clothing.

un•der•pass (ŭn′dər-păs′) *n.* A part of a road that passes underneath another road or a railroad.

un•der•pay (ŭn′dər-pā′) *v.* To pay less than is required or deserved.

un•der•pin•ning (ŭn′dər-pĭn′ĭng) *n.* **1.** Material or masonry used to support a structure. **2.** *often* **underpinnings. a.** A support or foundation. **b.** *Informal.* The legs. **—un′der•pin′** *v.*

un•der•play (ŭn′dər-plā′, ŭn′dər-plā′) *v.* **1.** To play down. **2.** To play (a role) in a restrained way.

un•der•priv•i•leged (ŭn′dər-prĭv′ə-lĭjd) *adj.* Socially or economically disadvantaged <*underprivileged* children>

un•der•pro•duc•tion (ŭn′dər-prə-dŭk′shən) *n.* Production of less than the usual quantity or below demand.

un•der•rate (ŭn′dər-rāt′) *v.* To rate too low : underestimate.

un•der•score (ŭn′dər-skôr′, -skōr′) *v.* **1.** To draw a line under. **2.** To emphasize. **—un′der•score′** *n.*

un•der•sea (ŭn′dər-sē′) *adj.* & *adv.* Under the surface of the sea. **—un′der•seas′** *adv.*

un•der•sec•re•tar•y (ŭn′dər-sĕk′rĭ-tĕr′ē) *n.* An official immediately subordinate, esp. to a cabinet member.

un•der•sell (ŭn′dər-sĕl′) *v.* To sell for less money than (a competitor).

un•der•shirt (ŭn′dər-shûrt′) *n.* A shirtlike undergarment.

un•der•shoot (ŭn′dər-sho͞ot′) *v.* **1.** To shoot or land short of (a target). **2.** To land short of (a runway) in piloting an aircraft.

un•der•shorts (ŭn′dər-shôrts′) *pl.n.* Short underpants.

un•der•shot (ŭn′dər-shŏt′) *adj.* **1.** Moved or turned by water passing underneath, as a water wheel. **2.** Projecting beyond an upper part <an *undershot* jaw>

un•der•side (ŭn′dər-sīd′) *n.* The side or surface that is on the bottom.

un•der•signed (ŭn′dər-sīnd′) *n., pl.* **undersigned.** One whose name is signed at the end of a document.

un•der•sized (ŭn′dər-sīzd′) *also* **un•der•size** (-sīz′) *adj.* Of a smaller size than is usual, expected, or normal.

un•der•skirt (ŭn′dər-skûrt′) *n.* A skirt, as a petticoat, worn under an outer skirt.

un•der•slung (ŭn′dər-slŭng′) *adj.* Suspended by springs attached below the axles. Used of a vehicle chassis.

un•der•stand (ŭn′dər-stănd′) *v.* **1.** To perceive and comprehend the meaning and significance of. **2.** To be thoroughly familiar with or expert in. **3.** To grasp the intended meaning of what is expressed by. **4.** To be tolerantly or sympathetically disposed. **5.** To find out in a roundabout way. **6.** To draw as a conclusion. **7.** To accept as agreed upon. **—un′der•stand′a•ble** *adj.* **—un′der•stand′a•bly** *adv.*

un•der•stand•ing (ŭn′dər-stăn′dĭng) *n.* **1.** Ability to comprehend : perception. **2.** Capacity to think, learn, judge, etc. **3.** Individual judgment or interpretation. **4.** Accord of thought or feeling. **5.** A mutual agreement esp. to reconcile differences. —*adj.* Disposed to kindness, compassion, tolerance, etc.

un•der•state (ŭn′dər-stāt′) *v.* **1.** To state as less than is the actual situation. **2.** To state unemphatically esp. for dramatic effect. **—un′der•state′ment** *n.*

un•der•stood (ŭn′dər-sto͝od′) *adj.* **1.** Agreed upon : settled. **2.** Implicit.

un•der•stud•y (ŭn′dər-stŭd′ē) *v.* **1.** To learn (another's role) so as to be able to substitute if necessary. **2.** To serve as an understudy to. **—un′der•stud′y** *n.*

un•der•take (ŭn′dər-tāk′) *v.* **1.** To set about doing, as a task. **2.** To obligate oneself : pledge. **3.** To guarantee.

un•der•tak•er (ŭn′dər-tā′kər) *n.* One who prepares the dead for burial and usu. serves as funeral director.

▲word history: The subject of death has always inspired euphemism; the word *undertaker* is one example. Derived from the verb *undertake,* "to take upon oneself," *undertaker* orig. denoted one who undertakes any kind of task. Around 1700, during a period of general refinement of speech and manners, the word *undertaker* was applied specifically to those who undertake to prepare the dead for the grave.

un•der•tak•ing (ŭn′dər-tā′kĭng) *n.* **1.** Something undertaken. **2.** A promise or guarantee. **3.** The business or duties of an undertaker.

un•der-the-count•er (ŭn′dər-*thə*-koun′tər) *adj.* Not lawful.

un•der•tone (ŭn′dər-tōn′) *n.* **1.** A low or quiet voice tone. **2.** A pale or subdued color, esp. one visible through another color. **3.** An underlying emotional quality <*undertones* of sadness>

un•der•tow (ŭn′dər-tō′) *n.* An underwater current running opposite to the surface current.

un•der•val•ue (ŭn′dər-văl′yo͞o) *v.* **1.** To place too little a value on. **2.** To hold in low regard or esteem.

un•der•wa•ter (ŭn′dər-wô′tər, -wŏt′ər) *adj.* Under the surface of water. **—un′der•wa′ter** *adv.*

un•der•wear (ŭn′dər-wâr′) *n.* Garments worn next to the skin : underclothes.

un•der•weight (ŭn′dər-wāt′) *adj.* Of less than the normal, usual, or requisite weight. **—un′der•weight′** *n.*

un•der•world (ŭn′dər-wûrld′) *n.* **1.** *Gk.* & *Rom. Myth.* The nether world, esp. the abode of the dead : Hades. **2.** The world of organized crime.

un•der•write (ŭn′dər-rīt′) *v.* **1.** To write at the end of, esp. to sign (a document). **2.** To agree to finance (an enterprise). **3.** To sign (an insurance policy) so as to assume liability in case of specified losses. **4.** To agree to purchase (stock in a new enterprise) usu. at a fixed date and price. **—un′der•writ′er** *n.*

un•de•sir•a•ble (ŭn′dĭ-zīr′ə-bəl) *adj.* Not desirable. **—un′de•sir′a•ble** *n.* **—un′de•sir′a•bly** *adv.*

un•dies (ŭn′dēz) *pl.n. Informal.* Women's or girls' underwear.

un•do (ŭn-do͞o′) *v.* **1.** To reverse, erase, or annul. **2.** To unfasten or loosen. **3.** To open by unwrapping. **4. a.** To cause the downfall of. **b.** To upset : confuse.

un•do•ing (ŭn-do͞o′ĭng) *n.* **1.** Reversal or annulment. **2.** Loosening or untying. **3. a.** Ruin. **b.** A cause of ruin : downfall.

un•doubt•ed (ŭn-dou′tĭd) *adj.* Not doubted or questioned : accepted completely. **—un•doubt′ed•ly** *adv.*

un•dress (ŭn-drĕs′) *v.* To take off the clothing of. —*n.* **1.** Casual attire. **2.** The state of being naked.

un•due (ŭn-do͞o′, -dyo͞o′) *adj.* **1.** Exceeding a normal or reasonable limit : excessive. **2.** Improper or unlawful.

un•du•lant (ŭn′jə-lənt, ŭn′dyə-, ŭn′də-) *adj.* Undulating : wavelike.

un•du•late (ŭn′jə-lāt′, ŭn′dyə-, ŭn′də-) *v.* **1.** To rise and fall or move from side to side in a smooth wavelike motion. **2.** To have a wavy look or shape. **—un′du•la′tion** *n.*

un•du•ly (ŭn-do͞o′lē, -dyo͞o′-) *adv.* **1.** To an excessive degree. **2.** Improperly.

un•dy•ing (ŭn′dī′ĭng) *adj.* Being without end : everlasting.

un•earned (ŭn-ûrnd′) *adj.* **1.** Not merited <*unearned* praise> **2.** Not acquired by labor or service.

un•earth (ŭn-ûrth′) **1.** To dig up out of the earth. **2.** To disclose : uncover.

un•earth•ly (ŭn-ûrth′lē) *adj.* **-li•er, -li•est. 1.** Not of the natural world : supernatural. **2.** Frighteningly unexplainable : weird. **3.** Unreasonable : absurd <an *unearthly* hour for visitors>

un•eas•y (ŭn-ē′zē) *adj.* **1.** Causing or feeling discomfort or distress. **2.** Not easy : difficult. **3.** Awkward or embarrassed. **4.** Restless. **5.** Unstable : uncertain. **—un•eas′i•ly** *adv.* **—un•eas′i•ness** *n.*

un•em•ployed (ŭn′ĕm-ploid′) *adj.* **1.** Not employed : out of work. **2.** Not put to use : inactive. **—un′em•ploy′ment** *n.*

un•e•qual (ŭn-ē′kwəl) *adj.* **1.** Not the same, as in quantity, size, value, etc. **2.** Having unbalanced sides or parts : asymmetric. **3.** Not even or consistent : variable. **4.** Lacking sufficient ability : inadequate.

un•e•qualed (ŭn-ē′kwəld) *adj.* Having no equal or match : unrivaled.

un•e•quiv•o•cal (ŭn′ĭ-kwĭv′ə-kəl) *adj.* Not doubtful or uncertain : clear. **—un′e•quiv′o•cal•ly** *adv.*

un•err•ing (ŭn-ûr′ĭng, -ĕr′-) *adj.* Consistently accurate. **—un′err′ing•ly** *adv.*

un•es•sen•tial (ŭn′ĭ-sĕn′shəl) *adj.* Dispensable. —*n.* Something dispensable.

un·e·ven (ŭn-ē′vən) *adj.* **1.** Having a rough, irregular surface. **2.** Deviating from the straight or parallel. **3.** Varying in uniformity or consistency. **4.** Not balanced or equitable : unfair. **5.** Not divisible by 2 <an *uneven* number> **—un·e′ven·ly** *adv.* **—un·e′ven·ness** *n.*

un·e·vent·ful (ŭn′ĭ-vĕnt′fəl) *adj.* Lacking in significant events. **—un′e·vent′ful·ly** *adv.* **—un′e·vent′ful·ness** *n.*

un·ex·am·pled (ŭn′ĭg-zăm′pəld) *adj.* Without parallel : unequaled.

un·ex·cep·tion·a·ble (ŭn′ĭk-sĕp′shə-nə-bəl) *adj.* Beyond objection or reproach. **—un′ex·cep′tion·a·bly** *adv.*

un·ex·pect·ed (ŭn′ĭk-spĕk′tĭd) *adj.* Not anticipated beforehand. **—un′ex·pect′ed·ly** *adv.* **—un′ex·pect′ed·ness** *n.*

un·fail·ing (ŭn-fā′lĭng) *adj.* **1.** Not running out : inexhaustible. **2.** Constant : dependable. **3.** Incapable of error : infallible. **—un·fail′ing·ly** *adv.*

un·fair (ŭn-fâr′) *adj.* **1.** Marked by a lack of justice or honesty : biased. **2.** Not ethical, esp. in business affairs. ☆***syns:*** INEQUITABLE, UNEQUAL, UNJUST **—un·fair′ly** *adv.* **—un·fair′ness** *n.*

un·faith·ful (ŭn-fāth′fəl) *adj.* **1.** Lacking in loyalty. **2.** Guilty of adultery. **3.** Not accurately reflecting the original. **—un·faith′ful·ly** *adv.* **—un·faith′ful·ness** *n.*

un·fa·mil·iar (ŭn′fə-mĭl′yər) *adj.* **1.** Not previously known : strange <an *unfamiliar* street> **2.** Not acquainted or conversant <*unfamiliar* with the topic> **—un′fa·mil·iar′i·ty** (-mĭl-yăr′ĭ-tē, -mĭl′ē-ăr′-) *n.*

un·fa·vor·a·ble (ŭn-fā′vər-ə-bəl, -fā′vrə-) *adj.* **1.** Not favorable or propitious. **2.** Negative : opposed. **—un·fa′vor·a·bly** *adv.*

un·feel·ing (ŭn-fē′lĭng) *adj.* **1.** Not sympathetic : hardhearted. **2.** Having no sensation : numb. **—un·feel′ing·ly** *adv.*

un·feigned (ŭn-fānd′) *adj.* Not pretended : authentic. **—un·feign′ed·ly** *adv.*

un·fet·ter (ŭn-fĕt′ər) *v.* To free from fetters or restraints, esp. to liberate.

un·fit (ŭn-fĭt′) *adj.* **1.** Not appropriate for a given purpose. **2.** Not qualified : incompetent. **3.** In poor mental or bodily health. *—v.* To disqualify. **—un·fit′ly** *adv.* **—un·fit′ness** *n.*

un·flap·pa·ble (ŭn-flăp′ə-bəl) *adj. Slang.* Not easily upset : cool and collected. **—un·flap′pa·bil′i·ty** *n.* **—un·flap′pa·bly** *adv.*

un·fledged (ŭn-flĕjd′) *adj.* **1.** Not yet having fully developed flight feathers. **2.** Lacking experience or maturity.

un·flinch·ing (ŭn-flĭn′chĭng) *adj.* Standing firm and unyielding : resolute. **—un·flinch′ing·ly** *adv.*

un·fold (ŭn-fōld′) *v.* **1.** To open up the folds of and spread out. **2.** To become gradually visible. **3.** To make known or develop gradually. **—un·fold′ment** *n.*

un·fore·seen (ŭn′fər-sēn′) *adj.* Not anticipated in advance : unexpected.

un·for·get·ta·ble (ŭn′fər-gĕt′ə-bəl) *adj.* Extremely memorable. **—un′for·get′ta·bly** *adv.*

un·for·mat·ted (ŭn-fôr′măt′ĭd) *adj. Computer Sci.* Designating input or output data not edited before display.

un·formed (ŭn-fôrmd′) *adj.* **1.** Having no definite form or structure : amorphous. **2.** Not yet fully developed : immature.

un·for·tu·nate (ŭn-fôr′chə-nĭt) *adj.* **1.** Having bad luck. **2.** Causing misfortune. **3.** Inappropriate <an *unfortunate* remark> ☆***syns:*** AWKWARD, INAPPROPRIATE, INFELICITOUS, UNHAPPY *—n.* A victim of misfortune. **—un·for′tu·nate·ly** *adv.*

un·found·ed (ŭn-foun′dĭd) *adj.* Having no basis in fact : groundless.

un·fre·quent·ed (ŭn′frĭ-kwĕn′tĭd, ŭn-frē′kwən-) *adj.* Infrequently visited <an *unfrequented* spot>

un·friend·ly (ŭn-frĕnd′lē) *adj.* **1.** Not friendly : aloof or hostile. **2.** Not favorable. **—un·friend′li·ness** *n.*

un·frock (ŭn-frŏk′) *v.* To deprive (a member of the clergy) of rightful privileges and functions.

un·furl (ŭn-fûrl′) *v.* To unfold or unroll.

un·gain·ly (ŭn-gān′lē) *adj.* **-li·er, -li·est.** Lacking grace or ease of movement : awkward. **—un·gain′li·ness** *n.*

un·god·ly (ŭn-gŏd′lē) *adj.* **1.** Lacking reverence for God : impious. **2.** Marked by wickedness : sinful. **3.** *Informal.* Outrageous : absurd <got up at an *ungodly* hour> **—un·god′li·ness** *n.*

un·gov·ern·a·ble (ŭn-gŭv′ər-nə-bəl) *adj.* Uncontrollable : unruly.

un·gra·cious (ŭn-grā′shəs) *adj.* **1.** Discourteous : rude. **2.** Not pleasant : disagreeable. **—un·gra′cious·ly** *adv.* **—un·gra′cious·ness** *n.*

un·grate·ful (ŭn-grāt′fəl) *adj.* **1.** Not thankful. **2.** Unpleasant : distasteful. **—un·grate′ful·ly** *adv.* **—un·grate′ful·ness** *n.*

un·guard·ed (ŭn-gär′dĭd) *adj.* **1.** Without protection or defense. **2.** Indiscreet.

un·guent (ŭng′gwənt) *n.* A soothing or healing salve : ointment.

un·gu·late (ŭng′gyə-lĭt, -lāt′) *adj.* Having hoofs. *—n.* An ungulate mammal.

un·hal·lowed (ŭn-hăl′ōd) *adj.* **1.** Not holy or consecrated. **2.** Impious : irreverent.

un·hand (ŭn-hănd′) *v.* To let go of.

un·hap·py (ŭn-hăp′ē) *adj.* **1.** Sad : sorrowful. **2.** Causing misfortune : unlucky. **3.** Not suitable : inappropriate. **4.** Not pleased or satisfied. **—un·hap′pi·ly** *adv.* **—un·hap′pi·ness** *n.*

un·health·y (ŭn-hĕl′thē) *adj.* **1.** In poor health : sick. **2.** Being a sign or symptom of poor health. **3.** Not contributing to health : unwholesome. **4.** Morally harmful. **—un·health′i·ly** *adv.* **—un·health′i·ness** *n.*

un·heard (ŭn-hûrd′) *adj.* **1.** Not heard. **2.** Not accorded a hearing : not listened to.

un·heard-of (ŭn-hûrd′ŭv′, -ŏv′) *adj.* Never before known or heard of, esp. unprecedented.

un·hinge (ŭn-hĭnj′) *v.* **1. a.** To take from hinges. **b.** To take the hinges from. **2.** To make mentally unbalanced.

un·ho·ly (ŭn′hō′lē) *adj.* **1.** Not holy or sacred. **2.** Morally bad : wicked. **3.** *Informal.* Outrageous : terrible <an *unholy* mess> **—un·ho′li·ness** *n.*

un·hook (ŭn-ho͝ok′) *v.* **1.** To release or remove from a hook. **2.** To loosen or unfasten the hooks of.

un·horse (ŭn-hôrs′) *v.* **1.** To unseat from a horse. **2.** To force from an occupied position, esp. to overthrow.

u·ni·cam·er·al (yo͞o′nĭ-kăm′ər-əl) *adj.* Having 1 legislative chamber.

u·ni·cel·lu·lar (yo͞o′nĭ-sĕl′yə-lər) *adj.* Consisting of a single cell, as a protozoan.

u·ni·corn (yo͞o′nĭ-kôrn′) *n.* A legendary animal resembling a horse, with a long spiraled horn in the center of its forehead.

unicorn plant *n.* A plant, *Proboscidea louisiana*, of the S U.S., having yellowish flowers mottled with purple and a beaked woody pod.

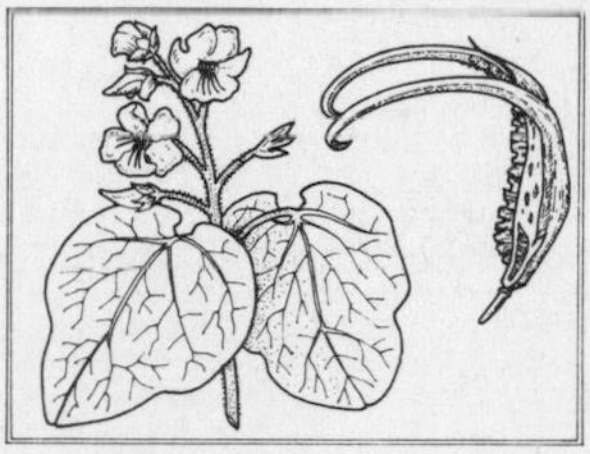

unicorn plant

u·ni·cy·cle (yo͞o′nĭ-sī′kəl) *n.* A 1-wheeled vehicle that is usu. pedaled.

un·i·den·ti·fied flying object (ŭn′ī-dĕn′tə-fīd′) *n.* An apparently flying object that cannot be identified or explained.

u·ni·form (yo͞o′nə-fôrm′) *adj.* **1.** Never changing or varying. **2.** Identical with another or others. *—n.* An outfit that distinguishes the wearer as belonging to a particular group. **—u′ni·for′mi·ty, u′ni·form′ness** *n.* **—u′ni·form′ly** *adv.*

u·ni·fy (yo͞o′nə-fī′) *v.* **-fied, -fy·ing.** To consolidate : unite. **—u′ni·fi·ca′tion** *n.* **—u′ni·fi′er** *n.*

u·ni·lat·er·al (yo͞o′nĭ-lăt′ər-əl) *adj.* **1.** Of, relating to, involving, or affecting only 1 side. **2.** Obligating only 1 of 2 or more persons, parties, or nations <a *unilateral* treaty> **—u′ni·lat′er·al·ly** *adv.*

un·im·peach·a·ble (ŭn′ĭm-pē′chə-bəl) *adj.* Beyond dispute or reproach : unquestionable <*unimpeachable* integrity> **—un′im·peach′a·bly** *adv.*

un·in·hib·it·ed (ŭn′ĭn-hĭb′ĭ-tĭd) *adj.* Without inhibitions, esp. exuberantly unconstrained. **—un′in·hib′it·ed·ly** *adv.*

un·in·tel·li·gent (ŭn′ĭn-tĕl′ə-jənt) *adj.* Showing a lack of intelligence.

un·in·tel·li·gi·ble (ŭn′ĭn-tel′ə-jə-bəl) *adj.* Difficult or impossible to comprehend <*unintelligible* speech> **—un′in·tel′li·gi·bly** *adv.*

un·in·ter·est·ed (ŭn-ĭn′trĭs-tĭd, -ĭn′tə-rĕs′tĭd) *adj.* **1.** Havng no concern with or share in something, esp. having no financial or property interest. **2.** Not interested. ☆***syns:*** DETACHED, INCURIOUS, INDIFFERENT, REMOTE, UNCONCERNED

un·ion (yo͞on′yən) *n.* **1. a.** The act or an instance of uniting. **b.** The state of being united. **c.** An alliance or confederation of persons, parties, or political entities for mutual interest or advantage. **2. a.** A marital partnership. **b.** A sexual uniting. **3.** An organized body of wage earners for the regulation and esp. upgrading of wages and working conditions. **4.** A device for joining or coupling pipes, rods, etc. **5.** A design on a flag signifying the union of 2 or more political entities. **6. Union.** The U.S. esp. during the Civil War.

un•ion•ism (yo͞on′yə-nĭz′əm) *n.* **1.** The theory, principle, or policy of forming or being loyal to a union. **2.** The principles or system of a union, esp. a labor or trade union. **—un′ion•ist** *n.*

un•ion•ize (yo͞on′yə-nīz′) *v.* **-ized, -iz•ing.** To form into or cause to become a member of a labor or trade union. **—un′ion•i•za′tion** *n.*

union jack *n.* **1.** A national flag composed entirely of a union. **2. Union Jack.** The national flag of the United Kingdom.

Union of Soviet Socialist Republics. Country of E Europe and N Asia, with coastlines on the Baltic and Black seas and the Arctic and Pacific oceans. *Cap.* Moscow. *Pop.* 264,486,000.

union shop *n.* An establishment whose employees are required to be or become union members.

u•nique (yo͞o-nēk′) *adj.* **1.** Being the only one. **2.** Being without an equal. ☆***syns:*** INCOMPARABLE, MATCHLESS, PEERLESS, UNEQUALED, UNPARALLELED, UNRIVALED **—u•nique′ly** *adv.*

u•ni•sex (yo͞o′nĭ-sĕks′) *adj.* Appropriate for or common to both sexes <*unisex* clothes>

u•ni•sex•u•al (yo͞o′nĭ-sĕk′sho͞o-əl) *adj.* Of, pertaining to, or confined to 1 sex.

u•ni•son (yo͞o′nĭ-sən, -zən) *n.* **1.** *Mus.* **a.** Sameness of pitch. **b.** The combination of tones or parts sounding simultaneously at the same pitch or in octaves. **2.** Simultaneous utterance of the same words by 2 or more persons. **3.** Harmonious agreement.

u•nit (yo͞o′nĭt) *n.* **1.** One considered to constitute part of a whole. **2.** An exact quantity used as a standard of measurement. **3.** Something that performs a particular function, as in a machine or system. **4.** The number 1.

U•ni•tar•i•an (yo͞o′nĭ-târ′ē-ən) *n.* A member of a Christian denomination that emphasizes freedom and tolerance in religious belief. **—U′ni•tar′i•an•ism** *n.*

u•ni•tar•y (yo͞o′nĭ-tĕr′ē) *adj.* **1.** Of or relating to a unit or units. **2.** Having the nature of a unit : whole.

u•nite (yo͞o-nīt′) *v.* **u•nit•ed, u•nit•ing. 1.** To bring or put together so as to make a whole. **2.** To join together for a common purpose. **3.** To become consolidated.

United Arab Emirates. Country of E Arabia, a federation of 7 sheikdoms on the Persian Gulf. *Cap.* Abu Dhabi. *Pop.* 180,200.

United Kingdom *also* **United Kingdom of Great Britain and Northern Ireland.** Country of W Europe, comprising England, Scotland, Wales, and Northern Ireland. *Cap.* London. *Pop.* 55,880,000.

United Nations *pl.n. (sing. or pl. in number).* An international organization comprising most of the countries of the world, formed in 1945 to promote peace, security, and economic development.

United States *also* **United States of America.** Country of C and NW North America, with coastlines on the Atlantic, Pacific, and Arctic oceans. *Cap.* Washington, D.C. *Pop.* 226,504,825.

unit pricing *n.* The pricing of goods based on cost per standard unit, as the ounce or pound.

u•ni•ty (yo͞o′nĭ-tē) *n., pl* **-ties. 1.** The state of being united into a whole. **2.** Agreement : accord. **3.** Unification of parts into a whole. **4.** Arrangement of elements in an artistic or literary work so that each contributes to the main theme. **5.** Unchanging singleness of purpose or action. **6.** *Math.* The smallest whole numerical unit : 1.

univ. *abbr.* **1.** universal. **2.** university.

u•ni•va•lent (yo͞o′nĭ-vā′lənt) *adj.* **1.** Having valence 1. **2.** Having a single valence.

u•ni•valve (yo͞o′nĭ-vălv′) *n.* A mollusk, as a snail, with a single shell.

u•ni•ver•sal (yo͞o′nə-vûr′səl) *adj.* **1.** Including, involving, or affecting the whole world : worldwide. **2.** Relating to, involving, or affecting all those belonging to a given class or group. **3.** Used by or common to all <a *universal* language> **4.** Of or relating to the universe : cosmic. **5.** Having or adjustable to a variety of sizes or uses. **—u′ni•ver•sal′i•ty** *n.* **—u′ni•ver′sal•ly** *adv.*

universal donor *n.* One having blood type O.

U•ni•ver•sal•ism (yo͞o′nə-vûr′sə-lĭz′əm) *n.* The theological doctrine of universal salvation. **—U′ni•ver′sal•ist** *n.*

universal joint *n.* A joint or coupling that permits machine parts not in the same line limited movement in any direction while transmitting rotary motion.

u•ni•verse (yo͞o′nə-vûrs′) *n.* **1.** All existing space and matter regarded as a whole. **2. a.** The planet earth. **b.** All humankind.

u•ni•ver•si•ty (yo͞o′nə-vûr′sĭ-tē) *n., pl.* **-ties.** An institution of higher learning that offers degrees in undergraduate, graduate, and professional school divisions.

un•just (ŭn-jŭst′) *adj.* Marked by a lack of justice or fairness. **—un•just′ly** *adv.*

un•kempt (ŭn-kĕmpt′) *adj.* **1.** Not brushed or combed. **2.** Untidy : messy.

un•kind (ŭn-kīnd′) *adj.* Lacking in concern, sympathy, or understanding. **—un•kind′li•ness** *n.* **—un•kind′ly** *adj.* & *adv.* **—un•kind′ness** *n.*

un•know•ing (ŭn-nō′ĭng) *adj.* Not informed or aware. **—un•know′ing•ly** *adv.*

un•known (ŭn-nōn′) *adj.* **1.** Not familiar : strange. **2.** Not identified or determined. **—un•known′** *n.*

un•law•ful (ŭn-lô′fəl) *adj.* **1.** Against the law. **2.** Immoral. **3.** Illegitimate. **—un•law′ful•ly** *adv.* **—un•law′ful•ness** *n.*

un•lead•ed (ŭn-lĕd′ĭd) *adj.* Containing no tetraethyl lead, as gasoline.

un•learn (ŭn-lûrn′) *v.* To forget.

un•learn•ed (ŭn-lûr′nĭd) *adj.* **1.** Having little or no education. **2.** (ŭn-lûrnd′). Not learned or acquired through training or studying <an *unlearned* response>

un•leash (ŭn-lēsh′) *v.* To loose from or as if from a leash.

un•less (ŭn-lĕs′) *conj.* Except on the condition or under the circumstances that.

un•let•tered (ŭn-lĕt′ərd) *adj.* Not educated, esp. unable to read and write.

un•like (ŭn-līk′) *adj.* **1.** Not alike : dissimilar. **2.** Not equal, as in quantity or strength. *—prep.* **1.** Different from <a flavor *unlike* any other> **2.** Not characteristic of <*unlike* them to be late> **—un•like′ness** *n.*

un•like•ly (ŭn-līk′lē) *adj.* **1.** Not likely or plausible. **2.** Likely to fail : not promising. ☆***syns:*** DOUBTFUL, IMPROBABLE **—un•like′li•hood, un•like′li•ness** *n.*

un•lim•ber (ŭn′lĭm′bər) *v.* To prepare for action.

un•load (ŭn-lōd′) *v.* **1. a.** To take the load or cargo from. **b.** To take (cargo) from. **2.a.** To unburden (one's mind) of something oppressive. **b.** To give vent to (troubles, problems, etc.). **3. a.** To take the charge from (a gun). **b.** To fire (a gun). **4.** To dispose of, esp. by selling in volume.

un•lock (ŭn-lŏk′) *v.* **1.a.** To open (a lock) esp. by turning a key. **b.** To open (a door, trunk, etc.) by unlocking. **2.** To make accessible <*unlock* a closed mind> **3.** To find a solution to <*unlock* a puzzle>

un•looked-for (ŭn-lo͝okt′fôr′) *adj.* Not expected : unforeseen.

un•loose (ŭn-lo͞os′) *also* **un•loos•en** (-lo͞o′sən) *v.* **1.** To let loose, as by unfastening or untying. **2.** To ease or release, as a firm grip.

un•luck•y (ŭn-lŭk′ē) *adj.* **1.** Having bad luck : unfortunate. **2.** Forecasting misfortune : inauspicious. **3.** Unsuitable or disappointing <an *unlucky* selection> **—un•luck′i•ly** *adv.* **—un•luck′i•ness** *n.*

un•make (ŭn-māk′) *v.* **1.** To reverse or nullify : undo. **2.** To deprive of status, rank, or power : depose. **3.** To cause the ruin of.

un•man•ly (ŭn-măn′lē) *adj.* **1.** Not brave. **2.** Effeminate.

un•manned (ŭn-mănd′) *adj.* Lacking or designed to operate without a crew <an *unmanned* spacecraft>

un•man•nered (ŭn-măn′ərd) *adj.* **1.** Having bad manners : rude. **2.** Without pretense or pause : unaffected.

un•man•ner•ly (ŭn-măn′ər-lē) *adj.* Ill-mannered. **—un•man′ner•li•ness** *n.*

un•mask (ŭn-măsk′) *v.* **1.** To take away a mask (from). **2.** To reveal the true nature of : expose.

un•mean•ing (ŭn-mē′nĭng) *adj.* Lacking meaning or sense.

un•men•tion•a•ble (ŭn-mĕn′shə-nə-bəl) *adj.* Unsuitable or improper as a subject of conversation. *—pl.n.* **unmentionables.** Underwear.

un•mer•ci•ful (ŭn-mûr′sĭ-fəl) *adj.* **1.** Without mercy : pitiless. **2.** Excessive : immoderate. **—un•mer′ci•ful•ly** *adv.* **—un•mer′ci•ful•ness** *n.*

un•mind•ful (ŭn-mīnd′fəl) *adj.* Inattentive : oblivious.

un•mis•tak•a•ble (ŭn′mĭ-stā′kə-bəl) *adj.* Clearly evident. **—un′mis•tak′a•bly** *adv.*

un•mit•i•gat•ed (ŭn-mĭt′ĭ-gā′tĭd) *adj.* **1.** Not lessened or relieved <*unmitigated* tension> **2.** Absolute : thoroughgoing <*unmitigated* impudence>

un•mor•al (ŭn-môr′əl, -mŏr′-) *adj.* Having no moral perception : amoral.

un•nat•u•ral (ŭn-năch′ər-əl, -năch′rəl) *adj.* **1.** Against natural law, esp. abnormal or unusual. **2.** Affected or artificial, as in behavior. **3.** Contrary to natural feelings : inhuman. **—un•nat′u•ral•ly** *adv.* **—un•nat′u•ral•ness** *n.*

un•nec•es•sar•y (ŭn-nĕs′ĭ-sĕr′ē) *adj.* Not necessary : uncalled-for. **—un•nec′es•sar′i•ly** *adv.*

un•nerve (ŭn-nûrv′) *v.* To deprive of courage or composure.

un•num•bered (ŭn-nŭm′bərd) *adj.* **1.** Too numerous to be counted. **2.** Not identified by a number.

un•ob•tru•sive (ŭn′əb-tro͞o′sĭv, -zĭv) *adj.* Not noticeable. **—un′ob•tru′sive•ly** *adv.*

un•oc•cu•pied (ŭn-ŏk′yə-pīd′) *adj.* **1.** Not occupied : empty. **2.** Doing little : idle.

un•or•gan•ized (ŭn-ôr′gə-nīzd′) *adj.* **1.** Not ordered, coordinated, or systematized. **2.** Not organized into a union.

un•pack (ŭn-păk′) *v.* **1.** To remove packed things (from). **2.** To take from a container, parcel, or packaging.

un•par•al•leled (ŭn-păr′ə-lĕld′) *adj.* Without equal : matchless.

un•par•lia•men•ta•ry (ŭn′pär-lə-mĕn′tə-rē, -mĕn′trē) *adj.* Not according to parliamentary practice.

un•peo•ple (ŭn-pē′pəl) *v.* To reduce sharply the population of.

un•pleas•ant (ŭn-plĕz′ənt) *adj.* Not pleasant : offensive. **—un•pleas′ant•ly** *adv.* **—un•pleas′ant•ness** *n.*

un•plug (ŭn-plŭg′) *v.* **1.** To withdraw a plug, stopper, or obstruction from. **2.** To disconnect (an electric appliance)

un•plumbed (ŭn-plŭmd′) *adj.* **1.** Not tested or measured with a plumb. **2.** Not explored or understood in depth.

un•pop•u•lar (ŭn-pŏp′yə-lər) *adj.* Not generally liked or approved of. **—un•pop′u•lar′i•ty** (-lăr′ĭ-tē) *n.*

un•prec•e•dent•ed (ŭn-prĕs′ĭ-dĕn′tĭd) *adj.* Not done or known before : novel.

un•pre•dict•a•ble (ŭn′prĭ-dĭk′tə-bəl) *adj.* Not capable of being known beforehand. **—un′pre•dict′a•bil′i•ty** *n.* **—un′pre•dict′a•bly** *adv.*

un•pre•pared (ŭn′prĭ-pârd′) *adj.* **1.** Not prepared or equipped. **2.** Not done or rehearsed in advance. **—un′pre•par′ed•ly** *adv.* **—un′pre•par′ed•ness** *n.*

un•pre•ten•tious (ŭn′prĭ-tĕn′shəs) *adj.* Not pretentious : modest.

un•prin•ci•pled (ŭn-prĭn′sə-pəld) *adj.* Unscrupulous.

un•print•a•ble (ŭn-prĭn′tə-bəl) *adj.* Improper or unfit for publication.

un•pro•fes•sion•al (ŭn′prə-fĕsh′ə-nəl) *adj.* **1.** Contrary to the standards or ethics of a profession. **2.** Lacking professional competence : amateurish.

un•prof•it•a•ble (ŭn-prŏf′ĭ-tə-bəl) *adj.* **1.** Producing no profit. **2.** Serving no purpose.

un•qual•i•fied (ŭn-kwŏl′ə-fīd′) *adj.* **1.** Lacking the requisite qualifications. **2.** Unreserved : absolute.

un•ques•tion•a•ble (ŭn-kwĕs′chə-nə-bəl) *adj.* Not open to doubt or dispute : certain. **—un•ques′tion•a•bly** *adv.*

un•qui•et (ŭn-kwī′ĭt) *adj.* **1.** Anxious : distressed. **2.** Violently disturbed : turbulent.

un•quote (ŭn′kwōt′) *n.* Used by a speaker to indicate the end of a quotation.

un•rav•el (ŭn-răv′əl) *v.* **1. a.** To disentangle (threads). **b.** To undo the knitted or woven fabric of. **2.** To clarify : solve.

un•read (ŭn-rĕd′) *adj.* **1.** Not read or studied. **2.** Not educated : unlearned.

un•read•a•ble (ŭn-rē′də-bəl) *adj.* **1.** Not legible. **2. a.** Too dull to read. **b.** Too difficult to understand.

un•re•al (ŭn-rē′əl, -rēl′) *adj.* Not real or substantial : illusory. **—un′re•al′i•ty** *n.*

un•rea•son•a•ble (ŭn-rē′zə-nə-bəl) *adj.* **1.** Not governed by reason : irrational or absurd. **2.** Exceeding reasonable limits : immoderate. **—un•rea′son•a•ble•ness** *n.* **—un•rea′son•a•bly** *adv.*

un•re•gen•er•ate (ŭn′rĭ-jĕn′ər-ĭt) *adj.* **1.** Not morally or spiritually reformed or regenerated. **2.** Stubborn : obstinate.

un•re•lent•ing (ŭn′rĭ-lĕn′tĭng) *adj.* **1.** Relentless : unyielding. **2.** Not lessening in intensity or pace. **—un′re•lent′ing•ly** *adv.*

un•re•li•a•ble (ŭn′rĭ-lī′ə-bəl) *adj.* Not to be depended on or trusted. **—un′re•li′a•bil′i•ty** *n.* **—un′re•li′a•bly** *adv.*

un•re•mit•ting (ŭn′rĭ-mĭt′ĭng) *adj.* Never letting up : continuous. **—un′re•mit′ting•ly** *adv.*

un•re•served (ŭn′rĭ-zûrvd′) *adj.* **1.** Not set aside for a specific person or use. **2.** Wholehearted. **3.** Not reticent : frank and open. **—un′re•serv′ed•ly** *adv.*

un•rest (ŭn-rĕst′) *n.* A state of turmoil.

un•re•strained (ŭn′rĭ-strānd′) *adj.* **1.** Not checked or controlled. **2.** Not forced or affected : natural.

un•ripe (ŭn-rīp′) *adj.* Not ripe or mature.

un•ri•valed (ŭn-rī′vəld) *adj.* Unequaled.

un•roll (ŭn-rōl′) *v.* **1.** To unwind (something rolled). **2.** To reveal : disclose.

un•ruf•fled (ŭn-rŭf′əld) *adj.* Not agitated or upset : calm.

un•ru•ly (ŭn-ro͞o′lē) *adj.* **-li•er, -li•est.** Difficult to control or subdue.

un•sad•dle (ŭn-săd′l) *v.* **1.** To take the saddle off. **2.** To unhorse.

un•sat•u•rat•ed (ŭn-săch′ə-rā′tĭd) *adj.* **1.** Of or relating to a compound, esp. of carbon, containing atoms that share more than 1 valence bond <*unsaturated* fats> **2.** Capable of dissolving more of a solute at a given temperature.

un•sa•vor•y (ŭn-sā′və-rē) *adj.* **1.** Tasting unpleasant or insipid. **2.** Not to one's liking : disagreeable. **3.** Morally repellent. **—un•sa′vor•i•ly** *adv.* **—un•sa′vor•i•ness** *n.*

un•scathed (ŭn-skāthd′) *adj.* Not injured or harmed.

un•schooled (ŭn-sko͞old′) *adj.* Not instructed or trained.

un•sci•en•tif•ic (ŭn-sī′ən-tĭf′ĭk) *adj.* Not conforming to the principles or methods of science. **—un•sci′en•tif′i•cal•ly** *adv.*

un•scram•ble (ŭn-skrăm′bəl) *v.* **1.** To straighten out : disentangle. **2.** To restore (a scrambled message) to intelligible form.

un•screw (ŭn-skro͞o′) *v.* **1.** To loosen by or as if by turning. **2.** To take out the screws from.

un•scru•pu•lous (ŭn-skro͞o′pyə-ləs) *adj.* Lacking scruples or principles : unprincipled. **—un•scru′pu•lous•ly** *adv.* **—un•scru′pu•lous•ness** *n.*

un•seal (ŭn-sēl′) *v.* To break open or remove the seal from.

un•sea•son•a•ble (ŭn-sē′zə-nə-bəl) *adj.* **1.** Not suitable for or typical of the season. **2.** Badly timed. **—un•sea′son•a•bly** *adv.*

un•seat (ŭn-sēt′) *v.* **1.** To remove from a seat or throw from a saddle. **2.** To force out of office : depose.

un•seem•ly (ŭn-sēm′lē) *adj.* Improper : unbecoming <*unseemly* behavior>

un•sel•fish (ŭn-sĕl′fĭsh) *adj.* Willing to give or share : generous. **—un•sel′fish•ly** *adv.* **—un•sel′fish•ness** *n.*

un•set•tle (ŭn-sĕt′l) *v.* **1.** To make unstable : disrupt. **2.** To make upset : disturb.

un•set•tled (ŭn-sĕt′əld) *adj.* **1.** Marked by disorder and unrest. **2.** Not decided : unresolved. **3.** Not paid as an account. **4.** Not populated. **5.** Not fixed or established, as in situation or character.

un•shak•a•ble (ŭn-shā′kə-bəl) *adj.* Not wavering : steadfast.

un•sheathe (ŭn-shēth′) *v.* To take from or as if from a sheath.

un•sight•ly (ŭn-sīt′lē) *adj.* Not pleasant to look at : unattractive or repulsive. **—un•sight′li•ness** *n.*

un•skilled (ŭn-skĭld′) *adj.* **1.** Having no skills or training, esp. in a given kind of work. **2.** Requiring no special skill <*unskilled* labor> **3.** Showing no skill : crude.

un•skill•ful (ŭn-skĭl′fəl) *adj.* Lacking in skill or proficiency : inexpert. **—un•skill′ful•ly** *adv.* **—un•skill′ful•ness** *n.*

un•so•cia•ble (ŭn-sō′shə-bəl) *adj.* Not disposed to social activities. **—un•so′cia•bil′i•ty** *n.* **—un•so′cia•bly** *adv.*

un•so•phis•ti•cat•ed (ŭn′sə-fĭs′tĭ-kā′tĭd) *adj.* **1.** Inexperienced in the ways of the world : naive. **2.** Not complex : simple.

un•sound (ŭn-sound′) *adj.* **1.** Not solidly made or placed. **2.** Unhealthy in mind or body. **3.** Founded on fallacy : illogical. **—un•sound′ly** *adv.* **—un•sound′ness** *n.*

un•spar•ing (ŭn-spâr′ĭng) *adj.* **1.** Liberal : generous. **2.** Pitiless : severe. **—un•spar′ing•ly** *adv.* **—un•spar′ing•ness** *n.*

un•speak•a•ble (ŭn-spē′kə-bəl) *adj.* **1.** Incapable of being expressed or described. **2.** Indescribably bad. ☆***syns:*** ABOMINABLE, FRIGHTFUL, REVOLTING, SHOCKING, SICKENING **—un•speak′a•bly** *adv.*

un•spo•ken (ŭn-spō′kən) *adj.* Not expressed in words.

un•spot•ted (ŭn-spŏt′ĭd) *adj.* **1.** Not marked or covered with spots. **2.** Free from moral blemish : unsullied.

un•sta•ble (ŭn-stā′bəl) *adj.* **1.** Not firmly or steadily fixed, made, etc. **2.** Tending to change or fluctuate. **3. a.** Of inconstant temperament : capricious. **b.** Mentally unbalanced or emotionally maladjusted. **4.** Decomposing readily <an *unstable* chemical compound> **5.** *Physics.* **a.** Decaying with relatively short lifetime, as a subatomic particle. **b.** Radioactive, as an atomic nucleus. **—un•sta′bly** *adv.*

un•stead•y (ŭn-stĕd′ē) *adj.* **1.** Not firm or secure : unstable. **2.** Inconstant : variable. **3.** Not consistent : erratic. **—un•stead′i•ly** *adv.* **—un•stead′i•ness** *n.*

un•stick (ŭn-stĭk′) *v.* To free from a stuck position.

un•stop (ŭn-stŏp′) *v.* **1.** To withdraw a stopper from. **2.** To remove a blockage from : open.

un•stressed (ŭn-strĕst′) *adj.* **1.** Not stressed or accented. Used of a syllable. **2.** Not given emphasis.

un•struc•tured (ŭn-strŭk′chərd) *adj.* **1.** Lacking form or arrangement. **2.** Lacking formal regulation, discipline, etc.

un•strung (ŭn′strŭng′) *adj.* **1.** Having the strings loosened or disconnected. **2.** Feeling nervous tension : upset.

un•stud•ied (ŭn-stŭd′ēd) *adj.* **1.** Not forced or contrived : natural. **2.** Not gained by study.

un•sub•stan•tial (ŭn′səb-stăn′shəl) *adj.* **1.** Lacking substance or reality. **2.** Lacking firmness or strength : flimsy. **3.** Lacking a factual basis : not valid.

un•suit•a•ble (ŭn-so͞o′tə-bəl) *adj.* Not suitable. ☆***syns:*** IMPROPER, INAPPROPRIATE, MALAPROPOS, UNBECOMING, UNFIT, UNSEEM-

LY **—un•suit'a•bil'i•ty, un•suit'a•ble•ness** *n.* **—un•suit'a•bly** *adv.*

un•sung (ŭn-sŭng') *adj.* **1.** Not sung. **2.** Not praised or celebrated, as in poetry.

un•tan•gle (ŭn-tăng'gəl) *v.* **1.** To free from tangles. **2.** To clear up : settle.

un•taught (ŭn-tôt') *adj.* **1.** Not educated : unlettered. **2.** Not acquired by study.

un•thank•ful (ŭn-thăngk'fəl) *adj.* **1.** Not thankful : ungrateful. **2.** Not appreciated : thankless.

un•think•a•ble (ŭn-thĭng'kə-bəl) *adj.* Inconceivable : unimaginable.

un•think•ing (ŭn-thĭng'kĭng) *adj.* Marked by or resulting from lack of forethought. **—un•think'ing•ly** *adv.*

un•ti•dy (ŭn-tī'dē) *adj.* Not tidy : messy. **—un•ti'di•ly** *adv.* **—un•ti'di•ness** *n.*

un•tie (ŭn-tī') *v.* **1.** To loosen or unfasten (something tied). **2.** To free from a bond or restraint. **3.** To straighten out : resolve.

un•til (ŭn-tĭl') *prep.* **1.** Up to the time of <jogged *until* dark> **2.** Before a given time <can't go *until* summer> *—conj.* **1.** Up to the time that <swam *until* it was noon> **2.** Before <won't come *until* my car is fixed> **3.** To the point or extent that <I worked *until* I was exhausted.>

un•time•ly (ŭn-tīm'lē) *adj.* **1.** Inopportune. **2.** Premature. **—un•time'li•ness** *n.* **—un•time'ly** *adv.*

un•to (ŭn'tōō) *prep.* To.

un•told (ŭn-tōld') *adj.* **1.** Not related or revealed, as secrets. **2.** Incalculable.

un•touch•a•ble (ŭn-tŭch'ə-bəl) *adj.* **1.** Not permitted to be touched. **2.** Incapable of being reached or obtained. *—n. often* **Untouchable.** A member of the lowest Hindu social class, whose touch was considered unclean by Hindus of higher castes.

un•to•ward (ŭn-tôrd', -tōrd', ŭn'tə-wôrd') *adj.* **1.** Not propitious : unfavorable. **2.** Unruly or obstinate.

un•true (ŭn-trōō') *adj.* **1.** Contrary to the truth : false. **2.** Departing from a standard : inexact. **3.** Not faithful : disloyal.

un•truth (ŭn-trōōth') *n.* **1.** Something untrue : falsehood. **2.** The state of being false. **—un•truth'•ful** *adj.* **—un•truth'ful•ly** *adv.* **—un•truth'ful•ness** *n.*

un•tu•tored (ŭn-tōō'tərd, -tyōō'-) *adj.* **1.** Not formally educated. **2.** Not learned : inborn. **3.** Unsophisticated : naive.

un•twist (ŭn-twĭst') *v.* To loosen or separate the twisted strands or parts of.

un•used (ŭn-yōōzd', -yōōst') *adj.* **1.** Not put to use. **2.** Never before used. **3.** Unaccustomed <*unused* to rich food>

un•u•su•al (ŭn-yōō'zhōō-əl) *adj.* Not usual : uncommon or extraordinary. **—un•u'su•al•ly** *adv.* **—un•u'su•al•ness** *n.*

un•ut•ter•a•ble (ŭn-ŭt'ər-ə-bəl) *adj.* **1.** Not capable of being expressed or described : inexpressible. **2.** Not pronounceable. **—un•ut'ter•a•bly** *adv.*

un•var•nished (ŭn-vär'nĭsht) *adj.* **1.** Not coated with varnish. **2.** Not embellished or disguised : plain.

un•veil (ŭn-vāl') *v.* **1.** To take a veil or other covering from. **2.** To uncover : reveal. **3.** To take off one's veil.

un•voiced (ŭn-voist') *adj.* **1.** Not uttered or expressed : unsaid. **2.** Uttered without vibrating the vocal cords : voiceless.

un•war•rant•a•ble (ŭn-wôr'ən-tə-bəl, -wŏr'-) *adj.* Not justifiable or excusable. **—un•war'rant•a•bly** *adv.*

un•war•rant•ed (ŭn-wôr'ən-tĭd, -wŏr'-) *adj.* Incapable of being justified or substantiated : groundless.

un•war•y (ŭn-wâr'ē) *adj.* Not guarded or cautious : gullible. **—un•war'i•ly** *adv.* **—un•war'i•ness** *n.*

un•well (ŭn-wĕl') *adj.* Not well : sick.

un•whole•some (ŭn-hōl'səm) *adj.* **1.** Not conducive to health : unhealthy. **2.** Morally harmful or corrupt. **—un•whole'some•ly** *adv.* **—un•whole'some•ness** *n.*

un•wield•y (ŭn-wēl'dē) *adj.* Hard to manage because of shape or size : clumsy.

un•will•ing (ŭn-wĭl'ĭng) *adj.* **1.** Not willing : loath. **2.** Marked by reluctance <an *unwilling* promise> **—un•will'ing•ly** *adv.* **—un•will'ing•ness** *n.*

un•wind (ŭn-wīnd') *v.* **1.** To undo (something rolled or coiled). **2.** To become unrolled or untwisted. **3.** To become free of tension : relax.

un•wise (ŭn-wīz') *adj.* Lacking wisdom or good judgment. **—un•wise'ly** *adv.*

un•wit•ting (ŭn-wĭt'ĭng) *adj.* **1.** Not intended : inadvertent. **2.** Unknowing : unaware. **—un•wit'ting•ly** *adv.*

un•wont•ed (ŭn-wôn'tĭd, -wōn'-, -wŭn'-) *adj.* Not customary or usual.

un•world•ly (ŭn-wûrld'lē) *adj.* **1.** Not of this world : spiritual rather than secular. **2.** Concerned with spiritual or religious matters. **3.** Unsophisticated : naive. **—un•world'li•ness** *n.*

un•wor•thy (ŭn-wûr'thē) *adj.* **1.** Not deserving <*unworthy* of praise> **2.** Not befitting : unbecoming <a deed *unworthy* of them> **3.** Base : despicable. **—un•wor'thi•ly** *adv.* **—un•wor'thi•ness** *n.*

un•writ•ten (ŭn-rĭt'n) *adj.* **1.** Not written down. **2.** Effective through custom or tradition <an *unwritten* rule>

un•yoke (ŭn-yōk') *v.* **1.** To free from a yoke. **2.** To disjoin : disconnect.

up (ŭp) *adv.* **1.** From a lower level or position to a higher one. **2.** In, to, or toward a higher level or position. **3.** To or into an upright position. **4. a.** Above a surface, as of ground or water. **b.** Above the horizon <The moon came *up.*> **5.** So as to be considered <brought the subject *up* again> **6.** In or toward a place or position considered as higher, as on a map, chart, or scale. **7.** To or at a greater charge or fee. **8.** Into an improved, intensified, or advanced state. **9.** With or to a higher volume : louder. **10.** Into a highly active state <A storm came *up.*> **11.** So as to uproot <pulling *up* carrots> **12.** Into parts or pieces <cut *up* the meat> **13.** Used as an intensive <tidied *up*> **14.** Completely : entirely <drank it all *up*> *—adj.* **1.** Moving or aimed upward <an *up* escalator> **2.** Being out of bed. **3.** Comparatively high <Prices are *up.*> **4.** *Informal.* Taking place : happening <Tell me what's *up.*> **5.** Under consideration. **6.** At an end <Time's *up* for today.> **7.** *Informal.* Highly informed <not *up* on politics> **8.** Being in advance of an opponent <*up* 2 holes in a golf match> **9.** *Baseball.* Being next at bat. **10.** Standing trial <*up* for homicide> *—prep.* **1.** To, toward, or at a higher point of or on <climbed *up* the hill> **2.** Toward or at a more distant point <lives *up* the block> **3.** Toward the source or origin of <*up* the Seine> *—n.* **1.** An upward slope. **2.** An upward movement or trend <a sudden *up* in prices> **3.** *Slang.* Excitement or euphoria. *—v.* **upped, up•ping. 1.** To cause to be greater <*upped* our chances of winning> **2.** To move or cause to move upward. **3.** *Informal.* To act abruptly <just *upped* and left home> **—on the up and up.** Open and aboveboard. **—up to. 1.** Involved in <What are you *up to*?> **2.** *Informal.* Ready or prepared for <not *up to* seeing people> **3.** The responsibility of <The choice is *up to* you.>

up-and-com•ing (ŭp'ən-kŭm'ĭng) *adj.* Having potential : promising.

U•pan•i•shad (ōō-păn'ĭ-shăd') *n.* One of a collection of philosophical discourses contributing to ancient Hindu theology.

up•beat (ŭp'bēt') *n. Mus.* An unaccented and esp. the final beat of a measure. *—adj. Informal.* Happy : optimistic.

up•braid (ŭp-brād') *v.* To reproach or criticize harshly. **—up•braid'er** *n.*

up•bring•ing (ŭp'brĭng'ĭng) *n.* The process of rearing and training a child.

up•com•ing (ŭp'kŭm'ĭng) *adj.* About to appear or take place.

up•coun•try (ŭp'kŭn'trē) *n.* The interior of a country. *—adj.* (ŭp'kŭn'trē). Of, relating to, located in, or coming from the upcountry. **—up•coun'try** *adv.*

up•date (ŭp-dāt') *v.* **1.** To bring up to date <*update* a news story> **2.** To modernize. **—up'date'** *n.*

up•draft (ŭp'drăft') *n.* A current of air flowing upward.

up•end (ŭp-ĕnd') *v.* **1.** To set on end. **2.** To overturn or defeat.

up-front (ŭp'frŭnt') *adj.* **1.** Straightforward : frank <an *up-front* discussion of grievances> **2.** Required in advance <*up-front* cash>

up•grade (ŭp'grād') *v.* To increase the rank, grade, or standard of. *—n.* An upward slope.

up•heav•al (ŭp-hē'vəl) *n.* **1.** The process or an instance of being lifted forcefully upward. **2.** An abrupt and violent change or tumult <a political *upheaval*> **3.** *Geol.* An uplifting of the earth's crust.

up•hill (ŭp'hĭl') *adj.* **1.** Going up an incline or hill. **2.** Prolonged and laborious : difficult. *—n.* An upward slope. *—adv.* (ŭp'hĭl'). **1.** Upward on an incline. **2.** Against adversity.

up•hold (ŭp-hōld') *v.* **1.** To raise or hold aloft. **2.** To keep from falling. **3.** To defend or affirm despite opposition <*upheld* our beliefs> **—up•hold'er** *n.*

up•hol•ster (ŭp-hōl'stər) *v.* To provide (furniture) with padding, cushions, a fabric covering, etc. **—up•hol'ster•er** *n.*

up•hol•ster•y (ŭp-hōl'stər-ē, -hōl'strē) *n., pl.* **-ies. 1.** An upholsterer's materials. **2.** The business or craft of upholstering.

up•keep (ŭp'kēp') *n.* **1.** Maintenance in proper operation and repair. **2.** The cost of maintenance.

up•land (ŭp'lənd, -lănd') *n.* The elevated areas of a country, region, or tract of land. **—up'land** *adj.* **—up'land•er** *n.*

up•lift (ŭp-lĭft') *v.* **1.** To lift or raise up. **2.** To elate. **3.** To elevate socially, morally, or intellectually. *—n.* (ŭp'lĭft'). **1.** A lifting up, esp. a geologic upheaval. **2.** A movement supporting social, moral, or intellectual improvement.

up•most (ŭp'mōst') *adj.* Uppermost.

up•on (ə-pŏn', ə-pôn') *prep.* On.

up•per (ŭp'ər) *adj.* **1.** Higher in location, position, or status. **2.**

Upper. Being a later division of a specific archaeological or geologic period. *—n.* **1.** The part of footwear above the sole. **2.** *Slang.* A drug used as a stimulant.

upper case *n.* The case of printing type containing the capital letters. **—up′per-case′** *adj.*

up•per-class (ŭp′ər-klăs′) *adj.* Of, belonging to, or typical of the upper and usu. highest social class.

up•per•class•man (ŭp′ər-klăs′mən) *n.* A junior or senior in a secondary school or college.

upper crust *n. Informal.* The pre-eminent social class or group.

up•per•cut (ŭp′ər-kŭt′) *n.* A short swinging blow aimed upward, as at an opponent's chin in boxing.

upper hand *n.* A controlling position : advantage.

up•per•most (ŭp′ər-mōst′) *adj.* Highest or foremost in position, place, rank, or influence. **—up′per•most′** *adv.*

Upper Vol•ta (vŏl′tə). Country of W Africa. *Cap.* Ouagadougou. *Pop.* 6,390,000.

up•pi•ty (ŭp′ĭ-tē) *adj. Informal.* Arrogant or snobbish.

up•raise (ŭp-rāz′) *v.* To uplift.

up•right (ŭp′rīt′) *adj.* **1.** In a vertical position or direction. **2.** Adhering to moral principles : honorable. *—n.* Something standing upright, as a building beam. **—up′right′** *adv.* **—up′right′ly** *adv.* **—up′right′ness** *n.*

upright piano *n.* A piano whose strings are mounted in a vertical direction.

up•ris•ing (ŭp′rī′zĭng) *n.* A revolt.

up•roar (ŭp′rôr′, -rōr′) *n.* A state of violent commotion : tumult. ☆*syns:* BROUHAHA, SENSATION, STIR, TO-DO

up•roar•i•ous (ŭp-rôr′ē-əs, -rōr′-) *adj.* **1.** Characterized by uproar. **2.** Boisterous <*uproarious* laughter> **3.** Hilarious <*uproarious* comedy> **—up•roar′i•ous•ly** *adv.* **—up•roar′i•ous•ness** *n.*

up•root (ŭp-ro͞ot′, -ro͝ot′) *v.* To unearth or detach completely by or as if by pulling up the roots. **—up•root′er** *n.*

up•set (ŭp-sĕt′) *v.* **-set, -set•ting. 1.** To overturn or cause to tip over. **2.** To throw into disorder or confusion : unsettle. **3.** To distress mentally, emotionally, or physically. **4.** To win a victory over, esp. unexpectedly. *—n.* (ŭp′sĕt′). **1.** An act of upsetting or the state of being upset. **2.** A disturbance of usual functioning, order, etc. **3.** A game or contest in which the favorite is unexpectedly defeated. *—adj.* (ŭp-sĕt′). **1.** Overturned : tipped over. **2.** Disordered : unsettled. **3.** Distressed : troubled. **—up•set′ter** *n.*

up•shot (ŭp′shŏt′) *n.* Outcome : result.

up•side-down *also* **upside down** (ŭp′sīd-doun′) *adv.* **1.** With the upper part or side on the bottom. **2.** In or into utter disorder or confusion. **—up′side-down′** *adj.*

up•stage (ŭp′stāj′) *adj. & adv.* At or toward the back part of a stage. *—v.* (ŭp-stāj′). **1.** To distract audience attention from (another actor), as by remaining upstage. **2.** *Informal.* To steal the show from or get the better of. **3.** *Informal.* To treat condescendingly.

up•stairs (up′stârz′) *adv.* **1.** To or on an upper floor. **2.** To or at a higher level or position. *—adj.* (ŭp′stârz′). Of, pertaining to, or situated on the upper floors. *—n. (sing. in number).* The upper section of a house or other building.

up•stand•ing (ŭp-stăn′dĭng, ŭp′stăn′-) *adj.* **1.** Erect. **2.** Morally upright.

up•start (ŭp′stärt′) *n.* One made self-important by new wealth or power.

up•state (ŭp′stāt′) *adv.* At, toward, or to the part of a state located inland or esp. N of a large city. **—up′state′** *adj. & n.*

up•stream (ŭp′strēm′) *adv.* **1.** At, toward, or to the source of a stream. **2.** Against the current. **—up′stream′** *adj.*

up•stroke (ŭp′strōk′) *n.* An upward stroke, as of a brush or pen.

up•surge (ŭp′sûrj′) *n.* An abrupt or rapid rise. **—up•surge′** *v.*

up•swept (ŭp′swĕpt′) *adj.* Swept upward <an *upswept* hairdo>

up•swing (ŭp′swĭng′) *n.* An upward swing or trend, esp. a noticeable increase.

up•take (ŭp′tāk′) *n.* **1.** A flue for the upward passage of smoke or air. **2.** *Informal.* Understanding : comprehension <slow on the *uptake*> **3.** An act or instance of absorbing esp. into living tissue.

up•tight *also* **up tight** (ŭp′tīt′) *adj. Slang.* **1.** Tense or nervous. **2.** Angry : outraged. **3.** Rigidly conventional.

up-to-date (ŭp′tə-dāt′) *adj.* **1.** Most recent : current <an *up-to-date* directory> **2.** In step with the times : modern. **—up′to-date′ness** *n.*

up•town (ŭp′toun′) *adv.* To, toward, or in the upper section of a city. *—n.* The section of a city located uptown. **—up′town′** *adj.*

up•turn (ŭp′tûrn′) *n.* An upward trend, as in business or prices. *—v.* (*also* ŭptûrn′). **1.** To dig up and turn over, as soil. **2.** To turn or direct upward.

up•ward (ŭp′wərd) *also* **up•wards** (-wərdz) *adv.* From a lower place, level, or position to or toward a higher one. *—adj.* **upward.** Directed toward a higher place or position. **—upwards (or upward) of.** More than <interviewed *upwards of* 50 candidates> **—up′ward•ly** *adv.*

up•wind (ŭp′wĭnd′) *adv. & adj.* In or toward the direction from which the wind is blowing.

u•ra•cil (yo͝or′ə-sĭl) *n.* A nitrogenous pyrimidine base that is a constituent of RNA.

u•rae•us (yo͞o-rē′əs) *n.* A figure of the sacred serpent depicted on the headdress of ancient Egyptian rulers and deities as an emblem of sovereignty.

U•ral (yo͝or′əl) *also* **U•rals** (-əlz). Mountain range of the U.S.S.R. forming the traditional boundary between Europe and Asia, extending c. 1,500 mi (2,400 km) S from the Arctic Ocean.

u•ra•ni•um (yo͞o-rā′nē-əm) *n. Symbol* **U** A heavy silvery-white radioactive metallic element used esp. in research and in nuclear fuels and weapons.

U•ra•nus (yo͝or′ə-nəs, yo͞o-rā′nəs) *n.* The 7th planet of the solar system in order of distance from the sun.

ur•ban (ûr′bən) *adj.* **1.** Of, pertaining to, or constituting a city. **2.** Typical of the city or city life.

ur•bane (ûr-bān′) *adj.* Polished and elegant in manner or style : suave. **—ur′bane′ly** *adv.* **—ur•ban′i•ty** (-băn′ĭ-tē) *n.*

▲word history: *Urban* and *urbane* are both derived from Latin *urbanus,* "belonging to a city," and they were once synonymous in meaning. *Urbane* was borrowed 1st, from Old French *urbain,* and it preserved the French pattern of stress. After *urban* was borrowed directly from Latin *urbanus, urbane* developed the more specialized sense of "refined, polite, elegant." These desirable qualities were considered to be characteristic of urban rather than country folk.

ur•ban•ite (ûr′bə-nīt′) *n.* One who lives in a city.

ur•ban•ize (ûr′bə-nīz′) *v.* **-ized, -iz•ing.** To impart an urban character to.

ur•chin (ûr′chĭn) *n.* A mischievous child.

u•re•a (yo͞o-rē′ə) *n.* A white chemical compound found in body fluids and esp. the urine of mammals.

u•re•mi•a (yo͞o-rē′mē-ə) *n.* A toxic condition resulting from abnormal accumulation of urea in the blood. **—u•re′mic** *adj.*

u•re•ter (yo͞o-rē′tər, yo͝or′ĭ-tər) *n.* Either of the ducts that carry urine from the kidneys to the bladder.

u•re•thra (yo͞o-rē′thrə) *n., pl.* **-thras** *or* **-thrae** (-thrē). The canal through which urine is discharged and that in the male also serves as the seminal duct. **—u•re′thral** *adj.*

urge (ûrj) *v.* **urged, urg•ing. 1.** To push or drive forcefully onward : impel. **2.** To plead with esp. insistently. **3.** To recommend strongly and persistently. ☆*syns:* EXHORT, PRESS, PROD, PROMPT. *—n.* An impelling force, influence, or impulse.

ur•gent (ûr′jənt) *adj.* **1.** Demanding immediate attention. **2.** Urging persistently. **—ur′gen•cy** *n.* **—ur′gent•ly** *adv.*

u•ric (yo͝or′ĭk) *adj.* Of, pertaining to, or present in urine.

uric acid *n.* A white crystalline compound, the end product of purine metabolism in humans and other primates, birds, terrestrial reptiles, and most insects.

u•ri•nal (yo͝or′ə-nəl) *n.* **1.** An upright wall fixture used by males for urinating. **2.** A receptacle for urine used esp. by bedridden persons.

u•ri•nal•y•sis (yo͝or′ə-năl′ĭ-sĭs) *n.* Laboratory analysis of urine.

u•ri•nar•y (yo͝or′ə-nĕr′ē) *adj.* **1.** Pertaining to, taking place in, or constituting organs for the production and excretion of urine. **2.** Of or pertaining to urine.

urinary bladder *n.* A muscular membranous sac in the forward part of the pelvic cavity for the temporary storage of urine before excretion.

u•ri•nate (yo͝or′ə-nāt′) *v.* **-nat•ed, -nat•ing.** To empty the bladder of urine.

u•rine (yo͝or′ĭn) *n.* A yellowish fluid secreted by the kidneys and containing dissolved bodily wastes.

urn (ûrn) *n.* **1.** A vaselike container used esp. to hold the ashes after cremation. **2.** A closed container with a spout, used for serving coffee or tea.

u•ro•gen•i•tal (yo͝or′ō-jĕn′ĭ-tl) *adj.* Of or pertaining to both the urinary and genital organs or their functions.

u•rol•o•gy (yo͞o-rŏl′ə-jē) *n.* The branch of medicine concerned with the urinary or urogenital tract. **—u•rol′o•gist** *n.*

Ur•sa Major (ûr′sə) *n.* A constellation of 7 stars that form the Big Dipper.

Ursa Minor *n.* A constellation of 7 stars that form the Little Dipper, with the star Polaris at the tip of the handle.

ur•sine (ûr′sīn′) *adj.* Of, pertaining to, or typical of a bear.

U•ru•guay (yo͝or′ə-gwī′, -gwā′). Country of South America, in the SE on the Atlantic. *Cap.* Montevideo. *Pop.* 2,763,964. **—U′ru•guay′an** *adj.* & *n.*

us (ŭs) *pron. The objective case of* WE. Used: **1.** As the direct object of a verb <The schedule exhausted *us.*> **2.** As the indirect object of a verb <They rented *us* the cottage.> **3.** As the object of a preposition <mailed a letter off to *us*>

U.S. or **US** *abbr.* United States.

U.S.A. or **USA** *abbr.* **1.** United States Army. **2.** United States of America.

us•a•ble *also* **use•a•ble** (yo͞o′zə-bəl) *adj.* **1.** Capable of being used. **2.** Fit for use. **—us′a•bil′i•ty** *n.* **—us′a•bly** *adv.*

us•age (yo͞o′sĭj, -zĭj) *n.* **1.** The act or way of using something. **2.** A customary or habitual way of doing something. **3.** The way in which language or its elements are used. **4.** A particular expression in speech or writing <a nonstandard *usage*>

use (yo͞oz) *v.* **used, us•ing. 1.** To put into action or service : employ for some purpose. **2.** To employ regularly <*uses* public transportation> **3.** To behave toward : treat. **4.** *Informal.* To exploit for one's advantage. **5.** To partake of as a habit <*uses* tobacco> **6.** Used in the past tense with *to* to denote earlier practice, fact, or state <They *used* to be rich.> **—use up.** To consume or exhaust totally. *—n.* (yo͞os). **1.** The act of using something. **2.** The state or fact of being used. **3.** The way of using : usage. **4. a.** The permission, privilege, or benefit of using something. **b.** The ability to use something, as an arm, leg, etc. **5.** Necessity or reason to use <had no more *use* for the car> **6.** The quality of being useful for some purpose : usefulness. **7.** The purpose for which something is used : function. **8.** Accustomed practice. **9.** *Law.* **a.** The enjoyment of property, as by occupying or utilizing it. **b.** The profit or benefit of property held in trust. **—used to.** Accustomed or habituated to <can't get *used to* the noise> **—us′er** *n.*

used (yo͞ozd) *adj.* Previously owned : secondhand <new and *used* appliances>

use•ful (yo͞os′fəl) *adj.* Of particular use or advantage : serviceable. **—use′ful•ly** *adv.* **—use′ful•ness** *n.*

use•less (yo͞os′lĭs) *adj.* **1.** Having little purpose or worth. **2.** Of no avail : futile <It's *useless* to worry.> **—use′less•ly** *adv.* **—use′less•ness** *n.*

ush•er (ŭsh′ər) *n.* **1.** One who conducts people to their seats, as in a theater or church. **2.** An official who goes before persons of rank in a procession. *—v.* **1.** To conduct : escort. **2.** To precede as an usher or forerunner. **3.** To begin or introduce <a party to *usher* in the new year>

U.S.S.R. or **USSR** *abbr.* Union of Soviet Socialist Republics.

u•su•al (yo͞o′zho͞o-əl) *adj.* **1.** Common : ordinary. **2.** Customary : regular. **—u′su•al•ly** *adv.* **—u′su•al•ness** *n.*

u•su•fruct (yo͞o′zə-frŭkt′, sə-) *n. Law.* The right to utilize and enjoy the profits and advantages of something, as property, belonging to another.

u•su•rer (yo͞o′zhər-ər) *n.* One who lends money at an excessive interest rate.

u•su•ri•ous (yo͞o-zho͝or′ē-əs) *adj.* Relating to, practicing, or being usury. **—u•su′ri•ous•ly** *adv.* **—u•su′ri•ous•ness** *n.*

u•surp (yo͞o-sûrp′, -zûrp′) *v.* To seize and hold illegally and by force. **—u′sur•pa′tion** *n.* **—u•surp′er** *n.*

u•su•ry (yo͞o′zhə-rē) *n., pl.* **-ries. 1.** The act or practice of lending money at excessive interest rates. **2.** An exorbitant or illegal rate of interest.

UT *abbr.* Utah (with Zip Code).

U•tah (yo͞o′tô′, -tä′). State of W U.S. *Cap.* Salt Lake City. *Pop.* 1,461,037. **—U′tah•an** *adj.* & *n.*

u•ten•sil (yo͞o-tĕn′səl) *n.* **1.** An implement or container for household and esp. kitchen use. **2.** A useful implement or tool.

u•ter•us (yo͞o′tər-əs) *n.* A hollow, muscular organ of female mammals, in which young develop and usu. are nourished prior to birth. **—u′ter•ine** (-ĭn, -tə-rīn′) *adj.*

u•tile (yo͞o′tl, yo͞o′tīl′) *adj.* Useful.

u•til•i•tar•i•an (yo͞o-tĭl′ĭ-târ′ē-ən) *adj.* **1.** Of, relating to, or based on utility. **2.** Stressing useful rather than aesthetic qualities. **3.** Adhering to or supporting utilitarianism. *—n.* A supporter of utilitarianism.

u•til•i•tar•i•an•ism (yo͞o-tĭl′ĭ-târ′ē-ə-nĭz′əm) *n.* The philosophical doctrine that action should be based on the usefulness of its effects and that only the useful is good or worthwhile.

u•til•i•ty (yo͞o-tĭl′ĭ-tē) *n., pl.* **-ties. 1.** The quality or state of being useful : usefulness. **2.** Something designed for practical use. **3.** A company that offers a governmentally regulated public service. **4.** A public service, as electricity, heat, or water, provided by a utility company.

u•til•ize (yo͞ot′l-īz′) *v.* **-ized, -iz•ing.** To put to use : make profitable use of. **—u′til•iz′a•ble** *adj.* **—u′til•i•za′tion** *n.*

ut•most (ŭt′mōst′) *adj.* **1.** Most distant : extreme. **2.** Of the greatest amount or degree. **—ut′most′** *n.*

u•to•pi•a (yo͞o-tō′pē-ə) *n.* **1.** *often* **Utopia.** A place in which there is sociopolitical perfection. **2.** An impractically idealistic goal or scheme, esp. for a perfect society. **—u•to′pi•an** *adj.* & *n.*

ut•ter¹ (ŭt′ər) *v.* **1.** To express verbally : speak. **2.** To produce as sound <*utter* a cry> **3.** To begin the circulation of (counterfeit money or a forgery). **—ut′ter•a•ble** *adj.* **—ut′ter•er** *n.*

ut•ter² (ŭt′ər) *adj.* Completely such, without qualification or exception. ☆***syns:*** ALL-OUT, ARRANT, COMPLETE, CONSUMMATE, FLAT, OUT-AND-OUT, OUTRIGHT, POSITIVE, PURE, SHEER, THOROUGH, TOTAL, UNMITIGATED, UNQUALIFIED

ut•ter•ance (ŭt′ər-əns) *n.* **1. a.** The act of uttering. **b.** The power or way of speaking. **2.** Something uttered.

ut•ter•ly (ŭt′ər-lē) *adv.* Completely.

ut•ter•most (ŭt′ər-mōst′) *adj.* Most distant or extreme : utmost. **—ut′ter•most** *n.*

U-turn (yo͞o′tûrn′) *n.* A turn in which the direction of travel is reversed <The driver made an illegal *U-turn.*>

u•vu•la (yo͞o′vyə-lə) *n.* The fleshy cone-shaped projection hanging above the back of the tongue. **—u′vu•lar** *adj.*

ux•o•ri•ous (ŭk-sôr′ē-əs, -sōr′-, ŭg-zôr′-, -zōr′-) *adj.* Unduly fond of or submissive to one's wife. **—ux•o′ri•ous•ly** *adv.* **—ux•o′ri•ous•ness** *n.*

Vv

v or **V** (vē) *n.,pl.* **v's** or **V's. 1.** The 22nd letter of the English alphabet. **2.** A speech sound represented by the letter *v.* **3.** Something with the shape of the letter V. **4.** The Roman numeral for 5.

v or **V** *abbr. Elect.* volt.

V *symbol for* VANADIUM.

V *abbr.* **1.** *Physics.* velocity. **2.** volume.

v. *abbr.* **1.** verb. **2.** verse. **3.** version. **4.** verso. **5.** versus. **6.** vide. **7.** volume (book). **8.** vowel.

VA *abbr.* Virginia (with Zip Code).

Va. *abbr.* Virginia.

va•can•cy (vā′kən-sē) *n., pl.* **-cies. 1.** The state of being unoccupied or vacant. **2.** An empty space. **3.** An unfilled or unoccupied office, position, or accommodation.

va•cant (vā′kənt) *adj.* **1.** Holding nothing : empty. **2.** Without an occupant or incumbent. **3.a.** Lacking intelligence. **b.** Expressionless : blank. **4.** Not filled with activity.

va•cate (vā′kāt′) *v.* **-cat•ed, -cat•ing. 1.** To cease to occupy : make vacant. **2.** *Law.* To make void.

va•ca•tion (vā-kā′shən) *n.* A period of time for pleasure, rest, or relaxation, esp. one with pay granted to an employee. *—v.* To take or spend a vacation.

va•ca•tion•land (vā-kā′shən-lănd′) *n.* A place with special attractions and facilities for vacationers.

vac•ci•nate (văk′sə-nāt′) *v.* **-nat•ed, -nat•ing.** To inoculate with a vaccine so as to produce immunity to an infectious disease, as smallpox.

vac•ci•na•tion (văk′sə-nā′shən) *n.* **1.** Inoculation with a vaccine. **2.** A scar on the skin caused by vaccinating.

vac•cine (văk-sēn′) *n.* A liquid suspension of weakened or killed microorganisms, as of bacteria or viruses, injected into a person or animal as protection against disease.

vac•il•late (văs′ə-lāt′) *v.* **-lat•ed, -lat•ing. 1.** To sway from side to side : oscillate. **2.** To show indecision : waver. **—vac′il•la′tion** *n.* **—vac′il•la′tor** *n.*

va•cu•i•ty (vă-kyo͞o′ĭ-tē) *n., pl.* **-ties. 1.** Complete absence of matter : emptiness. **2.** An empty space. **3.** Total lack of ideas. **4.** Something, esp. a remark, that is vacuous.

vac•u•ole (văk′yo͞o-ōl′) *n.* A small cavity in cell protoplasm.

vac•u•ous (văk′yo͞o-əs) *adj.* **1.** Empty : blank. **2. a.** Lacking intelligence : stupid. **b.** Pointless : inane. **—vac′u•ous•ly** *adv.*

vac•u•um (văk′yo͞o-əm, -yo͞om) *n., pl.* **-ums** *or* **-u•a** (-yo͞o-ə). **1.** A space empty of matter. **2.** A state of emptiness : void. *—v.* To clean with a vacuum cleaner.
vacuum bottle *n.* A flask or bottle with a vacuum between its inner and outer walls, designed to keep the contents, as a liquid, hot or cold.
vacuum cleaner *n.* An electrical appliance that cleans surfaces by suction.
vac•u•um-packed (văk′yo͞o-əm-păkt′, -yo͞om-, -yəm-) *adj.* Packed in a container that has had most of the air removed before being sealed.
vacuum tube *n.* An electron tube having an internal vacuum high enough to permit electrons to move with low interaction with any remaining gas molecules.
va•de me•cum (vä′dē mē′kəm) *n., pl.* **vade me•cums.** Something useful, as a manual, that one carries about constantly.
Va•duz (vä′do͞ots). Cap. of Liechtenstein, on the upper Rhine. *Pop.* 4,704.
vag•a•bond (văg′ə-bŏnd′) *n.* **1.** A homeless person who moves from place to place. **2.** A tramp. **—vag′a•bond′** *adj.*
va•gar•y (vā′gə-rē, və-gâr′ē) *n., pl.* **-ies.** A capricious or eccentric idea or action. **—va•gar′i•ous** *adj.*
va•gi•na (və-jī′nə) *n., pl.* **-nas** *or* **-nae** (-nē). *Anat.* The passage leading from the uterus to the vulva in female mammals. **—vag′i•nal** (văj′ə-nəl) *adj.*
vag•i•ni•tis (văj′ə-nī′tĭs) *n.* Inflammation of the vagina.
va•grant (vā′grənt) *n.* **1.** One who roams from place to place without a permanent home or job. **2.** One, as a drunkard, who lives on the streets and is considered a public nuisance. *—adj.* **1.** Roaming from place to place without a job. **2.** Moving in a random way. **—va′gran•cy** *n.*
vague (vāg) *adj.* **vagu•er, vagu•est. 1.** Not clearly outlined or expressed. **2.** Having an indefinite shape or form. **3.** Indistinctly perceived. ☆**syns:** CLOUDY, FOGGY, FUZZY, HAZY, INDEFINITE, INDISTINCT, MISTY, UNCLEAR **—vague′ly** *adv.*
vain (vān) *adj.* **1.** Not yielding the desired outcome : fruitless. **2.** Lacking substance or worth. **3.** Unduly proud of one's appearance or achievement. **—in vain. 1.** Fruitlessly. **2.** Irreverently <took the Lord's name *in vain*> **—vain′ly** *adv.*
vain•glo•ry (vān′glôr′ē, -glōr′ē) *n., pl.* **-ries. 1.** Boastful and unwarranted pride. **2.** Vain, pretentious display.
val•ance (văl′əns) *n.* **1.** A short ornamental curtain hanging from an edge, as of a bed. **2.** A decorative frame or drapery across the top of a window.
vale (vāl) *n.* A valley.
val•e•dic•tion (văl′ĭ-dĭk′shən) *n.* An act or expression of leave-taking.
val•e•dic•to•ri•an (văl′ĭ-dĭk-tôr′ē-ən, -tōr′) *n.* A student, usu. the one ranking highest in a graduating class, who delivers the valedictory at a commencement.
val•e•dic•to•ry (văl′ĭ-dĭk′tə-rē) *adj.* Of or constituting a farewell. *—n., pl.* **-ries.** A farewell speech, esp. one delivered by a valedictorian at a commencement exercise.
va•lence (vā′ləns) *also* **va•len•cy** (-lən-sē) *n., pl.* **-lenc•es** *also* **-len•cies** *n.* **1.** *Chem.* The capability of an atom or group of atoms to combine in particular proportions with other atoms or groups of atoms. **2.** A whole number used to represent this capability.
val•en•tine (văl′ən-tīn′) *n.* **1.** A person chosen as one's sweetheart on Valentine's Day. **2.** A usu. sentimental greeting card sent to one's valentine.
Valentine's Day or **Valentines Day** *n.* Feb. 14, when valentines are traditionally exchanged.
val•et (văl′ĭt, vă-lā′) *n.* **1.** A man's personal male attendant. **2.** A hotel employee who performs personal services for guests.
val•e•tu•di•nar•i•an (văl′ĭ-to͞od′n-âr′ē-ən, -tyo͞od′-) *n.* A weak or sickly person, esp. one constantly concerned with health matters. **—val′e•tu′di•nar′i•an•ism** *n.*
val•iant (văl′yənt) *adj.* Having or exhibiting valor. **—val′iance** *n.*
val•id (văl′ĭd) *adj.* **1.** Founded on truth or fact. **2.** Having legal force. **—va•lid′i•ty** (və-lĭd′ĭ-tē), **val′id•ness** *n.*
val•i•date (văl′ĭ-dāt′) *v.* **-dat•ed, -dat•ing. 1.** To declare or make legally valid. **2.** To verify : substantiate. **—val′i•da′tion** *n.*
va•lise (və-lēs′) *n.* A small suitcase.
Val•i•um (văl′ē-əm). A trademark for the tranquiler diazepam.
Val•let•ta (və-lĕt′ə). Cap. of Malta, in the NE. *Pop.* 14,042.
val•ley (văl′ē) *n., pl.* **-leys. 1.** An elongated lowland between mountain ranges or hills, often having a river running along the bottom. **2.** A channel formed by the joining of 2 roof slopes.
val•or (văl′ər) *n.* Bravery : courage. **—val′or•ous** *adj.*
val•our (văl′ər) *n. esp. Brit. var. of* VALOR.
val•u•a•ble (văl′yo͞o-ə-bəl, văl′yə-) *adj.* **1.** Of high monetary value. **2.** Of great importance or use. ☆**syns:** INVALUABLE, PRECIOUS, PRICELESS *—n. often* **valuables.** A personal possession of high monetary value.
val•u•ate (văl′yo͞o-āt′) *v.* **-at•ed, -at•ing.** To set a value on. **—val′u•a′tor** *n.*
val•u•a•tion (văl′yo͞o-ā′shən) *n.* **1.** An act or the process of assessing price or value. **2.** Assessed value or price.
val•ue (văl′yo͞o) *n.* **1.** An amount regarded as a fair equivalent for something, esp. goods or services. **2.** Material worth. **3.** Worth in importance or usefulness to the possessor. **4.** A standard or principle regarded as desirable or worthwhile. **5.** Precise meaning, as of a term. **6.** *Math.* A calculated or assigned numerical quantity. **7.** *Mus.* The relative length of a rest or tone. *—v.* **-ued, -u•ing. 1.** To determine or estimate the worth or value of. **2.** To regard highly. **3.** To rate according to usefulness, importance, or worth. **—val′ue•less** *adj.*
val•ue-ad•ded tax (văl′yo͞o-ăd′ĭd) *n.* A tax on the estimated market value of a product added at each stage of its manufacture and ult. passed on to the consumer.
valve (vălv) *n.* **1.** *Anat.* A membranous structure in a hollow organ or passage, as a vein or artery, that slows or prevents the backward movement of a fluid. **2. a.** A mechanical device that regulates the flow of gases, liquids, or loose materials by blocking and uncovering openings. **b.** The movable part of such a device. **c.** A device in a brass wind instrument used to vary the length of the column of air and thus control the pitch. **3.** *Biol.* Either of the paired hinged shells of many mollusks. **—valved** *adj.* **—val′vu•lar** (văl′vyə-lər) *adj.*
va•moose (vă-mo͞os′, və-) *v.* **-moosed, -moos•ing.** *Slang.* To leave hurriedly.
vamp[1] (vămp) *n.* **1.** The part of a shoe or boot that covers the instep and sometimes extends over the toes. **2.** An improvised musical accompaniment. *—v.* **1.** To provide (a shoe or boot) with a new vamp. **2.** To patch up (something old). **3.** *Mus.* To improvise.
vamp[2] (vămp) *n. Informal.* A woman who exploits or seduces men. **—vamp** *v.*
vam•pire (văm′pīr′) *n.* **1.** A reanimated corpse held to suck the blood of sleeping persons at night. **2.** One who preys on others. **3.** A tropical American bat erroneously thought to feed on the blood of living mammals. **—vam′pir•ism** *n.*
van[1] (văn) *n.* **1.** A large closed truck or wagon. **2.** *esp. Brit.* A closed railroad car for carrying freight or baggage.
van[2] (văn) *n.* The vanguard : forefront.
va•na•di•um (və-nā′dē-əm) *n. Symbol* **V** A white ductile metallic element.
Van Al•len belt (văn ăl′ən) *n.* Either of 2 zones surrounding the planet at various high altitudes in which atomic particles of high energies are trapped in the earth's magnetic field.
Van Bu•ren (văn byo͝or′ən), **Martin.** 1782–1862. 8th U.S. President (1837–41).
Van•cou•ver (văn-ko͞o′vər). City of SW B.C., Canada, on the Strait of Georgia opposite **Vancouver Is.** *Pop.* 410,188.
Van•dal (văn′dl) *n.* **1.** A member of a Germanic people that overran Gaul, Spain, and N Africa and sacked Rome in A.D. 455. **2. vandal.** One who maliciously destroys or defaces property. **—van′dal•ize′** *v.*
van•dal•ism (văn′dl-ĭz′əm) *n.* The malicious destruction or defacement of public or private property.
Van•dyke (văn-dīk′) *n.* A short, pointed beard.

Vandyke

vane (vān) *n.* **1.** A device that pivots on an elevated object, as a rooftop or spire, to indicate wind direction. **2.** One of a number of thin, rigid blades radially mounted along an axis that is used to turn or is turned by a fluid. **3.** One of the stabilizing fins attached to the tail of a missile.
van Gogh (văn gō′, gôKH′), **Vincent.** 1853–90. Dutch painter.
van•guard (văn′gärd′) *n.* **1.** An army or fleet's foremost position. **2.** The leading position in a movement or trend.
va•nil•la (və-nĭl′ə) *n.* **1.** A tropical American orchid of the genus *Vanilla,* esp. *V. planifolia,* cultivated for its long, narrow,

aromatic seedpods. **2.** A flavoring extract prepared from the seedpod of the vanilla.
van•ish (văn'ĭsh) *v.* **1.** To disappear, esp. quickly or in an unexplained way. **2.** To pass out of existence. **—van'ish•er** *n.*
van•i•ty (văn'ĭ-tē) *n., pl.* **-ties. 1.** Excessive pride : conceit. **2.** Lack of usefulness : worthlessness. **3.** Something vain or futile. **4.** A vanity case. **5.** A dressing table.
vanity case *n.* **1.** A woman's compact. **2.** A small case for toiletries or cosmetics.
vanity plate *n.* A usu. more expensive license plate for a motor vehicle having a combination of numbers or letters chosen by the vehicle's owner.
vanity press *n.* A publisher that publishes a book at the author's expense.
van•quish (văng'kwĭsh, văn'-) *v.* **1.** To defeat in battle. **2.** To overcome : suppress.
van•tage (văn'tĭj) *n.* **1.** Superiority in a conflict or competition. **2.** A strategic position providing superiority.
Va•nu•a•tu (vä'no͞o-ä'to͞o). Island country of the S Pacific. *Cap.* Vila. *Pop.* 112,596.
vap•id (văp'ĭd) *adj.* Lacking liveliness or interest. **—va•pid'i•ty** (vă-pĭd'ĭ-tē, və-), **vap'id•ness** *n.* **—vap'id•ly** *adv.*
va•por (vā'pər) *n.* **1.** A faintly visible suspension of fine particles of matter in the air, as mist or fog. **2.** The gaseous state of a substance that under normal circumstances is liquid or solid. **3. vapors.** *Archaic.* Hysteria. **—va'por•ish** *adj.*
va•por•ize (vā'pə-rīz') *v.* **-ized, -iz•ing.** To convert or be converted into vapor. **—va'por•i•za'tion** *n.* **—va'por•iz'er** *n.*
va•por•ous (vā'pər-əs) *adj.* **1.** Relating to or like vapor. **2. a.** Producing vapors. **b.** Giving off or full of vapors. **3.** Insubstantial or vague. **—va'por•ous•ly** *adv.*
vapor trail *n.* A contrail.
va•pour (vā'pər) *n.* & *v. esp. Brit. var. of* VAPOR.
†va•que•ro (vä-kâr'ō) *n., pl.* **-ros.** *SW U.S.* A cowboy.
var. *abbr.* variable.
var•i•a (vâr'ē-ə, văr'-) *n.* A miscellany, esp. of literary works.
var•i•a•ble (vâr'ē-ə-bəl) *adj.* **1.** Tending or apt to vary. **2.** Fickle : inconstant. *—n.* **1.** Something that varies. **2.** *Math.* **a.** A quantity that may assume any of a set of values. **b.** A symbol representing such a quantity. **—var'i•a•bil'i•ty, var'i•a•ble•ness** *n.* **—var'i•a•bly** *adv.*
variable field *n. Computer Sci.* A set of adjacent columns on a punchcard that can be varied in length.
variable logic *n. Computer Sci.* An internal machine logic that can be changed to match programming formats.
var•i•ance (vâr'ē-əns) *n.* **1. a.** Difference. **b.** A degree of variation. **2.** A difference of opinion. **3.** *Law.* A license to engage in an act contrary to a usual rule.
var•i•ant (vâr'ē-ənt) *adj.* **1.** Having or showing variation. **2.** Tending or apt to vary : variable. *—n.* Something that differs in form only slightly from something else <a spelling *variant*>
var•i•a•tion (vâr'ē-ā'shən) *n.* **1.** The process or result of varying. **2.** Extent or degree of varying. **3.** Something slightly different from another of the same type. **4.** *Mus.* An altered version of a given theme, with modifications in melody, key, or rhythm.
var•i•col•ored (vâr'ĭ-kŭl'ərd) *adj.* VARIEGATED 1.
var•i•cose (văr'ĭ-kōs') *adj.* Abnormally swollen and knotted <*varicose* veins>
var•ied (vâr'ēd) *adj.* **1.** Characterized by variety. **2.** Altered : modified.
var•i•e•gat•ed (vâr'ē-ĭ-gā'tĭd, vâr'ĭ-gā'-, văr'-) *adj.* **1.** Having streaks or marks of different colors. **2.** Marked by variety.
va•ri•e•ty (və-rī'ĭ-tē) *n., pl.* **-ties. 1.** The state or quality of being varied or various. **2.** A number of varied things, esp. of a particular group. **3.** A group set off from other groups by specific characteristics. **4.** A living thing, esp. a plant, belonging to a subdivision of a species.
var•i•ous (vâr'ē-əs) *adj.* **1. a.** Of diverse kinds. **b.** Different. **2.** Several. **3.** Versatile. **4.** Individual and separate. **—var'i•ous•ly** *adv.* **—var'i•ous•ness** *n.*
var•let (vär'lĭt) *n. Archaic.* **1.** A servant. **2.** A rascal : knave.
var•mint (vär'mĭnt) *n. Informal.* **1.** A dangerous or troublesome animal. **2.** A despised or obnoxious person.
var•nish (vär'nĭsh) *n.* **1.** An oil-based paint for coating a surface with a hard, transparent, shiny film. **2.** The smooth coating or gloss produced by applying varnish. **3.** A deceptively attractive outward appearance. **—var'nish** *v.*
var•si•ty (vär'sĭ-tē) *n., pl.* **-ties.** The best team representing a school or club.
var•y (vâr'ē) *v.* **-ied, -y•ing. 1.** To undergo or cause change : alter. **2.** To make different. **3.** To diverge : deviate.
vas•cu•lar (văs'kyə-lər) *adj. Biol.* Of, having, or forming vessels for the circulation of fluids, as blood or sap.
vas def•er•ens (văs' dĕf'ər-ənz, -ə-rĕnz') *n.* The duct in male vertebrate animals through which sperm passes from a testis to the ejaculatory duct.
vase (vās, vāz, väz) *n.* An open container for holding cut flowers.
va•sec•to•my (vă-sĕk'tə-mē) *n., pl.* **-mies.** A method of sterilization involving the surgical excision of a part of the vas deferens.
Vas•e•line (văs'ə-lēn'). A trademark for a petrolatum.
vas•o•con•stric•tion (văs'ō-kən-strĭk'shən) *n.* Constriction of a blood vessel. **—vas'o•con•stric'tor** *n.*
vas•o•dil•a•ta•tion (văs'ō-dĭl'ə-tā'shən, -dī'lə-) *n.* Dilatation of a blood vessel. **—vas'o•di•la'tor** (-dī-lā'tər, -dĭ-) *n.*
vas•sal (văs'əl) *n.* **1.** One who was granted land from a feudal lord in return for homage and military service. **2.** One who is subordinate or subservient to another. **—vas'sal•age** *n.*
vast (văst) *adj.* Very great in size or extent. **—vast'ly** *adv.* **—vast'ness** *n.*
vat (văt) *n.* A large tub or cask for storing or holding liquids.
vat•ic (văt'ĭk) *adj.* Prophetic : oracular.
Vat•i•can (văt'ĭ-kən) *n.* **1.** The official papal residence. **2.** The papal government.
Vatican City. Independent papal state within Rome, Italy. *Pop.* 723.
vaude•ville (vôd'vĭl', vōd'-, vô'də-) *n.* A stage show consisting of a number of short acts, as slapstick comedy, songs, and dances. **—vaude•vil'lian** *n.*
vault[1] (vôlt) *n.* **1. a.** An arched roof or ceiling. **b.** Something resembling a vault, as the sky. **2.** An underground room having arched walls and ceiling, as a storeroom. **3.** A room, as in a bank, for the safekeeping of valuables. **4.** A burial chamber. *—v.* To construct or supply with a vault.

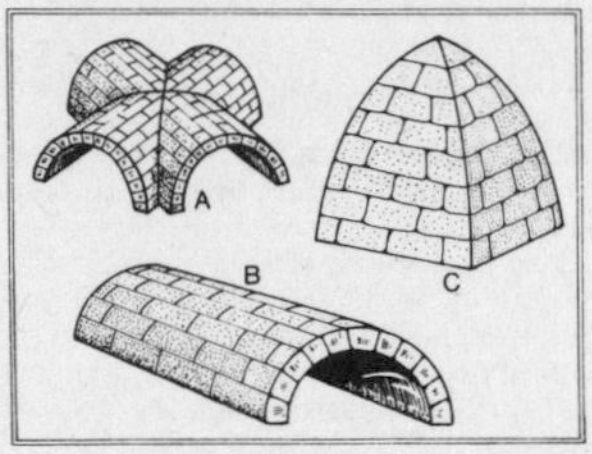

vault[1]
Three types of vaults: A. cross, B. barrel, C. cloister

vault[2] (vôlt) *v.* To leap or jump (over), esp. by holding a long pole or with the hands supported on the barrier. **—vault** *n.*
vaunt (vônt, vŏnt) *v.* To boast. **—vaunt** *n.* **—vaunt'ing•ly** *adv.*
vb. *abbr.* verb; verbal.
VCR *abbr.* videocassette recorder.
-'ve. Have <I've been invited.>
veal (vēl) *n.* The meat of a calf.
vec•tor (vĕk'tər) *n.* **1.** *Math.* A quantity that has magnitude and a direction. **2.** An organism that transmits disease-carrying germs. **—vec•to'ri•al** *adj.*
veep (vēp) *n. Slang.* A vice president.
veer (vîr) *v.* To shift from 1 course or direction to another. **—veer** *n.*
veg•an (vĕj'ən, -ăn') *n.* A strict vegetarian who uses no products derived from animals, as soap or leather. **—veg'an•ism** *n.*
veg•e•ta•ble (vĕj'tə-bəl, vĕj'ĭ-tə-) *n.* **1.** A plant, as the beet or spinach, raised for an edible part, as the root or leaves. **2.** One who leads a boring or passive life. **—veg'e•ta•ble** *adj.*
vegetable kingdom *n.* The category of living organisms that includes all plants.
veg•e•tar•i•an (vĕj'ĭ-târ'ē-ən) *n.* A person whose diet includes mainly plants and plant products and who eats no meat. *—adj.* **1.** Consuming only plants and plant products. **2.** Consisting only of plants and plant products. **—veg'e•tar'i•an•ism** *n.*
veg•e•tate (vĕj'ĭ-tāt') *v.* **-tat•ed, -tat•ing. 1.** To sprout or grow as a plant does. **2.** To lead a life characterized by little physical energy or mental effort.
veg•e•ta•tion (vĕj'ĭ-tā'shən) *n.* **1.** The act or process of vegetating. **2.** Plants or plant life in general.
veg•e•ta•tive (vĕj'ĭ-tā'tĭv) *adj.* **1.** Of, relating to, or typical of plants or plant growth. **2.** *Biol.* **a.** Of or capable of growth. **b.** Of or relating to growth or physical change rather than sexual processes.
ve•he•ment (vē'ə-mənt) *adj.* **1.** Marked by vigorous or forceful expression or intense emotion. **2.** Characterized by or full of vigor. **—ve'he•mence** *n.*
ve•hi•cle (vē'ĭ-kəl) *n.* **1.** A device, as a piece of mechanized equipment, for transporting goods, passengers, or equipment. **2.**

A medium, as a painting or novel, through which something is expressed or accomplished. **3.** A substance, as oil, in which paint pigments are mixed for application. **—ve·hic'u·lar** (vē-hĭk'yə-lər) *adj.*

veil (vāl) *n.* **1.** A piece of usu. fine, transparent cloth worn by women over the head, shoulders, and often part of the face. **2. a.** The part of a nun's headdress that frames the face and falls over the shoulders. **b.** The life or vows of a nun <took the *veil*> **3.** Something that conceals or screens. *—v.* To cover or conceal with or as if with a veil.

vein (vān) *n.* **1.** *Anat.* A vessel that transports blood toward the heart. **2.** One of the narrow branching tubes forming the framework of an insect's wing or a leaf. **3.** *Geol.* A deposit of an ore in the earth. **4.** A wavy streak of color, as in marble. **5.** A pervading quality or character. **6.** A manner or mode. *—v.* To fill or mark with veins.

Vel·cro (vĕl'krō'). A trademark for a fastening tape used esp. for clothing.

veldt (fĕlt, vĕlt) *n. So. Afr.* An open grazing area.

vel·lum (vĕl'əm) *n.* A fine parchment prepared from the skins of calf, lamb, or kid and used for writing on and for binding fine books.

ve·loc·i·ty (və-lŏs'ĭ-tē) *n., pl.* **-ties. 1.** Rapidity : speed. **2.** *Physics.* A vector quantity whose magnitude is a body's speed and whose direction is the body's direction of motion.

ve·loc·i·pede (və-lŏs'ə-pēd') *n.* **1.** An early bicycle propelled by pushing the feet along the ground. **2.** A tricycle.

velocipede

ve·lour *or* **ve·lours** (və-lo͝or') *n., pl.* **-lours** (-lo͝or'). A velvetlike fabric with a short thick nap.

ve·lum (vē'ləm) *n., pl.* **-la** (-lə). The soft back part of the palate. **—ve'lar** *adj.*

vel·vet (vĕl'vĭt) *n.* **1.** A fabric made usu. of silk or a synthetic fiber and having a smooth, dense pile. **2.** Something resembling velvet. **3.** The soft skin covering the growing antlers of a deer. **—vel'vet·y** *adj.*

vel·vet·een (vĕl'vĭ-tēn') *n.* A velvetlike cotton fabric.

ve·na ca·va (vē'nə kā'və) *n., pl.* **ve·nae ca·vae** (vē'nē kā'vē). Either of the 2 large veins that return blood to the right atrium of the heart in vertebrates that breathe air.

ve·nal (vē'nəl) *adj.* Open or susceptible to bribery. **—ve·nal'i·ty** (vē-năl'ĭ-tē) *n.*

vend (vĕnd) *v.* To sell.

vend·ee (vĕn-dē') *n.* A buyer.

vend·er *also* **ven·dor** (vĕn'dər) *n.* **1.** One that sells. **2.** A vending machine.

ven·det·ta (vĕn-dĕt'ə) *n.* A feud between families, esp. one involving revenge killings.

vending machine *n.* A coin-operated machine for dispensing merchandise.

ve·neer (və-nîr') *n.* **1.** A thin surface layer of a better material covering an inferior one. **2.** Superficial outward show. *—v.* To cover with a veneer.

ven·er·a·ble (vĕn'ər-ə-bəl) *adj.* **1.** Worthy of respect by reason of age, dignity, or position. **2.** Deserving respect for historic or religious associations. **—ven'er·a·bil'i·ty** *n.*

ven·er·ate (vĕn'ə-rāt') *v.* **-at·ed, -at·ing.** To regard with respect or deference. **—ven'er·a'tion** *n.*

venereal disease *n.* A contagious disease, as gonorrhea or syphilis, transmitted by sexual contact.

ve·ne·re·ol·o·gy (və-nîr'ē-ŏl'ə-jē) *n.* The study of venereal diseases. **—ve·ne're·ol'o·gist** *n.*

Ve·ne·tian blind (və-nē'shən) *n.* A blind with thin horizontal slats that can be set at a desired angle to control the amount of light that comes in between them.

Ven·e·zue·la (vĕn'ə-zwā'lə, -zwē'-). Country of N South America, on the Caribbean. *Cap.* Caracas. *Pop.* 11,300,000. **—Ven'e·zue'lan** *adj.* & *n.*

venge·ance (vĕn'jəns) *n.* The act of causing harm to another in retribution for a wrong or injury.

venge·ful (vĕnj'fəl) *adj.* Desiring vengeance. **—venge'ful·ness** *n.*

ve·ni·al (vē'nē-əl, vēn'yəl) *adj.* Easily forgiven or excused.

Ven·ice (vĕn'ĭs). City of NE Italy. *Pop.* 355,865. **—Ve·ne'tian** *adj.* & *n.*

ve·ni·re (və-nī'rē) *n.* A writ summoning persons to appear in court as jurors. **—ve·ni're·man** *n.*

ven·i·son (vĕn'ĭ-sən, -zən) *n.* The edible flesh of a deer.

ven·om (vĕn'əm) *n.* **1.** A poisonous secretion of an animal, as a snake or scorpion, usu. transmitted by a sting or bite. **2.** Malice : spite. **—ven'om·ous** *adj.*

ve·nous (vē'nəs) *adj.* **1.** Of or relating to veins. **2.** *Physiol.* Returning to the heart through a vein, esp. 1 of the larger veins.

vent[1] (vĕnt) *n.* **1.** A way of leaving a restricted space. **2.** An opening for the passage or escape of a liquid, gas, or vapor. *—v.* **1.** To give forceful expression to. **2.** To discharge through a vent. **3.** To provide with a vent.

vent[2] (vĕnt) *n.* A vertical slit in a garment, as a jacket or skirt.

ven·ti·late (vĕn'tl-āt') *v.* **-lat·ed, -lat·ing. 1.** To cause fresh air to circulate in. **2.** To provide with a vent. **3.** To expose to public examination or discussion. **—ven'ti·la'tion** *n.* **—ven'ti·la'tor** *n.*

ven·tral (vĕn'trəl) *adj.* **1.** Of, relating to, or near the belly. **2.** Of or relating to the lower surface of the body of an animal.

ven·tri·cle (vĕn'trĭ-kəl) *n.* A cavity in an anatomical organ, esp. either of the chambers of the heart that contract to pump blood into arteries. **—ven·tric'u·lar** (vĕn-trĭk'yə-lər) *adj.*

ven·tril·o·quism (vĕn-trĭl'ə-kwĭz'əm) *also* **ven·tril·o·quy** (-kwē) *n.* A means of producing vocal sounds so that they seem to come from a source other than the speaker, as from a mechanical or hand-operated dummy. **—ven·tril'o·quist** *n.*

ven·ture (vĕn'chər) *n.* **1.** A course of action involving risk or danger. **2.** Something at hazard in a venture. *—v.* **-tured, -tur·ing. 1.** To expose to risk or danger. **2.** To brave the dangers of. **3.** To dare to express <*ventured* an opinion> **—ven'tur·er** *n.* **—ven'ture·some, ven'tur·ous** *adj.*

ven·ue (vĕn'yo͞o) *n.* **1.** The locality where a crime or other cause of legal action occurs. **2.** The place where a gathering or public event, as a concert, is held.

Ve·nus (vē'nəs) *n.* The 2nd planet from the sun. **—Ve·nu'sian** (vĭ-no͞o'zhən, -nyo͞o'-) *adj.*

Ve·nus's-fly·trap (vē'nə-sĭz-flī'trăp') *n.* A plant, *Dionaea muscipula,* of boggy areas of the SE U.S., with hinged, spined leaf blades that close to entrap insects.

ve·ra·cious (və-rā'shəs) *adj.* **1.** Truthful : honest. **2.** True : accurate. **—ve·ra'cious·ly** *adv.* **—ve·ra'cious·ness** *n.*

ve·rac·i·ty (və-răs'ĭ-tē) *n., pl.* **-ties. 1.** Devotion to the truth. **2.** Accuracy.

ve·ran·dah or **ve·ran·da** (və-răn'də) *n.* A usu. roofed and often partly enclosed porch or balcony extending along the outside of a building.

verb (vûrb) *n.* **1.** The part of speech that expresses action, existence, or occurrence in most languages. **2.** Any of the words within this part of speech, as *be, walk,* or *think.*

ver·bal (vûr'bəl) *adj.* **1.** Of or relating to words. **2.** Having to do with words rather than with the ideas they represent. **3.** Expressed in speech. **4.** Word for word : literal. **5.** Relating to or derived from a verb. *—n.* A noun, adjective, or other word derived from a verb and retaining some of the verb's characteristics. **—ver'bal·ly** *adv.*

ver·bal·ize (vûr'bə-līz') *v.* **-ized, -iz·ing. 1.** To express in words. **2.** To convert into a verb. **—ver'bal·i·za'tion** *n.*

ver·ba·tim (vər-bā'tĭm) *adv.* & *adj.* Using precisely the same words : word for word.

ver·be·na (vər-bē'nə) *n.* A New World plant of the genus *Verbena,* with variously colored flower clusters.

ver·bi·age (vûr'bē-ĭj) *n.* **1.** More words than are needed : wordiness. **2.** The way in which one expresses oneself : wording.

ver·bose (vər-bōs') *adj.* Using or having more words than required. **—ver·bos'i·ty** (-bŏs'ĭ-tē) *n.*

ver·bo·ten (vər-bōt'n) *adj.* Forbidden.

ver·dant (vûr'dnt) *adj.* **1.** Covered with growing plants. **2.** Green in color. **—ver'dan·cy** *n.* **—ver'dant·ly** *adv.*

Ver·di (vâr'dē), **Giuseppe.** 1813–1901. Italian composer.

ver·dict (vûr'dĭkt) *n.* **1.** The decision arrived at by a jury at the end of a trial. **2.** A judgment.

ver·di·gris (vûr'dĭ-grēs', -grĭs) *n.* A green coating or crust of copper salts that forms on copper, brass, and bronze exposed to sea water or air for a long time.

ver·dure (vûr'jər) *n.* **1.** The green color of healthy growing plants. **2.** Vegetation.

verge[1] (vûrj) *n.* **1.** An edge or rim : brink. **2.** The point beyond which an action or condition is likely to start or happen. **3.** A staff or rod carried as a symbol of authority. *—v.* **verged, verg·ing.** To border on.

verge[2] (vûrj) *v.* **verged, verg•ing. 1.** To tend or incline. **2.** To be in transition.
ver•i•fy (vĕr′ə-fī′) *v.* **-fied, -fy•ing. 1.** To prove the truth of by presenting evidence or testimony. **2.** To test the accuracy of. **–ver′i•fi′a•ble** *adj.* **–ver′i•fi•ca′tion** *n.* **–ver′i•fi′er** *n.*
ver•i•ly (vĕr′ə-lē) *adv.* **1.** In fact : certainly. **2.** Assuredly : truly.
ver•i•si•mil•i•tude (vĕr′ĭ-sə-mĭl′ĭ-to͞od′, -tyo͞od′) *n.* **1.** The quality or state of appearing to be true : likelihood. **2.** Something appearing to be real or true.
ver•i•ta•ble (vĕr′ĭ-tə-bəl) *adj.* True : unquestionable. **–ver′i•ta•bly** *adv.*
ver•i•ty (vĕr′ĭ-tē) *n., pl.* **-ties. 1.** The quality or state of being real or true. **2.** A statement or principle regarded as established and permanent truth.
ver•mi•cel•li (vûr′mə-chĕl′ē, -sĕl′ē) *n.* Pasta in long strings thinner than spaghetti.
ver•mi•cide (vûr′mĭ-sīd′) *n.* An agent for killing worms. **–ver′mi•cid′al** *adj.*
ver•mi•form (vûr′mə-fôrm′) *adj.* Wormlike in shape.
vermiform appendix *n.* A slender, closed tube attached to the large intestine.
ver•mi•fuge (vûr′mə-fyo͞oj′) *n.* An agent that destroys or expels intestinal worms.
ver•mil•ion *also* **ver•mil•lion** (vər-mĭl′yən) *n.* A bright red.
ver•min (vûr′mĭn) *n., pl.* **vermin.** An insect or animal that is destructive, annoying, or harmful to health, as a cockroach or rat. **–ver′min•ous** *adj.*
Ver•mont (vər-mŏnt′). State of the NE U.S. *Cap.* Montpelier. *Pop.* 511,446.
ver•mouth (vər-mo͞oth′) *n.* A sweet red or dry white wine flavored with herbs.
ver•nac•u•lar (vər-năk′yə-lər) *n.* **1.** The normal spoken language of a country or region. **2.** The idiom of a specific profession or trade. **–ver•nac′u•lar** *adj.*
ver•nal (vûr′nəl) *adj.* Of, relating to, or happening in the spring. **–ver′nal•ly** *adv.*
ver•ni•er (vûr′nē-ər) *n.* A small auxiliary scale attached parallel to a main scale to indicate fractional parts of the smallest divisions of the larger scale.
vernier caliper *n.* A measuring instrument with an L-shaped frame with a linear scale along its longer arm and a L-shaped sliding attachment with a vernier scale.

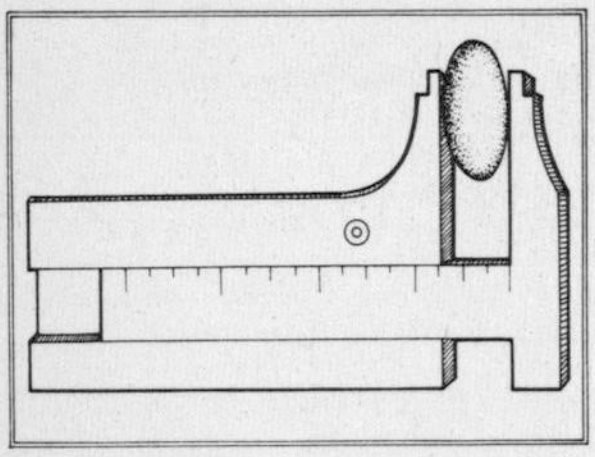

vernier caliper

Ve•ro•na (və-rō′nə). City of NE Italy. *Pop.* 269,763. **–Ver′o•nese′** *adj.* & *n.*
ve•ron•i•ca (və-rŏn′ĭ-kə) *n.* Any of various plants of the genus *Veronica,* including the speedwell.
ver•sa•tile (vûr′sə-təl, -tīl′) *adj.* **1.** Capable of doing many things. **2.** Having many functions or uses. **–ver′sa•til′i•ty** *n.*
verse[1] (vûrs) *n.* **1.** Writing that has meter or rhyme : poetry. **2. a.** A line of poetry. **b.** A stanza. **3.** A particular type of metrical composition, as blank verse. **4.** A subdivision of a chapter of the Bible.
verse[2] (vûrs) *v.* **versed, vers•ing.** To make familiar or skilled <*verse* oneself in economics>
ver•si•cle (vûr′sĭ-kəl) *n.* A short sentence chanted by a priest and followed by a congregational response.
ver•si•fy (vûr′sə-fī′) *v.* **-fied, -fy•ing. 1.** To put into verse form. **2.** To write verses. **–ver′si•fi•ca′tion** *n.* **–ver′si•fi′er** *n.*
ver•sion (vûr′zhən, -shən) *n.* **1.** A description or account told from a particular point of view. **2.** A translation of a written work, esp. the Bible. **3.** A particular form or variation. **4.** An adaptation of a work of literature or art into another medium.
ver•so (vûr′sō) *n., pl.* **-sos.** The left-hand page of a book.
ver•sus (vûr′səs) *prep.* **1.** Against <the Yankees *versus* the Orioles> **2.** In contrast with <compromise *versus* defeat>
ver•te•bra (vûr′tə-brə) *n., pl.* **-brae** (-brē) *or* **-bras.** Any of the bones or cartilaginous segments making up the spinal column. **–ver′te•bral** *adj.*
ver•te•brate (vûr′tə-brāt′, -brĭt) *adj.* **1.** Having a backbone. **2.** Of or typical of vertebrates. *–n.* A member of the subphylum Vertebrata that includes the fishes, amphibians, reptiles, birds, and mammals, all of which have a backbone.
ver•tex (vûr′tĕks′) *n., pl.* **-es** *or* **-ti•ces** (-tĭ-sēz′). **1.** The apex. **2. a.** The point at which the sides of an angle intersect. **b.** The point of a triangle opposite and farthest away from its base. **c.** A point on a polyhedron common to 3 or more sides.
ver•ti•cal (vûr′tĭ-kəl) *adj.* **1.** Being at right angles to the horizon. **2.** Directly overhead. ☆***syns:*** PERPENDICULAR, PLUMB, UPRIGHT *–n.* **1.** A vertical line or plane. **2.** A vertical position. **–ver′ti•cal′i•ty** (-kăl′ĭ-tē), **ver′ti•cal•ness** *n.*
ver•tig•i•nous (vər-tĭj′ə-nəs) *adj.* **1.** Turning about an axis. **2.** Affected by or likely to cause vertigo. **–ver•tig′i•nous•ly** *adv.*
ver•ti•go (vûr′tĭ-gō′) *n., pl.* **-goes** *or* **-gos.** The sensation of dizziness.
ver•vain (vûr′vān′) *n.* A plant of the genus *Verbena,* with spikes of small blue or white flowers.
verve (vûrv) *n.* **1.** Energy and vigor, esp. in artistic performance or composition. **2.** Liveliness : vitality.
ver•y (vĕr′ē) *adv.* **1.** To a high degree : extremely. **2.** Absolutely : truly <the *very* best we can buy> **3.** Exactly <the *very* same person> *–adj.* **-i•er, -i•est. 1.** Complete : absolute. **2.** Identical <the *very* complaints of yesterday> **3.** Used as an intensive to emphasize the importance of the thing mentioned <The *very* earth trembled.> **4.** Particularly suitable <the *very* thing for a cold> **5.** Mere <awed by the *very* mention of the name> **6.** Actual <caught in the *very* act>
very high frequency *n.* A band of radio frequencies ranging between 30 and 300 megahertz.
very low frequency *n.* A band of radio frequencies between 3 and 30 kilohertz.
ves•i•cant (vĕs′ĭ-kənt) *n.* A blistering agent, as mustard gas, used in chemical warfare. **–ves′i•cant** *adj.*
ves•i•cle (vĕs′ĭ-kəl) *n.* **1.** A small bladderlike cavity or cell. **2.** *Pathol.* A serum-filled blister. **–ve•sic′u•lar** (və-sĭk′yə-lər) *adj.*
ves•per (vĕs′pər) *n.* **1.** A bell for summoning people to vespers. **2. Vesper.** The evening star.
ves•pers *also* **Ves•pers** (vĕs′pərz) *pl.n.* A service of worship in the late afternoon or evening.
Ves•puc•ci (vĕs-po͞o′chē, -pyo͞o′-), **Amerigo.** 1451–1512. Italian navigator.
ves•sel (vĕs′əl) *n.* **1. a.** A hollow utensil used as a container, esp. for liquids. **b.** One regarded as an agent of some quality <a *vessel* of innocence> **2.** A craft, esp. one bigger than a rowboat, intended for navigation on water. **3.** *Anat.* A duct or other tube for circulating a bodily fluid.
vest (vĕst) *n.* **1.** A sleeveless and collarless garment, either open or fastening in front, worn over a shirt and often under a suit coat or jacket. **2.** *esp. Brit.* An undershirt. *–v.* **1.** To clothe or dress with or as if with ecclesiastical vestments. **2.** To place in the possession of. **3.** To place (e.g., authority) in the hands of.
ves•tal (vĕs′təl) *adj.* Chaste : virginal. *–n.* A woman who is a virgin.
vested interest *n.* **1.** A strong commitment to something, as an institution, from which one receives political or economic benefit. **2.** A group with a vested interest.
ves•ti•bule (vĕs′tə-byo͞ol′) *n.* **1.** A small entrance hall or passage. **2.** *Anat.* A cavity, chamber, or channel that serves as an approach or entrance to another cavity. **–ves•tib′u•lar** *adj.*
ves•tige (vĕs′tĭj) *n.* A visible sign of something that no longer exists.
ves•tig•i•al (vĕ-stĭj′ē-əl, -stĭj′əl) *adj.* **1.** Of, pertaining to, or being a vestige. **2.** *Biol.* Existing or persisting as a degenerate bodily structure. **–ves•tig′i•al•ly** *adv.*
vest•ment (vĕst′mənt) *n.* **1.** A garment, esp. a ceremonial or official robe. **2.** Any of the ritual robes worn by members of the clergy or assistants at religious services.
vest-pock•et (vĕst′pŏk′ĭt) *adj.* Relatively small : diminutive.
ves•try (vĕs′trē) *n., pl.* **-tries. 1.** A room in a church where the clergy don their vestments : sacristy. **2.** A church meeting room. **3.** A committee administering the affairs of an Episcopal parish.
ves•try•man (vĕs′trē-mən) *n.* A vestry member.
ves•ture (vĕs′chər) *n.* **1.** Clothing. **2.** Something that covers.
Ve•su•vi•us (və-so͞o′vē-əs). Active volcano, 4,190 ft (1,278 m), in W Italy.
vet (vĕt) *n. Informal.* **1.** A veterinarian. **2.** A veteran.
vetch (vĕch) *n.* A climbing plant of the genus *Vicia,* bearing pinnate leaves and small, usu. purplish flowers.
vet•er•an (vĕt′ər-ən, vĕt′rən) *n.* **1.** One with a long record of service in a particular activity or capacity. **2.** One who has served in the armed forces.
Veterans Day *n.* Nov. 11, a U.S. holiday commemorating the armistice ending World War I in 1918 and honoring veterans of the armed services.

vet·er·i·nar·i·an (vĕt′ər-ə-nâr′ē-ən, vĕt′rə-) *n.* One trained and qualified to give medical treatment to animals.
vet·er·i·nar·y (vĕt′ər-ə-nĕr′ē, vĕt′rə-) *adj.* Of, pertaining to, or being the science of the diagnosis and treatment of animals. —*n., pl.* **-ies.** A veterinarian.
ve·to (vē′tō) *n., pl.* **-toes. 1. a.** The right or power of a branch of government or of a governmental office to reject a bill passed by a legislature and thus delay or prevent its enactment. **b.** The exercise of this right. **2.** An authoritative rejection of a proposed act. —*v.* **-toed, -to·ing. 1.** To prevent enactment of (a legislative bill) by exercising the power of veto. **2.** To forbid.
vex (vĕks) *v.* **1.** To annoy or bother. **2.** To baffle. **3.** To discuss at length.
vex·a·tion (vĕk-sā′shən) *n.* **1.** An act of vexing or the state of being vexed. **2.** A source of annoyance. **—vex·a′tious** *adj.* **—vex·a′tious·ly** *adv.*
V format *n. Computer Sci.* A method of presenting output in which each record starts with an indication of its length.
vhf or **VHF** *abbr.* very high frequency.
vi·a (vī′ə, vē′ə) *prep.* By way of.
vi·a·ble (vī′ə-bəl) *adj.* **1.** Capable of living, as a newborn infant or a fetus arriving at a stage of development that will allow it to live. **2.** Capable of living or developing under favorable conditions. **3.** Capable of being successful or continuing to be effective. **—vi′a·bil′i·ty** *n.* **—vi′a·bly** *adv.*
vi·a·duct (vī′ə-dŭkt′) *n.* A bridge consisting of a series of arches for carrying a road or railroad over a wide valley or over other roads or railroads.

viaduct

vi·al (vī′əl) *n.* A small container, used esp. for liquids.
vi·and (vī′ənd) *n.* **1.** An item of food. **2. viands.** Provisions.
vibes (vībz) *pl.n.* **1.** *Informal.* A vibraphone. **2.** *Slang.* VIBRATIONS 4.
vi·brant (vī′brənt) *adj.* **1.** Displaying, marked by, or caused by vibration. **2.** Full of energy : vigorous. **—vi′brance, vi′bran·cy** *n.* **—vi′brant·ly** *adv.*
vi·bra·phone (vī′brə-fōn′) *n.* A percussion instrument resembling the marimba but with rotating disks and metal bars in the resonators to cause a vibrato. **—vi′bra·phon′ist** *n.*
vi·brate (vī′brāt′) *v.* **-brat·ed, -brat·ing. 1.** To move or cause to move back and forth rapidly. **2.** To produce a sound. **3.** To respond emotionally. **4.** To waver in making choices. **—vi′bra′tor** *n.* **—vi′bra·to′ry** (-brə-tôr′ē, -tōr′ē) *adj.*
vi·bra·tion (vī-brā′shən) *n.* **1.** The act of vibrating or state of being vibrated. **2.** *Physics.* Quick motion of a particle or of an elastic solid back and forth in a straight line on both sides of a center position. **3.** A single vibrating motion : quiver. **4. vibrations.** *Slang.* An emotional aura that can be instinctively sensed. **—vi·bra′tion·al** *adj.*
vi·bra·to (vĭ-brä′tō, vē-) *n., pl.* **-tos.** *Mus.* A tremulous or pulsating effect created in a vocal or instrumental tone by barely perceptible rapid variations in pitch.
vi·bur·num (vī-bûr′nəm) *n.* A shrub or tree of the genus *Viburnum,* bearing small white flower clusters and black or red berries.
vic·ar (vĭk′ər) *n.* **1.** A parish priest in the Church of England. **2.** A cleric in the Episcopal Church in charge of a chapel. **3.** One who serves as a substitute for another. **—vi·car′i·al** (vī-kâr′ē-əl) *adj.*
vic·ar·age (vĭk′ər-ĭj) *n.* **1.** The residence of a vicar. **2.** A vicar's benefice.
vicar general *n., pl.* **vicars general.** *Rom. Cath. Ch.* A priest acting as an administrative deputy to a bishop.
vi·car·i·ous (vī-kâr′ē-əs, vĭ-) *adj.* **1.** Endured or undergone by 1 person acting for another. **2.** Acting in place of someone else. **3.** Felt or experienced as if one were participating in the feelings or experience of another. **—vi·car′i·ous·ly** *adv.* **—vi·car′i·ous·ness** *n.*
vice¹ (vīs) *n.* **1.** A degrading or immoral habit or practice. **2.** Wicked or evil conduct. **3.** Sexual immorality, esp. prostitution. **4.** A personal failing.
vice² (vīs) *n. var. of* VISE.
vice³ (vīs) *n.* A person acting in the place of another <the *vice*-chairman> —*prep.* **vi·ce** (vī′sē). In place of.
vice admiral *n.* A U.S. naval officer ranking next beneath an admiral.
vice·ge·rent (vīs-jîr′ənt) *n.* One appointed by a head of state to act as an administrative deputy.
vi·cen·ni·al (vī-sĕn′ē-əl) *adj.* Occurring once every 20 years.
vice president *n.* **1.** An officer ranking next beneath a president and having authority to take his place in case of absence, illness, or death. **2.** A deputy of a president, esp. in a corporation, who is head of a department. **—vice-pres′i·den·cy** *n.*
vice·re·gal (vīs-rē′gəl) *adj.* Of or pertaining to a viceroy.
vice·roy (vīs′roi′) *n.* A governor of a country, colony, or province ruling as the representative of a sovereign. **—vice′roy′al·ty** *n.*
vice squad *n.* A police division whose task is to control gambling and prostitution.
vi·ce ver·sa (vī′sə vûr′sə, vīs vûr′-) *adv.* With the meaning or order reversed.
vi·chys·soise (vĭsh′ē-swäz′, vē′shē-) *n.* A creamy, thick potato soup made from chicken stock, flavored with leeks or onions, and usu. served cold.
vi·cin·i·ty (vĭ-sĭn′ĭ-tē) *n., pl.* **-ties. 1.** The state of being near in space or relationship. **2.** A surrounding area.
vi·cious (vĭsh′əs) *adj.* **1.** Addicted to vice or depravity : evil. **2.** Malicious : spiteful <*vicious* rumors> **3.** Marked by violence or ferocity <a *vicious* storm> **4.** Savagely aggressive : dangerous. **—vi′cious·ly** *adv.*
vi·cis·si·tude (vĭ-sĭs′ĭ-tōōd′, -tyōōd′) *n.* **1.** *often* **vicissitudes.** A change or variation. **2.** The quality of being changeable.
vic·tim (vĭk′tĭm) *n.* **1.** One harmed or killed by another. **2.** A living creature slain and offered to a deity as a sacrifice. **3.** One harmed by an act, circumstance, or condition <*victims* of disaster>
vic·tim·ize (vĭk′tə-mīz′) *v.* **-ized, -iz·ing. 1.** To subject to fraud. **2.** To make a victim of. **—vic′tim·i·za′tion** *n.*
vic·tor (vĭk′tər) *n.* One who vanquishes or defeats an adversary.
vic·to·ri·a (vĭk-tôr′ē-ə, -tōr′-) *n.* A light 4-wheeled horse-drawn carriage for 2 with a folding top and a raised seat in front for the driver.
Victoria. 1819–1901. Queen of England (1837–1901).
Victoria. 1. Cap. of B.C., Canada, on SE Vancouver Is. *Pop.* 62,551. **2.** Cap. of Hong Kong colony, on NW Hong Kong Is. *Pop.* 1,026,870. **3.** Cap. of the Seychelles, on NE Mahé Is. *Pop.* 13,622.
Victoria Day *n. Can.* The 1st Monday preceding May 25, a national holiday commemorating Queen Victoria's birthday.
Vic·to·ri·an (vĭk-tôr′ē-ən, -tōr′-) *adj.* **1.** Of or relating to the period of Queen Victoria's reign. **2.** Displaying qualities, as hypocrisy and moral severity, usu. associated with the time of Queen Victoria. —*n.* One belonging to or typical of the Victorian period.
vic·to·ri·ous (vĭk-tôr′ē-əs, -tōr′-) *adj.* **1.** Being the winner in a struggle or contest. **2.** Typical of or expressing victory. **—vic·to′ri·ous·ly** *adv.* **—vic·to′ri·ous·ness** *n.*
vic·to·ry (vĭk′tə-rē) *n., pl.* **-ries. 1.** Defeat of an enemy, as in wartime. **2.** Success in a struggle against an obstacle or opponent. ☆***syns:*** CONQUEST, TRIUMPH, WIN
vict·ual (vĭt′l) *n.* **1.** Food suitable for consumption. **2. victuals.** Items of food : provisions. **—vict′ual** *v.*
▲word history: *Victual* was borrowed from Old French *vitaille,* and until the 16th cent. the spelling of the word conformed to its pronunciation, which rhymes with *little.* During the Renaissance and the renewal of interest in classical languages and literature, scholars pedantically revised the spelling of English words to reflect their origins. *Victual* comes ult. from Late Latin *victualia,* "provisions." The pronunciation has never reflected this artificial respelling, and the form *vittle,* which adheres more closely to the actual sound of the word, is still sometimes seen.
vict·ual·er *also* **vict·ual·ler** (vĭt′l-ər) *n.* A supplier of provisions.
vi·cu·ña *or* **vi·cu·na** (vī-kōōn′yə, -kōō′nə, -kyōō′nə, və-) *n.* **1.** A llamalike ruminant mammal, *Vicugna vicugna,* of the Andes, with a fine, silky fleece. **2.** Cloth made from this fleece.
vi·de (vī′dē, vē′dā′). See. Used to direct a reader's attention <*Vide* page 31.>
vi·del·i·cet (vĭ-dĕl′ĭ-sĭt′, vī-) *adv.* That is to say : namely. Used to introduce examples or lists.
vid·e·o (vĭd′ē-ō′) *adj.* Of or relating to television, esp. to televised pictures. —*n.* **1.** The visual part of a telecast. **2.** Television.
vid·e·o·cas·sette (vĭd′ē-ō-kə-sĕt′, -kă-) *n.* A videotape recording in cassette form.

vid•e•o•disc *also* **vid•e•o•disk** (vĭd′ē-ō-dĭsk′) *n.* A disc recording of sounds and images, as of a film, that may be played on a television set.
video display terminal *n.* A video terminal.
video game *n.* A computerized game in which the player or players control images on a display screen.
Vid•e•o•phone (vĭd′ē-ō-fōn′). A trademark for a telephone equipped for both audio and video transmission.
Vid•e•o•scan (vĭd′ē-ō-skăn′). A trademark for a method of machine character recognition in which a video camera records the shapes of the characters to be recognized and then matches the shapes to data held in machine storage.
vid•e•o•tape (vĭd′ē-ō-tāp′) *n.* Magnetic tape for recording television programs. **—vid′e•o•tape′** *v.*
video terminal *n.* A computer input-output device utilizing a cathode-ray tube to display data on a screen.

video terminal

vie (vī) *v.* **vied, vy•ing.** To engage in a struggle or contest : contend. **—vi′er** *n.*
Vi•en•na (vē-ĕn′ə). Cap. of Austria, in the NE. *Pop.* 1,572,300. **—Vi′en•nese′** (-nēz′, -nēs′) *adj.* & *n.*
Vien•tiane (vyĕn-tyän′). Cap. of Laos, in the NC part. *Pop.* 174,229.
Vi•et•nam (vē-ĕt′näm′, -năm′, vyĕt′-). Country of SE Asia. *Cap.* Hanoi. *Pop.* 53,550,000. **—Vi•et′na•mese′** (-mēz′, -mēs′) *adj.* & *n.*
view (vyo͞o) *n.* **1.** The act of examining : inspection. **2.** A systematic survey. **3.** Opinion. **4.** The field of vision. **5.** A scene : vista. **6.** A picture of a scene. **7.** A way of seeing something, as from a particular position <an aerial *view* of the fortifications> **8.** An intention <wrote the book with a *view* to publication> *—v.* **1.** To see. **2. a.** To examine. **b.** To survey mentally : consider. **—view′er** *n.*
view finder *n.* FINDER 2.
view•point (vyo͞o′point′) *n.* A point of view.
vi•ges•i•mal (vī-jĕs′ə-məl) *adj.* **1.** Twentieth. **2.** Based on or relating to 20.
vig•il (vĭj′əl) *n.* **1.** A watch kept at night. **2.** The day before a religious festival, observed by devotional preparation.
vig•i•lance (vĭj′ə-ləns) *n.* Alert watchfulness. **—vig′i•lant** *adj.*
vig•i•lan•te (vĭj′ə-lăn′tē) *n.* A member of a group of volunteers that without authority assumes police powers, as pursuing and punishing criminal suspects.
vi•gnette (vĭn-yĕt′, vēn-) *n.* **1.** A decorative design at the opening or end of a book or a chapter of a book. **2.** An unbordered portrait that shades off into the surrounding color at the edges. **3.** A short, descriptive literary sketch.
vig•or (vĭg′ər) *n.* **1.** Physical strength or energy. **2.** Intensity.
vig•or•ous (vĭg′ər-əs) *adj.* **1.** Healthy and energetic : robust. **2.** Lively : forceful. **—vig′or•ous•ly** *adv.* **—vig′or•ous•ness** *n.*
vig•our (vĭg′ər) *n. esp. Brit. var. of* VIGOR.
Vi•king (vī′kĭng) *n.* One of a seafaring Scandinavian people who raided settlements on the coasts of N and W Europe from the 8th to the 10th cent.
Vi•la (vē′lə). Cap. of Vanuatu, in the SW Pacific. *Pop.* 17,400.
vile (vīl) *adj.* **vil•er, vil•est. 1.** Disgusting : loathsome. **2.** Objectionable : unpleasant. **3.** Miserable : wretched. **4.** Depraved : ignoble. **—vile′ly** *adv.* **—vile′ness** *n.*
vil•i•fy (vĭl′ə-fī′) *v.* **-fied, -fy•ing.** To defame : denigrate. **—vil′i•fi•ca′tion** *n.* **—vil′i•fi′er** *n.*
vil•la (vĭl′ə) *n.* **1.** An often large and luxurious house in the country. **2.** *esp. Brit.* A middle-class suburban house.
vil•lage (vĭl′ĭj) *n.* **1.** A small group of dwellings in a rural area. **2.** An incorporated community smaller than a town in some U.S. states. **3.** The inhabitants of a village. **—vil′lag•er** *n.*
vil•lain (vĭl′ən) *n.* **1.** A wicked or evil person. **2.** A fictional or dramatic character typically at odds with the hero. **3.** *var. of* VILLEIN. **—vil′lain•ous** *adj.*
vil•lain•y (vĭl′ə-nē) *n., pl.* **-ies. 1.** Villainous conduct. **2.** Baseness of character or mind. **3.** A treacherous or wicked act.
vil•lein *also* **vil•lain** (vĭl′ən) *n.* One of a class of feudal serfs holding the legal status of freemen in their dealings with everyone except their lord. **—vil′lein•age** *n.*
vil•lous (vĭl′əs) *also* **vil•lose** (-lōs′) *adj.* Covered with fine hairs or villi.
vil•lus (vĭl′əs) *n., pl.* **vil•li** (vĭl′ī′) **1.** *Anat.* A minute projection arising from a mucous membrane. **2.** *Bot.* A fine hairlike epidermal outgrowth.
vim (vĭm) *n.* Ebullient vitality.
vin•ai•grette (vĭn′ə-grĕt′) *n.* **1.** A small decorative bottle with a perforated top for holding an aromatic preparation such as smelling salts. **2.** A dressing of vinegar or lemon juice and oil flavored with herbs.
vin•ci•ble (vĭn′sə-bəl) *adj.* Capable of being vanquished or overcome.
vin•di•cate (vĭn′dĭ-kāt′) *v.* **-cat•ed, -cat•ing. 1.** To clear of blame or suspicion with corroboration or proof. **2.** To justify or support <*vindicate* one's faith> **3.** To justify or prove the value of, esp. in light of subsequent events. ☆***syns:*** ABSOLVE, AQUIT, CLEAR, EXONERATE **—vin′di•ca′tion** *n.* **—vin′di•ca′tor** *n.*
vin•dic•tive (vĭn-dĭk′tĭv) *adj.* **1.** Having or showing a desire for revenge. **2.** Meant to cause harm or pain. ☆***syns:*** REVENGEFUL, SPITEFUL, VENGEFUL **—vin•dic′tive•ly** *adv.* **—vin•dic′tive•ness** *n.*
vine (vīn) *n.* **1. a.** A plant with a flexible stem that grows along the ground or climbs or clings to a surface for support. **b.** The stem of such a plant. **2.** A grapevine.
vin•e•gar (vĭn′ĭ-gər) *n.* An impure dilute solution of acetic acid, obtained by fermentation and used in flavoring and preserving food. **—vin′e•gar•y** *adj.*
vin•e•gar•roon (vĭn′ĭ-gə-ro͞on′) *n.* A large nonvenomous scorpionlike arachnid, *Mastigoproctus giganteus,* that gives off a strong vinegary odor when disturbed.

vinnegarroon

vine•yard (vĭn′yərd) *n.* Ground planted with cultivated grapevines.
vin•i•cul•ture (vĭn′ĭ-kŭl′chər, vī′nĭ-) *n.* Cultivation of grapes : viticulture.
vi•no (vē′nō) *n., pl.* **-nos.** Wine.
vin or•di•naire (văɴ′ ôr-dē-nâr′) *n., pl.* **vins or•di•naires** (văɴ′ ôr-dē-nâr′) Inexpensive table wine.
vin•tage (vĭn′tĭj) *n.* **1.** The grapes or wine produced from a particular vineyard or district in 1 season. **2.** Wine identified as to year and vineyard or district of origin. **3.** The harvesting of a grape crop. **4.** A year or time of origin <a uniform of 1914 *vintage*> *—adj.* **1.** Of or relating to a vintage. **2.** Characterized by excellence and lasting popularity. **3.** Representative of the best <stories that were *vintage* Saroyan>
vint•ner (vĭnt′nər) *n.* **1.** A wine merchant. **2.** A wine maker.
vi•nyl (vī′nəl) *n.* Any of various tough, flexible, shiny plastics used esp. for coverings and clothing.
vi•ol (vī′əl) *n.* Any of a family of stringed instruments, chiefly of the 16th and 17th cent., with a fretted fingerboard, usu. 6 strings, and a flat back.
vi•o•la (vē-ō′lə) *n.* A stringed instrument of the violin family, somewhat bigger than a violin and having a deeper tone.
vi•o•la•ble (vī′ə-lə-bəl) *adj.* Capable of being violated.
vi•o•late (vī′ə-lāt′) *v.* **-lat•ed, -lat•ing. 1.** To break (e.g. a law). **2.** To injure the person or property of, esp. to rape. **3.** To desecrate. **—vi′o•la′tion** *n.* **—vi′o•la′tor** *n.*
vi•o•lence (vī′ə-ləns) *n.* **1.** Physical force employed so as to damage or injure. **2.** An instance of violent action. **3.** Intensity <the *violence* of the tornado> **4.** Damage or abuse, as to meaning or content <do *violence* to a song> **5.** Fervor : vehemence.
vi•o•lent (vī′ə-lənt) *adj.* **1.** Characterized or caused by great physical force. **2.** Having or showing great emotional force. **3.** Intense : severe. **4.** Caused by force rather than by natural causes <a *violent* death>
vi•o•let (vī′ə-lĭt) *n.* **1.** A low-growing plant of the genus *Viola,*

bearing flowers that are purplish-blue or occas. white or yellow. **2.** A bluish purple.

vi•o•lin (vī′ə-lĭn′) *n.* A stringed instrument played with a bow and having 4 strings and an unfretted fingerboard. **–vi′o•lin′ist** *n.*

vi•o•lon•cel•lo (vē′ə-lən-chĕl′ō) *n., pl.* **-los.** A cello. **–vi′o•lon•cel′list** *n.*

VIP (vē′ī-pē′) *n., pl.* **VIPs.** *Informal.* A very important person.

vi•per (vī′pər) *n.* **1.** A venomous snake of the family Viperidae, esp. a common Eurasian species, *Vipera berus.* **2.** A venomous or presumably venomous snake. **3.** A treacherous person. **–vi′per•ous** *adj.*

vi•ra•go (vĭ-rä′gō) *n., pl.* **-goes** *or* **-gos.** A noisy, overbearing woman.

vi•ral (vī′rəl) *adj.* Of, pertaining to, or resulting from a virus.

vir•e•o (vîr′ē-ō′) *n., pl.* **-os.** Any of various small New World birds of the genus *Vireo,* with greenish or grayish plumage.

Vir•gil (vûr′jəl). 70–19 B.C. Roman poet. **–Vir•gil′i•an** (-jĭl′ē-ən) *adj.*

vir•gin (vûr′jĭn) *n.* **1.** One who has never engaged in sexual intercourse. **2. Virgin.** The mother of Jesus. **3. Virgin.** VIRGO 2. *–adj.* **1.** Typical of or suitable for a virgin. **2.** In a natural or unchanged state <*virgin* forests> **3.** Extracted from the 1st pressing <*virgin* olive oil> **–vir•gin′i•ty** *n.*

vir•gin•al¹ (vûr′jə-nəl) *adj.* **1.** Of or pertaining to a virgin. **2.** Untouched : fresh.

vir•gin•al² (vûr′jə-nəl) *n. often* **virginals.** A small rectangular harpsichord without legs, popular in the 16th and 17th cent.

Vir•gin•ia (vər-jĭn′yə). State of the E U.S. *Cap.* Richmond. *Pop.* 5,346,279. **–Vir•gin′ian** *adj. & n.*

Virginia creeper *n.* A North American climbing vine, *Parthenocissus quinquefolia,* bearing compound leaves and bluish-black berries.

Virginia reel *n.* An American country dance in which couples perform various steps together to the instructions of a caller.

Virgin Islands. Islands of the West Indies E of Puerto Rico.

Virgin Islands of the United States. SW part of the Virgin Is., constituting a U.S. territory. *Cap.* Charlotte Amalie. *Pop.* 62,468.

Vir•go (vûr′gō, vîr′-) *n.* **1.** A constellation in the region of the celestial equator. **2. a.** The 6th sign of the zodiac. **b.** One born under this sign.

vir•gule (vûr′gyo͞ol) *n.* A diagonal mark (/) used esp. to denote alternatives, as in *and/or,* and to stand for the word *per,* as in *feet/second.*

vi•ri•cide (vī′rĭ-sīd′) *n.* An agent that destroys viruses.

vir•i•des•cent (vîr′ĭ-dĕs′ənt) *adj.* Green or somewhat green. **–vir′i•des′cence** *n.*

vir•ile (vîr′əl) *adj.* **1.** Typical of or appropriate to a man. **2.** Having or showing energy and vigor. **3.** Able to perform sexually as a male. **–vi•ril′i•ty** (vĭ-rĭl′ĭ-tē) *n.*

vi•rol•o•gy (vī-rŏl′ə-jē) *n.* The study of viruses and viral diseases. **–vi•rol′o•gist** *n.*

vir•tu (vər-to͞o′, vîr-) *n.* **1.** A knowledge or love of fine objects of art. **2.** Objects of art, esp. antiques.

vir•tu•al (vûr′cho͞o-əl) *adj.* Existing or resulting in effect though not in actual fact. **–vir′tu•al′i•ty** (-ăl′ĭ-tē) *n.*

vir•tue (vûr′cho͞o) *n.* **1. a.** Moral excellence. **b.** An example of moral excellence <the *virtue* of generosity> **2.** Chastity, esp. of a girl or woman. **3.** A particular beneficial quality : advantage. **4.** Effective power <believed in the *virtue* of meditation> **–by virtue of.** By reason of.

vir•tu•o•so (vûr′cho͞o-ō′sō) *n., pl.* **-sos** *or* **-si** (-sē). **1.** A musical performer of unusual excellence. **2.** One with outstanding talent in any field, esp. in the arts. **–vir′tu•os′i•ty** *n.*

vir•tu•ous (vûr′cho͞o-əs) *adj.* **1.** Displaying virtue : righteous. **2.** Chaste : pure.

vir•u•lent (vîr′yə-lənt, vîr′ə-) *adj.* **1.** Extremely poisonous or pathogenic. **2.** Bitterly hostile or malicious. **–vir′u•lence** *n.* **–vir′u•lent•ly** *adv.*

vi•rus (vī′rəs) *n.* **1.** Any of various submicroscopic pathogens consisting essentially of a particle of nucleic acid enclosed in protein and able to replicate only within a living cell. **2.** A corrupting influence.

vi•sa (vē′zə) *n.* An official authorization appended to a passport allowing entry into a specific country.

vis•age (vĭz′ĭj) *n.* The face or facial expression of a person.

vis-à-vis (vē′zə-vē′) *n., pl.* **vis-à-vis** (-vēz′, -vē′). One of 2 persons or things opposite or corresponding to the other. *–adv.* Face to face. *–prep.* **1.** Compared with. **2.** In relation to. **–vis′-à-vis′** *adj.*

vis•cer•a (vĭs′ər-ə) *pl.n.* The internal organs of the body, esp. those within the thorax and abdomen.

vis•cer•al (vĭs′ər-əl) *adj.* **1.** Relating to or located in the viscera. **2.** Profound : intense <*visceral* grief>

vis•cid (vĭs′ĭd) *adj.* **1.** Thick and sticky. **2.** Covered with a sticky coating. **–vis•cid′i•ty** (vĭ-sĭd′ĭ-tē) *n.* **–vis′cid•ly** *adv.*

vis•cose (vĭs′kōs′) *n.* A thick, brown solution made from cellulose and used in manufacturing rayon and cellophane. *–adj.* Viscous.

vis•cos•i•ty (vĭ-skŏs′ĭ-tē) *n., pl.* **-ties.** The condition or property of being viscous.

vis•count (vī′kount′) *n.* A peer ranking beneath an earl and above a baron. **–vis′count′cy** *n.* **–vis′count′ess** *n.*

vis•cous (vĭs′kəs) *adj.* **1.** Having relatively high resistance to flow. **2.** Having a heavy, gluey quality. **–vis′cous•ly** *adv.*

vise *also* **vice** (vīs) *n.* A clamping apparatus consisting of 2 jaws opened or closed by a screw or lever, used in carpentry or metalworking to hold a piece in position.

vis•i•bil•i•ty (vĭz′ĭ-bĭl′ə-tē) *n., pl.* **-ties. 1.** The fact, state, or degree of being visible. **2.** The range of vision under given weather conditions.

vis•i•ble (vĭz′ə-bəl) *adj.* **1.** Capable of being seen. **2.** Apparent. **–vis′i•bly** *adv.*

vi•sion (vĭzh′ən) *n.* **1.** The faculty of sight. **2.** Unusual ability in foreseeing what is going to happen. **3.** A mental image created by the imagination. **4.** A mystical experience of seeing a supernatural sight. **5.** One of great beauty.

vi•sion•ar•y (vĭzh′ə-nĕr′ē) *adj.* **1.** Marked by foresight. **2.** Having the nature of fantasies or dreams. **3.** Existing only in the imagination : not practicable. *–n., pl.* **-ies. 1.** One who has visions. **2.** One given to impractical ideas.

vis•it (vĭz′ĭt) *v.* **1.** To go or come to see (a person). **2.** To go or come to see (a place), as on a tour. **3.** To stay with as a guest. **4.** To afflict. **5.** To inflict punishment for <*visit* the sins of the fathers upon the children> **6.** *Informal.* To chat. **–vis′it** *n.* **–vis′i•tor, vis′i•tant** *n.*

vis•i•ta•tion (vĭz′ĭ-tā′shən) *n.* **1.** A visit, esp. an official one. **2.** A parent's right to visit a child or have a child as a visitor, as specified in a divorce or separation order. **3.** A punishment or blessing regarded as being divinely ordained.

visiting nurse *n.* A registered nurse employed by a hospital or public health agency to promote community health.

vi•sor *also* **vi•zor** (vī′zər) *n.* **1.** A piece projecting from the front of a cap to shade the eyes or protect against wind or rain. **2.** A fixed or movable shield against glare over the windshield of a motor vehicle. **3.** The front piece of the helmet of a suit of armor, able to be raised or lowered.

vis•ta (vĭs′tə) *n.* **1.** A distant view, esp. through a passage or opening. **2.** A mental view of a series of events.

vi•su•al (vĭzh′o͞o-əl) *adj.* **1.** Of or relating to the sense of sight. **2.** Visible. **3.** Done or controlled by using sight alone. **4.** Of or relating to communication of instruction by means of vision <*visual* aids>

vi•su•al•ize (vĭzh′o͞o-ə-līz′) *v.* **-ized, -iz•ing.** To form a mental image of. **–vi′su•al•i•za′tion** *n.* **–vi′su•al•iz′er** *n.*

vi•ta (vī′tə, vē′-) *n.* A résumé.

vi•tal (vīt′l) *adj.* **1.** Of or characteristic of life. **2.** Essential to life. **3.** Full of life : animated. **4.** Very important. **–vi′tal•ly** *adv.*

vi•tal•i•ty (vī-tăl′ĭ-tē) *n., pl.* **-ties. 1.** The characteristic that distinguishes the living from the nonliving. **2.** The capacity to grow or develop. **3.** Physical or intellectual vigor : energy.

vi•tal•ize (vīt′l-īz′) *v.* **-ized, -iz•ing. 1.** To endow with life. **2.** To invigorate. **–vi′tal•i•za′tion** *n.* **–vi′tal•iz′er** *n.*

vital signs *pl.n. Med.* A person's pulse rate, temperature, and respiratory rate.

vi•ta•min (vī′tə-mĭn) *n.* Any of various relatively complex organic substances that occur in small amounts in animal and plant tissue and are essential for the continuation of normal life functions.

▲word history: *Vitamin* was borrowed from German *Vitamine,* which is a compound of Latin *vita,* "life," and the scientific suffix *-amine,* "amine, an organic compound of nitrogen." It was at 1st believed that vitamins were based on amino acids. Although this was later found to be untrue, the name *vitamin* was kept.

vitamin A *n.* A vitamin or mixture of vitamins found esp. in fish-liver oils that is necessary for normal cell growth and sight.

vitamin B *n.* **1.** Vitamin B complex. **2.** A member of the vitamin B complex, esp. vitamin B_1.

vitamin B_1 *n.* Thiamine.

vitamin B_2 *n.* Riboflavin.

vitamin B_{12} *n.* A complex cobalt-containing compound occurring in liver and essential for normal blood formation.

vitamin B complex *n.* A related group of vitamins orig. held to be a single substance and found mainly in yeast, eggs, liver, and certain vegetables.

vitamin C *n.* Ascorbic acid.

vitamin D *n.* Any of several related sterols made active by exposure to ultraviolent light or obtained from milk, fish, and eggs and necessary for normal bone growth.
vitamin E *n.* Any of several related oils found mainly in grains and vegetable oils and used esp. in treating sterility.
vitamin G *n.* Riboflavin.
vitamin H *n.* Biotin.
vitamin K *n.* Any of several artificial or natural substances essential for the normal clotting of blood.
vi•ti•ate (vĭsh′ē-āt′) *v.* **-at•ed, -at•ing. 1.** To impair the quality or value of. **2.** To corrupt morally. **3.** To invalidate. **—vi′ti•a′tion** *n.* **—vi′ti•a′tor** *n.*
vit•i•cul•ture (vĭt′ĭ-kŭl′chər) *n.* Cultivation of grapes. **—vit′i•cul′tur•al** *adj.* **—vit′i•cul′tur•ist** *n.*
vit•re•ous (vĭt′rē-əs) *adj.* **1.** Relating to or similar to glass. **2.** Of or relating to the vitreous humor.
vitreous humor *n.* Clear gelatinous matter that fills the section of the eyeball between the retina and the lens.
vit•ri•fy (vĭt′rə-fī′) *v.* **-fied, -fy•ing.** To make into glass or a similar substance, esp. by heat fusion. **—vit′ri•fi•ca′tion** *n.*
vit•ri•ol (vĭt′rē-ōl′) *n.* **1.** *Chem.* **a.** Sulfuric acid. **b.** Any of various sulfates of metals. **2.** Bitter or sharp expression or feeling. **—vit′ri•ol′ic** *adj.*
vit•tles (vĭt′lz) *pl.n. nonstandard var. of* VICTUALS.
vi•tu•per•ate (vī-to͞o′pə-rāt′, -tyo͞o′-, vĭ-) *v.* **-at•ed, -at•ing.** To berate. **—vi•tu′per•a′tion** *n.* **—vi•tu′per•a•tive** *adj.*
vi•va (vē′və) *interj.* Used to express approval.
vi•va•ce (vē-vä′chā) *adv. & adj. Mus.* In a lively manner. Used as a direction.
vi•va•cious (vĭ-vā′shəs, vī-) *adj.* Filled with animation : lively. **—vi•va′cious•ly** *adv.* **—vi•va′cious•ness, vi•vac′i•ty** (vĭ-văs′ĭ-tē, vī-) *n.*
vi•var•i•um (vī-vâr′ē-əm) *n., pl.* **-ums** *or* **-i•a** (-ē-ə) An enclosure for keeping living animals for research or observation.
vi•va vo•ce (vī′və vō′sē) *adv. & adj.* By word of mouth.
viv•id (vĭv′ĭd) *adj.* **1.** Bright : brilliant. **2.** Having intensely bright colors. **3. a.** Evoking lifelike images in the mind. **b.** Active <a *vivid* imagination> **—viv′id•ly** *adv.*
viv•i•fy (vĭv′ə-fī′) *v.* **-fied, -fy•ing. 1.** To give or bring life to. **2.** To make livelier. **—viv′i•fi•ca′tion** *n.* **—viv′i•fi′er** *n.*
vi•vip•a•rous (vī-vĭp′ər-əs, vĭ-) *adj. Zool.* Giving birth to living offspring that develop inside the body of the mother rather than hatching from eggs. **—vi′vi•par′i•ty** (vī′və-păr′ĭ-tē, vĭv′ə-) *n.*
viv•i•sec•tion (vĭv′ĭ-sĕk′shən) *n.* Dissection of or operation on a living animal, esp. for scientific research. **—viv′i•sect′** *v.*
vix•en (vĭk′sən) *n.* **1.** A female fox. **2.** A shrewish woman. **—vix′en•ish** *adj.*
vi•zier *also* **vi•zir** (vĭ-zîr′) *n.* A high Moslem governmental official, esp. in the former Turkish Empire.
vi•zor (vī′zər) *n. var. of* VISOR.
V-neck (vē′nĕk′) *n.* A V-shaped neckline.
vo•ca•ble (vō′kə-bəl) *n.* A word regarded only as a sequence of letters or sounds instead of as a unit of meaning.
vo•cab•u•lar•y (vō-kăb′yə-lĕr′ē) *n., pl.* **-ies. 1.** A list of words and often phrases, usu. in an alphabetical arrangement and translated or defined. **2.** All the words of a language. **3.** All the words used and understood by a particular person.
vo•cal (vō′kəl) *adj.* **1.** Of, relating to, or composed for the human voice. **2.** Uttered by the voice. **3.** Having a voice and able to emit sound or speech. **4.** Full of voices. **5.** Speaking freely and loudly : outspoken. *—n.* **1.** A vocal sound. **2.** A popular piece of music for a singer. **—vo′cal•ly** *adv.*
vocal cords *pl.n.* The lower of 2 pairs of bands or folds in the larynx that vibrate when drawn together and when air is passed up from the lungs, thereby producing vocal sounds.
vo•cal•ic (vō-kăl′ĭk) *adj.* Relating to or being the nature of a vowel or vowels.
vo•cal•ist (vō′kə-lĭst) *n.* A singer.
vo•cal•ize (vō′kə-līz′) *v.* **-ized, -iz•ing. 1.** To give vocal expression to. **2.** To change (a consonant) into a vowel. **3.** To use the voice, esp. to sing. **—vo′cal•i•za′tion** *n.* **—vo′cal•iz′er** *n.*
vo•ca•tion (vō-kā′shən) *n.* **1.** A profession, esp. one to which an individual is particularly suited. **2.** A predisposition or urge to take up a particular type of work, esp. religious work. **—vo•ca′tion•al** *adj.*
voc•a•tive (vŏk′ə-tĭv) *adj.* Relating to or being a grammatical case, as in Latin, used to designate the one being addressed. **—voc′a•tive** *n.*
vo•cif•er•ate (vō-sĭf′ə-rāt′) *v.* **-at•ed, -at•ing.** To cry out or utter vehemently. **—vo•cif′er•a′tion** *n.*
vo•cif•er•ous (vō-sĭf′ər-əs) *adj.* Making an outcry. **—vo•cif′er•ous•ly** *adv.*
vod•ka (vŏd′kə) *n.* A colorless alcoholic liquor distilled from fermented wheat or rye mash, potatoes, or corn.
vogue (vōg) *n.* **1.** Prevailing fashion or style. **2.** Popularity. **—vogu′ish** *adj.*
voice (vois) *n.* **1.a.** The sound produced by the vocal organs of a vertebrate, esp. a human being. **b.** The ability to produce such sounds. **2.** A sound resembling vocal utterance. **3.** The specified quality or timbre of vocal sound <a *soft* voice> **4. a.** A medium or agency of expression <give *voice* to one's feelings> **b.** The opportunity to express an opinion or choice. **5.** *Gram.* A verb form showing the relation between the subject and the action expressed by the verb. **6. a.** Musical tone produced by vibrating vocal chords and resonated within the throat and head cavities. **b.** A singer <a choir of 300 *voices*> **c.** Any of the melodic parts in a vocal composition. *—v.* **voiced, voic•ing. 1.** To give voice to : utter. **2.** To pronounce with vibration of the vocal cords. **3.** *Mus.* To regulate the tone of (e.g., the pipes of an organ). **—voice′less** *adj.*
voice box *n.* The larynx.
voice-o•ver (vois′ō′vər) *n.* The voice of a film or television narrator who does not appear on camera.
void (void) *adj.* **1.** Containing no matter : empty. **2.** Unoccupied, as a position or a building : vacant. **3.** Devoid : lacking. **4.** Useless : ineffective. **5.** Lacking legal force : null. *—n.* **1.** An empty space. **2.** A feeling or state of emptiness or loneliness. *—v.* **1.** To make void or of no effect. **2. a.** To empty. **b.** To evacuate (body wastes). **3.** To vacate. **—void′a•ble** *adj.* **—void′er** *n.*
voile (voil) *n.* A sheer fabric used esp. for making light clothing and curtains.
vol. *abbr.* **1.** volume. **2.** volunteer.
vol•a•tile (vŏl′ə-tl, -tīl′) *adj.* **1.** Evaporating readily at normal pressures and temperatures. **2.** Changeable, esp.: **a.** Fickle. **b.** Given to violence. **c.** Ephemeral. **—vol′a•til′i•ty** (-tĭl′ĭ-tē) *n.* **—vol′a•til•ize′** *v.*
vol-au-vent (vō′lō-väN′) *n.* A small pastry shell with a filling, as of meat or fish.
vol•can•ic (vŏl-kăn′ĭk) *adj.* **1.** Relating to or produced by a volcano. **2.** Violent.
vol•can•ism (vŏl′kə-nĭz′əm) *also* **vul•can•ism** (vŭl′-) *n.* Volcanic force.
vol•ca•no (vŏl-kā′nō) *n., pl.* **-noes** *or* **-nos. 1.** A vent in the earth's crust through which molten rock, ash, and gases are ejected. **2.** A mountain formed by the materials ejected from a volcano.
vole (vōl) *n.* Any of various short-tailed rodents of the genus *Microtus* and related genera, similar to rats or mice.
Vol•ga (vŏl′gə). Longest river of Europe, rising NW of Moscow and flowing 2,290 mi (3,684.6 km) to the Caspian Sea.
vo•li•tion (və-lĭsh′ən) *n.* **1.** An act of choosing, using one's own will. **2.** A conscious choice. **3.** The power of choosing.
vol•ley (vŏl′ē) *n., pl.* **-leys. 1.a.** Simultaneous discharge of a number of missiles. **b.** The missiles so discharged. **2.** A bursting forth of many things at the same time or in rapid succession <a *volley* of oaths> **3.** A shot, esp. in tennis, in which the ball is hit before touching the ground. *—v.* **1.** To discharge or be discharged in a volley. **2.** To hit (e.g., a tennis ball) before it touches the ground. **—vol′ley•er** *n.*
vol•ley•ball (vŏl′ē-bôl′) *n.* A court game in which 1 team tries to score by making the ball hit the ground on the opposing team's side of a high net.
volt (vōlt) *n.* A unit of electric potential and electromotive force, equal to the difference of electric potential between 2 points measured between the ends of a conductor that has a resistance of 1 ohm and through which a current of 1 ampere is flowing.
volt•age (vōl′tĭj) *n.* Electromotive force, usu. expressed in volts.
vol•ta•ic (vŏl-tā′ĭk, vōl-, vôl-) *adj.* Relating to or designating electricity produced by chemical action.
Vol•taire (vōl-târ′, vŏl-). François Marie Arouet. 1694–1778. French author.
volte-face (vôlt′fäs′, vôl′tə-) *n.* A reversal : about-face.
volt•me•ter (vōlt′mē′tər) *n.* An instrument for measuring differences of electric potential in volts.
vol•u•ble (vŏl′yə-bəl) *adj.* Fluent in speech. **—vol′u•bil′i•ty, vol′u•ble•ness** *n.* **—vol′u•bly** *adv.*
vol•ume (vŏl′yo͞om, -yəm) *n.* **1.** A book. **2.** 1 book of a set. **3. a.** The size of a 3-dimensional object or region of space. **b.** The capacity of such a region or object. **4.** A quantity : amount. **5. a.** The loudness of a sound. **b.** A control, as on a radio, for regulating loudness.
vol•u•met•ric (vŏl′yə-mĕt′rĭk) *adj.* Of or relating to measurement of volume. **—vol′u•met′ri•cal•ly** *adv.*
vo•lu•mi•nous (və-lo͞o′mə-nəs) *adj.* **1.** Having great volume, size, or quantity. **2.** Filling or sufficient to fill many volumes. **3.** Consisting of many coils or folds.
vol•un•tar•y (vŏl′ən-tĕr′ē) *adj.* **1. a.** Arising from one's own

free will. **b.** Acting on one's own initiative. **2.** Acting willingly and without reward. **3.** *Law.* Intentional <*voluntary* manslaughter> ☆***syns:*** DELIBERATE, INTENTIONAL, WILLFUL —*n., pl.* **-ies.** Solo organ music played at a church service. **—vol'un•tar'i•ly** *adv.*
vol•un•teer (vŏl'ən-tîr') *n.* One who serves or acts of his or her own free will. —*v.* **1.** To offer or give of one's own accord. **2.** To offer oneself as a volunteer. **—vol'un•teer'ism** *n.*
vo•lup•tu•ar•y (və-lŭp'cho͞o-ĕr'ē) *n., pl.* **-ies.** One whose life is devoted to sensual pleasures. **—vo•lup'tu•ar'y** *adj.*
vo•lup•tu•ous (və-lŭp'cho͞o-əs) *adj.* **1.** Characterized by or giving sensual gratification. **2.** Given over to sensual pleasures. **—vo•lup'tu•ous•ness** *n.*
vo•lute (və-lo͞ot') *n.* A scroll-like decoration, as on a column.
vom•it (vŏm'ĭt) *v.* **1.** To eject the contents of the stomach through the mouth. **2.** To eject in a gush. —*n.* Matter ejected from the stomach by vomiting.
voo•doo (vo͞o'do͞o) *n.* **1.** A religious cult marked by a belief in sorcery, primitive deities, and fetishes. **2.** A spell or curse held to possess magic power. **—voo'doo•ism** *n.* **—voo'doo•is'tic** *adj.*
vo•ra•cious (vô-rā'shəs, və-) *adj.* **1.** Consuming or eager to consume large quantities of food. **2.** Avid : insatiable. **—vo•ra'cious•ly** *adv.* **—vo•rac'i•ty** (-răs'ĭ-te), **vo•ra'cious•ness** *n.*
vor•tex (vôr'tĕks') *n., pl.* **-es** *or* **-ti•ces** (-tĭ-sēz'). A mass of fluid whirling about an axis : whirlpool.
vo•ta•ry (vō'tə-rē) *n., pl.* **-ries. 1.** A person bound by religious vows : monk or nun. **2.** A fervent devotee to a religion or ideal.
vote (vōt) *n.* **1. a.** A choice made, as for a candidate for office or in a referendum, in or as if in an election. **b.** The way in which such a choice is indicated, as by a ballot. **2.** The number of votes cast in an election or to resolve an issue. **3.** A group of voters <the farm *vote*> **4.** The result of an election. **5.** The right to vote. —*v.* **vot•ed, vot•ing. 1.** To indicate one's preference by a vote. **2.** To bring into existence by a vote. **3.** To pronounce by general agreement. **—vote'less** *adj.* **—vot'er** *n.*
vo•tive (vō'tĭv) *adj.* Dedicated or performed in fulfillment of a vow.
vouch (vouch) *v.* **1.** To verify by supplying proof. **2.** To give a personal assurance. **3.** To corroborate.
vouch•er (vou'chər) *n.* **1.** One who vouches. **2.** A document giving proof of a business transaction.
vouch•safe (vouch-sāf', vouch'sāf') *v.* **-safed, -saf•ing.** To condescend to grant.
vow (vou) *n.* **1.** A solemn promise or pledge that commits one to act or behave in a particular way. **2.** A formal assertion. —*v.* **1.** To promise solemnly. **2.** To assert formally. **3.** To make a promise. **—take vows.** To enter a religious order.
vow•el (vou'əl) *n.* **1.** A speech sound produced by relatively free passage of breath through the larynx and mouth, usu. forming the central sound of a syllable. **2.** A letter that represents a vowel, as *a, e, i, o, u,* and sometimes *y.*
vox pop•u•li (vŏks' pŏp'yə-lī') *n.* Popular sentiment.
voy•age (voi'ĭj) *n.* A long journey, esp. on a ship. **—voy'age** *v.* **—voy'ag•er** *n.*
vo•ya•geur (voi'ə-zhûr', vwä'yä-) *n.* A woodsman or guide, esp. one who transports furs and supplies between isolated posts in the U.S. and Canadian NW.
vo•yeur (voi-yûr') *n.* One who habitually seeks sexual gratification from observing the sexual activities of others. **—vo•yeur'ism** *n.* **—vo'yeur•is'tic** *adj.* **—vo'yeur•is'ti•cal•ly** *adv.*
VP *or* **V.P.** *abbr.* vice president.
vs. *abbr.* versus.
VT *abbr.* Vermont (with Zip Code).
Vt. *abbr.* Vermont.
vul•can•ism (vŭl'kə-nĭz'əm) *n. var. of* VOLCANISM.
vul•ca•nite (vŭl'kə-nīt') *n.* A hard rubber made by vulcanization.
vul•can•ize (vŭl'kə-nīz') *v.* **-ized, -iz•ing.** To increase the strength and resilience of (e.g., rubber) by combination with additives, as sulfur, under heat and pressure. **—vul'can•i•za'tion** *n.* **—vul'can•iz'er** *n.*
vul•gar (vŭl'gər) *adj.* **1.** Of or associated with the great masses of people. **2.** Spoken by or expressed in language used by the common people. **3.** Deficient in taste or delicacy. **4.** Indecent. **—vul'gar•ly** *adv.*
vul•gar•i•an (vŭl-gâr'ē-ən) *n.* A vulgar person.
vul•gar•ism (vŭl'gə-rĭz'əm) *n.* **1.** An obscene word or expression. **2.** A word, phrase, or expression used chiefly by uncultivated persons.
vul•gar•i•ty (vŭl-găr'ĭ-tē) *n., pl.* **-ties. 1.** The quality or state of being vulgar. **2.** Something vulgar, as an act or expression.
vul•gar•ize (vŭl'gə-rīz') *v.* **-ized, -iz•ing. 1.** To make vulgar : debase. **2.** To popularize. **—vul'gar•i•za'tion** *n.*
vul•gate (vŭl'gāt', -gĭt) *n.* The Latin translation of the Bible made at the end of the 4th cent., now used in a revised form by the Roman Catholic Church.
vul•ner•a•ble (vŭl'nər-ə-bəl) *adj.* **1.** Susceptible to physical injury. **2.** Susceptible to attack. **3. a.** Subject to criticism or censure. **b.** Liable to yield to temptation or persuasion. **4.** Being in a position to receive greater penalties or bonuses. Used of a pair that has won 1 game of a rubber in bridge. **—vul'ner•a•bil'i•ty** *n.* **—vul'ner•a•bly** *adv.*
vul•pine (vŭl'pīn') *adj.* **1.** Of, relating to, or typical of a fox. **2.** Cunning.
vul•ture (vŭl'chər) *n.* **1.** A large carrion-eating bird of the New World family Cathartidae or Old World family Accipitridae, with dark plumage and a naked head and neck. **2.** A greedy person.

vulture

vul•va (vŭl'və) *n., pl.* **-vae** (-vē'). The external parts of the female genitalia. **—vul'val, vul'var** *adj.*

Ww

w *or* **W** (dŭb'əl-yo͞o) *n., pl.* **w's** *or* **W's. 1.** The 23rd letter of the English alphabet. **2.** A speech sound represented by the letter *w.* **3.** Something with the shape of the letter W.
w *abbr.* **1.** width. **2.** *also* **W** *or* **w.** *or* **W.** west; western.
W¹ *symbol for* TUNGSTEN.
W² *abbr.* **1.** *Elect.* watt. **2.** *also* **w** *Physics.* work.
w. *abbr.* **1.** week. **2.** width. **3.** wife. **4.** with.
W. *abbr.* Wednesday.
WA *abbr.* Washington (with Zip Code).
Wac (wăk) *n.* A member of the U.S. Women's Army Corps.
wack•y *also* **whack•y** (wăk'ē) *adj.* **-i•er, -i•est.** *Slang.* Eccentric or silly.
wad (wŏd) *n.* **1.** A small soft mass of fibrous material used for padding, stuffing, or packing. **2.** Material, as tobacco or chewing gum, pressed into a ball, roll, or lump. **3.** A flexible plug for holding shot or a gunpowder charge in place in a cartridge. **4.** *Informal.* **a.** A thick roll of papers or paper money. **b.** A sizable amount, esp. of money. **—wad** *v.*
wad•ding (wŏd'ĭng) *n.* **1.** Wads as a whole. **2.** A sheet of cotton or wool used for packing, padding, or stuffing. **3.** Material for shotgun wads.
wad•dle (wŏd'l) *v.* **-dled, -dling.** To take short steps and tilt slightly from side to side. **—wad'dle** *n.* **—wad'dler** *n.*
wad•dy¹ (wŏd'ē) *n., pl.* **-dies.** *Austral.* A heavy straight stick or club thrown as a weapon by aborigines. **—wad'dy** *v.*
†**wad•dy²** *also* **wad•die** (wŏd'ē) *n., pl.* **-dies.** *W U.S.* **1.** A cowboy. **2.** A rustler.
wade (wād) *v.* **wad•ed, wad•ing. 1.** To walk in or through a medium, as water or mud, that hampers movement. **2.** To make one's way with difficulty. **3.** To begin vigorously or resolutely.

wad•er (wā′dər) *n.* **1.** One that wades. **2.** A wading bird. **3.** **waders.** Waterproof hip boots or trousers worn esp. by fishermen.
wa•di (wä′dē) *n.* A dry valley, gully, or riverbed in N Africa or SW Asia that fills up only during the rainy season.
wading bird *n.* A long-legged bird, as a heron, that looks for food in shallow water.
Waf (wăf) *n.* A member of the Women in the Air Force.
wa•fer (wā′fər) *n.* **1.** A small flat crisp cookie, cracker, or candy. **2.** A very thin round piece of unleavened bread used in Communion.
waf•fle¹ (wŏf′əl) *n.* Pancake batter baked into a light crisp cake in a waffle iron.
waf•fle² (wŏf′əl) *v.* **-fled, -fling.** *Informal.* To use words evasively : equivocate.
waffle iron *n.* An electric appliance with 2 hinged metal plates marked with an indented pattern, as of squares, that are pressed into baking waffle batter.
waft (wäft, wăft) *v.* To move or drift gently by or as if by the motion of air or water. —*n.* **1.** Something conveyed through the air <a *waft* of perfume> **2.** A gentle breeze.
wag¹ (wăg) *v.* **wagged, wag•ging. 1.** To move or cause to move quickly and repeatedly from side to side or up and down. **2.** To move (the tongue) in conversation or chatter. ☆**syns:** LASH, SWITCH, WAGGLE, WAVE **—wag** *n.* **—wag′ger** *n.*
wag² (wăg) *n.* A witty, playful person : joker. **—wag′gish** *adj.*
wage (wāj) *n.* **1.** Remuneration for labor or services. **2. wages** *(sing. or pl. in number).* A fitting return or just desert. —*v.* **waged, wag•ing.** To begin or conduct (a war or campaign.)
wa•ger (wā′jər) *n.* A bet : stake. —*v.* To make a bet. **—wa′ger•er** *n.*
wag•ger•y (wăg′ə-rē) *n., pl.* **-ies. 1.** Whimsical playfulness : drollery. **2.** A playful act or remark : jest.
wag•gle (wăg′əl) *v.* **-gled, -gling.** To move quickly from side to side or back and forth : wag. **—wag′gle** *n.* **—wag′gly** *adj.*
Wag•ner (väg′nər), **(Wilhelm) Richard.** 1813–83. German composer. **—Wag•ne′ri•an** (väg-nîr′ē-ən) *adj.*
wag•on (wăg′ən) *n.* **1.** A 4-wheeled vehicle, esp. one drawn by horses and used for transporting loads or goods. **2. a.** A station wagon. **b.** A patrol wagon. **3.** A child's low 4-wheeled cart with a long handle.
wagon train *n.* A column of wagons traveling cross-country, as in pioneer days.
wag•tail (wăg′tāl′) *n.* A bird of the genus *Motacilla* or related genera, with a long, constantly wagging tail.

wagtail

wa•hi•ne (wä-hē′nē, -nā′) *n.* **1.** A Polynesian woman. **2.** A girl or woman surfer.
wa•hoo¹ (wä′ho͞o) *n., pl.* **-hoos.** A shrub or small tree, *Euonymus atropurpureus,* of E North America, with small purplish flowers and red fruit.
†**wa•hoo²** (wä′hoo′) *interj. esp. W U.S.* Used to express exuberance.
waif (wāf) *n.* **1. a.** A lost, homeless, or abandoned child. **b.** A young animal that has strayed. **2.** Something found and unclaimed, as an object cast up by the sea.
wail (wāl) *v.* **1.** To make a loud, mournful cry. **2.** To make a long, loud, high-pitched sound <sirens *wailing*> **—wail** *n.* **—wail′ful** *adj.* **—wail′ing•ly** *adv.*
wain (wān) *n.* **1.** A large open wagon for farm use. **2. Wain.** The Big Dipper.
wain•scot (wān′skət, -skŏt′, -skōt′) *n.* **1.** A usu. wooden facing or paneling applied to the walls of a room. **2.** The lower part of an interior wall when finished in a different material. **—wain′scot** *v.*
wain•scot•ing *also* **wain•scot•ting** (wān′skə-tĭng, -skŏt′ĭng, -skō′tĭng) *n.* **1.** A wainscot. **2.** Material for a wainscot.
wain•wright (wān′rīt′) *n.* One who builds and repairs wagons.
waist (wāst) *n.* **1.** The somewhat narrowed part of the body between the rib cage and the pelvis. **2. a.** The part of a garment that fits around the waist. **b.** A garment, as a blouse or bodice, worn on the upper body. **c.** A child's undershirt, to which other clothing may be fastened. **3.** The middle section or part of something, esp. when narrower than the rest. **—waist′ed** *adj.*
waist•band (wāst′bănd′) *n.* A cloth band, as on a skirt, that circles the waist.
waist•coat (wĕs′kĭt, wāst′kōt′) *n. esp. Brit.* A vest for men.
waist•line (wāst′līn′) *n.* **1. a.** The narrowest part of the waist. **b.** The measurement of this part. **2.** The juncture of the skirt and bodice of a dress.
wait (wāt) *v.* **1.** To remain inactive until something anticipated occurs. **2.** To put off until later. **3. a.** To be in attendance, as a waiter, waitress, or salesperson. **b.** To serve at meals <*wait* on table> **4.** To be prepared or ready <a hot meal *waiting*> —*n.* Time spent in waiting. **—in wait.** In hiding, awaiting a chance to attack.
wait•er (wā′tər) *n.* **1.** A man who serves at meals, as in a restaurant. **2.** A tray or salver.
wait•ing game (wā′tĭng) *n.* A strategy in which advantage is sought through the use of delaying tactics.
waiting room *n.* A room for the use of persons waiting, as to see a doctor.
wait•ress (wā′trĭs) *n.* A woman who serves at meals, as in a restaurant.
waive (wāv) *v.* **waived, waiv•ing. 1.** To relinquish (a right or claim) voluntarily. **2.** To dispense with or postpone.
waiv•er (wā′vər) *n.* **1.** The deliberate waiving of a right, claim, or privilege. **2.** A formal document indicating a waiver.
wake¹ (wāk) *v.* **woke** (wōk), **waked** (wākt) *or* **woke** *or* **wo•ken** (wō′kən), **wak•ing. 1.** To bring or come from sleep : awaken. **2.** To keep a vigil, esp. over a deceased person. **3.** To be or stay awake. **4.** To rouse to awareness : alert. **5.** To stir up : stimulate. —*n.* A vigil, esp. over a corpse before the burial.
wake² (wāk) *n.* **1.** The visible turbulence left by a vessel moving through water. **2.** A track or course left behind.
wake•ful (wāk′fəl) *adj.* **1.** Not sleeping, whether involuntarily or by choice : sleepless. **2.** Vigilant. **—wake′ful•ness** *n.*
wak•en (wā′kən) *v.* **1.** To awaken from sleep. **2.** To stir up from a dormant state.
wale (wāl) *n.* **1. a.** A ridge in some fabrics, as corduroy. **b.** The weave or texture of such fabric <a wide *wale*> **2.** A skin welt made by a lash or blow. —*v.* **waled, wal•ing.** To mark (the skin) with wales.
Wales (wālz). Principality of SW Great Britain, W of England; part of the United Kingdom. *Pop.* 2,774,700.
walk (wôk) *v.* **1.** To move or cause to go on foot over a surface at a pace slower than a run. **2.** To go or pass over, on, or through by walking. **3.** To behave in a certain way. **4.** *Baseball.* To advance or cause to advance to 1st base after 4 balls have been pitched. —*n.* **1.** The act or an example of walking. **2.** A distance to be walked. **3.** A place on which to walk. **4.** A way of walking : gait. **5.** *Baseball.* The automatic advance of a batter to 1st base after receiving 4 balls. **6. a.** A way of acting or living. **b.** Status or occupation. **—walk′er** *n.*
walk•a•way (wôk′ə-wā′) *n.* A contest, competition, or victory won with ease.
walk•ie-talk•ie (wô′kē-tô′kē) *n.* A portable, battery-operated radio transmitter and receiver.
walk-in (wôk′ĭn′) *adj.* Big enough to walk into, as a closet or refrigerator. —*n.* **1.** An easy win. **2.** One who walks in.
walking papers *pl.n. Informal.* Notice of dismissal.
walking stick *n.* **1.** A cane used in walking. **2.** Any of various insects of the family Phasmidae that look like twigs or sticks.
walk-on (wôk′ŏn′, -ôn′) *n.* A small role in a play, usu. without speaking lines.
walk•out (wôk′out′) *n.* **1.** A labor strike. **2.** The act of leaving a meeting, organization, etc., as a sign of disapproval.
walk•o•ver (wôk′ō′vər) *n.* A walkaway.
walk•up *also* **walk-up** (wôk′ŭp′) *n.* A building of several stories with no elevator or an apartment or office in such a building. **—walk′up** *adj.*
wall (wôl) *n.* **1.** A vertical structure or partition that serves to enclose or separate. **2.** A continuous defensive rampart. **3.** Something that rises, separates, surrounds, or protects like a wall. —*v.* To provide or close up with or as if with a wall.
wal•la•by (wŏl′ə-bē) *n., pl.* **-bies.** An Australian marsupial of the genus *Wallabia* or related genera that resembles the kangaroo but is gen. smaller.
wal•la•roo (wŏl′ə-ro͞o′) *n., pl.* **-roos.** A kangaroo, *Macropus robustus* or *Osphranter robustus,* of hilly regions of Australia.
wall•board (wôl′bôrd′, -bōrd′) *n.* A structural material, as paper-coated gypsum plaster, used in large sheets to cover inside walls and ceilings.
wal•let (wŏl′ĭt) *n.* A small flat folding case for carrying paper money, cards, etc.

wall•eye (wôl′ī′) *n.* **1. a.** An eye abnormally directed out to the side of the face. **b.** An eye with an opaque or white cornea. **2.** A North American freshwater food and game fish, *Stizostedium vitreum,* with large, conspicuous eyes. **—wall′eyed′** *adj.*

wall•flow•er (wôl′flou′ər) *n.* **1. a.** A widely cultivated European plant *Cheiranthus cheiri,* with fragrant yellow, orange, or brownish flowers. **b.** A similar plant, *Erysimum asperum,* of the W U.S. **2.** *Informal.* One who only looks on at a dance or party esp. from shyness or unpopularity.

Wal•loon (wŏ-lo͞on′) *n.* One of a French-speaking people of Celtic descent inhabiting S and SE Belgium.

wal•lop (wŏl′əp) *v.* **1.** To thrash soundly. **2.** To hit with a hard blow. *—n.* **1.** A hard blow. **2.** An impact. **—wal′lop•er** *n.*

wal•lop•ing (wŏl′ə-pĭng) *adj. Informal.* **1.** Very large. **2.** Very impressive. *—n.* A sound thrashing or defeat.

wal•low (wŏl′ō) *v.* **1.** To roll around in or as if in muddy water or deep mud. **2.** To take luxurious pleasure : revel. **3.** To be or become plentifully supplied with something. *—n.* A place where animals wallow.

wall•pa•per (wôl′pā′pər) *n.* Heavy colored or patterned paper used to cover interior walls. **—wall′pa′per** *v.*

wal•nut (wôl′nŭt′, -nət) *n.* **1.** Any of several trees of the genus *Juglans,* with round, sticky fruit that encloses an edible nut. **2.** The hard, dark-brown wood of a walnut, used esp. for furniture.

wal•rus (wôl′rəs, wŏl′-) *n.* A large Arctic marine mammal, *Odobenus rosmarus,* related to the seals and sea lions and having tough, wrinkled skin and large tusks.

waltz (wôlts) *n.* **1.** A gliding dance in ¾ time. **2.** Music to accompany the waltz. *—v.* **1.** To dance the waltz (with). **2.** To move or progress lightly or easily.

wam•pum (wŏm′pəm, wôm′-) *n.* **1.** Small strung beads of polished shells, once used by North American Indians as currency or jewelry. **2.** *Informal.* Money.

wan (wŏn) *adj.* **wan•ner, wan•nest. 1.** Abnormally pale. **2.** Weak or faint <a *wan* smile> **—wan′ly** *adv.* **—wan′ness** *n.*

wand (wŏnd) *n.* **1.** A thin rod carried in a procession : scepter. **2.** A thin rod used by a magician, diviner, or sorcerer.

wan•der (wŏn′dər) *v.* **1.** To move or travel about aimlessly : roam. **2.** To go in a roundabout or leisurely way. **3.** To stray from a given place, group, or topic. **4.** To think or speak disjointedly. **5.** To go astray morally. **—wan′der•er** *n.* **—wan′der•ing•ly** *adv.*

wandering jew *n.* A trailing plant native to tropical America, *Tradescantia fluminensis* or *Zebrina pendula,* with usu. variegated foliage.

wan•der•lust (wŏn′dər-lŭst′) *n.* A strong, persistent urge to travel.

wane (wān) *v.* **waned, wan•ing. 1.** To grow gradually less illuminated when passing from full to new <The moon *wanes.*> **2.** To decrease gradually : decline. **3.** To near an end. *—n.* **1.** The period during which the moon wanes. **2.** A gradual decrease or deterioration.

wan•gle (wăng′gəl) *v.* **-gled, -gling. 1.** To do or get by connivance. **2.** To manipulate, esp. by deception or fraud. **—wan′gler** *n.*

Wan•kel engine (väng′kəl, wăng′-) *n.* An internal-combustion engine in which a triangular rotor replaces the pistons.

want (wŏnt, wônt) *v.* **1.** To desire greatly : wish. **2.** To be deficient in : lack <The novel *wants* cohesiveness.> **3.** To need : require. **4.** To be needy. **5.** To seek with intent to capture. *—n.* **1.** Lack of a usual or necessary amount. **2.** Urgent need : impoverishment. **3.** A need, desire, or requirement. **4.** A character fault or flaw.

want ad *n.* A classified advertisement.

want•ing (wŏn′tĭng, wôn′-) *adj.* **1.** Not present. **2.** Below standards or expectations. **3.** Deficient <*wanting* in tact> *—prep.* **1.** Without. **2.** Minus : less.

wan•ton (wŏn′tən) *adj.* **1. a.** Lascivious : lewd. **b.** Suggesting sexuality. **2.** Cruel and merciless : inhumane. **3.** Unduly extravagant. **4.** Lacking sound reason or cause : unjust. **5.** Excessively playful : frolicsome. *—n.* A wanton person. **—wan′ton•ly** *adv.*

wap•i•ti (wŏp′ĭ-tē) *n., pl.* **-tis** or **wapiti.** A large North American deer, *Cervus canadensis.*

war (wôr) *n.* **1.** Armed conflict between nations, states, or factions. **2.** A determined struggle esp. for a specific goal <a *war* against illiteracy> **3.** A state of antagonism or discord. **4.** Military techniques or procedures as a science. *—v.* **warred, war•ring. 1.** To engage in armed conflict. **2.** To struggle or contend.

war•ble (wôr′bəl) *v.* **-bled, -bling.** To sing a sequence of melodious trilling sounds. **—war•ble** *n.*

war•bler (wôr′blər) *n.* **1.** Any of various small, often yellowish New World birds of the family Parulidae. **2.** Any of various small brownish or grayish Old World birds of the subfamily Silviinae.

war bonnet *n.* A headdress with a trailing feathered extension worn ceremonially by some North American Indians.

war crime *n. often* **war crimes.** A crime, as genocide, committed during wartime. **—war criminal** *n.*

ward (wôrd) *n.* **1. a.** A division in a hospital <a maternity *ward*> **b.** A room in a hospital usu. for 2 or more patients. **c.** A division in a penal institution. **2.** A division of a city or town for administrative and representative purposes. **3.** A minor or incompetent person under the protection of a legal guardian or a court. **4. a.** The state of being in custody. **b.** The act of guarding or protecting. **5.** A defense. *—v.* To avert <*ward* off an attack>

-ward or **-wards** *suff.* Direction toward <earth*ward*><north*ward*>

war dance *n.* A tribal dance performed before a battle or after a victory.

war•den (wôr′dn) *n.* **1.** The administrative head of a prison. **2.** An official whose duty it is to enforce certains laws and governmental orders <a fire *warden*> **3.** A churchwarden.

ward•er (wôr′dər) *n.* One employed to stand guard or keep watch.

ward heel•er (hē′lər) *n. Slang.* A local worker for a powerful political machine.

ward•robe (wôr′drōb′) *n.* **1.** A cabinet, closet, or room for clothes. **2.** All the clothing belonging to an individual.

ward•room (wôrd′ro͞om′, -ro͝om′) *n.* A room on a warship in which commissioned officers may dine and lounge.

ward•ship (wôrd′shĭp′) *n.* **1.** The state of being a ward or under a guardian's care. **2.** The act or right of guardianship : custody.

ware (wâr) *n.* **1.** Manufactured or handmade articles of the same general kind <table*ware*> **2.** Articles made of fired clay : pottery or ceramics. **3. wares.** Articles for sale : merchandise.

ware•house (wâr′hous′) *n.* A usu. large building for the storage of goods or merchandise. **—ware′house′** *v.*

war•fare (wôr′fâr′) *n.* **1.** Armed conflict between enemies. **2.** Struggle : discord.

war•head (wôr′hĕd′) *n.* The part of a projectile, as a bomb or guided missile, that houses the charge.

war•horse (wôr′hôrs′) *n.* **1.** A horse used in battle. **2.** *Informal.* A veteran esp. of military or political life.

war•like (wôr′līk′) *adj.* **1.** Inclined to fight or make war. **2.** Of or relating to war. **3.** Portending or indicating war.

war•lock (wôr′lŏk′) *n.* A male witch or wizard.

war•lord (wôr′lôrd′) *n.* A military commander exercising civil power in a given region, whether in nominal allegiance to the national government or in defiance of it.

warm (wôrm) *adj.* **1.** Neither cool nor very hot : moderately hot. **2. a.** Giving off a moderate amount of heat, as the sun. **b.** Helping to retain bodily heat <*warm* clothes> **3.** Feeling sensations of high bodily heat, as from vigorous exercise. **4.** Enthusiastic : ardent <*warm* praises> **5.** Marked by excitement or emotional tensions. **6.** Freshly made, as a trail or scent. **7.** Close to a goal, as in a game or search. **8.** *Informal.* Distressing or dangerous <made things *warm* for the suspect> **9.** Marked by warmth of color, tone, or feeling. *—v.* **1.** To make or become somewhat high in temperature. **2.** To make lively or spirited. **3.** To inspire with pleasant feelings. **4.** To become kindly disposed. **5.** To become gradually more ardent or animated, as in public speaking. **—warm up.** To make or become prepared for action, as by preliminary practicing or exercising. **—warm′er** *n.* **—warm′ish** *adj.* **—warm′ly** *adv.*

warm-blood•ed (wôrm′blŭd′ĭd) *adj.* Having a relatively constant warm body temperature unrelated to the temperature of the surroundings, as a bird or mammal. **—warm′-blood′ed•ness** *n.*

warm-heart•ed (wôrm′här′tĭd) *adj.* Marked by emotional warmth : kind and friendly. **—warm′heart′ed•ly** *adv.* **—warm′-heart′ed•ness** *n.*

war•mon•ger (wôr′mŭng′gər, -mŏng′-) *n.* One who favors or tries to stir up war. **—war′mon′ger•ing** *n.* & *adj.*

warmth (wôrmth) *n.* **1.** The quality or state of being warm. **2.** Kindness, friendliness, etc. **3.** Excitement or intensity.

warm-up (wôrm′ŭp′) *n.* An act, method, or time of warming up.

warn (wôrn) *v.* **1.** To alert to danger. **2.** To admonish or advise as to action or conduct. **3.** To direct to go or remain away. **4.** To notify or inform beforehand. ☆**syns:** ALERT, CAUTION, FOREWARN

warn•ing (wôr′nĭng) *n.* **1.** An intimation esp. of impending danger. **2. a.** A sign or notice of impending danger. **b.** The act of giving such a sign. *—adj.* Serving as a warning. **—warn′ing•ly** *adv.*

warp (wôrp) *v.* **1.** To distort or become bent out of shape, as wood. **2.** To deviate or cause to deviate from a proper course. **3.** *Naut.* To move (a vessel) by hauling on a line attached to a piling, anchor, or pier. —*n.* **1.** The state of being warped. **2.** A distortion or twist. **3.** The lengthwise threads in a woven fabric, crossed at right angles by the woof threads.

war paint *n.* **1.** Pigments applied to the face or body as a tribal ceremony before waging war. **2.** *Informal.* Make-up.

war•path (wôr′păth′, -päth′) *n.* **1.** The course taken by a band of North American Indians on an expedition of war. **2.** A hostile course or mood <on the *warpath*>

war•plane (wôr′plān′) *n.* An aircraft equipped for combat.

war•rant (wôr′ənt, wŏr′-) *n.* **1.** Authorization or justification. **2.** Something that assures, proves, or guarantees. **3.** A written authorization, esp. a legal writ authorizing a search, seizure, or arrest. **4.** A certificate of appointment to the rank of warrant officer. —*v.* **1.** To give proof of : bear witness to. **2.** To vouch for. **3. a.** To guarantee (a product) to be as represented. **b.** To guarantee (a buyer) insurance against damage or loss. **4.** To call for or merit. **5.** To grant authorization to. **—war′rant•a•ble** *adj.* **—war′ran•tee′** *n.* **—war′ran•tor** *n.*

warrant officer *n.* A military officer ranking below a commissioned officer and above a noncommissioned officer.

war•ran•ty (wôr′ən-tē, wŏr′-) *n., pl.* **-ties. 1.** Official authorization. **2.** Justification for a course of action. **3.** A legally binding written guarantee.

war•ren (wôr′ən, wŏr′-) *n.* **1.** A living and breeding area for rabbits. **2.** A crowded dwelling place or locality.

war•ri•or (wôr′ē-ər, wŏr′-) *n.* One who fights in a war, esp. a battle veteran.

War•saw (wôr′sô). Cap. of Poland, in the EC part. *Pop.* 1,576,600.

war•ship (wôr′shĭp′) *n.* A ship equipped for combat.

wart (wôrt) *n.* **1.** A small, usu. hard outgrowth on the skin, esp. one produced by a virus. **2.** A wartlike protuberance, as on a plant. **—wart′y** *adj.*

wart hog *n.* A wild African tusked hog, *Phacochoerus aethiopicus,* with wartlike swellings on the face.

wart hog

war•y (wâr′ē) *adj.* **-i•er, -i•est. 1.** Alert to danger : watchful. **2.** Marked by caution : careful. **—war′i•ly** *adv.* **—war′i•ness** *n.*

was (wŏz, wŭz; wəz *when unstressed*) *v. 1st & 3rd person sing. p.t. of* BE.

†**wash** (wŏsh, wôsh) *v.* **1.** To cleanse usu. with water and soap or detergent. **2.** To make oneself clean. **3.** To cleanse of moral corruption. **4.** To make somewhat wet. **5.** To flow over or along. **6.** To carry or be carried away by water. **7.** To erode or destroy by water. **8.** To cover (e.g., a canvas) with a thin, watery layer of paint or other coloring. **9.** To pour or shake water through to separate out valuable material. **10.** *Informal.* To hold up under inspection <Your story just won't *wash.*> —*n.* **1.** An act, process, or instance of washing or undergoing washing. **2.** A quantity of soiled or laundered clothes, linens, etc. **3. a.** A liquid used in cleansing or coating something. **b.** A thin coating, as of water color or whitewash. **4. a.** A turbulent rush or surge of air or water. **b.** The sound of this. **5.** Liquid refuse : swill. **6.** Soil erosion by the action of moving water. **7.** *W U.S.* The dry bed of a stream.

Wash. *abbr.* Washington.

wash•a•ble (wŏsh′ə-bəl, wô′shə-bəl) *adj.* Able to withstand washing without damage <a *washable* fabric>

wash-and-wear (wŏsh′ən-wâr′, wôsh′-) *adj.* Requiring little or no ironing after being washed <a *wash-and-wear* shirt>

wash•ba•sin (wôsh′bā′sĭn) *n.* A basin for washing : washbowl.

wash•board (wŏsh′bôrd′, -bōrd′, wôsh′-) *n.* A corrugated board on which clothes can be scrubbed clean.

wash•bowl (wŏsh′bōl′, wôsh′-) *n.* A water basin esp. for use in washing one's hands and face.

wash•cloth (wŏsh′klôth′, -klŏth′, wôsh′-) *n.* A small cloth for washing oneself.

washed-out (wŏsht′out′, wôsht′-) *adj.* **1. a.** Faded. **b.** Pale. **2.** *Informal.* Tired out.

wash•er (wŏsh′ər, wô′shər) *n.* **1.** One that washes, esp. a machine for washing clothes or dishes. **2.** A small disk or plate used under a nut or at an axle bearing to relieve friction or prevent leakage.

wash•er•wom•an (wŏsh′ər-wo͝om′ən, wô′shər-) *n.* A woman who launders clothes for a living : laundress.

wash•ing (wŏsh′ĭng, wô′shĭng) *n.* **1.** A batch of articles washed or to be washed : laundry. **2.** The material remaining after an ore has been washed. **3.** A thin coating or covering.

washing soda *n.* A hydrated carbonate of sodium, used as an all-purpose cleanser.

Wash•ing•ton (wŏsh′ĭng-tən, wôsh′-). State of the NW U.S., on the Pacific. *Cap.* Olympia. *Pop.* 4,130,163. **—Wash′ing•to′ni•an** (-tō′nē-ən) *n.*

Washington. 1. George. 1732–99. 1st U.S. President (1789–97). **2. Booker Taliaferro.** 1856–1915. Amer. educator.

wash•out (wŏsh′out′, wôsh′-) *n.* **1.** The removal or erosion of something by water. **2.** A total failure.

wash•room (wŏsh′ro͞om′, -ro͝om′, wôsh′-) *n.* A rest room or lavatory.

wash•stand (wŏsh′stănd′, wôsh′-) *n.* **1.** A small table with a basin and a pitcher of water for washing. **2.** A stationary washbowl, esp. in a bathroom.

wash•tub (wŏsh′tŭb′, wôsh′-) *n.* A tub for washing clothes.

wash•y (wŏsh′ē, wô′shē) *adj.* **-i•er, -i•est. 1.** Having a watery consistency : diluted. **2.** Lacking force, intensity, or definition.

was•n't (wŏz′ənt, wŭz′-). Was not.

wasp (wŏsp, wôsp) *n.* Any of numerous insects, chiefly of the superfamilies Vespoidea and Sphecoidea, having a slender body with a constricted abdomen, the female of which is capable of inflicting a painful sting.

Wasp or **WASP** (wŏsp, wôsp) *n.* A white American Protestant whose ancestors were Anglo-Saxon. **—Wasp′ish** *adj.*

wasp•ish (wŏs′pĭsh, wô′spĭsh) *adj.* **1.** Of or typical of a wasp. **2.** Easily vexed : snappish. **—wasp′ish•ness** *n.*

wasp waist *n.* A very narrow waist. **—wasp′-waist′ed** *adj.*

was•sail (wŏs′əl, wŏ-sāl′) *n.* **1. a.** An English toast given to someone's health in former times. **b.** The alcoholic beverage used in giving this toast. **2.** A festive occasion with much drinking. —*v.* To drink a wassail (to) : toast. **—was′sail•er** *n.*

Was•ser•mann test (wä′sər-mən) *n.* A blood test for syphilis.

wast•age (wā′stĭj) *n.* **1.** Loss by use, wear, decline, destruction, or wastefulness. **2.** Something wasted or lost by wear.

waste (wāst) *v.* **wast•ed, wast•ing. 1.** To use or expend carelessly or needlessly : squander. **2.** To grow or cause to grow gradually thinner or weaker, as from illness. **3. a.** To fail to use, as an opportunity. **b.** To be available without being put to use <Time is *wasting.*> **4.** To destroy completely : devastate. **5.** *Slang.* To murder. ☆***syns:*** CONSUME, DEVOUR, EXPEND, SQUANDER —*n.* **1. a.** The act or an example of wasting. **b.** The condition of being wasted. **2.** Gradual loss through wastefulness. **3.** Worthless or useless material that is produced as a by-product or discarded as refuse. **4.** Unusable digestive residue eliminated from the body. **5.** A barren region. **—wast′er** *n.* **—waste′ful** *adj.*

waste•bas•ket (wāst′băs′kĭt) *n.* A container for wastepaper or trash.

waste•land (wāst′lănd′) *n.* Uncultivated or uninhabited land, as a desert.

waste•pa•per (wāst′pā′pər) *n.* Discarded paper.

wast•rel (wā′strəl) *n.* **1.** One who wastes, esp. a spendthrift. **2.** A lazy person : idler.

watch (wŏch) *v.* **1.** To look at or observe attentively and usu. continuously. **2.** To wait expectantly <*watch* for a chance> **3.** To be on the alert. **4.** To keep guard or vigil. **5.** To keep informed about. **6.** To keep guard over : tend. ☆***syns:*** EYE, OBSERVE, SCRUTINIZE —*n.* **1.** The act of staying awake esp. to guard or attend. **2.** A period of attentive observation. **3.** One or several serving to guard or protect <a night *watch*> **4.** The post or period of duty of one who keeps watch. **5.** A small, portable timepiece worn or carried on the person. **6.** *Naut.* **a.** A designated period of time for certain crew members to be on duty. **b.** The crew members on duty during a given watch. **—watch′er** *n.*

watch•case wŏch′kās′) *n.* The casing for the mechanism of a watch.

watch•dog (wŏch′dôg′, -dŏg′) *n.* **1.** A dog trained to guard esp. private property against intruders. **2.** One who serves as a guardian or protector against waste, loss, or illegal practices.

watch•ful (wŏch′fəl) *adj.* Constantly on the alert, esp. for danger. **—watch′ful•ly** *adv.* **—watch′ful•ness** *n.*

watch•mak•er (wŏch′mā′kər) *n.* A maker or repairer of watches.

watch•man (wŏch′mən) *n.* One employed to keep watch : guard.

watch·tow·er (wŏch′tou′ər) *n.* A tower for a lookout or sentinel.

watch·word (wŏch′wûrd′) *n.* **1.** A secret word or phrase spoken to a guard to gain entrance. **2.** A slogan.

wa·ter (wô′tər, wŏt′ər) *n.* **1.** A clear liquid compound of hydrogen and oxygen that is essential for most plant and animal life. **2.** A form of water, as rain, ice, or steam. **3. a.** A body of water, as an ocean, lake, or river. **b.** An area or quantity of water, esp. ocean water near or controlled by a country. **4.** A bodily fluid, as urine or tears. **5.** A solution containing and resembling water <soda *water*> **6.** A pattern or finish, as of a fabric, marked by a wavy luster. **7. a.** Clearness and luster of a precious gem. **b.** Degree of completeness. Used esp. in the phrase *of the first water.* —*v.* **1.** To make wet by supplying with water. **2. a.** To give drinking water to. **b.** To get or take on water. **3.** To mix or dilute with or as if with water. **4.** To give a wavy finish or luster to the surface of (e.g., silk or metal). **5.** To produce or discharge a watery fluid.

water bed *n.* A bed consisting of a tough, heavy plastic bag filled with water.

wa·ter·borne (wô′tər-bôrn′, -bōrn′, wŏt′ər-) *adj.* Supported, transported, or transmitted by water.

water buffalo *n.* A large, often domesticated Asian or African buffalo, *Bubalus bubalis,* with spreading horns.

water chestnut *n.* A Chinese sedge, *Eleocharis tuberosa,* with an edible, succulent corm used esp. in Oriental cookery.

water closet *n.* A small room with a toilet and often a sink.

water color *also* **wa·ter·col·or** (wô′tər-kŭl′ər, wŏt′ər-) *n.* **1.** A paint in which water rather than oil is mixed with the coloring material. **2.** A picture done in water colors. **3.** The art or process of using water colors. **—water colorist** *n.*

wa·ter·course (wô′tər-kôrs′, -kōrs′, wŏt′ər-) *n.* **1.** A waterway. **2.** A channel through which water flows.

wa·ter·cress (wô′tər-krĕs′, wŏt′ər-) *n.* A freshwater plant, *Nasturtium officinale,* with pungent edible leaves.

wa·ter·fall (wô′tər fôl′, wŏt′ər) *n.* A natural stream of water descending from a steep height.

wa·ter·fowl (wô′tər-foul′, wŏt′ər-) *n.* **1.** A swimming bird usu. found in freshwater areas. **2.** Swimming birds as a group.

wa·ter·front (wô′tər-frŭnt′, wŏt′ər-) *n.* **1.** Land bordering a body of water, as a harbor or lake. **2.** The district of a town or city that borders the water, esp. a wharf district.

water gap *n.* A transverse gap in a mountain ridge through which a stream runs.

watering place *n.* A health resort with mineral springs for drinking, bathing, etc.

water lily *n.* An aquatic plant of the genus *Nymphaea,* with floating leaves and variously colored often fragrant flowers.

water line *n.* **1.** The line on a ship's hull to which the water surface rises. **2.** A line on a ship's hull indicating the depth to which the ship sinks when carrying cargo.

wa·ter-logged (wô′tər-lôgd′, -lŏgd′, wŏt′ər-) *adj.* So filled or saturated with water as to be heavy or unwieldy.

Wa·ter·loo (wô′tər-lo͞o′) *n.* **1.** Town of C Belgium; site of Napoleon's final defeat (1815). **2. waterloo.** A disastrous defeat.

wa·ter·mark (wô′tər-märk′, wŏt′ər-) *n.* **1.** A mark indicating the height to which water has risen, esp. the height of high and low tide. **2.** A very faintly visible design impressed on paper during manufacture. —*v.* To mark (paper) with a watermark.

wa·ter·mel·on (wô′tər-mĕl′ən, wŏt′ər-) *n.* A native African vine, *Citrullus vulgaris,* grown for its large, edible fruit, which has a hard green rind and sweet pink flesh.

water moccasin *n.* A venomous snake, *Agkistrodon piscivorus,* of lowlands and swampy areas of the S U.S.

water ouzel *n.* A small bird of the genus *Cinclus* that feeds along the bottom of swift-moving streams.

water polo *n.* A water sport with 2 teams of swimmers that try to push, throw, or carry a ball into the other's goal.

wa·ter·pow·er (wô′tər-pou′ər, wŏt′ər-) *n.* The energy of swift-moving water as used esp. for generating electricity.

wa·ter·proof (wô′tər-pro͞of′, wŏt′ər-) *adj.* Capable of keeping water from penetrating. —*n.* **1.** A waterproof fabric or material. **2.** *esp. Brit.* A raincoat : slicker. —*v.* To treat in order to make waterproof.

wa·ter-re·pel·lent (wô′tər-rĭ-pĕl′ənt, wŏt′ər-) *adj.* Treated to resist water but not completely waterproof.

wa·ter-re·sis·tant (wô′tər-rĭ-zĭs′tənt, wŏt′ər-) *adj.* Water-repellent.

wa·ter·shed (wô′tər-shĕd′, wŏt′ər-) *n.* **1.** A ridge between regions whose water drains into 2 different river systems. **2.** The region or area drained by a river system or other body of water. **3.** A critical point serving as a dividing line.

wa·ter·side (wô′tər-sīd′, wŏt′ər-) *n.* Land alongside a body of water.

wa·ter-ski *also* **water ski** (wô′tər-skē′, wŏt′ər-) *n.* One of a pair of short, broad skis worn while skimming over water behind a towing motorboat. **—wa′ter-ski′** *v.* **—wa′ter-ski′er** *n.*

wa·ter·spout (wô′tər-spout′, wŏt′ər-) *n.* **1.** A hole or pipe from which water is discharged. **2.** A tornado or whirlwind over an ocean or lake that appears as a whirling funnel-shaped column of spray and mist.

water strider *n.* An insect of the family Gerridae, with long, slender legs for supporting itself on the water surface.

water table *n.* The upper limit of a zone of underground rock that is entirely saturated with water.

wa·ter·tight (wô′tər-tīt′, wŏt′ər-) *adj.* **1.** Tight enough to prevent water from getting in. **2.** Incapable of being misinterpreted, thwarted, etc. : flawless.

wa·ter·way (wô′tər-wā′, wŏt′ər-) *n.* A navigable body of water.

water wheel *n.* A wheel propelled by falling or flowing water.

water wings *pl.n.* An inflatable device used to support one's body in water.

wa·ter·works (wô′tər-wûrks′, wŏt′ər-) *pl.n. (sing. or pl. in number).* A system of reservoirs, pipes, and pumping stations, that supplies water to a city or town.

wa·ter·y (wô′tə-rē, wŏt′ə-) *adj.* **-i·er, -i·est. 1.** Filled with or containing water. **2.** Resembling or reminiscent of water. **3.** Weak or thin : diluted. **4.** Lacking force or effectiveness. **—wa′ter·i·ness** *n.*

watt (wŏt) *n.* A unit of electrical power equal to 1 joule per sec.

watt·age (wŏt′ĭj) *n.* Amount of electrical power expressed in watts.

wat·tle (wŏt′l) *n.* **1.** Sticks and twigs, branches, reeds, etc., woven into a construction material, as for walls or fences. **2.** A fleshy, often vividly colored flap of skin hanging from the head or neck of certain birds and lizards.

wave (wāv) *v.* **waved, wav·ing. 1.** To move or cause to move back and forth or up and down : flap or flutter. **2.** To signal or express by waving <*wave* good-bye> **3.** To arrange or fall in curves or curls, as hair. —*n.* **1.** An undulating ridge or swell on the surface of water. **2.** An undulation or succession of rippling movements in or on a surface <*waves* of tall grass> **3.** A curve or an arrangement of curves, as in the hair. **4.** An up-and-down or back-and-forth movement. **5. a.** A sweeping or surging movement <*waves* of protest> **b.** A peak of activity <a buying *wave*> **6.** A persistent condition of unusually hot or cold weather. **7.** *Physics.* A disturbance or oscillation that passes energy from point to point in a medium or in space <a sound *wave*> **—wave′like** *adj.*

Wave (wāv) *n.* A member of the women's reserve of the U.S. Navy.

wave·band (wāv′bănd′) *n.* A range of radio frequencies.

wave·form (wāv′fôrm′) *n.* Mathematical representation of a wave.

wave·length (wāv′lĕngth′) *n.* The distance in a periodic wave between 2 points of corresponding phases.

wave·let (wāv′lĭt) *n.* A small wave.

wa·ver (wā′vər) *v.* **1.** To sway unsteadily back and forth. **2.** To be undecided or irresolute : vacillate. **3.** To weaken in force or purpose <My courage began to *waver.*> **4.** To have a trembling or quavering sound. **5.** To flicker or flutter, as candlelight. **—wa′ver** *n.* **—wa′ver·ing·ly** *adv.*

wav·y (wā′vē) *adj.* **-i·er, -i·est. 1.** Having or moving in waves. **2.** Characterized by wavelike or winding curves.

wax¹ (wăks) *n.* **1.** Any of various natural yellowish solid or soft, sticky substances, as beeswax, that when heated melt or soften easily. **2.** A waxy substance occurring naturally in the ears. **3.** A solid plastic or very thick liquid material, as paraffin. **4.** A commercial preparation containing wax and used esp. for shining surfaces. —*v.* To treat or shine with wax.

wax² (wăks) *v.* **1.** To grow gradually more illuminated when passing from new to full <The moon *waxes.*> **2.** To increase gradually, as in quantity or strength. **3.** To become <The weather *waxed* cool.>

wax bean *n.* A variety of snap bean with long, pale-yellow pods.

wax·en (wăk′sən) *adj.* **1.** Made of or coated with wax. **2.** Pale-yellow or very smooth like wax <a *waxen* complexion>

wax myrtle *n.* A shrub, *Myrica cerifera,* of the SE U.S., bearing with evergreen leaves and small, waxy berrylike fruit.

wax paper *or* **waxed paper** *n.* Paper treated against moisture with wax.

wax·wing (wăks′wĭng′) *n.* A crested bird of the genus *Bombycilla,* with brownish plumage and red-tipped wing feathers.

wax·work (wăks′wûrk′) *n.* **1.** A usu. life-size figure made of wax. **2. waxworks.** *(sing. or pl. in number).* An exhibition of waxwork representing famous persons.

wax•y (wăk′sē) *adj.* **-i•er, -i•est. 1.** Like wax in texture or appearance. **2.** Consisting of or full of wax. **—wax′i•ness** *n.*

†**way** (wā) *n.* **1.** A manner or fashion. **2.** A means, method, or technique. **3.** An aspect or feature. **4.** A characteristic or tendency. **5.** A customary manner of living, acting, or doing. **6.** A passage leading from one place to another. **7.** Progress toward a goal. **8.** Sufficient room for passing <make *way*> **9.** An extent of linear space : distance. **10.** Direction of movement or location. **11.** Facility : talent. **12.** Freedom to do as one likes. **13.** A course of conduct or action <did it the hard *way*> **14.** A condition or state of affairs <That's the *way* it is.> **15.** *Informal.* A district or locality. **—out of the way. 1.** Remote. **2.** Improper. **—under way.** Actively progressing.

way•bill (wā′bĭl′) *n.* A list of goods, charges, and shipping instructions accompanying a shipment.

way•far•er (wā′fâr′ər) *n.* One who travels, esp. on foot. **—way′far′ing** *adj.* & *n.*

way•lay (wā′lā′) *v.* **1.** To attack from ambush. **2.** To accost or intercept in an attempt to speak with. **—way′lay′er** *n.*

way-out (wā′out′) *adj. Slang.* Very unconventional : far-out.

ways and means *pl.n.* **1.** Ways of funding a specific project or accomplishing a specific goal. **2.** A committee in charge of ways and means.

way•side (wā′sīd′) *n.* Land at the immediate edge of a road.

way station *n.* An intermediate stop on a travel route.

way•ward (wā′wərd) *adj.* **1.** Willful : intractable <a *wayward* child> **2.** Capricious : unpredictable <a *wayward* breeze>

we (wē) *pron.* **1.** Used to refer to the person speaking or writing plus another or others. **2.** Used instead of *I* in an official capacity by a monarch or by an editor or writer. **3.** People in general.

weak (wēk) *adj.* **1.** Having little strength or energy : feeble. **2.** Easily damaged or broken : fragile. **3.** Marked by, indicative of, or resulting from insufficient intellect, character, strength, or will power. **4.** Lacking the usual or required strength <*weak* broth> **5.** Lacking the ability to function normally <*weak* lungs> **6.** Having inadequate capability or skills <a *weak* administrator> **7.** Unconvincing <a *weak* alibi> **8.** Not forceful or intense <a *weak* little voice><*weak* sunlight> **9.** Of or being a verb whose past tense and past participle are formed by adding *-ed, -d,* or *-t.* **—weak′ly** *adv.*

weak•en (wē′kən) *v.* To make or become weak. **—weak′en•er** *n.*

weak•fish (wēk′fĭsh′) *n.* A marine food and game fish of the genus *Cynoscion,* esp. *C. regalis* of N Atlantic waters.

weak-kneed (wēk′nēd′) *adj.* Lacking in courage or determination.

weak•ling (wēk′lĭng) *n.* One of weak constitution or character.

weak•ly (wēk′lē) *adj.* **-li•er, -li•est.** Feeble : sickly.

weak•ness (wēk′nĭs) *n.* **1.** The state or sensation or an instance of being weak. **2.** A defect or shortcoming. **3. a.** A particular fondness. **b.** An object of special liking.

weal[1] (wēl) *n.* Well-being : welfare.

weal[2] (wēl) *n.* A welt.

wealth (wĕlth) *n.* **1.** Abundance of riches, resources, or valuable possessions. **2.** An abundant amount <a *wealth* of information> **3.** All goods, property, and resources having monetary value.

wealth•y (wĕl′thē) *adj.* **-i•er, -i•est. 1.** Having much wealth : affluent. **2.** Richly supplied : abundant.

wean (wēn) *v.* **1.** To train (a young child or mammal) to stop nursing and take other nourishment. **2.** To rid of a dependence on something undesirable.

weap•on (wĕp′ən) *n.* **1.** An instrument or device used for offense or defense. **2.** A means employed to contend with another.

weap•on•ry (wĕp′ən-rē) *n.* **1.** Design and manufacture of weapons. **2.** Weapons.

wear (wâr) *v.* **wore** (wôr, wōr), **worn** (wôrn, wōrn), **wear•ing. 1.** To have on or put on, as clothes or accessories. **2.** To bear regularly on one's person <*wears* a mustache> **3.** To affect or display <always *wearing* a grin> **4.** To maintain in a certain way <*wore* my hair in pigtails> **5.** To damage or expend by or as if by excessive use, friction, or exposure to weather. **6.** To make by continual use or exposure. **7.** To exhaust or become exhausted. **8.** To hold up under long or hard use : last. **9.** To pass gradually <The day *wore* on.><The anesthetic *wore off.*> **—wear down.** To weaken the resistance of by constant pressure. *—n.* **1. a.** The act of wearing. **b.** The state of being worn : use. **2.** Clothing, esp. of a specific type or for a specific use <children's *wear*> <beach *wear*> **3.** Gradual depreciation or decline resulting from use or age. **4.** Durability. **—wear′a•bil′i•ty** *n.* **—wear′a•ble** *adj.*

wear and tear *n.* Depreciation, damage, or loss resulting from ordinary use.

wea•ri•some (wîr′ē-səm) *adj.* Causing fatigue : tedious. **—wea′ri•some•ly** *adv.*

wea•ry (wîr′ē) *adj.* **-ri•er, -ri•est. 1.** Feeling fatigued. **2.** Indicative of fatigue. **3.** Exhausted of patience. *—v.* **-ried, -ry•ing.** To make or become fatigued. **—wea′ri•ly** *adv.* **—wea′ri•ness** *n.*

wea•sel (wē′zəl) *n.* **1.** A long-tailed carnivorous mammal of the genus *Mustela,* with a long, slender body and short legs. **2.** A sneaky, devious person. *—v.* To speak or act evasively.

weath•er (wĕth′ər) *n.* **1.** The state of the atmosphere in terms of temperature, humidity, wind velocity, and barometric pressure. **2.** Stormy or disagreeable atmospheric conditions. *—v.* **1.** To subject to or resist the action of weather. **2.** To change through exposure to the weather. **3.** To survive successfully.

weath•er-beat•en (wĕth′ər-bēt′n) *adj.* **1.** Impaired by exposure to the elements. **2.** Tanned and leathery from being exposed to the weather <*weather-beaten* skin>

weath•er-bound (wĕth′ər-bound′) *adj.* Delayed or kept indoors by bad weather.

weath•er•cock (wĕth′ər-kŏk′) *n.* **1.** A weather vane often in the form of a cock. **2.** A fickle or changeable person.

weath•er•ize (wĕth′ə-rīz′) *v.* To make repairs and improvements on as a protective measure against cold weather.

weath•er•man (wĕth′ər-măn′) *n.* One who reports or forecasts the weather.

weath•er•proof (wĕth′ər-pro͞of′) *adj.* Capable of being exposed to weather without impairment. *—v.* To make weatherproof.

weather stripping *n.* A narrow piece of material fitted around doors and windows to make a seal against cold weather. **—weath′er-strip′** *v.*

weather vane *n.* A vane that turns to indicate the direction the wind is blowing.

weave (wēv) *v.* **wove** (wōv) or **weaved, wo•ven** (wō′vən), **weav•ing. 1.a.** To make (cloth) by interlacing woof and warp threads on a loom. **b.** To interlace (threads or strands) into cloth. **2.** To make (e.g, a basket or rug) by intertwining the materials of. **3.** To bring together into a whole. **4.** To wind or twine into a material or work. **5.** To spin (a spider's web). **6.** To make one's way by moving in and out. *—n.* A pattern or technique of weaving. **—weav′er** *n.*

web (wĕb) *n.* **1.** A fabric on or being taken from a loom. **2.** An interlacing of materials that forms a latticed or woven structure. **3.** A cobweb. **4.** Something intricately constructed, as an entanglement or snare. **5.** A complicated network <a *web* of electrical wires> **6.** A piece of skin or membrane, esp. one joining the toes of certain water birds. **7.** A thin metal sheet, plate, or strip in a structural element. *—v.* **webbed, web•bing. 1.** To cover, join, or provide with a web. **2.** To entangle in or as if in a web. **—webbed** *adj.*

web•bing (wĕb′ĭng) *n.* A strong closely woven fabric used esp. for seat belts, brake linings, or upholstery.

web-foot•ed (wĕb′fo͝ot′ĭd) *adj.* Having webbed feet.

Web•ster (wĕb′stər). **Noah.** 1758–1843. Amer. lexicographer.

wed (wĕd) *v.* **wed•ded, wed** or **wed•ded, wed•ding. 1.** To take as a spouse : marry. **2.** To unite (a couple) in marriage. **3.** To unite closely.

we'd (wēd). **1.** We had. **2.** We should. **3.** We would.

Wed. *abbr.* Wednesday.

wed•ding (wĕd′ĭng) *n.* **1.** A matrimonial ceremony or celebration. **2.** A marriage anniversary or its celebration. **3.** A joining together in close association.

wedge (wĕj) *n.* **1.** A tapered triangular piece of wood or metal used for splitting, tightening, securing, or levering. **2.** Something wedge-shaped. **3.** Something, as an action, idea, or policy that causes division or disruption among people. *—v.* **wedged, wedg•ing. 1.** To force apart or divide with or as if with a wedge. **2.** To make fast with a wedge. **3.** To squeeze into a limited space.

wed•lock (wĕd′lŏk′) *n.* The state of being married : marriage.

Wednes•day (wĕnz′dē, -dā′) *n.* The 4th day of the week.

wee (wē) *adj.* **we•er, we•est. 1.** Very small. **2.** Very early <the *wee* hours>

weed[1] (wēd) *n.* A plant held to have no value, esp. one growing plentifully and detrimentally in a garden, lawn, etc. *—v.* **1.** To remove or rid of weeds. **2.** To get rid of as undesirable or unfit. **—weed′er** *n.* **—weed′i•ness** *n.* **—weed′y** *adj.*

weed[2] (wēd) *n.* **1.** A symbol of mourning, as a black arm band. **2. weeds.** Black clothes worn by a widow in mourning. **3.** *often* **weeds.** A garment.

week (wēk) *n.* **1.** A period of 7 days, esp. a period that begins on a Sunday and ends the following Saturday. **2.** The school or business hours of a calendar week.

week•day (wēk′dā′) *n.* **1.** Any day of the week excluding Sunday. **2.** A day not included in the weekend.

week•end (wēk′ĕnd′) *n.* The end of the school or business week, esp. the period from Friday evening through Sunday evening. *–v.* To pass the weekend.

week•ly (wēk′lē) *adv.* **1.** Once a week or every week. **2.** By the week : per week. *–adj.* **1.** Done, taking place, or issued every week. **2.** Made or figured by the week. *–n., pl.* **-lies.** A newspaper or magazine issued once a week.

ween (wēn) *v.* **weened, ween•ing.** *Archaic.* To think : imagine.

weep (wēp) *v.* **wept** (wĕpt), **weep•ing. 1.** To express emotion, as sorrow or joy, by shedding tears : cry. **2.** To ooze or exude (drops of a liquid). *–n. often* **weeps.** A fit of weeping. **–weep′er** *n.*

weep•ing (wē′pĭng) *adj.* **1.** Shedding tears : tearful. **2.** Having long, slender, drooping branches <a *weeping* willow> *–n.* The act of shedding tears.

weep•y (wē′pē) *adj.* **-i•er, -i•est.** Given to weeping : tearful.

wee•vil (wē′vəl) *n.* Any of various beetles, chiefly of the family Curculionidae, that usu. have a downward-curving snout and are damaging to plants and plant products. **–wee′vil•y, wee′vil•ly** *adj.*

weft (wĕft) *n.* **1.** The horizontal threads in weaving : woof. **2.** Fabric that is woven.

weigh (wā) *v.* **1.** To find out the weight of by or as if by using a scale or similar instrument. **2.** To balance carefully in the mind : ponder. **3.** *Naut.* To hoist up (an anchor) prior to sailing. **4.** To have or be of a particular weight. **5.** To have influence or importance : count <testimony *weighing* in our favor> **6.** To burden : oppress.

weight (wāt) *n.* **1.** Heaviness or mass of an object as determined by weighing. **2. a.** The gravitational force exerted on an object. **b.** A unit measure of this force, as an ounce or pound. **c.** A system of such units. **3.** An object used chiefly to exert a downward force, as a solid used for making scientific measurements. **4.** An object, as a paperweight, for holding something down. **5.** A heavy object, as a barbell, used in weightlifting. **6.** A burden <the *weight* of many tasks> **7.** The greatest portion <the *weight* of the evidence> **8.** Authoritative influence or importance. *–v.* **1.** To make heavy with or as if with a weight. **2.** To burden or oppress.

weight•less (wāt′lĭs) *adj.* **1.** Having very little weight. **2.** Experiencing little or no gravitational force, as an orbiting object.

weight•lift•ing (wāt′lĭf′tĭng) *n.* The lifting of barbells for exercise or in athletic events.

weight•y (wā′tē) *adj.* **-i•er, -i•est. 1. a.** Having great weight : heavy. **b.** Fat. **2.** Of great importance. **3.** Burdensome. **4.** Authoritative. **–weight′i•ly** *adv.* **–weight′i•ness** *n.*

Wei•mar•an•er (vī′mä-rä′nər, wī′-) *n.* A large dog with a smooth grayish coat.

Weimaraner

weir (wîr) *n.* **1.** A dam built to direct or back up the flow of water. **2.** A fence or barrier, as of branches or net, placed in a stream to catch or retain fish.

weird (wîrd) *adj.* **1.** Having a mysterious or unearthly quality. **2.** Of an odd, bizarre, or inexplicable nature. ☆***syns:*** EERIE, UNCANNY, UNEARTHLY

▲word history: When Macbeth referred to the witches on the heath as the "weird sisters" he was not being insulting, he was being etymological and innovative at the same time. The phrase *weird sisters* orig. referred to the Fates, the 3 women of classical myth who controlled the destiny of each individual person. The phrase was also extended to include women who prophesied or possessed other attributes of the Fates. *Weird* by itself was a noun that orig. meant "fate" or "destiny" pure and simple, and in medieval times the word was used to translate *Parca,* the Latin word for "Fate." This use of *weird* lost currency during the modern period, surviving primarily in the phrase "weird sisters," where it was interpreted as an adjective. The great prestige of Shakespeare preserved this use of *weird,* which was extended to its current meaning by 19th-cent. poets and writers.

weird•ie *also* **weird•y** (wîr′dē) *n. pl.* **-ies.** *Slang.* A weirdo.

weird•o (wîr′dō) *n., pl.* **-oes.** *Slang.* One that is strange or bizarre.

wel•come (wĕl′kəm) *v.* **-comed, -com•ing. 1.** To greet or extend hospitality cordially to. **2.** To accept willingly or gladly <*welcome* an opportunity> *–n.* A warm greeting or reception. *–adj.* **1.** Greeted or received warmly. **2.** Pleasing : gratifying. **3.** Willingly invited or allowed. **4.** Used in the phrase "you're welcome" to acknowledge thanks. *–interj.* Used as a cordial greeting.

weld (wĕld) *v.* **1.** To unite (metal parts) by applying heat and sometimes pressure. **2.** To bring closely together : unite. *–n.* A union or joint formed by welding.

wel•fare (wĕl′fâr′) *n.* **1.** The state of being healthy, happy, or prosperous : general well-being. **2.** Organized efforts by a community or private agency to improve the circumstances of the poor. **3.** Governmental aid to the disadvantaged or disabled.

well[1] (wĕl) *n.* **1.** A deep excavation to obtain a natural deposit, as water, oil, or gas. **2.** A spring or fountain serving as a natural source of water. **3.** A valuable source of supply. **4.** A container or reservoir for a liquid. **5.** A vertical opening through floors, as for a staircase. **6.** An enclosure around the pumps in a ship's hold. *–v.* To rise to the surface and flow forth.

well[2] (wĕl) *adv.* **bet•ter** (bĕt′ər), **best** (bĕst). **1.** In a good or correct fashion : properly. **2.** With skill or proficiency : expertly. **3.** In a satisfactory or sufficient way <dined *well*> **4.** In an effective or successful way <communicates *well* with teenagers> **5.** Comfortably or affluently <too poor to live *well*> **6.** Favorably : positively <spoke *well* of you> **7.** Thoroughly : completely <*well* insulated> **8.** Exactly : clearly <I recall it *well.*> **9.** To a considerable extent or degree <*well* over 50> **10.** With reason or justification <can't very *well* refuse>. **11.** In all probability <They may *well* be lying.> **12.** Prudently : advisably <You would do *well* to keep quiet.> **13.** Closely : familiarly <knew them *well*> **14.** Attentively <listen *well*> *–adj.* **1. a.** In good health. **b.** Recovered or healed. **2.** In a satisfactory or agreeable state <All is *well* with us.> **3. a.** Prudent <It would be *well* not to interfere.> **b.** Fortunate <It is *well* that they left early.>

we'll (wēl). **1.** We will. **2.** We shall.

well-ap•point•ed (wĕl′ə-poin′tĭd) *adj.* Having a full array of suitable furnishings or equipment.

well-bal•anced (wĕl′băl′ənst) *adj.* **1.** Balanced evenly in amount, extent, or degree. **2.** Mentally sound : sensible.

well-be•ing (wĕl′bē′ĭng) *n.* The state of being gen. healthy, happy, or prosperous.

well-born (wĕl′bôrn′) *adj.* Of good ancestry or breeding stock.

well-bred (wĕl′brĕd′) *adj.* Having or indicating good breeding : polite and refined.

well-de•fined (wĕl′dĭ-fīnd′) *adj.* Having clearly defined lines or features.

well-dis•posed (wĕl′dĭ-spōzd′) *adj.* Inclined to be kindly, friendly, or receptive.

well-done (wĕl′dŭn′) *adj.* **1.** Done properly or proficiently. **2.** Cooked thoroughly.

well-fixed (wĕl′fĭkst′) *adj. Informal.* In good financial circumstances : well-to-do.

well-found•ed (wĕl′foun′dĭd) *adj.* Based on reliable judgment or evidence.

well-groomed (wĕl′gro͞omd′) *adj.* **1.** Neat, clean, and carefully dressed. **2.** Well cared for <a *well-groomed* horse>

well-ground•ed (wĕl′groun′dĭd) *adj.* **1.** Knowledgeable about the basics of a subject. **2.** Well-founded.

well-heeled (wĕl′hēld′) *adj. Slang.* Well-fixed : well-to-do.

Wel•ling•ton (wĕl′ĭng-tən). Cap. of New Zealand, on S North Is. *Pop.* 137,600.

well-knit (wĕl′nĭt′) *adj.* Strongly knit, esp. strongly and firmly constructed <a *well-knit* physique> <a *well-knit* play>

well-known (wĕl′nōn′) *adj.* **1.** Widely known. **2.** Fully known.

well-man•nered (wĕl′măn′ərd) *adj.* Having good manners : polite.

well-mean•ing (wĕl′mē′nĭng) *adj.* Meaning or meant to be helpful.

well-nigh (wĕl′nī′) *adv.* Very nearly.

well-off (wĕl′ôf′, -ŏf′) *adj.* Being in fortunate circumstances, esp. well-to-do.

well-read (wĕl′rĕd′) *adj.* Well informed through extensive reading.

well-spo•ken (wĕl′spō′kən) *adj.* **1.** Spoken with aptness or propriety. **2.** Speaking skillfully and esp. courteously.

well•spring (wĕl′sprĭng′) *n.* **1.** The source of a stream or spring. **2.** A source.

well-timed (wĕl′tīmd′) *adj.* Happening or done at a timely moment : opportune.

well-to-do (wĕl′tə-do͞o′) *adj.* Wealthy.
well-turned (wĕl′tûrnd′) *adj.* **1.** Nicely shaped or formed. **2.** Skillfully or appropriately expressed.
well-wish•er (wĕl′wĭsh′ər) *n.* One who extends good wishes.
well-worn (wĕl′wôrn′, -wōrn′) *adj.* **1.** Impaired from much use. **2.** Hackneyed from much repetition.
welsh (wĕlsh, wĕlch) *v. Slang.* **1.** To cheat by not paying a debt or bet. **2.** To neglect to discharge an obligation. **–welsh′er** *n.*
Welsh (wĕlsh) *n.* **1.** *(pl. in number).* The people inhabiting Wales. **2.** The Celtic language of Wales. **–Welsh** *adj.* **–Welsh′man** *n.*

▲word history: The Welsh are the descendants of the Celts who lived in Britain before the Roman and Germanic invasions. The Welsh called themselves the *Cymry,* but the invading Anglo-Saxons called them *Wealas,* which in Old English meant "foreigners." *Wealas* became *Wales* in Modern English; *Wælisc,* the adjective derived from *Wealas,* became modern *Welsh.*

Welsh cor•gi (kôr′gē) *n.* A short-legged dog orig. bred in Wales, with a long body and a foxlike head.
Welsh rabbit *also* **Welsh rarebit** *n.* A hot dish of melted cheese poured over toast or crackers.
welt (wĕlt) *n.* **1.** A strip of material, as leather, stitched into a shoe between the sole and the upper. **2.** A strip or cord sewn into a seam to reinforce or trim it. **3.** A ridge or slight swelling raised on the skin by a blow or lash or by an allergic reaction. *–v.* **1.** To provide with a welt. **2.** To beat or whip severely.
wel•ter (wĕl′tər) *v.* **1.** To wallow, roll, or toss about, as in mud or waves. **2.** To lie drenched in a liquid, esp. blood. **3.** To billow and swell, as the sea. *–n.* **1.** An agitated rolling and tossing : turbulence. **2. a.** Great confusion : turmoil. **b.** A disorderd mass or jumble.
wel•ter•weight (wĕl′tər-wāt′) *n.* A boxer or wrestler weighing 136 to 147 lb or approx. 62 to 67 kg.
wen (wĕn) *n.* A cyst containing oily secretions from the skin.
wench (wĕnch) *n. Archaic.* **1.** A young girl or woman. **2.** A woman servant. **3.** A prostitute.
wend (wĕnd) *v.* To go on (one's way).
went (wĕnt) *v. p.t. of* GO.
wept (wĕpt) *v. p.t. & p.p. of* WEEP.
were (wûr) *v.* **1.** *2nd person sing. p.t. of* BE. **2.** *1st, 2nd, & 3rd person pl. p.t. of* BE. **3.** *Past subjunctive of* BE.
we're (wîr). We are.
were•n't (wûrnt, wûr′ənt). Were not.
were•wolf (wîr′wo͝olf′, wûr′-, wâr′-) *n.* A person thought capable of taking on the form of a wolf.
wes•kit (wĕs′kĭt) *n.* A waistcoat : vest.
Wes•ley (wĕs′lē, wĕz′-), **John.** 1703–91. British founder of Methodism.
west (wĕst) *n.* **1. a.** The general direction opposite to sunrise. **b.** The point on the mariner's compass directly opposite to east. **2.** *often* **West.** An area or region lying in a western direction from a certain point. **3. West.** Europe and the Western Hemisphere : the Occident. *–adj.* Of, at, toward, or coming from the west. *–adv.* To or toward the west. **–west′er•ly** *adv. & adj.* **–west′ward** *adv. & adj.* **–west′wards** *adv.*
west•ern (wĕs′tərn) *adj.* **1.** Lying toward the west. **2.** Coming from the west. **3.** *often* **Western. a.** Of, pertaining to, typical of, or found in regions designated as western. **b.** Of, pertaining to, or typical of Europe and the Western Hemisphere. *–n. often* **Western.** A novel, film, or broadcast about frontier life in the American West. **–west′ern•er, West′ern•er** *n.*
West•ern•ize (wĕs′tər-nīz′) *v.* **-ized, -iz•ing.** To convert to the ways or ideas of the West. **–West′ern•i•za′tion** *n.*
Western Samoa. Island nation of the S Pacific. *Cap.* Apia. *Pop.* 160,000.
West In•dies (ĭn′dēz). Islands between SE North America and N South America, separating the Caribbean and the Atlantic.
West Vir•gin•ia (vûr-jĭn′yə). State of the EC U.S. *Cap.* Charleston. *Pop.* 1,949,644. **–West Vir•gin′ian** *adj. & n.*
wet (wĕt) *adj.* **wet•ter, wet•test. 1.** Covered or saturated with a liquid, esp. water. **2.** Marked by rain : rainy. **3.** Not yet dry or hardened, as paint or plaster. **4.** Permitting or favoring the sale of alcoholic beverages <a *wet* town> *–n.* **1.** Something wet, esp. water. **2.** Moisture : wetness. **3.** Rainy or snowy weather. **4.** One supporting the sale of liquor. *–v.* **wet** *or* **wet•ted, wet•ting.** To make or become wet. **–wet′ly** *adv.* **–wet′ness** *n.*
wet blanket *n. Informal.* One that dampens the enjoyment of others.
weth•er (wĕth′ər) *n.* A male sheep castrated before maturity.
wet•land (wĕt′lănd′) *n.* A wet, swampy lowland area.
wet nurse *n.* A woman who nurses and cares for another woman's child.
wet suit *n.* A tight-fitting permeable suit, as of rubber, worn esp. by skin divers.
we've (wēv). We have.
whack (hwăk, wăk) *v.* To strike with a sharp, resounding blow : slap. *–n.* **1.** A loud, hard blow or slap. **2.** The resounding noise made by a whack. **3.** *Informal.* An attempt : try. **–out of whack.** Not functioning properly.
whack•y (hwăk′ē, wăk′ē) *adj. var. of* WACKY.
whale¹ (hwāl, wāl) *n.* **1.** Any of various often very large marine mammals of the order Cetacea, having a gen. fishlike form, flippers, and a tail with horizontal flukes. **2.** *Informal.* An unusually impressive example <had a *whale* of a time> *–v.* **whaled, whal•ing.** To hunt whales.
whale² (hwāl, wāl) *v.* **whaled, whal•ing. 1.** To strike forcefully and repeatedly. **2.** To thrash about.
whale•boat (hwāl′bōt′, wāl′-) *n.* A long rowboat with pointed ends, formerly used in whaling.
whale•bone (hwāl′bōn′, wāl′-) *n.* **1.** The flexible, hornlike substance forming plates or strips in the upper jaw of certain large whales. **2.** A strip of whalebone used esp. to stiffen a corset.
whal•er (hwā′lər, wā′-) *n.* **1.** One engaged in whaling. **2.** A whaleboat.
whal•ing (hwā′lĭng, wāl-) *n.* The business or practice of hunting, killing, and processing whales.
wham (hwăm, wăm) *n.* **1.** A loud, hard blow. **2.** The sound of such a blow. *–v.* **whammed, wham•ming.** To hit or smash into loudly and forcefully.
wham•my (hwăm′ē, wăm′ē) *n., pl.* **-mies.** *Slang.* An evil spell : hex.
wharf (hwôrf, wôrf) *n., pl.* **wharves** (hwôrvz, wôrvz) *or* **wharfs.** A dock or pier at which ships are loaded or unloaded.
wharf•age (hwôr′fĭj, wôr′-) *n.* **1.** Permission to use a wharf. **2.** A charge or fee for such permission and use.
what (hwŏt, hwŭt, wŏt, wŭt; hwət, wət *when unstressed*) *pron.* **1.** Which thing, event, kind, character, etc. <*What* do you want?><*What's* this?><*What* is it to me?> **2. a.** That which <I saw *what* you did.> **b.** Whatever thing or anything that <Say *what* you want.> **3.** *Informal.* Something unspecified <Do you know *what*?> *–adj.* **1.** Which one or ones <*What* shirt will you wear?> **2.** As much or as many : whatever <solved *what* problems arose> **3.** How great, remarkable, etc. <*What* foolishness> *–adv.* **1.** In which way <*What* do you care?> **2.** Because of <busy *what* with job and school>
what•ev•er (hwŏt-ĕv′ər, hwŭt-, wŏt-, wŭt-) *pron.* **1.** Anything that <did *whatever* we could> **2.** No matter what <*Whatever* happens, be sure to call me.> **3.** *Informal.* Which thing or things : what <*Whatever* have they done?> *–adj.* Of any kind at all <no money *whatever*>
what•not (hwŏt′nŏt′, hwŭt′-, wŏt′-, wŭt′-) *n.* A set of open shelves for small objects.
what•so•ev•er (hwŏt′sō-ĕv′ər, hwŭt′-, wŏt′-, wŭt′-) *pron. & adj.* Whatever.
wheal (hwēl, wēl) *n.* A small acute swelling on the surface of the skin.
wheat (hwēt, wēt) *n.* **1.** A cereal grass of the genus *Triticum,* esp. *T. aestivum,* widely cultivated in many varieties for its commercially important grain. **2.** The grain of the wheat plant ground into flour. **–wheat′en** *adj.*
wheat germ *n.* The embryo of wheat kernels, rich in vitamins and used as a cereal or food supplement.
whee•dle (hwēd′l, wēd′l) *v.* **-dled, -dling.** To persuade or obtain by flattery or cajolery : coax. **–whee′dler** *n.* **–whee′dling•ly** *adv.*
wheel (hwēl, wēl) *n.* **1. a.** A disk or ring joined to a hub by spokes and designed to turn around a central axle or shaft. **b.** Something resembling a wheel in shape or function. **c.** Something having a wheel as its main part, esp. the steering device of a vehicle. **d.** *Informal.* A bicycle. **2. wheels.** Moving or energizing forces <the *wheels* of big business> **3.** A rotation around an axis. **4. wheels.** *Slang.* An automobile. **5.** *Slang.* One having great power or influence <a big *wheel* in politics> *–v.* **1.** To move or transport on or as if on wheels or in a vehicle. **2.** To turn or cause to turn around or as if around a central axis. **3.** To change direction esp. by pivoting. **4.** To reverse one's opinion or practice.
wheel•bar•row (hwēl′băr′ō, wēl′-) *n.* A usu. 1-wheeled vehicle with handles, used to transport small loads.
wheel•base (hwēl′bās′, wēl′-) *n.* The distance in inches from front to rear axle in an automotive vehicle.
wheel•chair (hwēl′châr′, wēl′-) *n.* A chair mounted on wheels esp. for the use of persons unable to walk by themselves.
wheel•er (hwē′lər, wē′-) *n.* Something that has wheels <a 2 *wheeler*>

wheel·er-deal·er (hwē′lər-dē′lər, wē′-) *n. Informal.* One who wheels and deals, esp. a shrewd businessman or politician.
wheel house *n.* A pilothouse.
wheel·wright (hwēl′rīt′, wēl′-) *n.* A builder and repairer of wheels.
wheeze (hwēz, wēz) *v.* **wheezed, wheez·ing.** To make a hoarse whistling sound in breathing. *—n.* **1.** A wheezing sound. **2.** An old joke or cliché. **—wheez′er** *n.*
wheez·y (hwē′zē, wē′-) *adj.* **-i·er, -i·est. 1.** Tending to wheeze. **2.** Having or making a wheezing sound. **—wheez′i·ly** *adv.* **—wheez′i·ness** *n.*
whelk (hwĕlk, wĕlk) *n.* Any of various large, sometimes edible marine snails of the family Buccinidae, with turreted shells.
whelp (hwĕlp, wĕlp) *n.* **1.** The young of a mammal such as a dog or wolf. **2.** An insolent or base young fellow. *—v.* To give birth to (whelps).
when (hwĕn, wĕn) *adv.* **1.** At what time <*When* will the train arrive?> **2.** At which time <a year *when* we traveled> *—conj.* **1.** At the time that <Start *when* I give the signal.> **2.** Every time that : whenever <afraid *when* they're alone> **3.** While on the contrary : although <playing *when* we should be working> **4.** Considering that : if <How can you succeed *when* you won't try!> *—pron.* What or which time <By *when* will it be ready?> *—n.* The time or date of an event.
whence (hwĕns, wĕns) *adv.* **1.** From what place, cause, or origin <*Whence* came all this money?> **2.** From which <the country *whence* we came> *—conj.* By reason of which.
when·ev·er (hwĕn-ĕv′ər, wĕn-) *adv.* At whatever time : when. *—conj.* At whatever or every time that.
when·so·ev·er (hwĕn′sō-ĕv′ər, wĕn′-) *adv. & conj.* At whatever time : whenever.
where (hwâr, wâr) *adv.* **1.** At or in what place <*Where* are you?> **2.** To or toward what place or end <*Where* is this discussion leading?> **3.** From what place or origin <*Where* did you hear that story?> *—conj.* **1. a.** At or in what place <don't know *where* they are> **b.** At or in which place <the house *where* we stayed> **2.** In or to a place in which or to which <went *where* we could find work> **3.** In or to whatever place or situation : wherever <my dog goes *where* I go.> **4.** While on the contrary : whereas <had 3 cars, *where* we had none> **5.** In a situation in which <useless *where* common sense is needed> *—n.* **1.** The location or occasion. **2.** What place <*Where* are you from?>
where·a·bouts (hwâr′ə-bouts′, wâr′-) *adv.* In, at, or near what location <*Whereabouts* can we find them?> *—n. (sing. or pl. in number).* Approximate location <just discovered its *whereabouts*>
where·as (hwâr-ăz′, wâr-) *conj.* **1.** It being the fact that : since. **2.** While on the contrary : although.
where·at (hwâr-ăt′, wâr-) *conj.* **1.** Toward or at which place. **2.** Whereupon.
where·by (hwâr-bī′, wâr-) *conj.* By or through which.
where·fore (hwâr′fôr′, -fōr′, wâr′-) *adv.* For what reason : why. *—n.* A reason.
where·in (hwâr-ĭn′, wâr-) *adv.* In what way : how. *—conj.* In which thing, location, or circumstance.
where·of (hwâr-ŏv′, -ŭv′, wâr-) *conj.* **1.** Of what. **2.** Of which or whom.
where·on (hwâr-ŏn′, -ôn′, wâr-) *conj.* On which or what.
where·so·ev·er (hwâr′sō-ĕv′ər, wâr′-) *conj. Archaic.* Wherever.
where·to (hwâr-tōō′, wâr-) *conj.* To which. *—adv.* To what place or end.
where·up·on (hwâr′ə-pŏn′, -pôn′, wâr′-) *conj.* **1.** On or upon which. **2.** Following and as a result of which.
wher·ev·er (hwâr-ĕv′ər, wâr-) *adv.* **1.** In or to whatever place. **2.** Where. Used as an intensive <*Wherever* did you disappear?> *—conj.* In or to whatever place or circumstance.
where·with (hwâr′wĭth′, -wĭth′, wâr′-) *conj.* With or by means of which.
where·with·al (hwâr′wĭth-ôl′, -wĭth-, wâr′-) *n.* The necessary means or resources, esp. money.
wher·ry (hwĕr′ē, wĕr′ē) *n., pl.* **-ries.** A light, swift rowboat used esp. in racing.
whet (hwĕt, wĕt) *v.* **whet·ted, whet·ting. 1.** To sharpen or hone. **2.** To stimulate <*whet* the appetite>
wheth·er (hwĕth′ər, wĕth′-) *conj.* **1.** Used in indirect questions to introduce an alternative <We need to know *whether* you'll come.> **2.** Used to introduce alternative possibilities <*Whether* we win or lose, we must play fair.> **3.** Either <succeeded *whether* by ability or luck.>
whet·stone (hwĕt′stōn′, wĕt′-) *n.* A stone for sharpening knives, scissors, etc.
whew (hwōō, hwyōō) *interj.* Used to express amazement, relief, or fatigue.
whey (hwā, wā) *n.* The watery part of milk that separates from the curds.
which (hwĭch, wĭch) *pron.* **1.** What one or ones <*Which* is yours?> **2.** The one or ones that <I just want that *which* is mine.> **3.** The one or ones previously named or implied <my car, *which* is old but dependable> **4.** Whatever one or ones : whichever <Buy *which* looks best.> *—adj.* **1.** What one or ones of. **2.** Any one of. **3.** Being the one or ones just mentioned.
which·ev·er (hwĭch-ĕv′ər, wĭch-) *pron.* Whatever one or ones which. *—adj.* Being anyone of which : no matter which.
which·so·ev·er (hwĭch′sō-ĕv′ər, wĭch′-) *pron. & adj.* Whichever.
whiff (hwĭf, wĭf) *n.* **1.** A slight gust, as of air or smoke. **2.** A slight passing smell. **3.** An inhalation, as of smoke or scent. *—v.* **1.** To carry or be conveyed in slight gusts : waft. **2.** To sniff : smell.
whif·fle·tree (hwĭf′əl-trē, wĭf′-) *n.* The pivoted crossbar to which the traces of a harness are hitched.
Whig (hwĭg, wĭg) *n.* **1.** A member of an 18th- and 19th-cent. English political party opposed to the Tories. **2.** A colonist who advocated independence from England during the American Revolution.
while (hwīl, wīl) *n.* **1.** A length of time <Let's walk a *while.*> **2.** Time or effort used <well worth her *while*> *—conj.* **1. a.** As long as <*While* you're up, please get me a drink.> **b.** During the time that <arrived *while* you were sleeping> **2.** At the same time that : although <*While* comfortable, we're not rich.> *—v.* **whiled, whil·ing.** To cause to pass, esp. agreeably <*whiled* away the summer day>
whi·lom (hwī′ləm, wī′-) *adv. Archaic.* At a former time : formerly.
whilst (hwīlst, wīlst) *conj.* While.
whim (hwĭm, wĭm) *n.* A sudden, capricious, or arbitrary notion or impulse.
whim·per (hwĭm′pər, wĭm′-) *v.* To cry with weak whining sounds. **—whim′per** *n.* **—whim′per·er** *n.*
whim·si·cal (hwĭm′zĭ-kəl, wĭm′-) *adj.* **1.** Full of whim, fancy, or caprice. **2.** Erratic or unpredictable. **—whim′si·cal′i·ty** (-kăl′ĭ-tē) *n.* **—whim′si·cal·ly** *adv.*
whim·sy *also* **whim·sey** (hwĭm′zē, wĭm′-) *n., pl.* **-sies** *also* **-seys 1.** A whimsical idea or fancy. **2.** Something quaint, fanciful, etc., esp. a fanciful style of humor.
whine (hwīn, wīn) *v.* **whined, whin·ing. 1.** To make a high-pitched, plaintive sound, as in pain or protest. **2.** To complain in a childish, irritating way. **3.** To make a continuous high-pitched sound, as an engine or machine. **—whine** *n.* **—whin′y** *adj.*
whin·ny (hwĭn′ē, wĭn′ē) *v.* **-nied, -ny·ing.** To neigh softly, as a horse does. **—whin′ny** *n.*
whip (hwĭp, wĭp) *v.* **whipped, whip·ping. 1.** To strike repeatedly, as with a lash or rod. **2.** To subject to punishment by or as if by whipping. **3.** To drive or impel to action by or as if by whipping. **4.** To beat into a froth or foam <*whip* egg whites> **5.** To move, pull, or grab abruptly <*whipped* out a pen> **6.** To bind (e.g., a rope) with cord to strengthen or prevent fraying. **7.** To defeat soundly. **8.** To move swiftly or nimbly. **9.** To thrash about like a lash. **—whip up. 1.** To stir up : excite <*whipped up* the crowd> **2.** To put together quickly, as a meal. *—n.* **1.** A pliable rod or lash used in whipping. **2.** A blow, motion, or stroke with or as if with a whip. **3.** A legislative member selected to enforce party discipline and ensure attendance. **4.** A dessert made with whipped cream or stiffly beaten egg whites. **—whip′per** *n.*
whip·cord (hwĭp′kôrd′, wĭp′-) *n.* **1.** A tough worsted fabric with a diagonally ribbed or corded surface. **2.** A strong thin twisted or braided cord esp. for making whiplashes. **3.** A tough cord of catgut.
whip·lash (hwĭp′lăsh′, wĭp′-) *n.* **1.** The lash of a whip. **2.** Injury to the neck or spine caused by an abrupt forward or backward jerking motion of the head, as in an automobile collision.
whip·per·snap·per (hwĭp′ər-snăp′ər, wĭp′-) *n.* One who is small, unimportant, or impertinent.
whip·pet (hwĭp′ĭt, wĭp′-) *n.* A short-haired, swift-running dog of a breed developed in England, resembling but smaller than the greyhound.
whipping boy *n.* One bearing blame for others : scapegoat.
whip·poor·will (hwĭp′ər-wĭl′, wĭp′-) *n.* A brownish nocturnal North American bird, *Caprimulgus vociferus.*
whip·saw (hwĭp′sô′, wĭp′-) *n.* A long narrow crosscut saw operated by 2 persons. *—v.* **1.** To saw with a whipsaw. **2.** To defeat or best in 2 ways at once.
whir (hwûr, wûr) *v.* **whirred, whir·ring.** To move or revolve rapidly with a buzzing or humming sound. *—n.* **1.** A sustained buzzing or vibrating sound. **2.** An excited bustle of activity.
whirl (hwûrl, wûrl) *v.* **1.** To spin, rotate, or twirl briskly. **2.** To wheel or pivot, changing direction. **3.** To have a spinning or

reeling sensation. **4.** To move or drive at a high speed. **5.** To move or drive in a circular course, esp. rapidly or forcefully. *—n.* **1.** A swift whirling or rotating motion. **2.** One that whirls or undergoes whirling. **3.** A rapid succession or round of events <the social *whirl*> **4.** A confused condition : tumult. **5.** *Informal.* A brief try : attempt <gave skiing a *whirl*> **—whirl'er** *n.*

whirl•i•gig (hwûr'lĭ-gĭg', wûr'-) *n.* **1.** A toy that whirls. **2.** A carousel. **3.** Something that constantly whirls or changes.

whirl•pool (hwûrl'po͞ol', wûrl'-) *n.* A rapid rotary current of water, as from the meeting of 2 tides.

whirl•wind (hwûrl'wĭnd', wûrl'-) *n.* **1.** A small often violently whirling column of air. **2.** A confused bustle or rush. *—adj.* Very fast or rushed <a *whirlwind* tour>

whirl•y•bird (hwûr'lē-bûrd', wûr'-) *n. Slang.* A helicopter.

whisk (hwĭsk, wĭsk) *v.* **1.** To move or cause to move with brisk little sweeping or brushing motions. **2.** To whip (eggs or cream) esp. by hand. **3.** To move quickly and spryly. *—n.* **1.** A brisk little sweeping motion. **2.** A whiskbroom. **3.** A hand utensil used to whip foods.

whisk•broom (hwĭsk'bro͞om', -bro͞om', wĭsk'-) *n.* A small short-handled broom used esp. as a clothes brush.

whisk•er (hwĭs'kər, wĭs'-) *n.* **1. a. whiskers.** The hair growing on a man's cheeks and chin and above the upper lip. **b.** A single hair of this growth. **2.** A long hair or bristle near the mouth of certain animals. **—whisk'ered, whisk'er•y** *adj.*

whis•key (hwĭs'kē, wĭs'-) *n., pl.* **-keys.** A liquor distilled from corn, rye, or barley.

whis•ky (hwĭs'kē, wĭs'-) *n. Scot. var. of* WHISKEY.

whis•per (hwĭs'pər, wĭs'-) *v.* **1.** To speak or say in a very low, muted voice. **2.** To tell in private or in secret. **3.** To make a soft rustling or hissing sound. *—n.* **1.** An act or instance of whispering. **2.** Soft low speech produced by whispering. **3.** A low rustling sound. **4.** A whispered message, esp. of gossip or scandal.

whist (hwĭst, wĭst) *n.* A card game played with 52 cards by 4 players in 2 teams.

whis•tle (hwĭs'əl, wĭs'-) *v.* **-tled, -tling. 1.** To make a clear shrill sound by forcing air through the teeth or through puckered lips or by blowing on or through an instrument or device. **2.** To make a high-pitched sound, esp. by rapid movement through the air. **3.** To make or express by whistling <*whistled* their approval> **4.** To summon or signal by whistling. *—n.* **1.** An instrument or device that uses a jet of air or steam to make a whistling sound. **2.** A sound produced by a device or by whistling through the teeth or lips. **3.** A whistling sound made by an animal or a moving projectile. **—whis'tler** *n.*

whistle stop *n.* **1.** A small town at which a train stops only on signal. **2.** A brief appearance of a candidate for office, as on the observation platform of a train.

whit (hwĭt, wĭt) *n.* The smallest bit.

white (hwīt, wīt) *n.* **1.** A color of maximum lightness that is the opposite of black. **2.** The white or light-colored part of something, as an egg or the eyeball. **3. whites.** White clothes, esp. as a part of an outfit or uniform. **4.** A member of the Caucasoid ethnic division. *—adj.* **whit•er, whit•est. 1.** Of or almost of the color white. **2.** Having a light color : pale. **3.** Of, relating to, or belonging to an ethnic group having skin color varying from very light to brown, esp. Caucasoid. **4.** Pale gray or silvery, as hair. **5.** Marked by snow <a *white* Christmas in Vermont> **6.** Ardent : impassioned. **7.** Morally unblemished : pure. **8.** Not written or printed on : blank. **9.** Ultraconservative in politics. **—white'ness** *n.*

white ant *n.* A termite.

white•bait (hwīt'bāt', wīt'-) *n.* The edible young of herring or other small fish.

white blood cell *n.* A leukocyte.

white•cap (hwīt'kăp', wīt'-) *n.* A wave capped with foam.

white-col•lar (hwīt'kŏl'ər, wīt'-) *adj.* Of or relating to workers whose occupations usu. do not involve manual labor.

white elephant *n.* **1.** A rare pale-colored Asian elephant sometimes venerated in parts of SE Asia. **2.** A possession of little practical value that requires much care and expense. **3.** Something no longer wanted by its owner but possibly of value to others.

white-faced (hwīt'fāst', wīt'-) *adj.* **1.** Having a pallid complexion. **2.** Having a white patch extending from the muzzle to the forehead <*white-faced* cattle>

white feather *n.* A sign of cowardice.

white•fish (hwīt'fĭsh', wīt'-) *n.* Any of various North American silvery freshwater food fishes of the genus *Coregonus.*

white flag *n.* A white flag or cloth raised to signal a truce or surrender.

white gold *n.* A pale alloy of gold and nickel that resembles platinum.

white•head (hwīt'hĕd') *n.* A small whitish bump under the skin, caused by retained secretion of a sebaceous gland.

white heat *n.* **1.** An intensely hot temperature at which a substance glows with a bright white light. **2.** A state of intense emotion. **—white'-hot'** *adj.*

White•horse (hwīt'hôrs'). Cap. of the Y.T., Canada, on the Yukon R. *Pop.* 13,311.

White House *n.* **1.** The executive branch of the U.S. government. **2.** The residence of the President of the U.S.

white lead *n.* A heavy white poisonous lead compound used in paint.

white lie *n.* A diplomatic untruth.

whit•en (hwīt'n, wīt'n) *v.* To make or become white. **—whit'en•er** *n.*

white noise *n.* Acoustical or electrical noise in which the intensity is the same at all frequencies within a given band.

white pine *n.* A timber tree of E North America that has needles in clusters of 5 and durable, easily worked wood.

white slave *n.* A woman forced into prostitution. **—white slavery** *n.*

white•wall (hwīt'wôl', wīt'-) *n.* An automotive tire with a white band on the visible side wall.

white•wash (hwīt'wŏsh', -wôsh', wīt'-) *n.* **1.** A preparation of lime and water and often whiting, size, or glue for whitening exterior walls, fences, etc. **2.** A glossing over or covering up, as of faults or crime. *—v.* **1.** To whiten with or as if with whitewash. **2.** To try to excuse or ignore (e.g., a fault).

whith•er (hwĭth'ər, wĭth'-) *adv.* **1.** To what place, end, or circumstance. **2.** To which designated place. **3.** Wherever.

whit•ing[1] (hwī'tĭng, wī'-) *n.* A pulverized chalk used esp. in paints and putty.

whit•ing[2] (hwī'tĭng, wī'-) *n.* A food fish, *Gadus merlangus,* of European Atlantic waters, related to the cod.

whit•ish (hwī'tĭsh, wī'-) *adj.* Somewhat white in color.

whit•low (hwĭt'lō, wĭt'-) *n.* A pus-filled infection near the nail of a finger or toe.

Whit•man (hwĭt'mən), **Walt.** 1819–92. Amer. poet.

Whit•ney (hwĭt'nē, wĭt'-). 2nd-highest mountain (14,495 ft/ 4,421 m) in the U.S., in E Calif.

Whit•sun•day (hwĭt'sŭn'dē, -sən-dā', wĭt'-) *n.* Pentecost.

whit•tle (hwĭt'l, wĭt'l) *v.* **-tled, -tling. 1. a.** To pare small bits or shavings from (wood) with a knife. **b.** To shape (an object) by whittling. **2.** To reduce or remove gradually as if by whittling. **—whit'tler** *n.*

whiz *also* **whizz** (hwĭz, wĭz). *—v.* **whizzed, whiz•zing. 1.** To make a whirring or hissing sound, as of a projectile speeding through air. **2.** To speed by. *—n., pl.* **whiz•zes. 1.** A whirring or hissing sound. **2.** *Slang.* One with notable expertise <a computer *whiz*>

who (ho͞o) *pron.* **1.** What or which individual or group <*Who* found it?> <*Who* are they?> **2.** The individual or group that <The students *who* left got jobs.>

WHO *abbr.* World Health Organization.

who'd (ho͞od). **1.** Who would. **2.** Who had.

who•dun•it (ho͞o-dŭn'ĭt) *n. Informal.* A detective or mystery story.

who•ev•er (ho͞o-ĕv'ər) *pron.* Whatever person <*Whoever* took it will be caught.>

whole (hōl) *adj.* **1.** Having no part or element missing : complete. **2.** Not divided into units or sections <a *whole* acre> **3.** In good health or condition : sound. **4.** Being the entire quantity, duration, or extent <laughed the *whole* time> **5.** *Math.* Not in fractional units : integral. *—n.* **1.** Something lacking no part or element. **2.** A complete entity, unity, or system. **—on the whole. 1.** All things considered. **2.** In general. **—whole'ness** *n.*

whole•heart•ed (hōl'här'tĭd) *adj.* Wholly committed, enthusiastic, or sincere.

whole number *n.* An integer.

whole•sale (hōl'sāl') *n.* The sale of goods in quantity esp. for resale by a retailer. *—adj.* **1.** Of, relating to, or involved in wholesaling. **2.** Sold in quantity, usu. at a lower price. **3.** Made or done indiscriminately. *—v.* **-saled, -sal•ing. 1.** To sell or be sold at wholesale. **2.** To engage in wholesale selling. **—whole'sale'** *adv.* **—whole'sal'er** *n.*

whole•some (hōl'səm) *adj.* **1.** Contributing or conducive to health or well-being <*wholesome* food> **2.** Having or indicating sound physical or mental health <a *wholesome* attitude> **—whole'some•ly** *adv.* **—whole'some•ness** *n.*

whole-wheat (hōl'hwēt', -wēt') *adj.* Made from ground wheat kernels from which no part has been removed.

who'll (ho͞ol). **1.** Who will. **2.** Who shall.

whol•ly (hō'lē, hōl'lē) *adv.* **1.** Entirely : totally. **2.** Exclusively : solely.

whom (ho͞om) *pron. objective case of* WHO.

whom•ev•er (ho͞om-ĕv'ər) *pron. objective case of* WHOEVER.

whom·so·ev·er (ho͞om′sō-ĕv′ər) *pron. objective case of* WHOSOEVER.
whoop (hwo͞op, ho͞op, wo͞op) *n.* **1.** A loud shout or hooting cry, as of excitement or triumph. **2.** The convulsive gasp typical of whooping cough. *—v.* **1.** To shout loudly. **2.** To utter with a whoop. **3.** To gasp convulsively, as in whooping cough. **4.** To urge or cheer on with a whoop. **—whoop′er** *n.*
whooping cough *n.* An infectious disease that causes spasms of coughing often followed by deep, noisy inspiration.
whooping crane *n.* A large, long-legged nearly extinct North American bird, *Grus americana,* with black and white plumage and a shrill, trumpeting cry.
whoops (hwo͝ops, wo͝ops, hwo͞ops, wo͞ops) *interj.* Used to express mild surprise or apology.
whoosh (hwo͞osh, wo͞osh, hwo͝osh, wo͝osh) *v.* To make a gushing, rushing, or hissing sound. **—whoosh** *n.*
whop (hwŏp, wŏp) *v.* **whopped, whop·ping. 1.** To beat : thrash. **2.** To defeat completely. *—n.* A heavy blow or thump.
whop·per (hwŏp′ər, wŏp′-) *n.* **1.** Something unusually large or extraordinary. **2.** A flagrant lie.
whop·ping (hwŏp′ĭng, wŏp′-) *adj.* Exceptionally large.
whore (hôr, hōr) *n.* A prostitute. **—whor′ish** *adj.* **—whor′ish·ly** *adv.*
whorl (hwôrl, wôrl, hwûrl, wûrl) *n.* **1.** Something having a coiled, curved, or spiral form, as a ridge of a fingerprint. **2.** An arrangement esp. of leaves or petals radiating from a single axis. **—whorled** *adj.*
who's (ho͞oz). **1.** Who is. **2.** Who has.
whose (ho͞oz) *pron. (sing. or pl. in number).* That which belongs to whom. *—adj.* Of or relating to whom or which.
who·so·ev·er (ho͞o′sō-ĕv′ər) *pron.* Whoever.
W-hr *abbr.* watt-hour.
why (hwī, wī) *adv.* For what purpose, reason, or cause <*Why* were they fired?> *—conj.* **1.** The reason, cause, or purpose for which <Do you know *why* they were fired?> **2.** For which <can guess the reason *why* it happened> *—n., pl.* **whys.** The reason or cause. *—interj.* Used to express mild indignation or surprise.
WI *abbr.* Wisconsin (with Zip Code)
Wich·i·ta (wĭch′ə-tô′). City of SC Kans. *Pop.* 279,272.
wick (wĭk) *n.* A cord or strand of soft fibers, as in a candle or an oil lamp, that draws up fuel to be burned.
wick·ed (wĭk′ĭd) *adj.* **1.** Morally bad : sinful. **2.** Marked by playful mischief. **3.** Causing harm, trouble, or distress. **4.** Obnoxious, as a vile odor. **—wick′ed·ly** *adv.*
wick·er (wĭk′ər) *n.* **1.** A small flexible shoot or rodlike twig, as of willow, used esp. in making baskets and furniture. **2.** Woven wicker : wickerwork.
wick·er·work (wĭk′ər-wûrk′) *n.* Articles, as baskets and furniture, made of wicker.
wick·et (wĭk′ĭt) *n.* **1.** A set of 3 upright sticks topped by 2 crossbars that forms the target of the bowler in cricket. **2.** A small usu. wire arch through which a player tries to hit the ball in croquet. **3.** A small door or gate, esp. one built in or near a larger one. **4.** A small windowlike opening, usu. with a grating, as at a box office.
wick·i·up (wĭk′ē-ŭp′) *n.* A temporary dwelling used by nomadic North American Indians, consisting of a frame hut covered with matting, bark, or brushwood.
wide (wīd) *adj.* **wid·er, wid·est. 1.** Extending over a large area : broad <a *wide* river> **2.** Measured across <paper 8 inches *wide*> **3.** Extensive in range or scope <a *wide* variety> **4.** Completely open or extended, as eyes or wings. **5.** Far from a goal, target, or truth. *—adv.* **1.** Over an extensive area. **2.** To the full extent. **3.** Deviating from the target : afield. **—wide′ly** *adv.* **—wide′ness** *n.*
wide-a·wake (wīd′ə-wāk′) *adj.* **1.** Fully awake. **2.** Observant : alert.
wide-eyed (wīd′īd′) *adj.* **1.** Having the eyes fully open. **2.** Astonished. **3.** Naive.
wid·en (wīd′n) *v.* To make or become wide. **—wid′en·er** *n.*
wide·spread (wīd′sprĕd′) *adj.* **1.** Fully opened or spread out. **2.** Prevalent.
wid·geon (wĭj′ən) *n., pl.* **widgeon** or **-geons.** A wild duck, esp. *Mareca americana* of North America, with brownish plumage and a light head patch.
wid·ow (wĭd′ō) *n.* A woman who has not remarried after her husband's death. *—v.* To cause to become a widow. **—wid′ow·hood′** *n.*
wid·ow·er (wĭd′ō-ər) *n.* A man who has not remarried after his wife's death. **—wid′ow·er·hood′** *n.*
width (wĭdth, wĭtth) *n.* **1.** The quality, state, or fact of being wide. **2.** The extent of something from side to side : breadth. **3.** Something, as a piece of fabric or lumber, that has a specified width.
wield (wēld) *v.* **1.** To handle (e.g., a weapon or tool) esp. skillfully. **2.** To employ (power or influence) affectively.
wie·ner (wē′nər) *n.* A frankfurter.
wife (wīf) *n., pl.* **wives** (wīvz). A married woman. **—wife′hood′** *n.* **—wife′ly** *adj.*
wig (wĭg) *n.* A covering of artificial or human hair for the head.
wig·gle (wĭg′əl) *v.* **-gled, -gling. 1.** To move or cause to move with rapid irregular side-to-side motions : jiggle. **2.** To proceed with a sinous motion : wriggle. **—wig′gle** *n.* **—wig′gler** *n.* **—wig′gly** *adj.*
wig·wam (wĭg′wŏm′) *n.* A dwelling used by North American Indians, typically consisting of an arched or cone-shaped framework covered with bark or hides.
wild (wīld) *adj.* **1.** Existing in a natural state : not cultivated or domesticated. **2.** Lacking discipline : unruly. **3.** Filled with or indicating intense, uncontrolled emotion. **4.** Marked by turbulence : stormy. **5.** Uncivilized : barbarous. **6.** Extravagant or outlandish <*wild* notions> **7.** Going astray of the mark or target. **8.** Representing any card desired rather than the actual one held or played <deuces *wild*> *—adv.* Out of control. *—n. often* **wilds.** A region not settled or cultivated by humans. **—wild′ly** *adv.* **—wild′ness** *n.*
wild·cat (wīld′kăt′) *n.* **1.** A small to medium-size wild feline, as an ocelot, lynx, or bobcat. **2.** One who is quick-tempered or fierce. **3.** An oil well drilled in an area not known to be productive. *—adj.* **1.** Having no certainty of profit or success. **2.** Undertaken without official authorization, as a labor strike. *—v.* **-cat·ted, -cat·ting.** To prospect for (oil or minerals) in an area regarded as unproductive. **—wild′cat′ter** *n.*
wil·de·beest (wĭl′də-bēst′, vĭl′-) *n.* The gnu.
wil·der·ness (wĭl′dər-nĭs) *n.* An unsettled and uncultivated region.
wild-eyed (wīld′īd′) *adj.* **1.** Having a wild look in the eyes. **2.** Impractical or extreme.
wild·fire (wīld′fīr′) *n.* A raging fire that spreads very quickly.
wild·fowl (wīld′foul′) *n.* A game bird, as a wild duck or goose.
wild-goose chase (wīld′go͞os′) *n.* Pursuit of something beyond reach or hope.
wild·life (wīld′līf′) *n.* Wild plants and animals, esp. wild animals living in their natural environment.
wild oat *n.* **1.** A native Eurasian grass, *Avena fatua,* related to the cultivated oat. **2. wild oats.** The excesses of youth.
wild rice *n.* A tall water grass of N North America, *Zizania aquatica,* that bears edible brownish grain.
wile (wīl) *n.* **1.** A stratagem or trick intended to entrap or deceive. **2.** A disarming or seductive manner. **3.** Deceitful cunning : guile. *—v.* **wiled, wil·ing. 1.** To entice with wiles. **2.** To while.
will¹ (wĭl) *n.* **1.** The mental power or capability of choosing or deciding. **2.** An example of making a deliberate choice or decision. **3.** Control exercised over oneself : self-discipline. **4.** Something desired or determined, esp. by one holding power or authority. **5.** Inclination, intention, or wish <held against my *will*> **6.** Determined purpose or desire <the *will* to succeed> **7.** Disposition or attitude toward others <good *will*> **8.** A legal document indicating the distribution of a person's possessions after his or her death. *—v.* **1.** To decide upon or bring about by an act of the will. **2.** To order or decide by or as if by decree. **3.** To bequeath in a legal will. **4.** To intend to do. **—at will.** Freely.
will² (wĭl) *v. p.t.* **would** (wo͝od). Used to indicate: **1.** Simple futurity <I *will* go tomorrow.> **2.** Likelihood or certainty <You *will* rue that decision.> **3.** Readiness to act : willingness <*Will* you lend me your car?> **4.** Intention or determination <I *will* come no matter what.> **5.** Required action or command <You *will* do the dishes.> **6.** Customary action <*would* shop for hours> **7.** *Informal.* Probability <That *will* be the lawyer.> **8.** To wish, want, or desire <Go where you *will.*>
Wil·lem·stad (vĭl′əm-stăt′). Cap. of the Netherlands Antilles, on the S coast of Curaçao. *Pop.* 50,000.
will·ful *also* **wil·ful** (wĭl′fəl) *adj.* **1.** Said or done deliberately. **2.** Stubborn. **—will′ful·ly** *adv.* **—will′ful·ness** *n.*
Wil·liam I (wĭl′yəm). "the Conqueror." 1027–87. King of England (1066–87).
Wil·liams (wĭl′yəmz), **Roger.** 1603?–83. English clergyman in America; founder of Rhode Island.
wil·lies (wĭl′ēz) *pl.n. Slang.* Feelings of nervousness.
will·ing (wĭl′ĭng) *adj.* **1.** Done, accepted, or given readily and voluntarily. **2.** Favorably inclined : ready. **3.** Acting or responding promptly. **4.** Volitional. **—will′ing·ly** *adv.* **—will′ing·ness** *n.*
wil·li·waw (wĭl′ē-wô′) *n.* A sudden violent rush of cold air blowing from a mountainous coast to the sea.
will-o'-the-wisp (wĭl′ə-*th*ə-wĭsp′) *n.* **1.** A light that glows over marshy ground at night. **2.** A misleading or deceptive goal.
wil·low (wĭl′ō) *n.* **1.** A deciduous tree or shrub of the genus

Salix, usu. with narrow leaves, flowers borne in catkins, slender, flexible twigs used in wickerwork, and strong, lightweight wood.
wil·low·y (wĭl′ō-ē) *adj.* **-i·er, -i·est. 1.** Flexible : pliant. **2.** Slender and graceful.
will power *n.* Power to carry out one's desires or decisions : strength of mind.
wil·ly-nil·ly (wĭl′ē-nĭl′ē) *adv.* & *adj.* Without consideration for one's wishes.
Wil·son (wĭl′sən), **(Thomas) Woodrow.** 1856–1924. 28th U.S. President (1913–21).
wilt (wĭlt) *v.* **1.** To become or cause to become limp or withered. **2.** To lose vigor or force. **3.** To deprive of energy or courage. ☆***syns:*** DROOP, FLAG, SAG —*n.* Any of various plant diseases marked by wilting or collapse.
wil·y (wī′lē) *adj.* **-i·er, -i·est.** Tricky : sly. **—wi′li·ness** *n.*
wim·ble (wĭm′bəl) *n.* A hand tool for boring holes. **—wim′ble** *v.*
wim·ple (wĭm′pəl) *n.* A cloth wound around the head and under the chin so that only the face is exposed, worn by women in medieval times and by some orders of nuns.

wimple

win (wĭn) *v.* **won** (wŭn), **win·ning. 1.** To gain victory in or as if in a contest. **2.** To gain by means of effort : earn <*win* fame> **3.** To receive for performance, as in a contest of skill or luck <*win* a prize> **4. a.** To gain the favor or support of <*won* the public> **b.** To cause (someone) to accept oneself in marriage. —*n.* A victory, esp. in a sports event. **—win′ner** *n.*
wince (wĭns) *v.* **winced, winc·ing.** To draw back or away involuntarily, as in pain.
winch (wĭnch) *n.* **1.** An apparatus for pulling or lifting, consisting of a drum around which a rope or cable attached to the load is wound as the load is moved. **2.** The crank used to turn a device such as a grindstone. **—winch** *v.* **—winch′er** *n.*
wind[1] (wĭnd) *n.* **1.** A natural or artificially produced movement of air. **2.** A prevailing influence : tendency. **3.** Air bearing a scent, as of game. **4. winds. a.** Wind instruments, as in an orchestra or band. **b.** The players of wind instruments. **5.** Intestinal gas : flatulence. **6. a.** Ability to breathe normally : respiration. **b.** Breath <had the *wind* knocked out of me> **7.** Empty or boastful words. **8.** An intimation or hint <got *wind* of their intentions> —*v.* **1.** To make short of breath <*winded* from the race> **2.** To perceive a scent of <The hounds *winded* a fox.> **3.** To allow (e.g., a horse) to rest in order to regain breath.
wind[2] (wīnd) *v.* **wound** (wound), **wind·ing. 1.** To wrap or be wrapped around something. **2.** To encircle in a series of coils. **3.** To move or proceed in a twisting course. **4.** To introduce indirectly : insinuate. **5.** To tighten the spring of <*wind* a watch> **6.** To turn, as a handle : crank. **7.** To lift or haul, as with a windlass or winch. ☆***syns:*** COIL, CURL, ENTWINE, SNAKE, SPIRAL, TWINE, TWIST, WEAVE **—wind up.** *Informal.* **1.** To end : finish. **2.** To experience a given outcome of a course of action <*wound up* a millionaire> **3.** To swing the arm before pitching a ball. —*n.* A turn or twist. **—wind′er** *n.*
wind[3] (wīnd, wĭnd) *v.* **wind·ed** (wīn′dĭd, wĭn′-) or **wound** (wound), **wind·ing.** To sound (e.g., a horn or trumpet) by blowing.
wind·age (wĭn′dĭj) *n.* The influence of the wind on the course of a projectile moving through the air.
wind·bag (wĭnd′băg′) *n. Slang.* A tiresomely or idly garrulous person.
wind-blown (wĭnd′blōn′) *adj.* **1.** Blown or scattered by the wind. **2.** Growing or shaped in a way determined by the prevailing winds. **3.** Seeming or looking as if blown by the wind.
wind·break (wĭnd′brāk′) *n.* Something, as a hedge or fence, serving to lessen the force of the wind.
Wind·break·er (wĭnd′brā′kər). A trademark for an outer jacket having close-fitting, often elastic cuffs and waistband.
wind·burn (wĭnd′bûrn′) *n.* Irritation of the skin caused by wind.
wind-chill factor (wĭnd′chĭl′) *n.* An air temperature with the same effect on exposed skin as a specified combination of temperature and wind speed.
wind·fall (wĭnd′fôl′) *n.* **1.** Something, as a tree or fruit, blown down by the wind. **2.** A sudden unlooked-for stroke of good luck.
wind·flow·er (wĭnd′flou′ər) *n.* ANEMONE 1.
Wind·hoek (vĭnt′ho͝ok′, -ho͞ok′). Cap. of Nambia, in the C part. Pop. 61,260.
wind·ing (wīn′dĭng) *adj.* **1.** Having a turning or twisting course. **2.** Spiral : curving. —*n.* Wire wound into a coil.
wind instrument (wĭnd) *n.* A musical instrument sounded by a current of air, esp. the player's breath.
wind·jam·mer (wĭnd′jăm′ər) *n.* A sailing ship or one of its crew members.
wind·lass (wĭnd′ləs) *n.* Any of various hauling or lifting machines similar to a winch and turned by a crank.
wind·mill (wĭnd′mĭl′) *n.* A mill or machine powered by the wind turning a wheel of adjustable blades or vanes.
win·dow (wĭn′dō) *n.* **1.** An opening, usu. framed and spanned with glass, built into a wall for light and air. **2.** A framework around a window : sash. **3.** A pane of glass : windowpane. **4.** A windowlike opening.
win·dow-dress·ing *also* **window dressing** (wĭn′dō-drĕs′ĭng) *n.* **1.** Decorative display of retail goods in store windows. **2.** A display made esp. to create a favorable but often false impression. **—win′dow-dress′er** *n.*
win·dow·pane (wĭn′dō-pān′) *n.* A pane of glass in a window.
win·dow-shop (wĭn′dō-shŏp′) *v.* To look at goods in store windows without going inside to buy. **—win′dow-shop′per** *n.* **—win′dow-shop′ping** *n.*
win·dow·sill (wĭn′dō-sĭl′) *n.* The sill at the bottom of a window opening.
Wind·sor (wĭn′zər). City of S Ont., Canada. *Pop.* 197,235.
wind·pipe (wĭnd′pīp′) *n.* The trachea.
wind·row (wĭnd′rō′) *n.* **1.** A row, as of leaves or snow, heaped up by the wind. **2.** A long row of cut hay or grain left to dry in a field before being bundled.
wind·shield (wĭnd′shēld′) *n.* A framed transparent screen located in front of the occupants of an automotive vehicle.
wind·sock (wĭnd′sŏk′) *n.* A large, conical, open-ended sleeve attached to a stand by a pivot so that it points in the direction of the wind blowing through it.
wind·storm (wĭnd′stôrm′) *n.* A storm with violent winds and very little rain.
wind·swept (wĭnd′swĕpt′) *adj.* Exposed to or driven by the wind.
wind tunnel (wĭnd) *n.* An enclosed chamber through which air is blown to study its effect on an aircraft, airfoil, etc.
wind-up (wīnd′ŭp′) *n.* **1. a.** The act of concluding : finish. **b.** A concluding part. **2.** *Baseball.* A pitcher's movements before pitching the ball.
wind·ward (wĭnd′wərd) *adj.* Facing or moving into the wind. —*n.* The point or side from which the wind blows. **—wind′ward** *adv.*
wind·y (wĭn′dē) *adj.* **-i·er, -i·est. 1. a.** Marked by or having much wind. **b.** Stormy : gusty. **2.** Exposed to the prevailing wind, esp. unsheltered. **3.** Tending toward or marked by prolonged, empty, or boastful talk. **—wind′i·ly** *adv.* **—wind′i·ness** *n.*
wine (wīn) *n.* **1. a.** The fermented juice of grapes, usu. containing 10–15% alcohol by volume. **b.** The fermented juice of various fruits or plants <blackberry *wine*> <rice *wine*> **2.** The dark purplish color of red wine. —*v.* **wined, win·ing.** To provide or entertain with drink or wine.
wine·glass (wīn′glăs′) *n.* A usu. stemmed glass for wine.
wine·grow·er (wīn′grō′ər) *n.* A vineyard owner and producer of wine. **—wine′grow′ing** *adj.* & *n.*
wine·press (wīn′prĕs′) *n.* A vat in which juice is expressed from grapes.
win·er·y (wī′nə-rē) *n., pl.* **-ies.** A wine-making establishment.
wing (wĭng) *n.* **1.** One of a pair of movable appendages that enable a bird, bat, or insect to fly. **2.** A plant or animal projection or part that resembles a wing. **3.** *Informal.* The human arm. **4.** One of a pair of airfoils positioned on each side of an aircraft fuselage to provide lift. **5.** Something resembling a wing esp. in form or function. **6.** An extension of a main building. **7.** A faction, as of a political party. **8.** *often* **wings.** The concealed area on either side of a stage for exits and entrances. **9.** A military aircraft unit or its pilots. **10.** The left or right flank of an army unit or navy fleet. **11.** A forward position or player, esp. in hockey. —*v.* **1.** To move on or as if on wings. **2.** To provide with wings. **3.** To do, gain, or accomplish by flying. **4.** To wound superficially. **—under (one's) wing.** In one's care. **—wing it.** *Informal.* To improvise. **—wing′less** *adj.* **—wing′like′** *adj.*
wing·ding (wĭng′dĭng′) *n. Slang.* A lively or extravagant party.

wing·ed *adj.* **1.** (wĭngd). Having wings or winglike projections or extensions. **2.** (wĭng′ĭd). **a.** Moving swiftly on or as if on wings. **b.** Elevated : sublime.

wing·span (wĭng′spăn′) *n.* Wingspread, esp. of an aircraft.

wing·spread (wĭng′sprĕd′) *n.* **1.** The distance between the tips of the fully spread wings, as of a bird or an insect. **2.** The distance between the extremities of an aircraft's wings.

wink (wĭngk) *v.* **1.** To close and open 1 eye deliberately, as to convey a message or signal. **2.** To shine or twinkle intermittently. **3.** To blink rapidly. **—wink at.** To ignore intentionally <*winked at* fraudulent practices> *—n.* **1. a.** The act of winking. **b.** A very short time, as that required for a wink. **2.** A brief sleep : nap.

win·ning (wĭn′ĭng) *adj.* **1.** Victorious in competition. **2.** Charming : captivating. *—n* **1.** Victory : triumph. **2.** *often* **winnings.** Something won, esp. money.

Win·ni·peg (wĭn′ə-pĕg′). Cap. of Man., Canada, in the S part. *Pop.* 610,000.

win·now (wĭn′ō) *v.* **1.** To remove by a stream of air <*winnow* chaff from grain> **2.** To examine closely and carefully : sift. **3.** To separate out (something good or bad) as if by winnowing. **—win′now·er** *n.*

win·o (wī′nō) *n., pl.* **-os.** *Slang.* One addicted to drinking wine, esp. cheap wine.

win·some (wĭn′səm) *adj.* Very pleasant or agreeable : charming. **—win′some·ly** *adv.* **—win′some·ness** *n.*

win·ter (wĭn′tər) *n.* The season between autumn and spring, usu. the coldest time of the year. *—adj.* **1.** Of, relating to, typical of, or taking place in the winter. **2.** Planted in the autumn for spring or summer harvest. *—v.* **1.** To spend the winter <*wintered* in Florida> **2.** To keep, feed, or care for (e.g., cattle) during the winter.

win·ter·green (wĭn′tər-grēn′) *n.* A low-growing plant, *Gaultheria procumbens,* of E North America, with spicy, edible red berries and aromatic evergreen leaves that yield an oil or flavoring.

win·ter·ize (wĭn′tə-rīz′) *v.* **-ized, -iz·ing.** To equip or make ready for winter weather <*winterize* a car>

win·ter·kill (wĭn′tər-kĭl′) *v.* To kill by or perish from exposure to winter cold.

win·ter·time (wĭn′tər-tīm′) *n.* The season of winter.

win·try (wĭn′trē) *also* **win·ter·y** (-tə-rē) **1.** Of or typical of winter. **2.** Cheerless and unfriendly <a *wintry* greeting> **—win′tri·ness** *n.*

wipe (wīp) *v.* **wiped, wip·ing. 1.** To clean or dry by rubbing. **2.** To rid of by or as if by rubbing <*wipe* away the dirt> **3.** To pass over a surface <*wipe* a dustcloth over a table> **—wipe out. 1.** To destroy completely. **2.** *Informal.* To kill. **—wipe** *n.* **—wip′er** *n.*

wire (wīr) *n.* **1.** A usu. pliable, slender metal rod or strand used mainly to conduct electricity or for structural support. **2.** Wires bundled or twisted together to form a cable. **3. a.** A telegraph or telephone wire or service. **b.** A telegram or cablegram. **4.** An active telephone connection <hold the *wire*> **5.** The finish line of a race. **6.** *often* **wires.** Hidden manipulative influences affecting a person or group <pulled *wires* to get the position> *—v.* **wired, wir·ing. 1.** To join or attach with or as if with wire. **2.** To install a system of electrical wires in. **3. a.** To convey (a message) by telegraph. **b.** To telegraph to.

wire-draw (wīr′drô′) *v.* **1.** To draw (metal) into wire. **2.** To draw out to great length or refinement.

wire-haired (wīr′hârd′) *adj.* Having a stiff, wiry coat of hair, as a dog.

wire·less (wīr′lĭs) *n.* **1.** A radio telegraph or telephone system operating by electromagnetic waves. **2.** *esp. Brit.* Radio or radio communications. *—adj.* Having no wires.

Wire·pho·to (wīr′fō′tō). A trademark for a photograph electrically transmitted over telephone wires.

wire·pull·er (wīr′po͝ol′ər) *n.* One who uses secret or underhand means to influence others and esp. to reach a goal.

wire·tap (wīr′tăp′) *n.* A hidden listening or recording device tapped into an electric circuit. *—v.* To install or monitor a wiretap. **—wire′tap′per** *n.*

wir·ing (wīr′ĭng) *n.* A system of electric wires, esp. for electricity in a building.

wir·y (wīr′ē) *adj.* **-i·er, -i·est. 1.** Resembling wire, as stiff or kinky hair. **2.** Lean but strong. **—wir′i·ness** *n.*

Wis·con·sin (wĭs-kŏn′sən). State of the NC U.S. *Cap.* Madison. *Pop.* 4,705,335.

wis·dom (wĭz′dəm) *n.* **1.** Insightful understanding of what is true, right, or enduring. **2.** Native good judgment <had the *wisdom* to leave well enough alone> **3.** The amassed learning of philosophers, scientists, and scholars.

wisdom tooth *n.* The last tooth on each side of both jaws in humans.

wise¹ (wīz) *adj.* **wis·er, wis·est. 1.** Having great learning. **2.** Having discernment : sagacious. **3.** Sensible : prudent. **4. a.** Having awareness or information : knowing. **b.** Cunning : shrewd. **5.** *Slang.* Offensively bold or impudent. **—wise′ly** *adv.*

wise² (wīz) *n.* Manner or fashion <in this *wise*>

-wise *suff.* **1.** In a given way, direction, or position <counterclock*wise*> **2.** *Informal.* Regarding <dollar*wise*>

wise·a·cre (wīz′ā′kər) *n. Informal.* One who pretends to be learned or clever.

wise·crack (wīz′krăk′) *n. Slang.* A witty or facetious remark. **—wise′crack′** *v.*

wish (wĭsh) *n.* **1.** A desire or longing for something. **2.** An expression of a wish <Make a *wish.*> **3.** Something desired. *—v.* **1.** To desire or long for : want. **2.** To make or express a wish for <*wished* us a safe trip> **3.** To bid <*wish* someone good night> **4.** To request or command <I *wish* you to go at once.> **5.** To force or impose upon another. **—wish′er** *n.*

wish·bone (wĭsh′bōn′) *n.* The forked bone anterior to the breastbone of the majority of birds.

wish·ful (wĭsh′fəl) *adj.* **1.** Expressing a wish : longing. **2.** In keeping with wishes rather than fact. **—wish′ful·ly** *adv.* **—wish′ful·ness** *n.*

wish·y-wash·y (wĭsh′ē-wŏsh′ē, -wô′shē) *adj.* **-i·er, -i·est.** *Informal.* **1.** Weak or watery. **2.** Weak-willed : indecisive.

wisp (wĭsp) *n.* **1.** A small bunch of hay or straw. **2. a.** A thin piece, strip, etc. <a *wisp* of hair> **b.** A faint streak <a *wisp* of smoke> **3.** One that is slender, frail, or evanescent. **—wisp′y** *adj.*

wis·te·ri·a (wĭ-stîr′ē-ə) *also* **wis·tar·i·a** (-stâr′-) *n.* A woody vine of the genus *Wisteria,* with long, drooping purplish or white flower clusters.

wist·ful (wĭst′fəl) *adj.* Filled with longing. **—wist′ful·ly** *adv.* **—wist′ful·ness** *n.*

wit (wĭt) *n.* **1. a.** The ability to use words cleverly and humorously. **b.** One having this ability. **c.** Inventive skill or imagination. **2.** *often* **wits. a.** Ability to reason and understand. **b.** Intact mental powers : sanity. **—at (one's) wits' end.** At the end of one's mental resources.

witch (wĭch) *n.* **1.** One thought to have magical powers, esp. a sorceress. **2.** An ugly old woman. **3.** *Informal.* An irresistibly fascinating woman or girl.

witch·craft (wĭch′krăft′) *n.* The use of magical powers : sorcery.

witch doctor *n.* One who practices magic esp. among primitive peoples.

witch·er·y (wĭch′ə-rē) *n., pl.* **-ies. 1.** The use of magic : witchcraft. **2.** Exceptional power to fascinate.

witch hazel *n.* **1.** A shrub of the genus *Hamamelis,* esp. *H. virginiana,* of E North America, with yellow flowers. **2.** A spicy-smelling alcoholic solution made from the bark and leaves of witch hazel that is used as a mild astringent.

witch hazel

witch-hunt (wĭch′hŭnt′) *n.* An intensive searching out and harassment of those with unpopular viewpoints <a political *witch-hunt*> **—witch′-hunt′ing** *n.*

witch·ing (wĭch′ĭng) *adj.* **1.** Pertaining to or suitable for witchcraft. **2.** Enchanting.

with (wĭth, wĭth) *prep.* **1.** In the company of <a cat *with* her kittens> **2.** Alongside <walk *with* your partner> **3.** Having, bearing, or wearing <a child *with* freckles> **4.** In a way marked by <drive *with* care> **5.** In the opinion or judgment of <It's O.K. *with* them if I stay.> **6.** In support of <We're *with* you on this issue.> **7.** Containing : including <tea *with* lemon> **8.** By means of <cooks *with* gas> **9.** In spite of : despite <*With* all our efforts, we're still broke.> **10.** At the same time as <sailed *with* high tide> **11.** In regard to : concerning <happy *with* my job> **12.** Compared to <on a par *with* classmates> **13.** Having been granted <We'll only marry *with* your approval.> **14.** In opposition or resistance to <fought *with* my brothers> **15.** As a result of <wept *with* relief> **16.** So as to join : to or onto <connect this piece *with* that one.> **17.** So as to be separated from <had to part *with* my savings.> **18.** In the passage of <got worse *with* each hour> **19.** In relation to <linked cancer *with* smoking> **20.** In the care or keeping of <left the car *with* me>

with•al (wĭth-ôl′, wĭth-) *adv.* **1.** Besides : as well. **2.** However : nevertheless. **3.** *Archaic.* With that : therewith.

with•draw (wĭth-drô′, wĭth-) *v.* **1.** To take back or away. **2.** To call back or retract <*withdrew* the complaint> **3.** To draw back : retreat. **4.** To end one's involvement in or use of something.

with•draw•al (wĭth-drô′əl, wĭth-) *n.* **1.** The act, process, or an instance of withdrawing. **2.** An emotional or psychological detachment. **3. a.** Discontinuation of the use of a habit-forming substance. **b.** The physical and emotional reactions that are manifested upon withdrawal.

with•drawn (wĭth-drôn′, wĭth-) *adj.* **1.** Isolated : remote. **2.** Retiring : shy. **3.** Emotionally detached.

withe (wĭth, wĭth, wīth) *n.* A strong, pliable twig used esp. as a rope or binding.

with•er (wĭth′ər) *v.* **1.** To shrivel or wilt from or as if from moisture loss. **2.** To lose or cause to lose freshness, force, or vigor. **3.** To render speechless or powerless.

with•ers (wĭth′ərz) *pl.n.* The part of a horse's back between the shoulder blades.

with•hold (wĭth-hōld′, wĭth-) *v.* **1.** To keep or hold back <*withhold* applause> **2.** To refrain from giving <*withhold* permission> **—with•hold′er** *n.*

withholding tax *n.* A tax on income withheld by one's employer.

with•in (wĭth-ĭn′, wĭth-) *adv.* **1.** In or into the inner part : inside. **2.** Indoors. **3.** In oneself : inwardly. *—prep.* **1.** In the inner part of : inside. **2.** Inside the limits or extent of in time, degree, or distance. **3.** Not exceeding the fixed limits of. **4.** In the area or domain of. *—n.* An inside place or area <change from *within*>

with-it (wĭth′ĭt) *adj. Slang.* Highly aware esp. of the latest trends.

†**with•out** (wĭth-out′, wĭth-) *adv.* **1.** On the outside. **2.** Not indoors. **3.** With something lacking <had to do *without*> *—prep.* **1.** With someone or something absent or lacking <went *without* me> <walks *without* help> **2.** On or to the outer side of. *—conj. Regional.* Unless.

with•stand (wĭth-stănd′, wĭth-) *v.* To resist or endure successfully.

wit•less (wĭt′lĭs) *adj.* Lacking intelligence or understanding. **—wit′less•ly** *adv.*

wit•ness (wĭt′nĭs) *n.* **1.** One who has personally seen, heard, or experienced something. **2.** Something that serves as proof or evidence. **3. a.** One who is requested to testify in court. **b.** One who is present at and can attest to a transaction. **4.** Affirmation : testimony <bear *witness*> *—v.* **1.** To be a witness of : see. **2.** To give proof or evidence of. **3.** To be the setting of <The town has *witnessed* much change.> **4.** To serve as a legal witness of <*witness* a will>

wit•ti•cism (wĭt′ĭ-sĭz′əm) *n.* A cleverly worded remark or saying.

wit•ty (wĭt′ē) *adj.* **-ti•er, -ti•est.** Cleverly humorous : amusing. **—wit′ti•ly** *adv.* **—wit′ti•ness** *n.*

wives (wīvz) *n. pl. of* WIFE.

wiz•ard (wĭz′ərd) *n.* **1.** One thought to have magical powers : sorcerer or magician. **2.** *Informal.* One with skill or expertise : whiz. **—wiz′ard•ry** *n.*

▲word history: *Wizard* is a compound word formed from the adjective *wise,* "learned, sensible," and the suffix *-ard.* The word orig. meant "a wise man, philosopher." The suffix *-ard,* however, almost always has a pejorative or disparaging sense, as in the words *coward, drunkard,* and *sluggard. Wizard* was therefore often used contemptuously to mean "a so-called wise man," and from this use it came to mean "sorcerer" and "male witch."

wiz•ened (wĭz′ənd) *adj.* Shriveled and withered : dried up.

wk. *abbr.* **1.** weak. **2.** week. **3.** work.

wkly. *abbr.* weekly.

woad (wōd) *n.* An Old World plant, *Isatis tinctoria,* with leaves yielding a blue dye.

wob•ble (wŏb′əl) *v.* **-bled, -bling. 1.** To move or cause to move with an unsteady rocking motion. **2.** To tremble or quaver <a voice *wobbling* with fear> **3.** To be indecisive : vacillate. **—wob′ble** *n.* **—wob′bli•ness** *n.* **—wob′bly** *adj.*

woe (wō) *n.* **1.** A state of deep sorrow : grief. **2.** Misfortune : adversity.

woe•be•gone (wō′bĭ-gôn′, -gŏn′) *adj.* Mournful or wretched, esp. in appearance.

woe•ful (wō′fəl) *adj.* **1.** Full of woe : sorrowful. **2.** Pertaining to or causing woe. **3.** Lamentable : deplorable. **—woe′ful•ly** *adv.*

wok (wŏk) *n.* A metal pan with a convex bottom used esp. for stir-frying.

woke (wōk) *v. var. p.t. of* WAKE[1].

wo•ken (wō′kən) *v. var. p.p. of* WAKE[1].

wold (wōld) *n.* An open rolling stretch of upland.

wolf (wŏŏlf) *n., pl.* **wolves** (wŏŏlvz). **1.** A carnivorous mammal, *Canis lupus,* of N regions, or *C. rufus* or *C. niger,* of SW North America, related to and resembling the dog. **2.** A fierce or predacious person. **3.** *Slang.* A man who ardently pursues women. *—v.* To eat quickly and greedily. **—wolf′ish** *adj.* **—wolf′ish•ly** *adv.*

wolf•hound (wŏŏlf′hound′) *n.* A large dog orig. used in wolf hunting.

wol•ver•ine (wŏŏl′və-rēn′) *n.* A carnivorous mammal, *Gulo gulo* or *G. luscus,* of N regions, with dark fur and a bushy tail.

wom•an (wŏŏm′ən) *n., pl.* **wom•en** (wĭm′ĭn). **1.** An adult human female. **2.** Women as a group : womankind. **3.** Characteristic feminine qualities. **4.** A woman servant or attendant.

wom•an•hood (wŏŏm′ən-hŏŏd′) *n.* **1.** The state of being an adult human female. **2.** Womanly qualities, feelings, etc. **3.** Women in general : womankind.

wom•an•ish (wŏŏm′ə-nĭsh) *adj.* **1.** Of, pertaining to, or typical of a woman. **2.** Regarded as appropriate in women but not in men : effeminate.

wom•an•kind (wŏŏm′ən-kīnd′) *n.* Women as a group.

wom•an•ly (wŏŏm′ən-lē) *adj.* **-li•er, -li•est.** Having qualities regarded as characteristic of and esp. admirable in women. **—wom′an•li•ness** *n.*

womb (wōōm) *n.* **1.** The mammalian organ of gestation : uterus. **2.** A place where something develops.

wom•bat (wŏm′băt′) *n.* An Australian marsupial, *Phascolomis ursinus* or *Lasiorhinus latifrons,* resembling a small bear.

wom•en (wĭm′ĭn) *n. pl. of* WOMAN.

wom•en•folk (wĭm′ĭn-fōk′) *pl.n.* **1.** Women in general. **2.** A particular group of women.

women's room *n.* A rest room for women.

won[1] (wŭn) *v. p.t. & p.p. of* WIN.

won[2] (wôn) *n., pl.* **won.** See CURRENCY TABLE.

won•der (wŭn′dər) *n.* **1. a.** One that excites amazement or admiration : marvel. **b.** The feeling aroused by something extraordinary or marvelous. **c.** The quality of arousing wonder. **2.** A feeling of uncertainty. *—v.* **1.** To feel amazement or admiration. **2.** To feel curiosity or uncertainty. **3.** To feel inquisitive or uncertain about.

won•der•ful (wŭn′dər-fəl) *adj.* **1.** Astonishing or marvelous. **2.** Exceptionally fine : excellent. **—won′der•ful•ly** *adv.*

won•der•land (wŭn′dər-lănd′) *n.* **1.** An imaginary realm filled with marvels. **2.** A place that arouses awe or admiration.

won•der•ment (wŭn′dər-mənt) *n.* **1.** A state or feeling of amazement. **2.** A cause of wonder : marvel. **3.** A state of being puzzled, uncertain, or curious.

won•drous (wŭn′drəs) *adj.* Remarkable : wonderful. *—adv. Archaic.* Wonderfully : amazingly. **—won′drous•ly** *adv.*

wont (wônt, wōnt) *adj.* **1.** Accustomed or used <was *wont* to speed> **2.** Apt or likely <is *wont* to be grumpy> *—n.* Habitual practice : custom.

won't (wōnt). Will not.

wont•ed (wôn′tĭd, wōn′-) *adj.* Accustomed : habitual.

won ton (wŏn′ tŏn′) *n., pl.* **won tons.** A noodle-dough dumpling filled with spiced minced pork, usu. served in soup.

woo (wōō) *v.* **1.** To court with the hope of marrying. **2.** To attempt to obtain or achieve <*woo* fame and fortune> **3.** To entreat insistently. **—woo′er** *n.*

wood (wŏŏd) *n.* **1. a.** The solid fibrous substance composing the main part of trees and shrubs below the outer covering. **b.** This substance used esp. for building material and fuel. **2.** *often* **woods.** A thick growth of trees somewhat smaller than a forest. **3.** An object, as a golf club, made of wood. *—adj.* **1.** Made of wood : wooden. **2.** Relating to wood as fuel or lumber. **3.** Inhabiting or growing naturally in woods. *—v.* **1.** To cover with a stand of trees. **2.** To furnish with wood, esp. for burning.

wood alcohol *n.* A flammable poisonous liquid used esp. as antifreeze.

wood•bine (wŏŏd′bīn′) *n.* Any of various climbing vines, as an Old World honeysuckle, *Lonicera periclymenum,* or the Virginia creeper.

wood•block (wŏŏd′blŏk′) *n.* A woodcut.

wood•chuck (wŏŏd′chŭk′) *n.* A common rodent, *Marmota monax,* of N and E North America, with a short-legged, heavy-set body and grizzled brownish fur.

wood•cock (wŏŏd′kŏk′) *n.* A game bird, *Scolopax rusticola* or *Philohela minor,* with short legs and a long bill.

wood•craft (wŏŏd′krăft′) *n.* **1.** Skill in making things from wood. **2.** Skill and experience in woods-related activities, as hunting, fishing, or camping.

wood·cut (wŏŏd′kŭt′) *n.* **1.** A wooden block whose surface is engraved with a design for printing. **2.** A print made from a woodcut.

wood·cut·ter (wŏŏd′kŭt′ər) *n.* One who cuts wood or trees esp. as a livelihood.

wood·ed (wŏŏd′ĭd) *adj.* Covered with trees or woods.

wood·en (wŏŏd′n) *adj.* **1.** Made or consisting of wood. **2.** Lacking in spirit or liveliness. **3.** Clumsy. **—wood′en·ly** *adv.*

wood·land (wŏŏd′lənd, -lănd′) *n.* Land with a cover of trees and shrubs.

wood·peck·er (wŏŏd′pĕk′ər) *n.* Any of various birds of the family Picidae, with strong claws and a chisellike bill for drilling through bark and wood.

wood·pile (wŏŏd′pīl′) *n.* A pile of wood, esp. when stacked for use as firewood.

wood·ruff (wŏŏd′rəf, -rŭf′) *n.* A plant of the genus *Asperula*, esp. the Eurasian variety *A. odorata*, with small white flowers and fragrant leaves used esp. in sachets.

wood·shed (wŏŏd′shĕd′) *n.* A shed for the storage of firewood.

woods·man (wŏŏdz′mən) *n.* One who lives, works, or spends much time in the woods, esp. one who is skilled in woodcraft.

woods·y (wŏŏd′zē) *adj.* **-i·er, -i·est.** Relating to or suggestive of the woods.

wood·wind (wŏŏd′wĭnd′) *n.* Any of a group of wind instruments, including the clarinet, oboe, flute, and bassoon.

wood·work (wŏŏd′wûrk′) *n.* Objects made of or work done in wood, esp. wooden moldings or doors.

wood·y (wŏŏd′ē) *adj.* **-i·er, -i·est. 1.** Of or containing wood. **2.** Typical or suggestive of wood. **3.** Abounding in trees : wooded.

woof (wŏŏf, wōōf) *n.* **1.** The threads that run crosswise in a woven fabric, at right angles to the warp threads. **2.** The texture of a woven fabric or the fabric itself.

woof·er (wŏŏf′ər) *n.* A loudspeaker that reproduces low-frequency sounds.

wool (wŏŏl) *n.* **1.** The soft, thick, often curly hair of some mammals, esp. sheep. **2.** Yarn, textiles, or garments made of wool. **3.** Something having the look or feel of wool.

wool·en *also* **wool·len** (wŏŏl′ən). *—adj.* Of, relating to, or made of wool. *—n. often* **woolens.** Wool textiles or garments.

wool·gath·er·ing (wŏŏl′găth′ər-ĭng) *n.* Idle indulgence in daydreams. **—wool′gath′er·er** *n.*

†wool·ly *also* **wool·y** (wŏŏl′ē). *adj.* **-li·er, -li·est** *also* **-i·er, -i·est. 1. a.** Of, relating to, or covered with wool. **b.** Like wool. **2.** Lacking clarity, as of thought. **3.** Marked by absence of law and order, as in American frontier times. *—n., pl.* **-lies** *also* **-ies. 1.** A garment made of wool. **2.** *W U.S. & Austral.* A sheep. **—wool′li·ness** *n.*

woolly bear *n.* The hairy caterpillar of a tiger moth, esp. that of *Isia isabella.*

woo·zy (wōō′zē, wŏŏz′ē) *adj.* **-zi·er, -zi·est. 1.** Dazed : confused. **2.** Dizzy or nauseated. **—woo′zi·ness** *n.*

Worces·ter·shire (wŏŏs′tər-shîr′, -shər). A trademark for a spicy soy and vinegar sauce.

word (wûrd) *n.* **1. a.** A meaningful speech sound or succession of speech sounds that can be represented by graphic symbols. **b.** A written or printed representation of a word. **2.** A remark or comment. **3. words.** An argument. **4.** An assurance. **5.** An order to do something. **6.** News <sent *word* of their discovery> **7.** A password or watchword. **8. words.** The lyrics of a musical composition. **9. Word.** The Bible or Gospel. *—v.* To express orally or in writing. **—word′less** *adj.* **—word′less·ly** *adv.*

word·age (wûr′dĭj) *n.* **1.** Words in general. **2.** The number of words used, as in a novel. **3.** Choice of words : wording.

word·book (wûrd′bŏŏk′) *n.* A dictionary or specialized vocabulary.

word·ing (wûr′dĭng) *n.* The way in which words and phrases are used.

word play *n.* A clever or witty use of words, esp. a pun.

word processing *n.* A system of producing typewritten documents, as business letters, by use of automated typewriters and electronic text-editing equipment. **—word processor** *n.*

Words·worth (wûrdz′wûrth′), **William.** 1770–1850. English poet.

word·y (wûr′dē) *adj.* **-i·er, -i·est.** Marked by too many words. ☆***syns:*** DIFFUSE, LONG-WINDED, PROLIX, VERBOSE **—word′i·ly** *adv.* **—word′i·ness** *n.*

wore (wôr, wōr) *v. p.t. of* WEAR.

work (wûrk) *n.* **1.** Physical or mental effort directed toward a goal. **2.** A job : employment <out of *work*> **3.** The activity that serves as one's regular source of livelihood : occupation. **4.** Something done as part of a job : task or duty. **5.** Quality of workmanship <careless *work*> **6. a.** Something brought about by an effort <the *work* of a mastermind> **b.** An act or deed, as of charity. **c. works.** The total production of a creative artist. **d. works.** Engineering structures, as bridges, roads, and dams. **7.** Something being produced, studied, or subjected to a process. **8. works** *(sing. in number).* A site of industry, as a factory or plant <iron *works*> **9. works.** The operating parts of a mechanism, as a clock. **10. the works.** *Slang.* Everything <ordered pizza with *the works*> **11.** The transfer of energy when a force is applied to a body. ☆***syns:*** BUSINESS, EMPLOYMENT, JOB, OCCUPATION *—v.* **1.** To engage in physical or mental exertion. **2.** To have a job. **3.** To function or cause to function, esp. effectively. **4.** To have an influence or effect <Guilt *worked* on my conscience.> **5.** To become through gradual or repeated stress, pressure, or movement <The masonry *worked* loose.> **6.** To make a passage or way steadily or forcibly. **7.** To move or contort, as from painful emotion. **8.** To be handled or processed, as metal. **9.** To bring about : achieve <*works* wonders with children> **10.** To cause to expend effort <*worked* the dancers hard> **11.** To form or shape. **12.** To solve (a math problem) by figuring and reasoning. **13.** To achieve (a particular state) in stages. **14.** To plan or arrange. **15.** To excite or provoke <*worked* myself into a rage> **—work out. 1.** To find a solution for. **2.** To prove effective or appropriate. **3.** To exercise esp. regularly and strenuously.

work·a·ble (wûr′kə-bəl) *adj.* **1.** Capable of being done : practicable. **2.** Capable of being shaped, molded, or dealt with. **—work′a·bil′i·ty, work′a·ble·ness** *n.*

work·a·day (wûr′kə-dā′) *adj.* **1.** Of, relating to, or suitable for working days : everyday. **2.** Commonplace : ordinary.

work·bench (wûrk′bĕnch′) *n.* A sturdy table used esp. by machinists or carpenters.

work·book (wûrk′bŏŏk′) *n.* **1.** A student's booklet of problems and exercises that is designed to be written in. **2.** A manual of instructions. **3.** A record book for work accomplished.

work·day (wûrk′dā′) *n.* **1.** A day that is part of one's workweek. **2.** The section of the day during which one works at a job.

work·er (wûr′kər) *n.* **1.** One that works <a slow *worker*> **2.** One who works for wages, esp. a manual or industrial laborer. **3.** A sterile ant, bee, or termite that performs specialized work in the colony.

work force *n.* **1.** The staff employed in a specific work project. **2.** All workers potentially available, as to a nation.

work·horse (wûrk′hôrs′) *n.* **1.** A horse used primarily for labor. **2.** One who works tirelessly, esp. at difficult tasks.

work·ing (wûr′kĭng) *adj.* **1.** Of, relating to, used for, or spent in work. **2.** Adequate or enough for use or work. **3.** Capable of being used to further activity or work.

work·load (wûrk′lōd′) *n.* The quantity of work assigned or accomplished in a specified time period.

work·man (wûrk′mən) *n.* **1.** One who performs usu. manual labor for wages. **2.** A skilled craftsman.

work·man·like (wûrk′mən-līk′) *adj.* Of or worthy of a skillful worker or craftsman.

work·man·ship (wûrk′mən-shĭp′) *n.* **1.** The craftsmanship of a workman. **2.** The quality of a craftsman's work.

work·out (wûrk′out′) *n.* **1.** A usu. strenuous period of exercise or practice. **2.** An arduous task.

work·room (wûrk′rōōm′, -rŏŏm′) *n.* A room used esp. for work done by hand.

work·shop (wûrk′shŏp′) *n.* **1.** A place where manual or industrial work is done. **2. a.** A group of people who meet regularly for a seminar in a particular field. **b.** A usu. short educational program in which small groups deal with specific problems.

work·ta·ble (wûrk′tā′bəl) *n.* A table for a particular task or activity.

work·week (wûrk′wēk′) *n.* The total number of hours, as 35 or 40, required to be worked in 1 week.

world (wûrld) *n.* **1.** The planet earth. **2.** All of creation : the universe. **3.** The earth and all that inhabit it. **4.** The human race. **5.** The public : society. **6.** A specific region of the earth. **7.** A sphere or domain <the insect *world*> **8.** A field or sphere of human interest or effort <the sports *world*> **9.** Individual existence, experience, etc. **10.** Secular life and its affairs. **11.** A great amount <a *world* of misfortune> **12.** A celestial body, esp. a planet <extraterrestrial *worlds*>

world·ly (wûrld′lē) *adj.* **-li·er, -li·est. 1.** Of or concerned with temporal rather than spiritual or religious matters. **2.** Worldly-wise. **—world′li·ness** *n.*

world·ly-wise (wûrld′lē-wīz′) *adj.* Having a shrewd understanding of human affairs : sophisticated.

world·wide (wûrld′wīd′) *adj.* Universal in scope or extent. **—world′wide′** *adv.*

worm (wûrm) *n.* **1.** Any of various invertebrates, as those of the phyla Annelida, Nematoda, or Platyhelminthes, that have a long, flexible rounded or flattened body. **2.** Any of various insect larvae, as caterpillars or grubs, that have a soft elongated body. **3.** Something like a worm in movement or appearance. **4.** A force that inwardly torments or corrupts. **5.** A contemptible person. **6. worms.** Infestation with intestinal worms or wormlike parasites. *—v.* **1.** To move or cause to move with or as if with the wriggling motion of a worm. **2.** To obtain by devious means <*wormed* a loan out of me> **3.** To rid (e.g., a cat) of intestinal worms. **—worm'y** *adj.*

worm-eat·en (wûrm'ēt'n) *adj.* **1.** Infested with or damaged by worms. **2.** Affected by decay : rotten. **3.** Out-of-date.

worm gear *n.* **1.** A gear consisting of a rotating threaded shaft and a worm wheel that mesh together. **2.** A worm wheel.

worm gear

worm wheel *n.* The toothed wheel that meshes with the rotating threaded shaft of a worm gear.

worm·wood (wûrm'wo͝od') *n.* **1.** An aromatic plant of the genus *Artemisia*, esp. the European variety *A. absinthium*, that yields a bitter extract used in making absinthe. **2.** Something harsh or embittering.

worn (wôrn, wōrn) *adj.* **1.** Affected or damaged by wear or use. **2.** Completely exhausted. **3.** Trite through overuse.

worn-out (wôrn'out', wōrn'-) *adj.* **1.** Worn or used up completely <*worn-out* clothes> **2.** Extremely tired.

wor·ri·some (wûr'ē-səm, wŭr'-) *adj.* **1.** Causing worry. **2.** Inclined to worry.

wor·ry (wûr'ē, wŭr'ē) *v.* **-ried, -ry·ing. 1.** To feel or cause to feel anxious or distressed. **2. a.** To grasp and tug at repeatedly <a dog *worrying* a bone> **b.** To press or handle absentmindedly <*worry* a sore tooth> **3.** To irritate : annoy. *—n., pl.* **-ries. 1.** Mental anxiety or distress. **2.** A cause or source of worry. **—wor'ri·er** *n.*

wor·ry·wart (wûr'ē-wôrt', wŭr'-) *n. Informal.* One who tends to worry a great deal.

worse (wûrs) *adj.* **1.** More inferior. **2.** In poorer health. **3.** More disagreeable or severe. *—adv.* To a worse extent. *—n.* Something worse <a turn for the *worse*>

wors·en (wûr'sən) *v.* To make or become worse.

wor·ship (wûr'shĭp) *n.* **1. a.** Reverence for a deity or sacred object. **b.** A set of religious forms by which this reverence is expressed. **2.** Intense devotion to or esteem for a person or thing. **3.** *often* **Worship.** *esp. Brit.* A title of respect for some officials, as magistrates or mayors. *—v.* **-shiped, -ship·ing** *or* **-shipped, -ship·ping. 1.** To venerate as a deity. **2.** To love, admire, or esteem devotedly. **3.** To attend a religious service. **—wor'ship·er** *n.*

wor·ship·ful (wûr'shĭp-fəl) *adj.* **1.** Reverent or adoring. **2.** *esp. Brit.* Honorable by virtue of position or rank. Used in titles of respect.

worst (wûrst) *adj.* **1.** Most inferior : least good. **2.** Most disagreeable or severe. **3.** Least desirable or satisfactory, esp. furthest from an ideal or standard. *—n.* One that is worst. *—adv.* In the worst way or degree. *—v.* To surpass : defeat.

wor·sted (wo͝os'tĭd, wûr'stĭd) *n.* **1.** Smooth, firmly twisted yarn made from long strands of wool. **2.** A firm, smooth fabric made from worsted.

wort (wûrt, wôrt) *n.* An herbaceous plant. Usu. used in combination.

worth (wûrth) *n.* **1.** The quality of something that gives value or usefulness. **2.** Personal value or merit. **3.** The monetary value of something. **4.** The amount that a certain sum of money will buy <a dollar's *worth* of candy> **5.** Wealth : affluence. *—prep.* **1.** Equal in value to. **2.** Having money or property amounting to. **3.** Deserving of <a job *worth* doing>

worth·less (wûrth'lĭs) *adj.* **1.** Without value or use. **2.** Contemptible : despicable.

worth·while (wûrth'hwīl', -wīl') *adj.* Deserving of the time, effort, or expense involved. **—worth'while'ness** *n.*

wor·thy (wûr'thē) *adj.* **-thi·er, -thi·est. 1.** Useful or valuable. **2.** Deserving respect : admirable. **3.** Meriting : deserving <*worthy* of attention> *—n., pl.* **-thies.** One who is respected or esteemed. **—wor'thi·ly** *adv.* **—wor'thi·ness** *n.*

would (wo͝od) *v. p.t. of* WILL[2].

would-be (wo͝od'bē') *adj.* Wishing or pretending to be <a *would-be* novelist>

would·n't (wo͝od'nt). Would not.

wound[1] (wo͞ond) *n.* **1.** An injury, esp. one in which the skin is lacerated or pierced. **2.** An emotional injury. *—v.* To injure by means of a wound.

wound[2] (wound) *v. p.t. & p.p. of* WIND[2].

wound[3] (wound) *v. var. p.t. & p.p. of* WIND[3].

wove (wōv) *v. var. p.t. of* WEAVE.

wo·ven (wō'vən) *v. p.p. of* WEAVE.

wow (wou) *interj.* Used to express surprise, amazement, excitement, etc. *—n. Informal.* An extraordinary success. *—v.* To affect strongly and usu. agreeably.

†**wrack** (răk) *n.* **1.** Total destruction. **2. a.** Wreckage, esp. of a ship cast ashore. **b.** *Regional.* Violent destruction of a vehicle or building. **3.** Seaweed forming a tangled mass. *—v.* **1.** To ruin : wreck. **2.** To have a violent effect on <*wracked* by sobs>

wraith (rāth) *n.* **1.** An apparition or ghost. **2.** One that is insubstantial or shadowy.

wran·gle (răng'gəl) *v.* **-gled, -gling. 1.** To quarrel noisily or angrily. **2.** To achieve by argument. **3.** To herd (livestock). **—wran'gle** *n.* **—wran'gler** *n.*

wrap (răp) *v.* **wrapped** *or* **wrapt, wrap·ping. 1.** To arrange or fold about in order to cover or protect something. **2.** To enclose, encase, or enfold. **3.** To package, esp. with paper. **4.** To wind, fold, or twine about something. **5.** To envelop esp. so as to conceal. **6.** To be or cause to be completely engrossed <*wrapped* in thought> **—wrap up. 1.** To finish : end. **2.** To give a brief summary of. ☆***syns:*** CLOAK, CLOTHE, ENFOLD, ENSHROUD, ENVELOP, ENWRAP, SHROUD, VEIL *—n.* **1.** A coat, shawl, etc., worn for warmth. **2.** A wrapper.

wrap·a·round (răp'ə-round') *n.* A dress or skirt open to the hem and fitted to the body by wrapping around.

wrap·per (răp'ər) *n.* **1.** One that wraps. **2. a.** Material in which something is wrapped. **b.** The tobacco leaf wrapped around a cigar. **3.** A loose robe.

wrap·ping (răp'ĭng) *n.* The material used for wrapping something.

wrap-up (răp'ŭp') *n.* A brief summary.

wrasse (răs) *n.* Any of numerous chiefly tropical, often brightly colored marine fishes of the family Labridae.

wrath (răth, räth) *n.* **1.** Violent anger : fury. **2. a.** A manifestation of wrath. **b.** Divine punishment for sin. **—wrath'ful** *adj.* **—wrath'ful·ly** *adv.*

wreak (rēk) *v.* **1.** To inflict (vengeance or punishment) upon another. **2.** To give expression to <*wreak* one's anger>

wreath (rēth) *n., pl.* **wreaths** (rēthz, rēths). **1.** A ringlike band or circular form, as of interwined flowers or pine boughs. **2.** A wreathlike ring or form.

wreathe (rēth) *v.* **wreathed, wreath·ing. 1.** To twist into a wreath or wreathlike contour. **2.** To move in coils or spirals. **3.** To take on or cause to take on the circular shape of a wreath.

wreck (rĕk) *v.* **1.** To damage or ruin by accident <*wrecked* the car> **2.** To tear down or blow up : demolish. **3.** To bring to a state of ruin. *—n.* **1.** The action of wrecking or state of being wrecked. **2. a.** Damaged remains, as of a wrecked ship or vehicle. **b.** A shipwreck. **c.** Cargo or debris washed ashore after a shipwreck. **3.** One in a disabled or ruined state.

wreck·age (rĕk'ĭj) *n.* **1.** The act of wrecking or state of being wrecked. **2.** The debris or remains of something wrecked.

wreck·er (rĕk'ər) *n.* **1. a.** One that wrecks. **b.** One engaged commercially in wrecking or demolishing something. **2. a.** A vehicle or ship that recovers or removes wrecks. **b.** A salvager of wrecked cargo.

wren (rĕn) *n.* A small, brownish bird of the family Troglodytidae that usu. holds its tail pointing upward.

wrench (rĕnch) *n.* **1.** An abrupt, forcible twisting movement. **2.** An injury, as to a muscle or joint, produced esp. by twisting. **3.** A tool for gripping, turning, or twisting an object such as a nut or bolt. *—v.* **1. a.** To twist or turn esp. violently. **b.** To twist and sprain <*wrenched* my ankle> **2.** To pull forcibly : wrest. **3.** To give emotional pain or anguish to. **4.** To distort the orig. meaning of. **—wrench'ing·ly** *adv.*

wrest (rĕst) *v.* **1.** To get by or as if by pulling with violent wrenching movements. **2.** To gain by or as if by force or violence. *—n.* A forcible twist or wrench.

wres·tle (rĕs'əl) *v.* **-tled, -tling. 1.** To struggle with an opponent in an attempt to throw or pin him down. **2.** To struggle to deal with or overcome <*wrestling* with unemployment> **3.** To strive against in a wrestling match. *—n.* An act or instance of wrestling. **—wres'tler** *n.*

wres·tling (rĕs'lĭng) *n.* A gymnastic exercise or competition between 2 contenders who attempt to throw each other by struggling hand-to-hand.

wretch (rĕch) *n.* **1.** An extremely unfortunate or miserable person. **2.** A vile or contemptible person.

wretch·ed (rĕch'ĭd) *adj.* **1.** Extremely unhappy : miserable. **2.** Of a poor or mean character <a *wretched* hovel> **3.** Extremely distressing : grievous <a *wretched* illness> **4.** Despicable : vile. **5.** Inferior in quality or competence. **–wretch'ed·ly** *adv.* **–wretch'ed·ness** *n.*

wrig·gle (rĭg'əl) *v.* **-gled, -gling. 1.** To turn or twist about sinuously. **2.** To go forward by turning and twisting, as a snake. **3.** To get into or out of by subtle or devious means. **–wrig'gle** *n.* **–wrig'gly** *adj.*

wrig·gler (rĭg'lər) *n.* **1.** One that wriggles. **2.** The larval or pupal stage of a mosquito.

Wright (rīt). **Wilbur** (1867–1912) and **Orville** (1871–1948). Amer. aviation pioneers.

wring (rĭng) *v.* **wrung** (rŭng), **wring·ing. 1.** To twist and squeeze by hand or machine, esp. to extract liquid. **2.** To obtain by or as if by forcible twisting or compressing <*wring* a confession out of a suspect> **3.** To twist or wrench forcibly <*wring* someone's neck> **4.** To twist or press together (one's hands) in distress. **5.** To affect with emotional pain or distress.

wring·er (rĭng'ər) *n.* One that wrings, esp. a device with rollers that press out water from wet clothes.

wrin·kle (rĭng'kəl) *n.* **1.** A small fold, ridge, or crease, as on fabric or the skin. **2.** *Informal.* An ingenious innovation. ☆***syns:*** ANGLE, GIMMICK, KICKER, TWIST *–v.* **-kled, -kling.** To form or cause to form wrinkles. **–wrin'kly** *adj.*

wrist (rĭst) *n.* **1.** The joint at which the hand and forearm come together. **2.** The arrangement of bones composing the wrist.

wrist·band (rĭst'bănd') *n.* The part of a sleeve or wrist watch encircling the wrist.

wrist watch *n.* A small timepiece worn on a band that encircles the wrist.

writ (rĭt) *n.* **1.** A written court order commanding an individual to perform or refrain from a specified act. **2.** Something written, esp. a formal document.

write (rīt) *v.* **wrote** (rōt), **writ·ten** (rĭt'n), **writ·ing. 1.** To form (symbols, letters, or words) on a surface, as with a pen or pencil. **2.** To inscribe the symbol, letters, or words of <*write* one's signature> **3.** To create and put down on paper. **4.** To communicate by writing <*wrote* the news to my family> **5.** To send a communication to <*write* me all the news> **–write in.** To vote for (a candidate not listed) by entering the name on the ballot. **–write off. 1.** To cancel as a loss <*write off* a debt> **2.** To make less in value.

write-in (rīt'ĭn') *n.* **1.** A vote cast by writing in the name of a candidate. **2.** A candidate whose name is written in.

writ·er (rī'tər) *n.* One who writes, esp. as an occupation : author.

writer's cramp *n.* A painful muscular spasm of the fingers or hand caused by prolonged writing.

write-up (rīt'ŭp') *n.* A written usu. favorable report or review, as in a newspaper.

writhe (rīth) *v.* **writhed, writh·ing. 1.** To twist or squirm, as in pain. **2.** To move with a twisting or contorted motion, as a snake. **3.** To suffer acutely.

writ·ing (rī'tĭng) *n.* **1.** Written mode <an order put in *writing*> **2.** Handwriting. **3.** A written work, esp. a literary composition. **4.** The art or occupation of a writer.

wrong (rông, rŏng) *adj.* **1.** Being in error : incorrect. **2. a.** Against moral standards or legal codes. **b.** Unethical or unjust. **3.** Not needed, wanted, or intended <dialed the *wrong* number> **4.** Unsuitable : inappropriate. **5.** Not conforming to a fixed usage, method, or procedure. **6.** Being the side or surface opposite to the right or more prominent side. *–adv.* **1.** In an erroneous way. **2.** In an immoral or unjust manner. *–n.* **1.** Something that is unjust, injurious, or immoral. **2.** The state of being mistaken or at fault. *–v.* **1.** To do wrong to : harm. **2.** To treat dishonorably or unfairly. ☆***syns:*** AGGRIEVE, OPPRESS, OUTRAGE, PERSECUTE **–wrong'er** *n.* **–wrong'ly** *adv.*

wrong·do·er (rông'do͞o'ər, rŏng') *n.* One who does wrong, esp. moral or legal wrong. **–wrong'do'ing** *n.*

wrong·ful (rông'fəl, rŏng'-) *adj.* **1.** Unethical : unjust. **2.** Unlawful : illegal. **–wrong'ful·ly** *adv.* **–wrong'ful·ness** *n.*

wrong-head·ed (rông'hĕd'ĭd, rŏng'-) *adj.* Obstinately wrong in judgment or opinion.

wrote (rōt) *v. p.t. of* WRITE.

wroth (rôth, rŏth) *adj.* Wrathful.

wrought (rôt) *adj.* **1.** Made or fashioned. **2.** Hammered into shape, as metal. **3.** Delicately or elaborately made. **4.** Emotionally agitated. Used with *up.*

wrought iron *n.* Commercial iron that is tough and malleable.

wrung (rŭng) *v. p.t.* & *p.p. of* WRING.

wry (rī) *adj.* **wri·er, wri·est** *also* **wry·er, wry·est. 1.a.** Abnormally bent to one side : crooked. **b.** Contorted to express distaste or displeasure <made a *wry* mouth> **2.** Ironically humorous. **–wry'ly** *adv.*

wt. *abbr.* weight.

Wu·han (wo͞o'hän'). City of EC China, on the Yangtze. *Pop.* 3,000,000.

wurst (wûrst, wo͝orst) *n.* Sausage.

WV *abbr.* West Virginia (with Zip Code).

W.Va. *abbr.* West Virginia.

WY *abbr.* Wyoming (with Zip Code).

wye (wī) *n.* The letter *y.*

Wyo. *abbr.* Wyoming.

Wy·o·ming (wī-ō'mĭng). State of the W U.S. *Cap.* Cheyenne. *Pop.* 470,816.

Xx

x *or* **X** (ĕks) *n., pl.* **x's** *or* **X's. 1.** The 24th letter of the English alphabet. **2.** Roman numeral for 10. **3.** An unknown or unnamed quantity. *–v.* **x'd, x'ing.** To cancel or delete with a series of x's.

x-ax·is (ĕks'ăk'sĭs) *n.* The horizontal axis of a graph or chart.

X-chro·mo·some (ĕks'krō'mə-sōm') *n.* The sex chromosome that is associated with female characteristics and occurs paired in the female and single in the male sex-chromosome pair.

Xe *symbol for* XENON.

xe·bec (zē'bĕk') *n.* A 3-masted sailing ship with both square and triangular sails used in the Mediterranean.

xen·o·lith (zĕn'ə-lĭth', zē'nə-) *n.* A rock fragment foreign to the igneous mass in which it occurs.

xe·non (zē'nŏn') *n. Symbol* **Xe** A colorless, odorless gaseous element found in extremely small quantities in the air.

xen·o·phobe (zĕn'ə-fōb', zē'nə-) *n.* One who fears, mistrusts, and dislikes foreigners or what is strange or foreign. **–xen'o·pho'bi·a** *n.* **–xen'o·pho'bic** *adj.*

xe·rog·ra·phy (zĭ-rŏg'rə-fē) *n.* A process for copying graphic material in which a negative image formed by a resinous powder on a charged plate is electrically transferred and fixed to a sheet of paper by means of heat. **–xe'ro·graph'ic** (zîr'ə-grăf'ĭk) *adj.*

xe·ro·phyte (zîr'ə-fīt') *n.* A plant adapted to growing in an environment providing limited moisture. **–xe'ro·phyt'ic** (-fĭt'ĭk) *adj.*

Xe·rox (zîr'ŏks'). A trademark for a photocopying process or machine using xerography.

Xerx·es (zûrk'sēz). 519?–465 B.C. King of Persia (486–465 B.C.).

XL *abbr.* extra large.

X·mas (krĭs'məs, ĕks'məs) *n.* Christmas.

▲word history: The character **x** in *Xmas* does not represent the letter *X* in the Roman alphabet but rather the Greek letter *chi.* The Greek form of *chi* is **x**. *Chi* is the first letter of the Greek form of *ChristKhristos* or *Christos.* The symbol **x** or *X* has been used as an abbreviation for *Christ* since earliest Christian times.

x-ra·di·a·tion (ĕks'rā'dē-ā'shən) *n.* **1.** Exposure to or treatment with x-rays. **2.** Radiation composed of x-rays.

x-ray *also* **X-ray** (ĕks'rā') *n.* **1. a.** A relatively high-energy photon with a very short wavelength. **b.** A stream of such photons, capable of penetrating solids and used in radiography, radiology, and research. **2.** A photograph taken with x-rays. *–v.* To treat with or photograph with x-rays.

▲word history: Wilhelm Roentgen, the German scientist who discovered x-rays, gave them the name *x-strahlen,* translated into English as "x-rays." He used x, the symbol for an unknown quantity, because he did not completely understand the nature of this kind of radiation.

x-ray astronomy *n.* Astronomy that deals with the properties of celestial bodies as indicated by the x-rays they emit.

x-ray star *n.* A celestial object resembling a star but emitting a major portion of its radiation in the form of x-rays.

xy•lem (zī'ləm) *n.* A woody tissue of vascular plants that conducts water and serves as a support, as for a stem.

xy•lo•phone (zī'lə-fōn') *n.* A musical instrument consisting of a mounted series of wooden bars graduated in length and played by striking with 2 small wooden mallets. **—xy'lo•phon'ist** *n.*

Yy

y or **Y** (wī) *n., pl.* **y's** or **Y's. 1.** The 25th letter of the English alphabet. **2.** Something with the shape of the letter Y.

y *abbr. Math.* ordinate.

y. *abbr.* year.

Y *symbol for* YTTRIUM.

-y[1] *suff.* **1.** Characterized by : consisting of <rainy> **2.** Like <summery> **3.** Tending or inclined toward <sleepy>

-y[2] *suff.* **1.** Condition : state : quality <jealousy> **2.a.** Activity <cookery> **b.** Instance of a specified action <inquiry> **3.a.** Place for an activity <tannery> **b.** Result or product of an activity <laundry> **4.** Collection : body : group <soldiery>

-y[3] *suff.* **1.** Small one <puppy> **2.** Dear one <daddy>

yab•ber (yăb'ər) *Austral.* —*n.* Jabber. —*v.* To jabber.

yacht (yät) *n.* A relatively small motor-driven or sailing vessel that usu. has graceful lines and is used esp. for pleasure cruises or racing. **—yacht** *v.*

yacht•ing (yä'tĭng) *n.* The activity or sport of cruising or racing in a yacht.

yachts•man (yäts'mən) *n.* Someone who owns or sails a yacht. **—yachts'man•ship'** *n.*

ya•hoo (yä'hōō, yā'-) *n., pl.* **-hoos.** A crude or boisterous person.

Yah•weh (yä'wā') *also* **Yah•veh** (-vā') *n.* The God of the ancient Hebrews.

yak[1] (yăk) *n.* A long-haired bovine mammal, *Bos grunniens,* of Tibet and the mountains of C Asia, often domesticated.

yak[2] *also* **yack** (yăk) *v.* **yakked, yak•king** *also* **yacked, yacking.** *Slang.* To chatter or talk persistently and at length. **—yak, yack** *n.*

y'all (yôl) *pron. var. of* YOU-ALL.

Ya•lu (yä'lōō). River forming part of the North Korea–China border.

†yam (yăm) *n.* **1.** A vine of the genus *Dioscorea* with a starchy edible root that is much used in the tropics as food. **2.** *S U.S.* A sweet potato with reddish flesh.

yam•mer (yăm'ər) *v.* **1.** To complain persistently : whine. **2.** To talk rapidly and often loudly : chatter. **—yam'mer** *n.*

Yang•tze (yăng'tsē'). Longest river of Asia, flowing c. 3,450 mi (5,550 km) from Tibet to the East China Sea.

yank (yăngk) *v.* To pull or jerk with a quick forceful movement. **—yank** *n.*

Yank (yăngk) *n. Informal.* A Yankee.

Yan•kee (yăng'kē) *n.* **1.a.** A native or resident of New England. **b.** A native or resident of the N U.S. **2.** A native or resident of the U.S. **—Yan'kee** *adj.*

Ya•oun•dé (yä-ōōn-dā'). Cap. of Cameroun, in the C part. *Pop.* 313,706.

yap (yăp) *v.* **yapped, yap•ping. 1.** To bark : yelp. **2.** *Slang.* To talk shrilly and relentessly : jabber. —*n.* **1.** A bark : yelp. **2.** *Slang.* **a.** Shrill, relentless talk : chatter. **b.** The mouth. **—yap'per** *n.*

yard[1] (yärd) *n.* **1.** See MEASUREMENT TABLE. **2.** A long, tapering spar that is attached at right angles to a mast to support and spread the head of a square sail.

yard[2] (yärd) *n.* **1.** A small area of ground adjacent to a building. **2.** An often enclosed area together with its buildings set aside for a specific activity or business. **3.** An area with a system of tracks where railroad trains are made up and cars are switched, serviced, or stored. **4.** An enclosed area for livestock.

yard•age (yär'dĭj) *n.* The amount, extent, or length of something measured in yards.

yard•arm (yärd'ärm') *n.* Either end of the yard supporting a square sail.

yard•man (yärd'mən) *n.* A man employed esp. in a railroad yard.

yard•mas•ter (yärd'măs'tər) *n.* A man in charge of a railroad yard.

yard•stick (yärd'stĭk') *n.* **1.** A graduated measuring stick 1 yd long. **2.** A standard for making a judgment or comparison.

▲word history: A yardstick is literally a "stick-stick," for the word *yard* is the descendant of Old English *gerd,* which meant simply "a stick." Since sticks make convenient measuring devices, a stick of a certain length of this unit varied over the centuries; the current length of a yard was fixed in the 14th cent., during the reign of Edward III. The compound *yardstick* is a relatively recent coinage in which the word *yard* is used in the sense "a unit of length."

yar•mul•ke (yär'məl-kə, yä'məl-) *n.* A skullcap worn by Jewish males.

yarn (yärn) *n.* **1.** A continuous strand consisting of twisted fibers, as of wool, used in knitting or weaving. **2.** *Informal.* A long, often elaborate tale of real or fictitious adventures.

yar•row (yăr'ō) *n.* A pungent-smelling plant, *Achillea millefolium,* with usu. white flower clusters.

yaw (yô) *v.* **1.** *Naut.* To veer erratically from an intended course. **2.** To move unsteadily : weave. **—yaw** *n.*

yawl (yôl) *n.* **1.** A 2-masted fore-and-aft-rigged sailboat with the shorter mast at the stern abaft the tiller. **2.** A ship's small boat.

yawn (yôn) *v.* **1.** To take a deep inward breath with the mouth open wide, as from fatigue or boredom. **2.** To be wide open : gape <a *yawning* chasm> **—yawn** *n.* **—yawn'er** *n.* **—yawn'ing•ly** *adv.*

yawp *also* **yaup** (yôp) *v.* **1.** To utter a harsh, hoarse sound : squawk. **2.** *Slang.* To talk loudly and stupidly. **—yawp** *n.* **—yawp'er** *n.*

yaws (yôz) *pl.n.* An infectious epidemic tropical skin disease marked by multiple pimples or pustules.

y-ax•is (wī'ăk'sĭs) *n.* The vertical axis of a graph or chart.

Yb *symbol for* YTTERBIUM.

Y-chro•mo•some (wī'krō'mə-sōm') *n.* The sex chromosome that is associated with male characteristics and occurs with 1 X-chromosome in the male sex-chromosome pair.

ye[1] (thē, yē) *adj. Archaic.* The.

▲word history: The word *ye*[1], which is sometimes used in pseudoarchaic phrases such as "ye olde curiosity shoppe," is actually a variant spelling of the definite article *the.* The variant arose from a confusion of the lower-case letter Y with the letter þ, called *thorn,* which was used in medieval times to represent the sounds now spelled with *th.* In early printed English books the common manuscript abbreviations *ye* for *the* and *yt* for *that* were retained. The form *ye* as a living word has now died out.

ye[2] (yē) *pron. Archaic.* YOU 1. Used esp. in literary or religious contexts and in certain dialects of English.

yea (yā) *adv.* **1.** Yes. **2.** Truly : indeed. —*n.* An affirmative vote or voter.

yeah (yĕ'ə, yă'ə, yā'ə) *adv. Informal.* Yes.

year (yîr) *n.* **1.** A period of time in the Gregorian calendar beginning on Jan. 1 and ending on Dec. 31 and consisting of 365 or 366 days. **2.** The period required for the earth to complete a revolution around the sun, consisting of 365 days, 5 hr, 49 min, and 12 sec. **3.** A period of time that is usu. shorter than but does not correspond to the calendar year <the academic *year*> **4. years.** Age <young in *years*> **5. years.** A long time <died *years* ago>

year•book (yîr'bŏŏk') *n.* **1.** A book published every year, esp. as a summary or report of facts. **2.** A book published as a record of the members and activities of the graduating class of a school.

year•ling (yîr'lĭng) *n.* An animal that is 1 year old or has not yet completed its 2nd year. —*adj.* Being 1 year old.

year•long (yîr'lông', -lŏng') *adj.* Continuing through a year.

year•ly (yîr'lē) *adv.* Once every year : annually. —*adj.* Occurring once every year : annual. **—year'ly** *n.*

yearn (yûrn) *v.* **1.** To feel a strong desire or craving : long <*yearn* for solitude> **2.** To feel sympathy, pity, or tenderness.

yearn•ing (yûr'nĭng) *n.* A strong or tender longing.

year-round (yîr'round') *adj.* Existing, operating, or used throughout the year.

yeast (yēst) *n.* **1.** Any of various unicellular fungi of the genus *Saccharomyces* and related genera, reproducing by budding and capable of fermenting carbohydrates. **2.** A froth produced by and containing yeast cells that is present in or added to sugary substances, as fruit juices, in the making of alcoholic beverages. **3.** A commercial preparation in powdered or compressed form that contains yeast cells and is used esp. as a leavening agent. **4.** A cause of ferment or activity.

yeast•y (yē'stē) *adj.* **-i•er, -i•est. 1.** Of, relating to, or similar to yeast. **2.** Marked by ferment or agitation : unsettled. **3.** Full of unrestrained enthusiasm : exuberant. **4.** Frothy : frivolous. **–yeast'i•ness** *n.*

Yeats (yāts), **William Butler.** 1865–1939. Irish poet and playwright.

yegg (yĕg) *n. Slang.* A safecracker.

yell (yĕl) *v.* To scream or cry out loudly, as in fright or surprise : shout. *–n.* **1.** A loud cry : shout. **2.** A rhythmic cheer used esp. to show support for an athletic team, as at a college football game.

yel•low (yĕl'ō) *n.* **1.** The color of dandelions or ripe lemons. **2.** Something of the color yellow as the yolk of an egg. **3. yellows.** Any of several plant diseases caused by viruses and marked by yellow discoloration of the foliage. *–adj.* **1.** Of the color yellow. **2.** Having a somewhat yellow skin or complexion. **3.** *Slang.* Cowardly. **4.** Featuring scandalous or sensational news items to attract or hold readers. *–v.* To make or become yellow. **–yel'low•ish** *adj.*

Yel•low (yĕl'ō). **1. Sea.** Arm of the Pacific, between the Chinese mainland and Korean Peninsula. **2.** River of N China, flowing c. 3,000 mi (4,830 km) to the Gulf of Bo Hai.

yel•low-bel•lied (yĕl'ō-bĕl'ēd) *adj. Slang.* Cowardly.

yellow birch *n.* A North American tree, *Betula lutea,* with yellowish bark and hard light-colored wood used for furniture.

yellow fever *n.* An acute infectious viral disease of warm regions that is transmitted by a mosquito and marked by fever, jaundice, and often hemorrhaging.

yellow jack *n.* **1.** Yellow fever. **2.** A yellow flag hoisted on a quarantined ship to warn of disease.

yellow jacket *n.* Any of several small wasps of the family Vespidae with yellow and black markings.

Yel•low•knife (yĕl'ō-nīf'). Cap. of N.W.T., Canada. *Pop.* 9,969.

yelp (yĕlp) *v.* To utter a sharp, short, shrill cry or bark. **–yelp** *n.*

Yem•en (yĕm'ən, yā'mən). **1.** *also* **North Yemen.** Country of SW Asia, at the SW tip of Arabia. *Cap.* Sana. *Pop.* 5,785,000. **2.** *also* **Southern Yemen.** Country of SW Asia, at the S edge of Arabia. *Cap.* Aden. *Pop.* 1,555,000.

yen[1] (yĕn) *v. Informal.* A longing : yearning. **–yen** *v.*

yen[2] (yĕn) *n., pl.* **yen.** See CURRENCY TABLE.

yen•ta (yĕn'tə) *n. Slang.* A prying, gossipy woman : busybody.

yeo•man (yō'mən) *n.* **1.** An independent farmer, esp. a member of a former class of English freeholding farmers ranking below the gentry. **2.** An officer or attendant in a noble or royal household. **3.** A petty officer who performs clerical duties.

yeo•man•ry (yō'mən-rē) *n.* The class of yeomen, esp. independent farmers.

yes (yĕs) *adv.* Used to express affirmation, agreement, or consent, to contradict a preceding negative statement, or to introduce a more precise or emphatic statement. *–n., pl.* **yes•es. 1.** An affirmative or consenting reply. **2.** An affirmative vote or voter.

ye•shi•va *or* **ye•shi•vah** (yə-shē'və) *n.* **1.** A school for the study of the Talmud. **2.** A Jewish day school that offers instruction in both religious and secular subjects.

yes man *n. Informal.* A toady.

yes•ter•day (yĕs'tər-dā', -dē) *n.* **1.** The day before today. **2.** Time in the recent past. *–adv.* **1.** On the day before today. **2.** Just a short while ago.

yes•ter•year (yĕs'tər-yîr') *n.* **1.** Last year. **2.** Time in the recent past.

yet (yĕt) *adv.* **1.** At this time : now <not time to eat *yet*> **2.** Up to now : thus far <hasn't arrived *yet*> **3.** As previously : still <is *yet* a young man> **4.** In addition : besides <made *yet* another mistake> **5.** Even <a *yet* more beautiful house> **6.** Nevertheless <poor *yet* happy> **7.** At a future time : eventually <may *yet* come to understand> *–conj.* Nevertheless : but.

yet•i (yĕt'ē) *n.* The abominable snowman.

yew (yo͞o) *n.* Any of several evergreen tres or shrubs of the genus *Taxus,* with poisonous flat, dark-green needles, often poisonous scarlet berries, and fine-grained wood used esp. in cabinetmaking.

Yid•dish (yĭd'ĭsh) *n.* A language derived from German and Hebrew and spoken by Jews, esp. in E Europe. **–Yid'dish** *adj.*

yield (yēld) *v.* **1.** To bring forth by a natural process : bear. **2.** To produce as gain or profit : return <bonds *yielding* 11%> **3.** To give up possession of : relinquish. **4.** To grant to another : concede <had to *yield* the right of way> **5.** To give way, as to force or persuasion : submit. **6.** To defer to the superiority of someone else. ☆**syns:** BOW, CAPITULATE, FOLD, SUBMIT, SUCCUMB, SURRENDER *–n.* An amount yielded or obtained.

yield•ing (yēl'dĭng) *adj.* **1.** Giving way readily to pressure : flexible. **2.** Docile.

yip (yĭp) *n.* A sharp, quick high-pitched bark. **–yip** *v.*

yipe (yīp) *also* **yipes** (yīps) *interj.* Used to express surprise, fear, or dismay.

yo•del (yōd'l) *v.* **-deled, -del•ing** *or* **-delled, -del•ling. 1.** To sing so that the voice alternates between chest voice and falsetto. **2.** To sing, call, or shout by yodeling. **–yo'del** *n.* **–yo'del•er** *n.*

yo•ga (yō'gə) *n.* **1.** *often* **Yoga.** A system of Hindu philosophy teaching control of the body and mind as a means of achieving spiritual insight and tranquillity. **2.** A system of exercises for promoting control of the body and mind.

yo•gi (yō'gē) *n., pl.* **-gis.** Someone who practices yoga.

yo•gurt *also* **yo•ghurt** (yō'gərt) *n.* An acidulous custardlike food made of milk fermented by bacteria.

yoke (yōk) *n.* **1.** A wooden bar with 2 U-shaped pieces that fit around the necks of a pair of draft animals working together. **2.** *pl.* **yoke.** A pair of draft animals coupled with a yoke. **3.** A frame placed across a person's shoulders to carry 2 equal loads 1 at each end. **4.** A vise or clamp that holds 2 parts together or in position. **5.** A shaped or fitted piece of a garment, esp. at the shoulders. **6.** Something that ties or connects : bond. **7.** Slavery : bondage. *–v.* **yoked, yok•ing. 1.** To join with or as if with a yoke : harness. **2.** To harness a draft animal to. **3.** To join together : bind.

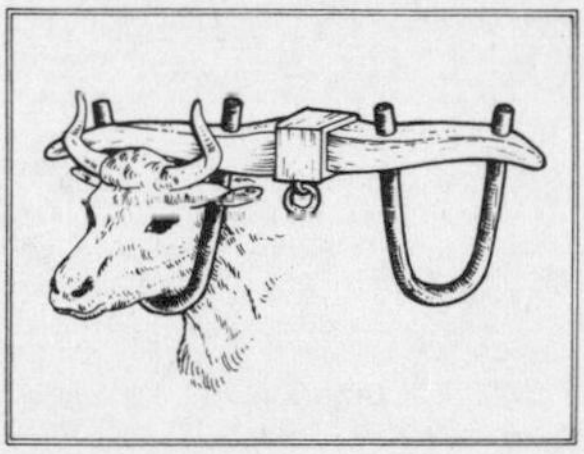

yoke

yo•kel (yō'kəl) *n.* An unsophisticated country person : bumpkin.

Yo•ko•ha•ma (yō'kə-hä'mə). City of SE Honshu, Japan. *Pop.* 2,773,322.

yolk (yōk) *n.* **1.** The rounded yellow inner mass of nutritive material in the egg of a bird or reptile. **2.** An oily substance found in unprocessed sheep's wool.

▲word history: The word *yolk,* meaning "the yellow part of an egg" is descended from Old English *geoloca. Geoloca* is a noun derived from the adjective *geolu,* the ancestor of *yellow. Yolk* and *yellow* are related to many other words such as *glass, gloaming, gleam,* and *gold,* denoting something bright, shining, or yellow-colored.

Yom Kip•pur (yŏm kĭp'ər, yōm' kĭ-po͝or') *n.* A Jewish holiday in Sept. or Oct., observed with prayer and fasting for the atonement of sins or wrongdoing.

†**yon** (yŏn) *adj. & adv.* Yonder. *–pron. Regional.* That one or those yonder.

yon•der (yŏn'dər) *adj.* Being at a distance but within sight. *–adv.* In, to, or at that place : over there.

Yon•kers (yŏng'kərz). City of Se N.Y., N of New York City. *Pop.* 195,351.

yore (yôr, yōr) *n.* Time long past.

you (yo͞o) *pron.* **1.** The person or persons addressed <I'll do what *you* say.><*You* are naughty children.> **2.** A person in general : one <*You* can't be too careful.>

†**you-all** (yo͞o-ôl') *also* **y'all** (yôl) *pron. SE U.S.* You. Used in addressing 2 or more persons or referring to 2 or more persons 1 of whom is addressed.

you'd (yo͞od). **1.** You had. **2.** You would.

you'll (yo͞ol). **1.** You will. **2.** You shall.

young (yŭng) *adj.* **1.** Being in the first or an early period of growth, life, or development. **2.** Having qualities associated with youth : youthful. **3.** Lacking experience. **4.** Recently begun or formed : new. *–n., pl.* **young. 1.** Young persons : youth. **2.** Offspring, esp. of animals. **–young'ish** *adj.* **–young'ness** *n.* **–young'ster** *n.*

Young (yŭng), **Brigham.** 1801–77. Amer. Mormon leader.

young•ling (yŭng′lĭng) *n.* A young person, plant, or animal.
your (yo͝or, yôr, yōr) *adj.* Of or relating to you or yourself.
you're (yo͝or). You are.
yours (yo͝orz, yôrz, yōrz) *pron.* That or those belonging to you.
your•self (yo͝or-sĕlf′, yôr-, yōr-, yər-) *pron., pl.* **-selves** (-sĕlvz′). That one identical with you. Used: **a.** Reflexively <Don't exert *yourself.*><Are you mumbling to *yourself?*> **b.** For emphasis <You should solve the problem *yourself.*>
youth (yo͞oth) *n., pl.* **youths** (yo͞oths, yo͞othz). **1.** The quality or state of being young. **2.** The time of life between childhood and adulthood. **3.a.** A young person, esp. a young man. **b.** Young people. **4.** The quality or state of being youthful.
youth•ful (yo͞oth′fəl) *adj.* **1.** Being still young. **2.** Of, pertaining to, or characteristic of youth. **3.** Having the freshness and energy typical of the young : vigorous. **–youth′ful•ly** *adv.* **–youth′ful•ness** *n.*
you've (yo͞ov). You have.
yowl (youl) *v.* To utter a long, loud, mournful howl or wail. **–yowl** *n.*
yo-yo (yō′yō) *n., pl.* **-yos.** A grooved spool wound around its center with string that is made to spin down from and reel up to the hand by winding and unwinding the string.
yt•ter•bi•um (ĭ-tûr′bē-əm) *n. Symbol* **Yb** A soft bright silvery rare-earth element.
yt•tri•um (ĭt′rē-əm) *n. Symbol* **Y** A silvery metallic element.
yu•an (yo͞o′än′) *n., pl.* **-an** or **-ans.** See CURRENCY TABLE.
Yu•ca•tán (yo͞o′kə-tăn′). Peninsula, mostly in SE Mexico, separating the Caribbean from the Gulf of Mexico.
yuc•ca (yŭk′ə) *n.* Any of various chiefly tropical New World plants of the genus *Yucca* with stiff, pointed leaves and a terminal cluster of white flowers.
Yu•go•sla•vi•a (yo͞o′gō-slä′vē-ə). Country of SE Europe, on the Adriatic. *Cap.* Belgrade. *Pop.* 21,560,000. **–Yu′go•sla′vi•an** *adj.* & *n.*
Yu•kon (yo͞o′kŏn′). **1.** River flowing c. 2,000 mi (3,220 km) S Y.T., Canada, through Alas. to the Bering Sea. **2.** Territory o NW Canada, E of Alas. *Cap.* Whitehorse. *Pop.* 21,836.
Yule or **yule** (yo͞ol) *n.* Christmas.
▲word history: The word *Yule, gēol* in Old English, was orig the name of a pagan Germanic religious festival held in midwin ter. After the English were converted to Christianity, the nam *Yule* was used for the feast of Christmas. The use of nativ words for Christian terms was encouraged in the Anglo-Saxor church; another example is the use of the name *Easter* for th feast of Christ's Resurrection.
Yule log *n.* A large log used for the foundation of the tradition al Christmas Eve fire.
Yule•tide or **yule•tide** (yo͞ol′tīd′) *n.* The Christmas season
yum•my (yŭm′ē) *adj.* **-mi•er, -mi•est.** *Slang.* Delicious : de lectable.

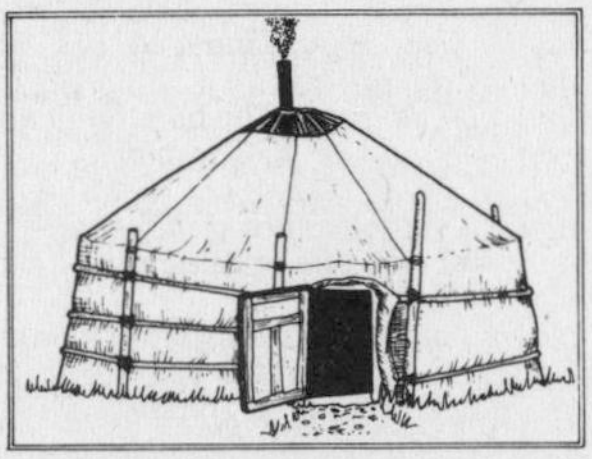

yurt

yurt (yûrt) *n.* A circular domed tent used by nomadic tribes o Siberia.

Zz

z or **Z** (zē) *n., pl.* **z's** or **Z's. 1.** The 26th letter of the English alphabet. **2.** A speech sound represented by the letter z. **3.** Something with the shape of the letter Z.
Zach•a•ri•as (zăk′ə-rī′əs) *n.* See BIBLE TABLE.
zaf•tig or **zof•tig** (zäf′tĭk, -tĭg) *adj. Slang.* **1.** Full-bosomed. **2.** Comfortably and pleasingly plump.
Za•greb (zä′grĕb′). City of NW Yugoslavia. *Pop.* 566,084.
zai•bat•su (zī′bät′so͞o) *n., pl.* **zaibatsu.** A powerful family-controlled commercial combine of Japan.
zaire (zîr, zä-îr′) *n.* See CURRENCY TABLE.
Zaire (zâr). Country of WC Africa. *Cap.* Kinshasa. *Pop.* 24,222,000.
Zam•be•zi (zăm-bē′zē). River c. 1,700 mi (2,735 km), of C and S Africa.
Zam•bi•a (zăm′bē-ə, zäm′-). Country of SC Africa. *Cap.* Lusaka. *Pop.* 5,834,000. **–Zam′bi•an** *adj.* & *n.*
za•ny (zā′nē) *n., pl.* **-nies. 1.** A buffoon : clown. **2.** A person given to silly or foolish behavior. *–adj.* **-ni•er, -ni•est. 1.** Of or typical of a zany : clownish. **2.** Outlandishly ludicrous : absurd. **–za′ni•ly** *adv.* **–za′ni•ness** *n.*
zap (zăp) *v.* **zapped, zap•ping.** *Slang.* To destroy or kill.
zeal (zēl) *n.* Enthusiastic and intensive interest, as in a cause or ideal : ardor.
zeal•ot (zĕl′ət) *n.* A zealous person, esp. a fanatical adherent of a cause.
zeal•ous (zĕl′əs) *adj.* Filled with, marked by, or motivated by zeal. **–zeal′ous•ly** *adv.* **–zeal′ous•ness** *n.*
ze•bra (zē′brə) *n.* Any of several horselike African mammals of the genus *Equus,* having conspicuous black or brown stripes on a whitish body.
ze•bu (zē′byo͞o, -bo͞o) *n.* A domesticated bovine mammal, *Bos indicus,* of Asia and Africa, having a prominent hump on the shoulders and a large dewlap.
Zech•a•ri•ah (zĕk′ə-rī′ə) *n.* See BIBLE TABLE.
zed (zĕd) *n. esp. Brit.* The letter z.
Zeit•geist (tsīt′gīst′) *n.* The moral and intellectual atmosphere characteristic of an epoch or age : spirit of the times.
Zen (zĕn) *n.* A Japanese form of Buddhism reaching enlightenment through meditation, contemplation, and intuition.
ze•nith (zē′nĭth) *n.* **1.** The point in the sky that is directly overhead. **2.** The highest point : apex : climax.
Ze•no (zē′nō). 342?–270? B.C. Greek Stoic philosopher.
ze•o•lite (zē′ə-līt′) *n.* Any of a group of hydrous aluminum silicate minerals or their corresponding synthetic compounds, used esp. as molecular filters and ion-exchange agents.
Zeph•a•ni•ah (zĕf′ə-nī′ə) *n.* See BIBLE TABLE.
zeph•yr (zĕf′ər) *n.* **1.** A gentle breeze. **2.** A light, soft fabric, yarn, or garment.
zep•pe•lin (zĕp′ə-lĭn) *n.* A rigid dirigible with a long, cylindrical frame supported by internal gas cells.
ze•ro (zîr′ō, zē′rō) *n., pl.* **-ros** or **-roes. 1.** The numerical symbol "0" : cipher. **2.** The cardinal number indicating the absence of quantity. **3. a.** The point, as on a thermometer, from which measurements or degrees are reckoned. **b.** The temperature indicated by the numeral 0 on a thermometer. **4.** One that is unimportant : nonentity. **5.** The lowest point. *–adj.* **1.** Of, pertaining to, or being a zero. **2.a.** Without measurable or determinable value. **b.** Lacking : absent. *–v.* **-roed, -ro•ing.** To point at, aim at, or close in on something.
▲word history: The word *zero,* "the numeral 0," is not only synonymous with the word *cipher* but is descended from the same Arabic source. The Arabic word *ṣifr* meant "empty" as well as "zero." *Zero* comes from the Italian form of *ṣifr, zefiro,* but *cipher* came into English through Medieval Latin *cifra.* Although *zero* was borrowed as a synonym of *cipher,* the 2 words have diverged in meaning. *Cipher* has developed the sense of "a code," whereas *zero* is used primarily as the name of the numeral, esp. in scientific use.
ze•ro-base (zîr′ō-bās′, zē′rō-) or **ze•ro-based** (-bāst′) *adj.* Having each expenditure or item justified as to need or cost.
zero hour *n.* The scheduled time for an action or operation to start.
zero population growth *n.* A rate of population increase limited to the number needed to replace the existing population.
zest (zĕst) *n.* **1.** An invigorating or keen quality : piquancy. **2.** Spirited enjoyment : relish. **3.** The outermost part of an orange or lemon rind, used as flavoring. **–zest′ful** *adj.* **–zest′ful•ly** *adv.* **–zest′y** *adj.*
Zhou En•lai (jō ĕn-lī′). 1898–1976. Chinese statesman.
zig•zag (zĭg′zăg′) *n.* **1.a.** A series of sharp turns in alternating directions. **b.** One of such a series. **2.** Something, as a pattern,

marked by zigzags. *—adj.* Shaped like or forming a zigzag. *—adv.* In a zigzag path, course, or pattern. **—zig'zag'** *v.*
zilch (zĭlch) *n. Slang.* Zero : nothing.
zil•lion (zĭl'yən) *n. Informal.* An extremely large but unspecified number.
Zim•bab•we (zĭm-bä'bwā). Country of SC Africa. *Cap.* Salisbury. *Pop.* 7,130,000. **—Zim•bab'we•an** *adj. & n.*
zinc (zĭngk) *n. Symbol* **Zn** A shiny bluish-white metallic element used to make a wide variety of alloys and to galvanize metals, as iron. *—v.* **zinced, zinc•ing** or **zincked, zinck•ing.** To coat with zinc : galvanize.
zinc ointment *n.* A salve containing approx. 20% zinc oxide, used in the treatment of skin disorders.
zinc oxide *n.* A white or yellowish powdery compound that is used as a pigment and in ointments and cosmetics.
zin•fan•del (zĭn'fən-dĕl') *n.* A dry red wine produced in California.
zing (zĭng) *n.* **1.** A high-pitched humming sound. **2.** Vigor : vivacity. **—zing** *v.*
zin•ni•a (zĭn'ē-ə) *n.* An American plant, *Zinnia elegans,* cultivated for its showy, colorful flowers.
Zi•on (zī'ən) *n.* **1. a.** The Jewish people. **b.** The homeland of the Jewish people as a symbol of Judaism. **2.** The city of God : heaven. **3.** Utopia.
Zi•on•ism (zī'ə-nĭz'əm) *n.* A movement or plan for establishing a Jewish national homeland and state in Palestine. **—Zi'on•ist** *n.* **—Zi'on•is'tic** *adj.*
zip (zĭp) *n.* **1.** A short sharp hissing sound. **2.** *Informal.* Vim : energy. **3.** *Slang.* Zero : nothing. *—v.* **zipped, zip•ping. 1.** To act or move with facility, energy, or speed. **2.** To fasten or unfasten with a zipper.
Zip Code *also* **zip code** *or* **ZIP Code.** A trademark for a system to expedite the delivery of mail by assigning a 5-digit number to each postal delivery area in the U.S.
zip•per (zĭp'ər) *n.* A fastener that consists of 2 strips of tape each with a row of metal or plastic teeth that are interlocked by means of a sliding tab.
zip•py (zĭp'ē) *adj.* **-pi•er, -pi•est.** Full of energy : brisk : lively.
zir•con (zûr'kŏn') *n.* A brown to colorless mineral, the transparent form of which is polished to form a gem.
zir•co•ni•um (zər-kō'nē-əm) *n. Symbol* **Zr** A shiny strong ductile metallic element used esp. in ceramics and alloys.
zit (zĭt) *n. Slang.* A pimple.
zith•er (zĭth'ər, zĭth'-) *n.* A musical instrument with 30 to 40 strings played with the fingertips or a plectrum.
zi•ti (zē'tē) *n., pl.* **ziti.** Medium-sized tubular pasta.
zlo•ty (zlô'tē) *n., pl.* **-ty** or **-tys.** See CURRENCY TABLE.
Zn *symbol for* ZINC.
zo•di•ac (zō'dē-ăk') *n.* **1.a.** A band of the celestial sphere that extends approx. 8° on both sides of the ecliptic and encompasses the apparent paths of the principal planets, the moon, and the sun. **b.** This band divided into 12 astrological signs, each bearing the name of a constellation. **2.** A figure or diagram representing the zodiac. **—zo•di'a•cal** (-dī'ə-kəl) *adj.*
zof•tig (zäf'tĭk, -tĭg) *adj. var. of* ZAFTIG.
zom•bie *also* **zom•bi** (zŏm'bē) *n., pl.* **-bies** *also* **-bis. 1.a.** A snake god of voodoo cults. **b.** A supernatural power that according to voodoo belief enters into and reanimates a corpse. **2.** A person who is thought to look or behave like a reanimated corpse.
zon•al (zō'nəl) *also* **zo•na•ry** (-nə-rē) *adj.* **1.** Of or pertaining to a zone. **2.** Divided into zones. **—zon'al•ly** *adv.*
zone (zōn) *n.* **1.** A region or area distinguished or set apart from adjacent or surrounding parts by some feature or characteristic. **2.** A section of an area established for a specific purpose <a residential *zone*> **3.** *Archaic.* A belt or girdle. *—v.* **zoned, zon•ing.** To divide, mark off, or designate into zones. **—zo•na'tion** *n.*
zonk (zôngk, zŏngk) *v. Slang.* **1.** To stupefy : stun. **2.** To intoxicate or render senseless with drugs or alcohol.
zoo (zo͞o) *n., pl.* **zoos. 1.** A public park or large enclosure where animals are kept for public display. **2.** Something characterized by rampant confusion or disorder.
zo•o•ge•og•ra•phy (zō'ə-jē-ŏg'rə-fē) *n.* Study of the geographic distribution of animals. **—zo'o•ge•og'ra•pher** *n.* **—zo'o•ge'o•graph'ic, zo'o•ge'o•graph'i•cal** *adj.*
zoological garden *n.* ZOO 1.
zo•ol•o•gy (zō-ŏl'ə-jē) *n.* The biological science that deals with animals, animal life, and the animal kingdom. **—zo'o•log'i•cal** (-ə-lŏg'ĭ-kəl) *adj.* **—zo•ol'o•gist** *n.*
zoom (zo͞om) *v.* **1.** To make or move with a continuous loud buzzing sound. **2.** To climb suddenly and sharply in an airplane. **3.** To move upward sharply <Expenses *zoomed.*> **4.** To move quickly toward or away from a photographic subject while keeping the subject in focus. **—zoom** *n.*
zoom lens *n.* A camera lens whose focal length can be rapidly changed to permit continuous change in the size of the image without loss of focus.
zo•o•mor•phism (zō'ə-môr'fĭz'əm) *n.* **1.** The attribution of the form, characteristics, or qualities of an animal to a deity. **2.** The use of animal forms in graphic representation. **—zo'o•mor'phic** *adj.*
zo•o•phyte (zō'ə-fīt') *n.* An invertebrate animal, such as a sea anemone or sponge, that remains attached to a surface and superficially resembles a plant. **—zo'o•phyt'ic** (-fĭt'ĭk) *adj.*
zo•o•spore (zō'ə-spôr', -spōr') *n.* A motile asexual spore.
zo•ri (zôr'ē, zōr'ē) *n., pl.* **zori.** A flat Japanese sandal held by means of a thong passing between the big toe and the 2nd toe.
Zo•ro•as•ter (zōr'ō-ăs'tər, zôr'-). 6th cent. B.C. Persian prophet.
Zo•ro•as•tri•an•ism (zôr'ō-ăs'trē-ə-nĭz'əm) *n.* The religion founded by Zoroaster. **—Zo'ro•as'tri•an** *n. & adj.*
Zou•ave (zo͞o-äv') *n.* A member of a French infantry unit, formerly composed of Algerian recruits, noted for their colorful oriental uniforms and precision drilling.
zounds (zoundz) *interj.* Used to express surprise, anger, or indignation.
zoy•si•a (zoi'sē-ə, -zē-ə) *n.* A creeping grass of the genus *Zoysia* used as a lawn grass.
Zr *symbol for* ZIRCONIUM.
zuc•chet•to (zo͞o-kĕt'ō, tso͞o-) *n., pl.* **-tos.** *Rom. Cath. Ch.* A small skullcap worn by ecclesiastics.
zuc•chi•ni (zo͞o-kē'nē) *n., pl.* **-ni.** A type of summer squash that is long and narrow in shape and has a dark-green rind.
Zu•rich (zo͝or'ĭk). City of NE Switzerland. *Pop.* 374,200.
zwie•back (swē'băk', swī'-, zwē'-, zwī'-) *n.* A usu. sweetened egg bread baked and then sliced and toasted.
zy•go•mat•ic bone (zī'gə-măt'ĭk) *n.* The cheekbone.
zy•gote (zī'gōt') *n.* A cell formed by the union of 2 gametes. **—zy•got'ic** (-gŏt'ĭk) *adj.* **—zy•got'i•cal•ly** *adv.*
zy•mur•gy (zī'mûr-jē) *n.* Technological chemistry that deals with fermentation processes, as in brewing.

Foreign Words and Phrases

à bas [Fr.] Down with.
ab incunabulis [Lat.] From the cradle : from the earliest stages.
à bon chat, bon rat [Fr.] A good cat deserves a good rat : tit for tat.
à bon marché [Fr.] At a bargain price.
ab ovo [Lat.] From the egg : from the very beginning : tediously. –Horace
à bras ouverts [Fr.] With open arms : warmly.
absit invidia [Lat.] May there be no envy : no offense intended. –Livy
absit omen [Lat.] May it not be an omen.
ab uno disce omnes [Lat.] From one learn to judge all. –Virgil
abusus non tollit usum [Lat.] Abuse does not detract from use : misuse does not invalidate proper use.
à coup sûr [Fr.] With sure stroke : confidently.
ad calendas Graecas [Lat.] At the Greek calends (i.e., never, since the Greeks had no calends).
ad captandum vulgus [Lat.] To win the crowd : appealing to popular sentiment.
ad extremum [Lat.] To the extreme : to the very end : at last.
ad finem [Lat.] At or toward the end : finally.
ad patres [Lat.] (Gathered) to one's fathers : dead.
ad utrumque paratus [Lat.] Ready for either (event).
advocatus diaboli [Lat.] Devil's advocate.
aegri somnia vana [Lat.] A sick man's empty dreams. –Horace
aequo animo [Lat.] With equanimity : serenely.
aetatis *or* **aetatis suae** [Lat.] At the age of. –Used before a date.
à fond [Fr.] At bottom : thoroughly.
age quod agis [Lat.] Do what you're doing : pay attention to your work.
à huis clos [Fr.] Behind closed doors.
aide-toi, le ciel t'aidera [Fr.] Heaven helps those who help themselves.
à l'abandon [Fr.] Carelessly : in confusion : at random.
à la belle étoile [Fr.] Under the open sky : under the stars.
à la bonne heure [Fr.] At a good time : splendid : all right.
à la page [Fr.] Up to date.
aliquando bonus dormitat Homerus [Lat.] Sometimes good Homer himself nods : even the great make mistakes. –Horace
alter idem [Lat.] Second self : alter ego.
a maximis ad minima [Lat.] From the greatest to the least.
âme damnée [Fr.] Lost soul : scapegoat.
à merveille [Fr.] Wonderfully : to perfection.
amicus humani generis [Lat.] Friend of the human race.
ami de cour [Fr.] Court friend : false or fair-weather friend.
anguis in herba [Lat.] Snake in the grass. –Virgil
animal bipes implume [Lat.] Two-legged featherless animal : human being.
anima mundi [Lat.] World spirit : force governing the physical universe.
à outrance [Fr.] To the bitter end : to the death.
après nous (or **moi) le déluge** [Fr.] After us (or me), the deluge.
arbiter elegantiarum [Lat.] Authority in matters of style and aesthetics.
ars est celare artem [Lat.] (True) art is to conceal art.
ars gratia artis [Lat.] Art for art's sake.
ars longa, vita brevis [Lat.] Art is long, life short.
à tort et à travers [Fr.] All wrong and crosswise : with no rhyme or reason.
au bout de son latin [Fr.] At the end of one's Latin : at the end of one's wits.
audentes fortuna juvat [Lat.] Fortune favors the bold. –Virgil
au fait [Fr.] Well-informed : expert : to the point : socially correct.
au pays des aveugles les borgnes sont rois [Fr.] In the land of the blind the one-eyed are kings.
aurea mediocritas [Lat.] The golden mean. –Horace
aussitôt dit, aussitôt fait [Fr.] No sooner said than done.
aut Caesar aut nullus [Lat.] Either Caesar or no one : nothing but the best.
autres temps, autres moeurs [Fr.] Other times, other customs.
aut vincere aut mori [Lat.] Conquer or die.
ave atque vale [Lat.] Hail and farewell. –Catullus
beatae memoriae [Lat.] Of blessed memory.
belle laide [Fr.] Woman whose unattractiveness is considered appealing.
bien-pensant [Fr.] Right-thinking : holding orthodox or conservative views.
bienséance [Fr.] Propriety : decorum : good breeding.
bis dat qui cito dat [Lat.] Who gives promptly gives twice.
bon gré, mal gré [Fr.] Whether willing or not : willy-nilly.
bonne à tout faire [Fr.] Maid of all work.
bonne chance [Fr.] Good luck.
brutum fulmen [Lat.] Harmless thunderbolt : empty bluster. –Pliny the Elder
cacoethes loquendi [Lat.] Irresistible compulsion to talk.
causa sine qua non [Lat.] Indispensable condition or cause.
caveat lector [Lat.] Let the reader beware.
ce n'est que le premier pas qui coûte [Fr.] The first step is always the hardest.
c'est la guerre [Fr.] That's war : that's what happens in war.
c'est la vie [Fr.] That's life : that's how it goes.
chacun à son goût [Fr.] Everyone to his own taste.
chacun à son métier [Fr.] Everyone to his own trade.
chacun pour soi [Fr.] Everyone for himself.
cherchez la femme [Fr.] Look for the woman : there's bound to be a woman involved.
che sarà sarà [Ital.] What will be will be.
cogito, ergo sum [Lat.] I think, therefore I am. –Descartes
comédie humaine [Fr.] Comedy of life : the whole variety of human life.
concordia discors [Lat.] Harmony in discord.
contemptus mundi [Lat.] Contempt for the world.
contra mundum [Lat.] Against the world : standing alone.
coup de foudre [Fr.] Thunderclap : sudden and surprising event : love at first sight.
coup de maître [Fr.] Masterstroke.
coup d'essai [Fr.] First attempt.
coûte que coûte [Fr.] At all costs.
credo quia absurdum est [Lat.] I believe it because it's absurd.
credo ut intelligam [Lat.] I believe so that I may understand. –St. Anselm
cri de cœur [Fr.] Heartfelt appeal or protest.
cui bono? [Lat.] Who is the beneficiary? : who will profit by it? –Cicero
cum grano salis [Lat.] With a grain of salt.
damnant quod no intelligunt [Lat.] They condemn what they do not understand.
damnosa hereditas [Lat.] Accursed inheritance : inheritance that brings more hardship than benefit.
danse macabre [Fr.] Dance of death.
de gustibus non est disputandum [Lat.] There is no arguing in matters of taste.
Dei gratia [Lat.] By the grace of God.
delenda est Carthago [Lat.] Carthage must be destroyed : let no obstacle stand in the way. –Cato the Elder
de mal en pis [Fr.] From bad to worse.
de mortuis nil nisi bonum [Lat.] (Say) nothing but good about the dead.
de profundis [Lat.] From the depths : cry of misery or despair.
desipere in loco [Lat.] To be frivolous at the proper time : to relax on occasion.
dialogue des sourds [Fr.] Dialogue of the deaf : conversation between people who do not listen to each other.
dies faustus [Lat.] Lucky day.
dies infaustus [Lat.] Unlucky day.
dies non [Lat.] Day on which no legal business is transacted.
Ding an sich [G.] Thing in itself : reality behind appearance. –Kant

dis aliter visum [Lat.] The gods deemed otherwise. –Virgil
disjecta membra [Lat.] Scattered remains : fragments of literary works.
divide et impera [Lat.] Divide and rule.
docendo discimus [Lat.] We learn by teaching.
dolce far niente [Ital.] Pleasant idleness.
dulce et decorum est pro patria mori [Lat.] It is sweet and proper to die for one's country. –Horace
dum vivimus vivamus [Lat.] Let us live while we have life.
ecce signum [Lat.] Behold the sign. –Used when introducing evidence or proof
écrasez l'infâme [Fr.] Crush the vile thing. –Voltaire
eheu fugaces labuntur anni [Lat.] Alas, the fleeting years slip by. –Horace
embarras de richesses [Fr.] Embarrassment of riches : abundance which is difficult to appreciate or choose from.
embarras du choix [Fr.] Embarrassment of choice : too much to choose from.
éminence grise [Fr.] Gray eminence : power behind the throne.
en ami [Fr.] In friendship : as a friend.
en clair [Fr.] In ordinary language : not in code.
en famille [Fr.] As one of the family : informally : at home.
enfants perdus [Fr.] Lost children : forlorn hope : troops occupying an indefensible position.
en pantoufles [Fr.] In slippers : in an informal manner : at ease.
en plein air [Fr.] In the open air : outdoors.
en plein jour [Fr.] In broad day : openly.
en règle [Fr.] In order : in proper form.
en suite [Fr.] In series : in succession : connected.
entre nous [Fr.] Between ourselves : confidentially.
épater les bourgeois [Fr.] Shock the middle classes : disconcert those of conventional tastes or beliefs.
errare humanum est [Lat.] To err is human.
esprit de l'escalier [Fr.] Staircase witticism : witty retort that one thinks of after the opportunity has passed. –Diderot
est modus in rebus [Lat.] There is a proper measure in things : there is a middle course in everything. –Horace
et hoc genus omne [Lat.] And everything of this kind.
et sic de similibus [Lat.] And so of like things.
et tu, Brute [Lat.] You too, Brutus –Attributed to Julius Caesar on recognizing his friend Brutus among his assassins
Ewig-Weibliche [G.] The eternal feminine. –Goethe
ex animo [Lat.] From the heart : genuinely.
exceptio probat regulam [Lat.] The exception proves the rule.
exceptis excipiendis [Lat.] With exceptions as appropriate.
ex more [Lat.] According to custom.
ex necessitate rei [Lat.] From the necessity of the case : necessarily.
ex nihilo nihil fit [Lat.] Nothing comes from nothing.
ex pede Herculem [Lat.] From the foot of Hercules (one may judge his size).
experto credite [Lat.] Believe one who knows from experience.
ex silentio [Lat.] From lack of evidence to the contrary.
ex voto [Lat.] In fulfillment of a vow.
fas est et ab hoste doceri [Lat.] It is proper to learn even from an enemy.
Fata viam invenient [Lat.] The Fates will find a way. –Virgil
faute de mieux [Fr.] For lack of anything better.
faux-naïf [Fr.] Person pretending to be naive.
femme savante [Fr.] Learned and cultured woman : bluestocking.
festina lente [Lat.] Make haste slowly : more haste, less speed.
fiat experimentum in corpore vili [Lat.] Let the experiment be performed on a worthless body.
fiat justitia, ruat caelum [Lat.] Let justice be done even if the heavens fall.
fils [Fr.] Son. –Used after a name to distinguish between father and son of the same name
finem respice [Lat.] Consider the end.
finis coronat opus [Lat.] The end crowns the work.
folie de grandeur (or **des grandeurs**) [Fr.] Delusion of grandeur.
fons et origo [Lat.] Source and origin.
forsan et haec olim meminisse juvabit [Lat.] Perhaps this too will be pleasant to remember someday. –Virgil
fortes fortuna juvat [Lat.] Fortune favors the brave.
fronti nulla fides [Lat.] There is no trusting to appearances. –Juvenal
gardez la foi [Fr.] Keep the faith.
guadeamus igitur [Lat.] Let us therefore rejoice.
gens du monde [Fr.] Worldly people : fashionable society.
gnōthi seauton [Gk.] Know thyself.
grand monde [Fr.] Fashionable society.
gravitas [Lat.] Solemn bearing : sober-mindedness.
guerre à outrance [Fr.] All-out war.
haut monde [Fr.] High society : the fashionable world.
hic et ubique [Lat.] Here, (there) and everywhere.
hinc illae lacrimae [Lat.] Hence those tears. –Terence
hoc age [Lat.] Do this : attend to your work.
hoc anno [Lat.] In this year.
hoc opus, hic labor est [Lat.] This is the work, this the labor : here is the real difficulty. –Virgil
homme d'affaires [Fr.] Businessman : agent : middleman.
homme d'esprit [Fr.] Man of wit.
homme du monde [Fr.] Man of the world : sophisticated or worldly-wise man.
homme moyen sensuel [Fr.] Average man : man on the street.
homo sum: humani nil a me alienum puto [Lat.] I am a man; nothing concerning mankind is alien to me.
honi soit qui mal y pense [Fr.] Shame to him who thinks evil of it.
honnête homme [Fr.] Honest man : decent and upright citizen.
horribile dictu [Lat.] Horrible to relate.
idée reçue [Fr.] Received idea : doctrine or opinion accepted without questioning.
ignotum per ignotius [Lat.] Explanation that is more obscure than the thing being explained.
il faut cultiver notre jardin [Fr.] We must cultivate our garden : let us tend to our own affairs. –Voltaire
in forma pauperis [Lat.] Not liable for costs on account of poverty.
in omnia paratus [Lat.] Ready for everything.
in pectore [Lat.] In one's heart : secretly : in private.
in perpetuum [Lat.] For ever : in perpetuity.
in rerum natura [Lat.] In the nature of things.
in saecula saeculorum [Lat.] For ever and ever.
integer vitae scelerisque purus [Lat.] Blameless of life and free of vice.
intra vires [Lat.] Within the authority or power (of a person or body).
in utero [Lat.] In the womb.
in utrumque paratus [Lat.] Ready for either (outcome). –Virgil
in vacuo [Lat.] In a vacuum : without reference to related arguments or circumstances.
in vino veritas [Lat.] In wine there is truth : a drunken person speaks the truth.
ira furor brevis est [Lat.] Anger is a brief madness. –Horace
j'accuse [Fr.] I accuse : bitter denunciation. –Émile Zola
jacta alea est (or **est alea**) [Lat.] The die is cast. –Julius Caesar
jeu de mots [Fr.] Play on words : pun.
jus canonicum [Lat.] Canon law.
jus divinum [Lat.] Divine law.
juste milieu [Fr.] Golden mean : happy medium.
j'y suis, j'y reste [Fr.] Here I am and here I stay.
Kinder, Kirche, Küche [G.] Children, church, kitchen. –Used to express conventional view of a woman's responsibilities
ktēma es aei [Gk.] A possession for all time : an artistic work of enduring value.
la belle dame sans merci [Fr.] The beautiful, merciless lady.
lacrimae rerum [Lat.] Tears for things : sadness of things : tragedy of life. –Virgil
laissez-aller or **laisser-aller** [Fr.] Lack of restraint in speech or manner.
lapsus calami [Lat.] Slip of the pen.
lapsus linguae [Lat.] Slip of the tongue.
l'art pour l'art [Fr.] Art for art's sake.
lasciate ogni speranza, voi ch'entrate [Ital.] Abandon all hope, ye who enter. –Dante
le cœur a ses raisons que la raison ne connaît point [Fr.] The heart has its reasons that reason knows nothing of.
le style, est l'homme même [Fr.] The style is the man himself. –Buffon
l'état, c'est moi [Fr.] I am the state. –Attributed to Louis XIV
lex talionis [Lat.] Law of retaliation : an eye for an eye.
littera scripta manet [Lat.] The written letter abides.

locus standi [Lat.] Recognized position : right to appear in court.
lucus a non lucendo [Lat.] Paradoxical explanation : explanation of something by the opposite of what it suggests.
magna est veritas et praevalebit [Lat.] Truth is great and will prevail.
malade imaginaire [Fr.] Imaginary invalid : hypochondriac. –Molière
mal du pays [Fr.] Homesickness.
mal du siècle [Fr.] World-weariness : disillusionment at the state of the world.
malgré tout [Fr.] In spite of everything.
malis avibus [Lat.] Under evil auspices.
mal vu [Fr.] Disapproved of : resented.
mauvaise honte [Fr.] False shame : painful shyness.
mauvais quart d'heure [Fr.] Bad quarter-hour : difficult but brief experience.
meden agan [Gk.] Nothing in excess.
medio tutissimus ibis [Lat.] The middle path is the safest. –Ovid
memoria technica [Lat.] System or device to assist memory.
mens rea [Lat.] Criminal intent.
mens sana in corpore sano [Lat.] A healthy mind in a healthy body. –Juvenal
meum et tuum [Lat.] Mine and yours. –Used to express principle of rights of property
miserere nobis [Lat.] Have mercy on us.
mole ruit sua [Lat.] It collapses from its own massiveness. –Horace
monstre sacré [Fr.] Sacred monster : celebrity notorious for his or her unorthodox life or opinions.
monumentum aere perennius [Lat.] A monument more lasting than bronze : immortal work of art or literature.
more suo [Lat.] In his (or her) own way.
morituri te salutant (or **salutamus)** [Lat.] Those (or we) who are about to die salute you. –Salutation to Emperor by Roman gladiators
multum in parvo [Lat.] Much in little : a great deal in a small space.
mutato nomine de te fabula narratur [Lat.] With the name changed the story applies to you. –Horace
naturam expellas furca, tamen usque recurret [Lat.] Though you drive nature out with a pitchfork, she will keep coming back. –Horace
natura non facit saltum [Lat.] Nature makes no leap : nature takes no shortcuts.
ne cede malis [Lat.] Yield not to misfortunes. –Virgil
ne quid nimis [Lat.] Nothing in excess. –Terence
nihil ad rem [Lat.] Beside the point : irrelevant.
nil admirari [Lat.] To remain unimpressed : composure of mind. –Horace
nil desperandum [Lat.] Never despair. –Horace
n'importe [Fr.] No matter : that's all right.
nolens volens [Lat.] Whether willing or not : willy-nilly.
non omnia possumus omnes [Lat.] We can't all do everything. –Virgil
non sum qualis eram [Lat.] I am not what I once was. –Horace
nosce te ipsum [Lat.] Know thyself.
nostalgie de la boue [Fr.] Nostalgia for the mud : longing for esp. sexual degradation.
novus homo [Lat.] New man : man newly ennobled : parvenu.
nuit blanche [Fr.] White night : sleepless night.
nulli secundus [Lat.] Second to none.
obscurum per obscurius [Lat.] Explanation that is more obscure than the thing being explained.
oderint dum metuant [Lat.] Let them hate, so long as they fear.
odi et amo [Lat.] I hate and I love.
omertà [Ital.] Submission : code of sworn silence and private revenge esp. among the criminal underworld.
omne ignotum pro magnifico [Lat.] Everything unknown is assumed to be grand : the unknown always appears more wonderful than it really is. –Tacitus
omnia mutantur, nos et mutamur in illis [Lat.] All things are changing, and we are changing with them.
omnia vincit amor [Lat.] Love conquers all. –Virgil
onus probandi [Lat.] Burden of proof.
orare est laborare, laborare est orare [Lat.] To pray is to work, to work is to pray.
ore rotundo [Lat.] With rounded mouth : eloquently. –Horace
O tempora O mores [Lat.] O times O morals : what corrupt times we live in
où sont les neiges d'antan? [Fr.] Where are the snows of yesteryear? –Villon
pallida Mors [Lat.] Pale Death.
panem et circenses [Lat.] Bread and circuses : benefits provided by a government to pacify the common populace.
panta rhei [Gk.] All things are in flux.
par avance [Fr.] In advance : beforehand : by anticipation.
parturient montes, nascetur ridiculus mus [Lat.] The mountains shall labor and bring forth a ridiculous mouse.
peine forte et dure [Fr.] Harsh and severe punishment : torture.
per angusta ad augusta [Lat.] Through hardships to greatness.
père [Fr.] Father. –Used after a name to distinguish between father and son of the same name
pereant qui ante nos nostra dixerunt [Lat.] A plague on those who have proclaimed our bright ideas before us
pereunt et imputantur [Lat.] (The hours) pass away and are reckoned against us. –Martial
peu de chose [Fr.] Small matter : trifle.
pièce justificative [Fr.] Justificatory paper : document serving as evidence.
pièce montée [Fr.] Set piece : food arranged in a decorative shape.
place aux dames [Fr.] Make room for the ladies.
plein air [Fr.] Open air : representation in painting of natural light or atmospheric conditions.
pleno jure [Lat.] With full authority.
plus ça change, plus c'est la même chose [Fr.] The more things change, the more they remain the same.
plus royaliste que le roi [Fr.] More royalist than the king.
poeta nascitur, non fit [Lat.] A poet is born, not made.
point de repère [Fr.] Point of reference.
post hoc, ergo propter hoc [Lat.] After this, therefore because of it : fallacious argument that because one thing precedes another it necessarily causes it.
pour encourager les autres [Fr.] To encourage the others (by frightening them). –Voltaire
pou stō [Gk.] Place to stand : base of operation. –Archimedes
pro bono publico [Lat.] For the public good.
pro rege, lege, et grege [Lat.] For the king, the law, and the people.
punica fide [Lat.] With Punic faith : treacherously.
pur sang [Fr.] Pure-blooded : of noble birth : through and through.
quand même [Fr.] All the same : even so : despite the consequences.
quantum mutatus ab illo [Lat.] How changed from what he once was.
qui facit per alium facit per se [Lat.] He who does something through another does it through himself (i.e., shares the responsibility).
quis custodiet ipsos custodes? [Lat.] Who shall guard the guardians themselves? –Juvenal
qui s'excuse s'accuse [Fr.] Who excuses himself accuses himself.
qui va là? [Fr.] Who goes there?
quoad hoc [Lat.] As to this : as far as this is concerned.
quod erat demonstrandum [Lat.] Which was to be demonstrated.
quos deus vult perdere prius dementat [Lat.] Those whom a god wishes to destroy he first drives mad.
quot homines, tot sententiae [Lat.] There are as many opinions as there are people. –Terence
quo vadis? [Lat.] Where are you going?
raison d'état [Fr.] Reason of state.
reculer pour mieux sauter [Fr.] To draw back so as to better leap forward : to retreat so as to better advance.
re infecta [Lat.] The business being unfinished : without accomplishing one's goal.
requiescat in pace [Lat.] May he (or she) rest in peace. –Used on tombstones
respice finem [Lat.] Look to the end : consider the final outcome.
revenons à nos moutons [Fr.] Let us return to our sheep : let's get back to the subject.
saeva indignatio [Lat.] Fierce indignation.
sal Atticum [Lat.] Attic salt : sharp wit.
salto mortale [Ital.] Deadly leap : full somersault : dangerous or crucial act.
sancta simplicitas [Lat.] Holy simplicity : well-meant naiveté.
sans pareil [Fr.] Without equal : peerless.

sans-souci [Fr.] Carefree pleasure : idle enjoyment.
sauve-qui-peut [Fr.] Save himself who can : general rout.
savoir-vivre [Fr.] Good breeding : correct social behavior.
scène à faire [Fr.] Obligatory scene : climactic scene.
secundum artem [Lat.] According to the art : in accord with the accepted procedure of a profession or craft.
secundum naturam [Lat.] According to nature : naturally. —Cicero
securus judicat orbis terrarum [Lat.] The verdict of the world is conclusive : the whole world can't be wrong.
se defendendo [Lat.] In self-defense.
se non è vero, è ben trovato [Ital.] Even if it isn't true, it's a wonderful invention.
sic itur ad astra [Lat.] Thus does one go to the stars : this is the way to fame and immortality. —Virgil
sic transit gloria mundi [Lat.] Thus passes away the glory of the world.
si jeunesse savait, si vieillesse pouvait [Fr.] If only youth knew, if only age could —Henri Estienne
silent leges inter arma [Lat.] The laws are silent in time of war. —Cicero
similia similibus curantur [Lat.] Like cures like.
similis simili gaudet [Lat.] Like takes pleasure in like.
si vis pacem, para bellum [Lat.] If you want peace, prepare for war.
solvitur ambulando [Lat.] It is solved by walking : the problem is solved by practical experiment.
splendide mendax [Lat.] Nobly untruthful : lying for an honorable cause.
spolia opima [Lat.] The richest spoils : supreme achievement : arms stripped from the defeated general by the victor.
suaviter in modo, fortiter in re [Lat.] Soft in manner, strong in deed.
sub specie aeternitatis [Lat.] In relation to eternal things : without reference to the changing conditions of everyday life.
succès de scandale [Fr.] Success gained through notoriety or scandal.
suggestio falsi [Lat.] Deliberate misrepresentation not involving a direct lie.
sunt lacrimae rerum [Lat.] There are tears for things : life is tragic. —Virgil
suo jure [Lat.] In one's own right.
suo loco [Lat.] In its rightful place.
suo Marte [Lat.] By one's own effort.
suppressio veri [Lat.] Suppression of the truth : misrepresentation by concealment.
suum cuique [Lat.] To each his own.
taedium vitae [Lat.] Weariness of life.
tant mieux [Fr.] So much the better.
tant pis [Fr.] So much the worse.
tempora mutantur, nos et mutamur in illis [Lat.] The times change, and we change with them.
tempus edax rerum [Lat.] Time, the devourer of all things. —Ovid
tempus fugit [Lat.] Time flies.
terra incognita [Lat.] Unknown territory.
timeo Danaos et dona ferentes [Lat.] I fear the Greeks even when they bring gifts. —Virgil
totidem verbis [Lat.] In so many words : in these exact words.
toties quoties [Lat.] As often as : on each occasion : repeatedly.
toto caelo [Lat.] By the whole extent of the heavens : as far apart as possible : diametrically opposed.
toujours la politesse [Fr.] It is always best to be polite.
toujours perdrix [Fr.] Always partridge : too much of a good thing.
tour d'horizon [Fr.] Circuit of the horizon : general survey.
tout à fait [Fr.] Entirely : altogether : quite.
tout bien ou rien [Fr.] Everything done properly or not at all : all or nothing.
tout comprendre, c'est tout pardonner [Fr.] To understand everything is to forgive everything.
tout court [Fr.] Briefly : simply : curtly.
tout de même [Fr.] All the same : nevertheless.
tout de suite [Fr.] Immediately : all at once.
tout ensemble [Fr.] All together : general effect.
tout le monde [Fr.] Everybody : everyone of importance.
trahison des clercs [Fr.] Betrayal by the intellectuals (in compromising their own standards). —Julien Benda
tranche de vie [Fr.] Slice of life.
truditur dies die [Lat.] Day shoves forth day : one day hurries after another.
ultima ratio regum [Lat.] The final argument of kings : war.
ultra vires [Lat.] Beyond the power or authority of a person or body.
uno animo [Lat.] With one mind : unanimously.
uomo universale [Ital.] Universal man : one of broad education and ability.
urbi et orbi [Lat.] To the city (Rome) and to the world. —Used formerly in papal proclamations
utile dulci [Lat.] The useful with the pleasurable. —Horace
uti possidetis [Lat.] As you possess : principle leaving belligerents in possession of what they have seized.
va-et-vient [Fr.] Coming and going : traffic : commotion.
vae victis [Lat.] Woe to the vanquished.
vale *or* **valete** [Lat.] Farewell.
varia lectio [Lat.] Variant reading.
varium et mutabile semper femina [Lat.] Woman is ever a fickle and changeable thing. —Virgil
vedi Napoli e poi mori [Ital.] See Naples and then die.
veni, vidi, vici [Lat.] I came, I saw, I conquered. —Attributed to Julius Caesar
ventre à terre [Fr.] Belly to the ground : at full speed.
verbatim et literatim [Lat.] Word for word and letter for letter.
verbum sapienti sat est [Lat.] A word to the wise is sufficient.
victor ludorum [Lat.] Winner of the games : athletic champion.
vieux jeu [Fr.] Old-fashioned.
vincit omnia veritas [Lat.] Truth conquers all.
virginibus puerisque [Lat.] For girls and boys. —Horace
vis medicatrix naturae [Lat.] Healing power of nature.
vita nuova [Ital.] New life. —Dante
vive la différence [Fr.] Long live the difference (between the sexes).
vixere fortes ante Agamemnona [Lat.] There lived brave men before Agamemnon. —Horace
vogue la galère [Fr.] Keep the galley rowing : keep on at all costs. —Rabelais
voilà tout [Fr.] That's all.
vox et praeterea nihil [Lat.] A voice and nothing more : empty words.
vox populi, vox Dei [Lat.] The voice of the people is the voice of God.
Wanderjahr [G.] Years of wandering : years spent gathering experience.
Weltbild [G.] Conception of the world.
Weltpolitik [G.] World politics : foreign policy or diplomacy.
Wunderkind [G.] Child prodigy.

A Concise Guide to Style and Diction

This section of the Dictionary discusses and illustrates the basic conventions of American capitalization, punctuation, and italicization. The section concludes with a guide to better diction in which clichés and redundant expressions are listed and discussed as an aid to those who wish to achieve clear and effective prose style.

I. Style Guide

Capitalization

Capitalize the following:

1. the first word of a sentence:

   Some spiders are poisonous; others are not.

   Are you my new neighbor?

2. the first word of a direct quotation, except when the quotation is split:

   Joyce asked, "Do you think that the lecture was interesting?"

   "No," I responded, "it was very boring."

   Tom Paine said, "The sublime and the ridiculous are often so nearly related, that it is difficult to class them separately."

3. the first word of each line in a poem in traditional verse:

   Half a league, half a league,
   Half a league onward,
   All in the valley of Death
   Rode the six hundred.

   —Alfred, Lord Tennyson

4. the names of people, of organizations and their members, of councils and congresses, and of historical periods and events:

   Marie Curie
   Benevolent and Protective Order of Elks
   an Elk
   Protestant Episcopal Church
   an Episcopalian
   the Democratic Party
   a Democrat
   the Nuclear Regulatory Commission
   the U.S. Senate
   the Middle Ages
   World War I
   the Battle of Britain

5. the names of places and geographic divisions, districts, regions, and locales:

Richmond	Continental Divide
Vermont	Middle East
Argentina	Far North
Seventh Avenue	Gulf States
London Bridge	East Coast
Arctic Circle	the North
Eastern Hemisphere	the South Shore

   Do not capitalize words indicating compass points unless a specific region is referred to: Turn north onto Interstate 91.

6. the names of rivers, lakes, mountains, and oceans:

Ohio River	Rocky Mountains
Lake Como	Atlantic Ocean

7. the names of ships, aircraft, satellites, and space vehicles:

   U.S.S. *Arizona*
   Spirit of St. Louis
   the spy satellite Ferret-D
   Voyager II
   the space shuttle Challenger

8. the names of nationalities, races, tribes, and languages:

Spanish	Bantu
Maori	Russian

9. words derived from proper names, except in their extended senses:

   the Byzantine Empire

   but

   byzantine office politics

10. words indicating family relationships when used with a person's name as a title:

    Aunt Toni and Uncle Jack

but

my aunt and uncle, Toni and Jack Walker

11. a title (i.e., civil, judicial, military, royal and noble, religious, and honorary) when preceding a name:

Justice Marshall	Lord Mountbatten
General Jackson	Pope John Paul II
Mayor Daley	Professor Jacobson
Queen Victoria	Senator Byrd

12. all references to the President and Vice President of the United States:

The President has entered the hall.

The Vice President presides over the Senate.

13. all key words in titles of literary, dramatic, artistic, and musical works:

the novel *The Old Man and the Sea*
the short story "Notes from Underground"
an article entitled "On Passive Verbs"
James Dickey's poem "In the Tree House at Night"
the play *Cat on a Hot Tin Roof*
Van Gogh's *Wheat Field and Cypress Trees*
Beethoven's *Emperor Concerto*

14. *the* in the title of a newspaper if it is a part of the title:

The Wall Street Journal

but

the New York *Daily News*

15. the first word in the salutation and in the complimentary close of a letter:

My dear Carol, Yours sincerely,

16. epithets and substitutes for the names of people and places:

Old Hickory	The Oval Office
Old Blood and Guts	the Windy City

17. words used in personifications:

When is not Death at watch
Within those secret waters?
What wants he but to catch
Earth's heedless sons and daughters?
—Edmund Blunden

18. the pronoun *I*:

I told them that I had heard the news.

19. names for the Deity and sacred works:

God	the Supreme Being
the Almighty	the Bible
Jesus	the Koran
Allah	the Talmud

20. days of the week, months of the year, holidays, and holy days:

Tuesday	Passover
May	Ramadan
Independence Day	Christmas

21. the names of specific courts:

The Supreme Court of the United States
the Massachusetts Appeals Court
the United States Court of Appeals for the First Circuit

22. the names of treaties, accords, pacts, laws, and specific amendments:

Panama Canal Treaty
Treaty of Paris
Geneva Accords
Warsaw Pact countries
Sherman Antitrust Law
Labor Management Relations Act
took the Fifth Amendment

23. registered trademarks and service marks:

Day-Glo Comsat

24. the names of geologic eras, periods, epochs, and strata and the names of prehistoric divisions:

Paleozoic Era	Age of Reptiles
Precambrian	Bronze Age
Pleistocene	Stone Age

25. the names of constellations, planets, and stars:

Milky Way	Jupiter
Southern Crown	Uranus
Saturn	Polaris

26. genus but not species names in binomial nomenclature:

Rana pipiens

27. New Latin names of classes, families, and all groups higher than genera in botanical and zoological nomenclature:

Nematoda

But do not capitalize derivatives from such names: nematodes.

28. many abbreviations and acronyms:

Dec.	M.F.A.
Tues.	UNESCO
Lt. Gen.	MIRV

Italicization

Use italics to:

1. indicate titles of books, plays, and epic poems:

War and Peace
The Importance of Being Earnest
Paradise Lost

2. indicate titles of magazines and newspapers:

New York magazine
The Wall Street Journal
the New York *Daily News*

3. set off the titles of motion pictures and radio and television programs:

Star Wars
All Things Considered
Masterpiece Theater

4. indicate titles of major musical compositions:

   Handel's *Messiah*
   Adam's *Giselle*

5. set off the names of paintings and sculpture:

   Mona Lisa *Pietà*

6. indicate words, letters, or numbers that are referred to:

   The word *hiss* is onomatopoeic.
   Can't means *won't* in your lexicon.
   You form your *n*'s like *u*'s.
   A *6* looks like an inverted *9*.

7. indicate foreign words and phrases not yet assimilated into English:

   C'est la vie was the response to my complaint.

8. indicate the names of plaintiff and defendant in legal citations:

   Roe v. *Doe*

9. emphasize a word or phrase:

   When you appear on the national news, you are *somebody*.

   Use this device sparingly.

10. distinguish New Latin names of genera, species, subspecies, and varieties in botanical and zoological nomenclature:

    Homo sapiens

11. set off the names of ships and aircraft but not space vehicles:

    U.S.S. *Arizona*
    Spirit of St. Louis
    Voyager II
    the space shuttle Challenger
    the spy satellite Ferret-D

Punctuation

Apostrophe

1. indicates the possessive case of singular and plural nouns, indefinite pronouns, and surnames combined with designations such as *Jr.*, *Sr.*, and *II*:

   my sister's husband
   my three sisters' husbands
   anyone's guess
   They answer each other's phones.
   John Smith, Jr.'s car

2. indicates joint possession when used with the last of two or more nouns in a series:

   Doe and Roe's report

3. indicates individual possession or authorship when used with each of two or more nouns in a series:

   Smith's, Roe's, and Doe's reports

4. indicates the plurals of words, letters, and figures used as such:

   60's and 70's *x*'s, *y*'s, and *z*'s

5. indicates omission of letters in contractions:

   aren't that's o'clock

6. indicates omission of figures in dates:

   the class of '63

Brackets

1. enclose words or passages in quoted matter to indicate insertion of material written by someone other than the author:

   A tough but nervous, tenacious but restless race [the Yankees]; materially ambitious, yet prone to introspection. . . . —Samuel Eliot Morison

2. enclose material inserted within matter already in parentheses:

   (Vancouver [B.C.] January 1, 19–)

Colon

1. introduces words, phrases, or clauses that explain, amplify, or summarize what has gone before:

   Suddenly I realized where we were: Rome.

   There are two cardinal sins from which all the others spring: impatience and laziness.
   —Franz Kafka

2. introduces a long quotation:

   In his original draft of the *Declaration of Independence*, Jefferson wrote: "We hold these truths to be sacred and undeniable; that all men are created equal and independent, that from that equal creation they derive rights inherent and inalienable. . . ."

3. introduces a list:

   We need the following items: pens, paper, pencils, blotters, and erasers.

4. separates chapter and verse numbers in Biblical references:

   James 1:4

5. separates city from publisher in footnotes and bibliographies:

   Boston: Houghton Mifflin, 1985.

6. separates hour and minute(s) in time designations:

   9:30 a.m. a 9:30 meeting

7. follows the salutation in a business letter:

   Gentlemen:

Comma

1. separates the clauses of a compound sentence connected by a coordinating conjunction:

   A difference exists between the musical works of Handel and Haydn, and it is a difference worth noting.

   The comma may be omitted in short compound sentences:

I heard what you said and I am furious.

I got out of the car and I walked and walked.

2. separates *and* or *or* from the final item in a series of three or more:

   Red, yellow, and blue may be mixed to produce all colors.

3. separates two or more adjectives modifying the same noun if *and* could be used between them without altering the meaning:

   a solid, heavy gait

   but

   a polished mahogany dresser

4. sets off nonrestrictive clauses or phrases (i.e., those that if eliminated would not affect the meaning of the sentences):

   The burglar, who had entered through the patio, went straight to the silver chest.

   The comma should not be used when a clause is restrictive (i.e., essential to the meaning of the sentence):

   The burglar who had entered through the patio went straight to the silver chest; the other burglar searched for the wall safe.

5. sets off words or phrases in apposition to a noun or noun phrase:

   Plato, the famous Greek philosopher, was a student of Socrates.

   The comma should not be used if such words or phrases precede the noun:

   The Greek philosopher Plato was a student of Socrates.

6. sets off transitional words and short expressions that require a pause in reading or speaking:

   Unfortunately, my friend was not well traveled.

   Did you, after all, find what you were looking for?

   I live with my family, of course.

7. sets off words used to introduce a sentence:

   No, I haven't been to Paris.

   Well, what do you think we should do now?

8. sets off a subordinate clause or a long phrase that precedes a principal clause:

   By the time we found the restaurant, we were starved.

   Of all the illustrations in the book, the most striking are those of the tapestries.

9. sets off short quotations and sayings:

   The candidate said, "Actions speak louder than words."

   "Talking of axes," said the Duchess, "chop off her head!" —Lewis Carroll

10. indicates omission of a word or words:

    To err is human; to forgive, divine.

11. sets off the year from the month in full dates:

    Nicholas II of Russia was shot on July 16, 1918.

    But note that when only the month and the year are used, no comma appears:

    Nicholas II of Russia was shot in July 1918.

12. sets off city and state in geographic names:

    Atlanta, Georgia, is the transportation center of the South.

    34 Beach Drive
    Bedford, VA 24523

13. separates series of four or more figures into thousands, millions, etc.:

    67,000 200,000

14. sets off words used in direct address:

    I tell you, folks, all politics is applesauce. —Will Rogers

    Thank you for your expert assistance, Dolores.

15. Separates a tag question from the rest of a sentence:

    You forgot your keys again, didn't you?

16. sets off sentence elements that could be misunderstood if the comma were not used:

    Some time after, the actual date for the project was set.

17. follows the salutation in a personal letter and the complimentary close in a business or personal letter:

    Dear Jessica, Sincerely yours,

18. sets off titles and degrees from surnames and from the rest of a sentence:

    Walter T. Prescott, Jr.
    Gregory A. Rossi, S.J.
    Susan P. Green, M.D., presented the case.

Dash

1. indicates a sudden break or abrupt change in continuity:

   "If—if you'll just let me explain—" the student stammered.

   And the problem—if there really is one—can then be solved.

2. sets apart an explanatory, a defining, or an emphatic phrase:

   Foods rich in protein—meat, fish, and eggs—should be eaten on a daily basis.

More important than winning the election, is governing the nation. That is the test of a political party—the acid, final test.

—Adlai E. Stevenson

3. sets apart parenthetical matter:

Wolsey, for all his faults—and he had many—was a great statesman, a man of natural dignity with a generous temperament. . . .

—Jasper Ridley

4. marks an unfinished sentence:

"But if my bus is late—" he began.

5. sets off a summarizing phrase or clause:

The vital measure of a newspaper is not its size but its spirit—that is its responsibility to report the news fully, accurately, and fairly.

—Arthur H. Sulzberger

6. sets off the name of an author or source, as at the end of a quotation:

A poet can survive everything but a misprint.

—Oscar Wilde

Ellipses

1. indicate, by three spaced points, omission of words or sentences within quoted matter:

Equipped by education to rule in the nineteenth century, . . . he lived and reigned in Russia in the twentieth century. —Robert K. Massie

2. indicate, by four spaced points, omission of words at the end of a sentence:

The timidity of bureaucrats when it comes to dealing with . . . abuses is easy to explain. . . .

—*New York*

3. indicate, when extended the length of a line, omission of one or more lines of poetry:

Roll on, thou deep and dark blue
ocean—roll!
. . . .
Man marks the earth with ruin—his
control
Stops with the shore.

—Lord Byron

4. are sometimes used as a device, as for example, in advertising copy:

To help you Move and Grow
with the Rigors of
Business in the 1980's. . .
and Beyond.

—*Journal of Business Strategy*

Exclamation Point

1. terminates an emphatic or exclamatory sentence:

Go home at once!
You've got to be kidding!

2. terminates an emphatic interjection:

Encore!

Hyphen

1. indicates that part of a word of more than one syllable has been carried over from one line to the next:

During the revolution, the nation was
beset with problems—looting, fighting, and famine.

2. joins the elements of some compounds:

great-grandparent
attorney-at-law
ne'er-do-well

3. joins the elements of compound modifiers preceding nouns:

high-school students
a fire-and-brimstone lecture
a two-hour meeting

4. indicates that two or more compounds share a single base:

four- and six-volume sets
eight- and nine-year olds

5. separates the prefix and root in some combinations; check the Dictionary when in doubt about the spelling:

anti-Nazi	re-form/reform
re-elect	re-cover/recover
co-author	re-creation/recreation

6. substitutes for the word *to* between typewritten inclusive words or figures:

pp. 145-155
the Boston-New York air shuttle

7. punctuates written-out compound numbers from 21 through 99:

forty-six years of age
a person who is forty-six
two hundred fifty-nine dollars

Parentheses

1. enclose material that is not essential to a sentence and that if not included would not alter its meaning:

After a few minutes (some say less) the blaze was extinguished.

2. often enclose letters or figures to indicate subdivisions of a series:

A movement in sonata form consists of the following elements: (1) the exposition, (2) the development, and (3) the recapitulation.

3. enclose figures following and confirming written-out numbers, especially in legal and business documents:

The fee for my services will be two thousand dollars ($2,000.00).

4. enclose an abbreviation for a term following the written-out term, when used for the first time in a text:

The patient is suffering from acquired immune deficiency syndrome (AIDS).

Period

1. terminates a complete declarative or mild imperative sentence:

   There could be no turning back as war's dark shadow settled irrevocably across the continent of Europe. —W. Bruce Lincoln

   Return all the books when you can.

   Would you kindly affix your signature here.

2. terminates sentence fragments:

   Gray clouds—and what looks like a veil of rain falling behind the East German headland. A pair of ducks. A tired or dying swan, head buried in its back feathers, sits on the sand a few feet from the water's edge. —Anthony Bailey

3. follows some abbreviations:

   Dec. Blvd.
   Rev. pp.
   St. Co.

Question Mark

1. punctuates a direct question:

   Have you seen the new play yet?

   Who goes there?

   but

   I wonder who said "Nothing is easy in war."

   I asked if they planned to leave.

2. indicates uncertainty:

   Ferdinand Magellan (1480?–1521)
   Plato (427?–347 B.C.)

Quotation Marks

1. Double quotation marks enclose direct quotations:

   "What was Paris like in the Twenties?" our daughter asked.

   "Ladies and Gentlemen," the Chief Usher said, "the President of the United States."

   Robert Louis Stevenson said that "it is better to be a fool than to be dead."

   When advised not to become a lawyer because the profession was already overcrowded, Daniel Webster replied, "There is always room at the top."

2. Double quotation marks enclose words or phrases to clarify their meaning or use or to indicate that they are being used in a special way:

   This was the border of what we often call "the West" or "the Free World."

   "The Windy City" is a name for Chicago.

3. Double quotation marks set off the translation of a foreign word or phrase:

   die Grenze, "the border"

4. Double quotation marks set off the titles of series of books, of articles or chapters in publications, of essays, of short stories and poems, of individual radio and television programs, and of songs and short musical pieces:

   "The Horizon Concise History" series

   an article entitled "On Reflexive Verbs in English"

   Chapter Nine, "The Prince and the Peasant"

   Pushkin's "The Queen of Spades"

   Tennyson's "Ode on the Death of the Duke of Wellington"

   "The Bob Hope Special"

   Schubert's "Death and the Maiden"

5. Single quotation marks enclose quotations within quotations:

   The blurb for the piece proclaimed, "Two years ago at Geneva, South Vietnam was virtually sold down the river to the Communists. Today the spunky little . . . country is back on its own feet, thanks to 'a mandarin in a sharkskin suit who's upsetting the Red timetable.' "

   —Frances FitzGerald

   Put commas and periods inside quotation marks; put semicolons and colons outside. Other punctuation, such as exclamation points and question marks, should be put inside the closing quotation marks only if part of the matter quoted.

Semicolon

1. separates the clauses of a compound sentence having no coordinating conjunction:

   Do not let us speak of darker days; let us rather speak of sterner days. —Winston Churchill

2. separates the clauses of a compound sentence in which the clauses contain internal punctuation, even when the clauses are joined by conjunctions:

   Skis in hand, we trudged to the lodge, stowed our lunches, and donned our boots; and the rest of our party waited for us at the lifts.

3. separates elements of a series in which items already contain commas:

   Among those at the diplomatic reception were the Secretary of State; the daughter of the Ambassador to the Court of St. James's, formerly of London; and two United Nations delegates.

4. separates clauses of a compound sentence joined by a conjunctive adverb, such as *however, nonetheless,* or *hence*:

   We insisted upon a hearing; however, the Grievance Committee refused.

5. may be used instead of a comma to signal longer pauses for dramatic effect:

But I want you to know that when I cross the river my last conscious thought will be of the Corps; and the Corps; and the Corps.

—General Douglas MacArthur

Virgule

1. separates successive divisions in an extended date:

   fiscal year 1983/84

2. represents *per*:

   35 km/hr 1,800 ft/sec

3. means *or* between the words *and* and *or*:

   Take water skis and/or fishing equipment when you visit the beach this summer.

4. separates two or more lines of poetry that are quoted and run in on successive lines of a text:

   The student actress had a memory lapse when she came to the lines "Double, double, toil and trouble/Fire burn and cauldron bubble/Eye of newt and toe of frog/Wool of bat and tongue of dog" and had to leave the stage in embarrassment.

II. Clichés

A *cliché* may be defined as "A trite or overused expression or idea." The English language abounds in clichés, many of which originated as metaphors, proverbs, or brief quotations. But historical changes in the language through the years have rendered many of these expressions meaningless. For instance, what does *fell* in *one fell swoop* mean? Others, such as *do one's thing* and *keep a low profile,* illustrate that such expressions age very fast through relentless use, and become stale. Since most clichés express rather clear meanings, the writer will have to determine whether it is a shade of meaning that is hard to convey by fresher wording. If the process of substitution is too difficult, use of some of the phrases that follow may be advisable; writing around the formulaic expression may produce something worse than hackneyed language, such as strained, wordy, or ambiguous discourse. But few on the following list are truly indispensable, and writers of fresh, original prose will avoid most of them.

absence makes the heart grow fonder
add insult to injury
age before beauty
agonizing reappraisal
agree to disagree
albatross around one's neck
all in a day's work
all in the same boat
all over but the shouting
all things being equal
all things to all men
all work and no play
apple of one's eye
apple-pie order
armed to the teeth
arms of Morpheus
as luck would have it
at a loss for words (*or* **never at a loss . . .**)
at first blush
at sixes and sevens
(an) **axe to grind**

bag and baggage
bark up the wrong tree
bated breath
bathed in tears
beard the lion in his den
beat a dead horse
beat a hasty retreat
beat around the bush
beg to disagree
beggar description
bend (*or* **lean**) **over backward**
best foot forward
best-laid plans
best of all possible worlds
better late than never
between the devil and the deep blue sea
beyond the call of duty
beyond the pale
bigger than all outdoors
bigger (*or* **larger**) **than life**
bite off more than one can chew
bite the bullet
blushing bride
blush of shame
boggle the mind
bolt from the blue
bone of contention
born with a silver spoon
bosom of the family
brave the elements
breathe a sigh of relief
bright and early
bright as a button
bright-eyed and bushy-tailed
bright future
bring home the bacon
brown as a berry
budding genius
bull in a china shop
burn the midnight oil
busy as a bee
butter wouldn't melt in one's mouth
by leaps and bounds
by the same token

calm before the storm
can't see the forest for the trees
carry (*or* **have**) **a chip on one's shoulder**
carry coals to Newcastle
(a) **case in point**
caught on the horns of a dilemma
caught red-handed
chip off the old block
clear as mud
(to) **coin a phrase**
cold as ice
conspicuous by one's absence
cool as a cucumber
cross the Rubicon
(a) **crying need**
cut a long story short
cut off one's nose to spite one's face
cynosure of all eyes

daily repast
dead as a doornail

defend to the death one's right to . . .
depths of despair
diamond in the rough
die in harness
die is cast
distaff side
do it up brown
do one's thing
dog in the manger
doom is sealed
doomed to disappointment
down in the dumps
down in the mouth
down one's alley
draw the line
drown one's sorrows
drunk as a lord (*or* skunk)
dull thud

early bird gets the worm
early to bed . . . to rise
ear to the ground
easier said than done
eat one's hat (*or* words)
epoch-making
eternal reward
eyes of the world

face the music
(the) fair sex
fall on deaf ears
far be it from me
(a) far cry
fast and loose
fate worse than death
fat's in the fire
feather in one's cap
feel one's oats
festive board
few and far between
few well-chosen words
fiddle while Rome burns
fight like a tiger
fill the bill
filthy lucre
fine and dandy
first and foremost
fit as a fiddle
flash in a the pan
flat as a flounder (*or* pancake)
flesh and blood
fly off the handle
fond farewell
food for thought
fools rush in
foot in one's mouth
foot the bill
foregone conclusion
forewarned is forearmed
free as a bird (*or* the air)
fresh as a daisy

generous to a fault
gentle as a lamb
get down to brass tacks
get one's back (*or* dander) up
(a) good time was had by all
goose that laid the golden egg
grain of salt
grand and glorious
graphic account
green-eyed monster
grin like a Cheshire cat
grind to a halt

hail fellow well met
hale and hearty
hand that rocks the cradle
handsome is as handsome does
handwriting on the wall
hapless victim
happy as a lark
happy pair
hard row to hoe
haughty stare
haul (*or* rake) over the coals
have a foot in the door
have a leg up
head over heels
heart of gold
heave a sigh of relief
hew to the line
high and dry
high as a kite
high on the hog
hit the nail on the head
hit the spot
hook, line, and sinker
hook or crook
hot as a firecracker (*or* pistol)
hue and cry
hungry as a bear (*or* lion)

if (the) truth be told
in full swing
in no uncertain terms
in on the ground floor
in seventh heaven
inspiring sight
in the final (*or* last) analysis
in the limelight
in the long run
in the nick of time
in this day and age
iron out a difficulty
irons in the fire
irony of fate
irreparable damage (*or* loss)
it goes without saying
it is interesting to note
it never rains but it pours
it's an ill wind
it's six of one and a half a dozen of the other
it stands to reason
it takes all kinds to make a world
it takes two to tango

jig is up
just deserts

keep a low profile
keep a stiff upper lip

knock into a cocked hat
knock on wood

labor of love
land of milk and honey
land-office business
last but not least
last straw
law unto one's self
lead to the altar
lean and hungry look
lean over backward
leave in the lurch
leave no stone unturned
left-handed compliment
lend a helping hand
let one's hair down
let the cat out of the bag
let well enough alone
lick into shape
lid of secrecy
like a house afire (*or* on fire)
like a newborn babe
limp as a dish rag
lock, stock, and barrel
long arm of the law
look a gift horse in the mouth
(as) luck would have it

mad as a hatter
mad as a hornet (*or* wet hen)
mad as a March hare
mad dash
make a clean breast of
make a long story short
make a virtue of necessity
make bricks without straw
make ends meet
make hay while the sun shines
make no bones about
mantle of snow
matter or life and death
meek as Moses
meet one's Waterloo
meets the eye
method in one's madness
milk of human kindness
mince words
mind one's *p*'s and *q*'s
miss the boat
moment of truth
monarch of all one surveys
month of Sundays
moot question (*or* point)
more easily said than done
more sinned against than sinning
more than meets the eye
(the) more the merrier
motley crew

naked truth
name is legion
necessary evil
needle in a haysack
needs no introduction
neither fish nor fowl
never say die
nip in the bud
none the worse for wear
no sooner said than done
not to be sneezed (*or* sniffed) at
not wisely but too well
nothing new under the sun

of a high order
on cloud nine
on one's uppers
on the ball (*or* stick)
on the best (*or* unimpeachable) authority
on the bum (*or* the fritz)
on the lam
on the other hand
on the q.t.
on the wagon
once in a blue moon
one fell swoop
one's own worst enemy
open secret
opportunity knocks
other side of the coin
other things being equal
out of the frying pan into the fire
over a barrel
overcome with emotion

paint the town red
pandemonium reigned
part and parcel
pay the piper
penny for one's thoughts
penny wise, pound foolish
perfect gentleman
pet peeve
pillar of society
pillar to post
pinch pennies
play fast and loose
play it by ear
play second fiddle
play the Devil's advocate
plumb the depths
(at this) point in time
point with pride
poor but honest
(the) powers that be
pretty as a picture
pretty kettle of fish
pretty penny
psychological moment
pull the wool over one's eyes
pure as the driven snow
put on the dog

quick as lightning (*or* a flash)
quiet as a mouse

rack one's brains
rain cats and dogs
raise Cain
raise the roof

ed-letter day
eign supreme
ender a decision
ing true
ipe old age
ub one the wrong way

adder but wiser
ad to relate
ave for a rainy day
eal one's fate (*or* doom)
econd to none
eething mass
ell like hot cakes
eparate the men from the boys
eparate the sheep from the goats
hoot from the hip
a) shot in the arm
hout from the rooftops
how one's hand
how the white feather
ick and tired
ight to behold
ing like a bird
keleton in one's closet
mall world
mell a rat
our grapes
ow one's wild oats
tagger the imagination
tart (*or* get) the ball rolling
teal one's thunder
tem to stern
tick in one's craw
tick out like a sore thumb
tick to one's guns
tick to one's knitting
tir up a hornet's nest
traight from the shoulder
traight and narrow
traw in the wind
traw that broke the camel's back
trong as an ox
tubborn as a mule
weat of one's brow
weet sixteen
weet smell of success

take a dim view of
take a rain check
take it easy
take the bull by the horns
take up the cudgels
talk through one's hat
tell someone who cares
that is to say
that's for sure
throw caution to the winds
throw in the towel (*or* sponge)
throw one's hat in the ring
throw the book at
time hangs heavy
time immemorial
time of one's life
tip the scales
tired as a dog
tit for tat
to tell the truth
to the manner born
too funny for words
too little, too late
trip the light fantastic
true blue
turn over a new leaf

uncharted seas
up the creek without a paddle
usually reliable sources

vale of tears
view with alarm

wash one's hands of
wax poetic
wear two hats
wee (*or* small) hours
wet to the skin
what makes the world go round
when all is said and done
when you come (right) down to it
while ignorance is bliss
wide-open spaces
wise as an owl
without further ado
wolf in sheep's clothing
work one's fingers to the bone

III. Redundant Expressions

Redundancy—the needless repetition of ideas—is one of the principal obstacles to writing clear, precise prose. The list below gives some common redundant expressions. The elements repeated in the phrases and in the brief definitions are italicized. To eliminate redundancy, delete the italic elements in the phrases.

anthracite *coal*
(= a hard *coal* having a high carbon content)

old **antique**
(= an object having special value because of its *age,* esp. a work of art or handicraft more than 100 years *old*)

ascend *upward*
(= to go or move *upward*)

assemble *together*
(= to bring or gather *together*)

pointed **barb**
(= a sharp *point* projecting in reverse direction to the main point of a weapon or tool)

first **beginning**
(= the *first* part)

big *in size*
(= of considerable *size*)

bisect *in two*
(= to cut *into two* equal parts)

blend *together*
(= to combine, mix, or go well *together*)

capitol *building*
(= a *building* in which a legislative body meets)

coalesce *together*
(= to grow or come *together* so as to form a whole)

collaborate *together* or *jointly*
(= to work *together,* esp. in a joint effort)

fellow **colleague**
(=a *fellow* member of a profession, staff, or academic faculty)

congregate *together*
(= to bring or come *together* in a crowd)

connect *together*
(= to join or fasten *together*)

consensus *of opinion*
(= collective *opinion*)

courthouse *building*
(= a *building* in which judicial courts or county government offices are housed)

habitual **custom**
(= a *habitual* practice)

descend *downward*
(= to move, slope, extend, or incline *downward*)

doctorate *degree*
(= the *degree* or status of a doctor)

endorse (a check) *on the back*
(= to write one's signature *on the back of,* e.g., a check)

erupt *violently*
(= to emerge *violently* or to become *violently* active)

explode *violently*
(= to burst *violently* from internal pressure)

real **fact**
(= something with *real,* demonstrable existence)

passing **fad**
(= a *passing* fashion)

few *in number*
(= amounting to or made up of a *small number*)

founder *and sink*
(= to *sink* beneath the water)

basic **fundamental**
(= a *basic* or essential part)

fuse *together*
(= to mix *together* by or as if by melting)

opening **gambit**
(= a remark intended to *open* a conversation)

gather *together*
(= to come *together* or cause to come *together*)

free **gift**
(= something bestowed voluntarily and *without compensation*)

past **history**
(= a narrative of *past* events; something that took place *in the past*)

hoist *up*
(= to raise or to haul *up* with or as if with a mechanical device)

current or *present* **incumbent**
(= one *currently* holding an office)

new **innovation**
(= something *new* or unusual)

join *together*
(= to bring or put *together* so as to make continuous or form a unit)

knots *per hour*
(= a unit of speed, one nautical mile *per hour,* approx. 1.15 statute miles *per hour*)

large *in size*
(= greater than average *in size*)

merge *together*
(= to blend or cause to blend *together* gradually)

necessary **need**
(= something *necessary* or wanted)

universal **panacea**
(= a remedy for *all* diseases, evils, or difficulties)

continue to **persist**
(= to *continue* in existence)

individual **person**
(= an *individual* human being)

advance **planning**
(= detailed methodology, programs, or schemes worked out *beforehand* for the accomplishment of an objective)

chief or *leading* or *main* **protagonist**
(= the *leading* character in a Greek drama or other literary form; a *leading* or *principal* figure)

original **prototype**
(= an *original* type, form, or instance that is a model on which later stages are based or judged)

protrude *out*
(= to push or thrust *outward*)

recall *back*
(= to summon *back* to awareness; to bring *back*)

recoil *back*
(= to kick or spring *back*; to shrink *back* in fear or loathing; to fall *back*)

new **recruit**
(= a *new* member of a body or organization, esp. of a military force)

recur *again* or *repeatedly*
(= to occur *again* or *repeatedly*)

temporary **reprieve**
(= *temporary* relief, as from danger or pain)

short *in length* or *height*
(= having very little *length* or *height*)

shuttle *back and forth*
(= to move, go, or travel *back and forth*)

skirt *around*
(= to move or pass *around* rather than across or through)

small *in size*
(= characterized by relatively little *size* or slight *dimensions*)

tall *in height*
(having greater than average *height*)

two **twins**
(= one of *two* offspring born at the same birth; one of *two* identical or similar persons, animals, or things)

completely **unanimous**
(= being in *complete* harmony, accord, or agreement)

visible *to the eye*
(= perceptible *to the eye*)

from **whence**
(= *from* where; *from* what place; *from* what origin or source)